PRONUNCIATION SYMBOLS

ə {
banana	silent	capital	collect	suppose	perplex
bun	lunch	putty	color	supper	pup
burn	learnt	pert	curl	serpent	purple

[in the words in the first line above, ə (called *schwa* \'shwä\) is spoken with very weak force; in the words in the second and third lines ə is spoken with stronger force]

a	ax, map
ā	age, vacation, day
ä	father, cot, cart
à	[a sound between \a\ and \ä\, as in an Eastern New England pronunciation of aunt, half]
au̇	out, now
b	baby, rib
ch	chin, match, nature \'nā-chər\
d	did, ladder
e	less
ē	seaweed, any, serial, cereal
f	fifty, cuff, phone
g	gift, pig, bigger
h	hat, ahead
i	trip
ī	life, buy, my
j	job, gem, edge
k	kin, cook, chasm
l	lily, mortal
m	murmur

n	nine, cotton
ng	sing, singer, finger, ink
ō	low, bone, cooperate
ȯ	moth, law, sort, all
ȯi	coin, destroy
p	pepper, lip
r	rarity
s	spice, less
sh	shy, dish, machine, mission, special
t	tight, latter
th	thin, ether
th	this, either
ü	boot, rule
u̇	foot, pull
v	give, vivid
w	we, away
y	you, yet
yü	few, union, mule, youth
yu̇	furious
z	zone, raise
zh	vision, beige

\ \ slant lines used in pairs to mark the beginning and end of a pronunciation: \'pen\

' mark at the beginning of a syllable that has primary (strongest) stress: \'pen-mən-ˌship\

ˌ mark at the beginning of a syllable that has secondary (next-strongest) stress: \'pen-mən-ˌship\

- mark of syllable division in pronunciations [the mark of syllable division in boldface entry words is a centered dot · and the position of the two kinds of division often does not agree, as in build·ing \'bil-ding\, spe·cial \'spesh-əl\, ca·ter \'kāt-ər\]

Symbol Names. In naming symbols we use the terms *bar, one-dot, two-dot,* and *plain*; thus ā is "bar a", th is "bar t-h", ȯ is "one-dot o", ü is "two-dot u", a is "plain a", th is "plain t-h". Call i "plain i" because the dot is not a diacritical mark. ə is called *schwa* \'shwä\.

Webster's Elementary Dictionary

A Merriam-Webster ®

AMERICAN BOOK COMPANY

New York   Cincinnati   Atlanta   Dallas

Registered User of the Trademark

Contents

The Story of Your Dictionary

Noah Webster.

EDWIN B. CHILD

This dictionary began with a man named Noah Webster. Webster was born in Hartford, Connecticut, in 1758. He grew up during the years that our nation was growing up. The young man loved his country, and he loved the language of its people.

When Webster became a teacher, he needed books for his pupils. But the only ones he could find were made in England. These books told about English ways of life. They taught the kind of English that was spoken in England. This was different from American English. So Noah Webster decided to write his own schoolbook.

This first book of Webster's is called the *Blue-Backed Speller*. It taught the sounds and letters as they were used by Americans. The stories in the *Speller* told about things that were important to Americans. The *Speller* soon became a best-seller. Thousands of families had it in their homes. The *Speller* is still sold today.

The First American Dictionaries

Webster was always taking notes on words. He listened to the way people said and used words in their speech. He read newspapers and books to see how words were used in writing. In 1806, Webster brought all his notes together. He published his first dictionary.

But there was still more work to do. Webster wanted to make a dictionary that would be like a huge schoolbook. It must be a dictionary that Americans everywhere could use and understand. So Webster worked for twenty-two more years. Then he published his *American Dictionary of the English Language*.

This dictionary was different in many ways from the dictionaries being used in England. Webster's dictionary

- had more words
- showed American pronunciation and spelling
- gave more exact definitions
- told more about where words came from

The Merriam-Webster Dictionaries

George and Charles Merriam were printers. After Webster died, they received the right to bring his dictionary up to date. The first new edition was published in 1847.

Since then, many new editions have been published. Each one is put together carefully, in the way Webster worked. Editors take many notes on the way people use words as they speak and write. Each new edition has in it:

- words that are new in our language
- words that have changed in use or meaning

You can see that the Merriam-Webster dictionaries are, in a way, as old as the United States. Yet the dictionaries are always new, too. The people who make them agree with Noah Webster. A useful dictionary is like a living language. Both are always growing and changing. 5a

3 : something that serves to compensate or make up for something else

²offset *vb* **offset**; **off·set·ting** : to make up for : BALANCE ⟨gains in one state *offset* losses in another⟩

off·shoot \'òf-,shüt\ *n* **1** : a branch of a main stem of a plant **2** : something arising or developing from or branching out of something else ⟨*offshoots* from the old trail⟩

¹off·shore \'òf-'shōr\ *adv* : from the shore : at a distance from the shore

²off·shore \'òf-,shōr\ *adj* **1** : coming or moving away from the shore ⟨an *offshore* breeze⟩ **2** : located off the shore ⟨*offshore* fisheries⟩

off·spring \'òf-,spring\ *n, pl* **offspring** *also* **off·springs** : the young of a person, animal, or plant : PROGENY

off·stage \'òf-'stāj\ *adv (or adj)* : off or away from the stage

off–the–rec·ord \,òf-thə-'rek-ərd\ *adj* : given or made in confidence and not for publication ⟨the candidate's *off-the-record* remarks⟩

oft \'òft\ *adv* : OFTEN

of·ten \'òf-ən, -tən\ *adv* : many times

of·ten·times \'òf-ən-,tīmz, 'òf-tən-\ *adv* : OFTEN

o·gle \'ō-gəl\ *vb* **o·gled**; **o·gling** : to look at in a flirting way ⟨*ogling* the pretty girls⟩

o·gre \'ō-gər\ *n* **1** : an ugly giant of fairy tales and folklore who eats people **2** : a dreaded person or object

oh \'ō\ *interj* **1** — used to express various emotions (as surprise or pain) **2** — used in direct address ⟨*Oh*, John, you forgot your cap⟩

¹-oid \,òid\ *n suffix* : something resembling a specified object or having a specified quality ⟨plan*toid*⟩

²-oid *adj suffix* : resembling : having the form or appearance of ⟨petal*oid*⟩

¹oil \'òil\ *n* **1** : any of numerous greasy combustible and usually liquid substances from plant, animal, or mineral sources that are not soluble in water and are used especially as lubricants, fuels, and food **2** : PETROLEUM **3** : artists' paints made of pigments and oil **4** : a painting in oils

²oil *vb* : to put oil on or in

oil·cloth \'òil-,klòth\ *n* : cloth treated with oil or paint so as to be waterproof and used for shelf and table coverings

oil·skin \'òil-,skin\ *n* **1** : an oiled waterproof cloth used for garments and coverings **2** *pl* : an oilskin suit of coat and trousers

oilskins

oil well *n* : a well from which petroleum is obtained

oil·y \'òi-lē\ *adj* **oil·i·er**; **oil·i·est** **1** : of, relating to, or containing oil **2** : covered or soaked with oil ⟨*oily* rags⟩ **3** : too smooth in manner ⟨an *oily* salesman⟩ — **oil·i·ness** *n*

oint·ment \'òint-mənt\ *n* : a semisolid usually greasy and medicated preparation for use on the skin

¹OK *or* **o·kay** \ō-'kā\ *adv (or adj)* : all right

²OK *or* **okay** *vb* **OK'd** *or* **o·kayed**; **OK'·ing** *or* **o·kay·ing** : APPROVE, AUTHORIZE

³OK *or* **okay** *n* : APPROVAL

o·ka·pi \ō-'kä-pē\ *n* : a giraffelike animal of the African forests

o·kra \'ō-krə\ *n* : a plant related to the hollyhocks and grown for its edible green pods which are used in soups and stews

¹old \'ōld\ *adj* **1** : dating from the distant past : ANCIENT ⟨an *old* custom⟩ **2** : being of long standing ⟨an *old* friend⟩ **3** : having existed for a specified length of time ⟨a girl three years *old*⟩ **4** : advanced in age ⟨an *old* man⟩ **5** : FORMER ⟨his *old* students⟩ **6** : showing the effects of age or use ⟨wore an *old* coat⟩

²old *n* : old or earlier time ⟨in days of *old*⟩

old·en \'ōl-dən\ *adj* : of or relating to a bygone era : ANCIENT

Old English *n* : the language of the English people from the earliest documents in the seventh century to about 1100

old–fash·ioned \'ōld-'fash-ənd\ *adj* **1** : of, relating to, or characteristic of a past era **2** : holding fast to old ways : CONSERVATIVE

Old French *n* : the French language from the ninth to the thirteenth century

Old Glory *n* : the flag of the United States

old·ish \'ōl-dish\ *adj* : somewhat old

old maid *n* **1** : an elderly unmarried woman **2** : a prim fussy person **3** : a card game in which the player holding the odd queen at the end is called an "old maid"

old·ster \'ōld-stər\ *n* : an old or elderly person

old–tim·er \'ōld-'tī-mər\ *n* **1** : VETERAN **2** : OLDSTER **3** : something old-fashioned : ANTIQUE

Old World *n* **1** : the eastern hemisphere **2** : the continent of Europe

old–world \'ōld-'wərld\ *adj* : OLD-FASHIONED, PICTURESQUE

o·le·o·mar·ga·rine \,ō-lē-ō-'mär-jə-rən\ *n* : MARGARINE

ol·fac·to·ry \äl-'fak-tə-rē\ *adj* : of, relating to, or concerned with the sense of smell ⟨the *olfactory* nerve⟩

ol·ive \'äl-iv\ *n* **1** : an oily fruit that is eaten

j job   ng sing   ō low   ò moth   òi coin   th thin   th this   ü boot   ù foot   y you   yü few   yù furious   zh vision

What Do You know About Dictionary Entries?

Number your paper from 1 to 10. These numerals go with the ones on the page at the left. Use that page to find your answers. After each numeral on your paper, write the word or phrase that makes the *best* ending for the sentence.

1. These words help you to find words on the page
   (a) alphabetically   (b) by meaning   (c) by length

2. This kind of dot can help you most in your
   (a) spelling   (b) writing   (c) speaking

3. **Offshore** is listed twice because it has different
   (a) importance   (b) pronunciation   (c) meanings or uses

4. This word shows that some dictionary entries are
   (a) old   (b) combinations of words   (c) slang

5. The part that is underlined shows you that **-oid** is a
   (a) whole word   (b) new word   (c) word part

6. The word underlined shows the main word in another
   (a) spelling   (b) word like it   (c) kind of meaning

7. The word *or* shows that there are different ways to
   (a) spell the word   (b) say the word   (c) use the word

8. This shows that the dictionary tells when to use
   (a) old words   (b) capital letters   (c) certain languages

9. The word in small capital letters tells where to turn for
   (a) more information   (b) other spellings   (c) pictures

10. The underlined letter tells how the word is used in
    (a) dictionaries   (b) speaking   (c) sentences

Where to find help in answering the questions:

Question 1 . . . . .page 11a   Question 6 . . . . .page 20a
Question 2 . . . . .page 14a   Question 7 . . . . .page 16a
Question 3 . . . . .page 15a   Question 8 . . . . .page 17a
Question 4 . . . . .page 14a   Question 9 . . . . .page 18a
Question 5 . . . . .page 19a   Question 10 . . . . . . .page 21a   7a

Finding a Word Quickly

The words in the dictionary follow one another in alphabetical order. All the words that begin with the letter *a* come first. Then come the words that begin with *b*. Then come words that begin with *c*, and so on.

Dividing the dictionary into thirds

Here is one way to help you find words in a hurry. Think of the dictionary as having three parts.

In the front part are words beginning with

a   b   c   d   e   f

In the middle part are words beginning with

g   h   i   j   k   l   m   n   o   p

In the back part are words beginning with

q   r   s   t   u   v   w   x   y   z

For fun and practice, try turning right to the listings that begin

d   y   c   p   b   l   r   j   e   t   f   q

Checkup 1

Copy each word on your paper. In what part of the dictionary does each one come? Write *Front*, *Middle*, or *Back* after each word.

1. very	6. dime	11. famous
2. ghost	7. waitress	12. ancient
3. effort	8. loud	13. moon
4. triumph	9. babble	14. safety
5. peculiar	10. zip	15. ready

Alphabetical order by second letters

Suppose you want to find the words **bend, bag, blue,** and **big.** All begin with the same letter, *b.* So which one comes first in the dictionary?

Look at the second letter in each word. You see that they are different: *e, a, l,* and *i.* The letter *a* comes first in the alphabet. Then comes *e.* Then come *i* and *l.* So that words would be listed in this order:

> **bag**
> **bend**
> **big**
> **blue**

Alphabetical order by third letters

Many words begin with the same *two* letters. Here are four that do: **bang, battle, ball,** and **back.** In what order would you find these words? Look at the third letter in each. They are different: *n, t, l,* and *c.*

You know that the letter *c* comes before the others in the alphabet. Then come *l, n,* and *t.* So the words would be listed in this order:

> **back**
> **ball**
> **bang**
> **battle**

Checkup 2

A. First and second letters. Put these words in alphabetical order:

creature
lodge
coil
custom
czar
week
garage
clog
cell
cycle

B. Third letters. Put these words in alphabetical order:

revolve
realize
resent
regular
rewrite
reed
reforest
rely
repose
rebuild

Alphabetical order by fourth and fifth letters

Look at these words: **ball** and **bald.** The first *three* letters are the same. So which word would come first in the dictionary? To find out, look at the *fourth* letters in each word: *l* and *d. D* comes first in the alphabet, so the words are listed in this order:

bald
ball

If the first four letters are the same, look at the *fifth* letters: **millstone, millipede, and millrace.** Which of these three words would be listed first? Why? Which would be listed last? Why?

Alphabetical order with spaces and hyphens

Many listings in the dictionary have spaces or hyphens in them. The same rules about alphabetical order are true for these listings:

alphabetize	**Old English**
alpha particle	**old-fashioned**

Alpha particle comes after **alphabetize,** because *p* comes after *b* in the alphabet. **Old English** comes before **old-fashioned,** because *e* comes before *f* in the alphabet.

Checkup 3

A. Fourth and fifth letters. Write these words in alphabetical order:

tourist
timepiece
tinsmith
towhead
tournament
tower
tinsel

B. Spaces and hyphens. Put these listings in alphabetical order:

warrant officer
woody
warm-blooded
wood pulp
water polo
warmth
warlike
worn-out

Guide words

Here is another way to help you find words quickly. At the top of almost any dictionary page you will see two words in dark type. Look at the top of page 96. There you see the words **coat** and **cog.** What words do you see at the top of page 229?

These words at the top of the page are called *guide words.* They help you find the word you are looking for.

The guide word on the left is the same as the first word alphabetically on the page. The guide word on the right is usually the same as the last word alphabetically on the page. All the words on that page are in alphabetical order between the two guide words.

Checkup 4

Guide words

A. Write these words on your paper. Find them in your dictionary. Next to each word, write the guide words that are on that dictionary page.

1. earthquake
2. mallard
3. recital
4. pavilion
5. institute

6. diamond
7. auction
8. tiptop
9. treat
10. curtail

B. Here are the guide words on one page: **fatal, fear.** Write each word below on your paper. If the word would be on the page with **fatal** and **fear**, write *yes* after it. If the word would come before that page, write *before.* If the word would come after that page, write *after.*

1. fathom
2. fashion
3. felony
4. fare
5. farther

6. feather
7. fauna
8. far-off
9. fawn
10. fealty

1. Alphabetical order by first letters. Write these words in alphabetical order:

prison   shake   litter   toast   open

2. The dictionary in three parts. Where are these words in the dictionary? Write *front, middle,* or *back* after each word.

(a) faraway   (d) queen   (g) pony
(b) nose   (e) trust   (h) steady
(c) dare   (f) jazz   (i) beneath

3. Alphabetical order by second letters. Write these words in alphabetical order:

drama   double   digit   devotion   duck

4. Alphabetical order by third letters. Write these words in alphabetical order:

emu   emerald   ember   employ   emit

5. Alphabetical order by fourth letters. Write these words in alphabetical order:

languor   lane   landlady   lance   lanky

6. Alphabetical order by fifth letters. Write these words in alphabetical order:

signature   signify   signboard   signpost   sign

7. Alphabetical order with spaces and hyphens. Write these in alphabetical order:

hi-fi   jack-in-the-box
highwayman   jackrabbit
higgledy-piggledy   jack-of-all-trades
Highland fling   jack-o'-lantern
high-handed   Jack Frost

8. Guide words. Copy these words. Next to each, write the guide words for the page it is on.

(a) spoonbill   (c) teddy bear   (e) charley horse
(b) fang   (d) flea   (f) beebread

Dictionary Games

A. Guide Word Race

Just the first word of a silly sentence is given below. You must find the next ten. Here's how:

On your paper, write *The* and the blanks, as you see them below. Then look up each word in the list. What guide word is on the left-hand side of the page where you find the word? Write the *guide word* in the blank.

Work with a partner or with a small group. Time yourselves. See who can finish first.

Silly sentence:

The ___ ___ ___ ___ ___ ___ ___ ___ ___ ___.
    1   2   3   4   5   6   7   8   9   10

List:

1. ¹**study**	5. ¹**calf**
2. **mane**	6., 7., and 8. **atop**
3. ¹**some**	9. ²**pitch**
4. **text**	10. ¹**give**

B. What's the Same?

In each group below, the words have something in common. Can you figure out what it is? Use your dictionary. Also, think back to what you have learned from pages 8a-11a.

If you wish, work with a partner or small group. See who can find the likenesses first.

Group 1	Group 2	Group 3
fish	gain	koala
ghost	oak	geranium
jacket	each	locket
hat	aback	spider
marine	machine	boxcar
inside	raccoon	squirrel
over	baby	anchor
port	la	spray gun

13a

Understanding Entries

daylight saving time *n* : time usually one hour ahead of standard time

day·time \'dā-ˌtīm\ *n* : the period of daylight

¹daze \'dāz\ *vb* **dazed**; **daz·ing** **1** : to stun by a sudden blow **2** : to dazzle with light

²daze *n* : a dazed state

¹daz·zle \'daz-əl\ *vb* **daz·zled**; **daz·zling** **1** : to confuse or be confused by too much light or by moving lights **2** : to bewilder, surprise, or excite admiration with a brilliant display — **daz·zler** \'daz-lər\ *n* — **daz·zling·ly** \'daz-ling-lē\ *adv*

²dazzle *n* : something dazzling : GLITTER

DDT \ˌdē-ˌdē-'tē\ *n* : a colorless insecticide that has no smell

de- *prefix* **1** : do the opposite of ⟨*de*activate⟩

Each *main entry* is in dark type at the far left of each column. It shows the right way to spell the word.

After the entry word comes information about it. The entry word and the information together are called an *entry*.

Most main entries are just one word such as **dazzle** or **daze**, above. Some main entries are made of capital letters, such as **DDT**. Others are parts of words, such as **de-**. You may remember that some main entries are made of two or more words. (See page 10a.) Find such an entry above. Sometimes the two words are written as one, as in **daytime.**

The centered dot

In many entry words, you see dots between word parts. These dots can help you in your writing. Sometimes you have to divide a word when you come to the end of a line. You use a hyphen (-) when you do that. The dot shows where you may use a hyphen correctly.

Checkup 5

The centered dot. Copy these words. Find them in the dictionary. Where are the centered dots? Draw lines to show where the word can be divided at the end of a line.

Example: dazzle   daz/zle

1. pajamas
2. cousin
3. restful
4. washer
5. engineer
6. gumdrop
7. courage
8. vegetable

Entries that are spelled alike

---

¹cue \'kyü\ *n* **1** : a word, phrase, or action in a play serving as a signal for the next actor to speak or act **2** : something serving as a signal or suggestion : HINT

²cue *n* : a straight tapering stick used in playing billiards and pool

¹cuff \'kəf\ *n* **1** : a band or turned-over piece at the end of a sleeve **2** : the turned-back hem of a trouser leg

²cuff *vb* : to strike especially with or as if with the palm of the hand : SLAP

³cuff *n* : SLAP

Look at the entries for **cue**. These words are spelled alike. But they have different meanings. Look at the entries for **¹cuff** and **²cuff**. Do they, too, have different meanings?

Now look at the entries for **²cuff** and **³cuff**. You can see that their meanings are much alike. But they are used in different ways in a sentence.

²Cuff is an action word. You would use it in a sentence such as this:

The little girl often *cuffs* her big brother.

³Cuff is a word that names something. You would use it in a sentence such as this:

My sister often gives me a *cuff* on the chin.

Many words are like **¹cue** and **²cue**, **²cuff** and **³cuff**. They are spelled alike. But they have different meanings or uses. Such words are called *homographs*.

As you can see, each homograph has its own entry. The entries are in a certain order. In this dictionary, the order shows which homograph came into our language first. For example, *cuff* meaning *part of a sleeve* came into English first. Later, *cuff* was used meaning *to hit someone*.

Checkup 6

Homographs

A. Find these words in your dictionary. On your paper, write *only* the ones that are homographs.

1. fuse	3. coax	5. irk
2. fly	4. cold	6. ill

B. Find these homographs. Write the meaning or meanings for the ones that came *first* into our language.

1. cull   2. hale   3. meal   4. fib

Different spellings and forms

cook·ie *or* cook·y \'kûk-ē\ *n, pl* cook·ies : a small sweet cake

²plow *or* plough *vb* 1 : to open, break up, or work with a plow ⟨*plow* a furrow⟩ ⟨*plow* the soil⟩ 2 : to move through or cut as a plow does

stream·lined \'strēm-'līnd\ *also* stream·line \-'līn\ *adj* 1 : designed or constructed to reduce resistance to motion through water or air or as if for this purpose ⟨a *streamlined* automobile⟩ 2 : SIMPLIFIED, COMPACT ⟨a *streamlined* version of a play⟩ 3 : MODERNIZED

Most words have only one correct spelling. But a few words can be spelled correctly in more than one way.

• An entry word may have the word *or* after it. Then comes another spelling or form of the word. Look at the entry for **cookie**. How else can it be spelled? Are the two spellings in alphabetical order? Then you know that both are correct. You may use either one and know that you are right.

• Look at the entry for the word **plow**. There are two spellings joined by *or*. But they are *not* in alphabetical order. This tells you that the first spelling is used more often. But both spellings are correct.

• When two words that mean the same and have similar pronunciations occur, they are usually different forms of the same word. Different forms, such as *toward* and *towards* are handled in the same way as different spellings.

• Sometimes two spellings or forms are joined by the word *also*. The word *also* lets you know that the first spelling or form is used *much* more than the second one.

Checkup 7

A. Two spellings. Write each word below on your paper. Next to the word, write another spelling for it.

1. caddie
2. orangutan
3. catalog
4. ax
5. gasoline

B. Two forms. Write each word on your paper. Next to it, write another form that it may sometimes have.

1. among
2. acoustic
3. king-size
4. inward
5. edgeways

Entries with capital letters

Au·gust \\'ȯ-gəst\\ *n* [taken into Old English from Latin *Augustus*, the month named after the Roman emperor Augustus Caesar] **:** the eighth month of the year

black–eyed Su·san \\ˌblak-ˌīd-'süz-n\\ *n* **:** a daisy with deep yellow or orange petals and a dark center

braille \\'brāl\\ *n, often cap* [named after its inventor, Louis Braille, a French teacher of the blind who was himself blind] **:** a system of printing for the blind in which the letters are represented by raised dots

french fry *n, often cap 1st F* **:** a strip of potato fried in deep fat ⟨steak and *french fries*⟩

French horn *n* **:** a musical instrument in the form of a long bent cone‑shaped tube flaring at one end and having a funnel‑shaped mouthpiece at the other

The dictionary shows you the right way to spell a word. It also shows you if the word usually begins with a capital letter. See the entry for **August**, at the left.

As you know, some main entries are made up of more than one word. Then the entry will show you if one or more of the words begins with a capital letter. Look at the entries above. Which ones have just one word that begins with a capital letter?

Sometimes, you have a choice about capital letters. See the entry for **french fry.** **French** comes from the name of a land and a people. So you may use a capital *F* (*French fry*) if you wish. The label *often cap 1st F* tells you this.

Now look at the entry for **braille**. As you can see, the word comes from a man's name. You are right if you use a capital *B* or a small *b*.

Checkup 8

Capital letters. Find these entry words. Write them on your paper. Use capital letters where they belong.

1. new world
2. adam's apple
3. t-shirt
4. sweet william
5. big dipper
6. neanderthal man
7. labor day
8. h-bomb
9. gila monster
10. central american

Cross-references

---

besought *past of* BESEECH
¹**best** \'best\ *adj, superlative of* GOOD **1** : good
or useful in the highest degree : most excellent
2 : MOST, LARGEST ⟨the *best* part of a week⟩
¹**calk** \'kȯk\ *var of* CAULK
dick·er \'dik-ər\ *vb* : BARGAIN, HAGGLE

In many main entries, you will find words in small capital letters. These words are called *cross-references*. To find out more about the entry word, turn to the cross-reference word.

For example, see the word **dicker,** above. The cross-references there are *bargain* and *haggle*. So, to find out more about the meaning of **dicker,** you would turn to those two words.

- Some cross-references have labels before them. Look at the entry above for **besought**. It says that it is the *past of* another word. You would turn to that word to find more about the meaning of **besought**. Or you may already know the meaning of *beseech* and not have to look it up.

- Look at the entry for ¹**best**. What label comes before the cross-reference?

- Look at the label before the cross-reference for ¹**calk**. The label is *var of*. You will see this label often in the dictionary. It tells you about another form or spelling of a word.

Checkup 9

Cross-references. Write these words on your paper. Use your dictionary. To what entries would you turn to find out more about each word? Write the cross-reference next to the word. (Be sure to read each entry carefully. You may find more than one cross-reference in it.)

1. ²nigh
2. ²herald
3. ¹blot
4. chute
5. man-of-war

6. ninny
7. nippy
8. ¹true
9. ²curl
10. helter-skelter

Word parts

---

bi- *prefix* **1** : two ⟨*bi*racial⟩ **2** : coming or occurring every two ⟨*bi*monthly⟩ **3** : into two parts ⟨*bi*sect⟩ **4** : twice : doubly : on both sides ⟨*bi*convex⟩
²-ese *n suffix, pl* **-ese** **1** : native or resident of a specified place or country ⟨Chin*ese*⟩ **2** : language of a particular place, country, or nationality ⟨Siam*ese*⟩ **3** : speech, literary style, or diction peculiar to a specified place, person, or group ⟨journal*ese*⟩
¹pro- *prefix* : located in front of or at the front of : front ⟨*pro*thorax⟩

Many entries are not whole words. They are parts of words. These word parts can be put together with root words to make new words. *Root words* are words or parts of words such as *month* in *bimonthly* and *-sect* in *bisect*. The dictionary tells you what each word part means.

● Some word parts come *before* the main word. These word parts are called *prefixes*. In the dictionary, a hyphen comes after each prefix.

Look at the entry for **bi-**, above. After the hyphen comes the label *prefix*. Read the entry. Does it tell you some words that have **bi-** in them?

● Some word parts come *after* the main word. These word parts are called *suffixes*. In the dictionary, a hyphen comes *before* each suffix. Look at the entry for the suffix **-ese**, above. What examples does it give of words that use this suffix?

Now look at the entry for **pro-**. Is it a suffix or a prefix? What two things tell you so?

Checkup 10

A. Prefixes. Here are some prefixes. For each one, write two words that use it. If you need help, use your dictionary.

1. un-
2. mis-
3. super-
4. multi-
5. non-

B. Suffixes. Here are some suffixes. For each one, write two words that use it. If you need help, use your dictionary.

1. -ly
2. -ment
3. -graph
4. -dom
5. -ful

Run-in and run-on entries

¹cot·ton \\'kät-n\\ *n* **1** : a soft fluffy material made up of twisted hairs that surrounds the seeds of a tall plant (**cotton plant**) related to the mallows and that is spun into yarn **2** : thread, yarn, or cloth made from cotton

¹hook \\'hùk\\ *n* **1** : a curved device (as a piece of bent metal) for catching, holding, or pulling something **2** : something that resembles a hook especially in shape — **by hook or by crook** : by any means : fairly or unfairly

hook 1

lov·a·ble \\'ləv-ə-bəl\\ *adj* : having a character that tends to make one loved — **lov·a·ble·ness** *n* — **lov·a·bly** \\-blē\\ *adv*

Look at the entry for **cotton**, at the left. Find the part of the entry that is in parentheses ( ) and dark type. This is called a *run-in entry*. A run-in entry is very close in meaning to the main entry.

Now read the entry for **lovable**. Toward the end, you will find two words in dark type. Each one has a light dash (-) before it. This kind of word is called a *run-on entry*.

Each run-on entry has a form of the main word in it. The main word here is **lovable**. If you did not know the meaning of **lovableness**, you could look up the suffix **-ness**. If you did not know the meaning of **lovably**, you could find the meaning of the suffix **-ly**. Then, you can always look back to the meaning of the main word.

Find the run-on entry in the entry for **¹hook**, above. There you see a main word in a phrase that people often use. What is the phrase? What does it mean? Many run-on entries are phrases of this kind.

Checkup 11

A. Run-in entries. Write these words on your paper. After each, write the run-in entries you find for it in the dictionary.

1. hemisphere
2. ¹bracket
3. ¹date
4. ¹pepper
5. adder

B. Run-on entries. Write these words on your paper. After each, write the run-on entry or entries you find for it.

1. delicate
2. length
3. ¹hand
4. follow
5. ¹firm

Part-of speech and other labels

---

ab·bre·vi·a·tion \ə-ˌbrē-vē-ˈā-shən\ *n* **1** : a making shorter **2** : a shortened form of a word or phrase used for brevity in writing

¹ca·per \ˈkā-pər\ *vb* : to leap about in a lively manner : PRANCE, FRISK

¹clean \ˈklēn\ *adj* **1** : free from dirt or foreign matter : not soiled ⟨*clean* clothes⟩ **2** : PURE, HONORABLE **3** : THOROUGH, COMPLETE ⟨a *clean* sweep⟩ **4** : SKILLFUL, SMART **5** : EVEN, SMOOTH ⟨a *clean* cut⟩ **6** : SHAPELY, TRIM ⟨a ship with *clean* lines⟩ **7** : cleanly in habits

may \mā\ *helping verb, past* **might** \mīt\; *pres sing & pl* **may** **1** : have permission to ⟨you *may* go now⟩ **2** : be in some degree likely to ⟨you *may* be right⟩ **3** — used to express a wish ⟨*may* you be happy⟩ **4** — used to express purpose ⟨we exercise so that we *may* be strong⟩

Look at the entry for **¹clean**. The label *adj.* is an abbreviation. It stands for a part of speech (*adjective*).

Almost every entry word is followed by a part-of-speech label. A few entry words have more than one. The label tells how the entry word works in a sentence.

For example, the label *vb* tells you that **¹caper** acts as a *verb*, or action word. You could use **¹caper** in a sentence such as this:

The little horse *capers* through the field.

Here are other part-of-speech labels. Which one follows the entry word **abbreviation**?

adv (adverb)	*n* (noun)
conj (conjunction)	*prep* (preposition)
inter (interjection)	*pron* (pronoun)

Look at the label after the entry word **may**, above. The label *helping verb* also helps you know how a word works in a sentence. You could use the word *may* with another verb:

The little horse *may caper* through the field.

Look at page 603 for a list of all the abbreviations and labels used in this dictionary.

Checkup 12

Part-of-speech labels. Write these words on your paper. Find them in the dictionary. Write the part-of-speech label out in full. Do not use abbreviations.

1. ¹off	3. or	5. ¹offer	7. ours
2. ²offer	4. oh	6. ²off	8. ¹old

Understanding Entries

1. Centered dots. Copy these words. Draw lines to show where a word can be divided at the end of a line.

(a) recess   (b) splinter   (c) coyote   (d) spoken

2. Homographs. Find these words. Write only the ones that are homographs. Write the number of times each one is listed.

(a) short   (b) even   (c) cad   (d) compound

3. Different spellings. Write all the spellings for each word. Is one spelling used more often? If so, draw a line under it.

(a) myna   (b) chili   (c) calorie   (d) luster

4. Capital letters. Write the words. Put capital letters where they belong.

(a) thanksgiving day   (b) old glory   (c) geiger counter
(d) japanese beetle   (e) welsh rabbit

5. Cross-references. Write these words. Use your dictionary. Write the cross-references you find at each entry.

(a) bandit   (b) also   (c) ¹spoke   (d) ¹shred

6. Prefixes and suffixes. Write these word parts. After each, write two words that use it. You may use your dictionary.

(a) re-   (b) -less   (c) de-   (d) -ist   (e) -ize

7. Run-in and run-on entries. Copy the words. Next to each write the run-in or run-on entries you find in the dictionary. Remember to put the run-in entries in parentheses (   ).

(a) javelin   (b) ton   (c) ¹short   (d) ¹loud   (e) get

8. Part-of-speech and other labels. Write each entry word. After each, write the label you find in the dictionary.

(a) ¹will   (b) ²tandem   (c) ¹dove   (d) ²list

Dictionary Games

A. Cross-reference Rewrites

There are ten pairs of words below. Look up each word, and you will find a cross-reference.

For example, here is one word pair: *perilous vestibule*. The cross-references for *perilous* are *hazardous* and *dangerous*. The cross-reference for *vestibule* is *lobby*. So you could rewrite *perilous vestibule* as *dangerous lobby*.

Follow the same steps. Rewrite each word pair below. If you wish, work with a partner and time yourselves.

1. [1]vertical jigger
2. opaque mitt
3. affluent jester
4. jaded hag
5. jocund [1]kid
6. [2]melancholy merchant
7. magical [3]sub
8. drear [3]pike
9. plaintive [1]sub
10. [1]madcap ninny

B. What's the Same?

In each group below, the words have something in common. If you use your dictionary, you can figure out what it is. Also, think back to what you have learned from pages 14a-21a.

Group 1	Group 2	Group 3
herd	[1]take	happiness
sour	get	joyful
gorge	[1]head	helpless
course	[1]sour	suggestive
tug	[2]official	renew
much	[1]look	disable
bank	expressive	unhappy
track	air-condition	prepay

23a

²accordion *adj* : folding or creased or hinged to fold like an accordion 〈a skirt with *accordion* pleats〉

ac·cost \ə-ˈkȯst\ *vb* : to approach and speak first to

¹ac·count \ə-ˈkau̇nt\ *n* **1** : a record of money received and money paid out **2** : a statement of business transactions **3** : an arrangement with a seller to supply credit **4** : an explanation of one's conduct **5** : a statement of facts or events : REPORT **6** : WORTH, VALUE **7** : a sum of money deposited in a bank and subject to withdrawal by the depositor — **on account of** : because of : for the sake of — **on no account** : under no circumstances — **on one's account** : for one's benefit

²account *vb* **1** : to think of as : CONSIDER 〈I *account* him lucky〉 **2** : to give an analysis or explanation **3** : to be the only or chief reason

ac·count·a·ble \ə-ˈkau̇nt-ə-bəl\ *adj* **1** : responsible for giving an account : ANSWERABLE **2** : capable of being accounted for : EXPLAINABLE — **ac·count·a·ble·ness** *n* — **ac·count·a·bly** \-blē\ *adv*

ac·count·ant \ə-ˈkau̇nt-nt\ *n* : a person skilled in accounting

ac·count·ing \ə-ˈkau̇nt-iŋ\ *n* : the skill or practice of recording and analyzing money transactions

ac·cred·it \ə-ˈkred-ət\ *vb* **1** : to authorize officially **2** : CREDIT

ac·cre·tion \ə-ˈkrē-shən\ *n* : growth especially by increase from outside

ac·cru·al \ə-ˈkrü-əl\ *n* **1** : the action or process of accruing **2** : something that accrues or has accrued

ac·crue \ə-ˈkrü\ *vb* **ac·crued**; **ac·cru·ing** **1** : to come by way of increase **2** : to accumulate over a period of time

ac·cu·mu·late \ə-ˈkyü-myə-ˌlāt\ *vb* **ac·cu·mu·lat·ed**; **ac·cu·mu·lat·ing** **1** : COLLECT, GATHER **2** : to increase in quantity, number, or amount

ac·cu·mu·la·tion \ə-ˌkyü-myə-ˈlā-shən\ *n* **1** : a collecting together : AMASSING **2** : COLLECTION, HEAP

ac·cu·ra·cy \ˈak-yə-rə-sē\ *n* : freedom from mistakes : EXACTNESS

ac·cu·rate \ˈak-yə-rət\ *adj* : free from mistakes : PRECISE 〈an *accurate* answer〉 — **ac·cu·rate·ly** *adv* — **ac·cu·rate·ness** *n*

ac·cu·sa·tion \ˌak-yə-ˈzā-shən\ *n* : a charge of wrongdoing

ac·cuse \ə-ˈkyüz\ *vb* **ac·cused**; **ac·cus·ing** : to charge a person with a fault or wrong and especially with a criminal offense — **ac·cus·er** *n*

ac·cus·tom \ə-ˈkəs-təm\ *vb* : to make familiar through use or experience

ac·cus·tomed \ə-ˈkəs-təmd\ *adj* **1** : CUSTOMARY, USUAL 〈his *accustomed* lunch hour〉 **2** : USED, WONT 〈*accustomed* to hard luck〉

¹ace \ˈās\ *n* [once spelled *as* in English, the same as in Latin from which it was taken; Latin *as* means "one single thing", "unit"] **1** : a playing card with one large pip in its center **2** : a point scored on a tennis serve that an opponent fails to touch **3** : a combat pilot who has brought down at least five enemy planes **4** : a person who excels at something

²ace *adj* : of first rank or quality

¹ache \ˈāk\ *vb* **ached**; **ach·ing** **1** : to suffer a dull continuous pain **2** : YEARN

²ache *n* : a dull continuous pain

a·chieve \ə-ˈchēv\ *vb* **a·chieved**; **a·chiev·ing** **1** : to bring to a successful end **2** : to get by means of one's own efforts : WIN

a·chieve·ment \ə-ˈchēv-mənt\ *n* **1** : the act of achieving **2** : something achieved especially by great effort or persistence

¹ac·id \ˈas-əd\ *adj* **1** : sour, sharp, or biting to the taste **2** : sour in temper : CROSS 〈*acid* remarks〉 **3** : of, relating to, or having the characteristics of an acid — **ac·id·ly** *adv*

²acid *n* **1** : a sour substance **2** : a sour-tasting hydrogen-containing compound whose water solution turns blue litmus paper red

a·cid·i·ty \ə-ˈsid-ət-ē\ *n, pl* **a·cid·i·ties** : TARTNESS

ac·knowl·edge \ak-ˈnäl-ij\ *vb* **ac·knowl·edged**; **ac·knowl·edg·ing** **1** : to own or admit the truth or existence of 〈*acknowledged* his mistake〉 **2** : to recognize the rights or authority of **3** : to make known that something has been received or noticed

syn ACKNOWLEDGE, ADMIT, CONFESS all mean to make public some private knowledge or information. ACKNOWLEDGE suggests disclosing what could have been kept secret 〈*acknowledged* the fact that she was afraid of dogs〉 ADMIT indicates telling with some unwillingness often as a result of outside insistence 〈finally *admitted* that a new dress wasn't absolutely necessary〉 CONFESS emphasizes the ideas of unwillingness and compulsion and adds to them the idea that a personal fault or failure is the subject of the disclosure 〈*confessed* that he was involved in the playground fight〉

ac·knowl·edged \ak-ˈnäl-ijd\ *adj* : generally recognized or accepted 〈an *acknowledged* leader〉

---

j job   ŋ sing   ō low   ȯ moth   ȯi coin   th thin   <u>th</u> this   ü boot   u̇ foot   y you   yü few   yu̇ furious   zh vision

What Do You Know About Finding Meanings?

Number your paper from 1 to 9. Each numeral goes with one on the dictionary page at the left. Use that page to find your answers. After each numeral, write the word or phrase that makes the *best* ending.

1. The phrase with a line under it gives the entry word's

    (a) uses   (b) definition   (c) pronunciation

2. The entry after numeral 2 has

    (a) 1 sense   (b) 3 senses   (c) 7 senses

3. The run-on entries after numeral 3 have

    (a) special meanings   (b) new uses   (c) certain histories

4. The phrase with a line under it gives an example of

    (a) an exception   (b) the word in use   (c) a run-in entry

5. The underlined words before numeral 5 tell the word's

    (a) senses   (b) history   (c) part of speech

6. The picture goes with ¹ace's

    (a) third definition   (b) first definition   (c) second definition

7. *The scientist put the powder in the acid.* The entry matching *acid* in the sentence above is

    (a) ²acid   (b) ¹acid   (c) neither one

8. The entry for the underlined word will tell more about

    (a) acidity   (b) different examples   (c) other chemicals

9. This paragraph helps to explain differences among

    (a) confessions   (b) entries   (c) synonyms

Where to find help in answering the questions:

Question 1 .....page 26a   Question 6 .....page 29a
Question 2 .....page 27a   Question 7 .....page 30a
Question 3 .....page 31a   Question 8 .....page 26a
Question 4 .....page 29a   Question 9 .....page 28a
Question 5 .page 36a, 37a

Finding the Right Meaning

dog·wood \'dȯg-ˌwu̇d\ *n* : any of a group of shrubs and small trees having clusters of small flowers often surrounded by four showy petallike leaves and in some cases having twigs with bright red-purple bark

dogwood

doi·ly \'dȯi-lē\ *n*, *pl* **doi·lies** : a small often ornamental mat used on a table

do·ings \'dü-ingz\ *n pl* : DEEDS, EVENTS

Just after the main entry you will see a colon (:) in dark type. Then comes the meaning of the main entry. Another word for *meaning* is *definition*, or *sense*.

● Look at the definitions for **dogwood** and **doily**. These are called *phrase definitions*.

● Look at the entry for **doings**. Just after the colon, you see words in small capital letters. These are called *synonymous cross-references*. Synonyms are words that are very much alike in meaning. As you learned on page 18a, a cross-reference tells you to turn to another word in the dictionary. So, to find the meaning of **doings**, look up its synonyms—**deeds**, and **events**.

A synonymous cross-reference may tell you to turn to a certain homograph. In the entry for **castle**, you will see ³ROOK. This means: turn to **³rook** to find one meaning of **¹castle**.

A synonymous cross-reference may tell you to look for a word with a certain numeral after it. On the next page, you will learn about the numerals in entries.

Checkup 13

Phrase definitions and synonymous cross-references. Write these words on your paper. Find their entries. Is the definition a phrase? Then write *P* next to the word. Is the definition a synonymous cross-reference? Then write the synonym or synonyms to which you should turn.

1. donation
2. oxygen
3. prude
4. ¹shoal
5. tiresome
6. facet
7. red corpuscle
8. ²throb

Words with more than one meaning

soothe \'süth\ *vb* **soothed; sooth·ing 1 :** to please by flattery or attention **2 :** RELIEVE **3 :** to calm down : REASSURE, COMFORT
sooth·say·er \'süth-‚sā-ər\ *n* : a person who claims to foretell events
soot·y \'sut-ē, 'sət-\ *adj* **soot·i·er; soot·i·est 1 :** soiled with soot **2 :** resembling soot especially in color
sop \'säp\ *vb* **sopped; sop·ping 1 :** to steep or dip in or as if in liquid : SOAK **2 :** to mop up (as water)
soph·o·more \'säf-ə-‚mōr\ *n* : a student in his second year at a college or high school

Many words have more than one meaning or sense. So, in the dictionary, they have more than one definition. Each definition has a numeral and a colon just before it. Look at the entry for **sooty**, at the left. How many definitions does it have?

In this dictionary, definitions come in a certain order. The order shows which meaning came into the language first, which second, and so on.

● Some words have only definitions that are phrases, like the definitions for **sooty**.

● Some words have definitions that are phrases, and other definitions that are synonyms. Look at definition 1 for **soothe**. Is it a phrase or a synonym? What is definition 2?

● Some definitions are made up of a phrase *and* a synonym. Definition 1 of **sop** is like that. Can you find another example in the entries shown above?

Checkup 14

A. Finding definitions. Write these words and find their entries. Tell how many definitions each word has.

1. desk
2. tell
3. ²command
4. gamely
5. ¹turn
6. ¹flight
7. ¹the
8. nominate
9. ¹sharp
10. dogwood

B. Kinds of definitions. Write and find these words. If the definitions are just phrases, write *P*. If they are phrases and synonyms, write *PS*.

1. nighthawk
2. column
3. gallantry
4. reed
5. corner
6. tenant
7. archer
8. blood

Synonymy paragraphs

¹jour·ney \ˈjər-nē\ *n, pl* **jour·neys** : travel from one place to another : TRIP
  syn JOURNEY, TRIP, TOUR all mean a going or traveling from one place to another. JOURNEY is a very general term but is likely to suggest covering a considerable distance with the possibility of danger and difficulty and adventure ⟨gathering supplies for the long *journey* across the desert⟩ TRIP may suggest relative ease, shortness, or swiftness of travel and applies especially to repeated journeys ⟨the farmer's weekly *trip* to the city⟩ TOUR applies to a usually roundabout journey planned and carried out for some purpose other than reaching a single destination ⟨a walking *tour*⟩ ⟨a lecture *tour*⟩
¹tour \ˈtu̇r\ *n* **1** : a period (as of duty) under an orderly schedule **2** : a trip usually ending at the starting point **syn** see JOURNEY

Look at the entry for **journey**. Find the label syn. This stands for *synonym*. The paragraph after the label is called a *synonymy paragraph*.

As you know, synonyms are words with meanings that are much alike—but not *exactly* alike. A synonymy paragraph tells about the small differences in meaning among the synonyms.

What three synonyms can you find out about in the synonymy paragraph above?

Look at the entry for **¹tour**, above. At the end is the label **syn**. Then comes the word *see* and a synonym, JOURNEY. This means that you will find a synonymy paragraph at the entry for **journey**. Many other entries are like this. They ask you to turn to a synonymy paragraph to find out more about a word's meaning.

Checkup 15

Synonymy paragraphs
A. Write these words and find the entries. Next to each word, tell what synonymy paragraph the entry sends you to.

1. ³close   3. ¹group   5. mislay
2. mythical   4. ¹toil   6. ²ape

B. The entry for each word below has a synonymy paragraph. Read the paragraphs carefully. Write the synonyms that each one tells about. Then use each synonym in a sentence of your own.

1. ¹game   2. careful   3. ²rare

Pictures and verbal illustrations

¹rest \'rest\ *n* **1** : REPOSE, SLEEP **2** : freedom from activity : QUIET **3** : a state of motionlessness or inactivity **4** : a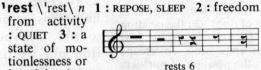
rests 6
place for resting or lodging **5** : a silence in music **6** : a character representing a musical silence **7** : something used for support ⟨a chin *rest* for a violin⟩
²rest *vb* **1** : to get rest by lying down : SLEEP **2** : to give rest to ⟨*rested* himself on the couch⟩ **3** : to lie dead **4** : to refrain from work or activity **5** : to sit or lie fixed or supported ⟨a house *rests* on its foundation⟩ **6** : DEPEND ⟨the success of the flight *rests* on the wind⟩ **7** : to fix or be fixed in trust or confidence ⟨*rested* her hopes on his promise⟩

Many entry words have pictures near them. These help you to know more about what the word means.

Sometimes the picture goes with just one of the definitions of the word. Look at the picture next to the entry **¹rest**, at the left. What numeral do you see in the label? This means that the picture goes with definition **6** of **¹rest**.

Verbal illustrations

An entry often shows you the entry word in phrases or sentences. These phrases and sentences are like word pictures. They help you to understand the different meanings the word can have.

Such phrases and sentences are called *verbal illustrations*. Each verbal illustration is inside angle brackets like these ⟨ ⟩.

How many verbal illustrations do you see in the entry for **²rest**, above?

Checkup 16

A. Pictures. Find the picture of each thing below. Copy the definition that goes with the picture.

1. magnet
2. frog
3. jack
4. horse
5. porpoise
6. measure

B. Verbal illustrations. Use the entry for **²rest**, above. Which definition fits each sentence best?

1. The fawn *rested* in the leaves.
2. The picnic day *rests* with the weather.

Homographs and words in context

¹**bay** \'bā\ *vb* : to bark with long deep tones

²**bay** *n* **1** : the baying of dogs **2** : the position of an animal or a person obliged to face pursuers when it is impossible to escape ⟨brought to *bay*⟩ **3** : the position of pursuers who are held off ⟨kept the hounds at *bay*⟩

³**bay** *n* **1** : a bay-colored horse **2** : a reddish brown

⁴**bay** *n* : a part of a large body of water making an indentation in the land

⁵**bay** *n* : the laurel or a related tree or shrub

As you read, you often find words that are new to you. Or you may find old words that seem to be used in a new way. Read these sentences:

1. The girl rode the bay through the field.

2. He heard Fido's bay.

3. The family went sailing on the bay.

4. There is a large bay growing in our yard.

On page 15a, you looked at some words that are spelled alike. But they had different meanings or uses. Such words, as you may remember, are called *homographs*. What are the homographs in the four sentences above?

You may know the meaning of the word **bay** in sentence 3. But what about the meanings of **bay** in sentences 1, 2, and 4? Study the sentences in which the word is used. That is, study the *context* of the word. Then look at the entries for **bay**. Which one best fits sentence 1? sentence 2? sentence 4?

Think of the context in which you hear or read a new word. The word may be a homograph. If so, knowing the context will help you find the right homograph and the right definition.

Checkup 17

Homographs and words in context. Copy each sentence below. Find the entries for the word that is underlined. Which homograph fits the word best in the context of the sentence? Write the number of the homograph after the sentence.

1. Her father was feeling very <u>cross</u> today.
2. The dye in this cloth is <u>fast</u>.
3. The teachers back us in our wish for a longer <u>recess</u>.
4. The Pirates will <u>trim</u> our team this year.

Run-on entries and idioms

¹fall \'fȯl\ *vb* **fell** \'fel\; **fall·en** \'fȯl-ən\; **fall·ing 1 :** to descend freely by the force of gravity ⟨an apple *fallen* from the tree⟩ **2 :** to come as if by dropping down ⟨night *fell*⟩ **3 :** to become lower (as in degree or pitch) ⟨the temperature *fell* ten degrees⟩ **4 :** to drop from an upright position **5 :** to drop down wounded or dead ⟨*fall* in battle⟩ **6 :** to become captured ⟨the city *fell* to the invaders⟩ **7 :** to decline in quantity, quality, or value ⟨prices *fell* on the stock exchange⟩ **8 :** to occur at a certain time ⟨*falls* on the first Monday of September⟩ **9 :** to pass from one condition of body or mind to another ⟨*fall* asleep⟩ ⟨*fall* ill⟩ — **fall back :** RETREAT — **fall in :** to take one's place in ranks — **fall out 1 :** QUARREL **2 :** to leave one's place in ranks — **fall short :** to be deficient

On page 20a, you looked at some entries called *run-on entries.* Many run-on entries are phrases such as **fall back.** Read the meaning of **fall back** in the entry at the left.

As you can see, the meaning of **fall back** is special. It does not come from the meaning of the separate words **fall** and **back.** It is the two words used together that take on the special meaning. Such phrases are called *idioms.* This dictionary gives the meanings of many idioms.

The English language has hundreds of idioms. To people who have heard them many times, idioms seem clear in meaning. To people who are just learning English, the meaning of idioms is not so clear. What might **fall out** mean to someone just learning English? What does this idiom really mean?

Checkup 18

Idioms

A. Write the idioms that you find at each entry below.

1. ¹set
2. ¹stand

3. carry
4. ¹draw

B. Write each idiom. After it, write the entry at which you found it. Then give the meaning of the idiom.

1. in order to
2. pull through
3. out of sorts

4. in common
5. on the contrary
6. on the sly

Prefixes and meaning

---

pre- *prefix* **1** : earlier than : before ⟨*pre*-historic⟩ : preparatory or prerequisite to ⟨a *pre*medical course⟩ **2** : in advance : beforehand ⟨*pre*pay⟩ **3** : in front of : front ⟨*pre*molar⟩

re- *prefix* **1** : again : anew ⟨*re*tell⟩ **2** : back : backward ⟨*re*call⟩

¹un- \ˌən, ˈən\ *prefix* **1** : not : IN-, NON- ⟨*un*skilled⟩ **2** : opposite of : contrary to ⟨*un*constitutional⟩ ⟨*un*believing⟩ ⟨*un*rest⟩

²un- *prefix* **1** : do the opposite of : reverse a specified action : DE- 1, DIS- 1 ⟨*un*dress⟩ ⟨*un*fold⟩ **2** : deprive of, remove a specified thing from, or free or release from ⟨*un*leash⟩ ⟨*un*hand⟩ **3** : cause to cease to be ⟨*un*man⟩

Some entries are not whole words but word parts. You saw some of them on page 19a.

Many of these word parts, as you may remember, are called *prefixes*. They come before a root word. They change the meaning of the root word in some way.

Read the two entries for **un-**. As you can see, this prefix can make a root word mean just the opposite. **Happy** can become **unhappy. Wise** can become **unwise.** Two synonyms for **un- –de-** and **dis- –**can do the same thing. Put the prefix **dis-** before the root word **agree.** What happens to the meaning of **agree?**

Many words with prefixes are in the dictionary. You can find entries for **prehistoric** and **recount**, for example. But many words with prefixes are not listed. Here are some that are not in this dictionary:

precook	rewind
pretest	reschedule
preview	retell

Suppose you want to know their meanings. You can find the meaning of the prefix. Then you can find the meaning of the root word. Then you build your own definition.

Checkup 19

Prefixes and meaning. The words below are not listed in your dictionary. Write each one on your paper. Find the definition of the prefix. Next, find the definition of the root word. Then write your own definition for the whole word.

1. misaddress   3. uncurious   5. disentwine
2. nonpublic   4. trimotor   6. bimotor

Suffixes and meaning

2-er \ər\ *also* **-i•er** \ē-ər, yər\ *or* **-yer** \yər\ *n suffix* **1** : a person occupationally connected with ⟨hat*ter*⟩ ⟨furr*ier*⟩ ⟨law*yer*⟩ **2** : a person or thing belonging to or associated with ⟨old= tim*er*⟩ **3** : a native of : resident of ⟨cottag*er*⟩ ⟨New York*er*⟩ **4** : one that has ⟨three-deck-*er*⟩ **5** : one that produces or yields ⟨pork*er*⟩ **6** : one that does or performs a specified action ⟨report*er*⟩ ⟨build*er*-upp*er*⟩ **7** : one that is a suitable object of a specified action ⟨broil*er*⟩ **8** : one that is ⟨foreign*er*⟩
-ness \nəs\ *n suffix* : state : condition : quality : degree ⟨good*ness*⟩ ⟨sick*ness*⟩

A suffix is a word part. As you learned on page 19a, a suffix comes *after* a root word.

Look at the entries for the suffix **-er**. (You see that it has other forms — **-ier** and **-yer**.) This suffix can build on the meaning of the root word. Add **-yer** to **law**, and you have **lawyer**.

A suffix usually changes the way a word works in a sentence. That is why a suffix usually has a part-of-speech label after it. Read this sentence. You can see that **build** is an action word, or verb:

She will *build* a house here.

What happens when the suffix **-er** is added to **build**? *Builder* becomes a word that names a person:

The woman is a *builder*.

How is **happy** used in this sentence?

The *happy* man was smiling.

How does the use of **happy** change when **-ness** is added?

His *happiness* made us feel good.

Many words with suffixes are not listed in the dictionary. Here is one that is not: **Americanize**. To find its meaning, you would find the meaning of the suffix **-ize**. Then you would put it with the meaning of the root word, **American**.

Checkup 20

Suffixes and meaning. Here are four suffixes: **-less**, **-er**, **-ful**, and **-ish**. Read each sentence. Choose a suffix to add to the underlined word. Then write a new sentence, using the word with the suffix.

1. The dog had no *home*.
2. The man liked to *write*.
3. She had great *hope* for her team.
4. Chauncey acted like a *child*.

Special meanings of plurals and capitalized words

---

³east *n* **1** : the direction of sunrise : the compass point opposite to west **2** *cap* : regions or countries east of a specified or implied point
fid·dle·stick \'fid-l-,stik\ *n* **1** : a violin bow **2** *pl* : NONSENSE — used as an interjection
gro·cer·y \'grō-sə-rē\ *n, pl* **gro·cer·ies** **1** : the trade, business, or store of a grocer **2** *pl* : the goods sold by grocers

---

Cat means just one cat. *Cats* means more than one cat. That is the way it is with the plurals of most words. (*Plural* means *more than one*.)

But a few words are different. The plural form can have a special meaning. The dictionary tells you about such words.

Look at the entry for **fiddlestick**, above. Now look at the definition for the plural form of the word. (The label *pl* means *plural*). What does **fiddlesticks** mean?

The plural of **grocery** is shown above. What does it mean? How is it different in meaning from the word **grocery**?

Capitalized words and meanings

A few words have a special meaning or use when you begin them with a capital letter. The dictionary points these words out to you.

Look at the entry for **³east**. (The label *cap* means *capitalized*.) Sometimes you may mean **east** as a whole part of the world. Then you would write it with a capital **E**.

Checkup 21

A. Special meanings of plurals. Copy the words that follow. After each one, write the special meaning of its plural.

1. ³slack
2. ¹letter
3. ¹minute
4. ¹glass
5. ²due

B. Special meanings of capitalized words. Copy the words below. Tell what the word means when it is capitalized.

1. pilgrim
2. capitol
3. puritan
4. dipper
5. continent

Usage notes and special labels

---

aer·o·drome \\'ar-ə-‚drōm\ *n*, *Brit* : AIRFIELD
a·ha \ä-'hä\ *interj* — used to express surprise, triumph, or scorn
¹de·cre·scen·do \‚dā-krə-'shen-dō\ *adv* (*or adj*) : with diminishing volume — used as a direction in music
thy \thī\ *adj*, *archaic* : of, relating to, or done by or to thee or thyself

---

Some entries have special notes to help you with meanings. These notes may begin with *used as, used in, used to,* or *usually.* A light dash comes before these *usage notes.*

Find the usage notes in the entries at the left. Which one tells about a word used in music? Which one tells about a sound you make when you are surprised?

Special labels

Some labels tell you that a word is not often used in the United States. Look at the entry for **aerodrome**, above. Find the label *Brit.* This label means *British.* The label lets you know that **aerodrome** is a word most often used by people in England.

Find the entry for **aeroplane**. What label do you see there? What do you think the label means?

A few words have this label: *archaic.* This means that the word is no longer in everyday use among most people. You can see the label in the entry for **thy**, above.

Checkup 22

A. Usage notes. Read through the entry for each word below. Find the usage note. Write each word and usage note on your paper.

1. ²fall
2. ¹knot
3. ¹farewell
4. ⁴fore

B. Special labels. Read the entry for each word below. Find the label. Write the word, label, and definition on your paper.

1. assurance
2. waistcoat
3. draught
4. ²lift

Etymologies: the stories of words

¹date \\'dāt\\ *n* [taken into English from Old French *date*, a word whose source was Greek *daktylos* meaning "finger" and then "date", because the fruit is shaped like a finger] : the sweet brownish edible fruit of an Old World palm (**date palm**)

¹nick·name \\'nik-,nām\\ *n* [in earlier English *a nekename* was the result of misunderstanding the phrase *an ekename*, which meant "an additional name", coming from *eke* "also"] **1** : a usually descriptive name given instead of or in addition to the one belonging to an individual **2** : a familiar form of a proper name

¹school \\'skül\\ *n* [from Old English *scōl*, taken from Latin *schola*, from Greek *scholē*, which meant originally "leisure" and then especially "leisure devoted to learning" and so finally "school"] **1** : a place for teaching and learning **2** : the body of teachers and pupils in a school **3** : a session of school **4** : SCHOOLHOUSE **5** : a body of persons who share the same opinions and beliefs

Each word in our language has a beginning and a history. This beginning and history make up the *etymology* of the word.

In this dictionary, the etymology is in square brackets [ ] in dark type. The brackets come before the colon and the definition of the word. Here are some things an etymology may show you:

1. Read the etymology for **nickname**, above. You can see that the word was used in another form in early England. It has been in our language a long time.

2. Read the etymology for **date**, above. It tells you that the word came into English from another language and how the borrowing took place.

3. Read the etymology of **school**. It came to us from other languages. It has also changed in meaning through the years.

As you see, an etymology may tell about (1) older English words, (2) words from other languages, and (3) words whose meanings have changed through the years.

Checkup 23

Etymologies. Find the etymology for each of the following words.

1. Gypsy
2. ¹flower
3. ²fawn
4. atom
5. democracy
6. ¹fence
7. ²pupil
8. poodle
9. porpoise
10. canopy

Etymologies: words coming into the language

as·tro·naut \\'as-trə-ˌnȯt\\ *n* [formed in English from Greek *astron* "star", found also in *astro*logy and *astro*nomy, and Greek *nautēs* "sailor"] : a traveler in a spacecraft

pa·ja·mas \\pə-'jä-məz, -'jam-əz\\ *n pl* [from Hindi *pājāma*, a compound of Persian *pā* "leg" and *jāma* "garment"] : a loose-fitting usually two-piece suit for lounging or sleeping

ra·dar \\'rā-ˌdär\\ *n* [from the first letters of *ra*dio *d*etecting *a*nd *r*anging] : a radio device for detecting the position of distant masses and the course of moving objects (as distant airplanes or ships)

watt \\'wät\\ *n* [named in honor of James *Watt* (1736-1819), the Scotch engineer who invented the modern steam engine] : a unit for measuring electric power

We are always adding new words to our language. The etymology of a word can tell you how it came into English. Here are some of the ways:

1. *Words from another language.* Some words come into English without a change. **Pajamas** is a word like that. Read its etymology. From what language does the word **pajamas** come?

2. *Words from people's names.* Look at the etymology of the word **watt**. Where did the word come from? Can you remember another word like this? Look back at page 17a.

3. *Words made up of letters from separate words.* Look at the etymology for **radar**. How was the word made?

4. *Words formed from other languages.* Scientists need many new words. They often make them by putting together words from other languages. Read the etymology for **astronaut**. What do the two parts of the word mean in Greek?

Checkup 24

Etymologies. Make two columns on your paper. Find the etymologies of the words below. Some words came into our language from an older kind of English. Write those words in the first column. Write the other words in the second column. Tell what language or languages they came from.

1. etymology
2. daisy
3. vinegar
4. orangutan
5. lady
6. czar
7. marmalade
8. happy
9. skipper
10. rather
11. decal
12. barn

Finding the Right Meaning

1. Different kinds of definitions. Write the words. Find their entries. If the definition is a phrase, write (P). If it is a cross-reference, write (CR).

(a) lockjaw   (b) stylus   (c) elegy   (d) afoul   (e) ¹aid

2. More than one meaning. Write each word. Tell how many definitions it has.

(a) ¹hang   (b) album   (c) ¹shoot   (d) locust   (e) ¹base

3. Synonmy paragraphs. Find the synonmy paragraphs at these entries. Write the synonyms each one tells about.

(a) ask   (b) scoff   (c) ²fake   (d) speak   (e) weak

4. Verbal illustrations. Find the entries for these words. (Note the definition number after each one.) Write the verbal illustration given for that definition.

(a) weigh **2**   (b) system **2**   (c) ²lodge **1**   (d) ¹trouble **4**

5. Homographs and words in context. Copy the words underlined. Write the numeral of the homograph that best fits it: The troll tripped the kid as it tramped over the bridge.

6. Idioms. Write the idioms that you find at these entries.

(a) ¹turn   (b) get   (c) ¹look   (d) ¹make   (e) ⁴wind

7. Prefixes and suffixes. Write your own definition for each word. Then use it in a sentence of your own.

(a) sweetish   (b) multicolored   (c) bendable   (d) nontoxic

8. Special labels. Write the special label or usage note that you find at each of these entries:

(a) ho   (b) ²inland **1**   (c) adios   (d) ¹monkey **1**

9. Etymologies. Write the etymology for each word.

(a) magnet   (b) science   (c) nucleus

Dictionary Games

A. Idiom Pictures

In each sentence below, the idiom is underlined. Work with each idiom in two ways:

First, suppose you do not know English very well. Suppose you do not know what the idiom means. Draw a picture to show what you might then think the sentence means.

Second, find the idiom in an entry in your dictionary. Read its meaning. Then rewrite the sentence. Use other words in place of the idiom to show that you know what the sentence means.

1. Hiram tried to keep up his good marks.
2. The neighbor's noisy car gets my goat.
3. Mr. George looked up to the principal.
4. Myra was carried away by the music.
5. She brings up her children carefully.
6. The speaker was over my head.
7. Helen drew out the information from Isabel.
8. The secretary will wind up the meeting.
9. Clarence takes in all the news.
10. The president put the bill through the House.

B. Etymology Game

Each sentence below has an underlined word. Find the etymology for that word. What was the meaning of the word in the language from which it came? Write the sentence over. Use that first meaning in place of the underlined word.

EXAMPLE: The movie was just mediocre.

The movie was just *halfway up the mountain.*

1. A caterpillar crawled up my arm.
2. There is too much garlic in this hamburger.
3. The lens fell out of my eyeglasses.
4. I can see the planet Mars.
5. We sat under the obelisk in the park.

39a

Pronunciation Symbols

ə
banana	mitten	capital	cotton	suppose	perplex
bun	lunch	putty	color	supper	pup
burn	learnt	pert	curl	serpent	purple

(In the words in the first line above, ə (called *schwa* \'shwä\) is spoken with weak force. In the words in the other lines ə is spoken with stronger force.)

a	ax, map	n	nine, cotton
ā	age, vacation, day	ng	sing, singer, finger, ink
ä	father, cot, cart	ō	low, bone, cooperate
ȧ	[a sound between \a\ and \ä\, as in an eastern New England pronunciation of aunt, half]	ȯ	moth, law, sort, all
		ȯi	coin, destroy
au̇	out, now	p	pepper, lip
b	baby, rib	r	rarity
ch	chin, match, nature \'nā-chər\	s	spice, less
		sh	shy, dish, machine, mission, special
d	did, ladder	t	tight, latter
e	less	th	thin, ether
ē	seaweed, any, serial, cereal	th	this, either
f	fifty, cuff, phone	ü	boot, rule
g	gift, pig, bigger	u̇	foot, pull
h	hat, ahead	v	give, vivid
i	trip	w	we, away
ī	life, buy, my	y	you, yet
j	job, gem, edge	yü	few, union, mule, youth
k	kin, cook, chasm	yu̇	furious
l	lily, pool, mortal	z	zone, raise
m	murmur	zh	vision, beige

\\ The slant lines mark the beginning and end of a pronunciation: \'pen\.

ˈ A high vertical mark is at the beginning of a syllable that has primary (strongest) stress: \'pen-mən-ˌship\.

ˌ A low vertical mark is at the beginning of a syllable that has secondary (next-strongest) stress: \'pen-mən-ˌship\.

- A hyphen separates syllables in pronunciation respellings: **build·ing** \'bil-ding\.

( ) Parentheses show that what is between may be in the pronunciation of the word at some times but not at others: \'fak-t(ə)-rē\.

What Do You Know About Pronunciation?

Look at page 40a. The part in color shows *pronunciation symbols*. Many of the symbols look like letters of the alphabet. But they are not letters. The symbols stand for *sounds* in our language. Each sound may be spelled in different ways.

The pronunciation symbols are also listed inside the front and back covers of this dictionary. Some of the symbols are along the bottom of the dictionary pages.

Find out how much you know about sounds and symbols.

1. List all the consonant symbols. For each, say the sample words. Next to each symbol, write two other words that have that sound.

2. List all the vowel symbols. Say the sample words for each. Then write two other words that have that sound.

3. What is the name of the symbol for which most examples are given on page 40a?

4. Look at the entry words and pronunciations. What does the centered dot tell you? What does the hyphen tell you?

   (a) **cam·el** \'kam-əl\   (b) **par·ty** \'pärt-ē\

5. Copy these pronunciations. Draw two lines under the syllables that receive strongest stress. Draw one line under the syllables that receive next-strongest stress.

   (a) \'biz-ē-,bäd-ē\   (b) \'sak-sə-,fōn\

6. Find the entries for these words. Tell how many correct pronunciations each one has:

   (a) status   (b) ¹half   (c) sumac

7. Find these homographs. Which pair is pronounced the same? Which ones are pronounced differently?

   (a) ¹appeal, ²appeal   (b) ¹project, ²project

Where to find help in answering the questions:

Question 1 .. pages 43a-44a
Question 2 .. pages 45a-46a
Question 3 .... page 45a
Question 4 .... page 42a
Question 5 ...... page 42a
Question 6 ...... page 47a
Question 7 ...... page 48a

41a

Pronouncing Words Correctly

cob·bler \'käb-lər\ *n* **1 :** a person who mends or makes shoes **2 :** a deep-dish fruit pie with a thick upper crust
cob·ble·stone \'käb-əl-,stōn\ *n* **:** a naturally rounded stone larger than a pebble and smaller than a boulder used especially in paving streets
co·bra \'kō-brə\ *n* **:** a very poisonous snake of Asia and Africa that puffs out the skin around its neck into a hood when excited
cob·web \'käb-,web\ *n* **1 :** the fine network spread by a spider **2 :** something resembling or suggesting a spider's web

A syllable is part of a spoken word. Some words, such as *pie,* have one syllable. Other words, such as *potato* and *peanut,* have more than one syllable.

The dictionary entry shows how many syllables a word has. Between two syllables is a *hypehn* (-). Look at the entry for **cobblestone.** Look between the slanted lines (\ \). How many syllables does **cobblestone** have?

Stress marks

When you say a word, you give the syllables different *stress.* Another word for *stress* is *loudness.* There are three stresses.

1. **Strong stress.** A high up-and-down mark at the beginning of a syllable shows strong stress on that syllable.

2. **Medium stress.** A low up-and-down mark at the beginning of a syllable shows it is said less loudly.

3. **Weak stress.** If a syllable has no up-and-down mark in front of it, then you know it has weak stress.

Checkup 25

A. Syllables. Find and write these words. Next to each, tell how many syllables.

1. stemmed
2. responsibility
3. wily
4. plaque
5. dillydally

B. Stress. Use the entries above. Write the entry word or words that have:

1. strong stress on 1st syllable
2. medium stress on 2nd syllable
3. weak stress on 2nd syllable

42a

The consonant symbols

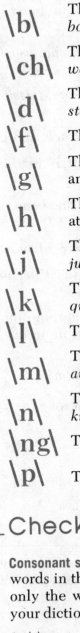

\b This symbol stands for the consonant sound heard in *boy,* and *robber.*

\ch The \ch\ sound is heard in words such as *church, watch, question,* and *pension.*

\d This stands for the sound heard in *dad, daddy,* and *stayed.*

\f This sound is in *fan, offer, telephone,* and *cough.*

\g This symbol stands for the sound in *go, egg, ghost,* and *guard.*

\h This sound is heard in *hat* and *behind.* It comes only at the beginning of syllables.

\j This stands for the sound in *jam, gem, page, fudge, judgment,* and *soldier.*

\k This sound is heard in *kite, cat, pick, chemist, ache, quite,* and *antique.*

\l This sound is heard in *lap,* and *pull.*

\m This symbol stands for the sound in *made, trimmer, autumn,* and *bomb.*

\n This stands for the sound in *net, winner, gnaw, knight,* and *pneumonia.*

\ng This stands for the sound in *sing,* and *rink.*

\p This stands for the sound heard in *pan,* and *happen.*

Checkup 26

Consonant symbols. Copy the consonant symbols. Say the words in the row after each symbol. Next to the symbol, write only the words that have that sound in them. You may use your dictionary.

1. \j\	giant	edge	gone	song	barge
2. \ch\	charm	catch	machine	rush	shake
3. \f\	graph	cough	offer	cage	of
4. \g\	gem	fudge	high	guard	trigger

The consonant symbols

\r\ — This stands for the sound heard in *brass, merry, rhubarb,* and *write.*

\s\ — This sound is heard in *say, miss, scene, psychology, cent,* and *quartz.*

\sh\ — This stands for the sound in *fish, sure, mission, special, nation,* and *machine.*

\t\ — This stands for the sound in *sat, attack,* and *walked.*

\th\ — This symbol is called *plain t-h.* It is in *thing* and *breath.*

\t̲h̲\ — This is called *bar t-h.* It is heard in *these* and *breathe.*

\v\ — This stands for the sound heard in *very, of,* or *Stephen.*

\w\ — This consonant sound is in *wait, twist persuade,* or *choir.* It comes only before vowels.

\y\ — This consonant sound is heard in *yes,* or *onion.* It is also the first of two sounds spelled *ue* in *cue, ew* in *few,* and *eu* in *feud.*

\z\ — This sound is heard in *zone, buzz,* or *busy.*

\zh\ — This stands for the sound in *vision* or *rouge.*

Checkup 27

Consonant symbols. Copy the consonant symbols. Say the words in the row after each symbol. Next to the symbol, write only the words that have that sound in them. You may use your dictionary.

1. \th\	hatch	them	think	bath	earth
2. \s\	cats	is	cost	easy	city
3. \t\	hopped	the	batter	watch	pretty
4. \t̲h̲\	heart	thank	breathe	that	through

The vowel symbols

\ə\ This stands for one of the sounds most used in English. The symbol is called *schwa*. The \ə\ sound is very common in unstressed syllables, as in *banana* and the first syllable of *above*. In stressed syllables it is pronounced as in both syllables of *humdrum* and the second syllable of *above*. Before \r\, the sound is as in *bird, fur, perceive, other*, and *hurry*.

\a\ *Plain a* stands for the sound in *fat*.

\ā\ *Bar a* stands for the sound in *age, main, vein, break, day, prey*, and *gauge*.

\ä\ *Two-dot a* stands for the sound in *cot*. Most speakers use this sound for the *a* in *cart* and *father*.

\à\ *One-dot a* stands for the vowel sound used by some speakers in *aunt* and *cart*, and in the first syllable of *father*.

\e\ *Plain e* stands for the sound in *met, said, says, death*, and *friend*.

\ē\ *Bar e* stands for the vowel sound in *feed, seat, field, he, key*, and *ever*.

Checkup 28

Vowel sounds. Copy the vowel symbols on the left. Say the words in the row after each symbol. Next to the symbol, write only the words that have that sound in them. You may use your dictionary.

1.	\ē\	steep	plead	bread	believe	debt
2.	\ā\	break	reign	wash	faint	bray
3.	\e\	steak	any	people	tent	thread
4.	\ä\	stop	trap	shawl	shout	lots
5.	\ə\	shut	push	away	come	worth
6.	\a\	plaid	slate	batter	wealthy	barrel

The vowel symbols

\i\   *Plain i* stands for the vowel sound in *sit, build, hymn,* and *sieve.* You can also hear it in the stressed syllable of *busy* and *women.*

\ī\   *Bar i* stands for the vowel sound in *light, height, try, buy, bite,* and *aisle.*

\ō\   *Bar o* stands for the vowel sound in *go, coat, though, beau, cone, sew,* and *bowl.*

\ȯ\   *One-dot o* stands for the vowel sound in *soft, corn, saw, all, caught, fought,* and *broad.*

\ü\   *Two-dot u* stands for the vowel sound in *flu, school, blue, youth, rule,* and *crew.*

\u̇\   *One-dot u* stands for the vowel sound in *pull, wood,* and in the first syllable of *sugar.*

\au̇\   Say the word *out.* Two vowels come together as part of one syllable \'au̇t\. Two vowels coming together this way form a *diphthong.* You hear the diphthong \au̇\ in *cow* and *sound,* too.

\ȯi\   This dictionary uses two diphthong symbols. One is \au̇\. The other is \ȯi\. This stands for the vowel sound in *join* and *boy.*

Checkup 29

Vowel symbols. Copy the symbols on the left. Say the words in the row after each symbol. Next to the symbol, write only the words that have that sound in them. You may use your dictionary.

1. \i\	might	gym	dine	dinner	fruit
2. \ō\	son	shone	on	float	blow
3. \u̇\	put	book	sure	moon	mule
4. \ī\	flier	siege	signal	guy	trial
5. \ȯ\	tall	ought	though	plow	broaden
6. \ü\	news	hood	butter	fool	ruler
7. \au̇\	pound	brown	loudly	youngster	daughter
8. \ȯi\	tortoise	employ	choir	coyote	chamois

Different pronunciations

> **²di·gest** \dī-'jest, də-\ *vb* **1** : to think over and arrange in the mind ⟨*digest* a lesson⟩ **2** : to change food into simpler forms that can be taken in and used by the body **3** : SUMMARIZE **4** : to become digested
>
> **gal·lant** *adj* **1** \'gal-ənt\ : NOBLE, BRAVE **2** \gə-'lant\ : very polite to women
>
> **¹route** \'rüt, 'raût\ *n* : an established, selected, or assigned course of travel
>
> **tur·quoise** \'tər-ˌkȯiz, -ˌkwȯiz\ *n* : a blue to greenish gray mineral used as a gem

Some words can be pronounced in different ways. The dictionary shows you these different ways. All of them are correct. But the first one usually is used more often.

Often, the different pronunciations are shown in full. Look at the entry for **¹route,** above. Say the word in the two ways. Which pronunciation do you use?

● Often, only part of a different pronunciation is shown. Look at the pronunciation for **²digest,** above. It shows you that the first part can also be pronounced \də-\. The hyphen *after* \də-\ means that the *last* part of the word is pronounced the same: \də-'jest\.

● Look at the pronunciation for **turquoise.** Find this part: \-ˌkwȯiz\. Notice the hyphen *before* it. This means that the *first* part of the word is pronounced the same: \'tər-ˌkwȯiz\.

● Look at the entry for **gallant.** You see two meanings. You also see two pronunciations. Some words are like this. The word may be pronounced in a different way when it is used with a special meaning.

Checkup 30

Different pronunciations. Find each word in your dictionary. Write all the pronunciations for each word. (Write each pronunciation out in full.) Put a circle around the pronunciation that *you* use.

1. depot	6. envelope
2. suggest	7. ¹adult
3. long-lived	8. ¹roof
4. chimpanzee	9. kilometer
5. Halloween	10. ¹water

Same spelling, different pronunciations

---

con·jure \'kän-jər, 'kən-jər; *in sense 1* kən-'jür\ *vb* **con·jured; con·jur·ing** **1** : to entreat earnestly or solemnly : BESEECH **2** : to summon by invocation or incantation **3** : to practice magical arts

¹des·ert \'dez-ərt\ *n* : a dry barren region where only a few special kinds of plants grow without an artificial water supply

²desert *adj* : of, relating to, or being a desert

³de·sert \di-'zərt\ *n* **1** : worthiness of reward or punishment ⟨rewarding each according to his *deserts*⟩ **2** : a just reward or punishment

⁴de·sert \di-'zərt\ *vb* **1** : to withdraw from **2** : to leave a person or a thing that one should stay with **3** : to fail in time of need   **syn** see ABANDON — **de·sert·er** *n*

You know that some entry words are spelled alike. But they have different meanings or uses. Such words are called *homographs*.

Most homographs are pronounced the same. Then the pronunciation is shown only once, for the first entry. See the entries for **¹desert** and **²desert**, above. **²Desert** is pronounced as **¹desert** is. So, no pronunciation is given for **²desert**.

Now look at the entries for **³desert** and **⁴desert**. Are they pronounced in the same way as **¹desert**? How do you know?

If homographs have different pronunciations, the dictionary will show these differences. If a word is pronounced in a special way for a special meaning, a note may tell you this, too. Look at the pronunciation for **conjure.** What does the pronunciation note tell you?

Checkup 31

Pronouncing homographs. There is a line under the homographs in each sentence pair below. Write the homographs on your paper. Find their entries in the dictionary.

Read each sentence carefully. Which homograph best fits the context of the sentence? Next to the homograph, write its numeral and its pronunciation.

1. (a) The ranger will *lead* us through the park.
   (b) The *lead* in this pencil is soft.
2. (a) Susan went fishing and caught a *bass.*
   (b) He sings *bass* in the school chorus.
3. (a) This food is easy to *digest.*
   (b) They borrowed a *digest* of the book.

Entries with parts of, or no, pronunciations

bi·car·bon·ate of soda \bī-'kär-bə-nət-, -ˌnāt-\ : SODIUM BICARBONATE

¹dear \'diər\ *adj* **1** : highly valued : LOVED **2** — used as a form of address in letters and sometimes in speech ⟨*Dear* Sir⟩ **3** : high-priced **4** : HEARTFELT, EARNEST — **dear·ness** *n*

ground crew *n* : the mechanics and technicians who maintain and service an airplane

nois·y \'nȯi-zē\ *adj* **nois·i·er; nois·i·est** : making noise : full of noises ⟨a *noisy* street⟩ — **nois·i·ly** \-zə-lē\ *adv* — **nois·i·ness** \-zē-nəs\ *n*

Find the run-on entries for **noisy**. As you see, *part* of each pronunciation is given. The missing syllables will be found in a word before it.

Look at the run-on entry **dearness**. No pronunciation is given. You could look up the pronunciation of the suffix **-ness**. And then, you could look at the pronunciation for **dear**. Then, on your own, you could figure out the pronunciation of **dearness**.

Many entries have more than one word. Sometimes, the pronunciation for only part of the entry is shown. Look at the entry for **bicarbonate of soda**. For which part is the pronunciation shown? How would you find the pronunciation for the other two words in the entry?

Some entries have no pronunciation at all. See the entry above for **ground crew**. Suppose you did not know how to say it. You could look up the entry for **ground**. Then you could look up the entry for **crew**.

Checkup 32

Parts of pronunciations. Write each entry and run-on entry below. For some of them, the dictionary shows no pronunciation. For others, the dictionary shows part of the pronunciation.

Figure out the *whole* pronunciation for each entry. Write the pronunciation on your paper.

1. sea dog
2. dimness
3. marksmanship
4. redwing blackbird
5. plasterer
6. nerve cell
7. crab apple
8. second lieutenant
9. mutually
10. responsibility

Pronouncing Words Correctly

1. Hyphens. Copy each word. Tell how many syllables it has. Then decide: Is the word divided in speaking as it is writing? If so, draw a circle around it.

(a) believe   (b) postage   (c) freedom   (d) factory

2. Stress marks. Copy these words. Find and copy their pronunciations. Draw two lines under syllables that have strong stress. Draw one under syllables with medium stress.

(a) bubble   (b) molecule   (c) herself   (d) reappear

3. Consonant symbols. Copy the pronunciations. Write the correct consonant symbol in place of each question mark.

(a) ledge \'le?\   (c) hatch \'ha?\
(b) descent \di-'?ent\   (d) know \'?ō\

4. Vowel symbols. Copy each word. After it write the symbol for the vowel sound or diphthong in the word.

(a) loud   (b) knee   (c) boot   (d) rag

5. Different pronunciations. Give all the pronunciations for each word. Write each pronunciation in full.

(a) ¹lever   (b) adios   (c) drama   (d) toward

6. Pronouncing homographs. Write the homographs on your paper. Next to each, write two ways it can be pronounced.

(a) record   (c) subject
(b) separate   (d) object

7. Parts of, or no, pronunciations. For each entry below, figure out the whole pronunciation. Write it on your paper.

(a) tree fern   (b) stalker   (c) equally   (d) boneless

Dictionary Games

A. Pronunciation Race

Play this with a partner. Time yourselves. Write each sentence below. Say the pronunciations at the left. Which one stands for the word that belongs in the blank? Write that *word* in the blank.

\\'bəg\ \beg\   1. Many dogs ____ for food.

\\'mēt-ər\ \\'mēt-ē-ər\   2. A unit of length is a ____.

\\'kȯil\ \\'kaȯl\   3. A ____ of rope is in the garage.

\\'fäks\ \\'fāks\   4. The jewels were all ____.

B. Riddles in Symbols

Here are some riddles. The answers are written with pronunciation symbols. Figure out and write each answer. Then match it with a riddle question.

1. What's light, but can't be held for ten minutes?
2. What has eyes but cannot see?
3. Why is your nose in the middle of your face?
4. What do you get from ducks and a cow?
5. How do you get into a locked house?
6. Why do birds fly south?
7. Why did the ball player put milk in his hat?
8. What has two tongues but can't talk?
9. Why is a giraffe's neck so long?
10. Why are fish so smart?

ANSWERS

a. \bi-'kȯz\ \it\ \iz\ \thə\ \\'sent-ər\

b. \it\ \iz\ \tü\ \\'fär\ \tə\ \\'wȯk\

c. \ə\ \pə-'tāt-ō\

d. \hē\ \wəz\ \thə\ \\'pich-ər\

e. \its\ \\'həd\ \iz\ \sō\ \\'fär\ \frəm\ its\ \\'bäd-ē\

f. \yər\ \\'breth\

g. \\'rən\ \ə-'raȯnd\ \ən-ˌtil\ \yü\ \är\ \\'ȯl\ \in\

h. \ə\ \\'paər\ \əv\ \\'shüz\

i. \thər\ \\'ȯl-wēz\ \in\ \\'skülz\

j. \\'kwak-ərs\ \and\ \\'milk\

51a

A Spelling Handbook

English spelling is not always easy. But you already
know much about it. And you
have learned about spelling
helps that are in this dictionary.

1. The pronunciation key. It
shows you that a sound can be
spelled in more than one way.
Suppose you *hear* the word
\'käl-ə-rə\. You know that the
sound \k\ sound can be spelled
with a *k*, a *c*, or a *ch*. So, you
know three places to begin
looking for the word with the
sound. \'käl-ə-rə\.

2. The dictionary itself. It
gives you the correct spelling
of a word. It also tells you if
the word has more than one
correct spelling.

A
Spelling
Handbook

3. This Spelling Handbook.
Here you can learn:

Finding Verb Forms

clothe \\'klōth\\ *vb* **clothed** *or* **clad** \\'klad\\; **cloth·ing** **1** : to cover with or as if with clothing : DRESS **2** : to provide with clothes ⟨fed and *clothed* his family⟩ **3** : to express by suitably significant language

bring \\'bring\\ *vb* **brought** \\'brȯt\\; **bring·ing** **1** : to cause to come with oneself by carrying or leading ⟨told to *bring* lunches⟩ ⟨*bring* your friend⟩ **2** : to cause to come into a particular state or condition **3** : to cause to arrive or come about ⟨heavy losses *brought* by the storm⟩ — **bring about** : to cause to take place : ACCOMPLISH — **bring forth** : to give birth to : PRODUCE — **bring to** : to restore to consciousness — **bring up** : REAR ⟨*bring up* a child⟩

Most verbs in English are *regular*. There is a present, or plain, form, such as *look*. To show the past, you add *-ed* (*looked*). Usually, you can use this past form as a *past participle*, too. That is, you can use it with a word such as *have* (*have looked*).

Then there is the *-ing* form for the verb (*looking*). This *-ing* form is called the *present participle*.

Not all verbs are regular, however. Some have special spellings or forms. They are *irregular*. The dictionary tells you about them. Look at the entry word **bring,** above. It is the present, or plain, form. Then comes the past form, **brought.** (If the past participle were different, it would come next.) Then comes the *-ing* form, **bringing.**

Some verbs have more than one form for the past or past participle. Look at the entry for **clothe.** You see the word *or* between two past forms. This means you can use either one.

Some verb forms are listed in their own alphabetical place:

taught *past of* TEACH

Checkup 33

Forms of verbs. Write each plain form on your paper. Find it in your dictionary. After it, write the past form. If the past participle form is different, write that next. (Is there more than one correct form for the past or past participle? If so, write them both.) Last, write the *-ing* form.

1. begin
2. sing
3. drive
4. fall
5. awake
6. draw
7. grind
8. strive
9. dive

53a

Finding Forms of Adjectives and Adverbs

¹good \'gủd\ *adj* **bet·ter** \'bet-ər\; **best** \'best\ **1** : suitable for its purpose : SATIS-FACTORY ⟨a *good* light for reading⟩ **2** : having or being over the required amount : FULL ⟨a *good* day's work⟩ **3** : CONSIDERABLE ⟨a *good* deal of trouble⟩ **4** : DESIRABLE, ATTRAC-TIVE ⟨a *good* job⟩ **5** : HELPFUL, KIND **6** : be-having well ⟨a *good* boy⟩ **7** : being honest and upright **8** : SOUND, RELIABLE ⟨*good* advice⟩ **9** : up to the standard : not bad ⟨*good* work⟩

sad \'sad\ *adj* **sad·der**; **sad·dest** **1** : filled with sorrow or unhappiness **2** : causing sorrow or gloom — **sad·ly** *adv* — **sad·ness** *n*

Most adjectives and adverbs are *regular*. The adjective *tall* is an example. To make the *comparative* form, you add -*er* (*taller*). To make the superlative form, you add -*est* (*tallest*).

Many regular adjectives and adverbs are longer words. Then the words *more* and *less* may be used in the comparative form (*more dangerous, less calmly*). *Most* and *least* may be used in the superlative form (*most dangerous, least calmly*).

Some adjectives and adverbs are *irregular*. The dictionary tells you about them. Look at the entry for the adjective **good**, above. What is the comparative form? What is the superlative form?

Some adjectives change in spelling when they take on new forms. The dictionary will show these spelling changes. Look at the entry for **sad**. How does the root word (**sad**) change when -*er* and -*est* are added?

Some adverbs and adjectives are homographs. So are their comparative and superlative forms. So the forms of just one may be shown:

> **³close** .... *adj* **clos·er**; **clos·est**
> **⁴close** .... *adv*

Checkup 34

A. Adjective forms. Write the comparative and superlative forms of these adjectives:

1. ¹pretty   3. big
2. ¹noble   4. beautiful

B. Adverb forms. Write the comparative and superlative forms of these adverbs:

1. ³well   3. ²free
2. ²much   4. ²deep

54a

Finding Plurals of Nouns

a·lum·nus \ə-'ləm-nəs\ *n, pl* **a·lum·ni** \-,nī\ : one who has attended or has graduated from a school, college, or university

¹**ba·by** \'bā-bē\ *n, pl* **ba·bies** **1** : a child too young to talk or walk **2** : a childish person **3** : the youngest of a group

bus \'bəs\ *n, pl* **bus·es** *or* **bus·ses** : a large motor-driven passenger vehicle

mice *pl of* MOUSE

mouse \'maùs\ *n, pl* **mice** \'mīs\ : a furry gnawing animal resembling but smaller than the related rats

sheep \'shēp\ *n, pl* **sheep** **1** : an animal related to the goat that is raised for its flesh, wool, and skin **2** : a timid weak defenseless person **3** : SHEEPSKIN

Plural means *more than one.* To show the plurals of most nouns, you add -*s* or -*es.*

Some nouns make their plurals in other ways. They are called *irregular plurals.* The dictionary will show them to you. Here are some examples:

A few nouns come from foreign languages and keep the foreign plural. See **alumnus,** above, as an example. What is its plural?

For some nouns, the root word changes when the plural is formed. Look at the entry for **baby,** above. How does the root change when the plural ending is added?

Some nouns have more than one plural. Can you find such a noun among the entries above?

For a few nouns, the plural form is just the same as the singular form. The noun **sheep** is like that.

A few nouns make their plurals by changing some of the middle letters of the singular form. See the word **mouse** as an example.

Some plural forms of nouns have their own listing, too. See **mice,** above.

Checkup 35

Plurals of nouns. Use your dictionary. Write the plural or plurals of each of these nouns.

1. dwarf	4. child	7. appendix
2. axis	5. overalls	8. ox
3. corps	6. goose	9. mother-in-law

Some Rules for Forming Plurals of Nouns

1. Most nouns form their plurals just by adding -s:

rug   rugs

This rule is true of:
- most nouns ending in silent -e: house   houses
- most nouns ending in a vowel plus -y: toy   toys
- most nouns ending in a vowel plus -o: duo   duos
- most nouns ending in -oo: kangaroo   kangaroos
- most nouns ending in -i: ski   skis
- most nouns ending in a consonant plus -o: piano   pianos

But some nouns ending in a consonant plus -o add -es:

hero   heroes   tomato tomatoes

Some nouns ending in a consonant plus -o add either -s or -es:

zero *or* zeroes

2. Most nouns ending in a consonant plus -y change the -y to -i and add -es:

sky   skies   party   parties

3. Most nouns ending in -s, -z, -x, -ch, or -sh add -es:

gas gases   buzz buzzes   box boxes
bush bushes   watch watches

4. Some nouns ending in -f change -f to -v and add -es:

leaf leaves   self selves

But some of these can also add just -s:

calf   calves *or* calfs

5. Some nouns ending in -fe change the -f- to -v- and add -s:

knife knives   life lives

6. To make plurals of letters, numerals, figures, and signs, add apostrophe and -s, or just -s:

A	A's *or* As
$	$'s *or* $s
1970	1970's *or* 1970s
OK	OK's *or* OKs

7. Some abbreviations are made by cutting off a word in some way. To form the plurals, you usually add -s without an apostrophe:

apt	apts
cap	caps
mt	mts

For some abbreviations, the plural form can be the same as the singular:

1 hr	4 hr *or* 4 hrs
1 mo	4 mo *or* 4 mos

8. A few nouns form their plurals in very special ways:

• by adding **-en** or **-ren:**

ox   oxen   child   children

• by changing a middle vowel:

foot	feet	woman	women
tooth	teeth	goose	geese

Some compounds have one of the words above at the end. The same spelling change takes place:

Englishman   Englishmen   forefoot   forefeet

9. Many nouns from foreign languages use the foreign plural:

alga   algae   index   indices

Most foreign nouns also use the English plural -s or -es:

formula	formulas *or* formulae
bandit	bandits *or* banditti

10. Some nouns are made of more than one word. A hyphen may or may not come between each word. Usually, the first word has the plural form:

man-of-war	men-of-war
rule of thumb	rules of thumb
sister-in-law	sisters-in-law

11. Some words have a plural form that is the same as the singular form. This is called the *zero plural*.

deer
sheep
cattle

Some nouns have a zero plural and a regular plural:

bear   bear or bears

Some nouns usually use the zero plural except when naming different kinds of types:

trouts of the Rocky Mountains
fishes of the Atlantic Ocean

Spelling Quiz 1

Write the plurals of the following nouns. You may use your dictionary to check your work.

1. turkey	11. quail
2. six	12. penny
3. patch	13. eyetooth
4. beau	14. fungus
5. history	15. louse
6. dormouse	16. cuckoo
7. shelf	17. twitch
8. foray	18. 1980
9. cupful	19. yr
10. staff	20. trio

Some Rules for Adding Suffixes

1. Many words do not change their forms when a suffix is added. These include:

   - most words ending in **-x**:

coax	coaxed	coaxing
six	sixteen	sixty

   - most words ending in **-c**:

     tropic   tropical

   If the **-c** stays hard, though, before **e-** or **i-**, a **-k-** is usually added:

   picnic   picnicking

   - most words ending in one or two unstressed vowels plus a consonant:

     credit   credited   crediting

   In British spelling, such words *may* double the final consonant. The dictionary shows these British spellings:

   travel   traveled *or* travelled

   - most words ending in a vowel plus **-y**:

play	played
gray	grayest

   - most words ending in a vowel (except **e** or **y**) when they add a suffix that begins with a vowel:

radio	radioing
ski	skied

2. Many words double the last letter before adding a suffix that begins with a vowel. These usually are words that end in one strongly-stressed vowel and a consonant:

bag	baggage
control	controlling

3. Most words that end in silent **-e** drop the **-e** before adding a suffix that begins with a vowel;

   curve   curving

4. Most words that end in a vowel plus **-e** drop the **-e** if the suffix begins with **a-** or **e-:**

argue   arguable

5. Most words that end in a consonant plus **-y** change the **-y** to **-i**, unless the suffix begins with **-i:**

fancy   fanciful   fancying

6. Many geographical and personal names end in **-a** or **-o.**
  ● If the name ends in **-a**, the -a is usually dropped before adding **-an** or **ian:**

America   American   Canada   Canadian

  ● If the name ends in **-o**, the **-o** is sometimes dropped before adding **-ian** or **-an:**

Puerto Rico   Puerto Rican

Spelling Quiz 2

Write each of the following words. Add the suffix shown in parentheses. You may use your Spelling Handbook and your dictionary to check your work.

1. refer (-ing)	11. mimic (-ed)
2. frolic (-ed)	12. nice (-ness)
3. valley (-s)	13. kind (-ness)
4. barter (-ing)	14. diagram (-er)
5. shop (-er)	15. lie (-ing)
6. face (-ing)	16. mighty (-est)
7. gully (-s)	17. decay (-ed)
8. imagine (-able)	18. final (-ly)
9. beauty (-ful)	19. misbehave (-ing)
10. India (-an)	20. boo (-ing)

A DICTIONARY OF
THE ENGLISH LANGUAGE

¹a \'ā\ *n, often cap* **1** : the first letter of the English alphabet **2** : a grade rating a student's work as superior

²a \ə, ā\ *indefinite article* **1** : some one not specified ⟨*a* man overboard⟩ **2** : the same : ONE ⟨two of *a* kind⟩ **3** : ANY ⟨too much for *a* man to bear⟩ **4** : in each ⟨an apple *a* day⟩

a- \ə\ *prefix* **1** : on : in : at ⟨*a*bed⟩ **2** : in a specified state, condition, or manner ⟨*a*fire⟩ **3** : in the act or process of

ab- *prefix* : from : departing from ⟨*ab*normal⟩

a·back \ə-'bak\ *adv* : by surprise

ab·a·cus \'ab-ə-kəs\ *n, pl* **ab·a·ci** \'ab-ə-ˌsī\ *or* **ab·a·cus·es** : an instrument for making calculations by sliding counters along rods or grooves

abacus

a·baft \ə-'baft\ *adv* : toward or at a ship's stern

ab·a·lo·ne \ˌab-ə-'lō-nē\ *n* : a sea mollusk related to the snails that has a flattened slightly spiral shell with a pearly lining

¹a·ban·don \ə-'ban-dən\ *vb* **1** : to give up completely : FORSAKE ⟨*abandon* a sinking ship⟩ **2** : to give (oneself) over to a feeling or emotion — **a·ban·don·ment** *n*

syn ABANDON, DESERT, FORSAKE all mean to leave behind or go away from. ABANDON stresses withdrawing protection or care from ⟨*abandon* a cat⟩ DESERT suggests leaving in violation of a duty or promise ⟨*desert* a sentry post⟩ FORSAKE implies breaking ties based largely on affection ⟨didn't *forsake* old friends when she moved away⟩

²abandon *n* **1** : a complete yielding to natural impulses **2** : ENTHUSIASM

a·ban·doned \ə-'ban-dənd\ *adj* **1** : DESERTED, FORSAKEN ⟨*abandoned* houses⟩ **2** : wholly given up to wickedness or vice

a·base \ə-'bās\ *vb* **a·based**; **a·bas·ing** : to lower in rank or position — **a·base·ment** *n*

a·bash \ə-'bash\ *vb* : to destroy the self-confidence of : EMBARRASS — **a·bash·ment** *n*

a·bate \ə-'bāt\ *vb* **a·bat·ed**; **a·bat·ing** : to reduce or decrease in degree, amount, or force : DIMINISH

a·bate·ment \ə-'bāt-mənt\ *n* : a deduction from the full amount of a tax

ab·at·toir \'ab-ə-ˌtwär\ *n* : SLAUGHTERHOUSE

ab·bess \'ab-əs\ *n* : the head of an abbey for women

ab·bey \'ab-ē\ *n, pl* **ab·beys** **1** : MONASTERY, CONVENT **2** : a church that once belonged to an abbey ⟨Westminster *Abbey*⟩

ab·bot \'ab-ət\ *n* : the head of an abbey for men

ab·bre·vi·ate \ə-'brē-vē-ˌāt\ *vb* **ab·bre·vi·at·ed**; **ab·bre·vi·at·ing** [from Latin *abbreviare* "to shorten", from *ad-*, a prefix meaning "to" or "toward", and *brevis* "brief"] : to make briefer : SHORTEN

ab·bre·vi·a·tion \ə-ˌbrē-vē-'ā-shən\ *n* **1** : a making shorter **2** : a shortened form of a word or phrase used for brevity in writing

ab·di·cate \'ab-di-ˌkāt\ *vb* **ab·di·cat·ed**; **ab·di·cat·ing** : to give up a position of power or authority ⟨the king *abdicated* his throne⟩

ab·di·ca·tion \ˌab-di-'kā-shən\ *n* : the giving up of a position of power or authority

ab·do·men \'ab-də-mən, ab-'dō-\ *n* **1** : the part of the body between the chest and the hips including the cavity in which the chief digestive organs lie **2** : the hind part of the body of an insect or related animal

ab·dom·i·nal \ab-'däm-ən-l\ *adj* : of, relating to, or located in the abdomen — **ab·dom·i·nal·ly** *adv*

ab·duct \ab-'dəkt\ *vb* : to take a person away by force : KIDNAP

a·beam \ə-'bēm\ *adv (or adj)* : on a line at right angles to a ship's keel

a·bed \ə-'bed\ *adv (or adj)* : in bed

ab·er·ra·tion \ˌab-ə-'rā-shən\ *n* : a deviating from what is normal or usual

---

ə abut   ər further   a ax   ā age   ä father cot   ȧ (see key page)   au̇ out   ch chin   e less   ē easy   g gift   i trip   ī life
j job   ng sing   ō low   o̤ moth   ȯi coin   th thin   th̲ this   ü boot   u̇ foot   y you   yü few   yu̇ furious   zh vision

a·bet \ə-'bet\ *vb* **a·bet·ted; a·bet·ting** **1** : to encourage or aid in doing wrong **2** : HELP, ASSIST — **a·bet·tor** *or* **a·bet·ter** *n*

a·bey·ance \ə-'bā-əns\ *n* : a state of temporary inactivity ⟨plans held in *abeyance*⟩

ab·hor \ab-'hȯr\ *vb* **ab·horred; ab·hor·ring** : to shrink from in disgust : LOATHE

ab·hor·rent \ab-'hȯr-ənt\ *adj* : DETESTABLE

a·bide \ə-'bīd\ *vb* **a·bode** \-'bōd\ *or* **a·bid·ed; a·bid·ing** **1** : to bear patiently : TOLERATE **2** : LAST, ENDURE **3** : to live in a place : DWELL — **abide by** : to accept the terms of : OBEY

a·bid·ing \ə-'bīd-ing\ *adj* : PERMANENT

a·bil·i·ty \ə-'bil-ət-ē\ *n, pl* **a·bil·i·ties** **1** : physical, mental, or legal power to do something **2** : SKILL **3** : natural talent or acquired proficiency

syn ABILITY, APTITUDE, TALENT all mean a capacity for doing something. ABILITY means no more than this and suggests nothing about the quality of the performance ⟨practice increased my *ability* to do magic tricks⟩ APTITUDE indicates a quickness to learn and often a special interest in certain activities ⟨showed a real *aptitude* for science⟩ TALENT implies an inborn capacity and great aptitude in a creative field ⟨a *talent* for writing⟩

-a·bil·i·ty *also* **-i·bil·i·ty** \ə-'bil-ət-ē\ *n suffix, pl* **-a·bil·i·ties** *also* **-i·bil·i·ties** : capacity, fitness, or tendency to act or be acted upon in a specified way ⟨read*ability*⟩

ab·ject \'ab-ˌjekt\ *adj* : low in spirit or hope : CRINGING ⟨an *abject* coward⟩ — **ab·ject·ly** *adv* — **ab·ject·ness** *n*

ab·jure \ab-'jūr\ *vb* **ab·jured; ab·jur·ing** : to renounce or reject solemnly

a·blaze \ə-'blāz\ *adj* **1** : being on fire **2** : radiant with color

a·ble \'ā-bəl\ *adj* **a·bler** \-blər\; **a·blest** \-bləst\ **1** : having enough power, skill, or resources to do something ⟨*able* to swim⟩ **2** : marked by skill or efficiency

-a·ble *also* **-i·ble** \ə-bəl\ *adj suffix* **1** : capable of, fit for, or worthy of being ⟨break*able*⟩ ⟨collect*ible*⟩ **2** : tending or liable to ⟨peace*able*⟩ ⟨perish*able*⟩ — **-a·bly** *also* **-i·bly** \ə-blē\ *adv suffix*

a·bloom \ə-'blüm\ *adj* : BLOOMING

a·bly \'ā-blē\ *adv* : in an able manner

ab·nor·mal \ab-'nȯr-məl\ *adj* : differing from and often inferior to what is normal : UNUSUAL ⟨an *abnormal* growth⟩ — **ab·nor·mal·ly** *adv*

syn ABNORMAL, UNUSUAL, ODD all mean being out of the ordinary. ABNORMAL implies being outside of a standard or average range ⟨*abnormal* pulse rate⟩ UNUSUAL may suggest being different in a desirable way ⟨an *unusual* person

with many talents⟩ ODD often indicates strangeness that is neither understood nor approved of ⟨an *odd* idea about how to treat animals⟩

¹a·board \ə-'bōrd\ *adv* : on, onto, or within a ship, a railway car, or a passenger vehicle

²aboard *prep* : ON, ONTO, WITHIN

¹a·bode \ə-'bōd\ *past of* ABIDE

²abode *n* : the place where one stays or lives

a·bol·ish \ə-'bäl-ish\ *vb* : to do away with : put an end to ⟨*abolish* slavery⟩

ab·o·li·tion \ˌab-ə-'lish-ən\ *n* : a complete doing away with ⟨the *abolition* of war⟩

A–bomb \'ā-ˌbäm\ *n* : ATOM BOMB

a·bom·i·na·ble \ə-'bäm-ə-nə-bəl\ *adj* DISGUSTING — **a·bom·i·na·bly** \-blē\ *adv*

a·bom·i·nate \ə-'bäm-ə-ˌnāt\ *vb* **a·bom·i·nat·ed; a·bom·i·nat·ing** : to hate intensely : LOATHE

a·bom·i·na·tion \ə-ˌbäm-ə-'nā-shən\ *n* **1** : something abominable **2** : DISGUST

ab·o·rig·i·ne \ˌab-ə-'rij-ə-nē\ *n, pl* **ab·o·rig·i·nes** : a member of the original race of inhabitants of a region : NATIVE

a·born·ing \ə-'bȯr-ning\ *adv* : while being born or produced

a·bor·tive \ə-'bȯrt-iv\ *adj* : failing to achieve the desired end — **a·bor·tive·ly** *adv*

a·bound \ə-'baund\ *vb* **1** : to be plentiful : TEEM **2** : to be fully supplied

¹a·bout \ə-'baut\ *adv* **1** : on all sides : AROUND **2** : APPROXIMATELY, NEARLY ⟨*about* an hour ago⟩ **3** : in succession ⟨turn *about* is fair play⟩ **4** : in the opposite direction

²about *prep* **1** : on every side of : AROUND ⟨trees *about* the house⟩ **2** : near to **3** : on the point of ⟨was just *about* to leave⟩ **4** : CONCERNING ⟨a story *about* dogs⟩

¹a·bove \ə-'bəv\ *adv* : in or to a higher place

²above *prep* **1** : higher than : OVER ⟨flying *above* the clouds⟩ **2** : superior to ⟨thought herself *above* her schoolmates⟩ **3** : more than

³above *adj* : said or written earlier

a·bove·board \ə-'bəv-ˌbōrd\ *adv* (*or adj*) : in a straightforward manner syn see STRAIGHTFORWARD

a·brade \ə-'brād\ *vb* **a·brad·ed; a·brad·ing** : to wear away by rubbing

¹a·bra·sive \ə-'brā-siv\ *adj* : having the effect of abrading

²abrasive *n* : a substance for grinding, smoothing, or polishing

a·breast \ə-'brest\ *adv* (*or adj*) **1** : side by side **2** : up to a standard or level

a·bridge \ə-'brij\ *vb* **a·bridged; a·bridg·ing** : to shorten by leaving out some parts ⟨*abridge* a dictionary⟩ syn see SHORTEN

a·bridg·ment *or* **a·bridge·ment** \ə-'brij-mənt\ *n* : a shortened form of a work

A DICTIONARY OF THE ENGLISH LANGUAGE

¹a \'ā\ *n, often cap* **1** : the first letter of the English alphabet **2** : a grade rating a student's work as superior

²a \ə, ā\ *indefinite article* **1** : some one not specified ⟨*a* man overboard⟩ **2** : the same : ONE ⟨two of *a* kind⟩ **3** : ANY ⟨too much for *a* man to bear⟩ **4** : in each ⟨an apple *a* day⟩

a- \ə\ *prefix* **1** : on : in : at ⟨*a*bed⟩ **2** : in a specified state, condition, or manner ⟨*a*fire⟩ **3** : in the act or process of

ab- *prefix* : from : departing from ⟨*ab*normal⟩

a·back \ə-'bak\ *adv* : by surprise

ab·a·cus \'ab-ə-kəs\ *n, pl* **ab·a·ci** \'ab-ə-ˌsī\ *or* **ab·a·cus·es** : an instrument for making calculations by sliding counters along rods or grooves

abacus

a·baft \ə-'baft\ *adv* : toward or at a ship's stern

ab·a·lo·ne \ˌab-ə-'lō-nē\ *n* : a sea mollusk related to the snails that has a flattened slightly spiral shell with a pearly lining

¹a·ban·don \ə-'ban-dən\ *vb* **1** : to give up completely : FORSAKE ⟨*abandon* a sinking ship⟩ **2** : to give (oneself) over to a feeling or emotion — **a·ban·don·ment** *n*

syn ABANDON, DESERT, FORSAKE all mean to leave behind or go away from. ABANDON stresses withdrawing protection or care from ⟨*abandon* a cat⟩ DESERT suggests leaving in violation of a duty or promise ⟨*desert* a sentry post⟩ FORSAKE implies breaking ties based largely on affection ⟨didn't *forsake* old friends when she moved away⟩

²abandon *n* **1** : a complete yielding to natural impulses **2** : ENTHUSIASM

a·ban·doned \ə-'ban-dənd\ *adj* **1** : DESERTED, FORSAKEN ⟨*abandoned* houses⟩ **2** : wholly given up to wickedness or vice

a·base \ə-'bās\ *vb* **a·based**; **a·bas·ing** : to lower in rank or position — **a·base·ment** *n*

a·bash \ə-'bash\ *vb* : to destroy the self-confidence of : EMBARRASS — **a·bash·ment** *n*

a·bate \ə-'bāt\ *vb* **a·bat·ed**; **a·bat·ing** : to reduce or decrease in degree, amount, or force : DIMINISH

a·bate·ment \ə-'bāt-mənt\ *n* : a deduction from the full amount of a tax

ab·at·toir \'ab-ə-ˌtwär\ *n* : SLAUGHTERHOUSE

ab·bess \'ab-əs\ *n* : the head of an abbey for women

ab·bey \'ab-ē\ *n, pl* **ab·beys** **1** : MONASTERY, CONVENT **2** : a church that once belonged to an abbey ⟨Westminster *Abbey*⟩

ab·bot \'ab-ət\ *n* : the head of an abbey for men

ab·bre·vi·ate \ə-'brē-vē-ˌāt\ *vb* **ab·bre·vi·at·ed**; **ab·bre·vi·at·ing** [from Latin *abbreviare* "to shorten", from *ad-*, a prefix meaning "to" or "toward", and *brevis* "brief"] : to make briefer : SHORTEN

ab·bre·vi·a·tion \ə-ˌbrē-vē-'ā-shən\ *n* **1** : a making shorter **2** : a shortened form of a word or phrase used for brevity in writing

ab·di·cate \'ab-di-ˌkāt\ *vb* **ab·di·cat·ed**; **ab·di·cat·ing** : to give up a position of power or authority ⟨the king *abdicated* his throne⟩

ab·di·ca·tion \ˌab-di-'kā-shən\ *n* : the giving up of a position of power or authority

ab·do·men \'ab-də-mən, ab-'dō-\ *n* **1** : the part of the body between the chest and the hips including the cavity in which the chief digestive organs lie **2** : the hind part of the body of an insect or related animal

ab·dom·i·nal \ab-'däm-ən-l\ *adj* : of, relating to, or located in the abdomen — **ab·dom·i·nal·ly** *adv*

ab·duct \ab-'dəkt\ *vb* : to take a person away by force : KIDNAP

a·beam \ə-'bēm\ *adv (or adj)* : on a line at right angles to a ship's keel

a·bed \ə-'bed\ *adv (or adj)* : in bed

ab·er·ra·tion \ˌab-ə-'rā-shən\ *n* : a deviating from what is normal or usual

---

ə abut   ər further   a ax   ā age   ä father cot   à (see key page)   aù out   ch chin   e less   ē easy   g gift   i trip   ī life
j job   ng sing   ō low   ò moth   òi coin   th thin   th this   ü boot   ù foot   y you   yü few   yù furious   zh vision

a·bet \ə-'bet\ *vb* **a·bet·ted; a·bet·ting** **1** : to encourage or aid in doing wrong **2** : HELP, ASSIST — **a·bet·tor** *or* **a·bet·ter** *n*

a·bey·ance \ə-'bā-əns\ *n* : a state of temporary inactivity ⟨plans held in *abeyance*⟩

ab·hor \ab-'hȯr\ *vb* **ab·horred; ab·hor·ring** : to shrink from in disgust : LOATHE

ab·hor·rent \ab-'hȯr-ənt\ *adj* : DETESTABLE

a·bide \ə-'bīd\ *vb* **a·bode** \-'bōd\ *or* **a·bid·ed; a·bid·ing** **1** : to bear patiently : TOLERATE **2** : LAST, ENDURE **3** : to live in a place : DWELL — **abide by** : to accept the terms of : OBEY

a·bid·ing \ə-'bīd-ing\ *adj* : PERMANENT

a·bil·i·ty \ə-'bil-ət-ē\ *n, pl* **a·bil·i·ties** **1** : physical, mental, or legal power to do something **2** : SKILL **3** : natural talent or acquired proficiency

syn ABILITY, APTITUDE, TALENT all mean a capacity for doing something. ABILITY means no more than this and suggests nothing about the quality of the performance ⟨practice increased my *ability* to do magic tricks⟩ APTITUDE indicates a quickness to learn and often a special interest in certain activities ⟨showed a real *aptitude* for science⟩ TALENT implies an inborn capacity and great aptitude in a creative field ⟨a *talent* for writing⟩

-a·bil·i·ty *also* **-i·bil·i·ty** \ə-'bil-ət-ē\ *n suffix, pl* **-a·bil·i·ties** *also* **-i·bil·i·ties** : capacity, fitness, or tendency to act or be acted upon in a specified way ⟨read*ability*⟩

ab·ject \'ab-ˌjekt\ *adj* : low in spirit or hope : CRINGING ⟨an *abject* coward⟩ — **ab·ject·ly** *adv* — **ab·ject·ness** *n*

ab·jure \ab-'ju̇r\ *vb* **ab·jured; ab·jur·ing** : to renounce or reject solemnly

a·blaze \ə-'blāz\ *adj* **1** : being on fire **2** : radiant with color

a·ble \'ā-bəl\ *adj* **a·bler** \-blər\; **a·blest** \-bləst\ **1** : having enough power, skill, or resources to do something ⟨*able* to swim⟩ **2** : marked by skill or efficiency

-a·ble *also* **-i·ble** \ə-bəl\ *adj suffix* **1** : capable of, fit for, or worthy of being ⟨break*able*⟩ ⟨collect*ible*⟩ **2** : tending or liable to ⟨peace*able*⟩ ⟨perish*able*⟩ — **-a·bly** *also* **-i·bly** \ə-blē\ *adv suffix*

a·bloom \ə-'blüm\ *adj* : BLOOMING

a·bly \'ā-blē\ *adv* : in an able manner

ab·nor·mal \ab-'nȯr-məl\ *adj* : differing from and often inferior to what is normal : UNUSUAL ⟨an *abnormal* growth⟩ — **ab·nor·mal·ly** *adv*

syn ABNORMAL, UNUSUAL, ODD all mean being out of the ordinary. ABNORMAL implies being outside of a standard or average range ⟨*abnormal* pulse rate⟩ UNUSUAL may suggest being different in a desirable way ⟨an *unusual* person

with many talents⟩ ODD often indicates strangeness that is neither understood nor approved of ⟨an *odd* idea about how to treat animals⟩

¹a·board \ə-'bōrd\ *adv* : on, onto, or within a ship, a railway car, or a passenger vehicle

²aboard *prep* : ON, ONTO, WITHIN

¹a·bode \ə-'bōd\ *past of* ABIDE

²abode *n* : the place where one stays or lives

a·bol·ish \ə-'bäl-ish\ *vb* : to do away with : put an end to ⟨*abolish* slavery⟩

ab·o·li·tion \ˌab-ə-'lish-ən\ *n* : a complete doing away with ⟨the *abolition* of war⟩

A–bomb \'ā-ˌbäm\ *n* : ATOM BOMB

a·bom·i·na·ble \ə-'bäm-ə-nə-bəl\ *adj* DISGUSTING — **a·bom·i·na·bly** \-blē\ *adv*

a·bom·i·nate \ə-'bäm-ə-ˌnāt\ *vb* **a·bom·i·nat·ed; a·bom·i·nat·ing** : to hate intensely : LOATHE

a·bom·i·na·tion \ə-ˌbäm-ə-'nā-shən\ *n* **1** : something abominable **2** : DISGUST

ab·o·rig·i·ne \ˌab-ə-'rij-ə-nē\ *n, pl* **ab·o·rig·i·nes** : a member of the original race of inhabitants of a region : NATIVE

a·born·ing \ə-'bȯr-ning\ *adv* : while being born or produced

a·bor·tive \ə-'bȯrt-iv\ *adj* : failing to achieve the desired end — **a·bor·tive·ly** *adv*

a·bound \ə-'bau̇nd\ *vb* **1** : to be plentiful : TEEM **2** : to be fully supplied

¹a·bout \ə-'bau̇t\ *adv* **1** : on all sides : AROUND **2** : APPROXIMATELY, NEARLY ⟨*about* an hour ago⟩ **3** : in succession ⟨turn *about* is fair play⟩ **4** : in the opposite direction

²about *prep* **1** : on every side of : AROUND ⟨trees *about* the house⟩ **2** : near to **3** : on the point of ⟨was just *about* to leave⟩ **4** : CONCERNING ⟨a story *about* dogs⟩

¹a·bove \ə-'bəv\ *adv* : in or to a higher place

²above *prep* **1** : higher than : OVER ⟨flying *above* the clouds⟩ **2** : superior to ⟨thought herself *above* her schoolmates⟩ **3** : more than

³above *adj* : said or written earlier

a·bove·board \ə-'bəv-ˌbōrd\ *adv (or adj)* : in a straightforward manner syn see STRAIGHTFORWARD

a·brade \ə-'brād\ *vb* **a·brad·ed; a·brad·ing** : to wear away by rubbing

¹a·bra·sive \ə-'brā-siv\ *adj* : having the effect of abrading

²abrasive *n* : a substance for grinding, smoothing, or polishing

a·breast \ə-'brest\ *adv (or adj)* **1** : side by side **2** : up to a standard or level

a·bridge \ə-'brij\ *vb* **a·bridged; a·bridg·ing** : to shorten by leaving out some parts ⟨*abridge* a dictionary⟩ syn see SHORTEN

a·bridg·ment *or* **a·bridge·ment** \ə-'brij-mənt\ *n* : a shortened form of a work

a·broad \ə-'bròd\ *adv (or adj)* **1** : over a wide area **2** : in the open : OUTDOORS **3** : in or to a foreign country **4** : in wide circulation

a·brupt \ə-'brəpt\ *adj* **1** : broken off **2** : SUDDEN **3** : STEEP — **a·brupt·ly** *adv* — **a·brupt·ness** *n*

ab·scess \'ab-,ses\ *n* : a collection of pus surrounded by inflamed tissue — **ab·scessed** \-,sest\ *adj*

ab·scond \ab-'skänd\ *vb* : to go away secretly and hide oneself

ab·sence \'ab-səns\ *n* **1** : a being away **2** : LACK, WANT

¹ab·sent \'ab-sənt\ *adj* **1** : not present : MISSING **2** : LACKING **3** : not attentive

²ab·sent \ab-'sent\ *vb* : to keep (oneself) away

ab·sen·tee \,ab-sən-'tē\ *n* : a person who is absent

ab·sent·mind·ed \,ab-sənt-'mīn-dəd\ *adj* : lost in thought and not paying attention to what is going on or to what one is doing — **ab·sent·mind·ed·ly** *adv* — **ab·sent·mind·ed·ness** *n*

ab·so·lute \'ab-sə-,lüt\ *adj* **1** : free from mixture or imperfection **2** : free from control, restriction, or qualification ⟨*absolute* power⟩ **3** : POSITIVE ⟨*absolute* proof⟩ — **ab·so·lute·ly** *adv* — **ab·so·lute·ness** *n*

ab·so·lu·tion \,ab-sə-'lü-shən\ *n* : a forgiving of sins

ab·solve \əb-'sälv\ *vb* **ab·solved; ab·solv·ing** : PARDON, FREE

ab·sorb \əb-'sòrb\ *vb* **1** : to take in or swallow up **2** : to suck up or drink in ⟨a sponge *absorbs* water⟩ **3** : to hold all one's interest

ab·sorb·en·cy \əb-'sòr-bən-sē\ *n* : the quality or state of being absorbent

ab·sorb·ent \əb-'sòr-bənt\ *adj* : able to absorb ⟨*absorbent* cotton⟩

ab·sorp·tion \əb-'sòrp-shən\ *n* **1** : the process of absorbing or being absorbed ⟨the *absorption* of water by soil⟩ ⟨the *absorption* of sound by a curtain⟩ **2** : complete attention

ab·stain \əb-'stān\ *vb* : to restrain oneself : REFRAIN ⟨*abstain* from voting⟩ **syn** see REFRAIN — **ab·stain·er** *n*

ab·sti·nence \'ab-stə-nəns\ *n* : a voluntary refraining especially from eating certain foods or drinking liquor

¹ab·stract \'ab-,strakt\ *adj* **1** : expressing a quality without reference to an actual person or thing that possesses it ⟨*honesty* is an *abstract* word⟩ **2** : hard to understand **3** : having little or no pictorial representation ⟨*abstract* painting⟩ — **ab·stract·ly** *adv* — **ab·stract·ness** *n*

²ab·stract \'ab-,strakt\ *n* : a brief statement of the main points or facts : SUMMARY

³ab·stract \ab-'strakt\ *vb* **1** : REMOVE, SEPARATE **2** : to make an abstract of

ab·strac·tion \ab-'strak-shən\ *n* **1** : the act of abstracting : the state of being abstracted **2** : an abstract idea **3** : an abstract work of art

ab·struse \ab-'strüs\ *adj* : hard to understand — **ab·struse·ly** *adv* — **ab·struse·ness** *n*

ab·surd \əb-'sərd\ *adj* : highly unreasonable or untrue : RIDICULOUS — **ab·surd·ly** *adv*

ab·surd·i·ty \əb-'sərd-ət-ē\ *n, pl* **ab·surd·i·ties** **1** : extreme unreasonableness : SILLINESS **2** : something that is absurd

a·bun·dance \ə-'bən-dəns\ *n* : a large quantity : PLENTY

a·bun·dant \ə-'bən-dənt\ *adj* : more than enough : PLENTIFUL — **a·bun·dant·ly** *adv*

¹a·buse \ə-'byüz\ *vb* **a·bused; a·bus·ing** **1** : to use wrongly : MISUSE ⟨*abuse* privileges⟩ **2** : to treat cruelly : MISTREAT ⟨*abuse* a horse by overworking it⟩ **3** : to blame or scold rudely

²a·buse \ə-'byüs\ *n* **1** : wrong, improper, or unfair treatment **2** : a corrupt practice **3** : harsh insulting language

a·bu·sive \ə-'byü-siv\ *adj* **1** : using or characterized by abuse **2** : physically injurious — **a·bu·sive·ly** *adv* — **a·bu·sive·ness** *n*

a·but \ə-'bət\ *vb* **a·but·ted; a·but·ting** : to touch along a border or with a projecting part

a·but·ment \ə-'bət-mənt\ *n* : something against which another thing rests its weight or pushes with force

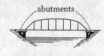

abutments

a·bys·mal \ə-'biz-məl\ *adj* : immeasurably deep : BOTTOMLESS — **a·bys·mal·ly** *adv*

a·byss \ə-'bis\ *n* : an extremely deep gulf or great space

a·ca·cia \ə-'kā-shə\ *n* : a shrub or small tree with ball-like or cylindrical flower clusters, leaves with many leaflets, and often thorny stems

ac·a·dem·ic \,ak-ə-'dem-ik\ *adj* **1** : of or relating to schools or colleges **2** : literary or general rather than technical ⟨took the *academic* course⟩ **3** : theoretical rather than practical — **ac·a·dem·i·cal·ly** \-i-kə-lē\ *adv*

acacia: leaf and flowers

a·cad·e·my \ə-'kad-ə-mē\ *n, pl* **a·cad·e·mies** **1** : a private high school **2** : a society of scholars, artists, or learned men

ac·cede \ak-'sēd\ *vb* **ac·ced·ed; ac·ced·ing** **1** : to adhere to an agreement **2** : CONSENT

ac·cel·er·ate \ak-'sel-ə-,rāt\ *vb* **ac·cel·er·at-**

ed; **ac·cel·er·at·ing** **1** : to bring about earlier : HASTEN **2** : to move or cause to move faster

ac·cel·er·a·tion \ak-ˌsel-ə-'rā-shən\ *n* : a speeding up

ac·cel·er·a·tor \ak-'sel-ə-ˌrāt-ər\ *n* : a pedal in an automobile for controlling the speed of the motor

¹ac·cent \'ak-ˌsent\ *n* **1** : a peculiar or characteristic manner of speech ⟨foreign *accent*⟩ **2** : increased force or emphasis given to a syllable of a word in speaking or to a beat in music **3** : a mark (as ' or ˌ) used in writing or printing to show the place of increased force or emphasis on a syllable

²ac·cent \ak-'sent\ *vb* **1** : to give increased force or emphasis : STRESS **2** : to mark with a written or printed accent

ac·cen·tu·ate \ak-'sen-chə-ˌwāt\ *vb* **ac·cen·tu·at·ed; ac·cen·tu·at·ing** **1** : ACCENT **2** : EMPHASIZE

ac·cept \ak-'sept\ *vb* **1** : to receive or take willingly ⟨*accept* a gift⟩ **2** : to agree to

ac·cept·a·ble \ak-'sep-tə-bəl\ *adj* **1** : worthy of being accepted ⟨an *acceptable* excuse⟩ **2** : SATISFACTORY, ADEQUATE ⟨plays an *acceptable* game of tennis⟩ — **ac·cept·a·ble·ness** *n* — **ac·cept·a·bly** \-blē\ *adv*

ac·cept·ance \ak-'sep-təns\ *n* **1** : the act of accepting **2** : the quality or state of being accepted or acceptable

ac·cess \'ak-ˌses\ *n* **1** : ADMITTANCE **2** : a way or means of approach ⟨*access* to the sea⟩

ac·ces·si·ble \ak-'ses-ə-bəl\ *adj* **1** : easy to approach ⟨a resort *accessible* by train or bus⟩ **2** : OBTAINABLE — **ac·ces·si·bly** \-blē\ *adv*

ac·ces·sion \ak-'sesh-ən\ *n* **1** : something added **2** : increase by something added **3** : a coming to high office or a position of power

¹ac·ces·so·ry \ak-'ses-ə-rē\ *n, pl* **ac·ces·so·ries** **1** : something of secondary or subordinate importance **2** : a person who helps another in wrongdoing

²accessory *adj* : aiding or contributing in a secondary way : SUPPLEMENTARY

ac·ci·dent \'ak-sə-dənt\ *n* **1** : something that happens by chance or without intention : MISHAP ⟨automobile *accident*⟩ **2** : CHANCE

ac·ci·den·tal \ˌak-sə-'dent-l\ *adj* **1** : happening by chance or unexpectedly ⟨an *accidental* discovery of oil⟩ **2** : not intended ⟨an *accidental* shooting⟩ — **ac·ci·den·tal·ly** *adv*

¹ac·claim \ə-'klām\ *vb* **1** : APPLAUD, PRAISE **2** : to welcome or proclaim with applause

²acclaim *n* : APPLAUSE, PRAISE

ac·cla·ma·tion \ˌak-lə-'mā-shən\ *n* : a loud eager expression of approval or praise

ac·cli·mate \ə-'klī-mət, 'ak-lə-ˌmāt\ *vb* **ac-**

cli·mat·ed; **ac·cli·mat·ing** : to adapt to a new climate or new surroundings

ac·cli·ma·tize \ə-'klī-mə-ˌtīz\ *vb* **ac·cli·ma·tized; ac·cli·ma·tiz·ing** : ACCLIMATE

ac·cliv·i·ty \ə-'kliv-ət-ē\ *n, pl* **ac·cliv·i·ties** : a steep upward slope

ac·co·lade \'ak-ə-ˌlād\ *n* : a recognition of merit

ac·com·mo·date \ə-'käm-ə-ˌdāt\ *vb* **ac·com·mo·dat·ed; ac·com·mo·dat·ing** **1** : to make fit or suitable : ADAPT **2** : to provide with something needed **3** : to hold without crowding

ac·com·mo·dat·ing \ə-'käm-ə-ˌdāt-ing\ *adj* : ready to help — **ac·com·mo·dat·ing·ly** *adv*

ac·com·mo·da·tion \ə-ˌkäm-ə-'dā-shən\ *n* **1** : something supplied for convenience or to satisfy a need **2** *pl* : hotel lodging and services

ac·com·pa·ni·ment \ə-'kəm-pə-nē-mənt\ *n* : subordinate music to support or complement a principal voice or instrument

ac·com·pa·nist \ə-'kəm-pə-nəst\ *n* : a musician who plays an accompaniment

ac·com·pa·ny \ə-'kəm-pə-nē\ *vb* **ac·com·pa·nied; ac·com·pa·ny·ing** **1** : to go with as a companion **2** : to play a musical accompaniment for **3** : to occur at the same time

syn ACCOMPANY, ESCORT both mean to go or come with. ACCOMPANY stresses closeness of association ⟨high winds *accompanied* the rain⟩ and equality of status ⟨*accompany* a friend to the dentist⟩ ESCORT adds the idea of protection often as a courtesy ⟨*escorted* the girls to their homes⟩ or as a mark of honor ⟨troops to *escort* the visiting royalty⟩

ac·com·plice \ə-'käm-pləs\ *n* : a partner in wrongdoing

ac·com·plish \ə-'käm-plish\ *vb* : to bring to a successful end : carry out : PERFORM

ac·com·plish·ment \ə-'käm-plish-mənt\ *n* **1** : COMPLETION **2** : something accomplished **3** : an acquired excellence or skill : ATTAINMENT

¹ac·cord \ə-'kord\ *vb* **1** : to bring into agreement **2** : GRANT, CONCEDE **3** : to be in harmony : AGREE

²accord *n* **1** : AGREEMENT, HARMONY **2** : WILLINGNESS ⟨went of his own *accord*⟩

ac·cord·ance \ə-'kord-ns\ *n* : AGREEMENT

ac·cord·ing·ly \ə-'kord-ing-lē\ *adv* **1** : in accordance **2** : CONSEQUENTLY, SO

ac·cord·ing to \ə-ˌkord-ing-tə, -tü\ *prep* **1** : in agreement or conformity with ⟨seated *according to* their ages⟩ **2** : as stated by ⟨*according to* the latest report⟩

¹ac·cor·di·on \ə-'kord-ē-ən\ *n* : a portable musical instrument with a bellows, keys, and reeds

accordion

²accordion *adj* : folding or creased or hinged to fold like an accordion ⟨a skirt with *accordion* pleats⟩

ac·cost \ə-'kȯst\ *vb* : to approach and speak first to

¹ac·count \ə-'kȧunt\ *n* **1** : a record of money received and money paid out **2** : a statement of business transactions **3** : an arrangement with a seller to supply credit **4** : an explanation of one's conduct **5** : a statement of facts or events : REPORT **6** : WORTH, VALUE **7** : a sum of money deposited in a bank and subject to withdrawal by the depositor — **on account of** : because of : for the sake of — **on no account** : under no circumstances — **on one's account** : for one's benefit

²account *vb* **1** : to think of as : CONSIDER ⟨I *account* him lucky⟩ **2** : to give an analysis or explanation **3** : to be the only or chief reason

ac·count·a·ble \ə-'kȧunt-ə-bəl\ *adj* **1** : responsible for giving an account : ANSWERABLE **2** : capable of being accounted for : EXPLAINABLE — **ac·count·a·ble·ness** *n* — **ac·count·a·bly** \-blē\ *adv*

ac·count·ant \ə-'kȧunt-nt\ *n* : a person skilled in accounting

ac·count·ing \ə-'kȧunt-ing\ *n* : the skill or practice of recording and analyzing money transactions

ac·cred·it \ə-'kred-ət\ *vb* **1** : to authorize officially **2** : CREDIT

ac·cre·tion \ə-'krē-shən\ *n* : growth especially by increase from outside

ac·cru·al \ə-'krü-əl\ *n* **1** : the action or process of accruing **2** : something that accrues or has accrued

ac·crue \ə-'krü\ *vb* **ac·crued**; **ac·cru·ing** **1** : to come by way of increase **2** : to accumulate over a period of time

ac·cu·mu·late \ə-'kyü-myə-ˌlāt\ *vb* **ac·cu·mu·lat·ed**; **ac·cu·mu·lat·ing** **1** : COLLECT, GATHER **2** : to increase in quantity, number, or amount

ac·cu·mu·la·tion \ə-ˌkyü-myə-'lā-shən\ *n* **1** : a collecting together : AMASSING **2** : COLLECTION, HEAP

ac·cu·ra·cy \'ak-yə-rə-sē\ *n* : freedom from mistakes : EXACTNESS

ac·cu·rate \'ak-yə-rət\ *adj* : free from mistakes : PRECISE ⟨an *accurate* answer⟩ — **ac·cu·rate·ly** *adv* — **ac·cu·rate·ness** *n*

ac·cu·sa·tion \ˌak-yə-'zā-shən\ *n* : a charge of wrongdoing

ac·cuse \ə-'kyüz\ *vb* **ac·cused**; **ac·cus·ing** : to charge a person with a fault or wrong and especially with a criminal offense — **ac·cus·er** *n*

ac·cus·tom \ə-'kəs-təm\ *vb* : to make familiar through use or experience

ac·cus·tomed \ə-'kəs-təmd\ *adj* **1** : CUSTOMARY, USUAL ⟨his *accustomed* lunch hour⟩ **2** : USED, WONT ⟨*accustomed* to hard luck⟩

¹ace \'ās\ *n* [once spelled *as* in English, the same as in Latin from which it was taken; Latin *as* means "one single thing", "unit"] **1** : a playing card with one large pip in its center **2** : a point scored on a tennis serve that an opponent fails to touch **3** : a combat pilot who has brought down at least five enemy planes **4** : a person who excels at something

ace

²ace *adj* : of first rank or quality

¹ache \'āk\ *vb* **ached**; **ach·ing** **1** : to suffer a dull continuous pain **2** : YEARN

²ache *n* : a dull continuous pain

a·chieve \ə-'chēv\ *vb* **a·chieved**; **a·chiev·ing** **1** : to bring to a successful end **2** : to get by means of one's own efforts : WIN

a·chieve·ment \ə-'chēv-mənt\ *n* **1** : the act of achieving **2** : something achieved especially by great effort or persistence

¹ac·id \'as-əd\ *adj* **1** : sour, sharp, or biting to the taste **2** : sour in temper : CROSS ⟨*acid* remarks⟩ **3** : of, relating to, or having the characteristics of an acid — **ac·id·ly** *adv*

²acid *n* **1** : a sour substance **2** : a sour-tasting hydrogen-containing compound whose water solution turns blue litmus paper red

a·cid·i·ty \ə-'sid-ət-ē\ *n, pl* **a·cid·i·ties** : TARTNESS

ac·knowl·edge \ak-'näl-ij\ *vb* **ac·knowl·edged**; **ac·knowl·edg·ing** **1** : to own or admit the truth or existence of ⟨*acknowledged* his mistake⟩ **2** : to recognize the rights or authority of **3** : to make known that something has been received or noticed

syn ACKNOWLEDGE, ADMIT, CONFESS all mean to make public some private knowledge or information. ACKNOWLEDGE suggests disclosing what could have been kept secret ⟨*acknowledged* the fact that she was afraid of dogs⟩ ADMIT indicates telling with some unwillingness often as a result of outside insistence ⟨finally *admitted* that a new dress wasn't absolutely necessary⟩ CONFESS emphasizes the ideas of unwillingness and compulsion and adds to them the idea that a personal fault or failure is the subject of the disclosure ⟨*confessed* that he was involved in the playground fight⟩

ac·knowl·edged \ak-'näl-ijd\ *adj* : generally recognized or accepted ⟨an *acknowledged* leader⟩

---

j job   ng sing   ō low   ȯ moth   ȯi coin   th thin   th this   ü boot   u̇ foot   y you   yü few   yu̇ furious   zh vision

ac·knowl·edg·ment \ak-'näl-ij-mənt\ *n* **1** : recognition or favorable notice of an act or achievement **2** : something done or given in recognition of something received

ac·me \'ak-mē\ *n* : the highest point : PEAK

ac·ne \'ak-nē\ *n* : a skin disorder in which skin glands and pores are inflamed and pimples and blackheads are present

ac·o·lyte \'ak-ə-ˌlīt\ *n* : a man or boy who assists the clergyman in a religious service

a·corn \'ā-ˌkȯrn, -kərn\ *n* : the nut of the oak tree

a·cous·tic \ə-'küs-tik\ *or* **a·cous·ti·cal** \-ti-kəl\ *adj* **1** : of or relating to hearing or sound **2** : deadening sound ⟨*acoustical* tile⟩

acorns

a·cous·tics \ə-'küs-tiks\ *n sing or pl* **1** : a science dealing with sound **2** : the qualities in a room or hall that make it easy or hard for a person in it to hear distinctly

ac·quaint \ə-'kwānt\ *vb* **1** : to cause to know socially ⟨became *acquainted* through mutual friends⟩ **2** : to cause to know firsthand : INFORM ⟨*acquaint* him with his duties⟩

ac·quaint·ance \ə-'kwānt-ns\ *n* **1** : personal knowledge **2** : a person one knows slightly

ac·qui·esce \ˌak-wē-'es\ *vb* **ac·qui·esced; ac·qui·esc·ing** : to accept, agree, or give implied consent by keeping silent or by not making objections

ac·qui·es·cence \ˌak-wē-'es-ns\ *n* : a tacit or passive accepting or agreeing

ac·qui·es·cent \ˌak-wē-'es-nt\ *adj* : acquiescing or disposed to acquiesce — **ac·qui·es·cent·ly** *adv*

ac·quire \ə-'kwīr\ *vb* **ac·quired; ac·quir·ing** : to come into possession of especially by one's own efforts : GAIN

ac·quire·ment \ə-'kwīr-mənt\ *n* **1** : the act of acquiring **2** : ATTAINMENT

ac·qui·si·tion \ˌak-wə-'zish-ən\ *n* **1** : ACQUIREMENT **2** : something acquired

ac·quis·i·tive \ə-'kwiz-ət-iv\ *adj* : eager to acquire : GREEDY — **ac·quis·i·tive·ly** *adv* — **ac·quis·i·tive·ness** *n*

ac·quit \ə-'kwit\ *vb* **ac·quit·ted; ac·quit·ting** **1** : to free from a charge of wrongdoing **2** : to conduct oneself : BEHAVE

ac·quit·tal \ə-'kwit-l\ *n* : the setting free of a person from a charge of wrongdoing

a·cre \'ā-kər\ *n* **1** *pl* : LANDS, ESTATE **2** : a measure of land area equal to 160 square rods or 4840 square yards

a·cre·age \'ā-kə-rij\ *n* : area in acres : ACRES

ac·rid \'ak-rəd\ *adj* **1** : sharp and biting in taste or odor **2** : bitterly irritating : CAUSTIC

ac·ri·mo·ni·ous \ˌak-rə-'mō-nē-əs\ *adj* : marked by acrimony — **ac·ri·mo·ni·ous·ly** *adv* — **ac·ri·mo·ni·ous·ness** *n*

ac·ri·mo·ny \'ak-rə-ˌmō-nē\ *n, pl* **ac·ri·mo·nies** : harsh or biting sharpness of language or feeling

ac·ro·bat \'ak-rə-ˌbat\ *n* : a person who performs gymnastic feats requiring skillful control of the body

ac·ro·bat·ic \ˌak-rə-'bat-ik\ *adj* : of or relating to acrobats or acrobatics

ac·ro·bat·ics \ˌak-rə-'bat-iks\ *n sing or pl* **1** : the art or performance of an acrobat **2** : a striking performance involving great agility or maneuverability ⟨airplane *acrobatics*⟩

a·crop·o·lis \ə-'kräp-ə-ləs\ *n* : the upper fortified part of an ancient Greek city

¹a·cross \ə-'krȯs\ *adv* **1** : so as to reach or pass from one side to the other ⟨boards sawed directly *across*⟩ **2** : to or on the opposite side

²across *prep* **1** : to or on the opposite side of ⟨lives *across* the street⟩ **2** : so as to intersect or pass at an angle ⟨lay one stick *across* another⟩

a·cros·tic \ə-'krȯs-tik\ *n* : a series of words of equal length arranged to read the same horizontally or vertically

```
H E A R T
E M B E R
A B U S E
R E S I N
T R E N D
```
acrostic

¹act \'akt\ *n* **1** : something that is done : DEED **2** : the doing of something ⟨caught in the *act* of stealing⟩ **3** : a law made by a governing body **4** : a main division of a play

²act *vb* **1** : to perform by action especially on the stage **2** : to play the part of ⟨*act* the hero in a play⟩ **3** : to conduct oneself : BEHAVE ⟨*acts* like a coward⟩ **4** : to take action : MOVE ⟨*act* quickly in an emergency⟩ **5** : to perform a specific function : SERVE **6** : to produce an effect : WORK ⟨the medicine *acts* on the heart⟩

act·ing \'ak-ting\ *adj* : serving for a short time only or in place of another

ac·tion \'ak-shən\ *n* **1** : a legal proceeding **2** : the working of one thing on another so as to produce a change ⟨the *action* of acids on metals⟩ **3** : the manner or method of performing : PERFORMANCE **4** : DEED, ACT **5** *pl* : BEHAVIOR **6** : BATTLE ⟨a soldier killed in *action*⟩ **7** : the plot of a play or a work of fiction

ac·ti·vate \'ak-tə-ˌvāt\ *vb* **ac·ti·vat·ed; ac·ti·vat·ing** : to make active or more active

ac·tive \'ak-tiv\ *adj* **1** : producing or involving action or movement **2** : quick in physical movement : LIVELY ⟨an *active* child⟩ **3** : engaged in an action or activity ⟨an *active* volcano⟩ — **ac·tive·ly** *adv*

ac·tiv·i·ty \ak-'tiv-ət-ē\ *n, pl* **ac·tiv·i·ties**

1 : vigorous or energetic action 2 : a natural or normal function 3 : an organized, supervised, often extracurricular recreation

ac·tor \'ak-tər\ *n* : a person who acts especially in a play or motion picture

ac·tress \'ak-trəs\ *n* : a female actor

ac·tu·al \'ak-chə-wəl\ *adj* : really existing or happening : not false

ac·tu·al·ly \'ak-chə-wə-lē\ *adv* : in fact

a·cu·men \ə-'kyü-mən\ *n* : mental keenness and penetration

a·cute \ə-'kyüt\ *adj* 1 : SHARP, POINTED 2 : mentally keen 3 : responsive to slight impressions or stimuli ⟨*acute* observer⟩ 4 : SEVERE ⟨*acute* distress⟩ 5 : developing quickly and lasting only a short time : not chronic ⟨*acute* illness⟩ 6 : CRITICAL, URGENT ⟨an *acute* situation that may well lead to war⟩ — **a·cute·ly** *adv* — **a·cute·ness** *n*

acute angle *n* : an angle that is less than a right angle

acute angle

ad \'ad\ *n* : ADVERTISEMENT

ad·age \'ad-ij\ *n* : an old familiar saying : PROVERB

¹**ad·a·mant** \'ad-ə-mənt\ *n* : a stone believed to be of impenetrable hardness

²**adamant** *adj* : unyielding especially in opposition : UNBENDING

Ad·am's apple \,ad-əmz-\ *n* : the enlargement formed in the front of a person's neck by cartilage in the throat

a·dapt \ə-'dapt\ *vb* : to make suitable or fit (as for a new use) — **a·dapt·er** *n*

a·dapt·a·ble \ə-'dap-tə-bəl\ *adj* : capable of being adapted or of adapting oneself

ad·ap·ta·tion \,ad-,ap-'tā-shən\ *n* 1 : a making suitable or fit 2 : adjustment to conditions of environment 3 : something adapted from something else

a·dapt·ed \ə-'dap-təd\ *adj* : SUITABLE

add \'ad\ *vb* 1 : to join or unite to something so as to enlarge, increase, or enhance it ⟨*add* a wing to the house⟩ 2 : to say something more 3 : to combine numbers into a single sum

ad·dend \'ad-,end\ *n* : a number that is to be added to another number

ad·den·dum \ə-'den-dəm\ *n, pl* **ad·den·da** \ə-'den-də\ : something added (as to a book)

ad·der \'ad-ər\ *n* 1 : a poisonous snake of Europe 2 : any of several harmless North American snakes (as the **puff adder**)

¹**ad·dict** \ə-'dikt\ *vb* : to devote or surrender (oneself) completely to something

²**ad·dict** \'ad-,ikt\ *n* : a person who is addicted (as to a drug)

ad·dic·tion \ə-'dik-shən\ *n* : the state of being addicted (as to the use of habit-forming drugs)

ad·di·tion \ə-'dish-ən\ *n* 1 : the act or process of adding 2 : the adding of numbers to obtain their sum 3 : something added ⟨an *addition* to a house⟩⟨a recent *addition* to the pitching staff⟩ — **in addition to** : over and above

ad·di·tion·al \ə-'dish-ən-l\ *adj* : ADDED, EXTRA — **ad·di·tion·al·ly** *adv*

ad·di·tive \'ad-ət-iv\ *adj* : relating to or produced by addition

ad·dle \'ad-l\ *vb* **ad·dled**; **ad·dling** 1 : to throw into confusion ⟨*addled* his brain⟩ 2 : to become rotten ⟨*addled* eggs⟩

¹**ad·dress** \ə-'dres\ *vb* 1 : to direct one's remarks to : speak or write to 2 : to mark directions for delivery on ⟨*address* a letter⟩

²**ad·dress** \ə-'dres, 'ad-,res\ *n* 1 : a formal speech : LECTURE 2 : the place where a person can usually be reached ⟨a business *address*⟩ 3 : the directions for delivery placed on mail

ad·dress·ee \,ad-,res-'ē\ *n* : the person to whom something is addressed

ad·e·noids \'ad-n-,óidz\ *n pl* : fleshy growths near the opening of the nose into the throat

¹**ad·ept** \'ad-,ept\ *n* : EXPERT

²**a·dept** \ə-'dept\ *adj* : highly skilled or trained ⟨*adept* at swimming⟩ **syn** see SKILLFUL — **a·dept·ly** *adv* — **a·dept·ness** *n*

ad·e·quate \'ad-i-kwət\ *adj* : enough to meet a need or to satisfy a requirement — **ad·e·quate·ly** *adv* — **ad·e·quate·ness** *n*

ad·here \ad-'hiər\ *vb* **ad·hered**; **ad·her·ing** 1 : to give support : maintain loyalty 2 : to stick fast : CLING 3 : to agree to accept as binding ⟨*adhere* to a treaty⟩

ad·her·ence \ad-'hir-əns\ *n* : steady or faithful attachment ⟨*adherence* to the truth⟩

ad·her·ent \ad-'hir-ənt\ *n* : a person who adheres to a belief, an organization, or a leader

ad·he·sion \ad-'hē-zhən\ *n* : the act or state of adhering

¹**ad·he·sive** \ad-'hē-siv\ *adj* 1 : tending to adhere : STICKY 2 : prepared for adhering — **ad·he·sive·ly** *adv* — **ad·he·sive·ness** *n*

²**adhesive** *n* : an adhesive substance

a·dieu \ə-'dü, -'dyü\ *n, pl* **a·dieus** *or* **a·dieux** \-'düz, -'dyüz\ : FAREWELL — often used as an interjection

a·di·os \,ad-ē-'ōs, ,äd-\ *interj* — used to express farewell

ad·ja·cent \ə-'jās-nt\ *adj* : situated or lying next or near — **ad·ja·cent·ly** *adv*

ad·jec·ti·val \,aj-ik-'tī-vəl\ *adj* : of, relating to, or functioning as an adjective ⟨an *adjectival* phrase⟩ — **ad·jec·ti·val·ly** *adv*

ad·jec·tive \'aj-ik-tiv\ *n* : a word used to modify a noun ⟨*blue* in "blue sky" is an *adjective*⟩

ad·join \ə-'jȯin\ *vb* **1** : ADD, ATTACH **2** : to be next to or in contact with

ad·journ \ə-'jərn\ *vb* : to bring or come to a close for an indefinite or stated period of time ⟨*adjourn* a meeting⟩ — **ad·journ·ment** *n*

ad·judge \ə-'jəj\ *vb* **ad·judged; ad·judg·ing** : to hold or pronounce to be : DEEM

ad·junct \'aj-,əngkt\ *n* : something joined or added to something else but not an essential part of it

ad·just \ə-'jəst\ *vb* **1** : to bring to a more satisfactory state : SETTLE ⟨*adjust* conflicts⟩ **2** : to move the parts of an instrument or a piece of machinery until they fit together in the best working order ⟨*adjust* the brakes on a car⟩ **3** : ADAPT, ACCOMMODATE ⟨*adjust* to a new school⟩ — **ad·just·er** *n*

ad·just·a·ble \ə-'jəs-tə-bəl\ *adj* : capable of being adjusted

ad·just·ment \ə-'jəst-mənt\ *n* **1** : the act or process of adjusting : the state of being adjusted **2** : a settlement of a claim or debt **3** : a means of adjusting one part to another

ad·ju·tant \'aj-ət-ənt\ *n* : a staff officer (as in the army) who assists a commanding officer

ad–lib \'ad-'lib\ *vb* **ad–libbed; ad–lib·bing** : to improvise lines, a speech, or music

ad·min·is·ter \əd-'min-əs-tər\ *vb* **1** : to direct the affairs of : MANAGE ⟨*administer* an athletic program⟩ **2** : to mete out : DISPENSE ⟨*administer* justice⟩ **3** : GIVE, SUPPLY

ad·min·is·tra·tion \əd-,min-əs-'trā-shən\ *n* **1** : the act or process of administering **2** : performance of executive duties **3** : the persons who direct affairs (as of a city or school)

ad·min·is·tra·tive \əd-'min-əs-,trāt-iv\ *adj* : of or relating to administration

ad·mi·ra·ble \'ad-mə-rə-bəl\ *adj* : deserving to be admired — **ad·mi·ra·bly** \-blē\ *adv*

ad·mi·ral \'ad-mə-rəl\ *n* : a commissioned officer in the navy ranking next below a fleet admiral

ad·mi·ral·ty \'ad-mə-rəl-tē\ *adj* : of or relating to maritime affairs ⟨*admiralty* law⟩

ad·mi·ra·tion \,ad-mə-'rā-shən\ *n* **1** : an object of esteem **2** : delighted or astonished approval

ad·mire \əd-'mīr\ *vb* **ad·mired; ad·mir·ing** **1** : to regard with admiration ⟨*admired* the scenery⟩ **2** : to esteem highly — **ad·mir·er** *n*

ad·mis·si·ble \əd-'mis-ə-bəl\ *adj* : deserving to be admitted or allowed : ALLOWABLE

ad·mis·sion \əd-'mish-ən\ *n* **1** : the act of admitting **2** : the right or permission to enter ⟨*admission* to college⟩ **3** : the price of entrance **4** : a granting of something that has not been proved ⟨an *admission* of guilt⟩

ad·mit \əd-'mit\ *vb* **ad·mit·ted; ad·mit·ting** **1** : PERMIT, ALLOW **2** : to allow to enter : let in **3** : to confess to   **syn** see ACKNOWLEDGE

ad·mit·tance \əd-'mit-ns\ *n* : permission to enter

ad·mix \ad-'miks\ *vb* : MIX, MINGLE

ad·mix·ture \ad-'miks-chər\ *n* **1** : MIXTURE **2** : something added in mixing

ad·mon·ish \ad-'män-ish\ *vb* **1** : to express warning or disapproval to ⟨*admonish* a student for talking⟩ **2** : to give friendly advice or encouragement   **syn** see REBUKE

ad·mo·ni·tion \,ad-mə-'nish-ən\ *n* : a gentle or friendly reproof or warning

a·do \ə-'dü\ *n* : FUSS, TROUBLE

a·do·be \ə-'dō-bē\ *n* **1** : brick made of earth or clay dried in the sun **2** : a building made of adobe

ad·o·les·cence \,ad-l-'es-ns\ *n* : the period of life between childhood and maturity

ad·o·les·cent \,ad-l-'es-nt\ *n* : a person who is growing up but not yet adult

a·dopt \ə-'däpt\ *vb* **1** : to take (a child of other parents) as one's own **2** : to take up and practice as one's own **3** : to accept and put into effect — **a·dopt·er** *n*

a·dop·tion \ə-'däp-shən\ *n* : the act of adopting : the state of being adopted

a·dor·a·ble \ə-'dȯr-ə-bəl\ *adj* **1** : deserving to be adored **2** : CHARMING, LOVELY — **a·dor·a·ble·ness** *n* — **a·dor·a·bly** \-blē\ *adv*

ad·o·ra·tion \,ad-ə-'rā-shən\ *n* : deep love

a·dore \ə-'dȯr\ *vb* **a·dored; a·dor·ing** **1** : WORSHIP **2** : to be extremely fond of — **a·dor·er** *n*

a·dorn \ə-'dȯrn\ *vb* : to decorate with ornaments : BEAUTIFY

   syn ADORN, DECORATE, EMBELLISH all mean to add something in order to improve the appearance. ADORN suggests the adding of a beautiful touch to something already attractive ⟨a lovely lawn *adorned* with occasional flower beds⟩ DECORATE may indicate adding design and color to relieve dullness or plainness ⟨*decorate* a room with gay pictures⟩ or to add a touch of festivity ⟨*decorate* the gym for a party⟩ EMBELLISH often stresses the adding of too much or unnecessary ornament ⟨*embellished* the book cover with so much design we couldn't find the title⟩

a·dorn·ment \ə-'dȯrn-mənt\ *n* : DECORATION

a·drift \ə-'drift\ *adv (or adj)* **1** : afloat without motive power, anchor, or mooring ⟨a ship *adrift* in the storm⟩ **2** : without guidance or purpose

a·droit \ə-'drȯit\ *adj* **1** : skillful with one's hands **2** : SHREWD, RESOURCEFUL — **a·droit·ly** *adv* — **a·droit·ness** *n*

---

ad·u·la·tion \ˌaj-ə-ˈlā-shən\ *n* : excessive praise

¹a·dult \ə-ˈdəlt, ˈad-ˌəlt\ *adj* : fully developed and mature

²adult *n* : an adult person or thing

a·dul·ter·ate \ə-ˈdəl-tə-ˌrāt\ *vb* a·dul·ter·at·ed; a·dul·ter·at·ing : to make impure or weaker by adding a foreign or inferior substance

¹ad·vance \əd-ˈvans\ *vb* ad·vanced; ad·vanc·ing 1 : to move forward 2 : to further the progress of ⟨sacrifices that *advance* freedom⟩ 3 : to promote in rank 4 : LEND ⟨*advanced* him five dollars⟩ 5 : PROPOSE ⟨*advance* a new plan⟩ 6 : to raise in rate : INCREASE

²advance *n* 1 : a forward movement 2 : IM-PROVEMENT 3 : a rise in price, value, or amount 4 : a first step : OFFER 5 : a provision (as of money) before a return is received ⟨asked for an *advance* on his salary⟩ — in ad-vance : BEFORE — in advance of : ahead of

ad·vanced \əd-ˈvanst\ *adj* 1 : being far along in years or progress ⟨an *advanced* civilization⟩ 2 : being beyond the elementary or introduc-tory level ⟨*advanced* mathematics⟩

ad·vance·ment \əd-ˈvans-mənt\ *n* : IM-PROVEMENT, PROMOTION

ad·van·tage \əd-ˈvant-ij\ *n* 1 : superiority of position or condition 2 : BENEFIT, GAIN ⟨the *advantages* of an education⟩ ⟨it's to your own *advantage*⟩ 3 : something that benefits its possessor ⟨speed is an *advantage* in sports⟩

ad·van·ta·geous \ˌad-vən-ˈtā-jəs, -ˌvan-\ *adj* : giving an advantage : HELPFUL **syn** see BENEFICIAL — ad·van·ta·geous·ly *adv* — ad-van·ta·geous·ness *n*

ad·vent \ˈad-ˌvent\ *n* : ARRIVAL

¹ad·ven·ture \əd-ˈven-chər\ *n* 1 : an under-taking that involves unknown dangers and risks 2 : an unusual experience

²adventure *vb* ad·ven·tured; ad·ven·tur·ing : RISK, VENTURE

ad·ven·tur·er \əd-ˈven-chər-ər\ *n* 1 : a per-son who engages in new and risky undertak-ings 2 : a person who tries to advance his for-tunes by questionable means

ad·ven·ture·some \əd-ˈven-chər-səm\ *adj* : inclined to take risks : DARING

ad·ven·tur·ous \əd-ˈven-chə-rəs\ *adj* 1 : DARING, BOLD 2 : DANGEROUS, RISKY — ad·ven·tur·ous·ly *adv* — ad·ven·tur·ous·ness *n*

ad·verb \ˈad-ˌvərb\ *n* : a word used to modify a verb, an adjective, or another adverb ⟨*almost* and *very* in "at almost three o'clock on a very hot day" are *adverbs*⟩

ad·ver·bi·al \ad-ˈvər-bē-əl\ *adj* : of, relating to, or functioning as an adverb — ad·ver·bi-al·ly *adv*

ad·ver·sar·y \ˈad-vər-ˌser-ē\ *n, pl* ad·ver·sar-ies : ANTAGONIST, OPPONENT

ad·verse \ad-ˈvərs\ *adj* 1 : acting against or in a contrary direction ⟨*adverse* winds⟩ 2 : UNFAVORABLE ⟨*adverse* circumstances⟩ — ad·verse·ly *adv* — ad·verse·ness *n*

ad·ver·si·ty \ad-ˈvər-sət-ē\ *n, pl* ad·ver·si·ties : hard times : MISFORTUNE

ad·ver·tise \ˈad-vər-ˌtīz\ *vb* ad·ver·tised; ad-ver·tis·ing 1 : to announce publicly especially by a printed notice or a broadcast 2 : to call to public attention especially by stressing desirable qualities in order to arouse a desire to buy or patronize 3 : to issue a notice or re-quest ⟨*advertise* for a lost dog⟩ —ad·ver·tis·er *n*

ad·ver·tise·ment \ˌad-vər-ˈtīz-mənt, ad-ˈvərt-əz-\ *n* : a notice advertising something

ad·ver·tis·ing \ˈad-vər-ˌtī-zing\ *n* 1 : AD-VERTISEMENTS 2 : the business of preparing advertisements

ad·vice \əd-ˈvīs\ *n* 1 : recommendation about a decision or course of action 2 : IN-FORMATION, REPORT

ad·vis·a·ble \əd-ˈvī-zə-bəl\ *adj* : reasonable or proper to do : WISE ⟨it is not *advisable* to swim after a meal⟩ — ad·vis·a·bly \-blē\ *adv*

ad·vise \əd-ˈvīz\ *vb* ad·vised; ad·vis·ing 1 : to give advice to : COUNSEL 2 : INFORM, NOTIFY ⟨were *advised* of bad flying conditions⟩ 3 : to take counsel : CONSULT — ad·vis·er *or* ad·vi·sor *n*

ad·vise·ment \əd-ˈvīz-mənt\ *n* : careful con-sideration ⟨take a matter under *advisement*⟩

ad·vi·so·ry \əd-ˈvī-zə-rē\ *adj* 1 : having the power or right to advise 2 : containing advice

¹ad·vo·cate \ˈad-və-kət, -ˌkāt\ *n* 1 : a person who pleads another's cause (as in court) 2 : a person who argues for or supports a cause or policy

²ad·vo·cate \ˈad-və-ˌkāt\ *vb* ad·vo·cat·ed; ad-vo·cat·ing : to speak in favor of

adz *or* adze \ˈadz\ *n* : a cutting tool that has a thin arched blade at right angles to the handle and is used for roughly shaping wood

-aemia — see -EMIA

ae·on \ˈē-ən, -ˌän\ *n* : a vast period of time : AGE

aer- *or* aero- *prefix* 1 : air : at-mosphere : gas ⟨*aerate*⟩ ⟨*aerosol*⟩ ⟨*aerospace*⟩ 2 : aviation ⟨*aerodrome*⟩

adz

aer·ate \ˈaər-ˌāt\ *vb* aer·at·ed; aer·at·ing 1 : to supply (blood) with oxygen by respira-tion 2 : to supply or impregnate with air 3 : to combine or charge with gas — aer·at·or *n*

aer·a·tion \aər-ˈā-shən\ *n* : the process of aerating

¹**aer·i·al** \'ar-ē-əl\ *adj* **1** : of, relating to, or occurring in the air **2** : operating overhead on elevated cables or rails ⟨an *aerial* railway⟩ **3** : AIRY **4** : of or relating to aircraft ⟨*aerial* navigation⟩ **5** : designed for use in, taken from, or operating from or against aircraft ⟨*aerial* camera⟩⟨*aerial* warfare⟩—**aer·i·al·ly** *adv*

²**aerial** *n* : a radio or television antenna

aer·ie \'aər-ē, 'iər-\ *n* : the nest of a bird (as an eagle) high on a rock

aer·o·drome \'ar-ə-ˌdrōm\ *n, Brit* : AIRFIELD

aer·o·nau·ti·cal \ˌar-ə-'nȯt-i-kəl\ *or* **aer·o·nau·tic** \-ik\ *adj* : of or relating to aeronautics ⟨*aeronautical* engineer⟩

aer·o·nau·tics \ˌar-ə-'nȯt-iks\ *n* : a science dealing with the operation of aircraft or with their design and manufacture

aer·o·plane \'ar-ə-ˌplān\ *chiefly Brit var of* AIRPLANE

aer·o·sol \'ar-ə-ˌsȯl\ *n* : a substance (as fog or a paint for spraying on) that consists of fine solid or liquid particles in gas

aer·o·space \'ar-ō-ˌspās\ *n* : the earth's atmosphere and the space beyond

aes·thet·ic \es-'thet-ik\ *adj* **1** : of or relating to beauty and what is beautiful **2** : appreciative of what is beautiful — **aes·thet·i·cal·ly** \-i-kə-lē\ *adv*

a·far \ə-'fär\ *adv* : from, at, or to a great distance ⟨saw the man *afar* off⟩

af·fa·ble \'af-ə-bəl\ *adj* : courteous and agreeable in conversation — **af·fa·bly** \-blē\ *adv*

af·fair \ə-'faər\ *n* **1** *pl* : BUSINESS ⟨government *affairs*⟩ **2** : something that relates to or involves one ⟨is no *affair* of mine⟩ **3** : EVENT, ACTIVITY ⟨social *affairs*⟩

¹**af·fect** \ə-'fekt\ *vb* **1** : to be fond of using or wearing ⟨*affect* bright colors⟩ **2** : ASSUME

²**affect** *vb* **1** : to attack or act on as a disease does **2** : to have an effect on : INFLUENCE

syn AFFECT, EFFECT are often confused, partly because both verbs have the same word *effect* as the corresponding noun. AFFECT applies to the changing or altering of something ⟨the climate *affected* his health⟩ EFFECT applies to the intentional achieving of a result ⟨the new teacher *effected* great improvement in the class⟩

af·fec·ta·tion \ˌaf-ˌek-'tā-shən\ *n* : an attitude or way of behaving assumed to impress others

af·fect·ed \ə-'fek-təd\ *adj* : not natural or genuine : ASSUMED ⟨*affected* manners⟩ — **af·fect·ed·ly** *adv* — **af·fect·ed·ness** *n*

af·fect·ing \ə-'fek-ting\ *adj* : arousing pity, sympathy, or sorrow ⟨an *affecting* story⟩

¹**af·fec·tion** \ə-'fek-shən\ *n* : a feeling of attachment : FONDNESS

²**affection** *n* : DISEASE, DISORDER

af·fec·tion·ate \ə-'fek-shə-nət\ *adj* : feeling or showing a great liking for a person or thing : LOVING — **af·fec·tion·ate·ly** *adv*

af·fi·ance \ə-'fī-əns\ *vb* **af·fi·anced; af·fi·anc·ing** : BETROTH, ENGAGE

af·fi·da·vit \ˌaf-ə-'dā-vət\ *n* : a sworn statement in writing

af·fil·i·ate \ə-'fil-ē-ˌāt\ *vb* **af·fil·i·at·ed; af·fil·i·at·ing** : to associate as a member or branch

af·fin·i·ty \ə-'fin-ət-ē\ *n, pl* **af·fin·i·ties** **1** : RELATIONSHIP, KINSHIP **2** : ATTRACTION

af·firm \ə-'fərm\ *vb* : to declare to be true : state with confidence : ASSERT

af·fir·ma·tion \ˌaf-ər-'mā-shən\ *n* : an act of affirming : ASSERTION

¹**af·firm·a·tive** \ə-'fər-mət-iv\ *adj* **1** : asserting that the fact is so **2** : POSITIVE

²**affirmative** *n* **1** : an expression (as the word *yes*) of agreement or assent **2** : the affirmative side in a debate or vote

¹**af·fix** \ə-'fiks\ *vb* : FASTEN, ATTACH

²**af·fix** \'af-ˌiks\ *n* : a sound or sequence of sounds or a letter or sequence of letters attached to the beginning or to the end of a word to change its meaning

af·flict \ə-'flikt\ *vb* : to cause pain and distress to : make miserable

af·flic·tion \ə-'flik-shən\ *n* **1** : the state of being afflicted **2** : something that causes pain and distress

af·flu·ence \'af-ˌlü-əns\ *n* : abundant wealth or property : RICHES

af·flu·ent \'af-ˌlü-ənt\ *adj* : WEALTHY, RICH

af·ford \ə-'fōrd\ *vb* **1** : to have money enough to buy ⟨unable to *afford* a new car⟩ **2** : to be able to do or to bear without serious harm ⟨no one can *afford* to waste his strength⟩ **3** : PROVIDE, FURNISH ⟨tennis *affords* good exercise⟩

af·fray \ə-'frā\ *n* : a noisy quarrel or fight

¹**af·front** \ə-'frənt\ *vb* : to offend by showing disrespect : INSULT

²**affront** *n* : INSULT

a·field \ə-'fēld\ *adv* **1** : to, in, or on the field **2** : away from home **3** : out of one's regular course

a·fire \ə-'fīr\ *adj* : being on fire : BURNING

a·flame \ə-'flām\ *adj* : FLAMING, GLOWING

a·float \ə-'flōt\ *adv (or adj)* **1** : being on board ship **2** : FLOATING, ADRIFT **3** : flooded with water ⟨a ship with decks *afloat*⟩

a·flut·ter \ə-'flət-ər\ *adj* **1** : FLUTTERING **2** : nervously excited

a·foot \ə-'fut\ *adv (or adj)* **1** : on foot ⟨traveled *afoot*⟩ **2** : in action : in progress

a·fore·men·tioned \ə-'fōr-ˌmen-chənd\ *adj* : mentioned before

a·fore·said \ə-'fōr-ˌsed\ *adj* : said or named before ⟨the *aforesaid* persons⟩

a·fore·thought \ə-'fōr-ˌthȯt\ *adj* : PREMEDITATED ⟨with malice *aforethought*⟩

a·foul \ə-'faủl\ *adj* : FOULED, TANGLED

afoul of *prep* : in or into conflict with

a·fraid \ə-'frād\ *adj* : filled with fear

a·fresh \ə-'fresh\ *adv* : from a new start

¹Af·ri·can \'af-ri-kən\ *adj* : of or relating to Africa or the Africans

²African *n* **1** : a native or inhabitant of Africa **2** : NEGRO

African violet *n* : a tropical African plant grown as a houseplant for its showy white, pink, or purple flowers and its velvety leaves

aft \'aft\ *adv* : toward or at the stern of a ship or the tail of an aircraft

¹af·ter \'af-tər\ *adv* : following in time or place

²after *prep* **1** : behind in place or time ⟨running *after* his brother⟩ ⟨got there *after* the others⟩ **2** : intent on the seizure, mastery, or achievement of ⟨go *after* the prisoner⟩

³after *conj* : following the time when

⁴after *adj* **1** : LATER **2** : located toward the rear

af·ter·ef·fect \'af-tər-ə-ˌfekt\ *n* **1** : an effect that follows its cause after some time has passed **2** : a secondary effect

af·ter·glow \'af-tər-ˌglō\ *n* : a glow remaining (as in the sky after sunset) where a light has disappeared

af·ter·life \'af-tər-ˌlīf\ *n* : an existence after death

af·ter·math \'af-tər-ˌmath\ *n* : CONSEQUENCE

af·ter·noon \ˌaf-tər-'nün\ *n* : the part of the day between noon and evening

af·ter·thought \'af-tər-ˌthȯt\ *n* : a later thought about something one has done or said

af·ter·ward \'af-tər-wərd\ *or* **af·ter·wards** \-wərdz\ *adv* : at a later time

a·gain \ə-'gen\ *adv* **1** : once more : ANEW ⟨he did it *again*⟩ **2** : on the other hand **3** : FURTHER **4** : in addition ⟨half as much *again*⟩

a·gainst \ə-'genst\ *prep* **1** : directly opposite : FACING **2** : opposed to ⟨war *against* poverty⟩ **3** : as protection from ⟨a shield *against* aggression⟩ **4** : in or into contact with

a·gape \ə-'gāp\ *adj* : having the mouth open in wonder or surprise

ag·ate \'ag-ət\ *n* **1** : a mineral consisting of quartz with colors arranged in stripes, cloudy masses, or mosslike forms **2** : a child's marble of agate or glass resembling agate

a·ga·ve \ə-'gä-vē\ *n* : a plant with sword‿ shaped spiny-edged leaves sometimes grown for its showy spike of flowers

¹age \'āj\ *n* **1** : the time from birth to a specified date ⟨a boy six years of *age*⟩ **2** : the time of life when a person receives full legal rights ⟨come of *age*⟩ **3** : the later part of life ⟨a mind as active in *age* as in youth⟩ **4** : normal lifetime **5** : a period of history ⟨the machine *age*⟩ **6** : a long period of time   **syn** see PERIOD

²age *vb* **aged** \'ājd\; **ag·ing** *or* **age·ing** **1** : to grow old or cause to grow old **2** : to become or cause to become mature or mellow

-age \ij\ *n suffix* **1** : aggregate : collection ⟨track*age*⟩ **2** : action : process ⟨haul*age*⟩ **3** : result of ⟨break*age*⟩ **4** : rate of ⟨leak*age*⟩ **5** : house or place of ⟨orphan*age*⟩ **6** : state : rank ⟨vassal*age*⟩ **7** : fee : charge ⟨post*age*⟩

aged \'ā-jəd *for 1*, 'ājd *for 2*\ *adj* **1** : very old ⟨an *aged* oak⟩ **2** : of age ⟨a boy *aged* ten⟩

age·less \'āj-ləs\ *adj* **1** : not growing old or showing the effects of age **2** : TIMELESS, ETERNAL — **age·less·ly** *adv*

a·gen·cy \'ā-jən-sē\ *n, pl* **a·gen·cies** **1** : a person or thing through which power is exerted or an end is achieved **2** : the office or function of an agent **3** : an establishment doing business for another ⟨automobile *agency*⟩ **4** : an administrative division of a government

a·gen·da \ə-'jen-də\ *n* : a list of things to be done or discussed : PROGRAM

a·gent \'ā-jənt\ *n* **1** : something that produces an effect ⟨cleansing *agents*⟩ **2** : MEANS, INSTRUMENT **3** : a person who acts or does business for another

ag·gran·dize \ə-'gran-ˌdīz, 'ag-rən-\ *vb* **ag·gran·dized**; **ag·gran·diz·ing** : to make great or greater (as in power or resources)

ag·gra·vate \'ag-rə-ˌvāt\ *vb* **ag·gra·vat·ed**; **ag·gra·vat·ing** **1** : to make worse or more severe ⟨*aggravate* an injury⟩ **2** : EXASPERATE, ANNOY

ag·gra·va·tion \ˌag-rə-'vā-shən\ *n* **1** : an increase in severity **2** : something that aggravates

¹ag·gre·gate \'ag-ri-gət\ *adj* : formed by the collection of units or particles into one mass or sum

²ag·gre·gate \'ag-ri-ˌgāt\ *vb* **ag·gre·gat·ed**; **ag·gre·gat·ing** **1** : to collect or gather into a mass or whole **2** : to amount to as a whole

³ag·gre·gate \'ag-ri-gət\ *n* **1** : a mass or body of units or parts **2** : the whole sum or amount

ag·gre·ga·tion \ˌag-ri-'gā-shən\ *n* **1** : the collecting of units or parts into a mass or whole **2** : a group, body, or mass composed of many distinct parts

ag·gres·sion \ə-'gresh-ən\ *n* **1** : an unprovoked attack **2** : the practice of making attacks

ag·gres·sive \ə-'gres-iv\ *adj* **1** : showing a readiness to attack others ⟨an *aggressive* dog⟩ **2** : practicing aggression ⟨an *aggressive* nation⟩ **3** : ENERGETIC, FORCEFUL — **ag·gres·sive·ly** *adv* — **ag·gres·sive·ness** *n*

ag·gres·sor \ə-'gres-ər\ *n* : a person or a country that makes an unprovoked attack

ag·grieved \ə-'grēvd\ *adj* **1** : troubled or distressed in spirit **2** : having a grievance

a·ghast \ə-'gast\ *adj* : struck with terror, amazement, or horror : SHOCKED

ag·ile \'aj-əl\ *adj* **1** : able to move quickly and easily **2** : mentally quick — **ag·ile·ly** *adv*

a·gil·i·ty \ə-'jil-ət-ē\ *n* : the ability to move quickly and easily

aging *pres part of* AGE

ag·i·tate \'aj-ə-ˌtāt\ *vb* **ag·i·tat·ed; ag·i·tat·ing** **1** : to move with an irregular rapid motion ⟨water *agitated* by wind⟩ **2** : to stir up : EXCITE ⟨*agitated* by bad news⟩ **3** : to attempt to arouse public feeling — **ag·i·ta·tor** *n*

ag·i·ta·tion \ˌaj-ə-'tā-shən\ *n* : the act of agitating : the state of being agitated

a·gleam \ə-'glēm\ *adj* : GLEAMING

a·glit·ter \ə-'glit-ər\ *adj* : GLITTERING

a·glow \ə-'glō\ *adj* : GLOWING

a·go \ə-'gō\ *adj (or adv)* : earlier than the present time ⟨a week *ago*⟩

a·gog \ə-'gäg\ *adj* : full of excitement : EAGER

ag·o·nize \'ag-ə-ˌnīz\ *vb* **ag·o·nized; ag·o·niz·ing** : to suffer or cause to suffer agony

ag·o·ny \'ag-ə-nē\ *n, pl* **ag·o·nies** **1** : intense pain of body or mind **2** : the last sufferings of a dying person

a·grar·i·an \ə-'grer-ē-ən\ *adj* **1** : of or relating to land or its ownership ⟨*agrarian* reforms⟩ **2** : of or relating to farmers or farming

a·gree \ə-'grē\ *vb* **a·greed; a·gree·ing** **1** : to give one's approval : CONSENT **2** : to have the same opinion : CONCUR **3** : ADMIT, CONCEDE ⟨*agreed* that he was wrong⟩ **4** : to be alike : CORRESPOND **5** : to get on well together **6** : to come to an understanding ⟨*agree* on a price⟩ **7** : to be fitting or healthful : SUIT

a·gree·a·ble \ə-'grē-ə-bəl\ *adj* **1** : PLEASING, PLEASANT ⟨an *agreeable* taste⟩ **2** : willing to agree ⟨*agreeable* to his suggestion⟩ — **a·gree·a·ble·ness** *n* — **a·gree·a·bly** \-blē\ *adv*

a·gree·ment \ə-'grē-mənt\ *n* **1** : the act or fact of having the same opinion : harmony of opinion or action **2** : a mutual arrangement or understanding

ag·ri·cul·tur·al \ˌag-ri-'kəl-chə-rəl\ *adj* : of, relating to, or used in agriculture

ag·ri·cul·ture \'ag-ri-ˌkəl-chər\ *n* : the cultivation of the soil, production of crops, and raising of livestock : FARMING

a·ground \ə-'graund\ *adv (or adj)* : with the bottom lodged on the ground or on the shore

ah \'ä\ *interj* — used to express delight, relief, regret, or contempt

a·ha \ä-'hä\ *interj* — used to express surprise, triumph, or scorn

a·head \ə-'hed\ *adv (or adj)* **1** : in or toward the front : LEADING **2** : into or for the future

ahead of *prep* **1** : in front or advance of **2** : in excess of

a·hoy \ə-'hoi\ *interj* — used in hailing

¹aid \'ād\ *vb* : HELP, ASSIST

²aid *n* **1** : ASSISTANCE **2** : ASSISTANT **3** : something that is of help or assistance

aide \'ād\ *n* : a person who acts as an assistant especially to a military officer

ail \'āl\ *vb* **1** : to be the matter with : TROUBLE ⟨wondered what *ailed* his family⟩ **2** : to suffer with something and especially ill health

ai·le·ron \'ā-lə-ˌrän\ *n* : a winglike portion of an airplane wing that is movable and sometimes external to it

ail·ment \'āl-mənt\ *n* : a disordered condition : SICKNESS

¹aim \'ām\ *vb* **1** : to point a weapon toward an object **2** : ASPIRE, INTEND ⟨we *aim* to please⟩ **3** : to direct to or toward a specified object or goal

²aim *n* **1** : the directing of a weapon or a missile at a mark **2** : GOAL, PURPOSE

aim·less \'ām-ləs\ *adj* : lacking purpose or aim — **aim·less·ly** *adv* — **aim·less·ness** *n*

¹air \'aər\ *n* **1** : the invisible mixture of odorless tasteless gases that surrounds the earth **2** : air that is compressed ⟨*air* sprayer⟩ **3** : AIRCRAFT ⟨*air* mechanic⟩ **4** : AVIATION ⟨*air* safety⟩ **5** : RADIO, TELEVISION ⟨gave a speech on the *air*⟩ **6** : outward appearance ⟨an *air* of mystery⟩ **7** *pl* : an artificial or affected manner ⟨put on *airs*⟩ **8** : MELODY, TUNE

²air *vb* **1** : to place in the air for cooling, refreshing, or cleansing ⟨*air* blankets⟩ **2** : to make known in public ⟨*aired* his opinions⟩

air base *n* : a base of operations for military aircraft

air–con·di·tion \ˌaər-kən-'dish-ən\ *vb* : to equip with an apparatus for washing air and controlling its humidity and temperature — **air conditioner** *n* — **air–con·di·tion·ing** *n*

air·craft \'aər-ˌkraft\ *n, pl* **aircraft** : a vehicle (as a balloon, airplane, or helicopter) for rising from the earth's surface and traveling through the air that is supported either by its own lightness or by the action of the air against its surfaces

air·drome \'aər-ˌdrōm\ *n* : AIRPORT

ə abut   ər further   a ax   ā age   ä father, cot   à (see key page)   au out   ch chin   e less   ē easy   g gift   i trip   ī life

air·drop \'aər-ˌdräp\ *n* : delivery of cargo or personnel by parachute from an airplane

air·field \'aər-ˌfēld\ *n* **1** : the landing field of an airport **2** : AIRPORT

air force *n* : the military organization of a nation for air warfare

air lane *n* : AIRWAY 2

air·lift \'aər-ˌlift\ *n* : a supply line operated by aircraft

air·line \'aər-ˌlīn\ *n* **1** : a system of transportation by aircraft **2** : a company operating an airline

air·lin·er \'aər-ˌlī-nər\ *n* : a large passenger airplane operating over an airline

airliner

¹air·mail \'aər-'māl\ *n* **1** : the system of transporting mail by airplanes **2** : mail transported by airplanes

²airmail *vb* : to send by airmail

air·man \'aər-mən\ *n, pl* **air·men** \-mən\ **1** : an enlisted man in the air force in one of the four ranks below a staff sergeant **2** : AVIATOR

airman basic *n* : an enlisted man of the lowest rank in the air force

air·plane \'aər-ˌplān\ *n* : a fixed-wing aircraft heavier than air that is driven by a propeller or by a rearward jet and supported by the action of the air against its wings

air·port \'aər-ˌpōrt\ *n* : a place either on land or water that is kept for the landing and takeoff of airplanes and for receiving and discharging passengers and cargo and that usually has facilities for the shelter, supply, and repair of airplanes

air·ship \'aər-ˌship\ *n* : an aircraft lighter than air that is kept in the air by a gas-filled container and has an engine, propeller, and rudder

air·sick \'aər-ˌsik\ *adj* : sick at the stomach while riding in an airplane because of the effects of irregular motion, speed, and altitude — **air·sick·ness** *n*

air·strip \'aər-ˌstrip\ *n* : a runway without air base or airport facilities (as hangars)

air·tight \'aər-'tīt\ *adj* : so tight that no air can get in or out — **air·tight·ness** *n*

air·wave \'aər-ˌwāv\ *n* : the medium of radio and television transmission

air·way \'aər-ˌwā\ *n* **1** : a passage for a current of air **2** : a regular route for airplanes **3** : AIRLINE

air·y \'aər-ē\ *adj* **air·i·er**; **air·i·est** **1** : of, relating to, or living in the air **2** : open to the air : BREEZY ⟨an *airy* room⟩ **3** : resembling air in lightness : DELICATE

aisle \'īl\ *n* : a passage between sections of seats (as in a church or theater)

a·jar \ə-'jär\ *adv* (*or adj*) : slightly open

a·kim·bo \ə-'kim-bō\ *adv* (*or adj*) : with hands on hips and elbows turned outward

a·kin \ə-'kin\ *adj* **1** : related by blood **2** : similar in kind : ALIKE

¹-al \əl, l\ *adj suffix* : of, relating to, or characterized by ⟨direction*al*⟩ ⟨fiction*al*⟩

²-al *n suffix* : action : process ⟨rehears*al*⟩

al·a·bas·ter \'al-ə-ˌbas-tər\ *n* : a fine-textured usually white and translucent stone used for carving

a la carte \ˌal-ə-'kärt, ˌä-lə-\ *adv* (*or adj*) : with a separate price for each item on the menu

a·lac·ri·ty \ə-'lak-rət-ē\ *n* : a cheerful readiness to do something : BRISKNESS

¹a·larm \ə-'lärm\ *n* **1** : a warning of danger **2** : a device (as a bell) that warns or signals people **3** : the fear caused by sudden danger

²alarm *vb* **1** : to warn of danger **2** : to arouse to a sense of danger : FRIGHTEN

a·las \ə-'las\ *interj* — used to express unhappiness, pity, or concern

al·ba·tross \'al-bə-ˌtrȯs\ *n* : a very large web-footed seabird

al·be·it \ȯl-'bē-ət, al-\ *conj* : even though

al·bi·no \al-'bī-nō\ *n, pl* **al·bi·nos** **1** : a person or an animal that lacks the normal coloring matter in skin, hair, and eyes **2** : a plant that lacks coloring matter

al·bum \'al-bəm\ *n* **1** : a book with blank pages in which to put photographs, stamps, or autographs **2** : one or more phonograph records or tape recordings carrying a major musical work or a group of related selections

al·co·hol \'al-kə-ˌhȯl\ *n* **1** : a colorless flammable liquid that is the intoxicating substance in fermented and distilled liquors (as beer, wine, or whiskey) **2** : a liquor (as beer, wine, or whiskey) containing alcohol

¹al·co·hol·ic \ˌal-kə-'hȯl-ik, -'häl-\ *adj* **1** : of, relating to, or containing alcohol ⟨*alcoholic* drinks⟩ **2** : affected with alcoholism

²alcoholic *n* : a person affected with alcoholism

al·co·hol·ism \'al-kə-ˌhȯl-ˌiz-əm\ *n* : an abnormal condition of body and mind caused by excessive use of alcoholic drinks

al·cove \'al-ˌkōv\ *n* : a nook or small recess opening off a larger room

al·der \'ȯl-dər\ *n* : a tree or shrub related to the birches

alder: leaves and cones

that has toothed leaves and grows in moist soil

ale \'āl\ *n* : an alcoholic drink made from malt and flavored with hops that is usually more bitter than beer

¹a·lert \ə-'lərt\ *adj* **1** : watchful and prompt to meet danger **2** : ACTIVE, BRISK — **a·lert·ly** *adv* — **a·lert·ness** *n*

²alert *n* **1** : a signal (as an alarm) of danger **2** : the period during which an alert is in effect — **on the alert** : watchful against danger

³alert *vb* : to call to a state of readiness : WARN

al·fal·fa \al-'fal-fə\ *n* : a plant with cloverlike leaves and purple flowers that is grown as a food for horses and cattle

al·ga \'al-gə\ *n, pl* **al·gae** \'al-,jē\ : any of a large group of lowly plants that are not divisible into roots, stems, and leaves, do not produce seeds, and include the seaweeds and related freshwater and land plants

¹a·li·as \'ā-lē-əs\ *adv* : otherwise known as

²alias *n* : an assumed name

¹al·i·bi \'al-ə-,bī\ *n, pl* **al·i·bis 1** : the plea made by a person accused of a crime that he was somewhere else when the crime was committed **2** : EXCUSE

²alibi *vb* **al·i·bied; al·i·bi·ing 1** : to offer an excuse **2** : to make an excuse for

¹a·li·en \'ā-lē-ən\ *adj* : FOREIGN

²alien *n* : a foreign-born resident who is not a citizen of the country in which he lives

a·li·en·ate \'ā-lē-ə,nāt\ *vb* **a·li·en·at·ed; a·li·en·at·ing** : to make hostile where love, loyalty, or attachment formerly existed : ESTRANGE

¹a·light \ə-'līt\ *vb* **a·light·ed** *also* **a·lit** \ə-'lit\; **a·light·ing 1** : to get down : DISMOUNT **2** : to descend from the air and settle : LAND

²alight *adj* : LIGHTED, AFLAME

a·lign \ə-'līn\ *vb* **1** : to bring into line ⟨*align* the wheels of an automobile⟩ **2** : to array on the side of or against a cause — **a·lign·er** *n* — **a·lign·ment** *n*

¹a·like \ə-'līk\ *adj* : SIMILAR — **a·like·ness** *n*

²alike *adv* : in the same manner

al·i·men·ta·ry \,al-ə-'ment-ə-rē\ *adj* : of or relating to food and nourishment

alimentary canal *n* : a long tube made up of the esophagus, stomach, and intestine into which food is taken and digested and from which wastes are passed out

al·i·mo·ny \'al-ə-,mō-nē\ *n* : an allowance paid by a man to a woman after her legal separation or divorce from him

alit *past of* ALIGHT

a·live \ə-'līv\ *adj* **1** : not dead or inanimate : LIVING **2** : being in force or operation : ACTIVE **3** : knowingly aware ⟨was *alive* to

the danger⟩ **4** : SWARMING — **a·live·ness** *n*

al·ka·li \'al-kə-,lī\ *n, pl* **al·ka·lies** *or* **al·ka·lis 1** : any of numerous substances that have a bitter taste and counteract acids **2** : a salt or a mixture of salts sometimes found in large amounts in the soil of dry regions

al·ka·line \'al-kə-,līn, -lən\ *adj* : of or relating to an alkali

¹all \'ol\ *adj* **1** : the whole of ⟨sat up *all* night⟩ **2** : the greatest possible ⟨told in *all* seriousness⟩ **3** : every one of ⟨*all* men will go⟩

²all *adv* **1** : WHOLLY, ALTOGETHER ⟨sat *all* alone⟩ **2** : so much ⟨is *all* the better for it⟩ **3** : for each side ⟨the score is two *all*⟩

³all *pron* **1** : the whole number or amount ⟨*all* of us⟩ ⟨*all* of the money⟩ **2** : EVERYTHING

Al·lah \'al-ə\ *n* : the Supreme Being of the Muslims

all–a·round \,ol-ə-'raund\ *adj* **1** : competent in many fields **2** : useful in many ways

al·lay \ə-'lā\ *vb* **1** : to make less severe ⟨*allay* pain⟩ **2** : to make quiet ⟨*allay* anxiety⟩

al·lege \ə-'lej\ *vb* **al·leged; al·leg·ing 1** : to state positively but without proof ⟨*allege* a man's guilt⟩ **2** : to offer as a reason or excuse

al·le·giance \ə-'lē-jəns\ *n* **1** : loyalty and service owed to one's country and government **2** : devotion or loyalty to a person, group, or cause **syn** see LOYALTY

al·le·lu·ia \,al-ə-'lü-yə\ *interj* : HALLELUJAH

al·ler·gic \ə-'lər-jik\ *adj* : of, relating to, or inducing allergy

al·ler·gy \'al-ər-jē\ *n, pl* **al·ler·gies** : a condition in which a person is made sick by something that is harmless to most people

al·le·vi·ate \ə-'lē-vē-,āt\ *vb* **al·le·vi·at·ed; al·le·vi·at·ing** : to make easier to be endured

al·ley \'al-ē\ *n, pl* **al·leys 1** : a narrow passageway between buildings **2** : a place for playing games in which balls are rolled

al·li·ance \ə-'lī-əns\ *n* **1** : a union or connection between families, groups, or individuals **2** : an association formed by two or more nations for their mutual assistance and protection **3** : a treaty of alliance

al·lied \ə-'līd, 'al-,īd\ *adj* **1** : CONNECTED, RELATED ⟨chemistry and *allied* subjects⟩ **2** : joined in alliance ⟨*allied* nations⟩

al·li·ga·tor \'al-ə-,gāt-ər\ *n* [from Spanish *el legarto* "the lizard"] : a large four-footed water animal related to the snakes and lizards

al·lit·er·ate \ə-'lit-ə-,rāt\ *vb* **al·lit·er·at·ed; al·lit·er·at·ing** : to form an alliteration

al·lit·er·a·tion \ə-,lit-ə-'rā-shən\ *n* : the repetition of a sound at the beginning of two or more neighboring words (as in "wild and woolly" or "babbling brook")

ə abut   ər further   a ax   ā age   ä father, cot   å (see key page)   au̇ out   ch chin   e less   ē easy   g gift   i trip   ī life

al·lo·cate \'al-ə-ˌkāt\ *vb* **al·lo·cat·ed; al·lo·cat·ing** : ALLOT, ASSIGN

al·lot \ə-'lät\ *vb* **al·lot·ted; al·lot·ting** : to distribute as a share or portion : ASSIGN

al·lot·ment \ə-'lät-mənt\ *n* **1** : the act of allotting **2** : something that is allotted

al·low \ə-'laù\ *vb* **1** : to assign as a share or suitable amount (as of time or money) **2** : to grant as a deduction or an addition **3** : ADMIT, CONCEDE **4** : PERMIT **5** : to make allowance ⟨*allow* for growth⟩

al·low·a·ble \ə-'laù-ə-bəl\ *adj* : not forbidden : PERMITTED — **al·low·a·bly** \-blē\ *adv*

al·low·ance \ə-'laù-əns\ *n* **1** : an allotted share **2** : a sum given as a reimbursement or bounty or for expenses ⟨a weekly *allowance*⟩ **3** : the taking into account of things that may partly excuse an offense or a mistake

al·loy \'al-ˌòi, ə-'lòi\ *n* **1** : a substance made of two or more metals melted together ⟨brass is an *alloy* of copper and zinc⟩ **2** : a metal mixed with a more valuable metal to add hardness or wearing quality

all–round \'òl-'raùnd\ *var of* ALL-AROUND

al·lude \ə-'lüd\ *vb* **al·lud·ed; al·lud·ing** : to make indirect reference : REFER

syn ALLUDE, REFER mean to call attention to or make mention of something. REFER indicates making an open and straightforward statement ⟨*referred* twice to the amount of talking in the class⟩ ALLUDE suggests the use of indirect statements and hints ⟨*alluded* to the bad manners shown by some of the class⟩

al·lure \ə-'lùr\ *vb* **al·lured; al·lur·ing** : to entice by charm or attraction

al·lure·ment \ə-'lùr-mənt\ *n* : ATTRACTION

al·lu·sion \ə-'lü-zhən\ *n* : an implied or indirect reference

¹al·ly \ə-'lī, 'al-ˌī\ *vb* **al·lied; al·ly·ing** : to form a connection between : join in an alliance

²al·ly \'al-ˌī, ə-'lī\ *n, pl* **al·lies** : one (as a person or a nation) associated or united with another in a common purpose ⟨*allies* in the war⟩ syn see PARTNER

al·ma·nac \'òl-mə-ˌnak\ *n* : a publication containing a calendar of days, weeks, and months and usually facts about the rising and setting of sun and moon and changes in the tides

al·might·y \òl-'mīt-ē\ *adj, often cap* : having absolute power over all ⟨*Almighty* God⟩

al·mond \'ä-mənd, 'am-ənd\ *n* : a nut that is the edible kernel of a small tree related to the peach

almond: leaves and fruit

al·most \'òl-ˌmōst\ *adv* : only a little less than : NEARLY

alms \'ämz\ *n, pl* **alms** : something and especially money given to help the poor : CHARITY

a·loft \ə-'lòft\ *adv (or adj)* **1** : at or to a great height **2** : in the air and especially in flight **3** : at, on, or to the top of the mast or the higher rigging of a ship

¹a·lone \ə-'lōn\ *adj* **1** : separated from others **2** : exclusive of anyone or anything else

²alone *adv* **1** : SOLELY, EXCLUSIVELY **2** : without company or help ⟨lives and works *alone*⟩

¹a·long \ə-'lòng\ *prep* **1** : on or near in a lengthwise direction ⟨walk *along* the street⟩ **2** : at a point on ⟨stopped *along* the way⟩

²along *adv* **1** : FORWARD, ON ⟨move *along*⟩ **2** : as a companion or associate ⟨brought his brother *along*⟩ **3** : throughout the time

a·long·shore \ə-'lòng-ˌshōr\ *adv (or adj)* : along the shore or coast

¹a·long·side \ə-'lòng-ˌsīd\ *adv* : along or by the side

²alongside *prep* : parallel to

¹a·loof \ə-'lüf\ *adv* : at a distance ⟨stood *aloof*⟩

²aloof *adj* : RESERVED ⟨a shy *aloof* manner⟩ — **a·loof·ly** *adv* — **a·loof·ness** *n*

a·loud \ə-'laùd\ *adv* : using the voice so as to be clearly heard ⟨read *aloud*⟩

al·pac·a \al-'pak-ə\ *n* : a South American animal related to the camel and llama that is raised for its fine long woolly hair which is woven into warm strong cloth

al·pha·bet \'al-fə-ˌbet\ *n* : the letters used in writing a language arranged in their regular order

alpaca

al·pha·bet·ic \ˌal-fə-'bet-ik\ *or* **al·pha·bet·i·cal** \-i-kəl\ *adj* : arranged in the order of the letters of the alphabet — **al·pha·bet·i·cal·ly** *adv*

al·pha·bet·ize \'al-fə-bə-ˌtīz\ *vb* **al·pha·bet·ized; al·pha·bet·iz·ing** : to arrange in alphabetical order

al·pha particle \'al-fə-\ *n* : a particle with a positive electric charge given off by a radioactive chemical element

al·read·y \òl-'red-ē\ *adv* **1** : before a stated or implied time : PREVIOUSLY **2** : so soon

al·so \'òl-sō\ *adv* : in addition : TOO

al·so–ran \'òl-sō-ˌran\ *n* : a contestant that does not win

al·tar \'òl-tər\ *n* **1** : a usually raised structure on which sacrifices are offered or incense is burned in worship **2** : a table used as a center of worship or ritual

al·tar·piece \'òl-tər-ˌpēs\ *n* : a work of art to decorate the space above and behind an altar

al·ter \'ȯl-tər\ vb : to change partly but not completely ⟨alter a dress⟩

al·ter·a·tion \ˌȯl-tə-'rā-shən\ n 1 : a making or becoming different in some respects 2 : the result of altering : MODIFICATION

al·ter·ca·tion \ˌȯl-tər-'kā-shən\ n : a noisy or angry dispute

¹**al·ter·nate** \'ȯl-tər-nət\ adj 1 : occurring or succeeding by turns ⟨alternate sunshine and rain⟩ 2 : arranged one above, beside, or next to another in a regular sequence ⟨alternate layers of cake and filling⟩ 3 : every other : every second — **al·ter·nate·ly** adv

²**al·ter·nate** \'ȯl-tər-ˌnāt\ vb **al·ter·nat·ed**; **al·ter·nat·ing** : to occur or cause to occur by turns

³**al·ter·nate** \'ȯl-tər-nət\ n : a person named to take the place of another whenever necessary ⟨alternates to a convention⟩

al·ter·nat·ing current n : an electric current that reverses its direction of flow regularly many times per second

al·ter·na·tion \ˌȯl-tər-'nā-shən\ n 1 : the act or process of alternating 2 : SUCCESSION 3 : regular reversal in direction of flow

¹**al·ter·na·tive** \ȯl-'tər-nət-iv\ adj 1 : offering or expressing a choice ⟨alternative plans⟩ 2 : ALTERNATE — **al·ter·na·tive·ly** adv

²**alternative** n 1 : a chance to choose between two things 2 : one of the things between which a choice is to be made syn see CHOICE

al·though \ȯl-'thō\ conj : in spite of the fact that : even though

al·ti·tude \'al-tə-ˌtüd, -ˌtyüd\ n 1 : height above a given level and especially above sea level 2 : the perpendicular distance from the base of a geometric figure to the vertex or to the side parallel to the base 3 : a high position or region syn see HEIGHT

al·to \'al-tō\ n, pl **al·tos** 1 : the lowest female singing voice 2 : a singer or an instrument (as a horn) having the range of an alto voice

al·to·geth·er \ˌȯl-tə-'geth-ər\ adv 1 : WHOLLY, ENTIRELY 2 : on the whole

al·tru·ism \'al-trù-ˌiz-əm\ n : unselfish interest in the welfare of others

al·um \'al-əm\ n 1 : either of two crystalline aluminum compounds that have a sweetish-sourish taste and puckering effect on the mouth and are used (as to stop bleeding) in medicine 2 : a crystalline aluminum compound used in paper manufacture, dyeing, and sewage treatment

a·lu·mi·num \ə-'lü-mə-nəm\ n : a silver-white light metallic chemical element that is very malleable, conducts electricity well, resists rustlike effects, is the most abundant metal in the earth's crust, and is used (as in aircraft) in the form of alloys for structural purposes and in cooking utensils

a·lum·nus \ə-'ləm-nəs\ n, pl **a·lum·ni** \-ˌnī\ : one who has attended or has graduated from a school, college, or university

al·ways \'ȯl-wēz, -wəz\ adv 1 : at all times 2 : FOREVER, PERPETUALLY

am \əm, am\ pres 1st sing of BE

a·main \ə-'mān\ adv 1 : with all one's might 2 : at full speed

a·mal·gam \ə-'mal-gəm\ n : a combination or mixture of different elements

a·mal·ga·mate \ə-'mal-gə-ˌmāt\ vb **a·mal·ga·mat·ed**; **a·mal·ga·mat·ing** : to unite into one body or organization

a·mal·ga·ma·tion \ə-ˌmal-gə-'mā-shən\ n : the combining of different elements into a single body

a·mass \ə-'mas\ vb : to collect into a mass or heap : ACCUMULATE ⟨amass a fortune⟩

¹**am·a·teur** \'am-ə-ˌtər, -ət-ər\ n [from French amateur, taken from Latin amator "lover", from amare "to love"; so called because an amateur likes doing what he does] 1 : a person who takes part in sports or occupations for pleasure and not for pay 2 : a person who engages in something without having experience or competence in it — **am·a·teur·ish** \ˌam-ə-'tər-ish\ adj

²**amateur** adj : of, relating to, or performed by amateurs : not professional

a·maze \ə-'māz\ vb **a·mazed**; **a·maz·ing** : to surprise or astonish greatly syn see SURPRISE

a·maze·ment \ə-'māz-mənt\ n : great surprise or astonishment

am·bas·sa·dor \am-'bas-ə-dər\ n : an official envoy of the highest rank sent to a foreign sovereign or government as the resident representative of his own sovereign or government — **am·bas·sa·dor·ship** \-ˌship\ n

am·ber \'am-bər\ n 1 : a hard yellowish to brownish translucent substance from trees long dead that takes a polish and is used for ornamental objects (as beads) 2 : a dark orange yellow

am·bi- \'am-bi\ prefix : both ⟨ambilateral⟩

am·bi·dex·trous \ˌam-bi-'dek-strəs\ adj : using both hands with equal ease — **am·bi·dex·trous·ly** adv

am·bi·ence \äm-'byäns\ n : a surrounding atmosphere : ENVIRONMENT

am·bi·gu·i·ty \ˌam-bə-'gyü-ət-ē\ n, pl **am·bi·gu·i·ties** : uncertainty or confusion of meaning (as of a word)

am·big·u·ous \am-'big-yə-wəs\ adj : capable of being understood in more than one way

---

ə abut　ər further　a ax　ā age　ä father, cot　á (see key page)　aù out　ch chin　e less　ē easy　g gift　i trip　ī life

⟨an *ambiguous* answer⟩ — **am·big·u·ous·ly** *adv*
am·bi·tion \am-'bish-ən\ *n* **1** : an eager desire for success, honor, or power ⟨full of *ambition*⟩ **2** : the aim or object for which one strives ⟨his *ambition* is to become a jet pilot⟩
am·bi·tious \am-'bish-əs\ *adj* **1** : stirred by or possessing ambition ⟨*ambitious* to be captain of the team⟩ **2** : showing ambition ⟨an *ambitious* plan⟩ — **am·bi·tious·ly** *adv*
¹am·ble \'am-bəl\ *vb* **am·bled; am·bling** : to go at an amble : SAUNTER
²amble *n* **1** : an easy gait of a horse in which the legs on the same side of the body move together **2** : a gentle easy gait
am·bu·lance \'am-byə-ləns\ *n* : a vehicle equipped for carrying sick or injured persons
¹am·bush \'am-,bush\ *vb* **1** : to station in ambush **2** : to attack from an ambush
²ambush *n* : a trap in which concealed persons lie in wait to attack by surprise
a·me·ba \ə-'mē-bə\ *var of* AMOEBA
a·me·lio·rate \ə-'mēl-yə-,rāt\ *vb* **a·me·lio·rat·ed; a·me·lio·rat·ing** : to make or grow better : IMPROVE
a·men \'ā-'men, 'ä-\ *interj* — used to express solemn agreement or hearty approval
a·me·na·ble \ə-'mē-nə-bəl, -'men-ə-\ *adj* **1** : ANSWERABLE ⟨*amenable* to the law⟩ **2** : RESPONSIVE ⟨*amenable* to discipline⟩
a·mend \ə-'mend\ *vb* **1** : to change for the better : IMPROVE **2** : to alter formally by modification, deletion, or addition
a·mend·ment \ə-'mend-mənt\ *n* **1** : a change for the better **2** : a formal alteration especially of a law, bill, or motion
a·mends \ə-'mendz\ *n sing or pl* : something done or given by a person to make up for a loss or injury he has caused ⟨make *amends*⟩
a·men·i·ty \ə-'men-ət-ē\ *n, pl* **a·men·i·ties** **1** : PLEASANTNESS **2** *pl* : the conventions observed in social intercourse
¹A·mer·i·can \ə-'mer-ə-kən\ *n* **1** : a native or inhabitant of North or South America **2** : a citizen of the United States
²American *adj* **1** : of or relating to North or South America or their inhabitants **2** : of or relating to the United States or its citizens
am·e·thyst \'am-ə-thəst\ *n* : a clear purple or bluish violet variety of crystallized quartz used as a jeweler's stone
a·mi·a·ble \'ā-mē-ə-bəl\ *adj* : having a friendly, sociable, and congenial disposition — **a·mi·a·bly** \-blē\ *adv*
am·i·ca·ble \'am-i-kə-bəl\ *adj* : FRIENDLY, PEACEABLE — **am·i·ca·bly** \-blē\ *adv*
a·mid \ə-'mid\ *or* **a·midst** \-'midst\ *prep* : in or into the middle of : AMONG

a·mid·ships \ə-'mid-,ships\ *adv* : in or near the middle of a ship
a·mi·no acid \ə-'mē-no-\ *n* : any of numerous acids that contain a group of elements consisting of nitrogen and hydrogen, include some which are the building blocks of protein, and are made by living plant or animal cells or obtained from the diet
¹a·miss \ə-'mis\ *adv* : in the wrong way
²amiss *adj* : WRONG ⟨something is *amiss* here⟩
am·i·ty \'am-ət-ē\ *n, pl* **am·i·ties** : FRIENDSHIP
am·me·ter \'am-,ēt-ər\ *n* : an instrument for measuring electric current in amperes
am·mo·nia \ə-'mō-nyə\ *n* **1** : a colorless gas that is a compound of nitrogen and hydrogen, has a sharp smell and taste, can be easily liquefied by cold and pressure, and is used in making ice, fertilizers, and explosives **2** : a solution of ammonia and water
am·mu·ni·tion \,am-yə-'nish-ən\ *n* **1** : projectiles fired from guns **2** : explosive items used in war
am·ne·sia \am-'nē-zhə\ *n* : an abnormal and usually complete loss of one's memory
a·moe·ba \ə-'mē-bə\ *n, pl* **a·moe·bas** *or* **a·moe·bae** \-bē\ : a tiny water animal consisting of a single cell that flows about and takes in food
a·mok \ə-'mək, -'mäk\ *adv* : in a murderously frenzied manner ⟨ran *amok*⟩

amoeba

a·mong \ə-'məng\ *also* **a·mongst** \-'məngst\ *prep* **1** : in or through the midst of ⟨*among* the trees⟩ **2** : in company with ⟨you're *among* friends⟩ **3** : through all of ⟨the report spread *among* the crowd⟩ **4** : in shares to each of ⟨candy divided *among* friends⟩ **syn** *see* BETWEEN
am·o·rous \'am-ə-rəs\ *adj* **1** : easily falling in love **2** : of, relating to, or caused by love — **am·o·rous·ly** *adv* — **am·o·rous·ness** *n*
¹a·mount \ə-'maunt\ *vb* **1** : to add up ⟨the bill *amounted* to ten dollars⟩ **2** : to be equivalent ⟨acts that *amount* to treason⟩
²amount *n* **1** : the total number or quantity **2** : a principal sum plus the interest on it
am·pere \'am-,piər\ *n* : a unit of electric current equivalent to a flow of one coulomb per second
am·per·sand \'am-pər-,sand\ *n* : a character & standing for the word *and*
am·phib·i·an \am-'fib-ē-ən\ *n* **1** : an amphibious animal **2** : any of a group of smooth-skinned cold-blooded animals including the frogs, toads, and salamanders **3** : an airplane designed to take off from and land on either land or water

am·phib·i·ous \am-'fib-ē-əs\ *adj* **1** : able to live both on land and in water ⟨*amphibious* animals⟩ **2** : adapted for both land and water ⟨*amphibious* vehicles⟩ **3** : made by joint action of land, sea, and air forces ⟨*amphibious* attack⟩ — **am·phib·i·ous·ly** *adv* — **am·phib·i·ous·ness** *n*

am·phi·the·a·ter \'am-fə-ˌthē-ət-ər\ *n* **1** : a round or oval building with seats rising in curved rows around an open space on which games and plays take place **2** : something (as a piece of level ground surrounded by hills) resembling an amphitheater

am·ple \'am-pəl\ *adj* **1** : more than adequate in size, scope, or capacity ⟨an *ample* fireplace⟩ **2** : enough to satisfy : ABUNDANT ⟨an *ample* supply of food⟩ — **am·ply** \-plē\ *adv*

am·pli·fi·ca·tion \ˌam-plə-fə-'kā-shən\ *n* **1** : an act, example, or product of amplifying **2** : something that amplifies

am·pli·fy \'am-plə-ˌfī\ *vb* **am·pli·fied; am·pli·fy·ing** **1** : to expand by the addition of details or illustration ⟨*amplify* a statement⟩ **2** : to make louder ⟨*amplify* the voice by using a megaphone⟩ — **am·pli·fi·er** *n*

am·pu·tate \'am-pyə-ˌtāt\ *vb* **am·pu·tat·ed; am·pu·tat·ing** : to cut off ⟨*amputate* a leg⟩

a·muck \ə-'mək\ *var of* AMOK

am·u·let \'am-yə-lət\ *n* : a small object worn as a charm against evil

a·muse \ə-'myüz\ *vb* **a·mused; a·mus·ing** **1** : to occupy with something pleasant ⟨*amuse* the child with a toy⟩ **2** : to please the sense of humor of ⟨the joke *amused* everyone⟩

syn ENTERTAIN, DIVERT: AMUSE implies merely keeping one interested with something pleasant; ENTERTAIN suggests supplying somewhat lavish or planned amusement; DIVERT emphasizes amusing for the purpose of directing one's attention away from something unpleasant

a·muse·ment \ə-'myüz-mənt\ *n* **1** : the condition of being amused **2** : pleasant diversion **3** : something that amuses or entertains

an \ən, an\ *indefinite article* : A — used before words beginning with a vowel sound ⟨*an* oak⟩

¹-an \ən\ *or* **-ian** *also* **-ean** \ē-ən, yən, ən\ *n suffix* **1** : one that belongs to ⟨Americ*an*⟩ ⟨Boston*ian*⟩ ⟨Europ*ean*⟩ **2** : one skilled in or specializing in ⟨magic*ian*⟩

²-an *or* **-ian** *also* **-ean** *adj suffix* **1** : of or relating to ⟨Americ*an*⟩ **2** : characteristic of : resembling ⟨Mozart*ean*⟩

a·nach·ro·nism \ə-'nak-rə-ˌniz-əm\ *n* **1** : an error in placing a person or thing in a period to which he or it does not belong **2** : a person or thing that is chronologically out of place

an·a·con·da \ˌan-ə-'kän-də\ *n* : a large South American snake of the boa family

an·aes·the·sia, an·aes·thet·ic *var of* ANES-THESIA, ANESTHETIC

a·nal·o·gy \ə-'nal-ə-jē\ *n, pl* **a·nal·o·gies** : resemblance in some particulars : SIMILARITY

a·nal·y·sis \ə-'nal-ə-səs\ *n, pl* **a·nal·y·ses** \-ə-ˌsēz\ **1** : separation of a thing into the parts or elements of which it is composed **2** : an examination of a thing to determine its parts or elements

an·a·lyst \'an-l-əst\ *n* : a person who analyzes or is skilled in analysis

an·a·lyt·ic \ˌan-l-'it-ik\ *or* **an·a·lyt·i·cal** \ˌan-l-'it-i-kəl\ *adj* : of, relating to, or skilled in analysis — **an·a·lyt·i·cal·ly** *adv*

an·a·lyze \'an-l-ˌīz\ *vb* **an·a·lyzed; an·a·lyz·ing** : to study or determine the nature and relationship of the parts of by analysis

an·ar·chist \'an-ər-kəst\ *n* **1** : a person who rebels against any authority, established order, or ruling power **2** : a person who uses violent means to overthrow the established order

an·ar·chy \'an-ər-kē\ *n* **1** : the condition of a society where there is no government or law and order **2** : a state of lawlessness, confusion, or disorder

a·nath·e·ma \ə-'nath-ə-mə\ *n* **1** : a solemn curse **2** : a person or thing that is cursed or intensely disliked

an·a·tom·i·cal \ˌan-ə-'täm-i-kəl\ *adj* : of or relating to anatomy

a·nat·o·my \ə-'nat-ə-mē\ *n* **1** : a science that deals with the structure of the body **2** : the structural makeup especially of a person or animal ⟨the *anatomy* of the cat⟩

-ance \əns\ *n suffix* **1** : action or process ⟨further*ance*⟩ ⟨perform*ance*⟩ **2** : quality or state ⟨resembl*ance*⟩ **3** : amount or degree ⟨conduct*ance*⟩

an·ces·tor \'an-ˌses-tər\ *n* **1** : one from whom an individual or kind of individual is descended : FOREFATHER **2** : FORERUNNER

an·ces·tral \an-'ses-trəl\ *adj* : of, relating to, or derived from an ancestor ⟨his *ancestral* home⟩ — **an·ces·tral·ly** *adv*

an·ces·try \'an-ˌses-trē\ *n, pl* **an·ces·tries** **1** : line of descent **2** : ANCESTORS

¹an·chor \'ang-kər\ *n* **1** : a heavy iron or steel device attached to a ship by a cable or chain and so made that when thrown overboard it digs into the earth and holds the ship in place **2** : something that secures or steadies

²anchor *vb* **1** : to hold or become held in place by means of an anchor ⟨*anchor* a ship⟩ **2** : to fasten securely ⟨*anchor* the cables of a bridge⟩

anchor

an·chor·age \'ang-kə-rij\ *n* **1** : a place where boats may be anchored **2** : a secure hold to resist a strong pull

¹an·cient \'ān-shənt\ *adj* **1** : very old ⟨*ancient* customs⟩ **2** : of or relating to a period of time long past or to those living in such a period

²ancient *n* **1** : an aged person **2** *pl* : the civilized peoples of ancient times and especially of Greece and Rome

-an·cy \ən-sē, -n-sē\ *n suffix, pl* **-an·cies** : quality or state ⟨buoy*ancy*⟩

and \ənd, and\ *conj* **1** : added to ⟨2 *and* 2 make 4⟩ **2** : as well as ⟨sports *and* studies⟩

and·i·ron \'an-,dī-ərn\ *n* : one of a pair of metal supports for firewood or a grate in a fireplace

an·ec·dote \'an-ik-,dōt\ *n* : a brief story of an interesting and usually biographical incident ⟨*anecdotes* about his fishing trip⟩

andirons

an·e·mom·e·ter \,an-ə-'mäm-ət-ər\ *n* : an instrument for measuring the speed of the wind

a·nem·o·ne \ə-'nem-ə-nē\ *n* : a spring-flowering plant related to the buttercup that has showy white or colored flowers

an·es·the·sia \,an-əs-'thē-zhə\ *n* : loss of feeling or sensation

¹an·es·thet·ic \,an-əs-'thet-ik\ *adj* : of, relating to, or capable of producing anesthesia

anemone

²anesthetic *n* : something that produces anesthesia

a·new \ə-'nü, -'nyü\ *adv* **1** : over again : AFRESH ⟨begin *anew*⟩ **2** : in a new or different form ⟨tear down and build *anew*⟩

an·gel \'ān-jəl\ *n* **1** : a spiritual being serving God especially as a messenger **2** : a winged figure of human form in art **3** : a person held to resemble (as in virtue or beauty) an angel

¹an·ger \'ang-gər\ *n* : a strong feeling of displeasure and usually of antagonism

²anger *vb* : to make angry

¹an·gle \'ang-gəl\ *n* **1** : the figure formed by two lines meeting at a point : the set of all points in the union of two rays having a common end point **2** : a sharp projecting corner **3** : ASPECT, VIEWPOINT ⟨consider a problem from a new *angle*⟩ **4** : an abruptly diverging course or direction

²angle *vb* **an·gled; an·gling** : to turn, move, or direct at an angle

³angle *vb* **an·gled; an·gling** **1** : to fish with hook and line **2** : to use sly means to get what one wants ⟨*angle* for a compliment⟩

an·gler \'ang-glər\ *n* : one who fishes with hook and line especially for sport

an·gle·worm \'ang-gəl-,wərm\ *n* : EARTHWORM

An·gli·can \'ang-gli-kən\ *n* : a member of the established Church of England or of one of the related churches in communion with it

an·gling \'ang-gling\ *n* : fishing with hook and line usually for sport

An·glo- \'ang-glō\ *prefix* **1** : English ⟨*Anglo-*Norman⟩ **2** : English and ⟨*Anglo-*Russian⟩

¹An·glo–Sax·on \,ang-glō-'sak-sən\ *n* **1** : a member of the German people conquering England in the fifth century A.D. **2** : a person of English ancestry

²Anglo–Saxon *adj* : of or relating to the Anglo-Saxons or their descendants

an·go·ra \ang-'gōr-ə\ *n* : cloth or yarn made from the soft silky hair of a special usually white domestic rabbit (**Angora rabbit**) or from the long lustrous wool of a goat (**Angora goat**)

an·gry \'ang-grē\ *adj* **an·gri·er; an·gri·est** **1** : feeling or showing anger : WRATHFUL **2** : painfully inflamed ⟨an *angry* rash⟩ — **an·gri·ly** \-grə-lē\ *adv*

an·guish \'ang-gwish\ *n* : extreme pain or distress of body or mind

an·guished \'ang-gwisht\ *adj* : full of anguish : TORMENTED ⟨an *anguished* cry⟩

an·gu·lar \'ang-gyə-lər\ *adj* **1** : having one or more angles **2** : sharp-cornered : POINTED ⟨an *angular* mountain peak⟩ **3** : being lean and bony ⟨his *angular* figure⟩

an·i·mal \'an-ə-məl\ *n* **1** : any of the great group of living beings (as jellyfishes, crabs, birds, and men) that differ from plants typically in being able to move about, in lacking cellulose cell walls, and in depending on plants and other animals as sources of food **2** : any of the animals lower than man in the natural order **3** : MAMMAL

¹an·i·mate \'an-ə-mət\ *adj* : having life

²an·i·mate \'an-ə-,māt\ *vb* **an·i·mat·ed; an·i·mat·ing** **1** : to give life to : make alive **2** : to give spirit and vigor to : ENLIVEN **3** : to make appear to move ⟨*animate* a cartoon⟩

an·i·mat·ed \'an-ə-,māt-əd\ *adj* **1** : ALIVE, LIVING **2** : full of vigor and spirit : LIVELY ⟨an *animated* discussion⟩ **3** : having the appearance or movement of something alive

an·i·ma·tion \,an-ə-'mā-shən\ *n* : SPIRIT

an·i·mos·i·ty \,an-ə-'mäs-ət-ē\ *n, pl* **an·i·mos·i·ties** : ILL WILL, RESENTMENT

an·i·mus \'an-ə-məs\ *n* : deep-seated hostility

an·kle \'ang-kəl\ *n* **1** : the joint between the foot and the leg **2** : the area containing the ankle joint

an·klet \'ang-klət\ *n* **1** : something (as an ornament) worn around the ankle **2** : a sock reaching slightly above the ankle

an·nals \'an-lz\ *n pl* **1** : a record of events arranged in yearly sequence **2** : historical records : HISTORY

an·neal \ə-'nēl\ *vb* : to soften and toughen (as glass or steel) by subjecting to heat and then cooling

¹an·nex \ə-'neks\ *vb* **1** : to attach as an addition : APPEND **2** : to incorporate (as a territory) within a political domain

²an·nex \'an-,eks\ *n* : something (as a wing of a building) annexed or appended

an·nex·a·tion \,an-,ek-'sā-shən\ *n* **1** : an annexing especially of new territory **2** : something annexed

an·ni·hi·late \ə-'nī-ə-,lāt\ *vb* **an·ni·hi·lat·ed; an·ni·hi·lat·ing** : to destroy entirely : put completely out of existence ⟨*annihilate* an army⟩

an·ni·ver·sa·ry \,an-ə-'vər-sə-rē\ *n, pl* **an·ni·ver·sa·ries** **1** : the annual return of the date of a notable event (as a wedding) **2** : the celebration of an anniversary

an·no·tate \'an-ə-,tāt\ *vb* **an·no·tat·ed; an·no·tat·ing** : to make or furnish critical or explanatory notes

an·nounce \ə-'naúns\ *vb* **an·nounced; an·nounc·ing** **1** : to make known publicly **2** : to give notice of the arrival or presence of **3** : to serve as an announcer

an·nounce·ment \ə-'naúns-mənt\ *n* **1** : the act of announcing **2** : a public notice announcing something

an·nounc·er \ə-'naún-sər\ *n* : a person who introduces radio or television programs, makes announcements, and gives the news and station identification

an·noy \ə-'nòi\ *vb* : to disturb or irritate especially by repeated disagreeable acts : VEX

an·noy·ance \ə-'nòi-əns\ *n* **1** : the act of annoying **2** : the feeling of being annoyed **3** : a source of vexation or irritation

¹an·nu·al \'an-yə-wəl\ *adj* **1** : occurring, done, produced, or issued once a year **2** : computed in terms of one year **3** : completing the life cycle in one growing season — **an·nu·al·ly** *adv*

²annual *n* **1** : a publication appearing once a year **2** : an annual plant

an·nu·i·ty \ə-'nü-ət-ē, -'nyü-\ *n, pl* **an·nu·i·ties** **1** : a sum of money paid at regular intervals **2** : an insurance contract providing for the payment of an annuity

an·nul \ə-'nəl\ *vb* **an·nulled; an·nul·ling** : to make ineffective or legally void ⟨*annul* a marriage⟩ — **an·nul·ment** *n*

an·ode \'an-,ōd\ *n* **1** : the positive electrode of an electrolytic cell **2** : the negative terminal of a battery that is delivering electric current **3** : the electron-collecting electrode of an electron tube

a·noint \ə-'nòint\ *vb* **1** : to rub or cover with oil or grease **2** : to apply oil to as a sacred rite — **a·noint·ment** *n*

a·nom·a·lous \ə-'näm-ə-ləs\ *adj* : departing from a general rule : ABNORMAL — **a·nom·a·lous·ly** *adv* — **a·nom·a·lous·ness** *n*

a·nom·a·ly \ə-'näm-ə-lē\ *n, pl* **a·nom·a·lies** : something anomalous : IRREGULARITY

a·non·y·mous \ə-'nän-ə-məs\ *adj* : of unknown or undeclared origin or authorship — **a·non·y·mous·ly** *adv*

¹an·oth·er \ə-'nəth-ər\ *adj* **1** : some other ⟨choose *another* day⟩ **2** : being one in addition : one more ⟨bring *another* cup⟩

²another *pron* **1** : one more ⟨got one homer in the first game and *another* in the second⟩ **2** : something different ⟨horseplay is one thing, but downright vandalism is *another*⟩

¹an·swer \'an-sər\ *n* **1** : something said or written in reply (as to a question) **2** : something done in return for something else ⟨the enemy's *answer* was a volley of shells⟩ **3** : a solution of a problem

²answer *vb* **1** : to speak or write in reply to **2** : to take responsibility ⟨*answered* for the children's safety⟩ **3** : CONFORM, CORRESPOND ⟨*answered* to the description⟩ **4** : SERVE ⟨this box will *answer* for a chair⟩ **syn** see SATISFY

an·swer·a·ble \'an-sə-rə-bəl\ *adj* **1** : RESPONSIBLE ⟨*answerable* for his actions⟩ **2** : capable of being answered

ant \'ant\ *n* : a small insect related to the bees and wasps that lives in colonies and forms nests in the ground or in wood in which it stores food and raises its young

ant- — see ANTI-

¹-ant \ənt\ *n suffix* **1** : one that performs or promotes a specified action ⟨cool*ant*⟩ **2** : thing that is acted upon in a specified manner ⟨inhal*ant*⟩

²-ant *adj suffix* **1** : performing a specified action or being in a specified condition ⟨propell*ant*⟩ **2** : promoting a specified action or process ⟨expector*ant*⟩

an·tag·o·nism \an-'tag-ə-,niz-əm\ *n* : active opposition or hostility

an·tag·o·nist \an-'tag-ə-nəst\ *n* : a person who opposes another especially in a contest or combat : OPPONENT

an·tag·o·nis·tic \an-,tag-ə-'nis-tik\ *adj* : showing antagonism : HOSTILE — **an·tag·o·nis·ti·cal·ly** \-ti-kə-lē\ *adv*

ə abut   ər further   a ax   ā age   ä father, cot   á (see key page)   aú out   ch chin   ē less   ē easy   g gift   i trip   ī life

an·tag·o·nize \an-'tag-ə-ˌnīz\ *vb* **an·tag·o-nized; an·tag·o·niz·ing** : to provoke the hostility of : arouse dislike or ill feeling

ant·arc·tic \ant-'ärk-tik\ *adj, often cap* : of or relating to the south pole or to the region around it ⟨*antarctic* explorers⟩

an·te- \'ant-i\ *prefix* **1** : before in time : earlier ⟨*ante*nuptial⟩ ⟨*ante*date⟩ **2** : in front of ⟨*ante*room⟩

ant·eat·er \'ant-ˌēt-ər\ *n* : any of several animals that have long noses and long sticky tongues and feed chiefly on ants

an·te·bel·lum \ˌant-i-'bel-əm\ *adj* : existing before a war and especially before the Civil War

an·te·ce·dent \ˌant-ə-'sēd-nt\ *n* **1** : a noun, pronoun, phrase, or clause referred to by a pronoun **2** : a preceding event or cause **3** *pl* : ANCESTORS

an·te·cham·ber \'ant-i-ˌchām-bər\ *n* : an outer room leading to another room

an·te·date \'ant-i-ˌdāt\ *vb* **an·te·dat·ed; an·te-dat·ing** **1** : to date with an earlier date than that on which the actual writing or signing is done **2** : to precede in time

an·te·lope \'ant-l-ˌōp\ *n* : any of a group of cud-chewing animals that have horns that extend upward and backward

an·ten·na \an-'ten-ə\ *n* **1** *pl* **an·ten·nae** \-'ten-ē\ : one of two or four threadlike movable feelers on the heads of insects, lobsters, or crabs **2** *pl* **an·ten·nas** : a metallic device (as a rod or wire) for sending out or receiving radio waves

antennae

an·ten·nule \an-'ten-yül\ *n* : a small antenna (as of a crayfish)

an·te·room \'ant-i-ˌrüm, -ˌrùm\ *n* : a room used as an entrance to another

an·them \'an-thəm\ *n* **1** : a sacred song usually sung by a church choir **2** : a song or hymn of praise or gladness

an·ther \'an-thər\ *n* : the enlargement at the tip of a flower's stamen that contains pollen

anther

ant·hill \'ant-ˌhil\ *n* : a mound of dirt thrown up by ants in digging their nest

an·thol·o·gy \an-'thäl-ə-jē\ *n, pl* **an·thol·o-gies** : a collection of literary pieces or passages

an·thra·cite \'an-thrə-ˌsīt\ *n* : a hard glossy coal that burns without much smoke

¹an·thro·poid \'an-thrə-ˌpòid\ *adj* : resembling man ⟨the *anthropoid* apes⟩

²anthropoid *n* : any of several large apes (as the gorilla) that have no tails and walk partly erect

an·ti- \'ant-i, 'an-ˌtī\ *or* **ant-** \ant\ *prefix*

1 : opposite in kind, position, or action ⟨*anti*climax⟩ **2** : hostile toward ⟨*anti*slavery⟩

an·ti·bi·ot·ic \ˌant-i-bī-'ät-ik\ *n* : a substance produced by living things and especially by bacteria and fungi that is used to kill or prevent the growth of harmful bacteria

an·ti·bod·y \'ant-i-ˌbäd-ē\ *n, pl* **an·ti·bod·ies** : a substance produced by the body that counteracts the effects of a disease germ or its poisons

an·tic \'ant-ik\ *n* : a ludicrous act or action

an·tic·i·pate \an-'tis-ə-ˌpāt\ *vb* **an·tic·i·pat·ed; an·tic·i·pat·ing** **1** : to be before in doing or acting : FORESTALL **2** : to foresee and provide for beforehand ⟨*anticipate* his wishes⟩ **3** : to look forward to ⟨*anticipate* his visit⟩

an·tic·i·pa·tion \an-ˌtis-ə-'pā-shən\ *n* **1** : a prior action that takes into account or forestalls a later action **2** : pleasurable expectation **3** : a picturing beforehand of a future event or state

an·ti·cy·clone \ˌant-i-'sī-ˌklōn\ *n* : a system of winds that rotates clockwise about a center of high atmospheric pressure

an·ti·dote \'ant-i-ˌdōt\ *n* : a remedy that counteracts the effects of poison

an·ti·freeze \'ant-i-ˌfrēz\ *n* : a substance added to the liquid in an automobile radiator to prevent its freezing

an·ti·mo·ny \'ant-ə-ˌmō-nē\ *n* : a silvery white metallic chemical element used in alloys

an·tip·a·thy \an-'tip-ə-thē\ *n, pl* **an·tip·a·thies** **1** : a deep-seated aversion or dislike **2** : a person or thing that arouses antipathy

an·ti·pov·er·ty \ˌant-i-'päv-ərt-ē\ *adj* : intended to relieve poverty

an·ti·quat·ed \'ant-ə-ˌkwāt-əd\ *adj* **1** : OLD-FASHIONED, OUTMODED **2** : advanced in age

¹an·tique \an-'tēk\ *adj* **1** : belonging to antiquity **2** : ANCIENT **3** : belonging to or resembling a former style or fashion

²antique *n* : an object (as a piece of furniture) made at an earlier period

an·tiq·ui·ty \an-'tik-wət-ē\ *n, pl* **an·tiq·ui·ties** **1** : ancient times **2** : very great age ⟨a castle of great *antiquity*⟩ **3** *pl* : relics or monuments of ancient times **4** *pl* : matters relating to the culture of ancient times

¹an·ti·sep·tic \ˌant-ə-'sep-tik\ *adj* : killing or making harmless the germs that cause decay or infection ⟨iodine is *antiseptic*⟩

²antiseptic *n* : an antiseptic substance

an·ti·so·cial \ˌant-i-'sō-shəl, ˌan-ˌtī-\ *adj* **1** : contrary or hostile to the well-being of society **2** : disliking the society of others

an·tith·e·sis \an-'tith-ə-səs\ *n, pl* **an·tith·e·ses** \-ə-ˌsēz\ **1** : the opposition or contrast of ideas **2** : the direct opposite

an·ti·tox·in \,ant-i-'täk-sən\ *n* : a substance formed in the blood of one exposed to a toxin of a disease germ that tends to counteract the toxin and is prepared in animals for use in treating some diseases (as diphtheria)

ant·ler \'ant-lər\ *n* : the entire horn or a branch of the horn of an animal of the deer family — **ant·lered** \-lərd\ *adj*

ant lion *n* : an insect larva with long jaws that digs a cone-shaped hole in which it waits to catch insects (as ants) on which it feeds

antler

an·to·nym \'an-tə-,nim\ *n* : a word of opposite meaning ⟨*hot* and *cold* are *antonyms*⟩

an·vil \'an-vəl\ *n* : an iron block on which pieces of metal are hammered into shape

anx·i·e·ty \ang-'zī-ət-ē\ *n, pl* **anx·i·e·ties** 1 : painful uneasiness of mind usually over an anticipated ill 2 : earnest desire or interest

anvil

anx·ious \'angk-shəs\ *adj* 1 : fearful of what may happen : WORRIED ⟨a mother *anxious* about her son's health⟩ 2 : desiring earnestly : EAGER ⟨*anxious* to make good⟩ — **anx·ious·ly** *adv*

¹an·y \'en-ē\ *adj* 1 : one taken at random ⟨*any* man you meet⟩ 2 : of whatever number or quantity ⟨needs *any* money he can get⟩

²any *pron* 1 : any individuals ⟨are *any* of you ready⟩ 2 : any amount ⟨is there *any* of it left⟩

³any *adv* : to any extent or degree : at all

an·y·bod·y \'en-ē-,bäd-ē\ *pron* : ANYONE

an·y·how \'en-ē-,hau̇\ *adv* 1 : in any way, manner, or order 2 : at any rate : in any case

an·y·more \,en-ē-'mōr\ *adv* : at the present time : NOWADAYS ⟨we never see him *anymore*⟩

an·y·one \'en-ē-,wən\ *pron* : any person at all

an·y·place \'en-ē-,plās\ *adv* : in any place

an·y·thing \'en-ē-,thing\ *pron* : a thing of any kind

an·y·way \'en-ē-,wā\ *adv* : ANYHOW

an·y·where \'en-ē-,hwear\ *adv* : in, at, or to any place

an·y·wise \'en-ē-,wīz\ *adv* : in any way whatever : at all

A 1 \'ā-'wən\ *adj* : of the finest quality

a·pace \ə-'pās\ *adv* : at a quick pace : FAST

a·part \ə-'pärt\ *adv* 1 : at a distance in space or time ⟨towns many miles *apart*⟩ 2 : as a separate unit ⟨considered *apart* from other points⟩ 3 : into two or more parts : to pieces

a·part·ment \ə-'pärt-mənt\ *n* 1 : a room or set of rooms used as a dwelling 2 : a building divided into individual dwelling units

ap·a·thet·ic \,ap-ə-'thet-ik\ *adj* : having or showing little or no feeling or interest : IMPASSIVE — **ap·a·thet·i·cal·ly** \-i-kə-lē\ *adv*

ap·a·thy \'ap-ə-thē\ *n* : lack of feeling or of interest : INDIFFERENCE

¹ape \'āp\ *n* 1 : a monkey that is usually large and tailless 2 : MIMIC

²ape *vb* **aped; ap·ing** : COPY, MIMIC **syn** see IMITATE

ap·er·ture \'ap-ər-,chu̇r\ *n* : an opening or open space : HOLE

a·pex \'ā-,peks\ *n, pl* **a·pex·es** *or* **a·pi·ces** \'ā-pə-,sēz\ : the highest point : PEAK

a·phid \'ā-fəd\ *n* : PLANT LOUSE

aph·o·rism \'af-ə-,riz-əm\ *n* : a short saying stating a general truth : MAXIM

a·piece \ə-'pēs\ *adv* : for each one

a·plomb \ə-'pläm\ *n* : complete composure

a·pol·o·get·ic \ə-,päl-ə-'jet-ik\ *adj* 1 : offered by way of excuse or apology 2 : expressing apology — **a·pol·o·get·i·cal·ly** \-i-kə-lē\ *adv*

a·pol·o·gize \ə-'päl-ə-,jīz\ *vb* **a·pol·o·gized; a·pol·o·giz·ing** : to make an apology

a·pol·o·gy \ə-'päl-ə-jē\ *n, pl* **a·pol·o·gies** 1 : a formal justification or defense 2 : an expression of regret (as for a discourteous remark) 3 : a poor substitute

syn APOLOGY, EXCUSE both refer to a statement offered about a wrong or error. The intent of an APOLOGY is to express regret; the intent of an EXCUSE is to remove or reduce blame; both suggest admitting involvement in the wrong, but the first word adds to that the acceptance of guilt

a·pos·tle \ə-'päs-əl\ *n* [from Greek *apostolos* "one who is sent off", from the prefix *apo-* "away" and *stellein* "to send"] 1 : one of the twelve close followers of Christ sent out to teach the gospel 2 : the first Christian missionary to a region 3 : one who first advocates an important belief or initiates a great reform — **a·pos·tle·ship** \-,ship\ *n*

a·pos·tro·phe \ə-'päs-trə-fē\ *n* : a mark ' used to show the omission of letters or figures (as in *can't* for *cannot* or *'76* for *1776*), the possessive case (as in *James's*), or the plural of letters or figures (as in *cross your t's*)

a·poth·e·car·y \ə-'päth-ə-,ker-ē\ *n, pl* **a·poth·e·car·ies** : DRUGGIST

ap·o·thegm \'ap-ə-,them\ *n* : APHORISM

ap·pall \ə-'pȯl\ *vb* : to overcome with fear or dread

ap·pall·ing *adj* : arousing horror and dismay

ap·pa·rat·us \,ap-ə-'rat-əs, -'rāt-\ *n, pl* **apparatus** *or* **ap·pa·rat·us·es** 1 : the equipment used to do a particular kind of work ⟨gymnasium *apparatus*⟩ **2** : an instrument or appliance for a specific operation

¹ap·par·el \ə-'par-əl\ *vb* **ap·par·eled** *or* **ap·par·elled**; **ap·par·el·ing** *or* **ap·par·el·ling** **1** : CLOTHE, DRESS **2** : ADORN, EMBELLISH

²apparel *n* : personal attire ⟨men's *apparel*⟩

ap·par·ent \ə-'par-ənt, -'per-\ *adj* **1** : open to view : VISIBLE ⟨a night in which many stars are *apparent*⟩ **2** : clear to the understanding : EVIDENT ⟨after his long day's work his reason for going to bed early is *apparent*⟩ **3** : appearing as real or true : SEEMING — **ap·par·ent·ly** *adv* — **ap·par·ent·ness** *n*

ap·pa·ri·tion \ˌap-ə-'rish-ən\ *n* **1** : an unusual or unexpected sight **2** : GHOST

¹ap·peal \ə-'pēl\ *n* **1** : a legal proceeding by which a case is brought to a higher court for a reexamination **2** : an earnest request : PLEA **3** : the power of arousing a sympathetic response : ATTRACTION ⟨the *appeal* of music⟩

²appeal *vb* **1** : to take action to have a case or decision reviewed by a higher court **2** : to make an earnest request **3** : to be pleasing or attractive ⟨a game that *appeals* to everybody⟩

ap·pear \ə-'piər\ *vb* **1** : to come into sight : become evident **2** : to present oneself formally ⟨*appear* in court⟩ **3** : to become clear to the mind **4** : to come out in printed form **5** : to come before the public on stage or screen **6** : SEEM, LOOK ⟨*appears* to be tired⟩

ap·pear·ance \ə-'pir-əns\ *n* **1** : the act or an instance of appearing ⟨a personal *appearance*⟩ **2** : outward aspect : LOOK ⟨the room has a cool *appearance*⟩ **3** : PHENOMENON

ap·pease \ə-'pēz\ *vb* **ap·peased**; **ap·peas·ing** **1** : to make calm or quiet : ALLAY **2** : to make concessions to usually at the sacrifice of principles — **ap·pease·ment** *n* — **ap·peas·er** *n*

ap·pel·la·tion \ˌap-ə-'lā-shən\ *n* : identifying or descriptive name or title : DESIGNATION

ap·pend \ə-'pend\ *vb* : to add as a supplement or appendix ⟨*append* a postscript⟩

ap·pend·age \ə-'pen-dij\ *n* : something (as a leg) attached to a larger or more important thing

ap·pen·di·ci·tis \ə-ˌpen-də-'sīt-əs\ *n* : inflammation of the intestinal appendix

ap·pen·dix \ə-'pen-diks\ *n, pl* **ap·pen·dix·es** *or* **ap·pen·di·ces** \-də-ˌsēz\ **1** : a part of a book giving additional and helpful information (as notes or tables) **2** : a small tubelike outgrowth from the intestine

ap·per·tain \ˌap-ər-'tān\ *vb* : to belong or be connected as a possession, part, or right

ap·pe·tite \'ap-ə-ˌtīt\ *n* **1** : a desire for food or drink **2** : TASTE ⟨an *appetite* for adventure⟩

ap·pe·tiz·er \'ap-ə-ˌtī-zər\ *n* : a food or drink that gives one an appetite and is usually served before a meal

ap·pe·tiz·ing \'ap-ə-ˌtī-zing\ *adj* : appealing to the appetite ⟨an *appetizing* smell⟩

ap·plaud \ə-'plȯd\ *vb* **1** : PRAISE **2** : to show approval especially by clapping the hands

ap·plause \ə-'plȯz\ *n* : approval expressed especially by clapping the hands

ap·ple \'ap-əl\ *n* : the round or oval fruit with red, yellow, or green skin of a spreading tree that is related to the rose

ap·pli·ance \ə-'plī-əns\ *n* **1** : a piece of equipment for making a machine or tool suitable for a special purpose **2** : a device designed for a particular use **3** : a piece of household or office equipment operated by gas or electricity

ap·pli·ca·ble \'ap-li-kə-bəl\ *adj* : capable of being put to use or put into practice

ap·pli·cant \'ap-li-kənt\ *n* : a person who applies for something (as admission to a school)

ap·pli·ca·tion \ˌap-lə-'kā-shən\ *n* **1** : the act or an instance of applying ⟨the *application* of paint to a house⟩ **2** : something put or spread on a surface ⟨hot *applications* on a sprained ankle⟩ **3** : ability to fix one's attention on a task **4** : a request made personally or in writing ⟨an *application* for a job⟩ **5** : capacity for practical use

ap·pli·ca·tor \'ap-lə-ˌkāt-ər\ *n* : a device for applying a substance (as medicine or polish)

ap·plied \ə-'plīd\ *adj* : put to practical use

ap·ply \ə-'plī\ *vb* **ap·plied**; **ap·ply·ing** **1** : to put to use ⟨*applied* his knowledge⟩ **2** : to lay or spread on ⟨*apply* a coat of paint⟩ **3** : to place in contact ⟨*apply* heat⟩ **4** : to give one's full attention ⟨*applied* himself to his work⟩ **5** : to have relevance or a valid connection ⟨this law *applies* to everyone⟩ **6** : to request personally or in writing ⟨*apply* for a job⟩

ap·point \ə-'pȯint\ *vb* **1** : to fix or set officially ⟨*appoint* a day for a meeting⟩ **2** : to name officially especially to an office or position ⟨the president *appoints* his cabinet⟩

ap·poin·tee \ə-ˌpȯin-'tē\ *n* : a person appointed to an office or position

ap·point·ive \ə-'pȯint-iv\ *adj* : of, relating to, or filled by appointment ⟨an *appointive* office⟩

ap·point·ment \ə-'pȯint-mənt\ *n* **1** : the act or an instance of appointing ⟨holds office by *appointment*⟩ **2** : a position or office to which a person is officially named **3** : an agreement to meet at a fixed time ⟨an eight-o'clock *appointment*⟩ **4** *pl* : FURNISHINGS, EQUIPMENT

ap·por·tion \ə-'pōr-shən\ *vb* : to divide and distribute proportionately — **ap·por·tion·ment** *n*

ap·po·si·tion \ˌap-ə-'zish-ən\ *n* : a grammatical construction in which a noun or noun equivalent is followed by another that explains it ⟨in "a biography of the poet Burns" *Burns* is in *apposition* with *poet*⟩

ap·pos·i·tive \ə-'päz-ət-iv\ *n* : the second of a pair of noun or noun equivalents in apposition ⟨in "a biography of the poet Burns" *Burns* is an *appositive*⟩

ap·prais·al \ə-'prā-zəl\ *n* : an act or instance of appraising

ap·praise \ə-'prāz\ *vb* **ap·praised; ap·prais·ing** : to set a value on ⟨a house *appraised* at $15,000⟩

ap·pre·cia·ble \ə-'prē-shə-bəl\ *adj* : large enough to be recognized and measured or to be felt — **ap·pre·cia·bly** \-blē\ *adv*

ap·pre·ci·ate \ə-'prē-shē-ˌāt\ *vb* **ap·pre·ci·at·ed; ap·pre·ci·at·ing** **1** : to evaluate the worth, quality, or significance of **2** : to admire greatly **3** : to be fully aware of **4** : to be grateful for **5** : to increase in number or value

ap·pre·ci·a·tion \ə-ˌprē-shē-'ā-shən\ *n* **1** : the act of appreciating **2** : awareness or understanding of worth or value **3** : a rise in value

ap·pre·cia·tive \ə-'prē-shət-iv\ *adj* : having or showing appreciation ⟨an *appreciative* audience⟩ — **ap·pre·cia·tive·ly** *adv*

ap·pre·hend \ˌap-ri-'hend\ *vb* **1** : SEIZE, ARREST ⟨*apprehend* a burglar⟩ **2** : to become aware of : PERCEIVE **3** : to anticipate with anxiety, dread, or fear **4** : UNDERSTAND

ap·pre·hen·sion \ˌap-ri-'hen-chən\ *n* **1** : CAPTURE, ARREST **2** : UNDERSTANDING, COMPREHENSION **3** : fear of what may be coming : dread of the future

ap·pre·hen·sive \ˌap-ri-'hen-siv\ *adj* : fearful of what may be coming — **ap·pre·hen·sive·ly** *adv* — **ap·pre·hen·sive·ness** *n*

¹ap·pren·tice \ə-'prent-əs\ *n* : a person who is learning a trade, art, or calling by practical experience under a skilled worker

²apprentice *vb* **ap·pren·ticed; ap·pren·tic·ing** : to bind or set at work as an apprentice

ap·pren·tice·ship \ə-'prent-əs-ˌship\ *n* **1** : service as an apprentice **2** : the period during which a person serves as an apprentice

¹ap·proach \ə-'prōch\ *vb* **1** : to come near or nearer : draw close **2** : to take preliminary steps toward

²approach *n* **1** : an act or instance of approaching **2** : a preliminary step **3** : a means (as a path or road) of access

ap·proach·a·ble \ə-'prō-chə-bəl\ *adj* : easy to meet or deal with

ap·pro·ba·tion \ˌap-rə-'bā-shən\ *n* **1** : the act of approving formally or officially **2** : PRAISE, COMMENDATION

¹ap·pro·pri·ate \ə-'prō-prē-ˌāt\ *vb* **ap·pro·pri·at·ed; ap·pro·pri·at·ing** **1** : to take possession of **2** : to set apart for a particular purpose or use

²ap·pro·pri·ate \ə-'prō-prē-ət\ *adj* : especially suitable or fitting : PROPER — **ap·pro·pri·ate·ly** *adv* — **ap·pro·pri·ate·ness** *n*

ap·pro·pri·a·tion \ə-ˌprō-prē-'ā-shən\ *n* **1** : an act or instance of appropriating **2** : a sum of money appropriated for a specific use

ap·prov·al \ə-'prü-vəl\ *n* : an act or instance of approving : APPROBATION — **on approval** : subject to a prospective buyer's acceptance or rejection ⟨goods sent *on approval*⟩

ap·prove \ə-'prüv\ *vb* **ap·proved; ap·prov·ing** **1** : to have or express a favorable opinion : think well of **2** : to accept as satisfactory

¹ap·prox·i·mate \ə-'präk-sə-mət\ *adj* : nearly correct or exact ⟨the *approximate* cost⟩ — **ap·prox·i·mate·ly** *adv*

²ap·prox·i·mate \ə-'präk-sə-ˌmāt\ *vb* **ap·prox·i·mat·ed; ap·prox·i·mat·ing** **1** : to bring near or close **2** : to come near : APPROACH

ap·prox·i·ma·tion \ə-ˌpräk-sə-'mā-shən\ *n* **1** : a coming near or close (as in value) **2** : a nearly exact estimate or figure

ap·pur·te·nance \ə-'pərt-n-əns\ *n* : something that belongs to or goes with another thing

ap·ri·cot \'ap-rə-ˌkät, 'ā-prə-\ *n* : a small oval orange-colored fruit resembling the related peach and plum

A·pril \'ā-prəl\ *n* : the fourth month of the year

a·pron \'ā-prən\ *n* [from the word *napron*, which was taken from French *naperon* "little cloth"; instead of *a napron* people thought it was *an apron*] **1** : a garment worn on the front of the body to protect the clothing **2** : a paved area for parking or handling airplanes

apt \'apt\ *adj* **1** : FITTING, SUITABLE ⟨an *apt* quotation⟩ **2** : having an habitual tendency : LIKELY ⟨is *apt* to become angry over trifles⟩ **3** : quick to learn ⟨a pupil *apt* in arithmetic⟩ — **apt·ly** *adv* — **apt·ness** *n*

ap·ti·tude \'ap-tə-ˌtüd, -ˌtyüd\ *n* **1** : capacity for learning **2** : natural ability : TALENT **syn** *see* ABILITY

aq·ua·cade \'ak-wə-ˌkād\ *n* : an elaborate water spectacle consisting of exhibitions of swimming, diving, and acrobatics accompanied by music

aq·ua·lung·er \'ak-wə-ˌləng-ər\ *n* : an underwater swimmer who uses a breathing device

aq·ua·ma·rine \ˌak-wə-mə-'rēn\ *n* : a bluish green gem

ə abut   ər further   a ax   ā age   ä father, cot   ȧ (see key page)   au̇ out   ch chin   e less   ē easy   g gift   i trip   ī life

aq·ua·plane \'ak-wə-ˌplān\ *n* : a board towed behind a motorboat and ridden by a person standing on it

aquaplane

a·quar·i·um \ə-'kwer-ē-əm\ *n*, *pl* **a·quar·i·ums** *or* **a·quar·i·a** \-ē-ə\ **1** : a container (as a tank or bowl) in which living water animals or water plants are kept **2** : a building in which water animals or water plants are exhibited

a·quat·ic \ə-'kwät-ik, -'kwat-\ *adj* **1** : growing or living in water ⟨*aquatic* animals⟩ **2** : performed in or on water ⟨*aquatic* sports⟩

aq·ue·duct \'ak-wə-ˌdəkt\ *n* : an artificial channel (as a structure that carries the water of a canal across a river or hollow) for carrying flowing water from place to place

a·que·ous \'ā-kwē-əs, 'ak-wē-\ *adj* **1** : of, relating to, or resembling water **2** : made of, by, or with water ⟨an *aqueous* solution⟩

aq·ui·line \'ak-wə-ˌlīn, -lən\ *adj* : curved like an eagle's beak ⟨an *aquiline* nose⟩

-ar \ər\ *adj suffix* : of or relating to ⟨molecul*ar*⟩

¹Ar·ab \'ar-əb\ *n* **1** : a native or inhabitant of Arabia **2** : a member of an Arabic-speaking people

²Arab *adj* : ARABIAN

¹A·ra·bi·an \ə-'rā-bē-ən\ *adj* : of or relating to Arabia or the Arabs

²Arabian *n* : ARAB

¹Ar·a·bic \'ar-ə-bik\ *adj* : of or relating to Arabia, the Arabs, or Arabic

²Arabic *n* : a language spoken in Arabia, Jordan, Lebanon, Syria, Iraq, and northern Africa

arabic numeral *n*, *often cap A* : one of the number symbols 1, 2, 3, 4, 5, 6, 7, 8, 9, and 0

ar·a·ble \'ar-ə-bəl\ *adj* : fit for or cultivated by plowing : suitable for producing crops

ar·bi·ter \'är-bət-ər\ *n* **1** : ARBITRATOR **2** : a person having absolute authority to judge and decide what is right or proper

ar·bi·trary \'är-bə-ˌtrer-ē\ *adj* **1** : depending on choice or discretion **2** : arising from or guided by ungoverned will, impulse, or caprice ⟨an *arbitrary* decision⟩ ⟨an *arbitrary* ruler⟩ **3** : selected at random — **ar·bi·trar·i·ly** \ˌär-bə-'trer-ə-lē\ *adv* — **ar·bi·trar·i·ness** \'är-bə-ˌtrer-ē-nəs\ *n*

ar·bi·trate \'är-bə-ˌtrāt\ *vb* **ar·bi·trat·ed; ar·bi·trat·ing** **1** : to settle a dispute after hearing and considering the arguments of both sides **2** : to refer a dispute to others for settlement

ar·bi·tra·tion \ˌär-bə-'trā-shən\ *n* : the settling of a dispute in which both sides present their arguments to a third person or group for decision

ar·bi·tra·tor \'är-bə-ˌtrāt-ər\ *n* : a person chosen to settle differences in a controversy

ar·bor \'är-bər\ *n* : a shelter of vines or branches or of lattice covered with growing vines

ar·bo·re·al \är-'bor-ē-əl\ *adj* **1** : of or relating to a tree **2** : living in or frequenting trees

ar·bo·re·tum \ˌär-bə-'rēt-əm\ *n*, *pl* **ar·bo·re·tums** *or* **ar·bo·re·ta** \-'rēt-ə\ : a place where trees and plants are grown for scientific and educational purposes

arbor

ar·bor·vi·tae \ˌär-bər-'vīt-ē\ *n* : any of several evergreen trees with tiny scalelike leaves on flat fan-shaped branches

ar·bu·tus \är-'byüt-əs\ *n* : a trailing spring-blossoming plant that bears clusters of small fragrant flowers with five white or pink petals

arc \'ärk\ *n* **1** : something that is curved **2** : a glowing light across a gap in an electric circuit or between electrodes **3** : a portion of a curved line between any two points on it

ar·cade \är-'kād\ *n* **1** : a row of arches with the columns that support them **2** : an arched or covered passageway often lined with shops

ar·cane \är-'kān\ *adj* : SECRET, MYSTERIOUS

arcade 1

¹arch \'ärch\ *n* **1** : a usually curved part of a structure that is over an opening and serves as a support (as for the wall above the opening) **2** : something resembling an arch ⟨the *arch* of the foot⟩ — **arched** \'ärcht\ *adj*

²arch *vb* **1** : to cover with an arch **2** : to form or shape into an arch

³arch *adj* : slyly mischievous : ROGUISH ⟨an *arch* look⟩ — **arch·ly** *adv* — **arch·ness** *n*

ar·chae·ol·o·gy *or* **ar·che·ol·o·gy** \ˌär-kē-'äl-ə-jē\ *n* : a science that deals with past human life and activities as shown by fossil relics and the monuments and artifacts left by ancient peoples

ar·cha·ic \är-'kā-ik\ *adj* **1** : of or relating to an earlier time : ANTIQUATED **2** : surviving from an earlier period

arch·an·gel \'ärk-ˌān-jəl\ *n* : a chief angel

arch·bish·op \'ärch-'bish-əp\ *n* : the bishop of highest rank in a group of dioceses

ar·cher \'är-chər\ *n* : a person who shoots with a bow and arrow

ar·cher·y \'är-chə-rē\ *n* **1** : shooting with bows and arrows **2** : a body of archers

ar·chi·pel·a·go \ˌär-kə-'pel-ə-ˌgō, ˌär-chə-\ *n*, *pl* **ar·chi·pel·a·goes** *or* **ar·chi·pel·a·gos** **1** : an expanse of water (as a sea) with many scattered islands **2** : a group of islands in an archipelago

ar·chi·tect \'är-kə-ˌtekt\ *n* : a person who designs buildings and oversees their construction

ar·chi·tec·tur·al \ˌär-kə-'tek-chə-rəl\ *adj* : of, relating to, or conforming to the rules of architecture — **ar·chi·tec·tur·al·ly** *adv*

ar·chi·tec·ture \'är-kə-ˌtek-chər\ *n* **1** : the art of making plans for buildings **2** : the style of building that architects produce or imitate ⟨a church of modern *architecture*⟩ **3** : architectural work : BUILDINGS

ar·chive \'är-ˌkīv\ *n* : a place in which public records or historical documents are preserved

arch·way \'ärch-ˌwā\ *n* **1** : a passage under an arch **2** : an arch over a passage

-ar·chy \ˌär-kē, ər-kē\ *n suffix, pl* **-ar·chies** : rule : government ⟨squire*archy*⟩

¹**arc·tic** \'ärk-tik\ *adj* **1** *often cap* : of or relating to the north pole or to the region around it ⟨*arctic* explorers⟩ **2** : very cold

²**arctic** *n* : a rubber overshoe reaching to the ankle or above

ar·dent \'ärd-nt\ *adj* **1** : characterized by warmth of feeling : PASSIONATE **2** : FIERY, HOT **3** : GLOWING, SHINING — **ar·dent·ly** *adv*

ar·dor \'ärd-ər\ *n* **1** : warmth of feeling **2** : ZEAL, EAGERNESS

ar·du·ous \'är-jə-wəs\ *adj* : DIFFICULT — **ar·du·ous·ly** *adv* — **ar·du·ous·ness** *n*

are \ər, är\ *pres 2d sing or pres pl of* BE

ar·e·a \'ar-ē-ə, 'er-\ *n* **1** : a flat surface or space **2** : a level piece of ground **3** : the amount of surface included within limits ⟨the *area* of a triangle⟩ **4** : REGION ⟨a farming *area*⟩ **5** : a field of activity or study

a·re·na \ə-'rē-nə\ *n* **1** : an enclosed area used for public entertainment **2** : a building containing an arena **3** : a sphere of activity

aren't \ärnt\ : are not

ar·gue \'är-gyü\ *vb* **ar·gued; ar·gu·ing 1** : to give reasons for or against ⟨*argue* in favor of lower taxes⟩ **2** : to debate or discuss some matter : DISPUTE ⟨*argue* about politics⟩ **3** : to persuade by giving reasons ⟨could not *argue* his father into getting a new car⟩ **syn** see DISCUSS — **ar·gu·er** *n*

ar·gu·ment \'är-gyə-mənt\ *n* **1** : a reason for or against something **2** : a discussion in which reasons for and against something are given **3** : a heated dispute : QUARREL

ar·gu·men·ta·tion \ˌär-gyə-mən-'tā-shən\ *n* : the art of formal discussion

ar·gu·men·ta·tive \ˌär-gyə-'ment-ət-iv\ *adj* : fond of arguing — **ar·gu·men·ta·tive·ly** *adv*

ar·id \'ar-əd\ *adj* **1** : DRY, BARREN **2** : not

having enough rainfall to support agriculture

a·right \ə-'rīt\ *adv* : RIGHTLY, CORRECTLY

a·rise \ə-'rīz\ *vb* **a·rose** \-'rōz\; **a·ris·en** \-'riz-n\; **a·ris·ing** \-'rī-zing\ **1** : to move upward : ASCEND ⟨mist *arose* from the valley⟩ **2** : to get up from sleep or after lying down **3** : to come into existence ⟨a dispute *arose* between the two leaders⟩

ar·is·toc·ra·cy \ˌar-əs-'täk-rə-sē\ *n, pl* **ar·is·toc·ra·cies 1** : a government that is in the hands of a noble or privileged class **2** : the noble or privileged class **3** : persons thought of as superior to the rest of the community in wealth, culture, or intelligence

a·ris·to·crat \ə-'ris-tə-ˌkrat\ *n* **1** : a member of an aristocracy **2** : a person who has the point of view and habits of a ruling class or of a class considered superior

a·ris·to·crat·ic \ə-ˌris-tə-'krat-ik\ *adj* : of, relating to, or characteristic of the aristocracy or of aristocrats — **a·ris·to·crat·i·cal·ly** \-i-kə-lē\ *adv*

¹**a·rith·me·tic** \ə-'rith-mə-ˌtik\ *n* **1** : a science that deals with real numbers and computations with them involving addition, subtraction, multiplication, and division **2** : an act or method of computing

²**ar·ith·met·ic** \ˌar-ith-'met-ik\ *or* **ar·ith·met·i·cal** \-i-kəl\ *adj* : of or relating to arithmetic

ar·ith·met·ic mean \ˌar-ith-ˌmet-ik-\ *n* : a quantity formed by adding quantities together and dividing by their number ⟨the *arithmetic mean* of 6, 4, and 5 is 5⟩

ark \'ärk\ *n* **1** : the ship in which Noah and his family were saved from the Flood **2** : a sacred chest in which the ancient Hebrews kept the two tablets of the Law **3** : a repository in a synagogue for the scrolls of the Law

¹**arm** \'ärm\ *n* **1** : a human upper limb especially between the shoulder and wrist **2** : something resembling an arm ⟨an *arm* of the sea⟩ ⟨the *arm* of a chair⟩ **3** : POWER, MIGHT ⟨the *arm* of the law⟩ **4** : a foreleg of a quadruped — **armed** \'ärmd\ *adj*

²**arm** *vb* **1** : to provide with weapons ⟨*arm* and equip a new regiment⟩ **2** : to provide with a means of defense ⟨*armed* with facts⟩

³**arm** *n* **1** : WEAPON, FIREARM **2** : a branch of an army or of the military forces **3** *pl* : the heraldic devices of a family or government **4** *pl* : active hostilities : WARFARE **5** *pl* : military service

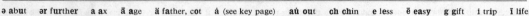

arms 3

ar·ma·da \är-'mäd-ə, -'mād-\ *n* **1** : a large fleet of warships **2** : a large force of moving objects (as planes)

---

ar·ma·dil·lo \ˌär-mə-'dil-ō\ *n, pl* **ar·ma·dil·los** : a small burrowing animal of Latin America and Texas whose head and body are protected by a hard bony armor

armadillo

ar·ma·ment \'är-mə-mənt\ *n* **1** : the military strength and equipment of a nation **2** : the supply of materials for war **3** : the process of preparing for war

ar·ma·ture \'är-mə-chər\ *n* : the part (as in a generator) acted on by the magnetic force

arm·chair \'ärm-ˌcheər\ *n* : a chair with arms

arm·ful \'ärm-ˌfùl\ *n, pl* **arm·fuls** \-ˌfùlz\ *or* **arms·ful** \'ärmz-ˌfùl\ : as much as a person's arm can hold

ar·mi·stice \'är-mə-stəs\ *n* : a pause in fighting brought about by agreement between the two sides : TRUCE

arm·let \'ärm-lət\ *n* : a bracelet or band for the upper arm

ar·mor \'är-mər\ *n* **1** : a covering (as of metal) to protect the body in battle **2** : a protective covering **3** : armored forces and vehicles (as tanks)

ar·mored \'är-mərd\ *adj* : protected by or equipped with armor ⟨an *armored* car⟩

ar·mo·ri·al \är-'mōr-ē-əl\ *adj* : of, relating to, or bearing heraldic arms

armor

ar·mo·ry \'är-mə-rē\ *n, pl* **ar·mo·ries** **1** : a supply of arms **2** : a place where arms are stored and where military reserve personnel are often trained **3** : a place where arms are manufactured

arm·pit \'ärm-ˌpit\ *n* : the hollow under a person's arm where the arm joins the shoulder

arm·rest \'ärm-ˌrest\ *n* : a support for the arm

ar·my \'är-mē\ *n, pl* **ar·mies** **1** : a large organized body of men and women trained for land warfare **2** *often cap* : the complete military organization of a nation for land warfare **3** : a great multitude **4** : a body of persons organized to advance a cause

a·ro·ma \ə-'rō-mə\ *n* : a distinctive and pleasant smell ⟨the *aroma* of coffee⟩

ar·o·mat·ic \ˌar-ə-'mat-ik\ *adj* : FRAGRANT

arose *past of* ARISE

¹a·round \ə-'raùnd\ *adv* **1** : in circumference ⟨a tree five feet *around*⟩ **2** : in or along a curving course **3** : on all sides ⟨papers lying *around*⟩ **4** : NEARBY **5** : here and there in various places ⟨travel *around* from state to state⟩ **6** : in rotation or succession ⟨pass the candy *around*⟩ **7** : in an opposite direction ⟨turn *around*⟩ **8** : APPROXIMATELY

²around *prep* **1** : in a curving course along the outside boundary of ⟨walk *around* the house⟩ **2** : on every side of ⟨fields *around* the city⟩ **3** : near to in amount or number ⟨selling at prices *around* five dollars⟩ **4** : NEAR

a·rouse \ə-'raùz\ *vb* **a·roused**; **a·rous·ing** **1** : to awaken from sleep **2** : to rouse to action : EXCITE

ar·peg·gio \är-'pej-ō, -'pej-ē-ˌō\ *n, pl* **ar·peg·gios** **1** : production of the tones of a chord in succession and not simultaneously **2** : a chord played in arpeggio

ar·raign \ə-'rān\ *vb* **1** : to call before a court to answer to an indictment **2** : ACCUSE, DENOUNCE — **ar·raign·ment** *n*

ar·range \ə-'rānj\ *vb* **ar·ranged**; **ar·rang·ing** **1** : to put in order and especially a particular order **2** : to make plans for : PREPARE ⟨*arrange* a program⟩ **3** : to come to an agreement about : SETTLE ⟨*arrange* a truce⟩ **4** : to make a musical arrangement of — **ar·rang·er** *n*

ar·range·ment \ə-'rānj-mənt\ *n* **1** : a putting in order : the order in which things are put ⟨the *arrangement* of furniture in a room⟩ **2** : PREPARATION, PLAN ⟨make *arrangements* for a trip⟩ **3** : something made by arranging ⟨a flower *arrangement*⟩ **4** : an adaptation of a piece of music to voices or instruments for which it was not originally written

ar·rant \'ar-ənt\ *adj* : THOROUGHGOING

¹ar·ray \ə-'rā\ *vb* **1** : to set in order : draw up ⟨soldiers *arrayed* for review⟩ **2** : to clothe or dress especially in rich or beautiful clothing

²array *n* **1** : regular order or arrangement **2** : a group of persons (as soldiers) drawn up in regular order **3** : rich or beautiful clothing **4** : an imposing group **5** : a group of mathematical elements (as numbers or letters) arranged in rows and columns

ar·rears \ə-'riərz\ *n pl* **1** : the state of being behind in the discharge of debts ⟨two months in *arrears*⟩ **2** : unpaid and overdue debts

¹ar·rest \ə-'rest\ *vb* **1** : to stop the progress or movement of : CHECK ⟨*arrest* a disease⟩ **2** : to take or keep in custody by authority of law ⟨*arrest* a man on suspicion of robbery⟩ **3** : to attract and hold the attention of

²arrest *n* : the act of taking or holding in custody by authority of law

ar·riv·al \ə-'rī-vəl\ *n* **1** : the act of arriving **2** : a person or thing that has arrived

ar·rive \ə-'rīv\ *vb* **ar·rived**; **ar·riv·ing** **1** : to reach a place and especially one's destination ⟨*arrive* home at six o'clock⟩ **2** : to gain an end or object ⟨*arrive* at a decision⟩ **3** : COME ⟨the time to leave finally *arrived*⟩ **4** : to attain success

ar·ro·gance \'ar-ə-gəns\ *n* : a sense of one's own importance that shows itself in an offensively proud manner : HAUGHTINESS

ar·ro·gant \'ar-ə-gənt\ *adj* : thinking too well of oneself or of one's own opinions — **ar·ro·gant·ly** *adv*

ar·row \'ar-ō\ *n* **1** : a missile made to be shot from a bow and usually having a slender shaft, a pointed head, and feathers at the butt **2** : a mark (as on a map) to indicate direction

ar·row·head \'ar-ō-,hed\ *n* : the pointed end of an arrow

arrow

ar·row·root \'ar-ō-,rüt, -,rüt\ *n* : a starch obtained from the potatolike roots of a tropical plant

ar·se·nal \'ärs-n-əl\ *n* **1** : a place where military equipment is made and stored **2** : STORE, REPERTORY

ar·se·nic \'ärs-n-ik\ *n* : a solid poisonous chemical element that is commonly steel gray, crystalline, and brittle

ar·son \'ärs-n\ *n* : the malicious burning of property (as a dwelling house)

art \'ärt\ *n* **1** : the power of doing something easily and skillfully ⟨the *art* of making friends⟩ **2** : an occupation that requires a natural skill in addition to training and practice ⟨the *art* of cooking⟩ **3** : the rules or ideas that a person must know in order to follow a profession or craft ⟨the *art* of medicine⟩ **4** : the study of drawing, painting, and sculpture **5** : the works produced by artists

ar·ter·y \'ärt-ə-rē\ *n, pl* **ar·ter·ies 1** : one of the branching tubes that carry blood from the heart to all parts of the body **2** : a channel (as a river or highway) of communication

ar·te·sian well \är-,tē-zhən-\ *n* **1** : a bored well from which water flows up like a fountain **2** : a deep-bored well

art·ful \'ärt-fəl\ *adj* **1** : performed with or showing art or skill ⟨*artful* workmanship⟩ **2** : CRAFTY, CUNNING — **art·ful·ly** *adv* — **art·ful·ness** *n*

ar·thro·pod \'är-thrə-,päd\ *n* : any of a large group of animals (as crabs, insects, and spiders) with a body made up of segments and with jointed limbs

ar·ti·choke \'ärt-ə-,chōk\ *n* : a tall plant of the aster family with a flower head cooked and eaten as a vegetable

artichoke

ar·ti·cle \'ärt-i-kəl\ *n* **1** : a distinct part of a written document (as a constitution) **2** : a nonfictional prose composition forming an independent part of a publication (as a magazine) ⟨an *article* on winter sports⟩ **3** : a word (as *a*, *an*, or *the*) used with a noun to limit or give definiteness to its application **4** : a member of a class of things ⟨*articles* of trade⟩

¹ar·tic·u·late \är-'tik-yə-lət\ *adj* **1** : INTELLIGIBLE **2** : able to express oneself effectively — **ar·tic·u·late·ly** *adv* — **ar·tic·u·late·ness** *n*

²ar·tic·u·late \är-'tik-yə-,lāt\ *vb* **ar·tic·u·lat·ed; ar·tic·u·lat·ing** : to speak clearly and distinctly

ar·tic·u·la·tion \är-,tik-yə-'lā-shən\ *n* : the making of articulate sounds (as in speaking)

ar·ti·fice \'ärt-ə-fəs\ *n* **1** : SKILL, INGENUITY **2** : an ingenious device or trick

ar·ti·fi·cial \,ärt-ə-'fish-əl\ *adj* **1** : not natural ⟨an *artificial* lake⟩ **2** : made by man to imitate nature ⟨*artificial* flowers⟩ **3** : not genuine ⟨*artificial* gaiety⟩ — **ar·ti·fi·cial·ly** *adv*

artificial respiration *n* : the forcing of air into and out of the lungs of a person whose breathing has stopped

ar·til·ler·y \är-'til-ə-rē\ *n* **1** : large caliber mounted firearms (as cannon or rockets) **2** : a branch of an army armed with artillery

ar·ti·san \'ärt-ə-zən\ *n* : a person (as a bricklayer or carpenter) who works at a trade requiring skill with the hands

art·ist \'ärt-əst\ *n* **1** : a person skilled in one of the arts (as painting, sculpture, music, or writing) **2** : a person showing unusual ability in an occupation requiring skill

ar·tis·tic \är-'tis-tik\ *adj* **1** : relating to or characteristic of art or artists **2** : showing taste in arrangement or execution — **ar·tis·ti·cal·ly** \-ti-kə-lē\ *adv*

art·ist·ry \'ärt-əs-trē\ *n* : artistic quality of effect or workmanship

art·less \'ärt-ləs\ *adj* **1** : lacking art, knowledge, or skill **2** : being simple and sincere : NATURAL — **art·less·ly** *adv* — **art·less·ness** *n*

¹-ary \,er-ē, ə-rē\ *n suffix, pl* **-aries** : thing or person belonging to or connected with ⟨functionary⟩

²-ary *adj suffix* : of, relating to, or connected with ⟨budgetary⟩

¹as \əz, az\ *conj* **1** : in an equal amount or degree with ⟨green *as* grass⟩ **2** : in the same way that ⟨farmed *as* his father before him had⟩ **3** : WHILE, WHEN ⟨spoke to me *as* I was leaving⟩ **4** : BECAUSE, SINCE

²as *adv* **1** : to the same degree or extent ⟨*as* deaf as a post⟩ **2** : for example

ə abut   ər further   a ax   ā age   ä father, cot   å (see key page)   aů out   ch chin   e less   ē easy   g gift   i trip   ī life

³as *pron* **1** : THAT ⟨the same price *as* before⟩ **2** : a fact that ⟨he is rich, *as* you know⟩

⁴as *prep* **1** : LIKE ⟨the audience rose *as* one man⟩ **2** : in the character or position of

as·bes·tos \as-'bes-təs, az-\ *n* : a grayish mineral that readily separates into long flexible fibers and is used in making various fireproof materials and articles

as·cend \ə-'send\ *vb* : to go up : RISE

  syn ASCEND, MOUNT, CLIMB all mean to move upward or toward the top. ASCEND indicates simply this and no more⟨*ascend* in an elevator⟩ MOUNT implies actually reaching the top ⟨*mount* a ladder⟩ CLIMB suggests physical effort and often the use of hands as well as feet ⟨*climb* a rope⟩

as·cend·an·cy \ə-'sen-dən-sē\ *n* : governing or controlling influence

as·cend·ant \ə-'sen-dənt\ *n* : a position of dominant power

as·cen·sion \ə-'sen-chən\ *n* : the act or process of ascending

as·cent \ə-'sent\ *n* **1** : the act of rising or mounting upward **2** : an upward slope : RISE

as·cer·tain \,as-ər-'tān\ *vb* : to learn with certainty ⟨*ascertain* the date of the game⟩

as·cet·ic \ə-'set-ik\ *adj* : practicing self-denial especially for religious reasons : AUSTERE

as·cribe \ə-'skrīb\ *vb* **as·cribed; as·crib·ing** : to refer to a supposed cause, source, or author : ATTRIBUTE

as·crip·tion \ə-'skrip-shən\ *n* : ATTRIBUTION

a·sex·u·al \'ā-'sek-shə-wəl\ *adj* : lacking sex

¹ash \'ash\ *n* : a common shade tree or timber tree with furrowed bark and winged seeds

²ash *n* **1** : the solid matter left when material is thoroughly burned **2** *pl* : a collection of ash left after something has been burned **3** *pl* : the remains of the dead human body

ash: leaf and fruit

a·shamed \ə-'shāmd\ *adj* **1** : feeling shame, guilt, or disgrace ⟨*ashamed* of his behavior⟩ **2** : kept back by anticipation of shame ⟨*ashamed* to beg⟩

ash·en \'ash-ən\ *adj* **1** : of the color of ashes **2** : deadly pale

a·shore \ə-'shōr\ *adv (or adj)* : on or to the shore

Ash Wednesday *n* : the first day of Lent

ash·y \'ash-ē\ *adj* **1** : of, relating to, or resembling ashes **2** : deadly pale

¹A·sian \'ā-zhən\ *adj* : of or relating to Asia or the Asians

²Asian *n* : a native or inhabitant of Asia

a·side \ə-'sīd\ *adv* **1** : to or toward the side

⟨stepped *aside*⟩ **2** : out of the way : AWAY **3** : away from one's thought ⟨joking *aside*⟩

aside from *prep* : with the exception of

as if *conj* **1** : the way it would be if ⟨it's *as if* nothing had changed⟩ **2** : the way one would do if ⟨he acts *as if* he'd never been away⟩ **3** : THAT ⟨it seems *as if* nothing ever changes⟩

as·i·nine \'as-n-,īn\ *adj* : STUPID, FOOLISH ⟨an *asinine* remark⟩ **syn** see SILLY

ask \'ask\ *vb* **1** : to seek information : INQUIRE **2** : to make a request ⟨*ask* for help⟩ **3** : to set as a price : DEMAND ⟨*ask* twenty dollars for a bicycle⟩ **4** : INVITE ⟨be *asked* to a party⟩ **5** : LOOK ⟨he is *asking* for trouble⟩

  syn ASK, REQUEST, BEG all mean to express a desire to someone thought able to satisfy it. ASK implies no more than a simple statement of the desire ⟨*ask* for a different seat⟩ REQUEST suggests some special attention to courtesy and is used when a favorable answer is expected ⟨*requested* less noise in the room⟩ BEG occurs mainly in set phrases of formal politeness ⟨*beg* one's pardon⟩ ⟨*beg* permission to go⟩

a·skance \ə-'skans\ *adv* **1** : with a side glance **2** : with distrust, suspicion, or disapproval

a·skew \ə-'skyü\ *adv (or adj)* : out of line

¹a·slant \ə-'slant\ *adv* : in a slanting direction

²aslant *prep* : over or across in a slanting direction

¹a·sleep \ə-'slēp\ *adj* **1** : SLEEPING **2** : lacking sensation : NUMB

²asleep *adv* : into a state of sleep

as of *prep* : starting on ⟨takes effect *as of* July 1⟩

as·par·a·gus \ə-'spar-ə-gəs\ *n* : a vegetable that consists of the thick young shoots of a perennial garden plant related to the lilies

as·pect \'as-,pekt\ *n* **1** : a position facing a particular direction **2** : a particular status or phase in which something appears or may be regarded **3** : LOOK, APPEARANCE

as·pen \'as-pən\ *n* : a poplar tree whose leaves flutter in the lightest breeze

as·per·i·ty \a-'sper-ət-ē\ *n, pl* **as·per·i·ties 1** : RIGOR, SEVERITY **2** : harshness of temper, manner, or tone

aspen leaves

as·per·sion \ə-'spər-zhən\ *n* : a mean, damaging, or untrue statement or implication ⟨cast *aspersions*⟩

as·phalt \'as-,fòlt\ *n* **1** : a dark-colored substance obtained from natural beds or from certain petroleums and tars **2** : any of various compositions of asphalt having different uses (as for pavement or for waterproof cement)

as·phyx·i·ate \as-'fik-sē-,āt\ *vb* **as·phyx·i-**

at·ed; as·phyx·i·at·ing : to cause (as a person) to become unconscious or die by cutting off the normal intake of oxygen whether by interfering with breathing or by replacing the oxygen of the air with another gas

as·pi·rant \'as-pə-rənt, ə-'spī-\ n : a person who aspires ⟨an *aspirant* to the presidency⟩

as·pi·ra·tion \,as-pə-'rā-shən\ n 1 : a strong desire to achieve something high or great 2 : an object of aspiration

as·pire \ə-'spīr\ vb as·pired; as·pir·ing 1 : to have a noble desire or ambition 2 : ASCEND

as·pi·rin \'as-pə-rən\ n : a white drug used as a remedy for pain and fever

ass \'as\ n 1 : an animal resembling but smaller than the related horse and having shorter hair in mane and tail and longer ears : DONKEY 2 : a dull stupid person

as·sail \ə-'sāl\ vb : to attack violently with blows or words

as·sail·ant \ə-'sā-lənt\ n : a person who assails : ATTACKER

as·sas·sin \ə-'sas-n\ n [from medieval Latin *assassinus*, taken from Arabic *hashshāsh* meaning "a user of the drug hashish"; the meaning "secret slayer" developed because of a group of Muslims who, while under the influence of hashish, murdered Crusaders] : a person who kills another person by a surprise or secret attack

as·sas·si·nate \ə-'sas-n-,āt\ vb as·sas·si·nat·ed; as·sas·si·nat·ing : to murder by a surprise or secret attack **syn** see KILL

as·sas·si·na·tion \ə-,sas-n-'ā-shən\ n : the act of assassinating

¹as·sault \ə-'sȯlt\ n 1 : a violent or sudden attack 2 : an unlawful attempt or threat to do harm to another

²assault vb : to make an assault on

¹as·say \'as-,ā, a-'sā\ n 1 : a test (as of gold) to determine characteristics (as weight or quality) 2 : analysis (as of a drug) to determine the presence of one or more ingredients

²as·say \a-'sā, 'as-,ā\ vb 1 : to analyze (as an ore) for one or more valuable components 2 : ESTIMATE 3 : to prove to be of a particular nature by means of an assay

as·sem·blage \ə-'sem-blij\ n : a collection of persons or things : GATHERING

as·sem·ble \ə-'sem-bəl\ vb as·sem·bled; as·sem·bling 1 : to collect into one place or group 2 : to fit together the parts of ⟨*assemble* a machine gun⟩ 3 : to meet together : CONVENE — as·sem·bler n

as·sem·bly \ə-'sem-blē\ n, pl as·sem·blies 1 : a gathering of persons : MEETING ⟨a school

assembly⟩ 2 cap : a legislative body 3 : the act of assembling : the state of being assembled 4 : a collection of parts that go to make up a complete unit

¹as·sent \ə-'sent\ vb : AGREE, CONCUR

²assent n : an act of assenting : AGREEMENT

as·sert \ə-'sərt\ vb 1 : to state clearly and strongly : declare positively ⟨*assert* an opinion in a loud voice⟩ 2 : MAINTAIN, DEFEND ⟨*assert* one's rights⟩ — assert oneself : to demand and insist that others recognize one's rights

as·ser·tion \ə-'sər-shən\ n 1 : the act of asserting 2 : a positive statement

as·ser·tive \ə-'sərt-iv\ adj : characterized by self-confidence and boldness in expressing opinions — as·sert·ive·ly adv — as·sert·ive·ness n

as·sess \ə-'ses\ vb 1 : to fix the rate or amount of ⟨the jury *assessed* damages of $5000⟩ 2 : to set a value on for purposes of taxation 3 : to lay a charge or tax on — as·ses·sor n

as·sess·ment \ə-'ses-mənt\ n 1 : the act of assessing 2 : the amount or value assessed

as·set \'as-,et\ n 1 pl : all the property (as cash, securities, real estate) of a person, corporation, or estate 2 : ADVANTAGE

as·si·du·i·ty \,as-ə-'dü-ət-ē, -'dyü-\ n : DILIGENCE

as·sid·u·ous \ə-'sij-ə-wəs\ adj : steadily attentive : DILIGENT — as·sid·u·ous·ly adv — as·sid·u·ous·ness n

as·sign \ə-'sīn\ vb 1 : to transfer to another 2 : to appoint to a post or duty 3 : PRESCRIBE ⟨*assign* lessons⟩ 4 : to fix authoritatively

as·sign·ment \ə-'sīn-mənt\ n 1 : the act of assigning ⟨the *assignment* of seats⟩ 2 : something assigned ⟨an *assignment* in arithmetic⟩

as·sim·i·late \ə-'sim-ə-,lāt\ vb as·sim·i·lat·ed; as·sim·i·lat·ing : to take something in and make it part of the thing it has joined or make it like the thing it has joined : ABSORB

as·sim·i·la·tion \ə-,sim-ə-'lā-shən\ n : the act or process of assimilating

¹as·sist \ə-'sist\ vb : to give aid : HELP

²assist n : an act of assisting

as·sist·ance \ə-'sis-təns\ n : AID, HELP

¹as·sist·ant \ə-'sis-tənt\ adj : serving as an assistant to another ⟨*assistant* manager⟩

²assistant n : a person who assists another

¹as·so·ci·ate \ə-'sō-shē-,āt\ vb as·so·ci·at·ed; as·so·ci·at·ing 1 : to join or come together as partners, friends, or companions 2 : to connect in thought 3 : UNITE

²as·so·ci·ate \ə-'sō-shē-ət, -shət\ n 1 : a fellow worker : PARTNER 2 : COMPANION

³as·so·ci·ate \ə-'sō-shē-ət, -shət\ adj

1 : closely joined with another (as in duties or responsibility) **2** : admitted to some but not to all rights and privileges ⟨*associate* member⟩

as·so·ci·a·tion \ə-ˌsō-sē-'ā-shən\ *n* **1** : the act of associating : the state of being associated **2** : an organization of persons with a common interest ⟨an athletic *association*⟩ **3** : a feeling, memory, or thought connected with a person, place, or thing

as·so·ci·a·tive \ə-'sō-shē-ˌāt-iv\ *adj* **1** : serving to associate ⟨*associative* nerve cells⟩ **2** : being a property of a mathematical operation (as addition or multiplication) in which the result is independent of the original grouping of the elements

as·sort \ə-'sȯrt\ *vb* **1** : CLASSIFY **2** : HARMONIZE

as·sort·ed \ə-'sȯrt-əd\ *adj* **1** : consisting of various kinds ⟨*assorted* chocolates⟩ **2** : MATCHED, SUITED ⟨an ill-*assorted* pair⟩ **syn** see MISCELLANEOUS

as·sort·ment \ə-'sȯrt-mənt\ *n* **1** : arrangement in classes **2** : a collection of assorted things or persons

as·suage \ə-'swāj\ *vb* **as·suaged; as·suag·ing** **1** : to lessen the intensity of : EASE **2** : SATISFY

as·sume \ə-'süm\ *vb* **as·sumed; as·sum·ing** **1** : to take upon oneself : UNDERTAKE ⟨*assume* new duties⟩ **2** : SEIZE, USURP **3** : to put on in appearance only : FEIGN ⟨an *assumed* manner⟩ **4** : to take for granted : SUPPOSE

as·sump·tion \ə-'səmp-shən\ *n* **1** : the act of assuming ⟨the *assumption* of power by a new administration⟩ **2** : something taken for granted ⟨the *assumption* that he will be here⟩

as·sur·ance \ə-'shùr-əns\ *n* **1** : the act of assuring : PLEDGE **2** : the state of being sure or certain **3** : SECURITY, SAFETY **4** *chiefly Brit* : INSURANCE **5** : SELF-CONFIDENCE **6** : AUDACITY, PRESUMPTION

as·sure \ə-'shùr\ *vb* **as·sured; as·sur·ing** **1** : INSURE **2** : to give confidence to **3** : to make sure or certain ⟨*assure* the success of the enterprise⟩ **4** : to inform positively

¹**as·sured** \ə-'shùrd\ *adj* **1** : made sure or certain **2** : CONFIDENT **3** : CONVINCED — **as·sur·ed·ness** \-'shùr-əd-nəs\ *n*

²**as·sured** \ə-'shùrd\ *n* : a person whose life or property is insured

as·sur·ed·ly \ə-'shùr-əd-lē\ *adv* : CERTAINLY

as·ta·tine \'as-tə-ˌtēn\ *n* : a radioactive chemical element produced artificially from bismuth

as·ter \'as-tər\ *n* : any of various mostly fall-blooming leafy-stemmed herbs related to the

aster

daisies that have showy white, pink, purple, or yellow flower heads

as·ter·isk \'as-tə-ˌrisk\ *n* : a character * used as a reference mark or to show the omission of letters or words

a·stern \ə-'stərn\ *adv* **1** : behind a ship or airplane **2** : at or toward the stern **3** : BACKWARD ⟨full speed *astern*⟩

as·ter·oid \'as-tə-ˌrȯid\ *n* : one of thousands of small planets in orbits between those of Mars and Jupiter with diameters from a fraction of a mile to nearly 500 miles

asth·ma \'az-mə\ *n* : a disorder of which labored breathing, wheezing, and coughing are symptoms

a·stir \ə-'stər\ *adj* **1** : being in a state of activity : STIRRING **2** : out of bed : UP

as to *prep* **1** : with reference to : ABOUT ⟨at a loss *as to* what caused the accident⟩ **2** : according to : BY ⟨graded *as to* size and color⟩

as·ton·ish \ə-'stän-ish\ *vb* : to strike with sudden wonder : AMAZE **syn** see SURPRISE

as·ton·ish·ment \ə-'stän-ish-mənt\ *n* : great surprise : AMAZEMENT

as·tound \ə-'staùnd\ *vb* : to fill with bewildered wonder : ASTONISH

a·stray \ə-'strā\ *adv (or adj)* **1** : off the right path or route **2** : into error : MISTAKEN

¹**a·stride** \ə-'strīd\ *adv* : with one leg on each side

²**astride** *prep* : with one leg on each side of

as·trin·gent \ə-'strin-jənt\ *adj* : able or tending to shrink body tissues ⟨an *astringent* lotion⟩ — **as·trin·gent·ly** *adv*

as·tro- \'as-trə, -trō\ *prefix* : star : heavens : astronomical ⟨*astro*physics⟩

as·trol·o·gy \ə-'sträl-ə-jē\ *n* : the telling of fortunes by the stars

as·tro·naut \'as-trə-ˌnȯt\ *n* [formed in English from Greek *astron* "star", found also in *astro*logy and *astro*nomy, and Greek *nautēs* "sailor"] : a traveler in a spacecraft

as·tro·nau·tics \ˌas-trə-'nȯt-iks\ *n* : the science of the construction and operation of spacecraft

as·tron·o·mer \ə-'strän-ə-mər\ *n* : a person who is skilled in astronomy

as·tro·nom·i·cal \ˌas-trə-'näm-i-kəl\ *or* **as·tro·nom·ic** \-ik\ *adj* **1** : of or relating to astronomy **2** : extremely or incomprehensibly large — **as·tro·nom·i·cal·ly** *adv*

as·tron·o·my \ə-'strän-ə-mē\ *n* : a science that collects, studies, and explains facts about the heavenly bodies

as·tute \ə-'stüt, -'styüt\ *adj* : shrewdly discerning — **as·tute·ly** *adv* — **as·tute·ness** *n*

a·sun·der \ə-'sən-dər\ *adv (or adj)* **1** : into

separate pieces ⟨torn *asunder*⟩ **2** : APART

as well as *prep* : BESIDES

a·sy·lum \ə-'sī-ləm\ *n* **1** : a place of refuge **2** : protection given especially to political fugitives **3** : an institution for the care of the needy or afflicted and especially of the insane

at \ət, at\ *prep* **1** — used to indicate a point in time or space ⟨be here *at* six⟩ ⟨he is *at* the hotel⟩ **2** — used to indicate a goal ⟨swing *at* the ball⟩ ⟨laughed *at* him⟩ **3** — used to indicate position or condition ⟨*at* rest⟩ **4** — used to indicate how or why something is done ⟨sold *at* auction⟩

ate past of EAT

¹-ate \ət, ‚āt\ *n suffix* **1** : one acted upon in a specified way ⟨distill*ate*⟩ **2** : chemical compound derived from a specified compound or element ⟨carbon*ate*⟩

²-ate *n suffix* : office : function : rank : group of persons holding a specified office or rank ⟨professor*ate*⟩

³-ate *adj suffix* **1** : acted on in a specified way : brought into or being in a specified state ⟨temper*ate*⟩ **2** : marked by having ⟨chord*ate*⟩

⁴-ate \‚āt\ *vb suffix* **1** : cause to be modified or affected by ⟨camphor*ate*⟩ **2** : cause to become ⟨activ*ate*⟩ : furnish with ⟨aer*ate*⟩

a·the·ist \'ā-thē-əst\ *n* : a person who believes there is no God

a·thirst \ə-'thərst\ *adj* **1** : THIRSTY **2** : EAGER

ath·lete \'ath-‚lēt\ *n* : a person who is trained in or good at games and exercises that require physical skill, endurance, and strength

athlete's foot *n* : a fungus infection of the foot marked by blisters, itching, and cracks between and under the toes

ath·let·ic \ath-'let-ik\ *adj* **1** : of, relating to, or characteristic of athletes or athletics **2** : VIGOROUS, ACTIVE **3** : STURDY, MUSCULAR

ath·let·ics \ath-'let-iks\ *n sing or pl* : games, sports, and exercises requiring strength and skill

¹a·thwart \ə-'thwȯrt\ *adv* : ACROSS

²athwart *prep* **1** : ACROSS **2** : in opposition to

-a·tion \'ā-shən\ *n suffix* **1** : action or process ⟨flirt*ation*⟩ **2** : something connected with an action or process ⟨discolor*ation*⟩

-a·tive \ət-iv, ‚āt-\ *adj suffix* **1** : of, relating to, or connected with ⟨authorit*ative*⟩ **2** : tending to ⟨talk*ative*⟩

at·las \'at-ləs\ *n* : a book of maps

at·mo·sphere \'at-mə-‚sfiər\ *n* **1** : the air surrounding the earth **2** : the air in a particular place ⟨the stuffy *atmosphere* of this room⟩ **3** : a surrounding influence or set of conditions ⟨the home *atmosphere*⟩

at·mo·spher·ic \‚at-mə-'sfiər-ik, -'sfer-\ *adj* : of or relating to the atmosphere

a·toll \'a-‚tȯl, -‚tȧl\ *n* : a ring-shaped coral island or string of islands consisting of a coral reef surrounding a lagoon

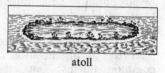
atoll

at·om \'at-əm\ *n* [from the Greek noun *atomos*, which was originally an adj., *atomos* "indivisible"; so called because it was believed to be the smallest particle into which matter could be divided] **1** : a tiny particle : BIT **2** : the smallest particle of an element that can exist alone or in combination

atom bomb *or* **atomic bomb** *n* : a bomb whose great power is due to the sudden release of the energy in the atomic nucleus

a·tom·ic \ə-'täm-ik\ *adj* **1** : of, relating to, or concerned with atoms, atomic energy, or atomic bombs **2** : extremely small : TINY

atomic energy *n* : energy that can be freed by changes (as by splitting of a heavy nucleus or fusion of light nuclei into heavier ones) in the nucleus of an atom

at·om·iz·er \'at-ə-‚mī-zər\ *n* : a device for spraying a liquid (as a perfume or disinfectant)

a·tone \ə-'tōn\ *vb* **a·toned**; **a·ton·ing** : to do something to make up for a wrong that has been done : make amends

a·tone·ment \ə-'tōn-mənt\ *n* : reparation for an offense or injury

atomizer

a·top \ə-'täp\ *prep* : on top of

a·tro·cious \ə-'trō-shəs\ *adj* **1** : savagely brutal, cruel, or wicked **2** : very bad — **a·tro·cious·ly** *adv* — **a·tro·cious·ness** *n*

a·troc·i·ty \ə-'träs-ət-ē\ *n, pl* **a·troc·i·ties** : an atrocious act, object, or situation

at·tach \ə-'tach\ *vb* **1** : to seize legally in order to secure payment of a debt **2** : to fasten or join one thing to another ⟨*attach* a bell to a bicycle⟩ **3** : to tie or bind by feelings of affection ⟨the boy was *attached* to his dog⟩ **4** : APPOINT ⟨*attach* an officer to a headquarters⟩ **5** : ATTRIBUTE ⟨*attach* no importance to it⟩

at·ta·ché \‚at-ə-'shā, ‚a-‚ta-\ *n* : a technical expert on the staff of an ambassador

at·tach·ment \ə-'tach-mənt\ *n* **1** : legal seizure of property **2** : connection by ties of affection or regard **3** : a device attached to a machine or implement **4** : a connection by which one thing is attached to another

¹at·tack \ə-'tak\ *vb* **1** : to set upon forcefully ⟨*attack* a snake with a stick⟩ **2** : to use unfriendly or bitter words against ⟨*attack* the mayor over the radio⟩ **3** : to begin to affect or to act upon harmfully ⟨the camp was *attacked* by fever⟩ **4** : to set to work on — **at·tack·er** *n*

²attack *n* **1** : the act of attacking : ASSAULT **2** : a setting to work **3** : a fit of sickness

at·tain \ə-'tān\ *vb* **1** : ACHIEVE, ACCOMPLISH ⟨*attain* an ambition⟩ **2** : to come into possession of **3** : to arrive at : REACH ⟨*attain* the top of the hill⟩ — **at·tain·a·ble** \ə-'tā-nə-bəl\ *adj*

at·tain·ment \ə-'tān-mənt\ *n* **1** : the act of attaining : the state of being attained **2** : AC-COMPLISHMENT ⟨a man of great *attainments*⟩

at·tar \'at-ər\ *n* : a fragrant floral oil

¹at·tempt \ə-'tempt\ *vb* **1** : to try to do or perform : make an effort ⟨*attempt* an escape⟩ **2** : to try to take by force **3** : ENDEAVOR

²attempt *n* : the act or an instance of attempting

at·tend \ə-'tend\ *vb* **1** : to care for : look after : take charge of ⟨*attend* to taking out the rubbish⟩ **2** : to wait on ⟨nurses *attend* the sick⟩ **3** : to go or stay with as a servant or companion ⟨a king *attended* by his court⟩ **4** : to be present at ⟨*attend* a party⟩ **5** : to pay attention

at·tend·ance \ə-'ten-dəns\ *n* **1** : the act of attending ⟨a prize for perfect *attendance*⟩ **2** : the number of persons present

¹at·tend·ant \ə-'ten-dənt\ *adj* : ACCOMPANY-ING ⟨*attendant* circumstances⟩

²attendant *n* : a person (as a companion or servant) who attends another

at·ten·tion \ə-'ten-chən\ *n* **1** : the act or the power of fixing one's mind on something : careful listening or watching ⟨give *attention* to a speaker⟩ **2** : careful consideration of something with a view to taking action on it ⟨a matter requiring *attention*⟩ **3** : an act of kindness, care, or courtesy **4** : a military position of readiness to act on the next command

at·ten·tive \ə-'tent-iv\ *adj* **1** : paying attention ⟨an *attentive* listener⟩ **2** : being thought-ful and courteous ⟨*attentive* to his mother⟩ — **at·ten·tive·ly** *adv* — **at·ten·tive·ness** *n*

at·test \ə-'test\ *vb* : to give proof of : testify to

at·tic \'at-ik\ *n* : a room or a space just under the roof of a building

¹at·tire \ə-'tīr\ *vb* **at·tired**; **at·tir·ing** **1** : DRESS, ARRAY **2** : to clothe in rich garments

²attire *n* **1** : DRESS, CLOTHES **2** : fine clothing

at·ti·tude \'at-ə-ˌtüd, -ˌtyüd\ *n* **1** : the ar-rangement of a body or figure : POSTURE **2** : a mental position or feeling regarding a fact or state **3** : the position of something in regard to something else

at·tor·ney \ə-'tər-nē\ *n, pl* **at·tor·neys** : a per-son who is appointed by another to transact

business and especially legal business for him

at·tract \ə-'trakt\ *vb* **1** : to draw to or toward oneself ⟨a magnet *attracts* iron⟩ **2** : to draw by appealing to interest or feeling

at·trac·tion \ə-'trak-shən\ *n* **1** : the act or power of attracting **2** : an attractive quality, object, or feature ⟨the *attractions* of a city⟩

at·trac·tive \ə-'trak-tiv\ *adj* : having the power or quality of attracting : PLEASING — **at·trac·tive·ly** *adv* — **at·trac·tive·ness** *n*

¹at·tri·bute \'at-rə-ˌbyüt\ *n* **1** : an inherent characteristic : a quality belonging to a par-ticular person or thing **2** : an object closely associated with a specific person, thing, or of-fice ⟨a scepter and crown are *attributes* of a king⟩ **3** : a word (as an adjective) ascribing a quality

²at·trib·ute \ə-'trib-yət\ *vb* **at·trib·ut·ed**; **at·trib·ut·ing** **1** : to explain as to cause or origin ⟨*attributes* his success to hard work⟩ **2** : to re-gard as a characteristic of a person or thing

at·tri·bu·tion \ˌat-rə-'byü-shən\ *n* : the act of attributing

at·trib·u·tive \ə-'trib-yət-iv\ *adj* : of, relating to, or being an attribute

at·tri·tion \ə-'trish-ən\ *n* : the act of wearing away or of weakening by or as if by friction

at·tune \ə-'tün, -'tyün\ *vb* **at·tuned**; **at·tun·ing** : to bring into harmony : TUNE

a·typ·i·cal \'ā-'tip-i-kəl\ *adj* : not typical : IR-REGULAR — **a·typ·i·cal·ly** *adv*

au·burn \'ȯ-bərn\ *adj* : of a reddish brown color ⟨*auburn* hair⟩

¹auc·tion \'ȯk-shən\ *n* : a public sale at which persons bid on property to be sold and the property is sold to the highest bidder

²auction *vb* : to sell at auction

auc·tion·eer \ˌȯk-shə-'niər\ *n* : an agent who sells goods for another at auction

au·da·cious \ȯ-'dā-shəs\ *adj* **1** : extremely bold : DARING **2** : IMPUDENT, INSOLENT — **au·da·cious·ly** *adv* — **au·da·cious·ness** *n*

au·dac·i·ty \ȯ-'das-ət-ē\ *n, pl* **au·dac·i·ties** **1** : BOLDNESS, DARING **2** : IMPUDENCE

au·di·ble \'ȯd-ə-bəl\ *adj* : loud enough to be heard — **au·di·bly** \-blē\ *adv*

au·di·ence \'ȯd-ē-əns\ *n* **1** : the act or state of hearing **2** : an assembled group that listens or watches (as at a concert or a game) **3** : a formal interview with a person of very high rank **4** : those of the general public who give attention to something said, done, or written

¹au·di·o \'ȯd-ē-ˌō\ *adj* **1** : of or relating to sound or its reproduction **2** : relating to or used in the transmission or reception of sound (as in radio or television)

²audio *n* **1** : the transmission, reception, or

---

reproduction of sound **2** : the section of television equipment that deals with sound

¹au·dit \'òd-ət\ *n* : a formal examination and verification of financial accounts

²audit *vb* : to make an audit of

¹au·di·tion \ò-'dish-ən\ *n* **1** : the power or sense of hearing **2** : a hearing especially for appraising an entertainer's merits

²audition *vb* : to test or try out in an audition

au·di·tor \'òd-ət-ər\ *n* **1** : HEARER, LISTENER **2** : a person authorized to audit accounts

au·di·to·ri·um \,òd-ə-'tōr-ē-əm\ *n* **1** : the part of a public building where an audience sits **2** : a hall used for public gatherings

au·di·to·ry \'òd-ə-,tōr-ē\ *adj* : of or relating to hearing

au·ger \'ò-gər\ *n* : a tool used for boring holes

aught \'òt\ *n* : ZERO, CIPHER

aug·ment \òg-'ment\ *vb* : to increase especially in size, amount, or degree

aug·men·ta·tion \,òg-mən-'tā-shən\ *n* : INCREASE, ENLARGE-MENT

auger

¹au·gur \'ò-gər\ *n* **1** : an official diviner of ancient Rome **2** : SOOTHSAYER

²augur *vb* **1** : to foretell especially from omens **2** : to give promise of

au·gu·ry \'ò-gyə-rē\ *n, pl* **au·gu·ries** **1** : divination from omens **2** : OMEN, PORTENT

au·gust \ò-'gəst\ *adj* : being stately and noble : MAJESTIC — **au·gust·ly** *adv* — **au·gust·ness** *n*

Au·gust \'ò-gəst\ *n* [taken into Old English from Latin *Augustus*, the month named after the Roman emperor Augustus Caesar] : the eighth month of the year

auk \'òk\ *n* : a diving seabird of the cold regions of the northern hemisphere with a heavy body and small wings

aunt \'ant, 'ant\ *n* **1** : a sister of one's father or mother **2** : the wife of one's uncle

au·ra \'òr-ə\ *n* : a distinctive atmosphere or impression surrounding a person or thing

au·ral \'òr-əl\ *adj* : of or relating to the ear or sense of hearing — **au·ral·ly** *adv*

au·ro·ra bo·re·al·is \ə-,rōr-ə-,bōr-ē-'al-əs\ *n* : streamers or arches of light in the sky at night that are held to be of electrical origin and appear especially in the arctic regions

aus·pic·es \'ò-spə-səz\ *n pl* : kindly patronage and guidance : SPONSORSHIP

aus·pi·cious \ò-'spish-əs\ *adj* **1** : promising success : FAVORABLE 〈an *auspicious* beginning〉 **2** : PROSPEROUS — **aus·pi·cious·ly** *adv*

aus·tere \ò-'stiər\ *adj* **1** : stern and forbidding especially in appearance and manner **2** : PLAIN 〈an *austere* room〉 — **aus·tere·ly** *adv*

aus·ter·i·ty \ò-'ster-ət-ē\ *n, pl* **aus·ter·i·ties** **1** : an austere act, manner, or attitude **2** : enforced or extreme economy

¹Aus·tra·lian \ò-'strāl-yən\ *n* : a native or inhabitant of Australia

²Australian *adj* : of or relating to Australia or the Australians

aut- \òt\ *or* **au·to-** \'òt-ə, 'òt-ō\ *prefix* **1** : self : same one 〈*auto*biography〉 **2** : automatic : self-regulating 〈*auto*-rifle〉

au·then·tic \ò-'thent-ik\ *adj* **1** : being really what it seems to be : GENUINE 〈an *authentic* signature〉 **2** : CORRECT, TRUE 〈a report *authentic* in every detail〉 — **au·then·ti·cal·ly** \-i-kə-lē\ *adv*

au·then·tic·i·ty \,ò-,then-'tis-ət-ē\ *n* : GENU-INENESS

au·thor \'ò-thər\ *n* **1** : a person who writes or composes a literary work (as a novel) **2** : one that originates or creates

au·thor·i·ta·tive \ə-'thòr-ə-,tāt-iv\ *adj* **1** : having or coming from authority 〈an *authoritative* order〉 **2** : having an air of authority : POSITIVE 〈an *authoritative* manner〉 — **au·thor·i·ta·tive·ly** *adv* — **au·thor·i·ta·tive·ness** *n*

au·thor·i·ty \ə-'thòr-ət-ē\ *n, pl* **au·thor·i·ties** **1** : a fact or statement used to support a position **2** : a person appealed to as an expert **3** : the right to give commands and the power to enforce obedience 〈parental *authority*〉 **4** : persons having powers of government 〈state *authorities*〉 **syn** see INFLUENCE

au·tho·rize \'ò-thə-,rīz\ *vb* **au·tho·rized**; **au·tho·riz·ing** **1** : to give authority to : EMPOWER 〈*authorize* a son to act for his father〉 **2** : to give legal or official approval to

au·thor·ship \'ò-thər-,ship\ *n* **1** : the profession of writing **2** : the origin of a piece of writing

au·to \'òt-ō\ *n, pl* **au·tos** : AUTOMOBILE

au·to·bi·og·ra·phy \,òt-ə-bī-'äg-rə-fē\ *n, pl* **au·to·bi·og·ra·phies** : the biography of a person written by himself

au·toc·ra·cy \ò-'täk-rə-sē\ *n, pl* **au·toc·ra·cies** : government by one person having unlimited power

au·to·crat \'òt-ə-,krat\ *n* : a person (as a monarch) who has unlimited power

au·to·crat·ic \,òt-ə-'krat-ik\ *adj* : of, relating to, or characteristic of an autocracy or an autocrat — **au·to·crat·i·cal·ly** \-i-kə-lē\ *adv*

¹au·to·graph \'òt-ə-,graf\ *n* : a person's signature written by hand

²autograph *vb* : to write one's signature in or on (as a book)

au·to·mate \'òt-ə-,māt\ *vb* **au·to·mat·ed**; **au·to·mat·ing** : to operate by automation

¹**au·to·mat·ic** \ˌȯt-ə-'mat-ik\ *adj* **1** : largely or wholly involuntary : of a reflex nature ⟨gave an *automatic* smile⟩ **2** : having a self≠ acting or self-regulating device ⟨an *automatic* machine⟩ — **au·to·mat·i·cal·ly** \-i-kə-lē\ *adv*

²**automatic** *n* **1** : an automatic machine **2** : an automatic firearm

au·to·ma·tion \ˌȯt-ə-'mā-shən\ *n* **1** : the method of making an apparatus, a process, or a system operate automatically **2** : automatic operation of an apparatus, process, or system by mechanical or electronic devices that take the place of human operators

au·tom·a·ton \ȯ-'täm-ət-ən\ *n, pl* **au·tom·a·tons** *or* **au·tom·a·ta** \-ət-ə\ **1** : a machine made to imitate the motions of a man or an animal **2** : a person who acts in a mechanical fashion

¹**au·to·mo·bile** \ˌȯt-ə-mō-'bēl\ *adj* : AUTOMO- TIVE

²**automobile** *n* : a usually four-wheeled auto- motive vehicle designed for passenger trans- portation on streets and roadways

au·to·mo·tive \ˌȯt-ə-'mōt-iv\ *adj* : SELF≠ PROPELLED

au·tumn \'ȯt-əm\ *n* : the season between summer and winter comprising in the northern hemisphere usually the months of September, October, and November or as reckoned astronomically extending from the September equinox to the December solstice

au·tum·nal \ȯ-'təm-nəl\ *adj* : of, relating to, or characteristic of autumn

¹**aux·il·ia·ry** \ȯg-'zil-yə-rē\ *adj* **1** : offering or providing help **2** : SUPPLEMENTARY

²**auxiliary** *n, pl* **aux·il·ia·ries** **1** : an auxiliary person, group, or device **2** : HELPING VERB

¹**a·vail** \ə-'vāl\ *vb* : to be of use or advantage

²**avail** *n* : help or benefit toward reaching a goal : USE ⟨effort was of little *avail*⟩

a·vail·a·ble \ə-'vā-lə-bəl\ *adj* **1** : that may be used : USABLE **2** : ACCESSIBLE, OBTAINABLE

av·a·lanche \'av-ə-ˌlanch\ *n* : a large mass of snow and ice or of earth or rock sliding down a mountainside or over a cliff

av·a·rice \'av-ə-rəs\ *n* : excessive desire for wealth or gain : GREED

av·a·ri·cious \ˌav-ə-'rish-əs\ *adj* : greedy of gain — **av·a·ri·cious·ly** *adv* — **av·a·ri·cious- ness** *n*

a·venge \ə-'venj\ *vb* **a·venged; a·veng·ing** : to take vengeance for — **a·veng·er** *n*

av·e·nue \'av-ə-ˌnü, -ˌnyü\ *n* **1** : PASSAGEWAY **2** : a way or means to an end **3** : a usually broad and attractive street

a·ver \ə-'vər\ *vb* **a·verred; a·ver·ring** : to de- clare positively : ASSERT

¹**av·er·age** \'av-ə-rij\ *n* **1** : ARITHMETIC MEAN **2** : something typical of a group, class, or series **3** : a measure of success in a game or sport ⟨batting *average*⟩

²**average** *adj* **1** : equaling or approximating an average ⟨the *average* age of the class is eleven⟩ **2** : ORDINARY, USUAL ⟨the *average* man⟩ **syn** see MEDIOCRE

³**average** *vb* **av·er·aged; av·er·ag·ing** **1** : to amount to on the average : be usually **2** : to find the average of .

a·ver·ment \ə-'vər-mənt\ *n* : AFFIRMATION

a·verse \ə-'vərs\ *adj* : having a feeling of dis- like or distaste ⟨*averse* to exercise⟩

a·ver·sion \ə-'vər-zhən\ *n* **1** : a strong dis- like **2** : something strongly disliked

a·vert \ə-'vərt\ *vb* **1** : to turn away ⟨*avert* one's eyes⟩ **2** : to prevent from happening

a·vi·ar·y \'ā-vē-ˌer-ē\ *n, pl* **a·vi·ar·ies** : a place (as a large cage) where birds are kept

a·vi·a·tion \ˌā-vē-'ā-shən\ *n* **1** : the operation of heavier-than-air aircraft (as airplanes) **2** : airplane manufacture and development

aviation cadet *n* : a student officer in the air force

a·vi·a·tor \'ā-vē-ˌāt-ər\ *n* : the pilot of an air- plane

a·vi·a·tress \'ā-vē-ˌā-trəs\ *n* : AVIATRIX

a·vi·a·trix \ˌā-vē-'ā-triks\ *n* : a woman aviator

av·id \'av-əd\ *adj* **1** : very eager : GREEDY ⟨*avid* for praise⟩ **2** : ENTHUSIASTIC ⟨an *avid* football fan⟩ — **av·id·ly** *adv*

a·vid·i·ty \ə-'vid-ət-ē\ *n* : extreme eagerness

av·o·ca·do \ˌav-ə-'käd-ō\ *n, pl* **av·o·ca·dos** : the green pulpy pear-shaped or egg-shaped fruit of a tropical American tree

av·o·ca·tion \ˌav-ə-'kā- shən\ *n* : a subordinate oc- cupation engaged in usually for pleasure : HOBBY

avocados

a·void \ə-'vȯid\ *vb* : to keep away from

a·void·ance \ə-'vȯid-ns\ *n* : a keeping away from or clear of something

a·vow \ə-'vaù\ *vb* : to declare or acknowledge openly and frankly

a·vow·al \ə-'vaù-əl\ *n* : an open declaration or acknowledgment

a·wait \ə-'wāt\ *vb* **1** : to wait for : EXPECT ⟨*await* a train⟩ **2** : to be ready or waiting for

¹**a·wake** \ə-'wāk\ *vb* **a·woke** \-'wōk\ *or* **a·waked; a·wak·ing** **1** : to arouse from sleep : wake up **2** : to become conscious or aware of something ⟨*awoke* to their danger⟩

²**awake** *adj* : not asleep : ALERT

a·wak·en \ə-'wā-kən\ *vb* : AWAKE — **a·wak- en·er** *n*

¹a·ward \ə-'wȯrd\ vb **1** : to give by judicial decision ⟨*award* damages⟩ **2** : to give or grant as a reward ⟨*award* a medal⟩

²award n **1** : the decision of arbitrators in a case submitted to them **2** : PRIZE

a·ware \ə-'waər\ adj : having or showing realization, perception, or knowledge : CONSCIOUS ⟨*aware* of what's what⟩ — **a·ware·ness** n

a·wash \ə-'wȯsh, -'wäsh\ adv (or adj) **1** : washed by waves or tide **2** : AFLOAT **3** : FLOODED

¹a·way \ə-'wā\ adv **1** : on the way ⟨get *away* early⟩ **2** : from this or that place ⟨go *away*⟩ **3** : in another place or direction ⟨turn *away*⟩ **4** : out of existence ⟨the echo died *away*⟩ **5** : from one's possession ⟨gave *away* a fortune⟩ **6** : without interruption or hesitation ⟨talk *away*⟩ **7** : FAR ⟨*away* back in 1910⟩

²away adj **1** : ABSENT, GONE ⟨be *away* from home⟩ **2** : DISTANT ⟨a lake ten miles *away*⟩

¹awe \'ȯ\ n **1** : profound and reverent dread of the supernatural **2** : a feeling of mingled fear, respect, and wonder

²awe vb awed; aw·ing : to fill with awe

aw·ful \'ȯ-fəl\ adj **1** : filling with awe ⟨an *awful* disaster⟩ **2** : extremely disagreeable or objectionable ⟨an *awful* cold⟩ **3** : very great

aw·ful·ly \'ȯ-flē, esp for 1 -fə-lē\ adv **1** : in a manner to inspire awe **2** : in a disagreeable or objectionable manner **3** : EXTREMELY

a·while \ə-'hwīl\ adv : for a while : for a short time ⟨sit down and rest *awhile*⟩

awk·ward \'ȯk-wərd\ adj **1** : not graceful : CLUMSY ⟨an *awkward* basketball player⟩ **2** : EMBARRASSING ⟨an *awkward* question⟩ **3** : difficult to use or handle — **awk·ward·ly** adv — **awk·ward·ness** n

awl \'ȯl\ n : a pointed tool for making small holes (as in leather or wood)

aw·ning \'ȯ-ning\ n : a roof-like cover (as of canvas) that serves as a shade or a shelter

awls

awoke past of AWAKE

a·wry \ə-'rī\ adv (or adj) **1** : turned or twisted to one side : ASKEW **2** : out of the right course : AMISS ⟨plans had gone *awry*⟩

ax or **axe** \'aks\ n : a tool that consists of a heavy head with a sharp edge fixed to a handle and is used for chopping and splitting wood

ax·i·om \'ak-sē-əm\ n **1** : MAXIM **2** : a proposition regarded as a self-evident truth

axes

ax·is \'ak-səs\ n, pl **ax·es** \'ak-,sēz\ : a straight line about which a body or a geometric figure rotates or may be supposed to rotate ⟨the earth's *axis*⟩

ax·le \'ak-səl\ n : a pin or shaft on or with which a wheel or pair of wheels turns

ax·on \'ak-,sän\ n : a long fiber that conducts impulses away from a nerve cell

¹aye \'ā\ adv : FOREVER, ALWAYS

²aye \'ī\ adv : YES

³aye \'ī\ n : an affirmative vote or voter

a·za·lea \ə-'zāl-yə\ n : a usually small rhododendron that sheds its leaves in the fall and has funnel-shaped white, orange, or reddish flowers

a·zure \'azh-ər\ n : the blue color of the clear sky

b \'bē\ n, often cap **1** : the second letter of the English alphabet **2** : a grade rating a student's work as good

¹baa \'ba, 'bä\ n : the cry of a sheep : BLEAT

²baa vb : to make the cry of a sheep

¹bab·ble \'bab-əl\ vb bab·bled; bab·bling **1** : to utter meaningless sounds ⟨*babbled* in his crib⟩ **2** : to talk foolishly **3** : to make the sound of a brook — **bab·bler** \-lər\ n

²babble n **1** : indistinct talk **2** : the sound of a brook

babe \'bāb\ n : BABY ⟨a *babe* in arms⟩

ba·boon \ba-'bün\ n : a large monkey of Africa and Asia with a doglike face

¹ba·by \'bā-bē\ n, pl **ba·bies** **1** : a child too young to talk or walk **2** : a childish person **3** : the youngest of a group

²baby adj : SMALL, YOUNG ⟨a *baby* deer⟩

³baby vb ba·bied; ba·by·ing : to treat as a baby

ba·by·hood \'bā-bē-,hud\ n : the time or condition of being a baby

ba·by·ish \'bā-bē-ish\ adj : having the characteristics of a baby

ba·by–sit \'bā-bē-,sit\ vb ba·by–sat \-,sat\; ba·by–sit·ting : to act as a baby-sitter

ba·by–sit·ter \'bā-bē-,sit-ər\ n : a person who takes care of a child during the temporary absence of the parents or usual guardians

bach·e·lor \'bach-ə-lər\ n : a man who has not married

bachelor's button n : a plant (as a cornflower) with flowers or flower heads suggesting buttons

bachelor's button

ba·cil·lus \bə-'sil-əs\ n, pl **ba·cil·li** \-'sil-,ī\ **1** : a rod-shaped bacterium

that forms internal spores **2** : a disease=
producing bacterium : GERM, MICROBE

¹back \'bak\ *n* **1** : the rear part of the
human body from the neck to the end of the
spine : the upper part of the body of an animal **2** : the part of something that is opposite
or away from the front or lower part **3** : a
player in a football backfield — **backed**
\'bakt\ *adj*

²back *adv* **1** : to or toward the rear ⟨the
crowd moved *back*⟩ **2** : in or to a former time,
condition, or place ⟨some years *back*⟩ ⟨went
back home⟩ **3** : under control ⟨kept *back* his
anger⟩ **4** : in return or reply ⟨to talk *back*⟩

³back *adj* **1** : located at the back ⟨*back* door⟩
2 : not yet paid : OVERDUE ⟨*back* rent⟩ **3** : no
longer current ⟨*back* number of a magazine⟩

⁴back *vb* **1** : to give support or help to **2** : to
move back — **back·er** *n*

back·bone \'bak-'bōn\ *n* **1** : the column of
bones in the back : SPINAL COLUMN **2** : the
sturdiest part of something **3** : firmness of
character

back·field \'bak-ˌfēld\ *n* : the football
players whose positions are behind the line
of scrimmage

¹back·fire \'bak-ˌfīr\ *n* **1** : a fire that is set to
check the spread of a forest fire or a grass fire
by burning off a strip of land ahead of it
2 : an improperly timed explosion of fuel
mixture in the cylinder of an engine

²backfire *vb* **back·fired; back·fir·ing 1** : to
make a backfire **2** : to have the opposite of
the desired effect ⟨the plan *backfired*⟩

back·ground \'bak-ˌgraund\ *n* **1** : the scenery, ground, or surface that is or appears to be
behind a main figure or object ⟨material with
flowers on a gray *background*⟩ **2** : a place
or position that attracts little attention ⟨keep
in the *background*⟩ **3** : the total of a person's
experience, knowledge, and education

¹back·hand \'bak-ˌhand\ *n* **1** : a stroke
made with the back of the
hand turned in the direction
in which the hand is moving
2 : handwriting in which the
letters slant to the left

²backhand *adj* : using or
made with a backhand

back·hand·ed \'bak-ˌhan-
dəd\ *adj* **1** : BACKHAND ⟨a
backhanded blow⟩ **2** : written in backhand
3 : not sincere : SARCASTIC

backhand 1

back of *prep* : BEHIND

¹back·ward \'bak-wərd\ *or* **back·wards**
\-wərdz\ *adv* **1** : toward the back or rear
⟨look *backward*⟩ **2** : with the back first ⟨ride

backward⟩ **3** : contrary to or in reverse of the
usual way ⟨count *backward*⟩ **4** : to a worse
condition

²backward *adj* **1** : turned backward ⟨a
backward glance⟩ **2** : SHY, BASHFUL **3** : slow
in learning or development ⟨a *backward* child⟩

back·wa·ter \'bak-ˌwȯt-ər, -ˌwät-\ *n* **1** : water held or turned back from its course **2** : a
backward stagnant place or condition

back·woods \'bak-'wùdz\ *n pl* **1** : forests
or partly cleared regions away from cities
2 : a remote area backward in culture

ba·con \'bā-kən\ *n* : salted and smoked meat
from the sides and the back of a pig

bac·te·ri·um \bak-'tir-ē-əm\ *n, pl* **bac·te·ri·a**
\-ē-ə\ : any of numerous microscopic plants
that are single cells and are important to man
because of their chemical activities and as
causes of disease

bad \'bad\ *adj* **worse** \'wərs\; **worst** \'wərst\
1 : not good : POOR ⟨*bad* weather⟩ **2** : not
favorable ⟨a *bad* impression⟩ **3** : SPOILED ⟨a
bad egg⟩ **4** : morally evil ⟨a *bad* man⟩
5 : not adequate ⟨*bad* lighting⟩ **6** : DISAGREE-
ABLE, UNPLEASANT ⟨a *bad* taste⟩ ⟨*bad* news⟩
7 : HARMFUL ⟨*bad* for the health⟩ **8** : SEVERE
⟨a *bad* cold⟩ **9** : not correct ⟨*bad* spelling⟩
10 : SICK, ILL ⟨a cold that made him feel *bad*⟩
11 : SORRY ⟨felt *bad* about his mistake⟩ —
bad·ly *adv* — **bad·ness** *n*

bade *past of* BID

badge \'baj\ *n* : a mark, sign, or emblem
worn to show that a person belongs to a
certain group, class, or rank

¹badg·er \'baj-ər\ *n* : a furry burrowing
mammal with short thick legs and long claws
on the front feet

²badger *vb* : to tease or annoy persistently

bad·min·ton \'bad-ˌmint-n\ *n* : a game in
which a shuttlecock is hit over a net by players
with light rackets

baf·fle \'baf-əl\ *vb* **baf·fled; baf·fling** : to
prevent from understanding or accomplishing
something by being confusing or difficult
syn BAFFLE, CONFUSE, PERPLEX all mean to
make or be obscure and puzzling. BAFFLE
suggests being so misled or bewildered that
success is doubtful ⟨this puzzle *baffles* me
completely; I give up⟩ CONFUSE may indicate
a temporary mix-up that can be straightened
out with time or effort ⟨at first fractions *confused* me, but now they seem easy⟩ PERPLEX
suggests an element of worry and uncertainty
and is often used of situations in which there
really is no definite or expected solution ⟨his
behavior *perplexes* me; one day he's my
friend and the next he isn't⟩

¹**bag** \'bag\ *n* **1** : a sack or pouch for holding something **2** : PURSE, HANDBAG **3** : SUITCASE

²**bag** *vb* **bagged**; **bag·ging** **1** : to bulge or swell like a full bag ⟨trousers that *bagged* at the knees⟩ **2** : to put into a bag **3** : to kill or capture in hunting ⟨*bagged* three deer⟩

bag·gage \'bag-ij\ *n* : the trunks, suitcases, and boxes that one takes on a trip

bag·gy \'bag-ē\ *adj* **bag·gi·er**; **bag·gi·est** : resembling a bag : hanging loosely

bag·pipe \'bag-ˌpīp\ *n* : a musical instrument played especially in Scotland that consists of a tube, a bag for air, and pipes from which the sound comes

bag·worm \'bag-ˌwərm\ *n* : a moth larva that lives in a silk case and feeds on leaves

bagpipe

¹**bail** \'bāl\ *n* : a promise or deposit of money required to free a prisoner until his trial

²**bail** *vb* : to gain the release of by giving bail

³**bail** *vb* : to dip and throw out water from ⟨*bail* out a boat⟩ — **bail out** : to jump with a parachute from an airplane in flight

¹**bait** \'bāt\ *vb* **1** : to torment by repeated attacks ⟨*baited* the speaker by whistling and shouting⟩ **2** : to place bait on or in

²**bait** *n* : something and especially food used to attract animals so that they may be caught on a hook or in a trap

bake \'bāk\ *vb* **baked**; **bak·ing** **1** : to cook or become cooked in a dry heat and especially in an oven **2** : to dry or harden by heat

bak·er \'bā-kər\ *n* : one that bakes and sells bread, cakes, or pastry

baker's dozen *n* : THIRTEEN

bak·er·y \'bā-kə-rē\ *n*, *pl* **bak·er·ies** : a place where bread, cakes, and pastry are made or sold

baking powder *n* : a powder used in baking cakes and biscuits to make the dough rise and become light

baking soda *n* : SODIUM BICARBONATE

¹**bal·ance** \'bal-əns\ *n* [taken from Old French *balance*, a noun derived from the Latin adj. *bilanx* "having two scales", a compound of the prefix *bi-* "bi-" and *lanx* "plate", "pan of a scale"] **1** : an instrument for weighing **2** : an equality between two sides or parts **3** : a steady position or condition ⟨kept his *balance* by holding out his arms⟩ **4** : equal total sums on the two sides of a bookkeeping account **5** : the amount by which one side of an account is greater than the other ⟨a

balance 1

balance of ten dollars on the credit side⟩ **6** : something left over : REMAINDER

²**balance** *vb* **bal·anced**; **bal·anc·ing** **1** : to make the two sides of (an account) add up to the same total **2** : to make equal in weight or number **3** : to weigh against one another : COMPARE ⟨*balance* the chances of the two teams⟩ **4** : to poise in or as if in balance

bal·co·ny \'bal-kə-nē\ *n*, *pl* **bal·co·nies** **1** : a platform enclosed by a low wall or a railing built out from the side of a building **2** : a gallery inside a building ⟨a theater *balcony*⟩

bald \'bȯld\ *adj* **1** : having no hair on the head **2** : not having a natural covering (as of trees, feathers, or leaves) ⟨a *bald* summit of a mountain⟩ **3** : BARE, PLAIN — **bald·ness** *n*

bald eagle *n* : the common North American eagle that when mature has white head and neck feathers

¹**bale** \'bāl\ *n* : a large bundle of goods tightly tied for storing or shipping ⟨a *bale* of cotton⟩

²**bale** *vb* **baled**; **bal·ing** : to put up in a bale

bald eagle

¹**balk** \'bȯk\ *n* **1** : HINDRANCE **2** : an illegal motion made by a baseball pitcher

²**balk** *vb* **1** : HINDER, CHECK ⟨*balked* our plans for a hike⟩ **2** : to stop short and refuse to go

balk·y \'bȯ-kē\ *adj* **balk·i·er**; **balk·i·est** : likely to balk ⟨a *balky* horse⟩

¹**ball** \'bȯl\ *n* **1** : a round body or mass ⟨a *ball* of twine⟩ **2** : a round or egg-shaped object used in a game or sport **3** : a game or sport (as baseball) played with a ball **4** : a solid usually round shot for a gun **5** : the rounded bulge at the base of the thumb or big toe ⟨the *ball* of the foot⟩ **6** : a pitched baseball not swung at by the batter that misses the strike zone

²**ball** *vb* : to form or gather into a ball

³**ball** *n* [from Latin *ballare* "to dance", which is also the source of the English words *ballad*, once meaning "a song sung while dancing", and *ballet*] : a large party for dancing

bal·lad \'bal-əd\ *n* **1** : a simple song **2** : a short poem suitable for singing that tells a story in simple language

¹**bal·last** \'bal-əst\ *n* **1** : something heavy carried in a ship to steady it **2** : something heavy put into the car of a balloon to steady it or control its ascent **3** : gravel, cinders, or crushed stone used in making a foundation (as of a road) ⟨*ballast* for railroad tracks⟩

²**ballast** *vb* : to provide with ballast

---

ball bearing *n* **1** : a bearing in which the revolving part turns on metal balls that roll easily in a groove **2** : one of the balls in a ball bearing

bal·let \'bal-,ā\ *n* **1** : a stage dance that tells a story in movement and pantomime **2** : a group that performs ballets

¹**bal·loon** \bə-'lün\ *n* **1** : a bag filled with heated air or with a gas that is lighter than air so as to rise and float above the ground **2** : a toy consisting of a baglike rubber case that can be blown up with air or gas

²**balloon** *vb* : to swell or puff out like a balloon

balloon 1

¹**bal·lot** \'bal-ət\ *n* **1** : an object and especially a printed sheet of paper used in voting **2** : the act of voting **3** : the right to vote **4** : the total number of votes cast at an election

²**ballot** *vb* : to vote or decide by ballot

ball·play·er \'bȯl-,plā-ər\ *n* : one that plays baseball especially professionally

ball–point pen \,bȯl-,pȯint-\ *n* : a pen having as the writing point a small steel ball that inks itself from an inner reservoir

ball·room \'bȯl-,rüm, -,rum\ *n* : a large room for dances

balm \'bäm\ *n* **1** : a fragrant healing or soothing preparation (as an ointment) **2** : something that comforts or refreshes **3** : a fragrant herb grown in gardens

balm·y \'bäm-ē\ *adj* **balm·i·er**; **balm·i·est** : gently soothing ⟨a *balmy* breeze⟩

bal·sa \'bȯl-sə\ *n* **1** : the very light but strong wood of a tropical American tree **2** : a raft or boat made of reeds

bal·sam \'bȯl-səm\ *n* **1** : a fragrant aromatic material that oozes from some plants **2** : BALM 1 **3** : a plant (as the evergreen **balsam fir** often used as a Christmas tree) that yields balsam

bal·us·ter \'bal-əs-tər\ *n* **1** : a short columnlike support forming one of the supports of a balustrade rail **2** : a banister post

bal·us·trade \'bal-əs-,trād\ *n* **1** : a row of balusters topped by a rail to serve as an open barrier (as along the edge of a terrace or a balcony) **2** : a stair rail

balusters 1

bam·boo \bam-'bü\ *n* : a tall treelike tropical grass with a hard jointed stem that is used in making furniture and in building

¹**ban** \'ban\ *vb* **banned**; **ban·ning** : to forbid or prohibit by official order

²**ban** *n* : an official order prohibiting something ⟨a *ban* on the sale of a book⟩

ba·nan·a \bə-'nan-ə\ *n* : a large treelike tropical plant with large leaves and flower clusters that develop into a bunch of fingerlike fruit that becomes yellow or ' red when ripe

banana plant

¹**band** \'band\ *n* **1** : something that binds, ties, or goes around ⟨a rubber *band*⟩ **2** : a strip of material around or across something ⟨a hat *band*⟩ **3** : a range of frequencies

²**band** *vb* **1** : to put a band on **2** : to unite in a group ⟨*banded* together for protection⟩

³**band** *n* **1** : a group of persons united for a common purpose ⟨a *band* of robbers⟩ **2** : a group of performers on various instruments especially of the wind and percussion type

¹**ban·dage** \'ban-dij\ *n* : a strip of material (as cloth) used in binding up injuries to the body

²**bandage** *vb* **ban·daged**; **ban·dag·ing** : to bind or cover with a bandage

ban·dan·na *or* **ban·dan·a** \ban-'dan-ə\ *n* : a large figured handkerchief usually having a red or blue background and often used as a scarf or kerchief

bandage

ban·dit \'ban-dət\ *n* : OUTLAW, ROBBER

band·stand \'band-,stand\ *n* : an outdoor platform used for band concerts

¹**bang** \'bang\ *vb* : to beat, strike, or shut with a loud noise

²**bang** *n* **1** : a violent blow **2** : a sudden loud noise

³**bang** *n* : hair cut short across the forehead

⁴**bang** *vb* : to cut (hair) short and squarely across

ban·ish \'ban-ish\ *vb* **1** : to compel to leave a country ⟨traitors *banished* by the king⟩ **2** : to drive away : DISMISS ⟨*banish* fears⟩

ban·ish·ment \'ban-ish-mənt\ *n* : a banishing from a country : EXILE

ban·is·ter \'ban-əs-tər\ *n* **1** : one of the slender posts used to support the handrail of a staircase **2** *pl* : a stair rail and its supporting posts **3** : the handrail of a staircase

ban·jo \'ban-jō\ *n, pl* **ban·jos** : a musical instrument with a

banjo

long fretted neck and drum-shaped body usually having five gut or metal strings plucked with the fingers

¹**bank** \'bangk\ *n* **1** : a mound or ridge of earth **2** : something shaped like a mound ⟨a *bank* of clouds⟩ **3** : an undersea elevation : SHOAL ⟨the *banks* of Newfoundland⟩ **4** : the rising ground at the edge of a river, lake, or sea ⟨the *banks* of the Hudson⟩

²**bank** *vb* **1** : to raise a bank around **2** : to heap up in a bank ⟨*banked* the snow against the door⟩ **3** : to build (a curve) with the road or track sloping upward from the inside edge **4** : to cover with fuel or ashes so as to reduce the speed of burning ⟨*bank* a fire⟩ **5** : to incline in turning so the edge nearer the inside of the curve is lower

³**bank** *n* : one of two or more rows of objects arranged one above another ⟨a *bank* of seats⟩

⁴**bank** *n* **1** : a place of business that lends, issues, exchanges, and takes care of money **2** : a small closed container into which coins may be dropped for savings **3** : a storage place for a reserve supply ⟨blood *bank*⟩

⁵**bank** *vb* **1** : to keep a bank **2** : to have an account in a bank ⟨*banks* locally⟩ **3** : to deposit in a bank ⟨*bank* ten dollars⟩

bank·er \'bang-kər\ *n* : one that is engaged in the business of a bank

bank·ing \'bang-king\ *n* : the business of a bank or banker

¹**bank·rupt** \'bangk-ˌrəpt\ *n* [from Old Italian *bancarotta* "bankruptcy", from *banca* "bench" and *rotta* "broken"; so called because it was once an Italian custom to smash the workbench of a banker without enough money to pay what he owed] : a person who becomes unable to pay his debts and whose property is by court order divided among his creditors

²**bankrupt** *adj* : unable to pay one's debts

³**bankrupt** *vb* : to make bankrupt

bank·rupt·cy \'bangk-ˌrəpt-sē\ *n, pl* **bank·rupt·cies** : the state of being bankrupt

¹**ban·ner** \'ban-ər\ *n* **1** : FLAG **2** : a piece of cloth with a design, a picture, or some writing on it

²**banner** *adj* : outstanding in excellence

ban·quet \'bang-kwət\ *n* : a formal dinner for many people at which speeches are made

ban·tam \'bant-əm\ *n* : a small domestic fowl that is often a miniature of a standard breed

¹**ban·ter** \'bant-ər\ *vb* : to make fun of by joking

²**banter** *n* : good-natured joking

ban·yan \'ban-yən\ *n* : a large East Indian

tree from whose branches roots grow downward into the ground and form new trunks

bap·tism \'bap-ˌtiz-əm\ *n* : the act of baptizing

bap·tize \bap-'tīz\ *vb* **bap·tized; bap·tiz·ing** [from Greek *baptizein* "to baptize", from *baptos* "dipped", from *baptein* "to dip"] **1** : to dip in water or sprinkle water on as a part of the ceremony of receiving into the Christian church **2** : to give a name to as in the ceremony of baptism : CHRISTEN

¹**bar** \'bär\ *n* **1** : a usually slender rigid piece (as of wood or metal) that has many uses (as for a lever, barrier, or fastener) **2** : a usually more or less rectangular solid piece or block of something ⟨a *bar* of soap⟩ ⟨a *bar* of chocolate⟩ **3** : something that obstructs or impedes passage or progress ⟨a *bar* to advancement⟩ **4** : a submerged or partly submerged bank along a shore or in a river **5** : a court of law **6** : the profession of law **7** : STRIPE **8** : a counter on which liquor is served **9** : a place of business for the sale of alcoholic drinks **10** : a vertical line across a musical staff marking equal measures of time

bar 10

²**bar** *vb* **barred; bar·ring** **1** : to fasten with a bar ⟨*bar* the doors⟩ **2** : to block off : OBSTRUCT ⟨*barred* by a chain across the road⟩ **3** : to shut out : PROHIBIT

³**bar** *prep* : with the exception of

barb \'bärb\ *n* : a sharp point that extends out and backward (as from the tip of an arrow or fishhook) — **barbed** \'bärbd\ *adj*

bar·bar·i·an \bär-'ber-ē-ən\ *n* **1** : an uncivilized person **2** : a person who lacks an appreciation of or feeling for culture

bar·bar·ic \bär-'bar-ik\ *adj* **1** : of or characteristic of barbarians : PRIMITIVE ⟨*barbaric* empires⟩ **2** : of crude style or taste

bar·ba·rous \'bär-bə-rəs\ *adj* **1** : UNCIVILIZED ⟨a *barbarous* tribe⟩ **2** : CRUEL, BRUTAL ⟨*barbarous* treatment of captives⟩ — **bar·ba·rous·ly** *adv*

¹**bar·be·cue** \'bär-bi-ˌkyü\ *n* **1** : a large animal roasted whole **2** : an outdoor social gathering at which food is barbecued and eaten

²**barbecue** *vb* **bar·be·cued; bar·be·cu·ing** **1** : to cook whole or in large pieces over or before an open source of heat **2** : to cook in a highly seasoned sauce

bar·ber \'bär-bər\ *n* : a person whose business is cutting hair and shaving or trimming beards

ə abut   ər further   a ax   ā age   ä father, cot   ȧ (see key page)   au̇ out   ch chin   e less   ē easy   g gift   i trip   ī life

bard \'bärd\ *n* **1** : a person in primitive societies skilled at composing and singing songs about heroes **2** : POET

¹bare \'baər\ *adj* **bar·er; bar·est** **1** : being without covering : NAKED ⟨trees *bare* of leaves⟩ **2** : EMPTY ⟨the cupboard was *bare*⟩ **3** : having just enough with nothing to spare : MERE ⟨elected by a *bare* majority⟩ **4** : PLAIN, SIMPLE ⟨the *bare* facts⟩ **syn** see NAKED

²bare *vb* **bared; bar·ing** : UNCOVER

bare·back \'baər-,bak\ *adv (or adj)* : on the bare back of a horse : without a saddle

bare·foot \'baər-,fut\ *adv (or adj)* : with the feet bare

bare·head·ed \'baər-'hed-əd\ *adv (or adj)* : with the head bare : without a hat

bare·ly \'baər-lē\ *adv* **1** : SCARCELY, HARDLY ⟨*barely* enough to eat⟩ **2** : not sufficiently

¹bar·gain \'bär-gən\ *n* **1** : an agreement between persons settling what each is to give and receive in a transaction ⟨make a *bargain* to mow a neighbor's lawn for two dollars a week⟩ **2** : something bought or offered for sale at a desirable price

²bargain *vb* : to talk over the terms of a purchase or agreement

barge \'bärj\ *n* : a broad flat-bottomed boat used chiefly in harbors and on rivers and canals ⟨a coal *barge*⟩

bar·i·tone \'bar-ə-,tōn\ *n* [the Greeks combined *barys* "heavy" and *tonos* "tone" to make *barytonos* "deep sounding"; from this adj. came the Italian noun *baritono* "baritone", and from this came English *baritone*] **1** : a male voice between bass and tenor **2** : a person who has a voice between bass and tenor **3** : a horn used in bands that is lower than the alto but higher than the tuba

¹bark \'bärk\ *vb* **1** : to utter a bark **2** : to shout or speak sharply ⟨*bark* out a command⟩

²bark *n* : the short loud noise uttered by a dog

³bark *n* : the outside covering of the trunk, branches, and roots of a tree

⁴bark *vb* **1** : to remove the bark from **2** : to rub or scrape the skin off ⟨*barked* his shin⟩

⁵bark *or* **barque** \'bärk\ *n* **1** : a small sailing boat **2** : a three-masted ship with foremast and mainmast square-rigged

bark·er \'bär-kər\ *n* : one that stands at the entrance to a show or a store and tries to attract customers to it

bar·ley \'bär-lē\ *n* : a cereal grass with flowers in dense spikes that is grown for its grain which is used mostly to feed farm animals or make malt

bar magnet *n* : a magnet in the shape of a bar

barley

barn \'bärn\ *n* [formed over 1000 years ago in England to mean "a place for storing grain", from *bere* "barley" and *ærn* "place"] : a building used for storing grain and hay and for housing farm animals (as cows)

bar·na·cle \'bär-nə-kəl\ *n* : a small saltwater shellfish that fastens itself on rocks or on wharves and ship bottoms

barn·storm \'bärn-,storm\ *vb* **1** : to tour through rural districts staging theatrical performances usually in one-night stands **2** : to travel from place to place making brief stops — **barn·storm·er** *n*

barn·yard \'bärn-,yärd\ *n* : the yard around a barn

ba·rom·e·ter \bə-'räm-ət-ər\ *n* : an instrument that measures air pressure and shows changes of the weather

bar·on \'bar-ən\ *n* : a member of the lowest grade of the British peerage

bar·on·ess \'bar-ə-nəs\ *n* **1** : the wife or widow of a baron **2** : a woman who holds the rank of a baron in her own right

barometer

bar·on·et \'bar-ə-nət\ *n* : a man holding a rank of honor below a baron but above a knight

ba·ro·ni·al \bə-'rō-nē-əl\ *adj* : belonging to or suitable for a baron

bar·racks \'bar-əks\ *n sing or pl* : a building or group of buildings in which soldiers live

bar·rage \bə-'räzh\ *n* : a barrier formed by continuous artillery or machine-gun fire directed upon a narrow strip of ground

bar·rel \'bar-əl\ *n* **1** : a round bulging container that is longer than it is wide and has flat ends **2** : the amount contained in a full barrel **3** : a cylindrical part ⟨a gun *barrel*⟩

¹bar·ren \'bar-ən\ *adj* **1** : not capable of bearing seed, fruit, or young ⟨*barren* plants⟩ **2** : growing only poor or scanty plants

²barren *n* : an area of barren land

bar·rette \bär-'et\ *n* : a clasp or bar used to hold a woman's hair in place

¹bar·ri·cade \'bar-ə-,kād\ *vb* **bar·ri·cad·ed; bar·ri·cad·ing** : to block off with a barricade

²barricade *n* : a hastily made barrier for protection against attack or for blocking the way

bar·ri·er \'bar-ē-ər\ *n* **1** : something (as a fence or railing or a natural obstacle) that blocks the way **2** : something that keeps apart or makes progress difficult

bar·ring \'bär-ing\ *prep* : EXCEPT

¹bar·row \'bar-ō\ *n* : a castrated male hog

²barrow *n* : a framework that has handles and sometimes a wheel and is used for carrying things

¹bar·ter \'bärt-ər\ *vb* : to trade by exchanging one thing for another without the use of money **syn** see SELL

barrow

²barter *n* : the exchange of goods without the use of money

bar·y·tone \'bar-ə-ˌtōn\ *var of* BARITONE

¹base \'bās\ *n* **1** : a thing or a part on which something rests : BOTTOM, FOUNDATION ⟨the *base* of a statue⟩ **2** : a main ingredient **3** : a supporting or carrying ingredient (as of a medicine or paint) **4** : a place where an army, navy, or similar force keeps its supplies or from which it starts its operations ⟨air force *base*⟩ **5** : a number with reference to which a system of numbers is constructed **6** : a starting place or goal in various games **7** : any of the four stations a runner in baseball must touch in order to score **8** : a chemical substance (as lime or ammonia) that reacts with an acid to form a salt and turns litmus paper blue

²base *vb* based; bas·ing : to put on a base

³base *adj* bas·er; bas·est **1** : of comparatively low value and relatively inferior in various properties ⟨*base* metals⟩ **2** : morally low : MEAN ⟨*base* conduct⟩ — **base·ness** *n*

base·ball \'bās-ˌbȯl\ *n* **1** : a game played with a bat and ball by two teams of nine players on a field with four bases that mark the course a runner must take to score **2** : the ball used in baseball

base·board \'bās-ˌbȯrd\ *n* : a line of boards or molding extending around the walls of a room and touching the floor

base·ment \'bās-mənt\ *n* : the floor or story in a building next below the main floor and partly or wholly below ground level

base on balls : an advance to first base given to a baseball batter who receives four balls

bash·ful \'bash-fəl\ *adj* : timid in the presence of others : SHY **syn** see SHY

ba·sic \'bā-sik\ *adj* **1** : of, relating to, or forming the base or foundation of a thing : FUNDAMENTAL, ESSENTIAL ⟨the *basic* facts⟩ **2** : relating to or characteristic of a chemical base — **ba·si·cal·ly** \-si-kə-lē\ *adv*

bas·il \'baz-əl\ *n* : an aromatic mint used in cooking

ba·sin \'bās-n\ *n* **1** : a wide shallow usually round dish or bowl for holding liquids **2** : the amount that a basin holds **3** : a

natural or artificial hollow or enclosure containing water ⟨a *basin* for anchoring ships⟩ **4** : the land drained by a river and its branches

ba·sis \'bā-səs\ *n, pl* ba·ses \-ˌsēz\ : FOUNDATION, BASE ⟨a story with a *basis* in fact⟩

bask \'bask\ *vb* : to lie in a pleasantly warm atmosphere ⟨*bask* in the sun⟩

bas·ket \'bas-kət\ *n* **1** : a container made by weaving together materials (as twigs, straw, or strips of wood) **2** : the contents of a basket ⟨berries for sale at forty cents a *basket*⟩ **3** : something that resembles a basket in shape or use **4** : a score in basketball

bas·ket·ball \'bas-kət-ˌbȯl\ *n* **1** : a game in which each of two teams tries to throw a round inflated ball through a raised basket-like goal **2** : the ball used in basketball

bas·ket·ry \'bas-kə-trē\ *n* **1** : the making of baskets **2** : objects made of interwoven twigs or reeds

bas–re·lief \ˌbä-ri-'lēf\ *n* : a sculpture in relief in which the design is raised very slightly from the background

¹bass \'bas\ *n, pl* bass *or* bass·es : any of numerous edible freshwater and sea fishes

²bass \'bās\ *n* **1** : a deep or low-pitched tone **2** : the part in music performed by the lowest voice or instrument **3** : the lowest male singing voice **4** : one who has a bass voice **5** : the lowest member of a family of instruments

bass drum \'bās-\ *n* : a large drum having two heads and giving a low booming sound of indefinite pitch

bass horn \'bās-\ *n* : TUBA

bas·soon \bə-'sün\ *n* : a musical instrument of low pitch in the form of a long doubled wooden tube with holes and keys and played by blowing into a long curved mouthpiece fitted with a double reed

bass viol \'bās-\ *n* : DOUBLE BASS

bass·wood \'bas-ˌwùd\ *n* : a pale wood with straight grain from the linden or a related tree

¹baste \'bāst\ *vb* bast·ed; bast·ing : to sew with long stitches so as to hold the work temporarily in place

²baste *vb* bast·ed; bast·ing : to moisten with melted butter or fat while roasting

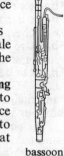
bassoon

¹bat \'bat\ *n* **1** : a stout solid stick : CLUB ⟨a baseball *bat*⟩ **2** : a sharp blow or slap **3** : a turn at batting

²bat *vb* bat·ted; bat·ting : to strike or hit with or as if with a bat

³bat *n* : a small furry animal that has a mouse-like body and long front limbs covered with skin so as to form wings

bat

batch \'bach\ *n* **1** : a quantity of something baked at one time ⟨a *batch* of cookies⟩ **2** : a quantity of material for use at one time or produced at one operation **3** : a group of persons or things ⟨a *batch* of letters⟩

bath \'bath, 'bȧth\ *n, pl* **baths** \'bathz, 'bȧthz\ **1** : a washing of the body **2** : water for bathing ⟨draw the *bath*⟩ **3** : a place, room, or building where persons may bathe **4** : a large container holding water for bathing **5** : a liquid in which objects are placed so that it can act upon them

bathe \'bāth\ *vb* **bathed; bath·ing 1** : to take a bath **2** : to go into a body of water (as the sea or a river) for pleasure : go swimming **3** : to give a bath to ⟨*bathe* the baby⟩ **4** : to apply a liquid to ⟨*bathe* the eyes⟩ **5** : to cover with or as if with a liquid ⟨a scene *bathed* by moonlight⟩ — **bath·er** *n*

bath·room \'bath-,rüm, 'bȧth-, -,rum\ *n* : a room containing a bathtub or shower and usually a washbowl and toilet

ba·ton \bə-'tän, ba-\ *n* **1** : a staff or stick carried as a symbol of office or authority **2** : a stick with which a leader directs an orchestra or band **3** : a rod with a ball on one end carried by a drum major or baton twirler

bat·tal·ion \bə-'tal-yən\ *n* **1** : a division of an army consisting of two or more companies **2** : a large body of persons organized to act together ⟨labor *battalions*⟩

¹bat·ter \'bat-ər\ *vb* **1** : to beat with repeated violent blows ⟨a shore *battered* by waves⟩ **2** : to wear down or injure by hard use

²batter *n* : a thin mixture made chiefly of flour and a liquid beaten together and used in making cakes and biscuits

³batter *n* : one whose turn it is to bat

bat·ter·ing ram \'bat-ə-ring-\ *n* **1** : an ancient military machine consisting of a heavy iron-tipped beam mounted in a frame and swung back and forth in order to batter down walls **2** : a beam or bar with handles used to batter down doors or walls

battering ram

bat·ter·y \'bat-ə-rē\ *n, pl* **bat·ter·ies 1** : two or more big guns forming a unit **2** : a single electric cell for furnishing electric current or a group of such cells ⟨a flashlight *battery*⟩ **3** : a number of machines or devices grouped together ⟨a *battery* of lights⟩ **4** : the pitcher and catcher of a baseball team

bat·ting \'bat-ing\ *n* **1** : the act of one who bats **2** : the use of or ability to use a bat **3** : cotton or wool in sheets used for stuffing quilts or packaging goods

¹bat·tle \'bat-l\ *n* **1** : a fight between armies, warships, or airplanes **2** : a fight between two persons or animals **3** : CONTEST ⟨a *battle* of wits⟩ **4** : WARFARE, FIGHTING

²battle *vb* **bat·tled; bat·tling** : to engage in battle : FIGHT

bat·tle–ax *or* **bat·tle–axe** \'bat-l-,aks\ *n* : an ax with a broad blade formerly used as a weapon

bat·tle·field \'bat-l-,fēld\ *n* : a place where a battle is fought or was once fought

bat·tle·ground \'bat-l-,graund\ *n* : BATTLEFIELD

bat·tle·ment \'bat-l-mənt\ *n* : a low wall (as at the top of a castle or tower) with open spaces to shoot through

bat·tle·ship \'bat-l-,ship\ *n* : a large warship having heavy armor and large guns

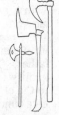

battle-axes

bau·ble \'bȯ-bəl\ *n* : TRINKET

¹bawl \'bȯl\ *vb* **1** : to shout or cry loudly ⟨*bawl* a command⟩ **2** : to weep noisily

²bawl *n* : a loud prolonged cry

¹bay \'bā\ *vb* : to bark with long deep tones

²bay *n* **1** : the baying of dogs **2** : the position of an animal or a person obliged to face pursuers when it is impossible to escape ⟨brought to *bay*⟩ **3** : the position of pursuers who are held off ⟨kept the hounds at *bay*⟩

³bay *n* **1** : a bay-colored horse **2** : a reddish brown

⁴bay *n* : a part of a large body of water making an indentation in the land

⁵bay *n* : the laurel or a related tree or shrub

bay·ber·ry \'bā-,ber-ē\ *n* : a shrub with leathery leaves and small bluish white waxy berries used in making candles : WAX MYRTLE

¹bay·o·net \'bā-ə-nət, ,bā-ə-'net\ *n* [from French *baïonette* "bayonet", named for Bayonne, the city in France where the first ones were made] : a weapon like a dagger in form made to fit on the end of a rifle

²bayonet *vb* **bay·o·net·ted; bay·o·net·ting** : to stab with a bayonet

bay·ou \'bī-ō, -ü\ *n* : a creek or branch stream having a slow current and flowing through marshy land

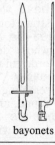

bayonets

bay window \'bā-\ *n* : a window or a set of windows in a compartment that projects outward from the wall of a building

ba·zaar \bə-'zär\ *n* **1** : an oriental marketplace containing rows of stalls or shops **2** : a large building where many kinds of goods are sold **3** : a fair for the sale of goods especially for charity

ba·zoo·ka \bə-'zü-kə\ *n* : a portable shoulder gun consisting of a tube open at both ends that shoots an explosive rocket able to pierce armor

be \bē\ *vb, past 1st & 3d sing* **was** \wəz, 'wəz, wäz\; *2d sing* **were** \wər, 'wər\; *pl* **were**; *past subjunctive* **were**; *past part* **been** \bin\; *pres part* **be·ing** \'bē-ing\; *pres 1st sing* **am** \əm, am\; *2d sing* **are** \ər, är\; *3d sing* **is** \iz\; *pl* **are**; *pres subjunctive* **be** **1** : to equal in meaning or identity ⟨that man *is* my father⟩ **2** : to have a specified character or quality ⟨the leaves *are* green⟩ **3** : to belong to the class of ⟨apes *are* mammals⟩ **4** : EXIST, LIVE ⟨once there *was* a knight⟩ **5** — used as a helping verb with other verbs ⟨the ball *was* thrown⟩ ⟨he *was* running⟩

be- *prefix* **1** : on : around : over ⟨*be*daub⟩ ⟨*be*smear⟩ **2** : provide with or cover with especially excessively ⟨*be*jeweled⟩ ⟨*be*whiskered⟩ **3** : about : to : upon ⟨*be*stride⟩ **4** : make : cause to be ⟨*be*little⟩ ⟨*be*fool⟩

¹beach \'bēch\ *n* : the shore of the sea or of a lake covered by sand or gravel

²beach *vb* : to drive ashore ⟨*beach* a boat⟩

beach·head \'bēch-,hed\ *n* : an area on an enemy-held shore occupied by an advance force to protect the later landing of troops or supplies

bea·con \'bē-kən\ *n* **1** : a guiding or warning light or fire on a high place **2** : a radio station that sends out signals for the guidance of aircraft

¹bead \'bēd\ *n* **1** : a small piece of material with a hole through it to be strung on a thread ⟨a string of glass *beads*⟩ **2** : a small round body ⟨a *bead* of sweat⟩ **3** : a small knob on a gun used in taking aim

²bead *vb* **1** : to cover with beads **2** : to string together like beads

bea·dle \'bēd-l\ *n* : a minor parish official whose duties include ushering and keeping order in church

bead·y \'bēd-ē\ *adj* **bead·i·er**; **bead·i·est** : resembling a bead especially in being small, round, and shiny ⟨*beady* eyes⟩

bea·gle \'bē-gəl\ *n* : a small short-legged hound with a smooth coat

beak \'bēk\ *n* **1** : the bill of a bird ⟨an eagle's *beak*⟩ **2** : a beaklike part or projection — **beaked** \'bēkt\ *adj*

beak 1

bea·ker \'bē-kər\ *n* **1** : a drinking vessel with a wide mouth **2** : a deep cup or glass with a wide mouth and usually a lip for pouring

¹beam \'bēm\ *n* **1** : a long heavy piece of timber or metal used as a main horizontal support of a building or a ship **2** : a ray or shaft of light **3** : a constant radio wave sent out from an airport to guide pilots along a course

²beam *vb* **1** : to send out beams of light **2** : to smile with joy **3** : to aim a radio broadcast by use of a special antenna

bean \'bēn\ *n* **1** : the edible seed or pod of a bushy or climbing garden plant related to the peas and clovers **2** : a seed or fruit resembling a bean ⟨coffee *beans*⟩

¹bear \'baər\ *n* **1** : a large heavy mammal with long shaggy hair and a very short tail **2** : a gruff or sullen person

²bear *vb* **bore** \'bōr\; **borne** \'bōrn\; **bear·ing** **1** : SUPPORT, CARRY ⟨*bear* a burden⟩ **2** : to have as a feature or characteristic ⟨*bear* marks of suffering⟩ **3** : to bring forth : give birth to : PRODUCE ⟨*bear* fruit⟩ ⟨*bear* children⟩ **4** : ENDURE ⟨could not *bear* pain⟩ **5** : PRESS ⟨*bear* down hard on your crayon⟩ **6** : to have relevance

bear·a·ble \'bar-ə-bəl\ *adj* : able to be borne

¹beard \'biərd\ *n* **1** : the hair on the face of a man **2** : a tuft like a beard

²beard *vb* : to face daringly : DEFY

bear·er \'bar-ər\ *n* **1** : one that bears, supports, or carries **2** : MESSENGER **3** : a person holding a check or order for payment

bear·ing \'baər-ing\ *n* **1** : the manner in which a person carries or conducts himself : BEHAVIOR ⟨he has the *bearing* of a soldier⟩ **2** : a part of a machine in which another part turns **3** : the position or direction of one point with respect to another or to the compass **4** *pl* : comprehension of one's position or situation ⟨lost his *bearings*⟩ **5** : RELATION, CONNECTION ⟨had no *bearing* on our decision⟩

beast \'bēst\ *n* **1** : a four-footed mammal (as a bear, deer, or rabbit) ⟨*beasts* of the field and fowls of the air⟩ **2** : a farm animal especially when kept for work ⟨oxen and horses used as *beasts* of burden⟩ **3** : a contemptible person

¹beat \'bēt\ *vb* **beat**; **beat·en** \'bēt-n\ *or* **beat**; **beat·ing** **1** : to strike again and again ⟨*beat* his dog⟩ ⟨*beat* a drum⟩ **2** : THROB, PULSATE ⟨heart still *beating*⟩ **3** : to flap against ⟨wings *beating* the air⟩ 4 : to mix by stirring ⟨*beat* two eggs⟩ 5 : DEFEAT, OVERCOME ⟨*beat* the enemy⟩ 6 : to measure or mark off by strokes ⟨*beat* time to the music⟩ — **beat·er** *n*

²beat *n* 1 : a blow or a stroke made again and again ⟨the *beat* of drums⟩ 2 : a single pulse or throb (as of the heart) 3 : a measurement of time or accent in music 4 : a course or round made regularly ⟨a policeman's *beat*⟩

³beat *adj* 1 : EXHAUSTED 2 : having lost one's morale 3 : of or relating to beatniks

beat·en \'bēt-n\ *adj* : worn smooth by treading ⟨a *beaten* path⟩

be·at·i·tude \bē-'at-ə-,tüd, -,tyüd\ *n* 1 : supreme bliss : BLESSEDNESS 2 : one of the statements made in the Sermon on the Mount (Matthew 5: 3–12) beginning "Blessed are"

beat·nik \'bēt-nik\ *n* [from ³*beat* and *-nik*, a Yiddish suffix used in English to mean "one who is"; *beatnik* means literally "one who is beat"] : a person who likes to defy conventions in behavior and dress and to express himself in outlandish ways

beau \'bō\ *n, pl* **beaux** \'bōz\ *or* **beaus** \'bōz\ 1 : a man of fashion : DANDY 2 : SUITOR

beau·te·ous \'byüt-ē-əs\ *adj* : BEAUTIFUL

beau·ti·ful \'byüt-i-fəl\ *adj* : pleasing to the eye or ear : LOVELY — **beau·ti·ful·ly** *adv*

beau·ti·fy \'byüt-ə-,fī\ *vb* **beau·ti·fied**; **beau·ti·fy·ing** : to make beautiful

beau·ty \'byüt-ē\ *n, pl* **beau·ties** 1 : the qualities of a person or a thing that give pleasure to the senses or to the mind ⟨the *beauty* of the landscape⟩ ⟨a poem of great *beauty*⟩ 2 : a beautiful person or thing

beauty shop *n* : a place of business for the care of women's hair, skin, and nails

bea·ver \'bē-vər\ *n* : an animal related to the rats and mice that has webbed hind feet and a broad flat tail, builds dams and houses of sticks and mud in water, and is prized for its soft rich durable fur

be·calm \bi-'käm\ *vb* : to bring to a stop because of lack of wind ⟨a ship *becalmed*⟩

became *past of* BECOME

be·cause \bi-'koz\ *conj* : for the reason that

because of *prep* : on account of : by reason of

beck \'bek\ *n* 1 : a beckoning gesture 2 : SUMMONS, COMMAND

beck·on \'bek-ən\ *vb* : to summon or signal to a person by a gesture (as a wave or nod)

be·come \bi-'kəm\ *vb* **be·came** \-'kām\; **become**; **be·com·ing** 1 : to come or grow to be ⟨a tadpole *becomes* a frog⟩ ⟨days that *become* shorter as summer ends⟩ 2 : to be suitable : SUIT ⟨a dress that *becomes* her⟩ — **become of** : to happen to ⟨what has *become of* my friend⟩

be·com·ing \bi-'kəm-ing\ *adj* : SUITABLE, ATTRACTIVE — **be·com·ing·ly** *adv*

¹bed \'bed\ *n* 1 : a piece of furniture on which one may sleep or rest 2 : a place for sleeping or resting ⟨make a *bed* in the grass⟩ 3 : a level piece of ground prepared for growing plants or flowers 4 : the bottom or base of something ⟨the *bed* of a river⟩ 5 : LAYER

²bed *vb* **bed·ded**; **bed·ding** 1 : to put to bed 2 : to go to bed 3 : to plant in beds

bed·bug \'bed-,bəg\ *n* : a small wingless blood-sucking insect sometimes found in houses and especially in beds

bed·clothes \'bed-,klō_thz\ *n pl* : coverings (as sheets and pillowcases) for a bed

bedbug

bed·ding \'bed-ing\ *n* 1 : BEDCLOTHES 2 : material for a bed

be·deck \bi-'dek\ *vb* : DECORATE, ADORN

be·dew \bi-'dü, -'dyü\ *vb* : to wet with or as if with dew ⟨cheeks *bedewed* with tears⟩

bed·fel·low \'bed-,fel-ō\ *n* : one who shares a bed with another

bed·lam \'bed-ləm\ *n* [*Bedlam*, an old form for *Bethlehem*, was the popular name for the Hospital of St. Mary of Bethlehem, an insane asylum in London; the word *bedlam* came to mean "an insane asylum"] : a place or scene of uproar and confusion

be·drag·gled \bi-'drag-əld\ *adj* : soiled from or as if from being dragged in dust or mud ⟨*bedraggled* clothes⟩

bed·rid·den \'bed-,rid-n\ *adj* : forced to stay in bed by sickness or weakness

bed·rock \'bed-'räk\ *n* : the solid rock underlying surface materials (as soil)

bed·roll \'bed-,rōl\ *n* : bedding rolled up for carrying

bed·room \'bed-,rüm, -,rùm\ *n* : a room to sleep in

bed·side \'bed-,sīd\ *n* : the place beside a bed

bed·spread \'bed-,spred\ *n* : a decorative top covering for a bed

bed·stead \'bed-,sted\ *n* : the framework of a bed

bed·time \'bed-,tīm\ *n* : time to go to bed

bee \'bē\ *n* 1 : a four-winged insect related to the wasps that gathers pollen and nectar from flowers from which it makes beebread and honey for food and that usually lives in large colonies 2 : a gathering of people for the purpose of doing something together

bee·bread \'bē-,bred\ *n* : a bitter yellowish brown food material prepared by bees from pollen and stored in their honeycomb

---

j job   ng sing   ō low   o moth   oi coin   th thin   th this   ü boot   ù foot   y you   yü few   yù furious   zh vision

beech \'bēch\ *n* : a tree with smooth gray bark, deep green leaves, and small triangular edible nuts

beef \'bēf\ *n, pl* **beeves** \'bēvz\ *or* **beefs** 1 : the flesh of a steer, cow, or bull 2 : a steer, cow, or bull especially when fattened for food

beef·steak \'bēf-ˌstāk\ *n* : a slice of beef suitable for broiling or frying

beech: leaves and fruit

bee·hive \'bē-ˌhīv\ *n* : a hive for honeybees

bee·line \'bē-ˌlīn\ *n* [so called from the belief that honey-laden bees return to their hives in a direct line] : a straight direct course

been *past part of* BE

beer \'biər\ *n* : an alcoholic drink made from malt and flavored with hops

bees·wax \'bēz-ˌwaks\ *n* : wax made by bees and used by them in building honeycomb

beet \'bēt\ *n* : a leafy plant with a thick juicy root that is used as a vegetable or as a source of sugar

bee·tle \'bēt-l\ *n* 1 : any of a group of insects with four wings the outer pair of which are stiff cases that cover the others when folded 2 : an insect (as a bug) that resembles a beetle

bee·tling \'bēt-ling\ *adj* : jutting out : OVERHANGING ⟨a *beetling* cliff⟩ ⟨*beetling* eyebrows⟩

beetle

beeves *pl of* BEEF

be·fall \bi-'fȯl\ *vb* **be·fell** \-'fel\; **be·fall·en** \-'fȯ-lən\; **be·fall·ing** 1 : to come to pass : HAPPEN 2 : to happen to

be·fit \bi-'fit\ *vb* **be·fit·ted**; **be·fit·ting** : to be suitable to or proper for

¹**be·fore** \bi-'fȯr\ *adv* 1 : in front : AHEAD ⟨go on *before*⟩ 2 : in the past : PREVIOUSLY ⟨have been here *before*⟩ 3 : EARLIER, SOONER ⟨come at six o'clock, not *before*⟩

²**before** *prep* 1 : in front of ⟨stand *before* a mirror⟩ 2 : in the presence of ⟨stood *before* the judge⟩ 3 : in advance of

³**before** *conj* 1 : ahead of the time when ⟨look *before* you leap⟩ 2 : more willingly than ⟨would starve *before* he'd steal⟩

be·fore·hand \bi-'fȯr-ˌhand\ *adv* : in advance : ahead of time

be·friend \bi-'frend\ *vb* : to act as a friend to : aid in a friendly way

beg \'beg\ *vb* **begged**; **beg·ging** 1 : to ask for money, food, or help as a charity ⟨*beg* in the streets⟩ 2 : to ask as a favor in an earnest or

polite way ⟨*beg* to be taken to the circus⟩ ⟨*beg* pardon⟩ **syn** see ASK

beg·gar \'beg-ər\ *n* 1 : one who lives by begging 2 : PAUPER

be·gin \bi-'gin\ *vb* **be·gan** \-'gan\; **be·gun** \-'gən\; **be·gin·ning** 1 : to do the first part of an action : START ⟨*begin* your homework⟩ 2 : to come into existence : ORIGINATE

be·gin·ner \bi-'gin-ər\ *n* : one who is doing something for the first time

be·gin·ning \bi-'gin-ing\ *n* 1 : the point at which something begins ⟨the *beginning* of the war⟩ 2 : first part ⟨the *beginning* of the song⟩ 3 : ORIGIN, SOURCE

be·gone \bi-'gȯn\ *vb* : to go away : DEPART — used especially in the imperative mood

be·go·nia \bi-'gōn-yə\ *n* [named in honor of Michel Bégon, a French governor and amateur botanist] : a juicy-stemmed plant with ornamental leaves and small waxy flowers

be·half \bi-'haf, -'häf\ *n* : SUPPORT, INTEREST

be·have \bi-'hāv\ *vb* **be·haved**; **be·hav·ing** 1 : to conduct oneself : ACT ⟨the children *behaved* well at the party⟩ 2 : to conduct oneself properly ⟨tell the boy to *behave*⟩

be·hav·ior \bi-'hāv-yər\ *n* 1 : the way in which a person conducts himself : DEPORTMENT 2 : the whole activity of something and especially a living being

be·head \bi-'hed\ *vb* : to cut off the head of

¹**be·hind** \bi-'hīnd\ *adv* 1 : in a place that is being or has been departed from ⟨leave your books *behind*⟩ ⟨stay *behind*⟩ 2 : at, to, or toward the back ⟨look *behind*⟩ ⟨fall *behind*⟩ 3 : not up to the general level ⟨*behind* in school⟩

²**behind** *prep* 1 : at, to, or toward the back of ⟨*behind* the door⟩ 2 : not up to the general level of ⟨*behind* his class⟩

be·hold \bi-'hōld\ *vb* **be·held** \-'held\; **be·hold·ing** : SEE, OBSERVE — **be·hold·er** *n*

beige \'bāzh\ *n* : a yellowish brown

be·ing \'bē-ing\ *n* 1 : EXISTENCE, LIFE 2 : a living thing

be·la·bor \bi-'lā-bər\ *vb* 1 : to keep working on to excess ⟨*belabor* the argument⟩ 2 : to beat hard

be·lat·ed \bi-'lāt-əd\ *adj* : delayed beyond the usual or expected time

¹**belch** \'belch\ *vb* 1 : to force out gas suddenly from the stomach through the mouth 2 : to throw out or be thrown out violently

²**belch** *n* : a belching of gas

bel·fry \'bel-frē\ *n, pl* **bel·fries** : a tower or room in a tower for a bell or set of bells

¹**Bel·gian** \'bel-jən\ *adj* : of or relating to Belgium or the Belgians

²**Belgian** *n* : a native or inhabitant of Belgium

be·lief \bə-'lēf\ *n* **1** : confidence that a person or thing exists or is true or trustworthy : FAITH, TRUST ⟨*belief* in Santa Claus⟩ ⟨*belief* in democracy⟩ **2** : religious faith : CREED **3** : something that is believed : OPINION

syn BELIEF and FAITH are often used interchangeably to refer to something accepted as real or true. BELIEF suggests an intellectual acceptance based on some sort of evidence ⟨as the facts became known, my *belief* in his innocence became stronger⟩ while FAITH suggests an emotional acceptance based mainly on unsupported trust and a will to believe ⟨I know his whole family well and have *faith* in his innocence⟩ BELIEF may suggest a personal involvement or commitment ⟨*belief* in God⟩ but often does not ⟨a *belief* in ghosts⟩ FAITH always carries the idea of personal commitment ⟨*faith* in his parents⟩ ⟨*faith* in prayer⟩

be·liev·a·ble \bə-'lē-və-bəl\ *adj* : capable of being believed

be·lieve \bə-'lēv\ *vb* **be·lieved; be·liev·ing** **1** : to have faith or confidence in the existence or efficacy of ⟨*believe* in ghosts⟩ ⟨*believes* in strenuous exercise⟩ **2** : to accept as true ⟨*believe* the report⟩ **3** : to accept the word of ⟨they didn't *believe* me⟩ **4** : THINK

be·liev·er \bə-'lē-vər\ *n* : one who has faith in a religion

be·lit·tle \bi-'lit-l\ *vb* **be·lit·tled; be·lit·tling** : to make (a person or a thing) seem little or unimportant

bell \'bel\ *n* **1** : a hollow usually cup-shaped metallic device that makes a ringing sound when struck ⟨church *bells*⟩ **2** : the stroke or sound of a bell that tells the hour **3** : the time indicated by the stroke of a bell **4** : a half hour on shipboard **5** : something shaped like a bell ⟨the *bell* of a trumpet⟩

bells 1

bell·boy \'bel-ˌbȯi\ *n* : a hotel or club employee who answers calls for service by bell or telephone and assists guests with luggage

bell·hop \'bel-ˌhäp\ *n* : BELLBOY

¹bel·lig·er·ent \bə-'lij-ə-rənt\ *adj* **1** : carrying on war **2** : showing a readiness to fight

²belligerent *n* **1** : a nation at war **2** : a person engaged in a fight

bell jar *n* : a bell-shaped usually glass vessel designed to cover objects or to contain gases or a vacuum

¹bel·low \'bel-ō\ *vb* : to give a loud deep roar like that of a bull : SHOUT, BAWL

²bellow *n* : a loud deep roar

bel·lows \'bel-ōz\ *n sing or pl* **1** : a device whose two sides can be spread apart and then pressed together to force air through a tube at one end **2** : a part of a camera that is pleated and can be extended

bellows 1

¹bel·ly \'bel-ē\ *n, pl* **bel·lies** **1** : ABDOMEN 1 **2** : the under part of an animal's body **3** : STOMACH **4** : an internal cavity (as of the human body) **5** : the thick part of a muscle

²belly *vb* **bel·lied; bel·ly·ing** : to swell out

be·long \bə-'lȯng\ *vb* **1** : to be in a proper situation ⟨this book *belongs* on the top shelf⟩ **2** : to be the property of a person or group of persons ⟨the watch *belongs* to me⟩ **3** : to be a part of : be connected with : go with

be·long·ings \bə-'lȯng-ingz\ *n pl* : the things that belong to a person : POSSESSIONS

be·lov·ed \bə-'ləv-əd, -'ləvd\ *adj* : greatly loved : very dear

¹be·low \bə-'lō\ *adv* : in or to a lower place

²below *prep* : lower than : BENEATH

¹belt \'belt\ *n* **1** : a strip of flexible material (as leather or cloth) worn around a person's body for holding in or supporting clothing or weapons or for ornament **2** : something resembling a belt : BAND, CIRCLE ⟨a *belt* of trees⟩ **3** : a flexible endless band running around wheels or pulleys and used for moving or carrying something ⟨a fan *belt* on an automobile⟩ **4** : a region suited to or characterized by certain products or activities ⟨the cotton *belt*⟩ — **belt·ed** \'bel-təd\ *adj*

²belt *vb* **1** : to put a belt on or around **2** : to beat with a belt : THRASH **3** : to strike hard

be·moan \bi-'mōn\ *vb* : to express grief over

bench \'bench\ *n* **1** : a long seat for two or more persons **2** : a long table for holding work and tools ⟨a carpenter's *bench*⟩ **3** : the position or rank of a judge

bench 1

¹bend \'bend\ *n* : a knot by which one rope is fastened to another

²bend *vb* **bent** \'bent\; **bend·ing** **1** : to pull taut or tense ⟨*bend* a bow⟩ **2** : to curve or cause a change of shape ⟨*bend* a wire into a circle and then *bend* it straight again⟩ **3** : to turn in a certain direction : DIRECT

³bend *n* : something that is bent : CURVE

¹be·neath \bi-'nēth\ *adv* : in a lower place

²beneath *prep* **1** : lower than : UNDER ⟨*beneath* the surface⟩ **2** : unworthy of

ben·e·dic·tion \ˌben-ə-'dik-shən\ *n* **1** : BLESSING **2** : the invocation of a blessing at the end of a meeting ⟨pronounced the *benediction*⟩

ben·e·fac·tor \'ben-ə-ˌfak-tər\ *n* [from Latin *benefactor* "one who does a favor", from the phrase *bene facere* "to do good"] : one who confers a benefit on another especially by giving money

ben·e·fi·cial \ˌben-ə-'fish-əl\ *adj* : producing good results : HELPFUL — **ben·e·fi·cial·ly** *adv*

syn BENEFICIAL, ADVANTAGEOUS, PROFITABLE all refer to something considered to be of value. BENEFICIAL applies to what is good in itself or promotes general well-being ⟨*beneficial* rains turned the fields green overnight⟩ ADVANTAGEOUS usually indicates a choice or preference ⟨an *advantageous* move in chess⟩ and applies to whatever helps further a particular end or purpose ⟨before breakfast is rarely an *advantageous* time to ask for special favors⟩ PROFITABLE refers to whatever gives a rewarding return and implies that something (as time or effort) has been invested ⟨acquired several new customers on a *profitable* business trip⟩⟨found the study of Latin *profitable* as an aid to learning English⟩

ben·e·fi·ci·ar·y \ˌben-ə-'fish-ē-ˌer-ē\ *n, pl* **ben·e·fi·ci·ar·ies** : a person who benefits or is expected to benefit from something

¹**ben·e·fit** \'ben-ə-ˌfit\ *n* 1 : something that does good to a person or thing : ADVANTAGE ⟨the *benefits* of sunshine⟩ 2 : money paid in time of death, sickness, or unemployment or in old age (as by an insurance company)

²**benefit** *vb* **ben·e·fit·ed** *or* **ben·e·fit·ted; ben·e·fit·ing** *or* **ben·e·fit·ting** 1 : to be useful or profitable to 2 : to receive benefit

be·nev·o·lence \bə-'nev-ə-ləns\ *n* : KINDNESS, GENEROSITY

be·nev·o·lent \bə-'nev-ə-lənt\ *adj* : having a desire to do good : KINDLY, CHARITABLE

be·nign \bi-'nīn\ *adj* 1 : of a gentle disposition 2 : FAVORABLE — **be·nign·ly** *adv*

¹**bent** \'bent\ *adj* 1 : changed by bending : no longer straight : CROOKED ⟨a *bent* pin⟩ 2 : strongly inclined : DETERMINED

²**bent** *n* : a strong inclination : a natural liking

be·queath \bi-'kwēth, -'kwēth\ *vb* 1 : to give or leave by means of a will ⟨her aunt *bequeathed* her some money⟩ 2 : to hand down ⟨knowledge *bequeathed* to later times⟩

be·quest \bi-'kwest\ *n* 1 : the act of bequeathing 2 : something given or left by a person in his will

be·reave \bi-'rēv\ *vb* **be·reaved** *or* **be·reft** \-'reft\; **be·reav·ing** : to deprive of some cherished person or thing usually by death

be·ret \bə-'rā\ *n* : a soft round flat cap of wool without a visor

berg \'bərg\ *n* : ICEBERG

ber·i·ber·i \ˌber-ē-'ber-ē\ *n* : a disease caused by lack of a vitamin in which there is weakness, wasting, and damage to nerves

¹**ber·ry** \'ber-ē\ *n, pl* **ber·ries** 1 : a small pulpy and usually edible fruit (as a strawberry) 2 : a simple fruit (as a grape or tomato) in which the ripened ovary wall is fleshy 3 : a dry seed (as of the coffee tree)

²**berry** *vb* **ber·ried; ber·ry·ing** : to gather berries

¹**berth** \'bərth\ *n* 1 : a place where a ship lies at anchor or at a wharf 2 : a bed on a ship, train, or airplane : BUNK 3 : POSITION, JOB

²**berth** *vb* : to bring or come into a berth

be·seech \bi-'sēch\ *vb* **be·sought** \-'sȯt\ *or* **be·seeched; be·seech·ing** : to ask earnestly

be·set \bi-'set\ *vb* **be·set; be·set·ting** 1 : to attack from all sides 2 : to hem in : SURROUND

be·set·ting \bi-'set-ing\ *adj* : constantly present ⟨a *besetting* sin⟩

be·side \bi-'sīd\ *prep* 1 : by the side of ⟨sat *beside* her⟩ 2 : compared with ⟨looks like a midget *beside* him⟩ 3 : in addition to ⟨anyone here *beside* you⟩ 4 : away from : not relevant to ⟨your remark is *beside* the point⟩ — **beside oneself** : very upset ⟨*beside herself* with worry⟩

¹**be·sides** \bi-'sīdz\ *adv* : in addition : ALSO ⟨had ice cream and cake and candy *besides*⟩

²**besides** *prep* : in addition to : other than

be·siege \bi-'sēj\ *vb* **be·sieged; be·sieg·ing** 1 : to surround with armed forces for the purpose of capturing : lay siege to 2 : to crowd around — **be·sieg·er** *n*

besought *past of* BESEECH

¹**best** \'best\ *adj, superlative of* GOOD 1 : good or useful in the highest degree : most excellent 2 : MOST, LARGEST ⟨the *best* part of a week⟩

²**best** *adv, superlative of* WELL 1 : in the best way 2 : MOST ⟨*best* able to do the work⟩

³**best** *n* 1 : a person or thing or part of a thing that is best 2 : one's greatest effort

⁴**best** *vb* : to get the better of : SURPASS, DEFEAT

be·stir \bi-'stər\ *vb* **be·stirred; be·stir·ring** : to stir up : rouse to action ⟨*bestir* yourself⟩

be·stow \bi-'stō\ *vb* : to present as a gift

¹**bet** \'bet\ *n* 1 : an agreement requiring the person whose guess proves wrong about the result of a contest or the outcome of an event to give something to the person whose guess proves right 2 : the money or thing risked in a bet

²**bet** *vb* **bet** *or* **bet·ted; bet·ting** 1 : to risk in a bet ⟨*bet* a dollar⟩ 2 : to be certain enough to bet ⟨*bet* it will rain⟩

be·ta particle \'bāt-ə-\ *n* : an electron ejected from the nucleus of an atom during radioactive decay

be·tide \bi-'tīd\ *vb* **be·tid·ed; be·tid·ing** : to happen to : BEFALL

be·tray \bi-'trā\ *vb* **1** : to give over to an enemy by treachery or fraud ⟨*betray* a fort⟩ **2** : to be unfaithful to : prove false to ⟨*betray* a friend⟩ **3** : REVEAL, SHOW ⟨*betrayed* fear⟩

be·troth \bi-'träth, -'troth, -'trōth, *or with* th\ *vb* : to promise to give in marriage

be·troth·al \bi-'trōth-əl, -'troth-, -'trōth-\ *n* : an engagement to be married

¹bet·ter \'bet-ər\ *adj, comparative of* GOOD **1** : preferable to another thing : more satisfactory : SUPERIOR **2** : GREATER ⟨the *better* part of a week⟩ **3** : improved in health

²better *adv, comparative of* WELL : in a superior or more excellent way

³better *n* **1** : a better person or thing ⟨a change for the *better*⟩ **2** : ADVANTAGE, VICTORY ⟨got the *better* of his opponent⟩

⁴better *vb* : IMPROVE — **bet·ter·ment** *n*

bet·tor *or* **bet·ter** \'bet-ər\ *n* : one that bets

¹be·tween \bi-'twēn\ *prep* **1** : by the efforts of each of ⟨*between* the two of them they licked the platter clean⟩ **2** : in the interval separating ⟨*between* the two desks⟩⟨*between* nine and ten o'clock⟩ **3** : SEPARATING, DISTINGUISHING ⟨the difference *between* soccer and football⟩ **4** : from among ⟨choose *between* two things⟩ **5** : CONNECTING ⟨a bond *between* friends⟩

  syn BETWEEN, AMONG are both used to show the relationship of things in terms of their position or distribution. BETWEEN is used of two objects ⟨divided the work *between* my brother and me⟩⟨rivalry *between* their school and ours⟩ AMONG usually indicates more than two objects ⟨divided the work *among* all of us⟩ ⟨rivalry *among* the schools⟩

²between *adv* : in a position between others

¹bev·el \'bev-əl\ *n* : a slant or slope of one surface or line against another

²bevel *vb* **bev·eled** *or* **bev·elled; bev·el·ing** *or* **bev·el·ling** : to cut or shape (an edge or surface) so as to form a bevel

bevel

bev·er·age \'bev-ə-rij\ *n* : a liquid that is drunk for food or pleasure

be·ware \bi-'waər\ *vb* : to be on one's guard

be·whis·kered \bi-'hwis-kərd\ *adj* : having whiskers ⟨a *bewhiskered* man⟩

be·wil·der \bi-'wil-dər\ *vb* : to fill with uncertainty : CONFUSE — **be·wil·der·ment** *n*

be·witch \bi-'wich\ *vb* **1** : to gain an influence over by means of magic or witchcraft **2** : CHARM, FASCINATE — **be·witch·ment** *n*

¹be·yond \bē-'änd\ *adv* : on or to the farther side

²beyond *prep* **1** : on the other side of ⟨*beyond* the ocean⟩ **2** : past the point of being affected by ⟨*beyond* help⟩ **3** : far past any power of ⟨lovely *beyond* description⟩

³beyond *n* : HEREAFTER

bi- *prefix* **1** : two ⟨*bi*racial⟩ **2** : coming or occurring every two ⟨*bi*monthly⟩ **3** : into two parts ⟨*bi*sect⟩ **4** : twice : doubly : on both sides ⟨*bi*convex⟩

¹bi·as \'bī-əs\ *n* **1** : a seam, cut, or stitching running in a slant across cloth **2** : an inclination to feel or act in a certain way : PREJUDICE

²bias *vb* **bi·ased** *or* **bi·assed; bi·as·ing** *or* **bi·as·sing** : to give a bias to : PREJUDICE

bib \'bib\ *n* **1** : a cloth or plastic shield tied under a child's chin to protect the clothes while eating **2** : the upper part of an apron

Bi·ble \'bī-bəl\ *n* [from Greek *biblia* "Bible", from *biblos* meaning both "papyrus" and "book"; so called because books were written on papyrus, and papyrus was exported from Byblos, an ancient city of Phoenicia] **1** : the book made up of the writings accepted by Christians as inspired by God **2** : a book containing the sacred writings of a religion

bib·li·cal \'bib-li-kəl\ *adj* : relating to, drawn from, or found in the Bible

bib·li·og·ra·phy \ˌbib-lē-'äg-rə-fē\ *n, pl* **bib·li·og·ra·phies** : a list of writings about an author or a subject

bi·car·bon·ate of soda \bī-'kär-bə-nət-, -ˌnāt-\ : SODIUM BICARBONATE

bi·ceps \'bī-ˌseps\ *n* : a large muscle of the upper arm

bick·er \'bik-ər\ *vb* : to quarrel in a petty way

bi·cus·pid \bī-'kəs-pəd\ *n* : either of the two double-pointed teeth on each side of each jaw of a person

¹bi·cy·cle \'bī-ˌsik-əl\ *n* : a light vehicle having two wheels one behind the other, a saddle seat, and pedals by which it is propelled

²bicycle *vb* **bi·cy·cled; bi·cy·cling** : to ride a bicycle

bi·cy·clist \'bī-ˌsik-ləst\ *n* : one that rides a bicycle

¹bid \'bid\ *vb* **bade** \'bad\ *or* **bid; bid·den** \'bid-n\ *or* **bid; bid·ding** **1** : ORDER, COMMAND ⟨a soldier is expected to do as he is *bidden*⟩ **2** : to express to ⟨*bade* her guests good-bye⟩ **3** : to make an offer for something (as a chair up for auction) — **bid·der** *n*

²bid *n* **1** : an offer to pay a certain sum for something or to perform certain work at a stated fee **2** : INVITATION

bide \'bīd\ *vb* **bode** \'bōd\ *or* **bid·ed** \'bīd-əd\; **bid·ed; bid·ing** : to wait or wait for ⟨*bide* a while⟩ ⟨*bided* his time⟩

¹bi·en·ni·al \bī-'en-ē-əl\ *adj* **1** : occurring

every two years **2** : growing leaves and shoots one year and flowers and fruit the next before dying — **bi·en·ni·al·ly** *adv*

²biennial *n* : a biennial plant

bier \'biər\ *n* : a stand on which a corpse or coffin is placed

big \'big\ *adj* **big·ger; big·gest 1** : large in size **2** : IMPORTANT — **big·ness** *n*

Big Dipper *n* : DIPPER 3

big·horn \'big-,hȯrn\ *n* : a grayish brown wild sheep of mountainous western North America

big tree *n* : a very large California sequoia with light soft brittle wood

bike \'bīk\ *n* : BICYCLE

bile \'bīl\ *n* : a thick bitter yellow or greenish fluid supplied by the liver to aid in digestion

bighorn

¹bill \'bil\ *n* **1** : the jaws of a bird together with their horny covering **2** : a part of an animal (as a turtle) that resembles the bill of a bird — **billed** \'bild\ *adj*

²bill *vb* : to touch bills together ⟨doves *billing* on a limb⟩

³bill *n* **1** : a draft of a law presented to a legislature for consideration ⟨the representative introduced a *bill* in Congress⟩ **2** : a record of goods sold, services performed, or work done with the cost involved ⟨a grocery *bill*⟩ **3** : a sign or placard advertising something **4** : a piece of paper money ⟨a dollar *bill*⟩

bills 1

⁴bill *vb* : to send a bill to

bill·board \'bil-,bōrd\ *n* : a flat surface on which outdoor advertisements are posted

¹bil·let \'bil-ət\ *n* **1** : a written order directing a person to provide lodging for a soldier **2** : lodging provided in accordance with a billet **3** : JOB ⟨a *billet* as a watchman⟩

²billet *vb* : to assign to a billet

bill·fold \'bil-,fōld\ *n* : a folding pocketbook especially for paper money : WALLET

bil·liards \'bil-yərdz\ *n* : a game played with solid balls and a cue on a large rectangular table

billfold

bil·lion \'bil-yən\ *n* **1** : a thousand millions **2** : a very large number ⟨*billions* of dollars⟩

¹bil·lionth \'bil-yənth\ *adj* : being last in a series of a billion

²billionth *n* : number 1,000,000,000 in a series

bill of fare : MENU

¹bil·low \'bil-ō\ *n* : a great wave

²billow *vb* **1** : to roll in great waves ⟨the *billowing* ocean⟩ **2** : to swell out ⟨*billowing* sails⟩

bil·ly \'bil-ē\ *n, pl* **bil·lies** : a heavy club (as of wood) carried by a policeman

bil·ly goat \'bil-ē-\ *n* : a male goat

bin \'bin\ *n* : a box or enclosed place used for storage ⟨a coal *bin*⟩

bind \'bīnd\ *vb* **bound** \'baůnd\; **bind·ing 1** : to fasten by tying **2** : to hold, restrain, or confine by force or obligation **3** : BANDAGE **4** : to fasten together and enclose in a cover

bind·er \'bīn-dər\ *n* **1** : a cover for holding together loose sheets of paper **2** : a machine that cuts grain and binds it into bundles

bind·ing \'bīn-ding\ *n* **1** : the cover and the fastenings of a book **2** : a narrow strip of fabric used along the edge of an article of clothing

¹bin·oc·u·lar \bə-'näk-yə-lər\ *adj* : of, using, or suited for the use of both eyes

²binocular *n* **1** : a binocular optical instrument (as a microscope) **2** : FIELD GLASS — usually used in plural

bio- *prefix* : living matter ⟨*biochemistry*⟩

bi·o·graph·i·cal \,bī-ə-'graf-i-kəl\ *adj* : of or relating to the history of people's lives

bi·og·ra·phy \bī-'äg-rə-fē\ *n, pl* **bi·og·ra·phies** : a written history of a person's life

bi·o·log·i·cal \,bī-ə-'läj-i-kəl\ *adj* : of or relating to biology

bi·ol·o·gist \bī-'äl-ə-jəst\ *n* : a specialist in biology

bi·ol·o·gy \bī-'äl-ə-jē\ *n* : a science that deals with living things and their relationships, distribution, and behavior

bi·ped \'bī-,ped\ *n* : a two-footed animal

bi·plane \'bī-,plān\ *n* : an airplane with two wings on each side of the body usually placed one above the other

birch \'bərch\ *n* : a tree with hard wood and a smooth bark that can be peeled off in thin layers

bird \'bərd\ *n* : an egg-laying animal that has wings and a body covered with feathers

bird·bath \'bərd-,bath, -,båth\ *n* : an artificial bath (as in a garden) for birds to bathe in

bird dog *n* : a dog trained to hunt or retrieve game birds

bird·house \'bərd-,haůs\ *n* **1** : an artificial nesting place for birds **2** : AVIARY

bird of prey : a bird (as an eagle or owl) that feeds almost entirely on meat taken by hunting

bird·seed \'bərd-,sēd\ *n* : a mixture of small seeds (as of hemp or millet) used chiefly for feeding cage birds

bird's–eye \'bərdz-,ī\ *adj* : seen from above as if by a flying bird ⟨a *bird's-eye* view⟩

birth \'bərth\ *n* **1** : the emergence of a new individual from the body of its parent **2** : the act of bringing into life **3** : a person's descent ⟨a man of noble *birth*⟩ **4** : BEGINNING, ORIGIN

birth·day \'bərth-,dā\ *n* **1** : the day on which a person is born **2** : a day of origin or beginning **3** : the return each year of the date on which a person was born or something began

birth·place \'bərth-,plās\ *n* : the place where a person was born or where something began

birth·right \'bərth-,rīt\ *n* : a right belonging to a person because of his birth

bis·cuit \'bis-kət\ *n* **1** : a crisp flat cake : CRACKER **2** : a small cake of raised dough baked in an oven

bi·sect \'bī-,sekt\ *vb* [formed in English from the prefix *bi-* "two" and the root *-sect* "to cut", from Latin *secare* "to cut"] **1** : to divide into two usually equal parts **2** : CROSS

bish·op \'bish-əp\ *n* **1** : a clergyman of high rank **2** : a piece in the game of chess

bis·muth \'biz-məth\ *n* : a heavy grayish white metallic chemical element that is used in alloys and medicine

bi·son \'bīs-n, 'bīz-\ *n* : a large shaggy-maned cud-chewing animal with short horns

¹bit \'bit\ *n* **1** : a part of a bridle that is put in the horse's mouth **2** : a tool with a cutting end or edge used for drilling or boring

bit 1

²bit *n* **1** : a small piece or quantity ⟨a *bit* of food⟩ **2** : a short time ⟨rest a *bit*⟩ **3** : SOMEWHAT ⟨a *bit* of a fool⟩

bits 2

bitch \'bich\ *n* : a female dog

¹bite \'bīt\ *vb* **bit** \'bit\; **bit·ten** \'bit-n\; **bit·ing** \'bīt-ing\ **1** : to seize, grip, or cut into with or as if with teeth ⟨*bite* an apple⟩ **2** : to wound or sting with a sharp-pointed organ connected with the mouth **3** : to cause to smart : STING ⟨pepper *bites* the mouth⟩ **4** : to take a bait : respond to a lure

²bite *n* **1** : a seizing of something with the teeth or the mouth **2** : a wound made by biting : STING ⟨a mosquito *bite*⟩ **3** : the amount taken by the teeth or mouth at one time ⟨a *bite* of food⟩ **4** : a sharp or biting sensation

bit·ing \'bīt-ing\ *adj* : producing bodily or mental distress : SHARP, SARCASTIC

bit·ter \'bit-ər\ *adj* **1** : sharp, biting, and unpleasant to the taste **2** : hard to bear : PAINFUL, SEVERE ⟨a *bitter* disappointment⟩ **3** : piercingly harsh : STINGING ⟨a *bitter* wind⟩ **4** : arising from anger, distress, or sorrow ⟨*bitter* tears⟩ — **bit·ter·ly** *adv* — **bit·ter·ness** *n*

bit·tern \'bit-ərn\ *n* : a brownish marsh bird which has a loud booming cry

bit·ter·sweet \'bit-ər-,swēt\ *n* **1** : a poisonous vine with purple flowers and red berries **2** : a woody climbing plant with orange seedcases that open and show the red-coated seeds

bi·tu·mi·nous coal \bə-,tü-mə-nəs-, -,tyü-\ *n* : a soft coal that gives much smoke when burned

bi·zarre \bə-'zär\ *adj* : STRANGE, GROTESQUE

blab \'blab\ *vb* **blabbed**; **blab·bing** **1** : to reveal secrets by careless talking **2** : TATTLE

¹black \'blak\ *adj* **1** : of the color black **2** : very dark ⟨a *black* night⟩ **3** : having dark skin, hair, and eyes ⟨the *black* races⟩ **4** : SOILED, DIRTY **5** : DISMAL, GLOOMY ⟨*black* despair⟩ **6** : SULLEN, HOSTILE ⟨*black* looks⟩

²black *n* **1** : a black pigment or dye **2** : the color of soot or coal : the opposite of white **3** : black clothing ⟨dressed in *black*⟩ **4** : a member of a dark-skinned race

³black *vb* : BLACKEN — **black out** : to lose consciousness or the ability to see for a short period

black–and–blue \,blak-ən-'blü\ *adj* : darkly discolored (as from a bruise)

black·ber·ry \'blak-,ber-ē\ *n, pl* **black·berries** : a black or dark purple sweet juicy edible berry of a bramble related to the raspberry

black·bird \'blak-,bərd\ *n* : any of several birds of which the males are largely black

black·board \'blak-,bōrd\ *n* : a dark smooth surface (as of slate) used for writing or drawing on with chalk or crayons

black·en \'blak-ən\ *vb* **1** : to make or become black **2** : DAMAGE

black–eyed Su·san \,blak-,īd-'süz-n\ *n* : a daisy with deep yellow or orange petals and a dark center

black·head \'blak-,hed\ *n* : a dark oily plug of hardened secretion blocking the opening of a skin gland

black·ish \'blak-ish\ *adj* : somewhat black

¹black·mail \'blak-,māl\ *n* **1** : the forcing of someone to pay money by threatening to reveal a secret that might bring disgrace on him **2** : money paid under threat of blackmail

²blackmail *vb* : to threaten with the disclosure of a secret unless money is paid — **black·mail·er** *n*

black·out \'blak-,aút\ *n* **1** : a period of darkness as a precaution against airplane raids in time of war **2** : a temporary loss of vision or consciousness

black-eyed Susan

black·smith \'blak-,smith\ *n* : a man who shapes iron by heating and hammering it

black·snake \'blak-,snāk\ *n* 1 : either of two dark-colored harmless snakes of the United States 2 : a long braided whip of rawhide

black·top \'blak-,täp\ *n* : a blackish road surface used for highways, parking lots, and play areas

black widow *n* : a poisonous spider having the female black with a red mark on the abdomen

blad·der \'blad-ər\ *n* 1 : a thin-walled pouch into which urine passes from the kidneys 2 : a bag or container that can be filled with air or gas

blade \'blād\ *n* 1 : a leaf of a plant and especially of a grass 2 : the broadened part of a leaf 3 : something that widens out like the blade of a leaf ⟨a shoulder *blade*⟩ ⟨the *blade* of a propeller⟩ ⟨the *blade* of a fan⟩ 4 : the cutting part of an instrument, tool, or machine ⟨a knife *blade*⟩ 5 : SWORD 6 : the runner of an ice skate — **blad·ed** \'blād-əd\ *adj*

blade of a paddle

¹blame \'blām\ *vb* **blamed**; **blam·ing** 1 : to find fault with 2 : to hold responsible ⟨*blamed* him for everything⟩ 3 : to place responsibility for ⟨don't *blame* it on me⟩

²blame *n* 1 : expression of disapproval ⟨receive both praise and *blame*⟩ 2 : responsibility for something that fails ⟨took the *blame* for the defeat⟩ — **blame·less** \'blām-ləs\ *adj*

blame·wor·thy \'blām-,wər-thē\ *adj* : deserving blame

blanch \'blanch\ *vb* 1 : WHITEN, BLEACH 2 : to scald in order to remove the skin from ⟨*blanch* almonds⟩ 3 : to turn pale

¹blank \'blangk\ *adj* 1 : not having any writing, printing, or marks ⟨a *blank* sheet of paper⟩ 2 : having empty spaces to be filled in ⟨a *blank* form⟩ 3 : appearing dazed or confused : EXPRESSIONLESS ⟨a *blank* look⟩

²blank *n* 1 : an empty space in a line of writing or printing 2 : a paper with empty spaces to be filled in ⟨an application *blank*⟩ 3 : a cartridge loaded with powder but no bullet

¹blan·ket \'blang-kət\ *n* 1 : a heavy woven usually woolen covering used for beds 2 : a covering layer ⟨a *blanket* of snow⟩

²blanket *vb* : to cover with a blanket

¹blare \'blaər\ *vb* **blared**; **blar·ing** 1 : to sound loud and harsh ⟨heard the trumpet *blare*⟩ 2 : to utter in a harsh noisy manner ⟨loudspeakers *blaring* advertisements⟩

²blare *n* : a harsh loud noise

¹blast \'blast\ *n* 1 : a strong gust of wind ⟨the icy *blasts* of winter⟩ 2 : a current of air or gas forced through an opening 3 : the sound made by a wind instrument ⟨the *blast* of a whistle⟩ 4 : EXPLOSION

²blast *vb* 1 : BLIGHT 2 : to shatter by an explosion

¹blaze \'blāz\ *n* 1 : an intense flame 2 : intense brightness accompanied by heat ⟨the *blaze* of the sun⟩ 3 : OUTBURST ⟨a *blaze* of anger⟩ 4 : a bright display ⟨a *blaze* of color⟩

²blaze *vb* **blazed**; **blaz·ing** 1 : to burn brightly 2 : to shine as if on fire

³blaze *n* : a mark made on a tree by chipping off a piece of the bark

⁴blaze *vb* **blazed**; **blaz·ing** 1 : to make a blaze on 2 : to mark by blazing trees ⟨*blaze* a trail⟩

¹bleach \'blēch\ *vb* : to make white by removing the color or stains from

²bleach *n* : a chemical used for bleaching

bleach·er \'blē-chər\ *n* : a usually uncovered steplike arrangement of planks providing seats for spectators — usually used in plural

bleak \'blēk\ *adj* 1 : exposed to wind or weather ⟨a *bleak* coast⟩ 2 : DREARY, CHEERLESS 3 : being cold and cutting ⟨a *bleak* wind⟩ — **bleak·ly** *adv* — **bleak·ness** *n*

¹bleat \'blēt\ *vb* : to utter the cry of a sheep, goat, or calf

²bleat *n* : the sound of bleating

bleed \'blēd\ *vb* **bled** \'bled\; **bleed·ing** 1 : to lose or shed blood ⟨a cut finger *bleeds*⟩ 2 : to feel pain or sympathy ⟨my heart *bleeds* for him⟩ 3 : to draw liquid (as blood or sap) from ⟨*bleed* a maple tree⟩

¹blem·ish \'blem-ish\ *vb* : to spoil by a flaw

²blemish *n* : a mark that makes something imperfect : FLAW

syn BLEMISH, DEFECT, FLAW all mean an imperfection of some kind. BLEMISH suggests something that mars or defaces an otherwise smooth or perfect surface ⟨one small *blemish* on the peach⟩ ⟨one day's tardiness was the only *blemish* on his attendance record⟩ DEFECT suggests a significant and often hidden shortcoming that spoils the perfection of something ⟨a rocket must be absolutely free of *defects*⟩ ⟨even a touch of the wrong color is considered a *defect* in a show dog⟩ FLAW may suggest a less significant defect ⟨a *flaw* in the motor that doesn't need repairing yet⟩ or a defect of continuity, as a crack or break ⟨an unseen *flaw* in the marble caused it to shatter⟩

¹blend \'blend\ *vb* 1 : to mix so thoroughly that the separate things mixed cannot be distinguished 2 : to shade into each other : MERGE, HARMONIZE **syn** see MIX

²blend n **1** : a thorough mixture : a product made by blending **2** : a word formed by combining parts of two or more other words so that they overlap ⟨*smog* is a *blend* of *smoke* and *fog*⟩

bless \'bles\ vb **blessed** \'blest\ or **blest**; **bless·ing** **1** : to make holy by religious rite or word : HALLOW ⟨*bless* an altar⟩ **2** : to ask divine favor or protection for ⟨*bless* a congregation in church⟩ **3** : to confer happiness or good fortune on ⟨*blessed* with good health⟩ **4** : PRAISE, HONOR ⟨*bless* the Lord⟩

bless·ed \'bles-əd, 'blest\ adj **1** : HOLY **2** : favored with blessings : HAPPY — **bless·ed·ness** \'bles-əd-nəs\ n

bless·ing \'bles-ing\ n **1** : the act of one who blesses **2** : APPROVAL ⟨gave his *blessing* to the plan⟩ **3** : something that makes one happy or content ⟨the *blessings* of peace⟩

blest \'blest\ adj : BLESSED

blew past of BLOW

¹blight \'blīt\ n **1** : a plant disease marked by withering without rotting **2** : an organism (as a germ or insect) that causes a plant blight

²blight vb : to injure or destroy by a blight

blimp \'blimp\ n : a small balloonlike airship

¹blind \'blīnd\ adj **1** : unable to see or nearly so : SIGHTLESS **2** : lacking in judgment or understanding **3** : closed at one end ⟨a *blind* alley⟩ **4** : having no opening ⟨a *blind* wall⟩ **5** : performed solely by the aid of instruments within an airplane ⟨*blind* flying⟩ — **blind·ly** adv — **blind·ness** n

²blind vb **1** : to make blind **2** : to make it impossible to see well : DAZZLE ⟨*blinded* by the lights of an approaching car⟩ **3** : to deprive of judgment or understanding

³blind n **1** : a device to hinder sight or keep out light ⟨window *blinds*⟩ **2** : a place of concealment ⟨shot the birds from a *blind*⟩

⁴blind adv : BLINDLY ⟨fly *blind*⟩

¹blind·fold \'blīnd-ˌfōld\ vb : to cover the eyes of with or as if with a bandage

²blindfold adj : prevented from seeing

³blindfold n : a bandage over the eyes

blind·man's buff \ˌblīnd-ˌmanz-'bəf\ n : a game in which a blindfolded player tries to catch and identify one of the other players

blink \'blingk\ vb **1** : to look with half-shut winking eyes **2** : to wink quickly ⟨*blink* back tears⟩ **3** : to shine with a light that goes or seems to go on and off ⟨lights *blinking*⟩

blink·er \'bling-kər\ n : a light that blinks

bliss \'blis\ n : great happiness : JOY — **bliss·ful** \-fəl\ adj — **bliss·ful·ly** adv

¹blis·ter \'blis-tər\ n **1** : a small raised area of the skin filled with a watery liquid **2** : a

swelling (as in paint) resembling a blister

²blister vb **1** : to develop a blister : rise in blisters ⟨his heel *blistered* on the hike⟩ ⟨*blistering* paint⟩ **2** : to cause blisters

blithe \'blīth, 'blīth\ adj **blith·er; blith·est** **1** : LIGHTHEARTED, CHEERFUL **2** : HEEDLESS — **blithe·ly** adv

bliz·zard \'bliz-ərd\ n **1** : a driving storm of wind and snow **2** : a long severe snowstorm

bloat \'blōt\ vb : to swell by filling with water or air : puff up

blob \'bläb\ n : a small lump or drop of something thick ⟨a *blob* of paint⟩

¹block \'bläk\ n **1** : a solid piece of some material (as stone or wood) usually with one or more flat sides ⟨building *blocks*⟩ **2** : something that stops or hinders passage or progress : OBSTRUCTION ⟨a traffic *block*⟩ **3** : a grooved pulley in a frame **4** : a number of things thought of as forming a group or unit ⟨a *block* of seats⟩ **5** : a large building divided into separate houses or shops : a number of houses or shops joined together ⟨an apartment *block*⟩ ⟨a business *block*⟩ **6** : a space enclosed by streets **7** : the length of one side of a block

blocks 3

²block vb **1** : to stop or hinder passage through : OBSTRUCT ⟨*block* the doorway with a bicycle⟩ **2** : to stop or hinder the passage of ⟨*block* a bill in Congress⟩ **3** : to hinder an opponent's play (as in football or basketball) **4** : to mark the chief lines of ⟨*block* out a plan⟩ **5** : to arrange (writing) in the shape of a block with none of the lines indented **6** : to support with blocks ⟨*block* up a car⟩

¹block·ade \blä-'kād\ n : the shutting off of a place (as by warships) to prevent the coming in or going out of persons or supplies

²blockade vb **block·ad·ed; block·ad·ing** : to close to traffic or commerce by a blockade

block·head \'bläk-ˌhed\ n : a stupid person

block·house \'bläk-ˌhaús\ n : a building of heavy timbers or of concrete built with holes in its sides through which persons inside may fire out at an enemy

blockhouse

¹blond \'bländ\ adj **1** : of a light color ⟨*blond* hair⟩ ⟨*blond* skin⟩ **2** : having light hair and skin

²blond or **blonde** \'bländ\ n : a blond person

blood \'bləd\ n **1** : the red fluid that circulates in the heart, arteries, capillaries, and veins of persons and animals **2** : relationship by descent from a common ancestor : RELA-

---

j job   ng sing   ō low   ȯ moth   ȯi coin   th thin   <u>th</u> this   ü boot   u̇ foot   y you   yü few   yu̇ furious   zh vision

TIVES ⟨ties of *blood*⟩ — **blood·ed** \'bləd-əd\ *adj*

blood bank *n* : blood stored for emergency use in transfusion

blood·hound \'bləd-,haund\ *n* : a hound with long drooping ears, a wrinkled face, and a keen sense of smell

blood pressure *n* : pressure that the blood exerts on the walls of blood vessels and especially arteries

blood·shed \'bləd-,shed\ *n* : SLAUGHTER

blood·shot \'bləd-,shät\ *adj* : being red and inflamed ⟨*bloodshot* eyes⟩

blood·stream \'bləd-,strēm\ *n* : the circulating blood in the living body

blood·suck·er \'bləd-,sək-ər\ *n* : an animal that sucks blood — **blood·suck·ing** \-,sək-ing\ *adj*

blood·thirst·y \'bləd-,thərs-tē\ *adj* : eager to shed blood : CRUEL — **blood·thirst·i·ly** \-tə-lē\ *adv* — **blood·thirst·i·ness** \-tē-nəs\ *n*

blood vessel *n* : an artery, vein, or capillary of the body

blood·y \'bləd-ē\ *adj* **blood·i·er; blood·i·est** **1** : smeared or stained with blood **2** : causing or accompanied by bloodshed

¹bloom \'blüm\ *n* **1** : FLOWER 1 **2** : flowers or amount of flowers **3** : the period or state of blooming **4** : a condition or time of beauty, freshness, and vigor ⟨the *bloom* of youth⟩ **5** : the rosy color of the cheek **6** : the delicate powdery coating on some fruits and leaves

²bloom *vb* **1** : to produce blooms : FLOWER **2** : to be in a state of youthful beauty and freshness

bloo·mers \'blü-mərz\ *n pl* **1** : short full pants with the legs gathered at the bottom formerly worn by girls for athletics **2** : underpants gathered at the knee worn chiefly by girls

¹blos·som \'bläs-əm\ *n* **1** : FLOWER 1 **2** : BLOOM 3

²blossom *vb* **1** : BLOOM **2** : to unfold like a blossom

¹blot \'blät\ *n* **1** : SPOT, STAIN **2** : DISGRACE, BLEMISH

²blot *vb* **blot·ted; blot·ting** **1** : SPOT, STAIN **2** : to conceal completely ⟨the fog *blotted* out the lighthouse⟩ **3** : to dry with a blotter

blotch \'bläch\ *n* **1** : a blemish on the skin **2** : a large irregular spot of color or ink — **blotched** \'blächt\ *adj*

blot·ter \'blät-ər\ *n* : a piece of blotting paper

blot·ting paper \'blät-ing-\ *n* : a soft spongy paper used to absorb wet ink

blouse \'blaus\ *n* **1** : a loose outer garment like a smock **2** : the jacket of a uniform **3** : a loose garment for women and children covering the body from the neck to the waist

¹blow \'blō\ *vb* **blew** \'blü\; **blown** \'blōn\; **blow·ing** **1** : to move or be moved especially rapidly or with power ⟨wind *blowing* from the north⟩ **2** : to send forth a strong current of air from the mouth or from a bellows ⟨*blow* on your hands⟩ **3** : to make a sound or cause to sound by blowing ⟨the whistle *blows*⟩ ⟨*blow* a trumpet⟩ **4** : to clear by forcing air through ⟨*blow* your nose⟩ **5** : to swell by forcing air into ⟨*blow* glass⟩ **6** : to destroy or be destroyed by an explosion ⟨*blow* up the bridge⟩

²blow *n* : a blowing of wind : GALE

³blow *n* **1** : a hard stroke with the fist, hand, or some object **2** : a sudden act : ATTACK **3** : a sudden happening that causes suffering or loss ⟨the death of her pet was a severe *blow*⟩

blow·gun \'blō-,gən\ *n* : a tube from which a dart may be shot by the force of the breath

blow·out \'blō-,aut\ *n* : a bursting of a container (as an automobile tire) by pressure of the contents on a weak spot

blow·pipe \'blō-,pīp\ *n* **1** : a small round tube for blowing air or gas into a flame so as to increase its heat **2** : BLOWGUN

blow·torch \'blō-,torch\ *n* : a small portable burner in which the flame is intensified by means of a blast of air or oxygen

blowtorch

¹blub·ber \'bləb-ər\ *n* : the fat of various sea mammals (as whales) from which oil can be obtained

²blubber *vb* : to weep noisily

¹blue \'blü\ *adj* **blu·er; blu·est** **1** : of the color blue **2** : low in spirits : MELANCHOLY

²blue *n* **1** : the color in the rainbow between green and violet : the color of the clear daytime sky **2** : something blue in color

blue·bell \'blü-,bel\ *n* : a plant with blue bell-shaped flowers

blue·ber·ry \'blü-,ber-ē\ *n, pl* **blue·ber·ries** : the edible blue berry of a bush having urn-shaped flowers and differing from the huckleberry in having many tiny seeds instead of ten small nutlike seeds

bluebell

blue·bird \'blü-,bərd\ *n* : any of several small North American songbirds more or less blue above

blue·bot·tle \'blü-,bät-l\ *n* : a large steel-blue hairy fly

blue·fish \'blü-,fish\ *n* : a very active and greedy saltwater fish used for food

blue·grass \'blü-,gras\ *n* : a grass with bluish green stems

blue jay \'blü-,jā\ *n* : any of several crested

and mostly blue American birds related to the crows

¹blue·print \'blü-ˌprint\ *n* **1** : a photographic print made with white lines on a blue background and used for copying maps and building plans **2** : a detailed outline of something to be accomplished : PLAN

²blueprint *vb* : to make a blueprint of

blues \'blüz\ *n pl* **1** : low spirits 〈overcome by the *blues*〉 **2** : a song expressing melancholy and composed in a style originating among the American Negroes

blue whale *n* : a very large whale that is probably the largest living animal

¹bluff \'bləf\ *adj* **1** : rising steeply with a broad front 〈a *bluff* coastline〉 **2** : frank and outspoken in a rough but good-natured manner — **bluff·ly** *adv* — **bluff·ness** *n*

²bluff *n* : a high steep bank : CLIFF

³bluff *vb* : to deceive or frighten by pretending to have strength or confidence that one does not really have — **bluff·er** *n*

⁴bluff *n* **1** : an act or instance of bluffing **2** : a person who bluffs

blu·ing *or* **blue·ing** \'blü-ing\ *n* : a preparation of blue or violet dyes used in laundering to counteract yellowing of white fabrics

blu·ish \'blü-ish\ *adj* : somewhat blue

¹blun·der \'blən-dər\ *vb* **1** : to move clumsily **2** : to make a mistake — **blun·der·er** *n*

²blunder *n* : a bad or stupid mistake **syn** see ERROR

blun·der·buss \'blən-dər-ˌbəs\ *n* : a short gun with a flaring muzzle formerly used for shooting at close range without taking exact aim

blunderbuss

¹blunt \'blənt\ *adj* **1** : having a thick edge or point : DULL 〈a *blunt* knife〉 **2** : abrupt or outspoken in speech or manners 〈disliked *blunt* criticism〉 — **blunt·ly** *adv*

²blunt *vb* : to make blunt

¹blur \'blər\ *n* : something vague or lacking definite outline 〈could see only a *blur*〉

²blur *vb* **blurred; blur·ring** **1** : to obscure by smearing **2** : to make indistinct or confused

blurt \'blərt\ *vb* : to utter suddenly and without thinking 〈*blurt* out a secret〉

¹blush \'bləsh\ *vb* **1** : to become red in the face from shame, modesty, or confusion **2** : to feel ashamed or embarrassed

²blush *n* **1** : a reddening of the face from shame, modesty, or confusion **2** : a rosy color

¹blus·ter \'bləs-tər\ *vb* **1** : to blow violently and noisily **2** : to talk or act in a noisy boastful way

²bluster *n* : noisy violent action or speech

bo·a \'bō-ə\ *n* : a large snake (as a python) that crushes its prey in its coils

boar \'bōr\ *n* **1** : a male pig **2** : a wild pig

¹board \'bōrd\ *n* **1** : a thin sawed piece of lumber that is comparatively broad and long **2** : a dining table **3** : meals furnished regularly for a price 〈room and *board*〉 **4** : a number of persons authorized to manage or direct something 〈the school *board*〉 **5** : a usually rectangular piece of rigid material used for some special purpose 〈a diving *board*〉 〈a game *board*〉 — **on board** : ABOARD

²board *vb* **1** : to go aboard 〈*boarded* the plane in New York〉 **2** : to cover with boards 〈the windows of the old house were *boarded* up〉 **3** : to provide with or be provided with regular meals for a price

board·er \'bōrd-ər\ *n* : a person who pays for meals or for meals and lodging at another's house

board·ing·house \'bōrd-ing-ˌhaus\ *n* : a house at which persons board

boarding school *n* : a school at which most of the pupils live during the term

board·walk \'bōrd-ˌwok\ *n* **1** : a walk made of planks **2** : a promenade constructed along a beach

¹boast \'bōst\ *n* **1** : an act of boasting **2** : a cause for boasting or pride

²boast *vb* **1** : to praise one's own possessions or accomplishments 〈*boasted* of his strength〉 **2** : to have and be proud of having

boast·ful \'bōst-fəl\ *adj* : inclined to boast : marked by boasting — **boast·ful·ly** *adv* — **boast·ful·ness** *n*

¹boat \'bōt\ *n* **1** : a small vessel propelled by oars or paddles or by sail or power **2** : SHIP

²boat *vb* : to use a boat

boat·house \'bōt-ˌhaus\ *n* : a house or shelter for boats

boat·man \'bōt-mən\ *n, pl* **boat·men** \-mən\ : a man who works on or deals in boats

boat·swain \'bōs-n\ *n* : a warrant officer on a warship or a petty officer on a merchantman who has charge of the hull, anchors, boats, and rigging

¹bob \'bäb\ *vb* **bobbed; bob·bing** **1** : to move or cause to move with a short jerky motion **2** : to appear suddenly 〈*bob* up again〉 **3** : to try to seize something with the teeth

²bob *n* : a short jerky up-and-down motion

³bob *n* **1** : a float used to buoy up the baited end of a fishing line **2** : a woman's or child's short haircut

⁴bob *vb* **bobbed; bob·bing** : to cut in the style of a bob 〈had her hair *bobbed*〉

---

bob·by pin \'bäb-ē-\ *n* : a flat metal hairpin with prongs that press close together

bob·cat \'bäb-,kat\ *n* : an American wildcat that is a small rusty brown variety of the lynx

bob·o·link \'bäb-ə-,lingk\ *n* : an American songbird related to the blackbirds

bob·sled \'bäb-,sled\ *n* : a sled made by joining two short sleds together

bob·tail \'bäb-,tāl\ *n* **1** : a short tail : a tail cut short **2** : an animal with a short tail

bob·white \bäb-'hwīt\ *n* : an American quail with gray, white, and reddish coloring

bode *past of* BIDE

bod·ice \'bäd-əs\ *n* : the upper part of a woman's dress

bod·i·ly \'bäd-l-ē\ *adj* : of or relating to the body ⟨*bodily* comfort⟩

body \'bäd-ē\ *n, pl* **bod·ies** **1** : the physical whole of a live or dead person or animal **2** : the trunk or main part of a person, animal, or plant **3** : the main or central part ⟨the *body* of a letter⟩ **4** : a group of persons or things united for some purpose ⟨a *body* of troops⟩ **5** : a mass or portion of matter distinct from other masses ⟨a *body* of water⟩ ⟨a *body* of cold air⟩ — **bod·ied** \'bäd-ēd\ *adj*

body·guard \'bäd-ē-,gärd\ *n* : a man or a group of men whose duty it is to protect a person

¹bog \'bäg, 'bȯg\ *n* : wet spongy ground that is usually acid and situated next to a body of water (as a pond)

²bog *vb* **bogged; bog·ging** : to sink or stick fast in a bog or as if in one ⟨the car *bogged* down⟩

bo·gey *or* **bo·gy** *or* **bo·gie** *n, pl* **bo·geys** *or* **bo·gies** **1** \'bùg-ē, 'bō-gē\ : GHOST, GOBLIN **2** \'bō-gē, 'bùg-ē\ : something one is afraid of without reason **3** \'bō-gē\ : a score of one over par on a hole in golf

Bo·he·mi·an \bō-'hē-mē-ən\ *n* **1** : a native or inhabitant of Bohemia **2** *often not cap* : a writer or artist living an unconventional life

¹boil \'bȯil\ *n* : a painful inflamed lump in the skin that contains pus and is caused by infection

²boil *vb* **1** : to heat or become heated to the temperature (**boiling point**) at which bubbles rise and break at the surface ⟨*boil* water⟩ **2** : to cook or become cooked in boiling water ⟨*boil* eggs⟩ **3** : to become excited

³boil *n* : the condition of something that is boiling

boil·er \'bȯi-lər\ *n* **1** : a container in which something is boiled **2** : a tank holding hot water **3** : a strong metal container used in making steam (as to heat buildings)

bois·ter·ous \'bȯis-tə-rəs\ *adj* : being rough and noisy — **bois·ter·ous·ly** *adv* — **bois·ter·ous·ness** *n*

bold \'bōld\ *adj* **1** : willing to meet danger or take risks : DARING **2** : too forward : IMPUDENT **3** : showing or requiring courage or daring ⟨a *bold* plan⟩ — **bold·ly** *adv* — **bold·ness** *n*

bold·face \'bōld-,fās\ *n* : a heavy black type — **bold–faced** \-,fāst\ *adj*

bo·le·ro \bə-'leər-ō\ *n, pl* **bo·le·ros** **1** : a Spanish dance in three-quarter time or the music for it **2** : a loose short jacket open at the front

boll \'bōl\ *n* : the seedpod of a plant (as cotton)

boll weevil *n* : a grayish insect that lays its eggs in cotton bolls

bo·lo \'bō-lō\ *n, pl* **bo·los** : a large single-edged knife of the Philippines

boll weevil

¹bol·ster \'bōl-stər\ *n* : a long pillow or cushion sometimes used to support bed pillows

²bolster *vb* : to support with or as if with a bolster ⟨help to *bolster* up his courage⟩

¹bolt \'bōlt\ *n* **1** : a stroke of lightning : THUNDERBOLT **2** : a sliding bar used to fasten a door **3** : the part of a lock worked by a key **4** : a metal pin or rod usually with a head at one end and a screw thread at the other that is used to hold something in place **5** : a roll of cloth or wallpaper

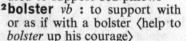
bolt 2

bolts 4

²bolt *vb* **1** : to move suddenly and rapidly ⟨he *bolted* from the room⟩ **2** : to run away ⟨the horse shied and *bolted*⟩ **3** : to fasten with a bolt **4** : to swallow hastily or without chewing ⟨don't *bolt* your food⟩

¹bomb \'bäm\ *n* **1** : a hollow case or shell containing explosive material and made to be dropped from an airplane, thrown by hand, or set off by a fuse **2** : a container in which a substance (as an insecticide) is stored under pressure and from which it is released in the form of a fine spray

²bomb *vb* : to attack with bombs

bom·bard \bäm-'bärd\ *vb* **1** : to attack with heavy fire from big guns : SHELL ⟨*bombard* a fort⟩ **2** : to attack repeatedly ⟨*bombard* a person with questions⟩

bomb·er \'bäm-ər\ *n* : an airplane designed for dropping bombs

bon·bon \'bän-,bän\ *n* : a candy usually with a chocolate coating and a creamy center

¹**bond** \'bänd\ *n* **1** : something that binds or confines **2** : a force or influence that unites ⟨a *bond* of friendship⟩ **3** : a legal agreement in which a person binds himself to pay a sum of money if he fails to meet stated requirements **4** : a certificate issued by a government or a corporation which binds the maker to pay a sum of money at a certain time

²**bond** *vb* : to cause to adhere

bond·age \'bän-dij\ *n* : SLAVERY

¹**bone** \'bōn\ *n* **1** : the hard material of which the skeleton of most animals is formed **2** : one of the hard pieces into which the bone of the skeleton is naturally divided ⟨broke a *bone* in his arm⟩ — **bone·less** \-ləs\ *adj*

²**bone** *vb* **boned**; **bon·ing** : to remove the bones from ⟨*bone* a fish⟩

bon·fire \'bän-ˌfīr\ *n* : a large fire built in the open air

bon·net \'bän-ət\ *n* **1** : a covering for the head usually tied under the chin by ribbons or strings and worn chiefly by small children **2** : the headdress of an American Indian

bon·ny *or* **bon·nie** \'bän-ē\ *adj* **bon·ni·er**; **bon·ni·est** *chiefly Brit* : HANDSOME, BEAUTIFUL

bo·nus \'bō-nəs\ *n* : something given to a person in addition to what is strictly due him

bon·y \'bō-nē\ *adj* **bon·i·er**; **bon·i·est** **1** : of or relating to bone ⟨a *bony* skeleton⟩ **2** : resembling bone especially in hardness ⟨*bony* material⟩ **3** : having bones and especially large or prominent bones ⟨a *bony* fish⟩

¹**boo** \'bü\ *interj* — used to express disapproval or to frighten children

²**boo** *n, pl* **boos** : a cry expressing disapproval

³**boo** *vb* : to attack with boos

boo·by \'bü-bē\ *n, pl* **boo·bies** **1** : a stupid person : DUNCE **2** : a large heavy seabird

booby trap *n* **1** : a trap set to catch a careless person **2** : a concealed explosive device attached to some harmless-looking object

¹**book** \'bük\ *n* **1** : a collection of sheets of paper bound together **2** : a literary composition of some length ⟨going to write a *book*⟩ **3** : a large subdivision of a literary work ⟨the *books* of the Bible⟩ **4** : a packet of small items bound together ⟨a *book* of matches⟩

²**book** *vb* : to make reservation for future use of ⟨*book* rooms at the hotel⟩

book·case \'bük-ˌkās\ *n* : a set of shelves to hold books

book·end \'bük-ˌend\ *n* : a support placed at the end of a row of books to keep them standing upright

book·keep·er \'bük-ˌkē-pər\ *n* : a person who keeps accounts for a business

book·keep·ing \'bük-ˌkē-ping\ *n* : the work of keeping business accounts

book·let \'bük-lət\ *n* : a little book usually having paper covers and few pages

book·mo·bile \'bük-mō-ˌbēl\ *n* : a truck with shelves of books serving as a traveling library

¹**boom** \'büm\ *n* **1** : a long pole used especially to stretch the bottom of a sail **2** : a long beam projecting from the mast of a derrick to support or guide something that is being lifted

boom

²**boom** *vb* **1** : to make a deep hollow rumbling sound ⟨the cannon *boomed*⟩ **2** : to increase or develop rapidly ⟨business *boomed* during the war⟩

³**boom** *n* **1** : a booming sound **2** : a rapid increase in activity or popularity

boo·mer·ang \'bü-mə-ˌrang\ *n* **1** : a curved club or stick that can be thrown so as to return to the thrower **2** : something that reacts with harm to its maker or doer ⟨the lie proved a *boomerang*⟩

boomer-
angs

boon \'bün\ *n* **1** : something asked or granted as a favor **2** : a timely benefit ⟨the steady rain came as a *boon* to the farmers⟩

¹**boost** \'büst\ *vb* **1** : to raise or push up from below : help to rise ⟨my brother *boosted* me through the window⟩ **2** : to increase in force, power, or amount ⟨*boost* aircraft production⟩ **3** : to promote the cause or interests of — **boost·er** *n*

²**boost** *n* : an act of boosting ⟨give me a *boost*⟩

¹**boot** \'büt\ *n* : a covering of leather or rubber for the foot and part of the leg

²**boot** *vb* : KICK ⟨*boot* the football around⟩

boot·ee *or* **boot·ie** \'büt-ē\ *n* : an infant's knitted or crocheted sock

boots

booth \'büth\ *n, pl* **booths** \'bü_th_z\ **1** : a covered stall or stand for selling or displaying goods at a fair, market, or exhibition **2** : a small enclosure giving privacy for one person ⟨a telephone *booth*⟩ **3** : a section of a restaurant consisting of a table between two backed benches

boo·ty \'büt-ē\ *n* **1** : goods seized from an enemy in war : PLUNDER **2** : GAIN, PRIZE

bo·rax \'bōr-ˌaks\ *n* : a crystalline compound of sodium, boron, and oxygen that occurs as a mineral or is manufactured and is used as a cleansing agent and water softener

¹bor·der \'bȯrd-ər\ *n* **1** : the outer edge of something ⟨the *border* of a lake⟩ **2** : BOUNDARY, FRONTIER **3** : an ornamental strip on or near the edge of a flat object

²border *vb* **1** : to put a border on ⟨*border* the garden with flowers⟩ **2** : to be close : be adjacent ⟨the United States *borders* on Canada⟩

¹bore \'bȯr\ *vb* **bored; bor·ing** **1** : to make a hole in especially with a tool that turns round : PIERCE ⟨*bore* a piece of wood⟩ **2** : to make by piercing or drilling ⟨*bore* a hole⟩ ⟨*bore* a well⟩ — **bor·er** *n*

²bore *n* **1** : a hole made by boring **2** : the size of a hole **3** : a cylindrical cavity (as in a gun barrel) **4** : the diameter of a cylinder

³bore *past of* BEAR

⁴bore *n* : a tiresome person or thing

⁵bore *vb* **bored; bor·ing** : to weary by being dull ⟨this story *bores* me⟩

bore·dom \'bȯrd-əm\ *n* : the state of being bored

bo·ric acid \,bȯr-ik-\ *n* : a weak acid containing boron used as an antiseptic

born \'bȯrn\ *adj* **1** : brought into life by birth **2** : having certain natural abilities or character from birth ⟨a *born* leader⟩

borne *past participle of* BEAR

bo·ron \'bȯr-,än\ *n* : a powdery or hard solid chemical element that melts at a very high temperature and is found in nature only in combination

bor·ough \'bər-ō\ *n* **1** : a self-governing town or village in some states **2** : one of the five political divisions of New York City

bor·row \'bär-ō\ *vb* **1** : to take or receive something with the promise of returning it **2** : to take for one's own use something originated by someone else : ADOPT ⟨*borrow* an idea⟩ — **bor·row·er** *n*

¹bos·om \'bùz-əm\ *n* **1** : the front of the human chest : the breasts of a woman **2** : the place of secret thoughts and feelings

²bosom *adj* : CLOSE, INTIMATE ⟨*bosom* friends⟩

¹boss \'bȯs\ *n* [from Dutch *baas* "master"] **1** : a person who directs or supervises workers : EMPLOYER, FOREMAN **2** : a person who exercises authority **3** : a political leader who controls a large number of votes

²boss *vb* **1** : DIRECT, SUPERVISE ⟨*boss* a job⟩ **2** : to give orders to ⟨don't *boss* me around⟩

boss·y \'bȯs-ē\ *adj* **boss·i·er; boss·i·est** : inclined to act like a boss : DICTATORIAL

bo·tan·i·cal \bə-'tan-i-kəl\ *adj* : of or relating to botany

bot·a·nist \'bät-n-əst\ *n* : a specialist in botany

bot·a·ny \'bät-n-ē\ *n* : a branch of biology dealing with plants

botch \'bäch\ *vb* : to do clumsily and unskillfully : SPOIL, BUNGLE

¹both \'bōth\ *adj* : the two : the one and the other of the ⟨*both* sisters are pretty⟩

²both *pron* : the one and the other : the two

³both *conj* : INCLUSIVELY, EQUALLY

¹both·er \'bäth-ər\ *vb* **1** : ANNOY, PESTER ⟨*bothered* by flies⟩ **2** : to cause anxiety to ⟨her illness *bothers* me⟩ **3** : to take trouble

²bother *n* **1** : a source of petty annoyance ⟨what a *bother* a cold can be⟩ **2** : FUSS

¹bot·tle \'bät-l\ *n* **1** : a glass, earthenware, or plastic container usually having a narrow neck and mouth and no handle **2** : the quantity held by a bottle

²bottle *vb* **bot·tled; bot·tling** **1** : to put into a bottle **2** : to shut up as if in a bottle

bot·tle·neck \'bät-l-,nek\ *n* : a place or condition where progress is held up

bot·tom \'bät-əm\ *n* **1** : the under surface of something ⟨*bottom* of a shelf⟩ **2** : a supporting surface or part : BASE ⟨chair *bottom*⟩ **3** : the bed of a body of water ⟨river *bottom*⟩ **4** : the lowest part of something ⟨*bottom* of the heap⟩ **5** : low land along a river ⟨Mississippi river *bottoms*⟩ — **bot·tomed** \-əmd\ *adj*

bot·tom·less \'bät-əm-ləs\ *adj* **1** : having no bottom **2** : very deep ⟨a *bottomless* pit⟩

bough \'baù\ *n* : a usually large or main branch of a tree

bought *past of* BUY

bouil·lon \'bü-,yän, 'bùl-yən\ *n* : a clear soup made from meat (as beef or chicken)

boul·der \'bōl-dər\ *n* : a detached and rounded or much-worn mass of rock

bou·le·vard \'bùl-ə-,värd\ *n* [Dutch *bolwerc* "bulwark" became French *boulevard*, the source of English *boulevard*, and meant both "boulevard" and "bulwark"; so called because the original boulevards were laid out on the sites where city fortifications had been torn down] : a broad avenue often having grass strips with trees along its center or sides

¹bounce \'baùns\ *vb* **bounced; bounc·ing** **1** : to spring backward after striking ⟨the ball *bounced* into the street⟩ **2** : to leap suddenly **3** : to cause to bounce ⟨*bounce* the ball⟩

²bounce *n* **1** : a sudden leap **2** : REBOUND

¹bound \'baùnd\ *adj* : going or intending to go ⟨homeward *bound*⟩ ⟨*bound* for the city⟩

²bound *n* **1** : a boundary line **2** : a point or a line beyond which a person or thing cannot go ⟨out of *bounds*⟩

³bound *vb* **1** : to form the boundary of ⟨a farm *bounded* by a river on one side⟩ **2** : to name the boundaries of ⟨*bound* Illinois⟩

⁴bound *past of* BIND

ə abut ər further a ax ā age ä father, cot à (see key page) aù out ch chin e less ē easy g gift i trip ī life

⁵bound *adj* **1** : FASTENED, TIED **2** : compelled by law or duty : OBLIGED ⟨*bound* in honor to repay⟩ **3** : covered with binding ⟨a *bound* book⟩ **4** : DETERMINED ⟨*bound* he would succeed⟩ **5** : CERTAIN, SURE ⟨*bound* to rain⟩

⁶bound *n* **1** : LEAP, SPRING **2** : BOUNCE

⁷bound *vb* : to move with a bound

bound·a·ry \'baun-də-rē\ *n, pl* **bound·a·ries** : something that marks or shows a limit or end : a dividing line

bound·less \'baund-ləs\ *adj* : having no limits : VAST ⟨*boundless* energy⟩

boun·te·ous \'baunt-ē-əs\ *adj* **1** : GENEROUS **2** : given plentifully — **boun·te·ous·ly** *adv*

boun·ti·ful \'baunt-i-fəl\ *adj* **1** : giving in abundance ⟨a *bountiful* host⟩ **2** : PLENTIFUL ⟨a *bountiful* feast⟩ — **boun·ti·ful·ly** *adv*

boun·ty \'baunt-ē\ *n, pl* **boun·ties** **1** : GENEROSITY **2** : generous gifts **3** : money given as a reward for killing certain destructive animals ⟨a state *bounty* on weasels⟩

bou·quet \bō-'kā, bü-\ *n* **1** : a bunch of flowers **2** : FRAGRANCE

bout \'baut\ *n* : a contest of skill or strength between two persons ⟨a wrestling *bout*⟩

¹bow \'bau\ *vb* **1** : to bend the head, body, or knee in greeting, reverence, respect, or submission **2** : SUBMIT, YIELD **3** : BEND

²bow *n* : a bending of the head or body to express respect, reverence, or greeting

³bow \'bō\ *n* **1** : a weapon used for shooting arrows and usually made of a strip of wood bent by a cord connecting the two ends **2** : something shaped in a curve like a bow **3** : a wooden rod with horsehairs stretched from end to end used for playing a musical instrument (as a violin) **4** : a knot made with one or more loops ⟨tie the ribbon in a *bow*⟩

⁴bow \'bō\ *vb* **1** : to bend into a bow **2** : to play with a bow ⟨*bowed* two strings at once⟩

⁵bow \'bau\ *n* : the forward part of a ship

bow·el \'bau-əl\ *n* **1** : INTESTINE — usually used in plural **2** : a part of the intestine

bow·er \'bau-ər\ *n* **1** : an attractive place for rest : RETREAT **2** : a shelter in a garden made of boughs of trees or vines : ARBOR

¹bowl \'bōl\ *n* **1** : a round hollowed dish without handles **2** : the contents of a bowl ⟨eat a *bowl* of cereal⟩ **3** : the bowl-shaped part of something (as a spoon or a pipe)

²bowl *n* **1** : a round ball for bowling **2** : the rolling of a ball

³bowl *vb* **1** : to roll a ball in bowling **2** : to move rapidly and smoothly as if rolling **3** : to hit with or as if with something rolled

bow·leg·ged \'bō-'leg-əd\ *adj* : having the legs bowed outward

bow·line \'bō-lən\ *n* : a knot used for making a loop that will not slip

bowl·ing \'bō-ling\ *n* : a game in which balls are rolled so as to knock down pins

bow·man \'bō-mən\ *n, pl* **bow·men** \-mən\ : ARCHER

bow·sprit \'bau-,sprit, 'bō-\ *n* : a large spar projecting forward from the bow of a ship

bowline

bow·string \'bō-,string\ *n* : the cord connecting the two ends of a bow

¹box \'bäks\ *n* : an evergreen shrub or small tree used for hedges

²box *n* **1** : a container usually having four sides, a bottom, and a cover **2** : the contents of a box ⟨eat a whole *box* of candy⟩ **3** : an enclosed place for one or more persons ⟨a sentry *box*⟩ ⟨a *box* in a theater⟩ **4** : a place on a baseball diamond where a given player has to stand ⟨batter's *box*⟩ ⟨pitcher's *box*⟩

³box *vb* : to enclose in or as if in a box

⁴box *n* : a blow with the hand : SLAP

⁵box *vb* **1** : to strike with the hand ⟨*box* his ears⟩ **2** : to engage in boxing

box·car \'bäks-,kär\ *n* : a roofed freight car usually having sliding doors in the sides

box elder *n* : an American maple with leaves divided into several leaflets

boxcar

¹box·er \'bäk-sər\ *n* : one that engages in the sport of boxing

²boxer *n* : a compact medium-sized short=haired usually fawn or brindle dog of German origin

box·ing \'bäk-sing\ *n* : fighting with the fists as a sport

boy \'boi\ *n* **1** : a male child from birth to young manhood **2** : a male servant

boy·hood \'boi-,hud\ *n* : the time or condition of being a boy

boy·ish \'boi-ish\ *adj* **1** : resembling a boy **2** : natural to boys ⟨*boyish* pranks⟩ — **boy·ish·ly** *adv* — **boy·ish·ness** *n*

boy scout *n* : a member of the Boy Scouts of America

¹brace \'brās\ *n* **1** : two of a kind ⟨a *brace* of quail⟩ **2** : a crank-shaped handle for holding and turning wood-boring bits **3** : something that braces ⟨a *brace* for a fence post⟩ ⟨a *brace* for a crippled leg⟩ **4** : a usually wire device worn on the teeth for changing faulty position **5** : a mark { or } or ‿ used to connect words or items to be considered together

brace 2

²brace *vb* **braced; brac·ing** **1** : to make strong, firm, or steady **2** : INVIGORATE, REFRESH ⟨a *bracing* breeze⟩ **3** : to take heart

brace·let \'brās-lət\ *n* : a decorative band or chain for the wrist or arm

brack·en \'brak-ən\ *n* : a large coarse branching fern

¹brack·et \'brak-ət\ *n* **1** : a support for a shelf usually attached to a wall **2** : a fixture or holder (as for an electric light) projecting from a wall **3** : one of a pair of marks [ ] (**square brackets**) used to enclose written or printed matter or in mathematics to enclose items to be treated together **4** : one of a pair of marks ⟨ ⟩ (**angle brackets**) used to enclose written or printed matter

bracket 1

²bracket *vb* **1** : to place within brackets **2** : to put into the same class : GROUP

brack·ish \'brak-ish\ *adj* : somewhat salty

brad \'brad\ *n* : a slender wire nail with a small longish but rounded head

brag \'brag\ *vb* **bragged; brag·ging** : BOAST

brag·gart \'brag-ərt\ *n* : one that brags

¹braid \'brād\ *vb* : to weave together into a braid : PLAIT ⟨wore her hair *braided*⟩

²braid *n* : a length of cord, ribbon, or hair formed of three or more strands twisted around one another

braille \'brāl\ *n, often cap* [named after its inventor, Louis Braille, a French teacher of the blind who was himself blind] : a system of printing for the blind in which the letters are represented by raised dots

¹brain \'brān\ *n* **1** : the part of the nervous system that is inside the skull, consists of grayish nerve cells and whitish nerve fibers, and is the organ of thought and nervous coordination **2** *pl* : a good mind : INTELLIGENCE

²brain *vb* **1** : to kill by smashing the skull **2** : to hit on the head

brain·storm \'brān-ˌstȯrm\ *n* **1** : a temporary mental upset or disturbance **2** : a sudden burst of inspiration : a startling idea

¹brake \'brāk\ *n* : a coarse fern often growing several feet high

²brake *n* : a thick growth of shrubs, small trees, or canes : THICKET

³brake *n* : a device for slowing up or stopping motion (as of a wheel) usually by friction

brake

⁴brake *vb* **braked; brak·ing** : to slow up or stop by using a brake

brake·man \'brāk-mən\ *n, pl* **brake·men** \-mən\ : a crew member on a train whose duties include inspecting the train and assisting the conductor

bram·ble \'bram-bəl\ *n* : any of a group of prickly-stemmed woody plants including the raspberries and blackberries and related to the roses

bran \'bran\ *n* : the broken coat of the seed of cereal grain separated (as by sifting) from the flour or meal

¹branch \'branch\ *n* **1** : a part of a tree that grows out from the trunk or from a large bough **2** : something extending from a main line or body like a branch ⟨a *branch* of a railroad⟩ **3** : PART, DIVISION ⟨the infantry *branch* of the army⟩ **4** : a subordinate office — **branched** \'brancht\ *adj*

²branch *vb* : to send out a branch : spread or divide into branches

¹brand \'brand\ *n* **1** : a charred or burning piece of wood **2** : a mark put on criminals with a hot iron : a mark of disgrace **3** : a mark made by burning (as on cattle) or by stamping or printing (as on manufactured goods) to show ownership, maker, or quality : TRADEMARK **4** : a kind, quality, or make of goods as known by the label ⟨a good *brand* of flour⟩

²brand *vb* **1** : to mark with a brand **2** : to mark or expose as bad or infamous

bran·dish \'bran-dish\ *vb* : to wave or shake in a threatening manner

brand–new \'bran-'nü, -'nyü\ *adj* : noticeably new and unused

bran·dy \'bran-dē\ *n, pl* **bran·dies** : an alcoholic liquor distilled from wine or fermented fruit juice

brass \'bras\ *n* **1** : an alloy made by combining copper and zinc **2** : the brass wind instruments of an orchestra or band — often used in plural

¹brave \'brāv\ *adj* **brav·er; brav·est** [Latin *barbarus* "barbarous" was altered to *bravo* in Spanish and Italian, and meant both "wild" and "courageous"; *bravo* was then taken by the French, spelled *brave*, and used only to mean "courageous"; English took both spelling and meaning from French] : FEARLESS, COURAGEOUS — **brave·ly** *adv*

²brave *n* : an American Indian warrior

³brave *vb* **braved; brav·ing** : to face or endure with courage ⟨*braved* the raging storm⟩

brav·er·y \'brā-və-rē\ *n, pl* **brav·er·ies** : COURAGE

¹brawl \'brȯl\ *vb* **1** : to quarrel noisily and roughly **2** : to make a loud confused noise

²brawl *n* : a noisy quarrel

brawn \'bròn\ *n* : muscular strength

¹bray \'brā\ *vb* : to make the loud harsh cry of a donkey

²bray *n* : a sound of braying

bra·zen \'brāz-n\ *adj* **1** : made of brass **2** : resembling brass in strength or color **3** : sounding harsh and loud ⟨*brazen* voices⟩ **4** : IMPUDENT, SHAMELESS ⟨a *brazen* girl⟩

Bra·zil nut \brə-ˌzil-\ *n* : a dark three-sided nut with a white kernel

¹breach \'brēch\ *n* **1** : a breaking of a law : a failure to observe an obligation : VIOLATION **2** : an opening made by breaking

²breach *vb* : to make a break in

¹bread \'bred\ *n* **1** : a baked food made from flour or meal **2** : FOOD ⟨our daily *bread*⟩

²bread *vb* : to cover with bread crumbs

bread·fruit \'bred-ˌfrüt\ *n* : a large round tropical fruit that when baked resembles bread

breadth \'bredth\ *n* **1** : distance measured from side to side : WIDTH **2** : COMPREHENSIVENESS, SCOPE

breadfruit

¹break \'brāk\ *vb* **broke** \'brōk\; **bro·ken** \'brō-kən\; **break·ing** **1** : to separate suddenly or forcibly into two or more parts : SMASH, SPLIT ⟨*break* a dish⟩⟨glass *breaks* easily⟩ **2** : to fail to keep ⟨*break* a law⟩ **3** : to force a way ⟨*break* into a house⟩ **4** : to bring to an end suddenly ⟨*break* a deadlock⟩ **5** : INTERRUPT, SUSPEND ⟨*broke* in with a question⟩ **6** : to make known ⟨*break* the news⟩ **7** : to develop or appear suddenly ⟨day *breaks*⟩ **8** : TAME **9** : to decrease the force of ⟨*break* a fall⟩ **10** : EXCEED ⟨*break* a record⟩

²break *n* **1** : an act of breaking ⟨make a *break* for freedom⟩⟨at *break* of day⟩ **2** : something produced by breaking ⟨a bad *break* in his leg⟩ **3** : a chance event ⟨a lucky *break*⟩

break·down \'brāk-ˌdaùn\ *n* : physical or mental collapse : FAILURE

break·er \'brā-kər\ *n* **1** : a person or thing that breaks ⟨a circuit *breaker*⟩ **2** : a wave that breaks on shore

¹break·fast \'brek-fəst\ *n* : the first meal of the day

²breakfast *vb* : to eat breakfast

break·neck \'brāk-ˌnek\ *adj* : likely to cause a broken neck ⟨*breakneck* speed⟩

break·wa·ter \'brāk-ˌwòt-ər, -ˌwät-\ *n* : a wall to protect a beach or a harbor from the sea

¹breast \'brest\ *n* **1** : a gland that secretes milk **2** : the front part of the body between the neck and the abdomen **3** : the seat of emotion — **breast·ed** \'bres-təd\ *adj*

²breast *vb* : to face or oppose bravely

breast·bone \'brest-ˌbōn\ *n* : the bony plate at the front and center of the breast

breast–feed \'brest-ˌfēd\ *vb* : to feed (a baby) from a mother's breast

breast·plate \'brest-ˌplāt\ *n* : a piece of armor for covering the breast

breast·work \'brest-ˌwərk\ *n* : a hastily built wall to serve as a defense in battle

breastplate

breath \'breth\ *n* **1** : air taken in or sent out by the lungs **2** : a slight breeze ⟨not a *breath* of air⟩ **3** : ease of breathing ⟨lost his *breath*⟩ — **out of breath** : breathing very rapidly as the result of strenuous exercise

breathe \'brēth\ *vb* **breathed**; **breath·ing** **1** : to draw air into and expel it from the lungs **2** : LIVE, EXIST **3** : to utter softly

breath·er \'brē-thər\ *n* : a pause for rest

breath·less \'breth-ləs\ *adj* **1** : not breathing : DEAD **2** : panting from exertion **3** : holding one's breath from excitement or fear

breath·tak·ing \'breth-ˌtā-king\ *adj* : EXCITING, THRILLING

breech·es \'brich-əz\ *n pl* **1** : short trousers fastening below the knee **2** : TROUSERS

¹breed \'brēd\ *vb* **bred** \'bred\; **breed·ing** **1** : to produce or increase (plants or animals) by sexual reproduction ⟨*breed* flowers for market⟩ **2** : to produce offspring by sexual reproduction **3** : to bring up : TRAIN ⟨was *bred* a farmer⟩⟨born and *bred* in this town⟩ **4** : to give rise to — **breed·er** *n*

²breed *n* **1** : a kind of plant or animal developed under domestication and differing from related kinds ⟨a beef *breed* of cattle⟩ **2** : CLASS, KIND

breed·ing \'brēd-ing\ *n* : training especially in manners : UPBRINGING ⟨his behavior shows good *breeding*⟩

breeze \'brēz\ *n* : a gentle wind

breez·y \'brē-zē\ *adj* **breez·i·er**; **breez·i·est** **1** : swept by breezes **2** : BRISK, LIVELY — **breez·i·ly** \-zə-lē\ *adv* — **breez·i·ness** \-zē-nəs\ *n*

brethren *pl of* BROTHER — used chiefly in formal or solemn address

brev·i·ty \'brev-ət-ē\ *n* : SHORTNESS

¹brew \'brü\ *vb* **1** : to prepare by steeping, boiling, and fermenting ⟨beer *brewed* from malt and hops⟩ **2** : to prepare by steeping in hot water ⟨*brew* the tea⟩ **3** : PLOT, PLAN ⟨*brewing* mischief⟩ **4** : to be in the process of formation ⟨a storm is *brewing*⟩ — **brew·er** *n*

²brew *n* : a brewed beverage ⟨a strong *brew*⟩

brew·er·y \'brü-ə-rē\ *n, pl* **brew·er·ies** : a place where malt liquors are brewed

bri·ar *var of* BRIER

¹bribe \'brīb\ *n* : something given or promised to a person in order to influence dishonestly his decision or action

²bribe *vb* **bribed; brib·ing** : to influence or attempt to influence by a bribe

brib·er·y \'brī-bə-rē\ *n, pl* **brib·er·ies** : the act or practice of bribing

¹brick \'brik\ *n* 1 : a building or paving material made from clay molded into blocks and baked 2 : a block made of brick 3 : a rectangular mass ⟨a *brick* of ice cream⟩

²brick *vb* : to close, face, or pave with bricks

brick·lay·er \'brik-,lā-ər\ *n* : a person who builds or paves with bricks

brid·al \'brīd-l\ *adj* : of or relating to a bride or a wedding

bride \'brīd\ *n* : a woman just married or about to be married

bride·groom \'brīd-,grüm\ *n* : a man just married or about to be married

brides·maid \'brīdz-,mād\ *n* : a woman who attends a bride at her wedding

¹bridge \'brij\ *n* 1 : a structure built over water, a low place, or an obstacle (as a railroad) for use as a passageway 2 : a platform above and across the deck of a ship for the captain or officer in charge 3 : something like a bridge (as in form) ⟨the *bridge* of the nose⟩

²bridge *vb* **bridged; bridg·ing** : to make a bridge over or across ⟨*bridge* a gap⟩

³bridge *n* : a card game for four players usually played in two forms (**contract bridge** and **auction bridge**)

¹bri·dle \'brīd-l\ *n* : a headstall with bit and reins by which a horse can be guided and controlled

²bridle *vb* **bri·dled; bri·dling** 1 : to put a bridle on 2 : RESTRAIN ⟨tried to *bridle* his anger⟩ 3 : to hold the head high and draw in the chin as an expression of resentment ⟨*bridle* at a criticism⟩

bridle

¹brief \'brēf\ *adj* 1 : SHORT ⟨a *brief* visit⟩ 2 : expressed in few words ⟨a *brief* answer to a question⟩ — **brief·ly** *adv*

²brief *vb* : to give final instructions to

briefs \'brēfs\ *n pl* : short snug underpants

bri·er \'brī-ər\ *n* : a plant (as the blackberry) with a thorny or prickly woody stem

brig \'brig\ *n* : a two-masted square-rigged sailing ship

bri·gade \bri-'gād\ *n* 1 : a body of soldiers consisting of two or more regiments 2 : a group of persons organized for acting together ⟨a fire *brigade*⟩

brig·a·dier general \,brig-ə-,diər-\ *n* : a commissioned officer (as in the army) ranking next below a major general

brig·and \'brig-ənd\ *n* : one who lives by plunder usually as a member of a band

bright \'brīt\ *adj* 1 : shedding much light : SHINING, GLOWING ⟨a *bright* fire⟩ ⟨a *bright* day⟩ 2 : very clear or vivid in color ⟨a *bright* red⟩ 3 : CLEVER, INTELLIGENT ⟨a *bright* boy⟩ 4 : LIVELY, CHEERFUL — **bright·ly** *adv* — **bright·ness** *n*

bright·en \'brīt-n\ *vb* : to make or become bright or brighter

bril·liance \'bril-yəns\ *n* : great brightness

bril·liant \'bril-yənt\ *adj* 1 : flashing with light : very bright : SPARKLING ⟨*brilliant* jewels⟩ 2 : DISTINGUISHED, SPLENDID ⟨a *brilliant* career⟩ 3 : very clever ⟨a *brilliant* student⟩ — **bril·liant·ly** *adv*

¹brim \'brim\ *n* 1 : the edge or rim of something hollow ⟨a cup filled to the *brim*⟩ 2 : the part of a hat that projects from the lower edge of the crown — **brim·less** \-ləs\ *adj*

²brim *vb* **brimmed; brim·ming** 1 : to be filled to the brim 2 : to reach or overflow the brim

brin·dled \'brin-dld\ *adj* : having dark streaks or spots on a gray or brownish background

brine \'brīn\ *n* 1 : water containing a great deal of salt 2 : OCEAN

bring \'bring\ *vb* **brought** \'brȯt\; **bring·ing** 1 : to cause to come with oneself by carrying or leading ⟨told to *bring* lunches⟩ ⟨*bring* your friend⟩ 2 : to cause to come into a particular state or condition 3 : to cause to arrive or come about ⟨heavy losses *brought* by the storm⟩ — **bring about** : to cause to take place : ACCOMPLISH — **bring forth** : to give birth to : PRODUCE — **bring to** : to restore to consciousness — **bring up** : REAR ⟨*bring up* a child⟩

brink \'bringk\ *n* 1 : the edge at the top of a steep place 2 : the point of onset : VERGE

brin·y \'brī-nē\ *adj* **brin·i·er; brin·i·est** : of or like brine : SALTY

brisk \'brisk\ *adj* 1 : very active : LIVELY 2 : INVIGORATING, REFRESHING — **brisk·ly** *adv* — **brisk·ness** *n*

¹bris·tle \'bris-əl\ *n* 1 : a short stiff hair ⟨a hog's *bristle*⟩ 2 : a stiff hair or something like a hair fastened in a brush

²bristle *vb* **bris·tled; bris·tling** 1 : to rise up and stiffen like bristles ⟨makes your hair *bristle*⟩ 2 : to show signs of anger or defiance ⟨*bristled* at the insult⟩ 3 : to appear as if covered with bristles

bris·tly \'bris-lē\ *adj* **bris·tli·er; bris·tli·est** : of, resembling, or set with bristles

britch·es \'brich-əz\ *n pl* : BREECHES

¹Brit·ish \'brit-ish\ *adj* : of or relating to Great Britain or the British

²British *n pl* : the people of Great Britain

brit·tle \'brit-l\ *adj* **brit·tler; brit·tlest** : hard but not tough : easily broken ⟨*brittle* glass⟩ — **brit·tle·ness** *n*

  syn BRITTLE, CRISP, FRAGILE all mean tending to break easily. BRITTLE refers to something hard and dry, often because of age, that lacks toughness or elasticity and is likely to shatter under pressure ⟨*brittle* twigs snapping under our feet⟩ ⟨old and *brittle* bones⟩ CRISP also suggests a hard dryness but adds to that the implication of freshness and a desirable lack of limpness ⟨*crisp* lettuce⟩ ⟨crackers no longer *crisp*⟩ ⟨a *crisp* new blouse⟩ FRAGILE applies to anything that is delicate in material or structure and may be easily broken ⟨a *fragile* carving in ivory⟩

broach \'brōch\ *vb* : to introduce as a topic of conversation ⟨*broach* a question⟩

broad \'brȯd\ *adj* **1** : not narrow : WIDE ⟨a *broad* stripe⟩ **2** : extending far and wide : SPACIOUS ⟨*broad* prairies⟩ **3** : OPEN, CLEAR ⟨*broad* daylight⟩ **4** : not limited ⟨a *broad* choice of subjects⟩ **5** : not detailed : GENERAL ⟨*broad* outlines⟩ — **broad·ly** *adv*

¹broad·cast \'brȯd-ˌkast\ *vb* **broadcast; broad·cast·ing** **1** : to scatter far and wide ⟨*broadcast* seed⟩ **2** : to make widely known **3** : to send out by radio or television from a transmitting station ⟨his speech will be *broadcast*⟩ — **broad·cast·er** *n*

²broadcast *adv* : so as to spread far and wide

³broadcast *n* **1** : an act of broadcasting **2** : the material broadcast by radio or television : a radio or television program

broad·cloth \'brȯd-ˌklȯth\ *n* **1** : a smooth glossy woolen cloth **2** : a fine cotton or silk cloth with a firm smooth surface

broad·en \'brȯd-n\ *vb* : to make or become broad or broader : WIDEN

broad–mind·ed \'brȯd-'mīn-dəd\ *adj* : free from prejudice : TOLERANT — **broad–mind·ed·ly** *adv* — **broad–mind·ed·ness** *n*

¹broad·side \'brȯd-ˌsīd\ *n* **1** : the part of a ship's side above the waterline **2** : a discharge of all of the guns that can be fired from the same side of a ship ⟨fire a *broadside*⟩

²broadside *adv* : with the broadside turned toward a given object or point

broad·sword \'brȯd-ˌsōrd\ *n* : a broad= bladed sword

bro·cade \brō-'kād\ *n* : a cloth with a raised design woven into it

broc·co·li \'bräk-ə-lē\ *n* : an open branching form of cauliflower whose green stalks and tops are cooked as a vegetable

broil \'brȯil\ *vb* **1** : to cook or be cooked by direct exposure to fire or flame **2** : to make or be extremely hot ⟨a *broiling* sun⟩

¹broke \'brōk\ *adj* : having no money

²broke *past of* BREAK

bro·ken \'brō-kən\ *adj* **1** : shattered into pieces ⟨*broken* glass⟩ **2** : having gaps or breaks ⟨a *broken* line⟩ **3** : not kept ⟨a *broken* promise⟩ **4** : imperfectly spoken

bro·ken·heart·ed \ˌbrō-kən-'härt-əd\ *adj* : crushed by sorrow

bro·ker \'brō-kər\ *n* : a person who acts as an agent for others in the purchase and sale of property

bro·mine \'brō-ˌmēn\ *n* : a chemical element that is usually seen as a deep red liquid giving off an irritating vapor of disagreeable odor

bron·chi·al \'bräng-kē-əl\ *adj* : relating to the branches **(bronchial tubes)** of the windpipe

bronchial tubes

bron·chi·tis \brän-'kīt-əs\ *n* : an inflammation of the bronchial tubes

bron·co \'bräng-kō\ *n, pl* **broncos** : a small half-wild horse of western North America used chiefly as a saddle horse or a pack animal

¹bronze \'bränz\ *n* **1** : an alloy of copper and tin and sometimes other elements **2** : a moderate yellowish brown

²bronze *vb* **bronzed; bronz·ing** : to make bronze in color

brooch \'brōch, 'brüch\ *n* : an ornamental pin or clasp for the clothing

¹brood \'brüd\ *n* **1** : the young of birds hatched at the same time ⟨a *brood* of chicks⟩ **2** : a group of young children or animals having the same mother : OFFSPRING

²brood *vb* **1** : to sit on eggs to hatch them **2** : to think long and anxiously about something : PONDER ⟨he *brooded* over his mistake⟩

brood·er \'brüd-ər\ *n* **1** : one that broods **2** : a building or a compartment that can be heated and is used for raising young fowl

brook \'brük\ *n* : a small stream — **brook·let** \-lət\ *n*

broom \'brüm, 'brům\ *n* **1** : a plant of the pea family with long slender branches along which grow many drooping yellow flowers **2** : a long-handled brush used for sweeping

brooms 2

broom·stick \'brüm-ˌstik, 'brům-\ *n* : the handle of a broom

broth \'bròth\ *n* : the liquid in which a meat, fish, or vegetable has been boiled

broth·er \'brəth-ər\ *n, pl* **broth·ers** *or* **breth·ren** \'breth-rən\ **1** : a boy or man related to another person by having the same parents **2** : a fellow member

broth·er·hood \'brəth-ər-ˌhùd\ *n* **1** : the state of being a brother **2** : an association of men for a particular purpose : FRATERNITY, TRADE UNION **3** : those who are engaged in the same business or profession

broth·er–in–law \'brəth-ər-ən-ˌlò\ *n, pl* **broth·ers-in-law** **1** : the brother of one's spouse **2** : the husband of one's sister

broth·er·ly \'brəth-ər-lē\ *adj* **1** : of or relating to brothers **2** : KINDLY, AFFECTIONATE

brought *past of* BRING

brow \'braù\ *n* **1** : EYEBROW **2** : the ridge on which the eyebrow grows **3** : FOREHEAD **4** : the upper edge of a steep slope

¹brown \'braùn\ *adj* **1** : of the color brown **2** : of dark or tanned complexion

²brown *n* : a color like that of coffee or chocolate that is a blend of red and yellow darkened by black

³brown *vb* : to make or become brown

brown·ie \'braù-nē\ *n* **1** : a cheerful goblin believed to perform helpful services by night **2** : a member of the Girl Scouts of the United States of America program for girls of the age range seven to nine **3** : a small rectangle of chocolate cake containing nuts

brown·ish \'braù-nish\ *adj* : somewhat brown

browse \'braùz\ *vb* **1** : to nibble young shoots and foliage ⟨*browsing* cattle⟩ **2** : to read here and there in a book or in a library

bru·in \'brü-ən\ *n* : BEAR

¹bruise \'brüz\ *vb* **bruised; bruis·ing** **1** : to injure the flesh (as by a blow) without breaking the skin **2** : to wound the feelings of

²bruise *n* : a black-and-blue spot on the body caused by a blow, bump, or fall

¹bru·net *or* **bru·nette** \brü-'net\ *adj* **1** : having a dark complexion **2** : having dark brown or black hair and eyes

²brunet *or* **brunette** *n* : a person with dark hair, eyes, and complexion

brunt \'brənt\ *n* : the main force of a blow or an attack ⟨the *brunt* of a storm⟩

¹brush \'brəsh\ *n* : BRUSHWOOD

²brush *n* **1** : a tool made of bristles set in a back or a handle and used for cleaning, smoothing, or painting **2** : a bushy tail ⟨a fox's *brush*⟩ **3** : an act of brushing **4** : a light stroke ⟨a *brush* of the hand⟩

brushes 1

³brush *vb* **1** : to scrub or smooth with a brush ⟨*brush* your hair⟩ **2** : to remove with or as if with a brush ⟨*brush* up the dirt⟩ **3** : to pass lightly across ⟨a twig *brushed* his cheek⟩

⁴brush *n*: a brief fight ⟨a *brush* with the enemy⟩

brush·wood \'brəsh-ˌwùd\ *n* **1** : branches and twigs cut from trees **2** : a heavy growth of small trees and bushes

brus·sels sprouts \ˌbrəs-əlz-\ *n pl, often cap* B : tiny green cabbagelike heads growing thickly on the stem of a plant of the cabbage family and cooked and eaten as a vegetable

bru·tal \'brüt-l\ *adj* : being cruel and inhuman — **bru·tal·ly** *adv*

syn BRUTAL and BRUTISH refer to human qualities or behavior thought of as beastlike. BRUTAL stresses cruelty and violence and indicates a reprehensible lack of humanity ⟨saved the dog from a *brutal* beating⟩ BRUTISH stresses crudeness and insensitivity, suggesting stupidity rather than cruelty as a major cause ⟨tried to overlook the *brutish* manners of the stranger⟩

bru·tal·i·ty \brü-'tal-ət-ē\ *n, pl* **bru·tal·i·ties** **1** : the quality of being brutal **2** : a brutal act or course of action

¹brute \'brüt\ *adj* **1** : not having human reasoning power ⟨the *brute* beasts⟩ **2** : not involving mental effort or reasoning

²brute *n* **1** : a four-footed animal especially when wild **2** : a brutal person

brut·ish \'brüt-ish\ *adj* : resembling a beast : lacking sensitivity : IRRATIONAL **syn** see BRUTAL

¹bub·ble \'bəb-əl\ *vb* **bub·bled; bub·bling** **1** : to form or produce bubbles ⟨stirred the drink to make it *bubble*⟩ **2** : to flow with a gurgle ⟨a *bubbling* brook⟩

²bubble *n* **1** : a tiny round body of air or gas in a liquid ⟨*bubbles* in boiling water⟩ **2** : a round body of air within a solid ⟨a *bubble* in glass⟩ **3** : a thin film of liquid filled with air or gas ⟨soap *bubbles*⟩

buc·ca·neer \ˌbək-ə-'niər\ *n* : PIRATE

¹buck \'bək\ *n* : the male of deer or antelopes or of goats, hares, rabbits, or rats

²buck *vb* **1** : to spring or plunge upward with head down and back arched ⟨a bronco *bucking*⟩ **2** : to charge or push against : RESIST

buck·board \'bək-ˌbōrd\ *n* : a lightweight four-wheeled carriage with a seat supported by a springy platform

buckboard

buck·et \'bək-ət\ *n* **1** : a pail for drawing up water from a well **2** : a container in which something is collected and carried ⟨a coal *bucket*⟩ **3** : the amount that a bucket can hold

buck·eye \'bək-ˌī\ *n* : a horse chestnut or a closely related tree or shrub

¹buck·le \'bək-əl\ *n* : a fastening for two loose ends of a strap or belt which is attached to one and through which the other is passed and held

²buckle *vb* **buck·led; buck·ling** **1** : to fasten with a buckle **2** : to apply oneself with vigor ⟨*buckle* down to business⟩ **3** : BEND, WARP, KINK ⟨the pavement *buckled* in the heat⟩

buck·ler \'bək-lər\ *n* : a shield worn on the arm

buck·shot \'bək-ˌshät\ *n* : coarse lead shot

buck·skin \'bək-ˌskin\ *n* : a soft pliable leather usually having a suede finish and used for gloves and shoe uppers

buck·wheat \'bək-ˌhwēt\ *n* : a plant with pinkish white flowers that is grown for its dark triangular seeds which are used as a cereal grain

buckwheat

¹bud \'bəd\ *n* **1** : a small growth at the tip or on the side of a stem that later develops into a flower, a leaf, or a new stem or branch **2** : a flower that has not fully opened **3** : a part that grows out from the body of an organism and develops into a new organism ⟨a *bud* on a yeast plant⟩ **4** : an early stage of development

²bud *vb* **bud·ded; bud·ding** **1** : to form or put forth buds **2** : to grow or reproduce by buds

bud·dy \'bəd-ē\ *n, pl* **bud·dies** : CHUM, PAL

budge \'bəj\ *vb* **budged; budg·ing** : to move or cause to move from one position to another

¹budg·et \'bəj-ət\ *n* **1** : a statement of estimated income and probable expenses for a period of time ⟨the government *budget*⟩ **2** : a plan for using money ⟨work out a *budget*⟩

²budget *vb* **1** : to include in a budget ⟨*budget* a dollar for carfare⟩ **2** : to plan as in a budget

¹buff \'bəf\ *n* **1** : a moderate orange yellow **2** : a stick or wheel with a soft surface for applying polishing material

²buff *vb* : to polish with or as if with a buff

buf·fa·lo \'bəf-ə-ˌlō\ *n, pl* **buffalo** *or* **buf·fa·loes** : any of several wild oxen and especially the American bison

¹buf·fet \'bəf-ət\ *n* : a blow with the hand

²buffet *vb* : to pound repeatedly : BATTER

³buf·fet \ˌbə-'fā, bü-\ *n* **1** : a sideboard often without a mirror **2** : a cupboard or set of shelves for the display of dishes and silver **3** : a meal set out on a buffet or table from which people may serve themselves

bug \'bəg\ *n* **1** : an insect or other lowly creeping or crawling animal **2** : any of a large group of four-winged insects that suck liquid food (as plant juices or blood) and have young which resemble the adults but lack wings **3** : FLAW, DEFECT ⟨try to get the *bugs* out of the TV set⟩ **4** : one who is enthusiastic about something ⟨he's a camera *bug*⟩

bug·a·boo \'bəg-ə-ˌbü\ *n, pl* **bug·a·boos** : BUGBEAR

bug·bear \'bəg-ˌbaər\ *n* **1** : an imaginary creature used to frighten children **2** : something of which one is afraid

bug·gy \'bəg-ē\ *n, pl* **bug·gies** : a light single-seated carriage usually drawn by one horse

buggy

bu·gle \'byü-gəl\ *n* [in earlier English *bugle* meant "a buffalo" and "an instrument made from a horn"; it was taken from Old French *bugle*, which was in turn taken from Latin *buculus* "young steer"] : an instrument like a trumpet but having no valves and used chiefly for giving military signals

bu·gler \'byü-glər\ *n* : a person who plays a bugle

¹build \'bild\ *vb* **built** \'bilt\; **build·ing** **1** : to make by putting together parts or materials : CONSTRUCT ⟨*build* a house⟩ ⟨*build* a bridge⟩ **2** : to produce or create gradually by effort ⟨*build* a winning team⟩ **3** : to progress toward a peak ⟨excitement *building* up⟩

²build *n* : form or kind of structure : PHYSIQUE

build·er \'bil-dər\ *n* : a person whose business is the building of houses and similar structures

build·ing \'bil-ding\ *n* **1** : a stationary structure built as a dwelling, shelter, or place for human activities or for storage ⟨an office *building*⟩ **2** : the art, work, or business of assembling materials into a structure

built-in \'bilt-'in\ *adj* : forming a permanent part of a structure ⟨*built-in* bookcases⟩

bulb \'bəlb\ *n* **1** : a plant underground resting form which consists of a short stem with one or more buds enclosed in thick fleshy leaves and from which a new plant can grow **2** : a plant structure (as a corm or tuber) that resembles a bulb **3** : a rounded more or less bulb-shaped object or part

bulb·ous \'bəl-bəs\ *adj* **1** : having a bulb **2** : resembling a bulb : ROUND, SWOLLEN

¹bulge \'bəlj\ *n* : a swelling part : a part that sticks out ⟨a *bulge* in a bag⟩

²bulge *vb* **bulged; bulg·ing** : to swell or bend outward ⟨*bulging* muscles⟩

bulk \'bəlk\ *n* **1** : greatness of size or volume ⟨hard to handle because of its *bulk*⟩ **2** : the largest or chief part

bulk·head \'bəlk-ˌhed\ *n* : an upright partition separating sections in a ship

bulk·y \'bəl-kē\ *adj* **bulk·i·er; bulk·i·est**
1 : having bulk **2** : being large and unwieldy

bull \'bùl\ *n* : the male of an animal of the ox
and cow family and of certain other large animals (as the elephant and the whale)

¹bull·dog \'bùl-ˌdȯg\ *n* : a short-haired
thickset powerful dog of English origin

²bulldog *vb* **bull·dogged; bull·dog·ging** : to
throw by seizing the horns and twisting the
neck ⟨*bulldog* a steer⟩

bull·doz·er \'bùl-ˌdō-zər\ *n* : a tractor-driven
machine having a broad horizontal blade for
pushing (as in clearing land of trees)

bul·let \'bùl-ət\ *n* : a shaped piece of metal
made to be shot from a firearm — **bul·let-
proof** \ˌbùl-ət-'prüf\ *adj*

bul·le·tin \'bùl-ət-n\ *n* : a short public notice
usually issued by an official source

bulletin board *n* : a board for posting bulle-
tins and announcements

bull·fight \'bùl-ˌfīt\ *n* : a public entertainment in which men excite, fight with, and
usually kill bulls in an arena (**bull ring**) —
bull·fight·er *n*

bull·finch \'bùl-ˌfinch\ *n* : a thick-billed red-
breasted European songbird often kept as a
cage bird

bull·frog \'bùl-ˌfrȯg, -ˌfräg\ *n* : a large heavy
frog that makes a booming or bellowing sound

bull·head \'bùl-ˌhed\ *n* : any of various
fishes that have a large head

bul·lion \'bùl-yən\ *n* : gold or silver metal in
bars or blocks

bull·ock \'bùl-ək\ *n* **1** : a young bull
2 : STEER, OX

bull's–eye \'bùlz-ˌī\ *n* **1** : the center of a
target **2** : a shot that hits the center of a
target

¹bul·ly \'bùl-ē\ *n, pl* **bul·lies** : one who constantly teases, hurts, or threatens smaller or
weaker persons

²bully *vb* **bul·lied; bul·ly·ing** : to act like a bully
toward

bul·rush \'bùl-ˌrəsh\ *n* : any of several large
rushes or sedges that grow in wet places

bul·wark \'bùl-wərk\ *n* **1** : a solid wall-like
structure built for defense against an enemy
2 : something that defends or protects ⟨free-
dom is one of the *bulwarks* of democracy⟩

bum \'bəm\ *n* **1** : a person who avoids work
and tries to live off others **2** : TRAMP, HOBO

bum·ble·bee \'bəm-bəl-ˌbē\ *n* : a large hairy
bee that makes a loud humming sound

¹bump \'bəmp\ *vb* **1** : to strike or knock
against something ⟨*bump* into a door⟩ **2** : to
move along unevenly : JOLT

²bump *n* **1** : a sudden heavy blow or jolt **2** : a
rounded swelling of flesh as from a blow
3 : an unevenness in a road surface

¹bump·er \'bəm-pər\ *n* : a bar across the
front or back of an automobile intended to
lessen the shock or damage from collision

²bumper *adj* : unusually large or fine

bun \'bən\ *n* : a sweetened roll or biscuit

¹bunch \'bənch\ *n* **1** : a number of things of
the same kind growing together ⟨a *bunch* of
grapes⟩ **2** : GROUP ⟨a *bunch* of children⟩

²bunch *vb* : to gather in a bunch

¹bun·dle \'bən-dl\ *n* : a number of things
fastened or wrapped together : PACKAGE

²bundle *vb* **bun·dled; bun·dling** : to make into a
bundle : WRAP

bung \'bəng\ *n* **1** : the stopper in the bunghole of a cask **2** : BUNGHOLE

bun·ga·low \'bəng-gə-ˌlō\ *n* : a one-story
house

bung·hole \'bəng-ˌhōl\ *n* : a hole for emptying or filling a cask

bun·gle \'bəng-gəl\ *vb* **bun·gled; bun·gling** : to
act, do, make, or work in a clumsy manner
⟨*bungled* the job⟩ — **bun·gler** *n*

¹bunk \'bəngk\ *n* **1** : a built-in bed that is
often one of a tier **2** : a sleeping place

²bunk *vb* : to occupy or share a bunk

bun·ny \'bən-ē\ *n, pl* **bun·nies** : RABBIT

¹bunt \'bənt\ *vb* **1** : to strike or push with the
horns or head : BUTT **2** : to push or tap a
baseball lightly without swinging the bat

²bunt *n* **1** : BUTT, PUSH **2** : a bunted baseball

¹bun·ting \'bənt-ing\ *n* : any of various stout-
billed birds of the size and habits of a sparrow

²bunting *n* **1** : a thin cloth used chiefly for
making flags and patriotic decorations
2 : flags or decorations made of bunting

¹buoy \'bü-ē, 'bȯi\ *n* **1** : a floating object
anchored in a body of water so
as to mark a channel or to
warn of danger **2** : LIFE BUOY

²buoy *vb* **1** : to keep from
sinking : keep afloat **2** : to
keep up the spirits of ⟨*buoyed*
up by the hope of success⟩

buoys 1

buoy·an·cy \'bȯi-ən-sē, 'bü-
yən-\ *n* **1** : the power of rising
and floating (as on water or in air) ⟨the *buoy-
ancy* of cork in water⟩ **2** : the power of a
liquid to hold up a floating body ⟨the *buoy-
ancy* of sea water⟩ **3** : LIGHTHEARTEDNESS

buoy·ant \'bȯi-ənt, 'bü-yənt\ *adj* **1** : able to
rise and float in the air or on the top of a
liquid ⟨*buoyant* cork⟩ **2** : able to keep a body
afloat **3** : CHEERFUL, LIVELY

bur *or* **burr** \'bər\ *n* **1** : a rough or prickly
covering or shell of a seed or fruit **2** : some-

thing that resembles a bur (as in sticking)

¹bur·den \'bərd-n\ *n* **1** : something carried : LOAD **2** : something that is hard to bear ⟨a heavy *burden* of sorrow⟩ **3** : the carrying of loads ⟨beast of *burden*⟩ **4** : the capacity of a ship for carrying cargo

²burden *vb* : to put a burden on

bur·den·some \'bərd-n-səm\ *adj* : so heavy or hard to bear as to be a burden

bur·dock \'bər-,däk\ *n* : a tall coarse weed related to the thistles that has purplish flower heads surrounded by prickles

bu·reau \'byůr-ō\ *n* **1** : a low chest of drawers with a mirror for use in a bedroom **2** : a subdivision of a government department ⟨the Weather *Bureau*⟩ **3** : a business office that provides services ⟨a travel *bureau*⟩

bur·glar \'bər-glər\ *n* : a person who is guilty of burglary

bur·glary \'bər-glə-rē\ *n, pl* **bur·glar·ies** : the breaking into a building with intent to steal

bur·i·al \'ber-ē-əl\ *n* : the placing of a dead body in a grave or a tomb

bur·lap \'bər-,lap\ *n* : a coarse fabric made usually from jute or hemp and used chiefly for bags and wrappings

bur·ly \'bər-lē\ *adj* **bur·li·er; bur·li·est** : strongly and heavily built — **bur·li·ness** *n*

¹burn \'bərn\ *vb* **burned** \'bərnd\ *or* **burnt** \'bərnt\; **burn·ing** **1** : to be on fire or to set on fire **2** : to destroy or be destroyed by fire or heat ⟨*burn* the trash⟩ ⟨a house that *burned* to the ground⟩ **3** : to make or produce by fire or heat ⟨*burn* a hole in a coat⟩ **4** : to give or cause to give light ⟨leave a light *burning* all night⟩ **5** : to injure or affect by or as if by fire or heat ⟨*burned* her finger⟩ **6** : to feel or cause to feel as if on fire ⟨*burn* with anger⟩

²burn *n* : an injury produced by burning

burn·er \'bər-nər\ *n* : the part of a stove or furnace where the flame or heat is produced

bur·nish \'bər-nish\ *vb* : to make shiny

bur·ro \'bər-ō\ *n, pl* **bur·ros** : a small donkey often used as a pack animal

¹bur·row \'bər-ō\ *n* : a hole in the ground made by an animal (as a rabbit or fox) for shelter or protection

²burrow *vb* **1** : to hide in or as if in a burrow **2** : to make a burrow **3** : to make one's way by or as if by digging

¹burst \'bərst\ *vb* **burst; burst·ing** **1** : to break open or in pieces (as by an explosion from within) ⟨bombs *bursting* in air⟩ ⟨buds *bursting* open⟩ **2** : to give way suddenly to an expression of emotion ⟨*burst* into tears⟩ **3** : to come or go suddenly ⟨*burst* into the room⟩ **4** : to be filled to the breaking point

²burst *n* **1** : a sudden outbreak ⟨a *burst* of laughter⟩ **2** : a sudden violent effort

bur·y \'ber-ē\ *vb* **bur·ied; bur·y·ing** **1** : to cover (a dead body) out of sight in a grave or tomb **2** : to place in the ground and cover over for concealment ⟨*buried* treasure⟩ **3** : to cover up : HIDE ⟨*buried* his face in his hands⟩

bus \'bəs\ *n, pl* **bus·es** *or* **bus·ses** : a large motor-driven passenger vehicle

bush \'bůsh\ *n* **1** : a usually low-growing and much-branched shrub **2** : a stretch of uncleared or sparsely inhabited country

bush·el \'bůsh-əl\ *n* **1** : a unit of dry capacity equal to four pecks or thirty-two quarts **2** : a container holding a bushel

bush·y \'bůsh-ē\ *adj* **bush·i·er; bush·i·est** **1** : overgrown with bushes **2** : being thick and spreading ⟨a *bushy* beard⟩

busi·ness \'biz-nəs\ *n* **1** : an activity that takes the greater part of the time, attention, or effort of a person or group : OCCUPATION **2** : a commercial enterprise **3** : the making, buying, and selling of goods or services **4** : AFFAIR ⟨mind your own *business*⟩ **syn** see TRADE

busi·ness·man \'biz-nəs-,man\ *n, pl* **busi·ness·men** \-,men\ : a man engaged in business especially in an executive capacity

¹bust \'bəst\ *n* : a piece of sculpture representing the upper part of the human figure including the head and neck

²bust *vb* **1** : HIT, PUNCH **2** : BREAK, DESTROY

¹bus·tle \'bəs-əl\ *vb* **bus·tled; bus·tling** : to move about with fussy or noisy activity

²bustle *n* : fussy or noisy activity

¹bus·y \'biz-ē\ *adj* **bus·i·er; bus·i·est** **1** : actively at work : not idle **2** : being used ⟨the line is *busy*⟩ **3** : full of activity ⟨a *busy* day⟩ — **bus·i·ly** \'biz-ə-lē\ *adv*

²busy *vb* **bus·ied; bus·y·ing** : to make or keep busy ⟨*busied* herself with dusting⟩

bus·y·bod·y \'biz-ē-,bäd-ē\ *n, pl* **bus·y·bod·ies** : a person who meddles in the affairs of others

¹but \bət\ *conj* **1** : yet nevertheless ⟨got cold *but* didn't snow⟩ **2** : while on the contrary ⟨likes to fish *but* his brother doesn't⟩ **3** : except that : UNLESS ⟨never rains *but* it pours⟩

syn BUT, HOWEVER, NEVERTHELESS all lead to a conclusion qualifying or altering an earlier thought. BUT marks opposition without emphasizing it ⟨he came late *but* didn't miss much⟩ HOWEVER may mark a weaker conclusion and often carries the tone of being merely an added comment ⟨he came late; he didn't, *however*, miss much⟩ NEVERTHELESS states the

bust

opposing conclusion fairly strongly, and indicates that what preceded had little bearing on the conclusion ⟨he came late; *nevertheless* he didn't miss much as it was a dull game⟩

²but *prep* : other than ⟨no one *but* us⟩

³but *adv* : ONLY, MERELY ⟨he is *but* a child⟩

¹butch·er \'bùch-ər\ *n* **1** : one whose business is killing animals for sale as food **2** : a dealer in meat **3** : one that kills in large numbers or brutally

²butcher *vb* **1** : to slaughter as a butcher does **2** : to make a mess of : BOTCH

but·ler \'bət-lər\ *n* : the chief male servant of a household

¹butt \'bət\ *vb* : to strike or thrust with the head or horns

²butt *n* : a blow or thrust with the head or horns

³butt *n* : a person who is a target for abuse or ridicule ⟨made the *butt* of the joke⟩

⁴butt *n* **1** : the thicker or bottom end of something ⟨the *butt* of a rifle⟩ **2** : an unused remainder ⟨a cigarette *butt*⟩

butte \'byüt\ *n* : an isolated hill with steep sides usually having a smaller summit than a mesa

¹but·ter \'bət-ər\ *n* **1** : the solid yellowish fatty food obtained from cream or milk by churning **2** : a substance resembling butter in texture and use ⟨apple *butter*⟩ ⟨peanut *butter*⟩

— butt

²butter *vb* : to spread with or as if with butter

but·ter·cup \'bət-ər-,kəp\ *n* : a common wild flower having bright yellow cup-shaped blossoms

but·ter·fat \'bət-ər-,fat\ *n* : the natural fat of milk that is the chief ingredient of butter

but·ter·fly \'bət-ər-,flī\ *n, pl* **but·ter·flies** : a day-flying slender-bodied insect with colored wings covered with tiny overlapping scales

buttercup

but·ter·milk \'bət-ər-,milk\ *n* : the liquid left after churning butter from milk or cream

but·ter·nut \'bət-ər-,nət\ *n* : an edible oily nut produced by an American tree related to the walnuts

but·ter·scotch \'bət-ər-,skäch\ *n* : a candy made from sugar, corn syrup, and water

but·tock \'bət-ək\ *n* **1** : the back of the hip which forms one of the fleshy parts on which a person sits **2** *pl* : RUMP

butternut: leaf and nuts

¹but·ton \'bət-n\ *n* **1** : a small knob or disk used for holding parts of a garment together or as an ornament **2** : something that resembles a button ⟨an electric light *button*⟩

²button *vb* : to close or fasten with buttons

but·ton·hole \'bət-n-,hōl\ *n* : a slit or loop for fastening a button

but·ton·wood \'bət-n-,wùd\ *n* : SYCAMORE 3

¹but·tress \'bət-rəs\ *n* **1** : a structure built against a wall or building to give support and strength **2** : something that supports, props, or strengthens

²buttress *vb* : to support with or as if with a buttress : PROP

bux·om \'bək-səm\ *adj* : vigorously or healthily plump

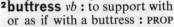
buttresses 1

¹buy \'bī\ *vb* **bought** \'bòt\; **buy·ing** : to get by paying for : PURCHASE — **buy·er** *n*

²buy *n* : something bought at a favorable price

¹buzz \'bəz\ *vb* **1** : to make a low humming sound like that of bees **2** : to be filled with a low hum or murmur ⟨a room that *buzzed* with excitement⟩ **3** : to fly an airplane low over

²buzz *n* : a sound of buzzing

buz·zard \'bəz-ərd\ *n* : a usually large and slow-flying bird of prey

buzz·er \'bəz-ər\ *n* : an electric signaling device that makes a buzzing sound

¹by \'bī\ *prep* **1** : NEAR ⟨stood *by* the door⟩ **2** : VIA ⟨left *by* the door⟩ **3** : PAST ⟨drove *by* the house⟩ **4** : AT, DURING ⟨travel *by* night⟩ **5** : no later than ⟨get here *by* ten o'clock⟩ **6** : through the means or direct agency of ⟨won it *by* cheating⟩ ⟨was seen *by* the others⟩ **7** : according to : in conformity with ⟨did it *by* the book⟩ **8** : with respect to ⟨an electrician *by* trade⟩ **9** : to the amount or extent of ⟨his horse won *by* a nose⟩ **10** : multiplied by ⟨a lot 150 feet *by* 200 feet⟩

²by *adv* **1** : near at hand ⟨stand *by*⟩ **2** : PAST ⟨walk *by*⟩ ⟨in days gone *by*⟩ **3** : ASIDE, AWAY ⟨put something *by* for a rainy day⟩

by and by \,bī-ən-'bī\ *adv* : after a while

by–and–by \,bī-ən-'bī\ *n* : a future time

by·gone \'bī-,gòn\ *adj* : gone by : PAST

by·gones \'bī-,gònz\ *n pl* : events that are over and done with ⟨let *bygones* be *bygones*⟩

¹by·pass \'bī-,pas\ *n* **1** : a passage to one side **2** : a road serving as an alternate route around a congested area

²bypass *vb* : to make a detour or circuit around

by·path \'bī-,path, -,pàth\ *n* : BYWAY

by–prod·uct \'bī-,präd-əkt\ *n* : something produced (as in manufacturing) in addition to the principal product

by·stand·er \'bī-,stan-dər\ *n* : a person present or standing near but taking no part in what is going on

by·way \'bī-,wā\ *n* : a road off the main highway that is little traveled

c \'sē\ *n, often cap* **1** : the third letter of the English alphabet **2** : the roman numeral 100 **3** : a grade rating a student's work as fair **cab** \'kab\ *n* **1** : a light closed horse-drawn carriage usually for hire **2** : TAXICAB **3** : the covered compartment for the engineer and operating controls of a locomotive or for the operator of a truck, tractor, or crane

cab

ca·ban·a \kə-'ban-ə, -yə\ *n* : a beach shelter usually with an open side facing the sea

cab·bage \'kab-ij\ *n* : a garden plant related to the turnips that has a dense head of leaves used as a vegetable

cab·in \'kab-ən\ *n* **1** : a private room on a ship **2** : a compartment below deck on a small boat for passengers or crew **3** : an airplane compartment for cargo, crew, or passengers **4** : a small one-story dwelling usually of simple construction

cab·i·net \'kab-ə-nət\ *n* **1** : a case or cupboard for keeping or displaying articles ⟨filing *cabinet*⟩ **2** : a group of persons who serve as advisers (as to the head of a country)

¹ca·ble \'kā-bəl\ *n* **1** : a very strong rope, wire, or chain **2** : CABLEGRAM **3** : a bundle of insulated wires to carry electric current

²cable *vb* **ca·bled; ca·bling 1** : to fasten or provide with a cable **2** : to telegraph by submarine cable

cables 1

ca·ble·gram \'kā-bəl-,gram\ *n* : a message sent by submarine cable

ca·boose \kə-'büs\ *n* : a car usually at the rear of a freight train for the use of the train crew and railroad workmen

ca·cao \kə-'kaù, kə-'kā-ō\ *n, pl* **ca·caos** : a South American tree with yellow flowers followed by fleshy yellow pods that contain fatty seeds from which chocolate is made

¹cache \'kash\ *n* **1** : a place for hiding, storing, or preserving supplies (as food)

2 : something hidden or stored in a cache

²cache *vb* **cached; cach·ing** : to place, hide, or store in a cache

¹cack·le \'kak-əl\ *vb* **cack·led; cack·ling 1** : to make the sharp broken noise or cry characteristic of a hen especially after laying **2** : to laugh or chatter noisily

²cackle *n* : a cackling sound

cac·tus \'kak-təs\ *n, pl* **cac·tus·es** *or* **cac·ti** \-,tī\ : any of a large group of flowering plants of dry regions that have fleshy stems and branches with scales or prickles

cad \'kad\ *n* : a person who deliberately behaves in an ungentlemanly way

ca·dav·er \kə-'dav-ər\ *n* : a dead body

¹cad·die *or* **cad·dy** \'kad-ē\ *n, pl* **cad·dies** : a person who carries a golfer's clubs

²caddie *or* **caddy** *vb* **cad·died; cad·dy·ing** : to serve as a caddie

cad·dis fly \'kad-əs-\ *n* : a four-winged insect with an aquatic larva that lives in a silk case covered with bits of wood or gravel

ca·dence \'kād-ns\ *n* **1** : the measure or beat of rhythmical motion or sound : RHYTHM **2** : the close of a strain of music

ca·den·za \kə-'den-zə\ *n* : a brilliant sometimes improvised passage usually toward the close of a musical composition

ca·det \kə-'det\ *n* **1** : a younger son or brother **2** : a student military officer

ca·fé *also* **ca·fe** \ka-'fā\ *n* **1** : BAR, SALOON **2** : RESTAURANT **3** : NIGHTCLUB

caf·e·te·ri·a \,kaf-ə-'tir-ē-ə\ *n* : a restaurant where the customers serve themselves or are served at a counter but take the food to tables

caf·feine \ka-'fēn\ *n* : a stimulating substance in coffee and tea

¹cage \'kāj\ *n* **1** : an openwork box or enclosure for confining an animal (as a bird) **2** : an enclosure like a cage in shape or purpose

²cage *vb* **caged; cag·ing** : to confine or keep in or as if in a cage

ca·gey *also* **ca·gy** \'kā-jē\ *adj* **ca·gi·er; ca·gi·est** : wary of being trapped or deceived

cais·son \'kā-,sän\ *n* **1** : a chest for ammunition usually mounted on two wheels **2** : a watertight box or chamber used for carrying on construction work under water or as a foundation

caisson 1

ca·jole \kə-'jōl\ *vb* **ca·joled; ca·jol·ing** : to coax or persuade especially by flattery or false promises : WHEEDLE

¹cake \'kāk\ *n* **1** : a small mass of food (as dough or batter, meat, or fish) baked or fried **2** : a baked food made from a mixture of flour, sugar, eggs, and flavoring **3** : a substance hardened or molded into a solid mass

²**cake** *vb* **caked; cak·ing 1** : ENCRUST **2** : to form or harden into a cake

ca·lam·i·ty \kə-'lam-ət-ē\ *n, pl* **ca·lam·i·ties 1** : great distress or misfortune **2** : an event that causes great harm or destruction

cal·ci·um \'kal-sē-əm\ *n* : a silver-white soft metallic chemical element that is an essential part of the bodies of most plants and animals

calcium carbonate *n* : a solid substance that is found as limestone and marble and in plant ashes, bones, and shells

cal·cu·late \'kal-kyə-ˌlāt\ *vb* **cal·cu·lat·ed; cal·cu·lat·ing** [Latin *calculare* "to figure" came from *calculus* "pebble" because pebbles were used in figuring; Latin *calculus*, like English *chalk* and *calcium*, derived from *calx* "limestone", "lime"] **1** : to determine by adding, subtracting, multiplying, or dividing : COMPUTE **2** : ESTIMATE **3** : to plan by careful thought **4** : RELY, DEPEND

cal·cu·lat·ing \'kal-kyə-ˌlāt-ing\ *adj* : marked by shrewd analysis of one's own interest or advantage : SCHEMING

cal·cu·la·tion \ˌkal-kyə-'lā-shən\ *n* **1** : the process or an act of calculating **2** : the result obtained by calculating **3** : CAUTION

cal·cu·la·tor \'kal-kyə-ˌlāt-ər\ *n* **1** : one that calculates **2** : a machine that solves mathematical problems

cal·dron \'kȯl-drən\ *n* : a large kettle or boiler

cal·en·dar \'kal-ən-dər\ *n* **1** : an arrangement of time into days, weeks, months, and years **2** : a sheet, folder, or book containing a record of an arrangement of time (as for a year) **3** : a list or schedule of coming events ⟨a church *calendar*⟩

¹**cal·en·der** \'kal-ən-dər\ *vb* : to press (as cloth or paper) between rollers or plates so as to make smooth or glossy or to thin into sheets

²**calender** *n* : a machine for calendering

¹**calf** \'kaf, 'kȧf\ *n, pl* **calves** \'kavz, 'kȧvz\ **1** : the young of the cow **2** : the young of various large animals (as the elephant, moose, or whale) **3** *pl* **calfs** : CALFSKIN

²**calf** *n, pl* **calves** : the fleshy back part of the leg below the knee

calf·skin \'kaf-ˌskin, 'kȧf-\ *n* : the skin of a calf or the fine leather made from it

cal·i·ber *or* **cal·i·bre** \'kal-ə-bər\ *n* **1** : the diameter of a projectile **2** : the diameter of the bore of a gun **3** : degree of mental ability or moral quality

cal·i·co \'kal-i-ˌkō\ *n, pl* **cal·i·coes** *or* **cal·i·cos** : cotton cloth especially with a colored pattern printed on one side

cal·i·per *or* **cal·li·per** \'kal-ə-pər\ *n* : an instrument with two adjustable legs used to measure the thickness of objects or distances between surfaces — usually used in plural ⟨a pair of *calipers*⟩

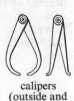

calipers (outside and inside)

ca·liph *or* **ca·lif** \'kā-ləf\ *n* : a successor of Muhammad as temporal and spiritual head of Islam — used as a title

cal·is·then·ics \ˌkal-əs-'then-iks\ *n sing or pl* [formed in English from Greek *kalos* "beautiful" and *sthenos* "strength"] : bodily exercise without apparatus to develop strength and grace

¹**calk** \'kȯk\ *var of* CAULK

²**calk** *n* : a tapered piece projecting downward from a shoe (as of a horse) to prevent slipping

³**calk** *vb* **1** : to furnish with calks **2** : to wound with a calk

¹**call** \'kȯl\ *vb* **1** : to speak in a loud distinct voice so as to be heard at a distance : CRY, SHOUT ⟨*call* for help⟩ **2** : to utter in a loud clear voice ⟨*call* out a command⟩ **3** : to announce with authority : PROCLAIM ⟨*call* a halt⟩ **4** : SUMMON ⟨*call* the children home⟩ **5** : to bring into action or discussion ⟨*call* up reserves⟩ **6** : to make a request or demand ⟨*call* for an investigation⟩ **7** : to get in touch with by telephone : make a telephone call **8** : to make a brief visit ⟨*call* on a neighbor⟩ **9** : to give a name to ⟨*called* him John⟩ **10** : to estimate as being ⟨*call* the distance ten miles⟩ — **call down** : REPRIMAND

²**call** *n* **1** : an act of calling with the voice : SHOUT, CRY **2** : a request or command to come or assemble : INVITATION, SUMMONS **3** : DEMAND, CLAIM **4** : REQUEST ⟨many *calls* for mystery books⟩ **5** : a brief visit ⟨a neighborly *call*⟩ **6** : a name or thing called **7** : the act of calling on the telephone

call·er \'kȯl-ər\ *n* : one that calls **syn** see VISITOR

call·ing \'kȯl-ing\ *n* **1** : a strong inner impulse toward a particular vocation (as the ministry) **2** : a person's customary vocation or profession ⟨follow the *calling* of a doctor⟩

cal·li·o·pe \kə-'lī-ə-pē\ *n* : a musical instrument consisting of a set of whistles played by keys arranged as in an organ

cal·lous \'kal-əs\ *adj* **1** : having a callus : HARDENED **2** : UNFEELING, INDIFFERENT

cal·lus \'kal-əs\ *n* : a hard thickened spot

¹**calm** \'käm\ *n* **1** : a period or condition of freedom from storm, wind, or turbulent water **2** : QUIET, PEACEFULNESS

²**calm** *adj* **1** : marked by calm : STILL ⟨a *calm* night⟩ **2** : free from agitation, excitement, or disturbance ⟨a *calm* reply⟩ — **calm·ly** *adv* — **calm·ness** *n*

³**calm** *vb* : to make or become calm

cal·o·rie *or* **cal·o·ry** \'kal-ə-rē\ *n, pl* **cal·o·ries** **1** : a unit for measuring heat equal to the heat required to raise the temperature of one gram of water one degree centigrade **2** : a unit equal to 1000 calories — used especially to indicate the value of foods for producing heat and energy in the human body

calve \'kav, 'kȧv\ *vb* **calved**; **calv·ing** : to give birth to a calf

calves *pl of* CALF

ca·lyp·so \kə-'lip-sō\ *n, pl* **ca·lyp·sos** : an improvised song usually satirizing current events in a rhythmic style of West Indies origin

ca·lyx \'kā-liks\ *n, pl* **ca·lyx·es** *or* **ca·ly·ces** \-lə-,sēz\ : the outer usually green or leaflike part of a flower made up of sepals

cam \'kȧm\ *n* : a rotating or sliding projection (as on a wheel) for receiving or imparting motion

cam·bi·um \'kam-bē-əm\ *n, pl* **cam·bi·ums** *or* **cam·bi·a** \-bē-ə\ : soft tissue in trees from which new wood and bark grow

came *past of* COME

cam·el \'kam-əl\ *n* : a large hoofed cud‑chewing animal used in the deserts of Asia and Africa for carrying burdens and for riding

cam·er·a \'kam-ə-rə\ *n* **1** : a box that has a lens on one side to let the light in and is used for taking pictures **2** : the part of a television sending apparatus in which the image to be sent out is formed

¹**cam·ou·flage** \'kam-ə-,fläzh\ *n* **1** : the disguising of military equipment or installations with paint, nets, or foliage : DISGUISE **2** : concealment by means of disguise **3** : behavior or a trick intended to deceive or hide

²**camouflage** *vb* **cam·ou·flaged**; **cam·ou·flag·ing** : to protect or disguise by camouflage

¹**camp** \'kamp\ *n* **1** : ground on which temporary shelters are erected **2** : a group of tents or huts **3** : TENT, CABIN **4** : a body of persons encamped

²**camp** *vb* **1** : to make or occupy a camp **2** : to live in a camp or outdoors — **camp·er** *n*

¹**cam·paign** \kam-'pān\ *n* **1** : a series of military operations forming one distinct stage in a war **2** : a series of activities designed to bring about a desired result ⟨an extensive advertising *campaign*⟩

²**campaign** *vb* : to take part in a campaign — **cam·paign·er** *n*

cam·pa·ni·le \,kam-pə-'nē-lē\ *n* : a usually freestanding bell tower

camp fire girl *n* : a member of a national organization for girls from seven to eighteen

cam·phor \'kam-fər\ *n* : a white volatile aromatic solid from the wood and bark of a tall Asiatic tree (**camphor tree**)

cam·po·ree \,kam-pə-'rē\ *n* : a gathering of boy or girl scouts from a given geographic area

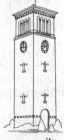

campanile

cam·pus \'kam-pəs\ *n* : the grounds and buildings of a university, college, or school

¹**can** \kən, kan\ *helping verb, past* **could** \kəd, kùd\; *pres sing & pl* **can** **1** : know how to ⟨he *can* read⟩ **2** : be able to ⟨he *can* lift 200 pounds⟩ **3** : be permitted by conscience or feeling to ⟨you *can* hardly blame him⟩ **4** : have permission to : MAY ⟨you *can* go now if you wish⟩

²**can** \'kan\ *n* **1** : a typically cylindrical metal container or receptacle ⟨garbage *can*⟩ **2** : the contents of a can ⟨a *can* of tomatoes⟩

³**can** \'kan\ *vb* **canned**; **can·ning** : to put in a can : preserve by sealing (as in an airtight can)

¹**Ca·na·di·an** \kə-'nād-ē-ən\ *adj* : of or relating to Canada or the Canadians

²**Canadian** *n* : a native or inhabitant of Canada

ca·nal \kə-'nal\ *n* **1** : an artificial waterway for boats or for irrigation of land **2** : a tube-like passage in the body

ca·nar·y \kə-'neər-ē\ *n, pl* **ca·nar·ies** : a small usually yellow songbird raised as a cage bird

can·cel \'kan-səl\ *vb* **can·celed** *or* **can·celled**; **can·cel·ing** *or* **can·cel·ling** **1** : to cross out or strike out with a line : DELETE ⟨*cancel* what has been written⟩ **2** : to wipe out : take back : WITHDRAW **3** : to match in force or effect : OFFSET, BALANCE ⟨a bad deed often *cancels* a good one⟩ **4** : to remove (a common divisor) from numerator and denominator : remove (equivalents) on opposite sides of an equation or account **5** : to deface (as a postage stamp) so as to invalidate for reuse

can·cel·la·tion \,kan-sə-'lā-shən\ *n* **1** : an act of canceling ⟨*cancellation* of a game⟩ **2** : a mark made to cancel something

can·cer \'kan-sər\ *n* : a spreading growth in or on a body often causing death

can·de·la·bra \,kan-də-'lä-brə, -'lab-rə\ *n* : CANDELABRUM

can·de·la·brum \,kan-də-'läbrəm, -'lab-rəm\ *n, pl* **can-**

candelabrum

---

j job   ng sing   ō low   ȯ moth   ȯi coin   th thin   th̲ this   ü boot   ů foot   y you   yü few   yů furious   zh vision de·la·bra \-'lä-brə, -'lab-rə\ *or* can·de·la·brums : a candlestick that has several branches for holding more than one candle

can·did \'kan-dəd\ *adj* 1 : not prejudiced : FAIR, JUST 2 : FRANK, STRAIGHTFORWARD 3 : relating to photography of human subjects acting naturally or spontaneously without being posed — can·did·ly *adv* — can·did·ness *n*

can·di·da·cy \'kan-də-də-sē\ *n, pl* can·di·da·cies : the state of being a candidate

can·di·date \'kan-də-‚dāt\ *n* [from Latin *candidatus*, literally, "one dressed in white" from *candidus* "white"; so called because candidates for office in ancient Rome wore white togas] : a person who offers himself or is proposed by others as a suitable person for an office or honor

can·died \'kan-dēd\ *adj* : preserved in or encrusted with sugar ⟨*candied* ginger⟩

¹can·dle \'kan-dl\ *n* : a stick of tallow or wax containing a wick and burned to give light

²candle *vb* can·dled; can·dling : to examine (as eggs) by holding between the eye and a light — can·dler *n*

can·dle·light \'kan-dl-‚līt\ *n* 1 : the light of a candle 2 : a soft artificial light 3 : the time when candles are lighted : TWILIGHT

can·dle·stick \'kan-dl-‚stik\ *n* : a holder for a candle

can·dor \'kan-dər\ *n* 1 : freedom from prejudice 2 : FRANKNESS, OUTSPOKENNESS

¹can·dy \'kan-dē\ *n, pl* can·dies 1 : crystallized sugar formed by boiling down sugar syrup 2 : a confection made of sugar often with flavoring and filling

²candy *vb* can·died; can·dy·ing 1 : to coat or become coated with sugar often by cooking 2 : to crystallize into sugar 3 : SWEETEN

¹cane \'kān\ *n* 1 : a slender and more or less flexible jointed plant stem 2 : a tall woody grass or reed (as sugarcane) 3 : WALKING STICK 4 : a rod for flogging

²cane *vb* caned; can·ing 1 : to beat with a cane 2 : to make or repair with cane

¹ca·nine \'kā-‚nīn\ *adj* 1 : of or relating to the dogs or to the group of animals (as wolves) to which the dog belongs 2 : resembling or typical of a dog

²canine *n* 1 : a pointed tooth next to the incisors 2 : a canine animal : DOG

can·is·ter \'kan-əs-tər\ *n* : a small box or can for holding a dry product (as tea)

canned \'kand\ *adj* 1 : preserved in a sealed can or jar 2 : recorded for radio or television reproduction

can·ner·y \'kan-ə-rē\ *n, pl* can·ner·ies : a factory where foods are canned

can·ni·bal \'kan-ə-bəl\ *n* 1 : a human being who eats human flesh 2 : an animal that eats other animals of its own kind

can·non \'kan-ən\ *n, pl* can·nons *or* cannon 1 : a heavy gun mounted on a carriage and fired from that position 2 : a heavy-caliber automatic gun on an airplane

can·non·ball \'kan-ən-‚bȯl\ *n* : a usually round solid missile for firing from a cannon

can·not \'kan-‚ät, kə-'nät\ : can not — cannot but : to be bound to : MUST

can·ny \'kan-ē\ *adj* can·ni·er; can·ni·est : watchful of one's own interest : CAUTIOUS — can·ni·ly \'kan-l-ē\ *adv*

¹ca·noe \kə-'nü\ *n* : a long light narrow boat with sharp ends and curved sides usually propelled by paddles

canoe

²canoe *vb* ca·noed; ca·noe·ing : to travel or transport in a canoe — ca·noe·ist *n*

can·on \'kan-ən\ *n* 1 : a rule or law of a church 2 : an official or authoritative list (as of the saints or of the books of the Bible) 3 : an accepted principle or rule ⟨the *canons* of good taste⟩ 4 : a musical composition for two or more voices in which one voice begins and then is imitated by others

can·o·py \'kan-ə-pē\ *n, pl* can·o·pies [originally in English a *canopy* was "a covering used for protection"; it was taken from medieval Latin *canopeum* "netting used to keep out mosquitoes", which came from Greek *kōnōpion*, a derivative of *kōnōps* "mosquito"] 1 : a covering fixed over a bed, throne, or shrine or carried on poles (as over a person of high rank) 2 : an overhanging shade or shelter

canopy 1

cant \'kant\ *n* 1 : the special vocabulary of a trade or profession 2 : insincere speech

can't \kant, kȧnt, kānt\ : can not

can·ta·loupe \'kant-l-‚ōp\ *n* : a muskmelon usually with a hard ridged or warty skin and reddish orange flesh

can·tan·ker·ous \kan-'tang-kə-rəs\ *adj* : ILL-NATURED, QUARRELSOME

can·ta·ta \kən-'tät-ə\ *n* : a poem or narrative set to music to be sung by a chorus and soloists

can·teen \kan-'tēn\ *n* 1 : a store (as in a camp or factory) in which food, drinks, and small supplies are sold 2 : a place of recreation for servicemen 3 : a small container for carrying liquid (as drinking water)

can·ter \'kant-ər\ *n* : a horse's gait resembling but slower than the gallop

can·ti·le·ver \'kant-l-,ē-vər, -,ev-ər\ *n* **1** : a projecting beam or similar structure fastened (as by being built into a wall) only at one end **2** : either of two structures that project from piers toward each other and when joined form a span in a bridge (**cantilever bridge**)

can·to \'kan-,tō\ *n, pl* **can·tos** : one of the major divisions of a long poem

can·ton \'kant-n, 'kan-,tän\ *n* **1** : a small territorial division of a country **2** : one of the political divisions of Switzerland

can·tor \'kant-ər\ *n* : a synagogue official who sings liturgical music and leads the congregation in prayer

can·vas \'kan-vəs\ *n* **1** : a strong cloth of hemp, flax, or cotton that is used for making tents and sails and as the material on which oil paintings are made **2** : something (as an oil painting) made of canvas or on canvas

can·vas·back \'kan-vəs-,bak\ *n* : a North American wild duck with reddish head and grayish back

¹can·vass \'kan-vəs\ *vb* : to go through (a district) or go to (persons) to solicit votes, contributions, or orders for goods or to determine public opinion or sentiment — **can·vass·er** *n*

²canvass *n* : an act of canvassing

can·yon *also* **ca·ñon** \'kan-yən\ *n* : a deep valley with high steep slopes

¹cap \'kap\ *n* **1** : a head covering (as for men and boys) that has a visor and no brim **2** : something that is like a cap in appearance, position, or use (a bottle *cap*) (the *cap* of a fountain pen) **3** : a paper or metal container holding an explosive charge

²cap *vb* **capped**; **cap·ping** **1** : to cover or provide with a cap (*cap* a bottle) **2** : to match with something equal or better

ca·pa·bil·i·ty \,kā-pə-'bil-ət-ē\ *n, pl* **ca·pa·bil·i·ties** **1** : the quality of being capable : CAPACITY, ABILITY **2** : the capacity for an indicated use or development

ca·pa·ble \'kā-pə-bəl\ *adj* **1** : having the ability, capacity, or power to do something **2** : of such a nature as to permit (*capable* of improvement) **3** : EFFICIENT, COMPETENT (a *capable* teacher) — **ca·pa·bly** \-blē\ *adv*

ca·pa·cious \kə-'pā-shəs\ *adj* : SPACIOUS

ca·pac·i·ty \kə-'pas-ət-ē\ *n, pl* **ca·pac·i·ties** **1** : the ability to hold or accommodate (the seating *capacity* of a room) **2** : a measure of content (a *capacity* of one gallon) **3** : POSITION

¹ca·par·i·son \kə-'par-ə-sən\ *n* **1** : an ornamental covering for a horse **2** : the clothing and ornaments worn by a person

²caparison *vb* : to adorn with rich and beautiful clothing

¹cape \'kāp\ *n* : a point of land that juts out into the sea or into a lake

²cape *n* : a sleeveless garment worn so as to hang over the shoulders, arms, and back

¹ca·per \'kā-pər\ *vb* : to leap about in a lively manner : PRANCE, FRISK

²caper *n* **1** : a gay bounding leap or spring **2** : PRANK, TRICK

¹cap·il·lar·y \'kap-ə-,ler-ē\ *adj* **1** : having a slender elongated form and a small bore (a *capillary* tube) **2** : being the action by which the surface of a liquid where it is in contact with a solid (as in a capillary tube) is elevated or depressed **3** : of or relating to a capillary

²capillary *n, pl* **cap·il·lar·ies** : one of the slender hairlike tubes that are the smallest blood vessels and connect arteries with veins

¹cap·i·tal \'kap-ət-l\ *adj* **1** : punishable by or resulting in death (a *capital* crime) (*capital* punishment) **2** : conforming to the series A, B, C, etc. rather than a, b, c, etc. (*capital* letters) **3** : first in importance or influence : CHIEF (the *capital* city of a country) **4** : of or relating to capital **5** : EXCELLENT

²capital *n* **1** : accumulated wealth especially as used to produce more wealth : net assets **2** : the total value of shares of stock issued by a company **3** : INVESTORS, CAPITALISTS **4** : ADVANTAGE, GAIN (they made *capital* out of his weakness) **5** : a capital letter (begin each sentence with a *capital*) **6** : a capital city

³capital *n* : the top part of an architectural column

cap·i·tal·ism \'kap-ət-l-,iz-əm\ *n* : a system under which the ownership of land and wealth is for the most part in the hands of private individuals

¹cap·i·tal·ist \'kap-ət-l-əst\ *n* **1** : a person who has capital and especially business capital **2** : a person who favors capitalism

²capitalist *or* **cap·i·tal·is·tic** \,kap-ət-l-'is-tik\ *adj* **1** : owning capital **2** : practicing or favoring capitalism (*capitalistic* nations) **3** : of or relating to capitalism or capitalists — **cap·i·tal·is·ti·cal·ly** \,kap-ət-l-'is-ti-kə-lē\ *adv*

cap·i·tal·i·za·tion \,kap-ət-l-ə-'zā-shən\ *n* **1** : the act or process of capitalizing **2** : the amount of money used as capital in business

cap·i·tal·ize \'kap-ət-l-,īz\ *vb* **cap·i·tal·ized**; **cap·i·tal·iz·ing** **1** : to write with a beginning capital letter or in capital letters **2** : to use as capital (as in a business) : furnish capital for a business **3** : to gain by turning something to advantage ⟨*capitalize* on another's mistakes⟩

cap·i·tal·ly \'kap-ət-l-ē\ *adv* : in a capital manner ⟨he got along *capitally* in school⟩

cap·i·tol \'kap-ət-l\ *n* **1** : the building in which a state legislature meets **2** *cap* : the building in Washington in which the United States Congress meets

ca·pit·u·late \kə-'pich-ə-ˌlāt\ *vb* **ca·pit·u·lat·ed; ca·pit·u·lat·ing** : to surrender usually on certain terms agreed upon in advance

ca·pon \'kā-ˌpän\ *n* : a castrated male chicken

ca·price \kə-'prēs\ *n* : a sudden unpredictable change in feeling, opinion, or action : WHIM

ca·pri·cious \kə-'prish-əs\ *adj* : moved or controlled by caprice : apt to change suddenly — **ca·pri·cious·ly** *adv* — **ca·pri·cious·ness** *n*

cap·size \'kap-ˌsīz\ *vb* **cap·sized; cap·siz·ing** : to turn over : UPSET ⟨*capsized* a canoe⟩

cap·stan \'kap-stən\ *n* : a mechanical device that consists of an upright revolving drum to which a rope is fastened and that is used especially on ships for moving or raising weights and for exerting pulling force

capstan

cap·sule \'kap-səl\ *n* **1** : a case enclosing the seeds or spores of a plant **2** : a case of edible material (as gelatin) enclosing medicine to be swallowed **3** : a closed compartment for travel in space

¹**cap·tain** \'kap-tən\ *n* **1** : a leader of a group : one in command ⟨the *captain* of a football team⟩ **2** : a commissioned officer in the navy ranking next below a rear admiral or a commodore **3** : a commissioned officer (as in the army) ranking next below a major **4** : the commanding officer of a ship

²**captain** *vb* : to be captain of : LEAD

cap·tion \'kap-shən\ *n* **1** : the heading especially of an article or document : TITLE **2** : the explanatory comment or designation accompanying an illustration or picture (as in a book) **3** : a motion-picture subtitle

cap·ti·vate \'kap-tə-ˌvāt\ *vb* **cap·ti·vat·ed; cap·ti·vat·ing** : to attract and win over : CHARM ⟨music that *captivated* the listeners⟩

¹**cap·tive** \'kap-tiv\ *adj* **1** : taken and held prisoner especially in war **2** : kept within bounds or under control : CONFINED ⟨a *captive* balloon⟩ **3** : of or relating to captivity

²**captive** *n* : one that is captive : PRISONER

cap·tiv·i·ty \kap-'tiv-ət-ē\ *n* : the state of being a prisoner or a captive

cap·tor \'kap-tər\ *n* : one that has captured a person or thing

¹**cap·ture** \'kap-chər\ *n* **1** : the act of capturing **2** : one that has been taken captive

²**capture** *vb* **cap·tured; cap·tur·ing** **1** : to take captive : WIN, GAIN ⟨*capture* a city⟩ **2** : to preserve in a relatively permanent form

car \'kär\ *n* **1** : a vehicle (as a railroad coach) moved on wheels **2** : the cage of an elevator

ca·rafe \kə-'raf\ *n* : a bottle with a flaring lip used to hold water or beverages

car·a·mel \'kar-ə-məl\ *n* **1** : burnt sugar used for coloring and flavoring **2** : a firm chewy candy

car·at \'kar-ət\ *n* : a unit of weight for precious stones equal to 200 milligrams

car·a·van \'kar-ə-ˌvan\ *n* **1** : a group of travelers (as merchants or pilgrims) traveling together on a long journey through desert or hostile regions **2** : a group of vehicles traveling together in a file **3** : VAN

car·a·vel \'kar-ə-ˌvel\ *n* : a small sailing ship of the fifteenth and sixteenth centuries with a broad bow and high stern and three or four masts

caravel

car·a·way \'kar-ə-ˌwā\ *n* : an herb related to the carrots that is grown for its strong-flavored seeds used especially as a seasoning

car·bine \'kär-ˌbēn, -ˌbīn\ *n* : a short light rifle

car·bo·hy·drate \ˌkär-bō-'hī-ˌdrāt\ *n* : an energy-rich nutrient composed of carbon, hydrogen, and oxygen

car·bol·ic acid \ˌkär-ˌbäl-ik-\ *n* : a poison present in coal tar and wood tar that is diluted and used as an antiseptic

car·bon \'kär-bən\ *n* : a chemical element in diamonds and graphite, in coal and petroleum, and in plant and animal bodies

carbon di·ox·ide \-dī-'äk-ˌsīd\ *n* : a heavy colorless gas that is formed by burning of fuels and by decay and that forms the simple raw material from which plants build up more complex compounds for their nourishment

carbon mon·ox·ide \-mə-'näk-ˌsīd\ *n* : a colorless odorless very poisonous gas formed by incomplete burning of carbon

carbon tet·ra·chlo·ride \-ˌtet-rə-'klōr-ˌīd\ *n* : a colorless nonflammable poisonous liquid used as a solvent of grease and as a fire extinguisher

car·bu·re·tor \'kär-bə-ˌrāt-ər\ *n* : the part of a motor or an engine in which liquid fuel (as gasoline) is mixed with air to make it explosive

car·cass \'kär-kəs\ *n* : the body of an animal dressed for meat

¹**card** \'kärd\ *vb* : to cleanse and untangle fibers and especially wool by combing with a card before spinning — **card·er** *n*

²card *n* : an instrument usually having bent wire teeth for combing fibers (as wool)

³card *n* 1 : PLAYING CARD 2 *pl* : a game played with cards 3 : a flat stiff piece of paper or thin pasteboard (as a postcard)

card·board \'kärd-ˌbōrd\ *n* : a stiff moderately thick pasteboard

car·di·ac \'kärd-ē-ˌak\ *adj* : of, relating to, or affecting the heart

¹car·di·nal \'kärd-n-əl\ *adj* : of first importance : MAIN, PRINCIPAL 〈*cardinal* principles〉

²cardinal *n* 1 : a high official of the Roman Catholic Church ranking next below the pope 2 : a bright red crested songbird with a loud whistling warble

cardinal flower *n* : the brilliant red flower of a North American plant that blooms in late summer

car·di·nal·i·ty \ˌkärd-n-'al-ət-ē\ *n, pl* **car·di·nal·i·ties** : the cardinal number of a mathematical sequence

cardinal number *n* : a number (as 1, 5, 22) that is used in simple counting and answers the question "how many?"

cardinal point *n* : one of the four principal points of the compass which are north, south, east, west

¹care \'keər\ *n* 1 : a heavy sense of responsibility : WORRY 〈weighed down by many *cares*〉 2 : serious attention : HEED 〈take *care* in crossing streets〉 3 : PROTECTION, SUPERVISION 〈under a doctor's *care*〉 4 : a person or thing that is the object of one's watchful attention

²care *vb* **cared; car·ing** 1 : to feel anxiety, interest, or concern : be troubled 〈doesn't *care* what happens〉 2 : to give care 〈*care* for the sick〉 3 : to have a liking, fondness, taste, or inclination 〈doesn't *care* for her〉

ca·reer \kə-'riər\ *n* 1 : the course followed or progress made by a person in his occupation or life's work 2 : an occupation or profession followed as a life's work

care·free \'keər-ˌfrē\ *adj* : free from care

care·ful \'keər-fəl\ *adj* 1 : using or taking care : WATCHFUL, CAUTIOUS 〈a *careful* driver〉 2 : made, done, or said with care — **care·ful·ly** *adv* — **care·ful·ness** *n*

syn CAREFUL, CAUTIOUS, WARY all refer to avoiding some kind of trouble. CAREFUL suggests maintaining an alert watchfulness in order to prevent mistakes or mishaps 〈he did *careful* work on his science workbook〉 CAUTIOUS suggests a tendency toward prudence that reduces the risk of future problems or difficulties 〈he was *cautious* in choosing words that wouldn't offend〉 WARY usually refers to an attitude of suspicion and fear of danger

rather than to a way of acting to avoid trouble 〈*wary* of the mountain road〉

care·less \'keər-ləs\ *adj* 1 : CAREFREE 2 : not taking proper care : HEEDLESS 〈a *careless* worker〉 3 : done, made, or said without due care — **care·less·ly** *adv* — **care·less·ness** *n*

¹ca·ress \kə-'res\ *n* : a tender or loving touch or embrace

²caress *vb* : to touch or stroke tenderly or lovingly

care·tak·er \'keər-ˌtā-kər\ *n* : a person who takes care of property for another person

car·fare \'kär-ˌfaər\ *n* : the fare charged for carrying a passenger (as on a streetcar)

car·go \'kär-gō\ *n, pl* **car·goes** *or* **car·gos** : the goods carried in a vehicle (as a ship)

car·i·bou \'kar-ə-ˌbü\ *n* : a large deer of northern and arctic North America that is closely related to the Old World reindeer

car·il·lon \'kar-ə-ˌlän, -lən\ *n* 1 : a set of bells sounded by hammers controlled by a keyboard 2 : a tune for use on a carillon

car·nage \'kär-nij\ *n* : SLAUGHTER

car·na·tion \kär-'nā-shən\ *n* : a showy fragrant usually white, pink, or red garden or greenhouse flower that is related to the pinks

car·ne·lian \kär-'nēl-yən\ *n* : a hard tough reddish quartz used as a gem

car·ni·val \'kär-nə-vəl\ *n* [from Italian *carnevale* "the season of festival before Lent", which was an alteration of earlier Italian *carnelevare*, a compound of *carne* "flesh" and *levare* "to remove"; so called because during Lent many Christians eat meat less often] 1 : a season or festival of merrymaking just before Lent 2 : a noisy merrymaking 3 : a traveling enterprise offering a variety of amusements 4 : an organized program of entertainment 〈a church fair and *carnival*〉

carnation

car·ni·vore \'kär-nə-ˌvōr\ *n* : a carnivorous animal

car·niv·o·rous \kär-'niv-ə-rəs\ *adj* : feeding on the flesh of animals

¹car·ol \'kar-əl\ *n* : a song of joy, praise, or devotion

²carol *vb* **car·oled** *or* **car·olled; car·ol·ing** *or* **car·ol·ling** 1 : to sing in a joyful manner 2 : to sing carols — **car·ol·er** *or* **car·ol·ler** *n*

¹car·om \'kar-əm\ *n* : a rebounding especially at an angle

²carom *vb* : to strike and rebound at an angle

¹carp \'kärp\ *vb* : to find fault

²carp *n* : a long-lived freshwater fish that sometimes weighs as much as forty pounds

car·pel \'kär-pəl\ *n* : one of the ring of parts that form the ovary of a flower

car·pen·ter \'kär-pən-tər\ *n* : a workman who builds or repairs wooden structures

car·pen·try \'kär-pən-trē\ *n* : the work or trade of a carpenter

¹car·pet \'kär-pət\ *n* **1** : a heavy woven fabric used especially as a floor covering **2** : a carpetlike covering ⟨a *carpet* of grass⟩

²carpet *vb* : to cover with or as if with a carpet

car·riage \'kar-ij\ *n* **1** : the act of carrying or being carried ⟨a box damaged in *carriage*⟩ **2** : manner of bearing the body : POSTURE **3** : the price or expense of carrying goods ⟨*carriage* prepaid⟩ **4** : a wheeled vehicle for carrying persons **5** : a wheeled support for carrying a load ⟨a gun *carriage*⟩ **6** : a movable part of a machine that carries or supports some other moving part

car·ri·er \'kar-ē-ər\ *n* **1** : a person or thing that carries ⟨mail *carrier*⟩ **2** : one engaged in transporting passengers or goods **3** : a bearer and transmitter of disease germs

car·ri·on \'kar-ē-ən\ *n* : dead and decaying flesh

car·rot \'kar-ət\ *n* : the yellow tapering edible root of a garden plant

car·ry \'kar-ē\ *vb* **car·ried**; **car·ry·ing** **1** : to take or transfer from one place to another : TRANSPORT, CONVEY ⟨*carry* a package⟩⟨*carry* a number in addition⟩ **2** : SUPPORT, MAINTAIN ⟨pillars that *carry* an arch⟩ **3** : WIN, CAPTURE ⟨*carry* an election⟩ **4** : to contain and direct the course of : CONDUCT ⟨a pipe *carrying* water⟩ **5** : to wear or have on one's person or within one ⟨*carry* a gun⟩ **6** : INVOLVE, IMPLY ⟨*carry* a guarantee⟩ **7** : to hold or bear the body or some part of it ⟨*carry* your head high⟩ **8** : to sing in correct pitch ⟨*carry* a tune⟩ **9** : to keep in stock for sale ⟨the grocer *carries* fresh fish⟩ **10** : PUBLISH ⟨the paper *carries* weather reports⟩ **11** : to penetrate to a distance ⟨his voice *carries* well⟩ — **carry away** : to arouse to a high degree of emotion or enthusiasm — **carry on** **1** : CONDUCT, MANAGE **2** : to behave in a foolish, excited, or improper manner **3** : to continue in spite of handicaps — **carry out** : to put into action or effect

car·ry·all \'kar-ē-ˌol\ *n* : a capacious bag or case

¹cart \'kärt\ *n* **1** : a heavy usually horse-drawn two-wheeled vehicle used for hauling **2** : a light usually two-wheeled vehicle

²cart *vb* : to carry in a cart — **cart·er** *n*

car·ti·lage \'kärt-l-ij\ *n* : an elastic tissue that makes up most of the skeleton of very young animals and is later mostly changed into bone

car·ti·lag·i·nous \ˌkärt-l-'aj-ə-nəs\ *adj* : of or relating to cartilage

car·ton \'kärt-n\ *n* : a cardboard container

car·toon \kär-'tün\ *n* **1** : a drawing or sketch (as in a newspaper) making persons or objects amusing or absurd **2** : COMIC STRIP

car·toon·ist \kär-'tü-nəst\ *n* : a person who draws cartoons

car·tridge \'kär-trij\ *n* **1** : a case or shell filled with an explosive for use in blasting **2** : a case or shell containing gunpowder and a bullet or shot for use in a firearm **3** : a container shaped like a cartridge

cartridge for
a rifle

cartridge for
a shotgun

cart·wheel \'kärt-ˌhwēl\ *n* **1** : a large coin (as a silver dollar) **2** : a sidewise handspring with arms and legs extended that suggests a turning wheel

carve \'kärv\ *vb* **carved**; **carv·ing** **1** : to cut with care especially artistically ⟨*carve* ivory⟩ **2** : to cut into pieces or slices **3** : to slice and serve meat at table — **carv·er** *n*

cas·cade \kas-'kād\ *n* : a steep usually small waterfall

cas·car·a \kas-'kar-ə\ *n* : the dried laxative bark of a western North American shrub

¹case \'kās\ *n* **1** : a particular instance, situation, or example ⟨a *case* of injustice⟩ **2** : a situation or an object requiring investigation, consideration, or action (as by the police) : a question to be settled in a court of law **3** : an inflectional form (as of a noun or pronoun) indicating its grammatical relation to other words **4** : FACT ⟨such is the *case*⟩ **5** : a convincing argument **6** : an instance of disease or injury ⟨a *case* of measles⟩ **7** : PATIENT

²case *n* **1** : a receptacle (as a box) for holding something **2** : a box and its contents ⟨a *case* of books⟩ **3** : an outer covering or housing **4** : the frame of a door or window

ca·sein \kā-'sēn\ *n* : a whitish to yellowish substance produced from milk especially by the action of acid and used in making paints and plastics

case·ment \'kās-mənt\ *n* **1** : a window sash opening on hinges **2** : a window with a casement

¹cash \'kash\ *n* **1** : ready money : CURRENCY **2** : money or its equivalent (as a check) paid for goods at the time of purchase or delivery

²cash *vb* : to pay or obtain cash for ⟨the bank will *cash* your check⟩

casement 2

cash·ew \'kash-ü\ *n* : the kidney-shaped edible nut of a tropical American tree

¹**cash·ier** \kash-'iər\ *n* : a person who has charge of money (as in a bank or business concern)

²**ca·shier** *vb* : to dismiss from service and especially in disgrace

cash·mere \'kazh-,miər, 'kash-\ *n* : a soft yarn or fabric originally made from the fine wool of an Indian goat

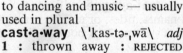

cashew: leaves, fruit, and nuts

cas·ing \'kā-sing\ *n* : something that encases

cask \'kask\ *n* **1** : a barrel-shaped container usually for liquids **2** : the amount contained in a cask

cas·ket \'kas-kət\ *n* **1** : a small box or chest (as for jewels) **2** : COFFIN

casque \'kask\ *n* : HELMET

cas·sa·va \kə-'sä-və\ *n* : a tropical plant with a fleshy edible root

cas·se·role \'kas-ə-,rōl\ *n* **1** : a covered dish in which food can be baked and served **2** : the food cooked and served in a casserole

cas·so·war·y \'kas-ə-,wer-ē\ *n, pl* **cas·so·war·ies** : a tall swift-running Australian bird with hairlike feathers and useless wings

¹**cast** \'kast\ *vb* **cast**; **cast·ing** **1** : THROW, FLING ⟨*cast* a stone⟩ ⟨*cast* a fishing line⟩ **2** : to throw out, off, or away : SHED, DISCARD ⟨snakes *cast* their skins⟩ **3** : DIRECT ⟨*cast* a glance⟩ ⟨*cast* doubt on his honesty⟩ **4** : to deposit formally ⟨*cast* a ballot⟩ **5** : ADD, COMPUTE ⟨*cast* a horoscope⟩ **6** : to assign actors or parts to actors for a play ⟨*cast* as the hero⟩ **7** : to give a special form to liquid material by pouring it into a mold and letting it harden : MOLD ⟨*cast* a statue in bronze⟩ ⟨*cast* steel⟩ **8** : to make by looping or catching up ⟨*cast* on fifty stitches⟩ — **cast about** : to search here and there — **cast lots** : to draw lots to determine a matter by chance

²**cast** *n* **1** : an act of casting : THROW, FLING **2** : the form in which a thing is constructed **3** : the characters or the actors in a play or story **4** : the distance to which a thing can be thrown **5** : a glance of the eyes : EXPRESSION **6** : something formed by casting in a mold or form ⟨a bronze *cast* of Lincoln⟩ **7** : a stiff surgical dressing of plaster hardened around a part of the body ⟨had a *cast* on his broken leg⟩ **8** : a tinge of color : SHADE ⟨a bluish *cast*⟩ **9** : SHAPE, APPEARANCE ⟨the sad *cast* of his face⟩ **10** : something (as the skin of an insect) thrown out or off, shed, or ejected

cas·ta·net \,kas-tə-'net\ *n* : a rhythm instrument that consists of two small ivory, wooden, or plastic shells fastened to the thumb and clicked by the fingers in accompaniment to dancing and music — usually used in plural

castanets

¹**cast·a·way** \'kas-tə-,wā\ *adj* **1** : thrown away : REJECTED **2** : cast adrift or ashore

²**castaway** *n* **1** : one that has been cast away or rejected **2** : a shipwrecked person

caste \'kast\ *n* **1** : one of the classes into which the people of India have been divided from the earliest times **2** : a division or class of society based on wealth, rank, or occupation **3** : social position : PRESTIGE

cast·er \'kas-tər\ *n* **1** : a person or thing that casts **2** : a small container (as for salt or pepper) with a perforated top **3** *or* **cas·tor** \'kas-tər\ : a small free-turning wheel used for supporting furniture

cas·ti·gate \'kas-tə-,gāt\ *vb* **cas·ti·gat·ed**; **cas·ti·gat·ing** : to punish or correct with words or blows

caster 3

cast·ing \'kas-ting\ *n* **1** : the act of a person or a thing that casts **2** : something that is cast in a mold ⟨a bronze *casting*⟩ **3** : something (as skin or feathers) that is cast out or off

cast iron *n* : a hard and brittle alloy of iron, carbon, and silicon shaped by being poured into a mold while it is molten

cas·tle \'kas-əl\ *n* **1** : a large fortified building or group of buildings usually having high walls with towers and a surrounding moat **2** : a large or imposing building **3** : ³ROOK

cast–off \'kast-,óf\ *adj* : DISCARDED

cast·off *n* : a cast-off person or thing

cas·tor oil \'kas-tər-\ *n* : a thick yellowish liquid extracted from the seeds (**castor beans**) of a tropical herb and used as a lubricant and as a cathartic

cas·trate \'kas-,trāt\ *vb* **cas·trat·ed**; **cas·trat·ing** : to deprive of the sex glands

ca·su·al \'kazh-ə-wəl\ *adj* **1** : happening unexpectedly or by chance : not planned or foreseen ⟨a *casual* meeting⟩ **2** : occurring without regularity : OCCASIONAL **3** : showing or feeling little concern : OFFHAND, NONCHALANT **4** : designed for informal use — **ca·su·al·ly** *adv*

ca·su·al·ty \'kazh-əl-tē\ *n, pl* **ca·su·al·ties** **1** : serious or fatal accident : DISASTER **2** : a military person lost (as by death) during warfare **3** : a person or thing injured, lost, or destroyed **4** : injury or death from accident

cat \'kat\ *n* **1** : a common furry flesh-eating

animal kept as a pet or for catching mice and rats **2** : any of the group of mammals (as lions, tigers, lynxes, and wildcats) to which the domestic cat belongs **3** : a malicious woman **4** : CAT-O'-NINE-TAILS

¹**cat·a·log** *or* **cat·a·logue** \'kat-l-ˌȯg\ *n* **1** : a list of names, titles, or articles arranged according to a system **2** : a book or file containing a catalog

²**catalog** *or* **catalogue** *vb* **1** : to make a catalog of **2** : to enter in a catalog — **cat·a·log·er** *or* **cat·a·logu·er** *n*

ca·tal·pa \kə-'tal-pə\ *n* : a broad-leaved tree of America and Asia bearing long pods

¹**cat·a·pult** \'kat-ə-ˌpəlt\ *n* **1** : an ancient military machine for hurling missiles (as stones and arrows) **2** : a device for launching an airplane from the deck of a ship **3** : SLINGSHOT

catapult 1

²**catapult** *vb* **1** : to throw or launch by or as if by a catapult **2** : to become catapulted

ca·tarrh \kə-'tär\ *n* : inflammation of mucous membrane especially when chronic

ca·tas·tro·phe \kə-'tas-trə-fē\ *n* **1** : a sudden calamity **2** : utter failure or ruin

cat·bird \'kat-ˌbərd\ *n* : a dark gray songbird that has a call like a cat's mewing

cat·boat \'kat-ˌbōt\ *n* : a sailboat with a single mast set far forward and a single large sail with a long boom

cat·call \'kat-ˌkȯl\ *n* : a sound like the cry of a cat or a noise expressing disapproval (as at a sports event)

catboat

¹**catch** \'kach\ *vb* **caught** \'kȯt\; **catch·ing** **1** : to capture or seize something in flight or motion **2** : to discover unexpectedly ⟨*caught* in the act⟩ **3** : to check suddenly **4** : to take hold of ⟨*catch* a ball⟩ **5** : to get entangled ⟨*catch* a sleeve on a nail⟩ **6** : to hold firmly : FASTEN ⟨a lock that will not *catch*⟩ **7** : to become seized or affected by ⟨*catch* fire⟩ ⟨*catch* a cold⟩ **8** : to take or get briefly or quickly ⟨*catch* a glimpse of a friend⟩ **9** : to be in time for : OVERTAKE ⟨*catch* the next bus⟩ **10** : to grasp by the senses or the mind **11** : to play catcher on a baseball team

²**catch** *n* **1** : something caught : the total quantity caught at one time ⟨a *catch* of fish⟩ **2** : the act of catching **3** : a game in which a ball is thrown and caught **4** : something that checks, fastens, or holds immovable ⟨a *catch*

on a door⟩ **5** : a round for three or more voices **6** : a concealed difficulty

catch·er \'kach-ər\ *n* **1** : a person or thing that catches **2** : a baseball player who plays behind home plate

catch·ing \'kach-ing\ *adj* **1** : INFECTIOUS, CONTAGIOUS **2** : ALLURING, CATCHY

catch·y \'kach-ē\ *adj* **catch·i·er; catch·i·est** **1** : likely to attract ⟨*catchy* music⟩ **2** : TRICKY

cat·e·chism \'kat-ə-ˌkiz-əm\ *n* **1** : a series of questions and answers used in giving instruction and especially religious instruction **2** : a set of formal questions

cat·e·go·ry \'kat-ə-ˌgōr-ē\ *n, pl* **cat·e·go·ries** : a class or division of things : KIND, VARIETY

ca·ter \'kāt-ər\ *vb* **1** : to provide a supply of food ⟨*cater* for parties⟩ **2** : to supply what is needed — **ca·ter·er** *n*

cat·er·pil·lar \'kat-ər-ˌpil-ər\ *n* [from Old French (northern dialect) *catepelose*, literally, "hairy cat"] : a wormlike often hairy larva of an insect (as a moth or butterfly)

cat·fish \'kat-ˌfish\ *n* : any of a group of usually large-headed fishes with feelers about the mouth

cat·gut \'kat-ˌgət\ *n* : a tough cord made from intestines of animals (as sheep) and used for strings of musical instruments and rackets and for sewing in surgery

ca·thar·tic \kə-'thärt-ik\ *n* : a strong laxative

ca·the·dral \kə-'thē-drəl\ *n* : the principal church of a district headed by a bishop

cath·o·lic \'kath-ə-lik\ *adj* **1** : general in scope : UNIVERSAL ⟨a man of *catholic* interests⟩ **2** *cap* : of or relating to the church of which the pope is head : Roman Catholic

Catholic *n* **1** : a member of a Christian church tracing its history back to the apostles **2** : a member of the Roman Catholic Church

cat·kin \'kat-kən\ *n* : a flower cluster (as of the willow and birch) in which the flowers grow in close circular rows along a slender stalk

cat·like \'kat-ˌlīk\ *adj* : resembling a cat : STEALTHY

cat·nap \'kat-ˌnap\ *n* : a very short light nap

catkins of birch tree

cat·nip \'kat-ˌnip\ *n* : a common plant of the mint family relished by cats

cat-o'-nine-tails \ˌkat-ə-'nīn-ˌtālz\ *n, pl* **cat-o'-nine-tails** : a whip made of nine knotted cords fastened to a handle

cat·sup \'kech-əp, 'kat-səp\ *n* : a seasoned sauce (as for meat) usually made of tomatoes

cat·tail \'kat-ˌtāl\ *n* : a tall marsh plant with long flat leaves and long furry spikes

cat·tle \'kat-l\ *n, pl* **cattle** : domesticated four-footed animals and especially cows, bulls, and calves that are kept as property

cat·walk \'kat-ˌwȯk\ *n* : a narrow walk or way (as along a bridge)

caught *past of* CATCH

caul·dron *var of* CALDRON

cau·li·flow·er \'kȯl-ə-ˌflau̇-ər\ *n* : a plant closely related to the cabbage that is grown for its edible white head of undeveloped flowers

¹caulk \'kȯk\ *vb* : to fill up a crack, seam, or joint so as to make it watertight

²caulk *var of* CALK

¹cause \'kȯz\ *n* **1** : a person or thing that brings about a result ⟨carelessness is the *cause* of many accidents⟩ **2** : a good or sufficient reason or ground for something ⟨a *cause* for rejoicing⟩ **3** : a matter or question to be decided **4** : something supported or deserving support ⟨a worthy *cause*⟩

syn CAUSE, REASON, MOTIVE all mean the explanation for an event or condition. CAUSE is the general term and can apply to anything that brings about or helps bring about a result ⟨investigated the *cause* of the disturbance⟩ REASON applies to a traceable or explainable cause of a particular result ⟨give the *reason* for your absence⟩ MOTIVE applies to the cause of a voluntary action and usually involves emotions or desires ⟨winning the scholarship was his *motive* for studying so hard⟩

²cause *vb* **caused; caus·ing** : to be the cause of

cause·way \'kȯz-ˌwā\ *n* : a raised road or way across wet ground or water

caus·tic \'kȯs-tik\ *adj* **1** : capable of destroying or eating away by chemical action : BURNING **2** : SHARP, BITING ⟨a *caustic* remark⟩

¹cau·tion \'kȯ-shən\ *n* **1** : WARNING **2** : carefulness in regard to danger : PRECAUTION

²caution *vb* : to advise caution to : WARN

cau·tious \'kȯ-shəs\ *adj* : CAREFUL, PRUDENT **syn** see CAREFUL — **cau·tious·ly** *adv*

cav·al·cade \ˌkav-əl-'kād\ *n* **1** : a procession of riders or carriages **2** : PAGEANT

¹cav·a·lier \ˌkav-ə-'liər\ *n* **1** : a mounted soldier **2** : a gay and gallant gentleman

²cavalier *adj* **1** : gay and easy in manner **2** : HAUGHTY, DISDAINFUL

cav·al·ry \'kav-əl-rē\ *n, pl* **cav·al·ries** : troops mounted on horseback or moving in motor vehicles

cav·al·ry·man \'kav-əl-rē-mən\ *n, pl* **cav·al·ry·men** \-mən\ : a cavalry soldier

cattails

¹cave \'kāv\ *n* : a hollowed-out place in the earth or in the side of a hill

²cave *vb* **caved; cav·ing** : to fall or cause to fall in or down : COLLAPSE ⟨the mine *caved* in⟩

cave·man \'kāv-ˌman\ *n, pl* **cave·men** \-ˌmen\ : an inhabitant of a cave especially during the Stone Age

cav·ern \'kav-ərn\ *n* : an underground chamber often of large or indefinite extent : CAVE

cav·ern·ous \'kav-ər-nəs\ *adj* **1** : having caverns or cavities **2** : of, relating to, or resembling a cavern ⟨a *cavernous* cellar⟩

cav·i·ty \'kav-ət-ē\ *n, pl* **cav·i·ties** : a hollow place : HOLE ⟨a *cavity* in a tooth⟩

ca·vort \kə-'vȯrt\ *vb* : to bound or frisk about

ca·vy \'kā-vē\ *n, pl* **ca·vies** : GUINEA PIG

¹caw \'kȯ\ *vb* : to utter a caw

²caw *n* : the cry of a crow or a raven

cay·enne pepper \ˌkī-'en-, ˌkā-'en-\ *n* : dried ripe hot peppers ground for use as seasoning

cay·use \'kī-ˌüs\ *n* : a native range horse of the western United States

cease \'sēs\ *vb* **ceased; ceas·ing** : to come or bring to an end : STOP, DISCONTINUE

cease·less \'sēs-ləs\ *adj* : CONSTANT

ce·cro·pi·a moth \si-ˌkrō-pē-ə-\ *n* : a silkworm moth that is the largest moth of the eastern United States

ce·dar \'sēd-ər\ *n* : any of a number of cone-bearing trees having fragrant durable wood

cede \'sēd\ *vb* **ced·ed; ced·ing** **1** : to yield or give up especially by treaty ⟨territory *ceded* by one country to another⟩ **2** : ASSIGN, TRANSFER

cedar: twigs bearing scalelike leaves and cones

ceil·ing \'sē-ling\ *n* **1** : the overhead inside lining of a room **2** : something that overhangs like a shelter **3** : the greatest height at which an airplane can operate efficiently **4** : the height above the ground of the base of the lowest layer of clouds **5** : a figure (as for rent, goods, or services) set as an upper limit

cel·e·brate \'sel-ə-ˌbrāt\ *vb* **cel·e·brat·ed; cel·e·brat·ing** **1** : to perform publicly and according to a certain rule or form ⟨*celebrate* Mass⟩ **2** : to observe in some special way (as by merrymaking or by staying away from business) **3** : PRAISE

cel·e·brat·ed \'sel-ə-ˌbrāt-əd\ *adj* : FAMOUS, RENOWNED

cel·e·bra·tion \ˌsel-ə-'brā-shən\ *n* **1** : the act of celebrating **2** : the activities or ceremonies for celebrating a special occasion

---

j job　**ng** sing　**ō** low　**ȯ** moth　**ȯi** coin　**th** thin　**th** this　**ü** boot　**u̇** foot　**y** you　**yü** few　**yu̇** furious　**zh** vision

ce·leb·ri·ty \sə-'leb-rət-ē\ *n, pl* **ce·leb·ri·ties**
1 : FAME **2** : a celebrated person

ce·ler·i·ty \sə-'ler-ət-ē\ *n* : rapidity of motion

cel·er·y \'sel-ə-rē\ *n* : a garden plant related
to the carrots and grown for its thick crisp
edible leafstalks

ce·les·ta \sə-'les-tə\ *n* : a keyboard instrument giving its tones from steel plates struck
by hammers

ce·les·tial \sə-'les-chəl\ *adj* **1** : of or relating
to the sky **2** : HEAVENLY, DIVINE

cell \'sel\ *n* **1** : a very small room or compartment (as in a prison or a monastery)
2 : a small enclosed part or division (as in a
honeycomb) **3** : a small mass of living matter
that consists of protoplasm, includes a nucleus, is enclosed in a membrane, and is the
structural unit of which all plants and animals
are made up **4** : a container with substances
prepared for generating an electric current by
chemical action or for use in electrolysis —
celled \'seld\ *adj*

cel·lar \'sel-ər\ *n* : a room or set of rooms
below the surface of the ground : BASEMENT

cel·list \'chel-əst\ *n* : a person who plays the
cello

cel·lo \'chel-ō\ *n, pl* **cel·los** : a stringed instrument like the violin but much larger and with
a deeper tone : VIOLONCELLO

cel·lo·phane \'sel-ə-ˌfān\ *n* : a thin transparent material made from cellulose and used
as a wrapping

cel·lu·lar \'sel-yə-lər\ *adj* : of, relating to, or
made up of cells (*cellular* tissue)

cel·lu·lose \'sel-yə-ˌlōs\ *n* : a substance that
is the chief part of the solid framework or cell
walls of plants, is commonly obtained as a
white fibrous substance (as from wood or cotton), and is used in making various products

Cel·si·us \'sel-sē-əs\ *adj* : CENTIGRADE

¹ce·ment \si-'ment\ *n* **1** : a powder that is
produced essentially from compounds of
aluminum, calcium, silicon, and iron heated
together and then ground, that combines with
water and hardens into a mass, and that is
used in mortar and concrete **2** : CONCRETE,
MORTAR **3** : a substance that by hardening
sticks things together firmly

²cement *vb* **1** : to join together with or as if
with cement **2** : to cover with concrete

cem·e·tery \'sem-ə-ˌter-ē\ *n, pl* **cem·e·ter·ies**
: a burial ground : GRAVEYARD

Ce·no·zo·ic \ˌsē-nə-'zō-ik\ *n* : an era of
geological history that extends from 70,000,000
years ago to the present time and is marked by
a rapid evolution of mammals and birds and
of flowering plants

cen·ser \'sen-sər\ *n* : a container in which
incense is burned

¹cen·sor \'sen-sər\ *n* : an official
who examines written or printed
matter or motion pictures in order to
prevent the publication or distribution of something considered objectionable

censer

²censor *vb* : to examine (as a book)
for the purpose of suppressing or removing
something considered harmful or dangerous
  syn CENSOR, CENSURE are not synonyms but
are frequently confused. CENSOR usually applies to written works that are thought to need
change or suppression (letters to or from
prisoners are *censored*) (*censored* the script
deleting references to the dictator) CENSURE
usually applies to people who are thought to
need adverse and usually public or official
criticism (the senate may *censure* a member for
misconduct)

¹cen·sure \'sen-chər\ *n* **1** : the act of finding
fault with, blaming, or condemning : unfriendly criticism **2** : an official reprimand

²censure *vb* **cen·sured**; **cen·sur·ing** : to find
fault with **syn** see CENSOR

cen·sus \'sen-səs\ *n* : an official count of the
population of a country, city, or town usually
with information about economic, educational, and social conditions

cent \'sent\ *n* [from Latin *centum* "hundred"]
1 : a hundredth part of the unit of the money
system in a number of different countries (in
the United States 100 *cents* equal one dollar)
2 : a coin, token, or note representing one cent

cen·taur \'sen-ˌtȯr\ *n* : a creature in Greek
mythology that was part man and part horse

cen·te·nar·i·an \ˌsent-n-'er-ē-ən\ *n* : a person
100 or more years old

¹cen·ten·ni·al \sen-'ten-ē-əl\ *n* : a 100th anniversary or a celebration of this event

²centennial *adj* : relating to a period of 100
years

¹cen·ter \'sent-ər\ *n* **1** : the middle point of a
circle or a sphere equally distant from every
point of the circumference **2** : the middle
point or part of something (the *center* of a
room) **3** : a point at which things meet or
from which they proceed **4** : a player occupying a middle position on a team

²center *vb* **1** : to place or fix at or around a
center or central area **2** : to collect at or
around one point

center of gravity : the point at which the entire weight of a body may be considered as
concentrated so that if supported at this point
the body would balance perfectly

cen·ter·piece \'sent-ər-ˌpēs\ *n* : a piece put in the center of something and especially an adornment (as flowers) for the table

centi- *prefix* : hundredth part ⟨*centi*meter⟩ — used in terms of the metric system

cen·ti·grade \'sent-ə-ˌgrād\ *adj* : relating to, conforming to, or having a thermometer scale on which the interval between the freezing point and the boiling point of water is divided into 100 degrees with 0° representing the freezing point and 100° the boiling point

cen·ti·gram \'sent-ə-ˌgram\ *n* : a unit of weight equal to 1/100 gram

cen·ti·li·ter \'sent-ə-ˌlēt-ər\ *n* : a unit of liquid capacity equal to 1/100 liter

cen·ti·me·ter \'sent-ə-ˌmēt-ər\ *n* : a unit of length equal to 1/100 meter

cen·ti·pede \'sent-ə-ˌpēd\ *n* : a small long= bodied many-legged animal related to the insects

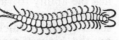

centipede

¹cen·tral \'sen-trəl\ *adj* **1** : containing or constituting the center : equally distant from certain points **2** : CHIEF, LEADING ⟨the *central* person in a story⟩ **3** : situated at, in, or near the center **4** : centrally placed to take the place of separate scattered units ⟨*central* heating⟩ — **cen·tral·ly** *adv*

²central *n* : a telephone exchange or operator

¹Central American *adj* : of or relating to Central America or the Central Americans

²Central American *n* : a native or inhabitant of Central America

cen·tral·i·za·tion \ˌsen-trə-lə-'zā-shən\ *n* : the act or process of centralizing

cen·tral·ize \'sen-trə-ˌlīz\ *vb* **cen·tral·ized; cen·tral·iz·ing** : to bring to a central point or under a single control

cen·trif·u·gal force \sen-ˌtrif-yə-gəl-\ *n* : the force that tends to cause a thing or parts of a thing to go outward from a center of rotation

cen·tu·ry \'sen-chə-rē\ *n, pl* **cen·tu·ries** : a period of 100 years

ce·ram·ic \sə-'ram-ik\ *n* **1** *pl* : the art of making things (as pottery or tiles) of baked clay **2** : a product produced by ceramics

¹ce·re·al \'sir-ē-əl\ *adj* [from Latin *cerealis*, literally, "of Ceres", from *Ceres*, goddess of agriculture in Roman mythology] **1** : relating to grain or the plants that produce it **2** : made of grain

²cereal *n* **1** : a plant (as a grass) that yields edible grain **2** : a food prepared from grain

cer·e·bel·lum \ˌser-ə-'bel-əm\ *n, pl* **cer·e·bel·lums** *or* **cer·e·bel·la** \-'bel-ə\ : a part of the brain concerned especially with the coordina-

tion of muscles and with keeping the body properly oriented

ce·re·bral \sə-'rē-brəl, 'ser-ə-brəl\ *adj* **1** : of or relating to the brain or mind **2** : of, relating to, or affecting the cerebrum

ce·re·brum \sə-'rē-brəm, 'ser-ə-brəm\ *n, pl* **ce·re·brums** *or* **ce·re·bra** \-brə\ : the enlarged front and upper part of the brain that is the center of higher and conscious mental activity

¹cer·e·mo·ni·al \ˌser-ə-'mō-nē-əl\ *adj* : of, relating to, or forming a ceremony

²ceremonial *n* : a ceremonial act, action, or system : RITUAL

cer·e·mo·ni·ous \ˌser-ə-'mō-nē-əs\ *adj* **1** : CEREMONIAL **2** : careful to observe forms and ceremonies — **cer·e·mo·ni·ous·ly** *adv*

cer·e·mo·ny \'ser-ə-ˌmō-nē\ *n, pl* **cer·e·mo·nies 1** : an act or series of acts performed in some regular order as required by law or settled by custom **2** : a conventional act of politeness or etiquette **3** : FORMALITY

ce·rise \sə-'rēs\ *n* : a moderate red

¹cer·tain \'sərt-n\ *adj* **1** : FIXED, SETTLED ⟨received a *certain* percentage of the profit⟩ **2** : proved to be true **3** : of a specific but unspecified character : PARTICULAR ⟨a *certain* town in Maine⟩ **4** : DEPENDABLE, RELIABLE ⟨a *certain* cure⟩ **5** : INDISPUTABLE, UNDENIABLE **6** : DESTINED ⟨*certain* to happen⟩ **7** : assured in mind or action — **cer·tain·ly** *adv*

²certain *pron* : certain ones

cer·tain·ty \'sərt-n-tē\ *n, pl* **cer·tain·ties 1** : something that is certain **2** : the quality or state of being certain ⟨answered with *certainty*⟩

cer·tif·i·cate \sər-'tif-i-kət\ *n* **1** : a written or printed statement testifying to the truth of something ⟨a vaccination *certificate*⟩ **2** : a document certifying that a person has fulfilled certain requirements (as of a school) **3** : a document showing ownership or debt

cer·ti·fi·ca·tion \ˌsərt-ə-fə-'kā-shən\ *n* **1** : the act of certifying : the state of being certified **2** : a certified statement

cer·ti·fy \'sərt-ə-ˌfī\ *vb* **cer·ti·fied; cer·ti·fy·ing 1** : VERIFY, CONFIRM ⟨*certify* a student for admission to a college⟩ **2** : to guarantee officially the quality or fitness of ⟨*certified* milk⟩ **3** : to guarantee a bank check as good by a statement to that effect stamped on its face

ce·ru·le·an \sə-'rü-lē-ən\ *adj* : somewhat resembling the blue of the sky

ces·sa·tion \se-'sā-shən\ *n* : CEASING

chafe \'chāf\ *vb* **chafed; chaf·ing 1** : IRRITATE, VEX **2** : to be irritated : FRET **3** : to warm by rubbing ⟨*chafed* his hands⟩ **4** : to rub so as to wear away or make sore

¹chaff \'chaf\ *n* **1** : the husks of grains and grasses separated from the seed in threshing **2** : something light and worthless

²chaff *n* : light jesting talk : BANTER

³chaff *vb* : to tease good-naturedly : BANTER

cha·grin \shə-'grin\ *n* : a feeling of annoyance caused by failure or disappointment

¹chain \'chān\ *n* **1** : a series of links or rings usually of metal **2** : something that confines or binds : BOND ⟨the *chains* of habit⟩ **3** : a series of things joined together as if by links ⟨a *chain* of mountains⟩ ⟨a *chain* of events⟩

chains 1

²chain *vb* : to fasten, bind, or connect with or as if with a chain

chair \'cheər\ *n* **1** : a seat with legs and a back for use by one person **2** : an official seat or a seat of authority or dignity ⟨take the *chair* at a meeting⟩ **3** : an office or position of authority or dignity **4** : CHAIRMAN

chair·man \'cheər-mən\ *n*, *pl* **chair·men** \-mən\ : an official who presides at a meeting — **chair·man·ship** \-ˌship\ *n*

chaise longue \'shāz-'lòng\ *n* : a long couch-like chair

chaise lounge \'shāz-'laùnj\ *n* : CHAISE LONGUE

cha·let \sha-'lā\ *n* **1** : a remote herdsman's hut in the Alps **2** : a Swiss dwelling with a wide roof overhang **3** : a cottage in chalet style

chalet 2

chal·ice \'chal-əs\ *n* : a drinking cup : GOBLET

¹chalk \'chòk\ *n* **1** : a soft white, gray, or buff limestone chiefly composed of very small sea shells **2** : a material like chalk especially when used in the form of a crayon

²chalk *vb* **1** : to rub, mark, write, or draw with chalk **2** : to record or add up with chalk

chalk·board \'chòk-ˌbòrd\ *n* : BLACKBOARD

chalk·y \'chòk-ē\ *adj* **chalk·i·er; chalk·i·est 1** : consisting of or characterized by chalk **2** : POWDERY **3** : having the color of chalk

¹chal·lenge \'chal-ənj\ *vb* **chal·lenged; chal·leng·ing 1** : to halt and demand a password from **2** : to take exception to : object to : DISPUTE **3** : to question the legality or legal qualifications of ⟨*challenge* a vote⟩ **4** : to invite to a contest : DARE, DEFY ⟨*challenged* him to a game of tennis⟩ — **chal·leng·er** *n*

²challenge *n* **1** : an exception taken to something as not being true, genuine, accurate, or justified or to a person (as a juror) as not being qualified or acceptable : PROTEST **2** : a sentry's demand to halt and prove identity

3 : a summons to a duel **4** : an invitation to compete in a contest or sport

cham·ber \'chām-bər\ *n* **1** : a room in a house and especially a bedroom **2** : an enclosed space, cavity, or compartment (as in a gun) **3** : a meeting hall of a government body (as an assembly) **4** : a room where a judge transacts business out of court **5** : the reception room of a person of rank or authority **6** : a group of people organized into a lawmaking body **7** : a voluntary board or council (as of businessmen)

cham·ber·lain \'chām-bər-lən\ *n* **1** : a chief officer in the household of a king or nobleman **2** : TREASURER ⟨city *chamberlain*⟩

cham·ber·maid \'chām-bər-ˌmād\ *n* : a maid who takes care of bedrooms (as in a hotel)

cha·me·leon \kə-'mēl-yən\ *n* : a lizard that has the ability to vary the color of its skin

cham·ois \'sham-ē\ *n*, *pl* **cham·ois** \-ē,-ēz\ **1** : a small goatlike antelope living on the highest mountains of Europe and Asia **2** : a soft yellowish leather made from the skin of the chamois or from sheepskin

chamois

¹champ \'champ\ *vb* **1** : to bite and chew noisily ⟨a horse *champing* his bit⟩ **2** : to show impatience of delay or restraint

²champ *n* : CHAMPION

¹cham·pi·on \'cham-pē-ən\ *n* **1** : a person who fights or speaks in behalf of another person or in behalf of a cause : DEFENDER **2** : a person formally acknowledged as better than all others in a sport or in a game of skill **3** : a person or a thing winning first place

²champion *vb* : to protect or fight for as a champion : DEFEND

cham·pi·on·ship \'cham-pē-ən-ˌship\ *n* **1** : the act of defending as a champion **2** : the position or title of champion **3** : a contest held to determine a champion

¹chance \'chans\ *n* **1** : the way in which things take place : the happening of events : FORTUNE ⟨occurred by *chance*⟩ **2** : OPPORTUNITY ⟨had a *chance* to travel⟩ **3** : RISK, GAMBLE ⟨take *chances*⟩ **4** : PROBABILITY **5** : a ticket in a raffle

²chance *vb* **chanced; chanc·ing 1** : to take place by chance : HAPPEN **2** : to come casually and unexpectedly ⟨*chanced* upon an old friend⟩ **3** : to leave to chance : RISK

³chance *adj* : happening by chance

chan·cel·lor \'chan-sə-lər\ *n* **1** : a high state official in various countries : the chief minister of state in some European countries

2 : the head of some universities **3** : a chief judge in some courts — **chan·cel·lor·ship** \-ₚship\ *n*

chan·de·lier \ₚshan-də-'liər\ *n* : a branched candlestick or lighting fixture that usually hangs from the ceiling

¹**change** \'chānj\ *vb* **changed; chang·ing** **1** : to make or become different : alter or be altered ⟨*change* the looks of a room⟩ ⟨*changing* autumn leaves⟩ **2** : to give a different position, course, or direction to : REVERSE ⟨*changed* his vote⟩ **3** : to replace with another : SWITCH, EXCHANGE ⟨*change* places⟩ **4** : to give or receive an equivalent sum in notes or coins of usually smaller denominations or of another currency ⟨*change* a ten-dollar bill⟩ **5** : to put fresh clothes or covering on ⟨*change* a bed⟩ **6** : to put on different clothes

²**change** *n* **1** : the act, process, or result of changing ⟨*change* of seasons⟩ **2** : a fresh set of clothes ⟨take several *changes* on your vacation⟩ **3** : money in small denominations received in exchange for an equivalent sum in larger denominations ⟨*change* for a dollar bill⟩ **4** : money returned when a payment exceeds the amount due ⟨wait for your *change*⟩ **5** : COINS

change·a·ble \'chān-jə-bəl\ *adj* : capable of change : VARIABLE

change·less \'chānj-ləs\ *adj* : UNCHANGING

¹**chan·nel** \'chan-l\ *n* **1** : the bed of a stream **2** : the deeper part of a waterway (as a river or harbor) **3** : a strait or a narrow sea ⟨the English *Channel*⟩ **4** : a closed course (as a tube) through which something flows **5** : a long groove or furrow **6** : a means by which something is passed or carried **7** : a range of frequencies of sufficient width for a single radio or television transmission

²**channel** *vb* **chan·neled** *or* **chan·nelled; chan·nel·ing** *or* **chan·nel·ling 1** : to form a channel in **2** : to direct into or through a channel

¹**chant** \'chant\ *vb* **1** : to sing especially in the way a chant is sung **2** : to recite or speak monotonously in the manner of a chant

²**chant** *n* **1** : a melody in which several words or syllables are sung on one tone **2** : SONG **3** : a rhythmic monotonous utterance

chan·tey *or* **chan·ty** \'shant-ē\ *n, pl* **chan·teys** *or* **chan·ties** : a song sung by sailors in rhythm with their work

chan·ti·cleer \ₚchant-ə-'kliər\ *n* : ¹COCK 1

cha·os \'kā-ₚäs\ *n* : complete confusion and disorder **syn** see CONFUSION

cha·ot·ic \kā-'ät-ik\ *adj* : in a state of chaos

¹**chap** \'chap\ *n* : FELLOW ⟨poor *chap*⟩

²**chap** *vb* **chapped; chap·ping** : to open in slits

: CRACK ⟨lips *chapped* by wind and cold⟩

chap·el \'chap-əl\ *n* **1** : a place of worship in a residence or institution **2** : a building or a room or recess for prayer or special religious services **3** : a service of worship or an assembly in a school or college

¹**chap·er·on** *or* **chap·er·one** \'shap-ə-ₚrōn\ *n* : a person (as a married woman) who accompanies and is responsible for a young woman or a group of young people (as at a dance)

²**chaperon** *or* **chaperone** *vb* **chap·er·oned; chap·er·on·ing** : to act as a chaperon : ESCORT

chap·lain \'chap-lən\ *n* **1** : a clergyman officially attached to a special group (as the army) **2** : a person chosen to conduct religious services (as for a club)

chaps \'shaps\ *n pl* : leather leggings resembling trousers without seats that are used especially by western ranch workers

chap·ter \'chap-tər\ *n* **1** : a main division of a book or story **2** : a local branch of a society

char \'chär\ *vb* **charred; char·ring 1** : to change to charcoal by burning **2** : to burn slightly : SCORCH **syn** see SINGE

char·ac·ter \'kar-ək-tər\ *n* **1** : a mark, sign, or symbol (as a letter or figure) used in writing or printing **2** : a distinguishing feature of a person or thing : CHARACTERISTIC **3** : the total sum of the distinguishing qualities of a person, group, or thing : NATURE **4** : a person having conspicuous often peculiar traits **5** : a person in a story or play **6** : REPUTATION **7** : moral excellence ⟨a man of *character*⟩

¹**char·ac·ter·is·tic** \ₚkar-ək-tə-'ris-tik\ *adj* : serving to mark the individual character of a person or thing : TYPICAL

²**characteristic** *n* : a special quality or appearance that makes one person or thing different from others

char·ac·ter·is·ti·cal·ly \ₚkar-ək-tə-'ris-ti-kə-lē\ *adv* : in a characteristic way : TYPICALLY

char·ac·ter·ize \'kar-ək-tə-ₚrīz\ *vb* **char·ac·ter·ized; char·ac·ter·iz·ing 1** : to indicate the character of a person or thing : DESCRIBE **2** : to be characteristic of

char·coal \'chär-ₚkōl\ *n* : a black or dark porous carbon made by charring animal or vegetable substances (as wood in a kiln from which most of the air is excluded)

¹**charge** \'chärj\ *vb* **charged; charg·ing 1** : LOAD, FILL ⟨*charge* a gun⟩ **2** : to give an electric charge to **3** : to restore the active materials in a storage battery by passage of an electric current through it **4** : to give a task, duty, or responsibility to **5** : COMMAND, ORDER **6** : ACCUSE, BLAME ⟨*charged* with speeding⟩ **7** : to rush against : ASSAULT,

j job   **ng** sing   **ō** low   **ȯ** moth   **ȯi** coin   **th** thin   **th̲** this   **ü** boot   **u̇** foot   **y** you   **yü** few   **yu̇** furious   **zh** vision

ATTACK **8** : to make liable for payment ⟨*charged* him $100⟩ **9** : to record as a debt or liability against ⟨*charged* his purchases⟩ **10** : to ask or set a price

²charge *n* **1** : the quantity (as of ammunition or fuel) required to load or fill something **2** : a quantity of electricity **3** : a task, duty, or order given to a person : OBLIGATION, REQUIREMENT **4** : MANAGEMENT, CUSTODY ⟨has *charge* of the building⟩ **5** : a person or thing given to a person to look after ⟨a nursemaid's young *charges*⟩ **6** : INSTRUCTION, COMMAND ⟨a judge's *charge* to a jury⟩ **7** : COST, PRICE ⟨storage *charges*⟩ **8** : a debit to an account **9** : ACCUSATION **10** : a rushing attack **syn** see PRICE

charg·er \'chär-jər\ *n* : a cavalry horse

char·i·ot \'char-ē-ət\ *n* : a two-wheeled vehicle of ancient times pulled by horses and used in war and in races and processions

char·i·ta·ble \'char-ət-ə-bəl\ *adj* **1** : liberal with money or help for poor and needy persons : GENEROUS **2** : given for

chariot

the needy : of service to the needy **3** : kindly in judging other people : FORGIVING

char·i·ty \'char-ət-ē\ *n, pl* **char·i·ties** **1** : love for one's fellowmen **2** : kindliness in judging others **3** : the giving of aid to the poor and suffering **4** : public aid for the poor **5** : an institution or fund for helping the needy

char·ley horse \'chär-lē-,hȯrs\ *n* : muscular pain and stiffness (as in a leg)

¹charm \'chärm\ *n* **1** : a word, action, or thing believed to have magic powers **2** : something worn or carried to keep away evil and bring good luck **3** : a small decorative object worn on a chain or bracelet **4** : physical grace or attractiveness

²charm *vb* **1** : to affect or influence by or as if by a magic spell ⟨*charm* a snake⟩ **2** : FASCINATE, DELIGHT ⟨sounds that *charm* the ear⟩ **3** : to protect by or as if by a charm ⟨leads a *charmed* life⟩ **4** : to attract by grace or beauty

charm·ing \'chär-ming\ *adj* : highly pleasing

¹chart \'chärt\ *n* **1** : MAP **2** : a map showing coasts, reefs, currents, and depths of water **3** : a sheet giving information in a table or lists or by means of diagrams

²chart *vb* **1** : to make a map or chart of ⟨*chart* the seas⟩ **2** : to lay out a plan for

¹char·ter \'chärt-ər\ *n* **1** : an official document granting rights or privileges (as to a colony, town, or college) from a ruler or a governing body **2** : CONSTITUTION ⟨United Nations *Charter*⟩ **3** : a contract by which the owners of a ship lease it to others

²charter *vb* **1** : to grant a charter to **2** : to hire (as a bus or a ship) for temporary use

char·wom·an \'chär-,wùm-ən\ *n, pl* **char·wom·en** \'chär-,wim-ən\ : a cleaning woman

¹chase \'chās\ *vb* **chased**; **chas·ing** **1** : to follow in order to capture or overtake ⟨*chase* a thief⟩ ⟨*chase* a bus⟩ **2** : HUNT ⟨*chase* the fox⟩ **3** : to drive away or out

syn CHASE, PURSUE, FOLLOW mean to go after something. CHASE suggests a swift pursuit to overtake something that is running away ⟨*chased* the dog that stole the bacon⟩ PURSUE adds to CHASE the idea of a longer, more persistent effort ⟨hounds *pursuing* the fox⟩ but may also be used in situations where actual swiftness is not involved ⟨police *pursued* the suspect for weeks before capturing him⟩ FOLLOW puts little or no emphasis on speed and may be used when there is no effort or intent to catch up ⟨a stray dog *followed* him for blocks⟩

²chase *n* **1** : the act of chasing : PURSUIT **2** : HUNTING **3** : something pursued

chasm \'kaz-əm\ *n* : a deep opening, split, or gap (as in the earth)

chas·sis \'shas-ē, 'chas-\ *n, pl* **chas·sis** \-ēz\ : a framework that supports the body (as of an automobile or airplane or the parts of a radio or television set)

chassis

chaste \'chāst\ *adj* **1** : pure in thought and act : MODEST **2** : simple or severe in design

chas·ten \'chās-n\ *vb* **1** : to correct by punishment or suffering : DISCIPLINE **2** : REFINE, PURIFY

chas·tise \chas-'tīz\ *vb* **chas·tised**; **chas·tis·ing** **1** : to inflict bodily punishment on (as by whipping) **2** : to censure severely

chas·ti·ty \'chas-tət-ē\ *n* : the quality or state of being chaste : personal purity and modesty

¹chat \'chat\ *vb* **chat·ted**; **chat·ting** **1** : CHATTER, PRATTLE **2** : to talk in a light, informal, or familiar manner

²chat *n* : an informal conversation

¹chat·ter \'chat-ər\ *vb* **1** : to utter quick speechlike but unintelligible sounds ⟨monkeys *chattering* in the trees⟩ **2** : to speak rapidly, thoughtlessly, or indistinctly : JABBER **3** : to click repeatedly or uncontrollably ⟨teeth *chattering* from the cold⟩ — **chat·ter·er** *n*

²chatter *n* : the act or sound of chattering

chat·ter·box \'chat-ər-,bäks\ *n* : a person who talks unceasingly : a constant chatterer

chat·ty \'chat-ē\ *adj* **chat·ti·er**; **chat·ti·est** **1** : TALKATIVE **2** : having the style and manner of light familiar conversation

chauf·feur \'shō-fər, shō-'fər\ *n* : a person employed to drive an automobile

¹**cheap** \'chēp\ *adj* 1 : of low cost or price : INEXPENSIVE ⟨a *cheap* watch⟩ 2 : worth little : of inferior quality 3 : gained with little effort 4 : lowered in one's own opinion ⟨feel *cheap*⟩ 5 : charging low prices — **cheap·ly** *adv*

²**cheap** *adv* : at low cost

cheap·en \'chē-pən\ *vb* : to make or become cheap or cheaper

¹**cheat** \'chēt\ *n* 1 : an act of cheating : DECEPTION, FRAUD 2 : a dishonest person

²**cheat** *vb* 1 : to deprive of something through deceit or fraud 2 : to practice fraud or trickery 3 : to violate rules (as of a game) dishonestly

¹**check** \'chek\ *n* 1 : a sudden stoppage of progress : ARREST, PAUSE 2 : something that delays, stops, or restrains : RESTRAINT, CURB 3 : a standard or guide for testing and evaluation 4 : EXAMINATION, INVESTIGATION 5 : a written order directing a bank to pay out money according to instructions on the order ⟨pay a bill by *check*⟩ 6 : a ticket or token showing the bearer's ownership, identity, or claim to something ⟨a baggage *check*⟩ 7 : a slip of paper showing the amount due : BILL ⟨a dinner *check*⟩ 8 : a pattern in squares 9 : a fabric with a design in squares 10 : a mark typically √ placed beside a written or printed item to show that something has been specially noted 11 : CRACK, BREAK

²**check** *vb* 1 : to bring to a sudden pause : slow down : STOP 2 : RESTRAIN, CURB ⟨*check* a horse⟩ 3 : to make sure of the correctness or satisfactoriness of : VERIFY 4 : to mark printing or writing with a check as specially noted or examined 5 : to mark with squares or checks ⟨a *checked* suit⟩ 6 : to leave or accept for safekeeping or for shipment ⟨*check* baggage⟩ 7 : to investigate conditions 8 : to correspond point for point : TALLY 9 : to develop small cracks (as in wood)

check·er·board \'chek-ər-,bōrd\ *n* : a board used in games (as checkers) and marked with sixty-four squares in two alternating colors

checkerboard

check·ers \'chek-ərz\ *n* : a game played on a checkerboard by two players each having twelve men

check·up \'chek-,əp\ *n* 1 : EXAMINATION 2 : a physical examination

cheek \'chēk\ *n* 1 : the side of the face below the eye and above and beside the mouth 2 : saucy speech or behavior : IMPUDENCE

¹**cheep** \'chēp\ *vb* : PEEP, CHIRP

²**cheep** *n* : CHIRP

¹**cheer** \'chiər\ *n* 1 : state of mind or heart : SPIRIT ⟨be of good *cheer*⟩ 2 : ANIMATION, GAIETY ⟨full of *cheer*⟩ 3 : food and drink for a feast : FARE 4 : something that gladdens ⟨words of *cheer*⟩ 5 : a shout of applause or encouragement ⟨three *cheers* for the team⟩

²**cheer** *vb* 1 : to give hope to : make happier : COMFORT ⟨*cheer* the sick⟩ 2 : to urge on especially with shouts or cheers ⟨*cheer* a team to victory⟩ 3 : to shout with joy, approval, or enthusiasm 4 : to grow or be cheerful

cheer·ful \'chiər-fəl\ *adj* : full of cheer : being pleasant and bright : GAY — **cheer·ful·ly** *adv* — **cheer·ful·ness** *n*

cheer·less \'chiər-ləs\ *adj* : being without cheer : GLOOMY, BLEAK

cheer·y \'chiər-ē\ *adj* **cheer·i·er**; **cheer·i·est** : gay in manner or effect : CHEERFUL — **cheer·i·ly** \-ə-lē\ *adv* — **cheer·i·ness** \-ē-nəs\ *n*

cheese \'chēz\ *n* : the curd of milk pressed and used as food

cheese·cloth \'chēz-,klȯth\ *n* : a thin loosely woven cotton cloth

chees·y \'chē-zē\ *adj* **chees·i·er**; **chees·i·est** : resembling or suggesting cheese

chef \'shef\ *n* 1 : a male head cook 2 : COOK

¹**chem·i·cal** \'kem-i-kəl\ *adj* : of or relating to chemistry or chemicals — **chem·i·cal·ly** *adv*

²**chemical** *n* 1 : a substance formed when two or more other substances act upon one another 2 : a substance prepared for use in the manufacture of another substance 3 : a substance that acts upon something else to cause a permanent change

chem·ist \'kem-əst\ *n* : one trained or engaged in chemistry

chem·is·try \'kem-əs-trē\ *n* 1 : a science that deals with the composition and properties of elements and substances made up of elements and of the changes they undergo 2 : chemical composition and properties

cher·ish \'cher-ish\ *vb* 1 : to hold dear ⟨*cherish* a friend⟩ 2 : to keep deeply in mind : cling to

cher·ry \'cher-ē\ *n, pl* **cher·ries** 1 : the round red or yellow fruit of a tree that is related to the plum 2 : a moderate red

cher·ub \'cher-əb\ *n* 1 *pl* **cher·u·bim** \-ə-,bim\ : ANGEL 2 *pl* **cher·ubs** : a painting or drawing of a beautiful child usually with wings 3 *pl* **cherubs** : a chubby rosy child

chess \'ches\ *n* : a game played on a board by two players each having sixteen pieces

chess positions

chest \'chest\ *n* 1 : a box, case, or boxlike container for storage, safekeeping, or shipping ⟨tool *chest*⟩ ⟨linen *chest*⟩ **2** : a public fund or treasury ⟨community *chest*⟩ **3** : the part of the body enclosed by the ribs and breastbone — **chest·ed** \'ches-təd\ *adj*

chest·nut \'ches-nət\ *n* **1** : a sweet edible nut borne in burs by a tree related to the beech **2** : a grayish brown

chev·ron \'shev-rən\ *n* : a sleeve badge of one or more bars or stripes usually indicating the wearer's rank or service (as in the armed forces)

chestnut burs

¹**chew** \'chü\ *vb* : to bite and grind with the teeth

²**chew** *n* **1** : the act of chewing **2** : something for chewing ⟨a *chew* of tobacco⟩

chew·ing gum \'chü-ing-\ *n* : gum usually of sweetened and flavored chicle prepared for chewing

chew·y \'chü-ē\ *adj* **chew·i·er**; **chew·i·est** : requiring chewing ⟨*chewy* candy⟩

¹**chic** \'shēk\ *n* : STYLISHNESS

²**chic** *adj* : STYLISH, SMART ⟨a *chic* costume⟩

chick \'chik\ *n* **1** : a young chicken **2** : CHILD

chick·a·dee \'chik-ə-dē\ *n* : a small bird with fluffy grayish feathers and usually a black cap

chick·en \'chik-ən\ *n* **1** : the common domestic fowl especially when young : a young hen or rooster **2** : the flesh of a chicken for use as food

chickadee

chick·en·heart·ed \,chik-ən-'härt-əd\ *adj* : COWARDLY, TIMID

chicken pox *n* : a contagious disease especially of children in which there is fever and the skin breaks out in watery blisters

chick·weed \'chik-,wēd\ *n* : a weedy plant related to the pinks that has small pointed leaves and whitish flowers

chi·cle \'chik-əl\ *n* : a gum obtained from the sap of a tropical American tree and used in making chewing gum

chide \'chīd\ *vb* **chid** \'chid\ *or* **chid·ed** \'chīd-əd\; **chid** *or* **chid·den** \'chid-n\ *or* **chided**; **chid·ing** : to find fault with : SCOLD

chickweed

¹**chief** \'chēf\ *n* : a person at the head : LEADER ⟨the *chief* of police⟩ — **in chief** : in the chief position or place ⟨editor *in chief*⟩

²**chief** *adj* **1** : highest in rank or authority ⟨*chief* executive⟩ **2** : most important : MAIN

chief·ly \'chēf-lē\ *adv* **1** : above all : PRINCIPALLY, ESPECIALLY **2** : for the most part

chief master sergeant *n* : a noncommissioned officer of the highest rank in the air force

chief petty officer *n* : a petty officer in the navy ranking next below a senior chief petty officer

chief·tain \'chēf-tən\ *n* : a chief especially of a band, tribe, or clan

chief warrant officer *n* : a warrant officer of senior rank

chig·ger \'chig-ər\ *n* : the six-legged larva of certain mites which clings to the skin and causes itching

chil·blain \'chil-,blān\ *n* : a red swollen itchy condition that occurs especially on the hands or feet and is caused by cold

chigger mite

child \'chīld\ *n, pl* **chil·dren** \'chil-drən\ **1** : an unborn or recently born person **2** : a young person of either sex between infancy and youth **3** : a son or daughter of human parents

child·birth \'chīld-,bərth\ *n* : the act or process of giving birth to offspring

child·hood \'chīld-,hůd\ *n* : the period of life between infancy and youth

child·ish \'chīl-dish\ *adj* **1** : of, resembling, or suitable to a child or children ⟨*childish* laughter⟩ **2** : FOOLISH, SILLY — **child·ish·ness** *n*
  syn CHILDISH, CHILDLIKE may both be applied to qualities in adults that are thought of as belonging normally to children. CHILDISH suggests those qualities which ought to have been outgrown and are not attractive in adults ⟨*childish* burst of temper⟩ ⟨*childish* disregard for others⟩ CHILDLIKE suggests qualities which adults rarely retain but are considered desirable or appealing at any age ⟨*childlike* innocence and trust⟩

child·like \'chīld-,līk\ *adj* : of, relating to, or resembling a child or childhood : SIMPLE, INNOCENT, TRUSTING syn see CHILDISH

chil·i *or* **chil·e** \'chil-ē\ *n, pl* **chil·ies** *or* **chil·es** **1** : a plant with small very hot red fruits **2** : a dish made of hot peppers and meat

¹**chill** \'chil\ *vb* **1** : to make or become cold or chilly **2** : to make cool especially without freezing ⟨*chilled* dessert⟩ **3** : to harden the surface of (as metal) by sudden cooling

²**chill** *adj* **1** : moderately but unpleasantly cold : RAW ⟨a *chill* wind⟩ **2** : not cordial

³**chill** *n* **1** : a feeling of coldness accompanied by shivering ⟨suffering from a *chill*⟩ **2** : moderate but disagreeable coldness ⟨a *chill* in the air⟩

chill·y \'chil-ē\ *adj* **chill·i·er**; **chill·i·est** : noticeably cold — **chill·i·ness** *n*

¹**chime** \'chīm\ *n* **1** : a set of bells musically

tuned **2** : the music from a set of bells ⟨heard the *chimes* every evening⟩ **3** : a musical sound suggesting that of bells

²chime *vb* **chimed; chim·ing 1** : to make bell= like sounds : ring chimes **2** : to be or act in accord or in harmony **3** : to call or indicate by chiming ⟨the clock *chimed* midnight⟩ — **chime in** : to break into or join in a conversation or discussion

chim·ney \'chim-nē\ *n, pl* **chim·neys 1** : a passage for smoke especially in the form of an upright structure of brick or stone extending above the roof of a building **2** : a glass tube around a lamp flame

chimney sweep *n* : a person who cleans soot from chimneys

chimney swift *n* : a small sooty-gray bird with long narrow wings that often attaches its nest to chimneys

chim·pan·zee \,chim-,pan-'zē, chim-'pan-zē\ *n* : an African ape that lives largely in trees and is smaller than the related gorilla

¹chin \'chin\ *n* : the part of the face below the mouth : the point of the lower jaw

²chin *vb* **chinned; chin·ning** : to raise oneself while hanging by the hands until the chin is level with the support

chi·na \'chī-nə\ *n* **1** : porcelain ware originally from the Orient **2** : pottery (as dishes) for domestic use

chin·chil·la \chin-'chil-ə\ *n* : a squirrellike South American animal hunted or raised for its soft silvery gray fur

¹Chi·nese \chī-'nēz\ *adj* : of or relating to China, the Chinese people, or Chinese

²Chinese *n, pl* **Chinese 1** : a native or inhabitant of China **2** : a group of related languages used by the Chinese

¹chip \'chip\ *n* **1** : a small piece (as of wood, stone, or glass) cut or broken off : FLAKE **2** : a thin crisp piece of food **3** : a flaw left after a small piece has been broken off

²chip *vb* **chipped; chip·ping** : to cut or break chips from : break off in small pieces — **chip in** : CONTRIBUTE

chip·munk \'chip-,məngk\ *n* : a small striped animal related to the squirrel

chip·ping sparrow \'chip-ing-\ *n* : a small North American sparrow that often nests about houses and has a weak chirp as a call

¹chirp \'chərp\ *n* : the short sharp sound made by crickets and some small birds

²chirp *vb* : to make a chirp

¹chis·el \'chiz-əl\ *n* : a metal tool with a sharp edge at the end of a usually flat piece used to chip away stone or wood

chisels

²chisel *vb* **chis·eled** *or* **chis·elled; chis·el·ing** *or* **chis·el·ling** : to cut or shape with a chisel

chiv·al·rous \'shiv-əl-rəs\ *adj* **1** : of or relating to chivalry **2** : marked by honor, generosity, and courtesy **3** : marked by especial courtesy and consideration to women

chiv·al·ry \'shiv-əl-rē\ *n* **1** : a body of knights **2** : the system, spirit, ways, or customs of knighthood **3** : chivalrous conduct

chlo·rine \'klōr-,ēn, -ən\ *n* : a chemical element that is a greenish yellow irritating gas of strong odor used as a bleach and as a disinfectant in water purification

¹chlo·ro·form \'klōr-ə-,fòrm\ *n* : a colorless heavy liquid used as a solvent or as an anesthetic

²chloroform *vb* : to make unconscious or kill with chloroform

chlo·ro·phyll \'klōr-ə-,fil\ *n* : the green coloring matter by means of which green plants produce carbohydrates from carbon dioxide and water

chock–full \'chäk-'fùl\ *adj* : full to the limit

choc·o·late \'chäk-ə-lət, 'chòk-\ *n* **1** : a food prepared from ground roasted cacao beans **2** : a beverage of chocolate in water or milk **3** : a candy coated with chocolate

¹choice \'chòis\ *n* **1** : the act of choosing : SELECTION **2** : the power of choosing : OPTION **3** : a person or thing chosen **4** : the best part **5** : a sufficient number and variety for wide or free selection

syn CHOICE, ALTERNATIVE, PREFERENCE all mean a selection that is to be or has been made. CHOICE is the general term suggesting the opportunity to choose freely and giving no hint as to how numerous or how desirable the possibilities may be ⟨he had his *choice* of how to spend the summer vacation⟩ ALTERNATIVE indicates a choice to be made from two possibilities, one of which must be selected ⟨his *alternative* to going to summer school was going to work⟩ PREFERENCE may suggest a choice to be made from several desirable possibilities ⟨he was given his *preference* of going any day of the week⟩

²choice *adj* : very fine : better than most

choir \'kwīr\ *n* **1** : an organized group of singers especially in a church **2** : the part of a church reserved for the singers

¹choke \'chōk\ *vb* **choked; chok·ing 1** : to hinder normal breathing by cutting off the supply of air ⟨*choked* by thick smoke⟩ **2** : to have the windpipe stopped entirely or partly : STRANGLE ⟨he *choked* on a bone⟩ **3** : to check the growth or action of **4** : CLOG, OBSTRUCT ⟨leaves *choked* the sewer⟩

²choke n **1** : something that chokes **2** : the act or sound of choking

choke·cher·ry \'chōk-ˌcher-ē\ n, pl **choke-cher·ries** : a wild cherry tree with long clusters of reddish black fruits that pucker the mouth

chokecherry: leaves and fruit

chol·er·a \'käl-ə-rə\ n : a destructive infectious disease of Asiatic origin marked by violent vomiting and dysentery

choose \'chüz\ vb **chose** \'chōz\; **cho·sen** \'chōz-n\; **choos·ing 1** : to select especially after consideration ⟨*choose* a leader⟩ **2** : DE-CIDE, PREFER **3** : to see fit : PLEASE

¹chop \'chäp\ vb **chopped; chop·ping 1** : to cut by striking especially repeatedly with something sharp ⟨*chop* down a tree⟩ **2** : to cut into small pieces : MINCE ⟨*chop* meat⟩ **3** : to strike quickly or repeatedly — **chop·per** n

²chop n **1** : a sharp downward blow or stroke (as with an ax) **2** : a small cut of meat often including a part of a rib ⟨a lamb *chop*⟩ **3** : a short quick motion (as of a wave)

¹chop·py \'chäp-ē\ adj **chop·pi·er; chop·pi·est** : CHANGEABLE, VARIABLE ⟨a *choppy* wind⟩

²choppy adj **chop·pi·er; chop·pi·est 1** : rough. with small waves **2** : JERKY, DISCONNECTED

chops \'chäps\ n pl : the fleshy covering of the jaws

chop·stick \'chäp-ˌstik\ n : one of two slender sticks used chiefly in oriental countries to lift food to the mouth

cho·ral \'kōr-əl\ adj : of, relating to, or sung or recited by a chorus or choir or in chorus

cho·rale or **cho·ral** \kə-'ral\ n **1** : a hymn or a hymn tune sung in unison **2** : CHORUS

¹chord \'kȯrd\ n : a combination of tones that blend harmoniously when sounded together

²chord n : a straight line joining two points on a curve

chore \'chōr\ n **1** pl : the regular light work about a household or farm **2** : a routine task or job **3** : a difficult or disagreeable task

cho·re·og·ra·phy \ˌkōr-ē-'äg-rə-fē\ n : the art of dancing or of arranging dances and especially ballets — **cho·re·og·ra·pher** \-fər\ n

cho·ris·ter \'kōr-əs-tər\ n : a singer in a choir

chor·tle \'chȯrt-l\ vb **chor·tled; chor·tling** : to laugh or chuckle especially in satisfaction

¹cho·rus \'kōr-əs\ n **1** : a company of singers : CHOIR **2** : a group of dancers and singers (as in a musical comedy) **3** : a part of a song or hymn that is repeated at intervals (as at the end of each stanza) **4** : a song intended to be sung by a group : group singing **5** : the main

part of a popular song **6** : sounds uttered by a group of persons or animals together

²chorus vb : to speak, sing, or sound at the same time or together

cho·sen \'chōz-n\ adj **1** : selected or marked for favor or special privilege ⟨a *chosen* few⟩ **2** : selected by God ⟨a *chosen* people⟩

chow \'chaú\ n : a thick-coated straight-legged muscular dog with a blue-black tongue and a short tail curled close to the back

chow·der \'chaúd-ər\ n : a soup or stew made of fish, clams, or a vegetable usually stewed in milk

chris·ten \'kris-n\ vb **1** : BAPTIZE **2** : to give a name to at baptism ⟨*christened* the baby Mary⟩ **3** : to name or dedicate (as a ship) in a ceremony suggestive of baptism

Chris·ten·dom \'kris-n-dəm\ n **1** : the entire body of Christians **2** : the part of the world in which Christianity prevails

chris·ten·ing \'kris-n-ing\ n : BAPTISM

¹Chris·tian \'kris-chən\ n **1** : a person who believes in Jesus and follows his teachings **2** : a member of a Christian church

²Christian adj **1** : of or relating to Jesus Christ or the religion based on his teachings **2** : of or relating to Christians ⟨a *Christian* nation⟩ **3** : befitting a Christian : KIND

Chris·ti·an·i·ty \ˌkris-chē-'an-ət-ē\ n **1** : CHRISTENDOM **2** : the religion of Christians

Christian name n : the name given to a person at birth or christening as distinct from the family name

Christ·mas \'kris-məs\ n : December 25 celebrated in commemoration of the birth of Christ

Christ·mas·tide \'kris-məs-ˌtīd\ n : the season of Christmas

chro·mi·um \'krō-mē-əm\ n : a blue-white metallic chemical element that does not rust quickly

chro·mo·some \'krō-mə-ˌsōm\ n : one of the rodlike bodies of a cell nucleus that contain genes and divide when the cell divides

chron·ic \'krän-ik\ adj **1** : continuing for a long time or recurring often ⟨a *chronic* disease⟩ **2** : HABITUAL — **chron·i·cal·ly** \-i-kə-lē\ adv

¹chron·i·cle \'krän-i-kəl\ n : an account or history of events in the order of their occurrence : HISTORY, NARRATIVE

²chronicle vb **chron·i·cled; chron·i·cling** : to record in or as if in a chronicle

chron·o·log·i·cal \ˌkrän-l-'äj-i-kəl\ adj : arranged in or according to the order of time ⟨*chronological* tables of American history⟩ — **chron·o·log·i·cal·ly** adv

chrys·a·lis \'kris-ə-ləs\ *n* : a moth or butterfly pupa that is enclosed in a firm protective case

chry·san·the·mum \kri-'san-thə-məm\ *n* : a plant related to the daisies that has deeply notched leaves and brightly colored often double flower heads

chrysalis

chub·by \'chəb-ē\ *adj* **chub·bi·er; chub·bi·est** : PLUMP ⟨a *chubby* baby⟩

¹chuck \'chək\ *vb* **1** : to give a pat or tap to **2** : TOSS ⟨*chuck* a ball back and forth⟩

²chuck *n* **1** : a pat or nudge under the chin **2** : TOSS, JERK

chuck–full \'chək-'fūl\ *var of* CHOCK-FULL

¹chuck·le \'chək-əl\ *vb* **chuck·led; chuck·ling** : to laugh inwardly or quietly

²chuckle *n* : a low quiet laugh

chuck wagon \'chək-\ *n* : a wagon carrying a stove and provisions for cooking

¹chug \'chəg\ *n* : a dull explosive sound

²chug *vb* **chugged; chug·ging** : to move or go with chugs ⟨a locomotive *chugging* along⟩

¹chum \'chəm\ *n* : a close friend : PAL

²chum *vb* **chummed; chum·ming** : to go about with someone as a friend

chum·my \'chəm-ē\ *adj* **chum·mi·er; chum·mi·est** : INTIMATE, SOCIABLE

chunk \'chəngk\ *n* : a short thick piece or lump (as of coal) : HUNK

church \'chərch\ *n* **1** : a building for public worship and especially Christian worship **2** : an organized body of religious believers **3** : public worship especially in a church

church·yard \'chərch-ˌyärd\ *n* : a yard that belongs to a church and is often used as a burial ground

¹churn \'chərn\ *n* : a container in which milk or cream is violently stirred in making butter

²churn *vb* **1** : to stir in a churn (as in making butter) **2** : to stir or shake violently

chute \'shüt\ *n* **1** : an inclined plane, trough, or passage down or through which things are slid or dropped **2** : PARACHUTE

ci·ca·da \sə-'kād-ə\ *n* : a stout-bodied insect with transparent wings that is related to the true bugs

-cide \ˌsīd\ *n suffix* **1** : killer ⟨insecti*cide*⟩ **2** : killing ⟨sui*cide*⟩

ci·der \'sīd-ər\ *n* : the juice pressed out of fruit (as apples) and used especially as a drink and in making vinegar

ci·gar \si-'gär\ *n* : a small tight roll of tobacco leaf for smoking

cicada

cig·a·rette \ˌsig-ə-'ret\ *n* : a small roll of cut tobacco wrapped in paper for smoking

¹cinch \'sinch\ *n* **1** : GIRTH 1 **2** : a sure or an easy thing

²cinch *vb* **1** : to fasten or tighten a girth on ⟨*cinch* up a horse⟩ **2** : to secure with or as if with a girth ⟨*cinch* a saddle in place⟩

cin·cho·na \sing-'kō-nə\ *n* : a South American tree whose bark yields quinine

cin·der \'sin-dər\ *n* **1** : SLAG **2** : a piece of partly burned coal or wood that is not burning **3** : a hot coal without flame **4** *pl* : ASHES

cin·e·ma \'sin-ə-mə\ *n* **1** : a motion-picture theater **2** : MOVIES

cin·na·mon \'sin-ə-mən\ *n* : a spice prepared from the aromatic bark of tropical trees related to the Old World laurel

cinnamon: leaves and flowers

¹ci·pher \'sī-fər\ *n* **1** : ZERO, NAUGHT **2** : a person of no worth or influence **3** : a method of secret writing or the alphabet or characters used in such writing **4** : a message in code

²cipher *vb* : to use figures in doing a problem in arithmetic : CALCULATE

¹cir·cle \'sər-kəl\ *n* **1** : a closed plane curve every point of which is equally distant from a point within it : the space inside such a closed curve **2** : something resembling a circle or part of a circle **3** : RING ⟨the children sat in a *circle*⟩ **4** : CYCLE, ROUND ⟨the wheel has come full *circle*⟩ **5** : a group of people bound by common interests

circle

²circle *vb* **cir·cled; cir·cling** **1** : to enclose in or as if in a circle **2** : to move or revolve around **3** : to move in or as if in a circle

cir·cuit \'sər-kət\ *n* **1** : a boundary around an enclosed space **2** : an enclosed space : REGION, AREA **3** : a moving around (as in a circle) : CIRCLING ⟨the *circuit* of the earth around the sun⟩ **4** : a regular tour (as by a judge) around an assigned territory : the course or route regularly traveled **5** : LEAGUE **6** : a chain of theaters at which productions are shown in turn **7** : the complete path or part of the path of an electric current

cir·cu·i·tous \ˌsər-'kyü-ət-əs\ *adj* **1** : marked by a circular or winding course ⟨a *circuitous* route⟩ **2** : ROUNDABOUT, INDIRECT

¹cir·cu·lar \'sər-kyə-lər\ *adj* **1** : having the form of a circle : ROUND ⟨a *circular* track⟩ **2** : passing or going around in a circle ⟨*circular*

motion⟩ **3** : ROUNDABOUT **4** : sent around to a number of persons ⟨a *circular* letter⟩

²**circular** *n* : a paper (as a leaflet containing an advertisement) intended for wide distribution

cir·cu·late \'sər-kyə-ˌlāt\ *vb* **cir·cu·lat·ed; cir·cu·lat·ing** **1** : to move around in a regular course ⟨blood *circulates* in the body⟩ **2** : to go, pass, or send about from place to place or from person to person ⟨money *circulates*⟩

cir·cu·la·tion \ˌsər-kyə-'lā-shən\ *n* **1** : motion around in a regular course : FLOW ⟨the *circulation* of air in a room⟩ **2** : passage from place to place or person to person ⟨coins in *circulation*⟩ **3** : the average number of copies (as of a newspaper) sold in a given period

cir·cu·la·to·ry \'sər-kyə-lə-ˌtōr-ē\ *adj* : of or relating to circulation (as of the blood)

circum- *prefix* : around : about ⟨*circum*polar⟩

cir·cum·fer·ence \sər-'kəm-fə-rəns\ *n* **1** : the line that goes around a circle **2** : a boundary line or circuit enclosing an area **3** : the distance around something

cir·cum·nav·i·gate \ˌsər-kəm-'nav-ə-ˌgāt\ *vb* **cir·cum·nav·i·gat·ed; cir·cum·nav·i·gat·ing** : to go completely around (as the earth) especially by water

cir·cum·po·lar \ˌsər-kəm-'pō-lər\ *adj* **1** : continually visible above the horizon ⟨*circumpolar* star⟩ **2** : surrounding or found in the vicinity of the north pole or south pole

cir·cum·stance \'sər-kəm-ˌstans\ *n* **1** : a fact or event that must be considered along with another fact or event **2** *pl* : surrounding conditions ⟨I can't under the *circumstances*⟩ **3** *pl* : condition or situation with respect to wealth ⟨in easy *circumstances*⟩ **4** : FORMALITY, CEREMONY **5** : a detail, incident, or fact in a chain of events **6** : CHANCE, FATE

cir·cum·vent \ˌsər-kəm-'vent\ *vb* **1** : to hem in **2** : to go around **3** : to gain an advantage over by trickery or deception

cir·cus \'sər-kəs\ *n* **1** : an enclosure often covered by a tent and used for entertaining spectators by a variety of exhibitions including riding, acrobatic feats, wild animal displays, and the performances of jugglers and clowns **2** : a circus performance : the performers and equipment of a circus

cir·rus \'sir-əs\ *n, pl* **cir·ri** \'sir-ˌī\ : a wispy white cloud formed at a very high altitude of tiny ice crystals

cis·tern \'sis-tərn\ *n* : an often underground artificial reservoir or tank for storing water

cit·a·del \'sit-əd-l\ *n* **1** : a fortress that commands a city **2** : STRONGHOLD

ci·ta·tion \sī-'tā-shən\ *n* **1** : an act or instance of quoting **2** : QUOTATION **3** : a formal statement of the achievements of a person receiving an award (as an honorary degree)

cite \'sīt\ *vb* **cit·ed; cit·ing** **1** : to quote as an example, authority, or proof **2** : to refer to especially in commendation or praise

cit·i·zen \'sit-ə-zən\ *n* **1** : an inhabitant of a city or town **2** : a person who owes allegiance to a government and is entitled to protection by it

cit·i·zen·ry \'sit-ə-zən-rē\ *n* : the whole body of citizens

cit·i·zen·ship \'sit-ə-zən-ˌship\ *n* : the state of being a citizen

cit·ron \'sit-rən\ *n* **1** : a citrus fruit resembling but larger than a lemon and having a thick rind that is preserved for use in cakes and puddings **2** : a small hard-fleshed watermelon used especially in pickles and preserves

cit·rus \'sit-rəs\ *adj* : of or relating to a group of often thorny trees and shrubs of warm regions whose fruits include the lemon, lime, orange, and grapefruit

citron 1

city \'sit-ē\ *n, pl* **cit·ies** **1** : an inhabited place of greater size or importance than a town **2** : the people of a city

civ·ic \'siv-ik\ *adj* : of or relating to a citizen, a city, or citizenship ⟨*civic* pride⟩ ⟨*civic* duty⟩

civ·ics \'siv-iks\ *n* : a study that deals with the rights and duties of citizens

civ·il \'siv-əl\ *adj* **1** : of or relating to citizens ⟨*civil* liberties⟩ **2** : of or relating to the state as an organized political body ⟨*civil* institutions⟩ **3** : of or relating to ordinary or civic affairs as distinguished from military or church affairs **4** : COURTEOUS, POLITE ⟨give a *civil* answer⟩ **5** : relating to legal proceedings in connection with private rights and obligations

syn CIVIL, POLITE, COURTEOUS all refer to the behavior of one person toward another. CIVIL suggests showing only enough proper or good behavior to avoid being actually rude ⟨his answers were *civil*, but he obviously wanted us to leave⟩ POLITE suggests adherence to a formal set of good manners but gives no information about the attitudes or feelings behind the outward behavior ⟨the boy was always *polite*, always did the proper thing, but lacked real warmth and friendliness⟩ COURTEOUS adds to POLITE the suggestion that behind the good manners lies a real thoughtfulness and regard for others ⟨a *courteous* child who seemed sensitive to the feelings of others⟩

¹**ci·vil·ian** \sə-'vil-yən\ *n* : a person not on active duty in a military, police, or fire-fighting force

²**civilian** *adj* : of or relating to a civilian

ci·vil·i·ty \sə-'vil-ət-ē\ *n, pl* **ci·vil·i·ties** : PO-LITENESS, COURTESY

civ·i·li·za·tion \,siv-ə-lə-'zā-shən\ *n* 1 : an advanced stage (as in art, science, and government) in social development 2 : the way of life of a people ⟨Greek *civilization*⟩

civ·i·lize \'siv-ə-,līz\ *vb* **civ·i·lized; civ·i·liz·ing** : to raise out of a savage state : EDUCATE

civil service *n* : all of the branches of the public service of a country that are not military, naval, legislative, or judicial

¹**clack** \'klak\ *vb* 1 : CHATTER, PRATTLE 2 : to make or cause to make a clatter

²**clack** *n* 1 : rapid continuous talk : CHATTER 2 : a sound of clacking

clad \'klad\ *adj* : CLOTHED, COVERED

¹**claim** \'klām\ *vb* 1 : to ask for as rightfully belonging to oneself 2 : to call for : RE-QUIRE ⟨matter that *claims* attention⟩ 3 : to state as a fact : MAINTAIN 4 : PROFESS

²**claim** *n* 1 : a demand for something due or believed to be due ⟨insurance *claim*⟩ 2 : a right to something usually in another's possession 3 : an assertion open to challenge 4 : something claimed ⟨a prospector's *claim*⟩

¹**clam** \'klam\ *n* : a shellfish somewhat like an oyster with a soft body and a hinged double shell

²**clam** *vb* **clammed; clam·ming** : to dig or gather clams

clam·bake \'klam-,bāk\ *n* : a party or gathering (as at the seashore) at which food (as clams or potatoes) is cooked usually on heated rocks covered by seaweed

clam

clam·ber \'klam-bər\ *vb* : to climb awkwardly (as by scrambling)

clam·my \'klam-ē\ *adj* **clam·mi·er; clam·mi·est** : being damp, soft, sticky, and usually cool — **clam·mi·ly** \'klam-ə-lē\ *adv* — **clam·mi·ness** \'klam-ē-nəs\ *n*

¹**clam·or** \'klam-ər\ *n* 1 : a noisy shouting 2 : a loud continuous noise 3 : vigorous protest or demand ⟨public *clamor* for a tax cut⟩

²**clamor** *vb* : to make a clamor

clam·or·ous \'klam-ə-rəs\ *adj* : full of clamor

¹**clamp** \'klamp\ *n* : a device that holds or presses parts together firmly

²**clamp** *vb* : to fasten or to hold together with or as if with a clamp

clamp

clan \'klan\ *n* 1 : a group (as in the Scottish Highlands) made up of households whose heads claim descent from a common ancestor 2 : a group of persons united by some common interest

¹**clang** \'klang\ *vb* : to make or cause to make a clang ⟨*clanging* bells⟩

²**clang** *n* : a loud ringing sound like that made by pieces of metal striking each other

¹**clank** \'klangk\ *vb* 1 : to make or cause to make a clank or series of clanks ⟨the radiator hissed and *clanked*⟩ 2 : to move with a clank

²**clank** *n* : a sharp short metallic ringing sound

¹**clap** \'klap\ *vb* **clapped; clap·ping** 1 : to strike noisily : SLAM, BANG ⟨*clap* two boards together⟩ ⟨the door *clapped* shut⟩ 2 : AP-PLAUD 3 : to strike with the open hand ⟨*clapped* his friend on the shoulder⟩ 4 : to put or place vigorously or hastily

²**clap** *n* 1 : a loud noisy crash made by or as if by the striking together of two hard surfaces 2 : a hard slap 3 : APPLAUSE

clap·board \'klab-ərd, -,ōrd\ *n* : a narrow board thicker at one edge than at the other used horizontally for the outside of wooden buildings

clap·per \'klap-ər\ *n* : one (as the tongue of a bell) that makes a clapping sound

clar·i·fy \'klar-ə-,fī\ *vb* **clar·i·fied; clar·i·fy·ing** 1 : to make or to become pure or clear ⟨*clarify* a liquid⟩ 2 : to make or become more readily understandable ⟨*clarify* a statement⟩

clar·i·net \,klar-ə-'net\ *n* : a single-reed woodwind instrument in the form of a cylindrical tube with moderately flaring end

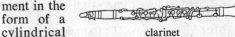
clarinet

¹**clar·i·on** \'klar-ē-ən\ *n* : a trumpet having very clear and shrill tones

²**clarion** *adj* : being loud and clear

clar·i·ty \'klar-ət-ē\ *n* : CLEARNESS

¹**clash** \'klash\ *vb* 1 : to make or cause to make a clash ⟨*clashing* cymbals⟩ 2 : to come into conflict : COLLIDE ⟨pickets *clashed* with the police⟩ 3 : to be out of harmony

²**clash** *n* 1 : a loud sharp usually metallic sound of collision ⟨the *clash* of swords⟩ 2 : a hostile encounter : COLLISION, CONFLICT

¹**clasp** \'klasp\ *n* 1 : a device for holding together two objects or two parts of something ⟨a belt *clasp*⟩ 2 : EMBRACE, GRASP

²**clasp** *vb* 1 : to fasten with or as if with a clasp 2 : EMBRACE 3 : GRASP

¹**class** \'klas\ *n* 1 : a group of persons or things of the same kind ⟨birds form a *class* of

animals⟩ **2** : a group or rank of society ⟨the working *class*⟩ **3** : a course of instruction ⟨a *class* in science⟩ **4** : a group of pupils meeting regularly for study or instruction **5** : the period during which a study group meets **6** : a body of students who are due to graduate at the same time **7** : a grouping of goods or services based on grade or quality

²class *vb* : CLASSIFY

¹clas·sic \'klas-ik\ *adj* **1** : serving as a standard of excellence **2** : TRADITIONAL **3** : of or relating to the ancient Greeks and Romans or their culture : CLASSICAL **4** : notable especially as the best or most typical example

²classic *n* **1** : a noted literary work or author of ancient Greece or Rome ⟨read the Greek *classics*⟩ **2** : a work (as of literature, music, or art) considered to be of lasting excellence **3** : something regarded as perfect of its kind

clas·si·cal \'klas-i-kəl\ *adj* **1** : of the highest class or degree of excellence : CLASSIC **2** : of or relating to the classics of literature, music, or art and especially to the ancient Greek and Roman classics **3** : concerned with a general study of the arts and sciences

clas·si·fi·ca·tion \ˌklas-ə-fə-'kā-shən\ *n* **1** : the act of classifying or arranging in classes **2** : orderly or systematic arrangement in classes ⟨a *classification* of plants⟩

clas·si·fy \'klas-ə-ˌfī\ *vb* **clas·si·fied; clas·si·fy·ing** : to group or arrange in classes

class·mate \'klas-ˌmāt\ *n* : a member of the same class in a school or college

class·room \'klas-ˌrüm, -ˌrum\ *n* : a room in a school or college in which classes meet

¹clat·ter \'klat-ər\ *vb* **1** : to make or cause to make a rattling sound ⟨dishes *clattering* in the kitchen⟩ **2** : to move or go with a clatter

²clatter *n* **1** : a rattling sound (as of hard bodies striking together) ⟨the *clatter* of pots and pans⟩ **2** : COMMOTION **3** : noisy chatter

clause \'klȯz\ *n* **1** : a separate distinct part of an article or document (as a will) **2** : a group of words having its own subject and predicate but forming only part of a complete sentence ⟨"when it rained" in "when it rained they went inside" is a *clause*⟩

¹claw \'klȯ\ *n* **1** : a sharp usually slender and curved nail on the finger or toe of an animal (as a cat or bird) **2** : a pointed or pincerslike structure at the end of a limb of a lower animal (as an insect, scorpion, or lobster) **3** : something that resembles a claw in shape or use

²claw *vb* : to rake, seize, or dig with claws

clay \'klā\ *n* **1** : an earthy material that is sticky and easily molded when wet and hard

and brittle when baked **2** : a plastic claylike substance used for modeling

¹clean \'klēn\ *adj* **1** : free from dirt or foreign matter : not soiled ⟨*clean* clothes⟩ **2** : PURE, HONORABLE **3** : THOROUGH, COMPLETE ⟨a *clean* sweep⟩ **4** : SKILLFUL, SMART **5** : EVEN, SMOOTH ⟨a *clean* cut⟩ **6** : SHAPELY, TRIM ⟨a ship with *clean* lines⟩ **7** : cleanly in habits

²clean *adv* **1** : so as to clean ⟨a new broom sweeps *clean*⟩ **2** : in a clean manner ⟨fight *clean*⟩ **3** : COMPLETELY ⟨went *clean* through⟩

³clean *vb* : to make or become clean ⟨*clean* a room⟩ ⟨*clean* up for supper⟩ — **clean·er** *n*

clean·li·ness \'klen-lē-nəs\ *n* : the condition of being clean : the habit of keeping clean

¹clean·ly \'klen-lē\ *adj* **clean·li·er; clean·li·est** **1** : careful to keep clean ⟨a *cleanly* animal⟩ **2** : habitually kept clean ⟨*cleanly* surroundings⟩

²clean·ly \'klēn-lē\ *adv* : in a clean manner

cleanse \'klenz\ *vb* **cleansed; cleans·ing** : to make clean

cleans·er \'klen-zər\ *n* : a preparation (as a scouring powder) used for cleaning

¹clear \'kliər\ *adj* **1** : free from clouds, haze, or mist ⟨a *clear* day⟩ **2** : BRIGHT, LUMINOUS ⟨*clear* sunlight⟩ **3** : SERENE, CALM ⟨a *clear* gaze⟩ **4** : free of blemishes **5** : easily seen through : TRANSPARENT ⟨*clear* glass⟩ **6** : easily heard, seen, or understood ⟨a *clear* voice⟩ **7** : free from doubt : SURE **8** : INNOCENT ⟨a *clear* conscience⟩ **9** : free from restriction, obstruction, or entanglement — **clear·ly** *adv* — **clear·ness** *n*

²clear *adv* **1** : in a clear manner **2** : WHOLLY

³clear *vb* **1** : to make or become clear ⟨the sky *cleared*⟩ **2** : to go away : DISPERSE ⟨the clouds *cleared* away⟩ **3** : to free from blame ⟨*cleared* his name⟩ **4** : to certify as trustworthy ⟨*cleared* for defense work⟩ **5** : EXPLAIN ⟨*clear* the matter up⟩ **6** : to free from obstruction : get rid of : REMOVE ⟨*clear* land of timber⟩ **7** : SETTLE ⟨*clear* an account⟩ **8** : NET **9** : to jump or go by without touching

⁴clear *n* : a clear space or part — **in the clear** : free from guilt or suspicion

clear·ance \'klir-əns\ *n* **1** : the act or process of clearing **2** : the distance by which one object avoids hitting or touching another

clear·ing \'kliər-ing\ *n* : a tract of land cleared of trees or bushes

cleat \'klēt\ *n* **1** : a wooden or metal device used to fasten a line or a rope **2** : a strip fastened on or across something to give strength, to provide a grip, or to prevent slipping ⟨the *cleats* on football shoes⟩

cleat 1

cleav·age \'klē-vij\ *n* **1** : the tendency of a rock or mineral to split readily in one or more directions **2** : the action of cleaving **3** : the state of being cleft

¹**cleave** \'klēv\ *vb* **cleaved** *or* **clove** \'klōv\; **cleav·ing** : to cling to a person or thing closely

²**cleave** *vb* **cleaved** *or* **cleft** \'kleft\ *or* **clove** \'klōv\; **cleaved** *or* **cleft** *or* **clo·ven** \'klō-vən\; **cleav·ing** : to separate or pierce by force (as with a cutting blow) : SPLIT, CUT

cleav·er \'klē-vər\ *n* **1** : a person or thing that cleaves **2** : a heavy knife used by butchers for cutting up meat

cleaver 2

clef \'klef\ *n* : a sign placed on the staff in writing music to show what pitch is represented by each line and space

¹**cleft** \'kleft\ *n* **1** : a space or opening made by splitting or cracking : CREVICE **2** : a usually V-shaped indentation resembling a cleft

²**cleft** *adj* : partially split or divided

clem·en·cy \'klem-ən-sē\ *n, pl* **clem·en·cies** **1** : MERCY, KINDNESS **2** : mildness of weather

clench \'klench\ *vb* **1** : CLINCH 1 **2** : to hold fast : CLUTCH **3** : to set or close tightly

cler·gy \'klər-jē\ *n, pl* **cler·gies** : the body of religious officials (as priests, ministers, and rabbis) especially prepared and authorized to conduct religious services

cler·gy·man \'klər-ji-mən\ *n, pl* **cler·gy·men** \-mən\ : a member of the clergy

cler·i·cal \'kler-i-kəl\ *adj* **1** : of, relating to, or characteristic of the clergy or a clergyman **2** : of or relating to a clerk or office worker

¹**clerk** \'klərk\ *n* **1** : a person employed to keep records or accounts (bank *clerk*) **2** : a salesman or saleswoman in a store

²**clerk** *vb* : to act or work as a clerk

clev·er \'klev-ər\ *adj* **1** : showing skill or resourcefulness (a *clever* trick) **2** : quick in learning (a *clever* child) **3** : marked by wit or ingenuity — **clev·er·ly** *adv* — **clev·er·ness** *n*

clew *var of* CLUE

¹**click** \'klik\ *n* : a slight sharp noise

²**click** *vb* **1** : to make or cause to make a click (*clicked* his tongue) **2** : to fit in or work together smoothly **3** : SUCCEED

cli·ent \'klī-ənt\ *n* **1** : a person who consults or employs the services of a professional man (as a lawyer) **2** : CUSTOMER

cli·en·tele \,klī-ən-'tel\ *n* : a group of clients

cliff \'klif\ *n* : a high steep face of rock

cli·mate \'klī-mət\ *n* : the average weather conditions of a particular place or region over a period of years

cli·max \'klī-,maks\ *n* : the time or part of something that is of greatest interest, excitement, or importance : the highest point

¹**climb** \'klīm\ *vb* **1** : to go up or down (as by grasping or clinging with hands and feet) **2** : to ascend in growth (as by twining) (a *climbing* vine) **3** : to rise gradually to a higher point (smoke *climbing* in the still air) **syn** *see* ASCEND — **climb·er** \'klī-mər\ *n*

²**climb** *n* **1** : a place where climbing is necessary **2** : the act of climbing

clime \'klīm\ *n* : CLIMATE

¹**clinch** \'klinch\ *vb* **1** : to turn over or flatten the protruding end of (as a driven nail) **2** : to fasten by clinching **3** : to establish as certain or true **4** : to seize or grasp one another (as in boxing)

²**clinch** *n* **1** : a fastening by means of a clinched nail, bolt, or rivet : the clinched part of a nail, bolt, or rivet **2** : an act or instance of clinching in boxing

cling \'kling\ *vb* **clung** \'kləng\; **cling·ing 1** : to hold fast or stick closely to a surface : STICK **2** : to hold fast by grasping or twining around (*cling* to the top of a ladder) **3** : to remain close (*clings* to her family)

clin·ic \'klin-ik\ *n* : a place (as in a hospital) where sick people able to get about are studied and treated (a dental *clinic*)

¹**clink** \'klingk\ *vb* : to make or cause to make a slight sharp short metallic sound

²**clink** *n* : a clinking sound

¹**clip** \'klip\ *vb* **clipped**; **clip·ping** : to fasten with a clip (*clip* the papers together)

²**clip** *n* : a device that grips, clasps, or hooks

³**clip** *vb* **clipped**; **clip·ping 1** : to cut or snip off (as with shears or scissors) (*clip* a hedge) (*clip* out a news item) **2** : to cut off or trim the hair or wool of (have a dog *clipped*) **3** : HIT, PUNCH

clips for papers

⁴**clip** *n* **1** : a two-bladed instrument for cutting especially the nails **2** : something (as the wool of a sheep) that is clipped off **3** : a sharp blow **4** : a rapid pace (moved along at a good *clip*)

clip·board \'klip-,bōrd\ *n* : a small board with a clip at the top for holding papers

clip·per \'klip-ər\ *n* **1** : a person who clips **2** *pl* : a device used for clipping especially hair or nails **3** : a fast sailing ship with an overhanging bow, tall masts, and a large sail area

clipboard

clip·ping \'klip-ing\ *n* : a piece clipped or cut

out or off of something ⟨a newspaper *clipping*⟩

clique \'klēk\ *n* : a small exclusive group of people

¹cloak \'klōk\ *n* **1** : a loose outer garment usually longer than a cape **2** : something that conceals or covers

²cloak *vb* : to cover or hide with a cloak

¹clock \'kläk\ *n* : a device for measuring or telling the time and especially one not intended to be worn or carried by a person

²clock *vb* **1** : to time a person or a performance by a timing device **2** : to register (as time, rate, or speed) on a recording device

³clock *n* : an ornamental figure on a stocking

clock·wise \'kläk-ˌwīz\ *adv* (*or adj*) : in the direction in which the hands of a clock turn

clock·work \'kläk-ˌwərk\ *n* : machinery (as in mechanical toys) similar to that making clocks go

clod \'kläd\ *n* **1** : a lump or mass especially of earth or clay **2** : a dull or stupid fellow

¹clog \'kläg\ *n* **1** : something that hinders or restrains **2** : a shoe having a thick usually wooden sole

²clog *vb* **clogged**; **clog·ging** **1** : HINDER, RE-STRAIN **2** : to prevent or obstruct passage through : choke up ⟨snow *clogged* the roads⟩

¹clois·ter \'klȯis-tər\ *n* **1** : MONASTERY, CON-VENT **2** : a covered usually arched passageway along or around the walls of a court

²cloister *vb* **1** : to shut away from the world **2** : to surround with a cloister

¹close \'klōz\ *vb* **closed**; **clos·ing** **1** : to stop up : fill up : stop access to ⟨*close* a gap⟩ **2** : SHUT **3** : to bring or come to an end : TERMINATE, COMPLETE ⟨*close* a meeting⟩ **4** : to bring together the parts or edges of ⟨a *closed* fist⟩ **5** : to draw near ⟨night *closed* in⟩ **6** : GRAPPLE

²close *n* : CONCLUSION, END

³close \'klōs\ *adj* **clos·er**; **clos·est** **1** : having no openings : CLOSED **2** : shut in with little space **3** : SECLUDED, SECRET **4** : SECRETIVE **5** : STRICT, RIGOROUS ⟨kept *close* watch⟩ **6** : STIFLING, SULTRY ⟨a hot *close* day⟩ **7** : not generous or liberal ⟨*close* with his money⟩ **8** : being near in time, place, relationship, or degree ⟨*close* neighbors⟩ **9** : SHORT **10** : MATCH-ING, BLENDING **11** : INTIMATE, FAMILIAR ⟨*close* friends⟩ **12** : CAREFUL, ACCURATE ⟨a *close* observer⟩ **13** : decided by a narrow margin ⟨a *close* contest⟩ **syn** see STINGY — **close·ly** *adv* — **close·ness** *n*

⁴close \'klōs\ *adv* : NEAR

closed \'klōzd\ *adj* **1** : not open : ENCLOSED **2** : characterized by mathematical elements that when subjected to an operation produce only elements of the same set ⟨whole numbers are *closed* under addition and multiplication⟩

¹clos·et \'kläz-ət\ *n* **1** : a small room for privacy **2** : a small room or compartment for clothing or household supplies ⟨clothes *closet*⟩

²closet *vb* **1** : to shut up in or as if in a closet **2** : to take into a private room for an interview

close–up \'klōs-ˌəp\ *n* : a photograph or movie shot taken at close range

clo·sure \'klō-zhər\ *n* **1** : an act of closing **2** : the condition or property of being closed **3** : something that closes

¹clot \'klät\ *n* : a lump made by some sub-stance thickening and sticking together

²clot *vb* **clot·ted**; **clot·ting** : to thicken into a clot

cloth \'klȯth\ *n*, *pl* **cloths** \'klȯthz, 'klȯths\ **1** : a pliable woven or knitted fabric (as of cot-ton, wool, linen, or silk) **2** : a piece of cloth used for a particular purpose ⟨a polishing *cloth*⟩ **3** : TABLECLOTH **4** : distinctive dress of a profession (as the clergy) **5** : CLERGY

clothe \'klōth\ *vb* **clothed** *or* **clad** \'klad\; **cloth·ing** **1** : to cover with or as if with clothing : DRESS **2** : to provide with clothes ⟨fed and *clothed* his family⟩ **3** : to express by suitably significant language

clothes \'klōz, 'klōthz\ *n pl* **1** : CLOTHING, DRESS **2** : BEDCLOTHES

clothes moth *n* : a small yellowish moth whose larvae feed on wool, fur, and feathers

clothes·pin \'klōz-ˌpin, 'klōthz-\ *n* : a forked piece of wood or plastic or a clamp for holding clothes in place on a line

clothespins

cloth·ing \'klō-thing\ *n* **1** : gar-ments in general : CLOTHES **2** : COVERING

¹cloud \'klaud\ *n* **1** : a visible mass of tiny bits of water or ice hanging in the air usually high above the earth **2** : a visible mass of small particles in the air ⟨a *cloud* of dust⟩ **3** : a large group massed together ⟨a *cloud* of mosquitoes⟩ **4** : something that has a dark or threatening look ⟨*clouds* of war⟩

²cloud *vb* **1** : to make or become cloudy **2** : to darken or conceal as if by a cloud

cloud·burst \'klaud-ˌbərst\ *n* : a sudden heavy rainfall

cloud·y \'klaud-ē\ *adj* **cloud·i·er**; **cloud·i·est** **1** : overspread with clouds : CLOUDED ⟨a *cloudy* sky⟩ **2** : CONFUSED ⟨*cloudy* thinking⟩ **3** : not clear ⟨a *cloudy* liquid⟩ — **cloud·i·ness** *n*

¹clout \'klaut\ *n* : a blow especially with the hand : a hard hit

²clout *vb* : to hit or strike forcefully

¹clove \'klōv\ *n* : the dried flower bud of a tropical tree used as a spice

²clove *past of* CLEAVE

cloven *past part of* CLEAVE

clo·ver \'klō-vər\ *n* : any of various hay and pasture plants having leaves with three leaflets and usually rounded red, white, yellow, or purple flower heads

clover

¹clown \'klaun\ *n* **1** : a rude ill-bred person **2** : a fool or comedian in an entertainment (as a play or circus)

²clown *vb* : to act like a clown : play the fool

¹club \'kləb\ *n* **1** : a heavy usually wooden stick used as a weapon **2** : a stick or bat used to hit a ball in various games ⟨golf *club*⟩ **3** : a group of people associated for a common purpose **4** : the meeting place of a club

²club *vb* **clubbed; club·bing 1** : to beat or strike with or as if with a club **2** : to unite for a common purpose ⟨*clubbed* together to buy a boat⟩

club·house \'kləb-,haús\ *n* **1** : a house occupied by a club **2** : locker rooms used by an athletic team

club moss *n* : a low often trailing evergreen plant that forms spores instead of seeds

¹cluck \'klək\ *vb* : to make or call with a cluck

²cluck *n* **1** : the call of the domestic hen especially to her chicks **2** : a brooding hen

clue \'klü\ *n* : something that guides a person in solving something difficult or perplexing

¹clump \'kləmp\ *n* **1** : a group of things clustered together ⟨a *clump* of bushes⟩ **2** : a compact mass **3** : a heavy tramping sound

²clump *vb* **1** : to tread clumsily and noisily **2** : to form or cause to form clumps

clum·sy \'kləm-zē\ *adj* **clum·si·er; clum·si·est 1** : lacking skill or grace : AWKWARD ⟨*clumsy* fingers⟩ **2** : lacking tact **3** : badly or awkwardly made or done — **clum·si·ly** \-zə-lē\ *adv* — **clum·si·ness** \-zē-nəs\ *n*

clung *past of* CLING

¹clus·ter \'kləs-tər\ *n* : a number of similar things growing, collected, or grouped closely together : BUNCH ⟨a *cluster* of houses⟩

²cluster *vb* : to grow, collect, or assemble in a cluster

¹clutch \'kləch\ *vb* **1** : to grasp or hold with or as if with the hands or claws **2** : SNATCH

²clutch *n* **1** : the claws or a hand in the act of grasping **2** : CONTROL, POWER **3** : a device for gripping an object **4** : a coupling for connecting and disconnecting a driving and a driven part in machinery **5** : a lever or pedal operating a clutch

¹clut·ter \'klət-ər\ *vb* : to throw into disorder : fill or cover with scattered things that hinder movement or reduce efficiency

²clutter *n* : a crowded or confused collection : DISORDER

co- *prefix* **1** : with : together : joint : jointly ⟨*co*exist⟩ ⟨*co*heir⟩ **2** : in or to the same degree ⟨*co*extensive⟩ **3** : fellow : partner ⟨*co*author⟩

¹coach \'kōch\ *n* **1** : a large four-wheeled horse-drawn carriage with a raised seat outside in front for the driver **2** : a railroad passenger car for day travel **3** : a class of passenger airplane transportation at a lower fare than first class **4** : a teacher who tutors students **5** : a person who instructs or trains a performer or team

coach 1

²coach *vb* : to act as coach

coach·man \'kōch-mən\ *n, pl* **coach·men** \-mən\ : a man whose business is driving a coach or carriage

co·ag·u·late \kō-'ag-yə-,lāt\ *vb* **co·ag·u·lat·ed; co·ag·u·lat·ing** : to gather into a thickened compact mass : CLOT

¹coal \'kōl\ *n* **1** : a piece of glowing or charred wood : EMBER **2** : a black solid mineral that is formed by the partial decay of vegetable matter under the influence of moisture and often increased pressure and temperature within the earth and is mined for use as a fuel

²coal *vb* **1** : to supply with coal **2** : to take on a supply of coal

coarse \'kōrs\ *adj* **1** : of ordinary or poor quality or appearance : COMMON, ROUGH ⟨*coarse* food⟩ ⟨*coarse* wool⟩ **2** : made up of large particles ⟨*coarse* sand⟩ **3** : ROUGH, HARSH ⟨*coarse* skin⟩ **4** : not refined : RUDE ⟨*coarse* language⟩ — **coarse·ly** *adv* — **coarse·ness** *n*

coars·en \'kōrs-n\ *vb* : to make or become coarse ⟨hands *coarsened* by hard labor⟩

¹coast \'kōst\ *n* : the land near a shore

²coast *vb* **1** : to sail along a coast **2** : to slide downhill by the force of gravity over snow or ice **3** : to move along (as on a bicycle when not pedaling) without applying power

coast·al \'kōst-l\ *adj* : of, relating to, or located on, near, or along a coast ⟨*coastal* trade⟩

coast·er \'kōs-tər\ *n* **1** : one that coasts **2** : a ship that trades from port to port along a coast **3** : a sled or small wagon used in coasting

coast guard *n* **1** : a military force that guards a coast **2** : a member of a coast guard

coast·wise \'kōst-,wīz\ *adv (or adj)* : along the coast ⟨*coastwise* shipping⟩

¹coat \'kōt\ *n* **1** : an outer garment varying in length and style according to fashion and use **2** : the outer covering (as fur or feathers) of an animal **3** : a layer of one substance covering another ⟨a *coat* of paint⟩ — **coat·ed** \-əd\ *adj*

²**coat** *vb* : to cover with a coat or layer

coat·ing \'kōt-ing\ *n* **1** : COAT, COVERING ⟨a thin *coating* of ice⟩ **2** : cloth for coats

coat of arms : the arms or emblems that a person wears or displays (as on a shield)

coat of mail : a garment of metal scales or rings worn as armor

co·au·thor \'kō-'ȯ-thər\ *n* : a joint or associate author

coax \'kōks\ *vb* **1** : to influence by gentle urging, caressing, or flattering **2** : to draw or gain by means of gentle urging or flattery

cob \'käb\ *n* **1** : CORNCOB **2** : a strong short-legged horse and especially one used for riding

co·balt \'kō-ˌbȯlt\ *n* : a tough shiny silver‑white metallic chemical element found with iron and nickel

cob·ble \'käb-əl\ *vb* **cob·bled**; **cob·bling** **1** : MEND, REPAIR **2** : to make or put together roughly or hastily

cob·bler \'käb-lər\ *n* **1** : a person who mends or makes shoes **2** : a deep-dish fruit pie with a thick upper crust

cob·ble·stone \'käb-əl-ˌstōn\ *n* : a naturally rounded stone larger than a pebble and smaller than a boulder used especially in paving streets

co·bra \'kō-brə\ *n* : a very poisonous snake of Asia and Africa that puffs out the skin around its neck into a hood when excited

cob·web \'käb-ˌweb\ *n* **1** : the fine network spread by a spider **2** : something resembling or suggesting a spider's web

co·caine \kō-'kān\ *n* : a drug obtained from the leaves of a South American shrub and used as a medicine to deaden pain and to cause sleep

¹**cock** \'käk\ *n* **1** : a male bird : ROOSTER **2** : a faucet or valve for regulating the flow of a liquid or a gas **3** : a cocked position of the hammer of a gun ⟨a rifle at half *cock*⟩

²**cock** *vb* **1** : to draw back the hammer of (a gun) in readiness for firing ⟨*cock* a pistol⟩ **2** : to turn or tip upward or to one side

³**cock** *n* : TILT, SLANT

⁴**cock** *n* : a small pile (as of hay)

⁵**cock** *vb* : to put (as hay) into cocks

cock·a·too \'käk-ə-ˌtü\ *n, pl* **cock·a·toos** : any of several large, noisy, and usually brightly colored crested parrots mostly of Australia

cock·le \'käk-əl\ *n* **1** : an edible shellfish with a heart-shaped double shell **2** : COCKLESHELL

cock·le·bur \'käk-əl-ˌbər, 'kək-\ *n* : a prickly‑fruited plant related to the thistles

cock·le·shell \'käk-əl-ˌshel\ *n* **1** : a shell of a cockle **2** : a light flimsy boat

cock·pit \'käk-ˌpit\ *n* **1** : an open space back of a decked area from which a small boat (as a yacht) is steered **2** : a space in an airplane for the pilot or pilot and passengers or pilot and crew

cockleshell

cock·roach \'käk-ˌrōch\ *n* : a troublesome insect found in houses and ships and active chiefly at night

cock·y \'käk-ē\ *adj* **cock·i·er**; **cock·i·est** : PERT, CONCEITED ⟨a *cocky* manner⟩

co·co \'kō-kō\ *n, pl* **co·cos** : the coconut palm or its fruit

co·coa \'kō-kō\ *n* **1** : chocolate ground to a powder after some of its fat is removed **2** : a drink made from cocoa powder

co·co·nut *or* **co·coa·nut** \'kō-kə-nət, -ˌnät\ *n* : the husk-covered nutlike fruit of a tall tropical palm (**coconut palm**)

co·coon \kə-'kün\ *n* : the silky covering which caterpillars make around themselves and in which they are protected while changing into butterflies or moths

cod \'käd\ *n, pl* **cod** : a large deep-water food fish found in the colder parts of the North Atlantic ocean

cod·dle \'käd-l\ *vb* **cod·dled**; **cod·dling** **1** : to cook slowly in water below the boiling point ⟨*coddle* eggs⟩ **2** : PAMPER

¹**code** \'kōd\ *n* **1** : a collection of laws systematically arranged ⟨criminal *code*⟩ **2** : a system of rules or principles ⟨the *code* of a gentleman⟩ **3** : a system of signals for communicating **4** : a system of letters or symbols used with special meanings

²**code** *vb* **cod·ed**; **cod·ing** : to put in the form of a code

cod·fish \'käd-ˌfish\ *n, pl* **codfish** *or* **cod·fish·es** : COD

codg·er \'käj-ər\ *n* : an odd or cranky fellow

co·erce \kō-'ərs\ *vb* **co·erced**; **co·erc·ing** : FORCE, COMPEL

cof·fee \'kȯf-ē\ *n* **1** : a drink made from the roasted and ground seeds of a tropical plant **2** : the seeds of the coffee plant

cof·fee·pot \'kȯf-ē-ˌpät\ *n* : a covered utensil for preparing or serving coffee

cof·fer \'kȯf-ər\ *n* **1** : a chest or box used especially for holding money and valuables **2** : TREASURY, FUNDS — usually used in plural

cof·fin \'kȯf-ən\ *n* : a box or case to hold a dead body

cog \'käg\ *n* : a tooth on the rim of a wheel in a mechanical device adjusted to fit the notches in another wheel or part and to give or receive motion

cog·i·tate \'käj-ə-ˌtāt\ *vb* **cog·i·tat·ed; cog·i·tat·ing** : to think over : PONDER, PLAN

cog·i·ta·tion \ˌkäj-ə-'tā-shən\ *n* : MEDITATION

cog·wheel \'käg-ˌhwēl\ *n* : a wheel with cogs on the rim

co·he·sion \kō-'hē-zhən\ *n* **1** : the action of sticking together **2** : the force of attraction between the molecules in a mass

cogwheel

¹coil \'kȯil\ *vb* **1** : to wind into rings or a spiral ⟨*coil* a rope⟩ **2** : to form or lie in a coil

²coil *n* **1** : a circle, a series of circles, or a spiral made by coiling **2** : something coiled

¹coin \'kȯin\ *n* **1** : a piece of metal issued by government authority as money **2** : metal money ⟨change these bills for *coin*⟩

²coin *vb* **1** : to make coins especially by stamping pieces of metal : MINT **2** : to make metal (as gold or silver) into coins **3** : CREATE

coin·age \'kȯi-nij\ *n* **1** : the act or process of coining **2** : something that is coined : COINS

co·in·cide \ˌkō-ən-'sīd\ *vb* **co·in·cid·ed; co·in·cid·ing** **1** : to happen at the same time **2** : to occupy the same space **3** : to agree exactly

co·in·ci·dence \kō-'in-sə-dəns\ *n* **1** : a coinciding in space or time **2** : two things that happen at the same time by accident but seem to have some connection

coke \'kōk\ *n* : gray lumps of fuel made by heating soft coal until some of its gases have passed off

col- — see COM-

col·an·der \'kəl-ən-dər\ *n* : a perforated utensil for draining foods

¹cold \'kōld\ *adj* **1** : having a low temperature or one decidedly below normal ⟨a *cold* day⟩ ⟨*cold* drinks⟩ **2** : lacking warmth of feeling : UNFRIENDLY **3** : suffering from lack of warmth ⟨feel *cold*⟩ — **cold·ly** *adv* — **cold·ness** *n*

colander

²cold *n* **1** : a condition of low temperature : cold weather **2** : the bodily feeling produced by lack of warmth : CHILL **3** : a bodily disorder popularly associated with chilling

cold–blood·ed \'kōld-'bləd-əd\ *adj* **1** : lacking or showing a lack of normal human feelings ⟨a *cold-blooded* criminal⟩ **2** : having a body temperature that varies with the temperature of the environment ⟨frogs are *cold-blooded* animals⟩ **3** : sensitive to cold

co·le·us \'kō-lē-əs\ *n* : a plant of the mint family grown for its many-colored leaves

col·ic \'käl-ik\ *n* : sharp pain in the bowels — **col·ick·y** \'käl-ə-kē\ *adj*

col·i·se·um \ˌkäl-ə-'sē-əm\ *n* : a large structure (as a stadium) for athletic contests or public entertainment

col·lab·o·rate \kə-'lab-ə-ˌrāt\ *vb* **col·lab·o·rat·ed; col·lab·o·rat·ing** **1** : to work jointly with others (as in writing a book) **2** : to cooperate with an enemy force occupying one's country

¹col·lapse \kə-'laps\ *vb* **col·lapsed; col·laps·ing** **1** : to break down completely : fall in **2** : to shrink together abruptly **3** : to suffer a physical or mental breakdown **4** : to fold together

²collapse *n* : the act or an instance of collapsing : BREAKDOWN

col·laps·i·ble \kə-'lap-sə-bəl\ *adj* : capable of collapsing or of being collapsed

¹col·lar \'käl-ər\ *n* **1** : a band, strap, or chain worn around the neck or the neckline of a garment **2** : a part of the harness of draft animals fitted over the shoulders **3** : something (as a ring or round flange to restrain motion or hold in place) resembling a collar — **col·lar·less** \-ləs\ *adj*

²collar *vb* **1** : to seize by the collar : CAPTURE, GRAB **2** : to put a collar on

col·lar·bone \ˌkäl-ər-'bōn\ *n* : a bone of the shoulder joined to the breastbone and the shoulder blade

col·league \'käl-ˌēg\ *n* : an associate in a profession : a fellow worker

col·lect \kə-'lekt\ *vb* **1** : to bring or come together into one body or place : ASSEMBLE, GATHER **2** : to gather from a number of sources ⟨*collect* stamps⟩ ⟨*collect* taxes⟩ **3** : to gain or regain control of ⟨*collected* his thoughts⟩ **4** : to receive payment for

col·lect·ed \kə-'lek-təd\ *adj* : CALM

col·lec·tion \kə-'lek-shən\ *n* **1** : the act or process of collecting or gathering together ⟨the *collection* of mail by the postman⟩ **2** : a group of persons or things assembled together and especially a group of specimens gathered for study or exhibition **3** : a gathering of money (as for charitable purposes)

col·lec·tive \kə-'lek-tiv\ *adj* **1** : having to do with a number of persons or things thought of as a whole **2** : done or shared by a number of persons as a group — **col·lec·tive·ly** *adv*

col·lec·tor \kə-'lek-tər\ *n* **1** : a person or thing that collects ⟨stamp *collector*⟩ **2** : a person whose business it is to collect money

col·lege \'käl-ij\ *n* : a school higher than a high school or an academy

col·le·giate \kə-'lē-jət\ *adj* **1** : having to do

with a college ⟨*collegiate* studies⟩ **2** : of, relating to, or characteristic of college students

col·lide \kə-'līd\ *vb* **col·lid·ed; col·lid·ing**
1 : to strike against each other **2** : CLASH

col·lie \'käl-ē\ *n* : a large usually long-coated dog of a Scottish breed used to herd sheep

col·li·sion \kə-'lizh-ən\ *n* : an act or instance of colliding : CRASH, CLASH

col·lo·qui·al \kə-'lō-kwē-əl\ *adj* : used in or characteristic of familiar and informal conversation

col·lo·qui·al·ism \kə-'lō-kwē-ə-,liz-əm\ *n* : a colloquial expression

co·logne \kə-'lōn\ *n* : a perfumed liquid composed of alcohol and fragrant oils

¹co·lon \'kō-lən\ *n* : the chief part of the large intestine

²colon *n* : a punctuation mark : used chiefly to direct attention to what follows (as a list, explanation, or quotation)

colo·nel \'kərn-l\ *n* : a commissioned officer (as in the army) ranking next below a brigadier general

¹co·lo·ni·al \kə-'lō-nē-əl\ *adj* **1** : of, relating to, or characteristic of a colony **2** *often cap* : of or relating to the original thirteen colonies that formed the United States

²colonial *n* : a member or inhabitant of a colony

col·o·nist \'käl-ə-nəst\ *n* **1** : an inhabitant of a colony **2** : a person who helps to found a colony

col·o·nize \'käl-ə-,nīz\ *vb* **col·o·nized; col·o·niz·ing** **1** : to establish a colony in or on **2** : to settle in a colony

col·on·nade \,käl-ə-'nād\ *n* : a row of columns alongside a building usually supporting the base of the roof structure

col·o·ny \'käl-ə-nē\ *n, pl* **col·o·nies** **1** : a group of people sent out by a state to a new territory : the territory inhabited by these people **2** : a distant territory belonging to or under the control of a nation **3** : a group of animals of one kind living together ⟨a *colony* of ants⟩ **4** : a group of individuals with common characteristics or interests situated in close association

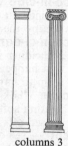
colonnade

¹col·or \'kəl-ər\ *n* **1** : the appearance of a thing apart from size and shape when light strikes it ⟨red is the *color* of blood⟩ **2** : a hue other than black, white, or gray ⟨dressed in bright *colors*⟩ **3** : outward show : APPEARANCE **4** : complexion tint **5** : BLUSH **6** *pl* : an identifying flag or pennant **7** *pl* : military service **8** : VIVIDNESS, INTEREST

²color *vb* **1** : to give color to ⟨a blush *colored* her cheeks⟩ **2** : to change the color of : PAINT, DYE **3** : MISREPRESENT, DISTORT **4** : to take on or change color : BLUSH

col·or·a·tion \,kəl-ə-'rā-shən\ *n* : use or arrangement of colors or shades : COLORING

col·ored \'kəl-ərd\ *adj* **1** : having color **2** : of a race other than the white : NEGRO

col·or·ful \'kəl-ər-fəl\ *adj* **1** : having striking colors **2** : full of variety or interest

col·or·ing \'kəl-ə-ring\ *n* **1** : the act of applying colors **2** : something that produces color ⟨vegetable *coloring*⟩ **3** : the effect produced by the use of color **4** : natural color : COMPLEXION ⟨a person of delicate *coloring*⟩ **5** : change of appearance (as by adding color)

col·or·less \'kəl-ər-ləs\ *adj* **1** : lacking color **2** : PALLID, BLANCHED **3** : DULL

co·los·sal \kə-'läs-əl\ *adj* : of very great size

colt \'kōlt\ *n* **1** : FOAL **2** : a young male horse

col·um·bine \'käl-əm-,bīn\ *n* : a plant related to the buttercups that has three-parted leaves and showy flowers usually with five petals ending in spurs

col·umn \'käl-əm\ *n* **1** : one of two or more vertical sections of a printed page ⟨a two-*column* page⟩ **2** : a special department (as in a newspaper) ⟨a sports *column*⟩ **3** : a pillar supporting a roof or gallery **4** : something resembling a column in shape, position, or use ⟨the spinal *column*⟩ ⟨a *column* of water⟩ ⟨a *column* of figures⟩ **5** : a long straight row (as of soldiers)

columns 3

col·um·nist \'käl-əm-nəst, -ə-məst\ *n* : a writer of a newspaper column

com- *or* **col-** *or* **con-** *prefix* : with : together : jointly — usually **com-** before *b, p,* or *m* ⟨*com*mingle⟩, **col-** before *l* ⟨*col*linear⟩, and **con-** before other sounds ⟨*con*centrate⟩

co·ma \'kō-mə\ *n* : a deep sleeplike state caused by sickness or injury

¹comb \'kōm\ *n* **1** : a toothed implement used to smooth and arrange the hair or worn in the hair to hold it in place **2** : a toothed instrument used for separating fibers (as of wool or flax) **3** : a fleshy crest with toothlike points on the head of a fowl and some related birds **4** : HONEYCOMB

comb 3

²comb *vb* **1** : to smooth, arrange, or untangle with a comb ⟨*combed* his hair⟩ **2** : to go over or through carefully in search of something

¹com·bat \kəm-'bat\ *vb* **com·bat·ed** *or* **com-**

bat·ted; **com·bat·ing** or **com·bat·ting** : to fight with : fight against : OPPOSE ⟨*combat* disease⟩

²**com·bat** \'käm-ˌbat\ *n* **1** : a fight or contest between individuals or groups **2** : CONFLICT, CONTROVERSY **3** : FIGHTING, ACTION ⟨soldiers lost in *combat*⟩

¹**com·bat·ant** \kəm-'bat-nt, 'käm-bət-ənt\ *n* : a person who takes part in a combat

²**combatant** *adj* : engaging in or ready to engage in combat

com·bi·na·tion \ˌkäm-bə-'nā-shən\ *n* **1** : a result or product of combining or being combined **2** : a union of persons or groups for a set purpose **3** : a series of letters or numbers which when dialed by a disk on a lock will operate or open the lock **4** : a union of different things

¹**com·bine** \kəm-'bīn\ *vb* **com·bined; com·bin·ing** : to join together so as to make or to seem one thing : UNITE, MIX

²**com·bine** \'käm-ˌbīn\ *n* **1** : a union of persons or groups of persons especially for a business or political advantage **2** : a machine that harvests and threshes grain

com·bus·ti·ble \kəm-'bəs-tə-bəl\ *adj* **1** : capable of being burned **2** : catching fire or burning easily

com·bus·tion \kəm-'bəs-chən\ *n* : the process of burning

come \'kəm, kəm\ *vb* **came** \'kām\; **come; com·ing** \'kəm-ing\ **1** : to move toward : APPROACH ⟨*come* here⟩ **2** : to reach the point of being or becoming ⟨the water *came* to a boil⟩ ⟨the rope *came* untied⟩ **3** : AMOUNT ⟨the bill *comes* to ten dollars⟩ **4** : to take place ⟨the holiday *comes* on Tuesday⟩ **5** : ORIGINATE, ARISE ⟨he *comes* from a good family⟩ **6** : to be obtainable or attainable ⟨these books *come* in four bindings⟩ **7** : EXTEND, REACH

co·me·di·an \kə-'mēd-ē-ən\ *n* **1** : an actor who plays comic roles **2** : an amusing person

com·e·dy \'käm-ə-dē\ *n, pl* **com·e·dies 1** : an amusing play that has a happy ending **2** : an amusing or ludicrous event

come·ly \'kəm-lē\ *adj* **come·li·er; come·li·est** : pleasing to the sight : good-looking

com·et \'käm-ət\ *n* : a celestial body that consists of a fuzzy head surrounding a bright part and often has a long tail that points away from the sun

¹**com·fort** \'kəm-fərt\ *n* **1** : acts or words that comfort **2** : the feeling of the one that is comforted **3** : something that makes a person comfortable

²**comfort** *vb* **1** : to give hope and strength to : CHEER **2** : to ease the grief or trouble of

com·fort·a·ble \'kəm-fərt-ə-bəl\ *adj* **1** : giving comfort ⟨a *comfortable* chair⟩ **2** : more than adequate ⟨a *comfortable* income⟩ **3** : physically at ease — **com·fort·a·bly** \-blē\ *adv*

com·fort·er \'kəm-fərt-ər\ *n* **1** : one that gives comfort **2** : a long narrow neck scarf **3** : QUILT, PUFF

com·ic \'käm-ik\ *adj* **1** : of, relating to, or characteristic of comedy **2** : LAUGHABLE

com·i·cal \'käm-i-kəl\ *adj* : causing mirth : FUNNY — **com·i·cal·ly** *adv*

comic book *n* : a magazine made up of a series of comic strips

comic strip *n* : a series of cartoons that tell a story or part of a story

com·ma \'käm-ə\ *n* : a punctuation mark , used chiefly to show separation of words or word groups within a sentence

¹**com·mand** \kə-'mand\ *vb* **1** : to direct with authority : ORDER **2** : to have power or control over : be commander of **3** : to have at one's disposal **4** : to demand as right or due : EXACT ⟨*commands* a high fee⟩ **5** : to overlook from an advantageous position

²**command** *n* **1** : the act of commanding **2** : an order given ⟨obey a *command*⟩ **3** : the ability to control and use : MASTERY ⟨a good *command* of the language⟩ **4** : the authority, right, or power to command : CONTROL **5** : the personnel, area, or unit under a commander **6** : a position from which military operations are directed

com·man·dant \'käm-ən-ˌdant, -ˌdänt\ *n* : a commanding officer

com·mand·er \kə-'man-dər\ *n* **1** : a person who commands **2** : a commissioned officer in the navy ranking next below a captain

commander in chief : one who holds supreme command of the armed forces of a nation

com·mand·ment \kə-'mand-mənt\ *n* : something given as a command and especially one of the Ten Commandments in the Bible

com·man·do \kə-'man-dō\ *n, pl* **com·man·dos** or **com·man·does 1** : a band or unit of troops trained for making surprise raids into enemy territory **2** : a member of a unit trained for making raids

com·mem·o·rate \kə-'mem-ə-ˌrāt\ *vb* **com·mem·o·rat·ed; com·mem·o·rat·ing 1** : to call or recall to mind **2** : CELEBRATE, OBSERVE **3** : to serve as a memorial of

com·mem·o·ra·tion \kə-ˌmem-ə-'rā-shən\ *n* **1** : the act of commemorating **2** : something (as a statue) that commemorates

com·mence \kə-'mens\ *vb* **com·menced; com·menc·ing** : BEGIN, START

com·mence·ment \kə-'mens-mənt\ *n* **1** : the

act or the time of commencing : BEGINNING **2** : graduation exercises

com·mend \kə-'mend\ vb **1** : to give into another's care : ENTRUST **2** : to speak of someone or something with approval : PRAISE

com·men·da·tion \ˌkäm-ən-'dā-shən\ n : PRAISE, APPROVAL

¹com·ment \'käm-ˌent\ n **1** : an expression of opinion either in speech or writing **2** : mention of something that deserves attention or notice **syn** see REMARK

²comment vb : to make a comment : REMARK

com·men·ta·tor \'käm-ən-ˌtāt-ər\ n **1** : a person who makes comments **2** : a person who talks on news events (as over radio)

com·merce \'käm-ərs, -ˌərs\ n : the buying and selling of goods especially on a large scale and between different places : TRADE

¹com·mer·cial \kə-'mər-shəl\ adj **1** : having to do with commerce **2** : having financial profit as the chief aim — **com·mer·cial·ly** adv

²commercial n : an advertisement broadcast on radio or television

com·mer·cial·ize \kə-'mər-shə-ˌlīz\ vb **com·mer·cial·ized; com·mer·cial·iz·ing** : to manage with the idea of making a profit

¹com·mis·sion \kə-'mish-ən\ n **1** : an order or instruction granting the power to perform various acts or duties : the right or duty thus authorized **2** : a certificate that gives military or naval rank and authority : the rank and authority so conferred **3** : authority to act as agent for another : a task or matter entrusted to an agent **4** : a group of persons given orders and authority to perform specified duties ⟨a park *commission*⟩ **5** : an act of committing (as a crime) **6** : a fee paid to an agent for transacting a piece of business

²commission vb **1** : to give a commission to **2** : to put a ship into service

commissioned officer n : a military or naval officer holding by a commission a rank of second lieutenant or ensign or a higher rank

com·mis·sion·er \kə-'mish-ə-nər\ n **1** : a member of a commission **2** : an official in charge of a government department

com·mit \kə-'mit\ vb **com·mit·ted; com·mit·ting** **1** : to put into charge or safekeeping : ENTRUST, CONSIGN **2** : to place in or send officially to a prison or mental institution **3** : to bring about : PERFORM ⟨*commit* a crime⟩ **4** : to pledge or assign to some particular course or use — **com·mit·ment** n

com·mit·tee \kə-'mit-ē\ n : a group of persons appointed or elected to consider some particular matter or to perform some duty

com·mod·i·ty \kə-'mäd-ət-ē\ n, pl **com·mod-**

i·ties : an article of trade or commerce including products of agriculture, mining, or manufacture

com·mo·dore \'käm-ə-ˌdōr\ n **1** : a commissioned officer in the navy ranking next below a rear admiral **2** : the chief officer of a yacht club **3** : the senior captain of a line of merchant ships

¹com·mon \'käm-ən\ adj **1** : having to do with, belonging to, or used by everybody : PUBLIC **2** : belonging to or shared by two or more individuals or by the members of a family or group ⟨a *common* ancestor⟩ **3** : GENERAL ⟨facts of *common* knowledge⟩ **4** : FREQUENT, FAMILIAR ⟨a *common* sight⟩ **5** : not above the average in rank, merit, or social position ⟨a *common* soldier⟩ **6** : PLAIN, PRACTICAL **7** : SECOND-RATE **8** : COARSE, VULGAR — **com·mon·ly** adv

²common n : land (as a park) owned and used in common by a community — **in common** : shared together

common cold n : an acute virus disease that causes inflammation and swelling of the nose and throat and usually excessive secretion of mucus and coughing and sneezing

common denominator n : a common multiple of the denominators of a number of fractions

com·mon·er \'käm-ə-nər\ n : one of the common people

common multiple n : a multiple of each of two or more numbers

¹com·mon·place \'käm-ən-ˌplās\ n : something that is very common or ordinary

²commonplace adj : not remarkable

common sense n : sound prudent judgment

com·mon·wealth \'käm-ən-ˌwelth\ n **1** : a political unit (as a nation or state) **2** : a state of the United States and especially Kentucky, Massachusetts, Pennsylvania, or Virginia

com·mo·tion \kə-'mō-shən\ n **1** : AGITATION **2** : noisy excitement and confusion

com·mune \kə-'myün\ vb **com·muned; com·mun·ing** : to communicate intimately

com·mu·ni·ca·ble \kə-'myü-ni-kə-bəl\ adj : capable of being communicated

com·mu·ni·cate \kə-'myü-nə-ˌkāt\ vb **com·mu·ni·cat·ed; com·mu·ni·cat·ing** **1** : to make known **2** : SPREAD, TRANSFER **3** : to get in touch (as by telephone) **4** : JOIN

com·mu·ni·ca·tion \kə-ˌmyü-nə-'kā-shən\ n **1** : the exchange (as by speech or letter) of information between persons **2** : MESSAGE **3** pl : a system of sending messages (as by telephone) **4** pl : a system of routes for moving troops, supplies, and vehicles

com·mu·nion \kə-'myü-nyən\ *n* **1** : an act or instance of communing or sharing **2** : a religious service or sacrament commemorating with bread and wine the last supper of Jesus Christ **3** : the act of receiving the sacrament **4** : COMMUNICATION **5** : a body of Christians having a common faith and discipline

com·mu·nism \'käm-yə-ˌniz-əm\ *n* **1** : a system of social organization in which property and goods are held in common **2** : a theory that advocates communism

com·mu·nist \'käm-yə-nəst\ *n* **1** : a person who believes in communism **2** *cap* : a member or follower of a Communist party or movement

com·mu·ni·ty \kə-'myü-nət-ē\ *n, pl* **com·mu·ni·ties** **1** : the people living in a particular place (as a village or city) : the area itself **2** : a natural group (as of kinds of plants and animals) living together and interdependent for various necessities of life **3** : a group of people with common interests living together ⟨a *community* of monks⟩ **4** : people in general : PUBLIC **5** : joint ownership or participation **6** : LIKENESS ⟨a *community* of ideas⟩

com·mu·ta·tive \'käm-yə-ˌtāt-iv\ *adj* : being a property of a mathematical operation (as addition or multiplication) in which the result of combining elements is independent of the order in which they are taken

com·mute \kə-'myüt\ *vb* **com·mut·ed; com·mut·ing** **1** : EXCHANGE, SUBSTITUTE **2** : to travel back and forth regularly — **com·mut·er** *n*

¹com·pact \kəm-'pakt, 'käm-ˌpakt\ *adj* **1** : closely united or packed : SOLID, FIRM **2** : arranged so as to save space ⟨a *compact* house⟩ **3** : not wordy : BRIEF— **com·pact·ly** *adv* — **com·pact·ness** *n*

²com·pact \'käm-ˌpakt\ *n* **1** : a small case for cosmetics **2** : a relatively small automobile

³com·pact \'käm-ˌpakt\ *n* : AGREEMENT

com·pan·ion \kəm-'pan-yən\ *n* [from Latin *companio* "comrade", from *com-*, a prefix meaning "together" and *panis* "bread"; so called because it was used originally of a companion at meals] **1** : a person or thing that accompanies another : COMRADE **2** : one of a pair of matching things **3** : a person employed to live with and serve another

com·pan·ion·ship \kəm-'pan-yən-ˌship\ *n* : FELLOWSHIP, COMPANY

com·pan·ion·way \kəm-'pan-yən-ˌwā\ *n* : a ship's stairway from one deck to another

com·pa·ny \'kəm-pə-nē\ *n, pl* **com·pa·nies** **1** : association with others : FELLOWSHIP **2** : COMPANIONS, ASSOCIATES ⟨known by the *company* you keep⟩ **3** : GUESTS, VISITORS ⟨have

company⟩ **4** : a group of persons or things **5** : a body of soldiers and especially an infantry unit normally led by a captain **6** : a band of musical or dramatic performers ⟨opera *company*⟩ **7** : the officers and men of a ship **8** : an association of persons carrying on a business enterprise

com·pa·ra·ble \'käm-pə-rə-bəl\ *adj* : capable or worthy of being compared

¹com·par·a·tive \kəm-'par-ət-iv\ *adj* **1** : of, relating to, or being the form of an adjective or adverb that shows a degree of comparison that is greater or less than its positive degree **2** : measured by comparisons : RELATIVE — **com·par·a·tive·ly** *adv*

²comparative *n* : the comparative degree or a comparative form in a language

com·pare \kəm-'pa(ə)r\ *vb* **com·pared; com·par·ing** **1** : to represent as similar : LIKEN ⟨*compare* an anthill to a town⟩ **2** : to examine for likenesses or differences ⟨*compare* two bicycles⟩ **3** : to be worthy of comparison **4** : to state the positive, comparative, and superlative forms of an adjective or adverb

syn COMPARE, CONTRAST mean to examine two or more things in order to show likenesses and differences. COMPARE suggests an intention of showing relative value ⟨*compare* the American, French, and English bikes⟩ and may stress an effort to find areas of similarity and of overlapping ⟨*compare* Caesar and Napoleon⟩ CONTRAST emphasizes a search for differences or even for opposite qualities ⟨*contrast* city life and rural life⟩

com·par·i·son \kəm-'par-ə-sən\ *n* **1** : the act of comparing : the condition of being compared **2** : an examination of two or more objects to find the likenesses and differences between them **3** : change in the form and meaning of an adjective or an adverb (as by adding *-er* or *-est* or by prefixing *more* or *most*) to show different levels of quality, quantity, or relation

com·part·ment \kəm-'pärt-mənt\ *n* **1** : one of the parts into which an enclosed space is divided **2** : a separate division or section

¹com·pass \'kəm-pəs\ *vb* **1** : to travel entirely around **2** : ACHIEVE, ACCOMPLISH

²compass *n* **1** : BOUNDARY, CIRCUMFERENCE **2** : an enclosed space **3** : RANGE, SCOPE ⟨within the *compass* of her voice⟩ **4** : a device for determining directions on the earth's surface by means of a magnetic needle that points

compass 4

toward the north **5** : a device that indicates direction by other than magnetic means **6** : an instrument for drawing circles or marking measurements consisting of two pointed legs joined at the top by a pivot — usually used in plural

com·pas·sion \kəm-'pash-ən\ *n* : sorrow or pity for another : SYMPATHY, MERCY

com·pas·sion·ate \kəm-'pash-ə-nət\ *adj* : having or showing compassion

com·pat·i·ble \kəm-'pat-ə-bəl\ *adj* : capable of existing together in harmony

com·pa·tri·ot \kəm-'pā-trē-ət\ *n* : a fellow countryman

com·pel \kəm-'pel\ *vb* **com·pelled; com·pel·ling** : to drive or urge by physical, moral, or intellectual means

com·pen·sate \'käm-pən-ˌsāt\ *vb* **com·pen·sat·ed; com·pen·sat·ing** **1** : to be equivalent to in value or effect : **2** : to make amends **3** : PAY

com·pen·sa·tion \ˌkäm-pən-'sā-shən\ *n* **1** : something that makes up for or is given to make up for something else **2** : SALARY

com·pete \kəm-'pēt\ *vb* **com·pet·ed; com·pet·ing** : to strive for the same thing (as a prize or a reward) for which another is striving

com·pe·tence \'käm-pət-əns\ *n* : the quality or state of being competent

com·pe·tent \'käm-pət-ənt\ *adj* : CAPABLE, QUALIFIED ⟨a *competent* teacher⟩

com·pe·ti·tion \ˌkäm-pə-'tish-ən\ *n* **1** : the act or process of competing **2** : a contest between rivals for the same thing : RIVALRY

com·pet·i·tive \kəm-'pet-ət-iv\ *adj* : relating to, characterized by, or based on competition

com·pet·i·tor \kəm-'pet-ət-ər\ *n* : one that competes especially in the selling of goods or services : RIVAL

com·pile \kəm-'pīl\ *vb* **com·piled; com·pil·ing** **1** : to collect into a volume or list **2** : to collect information from books or documents and arrange it in a new form

com·pla·cence \kəm-'plās-ns\ *n* : calm or secure satisfaction with one's self or lot

com·pla·cen·cy \kəm-'plās-n-sē\ *n* : COMPLACENCE

com·pla·cent \kəm-'plās-nt\ *adj* : marked by complacence

com·plain \kəm-'plān\ *vb* **1** : to express grief, pain, or discontent : find fault **2** : to make an accusation — **com·plain·er** *n*

com·plaint \kəm-'plānt\ *n* **1** : expression of grief, pain, or discontent ⟨sounds of *complaint*⟩ **2** : a cause or reason for complaining **3** : a bodily ailment or disease **4** : a formal charge against a person

¹com·ple·ment \'käm-plə-mənt\ *n* : something that completes or fills : the number required to complete or make perfect

²com·ple·ment \'käm-plə-ˌment\ *vb* : to form or serve as a complement to ⟨a hat that *complements* the costume⟩

¹com·plete \kəm-'plēt\ *adj* **1** : having no part lacking : ENTIRE ⟨a *complete* set of books⟩ **2** : FINISHED, ENDED **3** : THOROUGH, ABSOLUTE — **com·plete·ly** *adv* — **com·plete·ness** *n*

²complete *vb* **com·plet·ed; com·plet·ing** **1** : to bring to an end : FINISH ⟨*complete* a job⟩ **2** : to make whole or perfect

com·ple·tion \kəm-'plē-shən\ *n* : the act or process of completing : the condition of being complete ⟨a job near *completion*⟩

com·plex \käm-'pleks\ *adj* **1** : made up of two or more parts **2** : not simple

complex fraction *n* : a fraction with a fraction or mixed number in the numerator or denominator or both ⟨5/1¾ is a *complex fraction*⟩

com·plex·ion \kəm-'plek-shən\ *n* **1** : the color or appearance of the skin and especially of the face **2** : general appearance or impression : CHARACTER

com·plex·i·ty \kəm-'plek-sət-ē\ *n, pl* **com·plex·i·ties** **1** : the quality or condition of being complex ⟨the *complexity* of a problem⟩ **2** : something complex : COMPLICATION

com·pli·cate \'käm-plə-ˌkāt\ *vb* **com·pli·cat·ed; com·pli·cat·ing** : to make or become complex or difficult

com·pli·ca·tion \ˌkäm-plə-'kā-shən\ *n* **1** : a confused situation **2** : something that makes a situation more complex or difficult

¹com·pli·ment \'käm-plə-mənt\ *n* **1** : an act or expression of praise, approval, respect, or admiration **2** *pl* : best wishes : REGARDS

²com·pli·ment \'käm-plə-ˌment\ *vb* : to pay a compliment to

syn COMPLIMENT, PRAISE, FLATTER all mean to express approval or admiration directly to someone. COMPLIMENT usually refers to making a somewhat formal statement about a particular thing ⟨his teacher *complimented* him on his excellent essay⟩ PRAISE suggests a more general expression of approval and often a more casual and enthusiastic one ⟨*praised* the dog and gave him a treat whenever he learned a new trick⟩ FLATTER differs mainly in that it suggests insincerity on the part of the one who praises, and stresses an appeal to someone's vanity often for selfish or deceitful reasons ⟨he was wrong in thinking that *flattering* the teacher would get him better marks⟩

com·pli·men·ta·ry \ˌkäm-plə-'ment-ə-rē\ *adj*

ə abut   ər further   a ax   ā age   ä father, cot   ȧ (see key page)   aů out   ch chin   e less   ē easy   g gift   i trip   ī life

1 : expressing or containing a compliment
2 : given free as a courtesy or favor

com·ply \kəm-'plī\ *vb* **com·plied; com·ply·ing**
: to act in accordance with another's wishes or in obedience to a rule : YIELD, CONSENT

com·pose \kəm-'pōz\ *vb* **com·posed; com·pos·ing** 1 : to form by putting together ⟨*compose* a song⟩ 2 : to make up ⟨*composed* of four parts⟩ 3 : to put in order : SETTLE, CALM

com·posed \kəm-'pōzd\ *adj* : CALM, SELF-POSSESSED

com·pos·er \kəm-'pō-zər\ *n* 1 : one that composes 2 : a writer of music

com·pos·ite \kəm-'päz-ət\ *adj* : made up of various distinct parts or elements

composite number *n* : a number that is a product of two or more whole numbers each greater than 1

com·po·si·tion \ˌkäm-pə-'zish-ən\ *n* 1 : the act of composing (as by writing) 2 : the manner in which the parts of a thing are put together 3 : MAKEUP, CONSTITUTION ⟨the *composition* of rubber⟩ 4 : a literary, musical, or artistic production 5 : a short piece of writing done as an educational exercise

com·po·sure \kəm-'pō-zhər\ *n* : calmness especially of mind, bearing, or appearance

¹com·pound \käm-'paùnd\ *vb* 1 : to mix or unite together into a whole : COMBINE 2 : to form by combining parts

²com·pound \'käm-ˌpaùnd\ *adj* : made of or by the union of two or more parts

³com·pound \'käm-ˌpaùnd\ *n* : something that is formed by combining two or more parts, ingredients, or elements

⁴com·pound \'käm-ˌpaùnd\ *n* : an enclosure of European houses and commercial buildings especially in the Orient

com·pre·hend \ˌkäm-pri-'hend\ *vb* 1 : to understand fully 2 : to take in : INCLUDE

com·pre·hen·sion \ˌkäm-pri-'hen-chən\ *n* : power or ability to understand

com·pre·hen·sive \ˌkäm-pri-'hen-siv\ *adj* 1 : including much : FULL, INCLUSIVE ⟨a *comprehensive* description⟩ 2 : having the power to understand — **com·pre·hen·sive·ness** *n*

¹com·press \kəm-'pres\ *vb* 1 : to press or squeeze together 2 : to reduce the volume of by pressure ⟨a pump for *compressing* air⟩

²com·press \'käm-ˌpres\ *n* : a pad (as of folded cloth) applied firmly to a part of the body (as to check bleeding)

com·pres·sion \kəm-'presh-ən\ *n* : the process of compressing : the state of being compressed

com·pres·sor \kəm-'pres-ər\ *n* 1 : one that

compresses 2 : a machine for compressing something (as air)

com·prise \kəm-'prīz\ *vb* **com·prised; com·pris·ing** 1 : to be made up of : INCLUDE, CONTAIN 2 : to make up : CONSTITUTE

¹com·pro·mise \'käm-prə-ˌmīz\ *n* 1 : a settlement of a dispute reached by each party giving up part of his demands 2 : the thing agreed upon as a result of concessions

²compromise *vb* **com·pro·mised; com·pro·mis·ing** 1 : to settle by compromise 2 : to endanger the reputation of

com·pul·sion \kəm-'pəl-shən\ *n* 1 : an act of compelling : the state of being compelled 2 : a force that compels 3 : an irresistible impulse

com·pul·so·ry \kəm-'pəl-sə-rē\ *adj* 1 : ENFORCED, REQUIRED ⟨*compulsory* education⟩ 2 : having the power of compelling

com·pu·ta·tion \ˌkäm-pyə-'tā-shən\ *n* 1 : the act or action of computing : RECKONING 2 : a result obtained by computing

com·pute \kəm-'pyüt\ *vb* **com·put·ed; com·put·ing** : to determine by calculation : RECKON

com·put·er \kəm-'pyüt-ər\ *n* : an automatic electronic machine for computing

com·rade \'käm-ˌrad, -rəd\ *n* : COMPANION

¹con \'kän\ *vb* **conned; con·ning** 1 : to study carefully 2 : MEMORIZE

²con *adv* : on the negative side : AGAINST

³con *n* : an opposing argument, person, or position ⟨the pros and *cons* of the question⟩

con- — see COM-

con·cave \kän-'kāv\ *adj* : hollow or rounded inward like the inside of a bowl or circle

con·ceal \kən-'sēl\ *vb* 1 : to hide from sight ⟨a *concealed* weapon⟩ 2 : to keep secret

con·ceal·ment \kən-'sēl-mənt\ *n* 1 : the act of hiding : the state of being hidden 2 : a hiding place

con·cede \kən-'sēd\ *vb* **con·ced·ed; con·ced·ing** 1 : to grant as a right or privilege 2 : to admit to be true : ACKNOWLEDGE, YIELD ⟨*concede* defeat⟩ **syn** see GRANT

con·ceit \kən-'sēt\ *n* : excessive pride in oneself or one's ability : personal vanity

con·ceit·ed \kən-'sēt-əd\ *adj* : VAIN

con·ceiv·a·ble \kən-'sē-və-bəl\ *adj* : capable of being conceived, imagined, or understood

con·ceive \kən-'sēv\ *vb* **con·ceived; con·ceiv·ing** 1 : to form an idea of : IMAGINE ⟨unable to *conceive* how it happened⟩ 2 : THINK

con·cen·trate \'kän-sən-ˌtrāt\ *vb* **con·cen·trat·ed; con·cen·trat·ing** 1 : to bring or come to or direct toward a common center 2 : to increase in strength or reduce in bulk by removing something (as water) ⟨*concentrated* orange juice⟩ **3** : to fix one's powers, efforts, or attentions on one thing

con·cen·tra·tion \ˌkän-sən-'trā-shən\ *n* **1** : the act or process of concentrating : the state of being concentrated **2** : close mental attention to a subject

con·cept \'kän-ˌsept\ *n* **1** : THOUGHT, NOTION **2** : a general idea

¹con·cern \kən-'sərn\ *vb* **1** : to relate to : be about **2** : to be of interest or importance to : AFFECT **3** : to be a care, trouble, or distress to ⟨an illness that *concerned* her parents⟩ **4** : ENGAGE, OCCUPY

²concern *n* **1** : something that relates to or involves a person : AFFAIR **2** : INTEREST, ANXIETY **3** : a business organization ⟨a banking *concern*⟩

con·cerned \kən-'sərnd\ *adj* : DISTURBED

con·cern·ing \kən-'sər-ning\ *prep* : relating to : ABOUT ⟨news *concerning* friends⟩

con·cert \'kän-sərt, -ˌsərt\ *n* **1** : AGREEMENT, HARMONY **2** : a musical performance by several voices or instruments or by both

con·cer·ti·na \ˌkän-sər-'tē-nə\ *n* : a small musical instrument resembling an accordion

con·cer·to \kən-'chert-ō\ *n, pl* **con·cer·tos** : a musical composition usually in three movements in which one or more instruments stand out sharply against the orchestra

concertina

con·ces·sion \kən-'sesh-ən\ *n* **1** : the act or an instance of conceding or yielding **2** : something conceded : ACKNOWLEDGMENT, ADMISSION **3** : GRANT, LEASE ⟨a mining *concession*⟩

conch \'kängk, 'känch\ *n, pl* **conchs** \'kängks\ *or* **conch·es** \'kän-chəz\ : a sea animal related to the common snails that has a large thick spiral shell

con·cil·i·ate \kən-'sil-ē-ˌāt\ *vb* **con·cil·i·at·ed; con·cil·i·at·ing** **1** : to bring into agreement : RECONCILE ⟨tried to *conciliate* the enemy⟩ **2** : to gain the good-will or favor of

conch shell

con·cise \kən-'sīs\ *adj* : expressing much in few words : CONDENSED, BRIEF

con·clude \kən-'klüd\ *vb* **con·clud·ed; con·clud·ing** **1** : to bring or come to an end : FINISH ⟨*conclude* a speech⟩ **2** : to form an opinion **3** : to bring about as a result

con·clu·sion \kən-'klü-zhən\ *n* **1** : final decision reached by reasoning **2** : the last part of something : END **3** : RESULT, OUTCOME **4** : SETTLEMENT, ARRANGEMENT

con·clu·sive \kən-'klü-siv\ *adj* : DECISIVE, CONVINCING — **con·clu·sive·ly** *adv*

con·coct \kən-'käkt, kän-\ *vb* **1** : to prepare (as food) by combining various ingredients **2** : to make up : DEVISE ⟨*concoct* a plan⟩

con·cord \'kän-ˌkòrd\ *n* : HARMONY

con·course \'kän-ˌkōrs\ *n* **1** : a flocking, moving, or flowing together (as of persons or streams) : GATHERING **2** : a place where roads meet or people may pass or gather

¹con·crete \kän-'krēt\ *adj* **1** : ACTUAL, REAL **2** : made of or relating to concrete

²con·crete \'kän-ˌkrēt\ *n* : a hardened mixture of cement, sand, and water with gravel or broken stone used in construction (as of pavements and buildings)

con·cur \kən-'kər\ *vb* **con·curred; con·cur·ring** **1** : to act or happen together **2** : to be in agreement (as in action or opinion) : ACCORD

con·cus·sion \kən-'kəsh-ən\ *n* **1** : SHAKING **2** : bodily injury especially to the brain caused by a sudden jar (as from a blow)

con·demn \kən-'dem\ *vb* **1** : to declare to be wrong **2** : to pronounce guilty **3** : SENTENCE **4** : to declare to be unfit for use

con·dem·na·tion \ˌkän-ˌdem-'nā-shən\ *n* **1** : CENSURE, BLAME **2** : the act of judicially condemning **3** : the state of being condemned

con·den·sa·tion \ˌkän-ˌden-'sā-shən\ *n* **1** : the act or process of condensing **2** : something that has been condensed

con·dense \kən-'dens\ *vb* **con·densed; con·dens·ing** : to make or become more close, compact, concise, or dense : CONCENTRATE

con·de·scend \ˌkän-di-'send\ *vb* **1** : to stoop to a level considered less dignified or lower than one's own **2** : to grant favors with a superior air

¹con·di·tion \kən-'dish-ən\ *n* **1** : something agreed upon or required as necessary if some other thing is to be or to take place : PROVISION **2** *pl* : state of affairs : CIRCUMSTANCES **3** : station in life ⟨men of humble *condition*⟩ **4** : state of health or fitness

²condition *vb* **1** : to put into proper condition or into a desired condition **2** : to alter usually by training or to produce by such means

con·di·tion·al \kən-'dish-ən-l\ *adj* : subject to, implying, or dependent upon a condition

con·dor \'kän-dər\ *n* : a very large American vulture having a bare head and neck and a white neck ruff

¹con·duct \'kän-ˌdəkt\ *n* **1** : the act or manner of carrying on **2** : personal behavior

²con·duct \kən-'dəkt\ *vb* **1** : GUIDE, ESCORT **2** : DIRECT, LEAD ⟨*conduct* a business⟩ ⟨*conduct* an orchestra⟩ **3** : BEHAVE ⟨*conducted* him-

ə abut   ər further   a ax   ā age   ä father, cot   á (see key page)   aù out   ch chin   e less   ē easy   g gift   i trip   ī life

self well at the party⟩ **4** : to have the quality of transmitting light, heat, or sound

syn CONDUCT, DIRECT, MANAGE all mean to provide leadership or guidance for something. CONDUCT suggests leading in person something that moves or acts as a unit ⟨*conduct* an orchestra⟩ ⟨*conduct* a tour through the university⟩ DIRECT emphasizes guiding and providing the course for something that has many parts or elements ⟨*directed* the affairs of the Indian reservations⟩ MANAGE stresses the handling of many details while maneuvering something toward a desired result ⟨*managed* the fighter's career until he won the title⟩

con·duc·tion \kən-'dək-shən\ *n* **1** : the act of conveying **2** : transmission through a conductor

con·duc·tor \kən-'dək-tər\ *n* **1** : a person in charge of a public conveyance (as a bus) **2** : a person or thing that directs or leads **3** : a substance or body capable of transmitting electricity, heat, or sound

cone \'kōn\ *n* **1** : the scaly fruit of certain trees (as the pine or fir) **2** : a solid body tapering evenly to a point from a circular base **3** : something resembling a cone in shape **4** : an ice-cream holder **5** : a cell of the retina of the eye that is sensitive to colored light

cone 1

con·fec·tion \kən-'fek-shən\ *n* : a fancy dish or sweet : DELICACY, CANDY

con·fec·tion·er \kən-'fek-shə-nər\ *n* : a manufacturer of or dealer in confections (as candies)

cone 2

con·fec·tion·er·y \kən-'fek-shə-,ner-ē\ *n, pl* **con·fec·tion·er·ies** **1** : CANDIES **2** : a confectioner's business or place of business

con·fed·er·a·cy \kən-'fed-ə-rə-sē\ *n, pl* **con·fed·er·a·cies** **1** : a league of persons, parties, or states : ALLIANCE **2** *cap* : the eleven southern states that seceded from the United States in 1860 and 1861

¹**con·fed·er·ate** \kən-'fed-ə-rət\ *adj* **1** : united in a league : ALLIED **2** *cap* : of or relating to the Confederacy

²**confederate** *n* **1** : ALLY, ACCOMPLICE **2** *cap* : a soldier of or a person who sided with the Confederacy **syn** see PARTNER

³**con·fed·er·ate** \kən-'fed-ə-,rāt\ *vb* **con·fed·er·at·ed; con·fed·er·at·ing** : to unite in an alliance or confederacy

con·fer \kən-'fər\ *vb* **con·ferred; con·fer·ring** **1** : GRANT, BESTOW **2** : CONSULT, DISCUSS

con·fer·ence \'kän-fə-rəns\ *n* **1** : a meeting for discussion or exchange of opinions **2** : an association of athletic teams

con·fess \kən-'fes\ *vb* **1** : to make acknowledgment of **2** : to make known one's sins to God or to a priest **syn** see ACKNOWLEDGE

con·fes·sion \kən-'fesh-ən\ *n* **1** : an act of confessing **2** : an acknowledgment of guilt **3** : a formal statement of religious beliefs

con·fide \kən-'fīd\ *vb* **con·fid·ed; con·fid·ing** **1** : to have or show faith : TRUST **2** : to show confidence by imparting secrets ⟨*confided* in her friend⟩ **3** : to tell confidentially ⟨*confided* her secret to her mother⟩ **4** : ENTRUST

con·fi·dence \'kän-fə-dəns\ *n* **1** : TRUST, BELIEF ⟨have *confidence* in a person⟩ **2** : BOLDNESS, ASSURANCE **3** : reliance on another's secrecy or loyalty **4** : SECRET

con·fi·dent \'kän-fə-dənt\ *adj* : having or showing confidence — **con·fi·dent·ly** *adv*

con·fi·den·tial \,kän-fə-'den-chəl\ *adj* **1** : SECRET, PRIVATE ⟨*confidential* information⟩ **2** : INTIMATE, FAMILIAR **3** : trusted with secret matters — **con·fi·den·tial·ly** *adv*

¹**con·fine** \'kän-,fīn\ *n* : BOUNDARY, LIMIT

²**con·fine** \kən-'fīn\ *vb* **con·fined; con·fin·ing** **1** : to keep within limits ⟨*confined* the message to twenty words⟩ **2** : to shut up : IMPRISON **3** : to keep indoors — **con·fine·ment** *n*

con·firm \kən-'fərm\ *vb* **1** : to make firm or firmer (as in a habit, in faith, or in intention) : STRENGTHEN **2** : to make sure of the truth of ⟨*confirm* a suspicion⟩ **3** : APPROVE, ACCEPT **4** : to administer the rite of confirmation to

con·fir·ma·tion \,kän-fər-'mā-shən\ *n* **1** : an act of confirming **2** : a religious ceremony admitting a person to full privileges in a church or synagogue **3** : something that confirms

con·firmed \kən-'fərmd\ *adj* **1** : ESTABLISHED, SETTLED ⟨*confirmed* distrust of anything new⟩ **2** : HABITUAL, CHRONIC

con·fis·cate \'kän-fəs-,kāt\ *vb* **con·fis·cat·ed; con·fis·cat·ing** : to seize by or as if by public authority

con·fla·gra·tion \,kän-flə-'grā-shən\ *n* : a usually large disastrous fire

¹**con·flict** \'kän-,flikt\ *n* **1** : a prolonged struggle : BATTLE **2** : a clashing or sharp disagreement (as between ideas or interests)

²**con·flict** \kən-'flikt\ *vb* : to be in opposition

con·form \kən-'form\ *vb* **1** : to make or be like : AGREE, ACCORD **2** : OBEY

con·for·mi·ty \kən-'for-mət-ē\ *n, pl* **con·for·mi·ties** **1** : correspondence in form, manner, or character : AGREEMENT **2** : action in accordance with some specified or generally accepted standard or authority : OBEDIENCE

---

j job   ng sing   ō low   ȯ moth   ȯi coin   th thin   th this   ü boot   u̇ foot   y you   yü few   yu̇ furious   zh vision

con·found \kən-'faůnd, kän-\ *vb* : to throw into disorder : mix up : CONFUSE

con·front \kən-'frənt\ *vb* 1 : to face especially in challenge : OPPOSE ⟨*confront* an enemy⟩ 2 : to cause to face or meet

con·fuse \kən-'fyüz\ *vb* **con·fused; con·fus·ing** 1 : to make mentally unclear or uncertain : PERPLEX 2 : to disturb the composure of 3 : to fail to distinguish between ⟨teachers always *confused* the twins⟩ **syn** see BAFFLE

con·fu·sion \kən-'fyü-zhən\ *n* 1 : an act or instance of confusing 2 : the state of being confused : DISORDER 3 : EMBARRASSMENT

syn CONFUSION, DISORDER, CHAOS all mean a situation in which things are not in their right, logical, or normal place. CONFUSION suggests such a thorough intermingling or lack of structure that it becomes difficult to tell what the proper arrangement should be ⟨planned to write a book, but had nothing but a *confusion* of notes and ideas to work from⟩ DISORDER suggests a definite upsetting or lack of order but also stresses that there had been a proper structure that still remains apparent ⟨found the room in wild *disorder* after the robbery⟩ CHAOS indicates absolute confusion and strongly implies that the situation is hopeless in that no order or structure is possible ⟨all was *chaos* on the sinking ship⟩

con·geal \kən-'jēl\ *vb* 1 : to change from a fluid to a solid state by or as if by cold : FREEZE 2 : to make or become hard, stiff, or thick

con·ge·nial \kən-'jē-nyəl\ *adj* 1 : alike or sympathetic in nature, disposition, or tastes 2 : existing together harmoniously 3 : PLEASANT, AGREEABLE ⟨*congenial* work⟩

con·gest \kən-'jest\ *vb* : to make too crowded or full : CLOG ⟨a *congested* neighborhood⟩

¹con·glom·er·ate \kən-'gläm-ə-rət\ *adj* 1 : made up of parts from various sources or of various kinds 2 : densely clustered

²conglomerate *n* : a mass (as a rock) formed of fragments from various sources

con·grat·u·late \kən-'grach-ə-,lāt\ *vb* **con·grat·u·lat·ed; con·grat·u·lat·ing** : to express sympathetic pleasure to on account of success or good fortune : wish joy to ⟨*congratulate* the winner⟩

conglomerate

con·grat·u·la·tion \kən-,grach-ə-'lā-shən\ *n* 1 : the act of congratulating 2 : an expression of joy or pleasure at another's success or good fortune — usually used in plural

con·gre·gate \'käng-gri-,gāt\ *vb* **con·gre·gat·ed; con·gre·gat·ing** : to collect or gather into a crowd or group : ASSEMBLE

con·gre·ga·tion \,käng-gri-'gā-shən\ *n* 1 : a gathering or collection of persons or things 2 : an assembly of persons gathered especially for religious worship 3 : the membership of a church or synagogue

con·gress \'käng-grəs\ *n* 1 : a gathering or assembly especially of delegates for discussion and action : CONFERENCE 2 : the body of senators and representatives of a nation (as of a republic) forming its chief lawmaking body

con·gress·man \'käng-grəs-mən\ *n, pl* **con·gress·men** \-mən\ : a member of a congress and especially of the United States House of Representatives

con·gru·ent \kən-'grü-ənt, 'käng-grə-wənt\ *adj* : having the same size and shape

con·ic \'kän-ik\ *adj* 1 : CONICAL 2 : of or relating to a cone

con·i·cal \'kän-i-kəl\ *adj* : shaped like a cone

con·i·fer \'kän-ə-fər, 'kō-nə-\ *n* : any of a group of mostly evergreen trees and shrubs (as pines) with true cones

¹con·jec·ture \kən-'jek-chər\ *n* : GUESS

²conjecture *vb* **con·jec·tured; con·jec·tur·ing** : GUESS, SURMISE

con·junc·tion \kən-'jəngk-shən\ *n* 1 : a joining together : UNION 2 : a word or expression that joins together words or word groups

con·jure \'kän-jər, 'kən-jər; *in sense 1* kən-'jůr\ *vb* **con·jured; con·jur·ing** 1 : to entreat earnestly or solemnly : BESEECH 2 : to summon by invocation or incantation 3 : to practice magical arts

con·nect \kə-'nekt\ *vb* 1 : to join or link together ⟨*connect* two wires⟩ 2 : to attach by close personal relationship or association ⟨*connected* by marriage⟩ 3 : to associate in the mind — **con·nec·tor** *or* **con·nect·er** *n*

con·nec·tion \kə-'nek-shən\ *n* 1 : the act of connecting 2 : the fact or condition of being connected : RELATIONSHIP 3 : a thing that connects : BOND, LINK 4 : a person connected with others (as by kinship) 5 : a social, professional, or commercial relationship 6 : the act or the means of continuing a journey by transferring (as to another train)

con·nois·seur \,kän-ə-'sər\ *n* : a person competent to act as a judge in matters involving taste and appreciation

con·quer \'käng-kər\ *vb* 1 : to get or gain by force : win by fighting 2 : OVERCOME, SUBDUE

con·quer·or \'käng-kər-ər\ *n* : one that conquers : VICTOR

con·quest \'kän-,kwest\ *n* 1 : the act or process of conquering : VICTORY 2 : something that is conquered

con·quis·ta·dor \kŏng-'kēs-tə-,dŏr\ *n, pl*

con·quis·ta·do·res \-ˌkēs-tə-'dȯr-ēz\ *or* **con·quis·ta·dors** : a leader in the Spanish conquest especially of Mexico and Peru in the sixteenth century

con·science \'kän-chəns\ *n* : the sense of or sensitiveness to the rightness or wrongness of one's own acts and intentions together with a feeling of obligation to do right or be good

con·sci·en·tious \ˌkän-chē-'en-chəs\ *adj* 1 : guided by or agreeing with one's conscience 2 : CAREFUL ⟨a *conscientious* worker⟩

con·scious \'kän-chəs\ *adj* 1 : aware of facts or feelings 2 : known or felt by one's inner self 3 : mentally awake or active 4 : INTENTIONAL — **con·scious·ly** *adv*

con·scious·ness \'kän-chəs-nəs\ *n* 1 : the condition of being conscious 2 : the upper level of mental life involving conscious thought and the will

con·se·crate \'kän-sə-ˌkrāt\ *vb* **con·se·crat·ed; con·se·crat·ing** 1 : to declare to be sacred or holy : set apart or devote to the service of God ⟨*consecrate* a church⟩ 2 : to dedicate or devote to some particular purpose

con·sec·u·tive \kən-'sek-yət-iv\ *adj* : following one another in regular order without gaps

¹**con·sent** \kən-'sent\ *vb* : to give assent or approval : AGREE ⟨*consent* to a request⟩

²**consent** *n* : approval or acceptance of what is done or proposed by another person

con·se·quence \'kän-sə-ˌkwens\ *n* 1 : RESULT 2 : IMPORTANCE

con·se·quent \'kän-si-kwənt\ *adj* : following as a result or effect

con·se·quent·ly \'kän-sə-ˌkwent-lē\ *adv* : as a result : ACCORDINGLY

con·ser·va·tion \ˌkän-sər-'vā-shən\ *n* 1 : PROTECTION, PRESERVATION 2 : planned management of natural resources (as timber) to prevent waste, destruction, or neglect

¹**con·ser·va·tive** \kən-'sər-vət-iv\ *adj* 1 : favoring a policy of keeping things as they are : opposed to change 2 : MODERATE, CAUTIOUS

²**conservative** *n* : a person who holds conservative views : a cautious or discreet person

con·ser·va·to·ry \kən-'sər-və-ˌtōr-ē\ *n, pl* **con·ser·va·to·ries** 1 : GREENHOUSE 2 : a place of instruction in some special study (as music)

¹**con·serve** \kən-'sərv\ *vb* **con·served; con·serv·ing** 1 : to keep in a safe or sound condition : SAVE 2 : to preserve with sugar

²**con·serve** \'kän-ˌsərv\ *n* 1 : a candied fruit : SWEETMEAT 2 : a rich fruit preserve

con·sid·er \kən-'sid-ər\ *vb* 1 : to think over carefully : PONDER, REFLECT 2 : to regard highly : ESTEEM 3 : to think of in a certain way : regard as being : BELIEVE

con·sid·er·a·ble \kən-'sid-ə-rə-bəl\ *adj* 1 : worthy of consideration : IMPORTANT 2 : large in extent, amount, or quantity — **con·sid·er·a·bly** \-blē\ *adv*

con·sid·er·ate \kən-'sid-ə-rət\ *adj* : thoughtful of the rights and feelings of other persons

con·sid·er·a·tion \kən-ˌsid-ə-'rā-shən\ *n* 1 : careful thought : DELIBERATION 2 : thoughtfulness for other people 3 : MOTIVE, REASON 4 : RESPECT, REGARD 5 : a payment made in return for something

con·sign \kən-'sīn\ *vb* 1 : ENTRUST 2 : to give, transfer, or deliver formally 3 : to send (as goods) to an agent to be sold or cared for — **con·sign·ment** *n*

con·sist \kən-'sist\ *vb* 1 : to be contained : LIE 2 : to be made up or composed

con·sis·ten·cy \kən-'sis-tən-sē\ *n, pl* **con·sis·ten·cies** 1 : degree of denseness, firmness, or viscosity ⟨dough of the right *consistency*⟩ 2 : AGREEMENT, HARMONY 3 : UNIFORMITY

con·sis·tent \kən-'sis-tənt\ *adj* 1 : AGREEING, HARMONIOUS 2 : uniform throughout — **con·sis·tent·ly** *adv*

con·so·la·tion \ˌkän-sə-'lā-shən\ *n* 1 : the act of consoling : the state of being consoled 2 : comfort offered to lessen a person's misery or grief 3 : something that lessens disappointment

¹**con·sole** \kən-'sōl\ *vb* **con·soled; con·sol·ing** : to comfort in times of grief or distress

²**con·sole** \'kän-ˌsōl\ *n* 1 : the desklike part of an organ at which the organist sits and which contains the keyboard, stops, and pedals 2 : a flat surface or cabinet on which are dials and switches for controlling electrical or mechanical devices 3 : a radio, phonograph, or television cabinet that stands on the floor

con·sol·i·date \kən-'säl-ə-ˌdāt\ *vb* **con·sol·i·dat·ed; con·sol·i·dat·ing** 1 : to join together into one whole : UNITE 2 : STRENGTHEN

con·so·nant \'kän-sə-nənt\ *n* 1 : a speech sound (as \p\, \n\, or \s\) produced by narrowing or stoppage at one or more points in the breath channel 2 : a letter in the English alphabet other than *a, e, i, o,* and *u*

¹**con·sort** \'kän-ˌsȯrt\ *n* 1 : a wife or husband 2 : a ship accompanying another

²**con·sort** \kən-'sȯrt\ *vb* 1 : to keep company : ASSOCIATE 2 : ACCORD, HARMONIZE

con·spic·u·ous \kən-'spik-yə-wəs\ *adj* 1 : plainly visible 2 : attracting attention : PROMINENT, STRIKING **syn** *see* NOTICEABLE

con·spir·a·cy \kən-'spir-ə-sē\ *n, pl* **con·spir·a·cies** 1 : the act of conspiring or plotting 2 : an agreement among conspirators 3 : a group of conspirators **syn** *see* PLOT

---

j job **ng** sing **ō** low **ȯ** moth **ȯi** coin **th** thin **th** this **ü** boot **u̇** foot **y** you **yü** few **yu̇** furious **zh** vision

con·spir·a·tor \kən-'spir-ət-ər\ *n* : one that conspires : PLOTTER

con·spire \kən-'spīr\ *vb* **con·spired; con·spir·ing 1** : to make an agreement especially in secret to do some unlawful act : PLOT **2** : to act in harmony

con·sta·ble \'kän-stə-bəl, 'kən-\ *n* : POLICE-MAN

con·stan·cy \'kän-stən-sē\ *n* **1** : firmness in one's beliefs : STEADFASTNESS **2** : firmness and loyalty in one's personal relationships

con·stant \'kän-stənt\ *adj* **1** : FIRM, FAITHFUL ⟨*constant* friends⟩ **2** : FIXED, UNCHANGING **3** : occurring over and over again : CONTINUAL, REGULAR — **con·stant·ly** *adv*

con·stel·la·tion \ˌkän-stə-'lā-shən\ *n* : any of eighty-eight groups of stars forming patterns

con·ster·na·tion \ˌkän-stər-'nā-shən\ *n* : amazement or dismay that hinders or throws into confusion

con·sti·pate \'kän-stə-ˌpāt\ *vb* **con·sti·pat·ed; con·sti·pat·ing** : to cause constipation in

con·sti·pa·tion \ˌkän-stə-'pā-shən\ *n* : abnormally delayed or infrequent passage of dry hard matter from the bowels

¹con·stit·u·ent \kən-'stich-ə-wənt\ *n* **1** : one of the parts of which a thing is made up : ELEMENT, INGREDIENT **2** : VOTER, ELECTOR

²constituent *adj* **1** : serving to form or make up a unit or whole **2** : having power to elect or appoint or to make or revise a constitution ⟨a *constituent* assembly⟩

con·sti·tute \'kän-stə-ˌtüt, -ˌtyüt\ *vb* **con·sti·tut·ed; con·sti·tut·ing 1** : to appoint to an office or duty **2** : ESTABLISH, FIX ⟨*constituted* to help needy students⟩ **3** : to make up : FORM

con·sti·tu·tion \ˌkän-stə-'tü-shən, -'tyü-\ *n* **1** : the physical makeup of an individual **2** : the natural structure of something **3** : the basic principles and laws of a nation, state, or social group that determine the powers and duties of the government and guarantee certain rights to the people in it

¹con·sti·tu·tion·al \ˌkän-stə-'tü-shən-l, -'tyü-\ *adj* **1** : having to do with a person's physical or mental makeup **2** : of, relating to, or in accordance with the constitution (as of a nation)

²constitutional *n* : an exercise (as a walk) taken for one's health

con·strain \kən-'strān\ *vb* **1** : COMPEL, FORCE **2** : CONFINE **3** : RESTRAIN

con·straint \kən-'strānt\ *n* **1** : COMPULSION, RESTRAINT ⟨act under *constraint*⟩ **2** : a keeping back of one's natural feelings : EMBARRASSMENT

con·strict \kən-'strikt\ *vb* : to make narrower or smaller by drawing together : SQUEEZE

con·struct \kən-'strəkt\ *vb* : to make or form by combining parts : BUILD

con·struc·tion \kən-'strək-shən\ *n* **1** : the arrangement of words and the relationship between words in a sentence **2** : the process, art, or manner of constructing **3** : something built or put together : STRUCTURE ⟨a flimsy *construction*⟩ **4** : INTERPRETATION

con·struc·tive \kən-'strək-tiv\ *adj* **1** : fitted for or given to constructing **2** : helping to develop or improve something

con·strue \kən-'strü\ *vb* **con·strued; con·stru·ing** : to explain the sense or intention of

con·sul \'kän-səl\ *n* : an official appointed by a government to live in a foreign country in order to look after the commercial interests of citizens of his own country

con·sult \kən-'səlt\ *vb* **1** : to seek the opinion or advice of ⟨*consult* a doctor⟩ **2** : to seek information from ⟨*consult* an encyclopedia⟩ **3** : to have regard to **4** : CONFER

con·sul·ta·tion \ˌkän-səl-'tā-shən\ *n* **1** : a deliberation between physicians on a case or its treatment **2** : the act of consulting

con·sume \kən-'süm\ *vb* **con·sumed; con·sum·ing 1** : to destroy by or as if by fire **2** : to use up : SPEND **3** : to eat or drink up **4** : to take up one's interest or attention

con·sum·er \kən-'sü-mər\ *n* **1** : one that consumes **2** : one that buys and uses up goods

con·sump·tion \kən-'səmp-shən\ *n* **1** : the act or process of consuming and especially of using up something (as food or coal) **2** : a wasting away of the body especially from tuberculosis of the lungs

¹con·tact \'kän-ˌtakt\ *n* **1** : a meeting or touching of persons or things **2** : a social or business connection

²contact *vb* **1** : to come or bring into contact **2** : to get in touch or communication with

con·ta·gion \kən-'tā-jən\ *n* **1** : the passing of a disease from one person to another as a result of some contact between them **2** : a contagious disease **3** : the passing of a feeling or influence from one person to another

con·ta·gious \kən-'tā-jəs\ *adj* : spreading by contagion ⟨a *contagious* disease⟩

con·tain \kən-'tān\ *vb* **1** : to keep within limits : RESTRAIN, CHECK ⟨tried to *contain* his anger⟩ **2** : to hold within itself : ENCLOSE, INCLUDE **3** : to have within : HOLD

con·tain·er \kən-'tā-nər\ *n* : RECEPTACLE

con·tam·i·nate \kən-'tam-ə-ˌnāt\ *vb* **con·tam·i·nat·ed; con·tam·i·nat·ing 1** : to soil, stain, or infect by contact or association **2** : to make unfit for use by adding something harmful or unpleasant

con·tem·plate \'känt-əm-ˌplāt\ *vb* **con·tem·plat·ed; con·tem·plat·ing** 1 : MEDITATE 2 : to look forward to

con·tem·pla·tion \ˌkänt-əm-'plā-shən\ *n* 1 : concentration on spiritual things : MEDITATION 2 : the act of looking at or thinking about something for some time : STUDY 3 : EXPECTATION, INTENTION

¹**con·tem·po·rar·y** \kən-'tem-pə-ˌrer-ē\ *adj* 1 : living or occurring at the same period of time 2 : being of the same age 3 : LIVING, MODERN ⟨our *contemporary* writers⟩

²**contemporary** *n, pl* **con·tem·po·rar·ies** : a person that lives at the same time or is of about the same age as another

con·tempt \kən-'tempt\ *n* 1 : the act of despising : the state of mind of one who despises 2 : the state of being despised

con·tempt·i·ble \kən-'temp-tə-bəl\ *adj* : deserving contempt ⟨a *contemptible* lie⟩

con·temp·tu·ous \kən-'temp-chə-wəs\ *adj* : feeling or showing contempt : SCORNFUL

con·tend \kən-'tend\ *vb* 1 : COMPETE 2 : STRIVE, STRUGGLE ⟨*contend* against difficulties⟩ 3 : ARGUE, MAINTAIN — **con·tend·er** *n*

¹**con·tent** \kən-'tent\ *adj* : SATISFIED

²**content** *vb* : to make content : SATISFY

³**content** *n* : freedom from care or discomfort

⁴**con·tent** \'kän-ˌtent\ *n* 1 : something contained — usually used in plural ⟨the *contents* of a room⟩ 2 : the subject matter or topics treated (as in a book) — usually used in plural ⟨a table of *contents*⟩ 3 : the significant part or meaning (as of a book) 4 : CAPACITY

con·tent·ed \kən-'tent-əd\ *adj* : satisfied or showing satisfaction with one's possessions or one's lot in life ⟨a *contented* smile⟩

con·ten·tion \kən-'ten-chən\ *n* 1 : the act of contending : DISPUTE, STRIFE 2 : an idea or point for which a person argues or to which he holds (as in a debate or argument)

con·tent·ment \kən-'tent-mənt\ *n* : absence of worry or restlessness : peaceful satisfaction

¹**con·test** \kən-'test\ *vb* 1 : DISPUTE, CHALLENGE 2 : to struggle over or for

²**con·test** \'kän-ˌtest\ *n* 1 : a struggle for victory or superiority : COMPETITION ⟨a *contest* for a prize⟩ 2 : OPPOSITION, RIVALRY

con·tes·tant \kən-'tes-tənt\ *n* : one who takes part in a contest ⟨*contestant* in a spelling bee⟩

con·ti·nent \'känt-n-ənt\ *n* 1 : one of the great divisions of land (as North America, South America, Europe, Asia, Africa, Australia, or Antarctica) on the globe 2 *cap* : the continent of Europe

con·ti·nen·tal \ˌkänt-n-'ent-l\ *adj* : of or relating to a continent

con·tin·gent \kən-'tin-jənt\ *adj* 1 : liable but not certain to happen : POSSIBLE 2 : happening by chance : not planned 3 : CONDITIONAL 4 : dependent on something that may or may not occur

con·tin·u·al \kən-'tin-yə-wəl\ *adj* 1 : going on without interruption 2 : occurring in rapid succession — **con·tin·u·al·ly** *adv*

con·tin·u·ance \kən-'tin-yə-wəns\ *n* 1 : the act of continuing in a state, condition, or course of action 2 : unbroken succession

con·tin·u·a·tion \kən-ˌtin-yə-'wā-shən\ *n* 1 : extension or prolonging of a state or activity 2 : a going on after an interruption 3 : a thing or part by which something is continued

con·tin·ue \kən-'tin-yü\ *vb* **con·tin·ued; con·tin·u·ing** 1 : REMAIN, STAY ⟨*continue* in your present position⟩ 2 : ENDURE, LAST ⟨cold weather *continued*⟩ 3 : to go on in a course ⟨*continue* to study hard⟩ 4 : to go on or carry on after an interruption 5 : to allow or cause to remain especially in a position

con·ti·nu·i·ty \ˌkänt-n-'ü-ət-ē, -'yü-\ *n, pl* **con·ti·nu·i·ties** 1 : the quality or state of being continuous : duration without interruption 2 : an uninterrupted succession (as of actions)

con·tin·u·ous \kən-'tin-yə-wəs\ *adj* : continuing without break or interruption : CONTINUED, UNBROKEN — **con·tin·u·ous·ly** *adv*

con·tort \kən-'tȯrt\ *vb* : to twist into an unusual appearance or unnatural shape : DEFORM

con·tor·tion \kən-'tȯr-shən\ *n* 1 : a twisting or a being twisted out of shape 2 : a contorted shape or thing

con·tour \'kän-ˌtu̇r\ *n* 1 : the outline of a figure or body 2 : a line or a drawing representing an outline 3 : SHAPE, FORM

contra- *prefix* 1 : against : contrary : contrasting ⟨*contra*distinction⟩ 2 : pitched below normal bass ⟨*contra*octave⟩

con·tra·band \'kän-trə-ˌband\ *n* 1 : goods whose importing, exporting, or possession is forbidden by law 2 : smuggled goods

con·tra·bass \'kän-trə-ˌbās\ *n* : DOUBLE BASS

¹**con·tract** \'kän-ˌtrakt\ *n* 1 : a binding agreement 2 : a writing made to show the terms and conditions of a contract

²**con·tract** \kən-'trakt, *1 is also* 'kän-ˌtrakt\ *vb* 1 : to enter into an agreement : establish or make by contract 2 : to draw together : draw up 3 : SHORTEN, SHRINK ⟨metal *contracts* in cold weather⟩ 4 : to shorten (as a word) by omitting one or more sounds or letters 5 : GET, CATCH ⟨*contract* a cold⟩ 6 : FORM

con·trac·tion \kən-'trak-shən\ *n* 1 : the act or process of contracting : the state of being contracted 2 : a shortening of a word or word group by leaving out a sound or letter 3 : a form (as *don't*) produced by contraction

con·tra·dict \ˌkän-trə-'dikt\ *vb* 1 : to deny the truth of a statement : say the opposite of what someone else has said 2 : to be contrary or opposed to

con·tra·dic·tion \ˌkän-trə-'dik-shən\ *n* : a statement that contradicts another : DENIAL

con·tra·dic·to·ry \ˌkän-trə-'dik-tə-rē\ *adj* : involving, causing, or constituting a contradiction : OPPOSED ⟨*contradictory* reports⟩

con·tral·to \kən-'tral-tō\ *n, pl* **con·tral·tos** 1 : the lowest female singing voice 2 : a singer with a contralto voice 3 : the part sung by a contralto

con·trap·tion \kən-'trap-shən\ *n* [probably a blend of *contrivance, trap,* and *invention*] : DEVICE, GADGET

¹**con·trar·y** \'kän-ˌtrer-ē\ *n, pl* **con·trar·ies** : something opposite or contrary — **on the contrary** : just the opposite : NO

²**con·trar·y** \'kän-ˌtrer-ē, *3 is often* kən-'trear-ē\ *adj* 1 : exactly opposite : wholly different ⟨*contrary* opinions⟩ 2 : OPPOSED 3 : inclined to oppose or resist : WAYWARD

¹**con·trast** \'kän-ˌtrast\ *n* 1 : a person or thing that shows differences when compared 2 : difference or unlikeness (as in color, tone, or brightness) especially when sharp or striking between associated things

²**con·trast** \kən-'trast\ *vb* 1 : to show noticeable differences 2 : to compare two persons or things so as to show the differences between them **syn** see COMPARE

con·trib·ute \kən-'trib-yət\ *vb* **con·trib·ut·ed; con·trib·ut·ing** 1 : to give along with others 2 : to have a share in something : HELP 3 : to supply (as an article) for publication especially in a periodical

con·tri·bu·tion \ˌkän-trə-'byü-shən\ *n* 1 : the act of contributing 2 : the sum or thing contributed 3 : a writing for publication

con·trite \'kän-ˌtrīt, kən-'trīt\ *adj* 1 : sorrowful for some wrong that one has done : REPENTANT 2 : caused by repentance

con·triv·ance \kən-'trī-vəns\ *n* 1 : SCHEME, PLAN 2 : a mechanical device : APPLIANCE

con·trive \kən-'trīv\ *vb* **con·trived; con·triv·ing** 1 : PLAN, PLOT ⟨*contrive* a way to escape⟩ 2 : to form or make in some skillful or ingenious way : INVENT 3 : to bring about

¹**con·trol** \kən-'trōl\ *vb* **con·trolled; con·trol·ling** 1 : to check or test by parallel experiment or evidence ⟨*controlled* experiments⟩ 2 : to exercise restraining or directing influence over : REGULATE 3 : to have power over : RULE

²**control** *n* 1 : the power or authority to control or command 2 : ability to control ⟨anger that is out of *control*⟩ ⟨lose *control* of an automobile⟩ 3 : RESTRAINT, RESERVE 4 : REGULATION ⟨price *controls*⟩ 5 : a device used to regulate the operation of a machine, apparatus, or system ⟨a radio *control*⟩ 6 : something used in an experiment or study to provide a parallel case for checking results

con·tro·ver·sy \'kän-trə-ˌvər-sē\ *n, pl* **con·tro·ver·sies** : a discussion about a question over which there is strong disagreement

co·nun·drum \kə-'nən-drəm\ *n* : RIDDLE

con·va·lesce \ˌkän-və-'les\ *vb* **con·va·lesced; con·va·lesc·ing** : to regain health and strength gradually after sickness

con·va·les·cence \ˌkän-və-'les-ns\ *n* : the period during which one is convalescing

¹**con·va·les·cent** \ˌkän-və-'les-nt\ *adj* : passing through convalescence

²**convalescent** *n* : one that is convalescent

con·vec·tion \kən-'vek-shən\ *n* : the circulating motion in a gas (as air) or a liquid whereby the warmer portions rise and the colder portions sink ⟨heat transferred by *convection*⟩

con·vene \kən-'vēn\ *vb* **con·vened; con·ven·ing** 1 : ASSEMBLE, MEET ⟨the legislature *convened* on Tuesday⟩ 2 : to cause to assemble

con·ve·nience \kən-'vē-nyəns\ *n* 1 : FITNESS, SUITABLENESS 2 : personal comfort ⟨thought only of his own *convenience*⟩ 3 : a suitable or convenient time : OPPORTUNITY ⟨come at your earliest *convenience*⟩ 4 : something that gives comfort or advantage ⟨a house with modern *conveniences*⟩

con·ve·nient \kən-'vē-nyənt\ *adj* 1 : suited to a person's comfort or ease ⟨a *convenient* time⟩ ⟨a *convenient* house⟩ 2 : prepared or suited for a person's use ⟨*convenient* tools⟩ 3 : easy to reach — **con·ve·nient·ly** *adv*

con·vent \'kän-vənt, -ˌvent\ *n* 1 : a group of nuns living together and devoting themselves to a religious life 2 : a house or a set of buildings occupied by a community of nuns

con·ven·tion \kən-'ven-chən\ *n* 1 : AGREEMENT ⟨an international *convention*⟩ 2 : a rule, practice, or way of acting or doing things established by custom 3 : an assembly of persons gathered together for a common purpose ⟨a teachers' *convention*⟩

con·ven·tion·al \kən-'ven-chən-l\ *adj* 1 : behaving according to convention ⟨a very *conventional* man⟩ 2 : settled by or depending on convention : CUSTOMARY 3 : not original : COMMONPLACE, ORDINARY

con·ver·sa·tion \ˌkän-vər-'sā-shən\ *n* : an informal talking together : TALK

ə abut ər further a ax ā age ä father, cot à (see key page) aù out ch chin e less ē easy g gift i trip ī life

con·verse \kən-'vərs\ *vb* **con·versed; con-vers·ing** : TALK **syn** see SPEAK

con·ver·sion \kən-'vər-zhən\ *n* **1** : the act of converting : the state of being converted **2** : a change in the nature or form of a thing **3** : a spiritual change (as from a bad to a good life) in a person : a change of religious faith

¹con·vert \kən-'vərt\ *vb* **1** : to change from one belief, religion, view, or party to another : TURN **2** : to change from one form to another **3** : to exchange for an equivalent

²con·vert \'kän-ˌvərt\ *n* : one that has been converted

¹con·vert·i·ble \kən-'vərt-ə-bəl\ *adj* : capable of being converted into something else

²convertible *n* **1** : something that is convertible **2** : an automobile with a top that can be raised, lowered, or removed

con·vex \kän-'veks\ *adj* : rounded like the outside of a ball or circle

con·vey \kən-'vā\ *vb* **con·veyed; con·vey·ing** **1** : to carry from one place to another : TRANSPORT **2** : to serve as a means of transferring or transmitting ⟨pipes *convey* water⟩ **3** : IMPART, COMMUNICATE

con·vey·ance \kən-'vā-əns\ *n* **1** : the act of conveying **2** : something used to transport goods or passengers

¹con·vict \kən-'vikt\ *vb* : to prove or find guilty

²con·vict \'kän-ˌvikt\ *n* **1** : a person convicted of a crime **2** : a person serving a prison sentence usually for a long term

con·vic·tion \kən-'vik-shən\ *n* **1** : the act of convicting : the state of being convicted **2** : the state of mind of a person who is sure that what he believes or says is true **3** : a strong belief or opinion

con·vince \kən-'vins\ *vb* **con·vinced; con·vinc·ing** : to argue so as to make a person agree or believe : satisfy someone's objections

con·vinc·ing \kən-'vin-sing\ *adj* : having the power or the effect of overcoming objection **syn** see VALID — **con·vinc·ing·ly** *adv*

con·vulse \kən-'vəls\ *vb* **con·vulsed; con·vuls·ing** : to shake violently or with or as if with irregular spasms ⟨*convulsed* with laughter⟩

con·vul·sion \kən-'vəl-shən\ *n* **1** : an attack of violent involuntary muscular contractions : FIT **2** : a violent disturbance : UPHEAVAL

con·vul·sive \kən-'vəl-siv\ *adj* : constituting or producing a convulsion — **con·vul·sive·ly** *adv*

¹coo \'kü\ *vb* **cooed; coo·ing** **1** : to make the soft sound made by doves and pigeons or a similar sound **2** : to talk fondly or lovingly

²coo *n, pl* **coos** : the sound made in cooing

¹cook \'kuk\ *n* : a person who prepares food for eating

²cook *vb* **1** : to prepare (as by boiling, baking, or broiling) food for eating by the use of heat **2** : to undergo the process of being cooked **3** : to subject to the action of heat or fire

cook·book \'kuk-ˌbuk\ *n* : a book of cooking recipes and directions

cook·ie *or* **cook·y** \'kuk-ē\ *n, pl* **cook·ies** : a small sweet cake

cook·out \'kuk-ˌaut\ *n* : an outing at which a meal is cooked and served in the open

¹cool \'kül\ *adj* **1** : somewhat cold : not warm ⟨a *cool* day⟩ ⟨a *cool* room⟩ **2** : not admitting or retaining heat ⟨*cool* clothes⟩ **3** : CALM, COMPOSED **4** : not affectionate, friendly, or interested : INDIFFERENT — **cool·ly** *adv*

²cool *vb* : to make or become cool

³cool *n* : a cool time or place

cool·er \'kü-lər\ *n* : a container for cooling liquids

coon \'kün\ *n* : RACCOON

¹coop \'küp, 'kup\ *n* : a cage or small enclosure (as for chickens or small animals)

²coop *vb* : to shut up or keep in a coop

coo·per \'kü-pər, 'kup-ər\ *n* : one that makes or repairs wooden casks, tubs, or barrels

co·op·er·ate \kō-'äp-ə-ˌrāt\ *vb* **co·op·er·at·ed; co·op·er·at·ing** : to join others in doing something especially for mutual benefit

co·op·er·a·tion \kō-ˌäp-ə-'rā-shən\ *n* **1** : the act or process of cooperating **2** : association of individuals or groups for the purpose of mutual benefit

¹co·op·er·a·tive \kō-'äp-ə-rət-iv\ *adj* **1** : willing to cooperate or work with others ⟨show a *cooperative* spirit⟩ **2** : of, relating to, or organized as a cooperative ⟨a *cooperative* store⟩

²cooperative *n* : an association formed to enable its members to buy or sell to better advantage

¹co·or·di·nate \kō-'ord-n-ət\ *adj* : equal in rank or importance

²co·or·di·nate \kō-'ord-n-ˌāt\ *vb* **co·or·di·nat·ed; co·or·di·nat·ing** **1** : to make or become coordinate **2** : to work or cause to work together smoothly or harmoniously : ADJUST

co·or·di·na·tion \kō-ˌord-n-'ā-shən\ *n* : harmonious working together (as of parts)

cop \'käp\ *n* : POLICEMAN

cope \'kōp\ *vb* **coped; cop·ing** : to struggle or contend especially with some success

co·pi·lot \'kō-ˌpī-lət\ *n* : an assistant airplane pilot

co·pi·ous \'kō-pē-əs\ *adj* : very plentiful : ABUNDANT — **co·pi·ous·ly** *adv*

cop·per \'käp-ər\ *n* **1** : a tough reddish

metallic chemical element that is one of the best conductors of heat and electricity **2** : a copper or bronze coin

cop·per·head \'käp-ər-ˌhed\ *n* : a medium=sized mottled reddish brown poisonous snake of the eastern United States

cop·pice \'käp-əs\ *n* **1** : a thicket, grove, or growth of small trees **2** : forest that has grown from sprouts

co·pra \'kō-prə\ *n* : dried coconut meat

copse \'käps\ *n* : COPPICE

¹cop·y \'käp-ē\ *n, pl* **cop·ies** **1** : an exact likeness of an original work : IMITATION, REPRODUCTION ⟨a *copy* of a letter⟩⟨a *copy* of a painting⟩ **2** : one of the entire number of books, magazines, or papers made at the same printing **3** : something set up for imitation **4** : written or printed matter to be set up in type

²copy *vb* **cop·ied; copy·y·ing** **1** : to make a copy of : DUPLICATE **2** : IMITATE — **cop·i·er** *n*

¹cop·y·right \'käp-ē-ˌrīt\ *n* : the sole legal right to reproduce, publish, and sell the contents and form of a literary or artistic work

²copyright *vb* : to secure a copyright on

¹cor·al \'kȯr-əl\ *n* **1** : a stonelike or hornlike material consisting of the skeletons of tiny colonial sea animals related to the jellyfishes and including one kind that is red and used in jewelry **2** : one or a colony of the animals that form coral **3** : a deep pink

coral

²coral *adj* **1** : made of coral ⟨*coral* reef⟩ **2** : of the color of coral

coral snake *n* : a small poisonous American snake brightly ringed with red, black, and yellow or white

cord \'kȯrd\ *n* **1** : a heavy string or small rope **2** : something that resembles a cord **3** : a unit of wood cut for fuel equal to a pile of wood 8 feet long, 4 feet high, and 4 feet wide or 128 cubic feet **4** : a cordlike rib or ridge on cloth **5** : a ribbed fabric ⟨a summer suit of blue *cord*⟩ **6** : a small insulated cable used to connect an electrical appliance with an outlet

cord·ed \'kȯrd-əd\ *adj* **1** : having or drawn into ridges or cords ⟨a *corded* seam⟩ **2** : bound or wound about with cords

cor·dial \'kȯr-jəl\ *adj* : WARM, FRIENDLY ⟨a *cordial* welcome⟩ — **cor·dial·ly** *adv*

cor·di·al·i·ty \ˌkȯr-jē-'al-ət-ē\ *n, pl* **cor·di·al·i·ties** : cordial quality : warmth of regard

cor·du·roy \'kȯrd-ə-ˌrȯi\ *n* **1** : a heavy ribbed usually cotton cloth **2** *pl* : trousers made of corduroy **3** : a road built of logs laid side by side (as across a swampy place)

¹core \'kōr\ *n* **1** : the central part of some

fruits (as apples or pears) **2** : a central inmost part of something : CENTER

²core *vb* **cored; cor·ing** : to remove the core from ⟨*core* an apple⟩

¹cork \'kȯrk\ *n* **1** : the light but tough material which is the outer layer of bark of a tree (**cork oak**) and is used especially for stoppers and insulation **2** : a usually cork stopper for a bottle or jug

²cork *vb* : to stop with a cork ⟨*cork* a bottle⟩

¹cork·screw \'kȯrk-ˌskrü\ *n* : a pointed spiral piece of metal with a handle that is used to draw corks from bottles

²corkscrew *adj* : resembling a corkscrew

corm \'kȯrm\ *n* : a plant underground resting stage that is a thick rounded stem base with buds and scaly leaves

cor·mo·rant \'kȯr-mə-rənt\ *n* : a large black seabird with a long neck and a slender hooked beak

¹corn \'kȯrn\ *n* **1** : the seeds or grain of a cereal plant (as wheat or oats) **2** : INDIAN CORN **3** : a plant whose seeds are corn

²corn *vb* : to preserve by packing with salt or by soaking in salty water ⟨*corned* beef⟩

³corn *n* : a hardening and thickening of the skin (as on a person's toe)

corn·cob \'kȯrn-ˌkäb\ *n* : the woody core on which grains of Indian corn are borne

cor·ne·a \'kȯr-nē-ə\ *n* : the transparent outer layer of the front of the eye covering the pupil and iris

¹cor·ner \'kȯr-nər\ *n* **1** : the point or angle formed by the meeting of two edges or sides of a thing : the place near this point **2** : the place where two streets or roads come together **3** : a piece designed to mark, form, or protect a corner (as of a book) **4** : a place remote from ordinary life or affairs ⟨a quiet *corner* of a big city⟩ **5** : EDGE, END ⟨the four *corners* of the earth⟩ **6** : a position from which escape or retreat is difficult or impossible — **cor·nered** \-nərd\ *adj*

²corner *vb* : to drive into a corner : put in a difficult position ⟨*corner* a rat⟩

³corner *adj* **1** : situated at a corner **2** : used or fitted for use in or on a corner

cor·net \kȯr-'net\ *n* : a usually brass musical instrument similar to a trumpet

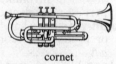
cornet

corn·flow·er \'kȯrn-ˌflau̇-ər\ *n* : a European plant related to the daisies that is often grown for its heads of showy blue, pink, or white flowers

cor·nice \'kȯr-nəs\ *n* **1** : the ornamental

projecting piece that forms the top edge of the front of a building or pillar   **2** : an ornamental molding placed where the walls meet the ceiling of a room

corn·meal \'kȯrn-'mēl\ *n* : meal ground from corn

corn·stalk \'kȯrn-ˌstȯk\ *n* : a stalk of Indian corn

corn·starch \'kȯrn-ˌstärch\ *n* : a fine starch made from corn and used as a thickening agent in cooking

corn syrup *n* : a syrup made from cornstarch and used chiefly in baked goods and candy

cor·nu·co·pi·a \ˌkȯr-nə-'kō-pē-ə, -nyə-\ *n* [from the Latin phrase *cornu copiae* "horn of plenty"]   **1** : a horn-shaped container overflowing with fruits and flowers used as a symbol of abundance   **2** : a container shaped like a horn or a cone

cornucopia

corn·y \'kȯr-nē\ *adj* **corn·i·er**; **corn·i·est** : tiresomely simple or sentimental : OLD-FASHIONED ⟨*corny* music⟩

co·rol·la \kə-'räl-ə\ *n* : the part of a flower that is formed by the petals

cor·o·nar·y \'kȯr-ə-ˌner-ē\ *adj* : of or relating to the heart or its blood vessels

cor·o·na·tion \ˌkȯr-ə-'nā-shən\ *n* : the act or ceremony of crowning a king or queen

cor·o·net \ˌkȯr-ə-'net\ *n* **1** : a small crown worn by a person of noble but not of royal rank ⟨a duke's *coronet*⟩   **2** : an ornamental wreath or band worn around the head

¹**cor·po·ral** \'kȯr-pə-rəl\ *adj* : of or relating to the body : BODILY ⟨*corporal* punishment⟩

²**corporal** *n* : a noncommissioned officer (as in the army) ranking next below a sergeant

cor·po·ra·tion \ˌkȯr-pə-'rā-shən\ *n* : a group of persons who are organized to carry on an activity (as a business) and are authorized by law to act as a single person

cor·po·re·al \kȯr-'pōr-ē-əl\ *adj* : having, consisting of, or relating to a physical material body

corps \'kōr\ *n, pl* **corps** \'kōrz\ **1** : an organized branch of a country's military forces ⟨Marine *Corps*⟩   **2** : a group of persons associated together or acting under common direction ⟨diplomatic *corps*⟩

corpse \'kȯrps\ *n* : a dead body

cor·pu·lent \'kȯr-pyə-lənt\ *adj* : very stout and heavy : extremely fat

cor·pus·cle \'kȯr-ˌpəs-əl\ *n* : one of the very small cells that float freely in the blood

¹**cor·ral** \kə-'ral\ *n* : an enclosure for keeping or capturing animals

²**corral** *vb* **cor·ralled**; **cor·ral·ling**   **1** : to confine in or as if in a corral   **2** : SURROUND, CAPTURE

¹**cor·rect** \kə-'rekt\ *vb* **1** : to make or set right ⟨*correct* a misspelled word⟩   **2** : to alter or adjust so as to bring to some standard or required condition   **3** : SCOLD, PUNISH ⟨*correct* a child for bad manners⟩   **4** : to show how a thing can be improved or made right

²**correct** *adj* **1** : conforming to an approved standard : PROPER ⟨*correct* dress for an evening wedding⟩   **2** : ACCURATE, RIGHT ⟨a *correct* answer⟩ — **cor·rect·ly** *adv* — **cor·rect·ness** *n*

cor·rec·tion \kə-'rek-shən\ *n* **1** : the act of correcting   **2** : a change that corrects something   **3** : REBUKE, PUNISHMENT

cor·re·spond \ˌkȯr-ə-'spänd\ *vb* **1** : to be like or equal (as in use, position, or amount) to something else : MATCH   **2** : ACCORD, AGREE   **3** : to communicate with a person by exchange of letters

cor·re·spond·ence \ˌkȯr-ə-'spän-dəns\ *n* **1** : agreement between particular things : HARMONY, LIKENESS   **2** : communication by means of letters : the letters exchanged

cor·re·spond·ent \ˌkȯr-ə-'spän-dənt\ *n* **1** : a person with whom another person communicates by letter   **2** : one who contributes news or comment to a newspaper or periodical especially from a distant place

cor·ri·dor \'kȯr-ə-dər\ *n* : a passage into which rooms open

cor·rode \kə-'rōd\ *vb* **cor·rod·ed**; **cor·rod·ing** : to eat away or be eaten away gradually (as by rust or acid)

cor·ro·sion \kə-'rō-zhən\ *n* : the process or effect of corroding

cor·ro·sive \kə-'rō-siv\ *adj* : corroding or likely to corrode

cor·ru·gate \'kȯr-ə-ˌgāt\ *vb* **cor·ru·gat·ed**; **cor·ru·gat·ing** : to make wrinkled : make with wavelike folds ⟨*corrugated* paper⟩

¹**cor·rupt** \kə-'rəpt\ *vb* **1** : to make corrupt : change from good to bad (as in morals, manners, or actions)   **2** : to influence a public official improperly (as by bribery)   **3** : TAINT

²**corrupt** *adj* **1** : morally bad   **2** : characterized by improper conduct ⟨a *corrupt* government⟩ — **cor·rupt·ly** *adv* — **cor·rupt·ness** *n*

cor·rup·tion \kə-'rəp-shən\ *n* **1** : physical decay or rotting   **2** : lack of honesty   **3** : the causing of other persons to do something wrong   **4** : a departure from what is pure or correct

cor·sage \kȯr-'säzh\ *n* : a bouquet of flowers to be worn or carried by a woman

corse·let *n* **1** \'kȯrs-lət\ *or* **cors·let** : the body armor worn by a knight especially on the upper part of the body 2 \ˌkȯr-sə-'let\ : a woman's corsetlike undergarment

cor·set \'kȯr-sət\ *n* : a usually close-fitting undergarment worn by women to support or give shape to waist and hips

co·ry·za \kə-'rī-zə\ *n* : COMMON COLD

cos·met·ic \käz-'met-ik\ *n* [from Greek *kosmētikos* "skilled in adornment", from *kosmein* meaning "to arrange" and "to adorn", from *kosmos* "order", the source of English *cosmos*] : a preparation (as a cream, lotion, or powder) intended to beautify especially the complexion

cos·mic \'käz-mik\ *adj* : of or relating to the whole universe

cosmic ray *n* : a stream of very penetrating high-speed particles that enter the earth's atmosphere from outer space

cos·mos \'käz-məs\ *n* 1 : the orderly universe 2 : a tall garden plant related to the daisies that has showy white, pink, or rose-colored flower heads

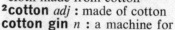

¹**cost** \'kȯst\ *n* 1 : the amount paid or charged for something : PRICE ⟨at a *cost* of three dollars per book⟩ 2 : loss or penalty incurred in gaining something ⟨the greatest *cost* of war⟩ **syn** see PRICE

cosmos

²**cost** *vb* **cost; cost·ing** 1 : to have a price of ⟨a ticket *costing* one dollar⟩ 2 : to cause one to pay, spend, or lose ⟨*cost* him his job⟩

cost·ly \'kȯst-lē\ *adj* **cost·li·er; cost·li·est** 1 : of great cost or value : EXPENSIVE, DEAR 2 : made at heavy expense or sacrifice

¹**cos·tume** \'käs-ˌtüm, -ˌtyüm\ *n* 1 : the prevailing fashion (as of a period, country, or class) in dress, personal adornments, and style of wearing the hair 2 : a suit or dress characteristic of a period, country, class, or occupation especially as worn on the stage or at a masquerade party 3 : a person's outer garments and especially a woman's dress with coat or jacket

²**costume** *vb* **cos·tumed; cos·tum·ing** : to provide with a costume : design costumes for

¹**cot** \'kät\ *n* : a small house : COTTAGE, HUT

²**cot** *n* : a narrow often collapsible bed (as of canvas stretched on a frame)

cote \'kōt, 'kät\ *n* : a shed or coop for small domestic animals (as sheep or pigeons)

cot·tage \'kät-ij\ *n* 1 : a small usually frame one-family house 2 : a small house for vacation use

cottage cheese *n* : a soft cheese made from soured skim milk

¹**cot·ton** \'kät-n\ *n* 1 : a soft fluffy material made up of twisted hairs that surrounds the seeds of a tall plant (**cotton plant**) related to the mallows and that is spun into yarn 2 : thread, yarn, or cloth made from cotton

cotton plant: leaves and flowers

²**cotton** *adj* : made of cotton

cotton gin *n* : a machine for removing seeds from cotton

cot·ton·mouth \'kät-n-ˌmau̇th\ *n* : MOCCASIN 2

cot·ton·seed \'kät-n-ˌsēd\ *n* : the seed of the cotton plant yielding a protein-rich meal and an oil used especially in cooking

cot·ton·tail \'kät-n-ˌtāl\ *n* : a small rabbit with a white tail

cot·ton·wood \'kät-n-ˌwu̇d\ *n* : any of several poplar trees having seeds with tufts of hairs resembling cotton and including some noted for their rapid growth

cottonwood leaves

couch \'kau̇ch\ *n* : a bed or sofa for resting or sleeping

cou·gar \'kü-gər\ *n* : a large tawny brown North American wild animal related to the domestic cat

cougar

¹**cough** \'kȯf\ *vb* 1 : to force air from the lungs with a sharp short noise or series of noises 2 : to get rid of by coughing ⟨*cough* up mucus⟩

²**cough** *n* 1 : a condition marked by repeated or frequent coughing 2 : an act or sound of coughing

could \kəd, ku̇d\ *past of* CAN — used as a helping verb in the past ⟨he *could* read at the age of five⟩ or as a polite or less forceful alternative to *can* in the present ⟨*could* you do this for me⟩

could·n't \'ku̇d-nt\ : could not

cou·lomb \'kü-ˌläm, -ˌlōm\ *n* : a unit of electric charge equal to the quantity of electricity transferred by a current of one ampere in one second

coun·cil \'kau̇n-səl\ *n* 1 : a group of persons called together to give advice or to make decisions : ASSEMBLY 2 : an official body of advisers or lawmakers ⟨city *council*⟩

coun·cil·or *or* **coun·cil·lor** \'kau̇n-sə-lər\ *n* : a member of a council

¹**coun·sel** \'kau̇n-səl\ *n* 1 : advice given ⟨a father's *counsel* to his son⟩ 2 : the discussion of reasons for or against a thing : an exchange of opinions ⟨take *counsel* with friends⟩ 3 *pl* **counsel** : a lawyer employed to manage a case in court : a lawyer appointed to advise and represent a client in legal matters

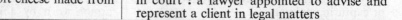

²counsel *vb* **coun·seled** *or* **coun·selled; coun·sel·ing** *or* **coun·sel·ling** **1** : to give counsel : AD-VISE ⟨*counsel* a student⟩ **2** : to seek counsel

coun·sel·or *or* **coun·sel·lor** \'kaún-sə-lər\ *n* **1** : ADVISER **2** : LAWYER **3** : a supervisor of campers or activities at a summer camp

¹count \'kaúnt\ *vb* **1** : to name or tell one by one in order to find the whole number in a collection ⟨*count* the apples in a box⟩ **2** : to name the numerals in regular order up to a particular point ⟨*count* ten⟩ **3** : to name the numbers in order one by one or by groups ⟨*count* to one hundred by fives⟩ **4** : to include in a reckoning or counting ⟨forty days *count-ing* Sundays⟩ **5** : CONSIDER, JUDGE ⟨*counts* himself lucky⟩ **6** : to include or exclude by or as if by counting ⟨*counted* himself out⟩ **7** : RELY, DEPEND ⟨can *count* on him⟩ **8** : RECK-ON, PLAN ⟨*count* on his coming⟩ **9** : to have value, force, or importance : be of account

²count *n* **1** : the act or process of counting **2** : a total obtained by counting ⟨a *count* of ten⟩ **3** : a particular charge in a legal declaration or indictment ⟨guilty on all *counts*⟩

³count *n* : a European nobleman whose rank corresponds to that of a British earl

¹coun·te·nance \'kaúnt-n-əns\ *n* **1** : the human face or expression of the face ⟨a kind *countenance*⟩ **2** : APPROVAL

²countenance *vb* **coun·te·nanced; coun·te·nanc·ing** : to extend approval or indulgence to

¹count·er \'kaúnt-ər\ *n* **1** : a piece (as of metal or ivory) used in counting or in games **2** : a level surface (as a table or board) over which business is transacted or food is served or on which goods are displayed or work is conducted

²count·er *n* **1** : one that counts **2** : a device for indicating a number or amount

³coun·ter \'kaúnt-ər\ *vb* **1** : to act in opposition to : OPPOSE **2** : RETALIATE

⁴coun·ter *adv* : in another or a contrary manner or direction ⟨go *counter* to advice⟩

⁵coun·ter *n* **1** : CONTRARY, OPPOSITE **2** : an answering or offsetting force or blow **3** : a stiffener used to give permanent shape to the upper of a shoe around the heel

⁶coun·ter *adj* : moving or acting in an opposite way : CONTRARY ⟨a *counter* offer⟩

coun·ter- *prefix* **1** : contrary : opposite ⟨*counter*clockwise⟩⟨*counter*march⟩ **2** : opposing : retaliatory ⟨*counter*irritant⟩ **3** : complementary : corresponding ⟨*counter*part⟩ **4** : duplicate : substitute ⟨*counter*foil⟩

coun·ter·act \ˌkaúnt-ər-'akt\ *vb* : to act in opposition so as to prevent something from acting in its own way

coun·ter·clock·wise \ˌkaúnt-ər-'kläk-ˌwīz\ *adv (or adj)* : in a direction opposite to that in which the hands of a clock rotate

¹coun·ter·feit \'kaúnt-ər-ˌfit\ *vb* **1** : to imitate or copy especially in order to deceive **2** : PRETEND — **coun·ter·feit·er** *n*

²counterfeit *adj* **1** : made in exact imitation of something genuine and intended to be passed off as genuine **2** : SHAM, FEIGNED

³counterfeit *n* : something made to imitate another thing with the desire to deceive

coun·ter·pane \'kaúnt-ər-ˌpān\ *n* : BED-SPREAD

coun·ter·part \'kaúnt-ər-ˌpärt\ *n* : a person or thing very closely like or corresponding to another person or thing

¹coun·ter·sign \'kaúnt-ər-ˌsīn\ *n* **1** : a signature confirming the genuineness of a document already signed by another **2** : a secret signal that must be given by a person wishing to pass a guard : PASSWORD

²countersign *vb* : to add one's signature to another's in order to confirm genuineness

count·ess \'kaúnt-əs\ *n* **1** : the wife or widow of a count or an earl **2** : a woman who holds the rank of a count or an earl in her own right

count·less \'kaúnt-ləs\ *adj* : too numerous to be counted ⟨*countless* grains of sand⟩

coun·try \'kən-trē\ *n, pl* **coun·tries** **1** : RE-GION, DISTRICT ⟨good farming *country*⟩ **2** : the territory of a nation : a land inhabited by a people with a common government **3** : a person's native or adopted land ⟨owe allegiance to our *country*⟩ **4** : the people of a nation ⟨a whole *country* in revolt⟩ **5** : rural regions as opposed to towns and cities

coun·try·man \'kən-trē-mən\ *n, pl* **coun·try·men** \-mən\ **1** : an inhabitant or native of a specified country **2** : a person born in the same country as another : a fellow citizen **3** : one living or raised in the country

coun·try·side \'kən-trē-ˌsīd\ *n* : a rural district or its people

coun·ty \'kaúnt-ē\ *n, pl* **coun·ties** : a division of a state or country for purposes of local government

coupe \kü-'pā, *2 is often* 'küp\ *n* **1** : a four-wheeled horse-drawn carriage with an enclosed body seating two persons and with an outside seat for the driver in front **2** : a two-door automobile with an enclosed body

¹cou·ple \'kəp-əl\ *vb* **cou·pled; cou·pling** **1** : to join or link together : CONNECT ⟨*coupled* freight cars⟩ **2** : to join in pairs

²couple *n* **1** : two persons who are paired together or closely associated **2** : two things of the same kind that are connected or that are thought of together : PAIR, BRACE

syn COUPLE, PAIR both mean two things having at least something in common. COUPLE refers to things that are in some way associated or related ⟨brought home a *couple* of friends⟩ but are not necessarily matched or part of a set ⟨found a *couple* of socks but they're not mates⟩ PAIR is used of things that belong or are used together ⟨a *pair* of horses⟩ and often refers to things that are actually one item in function ⟨a *pair* of pliers⟩

cou·plet \'kəp-lət\ *n* : two successive rhyming lines of verse

cou·pling \'kəp-ling\ *n* **1** : the act of bringing or coming together : PAIR-ING **2** : something that joins or connects two parts or things ⟨a car *coupling*⟩ ⟨a pipe *coupling*⟩

cou·pon \'kü-ˌpän, 'kyü-\ *n* **1** : a ticket or certificate or a detachable part that shows the right of the holder to receive some service, payment, or discount **2** : a part of a printed advertisement designed to be cut out for use as an order blank or inquiry form

coupling

cour·age \'kər-ij\ *n* : the quality of mind that enables one to meet danger and difficulties with firmness : BRAVERY, FEARLESSNESS

cou·ra·geous \kə-'rā-jəs\ *adj* : having or showing courage — **cou·ra·geous·ly** *adv*

¹course \'kōrs\ *n* **1** : motion from one point to another : progress in space or time ⟨the stars in their *course* through the sky⟩ ⟨during the *course* of a year⟩ **2** : the path over which something moves ⟨*course* of flight⟩ ⟨golf *course*⟩ **3** : direction of motion ⟨the *course* of a ship⟩ **4** : a natural channel for water ⟨followed the river's *course*⟩ **5** : method of procedure : CONDUCT, BEHAVIOR ⟨the easiest *course* is to withdraw⟩ **6** : a series of acts or proceedings arranged in regular order ⟨a *course* of lectures⟩ **7** : a series of studies leading to a diploma or a degree ⟨a four-year *course* in law⟩ **8** : a part of a meal served at one time ⟨finished the meat *course*⟩ **9** : a continuous level range of brick or masonry throughout a wall — **of course 1** : following the ordinary way of procedure **2** : as might be expected

²course *vb* **coursed**; **cours·ing 1** : to hunt with dogs ⟨*course* rabbits⟩ **2** : to run through or over **3** : to move rapidly : RACE

¹court \'kōrt\ *n* **1** : the residence of a sovereign or similar dignitary **2** : a sovereign's formal assembly of his advisers and officers as a governing power **3** : the family and retinue of a sovereign **4** : an open space wholly or partly surrounded by buildings **5** : a short street or lane **6** : a space arranged for playing one of various games ⟨tennis *court*⟩ ⟨basketball *court*⟩ **7** : a place where justice is administered **8** : the persons assembled to administer justice : a judge presiding at a trial **9** : a session held by a judge **10** : HOMAGE, COURTSHIP ⟨pay *court* to the king⟩

²court *vb* **1** : to try (as by attention or flattery) to gain or get the support of : SEEK ⟨*courting* favor with the authorities⟩ ⟨*court* the new voters⟩ **2** : to seem to be asking for : TEMPT **3** : to seek the affections of

cour·te·ous \'kərt-ē-əs\ *adj* : marked by respect for others : POLITE **syn** see CIVIL — **cour·te·ous·ly** *adv* — **cour·te·ous·ness** *n*

cour·te·sy \'kərt-ə-sē\ *n, pl* **cour·te·sies 1** : an act of politeness : POLITENESS **2** : a favor as distinguished from a right

court·house \'kōrt-ˌhaůs\ *n* **1** : a building in which courts of law are held **2** : a building in which county offices are housed

court·i·er \'kōrt-ē-ər\ *n* : a person in attendance at a royal court

court·ly \'kōrt-lē\ *adj* : suitable to a royal court : ELEGANT, POLITE ⟨*courtly* manners⟩

court·ship \'kōrt-ˌship\ *n* : the act or process of courting : WOOING

court·yard \'kōrt-ˌyärd\ *n* : a court or enclosure attached to a building (as a house)

cous·in \'kəz-n\ *n* **1** : a child of one's uncle or aunt **2** : a person belonging to an ethnically or culturally related group

cove \'kōv\ *n* **1** : a small sheltered inlet or bay **2** : a sheltered nook in hills or woods

cov·e·nant \'kəv-ə-nənt\ *n* : a formal binding agreement

¹cov·er \'kəv-ər\ *vb* **1** : to provide protection or security to or against : INSURE **2** : to maintain a check on especially by patrolling ⟨police *covering* the highways⟩ **3** : CONCEAL, SHELTER **4** : to place or spread something over : OVERSPREAD **5** : DOT, DAPPLE ⟨*covered* with freckles⟩ **6** : to place or set a cover or covering over **7** : to take into account ⟨a review *covering* the term's work⟩ **8** : to have as one's field of activity ⟨a reporter *covering* the courthouse⟩ **9** : to pass over or through

²cover *n* **1** : something that protects, shelters, or hides **2** : something that is placed over or about another thing : LID, TOP **3** : a binding or protecting case **4** : a tablecloth and tableware for one person **5** : a cloth used on a bed **6** : an envelope or wrapper for mail

cov·er·age \'kəv-ə-rij\ *n* **1** : the act or fact of covering : something that covers **2** : the number or amount covered : SCOPE

cov·er·all \'kəv-ər-ˌȯl\ *n* : a one-piece outer garment worn to protect one's clothes — usually used in plural

covered wagon *n* : a large long wagon with an arched canvas top

cov·er·ing \'kəv-ə-ring\ *n* : something (as a roof or an envelope) that covers or conceals

covered wagon

cov·er·let \'kəv-ər-lət\ *n* : BEDSPREAD

¹cov·ert \'kəv-ərt, 'kō-vərt\ *adj* 1 : SECRET, HIDDEN ⟨a *covert* glance⟩ 2 : SHELTERED

²covert *n* 1 : a hiding place (as a thicket that gives shelter to game animals) 2 : one of the feathers about the base of the quills on the wings and tail of a bird

cov·et \'kəv-ət\ *vb* 1 : to wish for enviously 2 : to long for something and especially something belonging to another person

cov·et·ous \'kəv-ət-əs\ *adj* : marked by a too eager desire for wealth or possessions or for something belonging to another person

cov·ey \'kəv-ē\ *n, pl* **cov·eys** 1 : a small flock (as of quail) 2 : COMPANY, GROUP

¹cow \'kaù\ *n* : the mature female of cattle or of an animal (as the moose) of which the male is called *bull*

²cow *vb* : to subdue the spirits or courage of : make afraid ⟨*cowed* by threats⟩

cow

cow·ard \'kaù-ərd\ *n* : a person who lacks courage or shows shameful fear

cow·ard·ice \'kaù-ərd-əs\ *n* : lack of courage to face danger : shameful fear

cow·ard·ly \'kaù-ərd-lē\ *adj* 1 : lacking courage : disgracefully timid 2 : characteristic of a coward — **cow·ard·li·ness** *n*

cow·bell \'kaù-ˌbel\ *n* : a bell hung about the neck of a cow to indicate its whereabouts

cow·bird \'kaù-ˌbərd\ *n* : a small American blackbird that lays its eggs in the nests of other birds

cow·boy \'kaù-ˌbòi\ *n* : one (as a mounted ranch hand) who tends or drives cattle

cow·catch·er \'kaù-ˌkach-ər\ *n* : a strong frame on the front of a railroad engine for throwing off obstructions

cow·er \'kaù-ər\ *vb* : to crouch down (as from fear or cold)

cow·girl \'kaù-ˌgərl\ *n* : a female cattle herder who works on a ranch or at a rodeo

cow·hand \'kaù-ˌhand\ *n* : one who works on a cattle ranch : COWBOY

cow·herd \'kaù-ˌhərd\ *n* : one who tends cows

cow·hide \'kaù-ˌhīd\ *n* 1 : the hide of a cow or leather made from it 2 : a coarse whip of rawhide or braided leather

cowl \'kaùl\ *n* : a hood or long hooded cloak especially of a monk

cow·lick \'kaù-ˌlik\ *n* : a turned-up tuft of hair that will not lie flat

cowl

cow·pox \'kaù-ˌpäks\ *n* : a disease of the cow that when given to man (as by vaccination) protects from smallpox

cow·punch·er \'kaù-ˌpən-chər\ *n* : COWBOY

cow·slip \'kaù-ˌslip\ *n* 1 : a common Old World primrose with yellow or purple flowers 2 : MARSH MARIGOLD

cox·swain \'käk-sən, -ˌswān\ *n* : the person who steers a boat or a racing shell

coy \'kòi\ *adj* [in earlier English this meant "quiet" as well as "shy"; it was taken from early French *coi* "calm", which came in turn from Latin *quietus* "quiet"] 1 : BASHFUL, SHY 2 : affecting shyness

coy·ote \'kī-ˌōt, kī-'ōt-ē\ *n* : a small wolf chiefly of western North America

¹co·zy \'kō-zē\ *adj* **co·zi·er; co·zi·est** 1 : SNUG, COMFORTABLE 2 : CAREFUL, CAUTIOUS — **co·zi·ly** \-zə-lē\ *adv* — **co·zi·ness** \-zē-nəs\ *n*

²cozy *n, pl* **co·zies** : a padded covering for a container (as a teapot) to keep the contents hot

¹crab \'krab\ *n* : a sea animal related to the lobsters but having a flattened shell and a small abdomen pressed against the underside of the body

crab

²crab *n* : a sour ill-tempered person

³crab *vb* **crabbed; crabbing** : to find fault : COMPLAIN

crab apple *n* 1 : a small wild sour apple 2 : a cultivated apple with small usually highly colored tart fruit

crab·bed \'krab-əd\ *adj* : PEEVISH, CROSS

crab·by \'krab-ē\ *adj* **crab·bi·er; crab·bi·est** : CROSS, ILL-NATURED

crab grass *n* : a weedy grass with coarse stems that root at the joints

¹crack \'krak\ *vb* 1 : to break or cause to break with a sudden sharp sound : SNAP 2 : to make a sound of cracking as if breaking ⟨*crack* a whip⟩ 3 : to break with or without completely separating into parts ⟨the ice *cracked* in several places⟩ 4 : to tell especially in a clever or witty way ⟨*crack* jokes⟩ 5 : to break down : FAIL ⟨*crack* under a strain⟩

---

j job   ng sing   ō low   ȯ moth   òi coin   th thin   th this   ü boot   ù foot   y you   yü few   yù furious   zh vision

6 : to become harsh : fail in tone ⟨his voice *cracked*⟩ 7 : to strike or receive a sharp blow

²crack *n* 1 : a sudden sharp noise 2 : a witty or sharp remark 3 : a narrow break or opening : FISSURE 4 : WEAKNESS, FLAW 5 : a broken tone of the voice 6 : MOMENT, INSTANT ⟨at the *crack* of dawn⟩ 7 : a sharp resounding blow 8 : ATTEMPT, TRY

³crack *adj* : of superior quality or ability

crack·er \'krak-ər\ *n* : a dry thin crisp bakery product made of flour and water

¹crack·le \'krak-əl\ *vb* **crack·led; crack·ling** 1 : to make small sharp sudden repeated noises 2 : to develop fine cracks in a surface

²crackle *n* 1 : the noise of repeated small cracks or reports (as of burning wood) 2 : a network of fine cracks on an otherwise smooth surface

crack–up \'krak-ˌəp\ *n* 1 : CRASH, WRECK ⟨*crack-up* of an airplane⟩ 2 : BREAKDOWN

¹cra·dle \'krād-l\ *n* 1 : a baby's bed or cot usually on rockers 2 : place of beginning or origin ⟨the *cradle* of civilization⟩ 3 : a framework or support resembling a baby's cradle in appearance or use 4 : a rocking device used in panning gold 5 : a support for a telephone receiver

²cradle *vb* **cra·dled; cra·dling** 1 : to place or keep in or as if in a cradle 2 : to nurse, train, or shelter in childhood 3 : to wash (as earth or sand) in a miner's cradle

craft \'kraft\ *n* 1 : DEXTERITY, SKILL 2 : an occupation or trade requiring manual or artistic skill ⟨carpentry is a *craft*⟩ 3 : skill in deceiving for a bad purpose : CUNNING 4 : the members of a trade or trade association 5 *pl usually* **craft** : a boat especially when of small size 6 *pl usually* **craft** : AIRCRAFT

crafts·man \'krafts-mən\ *n, pl* **crafts·men** \-mən\ 1 : a person who works at a trade or handicraft : ARTISAN 2 : a highly skilled worker in any field

craft·y \'kraf-tē\ *adj* **craft·i·er; craft·i·est** : skillful at deceiving others : CUNNING

crag \'krag\ *n* : a steep rugged rock or cliff

crag·gy \'krag-ē\ *adj* : having many crags

cram \'kram\ *vb* **crammed; cram·ming** 1 : to stuff or crowd in ⟨*cram* clothes into a bag⟩ 2 : to fill full ⟨barns *crammed* with hay⟩ 3 : to study hastily for a test 4 : to eat greedily

¹cramp \'kramp\ *n* 1 : a sudden painful involuntary tightening of a muscle 2 : sharp pain in the abdomen — usually used in plural

²cramp *vb* 1 : to affect with cramp ⟨the cold water *cramped* the swimmer⟩ 2 : to restrain from free action : HAMPER 3 : to turn the front wheels of a vehicle to right or left

cran·ber·ry \'kran-ˌber-ē\ *n, pl* **cran·ber·ries** : a sour bright red berry that is eaten in sauces and jelly and is the fruit of a trailing evergreen swamp plant related to the blueberries

¹crane \'krān\ *n* 1 : a tall wading bird resembling a heron but related to the rails 2 : a machine with a projecting swinging arm for lifting and carrying heavy weights 3 : a mechanical arm that swings freely from a center and is used to support or carry a weight

²crane *vb* **craned; cran·ing** : to stretch one's neck to see better

cra·ni·al \'krā-nē-əl\ *adj* : of or relating to the cranium

cra·ni·um \'krā-nē-əm\ *n, pl* **cra·ni·ums** *or* **cra·ni·a** \-nē-ə\ 1 : SKULL 2 : the part of the skull enclosing the brain

¹crank \'krangk\ *n* 1 : a bent armlike part with a handle that is turned to start or operate machinery 2 : a person who is very enthusiastic about a particular subject or hobby 3 : an eccentric person 4 : GROUCH

²crank *vb* : to start or operate by turning a crank

crank·y \'krang-kē\ *adj* **crank·i·er; crank·i·est** : IRRITABLE

cran·ny \'kran-ē\ *n, pl* **cran·nies** : a small narrow opening : SLIT, CREVICE

crape \'krāp\ *n* 1 : CREPE 2 : black crepe used as a sign of mourning

crap·pie \'kräp-ē\ *n* : either of two sunfishes native to the Great Lakes and Mississippi valley of which the larger and darker one (**black crappie**) is an important sport fish and the other (**white crappie**) is esteemed especially as a table fish

¹crash \'krash\ *vb* 1 : to break violently and noisily : SMASH 2 · to bring an airplane down in such a way that it is damaged in landing 3 : to make or cause to make a loud noise 4 : to move or force through noisily

²crash *n* 1 : a loud sound (as of things smashing) 2 : a breaking to pieces by or as if by collision : SMASH, COLLISION 3 : the crashing of an airplane 4 : a sudden decline or failure (as of a business or prices)

¹crate \'krāt\ *n* 1 : a container (as for fruits or vegetables) often with slats on the sides 2 : an enclosing framework for protecting something (as in shipment)

²crate *vb* **crat·ed; crat·ing** : to pack in a crate ⟨*crate* furniture for shipping⟩

crate 2

cra·ter \'krāt-ər\ *n* 1 : a bowl-shaped depression around the opening of a volcano or geyser 2 : a hole in the ground formed by an exploding shell, bomb, or mine or by the impact of a meteorite **3** : a small depression or larger circular walled structure on the moon

cra·vat \krə-'vat\ *n* : NECKTIE

crave \'krāv\ *vb* **craved; crav·ing** **1** : BEG, ENTREAT ⟨*craved* his pardon⟩ **2** : to long for ⟨*crave* rest⟩ **3** : REQUIRE, NEED ⟨*crave* food⟩

¹**cra·ven** \'krā-vən\ *adj* : COWARDLY

²**craven** *n* : COWARD

crav·ing \'krā-ving\ *n* : a great desire or longing (as for sweets)

craw \'krȯ\ *n* **1** : the crop of a bird **2** : the stomach of an animal

craw·fish \'krȯ-ˌfish\ *n, pl* **crawfish** : CRAYFISH

¹**crawl** \'krȯl\ *vb* **1** : to move slowly by drawing the body close to the ground or floor : CREEP **2** : to go very slowly or carefully **3** : to swarm with or have the sensation of swarming with creeping things

²**crawl** *n* **1** : the act or motion of crawling **2** : a racing stroke in swimming

cray·fish \'krā-ˌfish\ *n, pl* **crayfish** [an alteration (due to confusion with English *fish*) of earlier English *crevis*, taken from medieval French *crevice*, which itself probably came from early German *krebiz*, a word from the same source as English *crab*] **1** : a freshwater crustacean resembling but much smaller than the related lobster **2** : a spiny saltwater crustacean resembling a lobster but not having the very large claws

¹**cray·on** \'krā-ˌän, -ən\ *n* **1** : a stick of white or colored chalk or of colored wax used for writing or drawing **2** : a drawing made with crayons

²**crayon** *vb* : to draw or color with a crayon

¹**craze** \'krāz\ *vb* **crazed; craz·ing** : to make or become insane or as if insane

²**craze** *n* : FAD, MANIA

cra·zy \'krā-zē\ *adj* **cra·zi·er; cra·zi·est** **1** : mentally disordered : INSANE **2** : IMPRACTICAL, ERRATIC **3** : wildly excited

¹**creak** \'krēk\ *vb* : to make a long sharp grating or squeaking sound

²**creak** *n* : a rasping, squeaking, or grating noise

creak·y \'krē-kē\ *adj* **creak·i·er; creak·i·est** **1** : making a creaking sound **2** : apt to creak

¹**cream** \'krēm\ *n* **1** : the oily yellowish part of milk **2** : a food prepared with cream **3** : something (as a cosmetic) having the consistency of cream **4** : the choicest part **5** : a pale yellow

²**cream** *vb* **1** : to furnish, prepare, or treat with cream **2** : to rub or beat (as butter) until creamy

cream·er·y \'krē-mə-rē\ *n, pl* **cream·er·ies** : a place where butter and cheese are made or where dairy goods are sold or prepared

cream·y \'krē-mē\ *adj* **cream·i·er; cream·i·est** **1** : full of or containing cream **2** : resembling cream in nature, appearance, color, or taste

¹**crease** \'krēs\ *n* : a line or mark made by or as if by folding a pliable substance

²**crease** *vb* **creased; creas·ing** **1** : to make a crease in or on **2** : to become creased

cre·ate \krē-'āt\ *vb* **cre·at·ed; cre·at·ing** : to cause to exist : bring into existence : PRODUCE

cre·a·tion \krē-'ā-shən\ *n* **1** : the act of creating : the bringing of the world into existence out of nothing **2** : something created **3** : all created things : WORLD

cre·a·tive \krē-'āt-iv\ *adj* : able to create especially new and original things

cre·a·tor \krē-'āt-ər\ *n* **1** : one that creates or produces : MAKER **2** *cap* : ²GOD

crea·ture \'krē-chər\ *n* **1** : a living being **2** : a lower animal **3** : PERSON

cred·i·ble \'kred-ə-bəl\ *adj* : capable of being believed : deserving belief

¹**cred·it** \'kred-ət\ *n* **1** : the balance (as in a bank) in a person's favor **2** : time given for payment for goods on trust ⟨extended him thirty days' *credit*⟩ **3** : trust given to a customer for future payment for goods purchased ⟨buy on *credit*⟩ **4** : TRUST, BELIEF ⟨a story that deserves little *credit*⟩ **5** : good name : reputation for trustworthiness **6** : something that adds to a person's reputation or honor ⟨gave him *credit* for the discovery⟩ **7** : a source of honor ⟨a *credit* to his school⟩ **8** : official certification of the completion of a course of study **9** : a unit of academic work officially certified

²**credit** *vb* **1** : BELIEVE ⟨*credit* a statement⟩ **2** : to place in a person's favor on a financial record ⟨*credit* an account with ten dollars⟩ **3** : to give credit or honor to

cred·it·a·ble \'kred-ət-ə-bəl\ *adj* : worthy of esteem or praise ⟨a *creditable* attempt⟩

cred·i·tor \'kred-ət-ər\ *n* : a person to whom a debt is owed

cred·u·lous \'krej-ə-ləs\ *adj* : quick to believe especially without sufficient grounds

creed \'krēd\ *n* [this was *crēda* in Old English, taken from Latin *credo* "I believe", the first word of the Apostles' Creed] **1** : a statement of the essential beliefs of a religious faith **2** : a set of guiding principles or beliefs

creek \'krēk\ *n* **1** : a small stream of water usually larger than a brook and smaller than a river **2** : a narrow bay or inlet extending some distance into the land

---

j job　ng sing　ō low　ȯ moth　ȯi coin　th thin　th̲ this　ü boot　u̇ foot　y you　yü few　yu̇ furious　zh vision

creel \'krēl\ *n* : a wickerwork basket (as for carrying fish)

creel

¹**creep** \'krēp\ *vb* **crept** \'krept\; **creep·ing** **1** : to move along with the body close to the ground or floor : move slowly on hands and knees : CRAWL **2** : to move or advance slowly, timidly, or stealthily ⟨the tide *crept* up the beach⟩ **3** : to grow or spread along the ground or along a surface ⟨ivy *creeping* up a wall⟩ **4** : to feel as though insects were crawling on the body

²**creep** *n* **1** : a creeping movement **2** : a sensation as of insects crawling over the flesh : a feeling of horror — usually used in plural

creep·er \'krē-pər\ *n* **1** : one that creeps **2** : a small bird that creeps about trees and bushes in search of insects **3** : a plant (as ivy) that grows by creeping over surfaces

creep·y \'krē-pē\ *adj* **creep·i·er**; **creep·i·est** : having or causing a sensation as of insects creeping on the skin : EERIE

cre·mate \'krē-ˌmāt\ *vb* **cre·mat·ed**; **cre·mat·ing** : to reduce (as a dead body) to ashes by means of fire or great heat

crepe \'krāp\ *n* : a thin crinkled fabric (as of silk or wool)

crepe paper *n* : paper with a crinkled or puckered texture

¹**cre·scen·do** \kri-'shen-dō\ *n, pl* **cre·scen·dos** *or* **cre·scen·does** **1** : a swelling in volume of sound especially in music **2** : a crescendo musical passage

²**crescendo** *adv (or adj)* : with increasing volume — used as a direction in music

¹**cres·cent** \'kres-nt\ *n* **1** : the figure formed by the new moon **2** : the moon at a stage when it resembles a crescent **3** : something shaped like a crescent

²**crescent** *adj* : shaped like the new moon

crescent

cress \'kres\ *n* : any of several salad plants of the mustard group

crest \'krest\ *n* **1** : a showy tuft or process on the head of an animal (as a bird) **2** : an ornamental design or picture found on a coat of arms and also used as a decoration or marking (as on table silver) **3** : something suggesting a tuft especially in being the top of something — **crest·ed** \'kres-təd\ *adj*

crest·fall·en \'krest-ˌfól-ən\ *adj* **1** : having a drooping crest or hanging head : DEJECTED **2** : SHAMEFACED, HUMILIATED

crev·ice \'krev-əs\ *n* : a narrow opening that results from a split or crack : FISSURE

crew \'krü\ *n* **1** : a gathering of persons ⟨a happy *crew* on a picnic⟩ **2** : a group of persons associated in joint work ⟨a train *crew*⟩ **3** : the group of seamen who man a ship **4** : the oarsmen and steersman of a rowboat or racing shell **5** : the persons who man an airplane

crib \'krib\ *n* **1** : a manger for feeding animals **2** : a small bedstead with high sides for a child **3** : a building or bin for storing **4** : a translation or notes to aid a student sometimes in violation of rules

¹**crick·et** \'krik-ət\ *n* : a small leaping insect noted for the chirping notes made by the males

²**cricket** *n* : a game played on a large field with bats, ball, and wickets by two teams of eleven players each

cri·er \'krī-ər\ *n* : one who proclaims orders or announcements ⟨town *crier*⟩

crime \'krīm\ *n* **1** : the doing of an act forbidden by law : the failure to do an act required by law **2** : sinful conduct : an evil act

¹**crim·i·nal** \'krim-ən-l\ *adj* **1** : involving or being a crime ⟨a *criminal* act⟩ **2** : relating to crime or its punishment

²**criminal** *n* : one that has committed a crime

crimp·y \'krim-pē\ *adj* **crimp·i·er**; **crimp·i·est** : FRIZZY ⟨*crimpy* hair⟩

¹**crim·son** \'krim-zən\ *n* : a deep purplish red

²**crimson** *vb* : to make or become crimson

cringe \'krinj\ *vb* **cringed**; **cring·ing** **1** : to shrink in fear : WINCE, COWER **2** : to behave toward others with excessive humility

crin·kle \'kring-kəl\ *vb* **crin·kled**; **crin·kling** **1** : to form little waves or wrinkles on the surface : WRINKLE, RIPPLE **2** : RUSTLE

crin·kly \'kring-klē\ *adj* **crin·kli·er**; **crin·kli·est** **1** : WAVY, WRINKLED **2** : RUSTLING

¹**crip·ple** \'krip-əl\ *n* : a lame or disabled person

²**cripple** *vb* **crip·pled**; **crip·pling** **1** : to deprive of the use of a limb and especially of a leg : LAME **2** : to make useless or defective

cri·sis \'krī-səs\ *n, pl* **cri·ses** \'krī-ˌsēz\ **1** : a turning point for better or worse in an acute disease **2** : a decisive moment or turning point (as in the plot of a story) **3** : an unstable or critical time or state of affairs

¹**crisp** \'krisp\ *adj* **1** : CURLY, WAVY ⟨*crisp* hair⟩ **2** : easily crumbled : FLAKY, BRITTLE ⟨*crisp* pastry⟩ ⟨*crisp* snow⟩ **3** : FIRM, FRESH ⟨*crisp* lettuce⟩ **4** : SHARP, CLEAR ⟨a *crisp* illustration⟩ ⟨a *crisp* reply⟩ **5** : noticeably neat and spruce **6** : SPRIGHTLY, LIVELY ⟨a *crisp* retort⟩ **7** : FROSTY, SNAPPY ⟨*crisp* weather⟩ **8** : BRACING, INVIGORATING ⟨*crisp* autumn breezes⟩ **syn** see BRITTLE

²**crisp** *vb* : to make or become crisp

criss·cross \'kris-ˌkròs\ *vb* **1** : to mark with intersecting lines **2** : to go or pass back and forth

crit·ic \'krit-ik\ *n* **1** : a person who gives his judgment of the value, worth, beauty, or excellence of something **2** : one inclined to find fault or complain

crit·i·cal \'krit-i-kəl\ *adj* **1** : inclined to criticize especially unfavorably **2** : consisting of or involving criticism or critics ⟨*critical* writings⟩ **3** : using or involving careful judgment ⟨a *critical* examination of a patient⟩ **4** : of, relating to, or being a turning point or crisis ⟨the *critical* stage of a fever⟩ **5** : causing anxiety : CRUCIAL, DECISIVE ⟨a *critical* test⟩ — **crit·i·cal·ly** *adv*

crit·i·cism \'krit-ə-ˌsiz-əm\ *n* **1** : the act of criticizing and especially of finding fault **2** : a critical remark or observation **3** : a careful judgment or review especially by a critic

crit·i·cize \'krit-ə-ˌsīz\ *vb* **crit·i·cized**; **crit·i·ciz·ing** **1** : to examine and judge as a critic : EVALUATE **2** : to find fault with

¹croak \'krōk\ *vb* **1** : to make a deep harsh sound ⟨frogs *croaked*⟩ **2** : to speak in a hoarse throaty voice **3** : GRUMBLE

²croak *n* : a hoarse harsh sound or cry

¹cro·chet \krō-'shā\ *n* : needlework consisting of interlocked looped stitches formed with a single thread and a hooked needle

²crochet *vb* : to form a fabric of crochet

crock \'kräk\ *n* : a thick earthenware pot or jar

crock·er·y \'kräk-ə-rē\ *n* : EARTHENWARE

croc·o·dile \'kräk-ə-ˌdīl\ *n* : a very large thick-skinned long-tailed animal related to the alligator that crawls on short legs about tropical marshes and rivers

cro·cus \'krō-kəs\ *n* : a plant related to the irises that grows from a corm, has grasslike leaves, and is often planted for its bright white, yellow, or purple funnel-shaped spring flowers

crocus

crone \'krōn\ *n* : a withered old woman

cro·ny \'krō-nē\ *n, pl* **cro·nies** : a close companion : CHUM

¹crook \'krúk\ *n* **1** : an implement having a bent or hooked form ⟨a shepherd's *crook*⟩ **2** : THIEF, SWINDLER **3** : a curved or hooked part of a thing : BEND, CURVE

²crook *vb* : BEND, CURVE ⟨*crooked* his finger⟩

crook·ed \'krúk-əd\ *adj* **1** : having a crook or curve : BENT **2** : DISHONEST, CRIMINAL

croon \'krün\ *vb* : to hum or sing in a low soft voice ⟨*croon* a lullaby⟩

¹crop \'kräp\ *n* **1** : a short riding whip **2** : an enlargement at the lower end of the gullet of a bird or insect in which food is temporarily stored **3** : a close cut of the hair **4** : the amount gathered or harvested : HARVEST ⟨a *crop* of wheat⟩ **5** : BATCH, LOT

²crop *vb* **cropped**; **crop·ping** **1** : to remove (as by cutting or biting) the upper or outer parts of : CLIP, TRIM **2** : to grow or yield a crop (as of grain) : cause (land) to bear a crop **3** : HARVEST **4** : to come or appear unexpectedly ⟨problems *crop* up daily⟩

cro·quet \krō-'kā\ *n* : a game in which players drive wooden balls with mallets through a series of wickets set out on a lawn

cro·quette \krō-'ket\ *n* : a roll or ball of hashed meat, fish, or vegetables fried in deep fat

¹cross \'kròs\ *n* **1** : a structure consisting of a straight bar and a crossing bar **2** *often cap* : the structure on which Jesus was crucified used as a symbol of Christianity and of the Christian religion **3** : sorrow or suffering as a test of patience or virtue : AFFLICTION, TROUBLE ⟨had their *crosses* to bear⟩ **4** : an object shaped like a cross **5** : a figure or mark formed by the crossing of two straight lines **6** : a mixing of breeds, races, or kinds : the product of such a mixing

²cross *vb* **1** : to lie or be situated across **2** : INTERSECT **3** : to move, pass, or extend across or past : TRAVERSE ⟨*cross* a street⟩ **4** : to make the sign of the cross upon or over (as in prayer) **5** : to cancel by marking crosses on or by drawing a line through ⟨*cross* out a word⟩ **6** : to place or fold crosswise one over the other ⟨*crossed* his legs⟩ **7** : THWART, OPPOSE ⟨*crossed* his father's wishes⟩ **8** : to draw a line across ⟨*cross* your *t*'s⟩ **9** : to cause (an animal or plant) to breed with one of another kind : produce hybrids **10** : to meet and pass on the way

³cross *adj* **1** : lying, falling, or passing across ⟨a *cross* street⟩ **2** : CONTRARY, OPPOSED ⟨at *cross* purposes⟩ **3** : marked by bad temper

cross·bar \'kròs-ˌbär\ *n* : a bar, piece, or stripe placed crosswise or across

cross·bones \'kròs-ˌbōnz\ *n pl* : two leg or arm bones placed or pictured as lying across each other ⟨a skull and *crossbones*⟩

cross·bow \'kròs-ˌbō\ *n* : a short bow mounted crosswise near the end of a wooden stock that discharges stones and short square-headed arrows

crossbow

cross–eyed \'krȯs-'īd\ *adj* : having one or both eyes turned toward the nose

cross·ing \'krȯs-ing\ *n* **1** : a point where two lines, tracks, or streets cross each other **2** : a place provided for going across a street, railroad tracks, or a stream **3** : a voyage across a body of water

cross·piece \'krȯs-ˌpēs\ *n* : something placed crosswise of something else

cross–ref·er·ence \'krȯs-'ref-ə-rəns\ *n* : a reference made from one place to another (as in a book)

cross section *n* **1** : a cutting made across something (as a log or an apple) **2** : a representation of a cross section ⟨a *cross section* of a wire⟩ **3** : a number of persons or things selected from a group to represent or show the general nature of the whole

cross·walk \'krȯs-ˌwȯk\ *n* : a specially paved or marked path for pedestrians crossing a street or road

cross·wise \'krȯs-ˌwīz\ *also* **cross·ways** \-ˌwāz\ *adv* : so as to cross something : ACROSS

crotch \'kräch\ *n* : an angle formed by the spreading apart of two legs or branches or of a limb from its trunk ⟨the *crotch* of a tree⟩

¹crouch \'kraůch\ *vb* : to stoop or bend low with the limbs close to the body

²crouch *n* : the position of crouching

croup \'krüp\ *n* : a children's disease marked by a hoarse cough and hard breathing

¹crow \'krō\ *n* : a glossy black bird that has a harsh cry

²crow *vb* **1** : to make the loud shrill sound that a rooster makes **2** : to make sounds of delight **3** : GLOAT, BRAG

³crow *n* **1** : the cry of a rooster **2** : a triumphant cry

crow·bar \'krō-ˌbär\ *n* : an iron bar used as a lever (as for prying things apart)

¹crowd \'kraůd\ *vb* **1** : to press or push forward ⟨*crowd* into an elevator⟩ **2** : to press close to something : press or squeeze into a smaller space **3** : to collect in numbers : THRONG **4** : to fill or pack by pressing or thronging together

²crowd *n* **1** : a large number of persons collected together : THRONG **2** : POPULACE ⟨his books appealed to the *crowd*⟩ **3** : a group of people having a common interest : SET

¹crown \'kraůn\ *n* **1** : a wreath or band especially as a mark of victory or honor **2** : a royal headdress : DIADEM **3** : the highest part (as of a tree or mountain) **4** : the top of the head **5** : the top part of a hat **6** : the part of a tooth outside of the gum **7** : something resembling a crown **8** *cap* : royal power

or authority : MONARCH **9** : any of various coins (as an English coin worth five shillings) — **crowned** \'kraůnd\ *adj*

²crown *vb* **1** : to place a crown on : make sovereign : ENTHRONE **2** : to recognize officially as : HONOR, REWARD **3** : BESTOW, ADORN ⟨*crowned* with wisdom⟩ **4** : TOP, SURMOUNT **5** : to bring to a successful conclusion : COMPLETE, PERFECT **6** : to put an artificial crown on a damaged tooth

crow's nest *n* : a partly enclosed platform high on the mast of a ship for a lookout

cru·cial \'krü-shəl\ *adj* **1** : constituting a final or very important test or decision : DECISIVE ⟨a *crucial* battle⟩ **2** : DIFFICULT, TRYING

cru·ci·ble \'krü-sə-bəl\ *n* : a pot made of a substance that resists fire and used for holding something that is treated under great heat

cru·ci·fix \'krü-sə-ˌfiks\ *n* : a representation of Christ on the cross

cru·ci·fix·ion \ˌkrü-sə-'fik-shən\ *n* **1** : an act of crucifying **2** *cap* : the crucifying of Christ on the cross

cru·ci·fy \'krü-sə-ˌfī\ *vb* **cru·ci·fied; cru·ci·fy·ing** **1** : to put to death by nailing or binding the hands and feet to a cross **2** : to treat cruelly : TORTURE, PERSECUTE

crude \'krüd\ *adj* **crud·er; crud·est** **1** : in a natural state and not altered by processing : RAW ⟨*crude* oil⟩ ⟨*crude* sugar⟩ **2** : lacking refinement, good manners, or tact : VULGAR **3** : rough or inexpert in plan or execution : RUDE — **crude·ly** *adv* — **crude·ness** *n*

cru·el \'krü-əl\ *adj* **cru·el·er** *or* **cru·el·ler; cru·el·est** *or* **cru·el·lest** **1** : ready to hurt others : SAVAGE, MERCILESS **2** : showing savageness : causing suffering — **cru·el·ly** *adv*

cru·el·ty \'krü-əl-tē\ *n, pl* **cru·el·ties** **1** : an inclination to inflict pain **2** : cruel treatment

cru·et \'krü-ət\ *n* : a bottle for holding vinegar, oil, or sauce for table use

¹cruise \'krüz\ *vb* **cruised; cruis·ing** **1** : to travel by ship touching at a series of ports and not going directly to one port only ⟨*cruise* along the coast⟩ **2** : to travel for enjoyment **3** : to travel at the best operating speed ⟨an automobile *cruising* along the highway⟩

cruet

²cruise *n* : an act or instance of cruising

cruis·er \'krü-zər\ *n* **1** : a warship with less armor and armament than a battleship **2** : a police automobile equipped with radio for communicating with headquarters **3** : a motorboat with facilities for living aboard

crul·ler \'krəl-ər\ *n* : a small sweet cake made

of egg batter usually cut in strips or twists and fried in deep fat

¹crumb \'krəm\ *n* **1** : a small fragment especially of bread **2** : a little bit

²crumb *vb* **1** : to break into crumbs : CRUMBLE **2** : to cover or thicken with crumbs (as in cooking) **3** : to remove crumbs from

crum·ble \'krəm-bəl\ *vb* **crum·bled; crumbling 1** : to break into small pieces ⟨*crumble* bread⟩ **2** : to fall to pieces : fall into ruin

crum·bly \'krəm-blē\ *adj* **crum·bli·er; crum·bli·est** : easily crumbled

crum·ple \'krəm-pəl\ *vb* **crum·pled; crumpling 1** : to press or crush out of shape : WRINKLE, RUMPLE ⟨*crumple* paper⟩ **2** : to become crumpled **3** : COLLAPSE

¹crunch \'krənch\ *vb* : to chew, grind, or press with a crushing noise

²crunch *n* : an act or sound of crunching

¹cru·sade \krü-'sād\ *n* **1** *cap* : one of the military expeditions undertaken by Christian countries in the eleventh, twelfth, and thirteenth centuries to recover the Holy Land from the Turks **2** : a campaign for the improvement of conditions

²crusade *vb* **cru·sad·ed; cru·sad·ing** : to take part in a crusade

cru·sad·er \krü-'sād-ər\ *n* : one that takes part in a crusade

¹crush \'krəsh\ *vb* **1** : to squeeze together so as to bruise or destroy the natural shape or condition ⟨*crushed* his thumb⟩ ⟨*crush* grapes⟩ **2** : HUG, EMBRACE **3** : to break into fine pieces by pressure ⟨*crush* stone⟩ **4** : SUBDUE, OVERWHELM ⟨*crush* an enemy⟩ **5** : OPPRESS

²crush *n* **1** : an act of crushing **2** : a tightly packed crowd **3** : INFATUATION

crust \'krəst\ *n* **1** : the hardened outside surface of bread **2** : a hard dry piece of bread **3** : the cover or case of a pie **4** : a hard outer covering or surface layer **5** : the outer part of the earth composed of rocks

crus·ta·cean \ˌkrəs-'tā-shən\ *n* : any of a large group of mostly water animals (as crabs, lobsters, and shrimps) with a body made of segments, a firm outer shell, two pairs of antennae, and limbs that are jointed

crust·y \'krəs-tē\ *adj* **crust·i·er; crust·i·est 1** : having or being a crust **2** : SURLY

crutch \'krəch\ *n* **1** : a staff made with a piece at the top to fit under the armpit and used to support lame persons in walking **2** : something like a crutch in shape or use : PROP, SUPPORT

crutches

¹cry \'krī\ *vb* **cried; cry·ing** [from Old French *crier*, a modification of Latin *quiritare* "to shout out", literally, "to cry out for help from a citizen", from *Quirites* "Roman citizens"] **1** : to make a loud call or cry : SHOUT, EXCLAIM **2** : to shed tears : WEEP ⟨*cried* herself to sleep⟩ **3** : to utter a characteristic sound or call **4** : to proclaim publicly : call out

²cry *n, pl* **cries 1** : a loud call or shout (as of pain, fear, or joy) **2** : APPEAL **3** : a fit of weeping ⟨had a good *cry*⟩ **4** : the characteristic sound uttered by an animal

cry·ba·by \'krī-ˌbā-bē\ *n, pl* **cry·ba·bies** : one who cries easily or often

¹crys·tal \'krist-l\ *n* **1** : quartz that is colorless and transparent or nearly so **2** : something resembling crystal in transparency **3** : a body formed by a

crystals of snow

substance solidifying so that it has flat surfaces in regular even arrangement ⟨an ice *crystal*⟩ ⟨a salt *crystal*⟩ **4** : a clear colorless glass of superior quality **5** : the transparent cover over a clock or watch dial

²crystal *adj* : consisting of or resembling crystal : CLEAR

crys·tal·line \'kris-tə-lən\ *adj* **1** : made of crystal or composed of crystals **2** : resembling crystal : TRANSPARENT

crys·tal·lize \'kris-tə-ˌlīz\ *vb* **crys·tal·lized; crys·tal·liz·ing 1** : to form or to cause to form crystals or grains **2** : to become or cause to become settled and fixed in form

cub \'kəb\ *n* **1** : the young of various animals (as the bear, fox, or lion) **2** : CUB SCOUT

cub·by·hole \'kəb-ē-ˌhōl\ *n* : a snug or confined place (as for hiding or for storing things)

¹cube \'kyüb\ *n* **1** : a solid body having six equal square sides or faces **2** : the product obtained by taking a number three times as a factor ⟨27 is the *cube* of 3⟩

cube

²cube *vb* **cubed; cub·ing 1** : to take a number as a factor three times ⟨3 *cubed* is 27⟩ **2** : to form into a cube **3** : to cut into cubes

cu·bic \'kyü-bik\ *adj* **1** : having the form of a cube **2** : having three dimensions

cu·bi·cal \'kyü-bi-kəl\ *adj* **1** : CUBIC **2** : relating to volume

cu·bit \'kyü-bət\ *n* : a unit of length usually equal to about eighteen inches

cub scout *n* : a member of the Boy Scouts of America program for boys of the age range eight to ten

---

j job   ng sing   ō low   ȯ moth   ȯi coin   th thin   th this   ü boot   u̇ foot   y you   yü few   yu̇ furious   zh vision

cuck·oo \'kük-ü, 'kük-\ *n*, *pl* **cuck·oos**
1 : any of several related birds (as a grayish brown European bird) that mostly lay their eggs in the nests of other birds for them to hatch **2** : the call of the European cuckoo

cu·cum·ber \'kyü-ˌkəm-bər\ *n* : a long fleshy usually green-skinned vegetable that is used in salads and in making pickles and is the fruit of a vine related to the melons and gourds

cud \'kəd\ *n* : a portion of food brought up from the first stomach of some animals (as the cow and sheep) to be chewed again

cud·dle \'kəd-l\ *vb* **cud·dled; cud·dling 1** : to hold close for warmth or comfort or in affection **2** : to lie close : NESTLE, SNUGGLE

¹cudg·el \'kəj-əl\ *n* : a short heavy club

²cudgel *vb* **cudg·eled** *or* **cudg·elled; cudg·el·ing** *or* **cudg·el·ling** : to beat with or as if with a cudgel

¹cue \'kyü\ *n* **1** : a word, phrase, or action in a play serving as a signal for the next actor to speak or act **2** : something serving as a signal or suggestion : HINT

²cue *n* : a straight tapering stick used in playing billiards and pool

¹cuff \'kəf\ *n* **1** : a band or turned-over piece at the end of a sleeve **2** : the turned-back hem of a trouser leg

²cuff *vb* : to strike especially with or as if with the palm of the hand : SLAP

³cuff *n* : SLAP

cui·rass \kwi-'ras\ *n* : a piece of armor covering the body from the neck to the waist

¹cull \'kəl\ *vb* **1** : to select from a group **2** : to identify and remove the culls from

²cull *n* : something rejected from a group or lot as inferior or worthless

cul·mi·nate \'kəl-mə-ˌnāt\ *vb* **cul·mi·nat·ed; cul·mi·nat·ing** : to reach the highest point

cul·pa·ble \'kəl-pə-bəl\ *adj* : deserving blame

cul·prit \'kəl-prət\ *n* **1** : one accused of or charged with a crime or fault **2** : one guilty of a crime or fault : OFFENDER

cul·ti·vate \'kəl-tə-ˌvāt\ *vb* **cul·ti·vat·ed; cul·ti·vat·ing 1** : to prepare land for the raising of crops : TILL **2** : to raise or assist the growth of crops by tilling or by labor and care **3** : to improve or develop by careful attention, training, or study : devote time and thought to **4** : to seek the society and friendship of

cul·ti·vat·ed \'kəl-tə-ˌvāt-əd\ *adj* **1** : subjected to or produced under cultivation ⟨*cultivated* fruits⟩ **2** : REFINED, EDUCATED

cul·ti·va·tion \ˌkəl-tə-'vā-shən\ *n* **1** : the act or process of cultivating especially the soil **2** : CULTURE, REFINEMENT

cul·ti·va·tor \'kəl-tə-ˌvāt-ər\ *n* **1** : one (as a farmer) that cultivates something **2** : an implement for loosening the soil and killing weeds between rows of a crop

cul·tur·al \'kəl-chə-rəl\ *adj* : of or relating to culture — **cul·tur·al·ly** *adv*

cul·ture \'kəl-chər\ *n* **1** : CULTIVATION 1 **2** : the rearing or development (as of a product or crop) by careful attention ⟨grape *culture*⟩ **3** : the improvement of the mind, tastes, and manners through careful training : REFINEMENT **4** : a particular stage, form, or kind of civilization ⟨Greek *culture*⟩

cul·tured \'kəl-chərd\ *adj* **1** : CULTIVATED **2** : produced under artificial conditions

cul·vert \'kəl-vərt\ *n* : a drain or waterway crossing under a road or railroad

cum·ber·some \'kəm-bər-səm\ *adj* **1** : CLUMSY **2** : BURDENSOME

cum·brous \'kəm-brəs\ *adj* : CUMBERSOME

cu·mu·la·tive \'kyü-myə-lət-iv\ *adj* : increasing (as in force, strength, or amount) by one addition after another ⟨a *cumulative* effect⟩

cu·mu·lus \'kyü-myə-ləs\ *n*, *pl* **cu·mu·li** \-ˌlī\ : a massy cloud form having a flat base and rounded outlines often piled up like a mountain

¹cu·ne·i·form \kyù-'nē-ə-ˌfȯrm\ *adj* **1** : wedge-shaped **2** : composed of or written in wedge-shaped characters

²cuneiform *n* : cuneiform writing (as of ancient Assyria and Babylonia)

¹cun·ning \'kən-ing\ *adj* **1** : SKILLFUL, CLEVER **2** : cleverly deceitful : SLY, TRICKY ⟨a *cunning* thief⟩ **3** : prettily pleasing or attractive : CUTE ⟨a *cunning* baby⟩

²cunning *n* **1** : SKILL, DEXTERITY **2** : cleverness in gaining one's ends (as by deceit) : SLYNESS

cuneiform

¹cup \'kəp\ *n* **1** : a small open bowl-shaped drinking container or vessel usually with a handle ⟨a *cup* and saucer⟩ **2** : the contents of a cup : CUPFUL ⟨drink a *cup* of tea⟩ **3** : a large ornamental cup offered as a prize **4** : something resembling a cup in shape or use

²cup *vb* **cupped; cup·ping 1** : to curve into the shape of a cup **2** : to receive, place, or take in or as if in a cup

cup·board \'kəb-ərd\ *n* : a closet with shelves for dishes or food : a small closet

cup·cake \'kəp-ˌkāk\ *n* : a small cake baked in a cuplike mold

cup·ful \'kəp-ˌfùl\ *n*, *pl* **cup·fuls** \-ˌfùlz\ *or* **cups·ful** \'kəps-ˌfùl\ **1** : the amount held by a cup **2** : a half pint : eight ounces

cu·pid \\'kyü-pəd\\ *n* : an artistic representation of Cupid the Roman god of love often as a winged child with bow and arrow

cu·pid·i·ty \\kyù-'pid-ət-ē\\ *n* : GREED

cu·po·la \\'kyü-pə-lə, -ˌlō\\ *n* **1** : a rounded roof or ceiling : DOME **2** : a small structure built on top of a roof

cupola 2

cur \\'kər\\ *n* : a worthless or mongrel dog

cur·a·ble \\'kyùr-ə-bəl\\ *adj* : capable of being cured

cu·rate \\'kyùr-ət\\ *n* : a clergyman who assists the rector or vicar of a church

¹curb \\'kərb\\ *n* **1** : a chain or strap on a horse's bit used to check the horse by drawing against the lower jaw **2** : CHECK, RESTRAINT **3** : an enclosing border of stone often along the outer edge of a sidewalk

²curb *vb* : to control by or furnish with a curb

curb·ing \\'kər-bing\\ *n* **1** : the material for a curb **2** : CURB

curd \\'kərd\\ *n* : the thickened or solid part of milk

cur·dle \\'kərd-l\\ *vb* **cur·dled; cur·dling 1** : to change into curd **2** : SPOIL, SOUR

¹cure \\'kyùr\\ *n* **1** : a method or period of medical treatment **2** : recovery or relief from a disease **3** : REMEDY ⟨a *cure* for colds⟩

²cure *vb* **cured; cur·ing 1** : to restore to health or soundness : HEAL **2** : to prepare by a chemical or physical process for keeping or use ⟨*cure* pork in brine⟩ **3** : to undergo a curing process

cur·few \\'kər-ˌfyü\\ *n* [from early French *covrefeu* "a signal given to bank the hearth fire"; from *covrir* "to cover" and *feu* "fire"] **1** : an order or regulation requiring persons of a usually specified class to be off the streets at a stated time **2** : a signal (as the ringing of a bell) usually in the evening to announce the beginning of a curfew **3** : the time when a curfew is sounded

cu·ri·o \\'kyùr-ē-ˌō\\ *n, pl* **cu·ri·os** : a rare or unusual article : CURIOSITY

cu·ri·os·i·ty \\ˌkyùr-ē-'äs-ət-ē\\ *n, pl* **cu·ri·os·i·ties 1** : an eager desire to learn and often to learn what does not concern one **2** : something strange or unusual **3** : an object or article valued because of its strangeness or rarity

cu·ri·ous \\'kyùr-ē-əs\\ *adj* **1** : eager to learn : INQUISITIVE **2** : STRANGE, RARE **3** : ODD, ECCENTRIC ⟨*curious* ideas⟩ — **cu·ri·ous·ly** *adv*

syn CURIOUS, INQUISITIVE, PRYING all mean interested in finding out what is not one's personal concern. CURIOUS suggests an eager desire to learn how and why things happen or have happened and places no special emphasis on an objectionable interest in someone else's affairs ⟨he was *curious* about snakes and read several books about them⟩ ⟨she couldn't help feeling *curious* when a crowd gathered⟩ INQUISITIVE suggests a habitual and sometimes impertinent curiosity and often involves the asking of many, though not especially personal, questions ⟨an *inquisitive* youngster who found everything and everybody fascinating⟩ PRYING involves seeking personal information about others either to satisfy one's own curiosity ⟨*prying* neighbors who watch from behind curtained windows⟩ or for some special purpose ⟨he considered the questionnaire *prying* and refused to fill it in⟩ **syn** see in addition QUEER

¹curl \\'kərl\\ *vb* **1** : to twist or form into ringlets **2** : CURVE, COIL ⟨*curl* up in a chair⟩

²curl *n* **1** : a lock of hair that coils : RINGLET **2** : something having a spiral or winding form : COIL ⟨a *curl* of smoke⟩ **3** : the action of curling : the state of being curled

curl·y \\'kər-lē\\ *adj* **curl·i·er; curl·i·est 1** : tending to curl **2** : having curls

cur·rant \\'kər-ənt\\ *n* **1** : a small seedless raisin much used in baking and cooking **2** : a sour red or white edible berry produced by a low spreading shrub related to the gooseberry

cur·ren·cy \\'kər-ən-sē\\ *n, pl* **cur·ren·cies 1** : circulation as a medium of exchange **2** : general use or acceptance ⟨a belief that had wide *currency*⟩ **3** : money in circulation

¹cur·rent \\'kər-ənt\\ *adj* **1** : now passing ⟨the *current* month⟩ **2** : occurring in or belonging to the present time ⟨*current* events⟩ **3** : used as a medium of exchange **4** : generally accepted, used, or practiced ⟨*current* customs⟩

²current *n* **1** : a body of fluid or air moving in a specified direction **2** : the swiftest part of a stream **3** : general course or movement (as of events) **4** : a flow of charges of electricity

cur·ry \\'kər-ē\\ *vb* **cur·ried; cur·ry·ing 1** : to rub and clean the coat of ⟨*curry* a horse⟩ **2** : to prepare tanned leather by scraping, cleansing, smoothing, and coloring

¹curse \\'kərs\\ *n* **1** : a prayer that harm or injury may come upon someone **2** : a word or an expression used in cursing or swearing **3** : evil or misfortune that comes as if in answer to a curse : a cause of great harm or evil

²curse *vb* **cursed; curs·ing 1** : to call upon divine or supernatural power to send harm or evil upon **2** : to swear at **3** : SWEAR **4** : to bring unhappiness or evil upon : AFFLICT

curt \\'kərt\\ *adj* : short in language : BRIEF

cur·tail \\ˌkər-'tāl\\ *vb* : to shorten or reduce by cutting off the end or a part of **syn** see SHORTEN

---

j job   ng sing   ō low   ȯ moth   ȯi coin   th thin   <u>th</u> this   ü boot   ù foot   y you   yü few   yù furious   zh vision

¹cur·tain \'kərt-n\ *n* **1** : a hanging movable screen : a piece of material (as cloth) intended to darken, conceal, divide, or decorate **2** : something that covers, conceals, or separates like a curtain ⟨a *curtain* of fire⟩

²curtain *vb* **1** : to furnish with curtains **2** : to veil or shut off with a curtain

¹curt·sy *or* **curt·sey** \'kərt-sē\ *n, pl* **curt·sies** *or* **curt·seys** [an alteration of *courtesy*] : a bow made especially by women as a sign of respect that consists of a slight lowering of the body and bending of the knees

²curtsy *or* **curtsey** *vb* **curt·sied** *or* **curt·seyed**; **curt·sy·ing** *or* **curt·sey·ing** : to make a curtsy

cur·va·ture \'kər-və-ˌchủr\ *n* **1** : a curving or bending **2** : the condition of being curved

¹curve \'kərv\ *vb* **curved**; **curv·ing** **1** : to turn or change from a straight line or course ⟨the road *curved* to the left⟩ **2** : to cause to curve

²curve *n* **1** : a bending or turning without angles : BEND ⟨a *curve* in the road⟩ **2** : something curved **3** : a ball thrown so that it swerves from its normal course

¹cush·ion \'kủsh-ən\ *n* **1** : a soft pillow or pad to rest on or against **2** : something resembling a cushion in use, shape, or softness **3** : something that serves to soften or lessen the effects of disturbances or disorders

²cushion *vb* **1** : to place on or as if on a cushion **2** : to furnish with a cushion **3** : to soften or lessen the force or shock of

cusp \'kəsp\ *n* : a point or pointed end (as the crown of a tooth)

cus·pid \'kəs-pəd\ *n* : CANINE 1

cuss \'kəs\ *vb* : CURSE

cus·tard \'kəs-tərd\ *n* : a sweetened mixture of milk and eggs baked, boiled, or frozen

cus·to·di·an \ˌkəs-'tōd-ē-ən\ *n* : one that guards and protects or maintains : KEEPER

cus·to·dy \'kəs-tə-dē\ *n* **1** : immediate charge and control : CARE **2** : legal confinement

¹cus·tom \'kəs-təm\ *n* **1** : the usual way of doing things : the usual practice **2** *pl* : duties or taxes imposed by law on imports or exports **3** : support given to a business by its customers : CUSTOMERS **syn** see HABIT

²custom *adj* **1** : made or done to personal order **2** : specializing in custom work

cus·tom·ar·y \'kəs-tə-ˌmer-ē\ *adj* **1** : based on or established by custom **2** : commonly practiced or observed **syn** see USUAL

cus·tom·er \'kəs-tə-mər\ *n* : one that buys from or patronizes the same firm especially regularly

¹cut \'kət\ *vb* **cut**; **cut·ting** **1** : to penetrate or divide with or as if with an edged instrument : GASH, CLEAVE ⟨*cut* a finger⟩ ⟨*cut* a cake⟩

2 : to be able to be shaped or penetrated with an edged tool ⟨cheese *cuts* easily⟩ **3** : to experience the growth of through the gum ⟨the baby is *cutting* teeth⟩ **4** · to strike sharply (as with a whip) or at an angle : hurt the feelings **5** : to make less : REDUCE, SHORTEN ⟨*cut* prices⟩ ⟨*cut* a speech⟩ **6** : to turn sharply ⟨*cut* right to avoid collision⟩ **7** : to go quickly or by a short or direct route ⟨*cut* across the lawn⟩ **8** : to pass through or across : INTERSECT, CROSS ⟨lines that *cut* each other⟩ **9** : to divide into parts ⟨*cut* a deck of cards⟩ **10** : to refuse to recognize an acquaintance **11** : to cause to stop : STOP ⟨*cut* the motor⟩ ⟨*cut* the nonsense⟩ **12** : to make or form with or as if with an edged tool **13** : to record sounds on

²cut *n* **1** : something cut or cut off : SEGMENT ⟨a *cut* of pie⟩ ⟨a *cut* of beef⟩ **2** : SHARE ⟨took his *cut* of the winnings⟩ **3** : something produced by or as if by cutting : GASH, WOUND **4** : a passage made by cutting ⟨a railroad *cut*⟩ **5** : a pictorial illustration (as in a book) **6** : a gesture or expression that hurts the feelings ⟨an unkind *cut*⟩ **7** : a straight path or course **8** : STROKE, BLOW **9** : the way in which a thing is cut, formed, or made **10** : REDUCTION

cute \'kyüt\ *adj* **cut·er**; **cut·est** **1** : CLEVER, SHREWD **2** : attractive especially in a dainty or pretty way

cu·ti·cle \'kyüt-i-kəl\ *n* **1** : an outer layer (as of skin or a leaf) often secreted by the cells beneath **2** : a dead or hornlike layer of skin especially around a fingernail

cut·lass \'kət-ləs\ *n* : a short heavy curved sword

cut·ler·y \'kət-lə-rē\ *n, pl* **cut·ler·ies** **1** : edged or cutting tools (as knives and scissors) **2** : implements used in cutting, serving, and eating food

cut·let \'kət-lət\ *n* **1** : a small piece of meat cut for broiling or frying **2** : a piece of food shaped like a cutlet

cutlass

cut·out \'kət-ˌaủt\ *n* : something cut out or prepared for cutting out from something else ⟨a page of animal *cutouts*⟩

cut·ter \'kət-ər\ *n* **1** : one that cuts ⟨a diamond *cutter*⟩ ⟨a cookie *cutter*⟩ **2** : a boat used by warships for carrying passengers and stores to and from the shore **3** : a small one-masted sailing boat **4** : a small armed boat in the coast guard **5** : a small sleigh

cutter 5

cut·ting \'kət-ing\ *n* : a part (as a shoot) of a plant able to grow into a whole new plant

cut·tle·fish \'kət-l-ˌfish\ n : a ten-armed sea animal related to the squid and octopus

cut·up \'kət-ˌəp\ n : one who clowns or acts boisterously

cut·worm \'kət-ˌwərm\ n : a smooth-bodied moth caterpillar that feeds on the stems of plants at night

-cy \sē\ n suffix, pl **-cies** 1 : action : practice ⟨pira*cy*⟩ 2 : rank : office ⟨baronet*cy*⟩ ⟨chaplain*cy*⟩ 3 : body : class ⟨aristocra*cy*⟩ 4 : state : quality ⟨accura*cy*⟩ ⟨bankrupt*cy*⟩

cy·a·nide \'sī-ə-ˌnīd\ n : any of several compounds containing carbon and nitrogen and including two very poisonous substances

cy·cad \'sī-kəd\ n : a tropical tree resembling a palm but related to the conifers

¹cy·cle \'sī-kəl\ n 1 : a period of time taken up by a series of events or actions that repeat themselves regularly and in the same order ⟨the *cycle* of the seasons⟩ 2 : a complete round or series 3 : a long period of time : AGE 4 : BICYCLE 5 : TRICYCLE 6 : MOTORCYCLE

²cycle vb **cy·cled; cy·cling** : to ride a cycle

cy·clist \'sī-kləst\ n : one who rides a cycle and especially a bicycle

cy·clone \'sī-ˌklōn\ n 1 : a storm or system of winds that rotates about a center of low atmospheric pressure, advances at a speed of twenty to thirty miles an hour, and often brings abundant rain 2 : TORNADO

cyl·in·der \'sil-ən-dər\ n : a long round body either hollow or solid

cy·lin·dri·cal \sə-'lin-dri-kəl\ adj : having the shape of a cylinder

cym·bal \'sim-bəl\ n : one of a pair of concave brass plates that are clashed together to make a sharp ringing sound

cylinder

cy·no·sure \'sī-nə-ˌshur\ n : a center of attraction or attention

cy·press \'sī-prəs\ n : any of various evergreen cone-bearing trees related to the pines that have strong reddish moisture-resistant wood

cyst \'sist\ n 1 : an abnormal sac in a living body 2 : a covering (as of a spore) resembling a cyst

cy·to·plasm \'sīt-ə-ˌplaz-əm\ n : the protoplasm of a cell exclusive of the nucleus

czar \'zär\ n [from Polish *czar*, taken from Russian *tsar'* which in turn came from Gothic *kaisar;* the Gothic derived from Latin *Caesar* which originally was the name of several Roman emperors and later came to mean "emperor"] : the ruler of Russia until the 1917 revolution

cza·ri·na \zä-'rē-nə\ n : the wife of a czar

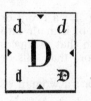

d \'dē\ n, often cap 1 : the fourth letter of the English alphabet 2 : the roman numeral 500 3 : a grade rating a student's work as poor

¹dab \'dab\ n 1 : a sudden poke 2 : a light quick touch

²dab vb **dabbed; dab·bing** 1 : to strike or touch lightly 2 : to apply with light or irregular strokes ⟨*dab* on paint⟩ — **dab·ber** n

³dab n : a small amount ⟨*dab* of butter⟩

dab·ble \'dab-əl\ vb **dab·bled; dab·bling** 1 : to wet by splashing : SPATTER 2 : to paddle in or as if in water 3 : to work without serious interest or effort — **dab·bler** \'dab-lər\ n

dace \'dās\ n, pl **dace** : any of several small carplike fishes

da·cha \'dä-chə\ n : a Russian country house

dachs·hund \'däks-ˌhunt\ n [from German *dachshund*, a compound of *dachs* "badger" and *hund* "dog", from the same source as English *hound*] : a small hound with a long body, very short legs, and long drooping ears

dachshund

dad \'dad\ n : FATHER

dad·dy \'dad-ē\ n, pl **dad·dies** : FATHER

dad·dy long·legs \ˌdad-ē-'lòng-ˌlegz\ n, pl **daddy longlegs** : a spiderlike insect with a small rounded body and long slender legs

daf·fo·dil \'daf-ə-ˌdil\ n : a plant that grows from a bulb and bears long slender leaves and yellow, white, or pinkish trumpet-shaped flowers with a scalloped edge and leaflike segments at the base

daft \'daft\ adj : FOOLISH, CRAZY — **daft·ly** adv — **daftness** n

daffodils

dag·ger \'dag-ər\ n 1 : a short knifelike weapon used for stabbing 2 : a mark † used in printed matter to refer the reader elsewhere or to indicate a death date

dahl·ia \'dal-yə\ n : a tall plant related to the daisies and widely grown for its showy flowers

¹dai·ly \'dā-lē\ adj 1 : occurring, done, produced, or issued every day or every weekday 2 : computed in terms of one day

daggers 1

²daily n, pl **dai·lies** : a daily newspaper

¹dain·ty \'dānt-ē\ n, pl **dain·ties** : DELICACY

²dainty adj **dain·ti·er; dain·ti·est** 1 : pleasing to the taste 2 : delicately pretty 3 : having or showing delicate taste — **dain·ti·ly** \'dānt-l-ē\ adv — **dain·ti·ness** \'dānt-ē-nəs\ n

dair·y \'deər-ē\ *n, pl* **dair·ies** **1** : a room or building where milk is stored or is made into butter and cheese **2** : a farm that produces milk **3** : a company or a store that sells or distributes milk products

dair·y·maid \'deər-ē-ˌmād\ *n* : a woman or girl who works in a dairy

dair·y·man \'deər-ē-mən\ *n, pl* **dair·y·men** \-mən\ : a man who operates a dairy farm or works in a dairy

da·is \'dā-əs\ *n* : a raised platform (as in a hall)

dai·sy \'dā-zē\ *n, pl* **dai·sies** [from Old English *dægesēage*, from *dæg* "day" and *ēage* "eye"] : any of a large group of plants with composite flower heads consisting of one or more rows of petallike white or colored ray flowers about a central disk of tiny often yellow flowers closely packed together

daisies

dale \'dāl\ *n* : VALLEY

dal·ly \'dal-ē\ *vb* **dal·lied; dal·ly·ing** **1** : to act playfully : TRIFLE, TOY **2** : to waste time **3** : LINGER, DAWDLE

dal·ma·tian \dal-'mā-shən\ *n, often cap* : a large dog of a breed having a white short-haired coat with black or brown spots

¹dam \'dam\ *n* : a female parent — used especially of a domestic animal

²dam *n* : a barrier (as across a stream) to hold back a flow of water

³dam *vb* **dammed; dam·ming** **1** : to make a dam across **2** : to hold back by a dam

¹dam·age \'dam-ij\ *n* **1** : loss or harm due to injury **2** *pl* : money demanded or paid according to law for injury or damage

²damage *vb* **dam·aged; dam·ag·ing** : to cause damage to

dam·ask \'dam-əsk\ *n* **1** : a reversible figured cloth used especially for household linen **2** : a tough steel (**damask steel**) decorated with wavy lines

dame \'dām\ *n* **1** : a woman of rank, station, or authority **2** : an elderly woman

¹damn \'dam\ *vb* **1** : to condemn to everlasting punishment especially in hell **2** : to condemn as bad or as a failure **3** : CURSE

²damn *n* **1** : the word *damn* used as a curse **2** : something of little value

dam·na·ble \'dam-nə-bəl\ *adj* **1** : deserving or liable to be condemned **2** : very bad : AWFUL — **dam·na·bly** \-blē\ *adv*

¹damned \'damd\ *adj* **1** : DAMNABLE **2** : EXTRAORDINARY ⟨the *damnedest* sight⟩

²damned *adv* : EXTREMELY, VERY

¹damp \'damp\ *n* **1** : a harmful gas or mixture of gases that occurs especially in coal mines **2** : MOISTURE

²damp *vb* **1** : DEADEN, CHECK **2** : DAMPEN

³damp *adj* : slightly wet : MOIST — **damp·ly** *adv* — **damp·ness** *n*

damp·en \'dam-pən\ *vb* **1** : to check in vigor or activity : DULL, DEADEN **2** : to make or become damp — **damp·en·er** *n*

damp·er \'dam-pər\ *n* **1** : one that checks, discourages, or deadens **2** : a valve or movable plate for regulating the flow of air

dam·sel \'dam-zəl\ *n* : GIRL, MAIDEN

¹dance \'dans\ *vb* **danced; danc·ing** **1** : to glide, step, or move through a series of movements usually in time to music **2** : to move about or up and down quickly and lightly **3** : to perform or take part in as a dancer **4** : to cause to dance — **danc·er** *n*

²dance *n* **1** : an act or round of dancing **2** : a social gathering for dancing **3** : a particular set of movements or steps for dancing usually in time to special music **4** : the art of dancing

dan·de·li·on \'dan-dl-ˌī-ən\ *n* : a weedy plant related to the daisies that has a whorl of long deeply toothed leaves often eaten as cooked greens or in salad and bright yellow flowers with hollow stems

dan·dle \'dan-dl\ *vb* **dan·dled; dan·dling** : to move up and down on one's knee or in one's arms in affectionate play ⟨*dandle* a baby⟩

dandelion

dan·druff \'dan-drəf\ *n* : a thin whitish scurf that forms on the scalp and comes off in small flakes

¹dan·dy \'dan-dē\ *n, pl* **dan·dies** **1** : a man who pays too much attention to his clothes **2** : something excellent in its class

²dandy *adj* **dan·di·er; dan·di·est** : very good

Dane \'dān\ *n* : a native or inhabitant of Denmark

dan·ger \'dān-jər\ *n* **1** : exposure to injury, harm, or evil : PERIL **2** : something that may cause injury or harm

syn DANGER, PERIL, RISK all imply possible loss of life or injury to one's well-being. DANGER, the more general term, refers to threatening trouble that may or may not be avoided ⟨we'll climb the mountain from the side that involves the least *danger*⟩ PERIL is a stronger word and carries the idea of more, deadlier, and less easily avoided pitfalls ⟨the *perils* of the western ski slope are great; many lose their lives on it⟩ RISK suggests the unavoidable dangers that one must accept in order to accomplish or participate in something ⟨mountain-climbing *risks*⟩

dan·ger·ous \'dān-jə-rəs\ *adj* **1** : exposing to danger ⟨*dangerous* work⟩ **2** : able or likely to injure — **dan·ger·ous·ly** *adv*

dan·gle \'dang-gəl\ *vb* **dan·gled**; **dan·gling** **1** : to hang loosely especially with a swinging or jerking motion : SWING **2** : to be a dependent **3** : to cause to dangle

¹Dan·ish \'dā-nish\ *adj* : of or relating to Denmark, the Danes, or Danish

²Danish *n* : the language of the Danes

dank \'dangk\ *adj* : disagreeably wet or moist — **dank·ly** *adv* — **dank·ness** *n*

dan·seuse \dän-'sərz\ *n* : a female ballet dancer

dap·per \'dap-ər\ *adj* **1** : neat and trim in dress or appearance **2** : alert and lively in movement and manners

dap·ple \'dap-əl\ *vb* **dap·pled**; **dap·pling** : to mark or become marked with rounded spots of a different color or shade ⟨*dappled* horse⟩

¹dare \'daər\ *vb* **dared**; **dar·ing** **1** : to have courage enough for some purpose : be bold enough to **2** : to challenge to perform an action especially as a proof of courage

²dare *n* : CHALLENGE ⟨took the *dare*⟩

dare·dev·il \'daər-,dev-əl\ *n* : a person so bold as to be reckless

¹dar·ing \'daər-ing\ *adj* : ready to take risks : BOLD, VENTURESOME — **dar·ing·ly** *adv*

syn DARING, RECKLESS, FOOLHARDY all mean exposing oneself to more danger than is sensible or necessary. DARING stresses fearlessness and a readiness to take chances ⟨the *daring* exploits of frontier heroes⟩ RECKLESS emphasizes a heedless disregard for consequences ⟨*reckless* driving that endangers lives⟩ FOOLHARDY stresses a foolish daring ⟨*foolhardy* attempts to swim the rapids⟩

²daring *n* : fearless boldness

¹dark \'därk\ *adj* **1** : being without light or without much light **2** : not light in color **3** : not bright and cheerful : GLOOMY **4** : being without knowledge and culture ⟨the *Dark Ages*⟩ **5** : HIDDEN, MYSTERIOUS —**dark·ish** *adj* — **dark·ly** *adv* — **dark·ness** *n*

²dark *n* **1** : absence of light : DARKNESS **2** : NIGHT, NIGHTFALL ⟨home before *dark*⟩ **3** : a dark or deep color **4** : IGNORANCE

dark·en \'där-kən\ *vb* **1** : to make or grow dark or darker **2** : BLACKEN, TARNISH **3** : to make or become gloomy — **dark·en·er** *n*

dark·room \'därk-,rüm, -,rùm\ *n* : a room protected from rays of light harmful in developing photographic plates and film

¹dar·ling \'där-ling\ *n* **1** : a dearly loved person **2** : FAVORITE

²darling *adj* **1** : dearly loved **2** : CHARMING

¹darn \'därn\ *vb* : to mend with interlacing stitches ⟨*darn* socks⟩

²darn *n* : a place that has been darned

³darn *n* : DAMN

¹dart \'därt\ *n* **1** : a small pointed missile **2** *pl* : a game in which darts are thrown at a target **3** : a quick sudden movement **4** : a stitched tapering fold in a garment

dart 1

²dart *vb* : to move or thrust suddenly and quickly ⟨a toad *darted* out its tongue⟩

¹dash \'dash\ *vb* **1** : to knock, hurl, or thrust violently **2** : SMASH, SHATTER **3** : SPLASH, SPATTER ⟨*dashed* cold water on his face⟩ **4** : DESTROY, RUIN ⟨his hopes were *dashed*⟩ **5** : to write or sketch rapidly or carelessly **6** : to move with sudden speed

²dash *n* **1** : a sudden burst or splash ⟨a *dash* of cold water⟩ **2** : a stroke of a pen **3** : a punctuation mark — used chiefly to indicate a break in the thought or structure of a sentence **4** : a small addition **5** : LIVELINESS, ENERGY **6** : a sudden rush or attempt ⟨a *dash* for the goal⟩ **7** : a short fast race ⟨100-yard *dash*⟩ **8** : a long click or buzz forming a letter or part of a letter (as in telegraphy) **9** : DASHBOARD

dash·board \'dash-,bōrd\ *n* : a panel across an automobile or airplane below the windshield usually containing dials and controls

dash·ing \'dash-ing\ *adj* : marked by smartness especially in dress and manners

das·tard \'das-tərd\ *n* : a mean and sneaky coward

das·tard·ly \'das-tərd-lē\ *adj* : of or resembling a dastard — **das·tard·li·ness** *n*

da·ta \'dāt-ə, 'dat-ə\ *n sing or pl* **1** : factual information about something used as a basis for calculation or reasoning **2** : DATUM

¹date \'dāt\ *n* [taken into English from Old French *date*, a word whose source was Greek *daktylos* meaning "finger" and then "date", because the fruit is shaped like a finger] : the sweet brownish edible fruit of an Old World palm (**date palm**)

²date *n* [the Romans wrote on their letters the place and date of sending, e.g., *data Romae Idibus Martiis* "given at Rome on the Ides of March"; the first word, *data*, literally, "given", came to be used to mean "date", and was taken into English in this meaning] **1** : the day, month, or year of a happening **2** : a statement giving the time of making something (as a coin, book, or building) **3** : the period to which something belongs **4** : APPOINTMENT **5** : a person of the opposite sex with whom one has a social engagement

---

j job   ng sing   ō low   ȯ moth   ȯi coin   th thin   th̲ this   ü boot   u̇ foot   y you   yü few   yu̇ furious   zh vision

³date *vb* **dat·ed; dat·ing 1 :** to find or show the date of **2 :** to write the date on ⟨*date* a letter⟩ **3 :** to make or have a date with **4 :** to belong to a time **5 :** to mark as old-fashioned or belonging to a past time ⟨his slang *dates* him⟩

da·tum \'dāt-əm, 'dat-\ *n, pl* **da·ta** \-ə\ *or* **datums :** a single piece of data **:** FACT

¹daub \'dȯb\ *vb* **1 :** to cover with something soft and sticky **:** SMEAR, PLASTER ⟨*daubed* with mud⟩ **2 :** to paint unskillfully — **daub·er** *n*

²daub *n* **1 :** a daubed spot **2 :** a crude picture

daugh·ter \'dȯt-ər\ *n* **1 :** a female offspring especially of human beings **2 :** a woman or girl derived from someone or something (as a country or race) — **daugh·ter·ly** *adj*

daugh·ter–in–law \'dȯt-ər-ən-ˌlȯ\ *n, pl* **daugh·ters–in–law :** the wife of one's son

daunt \'dȯnt\ *vb* **:** to lessen the courage of

daunt·less \'dȯnt-ləs\ *adj* **:** not to be dismayed — **daunt·less·ly** *adv* — **daunt·less·ness** *n*

dau·phin \'dȯ-fən\ *n* **:** the eldest son of a king of France

dav·en·port \'dav-ən-ˌpȯrt\ *n* **:** a large upholstered sofa

da·vit \'dā-vət, 'dav-ət\ *n* **:** one of a pair of posts fitted with ropes and pulleys and used for supporting and lowering a ship's boat

daw·dle \'dȯd-l\ *vb* **daw·dled; daw·dling 1 :** to spend time wastefully **:** linger idly **2 :** LOITER **syn** see DELAY — **daw·dler** \'dȯd-lər\ *n*

¹dawn \'dȯn\ *vb* **1 :** to begin to grow light in the morning **2 :** to begin to appear or develop **3 :** to begin to be understood

²dawn *n* **1 :** the first appearance of light in the morning **2 :** a first appearance **:** BEGINNING

day \'dā\ *n* **1 :** the time of light between sunrise and sunset **:** DAYLIGHT **2 :** the time the earth takes to make one turn on its axis **3 :** a period of twenty-four hours beginning at midnight **4 :** a stated period **:** AGE, TIME **5 :** a contest taking place on a certain day **6 :** the time set apart by custom or law for work

day·bed \'dā-ˌbed\ *n* **:** a couch with low head and foot pieces

day·break \'dā-ˌbrāk\ *n* **:** DAWN

¹day·dream \'dā-ˌdrēm\ *n* **:** a dreamy sequence of usually happy or pleasant imaginings about oneself or one's future

²daydream *vb* **:** to have a daydream — **day·dream·er** *n*

day·light \'dā-ˌlīt\ *n* **1 :** the light of day **2 :** DAWN ⟨from *daylight* to dark⟩ **3 :** understanding of something that has not been clear

daylight saving time *n* **:** time usually one hour ahead of standard time

day·time \'dā-ˌtīm\ *n* **:** the period of daylight

¹daze \'dāz\ *vb* **dazed; daz·ing 1 :** to stun by a sudden blow **2 :** to dazzle with light

²daze *n* **:** a dazed state

¹daz·zle \'daz-əl\ *vb* **daz·zled; daz·zling 1 :** to confuse or be confused by too much light or by moving lights **2 :** to bewilder, surprise, or excite admiration with a brilliant display — **daz·zler** \'daz-lər\ *n* — **daz·zling·ly** \'daz-ling-lē\ *adv*

²dazzle *n* **:** something dazzling **:** GLITTER

DDT \ˌdē-ˌdē-'tē\ *n* **:** a colorless insecticide that has no smell

de- *prefix* **1 :** do the opposite of ⟨*deactivate*⟩ **2 :** reverse of ⟨*de*-emphasis⟩ **3 :** remove or remove from a specified thing ⟨*delouse*⟩ **4 :** reduce ⟨*devalue*⟩ **5 :** get off of ⟨*detrain*⟩

dea·con \'dē-kən\ *n* **1 :** a clergyman in some Christian churches ranking just below a priest **2 :** a layman in some churches performing various duties (as assisting a minister)

¹dead \'ded\ *adj* **1 :** no longer living **:** LIFELESS **2 :** seemingly lifeless ⟨a *dead* faint⟩ **3 :** NUMB **4 :** very tired **5 :** never having lived **:** INANIMATE ⟨*dead* matter⟩ **6 :** lacking motion, activity, energy, or power to respond ⟨a *dead* tennis ball⟩ **7 :** no longer in use or effect **:** OBSOLETE ⟨a *dead* custom⟩ ⟨*dead* languages⟩ **8 :** lacking warmth, vigor, flavor, or animation **9 :** CERTAIN, EXACT ⟨a *dead* shot⟩ **10 :** being sudden and complete ⟨a *dead* stop⟩ **11 :** COMPLETE ⟨a *dead* loss⟩

²dead *n, pl* **dead 1 :** one that is dead ⟨the living and the *dead*⟩ **2 :** the time of greatest quiet

³dead *adv* **1 :** COMPLETELY, ABSOLUTELY ⟨*dead* right⟩ **2 :** completely and suddenly ⟨stopped *dead* in his tracks⟩ **3 :** DIRECTLY

dead·en \'ded-n\ *vb* **1 :** to take away some of the force of **:** lessen in strength **:** BLUNT, DULL **2 :** to make (as a wall) soundproof

dead end *n* **:** an end (as of a street) without an exit

dead heat *n* **:** a contest in which two or more contestants tie

dead letter *n* **1 :** something (as a law) that has lost its force without being formally abolished **2 :** a letter that cannot be delivered by the post office or returned to the sender

dead·line \'ded-ˌlīn\ *n* **:** a date or time before which something must be done

¹dead·lock \'ded-ˌläk\ *n* **:** a stopping of action because both sides in a struggle are equally strong and neither will give in

²deadlock *vb* **:** to bring or come to a deadlock

¹**dead·ly** \'ded-lē\ *adj* **dead·li·er; dead·li·est**
1 : causing or capable of causing death
⟨*deadly* weapons⟩   **2** : willing or aiming to
destroy ⟨*deadly* enemies⟩   **3** : extremely accurate ⟨*deadly* aim⟩   **4** : fatal to spiritual
progress   **5** : suggestive of death   **6** : EXTREME
⟨*deadly* seriousness⟩ — **dead·li·ness** *n*

²**deadly** *adv* **1** : in a way suggestive of death
⟨*deadly* pale⟩   **2** : EXTREMELY ⟨*deadly* dull⟩

dead march *n* : a solemn march for a funeral

dead·wood \'ded-,wud\ *n* **1** : wood dead on
the tree   **2** : useless personnel or material

deaf \'def\ *adj* **1** : wholly or partly unable to
hear   **2** : unwilling to hear — **deaf·ness** *n*

deaf·en \'def-ən\ *vb* **1** : to make deaf   **2** : to
stun with noise

deaf–mute \'def-,myüt\ *n* : a deaf person
who cannot speak

¹**deal** \'dēl\ *n* **1** : an indefinite quantity or
degree ⟨means a great *deal*⟩   **2** : a large
amount   **3** : the act or right of distributing
cards to players in a card game

²**deal** *vb* **dealt** \'delt\; **deal·ing** \'dē-ling\
1 : to give out in portions or shares
2 : DELIVER ⟨*dealt* him a blow⟩   **3** : to have to
do : TREAT ⟨a book that *deals* with airplanes⟩
4 : to take action ⟨*deal* harshly with law-
breakers⟩   **5** : to buy and sell regularly
: TRADE   **6** : to sell or distribute something as a
business — **deal·er** \'dē-lər\ *n*

³**deal** *n* **1** : an act of buying and selling
: BARGAINING   **2** : an agreement to do business   **3** : treatment received   **4** : a secret or
underhand agreement   **5** : BARGAIN

⁴**deal** *n* : wood or a board of fir or pine

deal·ing \'dē-ling\ *n* **1** : a business relation
2 : a way of acting or doing business

dean \'dēn\ *n* **1** : a clergyman in charge of a
cathedral church   **2** : the head of a division,
college, school, or faculty of a university   **3** : a
college or school official in charge of students
or studies   **4** : the senior member of a group
— **dean·ship** \-,ship\ *n*

¹**dear** \'diər\ *adj* **1** : highly valued : LOVED
2 — used as a form of address in letters and
sometimes in speech ⟨*Dear* Sir⟩   **3** : high=
priced   **4** : HEARTFELT, EARNEST — **dear·ness** *n*

²**dear** *adv* : at a high price

³**dear** *n* : a loved one : DARLING

dear·ly \'diər-lē\ *adv* **1** : FONDLY ⟨loved him
dearly⟩   **2** : KEENLY   **3** : at a high price

dearth \'dərth\ *n* : SCARCITY, LACK

death \'deth\ *n* **1** : the end of life : DYING
⟨sudden *death*⟩   **2** : the cause of loss of life
3 : the state of being dead   **4** : DESTRUCTION,
END ⟨the *death* of all hope⟩ — **death·less**
\-ləs\ *adj* — **death·like** \-,līk\ *adj*

death·bed \'deth-'bed\ *n* **1** : the bed in
which a person dies   **2** : the last hours of life

death·blow \'deth-'blō\ *n* : a fatal or crushing stroke or event

¹**death·ly** \'deth-lē\ *adj* **1** : FATAL   **2** : of,
relating to, or suggesting death

²**deathly** *adv* : in a way suggesting death

death's–head \'deths-,hed\ *n* : a human
skull

death·watch \'deth-,wäch\ *n* : a vigil kept
with a dead or dying person

deb \'deb\ *n* : DEBUTANTE

de·bar \di-'bär\ *vb* **de·barred; de·bar·ring** : to
bar from having or doing something

de·bark \di-'bärk\ *vb* : DISEMBARK

de·base \di-'bās\ *vb* **de·based; de·bas·ing** : to
lower in value, quality, character, or dignity
⟨*debase* coinage⟩ — **de·base·ment** *n*

de·bat·a·ble \di-'bāt-ə-bəl\ *adj* : open to
question or argument

¹**de·bate** \di-'bāt\ *n* **1** : a discussion or
argument carried on between two matched
sides according to fixed rules   **2** : DISCUSSION

²**debate** *vb* **de·bat·ed; de·bat·ing** **1** : to discuss
a question by giving arguments on both sides
: take part in a debate   **2** : CONSIDER, DISCUSS
syn see DISCUSS — **de·bat·er** *n*

¹**de·bauch** \di-'bȯch\ *vb* : to make corrupt

²**debauch** *n* : an occasion or period of de-
bauchery

de·bauch·er·y \di-'bȯch-ə-rē\ *n, pl* **de·bauch-
er·ies** : excessive indulgence in sensual
pleasures

de·bil·i·tate \di-'bil-ə-,tāt\ *vb* **de·bil·i·tat·ed;
de·bil·i·tat·ing** : to make feeble : WEAKEN

de·bil·i·ty \di-'bil-ət-ē\ *n, pl* **de·bil·i·ties** : a
weakened state especially of health

¹**deb·it** \'deb-ət\ *n* : an entry in an account
showing money paid out or owed

²**debit** *vb* : to enter as a debit

deb·o·nair \,deb-ə-'naər\ *adj* : gaily and
gracefully charming : LIGHTHEARTED —
deb·o·nair·ly *adv* — **deb·o·nair·ness** *n*

de·bris \də-'brē\ *n, pl* **de·bris** \-'brēz\ : fragments remaining from something broken
down or destroyed

debt \'det\ *n* **1** : SIN, TRESPASS   **2** : something
owed to another   **3** : the condition of owing
money in amounts greater than one can pay

debt·or \'det-ər\ *n* : one that owes a debt

de·but \'dā-,byü\ *n* **1** : a first public appearance   **2** : the formal entrance of a young
woman into society

deb·u·tante \'deb-yu-,tänt\ *n* : a young
woman making her debut

deca- *or* **dec-** *or* **deka-** *or* **dek-** *prefix* : ten
⟨*decagon*⟩

---

j job   **ng** sing   **ō** low   **ȯ** moth   **ȯi** coin   **th** thin   **th̲** this   **ü** boot   ** u̇** foot   **y** you   **yü** few   **yu̇** furious   **zh** vision

dec·ade \'dek-ˌād\ *n* **1** : a group or set of ten **2** : a period of ten years

dec·a·gon \'dek-ə-ˌgän\ *n* : a closed plane figure having ten angles and ten sides

de·cal \'dē-ˌkal\ *n* [short for earlier *decalcomania* which originally meant "the art of transferring pictures", taken from a French noun formed from *décalquer* "to copy by tracing" and *manie* "mania", "craze"] : a design made to be transferred (as to glass) from specially prepared paper

dec·a·logue \'dek-ə-ˌlóg\ *n, often cap* : the ten commandments of God given to Moses on Mount Sinai

de·camp \di-'kamp\ *vb* : to go away suddenly and usually secretly : run away

de·cant·er \di-'kant-ər\ *n* : an ornamental glass bottle used especially for serving wine

decanter

de·cap·i·tate \di-'kap-ə-ˌtāt\ *vb* **de·cap·i·tat·ed; de·cap·i·tat·ing** : to cut off the head of : BEHEAD

¹de·cay \di-'kā\ *vb* **1** : to pass (as by aging, weathering, or rotting) gradually from a healthy, sound, or intact condition to one that is imperfect : FAIL **2** : to undergo decay

²decay *n* **1** : a decayed condition : a gradual decline or failure **2** : a spontaneous change of a radioactive element into another form of the same element or into a different element

¹de·cease \di-'sēs\ *n* : DEATH

²decease *vb* **de·ceased; de·ceas·ing** : DIE

de·ce·dent \di-'sēd-nt\ *n* : a deceased person

de·ceit \di-'sēt\ *n* **1** : the act or practice of deceiving : DECEPTION **2** : a statement or act that misleads a person or causes him to believe what is false : TRICK **3** : DECEITFULNESS

de·ceit·ful \di-'sēt-fəl\ *adj* **1** : using or tending to use deceit **2** : marked by deceit — **de·ceit·ful·ly** *adv* — **de·ceit·ful·ness** *n*

de·ceive \di-'sēv\ *vb* **de·ceived; de·ceiv·ing** **1** : to cause to believe what is not true : MISLEAD **2** : to deal with dishonestly : CHEAT **3** : to use or practice deceit — **de·ceiv·er** *n*

de·cel·er·ate \dē-'sel-ə-ˌrāt\ *vb* **de·cel·er·at·ed; de·cel·er·at·ing** : to slow down

De·cem·ber \di-'sem-bər\ *n* : the twelfth month of the year

de·cen·cy \'dēs-n-sē\ *n, pl* **de·cen·cies** **1** : a being decent : modest or proper behavior **2** : something that is proper or becoming

de·cent \'dēs-nt\ *adj* **1** : being up to an accepted standard of good taste (as in speech, dress, or behavior) **2** : modestly clothed **3** : not obscene **4** : fairly good — **de·cent·ly** *adv*

de·cep·tion \di-'sep-shən\ *n* **1** : the act of deceiving or misleading **2** : TRICK, FRAUD

de·cep·tive \di-'sep-tiv\ *adj* : DECEIVING, MISLEADING — **de·cep·tive·ly** *adv*

deci- *prefix* : tenth part ⟨*deci*gram⟩

de·cide \di-'sīd\ *vb* **de·cid·ed; de·cid·ing** **1** : to make or give a judgment : SETTLE **2** : to come to a conclusion : make up one's mind **3** : to cause to decide

de·cid·ed \di-'sīd-əd\ *adj* **1** : CLEAR, UNMISTAKABLE ⟨a *decided* smell of gas⟩ **2** : FIRM, DETERMINED — **de·cid·ed·ly** *adv*

syn DECIDED, DECISIVE both refer to the settling of uncertain issues but they have different applications and are often confused. DECIDED stresses being unmistakably settled and no longer open to question ⟨suffered a *decided* defeat at Bull Run but won the war⟩ ⟨he had a *decided* mind and never doubted his position on any issue⟩ DECISIVE, on the other hand, stresses having the ability to decide or serving to decide an unsettled issue once and for all ⟨a *decisive* defeat from which they never recovered⟩ ⟨he had a *decisive* mind and could settle most disputes quickly and successfully⟩

de·cid·u·ous \di-'sij-ə-wəs\ *adj* : made up of or having a part that falls off at the end of a period of growth and use ⟨*deciduous* trees⟩

¹dec·i·mal \'des-ə-məl\ *adj* **1** : based on the number 10 : numbered or counting by tens **2** : expressed in or including a decimal fraction

²decimal *n* : a proper fraction in which the denominator is 10 or 10 multiplied one or more times by itself and is indicated by a point placed at the left of the numerator ⟨the *decimal* .2 = 2/10, the *decimal* .25 = 25/100, the *decimal* .025 = 25/1000⟩

dec·i·me·ter \'des-ə-ˌmēt-ər\ *n* : a unit of length equal to 1/10 meter

de·ci·pher \dē-'sī-fər\ *vb* **1** : to translate from secret writing (as code) **2** : to make out the meaning of something not clear or distinct

de·ci·sion \di-'sizh-ən\ *n* **1** : the act or result of deciding **2** : promptness and firmness in deciding : DETERMINATION

de·ci·sive \di-'sī-siv\ *adj* **1** : deciding or able to decide a question or dispute ⟨*decisive* proof⟩ **2** : showing decision **syn** see DECIDED — **de·ci·sive·ly** *adv* — **de·ci·sive·ness** *n*

¹deck \'dek\ *n* **1** : a floorlike platform extending from side to side of a ship **2** : something resembling the deck of a ship **3** : a pack of playing cards

²deck *vb* **1** : to dress or decorate especially in a striking manner **2** : to furnish with a deck

dec·la·ra·tion \ˌdek-lə-'rā-shən\ *n* **1** : an

act of declaring **2** : something declared or a document containing such a declaration ⟨the *Declaration* of Independence⟩

de·clar·a·tive \di-'klar-ət-iv\ *adj* : making a statement ⟨*declarative* sentence⟩

de·clare \di-'klaər\ *vb* **de·clared**; **de·clar·ing** **1** : to make known clearly to other persons : PROCLAIM **2** : to state positively

1de·cline \di-'klīn\ *vb* **de·clined**; **de·clin·ing** **1** : to bend or slope downward **2** : to draw to a close **3** : to refuse to accept

syn DECLINE, REFUSE, SPURN all mean to turn down someone or something. DECLINE is thought of as a courteous term and is often applied when something offered as a favor or benefit is not accepted ⟨*declined* the reward⟩ ⟨never *declines* a dinner invitation⟩ REFUSE often applies to the fact of rejecting a request for a favor or benefit ⟨*refused* to give him a job⟩ but does not itself imply either courtesy or rudeness ⟨he had to *refuse* my request⟩ ⟨he even *refused* to see me⟩ SPURN heavily emphasizes the idea of rude rejection and suggests a certain amount of scorn or contempt ⟨*spurned* all offers of help⟩ ⟨didn't like the way he *spurned* every one of my suggestions⟩

2decline *n* **1** : a gradual sinking and wasting away **2** : a change to a lower state or level **3** : the time when something is nearing its end **4** : a descending slope

de·cliv·i·ty \di-'kliv-ət-ē\ *n, pl* **de·cliv·i·ties** : a steep downward slope

de·code \dē-'kōd\ *vb* **de·cod·ed**; **de·cod·ing** : to change a message in code into ordinary language

de·com·pose \,dē-kəm-'pōz\ *vb* **de·com·posed**; **de·com·pos·ing** **1** : to separate a thing into its parts or into simpler compounds **2** : to break down in decaying

de·com·po·si·tion \,dē-,käm-pə-'zish-ən\ *n* **1** : the process of decomposing **2** : the state of being decomposed

dec·o·rate \'dek-ə-,rāt\ *vb* **dec·o·rat·ed**; **dec·o·rat·ing** **1** : to make more attractive by adding something beautiful or becoming : ADORN **2** : to award a decoration of honor to ⟨*decorate* a soldier for bravery⟩ **syn** see ADORN

dec·o·ra·tion \,dek-ə-'rā-shən\ *n* **1** : the act of decorating **2** : something that adorns or beautifies : ORNAMENT **3** : a badge of honor

dec·o·ra·tive \'dek-ə-rət-iv\ *adj* : serving to decorate : ORNAMENTAL

dec·o·ra·tor \'dek-ə-,rāt-ər\ *n* : a person who decorates especially the interiors of houses

de·co·rum \di-'kōr-əm\ *n* **1** : proper behavior **2** : ORDERLINESS

1de·coy \di-'kȯi, 'dē-,kȯi\ *n* [its origin is not absolutely certain; it is probably from Dutch *de kooi* "the cage", "the decoy"] : something (as an artificial bird) used to lead or lure into a trap or snare

decoy

2decoy *vb* : to lure by or as if by a decoy

1de·crease \di-'krēs\ *vb* **de·creased**; **de·creas·ing** : to grow or cause to grow less : DIMINISH

2de·crease \'dē-,krēs\ *n* : REDUCTION

1de·cree \di-'krē\ *n* : an order or decision given by a person or group in authority

2decree *vb* **de·creed**; **de·cree·ing** : to command or order by a decree

de·crep·it \di-'krep-ət\ *adj* : broken down with age : WORN-OUT

1de·cre·scen·do \,dā-krə-'shen-dō\ *adv (or adj)* : with diminishing volume — used as a direction in music

2decrescendo *n* **1** : a lessening in volume of sound **2** : a decrescendo musical passage

ded·i·cate \'ded-i-,kāt\ *vb* **ded·i·cat·ed**; **ded·i·cat·ing** **1** : to set apart for a certain purpose and especially for a sacred or serious purpose : DEVOTE **2** : to address or inscribe (as a book) as a compliment

ded·i·ca·tion \,ded-i-'kā-shən\ *n* **1** : an act of dedicating **2** : the inscription dedicating a book **3** : self-sacrificing devotion

de·duct \di-'dəkt\ *vb* : to take away an amount of something : SUBTRACT

de·duc·tion \di-'dək-shən\ *n* **1** : SUBTRACTION **2** : an amount deducted

1deed \'dēd\ *n* **1** : something done : ACT, ACTION ⟨a brave *deed*⟩ **2** : a legal document containing the record of a bargain or contract or especially of a transfer of real estate

2deed *vb* : to transfer by deed

deem \'dēm\ *vb* : THINK, JUDGE

1deep \'dēp\ *adj* **1** : reaching down far below the surface ⟨*deep* roots⟩ ⟨*deep* snow⟩ **2** : reaching far back from the front or outer part ⟨a *deep* forest⟩ **3** : hard to understand ⟨a *deep* book⟩ **4** : dark and rich in color ⟨a *deep* red⟩ **5** : completely occupied ⟨*deep* in study⟩ **6** : HEAVY, PROFOUND **7** : low or full in tone ⟨a *deep* voice⟩ — **deep·ly** *adv*

2deep *adv* **1** : to a great depth : DEEPLY ⟨drink *deep*⟩ **2** : far along in time

3deep *n* **1** : an extremely deep place or part ⟨the ocean *deeps*⟩ **2** : OCEAN ⟨the briny *deep*⟩

deep·en \'dē-pən\ *vb* : to make or to become deep or deeper

deep–seat·ed \'dēp-'sēt-əd\ *adj* **1** : situated far below the surface **2** : firmly established ⟨a *deep-seated* tradition⟩

deer \'diər\ *n, pl* **deer** : any of a group of cud-chewing mammals with cloven hoofs and in the male antlers that are often branched

deer·skin \'diər-ˌskin\ *n* : leather made from the skin of a deer or a garment made of such leather

de·face \di-'fās\ *vb* **de·faced; de·fac·ing** : to destroy or mar the face or surface of — **de·face·ment** *n* — **de·fac·er** *n*

de·fame \di-'fām\ *vb* **de·famed; de·fam·ing** : to injure or destroy the good name of

¹de·fault \di-'fȯlt\ *n* : failure to do something required by law or duty

²default *vb* : to fail to carry out an obligation or duty — **de·fault·er** *n*

¹de·feat \di-'fēt\ *vb* **1** : to bring to nothing **2** : to win victory over : BEAT, OVERCOME

²defeat *n* : loss of a contest : OVERTHROW

de·fect \'dē-ˌfekt, di-'fekt\ *n* : IMPERFECTION, FAULT **syn** see BLEMISH

de·fec·tive \di-'fek-tiv\ *adj* : lacking something essential : FAULTY

de·fend \di-'fend\ *vb* **1** : to protect from danger or harm **2** : to support or take the side of against opposition — **de·fend·er** *n*

syn DEFEND, PROTECT, SAFEGUARD all mean to keep secure or safe. DEFEND suggests acting against an actual or immediately threatening attack and often implies the use of force or violence ⟨kept a gun to *defend* himself against intruders⟩ PROTECT stresses the use of some kind of shield, bar, or covering that prevents possible attack ⟨used moats to *protect* the castle⟩ ⟨*protected* himself against radiation with special garments⟩ SAFEGUARD emphasizes the use of protective measures against not merely attack but any possible danger ⟨public health measures that *safeguard* the city from epidemics⟩

de·fense *or* **de·fence** \di-'fens\ *n* **1** : the act of defending **2** : something that defends or protects **3** : a defensive team — **de·fense·less** \-ləs\ *adj*

¹de·fen·sive \di-'fen-siv\ *adj* **1** : serving or intended to defend or protect **2** : of or relating to the attempt to keep an opponent from scoring (as in a game) — **de·fen·sive·ly** *adv*

²defensive *n* : a defensive position or attitude

¹de·fer \di-'fər\ *vb* **de·ferred; de·fer·ring** : to put off to a future time — **de·fer·ment** *n*

²defer *vb* **de·ferred; de·fer·ring** : to yield to the opinion, wishes, or will of another

def·er·ence \'def-ə-rəns\ *n* : courteous or respectful regard for the wishes of another

de·fi·ance \di-'fī-əns\ *n* **1** : an act of defying : CHALLENGE **2** : a willingness to resist

de·fi·ant \di-'fī-ənt\ *adj* : showing defiance — **de·fi·ant·ly** *adv*

de·fi·cien·cy \di-'fish-ən-sē\ *n, pl* **de·fi·cien·cies 1** : the state of being deficient : lack or shortage of something necessary **2** : lack or shortage of something essential to health

de·fi·cient \di-'fish-ənt\ *adj* : lacking something necessary for completeness

def·i·cit \'def-ə-sət\ *n* : a shortage especially in money needed

¹de·file \di-'fīl\ *vb* **de·filed; de·fil·ing 1** : to make filthy **2** : CORRUPT **3** : DISHONOR — **de·file·ment** *n*

²defile *n* : a narrow pass or gorge

de·fine \di-'fīn\ *vb* **de·fined; de·fin·ing 1** : to fix or mark the limits of **2** : to make distinct in outline **3** : to discover and explain the meaning of ⟨*define* a word⟩ — **de·fin·er** *n*

def·i·nite \'def-ə-nət\ *adj* **1** : having certain or distinct limits ⟨a *definite* period of time⟩ **2** : clear in meaning ⟨a *definite* answer⟩ — **def·i·nite·ly** *adv* — **def·i·nite·ness** *n*

definite article *n* : the article *the* used to show that the following noun refers to one or more particular persons or things

def·i·ni·tion \ˌdef-ə-'nish-ən\ *n* **1** : an act of defining **2** : a statement of the meaning of a word or a word group **3** : CLARITY

de·flate \di-'flāt\ *vb* **de·flated; de·flat·ing 1** : to let the air or gas out of something that has been blown up **2** : to cause to contract from an abnormally high level

de·flect \di-'flekt\ *vb* : to turn aside

de·for·est \dē-'fȯr-əst\ *vb* : to clear of forests

de·form \di-'fȯrm\ *vb* : to spoil the form or the natural appearance of

de·for·mi·ty \di-'fȯr-mət-ē\ *n, pl* **de·for·mi·ties 1** : the condition of being deformed **2** : a physical blemish or distortion **3** : a moral or aesthetic flaw

de·fraud \di-'frȯd\ *vb* : to deprive of something by deceiving : CHEAT

de·fray \di-'frā\ *vb* : to pay or provide for the payment of

de·frost \di-'frȯst\ *vb* **1** : to thaw out **2** : to free from ice — **de·frost·er** *n*

deft \'deft\ *adj* : quick and neat in action : SKILLFUL — **deft·ly** *adv* — **deft·ness** *n*

de·fy \di-'fī\ *vb* **de·fied; de·fy·ing 1** : to challenge to do something considered impossible : DARE **2** : to refuse boldly to obey or yield to **3** : to resist attempts at

deg·ra·da·tion \ˌdeg-rə-'dā-shən\ *n* **1** : an act of degrading **2** : DISGRACE, HUMILIATION

de·grade \di-'grād\ *vb* **de·grad·ed; de·grad·ing 1** : to reduce from a higher to a lower rank or degree **2** : to lower the character of

de·gree \di-'grē\ *n* **1** : a step in a series ⟨advanced by *degrees*⟩ **2** : extent of something as measured by a series of steps ⟨a man capable in the highest *degree*⟩ **3** : one of the three forms an adjective or adverb may have when it is compared **4** : a rank

degrees 7

or grade of official or social position ⟨persons of high *degree*⟩ **5** : a title given (as to students) by a college or university ⟨a *degree* of doctor of medicine⟩ **6** : one of the divisions marked on a measuring instrument (as a thermometer) **7** : a 360th part of the circumference of a circle **8** : a line or space of the staff in music or the interval between two adjacent notes

de·hu·mid·i·fy \,dē-hyü-'mid-ə-,fī\ *vb* **de·hu·mid·i·fied; de·hu·mid·i·fy·ing** : to remove moisture from — **de·hu·mid·i·fi·er** *n*

de·hy·drate \dē-'hī-,drāt\ *vb* **de·hy·drat·ed; de·hy·drat·ing** **1** : to take water from (as foods) **2** : to lose water or body fluids

de·ice \dē-'īs\ *vb* **de·iced; de·ic·ing** : to free or keep free of ice ⟨*deice* an airplane⟩ — **de·ic·er** *n*

de·i·fy \'dē-ə-,fī\ *vb* **de·i·fied; de·i·fy·ing** : to make a god of

deign \'dān\ *vb* : CONDESCEND

de·i·ty \'dē-ət-ē\ *n, pl* **de·i·ties** **1** *cap* : ²GOD **2** : GOD, GODDESS ⟨Roman *deities*⟩

de·ject·ed \di-'jek-təd\ *adj* : DEPRESSED, SAD — **de·ject·ed·ly** *adv*

de·jec·tion \di-'jek-shən\ *n* : SADNESS

deka- *or* **dek-** — see DECA-

¹de·lay \di-'lā\ *n* **1** : a putting off or postponing of something **2** : the time during which something is delayed

²delay *vb* **1** : to put off **2** : to stop or hinder for a time **3** : to move or act slowly

syn DELAY, LOITER, DAWDLE all mean to act so slowly that normal or expected progress is prevented. DELAY usually implies putting off the start of something rather than interrupting it in the middle ⟨their team *delayed* so long we didn't start until dusk⟩ LOITER suggests losing time while in progress toward some place rather than in doing a piece of work ⟨he *loitered* on the way to the store and found it closed⟩ DAWDLE emphasizes aimlessness and idleness that wastes time, often on purpose, during any sort of activity ⟨children *dawdling* on their way to bed⟩ ⟨outraged at workmen who *dawdle* on the job⟩

¹del·e·gate \'del-i-gət\ *n* : a person sent with power to act for another (as in a legislature)

²del·e·gate \'del-ə-,gāt\ *vb* **del·e·gat·ed; del-**

e·gat·ing **1** : to entrust to the care of another **2** : to send as one's representative

del·e·ga·tion \,del-ə-'gā-shən\ *n* **1** : the act of delegating **2** : one or more persons chosen to represent others

de·lete \di-'lēt\ *vb* **de·let·ed; de·let·ing** : to take out from something written especially by erasing, crossing out, or cutting out

de·le·tion \di-'lē-shən\ *n* **1** : an act of deleting **2** : something deleted

¹de·lib·er·ate \di-'lib-ə-rət\ *adj* **1** : decided upon as a result of careful thought **2** : weighing facts and arguments **3** : slow in action : not hurried **syn** see VOLUNTARY — **de·lib·er·ate·ly** *adv* — **de·lib·er·ate·ness** *n*

²de·lib·er·ate \di-'lib-ə-,rāt\ *vb* **de·lib·er·at·ed; de·lib·er·at·ing** : to consider carefully

de·lib·er·a·tion \di-,lib-ə-'rā-shən\ *n* **1** : careful consideration **2** : the quality of being deliberate

del·i·ca·cy \'del-i-kə-sē\ *n, pl* **del·i·ca·cies** **1** : something pleasing to eat because it is rare or a luxury **2** : FINENESS, DAINTINESS ⟨lace of great *delicacy*⟩ **3** : weakness of body : FRAILTY **4** : a state of affairs requiring very tactful handling **5** : refinement of feeling

del·i·cate \'del-i-kət\ *adj* **1** : satisfying or pleasing because of its fineness ⟨a *delicate* flavor⟩ ⟨*delicate* blossoms⟩ **2** : capable of sensing slight differences : very sensitive ⟨a *delicate* ear for music⟩ **3** : calling for fine skill or expert knowledge ⟨a *delicate* operation⟩ **4** : FRAIL, SICKLY ⟨a *delicate* child⟩ **5** : requiring tact — **del·i·cate·ly** *adv*

del·i·ca·tes·sen \,del-i-kə-'tes-n\ *n* : a store where ready-to-eat foods (as cooked meats and prepared salads) are sold

de·li·cious \di-'lish-əs\ *adj* : giving great pleasure especially to the taste or smell — **de·li·cious·ly** *adv* — **de·li·cious·ness** *n*

¹de·light \di-'līt\ *n* **1** : great pleasure or satisfaction : JOY **2** : something that gives great pleasure

²delight *vb* **1** : to take great pleasure **2** : to give joy or satisfaction to

de·light·ed \di-'līt-əd\ *adj* : highly pleased

de·light·ful \di-'līt-fəl\ *adj* : giving delight : highly pleasing — **de·light·ful·ly** *adv*

de·lir·i·ous \di-'lir-ē-əs\ *adj* **1** : suffering delirium **2** : wildly excited — **de·lir·i·ous·ly** *adv*

de·lir·i·um \di-'lir-ē-əm\ *n* **1** : a disordered condition of mind with confusion of thought and speech that often accompanies a high fever **2** : wild excitement

de·liv·er \di-'liv-ər\ *vb* **1** : to set free : SAVE, RESCUE ⟨*deliver* us from evil⟩ **2** : to hand over : CONVEY, TRANSFER ⟨*deliver* a letter⟩ ⟨this store *delivers*⟩ **3** : to help in childbirth **4** : UTTER, COMMUNICATE **5** : to send to an intended target — **de·liv·er·er** *n*

de·liv·er·ance \di-'liv-ə-rəns\ *n* **1** : an act of delivering or being delivered : a setting free **2** : a publicly expressed opinion

de·liv·er·y \di-'liv-ə-rē\ *n, pl* **de·liv·er·ies** **1** : a freeing from restraint **2** : the transfer of a thing from one place or person to another **3** : the act of giving birth **4** : speaking or manner of speaking (as of a formal speech) **5** : the manner of sending forth or throwing

dell \'del\ *n* : a small valley usually covered with trees

del·ta \'del-tə\ *n* [derived from *delta*, Δ, the fourth letter of the Greek alphabet, because of its shape] : a triangular or fan-shaped piece of land made by deposits of mud and sand at the mouth of a river

de·lude \di-'lüd\ *vb* **de·lud·ed; de·lud·ing** : to mislead the mind or judgment of : DECEIVE

¹del·uge \'del-yüj\ *n* **1** : a flooding of land by water : FLOOD **2** : a drenching rain **3** : an irresistible rush ⟨a *deluge* of mail⟩

²deluge *vb* **del·uged; del·ug·ing** **1** : FLOOD **2** : to overwhelm as if with a deluge

de·lu·sion \di-'lü-zhən\ *n* **1** : an act of deluding or being deluded **2** : a false belief that persists in spite of the facts

de·luxe \di-'lùks, -'ləks\ *adj* : extra fine, elegant, or luxurious ⟨*deluxe* hotel⟩

delve \'delv\ *vb* **delved; delv·ing** **1** : DIG **2** : to work hard looking for information in written records — **delv·er** *n*

¹de·mand \di-'mand\ *n* **1** : an act of demanding ⟨payable on *demand*⟩ **2** : an expressed desire to own or use something ⟨the *demand* for new cars⟩ **3** : an act of seeking or being sought after

²demand *vb* **1** : to ask or call for with authority ⟨*demand* an apology⟩ **2** : to ask earnestly or in the manner of a command ⟨the sentry *demanded* the password⟩ **3** : to call for : REQUIRE, NEED — **de·mand·er** *n*

¹de·mean \di-'mēn\ *vb* : to behave or conduct (oneself) usually in a proper way

²demean *vb* : DEBASE, LOWER

de·mean·or \di-'mē-nər\ *n* : outward manner or behavior : CONDUCT, BEARING

de·ment·ed \di-'ment-əd\ *adj* : INSANE, MAD — **de·ment·ed·ly** *adv*

de·mer·it \dē-'mer-ət\ *n* **1** : something that deserves blame **2** : a mark placed against a person's record for some fault or offense

demi- *prefix* **1** : half **2** : one that partly belongs to a specified type or class ⟨*demigod*⟩

dem·i·god \'dem-ē-,gäd\ *n* : one that is partly divine and partly human

dem·i·tasse \'dem-ē-,tas\ *n* : a small cup of black coffee

de·mo·bi·lize \di-'mō-bə-,līz\ *vb* **de·mo·bi·lized; de·mo·bi·liz·ing** **1** : to dismiss from military service ⟨*demobilized* soldiers⟩ **2** : to change from a state of war to a state of peace

de·moc·ra·cy \di-'mäk-rə-sē\ *n, pl* **de·moc·ra·cies** [from Greek *dēmokratia*, a compound of *dēmos* "people" and *kratos* "power", "authority"] **1** : government by the people **2** : government in which the highest power is held by the people and exercised directly or through representatives **3** : a political unit (as a nation) governed by the people themselves **4** : belief in or practice of the idea that all people are socially equal

dem·o·crat \'dem-ə-,krat\ *n* : one who believes in or practices democracy

dem·o·crat·ic \,dem-ə-'krat-ik\ *adj* **1** : of, relating to, or favoring political democracy **2** : believing in or practicing the idea that people are equal : disregarding social distinctions — **dem·o·crat·i·cal·ly** \-i-kə-lē\ *adv*

de·mol·ish \di-'mäl-ish\ *vb* **1** : to tear down **2** : to ruin completely : SMASH

de·mon \'dē-mən\ *n* **1** : an evil spirit : DEVIL **2** : a person of great energy or skill

de·mon·stra·ble \di-'män-strə-bəl\ *adj* : capable of being demonstrated or proved — **de·mon·stra·bly** \-blē\ *adv*

dem·on·strate \'dem-ən-,strāt\ *vb* **dem·on·strat·ed; dem·on·strat·ing** **1** : to show clearly **2** : to make clear or prove by reasoning **3** : to explain (as in teaching) by use of illustrative material (as examples) **4** : to show publicly the good qualities of an article or a product ⟨*demonstrate* a new car⟩ **5** : to make a public display (as of feelings or military force)

dem·on·stra·tion \,dem-ən-'strā-shən\ *n* **1** : an outward expression or display (as a show of feelings) **2** : a parade or a gathering to show public feeling **3** : an act or a means of demonstrating to the intelligence : PROOF **4** : a showing or trial of an article for sale to show its merits

de·mon·stra·tive \di-'män-strət-iv\ *adj* **1** : pointing out the one referred to and distinguishing it from others ⟨the *demonstrative* pronouns *this* and *that*⟩ **2** : showing feeling or sentiment without restraint

dem·on·stra·tor \'dem-ən-,strāt-ər\ *n* **1** : a person who makes or takes part in a demonstration **2** : a manufactured article used for purposes of demonstration

de·mor·al·ize \di-'mòr-ə-,līz\ *vb* **de·mor·al-**

ized; **de·mor·al·iz·ing** 1 : to corrupt in morals 2 : to weaken in discipline or spirit

de·mote \di-'mōt\ vb **de·mot·ed; de·mot·ing** : to reduce to a lower grade or rank

[1]**de·mur** \di-'mər\ vb **de·murred; de·mur·ring** : to make an objection : show unwillingness

[2]**demur** n : OBJECTION, HESITATION

de·mure \di-'myu̇r\ adj 1 : quietly modest in manner 2 : pretending to be modest : PRIM, COY — **de·mure·ly** adv — **de·mure·ness** n

den \'den\ n 1 : the shelter or resting place of a wild animal 2 : a hiding place (as for thieves) 3 : a dirty wretched place in which people live or gather 4 : a quiet snug room

de·na·ture \dē-'nā-chər\ vb **de·na·tured; de·na·tur·ing** 1 : to change the nature of : deprive of natural qualities 2 : to make alcohol poisonous for human consumption

den·drite \'den-ˌdrīt\ n : any of the usually branched fibers that carry nerve impulses toward a nerve cell body

de·ni·al \di-'nī-əl\ n 1 : a refusal to grant something asked for 2 : a refusal to admit the truth of a statement : CONTRADICTION 3 : a statement of disbelief or rejection 4 : a cutting down or limiting ⟨a *denial* of her appetite⟩

den·im \'den-əm\ n 1 : a firm often coarse cotton cloth 2 pl : overalls or trousers of usually blue denim

de·nom·i·na·tion \di-ˌnäm-ə-'nā-shən\ n 1 : a name or title especially for a class of things 2 : a religious body made up of a number of congregations having the same beliefs 3 : one of a series of related values each of which is called by a special name

de·nom·i·na·tor \di-'näm-ə-ˌnāt-ər\ n : the part of a fraction that is below the line ⟨5 is the *denominator* of the fraction 3/5⟩

de·note \di-'nōt\ vb **de·not·ed; de·not·ing** 1 : to mark out plainly : INDICATE ⟨the hands of a clock *denote* the time⟩ 2 : to make known 3 : to have the meaning of : MEAN, NAME

de·nounce \di-'nau̇ns\ vb **de·nounced; de·nounc·ing** 1 : to point out as deserving of blame or punishment 2 : to inform against : ACCUSE — **de·nounce·ment** n — **de·nounc·er** n

dense \'dens\ adj 1 : having its parts crowded together : THICK ⟨*dense* fog⟩ 2 : STUPID, DULL — **dense·ly** adv — **dense·ness** n

den·si·ty \'den-sət-ē\ n, pl **den·si·ties** 1 : the state of being dense : CLOSENESS, COMPACTNESS 2 : the quantity of something in each unit of volume or area 3 : STUPIDITY

[1]**dent** \'dent\ n 1 : a small notch or hollow made by a blow or by pressure on a smooth surface 2 : an impression or effect made usually against resistance

[2]**dent** vb 1 : to make a dent in or on 2 : to become marked by a dent

den·tal \'dent-l\ adj : of or relating to the teeth or dentistry — **den·tal·ly** adv

dental floss n : flat waxed thread used for cleaning between teeth

den·ti·frice \'dent-ə-frəs\ n : a powder, paste, or liquid used in cleaning the teeth

den·tin \'dent-n\ or **den·tine** \'den-ˌtēn\ n : a hard bony material composing the main part of a tooth

den·tist \'dent-əst\ n : one whose profession is the care, treatment, and repair of the teeth

den·tist·ry \'dent-əs-trē\ n : the profession or practice of a dentist

den·ture \'den-chər\ n : a set of false teeth

de·nude \di-'nüd, -'nyüd\ vb **de·nud·ed; de·nud·ing** : to strip of covering : lay bare

de·nun·ci·a·tion \di-ˌnən-sē-'ā-shən\ n 1 : an act of denouncing 2 : a public accusation

de·ny \di-'nī\ vb **de·nied; de·ny·ing** 1 : to declare not to be true : CONTRADICT ⟨*deny* a report⟩ 2 : to refuse to grant ⟨*deny* a request⟩ 3 : to refuse to acknowledge : DISOWN

de·o·dor·ant \dē-'ōd-ə-rənt\ n : a preparation that removes unpleasant odors

de·o·dor·ize \dē-'ōd-ə-ˌrīz\ vb **de·o·dor·ized; de·o·dor·iz·ing** : to remove odor and especially a bad odor from

de·part \di-'pärt\ vb 1 : to go away or go away from : LEAVE 2 : DIE 3 : to turn aside

de·part·ment \di-'pärt-mənt\ n : one of several distinct parts or divisions of an organization (as a government or college)

department store n : a store having separate departments for a wide variety of goods

de·par·ture \di-'pär-chər\ n 1 : a going away 2 : a setting out (as on a new course) 3 : a turning away or aside

de·pend \di-'pend\ vb 1 : to rely for support ⟨children *depend* on their parents⟩ 2 : to be determined by or based on some action or condition 3 : TRUST, RELY

de·pend·a·ble \di-'pen-də-bəl\ adj : RELIABLE — **de·pend·a·bly** \-blē\ adv

de·pend·ence \di-'pen-dəns\ n 1 : a condition of being influenced and determined by something else 2 : a state of being dependent on someone else 3 : RELIANCE, TRUST 4 : something on which a person depends or relies

[1]**de·pend·ent** \di-'pen-dənt\ adj 1 : hanging down 2 : relying on someone else for support 3 : subject to control by another

[2]**dependent** n : a person who depends upon another for support

---

j job   ng sing   ō low   ȯ moth   ȯi coin   th thin   t̲h this   ü boot   u̇ foot   y you   yü few   yu̇ furious   zh vision

de·pict \di-'pikt\ vb **1** : to represent by a picture **2** : to describe in words

de·plete \di-'plēt\ vb **de·plet·ed; de·plet·ing** : to reduce in amount by using up

de·plor·a·ble \di-'plōr-ə-bəl\ adj **1** : deserving to be deplored : REGRETTABLE **2** : very bad : WRETCHED — **de·plor·a·bly** \-blē\ adv

de·plore \di-'plōr\ vb **de·plored; de·plor·ing** **1** : to feel or express grief for **2** : to regret strongly **3** : to consider deserving of disapproval

de·port \di-'pōrt\ vb **1** : BEHAVE, CONDUCT **2** : to force to leave a country not one's own

de·port·ment \di-'pōrt-mənt\ n : BEHAVIOR

de·pose \di-'pōz\ vb **de·posed; de·pos·ing** **1** : to remove from a high office ⟨depose a king⟩ **2** : to make a statement under oath especially as a witness

¹de·pos·it \di-'päz-ət\ vb **1** : to place for safekeeping **2** : to put money in a bank **3** : to put down or give as a pledge that a purchase will be made or a service used ⟨deposit ten dollars on a new bicycle⟩ **4** : to lay down : PUT **5** : to let fall or sink

²deposit n **1** : the state of being deposited ⟨money on deposit⟩ **2** : money that is deposited in a bank **3** : something given as a pledge or as part payment ⟨a deposit of ten dollars on a new bicycle⟩ **4** : something laid or thrown down **5** : an accumulation of mineral matter in nature ⟨a coal deposit⟩

de·pos·i·tor \di-'päz-ət-ər\ n : a person who makes a deposit especially of money in a bank

de·pot \usu 'dep-,ō for 1 & 2, 'dē-,pō for 3\ n **1** : a place where military supplies are kept or where troops are assembled and trained **2** : STOREHOUSE **3** : a railroad or bus station

de·pre·ci·ate \di-'prē-shē-,āt\ vb **de·pre·ci·at·ed; de·pre·ci·at·ing** **1** : to lower the price or value of **2** : BELITTLE **3** : to fall in value

de·press \di-'pres\ vb **1** : to press down : cause to sink : LOWER ⟨depress a lever⟩ **2** : to lessen the activity or strength of ⟨bad weather had depressed sales⟩ **3** : to make low in spirits

de·pres·sion \di-'presh-ən\ n **1** : an act of depressing : a state of being depressed **2** : a depressed or hollowed place or part : HOLLOW ⟨depression in a road⟩ **3** : SADNESS, GLOOMINESS **4** : a period of reduced or lowered activity in business with widespread unemployment **syn** see MELANCHOLY

dep·ri·va·tion \,dep-rə-'vā-shən\ n **1** : an act or instance of depriving : LOSS **2** : the state of being deprived

de·prive \di-'prīv\ vb **de·prived; de·priv·ing** **1** : to take something away from ⟨deprived the king of his power⟩ **2** : to stop from having something ⟨deprived of sleep by street noises⟩

depth \'depth\ n **1** : a deep place in a body of water (as a sea or a lake) **2** : measurement from top to bottom or from front to back ⟨depth of a cupboard⟩ **3** : the innermost part of something : MIDDLE, MIDST ⟨depths of the jungle⟩ ⟨the depth of winter⟩ **4** : ABUNDANCE, COMPLETENESS ⟨depth of knowledge⟩ **5** : the quality of being deep

depth charge n : an explosive projectile for use under water especially against submarines

dep·u·ta·tion \,dep-yə-'tā-shən\ n **1** : the act of appointing a deputy **2** : a group of people appointed to represent others

dep·u·tize \'dep-yə-,tīz\ vb **dep·u·tized; dep·u·tiz·ing** : to appoint as deputy

dep·u·ty \'dep-yət-ē\ n, pl **dep·u·ties** : a person appointed to act for or in place of another

de·rail \di-'rāl\ vb : to cause to run off the rails — **de·rail·ment** n

de·range \di-'rānj\ vb **de·ranged; de·rang·ing** **1** : to put out of order : DISARRANGE, UPSET **2** : to make insane — **de·range·ment** n

der·by \'dər-bē\ n, pl **der·bies** **1** : a horse race for three-year-olds usually held annually **2** : a race or contest open to all **3** : a stiff felt hat with dome-shaped crown and narrow brim

derby 3

de·ride \di-'rīd\ vb **de·rid·ed; de·rid·ing** : to laugh at scornfully : make fun of : RIDICULE

de·ri·sion \di-'rizh-ən\ n : scornful or contemptuous ridicule

de·ri·sive \di-'rī-siv\ adj : expressing derision ⟨a derisive laugh⟩ — **de·ri·sive·ly** adv

der·i·va·tion \,der-ə-'vā-shən\ n **1** : the formation of a word from an earlier word or root **2** : ETYMOLOGY **3** : SOURCE, ORIGIN **4** : an act of deriving

¹de·riv·a·tive \di-'riv-ət-iv\ adj : derived from something else — **de·riv·a·tive·ly** adv

²derivative n **1** : a word formed by derivation **2** : something derived

de·rive \di-'rīv\ vb **de·rived; de·riv·ing** **1** : to receive or obtain from a source ⟨derive new ideas from reading⟩ **2** : to trace the derivation of **3** : to come from a certain source

der·mal \'dər-məl\ adj : of or relating to skin

der·mis \'dər-məs\ n : the inner sensitive layer of the skin

de·rog·a·to·ry \di-'räg-ə-,tōr-ē\ adj : intended to lower the reputation of a person or thing : DISPARAGING ⟨derogatory remarks⟩

der·rick \'der-ik\ *n* **1** : a machine for moving or hoisting heavy weights by means of a long beam fitted with pulleys and ropes **2** : a framework or tower over an oil well for supporting machinery

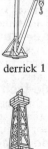

derrick 1

derrick 2

de·scend \di-'send\ *vb* **1** : to come or go down from a higher place or level to a lower one ⟨*descend* a hill⟩ ⟨rain *descended* in sheets of water⟩ **2** : to come down in sudden attack ⟨the enemy army *descended* upon the city⟩ **3** : to come down from an earlier time ⟨a custom *descended* from ancient times⟩ **4** : to come down from a stock or source : DERIVE ⟨*descended* from an ancient family⟩ **5** : to be handed down to an heir ⟨the property will *descend* to the son⟩ **6** : to sink in a social or moral scale : STOOP ⟨never thought he would *descend* to cheating⟩

de·scend·ant \di-'sen-dənt\ *n* : one who is descended from a particular ancestor or from a common stock

de·scent \di-'sent\ *n* **1** : a coming or going down **2** : ANCESTRY, BIRTH **3** : a downward slope ⟨a steep *descent*⟩ **4** : a sudden attack

de·scribe \di-'skrīb\ *vb* **de·scribed; de·scrib·ing 1** : to write or tell about : give an account of ⟨*describe* a football game⟩ **2** : to draw the outline of ⟨*describe* a circle⟩ — **de·scrib·er** *n*

de·scrip·tion \di-'skrip-shən\ *n* **1** : an account of something especially of a kind that presents a picture to a person who reads or hears it **2** : KIND, SORT

de·scrip·tive \di-'skrip-tiv\ *adj* : serving to describe — **de·scrip·tive·ly** *adv*

des·e·crate \'des-i-ˌkrāt\ *vb* **des·e·crat·ed; des·e·crat·ing** : to treat a sacred place or sacred object disrespectfully : PROFANE

de·seg·re·gate \dē-'seg-ri-ˌgāt\ *vb* **de·seg·re·gat·ed; de·seg·re·gat·ing** : to end segregation in : free of any law or practice setting apart members of a particular race in separate units

¹des·ert \'dez-ərt\ *n* : a dry barren region where only a few special kinds of plants grow without an artificial water supply

²desert *adj* : of, relating to, or being a desert

³de·sert \di-'zərt\ *n* **1** : worthiness of reward or punishment ⟨rewarding each according to his *deserts*⟩ **2** : a just reward or punishment

⁴de·sert \di-'zərt\ *vb* **1** : to withdraw from **2** : to leave a person or a thing that one should stay with **3** : to fail in time of need   **syn** see ABANDON — **de·sert·er** *n*

de·serve \di-'zərv\ *vb* **de·served; de·serv·ing** : to be worthy of : MERIT

de·serv·ed·ly \di-'zər-vəd-lē\ *adv* : according to merit : JUSTLY ⟨*deservedly* rewarded⟩

de·serv·ing \di-'zər-ving\ *adj* : WORTHY

¹de·sign \di-'zīn\ *vb* **1** : to think up and plan out mentally **2** : to set apart for or have as a special purpose : INTEND ⟨purchases *designed* to be used as gifts⟩ **3** : to make a pattern or sketch of — **de·sign·er** *n*

²design *n* **1** : PURPOSE, INTENTION **2** : a particular purpose : deliberate planning **3** : a secret purpose or scheme : PLOT **4** : a preliminary sketch or plan **5** : an arrangement of elements making up a structure or a work of art **6** : a decorative pattern

des·ig·nate \'dez-ig-ˌnāt\ *vb* **des·ig·nat·ed; des·ig·nat·ing 1** : to mark or point out : INDICATE, SHOW **2** : to appoint or choose for a special purpose : NAME ⟨*designate* a leader⟩ **3** : to call by a name or title

des·ig·na·tion \ˌdez-ig-'nā-shən\ *n* **1** : an act of designating **2** : a distinguishing name, sign, or title

de·sign·ing \di-'zī-ning\ *adj* : CRAFTY, SCHEMING

de·sir·a·ble \di-'zī-rə-bəl\ *adj* **1** : having pleasing qualities : ATTRACTIVE **2** : worth doing or seeking — **de·sir·a·bly** \-blē\ *adv*

¹de·sire \di-'zīr\ *vb* **de·sired; de·sir·ing 1** : to long for : wish earnestly ⟨*desire* peace⟩ **2** : to express a wish for : REQUEST

²desire *n* **1** : a strong wish : LONGING **2** : an expressed wish **3** : something desired

de·sir·ous \di-'zī-rəs\ *adj* : eagerly wishing

de·sist \di-'zist\ *vb* : to cease to act : STOP

desk \'desk\ *n* : a piece of furniture with a flat or sloping surface for use in writing or reading

¹des·o·late \'des-ə-lət\ *adj* **1** : DESERTED, ABANDONED ⟨*desolate* countryside⟩ **2** : being in a neglected condition or in ruins **3** : LONELY, WRETCHED **4** : CHEERLESS, GLOOMY

²des·o·late \'des-ə-ˌlāt\ *vb* **des·o·lat·ed; des·o·lat·ing** : to make or leave desolate

des·o·la·tion \ˌdes-ə-'lā-shən\ *n* **1** : the state of being desolated : DEVASTATION, RUIN **2** : GRIEF, SADNESS **3** : LONELINESS

¹de·spair \di-'spaər\ *vb* : to give up or lose all hope or confidence

²despair *n* **1** : loss of hope : a feeling of complete hopelessness **2** : a cause of hopelessness

des·patch \dis-'pach\ *var of* DISPATCH

des·per·ate \'des-pə-rət\ *adj* **1** : being beyond or almost beyond hope : causing despair **2** : reckless because of despair : RASH — **des·per·ate·ly** *adv* — **des·per·ate·ness** *n*

des·per·a·tion \ˌdes-pə-'rā-shən\ *n* : a state of despair or hopelessness leading to extreme recklessness

de·spic·a·ble \di-'spik-ə-bəl, 'des-pik-\ *adj* : CONTEMPTIBLE — **de·spic·a·bly** \-blē\ *adv*

de·spise \di-'spīz\ *vb* **de·spised; de·spis·ing** : to have a scornful dislike for

de·spite \di-'spīt\ *prep* : in spite of

de·spoil \di-'spȯil\ *vb* : to rob of possessions or belongings : PLUNDER — **de·spoil·er** *n*

de·spond·en·cy \di-'spän-dən-sē\ *n* : despondent condition : MELANCHOLY, DEJECTION

de·spond·ent \di-'spän-dənt\ *adj* : feeling extreme discouragement or depression : being in very low spirits — **de·spond·ent·ly** *adv*

des·pot \'des-pət\ *n* : one and especially a ruler having absolute power and authority

des·sert \di-'zərt\ *n* : a course of sweet food, fruit, or cheese served at the end of a meal

des·ti·na·tion \ˌdes-tə-'nā-shən\ *n* : a place which is set for the end of a journey or to which something is sent

des·tine \'des-tən\ *vb* **des·tined; des·tin·ing** **1** : to settle in advance ⟨a plan *destined* to fail⟩ **2** : to designate or dedicate in advance **3** : to be bound or directed

des·ti·ny \'des-tə-nē\ *n, pl* **des·ti·nies 1** : the fate or lot to which a person or thing is destined **2** : the course of events held to be arranged by a power greater than man's

syn DESTINY, FATE, DOOM all mean a condition or outcome decreed by some higher power or outside force. DESTINY suggests an unavoidable and inevitable path determined by the will of the gods, but does not indicate whether the path is good or bad ⟨he fled, but couldn't escape his *destiny*⟩ ⟨there are those who think it is their *destiny* to rule the world⟩ FATE is a less imposing word than DESTINY, may be used to refer to a course of events that is decreed by a lesser power and thus is less inevitable, and usually suggests, as DESTINY does not, an undesirable or unfortunate prospect ⟨my *fate* to always come in second⟩ ⟨the *fate* of the cat is in his hands⟩ DOOM is a thoroughly menacing word that suggests a grim and disastrous end ⟨a sense of approaching *doom* disheartened the 400 men of the brigade⟩

des·ti·tute \'des-tə-ˌtüt, -ˌtyüt\ *adj* **1** : lacking something needed or desirable ⟨a room *destitute* of comforts⟩ **2** : extremely poor

de·stroy \di-'strȯi\ *vb* **1** : to put an end to : do away with : RUIN **2** : KILL

de·stroy·er \di-'strȯi-ər\ *n* **1** : one that destroys **2** : a small fast warship armed with guns, depth charges, torpedoes, and sometimes rockets

de·struc·ti·ble \di-'strək-tə-bəl\ *adj* : capable of being destroyed

de·struc·tion \di-'strək-shən\ *n* **1** : an act or process of destroying something **2** : the state or fact of being destroyed : RUIN **3** : something that destroys

de·struc·tive \di-'strək-tiv\ *adj* **1** : causing destruction ⟨a *destructive* storm⟩ **2** : not constructive — **de·struc·tive·ly** *adv* — **de·struc·tive·ness** *n*

de·tach \di-'tach\ *vb* : to separate from something else or from others especially for a particular purpose and usually without violence or damage — **de·tach·a·ble** \-ə-bəl\ *adj*

de·tached \di-'tacht\ *adj* **1** : not joined or connected : SEPARATE **2** : not taking sides or being influenced by others : IMPARTIAL — **de·tach·ed·ly** \-'tach-əd-lē\ *adv*

de·tach·ment \di-'tach-mənt\ *n* **1** : SEPARATION **2** : a body of troops or ships sent on special duty **3** : a keeping apart : indifference to worldly concerns **4** : freedom from bias

¹de·tail \di-'tāl, 'dē-ˌtāl\ *n* **1** : a dealing with something item by item ⟨go into *detail*⟩ **2** : a small part : ITEM **3** : a soldier or group of soldiers selected for special duty

²detail *vb* **1** : to report in detail : give the details of **2** : to select for some special duty

de·tailed \di-'tāld, 'dē-ˌtāld\ *adj* : including many details

de·tain \di-'tān\ *vb* **1** : to hold or keep in or as if in custody **2** : to hold back **3** : to stop especially from proceeding : DELAY — **de·tain·ment** *n*

de·tect \di-'tekt\ *vb* : to discover the existence, presence, or fact of : find out : make out

¹de·tec·tive \di-'tek-tiv\ *adj* **1** : fitted for or used in detecting something ⟨*detective* device⟩ **2** : of or relating to detectives or their work

²detective *n* : an individual (as a policeman) whose business is solving crimes and catching criminals or gathering information that is not readily accessible

de·ten·tion \di-'ten-chən\ *n* **1** : the act of detaining : the state of being detained : CONFINEMENT **2** : a forced delay

de·ter \di-'tər\ *vb* **de·terred; de·ter·ring** : to discourage or prevent from doing something especially through fear (as of consequences)

¹de·ter·gent \di-'tər-jənt\ *adj* : CLEANSING

²detergent *n* **1** : a cleansing agent **2** : a soaplike cleansing substance

de·te·ri·o·rate \di-'tir-ē-ə-ˌrāt\ *vb* **de·te·ri·o·rat·ed; de·te·ri·o·rat·ing** : to make or become worse or of less value

de·ter·mi·na·tion \di-ˌtər-mə-'nā-shən\ *n* **1** : a coming to a decision or the decision or conclusion reached **2** : a settling or fixing of the position, extent, or character of something **3** : firm or fixed purpose : FIRMNESS

de·ter·mine \di-'tər-mən\ *vb* **de·ter·mined; de·ter·min·ing 1** : to fix or settle exactly and conclusively **2** : to make up one's mind : come to a decision **3** : to learn or find out exactly **4** : to be the cause of or reason for

de·ter·mined \di-'tər-mənd\ *adj* **1** : DECIDED, RESOLVED **2** : FIRM, RESOLUTE ⟨a very *determined* opponent⟩ — **de·ter·mined·ly** *adv*

de·test \di-'test\ *vb* : to dislike intensely

de·test·a·ble \di-'tes-tə-bəl\ *adj* : arousing or deserving strong dislike : ABOMINABLE, HATEFUL — **de·test·a·bly** \-blē\ *adv*

de·throne \di-'thrōn\ *vb* **de·throned; de·thron·ing** : to remove from a throne : DEPOSE — **de·throne·ment** *n*

¹**de·tour** \'dē-,tùr\ *n* : a roundabout way temporarily replacing part of a route regularly in use

²**detour** *vb* : to go by a detour

de·tract \di-'trakt\ *vb* : to take away (as from value or importance) : make of less worth

de·train \dē-'trān\ *vb* : to leave or cause to leave a railroad train — **de·train·ment** *n*

det·ri·ment \'det-rə-mənt\ *n* : injury or damage or its cause : HARM

dev·as·tate \'dev-əs-,tāt\ *vb* **dev·as·tat·ed; dev·as·tat·ing** : to reduce to ruin : lay waste

dev·as·ta·tion \,dev-əs-'tā-shən\ *n* : the action of devastating : the state of being devastated : DESOLATION, RUIN

de·vel·op \di-'vel-əp\ *vb* **1** : to unfold gradually or in detail : set forth by degrees **2** : to apply chemicals to exposed photographic material (as a film) in order to bring out the picture **3** : to bring out the possibilities of : IMPROVE **4** : to make more available or usable ⟨*develop* natural resources⟩ **5** : to acquire gradually ⟨*develop* a taste for reading⟩ **6** : to grow and differentiate toward maturity **7** : to become apparent — **de·vel·op·er** *n*

de·vel·op·ment \di-'vel-əp-mənt\ *n* **1** : the act or process of developing : a result of developing **2** : the state of being developed

de·vi·ate \'dē-vē-,āt\ *vb* **de·vi·at·ed; de·vi·at·ing** : to turn aside from a course, principle, standard, or topic

de·vice \di-'vīs\ *n* **1** : a piece of equipment or mechanism for a special purpose **2** : DESIRE, WILL **3** : an emblematic design (as on a shield or banner)

¹**dev·il** \'dev-əl\ *n* **1** *often cap* : the personal supreme spirit of evil **2** : an evil spirit : DEMON, FIEND **3** : a wicked or cruel person **4** : a reckless or dashing person ⟨a *devil* with

the ladies⟩ **5** : a wretched or pitiable person — **dev·il·ish** *adj or adv* — **dev·il·ish·ly** *adv*

²**devil** *vb* **dev·iled** *or* **dev·illed; dev·il·ing** *or* **dev·il·ling 1** : TEASE, ANNOY **2** : to chop fine and season highly ⟨*deviled* eggs⟩

dev·il·ment \'dev-əl-mənt\ *n* : reckless mischief

dev·il·ry \'dev-əl-rē\ *or* **dev·il·try** \-əl-trē\ *n, pl* **dev·il·ries** *or* **dev·il·tries 1** : something done with the help of the devil **2** : DEVILMENT

de·vise \di-'vīz\ *vb* **de·vised; de·vis·ing** : to think up : PLAN, INVENT — **de·vis·er** *n*

de·void \di-'vȯid\ *adj* : entirely lacking

de·vote \di-'vōt\ *vb* **de·vot·ed; de·vot·ing 1** : to set apart for a special purpose **2** : to give up to wholly or chiefly

de·vot·ed \di-'vōt-əd\ *adj* **1** : completely loyal ⟨his *devoted* supporters and admirers⟩ **2** : AFFECTIONATE, LOVING — **de·vot·ed·ly** *adv*

de·vo·tion \di-'vō-shən\ *n* **1** : a religious exercise or practice (as prayers) especially for use in private worship **2** : an act of devoting : the quality of being devoted ⟨years of *devotion* to music⟩ **3** : deep love or affection

de·vour \di-'vaùr\ *vb* **1** : to eat up greedily **2** : CONSUME ⟨buildings *devoured* by flames⟩ **3** : to take in eagerly by the senses or mind

de·vout \di-'vaùt\ *adj* **1** : devoted to religion **2** : warmly sincere and earnest ⟨*devout* thanks⟩ — **de·vout·ly** *adv* — **de·vout·ness** *n*

dew \'dü, 'dyü\ *n* : moisture condensed on the surfaces of cool bodies at night

dew·ber·ry \'dü-,ber-ē, 'dyü-\ *n, pl* **dew·ber·ries** : a sweet edible berry related to the blackberries that grows on a prickly trailing vine

dew·lap \'dü-,lap, 'dyü-\ *n* : a hanging fold of skin under the neck of various animals

dew point *n* : the temperature at which the moisture in the air begins to condense

dew·y \'dü-ē, 'dyü-\ *adj* **dew·i·er; dew·i·est** : moist with or suggestive of dew — **dew·i·ly** \-ə-lē\ *adv* — **dew·i·ness** \-ē-nəs\ *n*

dex·ter·i·ty \deks-'ter-ət-ē\ *n, pl* **dex·ter·i·ties 1** : skill and ease in physical activity **2** : mental skill or quickness

dex·ter·ous \'deks-tə-rəs\ *or* **dex·trous** \-trəs\ *adj* **1** : skillful and competent with the hands **2** : EXPERT **3** : done with skill — **dex·ter·ous·ly** *adv* — **dex·ter·ous·ness** *n*

di·a·be·tes \,dī-ə-'bēt-ēz, -'bēt-əs\ *n* : a disorder in which insulin is deficient and the blood and urine contain too much sugar

di·a·crit·i·cal mark \,dī-ə-,krit-i-kəl-\ *n* : a mark used with a letter or group of letters to indicate a sound value different from that given the unmarked or otherwise marked letter or group of letters

---

j job   ng sing   ō low   ȯ moth   ȯi coin   th thin   <u>th</u> this   ü boot   ù foot   y you   yü few   yù furious   zh vision

di·a·dem \'dī-ə-ˌdem\ *n* **1** : CROWN **2**/: a band for the head worn by some monarchs

di·ag·nose \'dī-əg-ˌnōs\ *vb* **di·ag·nosed; di·ag·nos·ing** : to recognize (as a disease) by signs and symptoms

di·ag·no·sis \ˌdī-əg-'nō-səs\ *n, pl* **di·ag·no·ses** \-ˌsēz\ : the art or act of identifying a disease from its signs and symptoms

¹di·ag·o·nal \dī-'ag-ən-l\ *adj* **1** : running from one corner to the opposite corner of a four-sided figure **2** : running in a slanting direction ⟨*diagonal* stripes⟩ — **di·ag·o·nal·ly** *adv*

²diagonal *n* **1** : a diagonal line **2** : a diagonal direction **3** : a diagonal pattern

¹di·a·gram \'dī-ə-ˌgram\ *n* : a drawing, sketch, plan, or chart that makes something clearer or easier to understand

²diagram *vb* **di·a·gramed** \'dī-ə-ˌgramd\ *or* **di·a·grammed; di·a·gram·ing** *or* **di·a·gram·ming** : to put in the form of a diagram

¹di·al \'dī-əl\ *n* **1** : the face of a watch or clock **2** : SUNDIAL **3** : a face or series of marks on which some measurement or other number is indicated usually by means of a pointer ⟨the *dial* of a pressure gauge⟩ **4** : a disk usually with a knob or slots that may be turned to operate something (as a telephone)

dial 1

²dial *vb* **di·aled** *or* **di·alled; di·al·ing** *or* **di·al·ling** : to use a dial so as to operate, select, or call

di·a·lect \'dī-ə-ˌlekt\ *n* **1** : a variety of a language belonging to a particular region **2** : a variety of a language used by the members of a particular occupation or class

di·a·logue *or* **di·a·log** \'dī-ə-ˌlòg\ *n* **1** : a conversation between two or more persons **2** : the parts of a book or play that represent conversation

di·am·e·ter \dī-'am-ət-ər\ *n* **1** : a straight line that joins two points of a circle and passes through the center **2** : the distance through the center of an object from one side to the other : THICKNESS ⟨the *diameter* of a tree trunk⟩

di·a·mond \'dī-ə-mənd\ *n* **1** : a very hard mineral that consists of crystallized carbon, is usually nearly colorless, and is used especially in jewelry **2** : a flat figure ◇ resembling one of the surfaces of certain cut diamonds **3** : INFIELD 1

di·a·per \'dī-ə-pər, 'dī-pər\ *n* : a piece of folded cloth drawn up between the legs of a baby and fastened about the waist

di·a·phragm \'dī-ə-ˌfram\ *n* **1** : a fleshy muscular wall separating the chest from the abdomen **2** : a thin circular plate (as in a microphone) that vibrates when sound strikes it

di·ar·rhe·a \ˌdī-ə-'rē-ə\ *n* : an abnormal frequency of bowel movement

di·a·ry \'dī-ə-rē\ *n, pl* **di·a·ries** **1** : a daily record especially of personal experiences and thoughts **2** : a book for keeping a diary

di·a·tom \'dī-ə-ˌtäm\ *n* : a tiny water plant that is a single cell in a two-parted shell

¹dice \'dīs\ *n, pl* **dice** : a small cube marked on each face with one to six spots and used usually in pairs in games

dice

²dice *vb* **diced; dic·ing** **1** : to play games with dice **2** : to cut into small cubes ⟨*dice* carrots⟩

dick·er \'dik-ər\ *vb* : BARGAIN, HAGGLE

¹dic·tate \'dik-ˌtāt\ *vb* **dic·tat·ed; dic·tat·ing** **1** : to speak or read for someone else to write down or for a machine to record ⟨*dictate* a letter⟩ **2** : to say with authority : ORDER

²dictate *n* : a statement made or direction given with authority : COMMAND

dic·ta·tion \dik-'tā-shən\ *n* **1** : the giving of arbitrary orders ⟨had always resented *dictation*⟩ **2** : the dictating of words **3** : something dictated or taken down from dictation

dic·ta·tor \'dik-ˌtāt-ər\ *n* **1** : a person who rules absolutely and often brutally and oppressively **2** : one that dictates — **dic·ta·tor·ship** \dik-'tāt-ər-ˌship\ *n*

dic·ta·to·ri·al \ˌdik-tə-'tōr-ē-əl\ *adj* : of, relating to, or characteristic of a dictator or a dictatorship

dic·tion \'dik-shən\ *n* **1** : choice of words especially with regard to correctness, clearness, and effectiveness **2** : ENUNCIATION

dic·tio·nary \'dik-shə-ˌner-ē\ *n, pl* **dic·tio·nar·ies** **1** : an alphabetically arranged book giving the meaning and usually the pronunciation of words **2** : an alphabetical reference book explaining words and phrases found in a particular field of knowledge ⟨medical *dictionary*⟩ ⟨biographical *dictionary*⟩ **3** : an alphabetical book listing words of one language with definitions in another

did *past of* DO

did·n't \'did-nt\ : did not

¹die \'dī\ *vb* **died; dy·ing** **1** : to stop living **2** : to pass out of existence ⟨a *dying* race of people⟩ **3** : to disappear gradually ⟨the wind *died* down⟩ **4** : LONG **5** : STOP

²die *n, pl* **dice** \'dīs\ *or* **dies** \'dīz\ **1** *pl* **dice** : DICE **2** *pl* **dies** : a device for forming or cutting material by pressure

¹di·et \'dī-ət\ *n* **1** : the food and drink that a person or animal usually takes **2** : the kind and amount of food selected or allowed with reference to a particular state (as ill health)

²diet *vb* : to eat or cause to eat less or according to certain rules — **di·et·er** *n*

di·e·tar·y \'dī-ə-,ter-ē\ *adj* : of or relating to a diet or to rules of diet

di·e·ti·tian *or* **di·e·ti·cian** \,dī-ə-'tish-ən\ *n* : a person trained to apply the principles of nutrition to the planning of food and meals

dif·fer \'dif-ər\ *vb* **1** : to be not the same : be unlike **2** : DISAGREE

dif·fer·ence \'dif-ə-rəns\ *n* **1** : unlikeness between two or more persons or things **2** : the degree or amount by which things differ in quantity or measure **3** : the number that is obtained by subtracting one number from another ⟨the *difference* between 4 and 6 is 2⟩ **4** : a disagreement in opinion

dif·fer·ent \'dif-ə-rənt\ *adj* **1** : not of the same kind **2** : not the same —**dif·fer·ent·ly** *adv*

dif·fer·en·ti·ate \,dif-ə-'ren-chē-,āt\ *vb* **dif·fer·en·ti·at·ed; dif·fer·en·ti·at·ing** **1** : to make or become different : undergo differentiation **2** : to recognize or state the difference between

dif·fer·en·ti·a·tion \,dif-ə-,ren-chē-'ā-shən\ *n* : the process of change by which immature living structures develop to maturity

dif·fi·cult \'dif-i-,kəlt\ *adj* **1** : hard to do or make ⟨a *difficult* climb⟩ **2** : hard to deal with, manage, or please **3** : hard to understand

dif·fi·cul·ty \'dif-i-,kəl-tē\ *n, pl* **dif·fi·cul·ties** **1** : difficult nature ⟨the *difficulty* of a task⟩ **2** : great effort **3** : something that is hard to do : OBSTACLE **4** : a trying situation

dif·fi·dent \'dif-ə-dənt\ *adj* **1** : lacking confidence **2** : RESERVED — **dif·fi·dent·ly** *adv*

¹dig \'dig\ *vb* **dug** \'dəg\; **dig·ging** **1** : to turn up the soil (as with a spade or hoe) **2** : to hollow out or form by removing earth ⟨*dig* a hole⟩ ⟨*dig* a cellar⟩ **3** : to uncover or seek by turning up earth ⟨*dig* potatoes⟩ ⟨*dig* for gold⟩ **4** : to bring to light : DISCOVER ⟨*dig* up information⟩ **5** : POKE, PROD ⟨*dug* him in the ribs⟩ **6** : to work hard — **dig·ger** *n*

²dig *n* **1** : THRUST, POKE **2** : a cutting remark

¹di·gest \'dī-,jest\ *n* : a body of information in condensed or shortened form

²di·gest \dī-'jest, də-\ *vb* **1** : to think over and arrange in the mind ⟨*digest* a lesson⟩ **2** : to change food into simpler forms that can be taken in and used by the body **3** : SUMMARIZE **4** : to become digested

di·gest·i·ble \dī-'jes-tə-bəl, də-\ *adj* : capable of being digested

di·ges·tion \dī-'jes-chən, də-\ *n* : the process or power of digesting something (as food)

di·ges·tive \dī-'jes-tiv, də-\ *adj* : of, relating to, or functioning in digestion

dig·it \'dij-ət\ *n* **1** : any of the numerals 1 to 9 and the symbol 0 **2** : FINGER, TOE

dig·ni·fied \'dig-nə-,fīd\ *adj* : having or showing dignity

dig·ni·fy \'dig-nə-,fī\ *vb* **dig·ni·fied; dig·ni·fy·ing** : to give dignity or distinction to

dig·ni·tar·y \'dig-nə-,ter-ē\ *n, pl* **dig·ni·tar·ies** : a person of high position or honor

dig·ni·ty \'dig-nət-ē\ *n, pl* **dig·ni·ties** **1** : the quality or state of being worthy, honored, or esteemed **2** : high rank, office, or position **3** : formal reserve (as of manner)

dike \'dīk\ *n* : a bank of earth thrown up from a ditch or heaped up to form a boundary or to control water

di·lap·i·dat·ed \də-'lap-ə-,dāt-əd\ *adj* : partly fallen into ruin or decay (as from neglect)

di·late \dī-'lāt\ *vb* **di·lat·ed; di·lat·ing** : to make or grow larger or wider : SWELL

dil·a·to·ry \'dil-ə-,tōr-ē\ *adj* **1** : tending or intended to cause delay **2** : not prompt — **dil·a·to·ri·ly** \,dil-ə-'tōr-ə-lē\ *adv*

di·lem·ma \də-'lem-ə\ *n* : a situation in which a person has to choose between things no one of which seems really desirable

dil·i·gence \'dil-ə-jəns\ *n* : careful and continued work : conscientious effort : INDUSTRY

dil·i·gent \'dil-ə-jənt\ *adj* : marked by steady and earnest care and effort ⟨a *diligent* search⟩ — **dil·i·gent·ly** *adv*

dill \'dil\ *n* : an herb related to the carrot with aromatic leaves and seeds used in flavoring pickles

dil·ly·dal·ly \'dil-ē-,dal-ē\ *vb* **dil·ly·dal·lied; dil·ly·dal·ly·ing** : to waste time (as by loitering)

¹di·lute \dī-'lüt, də-\ *vb* **di·lut·ed; di·lut·ing** : to make thinner or more liquid by admixture

²dilute *adj* : DILUTED — **di·lute·ness** *n*

di·lu·tion \dī-'lü-shən, də-\ *n* **1** : the act of diluting : the state of being diluted **2** : something (as a solution) that is diluted

¹dim \'dim\ *adj* **dim·mer; dim·mest** **1** : not bright or distinct : FAINT **2** : having no luster **3** : not seeing or understanding clearly — **dim·ly** *adv* — **dim·ness** *n*

²dim *vb* **dimmed; dim·ming** **1** : to make or become dim **2** : to reduce the light from

dime \'dīm\ *n* [from early French *dime* "tenth part", taken from Latin *decima*, which came from *decem* "ten"] : a United States coin worth ten cents

di·men·sion \də-'men-chən\ *n* **1** : measure in a straight line (as of length, width, or height) **2** : EXTENT, SCOPE

di·min·ish \də-'min-ish\ *vb* **1** : to make less or cause to seem less **2** : BELITTLE **3** : DWINDLE — **di·min·ish·ment** *n*

¹di·min·u·en·do \də-,min-yə-'wen-dō\ *adv (or adj)* : DECRESCENDO

²diminuendo *n* : DECRESCENDO

¹di·min·u·tive \də-'min-yət-iv\ *n* **1** : a word or form that indicates smallness and often the quality of being lovable or pitiable **2** : a diminutive object or individual

²diminutive *adj* **1** : being of small size **2** : extremely small : TINY ⟨a *diminutive* tree⟩

dim·i·ty \'dim-ət-ē\ *n, pl* **dim·i·ties** : a thin usually corded cotton cloth of plain weave in checks or stripes

dim·mer \'dim-ər\ *n* **1** : one that dims **2** *pl* : automobile headlights that have been dimmed

¹dim·ple \'dim-pəl\ *n* : a slight hollow spot or dent especially in the cheek or chin

²dimple *vb* **dim·pled**; **dim·pling** : to mark with or form dimples

¹din \'din\ *n* : loud confused noise

²din *vb* **dinned**; **din·ning** **1** : to make a din **2** : to impress by repeating over and over

di·nar \di-'när\ *n* : a coin of Yugoslavia or of any of various Muslim countries

dine \'dīn\ *vb* **dined**; **din·ing** **1** : to eat dinner ⟨*dine* out⟩ **2** : to give a dinner to

din·er \'dī-nər\ *n* **1** : a person eating dinner **2** : a railroad dining car or a restaurant in the shape of one

ding·dong \'ding-,dòng\ *n* : the sound of repeated strokes on a bell

dingh·y \'ding-ē, 'ding-kē\ *n, pl* **dingh·ies** **1** : a small light rowboat **2** : a rubber life raft

dinghy 1

din·gle \'ding-gəl\ *n* : a small narrow wooded valley

din·gy \'din-jē\ *adj* **din·gi·er**; **din·gi·est** : not fresh, bright, or light — **din·gi·ness** *n*

din·ner \'din-ər\ *n* **1** : the main meal of the day **2** : a formal banquet

di·no·saur \'dī-nə-,sòr\ *n* [a word formed by 19th century zoologists from Greek *deinos* "terrible" and *sauros* "lizard"] : a member of a group of huge reptiles that lived on the earth millions of years ago

dinosaur

dint \'dint\ *n* **1** : FORCE, POWER ⟨succeeded by *dint* of hard work⟩ **2** : DENT

¹di·oc·e·san \dī-'äs-ə-sən\ *adj* : of or relating to a diocese

²diocesan *n* : the bishop of a diocese

di·o·cese \'dī-ə-səs, -,sēz\ *n* : the district over which a bishop has authority

¹dip \'dip\ *vb* **dipped**; **dip·ping** **1** : to lower, sink, or thrust for a short time into a liquid ⟨*dipped* her fingers into water⟩ **2** : to take out with or as if with a ladle **3** : to lower and quickly raise again : drop or sink and quickly rise ⟨*dip* a flag⟩ **4** : to sink out of sight **5** : to slope or incline downward **6** : to make by plunging into a processing material

²dip *n* **1** : a plunge into water for sport or exercise **2** : an inclination downward : DROP **3** : something obtained by or used in dipping

diph·the·ri·a \dif-'thir-ē-ə\ *n* : an acute contagious disease in which the air passages become coated with a membrane that often obstructs breathing

diph·thong \'dif-,thòng\ *n* : two vowel sounds joined in one syllable to form one speech sound (as *ou* in *out* or *oi* in *oil*)

di·plo·ma \də-'plō-mə\ *n* : an official paper showing graduation from or a degree given by a school or college

di·plo·ma·cy \də-'plō-mə-sē\ *n* **1** : the business of carrying on negotiations between nations **2** : skill in dealing with others : TACT

dip·lo·mat \'dip-lə-,mat\ *n* **1** : a person engaged in or skilled in conducting official business between nations **2** : a person skilled in dealing tactfully with others

dip·lo·mat·ic \,dip-lə-'mat-ik\ *adj* **1** : of or relating to diplomats and their work **2** : TACTFUL — **dip·lo·mat·i·cal·ly** \-i-kə-lē\ *adv*

dip·per \'dip-ər\ *n* **1** : one that dips **2** : a ladle or scoop for dipping **3** *cap* : a group of seven stars in the northern sky arranged in a form resembling a dipper with the two stars that form the outer edge of the cup being in line with the North Star **4** *cap* : a group of seven stars in the northern sky similar to the Dipper but with the North Star forming the outer end of the handle

dipper 2

dire \'dīr\ *adj* **1** : very dreadful or terrible : HORRIBLE **2** : EXTREME ⟨in *dire* need⟩ — **dire·ly** *adv* — **dire·ness** *n*

¹di·rect \də-'rekt, dī-\ *vb* **1** : to put an address on (as a letter) **2** : TURN, AIM **3** : to point out the way **4** : LEAD, MANAGE ⟨*direct* a play⟩ **5** : ORDER, COMMAND **syn** see CONDUCT

²**direct** *adj* **1** : going from one point to another without turn or stop : STRAIGHT **2** : coming immediately from a source or cause ⟨*direct* result⟩ ⟨*direct* action⟩ **3** : being in a straight line of descent ⟨*direct* ancestor⟩ **4** : FRANK — **di·rect·ness** *n*

³**direct** *adv* : DIRECTLY

direct current *n* : an electric current flowing in one direction only

di·rec·tion \də-'rek-shən, dī-\ *n* **1** : SUPERVISION, MANAGEMENT **2** : an order or instruction to be followed **3** : the address on a letter or parcel **4** : the course along which something moves, lies, or points

di·rect·ly \də-'rekt-lē, dī-\ *adv* **1** : in a direct manner **2** : without delay : IMMEDIATELY

direct object *n* : an object that represents the primary goal or the result of the action of its verb ⟨*me* in "he hit me" is a *direct object*⟩

di·rec·tor \də-'rek-tər, dī-\ *n* : one that directs : MANAGER, SUPERVISOR

di·rec·to·ry \də-'rek-tə-rē, dī-\ *n, pl* **di·rec·to·ries** : a book containing names and addresses of the inhabitants of a place or of a class of persons ⟨telephone *directory*⟩

dire·ful \'dīr-fəl\ *adj* : DREADFUL, TERRIBLE — **dire·ful·ly** *adv*

dirge \'dərj\ *n* : a song or hymn of grief

dir·i·gi·ble \'dir-ə-jə-bəl\ *n* : AIRSHIP

dirk \'dərk\ *n* : DAGGER

dirt \'dərt\ *n* **1** : a filthy or soiling substance (as mud or dust) **2** : SOIL **3** : uncleanness in action or thought **4** : scandalous gossip

¹**dirt·y** \'dərt-ē\ *adj* **dirt·i·er; dirt·i·est 1** : not clean : SOILED, FILTHY **2** : LOW, UNFAIR ⟨a *dirty* trick⟩ **3** : INDECENT ⟨*dirty* talk⟩ **4** : FOGGY, STORMY ⟨*dirty* weather⟩ **5** : not clear in color ⟨a *dirty* red⟩ — **dirt·i·ness** *n*

²**dirty** *vb* **dirt·ied; dirt·y·ing** : to make or become dirty

dis- *prefix* **1** : do the opposite of ⟨*dis*establish⟩ **2** : deprive of ⟨*dis*able⟩ **3** : exclude or expel from ⟨*dis*bar⟩ **4** : opposite or absence of ⟨*dis*approval⟩ **5** : not ⟨*dis*agreeable⟩

dis·a·bil·i·ty \,dis-ə-'bil-ət-ē\ *n, pl* **dis·a·bil·i·ties 1** : lack of ability or power to do something **2** : a source of disability

dis·a·ble \dis-'ā-bəl\ *vb* **dis·a·bled; dis·a·bling** : to make unable or incapable : CRIPPLE — **dis·a·ble·ment** \-bəl-mənt\ *n*

dis·ad·van·tage \,dis-əd-'vant-ij\ *n* **1** : loss or damage especially to reputation or financial condition **2** : something that hinders success

dis·ad·van·ta·geous \,dis-,ad-,van-'tā-jəs\ *adj* : not favorable to success — **dis·ad·van·ta·geous·ly** *adv* — **dis·ad·van·ta·geous·ness** *n*

dis·a·gree \,dis-ə-'grē\ *vb* **dis·a·greed; dis·a-**

gree·ing 1 : to fail to agree : be unlike **2** : to differ in opinion ⟨*disagreed* over the price⟩ **3** : QUARREL **4** : to be unsuitable

dis·a·gree·a·ble \,dis-ə-'grē-ə-bəl\ *adj* **1** : UNPLEASANT, OFFENSIVE ⟨a *disagreeable* taste⟩ **2** : ILL-TEMPERED, PEEVISH ⟨a *disagreeable* child⟩ — **dis·a·gree·a·bly** \-blē\ *adv*

dis·a·gree·ment \,dis-ə-'grē-mənt\ *n* **1** : the act or fact of disagreeing **2** : the condition of being different **3** : a difference of opinion

dis·ap·pear \,dis-ə-'piər\ *vb* **1** : to cease to be visible : pass out of sight : VANISH **2** : to cease to be : become lost

dis·ap·pear·ance \,dis-ə-'pir-əns\ *n* : the act or fact of disappearing : VANISHING

dis·ap·point \,dis-ə-'pȯint\ *vb* : to fail to fulfill the hope or expectation of

dis·ap·point·ment \,dis-ə-'pȯint-mənt\ *n* **1** : the act of disappointing **2** : the condition or feeling of being disappointed **3** : one that disappoints

dis·ap·prov·al \,dis-ə-'prü-vəl\ *n* : unfavorable opinion or judgment : failure to approve

dis·ap·prove \,dis-ə-'prüv\ *vb* **dis·ap·proved; dis·ap·prov·ing** : to consider unfavorably : feel or express disapproval

dis·arm \dis-'ärm\ *vb* **1** : to take arms or weapons from ⟨*disarm* a prisoner⟩ **2** : to reduce the size and strength of the armed forces of a country **3** : to make harmless, peaceable, or friendly : win over ⟨a *disarming* smile⟩ — **dis·ar·ma·ment** \-'är-mə-mənt\ *n*

dis·ar·range \,dis-ə-'rānj\ *vb* **dis·ar·ranged; dis·ar·rang·ing** : to disturb the arrangement or order of — **dis·ar·range·ment** *n*

dis·ar·ray \,dis-ə-'rā\ *n* **1** : DISORDER, CONFUSION **2** : disorderly or incomplete dress

di·sas·ter \di-'zas-tər\ *n* [from an old Italian term *disastro* used in astrology to denote an evil influence due to the positions of stars and planets; it was formed from the prefix *dis-* "bad" and the noun *astro* "star"] : a sudden great misfortune : CALAMITY

di·sas·trous \di-'zas-trəs\ *adj* : accompanied by or resulting in disaster — **di·sas·trous·ly** *adv*

dis·band \dis-'band\ *vb* : to break up the organization of : DISPERSE — **dis·band·ment** *n*

dis·bar \dis-'bär\ *vb* **dis·barred; dis·bar·ring** : to deprive (a lawyer) of the rights and privileges of membership in the legal profession — **dis·bar·ment** *n*

dis·be·lief \,dis-bə-'lēf\ *n* : refusal or inability to believe (as a story) or accept as true

dis·be·lieve \,dis-bə-'lēv\ *vb* **dis·be·lieved; dis·be·liev·ing** : to hold not to be true or real : refuse to believe — **dis·be·liev·er** *n*

dis·burse \dis-'bərs\ *vb* **dis·bursed; dis·burs-**

ing : to pay out : EXPEND — **dis·burse·ment** *n*
disc *var of* DISK
¹dis·card \dis-'kärd\ *vb* **1** : to let go a playing card from one's hand **2** : to get rid of as useless or unwanted
²dis·card \'dis-,kärd\ *n* **1** : the act of discarding **2** : something discarded
dis·cern \dis-'ərn, diz-\ *vb* : to make out with the eyes or by the mind : DISTINGUISH
dis·cern·ing \dis-'ər-ning, diz-\ *adj* : having or showing insight and understanding : DISCRIMINATING — **dis·cern·ing·ly** *adv*
dis·cern·ment \dis-'ərn-mənt, diz-\ *n* : the power of discerning : keen insight
¹dis·charge \dis-'chärj\ *vb* **dis·charged; discharg·ing** **1** : to relieve of a load or a burden : UNLOAD **2** : SHOOT, FIRE 〈*discharge* a gun〉 **3** : to set free (as a prisoner) **4** : to dismiss from service 〈*discharge* an employee〉 〈*discharge* a soldier〉 **5** : to let go or let off **6** : to give forth the contents (as a fluid) **7** : to get rid of by paying or doing
²dis·charge \'dis-,chärj\ *n* **1** : the act of discharging, unloading, or releasing **2** : something (as a certificate of release from an obligation) that discharges **3** : a firing off **4** : a flowing out (as of blood or pus) **5** : dismissal especially from an office or from employment **6** : complete separation from military service
dis·ci·ple \di-'sī-pəl\ *n* : one that accepts and helps to spread his master's teachings
¹dis·ci·pline \'dis-ə-plən\ *n* **1** : strict training that corrects or strengthens **2** : PUNISHMENT **3** : control gained through obedience or strict training : orderly conduct **4** : a system of rules governing conduct
²discipline *vb* **dis·ci·plined; dis·ci·plin·ing** **1** : to punish or penalize for the sake of discipline **2** : to train in self-control or obedience **3** : to bring under control 〈*discipline* troops〉 **syn** see PUNISH
dis·claim \dis-'klām\ *vb* : to deny having a connection with or responsibility for
dis·close \dis-'klōz\ *vb* **dis·closed; dis·clos·ing** : to expose to view : make known : REVEAL
dis·clo·sure \dis-'klō-zhər\ *n* **1** : an act or instance of disclosing **2** : something disclosed
dis·col·or \dis-'kəl-ər\ *vb* : to change in color especially for the worse : STAIN, FADE
dis·col·or·a·tion \dis-,kəl-ə-'rā-shən\ *n* **1** : change of color **2** : a discolored spot
dis·com·fit \dis-'kəm-fət\ *vb* : to throw into confusion : UPSET 〈*discomfited* his enemies〉
dis·com·fort \dis-'kəm-fərt\ *n* : DISTRESS
dis·con·cert \,dis-kən-'sərt\ *vb* **1** : to throw into mental confusion **2** : to upset the composure of : EMBARRASS, FLUSTER

dis·con·nect \,dis-kə-'nekt\ *vb* : to undo or break the connection of 〈*disconnect* a hose〉
dis·con·nect·ed \,dis-kə-'nek-təd\ *adj* : not connected — **dis·con·nect·ed·ly** *adv*
dis·con·so·late \dis-'kän-sə-lət\ *adj* : being without hope or comfort : hopelessly sad : INCONSOLABLE — **dis·con·so·late·ly** *adv*
¹dis·con·tent \,dis-kən-'tent\ *vb* : to make dissatisfied
²discontent *n* : lack of contentment
dis·con·tent·ed \,dis-kən-'tent-əd\ *adj* : lacking contentment — **dis·con·tent·ed·ly** *adv*
dis·con·tin·ue \,dis-kən-'tin-yü\ *vb* **dis·con·tin·ued; dis·con·tin·u·ing** : to leave off : STOP
dis·cord \'dis-,kȯrd\ *n* **1** : lack of agreement or harmony **2** : an unpleasant combination of musical sounds **3** : a harsh sound
dis·cord·ant \dis-'kȯrd-nt\ *adj* **1** : DISAGREEING **2** : being without harmony
¹dis·count \'dis-,kaunt\ *n* : a reduction made from a regular price
²discount *vb* **1** : to reduce the amount of a bill, debt, or charge usually for cash or prompt payment **2** : to make allowance for exaggeration in 〈*discount* a friend's story〉
dis·cour·age \dis-'kər-ij\ *vb* **dis·cour·aged; dis·cour·ag·ing** **1** : to lessen the courage or confidence of : DISHEARTEN 〈*discouraged* by failure〉 **2** : to check or deter through fear of consequences **3** : to attempt to persuade not to do something
dis·cour·age·ment \dis-'kər-ij-mənt\ *n* **1** : an act of discouraging **2** : the condition of being discouraged **3** : something that discourages
¹dis·course \'dis-,kōrs\ *n* **1** : CONVERSATION, TALK **2** : a formal treatment of a subject
²dis·course \dis-'kōrs\ *vb* **dis·coursed; dis·cours·ing** : to talk especially at some length
dis·cour·te·ous \dis-'kərt-ē-əs\ *adj* : lacking courtesy : RUDE — **dis·cour·te·ous·ly** *adv*
dis·cour·te·sy \dis-'kərt-ə-sē\ *n, pl* **dis·cour·te·sies** **1** : RUDENESS **2** : a rude or impolite act
dis·cov·er \dis-'kəv-ər\ *vb* : to find out, see, or learn of especially for the first time : FIND — **dis·cov·er·er** *n*
dis·cov·er·y \dis-'kəv-ə-rē\ *n, pl* **dis·cov·er·ies** **1** : an act of discovering **2** : something discovered
¹dis·cred·it \dis-'kred-ət\ *vb* **1** : to refuse to accept as true **2** : to destroy confidence in
²discredit *n* **1** : loss of reputation 〈brought *discredit* on his family〉 **2** : DOUBT, DISBELIEF
dis·cred·it·a·ble \dis-'kred-ət-ə-bəl\ *adj* : causing discredit — **dis·cred·it·a·bly** \-blē\ *adv*

dis·creet \dis-'krēt\ *adj* : having or showing good judgment — **dis·creet·ly** *adv*

dis·cre·tion \dis-'kresh-ən\ *n* **1** : the quality of being discreet : CAUTION, PRUDENCE **2** : the power or right of free decision

dis·crim·i·nate \dis-'krim-ə-ˌnāt\ *vb* **dis·crim·i·nat·ed; dis·crim·i·nat·ing** **1** : to see and note differences : DISTINGUISH, DIFFERENTIATE **2** : to make a difference in favor of or against one person or thing as compared with others

dis·crim·i·nat·ing \dis-'krim-ə-ˌnāt-ing\ *adj* : marked by power of discrimination : DISCERNING — **dis·crim·i·nat·ing·ly** *adv*

dis·crim·i·na·tion \dis-ˌkrim-ə-'nā-shən\ *n* **1** : the act of discriminating **2** : the ability to discriminate and especially to make fine distinctions **3** : a difference and especially an unjust difference in the way one person or group is treated as compared with another

dis·crim·i·na·to·ry \dis-'krim-ə-nə-ˌtōr-ē\ *adj* : marked by unjust discrimination

dis·cuss \dis-'kəs\ *vb* **1** : to argue or consider fully and openly **2** : to talk about

syn DISCUSS, ARGUE, DEBATE all mean to talk about something that is at issue or in question. DISCUSS stresses the exchanging of information and ideas in an effort to arrive at the truth or reach a satisfactory solution ⟨the group read and then *discussed* new books⟩ ⟨we *discussed* possible ways of disposing of the kittens⟩ ARGUE stresses the stating of facts or ideas that support a conviction in an effort to convince others of its correctness ⟨*argued* in favor of his candidate⟩ and often suggests some heat or loss of temper ⟨they *argued* loudly about the civil war and almost came to blows⟩ DEBATE usually indicates a formal public arguing between two opposing sides, often according to fixed rules ⟨the candidates planned to *debate* the issues on television⟩

dis·cus·sion \dis-'kəsh-ən\ *n* **1** : conversation or debate for the purpose of understanding a question or subject **2** : a formal treatment of a topic (as in a lecture)

¹**dis·dain** \dis-'dān\ *n* : a feeling of contempt for something considered beneath oneself : SCORN — **dis·dain·ful** *adj* — **dis·dain·ful·ly** *adv*

²**disdain** *vb* **1** : to look upon with scorn or contempt **2** : to reject or refrain from because of disdain

dis·ease \diz-'ēz\ *n* **1** : a change in a living body (as of a person or plant) that interferes with the performance of its normal functions : ILLNESS **2** : a particular instance or kind of disease ⟨heart *disease*⟩ — **dis·eased** \-'ēzd\ *adj*

dis·em·bark \ˌdis-əm-'bärk\ *vb* : to go or put ashore from a ship

dis·en·chant \ˌdis-n-'chant\ *vb* : to free from a spell : DISILLUSION — **dis·en·chant·ment** *n*

dis·en·tan·gle \ˌdis-n-'tang-gəl\ *vb* **dis·en·tan·gled; dis·en·tan·gling** : to free from entanglement : straighten out — **dis·en·tan·gle·ment** \-gəl-mənt\ *n*

dis·fa·vor \dis-'fā-vər\ *n* **1** : DISAPPROVAL, DISLIKE **2** : the state of being regarded with dislike or displeasure

dis·fig·ure \dis-'fig-yər\ *vb* **dis·fig·ured; dis·fig·ur·ing** : to spoil the appearance of — **dis·fig·ure·ment** *n*

dis·fran·chise \dis-'fran-ˌchīz\ *vb* **dis·fran·chised; dis·fran·chis·ing** : to deprive of the right to vote — **dis·fran·chise·ment** \-ˌchīz-mənt, -chəz-\ *n*

¹**dis·grace** \dis-'grās\ *vb* **dis·graced; dis·grac·ing** : to bring shame to — **dis·grac·er** *n*

²**disgrace** *n* **1** : the condition of being out of favor : loss of respect **2** : SHAME, DISHONOR **3** : a cause of shame

dis·grace·ful \dis-'grās-fəl\ *adj* : bringing or deserving disgrace : SHAMEFUL — **dis·grace·ful·ly** *adv* — **dis·grace·ful·ness** *n*

dis·grun·tle \dis-'grənt-l\ *vb* **dis·grun·tled; dis·grun·tling** : to put in bad humor — **dis·grun·tle·ment** \-'grənt-l-mənt\ *n*

¹**dis·guise** \dis-'gīz\ *vb* **dis·guised; dis·guis·ing** **1** : to change the dress or looks of so as to conceal identity **2** : CONCEAL, ALTER

²**disguise** *n* **1** : clothing put on to conceal one's true identity or to counterfeit another's **2** : an outward form that hides or changes the true character or appearance of something

¹**dis·gust** \dis-'gəst\ *n* : a strong feeling of dislike or distaste : powerful aversion

²**disgust** *vb* : to cause disgust in : offend the senses or feelings of — **dis·gust·ed·ly** *adv*

dis·gust·ing \dis-'gəs-ting\ *adj* : causing disgust : REVOLTING — **dis·gust·ing·ly** *adv*

¹**dish** \'dish\ *n* [both *dish* and *disk* derive from Latin *discus* "quoit", "disk", "dish", which in turn is from Greek *diskos* "quoit", "anything quoit-shaped"] **1** : a concave vessel for serving food at table **2** : food served in a dish **3** : the amount of food that a dish holds

²**dish** *vb* **1** : to put into a dish or dishes **2** : to make concave like a dish

dis·heart·en \dis-'härt-n\ *vb* : DISCOURAGE — **dis·heart·en·ing·ly** *adv*

di·shev·eled *or* **di·shev·elled** \di-'shev-əld\ *adj* : marked by loose disorder : TOUSLED

dis·hon·est \dis-'än-əst\ *adj* **1** : not honest or trustworthy **2** : marked by fraud : DECEITFUL, CORRUPT — **dis·hon·est·ly** *adv*

dis·hon·es·ty \dis-'än-əs-tē\ *n* : lack of honesty : quality of being dishonest

j job   ng sing   ō low   ȯ moth   ȯi coin   th thin   <u>th</u> this   ü boot   u̇ foot   y you   yü few   yu̇ furious   zh vision

¹**dis·hon·or** \dis-'än-ər\ *n* **1** : loss of honor or reputation **2** : a cause of disgrace

²**dishonor** *vb* : to bring shame on : DISGRACE

dis·hon·or·a·ble \dis-'än-ə-rə-bəl\ *adj* : not honorable — **dis·hon·or·a·bly** \-blē\ *adv*

dis·il·lu·sion \,dis-ə-'lü-zhən\ *vb* : to free from illusion — **dis·il·lu·sion·ment** *n*

dis·in·fect \,dis-n-'fekt\ *vb* : to cleanse of germs that might cause disease

¹**dis·in·fect·ant** \,dis-n-'fek-tənt\ *n* : something that frees from infection

²**disinfectant** *adj* : serving to disinfect

dis·in·her·it \,dis-n-'her-ət\ *vb* : to prevent a person from inheriting property that would naturally be passed on to him

dis·in·te·grate \dis-'int-ə-,grāt\ *vb* **dis·in·te·grat·ed; dis·in·te·grat·ing** : to separate or break up into small parts or pieces

dis·in·te·gra·tion \dis-,int-ə-'grā-shən\ *n* : the act or process of disintegrating : the state of being disintegrated

dis·in·ter \,dis-n-'tər\ *vb* **dis·in·terred; dis·in·ter·ring** : to take out of the grave or tomb — **dis·in·ter·ment** *n*

dis·in·ter·est·ed \dis-'in-trəs-təd,-'int-ə-rəs-\ *adj* **1** : not interested **2** : free from selfish interest **syn** see UNINTERESTED — **dis·in·ter·est·ed·ly** *adv* — **dis·in·ter·est·ed·ness** *n*

dis·joint \dis-'jȯint\ *vb* **1** : DISCONNECT **2** : to take apart at the joints

dis·joint·ed \dis-'jȯint-əd\ *adj* : not clear and orderly — **dis·joint·ed·ly** *adv*

disk *or* **disc** \'disk\ *n* **1** : a flat round object in fact or appearance **2** *usu* **disc** : a phonograph record — **disk·like** \-,līk\ *adj*

¹**dis·like** \dis-'līk\ *vb* **dis·liked; dis·lik·ing** : to regard with dislike : DISAPPROVE

²**dislike** *n* : a feeling of distaste or disapproval

dis·lo·cate \'dis-lō-,kāt\ *vb* **dis·lo·cat·ed; dis·lo·cat·ing** **1** : to put out of its proper place : DISPLACE **2** : to displace a bone from its normal connections with another bone

dis·lodge \dis-'läj\ *vb* **dis·lodged; dis·lodg·ing** : to force out of a resting place or a place of hiding or defense

dis·loy·al \dis-'lȯi-əl\ *adj* : not loyal : FALSE, FAITHLESS — **dis·loy·al·ly** *adv*

dis·loy·al·ty \dis-'lȯi-əl-tē\ *n, pl* **dis·loy·al·ties** **1** : lack of loyalty **2** : a disloyal act

dis·mal \'diz-məl\ *adj* [from the obsolete English noun *dismal* meaning "days marked as unlucky on medieval calendars", from the medieval Latin phrase *dies mali* "evil days"] : GLOOMY, DREARY — **dis·mal·ly** *adv*

dis·man·tle \dis-'mant-l\ *vb* **dis·man·tled; dis·man·tling** **1** : to strip of furniture or equipment **2** : to tear down (as a building)

3 : to take to pieces temporarily (as for repairs) — **dis·man·tle·ment** \-'mant-l-mənt\ *n*

¹**dis·may** \dis-'mā\ *vb* : to cause to lose courage through fear or alarm : DAUNT

²**dismay** *n* **1** : loss of spirit or courage through fear **2** : a feeling of alarm or disappointment

dis·miss \dis-'mis\ *vb* **1** : to send away **2** : to discharge from office, service, or employment **3** : to put aside or out of mind

dis·miss·al \dis-'mis-əl\ *n* : the act of dismissing : the state or fact of being dismissed

dis·mount \dis-'maùnt\ *vb* **1** : to get down from something (as a horse or bicycle) **2** : to throw down from a horse : cause to fall off **3** : to take (as a cannon) from a carriage or mountings **4** : to take apart (as a machine)

dis·o·be·di·ence \,dis-ə-'bēd-ē-əns\ *n* : lack of obedience : neglect or refusal to obey

dis·o·be·di·ent \,dis-ə-'bēd-ē-ənt\ *adj* : neglecting or refusing to obey — **dis·o·be·di·ent·ly** *adv*

dis·o·bey \,dis-ə-'bā\ *vb* **dis·o·beyed; dis·o·bey·ing** : to refuse, neglect, or fail to obey

¹**dis·or·der** \dis-'ȯrd-ər\ *vb* **1** : to disturb the order of : DISARRANGE **2** : to disturb the regular or normal functioning of

²**disorder** *n* **1** : lack of order or of orderly arrangement : CONFUSION **2** : an abnormal physical or mental condition : SICKNESS, AILMENT **syn** see CONFUSION

dis·or·der·ly \dis-'ȯrd-ər-lē\ *adj* **1** : not observing the rules of law and order : UNRULY **2** : DISARRANGED — **dis·or·der·li·ness** *n*

dis·or·ga·nize \dis-'ȯr-gə-,nīz\ *vb* **dis·or·ga·nized; dis·or·ga·niz·ing** : to break up the regular arrangement or system of : CONFUSE

dis·own \dis-'ōn\ *vb* : to refuse to acknowledge as belonging to oneself : REPUDIATE

dis·par·age \dis-'par-ij\ *vb* **dis·par·aged; dis·par·ag·ing** **1** : to lessen or lower in reputation or opinion **2** : to speak of in a slighting manner : BELITTLE — **dis·par·age·ment** *n* — **dis·par·ag·ing·ly** *adv*

dis·pas·sion·ate \dis-'pash-ə-nət\ *adj* : not influenced by strong feeling : CALM, IMPARTIAL — **dis·pas·sion·ate·ly** *adv*

¹**dis·patch** \dis-'pach\ *vb* **1** : to send away promptly or rapidly to a particular place or for a particular purpose **2** : to attend to or dispose of speedily : get rid of ⟨*dispatch* some business⟩ **3** : to put to death — **dis·patch·er** *n*

²**dispatch** *n* **1** : the sending of a message or messenger **2** : MESSAGE **3** : an important official message **4** : an item of news sent in by a correspondent to a newspaper **5** : promptness or speed in performing a task

ə abut ər further a ax ā age ä father, cot à (see key page) aù out ch chin e less ē easy g gift i trip ī life

dis·pel \dis-'pel\ *vb* **dis·pelled**; **dis·pel·ling** : to drive away by scattering : clear away

dis·pense \dis-'pens\ *vb* **dis·pensed**; **dis·pens·ing** 1 : to deal out in portions : DISTRIBUTE ⟨*dispense* charity⟩ 2 : ADMINISTER ⟨*dispense* justice⟩ 3 : to put up or prepare medicine in a form ready for use — **dispense with** : to do or get along without

dis·pens·er \dis-'pen-sər\ *n* 1 : one that dispenses medicines 2 : a container so made as to release part of its contents without being fully opened

dis·perse \dis-'pərs\ *vb* **dis·persed**; **dis·pers·ing** : to break up and scatter

dis·pir·it \dis-'pir-ət\ *vb* : DISCOURAGE

dis·place \dis-'plās\ *vb* **dis·placed**; **dis·plac·ing** 1 : to remove from the usual or proper place 2 : to remove from office : DISCHARGE 3 : to take the place of : REPLACE — **dis·place·ment** *n*

¹**dis·play** \dis-'plā\ *vb* 1 : to spread out before the view 2 : to permit to be seen

²**display** *n* 1 : EXHIBITION, SHOWING 2 : an exhibition given for effect : exaggerated show

dis·please \dis-'plēz\ *vb* **dis·pleased**; **dis·pleas·ing** : to cause a feeling of disapproval and dislike : be offensive to

dis·plea·sure \dis-'plezh-ər\ *n* : a feeling of annoyance and dislike : DISSATISFACTION

dis·port \dis-'pōrt\ *vb* : to amuse oneself

dis·pos·al \dis-'pō-zəl\ *n* 1 : ARRANGEMENT 2 : a getting rid of ⟨trash *disposal*⟩ 3 : right or power to use : CONTROL

dis·pose \dis-'pōz\ *vb* **dis·posed**; **dis·pos·ing** 1 : to put in position : ARRANGE 2 : to incline in mind ⟨was *disposed* to help⟩ — **dis·pos·er** *n* — **dispose of** 1 : to deal with finally : SETTLE 2 : to get rid of

dis·po·si·tion \,dis-pə-'zish-ən\ *n* 1 : the act or power of disposing or managing 2 : ARRANGEMENT 3 : TENDENCY, INCLINATION 4 : natural attitude toward things

dis·proof \dis-'prüf\ *n* 1 : a proving that something is not as believed or stated 2 : evidence that disproves

dis·pro·por·tion \,dis-prə-'pōr-shən\ *n* : lack of proportion, symmetry, or proper relation

dis·pro·por·tion·ate \,dis-prə-'pōr-shə-nət\ *adj* : not in proper proportion — **dis·pro·por·tion·ate·ly** *adv*

dis·prove \dis-'prüv\ *vb* **dis·proved**; **dis·prov·ing** : to show to be false

dis·put·a·ble \dis-'pyüt-ə-bəl, 'dis-pyət-\ *adj* : open to dispute, debate, or contest : DEBATABLE — **dis·put·a·bly** \-blē\ *adv*

¹**dis·pute** \dis-'pyüt\ *vb* **dis·put·ed**; **dis·put·ing** 1 : ARGUE 2 : WRANGLE 3 : to deny the truth

or rightness of ⟨*dispute* a statement⟩ 4 : to fight about : CONTEST — **dis·put·er** *n*

²**dispute** *n* 1 : ARGUMENT, DEBATE 2 : QUARREL

dis·qual·i·fy \dis-'kwäl-ə-,fī\ *vb* **dis·qual·i·fied**; **dis·qual·i·fy·ing** : to make or declare unfit or ineligible

¹**dis·qui·et** \dis-'kwī-ət\ *vb* : to make uneasy or restless : DISTURB — **dis·qui·et·ing·ly** *adv*

²**disquiet** *n* : ANXIETY, UNEASINESS

¹**dis·re·gard** \,dis-ri-'gärd\ *vb* : to pay no heed or attention to **syn** see NEGLECT

²**disregard** *n* : the act of disregarding : the state of being disregarded : NEGLECT

dis·re·pair \,dis-ri-'paər\ *n* : the state of being in need of repair

dis·rep·u·ta·ble \dis-'rep-yət-ə-bəl\ *adj* : having a bad reputation : not respectable — **dis·rep·u·ta·bly** \-blē\ *adv*

dis·re·pute \,dis-ri-'pyüt\ *n* : low esteem

dis·re·spect \,dis-ri-'spekt\ *n* : lack of respect : DISCOURTESY — **dis·re·spect·ful** *adj* — **dis·re·spect·ful·ly** *adv*

dis·robe \dis-'rōb\ *vb* **dis·robed**; **dis·rob·ing** : UNDRESS

dis·rupt \dis-'rəpt\ *vb* 1 : to break apart 2 : to throw into disorder

dis·sat·is·fac·tion \di-,sat-əs-'fak-shən\ *n* : the state of being dissatisfied : DISCONTENT

dis·sat·is·fy \di-'sat-əs-,fī\ *vb* **dis·sat·is·fied**; **dis·sat·is·fy·ing** : to fail to satisfy : DISPLEASE

dis·sect \di-'sekt\ *vb* : to divide into separate parts especially for examination

dis·sem·i·nate \di-'sem-ə-,nāt\ *vb* **dis·sem·i·nat·ed**; **dis·sem·i·nat·ing** : to spread abroad as though sowing seed ⟨*disseminate* ideas⟩

dis·sen·sion \di-'sen-chən\ *n* : disagreement in opinion : DISCORD, QUARRELING

¹**dis·sent** \di-'sent\ *vb* : to differ in opinion

²**dissent** *n* : difference of opinion

dis·sent·er \di-'sent-ər\ *n* 1 : one that dissents 2 : NONCONFORMIST

dis·ser·vice \di-'sər-vəs\ *n* : HARM, INJURY

dis·sim·i·lar \di-'sim-ə-lər\ *adj* : UNLIKE

dis·si·pate \'dis-ə-,pāt\ *vb* **dis·si·pat·ed**; **dis·si·pat·ing** 1 : to break up and drive off : DISPERSE, DISPEL 2 : to scatter or waste foolishly : be wasteful : SQUANDER 3 : to drink to excess

dis·si·pat·ed \'dis-ə-,pāt-əd\ *adj* : indulging habitually and to excess in pleasures considered foolish or harmful

dis·so·ci·ate \di-'sō-shē-,āt\ *vb* **dis·so·ci·at·ed**; **dis·so·ci·at·ing** : to separate from association or connection with

dis·so·lute \'dis-ə-,lüt\ *adj* : loose in morals or conduct — **dis·so·lute·ly** *adv* — **dis·so·lute·ness** *n*

dis·solve \di-'zälv\ *vb* **dis·solved; dis·solv·ing**
1 : to mix or cause to mix with a liquid so that the result is a liquid of uniform nature ⟨sugar *dissolves* in water⟩ **2** : to bring to an end : TERMINATE **3** : to waste or fade away as if by melting or breaking up

dis·so·nance \'dis-ə-nəns\ *n* : DISCORD

dis·suade \di-'swād\ *vb* **dis·suad·ed; dis·suad·ing** : to advise against a course of action

dis·taff \'dis-ˌtaf\ *n, pl* **dis·taffs** : a staff for holding the flax, tow, or wool in spinning — **on the distaff side** : on the mother's side of a family

¹dis·tance \'dis-təns\ *n* **1** : the measure of separation between two points **2** : the quality or state of being distant : ALOOFNESS, RESERVE **3** : a distant point or region

²distance *vb* **dis·tanced; dis·tanc·ing** : to leave far behind (as in a race)

dis·tant \'dis-tənt\ *adj* **1** : separated in space or time : AWAY **2** : FAR-OFF **3** : not close in relationship ⟨*distant* cousins⟩ **4** : reserved or cold in personal relations — **dis·tant·ly** *adv*

dis·taste \dis-'tāst\ *n* : DISLIKE, AVERSION

dis·taste·ful \dis-'tāst-fəl\ *adj* **1** : unpleasant to the taste **2** : OFFENSIVE

dis·tend \dis-'tend\ *vb* : EXPAND, SWELL

dis·till *also* **dis·til** \dis-'til\ *vb* **dis·tilled; dis·till·ing** **1** : to fall or let fall in drops **2** : to obtain or extract by distillation **3** : to purify by distillation ⟨*distill* water⟩ — **dis·till·er** *n*

dis·til·la·tion \ˌdis-tə-'lā-shən\ *n* : the process of heating a liquid or solid until it sends off a gas or vapor and then cooling the gas or vapor until it becomes liquid

dis·tinct \dis-'tingkt\ *adj* **1** : distinguished from others : SEPARATE, DIFFERENT ⟨guilty of three *distinct* crimes⟩ **2** : clearly seen, heard, or understood ⟨a *distinct* sound⟩ — **dis·tinct·ly** *adv* — **dis·tinct·ness** *n*

dis·tinc·tion \dis-'tingk-shən\ *n* **1** : the act of distinguishing a difference **2** : something that makes a difference ⟨a room with a certain *distinction*⟩ **3** : a special recognition **4** : a mark or sign of special distinction **5** : HONOR ⟨served with great *distinction*⟩

dis·tinc·tive \dis-'tingk-tiv\ *adj* **1** : clearly marking a person or a thing as different from others **2** : CHARACTERISTIC **3** : having or giving style or distinction — **dis·tinc·tive·ly** *adv* — **dis·tinc·tive·ness** *n*

dis·tin·guish \dis-'ting-gwish\ *vb* **1** : to recognize one thing among others by some mark or characteristic **2** : to hear or see clearly : make out **3** : to make distinctions ⟨*distinguish* between right and wrong⟩ **4** : to set apart : mark as different **5** : to separate from others by a mark of honor : make outstanding

dis·tin·guish·a·ble \dis-'ting-gwish-ə-bəl\ *adj* : capable of being distinguished

dis·tin·guished \dis-'ting-gwisht\ *adj* : marked by distinction or excellence : FAMOUS

dis·tort \dis-'tȯrt\ *vb* **1** : to turn from the true meaning : MISREPRESENT ⟨*distorted* the facts of the case⟩ **2** : to twist out of natural or regular shape — **dis·tort·er** *n*

dis·tract \dis-'trakt\ *vb* **1** : to draw the mind or attention to something else **2** : to agitate or trouble in mind to a point of confusion

dis·trac·tion \dis-'trak-shən\ *n* **1** : the act of distracting : the state of being distracted **2** : complete confusion of mind : MADNESS, DESPAIR **3** : something that distracts attention **4** : DIVERSION, AMUSEMENT

¹dis·tress \dis-'tres\ *n* **1** : great suffering of body or mind : PAIN, ANGUISH **2** : a cause of suffering : MISFORTUNE, TROUBLE **3** : a condition of danger — **dis·tress·ful** *adj*

²distress *vb* : to cause distress to — **dis·tress·ing·ly** *adv*

dis·trib·ute \dis-'trib-yət\ *vb* **dis·trib·ut·ed; dis·trib·ut·ing** **1** : to divide among several or many : deal out **2** : to spread out so as to cover something **3** : to divide or separate especially into classes : SORT — **dis·trib·u·tor** *n*

dis·tri·bu·tion \ˌdis-trə-'byü-shən\ *n* **1** : the act of distributing **2** : the manner in which things are distributed **3** : something distributed

dis·trib·u·tive \dis-'trib-yət-iv\ *adj* **1** : of or relating to distribution **2** : being a property of multiplication whereby the same element is produced when operating on a whole as when operating on each part and collecting the results — **dis·trib·u·tive·ly** *adv*

¹dis·trict \'dis-ˌtrikt\ *n* **1** : a division of territory marked out for a special purpose ⟨school *district*⟩ **2** : a distinctive area or region

²district *vb* : to divide or organize into districts

¹dis·trust \dis-'trəst\ *vb* : to have no confidence in : MISTRUST, SUSPECT

²distrust *n* : a lack of trust or confidence : SUSPICION **syn** see DOUBT — **dis·trust·ful** *adj* — **dis·trust·ful·ly** *adv*

dis·turb \dis-'tərb\ *vb* **1** : to interfere with : INTERRUPT ⟨don't *disturb* him when he's resting⟩ **2** : to change the arrangement of : move from its place **3** : to trouble the mind of : make uneasy : UPSET **4** : to throw into disorder ⟨*disturb* the peace⟩ **5** : to put to inconvenience

dis·turb·ance \dis-'tər-bəns\ *n* **1** : the act of disturbing **2** : DISORDER, COMMOTION

dis·u·nite \ˌdis-yu̇-'nīt\ vb **dis·u·nit·ed; dis·u·nit·ing** : SEPARATE, DIVIDE

dis·use \dis-'yüs\ n : lack of use

dis·used \dis-'yüzd\ adj : no longer used

¹ditch \'dich\ n : a long narrow channel or trench dug in the earth

²ditch vb **1** : to dig a ditch in or around (as for drainage) **2** : to drive (as a car) into a ditch **3** : to get rid of : DISCARD **4** : to make a forced landing in an airplane on water

dith·er \'dith-ər\ n : a highly nervous or excited state

dit·ty \'dit-ē\ n, pl **dit·ties** : a short simple song

di·van \'dī-ˌvan\ n **1** : a low couch with no back or arms **2** : COUCH, SOFA

¹dive \'dīv\ vb **dived** or **dove** \'dōv\; **div·ing** **1** : to plunge into water headfirst **2** : SUBMERGE ⟨the submarine dived⟩ **3** : to descend or fall sharply **4** : to descend in an airplane at a steep angle **5** : to thrust suddenly into or at something : DART, LUNGE — **div·er** n

²dive n **1** : an act or instance of diving **2** : a sharp decline **3** : a disreputable bar

di·ver·gence \də-'vər-jəns, dī-\ n **1** : a drawing apart **2** : DIFFERENCE **3** : the acquisition of dissimilar characters by related organisms in unlike environments **4** : a departure from a course or standard

di·vers \'dī-vərz\ adj : VARIOUS

di·verse \dī-'vərs, də-\ adj : differing from one another : UNLIKE, SEPARATE — **di·verse·ly** adv — **di·verse·ness** n

di·ver·sion \də-'vər-zhən, dī-\ n **1** : an act or instance of diverting or turning aside **2** : something that diverts or amuses

di·ver·si·ty \də-'vər-sət-ē, dī-\ n, pl **di·ver·si·ties** **1** : the state of being diverse : UNLIKENESS **2** : an instance or a point of difference

di·vert \də-'vərt, dī-\ vb **1** : to turn aside : turn from one course or use to another **2** : to turn the attention away : DISTRACT **3** : AMUSE, ENTERTAIN **syn** see AMUSE

¹di·vide \də-'vīd\ vb **di·vid·ed; di·vid·ing** **1** : to separate into two or more parts or pieces ⟨divide an orange⟩ **2** : to give out in shares **3** : to cause to be separate **4** : to differ or cause to differ in opinion or interest **5** : to subject to mathematical division ⟨divide 10 by 2⟩ **6** : to branch off : FORK

²divide n : WATERSHED

div·i·dend \'div-ə-ˌdend\ n **1** : a sum or amount to be divided and distributed (as among owners of shares of stock) **2** : a number to be divided by another number

di·vid·er \də-'vīd-ər\ n : one that divides

div·i·na·tion \ˌdiv-ə-'nā-shən\ n : the practice of trying to foretell future events

¹di·vine \də-'vīn\ adj **1** : of or relating to God or a god ⟨divine will⟩ **2** : being in praise of God : RELIGIOUS, HOLY ⟨divine services⟩ **3** : GODLIKE, HEAVENLY **4** : excellent in the highest degree — **di·vine·ly** adv

²divine n **1** : CLERGYMAN **2** : one learned in divinity

³divine vb **di·vined; di·vin·ing** **1** : to discover or perceive through sympathetic feeling **2** : FORETELL, PROPHESY — **di·vin·er** n

di·vin·i·ty \də-'vin-ət-ē\ n, pl **di·vin·i·ties** **1** : the quality or state of being divine **2** : DEITY, GOD **3** : the study of religion : THEOLOGY

di·vis·i·ble \də-'viz-ə-bəl\ adj : capable of being divided or separated

di·vi·sion \də-'vizh-ən\ n **1** : the act or process of dividing : the state of being divided **2** : a part or portion of a whole **3** : a large self-contained military unit **4** : something that divides, separates, or marks off **5** : the operation of finding out how many times one number is contained in another

di·vi·sor \də-'vī-zər\ n : the number by which a dividend is divided

¹di·vorce \də-'vōrs\ n **1** : a complete legal breaking up of a marriage **2** : complete separation

²divorce vb **di·vorced; di·vorc·ing** **1** : to end a marriage or separate the partners in a marriage by divorce **2** : SEPARATE — **di·vorce·ment** n

di·vor·cée \də-ˌvōr-'sā\ n : a divorced woman

di·vulge \də-'vəlj, dī-\ vb **di·vulged; di·vulg·ing** : to make public : REVEAL, DISCLOSE

diz·zy \'diz-ē\ adj **diz·zi·er; diz·zi·est** **1** : having a sensation of whirling **2** : confused or unsteady in mind **3** : causing a feeling of being dizzy or giddy ⟨dizzy heights⟩ — **diz·zi·ly** \'diz-ə-lē\ adv — **diz·zi·ness** \'diz-ē-nəs\ n

¹do \dü\ vb **did** \did\; **done** \'dən\; **do·ing** \'dü-ing\; **does** \'dəz, dəz\ **1** : to carry out : ACCOMPLISH, PERFORM ⟨tell me what to do⟩ **2** : ACT, BEHAVE ⟨do as I say, not as I do⟩ **3** : to work at **4** : to deal with appropriately : take care of ⟨do the dishes⟩ **5** : to get along : FARE ⟨does well in school⟩ ⟨how do you do⟩ **6** : to bring or give to : RENDER ⟨did me a good turn⟩ **7** : FINISH ⟨when he had done⟩ **8** : to put forth : EXERT ⟨did his best⟩ **9** : TRAVEL **10** : to serve in prison ⟨had done six years for burglary⟩ **11** : to serve the purpose : SUIT ⟨this will do very well⟩ **12** — used as a helping verb (1) before the subject in a question ⟨does he work⟩, (2) in a negative statement ⟨I don't know⟩, (3) for emphasis ⟨he does know⟩, and (4) as a substitute for a preceding predicate ⟨he works harder than I *do⟩ — do away with* 1 : to get rid of 2 : KILL

²**do** \'dō\ *n* : the first note of the musical scale

doc·ile \'däs-əl\ *adj* : easily taught, led, or managed ⟨a *docile* child⟩ — **doc·ile·ly** *adv*

¹**dock** \'däk\ *n* : the solid part of an animal's tail

²**dock** *vb* 1 : to cut off the end of 2 : to take away a part of ⟨*dock* a man's wages⟩

³**dock** *n* 1 : an artificial basin to receive ships that has gates to keep the water in or out 2 : a slip or waterway usually between two piers to receive ships 3 : a wharf or platform for loading or unloading materials

⁴**dock** *vb* 1 : to haul or guide into a dock 2 : to come or go into a dock

⁵**dock** *n* : the place in a court where a prisoner stands or sits during trial

¹**doc·tor** \'däk-tər\ *n* : a person (as a licensed physician, surgeon, dentist, or veterinarian) skilled and specializing in the art of healing

²**doctor** *vb* : to treat in the manner of a physician : practice medicine

doc·trine \'däk-trən\ *n* 1 : something that is taught 2 : a principle or body of principles taught or recommended in a branch of knowledge or a system of beliefs (as of a church)

doc·u·ment \'däk-yə-mənt\ *n* : a written or printed paper furnishing information or used as proof of something else

¹**dodge** \'däj\ *vb* **dodged; dodg·ing** 1 : to move suddenly aside 2 : to avoid by moving quickly 3 : to avoid by trickery — **dodg·er** *n*

²**dodge** *n* 1 : a sudden movement to one side 2 : a trick by which to evade or deceive

do·do \'dōd-ō\ *n, pl* **do·does** *or* **do·dos** : a large heavy bird unable to fly and formerly living on some of the islands of the Indian ocean

doe \'dō\ *n* : the female of an animal (as a deer) the male of which is called *buck*

do·er \'dü-ər\ *n* : one that does

does·n't \'dəz-nt\ : does not

doff \'däf\ *vb* 1 : to take off 2 : LIFT

¹**dog** \'dòg\ *n* 1 : a flesh-eating domestic animal related to the wolves and foxes 2 : a device (as a metal bar with a hook at the end) for holding, gripping, or fastening something

²**dog** *vb* **dogged; dog·ging** 1 : to hunt or track like a hound 2 : to worry as if by dogs

dog·cart \'dòg-,kärt\ *n* 1 : a cart drawn by dogs 2 : a light one-horse carriage with two seats back to back

dog·catch·er \'dòg-,kach-ər\ *n* : an official assigned to catch and dispose of stray dogs

dog days *n pl* : the hot close part of summer from July to September

dog–eared \'dòg-,iərd\ *adj* : having a corner turned over ⟨a book with *dog-eared* pages⟩

dog·fish \'dòg-,fish\ *n* : any of several small gluttonous sharks often seen near shore

dog·ged \'dòg-əd\ *adj* : stubbornly determined — **dog·ged·ly** *adv* — **dog·ged·ness** *n*

dog·house \'dòg-,haùs\ *n* : a shelter for a dog — **in the doghouse** : in a state of disfavor

dog·ma \'dòg-mə\ *n* 1 : an opinion or belief held to be true beyond question 2 : a doctrine or body of doctrine laid down by a church

dog·mat·ic \dòg-'mat-ik\ *adj* 1 : of or relating to dogma 2 : very positive in manner of utterance — **dog·mat·i·cal·ly** \-i-kə-lē\ *adv*

¹**dog·trot** \'dòg-,trät\ *n* : a gentle trot

²**dogtrot** *vb* **dog·trot·ted; dog·trot·ting** : to move at a dogtrot

dog·wood \'dòg-,wùd\ *n* : any of a group of shrubs and small trees having clusters of small flowers often surrounded by four showy petallike leaves and in some cases having twigs with bright red-purple bark

dogwood

doi·ly \'dòi-lē\ *n, pl* **doi·lies** : a small often ornamental mat used on a table

do·ings \'dü-ingz\ *n pl* : DEEDS, EVENTS

dol·drums \'dōl-drəmz, 'däl-\ *n pl* 1 : a spell of low spirits or depression 2 : a part of the ocean near the equator noted for its calms

¹**dole** \'dōl\ *n* 1 : a giving out especially of food, clothing, or money to the needy 2 : something given out as charity 3 : a grant to the unemployed

²**dole** *vb* **doled; dol·ing** 1 : to give or distribute as a charity 2 : to give in small portions

dole·ful \'dōl-fəl\ *adj* : full of grief : SAD — **dole·ful·ly** *adv* — **dole·ful·ness** *n*

doll \'däl\ *n* : a small figure of a human being used especially as a child's plaything

dol·lar \'däl-ər\ *n* : any of various coins or pieces of paper money (as of the United States or Canada) equal to 100 cents

doll·y \'däl-ē\ *n, pl* **doll·ies** 1 : DOLL 2 : a platform on a roller or on wheels for moving heavy objects

dol·phin \'däl-fən\ *n* 1 : a small long-nosed whale with teeth 2 : either of two large food fishes of the sea

dolt \'dōlt\ *n* : a stupid fellow — **dolt·ish** *adj* — **dolt·ish·ly** *adv* — **dolt·ish·ness** *n*

dolphin 1

-dom \dəm\ *n suffix* 1 : dignity : office ⟨duke*dom*⟩ 2 : realm : jurisdiction ⟨king*dom*⟩ 3 : geographical area ⟨Anglo-Saxon*dom*⟩ 4 : state or fact of being ⟨free*dom*⟩ 5 : those having a specified office, occupation, interest, or character ⟨official*dom*⟩

do·main \dō-'mān\ *n* **1** : territory under rule or control (as of a king or government) **2** : a sphere of influence or activity

dome \'dōm\ *n* **1** : a large roof or ceiling shaped like a hemisphere **2** : something shaped like a dome — **domed** \'dōmd\ *adj*

dome

¹do·mes·tic \də-'mes-tik\ *adj* **1** : of or relating to a household, family, or home ⟨*domestic* life⟩ **2** : of or relating to or made in one's own country : not foreign : NATIVE **3** : living with or under the care of man : TAME — **do·mes·ti·cal·ly** \-ti-kə-lē\ *adv*

²domestic *n* : a household servant

do·mes·ti·cate \də-'mes-ti-ˌkāt\ *vb* **do·mes·ti·cat·ed; do·mes·ti·cat·ing** : to bring under the control and adapt to the use of man

dom·i·cile \'däm-ə-ˌsīl\ *n* : a dwelling place

dom·i·nance \'däm-ə-nəns\ *n* : the state or fact of being dominant

dom·i·nant \'däm-ə-nənt\ *adj* : controlling or being over all others — **dom·i·nant·ly** *adv*

dom·i·nate \'däm-ə-ˌnāt\ *vb* **dom·i·nat·ed; dom·i·nat·ing** : to have a commanding position over : RULE, CONTROL

dom·i·neer \ˌdäm-ə-'niər\ *vb* **1** : to rule in an arrogant manner **2** : to be overbearing

do·min·ion \də-'min-yən\ *n* **1** : highest authority : power of governing : RULE **2** : a territory governed ⟨the *dominions* of a king⟩

dom·i·no \'däm-ə-ˌnō\ *n, pl* **dom·i·noes** *or* **dom·i·nos** **1** : a masquerade costume consisting of a robe with a hood usually worn with a half mask **2** : one of the flat oblong dotted pieces used in playing a game (**dominoes**)

don \'dän\ *vb* **donned; don·ning** : to put on

do·nate \'dō-ˌnāt\ *vb* **do·nat·ed; do·nat·ing** : to make a gift of : CONTRIBUTE, PRESENT

do·na·tion \dō-'nā-shən\ *n* : GIFT

done *past part of* DO

don·jon \'dän-jən\ *n* : a large inner tower in a medieval castle

don·key \'däng-kē\ *n, pl* **donkeys** **1** : ASS 1 **2** : a silly or stupid person

donjon

do·nor \'dō-nər\ *n* : one that gives, donates, or presents — **do·nor·ship** \-ˌship\ *n*

don't \'dōnt\ : do not

¹doo·dle \'düd-l\ *vb* **doo·dled; doo·dling** : to draw or scribble without thought especially while attending to something else — **doo·dler** \'düd-lər\ *n*

²doodle *n* : something produced by doodling

doo·dle·bug \'düd-l-ˌbəg\ *n* : ANT LION

¹doom \'düm\ *n* **1** : JUDGMENT, SENTENCE **2** : destiny or fate especially of an unhappy kind **3** : RUIN, DEATH **syn** *see* DESTINY

²doom *vb* **1** : to give judgment against : CONDEMN **2** : to fix the fate of : DESTINE **3** : to ensure the failure of

dooms·day \'dümz-ˌdā\ *n* : the day of final judgment : the end of the world

door \'dōr\ *n* **1** : a usually swinging or sliding frame or barrier by which an entrance (as into a house) is closed and opened **2** : a doorlike part of a piece of furniture **3** : DOORWAY

door·man \'dōr-ˌman\ *n, pl* **door·men** \-ˌmen\ : one who tends a door (as of a hotel)

door·step \'dōr-ˌstep\ *n* : a step or series of steps before an outer door

door·way \'dōr-ˌwā\ *n* : the opening or passage that a door closes

door·yard \'dōr-ˌyärd\ *n* : a yard outside the door of a house

dope \'dōp\ *n* **1** : a thick liquid or pasty preparation **2** : a narcotic preparation **3** : a stupid person **4** : INFORMATION

dorm \'dȯrm\ *n* : DORMITORY

dor·mant \'dȯr-mənt\ *adj* : being in a resting or temporarily inactive state

dor·mer \'dȯr-mər\ *n* **1** : a window placed upright in a sloping roof **2** : the projecting structure containing a dormer window

dormer

dor·mi·to·ry \'dȯr-mə-ˌtōr-ē\ *n, pl* **dor·mi·to·ries** **1** : a sleeping room especially for a number of persons **2** : a residence hall having a number of sleeping rooms

dor·mouse \'dȯr-ˌmaus\ *n, pl* **dor·mice** \-ˌmīs\ : a small European squirrellike animal that lives in trees and feeds on nuts

dor·sal \'dȯr-səl\ *adj* : of, relating to, or being on or near the surface of the body that in man is the back but in most animals is the upper surface ⟨a fish's *dorsal* fin⟩ — **dor·sal·ly** *adv*

do·ry \'dōr-ē\ *n, pl* **do·ries** : a flat-bottomed boat with high sides that curve upward and outward and a sharp bow

¹dose \'dōs\ *n* : the measured amount of a medicine to be taken at one time

²dose *vb* **dosed; dos·ing** : to give medicine to

¹dot \'dät\ *n* **1** : a small point, mark, or spot **2** : a point in time **3** : a short click forming a letter or part of a letter (as in telegraphy)

²dot *vb* **dot·ted; dot·ting** : to mark with or as if with dots ⟨*dotted* his i's⟩

dote \'dōt\ *vb* **dot·ed; dot·ing** **1** : to be weak-minded especially from old age **2** : to be foolishly fond — **dot·er** *n* — **dot·ing·ly** *adv*

¹dou·ble \'dəb-əl\ *adj* **1** : TWOFOLD, DUAL

2 : consisting of two parts or members 3 : being twice as great or as many 4 : folded in two 5 : having more than the usual number of petals ⟨*double* roses⟩

²**double** *n* 1 : something that is twice another 2 : a hit in baseball that enables the batter to reach second base 3 : one that closely resembles another 4 : a sharp turn : REVERSAL 5 : FOLD

³**double** *adv* 1 : DOUBLY 2 : two together

⁴**double** *vb* **dou·bled; dou·bling** 1 : to make or become twice as great or as many : multiply by two 2 : to make of two thicknesses : FOLD 3 : CLENCH ⟨*doubled* his fist⟩ 4 : to become bent or folded usually in the middle 5 : to sail around (as a cape) by reversing direction 6 : to take the place of another 7 : to turn sharply especially back over the same course

double bass \ˌdəb-əl-ˈbās\ *n* : an instrument of the viol family larger than a cello and having a deep bass tone

dou·ble·head·er \ˌdəb-əl-ˈhed-ər\ *n* : two games played one right after the other on the same day

dou·ble–joint·ed \ˌdəb-əl-ˈjȯint-əd\ *adj* : having a joint that permits unusual freedom of movement of the parts that are joined

double bass

double play *n* : a play in baseball by which two base runners are put out

dou·blet \ˈdəb-lət\ *n* : a man's close-fitting jacket worn in Europe especially in the sixteenth century

dou·ble–talk \ˈdəb-əl-ˌtȯk\ *n* : language that appears to be sensible but is actually a mixture of sense and nonsense

dou·bloon \ˌdəb-ˈlün\ *n* : an old gold coin of Spain and Spanish America

dou·bly \ˈdəb-lē\ *adv* 1 : to twice the degree 2 : in a twofold manner

¹**doubt** \ˈdaút\ *vb* 1 : to be undecided in opinion about 2 : to be inclined not to believe or to believe in : DISTRUST 3 : to consider unlikely — **doubt·er** *n* — **doubt·ing·ly** *adv*

²**doubt** *n* 1 : uncertainty of belief or opinion 2 : the condition of being not yet decided 3 : DISTRUST 4 : an inclination not to believe **syn** DOUBT, DISTRUST, SUSPICION all mean a feeling of uncertainty about someone or something. DOUBT may imply uncertainty about the validity, truth, or reality of something, often leaving one unable to make a decision ⟨he was in *doubt* about the value of a class trip⟩ DISTRUST usually implies a lack of confidence in a person that is supported by some evidence

⟨we learned that his *distrust* was a result of having once been cheated⟩ SUSPICION usually suggests vague doubt, usually about someone's good intentions, and often with only slight evidence to support one's doubt ⟨we warned him to keep his *suspicions* to himself⟩

doubt·ful \ˈdaút-fəl\ *adj* 1 : not clear or certain as to fact ⟨a *doubtful* claim⟩ 2 : questionable in character ⟨*doubtful* intentions⟩ 3 : undecided in mind 4 : not certain in outcome ⟨a still *doubtful* battle⟩ — **doubt·ful·ly** *adv*

¹**doubt·less** \ˈdaút-ləs\ *adv* 1 : without doubt : CERTAINLY 2 : PROBABLY

²**doubtless** *adj* : free from doubt : CERTAIN

dough \ˈdō\ *n* 1 : a soft mass of moistened flour or meal thick enough to knead or roll 2 : a soft pasty mass similar to dough

dough·nut \ˈdō-ˌnət\ *n* : a small usually ring-shaped cake fried in fat

dough·ty \ˈdaút-ē\ *adj* **dough·ti·er; dough·ti·est** : being strong and valiant — **dough·ti·ly** \ˈdaút-l-ē\ *adv* — **dough·ti·ness** \ˈdaút-ē-nəs\ *n*

dough·y \ˈdō-ē\ *adj* **dough·i·er; dough·i·est** : resembling dough : PASTY

dour \ˈdaúr, ˈdúr\ *adj* 1 : STERN, SEVERE 2 : sour or sullen in looks — **dour·ly** *adv* — **dour·ness** *n*

douse \ˈdaús\ *vb* **doused; dous·ing** 1 : to plunge into water 2 : to throw a liquid over 3 : to put out : EXTINGUISH ⟨*douse* a light⟩

¹**dove** \ˈdəv\ *n* : any of various mostly small pigeons

²**dove** \ˈdōv\ *past of* DIVE

dowd·y \ˈdaúd-ē\ *adj* **dowd·i·er; dowd·i·est** : not neatly or becomingly dressed or cared for : SHABBY, UNTIDY — **dowd·i·ly** \ˈdaúd-l-ē\ *adv* — **dowd·i·ness** \ˈdaúd-ē-nəs\ *n*

dow·el \ˈdaú-əl\ *n* : a pin or peg used for fastening together two pieces of wood

¹**down** \ˈdaún\ *n* : a rolling grassy upland — usually used in plural

²**down** *adv* 1 : toward or in a lower position 2 : to a lying or sitting position 3 : toward or to the ground, floor, or bottom 4 : in cash ⟨five dollars *down*⟩ 5 : in a direction opposite to up 6 : to or in a lower or worse condition 7 : from a past time ⟨heirlooms handed *down*⟩ 8 : to or in a state of less activity ⟨quiet *down*⟩

³**down** *adj* 1 : being in a low position 2 : directed or going downward ⟨the *down* car⟩ 3 : being at a lower level ⟨sales were *down*⟩ 4 : DOWNCAST, DEPRESSED 5 : paid in part at the time of purchase ⟨a *down* payment⟩

⁴**down** *prep* : in a descending direction in, on, along, or through

⁵**down** *n* : a low or falling period (as in one's life) ⟨had had his ups and *downs*⟩

⁶down *vb* : to go or cause to go or come down

⁷down *n* **1** : soft fluffy feathers (as of young birds) **2** : something soft and fluffy like down — **down·like** \-,līk\ *adj*

down·cast \'daun-,kast\ *adj* **1** : DISCOURAGED, DEJECTED **2** : directed down

down·fall \'daun-,fȯl\ *n* **1** : a heavy fall (as of rain) **2** : a sudden fall (as from high rank) : RUIN — **down·fall·en** \-,fȯl-ən\ *adj*

¹down·grade \'daun-,grād\ *n* **1** : a downward slope (as of a road) **2** : a decline toward a worse condition

²downgrade *vb* **down·grad·ed; down·grad·ing** : to lower in grade, rank, position, or status

down·heart·ed \'daun-'härt-əd\ *adj* : DEJECTED, DISCOURAGED — **down·heart·ed·ly** *adv* — **down·heart·ed·ness** *n*

¹down·hill \'daun-'hil\ *adv* : DOWNWARD

²downhill *adj* : sloping downhill

down·pour \'daun-,pōr\ *n* : a heavy rain

¹down·right \'daun-,rīt\ *adv* : THOROUGHLY

²downright *adj* **1** : ABSOLUTE, COMPLETE ⟨a *downright* lie⟩ **2** : PLAIN, BLUNT

down·stage \'daun-'stāj\ *adv (or adj)* : toward or at the front of a theatrical stage

¹down·stairs \'daun-'staərz\ *adv* : down the stairs : on or to a lower floor

²down·stairs \'daun-,staərz\ *adj* : situated on a lower floor or on the main or ground floor

³down·stairs \'daun-'staərz\ *n* : the lower floor or floors of a house

down·stream \'daun-'strēm\ *adv* : in the direction of flow of a stream

¹down·town \'daun-'taun\ *adv* : to, toward, or in the lower part or business center of a town or city ⟨had lunch *downtown*⟩

²down·town \'daun-,taun\ *adj* **1** : located downtown **2** : of or relating to the business center of a city

down·trod·den \'daun-'träd-n\ *adj* : crushed by superior power : OPPRESSED

¹down·ward \'daun-wərd\ *also* **down·wards** \-wərdz\ *adv* **1** : from a higher place or condition to a lower **2** : from an earlier time

²downward *adj* : directed toward or situated in a lower place or condition : DESCENDING

down·wind \'daun-'wind\ *adv (or adj)* : in the direction toward which the wind is blowing

down·y \'dau-nē\ *adj* **down·i·er; down·i·est** **1** : resembling down **2** : covered with down **3** : SOFT, SOOTHING

dow·ry \'dau-rē\ *n, pl* **dow·ries** : the property that a woman brings to her husband in marriage

¹doze \'dōz\ *vb* **dozed; doz·ing** : to sleep lightly — **doz·er** *n*

²doze *n* : a light sleep

doz·en \'dəz-n\ *n, pl* **doz·ens** *or* **dozen** : a group of twelve

¹drab \'drab\ *n* : a light olive brown

²drab *adj* **drab·ber; drab·best** **1** : of the color drab **2** : DULL, MONOTONOUS ⟨a *drab* life⟩ — **drab·ly** *adv* — **drab·ness** *n*

drach·ma \'drak-mə\ *n* : a coin of Greece

¹draft \'draft, 'dråft\ *n* **1** : the act of drawing or hauling : the thing or amount that is drawn **2** : the act or an instance of drinking or inhaling : the portion drunk or inhaled in one such act **3** : a medicine prepared for drinking **4** : a representation of something in words or lines : DESIGN, PLAN **5** : a preliminary sketch, outline, or version **6** : the act of drawing out (as from a cask) : a portion of liquid drawn out **7** : the depth of water a ship requires in order to float **8** : a selection of persons for compulsory military service **9** : an order (as a check) from one person or party to another directing the payment of money **10** : a current of air **11** : a device to regulate an air supply

²draft *adj* **1** : used for drawing loads ⟨*draft* animal⟩ **2** : PRELIMINARY, TENTATIVE ⟨a *draft* treaty⟩ **3** : being on draft **4** : DRAWN

³draft *vb* **1** : to select especially for compulsory military service **2** : to draw up a preliminary sketch, version, or plan of **3** : COMPOSE, PREPARE — **draft·er** *n*

drafts·man \'drafts-mən, 'dråfts-\ *n, pl* **drafts·men** \-mən\ : one who draws plans (as for buildings) — **drafts·man·ship** \-,ship\ *n*

draft·y \'draf-tē, 'dråf-\ *adj* **draft·i·er; draft·i·est** : exposed to a draft or current of air ⟨a *drafty* hall⟩ — **draft·i·ness** *n*

¹drag \'drag\ *n* **1** : something (as a sledge for carrying heavy loads) that is dragged, pulled, or drawn along or over a surface **2** : something used to drag with (as a device for dragging under water to catch something) **3** : something that hinders progress

²drag *vb* **dragged; drag·ging** **1** : to haul especially slowly or heavily ⟨*drag* a trunk across a room⟩ **2** : to move with painful slowness or difficulty **3** : to pass or cause to pass slowly ⟨the hot afternoon *dragged* on⟩ **4** : to hang or lag behind **5** : to trail along on the ground **6** : to search or fish with a drag

drag·gle \'drag-əl\ *vb* **drag·gled; drag·gling** **1** : to wet and soil by dragging **2** : to follow slowly : STRAGGLE

drag·net \'drag-,net\ *n* **1** : a net to be drawn along in order to catch something **2** : a network of planned actions for pursuing and catching ⟨a police *dragnet*⟩

drag·on \'drag-ən\ *n* : an imaginary animal

usually pictured as a huge winged scaly serpent

drag·on·fly \'drag-ən-,flī\ *n, pl* **drag·on·flies**
: a large four-winged in-
sect with a long slender
body

¹dra·goon \drə-'gün\ *n*
: a mounted soldier : CAV-
ALRYMAN

dragonfly

²dragoon *vb* : to force or
try to force to submit by violent measures

¹drain \'drān\ *vb* **1** : to draw off or flow off
gradually or completely ⟨*drain* water from a
tank⟩ **2** : to make or become gradually dry or
empty ⟨*drain* a swamp⟩ **3** : to discharge surface or surplus water **4** : EXHAUST

²drain *n* **1** : a means of draining (as a pipe,
channel, or sewer) **2** : the act of draining
3 : a gradual using up or withdrawal

drain·age \'drā-nij\ *n* **1** : an act of draining
2 : something that is drained off **3** : a method
of draining : system of drains

drain·pipe \'drān-,pīp\ *n* : a pipe for drainage

drake \'drāk\ *n* : a male duck

dra·ma \'drä-mə, 'dram-ə\ *n* **1** : a composition in verse or prose for theatrical presentation **2** : dramatic art, literature, or affairs

dra·mat·ic \drə-'mat-ik\ *adj* **1** : of or relating to the drama **2** : characteristic of the
drama : VIVID — **dra·mat·i·cal·ly** \-i-kə-lē\ *adv*

dram·a·tist \'dram-ət-əst\ *n* : PLAYWRIGHT

dram·a·tize \'dram-ə-,tīz\ *vb* **dram·a·tized**;
dram·a·tiz·ing **1** : to make into a drama **2** : to
present or represent in a dramatic manner

drank *past of* DRINK

¹drape \'drāp\ *vb* **draped**; **drap·ing** **1** : to
decorate or cover with or as if with folds of
cloth **2** : to arrange or hang in flowing lines

²drape *n* **1** : CURTAIN **2** : arrangement in or
of folds **3** : the cut or hang of clothing

drap·er·y \'drā-pə-rē\ *n, pl* **drap·er·ies** **1** : a
fabric used for decoration usually hanging in
folds and arranged in a graceful design
2 : hangings of heavy fabric used as a curtain

dras·tic \'dras-tik\ *adj* : acting rapidly and
violently : extreme in effect : HARSH, SEVERE
— **dras·ti·cal·ly** \-ti-kə-lē\ *adv*

draught \'draft, 'dråft\ *chiefly Brit var of*
DRAFT

¹draw \'drȯ\ *vb* **drew** \'drü\; **drawn** \'drȯn\;
draw·ing **1** : to cause to move by pulling
: cause to follow **2** : to move or go especially
steadily or gradually ⟨day was *drawing* to a
close⟩ **3** : ATTRACT ⟨*draw* a crowd⟩ **4** : to call
forth : PROVOKE ⟨*draw* enemy fire⟩ **5** : INHALE
⟨*draw* a deep breath⟩ **6** : to bring or pull out
⟨*draw* a sword⟩ **7** : to bring or get from a

source ⟨*draw* a pail of water⟩ **8** : to extract
the essence of ⟨*draw* tea⟩ ⟨let the tea *draw*⟩
9 : to require (a specified depth) to float in
10 : to take a card (as from a deck) **11** : to
take or receive at random ⟨*draw* lots⟩ ⟨*drew*
the winning number⟩ **12** : to bend a bow by
pulling back the string **13** : to cause to shrink
or pucker : WRINKLE **14** : to change shape by
or as if by pulling ⟨face *drawn* with pain⟩
15 : to leave a contest undecided : TIE **16** : to
produce a likeness of by making lines on a
surface : SKETCH **17** : to write out in proper
form ⟨*draw* a check⟩ **18** : FORMULATE
19 : INFER **20** : to produce or make use of a
current of air ⟨the furnace *draws* well⟩ —
draw on : APPROACH ⟨night *drew on*⟩ — **draw
out 1** : EXTRACT, REMOVE **2** : to cause to
speak freely — **draw up 1** : to arrange (as a
body of troops) in order **2** : to straighten
oneself to an erect posture **3** : STOP

²draw *n* **1** : the act or the result of drawing ⟨a
lucky *draw*⟩ ⟨quick on the *draw*⟩ **2** : a tie
game or contest **3** : something that draws
attention **4** : a gully shallower than a ravine

draw·back \'drȯ-,bak\ *n* : HANDICAP

draw·bridge \'drȯ-,brij\ *n* : a bridge made to
be drawn up, down, or
aside to permit or hinder
passage

draw·er \'drȯ-ər, 'drȯr\ *n*
1 : one that draws **2** : a
sliding boxlike compart-
ment (as in a desk) ⟨ches
of *drawers*⟩ **3** *pl* : an undergarment for the lower
part of the body

drawbridge

draw·ing \'drȯ-ing\ *n* **1** : an act or instance of
drawing lots (as in a raffle) **2** : the act or art
of making a figure, plan, or sketch by means
of lines **3** : a representation made by drawing

drawing card *n* : something that attracts a
great deal of attention or patronage

drawing room *n* : a formal room for receiving company

¹drawl \'drȯl\ *vb* : to speak slowly with vowel
sounds drawn out beyond their usual length
— **drawl·er** *n*

²drawl *n* : a drawling manner of speaking

draw·string \'drȯ-,string\ *n* : a string, cord,
or tape for use in closing a bag or controlling fullness in garments or curtains

dray \'drā\ *n* : a strong low cart or wagon
without sides for hauling heavy loads

dray·man \'drā-mən\ *n, pl* **dray·men** \-mən\
: a driver of a dray

¹dread \'dred\ *vb* **1** : to fear greatly **2** : to
feel extreme reluctance to meet or face

²**dread** *n* : great fear especially of harm to come

³**dread** *adj* **1** : causing great fear or anxiety **2** : inspiring awe

dread·ful \'dred-fəl\ *adj* **1** : inspiring dread : FEARFUL **2** : extremely distasteful, unpleasant, or shocking — **dread·ful·ly** *adv* — **dread·ful·ness** *n*

dread·nought \'dred-ˌnȯt\ *n* : a very large battleship

¹**dream** \'drēm\ *n* **1** : a series of thoughts, pictures, or feelings occurring during sleep **2** : a dreamlike vision or experience : DAYDREAM, REVERIE **3** : something notable for its pleasing quality **4** : a longed-for goal : IDEAL — **dream·like** \-ˌlīk\ *adj*

²**dream** *vb* **dreamed** \'dremt, 'drēmd\ *or* **dreamt** \'dremt\; **dream·ing** \'drē-ming\ **1** : to have a dream or dreams **2** : to indulge in daydreams **3** : to think of as happening or possible — **dream·er** \'drē-mər\ *n*

dream·land \'drēm-ˌland\ *n* : a delightful country existing only in imagination or in dreams

dream·less \'drēm-ləs\ *adj* : having no dreams ⟨a *dreamless* sleep⟩ — **dream·less·ly** *adv* — **dream·less·ness** *n*

dream·y \'drē-mē\ *adj* **dream·i·er**; **dream·i·est** **1** : full of dreams : given to dreaming **2** : having the quality of a dream **3** : being quiet and soothing ⟨*dreamy* music⟩ — **dream·i·ly** \-mə-lē\ *adv* — **dream·i·ness** \-mē-nəs\ *n*

drear \'driər\ *adj* : DREARY

drea·ry \'driər-ē\ *adj* **drea·ri·er**; **drea·ri·est** : DISMAL, GLOOMY — **drea·ri·ly** \'drir-ə-lē\ *adv* — **drea·ri·ness** \'drir-ē-nəs\ *n*

¹**dredge** \'drej\ *n* **1** : a heavy iron frame with a net attached to be dragged (as for gathering oysters) over the sea bottom **2** : a machine for scooping up or removing earth usually by buckets on an endless chain or by a suction tube **3** : a barge used in dredging

dredge 2

²**dredge** *vb* **dredged**; **dredg·ing** : to dig or gather with or as if with a dredge — **dredg·er** *n*

dregs \'dregz\ *n pl* **1** : worthless sediment contained in a liquid : LEES, GROUNDS **2** : the worst or most useless part

drench \'drench\ *vb* : to wet thoroughly

¹**dress** \'dres\ *vb* **1** : to make or set straight : ALIGN **2** : to straighten a line of soldiers (as on parade) **3** : to put clothes on : CLOTHE **4** : to wear formal or fancy clothes **5** : to trim or decorate for display ⟨*dress* a shop window⟩ **6** : to treat with remedies and bandage ⟨*dress* a wound⟩ **7** : to arrange by combing and brushing or by curling ⟨*dress* hair⟩ **8** : to kill and prepare for use or for market **9** : to apply fertilizer to **10** : SMOOTH, FINISH

²**dress** *n* **1** : CLOTHING ⟨evening *dress*⟩ **2** : an outer garment for a woman or child

¹**dress·er** \'dres-ər\ *n* **1** : a cupboard for dishes and cooking utensils **2** : a chest of drawers or bureau with a mirror

²**dresser** *n* : one that dresses

dress·ing \'dres-ing\ *n* **1** : the act or process of one who dresses **2** : a sauce added to certain foods (as salads) **3** : a seasoned mixture used as a stuffing (as for a turkey) **4** : material used to cover an injury **5** : fertilizing material

dressing table *n* : a low table or stand with a mirror for use by a person while dressing

dress·mak·er \'dres-ˌmā-kər\ *n* : one that does dressmaking

dress·mak·ing \'dres-ˌmā-king\ *n* : the process or the occupation of making dresses

dress·y \'dres-ē\ *adj* **dress·i·er**; **dress·i·est** **1** : showy in dress **2** : SMART, STYLISH

drew *past of* DRAW

¹**drib·ble** \'drib-əl\ *vb* **drib·bled**; **drib·bling** **1** : to fall or let fall in small drops : TRICKLE **2** : SLOBBER, DROOL **3** : to propel by bouncing, tapping, or kicking ⟨*dribble* a basketball⟩

²**dribble** *n* **1** : a trickling flow **2** : a drizzling shower **3** : the act of dribbling a ball

drib·let \'drib-lət\ *n* **1** : a trifling sum or part **2** : a falling drop

dri·er *or* **dry·er** \'drī-ər\ *n* **1** : something that removes or absorbs moisture **2** : a substance that speeds up the drying of oils, paints, and inks **3** *usu* **dryer** : a device for drying ⟨a clothes *dryer*⟩

¹**drift** \'drift\ *n* **1** : the motion or course of something drifting **2** : a mass of matter (as snow or sand) piled in a heap by the wind **3** : general intention, tendency, or meaning

²**drift** *vb* **1** : to float or to be driven along by winds, waves, or currents **2** : to move along without effort ⟨*drift* through life⟩ **3** : to pile up in drifts — **drift·er** *n*

drift·wood \'drift-ˌwu̇d\ *n* : wood drifting on water or washed ashore

¹**drill** \'dril\ *vb* **1** : to bore with a drill **2** : to instruct and exercise by repetition — **drill·er** *n*

²**drill** *n* **1** : a tool for making holes in hard substances **2** : the training of soldiers (as in marching) **3** : regular strict training and instruction in a subject

³**drill** *n* : a farming implement for making holes or furrows and planting seeds in them

drill

⁴drill vb : to sow seeds with or as if with a drill

⁵drill n : a strong heavy cotton cloth with a diagonal weave

drill·mas·ter \'dril-,mas-tər\ n : one that drills especially soldiers

dri·ly \'drī-lē\ var of DRYLY

¹drink \'dringk\ vb **drank** \'drangk\; **drunk** \'drəngk\; **drink·ing** 1 : to swallow liquid 2 : to absorb a liquid ⟨plants *drink* up water⟩ 3 : to take in through the senses ⟨*drank* in the beautiful scenery⟩ 4 : to drink alcoholic liquor especially to excess — **drink·er** n

²drink n 1 : BEVERAGE 2 : alcoholic liquor

drink·a·ble \'dring-kə-bəl\ adj : suitable or safe for drinking

¹drip \'drip\ vb **dripped** or **dript**; **drip·ping** 1 : to fall or let fall in drops 2 : to let fall drops of liquid ⟨a *dripping* faucet⟩

²drip n 1 : a falling in drops 2 : dripping liquid 3 : the sound made by falling drops

¹drive \'drīv\ vb **drove** \'drōv\; **driv·en** \'driv-ən\; **driv·ing** \'drī-ving\ 1 : to urge, push, or force onward 2 : to direct the movement or course of 3 : to go or transport in a vehicle under one's own direction ⟨*drive* into town⟩ 4 : to set or keep in motion or operation ⟨machines *driven* by electricity⟩ 5 : to carry through : CONCLUDE ⟨*drive* a bargain⟩ 6 : to force or compel to work or to act ⟨*driven* by hunger to steal⟩ 7 : to bring into a specified condition — **driv·er** \'drī-vər\ n

²drive n 1 : a trip in a carriage or automobile 2 : a collecting and driving together of animals 3 : the act of driving a ball 4 : DRIVE-WAY 5 : a public road for driving (as in a park) 6 : an organized usually intensive effort to carry out a purpose 7 : the means for giving motion to a machine or machine part

drive–in \'drīv-,in\ adj : arranged and equipped so as to accommodate patrons while they remain in their automobiles

¹driv·el \'driv-əl\ vb **driv·eled** or **driv·elled**; **driv·el·ing** or **driv·el·ling** 1 : DROOL, SLOBBER 2 : to talk stupidly, carelessly, or in a silly or childish way — **driv·el·er** or **driv·el·ler** n

²drivel n 1 : saliva drooling from the mouth 2 : foolish talk

drive·way \'drīv-,wā\ n : a private road leading from the street to a house or garage

¹driz·zle \'driz-əl\ vb **driz·zled**; **driz·zling** : to rain in very small drops

²drizzle n : a fine misty rain

driz·zly \'driz-lē\ adj **driz·zli·er**; **driz·zli·est** : DRIZZLING

droll \'drōl\ adj : being odd and amusing in character or effect — **droll·ness** n — **drol·ly** \'drōl-lē\ adv

droll·er·y \'drō-lə-rē\ n, pl **droll·er·ies** 1 : something droll 2 : droll behavior or humor

drom·e·dar·y \'dräm-ə-,der-ē\ n, pl **drom·e·dar·ies** 1 : a speedy camel trained for riding 2 : the camel of western Asia and northern Africa that has but one hump

¹drone \'drōn\ n 1 : a male bee 2 : a lazy person : one who lives on the labor of others

²drone vb **droned**; **dron·ing** : to make or to speak with a low dull monotonous hum

³drone n : a deep humming sound

drool \'drül\ vb 1 : to let liquid flow from the mouth : SLOBBER 2 : to talk foolishly : DRIVEL

¹droop \'drüp\ vb 1 : to sink, bend, or hang down ⟨flowers *drooping* in the hot sun⟩ 2 : to grow weak with grief or disappointment

²droop n : the condition or appearance of drooping

¹drop \'dräp\ n 1 : the amount of liquid that falls naturally in one rounded mass 2 pl : a dose of medicine measured by drops 3 : something (as a pendant or a small round candy) that resembles a liquid drop 4 : an instance of dropping 5 : the distance of a fall 6 : a slot into which something is to be dropped

²drop vb **dropped**; **drop·ping** 1 : to fall or let fall in drops 2 : to let fall ⟨*drop* a book⟩ ⟨*drop* anchor⟩ 3 : LOWER ⟨*dropped* his voice⟩ 4 : SEND ⟨*drop* me a note about it⟩ 5 : to let go : DISMISS ⟨*drop* a subject⟩ 6 : to knock down : cause to fall 7 : to go lower 8 : to come or go unexpectedly or informally ⟨*drop* in on a friend⟩ 9 : to pass into a less active state ⟨*drop* off to sleep⟩ 10 : to withdraw from membership or from taking part ⟨*drop* out of school⟩ 11 : LOSE

drop·kick \'dräp-'kik\ n : a kick made by dropping a football and kicking it as it starts to rebound

drop·out \'dräp-,aut\ n : one that drops out especially from school or a training program

drop·per \'dräp-ər\ n 1 : one that drops 2 : a short glass tube with a rubber bulb used to measure out liquids by drops

dross \'dräs\ n : waste matter : REFUSE

drought \'draut\ or **drouth** \'drauth\ n 1 : lack of rain or water 2 : a long period of dry weather

¹drove \'drōv\ n 1 : a group of animals being driven or moving in a body 2 : a crowd of people moving or acting together

²drove past of DRIVE

drov·er \'drō-vər\ n : one that drives cattle or sheep

drown \'draun\ vb 1 : to suffocate in a liquid and especially in water 2 : to cover with water : FLOOD **3** : OVERPOWER, OVERCOME

¹drowse \'draúz\ *vb* **drowsed; drows·ing** : to be half asleep : sleep lightly

²drowse *n* : a light sleep : DOZE

drows·y \'draú-zē\ *adj* **drows·i·er; drows·i·est 1** : ready to fall asleep **2** : making one sleepy ⟨the *drowsy* buzz of bees⟩ — **drows·i·ly** \-zə-lē\ *adv* — **drows·i·ness** \-zē-nəs\ *n*

drub \'drəb\ *vb* **drubbed; drub·bing 1** : to beat severely **2** : to defeat decisively

¹drudge \'drəj\ *vb* **drudged; drudg·ing** : to work hard at a tiresome task — **drudg·er** *n*

²drudge *n* : a person who drudges

drudg·er·y \'drəj-ə-rē\ *n, pl* **drudg·er·ies** : hard tiresome work

¹drug \'drəg\ *n* **1** : a substance used as a medicine or in making medicines **2** : an article for which there is no demand **3** : medicine used to deaden pain or bring sleep

²drug *vb* **drugged; drug·ging 1** : to poison with or as if with a drug ⟨the wine was *drugged*⟩ **2** : to dull a person's senses with drugs

drug·gist \'drəg-əst\ *n* : one who sells drugs and medicines : PHARMACIST

drug·store \'drəg-,stōr\ *n* : a retail shop where medicines and miscellaneous articles are sold : PHARMACY

¹drum \'drəm\ *n* **1** : a musical instrument usually consisting of a metal or wooden cylinder with flat ends covered by tightly drawn skin **2** : a sound of or like a drum **3** : a drum-shaped object

drums

²drum *vb* **drummed; drum·ming 1** : to beat a drum **2** : to beat, throb, or sound like a drum **3** : to gather together by or as if by beating a drum ⟨*drum* up customers⟩ **4** : to drive or force by steady or repeated effort **5** : to beat or tap rhythmically

drum major *n* : the marching leader of a band or drum corps

drum ma·jor·ette \,drəm-,mā-jə-'ret\ *n* : a female drum major

drum·mer \'drəm-ər\ *n* **1** : one that plays a drum **2** : a traveling salesman

drum·stick \'drəm-,stik\ *n* **1** : a stick for beating a drum **2** : the lower section of the leg of a fowl

¹drunk \'drəngk\ *past part of* DRINK

²drunk *adj* **1** : being so much under the influence of alcohol that normal thinking and acting become difficult or impossible **2** : controlled by some feeling as if under the influence of alcohol ⟨*drunk* with power⟩

³drunk *n* **1** : a period of excessive drinking **2** : a drunken person

drunk·ard \'drəng-kərd\ *n* : a person who is often drunk

drunk·en \'drəng-kən\ *adj* **1** : DRUNK **2** : given to excessive use of alcohol **3** : resulting from intoxication ⟨a *drunken* sleep⟩ — **drunk·en·ly** *adv* — **drunk·en·ness** *n*

¹dry \'drī\ *adj* **dri·er; dri·est 1** : free or freed from water or liquid : not wet or moist **2** : having little or no rain ⟨*dry* spell⟩ ⟨*dry* climate⟩ **3** : lacking freshness : STALE **4** : not being in or under water ⟨*dry* land⟩ **5** : THIRSTY **6** : no longer liquid or sticky ⟨the paint is *dry*⟩ **7** : containing no liquid : EMPTY ⟨*dry* creek⟩ ⟨*dry* fountain pen⟩ **8** : not giving milk ⟨*dry* cow⟩ **9** : not producing phlegm ⟨*dry* cough⟩ **10** : marked by a matter-of-fact expression ⟨*dry* humor⟩ **11** : DULL, UNINTERESTING ⟨*dry* lecture⟩ **12** : not sweet ⟨*dry* wines⟩ — **dry·ly** *adv* — **dry·ness** *n*

²dry *vb* **dried; dry·ing** : to make or become dry

dry cell *n* : a small cell producing electricity by means of chemicals that cannot be spilled

dry·er *var of* DRIER

dry goods \'drī-,gùdz\ *n pl* : cloth goods as distinguished from hardware and groceries

dry–shod \'drī-'shäd\ *adj* : having dry shoes

du·al \'dü-əl, 'dyü-\ *adj* **1** : consisting of two parts : having two like parts : DOUBLE **2** : fitted for operation by either or both of two agents ⟨*dual*-control cars⟩ — **du·al·ly** *adv*

¹dub \'dəb\ *vb* **dubbed; dub·bing 1** : to confer knighthood upon **2** : NAME, NICKNAME

²dub *vb* **dubbed; dub·bing** : to add sound effects to a film or broadcast

du·bi·ous \'dü-bē-əs, 'dyü-\ *adj* **1** : causing doubt : UNCERTAIN **2** : feeling doubt **3** : QUESTIONABLE — **du·bi·ous·ly** *adv*

duc·at \'dək-ət\ *n* : any of various gold coins in former use

duch·ess \'dəch-əs\ *n* **1** : the wife or widow of a duke **2** : a woman who holds the rank of a duke in her own right

¹duck \'dək\ *n* : any of a group of swimming birds that have broad flat bills and are smaller than the related geese and swans

²duck *vb* **1** : to push or pull under water for a moment **2** : to lower the head or body suddenly **3** : BOW, BOB **4** : DODGE ⟨*duck* a blow⟩ **5** : to evade a duty, question, or responsibility

³duck *n* **1** : a canvaslike usually cotton fabric **2** *pl* : clothes (as trousers) made of duck

duck·bill \'dək-,bil\ *n* : a small web-footed egg-laying mammal of Australia with a bill like that of a duck

duck·ling \'dək-ling\ *n* : a young duck

duck·weed \'dək-,wēd\ *n* : a very small free-floating stemless water plant

duct \'dəkt\ *n* : a pipe, tube, or vessel that carries something (as a bodily secretion, water, or hot air) — **duct·less** \-ləs\ *adj*

ductless gland *n* : any of several glands of which the secretions pass into the blood rather than being discharged through ducts

dud \'dəd\ *n* **1** *pl* : CLOTHES **2** : a complete failure **3** : a missile that fails to explode

dude \'düd, 'dyüd\ *n* : a man who pays excessive attention to his clothes

¹due \'dü, 'dyü\ *adj* **1** : owed or owing as a debt or a right **2** : PROPER, SUITABLE ⟨in *due* course⟩ **3** : being a consequence or result : OWING — used with *to* ⟨accidents *due* to carelessness⟩ **4** : SCHEDULED, APPOINTED

²due *n* **1** : something owed as a debt or as a right **2** *pl* : a regular or legal charge or fee

³due *adv* : DIRECTLY ⟨*due* north⟩

¹du·el \'dü-əl, 'dyü-\ *n* **1** : a combat between two persons fought with deadly weapons by agreement and in the presence of witnesses **2** : a contest between two opponents

²duel *vb* **du·eled** *or* **du·elled; du·el·ing** *or* **du·el·ling** : to fight in a duel — **du·el·ist** *n*

du·et \dü-'et, dyü-\ *n* : a composition for two performers

due to *prep* : because of

dug *past of* DIG

dug·out \'dəg-,aut\ *n* **1** : a boat made by hollowing out a log **2** : a shelter dug in the side of a hill or in the ground or in the side of a trench **3** : a low shelter facing a baseball diamond and containing the players' bench

duke \'dük, 'dyük\ *n* : a member of the highest grade of the British peerage

¹dull \'dəl\ *adj* **1** : mentally slow : STUPID **2** : lacking zest : LISTLESS ⟨was feeling *dull*⟩ **3** : slow in action : SLUGGISH ⟨business was *dull*⟩ **4** : not sharp in edge or point : BLUNT **5** : lacking brilliance or luster ⟨a *dull* finish⟩ **6** : not clear and ringing ⟨*dull* sound⟩ **7** : CLOUDY, OVERCAST **8** : not interesting : TIRESOME **9** : not vivid : having a grayish tinge ⟨a *dull* red⟩ — **dull·ness** *or* **dul·ness** *n* — **dul·ly** *adv*

²dull *vb* : to make or become dull

dull·ard \'dəl-ərd\ *n* : a stupid person

du·ly \'dü-lē, 'dyü-\ *adv* : in a due or fit manner, time, or degree

dumb \'dəm\ *adj* **1** : lacking the normal power of speech ⟨deaf and *dumb* persons⟩ **2** : naturally unable to speak ⟨*dumb* animals⟩ **3** : not willing to speak : SILENT **4** : STUPID, FOOLISH — **dumb·ly** *adv* — **dumb·ness** *n*

dumb·bell \'dəm-,bel\ *n* **1** : a weight consisting of two

dumbbell

rounded ends or discs joined by a short bar and usually used in pairs for physical exercise **2** : a stupid person

dumb·found *or* **dum·found** \,dəm-'faund\ *vb* : to strike dumb with astonishment : AMAZE

dumb·wait·er \'dəm-,wāt-ər\ *n* : a small elevator for conveying food and dishes or small goods from one story to another

dum·my \'dəm-ē\ *n, pl* **dum·mies 1** : a person who lacks or seems to lack the power of speech **2** : a stupid person **3** : an imitation of something to be used as a substitute ⟨*dummies* in a store window⟩

¹dump \'dəmp\ *vb* : to let fall in a heap

²dump *n* **1** : a place for dumping something (as trash) **2** : a place for storage of reserve military materials or the materials stored **3** : a slovenly or dilapidated place

dump·ling \'dəmp-ling\ *n* **1** : a small mass of dough cooked by boiling or steaming **2** : a dessert of fruit baked in biscuit dough

dumps \'dəmps\ *n pl* : low spirits

dump·y \'dəm-pē\ *adj* **dump·i·er; dump·i·est** : short and thick in build — **dump·i·ness** *n*

¹dun \'dən\ *n* : a slightly brownish dark gray

²dun *vb* **dunned; dun·ning** : to make repeated demands for payment

dunce \'dəns\ *n* : a stupid person

dune \'dün, 'dyün\ *n* : a hill or ridge of sand piled up by the wind

dung \'dəng\ *n* : MANURE

dun·ga·ree \,dəng-gə-'rē\ *n* **1** : a heavy coarse cotton cloth **2** *pl* : trousers or work clothes made of dungaree

dun·geon \'dən-jən\ *n* : a close dark usually underground prison

dung·hill \'dəng-,hil\ *n* : a manure pile

dunk \'dəngk\ *vb* : to dip (as bread) into liquid (as coffee or tea)

du·o \'dü-ō, 'dyü-\ *n, pl* **du·os 1** : a duet especially for two performers at two pianos **2** : PAIR

¹dupe \'düp, 'dyüp\ *n* : one who has been or is easily deceived or cheated

²dupe *vb* **duped; dup·ing** : to make a dupe of

du·plex \'dü-,pleks, 'dyü-\ *adj* : DOUBLE

¹du·pli·cate \'dü-pli-kət, 'dyü-\ *adj* **1** : having two parts exactly the same or alike : DOUBLE **2** : being the same as another

²duplicate *n* : a thing that is exactly like another : COPY ⟨a sale of library *duplicates*⟩

³du·pli·cate \'dü-pli-,kāt, 'dyü-\ *vb* **du·pli·cat·ed; du·pli·cat·ing 1** : to make double **2** : to make an exact copy of

du·ra·bil·i·ty \,dur-ə-'bil-ət-ē, ,dyur-\ *n* : ability to last or to stand hard or continued use

du·ra·ble \'dur-ə-bəl, 'dyur-\ *adj* : able to

last a long time **syn** see LASTING — **du·ra·ble·ness** *n* — **du·ra·bly** \-blē\ *adv*

du·ra·tion \du̇·'rā-shən, dyu̇-\ *n* : the time during which something exists or lasts

dur·ing \ˌdu̇r-ing, ˌdyu̇r-\ *prep* **1** : throughout the course of ⟨*during* the last century⟩ **2** : at some point in the course of

dusk \'dəsk\ *n* **1** : the darker part of twilight especially at night **2** : partial darkness

dusk·y \'dəs-kē\ *adj* **dusk·i·er; dusk·i·est 1** : somewhat dark in color : BLACKISH **2** : somewhat dark : DIM — **dusk·i·ness** *n*

¹dust \'dəst\ *n* **1** : fine dry powdery particles (as of earth) : a fine powder **2** : the earthy remains of bodies once alive **3** : something worthless **4** : the surface of the ground — **dust·less** \-ləs\ *adj*

²dust *vb* **1** : to free from dust : brush or wipe away dust **2** : to sprinkle with fine particles **3** : to sprinkle in the form of dust

dust·er \'dəs-tər\ *n* **1** : one that dusts **2** : a garment to protect clothing from dust

dust·pan \'dəst-ˌpan\ *n* : a shovel-shaped pan for sweepings

dust storm *n* : a violent dust=bearing wind moving across a dry region

dustpan

dust·y \'dəs-tē\ *adj* **dust·i·er; dust·i·est 1** : filled or covered with dust **2** : resembling dust

¹Dutch \'dəch\ *adj* : of or relating to the Netherlands, the Dutch people, or Dutch

²Dutch *n* **1 Dutch** *pl* : the people of the Netherlands **2** : the language of the Dutch

Dutch door *n* : a door divided so that the lower part can be shut while the upper part remains open

Dutch treat *n* : a treat for which each person pays his own way

du·ti·a·ble \'düt-ē-ə-bəl, 'dyüt-\ *adj* : subject to a duty ⟨*dutiable* imports⟩

Dutch door

du·ti·ful \'düt-i-fəl, 'dyüt-\ *adj* : having or showing a sense of duty ⟨a *dutiful* son⟩ — **du·ti·ful·ly** *adv* — **du·ti·ful·ness** *n*

du·ty \'düt-ē, 'dyüt-\ *n, pl* **du·ties 1** : conduct due to parents and superiors **2** : the action required by one's position or occupation **3** : something a person is morally bound to do **4** : a tax especially on imports into a country **5** : the service required of a machine or a manufactured article **syn** see OBLIGATION

¹dwarf \'dwȯrf\ *n, pl* **dwarfs** \'dwȯrfs\ *also* **dwarves** \'dwȯrvz\ **1** : a person, animal, or plant much below normal size **2** : a small legendary manlike being usually pictured as deformed and ugly

²dwarf *vb* **1** : to hinder from growing to natural size : STUNT ⟨*dwarf* a tree⟩ **2** : to cause to appear smaller

³dwarf *adj* : of less than the usual size

dwell \'dwel\ *vb* **dwelt** \'dwelt\ *or* **dwelled** \'dweld\; **dwell·ing 1** : to stay for a while : REMAIN, LINGER **2** : to live in a place : RESIDE **3** : to keep the attention directed **4** : to write or speak at length — **dwell·er** *n*

dwell·ing \'dwel-ing\ *n* : HOUSE, RESIDENCE

dwin·dle \'dwin-dəl\ *vb* **dwin·dled; dwin·dling** : to make or become less : waste away

¹dye \'dī\ *n* **1** : a color produced by dyeing **2** : a material used for dyeing

²dye *vb* **dyed; dye·ing 1** : to give a new color to especially by treating with a dye **2** : to take up color from dyeing — **dy·er** *n*

dye·stuff \'dī-ˌstəf\ *n* : material used for dyeing

dying *pres part of* DIE

dyke *var of* DIKE

dy·nam·ic \dī-'nam-ik\ *adj* [from Greek *dynamikos* "powerful", from *dynamis* "power"] : full of energy : ACTIVE, FORCEFUL

¹dy·na·mite \'dī-nə-ˌmīt\ *n* : an explosive much used in blasting

²dynamite *vb* **dy·na·mit·ed; dy·na·mit·ing** : to blow up with dynamite — **dy·na·mit·er** *n*

dy·na·mo \'dī-nə-ˌmō\ *n, pl* **dy·na·mos** : a machine for producing electric current : GENERATOR

dynamo

dy·nas·ty \'dī-nəs-tē\ *n, pl* **dy·nas·ties** : a series of rulers of the same family or line of descent

dys·en·ter·y \'dis-n-ˌter-ē\ *n* : a disease marked by severe diarrhea with the passage of mucus and blood

dys·tro·phy \'dis-trə-fē\ *n* : a disorder of nerves and muscles often with wasting away of body tissue

e \'ē\ *n, often cap* **1** : the fifth letter of the English alphabet **2** : a grade rating a student's work as poor and usually constituting a conditional pass

¹each \'ēch\ *adj* : being one of two or more considered separately

²each *pron* : each one

³each *adv* : to or for each : APIECE

each other *pron* : each the other : one another

ea·ger \'ē-gər\ *adj* : desiring very much : IMPATIENT — **ea·ger·ly** *adv* — **ea·ger·ness** *n*

ea·gle \'ē-gəl\ *n* : any of several large birds of prey noted for keenness of vision and powers of flight

ea·glet \'ē-glət\ *n* : a young eagle

-ean — see -AN

¹ear \'iər\ *n* **1** : the organ of hearing **2** : the sense of hearing ⟨a good *ear* for music⟩ **3** : willing or sympathetic attention ⟨give *ear* to a request⟩ **4** : something that resembles an ear in shape or position — **eared** \'iərd\ *adj*

²ear *n* : the seed-bearing spike of a cereal grass (as wheat, rice, or Indian corn)

ear·ache \'iər-,āk\ *n* : an ache or pain in the ear

ear·drum \'iər-,drəm\ *n* : the membrane that separates the outer and middle parts of the ear and vibrates when sound waves strike it

earl \'ərl\ *n* : a member of the British peerage ranking below a marquess and above a viscount

ear of corn

¹ear·ly \'ər-lē\ *adv* **ear·li·er**; **ear·li·est** **1** : at or near the beginning of a period of time or a series ⟨get up *early*⟩ **2** : before the usual time

²early *adj* **ear·li·er**; **ear·li·est** : occurring near the beginning or before the usual time

ear·muff \'iər-,məf\ *n* : one of a pair of pads joined by a flexible band and worn to protect the ears from cold

earn \'ərn\ *vb* **1** : to deserve as a result of labor or service **2** : to get for services given

ear·nest \'ər-nəst\ *adj* : not light or playful : SERIOUS ⟨an *earnest* plea for help⟩ **syn** see SERIOUS — **ear·nest·ly** *adv* — **ear·nest·ness** *n*

earn·ings \'ər-ningz\ *n pl* : money received as wages or gained as profit

ear·phone \'iər-,fōn\ *n* : a device that converts electrical energy into sound and is worn over the opening of the ear or inserted into it

ear·ring \'iər-,ring\ *n* : an ornament worn on the ear

ear·shot \'iər-,shät\ *n* : the range within which an unaided human voice can be heard

earth \'ərth\ *n* **1** : SOIL, DIRT **2** : the land as distinguished from the sea and the air **3** *often cap* : the planet that we live on

earth·en \'ər-thən\ *adj* : made of earth

earth·en·ware \'ər-thən-,waər\ *n* : dishes, bowls, and ornaments of baked clay

earth·ly \'ərth-lē\ *adj* **1** : having to do with or belonging to the earth : not heavenly ⟨*earthly* joys⟩ **2** : POSSIBLE, IMAGINABLE

earth·quake \'ərth-,kwāk\ *n* : a shaking or trembling of a portion of the earth

earth·worm \'ərth-,wərm\ *n* : a worm with a long body made up of similar segments that lives in damp soil

earth·y \'ər-thē\ *adj* **earth·i·er**; **earth·i·est** **1** : consisting of or resembling earth **2** : PRACTICAL **3** : not polite : COARSE ⟨*earthy* humor⟩

ear·wig \'iər-,wig\ *n* [from Old English *ēarwicga*, a compound of *ēare* "ear" and *wicga* "insect"; probably so called from the belief that the insect crawls into human ears] : an insect with long slender feelers and a large forcepslike organ at the end of its abdomen

earwig

¹ease \'ēz\ *n* **1** : freedom from pain or trouble : comfort of body or mind ⟨a life of *ease*⟩ **2** : freedom from any sense or feeling of difficulty or embarrassment

²ease *vb* **eased**; **eas·ing** **1** : to free from discomfort or worry : RELIEVE **2** : to make less tight : LOOSEN **3** : to move very carefully

ea·sel \'ē-zəl\ *n* : a frame for holding a flat surface in an upright position

eas·i·ly \'ē-zə-lē\ *adv* **1** : in an easy manner : without difficulty ⟨won the race *easily*⟩ **2** : without doubt or question

¹east \'ēst\ *adv* : to or toward the east

²east *adj* : situated toward or coming from the east

³east *n* **1** : the direction of sunrise : the compass point opposite to west **2** *cap* : regions or countries east of a specified or implied point

east·bound \'ēst-,baund\ *adj* : going east

Eas·ter \'ēs-tər\ *n* : a church festival observed in memory of the Resurrection

Easter lily *n* : a white garden lily that blooms in spring

east·er·ly \'ēs-tər-lē\ *adv* (*or adj*) **1** : from the east ⟨an *easterly* wind⟩ **2** : toward the east

east·ern \'ēs-tərn\ *adj* **1** *often cap* : of or relating to a region usually called East **2** : lying toward or coming from the east

¹east·ward \'ēst-wərd\ *adv* (*or adj*) : toward the east

²eastward *n* : an eastward direction or part

eas·y \'ē-zē\ *adj* **eas·i·er**; **eas·i·est** **1** : not hard to do or get : not difficult ⟨an *easy* lesson⟩ **2** : not hard to please ⟨an *easy* teacher⟩ **3** : COMFORTABLE ⟨*easy* chair⟩ **4** : showing ease : NATURAL ⟨an *easy* manner⟩ **5** : free from pain, trouble, or worry ⟨an *easy* mind⟩

eat \'ēt\ *vb* **ate** \'āt\; **eat·en** \'ēt-n\; **eat·ing** **1** : to chew and swallow food **2** : to take a meal or meals ⟨*eat* at home⟩ **3** : to use up or destroy : wear away — **eat·er** *n*

¹eat·a·ble \'ēt-ə-bəl\ *adj* : fit to be eaten

²eat·a·ble *n* **1** : something eatable **2** *pl* : FOOD

eaves \'ēvz\ *n pl* : the overhanging lower edge of a roof

eaves·drop \'ēvz-ˌdräp\ *vb* **eaves·dropped**; **eaves·drop·ping** : to listen secretly to private conversation

eaves

¹ebb \'eb\ *n* **1** : the flowing out of the tide **2** : a passing from a high to a low point : a time of decline

²ebb *vb* **1** : to flow out or away : RECEDE **2** : WEAKEN, DECLINE

¹eb·o·ny \'eb-ə-nē\ *n, pl* **eb·o·nies** : a hard heavy durable wood obtained from various tropical trees related to the persimmon

²ebony *adj* **1** : made of or resembling ebony **2** : BLACK

¹ec·cen·tric \ek-'sen-trik\ *adj* **1** : acting or thinking in a strange way ⟨an *eccentric* old man⟩ **2** : QUEER, UNUSUAL ⟨*eccentric* actions⟩

²eccentric *n* : an eccentric person

ec·cle·si·as·ti·cal \i-ˌklē-zē-'as-ti-kəl\ *adj* : of or relating to the church or its affairs

¹ech·o \'ek-ō\ *n, pl* **ech·oes** : the repetition of a sound already heard caused by the throwing back of the sound waves

²echo *vb* **1** : to send back or repeat a sound **2** : to repeat the words of someone else

é·clair \ā-'klaər\ *n* : an oblong pastry with whipped cream or custard filling

¹e·clipse \i-'klips\ *n* **1** : a complete or partial hiding of the sun caused by the moon's passing between the sun and the earth **2** : a darkening of the moon caused by the moon's entering the shadow of the earth **3** : the obscuring of any celestial body by another **4** : a falling into decline or disgrace

²eclipse *vb* **e·clipsed**; **e·clips·ing** **1** : to cause an eclipse of **2** : to make appear less bright by hiding or by outshining

ec·o·nom·ic \ˌek-ə-'näm-ik, ˌē-kə-\ *adj* **1** : of or relating to the science of economics **2** : of, relating to, or based on the production, distribution, and consumption of goods and services

ec·o·nom·i·cal \ˌek-ə-'näm-i-kəl, ˌē-kə-\ *adj* : managing or managed without waste : THRIFTY — **ec·o·nom·i·cal·ly** *adv*

ec·o·nom·ics \ˌek-ə-'näm-iks, ˌē-kə-\ *n* : the science that studies and explains facts about the production, distribution, and consumption of goods and services

e·con·o·mize \i-'kän-ə-ˌmīz\ *vb* **e·con·o·mized**; **e·con·o·miz·ing** **1** : to be economical : be thrifty **2** : to reduce expenses : SAVE

e·con·o·my \i-'kän-ə-mē\ *n, pl* **e·con·o·mies** [from early French *yconomie* "management of household expenses", derived from Greek *oikonomia*, a compound from *oikos* "house" and *nemein* "to manage"] : the practice of economizing : the careful use of money and goods : THRIFT

ec·sta·sy \'ek-stə-sē\ *n, pl* **ec·sta·sies** : very great happiness : extreme delight

ec·stat·ic \ek-'stat-ik\ *adj* **1** : full of joy and rapture : deeply happy **2** : causing ecstasy

¹-ed \d *after a vowel or* b, g, j, l, m, n, ng, r, th, v, z, zh; əd, id *after* d, t; t *after other sounds*\ *vb suffix or adj suffix* **1** — used to form the past participle of verbs ⟨end*ed*⟩ ⟨fad*ed*⟩ ⟨tri*ed*⟩ ⟨patt*ed*⟩ **2** : having : characterized by ⟨cultur*ed*⟩ ⟨two-stori*ed*⟩ **3** : having the characteristics of ⟨bigot*ed*⟩

²-ed *vb suffix* — used to form the past tense of verbs ⟨judg*ed*⟩ ⟨deni*ed*⟩ ⟨dropp*ed*⟩

¹ed·dy \'ed-ē\ *n, pl* **ed·dies** : a current of air or water running contrary to the main current or in a circle

²eddy *vb* **ed·died**; **ed·dy·ing** : to move in an eddy

¹edge \'ej\ *n* **1** : the cutting side of a blade **2** : the line where a surface ends : MARGIN, BORDER — **edged** \'ejd\ *adj* — **on edge** : NERVOUS, TENSE

²edge *vb* **edged**; **edg·ing** **1** : to give an edge to **2** : to move slowly and little by little

edge·ways \'ej-ˌwāz\ *or* **edge·wise** \-ˌwīz\ *adv* : with the edge foremost : SIDEWAYS

ed·i·ble \'ed-ə-bəl\ *adj* : fit or safe to eat

e·dict \'ē-ˌdikt\ *n* : a command or law given or made by an authority (as a ruler)

ed·i·fice \'ed-ə-fəs\ *n* : a large or impressive building (as a church)

ed·it \'ed-ət\ *vb* **1** : to correct, revise, and prepare for publication : collect and arrange material to be printed ⟨*edit* a book of poems⟩ **2** : to be in charge of the publication of something (as an encyclopedia or a newspaper) that is the work of many writers

e·di·tion \i-'dish-ən\ *n* **1** : the form in which a book is published ⟨an illustrated *edition*⟩ **2** : the whole number of copies of a book, magazine, or newspaper published at one time

ed·i·tor \'ed-ət-ər\ *n* **1** : a person who edits **2** : a person who writes editorials

¹ed·i·to·ri·al \ˌed-ə-'tōr-ē-əl\ *adj* **1** : of or relating to an editor ⟨an *editorial* office⟩ **2** : being or resembling an editorial

²editorial *n* : a newspaper or magazine article that gives the opinions of editor or publisher

ed·u·cate \'ej-ə-ˌkāt\ *vb* **ed·u·cat·ed**; **ed·u·cat·ing** **1** : to provide schooling for **2** : to develop mentally and morally especially by formal instruction : TRAIN

ed·u·ca·tion \ˌej-ə-'kā-shən\ *n* **1** : the act or process of educating : training through study or instruction : SCHOOLING **2** : knowledge, skill, and development gained from study or training **3** : the study or science of the methods and problems of teaching

ed·u·ca·tion·al \ˌej-ə-'kā-shən-l\ *adj* **1** : having to do with education **2** : offering information or something of value in learning ⟨*educational* film⟩ — **ed·u·ca·tion·al·ly** *adv*

¹-ee \'ē, ˌē\ *n suffix* **1** : recipient or beneficiary of a specified action or thing ⟨appointee⟩ ⟨grantee⟩ ⟨patentee⟩ **2** : person that performs a specified action ⟨escapee⟩

²-ee *n suffix* **1** : a particular and especially a small kind of ⟨bootee⟩ **2** : one resembling or suggestive of ⟨goatee⟩

eel \'ēl\ *n* : a long snakelike fish with a smooth slimy skin

e'en \ēn\ *adv* : EVEN

-eer \'iər\ *n suffix* : one that is concerned with or conducts or produces professionally ⟨auctioneer⟩ ⟨pamphleteer⟩

e'er \eər\ *adv* : EVER

ee·rie *also* **ee·ry** \'iər-ē\ *adj* **ee·ri·er; ee·ri·est** : arousing fear and uneasiness : STRANGE

ef·face \i-'fās\ *vb* **ef·faced; ef·fac·ing** : to erase or blot out completely ⟨*efface* an inscription⟩ ⟨*efface* unpleasant memories⟩

¹ef·fect \i-'fekt\ *n* **1** : an event, condition, or state of affairs that is produced by a cause : the result of something that has been done or has happened : OUTCOME **2** : EXECUTION, OPERATION ⟨the law went into *effect* today⟩ **3** : REALITY, FACT **4** : the act of making a particular impression **5** : INFLUENCE ⟨the *effect* of climate on growth⟩ **6** *pl* : GOODS, POSSESSIONS ⟨household *effects*⟩

²effect *vb* : to bring about **syn** see AFFECT

ef·fec·tive \i-'fek-tiv\ *adj* **1** : producing a desired effect : likely to bring about a desired result ⟨*effective* measures to reduce traffic accidents⟩ **2** : IMPRESSIVE ⟨an *effective* speech⟩ **3** : being in actual operation ⟨the law will become *effective* next year⟩ — **ef·fec·tive·ly** *adv* — **ef·fec·tive·ness** *n*

ef·fec·tu·al \i-'fek-chə-wəl\ *adj* : producing or able to produce a desired effect

ef·fi·ca·cy \'ef-i-kə-sē\ *n, pl* **ef·fi·ca·cies** : power to produce effects : efficient action

ef·fi·cien·cy \i-'fish-ən-sē\ *n, pl* **ef·fi·cien·cies** : the quality or degree of being efficient

ef·fi·cient \i-'fish-ənt\ *adj* : capable of accomplishing what is undertaken especially without waste — **ef·fi·cient·ly** *adv*

ef·fort \'ef-ərt\ *n* **1** : hard work of mind or body : EXERTION **2** : ATTEMPT, TRY

ef·fort·less \'ef-ərt-ləs\ *adj* : showing or requiring little or no effort — **ef·fort·less·ly** *adv*

¹egg \'eg\ *vb* : URGE, ENCOURAGE

²egg *n* **1** : a hard-shelled oval or rounded body by which a bird reproduces and from which its young hatches out **2** : an egg cell usually together with its protective coverings

egg cell *n* : a cell that is produced by an ovary and when fertilized by a sperm cell can develop into an embryo and finally a new mature being

egg·plant \'eg-ˌplant\ *n* : an oval vegetable with a usually glossy purplish skin and white flesh that is the fruit of a plant related to the tomato

eggplant

egg·shell \'eg-ˌshel\ *n* : the shell of an egg

e·gret \'ē-grət, i-'gret\ *n* : any of various herons that have long plumes during the breeding season

¹E·gyp·tian \i-'jip-shən\ *adj* : of or relating to Egypt, the people of Egypt, or Egyptian

²Egyptian *n* **1** : a native or inhabitant of Egypt **2** : the language of the ancient Egyptians

ei·der \'īd-ər\ *n* : a large northern sea duck that is mostly white above and black below and has very soft down

ei·der·down \'īd-ər-ˌdaủn\ *n* **1** : the down of the eider used for filling quilts and pillows **2** : a quilt filled with down

¹eight \'āt\ *adj* : being one more than seven

²eight *n* **1** : one more than seven **2** : the eighth in a set or series

¹eigh·teen \ā-'tēn\ *adj* : being one more than seventeen

²eighteen *n* : one more than seventeen

¹eigh·teenth \ā-'tēnth\ *adj* : being next after the seventeenth

²eighteenth *n* : number eighteen in a series

¹eighth \'ātth\ *adj* : being next after the seventh

²eighth *n* **1** : number eight in a series **2** : one of eight equal parts

¹eight·i·eth \'āt-ē-əth\ *adj* : being next after the seventy-ninth

²eightieth *n* : number eighty in a series

¹eight·y \'āt-ē\ *adj* : being eight times ten

²eighty *n* : eight times ten

¹ei·ther \'ē-thər, 'ī-\ *adj* **1** : each of two : EACH ⟨flowers on *either* side of the road⟩ **2** : one or the other ⟨take *either* road⟩

²either *pron* : the one or the other

³either *conj* — used before two or more words or phrases of which the last is preceded by *or* to show that they represent different choices or possibilities ⟨a statement is *either* true or false⟩

e·jac·u·late \i-'jak-yə-‚lāt\ *vb* **e·jac·u·lat·ed; e·jac·u·lat·ing** : EXCLAIM

e·ject \i-'jekt\ *vb* : to drive or throw forth or out ⟨*eject* a disorderly person from a meeting⟩

eke out \'ēk-‚aút\ *vb* **eked out; ek·ing out** **1** : to add to bit by bit ⟨*eked out* a small income by sewing⟩　**2** : to gain by scanty and uncertain means ⟨*eked out* a living⟩

¹e·lab·o·rate \i-'lab-ə-rət\ *adj* : worked out with great care or with much detail

²e·lab·o·rate \i-'lab-ə-‚rāt\ *vb* **e·lab·o·rat·ed; e·lab·o·rat·ing** : to work out in detail

e·lapse \i-'laps\ *vb* **e·lapsed; e·laps·ing** : to slip or glide away : go by : PASS

¹e·las·tic \i-'las-tik\ *adj* : capable of returning to original shape or size after being stretched, pressed, or squeezed together : SPRINGY

²elastic *n* **1** : an elastic fabric made of yarns containing rubber　**2** : a rubber band

e·las·tic·i·ty \i-‚las-'tis-ət-ē\ *n* : the quality or state of being elastic

e·late \i-'lāt\ *vb* **e·lat·ed; e·lat·ing** : to fill with joy or pride

e·la·tion \i-'lā-shən\ *n* : a lifting up of the mind or spirit : the state of being elated

¹el·bow \'el-‚bō\ *n* **1** : the joint of the arm or of the same part of an animal's forelimb　**2** : the outer part of the bent arm　**3** : a part (as of a pipe) bent like an elbow

elbows 3

²elbow *vb* : to push or force a passage with the elbows

¹el·der \'el-dər\ *n* : a shrub or small tree related to the honeysuckles that has flat clusters of white flowers followed by berrylike fruits

²elder *adj* : OLDER ⟨an *elder* brother⟩

³elder *n* **1** : one who is older　**2** : a person having authority because of age and experience ⟨*elders* of the village⟩　**3** : an official in certain churches

el·der·ber·ry \'el-dər-‚ber-ē\ *n, pl* **el·der·ber·ries** : the juicy black or red fruit of the elder

el·der·ly \'el-dər-lē\ *adj* : somewhat old : past middle age

el·dest \'el-dəst\ *adj* : OLDEST

¹e·lect \i-'lekt\ *adj* : chosen for office but not yet holding office ⟨the president-*elect*⟩

²elect *vb* **1** : to select by vote ⟨*elect* a chairman⟩　**2** : to choose between alternatives ⟨the home team *elected* to kick off⟩

elderberries

e·lec·tion \i-'lek-shən\ *n* : an electing or being elected especially by vote

e·lec·tive \i-'lek-tiv\ *adj* : chosen or filled by popular election ⟨an *elective* political office⟩

e·lec·tor \i-'lek-tər\ *n* : one qualified or entitled to vote in an election

electr- *or* **electro-** *prefix* **1** : electricity ⟨*electro*meter⟩　**2** : electric ⟨*electro*de⟩　**3** : electric and ⟨*electro*chemical⟩　**4** : electrically ⟨*electro*positive⟩

e·lec·tric \i-'lek-trik\ *or* **e·lec·tri·cal** \-tri-kəl\ *adj* [from *electricus* meaning "produced from amber by friction", "electric" in the Latin of modern science, taken from the old Latin noun *electrum* "amber", from Greek *ēlektron*]　**1** : of or relating to electricity or its use ⟨an *electric* current⟩ ⟨*electrical* engineering⟩　**2** : heated, moved, produced, or operated by electricity ⟨an *electric* iron⟩ ⟨an *electric* locomotive⟩　**3** : having an effect like an electric shock : THRILLING — **e·lec·tri·cal·ly** *adv*

electric eel *n* : a large eellike South American fish that produces enough electricity to give a person a severe shock

e·lec·tri·cian \i-‚lek-'trish-ən\ *n* : one who installs, operates, or repairs electrical equipment

e·lec·tric·i·ty \i-‚lek-'tris-ət-ē\ *n* **1** : an important form of energy that is found in nature but that can be artificially produced by rubbing together two unlike things (as glass and silk), by the action of chemicals, or by means of a dynamo　**2** : electric current

e·lec·tri·fy \i-'lek-trə-‚fī\ *vb* **e·lec·tri·fied; e·lec·tri·fy·ing** **1** : to charge with electricity　**2** : to equip for use of electric power ⟨*electrify* a railroad⟩　**3** : to supply with electric power　**4** : to excite suddenly and sharply : THRILL

e·lec·tro·cute \i-'lek-trə-‚kyüt\ *vb* **e·lec·tro·cut·ed; e·lec·tro·cut·ing** : to kill by an electric shock

e·lec·trode \i-'lek-‚trōd\ *n* : a conductor (as a metal or carbon) used to make electrical contact with a part of an electrical circuit that is not metallic

e·lec·trol·y·sis \i-‚lek-'träl-ə-səs\ *n* : the producing of chemical changes by passage of an electric current through a liquid

e·lec·tro·lyte \i-'lek-trə-‚līt\ *n* : a substance (as an acid or salt) that when dissolved in something (as water) conducts an electric current

e·lec·tro·lyt·ic \i-‚lek-trə-'lit-ik\ *adj* : of or relating to electrolysis or an electrolyte

e·lec·tro·mag·net \i-‚lek-trō-'mag-nət\ *n* : a piece of soft iron encircled by a coil of wire through which an electric current is passed to magnetize the iron

---

j job　　ng sing　　ō low　　ȯ moth　　ȯi coin　　th thin　　th̲ this　　ü boot　　ú foot　　y you　　yü few　　yú furious　　zh vision

e·lec·tro·mag·net·ic wave \i-ˌlek-trō-mag-ˌnet-ik-\ *n* : a wave (as a radio wave or wave of light) that travels at the speed of light and consists of a combined electric and magnetic effect

e·lec·tron \i-ˈlek-ˌträn\ *n* : a very small particle that has a negative charge of electricity and forms the part of an atom outside the nucleus

e·lec·tron·ic \i-ˌlek-ˈträn-ik\ *adj* : of or relating to electrons or to the devices of electronics

e·lec·tron·ics \i-ˌlek-ˈträn-iks\ *n* : a science that deals with the giving off, behavior, and effects of electrons in vacuums, gases, and semiconductors and with devices using such electrons

electron tube *n* : a device in which conduction of electricity by electrons takes place through a vacuum or a gas within a sealed container and which has various uses (as in radio and television)

e·lec·tro·scope \i-ˈlek-trə-ˌskōp\ *n* : an instrument for detecting the presence of an electric charge on a body and for determining whether the charge is positive or negative

el·e·gance \ˈel-i-gəns\ *n* **1** : refined gracefulness **2** : tasteful richness of design or ornamentation

el·e·gant \ˈel-i-gənt\ *adj* : showing good taste (as in dress or manners) : marked by beauty and refinement — **el·e·gant·ly** *adv*

el·e·gy \ˈel-ə-jē\ *n, pl* **el·e·gies** : a sad or mournful poem usually expressing sorrow for one who is dead

el·e·ment \ˈel-ə-mənt\ *n* **1** : one of the parts of which something is made up **2** : one of the simplest principles of a study : something that must be learned before one can advance ⟨the *elements* of arithmetic⟩ **3** : a member of a given mathematical set **4** : any of more than 100 substances that cannot by ordinary chemical means be separated into different substances ⟨gold and carbon are *elements*⟩

el·e·men·ta·ry \ˌel-ə-ˈment-ə-rē\ *adj* : of or relating to the beginnings or first principles of a subject ⟨*elementary* arithmetic⟩

el·e·phant \ˈel-ə-fənt\ *n* : a huge thickset mammal with the snout prolonged as a trunk and two long curved tusks

el·e·vate \ˈel-ə-ˌvāt\ *vb* **el·e·vat·ed; el·e·vat·ing** : to lift up : RAISE ⟨*elevate* a flag⟩

el·e·va·tion \ˌel-ə-ˈvā-shən\ *n* **1** : the act of elevating : the condition of being elevated **2** : a raised place (as a hill) **3** : height especially above sea level : ALTITUDE ⟨a hill with an *elevation* of 1500 feet⟩ **syn** see HEIGHT

el·e·va·tor \ˈel-ə-ˌvāt-ər\ *n* **1** : an endless belt or chain conveyer for raising material **2** : a cage or platform that can be raised or lowered for carrying persons or goods from one level to another **3** : a building for storing grain **4** : a winglike device on an airplane to produce motion up or down

elevator

¹e·lev·en \i-ˈlev-ən\ *adj* : being one more than ten

²eleven *n* **1** : one more than ten **2** : a football team

¹e·lev·enth \i-ˈlev-ənth\ *adj* : being next after the tenth

²eleventh *n* : number eleven in a series

elf \ˈelf\ *n, pl* **elves** \ˈelvz\ : a small often mischievous fairy or sprite

elf·in \ˈel-fən\ *adj* **1** : of or relating to elves **2** : having a strange beauty or charm

e·lic·it \i-ˈlis-ət\ *vb* : to draw forth or bring out something not yet known or told often by skillful questioning or discussion

el·i·gi·ble \ˈel-i-jə-bəl\ *adj* : qualified to be chosen : satisfying all requirements

e·lim·i·nate \i-ˈlim-ə-ˌnāt\ *vb* **e·lim·i·nat·ed; e·lim·i·nat·ing** : to get rid of : do away with

e·lim·i·na·tion \i-ˌlim-ə-ˈnā-shən\ *n* : an eliminating or expelling especially of waste from the body

elk \ˈelk\ *n* **1** : a large deer of Europe and Asia with broad spreading antlers like those of a moose **2** : a large North American deer with curved antlers having many branches

el·lipse \i-ˈlips\ *n* : a closed curve having the shape of an elongated circle

el·lip·tic \i-ˈlip-tik\ *or* **el·lip·ti·cal** \-ti-kəl\ *adj* : of or resembling an ellipse : OVAL

ellipses

elm \ˈelm\ *n* : a tall shade tree with a broad rather flat top and spreading branches

el·o·cu·tion \ˌel-ə-ˈkyü-shən\ *n* : the art of reading or speaking effectively in public

e·lo·de·a \i-ˈlōd-ē-ə\ *n* : a common floating water plant with small green leaves

elm leaves

e·lon·gate \i-ˈlȯng-ˌgāt\ *vb* **e·lon·gat·ed; e·lon·gat·ing** **1** : to extend the length of **2** : to grow in length

e·lope \i-ˈlōp\ *vb* **e·loped; e·lop·ing** : to run away to be married — **e·lope·ment** *n*

el·o·quence \ˈel-ə-kwəns\ *n* **1** : speaking or writing that has force and ease **2** : the art

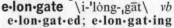

or power of speaking or writing forcefully or persuasively

el·o·quent \'el-ə-kwənt\ *adj* **1** : expressing oneself or expressed with ease and force ⟨an *eloquent* speaker⟩ **2** : movingly expressive or revealing ⟨an *eloquent* look⟩ — **el·o·quent·ly** *adv*

¹else \'els\ *adv* **1** : in a different manner or place or at a different time ⟨nowhere *else* to go⟩ **2** : if not : OTHERWISE

²else *adj* **1** : being other and different ⟨ask someone *else*⟩ **2** : being in addition : MORE

else·where \'els-,hweər\ *adv* : in or to another place

e·lude \i-'lüd\ *vb* **e·lud·ed; e·lud·ing** : to avoid or escape by being quick, skillful, or tricky

e·lu·sive \i-'lü-siv\ *adj* **1** : skillful in eluding **2** : hard to comprehend or define

elves *pl of* ELF

em- — see EN-

e·man·ci·pate \i-'man-sə-,pāt\ *vb* **e·man·ci·pat·ed; e·man·ci·pat·ing** : to set free from restraint or slavery : LIBERATE

e·man·ci·pa·tion \i-,man-sə-'pā-shən\ *n* : a setting free ⟨the *emancipation* of slaves⟩

em·balm \im-'bäm\ *vb* : to treat a dead body so as to preserve it from decay — **em·balm·er** *n*

em·bark \im-'bärk\ *vb* **1** : to go on or put on board a ship or an airplane **2** : to begin some enterprise or undertaking

em·bar·rass \im-'bar-əs\ *vb* **1** : HAMPER, HINDER **2** : to make confused or upset in mind — **em·bar·rass·ment** *n*

syn EMBARRASS, HUMILIATE both mean to make uncomfortable or unhappy from a feeling of shame or loss of confidence. EMBARRASS implies the causing of a confused and uncertain state of mind that makes it difficult to speak and act freely and naturally ⟨most people are *embarrassed* by direct compliments⟩ HUMILIATE implies the producing of a deeper and more lasting feeling of shame and a loss of self-respect ⟨the boy was *humiliated* by the teacher's ridicule of him in class⟩

em·bas·sy \'em-bə-sē\ *n, pl* **em·bas·sies 1** : an ambassador and his assistants **2** : the residence or office of an ambassador

em·bed \im-'bed\ *vb* **em·bed·ded; em·bed·ding** : to set solidly in or as if in a bed

em·bel·lish \im-'bel-ish\ *vb* : to add ornamental details to : ADORN, DECORATE **syn** see ADORN — **em·bel·lish·ment** *n*

em·ber \'em-bər\ *n* : a glowing piece of coal or wood in the ashes from a fire

em·bez·zle \im-'bez-əl\ *vb* **em·bez·zled; em·bez·zling** : to take for one's own use property (as money) entrusted to one's care : STEAL

em·bit·ter \im-'bit-ər\ *vb* : to make bitter or more bitter : arouse bitter feeling in

em·blem \'em-bləm\ *n* : an object or a likeness of an object used to suggest a thing that cannot be pictured : SYMBOL

syn EMBLEM, SYMBOL, TOKEN all mean a visible thing that stands for something that cannot be pictured. EMBLEM usually applies to an object or a pictorial device that represents a group such as a family, an organization, or a nation ⟨the eagle is one of our national *emblems*⟩ SYMBOL may apply to anything that serves as an outward sign for something else and especially for something ideal, abstract, or spiritual ⟨the lion is the *symbol* of courage⟩ TOKEN applies to an object or an act that gives evidence of the existence of something else ⟨an engagement ring is a *token* of a promise to marry⟩

em·blem·at·ic \,em-blə-'mat-ik\ *adj* : of, relating to, or constituting an emblem

em·bod·y \im-'bäd-ē\ *vb* **em·bod·ied; em·bod·y·ing 1** : to bring together so as to form a body or system ⟨the basic laws of the United States are *embodied* in its constitution⟩ **2** : to make a part of a body or system ⟨*embody* a new law in a state constitution⟩ **3** : to represent in visible form

em·bold·en \im-'bōl-dən\ *vb* : to make bold

em·boss \im-'bäs, -'bȯs\ *vb* : to ornament with a pattern having a raised surface

¹em·brace \im-'brās\ *vb* **em·braced; em·brac·ing** [from early French *embracer*, from *en-* "in" and *brace* "two arms"] **1** : to clasp in the arms : HUG **2** : ENCIRCLE, ENCLOSE ⟨low hills *embraced* the valley⟩ **3** : to take up : ADOPT, WELCOME ⟨*embrace* an opportunity⟩ **4** : to take in : INCLUDE

²embrace *n* : an encircling with the arms

em·broi·der \im-'brȯid-ər\ *vb* **1** : to make or fill in a design with needlework ⟨*embroider* a flower on a towel⟩ **2** : to ornament with needlework **3** : to add to the interest of (as a story) with details far beyond the truth

em·broi·der·y \im-'brȯid-ə-rē\ *n, pl* **em·broi·der·ies 1** : needlework done to decorate cloth **2** : the act or art of embroidering

em·bry·o \'em-brē-,ō\ *n, pl* **em·bry·os 1** : an animal in the earliest stages of growth when its essential structures are being formed **2** : the rudimentary plant contained in a seed

e·mend \ē-'mend\ *vb* : to make corrections in (a text) by alterations

¹em·er·ald \'em-ə-rəld\ *n* : a rich green precious stone

²emerald *adj* : brightly or richly green

e·merge \i-'mərj\ *vb* **e·merged; e·merg·ing**

1 : to come into view (as from water or fog) 2 : to become known especially as a result of study or questioning

e·mer·gen·cy \i-'mər-jən-sē\ *n, pl* **e·mer·gen·cies** : an unexpected state of affairs calling for prompt action

em·er·y \'em-ə-rē\ *n* : a mineral used in the form of powder or grains for polishing and grinding

¹**e·met·ic** \i-'met-ik\ *n* : something (as a drug) that causes vomiting

²**emetic** *adj* : causing vomiting

-e·mi·a *or* **-ae·mi·a** \'ē-mē-ə\ *n suffix* : condition of having a specified disorder of the blood ⟨leuk*emia*⟩

em·i·grant \'em-i-grənt\ *n* : a person who emigrates

em·i·grate \'em-ə-ˌgrāt\ *vb* **em·i·grat·ed; em·i·grat·ing** : to leave a country or region to settle somewhere else

em·i·gra·tion \ˌem-ə-'grā-shən\ *n* : a going away from one region or country to live in another

em·i·nence \'em-ə-nəns\ *n* 1 : the condition of being eminent 2 : a natural elevation

em·i·nent \'em-ə-nənt\ *adj* : standing above others in rank, merit, or virtue

em·is·sar·y \'em-ə-ˌser-ē\ *n, pl* **em·is·sar·ies** : REPRESENTATIVE, ENVOY

e·mit \ē-'mit\ *vb* **e·mit·ted; e·mit·ting** : to give out : send forth ⟨*emit* light⟩ ⟨*emit* a shriek⟩

e·mo·tion \i-'mō-shən\ *n* 1 : strong feeling : EXCITEMENT ⟨speak with *emotion*⟩ 2 : a mental and bodily reaction (as anger or fear) marked by strong feeling

e·mo·tion·al \i-'mō-shən-l\ *adj* 1 : of or relating to the emotions ⟨an *emotional* upset⟩ 2 : inclined to show or express emotion ⟨an *emotional* person⟩ 3 : appealing to or arousing emotion — **e·mo·tion·al·ly** *adv*

em·per·or \'em-pər-ər\ *n* : the sovereign ruler of an empire

em·pha·sis \'em-fə-səs\ *n, pl* **em·pha·ses** \-ˌsēz\ 1 : a forcefulness of expression that gives special importance to something 2 : special force given to one or more words or syllables in speaking or reading 3 : special importance given to something

em·pha·size \'em-fə-ˌsīz\ *vb* **em·pha·sized; em·pha·siz·ing** : to give emphasis to : STRESS

em·phat·ic \im-'fat-ik\ *adj* : marked by or spoken with emphasis ⟨an *emphatic* gesture⟩

em·pire \'em-ˌpīr\ *n* 1 : a group of territories or peoples under one ruler ⟨the Roman *empire*⟩ 2 : a country whose ruler is called an emperor 3 : the power or rule of an emperor

¹**em·ploy** \im-'plòi\ *vb* 1 : to make use of ⟨*employ* bricks in building⟩ 2 : to use the services of : hire for wages or salary

²**employ** *n* : EMPLOYMENT

em·ploy·ee *or* **em·ploy·e** \im-ˌplòi-'ē\ *n* : a person who works for pay in the service of an employer

em·ploy·er \im-'plòi-ər\ *n* : one that employs others

em·ploy·ment \im-'plòi-mənt\ *n* 1 : the act of employing : the state of being employed 2 : OCCUPATION, ACTIVITY

em·pow·er \im-'paù-ər\ *vb* : to give official authority or legal power to

em·press \'em-prəs\ *n* 1 : the wife of an emperor 2 : a woman who is the ruler of an empire in her own right

¹**emp·ty** \'emp-tē\ *adj* **emp·ti·er; emp·ti·est** 1 : containing nothing 2 : UNOCCUPIED, VACANT ⟨*empty* house⟩ — **emp·ti·ness** *n*

syn EMPTY, VACANT both apply to things that do not contain what they can or usually do contain or hold. EMPTY is the opposite of *full* and implies that a thing has nothing at all in it ⟨an *empty* box⟩ ⟨an *empty* bottle⟩ VACANT is the opposite of *occupied* and describes something that is temporarily unoccupied ⟨the king's death left the throne *vacant*⟩

²**empty** *vb* **emp·tied; emp·ty·ing** 1 : to make empty : remove the contents of ⟨*empty* a barrel⟩ 2 : to transfer by emptying ⟨*empty* the flour from the bag⟩ 3 : to become empty 4 : DISCHARGE ⟨the river *empties* into the gulf⟩

emp·ty–hand·ed \ˌemp-tē-'han-dəd\ *adj* 1 : having nothing in the hands 2 : having acquired or gained nothing

e·mu \'ē-ˌmyü\ *n* : a swift-running Australian bird resembling but smaller than the related ostrich

em·u·late \'em-yə-ˌlāt\ *vb* **em·u·lat·ed; em·u·lat·ing** : to strive to equal or excel ⟨*emulate* great men⟩

em·u·la·tion \ˌem-yə-'lā-shən\ *n* : ambition or endeavor to equal or excel

emu

e·mul·si·fy \i-'məl-sə-ˌfī\ *vb* **e·mul·si·fied; e·mul·si·fy·ing** : to make an emulsion of

e·mul·sion \i-'məl-shən\ *n* 1 : a material consisting of a mixture of liquids so that fine drops of one liquid are scattered throughout the other ⟨an *emulsion* of oil in water⟩ 2 : a coating on photographic films and paper containing a chemical that light affects in such a way as to produce a picture

en- *also* **em-** *prefix* 1 : put into or on to ⟨en-

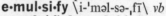

case⟩ ⟨en*throne*⟩ : go into or on to ⟨en*train*⟩
2 : cause to be ⟨en*slave*⟩ **3** : provide with
⟨em*power*⟩ — in all senses usually *em-* before
b, *m*, or *p*

¹-en \ən, -n\ *also* **-n** \n\ *adj suffix* : made of
: consisting of ⟨earth*en*⟩ ⟨wool*en*⟩ ⟨silver*n*⟩

²-en *vb suffix* **1** : become or cause to be
⟨sharp*en*⟩ **2** : cause or come to have ⟨length-
en⟩

en·a·ble \in-'ā-bəl\ *vb* **en·a·bled; en·a·bling** : to
give strength, power, or ability to : make able

en·act \in-'akt\ *vb* **1** : to make into law
2 : to act the part of (as in a play) — **en·act-
ment** *n*

¹e·nam·el \i-'nam-əl\ *vb* **e·nam·eled** *or*
e·nam·elled; e·nam·el·ing *or* **e·nam·el·ling** : to
cover with or as if with enamel

²enamel *n* **1** : a glasslike substance used for
coating the surface of metal, glass, and pottery
2 : the hard outer surface of the teeth **3** : a
paint that forms a hard glossy coat

en·camp \in-'kamp\ *vb* : to set up and occupy
a camp

en·camp·ment \in-'kamp-mənt\ *n* **1** : the
act of making a camp **2** : CAMP

en·case \in-'kās\ *vb* **en·cased; en·cas·ing** : to
enclose in or as if in a case

-ence \əns, -ns\ *n suffix* : action or process
⟨emerg*ence*⟩ ⟨refer*ence*⟩

en·chant \in-'chant\ *vb* **1** : to put under a
spell by or as if by charms or magic **2** : to
please greatly : DELIGHT — **en·chant·ment** *n*

en·chant·ing \in-'chant-ing\ *adj* : very attractive : CHARMING

en·chant·ress \in-'chan-trəs\ *n* : a woman
who enchants : WITCH, SORCERESS

en·cir·cle \in-'sər-kəl\ *vb* **en·cir·cled; en·cir-
cling** **1** : to form a circle around : SURROUND
2 : to pass completely around

en·close \in-'klōz\ *vb* **en·closed; en·clos·ing**
1 : to close in all around : shut in ⟨a porch *enclosed* with glass⟩ **2** : to put in the same parcel
or envelope with something else ⟨*enclose* a
snapshot with a letter⟩ **3** : SURROUND

en·clo·sure \in-'klō-zhər\ *n* **1** : the act of
enclosing **2** : an enclosed space **3** : something
(as a fence) that encloses **4** : something enclosed (as in a letter)

en·code \in-'kōd\ *vb* **en·cod·ed; en·cod·ing** : to
convert (a message) into code

en·com·pass \in-'kəm-pəs\ *vb* **1** : ENCIRCLE
2 : INCLUDE

¹en·core \'än-ˌkōr\ *n* **1** : the demand for the
repetition of an item on a program expressed
by applause from an audience **2** : a further
appearance or performance given in response
to applause

²encore *vb* **en·cored; en·cor·ing** : to call for an
encore

¹en·coun·ter \in-'kaunt-ər\ *vb* **1** : to meet in
opposition : FIGHT **2** : to come face to face
with : come upon ⟨*encounter* stormy weather⟩

²encounter *n* **1** : a hostile meeting : COMBAT
2 : a meeting face to face especially by chance

en·cour·age \in-'kər-ij\ *vb* **en·cour·aged; en-
cour·ag·ing** **1** : to give courage, spirit, or hope
to : HEARTEN **2** : to give help to : AID

en·cour·age·ment \in-'kər-ij-mənt\ *n*
1 : the act of encouraging : the state of being
encouraged **2** : something that encourages

en·croach \in-'krōch\ *vb* **1** : to enter or force
oneself gradually upon another's property or
rights : TRESPASS **2** : to go beyond the usual
or proper limits

en·crust \in-'krəst\ *vb* : to cover with a crust

en·cum·ber \in-'kəm-bər\ *vb* **1** : to weigh
down : BURDEN **2** : HINDER, HAMPER

-en·cy \ən-sē, -n-sē\ *n suffix, pl* **-en·cies** : quality or state ⟨despond*ency*⟩

en·cy·clo·pe·di·a \in-ˌsī-klə-'pēd-ē-ə\ *n* : a
work containing information on all branches
of learning in articles arranged alphabetically
by subject

¹end \'end\ *n* **1** : the part near the boundary
of an area ⟨the south *end* of a town⟩ **2** : the
point that marks the limit or extent of something **3** : the last point or part of a thing
lengthwise ⟨lay two boards *end* to *end*⟩ ⟨the
front *end* of a car⟩ **4** : DEATH, DESTRUCTION
⟨met his *end* bravely⟩ **5** : something aimed at
: PURPOSE **6** : something left over : REMNANT
⟨*ends* of meat⟩ **7** : a football player stationed
at the end of the line

²end *vb* : to bring or come to an end : STOP

en·dan·ger \in-'dān-jər\ *vb* : RISK

en·dear \in-'diər\ *vb* : to make dear or be-
loved ⟨his humor *endeared* him to the public⟩

en·dear·ment \in-'diər-mənt\ *n* : a word or
an act that shows love or affection

¹en·deav·or \in-'dev-ər\ *vb* : to make an effort : work for a certain end : TRY

²endeavor *n* : a serious determined effort

end·ing \'en-ding\ *n* : the final part : END

en·dive \'en-ˌdīv\ *n* : either of two common
salad plants

end·less \'end-ləs\ *adj* **1** : being or seeming
to be without end **2** : joined at the ends
: CONTINUOUS ⟨an *endless* belt⟩ ⟨*endless* prai-
rie⟩ — **end·less·ly** *adv* — **end·less·ness** *n*

en·do·crine gland \ˌen-də-krən-, -ˌkrīn-\ *n*
: DUCTLESS GLAND

en·dorse \in-'dȯrs\ *vb* **en·dorsed; en·dors·ing**
1 : to sign one's name on the back of a paper
for some special purpose ⟨*endorse* a check⟩

2 : to give one's support to ⟨*endorse* a candidate⟩ — **en·dorse·ment** *n*

en·dow \in-'daù\ *vb* **1** : to furnish with money for support or maintenance ⟨*endow* a hospital⟩ **2** : to furnish with something freely or naturally ⟨man is *endowed* with reason⟩

en·dow·ment \in-'daù-mənt\ *n* : the providing of a permanent fund for support or the fund provided

end·point \'end-ˌpòint\ *n* : either of two points that mark the ends of a line segment or a point that marks the end of a ray

end run *n* : a football play in which a back tries to run wide around the end

en·dur·ance \in-'dùr-əns, -'dyùr-\ *n* : the ability to withstand strain, suffering, or hardship

en·dure \in-'dùr, -'dyùr\ *vb* **en·dured**; **en·dur·ing** **1** : to continue in existence : LAST ⟨a civilization that has *endured* for centuries⟩ **2** : to bear (as pain) patiently or firmly

end·ways \'end-ˌwāz\ *adv* **1** : on end **2** : with the end forward **3** : LENGTHWISE

en·e·ma \'en-ə-mə\ *n* : the injection of liquid into the bowel or the liquid injected

en·e·my \'en-ə-mē\ *n, pl* **en·e·mies** **1** : one that hates another : one that attacks or tries to harm another **2** : something that harms or threatens **3** : a nation with which one's own country is at war or a person belonging to such a nation

en·er·get·ic \ˌen-ər-'jet-ik\ *adj* : full of energy : ACTIVE, VIGOROUS

en·er·gy \'en-ər-jē\ *n, pl* **en·er·gies** **1** : power or capacity to be active : strength of body or mind to do things or to work **2** : the capacity for doing work ⟨the *energy* of electricity⟩

en·fold \in-'fōld\ *vb* **1** : to wrap up or cover with folds **2** : EMBRACE

en·force \in-'fōrs\ *vb* **en·forced**; **en·forc·ing** **1** : FORCE, COMPEL ⟨*enforce* obedience to a law⟩ **2** : to put into force ⟨*enforce* a law⟩ — **en·force·ment** *n*

en·gage \in-'gāj\ *vb* **en·gaged**; **en·gag·ing** **1** : to bind oneself to do something : PROMISE **2** : to pledge to be married **3** : to hold or occupy the attention **4** : to arrange for the services or use of ⟨*engage* a plumber⟩ ⟨*engage* a room in a hotel⟩ **5** : to take part in something : busy oneself ⟨*engage* in a sport⟩ **6** : to enter into conflict or battle with ⟨*engage* the enemy⟩ **7** : to interlock with : MESH

en·gaged \in-'gājd\ *adj* **1** : OCCUPIED, EMPLOYED ⟨*engaged* in conversation⟩ **2** : pledged to be married ⟨an *engaged* couple⟩

en·gage·ment \in-'gāj-mənt\ *n* **1** : the act of engaging : the state of being engaged

2 : EMPLOYMENT ⟨a week's *engagement* at the theater⟩ **3** : a promise to be present at a certain time and place **4** : BATTLE

en·gag·ing \in-'gā-jing\ *adj* : ATTRACTIVE

en·gen·der \in-'jen-dər\ *vb* : to cause to exist or develop : PRODUCE

en·gine \'en-jən\ *n* **1** : a mechanical tool or device ⟨tanks, planes, and other *engines* of war⟩ ⟨a fire *engine*⟩ **2** : a machine for running, driving, moving, or operating something especially by using the energy of steam, gasoline, or oil **3** : LOCOMOTIVE

¹en·gi·neer \ˌen-jə-'niər\ *n* **1** : a member of a military group devoted to engineering work **2** : a person who specializes in engineering ⟨a chemical *engineer*⟩ ⟨an electrical *engineer*⟩ ⟨a mining *engineer*⟩ **3** : a person who runs or supervises an engine or an apparatus

²engineer *vb* **1** : to plan, build, or manage as an engineer **2** : to guide the course of

en·gi·neer·ing \ˌen-jə-'niər-ing\ *n* : a science by which the properties of matter and the sources of energy in nature are made useful to man in structures (as roads and dams), machines (as automobiles and computers), and products (as plastics and radios)

¹En·glish \'ing-glish\ *adj* : of or relating to England, the English people, or English

²English *n* **1** : the language of England, the United States, and some other countries now or formerly under British rule **2 English** *pl* : the people of England **3** : a sideways spin given to a ball (as in pool or bowling)

English horn *n* : a musical instrument like an oboe but giving tones lower in pitch

en·grave \in-'grāv\ *vb* **en·graved**; **en·grav·ing** **1** : to cut or carve (letters, figures, or designs) on a hard surface **2** : to cut wood, metal, or stone in preparation for printing : print from a cut surface ⟨an invitation *engraved* on white cards⟩ — **en·grav·er** *n*

en·grav·ing \in-'grā-ving\ *n* **1** : the art of cutting letters, pictures, or patterns in wood, stone, or metal **2** : a print made from an engraved surface

en·gross \in-'grōs\ *vb* : to take up the whole interest of ⟨be *engrossed* in a puzzle⟩

English
horn

en·gulf \in-'gəlf\ *vb* : to flow completely over : swallow up

en·hance \in-'hans\ *vb* **en·hanced**; **en·hanc·ing** : to make or become greater (as in value)

e·nig·ma \i-'nig-mə\ *n* : RIDDLE, PUZZLE

en·joy \in-'jòi\ *vb* **1** : to take pleasure or satisfaction in ⟨*enjoy* camping⟩ **2** : to have and use for one's benefit ⟨*enjoy* good health⟩

ə abut　ər further　a ax　ā age　ä father, cot　á (see key page)　aù out　ch chin　e less　ē easy　g gift　i trip　ī life

en·joy·a·ble \in-'jȯi-ə-bəl\ *adj* : DELIGHTFUL

en·joy·ment \in-'jȯi-mənt\ *n* **1** : the condition of enjoying something **2** : PLEASURE, SATISFACTION **3** : something that gives pleasure

en·large \in-'lärj\ *vb* **en·larged; en·larg·ing** : to make or grow larger : EXPAND, INCREASE

en·large·ment \in-'lärj-mənt\ *n* **1** : an act of enlarging **2** : the state of being enlarged **3** : a photographic print made larger than the negative

en·light·en \in-'līt-n\ *vb* : to give knowledge to : free from ignorance : INFORM

en·list \in-'list\ *vb* **1** : to enroll for military or naval service **2** : to obtain the help of ⟨*enlist* friends in a cause⟩ — **en·list·ment** *n*

en·list·ed \in-'lis-təd\ *adj* : of, relating to, or constituting the part of a military or naval force below commissioned or warrant officers

en·liv·en \in-'lī-vən\ *vb* : to put life or spirit into : make active, cheerful, or gay

en·mi·ty \'en-mət-ē\ *n, pl* **en·mi·ties** : ILL WILL, HATRED

e·nor·mous \i-'nȯr-məs\ *adj* : extraordinarily large : HUGE — **e·nor·mous·ly** *adv*

¹e·nough \i-'nəf\ *adj* : equal to the needs or demands : SUFFICIENT

²enough *adv* : in sufficient amount or degree

³enough *n* : a sufficient amount

en·quire \in-'kwīr\, **en·qui·ry** \'in-,kwī-rē, -kwə-\ *var of* INQUIRE, INQUIRY

en·rage \in-'rāj\ *vb* **en·raged; en·rag·ing** : to fill with rage : ANGER

en·rich \in-'rich\ *vb* **1** : to make rich **2** : ORNAMENT, ADORN ⟨a ceiling *enriched* with paintings⟩ **3** : to improve the quality of food by adding vitamins and minerals **4** : to make more fertile ⟨*enrich* soil with fertilizer⟩

en·roll *or* **en·rol** \in-'rōl\ *vb* **en·rolled; en·roll·ing** : to enter on a roll or list : REGISTER

en·roll·ment *or* **en·rol·ment** \in-'rōl-mənt\ *n* **1** : the act of enrolling or being enrolled **2** : the number of persons enrolled

en route \än-'rüt\ *adv* : on or along the way

en·shrine \in-'shrīn\ *vb* **en·shrined; en·shrin·ing** **1** : to enclose in or as if in a shrine **2** : to cherish as if sacred

en·sign \'en-sən, *1 is also* -,sīn\ *n* **1** : a flag flown as the symbol of nationality **2** : a commissioned officer in the navy ranking next below a lieutenant junior grade

ensign of Great Britain

en·slave \in-'slāv\ *vb* **en·slaved; en·slav·ing** : to make a slave of

en·sue \in-'sü\ *vb* **en·sued; en·su·ing** : to come after in time or as a result : FOLLOW

en·sure \in-'shu̇r\ *vb* **en·sured; en·sur·ing** : to make certain or safe : GUARANTEE

en·tan·gle \in-'tang-gəl\ *vb* **en·tan·gled; en·tan·gling** **1** : to make tangled or confused **2** : to catch in a tangle : SNARE — **en·tan·gle·ment** \-gəl-mənt\ *n*

en·ter \'ent-ər\ *vb* **1** : to come or go in or into ⟨*enter* a room⟩ **2** : PIERCE, PENETRATE **3** : to cause to go into or be admitted to ⟨*enter* a child in kindergarten⟩ **4** : to become a member of : JOIN ⟨*enter* the hikers' club⟩ **5** : to take an active part ⟨*enter* into the spirit of the party⟩ **6** : to set down in a book or list

en·ter·prise \'ent-ər-,prīz\ *n* **1** : an undertaking calling for courage and energy : VENTURE **2** : willingness to undertake projects **3** : a business organization

en·ter·pris·ing \'ent-ər-,prī-zing\ *adj* : bold, active, and energetic in undertaking or experimenting

en·ter·tain \,ent-ər-'tān\ *vb* **1** : to receive and provide for especially in one's home : have as a guest ⟨*entertain* friends over the weekend⟩ **2** : to have in mind ⟨*entertain* kind thoughts⟩ **3** : to provide amusement for **syn** *see* AMUSE

en·ter·tain·er \,ent-ər-'tā-nər\ *n* : one who performs for public entertainment

en·ter·tain·ment \,ent-ər-'tān-mənt\ *n* **1** : AMUSEMENT, RECREATION ⟨played the piano for his own *entertainment*⟩ **2** : a means of amusement or recreation (as a show)

en·thrall *or* **en·thral** \in-'thrȯl\ *vb* **en·thralled; en·thrall·ing** **1** : to make a slave of **2** : to hold spellbound : CHARM

en·throne \in-'thrōn\ *vb* **en·throned; en·thron·ing** **1** : to seat on a throne **2** : to place in a high position

en·thu·si·asm \in-'thü-zē-,az-əm, -'thyü-\ *n* : strong feeling for a cause or a subject

en·thu·si·ast \in-'thü-zē-,ast, -'thyü-\ *n* : a person filled with enthusiasm for something

en·thu·si·as·tic \in-,thü-zē-'as-tik, -,thyü-\ *adj* : full of enthusiasm : EAGER, ARDENT

en·thu·si·as·ti·cal·ly \in-,thü-zē-'as-ti-kə-lē, -,thyü-\ *adv* : with enthusiasm : EAGERLY

en·tice \in-'tīs\ *vb* **en·ticed; en·tic·ing** : to attract by arousing hope or desire : TEMPT

en·tire \in-'tīr\ *adj* : complete in all parts : having nothing left out — **en·tire·ly** *adv*

en·ti·re·ty \in-'tī-rət-ē, -'tīr-tē\ *n, pl* **en·ti·re·ties** **1** : a state of completeness **2** : the sum total : WHOLE

en·ti·tle \in-'tīt-l\ *vb* **en·ti·tled; en·ti·tling** **1** : to give a right or claim to ⟨buying a ticket *entitles* you to a seat⟩ **2** : to give a title to

en·trails \'en-trəlz\ *n pl* : the internal parts of an animal : INTESTINE

ǐ job   ng sing   ō low   ȯ moth   ȯi coin   th thin   th̲ this   ü boot   u̇ foot   y you   yü few   yu̇ furious   zh vision

¹en·trance \'en-trəns\ *n* **1** : the act of entering **2** : a door, gate, or way for entering **3** : permission to enter : ADMITTANCE

²en·trance \in-'trans\ *vb* **en·tranced; en·tranc·ing** **1** : to put into a trance **2** : to fill with delight and wonder

en·trant \'en-trənt\ *n* : one that enters a contest or competition

en·trap \in-'trap\ *vb* **en·trapped; en·trap·ping** : to catch in or as if in a trap

en·treat \in-'trēt\ *vb* : to ask earnestly : BEG

en·treat·y \in-'trēt-ē\ *n, pl* **en·treat·ies** : earnest request

en·trench \in-'trench\ *vb* **1** : to surround with a trench **2** : to establish in a strong defensive position ⟨*entrenched* customs⟩ **3** : ENCROACH, TRESPASS

en·trust \in-'trəst\ *vb* **1** : to give into the care of another (as for safekeeping) ⟨*entrust* your savings to a bank⟩ **2** : to give custody, care, or charge of something to as a trust

en·try \'en-trē\ *n, pl* **en·tries** **1** : the act of entering : ENTRANCE **2** : a place through which entrance is made : HALL, VESTIBULE **3** : the act of making (as in a book or a list) a written record of something **4** : something entered in a list or a record ⟨dictionary *entries*⟩ **5** : a person or thing entered in a contest or race

en·twine \in-'twīn\ *vb* **en·twined; en·twin·ing** : to twist or twine together or around

e·nu·mer·ate \i-'nü-mə-ˌrāt, -'nyü-\ *vb* **e·nu·mer·at·ed; e·nu·mer·at·ing** **1** : to count over **2** : to name one after another : LIST

e·nun·ci·ate \ē-'nən-sē-ˌāt\ *vb* **e·nun·ci·at·ed; e·nun·ci·at·ing** **1** : ANNOUNCE, PROCLAIM **2** : to pronounce words or parts of words *syn* see PRONOUNCE

e·nun·ci·a·tion \ē-ˌnən-sē-'ā-shən\ *n* : clearness of pronunciation

en·vel·op \in-'vel-əp\ *vb* : to put a covering completely around : wrap up or in

en·ve·lope \'en-və-ˌlōp, 'än-\ *n* : an enclosing cover or wrapper (as for a letter)

en·vi·ous \'en-vē-əs\ *adj* : feeling or showing envy — **en·vi·ous·ly** *adv* — **en·vi·ous·ness** *n*

syn ENVIOUS, JEALOUS are alike in suggesting discontent or injured feelings at another's success or possession of something desirable. ENVIOUS stresses the element of discontent and inward dissatisfaction rather than outward spite ⟨so *envious* of his brother's good grades that he cheated to improve his own⟩ JEALOUS stresses envy turned outward against the person possessing what is desired or even against the thing itself ⟨so *jealous* of his brother that he accused him of getting his good grades by cheating on exams⟩

en·vi·ron·ment \in-'vī-rən-mənt\ *n* : the conditions or influences that affect one's growth and development : SURROUNDINGS

en·voy \'en-ˌvȯi, 'än-\ *n* **1** : MESSENGER **2** : a representative sent by one government to another

¹en·vy \'en-vē\ *n, pl* **en·vies** **1** : a feeling of discontent at the sight of another's good fortune together with a desire to have the same good fortune oneself ⟨filled with *envy* at seeing his playmate's presents⟩ **2** : a person or a thing that is envied ⟨the *envy* of all his friends⟩

²envy *vb* **en·vied; en·vy·ing** : to feel envy toward or because of

en·zyme \'en-ˌzīm\ *n* : one of the substances produced by body cells that help bodily chemical activities (as digestion) to take place but are not destroyed in so doing

e·o·hip·pus \ˌē-ō-'hip-əs\ *n* : a primitive extinct horse with four toes on each front foot

e·on *var of* AEON

¹ep·ic \'ep-ik\ *adj* : of, relating to, or characteristic of an epic

²epic *n* : a long poem that tells the story of a hero and his deeds

¹ep·i·dem·ic \ˌep-ə-'dem-ik\ *adj* : spreading widely and affecting large numbers of people at the same time ⟨an *epidemic* disease⟩

²epidemic *n* **1** : a rapidly spreading attack of disease **2** : something that spreads or develops rapidly like an epidemic disease

ep·i·der·mis \ˌep-ə-'dər-məs\ *n* **1** : a thin outer insensitive layer of skin covering the dermis **2** : any of various thin outer layers of plants or animals

ep·i·sode \'ep-ə-ˌsōd\ *n* : an event or one of a series of events that stands out clearly in one's life, in history, or in a story

e·pis·tle \i-'pis-əl\ *n* : a formal letter

ep·i·taph \'ep-ə-ˌtaf\ *n* : an inscription (as on a tombstone) in memory of a dead person

ep·och \'ep-ək\ *n* **1** : an event or time that is the starting point of a new period in history ⟨marked an *epoch* in American history⟩ **2** : a period marked by unusual or important events

¹e·qual \'ē-kwəl\ *adj* **1** : exactly the same in number, amount, degree, rank, or quality ⟨an *equal* number of apples and oranges⟩ ⟨officers of *equal* rank⟩ **2** : evenly balanced ⟨an *equal* contest⟩ **3** : having enough strength, ability, or means : ADEQUATE ⟨*equal* to a difficult task⟩ *syn* see IDENTICAL — **e·qual·ly** *adv*

²equal *n* : one that is equal to another

³equal *vb* **e·qualed** *or* **e·qualled; e·qual·ing** *or* **e·qual·ling** : to be equal to : MATCH

e·qual·i·ty \i-'kwäl-ət-ē\ *n, pl* **e·qual·i·ties** : the condition or state of being equal

ə abut   ər further   a ax   ā age   ä father, cot   à (see key page)   au̇ out   ch chin   e less   ē easy   g gift   i trip   ī life

e·qual·ize \'ē-kwə-ˌlīz\ *vb* **e·qual·ized; e·qual-iz·ing** **1** : to make equal **2** : to make even

e·qua·tion \i-'kwā-zhən\ *n* **1** : a statement of the equality of two mathematical expressions **2** : an expression representing a chemical reaction by means of chemical symbols

e·qua·tor \i-'kwāt-ər\ *n* : an imaginary circle around the earth everywhere equally distant from the north pole and the south pole

e·qua·to·ri·al \ˌē-kwə-'tōr-ē-əl\ *adj* **1** : of, relating to, or lying near the equator **2** : resembling conditions at or near the equator

e·ques·tri·an \i-'kwes-trē-ən\ *adj* **1** : of or relating to horses, horsemen, or horsemanship **2** : mounted on horseback **3** : representing a person on horseback

e·qui·lat·er·al \ˌē-kwə-'lat-ə-rəl\ *adj* : having all sides of equal length ⟨an *equilateral* triangle⟩

e·qui·lib·ri·um \ˌē-kwə-'lib-rē-əm\ *n* : a state of balance between opposing weights, forces, or influences : physical or mental balance

e·qui·nox \'ē-kwə-ˌnäks\ *n* : either of the two times each year when the sun's center crosses the equator and day and night (as on March 21 and September 23) are everywhere of equal length

e·quip \i-'kwip\ *vb* **e·quipped; e·quip·ping** : to supply for a special purpose : fit out

e·quip·ment \i-'kwip-mənt\ *n* **1** : an act of equipping or fitting out **2** : supplies and tools needed for a special purpose

¹e·quiv·a·lent \i-'kwiv-ə-lənt\ *adj* : alike or equal in number, value, or meaning **syn** see IDENTICAL

²equivalent *n* : something equivalent

¹-er \ər\ *adj suffix or adv suffix* — used to form the comparative degree of adjectives and adverbs of one syllable ⟨hott*er*⟩ ⟨dri*er*⟩ and of some adjectives and adverbs of two or more syllables ⟨complet*er*⟩ ⟨earli*er*⟩

²-er \ər\ *also* **-i·er** \ē-ər, yər\ *or* **-yer** \yər\ *n suffix* **1** : a person occupationally connected with ⟨hatt*er*⟩ ⟨furr*ier*⟩ ⟨law*yer*⟩ **2** : a person or thing belonging to or associated with ⟨old-tim*er*⟩ **3** : a native of : resident of ⟨cottag*er*⟩ ⟨New York*er*⟩ **4** : one that has ⟨three-deck*er*⟩ **5** : one that produces or yields ⟨pork*er*⟩ **6** : one that does or performs a specified action ⟨report*er*⟩ ⟨build*er*-upper⟩ **7** : one that is a suitable object of a specified action ⟨broil*er*⟩ **8** : one that is ⟨foreign*er*⟩

e·ra \'ir-ə\ *n* **1** : a period of time reckoned from some special date or event ⟨the Christian *era*⟩ **2** : an important or distinctive period of history ⟨the colonial *era*⟩ **syn** see PERIOD

e·rad·i·cate \i-'rad-ə-ˌkāt\ *vb* **e·rad·i·cat·ed;**

e·rad·i·cat·ing : to remove by or as if by tearing up by the roots : destroy completely

e·rase \i-'rās\ *vb* **e·rased; e·ras·ing** : to rub out or scratch out ⟨*erase* a chalk mark⟩

e·ras·er \i-'rā-sər\ *n* : a sharp tool or a piece of rubber, felt, or cloth used for erasing marks

e·ra·sure \i-'rā-shər\ *n* **1** : an act of erasing **2** : something erased

ere \eər\ *prep or conj* : BEFORE

¹e·rect \i-'rekt\ *adj* : being straight up and down — **e·rect·ly** *adv* — **e·rect·ness** *n*

²erect *vb* **1** : BUILD ⟨*erect* a tower⟩ **2** : to set upright ⟨*erect* a flagpole⟩ — **e·rec·tor** *n*

er·mine \'ər-mən\ *n* : a weasel of northern regions that is valued for its winter coat of white fur with a black-tipped tail

e·rode \i-'rōd\ *vb* **e·rod·ed; e·rod-ing** : to eat into : wear away : destroy by wearing away ⟨a shore *eroded* by the sea⟩

ermine

e·ro·sion \i-'rō-zhən\ *n* : the act of eroding : the state of being eroded

err \'eər, 'ər\ *vb* **1** : to make a mistake **2** : to do wrong : SIN

er·rand \'er-ənd\ *n* **1** : a short trip taken to attend to some business **2** : the business done on an errand

er·rant \'er-ənt\ *adj* **1** : wandering in search of adventure ⟨an *errant* knight⟩ **2** : ERRING

er·rat·ic \i-'rat-ik\ *adj* : not following the usual or expected course : QUEER, ODD

er·ro·ne·ous \i-'rō-nē-əs\ *adj* : INCORRECT

er·ror \'er-ər\ *n* : a failure in correctness or accuracy : MISTAKE ⟨an *error* in adding figures⟩

syn ERROR, MISTAKE, BLUNDER all mean an act or statement that is not right or true or proper. ERROR suggests a failure to keep to a true course or follow a model accurately ⟨an *error* in reasoning⟩ ⟨a spelling *error*⟩ MISTAKE often implies an error made because of an excusable misunderstanding or an inability to foresee the result of choice or decision ⟨can often learn from the *mistakes* of others⟩ BLUNDER implies a mistake made through stupidity or ignorance or carelessness ⟨a translation full of comical *blunders*⟩

e·rupt \i-'rəpt\ *vb* **1** : to burst forth or cause to burst forth ⟨lava *erupting* from a volcano⟩ **2** : to break through a surface **3** : to break out (as with a skin rash)

e·rup·tion \i-'rəp-shən\ *n* **1** : a bursting forth ⟨*eruption* of lava from a volcano⟩ **2** : a breaking out (as of a skin rash) **3** : a product (as a rash) of erupting

-er·y \ə-rē, rē\ *n suffix, pl* **-er·ies** **1** : qualities collectively : character : -NESS ⟨snobb*ery*⟩

2 : art : practice ⟨cook*ery*⟩ **3** : place of doing, keeping, producing, or selling ⟨fish*ery*⟩ ⟨bak*ery*⟩ **4** : collection : aggregate ⟨fin*ery*⟩ **5** : state or condition ⟨slav*ery*⟩

¹-es \əz, iz *after* s, z, sh, ch; z *after* v *or a vowel*\ *n pl suffix* **1** — used to form the plural of most nouns that end in *s* ⟨glass*es*⟩, *z* ⟨fuzz*es*⟩, sh ⟨bush*es*⟩, ch ⟨peach*es*⟩, or a final *y* that changes to *i* ⟨lad*ies*⟩ and of some nouns ending in *f* that changes to *v* ⟨loa*ves*⟩ **2** : ¹-s 2

²-es *vb suffix* — used to form the third person singular present of most verbs that end in *s* ⟨bless*es*⟩, *z* ⟨fizz*es*⟩, sh ⟨hush*es*⟩, ch ⟨catch*es*⟩, or a final *y* that changes to *i* ⟨def*ies*⟩

es·ca·la·tor \'es-kə-ˌlāt-ər\ *n* : a moving stairway arranged like an endless belt

es·ca·pade \'es-kə-ˌpād\ *n* : a mischievous adventure : PRANK

¹es·cape \is-'kāp\ *vb* **es·caped; es·cap·ing** **1** : to get away : get free or clear ⟨*escape* from a burning building⟩ **2** : to keep free of : AVOID **3** : to leak out from some enclosed place

²escape *n* **1** : the act of escaping ⟨a daring *escape* from prison⟩ **2** : a means of escaping

¹es·cort \'es-ˌkȯrt\ *n* : a person or group of persons accompanying another to give protection or to show honor or courtesy

²es·cort \is-'kȯrt\ *vb* : to accompany as an escort **syn** see ACCOMPANY

¹-ese \'ēz\ *adj suffix* : of, relating to, or originating in a certain place or country ⟨Japan*ese*⟩

²-ese *n suffix, pl* **-ese** **1** : native or resident of a specified place or country ⟨Chin*ese*⟩ **2** : language of a particular place, country, or nationality ⟨Siam*ese*⟩ **3** : speech, literary style, or diction peculiar to a specified place, person, or group ⟨journal*ese*⟩

Es·ki·mo \'es-kə-ˌmō\ *n, pl* **Es·ki·mos** : a member of a group of peoples of northern Canada, Greenland, Alaska, and northeastern Siberia

Eskimo dog *n* : a sled dog of northern North America

e·soph·a·gus \i-'säf-ə-gəs\ *n, pl* **e·soph·a·gi** \-ˌgī, -ˌjī\ : the tube that leads from the mouth through the throat to the stomach

Eskimo dog

es·pe·cial \is-'pesh-əl\ *adj* : SPECIAL ⟨pay *especial* attention to spelling⟩ — **es·pe·cial·ly** *adv*

es·pi·o·nage \'es-pē-ə-ˌnäzh\ *n* : the practice of spying : the use of spies

es·py \is-'pī\ *vb* **es·pied; es·py·ing** : to catch sight of

-ess \əs\ *n suffix* : female ⟨author*ess*⟩

¹es·say \e-'sā\ *vb* : ATTEMPT, TRY

²es·say \'es-ˌā, *1 also* e-'sā\ *n* **1** : ATTEMPT **2** : a usually short piece of writing dealing with a subject from a personal point of view

es·say·ist \'es-ˌā-əst\ *n* : a writer of essays

es·sence \'es-ns\ *n* **1** : the basic nature or quality of a thing ⟨the *essence* of love⟩ **2** : a substance made from a plant or drug and having its special qualities **3** : PERFUME

¹es·sen·tial \i-'sen-chəl\ *adj* **1** : forming or belonging to the basic part of something ⟨free speech is an *essential* right of citizenship⟩ **2** : important in the highest degree : NECESSARY — **es·sen·tial·ly** *adv*

²essential *n* : something that is essential

-est \əst\ *adj suffix or adv suffix* — used to form the superlative degree of adjectives and adverbs of one syllable ⟨fatt*est*⟩ ⟨lat*est*⟩ and of some adjectives and adverbs of two or more syllables ⟨lucki*est*⟩ ⟨often*est*⟩

es·tab·lish \is-'tab-lish\ *vb* **1** : to set up : FOUND ⟨*establish* a colony⟩ **2** : to place beyond doubt : PROVE

established church *n* : a church recognized by law as the official church of a nation and supported by civil authority

es·tab·lish·ment \is-'tab-lish-mənt\ *n* **1** : the act of establishing **2** : a place set up for residence or for business

es·tate \is-'tāt\ *n* **1** : STATE, CONDITION ⟨reach man's *estate*⟩ **2** : the property of all kinds that a person leaves at his death **3** : a large country house on extensive grounds

¹es·teem \is-'tēm\ *n* : high regard

²esteem *vb* : to think well of : regard highly

es·thet·ic *var of* AESTHETIC

¹es·ti·mate \'es-tə-ˌmāt\ *vb* **es·ti·mat·ed; es·ti·mat·ing** : to give or form a general idea of the value, size, or cost of something : JUDGE

²es·ti·mate \'es-tə-mət\ *n* **1** : an opinion or judgment of the value or quality of something **2** : a rough calculation of size or cost

es·ti·ma·tion \ˌes-tə-'mā-shən\ *n* **1** : the making of an estimate : JUDGMENT, RECKONING **2** : favorable opinion : ESTEEM

es·trange \is-'trānj\ *vb* **es·tranged; es·trang·ing** : to cause to become separated or hostile ⟨*estranged* by a quarrel⟩ — **es·trange·ment** *n*

et cet·er·a \et-'set-ə-rə\ : and others of the same kind : and so forth : and so on

etch \'ech\ *vb* **1** : to produce designs or figures on metal or glass by lines eaten into the substance by acid **2** : to impress sharply

etch·ing \'ech-ing\ *n* **1** : the art or process of producing drawings or pictures by means of impressions taken from etched plates **2** : an impression in ink from an etched plate

e·ter·nal \i-'tərn-l\ *adj* **1** : lasting forever

: having no beginning and no end **2** : continuing without interruption : CEASELESS

e·ter·ni·ty \i-'tər-nət-ē\ *n, pl* **e·ter·ni·ties**
1 : endless duration **2** : the state after death
3 : seeming endlessness

-eth — see -TH

e·ther \'ē-thər\ *n* **1** : the upper regions of
space : the clear sky **2** : a light flammable
liquid used as a solvent of fats and as an
anesthetic

e·the·re·al \i-'thir-ē-əl\ *adj* **1** : HEAVENLY
⟨*ethereal* spirits⟩ **2** : AIRY, DELICATE

eth·i·cal \'eth-i-kəl\ *adj* **1** : of or relating to
ethics **2** : following accepted rules of personal
or professional behavior

eth·ics \'eth-iks\ *n sing or pl* **1** : a branch of
philosophy dealing with questions of what is
good and bad and with moral duty and obligation **2** : the principles of moral behavior governing an individual or a group

eth·nic \'eth-nik\ *adj* : of or relating to races
or large groups of people classed according to
common traits and customs — **eth·ni·cal·ly**
\-ni-kə-lē\ *adv*

et·i·quette \'et-i-kət, -,ket\ *n* : the rules governing the way in which people behave socially
or professionally or the way in which a ceremony is conducted ⟨flag *etiquette*⟩

-ette \'et\ *n suffix* **1** : little one ⟨kitchen*ette*⟩
2 : female ⟨farmer*ette*⟩ **3** : imitation ⟨leather-
ette⟩

é·tude \'ā-,tüd, -,tyüd\ *n* : a piece of music
for practice to develop skill : STUDY

et·y·mol·o·gy \,et-ə-'mäl-ə-jē\ *n, pl* **et·y·mol-
o·gies** [from Greek *etymologia*, a compound of
etymon "literal meaning of a word according
to its origin" and *-logia* "-logy"; Greek
etymon derives from *etymos* "true"] : the
history of a word shown by tracing it or its
parts back to the earliest known forms and
meanings both in its own language and any
other language from which it may have been
taken

eu·ca·lyp·tus \,yü-kə-'lip-təs\ *n, pl* **eu·ca·lyp-
ti** \-,tī\ *or* **eu·ca·lyp·tus·es** : a tree of a kind
found mainly in western Australia and important for timber, gum, and oil

Eu·cha·rist \'yü-kə-rəst\ *n* : COMMUNION

¹Eu·ro·pe·an \,yùr-ə-'pē-ən\ *adj* : of or relating to Europe or the Europeans

²European *n* : a native or inhabitant of
Europe

e·vac·u·ate \i-'vak-yə-,wāt\ *vb* **e·vac·u·at·ed;
e·vac·u·at·ing** **1** : to make empty : empty out
2 : to discharge waste matter from the body
3 : to remove or withdraw troops or people
from a place of danger ⟨*evacuate* a city⟩

e·vade \i-'vād\ *vb* **e·vad·ed; e·vad·ing** : to get
away from or avoid by skill or trickery

e·val·u·ate \i-'val-yə-,wāt\ *vb* **e·val·u·at·ed;
e·val·u·at·ing** : to find or estimate the value of

e·val·u·a·tion \i-,val-yə-'wā-shən\ *n* : the act
or result of evaluating

e·van·ge·list \i-'van-jə-ləst\ *n* : a preacher
who goes about from place to place trying to
awaken religious enthusiasm

e·vap·o·rate \i-'vap-ə-,rāt\ *vb* **e·vap·o·rat·ed;
e·vap·o·rat·ing** **1** : to change into vapor ⟨a
liquid that *evaporates* quickly⟩ **2** : to vanish
without being seen to go **3** : to remove some
of the water from something (as by heating)

e·vap·o·ra·tion \i-,vap-ə-'rā-shən\ *n* : the
process of evaporating

e·va·sion \i-'vā-zhən\ *n* : the act of evading

e·va·sive \i-'vā-siv\ *adj* : tending to evade
: not straightforward — **e·va·sive·ness** *n*

eve \'ēv\ *n* **1** : EVENING **2** : the evening or
day before a special day **3** : the period just
before an important event

¹e·ven \'ē-vən\ *adj* **1** : FLAT, SMOOTH ⟨a
house built on *even* ground⟩ **2** : REGULAR,
STEADY ⟨*even* breathing⟩ **3** : being on the same
line or level ⟨water *even* with the rim of a
glass⟩ **4** : equal in size, number, or amount
⟨bread cut in *even* slices⟩ **5** : EQUAL, FAIR ⟨an
even trade⟩ **6** : capable of being divided by
two without a remainder **syn** see LEVEL —
e·ven·ly *adv* — **e·ven·ness** *n*

²even *adv* **1** : EXACTLY, PRECISELY ⟨*even* as the
clock struck⟩ **2** : FULLY, QUITE ⟨faithful *even*
to death⟩ **3** : STILL, YET ⟨tried to do *even* bet-
ter⟩ **4** : INDEED

³even *vb* : to make even or equal

eve·ning \'ēv-ning\ *n* : the latter part of the
day and early part of the night

evening star *n* : a bright planet (as Venus)
seen in the western sky after sunset

e·vent \i-'vent\ *n* **1** : something that happens
: OCCURRENCE ⟨review the *events* of the past
year⟩ **2** : a social occasion **3** : the fact of
happening ⟨in the *event* of rain⟩ **4** : a contest in
a program of sports **syn** see INCIDENT

e·vent·ful \i-'vent-fəl\ *adj* : marked by many
events or by an important event

e·ven·tide \'ē-vən-,tīd\ *n* : EVENING

e·ven·tu·al \i-'ven-chə-wəl\ *adj* : coming as a
result or at some later time ⟨*eventual* success⟩
— **e·ven·tu·al·ly** *adv*

ev·er \'ev-ər\ *adv* **1** : at all times : ALWAYS
⟨*ever* faithful⟩ **2** : at any time ⟨has this *ever*
been done before⟩ **3** : in any case : at all

¹ev·er·green \'ev-ər-,grēn\ *adj* : having
foliage that stays green through more than
one growing season

²**evergreen** *n* **1** : an evergreen plant (as a pine or a laurel) **2** *pl* : branches and leaves of evergreens used for decorations

ev·er·last·ing \ˌev-ər-'las-ting\ *adj* **1** : lasting forever : ETERNAL ⟨*everlasting* fame⟩ **2** : going on for a long time or for too long a time — **ev·er·last·ing·ly** *adv*

ev·er·more \ˌev-ər-'mōr\ *adv* : FOREVER

ev·ery \'ev-rē\ *adj* : each of a group or series without leaving out any

ev·ery·bod·y \'ev-ri-ˌbäd-ē\ *pron* : every person

ev·ery·day \'ev-rē-ˌdā\ *adj* : used or suitable for every day or every ordinary day : USUAL

ev·ery·one \'ev-rē-wən, -ˌwən\ *pron* : every person

ev·ery·thing \'ev-rē-ˌthing\ *pron* : every thing : all that exists

ev·ery·where \'ev-rē-ˌhwear\ *adv* : in every place : in all places

e·vict \i-'vikt\ *vb* : to put out from property by legal means

ev·i·dence \'ev-ə-dəns\ *n* **1** : an outward sign or indication : PROOF ⟨find *evidence* of a robbery⟩ **2** : material presented to a court to find out the truth of a matter : TESTIMONY

ev·i·dent \'ev-ə-dənt\ *adj* : clear to the sight and to the mind : PLAIN — **ev·i·dent·ly** \-dənt-lē, -ˌdent-\ *adv*

¹**e·vil** \'ē-vəl\ *adj* **1** : not good morally : WICKED ⟨*evil* ruler⟩ ⟨*evil* deeds⟩ **2** : causing harm : tending to injure ⟨*evil* teeth of a shark⟩

²**evil** *n* **1** : something that brings sorrow, distress, or destruction ⟨the *evils* of poverty⟩ **2** : moral wrongdoing : WICKEDNESS

e·voke \i-'vōk\ *vb* **e·voked; e·vok·ing** : to call forth : summon up

ev·o·lu·tion \ˌev-ə-'lü-shən\ *n* **1** : the process of development of an animal or a plant **2** : the theory that the various kinds of existing animals and plants have developed from previously existing kinds

e·volve \i-'välv\ *vb* **e·volved; e·volv·ing** : to grow or develop out of something

ewe \'yü\ *n* : a female sheep

ex- \'eks\ *prefix* **1** : out of : outside ⟨*exter*-ritorial⟩ **2** : former ⟨*ex*-president⟩

¹**ex·act** \ig-'zakt\ *vb* : DEMAND, REQUIRE

²**exact** *adj* : showing strict agreement with fact : ACCURATE — **ex·act·ly** *adv* — **ex·act·ness** *n*

ex·act·ing \ig-'zak-ting\ *adj* : making many or difficult demands upon a person : TRYING

ex·ag·ger·ate \ig-'zaj-ə-ˌrāt\ *vb* **ex·ag·ger·at·ed; ex·ag·ger·at·ing** [from Latin *exaggerare*, literally, "to heap up", from *ex-* "out" and *agger* "heap"] : to enlarge a fact or statement beyond what is actual or true

ex·ag·ger·a·tion \ig-ˌzaj-ə-'rā-shən\ *n* **1** : the act of exaggerating **2** : an exaggerated statement

ex·alt \ig-'zòlt\ *vb* **1** : to raise in rank, dignity, or power **2** : to praise highly : WORSHIP

ex·am \ig-'zam\ *n* : EXAMINATION

ex·am·i·na·tion \ig-ˌzam-ə-'nā-shən\ *n* **1** : the act of examining or being examined ⟨go to the doctor for a physical *examination*⟩ **2** : a test given to determine progress, fitness, or knowledge ⟨a college entrance *examination*⟩

ex·am·ine \ig-'zam-ən\ *vb* **ex·am·ined; ex·am·in·ing** **1** : to look at or inspect carefully **2** : to question closely

ex·am·ple \ig-'zam-pəl\ *n* **1** : a sample of something taken to show what the whole is like : INSTANCE **2** : a problem to be solved in order to show how a rule works ⟨an *example* in arithmetic⟩ **3** : something to be imitated : MODEL ⟨set a good *example*⟩ **4** : something that is a warning to others

ex·as·per·ate \ig-'zas-pə-ˌrāt\ *vb* **ex·as·per·at·ed; ex·as·per·at·ing** : to make angry

ex·as·per·a·tion \ig-ˌzas-pə-'rā-shən\ *n* : extreme annoyance : ANGER

ex·ca·vate \'eks-kə-ˌvāt\ *vb* **ex·ca·vat·ed; ex·ca·vat·ing** **1** : to hollow out : form a hole in ⟨*excavate* the side of a hill⟩ **2** : to make by hollowing out **3** : to dig out

ex·ca·va·tion \ˌeks-kə-'vā-shən\ *n* **1** : the act of excavating **2** : a hollowed-out place formed by excavating

ex·ceed \ik-'sēd\ *vb* **1** : to go or be beyond the limit of ⟨*exceed* the speed limit⟩ **2** : to be greater than

ex·ceed·ing·ly \ik-'sēd-ing-lē\ *adv* : to an unusual degree : VERY

ex·cel \ik-'sel\ *vb* **ex·celled; ex·cel·ling** : to outdo others : SURPASS

ex·cel·lence \'ek-sə-ləns\ *n* **1** : high quality or merit **2** : an excellent quality

ex·cel·lent \'ek-sə-lənt\ *adj* : extremely good of its kind — **ex·cel·lent·ly** *adv*

¹**ex·cept** \ik-'sept\ *vb* : to leave out from a number or a whole : OMIT

²**except** *prep* **1** : not including ⟨daily *except* Sundays⟩ **2** : other than : BUT

³**except** *conj* : ONLY, BUT

ex·cep·tion \ik-'sep-shən\ *n* **1** : the act of excepting or leaving out **2** : something that is excepted **3** : OBJECTION, COMPLAINT

ex·cep·tion·al \ik-'sep-shən-l\ *adj* **1** : forming an exception : UNUSUAL ⟨an *exceptional* amount of rain⟩ **2** : better than average : SUPERIOR — **ex·cep·tion·al·ly** *adv*

¹**ex·cess** \ik-'ses, 'ek-ˌses\ *n* **1** : a state of being more than enough : an exceeding of what

is needed or allowed ⟨eat to *excess*⟩ **2** : the amount by which a quantity exceeds what is needed or allowed

²excess *adj* : more than is usual or permitted

ex·ces·sive \ik-'ses-iv\ *adj* : showing excess — **ex·ces·sive·ly** *adv*

¹ex·change \iks-'chānj\ *n* **1** : a giving or taking of one thing in return for another : TRADE ⟨a fair *exchange*⟩ **2** : the act of substituting one thing for another **3** : the act of giving and receiving between two groups ⟨an *exchange* of students between two countries⟩ ⟨an *exchange* of courtesies⟩ **4** : a place where goods or services are exchanged

²exchange *vb* **ex·changed; ex·chang·ing** : to give in exchange : TRADE, SWAP

ex·cit·a·ble \ik-'sīt-ə-bəl\ *adj* : easily excited

ex·cite \ik-'sīt\ *vb* **ex·cit·ed; ex·cit·ing** **1** : to increase the activity of **2** : to stir up : ROUSE

ex·cite·ment \ik-'sīt-mənt\ *n* **1** : the state of being excited : AGITATION **2** : something that excites, arouses, or stirs up

ex·claim \iks-'klām\ *vb* : to cry out or speak out suddenly or with strong feeling

ex·cla·ma·tion \,eks-klə-'mā-shən\ *n* **1** : a sharp or sudden cry expressing some strong feeling **2** : strong expression of protest or complaint

exclamation point *n* : a punctuation mark ! used chiefly to show a forceful way of speaking or strong feeling

ex·clam·a·to·ry \iks-'klam-ə-,tōr-ē\ *adj* : containing or using exclamation

ex·clude \iks-'klüd\ *vb* **ex·clud·ed; ex·clud·ing** : to shut out : keep out

ex·clu·sion \iks-'klü-zhən\ *n* : the act of excluding : the state of being excluded

ex·clu·sive \iks-'klü-siv\ *adj* **1** : excluding or inclined to exclude (as from ownership, membership, or privileges) ⟨an *exclusive* neighborhood⟩ **2** : SOLE, SINGLE ⟨his family has *exclusive* use of a bathing beach⟩ **3** : COMPLETE, ENTIRE ⟨give me your *exclusive* attention⟩ **4** : not inclusive — **ex·clu·sive·ly** *adv*

ex·crete \eks-'krēt\ *vb* **ex·cret·ed; ex·cret·ing** : to separate and give off waste matter from the body usually as urine or sweat

ex·cre·tion \eks-'krē-shən\ *n* **1** : the process of excreting **2** : waste material excreted

ex·cre·to·ry \'eks-krə-,tōr-ē\ *adj* : of, relating to, or functioning in excretion

ex·cur·sion \iks-'kər-zhən\ *n* **1** : a brief pleasure trip **2** : a trip (as on a train or airplane) at special reduced rates

ex·cus·a·ble \iks-'kyü-zə-bəl\ *adj* : capable of being excused

¹ex·cuse \iks-'kyüz\ *vb* **ex·cused; ex·cus·ing**

1 : to make apology for : try to remove blame from ⟨*excused* himself for being late⟩ **2** : to free or let off from doing something ⟨*excuse* a pupil from reciting⟩ **3** : to serve as an acceptable reason or explanation for something said or done : JUSTIFY

syn EXCUSE, PARDON, FORGIVE all mean to refrain from punishing or blaming. EXCUSE indicates passing over a fault or failure because of special reasons or circumstances ⟨his lateness was *excused* because of a traffic jam⟩ PARDON implies freeing from penalty or punishment even though guilt is proved or admitted ⟨the new king *pardoned* all the prisoners⟩ FORGIVE adds the suggestion of putting aside any resentment or desire for revenge ⟨it is often easier to *forgive* our enemies than our friends⟩

²ex·cuse \iks-'kyüs\ *n* **1** : the act of excusing **2** : something offered as a reason for being excused **3** : something that excuses or is a reason for excusing **syn** see APOLOGY

ex·e·cute \'ek-sə-,kyüt\ *vb* **ex·e·cut·ed; ex·e·cut·ing** **1** : to put into effect : carry out to completion : PERFORM ⟨*execute* a plan⟩ **2** : to put to death according to a legal order **3** : to make in accordance with a plan or design

ex·e·cu·tion \,ek-sə-'kyü-shən\ *n* **1** : the act or process of executing : a carrying through of something to its finish **2** : a putting to death as a legal penalty **3** : the way in which a work of art is made or performed

¹ex·ec·u·tive \ig-'zek-yət-iv\ *adj* **1** : fitted for executing or carrying out things to completion ⟨*executive* ability⟩ **2** : having to do with managing or directing affairs **3** : relating to the execution of the laws

²executive *n* **1** : the branch of government that puts laws into action **2** : a person who manages or directs ⟨a sales *executive*⟩

ex·em·pli·fy \ig-'zem-plə-,fī\ *vb* **ex·em·pli·fied; ex·em·pli·fy·ing** : to show by example

¹ex·empt \ig-'zempt\ *adj* : free or released from some requirement to which other persons are subject

²exempt *vb* : to make exempt : EXCUSE

ex·emp·tion \ig-'zemp-shən\ *n* **1** : the act of exempting : the state of being exempt **2** : one that exempts or is exempted

¹ex·er·cise \'ek-sər-,sīz\ *n* **1** : the act of exercising : a putting into action, use, or practice ⟨the *exercise* of patience⟩ **2** : bodily exertion for the sake of health ⟨go walking for *exercise*⟩ **3** : a school lesson or other task performed to develop skill : practice work : DRILL ⟨finger *exercises*⟩ **4** *pl* : a program of songs, speeches, and announcing of awards and honors ⟨graduation *exercises*⟩

---

j job   ng sing   ō low   ȯ moth   ȯi coin   th thin   th̲ this   ü boot   u̇ foot   y you   yü few   yu̇ furious   zh vision

²exercise vb **ex·er·cised; ex·er·cis·ing 1 :** to put into use **: EXERT** ⟨*exercise* authority⟩ **2 :** to use repeatedly in order to train or develop ⟨*exercise* a muscle⟩ **3 :** to exert oneself for the sake of health or training

ex·ert \ig-'zərt\ vb **1 :** to put forth (as strength or ability) : bring into play **2 :** to put (oneself) into action or to tiring effort

ex·er·tion \ig-'zər-shən\ n **1 :** the act of exerting ⟨with the *exertion* of a little more effort the game might have been won⟩ **2 :** use of strength or ability

ex·hale \eks-'hāl\ vb **ex·haled; ex·hal·ing :** to breathe out : send forth : give off

¹ex·haust \ig-'zȯst\ vb **1 :** to draw out or let out completely ⟨*exhaust* the water from a tank⟩ **2 :** to use up completely **3 :** to tire out **: FATIGUE syn** see TIRE

²exhaust n **:** the escape of used steam or gas from an engine : the gas that escapes from an engine

ex·haus·tion \ig-'zȯs-chən\ n **1 :** the act of exhausting **2 :** the condition of being exhausted

¹ex·hib·it \ig-'zib-ət\ vb **1 :** to show outwardly or by signs **: REVEAL** ⟨*exhibit* interest in something⟩ **2 :** to put on display ⟨*exhibit* a collection of paintings⟩ **syn** see SHOW

²exhibit n **1 :** an article or collection shown in an exhibition **2 :** an article presented as evidence in a law court

ex·hi·bi·tion \ˌek-sə-'bish-ən\ n **1 :** the act of exhibiting **2 :** a public showing (as of works of art or athletic skill)

ex·hil·a·rate \ig-'zil-ə-ˌrāt\ vb **ex·hil·a·rat·ed; ex·hil·a·rat·ing :** to make cheerful or lively

ex·hort \ig-'zȯrt\ vb **:** to try to arouse by words or advice : urge strongly

¹ex·ile \'eg-ˌzīl, 'ek-ˌsīl\ n **1 :** the sending or forcing of a person away from his own country or the situation of a person who is sent away **2 :** a person who is expelled from his own country

²exile vb **ex·iled; ex·il·ing :** to banish or expel from one's own country

ex·ist \ig-'zist\ vb **1 :** to have actual being : be real ⟨wonder if other worlds than ours *exist*⟩ **2 :** to continue to live ⟨how long can a man *exist* without water⟩ **3 :** to be found

ex·ist·ence \ig-'zis-təns\ n **1 :** the fact or the condition of being or of being real ⟨the largest animal in *existence*⟩ **2 :** way of living

ex·it \'eg-zət, 'ek-sət\ n **1 :** the act of going out of or away from a place **: DEPARTURE 2 :** a way of getting out of a place

ex·o·dus \'ek-sə-dəs\ n **:** the going out or away of a large number of people

ex·or·bi·tant \ig-'zȯr-bət-ənt\ adj **:** going beyond the limits of what is fair, reasonable, or expected **: EXCESSIVE** ⟨*exorbitant* prices⟩

ex·o·sphere \'ek-sō-ˌsfiər\ n **:** the outer fringe region of the atmosphere

ex·ot·ic \ig-'zät-ik\ adj **:** introduced from a foreign country **: STRANGE** ⟨an *exotic* flower⟩

ex·pand \iks-'pand\ vb **1 :** to open wide **: UNFOLD 2 :** to take up or cause to take up more space **: ENLARGE, SWELL** ⟨metals *expand* under heat⟩ **3 :** to work out in greater detail

ex·panse \iks-'pans\ n **:** a wide space, area, or stretch ⟨a vast *expanse* of desert⟩

ex·pan·sion \iks-'pan-chən\ n **:** the act of expanding or being expanded **: ENLARGEMENT**

ex·pect \iks-'pekt\ vb **1 :** to look for or look forward to something that ought to or probably will happen ⟨*expect* rain⟩ ⟨*expects* to go to town tomorrow⟩ **2 :** to consider as obliged

ex·pec·ta·tion \ˌeks-ˌpek-'tā-shən\ n **1 :** a looking forward to or waiting for something **2 :** prospect for inheritance

ex·pe·di·ent \iks-'pēd-ē-ənt\ adj **:** suitable for bringing about a desired result often without regard to fairness or rightness — **ex·pe·di·ent·ly** adv

ex·pe·di·tion \ˌeks-pə-'dish-ən\ n **1 :** a journey for a particular purpose (as for war or exploring) **2 :** the people making an expedition

ex·pel \iks-'pel\ vb **ex·pelled; ex·pel·ling :** to drive or force out : put out

ex·pend \iks-'pend\ vb **1 :** to pay out **: SPEND 2 :** to use up

ex·pen·di·ture \iks-'pen-di-chər\ n **1 :** the act of spending (as money, time, or energy) **2 :** something that is spent

ex·pense \iks-'pens\ n **1 :** something spent or required to be spent **: COST** ⟨*expenses* of a trip⟩ **2 :** a cause for spending

ex·pen·sive \iks-'pen-siv\ adj **:** high-priced — **ex·pen·sive·ly** adv

¹ex·pe·ri·ence \iks-'pir-ē-əns\ n **1 :** the actual living through an event or events ⟨learn by *experience*⟩ **2 :** the skill or knowledge gained by actually doing or feeling a thing ⟨a job that requires men with *experience*⟩ **3 :** something that one has actually done or lived through ⟨a soldier's *experiences* in war⟩

²experience vb **ex·pe·ri·enced; ex·pe·ri·enc·ing :** to have experience of **: UNDERGO, FEEL**

ex·pe·ri·enced \iks-'pir-ē-ənst\ adj **:** made skillful or wise through experience

¹ex·per·i·ment \iks-'per-ə-mənt\ n **:** a trial or test made to find out about something

²ex·per·i·ment \iks-'per-ə-ˌment\ vb **:** to make experiments

ex·per·i·men·tal \iks-ˌper-ə-'ment-l\ adj

1 : of, relating to, or based on experiment ⟨an *experimental* science⟩ **2** : used as a means of trying or testing

¹ex·pert \'eks-ˌpərt, iks-'pərt\ *adj* : showing special skill or knowledge gained from experience or training **syn** see SKILLFUL — **ex·pert·ly** *adv* — **ex·pert·ness** *n*

²ex·pert \'eks-ˌpərt\ *n* : one who has special skill or knowledge of a subject

ex·pi·ra·tion \ˌeks-pə-'rā-shən\ *n* : an act or instance of expiring

ex·pire \iks-'pīr\ *vb* **ex·pired; ex·pir·ing 1** : DIE **2** : to come to an end ⟨when his term of office *expires*⟩ **3** : to breathe out : EXHALE

ex·plain \iks-'plān\ *vb* **1** : to make understandable **2** : to give the reasons for or cause of — **ex·plain·a·ble** \-'plā-nə-bəl\ *adj*

ex·pla·na·tion \ˌeks-plə-'nā-shən\ *n* **1** : the act or process of explaining **2** : something that explains : a statement that makes clear

ex·plan·a·to·ry \iks-'plan-ə-ˌtȯr-ē\ *adj* : giving explanation : helping to explain

ex·plic·it \iks-'plis-ət\ *adj* : so clear in statement that there is no doubt about the meaning

ex·plode \iks-'plōd\ *vb* **ex·plod·ed; ex·plod·ing 1** : to cause to be given up or rejected ⟨science has *exploded* many old ideas⟩ **2** : to burst or cause to burst violently and noisily ⟨*explode* a bomb⟩ **3** : to burst forth (as with anger or laughter)

¹ex·ploit \'eks-ˌplȯit\ *n* : a notable act

²ex·ploit \iks-'plȯit\ *vb* **1** : to get the value or use out of ⟨*exploit* a coal mine⟩ **2** : to make use of unfairly for one's own advantage

ex·plo·ra·tion \ˌeks-plə-'rā-shən\ *n* : the act or an instance of exploring

ex·plore \iks-'plōr\ *vb* **ex·plored; ex·plor·ing 1** : to search through or into : examine closely **2** : to go into or through for purposes of discovery

ex·plor·er \iks-'plōr-ər\ *n* **1** : one that explores **2** : a traveler seeking new geographical or scientific information

ex·plo·sion \iks-'plō-zhən\ *n* **1** : the act of exploding : a sudden and noisy bursting (as of a bomb) **2** : a sudden outburst of feeling

¹ex·plo·sive \iks-'plō-siv\ *adj* **1** : able to cause explosion ⟨the *explosive* power of gunpowder⟩ **2** : likely to explode ⟨an *explosive* temper⟩ — **ex·plo·sive·ly** *adv*

²explosive *n* : an explosive substance

ex·po·nent \iks-'pō-nənt\ *n* : a numeral written above and to the right of a number to indicate how many times the number is to be used as a factor ⟨the *exponent* 3 in 10^3 indicates $10 \times 10 \times 10$⟩

¹ex·port \eks-'pōrt\ *vb* : to send or carry abroad especially for sale in foreign countries

²ex·port \'eks-ˌpōrt\ *n* **1** : something that is exported **2** : the act of exporting

ex·pose \iks-'pōz\ *vb* **ex·posed; ex·pos·ing 1** : to lay open (as to attack or danger) : leave without protection, shelter, or care **2** : to let light strike the photographic film or plate in taking a picture **3** : to make known ⟨*expose* a dishonest scheme⟩ **4** : to put where it can be seen : display for sale

ex·po·si·tion \ˌeks-pə-'zish-ən\ *n* **1** : EXPLANATION **2** : a public display : EXHIBITION

ex·po·sure \iks-'pō-zhər\ *n* **1** : an act of uncovering or laying open ⟨the *exposure* of a plot⟩ **2** : a being exposed ⟨suffer from *exposure* to the cold⟩ **3** : position with respect to direction ⟨a room with a southern *exposure*⟩ **4** : the act of letting light strike a photographic film or the time during which a film is exposed **5** : a section of a roll of film for one picture

ex·pound \iks-'paúnd\ *vb* : EXPLAIN

¹ex·press \iks-'pres\ *adj* **1** : clearly stated ⟨an *express* reply⟩ **2** : SPECIAL ⟨go to town for an *express* purpose⟩ **3** : sent with speed

²express *n* **1** : a system for the special transportation of goods ⟨send a package by *express*⟩ **2** : a vehicle (as a train or elevator) run at special speed with few or no stops

³express *vb* **1** : to make known especially in words ⟨*express* disapproval⟩ **2** : to represent by a sign or symbol **3** : to send by express

ex·pres·sion \iks-'presh-ən\ *n* **1** : the act or process of expressing especially in words ⟨to be better at understanding than at *expression*⟩ **2** : a significant word or saying ⟨use a common *expression*⟩ **3** : a way of speaking, singing, or playing so as to show mood or feeling ⟨read with *expression*⟩ **4** : LOOK, APPEARANCE — **ex·pres·sion·less** \-ləs\ *adj*

ex·pres·sive \iks-'pres-iv\ *adj* : expressing something : full of expression — **ex·pres·sive·ly** *adv* — **ex·pres·sive·ness** *n*

ex·press·way \iks-'pres-ˌwā\ *n* : a high-speed divided highway for through traffic

ex·pul·sion \iks-'pəl-shən\ *n* : the act of expelling : the state of being expelled

ex·quis·ite \eks-'kwiz-ət, 'eks-kwiz-\ *adj* **1** : delicately beautiful : DELIGHTFUL **2** : KEEN, INTENSE ⟨*exquisite* pain⟩ **3** : FINE, DELICATE ⟨*exquisite* sense of humor⟩ — **ex·quis·ite·ly** *adv*

ex·tend \iks-'tend\ *vb* **1** : to stretch out : LENGTHEN ⟨*extend* a road⟩ **2** : to straighten out : stretch forth ⟨*extended* his hand in greeting⟩ **3** : ENLARGE, WIDEN **4** : to hold out

ex·ten·sion \iks-'ten-chən\ *n* **1** : a stretching out : an increase in length or time **2** : a part forming an addition or enlargement

---

j job   ng sing   ō low   ȯ moth   ȯi coin   th thin   th̲ this   ü boot   u̇ foot   y you   yü few   yu̇ furious   zh vision

ex·ten·sive \iks-'ten-siv\ *adj* : having wide extent : BROAD, WIDESPREAD

ex·tent \iks-'tent\ *n* **1** : the distance, range, or space through which something extends : SIZE, LENGTH **2** : degree of greatness, largeness, smallness, or importance

¹ex·te·ri·or \eks-'tir-ē-ər\ *adj* : EXTERNAL

²exterior *n* : an exterior part or surface

ex·ter·mi·nate \iks-'tər-mə-ˌnāt\ *vb* **ex·ter·mi·nat·ed; ex·ter·mi·nat·ing** : to get rid of completely : wipe out ⟨*exterminate* rats⟩

¹ex·ter·nal \eks-'tərn-l\ *adj* : having to do with the outside : OUTSIDE

²external *n* : something external : APPEARANCE ⟨judging others by *externals*⟩

ex·tinct \iks-'tingkt\ *adj* **1** : no longer active ⟨an *extinct* volcano⟩ **2** : no longer existing

ex·tinc·tion \iks-'tingk-shən\ *n* : an act of extinguishing or being extinguished

ex·tin·guish \iks-'ting-gwish\ *vb* **1** : to cause to cease burning **2** : DESTROY — **ex·tin·guish·er** *n*

ex·tol \iks-'tōl\ *vb* **ex·tolled; ex·tol·ling** : to praise highly : GLORIFY

¹ex·tra \'eks-trə\ *adj* : being beyond or greater than what is usual, expected, or due

²extra *n* **1** : something extra or additional **2** : an additional payment or charge **3** : a special edition of a newspaper **4** : a person hired for a group scene (as in an opera)

³extra *adv* : beyond the usual size, amount, or degree ⟨*extra* large eggs⟩

extra- *prefix* : outside : beyond ⟨*extra*judicial⟩

¹ex·tract \iks-'trakt\ *vb* **1** : to pull out : draw out ⟨*extract* a tooth⟩ **2** : to get out by pressing, distilling, or by some chemical process ⟨*extract* juice from apples⟩ **3** : to choose and take out ⟨*extract* a few lines from a poem⟩

²ex·tract \'eks-ˌtrakt\ *n* **1** : a selection from a writing **2** : a product obtained by extraction

ex·trac·tion \iks-'trak-shən\ *n* **1** : an act of extracting or pulling out ⟨the *extraction* of a tooth⟩ **2** : ORIGIN, DESCENT ⟨a man of French *extraction*⟩ **3** : something extracted : EXTRACT

ex·tra·cur·ric·u·lar \ˌeks-trə-kə-'rik-yə-lər\ *adj* : of or relating to those activities (as athletics) that form part of the life of students but are not part of the courses of study

ex·traor·di·nar·y \iks-'trȯrd-n-ˌer-ē, ˌeks-trə-'ȯrd-\ *adj* : UNUSUAL, REMARKABLE — **ex·traor·di·nar·i·ly** \iks-ˌtrȯrd-n-'er-ə-lē, ˌeks-trə-ˌȯrd-n-'er-\ *adv*

ex·trav·a·gance \iks-'trav-ə-gəns\ *n* **1** : the wasteful or careless spending of money **2** : a going beyond what is reasonable or suitable (as in dress, speech, or behavior) **3** : an extravagant action or thing

ex·trav·a·gant \iks-'trav-ə-gənt\ *adj* **1** : going beyond the usual bounds : EXCESSIVE ⟨*extravagant* praise⟩ **2** : wasteful especially of money **3** : too high ⟨*extravagant* prices⟩ — **ex·trav·a·gant·ly** *adv*

¹ex·treme \iks-'trēm\ *adj* **1** : existing in the highest or greatest possible degree ⟨*extreme* heat⟩ ⟨*extreme* poverty⟩ **2** : FARTHEST, UTMOST ⟨the *extreme* tip⟩ — **ex·treme·ly** *adv*

²extreme *n* **1** : something as far as possible from the center or from its opposite ⟨*extremes* of heat and cold⟩ **2** : the greatest possible degree : an excessive degree

ex·trem·i·ty \iks-'trem-ət-ē\ *n, pl* **ex·trem·i·ties** **1** : the farthest limit, point, or part ⟨the northern *extremity* of the island⟩ **2** : an end part of a limb of the body (as a human foot) **3** : an extreme degree of pain, danger, or misery

ex·tri·cate \'eks-trə-ˌkāt\ *vb* **ex·tri·cat·ed; ex·tri·cat·ing** : to free from entanglement, danger, or difficulty

ex·ult \ig-'zəlt\ *vb* [the original English meaning, now obsolete, was "to leap for joy", and came from Latin *exsultare*, literally, "to leap up", a compound of *ex-* "out" and *saltare* "to leap"] : to be in high spirits : REJOICE

ex·ult·ant \ig-'zəlt-nt\ *adj* : EXULTING, JOYFUL — **ex·ult·ant·ly** *adv*

-ey — see -Y

¹eye \'ī\ *n* **1** : the organ of seeing **2** : the ability to see **3** : power to appreciate ⟨a keen *eye* for a bargain⟩ **4** : LOOK, GLANCE **5** : close attention : WATCH ⟨keep an *eye* on a store for the owner⟩ **6** : OPINION, JUDGMENT ⟨guilty in the *eyes* of the law⟩ **7** : something (as the hole in a needle) like or suggesting an eye ⟨hook and *eye*⟩ **8** : the center of something ⟨the *eye* of a hurricane⟩ — **eyed** \'īd\ *adj* — **eye·less** \'ī-ləs\ *adj*

eye 7

²eye *vb* **eyed; eye·ing** *or* **ey·ing** : to look at

eye·ball \'ī-ˌbȯl\ *n* : the whole eye

eye·brow \'ī-ˌbrau̇\ *n* : the arch or ridge over the eye : the hair on the ridge over the eye

eye·glass \'ī-ˌglas\ *n* **1** : a glass lens used to improve faulty eyesight **2** *pl* : a pair of glass lenses mounted in a frame : GLASSES

eyeglasses

eye·hole \'ī-ˌhōl\ *n* **1** : the opening in the skull for the eye **2** : a hole (as in a mask) to see through

eye·lash \'ī-ˌlash\ *n* : a single hair of the fringe on the eyelid

eye·let \'ī-lət\ *n* **1** : a small hole (as in cloth or leather) for a lacing or rope **2** : a metal ring to line an eyelet

eye·lid \'ī-,lid\ *n* : a movable cover of skin over an eye

eye·piece \'ī-,pēs\ *n* : the lens or combination of lenses at the eye end of an optical instrument (as a microscope or telescope)

eye·sight \'ī-,sīt\ *n* : SIGHT, VISION

eye·strain \'ī-,strān\ *n* : a tired or irritated state of the eyes (as from too much use)

eye·tooth \'ī-'tüth\ *n, pl* **eye·teeth** \-'tēth\ : a canine tooth of the upper jaw

ey·rie \'ī-rē\ *var of* AERIE

f \'ef\ *n, often cap* **1** : the sixth letter of the English alphabet **2** : a grade rating a student's work as failing

fa \'fä\ *n* : the fourth note of the musical scale

fa·ble \'fā-bəl\ *n* **1** : a story that is not true **2** : a story in which animals speak and act like people

fab·ric \'fab-rik\ *n* **1** : STRUCTURE, FRAMEWORK ⟨the *fabric* of society⟩ **2** : CLOTH **3** : a material that resembles cloth

fab·ri·cate \'fab-ri-,kāt\ *vb* **fab·ri·cat·ed; fab·ri·cat·ing** **1** : MAKE, MANUFACTURE **2** : INVENT, CREATE **3** : to make up in order to deceive someone ⟨*fabricate* a story⟩

fab·u·lous \'fab-yə-ləs\ *adj* **1** : told in or based on fable **2** : resembling a fable

syn FABULOUS, LEGENDARY, MYTHICAL all refer to something either actually unreal or so unusual as to seem unreal. FABULOUS is sometimes used of extraordinary or unbelievable aspects of real life ⟨the expedition brought *fabulous* treasures up from the bottom of the sea⟩ LEGENDARY is used to describe those things which have some basis in reality yet have become so colored by exaggeration and popular tradition that it is impossible to separate the fact from the fiction; MYTHICAL is used of things which have no direct basis in reality yet are commonly thought of as real ⟨the exciting world where a *legendary* saint slays a *mythical* dragon⟩

fa·cade \fə-'säd\ *n* : the face or front of a building

¹face \'fās\ *n* **1** : the front part of the human head **2** : PRESENCE ⟨in the *face* of danger⟩ **3** : facial expression ⟨put on a sad *face*⟩ **4** : outward appearance ⟨looks easy

facade

on the *face* of it⟩ **5** : BOLDNESS **6** : GRIMACE ⟨made a *face*⟩ **7** : DIGNITY, PRESTIGE ⟨afraid to lose *face*⟩ **8** : a front, upper, or outer surface **9** : one of the plane surfaces that bound a geometric solid ⟨a *face* of a prism⟩

²face *vb* **faced; fac·ing** **1** : to cover the front or surface of ⟨a building *faced* with marble⟩ **2** : to have the front or face toward ⟨the house *faces* east⟩ **3** : to oppose firmly

fac·et \'fas-ət\ *n* : one of the small surfaces of a cut gem

fa·ce·tious \fə-'sē-shəs\ *adj* : not serious : HUMOROUS

facet

facet

fa·cial \'fā-shəl\ *adj* : of or relating to the face — **fa·cial·ly** *adv*

fa·cil·i·tate \fə-'sil-ə-,tāt\ *vb* **fa·cil·i·tat·ed; fa·cil·i·tat·ing** : to make easier

fa·cil·i·ty \fə-'sil-ət-ē\ *n, pl* **fa·cil·i·ties** **1** : freedom from difficulty : EASE ⟨small enough to be handled with *facility*⟩ **2** : ease in performance : APTITUDE ⟨shows *facility* in reading⟩ **3** : something that makes an action, operation, or course of conduct easier ⟨modern library *facilities*⟩ **4** : something (as a hospital) that is built or installed to serve a particular purpose

fac·sim·i·le \fak-'sim-ə-lē\ *n* [from the Latin phrase *fac simile* "make similar"] : an exact copy ⟨a *facsimile* of a document⟩

fact \'fakt\ *n* **1** : something that has been done : DEED **2** : the quality of being actual ⟨a question of *fact*⟩ **3** : a statement about something that exists or is done

¹fac·tor \'fak-tər\ *n* **1** : a person who does business for another **2** : something that helps produce a result **3** : GENE **4** : any of the numbers that when multiplied together form a product

²factor *vb* : to find the factors of a number

fac·to·ry \'fak-tə-rē\ *n, pl* **fac·to·ries** : a place where goods are manufactured

fac·tu·al \'fak-chə-wəl\ *adj* **1** : of or relating to facts **2** : based on facts — **fac·tu·al·ly** *adv*

fac·ul·ty \'fak-əl-tē\ *n, pl* **fac·ul·ties** **1** : ability to do something : TALENT ⟨a *faculty* for making friends⟩ **2** : one of the powers of the mind or body ⟨the *faculty* of hearing⟩ **3** : the teachers in a school or college

fad \'fad\ *n* : a practice or interest followed for a time

fade \'fād\ *vb* **fad·ed; fad·ing** **1** : WITHER ⟨a *faded* flower⟩ **2** : to lose or cause to lose brilliance of color **3** : to grow dim or faint

Fahr·en·heit \'far-ən-,hīt\ *adj* : relating to, conforming to, or having a thermometer scale on which the boiling point of water is at 212 degrees above the zero of the scale and the freezing point is at 32 degrees above zero

j job   ng sing   ō low   ȯ moth   ȯi coin   th thin   th this   ü boot   u̇ foot   y you   yü few   yu̇ furious   zh vision

¹fail \'fāl\ *vb* **1** : to lose strength : WEAKEN ⟨*failing* in health⟩ **2** : to die away **3** : to stop functioning ⟨the engine *failed*⟩ **4** : to fall short ⟨*failed* in his duty⟩ **5** : to be or become absent or inadequate ⟨the water supply *failed*⟩ **6** : to be unsuccessful ⟨*failed* the test⟩ **7** : to become bankrupt ⟨the business *failed*⟩ **8** : DISAPPOINT, DESERT **9** : NEGLECT

²fail *n* : FAILURE ⟨promised to go without *fail*⟩

fail·ing \'fā-ling\ *n* : WEAKNESS, SHORTCOMING **syn** see FAULT

fail·ure \'fāl-yər\ *n* **1** : a failing to do or perform ⟨*failure* to keep his word⟩ **2** : a state of being unable to perform a normal function adequately ⟨heart *failure*⟩ **3** : a lack of success ⟨*failure* in a test⟩ **4** : BANKRUPTCY **5** : a falling short ⟨crop *failure*⟩ **6** : a breaking down **7** : a person or thing that has failed

¹faint \'fānt\ *adj* **1** : lacking courage : COWARDLY **2** : being weak or dizzy and likely to faint ⟨feel *faint*⟩ **3** : lacking vigor or strength : FEEBLE ⟨a *faint* attempt⟩ **4** : not distinct : DIM — **faint·ly** *adv* — **faint·ness** *n*

²faint *vb* : to lose consciousness

³faint *n* : an act or condition of fainting

faint·heart·ed \'fānt-'härt-əd\ *adj* : TIMID

¹fair \'faər\ *adj* **1** : attractive in appearance : BEAUTIFUL ⟨our *fair* city⟩ **2** : CLEAN, PURE ⟨the city's *fair* name⟩ **3** : not stormy or cloudy ⟨*fair* weather⟩ **4** : JUST, IMPARTIAL ⟨received *fair* treatment⟩ **5** : conforming with the rules ⟨*fair* play⟩ **6** : being within the foul lines ⟨*fair* ball⟩ **7** : not dark : BLOND ⟨*fair* hair⟩ **8** : ADEQUATE, AVERAGE ⟨a *fair* grade in spelling⟩ **syn** see MEDIOCRE — **fair·ness** *n*

²fair *adv* : in a fair manner ⟨play *fair*⟩

³fair *n* [from medieval Latin *feria*, from Latin *feriae* "holidays"] **1** : a gathering of buyers and sellers at a particular time and place for trade **2** : a competitive exhibition (as of livestock or farm products) usually along with entertainment and amusements ⟨county *fair*⟩ **3** : a sale of articles for a charitable purpose

fair·ground \'faər-,graund\ *n* : an area set aside for fairs, circuses, or exhibitions

fair·ly \'faər-lē\ *adv* **1** : ABSOLUTELY, QUITE ⟨*fairly* bursting with pride⟩ **2** : in a fair manner : JUSTLY **3** : MODERATELY, RATHER

¹fair·y \'faər-ē\ *n, pl* **fair·ies** : an imaginary being who has the form of a very tiny human being and has magic powers

²fairy *adj* : of, relating to, or resembling a fairy

fair·y·land \'faər-ē-,land\ *n* **1** : the land of fairies **2** : a place of delicate charm

fairy tale *n* **1** : a story about fairies **2** : a made-up story : FIB

faith \'fāth\ *n* **1** : allegiance to duty or to a

person : LOYALTY **2** : belief in God **3** : complete confidence : TRUST **4** : a system of religious beliefs : RELIGION **syn** see BELIEF

faith·ful \'fāth-fəl\ *adj* **1** : DEPENDABLE ⟨a *faithful* worker⟩ **2** : LOYAL, DEVOTED ⟨a *faithful* friend⟩ **3** : true to the facts : ACCURATE — **faith·ful·ly** *adv* — **faith·ful·ness** *n*

faith·less \'fāth-ləs\ *adj* : false to promises — **faith·less·ly** *adv* — **faith·less·ness** *n*

¹fake \'fāk\ *vb* **faked; fak·ing** **1** : to treat so as to give a false appearance ⟨*faked* the figures to make it look as if he had won⟩ **2** : COUNTERFEIT ⟨*fake* a signature⟩ **3** : PRETEND

²fake *n* : a person or thing that is not really what is pretended

syn FAKE, FRAUD, IMITATION all mean a less valuable copy of an original model. IMITATION can mean merely this, with no hint of deception involved ⟨glazed green pottery made in *imitation* of jade⟩ FAKE carries the idea of intent to deceive, at least as far as hoping that the imitation will be taken as real ⟨played the part so well you hardly knew the British accent was a *fake*⟩ FRAUD adds the aspect of mischievous or criminal intent ⟨the paintings, sold as original Rembrandts, turned out to be *frauds* done by an unknown⟩

³fake *adj* : SHAM, COUNTERFEIT

fal·con \'fal-kən, 'fòl-\ *n* **1** : a hawk trained for use in hunting small game **2** : any of several long-winged swift-flying small hawks

fal·con·ry \'fal-kən-rē, 'fòl-\ *n* : the art or sport of hunting with a falcon

¹fall \'fòl\ *vb* **fell** \'fel\; **fall·en** \'fòl-ən\; **fall·ing** **1** : to descend freely by the force of gravity ⟨an apple *fallen* from the tree⟩ **2** : to come as if by dropping down ⟨night *fell*⟩ **3** : to become lower (as in degree or pitch) ⟨the temperature *fell* ten degrees⟩ **4** : to drop from an upright position **5** : to drop down wounded or dead ⟨*fall* in battle⟩ **6** : to become captured ⟨the city *fell* to the invaders⟩ **7** : to decline in quantity, quality, or value ⟨prices *fell* on the stock exchange⟩ **8** : to occur at a certain time ⟨*falls* on the first Monday of September⟩ **9** : to pass from one condition of body or mind to another ⟨*fall* asleep⟩ ⟨*fall* ill⟩ — **fall back** : RETREAT — **fall in** : to take one's place in ranks — **fall out** **1** : QUARREL **2** : to leave one's place in ranks — **fall short** : to be deficient

²fall *n* **1** : the act of falling ⟨a *fall* from a horse⟩ **2** : AUTUMN **3** : a thing or quantity that falls ⟨a heavy *fall* of snow⟩ **4** : RUIN, DOWNFALL ⟨the *fall* of Rome⟩ **5** : WATERFALL — usually used in plural ⟨Niagara *Falls*⟩ **6** : a decrease in size, quantity, degree, or value ⟨a

fall in prices⟩ **7** : the distance something falls
fal·la·cious \fə-'lā-shəs\ *adj* : MISTAKEN
fal·la·cy \'fal-ə-sē\ *n, pl* **fal·la·cies 1** : a false
or mistaken idea **2** : false reasoning
fall·out \'fȯl-ˌau̇t\ *n* : the often radioactive
particles resulting from the explosion of an
atomic bomb and falling through the atmosphere
¹fal·low \'fal-ō\ *n* : land for crops that lies
idle
²fallow *vb* : to till without planting a crop
³fallow *adj* : left untilled or unplanted
fallow deer *n* : a small European deer with
broad antlers and a pale yellowish coat
spotted with white in summer
¹false \'fȯls\ *adj* **fals·er; fals·est 1** : not
genuine ⟨*false* documents⟩ ⟨*false* teeth⟩
2 : intentionally untrue ⟨*false* testimony⟩
3 : not true ⟨an argument based on *false* con-
cepts⟩ **4** : not faithful or loyal ⟨*false* friends⟩
5 : not consistent with the true facts ⟨a *false*
claim⟩ — **false·ly** *adv* — **false·ness** *n*
²false *adv* : in a false manner : TREACHEROUSLY
false·hood \'fȯls-ˌhu̇d\ *n* **1** : LIE **2** : the
practice of lying ⟨given to *falsehood*⟩
fal·set·to \fȯl-'set-ō\ *n, pl* **fal·set·tos** : an artificially high voice
fal·si·fy \'fȯl-sə-ˌfī\ *vb* **fal·si·fied; fal·si·fy·ing**
: to make false ⟨*falsified* the report card⟩
fal·si·ty \'fȯl-sət-ē\ *n, pl* **fal·si·ties 1** : something false **2** : the quality or state of being
false
fal·ter \'fȯl-tər\ *vb* **1** : to move unsteadily
: WAVER **2** : to hesitate in speech : STAMMER
3 : to hesitate in purpose or action
fame \'fām\ *n* : the fact or condition of being
known to the public : RENOWN
famed \'fāmd\ *adj* : FAMOUS, RENOWNED
fa·mil·ial \fə-'mil-yəl\ *adj* : of, relating to, or
typical of a family
¹fa·mil·iar \fə-'mil-yər\ *n* **1** : COMPANION
2 : one who frequents a place
²familiar *adj* **1** : closely acquainted : INTI-
MATE ⟨*familiar* friends⟩ **2** : INFORMAL, CASUAL
⟨spoke in a *familiar* manner⟩ **3** : overly intimate : PRESUMPTUOUS **4** : frequently seen or
experienced **5** : having a good knowledge
fa·mil·iar·i·ty \fə-ˌmil-'yar-ət-ē\ *n, pl* **fa·mil-
iar·i·ties 1** : INTIMACY **2** : close acquaintance with or knowledge of something **3** : IN-
FORMALITY **4** : IMPROPRIETY
fa·mil·iar·ize \fə-'mil-yə-ˌrīz\ *vb* **fa·mil·iar-
ized; fa·mil·iar·iz·ing** : to make familiar
fam·i·ly \'fam-ə-lē\ *n, pl* **fam·i·lies** [from
Latin *familia* "household, including servants
as well as relatives of the householder", from
famulus "servant"] **1** : a group of persons

descended from the same ancestor **2** : a group
of persons living under one roof or one head
3 : a group of things having common characteristics ⟨a *family* of languages⟩ **4** : a social
group made up of parents and their children
5 : a group of related kinds of plants or animals ⟨peaches, apples, and roses all belong to
the rose *family*⟩
fam·ine \'fam-ən\ *n* **1** : an extreme general
lack of food **2** : a great shortage
fam·ish \'fam-ish\ *vb* **1** : STARVE **2** : to suffer from hunger
fa·mous \'fā-məs\ *adj* : much talked about
syn FAMOUS, RENOWNED, NOTORIOUS all refer
to what is widely known. FAMOUS means no
more than this, and gives no hint as to the
cause or permanence of the fame ⟨the most
famous actor in America⟩ RENOWNED indicates
a praiseworthy reputation associated with
honorable and outstanding accomplishments
⟨*renowned* for his stand against tyranny⟩ ⟨was
renowned as both a poet and playwright⟩
NOTORIOUS denotes a dishonorable fame often
acquired as a result of scandal or evil deeds ⟨a
notorious band of outlaws⟩
fa·mous·ly \'fā-məs-lē\ *adv* : very well
¹fan \'fan\ *n* **1** : a device (as a hand-waved
triangular blade or a mecha-
nism with rotating blades) for
producing a current of air
2 : something resembling a fan
²fan *vb* **fanned; fan·ning 1** : to
move air with a fan **2** : to
direct a current of air upon
with a fan
³fan *n* : an enthusiastic follower or admirer
¹fa·nat·ic \fə-'nat-ik\ *adj*
[from Latin *fanaticus* "in-
spired by a god", "frenzied", from *fanum*
"temple"] : unreasonably enthusiastic or devoted
²fanatic *n* : one who is fanatic
fan·ci·ful \'fan-si-fəl\ *adj* **1** : full of fancy ⟨a
fanciful tale⟩ **2** : coming from fancy rather
than reason ⟨a *fanciful* scheme for getting
rich⟩ — **fan·ci·ful·ly** *adv* — **fan·ci·ful·ness** *n*
¹fan·cy \'fan-sē\ *n, pl* **fan·cies 1** : the power
of the mind to think of things that are not
present or real : IMAGINATION **2** : LIKING ⟨took
a *fancy* to her⟩ **3** : NOTION, IDEA
²fancy *vb* **fan·cied; fan·cy·ing 1** : LIKE, ENJOY
⟨*fancies* candied apples⟩ **2** : IMAGINE ⟨well,
fancy that⟩ **3** : to believe without evidence
³fancy *adj* **fan·ci·er; fan·ci·est 1** : not plain or
ordinary ⟨a *fancy* dress⟩ **2** : being above the
average (as in quality or price) ⟨*fancy* fruits⟩

fans 1

3 : executed with superior skill and grace ⟨*fancy* diving⟩ — **fan·ci·ly** \'fan-sə-lē\ *adv* — **fan·ci·ness** \-sē-nəs\ *n*

fang \'fang\ *n* 1 : a long sharp tooth by which animals seize and hold their prey 2 : one of the usually two long hollow or grooved teeth by which a poisonous snake injects its venom — **fanged** \'fangd\ *adj*

fangs

fan·tas·tic \fan-'tas-tik\ *adj* 1 : produced by the fancy : resembling something produced by the fancy ⟨a *fantastic* scheme⟩ 2 : hardly believable — **fan·tas·ti·cal·ly** \-ti-kə-lē\ *adv*

fan·ta·sy \'fant-ə-sē\ *n, pl* **fan·ta·sies** 1 : IMAGINATION 2 : something produced by the imagination

¹far \'fär\ *adv* **far·ther** \'fär-thər\ *or* **fur·ther** \'fər-\; **far·thest** \'fär-thəst\ *or* **fur·thest** \'fər-\ 1 : at or to a great distance in space or time ⟨*far* from home⟩ ⟨read *far* into the night⟩ 2 : by a great interval ⟨*far* better⟩ 3 : to or at a definite distance, point, or degree ⟨as *far* as I know⟩ 4 : to an advanced point or extent

²far *adj* **far·ther** *or* **fur·ther**; **far·thest** *or* **fur·thest** 1 : very distant in space or time ⟨a *far* country⟩ 2 : LONG 3 : the more distant of two

far·a·way \ˌfär-ə-ˌwā\ *adj* 1 : DISTANT 2 : DREAMY ⟨a *faraway* look⟩

¹fare \'faər\ *vb* **fared**; **far·ing** 1 : GO, TRAVEL ⟨*fare* forth on a journey⟩ 2 : to get along

²fare *n* 1 : the money a person pays to travel (as on a bus) 2 : PASSENGER 3 : FOOD

¹fare·well \faər-'wel\ *n* : an expression of good wishes at parting — often used as an interjection

²fare·well \ˌfaər-ˌwel\ *adj* : of or relating to leave-taking : FINAL ⟨a *farewell* speech⟩

far-fetched \'fär-'fecht\ *adj* : IMPROBABLE

¹farm \'färm\ *n* 1 : a piece of land used for raising crops or animals 2 : a tract of water where fish or oysters are grown

²farm *vb* : to run or work on a farm — **farm·er** *n*

farm·hand \'färm-ˌhand\ *n* : a farm laborer

farm·house \'färm-ˌhaùs\ *n* : the dwelling house of a farm

farm·yard \'färm-ˌyärd\ *n* : the yard around or enclosed by farm buildings

far-off \'fär-'òf\ *adj* : remote in time or space

far·sight·ed \'fär-'sīt-əd\ *adj* 1 : able to see distant things more clearly than near ones 2 : able to judge how something will work out in the future — **far·sight·ed·ness** *n*

¹far·ther \'fär-thər\ *adv* 1 : at or to a greater distance or more advanced point 2 : more completely

²farther *adj* : more distant

¹far·thest \'fär-thəst\ *adj* : most distant

²farthest *adv* 1 : to or at the greatest distance in space or time 2 : to the most advanced point

far·thing \'fär-thing\ *n* : a British coin worth one quarter of a penny

fas·ci·nate \'fas-n-ˌāt\ *vb* **fas·ci·nat·ed**; **fas·ci·nat·ing** 1 : to grip the attention of : hold spellbound 2 : to attract greatly

fas·cism \'fash-ˌiz-əm\ *n* : a political philosophy, movement, or regime marked by severe economic and social regimentation and forcible suppression of opposition

fas·cist \'fash-əst\ *n, often cap* : one who adheres to, advocates, or practices fascism

¹fash·ion \'fash-ən\ *n* 1 : the make or form of something 2 : MANNER, WAY 3 : the prevailing style of a thing at a particular time

²fashion *vb* : to give shape or form to : MOLD

fash·ion·a·ble \'fash-ə-nə-bəl\ *adj* : following the fashion or established style : STYLISH — **fash·ion·a·bly** \-blē\ *adv*

¹fast \'fast\ *adj* 1 : firmly fixed ⟨tent pegs *fast* in the ground⟩ 2 : firmly loyal ⟨*fast* friends⟩ 3 : marked by quick motion, operation, or effect ⟨a *fast* train⟩ ⟨a *fast* ball⟩ 4 : taking a short time ⟨a *fast* trip⟩ 5 : indicating ahead of the correct time ⟨a watch that is *fast*⟩ 6 : that will not fade ⟨*fast* colors⟩

²fast *adv* 1 : in a fast or fixed manner ⟨stuck *fast* in the mud⟩ 2 : SOUNDLY, DEEPLY ⟨*fast* asleep⟩ 3 : SWIFTLY ⟨run *faster* than a rabbit⟩

³fast *vb* 1 : to abstain from food 2 : to eat sparingly or abstain from some foods

⁴fast *n* 1 : the act of fasting 2 : a period of fasting

fas·ten \'fas-n\ *vb* 1 : to attach or join by or as if by pinning, tying, or nailing ⟨*fasten* clothes on a line⟩ 2 : to fix securely 3 : to become fixed or joined — **fas·ten·er** *n*

fas·ten·ing \'fas-n-ing\ *n* : something that fastens

fas·tid·i·ous \fas-'tid-ē-əs\ *adj* : hard to please : very particular

¹fat \'fat\ *adj* **fat·ter**; **fat·test** [from Old English *fætt*, past participle of *fætan* "to cram"] 1 : PLUMP, FLESHY ⟨a *fat* man⟩ 2 : OILY, GREASY ⟨*fat* meat⟩ 3 : well stocked ⟨a *fat* purse⟩ 4 : PROFITABLE ⟨a *fat* job⟩

²fat *n* 1 : animal or plant tissue containing much greasy or oily matter 2 : any of numerous compounds of carbon, hydrogen, and oxygen that are the chief constituents of animal or plant fat, are soluble in ether but not in water, and are important to nutrition as sources of energy 3 : a solid fat as distinguished from an oil **4** : the best or richest part ⟨the *fat* of the land⟩

fa·tal \'fāt-l\ *adj* **1** : causing death : MORTAL **2** : FATEFUL — **fa·tal·ly** *adv*

fa·tal·i·ty \fā-'tal-ət-ē\ *n, pl* **fa·tal·i·ties** : a death resulting from a disaster or accident

¹fate \'fāt\ *n* [from Latin *fatum*, literally, "that which has been spoken", derived from the past participle of *fari* "to speak"] **1** : a power beyond men's control that is held to determine what happens : DESTINY ⟨blamed his failure on *fate*⟩ **2** : something that happens as though determined by fate : FORTUNE **3** : OUTCOME, END **syn** see DESTINY

²fate *vb* **fat·ed; fat·ing** : DESTINE, DOOM

fate·ful \'fāt-fəl\ *adj* : having or marked by serious consequences ⟨a *fateful* decision⟩ ⟨that *fateful* day⟩ — **fate·ful·ly** *adv* — **fate·ful·ness** *n*

¹fa·ther \'fä-thər\ *n* **1** : a male parent **2** *cap* : ²GOD **3** : FOREFATHER **4** : one who cares for another as a father might **5** : one deserving the respect and love given to a father **6** : ORIGINATOR, AUTHOR **7** : PRIEST — used especially as a title — **fa·ther·hood** \-ˌhùd\ *n*

²father *vb* **1** : to become the father of **2** : to care for as a father

fa·ther–in–law \'fä-thər-ən-ˌlȯ\ *n, pl* **fa·thers–in–law** : the father of one's spouse

fa·ther·land \'fä-thər-ˌland\ *n* : one's native land

fa·ther·less \'fä-thər-ləs\ *adj* : having no living father

fa·ther·ly \'fä-thər-lē\ *adj* **1** : of or resembling a father ⟨a *fatherly* old man⟩ **2** : showing the affection or concern of a father

¹fath·om \'fath-əm\ *n* [from Old English *fæthm* meaning "the length of the outstretched arms"] : a unit of length equal to six feet used chiefly in measuring the depth of water

²fathom *vb* **1** : to measure the depth of water by means of a special line **2** : to penetrate and come to understand ⟨can't *fathom* his reasons⟩

¹fa·tigue \fə-'tēg\ *n* : WEARINESS

²fatigue *vb* **fa·tigued; fa·tigu·ing** : to tire by work or exertion **syn** see TIRE

fat·ten \'fat-n\ *vb* : to make or become fat

fat·ty \'fat-ē\ *adj* **fat·ti·er; fat·ti·est** : containing or resembling fat

fau·cet \'fȯ-sət\ *n* : a fixture for regulating the amount of liquid that runs out of a pipe or tank

fault \'fȯlt\ *n* **1** : a weakness in character : FAILING ⟨loved him in spite of his *faults*⟩ **2** : IMPERFECTION, FLAW ⟨a *fault* in the weaving of the cloth⟩ **3** : MISTAKE ⟨found a *fault* in the text⟩ **4** : responsibility

faucet

for something wrong ⟨your own *fault*⟩ **5** : a crack in the earth's crust with a displacing of rock masses

syn FAULT, FAILING, FOIBLE mean a weakness or imperfection of character. FAULT may be serious or minor and indicates a failure to meet some standard of perfection in habit or disposition ⟨her quick temper was the *fault* that often got her into trouble⟩ FAILING suggests a minor shortcoming in character ⟨their chief *failing* is feeling too proud of themselves after a victory⟩ FOIBLE suggests a harmless or even endearing weakness ⟨a weakness for cats was Mother's *foible*, so the house usually swarmed with them⟩ — **at fault** : liable to blame : RESPONSIBLE

fault·less \'fȯlt-ləs\ *adj* : free from fault : PERFECT — **fault·less·ly** *adv* — **fault·less·ness** *n*

fault·y \'fȯl-tē\ *adj* **fault·i·er; fault·i·est** : marked by fault, blemish, or defect : IMPERFECT — **fault·i·ly** \-tə-lē\ *adv* — **fault·i·ness** \-tē-nəs\ *n*

faun \'fȯn\ *n* : a Roman god of country life represented as part goat and part man

fau·na \'fȯ-nə\ *n* : the animal life characteristic of a region, period, or special environment

¹fa·vor \'fā-vər\ *n* **1** : APPROVAL, LIKING ⟨look with *favor* on a plan⟩ **2** : preference for one side over the other : PARTIALITY ⟨showed *favor* toward the older sister⟩ **3** : an act of kindness **4** : a small gift or decorative item

²favor *vb* **1** : to regard with favor ⟨*favors* a bill to cut taxes⟩ **2** : OBLIGE ⟨please *favor* me with an early reply⟩ **3** : to prefer especially unfairly **4** : to make possible or easier **5** : to look like

fa·vor·a·ble \'fā-və-rə-bəl\ *adj* **1** : showing favor ⟨a *favorable* opinion⟩ **2** : HELPFUL, PROMISING ⟨*favorable* weather⟩ — **fa·vor·a·ble·ness** *n* — **fa·vor·a·bly** \-blē\ *adv*

¹fa·vor·ite \'fā-və-rət\ *n* : a person or a thing that is favored above others

²favorite *adj* : being a favorite : best-liked

¹fawn \'fȯn\ *vb* **1** : to show affection — used especially of a dog **2** : to try to win favor by behavior that shows lack of self-respect

²fawn *n* [from early French *faon* "young of any animal", derived from Latin *fetus* "offspring"] **1** : a young deer **2** : a light grayish brown

fay \'fā\ *n* : FAIRY, ELF

faze \'fāz\ *vb* **fazed; faz·ing** : DAUNT

fe·al·ty \'fē-əl-tē\ *n* : LOYALTY, ALLEGIANCE

¹fear \'fiər\ *n* : a strong unpleasant feeling caused by being aware of danger or expecting something bad to happen

²**fear** *vb* : to be afraid of : have fear

fear·ful \'fiər-fəl\ *adj* **1** : causing fear ⟨the *fearful* roar of a lion⟩ **2** : filled with fear ⟨*fearful* of danger⟩ **3** : showing or caused by fear — **fear·ful·ly** *adv* — **fear·ful·ness** *n*

fear·less \'fiər-ləs\ *adj* : free from fear : BRAVE — **fear·less·ly** *adv* — **fear·less·ness** *n*

fear·some \'fiər-səm\ *adj* **1** : causing fear **2** : TIMID

fea·si·ble \'fē-zə-bəl\ *adj* : capable of being done or carried out ⟨a *feasible* plan⟩

¹**feast** \'fēst\ *n* **1** : an elaborate meal **2** : a religious festival

²**feast** *vb* **1** : to eat plentifully **2** : DELIGHT

feat \'fēt\ *n* : an act or deed showing courage, strength, or skill

¹**feath·er** \'feth-ər\ *n* **1** : one of the light horny outgrowths that make up the outer covering of a bird **2** : the same kind or sort ⟨birds of a *feather*⟩ — **feath·ered** \-ərd\ *adj* — **feath·er·less** \-ər-ləs\ *adj*

²**feather** *vb* **1** : to cover or clothe with feathers **2** : to grow or form feathers

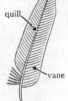

quill

vane

feather 1

feather bed *n* **1** : a mattress filled with feathers **2** : a bed with a feather mattress

feath·er·y \'feth-ə-rē\ *adj* **1** : resembling a feather or tuft of feathers ⟨a *feathery* palm tree⟩ **2** : covered with feathers

¹**fea·ture** \'fē-chər\ *n* **1** : a single part (as the nose or the mouth) of the face **2** : something especially noticeable **3** : a main attraction

²**feature** *vb* **fea·tured; fea·tur·ing 1** : to be a feature of **2** : to give prominence to

Feb·ru·ar·y \'feb-yə-,wer-ē, 'feb-rə-, 'feb-ə-\ *n* : the second month of the year

fe·ces \'fē-,sēz\ *n pl* : bodily waste that passes out from the intestine

fed·er·al \'fed-ə-rəl\ *adj* : of or relating to a nation formed by the union of several states or nations

fee \'fē\ *n* **1** : a fixed charge ⟨admission *fee*⟩ **2** : a charge for services ⟨a doctor's *fee*⟩

fee·ble \'fē-bəl\ *adj* **fee·bler** \-blər\; **fee·blest** \-bləst\ **1** : lacking in strength **2** : not loud ⟨a *feeble* cry⟩ **syn** see WEAK — **fee·ble·ness** \-bəl-nəs\ *n* — **fee·bly** \-blē\ *adv*

¹**feed** \'fēd\ *vb* **fed** \'fed\; **feed·ing 1** : to give food to or give as food ⟨*fed* the baby⟩ ⟨*fed* cereal to the baby⟩ **2** : to consume food : EAT — used especially of lower animals ⟨cattle *feeding* on hay⟩ **3** : to furnish with something necessary (as to growth or operation) ⟨*feed* plants with fertilizer⟩ — **feed·er** *n*

²**feed** *n* : food especially for livestock

¹**feel** \'fēl\ *vb* **felt** \'felt\; **feel·ing 1** : to get knowledge of through physical contact ⟨*feel* cold⟩ **2** : to examine or test by touching **3** : to be aware of **4** : to seem especially to the sense of touch **5** : to sense oneself to be a certain way ⟨*felt* sick⟩

²**feel** *n* **1** : SENSATION, FEELING **2** : the quality or properties of something determined through or as if through touch

feel·er \'fē-lər\ *n* **1** : a long flexible structure (as an insect's antenna) that is an organ of touch **2** : a proposal or remark made to find out the views of other people

feelers

feel·ing \'fē-ling\ *n* **1** : the sense by which a person knows whether things are hard or soft, hot or cold, heavy or light **2** : a sensation of temperature or pressure ⟨a *feeling* of cold⟩ ⟨a *feeling* of pain⟩ **3** : a state of mind ⟨a *feeling* of joy⟩ **4** *pl* : general emotional condition ⟨hurt his *feelings*⟩ **5** : the condition of being aware of something **6** : OPINION **7** : SYMPATHY

feet *pl of* FOOT

feign \'fān\ *vb* : to make believe : PRETEND

¹**feint** \'fānt\ *n* : a pretended blow or attack at one point to distract attention from the point one really intends to attack

²**feint** *vb* : to make a feint

fe·lic·i·ty \fi-'lis-ət-ē\ *n* : great happiness

¹**fe·line** \'fē-,līn\ *adj* **1** : of or relating to cats or the cat family **2** : suggesting a cat

²**feline** *n* : a feline animal : CAT

¹**fell** \'fel\ *vb* : to cut or knock down

²**fell** *past of* FALL

³**fell** *adj* : CRUEL, DEADLY

¹**fel·low** \'fel-ō\ *n* **1** : COMRADE, ASSOCIATE **2** : an equal in rank, power, or character **3** : one of a pair : MATE **4** : MAN, BOY

²**fellow** *adj* : being a companion, mate, or associate

fel·low·man \,fel-ō-'man\ *n, pl* **fel·low·men** \-'men\ : a kindred human being

fel·low·ship \'fel-ō-,ship\ *n* **1** : friendly relationship existing among persons **2** : a group with similar interests

fel·on \'fel-ən\ *n* : CRIMINAL

fel·o·ny \'fel-ə-nē\ *n, pl* **fel·o·nies** : a very serious crime — **fe·lo·ni·ous** \fə-'lō-nē-əs\ *adj*

¹**felt** \'felt\ *n* : a heavy cloth or hat material made by rolling and pressing together fibers

²**felt** *past of* FEEL

¹**fe·male** \'fē-,māl\ *n* : one that is female

²**female** *adj* **1** : of, relating to, or being the sex that bears young or lays eggs **2** : bearing a pistil but no stamens **3** : of, relating to,

or suitable for females — **fe·male·ness** *n*

fem·i·nine \'fem-ə-nən\ *adj* : of or relating to women or girls

fen \'fen\ *n* : low land covered by water

¹fence \'fens\ *n* [from earlier *fens* "a means of protection", short for *defens* "defense"] : a barrier (as of wood or wire) to prevent escape or entry or to mark a boundary

²fence *vb* **fenced; fenc·ing** **1** : to enclose with a fence **2** : to practice fencing — **fenc·er** *n*

fenc·ing \'fen-sing\ *n* : the art or sport of fighting with swords or foils

fend \'fend\ *vb* **1** : REPEL **2** : to try to get along without help ⟨*fended* for himself⟩

fend·er \'fen-dər\ *n* **1** : a frame on the lower front of a locomotive or streetcar to catch or throw off anything that is hit **2** : a guard over an automobile wheel **3** : a low metal frame in front of a fireplace

fender 3

¹fer·ment \fər-'ment\ *vb* : to cause or undergo fermentation

²fer·ment \'fər-ˌment\ *n* **1** : something (as yeast) that brings about fermentation **2** : a state of excitement

fer·men·ta·tion \ˌfər-mən-'tā-shən\ *n* : a chemical breaking down of an organic material that is controlled by an enzyme and usually does not require oxygen

fern \'fərn\ *n* : a flowerless plant with leaves divided into many parts

fe·ro·cious \fə-'rō-shəs\ *adj* : FIERCE, SAVAGE — **fe·ro·cious·ly** *adv* — **fe·ro·cious·ness** *n*

fe·roc·i·ty \fə-'räs-ət-ē\ *n, pl* **fe·roc·i·ties** : the quality or state of being ferocious

¹fer·ret \'fer-ət\ *n* : a partly domesticated pale-colored European polecat sometimes kept for hunting vermin (as rats)

²ferret *vb* **1** : to drive out of a hiding place **2** : to find by keen searching

Fer·ris wheel \'fer-əs\ *n* : an amusement device consisting of a large upright power-driven wheel carrying seats around its rim

¹fer·ry \'fer-ē\ *vb* **fer·ried; fer·ry·ing** **1** : to carry by boat over a body of water **2** : to cross by a ferry **3** : to deliver an airplane under its own power **4** : to transport in an airplane

Ferris wheel

²ferry *n, pl* **fer·ries** **1** : a place where persons or things are ferried **2** : FERRY-BOAT

fer·ry·boat \'fer-ē-ˌbōt\ *n* : a boat used to ferry passengers, vehicles, or goods

fer·tile \'fərt-l\ *adj* **1** : producing vegetation or crops plentifully **2** : capable of developing and growing ⟨a *fertile* egg⟩

fer·til·i·ty \ˌfər-'til-ət-ē\ *n* : the condition of being fertile

fer·til·i·za·tion \ˌfərt-l-ə-'zā-shən\ *n* **1** : an act or process of making fertile **2** : union of an egg cell and a sperm cell to form the first stage of an embryo

fer·til·ize \'fərt-l-ˌīz\ *vb* **fer·til·ized; fer·til·iz·ing** : to make fertile or more fertile

fer·til·iz·er \'fərt-l-ˌī-zər\ *n* : material added to soil to make it more fertile

fer·vent \'fər-vənt\ *adj* : warm in feeling : ARDENT — **fer·vent·ly** *adv*

fer·vid \'fər-vəd\ *adj* : ARDENT, PASSIONATE — **fer·vid·ly** *adv*

fer·vor \'fər-vər\ *n* : fervid emotion or words

fes·ter \'fes-tər\ *vb* : to become painfully inflamed usually with the formation of pus

fes·ti·val \'fes-tə-vəl\ *n* **1** : a time of celebration ⟨a harvest *festival*⟩ **2** : a season or program of cultural events or entertainment

fes·tive \'fes-tiv\ *adj* **1** : having to do with a feast or festival **2** : marked by festivity

fes·tiv·i·ty \fes-'tiv-ət-ē\ *n, pl* **fes·tiv·i·ties** **1** : JOYOUSNESS, GAIETY **2** : festive activity

¹fes·toon \fes-'tün\ *n* : a decorative chain or strip hanging from two points

²festoon *vb* : to hang or form festoons on

festoon

fetch \'fech\ *vb* **1** : to go after and bring back **2** : to bring as a price : sell for

fetch·ing \'fech-ing\ *adj* : ATTRACTIVE, PLEASING — **fetch·ing·ly** *adv*

fet·id \'fet-əd\ *adj* : having a bad odor

¹fet·ter \'fet-ər\ *n* **1** : a shackle for the feet **2** : something that hampers : RESTRAINT

²fetter *vb* **1** : to put fetters on **2** : to restrain from motion or action

fe·tus \'fēt-əs\ *n* : an animal not yet born or hatched but more developed than an embryo

¹feud \'fyüd\ *n* : a long bitter quarrel carried on especially between families or clans and marked by acts of violence and revenge

²feud *vb* : to carry on a feud

feu·dal \'fyüd-l\ *adj* : of or relating to feudalism

feu·dal·ism \'fyüd-l-ˌiz-əm\ *n* : a system of government existing in medieval Europe in which a vassal rendered service to a lord and received protection and land in return

fe·ver \'fē-vər\ *n* **1** : a rise of body temperature above normal **2** : a disease characterized by fever

fe·ver·ish \'fē-və-rish\ *adj* **1** : marked by

fever **2** : of, relating to, or being fever **3** : EXCITED ⟨*feverish* activity⟩ — **fe·ver·ish·ly** *adv* — **fe·ver·ish·ness** *n*

¹few \'fyü\ *pron* : not many : a small number

²few *adj* **1** : amounting to a small number **2** : not many but some ⟨caught a *few* fish⟩

³few *n* : a small number of individuals

fez \'fez\ *n, pl* **fez·zes** : a round flat-crowned red felt hat that usually has a tassel

fi·as·co \fē-'as-kō\ *n, pl* **fi·as·cos** : a complete failure

¹fib \'fib\ *n* : a petty lie

²fib *vb* **fibbed**; **fib·bing** : to tell a fib — **fib·ber** *n*

fi·ber *or* **fi·bre** \'fī-bər\ *n* : a long slender threadlike structure especially when capable of being spun into yarn

fez

fi·brous \'fī-brəs\ *adj* : containing, consisting of, or resembling fibers ⟨*fibrous* roots⟩

-fi·ca·tion \fə-'kā-shən\ *n suffix* : the act or process of or the result of ⟨ampli*fication*⟩

fick·le \'fik-əl\ *adj* : INCONSTANT, CHANGE-ABLE — **fick·le·ness** *n*

fic·tion \'fik-shən\ *n* **1** : something told or written that is not fact **2** : a made-up story

fic·tion·al \'fik-shən-l\ *adj* : of or relating to fiction — **fic·tion·al·ly** *adv*

fic·ti·tious \fik-'tish-əs\ *adj* : not real

¹fid·dle \'fid-l\ *n* : VIOLIN

²fiddle *vb* **fid·dled**; **fid·dling** **1** : to play on a fiddle **2** : to move the hands or fingers restlessly ⟨kept *fiddling* with a wedding ring⟩ **3** : to spend time in aimless activity ⟨*fiddled* around and got nothing done⟩ **4** : MEDDLE, TAMPER — **fid·dler** \'fid-lər\ *n*

fid·dle·stick \'fid-l-ˌstik\ *n* **1** : a violin bow **2** *pl* : NONSENSE — used as an interjection

fi·del·i·ty \fə-'del-ət-ē, fī-\ *n* : FAITHFULNESS

fidg·et \'fij-ət\ *vb* : to move or act restlessly or nervously

fidg·ets \'fij-əts\ *n pl* : uneasiness or restlessness shown by nervous movements

fidg·et·y \'fij-ət-ē\ *adj* : NERVOUS, UNEASY

fief \'fēf\ *n* : an estate given to a vassal by a feudal lord

¹field \'fēld\ *n* **1** : a piece of open, cleared, or cultivated land **2** : a piece of land put to a special use or yielding a special product ⟨a baseball *field*⟩ ⟨an oil *field*⟩ **3** : an open space or expanse **4** : a sphere or range of activity or influence ⟨the *field* of science⟩ **5** : a background on which something is drawn, painted, or mounted

²field *vb* : to catch, stop, or throw a ball as a fielder

³field *adj* : of or relating to a field

field·er \'fēl-dər\ *n* : a defensive player in baseball

field glass *n* : a hand-held optical instrument for use outdoors usually consisting of two telescopes on a single frame — usually used in plural

field glasses

field goal *n* : a score in football made by a dropkick or place-kick during ordinary play

fiend \'fēnd\ *n* **1** : DEMON, DEVIL **2** : an extremely wicked or cruel person

fierce \'fiərs\ *adj* **fierc·er**; **fierc·est** **1** : violently hostile or aggressive in temperament ⟨a *fierce* animal⟩ **2** : marked by intense zeal or vehemence **3** : wild or menacing in aspect — **fierce·ly** *adv* — **fierce·ness** *n*

fi·er·y \'fī-ə-rē, 'fīr-ē\ *adj* **fi·er·i·er**; **fi·er·i·est** **1** : BURNING, FLAMING ⟨a *fiery* furnace⟩ **2** : hot like a fire **3** : full of spirit

fi·es·ta \fē-'es-tə\ *n* : HOLIDAY, FESTIVAL

fife \'fīf\ *n* : a small shrill musical instrument like a flute

¹fif·teen \fif-'tēn\ *adj* : being one more than fourteen

fife

²fifteen *n* : one more than fourteen

¹fif·teenth \fif-'tēnth\ *adj* : being next after the fourteenth

²fifteenth *n* : number fifteen in a series

¹fifth \'fifth\ *adj* : being next after the fourth

²fifth *n* **1** : number five in a series **2** : one of five equal parts

¹fif·ti·eth \'fif-tē-əth\ *adj* : being next after the forty-ninth

²fiftieth *n* : number fifty in a series

¹fif·ty \'fif-tē\ *adj* : being five times ten

²fifty *n* : five times ten

fig \'fig\ *n* : the oblong or pear-shaped edible fruit of a tree related to the mulberry

¹fight \'fīt\ *vb* **fought** \'fȯt\; **fight·ing** **1** : to take part in a fight : fight with **2** : OPPOSE ⟨*fight* crime⟩ — **fight·er** *n*

²fight *n* **1** : a meeting in battle or in physical combat **2** : a verbal disagreement **3** : strength or disposition for fighting ⟨full of *fight*⟩

fig: fruit and leaves

¹fig·ure \'fig-yər\ *n* **1** : a symbol (as 1, 2, 3) that stands for a number : NUMERAL **2** *pl* : calculations using arithmetic ⟨has a good head for *figures*⟩ **3** : value or price expressed in figures ⟨the painting was sold for a high *figure*⟩ **4** : the shape or outline of something

figure 189 **financed**

5 : bodily shape especially of a person ⟨a slender *figure*⟩ **6** : a drawing or diagram illustrating a printed text **7** : PATTERN, DESIGN **8** : a series of movements in a dance **9** : an outline traced by a series of movements (as by an ice skater) **10** : a prominent person

²**figure** *vb* **fig·ured; fig·ur·ing** : to find out by using figures : CALCULATE ⟨*figure* the cost⟩ — **figure out** : to work out mentally

fig·ured \'fig-yərd\ *adj* : decorated with figures ⟨*figured* cloth⟩

fig·ure·head \'fig-yər-,hed\ *n* : a figure, statue, or bust on the bow of a ship

figure of speech : an expression that uses words in other than a plain or literal way

fil·a·ment \'fil-ə-mənt\ *n* : a fine thread : a slender threadlike object (as the fine wire in an electric bulb)

filament

fil·bert \'fil-bərt\ *n* [formed as *philber* in Anglo-French, the variety of French spoken in England after the Norman conquest; named after St. Philibert, an abbot whose feast day falls in the nutting season] : HAZEL, HAZELNUT

filch \'filch\ *vb* : STEAL, PILFER

¹**file** \'fīl\ *n* : a steel tool with sharp ridges or teeth for smoothing or rubbing down hard substances

²**file** *vb* **filed; fil·ing** : to rub, smooth, or cut away with a file

³**file** *vb* **filed; fil·ing** **1** : to arrange in order ⟨*file* cards in alphabetical order⟩ **2** : to enter or record officially

⁴**file** *n* **1** : a device (as a folder or cabinet) for keeping papers or records **2** : a collection of papers or records kept in a file

⁵**file** *n* : a row of persons or things arranged one behind the other ⟨walk in single *file*⟩

⁶**file** *vb* **filed; fil·ing** : to march or proceed in a file ⟨*file* out of the building⟩

fil·i·al \'fil-ē-əl\ *adj* **1** : of or befitting a son or daughter ⟨*filial* obedience⟩ **2** : being or having the relation of offspring

Fil·i·pi·no \,fil-ə-'pē-nō\ *n, pl* **Fil·i·pi·nos** : a native or inhabitant of the Philippines

¹**fill** \'fil\ *vb* **1** : to make or become full ⟨*fill* a basket⟩ **2** : to occupy fully : take up whatever space there is ⟨bicycles *filled* the sidewalk⟩ **3** : to spread through ⟨laughter *filled* the room⟩ **4** : to stop up : PLUG ⟨*fill* a crack⟩ ⟨*fill* a tooth⟩ **5** : to have and do the duties of ⟨*fill* the office of president⟩ **6** : to supply according to directions — **fill in** : SUBSTITUTE

²**fill** *n* **1** : a quantity that satisfies ⟨ate his *fill*⟩ **2** : material for filling

files

fill·er \'fil-ər\ *n* **1** : one that fills **2** : a material used for filling

fil·let \'fil-ət, fi-'lā\ *n* : a piece of lean boneless meat or fish

fill·ing \'fil-ing\ *n* : a substance used to fill something else ⟨a *filling* for a tooth⟩

filling station *n* : a place where gasoline and oil for automobiles are sold at retail

fil·ly \'fil-ē\ *n, pl* **fil·lies** : a female foal : a young female horse

¹**film** \'film\ *n* **1** : a thin skin or membrane **2** : a thin coating or layer ⟨a *film* of ice⟩ **3** : a roll of material prepared for taking pictures **4** : MOTION PICTURE

²**film** *vb* **1** : to cover or become covered with film **2** : to photograph on a film **3** : to make a motion picture

film·y \'fil-mē\ *adj* **film·i·er; film·i·est** : of, resembling, or made of film

¹**fil·ter** \'fil-tər\ *n* **1** : a device or a mass of material (as sand) with tiny openings through which a gas or liquid is passed to separate out something which it contains ⟨a *filter* for removing dust and soot from the air⟩ **2** : a transparent material that absorbs light of some colors and is used for modifying light (as in photography)

²**filter** *vb* **1** : to pass through a filter ⟨*filter* water⟩ **2** : to remove by means of a filter

filth \'filth\ *n* : disgusting dirt : foul matter

filth·y \'fil-thē\ *adj* **filth·i·er; filth·i·est** : disgustingly dirty — **filth·i·ness** *n*

fil·tra·tion \fil-'trā-shən\ *n* : the process of filtering

fin \'fin\ *n* **1** : any of the thin extensions of the body of a water animal and especially a fish that are used in propelling or guiding the body through the water **2** : a fin-shaped part

¹**fi·nal** \'fīn-l\ *adj* **1** : not to be changed : CONCLUSIVE ⟨the judges' decisions are *final*⟩ **2** : coming or happening at the end ⟨*final* examination⟩ **syn** see LAST — **fi·nal·ly** *adv*

²**final** *n* **1** : a deciding match or game **2** : a final examination in a course

fi·na·le \fə-'nal-ē\ *n* : the close or end of something (as a musical composition)

fi·nal·i·ty \fī-'nal-ət-ē\ *n, pl* **fi·nal·i·ties** **1** : the condition of being final **2** : something final

¹**fi·nance** \fə-'nans, 'fī-,nans\ *n* **1** : money available to a government or business ⟨the city's *finances*⟩ **2** : the system that includes the circulation of money, the granting of credit, the making of investments, and the providing of banks

²**finance** *vb* **fi·nanced; fi·nanc·ing** : to provide money for ⟨*finance* a trip⟩

fi·nan·cial \fə-'nan-chəl, fī-\ *adj* : having to do with finance or with finances — **fi·nan·cial·ly** *adv*

fin·an·cier \ˌfin-ən-'siər\ *n* **1** : one skilled in managing large funds **2** : a person with large sums of money to invest

finch \'finch\ *n* : a small seed-eating songbird (as the sparrow, bunting, or canary)

¹find \'fīnd\ *vb* **found** \'faund\; **find·ing** **1** : to come upon ⟨*found* a dime on the sidewalk⟩ **2** : to come upon by searching, study, or effort ⟨*find* the answer to a problem⟩ **3** : to decide on **4** : to know by experience ⟨people *found* the boy honest⟩ **5** : to gain or regain the use of ⟨*found* her voice again⟩ — **find fault** : to criticize unfavorably — **find out** **1** : to learn by study or observation **2** : DETECT, DISCOVER

²find *n* : something found

find·er \'fīn-dər\ *n* **1** : one that finds **2** : a device on a camera that shows the view being photographed

¹fine \'fīn\ *n* : a sum of money imposed as a punishment

²fine *vb* **fined; fin·ing** : to set a fine on

³fine *adj* **fin·er; fin·est** **1** : very small or thin ⟨*fine* print⟩ **2** : not coarse ⟨*fine* sand⟩ **3** : superior in quality or appearance ⟨a *fine* man⟩ — **fine·ly** *adv* — **fine·ness** *n*

⁴fine *adv* : very well ⟨doing *fine*⟩

fin·er·y \'fī-nə-rē\ *n, pl* **fin·er·ies** : showy clothes or ornaments

¹fin·ger \'fing-gər\ *n* **1** : one of the five divisions of the end of the hand including the thumb **2** : something that resembles or does the work of a finger **3** : the part of a glove into which a finger goes

²finger *vb* **1** : to touch with the fingers : HANDLE **2** : to perform with the fingers

fin·ger·ling \'fing-gər-ling\ *n* : a young fish

fin·ger·nail \'fing-gər-ˌnāl\ *n* : the hard covering at the end of a finger

¹fin·ger·print \'fing-gər-ˌprint\ *n* : the pattern of marks made by pressing a finger or thumb on a surface especially when such a pattern is made in ink for the purpose of identifying a person

fingerprint

²fingerprint *vb* : to take fingerprints of

fin·i·cal \'fin-i-kəl\ *adj* : FINICKY

fin·ick·y \'fin-i-kē\ *adj* : too particular in taste or standards : FUSSY — **fin·ick·i·ness** *n*

¹fin·ish \'fin-ish\ *vb* **1** : to bring or come to an end : COMPLETE, TERMINATE **2** : to put a final coat or surface on

²finish *n* **1** : END, CONCLUSION ⟨a close *finish* in a race⟩ **2** : the treatment given a surface or the appearance given by finishing

fi·nite \'fī-ˌnīt\ *adj* : having definite limits

Finn \'fin\ *n* : a native or inhabitant of Finland

finned \'find\ *adj* : having fins

¹Finn·ish \'fin-ish\ *adj* : of or relating to Finland, the Finns, or Finnish

²Finnish *n* : the language of the Finns

fiord \fē-'ord\ *var of* FJORD

fir \'fər\ *n* : a tall cone-shaped tree related to the pine that yields useful lumber

¹fire \'fīr\ *n* **1** : the light and heat and especially the flame produced by burning **2** : fuel that is burning (as in a fireplace or stove) **3** : the destructive burning of something (as a building or a forest) **4** : LIVELINESS, ENTHUSIASM **5** : the discharge of firearms ⟨rifle *fire*⟩ — **on fire** : BURNING — **under fire** **1** : exposed to the firing of enemy guns **2** : under attack

fir: needles and cone

²fire *vb* **fired; fir·ing** **1** : to set on fire ⟨vandals *fired* the barn⟩ **2** : STIR, ENLIVEN ⟨a story to *fire* the imagination⟩ **3** : to dismiss from employment **4** : to set off : EXPLODE ⟨*fire* a firecracker⟩ **5** : DISCHARGE ⟨*fire* a gun⟩ **6** : to subject to intense heat ⟨*fire* pottery⟩

fire·arm \'fīr-ˌärm\ *n* : a small weapon from which shot is discharged by gunpowder

fire·boat \'fīr-ˌbōt\ *n* : a ship equipped to fight fires

fire·bug \'fīr-ˌbəg\ *n* : a person who sets destructive fires deliberately

fire·crack·er \'fīr-ˌkrak-ər\ *n* : a paper tube containing an explosive to be fired in celebrations

fire engine *n* **1** : an apparatus for throwing water on a fire to put it out **2** : a truck equipped to fight fires

fire escape *n* : a stairway or ladder that provides a means of escape from a building in case of fire

fire extinguisher *n* : something (as a metal container filled with chemicals) that is used to put out a fire

fire·fly \'fīr-ˌflī\ *n, pl* **fire·flies** : a small beetle producing a soft light

fire·house \'fīr-ˌhaus\ *n* : FIRE STATION

fire·man \'fīr-mən\ *n, pl* **fire·men** \-mən\ **1** : a man whose business is to put out fires **2** : a man who tends a fire

fire·place \'fīr-ˌplās\ *n* : a rectangular opening made in a chimney to hold an open fire

fireplace

fire·plug \'fīr-ˌpləg\ *n* : a hydrant to which a large hose may be attached to draw water for fighting fires

fire·proof \'fīr-'prüf\ *adj* : not easily burned : made safe against fire

fire·side \'fīr-ˌsīd\ *n* 1 : a place near the fire or hearth 2 : HOME

fire station *n* : a building housing fire engines and usually firemen

fire·wood \'fīr-ˌwùd\ *n* : wood cut for fuel

fire·work \'fīr-ˌwərk\ *n* 1 : a device designed to make a display of light or noise by the combustion of explosive or flammable materials 2 *pl* : a display of fireworks

¹**firm** \'fərm\ *adj* 1 : HARD, SOLID ⟨*firm* flesh⟩ ⟨*firm* ground⟩ 2 : not easily shaken : LOYAL ⟨*firm* friends⟩ 3 : POSITIVE, DETERMINED — **firm·ly** *adv* — **firm·ness** *n*

²**firm** *n* 1 : the name under which a company does business 2 : a partnership of two or more persons in a business

fir·ma·ment \'fər-mə-mənt\ *n* : HEAVENS

¹**first** \'fərst\ *adj* 1 : being number one ⟨the *first* day of the week⟩ 2 : preceding all others

²**first** *adv* 1 : before any other ⟨reached the goal *first*⟩ 2 : for the first time

³**first** *n* 1 : number one in a series 2 : something that is first

first aid *n* : care or treatment given to an ill or injured person before regular medical aid can be obtained

first·hand \'fərst-'hand\ *adj* (*or adv*) : coming directly from the original source

first lieutenant *n* : a commissioned officer (as in the army) ranking next below a captain

first–rate \'fərst-'rāt\ *adj* : of the first order of size, importance, or quality

first sergeant *n* : MASTER SERGEANT 1

firth \'fərth\ *n* : a narrow arm of the sea

¹**fish** \'fish\ *n, pl* **fish** *or* **fish·es** 1 : an aquatic animal — usually used in combination ⟨star*fish*⟩ ⟨shell*fish*⟩ 2 : any of a large group of vertebrate animals that live in water, breathe with gills, and have fins and scales

²**fish** *vb* 1 : to attempt to catch fish 2 : to search for something that is buried or hidden

fish·er·man \'fish-ər-mən\ *n, pl* **fish·er·men** \-mən\ : a person who fishes

fish·er·y \'fish-ə-rē\ *n, pl* **fish·er·ies** 1 : the business of catching fish 2 : a place for catching fish

fish·hook \'fish-ˌhùk\ *n* : a hook used for catching fish

fish·y \'fish-ē\ *adj* **fish·i·er**; **fish·i·est** 1 : of or resembling fish ⟨a *fishy* odor⟩ 2 : inspiring doubt : QUESTIONABLE ⟨the story sounds *fishy* to me⟩

fishhooks

fis·sion \'fish-ən\ *n* 1 : a splitting or breaking into parts 2 : a method of reproduction in which a living cell or body divides into two or more parts each of which grows into a whole new individual 3 : the splitting of an atomic nucleus resulting in the release of large amounts of energy

fis·sure \'fish-ər\ *n* : a narrow opening or crack ⟨a *fissure* in rock⟩

fist \'fist\ *n* : the hand with the fingers doubled tight into the palm

¹**fit** \'fit\ *n* : a sudden attack or outburst

²**fit** *adj* **fit·ter**; **fit·test** 1 : good enough 2 : mentally and physically sound : HEALTHY ⟨feel *fit*⟩ — **fit·ly** *adv* — **fit·ness** *n*

³**fit** *vb* **fit·ted**; **fit·ting** 1 : to be suitable for or to ⟨dressed to *fit* the occasion⟩ 2 : to be the right shape or size 3 : to bring to a required shape or size ⟨have a suit *fitted*⟩ 4 : SUPPLY

⁴**fit** *n* 1 : the way something fits 2 : a piece of clothing that fits

fit·ful \'fit-fəl\ *adj* : not regular : RESTLESS

¹**fit·ting** \'fit-ing\ *adj* : SUITABLE, PROPER — **fit·ting·ly** *adv*

²**fitting** *n* : a small often standardized accessory part ⟨a pipe *fitting*⟩

¹**five** \'fīv\ *adj* : being one more than four

²**five** *n* 1 : one more than four 2 : the fifth in a set or series

¹**fix** \'fiks\ *vb* 1 : to make firm, stable, or fast ⟨*fix* a machine in place⟩ 2 : to change into a stable or available form ⟨bacteria that *fix* nitrogen⟩ 3 : to set definitely : ESTABLISH 4 : to get ready : PREPARE ⟨*fixed* a nice breakfast for herself⟩ 5 : REPAIR, MEND

²**fix** *n* : an unpleasant or difficult position

fixed \'fikst\ *adj* 1 : securely placed or fastened 2 : SETTLED, FINAL ⟨a *fixed* price⟩ 3 : INTENT — **fix·ed·ly** \'fik-səd-lē\ *adv*

fixed star *n* : a star so distant that its motion can be measured only by very precise observations over long periods

fix·ture \'fiks-chər\ *n* : something attached as a permanent part ⟨bathroom *fixtures*⟩

¹**fizz** \'fiz\ *vb* : to make a hissing sound

²**fizz** *n* : a hissing or sputtering sound

¹**fiz·zle** \'fiz-əl\ *vb* **fiz·zled**; **fiz·zling** 1 : FIZZ 2 : to fail after a good start

²**fizzle** *n* : FAILURE

fjord \fē-'órd\ *n* : a narrow inlet of the sea between cliffs or steep slopes

flab·by \'flab-ē\ *adj* **flab·bi·er; flab·bi·est** : not hard and firm : SOFT — **flab·bi·ness** *n*

¹flag \'flag\ *n* : a piece of fabric of a special design or color that is used as a symbol (as of a nation) or as a signaling device

²flag *vb* **flagged; flag·ging** : to signal with a flag

³flag *vb* **flagged; flag·ging** : to become feeble

fla·gel·lum \flə-'jel-əm\ *n, pl* **fla·gel·la** \-'jel-ə\ : a long whiplike structure by which some microorganisms move

flag·man \'flag-mən\ *n, pl* **flag·men** \-mən\ : a person who signals with a flag

flag·on \'flag-ən\ *n* : a container for liquids usually having a handle, spout, and lid

flag·pole \'flag-,pōl\ *n* : a pole to raise a flag on

fla·grant \'flā-grənt\ *adj* : so bad as to be impossible to overlook ⟨a *flagrant* violation of the rules⟩ — **fla·grant·ly** *adv*

flagon

flag·ship \'flag-,ship\ *n* : the ship carrying the commander of a fleet or squadron and flying his flag

flag·staff \'flag-,staf\ *n, pl* **flag·staffs** : FLAGPOLE

flag·stone \'flag-,stōn\ *n* : a piece of hard flat rock used for paving

¹flail \'flāl\ *n* : a tool for threshing grain by hand

²flail *vb* : to hit with or as if with a flail

flail

flair \'flaər\ *n* : natural ability

¹flake \'flāk\ *n* : a small thin flattened piece

²flake *vb* **flaked; flak·ing** : to form or separate into flakes

flak·y \'flā-kē\ *adj* **flak·i·er; flak·i·est** : tending to flake ⟨*flaky* pie crust⟩ — **flak·i·ness** *n*

flam·boy·ant \flam-'bói-ənt\ *adj* : given to dashing display — **flam·boy·ant·ly** *adv*

¹flame \'flām\ *n* **1** : the glowing gaseous part of a fire ⟨the *flame* of a candle⟩ **2** : a condition or appearance suggesting a flame

²flame *vb* **flamed; flam·ing** : to burn with or as if with a flame

flame·throw·er \'flām-,thrō-ər\ *n* : a device that shoots a burning stream of fuel

fla·min·go \flə-'ming-gō\ *n, pl* **fla·min·gos** *or* **fla·min·goes** : a very long-legged and long-necked water bird with scarlet wings and a broad bill bent downward at the end

flam·ma·ble \'flam-ə-bəl\ *adj* : capable of being easily set on fire and of burning with extreme rapidity ⟨a *flammable* liquid⟩

¹flank \'flangk\ *n* **1** : the fleshy part of the side between the ribs and the hip **2** : SIDE **3** : the right or left side of a formation

²flank *vb* **1** : to pass around the flank of **2** : to be situated at the side of

flank·er \'flang-kər\ *n* : a football player stationed wide of the formation

flan·nel \'flan-l\ *n* : a soft cloth made of wool or cotton

¹flap \'flap\ *n* **1** : a stroke with something broad and flat ⟨a *flap* of the hand⟩ **2** : something broad and limber that hangs loose **3** : the motion made by something hanging loose and moving back and forth

²flap *vb* **flapped; flap·ping** **1** : to strike with a flap **2** : to move with a beating or fluttering motion ⟨birds *flapping* their wings⟩

flap·jack \'flap-,jak\ *n* : GRIDDLE CAKE

flap·per \'flap-ər\ *n* : a young woman especially of the 1920s who shows bold freedom from conventions in conduct and dress

¹flare \'flaər\ *vb* **flared; flar·ing** **1** : to burn with an unsteady flame **2** : to flame up brightly **3** : to become angry ⟨*flared* up at the remark⟩ **4** : to spread outward

²flare *n* **1** : an unsteady glaring light **2** : a blaze of light used to signal, illuminate, or attract attention **3** : a device or material used to produce a flare **4** : a sudden outburst (as of sound or anger) **5** : a spreading outward : a part that spreads outward

¹flash \'flash\ *vb* **1** : to break forth in or like a sudden flame ⟨lightning *flashed*⟩ **2** : to send out in flashes ⟨*flash* a message⟩ **3** : to come or pass very suddenly ⟨a car *flashing* by⟩ **4** : to make a sudden display (as of feeling)

²flash *n* **1** : a sudden burst (as of light) ⟨a *flash* of lightning⟩ **2** : a very short time

³flash *adj* : beginning suddenly and lasting only a short time ⟨*flash* fire⟩ ⟨*flash* floods⟩

flash·light \'flash-,līt\ *n* **1** : a sudden bright light used in photography **2** : a small battery-operated portable electric light

flash·y \'flash-ē\ *adj* **flash·i·er; flash·i·est** : SHOWY, GAUDY ⟨*flashy* clothes⟩

flask \'flask\ *n* : a bottle-shaped container with a flat or rounded body

¹flat \'flat\ *adj* **flat·ter; flat·test** **1** : having a smooth level surface ⟨a *flat* rock⟩ **2** : spread out on or along a surface ⟨*flat* on the ground⟩ **3** : having a broad smooth surface and little thickness ⟨a phonograph record is *flat*⟩ **4** : DOWNRIGHT, POSITIVE ⟨a *flat* refusal⟩ **5** : UNCHANGING, FIXED ⟨charge a *flat* rate for service⟩ **6** : DULL, UNINTERESTING ⟨a *flat* story⟩ ⟨soup that tastes *flat*⟩ **7** : DEFLATED ⟨a *flat* tire⟩ **8** : lower than the true musical

ə abut   ər further   a ax   ā age   ä father, cot   á (see key page)   aù out   ch chin   e less   ē easy   g gift   i trip   ī life

pitch **9** : lower by a half step in music **10** : free from gloss : DULL **syn** see LEVEL — **flat·ly** *adv* —**flat·ness** *n*

²**flat** *n* **1** : a level place : PLAIN **2** : a flat part or surface **3** : a flat musical tone or note **4** : a sign ♭ meaning that the pitch of a musical note is to be lower by a half step **5** : a deflated tire

³**flat** *adv* **1** : EXACTLY ⟨four minutes *flat*⟩ **2** : below the true musical pitch ⟨sang *flat*⟩

⁴**flat** *n* : an apartment on one floor

flat·boat \'flat-ˌbōt\ *n* : a large flat-bottomed boat with square ends

flat·fish \'flat-ˌfish\ *n* : a fish (as the flounder) that swims on its side and has both eyes on the upper side

flat·i·ron \'flat-ˌī-ərn\ *n* : an iron for pressing clothes

flat·ten \'flat-n\ *vb* : to make or become flat

flat·ter \'flat-ər\ *vb* **1** : to praise without sincerity **2** : to represent too favorably ⟨a picture that *flatters* her⟩ **syn** see COMPLIMENT — **flat·ter·er** *n* — **flat·ter·ing·ly** *adv*

flat·ter·y \'flat-ə-rē\ *n, pl* **flat·ter·ies** : praise that is false

flat·top \'flat-ˌtäp\ *n* : a warship for carrying and launching airplanes

flaunt \'flȯnt\ *vb* **1** : to wave or flutter showily **2** : to make an impudent show of

  syn FLAUNT, FLOUT are not synonyms but are often confused, probably because of their similarity of sound and because they both are used to express a similar attitude of mind. FLAUNT means to display something in an offensive or brazen manner ⟨*flaunts* his disregard for the rules by breaking them openly⟩ ⟨*flaunts* her money in the face of the poor⟩ FLOUT means to disregard or ignore something, also in an offensive or brazen manner ⟨*flouts* the rules and laughs at those who abide by them⟩ ⟨*flouts* good manners by making a display of her money⟩

¹**fla·vor** \'flā-vər\ *n* **1** : the quality of something that affects the sense of taste **2** : a substance added to food to give it a desired taste — **fla·vored** \-vərd\ *adj*

²**flavor** *vb* : to give or add a flavor to

fla·vor·ing \'flā-və-ring\ *n* : FLAVOR 2

flaw \'flȯ\ *n* : an imperfect part : FAULT, DEFECT **syn** see BLEMISH

flax \'flaks\ *n* : a blue-flowered plant grown for its fiber from which linen is made and for its seed which yields oil and livestock feed

flax

flax·en \'flak-sən\ *adj* **1** : made of flax **2** : resembling flax in color : of light straw color

flax·seed \'flak-ˌsēd\ *n* : the seed of flax used as a source of linseed oil and medicinally

flay \'flā\ *vb* **1** : to strip off the skin or surface of something **2** : to scold severely

flea \'flē\ *n* : a small hard-bodied blood-sucking insect without wings

¹**fleck** \'flek\ *vb* : to mark with small streaks or spots ⟨bananas *flecked* with brown⟩

flea

²**fleck** *n* **1** : SPOT, MARK **2** : FLAKE, PARTICLE

fledg·ling \'flej-ling\ *n* : a young bird that has just grown the feathers needed to fly

flee \'flē\ *vb* **fled** \'fled\; **flee·ing** **1** : to run (as from danger) **2** : to pass away swiftly

¹**fleece** \'flēs\ *n* : the coat of wool that covers an animal (as a sheep)

²**fleece** *vb* **fleeced**; **fleec·ing** **1** : to remove the fleece from : SHEAR **2** : to strip of money or property by fraud

fleec·y \'flē-sē\ *adj* **fleec·i·er**; **fleec·i·est** : covered with, made of, or resembling fleece

¹**fleet** \'flēt\ *n* **1** : a group of warships under one command **2** : a country's navy **3** : a group of ships or vehicles that move together or are under one management ⟨fishing *fleet*⟩

²**fleet** *adj* : SWIFT, FAST ⟨*fleet* of foot⟩ — **fleet·ly** *adv* — **fleet·ness** *n*

fleet admiral *n* : a commissioned officer of the highest rank in the navy

flesh \'flesh\ *n* **1** : the soft and especially the edible muscular parts of an animal's body : MEAT **2** : a fleshy edible plant part (as the pulp of a fruit) — **fleshed** \'flesht\ *adj*

flesh·y \'flesh-ē\ *adj* **flesh·i·er**; **flesh·i·est** **1** : resembling or consisting of flesh **2** : CORPULENT

flew *past of* FLY

flex \'fleks\ *vb* : to bend especially repeatedly

flex·i·bil·i·ty \ˌflek-sə-'bil-ət-ē\ *n* : the quality or state of being flexible

flex·i·ble \'flek-sə-bəl\ *adj* : capable of being flexed : not stiff — **flex·i·bly** \-blē\ *adv*

¹**flick** \'flik\ *n* : a light snapping stroke

²**flick** *vb* **1** : to strike lightly with a quick sharp motion **2** : DART, FLIT

¹**flick·er** \'flik-ər\ *vb* **1** : to waver unsteadily like a flame in the wind **2** : to burn unsteadily ⟨a *flickering* candle⟩

²**flicker** *n* **1** : a flickering light **2** : a brief stirring ⟨a *flicker* of the eyelids⟩

³**flicker** *n* : a large insect-eating North American woodpecker

fli·er \'flī-ər\ *n* : one that flies : AVIATOR

¹**flight** \'flīt\ *n* **1** : an act or instance of

passing through the air by the use of wings **2** : a passing through the air or space ⟨a balloon *flight*⟩ ⟨the *flight* of a rocket to the moon⟩ **3** : the distance covered in a flight **4** : an airplane making a scheduled flight ⟨a four o'clock *flight*⟩ **5** : a group of similar things flying through the air together ⟨a *flight* of ducks⟩ ⟨a *flight* of bombers⟩ **6** : a passing above or beyond ordinary limits ⟨a *flight* of fancy⟩ **7** : a continuous series of stairs (as from one floor to another)

²**flight** *n* : the act of running away

flight·less \'flīt-ləs\ *adj* : unable to fly

flight·y \'flīt-ē\ *adj* **flight·i·er; flight·i·est** **1** : easily excited : SKITTISH ⟨a *flighty* horse⟩ **2** : SILLY, GIDDY — **flight·i·ness** *n*

flim·sy \'flim-zē\ *adj* **flim·si·er; flim·si·est** : having little strength or substance ⟨*flimsy* material that tears easily⟩ — **flim·si·ly** \-zə-lē\ *adv* — **flim·si·ness** \-zē-nəs\ *n*

¹**flinch** \'flinch\ *vb* : to draw back from or as if from pain : WINCE

²**flinch** *n* : an act of flinching

¹**fling** \'fling\ *vb* **flung** \'fləng\; **fling·ing** **1** : to move or rush suddenly **2** : to throw or swing forcefully or recklessly

²**fling** *n* **1** : an act of flinging **2** : a time of freedom for pleasure

flint \'flint\ *n* : a very hard stone that produces a spark when struck with steel

flint·lock \'flint-ˌläk\ *n* : an old-fashioned firearm using a flint for striking a spark to fire the charge

flint·y \'flint-ē\ *adj* **flint·i·er; flint·i·est** **1** : made of flint **2** : very hard ⟨a *flinty* heart⟩

¹**flip** \'flip\ *vb* **flipped; flip·ping** **1** : TOSS ⟨*flip* a coin⟩ **2** : FLICK, JERK ⟨*flip* a light switch⟩

²**flip** *n* : an act of flipping : TOSS

flip·pant \'flip-ənt\ *adj* : not serious : SAUCY, FRESH — **flip·pant·ly** *adv*

flip·per \'flip-ər\ *n* : a broad flat limb (as of a seal) adapted for swimming

¹**flirt** \'flərt\ *vb* : to play at making love

²**flirt** *n* : a person who flirts

flit \'flit\ *vb* **flit·ted; flit·ting** : to move in quick irregular darts

fliv·ver \'fliv-ər\ *n* : a small cheap old automobile

¹**float** \'flōt\ *n* **1** : something that floats in or on the surface of a liquid **2** : a cork or bob that holds up the baited end of a fishing line **3** : a floating platform anchored near a shore for the use of swimmers or boats **4** : a hollow ball that controls the flow or level of the liquid it floats on (as in a tank) **5** : a vehicle with a platform used to carry an exhibit in a parade

²**float** *vb* **1** : to rest on the surface of a liquid

⟨cork will *float*⟩ **2** : to drift along or through or as if along or through a liquid ⟨*floating* down the river on a raft⟩ **3** : to cause to float — **float·er** *n*

¹**flock** \'fläk\ *n* **1** : a group of animals (as geese or sheep) living or kept together **2** : a group over which someone watches

²**flock** *vb* : to gather or move in a crowd

floe \'flō\ *n* : a sheet or mass of floating ice

flog \'fläg\ *vb* **flogged; flog·ging** : to beat severely with a rod or whip

¹**flood** \'fləd\ *n* **1** : a great flow of water that rises and spreads over the land **2** : the flowing in of the tide **3** : a great quantity

²**flood** *vb* **1** : to cover or fill with water **2** : to fill as if with a flood

flood·light \'fləd-ˌlīt\ *n* : a lamp that gives a bright broad beam of light

flood·plain \'fləd-ˌplān\ *n* : low flat land along a stream that is flooded when the stream overflows

flood·wa·ter \'fləd-ˌwȯt-ər, -ˌwät-\ *n* : the water of a flood

¹**floor** \'flōr\ *n* **1** : the part of a room on which one stands **2** : a ground surface ⟨the ocean *floor*⟩ **3** : a story of a building

²**floor** *vb* **1** : to cover or provide with a floor ⟨*floor* a garage with concrete⟩ **2** : to strike down **3** : SHOCK, OVERWHELM

floor·board \'flōr-ˌbōrd\ *n* **1** : a board in a floor **2** : the floor of an automobile

floor·ing \'flōr-ing\ *n* **1** : FLOOR **2** : material for floors

¹**flop** \'fläp\ *vb* **flopped; flop·ping** **1** : to flap about ⟨a fish *flopping* on the deck⟩ **2** : to throw oneself heavily or awkwardly **3** : FAIL

²**flop** *n* **1** : the act or sound of flopping **2** : FAILURE

flop·py \'fläp-ē\ *adj* **flop·pi·er; flop·pi·est** : being soft and flexible ⟨a hat with a *floppy* brim⟩

flo·ra \'flōr-ə\ *n* : the plant life characteristic of a region, period, or special environment

flo·ral \'flōr-əl\ *adj* : of or relating to flowers

flo·ret \'flōr-ət\ *n* : a small flower

flor·in \'flȯr-ən\ *n* : a gold or silver coin of various countries (as England)

flo·rist \'flōr-əst\ *n* : a person who deals in flowers and ornamental plants

floss \'fläs\ *n* **1** : soft thread used in embroidery **2** : a silky substance

flo·til·la \flō-'til-ə\ *n* : a fleet of ships and usually of small ships

¹**flounce** \'flaůns\ *vb* **flounced; flounc·ing** : to move with exaggerated jerky motions

²**flounce** *n* : an act of flouncing

³**flounce** *n* : a strip of fabric attached by its upper edge to an article of clothing (as a skirt)

¹floun·der \'flaun-dər\ *n* : a flatfish used for food

²flounder *vb* **1** : to struggle to move or get footing ⟨*floundering* in the mud⟩ **2** : to move or progress clumsily

flour \'flaur\ *n* : the finely ground meal of a cereal grain and especially of wheat

¹flour·ish \'flər-ish\ *vb* **1** : to grow vigorously : THRIVE ⟨plants *flourish* in this rich soil⟩ **2** : to achieve success : PROSPER **3** : to make sweeping movements (as with a pen)

²flourish *n* **1** : a fancy bit of decoration added to handwriting or to a musical passage **2** : a sweeping motion

flout \'flaut\ *vb* : to disregard scornfully ⟨*flouted* her mother's advice⟩ **syn** see FLAUNT

¹flow \'flō\ *vb* **1** : to move in a stream **2** : to glide along smoothly **3** : to hang loose and waving

²flow *n* **1** : an act of flowing **2** : the flowing in of the tide **3** : a smooth even movement **4** : STREAM, CURRENT **5** : the quantity that flows in a specified time

¹flow·er \'flau-ər\ *n* [from earlier English *flour* meaning "flower", "the best of anything", "flour", from Old French *flor*, from Latin *flor-*, stem of *flos*] **1** : a plant shoot that is specialized for the bearing of seed **2** : a plant grown chiefly for its blossoms **3** : the best part or example **4** : a state of flourishing — **flow·ered** \-ərd\ *adj* — **flow·er·less** \-ər-ləs\ *adj*

stamen   petal

sepal   pistil

flower

²flower *vb* **1** : to produce flowers : BLOOM **2** : FLOURISH

flow·er·ing plant \'flau-ə-ring-\ *n* : a seed plant whose seeds are produced in the ovary of a flower

flow·er·pot \'flau-ər-,pät\ *n* : a pot in which to grow plants

flow·er·y \'flau-ə-rē\ *adj* **1** : having many flowers **2** : full of fine words ⟨*flowery* language⟩ — **flow·er·i·ness** *n*

flown *past part of* FLY

flu \'flü\ *n* **1** : INFLUENZA **2** : any of several virus diseases resembling a cold

fluc·tu·ate \'flək-chə-,wāt\ *vb* **fluc·tu·at·ed; fluc·tu·at·ing** : to move up and down or back and forth like a wave

flue \'flü\ *n* : an enclosed passage (as in a chimney) for smoke or air

flu·en·cy \'flü-ən-sē\ *n* : the quality or state of being fluent in speech

flu·ent \'flü-ənt\ *adj* **1** : ready or easy in speech ⟨a *fluent* speaker⟩ ⟨*fluent* in Spanish⟩ **2** : EFFORTLESS, SMOOTH — **flu·ent·ly** *adv*

¹fluff \'fləf\ *n* : DOWN, NAP

²fluff *vb* : to make or become fluffy

fluff·y \'fləf-ē\ *adj* **fluff·i·er; fluff·i·est** : covered or filled with fluff : soft and downy like fluff — **fluff·i·ness** *n*

¹flu·id \'flü-əd\ *adj* **1** : capable of flowing like a liquid or gas **2** : being smooth and easy — **flu·id·ly** *adv*

²fluid *n* : a substance tending to flow and to conform to the outline of its container

flung *past of* FLING

flunk \'fləngk\ *vb* : FAIL ⟨*flunk* a test⟩

flu·o·res·cent lamp \,flü-ə-,res-nt-\ *n* : an electric light in the form of a frosted glass tube that produces a cool white light like daylight

flu·o·rine \'flü-ə-,rēn, -rən\ *n* : a yellowish flammable irritating gaseous chemical element

¹flur·ry \'flər-ē\ *n, pl* **flur·ries** **1** : a gust of wind **2** : a brief light snowfall **3** : a brief outburst ⟨a *flurry* of excitement⟩

²flurry *vb* **flur·ried; flur·ry·ing** : EXCITE, FLUSTER

¹flush \'fləsh\ *vb* : to begin or cause to begin flight suddenly ⟨a hunting dog *flushing* quail⟩

²flush *n* **1** : an act of flushing **2** : BLUSH

³flush *vb* **1** : BLUSH ⟨*flushed* with pleasure⟩ **2** : to pour water over or through

⁴flush *adj* : even with the surface that joins it

⁵flush *adv* : so as to be flush

¹flus·ter \'fləs-tər\ *vb* : to make nervous and confused : UPSET

²fluster *n* : a state of nervous confusion

¹flute \'flüt\ *n* : a musical instrument in the form of a hollow slender tube open at only one end that is played by blowing across a hole near the closed end

flute

²flute *vb* **flut·ed; flut·ing** **1** : to play on a flute **2** : to make a sound like that of a flute

flut·ist \'flüt-əst\ *n* : a flute player

¹flut·ter \'flət-ər\ *vb* **1** : to move the wings rapidly without flying at all or flying in short flights ⟨butterflies *flutter*⟩ **2** : to move with a quick flapping motion ⟨a flag *fluttering* in the wind⟩ **3** : to move about with great bustle and show but without accomplishing much

²flutter *n* : an act of fluttering

¹fly \'flī\ *vb* **flew** \'flü\; **flown** \'flōn\; **fly·ing** **1** : to move in or pass through the air with wings ⟨birds *fly*⟩ **2** : to move through the air or before the wind ⟨paper *flying* in all directions⟩ **3** : to float or cause to float, wave, or soar in the wind ⟨*fly* a kite⟩ ⟨*fly* a flag⟩ **4** : to run away : FLEE **5** : to move or pass swiftly **6** : to operate or travel in an airplane

²fly *n, pl* **flies**　**1** : a flap of material to cover a fastening in a garment　**2** : the outer canvas of a tent that has a double top　**3** : a baseball hit high in the air

³fly *n, pl* **flies**　**1** : a winged insect　**2** : any of a large group of mostly stout-bodied two-winged insects (as the common housefly)　**3** : a fishhook made to look like an insect

fly 3

fly·catch·er \'flī-ˌkach-ər\ *n* : a small bird that eats flying insects

fly·er *var of* FLIER

fly·ing boat \'flī-ing-\ *n* : a seaplane with a hull built for floating

flying colors *n pl* : complete success

flying fish *n* : a fish with large fins that enable it to jump from the water and move for a distance through the air

fly·pa·per \'flī-ˌpā-pər\ *n* : paper coated to catch and kill flies

fly·speck \'flī-ˌspek\ *n* : a spot left by a fly on a surface

fly·way \'flī-ˌwā\ *n* : a course regularly followed by migratory birds

¹foal \'fōl\ *n* : a young animal of the horse family especially while less than one year old

²foal *vb* : to give birth to a foal

¹foam \'fōm\ *n* : a light frothy mass that forms in or on the surface of liquids or in the mouths or on the skins of animals

²foam *vb* : to produce or form foam

foam·y \'fō-mē\ *adj* **foam·i·er; foam·i·est** : covered with or resembling foam — **foam·i·ness** *n*

fo·cal \'fō-kəl\ *adj* : of, relating to, or having a focus

¹fo·cus \'fō-kəs\ *n, pl* **fo·cus·es** *or* **fo·ci** \'fō-ˌsī\　**1** : a point at which rays (as of light, heat, or sound) meet after being reflected or bent : the point at which an image is formed　**2** : the distance from a lens or mirror to a focus　**3** : an adjustment (as of a person's eyes or glasses) that gives clear vision ⟨bring into *focus*⟩　**4** : the center of activity, attraction, or attention

²focus *vb* **fo·cused** *or* **fo·cussed; fo·cus·ing** *or* **fo·cus·sing**　**1** : to bring or come to a focus ⟨*focus* rays of light⟩　**2** : CONCENTRATE, CENTER　**3** : to adjust the focus of ⟨*focus* the eyes⟩

fod·der \'fäd-ər\ *n* : coarse dry food (as stalks of corn) for livestock

foe \'fō\ *n* : an enemy especially in war

¹fog \'fȯg, 'fäg\ *n*　**1** : fine particles of water suspended in the air at or near the ground : a cloud at ground level　**2** : a murky condition of the air　**3** : a bewildered state

²fog *vb* **fogged; fog·ging** : to cover or become covered with fog

fog·gy \'fȯg-ē, 'fäg-\ *adj* **fog·gi·er; fog·gi·est**　**1** : filled with fog　**2** : CONFUSED, MUDDLED — **fog·gi·ness** *n*

fog·horn \'fȯg-ˌhȯrn, 'fäg-\ *n* : a loud horn sounded in a fog to give warning

fo·gy \'fō-gē\ *n, pl* **fo·gies** : a person with old-fashioned ideas ⟨an old *fogy*⟩

foi·ble \'fȯi-bəl\ *n* : a minor weakness or failing　**syn** see FAULT

¹foil \'fȯil\ *vb* : DEFEAT

²foil *n* : a fencing weapon having a light flexible blade with a blunt point

³foil *n*　**1** : a very thin sheet of metal ⟨aluminum *foil*⟩　**2** : something that makes another thing seem more noticeable by contrast in color or quality

foil

¹fold \'fōld\ *n*　**1** : an enclosure or shelter for sheep　**2** : a group of people with a common faith or interest ⟨welcome a newcomer to the *fold*⟩

²fold *vb* : to pen up sheep in a fold

³fold *vb*　**1** : to double something over itself ⟨*fold* a blanket⟩　**2** : to clasp together ⟨*folded* his hands⟩　**3** : ENCLOSE, EMBRACE

⁴fold *n*　**1** : a doubling of something over on itself　**2** : a part doubled or laid over another part : BEND ⟨a *fold* in a rock⟩

-fold \ˌfōld\ *suffix*　**1** : multiplied by a specified number : times — in adjectives ⟨a twelve*fold* increase⟩ and adverbs ⟨repay you ten*fold*⟩　**2** : having so many parts ⟨a three*fold* problem⟩

fold·er \'fōl-dər\ *n*　**1** : one that folds　**2** : a booklet of folded sheets　**3** : a folded cover or large envelope for loose papers

fo·li·age \'fō-lē-ij\ *n* : the leaves of a plant (as a tree) — **fo·li·aged** \-ijd\ *adj*

folder 3

¹folk \'fōk\ *n, pl* **folk** *or* **folks**　**1** : people in general : persons as a group ⟨country *folk*⟩ ⟨old *folks*⟩　**2** : the persons of one's own family ⟨visiting her *folks* this week⟩

²folk *adj* : originating among the common people ⟨*folk* dance⟩

folk·lore \'fōk-ˌlōr\ *n* : customs, beliefs, stories, and sayings of a people handed down from generation to generation

folk singer *n* : a person who sings songs (**folk songs**) that have originated or are traditional among the common people

folks·y \'fōk-sē\ *adj* **folks·i·er; folks·i·est** : casual or informal in manner or style

fol·low \'fäl-ō\ *vb*　**1** : to go or come after or

behind ⟨the dog *followed* his master⟩ **2** : to take as a leader : OBEY ⟨*follow* your conscience⟩ ⟨*follow* instructions⟩ **3** : PURSUE ⟨*follow* a clue⟩ **4** : to proceed along ⟨*follow* a path⟩ **5** : to attend to as a regular business or profession ⟨*follow* the sea⟩ **6** : to come after in order of rank or natural sequence ⟨two *follows* one⟩ **7** : to keep one's eyes or attention fixed on ⟨*follow* a speech⟩ **8** : to result from ⟨disaster *followed* the general's blunder⟩ **syn** see CHASE — **fol·low·er** \ˈfäl-ə-wər\ *n* — **follow suit 1** : to play a card of the same suit as the card led **2** : to do the same thing someone else has just done — **follow through** : to complete an action (as throwing a ball or swinging a golf club) — **follow up** : to show continued interest in often by taking further action

¹fol·low·ing \ˈfäl-ə-wing\ *adj* : NEXT

²following *n* : a group of followers

fol·ly \ˈfäl-ē\ *n, pl* **fol·lies 1** : the state of being foolish **2** : a foolish act or idea

fo·ment \fō-ˈment\ *vb* : to stir up

fond \ˈfänd\ *adj* **1** : strongly attracted ⟨*fond* of candy⟩ **2** : AFFECTIONATE, LOVING ⟨a *fond* father⟩ — **fond·ly** *adv* — **fond·ness** *n*

fon·dle \ˈfän-dəl\ *vb* **fon·dled; fon·dling** : to touch or handle in a tender or loving manner

font \ˈfänt\ *n* : a basin to hold water for baptizing

food \ˈfüd\ *n* **1** : material containing carbohydrates, fats, proteins, and supplements (as minerals and vitamins) that is taken in by and used in the living body for growth and repair and as a source of energy for functional activities **2** : inorganic substances absorbed by green plants and used to build organic nutrients **3** : organic materials formed by plants and used in their growth and activities **4** : food in solid form as distinguished from drink

font

food·stuff \ˈfüd-ˌstəf\ *n* : a substance with food value

¹fool \ˈfül\ *n* **1** : a person who lacks sense or judgment **2** : a person formerly kept in royal courts to amuse people : JESTER

²fool *vb* **1** : to spend time idly ⟨just *fooling* around⟩ **2** : to meddle with thoughtlessly ⟨don't *fool* with that gun⟩ **3** : to speak or act in jest : JOKE ⟨was only *fooling*⟩ **4** : TRICK

fool·har·dy \ˈfül-ˌhärd-ē\ *adj* **fool·har·di·er; fool·har·di·est** : RASH **syn** see DARING

fool·ish \ˈfü-lish\ *adj* : showing or arising from folly or lack of judgment : SENSELESS **syn** see SILLY — **fool·ish·ly** *adv* — **fool·ish·ness** *n*

fool·proof \ˈfül-ˈprüf\ *adj* : so simple, plain,

or reliable as to leave no chance of error or failure ⟨*foolproof* directions⟩

¹foot \ˈfut\ *n, pl* **feet** \ˈfēt\ **1** : the end part of the leg of an animal or of man : the part of an animal on which it stands or moves **2** : a unit of length equal to twelve inches **3** : a group of syllables forming the basic unit of verse meter **4** : something like a foot in position or use — **on foot** : by walking

²foot *vb* **1** : to go on foot **2** : PAY

foot·ball \ˈfut-ˌbȯl\ *n* **1** : a game played with an inflated ball on a large field by two teams of eleven men each **2** : the ball used in football

foot·ed \ˈfut-əd\ *adj* **1** : having a foot or feet ⟨a *footed* goblet⟩ **2** : having such or so many feet ⟨four-*footed* animals⟩

foot·fall \ˈfut-ˌfȯl\ *n* **1** : FOOTSTEP **2** : the sound of a footstep

foot·hill \ˈfut-ˌhil\ *n* : a hill at the foot of higher hills

foot·hold \ˈfut-ˌhōld\ *n* : a place where the foot may be put (as for climbing)

foot·ing \ˈfut-ing\ *n* **1** : the placing of one's feet so as to be able to stand securely **2** : FOOTHOLD **3** : the position that one person or group occupies in relation to another

foot·lights \ˈfut-ˌlīts\ *n pl* : a row of lights set across the front of a stage floor

foot·man \ˈfut-mən\ *n, pl* **foot·men** \-mən\ : a male servant who admits visitors and waits on table

foot·note \ˈfut-ˌnōt\ *n* : a note at the bottom of a page of text

foot·path \ˈfut-ˌpath, -ˌpȧth\ *n* : a path for people on foot

foot·print \ˈfut-ˌprint\ *n* : an impression left by a foot

foot·sore \ˈfut-ˌsōr\ *adj* : having sore feet from much walking

foot·step \ˈfut-ˌstep\ *n* **1** : a step or tread of the foot **2** : the distance covered by a step **3** : FOOTPRINT **4** : a step for going up or down

foot·stool \ˈfut-ˌstül\ *n* : a low stool to support the feet

foot·work \ˈfut-ˌwərk\ *n* : the management of the feet (as in boxing)

fop \ˈfäp\ *n* : a man who is vain about his dress or appearance

¹for \fər, fȯr\ *prep* **1** : in preparation toward ⟨wash up *for* supper⟩ **2** : toward the goal of ⟨time *for* study⟩ **3** : in order to reach ⟨run *for* cover⟩ **4** : as being ⟨took him *for* a fool⟩ **5** : because of ⟨cried *for* joy⟩ **6** — used to indicate a recipient ⟨a letter *for* you⟩ **7** : in support of ⟨fought *for* his country⟩ **8** : directed at ⟨a cure *for* what ails you⟩ **9** : in ex-

change as equal to ⟨paid ten dollars *for* a hat⟩
10 : CONCERNING ⟨a stickler *for* details⟩
11 : CONSIDERING ⟨tall *for* his age⟩ **12** : through
the period of ⟨served *for* three years⟩
²for *conj* : BECAUSE
¹for·age \'for-ij\ *n* : food (as pasture) for
browsing or grazing animals
²forage *vb* **for·aged; for·ag·ing** : SEARCH
for·ay \'for-ā\ *n* : RAID
for·bear \for-'baər\ *vb* **for·bore** \-'bōr\; **for-
borne** \-'bōrn\; **for·bear·ing** **1** : to hold back
⟨*forbear* from striking back⟩ **2** : to control
oneself when provoked **syn** see REFRAIN
for·bid \fər-'bid\ *vb* **for·bade** \-'bad\ *or* **for-
bad; for·bid·den** \-'bid-n\; **for·bid·ding** : to
order not to do something
for·bid·ding \fər-'bid-ing\ *adj* : tending to
frighten or discourage : DISAGREEABLE
¹force \'fōrs\ *n* **1** : STRENGTH, ENERGY ⟨the
force of a blow⟩ ⟨the *force* of the wind⟩
2 : legal efficacy ⟨a law that is still in *force*⟩
3 : a body of men gathered together or trained
for action ⟨a police *force*⟩ ⟨the armed *forces*⟩
4 : power or violence used on a person or
thing ⟨opened the door by *force*⟩ **5** : an influence (as a push or pull) that tends to produce a change in the speed or direction of
motion of something ⟨the *force* of gravity⟩
²force *vb* **forced; forc·ing** **1** : to compel by any
means ⟨*force* men to work⟩ **2** : to get or gain
against resistance **3** : to break open by force
4 : to hasten the development of
force·ful \'fōrs-fəl\ *adj* : having much force
— **force·ful·ly** *adv* — **force·ful·ness** *n*
for·ceps \'for-səps\ *n, pl* **forceps** : an instrument for grasping, holding, or
pulling on objects especially in
delicate operations (as by a
jeweler or surgeon)
forc·i·ble \'fōr-sə-bəl\ *adj*
1 : got, made, or done by force
or violence ⟨a *forcible* entrance⟩ **2** : showing
force or energy — **for·ci·bly** \-blē\ *adv*
¹ford \'fōrd\ *n* : a shallow place in a body of
water where one can wade across
²ford *vb* : to cross by wading
¹fore \'fōr\ *adv* : in or toward the front
²fore *adj* : being or coming before in time,
place, or order
³fore *n* : FRONT ⟨came to the *fore*⟩
⁴fore *interj* — used by a golfer to warn someone within range of his ball
fore- *prefix* **1** : earlier : beforehand ⟨*foresee*⟩
2 : occurring earlier : occurring beforehand
⟨*forepayment*⟩ **3** : situated at the front : in
front ⟨*fore*leg⟩ **4** : front part of something
specified ⟨*forearm*⟩

forceps

fore–and–aft \,for-ən-'aft\ *adj* : being in line
with the length of a ship ⟨*fore-and-aft* sails⟩
¹fore·arm \for-'ärm\ *vb* : to arm beforehand
²fore·arm \'for-,ärm\ *n* : the part of the arm
between the elbow and the wrist
fore·bear \'for-,baər\ *n* : ANCESTOR
fore·bod·ing \for-'bōd-ing\ *n* : a feeling that
something bad is going to happen
¹fore·cast \'for-,kast\ *vb* **forecast** *or* **fore-
cast·ed; fore·cast·ing** : FORETELL, PREDICT
syn see FORETELL — **fore·cast·er** *n*
²forecast *n* : a prediction of a future happening or condition ⟨weather *forecast*⟩
fore·cas·tle \'fōk-səl\ *n* **1** : the upper deck
of a ship in front of the foremast **2** : the part
of a merchantman having crew quarters forward
fore·fa·ther \'for-,fä-ther\ *n* : ANCESTOR
fore·fin·ger \'for-,fing-gər\ *n* : INDEX FINGER
fore·foot \'for-,fut\ *n, pl* **fore·feet** \-,fēt\
: one of the front feet of a four-footed animal
fore·front \'for-,frənt\ *n* : the place of greatest activity or interest
forego *var of* FORGO
fore·go·ing \for-'gō-ing\ *adj* : going before
fore·gone \,for-,gon\ *adj* : determined in advance ⟨a *foregone* conclusion⟩
fore·ground \'for-,graund\ *n* : the part of a
picture or scene that seems to be nearest to and
in front of the person looking at it
¹fore·hand \'for-,hand\ *n* : a stroke (as in
tennis) made with the palm of the hand
turned in the direction in which the hand is
moving
²forehand *adj* : using or made with a forehand
fore·head \'for-əd, 'for-,hed\ *n* : the part of
the face above the eyes
for·eign \'for-ən\ *adj* [from Old French
forein, derived from Latin *foranus* "on the outside", from *foris* "outside"] **1** : situated outside of a place or country and especially outside of one's own country ⟨*foreign* nations⟩
2 : belonging to a place or country other than
the one under consideration ⟨many Danes
speak *foreign* languages⟩ **3** : not pertinent
4 : relating to or dealing with other nations
for·eign·er \'for-ə-nər\ *n* : a person who belongs to a foreign country
fore·leg \'for-,leg\ *n* : a front leg
fore·limb \'for-,lim\ *n* : an arm, fin, wing, or
leg that is or occupies the position of a foreleg
fore·man \'for-mən\ *n, pl* **fore·men** \-mən\
: a chief man in a group (as of workmen)
fore·mast \'for-,mast, -məst\ *n* : the mast
nearest the bow of the ship
¹fore·most \'for-,mōst\ *adj* : first in time,
place, or order : most important

²fore·most *adv* : in the first place

fore·noon \'fōr-,nün\ *n* : MORNING

fore·quar·ter \'fōr-,kwȯrt-ər\ *n* : the front half of a whole side of the body or carcass of a four-footed animal ⟨a *forequarter* of beef⟩

fore·run·ner \'fōr-,rən-ər\ *n* **1** : one that goes before **2** : ANCESTOR

fore·see \fōr-'sē\ *vb* **fore·saw** \-'sȯ\; **fore·seen** \-'sēn\; **fore·see·ing** : to see or have knowledge of beforehand : EXPECT

fore·shad·ow \fōr-'shad-ō\ *vb* : to give a hint or suggestion of beforehand

fore·sight \'fōr-,sīt\ *n* **1** : the act or power of foreseeing **2** : care or provision for the future : PRUDENCE

for·est \'fȯr-əst\ *n* : a dense growth of trees and underbrush covering a large area — **for·est·ed** \-əs-təd\ *adj*

fore·stall \fōr-'stȯl\ *vb* : to keep out, hinder, or prevent by measures taken in advance

for·est·ry \'fȯr-əs-trē\ *n* : the science and practice of caring for forests — **for·est·er** \-tər\ *n*

fore·tell \fōr-'tel\ *vb* **fore·told** \-'tōld\; **fore·tell·ing** : to tell of a thing before it happens
syn FORETELL, PREDICT, FORECAST all mean to tell about or announce something before it happens. FORETELL often suggests knowing the future through some supernatural power ⟨shabby women on the midway who *foretell* the future for fifty cents⟩ PREDICT may imply a fairly exact statement based on sufficient information and scientific methods ⟨*predicted* the exact spot where the space capsule would land⟩ FORECAST normally is used when announcing probabilities rather than near certainties ⟨*forecast* the week's weather⟩

fore·thought \'fōr-,thȯt\ *n* : thought or care taken before something happens

for·ev·er \fə-'rev-ər\ *adv* **1** : for a limitless time : EVERLASTINGLY **2** : at all times

for·ev·er·more \fə-,rev-ər-'mōr\ *adv* : FOREVER

fore·word \'fōr-,wərd\ *n* : PREFACE

¹for·feit \'fȯr-fət\ *n* : something forfeited

²forfeit *vb* : to lose or lose the right to something through a fault, error, or crime

¹forge \'fōrj\ *n* : a furnace or a place with a furnace where metal is shaped and worked by heating and hammering

²forge *vb* **forged**; **forg·ing** **1** : to shape and work metal by heating and hammering **2** : to produce something that is not genuine : COUNTERFEIT ⟨*forge* a check⟩ — **forg·er** *n*

³forge *vb* **forged**; **forg·ing** : to move forward slowly but steadily

forg·er·y \'fōr-jə-rē\ *n, pl* **forg·er·ies** **1** : the

crime of falsely making or changing a written paper or signing someone else's name **2** : something that has been forged

for·get \fər-'get\ *vb* **for·got** \-'gät\; **for·got·ten** \-'gät-n\ *or* **for·got**; **for·get·ting** **1** : to be unable to think of or recall ⟨*forgot* her name⟩ **2** : to fail to think of ⟨*forgot* to pay the bill⟩

for·get·ful \fər-'get-fəl\ *adj* : forgetting easily — **for·get·ful·ly** *adv* — **for·get·ful·ness** *n*

for·get–me–not \fər-'get-mē-,nät\ *n* : a small low plant with blue flowers

for·give \fər-'giv\ *vb* **for·gave** \-'gāv\; **for·giv·en** \-'giv-ən\; **for·giv·ing** : to cease to feel anger or resentment against **syn** see EXCUSE

for·give·ness \fər-'giv-nəs\ *n* : PARDON

for·go *or* **fore·go** \fȯr-'gō, fōr-\ *vb* **for·went** *or* **fore·went** \-'went\; **for·gone** *or* **fore·gone** \-'gȯn\; **for·go·ing** *or* **fore·go·ing** : to go without : give up ⟨*forgo* an opportunity⟩

¹fork \'fȯrk\ *n* **1** : an implement having a handle and two or more prongs for taking up (as in eating), pitching, or digging **2** : something that resembles a fork in shape **3** : the place where something divides or branches ⟨a *fork* in the road⟩ **4** : one of the parts into which something divides or branches ⟨the left *fork*⟩ — **forked** \'fȯrkt, 'fȯr-kəd\ *adj*

forks 1

²fork *vb* **1** : to divide into branches **2** : to pitch or raise with a fork

for·lorn \fər-'lȯrn\ *adj* : DESERTED, WRETCHED — **for·lorn·ly** *adv*

¹form \'fȯrm\ *n* **1** : the shape and structure of something **2** : a set or fixed way of doing something ⟨different *forms* of worship⟩ **3** : manner of doing something ⟨such behavior is bad *form*⟩ ⟨shows good *form* in swimming⟩ **4** : a mold in which concrete is placed to set **5** : KIND, VARIETY ⟨early *forms* of plant life⟩ ⟨coal is one *form* of carbon⟩ **6** : one of the different pronunciations or spellings a word may have in inflection or compounding

²form *vb* **1** : to give form or shape to **2** : TRAIN, INSTRUCT ⟨education *forms* the mind⟩ **3** : GET, DEVELOP **4** : to make up

¹for·mal \'fȯr-məl\ *adj* : following established form, custom, or rule — **for·mal·ly** *adv*

²formal *n* : something formal in character

for·mal·i·ty \fȯr-'mal-ət-ē\ *n, pl* **for·mal·i·ties** **1** : the quality or state of being formal **2** : a set or customary way of doing something

for·ma·tion \fȯr-'mā-shən\ *n* **1** : a forming of something ⟨the *formation* of good habits⟩ **2** : something that is formed ⟨cloud *formation*⟩ **3** : an arrangement of persons, ships, or airplanes ⟨battle *formation*⟩ ⟨punt *formation*⟩

---

for·mer \'fȯr-mər\ *adj* : coming before in time : EARLIER ⟨a *former* president⟩

for·mer·ly \'fȯr-mər-lē\ *adv* : at an earlier time

for·mi·da·ble \'fȯr-mə-də-bəl\ *adj* **1** : exciting fear, dread, or awe **2** : imposing serious difficulties

form·less \'fȯrm-ləs\ *adj* : having no regular form or shape — **form·less·ly** *adv* — **form·less·ness** *n*

for·mu·la \'fȯr-myə-lə\ *n* **1** : a set of directions giving proportions of the substances for the preparation of something (as a medicine) **2** : a milk mixture or substitute for a baby **3** : a general fact or rule expressed in symbols ⟨a *formula* for finding the perimeter of a triangle⟩ **4** : an expression in symbols giving the makeup of a substance ⟨the *formula* for water is H_2O⟩ **5** : a set form or method

for·mu·late \'fȯr-myə-,lāt\ *vb* **for·mu·lat·ed**; **for·mu·lat·ing** : to state definitely and clearly

for·sake \fər-'sāk\ *vb* **for·sook** \-'sùk\; **for·sak·en** \-'sā-kən\; **for·sak·ing** : to give up : QUIT, ABANDON   **syn** *see* ABANDON

for·sooth \fər-'süth\ *adv* : in truth : INDEED

for·syth·i·a \fər-'sith-ē-ə\ *n* : a bush with yellow bell-shaped flowers that appear in early spring

fort \'fōrt\ *n* : a strong or fortified place especially when occupied by soldiers

¹forte \'fōrt\ *n* : something at which a person is particularly good

²for·te \'fȯr-,tā\ *adv (or adj)* : LOUDLY — used as a direction in music

forth \'fōrth\ *adv* **1** : FORWARD ⟨from that time *forth*⟩ **2** : out into view

forth·com·ing \fōrth-'kəm-ing\ *adj* **1** : being about to appear : APPROACHING **2** : ready or available when needed

forth·right \'fōrth-,rīt\ *adj* : DIRECT, STRAIGHTFORWARD ⟨a *forthright* answer⟩ **syn** *see* STRAIGHTFORWARD — **forth·right·ly** *adv*

forth·with \fōrth-'with, -'with\ *adv* : IMMEDIATELY

¹for·ti·eth \'fȯrt-ē-əth\ *adj* : being next after the thirty-ninth

²fortieth *n* : number forty in a series

for·ti·fi·ca·tion \,fȯrt-ə-fə-'kā-shən\ *n* **1** : the act of fortifying **2** *pl* : defensive works

for·ti·fy \'fȯrt-ə-,fī\ *vb* **for·ti·fied**; **for·ti·fy·ing** : to make strong (as by building defenses)

for·ti·tude \'fȯrt-ə-,tüd, -,tyüd\ *n* : strength of mind that enables a person to meet and endure trouble

fort·night \'fȯrt-,nīt\ *n* [an alteration of earlier English *fourtenight*, which developed from the Old English phrase *fēowertȳne niht* "fourteen nights"] : two weeks

for·tress \'fȯr-trəs\ *n* : a fortified place

for·tu·nate \'fȯr-chə-nət\ *adj* **1** : coming or happening by good luck : bringing unexpected happiness **2** : receiving some unexpected good : LUCKY — **for·tu·nate·ly** *adv*

for·tune \'fȯr-chən\ *n* **1** : CHANCE, LUCK **2** : what happens to a person : good or bad luck **3** : a person's destiny or fate **4** : RICHES

for·tune–tell·er \'fȯr-chən-,tel-ər\ *n* : a person who claims to foretell future events

¹for·ty \'fȯrt-ē\ *adj* : being four times ten

²forty *n* : four times ten

for·ty–nin·er \,fȯrt-ē-'nī-nər\ *n* : a person in the California gold rush of 1849

fo·rum \'fōr-əm\ *n* **1** : the marketplace or public place of an ancient Roman city serving as the center for public business **2** : a program of open discussion

¹for·ward \'fȯr-wərd\ *adj* **1** : near, at, or belonging to the front part ⟨a ship's *forward* gun⟩ **2** : tending to push oneself ⟨a pert *forward* young woman⟩ **3** : moving, tending, or leading to a position in front

²forward *adv* : to or toward what is in front

³forward *n* : a player at or near the front of his team (as in basketball)

⁴forward *vb* **1** : to help onward : ADVANCE **2** : to send on or ahead ⟨*forward* a letter⟩

for·wards \'fȯr-wərdz\ *adv* : FORWARD

fos·sil \'fäs-əl\ *n* : a trace, print, or remains of a plant or animal of a past age preserved in earth, rock, or clay

¹fos·ter \'fȯs-tər\ *adj* : giving, receiving, or sharing parent's care even though not related by blood or legal ties ⟨*foster* parent⟩

²foster *vb* **1** : to give parental care to **2** : to promote the growth and development of

fought *past of* FIGHT

¹foul \'faùl\ *adj* **1** : offensive in looks, taste, or smell ⟨a *foul* sewer⟩ **2** : clogged or covered with dirt **3** : INDECENT, ABUSIVE ⟨*foul* language⟩ **4** : being wet and stormy ⟨*foul* weather⟩ **5** : UNFAIR, DISHONORABLE ⟨would use fair means or *foul*⟩ **6** : violating a rule in a game or sport ⟨a *foul* blow in boxing⟩ **7** : being outside the foul lines ⟨hit a *foul* ball⟩ — **foul·ly** \'faùl-lē\ *adv* — **foul·ness** *n*

²foul *n* **1** : a breaking of the rules in a game or sport **2** : a foul ball in baseball

³foul *vb* **1** : to make or become foul or filthy ⟨*foul* the air⟩ ⟨*foul* a stream⟩ **2** : to commit a foul (as in basketball) ⟨*fouled* an opponent⟩ **3** : to hit a foul ball ⟨*fouled* to the catcher⟩ **4** : to become entangled : ENTANGLE

foul line *n* : either of two straight lines running from the rear corner of home plate through first and third base to the boundary of a baseball field

foul play *n* : VIOLENCE

¹found \'faund\ *past of* FIND

²found *vb* : ESTABLISH ⟨*found* a college⟩

foun·da·tion \faun-'dā-shən\ *n* **1** : the act of founding **2** : the support upon which something rests ⟨the *foundation* of a building⟩

¹found·er \'faun-dər\ *n* : one that founds

²foun·der \'faun-dər\ *vb* : to go down : SINK

found·ling \'faund-ling\ *n* : an infant found after being abandoned by unknown parents

found·ry \'faun-drē\ *n, pl* **found·ries** : a building or factory where metals are cast

foun·tain \'faunt-n\ *n* **1** : a spring of water **2** : SOURCE **3** : an artificially produced jet of water or the fixture from which it rises

fountain pen *n* : a pen with a reservoir that automatically feeds the writing point with ink

¹four \'fōr\ *adj* : being one more than three

²four *n* **1** : one more than three **2** : the fourth in a set or series

four·fold \'fōr-,fōld\ *adj* : being four times as great or as many

four–post·er \'fōr-'pōs-tər\ *n* : a bed with tall corner posts originally designed to support curtains or a canopy

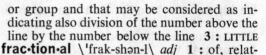

four·score \'fōr-,skōr\ *adj* : EIGHTY

¹four·teen \fōr-'tēn\ *adj* : being one more than thirteen

four-poster

²fourteen *n* : one more than thirteen

¹four·teenth \fōr-'tēnth\ *adj* : being next after the thirteenth

²fourteenth *n* : number fourteen in a series

¹fourth \'fōrth\ *adj* : being next after the third

²fourth *n* **1** : number four in a series **2** : one of four equal parts

fowl \'faul\ *n, pl* **fowl** *or* **fowls** **1** : BIRD ⟨wild *fowls*⟩ **2** : a common domestic rooster or hen **3** : the flesh of a mature domestic fowl for use as food

fox \'fäks\ *n* : a wild animal closely related to the dog that has a sharp muzzle, pointed ears, and long bushy tail

fox·y \'fäk-sē\ *adj* **fox·i·er; fox·i·est** : resembling a fox : WILY, CLEVER — **fox·i·ly** \-sə-lē\ *adv* — **fox·i·ness** \-sē-nəs\ *n*

foy·er \'fòi-ər, 'fòi-,ā\ *n* **1** : a lobby especially in a theater **2** : an entrance hall

fra·cas \'frā-kəs\ *n* : a noisy quarrel : BRAWL

frac·tion \'frak-shən\ *n* **1** : a part of a whole : FRAGMENT **2** : a number (as ½, ⅔, 17/100) that indicates one or more equal parts of a whole

or group and that may be considered as indicating also division of the number above the line by the number below the line **3** : LITTLE

frac·tion·al \'frak-shən-l\ *adj* **1** : of, relating to, or being a fraction **2** : relatively small

¹frac·ture \'frak-chər\ *n* **1** : a breaking or being broken (as of a bone) **2** : damage or an injury caused by breaking

²fracture *vb* **frac·tured; frac·tur·ing** : to cause a fracture in : BREAK ⟨*fracture* a leg⟩

frag·ile \'fraj-əl\ *adj* : easily broken : DELICATE   **syn** *see* BRITTLE

frag·ment \'frag-mənt\ *n* : a part broken off or incomplete

frag·men·tar·y \'frag-mən-,ter-ē\ *adj* : consisting of fragments : INCOMPLETE

fra·grance \'frā-grəns\ *n* : a sweet or pleasant smell

fra·grant \'frā-grənt\ *adj* : sweet or pleasant in smell — **fra·grant·ly** *adv*

frail \'frāl\ *adj* : FRAGILE, WEAK   **syn** *see* WEAK

frail·ty \'frāl-tē\ *n, pl* **frail·ties** **1** : the quality or state of being weak **2** : a fault due to weakness of character

¹frame \'frām\ *vb* **framed; fram·ing** **1** : FORM, CONSTRUCT **2** : to enclose in a frame

²frame *n* **1** : the physical makeup of an animal and especially a human body : PHYSIQUE **2** : an arrangement of parts that give form or support to something ⟨the bony *frame* of the body⟩ ⟨the *frame* of a house⟩ **3** : an open case or structure for holding or enclosing something ⟨window *frame*⟩ ⟨picture *frame*⟩ **4** : a particular state or disposition

frame of a roof

³frame *adj* : having a wooden frame

frame·work \'frām-,wərk\ *n* : STRUCTURE

franc \'frangk\ *n* : a small coin (as of France, Belgium, or Switzerland)

Fran·co- \'frang-kō\ *prefix* : French and ⟨*Franco*-German⟩ : French ⟨*Franco*phile⟩

¹frank \'frangk\ *adj* : free in expressing one's feelings and opinions : OUTSPOKEN — **frank·ly** *adv* — **frank·ness** *n*

²frank *vb* : to mark a piece of mail with a frank ⟨*franked* envelopes⟩

³frank *n* : an official mark (as a signature) on mail indicating that it can be mailed free

frank·furt·er \'frangk-fərt-ər\ *n* : a beef or beef and pork sausage

frank·in·cense \'frang-kən-,sens\ *n* : a fragrant gum that is burned as incense

fran·tic \'frant-ik\ *adj* : wildly excited

fran·ti·cal·ly \'frant-i-kə-lē\ *adv* : in a frantic manner

fra·ter·nal \frə-'tərn-l\ *adj* **1** : having to do with brothers **2** : composed of members banded together like brothers

fra·ter·ni·ty \frə-'tər-nət-ē\ *n, pl* **fra·ter·ni·ties** : a society or club of boys or men (as in a college)

fraud \'frȯd\ *n* **1** : TRICKERY, DECEIT **2** : an act of deceiving : TRICK **3** : a person who pretends to be what he is not **syn** see FAKE

fraud·u·lent \'frȯ-jə-lənt\ *adj* : based on or done by fraud — **fraud·u·lent·ly** *adv*

fraught \'frȯt\ *adj* : full of promise or menace

¹fray \'frā\ *n* : FIGHT, BRAWL

²fray *vb* : to wear out in shreds

fraz·zle \'fraz-əl\ *n* : a worn-out or nervous condition ⟨mothers worn to a *frazzle*⟩

¹freak \'frēk\ *n* : a strange, abnormal, or unusual person, thing, or event ⟨circus *freaks*⟩

²freak *adj* : having the nature of a freak

¹freck·le \'frek-əl\ *n* : a small brownish spot on the skin

²freckle *vb* **freck·led; freck·ling** : to mark or become marked with freckles ⟨a *freckled* face⟩

¹free \'frē\ *adj* **fre·er** \'frē-ər\; **fre·est** \'frē-əst\ **1** : having liberty : not being a slave ⟨a *free* man⟩ **2** : not controlled by others ⟨a *free* country⟩ **3** : released or not suffering from something unpleasant or painful ⟨*free* from worry⟩ **4** : given without charge ⟨a *free* ticket⟩ **5** : not held back by fear or distrust : OPEN ⟨a *free* expression of opinion⟩ **6** : not obstructed : OPEN, CLEAR — **free·ly** *adv*

²free *adv* **1** : FREELY **2** : without charge

³free *vb* **freed; free·ing** : to make or set free

free·boot·er \'frē-ˌbüt-ər\ *n* : PIRATE

freed·man \'frēd-mən\ *n, pl* **freed·men** \-mən\ : a man who has been freed from slavery

—**free·dom** \'frēd-əm\ *n* **1** : the condition of being free : LIBERTY, INDEPENDENCE **2** : EASE ⟨*freedom* of movement⟩ **3** : FRANKNESS, OUTSPOKENNESS ⟨speak with too much *freedom*⟩ **4** : free and unrestricted use

free·hand \'frē-ˌhand\ *adj* : done without mechanical aids ⟨a *freehand* drawing⟩

free·man \'frē-mən\ *n, pl* **free·men** \-mən\ : a free person : one who is not a slave

free·stand·ing \'frē-'stan-ding\ *adj* : standing alone or on its own foundation free of architectural or supporting frame or attachment

¹freeze \'frēz\ *vb* **froze** \'frōz\; **fro·zen** \'frōz-n\; **freez·ing** **1** : to harden into or be hardened into ice or a similar solid by loss of heat ⟨the river *froze* over⟩ ⟨*freeze* cream⟩ **2** : to chill or become chilled with cold ⟨it's *freezing* in here⟩ **3** : to damage by frost ⟨plants *frozen* by heavy frost⟩ **4** : to clog or become clogged by ice ⟨water pipes *frozen* overnight⟩ **5** : to become fixed or motionless

²freeze *n* **1** : very cold weather **2** : an act or instance of freezing **3** : the state of being frozen

freez·er \'frē-zər\ *n* : a refrigerating device used to freeze food or keep it frozen

freezing point *n* : the temperature at which a liquid becomes solid

¹freight \'frāt\ *n* **1** : the amount paid (as to a railroad or a steamship company) for carrying goods **2** : goods or cargo carried by a ship, train, truck, or airplane **3** : the carrying (as by truck) of goods from one place to another **4** : a train that carries freight

²freight *vb* : to send by freight

freight·er \'frāt-ər\ *n* : a ship or airplane for freight

¹French \'french\ *adj* : of or relating to France, the French people, or French

²French *n* **1** **French** *pl* : the people of France **2** : the language of the French

french fry *n, often cap 1st F* : a strip of potato fried in deep fat ⟨steak and *french fries*⟩

French horn *n* : a musical instrument in the form of a long bent cone-shaped tube flaring at one end and having a funnel-shaped mouthpiece at the other

fren·zied \'fren-zēd\ *adj* : very excited and agitated : FRANTIC

French horn

fren·zy \'fren-zē\ *n, pl* **fren·zies** : intense and wild activity

fre·quen·cy \'frē-kwən-sē\ *n, pl* **fre·quen·cies** **1** : repeated occurrence **2** : rate of occurrence

¹fre·quent \'frē-kwənt\ *adj* : often repeated ⟨*frequent* trips to town⟩ — **fre·quent·ly** *adv*

²fre·quent \frē-'kwent\ *vb* : to visit often

fresh \'fresh\ *adj* **1** : not salt ⟨*fresh* water⟩ **2** : PURE, BRISK ⟨*fresh* air⟩ ⟨a *fresh* breeze⟩ **3** : not frozen : not canned or pickled ⟨*fresh* vegetables⟩ **4** : not sour : not stale : not decayed ⟨*fresh* bread⟩ ⟨*fresh* milk⟩ **5** : NEW, ANOTHER ⟨make a *fresh* start⟩ **6** : newly made or received ⟨had a *fresh* wound⟩ ⟨*fresh* news⟩ **7** : IMPUDENT ⟨*fresh* talk⟩ ⟨*fresh* young thing⟩ **syn** see NEW — **fresh·ly** *adv* —**fresh·ness** *n*

fresh·en \'fresh-ən\ *vb* **1** : to make or become fresh : REFRESH ⟨took a shower to *freshen* up⟩ **2** : to grow brisk or strong ⟨the wind *freshened*⟩ **3** : to brighten in appearance

fresh·et \'fresh-ət\ *n* : a sudden overflowing of a stream

fresh·man \'fresh-mən\ *n, pl* **fresh·men**

\-mən\ : a first year student (as in college)

fresh·wa·ter \ˌfresh-ˌwȯt-ər, -ˌwät-\ *adj* : of, relating to, or living in fresh water

¹fret \ˈfret\ *vb* **fret·ted; fret·ting** : to become irritated : WORRY ⟨*fret* over a problem⟩

²fret *n* : an irritated or worried state

³fret *n* : a decorative design consisting of short lines or bars

⁴fret *n* : one of a series of ridges fixed across the fingerboard of a stringed musical instrument — **fret·ted** *adj*

frets

fret·ful \ˈfret-fəl\ *adj* : IRRI-TABLE — **fret·ful·ly** *adv* — **fret·ful·ness** *n*

fri·ar \ˈfrī-ər\ *n* : a member of a Roman Catholic religious order for men

fric·tion \ˈfrik-shən\ *n* **1** : the rubbing of one thing against another **2** : resistance to motion between bodies in contact (as when one body is slid past another) **3** : the clashing of persons or groups with different views

Fri·day \ˈfrīd-ē\ *n* : the sixth day of the week

friend \ˈfrend\ *n* **1** : a person who has a real liking for and confidence in another person **2** : a person who is not an enemy ⟨*friend* or foe⟩ **3** : a person who aids or favors something — **friend·less** \-ləs\ *adj*

friend·ly \ˈfrend-lē\ *adj* **friend·li·er; friend·li·est 1** : showing friendship **2** : not hostile — **friend·li·ness** *n*

friend·ship \ˈfrend-ˌship\ *n* : the state of being friends : FRIENDLINESS

frieze \ˈfrēz\ *n* : an ornamental band or stripe (as around a building)

frig·ate \ˈfrig-ət\ *n* : a square-rigged warship

fright \ˈfrīt\ *n* **1** : sudden terror : FEAR, ALARM **2** : something that frightens or is ugly or shocking

fright·en \ˈfrīt-n\ *vb* : to make afraid : TERRIFY, SCARE — **fright·en·ing·ly** *adv*

fright·ful \ˈfrīt-fəl\ *adj* **1** : causing fear or alarm ⟨a *frightful* scream⟩ **2** : SHOCKING, STARTLING ⟨the *frightful* cost of war⟩ — **fright·ful·ly** *adv* — **fright·ful·ness** *n*

frig·id \ˈfrij-əd\ *adj* **1** : freezing cold **2** : not friendly — **frig·id·ly** *adv* — **frig·id·ness** *n*

fri·gid·i·ty \fri-ˈjid-ət-ē\ *n* : the quality or state of being frigid

frill \ˈfril\ *n* : an ornamental addition

frill·y \ˈfril-ē\ *adj* **frill·i·er; frill·i·est** : having frills ⟨*frilly* clothes⟩

¹fringe \ˈfrinj\ *n* **1** : a border or trimming made by or made to look like the loose ends of the cloth **2** : something like a fringe

²fringe *vb* **fringed; fring·ing 1** : to decorate with a fringe **2** : to serve as a fringe for

frisk \ˈfrisk\ *vb* **1** : to jump, skip, or dance in a lively or playful way ⟨dogs *frisking* about⟩ **2** : to search a person for concealed weapons

frisk·y \ˈfris-kē\ *adj* **frisk·i·er; frisk·i·est** : PLAYFUL, LIVELY

¹frit·ter \ˈfrit-ər\ *n* : a small quantity of fried batter often containing fruit or meat

²fritter *vb* : to waste on unimportant things

fri·vol·i·ty \fri-ˈväl-ət-ē\ *n, pl* **fri·vol·i·ties 1** : the quality or state of being frivolous **2** : something frivolous

friv·o·lous \ˈfriv-ə-ləs\ *adj* **1** : of little importance : TRIVIAL ⟨a *frivolous* matter⟩ **2** : lacking in seriousness : PLAYFUL

frizz·y \ˈfriz-ē\ *adj* **frizz·i·er; frizz·i·est** : tightly curled ⟨*frizzy* hair⟩

fro \ˈfrō\ *adv* : BACK, AWAY — used in the phrase *to and fro*

frock \ˈfräk\ *n* : a woman's or girl's dress

frog \ˈfrȯg, ˈfräg\ *n* **1** : a smooth-skinned tailless web-footed animal that spends more of its time in water than the related toad **2** : a condition in the throat that produces hoarseness **3** : an ornamental fastening for a garment

frog 3

frog·man \ˈfrȯg-ˌman, ˈfräg-\ *n, pl* **frog·men** \-ˌmen\ : a swimmer equipped to stay under water for extended periods of time

¹frol·ic \ˈfräl-ik\ *vb* **frol·icked; frol·ick·ing** : to play about happily : ROMP

²frolic *n* **1** : a playful mischievous action **2** : FUN, MERRIMENT

frol·ic·some \ˈfräl-ik-səm\ *adj* : full of gaiety

from \frəm, ˈfräm\ *prep* — used to indicate a starting place, source, or point of separation ⟨a man *from* Chicago⟩ ⟨read aloud *from* a book⟩ ⟨the boat tore loose *from* its moorings⟩

frond \ˈfränd\ *n* : a large much-divided leaf (as of a palm or fern) or leaflike part

¹front \ˈfrənt\ *n* **1** : a region in which active warfare is taking place **2** : the forward part or surface **3** : the boundary between air masses of different temperatures ⟨cold *front*⟩

²front *vb* : FACE ⟨the cottage *fronts* on the lake⟩

³front *adj* : of, relating to, or situated at the front

front·al \ˈfrənt-l\ *adj* : having to do with or directed at the front ⟨a *frontal* attack⟩

fron·tier \ˌfrən-ˈtiər\ *n* **1** : a border between two countries **2** : the edge of the settled part of a country

fron·tiers·man \ˌfrən-ˈtiərz-mən\ *n, pl* **fron·tiers·men** \-mən\ : a man living on the frontier

fron·tis·piece \ˈfrənt-əs-ˌpēs\ *n* : an illustration at the front of a book

¹frost \ˈfrȯst\ *n* **1** : temperature cold enough

to cause freezing   **2** : a covering of tiny ice crystals on a cold surface formed from the water vapor in the air

²frost *vb* : to cover with frost or with something like frost ⟨*frost* a cake⟩

frost·bite \'fròst-,bīt\ *n* : the freezing of a part of the body

frost·ing \'fròs-ting\ *n* **1** : ICING **2** : a dull finish on glass

frost·y \'fròs-tē\ *adj* **frost·i·er; frost·i·est 1** : FREEZING, COLD ⟨a *frosty* evening⟩ **2** : covered with or appearing to be covered with frost ⟨a *frosty* glass⟩ — **frost·i·ly** \-tə-lē\ *adv* — **frost·i·ness** \-tē-nəs\ *n*

¹froth \'fròth\ *n* **1** : bubbles formed in or on liquids **2** : something light or of little value

²froth *vb* : to produce or form froth

froth·y \'fròth-ē\ *adj* **froth·i·er; froth·i·est** : full of or consisting of froth — **froth·i·ness** *n*

¹frown \'fraùn\ *vb* **1** : to wrinkle the forehead (as in anger, displeasure, or thought) **2** : to look with disapproval

²frown *n* : a wrinkling of the brow

froze *past of* FREEZE

frozen *past part of* FREEZE

fru·gal \'frü-gəl\ *adj* : showing economy in the use of resources — **fru·gal·ly** *adv*

¹fruit \'früt\ *n* [from Old French *fruit*, a modification of Latin *fructus* "use", "fruit", from *frui* "to enjoy", "to have the use of"] **1** : a pulpy or juicy plant part (as rhubarb or a strawberry) that is typically eaten as a dessert and distinguished from a vegetable **2** : a reproductive body of a seed plant that consists of the ripened ovary of a flower with its included seeds **3** : PRODUCT, RESULT — **fruit·ed** \-əd\ *adj*

²fruit *vb* : to bear or cause to bear fruit

fruit·cake \'früt-,kāk\ *n* : a rich cake containing nuts, dried or candied fruits, and spices

fruit·ful \'früt-fəl\ *adj* **1** : producing fruit abundantly **2** : bringing results ⟨a *fruitful* idea⟩ — **fruit·ful·ly** *adv* — **fruit·ful·ness** *n*

fruit·ing body \,früt-ing-\ *n* : a plant organ specialized for producing spores

fruit·less \'früt-ləs\ *adj* **1** : not bearing fruit **2** : UNSUCCESSFUL — **fruit·less·ly** *adv* — **fruit·less·ness** *n*

fruit·y \'früt-ē\ *adj* **fruit·i·er; fruit·i·est** : relating to or suggesting fruit

frus·trate \'frəs-,trāt\ *vb* **frus·trat·ed; frus·trat·ing** : to prevent from carrying out a purpose

frus·tra·tion \,frəs-'trā-shən\ *n* : DISAPPOINT-MENT, DEFEAT

¹fry \'frī\ *vb* **fried; fry·ing** : to cook in fat

²fry *n, pl* **fry** **1** : recently hatched or very young fishes **2** : PERSONS, INDIVIDUALS ⟨small *fry*⟩

fudge \'fəj\ *n* : a soft creamy candy often containing chocolate and nuts

¹fu·el \'fyü-əl\ *n* : a substance (as coal) that can be burned to produce heat or power

²fuel *vb* **fu·eled** *or* **fu·elled; fu·el·ing** *or* **fu·el·ling** : to supply with or take on fuel

¹fu·gi·tive \'fyü-jət-iv\ *adj* : running away or trying to escape ⟨a *fugitive* slave⟩

²fugitive *n* : a person who is running away

¹-ful \fəl\ *adj suffix* **1** : full of ⟨event*ful*⟩ **2** : characterized by ⟨peace*ful*⟩ **3** : having the qualities of ⟨master*ful*⟩ **4** : -ABLE ⟨mourn*ful*⟩

²-ful \,fùl\ *n suffix* : number or quantity that fills or would fill ⟨room*ful*⟩

ful·crum \'fùl-krəm, 'fəl-\ *n, pl* **ful·crums** *or* **ful·cra** \-krə\ : the support on which a lever turns in lifting something

ful·fill *or* **ful·fil** \fùl-'fil\ *vb* **ful·filled; ful·fill·ing** : to put into effect   **syn** see SATISFY — **ful·fill·ment** *n*

¹full \'fùl\ *adj* **1** : containing as much as possible or normal : FILLED ⟨a *full* glass⟩ **2** : being complete ⟨waited a *full* year⟩ **3** : plump and rounded in outline ⟨a *full* face⟩ **4** : having an abundance of material ⟨a *full* skirt⟩ — **full·ness** *n*

²full *adv* : COMPLETELY, ENTIRELY

³full *n* : the highest or fullest state or degree

full·back \'fùl-,bak\ *n* : a back on a football team

full moon *n* : the moon with its whole disk illuminated

ful·ly \'fùl-ē\ *adv* **1** : COMPLETELY **2** : at least ⟨*fully* half of them⟩

¹fum·ble \'fəm-bəl\ *vb* **fum·bled; fum·bling** : to handle something clumsily

²fumble *n* : an act of fumbling

¹fume \'fyüm\ *n* : a disagreeable smoke, vapor, or gas — usually used in plural

²fume *vb* **fumed; fum·ing** **1** : to give off fumes **2** : to show bad temper

fu·mi·gate \'fyü-mə-,gāt\ *vb* **fu·mi·gat·ed; fu·mi·gat·ing** : to disinfect by exposing to smoke, vapor, or gas

fun \'fən\ *n* **1** : something that provides amusement or enjoyment **2** : AMUSEMENT

¹func·tion \'fəngk-shən\ *n* **1** : the action or purpose for which a thing exists or is used **2** : an impressive ceremony or social affair

²function *vb* : to fulfill its purpose : WORK

fund \'fənd\ *n* **1** : SUPPLY ⟨a *fund* of jokes⟩ **2** : a sum of money to be used for a special purpose ⟨a book *fund*⟩ **3** : available money — usually used in plural ⟨out of *funds*⟩

---

¹**fun·da·men·tal** \,fən-də-'ment-l\ *adj* : having to do with the foundation : BASIC, ESSENTIAL — **fun·da·men·tal·ly** *adv*

²**fundamental** *n* : a basic or essential part

fu·ner·al \'fyü-nə-rəl\ *n* : the ceremonies held for a dead person (as before burial)

fun·gi·cide \'fən-jə-,sīd\ *n* : a substance used to kill fungi — **fun·gi·cid·al** \,fən-jə-'sīd-l\ *adj*

fun·gous \'fəng-gəs\ *or* **fun·gal** \-gəl\ *adj* : of, relating to, or caused by fungi

fun·gus \'fəng-gəs\ *n, pl* **fun·gi** \'fən-,jī\ *also* **fun·gus·es** : any of a large group of plants (as mushrooms, molds, and rusts) that have no chlorophyll and must live on other plants or animals or on decaying material

fun·nel \'fən-l\ *n* **1** : a utensil usually shaped like a hollow cone with a tube extending from the point and used to catch and direct a downward flow (as of liquid) **2** : a large pipe for the escape of smoke or for ventilation (as on a ship)

funnel 1

fun·ny \'fən-ē\ *adj* **fun·ni·er; fun·ni·est** **1** : causing laughter **2** : STRANGE

fur \'fər\ *n* **1** : a piece of the dressed pelt of an animal used on clothing **2** : an article of clothing made with fur **3** : the hairy coat of a mammal especially when fine, soft, and thick

fu·ri·ous \'fyur-ē-əs\ *adj* : being in a fury : ANGRY, FIERCE — **fu·ri·ous·ly** *adv*

furl \'fərl\ *vb* : to wrap or roll close to or around something ⟨*furl* a flag⟩

fur·long \'fər-,lȯng\ *n* : a unit of length equal to 220 yards or ⅛ of a mile

fur·lough \'fər-lō\ *n* : a leave of absence from duty ⟨a soldier's *furlough*⟩

fur·nace \'fər-nəs\ *n* : an enclosed place in which heat is produced (as for heating a house or for melting metals)

fur·nish \'fər-nish\ *vb* : to supply with what is needed or wanted

fur·nish·ings \'fər-nish-ingz\ *n pl* : articles of furniture for a room

fur·ni·ture \'fər-ni-chər\ *n* : movable articles used to furnish a room

fur·ri·er \'fər-ē-ər\ *n* : a dealer in furs

¹**fur·row** \'fər-ō\ *n* **1** : a trench made by or as if by a plow **2** : a narrow groove : WRINKLE

²**furrow** *vb* **1** : to make furrows in **2** : to form furrows

fur·ry \'fər-ē\ *adj* **fur·ri·er; fur·ri·est** **1** : resembling fur **2** : covered with fur

¹**fur·ther** \'fər-thər\ *adv* **1** : ¹FARTHER 1 **2** : in addition **3** : to a greater degree or extent

²**further** *adj* **1** : ²FARTHER **2** : going or extending beyond : ADDITIONAL ⟨*further* study⟩

³**further** *vb* : to help forward : PROMOTE

fur·ther·more \'fər-thər-,mōr\ *adv* : MOREOVER, BESIDES

fur·ther·most \'fər-thər-,mōst\ *adj* : most distant : FARTHEST

fur·thest \'fər-thəst\ *adv (or adj)* : FARTHEST

fur·tive \'fərt-iv\ *adj* : done by stealth : SLY **syn** see SECRET — **fur·tive·ly** *adv* — **fur·tive·ness** *n*

fu·ry \'fyur-ē\ *n, pl* **fu·ries** **1** : violent anger : RAGE **2** : a violent person **3** : FIERCENESS ⟨the *fury* of the storm⟩

¹**fuse** \'fyüz\ *n* **1** : a combustible cord for setting off an explosive by transmitting fire to it **2** *usu* **fuze** : a device for setting off a projectile, bomb, or torpedo

²**fuse** *vb* **fused; fus·ing** **1** : to change into a liquid or plastic state by heat **2** : to unite by or as if by melting together

³**fuse** *n* : a device having a metal wire or strip that melts and breaks an electrical circuit when the current becomes too strong

fu·se·lage \'fyü-sə-,läzh, -zə-\ *n* : the central body part of an airplane that holds the crew, passengers, and cargo

fuselage

fu·sion \'fyü-zhən\ *n* **1** : a fusing or melting together **2** : union by or as if by melting **3** : union of atomic nuclei to form heavier nuclei resulting in the release of enormous quantities of energy

¹**fuss** \'fəs\ *n* **1** : needless bustle or excitement : COMMOTION **2** : a state of agitation especially over a trivial matter

²**fuss** *vb* : to make a fuss

fuss·y \'fəs-ē\ *adj* **fuss·i·er; fuss·i·est** **1** : inclined to fuss ⟨a *fussy* child⟩ **2** : requiring much attention to details ⟨a *fussy* job⟩ **3** : too particular ⟨*fussy* about his food⟩

fu·tile \'fyüt-l\ *adj* : having no result or effect : USELESS — **fu·tile·ly** *adv* — **fu·tile·ness** *n*

fu·til·i·ty \fyü-'til-ət-ē\ *n* : the quality or state of being futile

¹**fu·ture** \'fyü-chər\ *adj* : coming after the present ⟨*future* events⟩

²**future** *n* : future time

fu·tu·ri·ty \fyü-'tur-ət-ē, -'tyur-\ *n* **1** : FUTURE **2** : the quality or state of being future

fuze \'fyüz\ *var of* FUSE

fuzz \'fəz\ *n* : fine light particles or fibers

fuzz·y \'fəz-ē\ *adj* **fuzz·i·er; fuzz·i·est** **1** : covered with or resembling fuzz **2** : not clear : INDISTINCT — **fuzz·i·ly** \'fəz-ə-lē\ *adv* — **fuzz·i·ness** \'fəz-ē-nəs\ *n*

-fy \,fī\ *vb suffix* **-fied; -fy·ing** **1** : make : form into ⟨solidi*fy*⟩ **2** : invest with the attributes of : make similar to ⟨beauti*fy*⟩

g \'jē\ *n, often cap* **1** : the seventh letter of the English alphabet **2** : a unit of force equal to a person's weight ⟨an astronaut during takeoff of his rocket vehicle may experience ten *G's*⟩

¹gab \'gab\ *vb* **gabbed; gab·bing** : to talk or chatter idly

²gab *n* : idle talk

gab·ar·dine \'gab-ər-ˌdēn\ *n* : a firm fabric with diagonal ribs and a hard smooth finish

¹gab·ble \'gab-əl\ *vb* **gab·bled; gab·bling** : to talk fast or without meaning : JABBER, CHATTER

²gabble *n* : loud or rapid talk that has no meaning

gab·by \'gab-ē\ *adj* **gab·bi·er; gab·bi·est** : full of idle talk or chatter : TALKATIVE

gab·er·dine \'gab-ər-ˌdēn\ *n* : GABARDINE

ga·ble \'gā-bəl\ *n* : the triangular part of an outside wall of a building formed by the sides of the roof sloping down from the ridgepole to the eaves

gad \'gad\ *vb* **gad·ded; gad·ding** : to roam about : go around restlessly

gad·a·bout \'gad-ə-ˌbaut\ *n* : a person who flits about in social activity

gad·fly \'gad-ˌflī\ *n, pl* **gad·flies** : a person who intentionally does a lot of criticizing and thus provokes or stimulates people

gadg·et \'gaj-ət\ *n* : an interesting, unfamiliar, or unusual device

gaff \'gaf\ *n* **1** : a spear for fishing **2** : an iron hook with a handle used in lifting heavy fish from the water **3** : something difficult to bear ⟨a person unable to stand the *gaff*⟩　　gaff 2

gaf·fer \'gaf-ər\ *n* : an old man

¹gag \'gag\ *vb* **gagged; gag·ging** **1** : to prevent from speaking by filling the mouth **2** : to cause to retch : RETCH

²gag *n* **1** : something that gags **2** : JOKE

gage *var of* GAUGE

gai·e·ty \'gā-ət-ē\ *n, pl* **gai·e·ties** : the state of being gay

gai·ly \'gā-lē\ *adv* **1** : in a gay or lively manner **2** : BRIGHTLY ⟨*gaily* dressed⟩

¹gain \'gān\ *n* **1** : PROFIT, ADVANTAGE ⟨share in the *gains*⟩ **2** : INCREASE, ADDITION ⟨a *gain* in weight⟩ **3** : the getting of money

²gain *vb* **1** : GET, ACQUIRE ⟨*gain* experience⟩ **2** : WIN ⟨*gained* the victory⟩ **3** : ACHIEVE ⟨*gain* strength⟩ **4** : to arrive at : REACH **5** : PROFIT

gain·er \'gā-nər\ *n* **1** : one that gains **2** : a backward somersault made from the takeoff position for a front dive

gain·ful \'gān-fəl\ *adj* : producing gain

gain·say \gān-'sā\ *vb* **gain·said** \-'sād, -'sed\; **gain·say·ing** : to speak against : CONTRADICT

gait \'gāt\ *n* : manner of walking or running

gai·ter \'gāt-ər\ *n* : a covering of cloth or leather for the leg from knee to instep or for the ankle and instep

¹ga·la \'gā-lə\ *n* : a gay celebration : FESTIVITY

²gala *adj* : suitable for festivities : FESTIVE

ga·lac·tic \gə-'lak-tik\ *adj* : of or relating to a galaxy ⟨*galactic* light⟩

gal·ax·y \'gal-ək-sē\ *n, pl* **gal·ax·ies** **1** : MILKY WAY GALAXY **2** : one of billions of collections each including stars, gas, and dust that make up the universe

gale \'gāl\ *n* **1** : a strong wind **2** : a wind of from thirty-two to sixty-three miles per hour **3** : OUTBURST ⟨*gales* of laughter⟩

ga·le·na \gə-'lē-nə\ *n* : a bluish gray mineral that is the principal ore of lead

¹gall \'gol\ *n* **1** : bile especially when stored in a small sac (**gall bladder**) attached to the liver **2** : bitterness of spirit : RANCOR **3** : IMPUDENCE

²gall *n* : a sore spot (as on a horse's back) caused by chafing

³gall *vb* **1** : to make sore by chafing **2** : ANNOY

⁴gall *n* : a swelling or growth on a twig or leaf

gal·lant *adj* **1** \'gal-ənt\ : NOBLE, BRAVE **2** \gə-'lant\ : very polite to women

gal·lant·ry \'gal-ən-trē\ *n, pl* **gal·lan·tries** **1** : COURAGE, BRAVERY **2** : a gallant speech or act **3** : polite attention shown to women

gal·le·on \'gal-ē-ən\ *n* : a large sailing ship of the time of Columbus and later

gal·ler·y \'gal-ə-rē\ *n, pl* **gal·ler·ies** **1** : a long narrow room or hall usually with windows along one side **2** : an indoor balcony (as in a theater or church) **3** : a gallerylike room or hall used for a special purpose (as showing pictures)

galleon

gal·ley \'gal-ē\ *n, pl* **gal·leys** **1** : a large low ship of ancient and medieval times propelled by oars and sails **2** : the kitchen of a ship

galley slave *n* : a person forced to row on a galley

gal·li·vant \'gal-ə-ˌvant\ *vb* : to gad about

gal·lon \'gal-ən\ *n* : a unit of liquid capacity equal to four quarts

¹gal·lop \'gal-əp\ *n* **1** : a fast springing natural gait of a quadruped and especially a horse **2** : a ride or run at a gallop

²gallop *vb* : to go or cause to go at a gallop

gal·lows \'gal-ōz\ *n, pl* **gallows** *or* **gal·lows·es** : a wooden framework from which criminals are hanged

gall·stone \'gȯl-ˌstōn\ *n* : a hard pebblelike mass formed in the gall bladder or bile passages

ga·losh \gə-'läsh\ *n* : an overshoe for wear in snow or wet weather

gal·va·nize \'gal-və-ˌnīz\ *vb* **gal·va·nized; gal·va·niz·ing 1** : to stimulate or excite by or as if by an electric shock **2** : to coat with zinc for protection ⟨*galvanized* iron⟩

¹**gam·ble** \'gam-bəl\ *vb* **gam·bled; gam·bling 1** : to play a game of chance for money or some other stake : BET **2** : to take risks for the sake of uncertain gains

²**gamble** *n* **1** : the act of gambling **2** : a risky undertaking

gam·bler \'gam-blər\ *n* : a person who gambles a great deal

gam·bol \'gam-bəl\ *vb* **gam·boled** *or* **gam·bolled; gam·bol·ing** *or* **gam·bol·ling** : to skip about playfully

¹**game** \'gām\ *n* **1** : SPORT, FUN ⟨make *game* of someone⟩ **2** : AMUSEMENT ⟨the children's *game* of tag⟩ **3** : a contest carried on according to set rules for amusement, exercise, or reward **4** : materials for playing a game **5** : animals hunted for sport or for food **6** : the edible flesh of game animals

syn GAME, PLAY, SPORT mean an activity engaged in for fun rather than to accomplish something. PLAY refers to activity of this sort, mental or physical; GAME indicates play that involves winning or losing according to fixed rules; SPORT suggests play that takes place outdoors and emphasizes physical action and skill

²**game** *adj* **gam·er; gam·est 1** : COURAGEOUS, PLUCKY **2** : of or relating to animals that are hunted ⟨the *game* laws⟩

game·cock \'gām-ˌkäk\ *n* : a rooster trained for fighting

game·keep·er \'gām-ˌkē-pər\ *n* : a person in charge of the breeding and protection of game animals or birds on a private preserve

gamecock

game·ly \'gām-lē\ *adv* : with pluck or spirit : BRAVELY ⟨fought *gamely*⟩

game·ness \'gām-nəs\ *n* : PLUCK, SPIRIT

game warden *n* : a man who enforces the fishing and hunting laws

gam·ing \'gā-ming\ *n* : GAMBLING

gam·ma rays \ˌgam-ə-\ *n pl* : very penetrating radiation of the same nature as X rays but of shorter wavelength

gam·mer \'gam-ər\ *n* : an old woman

gam·ut \'gam-ət\ *n* **1** : the whole series of musical notes **2** : a whole range or series

gam·y \'gā-mē\ *adj* **gam·i·er; gam·i·est 1** : GAME, PLUCKY **2** : having the flavor of game especially when slightly tainted

gan·der \'gan-dər\ *n* : a male goose

gang \'gang\ *n* **1** : a number of persons working or going about together **2** : a group of persons associated or acting together for lawless or criminal purposes

syn GANG, GROUP both refer to a band of people who associate with each other fairly regularly. GANG suggests lack of organization or fixed membership and stresses the idea of people of similar age and habits who go around together ⟨some of the *gang* had to stay after school⟩ GROUP indicates a somewhat more organized association based on an interest or purpose held in common ⟨went to the fair as a *group*⟩

gan·gli·on \'gang-glē-ən\ *n, pl* **gan·gli·a** \-glē-ə\ : a mass of nerve cells especially outside the brain or spinal cord

gang·plank \'gang-ˌplangk\ *n* : a movable passageway from a ship to the shore

gan·grene \'gang-ˌgrēn\ *n* : death of body tissue when deprived of blood

gang·way \'gang-ˌwā\ *n* **1** : a passage into, through, or out of an enclosed space **2** : GANGPLANK

gangplank

gan·net \'gan-ət\ *n* : a large fish-eating bird that spends much time far from land

gan·try \'gan-trē\ *n, pl* **gan·tries 1** : a movable structure for preparing a rocket for launching **2** : a structure over railroad tracks for displaying signals

gap \'gap\ *n* **1** : an opening made by a break or a parting : BREAK, CLEFT **2** : a mountain pass **3** : a break or separation in continuity

¹**gape** \'gāp\ *vb* **gaped; gap·ing 1** : to open the mouth wide especially in sleepiness or surprise **2** : to stare with open mouth **3** : to open or part widely

²**gape** *n* : an act or instance of gaping

¹**ga·rage** \gə-'räzh, -'räj\ *n* **1** : a building where automobiles are housed **2** : a repair shop for automobiles

²**garage** *vb* **ga·raged; ga·rag·ing** : to keep or put in a garage

¹**garb** \'gärb\ *n* : fashion or style of dress

²**garb** *vb* : CLOTHE, DRESS

gar·bage \'gär-bij\ *n* : waste food and especially that thrown out from a kitchen

gar·ble \'gär-bəl\ *vb* **gar·bled; gar·bling** : to distort the meaning or sound of

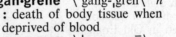

¹gar·den \'gärd-n\ *n* **1** : a piece of ground in which fruits, flowers, or vegetables are grown **2** : an enclosure for the exhibition of plants or animals ⟨a botanical *garden*⟩

²garden *vb* : to make or work in a garden

gar·den·er \'gärd-n-ər\ *n* : a person who gardens especially for pay

gar·de·nia \gär-'dē-nyə\ *n* : a large sweet‌smelling white or yellowish flower

gar·den·ing \'gärd-n-ing\ *n* : the laying out and cultivating of gardens

¹gar·gle \'gär-gəl\ *vb* **gar·gled; gar·gling** : to rinse the throat with a liquid kept in motion by air forced through it from the lungs

²gargle *n* **1** : a liquid used in gargling **2** : a gargling sound

gar·goyle \'gär-ˌgȯil\ *n* : a waterspout of a strange or grotesque shape jutting out at the roof or eaves of a building

gargoyle

gar·ish \'gaər-ish\ *adj* : extremely bright : GAUDY

¹gar·land \'gär-lənd\ *n* : a wreath or rope of leaves or flowers

²garland *vb* : to form into or decorate with a garland

gar·lic \'gär-lik\ *n* [a compound formed in Old English as *gārlēac*, from *gār* "spear" and *lēac* "leek"] : a plant related to the onion and grown for its pungent bulbs used in cooking

garland

gar·ment \'gär-mənt\ *n* : an article of clothing

¹gar·ner \'gär-nər\ *n* : a storage place for grain

²garner *vb* : to gather in : store up

gar·net \'gär-nət\ *n* [taken from early French *grenat* "garnet", from the adj. *grenat* meaning "red like a pomegranate", which was derived from the term *pomme grenate* meaning "pomegranate", literally, "seedy apple"] : a deep red mineral used as a gem

¹gar·nish \'gär-nish\ *vb* : to add decorative or savory touches to

²garnish *n* : something used in garnishing

gar·ret \'gar-ət\ *n* : a room or unfinished part of a house just under the roof

¹gar·ri·son \'gar-ə-sən\ *n* : a place in which troops are regularly stationed

²garrison *vb* **1** : to furnish (as a fort or town) with troops for defense **2** : to protect with forts and soldiers

gar·ru·lous \'gar-ə-ləs\ *adj* : very talkative

gar·ter \'gärt-ər\ *n* : a band or strap worn to hold up a stocking or sock

garter snake *n* : any of numerous harmless

American snakes with stripes along the back

¹gas \'gas\ *n, pl* **gas·es** **1** : an airlike substance (as oxygen or hydrogen) having no fixed shape and tending to expand without limit **2** : a gas or a mixture of gases used as a fuel or as an anesthetic **3** : a gaseous or liquid substance that poisons the air or makes breathing difficult **4** : GASOLINE

²gas *vb* **gassed; gas·sing; gas·ses** **1** : to treat with gas **2** : to poison with gas **3** : to supply with gas

gas·e·ous \'gas-ē-əs\ *adj* : of or relating to gas

¹gash \'gash\ *vb* : to make a long deep cut in

²gash *n* : a deep cut

gas mask *n* : a face covering connected to a device for purifying air and used to protect the face and lungs against poison gas

gas·o·line *or* **gas·o·lene** \ˌgas-ə-'lēn\ *n* : a flammable liquid made especially from gas found in the earth and petroleum and used as an automobile fuel

¹gasp \'gasp\ *vb* **1** : to breathe with difficulty : PANT ⟨*gasping* after a race⟩ **2** : to utter with quick difficult breaths

²gasp *n* **1** : the act of gasping **2** : something gasped out ⟨a *gasp* of surprise⟩

gas·tric juice \'gas-trik-\ *n* : an acid digestive liquid secreted by the stomach

gate \'gāt\ *n* **1** : an opening in a wall or fence often with a movable frame or door for closing it **2** : a part of a barrier (as a fence) that opens and closes like a door

¹gath·er \'gath-ər\ *vb* **1** : to bring or come together : COLLECT, ASSEMBLE **2** : to pick out and collect ⟨*gather* fruit⟩ **3** : to gain gradually ⟨*gather* speed⟩ **4** : to get an impression : UNDERSTAND **5** : to draw together in folds

²gather *n* : a puckering in cloth made by gathering

gath·er·ing \'gath-ə-ring\ *n* : an assembly of people

gau·cho \'gaů-chō\ *n, pl* **gau·chos** : a South American cowboy

gaud·y \'gȯd-ē\ *adj* **gaud·i·er; gaud·i·est** : being gay and showy

¹gauge \'gāj\ *n* **1** : measurement according to some standard **2** : DIMENSIONS, SIZE **3** : an instrument for measuring, testing, or registering ⟨a rain *gauge*⟩ ⟨a steam *gauge*⟩

gauge for steam

²gauge *vb* **gauged; gaug·ing** **1** : to measure exactly ⟨*gauge* rainfall⟩ **2** : to determine the capacity or contents of **3** : ESTIMATE, JUDGE

gaunt \'gȯnt\ *adj* **1** : very thin and bony (as

from illness or starvation) **2** : DESOLATE, GRIM ⟨the *gaunt* walls of a prison⟩ **syn** see THIN

¹gaunt·let \'gȯnt-lət\ *n* **1** : a glove made partly or wholly of small metal plates and worn as part of a suit of armor **2** : a glove with a flaring cuff that covers the wrist and part of the arm **3** : a challenge to combat

gauntlet 1

²gauntlet *n* : a double file of men armed with weapons (as clubs) with which to strike at someone forced to run between them

gauze \'gȯz\ *n* : a thin transparent fabric

gauz·y \'gȯ-zē\ *adj* **gauz·i·er; gauz·i·est** : being thin and transparent like gauze

gave *past of* GIVE

gav·el \'gav-əl\ *n* : a hammer or mallet with which the person presiding calls a meeting to order

¹gawk \'gȯk\ *vb* : to gape or stare stupidly

²gawk *n* : a stupid clumsy person

gavel

gawk·y \'gȯ-kē\ *adj* **gawk·i·er; gawk·i·est** : AWKWARD, CLUMSY — **gawk·i·ly** \-kə-lē\ *adv* — **gawk·i·ness** \-kē-nəs\ *n*

gay \'gā\ *adj* **gay·er; gay·est** **1** : MERRY **2** : being bright and showy

¹gaze \'gāz\ *vb* **gazed; gaz·ing** : to fix the eyes in a steady look

²gaze *n* : a long steady look

ga·zelle \gə-'zel\ *n* : a swift graceful antelope with soft bright eyes

ga·zette \gə-'zet\ *n* **1** : NEWSPAPER **2** : a journal giving official information

gaz·et·teer \ˌgaz-ə-'tiər\ *n* : a geographical dictionary

¹gear \'giər\ *n* **1** : EQUIPMENT **2** : a group of parts that performs a specific function in a machine ⟨steering *gear*⟩ **3** : a toothed wheel : COGWHEEL **4** : the position the gears of a machine are in when they are ready to work **5** : one of the adjustments in a motor vehicle that determine the direction of travel and the relative speed between the engine and the motion of the vehicle ⟨reverse *gear*⟩ ⟨second *gear*⟩

²gear *vb* **1** : to make ready for effective operation **2** : to adjust to match something

gear·shift \'giər-ˌshift\ *n* : a mechanism by which gears are connected and disconnected

gee \'jē\ *interj* — used to express surprise or enthusiasm

geese *pl of* GOOSE

Gei·ger counter \ˌgī-gər-\ *n* : an instrument for detecting the presence of cosmic rays or radioactive substances

gei·sha \'gā-shə\ *n, pl* **geisha** *or* **gei·shas** : a

Japanese girl who is trained to entertain men (as with conversation or music)

gel·a·tin \'jel-ət-n\ *n* **1** : a substance that is obtained from animal tissues by boiling and becomes jellylike in water **2** : a dessert made with gelatin

gem \'jem\ *n* **1** : JEWEL **2** : a usually precious stone cut and polished for ornament

gen·der \'jen-dər\ *n* **1** : SEX **2** : any of two or more classes of words (as nouns or pronouns) or of forms of words (as adjectives) in a language that are partly arbitrary but also partly based on distinguishable characteristics (as sex) and that determine agreement with and selection of other words or grammatical forms

gene \'jēn\ *n* : a specialized structure in a cell nucleus that carries hereditary characters from parent to offspring

genera *pl of* GENUS

¹gen·er·al \'jen-ə-rəl\ *adj* **1** : having to do with all ⟨a matter of *general* interest⟩ **2** : not specific or detailed **3** : not specialized

²general *n* : a commissioned officer ranking next below a general of the army or a general of the air force

gen·er·a·lis·si·mo \ˌjen-ə-rə-'lis-ə-ˌmō\ *n, pl* **gen·er·a·lis·si·mos** : the chief commander of an army

gen·er·al·i·za·tion \ˌjen-ə-rə-lə-'zā-shən\ *n* **1** : the act of generalizing about something **2** : a general observation or statement

gen·er·al·ize \'jen-ə-rə-ˌlīz\ *vb* **gen·er·al·ized; gen·er·al·iz·ing** : to put in the form of a general rule : draw or state a general conclusion from a number of particular items or instances

gen·er·al·ly \'jen-ə-rə-lē\ *adv* : USUALLY

general of the air force : a commissioned officer of the highest rank in the air force

general of the army : a commissioned officer of the highest rank in the army

gen·er·al·ship \'jen-ə-rəl-ˌship\ *n* **1** : office or duties of office of a general **2** : military skill as a high commander **3** : LEADERSHIP

gen·er·ate \'jen-ə-ˌrāt\ *vb* **gen·er·at·ed; gen·er·at·ing** : to cause to come into being

gen·er·a·tion \ˌjen-ə-'rā-shən\ *n* **1** : a step in a line of descent ⟨a family that has lived in the same house for four *generations*⟩ **2** : everyone born about the same time ⟨the younger *generation*⟩ **3** : the act of generating

gen·er·a·tor \'jen-ə-ˌrāt-ər\ *n* : DYNAMO

gen·er·os·i·ty \ˌjen-ə-'räs-ət-ē\ *n, pl* **gen·er·os·i·ties** **1** : willingness or readiness to give or to share **2** : a generous act or gift

gen·er·ous \'jen-ə-rəs\ *adj* **1** : free in giving : not mean or stingy **2** : ABUNDANT — **gen·er·ous·ly** *adv*

gen·e·sis \'jen-ə-səs\ *n, pl* **gen·e·ses** \-,sēz\ : a coming into being : BEGINNING

ge·net·i·cist \jə-'net-ə-səst\ *n* : a specialist in genetics

ge·net·ics \jə-'net-iks\ *n* : a science dealing with heredity and the variation of living things

ge·nial \'jē-nyəl\ *adj* : pleasantly cheerful

ge·nial·ly \'jē-nyə-lē\ *adv* : in a genial way

ge·nie \'jē-nē\ *n* : a magic spirit that often takes human form and serves his summoner

gen·i·tal \'jen-ə-tl\ *adj* : of or relating to reproduction or sex

ge·nius \'jē-nyəs\ *n* 1 : great natural ability ⟨a man of *genius*⟩ 2 : a highly gifted person

gen·tian \'jen-chən\ *n* : an herb with smooth opposite leaves and usually blue flowers

¹gen·tile \'jen-,tīl\ *n, often cap* : a person who is not Jewish

²gentile *adj, often cap* : of or relating to people not Jewish

gen·til·i·ty \jen-'til-ət-ē\ *n* 1 : good birth and family 2 : the qualities characteristic of a well-bred person 3 : good manners

gen·tle \'jent-l\ *adj* **gen·tler; gen·tlest** 1 : of good family 2 : not harsh or stern : MILD 3 : easily handled : not wild 4 : MODERATE ⟨a *gentle* slope⟩ — **gen·tle·ness** \'jent-l-nəs\ *n*

gen·tle·folk \'jent-l-,fōk\ *n pl* : persons of good family and breeding

gen·tle·man \'jent-l-mən\ *n, pl* **gen·tle·men** \-mən\ 1 : a man of good though not noble family 2 : a well-bred man of good education and social position 3 : MAN — used in the plural when addressing a group of men

gen·tle·man·ly \'jent-l-mən-lē\ *adj* : characteristic of or befitting a gentleman

gentleman's agreement *n* : an agreement that has no legal force but that is kept because of the honesty of those who make it

gen·tle·wom·an \'jent-l-,wum-ən\ *n, pl* **gen·tle·wom·en** \-,wim-ən\ 1 : a woman of good family or breeding 2 : a woman attending a lady of rank

gen·tly \'jent-lē\ *adv* : in a gentle manner

gen·try \'jen-trē\ *n* 1 : people of good birth, breeding, and education 2 : people of a designated class : FOLKS

gen·u·flect \'jen-yə-,flekt\ *vb* : to kneel on one knee and rise again as an act of reverence

gen·u·ine \'jen-yə-wən\ *adj* 1 : actually what it seems to be : REAL ⟨*genuine* gold⟩ 2 : SINCERE, HONEST — **gen·u·ine·ness** *n*

ge·nus \'jē-nəs\ *n, pl* **gen·er·a** \'jen-ə-rə\ 1 : a class of generally similar things that show differences by which they can be separated into smaller groups 2 : a group of plants or animals related in structure and heredity that

can be further divided into species

geo- *prefix* : geographical ⟨*geo*chemistry⟩

ge·o·chem·is·try \,jē-ō-'kem-əs-trē\ *n* : chemistry that deals with the earth's crust

ge·o·des·ic \,jē-ə-'des-ik\ *n* : the shortest line between two points on a surface

ge·og·ra·pher \jē-'äg-rə-fər\ *n* : a specialist in geography

ge·o·graph·ic \,jē-ə-'graf-ik\ *or* **ge·o·graph·i·cal** \-i-kəl\ *adj* : of or relating to geography

ge·og·ra·phy \jē-'äg-rə-fē\ *n* 1 : a science that deals with the natural features of the earth and its climate, products, and inhabitants 2 : the natural features of an area

ge·o·log·ic \,jē-ə-'läj-ik\ *or* **ge·o·log·i·cal** \-i-kəl\ *adj* : of or relating to geology

ge·ol·o·gist \jē-'äl-ə-jəst\ *n* : a specialist in geology

ge·ol·o·gy \jē-'äl-ə-jē\ *n* 1 : a science that deals with the history of the earth and its life especially as recorded in rocks 2 : the geologic features (as mountains or plains) of an area

ge·o·mag·net·ic \,jē-ō-mag-'net-ik\ *adj* : of or relating to the magnetism of the earth

ge·o·met·ric \,jē-ə-'met-rik\ *adj* : of or relating to geometry

ge·om·e·try \jē-'äm-ə-trē\ *n* : a branch of mathematics that deals with points, lines, angles, surfaces, and solids

ge·o·phys·i·cist \,jē-ə-'fiz-ə-səst\ *n* : a specialist in the physics of the earth

ge·ra·ni·um \jə-'rā-nē-əm\ *n* : an herb often grown for its bright flowers

ger·bil \'jər-bəl\ *n* : a small Old World leaping desert rodent

geranium

germ \'jərm\ *n* 1 : a bit of living matter capable of forming a new individual 2 : something from which something else develops ⟨the *germ* of an idea⟩ 3 : MICROBE

¹Ger·man \'jər-mən\ *n* 1 : a native or inhabitant of Germany 2 : the language of the Germans

²German *adj* : of or relating to Germany, the German people, or German

ger·ma·ni·um \jər-'mā-nē-əm\ *n* : a white hard brittle element used as a semiconductor

German silver *n* : an alloy of copper, zinc, and nickel

germ cell *n* : a reproductive cell (as an egg or sperm cell)

ger·mi·cide \'jər-mə-,sīd\ *n* : a substance that destroys germs

ger·mi·nate \'jər-mə-,nāt\ *vb* **ger·mi·nat·ed; ger·mi·nat·ing** : SPROUT

ger·mi·na·tion \,jər-mə-'nā-shən\ *n* : a beginning of development : SPROUTING

germ plasm *n* : the seat of heredity : GENES

ges·tic·u·late \jes-'tik-yə-,lāt\ *vb* **ges·tic·u·lat·ed; ges·tic·u·lat·ing** : to make gestures especially when speaking

¹ges·ture \'jes-chər\ *n* **1** : an act and especially a motion of the body that expresses an idea or a feeling **2** : something said or done for effect and not to be taken seriously

²gesture *vb* **ges·tured; ges·tur·ing** : to make a gesture

get \'get\ *vb* **got** \'gät\; **got** *or* **got·ten** \'gät-n\; **get·ting** \'get-iŋ\ **1** : to gain possession of (as by receiving, acquiring, earning, buying, or winning) ⟨*get* his hat⟩ ⟨*get* a present⟩ **2** : ARRIVE ⟨*get* home early⟩ **3** : GO, MOVE ⟨*get* out⟩ ⟨*get* about on crutches⟩ **4** : BECOME ⟨*get* angry⟩ ⟨it is *getting* warmer⟩ **5** : CATCH ⟨he'll *get* pneumonia⟩ **6** : to cause to be done ⟨*get* your hair cut⟩ **7** : PERSUADE — **get ahead** : to achieve success (as in business) — **get along 1** : MANAGE **2** : to stay on good terms — **get around 1** : to get the better of **2** : EVADE — **get at 1** : to reach effectively **2** : to influence corruptly **3** : to turn one's attention to **4** : to try to prove or make clear — **get away with** : to accomplish or perform without suffering unpleasant consequences — **get back at** : to get even with — **get even** : to get revenge — **get even with** : to pay back for a real or imagined injury — **get in** : to manage to perform, do, or finish — **get one's goat** : to make one angry or annoyed — **get over** : to recover from — **get wind of** : to become aware of : hear about

gey·ser \'gī-zər\ *n* [from *Geysir*, the name of a geyser in Iceland, from Icelandic *geysa* "to gush"] : a spring that now and then shoots up hot water and steam

ghast·ly \'gast-lē\ *adj* **ghast·li·er; ghast·li·est 1** : HORRIBLE, SHOCKING ⟨a *ghastly* crime⟩ **2** : resembling a ghost : PALE ⟨a *ghastly* face⟩

ghet·to \'get-ō\ *n, pl* **ghet·tos** *or* **ghet·toes** : a quarter of a city in which members of a minority group live because of social, legal, or economic pressure

ghost \'gōst\ *n* : the spirit thought of as living in an unseen world of the dead or as appearing in physical form to living people

ghost·ly \'gōst-lē\ *adj* **ghost·li·er; ghost·li·est** : of or appropriate to a ghost

ghost town *n* : a town deserted because of the exhaustion of some nearby natural resource

ghoul \'gül\ *n* **1** : a legendary evil being that robs graves and feeds on corpses **2** : a despicable person (as a grave robber) whose activities resemble those of a ghoul

¹gi·ant \'jī-ənt\ *n* **1** : an imaginary manlike monster of great size and strength **2** : a person or thing that is very large or powerful

²giant *adj* : much larger than ordinary : HUGE

gib·ber·ish \'jib-ə-rish\ *n* : rapid confused meaningless talk

gib·bet \'jib-ət\ *n* : a gallows from which the bodies of executed criminals are hung as a warning

gib·bon \'gib-ən\ *n* : a tailless ape of southeastern Asia and the East Indies

¹gibe \'jīb\ *vb* **gibed; gib·ing** : JEER

²gibe *n* : JEER

gib·let \'jib-lət\ *n* : an edible inner organ (as the heart or liver) of a fowl ⟨*giblet* gravy⟩

gid·dy \'gid-ē\ *adj* **gid·di·er; gid·di·est 1** : having a feeling of whirling or reeling about : DIZZY **2** : causing dizziness ⟨a *giddy* height⟩ **3** : FRIVOLOUS — **gid·di·ness** *n*

gift \'gift\ *n* **1** : a special ability : TALENT ⟨a *gift* for music⟩ **2** : a thing that is given : PRESENT **3** : the act or power of giving

gift·ed \'gif-təd\ *adj* : TALENTED

gig \'gig\ *n* **1** : a light two-wheeled one-horse carriage **2** : a long light boat for a ship's captain

gi·gan·tic \jī-'gant-ik\ *adj* : resembling a giant (as in size, weight, or strength)

gig·gle \'gig-əl\ *vb* **gig·gled; gig·gling** : to laugh in a high-pitched voice and with repeated short catches of the breath

gig·gly \'gig-lē\ *adj* : inclined to giggle a lot

Gi·la monster \,hē-lə-\ *n* : a large black and orange venomous lizard of the southwestern United States

gild \'gild\ *vb* **gild·ed** *or* **gilt** \'gilt\; **gild·ing 1** : to cover with a thin coating of gold **2** : to make attractive ⟨*gild* a story⟩

¹gill \'jil\ *n* : a unit of liquid capacity equal to a quarter of a pint

²gill \'gil\ *n* : an organ (as of a fish) for taking oxygen from water

¹gilt \'gilt\ *n* : gold or something like gold applied to a surface

²gilt *adj* : of a golden color

³gilt *n* : a young female hog

gim·let \'gim-lət\ *n* : a small tool for boring

¹gin \'jin\ *n* : a machine to separate seeds from cotton

²gin *vb* **ginned; gin·ning** : to separate seeds from cotton in a gin

³gin *n* : a distilled alcoholic liquor flavored with juniper berries

gin·ger \'jin-jər\ *n* : a spice obtained from the hot aromatic root of a tropical plant and used to season foods (as cookies) or as medicine

gimlet

ginger ale *n* : a nonalcoholic drink flavored with ginger

gin·ger·bread \'jin-jər-,bred\ *n* : a molasses cake flavored with ginger

¹**gin·ger·ly** \'jin-jər-lē\ *adj* : very cautious

²**gingerly** *adv* : very cautiously

gin·ger·snap \'jin-jər-,snap\ *n* : a thin brittle cookie flavored with ginger

ging·ham \'ging-əm\ *n* : a clothing fabric usually of yarn-dyed cotton in plain weave

gip·sy *var of* GYPSY

gi·raffe \jə-'raf\ *n* : a cud-chewing long-necked spotted mammal of Africa

gird \'gərd\ *vb* **gird·ed** *or* **girt** \'gərt\; **gird·ing** 1 : to encircle or fasten with or as if with a belt or cord 2 : to prepare or brace oneself

gird·er \'gərd-ər\ *n* : a horizontal main supporting beam ⟨a *girder* of a bridge⟩

¹**gir·dle** \'gərd-l\ *n* 1 : something (as a belt or sash) that encircles or binds 2 : a light corset worn below the waist

²**girdle** *vb* **gir·dled**; **gir·dling** 1 : to bind with or as if with a girdle, belt, or sash : ENCIRCLE 2 : to strip a ring of bark from a tree trunk

girl \'gərl\ *n* 1 : a female child or young woman 2 : a female servant

girl·hood \'gərl-,hud\ *n* : the state or time of being a girl

girl·ish \'gər-lish\ *adj* : typical of or suitable for a girl ⟨*girlish* laughter⟩

girl scout *n* : a member of the Girl Scouts of the United States of America

girth \'gərth\ *n* 1 : a band put around the body of an animal to hold something (as a saddle) on its back 2 : the measure or distance around something ⟨a man of huge *girth*⟩ ⟨the *girth* of a tree⟩

girth

gist \'jist\ *n* : the main point of a matter

¹**give** \'giv\ *vb* **gave** \'gāv\; **giv·en** \'giv-ən\; **giv·ing** 1 : to hand over to be kept : PRESENT ⟨*give* a friend a Christmas present⟩ 2 : PAY 3 : UTTER ⟨*give* a yell⟩ ⟨*give* a speech⟩ 4 : FURNISH, PROVIDE ⟨a candle that *gives* light⟩ ⟨*give* a party⟩ 5 : to cause to have ⟨*give* someone a lot of trouble⟩ 6 : GRANT, ALLOW ⟨*give* permission⟩ 7 : to yield slightly — **give in** : SURRENDER, YIELD ⟨*give in* to a repeated request⟩ — **give up** 1 : to part with : STOP, ABANDON ⟨finally *gave up* the idea⟩ 2 : to stop trying or opposing : QUIT ⟨refused to *give up* despite the losses⟩ — **give way** 1 : to yield oneself without restraint or control 2 : to break down : COLLAPSE

²**give** *n* : a yielding or giving way : SPRING

giv·en \'giv-ən\ *adj* 1 : DISPOSED, INCLINED ⟨one *given* to outbursts of temper⟩ 2 : STATED

given name *n* : a first name (as *John*)

giz·zard \'giz-ərd\ *n* : a muscular enlargement of the digestive tube (as of a bird) in which food is churned and ground small

gla·cial \'glā-shəl\ *adj* 1 : extremely cold 2 : of or relating to glaciers

gla·cier \'glā-shər\ *n* : a large body of ice moving slowly down a slope or over a wide area of land

glad \'glad\ *adj* **glad·der**; **glad·dest** 1 : HAPPY, JOYFUL 2 : bringing or arousing joy ⟨*glad* tidings⟩ 3 : GAY, BRIGHT

glad·den \'glad-n\ *vb* : to make glad

glade \'glād\ *n* : a grassy open space in a forest

glad·i·a·tor \'glad-ē-,āt-ər\ *n* : one of a pair of armed men forced to fight to the death for the entertainment of the public in ancient Rome

glad·i·o·lus \,glad-ē-'ō-ləs\ *n, pl* **glad·i·o·li** \-lē, -,lī\ *or* **gladiolus** *or* **glad·i·o·lus·es** : a plant with stiff sword-shaped leaves and spikes of brilliantly colored flowers

glad·ly \'glad-lē\ *adv* : WILLINGLY, CHEERFULLY, JOYFULLY

glad·ness \'glad-nəs\ *n* : JOY, HAPPINESS

glad·some \'glad-səm\ *adj* : giving or showing joy

glam·or·ous \'glam-ə-rəs\ *adj* : full of glamour

glam·our *or* **glam·or** \'glam-ər\ *n* 1 : charm or attractiveness especially when it is deceptive 2 : alluring or fascinating personal attraction

¹**glance** \'glans\ *vb* **glanced**; **glanc·ing** 1 : to strike at an angle and fly off to one side 2 : to give a hasty look

²**glance** *n* : a quick look : GLIMPSE

gland \'gland\ *n* : an organ in the body that prepares a substance to be used by the body or discharged from it ⟨a saliva *gland*⟩

glan·du·lar \'glan-jə-lər\ *adj* : of, resembling, or having to do with glands

¹**glare** \'glaər\ *vb* **glared**; **glar·ing** 1 : to shine with a dazzling light 2 : to look fiercely or angrily

²**glare** *n* 1 : a bright dazzling light 2 : a fierce look

glar·ing \'glaər-ing\ *adj* 1 : dazzlingly bright ⟨*glaring* sunlight⟩ 2 : FIERCE, ANGRY ⟨a *glaring* look⟩ 3 : very conspicuous : OBVIOUS

¹**glass** \'glas\ *n* 1 : a hard brittle usually transparent substance commonly made from sand heated with chemicals 2 : something (as

gladiolus

a mirror or a water tumbler) made of glass
3 *pl* : a pair of glass lenses used to correct
faulty eyesight **4** : the contents of a glass

²glass *vb* : to fit or protect with glass

glass·blow·ing \'glas-ˌblō-ing\ *n* : the art of
shaping a mass of melted glass by blowing air
into it through a tube

glass·ful \'glas-ˌfùl\ *n* : the amount a glass
will hold

glass·ware \'glas-ˌwaər\ *n* : articles of glass

glass·y \'glas-ē\ *adj* **glass·i·er; glass·i·est**
1 : resembling glass (as in smoothness)
2 : DULL, LIFELESS ⟨*glassy* eyes⟩

¹glaze \'glāz\ *vb* **glazed; glaz·ing** **1** : to furnish or fit with glass ⟨*glaze* a window⟩ **2** : to
cover with a glassy surface ⟨*glaze* pottery⟩
3 : to coat with crystallized sugar **4** : to become glazed or glassy in appearance

²glaze *n* **1** : something used for glazing **2** : a
glassy surface or coating

gla·zier \'glā-zhər\ *n* : a person who sets
glass in window frames

¹gleam \'glēm\ *n* : a moderate brightness

²gleam *vb* : to send out gleams

glean \'glēn\ *vb* **1** : to gather from a field or
vineyard what is left by the reapers **2** : to
gather little by little with patient effort

glee \'glē\ *n* **1** : JOY **2** : a song without an
accompaniment for three or four voices

glee club *n* : a singing group organized especially as a social activity in a school or college

glee·ful \'glē-fəl\ *adj* : MERRY, JOYOUS

glen \'glen\ *n* : a narrow hidden valley

glib \'glib\ *adj* : speaking or spoken with
careless ease and often with too little regard
for the truth — **glib·ly** *adv* — **glib·ness** *n*

¹glide \'glīd\ *vb* **glid·ed; glid·ing** : to move
with a smooth and silent motion

²glide *n* : a smooth and silent motion

glid·er \'glīd-ər\ *n* **1** : an aircraft similar to
an airplane but without an engine **2** : a porch
seat hung from an upright frame (as by chains)

¹glim·mer \'glim-ər\ *vb* : to shine faintly and
unsteadily

²glimmer *n* : a feeble unsteady light

¹glimpse \'glimps\ *vb* **glimpsed; glimps·ing**
: to catch a quick view of

²glimpse *n* : a short hurried view

¹glint \'glint\ *vb* : GLITTER, GLEAM, FLASH

²glint *n* : a brief flash

glis·ten \'glis-n\ *vb* : to shine with a soft
luster or sparkle

¹glit·ter \'glit-ər\ *vb* **1** : to sparkle brightly
2 : to sparkle with light that is harsh and cold
3 : to be very bright and showy

²glitter *n* : sparkling brilliance

gloam·ing \'glō-ming\ *n* : TWILIGHT, DUSK

gloat \'glōt\ *vb* : to gaze at or think about
something with great satisfaction and especially with mean or greedy satisfaction

glob \'gläb\ *n* : a small drop : BLOB

glob·al \'glō-bəl\ *adj* **1** : resembling a globe
in shape **2** : having to do with the whole earth

globe \'glōb\ *n* **1** : a round object : BALL,
SPHERE ⟨a *globe* for a lamp⟩
2 : EARTH **3** : a round model of
the earth or heavens

globe–trot·ter \'glōb-ˌträt-ər\
n : one that travels widely

glob·u·lar \'gläb-yə-lər\ *adj*
: shaped like a globe : ROUND

glob·ule \'gläb-yül\ *n* : a small
round particle (as of water)

globe 3

glock·en·spiel \'gläk-ən-ˌspēl\ *n* : a musical
instrument consisting of a series of metal bars
played with hammers

gloom \'glüm\ *n* **1** : partial or total darkness
2 : SADNESS **syn** see MELANCHOLY

gloom·y \'glü-mē\ *adj* **gloom·i·er; gloom·i·est**
1 : DUSKY, DIM ⟨a *gloomy* cave⟩ **2** : SAD
3 : causing gloom : DEPRESSING — **gloom·i·ly**
\-mə-lē\ *adv* — **gloom·i·ness** \-mē-nəs\ *n*

glo·ri·fi·ca·tion \ˌglōr-ə-fə-'kā-shən\ *n* : the
act of glorifying : the state of being glorified

glo·ri·fy \'glōr-ə-ˌfī\ *vb* **glo·ri·fied; glo·ri·fy·ing**
1 : WORSHIP, ADORE ⟨*glorify* God⟩ **2** : to give
honor and praise to ⟨*glorify* a hero⟩ **3** : to
show in a very favorable way ⟨*glorify* war⟩

glo·ri·ous \'glōr-ē-əs\ *adj* **1** : NOBLE, PRAISE-
WORTHY ⟨*glorious* deeds⟩ **2** : SPLENDID, MAG-
NIFICENT ⟨a *glorious* victory⟩ **3** : DELIGHTFUL

¹glo·ry \'glōr-ē\ *n, pl* **glo·ries** **1** : praise,
honor, and admiration given to a person by
others **2** : something that brings honor,
praise, or fame ⟨the *glories* of Greece⟩
3 : BRILLIANCE, SPLENDOR **4** : HEAVEN

²glory *vb* **glo·ried; glo·ry·ing** : to rejoice
proudly : be proud or boastful

¹gloss \'gläs\ *n* **1** : brightness from a smooth
surface : LUSTER, SHEEN **2** : an outwardly attractive appearance : outward show

²gloss *vb* **1** : to give a gloss to **2** : to smooth
over : explain away ⟨*gloss* over a mistake⟩

glos·sa·ry \'gläs-ə-rē\ *n, pl* **glos·sa·ries** : a
special dictionary (as of the hard or unusual
words used in a particular book)

gloss·y \'gläs-ē\ *adj* **gloss·i·er; gloss·i·est**
: smooth and shining on the surface

glove \'gləv\ *n* : a covering for the hand
made with a division for each finger

¹glow \'glō\ *vb* **1** : to shine with an intense
heat : give off light and heat without flame
2 : to show strong bright color **3** : to be or to
look warm and flushed (as with exercise)

²glow *n* **1** : light such as comes from something that is intensely hot but not flaming **2** : brightness or warmth of color ⟨a rosy *glow* in the sky⟩ **3** : a feeling of physical warmth (as from exercise) **4** : warmth of feeling

glow·er \ˈglau̇-ər\ *vb* : to stare angrily : SCOWL

glow·worm \ˈglō-ˌwərm\ *n* : an insect or insect larva that gives off light

glu·cose \ˈglü-ˌkōs\ *n* [from French *glucose*, a modification of Greek *gleukos* "juice of grapes"] : a sugar that occurs in plant saps and fruits and is the usual form in which carbohydrate is assimilated into the animal body

¹glue \ˈglü\ *n* : a strong adhesive substance (as one made by boiling animal skins, bones, and hoofs)

²glue *vb* **glued; glu·ing** : to stick with glue

glu·ey \ˈglü-ē\ *adj* **glu·i·er; glu·i·est** : covered with glue : sticky like glue

glum \ˈgləm\ *adj* **glum·mer; glum·mest** **1** : gloomily silent **2** : DISMAL — **glum·ly** *adv* — **glum·ness** *n*

¹glut \ˈglət\ *vb* **glut·ted; glut·ting** **1** : to make quite full : fill completely **2** : to flood with goods so that supply exceeds demand

²glut *n* : an excessive quantity

glu·ti·nous \ˈglüt-n-əs\ *adj* : resembling glue : STICKY — **glu·ti·nous·ly** *adv*

glut·ton \ˈglət-n\ *n* : a person who overeats — **glut·ton·ous** *adj* — **glut·ton·ous·ly** *adv*

glut·ton·y \ˈglət-n-ē\ *n, pl* **glut·ton·ies** : excess in eating or drinking

glyc·er·in \ˈglis-ə-rən\ *n* : a sweet syruplike liquid that occurs in various oils and fats, is a by-product in the making of soaps, and is used as a moistening substance and a solvent

G–man \ˈjē-ˌman\ *n, pl* **G–men** \-ˌmen\ : a special agent of the Federal Bureau of Investigation

gnarled \ˈnärld\ *adj* : being knotty, twisted, and rugged ⟨a *gnarled* old oak⟩

gnash \ˈnash\ *vb* : to strike or grind (the teeth) together (as in anger or pain)

gnat \ˈnat\ *n* : a very small two-winged fly

gnaw \ˈnȯ\ *vb* **gnawed; gnaw·ing** : to bite so as to wear away little by little : bite or chew upon ⟨the dog *gnawed* the bone⟩

gnome \ˈnōm\ *n* : one of an imaginary race of dwarfs believed to live inside the earth and guard treasure

gnat

gnu \ˈnü, ˈnyü\ *n, pl* **gnu** *or* **gnus** : a large African antelope with an oxlike head, short mane and flowing tail, and curving horns

go \ˈgō\ *vb* **went** \ˈwent\; **gone** \ˈgȯn\; **go·ing** \ˈgō-ing\; **goes** **1** : to pass from one place or point to another : MOVE, PROCEED **2** : to move away : LEAVE ⟨people coming and *going*⟩ **3** : to pass away : be spent : DISAPPEAR ⟨money *goes* more easily than it comes⟩ **4** : to continue its course or action : RUN ⟨some machines *go* by electricity⟩ **5** : to make its own special sound ⟨a kitten *goes* like this⟩ **6** : to be suitable : BELONG ⟨a tie that *goes* with his suit⟩ **7** : to prove ultimately to be : work out

¹goad \ˈgōd\ *n* **1** : a pointed rod used to urge on an animal **2** : something that urges

²goad *vb* : to urge on with a goad

goal \ˈgōl\ *n* **1** : the point at which a race or journey is to end **2** : AIM, PURPOSE ⟨reached his *goal* in life⟩ **3** : a place toward which play is directed (as in football) in order to score

goal·ie \ˈgō-lē\ *n* : a player who defends the goal

goal·keep·er \ˈgōl-ˌkē-pər\ *n* : GOALIE

goal·tend·er \ˈgōl-ˌten-dər\ *n* : GOALIE

goat \ˈgōt\ *n* : a horned cud-chewing mammal related to but more nimble than the sheep — **goatlike** \-ˌlīk\ *adj*

goa·tee \gō-ˈtē\ *n* : a small beard trimmed to a point

goat·herd \ˈgōt-ˌhərd\ *n* : one who tends goats

goat·skin \ˈgōt-ˌskin\ *n* : the skin of a goat used for making leather

¹gob \ˈgäb\ *n* : LUMP, MASS ⟨a *gob* of mud⟩

²gob *n* : SAILOR

gob·bet \ˈgäb-ət\ *n* : LUMP, MASS

¹gob·ble \ˈgäb-əl\ *vb* **gob·bled; gob·bling** : to eat hastily or greedily

²gobble *vb* **gob·bled; gob·bling** : to make a gobble

³gobble *n* : the throaty sound of a turkey

gob·ble·dy·gook \ˌgäb-əl-dē-ˈgu̇k\ *n* : wordy and generally unintelligible talk

gob·bler \ˈgäb-lər\ *n* : a male turkey

go–be·tween \ˈgō-bə-ˌtwēn\ *n* : a person who acts as a messenger or peacemaker

gob·let \ˈgäb-lət\ *n* : a drinking glass with a foot and stem

gob·lin \ˈgäb-lən\ *n* : an ugly imaginary creature with evil or mischievous ways

goblet

¹god \ˈgäd\ *n* **1** : a being possessing more than human powers ⟨ancient peoples worshiped many *gods*⟩ **2** : a natural or man-made physical object worshiped as divine **3** : something held to be the most important thing in existence

²God *n* : the Being regarded as the holy and sovereign power creating and sustaining all things of the universe

god·child \ˈgäd-ˌchīld\ *n, pl* **god·chil·dren**

\-,chil-drən\ : a person for whom another person stands as sponsor at baptism

god·dess \'gäd-əs\ *n* : a female god

god·fa·ther \'gäd-,fä-thər\ *n* : a man who stands as sponsor for a child at its baptism

god·less \'gäd-ləs\ *adj* **1** : not acknowledging the existence of God **2** : WICKED, EVIL — **god·less·ness** *n*

god·like \'gäd-,līk\ *adj* : resembling or suitable for God or a god

god·ly \'gäd-lē\ *adj* **god·li·er; god·li·est** : RELIGIOUS, PIOUS — **god·li·ness** *n*

god·moth·er \'gäd-,məth-ər\ *n* : a woman who stands as sponsor for a child at its baptism

god·par·ent \'gäd-,par-ənt\ *n* : a sponsor at baptism

god·send \'gäd-,send\ *n* : some badly needed thing that comes unexpectedly

go–get·ter \'gō-,get-ər\ *n* : a very aggressive enterprising person : HUSTLER

gog·gle \'gäg-əl\ *vb* **gog·gled; gog·gling** : to roll the eyes : SQUINT, STARE

gog·gle–eyed \,gäg-əl-'īd\ *adj* : having bulging or rolling eyes

gog·gles \'gäg-əlz\ *n pl* : eyeglasses worn to protect the eyes (as from dust, sun, or wind)

go·ings–on \,gō-ingz-'ȯn, -'än\ *n pl* : HAPPENINGS, EVENTS

goi·ter \'gȯit-ər\ *n* : a swelling on the front of the neck due to enlargement of the thyroid gland

gold \'gōld\ *n* **1** : a malleable yellow metallic chemical element used especially in coins and jewelry **2** : gold coins **3** : MONEY **4** : a deep yellow

¹gold·brick \'gōld-,brik\ *n* : a person (as a soldier) who shirks assigned work

²goldbrick *vb* : to avoid or try to avoid assigned work because of laziness

gold·en \'gōl-dən\ *adj* **1** : resembling, made of, or containing gold **2** : of the color of gold **3** : PRECIOUS, EXCELLENT **4** : being prosperous and happy : FLOURISHING ⟨a *golden* age⟩

gold·en·rod \'gōl-dən-,räd\ *n* : a tall stiff-stemmed plant topped with rows of tiny yellow flower heads on slender branches

golden rule *n* : a rule that one should do to others as he would have others do to him

gold·finch \'gōld-,finch\ *n* **1** : a European finch with a yellow patch on each wing **2** : an American finch resembling the canary

gold·fish \'gōld-,fish\ *n* : a small usually golden yellow or orange carp often kept in aquariums

gold·smith \'gōld-,smith\ *n* : a person who makes or deals in articles of gold

golf \'gälf\ *n* : a game played on an outdoor course with a small ball (**golf ball**) and a set of clubs (**golf clubs**)

golf·er \'gäl-fər\ *n* : a person who plays golf

gon·do·la \'gän-də-lə\ *n* **1** : a long narrow boat used in the canals of Venice **2** : a freight car with no top **3** : an enclosure suspended from a balloon for carrying passengers or instruments

gondola 1

gone \'gȯn\ *adj* **1** : no longer present ⟨he is *gone*⟩ **2** : PAST ⟨those days are *gone* forever⟩ **3** : ADVANCED **4** : SINKING, WEAK

gon·er \'gȯ-nər\ *n* : a hopeless case

gong \'gäng\ *n* : a metallic disk that produces a harsh ringing tone when struck

¹good \'gud\ *adj* **bet·ter** \'bet-ər\; **best** \'best\ **1** : suitable for its purpose : SATISFACTORY ⟨a *good* light for reading⟩ **2** : having or being over the required amount : FULL ⟨a *good* day's work⟩ **3** : CONSIDERABLE ⟨a *good* deal of trouble⟩ **4** : DESIRABLE, ATTRACTIVE ⟨a *good* job⟩ **5** : HELPFUL, KIND **6** : behaving well ⟨a *good* boy⟩ **7** : being honest and upright **8** : SOUND, RELIABLE ⟨*good* advice⟩ **9** : up to the standard : not bad ⟨*good* work⟩

²good *n* **1** : something good **2** : WELFARE, BENEFIT ⟨for his own *good*⟩ **3** *pl* : WARES **4** *pl* : personal property **5** *pl* : YARD GOODS

good–bye *or* **good–by** \gud-'bī\ *n* : a concluding remark at parting — often used as an interjection

Good Friday *n* : the Friday before Easter observed as the anniversary of the crucifixion of Christ

good–heart·ed \'gud-'härt-əd\ *adj* : having a kindly generous disposition — **good–heart·ed·ly** *adv* — **good–heart·ed·ness** *n*

good–hu·mored \'gud-'hyü-mərd\ *adj* : CHEERFUL — **good–hu·mored·ly** *adv* — **good–hu·mored·ness** *n*

good·ly \'gud-lē\ *adj* **good·li·er; good·li·est** **1** : of pleasing appearance ⟨a *goodly* person⟩ **2** : LARGE, CONSIDERABLE ⟨a *goodly* number⟩

good–na·tured \'gud-'nā-chərd\ *adj* : not easily offended — **good–na·tured·ly** *adv*

good·ness \'gud-nəs\ *n* : the quality or state of being good : excellence of character

good–sized \'gud-'sīzd\ *adj* : large enough

good–tem·pered \'gud-'tem-pərd\ *adj* : having a good temper

good·will \'gud-'wil\ *n* **1** : good intention **2** : kindly feeling **3** : the value of the trade a business has built up

good·y \'gůd-ē\ *n, pl* **good·ies** : something especially good to eat

¹goof \'güf\ *n* **1** : a ridiculous stupid person **2** : BLUNDER

²goof *vb* : to make a blunder

goose \'güs\ *n, pl* **geese** \'gēs\ **1** : a web=footed water bird larger than a duck and smaller than a swan but resembling both **2** : a female goose as distinguished from a gander **3** : the flesh of a goose used as food **4** : a silly person : SIMPLETON

goose·ber·ry \'güs-,ber-ē\ *n, pl* **goose·ber·ries** : the sour berry of a thorny bush related to the currant

goose·flesh \'güs-,flesh\ *n* : a roughening of the skin caused by cold or fear

goose pimples *n pl* : GOOSEFLESH

go·pher \'gō-fər\ *n* **1** : a rat-sized burrowing animal with strong claws on the forefeet and very large outside cheek pouches **2** : a striped ground squirrel of the prairies **3** : a burrowing American land tortoise

¹gore \'gōr\ *n* : clotted blood : BLOOD

²gore *vb* **gored**; **gor·ing** : to pierce or wound with a horn or tusk

¹gorge \'gȯrj\ *n* **1** : THROAT **2** : a narrow passage (as between two mountains)

²gorge *vb* **gorged**; **gorg·ing** : to eat greedily

gor·geous \'gȯr-jəs\ *adj* [early French *gorge* "throat" was the source of *gorgias* "neckerchief"; from this came the adj. *gorgias* "fond of fine dress", "elegant", which was taken into English as *gorgeous*] : splendidly beautiful — **gor·geous·ly** *adv* — **gor·geous·ness** *n*

go·ril·la \gə-'ril-ə\ *n* : the largest of the manlike apes

gor·y \'gōr-ē\ *adj* **gor·i·er**; **gor·i·est** : covered with gore

gos·ling \'gäz-ling\ *n* : a young goose

gos·pel \'gäs-pəl\ *n* [from Old English *gōdspel*, a compound of *gōd* "good" and *spell* "tidings"] **1** : the teachings of Christ and the apostles **2** : something told or accepted as being absolutely true

¹gos·sa·mer \'gäs-ə-mər\ *n* **1** : a fine film of cobweb **2** : a very thin gauzelike fabric

²gossamer *adj* : being very light and flimsy

¹gos·sip \'gäs-əp\ *n* **1** : a person who goes about tattling **2** : idle talk or rumors

²gossip *vb* : to spread gossip

got *past of* GET

gotten *past part of* GET

¹gouge \'gaůj\ *n* **1** : a chisel with a curved blade for scooping or cutting holes **2** : a hole or groove made with or as if with a gouge   gouge

²gouge *vb* **gouged**; **goug·ing** : to scoop out with or as if with a gouge

gou·lash \'gü-,läsh\ *n* : a beef stew with onion, påprika, and sometimes caraway

gourd \'gōrd\ *n* : the hard-shelled many=seeded fruit of a vine related to the pumpkin and melon

gour·met \'gůr-,mā\ *n* : a connoisseur in eating and drinking

gov·ern \'gəv-ərn\ *vb* **1** : DIRECT, CONTROL **2** : RULE **3** : DETERMINE, DECIDE

gov·ern·a·ble \'gəv-ər-nə-bəl\ *adj* : capable of being governed

gov·ern·ess \'gəv-ər-nəs\ *n* : a woman who teaches and trains a child especially in a private home

gov·ern·ment \'gəv-ərn-mənt\ *n* **1** : control and direction of affairs (as of a city, state, or nation) **2** : the method or system of control : the established form of political rule ⟨democratic *government*⟩ **3** : the persons making up the governing body

gov·ern·men·tal \,gəv-ərn-'ment-l\ *adj* : of or relating to government or the government

gov·er·nor \'gəv-ər-nər\ *n* **1** : a person who governs **2** : a device attached to an engine for automatically controlling its speed

gov·er·nor·ship \'gəv-ər-nər-,ship\ *n* **1** : the office or position of governor **2** : the term of office of a governor

gown \'gaůn\ *n* **1** : a woman's dress ⟨a dinner *gown*⟩ **2** : a loose robe

¹grab \'grab\ *vb* **grabbed**; **grab·bing** : SNATCH

²grab *n* **1** : the act of grabbing **2** : something grabbed

¹grace \'grās\ *n* **1** : KINDNESS, FAVOR **2** *pl* : the condition of being in favor ⟨in his good *graces*⟩ **3** : a short prayer before or after a meal **4** : a sense of what is proper ⟨accept criticism with good *grace*⟩ **5** : a pleasing and attractive quality, manner, or feature ⟨social *graces*⟩ **6** : easy flowing action : beauty of movement **7** : a musical decoration (as a trill)

²grace *vb* **graced**; **grac·ing** **1** : HONOR, FAVOR **2** : to adorn or to make more attractive

grace·ful \'grās-fəl\ *adj* **1** : showing grace or beauty in form or action **2** : nicely done — **grace·ful·ly** *adv* — **grace·ful·ness** *n*

grace·less \'grās-ləs\ *adj* : having no grace or charm (as from lack of feeling for what is fitting) — **grace·less·ly** *adv* — **grace·less·ness** *n*

gra·cious \'grā-shəs\ *adj* **1** : full of grace or charm **2** : KINDLY, COURTEOUS — **gra·cious·ly** *adv* — **gra·cious·ness** *n*

grack·le \'grak-əl\ *n* : a large blackbird with shiny feathers that show changeable green, purple, and bronze colors

¹grade \'grād\ *n* **1** : position in a scale of rank, of quality, or of order ⟨hold a high *grade* in the army⟩ ⟨leather of the highest *grade*⟩ **2** : a class of things that are of the same rank, quality, or order **3** : a division of the school course representing a year's work ⟨finish the fourth *grade*⟩ **4** : the group of pupils in a school grade **5** *pl* : the elementary school system ⟨teach in the *grades*⟩ **6** : a mark or rating especially in school ⟨get a *grade* of ninety in a test⟩ **7** : the degree of slope (as of a road or railroad track) : SLOPE

²grade *vb* **grad·ed; grad·ing** **1** : to arrange in grades : SORT ⟨*grade* apples⟩ **2** : to make level or evenly sloping ⟨*grade* a highway⟩ **3** : to give a grade to or assign to a grade **4** : to form a series having only slight differences

grade school *n* : a school including the first six or the first eight grades

grad·u·al \'graj-ə-wəl\ *adj* : proceeding by steps or degrees — **grad·u·al·ly** *adv*

¹grad·u·ate \'graj-ə-wət\ *n* : a person who has completed the required course of study in a college or school

²grad·u·ate \'graj-ə-ˌwāt\ *vb* **grad·u·at·ed; grad·u·at·ing** **1** : to become a graduate : finish a course of study **2** : to mark with degrees of measurement

grad·u·a·tion \ˌgraj-ə-'wā-shən\ *n* : a graduating or a being graduated

Graeco- — see GRECO-

¹graft \'graft\ *vb* **1** : to insert a shoot from one plant into another plant so they are joined and grow together **2** : to join one thing to another as if by grafting ⟨*graft* skin or bone⟩ **3** : to get money or some advantage by dishonest means — **graft·er** *n*

²graft *n* **1** : a grafted plant **2** : the act of grafting **3** : something (as skin or a shoot) used in grafting **4** : money or advantage acquired dishonestly and especially by betraying a public trust

graft

¹grain \'grān\ *n* **1** : the seed or seedlike fruit of cereal grasses (as wheat, Indian corn, or oats) **2** : cereal grasses or plants **3** : a small hard particle ⟨a *grain* of sand⟩ **4** : a tiny amount : BIT ⟨a *grain* of sense⟩ **5** : a unit of weight equal to 0.0648 gram **6** : the arrangement of fibers in wood — **grained** \'grānd\ *adj*

²grain *vb* : to paint in imitation of the grain (as of wood or marble)

grain·field \'grān-ˌfēld\ *n* : a field where grain is grown

gram *or* **gramme** \'gram\ *n* : a unit of weight in the metric system equal to 1/1000 kilogram

-gram \ˌgram\ *n suffix* : drawing : writing : record ⟨tele*gram*⟩

gram·mar \'gram-ər\ *n* **1** : the study of the classes of words and their uses and relations in the sentence **2** : the facts of language with which grammar deals **3** : speech or writing judged according to the rules of grammar

gram·mat·i·cal \grə-'mat-i-kəl\ *adj* : of, relating to, or conforming to the rules of grammar — **gram·mat·i·cal·ly** *adv*

gra·na·ry \'grā-nə-rē, 'gran-ə-\ *n, pl* **gra·na·ries** : a storehouse for grain

grand \'grand\ *adj* **1** : higher in rank than others of the same class : FOREMOST, PRINCIPAL ⟨the *grand* prize⟩ **2** : great in size ⟨a *grand* mountain⟩ **3** : INCLUSIVE, COMPLETE ⟨a *grand* total⟩ **4** : showing wealth or high social standing **5** : IMPRESSIVE, STATELY ⟨a *grand* view⟩ — **grand·ly** *adv* — **grand·ness** *n*

grand·aunt \'grand-'ant, -'ant\ *n* : an aunt of one's father or mother

grand·child \'grand-ˌchīld\ *n, pl* **grand·chil·dren** \-ˌchil-drən\ : a son's or daughter's child

grand·daugh·ter \'gran-ˌdot-ər\ *n* : a son's or daughter's daughter

gran·dee \gran-'dē\ *n* : a man of high rank or station especially in Spain or Portugal

gran·deur \'gran-jər\ *n* : impressive greatness (as of power, position, or character)

grand·fa·ther \'grand-ˌfä-thər\ *n* **1** : a father's or mother's father **2** : ANCESTOR — **grand·fa·ther·ly** *adj*

grandfather clock *n* : a tall pendulum clock standing directly on the floor

grand·moth·er \'grand-ˌməth-ər\ *n* **1** : a father's or mother's mother **2** : a female ancestor — **grand·moth·er·ly** *adj*

grand·neph·ew \'grand-ˌnef-yü\ *n* : a grandson of one's brother or sister

grand·niece \'grand-'nēs\ *n* : a granddaughter of one's brother or sister

grand·par·ent \'grand-ˌpar-ənt\ *n* : a parent's parent : GRANDFATHER, GRANDMOTHER

grandfather clock

grand·son \'grand-ˌsən\ *n* : a son's or daughter's son

grand·stand \'grand-ˌstand\ *n* : the principal stand (as on an athletic field) for spectators

grand·un·cle \'grand-'əng-kəl\ *n* : an uncle of one's father or mother : GREAT-UNCLE

gran·ite \'gran-ət\ *n* : a very hard igneous rock that is much used for building

gran·ny \'gran-ē\ *n, pl* **gran·nies** **1** : GRANDMOTHER **2** : a fussy person

granny knot *n* : an insecure knot often made instead of a square knot

granny knot

¹**grant** \'grant\ *vb* **1** : to agree to ⟨*grant* a request⟩ **2** : GIVE ⟨*granted* her a 4-year scholarship⟩ **3** : to admit as true something not yet proved

  syn GRANT, CONCEDE both mean to give or give up something in response to a desire that may or may not be expressed. GRANT suggests giving willingly and as a favor something that could rightfully be withheld ⟨*granted* them the afternoon off because of the heat⟩ CONCEDE implies giving up something unwillingly because one should or must ⟨*conceded* the chess game when he realized he could not win⟩

²**grant** *n* **1** : the act of granting **2** : GIFT

grape \'grāp\ *n* : a smooth-skinned juicy berry that grows in clusters on a woody vine in colors ranging from green or white to deep red, purple, or black

grape·fruit \'grāp-,früt\ *n* : a large yellow-skinned fruit related to the orange and lemon

grape·shot \'grāp-,shät\ *n* : a cluster of small iron balls used as a cannon charge

grape·vine \'grāp-,vīn\ *n* : a woody vine grown for its grapes

graph \'graf\ *n* : a diagram that by means of dots and lines shows a system of relationships between things ⟨a *graph* showing the rise and fall in temperature during a period of time⟩

graph

-graph \,graf\ *n suffix* **1** : something written ⟨mono*graph*⟩ **2** : instrument for making or transmitting records ⟨phono*graph*⟩

graph·ic \'graf-ik\ *adj* **1** : being written, drawn, printed, or engraved **2** : clearly and vividly told or described ⟨a *graphic* account of an accident⟩ **3** : of or relating to the pictorial arts or printing **4** : relating to or being in the form of a graph ⟨a *graphic* record of the weather⟩ — **graph·i·cal·ly** \-i-kə-lē\ *adv*

  syn GRAPHIC, VIVID, PICTURESQUE all mean giving a clear visual impression in words. GRAPHIC stresses evoking a picture that seems lifelike because of unusual clarity and sharpness of detail ⟨a *graphic* description of the ninth inning⟩ VIVID suggests the imprinting of a strong or lasting impression of reality ⟨the book makes *vivid* the struggle between Indian and settler⟩ PICTURESQUE implies the presenting of a colorful and effective picture without regard for reality ⟨the *picturesque* images of poetry⟩

graph·ite \'graf-,īt\ *n* : a soft black carbon used in making lead pencils and as a lubricant

-g·ra·phy \g-rə-fē\ *n suffix, pl* **-g·ra·phies** : writing or representation in a specified manner or by a specified means or of a specified object ⟨photo*graphy*⟩ ⟨steno*graphy*⟩

grap·nel \'grap-nl\ *n* : a small anchor with four or more claws that can be used to anchor a boat or to grapple an object (as another boat or something under water)

grapnel

¹**grap·ple** \'grap-əl\ *n* **1** : the act of grappling or seizing **2** : an implement for grappling

²**grapple** *vb* **grap·pled; grap·pling** **1** : to seize or hold with some implement (as a hook) **2** : to get a tight grip on : STRUGGLE

¹**grasp** \'grasp\ *vb* **1** : to seize and hold with or as if with the hand : GRIP ⟨*grasp* a bat⟩ **2** : to make the motion of seizing : CLUTCH **3** : to seize with the mind : UNDERSTAND

²**grasp** *n* **1** : the act of grasping : a grip of the hand : EMBRACE **2** : POSSESSION, CONTROL ⟨a land in the *grasp* of a tyrant⟩ **3** : the power of seizing and holding : REACH **4** : UNDERSTANDING, KNOWLEDGE

grasp·ing \'gras-ping\ *adj* : GREEDY

grass \'gras\ *n* **1** : herbs suitable for or eaten by grazing animals **2** : any of a large natural group of green plants with jointed stems, long slender leaves, and spikes or spikelike clusters of flowers **3** : GRASSLAND

grass·hop·per \'gras-,häp-ər\ *n* : a common leaping plant-eating insect

grass·land \'gras-,land\ *n* : land covered with herbs (as grass) rather than shrubs and trees

grasshopper

grass·y \'gras-ē\ *adj* **grass·i·er; grass·i·est** : of, resembling, or covered with grass

¹**grate** \'grāt\ *n* **1** : a frame containing parallel or crossed bars (as in a window) **2** : a frame of iron bars for holding burning fuel

²**grate** *vb* **grat·ed; grat·ing** **1** : to make into small particles by rubbing against something rough ⟨*grate* the cheese⟩ **2** : to grind or rub against something with a rasping noise **3** : to have a harsh rasping effect

grate·ful \'grāt-fəl\ *adj* **1** : THANKFUL, APPRECIATIVE **2** : PLEASING, WELCOME — **grate·ful·ly** *adv* — **grate·ful·ness** *n*

grat·er \'grāt-ər\ *n* : a tool or utensil with a rough surface for grating

grat·i·fi·ca·tion \,grat-ə-fə-'kā-shən\ *n* **1** : the act of gratifying : the state of being gratified **2** : something that gratifies

grat·i·fy \'grat-ə-,fī\ *vb* **grat·i·fied; grat·i·fy-**

ing : to give pleasure or satisfaction to

grat·ing \'grāt-ing\ *n* : GRATE

grat·i·tude \'grat-ə-ˌtüd, -ˌtyüd\ *n* : the condition of being grateful : THANKFULNESS

gra·tu·i·ty \grə-'tü-ət-ē, -'tyü-\ *n, pl* **gra·tu·i·ties** : [7]TIP

[1]**grave** \'grāv\ *n* : a hole in the ground for burying a dead body

[2]**grave** *adj* **grav·er; grav·est** [from Latin *gravis* meaning both "heavy in weight" and "burdensome"] **1** : deserving serious consideration : IMPORTANT **2** : SOLEMN, SERIOUS — **grave·ly** *adv* — **grave·ness** *n*

grav·el \'grav-əl\ *n* : small fragments of rock and pebbles coarser than sand

grav·el·ly \'grav-ə-lē\ *adj* **1** : containing or consisting of gravel **2** : having a harsh grating sound ⟨a *gravelly* voice⟩

grave·stone \'grāv-ˌstōn\ *n* : a monument marking a grave

grave·yard \'grāv-ˌyärd\ *n* : CEMETERY

gra·vim·e·ter \gra-'vim-ət-ər\ *n* : an instrument for measuring the force of gravity

grav·i·tate \'grav-ə-ˌtāt\ *vb* **grav·i·tat·ed; grav·i·tat·ing** : to move as though drawn toward something

grav·i·ta·tion \ˌgrav-ə-'tā-shən\ *n* **1** : the act or process of gravitating **2** : a force of attraction that tends to draw particles or bodies together

grav·i·ty \'grav-ət-ē\ *n, pl* **grav·i·ties** **1** : the condition of being grave : SERIOUSNESS **2** : the gravitation attraction of bodies toward the center of the earth **3** : GRAVITATION

gra·vy \'grā-vē\ *n, pl* **gra·vies** : a sauce for meat, fish, or vegetables

[1]**gray** \'grā\ *adj* **1** : of the color gray **2** : having gray hair **3** : DISMAL — **gray·ness** *n*

[2]**gray** *n* **1** : something gray in color **2** : a neutral color ranging between black and white

[3]**gray** *vb* : to make or become gray

gray·beard \'grā-ˌbiərd\ *n* : an old man

gray·ish \'grā-ish\ *adj* : somewhat gray

gray·ling \'grā-ling\ *n* : a slender freshwater fish similar in habits to the trout

[1]**graze** \'grāz\ *vb* **grazed; graz·ing** **1** : to eat grass **2** : to supply with grass or pasture

[2]**graze** *vb* **grazed; graz·ing** **1** : to rub or touch lightly in passing : barely touch **2** : to scratch or scrape by rubbing against something

[3]**graze** *n* : a scrape or rub caused by grazing

[1]**grease** \'grēs\ *n* **1** : a more or less solid substance extracted from animal fat by melting **2** : oily matter **3** : a thick lubricant

[2]**grease** \'grēs, 'grēz\ *vb* **greased; greas·ing** **1** : to smear with grease **2** : to lubricate with grease

grease·paint \'grēs-ˌpānt\ *n* : actors' makeup

greas·y \'grē-sē, -zē\ *adj* **greas·i·er; greas·i·est** **1** : smeared with grease : containing grease **2** : resembling grease or oil : SLIPPERY

great \'grāt\ *adj* **1** : large in size : not small or little : BIG **2** : large in number : NUMEROUS ⟨a *great* crowd⟩ **3** : long continued ⟨a *great* while⟩ **4** : much beyond the average or ordinary : MIGHTY, HEAVY ⟨a *great* weight⟩ **5** : EMINENT, IMPORTANT ⟨a *great* artist⟩ **6** : remarkable in knowledge of or skill in something ⟨*great* at diving⟩ — **great·ness** *n*

great–aunt \'grāt-'ant, -'änt\ *n* : GRANDAUNT

great–coat \'grāt-ˌkōt\ *n* : a heavy overcoat

great–grand·child \'grāt-'grand-ˌchīld\ *n, pl* **great–grand·chil·dren** \-ˌchil-drən\ : a son's or daughter's grandson (**great–grand·son**) or granddaughter (**great–grand·daugh·ter**)

great–grand·par·ent \'grāt-'grand-ˌpar-ənt\ *n* : a parent's grandfather (**great–grand·fa·ther**) or grandmother (**great–grand·moth·er**)

great·ly \'grāt-lē\ *adv* **1** : to a great extent or degree **2** : in a great manner : NOBLY

great–un·cle \'grāt-'əng-kəl\ *n* : GRAND-UNCLE

grebe \'grēb\ *n* : any of a group of swimming and diving birds related to the loons

Gre·cian \'grē-shən\ *adj* : GREEK

Gre·co- *or* **Grae·co-** \'grē-kō\ *prefix* **1** : Greece : Greeks ⟨*Greco*mania⟩ **2** : Greek and ⟨*Graeco*-Roman⟩

greed \'grēd\ *n* : greedy desire or hunger

greed·y \'grēd-ē\ *adj* **greed·i·er; greed·i·est** **1** : having a keen appetite for food or drink : very hungry **2** : having an eager and often selfish desire or longing — **greed·i·ly** \'grēd-l-ē\ *adv* — **greed·i·ness** \'grēd-ē-nəs\ *n*

[1]**Greek** \'grēk\ *n* **1** : a native or inhabitant of Greece **2** : the language of the Greeks

[2]**Greek** *adj* : of or relating to Greece, the Greek people, or Greek

[1]**green** \'grēn\ *adj* **1** : of the color green **2** : covered with green vegetation ⟨*green* fields⟩ **3** : consisting of green plants or of the leafy parts of plants ⟨a *green* salad⟩ **4** : not ripe ⟨*green* bananas⟩ **5** : not fully processed or treated ⟨*green* lumber⟩ **6** : lacking training or experience — **green·ly** *adv* — **green·ness** *n*

[2]**green** *n* **1** : the color in the rainbow between blue and yellow : the color of growing fresh grass **2** : something green in color **3** *pl* : leafy parts of plants used for decoration or food **4** : a grassy plain or plot

green·er·y \'grē-nə-rē\ *n, pl* **green·er·ies** : green plants or foliage : VERDURE

green·horn \'grēn-ˌhȯrn\ *n* : an inexperienced or easily tricked person

---

j job   ng sing   ō low   ȯ moth   ȯi coin   th thin   th this   ü boot   u̇ foot   y you   yü few   yu̇ furious   zh vision

green·house \'grēn-ˌhaus\ *n* : a glass-enclosed building for growing plants : HOTHOUSE

green·ish \'grē-nish\ *adj* : somewhat green

greenhouse

green·ling \'grēn-ling\ *n* : any of a group of food and sport fishes of the Pacific coast

green manure *n* : a leafy crop (as of clover) plowed under to improve the soil

green·sward \'grēn-ˌsword\ *n* : turf green with grass

green thumb *n* : an unusual ability to make plants grow

green·wood \'grēn-ˌwud\ *n* : a forest green with foliage

greet \'grēt\ *vb* 1 : to address in a friendly courteous manner : WELCOME 2 : to receive or react to in a certain way ⟨*greeted* the announcement with boos⟩ 3 : to present itself to ⟨a pretty scene *greeted* them⟩ — **greet·er** *n*

greet·ing \'grēt-ing\ *n* 1 : an expression of pleasure on meeting someone 2 : a friendly message from a person who is absent

gre·gar·i·ous \gri-'gar-ē-əs\ *adj* : tending to live together with or associate with others of one's own kind ⟨*gregarious* insects⟩ — **gre·gar·i·ous·ly** *adv* — **gre·gar·i·ous·ness** *n*

gre·nade \grə-'nād\ *n* : a small bomb designed to be thrown by hand

gren·a·dier \ˌgren-ə-'diər\ *n* : a member of a European regiment formerly armed with grenades

grew *past of* GROW

grey \'grā\ *var of* GRAY

grey·hound \'grā-ˌhaund\ *n* : a tall graceful swift dog with a smooth coat and keen eyesight

grid \'grid\ *n* 1 : a network-like group of electrical conductors 2 : a network of horizontal and perpendicular lines (as for helping locate places on a map)

greyhound

grid·dle \'grid-l\ *n* : a flat surface or pan on which food is cooked by dry heat

griddle cake *n* : a flat cake made of thin batter and cooked on both sides on a griddle

grid·i·ron \'grid-ˌī-ərn\ *n* 1 : an iron utensil with parallel bars for broiling food 2 : something (as a network of pipes) resembling a gridiron 3 : a football field

grief \'grēf\ *n* 1 : deep sorrow : DISTRESS 2 : a cause of sorrow 3 : MISHAP, DISASTER

griev·ance \'grē-vəns\ *n* 1 : a cause of uneasiness or annoyance 2 : COMPLAINT

grieve \'grēv\ *vb* **grieved; griev·ing** 1 : to cause grief or sorrow to 2 : to feel grief

griev·ous \'grē-vəs\ *adj* 1 : causing suffering : DISTRESSING ⟨*grievous* news⟩ 2 : SERIOUS, DEPLORABLE ⟨a *grievous* error⟩ 3 : full of or expressing grief ⟨a *grievous* cry⟩

¹**grill** \'gril\ *vb* 1 : to broil on a grill 2 : to question intensely

²**grill** *n* 1 : a gridiron for broiling food 2 : a dish of broiled meat or fish 3 : a restaurant specializing in broiled foods

grille *or* **grill** \'gril\ *n* : an often decorative grating forming a barrier or screen

grim \'grim\ *adj* **grim·mer; grim·mest** 1 : SAVAGE, CRUEL 2 : harsh in appearance : STERN ⟨a *grim* look⟩ 3 : UNYIELDING ⟨*grim* determination⟩ 4 : GHASTLY, FRIGHTFUL — **grim·ly** *adv* — **grim·ness** *n*

¹**grim·ace** \'grim-əs, gri-'mās\ *n* : a twisting of the face in disgust

²**grimace** *vb* **grim·aced; grim·ac·ing** : to distort the face

¹**grime** \'grīm\ *vb* **grimed; grim·ing** : to soil deeply

²**grime** *n* : dirt rubbed into a surface

grim·y \'grī-mē\ *adj* **grim·i·er; grim·i·est** : full of grime : DIRTY

¹**grin** \'grin\ *vb* **grinned; grin·ning** : to draw back the lips and show the teeth

²**grin** *n* : the act of grinning

¹**grind** \'grīnd\ *vb* **ground** \'graund\; **grinding** 1 : to make or be made into powder by rubbing : crush into small bits 2 : to wear down, polish, or sharpen by friction ⟨*grind* an ax⟩ 3 : to rub together with a grating noise : GRIT ⟨*grind* the teeth⟩ 4 : to operate or produce by turning a crank

²**grind** *n* 1 : an act of grinding 2 : steady hard work ⟨found his lessons a *grind*⟩

grind·stone \'grīn-ˌstōn\ *n* : a flat round stone that turns on an axle and is used for sharpening tools and for shaping and smoothing

¹**grip** \'grip\ *vb* **gripped; grip·ping** 1 : to grasp firmly 2 : to hold the interest of

²**grip** *n* 1 : a strong grasp or hold ⟨a *grip* of the hand⟩ 2 : a special way (as among members of a secret society) of clasping the hand 3 : strength or power in holding ⟨the *grip* of a disease⟩ 4 : HANDLE 5 : a small suitcase

grindstone

grippe \'grip\ *n* : an acute feverish disease similar to or the same as influenza

gris·ly \'griz-lē\ *adj* **gris·li·er; gris·li·est** : HORRIBLE, GHASTLY

grist \'grist\ *n* : grain to be ground or that is already ground

gris·tle \'gris-əl\ *n* : CARTILAGE — **gris·tli·ness** \'gris-lē-nəs\ *n* — **gris·tly** \'gris-lē\ *adj*

grist·mill \'grist-,mil\ *n* : a mill for grinding grain

¹grit \'grit\ *n* **1** : rough hard particles especially of sand **2** : firmness of mind or spirit

²grit *vb* **grit·ted**; **grit·ting** : GRIND, GRATE

grits \'grits\ *n pl* : coarsely ground hulled grain

grit·ty \'grit-ē\ *adj* **grit·ti·er**; **grit·ti·est 1** : containing or resembling grit **2** : courageously persistent : PLUCKY — **grit·ti·ness** *n*

griz·zled \'griz-əld\ *adj* : streaked or mixed with gray

griz·zly \'griz-lē\ *adj* **griz·zli·er**; **griz·zli·est** : GRAYISH, GRIZZLED

grizzly bear *n* : a large powerful bear of western North America usually brownish yellow

¹groan \'grōn\ *vb* **1** : to make a deep moaning sound **2** : to creak under a strain **3** : to utter with or as if with groans

²groan *n* : a low moaning sound

gro·cer \'grō-sər\ *n* : a dealer in foods

gro·cer·y \'grō-sə-rē\ *n, pl* **gro·cer·ies 1** : the trade, business, or store of a grocer **2** *pl* : the goods sold by grocers

grog·gy \'gräg-ē\ *adj* **grog·gi·er**; **grog·gi·est** : weak and dazed and unsteady on the legs — **grog·gi·ly** \'gräg-ə-lē\ *adv* — **grog·gi·ness** \'gräg-ē-nəs\ *n*

groin \'gròin\ *n* : the fold or area where the abdomen joins the thigh

grom·met \'gräm-ət\ *n* **1** : a ring of rope **2** : an eyelet of firm material to strengthen or protect an opening

¹groom \'grüm\ *n* **1** : a male servant especially in charge of horses **2** : BRIDEGROOM

²groom *vb* **1** : to make neat and attractive (as by cleaning and brushing) ⟨*groom* a dog⟩ **2** : to make fit or ready ⟨*groom* a candidate for office⟩

¹groove \'grüv\ *n* **1** : a narrow channel or long hollow (as made by cutting or grinding) **2** : a fixed routine — **grooved** \'grüvd\ *adj*

²groove *vb* **grooved**; **groov·ing** : to form a groove in

grope \'grōp\ *vb* **groped**; **grop·ing** : to search for by feeling (as in the dark) : feel one's way

gros·beak \'grōs-,bēk\ *n* : a finch with a strong conical bill

¹gross \'grōs\ *adj* **1** : THICK, BULKY ⟨*gross* vegetation⟩ **2** : WHOLE, ENTIRE ⟨*gross* earnings⟩ **3** : COARSE, VULGAR ⟨*gross* words⟩ **4** : GLARING, OBVIOUS ⟨a *gross* injustice⟩

²gross *n* : the whole before any deductions

³gross *n, pl* **gross** : twelve dozen

gro·tesque \grō-'tesk\ *adj* [from early Italian (*pittura*) *grottesca* "fantastic (painting)", originally just "cave painting", from *grotto* "cave"] : absurdly awkward or incongruous : FANTASTIC

grot·to \'grät-ō\ *n, pl* **grot·toes 1** : CAVE, CAVERN **2** : an artificial cavelike structure

¹grouch \'graùch\ *n* **1** : a fit of bad temper **2** : a sulky person

²grouch *vb* : SULK, GRUMBLE

grouch·y \'graù-chē\ *adj* **grouch·i·er**; **grouch·i·est** : SURLY, IRRITABLE — **grouch·i·ly** \-chə-lē\ *adv* — **grouch·i·ness** \-chē-nəs\ *n*

¹ground \'graùnd\ *n* **1** : the surface of the earth : SOIL **2** : a particular region or piece of land ⟨a hunting *ground*⟩ **3** : LAND ⟨own a house with a fair amount of *ground* around it⟩ **4** *pl* : the gardens and lawns around a house ⟨well-kept *grounds*⟩ **5** : an area or distance ⟨gain *ground*⟩ **6** : the bottom of a body of water ⟨the boat struck *ground*⟩ **7** *pl* : the material from a liquid that settles to the bottom : SEDIMENT ⟨coffee *grounds*⟩ **8** : the basis on which something rests ⟨*ground* for complaint⟩ **9** : the surface or background upon which something is made or displayed

²ground *vb* **1** : to force or bring down to the ground ⟨planes *grounded* by a storm⟩ **2** : to run or cause to run aground **3** : to instruct in basic knowledge or understanding

³ground *past of* GRIND

ground cover *n* : low plants that cover and protect the ground

ground crew *n* : the mechanics and technicians who maintain and service an airplane

ground·er \'graùn-dər\ *n* : a baseball hit on the ground

ground·hog \'graùnd-,hòg, -,häg\ *n* : WOODCHUCK

ground·less \'graùnd-ləs\ *adj* : being without foundation or reason ⟨*groundless* fears⟩

ground swell *n* : a broad deep ocean swell caused by a distant storm or earthquake

ground·work \'graùnd-,wərk\ *n* : BASIS

¹group \'grüp\ *n* : a number of persons or things that form one whole **syn** see GANG

²group *vb* : to arrange or combine in a group

¹grouse \'graùs\ *n, pl* **grouse** : a ground-dwelling game bird resembling domestic fowls

²grouse *vb* **groused**; **grous·ing** : GROUCH

grove \'grōv\ *n* : a small wood

grov·el \'gräv-əl\ *vb* **grov·eled** *or* **grov·elled**; **grov·el·ing** *or* **grov·el·ling 1** : to creep or lie face down on the ground (as in fear) **2** : CRINGE — **grov·el·er** *or* **grov·el·ler** *n*

grow \'grō\ *vb* **grew** \'grü\; **grown** \'grōn\; **grow·ing 1** : to spring up and develop to maturity ⟨the wheat is *growing* well⟩ **2** : to be able to grow in a particular situation ⟨most algae *grow* in water⟩ ⟨oranges *grow* in the tropics⟩ **3** : to be related in some way by reason of growing ⟨tree branches *grown* together⟩ **4** : INCREASE, EXPAND ⟨the city is *growing* rapidly⟩ **5** : BECOME ⟨*grow* old⟩ **6** : to cause to grow : RAISE — **grow·er** *n*

¹**growl** \'graùl\ *vb* **1** : to make a deep throaty sound (as of a dog) **2** : GRUMBLE **3** : to make a rumbling noise

²**growl** *n* **1** : a deep threatening sound **2** : a grumbling or muttered complaint **3** : RUMBLE

grown \'grōn\ *adj* : having reached full growth : MATURE ⟨a *grown* man⟩

¹**grown–up** \'grōn-,əp\ *adj* : ADULT

²**grown–up** *n* : an adult person

growth \'grōth\ *n* **1** : a stage or condition in growing : SIZE ⟨reach his full *growth*⟩ **2** : a process of growing ⟨*growth* of a crystal⟩ **3** : a progressive development or increase ⟨the *growth* of wealth⟩ **4** : something (as a covering of plants) produced by growing

¹**grub** \'grəb\ *vb* **grubbed**; **grub·bing 1** : to root out by digging : DIG ⟨*grub* up roots⟩ **2** : to work hard : DRUDGE

²**grub** *n* **1** : a soft thick wormlike larva (as of a beetle) **2** : FOOD

grub·by \'grəb-ē\ *adj* **grub·bi·er**; **grub·bi·est** : GRIMY, DIRTY — **grub·bi·ly** \'grəb-ə-lē\ *adv* — **grub·bi·ness** \'grəb-ē-nəs\ *n*

¹**grub·stake** \'grəb-,stāk\ *n* : supplies or funds furnished a prospector for a promise of a share in his finds

²**grubstake** *vb* **grub·staked**; **grub·stak·ing** : to provide with a grubstake

¹**grudge** \'grəj\ *vb* **grudged**; **grudg·ing** : to be unwilling to give ⟨*grudge* a person his success⟩

²**grudge** *n* : a feeling of ill will ⟨hold a *grudge*⟩

gru·el \'grü-əl\ *n* : a thin porridge

gru·el·ing *or* **gru·el·ling** \'grü-ə-ling\ *adj* : requiring extreme effort : EXHAUSTING

grue·some \'grü-səm\ *adj* : horribly repulsive : GHASTLY — **grue·some·ly** *adv* — **grue·some·ness** *n*

gruff \'grəf\ *adj* : rough in speech or manner : HARSH — **gruff·ly** *adv* — **gruff·ness** *n*

¹**grum·ble** \'grəm-bəl\ *vb* **grum·bled**; **grum·bling 1** : to murmur or mutter in discontent **2** : RUMBLE

²**grumble** *n* **1** : the act of grumbling **2** : RUMBLE

grump·y \'grəm-pē\ *adj* **grump·i·er**; **grump·i·est** : SURLY, CROSS — **grump·i·ly** \-pə-lē\ *adv* — **grump·i·ness** \-pē-nəs\ *n*

¹**grunt** \'grənt\ *n* : a deep short throat sound (as of a hog)

²**grunt** *vb* : to make a grunt — **grunt·er** *n*

¹**guar·an·tee** \,gar-ən-'tē\ *n* **1** : a person who guarantees something **2** : the act of guaranteeing **3** : something that is given or held as a security ⟨a car sold with a written *guarantee*⟩

²**guarantee** *vb* **guar·an·teed**; **guar·an·tee·ing 1** : to promise to answer for the debt or duty of another person ⟨*guarantee* that a loan will be repaid⟩ **2** : to make oneself responsible for

guar·an·tor \,gar-ən-'tòr\ *n* : a person who gives a guarantee

¹**guard** \'gärd\ *n* **1** : a position (as in fencing and boxing) of defense **2** : the act or duty of keeping watch **3** : a person or a body of persons that guards against injury or danger **4** : a device giving protection **5** : a football lineman stationed next to the center

²**guard** *vb* **1** : PROTECT, DEFEND **2** : to watch over : stand guard **3** : to take precautions

guard·ed \'gärd-əd\ *adj* **1** : PROTECTED **2** : CAUTIOUS ⟨a *guarded* answer⟩

guard·house \'gärd-,haùs\ *n* **1** : a building occupied by a guard or used as a headquarters by soldiers on guard duty **2** : a military jail

guard·i·an \'gärd-ē-ən\ *n* **1** : a person who guards or preserves : CUSTODIAN, CARETAKER **2** : a person who legally has the care of another person or of his property — **guard·i·an·ship** \-,ship\ *n*

guard·room \'gärd-,rüm, -,rùm\ *n* **1** : a room used by a military guard while on duty **2** : a room for confining military prisoners

guards·man \'gärdz-mən\ *n*, *pl* **guards·men** \-mən\ : a member of a military body called *guard* or *guards*

gu·ber·na·to·ri·al \,gü-bər-nə-'tōr-ē-əl, ,gyü-\ *adj* : of, relating to, or concerned with a governor or a governorship

gudg·eon \'gəj-ən\ *n* : any of several small fishes

guer·ril·la *or* **gue·ril·la** \gə-'ril-ə\ *n* : a member of a band of persons carrying on warfare but not part of a regular army

¹**guess** \'ges\ *vb* **1** : to judge without certain knowledge ⟨*guess* at a person's weight⟩ **2** : to discover or solve correctly ⟨*guess* a riddle⟩ **3** : SUPPOSE, BELIEVE — **guess·er** *n*

²**guess** *n* : an opinion formed by guessing

guess·work \'ges-,wərk\ *n* : work done by guess and not accurately or scientifically

guest \'gest\ *n* **1** : a person entertained in one's house or at one's table **2** : a patron of a hotel, inn, or restaurant **syn** see VISITOR

¹**guf·faw** \,gə-'fò\ *n* : a loud burst of laughter

²**guffaw** *vb* : to laugh noisily or coarsely

guid·ance \'gīd-ns\ *n* : the act or process of guiding or being guided : DIRECTION

¹**guide** \'gīd\ *n* **1** : one that guides **2** : a

person who leads or directs another **3** : a device for directing or steadying the motion of something (as on a machine) **4** : GUIDEBOOK

²guide *vb* **guid·ed; guid·ing 1** : to show the way to : CONDUCT **2** : DIRECT, INSTRUCT

guide·book \'gīd-ˌbuk\ *n* : a book of information for travelers

guide·post \'gīd-ˌpōst\ *n* : a post with signs on it to direct travelers

guide word *n* : either of the terms to right and left of the head of a page of an alphabetical reference work (as a dictionary) usually indicating the first and last entries on the page

guild \'gild\ *n* : an association of persons with similar aims or common interests

guil·der \'gil-dər\ *n* : GULDEN

guile \'gīl\ *n* : crafty cunning : DECEIT — **guile·ful** *adj* — **guile·ful·ly** *adv*

guile·less \'gīl-ləs\ *adj* : free from deceit or cunning — **guile·less·ly** *adv* — **guile·less·ness** *n*

¹guil·lo·tine \'gil-ə-ˌtēn\ *n* : a machine for cutting off a person's head by means of a heavy blade sliding in two upright grooved posts

²guillotine *vb* **guil·lo·tined; guil·lo·tin·ing** : to behead with a guillotine

guillotine

guilt \'gilt\ *n* **1** : the fact of having committed an offense and especially one that is punishable by law **2** : guilty conduct **3** : a feeling of responsibility for blameworthy acts — **guilt·less** \-ləs\ *adj*

guilt·y \'gil-tē\ *adj* **guilt·i·er; guilt·i·est 1** : having committed an offense **2** : showing or conscious of guilt ⟨a *guilty* expression⟩ — **guilt·i·ly** \-tə-lē\ *adv* — **guilt·i·ness** \-tē-nəs\ *n*

guin·ea \'gin-ē\ *n* : an old English gold coin

guinea fowl *n* : an African bird related to the pheasants that has a bare head and neck and white-speckled usually dark gray feathers

guinea pig *n* : a stocky short-eared rodent with a very short tail

guise \'gīz\ *n* **1** : a form or style of dress **2** : external appearance : SEMBLANCE

gui·tar \gə-'tär\ *n* : a six-stringed musical instrument played by plucking the strings

gulch \'gəlch\ *n* : a deep steep-sided ravine

gul·den \'gul-dən\ *n* : a coin of the Netherlands : GUILDER

gulf \'gəlf\ *n* **1** : a part of an ocean or sea extending into the land ⟨the *Gulf* of Mexico⟩ **2** : CHASM, ABYSS **3** : a wide separation (as in age or interests)

guitar

¹gull \'gəl\ *n* : a web-footed water bird usually blue-gray or whitish in color with a thick strong bill

²gull *vb* : to make a dupe of : DECEIVE

³gull *n* : a person easily deceived : DUPE

gull

gul·let \'gəl-ət\ *n* : THROAT, ESOPHAGUS

gull·i·ble \'gəl-ə-bəl\ *adj* : easily deceived

gul·ly \'gəl-ē\ *n, pl* **gul·lies** : a ditch or watercourse worn by water running (as after rains)

gully erosion *n* : soil erosion caused by running water

¹gulp \'gəlp\ *vb* **1** : to swallow eagerly or in large amounts at a time **2** : to keep back as if by swallowing ⟨*gulp* down a sob⟩ **3** : to catch the breath as if after a long drink

²gulp *n* : the act of gulping : SWALLOW

¹gum \'gəm\ *n* : the flesh along the jaws of animals at the roots of the teeth

²gum *n* **1** : a sticky substance obtained from plants that hardens on drying **2** : a gumlike substance (as glue) **3** : CHEWING GUM

³gum *vb* **gummed; gum·ming** : to smear, stick together, or stiffen with gum

gum·boil \'gəm-ˌboil\ *n* : an abscess in the gum

gum·drop \'gəm-ˌdräp\ *n* : a gumlike candy

gum·my \'gəm-ē\ *adj* **gum·mi·er; gum·mi·est 1** : consisting of, containing, or covered with gum **2** : STICKY

gump·tion \'gəmp-shən\ *n* **1** : shrewd common sense **2** : SPIRIT, COURAGE

¹gun \'gən\ *n* **1** : CANNON **2** : a portable firearm (as a rifle, shotgun, or pistol) **3** : something suggesting a gun in shape or function **4** : a discharge of a gun (as in a salute)

²gun *vb* **gunned; gun·ning** : to hunt with a gun

gun·boat \'gən-ˌbōt\ *n* : a small lightly armed ship for use in shallow waters

gun·fire \'gən-ˌfīr\ *n* : the firing of guns

gun·lock \'gən-ˌläk\ *n* : the device on some firearms by which the charge is exploded

gun·ner \'gən-ər\ *n* **1** : a person who operates a gun **2** : HUNTER

gun·ner·y \'gən-ə-rē\ *n* : the use of guns

gun·ny \'gən-ē\ *n, pl* **gun·nies 1** : coarse jute sacking **2** : BURLAP

gun·pow·der \'gən-ˌpaud-ər\ *n* : an explosive powder used in guns and blasting

gun·shot \'gən-ˌshät\ *n* **1** : a shot from a gun **2** : the effective range of a gun

gun·wale \'gən-l\ *n* : the upper edge of a ship's or boat's side

gup·py \'gəp-ē\ *n, pl* **gup·pies** : a small tropical minnow often kept as an aquarium fish

¹**gur·gle** \'gər-gəl\ *vb* **gur·gled; gur·gling**
1 : to run or flow in a broken irregular noisy
current **2** : to sound like a liquid flowing with
a gurgle

²**gurgle** *n* : a sound of or like gurgling water

¹**gush** \'gəsh\ *vb* **1** : to burst forth or pour
forth violently **2** : to make an exaggerated
show of affection or enthusiasm

²**gush** *n* : a sudden free pouring out

gush·er \'gəsh-ər\ *n* : an oil well with a large
natural flow

gus·set \'gəs-ət\ *n* : a triangular piece inserted (as into a garment or glove) to give
width or strength

gust \'gəst\ *n* **1** : a sudden brief rush of
wind **2** : a sudden outburst of feeling

gust·y \'gəs-tē\ *adj* **gust·i·er; gust·i·est** : WINDY

¹**gut** \'gət\ *n* **1** : ENTRAILS — usually used in
plural **2** : the digestive canal : a part of the
digestive canal **3** : CATGUT **4** *pl* : COURAGE

²**gut** *vb* **gut·ted; gut·ting 1** : to remove the
entrails from **2** : to destroy or remove the
inside of

¹**gut·ter** \'gət-ər\ *n* **1** : a channel worn by
running water **2** : a channel
at the eaves of a house or at a
roadside for carrying off rain
or water

²**gutter** *vb* **1** : to form gutters
in **2** : to flow in streams
3 : to melt away rapidly by becoming channeled down the
sides

gutter

¹**guy** \'gī\ *n* : a rope, chain, rod, or wire
(**guy wire**) attached to something to steady it

²**guy** *n* : PERSON, FELLOW

³**guy** *vb* : to make fun of

gym \'jim\ *n* : GYMNASIUM

gym·na·si·um \jim-'nā-zē-əm\ *n* [Greek
gymnos "naked" gave rise to the verb
gymnazein "to exercise naked", from which
came *gymnasion* "exercise yard"] : a place or
building for athletic exercises

gym·nast \'jim-,nast\ *n* : a person who is
skilled in gymnastics

gym·nas·tic \jim-'nas-tik\ *adj* : of or relating
to gymnastics

gym·nas·tics \jim-'nas-tiks\ *n sing or pl*
: physical exercises for developing skill,
strength, and control in the use of the body

Gyp·sy \'jip-sē\ *n, pl* **Gyp·sies** [this is a
shortened and altered form of *Egyptian*, because when Gypsies first came to England
they were thought to be from Egypt] : a
member of a wandering race originally from
India

gypsy moth *n* : a moth whose caterpillar has
a grayish mottled appearance and does great
damage to fruit trees

gy·rate \'jī-,rāt\ *vb* **gy·rat·ed; gy·rat·ing** : to
revolve around a center : SPIN ⟨a top *gyrates*⟩

gy·ro·scope \'jī-rə-,skōp\ *n* : a heavy wheel
mounted to spin rapidly about an axis that
is free to turn in various directions

gy·ro·scop·ic \,jī-rə-'skäp-ik\ *adj* : of or
relating to a gyroscope

h \'āch\ *n, often cap* : the
eighth letter of the English
alphabet

ha \'hä\ *interj* — used to express surprise, joy, grief, or
doubt

hab·er·dash·er \'hab-ər-
,dash-ər\ *n* : a dealer in men's wear (as
gloves, neckties, socks, and shirts)

hab·er·dash·er·y \'hab-ər-,dash-ə-rē\ *n, pl*
hab·er·dash·er·ies 1 : goods sold by a haberdasher **2** : a haberdasher's shop

hab·it \'hab-ət\ *n* **1** : DRESS, COSTUME ⟨a riding *habit*⟩ **2** : a usual way of behaving ⟨the
habits of a wild animal⟩ **3** : a way of acting or
doing that has become fixed by frequent
repetition **4** : characteristic way of growing
⟨trees of spreading *habit*⟩

syn HABIT, PRACTICE, CUSTOM all refer to a
way of acting that has become fixed through
repetition. HABIT indicates individual behavior so fixed that it occurs without thought
and often without intention ⟨woke at seven
through *habit*⟩ PRACTICE suggests a way of
acting that a person maintains with regularity
and through choice ⟨father's *practice* of walking to work on nice days⟩ CUSTOM is used of a
practice so long associated with a particular
group that it has become part of the group's
tradition ⟨by *custom* men wear neckties on
formal occasions⟩

hab·it·a·ble \'hab-ət-ə-bəl\ *adj* : suitable or
fit to live in ⟨a *habitable* house⟩

hab·i·tat \'hab-ə-,tat\ *n* [from Latin *habitat*
"it inhabits"] : the place where a plant or
animal grows or lives naturally

hab·i·ta·tion \,hab-ə-'tā-shən\ *n* **1** : the act
of inhabiting **2** : a dwelling place

ha·bit·u·al \hə-'bich-ə-wəl\ *adj* **1** : according to habit **2** : doing or acting by force of
habit **3** : REGULAR **syn** see USUAL — **ha·bit·u-**
al·ly *adv* — **ha·bit·u·al·ness** *n*

ha·ci·en·da \,hä-sē-'en-də\ *n* **1** : a large

estate in a Spanish-speaking country **2** : the main building of a farm or ranch

¹hack \'hak\ *vb* **1** : to cut with repeated irregular blows **2** : to cough in a short broken manner

²hack *n* **1** : NICK **2** : a short broken cough

³hack *n* **1** : a horse let out for hire or used for varied work **2** : HACKNEY 2 **3** : a person who does routine or tedious literary work for pay

hack·les \'hak-əlz\ *n pl* **1** : hairs (as on the neck of a dog) that can be erected **2** : TEMPER

hack·ney \'hak-nē\ *n, pl* **hack·neys** **1** : a horse for ordinary riding or driving **2** : a carriage or automobile for hire

hack·neyed \'hak-nēd\ *adj* : worn out from too long or too much use : COMMONPLACE

hack·saw \'hak-ˌso\ *n* : a fine-tooth saw with blade stretched tight in a bow-shaped frame for cutting hard materials

hacksaw

had *past of* HAVE

had·dock \'had-ək\ *n* : a food fish related to but smaller than the cod

had·n't \'had-nt\ : had not

haf·ni·um \'haf-nē-əm\ *n* : a gray metallic chemical element

haft \'haft\ *n* : the handle of a weapon or tool

hag \'hag\ *n* **1** : WITCH **2** : an ugly old woman

hag·gard \'hag-ərd\ *adj* : having a hungry, tired, or worried look

¹hag·gle \'hag-əl\ *vb* **hag·gled**; **hag·gling** : to argue especially over a bargain or price — **hag·gler** \'hag-lər\ *n*

²haggle *n* : an act or instance of haggling

ha–ha \hä-'hä\ *interj* — used to express amusement or derision

¹hail \'hāl\ *n* **1** : small lumps of ice and snow that fall from the clouds sometimes during thunderstorms **2** : VOLLEY ⟨a *hail* of bullets⟩

²hail *vb* **1** : to fall as hail **2** : to pour down like hail

³hail *interj* — used to express enthusiastic approval

⁴hail *vb* **1** : GREET, WELCOME **2** : to call out to ⟨*hail* a taxi⟩ — **hail from** : to come from

⁵hail *n* **1** : an exclamation of greeting, approval, or praise **2** : hearing distance

hail·stone \'hāl-ˌstōn\ *n* : a pellet of hail

hail·storm \'hāl-ˌstorm\ *n* : a storm accompanied by hail

hair \'haər\ *n* **1** : a threadlike growth from the skin of a person or lower animal **2** : a growth of hairs (as the fur of a fox) **3** : something (as a growth on a leaf) resembling an animal hair — **haired** \'haərd\ *adj* — **hairless** \'haər-ləs\ *adj*

hair·breadth \'haər-ˌbredth\ *or* **hairs·breadth** \'haərz-\ *n* : a very small distance

hair·brush \'haər-ˌbrəsh\ *n* : a brush for the hair

hair·cloth \'haər-ˌkloth\ *n* : a stiff wiry fabric (as of horsehair) used especially for upholstery

hairbrushes

hair·cut \'haər-ˌkət\ *n* : the act, process, or style of cutting the hair

hair·do \'haər-ˌdü\ *n, pl* **hair·dos** : a way of arranging a woman's hair

hair·dress·er \'haər-ˌdres-ər\ *n* : one who dresses or cuts women's hair — **hair·dress·ing** *n*

hair·pin \'haər-ˌpin\ *n* : a U-shaped pin for holding the hair in place

hair–rais·er \'haər-ˌrā-zər\ *n* : THRILLER

hair–rais·ing \'haər-ˌrā-zing\ *adj* : causing terror, excitement, or astonishment

hair·spring \'haər-ˌspring\ *n* : a very slender spring used in watches

hairy \'haər-ē\ *adj* **hair·i·er**; **hair·i·est** : covered with hair — **hair·i·ness** *n*

hal·cy·on \'hal-sē-ən\ *adj* : CALM, PEACEFUL

¹hale \'hāl\ *adj* : being strong and healthy

²hale *vb* **haled**; **hal·ing** **1** : HAUL, PULL **2** : to compel to go ⟨*haled* him into court⟩

¹half \'haf, 'hàf\ *n, pl* **halves** \'havz, 'hàvz\ **1** : one of two equal parts into which something can be divided **2** : a part of a thing that is about equal to the remainder ⟨the larger *half* of an apple⟩ **3** : one of a pair

²half *adj* **1** : being one of two equal parts **2** : amounting to nearly half : PARTIAL **3** : of half the usual size or extent

³half *adv* **1** : to the extent of half ⟨*half* full⟩ **2** : not completely ⟨*half* persuaded⟩

half·back \'haf-ˌbak, 'hàf-\ *n* : a back on a football team

half–breed \'haf-ˌbrēd, 'hàf-\ *n* : a person born of parents of different races

half brother *n* : a brother by one parent only

half·heart·ed \'haf-'härt-əd, 'hàf-\ *adj* : lacking spirit or interest — **half·heart·ed·ly** *adv* — **half·heart·ed·ness** *n*

half–knot \'haf-ˌnät, 'hàf-\ *n* : a knot joining the ends of two cords and used in tying other knots

half–life \'haf-ˌlīf, 'hàf-\ *n* : the time required for half of the atoms of a radioactive substance to become disintegrated

half sister *n* : a sister by one parent only

¹half·way \'haf-'wā, 'hàf-\ *adv* : at or to half the distance ⟨open the door *halfway*⟩

²halfway *adj* **1** : midway between two points **2** : PARTIAL ⟨*halfway* measures⟩

half–wit \'haf-ˌwit, 'håf-\ *n* : a foolish person
: DUNCE — **half–wit·ted** \-'wit-əd\ *adj*

hal·i·but \'hal-ə-bət\ *n* : a very large flatfish
much used for food

hall \'hȯl\ *n* **1** : a large building used for
public purposes ⟨city *hall*⟩ **2** : a building
(as of a college) set apart for a special purpose
⟨Science *Hall*⟩ **3** : an entrance room
4 : CORRIDOR **5** : AUDITORIUM

hal·le·lu·jah \ˌhal-ə-'lü-yə\ *interj* [from Hebrew *halălūyāh* "praise ye the Lord"] — used
to express praise, joy, or thanks

hal·low \'hal-ō\ *vb* : to set apart for holy
purposes : treat as sacred

Hal·low·een \ˌhal-ə-'wēn, ˌhäl-\ *n* : October
31 observed with merrymaking and the playing of pranks by children during the evening

hal·lu·ci·na·tion \hə-ˌlüs-n-'ā-shən\ *n* : the
perceiving of objects or the experiencing of
feelings that have no reality usually as the
result of mental disorder or as the effect of a
drug

hall·way \'hȯl-ˌwā\ *n* **1** : an entrance hall
2 : CORRIDOR

ha·lo \'hā-lō\ *n, pl* **ha·los** *or* **ha·loes** **1** : a
circle of light around the sun or
moon caused by the presence of
tiny ice crystals in the air **2** : a
circle drawn or painted around
the head of a person in a picture
as a symbol of holiness

halo 2

hal·o·gen \'hal-ə-jən\ *n* : any of
the five elements fluorine, chlorine, bromine,
iodine, and astatine

¹halt \'hȯlt\ *adj* : LAME, CRIPPLED

²halt *vb* **1** : to walk lamely : LIMP **2** : to be in
doubt about what to do : HESITATE **3** : to go
slowly and with frequent stops

³halt *n* : STOP ⟨call a *halt*⟩

⁴halt *vb* **1** : to stop or cause to stop marching
or traveling **2** : END

hal·ter \'hȯl-tər\ *n* **1** : a rope or strap for
leading or tying an animal
2 : a headstall to which a halter
may be attached **3** : a rope for
hanging a person **4** : a brief
blouse usually without a back
and fastened by straps around
the neck and waist

halter 2

halve \'hav, 'håv\ *vb* **halved; halv·ing** **1** : to
divide into two equal parts : share equally
⟨*halve* an apple⟩ **2** : to reduce to one half

halves *pl of* HALF

hal·yard \'hal-yərd\ *n* : a rope for raising or
lowering sails

ham \'ham\ *n* **1** : a buttock with its associated thigh **2** : a cut of meat consisting of a
thigh usually of pork **3** : an unskillful but
showy performer **4** : an operator of an
amateur radio station

ham·burg·er \'ham-ˌbər-gər\ *or* **ham·burg**
\-ˌbərg\ *n* **1** : ground beef **2** : a sandwich
made of a ground-beef patty in a split bun

ham·let \'ham-lət\ *n* : a small village

¹ham·mer \'ham-ər\ *n* **1** : a tool consisting
of a head fastened crosswise to a
handle and used for pounding (as
in driving nails) **2** : something
that resembles a hammer **3** : a
heavy metal ball with a flexible
handle thrown for distance in a
track-and-field contest (**hammer throw**)

hammer

²hammer *vb* **1** : to strike with a hammer
2 : to fasten (as by nailing) with a hammer
3 : to produce by means of repeated blows

ham·mock \'ham-ək\ *n* : a swinging couch
usually made of canvas or netting

ham·my \'ham-ē\ *adj* **ham·mi·er; ham·mi·est**
: characteristic of a ham actor

¹ham·per \'ham-pər\ *vb* : to keep from moving or acting freely ⟨*hampered* by heavy fog⟩

²hamper *n* : a large basket usually with a
cover ⟨clothes *hamper*⟩ ⟨picnic *hamper*⟩

ham·ster \'ham-stər\ *n* : a stocky short-tailed
rodent with large cheek pouches

ham·string \'ham-ˌstring\ *vb* **ham·strung**
\-ˌstrəng\; **ham·string·ing** **1** : to cripple by
cutting the leg tendons **2** : to make ineffective
or powerless : CRIPPLE

¹hand \'hand\ *n* **1** : the end part of the arm
adapted (as in man) for handling, grasping,
and holding **2** : a bodily structure (as the
large claw of a lobster) resembling the human
hand in function or form **3** : something
resembling a hand ⟨*hands* of a clock⟩ **4** : POS-
SESSION, CONTROL ⟨in the *hands* of the enemy⟩
5 : SIDE, ASPECT ⟨on the one *hand* and on the
other⟩ **6** : a pledge especially of marriage
7 : HANDWRITING **8** : ABILITY, SKILL ⟨tried
his *hand* at painting⟩ **9** : a unit of measure
equal to four inches ⟨a horse fifteen *hands*
high⟩ **10** : ASSISTANCE ⟨lend a *hand*⟩ **11** : a
part or share in doing something ⟨take a *hand*
in the work⟩ **12** : an outburst of applause
13 : the cards held by a player in a card game
14 : a hired worker : LABORER — **at hand**
: near in time or place — **by hand** : with
the hands — **in hand** **1** : in one's possession
or control **2** : in preparation — **off one's
hands** : out of one's care or charge — **on
hand** **1** : in present possession **2** : PRESENT
—**out of hand** : out of control — **to hand**
1 : into possession **2** : within reach **3** : into
control or subjection

²hand *vb* : to give or pass with the hand — **hand down** : to pass along in succession

hand·bag \'hand-ˌbag\ *n* : a woman's bag used for carrying money and small personal articles : PURSE

hand·ball \'hand-ˌbȯl\ *n* : a game played by hitting a small rubber ball against a wall or board with the hand

hand·bill \'hand-ˌbil\ *n* : a small printed sheet (as of advertising) distributed by hand

hand·book \'hand-ˌbu̇k\ *n* : a small book of facts usually about a particular subject

hand·car \'hand-ˌkär\ *n* : a small four-wheeled railroad car propelled by a hand-operated mechanism or by a small motor

hand·cart \'hand-ˌkärt\ *n* : a cart drawn or pushed by hand

hand·clasp \'hand-ˌklasp\ *n* : HANDSHAKE

hand·craft \'hand-ˌkraft\ *n* : HANDICRAFT

¹hand·cuff \'hand-ˌkəf\ *vb* : to put handcuffs on

²handcuff *n* : a ringlike metal clasp that can be locked around a person's wrist

hand·ed \'han-dəd\ *adj* : having such or so many hands ⟨a right-*handed* boy⟩

handcuffs

hand·ful \'hand-ˌfu̇l\ *n, pl* **hand·fuls** \-ˌfu̇lz\ *or* **hands·ful** \'handz-ˌfu̇l\ **1** : as much or as many as the hand will grasp **2** : FEW

¹hand·i·cap \'han-di-ˌkap\ *n* **1** : a contest in which one who is more skilled is given a disadvantage and one who is less skilled is given an advantage **2** : the disadvantage or advantage given in a contest **3** : a disadvantage that makes progress or success difficult

²handicap *vb* **hand·i·capped; hand·i·cap·ping** **1** : to give a handicap to **2** : to put at a disadvantage

hand·i·craft \'han-di-ˌkraft\ *n* **1** : an occupation (as weaving or pottery making) that requires skill with the hands **2** : articles made by one working at handicraft

hand·i·ly \'han-də-lē\ *adv* : in a handy manner : EASILY, CONVENIENTLY

hand·i·work \'han-di-ˌwərk\ *n* **1** : work done by the hands **2** : work one has done himself

hand·ker·chief \'haŋ-kər-chif\ *n, pl* **hand·ker·chiefs** : a small usually square piece of cloth used for wiping the face, nose, or eyes

¹han·dle \'han-dəl\ *n* : the part by which something (as a dish or tool) is picked up or held — **han·dled** \-dəld\ *adj*

²handle *vb* **han·dled; han·dling** **1** : to touch, feel, hold, or move with the hand **2** : to manage with the hands **3** : to deal with (as in

writing or speaking) **4** : CONTROL, DIRECT **5** : to deal with or act on **6** : to deal or trade in — **han·dler** \-dlər\ *n*

han·dle·bar \'han-dəl-ˌbär\ *n* : a bar (as on a bicycle) that has a handle at each end and is used for steering

hand·made \'hand-'mād\ *adj* : made by hand rather than by machine

hand·maid \'hand-ˌmād\ *n* : a female servant or attendant

hand·maid·en \'hand-ˌmād-n\ *n* : HANDMAID

hand organ *n* : a small musical instrument cranked by hand

hand·out \'hand-ˌau̇t\ *n* : a portion (as of food) given to a beggar

hand·rail \'hand-ˌrāl\ *n* : a rail to be grasped by the hand for support

hands down \'handz-'dau̇n\ *adv* : without question : EASILY ⟨won the race *hands down*⟩

hand·shake \'hand-ˌshāk\ *n* : a clasping of right hands by two people (as in greeting)

hand·some \'han-səm\ *adj* **hand·som·er; hand·som·est** **1** : CONSIDERABLE ⟨a *handsome* sum⟩ **2** : GENEROUS ⟨*handsome* tip⟩ **3** : having a pleasing and impressive appearance

hand·spring \'hand-ˌspriŋ\ *n* : a feat of tumbling in which the body turns forward or backward in a full circle from a standing position and lands first on the hands and then on the feet

hand–to–hand \ˌhand-tə-'hand\ *adj* : being at very close quarters ⟨*hand-to-hand* combat⟩

hand·work \'hand-ˌwərk\ *n* : work done by hand and not by machine

hand·wo·ven \'hand-'wō-vən\ *adj* : produced on a hand-operated loom

hand·writ·ing \'hand-ˌrīt-iŋ\ *n* **1** : writing done by hand **2** : a person's own writing

hand·y \'han-dē\ *adj* **hand·i·er; hand·i·est** **1** : conveniently near **2** : easily used or managed **3** : skillful in using the hands

hand·y·man \'han-dē-ˌman\ *n, pl* **hand·y·men** \-ˌmen\ : a man who does odd jobs

¹hang \'haŋ\ *vb* **hung** \'həŋ\ *also* **hanged; hang·ing** **1** : to fasten or be fastened to something without support from below : SUSPEND ⟨*hang* curtains⟩ **2** : to put or be put to death by suspending (as from a gallows) by a rope tied around the neck **3** : to fasten so as to allow free motion forward and backward ⟨*hang* a door⟩ **4** : to cause to droop : DROOP ⟨*hang* one's head⟩ — **hang on to** : to hold or keep with determination — **hang out** : to habitually spend one's time in idleness

²hang *n* **1** : the manner in which a thing hangs **2** : MEANING **3** : KNACK

hang·ar \'hang-ər\ *n* : a shelter for housing and repairing airplanes

hang·dog \'hang-ˌdòg\ *adj* : ASHAMED, GUILTY ⟨a *hangdog* look⟩

hangar

hang·er \'hang-ər\ *n* 1 : one that hangs 2 : a device on which something hangs

hang·man \'hang-mən\ *n, pl* **hang·men** \-mən\ : a man who hangs condemned criminals

hang·nail \'hang-ˌnāl\ *n* : a bit of skin hanging loose about a fingernail

hang·out \'hang-ˌaùt\ *n* : a place where a person spends much time or goes frequently

hang·o·ver \'hang-ˌō-vər\ *n* 1 : something (as a surviving custom) that remains from what is past 2 : disagreeable physical effects following heavy drinking

hank \'hangk\ *n* : a coiled or looped bundle

han·ker \'hang-kər\ *vb* : to have a great desire ⟨*hankering* for candy⟩

han·som \'han-səm\ *n* : a light two-wheeled covered carriage with the driver's seat elevated at the rear

Ha·nuk·kah \'hä-nə-kə\ *n* : an eight-day Jewish holiday celebrated in commemoration of the rededication of the Temple

hap·haz·ard \hap-'haz-ərd\ *adj* : marked by lack of plan, order, or direction — **hap·haz·ard·ly** *adv* — **hap·haz·ard·ness** *n*

hap·less \'hap-ləs\ *adj* : UNFORTUNATE

hap·pen \'hap-ən\ *vb* 1 : to occur or come about by chance 2 : to take place 3 : CHANCE 4 : to come especially by way of injury or harm ⟨nothing will *happen* to you⟩

hap·pen·ing \'hap-ə-ning\ *n* : something that happens : OCCURRENCE

hap·pi·ly \'hap-ə-lē\ *adv* : in a happy way

hap·pi·ness \'hap-ē-nəs\ *n* : CONTENTMENT

hap·py \'hap-ē\ *adj* **hap·pi·er; hap·pi·est** [*happy* developed from earlier English *hap* "chance", "fortune", "happening", from Old Norse *happ* "good luck"] 1 : FORTUNATE, LUCKY 2 : FITTING, SUITABLE ⟨a *happy* choice⟩ 3 : enjoying one's condition : CONTENT 4 : JOYOUS 5 : PLEASED

hap·py–go–luck·y \ˌhap-ē-gō-'lək-ē\ *adj* : free from care

¹**ha·rangue** \hə-'rang\ *n* 1 : a pretentious ranting speech or writing 2 : LECTURE

²**harangue** *vb* **ha·rangued; ha·rangu·ing** : to make or address in a harangue

ha·rass \hə-'ras, 'har-əs\ *vb* 1 : to lay waste (as an enemy's country) 2 : to worry and hinder by repeated attacks 3 : to trouble or annoy continually — **ha·rass·ment** *n*

har·bin·ger \'här-bən-jər\ *n* : one that announces or shows what is coming

¹**har·bor** \'här-bər\ *n* 1 : a place of safety and comfort : REFUGE 2 : a part of a body of water (as a sea or lake) so protected as to be a place of safety for ships : PORT

²**harbor** *vb* 1 : to give shelter or refuge to 2 : to hold a thought or feeling of

¹**hard** \'härd\ *adj* 1 : not easily cut, pierced, or divided into parts : not soft 2 : strong in alcoholic content 3 : containing substances that prevent the forming of a lather with soap 4 : difficult to endure 5 : UNFEELING 6 : SEVERE, HARSH 7 : carried on diligently ⟨hours of *hard* study⟩ 8 : DILIGENT, ENERGETIC 9 : sounding as in *cold* and *geese* — used of *c* and *g* 10 : difficult to do or to understand

²**hard** *adv* 1 : with energy, great effort, or strain 2 : VIOLENTLY 3 : with pain, bitterness, or resentment ⟨took his defeat *hard*⟩

hard·en \'härd-n\ *vb* 1 : to make or become hard or harder 2 : to make or become hardy or strong 3 : to make or become stubborn or unfeeling — **hard·en·er** *n*

hard·head·ed \'härd-'hed-əd\ *adj* 1 : STUBBORN 2 : marked by sound judgment — **hard·head·ed·ly** *adv* — **hard·head·ed·ness** *n*

hard·heart·ed \'härd-'härt-əd\ *adj* : without pity : UNFEELING — **hard·heart·ed·ly** *adv* — **hard·heart·ed·ness** *n*

har·di·hood \'härd-ē-ˌhùd\ *n* 1 : resolute courage and fortitude 2 : VIGOR

har·di·ness \'härd-ē-nəs\ *n* : the quality or state of being hardy

hard·ly \'härd-lē\ *adv* : only just : BARELY

hard·ness \'härd-nəs\ *n* : the quality or state of being hard

hard palate *n* : the bony front part of the roof of the mouth

hard·ship \'härd-ˌship\ *n* : something (as a loss or injury) that is hard to bear

hard·tack \'härd-ˌtak\ *n* : a hard biscuit made of flour and water without salt

hard·ware \'härd-ˌwaər\ *n* : articles (as cutlery, utensils, or tools) made of metal

¹**hard·wood** \'härd-ˌwùd\ *n* : the typically hard wood of a tree belonging to the group bearing broad leaves as distinguished from the wood of a conifer

²**hardwood** *adj* 1 : having or made of hardwood ⟨*hardwood* trees⟩ ⟨*hardwood* floors⟩ 2 : consisting of mature woody tissue

hard–wood·ed \'härd-'wùd-əd\ *adj* 1 : having hard wood that is difficult to work with 2 : HARDWOOD 1

har·dy \'härd-ē\ *adj* **har·di·er; har·di·est**

1 : BOLD, BRAVE   **2** : able to endure fatigue, hardship, or severe weather

hare \'haər\ *n* : a swift timid long-eared mammal like a rabbit but having young that are open-eyed and furry at birth

hare·brained \'haər-'brānd\ *adj* : FLIGHTY, FOOLISH

hark \'härk\ *vb* : LISTEN, HEARKEN

har·ken *var of* HEARKEN

¹harm \'härm\ *n* **1** : INJURY, DAMAGE **2** : MISCHIEF ⟨meant no *harm*⟩

²harm *vb* : to cause harm to : HURT

harm·ful \'härm-fəl\ *adj* : causing harm : IN-JURIOUS — **harm·ful·ly** *adv* — **harm·ful·ness** *n*

harm·less \'härm-ləs\ *adj* : not harmful — **harm·less·ly** *adv* — **harm·less·ness** *n*

har·mon·ic \här-'män-ik\ *adj* : of or relating to musical harmony as opposed to melody or rhythm — **har·mon·i·cal·ly** \-i-kə-lē\ *adv*

har·mon·i·ca \här-'män-i-kə\ *n* : a small musical instrument held in the hand and played by the mouth : MOUTH ORGAN

harmonica

har·mo·ni·ous \här-'mō-nē-əs\ *adj* **1** : pleasant-sounding : MELODIOUS   **2** : combining so as to produce a pleasing effect   **3** : marked by harmony in action or feeling — **har·mo·ni·ous·ly** *adv* — **har·mo·ni·ous·ness** *n*

har·mo·nize \'här-mə-ˌnīz\ *vb* **har·mo·nized**; **har·mo·niz·ing** **1** : to play or sing in harmony **2** : to be in harmony **3** : to bring into harmony or agreement — **har·mo·niz·er** *n*

har·mo·ny \'här-mə-nē\ *n, pl* **har·mo·nies** **1** : the combination of musical tones into chords and progressions of chords   **2** : a pleasing arrangement of parts   **3** : AGREE-MENT, ACCORD

¹har·ness \'här-nəs\ *n* : an arrangement of straps and fastenings placed on an animal so as to control it or adapt it to pulling a load

²harness *vb* **1** : to put a harness on   **2** : to put to work : UTILIZE ⟨*harness* a waterfall⟩

¹harp \'härp\ *n* : a musical instrument con-sisting of a triangular frame set with strings that are plucked by the fingers

²harp *vb* **1** : to play on a harp   **2** : to refer to something over and over again

harp·ist \'här-pəst\ *n* : one who plays the harp

¹har·poon \här-'pün\ *n* : a barbed spear used especially for hunting whales and large fish

²harpoon *vb* : to strike with a harpoon

harp·si·chord \'härp-si-ˌkȯrd\ *n* : a wire-stringed musical in-strument with a keyboard

harpsichord

¹har·row \'har-ō\ *n* : a heavy frame set with metal teeth or disks used in farming for breaking up soil and smoothing it over

²harrow *vb* **1** : to draw a harrow over **2** : DISTRESS, TORMENT

har·ry \'har-ē\ *vb* **har·ried**; **har·ry·ing** **1** : RAID, PILLAGE   **2** : HARASS, TORMENT

harsh \'härsh\ *adj* **1** : disagreeable to the touch   **2** : causing discomfort : UNPLEASANT ⟨a *harsh* wind⟩ ⟨a *harsh* voice⟩   **3** : SEVERE, STERN — **harsh·ly** *adv* — **harsh·ness** *n*

har·um–scar·um \ˌhar-əm-'skar-əm\ *adj* : RECKLESS, IRRESPONSIBLE

¹har·vest \'här-vəst\ *n* **1** : the season when grains and fruits are gathered   **2** : the gather-ing of a crop   **3** : a ripe crop (as of grain)

²harvest *vb* : to gather in a crop : REAP

har·vest·er \'här-vəs-tər\ *n* **1** : one that gathers by or as if by harvesting   **2** : a machine for harvesting field crops

has *pres 3d sing of* HAVE

¹hash \'hash\ *vb* : to chop into small pieces — **hash over** : to talk over : DISCUSS

²hash *n* **1** : cooked meat and vegetables chopped together and browned   **2** : JUMBLE

hash·ish \'hash-ˌēsh\ *n* : a drug from the hemp plant that causes addiction

has·n't \'haz-nt\ : has not

hasp \'hasp\ *n* : a fastener (as for a door) consisting of a hinged metal strap that fits over a staple and is held by a pin or padlock

hasp

has·sle \'has-əl\ *n* **1** : a heated argument   **2** : a violent skirmish

has·sock \'has-ək\ *n* : a tightly stuffed cushion used as a seat or leg rest

haste \'hāst\ *n* **1** : rapidity of motion or action : SPEED   **2** : rash action

syn HASTE, HURRY, SPEED all refer to quickness of action and the first two both carry the idea of urgency and some confusion. HASTE adds to this idea the aspect of carelessness or rash-ness ⟨in her *haste* she kept dropping things⟩ while HURRY suggests quickness prompted by an actual need to save time ⟨finished the game in a *hurry* because dinner was ready⟩ SPEED suggests swiftness of movement without accompanying confusion and often with desirable results ⟨plays shortstop with *speed* and precision⟩

has·ten \'hās-n\ *vb* : to make haste : HURRY

hast·y \'hās-tē\ *adj* **hast·i·er**; **hast·i·est** **1** : done or made quickly : HURRIED ⟨a *hasty* trip⟩   **2** : made, done, or decided without proper care and thought ⟨a *hasty* decision⟩ **3** : QUICK-TEMPERED — **hast·i·ly** \-tə-lē\ *adv*

hat \'hat\ *n* : a covering for the head usually having a crown and brim

¹hatch \'hach\ *n* **1** : an opening in the deck of a ship or in the floor or roof of a building **2** : a small door or opening (as in an airplane) ⟨escape *hatch*⟩ **3** : the covering for a hatch

²hatch *vb* **1** : to produce from eggs **2** : to come forth from an egg **3** : ORIGINATE

hatch·er·y \'hach-ə-rē\ *n*, *pl* **hatch·er·ies** : a place for hatching eggs ⟨a chick *hatchery*⟩

hatch·et \'hach-ət\ *n* : a short-handled ax to be used with one hand

hatch·way \'hach-,wā\ *n* : a hatch usually having a ladder or stairs

hatchet

¹hate \'hāt\ *n* **1** : intense hostility : HATRED **2** : an object of hatred

²hate *vb* **hat·ed; hat·ing** : to feel extreme dislike and enmity

hate·ful \'hāt-fəl\ *adj* **1** : full of hate **2** : arousing or deserving hatred ⟨a *hateful* crime⟩ — **hate·ful·ly** *adv* — **hate·ful·ness** *n*

ha·tred \'hā-trəd\ *n* : ILL WILL, HATE

hat·ter \'hat-ər\ *n* : one that makes, sells, or cleans and repairs hats

haugh·ty \'hȯt-ē\ *adj* **haugh·ti·er; haugh·ti·est** : inclined to look down on others : ARROGANT — **haugh·ti·ly** \'hȯt-l-ē\ *adv* — **haugh·ti·ness** \'hȯt-ē-nəs\ *n*

¹haul \'hȯl\ *vb* **1** : to pull or draw with force **2** : to transport in a vehicle

²haul *n* **1** : PULL **2** : an amount collected ⟨a burglar's *haul*⟩ **3** : the distance or route over which a load is transported

haunch \'hȯnch\ *n* **1** : HIP **2** : HIND-QUARTER

¹haunt \'hȯnt\ *vb* **1** : to visit often **2** : to come to mind frequently ⟨the song *haunted* him⟩ **3** : to visit or inhabit as a ghost

²haunt *n* : a place repeatedly visited

have \hav, həv, əv\ *vb*, *past & past part* **had** \had, həd, əd\; *pres part* **hav·ing** \'hav-ing\; *pres 3d sing* **has** \haz, həz, əz\ **1** : POSSESS, OWN **2** : to consist of **3** : BEAR, WEAR **4** : to be forced or feel obliged to ⟨*have* to stay⟩ **5** : to be in relationship to ⟨*have* the sun at your back⟩ **6** : OBTAIN, RECEIVE **7** : ACCEPT **8** : to be marked by ⟨*has* red hair⟩ **9** : SHOW, EXERCISE ⟨*have* mercy⟩ **10** : EXPERIENCE ⟨*has* a cold⟩ **11** : to carry on ⟨*had* a fight⟩ **12** : to hold in the mind ⟨*have* doubts⟩ **13** : to cause to do or be done ⟨*had* his hair cut⟩ **14** : AL-LOW **15** : to give birth to **16** : to partake of ⟨*have* dinner⟩ **17** — used as a helping verb with the past participle of another verb ⟨*has* gone home⟩ ⟨*had* already eaten⟩

ha·ven \'hā-vən\ *n* : HARBOR, SHELTER

have·n't \'hav-ənt\ : have not

hav·er·sack \'hav-ər-,sak\ *n* [from French *havresac* "haversack", taken from German *habersack* "bag for oats", a compound of *haber* "oats" and *sack* "bag"] : a bag worn over one shoulder for carrying supplies

hav·oc \'hav-ək\ *n* **1** : wide destruction **2** : great confusion and disorder

haw \'hȯ\ *n* : a hawthorn berry

¹hawk \'hȯk\ *n* : a bird of prey that has a strong hooked bill and sharp curved claws and is smaller than most eagles

²hawk *vb* : to hunt birds by means of a trained hawk — **hawk·er** *n*

³hawk *vb* : to offer for sale by calling out in the street ⟨*hawk* fruit⟩ — **hawk·er** *n*

⁴hawk *vb* : to make a harsh coughing sound in clearing the throat

haw·ser \'hȯ-zər\ *n* : a large rope for towing or mooring a ship

haw·thorn \'hȯ-,thȯrn\ *n* : any of several spiny shrubs or small trees with shiny leaves, white, pink, or red flowers, and small red fruits

¹hay \'hā\ *n* : any of various grasses cut and dried for use as fodder

²hay *vb* : to cut grass for hay

hawthorn

hay·cock \'hā-,käk\ *n* : a cone-shaped pile of hay

hay fever *n* : a sickness like a cold usually affecting people sensitive to plant pollen

hay·fork \'hā-,fȯrk\ *n* : a hand or mechanically operated fork for loading or unloading hay

hay·loft \'hā-,lȯft\ *n* : a loft in a barn or stable for storing hay

hay·mow \'hā-,maù\ *n* : HAYLOFT

hay·rick \'hā-,rik\ *n* : a large pile or stack of hay kept in the open air

hay·wire \'hā-,wīr\ *adj* **1** : being out of order **2** : emotionally or mentally upset

¹haz·ard \'haz-ərd\ *n* [this originally meant "a game of chance played with dice", taken from early French *hasard*, which came from Arabic *az-zahr* "the die"] **1** : DANGER, PERIL **2** : a source of danger ⟨a fire *hazard*⟩

²hazard *vb* : RISK, VENTURE

haz·ard·ous \'haz-ərd-əs\ *adj* : DANGEROUS — **haz·ard·ous·ly** *adv* — **haz·ard·ous·ness** *n*

¹haze \'hāz\ *vb* **hazed; haz·ing** : to make or become hazy or cloudy

²haze *n* : fine dust, smoke, or fine particles of water in the air

³haze *vb* **hazed; haz·ing** : to harass by humiliating and abusive tricks

ha·zel \\'hā-zəl\\ *n* **1** : a shrub or small tree that bears an eatable nut **2** : a light brown

ha·zel·nut \\'hā-zəl-ˌnət\\ *n* : the nut of a hazel

haz·y \\'hā-zē\\ *adj* **haz·i·er; haz·i·est 1** : partly concealed by haze **2** : not clear in thought or meaning : VAGUE — **haz·i·ly** \\-zə-lē\\ *adv* — **haz·i·ness** \\-zē-nəs\\ *n*

H–bomb \\'āch-ˌbäm\\ *n* : HYDROGEN BOMB

he \\hē, ē\\ *pron* **1** : that male one **2** : a or the person : ONE ⟨*he* who hesitates is lost⟩

¹head \\'hed\\ *n* **1** : the part of the body containing the brain, eyes, ears, nose, and mouth **2** : MIND ⟨a good *head* for figures⟩ **3** : mental or emotional control ⟨kept a level *head* in time of danger⟩ **4** : the side of a coin or medal bearing a head **5** : each one among a number ⟨count *heads*⟩ **6** *pl* **head** : a unit of number ⟨thirty *head* of cattle⟩ **7** : an upper or higher part or position ⟨*head* of a bed⟩ **8** : the source of a stream **9** : DIRECTOR, LEADER **10** : a compact mass of plant parts (as leaves or flowers) ⟨a *head* of cabbage⟩ **11** : a leading element (as of a procession) **12** : the uppermost extremity or projecting part of an object : TOP **13** : the place of leadership or honor **14** : CRISIS — **out of one's head** : DELIRIOUS — **over one's head** : beyond one's understanding

²head *adj* **1** : PRINCIPAL **2** : located at the head **3** : coming from in front ⟨*head* wind⟩

³head *vb* **1** : to provide with or form a head ⟨this cabbage *heads* early⟩ **2** : to be or put oneself at the head of **3** : to get in front of especially so as to stop ⟨*head* off the runaway⟩ **4** : to be at the beginning of **5** : to go or cause to go in a certain direction

head·ache \\'hed-ˌāk\\ *n* **1** : pain in the head **2** : something that annoys or baffles

head·band \\'hed-ˌband\\ *n* : a band worn on or around the head

head·dress \\'hed-ˌdres\\ *n* : a covering or ornament for the head

head·ed \\'hed-əd\\ *adj* : having a head or heading

head·first \\'hed-'fərst\\ *adv* : with the head foremost ⟨fell *headfirst* down the stairs⟩

head·gear \\'hed-ˌgiər\\ *n* : a covering or protective device for the head

head·ing \\'hed-ing\\ *n* : something that stands at the head, top, or beginning

head·land \\'hed-lənd\\ *n* : a point of high land jutting out into the sea

head·light \\'hed-ˌlīt\\ *n* : a light at the front of a vehicle

¹head·line \\'hed-ˌlīn\\ *n* : a title over an item or article in a newspaper

²headline *vb* **head·lined; head·lin·ing 1** : to provide with a headline **2** : PUBLICIZE

¹head·long \\'hed-'long\\ *adv* **1** : HEADFIRST **2** : RASHLY, HASTILY

²headlong *adj* **1** : RASH, HASTY **2** : plunging headfirst ⟨a *headlong* dive⟩

head·mas·ter \\'hed-ˌmas-tər\\ *n* : a man who heads the staff of a private school

head·phone \\'hed-ˌfōn\\ *n* : an earphone held over the ear by a band worn on the head

head·piece \\'hed-ˌpēs\\ *n* : a protective or defensive covering for the head

head·quar·ters \\'hed-ˌkwȯrt-ərz\\ *n sing or pl* **1** : a place from which a commander exercises command **2** : the center of authority

head·stall \\'hed-ˌstȯl\\ *n* : the part of a bridle or halter that fits around the head

head·stone \\'hed-ˌstōn\\ *n* : a stone at the head of a grave

head·strong \\'hed-ˌstrȯng\\ *adj* **1** : not easily controlled **2** : caused by stubbornness

head·wait·er \\'hed-'wāt-ər\\ *n* : the head of the dining-room staff of a restaurant or hotel

head·wa·ters \\'hed-ˌwȯt-ərz, -ˌwät-\\ *n pl* : the source and upper part of a stream

head·way \\'hed-ˌwā\\ *n* **1** : forward motion (as of a ship) **2** : PROGRESS **3** : clear space (as under an arch)

head·work \\'hed-ˌwərk\\ *n* : mental work or effort : THINKING

head·y \\'hed-ē\\ *adj* **head·i·er; head·i·est 1** : WILLFUL **2** : likely to make one dizzy

heal \\'hēl\\ *vb* **1** : CURE **2** : to return to a sound or healthy condition — **heal·er** *n*

health \\'helth\\ *n* **1** : the condition of being free from illness or disease **2** : the general condition of the body ⟨his *health* is poor⟩

health·ful \\'helth-fəl\\ *adj* **1** : serving to build up health : good for the health **2** : enjoying good health **syn** see HEALTHY — **health·ful·ly** *adv* — **health·ful·ness** *n*

health·y \\'hel-thē\\ *adj* **health·i·er; health·i·est 1** : being sound and well : free from disease **2** : showing good health **3** : aiding or building up health ⟨*healthy* exercise⟩ — **health·i·ly** \\-thə-lē\\ *adv* — **health·i·ness** \\-thē-nəs\\ *n*

  syn HEALTHY, HEALTHFUL, WHOLESOME all refer to well-being. HEALTHY is used to describe the physical condition of a living thing ⟨*healthy* children⟩ ⟨*healthy* rose bushes⟩ HEALTHFUL and WHOLESOME describe the conditions that create or sustain good health but the first may be preferred when referring to physical health ⟨*healthful* climate⟩ ⟨*healthful* meals⟩ while the second may be preferred when referring to mental health or character ⟨*wholesome* books⟩ ⟨*wholesome* sports⟩

¹heap \\'hēp\\ *n* **1** : a piled-up mass ⟨a

rubbish *heap*⟩ ⟨a *heap* of earth⟩ **2** : a large number or amount ⟨*heaps* of fun⟩

²heap *vb* **1** : to throw or lay in a heap : make into a pile **2** : to give in large amounts ⟨*heap* a plate with food⟩ **3** : to fill more than full

hear \'hiər\ *vb* **heard** \'hərd\; **hear·ing** \'hiər-ing\ **1** : to take in through the ear **2** : to gain knowledge of by hearing : LEARN **3** : to listen to with attention ⟨*hear* both sides of a story⟩ **4** : to get news — **hear·er** \'hir-ər\ *n*

hear·ing \'hiər-ing\ *n* **1** : the act or power of taking in sound through the ear : the sense by which a person hears **2** : EARSHOT **3** : a chance to be heard ⟨give both sides a fair *hearing*⟩

hearing aid *n* : an electronic device used by a partly deaf person to make sounds louder

hear·ken \'här-kən\ *vb* : LISTEN

hear·say \'hiər-ˌsā\ *n* : RUMOR

hearse \'hərs\ *n* : a vehicle for carrying the dead to the grave

heart \'härt\ *n* **1** : a hollow organ of the body the walls of which expand and contract so as to keep the blood moving through the arteries and veins **2** : something resembling a heart in shape **3** : the part nearest the center **4** : the most essential part **5** : human feelings : KINDNESS **6** : COURAGE, SPIRIT **7** : MOOD **8** : MEMORY

heart 2

heart·ache \'härt-ˌāk\ *n* : SORROW

heart·beat \'härt-ˌbēt\ *n* : one complete pulsation of the heart

heart·break \'härt-ˌbrāk\ *n* : crushing grief

heart·break·ing \'härt-ˌbrā-king\ *adj* : causing intense sorrow or distress

heart·bro·ken \'härt-ˌbrō-kən\ *adj* : overcome by sorrow

heart·en \'härt-n\ *vb* : to cheer up

heart·felt \'härt-ˌfelt\ *adj* : SINCERE

hearth \'härth\ *n* **1** : an area (as of brick) in front of a fireplace **2** : the floor of a fireplace **3** : HOME

hearth·side \'härth-ˌsīd\ *n* : FIRESIDE

hearth·stone \'härth-ˌstōn\ *n* **1** : a stone forming a hearth **2** : HOME

hearth

heart·i·ly \'härt-l-ē\ *adv* **1** : with sincerity, goodwill, or enthusiasm **2** : COMPLETELY

heart·i·ness \'härt-ē-nəs\ *n* : the quality or state of being hearty

heart·less \'härt-ləs\ *adj* : UNFEELING, CRUEL — **heart·less·ly** *adv* — **heart·less·ness** *n*

heart·rend·ing \'härt-ˌren-ding\ *adj* : causing deep grief or distress

hearts·ease \'härts-ˌēz\ *n* : peace of mind

heart·sick \'härt-ˌsik\ *adj* : DEPRESSED

heart·wood \'härt-ˌwůd\ *n* : the usually dark-colored wood in the center of a tree

heart·y \'härt-ē\ *adj* **heart·i·er**; **heart·i·est** **1** : SINCERE, CORDIAL ⟨a *hearty* welcome⟩ **2** : STRONG, HEALTHY **3** : having a good appetite **4** : being abundant and satisfying

¹heat \'hēt\ *vb* **1** : to make or become warm or hot **2** : EXCITE

²heat *n* **1** : a condition of being hot : WARMTH **2** : high temperature **3** : a form of energy that causes a body to rise in temperature **4** : intensity of feeling or action **5** : a single race in a contest that includes two or more races

heat·ed \'hēt-əd\ *adj* **1** : HOT **2** : ANGRY ⟨*heated* words⟩ — **heat·ed·ly** *adv*

heat·er \'hēt-ər\ *n* : a device for heating

heath \'hēth\ *n* **1** : any of a group of low, woody, and often evergreen plants that grow on barren sour wet soil **2** : a usually open level stretch of land on which heaths can grow

¹hea·then \'hē-thən\ *adj* **1** : of or relating to the heathen **2** : FOREIGN, UNCIVILIZED

²heathen *n, pl* **hea·thens** *or* **hea·then** **1** : a person who does not acknowledge and worship the God of the Bible : PAGAN **2** : an uncivilized person

heath·er \'heth-ər\ *n* : a pink-flowered evergreen heath of northern and mountainous areas with needle-like leaves

heather

¹heave \'hēv\ *vb* **heaved** *or* **hove** \'hōv\; **heav·ing** **1** : to raise with an effort : LIFT ⟨*heave* a trunk onto a truck⟩ **2** : THROW, HURL ⟨*heave* a rock⟩ **3** : to utter with an effort ⟨*heave* a sigh⟩ **4** : to rise and fall repeatedly ⟨the runner's chest was *heaving*⟩ **5** : to be thrown or raised up

²heave *n* **1** : an effort to lift or raise **2** : a forceful throw **3** : an upward motion (as of the chest in breathing)

heav·en \'hev-ən\ *n* **1** : SKY — usually used in plural **2** *often cap* : the dwelling place of God and of the blessed dead **3** *cap* : ²GOD **4** : a place or condition of supreme happiness

heav·en·ly \'hev-ən-lē\ *adj* **1** : of or relating to heaven or the heavens ⟨*heavenly* bodies such as the sun, moon, and stars⟩ **2** : DIVINE, BLESSED **3** : supremely delightful

heav·i·ly \'hev-ə-lē\ *adv* **1** : with or as if with weight ⟨bear down *heavily*⟩ **2** : in a slow and difficult manner **3** : SEVERELY **4** : THICKLY ⟨*heavily* populated district⟩

heav·y \'hev-ē\ *adj* **heav·i·er**; **heav·i·est** **1** : having great weight : hard to lift or carry **2** : hard to endure ⟨a *heavy* sorrow⟩ **3** : DEEP,

PROFOUND ⟨a *heavy* sleep⟩ **4 :** burdened by something weighty or oppressive ⟨a *heavy* heart⟩ **5 :** lacking vitality **6 :** unusually great in volume or force **7 :** not properly raised or leavened — **heav·i·ness** *n*

¹He·brew \'hē-brü\ *adj* : of or relating to the Hebrew peoples or Hebrew

²Hebrew *n* **1 :** a member of any of a group of peoples including the ancient Jews **2 :** JEW **3 :** the language of the Hebrews

heck·le \'hek-əl\ *vb* **heck·led; heck·ling** : to interrupt and annoy with questions or comments — **heck·ler** \'hek-lər\ *n*

hec·tic \'hek-tik\ *adj* : filled with excitement or confusion ⟨a *hectic* day of shopping⟩

hec·to·me·ter \'hek-tə-,mēt-ər\ *n* : a unit of length in the metric system equal to 100 meters

hec·tor \'hek-tər\ *vb* **1 :** SWAGGER **2 :** to intimidate by bluster or personal pressure

he'd \hēd, ēd\ : he had : he would

¹hedge \'hej\ *n* : a fence or boundary made up of a thick growth of shrubs or low trees

²hedge *vb* **hedged; hedg·ing 1 :** to surround or protect with a hedge **2 :** to avoid giving a direct or definite answer or promise

hedge·hog \'hej-,hog, -,häg\ *n* **1 :** a European insect-eating mammal having sharp spines mixed with the hair on its back and able to roll itself up into a ball **2 :** PORCUPINE

hedge·hop \'hej-,häp\ *vb* **hedge·hopped; hedge·hop·ping** : to fly an airplane very close to the ground — **hedge·hop·per** *n*

hedge·row \'hej-,rō\ *n* : a hedge of shrubs or trees around a field

¹heed \'hēd\ *vb* : to pay attention to : MIND

²heed *n* : ATTENTION ⟨pay *heed* to a warning⟩ — **heed·ful** *adj* — **heed·ful·ly** *adv*

heed·less \'hēd-ləs\ *adj* : taking no notice : being without heed : CARELESS, THOUGHTLESS — **heed·less·ly** *adv* — **heed·less·ness** *n*

¹heel \'hēl\ *n* **1 :** the back part of the human foot behind the arch and below the ankle **2 :** the part of an animal's limb corresponding to a heel **3 :** one of the crusty ends of a loaf of bread **4 :** a part (as of a stocking) that covers the human heel **5 :** the solid part of a shoe that supports the heel **6 :** a rear, low, or bottom part **7 :** a contemptible person — **heel·less** \'hēl-ləs\ *adj*

²heel *vb* : to tilt to one side : LIST

heft \'heft\ *vb* : to test the weight of by lifting

heft·y \'hef-tē\ *adj* **heft·i·er; heft·i·est** : HEAVY

heif·er \'hef-ər\ *n* : a young cow

height \'hīt\ *n* **1 :** the highest point : the greatest degree **2 :** the distance from the bottom to the top of something standing upright **3 :** extent of distance upward

syn HEIGHT, ALTITUDE, ELEVATION all refer to a vertical measurement of something. HEIGHT is a general term and can be used in reference to low or high things ⟨barely the *height* of a grasshopper⟩ ⟨two boys the same *height*⟩ ALTITUDE is used to indicate the distance of something above a standard level ⟨planes flying at *altitudes* of nearly 20,000 feet⟩ ELEVATION often refers to the height of something in relation to nearby levels ⟨placed the observatory on a suitable *elevation*⟩

height·en \'hīt-n\ *vb* **1 :** to increase in amount or degree ⟨*heightened* the man's interest⟩ **2 :** to make or become high or higher

hei·nous \'hā-nəs\ *adj* : hatefully or shockingly evil : ATROCIOUS ⟨a *heinous* offense⟩ — **hei·nous·ly** *adv* — **hei·nous·ness** *n*

heir \'aər\ *n* **1 :** a person who inherits or is entitled to inherit property after the death of its owner **2 :** a person who has legal claim to a title or a throne when the person holding it dies

heir·ess \'ar-əs\ *n* : a female heir

heir·loom \'aər-,lüm\ *n* : a piece of personal property handed down from one generation to another usually by inheritance

held *past of* HOLD

hel·i·cop·ter \'hel-ə-,käp-tər\ *n* [formed in French as *hélicoptère*, from Greek *helix* "spiral" and *pteron* "wing"] : an aircraft supported in the air by propellers revolving on a vertical axis

hel·i·port \'hel-ə-,pōrt, 'hē-lə-\ *n* : a landing and takeoff place for a helicopter

he·li·um \'hē-lē-əm\ *n* : a very light gaseous chemical element that is found in various natural gases, will not burn, and is used in balloons

hell \'hel\ *n* **1 :** an abode of souls after death **2 :** a place or state of punishment for the wicked after death : the home of evil spirits **3 :** a place or state of misery or wickedness **4 :** something tormenting — **hell·ish** *adj*

he'll \hēl, ēl\ : he shall : he will

hell·ben·der \'hel-,ben-dər\ *n* : a large American salamander that lives in water

hel·lo \hə-'lō, he-\ *interj* — used as a greeting or to express surprise

helm \'helm\ *n* **1 :** a lever or wheel for steering a ship **2 :** a position of control

hel·met \'hel-mət\ *n* : a protective covering for the head

¹help \'help\ *vb* **1 :** to provide with what is useful in achieving an end : AID, ASSIST **2 :** to give relief from pain or

helmet for diver

disease ⟨rest *helps* a cold⟩ 3 : PREVENT, AVOID ⟨a mistake that could not be *helped*⟩ 4 : SERVE

²**help** *n* 1 : an act or instance of helping : AID 2 : the state of being helped ⟨a situation that is beyond *help*⟩ 3 : a person or a thing that helps 4 : a body of hired helpers

help·er \'hel-pər\ *n* 1 : one that helps 2 : a person who helps with manual labor

help·ful \'help-fəl\ *adj* : furnishing help — **help·ful·ly** *adv* — **help·ful·ness** *n*

help·ing \'hel-ping\ *n* : a serving of food

helping verb *n* : a verb that accompanies another verb to express person, number, mood, or tense

help·less \'help-ləs\ *adj* 1 : lacking protection or support 2 : unable to help oneself — **help·less·ly** *adv* — **help·less·ness** *n*

hel·ter–skel·ter \,hel-tər-'skel-tər\ *adv* 1 : PELL-MELL 2 : HAPHAZARDLY

¹**hem** \'hem\ *n* : a border of a cloth article made by folding back an edge and sewing it down

²**hem** *vb* **hemmed; hem·ming** 1 : to finish with or make a hem 2 : CONFINE, SURROUND

hemi- *prefix* : half ⟨*hemi*sphere⟩

hem·i·sphere \'hem-ə-,sfiər\ *n* 1 : one of the halves of the earth as divided by the equator into northern and southern parts (**northern hemisphere, southern hemisphere**) or by a meridian into two parts so that one half (**eastern hemisphere**) to the east of the Atlantic ocean includes Europe, Asia, and Africa and the half (**western hemisphere**) to the west includes North and South America and surrounding waters 2 : a half of a sphere

hem·i·spher·ic \,hem-ə-'sfiər-ik, -'sfer-\ *or* **hem·i·spher·i·cal** \-'sfir-i-kəl, -'sfer-\ *adj* : of or relating to a hemisphere

hem·lock \'hem-,läk\ *n* 1 : a poisonous plant of the carrot family 2 : an evergreen tree of the pine family

he·mo·glo·bin \'hē-mə-,glō-bən\ *n* : the coloring matter of the red blood cells that carry oxygen from the lungs to the tissues

hemlock 2: needles and cone

hemp \'hemp\ *n* : a tall plant widely grown for its tough woody fiber that is used in making cloth, matting, and rope

hen \'hen\ *n* 1 : a female domestic fowl 2 : a female bird

hence \'hens\ *adv* 1 : from this place 2 : from this time 3 : as a result : THEREFORE

hence·forth \'hens-,fōrth\ *adv* : from this time on

hence·for·ward \hens-'fōr-wərd\ *adv* : HENCEFORTH

hen 1

hench·man \'hench-mən\ *n, pl* **hench·men** \-mən\ 1 : a trusted follower or supporter 2 : a political follower serving for his own advantage

hen·pecked \'hen-,pekt\ *adj* : constantly scolded and usually dominated by one's wife

hepta- *or* **hept-** *prefix* : seven ⟨*hepta*meter⟩

hep·ta·gon \'hep-tə-,gän\ *n* : a closed plane figure having seven angles and seven sides

¹**her** \hər, ər\ *adj* : of or relating to her or herself ⟨*her* book⟩ ⟨*her* illness⟩

²**her** *pron, objective case of* SHE

¹**her·ald** \'her-əld\ *n* 1 : an official crier or messenger 2 : HARBINGER 3 : one that conveys news or proclaims

²**herald** *vb* 1 : to give notice of : ANNOUNCE 2 : PUBLICIZE 3 : GREET, HAIL

he·ral·dic \he-'ral-dik\ *adj* : of or relating to heralds or heraldry

her·ald·ry \'her-əl-drē\ *n* : the art or science of tracing a person's forebears and determining what coat of arms his family is entitled to have

herb \'ərb, 'hərb\ *n* 1 : a plant with soft stems that die down at the end of the growing season 2 : a plant or plant part used in medicine or in seasoning foods

her·biv·o·rous \,hər-'biv-ə-rəs\ *adj* [formed as modern Latin *herbivorus*, from Latin *herba* "grass", "vegetation" and *-vorus*, a Latin form meaning "feeding on", "devouring"] : eating or living on plants

¹**herd** \'hərd\ *n* : a number of animals of one kind kept or living together ⟨a *herd* of cows⟩

²**herd** *vb* 1 : to gather or join in a herd 2 : to form into or move as a herd ⟨*herd* cattle⟩

herd·er \'hərd-ər\ *n* : HERDSMAN

herds·man \'hərdz-mən\ *n, pl* **herds·men** \-mən\ : a man who owns or tends a flock or herd

¹**here** \'hiər\ *adv* 1 : in or at this place ⟨stand *here*⟩ 2 : NOW ⟨*here* it is Monday again⟩ 3 : to or into this place : HITHER

²**here** *n* : this place

here·a·bouts \'hiər-ə-,bauts\ *or* **here·a·bout** \-,baut\ *adv* : near or around this place

¹**here·af·ter** \hiər-'af-tər\ *adv* 1 : after this 2 : in some future time or state

²**hereafter** *n* 1 : FUTURE 2 : life after death

here·by \hiər-'bī\ *adv* : by means of this

he·red·i·tar·y \hə-'red-ə-,ter-ē\ *adj* 1 : capable of being passed from parent to child ⟨*hereditary* disease⟩ 2 : received or passing from an ancestor to his heir

he·red·i·ty \hə-'red-ət-ē\ *n, pl* **he·red·i·ties** : the passing on of characteristics (as looks or ability) from parents to offspring

ə abut ər further a ax ā age ä father, cot à (see key page) aù out ch chin e less ē easy g gift i trip ī life

here·in \hiər-'in\ *adv* : in this

here·of \hiər-'əv, -'äv\ *adv* : of this

here·on \hiər-'òn, -'än\ *adv* : on this

her·e·sy \'her-ə-sē\ *n, pl* **her·e·sies** 1 : the holding of religious beliefs contrary to church doctrine 2 : an opinion contrary to a generally accepted belief

her·e·tic \'her-ə-ˌtik\ *n* : a person who believes or teaches something contrary to accepted beliefs (as of a church)

he·ret·i·cal \hə-'ret-i-kəl\ *adj* : of, relating to, or characterized by heresy

here·to \hiər-'tü\ *adv* : to this document

here·to·fore \'hiər-tə-ˌfòr\ *adv* : HITHERTO

here·up·on \'hiər-ə-ˌpòn, -ˌpän\ *adv* : on this : immediately after this

here·with \hiər-'with, -'with\ *adv* : with this

her·i·tage \'her-ət-ij\ *n* : something that is passed on from one's ancestors : BIRTHRIGHT

her·mit \'hər-mət\ *n* [the Greek adj. *erēmitēs* "living in the desert", from *erēmos* "lonely", was used as a noun meaning "hermit" in later Greek; this noun, via Latin and French, became English *hermit*] : one who lives apart from others especially for religious reasons

he·ro \'hē-rō\ *n, pl* **he·roes** 1 : a person who is remembered and honored for his courageous life and deeds ⟨*heroes* of a nation's history⟩ 2 : one who shows great courage 3 : the chief male character in a story, play, or poem

he·ro·ic \hi-'rō-ik\ *adj* 1 : of, relating to, or resembling heroes 2 : BRAVE, COURAGEOUS ⟨a *heroic* rescue⟩ — **he·ro·i·cal·ly** \-i-kə-lē\ *adv*

her·o·ine \'her-ə-wən\ *n* 1 : a woman of heroic achievements or qualities 2 : the chief female character in a story, poem, or play

her·o·ism \'her-ə-ˌwiz-əm\ *n* 1 : heroic conduct 2 : the qualities of a hero

her·on \'her-ən\ *n* : a long-necked long-legged wading bird that feeds on frogs, lizards, and small fish

her·ring \'her-ing\ *n* : a widely used food fish of the north Atlantic ocean

hers \'hərz\ *pron* : one or the one belonging to her : some or the ones belonging to her

her·self \hər-'self, ər-\ *pron* : her own self ⟨she hurt *herself*⟩ ⟨she *herself* did it⟩

he's \hēz, ēz\ : he is : he has

hes·i·tan·cy \'hez-ə-tən-sē\ *n, pl* **hes·i·tan·cies** 1 : the quality or state of being hesitant : INDECISION, RELUCTANCE 2 : an act or instance of hesitating

hes·i·tant \'hez-ə-tənt\ *adj* : feeling or showing hesitation — **hes·i·tant·ly** *adv*

heron

hes·i·tate \'hez-ə-ˌtāt\ *vb* **hes·i·tat·ed; hes·i·tat·ing** 1 : to stop or pause because of forgetfulness or uncertainty 2 : STAMMER

hes·i·ta·tion \ˌhez-ə-'tā-shən\ *n* 1 : an act or instance of hesitating 2 : STAMMERING

hew \'hyü\ *vb* **hewed** or **hewn** \'hyün\; **hewing** 1 : to chop down : CHOP ⟨*hew* logs⟩ 2 : to make or shape by cutting with an ax

hex \'heks\ *n* [from Pennsylvania German *hexe* "to practice witchcraft", from German *hexe* "witch"] 1 : SPELL, JINX 2 : a person who practices witchcraft

hexa- or **hex-** *prefix* : six ⟨*hexa*gon⟩

hex·a·gon \'hek-sə-ˌgän\ *n* : a closed plane figure having six angles and six sides

hex·ag·o·nal \hek-'sag-ən-l\ *adj* : six-sided — **hex·ag·o·nal·ly** *adv*

hey \'hā\ *interj* — used especially to call attention or to express surprise or joy

hexagon

hey·day \'hā-ˌdā\ *n* : the time of greatest strength, vigor, or prosperity

hi \'hī\ *interj* — used as an informal greeting

hi·ber·nate \'hī-bər-ˌnāt\ *vb* **hi·ber·nat·ed; hi·ber·nat·ing** [from Latin *hibernare* "to pass the winter", from *hibernus* "of winter"] : to pass the winter in a torpid or resting state — **hi·ber·na·tor** *n*

hi·ber·na·tion \ˌhī-bər-'nā-shən\ *n* : the state of one that hibernates

¹**hic·cup** \'hik-ˌəp\ *n* : a gulping sound caused by sudden movements of muscles active in breathing

²**hiccup** *vb* **hic·cuped** *also* **hic·cupped; hic·cup·ing** *also* **hic·cup·ping** : to make a hiccup : have hiccups

hick·o·ry \'hik-ə-rē\ *n, pl* **hick·o·ries** : a tall tree related to the walnuts that has strong tough elastic wood and bears a hard-shelled edible nut (**hickory nut**)

¹**hide** \'hīd\ *vb* **hid** \'hid\; **hid·den** \'hid-n\ *or* **hid; hid·ing** \'hīd-ing\ 1 : to put or remain out of sight : CONCEAL 2 : to keep secret 3 : to screen from view ⟨clouds *hiding* the sun⟩

hickory leaf

²**hide** *n* : the raw or dressed skin of an animal

³**hide** *vb* **hid·ed** \'hīd-əd\; **hid·ing** : FLOG

hide–and–go–seek \ˌhīd-n-gō-'sēk\ *n* : HIDE-AND-SEEK

hide–and–seek \ˌhīd-n-'sēk\ *n* : a game in which one player covers his eyes and after giving the others time to hide goes looking for them

hide·a·way \'hīd-ə-ˌwā\ *n* : RETREAT, HIDEOUT

hid·e·ous \'hid-ē-əs\ *adj* : horribly ugly or disgusting : FRIGHTFUL — **hid·e·ous·ly** *adv* — **hid·e·ous·ness** *n*

hide·out \'hīd-,aut\ *n* : a place of concealment or refuge

¹**hid·ing** \'hīd-ing\ *n* : a state or place of concealment

²**hiding** *n* : FLOGGING, WHIPPING

hie \'hī\ *vb* **hied; hy·ing** *or* **hie·ing** : HURRY

hi·er·o·glyph·ic \,hī-ə-rə-'glif-ik\ *n* : a character in the picture writing of the ancient Egyptians

hi–fi \'hī-'fī\ *adj* : characterized by or relating to the reproduction of sound with a high degree of fidelity to the original

hieroglyphics

hig·gle·dy–pig·gle·dy \,hig-əl-dē-'pig-əl-dē\ *adv* (*or adj*) : in confusion : TOPSY-TURVY

¹**high** \'hī\ *adj* **1** : extending to a great distance above the ground **2** : having a specified elevation : TALL **3** : of greater degree, size, or amount than average **4** : of more than usual importance **5** : STRONG, POWERFUL ⟨*high* winds⟩ **6** : pitched or sounding above some other sound **7** : EXPENSIVE

²**high** *adv* : at or to a high place or degree

³**high** *n* **1** : an elevated place **2** : a region in which the pressure of the atmosphere is high as shown by a barometer **3** : a high point or level **4** : the arrangement of gears in an automobile giving the highest speed of travel

high·brow \'hī-,brau\ *n* : a person of superior learning or culture

high·fa·lu·tin \,hī-fə-'lüt-n\ *adj* : PRETENTIOUS, POMPOUS

high–hand·ed \'hī-'han-dəd\ *adj* : OVERBEARING ⟨*high-handed* actions⟩ — **high–hand·ed·ly** *adv* — **high–hand·ed·ness** *n*

high–hat \'hī-'hat\ *adj* : characteristic of a snob

high jump *n* : a jump for height in a track-and-field contest

high·land \'hī-lənd\ *n* : high or hilly country : a high plateau

Highland fling *n* : a lively Scottish folk dance

¹**high·light** \'hī-,līt\ *n* : an event or detail of major interest ⟨*highlights* of the trip⟩

²**highlight** *vb* **1** : to throw a strong light on **2** : EMPHASIZE ⟨a speech *highlighting* his concern⟩ **3** : to constitute a highlight of

high·ly \'hī-lē\ *adv* **1** : to a high degree : very much **2** : with much approval

high·ness \'hī-nəs\ *n* : the quality or state of being high — used as a title (as for a king)

high school *n* : a secondary school usually comprising the ninth to twelfth or tenth to twelfth grades

high seas *n pl* : the open part of a sea or ocean

high–spir·it·ed \'hī-'spir-ət-əd\ *adj* : LIVELY

high–strung \'hī-'strəng\ *adj* : highly sensitive or nervous

high tide *n* : the tide when the water is at its greatest height

high·way \'hī-,wā\ *n* : a main road

high·way·man \'hī-,wā-mən\ *n*, *pl* **high·way·men** \-mən\ : a person who robs travelers on a road

¹**hike** \'hīk\ *vb* **hiked; hik·ing** : to take a long walk — **hik·er** *n*

²**hike** *n* : a long walk especially for pleasure or exercise

hi·lar·i·ous \hi-'lar-ē-əs, hī-\ *adj* : marked by or providing hilarity — **hi·lar·i·ous·ly** *adv* — **hi·lar·i·ous·ness** *n*

hi·lar·i·ty \hi-'lar-ət-ē, hī-\ *n* : noisy merriment

¹**hill** \'hil\ *n* **1** : a usually rounded elevation of land lower than a mountain **2** : a little heap or mound of earth **3** : several seeds or plants planted in a group rather than a row

²**hill** *vb* **1** : to form into a heap **2** : to draw earth around the roots or base of ⟨*hilled* his corn⟩

hill·bil·ly \'hil-,bil-ē\ *n*, *pl* **hill·bil·lies** : a person from a backwoods area

hill·ock \'hil-ək\ *n* : a small hill

hill·side \'hil-,sīd\ *n* : the part of a hill between the summit and the foot

hill·top \'hil-,täp\ *n* : the highest part of a hill

hill·y \'hil-ē\ *adj* **hill·i·er; hill·i·est** **1** : having many hills ⟨a *hilly* city⟩ **2** : STEEP

hilt \'hilt\ *n* : a handle especially of a sword or dagger

him \him, im\ *pron*, *objective case of* HE

hilt

him·self \him-'self, im-\ *pron* : his own self ⟨he hurt *himself*⟩ ⟨he *himself* did it⟩

hind \'hīnd\ *adj* : being at the end or back : REAR

hin·der \'hin-dər\ *vb* **1** : to make slow or difficult : HAMPER **2** : PREVENT

hind·quar·ter \'hīnd-,kwȯrt-ər\ *n* : the back half of a complete side of a four-footed animal or carcass

hin·drance \'hin-drəns\ *n* : something that hinders

hind·sight \'hīnd-,sīt\ *n* : understanding of an event after it has happened

¹**hinge** \'hinj\ *n* : a jointed piece on which a door, gate, or lid turns or swings

²**hinge** *vb* **hinged; hing·ing** **1** : to

hinges

attach by or furnish with hinges **2** : DEPEND

hin·ny \'hin-ē\ *n, pl* **hin·nies** : an animal whose father is a horse and whose mother is a donkey

¹hint \'hint\ *n* **1** : a suggestion made in an indirect or concise manner ⟨helpful *hints* for new students⟩ **2** : a slight indication ⟨a *hint* of spring⟩ **3** : a very small amount

²hint *vb* : to bring to mind by or give a hint

hin·ter·land \'hint-ər-,land\ *n* **1** : a region behind a coast **2** : a region remote from cities

hip \'hip\ *n* : the part of the body that curves out below the waist on each side

hip·po·pot·a·mus \,hip-ə-'pät-ə-məs\ *n, pl* **hip·po·pot·a·mus·es** *or* **hip·po·pot·a·mi** \-,mī\ [from Greek *hippopotamos*, a compound of *hippos* "horse" and *potamos* "river"] : a large herbivorous hoglike animal with thick hairless skin that lives in African rivers

¹hire \'hīr\ *n* **1** : money paid for wages or rental price ⟨a laborer worthy of his *hire*⟩ **2** : the act of hiring ⟨a truck for *hire*⟩

²hire *vb* **hired**; **hir·ing** **1** : to employ for pay **2** : to obtain the temporary use of for pay **3** : to take employment ⟨*hired* out as a cook⟩

¹his \hiz, iz\ *adj* : of or relating to him or himself ⟨*his* desk⟩ ⟨*his* turn⟩

²his \'hiz\ *pron* : one or the one belonging to him : some or the ones belonging to him

¹hiss \'his\ *vb* **1** : to make a hiss ⟨a snake *hissed*⟩ **2** : to show dislike by hissing

²hiss *n* **1** : a sound made by drawing out the sound of the letter *s* usually as a sign of dislike or contempt **2** : a sound like a prolonged *s* sound ⟨the *hiss* of steam⟩

his·to·ri·an \his-'tōr-ē-ən\ *n* : a scholarly writer of histories

his·tor·ic \his-'tȯr-ik\ *adj* : famous in history : HISTORICAL ⟨*historic* event⟩

his·tor·i·cal \his-'tȯr-i-kəl\ *adj* **1** : of or relating to history : based on history ⟨*historical* writings⟩ **2** : known to be true ⟨*historical* fact⟩ — **his·tor·i·cal·ly** *adv*

his·to·ry \'his-tə-rē\ *n, pl* **his·to·ries** **1** : an account of events : NARRATIVE **2** : a written account of past events **3** : a branch of knowledge that records and explains past events **4** : the events that form the subject matter of a history : past events

¹hit \'hit\ *vb* **hit**; **hit·ting** **1** : to come or cause to come in contact with especially with force **2** : to strike or cause to strike something aimed at ⟨the arrow *hit* the target⟩ **3** : to affect as if by a blow ⟨*hit* hard by the disappointment⟩ **4** : to come upon by chance or by searching ⟨*hit* upon the right answer⟩ **5** : REACH ⟨prices *hit* a new high⟩ — **hit·ter** *n*

²hit *n* **1** : BLOW **2** : COLLISION **3** : something very successful **4** : a batted baseball that enables the batter to reach base safely

¹hitch \'hich\ *vb* **1** : to move by jerks **2** : to fasten by or as if by a hook or knot **3** : HITCH-HIKE

²hitch *n* **1** : a jerky movement or pull ⟨gave his trousers a *hitch*⟩ **2** : an unexpected stop or obstacle ⟨plans went off without a *hitch*⟩ **3** : a knot used for a temporary fastening

hitch·hike \'hich-,hīk\ *vb* **hitch·hiked**; **hitch·hik·ing** : to travel by securing free rides from passing vehicles — **hitch·hik·er** *n*

hitches 3

hith·er \'hith-ər\ *adv* : to this place

hith·er·to \'hith-ər-,tü\ *adv* : up to this time

hive \'hīv\ *n* **1** : a container for housing honeybees **2** : a colony of bees **3** : a center of activity : a large number of busy people

ho \'hō\ *interj* — used to express surprise, attract attention, or give warning

hive 1

¹hoard \'hōrd\ *n* : an accumulation usually of something of value put aside for safekeeping and often hidden

²hoard *vb* : to accumulate and store away — **hoard·er** *n*

hoar·frost \'hōr-,frȯst\ *n* : FROST 2

hoarse \'hōrs\ *adj* **hoars·er**; **hoars·est** **1** : harsh in sound **2** : having a rough grating voice — **hoarse·ly** *adv* — **hoarse·ness** *n*

hoar·y \'hōr-ē\ *adj* **hoar·i·er**; **hoar·i·est** : gray or white with age

¹hoax \'hōks\ *vb* : to trick into accepting as genuine something that is false

²hoax *n* **1** : an act intended to fool or deceive **2** : something false passed off as genuine

¹hob \'häb\ *n* : MISCHIEF, TROUBLE ⟨raise *hob*⟩

²hob *n* : a projection at the back or side of a fireplace on which something may be kept warm

¹hob·ble \'häb-əl\ *vb* **hob·bled**; **hob·bling** **1** : to walk with difficulty : LIMP **2** : to make movement difficult by tying the legs

²hobble *n* **1** : a limping walk **2** : something used to hobble an animal

hob·by \'häb-ē\ *n, pl* **hob·bies** : an interest or activity engaged in for relaxation

hob·by·horse \'häb-ē-,hȯrs\ *n* **1** : a stick with a horse's head on which children pretend to ride **2** : ROCKING HORSE **3** : a toy horse suspended by springs from a frame

hob·gob·lin \'häb-,gäb-lən\ *n* **1** : a mischievous elf or goblin **2** : BOGEY

hob·nail \'häb-,nāl\ *n* : a short large-headed

nail used to stud soles of heavy shoes as a protection against wear — **hob·nailed** \-,nāld\ *adj*

ho·bo \'hō-bō\ *n, pl* **ho·boes** : TRAMP

hock·ey \'häk-ē\ *n* : a game played on ice or in a field by two teams who try to drive a puck or ball through a goal by hitting it with a curved stick

hod \'häd\ *n* **1** : a long-handled wooden tray or trough used to carry mortar or bricks **2** : a bucket for holding or carrying coal

hodge·podge \'häj-,päj\ *n* : MIXTURE, JUMBLE

hod 1

¹hoe \'hō\ *n* : a long-handled tool with a thin flat blade used for weeding and hilling

²hoe *vb* **hoed**; **hoe·ing** : to weed or loosen the soil around plants with a hoe

¹hog \'hòg, 'häg\ *n* : an adult domestic swine

²hog *vb* **hogged**; **hog·ging** : to take more than one's share

ho·gan \'hō-,gän\ *n* : an earth-covered dwelling of some American Indians

hog·gish \'hòg-ish, 'häg-\ *adj* : SELFISH, GREEDY — **hog·gish·ly** *adv* — **hog·gish·ness** *n*

hogan

hogs·head \'hògz-,hed, 'hägz-\ *n* **1** : a very large cask **2** : a unit of liquid measure equal to sixty-three gallons

¹hoist \'hòist\ *vb* : to lift up especially with a pulley : RAISE

²hoist *n* **1** : LIFT, BOOST **2** : a lifting apparatus especially for heavy loads

¹hold \'hōld\ *vb* **held** \'held\; **hold·ing** **1** : to have or keep in one's possession or under one's control ⟨*hold* a fort⟩ ⟨*hold* territory⟩ **2** : to impose restraint upon : limit in motion or action ⟨*hold* the dogs⟩ **3** : to bind legally or morally ⟨*hold* a man responsible for his actions⟩ **4** : to have or keep in the grasp ⟨*hold* a book⟩ **5** : SUPPORT ⟨a floor that will *hold* ten tons⟩ **6** : to receive and retain : CONTAIN ⟨a jar that *holds* a quart⟩ **7** : to have in mind ⟨*hold* opposing opinions⟩ **8** : CONSIDER, REGARD **9** : to carry on by group action ⟨*hold* a meeting⟩ **10** : to continue in the same way or state : LAST ⟨believes the good weather will *hold*⟩ **11** : to keep a connection with something : remain fastened ⟨the anchor *held* in the rough sea⟩ **12** : to bear or carry oneself

²hold *n* **1** : the act or manner of holding : GRIP **2** : INFLUENCE, POWER **3** : a prolonged note or rest in music

³hold *n* **1** : the part of a ship below decks where the cargo is stored **2** : the cargo compartment of an airplane

hold·er \'hōl-dər\ *n* : one that holds

hold·up \'hōld-,əp\ *n* **1** : a robbery at the point of a gun **2** : DELAY

hole \'hōl\ *n* **1** : an opening into or through something **2** : HOLLOW, CAVITY **3** : DEN, BURROW — **in the hole** : in debt

hol·i·day \'häl-ə-,dā\ *n* **1** : a day of freedom from work especially when observed in commemoration of an event **2** : VACATION

ho·li·ness \'hō-lē-nəs\ *n* **1** : the quality or state of being holy **2** — used as a title for various high religious dignitaries ⟨His *Holiness* the Pope⟩

¹hol·ler \'häl-ər\ *vb* : to cry out : SHOUT

²holler *n* : SHOUT, CRY

¹hol·low \'häl-ō\ *adj* **1** : curved inward : SUNKEN **2** : having a hole inside : not solid throughout **3** : sounding like a sound made in an empty place ⟨a *hollow* roar⟩ **4** : not sincere — **hol·low·ly** *adv* — **hol·low·ness** *n*

²hollow *vb* : to make or become hollow

³hollow *n* **1** : a low spot in a surface ⟨*hollow* of the hand⟩ **2** : VALLEY **3** : CAVITY

hol·ly \'häl-ē\ *n, pl* **hol·lies** : an evergreen tree or shrub with prickly-edged shiny leaves and red berries much used for Christmas decorations

holly: leaves and berries

hol·ly·hock \'häl-ē-,häk\ *n* : a tall leafy-stemmed plant having large rounded leaves and spikelike clusters of showy flowers

hol·o·caust \'häl-ə-,kòst\ *n* [from Greek *holokauston*, literally, "something burnt whole", a compound of *holos* "whole" and *kaustos* "burnt", which is also the source of English *caustic*] : a thorough destruction especially by fire

hol·ster \'hōl-stər\ *n* : a leather case for a pistol usually worn at the belt or attached to a saddle

ho·ly \'hō-lē\ *adj* **ho·li·er**; **ho·li·est** **1** : set apart for the service of God or of a divine being : SACRED, HALLOWED ⟨a *holy* temple⟩ ⟨a *holy* day⟩ **2** : commanding complete devotion **3** : spiritually pure

holster

hom- *or* **homo-** *prefix* : one and the same : similar : alike ⟨*homo*graph⟩

hom·age \'häm-ij\ *n* **1** : a feudal ceremony by which a man pledges allegiance to a lord and becomes his vassal **2** : RESPECT, HONOR

¹home \'hōm\ *n* **1** : the house in which one lives or in which one's family lives **2** : one's native place **3** : HABITAT **4** : a place for the care of persons unable to care for themselves **5** : the social unit formed by a family living together **6** : a dwelling house ⟨new *homes* for sale⟩ **7** : the goal or point to be reached in some games — **home·less** \-ləs\ *adj*

²home *adv* **1** : to or at home **2** : to the place where it belongs ⟨drive a nail *home*⟩

home·land \'hōm-,land\ *n* : native land

home·like \'hōm-,līk\ *adj* : resembling a home (as in coziness or wholesomeness)

home·ly \'hōm-lē\ *adj* **home·li·er; home·li·est 1** : PLAIN, SIMPLE **2** : not handsome

home·made \'hōm-'mād\ *adj* : made in the home or on the premises ⟨*homemade* bread⟩

home·mak·er \'hōm-,mā-kər\ *n* : one who manages a household especially as a wife and mother — **home·mak·ing** \-,mā-king\ *n or adj*

home plate *n* : the base that a baseball runner must touch to score

hom·er \'hō-mər\ *n* : HOME RUN

home·room \'hōm-,rüm, -,rùm\ *n* : a schoolroom where pupils of the same class report at the opening of school

home run *n* : a hit in baseball that enables the batter to go around all the bases and score

home·sick \'hōm-,sik\ *adj* : longing for home — **home·sick·ness** *n*

¹home·spun \'hōm-,spən\ *adj* **1** : spun or made at home **2** : made of homespun **3** : SIMPLE, HOMELY ⟨*homespun* humor⟩

²homespun *n* : a loosely woven usually woolen or linen fabric originally made from homespun yarn

¹home·stead \'hōm-,sted\ *n* **1** : a home and the land around it **2** : a tract of land acquired from United States public lands by filing a record and living on and cultivating it

²homestead *vb* : to acquire or settle as a homestead under a homestead law

home·stead·er \'hōm-,sted-ər\ *n* : one who holds a homestead especially under laws (**homestead laws**) authorizing the sale of public lands in parcels of one hundred sixty acres to settlers

home·stretch \'hōm-'strech\ *n* **1** : the last part of a racecourse **2** : a final stage

home·ward \'hōm-wərd\ *or* **home·wards** \-wərdz\ *adv* (*or adj*) : toward home

home·work \'hōm-,wərk\ *n* : work (as school lessons) to be done at home

hom·ey \'hō-mē\ *adj* **hom·i·er; hom·i·est** : COZY — **hom·ey·ness** *or* **hom·i·ness** *n*

hom·i·cide \'häm-ə-,sīd\ *n* : a killing of one human being by another

hom·ing pigeon \,hō-ming-\ *n* : a racing pigeon trained to return home

hom·i·ny \'häm-ə-nē\ *n* : hulled corn with the germ removed

ho·mo \'hō-mō\ *n* : MAN 4

homo- — see HOM-

ho·mog·e·nize \hō-'mäj-ə-,nīz\ *vb* **ho·mog·e·nized; ho·mog·e·niz·ing** : to reduce the particles in (as milk or paint) to uniform size and distribute them evenly throughout the liquid

hom·o·graph \'häm-ə-,graf\ *n* : one of two or more words spelled alike but different in meaning or origin or pronunciation ⟨the noun *conduct* and the verb *conduct* are *homographs*⟩

hom·o·nym \'häm-ə-,nim\ *n* **1** : HOMOPHONE **2** : HOMOGRAPH **3** : one of two or more words spelled and pronounced alike but different in meaning ⟨the noun *quail* and the verb *quail* are *homonyms*⟩

hom·o·phone \'häm-ə-,fōn\ *n* : one of two or more words pronounced alike but different in meaning or origin or spelling ⟨*to, too,* and *two* are *homophones*⟩

hone \'hōn\ *vb* **honed; hon·ing** : to sharpen with or as if with a fine abrasive stone

hon·est \'än-əst\ *adj* **1** : free from fraud or deception : REAL ⟨an *honest* plea⟩ **2** : being fair and straightforward : TRUSTWORTHY, TRUTHFUL **3** : OPEN, FRANK — **hon·est·ly** *adv*

hon·es·ty \'än-əs-tē\ *n* : fairness and straightforwardness in conduct or speech

hon·ey \'hən-ē\ *n* **1** : a sweet sticky fluid made by bees from the liquid drawn from flowers **2** : something superlative ⟨a *honey* of a coat⟩ **3** : SWEETNESS

hon·ey·bee \'hən-ē-,bē\ *n* : a bee whose honey is used by man as food

¹hon·ey·comb \'hən-ē-,kōm\ *n* **1** : a mass of wax cells built by honeybees in their nest to contain young bees and stores of honey **2** : something resembling a honeycomb in structure or appearance

honeybee

²honeycomb *vb* : to make or become full of holes like a honeycomb

hon·ey·dew \'hən-ē-,dü, -,dyü\ *n* : a sweet liquid given off by plant lice and eaten by ants

¹hon·ey·moon \'hən-ē-,mün\ *n* **1** : a holiday taken by a newly married couple **2** : a period of harmony especially just after marriage

²honeymoon *vb* : to have a honeymoon — **hon·ey·moon·er** *n*

hon·ey·suck·le \'hən-ē-,sək-əl\ *n* : a climbing vine or a bush with tube-shaped and fragrant white, yellow, or red flowers

¹honk \'hängk\ *n* **1** : the cry of a goose **2** : a sound resembling the cry of a goose ⟨the *honk* of a horn⟩

²honk *vb* : to make a honk

honeysuckle

¹hon·or \'än-ər\ *n* **1** : good name : public esteem **2** : outward respect : RECOGNITION ⟨a dinner in *honor* of a new coach⟩ **3** : PRIVILEGE **4** : a person of superior standing — used especially as a title ⟨His *Honor* the Mayor⟩ **5** : a person whose worth brings respect or fame ⟨an *honor* to his profession⟩ **6** : an evidence or symbol of distinction **7** : excellence of character : ethical conduct

²honor *vb* **1** : RESPECT ⟨*honor* your parents⟩ **2** : to confer honor on

hon·or·a·ble \'än-ə-rə-bəl\ *adj* **1** : accompanied with marks of honor ⟨an *honorable* burial⟩ **2** : doing credit to the possessor **3** : ETHICAL, UPRIGHT — **hon·or·a·bly** \-blē\ *adv*

hon·or·ary \'än-ə-ˌrer-ē\ *adj* : given or done as an honor ⟨an *honorary* office⟩

¹hood \'hùd\ *n* **1** : a covering for the head and neck and sometimes the face **2** : something that resembles a hood **3** : the movable covering for an automobile engine

²hood *vb* : to cover with a hood : HIDE — **hood·ed** \'hùd-əd\ *adj*

-hood \ˌhùd\ *n suffix* **1** : state : condition : quality : character ⟨boy*hood*⟩ ⟨hardi*hood*⟩ ⟨false*hood*⟩ **2** : individuals sharing a specified state or character ⟨brother*hood*⟩

hood·lum \'hüd-ləm\ *n* **1** : THUG **2** : a young ruffian

hood·wink \'hùd-ˌwingk\ *vb* : to deceive by false appearance

hoof \'hùf, 'hüf\ *n, pl* **hooves** \'hùvz, 'hüvz\ *or* **hoofs** **1** : a covering of horn that protects the ends of the toes of some animals (as horses, oxen, or swine) **2** : a hoofed foot especially of a horse

hoofed \'hùft, 'hüft\ *adj* : having hoofs

¹hook \'hùk\ *n* **1** : a curved device (as a piece of bent metal) for catching, holding, or pulling something **2** : something that resembles a hook especially in shape — **by hook or by crook** : by any means : fairly or unfairly

hook 1

²hook *vb* **1** : to bend in the shape of a hook **2** : to catch or fasten with a hook ⟨*hook* a fish⟩

hook·worm \'hùk-ˌwərm\ *n* : a small worm that lives in the bowel and makes people sick by sucking their blood

hoop \'hùp, 'hüp\ *n* **1** : a circular strip used for holding together the staves of a barrel or tub or as a plaything **2** : a circular figure or object ⟨embroidery *hoops*⟩ **3** : a circle or framework of circles of flexible material (as wire) used for expanding a woman's skirt

¹hoot \'hüt\ *vb* **1** : to utter a loud shout usually in contempt **2** : to make the natural throat noise of an owl or a similar cry **3** : to express by hoots ⟨*hooted* disapproval⟩

²hoot *n* **1** : a sound of hooting **2** : a very small amount ⟨doesn't care a *hoot*⟩

¹hop \'häp\ *vb* **hopped; hop·ping** **1** : to move by short quick jumps **2** : to jump on one foot **3** : to jump over ⟨*hop* a puddle⟩ **4** : to get aboard by or as if by hopping ⟨*hop* a bus⟩ **5** : to make a quick trip especially by air

²hop *n* **1** : an instance of hopping **2** : DANCE **3** : a short trip especially by air

³hop *n* **1** : a twining vine whose greenish flowers look like cones **2** *pl* : the dried flowers of the hop plant used chiefly in making beer and ale and in medicine

hops

¹hope \'hōp\ *vb* **hoped; hop·ing** : to desire especially with anticipation that the wish will be fulfilled

²hope *n* **1** : TRUST, RELIANCE **2** : desire accompanied by expectation of fulfillment **3** : a source of hope **4** : something hoped for

hope·ful \'hōp-fəl\ *adj* **1** : full of hope **2** : PROMISING — **hope·ful·ly** *adv* — **hope·ful·ness** *n*

hope·less \'hōp-ləs\ *adj* **1** : having no hope ⟨*hopeless* about the future⟩ **2** : offering no hope — **hope·less·ly** *adv* — **hope·less·ness** *n*

hop·per \'häp-ər\ *n* **1** : one that hops **2** : an insect that moves by leaping **3** : a usually funnel-shaped chute or box for delivering material (as grain or coal) into a machine or a bin **4** : a tank holding liquid and having a device for releasing its contents through a pipe

hop·scotch \'häp-ˌskäch\ *n* : a game in which a player tosses a stone into areas of a figure drawn on the ground and hops through the figure and back to regain the stone

horde \'hōrd\ *n* **1** : a nomadic people or tribe **2** : MULTITUDE, SWARM ⟨a *horde* of ants⟩

ho·ri·zon \hə-'rīz-n\ *n* **1** : the line where the earth or sea seems to meet the sky **2** : the range of a person's outlook or experience

¹hor·i·zon·tal \ˌhòr-ə-'zänt-l\ *adj* : parallel to the horizon : LEVEL — **hor·i·zon·tal·ly** *adv*

²horizontal *n* : something (as a line or plane) that is horizontal

horn \'hòrn\ *n* **1** : one of the hard bony growths on the head of hoofed animals (as cattle, goats, or sheep) **2** : the material of which horns are composed or a similar material ⟨a *horn*-handled knife⟩ **3** : something made from a horn ⟨a hunting *horn*⟩ **4** : something shaped like a horn **5** : a wind instrument somewhat like a horn in shape **6** : a usually electrical device that makes a noise like that of a horn — **horned** \ˈhȯrnd\ *adj* — **horn·less** \ˈhȯrn-ləs\ *adj* — **horn·like** \-ˌlīk\ *adj*

horn·book \ˈhȯrn-ˌbùk\ *n* : a child's primer consisting of a sheet of paper protected by a sheet of transparent horn

horned toad *n* : a small harmless lizard with scales and hornlike spines

hor·net \ˈhȯr-nət\ *n* : a large wasp that can give a severe sting

horn of plenty : CORNUCOPIA

horn·pipe \ˈhȯrn-ˌpīp\ *n* **1** : a lively folk dance of the British Isles **2** : a tune in the rhythm of a hornpipe

hornet

horn·y \ˈhȯr-nē\ *adj* **horn·i·er; horn·i·est 1** : made of or resembling horn **2** : having horns

hor·ri·ble \ˈhȯr-ə-bəl\ *adj* : marked by or arousing horror : TERRIBLE, DREADFUL — **hor·ri·bly** \-blē\ *adv*

hor·rid \ˈhȯr-əd\ *adj* **1** : HIDEOUS, SHOCKING **2** : REPULSIVE, OFFENSIVE — **hor·rid·ly** *adv*

hor·ri·fy \ˈhȯr-ə-ˌfī\ *vb* **hor·ri·fied; hor·ri·fy·ing** : to cause to feel horror

hor·ror \ˈhȯr-ər\ *n* **1** : painful and intense fear, dread, or dismay **2** : intense aversion **3** : the quality of inspiring horror **4** : something that inspires horror

horse \ˈhȯrs\ *n* **1** : a large hoofed mammal that feeds on grasses and is used as a work animal and for riding **2** : a frame that supports something (as wood while being cut) **3** : a piece of gymnasium equipment used for vaulting exercises **4 horse** *pl* : soldiers on horseback : CAVALRY — **horse·less** \-ləs\ *adj* — **from the horse's mouth** : from the original source

horse 3

¹horse·back \ˈhȯrs-ˌbak\ *n* : the back of a horse

²horseback *adv* : on horseback

horse·car \ˈhȯrs-ˌkär\ *n* **1** : a streetcar drawn by horses **2** : a car for transporting horses

horse chestnut *n* : a shiny brown nut that is unfit to eat and is the fruit of a tall tree with leaves divided into fingerlike parts and cone-shaped flower clusters

horse chestnut: leaves and blossoms

horse·fly \ˈhȯrs-ˌflī\ *n, pl* **horse·flies** : a large swift two-winged fly the females of which suck blood from animals

horse·hair \ˈhȯrs-ˌhaər\ *n* **1** : the hair of a horse especially from the mane or tail **2** : cloth made from horsehair

horse latitudes *n pl* : either of two regions in the neighborhoods of 30° north and 30° south of the equator marked by calms and light changeable winds

horse·man \ˈhȯrs-mən\ *n, pl* **horse·men** \-mən\ **1** : a horseback rider **2** : a person skilled in managing horses **3** : a breeder or raiser of horses — **horse·man·ship** \-ˌship\ *n*

horse opera *n* : a motion picture or radio or television play usually about western cowboys

horse·play \ˈhȯrs-ˌplā\ *n* : boisterous play

horse·pow·er \ˈhȯrs-ˌpaù-ər\ *n* : a unit of power that equals the work done in raising 550 pounds one foot in one second

horse·rad·ish \ˈhȯrs-ˌrad-ish\ *n* : a relish made from the pungent root of an herb of the mustard family

horse·shoe \ˈhȯrs-ˌshü\ *n* **1** : a protective iron plate that is nailed to the rim of a horse's hoof **2** : something shaped like a horseshoe **3** *pl* : a game in which horseshoes are tossed at a stake in the ground

horseshoes

horse·whip \ˈhȯrs-ˌhwip\ *vb* **horse·whipped; horse·whip·ping** : to flog with a whip made to be used on a horse

horse·wom·an \ˈhȯrs-ˌwùm-ən\ *n, pl* **horse·wom·en** \-ˌwim-ən\ : a woman skilled in riding horseback or in managing horses

hors·ey *or* **hors·y** \ˈhȯr-sē\ *adj* **hors·i·er; hors·i·est** : of or relating to horses or horsemen

ho·san·na \hō-ˈzan-ə\ *interj* — used as a cry of acclamation or adoration

¹hose \ˈhōz\ *n, pl* **hose** *or* **hos·es 1** *pl* **hose** : STOCKING, SOCK **2** : a flexible tube for carrying fluid

²hose *vb* **hosed; hos·ing** : to spray, water, or wash with a hose

ho·sier·y \ˈhō-zhə-rē\ *n* : STOCKINGS, SOCKS

hos·pit·a·ble \häs-ˈpit-ə-bəl, ˈhäs-pit-\ *adj* **1** : generous and kindly in entertaining guests **2** : readily receptive to something new — **hos·pit·a·bly** \-blē\ *adv*

hos·pi·tal \ˈhäs-ˌpit-l\ *n* : a place where the sick and injured are cared for

hos·pi·tal·i·ty \ˌhäs-pə-ˈtal-ət-ē\ *n* : generous and kindly treatment of guests

hos·pi·tal·ize \ˈhäs-ˌpit-l-ˌīz\ *vb* **hos·pi·tal·ized; hos·pi·tal·iz·ing** : to place in a hospital for care and treatment — **hos·pi·tal·i·za·tion** \ˌhäs-ˌpit-l-ə-ˈzā-shən\ *n*

---

j job ng sing ō low ȯ moth ȯi coin th thin th this ü boot ù foot y you yü few yủ furious zh vision

¹host \'hōst\ *n* **1** : ARMY **2** : MULTITUDE

²host *n* : one who receives or entertains guests

³host *n, often cap* : the bread used in the Eucharist

hos·tage \'häs-tij\ *n* : a person given or held as a pledge that promises will be kept

hos·tel \'häst-l\ *n* **1** : INN **2** : a supervised lodging for use by young travelers

hos·tel·ry \'häst-l-rē\ *n, pl* **hos·tel·ries** : INN

host·ess \'hōs-təs\ *n* : a woman who acts as host (as in a restaurant)

hos·tile \'häst-l\ *adj* **1** : of or relating to an enemy **2** : showing ill will : UNFRIENDLY

hos·til·i·ty \häs-'til-ət-ē\ *n, pl* **hos·til·i·ties 1** : a hostile state, attitude, or action **2** *pl* : acts of warfare

hos·tler \'häs-lər\ *n* : one who takes care of horses (as at a stable)

hot \'hät\ *adj* **hot·ter; hot·test 1** : having a high temperature ⟨a *hot* stove⟩ ⟨a *hot* day⟩ **2** : ARDENT, FIERY ⟨a *hot* temper⟩ **3** : having or causing the sensation of an uncomfortable degree of body heat **4** : newly made or received ⟨*hot* news⟩ **5** : close to something sought **6** : suggestive of heat or of burning ⟨*hot* mustard⟩ **7** : RADIOACTIVE **8** : STOLEN ⟨*hot* jewels⟩ — **hot·ly** *adv* — **hot·ness** *n*

hot·bed \'hät-,bed\ *n* : a bed of heated earth in a glass-covered frame for growing tender plants early in the season

hot dog \'hät-,dȯg\ *n* : a cooked frankfurter usually served in a long split roll

ho·tel \hō-'tel\ *n* : a place that provides lodging and meals for the public : INN

hot·foot \'hät-,fu̇t\ *vb* : HURRY

hot·head·ed \'hät-'hed-əd\ *adj* : RASH, FIERY

hot·house \'hät-,hau̇s\ *n* : a heated glass-enclosed building for growing plants

hot plate \'hät-,plāt\ *n* : a simple often portable gas or electric heater

hot rod *n* : an automobile rebuilt for high speed and fast acceleration

hot water *n* : a distressing predicament

¹hound \'hau̇nd\ *n* : a dog with drooping ears and deep bark that is used in hunting and follows game by the sense of smell

²hound *vb* : to hunt or pursue relentlessly

hour \'au̇r\ *n* **1** : one of the twenty-four divisions of a day : sixty minutes **2** : the time of day **3** : a fixed or particular time **4** : a measure of distance reckoned by the amount of time it takes to cover it

hour·glass \'au̇r-,glas\ *n* : a device for measuring time in which sand runs from the upper into the lower part of a glass in an hour

hourglass

¹hour·ly \'au̇r-lē\ *adv* **1** : at or during every hour ⟨planes leaving *hourly*⟩ **2** : FREQUENTLY, CONTINUALLY

²hourly *adj* **1** : occurring every hour **2** : FREQUENT, CONTINUAL

¹house \'hau̇s\ *n, pl* **hous·es** \'hau̇-zəz\ **1** : a place built for human inhabitants **2** : something (as a nest or den) used by an animal for shelter **3** : a building in which something is stored ⟨tool *house*⟩ **4** : HOUSEHOLD **5** : FAMILY ⟨the ' *house* of Windsor⟩ **6** : a body of persons assembled to make the laws for a country ⟨two *houses* of the United States Congress⟩ **7** : a business firm **8** : the audience in a theater or concert hall

²house \'hau̇z\ *vb* **1** : to provide with living quarters or shelter **2** : CONTAIN

house·boat \'hau̇s-,bōt\ *n* : a barge fitted for use as a dwelling or for leisurely cruising

house·boy \'hau̇s-,bȯi\ *n* : a boy or man hired to act as a general household servant

house·fly \'hau̇s-,flī\ *n, pl* **house·flies** : a two-winged fly that is common about houses and often carries disease germs

housefly

¹house·hold \'hau̇s-,hōld\ *n* : all the persons who live as a family in one house

²household *adj* **1** : of or relating to a household **2** : FAMILIAR

house·hold·er \'hau̇s-,hōl-dər\ *n* : one who occupies a dwelling alone or as the head of a household

house·keep·er \'hau̇s-,kē-pər\ *n* : a woman employed to take care of a house

house·keep·ing \'hau̇s-,kē-ping\ *n* : the care and management of a house

house·moth·er \'hau̇s-,məth-ər\ *n* : a woman who acts as hostess, chaperon, and often housekeeper in a residence for young people

house·plant \'hau̇s-,plant\ *n* : a plant grown or kept indoors

house·top \'hau̇s-,täp\ *n* : ROOF

house·warm·ing \'hau̇s-,wȯr-ming\ *n* : a party to celebrate moving into a new home

house·wife \'hau̇s-,wīf\ *n, pl* **house·wives** \-,wīvz\ : a married woman in charge of a household

house·work \'hau̇s-,wərk\ *n* : the work of housekeeping

hous·ing \'hau̇-zing\ *n* **1** : SHELTER **2** : DWELLINGS ⟨*housing* for the aged⟩ **3** : ENCLOSURE ⟨a lamp *housing*⟩

hove *past of* HEAVE

hov·el \'həv-əl, 'häv-\ *n* : a small mean usually dirty house

hov·er \'həv-ər\ vb **1** : to hang fluttering in the air or on the wing **2** : to move to and fro near a place ⟨waiters *hovered* about⟩

how \'haù\ adv **1** : in what way : by what means ⟨study *how* plants grow⟩ **2** : for what reason ⟨*how* could he do such a thing⟩ **3** : to what degree, number, or amount ⟨wonder *how* much apples cost⟩ **4** : in what state or condition ⟨*how* are you⟩ — **how about** : what do you say to or think of ⟨*how about* that⟩

how·dah \'haùd-ə\ n : a usually covered seat for use on the back of an elephant

how·ev·er \haù-'ev-ər\ adv **1** : to whatever degree or extent **2** : in whatever way **3** : in spite of that syn see BUT

howdah

¹howl \'haùl\ vb **1** : to emit a loud long mournful sound characteristic of dogs ⟨wind *howling* through the trees⟩ **2** : to cry out loudly (as with pain)

²howl n **1** : a loud long mournful sound characteristic of dogs **2** : a long loud cry (as of distress, disappointment, or rage) **3** : COMPLAINT **4** : something that causes laughter

hub \'həb\ n **1** : the center of a wheel, propeller, or fan **2** : a center of activity

hub·bub \'həb-ˌəb\ n : UPROAR, DIN

huck·le·ber·ry \'hək-əl-ˌber-ē\ n, pl **huck·le·ber·ries** : a dark edible berry with bony seeds that is related to the blueberry

hub

huck·ster \'hək-stər\ n **1** : a person who sells goods along the street or from door to door **2** : a writer of advertising especially for radio or television

¹hud·dle \'həd-l\ vb **hud·dled**; **hud·dling** **1** : to crowd, push, or pile together ⟨people *huddled* in a doorway⟩ **2** : CONFER **3** : to curl up ⟨*huddled* by the fire⟩

²huddle n **1** : a closely packed group **2** : MEETING, CONFERENCE

hue \'hyü\ n **1** : COLOR ⟨flowers of every *hue*⟩ **2** : a shade or modification of a color

¹huff \'həf\ vb **1** : to emit puffs (as of air or steam) **2** : to behave indignantly ⟨*huffed* off in anger⟩ **3** : to make angry

²huff n : a fit of anger or resentment

huff·y \'həf-ē\ adj **huff·i·er**; **huff·i·est** **1** : easily offended : TOUCHY **2** : SULKY — **huff·i·ly** \'həf-ə-lē\ adv — **huff·i·ness** \'həf-ē-nəs\ n

¹hug \'həg\ vb **hugged**; **hug·ging** **1** : to clasp in the arms : EMBRACE **2** : to keep close to

²hug n : a close embrace

huge \'hyüj\ adj : very large : VAST, ENORMOUS

hulk \'həlk\ n **1** : a heavy clumsy ship **2** : a person or thing that is bulky or clumsy **3** : the remains of an old or wrecked ship

hulk·ing \'həl-king\ adj : HUSKY, MASSIVE

¹hull \'həl\ n **1** : the outside covering of a fruit or seed **2** : the frame or body of a ship or airship

²hull vb : to remove the hulls of — **hull·er** n

hul·la·ba·loo \'həl-ə-bə-ˌlü\ n, pl **hul·la·ba·loos** : a confused noise : HUBBUB

¹hum \'həm\ vb **hummed**; **hum·ming** **1** : to utter a long *m*-like sound with the mouth closed **2** : to make the natural noise of an insect in motion **3** : to sing with closed lips **4** : to give forth a low murmur of sounds ⟨a street *humming* with activity⟩ **5** : to be busily active

²hum n : the act or an instance of humming

¹hu·man \'hyü-mən\ adj **1** : of, relating to, being, or characteristic of man **2** : having human form or characteristics

syn HUMAN, HUMANE both refer to whatever relates or belongs to mankind. HUMAN applies to whatever is characteristic of people in general ⟨*human* emotions⟩ HUMANE applies to an attitude of sympathy and compassion thought of as typical of mankind at its highest level ⟨*humane* treatment of prisoners⟩

²human n : a human being

hu·mane \hyü-'mān\ adj : KIND, SYMPATHETIC ⟨a *humane* judge⟩ syn see HUMAN — **hu·mane·ly** adv — **hu·mane·ness** n

¹hu·man·i·tar·i·an \hyü-ˌman-ə-'ter-ē-ən\ n : a person who promotes human welfare and social reform

²humanitarian adj : of, relating to, or characteristic of humanitarians

hu·man·i·ty \hyü-'man-ət-ē\ n, pl **hu·man·i·ties** **1** : KINDNESS, SYMPATHY **2** : the quality or state of being human **3** pl : the branches of learning having primarily a cultural character **4** : the human race : MANKIND

hu·man·ly \'hyü-mən-lē\ adv **1** : within the range of human capacity ⟨a task not *humanly* possible⟩ **2** : in a human manner

¹hum·ble \'həm-bəl\ adj **hum·bler**; **hum·blest** [from Old French *humble*, there taken from Latin *humilis* "low", "humble", derived from *humus* "earth"] **1** : not bold or proud : MODEST **2** : expressing a spirit of deference ⟨*humble* apologies⟩ **3** : low in rank or condition : LOWLY — **hum·bly** \-blē\ adv

²humble vb **hum·bled**; **hum·bling** **1** : to make humble **2** : to destroy the power of

¹hum·bug \'həm-ˌbəg\ n **1** : FRAUD, SHAM **2** : NONSENSE

²humbug vb **hum·bugged**; **hum·bug·ging** : DECEIVE ⟨was *humbugged* into believing it⟩

---

j job   ng sing   ō low   ȯ moth   ȯi coin   th thin   th̲ this   ü boot   u̇ foot   y you   yü few   yu̇ furious   zh vision

hum·ding·er \'həm-'ding-ər\ *n* : something of striking excellence

hum·drum \'həm-,drəm\ *adj* : MONOTONOUS

hu·mid \'hyü-məd\ *adj* : DAMP ⟨*humid* day⟩

hu·mid·i·fy \hyü-'mid-ə-,fī\ *vb* **hu·mid·i·fied**; **hu·mid·i·fy·ing** : to make (as the air of a room) humid — **hu·mid·i·fi·er** *n*

hu·mid·i·ty \hyü-'mid-ət-ē\ *n, pl* **hu·mid·i·ties** 1 : DAMPNESS, MOISTURE 2 : the amount of moisture in the air

hu·mil·i·ate \hyü-'mil-ē-,āt\ *vb* **hu·mil·i·at·ed**; **hu·mil·i·at·ing** : to lower the pride or self≈ respect of : HUMBLE **syn** see EMBARRASS

hu·mil·i·a·tion \hyü-,mil-ē-'ā-shən\ *n* 1 : the state of being humiliated 2 : an instance of being humiliated

hu·mil·i·ty \hyü-'mil-ət-ē\ *n* : MEEKNESS

hum·ming·bird \'həm-ing-,bərd\ *n* : a very small brilliantly colored American bird whose wings make a humming sound in flight

hum·mock \'həm-ək\ *n* 1 : a rounded mound of earth : KNOLL 2 : a ridge or pile of ice — **hum·mock·y** *adj*

¹**hu·mor** \'hyü-mər\ *n* 1 : state of mind : MOOD 2 : the amusing side of things ⟨the *humor* of a situation⟩ 3 : the faculty to see or tell the amusing side of things

²**humor** *vb* : to comply with the wishes of

hu·mor·ist \'hyü-mə-rəst\ *n* : a person who writes or talks with humor

hu·mor·ous \'hyü-mə-rəs\ *adj* : full of humor : FUNNY — **hu·mor·ous·ly** *adv*

hump \'həmp\ *n* 1 : a rounded bulge or lump (as on the back of a camel) 2 : a difficult part (as of an undertaking) — **humped** \'həmpt\ *adj*

hump·back \'həmp-,bak\ *n* 1 : a humped back 2 : HUNCHBACK 2 — **hump·backed** \-'bakt\ *adj*

hu·mus \'hyü-məs\ *n* : the dark rich part of earth formed by decaying matter

¹**hunch** \'hənch\ *vb* 1 : to thrust oneself forward by jerks 2 : to take a bent or crooked posture 3 : to thrust into a hump

²**hunch** *n* 1 : PUSH 2 : HUMP 3 : a strong feeling about what will happen : INTUITION

hunch·back \'hənch-,bak\ *n* 1 : HUMPBACK 1 2 : a person with a humped or crooked back

¹**hun·dred** \'hən-drəd\ *n* 1 : ten times ten 2 : a very large number ⟨*hundreds* of times⟩

²**hundred** *adj* : being 100

¹**hun·dredth** \'hən-drədth\ *adj* : being next after the ninety-ninth

²**hundredth** *n* : number 100 in a series

hung *past of* HANG

¹**hun·ger** \'həng-gər\ *n* 1 : a desire or a need for food 2 : a strong desire

²**hunger** *vb* 1 : to feel or suffer hunger 2 : to have a strong desire

hun·gry \'həng-grē\ *adj* **hun·gri·er**; **hun·gri·est** 1 : feeling or showing hunger 2 : having a strong desire — **hun·gri·ly** \-grə-lē\ *adv*

hunk \'həngk\ *n* : a large lump or piece

¹**hunt** \'hənt\ *vb* 1 : to pursue for food or as a sport ⟨*hunt* deer⟩ 2 : to try to find

²**hunt** *n* 1 : an act, practice, or instance of hunting 2 : a group of persons engaged in hunting

hunt·er \'hənt-ər\ *n* 1 : a person who hunts game 2 : a dog or horse used or trained for hunting 3 : a person who searches for something ⟨a bargain *hunter*⟩

hunts·man \'hənts-mən\ *n, pl* **hunts·men** \-mən\ : HUNTER 1

¹**hur·dle** \'hərd-l\ *n* 1 : a movable frame (as of woven twigs) for enclos- ing land or livestock 2 : a barrier to be jumped in a race (**hur·dles**) 3 : OBSTACLE

²**hurdle** *vb* **hur·dled**; **hur·dling** 1 : to leap over while running 2 : OVERCOME ⟨difficulties to be *hurdled*⟩

hurdle 2

hur·dy–gur·dy \,hərd- -ē-'gərd-ē\ *n, pl* **hur·dy–gur- dies** : a musical instrument in which the sound is produced by turning a crank

hurl \'hərl\ *vb* : to throw violently : FLING

hur·rah \hə-'rȯ, -'rä\ *interj* — used to express joy, triumph, or approval

hur·ri·cane \'hər-ə-,kān, 'hər-i-kən\ *n* : a violent windstorm that originates over the sea in warm climates, blows about a center of low pressure, has winds seventy-three miles per hour or greater, and is usually accompanied by rain, thunder, and lightning

hur·ried \'hər-ēd\ *adj* 1 : going or working with speed : FAST ⟨the *hurried* life of the city⟩ 2 : done in a hurry — **hur·ried·ly** *adv*

¹**hur·ry** \'hər-ē\ *vb* **hur·ried**; **hur·ry·ing** 1 : to carry or cause to go with haste 2 : to move or act with haste 3 : to speed up ⟨*hurried* the repair job⟩

²**hurry** *n, pl* **hur·ries** : a state of eagerness or urgency : extreme haste **syn** see HASTE

¹**hurt** \'hərt\ *vb* **hurt**; **hurt·ing** 1 : to feel or cause pain 2 : to do harm to : DAMAGE 3 : DIS- TRESS, OFFEND 4 : HAMPER

²**hurt** *n* 1 : a bodily injury or wound 2 : SUF- FERING, ANGUISH ⟨his sympathy eased her *hurt*⟩ 3 : HARM, WRONG — **hurt·ful** \-fəl\ *adj*

hur·tle \'hərt-l\ *vb* **hur·tled**; **hur·tling** 1 : to rush suddenly or violently ⟨rocks *hurtled* down the hill⟩ 2 : to drive or throw violently

¹hus·band \'həz-bənd\ *n* : a married man

²husband *vb* : to manage with thrift : use carefully ⟨*husbanded* his money and resources⟩

hus·band·ry \'həz-bən-drē\ *n* **1** : the management or wise use of resources : THRIFT **2** : FARMING, AGRICULTURE

¹hush \'həsh\ *vb* : to make or become quiet, calm, or still : SOOTHE ⟨*hush* a baby⟩

²hush *n* : STILLNESS, QUIET

hush–hush \'həsh-,həsh\ *adj* : SECRET, CONFIDENTIAL

¹husk \'həsk\ *n* : the outer covering of a fruit or seed (as of corn, grain, or coconuts)

²husk *vb* : to strip the husk from — **husk·er** *n*

husk·ing \'həs-king\ *n* : a gathering of farm families to husk corn

¹husk·y \'həs-kē\ *adj* **husk·i·er; husk·i·est** : HOARSE — **husk·i·ly** \-kə-lē\ *adv* — **husk·i·ness** \-kē-nəs\ *n*

²husky *adj* **husk·i·er; husk·i·est** : BURLY, ROBUST — **husk·i·ness** *n*

³husky *n, pl* **husk·ies** : one that is husky

⁴hus·ky \'həs-kē\ *n, pl* **hus·kies** : a strong thick-coated dog used to pull sleds in the arctic

¹hus·tle \'həs-əl\ *vb* **hus·tled; hus·tling** **1** : to push, crowd, or force forward roughly ⟨*hustled* the prisoner to jail⟩ **2** : HURRY

²hustle *n* : energetic activity

hus·tler \'həs-lər\ *n* : an energetic person who works fast

hut \'hət\ *n* : a small rude and often temporary dwelling

hutch \'həch\ *n* **1** : a chest or compartment for storage **2** : a low cupboard usually surmounted with open shelves **3** : a pen or coop for an animal **4** : HUT, SHACK

hy·a·cinth \'hī-ə-sinth\ *n* : a plant of the lily family with spikes of fragrant bell-shaped flowers

¹hy·brid \'hī-brəd\ *n* **1** : an animal or plant whose parents differ in some hereditary characteristic or belong to different groups (as breeds, races, or species) **2** : something of mixed origin or composition

hyacinth

²hybrid *adj* : of or relating to a hybrid : of mixed origin

hydr- *or* **hydro-** *prefix* **1** : water ⟨*hydr*ous⟩ ⟨*hydro*electric⟩ **2** : hydrogen ⟨*hydro*carbon⟩

hy·drant \'hī-drənt\ *n* **1** : a pipe with a spout through which water may be drawn from the main pipes ⟨a fire *hydrant*⟩ **2** : FAUCET

hy·drau·lic \hī-'drȯ-lik\ *adj* **1** : operated, moved, or brought about by means of water **2** : operated by liquid forced through a small

hole or through a tube ⟨*hydraulic* brakes⟩ — **hy·drau·li·cal·ly** \-li-kə-lē\ *adv*

hy·dro·car·bon \,hī-drə-'kär-bən\ *n* : a substance containing only carbon and hydrogen

hy·dro·chlo·ric acid \,hī-drə-,klȯr-ik-\ *n* : a strong liquid formed by dissolving in water a gas made up of hydrogen and chlorine

hy·dro·e·lec·tric \,hī-drō-i-'lek-trik\ *adj* : relating to or used in the making of electricity by waterpower

hy·dro·gen \'hī-drə-jən\ *n* : a colorless, odorless, and tasteless flammable gas that is the lightest of the chemical elements

hydrogen bomb *n* : a bomb whose great power is due to the sudden release of energy when the central portions of hydrogen atoms unite

hydrogen per·ox·ide \,hī-drə-jən-pə-'räk-,sīd\ *n* : a liquid containing hydrogen and oxygen used for bleaching and as an antiseptic

hy·dro·pho·bi·a \,hī-drə-'fō-bē-ə\ *n* : a deadly disease of dogs and some other animals that may be passed on to a person by the bite of an infected animal : RABIES

hy·dro·plane \'hī-drə-,plān\ *n* **1** : a speedboat whose hull is wholly or partly raised as it glides over the water **2** : SEAPLANE

hy·e·na \hī-'ē-nə\ *n* : a large flesh-eating mammal of Asia and Africa

hy·giene \'hī-,jēn\ *n* **1** : a science that deals with the bringing about and preservation of good health in the individual and the group **2** : conditions or practices essential to health

hy·gi·en·ic \,hī-jē-'en-ik, hī-'jen-ik\ *adj* : of, relating to, or conducive to health or hygiene — **hy·gi·en·i·cal·ly** \-i-kə-lē\ *adv*

hy·gien·ist \hī-'jē-nəst\ *n* : a person skilled in hygiene and especially in a specified branch of hygiene ⟨dental *hygienist*⟩

hy·gro·graph \'hī-grə-,graf\ *n* : an instrument for recording automatically variations in the humidity of the atmosphere

hy·grom·e·ter \hī-'gräm-ət-ər\ *n* : an instrument for measuring the humidity of the atmosphere

hying *pres part of* HIE

hymn \'him\ *n* : a song of praise especially to God

hym·nal \'him-nəl\ *n* : a book of hymns

hymn·book \'him-,bu̇k\ *n* : HYMNAL

hyper- *prefix* **1** : above : beyond : SUPER- ⟨*hyper*physical⟩ **2** : excessively ⟨*hyper*sensitive⟩ **3** : excessive ⟨*hyper*tension⟩

hy·per·sen·si·tive \,hī-pər-'sen-sət-iv\ *adj* : very sensitive ⟨*hypersensitive* to cold⟩

hy·pha \'hī-fə\ *n, pl* **hy·phae** \-,fē\ : one of the fine threads that make up the body of a fungus

¹hy·phen \'hī-fən\ *n* : a mark - used to divide or to compound words or word elements

²hyphen *vb* : to connect or mark with a hyphen

hy·phen·ate \'hī-fə-ˌnāt\ *vb* **hy·phen·at·ed; hy·phen·at·ing** : HYPHEN

hyp·no·tism \'hip-nə-ˌtiz-əm\ *n* : the act of putting a person or animal into a state resembling sleep in which he is responsive to suggestions of the hypnotizer

hyp·no·tist \'hip-nə-təst\ *n* : a person who practices hypnotism

hyp·no·tize \'hip-nə-ˌtīz\ *vb* **hyp·no·tized; hyp·no·tiz·ing** : to affect by or as if by hypnotism — **hyp·no·tiz·er** *n*

hy·po \'hī-pō\ *n* : a chemical used in photography to make an image permanent

hy·poc·ri·sy \hi-'päk-rə-sē\ *n, pl* **hy·poc·ri·sies** : a pretending to be what one is not or to believe or feel what one does not

hyp·o·crite \'hip-ə-ˌkrit\ *n* : a person who pretends to be something other than he is or better than he really is

hy·pot·e·nuse \hī-'pät-n-ˌüs, -ˌyüs\ *n* : the side of a right-angled triangle that is opposite the right angle

hy·poth·e·sis \hī-'päth-ə-səs\ *n, pl* **hy·poth·e·ses** \-ə-ˌsēz\ : something not proved but assumed to be true for purposes of argument or further study or investigation

hypotenuse

hy·po·thet·i·cal \ˌhī-pə-'thet-i-kəl\ *adj* **1**: ASSUMED **2** : of or depending on supposition — **hy·po·thet·i·cal·ly** *adv*

hys·ter·i·a \his-'ter-ē-ə\ *n* **1** : a nervous disorder marked by loss of control over the emotions **2** : a wild uncontrolled outburst of emotion (as fear) — **hys·ter·i·cal** \-'ter-i-kəl\ *adj* — **hys·ter·i·cal·ly** *adv*

hys·ter·ics \his-'ter-iks\ *n sing or pl* : a fit of uncontrollable laughter or crying : HYSTERIA

i \'ī\ *n, often cap* **1** : the ninth letter of the English alphabet **2** : the roman numeral 1 **3** : a grade rating a student's work as incomplete

I \ī\ *pron* : the person speaking or writing

-ial \ē-əl, yəl, əl\ *adj suffix* : ¹-AL ⟨aer*ial*⟩

-ian — see -AN

i·bex \'ī-ˌbeks\ *n* : a wild goat of the Old World having backward-curving horns

-ibility — see -ABILITY

i·bis \'ī-bəs\ *n* : a bird related to the herons but having a slender down-curved bill

-ible — see -ABLE

-ic \ik\ *adj suffix* **1** : of, relating to, or having the character or form of : being ⟨angel*ic*⟩ **2** : derived from, consisting of, or containing ⟨alcohol*ic*⟩ **3** : in the manner of : characteristic of ⟨Puritan*ic*⟩ **4** : associated or dealing with : utilizing ⟨electron*ic*⟩ **5** : characterized by : exhibiting : affected with ⟨allerg*ic*⟩

-i·cal \i-kəl\ *adj suffix* : -IC ⟨symmetr*ical*⟩

¹ice \'īs\ *n* **1** : frozen water **2** : a substance resembling ice **3** : a frozen dessert

²ice *vb* **iced; ic·ing 1** : to coat or become coated with ice : change into ice **2** : to chill or supply with ice **3** : to cover with icing

ice·berg \'īs-ˌbərg\ *n* : a large mass of ice that has been detached from a glacier and is floating in the sea

ice·boat \'īs-ˌbōt\ *n* : a boatlike frame on runners propelled on ice by sails

ice·bound \'īs-ˌbaund\ *adj* : surrounded or obstructed by ice ⟨an *icebound* river⟩

ice·box \'īs-ˌbäks\ *n* : a box which is kept cool by ice and in which food is kept

iceboat

ice·break·er \'īs-ˌbrā-kər\ *n* : a ship equipped to make and maintain a channel through ice

ice cap *n* : a large relatively level glacier flowing outward in all directions from its center

ice-cold \'īs-'kōld\ *adj* : extremely cold

ice cream *n* : a frozen food containing cream or butterfat, flavoring, sweetening, and usually eggs

ice·man \'īs-ˌman\ *n, pl* **ice·men** \-ˌmen\ : one who sells or delivers ice

ice sheet *n* : ICE CAP

ice-skate \'īs-ˌskāt\ *vb* : to skate on ice — **ice skat·er** *n*

i·ci·cle \'ī-ˌsik-əl\ *n* : a hanging mass of ice formed from dripping water

ic·ing \'ī-sing\ *n* : a coating for baked goods usually containing sugar and butter

i·con \'ī-ˌkän\ *n* : a religious image painted on a wood panel

-ics \iks\ *n sing or pl suffix* **1** : study : knowledge : skill : practice ⟨electron*ics*⟩ **2** : characteristic actions or qualities ⟨acrobat*ics*⟩

ic·y \'ī-sē\ *adj* **ic·i·er; ic·i·est 1** : covered with, full of, or consisting of ice ⟨*icy* roads⟩ **2** : intensely cold **3** : UNFRIENDLY — **ic·i·ly** \'ī-sə-lē\ *adv* — **ic·i·ness** \'ī-sē-nəs\ *n*

I'd\īd\ : I had : I should : I would

i·de·a \ī-'dē-ə\ *n* **1** : a plan of action : IN-TENTION ⟨his *idea* is to study law⟩ **2** : something imagined or pictured in the mind : NOTION **3** : a central meaning or purpose

¹**i·de·al** \ī-'dē-əl\ *adj* **1** : existing only in the mind **2** : PERFECT — **i·de·al·ly** *adv*

²**ideal** *n* **1** : a standard of perfection, beauty, or excellence **2** : a perfect type **3** : GOAL

i·de·al·ism \ī-'dē-ə-,liz-əm\ *n* **1** : the practice of forming or living according to ideals **2** : the ability or tendency to see things as one believes they should be rather than as they are

i·de·al·ist \ī-'dē-ə-ləst\ *n* : one guided by ideals

i·de·al·is·tic \ī-,dē-ə-'lis-tik\ *adj* : of or relating to ideals : practicing idealism

i·de·al·ize \ī-'dē-ə-,līz\ *vb* **i·de·al·ized; i·de·al·iz·ing** : to think of or represent as ideal

i·den·ti·cal \ī-'dent-i-kəl\ *adj* **1** : SAME **2** : being exactly alike or equal

syn IDENTICAL, EQUIVALENT, EQUAL refer to being alike in all or certain respects. IDENTICAL implies being exactly the same in all or all specified qualities ⟨all aspirin is *identical* in chemical composition⟩ EQUIVALENT refers to amounting to the same thing in significance or result ⟨she finds one of these pink pills *equivalent* to two aspirin tablets⟩ EQUAL implies being the same in some specific way, particularly in number or amount ⟨one aspirin tablet is *equal* to five grains⟩

i·den·ti·fi·ca·tion \ī-,dent-ə-fə-'kā-shən\ *n* **1** : an act of identifying : the state of being identified **2** : evidence of identity

i·den·ti·fy \ī-'dent-ə-,fī\ *vb* **i·den·ti·fied; i·den·ti·fy·ing** **1** : to regard as identical **2** : ASSO-CIATE **3** : to establish the identity of

i·den·ti·ty \ī-'dent-ət-ē\ *n, pl* **i·den·ti·ties** **1** : the fact or condition of being identical : SAMENESS **2** : INDIVIDUALITY **3** : the fact of being the same person or thing as one described or known to exist

id·i·o·cy \'id-ē-ə-sē\ *n, pl* **id·i·o·cies** **1** : extreme lack of intelligence **2** : something notably stupid or foolish

id·i·ot \'id-ē-ət\ *n* [from Latin *idiota* "ignorant person", from Greek *idiōtēs* meaning originally "a person in private life with no official position", then "one who is not an expert", and finally "ignorant person", from *idios* "one's own", "private"] **1** : a person of very low intelligence **2** : a silly or foolish person

id·i·ot·ic \,id-ē-'ät-ik\ *adj* : characterized by idiocy — **id·i·ot·i·cal·ly** \-i-kə-lē\ *adv*

¹**i·dle** \'īd-l\ *adj* **i·dler** \'īd-lər\; **i·dlest** \'īd-ləst\ **1** : not based on facts : WORTHLESS

2 : not employed **3** : LAZY — **i·dle·ness** \'īd-l-nəs\ *n* — **i·dly** \'īd-lē\ *adv*

²**idle** *vb* **i·dled** \'īd-ld\; **i·dling** \'īd-ling\ **1** : to spend time doing nothing : move idly **2** : to run without being connected for doing useful work **3** : WASTE — **i·dler** \'īd-lər\ *n*

i·dol \'īd-l\ *n* **1** : an image of a god used as an object of worship **2** : one that is very greatly loved and admired

i·dol·a·try \ī-'däl-ə-trē\ *n, pl* **i·dol·a·tries** **1** : the worship of a physical object as a god **2** : excessive attachment or devotion

i·dol·ize \'īd-l-,īz\ *vb* **i·dol·ized; i·dol·iz·ing** : to make an idol of : love or admire to excess

-ie *also* **-y** \ē\ *n suffix, pl* **-ies** : little one ⟨lass*ie*⟩

-ier — see -ER

if \if\ *conj* **1** : in the event that ⟨*if* it rains we'll stay home⟩ **2** : WHETHER ⟨see *if* he left⟩

-if·er·ous \'if-ə-rəs\ *adj suffix* : bearing : producing ⟨carbon*iferous*⟩

-i·fy \ə-,fī\ *vb suffix* **-i·fied; -i·fy·ing** : -FY

ig·loo \'ig-lü\ *n, pl* **ig·loos** : an Eskimo house often made of blocks of snow and in the shape of a dome

ig·ne·ous \'ig-nē-əs\ *adj* : formed by hardening of melted mineral matter ⟨*igneous* rock⟩

igloo

ig·nite \ig-'nīt\ *vb* **ig·nit·ed; ig·nit·ing** **1** : to set on fire : LIGHT **2** : to catch fire

ig·ni·tion \ig-'nish-ən\ *n* **1** : the act or action of igniting **2** : the process or means (as an electric spark) of igniting a fuel mixture

ig·no·ble \ig-'nō-bəl\ *adj* **1** : not of noble birth **2** : not honorable : BASE, MEAN ⟨an *ignoble* act⟩ — **ig·no·bly** \-blē\ *adv*

ig·no·rance \'ig-nə-rəns\ *n* : the state of being ignorant

ig·no·rant \'ig-nə-rənt\ *adj* **1** : having no knowledge or little knowledge : not educated **2** : UNAWARE **3** : resulting from or showing lack of knowledge — **ig·no·rant·ly** *adv*

syn IGNORANT, ILLITERATE, STUPID all refer to lack of knowledge or understanding. IG-NORANT suggests lack of education in general or in a particular subject but indicates no lack of intelligence ⟨completely *ignorant* of the principles of physics⟩ ILLITERATE is normally associated with ignorance in the area of language but may indicate anything from actual inability to read and write ⟨*illiterate* men unable to fill out applications⟩ to a lack of familiarity with literature ⟨can term *illiterate* those who haven't read Shakespeare⟩ STUPID suggests actual lack of intelligence and may be applied to those with as well as those without an education 〈the dogs seemed to be *stupid* because they had not been trained〉

ig·nore \ig-'nōr\ *vb* **ig·nored; ig·nor·ing** : to refuse to take notice of 〈*ignore* a rude remark〉

i·gua·na \i-'gwä-nə\ *n* : an extremely large tropical American lizard with a crest of erect scales along the back

i·kon *var of* ICON

il- — see IN-

¹ill \'il\ *adj* **worse** \'wərs\; **worst** \'wərst\ **1** : showing evil intention 〈*ill* deeds〉 **2** : causing suffering or distress 〈*ill* weather〉 **3** : not normal or sound 〈*ill* health〉 **4** : not in good health 〈an *ill* person〉 **5** : UNFORTUNATE, UNLUCKY 〈an *ill* omen〉 **6** : UNKIND : UNFRIENDLY 〈*ill* feeling〉 **7** : not right or proper

²ill *adv* **worse; worst** **1** : with displeasure 〈the remark was *ill* received〉 **2** : HARSHLY 〈*ill* treated〉 **3** : HARDLY, SCARCELY 〈can *ill* afford it〉 **4** : BADLY, POORLY 〈*ill* equipped〉

³ill *n* **1** : EVIL 〈for good or *ill*〉 **2** : SICKNESS **3** : TROUBLE **4** : something that expresses an unfavorable feeling

I'll \ī l\ : I shall : I will

ill–bred \'il-'bred\ *adj* : badly brought up

il·le·gal \i-'lē-gəl\ *adj* : not lawful — **il·le·gal·ly** *adv*

il·le·gal·i·ty \,il-ē-'gal-ət-ē\ *n* : the quality or state of being illegal

il·leg·i·ble \i-'lej-ə-bəl\ *adj* : not legible — **il·leg·i·bly** \-blē\ *adv*

il·le·git·i·mate \,il-i-'jit-ə-mət\ *adj* : not legitimate — **il·le·git·i·mate·ly** *adv*

il·lic·it \i-'lis-ət\ *adj* : not permitted : UNLAWFUL — **il·lic·it·ly** *adv*

il·lit·er·a·cy \i-'lit-ə-rə-sē\ *n* : the quality or state of being illiterate

¹il·lit·er·ate \i-'lit-ə-rət\ *adj* **1** : unable to read or write **2** : showing lack of education syn see IGNORANT — **il·lit·er·ate·ly** *adv*

²illiterate *n* : an illiterate person

ill–man·nered \'il-'man-ərd\ *adj* : not polite

ill–na·tured \'il-'nā-chərd\ *adj* : CROSS, SURLY — **ill–na·tured·ly** *adv*

ill·ness \'il-nəs\ *n* : SICKNESS

il·log·i·cal \i-'läj-i-kəl\ *adj* : not according to good reasoning — **il·log·i·cal·ly** *adv*

ill–tem·pered \'il-'tem-pərd\ *adj* : ILL-NATURED

ill–treat \'il-'trēt\ *vb* : to treat cruelly

ill–treat·ment \'il-'trēt-mənt\ *n* : cruel or improper treatment

il·lu·mi·nate \i-'lü-mə-,nāt\ *vb* il·lu·mi·nat-ed; il·lu·mi·nat·ing **1** : to supply or brighten with light : light up **2** : to make clear

il·lu·mi·na·tion \i-,lü-mə-'nā-shən\ *n* **1** : the action of illuminating : the state of being illuminated **2** : the quantity of light furnished

il·lu·mine \i-'lü-mən\ *vb* **il·lu·mined; il·lu·min·ing** : ILLUMINATE

ill–use \'il-'yüz\ *vb* : to use cruelly or badly

il·lu·sion \i-'lü-zhən\ *n* [meaning "the act of deceiving" in obsolete English, this came from Latin *illusio* "the act of mocking", from *illudere* "to mock at", a compound of the prefix *in-* "against" and *ludere* "to play", "to mock"] **1** : a misleading image presented to the eye **2** : the state or fact of being led to accept as true something unreal or imagined **3** : a mistaken idea

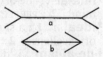

illusion: *a* is equal to *b* but seems longer

il·lu·sive \i-'lü-siv\ *adj* : ILLUSORY

il·lu·so·ry \i-'lü-sə-rē\ *adj* : based on or producing illusion : DECEPTIVE, UNREAL

il·lus·trate \'il-əs-,trāt\ *vb* **il·lus·trat·ed; il·lus·trat·ing** **1** : to explain or make clear (as by examples) **2** : to supply or decorate with pictures or diagrams **3** : to serve as an example

il·lus·tra·tion \,il-əs-'trā-shən\ *n* **1** : the action of illustrating : the condition of being illustrated **2** : an example or instance designed to make something clear **3** : a picture or diagram that explains or decorates

il·lus·tra·tive \i-'ləs-trət-iv\ *adj* : serving or designed to illustrate 〈*illustrative* examples〉

il·lus·tra·tor \'il-əs-,trāt-ər\ *n* : one that illustrates : an artist that makes illustrations

il·lus·tri·ous \i-'ləs-trē-əs\ *adj* : EMINENT

ill will *n* : unfriendly feeling

il·ly \'il-lē\ *adv* : BADLY, ILL 〈*illy* chosen〉

im- — see IN-

I'm \īm\ : I am

¹im·age \'im-ij\ *n* **1** : a likeness or imitation of a person or thing **2** : a picture of an object formed by a device (as a mirror or lens) **3** : a mental picture or conception : IMPRESSION, IDEA **4** : a person strikingly like another

²image *vb* **im·aged; im·ag·ing** **1** : to describe in vivid language **2** : REFLECT, MIRROR

i·mag·i·na·ble \i-'maj-ə-nə-bəl\ *adj* : capable of being imagined

i·mag·i·nary \i-'maj-ə-,ner-ē\ *adj* : existing only in imagination : not real

i·mag·i·na·tion \i-,maj-ə-'nā-shən\ *n* **1** : the act or power of forming a mental picture of something not present to the senses and especially of a person or situation one has not previously known **2** : creative ability **3** : a creation of the mind

i·mag·i·na·tive \i-'maj-ə-nət-iv\ *adj* **1** : of or relating to imagination **2** : having a lively imagination — **i·mag·i·na·tive·ly** *adv*

i·mag·ine \i-'maj-ən\ *vb* **i·mag·ined; i·mag·in-ing** **1** : to form a mental picture of **2** : SUPPOSE

¹**im·be·cile** \'im-bə-səl\ *n* : a person of very low intelligence unable to care for himself without help

²**imbecile** *or* **im·be·cil·ic** \,im-bə-'sil-ik\ *adj* : of very low intelligence : very stupid

im·be·cil·i·ty \,im-bə-'sil-ət-ē\ *n, pl* **im·be·cil-i·ties** **1** : the quality or state of being imbecile **2** : utter foolishness **3** : something that is extremely foolish

imbed *var of* EMBED

im·bibe \im-'bīb\ *vb* **im·bibed; im·bib·ing** : DRINK

im·i·tate \'im-ə-,tāt\ *vb* **im·i·tat·ed; im·i·tat-ing** **1** : to follow as a pattern, model, or example **2** : to be or appear similar to : RESEMBLE **3** : to copy exactly : MIMIC

syn IMITATE, MIMIC, APE all refer to copying or following a model. IMITATE implies no more than this though it may suggest allowance for some variation ⟨*imitated* the television commercials in their school skit⟩ MIMIC implies a very close copying often for the purpose of poking fun at or ridiculing someone ⟨children *mimicking* the teacher's manner⟩ APE indicates a slavish and often inferior imitating of one regarded as superior ⟨hated the landlords but *aped* their ways⟩

¹**im·i·ta·tion** \,im-ə-'tā-shən\ *n* **1** : an act of imitating **2** : COPY **syn** see FAKE

²**imitation** *adj* : resembling something else especially of a better quality : SYNTHETIC

im·i·ta·tive \'im-ə-,tāt-iv\ *adj* **1** : marked by imitation **2** : inclined to imitate

im·mac·u·late \i-'mak-yə-lət\ *adj* **1** : being without stain or blemish : PURE **2** : spotlessly clean — **im·mac·u·late·ly** *adv*

im·ma·te·ri·al \,im-ə-'tir-ē-əl\ *adj* **1** : not consisting of matter **2** : UNIMPORTANT

im·ma·ture \,im-ə-'tu̇r, -'tyu̇r\ *adj* : not yet fully grown or ripe — **im·ma·ture·ly** *adv*

im·mea·sur·a·ble \i-'mezh-ə-rə-bəl\ *adj* : not capable of being measured : BOUNDLESS — **im·mea·sur·a·bly** \-blē\ *adv*

im·me·di·ate \i-'mēd-ē-ət\ *adj* **1** : being next in line or relationship ⟨the king's *immediate* heir⟩ **2** : closest in importance **3** : acting directly without anything intervening **4** : not distant or separated : NEXT **5** : close in time **6** : made or done at once

im·me·di·ate·ly \i-'mēd-ē-ət-lē\ *adv* **1** : with nothing between **2** : without delay

im·mense \i-'mens\ *adj* **1** : very great in size or degree **2** : EXCELLENT — **im·mense·ly** *adv*

im·men·si·ty \i-'men-sət-ē\ *n, pl* **im·men·si-ties** : the quality or state of being immense

im·merse \i-'mərs\ *vb* **im·mersed; im·mers-ing** **1** : to plunge into something (as a fluid) that surrounds or covers **2** : to engage or involve deeply : ABSORB ⟨*immersed* in thought⟩

im·mi·grant \'im-i-grənt\ *n* : one that immigrates

im·mi·grate \'im-ə-,grāt\ *vb* **im·mi·grat·ed; im·mi·grat·ing** : to enter a country to take up permanent residence

im·mi·gra·tion \,im-ə-'grā-shən\ *n* : an act or instance of immigrating

im·mi·nence \'im-ə-nəns\ *n* : the quality or state of being imminent

im·mi·nent \'im-ə-nənt\ *adj* : ready to take place — **im·mi·nent·ly** *adv*

im·mo·bile \i-'mō-bəl\ *adj* : FIXED

im·mo·bil·i·ty \,im-ō-'bil-ət-ē\ *n* : the quality or state of being immobile

im·mo·bi·li·za·tion \i-,mō-bə-lə-'zā-shən\ *n* : the act of immobilizing : the state of being immobilized

im·mo·bi·lize \i-'mō-bə-,līz\ *vb* **im·mo·bi-lized; im·mo·bi·liz·ing** : to make immobile

im·mod·est \i-'mäd-əst\ *adj* : not modest ⟨*immodest* conduct⟩ — **im·mod·est·ly** *adv*

im·mod·es·ty \i-'mäd-əs-tē\ *n* : lack of modesty

im·mor·al \i-'mȯr-əl\ *adj* : not moral : WICKED — **im·mor·al·ly** *adv*

im·mo·ral·i·ty \,im-ȯ-'ral-ət-ē\ *n, pl* **im·mo·ral·i·ties** **1** : the quality or state of being immoral **2** : an immoral act or practice

¹**im·mor·tal** \i-'mȯrt-l\ *adj* : living or lasting forever — **im·mor·tal·ly** *adv*

²**immortal** *n* **1** : an immortal being **2** : a person of lasting fame

im·mor·tal·i·ty \,im-ȯr-'tal-ət-ē\ *n* **1** : the quality or state of being immortal : endless life **2** : lasting fame or glory

im·mor·tal·ize \i-'mȯrt-l-,īz\ *vb* **im·mor·tal-ized; im·mor·tal·iz·ing** : to make immortal

im·mov·a·ble \i-'mü-və-bəl\ *adj* **1** : incapable of being moved : firmly settled or fastened **2** : STEADFAST — **im·mov·a·bly** \-blē\ *adv*

im·mune \i-'myün\ *adj* **1** : EXEMPT **2** : having a special power to resist

im·mu·ni·ty \i-'myü-nət-ē\ *n, pl* **im·mu·ni·ties** **1** : FREEDOM, EXEMPTION ⟨*immunity* from a tax⟩ **2** : power to resist infection either natural or acquired (as by vaccination)

im·mu·ni·za·tion \,im-yə-nə-'zā-shən\ *n* : treatment (as with a vaccine) in order to produce immunity to a disease

im·mu·nize \'im-yə-,nīz\ *vb* **im·mu·nized; im·mu·niz·ing** : to make immune

im·mu·ta·ble \i-'myüt-ə-bəl\ *adj* : not capable of change — **im·mu·ta·bly** \-blē\ *adv*

imp \'imp\ *n* **1** : a small demon **2** : a mischievous child

im·pact \'im-ˌpakt\ *n* **1** : a striking together of two bodies **2** : a forceful effect

im·pair \im-'paər\ *vb* : to make less (as in quantity, value, or strength) : DAMAGE

im·pale \im-'pāl\ *vb* **im·paled; im·pal·ing** : to pierce with something pointed

im·part \im-'pärt\ *vb* **1** : to give or grant a share of **2** : to communicate knowledge of

im·par·tial \im-'pär-shəl\ *adj* : not partial or biased : FAIR, JUST — **im·par·tial·ly** *adv*

im·par·ti·al·i·ty \im-ˌpär-shē-'al-ət-ē\ *n* : the quality or state of being impartial : FAIRNESS

im·pass·a·ble \im-'pas-ə-bəl\ *adj* : not capable of being passed, crossed, or traveled

im·passe \'im-ˌpas\ *n* : DEADLOCK

im·pas·sioned \im-'pash-ənd\ *adj* : filled with passion or zeal : showing intense feeling

im·pas·sive \im-'pas-iv\ *adj* : not feeling or showing an emotion — **im·pas·sive·ly** *adv*

im·pa·tience \im-'pā-shəns\ *n* **1** : lack of patience **2** : restless or eager desire

im·pa·tient \im-'pā-shənt\ *adj* **1** : not patient **2** : showing or arising from impatience **3** : restlessly eager — **im·pa·tient·ly** *adv*

im·peach \im-'pēch\ *vb* **1** : to bring official charges against a public officer for misconduct of his office **2** : to throw discredit upon

im·pec·ca·ble \im-'pek-ə-bəl\ *adj* : free from fault or blame — **im·pec·ca·bly** \-blē\ *adv*

im·pe·cu·ni·ous \ˌim-pi-'kyü-nē-əs\ *adj* : having little or no money

im·pede \im-'pēd\ *vb* **im·ped·ed; im·ped·ing** : to interfere with the progress of : HINDER

im·ped·i·ment \im-'ped-ə-mənt\ *n* **1** : something that impedes **2** : a defect in speech

im·pel \im-'pel\ *vb* **im·pelled; im·pel·ling** : to urge or drive forward or into action : FORCE

im·pend \im-'pend\ *vb* **1** : to hover threateningly **2** : to be about to occur

im·pend·ing \im-'pen-ding\ *adj* : threatening to occur soon : APPROACHING

im·pen·e·tra·ble \im-'pen-ə-trə-bəl\ *adj* **1** : not capable of being penetrated or pierced **2** : incapable of being understood — **im·pen·e·tra·bly** \-blē\ *adv*

im·pen·i·tence \im-'pen-ə-təns\ *n* : the quality or state of being impenitent

im·pen·i·tent \im-'pen-ə-tənt\ *adj* : not penitent

im·per·a·tive \im-'per-ət-iv\ *adj* **1** : expressing a command, request, or strong encouragement ⟨*imperative* sentence⟩ **2** : not to be avoided or evaded : URGENT

im·per·cep·ti·ble \ˌim-pər-'sep-tə-bəl\ *adj* **1** : not perceptible by the senses or by the

mind **2** : extremely slight or gradual — **im·per·cep·ti·bly** \-blē\ *adv*

im·per·fect \im-'pər-fikt\ *adj* : not perfect : DEFECTIVE, INCOMPLETE — **im·per·fect·ly** *adv*

im·per·fec·tion \ˌim-pər-'fek-shən\ *n* **1** : the quality or state of being imperfect **2** : FAULT

im·pe·ri·al \im-'pir-ē-əl\ *adj* [from Latin *imperialis*, derived from *imperium*, "absolute authority", "empire", from *imperare* "to command"] **1** : of or relating to an empire or an emperor ⟨an *imperial* decree⟩ **2** : SOVEREIGN, REGAL — **im·pe·ri·al·ly** *adv*

im·per·il \im-'per-əl\ *vb* **im·per·iled** *or* **im·per·illed; im·per·il·ing** *or* **im·per·il·ling** : to bring into peril : ENDANGER

im·pe·ri·ous \im-'pir-ē-əs\ *adj* **1** : showing pride or superiority : COMMANDING **2** : ARROGANT **3** : URGENT — **im·pe·ri·ous·ly** *adv*

im·per·ish·a·ble \im-'per-ish-ə-bəl\ *adj* : not perishable — **im·per·ish·a·bly** \-blē\ *adv*

im·per·ma·nent \im-'pər-mə-nənt\ *adj* : not permanent

im·per·son·al \im-'pərs-n-əl\ *adj* : not referring or belonging to any particular person — **im·per·son·al·ly** *adv*

im·per·son·ate \im-'pərs-n-ˌāt\ *vb* **im·per·son·at·ed; im·per·son·at·ing** : to pretend to be another person ⟨*impersonate* a policeman⟩

im·per·son·a·tion \im-ˌpərs-n-'ā-shən\ *n* : the act of impersonating

im·per·ti·nence \im-'pərt-n-əns\ *n* : the quality or state of being impertinent

im·per·ti·nent \im-'pərt-n-ənt\ *adj* **1** : not pertinent **2** : RUDE — **im·per·ti·nent·ly** *adv*

im·per·turb·a·bil·i·ty \ˌim-pər-ˌtər-bə-'bil-ət-ē\ *n* : the quality or state of being calm

im·per·turb·a·ble \ˌim-pər-'tər-bə-bəl\ *adj* : marked by extreme calm and steadiness : SERENE — **im·per·turb·a·bly** \-blē\ *adv*

im·per·vi·ous \im-'pər-vē-əs\ *adj* **1** : not allowing entrance or passage ⟨a coat *impervious* to rain⟩ **2** : not capable of being disturbed

im·pet·u·ous \im-'pech-ə-wəs\ *adj* : IMPULSIVE — **im·pet·u·ous·ly** *adv*

im·pi·e·ty \im-'pī-ət-ē\ *n, pl* **im·pi·e·ties** **1** : the quality or state of being impious **2** : an impious act

im·pinge \im-'pinj\ *vb* **im·pinged; im·ping·ing** **1** : to strike or dash sharply ⟨sounds *impinge* on the ear⟩ **2** : ENCROACH, INFRINGE

im·pi·ous \'im-pē-əs\ *adj* : not pious : IRREVERENT, PROFANE — **im·pi·ous·ly** *adv*

imp·ish \'im-pish\ *adj* : MISCHIEVOUS ⟨an *impish* glance⟩ — **imp·ish·ly** *adv*

im·plac·a·ble \im-'plak-ə-bəl, -'plā-kə-\ *adj* : not capable of being appeased, pacified, or changed — **im·plac·a·bly** \-blē\ *adv*

im·plant \im-'plant\ *vb* : to fix or set securely or deeply : INCULCATE

¹**im·ple·ment** \'im-plə-mənt\ *n* : an article serving to equip ⟨*implements* of war⟩

²**im·ple·ment** \'im-plə-ˌment\ *vb* : to carry out : FULFILL ⟨*implement* a plan⟩

im·pli·cate \'im-plə-ˌkāt\ *vb* **im·pli·cat·ed; im·pli·cat·ing** : to bring into connection

im·pli·ca·tion \ˌim-plə-'kā-shən\ *n* **1** : the act of implicating : the state of being implicated **2** : the act of implying **3** : something implied

im·plic·it \im-'plis-ət\ *adj* **1** : understood though not directly stated or expressed **2** : COMPLETE, UTTER — **im·plic·it·ly** *adv*

im·plore \im-'plōr\ *vb* **im·plored; im·plor·ing** : to call upon in supplication : BESEECH

im·ply \im-'plī\ *vb* **im·plied; im·ply·ing** : to indicate or express indirectly : SUGGEST

syn IMPLY, INFER are sometimes used as synonyms but to most educated users the two words are complementary rather than synonymous. IMPLY means o hint at a fact or idea by indirect statements or actions, and is an actual synonym of *suggest* ⟨he *implied* that he would like to have one of the kittens⟩ INFER means to arrive at a conclusion by reasoning from evidence or what seems to be evidence ⟨from what he said I *inferred* that he wanted a kitten⟩

im·po·lite \ˌim-pə-'līt\ *adj* : not polite — **im·po·lite·ly** *adv* — **im·po·lite·ness** *n*

¹**im·port** \im-'pōrt\ *vb* **1** : MEAN **2** : MATTER **3** : to bring (as merchandise) into a country especially for selling ⟨*import* coffee⟩

²**im·port** \'im-ˌpōrt\ *n* **1** : MEANING **2** : IMPORTANCE **3** : something imported

im·por·tance \im-'pòrt-ns\ *n* : the quality or state of being important : SIGNIFICANCE

im·por·tant \im-'pòrt-nt\ *adj* **1** : marked by or possessing weight or consequence : SIGNIFICANT **2** : showing a feeling of personal importance — **im·por·tant·ly** *adv*

im·por·ta·tion \ˌim-ˌpōr-'tā-shən\ *n* **1** : the act or practice of importing **2** : IMPORT

im·por·tu·nate \im-'pòr-chə-nət\ *adj* : troublesomely urgent — **im·por·tu·nate·ly** *adv*

im·por·tune \ˌim-pər-'tün, -'tyün\ *vb* **im·por·tuned; im·por·tun·ing** : to beg or urge with troublesome persistence

im·pose \im-'pōz\ *vb* **im·posed; im·pos·ing** **1** : to establish or apply as a charge or penalty ⟨*impose* a tax⟩ **2** : to make prevail by force **3** : to use trickery to get what one wants **4** : to take unfair advantage of something

im·pos·ing \im-'pō-zing\ *adj* : impressive because of size, dignity, or grandeur

im·pos·si·bil·i·ty \im-ˌpäs-ə-'bil-ət-ē\ *n, pl* **im·pos·si·bil·i·ties** **1** : the quality or state of being impossible **2** : something impossible

im·pos·si·ble \im-'päs-ə-bəl\ *adj* **1** : incapable of being or of occurring **2** : HOPELESS ⟨an *impossible* situation⟩ **3** : extremely undesirable — **im·pos·si·bly** \-blē\ *adv*

im·pos·tor \im-'päs-tər\ *n* : one that represents himself as being someone else

im·pos·ture \im-'päs-chər\ *n* : the act or conduct of an impostor

im·po·tence \'im-pə-təns\ *n* : the quality or state of being impotent

im·po·tent \'im-pə-tənt\ *adj* : lacking in power or strength — **im·po·tent·ly** *adv*

im·pound \im-'paùnd\ *vb* **1** : to shut up in or as if in a pound ⟨*impound* cattle⟩ **2** : to seize and hold in legal custody ⟨*impound* funds⟩ **3** : to collect (water) in a reservoir

im·pov·er·ish \im-'päv-ə-rish\ *vb* **1** : to make poor **2** : to use up the strength, richness, or fertility of ⟨*impoverished* soil⟩

im·prac·ti·ca·ble \im-'prak-ti-kə-bəl\ *adj* : not practicable ⟨economically *impracticable*⟩

im·prac·ti·cal \im-'prak-ti-kəl\ *adj* : not practical — **im·prac·ti·cal·ly** *adv*

im·pre·cise \ˌim-pri-'sīs\ *adj* : not precise — **im·pre·cise·ly** *adv*

im·preg·na·ble \im-'preg-nə-bəl\ *adj* : UNCONQUERABLE

im·preg·nate \im-'preg-ˌnāt\ *vb* **im·preg·nat·ed; im·preg·nat·ing** **1** : to make fertile or fruitful **2** : to cause (a material or substance) to be filled or saturated

im·pre·sa·ri·o \ˌim-prə-'sä-rē-ˌō\ *n, pl* **im·pre·sa·ri·os** : one who puts on an entertainment (as an opera or concert)

¹**im·press** \im-'pres\ *vb* **1** : PRESS, STAMP **2** : to produce a clear impression of **3** : to influence or affect strongly

²**im·press** \'im-ˌpres\ *n* **1** : the act of impressing **2** : IMPRINT **3** : a distinctive mark : STAMP **4** : IMPRESSION, EFFECT

im·pres·sion \im-'presh-ən\ *n* **1** : the act or process of impressing **2** : an effect produced by impressing **3** : an image impressed on the senses or on the mind **4** : a vague or indefinite recollection or belief

im·pres·sion·a·ble \im-'presh-ə-nə-bəl\ *adj* : capable of being easily impressed

im·pres·sive \im-'pres-iv\ *adj* : having the power to impress the mind or feelings ⟨an *impressive* speech⟩ — **im·pres·sive·ly** *adv*

¹**im·print** \im-'print\ *vb* **1** : to mark by pressure : STAMP **2** : to fix firmly

²**im·print** \'im-ˌprint\ *n* : something imprinted or printed : IMPRESSION

j job   ng sing   ō low   ò moth   òi coin   th thin   th this   ü boot   ù foot   y you   yü few   yù furious   zh vision

im·pris·on \im-'priz-n\ *vb* : to put in prison
im·pris·on·ment \im-'priz-n-mənt\ *n* : the act of imprisoning : the state of being imprisoned
im·prob·a·bil·i·ty \im-,präb-ə-'bil-ət-ē\ *n* : the quality or state of being improbable
im·prob·a·ble \im-'präb-ə-bəl\ *adj* : not probable — **im·prob·a·bly** \-blē\ *adv*
im·promp·tu \im-'prämp-tü, -tyü\ *adj* [from French *impromptu,* taken from the Latin phrase *in promptu* "in readiness"] : made or done without previous study or preparation ⟨an *impromptu* speech⟩
im·prop·er \im-'präp-ər\ *adj* : not proper, fit, suitable, or correct **syn** see INAPPROPRIATE — **im·prop·er·ly** *adv*
improper fraction *n* : a fraction whose numerator is equal to or larger than the denominator ⟨13/4 is an *improper fraction*⟩
im·pro·pri·e·ty\ ,im-prə-'prī-ət-ē\ *n, pl* **im·pro·pri·e·ties** : an improper act or remark
im·prove \im-'prüv\ *vb* **im·proved; im·prov·ing** **1** : to make greater in amount or value : make better **2** : to grow better **3** : to make good use of — **im·prov·er** *n*
im·prove·ment \im-'prüv-mənt\ *n* **1** : the act or process of improving **2** : increased value or excellence **3** : something that adds to the value or appearance (as of a house)
im·prov·i·sa·tion \im-,präv-ə-'zā-shən\ *n* **1** : the act or art of improvising **2** : something that is improvised
im·pro·vise \,im-prə-'vīz\ *vb* **im·pro·vised; im·pro·vis·ing** **1** : to compose, recite, or sing without previous study or preparation **2** : to make, invent, or arrange offhand
im·pru·dence \im-'prüd-ns\ *n* : the quality or state of being imprudent
im·pru·dent \im-'prüd-nt\ *adj* : not prudent — **im·pru·dent·ly** *adv*
im·pu·dence \'im-pyə-dəns\ *n* : impudent behavior or speech : INSOLENCE, DISRESPECT
im·pu·dent \'im-pyə-dənt\ *adj* : BOLD, SAUCY — **im·pu·dent·ly** *adv*
im·pulse \'im-,pəls\ *n* **1** : a force that starts a body into motion **2** : the motion produced by a starting force **3** : a sudden arousing of the mind and spirit to do something **4** : the wave of change that sweeps along a stimulated nerve and conveys information to the brain
im·pul·sive \im-'pəl-siv\ *adj* : acting or liable to act on impulse — **im·pul·sive·ly** *adv*
im·pure \im-'pyùr\ *adj* **1** : not pure : UNCLEAN, DIRTY **2** : mixed with some other and usually inferior substance — **im·pure·ly** *adv*
im·pu·ri·ty \im-'pyùr-ət-ē\ *n, pl* **im·pu·ri·ties**

1 : the quality or state of being impure
2 : something that is or makes impure
im·pute \im-'pyüt\ *vb* **im·put·ed; im·put·ing** : to lay the responsibility or blame for
¹in \in\ *prep* **1** : enclosed or surrounded by : WITHIN ⟨swim *in* the lake⟩ **2** : INTO 1 ⟨ran *in* the house⟩ **3** : DURING ⟨*in* the summer⟩ **4** : WITH ⟨written *in* pencil⟩ **5** — used to indicate one's situation or state ⟨*in* luck⟩ ⟨*in* trouble⟩ **6** — used to show manner or purpose ⟨*in* a hurry⟩ ⟨said *in* reply⟩ **7** : INTO 2 ⟨broke *in* pieces⟩
²in *adv* **1** : to or toward the inside ⟨went *in* and closed the door⟩ **2** : to or toward some particular place ⟨flew *in* yesterday⟩ **3** : NEAR ⟨play close *in*⟩ **4** : into the midst of something ⟨mix *in* the flour⟩ **5** : to or at its proper place ⟨fit a piece *in*⟩ **6** : on the inner side : WITHIN ⟨everyone is *in*⟩ **7** : at hand or on hand ⟨after harvests are *in*⟩
³in *adj* **1** : being inside or within ⟨the *in* part⟩ **2** : directed or bound inward ⟨the *in* train⟩
¹in- *or* **il-** *or* **im-** *or* **ir-** *prefix* : not : NON-, UN- — usually *il*- before *l* ⟨*il*logical⟩ and *im*- before *b, m,* or *p* ⟨*im*balance⟩ ⟨*im*moral⟩ ⟨*im*practical⟩ and *ir*- before *r* ⟨*ir*reducible⟩ and *in*- before other sounds ⟨*in*conclusive⟩
²in- *or* **il-** *or* **im-** *or* **ir-** *prefix* **1** : in : within : into : toward : on ⟨*il*luminate⟩ — usually *il*- before *l, im*- before *b, m,* or *p, ir*- before *r,* and *in*- before other sounds **2** : EN- ⟨*im*peril⟩
-in \ən\ *n suffix* : chemical compound ⟨insul*in*⟩ ⟨penicill*in*⟩
in·a·bil·i·ty \,in-ə-'bil-ət-ē\ *n* : the condition of being unable : lack of ability
in·ac·ces·si·bil·i·ty \,in-ak-,ses-ə-'bil-ət-ē\ *n* : the quality or state of being inaccessible
in·ac·ces·si·ble \,in-ak-'ses-ə-bəl\ *adj* : not accessible
in·ac·cu·ra·cy \in-'ak-yə-rə-sē\ *n, pl* **in·ac·cu·ra·cies** **1** : lack of accuracy **2** : MISTAKE
in·ac·cu·rate \in-'ak-yə-rət\ *adj* : not accurate : not exact — **in·ac·cu·rate·ly** *adv*
in·ac·tive \in-'ak-tiv\ *adj* : not active : IDLE
in·ac·tiv·i·ty \,in-ak-'tiv-ət-ē\ *n* : an inactive state
in·ad·e·qua·cy \in-'ad-i-kwə-sē\ *n, pl* **in·ad·e·qua·cies** : DEFICIENCY, FAULT
in·ad·e·quate \in-'ad-i-kwət\ *adj* : not adequate : INSUFFICIENT
in·ad·ver·tence \,in-əd-'vərt-ns\ *n* **1** : INATTENTION **2** : OVERSIGHT
in·ad·ver·tent \,in-əd-'vərt-nt\ *adj* **1** : CARELESS, HEEDLESS ⟨an *inadvertent* remark⟩ **2** : UNINTENTIONAL — **in·ad·ver·tent·ly** *adv*
in·ad·vis·a·ble \,in-əd-'vī-zə-bəl\ *adj* : not advisable : UNWISE

in·a·lien·a·ble \in-'āl-yə-nə-bəl\ *adj* : not capable of being taken away, given up, or transferred ⟨*inalienable* rights⟩

i·nane \i-'nān\ *adj* : lacking meaning or point : SILLY ⟨*inane* remarks⟩ — **i·nane·ly** *adv*

in·an·i·mate \in-'an-ə-mət\ *adj* : not animate or animated : LIFELESS, DULL

in·a·ni·tion \,in-ə-'nish-ən\ *n* : a weak state from or as if from lack of food and water

i·nan·i·ty \i-'nan-ət-ē\ *n* : the quality or state of being inane

in·ap·pro·pri·ate \,in-ə-'prō-prē-ət\ *adj* : not appropriate — **in·ap·pro·pri·ate·ly** *adv*

syn INAPPROPRIATE, IMPROPER, UNSEEMLY all refer to something considered unsuitable. INAPPROPRIATE usually refers to something that is not objectionable itself but is unsuitable only because it is out of place in a particular situation ⟨food that is *inappropriate* for a baby⟩ IMPROPER suggests something that is considered unsuitable in itself, often representing a violation of the rules of social behavior or good taste ⟨such sauciness was *improper*⟩ ⟨skirts at an *improper* length⟩ UNSEEMLY carries much the same implications but is somewhat milder in the disapproval implied ⟨loudness that is *unseemly* in public places⟩ and may stress offense against refined taste rather than good taste in general ⟨*unseemly* piles of debris around the yard⟩

in·as·much as \,in-əz-'məch-əz\ *conj* : SINCE

in·at·ten·tion \,in-ə-'ten-chən\ *n* : failure to pay attention

in·at·ten·tive \,in-ə-'tent-iv\ *adj* : not attentive — **in·at·ten·tive·ly** *adv*

in·au·di·ble \in-'öd-ə-bəl\ *adj* : not capable of being heard — **in·au·di·bly** \-blē\ *adv*

in·au·gu·ral \in-'ö-gyə-rəl\ *adj* 1 : of or relating to an inauguration 2 : marking a beginning ⟨the *inaugural* meeting of a club⟩

in·au·gu·rate \in-'ö-gyə-,rāt\ *vb* **in·au·gu·rat·ed; in·au·gu·rat·ing** [from Latin *inaugurare* "to inaugurate", from the prefix *in-* "²in-" and *augurare* "to practice augury"; so called because the Romans consulted omens at the time of inaugurations] 1 : to introduce into office with suitable ceremonies : INSTALL 2 : to celebrate the opening of 3 : BEGIN

in·au·gu·ra·tion \in-,ö-gyə-'rā-shən\ *n* : an act or ceremony of inaugurating

in·born \'in-'börn\ *adj* : NATURAL

in·breed \'in-'brēd\ *vb* **in·bred** \-'bred\; **in·breed·ing** : to breed with closely related individuals

in·can·des·cent \,in-kən-'des-nt\ *adj* : white or glowing with intense heat : SHINING

incandescent lamp *n* : a lamp whose light is produced by the glow of a wire heated by an electric current

incandescent lamp

in·can·ta·tion \,in-,kan-'tā-shən\ *n* 1 : the use of spells or charms spoken or sung in magic ceremonies 2 : the form of words used in an incantation

in·ca·pa·ble \in-'kā-pə-bəl\ *adj* : lacking ability or qualification for the purpose or end in view

in·ca·pac·i·tate \,in-kə-'pas-ə-,tāt\ *vb* **in·ca·pac·i·tat·ed; in·ca·pac·i·tat·ing** : DISABLE

in·ca·pac·i·ty \,in-kə-'pas-ət-ē\ *n, pl* **in·ca·pac·i·ties** : lack of ability or power

in·car·cer·ate \in-'kär-sə-,rāt\ *vb* **in·car·cer·at·ed; in·car·cer·at·ing** : IMPRISON

incase *var of* ENCASE

¹**in·cense** \'in-,sens\ *n* 1 : material used to produce a perfume when burned 2 : the perfume exhaled by burning incense

²**in·cense** \in-'sens\ *vb* **in·censed; in·cens·ing** : to make very angry

in·cen·tive \in-'sent-iv\ *n* : something that arouses or spurs one on to action or effort

in·ces·sant \in-'ses-nt\ *adj* : continuing without interruption — **in·ces·sant·ly** *adv*

¹**inch** \'inch\ *n* : a unit of length equal to 1/36 yard or 2.54 centimeters

²**inch** *vb* : to move by small degrees

¹**in·ci·dent** \'in-sə-dənt\ *n* 1 : HAPPENING 2 : an accompanying minor occurrence

syn INCIDENT, OCCURRENCE, EVENT all mean something that happens. OCCURRENCE suggests a happening that is neither planned nor intended and is often unexpected, but says little about its importance ⟨the *occurrence* of a typhoid epidemic⟩ ⟨the *occurrence* of a second day of rain⟩ INCIDENT also suggests lack of plan or intent, but is normally used of a brief occurrence of little long-range significance ⟨she had already forgotten the *incident* that hurt her feelings yesterday⟩ ⟨*incidents* that were troublesome but didn't ruin the picnic⟩ EVENT, on the other hand, carries no indication of whether intent or planning is involved but does indicate a happening of some importance that may have far-reaching results for those involved ⟨winning the contest was the *event* that kept his interest in electricity alive⟩

²**incident** *adj* : occurring or likely to occur in connection with some other event

¹**in·ci·den·tal** \,in-sə-'dent-l\ *adj* : occurring by chance or as a minor consequence : CASUAL

²**incidental** *n* 1 : something that is incidental 2 *pl* : minor items (as of expense) that are not individually accounted for

in·ci·den·tal·ly \,in-sə-'dent-l-ē\ *adv* **1** : by chance : CASUALLY **2** : by way of interjection

in·cin·er·ate \in-'sin-ə-,rāt\ *vb* **in·cin·er·at·ed; in·cin·er·at·ing** : to burn to ashes

in·cin·er·a·tor \in-'sin-ə-,rāt-ər\ *n* : a furnace or a container for burning waste materials

in·cip·i·ent \in-'sip-ē-ənt\ *adj* : beginning to be apparent

in·cise \in-'sīz\ *vb* **in·cised; in·cis·ing** : to cut into : CARVE, ENGRAVE

incinerators

in·ci·sion \in-'sizh-ən\ *n* : a cutting into something or the cut or wound that results

in·ci·sor \in-'sī-zər\ *n* : a tooth (as any of the four front teeth of the human upper or lower jaw) for cutting

in·cite \in-'sīt\ *vb* **in·cit·ed; in·cit·ing** : to move to action : stir up : ROUSE

in·ci·vil·i·ty \,in-sə-'vil-ət-ē\ *n, pl* **in·ci·vil·i·ties** **1** : RUDENESS, IMPOLITENESS **2** : a rude or discourteous act

in·clem·ent \in-'klem-ənt\ *adj* **1** : HARSH, SEVERE ⟨an *inclement* judge⟩ **2** : STORMY

in·cli·na·tion \,in-klə-'nā-shən\ *n* **1** : an act or the action of bending or inclining : NOD **2** : TENDENCY, LIKING **3** : SLANT, TILT

¹in·cline \in-'klīn\ *vb* **in·clined; in·clin·ing** **1** : to cause to bend : BOW **2** : to lean in one's mind : TEND **3** : LEAN, SLOPE

²in·cline \'in-,klīn\ *n* : SLOPE

in·clined \in-'klīnd\ *adj* **1** : having inclination : WILLING **2** : SLOPING, SLANTING

inclose, inclosure *var of* ENCLOSE, ENCLOSURE

in·clude \in-'klüd\ *vb* **in·clud·ed; in·clud·ing** : to take in or comprise as part of a whole

in·clu·sion \in-'klü-zhən\ *n* **1** : an act of including : the state of being included **2** : something included

in·clu·sive \in-'klü-siv\ *adj* **1** : CONTAINING, COVERING **2** : BROAD **3** : including one or more limits or extremes — **in·clu·sive·ly** *adv* — **in·clu·sive·ness** *n*

in·cog·ni·to \,in-,käg-'nēt-ō, in-'käg-nə-,tō\ *adv (or adj)* : with one's identity concealed

in·co·her·ence \,in-kō-'hir-əns\ *n* : the quality or state of being incoherent

in·co·her·ent \,in-kō-'hir-ənt\ *adj* **1** : not sticking closely or compactly together : LOOSE **2** : not clearly or logically connected : RAMBLING — **in·co·her·ent·ly** *adv*

in·come \'in-,kəm\ *n* : a gain usually measured in money that comes in from labor, business, or property

income tax *n* : a tax on the net income of an individual or business concern

in·com·ing \'in-,kəm-ing\ *adj* : coming in

in·com·mu·ni·ca·ble \,in-kə-'myü-ni-kə-bəl\ *adj* : not communicable

in·com·pa·ra·ble \in-'käm-pə-rə-bəl\ *adj* **1** : eminent beyond comparison : MATCHLESS **2** : not suitable for comparison

in·com·pa·ra·bly \in-'käm-pə-rə-blē\ *adv* : to an incomparable degree

in·com·pat·i·bil·i·ty \,in-kəm-,pat-ə-'bil-ət-ē\ *n, pl* **in·com·pat·i·bil·i·ties** : the state or an instance of being incompatible

in·com·pat·i·ble \,in-kəm-'pat-ə-bəl\ *adj* : not capable of being brought together in harmonious or agreeable relations — **in·com·pat·i·bly** \-blē\ *adv*

in·com·pe·tence \in-'käm-pət-əns\ *n* : the state or fact of being incompetent

in·com·pe·tent \in-'käm-pət-ənt\ *adj* : not competent — **in·com·pe·tent·ly** *adv*

in·com·plete \,in-kəm-'plēt\ *adj* : not complete : not finished — **in·com·plete·ly** *adv*

in·com·pre·hen·si·ble \,in-,käm-pri-'hen-sə-bəl\ *adj* : not understandable : UNINTELLIGIBLE — **in·com·pre·hen·si·bly** \-blē\ *adv*

in·con·ceiv·a·ble \,in-kən-'sē-və-bəl\ *adj* **1** : impossible to imagine or conceive **2** : hard to believe — **in·con·ceiv·a·bly** \-blē\ *adv*

in·con·gru·ous \in-'käng-grə-wəs\ *adj* : not harmonious, appropriate, or proper ⟨*incongruous* colors⟩ — **in·con·gru·ous·ly** *adv*

in·con·se·quen·tial \,in-,kän-sə-'kwen-chəl\ *adj* : UNIMPORTANT — **in·con·se·quen·tial·ly** *adv*

in·con·sid·er·a·ble \,in-kən-'sid-ə-rə-bəl\ *adj* : not worth considering : TRIVIAL

in·con·sid·er·ate \,in-kən-'sid-ə-rət\ *adj* : not showing consideration for others

in·con·sis·tent \,in-kən-'sis-tənt\ *adj* **1** : not being in agreement **2** : not logical

in·con·sol·a·ble \,in-kən-'sō-lə-bəl\ *adj* : not capable of being consoled — **in·con·sol·a·bly** \-blē\ *adv*

in·con·spic·u·ous \,in-kən-'spik-yə-wəs\ *adj* : not conspicuous — **in·con·spic·u·ous·ly** *adv*

in·con·stant \in-'kän-stənt\ *adj* : not constant : CHANGEABLE

in·con·test·a·ble \,in-kən-'tes-tə-bəl\ *adj* : INDISPUTABLE

in·con·tro·vert·i·ble \,in-,kän-trə-'vərt-ə-bəl\ *adj* : INDISPUTABLE

¹in·con·ve·nience \,in-kən-'vē-nyəns\ *n* **1** : the quality or state of being inconvenient : DISCOMFORT **2** : something inconvenient

²inconvenience *vb* **in·con·ve·nienced; in·con·ve·nienc·ing** : to cause inconvenience to

in·con·ve·nient \,in-kən-'vē-nyənt\ *adj* : not convenient — **in·con·ve·nient·ly** *adv*

in·cor·po·rate \in-'kȯr-pə-,rāt\ *vb* **in·cor·po·rat·ed; in·cor·po·rat·ing** 1 : to join or unite closely into a single mass or body 2 : to form into a legal body

in·cor·po·rat·ed \in-'kȯr-pə-,rāt-əd\ *adj* : formed into a corporation (as by charter)

in·cor·po·ra·tion \in-,kȯr-pə-'rā-shən\ *n* : an act of incorporating : the state of being incorporated

in·cor·po·re·al \,in-kȯr-'pōr-ē-əl\ *adj* : not corporeal — **in·cor·po·re·al·ly** *adv*

in·cor·rect \,in-kə-'rekt\ *adj* 1 : not correct : not accurate or true : WRONG 2 : IMPROPER — **in·cor·rect·ly** *adv* — **in·cor·rect·ness** *n*

in·cor·ri·gi·ble \in-'kȯr-ə-jə-bəl\ *adj* : not capable of being corrected or reformed — **in·cor·ri·gi·bly** \-blē\ *adv*

in·cor·rupt·i·ble \,in-kə-'rəp-tə-bəl\ *adj* 1 : not subject to decay 2 : not capable of being bribed or morally corrupted — **in·cor·rupt·i·bly** \-blē\ *adv*

¹**in·crease** \in-'krēs\ *vb* **in·creased; in·creas·ing** : to make or become greater (as in size)

²**in·crease** \'in-,krēs\ *n* 1 : the act of increasing 2 : something added (as by growth)

in·creas·ing·ly \in-'krē-sing-lē\ *adv* : to an increasing degree : more and more

in·cred·i·ble \in-'kred-ə-bəl\ *adj* : too extraordinary or improbable to be believed — **in·cred·i·bly** \-blē\ *adv*

in·cre·du·li·ty \,in-kri-'dü-lət-ē, -'dyü-\ *n* : the quality or state of being incredulous

in·cred·u·lous \in-'krej-ə-ləs\ *adj* 1 : not credulous : SKEPTICAL 2 : expressing lack of belief — **in·cred·u·lous·ly** *adv*

in·crim·i·nate \in-'krim-ə-,nāt\ *vb* **in·crim·i·nat·ed; in·crim·i·nat·ing** : to charge with a crime or fault : ACCUSE

incrust *var of* ENCRUST

in·cu·bate \'ing-kyə-,bāt\ *vb* **in·cu·bat·ed; in·cu·bat·ing** 1 : to sit upon eggs to hatch them by warmth 2 : to keep under conditions favorable for hatching or development

in·cu·ba·tion \,ing-kyə-'bā-shən\ *n* 1 : an act of incubating : the state of being incubated 2 : the time between infection with disease germs and the appearance of disease symptoms

in·cu·ba·tor \'ing-kyə-,bāt-ər\ *n* 1 : an apparatus that supplies enough heat to hatch eggs artificially 2 : an apparatus to help the growth of tiny newborn babies

in·cul·cate \in-'kəl-,kāt, 'in-,kəl-\ *vb* **in·cul·cat·ed; in·cul·cat·ing** : to teach and impress upon the mind by frequent repetition

¹**in·cum·bent** \in-'kəm-bənt\ *n* : the holder of an office or position

²**incumbent** *adj* : OBLIGATORY

incumber *var of* ENCUMBER

in·cur \in-'kər\ *vb* **in·curred; in·cur·ring** 1 : to meet with 2 : to become liable or subject to

in·cur·a·ble \in-'kyùr-ə-bəl\ *adj* : not capable of being cured — **in·cur·a·bly** \-blē\ *adv*

in·cu·ri·ous \in-'kyùr-ē-əs\ *adj* : not curious or inquisitive : UNINTERESTED

in·debt·ed \in-'det-əd\ *adj* : being in debt : owing something — **in·debt·ed·ness** *n*

in·de·cen·cy \in-'dēs-n-sē\ *n, pl* **in·de·cen·cies** 1 : lack of decency 2 : an indecent act or word

in·de·cent \in-'dēs-nt\ *adj* : not decent

in·de·ci·sion \,in-di-'sizh-ən\ *n* : a wavering between two or more courses of action

in·de·ci·sive \,in-di-'sī-siv\ *adj* 1 : not decisive or final ⟨an *indecisive* battle⟩ 2 : characterized by indecision ⟨an *indecisive* person⟩ — **in·de·ci·sive·ly** *adv* — **in·de·ci·sive·ness** *n*

in·deed \in-'dēd\ *adv* : in fact : TRULY

in·de·fen·si·ble \,in-di-'fen-sə-bəl\ *adj* : not capable of being defended

in·def·i·nite \in-'def-ə-nət\ *adj* 1 : not clear or fixed in meaning or details 2 : not fixed or limited — **in·def·i·nite·ly** *adv*

indefinite article *n* : either of the articles *a* or *an* used to show that the following noun refers to any person or thing of the kind named

in·del·i·ble \in-'del-ə-bəl\ *adj* 1 : not capable of being erased, removed, or blotted out ⟨an *indelible* impression⟩ 2 : making marks not easily erased — **in·del·i·bly** \-blē\ *adv*

in·del·i·ca·cy \in-'del-i-kə-sē\ *n, pl* **in·del·i·ca·cies** : the state or an instance of being indelicate

in·del·i·cate \in-'del-i-kət\ *adj* : not delicate : COARSE, TACTLESS — **in·del·i·cate·ly** *adv*

in·dent \in-'dent\ *vb* 1 : to make a toothlike cut or cuts on an edge 2 : to set (as a line of a paragraph) in from the margin

in·den·ta·tion \,in-,den-'tā-shən\ *n* 1 : NOTCH 2 : a deep recess (as in a coast) 3 : the state of being indented 4 : DENT

in·den·tion \in-'den-chən\ *n* : an indentation especially in printing

in·de·pend·ence \,in-də-'pen-dəns\ *n* : the quality or state of being independent

Independence Day *n* : July 4 observed as a legal holiday in commemoration of the adoption of the Declaration of Independence in 1776

¹**in·de·pend·ent** \,in-də-'pen-dənt\ *adj* 1 : not under another's control or rule 2 : not having connections with another : SEPARATE 3 : not supported by another 4 : not easily influenced — **in·de·pend·ent·ly** *adv*

---

j job   ng sing   ō low   ȯ moth   ȯi coin   th thin   th̲ this   ü boot   ù foot   y you   yü few   yu̇ furious   zh vision

²independent *n* : one that is independent

in·de·scrib·a·ble \ˌin-di-'skrī-bə-bəl\ *adj* : incapable of being adequately described — **in·de·scrib·a·bly** \-blē\ *adv*

in·de·struc·ti·bil·i·ty \ˌin-di-ˌstrək-tə-'bil-ət-ē\ *n* : the quality or state of being indestructible

in·de·struc·ti·ble \ˌin-di-'strək-tə-bəl\ *adj* : incapable of being destroyed — **in·de·struc·ti·bly** \-blē\ *adv*

¹in·dex \'in-ˌdeks\ *n, pl* **in·dex·es** *or* **in·di·ces** \'in-də-ˌsēz\ **1** : an alphabetized list of names or topics (as in a book) giving the place where each is to be found ⟨card *index*⟩ **2** : POINTER, INDICATOR **3** : SIGN, INDICATION

²index *vb* **1** : to provide with an index **2** : to list in an index

index finger *n* : the finger next to the thumb

¹In·di·an \'in-dē-ən\ *n* **1** : a native or inhabitant of India **2** : a member of any of the aboriginal peoples of North and South America except the Eskimo **3** : an American Indian language

²Indian *adj* **1** : of or relating to India or its peoples **2** : of or relating to the American Indians or their languages

Indian club *n* : a wooden club used in gymnastics

Indian corn *n* : a tall American cereal grass widely grown for its large ears of grain which are used as food or for feeding livestock : MAIZE

Indian pipe *n* : a waxy white leafless woodland herb with nodding flowers

Indian summer *n* : a period of mild weather in late autumn or early winter

Indian club

in·di·cate \'in-də-ˌkāt\ *vb* **in·di·cat·ed; in·di·cat·ing** **1** : to point out or point to **2** : to state or express briefly

in·di·ca·tion \ˌin-də-'kā-shən\ *n* **1** : the act of indicating **2** : something that indicates

in·dic·a·tive \in-'dik-ət-iv\ *adj* **1** : representing a denoted act or state as an objective fact ⟨a verb in the *indicative* mood⟩ **2** : pointing out

in·di·ca·tor \'in-də-ˌkāt-ər\ *n* **1** : one that indicates **2** : POINTER, DIAL, GAUGE

indicator

in·dict \in-'dīt\ *vb* : to charge with an offense or crime : ACCUSE — **in·dict·ment** *n*

in·dif·fer·ence \in-'dif-ə-rəns\ *n* **1** : the condition or fact of being indifferent **2** : lack of importance

in·dif·fer·ent \in-'dif-ə-rənt\ *adj* **1** : having no choice or preference ⟨*indifferent* to heat or cold⟩ **2** : showing neither interest nor dislike **3** : neither good nor bad — **in·dif·fer·ent·ly** *adv*

in·di·gest·i·ble \ˌin-dī-'jes-tə-bəl, -də-\ *adj* : not digestible : not easily digested

in·di·ges·tion \ˌin-dī-'jes-chən, -də-\ *n* : discomfort caused by slow or painful digestion

in·dig·nant \in-'dig-nənt\ *adj* : filled with or marked by indignation — **in·dig·nant·ly** *adv*

in·dig·na·tion \ˌin-dig-'nā-shən\ *n* : anger aroused by something unjust or unworthy

in·dig·ni·ty \in-'dig-nət-ē\ *n, pl* **in·dig·ni·ties** **1** : an act that offends against one's dignity or self-respect **2** : humiliating treatment

in·di·go \'in-di-ˌgō\ *n, pl* **in·di·gos** *or* **in·di·goes** **1** : a blue dye made artificially and formerly obtained from plants (**indigo plants**) **2** : a dark grayish blue

in·di·rect \ˌin-də-'rekt, -dī-\ *adj* **1** : not straight : not the shortest ⟨an *indirect* route⟩ **2** : not straightforward ⟨*indirect* methods⟩ **3** : not having a plainly seen connection ⟨an *indirect* cause⟩ **4** : not straight to the point — **in·di·rect·ly** *adv* — **in·di·rect·ness** *n*

indirect object *n* : an object that represents the secondary goal of the action of its verb ⟨*me* in "he gave me the book" is an *indirect object*⟩

in·dis·creet \ˌin-dis-'krēt\ *adj* : not discreet : IMPRUDENT — **in·dis·creet·ly** *adv*

in·dis·cre·tion \ˌin-dis-'kresh-ən\ *n* . **1** : lack of discretion **2** : an indiscreet act or remark

in·dis·crim·i·nate \ˌin-dis-'krim-ə-nət\ *adj* : showing lack of discrimination

in·dis·pens·a·bil·i·ty \ˌin-dis-ˌpen-sə-'bil-ət-ē\ *n* : the quality or state of being indispensable

in·dis·pens·a·ble \ˌin-dis-'pen-sə-bəl\ *adj* : absolutely necessary ⟨an *indispensable* employee⟩ — **in·dis·pens·a·bly** \-blē\ *adv*

in·dis·posed \ˌin-dis-'pōzd\ *adj* **1** : slightly ill : somewhat unwell **2** : UNWILLING

in·dis·po·si·tion \ˌin-ˌdis-pə-'zish-ən\ *n* : the condition of being indisposed : a slight illness

in·dis·put·a·ble \ˌin-dis-'pyüt-ə-bəl, in-'dis-pyət-\ *adj* : not disputable : UNQUESTIONABLE — **in·dis·put·a·bly** \-blē\ *adv*

in·dis·sol·u·ble \ˌin-di-'säl-yə-bəl\ *adj* : not capable of being dissolved, broken up, or decomposed — **in·dis·sol·u·bly** \-blē\ *adv*

in·dis·tinct \ˌin-dis-'tingkt\ *adj* : not distinct — **in·dis·tinct·ly** *adv* — **in·dis·tinct·ness** *n*

in·dis·tin·guish·a·ble \ˌin-dis-'ting-gwish-ə-bəl\ *adj* : not capable of being clearly distinguished — **in·dis·tin·guish·a·bly** \-blē\ *adv*

¹in·di·vid·u·al \ˌin-də-'vij-ə-wəl\ *adj* [originally meaning "inseparable" in English, this was taken from medieval Latin *individualis* "inseparable", a compound from earlier Latin *in-* "un-" and *dividere* "to divide"] **1** : of or relating to an individual **2** : intended for one person **3** : PARTICULAR, SEPARATE **4** : having marked individuality — **in·di·vid·u·al·ly** *adv*

²individual *n* **1** : a single member of a class or species **2** : PERSON

in·di·vid·u·al·i·ty \ˌin-də-ˌvij-ə-ˈwal-ət-ē\ *n*, *pl* **in·di·vid·u·al·i·ties** **1** : the qualities that mark one person or thing off from all others **2** : the condition of having separate existence

in·di·vis·i·bil·i·ty \ˌin-də-ˌviz-ə-ˈbil-ət-ē\ *n* : the quality or state of being indivisible

in·di·vis·i·ble \ˌin-də-ˈviz-ə-bəl\ *adj* : not capable of being divided or separated — **in·di·vis·i·bly** \-blē\ *adv*

in·doc·tri·nate \in-ˈdäk-trə-ˌnāt\ *vb* **in·doc·tri·nat·ed; in·doc·tri·nat·ing** **1** : INSTRUCT, TEACH **2** : to instill with a partisan opinion, principle, or point of view

in·doc·tri·na·tion \in-ˌdäk-trə-ˈnā-shən\ *n* : the act or process of indoctrinating

in·do·lence \ˈin-də-ləns\ *n* : LAZINESS

in·do·lent \ˈin-də-lənt\ *adj* : LAZY, IDLE

in·dom·i·ta·ble \in-ˈdäm-ət-ə-bəl\ *adj* : UNCONQUERABLE — **in·dom·i·ta·bly** \-blē\ *adv*

in·door \ˌin-ˌdōr\ *adj* : of or relating to the inside of a building : done, living, or belonging within doors ⟨an *indoor* job⟩

in·doors \ˈin-ˈdōrz\ *adv* : in or into a building ⟨games to be played *indoors*⟩

indorse, indorsement *var of* ENDORSE, ENDORSEMENT

in·du·bi·ta·ble \in-ˈdü-bət-ə-bəl, -ˈdyü-\ *adj* : UNQUESTIONABLE — **in·du·bi·ta·bly** \-blē\ *adv*

in·duce \in-ˈdüs, -ˈdyüs\ *vb* **in·duced; in·duc·ing** **1** : to lead on to do something : PERSUADE, INFLUENCE **2** : to bring about : CAUSE **3** : to produce (as an electric current) by induction

in·duce·ment \in-ˈdüs-mənt, -ˈdyüs-\ *n* **1** : the act of inducing **2** : something that induces

in·duct \in-ˈdəkt\ *vb* **1** : to place in office : INSTALL **2** : to enroll into military service in accordance with a draft law

in·duc·tion \in-ˈdək-shən\ *n* **1** : the act or process of inducting **2** : the production of an electrical or magnetic effect through influence exerted by a nearby magnet, electrical current, or electrically charged body

in·dulge \in-ˈdəlj\ *vb* **in·dulged; in·dulg·ing** **1** : to give in to one's own or another's desires : HUMOR **2** : to allow oneself the pleasure of having or doing something

in·dul·gence \in-ˈdəl-jəns\ *n* **1** : the act of indulging : the state of being indulgent **2** : an indulgent act **3** : something indulged in

in·dul·gent \in-ˈdəl-jənt\ *adj* : indulging or characterized by indulgence : LENIENT **syn** see TOLERANT — **in·dul·gent·ly** *adv*

in·dus·tri·al \in-ˈdəs-trē-əl\ *adj* **1** : of, relating to, or engaged in industry ⟨*industrial* work⟩ **2** : having highly developed industries ⟨*industrial* nations⟩ — **in·dus·tri·al·ly** *adv*

in·dus·tri·al·ist \in-ˈdəs-trē-ə-ləst\ *n* : a person owning or engaged in the management of an industry

in·dus·tri·al·ize \in-ˈdəs-trē-ə-ˌlīz\ *vb* **in·dus·tri·al·ized; in·dus·tri·al·iz·ing** : to make or become industrial

in·dus·tri·ous \in-ˈdəs-trē-əs\ *adj* : DILIGENT, BUSY — **in·dus·tri·ous·ly** *adv*

in·dus·try \ˈin-dəs-trē\ *n*, *pl* **in·dus·tries** **1** : the habit of working hard and steadily **2** : a branch of business or manufacturing **3** : manufacturing activity

¹-ine \ˌīn, ən, ˌēn\ *adj suffix* : of, relating to, or like ⟨alkal*ine*⟩ ⟨opal*ine*⟩

²-ine \ˌēn, ən, ˌīn\ *n suffix* **1** : chemical element, compound, or mixture ⟨chlor*ine*⟩ ⟨gasol*ine*⟩ ⟨iod*ine*⟩ **2** : -IN

in·ed·i·ble \in-ˈed-ə-bəl\ *adj* : not fit to eat

in·ef·fa·ble \in-ˈef-ə-bəl\ *adj* : INDESCRIBABLE — **in·ef·fa·bly** \-blē\ *adv*

in·ef·fec·tive \ˌin-ə-ˈfek-tiv\ *adj* : not producing the desired effect — **in·ef·fec·tive·ly** *adv*

in·ef·fec·tu·al \ˌin-ə-ˈfek-chə-wəl\ *adj* : not producing the proper or usual effect : FUTILE — **in·ef·fec·tu·al·ly** *adv*

in·ef·fi·cien·cy \ˌin-ə-ˈfish-ən-sē\ *n*, *pl* **in·ef·fi·cien·cies** : the state or an instance of being inefficient

in·ef·fi·cient \ˌin-ə-ˈfish-ənt\ *adj* **1** : not producing the effect intended or desired : not effective **2** : not competent or capable — **in·ef·fi·cient·ly** *adv*

in·e·las·tic \ˌin-ə-ˈlas-tik\ *adj* : not elastic

in·el·i·gi·bil·i·ty \in-ˌel-ə-jə-ˈbil-ət-ē\ *n* : the condition or fact of being ineligible

in·el·i·gi·ble \in-ˈel-ə-jə-bəl\ *adj* : not eligible

in·ept \in-ˈept\ *adj* **1** : out of place **2** : lacking in skill or aptitude — **in·ept·ly** *adv*

in·e·qual·i·ty \ˌin-i-ˈkwäl-ət-ē\ *n*, *pl* **in·e·qual·i·ties** **1** : the quality of being unequal or uneven **2** : an instance of being uneven

in·ert \in-ˈərt\ *adj* : not having the power to move itself — **in·ert·ly** *adv* — **in·ert·ness** *n*

in·er·tia \in-ˈər-shə\ *n* **1** : a property of matter by which it remains at rest or in motion in the same straight line unless acted upon by some external force **2** : the disposition not to move or change

---

j job ng sing ō low ȯ moth ȯi coin th thin th this ü boot u̇ foot y you yü few yu̇ furious zh vision

in·er·tial \in-'ər-shəl\ *adj* : of or relating to inertia

in·es·cap·a·ble \,in-is-'kā-pə-bəl\ *adj* : IN-EVITABLE — **in·es·cap·a·bly** \-blē\ *adv*

in·ev·i·ta·bil·i·ty \in-,ev-ət-ə-'bil-ət-ē\ *n* : the quality or state of being inevitable

in·ev·i·ta·ble \in-'ev-ət-ə-bəl\ *adj* : incapable of being avoided — **in·ev·i·ta·bly** \-blē\ *adv*

in·ex·act \,in-ig-'zakt\ *adj* : not precisely correct or true : INACCURATE — **in·ex·act·ly** *adv* — **in·ex·act·ness** *n*

in·ex·cus·a·ble \,in-iks-'kyü-zə-bəl\ *adj* : not to be excused — **in·ex·cus·a·bly** \-blē\ *adv*

in·ex·haust·i·ble \,in-ig-'zòs-tə-bəl\ *adj* : plentiful enough not to give out or be used up — **in·ex·haust·i·bly** \-blē\ *adv*

in·ex·o·ra·ble \in-'ek-sə-rə-bəl\ *adj* : RELENT-LESS — **in·ex·o·ra·bly** \-blē\ *adv*

in·ex·pe·di·ent \,in-iks-'pēd-ē-ənt\ *adj* : not expedient : UNWISE

in·ex·pen·sive \,in-iks-'pen-siv\ *adj* : CHEAP — **in·ex·pen·sive·ly** *adv* — **in·ex·pen·sive·ness** *n*

in·ex·pe·ri·ence \,in-iks-'pir-ē-əns\ *n* : lack of experience

in·ex·pe·ri·enced \,in-iks-'pir-ē-ənst\ *adj* : being without experience

in·ex·pert \in-'eks-,pərt, ,in-iks-'pərt\ *adj* : not expert : UNSKILLED — **in·ex·pert·ly** *adv* — **in·ex·pert·ness** *n*

in·ex·plic·a·ble \,in-iks-'plik-ə-bəl, in-'eks-plik-\ *adj* : incapable of being explained or interpreted — **in·ex·plic·a·bly** \-blē\ *adv*

in·ex·press·i·ble \,in-iks-'pres-ə-bəl\ *adj* : being beyond one's power to express : INDE-SCRIBABLE — **in·ex·press·i·bly** \-blē\ *adv*

in·ex·pres·sive \,in-iks-'pres-iv\ *adj* : lacking expression or meaning — **in·ex·pres·sive·ly** *adv* — **in·ex·pres·sive·ness** *n*

in·fal·li·ble \in-'fal-ə-bəl\ *adj* 1 : not capable of being wrong 2 : not liable to fail, deceive, or disappoint — **in·fal·li·bly** \-blē\ *adv*

in·fa·mous \'in-fə-məs\ *adj* 1 : having an evil reputation ⟨an *infamous* person⟩ 2 : DE-TESTABLE — **in·fa·mous·ly** *adv*

in·fa·my \'in-fə-mē\ *n, pl* **in·fa·mies** 1 : an evil reputation 2 : an infamous act

in·fan·cy \'in-fən-sē\ *n, pl* **in·fan·cies** 1 : early childhood 2 : a beginning or early period of existence ⟨the *infancy* of our country⟩

¹**in·fant** \'in-fənt\ *n* [from Latin *infant-*, stem of *infans*, originally an adj. meaning "in-capable of speech", from *in-* "un-" and *fans* "speaking"] 1 : a child in the first period of life 2 : a person under the age of twenty-one

²**infant** *adj* 1 : of or relating to infancy 2 : intended for young children ⟨*infant* food⟩

in·fan·tile \'in-fən-,tīl\ *adj* : CHILDISH

infantile paralysis *n* : POLIOMYELITIS

in·fan·try \'in-fən-trē\ *n, pl* **in·fan·tries** 1 : soldiers trained, armed, and equipped to fight on foot 2 : a branch of an army com-posed of infantry

in·fat·u·at·ed \in-'fach-ə-,wāt-əd\ *adj* : hav-ing a foolish or very strong love or admiration

in·fat·u·a·tion \in-,fach-ə-'wā-shən\ *n* : the state of being infatuated

in·fect \in-'fekt\ *vb* 1 : to cause disease germs to be present in or on ⟨*infected* bedding⟩ 2 : to pass on a germ or disease to 3 : to enter and cause disease in ⟨bacteria that *infect* wounds⟩ 4 : to cause to share one's feelings

in·fec·tion \in-'fek-shən\ *n* 1 : the act or process of infecting : the state of being in-fected 2 : a contagious or infectious disease

in·fec·tious \in-'fek-shəs\ *adj* 1 : passing from one to another in the form of a germ 2 : capable of being easily spread

in·fer \in-'fər\ *vb* **in·ferred**; **in·fer·ring** 1 : to derive as a conclusion 2 : GUESS 3 : to point out 4 : HINT, SUGGEST **syn** see IMPLY

in·fer·ence \'in-fə-rəns\ *n* 1 : the act or process of inferring 2 : something inferred

¹**in·fe·ri·or** \in-'fir-ē-ər\ *adj* 1 : situated lower down (as in rank or importance) 2 : of little or less importance, value, or merit

²**inferior** *n* : an inferior person or thing

in·fe·ri·or·i·ty \in-,fir-ē-'òr-ət-ē\ *n* 1 : the state of being inferior 2 : a sense of being inferior

in·fer·nal \in-'fərn-l\ *adj* 1 : of or relating to hell ⟨the *infernal* regions⟩ 2 : HELLISH, DEVILISH — **in·fer·nal·ly** *adv*

in·fer·tile \in-'fərt-l\ *adj* : not fertile

in·fest \in-'fest\ *vb* : to spread or swarm in or over in a troublesome manner

in·fi·del \'in-fəd-l\ *n* [from Latin *infidelis* "unbelieving", a compound of *in-* "not" and *fidelis* "faithful", from *fides* "faith", the source also of English *faith* and *fidelity*] : a person who does not believe in a particular religion : UNBELIEVER

in·fi·del·i·ty \,in-fə-'del-ət-ē\ *n, pl* **in·fi·del·i·ties** 1 : lack of belief in a particular religion 2 : UNFAITHFULNESS, DISLOYALTY

in·field \'in-,fēld\ *n* 1 : the diamond-shaped part of a baseball field enclosed by the bases and home plate 2 : the players in the infield

in·field·er \'in-,fēl-dər\ *n* : a baseball player who plays in the infield

in·fi·nite \'in-fə-nət\ *adj* 1 : being without limits of any kind 2 : seeming to be with-out limits — **in·fi·nite·ly** *adv*

in·fin·i·tive \in-'fin-ət-iv\ *n* : a verb form

serving as a noun or as a modifier and at the same time showing certain characteristics of a verb ⟨"to run" in "able to run fast" is an *infinitive*⟩

in·fin·i·ty \in-'fin-ət-ē\ *n, pl* **in·fin·i·ties** **1** : the quality of being infinite **2** : unlimited extent of time, space, or quantity **3** : an indefinitely great number or amount

in·firm \in-'fərm\ *adj* : physically weak or frail : feeble from age

in·fir·ma·ry \in-'fər-mə-rē\ *n, pl* **in·fir·ma·ries** : a place for the care and housing of infirm or sick people

in·fir·mi·ty \in-'fər-mət-ē\ *n, pl* **in·fir·mi·ties** : the condition of being infirm : WEAKNESS

in·flame \in-'flām\ *vb* **in·flamed; in·flam·ing** **1** : to set on fire : KINDLE **2** : to excite to excessive action or feeling **3** : to cause to redden or grow hot (as from anger) **4** : to cause or become affected with inflammation

in·flam·ma·ble \in-'flam-ə-bəl\ *adj* **1** : FLAMMABLE **2** : easily inflamed : EXCITABLE

in·flam·ma·tion \,in-flə-'mā-shən\ *n* **1** : the act of inflaming : the state of being inflamed **2** : a bodily response to injury characterized by heat, redness, and swelling

in·flam·ma·to·ry \in-'flam-ə-,tōr-ē\ *adj* **1** : tending to excite anger or disorder ⟨an *inflammatory* speech⟩ **2** : causing or accompanied by inflammation ⟨an *inflammatory* disease⟩

in·flat·a·ble \in-'flāt-ə-bəl\ *adj* : capable of being inflated ⟨an *inflatable* toy⟩

in·flate \in-'flāt\ *vb* **in·flat·ed; in·flat·ing** **1** : to swell with air or gas ⟨*inflate* a balloon⟩ **2** : to cause to increase or expand beyond proper limits ⟨*inflated* prices⟩

in·fla·tion \in-'flā-shən\ *n* : an act of inflating : a state of being inflated

in·flect \in-'flekt\ *vb* **1** : to change a word by inflection **2** : to change or vary the pitch of the voice

in·flec·tion \in-'flek-shən\ *n* **1** : a change in the pitch of the voice **2** : a change in the form of a word marking a grammatical distinction (as of number, person, or tense)

in·flec·tion·al \in-'flek-shən-l\ *adj* : of or relating to inflection ⟨*darkened* and *darkening* are *inflectional* forms of the verb *darken*⟩

in·flex·i·ble \in-'flek-sə-bəl\ *adj* **1** : not easily bent or twisted : RIGID **2** : not easily influenced or persuaded : FIRM

in·flict \in-'flikt\ *vb* **1** : to give (as blows) by or as if by striking ⟨*inflict* a wound⟩ **2** : to cause to be endured ⟨*inflict* punishment⟩

in·flic·tion \in-'flik-shən\ *n* **1** : the act of inflicting **2** : something inflicted

in·flo·res·cence \,in-flə-'res-ns\ *n* : the arrangement of flowers on a stalk

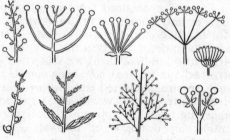

inflorescences of various forms

¹in·flu·ence \'in-,flü-əns\ *n* **1** : the act or power of producing an effect without apparent force or direct authority **2** : a person or thing that influences

syn INFLUENCE, PRESTIGE, AUTHORITY all mean power that can be exerted over the mind or behavior of others. INFLUENCE suggests power that may be exercised or felt unknowingly ⟨the *influence* of the extreme heat on the people's tempers⟩ and carries no special indication of whether the effect is a good or bad one ⟨wondered what kind of *influence* the new principal would have⟩ PRESTIGE indicates an influence that is knowingly received and acquires its force from the excellence or superior position of the source ⟨one whose *prestige* as a statesman gave his words added weight⟩ AUTHORITY implies quite direct and often considerable power over people's thoughts or actions but gives no indication of the source of or reason for the power ⟨spoke with *authority* on the subject of France since he was a Frenchman⟩

²influence *vb* **in·flu·enced; in·flu·enc·ing** : to have an influence on : affect by influence

in·flu·en·tial \,in-flü-'en-chəl\ *adj* : having or exerting influence

in·flu·en·za \,in-flü-'en-zə\ *n* [from Italian *influenza*, literally, "influence"; so called from the belief that epidemics were due to the influence of the stars] : a very contagious virus disease resembling a severe feverish cold

in·form \in-'fòrm\ *vb* **1** : to let a person know something **2** : to give information so as to accuse or cast suspicion — **in·form·er** *n*

in·for·mal \in-'fòr-məl\ *adj* **1** : being without formality or ceremony ⟨an *informal* party⟩ **2** : appropriate for ordinary or casual use ⟨*informal* clothes⟩ — **in·for·mal·ly** *adv*

in·for·mal·i·ty \,in-fòr-'mal-ət-ē\ *n, pl* **in·for·mal·i·ties** **1** : the quality or state of being informal **2** : an informal act

in·form·ant \in-'for-mənt\ *n* : INFORMER

in·for·ma·tion \ˌin-fər-'mā-shən\ *n* **1** : the communication or reception of knowledge **2** : knowledge obtained from investigation, study, or instruction : FACTS **3** : NEWS

in·for·ma·tive \in-'for-mət-iv\ *adj* : imparting knowledge : INSTRUCTIVE

in·frac·tion \in-'frak-shən\ *n* : VIOLATION

in·fra·red \ˌin-frə-'red\ *adj* : lying outside the visible spectrum at its red end ⟨*infrared* rays⟩

in·fre·quent \in-'frē-kwənt\ *adj* **1** : seldom happening : RARE **2** : placed or occurring at considerable distances or intervals — **in·fre·quent·ly** *adv*

in·fringe \in-'frinj\ *vb* **in·fringed**; **in·fring·ing** **1** : to fail to obey or heed : VIOLATE ⟨*infringe* a law⟩ **2** : to go further than is right or fair to another — **in·fringe·ment** *n*

in·fu·ri·ate \in-'fyùr-ē-ˌāt\ *vb* **in·fu·ri·at·ed**; **in·fu·ri·at·ing** : to make furious : ENRAGE

in·fuse \in-'fyüz\ *vb* **in·fused**; **in·fus·ing** **1** : to put in as if by pouring ⟨*infused* courage into his followers⟩ **2** : INSPIRE **3** : to steep (as tea) in water without boiling — **in·fu·sion** \in-'fyü-zhən\ *n*

¹-ing \ing\ *vb suffix or adj suffix* — used to form the present participle ⟨sail*ing*⟩ and sometimes to form adjectives not derived from a verb ⟨hulk*ing*⟩

²-ing *n suffix* **1** : action or process ⟨sleep*ing*⟩ ⟨meet*ing*⟩ **2** : product or result of an action or process ⟨engrav*ing*⟩ ⟨earn*ings*⟩ **3** : something used in or connected with making or doing ⟨bedd*ing*⟩ ⟨roof*ing*⟩

in·ge·nious \in-'jē-nyəs\ *adj* [from Latin *ingenium* "innate ability", a compound of *in-* "in" and the root *gen-* meaning "birth"] **1** : marked by especial aptitude at discovering, inventing, or contriving **2** : cleverly planned, made, or done — **in·ge·nious·ly** *adv*

in·ge·nu·i·ty \ˌin-jə-'nü-ət-ē, -'nyü-\ *n, pl* **in·ge·nu·i·ties** : SKILL, CLEVERNESS

in·gen·u·ous \in-'jen-yə-wəs\ *adj* **1** : FRANK, STRAIGHTFORWARD **2** : NAÏVE — **in·gen·u·ous·ly** *adv* — **in·gen·u·ous·ness** *n*

in·glo·ri·ous \in-'glōr-ē-əs\ *adj* **1** : not glorious **2** : SHAMEFUL — **in·glo·ri·ous·ly** *adv*

in·got \'ing-gət\ *n* : a mass of metal cast into a convenient shape (as for storage)

in·grate \'in-ˌgrāt\ *n* : an ungrateful person

in·gra·ti·ate \in-'grā-shē-ˌāt\ *vb* **in·gra·ti·at·ed**; **in·gra·ti·at·ing** : to gain favor by deliberate effort

in·gra·ti·at·ing \in-'grā-shē-ˌāt-ing\ *adj* **1** : PLEASING ⟨an *ingratiating* smile⟩ **2** : FLATTERING — **in·gra·ti·at·ing·ly** *adv*

in·grat·i·tude \in-'grat-ə-ˌtüd, -ˌtyüd\ *n* : lack of gratitude or thankfulness

in·gre·di·ent \in-'grēd-ē-ənt\ *n* : one of the substances that make up a mixture

in·hab·it \in-'hab-ət\ *vb* : to live or dwell in

in·hab·it·ant \in-'hab-ət-ənt\ *n* : one who lives permanently in a place

in·hal·ant \in-'hā-lənt\ *n* : something (as a medicated spray) that is inhaled

in·ha·la·tion \ˌin-ə-'lā-shən, -hə-\ *n* : the act or an instance of inhaling

in·hale \in-'hāl\ *vb* **in·haled**; **in·hal·ing** **1** : to draw in by breathing **2** : to breathe in

in·har·mo·ni·ous \ˌin-här-'mō-nē-əs\ *adj* : not harmonious — **in·har·mo·ni·ous·ly** *adv*

in·her·ent \in-'hir-ənt\ *adj* : belonging to or being a part of the essential character of a person or thing — **in·her·ent·ly** *adv*

in·her·it \in-'her-ət\ *vb* **1** : to receive especially from one's parents or ancestors **2** : to receive by birth

in·her·it·ance \in-'her-ət-əns\ *n* **1** : the act of inheriting **2** : something inherited

in·hib·it \in-'hib-ət\ *vb* **1** : to prohibit or restrain from doing something **2** : to discourage from free or spontaneous activity

in·hos·pit·a·ble \ˌin-ˌhäs-'pit-ə-bəl, in-'häs-pit-\ *adj* : not showing hospitality — **in·hos·pit·a·bly** \-blē\ *adv*

in·hu·man \in-'hyü-mən\ *adj* **1** : lacking pity or kindness **2** : of or suggesting a class of beings that are not human — **in·hu·man·ly** *adv*

in·hu·mane \ˌin-hyü-'mān\ *adj* : not humane

in·hu·man·i·ty \ˌin-hyü-'man-ət-ē\ *n* : the quality or state of being cruel or barbarous

in·im·i·cal \in-'im-i-kəl\ *adj* **1** : HOSTILE, UNFRIENDLY **2** : HARMFUL

in·im·i·ta·ble \in-'im-ət-ə-bəl\ *adj* : not capable of being imitated : MATCHLESS — **in·im·i·ta·bly** \-blē\ *adv*

in·iq·ui·tous \in-'ik-wət-əs\ *adj* : WICKED

in·iq·ui·ty \in-'ik-wət-ē\ *n, pl* **in·iq·ui·ties** **1** : great injustice : WICKEDNESS **2** : SIN

¹i·ni·tial \i-'nish-əl\ *adj* **1** : of or relating to the beginning : EARLIEST ⟨an *initial* effort⟩ **2** : placed or standing at the beginning : FIRST

²initial *n* **1** : the first letter of a name **2** : a large letter beginning a text or a paragraph

³initial *vb* **i·ni·tialed** *or* **i·ni·tialled**; **i·ni·tial·ing** *or* **i·ni·tial·ling** : to mark with an initial

i·ni·ti·ate \i-'nish-ē-ˌāt\ *vb* **i·ni·ti·at·ed**; **i·ni·ti·at·ing** **1** : to set going **2** : to begin the instruction of in something **3** : to admit into a club or society by special ceremonies

i·ni·ti·a·tion \i-ˌnish-ē-'ā-shən\ *n* **1** : the act or an instance of initiating : the process of being initiated **2** : the ceremonies with which a person is made a member of a club or society

i·ni·tia·tive \i-'nish-ət-iv\ *n* **1** : an introductory step or movement **2** : energy displayed in initiating action : ENTERPRISE

in·ject \in-'jekt\ *vb* **1** : to throw, drive, or force into something **2** : to force a fluid into (as a part of the body) for medical reasons

in·jec·tion \in-'jek-shən\ *n* **1** : an act or instance of injecting **2** : something injected

in·junc·tion \in-'jəngk-shən\ *n* : ORDER

in·jure \'in-jər\ *vb* **in·jured; in·jur·ing 1** : to do an injustice to : WRONG **2** : HURT, DAMAGE

in·ju·ri·ous \in-'jùr-ē-əs\ *adj* : causing injury

in·ju·ry \'in-jə-rē\ *n, pl* **in·ju·ries 1** : an act that damages or hurts : DAMAGE **2** : hurt, damage, or loss sustained

in·jus·tice \in-'jəs-təs\ *n* **1** : violation of a person's rights **2** : an unjust act or deed

¹**ink** \'ingk\ *n* : a usually liquid material for writing or printing

²**ink** *vb* : to put ink on

ink·horn \'ingk-ˌhòrn\ *n* : a small bottle (as of horn) for holding ink

in·kling \'ing-kling\ *n* **1** : HINT, INTIMATION **2** : a vague notion

ink·stand \'ingk-ˌstand\ *n* : INKWELL

ink·well \'ingk-ˌwel\ *n* : a container for ink

ink·y \'ing-kē\ *adj* **ink·i·er; ink·i·est 1** : consisting of or resembling ink ⟨*inky* darkness⟩ **2** : soiled with or as if with ink ⟨*inky* hands⟩

in·laid \'in-'lād\ *adj* **1** : set into a surface in a decorative design **2** : decorated with a design or material set into a surface

¹**in·land** \'in-ˌland\ *n* : the part of a country away from the coast or boundaries

²**inland** *adj* **1** *chiefly Brit* : not foreign : DOMESTIC ⟨*inland* revenue⟩ **2** : of or relating to the interior of a country

³**inland** *adv* : into or toward the interior

in–law \'in-ˌlò\ *n* : a relative by marriage

¹**in·lay** \'in-'lā\ *vb* **in·laid** \-'lād\; **in·lay·ing** : to set into a surface for decoration or reinforcement

²**in·lay** \'in-ˌlā\ *n* : inlaid work or material used in inlaying

in·let \'in-ˌlet\ *n* **1** : an act of letting in **2** : an indentation in a shoreline : BAY **3** : an opening for intake

in·mate \'in-ˌmāt\ *n* **1** : one of a group occupying a single residence **2** : a person confined in an institution (as an asylum or prison)

in me·mo·ri·am \ˌin-mə-'mōr-ē-əm\ *prep* : in memory of

in·most \'in-ˌmōst\ *adj* : INNERMOST

inn \'in\ *n* : a place that provides lodging and food for travelers : HOTEL

in·ner \'in-ər\ *adj* **1** : situated farther in **2** : of or relating to the mind or spirit

inner ear *n* : the inner hollow part of the ear that contains sense organs which perceive sound and help keep the body properly balanced

in·ner·most \'in-ər-ˌmōst\ *adj* : farthest inward : INMOST

in·ning \'in-ing\ *n* **1** : a baseball team's turn at bat that ends with the third out **2** : a division of a baseball game that consists of a turn at bat for each team

inn·keep·er \'in-ˌkē-pər\ *n* : the landlord of an inn

in·no·cence \'in-ə-səns\ *n* **1** : freedom from guilt, sin, or blame **2** : freedom from guile or cunning : SIMPLICITY

in·no·cent \'in-ə-sənt\ *adj* **1** : free from sin **2** : free from guilt or blame **3** : free from evil influence or effect — **in·no·cent·ly** *adv*

in·noc·u·ous \i-'näk-yə-wəs\ *adj* **1** : HARMLESS **2** : INOFFENSIVE **3** : INSIGNIFICANT

in·no·va·tion \ˌin-ə-'vā-shən\ *n* **1** : the introduction of something new **2** : a new idea, method, or device : NOVELTY

in·nu·mer·a·ble \i-'nü-mə-rə-bəl, -'nyü-\ *adj* : too many to be counted

in·oc·u·late \in-'äk-yə-ˌlāt\ *vb* **in·oc·u·lat·ed; in·oc·u·lat·ing** : to inject a serum, vaccine, or weakened germ into to protect against or treat a disease

in·oc·u·la·tion \in-ˌäk-yə-'lā-shən\ *n* **1** : the act or an instance of inoculating **2** : material used in inoculating

in·of·fen·sive \ˌin-ə-'fen-siv\ *adj* **1** : not harmful **2** : PEACEABLE **3** : not offensive

in·op·por·tune \in-ˌäp-ər-'tün, -'tyün\ *adj* : INCONVENIENT, UNSEASONABLE

in·quest \'in-ˌkwest\ *n* : an official inquiry into the cause of a death

in·quire \in-'kwīr\ *vb* **in·quired; in·quir·ing 1** : to ask about : ASK ⟨*inquire* the way⟩ **2** : to make an examination or investigation — **in·quir·er** *n* — **in·quir·ing·ly** *adv*

in·qui·ry \'in-ˌkwī-rē, -kwə-\ *n, pl* **in·qui·ries 1** : the act of inquiring **2** : a request for information **3** : a thorough examination

in·quis·i·tive \in-'kwiz-ət-iv\ *adj* **1** : habitually seeking information **2** : inclined to ask questions : PRYING **syn** see CURIOUS — **in·quis·i·tive·ly** *adv* — **in·quis·i·tive·ness** *n*

in·sane \in-'sān\ *adj* **1** : unsound in mind **2** : used by or for the insane — **in·sane·ly** *adv*

in·san·i·ty \in-'san-ət-ē\ *n, pl* **in·san·i·ties** : the condition of being insane : mental illness

in·sa·tia·ble \in-'sā-shə-bəl\ *adj* : incapable of being satisfied

in·scribe \in-'skrīb\ *vb* **in·scribed; in·scrib·ing 1** : to write, engrave, or print as a lasting

---

j job ng sing ō low ò moth òi coin th thin th̲ this ü boot ù foot y you yü few yù furious zh vision

record **2** : to write, engrave, or print characters on or in ⟨*inscribe* a book⟩

in·scrip·tion \in-'skrip-shən\ *n* **1** : something that is inscribed **2** : the dedication of a book or work of art **3** : the act of inscribing

in·sect \'in-ˌsekt\ *n* **1** : a very small usually

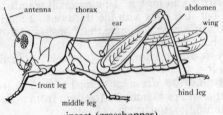

insect (grasshopper)

winged animal that has six jointed legs and a body formed of three parts ⟨flies, bees, and beetles are true *insects*⟩ **2** : an animal (as a spider) similar to the true insects

in·sec·ti·cide \in-'sek-tə-ˌsīd\ *n* : a chemical used to kill insects

in·se·cure \ˌin-si-'kyùr\ *adj* : not safe or secure — **in·se·cure·ly** *adv*

in·se·cu·ri·ty \ˌin-si-'kyùr-ət-ē\ *n* : the quality or state of being insecure

in·sen·si·ble \in-'sen-sə-bəl\ *adj* **1** : not endowed with consciousness : INANIMATE ⟨*insensible* rocks⟩ **2** : deprived of consciousness **3** : not able to feel ⟨*insensible* to pain⟩ **4** : so small or gradual as to be imperceptible or scarcely perceptible **5** : being unaware or indifferent — **in·sen·si·bly** \-blē\ *adv*

in·sen·si·tive \in-'sen-sət-iv\ *adj* : not sensitive : lacking feeling — **in·sen·si·tive·ly** *adv*

in·sen·si·tiv·i·ty \in-ˌsen-sə-'tiv-ət-ē\ *n* : lack of sensitivity

in·sen·ti·ence \in-'sen-chē-əns\ *n* : the quality or state of being insentient

in·sen·ti·ent \in-'sen-chē-ənt\ *adj* : lacking perception, consciousness, or animation

in·sep·a·ra·bil·i·ty \in-ˌsep-ə-rə-'bil-ət-ē\ *n* : the quality or state of being inseparable

in·sep·a·ra·ble \in-'sep-ə-rə-bəl\ *adj* : incapable of being separated — **in·sep·a·ra·bly** \-blē\ *adv*

¹**in·sert** \in-'sərt\ *vb* **1** : to put or thrust in **2** : to set in and make fast

²**in·sert** \'in-ˌsərt\ *n* : something that is inserted or is for insertion

in·ser·tion \in-'sər-shən\ *n* **1** : the act or process of inserting **2** : something inserted

¹**in·set** \'in-ˌset\ *n* : something that is inset

²**inset** *vb* **in·set** *or* **in·set·ted; in·set·ting** : to set in : INSERT

¹**in·side** \in-'sīd\ *n* **1** : an inner side or surface : the part within : INTERIOR ⟨the *inside* of

a box⟩ **2** : ENTRAILS — usually used in plural

²**inside** *adj* **1** : of, relating to, or being on the inside ⟨an *inside* wall⟩ **2** : included or enclosed in something **3** : measured from within **4** : relating or known to a select group

³**inside** *prep* **1** : to or on the inside of ⟨*inside* the house⟩ **2** : before the end of : WITHIN

⁴**inside** *adv* **1** : on the inner side ⟨cleaned his car *inside* and out⟩ **2** : in or into the interior

in·sid·er \in-'sīd-ər\ *n* : a person having firsthand information

in·sight \'in-ˌsīt\ *n* : the power or act of seeing into a situation : UNDERSTANDING

in·sig·ni·a \in-'sig-nē-ə\ *or* **in·sig·ne** \-nē\ *n, pl* **insignia** *or* **in·sig·ni·as** : a distinguishing mark (as of authority, office, or honor) : BADGE, EMBLEM

insignia of U.S. Army Medical Corps

in·sig·nif·i·cance \ˌin-sig-'nif-i-kəns\ *n* : the quality or state of being insignificant

in·sig·nif·i·cant \ˌin-sig-'nif-i-kənt\ *adj* : not significant — **in·sig·nif·i·cant·ly** *adv*

in·sin·cere \ˌin-sin-'siər\ *adj* : not sincere — **in·sin·cere·ly** *adv*

in·sin·cer·i·ty \ˌin-sin-'ser-ət-ē\ *n* : lack of sincerity

in·sin·u·ate \in-'sin-yə-ˌwāt\ *vb* **in·sin·u·at·ed; in·sin·u·at·ing** **1** : to introduce gently, slowly, or indirectly **2** : HINT, IMPLY

in·sin·u·at·ing \in-'sin-yə-ˌwāt-ing\ *adj* **1** : tending gradually to cause doubt, distrust, or change of outlook **2** : winning favor and confidence by imperceptible degrees

in·sin·u·a·tion \in-ˌsin-yə-'wā-shən\ *n* **1** : a sly or indirect suggestion **2** : the gaining of favor by gentle or artful means

in·sip·id \in-'sip-əd\ *adj* **1** : lacking taste or flavor : TASTELESS **2** : lacking in qualities that interest, stimulate, or challenge : DULL

in·sist \in-'sist\ *vb* **1** : to place special emphasis or great importance ⟨*insists* on punctuality⟩ **2** : to request urgently

in·sist·ence \in-'sis-təns\ *n* : PERSISTENCE

in·sist·ent \in-'sis-tənt\ *adj* : compelling attention : PERSISTENT— **in·sist·ent·ly** *adv*

in·so·lence \'in-sə-ləns\ *n* : lack of respect for rank or position : a haughty attitude

in·so·lent \'in-sə-lənt\ *adj* : exhibiting insolence — **in·so·lent·ly** *adv*

in·sol·u·bil·i·ty \in-ˌsäl-yə-'bil-ət-ē\ *n* : the quality or state of being insoluble

in·sol·u·ble \in-'säl-yə-bəl\ *adj* **1** : having no solution or explanation ⟨an *insoluble* problem⟩ **2** : difficult or impossible to dissolve ⟨*insoluble* in water⟩ — **in·sol·u·bly** \-blē\ *adv*

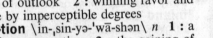

in·spect \in-'spekt\ *vb* **1** : to examine closely **2** : to view and examine (as troops) officially

in·spec·tion \in-'spek-shən\ *n* : the act of inspecting : EXAMINATION

in·spec·tor \in-'spek-tər\ *n* : a person employed to make inspections

in·spi·ra·tion \,in-spə-'rā-shən\ *n* **1** : the act of breathing in **2** : the act or power of moving the intellect or emotions ⟨the *inspiration* of music⟩ **3** : the quality or state of being inspired **4** : something that is inspired **5** : an inspiring agent or influence

in·spire \in-'spīr\ *vb* **in·spired; in·spir·ing** **1** : to move or guide by divine influence **2** : to give inspiration to : ENCOURAGE **3** : AROUSE **4** : to bring about **5** : INHALE

in·sta·bil·i·ty \,in-stə-'bil-ət-ē\ *n* : the quality or state of being unstable

in·stall \in-'stol\ *vb* **1** : to place formally in office **2** : to establish in an indicated position **3** : to set up for use or service

in·stal·la·tion \,in-stə-'lā-shən\ *n* **1** : the act of installing : the state of being installed **2** : something that is installed for use

¹**in·stall·ment** *or* **in·stal·ment** \in-'stol-mənt\ *n* : INSTALLATION 1

²**installment** *n* : one of several parts

in·stance \'in-stəns\ *n* **1** : SUGGESTION, REQUEST **2** : EXAMPLE **3** : OCCASION, CASE

¹**in·stant** \'in-stənt\ *n* : MOMENT

²**instant** *adj* **1** : closely following in time **2** : partially prepared by the manufacturer to make final preparation easy ⟨*instant* cake mix⟩ **3** : immediately soluble in water

in·stan·ta·ne·ous \,in-stən-'tā-nē-əs\ *adj* : done or occurring in an instant or without delay — **in·stan·ta·ne·ous·ly** *adv*

in·stant·ly \'in-stənt-lē\ *adv* : IMMEDIATELY

in·stead \in-'sted\ *adv* : as a substitute or alternative

instead of *prep* : as a substitute for or alternative to ⟨called *instead of* writing⟩

in·step \'in-,step\ *n* : the arched middle part of the human foot in front of the ankle joint

in·sti·gate \'in-stə-,gāt\ *vb* **in·sti·gat·ed; in·sti·gat·ing** : PROVOKE, INCITE

in·still \in-'stil\ *vb* : to impart gradually

in·stinct \'in-,stingkt\ *n* **1** : a natural aptitude or knack **2** : a largely hereditary act or course of action in response to an external stimulus that is unlearned and usually invariable **3** : behavior based on reactions below the conscious level

in·stinc·tive \in-'stingk-tiv\ *adj* : of or relating to instinct : resulting from instinct — **in·stinc·tive·ly** *adv*

¹**in·sti·tute** \'in-stə-,tüt, -,tyüt\ *vb* **in·sti·tut·ed; in·sti·tut·ing** **1** : to set up : ESTABLISH, FOUND **2** : INAUGURATE, BEGIN

²**institute** *n* **1** : an organization for the promotion of a cause ⟨an *institute* for the blind⟩ **2** : an educational institution **3** : a meeting or brief series of meetings for instruction

in·sti·tu·tion \,in-stə-'tü-shən, -'tyü-\ *n* **1** : the act of instituting : ESTABLISHMENT **2** : an established custom, practice, or law **3** : an established society or corporation

in·sti·tu·tion·al \,in-stə-'tü-shən-l, -'tyü-\ *adj* : of or relating to an institution

in·struct \in-'strəkt\ *vb* **1** : to impart knowledge to : TEACH **2** : to give information to **3** : to give directions or commands to

in·struc·tion \in-'strək-shən\ *n* **1** : LESSON **2** : ORDER **3** *pl* : DIRECTIONS **4** : the action or practice of an instructor or teacher

in·struc·tive \in-'strək-tiv\ *adj* : giving knowledge — **in·struc·tive·ly** *adv*

in·struc·tor \in-'strək-tər\ *n* : TEACHER

in·struc·tress \in-'strək-trəs\ *n* : a female instructor

in·stru·ment \'in-strə-mənt\ *n* **1** : a means whereby something is achieved, performed, or furthered **2** : TOOL, UTENSIL ⟨a surgical *instrument*⟩ **3** : a device used to produce music **4** : a formal legal document (as a deed) **5** : a measuring device **6** : a device used in flying an airplane especially when the device is the sole means of directing it

in·stru·men·tal \,in-strə-'ment-l\ *adj* **1** : acting as an instrument or means ⟨*instrumental* in organizing a club⟩ **2** : of or relating to an instrument : designed for or performed with or on an instrument — **in·stru·men·tal·ly** *adv*

in·stru·men·tal·ist \,in-strə-'ment-l-əst\ *n* : a player on a musical instrument

in·sub·or·di·nate \,in-sə-'bord-n-ət\ *adj* : unwilling to submit to authority : DISOBEDIENT

in·sub·or·di·na·tion \,in-sə-,bord-n-'ā-shən\ *n* : failure to obey authority

in·sub·stan·tial \,in-səb-'stan-chəl\ *adj* **1** : lacking reality **2** : lacking firmness or solidity — **in·sub·stan·tial·ly** *adv*

in·suf·fer·a·ble \in-'səf-ə-rə-bəl\ *adj* : incapable of being endured : INTOLERABLE ⟨*insufferable* wrongs⟩ — **in·suf·fer·a·bly** \-blē\ *adv*

in·suf·fi·cien·cy \,in-sə-'fish-ən-sē\ *n*, *pl* **in·suf·fi·cien·cies** **1** : the quality or state of being insufficient **2** : something insufficient

in·suf·fi·cient \,in-sə-'fish-ənt\ *adj* : not sufficient : INADEQUATE — **in·suf·fi·cient·ly** *adv*

in·su·late \'in-sə-,lāt\ *vb* **in·su·lat·ed; in·su·lat·ing** **1** : to place in a detached situation : ISOLATE **2** : to separate a conductor of electricity, heat, or sound from other conducting bodies by means of something that will not conduct electricity, heat, or sound

in·su·la·tion \,in-sə-'lā-shən\ *n* **1** : the act of insulating : the state of being insulated **2** : material used in insulating

in·su·la·tor \'in-sə-,lāt-ər\ *n* **1** : one that insulates **2** : a material (as rubber or glass) that is a poor conductor of electricity or a device made of such material

insulator 2

in·su·lin \'in-sə-lən\ *n* : a fluid from the pancreas that prevents or controls diabetes

¹in·sult \in-'səlt\ *vb* : to treat with insolence or contempt **syn** see OFFEND

²in·sult \'in-,səlt\ *n* : an act or speech showing disrespect or contempt

in·su·per·a·ble \in-'sü-pə-rə-bəl\ *adj* : INSURMOUNTABLE — **in·su·per·a·bly** \-blē\ *adv*

in·sur·ance \in-'shùr-əns\ *n* **1** : the act of insuring : the state of being insured **2** : the business of insuring persons or property **3** : coverage by contract whereby one party undertakes to guarantee another against loss by a specified event or peril **4** : the sum for which something is insured

in·sure \in-'shùr\ *vb* **in·sured; in·sur·ing** **1** : to give or procure insurance on or for **2** : to make certain ⟨*insure* the comfort of a guest⟩ — **in·sured** \-'shùrd\ *n* — **in·sur·er** *n*

¹in·sur·gent \in-'sər-jənt\ *n* : REBEL

²insurgent *adj* : REBELLIOUS

in·sur·mount·a·ble \,in-sər-'maùnt-ə-bəl\ *adj* : incapable of being surmounted or overcome — **in·sur·mount·a·bly** \-blē\ *adv*

in·sur·rec·tion \,in-sə-'rek-shən\ *n* : an act or instance of revolting against civil authority or an established government

in·sus·cep·ti·ble \,in-sə-'sep-tə-bəl\ *adj* : not susceptible

in·tact \in-'takt\ *adj* : not touched especially by anything that harms **syn** see PERFECT

in·take \'in-,tāk\ *n* **1** : a place where liquid or air is taken into something (as a pump) **2** : the act of taking in **3** : something taken in

¹in·tan·gi·ble \in-'tan-jə-bəl\ *adj* **1** : incapable of being touched **2** : incapable of being thought of as matter or substance

²intangible *n* : something intangible

in·te·ger \'int-i-jər\ *n* : a number that is a natural number (as 1, 2, or 3), the negative of a natural number (as -1, -2, -3), or 0

in·te·gral \'int-i-grəl\ *adj* **1** : essential to completeness ⟨an *integral* part⟩ **2** : composed of parts that make up a whole

in·te·grate \'int-ə-,grāt\ *vb* **in·te·grat·ed; in-**

te·grat·ing **1** : to form into a whole : UNITE **2** : to incorporate into a larger unit **3** : to bring into common and equal membership

in·te·gra·tion \,int-ə-'grā-shən\ *n* : the act, the process, or an instance of integrating

in·teg·ri·ty \in-'teg-rət-ē\ *n* **1** : SOUNDNESS **2** : COMPLETENESS **3** : utter honesty and sincerity ⟨a person of *integrity*⟩

in·tel·lect \'int-l-,ekt\ *n* **1** : the power of knowing **2** : the capacity for thought especially when highly developed **3** : a person of notable intellect

¹in·tel·lec·tu·al \,int-l-'ek-chə-wəl\ *adj* **1** : of or relating to the intellect or understanding ⟨*intellectual* processes⟩ **2** : having intellect to a high degree **3** : requiring study and thought ⟨*intellectual* work⟩ — **in·tel·lec·tu·al·ly** *adv*

²intellectual *n* : an intellectual person

in·tel·li·gence \in-'tel-ə-jəns\ *n* **1** : the ability to learn and understand **2** : mental acuteness : INTELLECT **3** : INFORMATION, NEWS **4** : an agency engaged in obtaining information concerning an enemy or possible enemy

in·tel·li·gent \in-'tel-ə-jənt\ *adj* : having or showing intelligence — **in·tel·li·gent·ly** *adv*

in·tel·li·gi·ble \in-'tel-ə-jə-bəl\ *adj* : capable of being understood — **in·tel·li·gi·bly** \-blē\ *adv*

in·tem·per·ance \in-'tem-pə-rəns\ *n* : lack of moderation (as in satisfying an appetite)

in·tem·per·ate \in-'tem-pə-rət\ *adj* **1** : not moderate or mild ⟨*intemperate* weather⟩ **2** : lacking or showing lack of restraint or self-control — **in·tem·per·ate·ly** *adv*

in·tend \in-'tend\ *vb* : to have in mind as a purpose or aim : PLAN ⟨*intend* to do better⟩

in·tense \in-'tens\ *adj* **1** : existing in an extreme degree ⟨*intense* heat⟩ **2** : done with great zeal or energy **3** : showing strong feeling ⟨an *intense* person⟩ — **in·tense·ly** *adv*

in·ten·si·fi·ca·tion \in-,ten-sə-fə-'kā-shən\ *n* : the act or process of intensifying

in·ten·si·fy \in-'ten-sə-,fī\ *vb* **in·ten·si·fied; in·ten·si·fy·ing** : to make or become intense or more intensive : SHARPEN

in·ten·si·ty \in-'ten-sət-ē\ *n, pl* **in·ten·si·ties** **1** : extreme degree of strength or force **2** : the degree or amount of a quality or condition

¹in·ten·sive \in-'ten-siv\ *adj* **1** : marked by special effort : THOROUGH **2** : serving to give emphasis — **in·ten·sive·ly** *adv*

²intensive *n* : an intensive word or prefix

¹in·tent \in-'tent\ *n* **1** : PURPOSE, INTENTION ⟨with *intent* to kill⟩ **2** : MEANING, SIGNIFICANCE

²intent *adj* **1** : directed with keen or eager attention **2** : closely occupied **3** : DETERMINED, SET — **in·tent·ly** *adv* — **in·tent·ness** *n*

in·ten·tion \in-'ten-chən\ *n* **1** : a determination to act in a certain way **2** : PURPOSE, AIM **3** : MEANING, SIGNIFICANCE

in·ten·tion·al \in-'ten-chən-l\ *adj* : done by intention or design : not accidental **syn** see VOLUNTARY — **in·ten·tion·al·ly** *adv*

in·ter \in-'tər\ *vb* **in·terred; in·ter·ring** [this came, by way of French, from the Latin phrase *in terra* "in the earth"] : BURY

inter- *prefix* **1** : between : among : together ⟨*inter*mix⟩ ⟨*inter*twine⟩ **2** : mutual : mutually : reciprocal : reciprocally ⟨*inter*relation⟩ ⟨*inter*communication⟩ **3** : located or occurring between ⟨*inter*lining⟩ ⟨*inter*glacial⟩ **4** : carried on between ⟨*inter*national⟩ **5** : shared by or derived from two or more ⟨*inter*faith⟩

in·ter·act \,int-ər-'akt\ *vb* : to act upon one another

in·ter·ac·tion \,int-ər-'ak-shən\ *n* : mutual or reciprocal action or influence

in·ter·cede \,int-ər-'sēd\ *vb* **in·ter·ced·ed; in·ter·ced·ing** **1** : to act as a go-between between unfriendly parties **2** : to plead in behalf of another

in·ter·cept \,int-ər-'sept\ *vb* : to stop or interrupt the progress of — **in·ter·cep·tor** *n*

in·ter·ces·sion \,int-ər-'sesh-ən\ *n* : the act of interceding

in·ter·ces·sor \,int-ər-'ses-ər\ *n* : one that intercedes

¹**in·ter·change** \,int-ər-'chānj\ *vb* **in·ter·changed; in·ter·chang·ing** : to put each in the place of the other : EXCHANGE

²**in·ter·change** \'int-ər-,chānj\ *n* **1** : the act or an instance of interchanging **2** : a highway junction that permits passage between highways without crossing traffic streams

in·ter·change·a·ble \,int-ər-'chān-jə-bəl\ *adj* : capable of being interchanged — **in·ter·change·a·bly** \-blē\ *adv*

in·ter·course \'int-ər-,kōrs\ *n* : connection between persons or groups

in·ter·de·pend·ence \,int-ər-di-'pen-dəns\ *n* : the quality or state of being interdependent

in·ter·de·pend·ent \,int-ər-di-'pen-dənt\ *adj* : depending upon one another — **in·ter·de·pend·ent·ly** *adv*

¹**in·ter·est** \'in-trəst, 'int-ə-rəst\ *n* **1** : a right, title, or legal share in something ⟨have an *interest* in a business⟩ **2** : WELFARE, BENEFIT ⟨in the common *interest*⟩ **3** : the money paid by a borrower for the use of borrowed money **4** *pl* : a group financially interested in an industry or enterprise ⟨mining *interests*⟩ **5** : readiness to be concerned with or moved by something **6** : the quality of a thing that arouses special attention

²**interest** *vb* **1** : to involve the interest of

2 : to persuade to participate or take part **3** : to arouse or hold the interest of

in·ter·est·ed \'in-trəs-təd, 'int-ə-rəs-\ *adj* : having or showing interest

in·ter·est·ing \'in-trəs-tiŋ, 'int-ə-rəs-\ *adj* : holding the attention : arousing interest — **in·ter·est·ing·ly** *adv*

in·ter·fere \,int-ər-'fiər\ *vb* **in·ter·fered; in·ter·fer·ing** **1** : to come in collision or be in opposition : CLASH **2** : to take a part in the concerns of others : MEDDLE **syn** see MEDDLE

in·ter·fer·ence \,int-ər-'fir-əns\ *n* **1** : the act or process of interfering **2** : something that interferes

in·ter·im \'in-tə-rəm\ *n* : a time intervening

¹**in·te·ri·or** \in-'tir-ē-ər\ *adj* **1** : lying, occurring, or functioning within the limits : INNER **2** : far from the border or shore

²**interior** *n* : the inner part of a thing

in·ter·ject \,int-ər-'jekt\ *vb* : to throw in between or among other things : INSERT

in·ter·jec·tion \,int-ər-'jek-shən\ *n* **1** : an interjecting of something **2** : something interjected **3** : a word or cry (as *ouch*) expressing sudden or strong feeling

in·ter·lace \,int-ər-'lās\ *vb* **in·ter·laced; in·ter·lac·ing** : to unite by or as if by lacing together

in·ter·lard \,int-ər-'lärd\ *vb* : INTERSPERSE

in·ter·line \,int-ər-'līn\ *vb* **in·ter·lined; in·ter·lin·ing** : to insert between lines already written or printed (as in making corrections)

in·ter·lock \,int-ər-'läk\ *vb* : to lock together

in·ter·lop·er \,int-ər-'lō-pər\ *n* : INTRUDER

in·ter·lude \'int-ər-,lüd\ *n* **1** : an entertainment between the acts of a play **2** : an intervening period or event : INTERVAL **3** : a musical composition inserted between parts of a longer composition or of a drama

in·ter·mar·riage \,int-ər-'mar-ij\ *n* : marriage between members of different groups

in·ter·mar·ry \,int-ər-'mar-ē\ *vb* **in·ter·married; in·ter·mar·ry·ing** : to become connected by intermarriage

in·ter·med·dle \,int-ər-'med-l\ *vb* **in·ter·med·dled; in·ter·med·dling** : MEDDLE

in·ter·me·di·ar·y \,int-ər-'mēd-ē-,er-ē\ *n, pl* **in·ter·me·di·ar·ies** : GO-BETWEEN

¹**in·ter·me·di·ate** \,int-ər-'mēd-ē-ət\ *adj* : being or occurring at the middle place or degree or between extremes — **in·ter·me·di·ate·ly** *adv*

²**intermediate** *n* : something that is intermediate

in·ter·ment \in-'tər-mənt\ *n* : BURIAL

in·ter·mez·zo \,int-ər-'met-sō, -'med-zō\ *n, pl* **in·ter·mez·zi** \-sē, -zē\ *or* **in·ter·mez·zos** : a short musical piece connecting major sections of a long musical work

in·ter·mi·na·ble \in-'tər-mə-nə-bəl\ *adj* : END-
LESS — **in·ter·mi·na·bly** \-blē\ *adv*

in·ter·min·gle \,int-ər-'ming-gəl\ *vb* **in·ter·-
min·gled; in·ter·min·gling** : to mix together

in·ter·mis·sion \,int-ər-'mish-ən\ *n* **1** : IN-
TERRUPTION ⟨continuing without *intermission*⟩
2 : a temporary halt (as between acts of a play)

in·ter·mit·tent \,int-ər-'mit-nt\ *adj* : coming
and going at intervals — **in·ter·mit·tent·ly** *adv*

in·ter·mix \,int-ər-'miks\ *vb* : INTERMINGLE

¹in·tern \'in-,tərn\ *vb* : to confine especially
during a war — **in·tern·ment** \in-'tərn-mənt\ *n*

²in·tern *or* **in·terne** \'in-,tərn\ *n* : a medical
school graduate getting practical experience
in a hospital — **in·tern·ship** \-,ship\ *n*

³in·tern \'in-,tərn\ *vb* : to act as an intern

in·ter·nal \in-'tərn-l\ *adj* **1** : existing or
situated within something : INTERIOR, INNER
2 : having to do with the inside of the body
3 : of or relating to the domestic affairs of a
country — **in·ter·nal·ly** *adv*

in·ter·na·tion·al \,int-ər-'nash-ən-l\ *adj* : of,
relating to, or affecting two or more nations
— **in·ter·na·tion·al·ly** *adv*

in·ter·nec·ine \,int-ər-'nes-,ēn, -'nē-,sīn\ *adj*
1 : marked by great slaughter **2** : of or
relating to conflict within a group

in·tern·ee \,in-,tər-'nē\ *n* : an interned person

in·ter·plan·e·tary \,int-ər-'plan-ə-,ter-ē\ *adj*
: existing, carried on, or operating between
planets ⟨*interplanetary* space⟩

in·ter·play \'int-ər-,plā\ *n* : INTERACTION

in·ter·po·late \in-'tər-pə-,lāt\ *vb* **in·ter·po·-
lat·ed; in·ter·po·lat·ing** **1** : to alter by inserting
new matter ⟨*interpolate* a text⟩ **2** : to insert
(as words) into a text or a conversation

in·ter·pose \,int-ər-'pōz\ *vb* **in·ter·posed; in·-
ter·pos·ing** **1** : to put between **2** : to introduce
between parts of a conversation ⟨*interpose* a
question⟩ **3** : to be or come between

in·ter·po·si·tion \,int-ər-pə-'zish-ən\ *n* **1** : the
act of interposing : the state of being interposed **2** : something that is interposed

in·ter·pret \in-'tər-prət\ *vb* **1** : to tell the
meaning of : TRANSLATE, EXPLAIN **2** : to
understand according to one's own belief,
judgment, or interest **3** : to bring out the
meaning of — **in·ter·pret·er** *n*

in·ter·pre·ta·tion \in-,tər-prə-'tā-shən\
n : the act or the result of interpreting

in·ter·pre·ta·tive \in-'tər-prə-,tāt-iv\ *adj* : designed or serving to interpret

in·ter·pre·tive \in-'tər-prət-iv\ *adj* : INTER-
PRETATIVE

in·ter·ra·cial \,int-ər-'rā-shəl\ *adj* : of or involving members of different races

in·ter·re·late \,int-ər-ri-'lāt\ *vb* **in·ter·re·lat·-**

ed; **in·ter·re·lat·ing** : to bring into or have a
mutual relationship

in·ter·re·la·tion \,int-ər-ri-'lā-shən\ *n* : mutual relation — **in·ter·re·la·tion·ship** \-,ship\ *n*

in·ter·ro·gate \in-'ter-ə-,gāt\ *vb* **in·ter·ro·gat·-
ed; in·ter·ro·gat·ing** : to question formally and
systematically ⟨*interrogate* a prisoner⟩

in·ter·ro·ga·tion \in-,ter-ə-'gā-shən\ *n* : the
act of interrogating

interrogation point *n* : QUESTION MARK

in·ter·rog·a·tive \,int-ə-'räg-ət-iv\ *adj* : asking a question ⟨*interrogative* sentence⟩

in·ter·rog·a·to·ry \,int-ə-'räg-ə-,tōr-ē\ *adj*
: containing or expressing a question

in·ter·rupt \,int-ə-'rəpt\ *vb* **1** : to stop or
hinder by breaking in **2** : to break the uniformity or continuity of

in·ter·rup·tion \,int-ə-'rəp-shən\ *n* **1** : an
act of interrupting : a state of being interrupted **2** : INTERMISSION, PAUSE

in·ter·scho·las·tic \,int-ər-skə-'las-tik\ *adj*
: existing or carried on between schools

in·ter·sect \,int-ər-'sekt\ *vb* : to cut or divide
by passing through or across : CROSS

in·ter·sec·tion \,int-ər-'sek-shən\ *n* **1** : the
act or process of intersecting **2** : the place or
point where two or more things (as streets)
intersect : CROSSING **3** : the set of mathematical elements common to two sets

in·ter·sperse \,int-ər-'spərs\ *vb* **in·ter·spersed;
in·ter·spers·ing** **1** : to insert here and there
2 : to vary with things inserted here and there

in·ter·state \,int-ər-'stāt\ *adj* : relating to,
including, or connecting two or more states

in·ter·stel·lar \,int-ər-'stel-ər\ *adj* : existing
or taking place among the stars

in·ter·stice \in-'tər-stəs\ *n* : CREVICE

in·ter·twine \,int-ər-'twīn\ *vb* **in·ter·twined;
in·ter·twin·ing** : to twine or cause to twine
about one another : INTERLACE

in·ter·val \'int-ər-vəl\ *n* **1** : a space of time
between events or states ⟨an *interval* between
games⟩ **2** : a space between things **3** : the difference in pitch between two tones

in·ter·vene \,int-ər-'vēn\ *vb* **in·ter·vened; in·-
ter·ven·ing** **1** : to happen or come between
points of time or between events **2** : to come
in or between in order to stop, settle, or change
3 : to be or lie between

in·ter·ven·tion \,int-ər-'ven-chən\ *n* : the act
or fact of intervening

¹in·ter·view \'int-ər-,vyü\ *n* **1** : a formal
meeting for the purpose of giving or securing
information or advice : CONSULTATION **2** : a
written account of an interview for publication

²interview *vb* : to meet and question in an
interview — **in·ter·view·er** *n*

---

in·ter·weave \,int-ər-'wēv\ *vb* **in·ter·wove** \-'wōv\; **in·ter·wo·ven** \-'wō-vən\; **in·ter·weav·ing** **1** : to weave together **2** : INTER-MINGLE

in·tes·ti·nal \in-'tes-tən-l\ *adj* : of or relating to the intestine

in·tes·tine \in-'tes-tən\ *n* : the lower tubular part of the alimentary canal in which most of the digestion and absorption of food occurs and through which waste matter passes to be discharged

in·ti·ma·cy \'int-ə-mə-sē\ *n, pl* **in·ti·ma·cies** : the state or an instance of being intimate

¹**in·ti·mate** \'int-ə-ˌmāt\ *vb* **in·ti·mat·ed**; **in·ti·mat·ing** : SUGGEST, HINT

²**in·ti·mate** \'int-ə-mət\ *adj* **1** : belonging to one's deepest nature : PERSONAL, PRIVATE ⟨an *intimate* diary⟩ **2** : marked by very close association ⟨*intimate* friends⟩ **3** : suggesting informal warmth or privacy : COZY **4** : marked by detailed information and understanding — **in·ti·mate·ly** *adv*

³**in·ti·mate** \'int-ə-mət\ *n* : an intimate friend

in·ti·ma·tion \,int-ə-'mā-shən\ *n* **1** : the act of intimating **2** : an indirect suggestion

in·tim·i·date \in-'tim-ə-ˌdāt\ *vb* **in·tim·i·dat·ed**; **in·tim·i·dat·ing** : to make timid or fearful

in·tim·i·da·tion \in-ˌtim-ə-'dā-shən\ *n* : the act of intimidating : the state of being intimidated

in·to \'in-tə, -tü\ *prep* **1** : to the inside of ⟨ran *into* the house⟩ **2** : to the state, condition, or form of ⟨got *into* trouble⟩ **3** : AGAINST ⟨ran *into* a wall⟩

in·tol·er·a·ble \in-'täl-ə-rə-bəl\ *adj* : UNBEARABLE — **in·tol·er·a·bly** \-blē\ *adv*

in·tol·er·ance \in-'täl-ə-rəns\ *n* : the quality or state of being intolerant

in·tol·er·ant \in-'täl-ə-rənt\ *adj* : not tolerant — **in·tol·er·ant·ly** *adv*

in·to·na·tion \,in-tə-'nā-shən\ *n* **1** : the act of intoning **2** : something intoned **3** : the rise and fall in pitch of the voice in speech

in·tone \in-'tōn\ *vb* **in·toned**; **in·ton·ing** : to utter in musical or prolonged tones : CHANT

in·tox·i·cant \in-'täk-si-kənt\ *n* : something (as an alcoholic drink) that intoxicates

in·tox·i·cate \in-'täk-sə-ˌkāt\ *vb* **in·tox·i·cat·ed**; **in·tox·i·cat·ing** **1** : to make drunk **2** : to make wildly excited

in·tox·i·ca·tion \in-ˌtäk-sə-'kā-shən\ *n* **1** : an abnormal state that is or is like a poisoning ⟨intestinal *intoxication*⟩ **2** : DRUNKENNESS

in·trac·ta·ble \in-'trak-tə-bəl\ *adj* : OBSTINATE

in·tra·mu·ral \,in-trə-'myùr-əl\ *adj* : being or occurring within the limits (as of a school) ⟨*intramural* sports⟩

in·tran·si·tive \in-'trans-ət-iv, -'tranz-\ *adj* : not having or containing a direct object

intrench *var of* ENTRENCH

in·trep·id \in-'trep-əd\ *adj* : resolutely fearless and daring — **in·trep·id·ly** *adv*

in·tri·ca·cy \'in-tri-kə-sē\ *n, pl* **in·tri·ca·cies** **1** : the quality or state of being intricate **2** : something intricate

in·tri·cate \'in-tri-kət\ *adj* : very difficult to follow, understand, or arrange : COMPLICATED — **in·tri·cate·ly** *adv*

¹**in·trigue** \in-'trēg\ *vb* **in·trigued**; **in·trigu·ing** **1** : to carry on an intrigue : PLOT **2** : to arouse the interest, desire, or curiosity of

²**in·trigue** \'in-ˌtrēg, in-'trēg\ *n* : a secret and involved scheme **syn** see PLOT

in·trigu·ing \in-'trē-ging\ *adj* : arousing the interest to a marked degree

in·tro·duce \,in-trə-'düs, -'dyüs\ *vb* **in·tro·duced**; **in·tro·duc·ing** **1** : to bring into practice or use **2** : to lead or bring in especially for the first time **3** : to cause to be acquainted : PRESENT **4** : to bring forward for discussion **5** : to put in : INSERT — **in·tro·duc·er** *n*

in·tro·duc·tion \,in-trə-'dək-shən\ *n* **1** : the action of introducing **2** : something introduced **3** : the part of a book that leads up to and explains what will be found in the main part : PREFACE **4** : the act of making persons known to each other

in·tro·duc·to·ry \,in-trə-'dək-tə-rē\ *adj* : serving to introduce : PRELIMINARY

in·trude \in-'trüd\ *vb* **in·trud·ed**; **in·trud·ing** **1** : to bring in or introduce without permission **2** : to come or go in without invitation or welcome — **in·trud·er** *n*

in·tru·sion \in-'trü-zhən\ *n* : the act of intruding : the state of being intruded

intrust *var of* ENTRUST

in·tu·i·tion \,in-tù-'ish-ən, -tyù-\ *n* : a knowing or something known without conscious reasoning

in·un·date \'in-ən-ˌdāt\ *vb* **in·un·dat·ed**; **in·un·dat·ing** : to cover with a flood : OVERFLOW

in·un·da·tion \,in-ən-'dā-shən\ *n* : FLOOD

in·ure \in-'ùr, -'yùr\ *vb* **in·ured**; **in·ur·ing** : to make less sensitive : HARDEN ⟨*inured* to cold⟩

in·vade \in-'vād\ *vb* **in·vad·ed**; **in·vad·ing** **1** : to enter for conquest or plunder **2** : to encroach on ⟨his rights were *invaded*⟩ — **in·vad·er** *n*

¹**in·val·id** \in-'val-əd\ *adj* : not valid

²**in·va·lid** \'in-və-ləd\ *adj* **1** : SICKLY **2** : of or relating to one that is sick ⟨*invalid* diet⟩

³**in·va·lid** \'in-və-ləd\ *n* : a sickly or disabled person — **in·va·lid·ism** \-ˌiz-əm\ *n*

in·val·i·date \in-'val-ə-ˌdāt\ *vb* **in·val·i·dat·ed**; **in·val·i·dat·ing** : to make invalid

in·val·u·a·ble \in-'val-yə-wə-bəl\ *adj* : having value too great to be estimated : PRICELESS

in·var·i·a·bil·i·ty \in-,ver-ē-ə-'bil-ət-ē\ *n* : the quality or state of being invariable

in·var·i·a·ble \in-'ver-ē-ə-bəl\ *adj* : not changing or capable of change — **in·var·i·a·bly** \-blē\ *adv*

in·va·sion \in-'vā-zhən\ *n* : an act of invading

in·vec·tive \in-'vek-tiv\ *n* : insulting or abusive language

in·veigh \in-'vā\ *vb* : RAIL

in·vei·gle \in-'vā-gəl, -'vē-\ *vb* **in·vei·gled; in·vei·gling** : to win over or acquire by flattery

in·vent \in-'vent\ *vb* [from Latin *invenire* "to come upon", "to find", from *in-* "²in-" and *venire* "to come"] **1** : to think up : make up **2** : to create or produce for the first time

in·ven·tion \in-'ven-chən\ *n* **1** : something invented **2** : the act or process of inventing

in·ven·tive \in-'vent-iv\ *adj* : gifted with the skill and imagination to invent

in·ven·tor \in-'vent-ər\ *n* : one that invents

¹in·ven·to·ry \'in-vən-,tōr-ē\ *n, pl* **in·ven·to·ries** **1** : an itemized list (as of goods on hand) **2** : the act or process of making an inventory

²inventory *vb* **in·ven·to·ried; in·ven·to·ry·ing** : to make an inventory of

¹in·verse \in-'vərs\ *adj* **1** : opposite in order, nature, or effect **2** : being a mathematical operation that is opposite in effect to another operation — **in·verse·ly** *adv*

²inverse *n* : something inverse

in·vert \in-'vərt\ *vb* **1** : to turn inside out or upside down **2** : to reverse the order or position of

¹in·ver·te·brate \in-'vərt-ə-brət\ *adj* : having no backbone

²invertebrate *n* : an invertebrate animal

¹in·vest \in-'vest\ *vb* **1** : to install formally in an office or honor **2** : to furnish with power or authority **3** : to cover completely **4** : BESIEGE **5** : to endow with a quality

²invest *vb* : to place money in order to earn a financial return — **in·ves·tor** *n*

in·ves·ti·gate \in-'ves-tə-,gāt\ *vb* **in·ves·ti·gat·ed; in·ves·ti·gat·ing** : to observe or study by systematic examination — **in·ves·ti·ga·tor** *n*

in·ves·ti·ga·tion \in-,ves-tə-'gā-shən\ *n* : the act or process of investigating

in·ves·ti·ture \in-'ves-tə-,chùr\ *n* : the act of establishing in office

¹in·vest·ment \in-'vest-mənt\ *n* **1** : INVESTITURE **2** : BLOCKADE, SIEGE

²investment *n* **1** : the outlay of money for income or profit **2** : the sum of money invested **3** : the property in which money is invested

in·vig·o·rate \in-'vig-ə-,rāt\ *vb* **in·vig·o·rat·ed; in·vig·o·rat·ing** : to give life and energy to

in·vin·ci·bil·i·ty \in-,vin-sə-'bil-ət-ē\ *n* : the quality or state of being invincible

in·vin·ci·ble \in-'vin-sə-bəl\ *adj* : incapable of being defeated, overcome, or subdued — **in·vin·ci·bly** \-blē\ *adv*

in·vi·o·la·ble \in-'vī-ə-lə-bəl\ *adj* **1** : too sacred to be violated **2** : incapable of being harmed or destroyed by violence

in·vi·o·late \in-'vī-ə-lət\ *adj* : not violated

in·vis·i·bil·i·ty \in-,viz-ə-'bil-ət-ē\ *n* : the quality or state of being invisible

in·vis·i·ble \in-'viz-ə-bəl\ *adj* **1** : incapable of being seen ⟨the *invisible* wind⟩ **2** : HIDDEN **3** : IMPERCEPTIBLE, INCONSPICUOUS — **in·vis·i·ble·ness** *n* — **in·vis·i·bly** \-blē\ *adv*

in·vi·ta·tion \,in-və-'tā-shən\ *n* **1** : the act of inviting **2** : the written, printed, or spoken expression by which a person is invited

in·vite \in-'vīt\ *vb* **in·vit·ed; in·vit·ing** **1** : EN-TICE, TEMPT **2** : to increase the likelihood of **3** : to request the presence or participation of **4** : ENCOURAGE, WELCOME

in·vit·ing \in-'vīt-ing\ *adj* : ATTRACTIVE, TEMPTING — **in·vit·ing·ly** *adv*

in·vo·ca·tion \,in-və-'kā-shən\ *n* **1** : a prayer or supplication especially at the beginning of a service **2** : INCANTATION

¹in·voice \'in-,vȯis\ *n* : an itemized list of goods shipped usually specifying the price and the terms of sale : BILL

²invoice *vb* **in·voiced; in·voic·ing** : to make an invoice of : BILL

in·voke \in-'vōk\ *vb* **in·voked; in·vok·ing** **1** : to call on for aid or protection (as in prayer) **2** : to call forth by magic : CONJURE **3** : to appeal to as an authority or for support

in·vol·un·tar·y \in-'väl-ən-,ter-ē\ *adj* **1** : not made or done willingly or from choice **2** : not under the control of the will — **in·vol·un·tar·i·ly** \,in-,väl-ən-'ter-ə-lē\ *adv*

in·volve \in-'välv\ *vb* **in·volved; in·volv·ing** **1** : to draw in as a participant : ENGAGE **2** : to make difficult **3** : INCLUDE **4** : to require as a necessary accompaniment — **in·volve·ment** *n*

in·volved \in-'välvd\ *adj* : COMPLICATED

in·vul·ner·a·bil·i·ty \in-,vəl-nə-rə-'bil-ət-ē\ *n* : the quality or state of being invulnerable

in·vul·ner·a·ble \in-'vəl-nə-rə-bəl\ *adj* **1** : incapable of being injured or damaged **2** : immune to or proof against attack — **in·vul·ner·a·bly** \-blē\ *adv*

¹in·ward \'in-wərd\ *adj* **1** : situated on the inside : INNER **2** : MENTAL, SPIRITUAL **3** : directed toward the interior ⟨an *inward* flow⟩

²inward *or* **in·wards** \-wərdz\ *adv* **1** : toward

the center or interior ⟨slope *inward*⟩ **2** : toward the inner being ⟨turned his thoughts *inward*⟩

in·ward·ly \'in-wərd-lē\ *adv* **1** : MENTALLY, SPIRITUALLY **2** : INTERNALLY **3** : to oneself : PRIVATELY **4** : toward the center or interior

in·weave \'in-'wēv\ *vb* **in·wove** \-'wōv\; **in·wo·ven** \-'wō-vən\ : INTERWEAVE

i·o·dine \'ī-ə-ˌdīn, -əd-n\ *n* **1** : a chemical element found in seawater and seaweeds and used especially in medicine and photography **2** : a solution of iodine in alcohol used as an antiseptic

i·o·dize \'ī-ə-ˌdīz\ *vb* **i·o·dized; i·o·diz·ing** : to add iodine to ⟨*iodized* salt⟩

i·on \'ī-ən, 'ī-ˌän\ *n* : an atom or group of atoms that carries an electric charge

-ion *n suffix* **1** : act or process ⟨construc*tion*⟩ **2** : result of an act or process ⟨regula*tion*⟩ ⟨erup*tion*⟩ **3** : state or condition ⟨perfec*tion*⟩

i·on·ize \'ī-ə-ˌnīz\ *vb* **i·on·ized; i·on·iz·ing** : to convert into ions

i·on·o·sphere \ī-'än-ə-ˌsfiər\ *n* : the part of the earth's atmosphere beginning at an altitude of about 25 miles and extending outward 250 miles or more and containing electrically charged particles

i·o·ta \ī-'ōt-ə\ *n* : a tiny amount : JOT

-ious *adj suffix* : -OUS ⟨capa*cious*⟩

ir- — see IN-

i·ras·ci·ble \i-'ras-ə-bəl, ī-\ *adj* : easily provoked to anger

i·rate \ī-'rāt\ *adj* : ANGRY — **i·rate·ly** *adv* — **i·rate·ness** *n*

¹ire \'īr\ *n* : ANGER, WRATH

²ire *vb* **ired; ir·ing** : to provoke to anger

ir·i·des·cence \ˌir-ə-'des-ns\ *n* : a play of colors producing rainbow effects

ir·i·des·cent \ˌir-ə-'des-nt\ *adj* : having iridescence — **ir·i·des·cent·ly** *adv*

i·rid·i·um \i-'rid-ē-əm\ *n* : a hard brittle heavy metallic chemical element

i·ris \'ī-rəs\ *n* **1** : the colored part around the pupil of an eye **2** : a plant with swordlike leaves and flowers in six parts with three drooping and three upright

¹I·rish \'ī-rish\ *adj* : of or relating to Ireland, the Irish people, or Irish

²Irish *n* **1** Irish *pl* : the people of Ireland **2** : a language of Ireland

irk \'ərk\ *vb* : to make weary, irritated, or bored : ANNOY

irk·some \'ərk-səm\ *adj* : TIRESOME, TEDIOUS, ANNOYING — **irk·some·ness** *n*

iris 1

iris 2

¹i·ron \'ī-ərn\ *n* **1** : a heavy silver-white metallic chemical element that rusts easily, is strongly attracted by magnets, occurs in meteorites and combined in minerals, and is vital to biological processes **2** : something (as a handcuff) made of metal and especially of iron **3** : FLATIRON

²iron *adj* **1** : made of or relating to iron **2** : resembling iron (as in hardness)

³iron *vb* : to smooth or press with a heated flatiron — **i·ron·er** *n*

i·ron·ic \ī-'rän-ik\ *or* **i·ron·i·cal** \-i-kəl\ *adj* : relating to, containing, or showing irony — **i·ron·i·cal·ly** *adv*

iron lung *n* : an apparatus in which a person whose breathing is damaged (as by poliomyelitis) can be placed to help him breathe

i·ron·mon·ger \'ī-ərn-ˌməng-gər\ *n* : a dealer in iron and hardware

i·ron·wood \'ī-ərn-ˌwùd\ *n* : a tree or shrub with unusually strong tough heavy wood

i·ron·work \'ī-ərn-ˌwərk\ *n* **1** : work in iron **2** *pl* : a mill where iron or steel is smelted or heavy iron or steel products are made

i·ro·ny \'ī-rə-nē\ *n, pl* **i·ro·nies** **1** : the use of words to express the opposite of what one really means **2** : a result contrary to what was expected

ir·ra·di·ance \i-'rād-ē-əns\ *n* : something emitted like rays of light

ir·ra·di·ate \i-'rād-ē-ˌāt\ *vb* **ir·ra·di·at·ed; ir·ra·di·at·ing** **1** : to cast rays of light on **2** : to affect or treat with radiations (as X rays)

ir·ra·di·a·tion \i-ˌrād-ē-'ā-shən\ *n* **1** : emission of radiant energy (as heat) **2** : exposure to irradiation (as of X rays)

ir·ra·tio·nal \i-'rash-ən-l\ *adj* **1** : incapable of reasoning **2** : not based on reason ⟨*irrational* fears⟩ — **ir·ra·tio·nal·ly** *adv*

irrational number *n* : a real number that is not expressible as the quotient of two integers ⟨the square root of 2 is an *irrational number*⟩

ir·rec·on·cil·a·ble \i-ˌrek-ən-'sī-lə-bəl\ *adj* : impossible to reconcile or harmonize

ir·re·cov·er·a·ble \ˌir-i-'kəv-ə-rə-bəl\ *adj* : not capable of being recovered or rectified

ir·re·deem·a·ble \ˌir-i-'dē-mə-bəl\ *adj* : not capable of being redeemed

ir·re·duc·i·ble \ˌir-i-'düs-ə-bəl, -'dyüs-\ *adj* : not capable of being reduced

ir·re·fut·a·ble \ˌir-i-'fyüt-ə-bəl, i-'ref-yət-\ *adj* : impossible to refute : INDISPUTABLE

ir·reg·u·lar \i-'reg-yə-lər\ *adj* **1** : not regular **2** : lacking perfect symmetry or evenness ⟨*irregular* flowers⟩ **3** : lacking continuity or regularity of occurrence — **ir·reg·u·lar·ly** *adv*

ir·reg·u·lar·i·ty \i-ˌreg-yə-'lar-ət-ē\ *n, pl* **ir-**

reg·u·lar·i·ties 1 : the quality or state of being irregular 2 : something irregular

ir·rel·e·vance \i-'rel-ə-vəns\ n 1 : the quality or state of being irrelevant 2 : something irrelevant

ir·rel·e·vant \i-'rel-ə-vənt\ adj : not relevant — **ir·rel·e·vant·ly** adv

ir·re·li·gious \,ir-i-'lij-əs\ adj : lacking religious emotions or practices

ir·rep·a·ra·ble \i-'rep-ə-rə-bəl\ adj : not capable of being repaired, regained, or remedied — **ir·rep·a·ra·bly** \-blē\ adv

ir·re·place·a·ble \,ir-i-'plā-sə-bəl\ adj : not capable of being replaced

ir·re·press·i·ble \,ir-i-'pres-ə-bəl\ adj : impossible to repress or control

ir·re·proach·a·ble \,ir-i-'prō-chə-bəl\ adj : being beyond reproach : BLAMELESS

ir·re·sist·i·ble \,ir-i-'zis-tə-bəl\ adj : impossible to resist — **ir·re·sist·i·bly** \-blē\ adv

ir·res·o·lute \i-'rez-ə-,lüt\ adj : uncertain how to act or proceed — **ir·res·o·lute·ly** adv

ir·res·o·lu·tion \i-,rez-ə-'lü-shən\ n 1 : DOUBT, UNCERTAINTY 2 : INDECISION

ir·re·spec·tive of \,ir-i-'spek-tiv-əv\ prep : without regard to

ir·re·spon·si·bil·i·ty \,ir-i-,spän-sə-'bil-ət-ē\ n : the quality or state of being irresponsible

ir·re·spon·si·ble \,ir-i-'spän-sə-bəl\ adj 1 : not to be held responsible 2 : having or showing little or no sense of responsibility — **ir·re·spon·si·bly** \-blē\ adv

ir·re·triev·a·ble \,ir-i-'trē-və-bəl\ adj : IRRECOVERABLE — **ir·re·triev·a·bly** \-blē\ adv

ir·rev·er·ence \i-'rev-ə-rəns\ n 1 : lack of reverence 2 : an irreverent act or utterance

ir·rev·er·ent \i-'rev-ə-rənt\ adj : not reverent : DISRESPECTFUL — **ir·rev·er·ent·ly** adv

ir·re·vers·i·ble \,ir-i-'vər-sə-bəl\ adj : incapable of being reversed

ir·rev·o·ca·ble \i-'rev-ə-kə-bəl\ adj : incapable of being revoked or recalled — **ir·rev·o·ca·bly** \-blē\ adv

ir·ri·gate \'ir-ə-,gāt\ vb **ir·ri·gat·ed; ir·ri·gat·ing** 1 : to supply (as land) with water by artificial means 2 : to flush with a liquid

ir·ri·ga·tion \,ir-ə-'gā-shən\ n : an act or process of irrigating

ir·ri·ta·bil·i·ty \,ir-ət-ə-'bil-ət-ē\ n : the quality or state of being irritable

ir·ri·ta·ble \'ir-ət-ə-bəl\ adj : capable of being irritated — **ir·ri·ta·bly** \-blē\ adv

¹ir·ri·tant \'ir-ə-tənt\ adj : IRRITATING

²irritant n : something that irritates

ir·ri·tate \'ir-ə-,tāt\ vb **ir·ri·tat·ed; ir·ri·tat·ing** 1 : to cause anger or impatience in : ANNOY 2 : to make sensitive or sore

ir·ri·ta·tion \,ir-ə-'tā-shən\ n 1 : the act of irritating : the state of being irritated 2 : something that irritates

is \iz\ pres 3d sing of BE

is- or **i·so-** prefix : equal : uniform ⟨isobar⟩

-ish \ish\ adj suffix 1 : of, relating to, or being ⟨Finnish⟩ 2 : characteristic of ⟨boyish⟩ ⟨mulish⟩ 3 : somewhat ⟨purplish⟩ 4 : being approximately ⟨fortyish⟩ ⟨eightish⟩

i·sin·glass \'īz-n-,glas\ n 1 : a gelatin obtained from the air bladders of fishes (as sturgeons) 2 : mica in thin sheets

Is·lam \is-'läm\ n : a religion marked by belief in Allah as the sole deity, in Muhammad as his prophet, and in the Koran

is·land \'ī-lənd\ n 1 : an area of land surrounded by water and smaller than a continent 2 : something suggesting an island by its isolated position

is·land·er \'ī-lən-dər\ n : an inhabitant of an island

isle \'īl\ n : a usually small island

is·let \'ī-lət\ n : a little island

-ism \,iz-əm\ n suffix 1 : act : practice : process ⟨baptism⟩ ⟨criticism⟩ 2 : manner of action or behavior characteristic of a specified person or thing ⟨despotism⟩ ⟨heroism⟩ 3 : state : condition ⟨paganism⟩ ⟨alcoholism⟩ 4 : doctrine : theory : cult : system ⟨Buddhism⟩ ⟨socialism⟩

is·n't \'iz-nt\ : is not

iso- — see IS-

i·so·bar \'ī-sə-,bär\ n : a line on a map to indicate areas having the same atmospheric pressure

i·so·late \'ī-sə-,lāt\ vb **i·so·lat·ed; i·so·lat·ing** : to place or keep apart from others

i·so·la·tion \,ī-sə-'lā-shən\ n : the act of isolating : the condition of being isolated

i·sos·ce·les triangle \ī-,säs-ə-,lēz-\ n : a triangle having two sides of equal length

¹Is·rae·li \iz-'rā-lē\ adj : of or relating to the Republic of Israel or its people

²Israeli n : a native or inhabitant of the Republic of Israel

Is·ra·el·ite \'iz-rē-ə-,līt\ n : a member of the Hebrew people descended from Jacob

is·su·ance \'ish-ù-əns\ n : the act of issuing

¹is·sue \'ish-ü\ n 1 : the action of going, coming, or flowing out : EMERGENCE 2 : OFFSPRING, PROGENY 3 : OUTCOME, RESULT 4 : a matter in dispute 5 : a discharge (as of blood) from the body 6 : the act of giving out officially ⟨an issue of supplies⟩ 7 : the thing or quantity of things given out at one time

²issue vb **is·sued; is·su·ing** 1 : to go, come, or flow out 2 : RESULT 3 : to give out officially 4 : to send out for sale or circulation

-ist \əst\ *n suffix* **1** : one that performs a specified action ⟨cyc*list*⟩ : one that makes or produces ⟨nove*list*⟩ **2** : one that plays a specified musical instrument or operates a specified mechanical contrivance ⟨harp*ist*⟩ ⟨automobil*ist*⟩ **3** : one that specializes in a specified art or science or skill ⟨geolog*ist*⟩ **4** : one that follows or advocates a specified doctrine or system or code of behavior ⟨socia*list*⟩

isth·mus \'is-məs\ *n* : a neck of land separating two bodies of water and connecting two larger areas of land

¹it \it, ət\ *pron* **1** : the act, thing, or matter mentioned before **2** : the general state of affairs ⟨how's *it* going⟩ **3** — used with little meaning of its own in certain kinds of sentences ⟨*it*'s snowing⟩ ⟨footed *it* home⟩

²it \'it\ *n* : the player in a game (as tag) who performs a function essential to the nature of the game

¹I·tal·ian \i-'tal-yən\ *n* **1** : a native or inhabitant of Italy **2** : the language of the Italians

²Italian *adj* : of or relating to Italy, the Italian people, or Italian

¹i·tal·ic \i-'tal-ik\ *adj* : of or relating to a type style with characters that slant upward to the right (as in "*these characters are italic*")

²italic *n* : an italic character or type

i·tal·i·cize \i-'tal-ə-ˌsīz\ *vb* **i·tal·i·cized; i·tal·i·ciz·ing** **1** : to print in italics **2** : UNDERLINE

¹itch \'ich\ *vb* : to have or cause an itch

²itch *n* **1** : an uneasy irritating sensation in the skin **2** : a skin disorder accompanied by an itch **3** : a restless usually constant desire

itch·y \'ich-ē\ *adj* **itch·i·er; itch·i·est** : ITCHING

it'd \ˌit-əd\ : it had : it would

-ite \ˌīt\ *n suffix* **1** : native : resident ⟨Brooklyn*ite*⟩ **2** : descendant ⟨Adam*ite*⟩ **3** : adherent : follower ⟨Wagner*ite*⟩

i·tem \'īt-əm\ *n* **1** : a separate part in a list, account, or series **2** : a brief piece of news

i·tem·i·za·tion \ˌīt-ə-mə-'zā-shən\ *n* : the act or an instance of itemizing

i·tem·ize \'īt-ə-ˌmīz\ *vb* **i·tem·ized; i·tem·iz·ing** : LIST

it·er·ate \'it-ə-ˌrāt\ *vb* **it·er·at·ed; it·er·at·ing** : REITERATE, REPEAT

it·er·a·tion \ˌit-ə-'rā-shən\ *n* : REPETITION

it·er·a·tive \'it-ə-ˌrāt-iv\ *adj* : marked by or involving repetition

¹i·tin·er·ant \ī-'tin-ə-rənt\ *adj* : traveling from place to place

²itinerant *n* : one that travels about

-itis \'īt-əs\ *n suffix* : inflammation of ⟨tonsill*itis*⟩ ⟨appendic*itis*⟩

it'll \ˌit-l\ : it shall : it will

its \its\ *adj* : of or relating to it or itself

it's \its\ **1** : it is **2** : it has

it·self \it-'self\ *pron* : its own self

-i·ty \ət-ē\ *n suffix, pl* **-i·ties** : quality : state : degree ⟨alkalin*ity*⟩

-i·um \ē-əm\ *n suffix* : chemical element ⟨sod*ium*⟩

-ive \iv\ *adj suffix* : that performs or tends toward an indicated action ⟨correct*ive*⟩

i·vo·ry \'ī-və-rē\ *n, pl* **i·vo·ries** **1** : the hard creamy-white substance that composes the tusks of an elephant **2** : a pale yellow

i·vy \'ī-vē\ *n, pl* **i·vies** **1** : a woody vine with evergreen leaves, small yellowish flowers, and black berries often found growing on buildings **2** : a plant that resembles ivy

ivy

-i·za·tion \ə-'zā-shən, ī-; *the second is to be understood at entries*\ *n suffix* : action : process : state ⟨social*ization*⟩

-ize \ˌīz\ *vb suffix* **-ized; -iz·ing** **1** : cause to be or conform to or resemble ⟨American*ize*⟩ : form or cause to be formed into ⟨crystall*ize*⟩ ⟨union*ize*⟩ **2** : subject to a specified action ⟨bapt*ize*⟩ **3** : saturate, treat, or combine with ⟨macadam*ize*⟩ **4** : treat like ⟨idol*ize*⟩ **5** : engage in a specified activity ⟨philosoph*ize*⟩

iz·zard \'iz-ərd\ *n* : the letter *z*

j \'jā\ *n, often cap* : the tenth letter of the English alphabet

¹jab \'jab\ *vb* **jabbed; jab·bing** : to thrust quickly or abruptly with or as if with something sharp : POKE

²jab *n* : a quick thrust or poke

¹jab·ber \'jab-ər\ *vb* : to talk rapidly, indistinctly, or so as not to be understandable

²jabber *n* : confused talk : CHATTER

jab·ber·wock·y \'jab-ər-ˌwäk-ē\ *n* : meaningless speech or writing

¹jack \'jak\ *n* **1** : a playing card bearing the figure of a man **2** : a device for exerting pressure or lifting a heavy body a short distance **3** : a small six-pointed metal object used in a children's game (**jacks**) **4** : a small national flag flown by a ship **5** : a socket in an electric circuit used with a plug to make a connection with another circuit

jack 2

²jack \vb\ **1** : to move or lift by or as if by a jack **2** : INCREASE ⟨*jacked* the price up⟩

jack·al \'jak-əl, -,ȯl\ *n* : any of several Old World wild dogs similar to but smaller than wolves

jack·ass \'jak-,as\ *n* **1** : a male ass : DONKEY **2** : a stupid person : FOOL

jack·daw \'jak-,dȯ\ *n* : a European bird somewhat like a crow

jack·et \'jak-ət\ *n* [from Old French *jaquet* "short jacket", from *jacque* "peasant"; perhaps so called because such jackets were commonly worn by peasants] **1** : a short coat : a short coatlike garment with or without sleeves **2** : an outer covering or casing ⟨a book *jacket*⟩

Jack Frost \'jak-'frȯst\ *n* : frost or frosty weather personified

jack–in–the–box \'jak-ən-thə-,bäks\ *n, pl* **jack–in–the–box·es** *or* **jacks–in–the–box** : a small box out of which a toy head springs when the lid is raised

jack–in–the–pul·pit \,jak-ən-thə-'pul-,pit\ *n, pl* **jack–in–the–pul·pits** *or* **jacks–in–the–pul·pit** : a plant that grows in moist shady woods and bears tiny yellowish flowers on a spike protected by a hoodlike leaf

¹jack·knife \'jak-,nīf\ *n, pl* **jack·knives** \-,nīvz\ : a large pocketknife

²jackknife *vb* **jack·knifed; jack·knif·ing** : to double up like a jackknife

jack–of–all–trades \,jak-əv-'ȯl-,trādz\ *n, pl* **jacks–of–all–trades** : a person who has some ability at many trades

jack–o'–lan·tern \'jak-ə-,lant-ərn\ *n* : a lantern made of a pumpkin cut to look like a human face

jack·pot \'jak-,pät\ *n* : an impressive often unexpected success or reward

jack-o'-lantern

jack·rab·bit \'jak-,rab-ət\ *n* : a North American hare having very long ears and long hind legs

jade \'jād\ *n* : a hard usually green stone used in making jewelry

jad·ed \'jād-əd\ *adj* : TIRED, EXHAUSTED

jag·ged \'jag-əd\ *adj* : sharply notched : ROUGH ⟨a *jagged* edge⟩ — **jag·ged·ly** *adv*

jag·uar \'jag-,wär\ *n* : a large brownish yellow black-spotted animal of the cat family found from Texas to Paraguay

¹jail \'jāl\ *n* : PRISON

²jail *vb* : to confine in or as if in a jail

jail·bird \'jāl-,bərd\ *n* : a person who is or has been confined in jail

jail·break \'jāl-,brāk\ *n* : a forcible escape from jail

jail·er *or* **jail·or** \'jā-lər\ *n* : a keeper of a jail

ja·lop·y \jə-'läp-ē\ *n, pl* **ja·lop·ies** : a dilapidated old automobile or airplane

¹jam \'jam\ *vb* **jammed; jam·ming 1** : to crowd, squeeze, or wedge into a tight position **2** : to push hard and suddenly **3** : CRUSH, BRUISE **4** : to be or cause to be wedged or stuck so as not to work **5** : to cause interference in (radio or radar signals)

²jam *n* **1** : a crowded mass that hinders or blocks **2** : a difficult state of affairs

³jam *n* : a food made by boiling fruit with sugar until it is thick

jamb \'jam\ *n* : an upright piece forming the side of an opening

jam·bo·ree \,jam-bə-'rē\ *n* **1** : a large festive gathering **2** : a national or international camping assembly of boy scouts

jamb

¹jan·gle \'jang-gəl\ *vb* **jan·gled; jan·gling** : to make or cause to make a harsh sound

²jangle *n* : discordant sound

jan·i·tor \'jan-ət-ər\ *n* : a person who has the care of a building (as a school)

Jan·u·ar·y \'jan-yə-,wer-ē\ *n* [taken into Old English from Latin *Januarius*, the first month of the ancient Roman year, and thus named after *Janus*, god of doors and gateways] : the first month of the year

¹Jap·a·nese \,jap-ə-'nēz\ *adj* : of or relating to Japan, the Japanese people, or Japanese

²Japanese *n, pl* **Japanese 1** : a native or inhabitant of Japan **2** : the language of the Japanese

Japanese beetle *n* : a small lustrous green or brown Asiatic beetle that is established in the United States where it is a destructive pest with larvae that feed on roots and adults that eat leaves and fruits

¹jar \'jär\ *vb* **jarred; jar·ring 1** : to make a harsh or discordant sound **2** : to have a harsh or disagreeable effect **3** : SHAKE, VIBRATE

²jar *n* **1** : a harsh sound **2** : JOLT **3** : SHOCK

³jar *n* : a broad-mouthed container usually of glass or earthenware

jar·gon \'jär-gən, -,gän\ *n* **1** : the special vocabulary or idiom of a particular activity or group **2** : obscure and often pretentious language

jas·mine \'jaz-mən\ *n* : any of various mostly climbing plants of warm regions noted for their fragrant flowers

jas·per \'jas-pər\ *n* : an opaque usually red, green, brown, or yellow stone used for making ornamental objects (as vases)

jasmine

¹jaunt \'jȯnt\ *vb* : to make a short trip for pleasure

²jaunt *n* : a short pleasure trip

jaun·ty \'jȯnt-ē\ *adj* **jaun·ti·er; jaun·ti·est** [French *gentil* "noble" meant also "stylish"; it was taken into English as *jaunty* which originally meant "stylish"] : sprightly in manner or appearance : PERKY, LIVELY — **jaun·ti·ly** \'jȯnt-l-ē\ *adv* — **jaun·ti·ness** \'jȯnt-ē-nəs\ *n*

Ja·va man \ˌjä-və-\ *n* : a small-brained prehistoric man known from skulls found in Java

jav·e·lin \'jav-lən, 'jav-ə-lən\ *n* **1** : a light spear **2** : a slender wooden shaft thrown for distance in a track-and-field contest (**javelin throw**)

jaw \'jȯ\ *n* **1** : either of the bony structures that support the soft parts of the mouth and usually bear teeth on their edge **2** : a part of an invertebrate animal (as an insect) that resembles or functions like a jaw **3** : one of a pair of moving parts that open and close for holding or crushing something ⟨*jaws* of a vise⟩

jay \'jā\ *n* : a noisy bird related to but more brightly colored than the crow

jay·walk \'jā-ˌwȯk\ *vb* : to cross a street in such a place or in such a way as to disregard traffic regulations — **jay·walk·er** *n*

jazz \'jaz\ *n* : American music marked by lively rhythms in which the accented notes often fall on beats that are usually not accented

jeal·ous \'jel-əs\ *adj* **1** : demanding complete devotion **2** : feeling a spiteful envy toward one who is or may be more successful than oneself **3** : VIGILANT ⟨*jealous* of his rights⟩ **syn** see ENVIOUS — **jeal·ous·ly** *adv*

jeal·ou·sy \'jel-ə-sē\ *n, pl* **jeal·ou·sies 1** : a jealous disposition, attitude, or feeling **2** : zealous vigilance

jeans \'jēnz\ *n pl* : pants made of a heavy cotton cloth

¹jeer \'jiər\ *vb* **1** : to speak or cry out in derision **2** : DERIDE **syn** see SCOFF

²jeer *n* : a jeering remark or sound : TAUNT

Je·ho·vah \ji-'hō-və\ *n* : ²GOD

jell \'jel\ *vb* **1** : to come to the consistency of jelly **2** : to take shape ⟨an idea *jelled*⟩

¹jel·ly \'jel-ē\ *n, pl* **jel·lies** : a soft somewhat elastic food made from fruit juice boiled with sugar, from meat juices, or from gelatin

²jelly *vb* **jel·lied; jel·ly·ing 1** : to bring or come to the consistency of jelly **2** : to make jelly

jel·ly·fish \'jel-ē-ˌfish\ *n* : a free-swimming sea animal related to the corals that has a jellylike saucer-shaped body

jen·net \'jen-ət\ *n* : a female donkey

jeop·ar·dize \'jep-ər-ˌdīz\ *vb* **jeop·ar·dized; jeop·ar·diz·ing** : to expose to danger : RISK

jeop·ar·dy \'jep-ər-dē\ *n* : DANGER

¹jerk \'jərk\ *vb* **1** : to give a quick sharp pull or twist to **2** : to move with jerks ⟨*jerk* to attention⟩ **3** : to mix and dispense (sodas)

²jerk *n* **1** : a short quick pull or twist **2** : a stupid, foolish, or eccentric person

jer·kin \'jər-kən\ *n* : a close-fitting hip-length sleeveless jacket

jerk·y \'jər-kē\ *adj* **jerk·i·er; jerk·i·est** : moving by sudden starts and stops — **jerk·i·ly** \-kə-lē\ *adv* — **jerk·i·ness** \-kē-nəs\ *n*

jer·sey \'jər-zē\ *n, pl* **jer·seys 1** : a knitted fabric of wool, cotton, nylon, rayon, or silk **2** : a close-fitting knitted garment (as a shirt)

jes·sa·mine \'jes-ə-mən\ *n* : JASMINE

¹jest \'jest\ *n* **1** : JOKE **2** : a witty remark **3** : a frivolous mood or manner ⟨many a true word is spoken in *jest*⟩ **4** : LAUGHINGSTOCK

²jest *vb* : JOKE, BANTER

jest·er \'jes-tər\ *n* **1** : a court fool : CLOWN **2** : a person given to jesting

Je·sus \'jē-zəs\ *n* : the founder of the Christian religion

¹jet \'jet\ *n* **1** : a black coallike mineral that is often used for jewelry **2** : a very dark black

²jet *vb* **jet·ted; jet·ting** : SPURT

³jet *n* **1** : a rush of liquid, gas, or vapor through a narrow opening or a nozzle **2** : a nozzle for a jet of gas or liquid **3** : JET ENGINE **4** : JET AIRPLANE

jet airplane *n* : an airplane powered by a jet engine

jet engine *n* : an engine in which fuel burns to produce a jet of heated air and gases that shoot out from the rear and result in propelling the engine forward

jet plane *n* : JET AIRPLANE

jet–pro·pelled \ˌjet-prə-'peld\ *adj* : propelled by a jet engine

jet·sam \'jet-səm\ *n* : goods thrown overboard to lighten a ship in distress

jet stream *n* : high-speed winds blowing from a westerly direction several miles above the earth's surface

jet·ti·son \'jet-ə-sən\ *vb* : to discard especially from a ship or airplane

jet·ty \'jet-ē\ *n, pl* **jet·ties 1** : a pier built to influence the current or tide or to protect a harbor **2** : a landing wharf

Jew \'jü\ *n* : a person who is a descendant of the ancient Hebrews or whose religion is Judaism

jew·el \'jü-əl\ *n* **1** : an ornament of precious metal often set with precious stones and worn as an accessory of dress **2** : GEM **3** : a bearing in a watch made of crystal or a precious stone **4** : a person who is highly esteemed

jew·el·er or **jew·el·ler** \'jü-ə-lər\ n : a person who makes or deals in jewelry and related articles (as silverware)

jew·el·ry \'jü-əl-rē\ n : ornamental pieces (as rings or necklaces) worn on the person

jew·fish \'jü-ˌfish\ n : a very large dark rough‑scaled sea fish

Jew·ish \'jü-ish\ adj : of or relating to the Jews or Judaism

Jew's harp or **Jews' harp** \'jüz-ˌhärp\ n : a small lyre-shaped instrument that when placed between the teeth gives tones from a metal tongue struck by the finger

Jew's harp

jib \'jib\ n : a three-cornered sail extending forward from the foremast

¹jibe \'jīb\ vb jibed; jib·ing **1** : to shift suddenly from side to side **2** : to change the course of a boat so that the sail jibes

²jibe var of GIBE

³jibe vb jibed; jib·ing : to be in agreement

jif·fy \'jif-ē\ n : MOMENT, INSTANT

¹jig \'jig\ n : a lively dance

²jig vb jigged; jig·ging : to dance a jig

jig·ger \'jig-ər\ n : GADGET

¹jig·gle \'jig-əl\ vb jig·gled; jig·gling : to move or cause to move with quick little jerks

²jiggle n : a jiggling motion

jig·saw \'jig-ˌsȯ\ n : a machine saw used to cut curved and irregular lines or openwork patterns

jigsaw puzzle n : a puzzle made by sawing a picture into small pieces that may be fitted together

jigsaw

jim·my \'jim-ē\ vb jim·mied; jim·my·ing : to force open with or as if with a short crowbar

jim·son·weed \'jim-sən-ˌwēd\ n : a coarse poisonous weedy plant related to the potato that is sometimes grown for its showy trumpet-shaped white or purple flowers

¹jin·gle \'jing-gəl\ vb jin·gled; jin·gling : to make or cause to make a light clinking sound

²jingle n **1** : a light clinking sound **2** : a catchy repetition of sounds in a poem **3** : a short verse or song marked by catchy repetition — **jin·gly** \'jing-glē\ adj

jin·rik·i·sha \jin-'rik-ˌshȯ\ n : a small two-wheeled hooded carriage pulled by one man and used originally in Japan

jinrikisha

jinx \'jingks\ n : one that brings bad luck

jit·ney \'jit-nē\ n, pl **jit·neys** : a small bus that carries passengers over a regular route

jit·ters \'jit-ərz\ n pl : extreme nervousness — **jit·ter·y** \-ə-rē\ adj

job \'jäb\ n **1** : a piece of work **2** : a piece of work undertaken on order at a stated rate **3** : something produced by or as if by work ⟨can do a better job⟩ **4** : a regular paying employment ⟨has a good job⟩ **5** : a specific duty or function — **job·less** \-ləs\ adj

jock·ey \'jäk-ē\ n, pl **jock·eys** **1** : a professional rider in a horse race **2** : OPERATOR

jo·cose \jō-'kōs\ adj : MERRY, JOKING

joc·u·lar \'jäk-yə-lər\ adj : given to jesting

joc·und \'jäk-ənd\ adj : MERRY, JOYFUL

¹jog \'jäg\ vb jogged; jog·ging **1** : to give a slight shake or push to : NUDGE **2** : to rouse to alertness **3** : to move up and down or about with a short heavy motion **4** : to move at a slow jolting gait

²jog n **1** : a slight shake or push **2** : a slow jolting gait

³jog n **1** : an irregularity in a line or surface **2** : a short change in direction ⟨a jog in a road⟩

jog·gle \'jäg-əl\ vb jog·gled; jog·gling : to shake or cause to shake slightly : JOG

john·ny·cake \'jän-ē-ˌkāk\ n : a bread made of cornmeal, water or milk, and leavening with or without flour, shortening, and eggs

join \'jȯin\ vb **1** : to come, bring, or fasten together **2** : ADJOIN **3** : to come or bring into close association **4** : to come into the company of **5** : to become a member of **6** : to take part in a collective activity

¹joint \'jȯint\ n **1** : a part of an animal's body where two pieces (as bones) of the skeleton come together usually in a way that allows motion **2** : the part between two joints **3** : a large piece of meat for roasting **4** : a place where two things or parts are connected — **joint·ed** \-əd\ adj

²joint adj **1** : UNITED, COMBINED **2** : done by or shared by two or more — **joint·ly** adv

³joint vb **1** : to unite by or provide with a joint **2** : to separate the joints of

joist \'jȯist\ n : any of the small timbers or metal beams laid crosswise in a building to support the floor or ceiling

floor
joists

¹joke \'jōk\ n **1** : something said or done to cause laughter : JEST **2** : a brief story with a humorous climax **3** : the humorous part of something **4** : KIDDING **5** : PRACTICAL JOKE **6** : a trivial or trifling matter

²joke vb joked; jok·ing : to speak or act without seriousness : make jokes

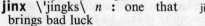

jok·er \'jō-kər\ *n* **1** : a person who jokes **2** : an extra card used in some card games

jok·ing·ly \'jō-king-lē\ *adv* : in a joking manner

jol·li·ty \'jäl-ət-ē\ *n* : GAIETY, MERRIMENT

¹jol·ly \'jäl-ē\ *adj* **jol·li·er; jol·li·est** **1** : full of fun **2** : very pleasant ⟨a *jolly* fire⟩

²jolly *adv* : VERY ⟨a *jolly* good time⟩

³jolly *vb* **jol·lied; jol·ly·ing** **1** : to engage in good-natured banter **2** : to put in good humor especially in order to gain an end

¹jolt \'jōlt\ *vb* **1** : to move or cause to move with a sudden jerky motion **2** : to disturb the composure of ⟨bad news *jolts* people⟩

²jolt *n* **1** : an abrupt jerky blow or movement **2** : a sudden shock (as of surprise)

jon·quil \'jän-kwəl\ *n* : a plant resembling the related daffodil but having fragrant yellow or white flowers with a short central tube

jonquil

josh \'jäsh\ *vb* : TEASE, JOKE

jos·tle \'jäs-əl\ *vb* **jos·tled; jos·tling** : to knock against so as to jar : push roughly ⟨*jostled* by a crowd⟩

¹jot \'jät\ *n* : the least bit : IOTA

²jot *vb* **jot·ted; jot·ting** : to write briefly or hurriedly : make a note of

jounce \'jaùns\ *vb* **jounced; jounc·ing** : to move, fall, drop, or bounce so as to shake

jour·nal \'jərn-l\ *n* **1** : a brief account of daily events : DIARY **2** : a daily record (as of business transactions) **3** : a periodical dealing especially with current events

jour·nal·ism \'jərn-l-,iz-əm\ *n* **1** : the business of writing for, editing, or publishing periodicals (as newspapers) **2** : writing designed for or characteristic of newspapers or popular magazines

jour·nal·ist \'jərn-l-əst\ *n* : an editor of or writer for a periodical

¹jour·ney \'jər-nē\ *n, pl* **jour·neys** : travel from one place to another : TRIP

syn JOURNEY, TRIP, TOUR all mean a going or traveling from one place to another. JOURNEY is a very general term but is likely to suggest covering a considerable distance with the possibility of danger and difficulty and adventure ⟨gathering supplies for the long *journey* across the desert⟩ TRIP may suggest relative ease, shortness, or swiftness of travel and applies especially to repeated journeys ⟨the farmer's weekly *trip* to the city⟩ TOUR applies to a usually roundabout journey planned and carried out for some purpose other than reaching a single destination ⟨a walking *tour*⟩ ⟨a lecture *tour*⟩

²jour·ney *vb* **jour·neyed; jour·ney·ing** **1** : to go on a journey : TRAVEL **2** : to travel over or through : TRAVERSE — **jour·ney·er** *n*

jour·ney·man \'jər-nē-mən\ *n, pl* **jour·ney·men** \-mən\ : a worker who has learned a trade and usually works for another person by the day

¹joust \'jaùst, 'jəst\ *n* : a combat on horseback between two knights with lances

²joust *vb* : to engage in a joust : TILT

jo·vi·al \'jō-vē-əl\ *adj* : JOLLY, MERRY — **jo·vi·al·ly** *adv*

¹jowl \'jaùl\ *n* **1** : JAW : the lower jaw especially **2** : CHEEK

²jowl *n* : loose flesh (as a double chin) hanging from the lower jaw and throat

joy \'jòi\ *n* **1** : a feeling of great pleasure or happiness that comes from success, good fortune, or a sense of well-being **2** : something that gives great pleasure or happiness

joy·ful \'jòi-fəl\ *adj* : feeling, causing, or showing joy — **joy·ful·ly** *adv* — **joy·ful·ness** *n*

joy·ous \'jòi-əs\ *adj* : JOYFUL ⟨a *joyous* occasion⟩ — **joy·ous·ly** *adv* — **joy·ous·ness** *n*

ju·bi·lant \'jü-bə-lənt\ *adj* : expressing great joy especially with shouting : noisily happy

ju·bi·lee \'jü-bə-,lē\ *n* **1** : a fiftieth anniversary **2** : time of celebration

Ju·da·ism \'jüd-ə-,iz-əm, 'jüd-ē-\ *n* : a religion developed among the ancient Hebrews that emphasizes belief in one God and adherence to the moral laws of the Old Testament

¹judge \'jəj\ *vb* **judged; judg·ing** **1** : to form an authoritative opinion **2** : to decide as a judge : TRY **3** : to reach a conclusion after inquiry and deliberation : CONSIDER **4** : THINK

²judge *n* **1** : a public official authorized to decide questions brought before a court **2** : a person appointed to decide in a contest or competition **3** : one who gives an authoritative opinion : CRITIC

judg·ment *or* **judge·ment** \'jəj-mənt\ *n* **1** : a formal decision or opinion (as of a court) given after judging **2** : an opinion or estimate formed by discerning and comparing **3** : the capacity for judging

ju·di·cial \jü-'dish-əl\ *adj* : of or relating to the administration of justice or the judiciary — **ju·di·cial·ly** *adv*

ju·di·cious \jü-'dish-əs\ *adj* : having, exercising, or characterized by sound judgment : WISE — **ju·di·cious·ly** *adv* — **ju·di·cious·ness** *n*

jug \'jəg\ *n* : a large deep usually earthenware or glass container with a narrow mouth and a handle

jug

jug·gle \'jəg-əl\ *vb* **jug·gled; jug-**

gling **1** : to keep several objects in motion in the air at the same time **2** : to mix things up so as to deceive **3** : to hold or balance insecurely — **jug·gler** \'jəg-lər\ n

juice \'jüs\ n : liquid material that can be pressed out of cells and tissues of a plant or animal : a natural fluid of a living body

juic·y \'jü-sē\ adj **juic·i·er; juic·i·est** : having much juice — **juic·i·ness** n

Ju·ly \jú-'lī\ n [taken into Old English from Latin *Julius*, the month named after the Roman dictator Julius Caesar] : the seventh month of the year

¹jum·ble \'jəm-bəl\ vb **jum·bled; jum·bling** : to mix in a confused mass

²jumble n : a disorderly mass or pile

jum·bo \'jəm-bō\ n, pl **jum·bos** : something very large of its kind

¹jump \'jəmp\ vb **1** : to spring into the air : LEAP **2** : to give a sudden movement : START **3** : to rise or cause to rise abruptly in rank, status, or condition **4** : to undergo or cause a sudden sharp increase ⟨prices *jumped*⟩ **5** : to make a sudden attack ⟨*jumped* on him for being late⟩ **6** : to pass over or cause to pass over with or as if with a leap **7** : ANTICIPATE ⟨*jumped* the gun⟩ **8** : to get aboard **9** : to depart from a normal course

²jump n **1** : an act or instance of jumping : LEAP **2** : a sports competition featuring a leap, spring, or bound **3** : a sudden involuntary movement : START **4** : a sharp sudden increase **5** : an initial advantage

jump·er \'jəm-pər\ n **1** : a loose blouse or jacket worn especially by workmen **2** : a sleeveless dress worn usually with a blouse

jump·ing jack \'jəm-ping-,jak\ n : a toy figure of a man jointed and made to jump or dance by means of strings or a sliding stick

jump·y \'jəm-pē\ adj **jump·i·er; jump·i·est** : NERVOUS, JITTERY

jun·co \'jəng-kō\ n, pl **jun·cos** or **jun·coes** : a small usually pink-billed and mostly gray American finch

junc·tion \'jəngk-shən\ n **1** : an act of joining **2** : a place or point of meeting

June \'jün\ n : the sixth month of the year

jun·gle \'jəng-gəl\ n **1** : a thick or tangled growth of vegetation **2** : a tract of land especially in a tropical region covered with thick tangled vegetation

¹ju·nior \'jü-nyər\ n **1** : a person who is younger or lower in rank than another **2** : a student in his next-to-last year (as at high school)

²junior adj **1** : YOUNGER **2** : lower in rank **3** : of or relating to juniors ⟨*junior* class⟩

ju·ni·per \'jü-nə-pər\ n : any of various evergreen trees and shrubs related to the pines but having tiny berrylike cones

¹junk \'jəngk\ n **1** : old iron, glass, paper, or waste : RUBBISH **2** : a shoddy product

²junk vb : to get rid of as worthless : SCRAP

³junk n : a sailing ship of Chinese waters

Ju·pi·ter \'jü-pət-ər\ n : the planet that is fifth in order of distance from the sun and is the largest of the planets with a diameter of about 86,800 miles

junk

ju·ris·dic·tion \,jùr-əs-'dik-shən\ n **1** : the power, right, or authority to interpret and apply the law **2** : the authority of a sovereign power to govern or to make laws **3** : the limits or territory within which authority may be exercised

ju·ror \'jùr-ər\ n : a member of a jury

ju·ry \'jùr-ē\ n, pl **ju·ries** **1** : a body of persons sworn to inquire into and test a matter submitted to them and to give their verdict according to the evidence presented **2** : a committee that judges and awards prizes at an exhibition or contest

¹just \'jəst\ adj **1** : well-founded : REASONABLE **2** : conforming to a standard of correctness **3** : morally right or good **4** : DESERVED **5** : legally right — **just·ly** adv

²just \jəst, 'jəst\ adv **1** : EXACTLY **2** : very recently **3** : BARELY **4** : IMMEDIATELY ⟨*just* east of here⟩ **5** : ONLY **6** : QUITE, VERY

jus·tice \'jəs-təs\ n **1** : just or righteous action, management, or treatment **2** : JUDGE **3** : the carrying out of law ⟨a court of *justice*⟩ **4** : FAIRNESS, HONESTY **5** : RIGHTFULNESS

jus·ti·fi·a·ble \'jəs-tə-,fī-ə-bəl\ adj : capable of being justified — **jus·ti·fi·a·bly** \-blē\ adv

jus·ti·fi·ca·tion \,jəs-tə-fə-'kā-shən\ n **1** : the act or an instance of justifying **2** : something that justifies

jus·ti·fy \'jəs-tə-,fī\ vb **jus·ti·fied; jus·ti·fy·ing** **1** : to prove or show to be just, right, or reasonable **2** : to release from the guilt of sin

jut \'jət\ vb **jut·ted; jut·ting** : to shoot or cause to shoot out, up, or forward : PROJECT

jute \'jüt\ n : a strong glossy fiber from a tropical plant used chiefly for making sacks and twine

¹ju·ve·nile \'jü-və-,nīl, -vən-l\ adj **1** : showing incomplete development : IMMATURE **2** : of, relating to, or characteristic of children or young people **syn** see YOUTHFUL

²juvenile n **1** : a young person : YOUTH **2** : a book for young people

k \'kā\ *n, often cap* : the eleventh letter of the English alphabet

kale \'kāl\ *n* : a hardy cabbage with wrinkled leaves that do not form a compact head

ka·lei·do·scope \kə-'līd-ə-ˌskōp\ *n* [formed from the Greek words *kalos* "beautiful" and *eidos* "shape" with the addition of *-scope*, a root of Greek origin used only in combination; English *-scope* means "an instrument for viewing" and comes from Greek *skopein* "to look at"] **1** : a device containing loose bits of colored glass between two flat plates and two plane mirrors so placed that changes in position of the bits of glass are reflected in an endless variety of patterns **2** : a changing pattern or scene

kan·ga·roo \ˌkang-gə-'rü\ *n, pl* **kan·ga·roos** : any of numerous leaping plant-eating mammals of Australia and nearby islands with long powerful hind legs, a thick tail used as a support in standing or walking, and in the female a pouch on the abdomen in which the young are carried

kangaroo

ka·o·lin \'kā-ə-lən\ *n* : a very pure white clay used in making porcelain

kar·at \'kar-ət\ *n* : a unit of fineness for gold

ka·ty·did \'kāt-ē-ˌdid\ *n* : any of several large green American grasshoppers with males that make shrill noises

kay·ak \'kī-ˌak\ *n* **1** : an Eskimo canoe made of a frame covered with skins except for a small opening in the center **2** : a small canvas-covered canoe

kayak 1

ka·zoo \kə-'zü\ *n, pl* **ka·zoos** : a toy musical instrument consisting of a tube with a membrane sealing one end and a side hole into which one sings or hums

¹keel \'kēl\ *n* : a timber or plate running lengthwise along the center of the bottom of a ship and usually projecting from the bottom

²keel *vb* **1** : to turn over **2** : to fall in a faint

¹keen \'kēn\ *adj* **1** : having a fine edge or point : SHARP ⟨a *keen* knife⟩ **2** : CUTTING, STINGING ⟨a *keen* wind⟩ **3** : STRONG, ACUTE ⟨a *keen* sense of smell⟩ **4** : EAGER, ENTHUSIASTIC **5** : having or showing mental sharpness — **keen·ly** *adv* — **keen·ness** *n*

²keen *vb* : to lament with a keen

³keen *n* : a lamentation for the dead uttered in a loud wailing voice

¹keep \'kēp\ *vb* **kept** \'kept\; **keep·ing** **1** : to perform as a duty : FULFILL, OBSERVE ⟨*keep* a promise⟩ ⟨*keep* a holiday⟩ **2** : GUARD ⟨*keep* us from harm⟩ **3** : to have the care of : TEND, SUPPORT **4** : to continue doing something **5** : to have in one's service or at one's disposal ⟨*keep* a maid⟩ ⟨*keep* a car⟩ **6** : to preserve a record in ⟨*keep* a diary⟩ **7** : to have on hand regularly for sale ⟨*keep* neckties⟩ **8** : to continue to have in one's possession or power **9** : HOLD, DETAIN **10** : to hold back : WITHHOLD ⟨*keep* a secret⟩ **11** : to remain or cause to remain in a given place, situation, or condition ⟨*keep* off the grass⟩ ⟨*kept* him waiting⟩ **12** : to continue in an unspoiled condition **13** : REFRAIN ⟨unable to *keep* from talking⟩ — **keep up** **1** : MAINTAIN, SUSTAIN ⟨*keep* standards *up*⟩ **2** : to keep adequately informed **3** : to continue without interruption **4** : to stay even with others (as in a race)

²keep *n* **1** : the strongest part of a medieval castle **2** : the means or provisions by which one is kept ⟨had to earn his *keep*⟩ — **for keeps** **1** : with the understanding that one may keep what he has won **2** : PERMANENTLY

keep·er \'kē-pər\ *n* : a person who watches, guards, or takes care of something : WARDEN

keep·ing \'kē-ping\ *n* **1** : CARE, CHARGE **2** : OBSERVANCE **3** : AGREEMENT, HARMONY

keep·sake \'kēp-ˌsāk\ *n* : something kept or given to be kept in memory of the giver

keg \'keg\ *n* **1** : a small barrel holding thirty gallons or less **2** : the contents of a keg

kelp \'kelp\ *n* **1** : a large coarse brown seaweed **2** : ashes of seaweed used especially as a source of iodine

kel·pie \'kel-pē\ *n* : an Australian sheep dog

ken \'ken\ *n* **1** : range of vision : SIGHT **2** : range of understanding

ken·nel \'ken-l\ *n* **1** : a shelter for a dog **2** : a place where dogs are bred

kept *past of* KEEP

ker·chief \'kər-chəf\ *n, pl* **ker·chiefs** **1** : a square of cloth worn by women as a head covering or as a scarf **2** : HANDKERCHIEF 1

ker·nel \'kərn-l\ *n* **1** : the inner softer part of a seed, fruit stone, or nut **2** : the whole grain or seed of a cereal

ker·o·sene *or* **ker·o·sine** \'ker-ə-ˌsēn\ *n* : a thin oil obtained from petroleum and used as a fuel and solvent

ketch \'kech\ *n* : a fore-and-aft rigged ship with two masts

ketch·up \'kech-əp\ *var of* CATSUP

ket·tle \'ket-l\ *n* **1** : a pot for boiling liquids **2** : TEAKETTLE

---

j job　　ng sing　　ō low　　ȯ moth　　ȯi coin　　th thin　　th͟ this　　ü boot　　u̇ foot　　y you　　yü few　　yu̇ furious　　zh vision

ket·tle·drum \'ket-l-ˌdrəm\ *n* : a brass or copper kettle-shaped drum with parchment stretched across the top and capable of being tuned to definite pitches

kettledrum

¹key \'kē\ *n* **1** : an instrument by which the bolt of a lock (as on a door) is turned **2** : a device having the form or function of a key ⟨a *key* for opening a can of meat⟩ **3** : a means of gaining or preventing entrance, possession, or control **4** : something (as a map legend) that gives an explanation : SOLUTION **5** : one of the levers with a flat surface that is pressed by a finger in operating or playing an instrument (as a typewriter, piano, or clarinet) **6** : a leading individual or principle ⟨the *key* to the situation⟩ **7** : a system of seven musical tones arranged in relation to a keynote from which the system is named ⟨the *key* of C⟩ **8** : characteristic style or tone (as of thought) **9** : a small switch for opening or closing an electric circuit

²key *vb* **keyed; key·ing 1** : LOCK, SECURE **2** : to regulate the musical pitch of **3** : HARMONIZE **4** : to make nervous or tense

³key *adj* : of basic importance

⁴key *n* : a low island or reef ⟨the Florida *keys*⟩

key·board \'kē-ˌbōrd\ *n* **1** : a row of keys (as on a piano) **2** : the whole arrangement of keys (as on a typewriter)

key·hole \'kē-ˌhōl\ *n* : a hole for receiving a key

key·note \'kē-ˌnōt\ *n* **1** : the first and harmonically fundamental tone of a scale **2** : the fundamental fact, idea, or mood

key·stone \'kē-ˌstōn\ *n* **1** : the wedge-shaped piece at the crown of an arch that locks the other pieces in place **2** : something on which associated things depend for support

keystone

khak·i \'kak-ē, 'kä-kē\ *n* **1** : a light yellowish brown **2** : a khaki-colored cloth used especially for military uniforms

khan \'kän, 'kan\ *n* **1** : a Mongol leader **2** : a local chieftain or man of rank in some countries of central Asia

kib·itz·er \'kib-ət-sər\ *n* : a person who looks on and often offers unwanted advice or comment especially at a card game

¹kick \'kik\ *vb* **1** : to strike out or hit with the foot **2** : to object strongly : PROTEST **3** : to spring back when fired — **kick off 1** : to make a kickoff **2** : BEGIN

²kick *n* **1** : a blow or thrust with the foot **2** : a sudden propelling (as of a ball) with the foot **3** : the recoil of a gun **4** : a feeling or expression of objection **5** : a stimulating effect (as of pleasure)

kick·off \'kik-ˌȯf\ *n* : a kick that puts the ball into play (as in football or soccer)

¹kid \'kid\ *n* **1** : the young of a goat or a related animal **2** : the flesh, fur, or skin of a kid or something (as leather) made from one of these **3** : CHILD, YOUNGSTER — **kid·dish** *adj*

²kid *vb* **kid·ded; kid·ding 1** : to deceive or trick as a joke **2** : TEASE — **kid·der** *n*

kid·nap \'kid-ˌnap\ *vb* **kid·napped** *or* **kid·naped** \-ˌnapt\; **kid·nap·ping** *or* **kid·nap·ing** : to carry away a person by unlawful force or by fraud and against his will — **kid·nap·per** *or* **kid·nap·er** *n*

kid·ney \'kid-nē\ *n, pl* **kid·neys** : either of a pair of organs near the backbone that excrete waste from the body in the form of urine

kidney bean *n* : a common garden bean especially when having large dark red seeds

¹kill \'kil\ *vb* **1** : to deprive of life : put to death : SLAY **2** : DESTROY, RUIN ⟨*kill* all chance of success⟩ **3** : to use up ⟨*kill* time⟩ **4** : DEFEAT ⟨*kill* a proposed law⟩ — **kill·er** *n*

syn KILL, MURDER, ASSASSINATE all mean to deprive of life. KILL simply states the fact of causing death, gives no hint of motive or manner, and is the only one used of living things other than humans ⟨auto accidents *killed* hundreds over the weekend⟩ ⟨crops *killed* by the drought⟩ MURDER means to kill a human illegally and normally involves an act done in secrecy with a selfish motive ⟨*murdered* the shopkeeper for the few dollars in his cash drawer⟩ ASSASSINATE is applied to the murdering of an individual who holds power, and is usually thought of as the act of a fanatic who kills to further a cause or ideal ⟨foiled the effort to *assassinate* the king⟩

²kill *n* **1** : an act of killing **2** : an animal killed (as for prey) ⟨a lion devouring its *kill*⟩

kill·deer \'kil-ˌdiər\ *n* : a North American plover with a shrill plaintive call

kil·li·fish \'kil-ē-ˌfish\ *n* : any of various tiny fishes

kill·joy \'kil-ˌjȯi\ *n* : one who spoils the pleasure of others

kiln \'kiln, 'kil\ *n* : a furnace or oven for hardening, burning, or drying something (as bricks or pottery)

ki·lo \'kē-lō, 'kē-ˌlō\ *n, pl* **ki·los 1** : KILOGRAM **2** : KILOMETER

kilo- *prefix* : thousand ⟨*kilo*gram⟩

ki·lo·gram \'kē-lə-ˌgram, 'kil-ə-\ *n* : a metric unit of weight equal to 1000 grams or about two pounds three ounces

ki·lo·me·ter \kil-'äm-ət-ər, 'kil-ə-ˌmēt-ər\ *n* : a metric unit of length equal to 1000 meters or about ⅝ mile

kilo·watt \'kil-ə-ˌwät\ *n* : a unit of electrical power equal to 1000 watts

kilt \'kilt\ *n* : a knee-length pleated skirt usually of tartan worn by men in Scotland

kil·ter \'kil-tər\ *n* : proper condition

ki·mo·no \kə-'mō-nə\ *n, pl* **ki·mo·nos** **1** : a loose robe with wide sleeves and a broad sash traditionally worn as an outer garment by the Japanese **2** : a loose dressing gown worn chiefly by women

kin \'kin\ *n* **1** : an individual's relatives **2** : KINSMAN

-kin \kən\ *also* **-kins** \kənz\ *n suffix* : little ⟨lamb*kin*⟩ ⟨baby*kins*⟩

¹kind \'kīnd\ *n* **1** : a natural group ⟨a bird of the hawk *kind*⟩ **2** : a group united by common traits or interests : CATEGORY ⟨*kinds* of insects⟩ **3** : VARIETY ⟨all *kinds* of people⟩ **4** : essential quality or character

²kind *adj* **1** : having the will to do good and to bring happiness to others : CONSIDERATE **2** : showing or growing out of gentleness or goodness of heart ⟨a *kind* act⟩

kin·der·gar·ten \'kin-dər-ˌgärt-n\ *n* : a school or a class for very young children

kind·heart·ed \'kīnd-'härt-əd\ *adj* : having or showing a kind and sympathetic nature — **kind·heart·ed·ly** *adv* — **kind·heart·ed·ness** *n*

kin·dle \'kin-dəl\ *vb* **kin·dled; kin·dling** **1** : to set on fire : LIGHT **2** : AROUSE, EXCITE

kin·dling \'kin-dling\ *n* : easily combustible material for starting a fire

¹kind·ly \'kīn-dlē\ *adj* **kind·li·er; kind·li·est** **1** : of an agreeable or beneficial nature ⟨a *kindly* climate⟩ **2** : of a sympathetic or generous nature ⟨*kindly* men⟩ — **kind·li·ness** *n*

²kindly *adv* **1** : READILY **2** : in a kind manner **3** : in an appreciative manner **4** : COURTEOUSLY, OBLIGINGLY

kind·ness \'kīnd-nəs\ *n* **1** : a kind deed : FAVOR **2** : the quality or state of being kind

¹kin·dred \'kin-drəd\ *n* **1** : a group of related individuals **2** : a person's relatives

²kindred *adj* : of like nature or character

kin·folk \'kin-ˌfōk\ *n* : RELATIVES

king \'king\ *n* **1** : a male ruler of a country who usually inherits his position and rules for life : SOVEREIGN **2** : a chief among competitors ⟨an oil *king*⟩ **3** : the chief piece in the game of chess **4** : a card bearing the figure of a king **5** : a piece in checkers that has

reached the opponent's back row — **king·ly** *adj*

king·dom \'king-dəm\ *n* **1** : a country whose ruler is a king or queen : MONARCHY **2** : one of the three great divisions (**animal kingdom, plant kingdom, mineral kingdom**) into which all natural objects are grouped

king·fish·er \'king-ˌfish-ər\ *n* : any of a group of usually crested and bright-colored birds with a short tail and long sharp bill

king·let \'king-lət\ *n* : a small bird resembling a warbler

king–size \'king-ˌsīz\ *or* **king–sized** \-ˌsīzd\ *adj* : unusually long or large

¹kink \'kingk\ *n* **1** : a short tight twist or curl (as in a thread or rope) **2** : CRAMP ⟨a *kink* in my back⟩ **3** : an imperfection that causes difficulties in operation ⟨getting the *kinks* out of the engine⟩ — **kink·y** *adj*

kink 1

²kink *vb* : to form or cause to form a kink in

-kins — see -KIN

kin·ship \'kin-ˌship\ *n* : the quality or state of being kin : RELATIONSHIP

kins·man \'kinz-mən\ *n, pl* **kins·men** \-mən\ : a relative usually by birth

¹kiss \'kis\ *vb* **1** : to touch with the lips as a mark of affection or greeting **2** : to touch gently or lightly ⟨wind *kissing* the trees⟩

²kiss *n* **1** : a caress with the lips **2** : a gentle touch or contact

kit \'kit\ *n* **1** : a set of articles for personal use ⟨a travel *kit*⟩ **2** : a set of tools or supplies

kitch·en \'kich-ən\ *n* : a room in which cooking is done

kitch·en·ette \ˌkich-ən-'et\ *n* : a small kitchen

kitchen garden *n* : a plot where vegetables are grown for household use

kite \'kīt\ *n* **1** : a hawk with long narrow wings and deeply forked tail that feeds mostly on insects and small reptiles **2** : a light covered frame designed to be flown in the air at the end of a long string

kith \'kith\ *n* : familiar friends and neighbors or relatives ⟨his *kith* and kin⟩

kit·ten \'kit-n\ *n* : a young cat — **kit·ten·ish** *adj*

kit·ty \'kit-ē\ *n, pl* **kit·ties** : CAT, KITTEN

ki·wi \'kē-wē\ *n* : a New Zealand bird that is unable to fly

knack \'nak\ *n* **1** : a clever or skillful way of doing something : TRICK ⟨a *knack* to wrapping a package neatly⟩ **2** : a natural ability for doing

kiwi

a specified thing ⟨a *knack* for making friends⟩

knap·sack \'nap-,sak\ *n* : a usually canvas or leather bag or case strapped on the back and used especially for supplies (as on a hike)

knave \'nāv\ *n* **1** : ROGUE 1 **2** : JACK 1

knead \'nēd\ *vb* **1** : to work and press into a mass with or as if with the hands ⟨*knead* dough⟩ **2** : MASSAGE — **knead·er** *n*

knee \'nē\ *n* **1** : the joint or region in which the thigh and lower leg come together **2** : something resembling a knee **3** : the part of a garment covering the knee

knee·cap \'nē-,kap\ *n* : a thick flat movable bone forming the front part of the knee

kneel \'nēl\ *vb* **knelt** \'nelt\ *or* **kneeled** \'nēld\; **kneel·ing** : to bend the knee : fall or rest on the knees

¹knell \'nel\ *vb* **1** : to ring (a bell) slowly and solemnly : TOLL **2** : to sound in an ominous manner or with an ominous effect **3** : to summon, announce, or proclaim by a knell

²knell *n* **1** : a stroke or sound of a bell especially when rung slowly for a death, funeral, or disaster **2** : an indication (as a sound) of the end or failure of something

knew *past of* KNOW

knick·ers \'nik-ərz\ *n pl* : loose-fitting short pants gathered at the knee

knick·knack \'nik-,nak\ *n* : a small trivial article intended for ornament

¹knife \'nīf\ *n, pl* **knives** \'nīvz\ **1** : a cutting instrument consisting of a sharp blade fastened to a handle **2** : a cutting blade in a machine

²knife *vb* **knifed; knif·ing** : to stab, slash, or wound with a knife

¹knight \'nīt\ *n* **1** : a mounted warrior of feudal times serving a king and usually awarded a special military rank and sworn to obey certain rules of conduct **2** : a man honored by a sovereign for merit and in Great Britain ranking below a baronet **3** : one of the pieces in the game of chess — **knight·ly** *adj*

knives

²knight *vb* : to confer the rank of knight on

knight·hood \'nīt-,hùd\ *n* **1** : the rank, dignity, or profession of a knight **2** : the qualities befitting a knight : CHIVALRY **3** : knights as a class or body

knit \'nit\ *vb* **knit** *or* **knit·ted; knit·ting** **1** : to form a fabric by interlacing yarn or thread in connected loops with needles (**knitting needles**) ⟨*knit* a sweater⟩ **2** : to draw or come together closely as if knitted : unite firmly ⟨wait for a broken bone to *knit*⟩ **3** : WRINKLE **4** : to bind closely — **knit·ter** *n*

knob \'näb\ *n* **1** : a rounded swelling **2** : a small rounded handle **3** : a rounded hill

¹knock \'näk\ *vb* **1** : to strike with a sharp blow **2** : COLLIDE, BUMP **3** : to make a pounding noise **4** : to find fault with

²knock *n* **1** : a sharp blow **2** : a severe misfortune or hardship **3** : a pounding noise ⟨a *knock* in an automobile engine⟩

knock·er \'näk-ər\ *n* **1** : a person or a thing that knocks **2** : a device hinged to a door for use in knocking

knock–knee \'näk-'nē\ *n* : a condition in which the legs curve inward at the knee — **knock–kneed** \-'nēd\ *adj*

knoll \'nōl\ *n* : a small round hill

knocker 2

¹knot \'nät\ *n* **1** : an interlacing (as of string or ribbon) that forms a lump or knob **2** : PROBLEM **3** : a bond of union ⟨the marriage *knot*⟩ **4** : the inner end of a branch enclosed in a plant stem or a section of this in sawed lumber **5** : a cluster of persons or things **6** : an ornamental bow of ribbon **7** : one nautical mile per hour — used as a unit for expressing the speed of ships and airplanes

knots

²knot *vb* **knot·ted; knot·ting** **1** : to tie in or with a knot **2** : to unite closely or intricately

knot·hole \'nät-,hōl\ *n* : a hole in wood where a knot has come out

knot·ty \'nät-ē\ *adj* **knot·ti·er; knot·ti·est** **1** : full of knots **2** : DIFFICULT, PUZZLING

know \'nō\ *vb* **knew** \'nü, 'nyü\; **known** \'nōn\; **know·ing** **1** : to perceive directly : have understanding of ⟨*know* yourself⟩ **2** : to recognize the nature of ⟨*knew* him to be honest⟩ **3** : to recognize as being the same as something previously known ⟨*knew* him by his walk⟩ **4** : to be acquainted or familiar with ⟨*knows* the city well⟩ **5** : to be aware of the truth of ⟨*know* that the earth is round⟩ **6** : to have a practical understanding of ⟨*knows* how to write⟩ **7** : to have information or knowledge ⟨ask someone who *knows*⟩

know·ing \'nō-ing\ *adj* **1** : having or showing special knowledge, information, or intelligence **2** : shrewdly and keenly alert **3** : DELIBERATE, INTENTIONAL — **know·ing·ly** *adv*

knowl·edge \'näl-ij\ *n* **1** : understanding and skill gained by actual experience ⟨a *knowledge* of carpentry⟩ **2** : the state of being aware of something or of having information **3** : range of information **4** : something learned and kept in the mind : LEARNING ⟨a man with a vast *knowledge* of history⟩

knuck·le \'nək-əl\ *n* : the rounded lump formed by the ends of two bones (as of a finger) where they come together in a joint

ko·a·la \kō-'ä-lə\ *n* : a tailless Australian animal with thick fur and long hairy ears, sharp claws for climbing, and a pouch like the kangaroo's for carrying its young

koala

kohl·rab·i \kōl-'rab-ē, -'rä-bē\ *n* : a cabbage that forms no head but has a fleshy edible stem

kook·a·bur·ra \'kùk-ə-‚bər-ə\ *n* : an Australian kingfisher that has a call resembling loud laughter

Ko·ran \kə-'ran\ *n* : a book of writings accepted by Muslims as revelations made to Muhammad by Allah

krill \'kril\ *n* : tiny floating sea creatures that are a chief food of whales

krim·mer \'krim-ər\ *n* : a gray curly fur from the pelt of young lambs

kum·quat \'kəm-‚kwät\ *n* [from Chinese *kam kwat*, literally "golden orange"] : a small citrus fruit with sweet rind and sour pulp that is used mostly in preserves

l \'el\ *n*, *often cap* **1** : the twelfth letter of the English alphabet **2** : the roman numeral 50

la \'lä\ *n* : the sixth note of the musical scale

¹la·bel \'lā-bəl\ *n* **1** : a slip (as of paper or cloth) attached to something and giving information (as contents or destination) about it **2** : a descriptive or identifying word or phrase ⟨part-of-speech *label*⟩

²label *vb* **la·beled** *or* **la·belled**; **la·bel·ing** *or* **la·bel·ling** **1** : to attach a label or tag to **2** : to name or describe by or as if by a label

la·bi·al \'lā-bē-əl\ *adj* : of or relating to the lips

¹la·bor \'lā-bər\ *n* **1** : TOIL, WORK ⟨rest from *labor*⟩ **2** : the physical activity involved in giving birth to offspring **3** : something that requires toil or work : TASK **4** : workers as a body or class **syn** see WORK

²labor *vb* **1** : to exert oneself : WORK, TOIL **2** : to move slowly or heavily ⟨a truck *laboring* up the hill⟩ **3** : to pitch or roll heavily

lab·o·ra·to·ry \'lab-rə-‚tōr-ē, 'lab-ə-rə-\ *n, pl*

lab·o·ra·to·ries : a room or building in which scientific experiments and tests are carried on

Labor Day *n* : the first Monday in September observed as a legal holiday in recognition of the workingman

la·bored \'lā-bərd\ *adj* : produced or done with toil or difficulty ⟨*labored* breathing⟩

la·bor·er \'lā-bər-ər\ *n* : one that works on jobs requiring strength rather than skill

la·bo·ri·ous \lə-'bōr-ē-əs\ *adj* **1** : INDUSTRIOUS **2** : requiring much labor — **la·bo·ri·ous·ly** *adv*

¹lace \'lās\ *n* [from Old French *laz* "knotted cord", from Latin *laqueus* "snare"] **1** : a string or cord passed through holes and used to draw or hold together opposite edges (as in shoes) **2** : an openwork fabric of thread or cord usually with a design

²lace *vb* **laced**; **lac·ing** : to fasten with a lace

lac·er·ate \'las-ə-‚rāt\ *vb* **lac·er·at·ed**; **lac·er·at·ing** : to tear roughly : injure by tearing

lac·er·a·tion \‚las-ə-'rā-shən\ *n* : a lacerated place or wound

¹lack \'lak\ *n* **1** : the fact or state of being wanting or deficient : NEED **2** : something that is lacking or is needed

²lack *vb* : to need, want, or be without

lack·a·dai·si·cal \‚lak-ə-'dā-zi-kəl\ *adj* : LANGUID, LISTLESS

lack·ey \'lak-ē\ *n, pl* **lack·eys** **1** : FOOTMAN **2** : TOADY

la·con·ic \lə-'kän-ik\ *adj* : sparing of words

¹lac·quer \'lak-ər\ *n* : any of numerous varnishlike preparations that dry rapidly to form a glossy film (as on wood or metal)

²lacquer *vb* : to coat with lacquer

la·crosse \lə-'krós\ *n* : an outdoor game of ball played with a long-handled netlike racket

lacrosse racket

lac·y \'lā-sē\ *adj* **lac·i·er**; **lac·i·est** : resembling or consisting of lace

lad \'lad\ *n* : BOY, YOUTH

lad·der \'lad-ər\ *n* : a device used for climbing usually consisting of two long pieces of wood, rope, or metal joined at short distances by horizontal pieces

lad·die \'lad-ē\ *n* : LAD, BOY

lad·en \'lād-n\ *adj* : LOADED, BURDENED ⟨a truck *laden* with gravel⟩

ladder

¹la·dle \'lād-l\ *n* : a long-handled cuplike spoon or dipper used in dipping

²ladle *vb* **la·dled**; **la·dling** : to dip up : take up and carry in a ladle

la·dy \'lād-ē\ *n, pl* **la·dies** [from Old English *hlǣfdīge*, originally "mistress of a household", from *hlāf* "loaf" and *-dīge* "kneader"] **1** : a woman of property, rank, or authority **2** : a woman of superior social position or of refinement and gentle manners **3** : WOMAN **4** : WIFE

la·dy·bird \'lād-ē-,bərd\ *n* : LADYBUG

la·dy·bug \'lād-ē-,bəg\ *n* : a small rounded often brightly colored beetle that feeds mostly on plant lice

la·dy·like \'lād-ē-,līk\ *adj* : WELL=BRED

la·dy·ship \'lād-ē-,ship\ *n* : the rank or dignity of a lady — used as a title ⟨her *Ladyship* is not at home⟩

ladybug

lady's slipper *or* **lady slipper** *n* : any of several North American wild orchids whose flowers suggest a slipper in shape

¹lag \'lag\ *vb* **lagged; lag·ging** : to move slowly : fall behind : LOITER

²lag *n* : the act or the amount of lagging

¹lag·gard \'lag-ərd\ *adj* **1** : SLOW, LOITERING **2** : BACKWARD, DULL

lady's slipper

²laggard *n* : a person who lags

la·goon \lə-'gün\ *n* : a shallow channel or pond near or connected to a larger body of water

laid *past of* LAY

lain *past part of* LIE

lair \'laər\ *n* : the den or resting place of a wild animal

lake \'lāk\ *n* : a large inland body of standing water

¹lamb \'lam\ *n* : a young sheep usually less than one year old

²lamb *vb* : to bring forth a lamb

lamb·kin \'lam-kən\ *n* : a young lamb

¹lame \'lām\ *adj* **lam·er; lam·est** **1** : having a part and especially a limb so disabled as to make movement difficult **2** : WEAK, PAINFUL ⟨a *lame* back⟩ **3** : LIMPING, HALTING **4** : UNSATISFACTORY — **lame·ly** *adv* — **lame·ness** *n*

²lame *vb* **lamed; lam·ing** : to make or become lame ⟨*lamed* himself in a fall⟩

¹la·ment \lə-'ment\ *vb* **1** : to mourn aloud : WAIL **2** : to express sorrow for

²lament *n* **1** : a crying out in grief : WAILING **2** : DIRGE, ELEGY

lam·en·ta·ble \'lam-ən-tə-bəl\ *adj* : SORROWFUL, PITIFUL

lam·en·ta·tion \,lam-ən-'tā-shən\ *n* : the act of lamenting or mourning

lam·i·nat·ed \'lam-ə-,nāt-əd\ *adj* : composed of layers of firmly united material

lamp \'lamp\ *n* **1** : a vessel with a wick for burning a flammable liquid (as oil) to produce light **2** : a device for producing light or heat by electricity or gas ⟨an electric *lamp*⟩

lamp·black \'lamp-,blak\ *n* : a finely powdered deep black soot made by incomplete burning of material and used especially as a pigment

lam·prey \'lam-prē\ *n, pl* **lam·preys** : a water animal resembling an eel but having a sucking mouth with no jaws

lance \'lans\ *n* : a long-handled weapon with a sharp steel head formerly used by light=armed cavalry soldiers

¹land \'land\ *n* **1** : the solid part of the surface of the earth **2** : a part of the earth's surface (as a country or a farm) considered by itself **3** : REALM, DOMAIN ⟨the *land* of Egypt⟩ **4** *pl* : territorial possessions **5** : the people of a country : NATION — **land·less** \-ləs\ *adj*

²land *vb* **1** : to set or go ashore from a ship **2** : to cause to reach or come to rest in a particular place ⟨*land* an arrow in the target⟩ **3** : CATCH ⟨*land* a fish⟩ **4** : to gain by effort **5** : to alight or cause to alight on a surface

land breeze *n* : a breeze blowing toward the sea

land·hold·er \'land-,hōl-dər\ *n* : a holder or owner of land

land·ing \'lan-ding\ *n* **1** : the act of coming to land **2** : a place for discharging or taking on passengers and cargo **3** : the level part of a staircase (as at the end of a flight of stairs)

landing field *n* : a field where aircraft may land and take off

landing strip *n* : AIRSTRIP

land·la·dy \'land-,lād-ē\ *n, pl* **land·la·dies** **1** : a woman who owns land or houses that she rents **2** : a woman who runs an inn or rooming house

land·locked \'land-,läkt\ *adj* **1** : shut in or nearly shut in by land ⟨a *landlocked* harbor⟩ **2** : confined to fresh water by some barrier

land·lord \'land-,lòrd\ *n* **1** : the owner or holder of land or houses that he leases or rents **2** : a man who runs an inn or rooming house

land·mark \'land-,märk\ *n* **1** : an object marking a boundary or serving as a guide **2** : a very important event

land·own·er \'land-,ō-nər\ *n* : an owner of land

¹land·scape \'land-,skāp\ *n* **1** : a stretch of land that can be seen in one glance **2** : a picture of natural scenery

²landscape *vb* **land·scaped; land·scap·ing** : to

improve the natural beauties of a tract of land by grading, clearing, or gardening

land·slide \'land-ˌslīd\ *n* **1** : the slipping down of a mass of rocks or earth on a steep slope **2** : the mass of material that moves in a landslide **3** : an overwhelming election victory

lane \'lān\ *n* **1** : a narrow way or road (as between fences or hedges) not used as a highway **2** : a special route (as for ships) **3** : a strip of road used for a single line of traffic

lan·guage \'lang-gwij\ *n* **1** : the speech of human beings **2** : the particular words and expressions used and understood in common by a large group of people ⟨the English *language*⟩ **3** : the special words used by particular groups of people ⟨the *language* of medicine⟩ **4** : a means of expressing ideas or feelings ⟨sign *language*⟩ **5** : the form, style, or manner of using words ⟨forceful *language*⟩ **6** : the study of languages

lan·guid \'lang-gwəd\ *adj* **1** : WEAK **2** : sluggish in character or disposition : LISTLESS **3** : SLOW — **lan·guid·ly** *adv* —**lan·guid·ness** *n*

lan·guish \'lang-gwish\ *vb* : to become weak — **lan·guish·er** *n* — **lan·guish·ing** *adj* — **lan·guish·ing·ly** *adv* — **lan·guish·ment** *n*

lan·guor \'lang-gər, 'lang-ər\ *n* **1** : weakness or weariness of body or mind **2** : a state of dreamy inactivity — **lan·guor·ous** *adj* — **lan·guor·ous·ly** *adv*

lank \'langk\ *adj* **1** : not well filled out : THIN ⟨*lank* cattle⟩ **2** : hanging straight and limp without spring or curl ⟨*lank* hair⟩ — **lank·ly** *adv* — **lank·ness** *n*

lank·y \'lang-kē\ *adj* **lank·i·er; lank·i·est** : being tall, thin, and usually loose-jointed — **lank·i·ly** \-kə-lē\ *adv* — **lank·i·ness** \-kē-nəs\ *n*

lan·tern \'lant-ərn\ *n* **1** : a usually portable light with a protective covering **2** : PROJECTOR

lantern jaw *n* **1** : an undershot jaw **2** : a long thin jaw

lan·yard \'lan-yərd\ *n* **1** : a short rope or cord used as a fastening on ships **2** : a cord around the neck for holding a knife or whistle **3** : a strong cord with a hook at one end used in firing cannon

lanterns

¹lap \'lap\ *n* **1** : a part of a garment that overlaps another **2** : the part of the clothing that is over the knees and thighs when a person sits down **3** : the front part of a person between the waist and the knees when seated **4** : CIRCUMSTANCES, CONDITIONS

²lap *vb* **lapped; lap·ping** **1** : FOLD ⟨*lap* cloth in

making a seam⟩ **2** : to lay over or near something else so as to partly cover it : OVERLAP

³lap *n* **1** : the part of something that overlaps another part **2** : one full circuit around a racetrack **3** : a stage in a journey

⁴lap *vb* **lapped; lap·ping** **1** : to scoop up food or drink with the tip of the tongue **2** : to splash gently

⁵lap *n* : the act or sound of lapping

lap·board \'lap-ˌbōrd\ *n* : a board used on the lap as a table or desk

lap·dog \'lap-ˌdȯg\ *n* : a small dog that may be held in the lap

la·pel \lə-'pel\ *n* : the part of the front of a collar that is turned back ⟨coat *lapels*⟩

lap·ful \'lap-ˌfu̇l\ *n, pl* **lap·fuls** \-ˌfu̇lz\ *or* **laps·ful** \'laps-ˌfu̇l\ : as much as the lap can hold or support

¹lapse \'laps\ *n* **1** : a slight error or slip (as of the tongue or pen) **2** : a gradual slipping or falling away from a higher to a lower rank or condition **3** : a gradual passing away (as of time) **4** : the ending of a right or privilege by failure to meet requirements

²lapse *vb* **lapsed; laps·ing** **1** : to slip, pass, or fall gradually ⟨*lapse* into silence⟩ **2** : to fall into disuse ⟨a custom that had *lapsed*⟩ **3** : to come to an end — **laps·er** *n*

lar·board \'lär-bərd\ *n* : ³PORT

lar·ce·ny \'lärs-n-ē\ *n, pl* **lar·ce·nies** : the unlawful carrying away of private property without the owner's consent : THEFT

larch \'lärch\ *n* : a tree related to the pine that sheds its needles each fall

¹lard \'lärd\ *vb* **1** : to insert pork or bacon into (meat) before cooking **2** : to smear with lard, fat, or grease

²lard *n* : a white soft fat obtained from fatty tissue of the hog by heating

larch: needles and cones

lar·der \'lärd-ər\ *n* : a place where foods (as meat) are kept

large \'lärj\ *adj* **larg·er; larg·est** : greater, bigger, more extended, or more powerful than usual — **large·ness** *n* — **at large** **1** : at liberty : FREE **2** : in general ⟨the public *at large*⟩ **3** : representing a whole state or district

large–heart·ed \'lärj-'härt-əd\ *adj* : GENEROUS, SYMPATHETIC

large intestine *n* : the wide lower part of the intestine from which water is absorbed and in which feces are made ready for discharge

large·ly \'lärj-lē\ *adv* : in the main : CHIEFLY

larg·ish \'lär-jish\ *adj* : rather large

lar·i·at \'lar-ē-ət\ *n* : a long light rope to catch livestock or picket grazing animals : LASSO

---

j job   ng sing   ō low   ȯ moth   ȯi coin   th thin   th this   ü boot   u̇ foot   y you   yü few   yu̇ furious   zh vision

¹lark \'lärk\ *n* **1** : a small mostly brownish European songbird **2** : any of various mostly dull-colored birds that live on the ground

²lark *n* : a merry adventure : PRANK

lark·spur \'lärk-,spər\ *n* : an erect branching plant related to the buttercups that is often grown for its showy spikes of blue, pink, or white flowers

lar·va \'lär-və\ *n, pl* **lar·vae** \-,vē\ **1** : a young wingless and often wormlike form (as a grub or caterpillar) in which many insects hatch from the egg **2** : an early form of any animal that at birth or hatching is fundamentally unlike its parents

larvae

lar·ynx \'lar-ingks\ *n, pl* **la·ryn·ges** \lə-'rin-,jēz\ *or* **lar·ynx·es** : the upper part of the windpipe that contains the vocal cords

la·ser \'lā-zər\ *n* : a device that produces a very powerful beam of light

¹lash \'lash\ *vb* **1** : to move violently or suddenly **2** : to strike with a whip — **lash·er** *n*

²lash *n* **1** : a stroke with a whip or switch **2** : a sudden swinging blow **3** : the part of a whip above the handle **4** : something used for whipping **5** : EYELASH

³lash *vb* : to bind with a rope, cord, or chain

lash·ing \'lash-ing\ *n* : something used for binding, wrapping, or fastening

lass \'las\ *n* : GIRL

lass·ie \'las-ē\ *n* : LASS, GIRL

las·si·tude \'las-ə-,tüd, -,tyüd\ *n* : the condition of being listless or weary : lack of energy

¹las·so \'las-ō, la-'sü\ *n, pl* **las·sos** *or* **las·soes** : a rope or long leather thong with a slipknot for catching animals

²lasso *vb* : to catch with a lasso

¹last \'last\ *vb* : CONTINUE, ENDURE — **last·er** *n*

²last *adj* **1** : following all the rest : FINAL **2** : most recent (*last* week) **3** : lowest in rank or position **4** : most unlikely

lasso

syn LAST, FINAL, ULTIMATE mean following all the others. LAST suggests being the end of a series but does not always imply that the series is complete or permanently ended (the *last* page of the book) (the *last* leaf on the tree) (down to his *last* dollar) FINAL applies to something that definitely closes a series and is often deciding or conclusive in character (the judge's decision is *final*) (the *final* round of a tournament) ULTIMATE commonly applies to what is the highest or most complete stage in a process of development (the *ultimate* leveling of mountains by erosion)

³last *adv* **1** : at the end **2** : most recently

⁴last *n* : a person or thing that is last

⁵last *n* : a foot-shaped wood or metal block on which shoes are made

last·ing \'las-ting\ *adj* : existing or continuing a long while : ENDURING — **last·ing·ly** *adv* — **last·ing·ness** *n*

syn LASTING, PERMANENT, DURABLE mean enduring so long as to seem fixed or established. LASTING stresses continuing existence or effectiveness that is often surprising or remarkable (the great and *lasting* popularity of Shakespeare's plays) PERMANENT applies to things that are planned or intended to remain unchanged indefinitely (marriage is a *permanent* relation) (replacing the tents of an army camp with *permanent* barracks) DURABLE implies having the power to withstand destruction by use or decay (a *durable* pavement)

last·ly \'last-lē\ *adv* : in conclusion

¹latch \'lach\ *n* : a movable piece of metal or wood that holds a door or gate closed

²latch *vb* : to fasten by means of a latch

¹late \'lāt\ *adj* **lat·er; lat·est** **1** : coming or doing something after the usual or proper time : TARDY **2** : toward the end or close (as of a day or night) (a *late* hour) **3** : having recently died or left a certain position **4** : RECENT — **late·ness** *n*

²late *adv* **lat·er; lat·est** : after the usual or proper time

late·com·er \'lāt-,kəm-ər\ *n* **1** : one who arrives late **2** : a recent arrival

late·ly \'lāt-lē\ *adv* : RECENTLY

la·tent \'lāt-nt\ *adj* : present but not visible or active (*latent* infection) — **la·tent·ly** *adv*

¹lat·er·al \'lat-ə-rəl\ *adj* : situated on or directed toward the side — **lat·er·al·ly** *adv*

²lateral *n* : a pass in football that does not go toward the opponent's goal

la·tex \'lā-,teks\ *n* : a milky plant juice

lath \'lath\ *n, pl* **laths** \'lathz, 'laths\ : a thin strip of wood used as a base for plaster

lathe \'lāth\ *n* : a machine in which a piece of material is held and turned while being shaped by a usually fixed tool

¹lath·er \'lath-ər\ *n* **1** : the foam or froth made by stirring soap and water together **2** : foam from sweating

lathe

²lather *vb* **1** : to spread lather over **2** : to form a lather (this soap doesn't *lather* well)

¹Lat·in \'lat-n\ *adj* : of or relating to ancient Latium, Latin, or the Latin peoples

²Latin *n* **1** : a native or inhabitant of ancient Latium **2** : the language of the ancient

Romans **3** : a member of a people whose language and customs have descended from the ancient Romans

Latin–American *adj* : of or relating to the Latin countries of the Americas south of the United States or to their inhabitants

Latin American *n* : a native or inhabitant of a Latin-American country

lat·i·tude \'lat-ə-ˌtüd, -ˌtyüd\ *n* **1** : freedom to act or speak as one wishes **2** : REGION, LOCALITY ⟨cold *latitudes*⟩ **3** : the distance north or south of the equator measured in degrees ⟨imaginary circles drawn around the earth parallel to the equator indicate places having the same *latitude*⟩

hemisphere marked with parallels of latitude

lat·ter \'lat-ər\ *adj* **1** : more recent : LATER **2** : of or relating to the end : FINAL **3** : of, relating to, or being the second of two things referred to

lat·tice \'lat-əs\ *n* **1** : a framework of thin strips of wood or metal crossed to form a network **2** : a window or gate having a lattice

¹laud \'lȯd\ *n* : ACCLAIM, PRAISE

²laud *vb* : EXTOL, PRAISE

lattice 1

¹laugh \'laf, 'làf\ *vb* **1** : to show amusement, joy, or scorn by smiling and making explosive sounds (as chuckling) in the throat **2** : to influence a person in some way by laughter or scorn

²laugh *n* : the act or sound of laughing

laugh·a·ble \'laf-ə-bəl, 'làf-\ *adj* : FUNNY, RIDICULOUS — **laugh·a·ble·ness** *n* — **laugh·a·bly** \-blē\ *adv*

syn LAUGHABLE, LUDICROUS, RIDICULOUS all mean causing or fit to cause laughter. LAUGHABLE applies to almost anything fit to provoke laughter ⟨the *laughable* antics of the kittens⟩ LUDICROUS applies to what is so obviously or hopelessly absurd, illogical, inaccurate, or inadequate that it calls forth both laughter and scorn ⟨man's early attempts to fly in *ludicrous* contraptions⟩ RIDICULOUS implies arousing laughter through being absurd or foolish but perhaps chiefly through being contrary to good sense or good judgment or good taste ⟨he gave us some *ridiculous* excuse for not going with us⟩ ⟨a *ridiculous* little hat⟩

laugh·ing·stock \'laf-ing-ˌstäk, 'làf-\ *n* : an object of ridicule

laugh·ter \'laf-tər, 'làf-\ *n* : the action or sound of laughing

¹launch \'lȯnch\ *vb* **1** : THROW, HURL ⟨*launch* a spear⟩ **2** : to cause to slide into the water : set afloat ⟨*launch* a ship⟩ **3** : to shove or send off especially with force ⟨*launch* an aircraft⟩ ⟨*launch* a rocket⟩ **4** : to give a start to **5** : to set out (as upon the sea)

²launch *n* : an act of launching

³launch *n* : an open or partly decked motorboat used for pleasure or transportation

laun·der \'lȯn-dər\ *vb* : to wash or wash and iron clothes — **laun·der·er** *n*

laun·dress \'lȯn-drəs\ *n* : a woman whose work is laundering

laun·dry \'lȯn-drē\ *n, pl* **laun·dries** **1** : clothes or linens that have been or are to be laundered **2** : a place where laundering is done

laun·dry·man \'lȯn-drē-mən\ *n, pl* **laun·dry·men** \-mən\ : a man who operates or works in or for a laundry

lau·rel \'lȯr-əl\ *n* **1** : a small evergreen European tree with foliage used in ancient times to crown victors (as in sport contests) **2** : any of various plants (as the showy-flowered American **mountain laurel**) that resemble the European laurel **3** : a crown of laurel as a mark of honor

mountain laurel

la·va \'lä-və\ *n* **1** : melted rock coming from a volcano **2** : lava that has cooled and hardened

lav·a·to·ry \'lav-ə-ˌtōr-ē\ *n, pl* **lav·a·to·ries** **1** : a basin or bowl for washing **2** : a room for washing the hands and face **3** : TOILET

lav·en·der \'lav-ən-dər\ *n* **1** : a European mint with narrow somewhat woolly leaves and spikes of small sweet-smelling pale violet flowers **2** : a pale purple

¹lav·ish \'lav-ish\ *adj* **1** : spending or giving more than is necessary : EXTRAVAGANT ⟨*lavish* with money⟩ **2** : spent, produced, or given freely — **lav·ish·ly** *adv* — **lav·ish·ness** *n*

²lavish *vb* : to spend, use, or give freely

law \'lȯ\ *n* **1** : a custom or rule that a nation or group of people agrees to follow **2** : the whole collection of customs and rules ⟨the *law* of the land⟩ **3** : a rule or principle that always works in the same way under the same conditions ⟨the *law* of gravity⟩ **4** : an act or bill passed by some authority (as a legislature) **5** *cap* : the first part of the Jewish scriptures **6** : trial in a court ⟨go to *law*⟩ **7** : the profession of a lawyer

law–a·bid·ing \'lȯ-ə-ˌbīd-ing\ *adj* : obedient to the law

law·break·er \'lȯ-ˌbrā-kər\ *n* : a person who breaks the law

law·ful \'lo-fəl\ *adj* **1** : permitted by law **2** : recognized by law — **law·ful·ly** *adv* — **law·ful·ness** *n*

law·less \'lo-ləs\ *adj* **1** : having no laws : not based on or regulated by law ⟨a *lawless* frontier society⟩ **2** : uncontrolled by existing law : UNRULY — **law·less·ly** *adv* — **law·less·ness** *n*

law·mak·er \'lo-ˌmā-kər\ *n* : one who takes part in the framing of laws : LEGISLATOR — **law·mak·ing** \-ˌmā-king\ *adj or n*

¹lawn \'lon\ *n* : a sheer linen or cotton fabric used for handkerchiefs and dresses

²lawn *n* : ground (as around a house) covered with grass that is kept mowed

lawn mower *n* : a machine used to clip the grass on lawns

lawn tennis *n* : tennis played on a grass court

law·suit \'lo-ˌsüt\ *n* : a case before a court of law

law·yer \'lo-yər\ *n* : a person whose profession is to conduct lawsuits for clients or to give advice about legal rights and obligations

lax \'laks\ *adj* **1** : not firm or tight : LOOSE **2** : not exact or strict ⟨*lax* discipline⟩ — **lax·ly** *adv* — **lax·ness** *n*

¹lax·a·tive \'lak-sət-iv\ *adj* **1** : tending to loosen or relax **2** : relieving constipation

²laxative *n* : a usually mild laxative medicine

¹lay \'lā\ *vb* **laid** \'lād\; **lay·ing** **1** : to bring down (as with force) ⟨trees *laid* low by the gale⟩ **2** : to put, place, or set down ⟨*laid* his hat on the table⟩ **3** : to produce an egg **4** : to calm or quiet down : cause to disappear ⟨*laid* his fears⟩ **5** : to spread over a surface ⟨*lay* a pavement⟩ **6** : PREPARE, ARRANGE ⟨*lay* plans⟩ **7** : to put to : APPLY ⟨*lay* siege to the city⟩ **8** : to bring to a specified condition

²lay *n* : the way a thing lies in relation to something else ⟨the *lay* of the land⟩

³lay *past of* LIE

lay·er \'lā-ər\ *n* **1** : one that lays **2** : one thickness of something laid over another

lay·ette \lā-'et\ *n* : a complete outfit of clothes and equipment for a newborn baby

lay·man \'lā-mən\ *n, pl* **lay·men** \-mən\ **1** : a person who is not a clergyman **2** : a person not a member of a particular profession

la·zy \'lā-zē\ *adj* **la·zi·er; la·zi·est** **1** : not willing to act or work **2** : SLOW, SLUGGISH — **la·zi·ly** \-zə-lē\ *adv* — **la·zi·ness** \-zē-nəs\ *n*

leach \'lēch\ *vb* **1** : to treat (as soil) with a liquid solvent (as water) in order to remove a soluble part **2** : to remove (as a soluble salt) by leaching

¹lead \'lēd\ *vb* **led** \'led\; **lead·ing** **1** : to guide on a way especially by going ahead **2** : to be at the head of ⟨*lead* the class⟩ **3** : to go through : LIVE ⟨*lead* a happy life⟩ **4** : to reach or go in a certain direction

²lead *n* **1** : position at the front ⟨take the *lead*⟩ **2** : the distance that a person or thing is ahead **3** : something that acts as a guide or clue

³lead \'led\ *n* **1** : a heavy soft gray metallic element that is easily bent and shaped **2** : something made of lead or an alloy of lead **3** : BULLETS, AMMUNITION ⟨a shower of *lead*⟩ **4** : a long thin piece of carbon or other substance used in pencils

lead·en \'led-n\ *adj* **1** : made of lead **2** : heavy as lead **3** : of the color of lead — **lead·en·ly** *adv* — **lead·en·ness** *n*

lead·er \'lēd-ər\ *n* : one that leads or is fitted to lead — **lead·er·ship** \-ˌship\ *n*

¹leaf \'lēf\ *n, pl* **leaves** \'lēvz\ **1** : one of the

leaves of various shapes

green usually flat parts that grow from a stem or twig of a plant and together make up the foliage **2** : a modified leaf (as a flower petal) **3** : a single sheet of a book making two pages **4** : the movable part of the top of a table — **leaf·less** \'lēf-ləs\ *adj* — **leaf·like** \-ˌlīk\ *adj*

²leaf *vb* **1** : to send forth leaves **2** : to turn the leaves of a book

leaf·let \'lēf-lət\ *n* **1** : a young leaf **2** : a division of a compound leaf **3** : PAMPHLET

leaf·stalk \'lēf-ˌstok\ *n* : PETIOLE

leaf·y \'lē-fē\ *adj* **leaf·i·er; leaf·i·est** : having, covered with, or resembling leaves

¹league \'lēg\ *n* **1** : an association or alliance of nations for a common purpose **2** : an association of persons or groups united for common interests or goals **3** : CLASS, CATEGORY

²league *vb* **leagued; leagu·ing** : to form a league

¹leak \'lēk\ *vb* **1** : to enter or escape or let enter or escape usually by accident ⟨fumes *leaking* in⟩ **2** : to make or become known

²leak *n* **1** : a crack or hole that accidentally lets fluid in or out **2** : something that accidentally or secretly causes or permits loss **3** : the act of leaking : LEAKAGE

leak·age \'lē-kij\ *n* **1** : the act or process of leaking **2** : the thing or amount that leaks

leak·y \'lē-kē\ *adj* **leak·i·er; leak·i·est** : permitting fluid to leak in or out — **leak·i·ness** *n*

¹lean \'lēn\ *vb* **1** : to tip or bend from a straight position ⟨a tree that *leans* badly⟩ ⟨*lean* the ladder against the wall⟩ **2** : to bend or stoop for support ⟨*lean* on me⟩ **3** : DEPEND, RELY **4** : to incline in opinion, taste, or desire

²lean *n* : INCLINATION

³lean *adj* **1** : lacking or deficient in flesh ⟨*lean* cattle⟩ **2** : containing little or no fat ⟨*lean* meat⟩ **3** : lacking in fullness or richness ⟨a *lean* harvest⟩ **syn** see THIN — **lean·ness** *n*

lean–to \'lēn-,tü\ *n, pl* **lean–tos** **1** : a building having a roof with only one slope usually joined to another building **2** : a rude shelter leaning against posts, rocks, or trees

lean-to

¹leap \'lēp\ *vb* **leaped** *or* **leapt** \'lēpt, 'lept\; **leap·ing** \'lē-ping\ **1** : to spring or cause to spring from a surface : JUMP ⟨*leaped* from his chair⟩ **2** : to move, act, or pass quickly — **leap·er** \'lē-pər\ *n*

²leap *n* **1** : an act of leaping : JUMP **2** : a place leaped over **3** : a distance leaped

leap·frog \'lēp-,fròg, -,fräg\ *n* : a game in which one player bends down and another leaps over him

leap year *n* : a year of 366 days with February 29 as the extra day

learn \'lərn\ *vb* **learned** \'lərnd\ *also* **learnt** \'lərnt\; **learn·ing** **1** : to gain knowledge of or skill in (as by study or experience) ⟨*learn* algebra⟩ **2** : MEMORIZE **3** : to become able through practice ⟨a baby *learning* to walk⟩ **4** : to find out ⟨*learned* what had happened⟩ **5** : to acquire knowledge — **learn·er** *n*

learn·ed \'lər-nəd\ *adj* : possessing or displaying knowledge or learning

learn·ing \'lər-ning\ *n* **1** : the act of one that learns **2** : knowledge or skill gained by instruction or study

¹lease \'lēs\ *n* **1** : an agreement to hand over real estate for a period of time in exchange for rent or services **2** : the period of time for which real estate is leased **3** : a piece of land or property that is leased

²lease *vb* **leased; leas·ing** : to grant or get the use of (real estate or property) in exchange for services or rent

¹leash \'lēsh\ *n* : a strap, cord, or chain to hold an animal

²leash *vb* : to put on a leash

¹least \'lēst\ *adj* : SMALLEST, SHORTEST

²least *n* : the smallest or lowest amount or degree ⟨doesn't care in the *least* about her⟩

³least *adv* : in or to the smallest degree

¹leath·er \'leth-ər\ *n* **1** : the tanned skin of an animal **2** : something made of leather

²leather *vb* : to cover with leather

leath·er·y \'leth-ə-rē\ *adj* : resembling leather

¹leave \'lēv\ *vb* **left** \'left\; **leav·ing** **1** : to allow or cause to remain behind ⟨*left* his books at home⟩ **2** : to have remaining ⟨a wound that *left* a scar⟩ ⟨taking 7 from 10 *leaves* 3⟩ **3** : to give by will ⟨*left* property to his wife⟩ **4** : to let stay without interference ⟨*leave* him alone⟩ **5** : to go away from ⟨*leave* the house⟩ **6** : to give up **7** : DELIVER ⟨*leave* a message⟩

²leave *n* **1** : PERMISSION ⟨ask *leave* to be absent⟩ **2** : authorized absence from duty or employment **3** : the act of leaving and saying good-bye ⟨take *leave* of her⟩ **4** : a period of time during which a person is allowed to be absent from duties

³leave *vb* **leaved; leav·ing** : LEAF

leaved \'lēvd\ *adj* : having leaves

¹leav·en \'lev-ən\ *n* **1** : a substance (as yeast) used to produce fermentation (as in dough) **2** : something that modifies or lightens a mass or aggregate

²leaven *vb* : to raise (dough) with a leaven

leaves *pl of* LEAF

¹lec·ture \'lek-chər\ *n* **1** : an instructive talk or address **2** : SCOLDING

²lecture *vb* **lec·tured; lec·tur·ing** **1** : to give or deliver a lecture **2** : SCOLD — **lec·tur·er** *n*

led *past of* LEAD

ledge \'lej\ *n* **1** : a shelflike piece projecting from a top or an edge ⟨the outer *ledge* of a window⟩ **2** : an overhanging shelf of rock

¹lee \'lē\ *n* **1** : a protecting shelter **2** : the side (as of a ship) sheltered from the wind

²lee *adj* : of or relating to the lee

leech \'lēch\ *n* **1** : a bloodsucking worm related to the earthworm **2** : a person who clings like a leech to another for personal gain

leek \'lēk\ *n* : a garden herb related to the onion and grown for its thick mildly pungent stems

¹leer \'liər\ *vb* : to look with a leer

²leer *n* : a sly sneering sidelong glance

leer·y \'liər-ē\ *adj* : SUSPICIOUS, WARY

lees \'lēz\ *n pl* : the settlings of liquor during fermentation and aging

¹lee·ward \'lē-wərd\ *adj* : situated away from the wind

²leeward *n* : the lee side

¹left \'left\ *adj* [from Old English *left*, an adjective originally meaning "weak"; it came to mean "left" because the left hand is the weaker one in most people] **1** : on the same side of the body as the heart ⟨the *left* leg⟩ ⟨the *left* hand⟩ **2** : located nearer to the left side of the body than to the right

²left *n* : the part on the left side

³left *past of* LEAVE

left–hand \ˌleft-ˌhand\ *adj* **1** : situated on the left **2** : LEFT-HANDED

left–hand·ed \ˈleft-ˈhan-dəd\ *adj* **1** : using the left hand more skillfully than the right **2** : done or made with or for the left hand

left·o·ver \ˈleft-ˌō-vər\ *n* : food left over from one meal and served at another

leg \ˈleg\ *n* **1** : one of the limbs of an animal that support the body and are used in walking and running **2** : the part of the leg between the knee and the foot **3** : something like a leg in shape or use ⟨the *legs* of a table⟩ **4** : the part of a garment that covers the leg **5** : a stage of a journey ⟨the first *leg* of a trip⟩ **6** : either side of a triangle as distinguished from the base or hypotenuse

leg 6

leg·a·cy \ˈleg-ə-sē\ *n, pl* **leg·a·cies** : something left to a person by or as if by a will

le·gal \ˈlē-gəl\ *adj* **1** : of or relating to law or lawyers **2** : established by or according to law : LAWFUL — **le·gal·ly** *adv*

le·gal·i·ty \li-ˈgal-ət-ē\ *n, pl* **le·gal·i·ties** : the quality or state of being legal : LAWFULNESS

le·gal·ize \ˈlē-gə-ˌlīz\ *vb* **le·gal·ized; le·gal·iz·ing** **1** : to make legal ⟨*legalized* gambling⟩ **2** : to give legal validity to — **le·gal·i·za·tion** \ˌlē-gə-lə-ˈzā-shən\ *n*

leg·ate \ˈleg-ət\ *n* : an official representative

leg·a·tee \ˌleg-ə-ˈtē\ *n* : a person to whom a legacy is bequeathed

leg·end \ˈlej-ənd\ *n* [from Latin *legenda* "something to be read", from *legere* "to read"] **1** : an old story that is widely accepted as true but cannot be proved to be so **2** : an inscription or title on an object

leg·end·ar·y \ˈlej-ən-ˌder-ē\ *adj* : of, relating to, or characteristic of a legend **syn** *see* FABULOUS

leg·er·de·main \ˌlej-ər-də-ˈmān\ *n* **1** : SLEIGHT OF HAND **2** : an artful trick

legged \ˈleg-əd, ˈlegd\ *adj* : having legs

leg·ging \ˈleg-ən, ˈleg-ing\ *n* : a long heavy outer stocking or gaiter ⟨a pair of *leggings*⟩

leg·i·ble \ˈlej-ə-bəl\ *adj* : clear enough to be read : PLAIN — **leg·i·bly** \-blē\ *adv*

le·gion \ˈlē-jən\ *n* **1** : a body of from 3000 to 6000 soldiers forming the chief army unit in ancient Rome **2** : ARMY **3** : a very great number ⟨has a *legion* of admirers⟩

leg·is·late \ˈlej-əs-ˌlāt\ *vb* **leg·is·lat·ed; leg·is-**

lat·ing : to make or enact laws — **leg·is·la·tor** *n*

leg·is·la·tion \ˌlej-əs-ˈlā-shən\ *n* **1** : the action of making laws **2** : the laws that are made

leg·is·la·tive \ˈlej-əs-ˌlāt-iv\ *adj* **1** : having the power or authority to make laws **2** : of or relating to legislation — **leg·is·la·tive·ly** *adv*

leg·is·la·ture \ˈlej-əs-ˌlā-chər\ *n* : a body of persons having the power to make, alter, or repeal laws

le·git·i·ma·cy \li-ˈjit-ə-mə-sē\ *n* : the quality or state of being legitimate

le·git·i·mate \li-ˈjit-ə-mət\ *adj* **1** : recognized by the law as rightful : LAWFUL ⟨a *legitimate* heir⟩ **2** : conforming to what is right ⟨a *legitimate* excuse⟩ — **le·git·i·mate·ly** *adv*

le·git·i·mize \li-ˈjit-ə-ˌmīz\ *vb* **le·git·i·mized; le·git·i·miz·ing** : to make legitimate or lawful

leg·less \ˈleg-ləs\ *adj* : having no legs

leg·ume \ˈleg-ˌyüm\ *n* : any of a large group of plants (as peas, beans, and clover) with fruits that are pods and root nodules containing bacteria that fix nitrogen

lei·sure \ˈlē-zhər\ *n* **1** : freedom from work ⟨a time of *leisure*⟩ **2** : time at one's command

lei·sure·ly \ˈlē-zhər-lē\ *adj* : UNHURRIED

lem·on \ˈlem-ən\ *n* : an oval yellow fruit with a sour juice that is related to the orange and borne on a small spiny citrus tree

lem·on·ade \ˌlem-ən-ˈād\ *n* : a drink made of lemon juice, sugar, and water

lend \ˈlend\ *vb* **lent** \ˈlent\; **lend·ing** **1** : to allow the use of something on the condition that it be returned **2** : to give temporarily ⟨*lend* assistance⟩ **3** : to make a loan or loans

length \ˈlength\ *n* **1** : the longest or the longer dimension of an object **2** : the distance from end to end ⟨a *length* of two feet⟩ **3** : extent in time ⟨the *length* of a visit⟩ **4** : one of certain pieces that may be joined together ⟨three *lengths* of pipe⟩ **5** : the sound of a vowel or syllable as it is affected by the time it takes to pronounce it — **at length** **1** : very fully ⟨tell a story *at length*⟩ **2** : at the end

length·en \ˈleng-thən\ *vb* : to make or become longer ⟨*lengthen* a dress⟩

length·ways \ˈlength-ˌwāz\ *adv* : LENGTH-WISE

¹length·wise \ˈlength-ˌwīz\ *adv* : in the direction of the length ⟨fold the paper *lengthwise*⟩

²lengthwise *adj* : moved, placed, or directed lengthwise ⟨a *lengthwise* fold in the paper⟩

length·y \ˈleng-thē\ *adj* **length·i·er; length·i·est** : very long — **length·i·ly** \-thə-lē\ *adv* — **length·i·ness** \-thē-nəs\ *n*

le·ni·ent \ˈlē-nē-ənt\ *adj* : not harsh or severe **syn** *see* TOLERANT — **le·ni·ent·ly** *adv*

lens \'lenz\ *n* [from Latin *lens* "lentil"; so named because a convex lens is shaped like a lentil] **1** : a transparent substance (as glass) whose two opposite surfaces (as in a camera or a pair of eyeglasses) are either both curved or one curved and the other flat and whose purpose is to change the direction of the rays of light passing through it so that they will come together and form a clear image **2** : a part of the eye that focuses rays of light so as to form clear images

Lent \'lent\ *n* : a period of penitence and fasting observed on the forty weekdays from Ash Wednesday to Easter by many churches

len·til \'lent-l\ *n* : the flattened round edible seed of a plant related to the pea

leop·ard \'lep-ərd\ *n* : a large spotted cat of Asia and Africa that is tawny with black spots

le·sion \'lē-zhən\ *n* : an abnormal spot or area of the body caused by sickness or injury

¹less \'les\ *adj* **1** : not so much : a smaller amount of ⟨we need *less* talk and more work⟩ **2** : FEWER ⟨*less* than ten people showed up⟩ **3** : of lower rank, degree, or importance

²less *adv* : to a lesser extent or degree

³less *prep* : diminished by : MINUS

⁴less *n* **1** : a smaller number or amount **2** : something of less importance

-less \ləs\ *adj suffix* **1** : destitute of : not having ⟨child*less*⟩ ⟨pain*less*⟩ **2** : unable to be acted on or to act in a specified way ⟨resist*less*⟩ ⟨cease*less*⟩

less·en \'les-n\ *vb* : to make or become less

¹less·er \'les-ər\ *adj* : less in importance

²lesser *adv* : LESS ⟨*lesser*-known⟩

les·son \'les-n\ *n* **1** : a portion of Scripture read in a church service **2** : a reading or exercise assigned for study **3** : something learned or taught

lest \'lest\ *conj* : for fear that

¹let \'let\ *n* : HINDRANCE, OBSTACLE ⟨go ahead without *let* or hindrance⟩

²let *vb* let; let·ting **1** : to cause to : MAKE ⟨*let* it be known⟩ **2** : RENT, LEASE ⟨rooms to *let*⟩ **3** : to allow or permit to ⟨*let* him go⟩ **4** : to allow to go or pass ⟨*let* me through⟩

-let \lət\ *n suffix* **1** : small one ⟨book*let*⟩ **2** : article worn on ⟨wrist*let*⟩

let's \lets\ : let us

¹let·ter \'let-ər\ *n* **1** : one of the characters of the alphabet : one of the symbols in writing or print that stand for speech sounds **2** : a written or printed communication (as one sent through the mail) **3** *pl* : LITERATURE ⟨men of *letters*⟩ **4** : the strict or outward meaning ⟨the *letter* of the law⟩

²letter *vb* : to mark with letters

let·ter·ing \'let-ə-ring\ *n* : letters used in an inscription

let·tuce \'let-əs\ *n* : a garden plant related to the daisies that has large crisp leaves eaten in salad

leu·ke·mi·a \lü-'kē-mē-ə\ *n* : a dangerous disease in which too many white blood cells are produced

lev·ee \'lev-ē\ *n* **1** : a bank built along a river to prevent flooding **2** : a river landing place : PIER

¹lev·el \'lev-əl\ *n* **1** : a device used (as by surveyors) to find a horizontal line or plane **2** : a horizontal position **3** : a horizontal line or surface taken as a point from which measurements are made **4** : a level surface : a level floor **5** : a step or stage in height, position, or rank

²level *vb* lev·eled *or* lev·elled; lev·el·ing *or* lev·el·ling : to make or become level, flat, or even — lev·el·er *or* lev·el·ler *n*

³level *adj* **1** : having a flat even surface ⟨a *level* lawn⟩ **2** : on a line with the floor or even ground : HORIZONTAL ⟨in a *level* position⟩ **3** : of the same height or rank : EVEN **4** : steady and cool in judgment — lev·el·ly *adv* — lev·el·ness *n*

syn LEVEL, FLAT, EVEN mean having a surface like that of a calm body of water. LEVEL applies especially to a surface or a line that does not slant up or down ⟨a *level* stretch of road between two hills⟩ FLAT applies to a surface that is free from curves or bumps or hollows but is not necessarily horizontal ⟨a perfectly *flat* wall⟩ ⟨iron clothes on a *flat* surface⟩ EVEN stresses the lack of breaks or irregularities of a line or surface but does not necessarily imply straightness or levelness ⟨trimmed the top of the hedge to make it *even*⟩

¹lev·er \'lev-ər, 'lē-vər\ *n* **1** : a bar used for prying or moving something : CROWBAR **2** : a rigid bar capable of turning about a point or axis and used for transmitting and changing force and motion **3** : a projecting piece by which something is operated or adjusted ⟨gearshift *lever*⟩

²lever *vb* : to raise or move with a lever

¹lev·y \'lev-ē\ *n, pl* lev·ies **1** : a collection (as of taxes) by legal authority **2** : the calling of troops into service **3** : something levied

²levy *vb* lev·ied; lev·y·ing **1** : to collect legally (as taxes) **2** : to raise or collect troops for service **3** : to carry on : WAGE ⟨*levy* war⟩ **4** : to impose (as a fine) by legal authority

li·a·ble \'lī-ə-bəl\ *adj* **1** : bound by law or by

---

j job   ng sing   ō low   ȯ moth   ȯi coin   th thin   th this   ü boot   u̇ foot   y you   yü few   yu̇ furious   zh vision

what is right : RESPONSIBLE ⟨*liable* for damage⟩
2 : exposed to (as danger or accident) : APT

li·ar \'lī-ər\ *n* : a person who tells lies

¹li·bel \'lī-bəl\ *n* : something (as a remark or statement) either spoken or written that hurts a person's good name

²libel *vb* **li·beled** *or* **li·belled; li·bel·ing** *or* **li·bel·ling** : to injure by a libel — **li·bel·er** *or* **li·bel·ler** *n*

lib·er·al \'lib-ə-rəl\ *adj* **1** : not stingy : GENEROUS ⟨a *liberal* giver⟩ **2** : ABUNDANT, AMPLE ⟨a *liberal* sum⟩ **3** : not strict **4** : BROAD ⟨a *liberal* education⟩ — **lib·er·al·ly** *adv*

lib·er·ate \'lib-ə-‚rāt\ *vb* **lib·er·at·ed; lib·er·at·ing** : to set free

lib·er·ty \'lib-ərt-ē\ *n, pl* **lib·er·ties 1** : the condition of those who are free and independent : FREEDOM **2** : power to do what one pleases : freedom from control ⟨give a child some *liberty*⟩ **3** : the state of being free or not busy : LEISURE **4** : the act of a person who is too free, bold, or familiar

li·brar·i·an \lī-'brer-ē-ən\ *n* : a person in charge of a library

li·brar·y \'lī-‚brer-ē\ *n, pl* **li·brar·ies 1** : a place in which literary and artistic materials and especially books are kept for use and not for sale **2** : a collection of literary or artistic materials (as books or prints)

li·bret·to \lə-'bret-ō\ *n, pl* **li·bret·tos** *or* **li·bret·ti** \-'bret-ē\ : the story and the words of an opera

lice *pl of* LOUSE

¹li·cense *or* **li·cence** \'līs-ns\ *n* **1** : permission granted by competent authority to do something **2** : a paper showing legal permission ⟨a driver's *license*⟩ **3** : liberty of action especially when carried too far

²license *or* **licence** *vb* **li·censed** *or* **li·cenced; li·cens·ing** *or* **li·cenc·ing** : to permit or authorize by license

li·chen \'lī-kən\ *n* : a complex plant made up of an alga and a fungus growing as a unit

¹lick \'lik\ *vb* **1** : to draw or pass the tongue over ⟨*lick* a spoon⟩ **2** : to touch or pass over like a tongue ⟨flames *licking* a wall⟩ **3** : BEAT, WHIP **4** : DEFEAT, OVERCOME

²lick *n* **1** : the act of licking **2** : a small quantity ⟨never did a *lick* of work⟩ **3** : a place (**salt lick**) where salt is found on the surface and animals come to lick it up

lic·o·rice \'lik-ə-rish, -rəs\ *n* [the Greeks combined *glykys* "sweet" and *rhiza* "root" to make *glykyrrhiza* "licorice", which was then taken into Latin as *glycyrrhiza,* altered to *liquiritia* in later Latin, and eventually taken into English as *licorice*] : the dried root of a

European plant related to the peas or an extract of it used in medicine and in candy

lid \'lid\ *n* **1** : a movable cover ⟨the *lid* of a box⟩ **2** : EYELID — **lid·ded** \'lid-əd\ *adj* — **lid·less** \'lid-ləs\ *adj*

¹lie \'lī\ *vb* **lay** \'lā\; **lain** \'lān\; **ly·ing** \'lī-ing\ **1** : to stretch out or be stretched out (as on a bed or the ground) **2** : to be or remain in a flat position ⟨snow *lying* on the fields⟩ **3** : to be located or placed ⟨Ohio *lies* west of Pennsylvania⟩ **4** : to be or remain

²lie *vb* **lied; ly·ing** : to make an untrue statement with intent to deceive

³lie *n* : something said or done in the hope of deceiving : FALSEHOOD, UNTRUTH

¹liege \'lēj\ *adj* **1** : having the right to receive service and allegiance ⟨*liege* lord⟩ **2** : owing or giving service to a lord

²liege *n* **1** : VASSAL **2** : a feudal superior

lieu·ten·ant \lü-'ten-ənt\ *n* **1** : an officer who takes the place of an absent superior **2** : a commissioned officer (as in the army) ranking next below a captain **3** : a commissioned officer in the navy ranking next below a lieutenant commander

lieutenant colonel *n* : a commissioned officer (as in the army) ranking next below a colonel

lieutenant commander *n* : a commissioned officer in the navy ranking next below a commander

lieutenant general *n* : a commissioned officer (as in the army) ranking next below a general

lieutenant junior grade *n* : a commissioned officer in the navy ranking next below a lieutenant

life \'līf\ *n, pl* **lives** \'līvz\ **1** : the quality by which animals and plants differ from such things as rocks, earth, and water : a quality that animals and plants lose when they die **2** : the sequence of physical and mental experiences that make up the existence of an individual **3** : BIOGRAPHY **4** : the period during which a person or thing is alive or exists **5** : a way of living ⟨the *life* of the ant⟩ **6** : a living being : PERSON ⟨many *lives* being saved by quick action⟩ **7** : LIVELINESS, SPIRIT

life belt *n* : a life preserver in the form of a buoyant belt

life·boat \'līf-‚bōt\ *n* : a strong boat especially designed for use in saving lives at sea

life buoy *n* : a float consisting of a ring of buoyant material to support a person who has fallen into the water

life buoy

life·guard \'līf-,gärd\ *n* : a guard employed at a bathing resort to save persons from drowning

life·less \'līf-ləs\ *adj* : having no life

life·like \'līf-,līk\ *adj* : accurately representing·or imitating real life

life·long \'līf-,lòng\ *adj* : continuing through life ⟨a *lifelong* friendship⟩

life preserver *n* : something (as a jacket lined with cork or capable of being inflated or a buoyant belt) used to keep a person from drowning

life preserver

life raft *n* : a raft usually made of wood or an inflatable material and designed for use by people forced into the water

life·sav·er \'līf-,sā-vər\ *n* : one trained in lifesaving

life·sav·ing \'līf-,sā-ving\ *n* : the art or practice of saving lives especially of drowning persons

life–size \'līf-'sīz\ *or* **life–sized** \-'sīzd\ *adj* : of natural size : of the size of the original

life·time \'līf-,tīm\ *n* : the time that a life continues : the length of one's life

¹lift \'lift\ *vb* **1** : to raise from a lower to a higher position, rate, or amount : ELEVATE **2** : to move from one place to another **3** : RISE, ASCEND **4** : to disperse upward ⟨until the fog *lifts*⟩ — **lift·er** *n*

²lift *n* **1** : the amount that may be lifted at one time : LOAD **2** : the action or an instance of lifting **3** : help especially in the form of a ride ⟨give a person a *lift*⟩ **4** : one of the layers forming the heel of a shoe **5** : the distance or extent to which something rises **6** *chiefly Brit* : ELEVATOR **7** : an upward force (as on an airplane wing) that opposes the pull of gravity

lig·a·ment \'lig-ə-mənt\ *n* : a tough band of tissue or fibers that holds bones together or keeps an organ in place in the body

¹light \'līt\ *n* **1** : the condition that enables one to see : the opposite of darkness **2** : the bright form of energy given off by something (as the sun) that enables one to see objects **3** : a source (as the sun) of light **4** : DAYLIGHT **5** : public view or knowledge ⟨facts brought to *light*⟩ **6** : an inner glow or brightness (as in the face) **7** : a particular aspect or appearance presented to view

²light *adj* **1** : having light : BRIGHT ⟨a *light* room⟩ **2** : not dark or deep in color

³light *vb* **light·ed** *or* **lit** \'lit\; **light·ing** **1** : to burn or cause to burn : KINDLE ⟨*light* the gas⟩ **2** : to conduct with a light : GUIDE **3** : ILLUMINATE **4** : to make or become bright

⁴light *adj* **1** : having little weight : not heavy **2** : not hard to bear, do, pay, or digest ⟨*light* punishment⟩ **3** : not strong or violent ⟨a *light* breeze⟩ **4** : active or nimble in motion ⟨*light* on her feet⟩ **5** : SLIGHT, MODERATE ⟨a *light* case of measles⟩ **6** : not burdened by care or suffering : HAPPY ⟨a *light* heart⟩ **7** : not serious in mood **8** : not soggy or heavy — **light·ly** *adv* — **light·ness** *n*

⁵light *adv* : with little baggage ⟨travel *light*⟩

⁶light *vb* **light·ed** *or* **lit** \'lit\; **light·ing** **1** : to dismount or get down (as from a horse) **2** : PERCH, SETTLE ⟨a bird *lighting* on a twig⟩ **3** : to come by chance : HAPPEN

¹light·en \'līt-n\ *vb* **1** : to make or grow light : BRIGHTEN **2** : to grow bright with lightning — **light·en·er** *n*

²lighten *vb* : to make or become less heavy — **light·en·er** *n*

light·face \'līt-,fās\ *n* : a type having light thin lines (as in this) — **light·faced** \-,fāst\ *adj*

light·heart·ed \'līt-'härt-əd\ *adj* : free from worry : GAY, MERRY — **light·heart·ed·ly** *adv* — **light·heart·ed·ness** *n*

light·house \'līt-,haùs\ *n* : a tower with a powerful light at the top that is built on the shore to guide navigators at night

light·ing \'līt-ing\ *n* **1** : ILLUMINATION **2** : an artificial supply of light or the apparatus providing it

lighthouse

light·ning \'līt-ning\ *n* : the flashing of light caused by the passing of electricity from one cloud to another or between a cloud and the earth

lightning bug *n* : FIREFLY

light·proof \'līt-'prüf\ *adj* : not admitting light ⟨*lightproof* box⟩

light·weight \'līt-,wāt\ *adj* : having less than average weight

lik·a·ble *or* **like·a·ble** \'lī-kə-bəl\ *adj* : so pleasant or agreeable as to be liked — **lik·a·ble·ness** *n*

¹like \'līk\ *vb* **liked**; **lik·ing** **1** : to have a liking for : ENJOY ⟨*like* games⟩ **2** : to feel toward : REGARD **3** : PREFER, CHOOSE

²like *n* : LIKING, PREFERENCE

³like *adj* **1** : ALIKE, SIMILAR **2** : resembling or similar to that or those of — used after the word modified ⟨dog*like* devotion⟩ **3** : similar to : RESEMBLING — used after the word modified ⟨a man*like* creature⟩

⁴like *prep* **1** : similar or similarly to ⟨he's a lot *like* his father⟩ ⟨she acts *like* a fool⟩ **2** : typical of ⟨it would be just *like* him to leave without paying⟩ **3** : inclined to ⟨looks

like rain⟩ **4** : such as ⟨a subject *like* physics⟩
⁵like *n* : COUNTERPART, EQUAL
⁶like *conj* **1** : in the same way that : AS **2** : as
if ⟨it looks *like* we're going to get some rain⟩
like·li·hood \'līk-lē-ˌhůd\ *n* : PROBABILITY
like·ly \'līk-lē\ *adj* **1** : probably such as
: probably sure ⟨that bomb is *likely* to ex-
plode⟩ **2** : seeming like the truth : BELIEVABLE
3 : PROMISING **syn** see PROBABLE
lik·en \'lī-kən\ *vb* : COMPARE
like·ness \'līk-nəs\ *n* **1** : RESEMBLANCE
2 : APPEARANCE **3** : COPY, PORTRAIT
like·wise \'līk-ˌwīz\ *adv* **1** : in like manner
⟨do *likewise*⟩ **2** : ALSO ⟨you *likewise*⟩
lik·ing \'lī-king\ *n* : favorable regard
li·lac \'lī-lək\ *n* **1** : a bush having clusters of
fragrant grayish pink, purple,
or white flowers **2** : a moderate
purple
¹lilt \'lilt\ *vb* : to sing or play in
a lively cheerful manner —
lilt·ing·ly *adv*

lilac

²lilt *n* **1** : a gay lively tune
2 : a swinging movement
lil·y \'lil-ē\ *n, pl* **lil·ies** : a leafy-stemmed herb
that grows from a bulb and has funnel-shaped
flowers (as the white **Easter lily** or the orange
tiger lily)
lily of the valley : a low herb related to the
lilies that has usually two leaves and a stalk
of fragrant nodding bell-shaped flowers
li·ma bean \ˌlī-mə-\ *n* : a bean with flat pale
green or white seeds
limb \'lim\ *n* **1** : one of the
projecting paired parts (as wings
or legs) of an animal body that
are used especially in moving or
grasping **2** : a large branch of a tree — **limbed**
\'limd\ *adj* — **limb·less** \'lim-ləs\ *adj*

lima beans
in pod

¹lim·ber \'lim-bər\ *adj* : bending easily
— **lim·ber·ly** *adv* — **lim·ber·ness** *n*
²limber *vb* : to make or become limber
¹lime \'līm\ *n* : a white substance made by
heating limestone, shells, or bones that is used
in making mortar, cement, fertilizers, and
medicines
²lime *vb* **limed; lim·ing** : to treat or cover
with lime ⟨*lime* a garden⟩
³lime *n* : a small greenish yellow green-fleshed
fruit that is related to the lemon and orange
lim·er·ick \'lim-ə-rik\ *n* : a humorous poem
five lines long
lime·stone \'līm-ˌstōn\ *n* : a rock formed
chiefly from animal remains (as shells or
coral) that is used in building and gives lime
when burned
lime·wa·ter \'līm-ˌwȯt-ər, -ˌwät-\ *n* : a

colorless calcium-containing water solution
that turns white when carbon dioxide is
blown through it
¹lim·it \'lim-ət\ *n* **1** : a boundary line
⟨within the city *limits*⟩ **2** : a point beyond
which a person or thing cannot go
²limit *vb* : to set bounds or limits to
lim·i·ta·tion \ˌlim-ə-'tā-shən\ *n* **1** : an act or
instance of limiting **2** : the quality or state of
being limited **3** : BOUNDARY, RESTRAINT
lim·it·less \'lim-ət-ləs\ *adj* : having no limits
limn \'lim\ *vb* **1** : DRAW, PAINT **2** : PORTRAY
¹limp \'limp\ *vb* : to walk lamely
²limp *n* : a limping movement or gait
³limp *adj* **1** : having no defined shape : SLACK
2 : not stiff or rigid **3** : lacking firmness or
strength — **limp·ly** *adv* — **limp·ness** *n*
lim·y \'lī-mē\ *adj* **lim·i·er; lim·i·est** : containing lime or limestone
lin·den \'lin-dən\ *n* : a shade tree with heart⹀
shaped toothed leaves, droop-
ing clusters of yellowish white
flowers, and hard pealike fruit
¹line \'līn\ *vb* **lined; lin·ing**
: to cover the inner surface of
⟨*line* a coat⟩ ⟨*line* a clothes
closet with cedar⟩

linden: fruit
and leaves

²line *n* **1** : THREAD, CORD, ROPE
⟨the fisherman put out his
lines⟩ **2** : the marked bounds or limits of a
place or a lot ⟨the town *line*⟩ **3** : piping for
carrying a fluid (as steam, water, or oil)
4 : the wire connecting one telegraph or
telephone station with another or the principal
outdoor wires of an electric power system
5 : the track of a railway **6** : a system of
transportation **7** : a geometric element produced by moving a point : a set of points
8 : a long narrow mark (as one drawn by a
pencil) **9** : AGREEMENT, HARMONY ⟨bring their
ideas into *line*⟩ **10** : WRINKLE, CREASE
11 : OUTLINE, CONTOUR ⟨a ship's *lines*⟩ **12** : a
plan for making or doing something ⟨a
story along the same *lines*⟩ **13** : a row of
letters or words across a page or column
14 : a course of conduct or thought ⟨a political
line⟩ ⟨in the *line* of duty⟩ **15** : FAMILY ⟨born
of a royal *line*⟩ **16** : a row of similar things ⟨a
line of houses⟩ **17** : the football players whose
positions are along the line of scrimmage
18 : the direction followed by something in
motion : ROAD, ROUTE ⟨a *line* of flight⟩
19 *pl* : the words of a part in a play
³line *vb* **lined; lin·ing** **1** : to mark or cover with
a line **2** : to place or be placed in a line along
3 : to array or form in a line
lin·e·age \'lin-ē-ij\ *n* **1** : the line of ancestors

from whom a person is descended **2** : the line of descendants from a common ancestor

lin·e·ar \'lin-ē-ər\ *adj* **1** : of, resembling, or relating to a line : STRAIGHT **2** : involving a single dimension

line drive *n* : a baseball hit in the air on a line almost parallel to and usually not far above the ground

line·man \'līn-mən\ *n, pl* **line·men** \-mən\ : a football player in the line

lin·en \'lin-ən\ *n* **1** : lustrous durable cloth or yarn made from flax **2** : household articles (as tablecloths or sheets) or clothing (as shirts or underwear) made of linen cloth or a similar fabric

line of scrimmage : an imaginary line in football parallel to the goal lines and running through the place where the ball is laid before each scrimmage

¹lin·er \'lī-nər\ *n* : a ship or airplane of a regular transportation line ⟨an ocean *liner*⟩

²liner *n* **1** : one that lines or covers the inner surface of something **2** : something used to line or back an inner surface

-ling \ling\ *n suffix* **1** : one connected with or being ⟨nest*ling*⟩ **2** : young, small, or inferior one ⟨duck*ling*⟩ ⟨prince*ling*⟩

lin·ger \'ling-gər\ *vb* : to be slow in leaving or quitting : DELAY, LOITER

lin·guis·tics \ling-'gwis-tiks\ *n* : the study of human speech including the units, nature, structure, and development of language or a language

lin·ing \'lī-ning\ *n* : material that lines the inner surface of something ⟨a removable coat *lining*⟩

¹link \'lingk\ *n* **1** : a single ring or division of a chain **2** : BOND, TIE ⟨the *link* of friendship⟩

²link *vb* : to join with or as if with links ⟨the towns now *linked* by the expressway⟩

links \'lingks\ *n pl* : a golf course

lin·net \'lin-ət\ *n* : a common small European finch popular as a cage bird

li·no·le·um \lə-'nō-lē-əm\ *n* : a floor covering with a canvas back and a surface of hardened linseed oil and cork dust

lin·seed \'lin-ˌsēd\ *n* : FLAXSEED

linseed oil *n* : a yellowish oil obtained from flaxseed

lint \'lint\ *n* **1** : linen made into a soft fleecy substance for use in dressing wounds **2** : fine ravelings from cloth or yarn **3** : COTTON 1

lin·tel \'lint-l\ *n* : a horizontal piece or part across the top of an opening (as of a door) to

lintel

carry the weight of the structure above it

li·on \'lī-ən\ *n* : a large tawny flesh-eating animal of the cat family that has a tufted tail and in the male a shaggy mane and that inhabits Africa and southern Asia to western India

li·on·ess \'lī-ə-nəs\ *n* : a female lion

lip \'lip\ *n* **1** : either of the two fleshy folds that surround the mouth **2** : a fleshy edge or margin (as of a flower or a wound) **3** : the edge of a hollow vessel especially where it flares slightly — **lip·less** \-ləs\ *adj* — **lip·like** \-ˌlīk\ *adj* — **lipped** \'lipt\ *adj*

lip·stick \'lip-ˌstik\ *n* : a waxy solid colored cosmetic in stick form for the lips

liq·ue·fy \'lik-wə-ˌfī\ *vb* **liq·ue·fied**; **liq·ue·ry·ing** : to change a solid substance or a gas into a liquid form

¹liq·uid \'lik-wəd\ *adj* **1** : flowing freely like water **2** : neither solid nor gaseous **3** : being musical and free from harshness **4** : consisting of or capable of ready conversion into cash — **liq·uid·ly** *adv* — **liq·uid·ness** *n*

²liquid *n* : a liquid substance

liq·uor \'lik-ər\ *n* **1** : a liquid substance or solution ⟨*liquor* from boiled meat⟩ **2** : a distilled alcoholic drink (as brandy or gin)

li·ra \'lir-ə\ *n, pl* **li·re** \'lē-ˌrā\ : a coin of Italy

¹lisp \'lisp\ *vb* **1** : to pronounce the letters *s* and *z* by giving them the sounds of *th* **2** : to speak imperfectly

²lisp *n* : the act or habit of lisping

¹list \'list\ *n* : a record or catalog of names or items

²list *vb* : to enter or enroll in a list

³list *vb* : to lean to one side ⟨a *listing* ship⟩

⁴list *n* : a leaning over to one side

lis·ten \'lis-n\ *vb* **1** : to pay attention in order to hear **2** : to give heed — **lis·ten·er** *n*

list·less \'list-ləs\ *adj* : having no desire, interest, or wish to do things : INDIFFERENT — **list·less·ly** *adv* — **list·less·ness** *n*

lists \'lists\ *n pl* : a field for knights to fight on in a tournament

lit *past of* LIGHT

li·ter \'lēt-ər\ *n* : a metric unit of liquid capacity equal to 1.057 quarts

lit·er·al \'lit-ə-rəl\ *adj* **1** : following the ordinary or usual meaning of the words ⟨the *literal* meaning of a passage⟩ **2** : true to fact ⟨a *literal* account⟩ — **lit·er·al·ly** *adv* — **lit·er·al·ness** *n*

lit·er·ary \'lit-ə-ˌrer-ē\ *adj* : of or relating to literature

lit·er·ate \'lit-ə-rət\ *adj* **1** : EDUCATED, CULTURED **2** : able to read and write

lit·er·a·ture \'lit-ə-rə-ˌchur\ *n* **1** : the production of written works having excellence of form or expression and dealing with ideas of permanent or universal interest **2** : writings in prose or verse

lithe \'līth, 'līth\ *adj* : LIMBER, SUPPLE — **lithe·ly** *adv* — **lithe·ness** *n*

lith·o·sphere \'lith-ə-ˌsfiər\ *n* : the outer part of the solid earth

lit·mus paper \'lit-məs-\ *n* : paper treated with coloring matter that turns red in acid solutions and blue in alkaline solutions

¹lit·ter \'lit-ər\ *n* **1** : a covered and curtained couch provided with shafts and used for carrying a single passenger **2** : a stretcher for carrying sick or wounded persons **3** : the young born (as to a dog or sow) at a single time ⟨a *litter* of pigs⟩ **4** : material (as straw or hay) used as bedding for animals **5** : things scattered about in confusion

litter 1

²litter *vb* **1** : to cover with litter **2** : to put into a disordered condition ⟨a room *littered* with toys⟩ **3** : to bring forth a litter of young

¹lit·tle \'lit-l\ *adj* **lit·tler** \'lit-lər\ *or* **less** \'les\; **lit·tlest** \'lit-ləst\ *or* **least** \'lēst\ **1** : small in size or extent ⟨a *little* body⟩ **2** : short in duration ⟨spend *little* time⟩ **3** : small in quantity : not much ⟨*little* food to eat⟩ **4** : small in dignity or importance ⟨a *little* matter⟩ **5** : not liberal or generous : NARROW, MEAN — **lit·tle·ness** \'lit-l-nəs\ *n*

²little *adv* **less** \'les\; **least** \'lēst\ : in a very small quantity or degree : SLIGHTLY

³little *n* : something small (as in amount)

Little Dipper *n* : DIPPER 4

li·tur·gi·cal \lə-'tər-ji-kəl\ *adj* : of, relating to, or having the characteristics of liturgy

¹live \'liv\ *vb* **lived**; **liv·ing** **1** : to be alive **2** : to continue in life ⟨*live* to a great age⟩ **3** : SUBSIST **4** : DWELL **5** : to pass one's life

²live \'līv\ *adj* **1** : not dead : ALIVE **2** : BURNING, GLOWING ⟨*live* coals⟩ **3** : not burned or exploded ⟨a *live* cartridge⟩ **4** : ENERGETIC, ALERT **5** : of present and immediate interest **6** : charged with an electric current

live·li·hood \'līv-lē-ˌhùd\ *n* : the means of supporting life ⟨an honest *livelihood*⟩

live·long \ˌliv-ˌlòng\ *adj* : WHOLE, ENTIRE

live·ly \'līv-lē\ *adj* **1** : full of life : ACTIVE ⟨a *lively* puppy⟩ **2** : KEEN ⟨a *lively* interest⟩ **3** : ANIMATED ⟨*lively* music⟩ **4** : showing activity or vigor ⟨a *lively* manner⟩ **5** : rebounding quickly ⟨a *lively* ball⟩ — **live·li·ness** *n*

liv·en \'līv-ən\ *vb* : to make or become lively

live oak \'līv-ˌōk\ *n* : any of several American oaks with evergreen leaves

liv·er \'liv-ər\ *n* : a large gland of vertebrates (as fishes and man) that has a rich blood supply, secretes bile, and helps maintain the chemical balance of the blood

liv·er·ied \'liv-ə-rēd\ *adj* : wearing a livery

liv·er·y \'liv-ə-rē\ *n, pl* **liv·er·ies** **1** : a special uniform worn by the servants of a wealthy household ⟨a footman in *livery*⟩ **2** : the particular clothing worn to distinguish some association of persons ⟨the *livery* of a school⟩ **3** : the care and stabling of horses for pay **4** : the keeping of horses and vehicles for hire or a place (**livery stable**) engaged in this

lives *pl of* LIFE

live·stock \'līv-ˌstäk\ *n* : animals kept or raised especially on a farm and for profit

live wire *n* : an alert active aggressive person

liv·id \'liv-əd\ *adj* **1** : discolored like bruised flesh **2** : ashy pale ⟨*livid* with rage⟩ — **liv·id·ly** *adv* — **liv·id·ness** *n*

¹liv·ing \'liv-ing\ *adj* **1** : not dead : ALIVE ⟨*living* authors⟩ **2** : ACTIVE ⟨*living* faith⟩ **3** : true to life ⟨the *living* image of his father⟩

²living *n* **1** : the condition of being alive **2** : conduct or manner of life ⟨right *living*⟩ **3** : a means of subsistence

living room *n* : a room in a house intended for the general use of the dwellers

liz·ard \'liz-ərd\ *n* : a usually harmless, four-legged, and small or medium-sized reptile with a scaly skin, movable eyelids, and a long tapering tail

lizard

lla·ma \'lä-mə\ *n* : a South American cud-chewing hoofed animal

lo \'lō\ *interj* — used to call attention or to express wonder or surprise

¹load \'lōd\ *n* **1** : something taken up and carried : BURDEN **2** : a mass or weight supported by something **3** : something that weighs down the mind or spirits **4** : a charge for a firearm **5** : the quantity of material loaded into a device at one time **6** : a device or group of devices using electric power

²load *vb* **1** : to put a load in or on ⟨*load* a truck⟩ **2** : to weigh down with a burden ⟨a mind *loaded* with care⟩ **3** : to supply abundantly ⟨*load* a man with honors⟩ **4** : to place or insert a load into ⟨*load* film into a camera⟩ — **load·er** *n*

load·star *var of* LODESTAR

load·stone *var of* LODESTONE

¹loaf \'lōf\ *n, pl* **loaves** \'lōvz\ **1** : a shaped or molded mass of bread **2** : a regularly molded often rectangular mass **3** : ground or flaked meat or fish baked in the form of a loaf ⟨salmon *loaf*⟩ ⟨veal *loaf*⟩

²loaf *vb* : to spend time in idleness : LOUNGE, LOITER ⟨*loaf* on the beach⟩ — **loaf·er** *n*

loam \'lōm\ *n* : a usually mellow soil with suitable proportions of silt, clay, and sand for good plant growth

loam·y \'lō-mē\ *adj* : made up of or resembling loam

¹loan \'lōn\ *n* **1** : money lent at interest **2** : something furnished for the borrower's temporary use **3** : the granting of the temporary use of something

²loan *vb* : LEND

loath \'lōth, 'lōth\ *adj* : UNWILLING

loathe \'lōth\ *vb* **loathed; loath·ing** : to dislike greatly

loath·ing \'lō-thing\ *n* : extreme disgust

loath·some \'lōth-səm, 'lōth-\ *adj* : causing loathing : DISGUSTING ⟨a *loathsome* sight⟩ — **loath·some·ly** *adv* — **loath·some·ness** *n*

loaves *pl of* LOAF

¹lob \'läb\ *vb* **lobbed; lob·bing** : to propel (as a ball) by hitting or throwing easily in a high arc

²lob *n* : a lobbed throw or shot (as in tennis)

lob·by \'läb-ē\ *n, pl* **lob·bies** : a hall or passage especially when large enough to serve as a waiting room ⟨the *lobby* of a hotel⟩

lobe \'lōb\ *n* : a rounded projection or division ⟨a *lobe* of a leaf⟩

lob·ster \'läb-stər\ *n* : a large edible sea crustacean with five pairs of legs the first of which usually forms large claws

¹lo·cal \'lō-kəl\ *adj* **1** : of or relating to place or position in space **2** : having to do with some particular place : not general or widespread ⟨*local* news⟩ **3** : making all the stops on a run ⟨a *local* train⟩ — **lo·cal·ly** *adv*

lobster

²local *n* **1** : a local train or other public conveyance **2** : a local branch or lodge

lo·cal·i·ty \lō-'kal-ət-ē\ *n, pl* **lo·cal·i·ties** : a particular district : NEIGHBORHOOD

lo·cal·ize \'lō-kə-,līz\ *vb* **lo·cal·ized; lo·cal·iz·ing** : to make or become local

lo·cate \'lō-,kāt\ *vb* **lo·cat·ed; lo·cat·ing** **1** : to state and fix exactly the place or limits of ⟨*locate* a mining claim⟩ **2** : to settle or establish in a particular spot **3** : to search for and discover the position of

lo·ca·tion \lō-'kā-shən\ *n* **1** : the act or process of locating **2** : a situation or place especially for a building (as a residence)

¹lock \'läk\ *n* **1** : a tress or ringlet of hair **2** : a tuft of something (as hair or wool)

²lock *n* **1** : a fastening (as for a door) in which a bolt is operated (as by a key) **2** : the mechanism for exploding the charge or cartridge of a firearm **3** : an enclosure (as in a canal) with gates at each end used in raising or lowering boats as they pass from level to level

lock 1

³lock *vb* **1** : to fasten with or as if with a lock **2** : to shut in or out ⟨*lock* a person in⟩ **3** : to make fast by the linking of parts together

lock·er \'läk-ər\ *n* : a cabinet, compartment, or chest for personal use or for storing frozen food at a low temperature

lock·et \'läk-ət\ *n* : a small ornamental case for holding a picture or a lock of hair

lock·jaw \'läk-,jò\ *n* : TETANUS

lock·smith \'läk-,smith\ *n* : a workman who makes or mends locks

lo·co·mo·tion \,lō-kə-'mō-shən\ *n* : the act or power of moving from place to place

locket

¹lo·co·mo·tive \,lō-kə-'mōt-iv\ *n* **1** : an engine that moves under its own power **2** : an engine that hauls cars on a railroad

²locomotive *adj* : having to do with an engine that moves under its own power

lo·cust \'lō-kəst\ *n* **1** : a grasshopper especially when traveling in vast swarms and destroying vegetation in its course **2** : CICADA **3** : a hardwood tree of the legume group with feathery compound leaves and drooping flower clusters

lode·star \'lōd-,stär\ *n* : a guiding star

lode·stone \'lōd-,stōn\ *n* **1** : a rocklike substance having magnetic properties **2** : something that strongly attracts

¹lodge \'läj\ *vb* **lodged; lodg·ing** **1** : to provide temporary quarters for ⟨*lodge* guests for the night⟩ **2** : to settle in a place **3** : to come to rest ⟨the bullet *lodged* in a tree⟩ **4** : to deposit for safekeeping **5** : FILE

²lodge *n* **1** : a house set apart for residence in a special season or by an employee on an estate ⟨hunting *lodge*⟩ ⟨caretaker's *lodge*⟩ **2** : a den or lair of wild animals **3** : the meeting place of the branch of a fraternal organization or the members of such a branch

lodg·er \'läj-ər\ *n* : one that occupies a rented room in another's house

lodg·ing \'läj-ing\ *n* **1** : a temporary dwelling or sleeping place **2** *pl* : a room or rooms in the house of another person rented as a dwelling place

---

j job ng sing ō low ȯ moth ȯi coin th thin th this ü boot u̇ foot y you yü few yu̇ furious zh vision

loft \'lóft\ *n* **1** : an upper room or upper story of a building : ATTIC **2** : a gallery in a church **3** : an upper part of a barn

loft·y \'lóf-tē\ *adj* **loft·i·er; loft·i·est 1** : PROUD ⟨a *lofty* air⟩ **2** : of high rank or quality ⟨*lofty* lineage⟩ **3** : rising high : TOWERING — **loft·i·ly** \-tə-lē\ *adv* — **loft·i·ness** \-tē-nəs\ *n*

¹log \'lóg, 'läg\ *n* **1** : a bulky piece of un-shaped timber : a long piece of a tree trunk or of a large branch trimmed and ready for sawing **2** : an apparatus for measuring a ship's speed **3** : the daily record of a ship's speed and progress **4** : the record of a ship's voyage or of an aircraft's flight **5** : a record of performance (as of a piece of equipment)

²log *vb* **logged; log·ging 1** : to engage in cutting and transporting logs for timber **2** : to enter details of or about in a log

log·ger·head \'lóg-ər-,hed, 'läg-\ *n* : a very large sea turtle found in the warmer parts of the Atlantic ocean — **at loggerheads** : in a state of quarrelsome disagreement

log·ic \'läj-ik\ *n* **1** : a science that deals with the rules and tests of sound thinking and reasoning **2** : sound reasoning

log·i·cal \'läj-i-kəl\ *adj* **1** : having to do with logic **2** : according to the rules of logic ⟨a *logical* argument⟩ **3** : according to what is reasonably expected ⟨the *logical* result⟩ — **log·i·cal·ly** *adv* — **log·i·cal·ness** *n*

-l·o·gy \l-ə-jē\ *n suffix* : doctrine : theory : science

loin \'lóin\ *n* **1** : the part of the body between the hip and the lower ribs **2** : a portion (as of beef or pork) from the hipbone to the ribs

loi·ter \'lóit-ər\ *vb* **1** : LINGER **2** : to hang around idly **syn** see DELAY — **loi·ter·er** *n*

loll \'läl\ *vb* **1** : to hang loosely : DANGLE, DROOP **2** : to lie around in a lazy manner

lol·li·pop *or* **lol·ly·pop** \'läl-ē-,päp\ *n* : a lump of hard candy on the end of a stick

lone \'lōn\ *adj* **1** : SOLITARY ⟨a *lone* sentinel⟩ **2** : SOLE, ONLY **3** : ISOLATED

lone·ly \'lōn-lē\ *adj* **lone·li·er; lone·li·est 1** : being without company : LONE **2** : not often visited **3** : LONESOME — **lone·li·ness** *n*

lone·some \'lōn-səm\ *adj* **1** : sad from lack of companionship **2** : not often visited or traveled over : REMOTE **3** : LONE — **lone·some·ly** *adv* — **lone·some·ness** *n*

¹long \'lóng\ *adj* **long·er** \'lóng-gər\; **long·est** \'lóng-gəst\ **1** : of great extent from end to end : not short **2** : lasting for a considerable time : not brief ⟨a *long* program at assembly⟩ **3** : stretched out to a given measure, degree, or time ⟨a yard *long*⟩ ⟨an hour *long*⟩ **4** : forming the greatest measurement in contrast to width or weight **5** : of, relating to, or being *a, e, i, o, oo, u* pronounced as in *ale, eve, ice, old, food,* and *cube*

²long *adv* **1** : for or during a long time ⟨were you away *long*⟩ **2** : at a distant point of time

³long *n* : a long time

⁴long *vb* : to wish for something earnestly and with deep feeling : YEARN — **long·ing·ly** *adv*

long·hand \'lóng-,hand\ *n* : HANDWRITING

long·horn \'lóng-,hórn\ *n* : any of the long-horned cattle of Spanish origin formerly common in the south-western United States

longhorn

long–horned \'lóng-'hórnd\ *adj* : having long horns or antennae ⟨a *long-horned* grasshopper⟩

long·ing \'lóng-ing\ *n* : an eager desire : YEARNING

long·ish \'lóng-ish\ *adj* : somewhat long

lon·gi·tude \'län-jə-,tüd, -,tyüd\ *n* : distance measured by degrees east or west from a line drawn between the north and south poles and usually running through Greenwich, England ⟨the *longitude* of New York is 74 degrees west of Greenwich⟩

hemisphere marked with meridians of longitude

lon·gi·tu·di·nal \,län-jə-'tüd-n-əl, -'tyüd-\ *adj* : placed or running lengthwise — **lon·gi·tu·di·nal·ly** *adv*

long–lived \'lóng-'līvd, -'livd\ *adj* : living or lasting long

long–range \'lóng-'rānj\ *adj* **1** : capable of traveling or shooting great distances **2** : lasting over or providing for a long period

long·shore·man \'lóng-'shōr-mən\ *n, pl* **long·shore·men** \-mən\ : a dock worker who loads and unloads cargo

long·sight·ed \'lóng-'sīt-əd\ *adj* : FARSIGHTED — **long·sight·ed·ness** *n*

long–suf·fer·ing \'lóng-'səf-ə-ring\ *n* : long and patient endurance of offense

¹look \'lúk\ *vb* **1** : to exercise the power of vision : SEE **2** : EXPECT **3** : to have an appearance that befits ⟨*looks* the part⟩ **4** : SEEM ⟨*looks* thin⟩ **5** : to direct one's attention : HEED **6** : POINT, FACE **7** : to show a tendency — **look after** : to take care of — **look down on** : to treat with contempt — **look up** : to search for — **look up to** : RESPECT

²look *n* **1** : an act of looking : GLANCE ⟨take a *look* around⟩ **2** : the state or form in which something appears : ASPECT ⟨a healthy *look*⟩

looking glass *n* : MIRROR

look·out \'lúk-,aút\ *n* **1** : a careful watch for

some development or happening ⟨on the *lookout*⟩ **2** : an elevated place or structure affording a wide view for observation **3** : a person engaged in watching

¹loom \'lüm\ *n* : a frame or machine for weaving cloth

²loom *vb* : to come into sight in an unnaturally large or indistinct form

loon \'lün\ *n* : any of several fish-eating diving birds with webbed feet, black head, and white-spotted black back

¹loop \'lüp\ *n* **1** : a fold or doubling in a thread or rope through which another thread or rope can be passed or into which a hook can be caught **2** : a loop-shaped figure, bend, or course ⟨a *loop* in a river⟩

²loop *vb* : to make a loop or loops in

loop·hole \'lüp-,hōl\ *n* **1** : a small opening (as in the wall of a blockhouse) through which a gun may be fired **2** : a small opening that offers a means of escape

¹loose \'lüs\ *adj* **loos·er; loos·est 1** : not tightly set or fastened ⟨a *loose* board⟩ **2** : not tightly drawn : SLACK, LAX ⟨a *loose* belt⟩ **3** : FREE, UNATTACHED ⟨a boat breaking *loose* from its moorings⟩ **4** : not brought together in a package or binding ⟨*loose* coffee⟩ **5** : DISCONNECTED, RANDOM ⟨*loose* paragraphs⟩ **6** : lacking in restraint or power of restraint ⟨*loose* conduct⟩ **7** : having wide meshes ⟨a cloth of *loose* weave⟩ **8** : not exact, precise, or accurate — **loose·ly** *adv* — **loose·ness** *n*

²loose *vb* **loosed; loos·ing 1** : to make loose : UNTIE **2** : RELAX, SLACKEN **3** : to set free

³loose *adv* : LOOSELY

loose–joint·ed \'lüs-'jȯint-əd\ *adj* : moving with unusual freedom or ease

loos·en \'lüs-n\ *vb* **1** : to free from tightness or firmness **2** : to become loose

¹loot \'lüt\ *n* : PLUNDER

²loot *vb* : PLUNDER — **loot·er** *n*

¹lope \'lōp\ *n* : an easy fast bounding gait

²lope *vb* **loped; lop·ing** : to go or ride at a lope

lop·sid·ed \'läp-'sīd-əd\ *adj* : UNBALANCED — **lop·sid·ed·ly** *adv* — **lop·sid·ed·ness** *n*

lo·quat \'lō-,kwät\ *n* : the yellow plumlike fruit of an Asiatic evergreen tree

¹lord \'lȯrd\ *n* [from one of the oldest recorded English words (probably 8th century), the compound *hlāford* "master of a household", "Lord", from *hlāf* "loaf" and *weard* "keeper"] **1** : one having power and authority over others **2** *cap* : ²GOD **3** *cap* : JESUS **4** : a feudal tenant holding directly of the king **5** : a British nobleman or a bishop in the Church of England entitled to sit in the House of Lords — used as a title

²lord *vb* : to act like a lord toward others — used in the expression *lord it*

lord·ship \'lȯrd-,ship\ *n* : the rank or dignity of a lord — used as a title ⟨his *Lordship* is not at home⟩

lore \'lōr\ *n* : traditional knowledge or belief

lorn \'lȯrn\ *adj* : left alone : FORSAKEN

lose \'lüz\ *vb* **lost** \'lȯst\; **los·ing** \'lü-zing\ **1** : to be unable to find or have at hand : MISLAY ⟨*lost* her purse⟩ **2** : to be deprived of ⟨*lost* his sight⟩ ⟨*lose* money⟩ **3** : to fail to achieve success **4** : to fail to use to best advantage **5** : to go astray from

loss \'lȯs\ *n* **1** : RUIN, DESTRUCTION ⟨the *loss* of a ship⟩ **2** : failure to keep in one's possession ⟨the *loss* of property⟩ **3** : something that is lost **4** : failure to win

¹lost \'lȯst\ *past of* LOSE

²lost *adj* **1** : not used, won, or claimed **2** : unable to find the way **3** : ruined or destroyed physically or morally **4** : no longer possessed or known **5** : ABSORBED, RAPT

lot \'lät\ *n* **1** : an object used in deciding something by chance or the use of such an object to decide something ⟨draw *lots*⟩ ⟨choose by *lot*⟩ **2** : FATE ⟨it fell to his *lot* to do the hard work⟩ **3** : a piece or plot of land **4** : a considerable amount or number

loth \'lōth, 'lōth\ *var of* LOATH

lo·tion \'lō-shən\ *n* : a liquid preparation used for healing or as a cosmetic

lot·ter·y \'lät-ə-rē\ *n, pl* **lot·ter·ies** : a scheme for distributing prizes by lot

lo·tus \'lōt-əs\ *n* **1** : a fruit in Greek legend causing dreamy contentment and forgetfulness **2** : any of various water lilies **3** : any of several erect plants related to the clovers and sometimes grown for hay or pasture

lotus 2

¹loud \'laud\ *adj* **1** : not low, soft, or quiet in sound : NOISY ⟨a *loud* cry⟩ **2** : striking or quick to be noticed by reason of noise, force, or vigor of expression ⟨a *loud* complaint⟩ **3** : too bright, striking, or intense to please ⟨*loud* clothes⟩ — **loud·ly** *adv* — **loud·ness** *n*

²loud *adv* : LOUDLY

loud·speak·er \'laud-'spē-kər\ *n* : a device similar to a telephone receiver in operation but producing sounds loud enough to be easily heard at a distance

¹lounge \'launj\ *vb* **lounged; loung·ing 1** : to move or act in a lazy, slow, or listless way **2** : to stand, sit, or lie in a relaxed manner

²lounge *n* **1** : a comfortable sitting room **2** : SOFA, COUCH

louse \'laús\ *n, pl* **lice** \'līs\ **1** : a small wingless usually flat insect that lives on the bodies of warm-blooded animals **2** : any of several small insects (as a plant louse) or related jointed-bodied animals (as a wood louse)

lous·y \'laú-zē\ *adj* **lous·i·er; lous·i·est** : infested with lice

lov·a·ble \'lǝv-ǝ-bǝl\ *adj* : having a character that tends to make one loved — **lov·a·ble·ness** *n* — **lov·a·bly** \-blē\ *adv*

¹love \'lǝv\ *n* **1** : warm affection (as of a child for his mother) **2** : LIKING, FONDNESS

²love *vb* **loved; lov·ing 1** : to feel warm affection for **2** : to enjoy greatly — **lov·er** *n*

love·bird \'lǝv-,bǝrd\ *n* : any of several small usually gray or green parrots that show great affection for their mates

love·ly \'lǝv-lē\ *adj* **love·li·er; love·li·est** : delicately beautiful — **love·li·ness** *n*

lov·ing \'lǝv-ing\ *adj* : feeling or showing love : AFFECTIONATE — **lov·ing·ly** *adv*

¹low \'lō\ *vb* : to make the calling sound of a cow : MOO

²low *n* : the mooing of a cow : MOO

³low *adj* **1** : not high : not tall ⟨a *low* building⟩ **2** : lying below the usual level : going below the usual level ⟨*low* ground⟩ ⟨a *low* bow⟩ **3** : sounding below some other sound : not loud : DEEP ⟨a *low* whisper⟩ **4** : FEEBLE, WEAK ⟨left *low* by a fever⟩ **5** : GLOOMY ⟨in *low* spirits⟩ **6** : less than usual (as in quantity or value) ⟨*low* prices⟩ ⟨*low* pressure⟩ **7** : COARSE, VULGAR ⟨*low* talk⟩ **8** : not favorable : POOR ⟨a *low* opinion of someone⟩ — **low·ness** *n*

⁴low *n* **1** : something that is low **2** : a region in which the pressure of the atmosphere is low as shown by a barometer **3** : the arrangement of gears in an automobile giving the lowest speed of travel

⁵low *adv* : so as to be low ⟨fly *low*⟩ ⟨sing *low*⟩

¹low·er \'lō-ǝr\ *adj* **1** : being below the other of two similar persons or things ⟨the *lower* floor⟩ **2** : not so far advanced

²lower *vb* **1** : to let down : pull down ⟨*lower* a flag⟩ **2** : to make less (as in value or amount) ⟨*lower* the price of eggs⟩ **3** : to make lower the aim or direction of ⟨*lower* the lights on a car⟩ **4** : to reduce the height of

low·land \'lō-lǝnd\ *n* : low flat country

¹low·ly \'lō-lē\ *adv* : HUMBLY, MEEKLY

²lowly *adj* **low·li·er; low·li·est** : of low rank : MODEST, HUMBLE — **low·li·ness** *n*

loy·al \'lói-ǝl\ *adj* **1** : faithful to one's country **2** : faithful to a friend or group — **loy·al·ly** *adv*

loy·al·ty \'lói-ǝl-tē\ *n, pl* **loy·al·ties** : the quality or state of being loyal : FAITHFULNESS

syn LOYALTY, ALLEGIANCE mean faithfulness to whatever one is bound to by duty or by a pledge or promise. LOYALTY implies a personal or emotional attachment and often a resisting of temptation to desert or betray ⟨she showed a fierce *loyalty* to her brother and would not listen to any criticism of him⟩ ALLEGIANCE stresses obligation or duty owed to something other than a person ⟨pledge *allegiance* to the flag⟩

loz·enge \'läz-nj\ *n* **1** : a diamond-shaped figure **2** : a small often medicated candy

lu·bri·cant \'lü-bri-kǝnt\ *n* : something (as oil or grease) that lubricates

lu·bri·cate \'lü-brǝ-,kāt\ *vb* **lu·bri·cat·ed; lu·bri·cat·ing 1** : to make smooth or slippery **2** : to apply oil or grease to ⟨*lubricate* a car⟩

lozenge

lu·bri·ca·tion \,lü-brǝ-'kā-shǝn\ *n* : the act or process of lubricating or being lubricated

lu·cid \'lü-sǝd\ *adj* **1** : CLEAR ⟨*lucid* water⟩ **2** : showing a sane and normal state of mind **3** : easily understood — **lu·cid·ly** *adv* — **lu·cid·ness** *n*

luck \'lǝk\ *n* **1** : something that happens to a person apparently by chance **2** : the accidental way events occur **3** : good fortune

luck·y \'lǝk-ē\ *adj* **luck·i·er; luck·i·est 1** : favored by luck : FORTUNATE ⟨a *lucky* person⟩ **2** : producing a good result apparently by chance ⟨a *lucky* hit⟩ **3** : thought of as bringing luck — **luck·i·ly** \'lǝk-ǝ-lē\ *adv*

lu·di·crous \'lü-dǝ-krǝs\ *adj* : comically ridiculous syn see LAUGHABLE — **lu·di·crous·ly** *adv* — **lu·di·crous·ness** *n*

lug \'lǝg\ *vb* **lugged; lug·ging** : to carry or haul with difficulty

lug·gage \'lǝg-ij\ *n* : BAGGAGE

luke·warm \'lük-'wòrm\ *adj* **1** : neither hot nor cold **2** : not enthusiastic

¹lull \'lǝl\ *vb* : to make or become quiet

²lull *n* : a period of calm (as in a storm)

lul·la·by \'lǝl-ǝ-,bī\ *n, pl* **lul·la·bies** : a song for lulling babies to sleep

¹lum·ber \'lǝm-bǝr\ *n* **1** : surplus or disused articles (as furniture) that are stored away **2** : timber especially when sawed into boards

²lumber *vb* : to cut logs : saw logs into lumber

³lumber *vb* : to move clumsily

lum·ber·jack \'lǝm-bǝr-,jak\ *n* : a man who works at lumbering

lum·ber·man \'lǝm-bǝr-mǝn\ *n, pl* **lum·ber·men** \-mǝn\ : LUMBERJACK

lum·ber·yard \'lǝm-bǝr-,yärd\ *n* : a place where a stock of lumber is kept for sale

lu·mi·nous \'lü-mə-nəs\ *adj* **1** : SHINING, BRIGHT **2** : easily understood : CLEAR — **lu·mi·nous·ly** *adv*

¹lump \'ləmp\ *n* **1** : a small irregular mass : CHUNK ⟨a *lump* of coal⟩ **2** : SWELLING

²lump *vb* **1** : to form into a lump **2** : to group together

lu·nar \'lü-nər\ *adj* **1** : of or relating to the moon **2** : measured by the revolutions of the moon ⟨a *lunar* month⟩

¹lu·na·tic \'lü-nə-,tik\ *adj* **1** : INSANE, CRAZY **2** : set apart for or used by insane persons ⟨a *lunatic* asylum⟩

²lunatic *n* : an insane person

¹lunch \'lənch\ *n* **1** : a light meal **2** : the regular midday meal **3** : food prepared for lunch ⟨a picnic *lunch*⟩

²lunch *vb* : to eat lunch

lun·cheon \'lən-chən\ *n* **1** : LUNCH **2** : a formal lunch

lung \'ləng\ *n* : one of the two baglike organs in the chest that form the special breathing apparatus of air-breathing animals

¹lunge \'lənj\ *vb* **lunged; lung·ing** : to make or cause to make a lunge — **lung·er** *n*

²lunge *n* **1** : a sudden thrust (as with a sword) **2** : a sudden plunging forward

lung·fish \'ləng-,fish\ *n* : any of several fishes that breathe with lunglike sacs as well as with gills

lu·pine \'lü-pən\ *n* : a plant related to the clovers that has tall spikes of showy pea-like flowers

¹lurch \'lərch\ *n* **1** : a sudden roll of a ship to one side **2** : a swaying staggering movement or gait

²lurch *vb* : to move with a lurch

¹lure \'lür\ *n* **1** : something that tempts, entices, or draws one on : ATTRACTION, APPEAL **2** : an artificial bait for catching fish

²lure *vb* **lured; lur·ing** : to tempt or lead away by offering some pleasure or advantage : ENTICE ⟨*lured* by gold⟩

lures 2

lu·rid \'lür-əd\ *adj* **1** : ghastly pale **2** : appearing like glowing fire seen through smoke ⟨*lurid* flames⟩ **3** : SENSATIONAL ⟨a *lurid* story⟩ — **lu·rid·ly** *adv* — **lu·rid·ness** *n*

lurk \'lərk\ *vb* **1** : to stay in or about a place secretly **2** : to move secretly : SNEAK

syn LURK, SKULK, SNEAK all mean to act so as to escape the notice of others. LURK implies waiting in concealment often in order to attack by surprise ⟨submarines *lurking* near the harbor⟩ SKULK has a stronger suggestion of moving about unseen through fear or shame or cowardice ⟨fugitives *skulking* in cellars and woods⟩ SNEAK implies entering or leaving a place unseen and especially unheard ⟨*sneaking* out of the house after his parents were asleep⟩

lus·cious \'ləsh-əs\ *adj* **1** : very sweet and pleasing to taste and smell **2** : delightful to hear, see, or feel — **lus·cious·ly** *adv* — **lus·cious·ness** *n*

lush \'ləsh\ *adj* **1** : very juicy and fresh ⟨*lush* grass⟩ **2** : covered with luxuriant growth ⟨*lush* pastures⟩ — **lush·ly** *adv* — **lush·ness** *n*

lus·ter *or* **lus·tre** \'ləs-tər\ *n* **1** : a shine or sheen by reflected light : GLOSS ⟨the *luster* of silk⟩ **2** : BRIGHTNESS, GLITTER **3** : SPLENDOR

lus·trous \'ləs-trəs\ *adj* : having luster

lute \'lüt\ *n* : an old stringed instrument like the mandolin but played by plucking the strings with the fingers

lute

lux·u·ri·ant \,ləg-'zhùr-ē-ənt, ,lək-'shùr-\ *adj* : growing plentifully and freely ⟨a *luxuriant* growth of plants⟩ — **lux·u·ri·ant·ly** *adv*

lux·u·ri·ous \,ləg-'zhùr-ē-əs, ,lək-'shùr-\ *adj* **1** : inclined to luxury **2** : extravagantly elegant and comfortable — **lux·u·ri·ous·ly** *adv* — **lux·u·ri·ous·ness** *n*

lux·u·ry \'lək-shə-rē, 'ləg-zhə-\ *n, pl* **lux·u·ries** **1** : use or possession of costly food, dress, or something that pleases a person's appetite or desire : rich surroundings ⟨live in *luxury*⟩ **2** : something desirable but costly or hard to get **3** : something that adds but is not necessary to one's pleasure or comfort

¹-ly \lē\ *adj suffix* **1** : like in appearance, manner, or nature ⟨queen*ly*⟩ ⟨father*ly*⟩ **2** : characterized by regular recurrence in specified units of time : every ⟨hour*ly*⟩

²-ly *adv suffix* **1** : in a specified manner ⟨slow*ly*⟩ **2** : from a specified point of view ⟨grammatical*ly*⟩

lye \'lī\ *n* : a sodium-containing crystalline substance that dissolves in water to form a strong solution and is used in cleaning and the making of soap

lying *pres part of* LIE

lymph \'limf\ *n* : a nearly colorless fluid resembling the plasma of blood that contains colorless cells and circulates in vessels that finally discharge it into the blood

lym·phat·ic \lim-'fat-ik\ *adj* : of or relating to lymph ⟨*lymphatic* duct⟩

lynx \'lingks\ *n, pl* **lynx** *or* **lynx·es** : any of several wildcats with rather long legs, a short tail, and often tufted ears

lyre \'līr\ *n* : a stringed musical instrument used by the ancient Greeks

lyre·bird \'līr-,bərd\ *n* : an Australian bird the male of which has long tail feathers that can be spread out in the form of a lyre

lyre

¹lyr·ic \'lir-ik\ *adj* **1** : suitable for singing : MUSICAL **2** : expressing personal emotion

²lyric *n* : a lyric poem

lyr·i·cal \'lir-i-kəl\ *adj* : LYRIC

m \'em\ *n, often cap* **1** : the thirteenth letter of the English alphabet **2** : the roman numeral 1000

ma \'mä, 'mȯ\ *n* : MOTHER

ma'am \'mam\ *n* : MADAM

mac·ad·am \mə-'kad-əm\ *n* : a road surface of small closely packed broken stone

ma·caque \mə-'kak, -'käk\ *n* : any of several mostly Asiatic short-tailed monkeys

mac·a·ro·ni \,mak-ə-'rō-nē\ *n, pl* **mac·a·ro·nis** *or* **mac·a·ro·nies** : a food made of flour paste dried in the form of tubes

mac·a·roon \,mak-ə-'rün\ *n* : a small cake made of the white of eggs, sugar, and ground almonds or coconut

ma·caw \mə-'kȯ\ *n* : a large parrot of Central and South America with a long tail, a harsh voice, and brilliant plumage

¹mace \'mās\ *n* : a staff carried before certain officials as a sign of authority

²mace *n* : a spice consisting of the dried outer covering of the nutmeg

ma·chet·e \mə-'shet-ē\ *n* : a large heavy knife used for cutting sugarcane and underbrush and as a weapon

machete

mach·i·na·tion \,mak-ə-'nā-shən, ,mash-\ *n* : a scheme to do harm : PLOT

¹ma·chine \mə-'shēn\ *n* **1** : VEHICLE **2** : AUTOMOBILE **3** : a combination of parts that transmits forces, motion, and energy in a way that does some desired work 〈a sewing *machine*〉 **4** : an organized group of persons that under the leadership of a boss or a small clique controls the policies and activities of a political party

²machine *adj* **1** : characterized by the widespread use of machinery 〈the *machine* age〉 **2** : produced by or as if by machinery 〈*machine* products〉

³machine *vb* **ma·chined; ma·chin·ing** : to shape or finish by machine-operated tools

machine gun *n* : an automatic gun for continuous firing

ma·chin·er·y \mə-'shē-nə-rē\ *n* **1** : MACHINES 〈the *machinery* in a factory〉 **2** : the working parts of a machine **3** : the organization or system by which something is done 〈the *machinery* of government〉

machine shop *n* : a workshop in which metal articles are machined and assembled

ma·chin·ist \mə-'shē-nəst\ *n* : one who makes or works on machines and engines

mack·er·el \'mak-ə-rəl\ *n, pl* **mackerel** *or* **mack·er·els** : a North Atlantic food fish that is green with blue bars above and silvery below

mackerel

mack·i·naw \'mak-ə-,nȯ\ *n* : a short heavy woolen plaid coat

ma·cron \'mā-,krän\ *n* : a mark ‾ placed over a vowel to show that the vowel is long

mad \'mad\ *adj* **mad·der; mad·dest** **1** : disordered in mind : CRAZY, INSANE **2** : being rash and foolish 〈a *mad* promise〉 **3** : FURIOUS, ENRAGED 〈make the bull *mad*〉 **4** : carried away by enthusiasm 〈*mad* about dancing〉 **5** : wildly gay 〈in a *mad* mood〉 **6** : having hydrophobia 〈a *mad* dog〉 — **mad·ly** *adv* — **mad·ness** *n*

mackinaw

mad·am \'mad-əm\ *n, pl* **mes·dames** \mā-'däm\ — used as a form of polite address to a lady 〈*Madam*, may I help you〉

ma·dame \mə-'dam, 'mad-əm\ *n, pl* **mes·dames** \mā-'däm\ — used as a title equivalent to *Mrs.* for a married woman not of English-speaking nationality

¹mad·cap \'mad-,kap\ *adj* : WILD, RECKLESS

²madcap *n* : a madcap person

mad·den \'mad-n\ *vb* : to make mad

made *past of* MAKE

ma·de·moi·selle \,mad-ə-mə-'zel\ *n, pl* **ma·de·moi·selles** \-'zelz\ *or* **mes·de·moi·selles** \,mād-ə-mə-'zel\ — used as a title equivalent to *Miss* for an unmarried woman not of English-speaking and especially of French nationality

made–up \'mād-'əp\ *adj* : fancifully conceived or falsely devised 〈a *made-up* story〉

mad·house \'mad-,haûs\ *n* **1** : an asylum for insane persons **2** : a place or scene of confusion

mag·a·zine \'mag-ə-ˌzēn\ *n* [from early French *magazin*, taken from Arabic *makhzan* "storehouse"] **1** : a storehouse or warehouse for military supplies **2** : a place for keeping explosives in a fort or ship **3** : a container in a gun for holding cartridges **4** : a publication issued at regular intervals

mag·got \'mag-ət\ *n* : a soft-bodied legless grub that is the larva of a two-winged fly

¹mag·ic \'maj-ik\ *n* **1** : the use of charms and spells believed to have supernatural power over natural forces **2** : a seemingly mysterious power ⟨the *magic* of a great name⟩ **3** : something that charms ⟨the *magic* of her voice⟩ **4** : SLEIGHT OF HAND

²magic *adj* **1** : of or relating to magic **2** : having effects that seem to be caused by magic **3** : ENCHANTING

mag·i·cal \'maj-i-kəl\ *adj* : MAGIC

ma·gi·cian \mə-'jish-ən\ *n* **1** : a person skilled in magic **2** : a sleight-of-hand performer

magic lantern *n* : an early type of slide projector

mag·is·trate \'maj-əs-ˌtrāt\ *n* **1** : a person holding executive power in government **2** : a local official holding judicial power

magic lantern

mag·ma \'mag-mə\ *n* : molten rock within the earth

mag·na·nim·i·ty \ˌmag-nə-'nim-ət-ē\ *n* : the quality of being magnanimous

mag·nan·i·mous \mag-'nan-ə-məs\ *adj* [from Latin *magnanimus*, a compound of *magnus* "great" and *animus* "spirit"] **1** : having a lofty and courageous spirit **2** : GENEROUS — **mag·nan·i·mous·ly** *adv*

mag·ne·si·um \mag-'nē-zē-əm\ *n* : a silver-white metallic chemical element that is lighter than aluminum and is used in lightweight alloys

mag·net \'mag-nət\ *n* [from Latin *magnet-*, stem of *magnes* "lodestone", taken from the Greek phrase *Magnēs lithos*, literally, stone of Magnesia, an ancient city in Asia Minor] **1** : a piece of iron-containing material that has the natural ability to attract iron **2** : a piece of iron, steel, or alloy having the ability to attract iron artificially given to it

magnet 2

mag·net·ic \mag-'net-ik\ *adj* **1** : of or relating to a magnet or magnetism **2** : having the properties of a magnet **3** : of or relating to the earth's magnetism **4** : gifted with great personal attractiveness

magnetic field *n* : the portion of space near a magnetic body or a body carrying an electric current within which forces due to the body or current can be detected

magnetic needle *n* : a narrow strip of magnetized steel that is free to swing horizontally or vertically to show the direction of the earth's magnetism

magnetic pole *n* **1** : either of the poles of a magnet **2** : either of two small regions which are located respectively in the polar areas of the northern and southern hemispheres and toward which the compass needle points from any direction throughout adjacent regions

mag·ne·tism \'mag-nə-ˌtiz-əm\ *n* **1** : the power to attract as possessed by a magnet **2** : the science that deals with magnetic occurrences or conditions **3** : the power to attract the interest or affection of others : personal charm

mag·ne·tize \'mag-nə-ˌtīz\ *vb* **mag·ne·tized**; **mag·ne·tiz·ing** : to cause to be magnetic

mag·ne·to \mag-'nēt-ō\ *n, pl* **mag·ne·tos** : a small dynamo used especially to produce the spark in some gasoline engines

mag·nif·i·cent \mag-'nif-ə-sənt\ *adj* : having grandeur and beauty : SPLENDID ⟨*magnificent* palaces⟩ — **mag·nif·i·cent·ly** *adv*

mag·ni·fy \'mag-nə-ˌfī\ *vb* **mag·ni·fied**; **mag·ni·fy·ing** **1** : to enlarge in fact or appearance ⟨a microscope *magnifies* an object seen through it⟩ **2** : to increase the importance of : EXAGGERATE ⟨*magnify* a fault⟩

magnifying glass *n* : a lens that magnifies an object seen through it

mag·ni·tude \'mag-nə-ˌtüd, -ˌtyüd\ *n* **1** : greatness in size : BIGNESS **2** : greatness in influence or effect ⟨the *magnitude* of the scheme⟩ **3** : QUANTITY, NUMBER

mag·no·lia \mag-'nōl-yə\ *n* : one of several trees or tall shrubs having showy white, pink, yellow, or purple flowers that appear before or sometimes with the leaves and having a cone-shaped fruit

magnolia

mag·pie \'mag-ˌpī\ *n* : a noisy black-and-white bird related to the jays

ma·hog·a·ny \mə-'häg-ə-nē\ *n* : a durable lustrous reddish brown wood that is used especially for furniture and is obtained from several tropical trees

maid \'mād\ *n* **1** : an unmarried girl or woman : MAIDEN **2** : a female servant

¹maid·en \'mād-n\ *adj* **1** : UNMARRIED ⟨a *maiden* aunt⟩ **2** : of or suitable to a maiden **3** : FIRST ⟨a *maiden* voyage⟩

²**maiden** *n* : an unmarried girl or woman

maid·en·hair \'mād-n-ˌhaər\ *n* : a fern with slender stems and delicate, much divided, and often feathery leaves

maid·en·hood \'mād-n-ˌhùd\ *n* : the condition or time of being a maiden

maiden name *n* : the surname of a woman before she is married

maidenhair

maid of honor   **1** : an unmarried lady who attends a queen or princess   **2** : an unmarried woman serving as the principal female attendant of a bride at her wedding

¹**mail** \'māl\ *n*   **1** : letters, parcels, and papers sent under public authority from one person to another through the agency of the post office   **2** : the whole system used in the public sending and delivery of mail ⟨do business by *mail*⟩   **3** : that which comes in the mail

²**mail** *vb* : to send by mail : put in a box to be collected and sent by mail

³**mail** *n* : a fabric of interlocked metal rings used as armor

mail·box \'māl-ˌbäks\ *n* **1** : a public box in which to place outgoing mail   **2** : a private box for the delivery of incoming mail

mail

mail·man \'māl-ˌman\ *n, pl* **mail·men** \-ˌmen\ : one who delivers mail or collects it from public mailboxes

maim \'mām\ *vb* : to deprive of the use of a part of the body (as a leg, arm, or toe) : wound seriously : CRIPPLE

¹**main** \'mān\ *n*   **1** : physical strength : FORCE ⟨with might and *main*⟩   **2** : HIGH SEAS   **3** : a principal line, tube, or pipe of a utility system ⟨water *main*⟩ ⟨gas *main*⟩ — **in the main** : for the most part

²**main** *adj*   **1** : first in size, rank, or importance : CHIEF ⟨*main* part⟩ ⟨*main* street⟩   **2** : SHEER, UTTER ⟨by *main* force⟩ — **main·ly** *adv*

main·land \'mān-ˌland\ *n* : a continent or the main part of a continent as distinguished from an offshore island or sometimes from a cape or peninsula

main·mast \'mān-ˌmast,-məst\ *n* : the principal mast of a sailing ship

main·sail \'mān-ˌsāl, -səl\ *n* : the principal sail on the mainmast

mainsail

main·sheet \'mān-ˌshēt\ *n* : a rope by which the mainsail is trimmed and secured

main·spring \'mān-ˌspring\ *n*   **1** : the principal spring in a mechanism (as a watch or clock)   **2** : the chief motive or cause

main·stay \'mān-ˌstā\ *n*   **1** : the large strong rope from the maintop of a ship usually to the foot of the foremast   **2** : a chief support ⟨the *mainstay* of the family⟩

main·tain \mān-'tān\ *vb* [from Old French *maintenir*, taken from medieval Latin *manutenēre*, which was formed from the Latin phrase *manu tenēre* "to hold in the hand"] **1** : to keep in a particular state or condition ⟨*maintain* a room as it was years ago⟩   **2** : to defend by argument ⟨*maintain* a position⟩   **3** : to carry on : CONTINUE ⟨*maintain* a correspondence⟩   **4** : to provide for : SUPPORT ⟨*maintained* his family by working⟩

main·te·nance \'mānt-n-əns\ *n*   **1** : the act of maintaining or being maintained ⟨*maintenance* of law and order⟩   **2** : supply of necessities and conveniences ⟨allowance for the family's *maintenance*⟩   **3** : UPKEEP ⟨workmen in charge of *maintenance*⟩

main·top \'mān-ˌtäp\ *n* : a platform around the head of a mainmast

maize \'māz\ *n* : INDIAN CORN

ma·jes·tic \mə-'jes-tik\ *adj* : being stately and dignified : NOBLE — **ma·jes·ti·cal·ly** \-ti-kə-lē\ *adv*

maj·es·ty \'maj-əs-tē\ *n, pl* **maj·es·ties** **1** : royal dignity or authority   **2** : STATELINESS   **3** : the person of a sovereign — used as a title for a king, queen, emperor, or empress ⟨may it please your *Majesty*⟩

¹**ma·jor** \'mā-jər\ *adj* : greater in number, quantity, rank, or importance ⟨the *major* part of the cost⟩ ⟨the *major* leagues⟩

²**major** *n* : a commissioned officer (as in the army) ranking next below a lieutenant colonel

major general *n* : a commissioned officer (as in the army) ranking next below a lieutenant general

ma·jor·i·ty \mə-'jòr-ət-ē\ *n, pl* **ma·jor·i·ties** **1** : the age at which one is given full civil rights   **2** : a number greater than half of a total   **3** : the amount by which a majority exceeds a minority ⟨winning by fifty-one to forty-nine, a *majority* of two⟩   **4** : a group or party that makes up the greater part of a whole body of persons ⟨the *majority* chose a leader⟩

¹**make** \'māk\ *vb* **made** \'mād\; **mak·ing** **1** : to cause to exist or occur ⟨*make* trouble⟩ **2** : to form or put together out of material or parts ⟨*make* a dress⟩ ⟨*make* a chair⟩ **3** : to be combined to produce ⟨two and two *make* four⟩ **4** : to set in order : PREPARE ⟨*make* a bed⟩ **5** : to cause to be or become ⟨*made* him

president⟩ **6** : to carry on : DO, PERFORM ⟨*make* a bow⟩ ⟨*make* war⟩ **7** : to produce by action ⟨*make* a mess of a job⟩ **8** : COMPEL ⟨*make* him go to bed⟩ **9** : GAIN, GET ⟨*make* money⟩ ⟨*make* friends⟩ **10** : to act so as to be ⟨*make* merry⟩ ⟨*make* ready⟩ ⟨*make* sure⟩ **11** : to complete (an electric circuit) — **mak·er** *n* — **make believe** : PRETEND — **make good** **1** : FULFILL, COMPLETE ⟨*made good* his promise⟩ ⟨*made good* his escape⟩ **2** : SUCCEED ⟨*made good* in the job⟩ — **make out** **1** : to draw up in writing ⟨*make out* a list⟩ **2** : UNDERSTAND ⟨I can't *make* it *out*⟩ **3** : SUCCEED ⟨I hope you *make out* well⟩ — **make up** **1** : CONSTRUCT, COMPOSE ⟨*make up* a poem⟩ **2** : to combine to produce a whole ⟨nine players *make up* a team⟩ **3** : to act as compensation ⟨this will *make up* for your loss⟩ **4** : to become reconciled ⟨they quarreled and then *made up*⟩ **5** : to put on makeup

²make *n* **1** : the way in which a thing is made : STRUCTURE **2** : KIND, BRAND ⟨a good *make* of car⟩

¹make–be·lieve \'māk-bə-ˌlēv\ *n* : a pretending to believe (as in children's play)

²make–believe *adj* : PRETENDED, IMAGINARY

¹make·shift \'māk-ˌshift\ *n* : a thing temporarily substituted for another

²makeshift *adj* : serving as a temporary substitute ⟨used a folded coat as a *makeshift* pillow⟩

make·up \'māk-ˌəp\ *n* **1** : the way the parts or elements of something are put together or joined : COMPOSITION **2** : materials used in changing one's appearance for a part on the stage **3** : COSMETICS

mal- *prefix* **1** : bad : badly ⟨*mal*practice⟩ ⟨*mal*odorous⟩ **2** : abnormal : abnormally ⟨*mal*formation⟩ ⟨*mal*formed⟩

mal·ad·just·ed \ˌmal-ə-'jəs-təd\ *adj* : not properly adjusted ⟨a *maladjusted* student⟩

mal·a·dy \'mal-ə-dē\ *n, pl* **mal·a·dies** : a disease or disorder of either body or mind

ma·lar·i·a \mə-'ler-ē-ə\ *n* [this originally meant, in English, "air infected with some substance capable of causing disease", and was taken from Italian *malaria*, formed from the phrase *mala aria* "bad air"] : a disease marked by chills and fever and transmitted through the bite of one kind of mosquito

¹male \'māl\ *adj* **1** : of, relating to, or being the sex that fathers young **2** : bearing stamens but no pistil ⟨a *male* flower⟩ **3** : of, relating to, or suitable for males ⟨a *male* voice⟩ — **male·ness** *n*

²male *n* : one that is male

mal·for·ma·tion \ˌmal-fȯr-'mā-shən\ *n* : a faulty or quite irregular formation or structure

mal·ice \'mal-əs\ *n* : ILL WILL

ma·li·cious \mə-'lish-əs\ *adj* **1** : feeling strong ill will : MEAN, SPITEFUL ⟨a *malicious* old witch⟩ **2** : carried on with or caused by malice ⟨*malicious* gossip⟩ — **ma·li·cious·ly** *adv*

¹ma·lign \mə-'līn\ *adj* : operating to injure or hurt ⟨hindered by *malign* influences⟩

²malign *vb* : to speak evil of : SLANDER

ma·lig·nant \mə-'lig-nənt\ *adj* **1** : evil in effect : INJURIOUS **2** : MALICIOUS **3** : likely to cause death : DEADLY — **ma·lig·nant·ly** *adv*

mal·lard \'mal-ərd\ *n* : a common wild duck of the northern hemisphere that is the ancestor of the domesticated ducks

mal·le·a·ble \'mal-ē-ə-bəl\ *adj* : capable of being beaten out, extended, or shaped by hammer blows

mal·let \'mal-ət\ *n* **1** : a short-handled hammer with a barrel-shaped head of wood or soft material used for driving a tool (as a chisel) or for striking a surface without denting it mallet 1 **2** : a club with a long handle and a cylindrical head ⟨croquet *mallet*⟩

mal·low \'mal-ō\ *n* : a tall plant related to the hollyhock that has usually lobed leaves and white, rose, or purplish five-petaled flowers followed by disk-shaped fruit mallow

mal·nu·tri·tion \ˌmal-nu̇-'trish-ən, -nyu̇-\ *n* : faulty nourishment

malt \'mȯlt\ *n* **1** : grain and especially barley steeped in water until it has sprouted **2** : MALTED MILK

malt·ed milk \ˌmȯl-təd-\ *n* **1** : a powder prepared from dried milk and cereals **2** : a beverage made by dissolving malted milk in a liquid (as milk)

mal·treat \mal-'trēt\ *vb* : to treat unkindly or roughly : ABUSE

mam·ma *or* **ma·ma** \'mä-mə\ *n* : MOTHER

mam·mal \'mam-əl\ *n* : a warm-blooded animal that has a backbone, two pairs of limbs, and a more or less complete covering of hair and nourishes its young with milk

¹mam·moth \'mam-əth\ *n* : a very large hairy extinct elephant with tusks that curve upward

²mammoth *adj* : very large : HUGE ⟨a *mammoth* stadium⟩ mammoth

mam·my \'mam-ē\ *n, pl* **mam·mies** **1** : MAMMA **2** : a Negro woman serving as a nurse to white children

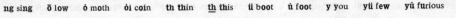
j job **ng** sing **ō** low **ȯ** moth **ȯi** coin **th** thin <u>**th**</u> this **ü** boot **u̇** foot **y** you **yü** few **yu̇** furious **zh** vision

especially formerly in the southern states of the United States

¹man \'man\ *n, pl* **men** \'men\ **1** : a human being : PERSON **2** : an adult male human being **3** : the human race : MANKIND **4** : a member of the natural family to which human beings belong including both modern man and extinct related forms **5** : HUSBAND ⟨*man* and wife⟩ **6** : an adult male servant or employee **7** : one of the pieces with which various games (as chess or checkers) are played

²man *vb* **manned; man·ning** : to supply with men for management or operation ⟨*man* the lifeboats⟩

man·age \'man-ij\ *vb* **man·aged; man·ag·ing 1** : to oversee and make decisions about : CONTROL, DIRECT ⟨*manage* a factory⟩ **2** : to achieve one's purpose : CONTRIVE ⟨I'll *manage* somehow⟩ ⟨he always *manages* to win⟩ **syn** see CONDUCT

man·age·ment \'man-ij-mənt\ *n* **1** : DIRECTION, CONTROL **2** : those who manage ⟨*management* and labor could not agree⟩

man·ag·er \'man-ij-ər\ *n* : a person who manages : DIRECTOR — **man·ag·er·ship** \-,ship\ *n*

man·da·rin \'man-də-rən\ *n* : one of the higher public officials under the Chinese Empire

man·date \'man-,dāt\ *n* **1** : an order entitled to be obeyed : COMMAND **2** : the instruction given by voters to their elected representatives

man·di·ble \'man-də-bəl\ *n* **1** : a lower jaw often with its soft parts **2** : either the upper or lower segment of the bill of a bird **3** : either of the first pair of mouth appendages of some invertebrates (as an insect or crustacean) that often form biting organs

man·do·lin \,man-də-'lin, 'man-dl-ən\ *n* : a musical instrument that has from four to six pairs of strings and is played by plucking with a pick

mane \'mān\ *n* : a mantle of long heavy hair growing from the neck or shoulders of an animal (as a horse or lion) — **maned** \'mānd\ *adj*

mandolin

¹ma·neu·ver \mə-'nü-vər, -'nyü-\ *n* [from Old French *maneuvre* "work done by hand", taken from medieval Latin *manuopera*, a word derived from the Latin phrase *manu operare* "to work by hand"] **1** : a planned movement of troops or ships **2** : a training exercise by armed forces **3** : skillful action or management ⟨avoided a collision by a quick *maneuver*⟩

²maneuver *vb* **1** : to move in a maneuver **2** : to perform a maneuver **3** : to guide skillfully — **ma·neu·ver·a·bil·i·ty** \-,nü-və-rə-'bil-ət-ē, -,nyü-\ *n* — **ma·neu·ver·a·ble** \-'nü-və-rə-bəl, -'nyü-\ *adj*

man·ga·nese \'mang-gə-,nēz\ *n* : a grayish white brittle metallic chemical element that resembles iron

mange \'mānj\ *n* : a contagious skin disease usually of domestic animals marked by itching and loss of hair

man·ger \'mān-jər\ *n* : an open box in which food for farm animals is placed

¹man·gle \'mang-gəl\ *vb* **man·gled; man·gling 1** : to cut, bruise, or hack with repeated blows **2** : to spoil in making or performing ⟨*mangle* a speech⟩

²mangle *n* : a machine for ironing clothes by the pressure of heated rollers

man·go \'mang-gō\ *n, pl* **man·goes** *or* **man·gos** : a juicy somewhat acid yellow or reddish tropical fruit borne by an evergreen tree related to the sumac

mangoes

mang·y \'mān-jē\ *adj* **mang·i·er; mang·i·est 1** : affected with or resulting from mange **2** : SHABBY, SEEDY

man·hole \'man-,hōl\ *n* : a hole (as in a pavement or tank) made to allow a man to pass through

man·hood \'man-,hùd\ *n* **1** : manly qualities : COURAGE **2** : the state of being an adult male **3** : MEN ⟨the *manhood* of a nation⟩

ma·ni·a \'mā-nē-ə\ *n* **1** : INSANITY, MADNESS **2** : unreasonable enthusiasm : CRAZE

ma·ni·ac \'mā-nē-,ak\ *n* : a violently crazy person

¹man·i·cure \'man-ə-,kyùr\ *n* **1** : MANICURIST **2** : a treatment for the care of the hands and nails

²manicure *vb* **man·i·cured; man·i·cur·ing** : to give a manicure to

man·i·cur·ist \'man-ə-,kyùr-əst\ *n* : one who gives manicures

¹man·i·fest \'man-ə-,fest\ *adj* : clear to the senses or to the mind : easy to recognize : OBVIOUS ⟨his relief was *manifest*⟩

²manifest *vb* : to show plainly : DISPLAY ⟨*manifest* interest⟩

man·i·fes·ta·tion \,man-ə-fəs-'tā-shən\ *n* **1** : the act of manifesting **2** : that which makes clear : EVIDENCE ⟨the first *manifestations* of spring⟩

man·i·fold \'man-ə-,fōld\ *adj* : of many and various kinds ⟨*manifold* activities⟩

man·i·kin *or* **man·ni·kin** \'man-i-kən\ *n* : a

form representing the human figure used especially for displaying clothes

ma·nip·u·late \mə-'nip-yə-,lāt\ *vb* **ma·nip·u·lat·ed; ma·nip·u·lat·ing** 1 : to treat or operate with the hands or by mechanical means and especially with skill ⟨*manipulate* the levers of a machine⟩ 2 : to manage skillfully and especially with intent to deceive ⟨*manipulated* the accounts⟩

man·kind *n* 1 \'man-'kīnd\ : the human race 2 \-,kīnd\ : men as distinguished from women

man·ly \'man-lē\ *adj* **man·li·er; man·li·est** : having qualities that suit a man : BRAVE, RESOLUTE — **man·li·ness** *n*

man–made \'man-'mād\ *adj* : made by man rather than nature ⟨*man-made* systems⟩

man·na \'man-ə\ *n* : food supplied by a miracle to the Israelites in the wilderness

man·ner \'man-ər\ *n* 1 : KIND, SORT ⟨what *manner* of man is he⟩ 2 : a way of acting ⟨worked in a brisk *manner*⟩ 3 *pl* : behavior toward or in the presence of other people ⟨she has good *manners*⟩

man·ner·ism \'man-ə-,riz-əm\ *n* : a peculiar manner of action or expression frequently used by a person

ma·noeu·vre \mə-'nü-vər, -'nyü-\ *var of* MANEUVER

man–of–war \,man-əv-'wȯr\ *n, pl* **men–of–war** \,men-\ : WARSHIP

man·or \'man-ər\ *n* : a large estate

man·sion \'man-chən\ *n* : a large stately house

man·slaugh·ter \'man-,slȯt-ər\ *n* : the unlawful killing of a person without intending to do it

man·tel \'mant-l\ *n* : the beam, stone, arch, or shelf above a fireplace

man·tel·piece \'mant-l-,pēs\ *n* 1 : a mantel with its side elements 2 : the shelf of a mantel

man·tis \'mant-əs\ *n, pl* **man·tis·es** *or* **man·tes** \'man-,tēz\ [from Greek *mantis*, literally, "prophet"; so called because the raised forelimbs suggest an attitude of prayer] : an insect related to the grasshoppers and roaches that feeds on other insects which are clasped in the raised forelimbs

mantis

man·tle \'mant-l\ *n* 1 : a loose sleeveless outer garment 2 : something that covers or envelops ⟨a *mantle* of snow⟩ 3 : a fold or lobe of the body wall of a mollusk that secretes the shell material 4 : the part of the earth's interior beneath the lithosphere and above the central core

²mantle *vb* **man·tled; man·tling** : to cover with or as if with a mantle ⟨the summit of the mountain was *mantled* in clouds⟩

¹man·u·al \'man-yə-wəl\ *adj* 1 : of or relating to the hands ⟨*manual* dexterity⟩ 2 : done or operated by the hands ⟨*manual* labor⟩ ⟨a *manual* gearshift⟩ — **man·u·al·ly** *adv*

²manual *n* : HANDBOOK ⟨a scout *manual*⟩

manual training *n* : training in work done with the hands and in practical arts ⟨woodworking is usually part of *manual training*⟩

¹man·u·fac·ture \,man-yə-'fak-chər\ *n* 1 : the making of products by hand or machinery 2 : PRODUCTION ⟨the *manufacture* of blood in the body⟩

²manufacture *vb* **man·u·fac·tured; man·u·fac·tur·ing** : to make from raw materials by hand or machinery — **man·u·fac·tur·er** *n*

ma·nure \mə-'nu̇r, -'nyu̇r\ *n* : material (as animal wastes) used to fertilize land

man·u·script \'man-yə-,skript\ *n* 1 : something written by hand or typewritten ⟨the *manuscript* of a book⟩ 2 : HANDWRITING

¹man·y \'men-ē\ *adj* **more** \'mȯr\; **most** \'mōst\ : amounting to a large number: not few

²many *pron* : a large number ⟨*many* of them were late⟩

³many *n* : a large number ⟨a good *many* of the books were novels⟩

¹map \'map\ *n* 1 : a picture or chart showing features of the surface of the earth, other planets, or the moon 2 : a picture or chart of the sky showing the position of stars and planets

²map *vb* **mapped; map·ping** 1 : to make a map of ⟨*map* the heavens⟩ 2 : to plan in detail ⟨*map* out a campaign⟩

ma·ple \'mā-pəl\ *n* : any of a group of trees having deeply notched leaves, two-winged fruits, and hard pale wood and including some whose sap is evaporated to a sweet syrup (**maple syrup**) and a brownish sugar (**maple sugar**)

mar \'mär\ *vb* **marred; mar·ring** : to make a blemish on : DAMAGE, SPOIL

mar·a·thon \'mar-ə-,thän\ *n* [from *Marathon*, Greece, site of a victory of Greeks over Persians in 490 B.C., the news of which was reputed to have been carried to Athens by a long-distance runner] 1 : a long-distance running race 2 : an endurance contest

¹mar·ble \'mär-bəl\ *n* 1 : limestone that is more or less crystallized by natural processes, is capable of taking a high polish, and is used in architecture and sculpture 2 : a little ball (as of glass) used in a children's game (**marbles**)

²marble *adj* : made of or resembling marble

¹march \'märch\ *vb* **1** : to move or cause to move with a regular stride and especially in step with others ⟨*march* in a parade⟩ **2** : to travel steadily : PROGRESS ⟨science *marches* on⟩ — **march·er** *n*

²march *n* **1** : the action of marching **2** : the distance covered in marching ⟨a long day's *march*⟩ **3** : a regular even step used in marching **4** : a piece of music used to accompany marching

March \'märch\ *n* : the third month of the year

mar·chio·ness \'mär-shə-nəs\ *n* **1** : the wife or widow of a marquess **2** : a woman who holds the rank of a marquess in her own right

mare \'maər\ *n* : an adult female of the horse or a related animal (as a zebra or ass)

mar·ga·rine \'mär-jə-rən\ *n* : a food product manufactured usually from vegetable oils and skim milk and used as a spread or cooking fat

mar·gin \'mär-jən\ *n* **1** : the part of a page outside the main body of printed or written matter **2** : BORDER, EDGE **3** : an extra amount (as of time or money) allowed for use if needed ⟨we have a *margin* of five minutes⟩

mar·gue·rite \ˌmär-gə-'rēt\ *n* : a chrysanthemum with single flowers

mar·i·gold \'mar-ə-ˌgōld\ *n* : any of several plants related to the daisies that are grown for their showy yellow or brownish red and yellow flower heads

marigold

mar·i·hua·na *or* **mar·i·jua·na** \ˌmar-ə-'wä-nə\ *n* : a drug from the hemp plant

ma·ri·na \mə-'rē-nə\ *n* : a dock or basin providing moorings for motorboats and yachts

¹ma·rine \mə-'rēn\ *adj* **1** : of or relating to the sea ⟨*marine* paintings⟩ ⟨fish and other *marine* animals⟩ **2** : of or relating to the navigation of the sea : NAUTICAL ⟨*marine* charts⟩

²marine *n* **1** : the ships of a country ⟨the merchant *marine*⟩ **2** : one of a class of soldiers serving on shipboard or in close cooperation with a naval force

mar·i·ner \'mar-ə-nər\ *n* : SEAMAN, SAILOR

mar·i·o·nette \ˌmar-ē-ə-'net\ *n* : a doll that can be made to move or act in a play by means of strings or by hand : PUPPET

mar·i·tal \'mar-ət-l\ *adj* : MATRIMONIAL

mar·i·time \'mar-ə-ˌtīm\ *adj* **1** : of or relating to ocean navigation or commerce ⟨*maritime* law⟩ **2** : bordering on or living near the sea ⟨*maritime* nations⟩

¹mark \'märk\ *n* **1** : something designed or serving to record position ⟨high-water *mark*⟩ **2** : something aimed at : TARGET **3** : SIGN, INDICATION ⟨a *mark* of friendship⟩ **4** : a written or printed symbol ⟨price *mark*⟩ ⟨punctuation *mark*⟩ **5** : a grade or score showing the quality of work or conduct ⟨good *marks* in school⟩ **6** : a blemish (as a scratch or stain) made on a surface ⟨the blow left a *mark*⟩

²mark *vb* **1** : to set apart by a line or boundary ⟨*mark* off a tennis court⟩ **2** : to make a mark on ⟨*mark* the top with a cross⟩ **3** : to decide and indicate by marks the value or quality of : GRADE ⟨*mark* the tests⟩ **4** : to be a sign of : CHARACTERIZE, DISTINGUISH ⟨a disease *marked* by fever⟩ **5** : to take notice of : OBSERVE ⟨*mark* my words⟩ — **mark·er** *n*

³mark *n* : a coin of Germany which is the basic unit of German money

marked \'märkt\ *adj* **1** : having a mark or marks **2** : NOTICEABLE ⟨speaks with a *marked* accent⟩

¹mar·ket \'mär-kət\ *n* **1** : a meeting of people at a stated time and place to buy and sell things **2** : a public place where a market is held **3** : a retail store where provisions are sold ⟨meat *market*⟩ **4** : the region in which something can be sold ⟨*markets* for American cotton⟩

²market *vb* : to buy or sell in a market

mar·ket·place \'mär-kət-ˌplās\ *n* : an open square or place in a town where markets or public sales are held

mark·ing \'mär-king\ *n* **1** : MARK **2** : arrangement or pattern of marks (as on an animal's coat)

marks·man \'märks-mən\ *n, pl* **marks·men** \-mən\ : one who shoots well — **marks·man·ship** \-ˌship\ *n*

mar·ma·lade \'mär-mə-ˌlād\ *n* [from Portuguese *marmelada* "quince conserve", from *marmelo* "quince", a derivative of Greek *melimēlon* "sweet apple", a compound of *meli* "honey" and *mēlon* "apple"] : a jam made usually from citrus fruits and containing pieces of fruit and fruit rind ⟨orange *marmalade*⟩

mar·mo·set \'mär-mə-ˌset\ *n* : a small monkey of South and Central America with soft fur and a bushy ringed tail

mar·mot \'mär-mət\ *n* : a stocky short-legged animal with coarse fur and bushy tail that is related to the squirrels and the rats : WOODCHUCK

¹ma·roon \mə-'rün\ *vb* : to put ashore and abandon on a lonely island or coast

²maroon *n* : a dark red

mar·quess \'mär-kwəs\ *n* : a member of the British peerage ranking below a duke and above an earl

mar·quis \'mär-kwəs\ *n* : MARQUESS

mar·quise \mär-'kēz\ *n* : MARCHIONESS

mar·riage \'mar-ij\ *n* **1** : the legal relationship into which a man and a woman enter with the purpose of making a home and raising a family **2** : WEDDING

mar·row \'mar-ō\ *n* : a soft tissue rich in fat and blood vessels that fills the cavities of most bones

mar·ry \'mar-ē\ *vb* **mar·ried; mar·ry·ing 1** : to join in marriage as husband and wife ⟨they were *married* by a priest⟩ **2** : to give in marriage ⟨*married* his daughter to a lawyer⟩ **3** : to take for husband or wife ⟨he *married* his secretary⟩ **4** : to enter into a marriage relationship ⟨decide to *marry*⟩

Mars \'märz\ *n* : the planet that is fourth in order of distance from the sun, is conspicuous for its redness, and has a diameter of about 4200 miles

marsh \'märsh\ *n* : an area of soft wet land usually overgrown with grasses and sedges

¹mar·shal \'mär-shəl\ *n* **1** : a person who arranges and directs ceremonies ⟨*marshal* of the parade⟩ **2** : an officer of the highest rank in some military forces **3** : a federal official having duties similar to those of a sheriff **4** : the head of some municipal departments ⟨fire *marshal*⟩

²marshal *vb* **mar·shaled** *or* **mar·shalled; mar·shal·ing** *or* **mar·shal·ling** : to arrange in order ⟨*marshal* troops⟩

marsh·mal·low \'märsh-,mel-ō, -,mal-\ *n* : a confection made from corn syrup, sugar, and gelatin beaten to a light creamy paste

marsh marigold *n* : a swamp plant with shiny leaves and bright yellow flowers resembling buttercups

marsh·y \'mär-shē\ *adj* **marsh·i·er; marsh·i·est** : resembling or constituting marsh

mar·su·pi·al \mär-'sü-pē-əl\ *n* : a mammal (as a kangaroo or opossum) that carries its young in a pouch on the mother's abdomen

mart \'märt\ *n* : a trading place : MARKET

mar·ten \'märt-n\ *n* : a slender flesh-eating animal larger than the related weasels that is sought for its soft gray or brown fur

mar·tial \'mär-shəl\ *adj* : having to do with or suitable for war ⟨a *martial* tune⟩

mar·tin \'märt-n\ *n* **1** : a European swallow with a forked tail **2** : any of several birds (as the American

marten

purple martin) resembling or related to the true martin

¹mar·tyr \'märt-ər\ *n* : a person who suffers greatly or dies rather than give up his religion or principles

²martyr *vb* : to put to death for clinging to a belief

¹mar·vel \'mär-vəl\ *n* : something that causes wonder or astonishment

²marvel *vb* **mar·veled** *or* **mar·velled; mar·vel·ing** *or* **mar·vel·ling** : to be struck with astonishment or wonder ⟨I *marvel* at your skill⟩

mar·vel·ous *or* **mar·vel·lous** \'mär-və-ləs\ *adj* **1** : causing wonder or astonishment **2** : SPLENDID ⟨we had a *marvelous* time⟩ — **mar·vel·ous·ly** *adv*

mas·cot \'mas-,kät, -kət\ *n* : a person, animal, or object believed to bring good luck

mas·cu·line \'mas-kyə-lən\ *adj* **1** : of the male sex **2** : characteristic of or belonging to men : MANLY ⟨a *masculine* voice⟩

¹mash \'mash\ *n* **1** : crushed malt or grain meal steeped and stirred in hot water to produce wort **2** : a mixture of ground feeds used for feeding livestock **3** : a mass of something made soft and pulpy by beating or crushing

²mash *vb* : to reduce to a soft pulpy mass ⟨*mashed* potatoes⟩

¹mask \'mask\ *n* **1** : a cover for the face used for disguise or protection ⟨a Halloween *mask*⟩ ⟨a catcher's *mask*⟩ **2** : something that disguises or conceals : PRETENSE ⟨under a *mask* of friendship⟩ **3** : a copy of a face molded in wax or plaster ⟨a death *mask*⟩

mask 1

²mask *vb* : CONCEAL, DISGUISE

ma·son \'mās-n\ *n* : a person who builds or works with stone, brick, or cement

ma·son·ry \'mās-n-rē\ *n, pl* **ma·son·ries 1** : the art, trade, or occupation of a mason **2** : the work done by a mason ⟨good *masonry*⟩ **3** : something built of stone, brick, or concrete

masque \'mask\ *n* **1** : MASQUERADE **2** : an old form of dramatic entertainment in which the actors wore masks

¹mas·quer·ade \,mas-kə-'rād\ *n* **1** : a party (as a dance) at which people wear masks and costumes **2** : a pretending by disguise to be something one is not

²masquerade *vb* **mas·quer·ad·ed; mas·quer·ad·ing 1** : to disguise oneself **2** : to pass oneself off as something one is not : POSE ⟨*masqueraded* as an expert⟩ — **mas·quer·ad·er** *n*

¹mass \'mas\ *n* **1** : an amount of something that holds or clings together ⟨a *mass* of iron ore⟩   **2** : SIZE, BULK ⟨an elephant's huge *mass*⟩ **3** : the principal part : main body ⟨the great *mass* of voters⟩   **4** : a large quantity or number ⟨a *mass* of figures⟩   **5** *pl* : the body of ordinary or common people

²mass *vb* : to collect into a mass

Mass \'mas\ *n* : a religious service in celebration of the Eucharist

¹mas·sa·cre \'mas-ə-kər\ *vb* **mas·sa·cred; mas·sa·cring** : to kill in a massacre : SLAUGHTER

²massacre *n* : the violent and cruel killing of a number of persons

¹mas·sage \mə-'säzh\ *n* : treatment of the body by rubbing, kneading, and tapping

²massage *vb* **mas·saged; mas·sag·ing** : to give massage to

mas·sive \'mas-iv\ *adj* : very large, heavy, and solid

mass·y \'mas-ē\ *adj* **mass·i·er; mass·i·est** : MASSIVE

mast \'mast\ *n*   **1** : a long pole that rises from the bottom of a ship and supports the sails and rigging   **2** : a vertical or nearly vertical tall pole ⟨a *mast* on a derrick⟩ ⟨a *mast* for a television antenna⟩ — **mast·ed** \'mas-təd\ *adj*

mast

mast of a derrick

¹mas·ter \'mas-tər\ *n*   **1** : a male teacher   **2** : an artist or performer of great skill   **3** : one having authority over another person or thing ⟨the slave's *master*⟩ ⟨*master* of a ship⟩   **4** : EMPLOYER   **5** — used as a title for a boy too young to be called *mister*

²master *vb*   **1** : to get control of ⟨*master* your temper⟩   **2** : to become skillful at ⟨*master* arithmetic⟩

master chief petty officer *n* : a petty officer of the highest rank in the navy

mas·ter·ful \'mas-tər-fəl\ *adj*   **1** : inclined to take control or dominate   **2** : highly skillful : MASTERLY

mas·ter·ly \'mas-tər-lē\ *adj* : showing the knowledge or skill of a master ⟨a *masterly* performance⟩

mas·ter·piece \'mas-tər-ˌpēs\ *n* : a work done or made with unusual skill

master sergeant *n*   **1** : a noncommissioned officer (as in the army) ranking next below a sergeant major   **2** : a noncommissioned officer in the air force ranking next below a senior master sergeant

mas·ter·y \'mas-tə-rē\ *n, pl* **mas·ter·ies** **1** : the position or authority of a master **2** : VICTORY ⟨gained the *mastery* over his opponents⟩   **3** : skill that makes one master of something

mast·head \'mast-ˌhed\ *n* : the top of a mast

mas·ti·cate \'mas-tə-ˌkāt\ *vb* **mas·ti·cat·ed; mas·ti·cat·ing** : CHEW

mas·tiff \'mas-təf\ *n* : a very large deep-chested powerful dog with a smooth coat

¹mat \'mat\ *n*   **1** : a piece of coarse fabric made of woven or braided rushes, straw, or wool and used as a floor or seat covering **2** : a piece of material in front of a door to wipe the shoes on   **3** : a piece of material (as leather, woven straw, or cloth) used under dishes or vases or as an ornament   **4** : a pad or cushion for gymnastics or wrestling   **5** : something made up of many intertwined or tangled strands ⟨a *mat* of weeds⟩

²mat *vb* **mat·ted; mat·ting** : to form into a tangled mat

mat·a·dor \'mat-ə-ˌdȯr\ *n* : a bullfighter who plays the principal part in a bullfight

¹match \'mach\ *n*   **1** : a person or thing that is equal to or as good as another ⟨we are a *match* for the enemy⟩   **2** : a thing that is exactly like another thing ⟨this cloth is a *match* for that⟩   **3** : two people or things that go well together   **4** : MARRIAGE ⟨made a good *match*⟩   **5** : a contest between two parties or teams ⟨tennis *match*⟩ ⟨boxing *match*⟩

²match *vb*   **1** : to place in competition ⟨*matched* his strength with his rival's⟩   **2** : to choose something that is the same as another or goes with it ⟨try to *match* this material⟩ **3** : to be the same or suitable to one another ⟨the colors *match*⟩   **4** : to toss coins and compare exposed faces

³match *n*   **1** : a wick or cord that is made to burn evenly and is used for lighting a charge of powder   **2** : a short slender piece of wood or of pressed paper tipped with a mixture that produces fire when scratched

match·book \'mach-ˌbůk\ *n* : a small folder containing rows of paper matches

match·less \'mach-ləs\ *adj* : having no equal : better than any other of the same kind — **match·less·ly** *adv*

match·lock \'mach-ˌläk\ *n* : a musket with a hole in the breech into which a slow-burning cord is lowered to ignite the charge

¹mate \'māt\ *n*   **1** : COMPANION, COMRADE **2** : an officer on a merchant ship who ranks below the captain   **3** : either member of a married couple   **4** : either member of a breeding pair of animals   **5** : either of two matched objects or individuals ⟨couldn't find the *mate* to the glove⟩

²mate *vb* **mat·ed; mat·ing** : to join as mates : MARRY

¹ma·te·ri·al \mə-'tir-ē-əl\ *adj*   **1** : of, relating to, or made of matter : PHYSICAL ⟨a baseball is a *material* thing⟩ **2** : of or relating to a person's bodily needs or wants : BODILY ⟨money buys *material* comforts⟩ **3** : making a difference : IMPORTANT ⟨exercise is *material* to his health⟩ — **ma·te·ri·al·ly** *adv*

²material *n* **1** : the elements, substance, or parts of which something is composed or can be made ⟨dress *material*⟩ **2** *pl* : apparatus needed for doing something ⟨writing *materials*⟩

ma·te·ri·al·ize \mə-'tir-ē-ə-,līz\ *vb* **ma·te·ri·al·ized; ma·te·ri·al·iz·ing 1** : to cause to take on a physical form ⟨the medium claimed to *materialize* the spirits of the dead⟩ **2** : to become actual fact ⟨their hopes never *materialized*⟩

ma·ter·nal \mə-'tərn-l\ *adj* **1** : of, relating to, or characteristic of a mother ⟨*maternal* love⟩ **2** : related through one's mother ⟨a *maternal* aunt⟩ — **ma·ter·nal·ly** *adv*

math \'math\ *n* : MATHEMATICS

math·e·mat·i·cal \,math-ə-'mat-i-kəl\ *adj* **1** : of or having to do with mathematics **2** : EXACT ⟨*mathematical* precision⟩ — **math·e·mat·i·cal·ly** *adv*

math·e·ma·ti·cian \,math-ə-mə-'tish-ən\ *n* : a specialist or expert in mathematics

math·e·mat·ics \,math-ə-'mat-iks\ *n* : the science that studies and explains numbers, quantities, measurements, and the relations between them

mat·i·née \,mat-n-'ā\ *n* [from French *matinée*, literally, "morning", derived from Latin *matutinus* "of the morning", from *Matuta*, Roman goddess of morning] : a musical or dramatic performance in the afternoon

mat·ri·mo·ni·al \,mat-rə-'mō-nē-əl\ *adj* : of or relating to matrimony

mat·ri·mo·ny \'mat-rə-,mō-nē\ *n, pl* **mat·ri·mo·nies** : MARRIAGE

ma·tron \'mā-trən\ *n* **1** : a married woman **2** : a woman who is in charge of the household affairs of an institution **3** : a woman who supervises women prisoners in a police station or jail

¹mat·ter \'mat-ər\ *n* **1** : a subject of interest ⟨a *matter* for careful thought⟩ **2** : something to be dealt with ⟨a serious *matter*⟩ **3** : TROUBLE, DIFFICULTY ⟨what's the *matter*⟩ **4** : the substance things are made of : something that occupies space and has weight **5** : material substance of a particular kind or function ⟨coloring *matter*⟩ ⟨gray *matter* of the brain⟩ **6** : PUS **7** : AMOUNT, QUANTITY ⟨a *matter* of ten cents⟩ **8** : MAIL ⟨third class *matter*⟩ — **no matter** : it makes no difference

²matter *vb* : to be of importance ⟨it does not *matter*⟩

mat·ter–of–fact \,mat-ər-ə-'fakt\ *adj* : adhering to or concerned with fact

mat·ting \'mat-ing\ *n* : material for mats

mat·tress \'mat-rəs\ *n* [from Old French *materas*, derived from Arabic *maṭraḥ* "place where something is thrown"] **1** : a part of a bed made of a springy material (as hair, cotton, or rubber) encased in strong cloth and placed on the bed springs **2** : a sack that can be filled with air and used as a mattress

¹ma·ture \mə-'tùr, -'tyùr\ *adj* **1** : fully grown : RIPE **2** : characteristic of a mature person ⟨a *mature* outlook⟩

²mature *vb* **ma·tured; ma·tur·ing 1** : to bring to maturity : COMPLETE **2** : to grow to maturity

ma·tu·ri·ty \mə-'tùr-ət-ē, -'tyùr-\ *n* : the condition of being mature : full development

¹maul \'mòl\ *n* : a heavy hammer used especially for driving wedges or posts

²maul *vb* **1** : BEAT, BRUISE **2** : to handle roughly

mauve \'mōv\ *n* : a moderate purple, violet, or lilac

maw \'mò\ *n* **1** : the place where food is deposited by swallowing : STOMACH **2** : the throat, gullet, or jaws especially of a gluttonous animal

maul

max·im \'mak-səm\ *n* : a general truth or a rule of conduct expressed in a few words

¹max·i·mum \'mak-sə-məm\ *n, pl* **max·i·mums** *or* **max·i·ma** \-sə-mə\ : the highest value : greatest amount ⟨we had to pay the *maximum*⟩

²maximum *adj* : as great as possible in amount or degree ⟨*maximum* efficiency⟩

may \'mā\ *helping verb, past* **might** \'mīt\; *pres sing & pl* **may 1** : have permission to ⟨you *may* go now⟩ **2** : be in some degree likely to ⟨you *may* be right⟩ **3** — used to express a wish ⟨*may* you be happy⟩ **4** — used to express purpose ⟨we exercise so that we *may* be strong⟩

May \'mā\ *n* : the fifth month of the year

may·be \'mā-bē\ *adv* : PERHAPS

mayn't \'mā-ənt, mānt\ : may not

may·on·naise \'mā-ə-,nāz\ *n* : a salad dressing consisting chiefly of yolk of egg, oil, and vinegar or lemon juice

may·or \'mā-ər\ *n* : an official elected to serve as head of a city or borough

maze \'māz\ *n* : a confusing network of paths or passages

me \mē\ *pron, objective case of* I

mead \'mēd\ *n* : a fermented drink made from honey and water

mead·ow \'med-ō\ *n* : usually moist and low-lying land devoted to grass (as for hay)

mead·ow·lark \'med-ō-ˌlärk\ *n* : a bird about the size of a robin and with brownish upper parts and a yellow breast

mea·ger *or* **mea·gre** \'mē-gər\ *adj* 1 : having little flesh : THIN 2 : INSUFFICIENT ⟨a *meager* diet⟩

syn MEAGER, SKIMPY, SCANTY all mean so small in size or amount as to fall short of what is normal or necessary. MEAGER suggests the absence of elements necessary to a thing's richness or effectiveness ⟨a *meager* meal of broth and bread⟩ ⟨a *meager* vocabulary prevented him from expressing himself well⟩ SKIMPY emphasizes a lack in quantity or size that is the result of excessive thrift or stinginess ⟨bargain sheets that were so *skimpy* we couldn't tuck them in⟩ SCANTY suggests an insufficiency of supply that is likely to cause loss or hardship ⟨*scanty* dress for a freezing day⟩ ⟨the *scanty* supply of oil wouldn't last the winter⟩

¹meal \'mēl\ *n* 1 : the food eaten or prepared for eating at one time 2 : the act or time of eating

²meal *n* 1 : usually coarsely ground seeds of a cereal grass and especially of Indian corn 2 : something like meal in texture

meal·y \'mē-lē\ *adj* **meal·i·er; meal·i·est** : resembling meal : CRUMBLY — **meal·i·ness** *n*

¹mean \'mēn\ *adj* 1 : of low birth or station : HUMBLE 2 : ORDINARY, INFERIOR ⟨a man of no *mean* ability⟩ 3 : POOR, SHABBY ⟨live in *mean* surroundings⟩ 4 : not honorable or worthy ⟨*mean* to his brother⟩ 5 : STINGY 6 : of a troublesome disposition ⟨a *mean* horse⟩ — **mean·ly** *adv* — **mean·ness** *n*

²mean *vb* **meant** \'ment\; **mean·ing** \'mē-ning\ 1 : to have in mind as one's purpose : INTEND ⟨*mean* to be kind⟩ 2 : to intend for a particular purpose or use ⟨a book *meant* for children⟩ 3 : to serve to indicate or show : DENOTE ⟨what does this word *mean*⟩ ⟨those clouds *mean* rain⟩

³mean *n* 1 : the middle point or course between extremes : MODERATION ⟨follow the golden *mean*⟩ 2 : ARITHMETIC MEAN 3 *pl* : something that helps a person to get what he wants ⟨use every *means* you can think of⟩ 4 *pl* : WEALTH — **by all means** : CERTAINLY — **by any means** : in any way : at all — **by means of** : through the use of — **by no means** : certainly not

⁴mean *adj* : lying midway between extremes : AVERAGE ⟨*mean* temperature⟩

me·an·der \mē-'an-dər\ *vb* 1 : to follow a winding course ⟨a brook *meandering* through the fields⟩ 2 : to wander without aim or purpose ⟨*meander* around town⟩

mean·ing \'mē-ning\ *n* 1 : the sense a person intends to express especially in language 2 : INTENTION, PURPOSE

mean·ing·ful \'mē-ning-fəl\ *adj* : having a meaning or purpose

mean·ing·less \'mē-ning-ləs\ *adj* : lacking sense or significance

¹mean·time \'mēn-ˌtīm\ *n* : the time between two events

²meantime *adv* : in the meantime

¹mean·while \'mēn-ˌhwīl\ *n* : MEANTIME

²meanwhile *adv* : during the time between two events

mea·sles \'mē-zəlz\ *n sing or pl* 1 : an acute contagious disease marked by fever and red spots on the skin 2 : any of several diseases (as the mild **German measles**) resembling true measles

mea·sly \'mēz-lē\ *adj* **mea·sli·er; mea·sli·est** : so small or insignificant as to be rejected with scorn

mea·sur·a·ble \'mezh-ə-rə-bəl\ *adj* : capable of being measured

¹mea·sure \'mezh-ər\ *n* 1 : AMOUNT, EXTENT, DEGREE ⟨succeed in large *measure*⟩ 2 : the dimensions, capacity, or quantity of something as fixed by measuring ⟨made to *measure*⟩ 3 : something (as a yardstick or cup) used in measuring 4 : a unit used in measuring 5 : a system of measuring ⟨liquid *measure*⟩ 6 : the part of the musical staff between two bars 7 : a means used to accomplish a purpose ⟨take *measures* to stop it⟩ 8 : a legislative bill or act

measure 3

²measure *vb* **mea·sured; mea·sur·ing** 1 : to find out the dimensions, degree, or amount of by comparison with accepted standards ⟨*measure* the cloth with the tape measure⟩ 2 : ESTIMATE ⟨*measure* the distance with the eye⟩ 3 : to bring into comparison ⟨*measured* his skill against an opponent's⟩ 4 : to serve as a measure of ⟨a thermometer *measures* temperature⟩ 5 : to have as its measurement ⟨the cloth *measures* ten yards⟩

mea·sure·ment \'mezh-ər-mənt\ *n* 1 : the act of measuring 2 : the extent, size, capacity, or amount of something as fixed by measuring 3 : a system of measures

meat \'mēt\ *n* 1 : food especially when solid

and distinguished from drink **2** : the edible part of something as distinguished from a covering (as a hull or shell) ⟨nut *meats*⟩ **3** : animal and especially mammal tissue for use as food

me·chan·ic \mi-'kan-ik\ *n* : a manual worker and especially one who makes or repairs machines

me·chan·i·cal \mi-'kan-i-kəl\ *adj* **1** : of or relating to machinery ⟨*mechanical* engineering⟩ **2** : made or operated by a machine ⟨a *mechanical* toy⟩ **3** : done or produced as if by a machine : lacking a personal touch ⟨sing in a *mechanical* way⟩ — **me·chan·i·cal·ly** *adv*

me·chan·ics \mi-'kan-iks\ *n sing or pl* **1** : a science dealing with the action of forces on bodies **2** : details of operation or procedure ⟨the *mechanics* of a watch⟩ ⟨the *mechanics* of writing plays⟩

mech·a·nism \'mek-ə-ˌniz-əm\ *n* **1** : a mechanical device **2** : the parts by which a machine operates ⟨the *mechanism* of a watch⟩ **3** : the parts or steps that make up a process or activity ⟨the *mechanism* of democratic government⟩

mech·a·nize \'mek-ə-ˌnīz\ *vb* **mech·a·nized**; **mech·a·niz·ing** **1** : to make mechanical **2** : to make automatic **3** : to equip with machinery

med·al \'med-l\ *n* : a piece of metal often in the form of a coin with design and words in honor of a special event, a person, or an achievement

me·dal·lion \mə-'dal-yən\ *n* **1** : a large medal **2** : something (as an oval portrait) resembling a large medal

medal

med·dle \'med-l\ *vb* **med·dled**; **med·dling** : to interfere in or pry into another's affairs

syn MEDDLE, INTERFERE, TAMPER all mean to intrude in a rude or improper manner. MEDDLE stresses the aspect of prying into something that isn't one's own affair, usually without permission and in an annoying fashion ⟨my questions were just meant to be friendly, but the neighbors thought I was *meddling*⟩ INTERFERE emphasizes an active meddling that seriously affects or influences the person or situation intruded upon ⟨he was warned that if he *interfered* with the nest the bird wouldn't stay to hatch the eggs⟩ TAMPER implies making undesirable or improper changes in something that should have been left alone, and may indicate that a secret or underhanded method was involved ⟨someone had *tampered* with the lock on the cabin door⟩ ⟨the test papers had been *tampered* with⟩

med·dle·some \'med-l-səm\ *adj* : inclined to meddle

media *pl of* MEDIUM

med·i·cal \'med-i-kəl\ *adj* : of or relating to the science or practice of medicine or to the treatment of disease — **med·i·cal·ly** *adv*

med·i·cate \'med-ə-ˌkāt\ *vb* **med·i·cat·ed**; **med·i·cat·ing** **1** : to treat with medicine ⟨*medicate* a sore throat⟩ **2** : to add medicinal material to ⟨*medicated* soap⟩

med·i·ca·tion \ˌmed-ə-'kā-shən\ *n* **1** : the act or process of medicating **2** : medicinal material

me·dic·i·nal \mə-'dis-n-əl\ *adj* : used or tending to relieve or cure disease — **me·dic·i·nal·ly** *adv*

med·i·cine \'med-ə-sən\ *n* **1** : a substance or preparation used in treating disease **2** : a science or art dealing with the prevention, cure, or relief of disease

me·di·e·val *or* **me·di·ae·val** \ˌmēd-ē-'ē-vəl, ˌmed-\ *adj* [formed in English from Latin *medius* "middle" and *aevum* "age"] : of or relating to the Middle Ages

me·di·o·cre \ˌmēd-ē-'ō-kər\ *adj* [from Latin *mediocris*, literally, "halfway up the mountain", from *medius* "middle" and *ocris* "stony mountain"] : neither good nor bad : ORDINARY, COMMONPLACE

syn MEDIOCRE, AVERAGE, FAIR all mean being about midway between good and bad. MEDIOCRE emphasizes being clearly less than good or satisfactory, and is the most disparaging of the terms ⟨plays at best a *mediocre* game of tennis and finds few partners⟩ AVERAGE stresses the aspect of being in no way exceptional or outstanding, of being clearly neither inferior nor superior ⟨plays an *average* game of tennis, as most of us do⟩ FAIR, though applied to that which is neither excellent nor poor, usually suggests being better than average, definitely removed from the best but still not deserving disapproval or rejection ⟨plays a *fair* game of tennis, especially for one so young⟩

med·i·tate \'med-ə-ˌtāt\ *vb* **med·i·tat·ed**; **med·i·tat·ing** **1** : to consider carefully : INTEND **2** : to spend time in quiet thinking : MUSE, REFLECT

med·i·ta·tion \ˌmed-ə-'tā-shən\ *n* : close and continued thought : REFLECTION

Med·i·ter·ra·ne·an \ˌmed-ə-tə-'rā-nē-ən\ *adj* : of or relating to the Mediterranean sea or to the lands or peoples surrounding it

¹me·di·um \'mēd-ē-əm\ *n, pl* **me·di·ums** *or* **me·di·a** \-ē-ə\ **1** : something that is between or in the middle **2** : the means by which or through which something is done ⟨money is a *medium* of exchange⟩ **3** : the substance in which something lives or acts ⟨the *medium* of air⟩ **4** : a person through whom other persons seek to communicate with the spirits of the dead

²medium *adj* : intermediate in amount, quality, position, or degree ⟨*medium* size⟩

med·ley \'med-lē\ *n, pl* **med·leys** **1** : MIXTURE, JUMBLE **2** : a musical composition made up of parts from other pieces

me·dul·la ob·lon·ga·ta \mə-'dəl-ə-,äb-,lòng-'gät-ə\ *n* : the last part of the brain that joins the spinal cord and is concerned especially with control of involuntary vital functions (as breathing and beating of the heart)

meed \'mēd\ *n* : something deserved or earned : REWARD ⟨received his *meed* of praise⟩

meek \'mēk\ *adj* **1** : enduring injury with patience and without resentment **2** : lacking spirit or self-confidence — **meek·ly** *adv* — **meek·ness** *n*

¹meet \'mēt\ *vb* **met** \'met\; **meet·ing** **1** : to come upon or across ⟨*met* a friend⟩ **2** : JOIN, CROSS ⟨where two roads *meet*⟩ **3** : to go to a place where a person is or will be ⟨arrange to *meet* at the drugstore⟩ **4** : to make the acquaintance of ⟨*met* some nice people⟩ **5** : to come together as opponents ⟨they *met* in the finals⟩ **6** : to struggle against ⟨*meet* competition⟩ **7** : ENDURE, EXPERIENCE ⟨*meet* failure bravely⟩ **8** : to come together : ASSEMBLE ⟨the club *meets* tonight⟩ **9** : to become noticed by ⟨strange sounds *met* his ears⟩ **10** : SATISFY ⟨*meet* the requirements⟩ ⟨*meets* his bills⟩

²meet *n* : a meeting to engage in competitive sports ⟨track *meet*⟩

meet·ing \'mēt-ing\ *n* **1** : the act of persons or things that meet **2** : ASSEMBLY, GATHERING **3** : the place where two things come together : JUNCTION

meet·ing·house \'mēt-ing-,haus\ *n* : a building used for public assembly and especially for Protestant worship

meg·a·phone \'meg-ə-,fōn\ *n* : a cone-shaped device used to direct the voice and increase its loudness

¹mel·an·chol·y \'mel-ən-,käl-ē\ *n* [from Greek *melancholia*, literally, "black bile"; so called because a gloomy disposition was thought to be the result of too much dark bile in the system] : low spirits : a gloomy mood

megaphone

syn MELANCHOLY, DEPRESSION, GLOOM all mean a mood of low spirits or sadness. MELANCHOLY suggests a not necessarily unpleasant state of mind that mingles sadness and thoughtfulness but avoids grief or heaviness ⟨a fit of *melancholy* accompanied the end of summer⟩ DEPRESSION applies to a discouraged and listless mood that is usually temporary and often stems from some understandable cause ⟨a state of *depression* followed his illness⟩ GLOOM emphasizes a mood of depression or sadness that may approach despair and that is often difficult to throw off ⟨the *gloom* that followed their dog's death affected the whole family⟩

²melancholy *adj* : low in spirits : SAD

¹mel·low \'mel-ō\ *adj* **1** : tender and sweet because of ripeness ⟨a *mellow* peach⟩ **2** : made gentle and sweet by age ⟨*mellow* wines⟩ ⟨a *mellow* character⟩ **3** : being clear, full, and pure : not coarse ⟨a *mellow* sound⟩ ⟨a *mellow* color⟩ — **mel·low·ness** *n*

²mellow *vb* : to make or become mellow

me·lo·di·ous \mə-'lōd-ē-əs\ *adj* : agreeable to the ear because of its melody : TUNEFUL — **me·lo·di·ous·ly** *adv* — **me·lo·di·ous·ness** *n*

mel·o·dy \'mel-ə-dē\ *n, pl* **mel·o·dies** **1** : pleasing arrangement of sounds **2** : a series of musical tones arranged to make a pleasing effect : TUNE **3** : the leading part in a musical composition

mel·on \'mel-ən\ *n* : the usually sweet juicy-fleshed edible fruit (as a watermelon) of a vine related to the gourds

melt \'melt\ *vb* **1** : to change from a solid to a liquid usually through the application of heat ⟨*melt* sugar⟩ ⟨snow *melts*⟩ **2** : to grow less : DISAPPEAR ⟨clouds *melting* away⟩ **3** : to make or become gentle : SOFTEN ⟨kindness that *melts* the heart⟩ **4** : to lose distinct outline ⟨sky *melting* into sea⟩

melting point *n* : the temperature at which a solid melts

mem·ber \'mem-bər\ *n* **1** : a part (as an arm, leg, leaf, or branch) of a person, animal, or plant **2** : one of the individuals (as persons) or units (as species) making up a group **3** : a part of a structure ⟨a horizontal *member* of a bridge⟩

mem·ber·ship \'mem-bər-,ship\ *n* **1** : the condition or fact of being a member **2** : the whole number of members

mem·brane \'mem-,brān\ *n* : a thin soft flexible layer especially of animal or plant tissue

mem·bra·nous \'mem-brə-nəs\ *adj* : being or resembling membrane

me·men·to \mi-'ment-ō\ *n, pl* **me·men·tos** *or* **me·men·toes** : something that serves as a reminder ⟨*mementos* of a trip to Europe⟩

mem·o·ra·ble \'mem-ə-rə-bəl\ *adj* : worth

remembering : not easily forgotten — **mem·o·ra·bly** \-blē\ *adv*

mem·o·ran·dum \ˌmem-ə-'ran-dəm\ *n, pl* **mem·o·ran·dums** *or* **mem·o·ran·da** \-də\ **1** : an informal record or communication **2** : a written reminder

¹me·mo·ri·al \mə-'mōr-ē-əl\ *adj* : serving to preserve the memory of a person or event ⟨a *memorial* service⟩

²memorial *n* : something by which the memory of a person or an event is kept alive : MONUMENT ⟨the Lincoln *Memorial*⟩

Memorial Day *n* : May 30 observed as a legal holiday in commemoration of dead servicemen

mem·o·rize \'mem-ə-ˌrīz\ *vb* **mem·o·rized; mem·o·riz·ing** : to learn by heart : commit to memory

mem·o·ry \'mem-ə-rē\ *n, pl* **mem·o·ries** **1** : the power or process of remembering **2** : the store of things learned and retained ⟨recite from *memory*⟩ **3** : REMEMBRANCE ⟨in *memory* of a great man⟩ **4** : something remembered ⟨a pleasant *memory*⟩ **5** : the time within which past events are remembered ⟨within the *memory* of living man⟩

men *pl of* MAN

¹men·ace \'men-əs\ *n* : THREAT, DANGER ⟨the *menace* of disease⟩

²menace *vb* **men·aced; men·ac·ing** : THREATEN

me·nag·er·ie \mə-'naj-ə-rē\ *n* : a collection of caged wild animals

¹mend \'mend\ *vb* **1** : IMPROVE, CORRECT ⟨*mend* your manners⟩ **2** : to restore to a whole condition ⟨*mend* shoes⟩ **3** : to improve in health — **mend·er** *n*

syn MEND, PATCH, REPAIR all mean to make usable again something that has been damaged. MEND suggests making whole or sound something that has been broken or injured ⟨*mended* the butterfly net⟩ ⟨the broken wing finally *mended*⟩ PATCH refers to mending a hole or tear by the addition of the same or similar material ⟨*patched* the tube with rubber cement⟩ and may indicate a hurried and careless job that will serve only temporarily ⟨*patch* the screen until it can be replaced⟩ REPAIR indicates a returning to wholeness, but usually suggests, unlike the other words, a complete success in restoring to soundness a complex thing that has been seriously damaged ⟨*repaired* his car⟩

²mend *n* **1** : the process of improving ⟨a broken leg on the *mend*⟩ **2** : a mended place

men·folk \'men-ˌfōk\ *or* **men·folks** \-ˌfōks\ *n pl* : the men of a family or community

men·ha·den \men-'hād-n\ *n* : a fish of the herring family found off the Atlantic coast of the United States

¹me·ni·al \'mē-nē-əl\ *adj* : of, relating to, or suitable for servants ⟨*menial* tasks⟩

²menial *n* : a domestic servant

men–of–war *pl of* MAN-OF-WAR

men·stru·a·tion \ˌmen-strə-'wā-shən, men-'strā-shən\ *n* : a periodic discharge of bloody fluid from the uterus

-ment \mənt\ *n suffix* **1** : result, object, or means of a specified action ⟨embank*ment*⟩ ⟨entangle*ment*⟩ ⟨entertain*ment*⟩ **2** : action : process ⟨encircle*ment*⟩ ⟨develop*ment*⟩ **3** : place of a specified action ⟨encamp*ment*⟩ **4** : state : condition ⟨amaze*ment*⟩

men·tal \'ment-l\ *adj* **1** : of or relating to the mind **2** : carried on in the mind ⟨*mental* arithmetic⟩ — **men·tal·ly** *adv*

men·tal·i·ty \men-'tal-ət-ē\ *n, pl* **men·tal·i·ties** **1** : mental power : keenness or breadth of mind **2** : mode of thinking ⟨I can't understand his *mentality*⟩

men·thol \'men-ˌthȯl\ *n* : a white crystalline soothing substance from oils of mint

¹men·tion \'men-chən\ *n* : a brief reference to something : a passing remark

²mention *vb* : to refer to : speak about briefly

men·u \'men-yü\ *n* **1** : a list of dishes served at a meal **2** : the dishes or kinds of food served at a meal

¹me·ow \mē-'au̇\ *n* : the sound made by a cat

²meow *vb* : to utter a meow

mer·can·tile \'mər-kən-ˌtēl, -ˌtīl\ *adj* : of or relating to merchants or trade

¹mer·ce·nar·y \'mərs-n-ˌer-ē\ *n, pl* **mer·ce·nar·ies** : a soldier from a foreign country hired to fight in an army

²mercenary *adj* **1** : doing something only for the pay or reward **2** : greedy for money

mer·chan·dise \'mər-chən-ˌdīz, -ˌdīs\ *n* : goods that are bought and sold in trade

mer·chant \'mər-chənt\ *n* **1** : a person who carries on trade especially on a large scale or with foreign countries **2** : STOREKEEPER

mer·chant·man \'mər-chənt-mən\ *n, pl* **mer·chant·men** \-mən\ : a ship used in trading

merchant marine *n* **1** : the trading ships of a nation **2** : the persons manning a merchant marine

mer·ci·ful \'mər-si-fəl\ *adj* : having or showing mercy : COMPASSIONATE — **mer·ci·ful·ly** *adv*

mer·ci·less \'mər-si-ləs\ *adj* : having no mercy : PITILESS — **mer·ci·less·ly** *adv* — **mer·ci·less·ness** *n*

mer·cu·ric \ˌmər-'kyu̇r-ik\ *adj* : of, relating to, or containing mercury ⟨a *mercuric* compound⟩

mer·cu·ry \'mər-kyə-rē\ *n, pl* **mer·cu·ries**

---

j job   ng sing   ō low   ȯ moth   ȯi coin   th thin   <u>th</u> this   ü boot   u̇ foot   y you   yü few   yu̇ furious   zh vision

1 : a heavy silver-white metallic chemical element that is liquid at ordinary temperatures **2** : the column of mercury in a thermometer or barometer **3** *cap* : the planet that is nearest the sun and has a diameter of about 2900 miles

mer·cy \'mər-sē\ *n, pl* **mer·cies** **1** : kind and gentle treatment of an offender, an opponent, or some unfortunate person **2** : a kind sympathetic disposition : willingness to forgive, spare, or help **3** : BLESSING ⟨the *mercies* of God⟩ **4** : a fortunate circumstance ⟨it's a *mercy* that he arrived in time⟩

mere \'miər\ *adj, superlative* **mer·est** : nothing more than : SIMPLE ⟨*mere* rumors⟩

mere·ly \'miər-lē\ *adv* : SIMPLY, ONLY

mer·gan·ser \mər-'gan-sər\ *n* : a fish-eating wild duck with a slender hooked beak and usually a crested head

merge \'mərj\ *vb* **merged; merg·ing** **1** : to be or cause to be swallowed up or absorbed in something else **2** : COMBINE, UNITE

merg·er \'mər-jər\ *n* : a combination of two or more business concerns into one

me·rid·i·an \mə-'rid-ē-ən\ *n* **1** : the highest point attained **2** : an imaginary semicircle on the earth reaching from north to south pole and passing through any particular place between **3** : a representation of a meridian on a map or globe numbered according to degrees of longitude

me·ringue \mə-'rang\ *n* **1** : a mixture of beaten white of egg and sugar put on pies or cakes and browned **2** : a shell made of baked meringue and filled with fruit or ice cream

me·ri·no \mə-'rē-nō\ *n, pl* **me·ri·nos** **1** : a sheep of a breed noted for production of a heavy fleece of white fine wool **2** : a fine soft fabric resembling cashmere **3** : a fine wool and cotton yarn

merino 1

¹mer·it \'mer-ət\ *n* **1** : the condition or fact of deserving well or ill ⟨each according to his *merit*⟩ **2** : WORTH, EXCELLENCE ⟨a suggestion having considerable *merit*⟩ **3** : a quality worthy of praise : VIRTUE ⟨the *merit* of honesty⟩

²merit *vb* : DESERVE, EARN

mer·i·to·ri·ous \,mer-ə-'tōr-ē-əs\ *adj* : deserving reward or honor : PRAISEWORTHY — **mer·i·to·ri·ous·ly** *adv*

mer·maid \'mər-,mād\ *n* : an imaginary sea creature usually represented with a woman's body and a fish's tail

mer·man \'mər-,man\ *n, pl* **mer·men** \-,men\ : an imaginary sea creature usually represented with a man's body and a fish's tail

mer·ri·ment \'mer-i-mənt\ *n* : GAIETY, MIRTH

mer·ry \'mer-ē\ *adj* **mer·ri·er; mer·ri·est** **1** : full of good humor and good spirits : JOYOUS **2** : marked by gaiety or festivity ⟨a *merry* Christmas⟩ — **mer·ri·ly** \'mer-ə-lē\ *adv*

mer·ry–go–round \'mer-ē-gō-,raund\ *n* : a circular revolving platform fitted with seats and figures of animals on which people sit for a ride

merry-go-round

mer·ry·mak·er \'mer-ē-,mā-kər\ *n* : one engaging in merrymaking

mer·ry·mak·ing \'mer-ē-,mā-king\ *n* **1** : merry activity **2** : a festive occasion : PARTY

me·sa \'mā-sə\ *n* : a flat-topped hill or small plateau with steep sides

mesdames *pl of* MADAM *or of* MADAME

mesdemoiselles *pl of* MADEMOISELLE

¹mesh \'mesh\ *n* **1** : one of the spaces enclosed by the threads of a net or the wires of a sieve or screen **2** : NET, NETWORK **3** : the coming or fitting together of the teeth of two sets of gears

²mesh *vb* **1** : to catch in or as if in a mesh : ENTANGLE **2** : to fit together : INTERLOCK ⟨gear teeth that *mesh*⟩

Mes·o·zo·ic \,mez-ə-'zō-ik, ,mes-\ *n* : an era of geological history that extends from the Paleozoic to the Cenozoic and is marked by the existence of dinosaurs and by the appearance of the first birds and mammals and of flowering plants

mes·quite \məs-'kēt\ *n* : a spiny shrub or small tree of the southwestern United States and Mexico that is related to the clovers

¹mess \'mes\ *n* **1** : a dish of soft or liquid food **2** : a group of people (as military personnel) who regularly eat together **3** : the meal eaten by a mess **4** : a state of confusion or disorder ⟨left things in a *mess*⟩

²mess *vb* **1** : to take meals with a mess **2** : to make dirty or untidy ⟨*messed* the place up⟩ **3** : BUNGLE **4** : PUTTER

mes·sage \'mes-ij\ *n* **1** : a communication in writing, in speech, or by signals **2** : a messenger's errand

mes·sen·ger \'mes-n-jər\ *n* : one that carries a message or does an errand

mess·y \'mes-ē\ *adj* **mess·i·er; mess·i·est** : UNTIDY — **mess·i·ly** \'mes-ə-lē\ *adv* — **mess·i·ness** \'mes-ē-nəs\ *n*

met *past of* MEET

met·a·bol·ic \,met-ə-'bäl-ik\ *adj* : of or relating to metabolism — **met·a·bol·i·cal·ly** \-i-kə-lē\ *adv*

me·tab·o·lism \mə-'tab-ə-ˌliz-əm\ *n* : the processes by which a living being uses food to obtain energy and build tissue and disposes of outworn or waste material

¹met·al \'met-l\ *n* **1** : a substance (as gold, tin, copper, or bronze) that has a more or less shiny appearance, is a good conductor of electricity and heat, and is usually capable of being made into a wire or hammered into a thin sheet **2** : a chemical element (as iron) that shows the properties of a metal as distinguished from an alloy (as bronze) **3** : TEMPER, METTLE ⟨a man of stern *metal*⟩

²metal *adj* : made of metal

me·tal·lic \mə-'tal-ik\ *adj* **1** : of, relating to, or being a metal **2** : containing or made of metal

met·al·lur·gi·cal \ˌmet-l-'ər-ji-kəl\ *adj* : of or relating to metallurgy

met·al·lur·gy \'met-l-ˌər-jē\ *n* : the science of extracting metals from their ores and preparing them for use

met·a·mor·phic \ˌmet-ə-'mȯr-fik\ *adj* : formed by the action of pressure, heat, and water with a resulting more compact and crystalline form ⟨a *metamorphic* rock⟩

met·a·mor·pho·sis \ˌmet-ə-'mȯr-fə-səs\ *n*, *pl* **met·a·mor·pho·ses** \-fə-ˌsēz\ : a sudden and drastic change especially in appearance or structure ⟨*metamorphosis* of a caterpillar into a butterfly⟩

met·a·phor \'met-ə-ˌfȯr\ *n* : a figure of speech in which a word denoting one object is used in place of another to suggest a likeness between them (as in "the ship plows the sea")

mete \'mēt\ *vb* **met·ed; met·ing** : ALLOT ⟨*mete* out punishment⟩

me·te·or \'mēt-ē-ər\ *n* : one of the small particles of matter in the solar system observable directly only when it enters the earth's atmosphere where friction may cause it to glow and form a streak of light

me·te·or·ic \ˌmēt-ē-'ȯr-ik\ *adj* **1** : of or relating to a meteor or group of meteors **2** : resembling a meteor in speed or in sudden and temporary brilliance ⟨a *meteoric* career⟩

me·te·or·ite \'mēt-ē-ə-ˌrīt\ *n* : a meteor that reaches the surface of the earth

me·te·o·rol·o·gist \ˌmēt-ē-ə-'räl-ə-jəst\ *n* : a specialist in meteorology

me·te·o·rol·o·gy \ˌmēt-ē-ə-'räl-ə-jē\ *n* : a science that deals with the atmosphere and with weather and weather forecasting

¹me·ter \'mēt-ər\ *n* **1** : a systematic rhythm in poetry **2** : the basic rhythmical pattern in music

²meter *n* : a measure of length that is equal to 39.37 inches and is the basis of the metric system

³meter *n* : an instrument for measuring and sometimes recording the amount of something ⟨light *meter*⟩ ⟨gas *meter*⟩

-m·et·er \m-ət-ər\ *n suffix* : instrument or means of measuring ⟨baro*meter*⟩

meth·od \'meth-əd\ *n* [from Greek *methodos*, literally, "pursuit after", from *meta-* "after", "in search of" and *hodos* "way"] **1** : a regular way of doing something ⟨a *method* of teaching⟩ **2** : orderly arrangement : REGULARITY ⟨a pupil whose work lacks *method*⟩

me·thod·i·cal \mə-'thäd-i-kəl\ *adj* **1** : characterized by or performed or arranged by method or order **2** : habitually following a method : SYSTEMATIC — **me·thod·i·cal·ly** *adv*

met·ric \'met-rik\ *adj* **1** : of or relating to measurement **2** : of or relating to the metric system

-met·ric \'met-rik\ *or* **-met·ri·cal** \'met-ri-kəl\ *adj suffix* **1** : of, employing, or obtained by such a meter ⟨baro*metric*⟩ **2** : of or relating to such an art, process, or science of measuring ⟨geo*metric*⟩

met·ri·cal \'met-ri-kəl\ *adj* **1** : of or relating to meter (as in poetry or music) **2** : METRIC

metric system *n* : a decimal system of weights and measures in which the meter is the unit of length and the kilogram is the unit of weight

met·ro·nome \'met-rə-ˌnōm\ *n* : an instrument that produces a regularly repeated tick to help a music pupil play in exact time

me·trop·o·lis \mə-'träp-ə-ləs\ *n* **1** : the chief or capital city of a country, state, or region **2** : a large or important city

met·ro·pol·i·tan \ˌmet-rə-'päl-ət-n\ *adj* : of, relating to, or characteristic of a metropolis ⟨in the *metropolitan* area⟩

metronome

met·tle \'met-l\ *n* : SPIRIT, COURAGE — **on one's mettle** : challenged or aroused to do one's best

¹mew \'myü\ *vb* : to utter a meow or a similar sound ⟨*mewing* sea gulls⟩

²mew *n* : MEOW

mewl \'myül\ *vb* : to cry weakly : WHIMPER

¹Mex·i·can \'mek-si-kən\ *adj* : of or relating to Mexico or the Mexicans

²Mexican *n* : a native or inhabitant of Mexico

mi \'mē\ *n* : the third note of the musical scale

mi·ca \'mī-kə\ *n* : a mineral that readily separates into very thin transparent sheets

mice *pl of* MOUSE

micr- *or* **micro-** *prefix* **1** : small : minute

⟨*micro*film⟩   **2** : enlarging : magnifying or amplifying ⟨*micro*phone⟩ ⟨*micro*scope⟩ **3** : one millionth part of a specified unit ⟨*micro*gram⟩

mi·crobe \'mī-ˌkrōb\ *n* : GERM, MICRO-ORGANISM

mi·cro·film \'mī-krə-ˌfilm\ *n* : a film bearing a photographic record (as of printing or a drawing) that is of smaller size than the original matter

mi·crom·e·ter \mī-'kräm-ət-ər\ *n* **1** : an instrument used with a telescope or microscope for measuring very small distances **2** : MICROMETER CALIPER

micrometer caliper *n* : an instrument having a spindle moved by fine screw threads for making precise measurements

micrometer caliper

mi·cro·or·gan·ism \ˌmī-krō-'òr-gə-ˌniz-əm\ *n* : an organism (as a bacterium) of microscopic or less than microscopic size

mi·cro·phone \'mī-krə-ˌfōn\ *n* : an instrument in which sound is converted into an electrical effect for the purpose of transmitting or recording (as in radio, television, or tape recording)

mi·cro·scope \'mī-krə-ˌskōp\ *n* : an instrument with a lens used to aid a person in seeing an extremely small object by enlarging the image of it

mi·cro·scop·ic \ˌmī-krə-'skäp-ik\ *adj* **1** : of, relating to, or conducted with the microscope ⟨a *microscopic* examination⟩ **2** : so small as to be visible only through a microscope : very tiny — **mi·cro·scop·i·cal·ly** \-i-kə-lē\ *adv*

microscope

¹mid \'mid\ *adj* **1** : being the part in the middle ⟨in *mid* ocean⟩ ⟨*mid*-August⟩ **2** : occupying a middle position ⟨the *mid* finger⟩

²mid *prep* : AMID

mid·day \'mid-ˌdā\ *n* : NOON

¹mid·dle \'mid-l\ *adj* **1** : equally distant from the ends : CENTRAL ⟨the *middle* house in the row⟩ **2** : being at neither extreme ⟨of *middle* size⟩

²middle *n* : the middle part, point, or position : CENTER ⟨in the *middle* of the room⟩

middle age *n* : the period of life from about forty to sixty years of age — **mid·dle–aged** \ mid-l-'ājd\ *adj*

Middle Ages *n pl* : the period of time between ancient and modern times : the period from about A.D. 500 to 1500

mid·dy \'mid-ē\ *n, pl* **mid·dies** **1** : MIDSHIP-MAN **2** : a loose blouse for women and children with a collar cut wide and square in the back

midge \'mij\ *n* : a very small fly or gnat

midg·et \'mij-ət\ *n* : one (as a person) that is much smaller than usual or normal

middy 2

mid·most \'mid-ˌmōst\ *adj* : being in the exact middle

mid·night \'mid-ˌnīt\ *n* : the middle of the night : twelve o'clock at night

mid·rib \'mid-ˌrib\ *n* : the main or central vein of a leaf

mid·riff \'mid-ˌrif\ *n* **1** : DIAPHRAGM 1 **2** : the middle region of the human torso

mid·ship·man \'mid-ˌship-mən\ *n, pl* **mid·ship·men** \-mən\ : a student naval officer

¹midst \'midst\ *n* **1** : the inside or central part : MIDDLE **2** : the condition of being surrounded ⟨in the *midst* of dangers⟩

²midst *prep* : in the midst of

mid·sum·mer \'mid-'səm-ər\ *n* **1** : the middle of summer **2** : the period about June 22

mid·way \'mid-ˌwā, -'wā\ *adv (or adj)* : in the middle of the way or distance : HALFWAY

mid·week \'mid-ˌwēk\ *n* : the middle of the week

mid·win·ter \'mid-'wint-ər\ *n* **1** : the middle of winter **2** : the period about December 22

mid·year \'mid-ˌyiər\ *n* **1** : the middle of a year **2** : an examination (as in a college) held at midyear

mien \'mēn\ *n* : the manner, looks, or bearing of a person : AIR ⟨a man of kindly *mien*⟩

¹might \'mīt\ *past of* MAY — used as a helping verb to express remote possibility ⟨it *might* rain, but I doubt it⟩

²might \'mīt\ *n* : power to do something : FORCE

might·n't \'mīt-nt\ : might not

¹might·y \'mīt-ē\ *adj* **might·i·er; might·i·est** **1** : POWERFUL, STRONG ⟨a *mighty* nation⟩ **2** : done by might : showing great power ⟨*mighty* deeds⟩ **3** : great in influence or size ⟨a *mighty* famine⟩ — **might·i·ly** \'mīt-l-ē\ *adv*

²mighty *adv* : VERY, EXTREMELY ⟨he was *mighty* proud⟩

mi·grant \'mī-grənt\ *n* : one (as a bird) that migrates

mi·grate \'mī-ˌgrāt\ *vb* **mi·grat·ed; mi·grat·ing** **1** : to move from one country or region to another **2** : to pass usually periodically from one region to another ⟨birds *migrating* south for the winter⟩

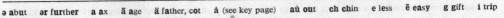

mi·gra·tion \mī-'grā-shən\ *n* **1** : the act of migrating **2** : a group of individuals that are migrating

mi·gra·to·ry \'mī-grə-ˌtōr-ē\ *adj* : of, relating to, or characterized by migration ⟨*migratory* workers⟩ ⟨*migratory* birds⟩

milch \'milk, 'milch\ *adj* : giving milk : kept for milking ⟨a *milch* cow⟩

mild \'mīld\ *adj* **1** : gentle in nature or behavior **2** : moderate in action or effect : not strong ⟨a *mild* drug⟩ ⟨*mild* weather⟩ — **mild·ly** *adv* — **mild·ness** *n*

¹mil·dew \'mil-ˌdü, -ˌdyü\ *n* **1** : a thin whitish growth of fungus on decaying matter or living plants **2** : a fungus that grows as a mildew

²mildew *vb* : to become covered with or affected by mildew

mile \'mīl\ *n* **1** : a measure of distance (**statute mile**) equal to 5280 feet **2** : a measure of distance (**geographical mile** or **nautical mile**) equal to about 6076 feet

mile·age \'mī-lij\ *n* **1** : an allowance for traveling expenses at a certain rate per mile **2** : distance or distance covered in miles **3** : the number of miles that something (as a car or tire) will travel before wearing out

mile·post \'mīl-ˌpōst\ *n* : a post showing the distance in miles to a stated place

mile·stone \'mīl-ˌstōn\ *n* **1** : a stone serving as a milepost **2** : an important point in progress or development

milestone

¹mil·i·tary \'mil-ə-ˌter-ē\ *adj* **1** : of or relating to soldiers, the army, or war ⟨*military* drill⟩ **2** : carried on by soldiers : supported by armed force ⟨a *military* government⟩

²military *n*, *pl* **military** : members of the armed forces

mi·li·tia \mə-'lish-ə\ *n* : a body of citizens with some military training but not called into active service except in emergencies

¹milk \'milk\ *n* **1** : a whitish liquid secreted by the breasts or udder of a female mammal as food for her young **2** : a liquid (as a plant juice) resembling milk

²milk *vb* : to draw off the milk of (as by pressing or sucking) ⟨*milk* a cow⟩

milk·man \'milk-ˌman, -mən\ *n*, *pl* **milk·men** \-ˌmen\ : a man who sells or delivers milk

milk shake *n* : a drink made of milk, a flavoring syrup, and sometimes ice cream shaken or mixed thoroughly

milk tooth *n* : one of the first and temporary teeth that in man number twenty

milk·weed \'milk-ˌwēd\ *n* : any of a group of plants with milky juice and flowers in dense clusters

milk·y \'mil-kē\ *adj* **milk·i·er**; **milk·i·est** **1** : resembling milk in color or consistency **2** : full of or containing milk — **milk·i·ness** *n*

Milky Way *n* **1** : a broad band of light that stretches across the sky and is caused by the light of a vast number of faint stars **2** : MILKY WAY GALAXY

Milky Way galaxy *n* : the galaxy of which the sun and the solar system are a part and which contains the stars that comprise the Milky Way

¹mill \'mil\ *n* **1** : a building in which grain is ground into flour **2** : a machine used in treating (as by grinding, crushing, stamping, cutting, or finishing) raw material **3** : a factory using machines ⟨a steel *mill*⟩ ⟨a cotton *mill*⟩

²mill *vb* **1** : to grind into flour or powder **2** : to shape or finish by means of a rotary cutter **3** : to give a raised rim to (a coin) **4** : to move about in a circle or in a disorderly mass ⟨cattle *milling* about⟩

³mill *n* : one tenth of a cent

mill·er \'mil-ər\ *n* **1** : a person who works in or runs a flour mill **2** : a moth whose wings seem to be covered with flour or dust

mil·let \'mil-ət\ *n* : an annual cereal and forage grass with clusters of small usually white seeds

milli- *prefix* : thousandth ⟨*milli*meter⟩

mil·li·gram \'mil-ə-ˌgram\ *n* : a metric unit of weight equal to 1/1000 gram

mil·li·me·ter \'mil-ə-ˌmēt-ər\ *n* : a metric unit of length equal to 1/1000 meter

mil·li·ner \'mil-ə-nər\ *n* : a person who makes, trims, or sells women's hats

¹mil·lion \'mil-yən\ *n* **1** : ten times 100,000 **2** : a very large number ⟨*millions* of mosquitoes⟩

²million *adj* : being 1,000,000

mil·lion·aire \ˌmil-yən-'aər\ *n* : a person who is worth a million dollars or more

¹mil·lionth \'mil-yənth\ *adj* : being last in a series of a million

²millionth *n* : number 1,000,000 in a series

mil·li·pede \'mil-ə-ˌpēd\ *n* : a long-bodied animal related to the centipedes that has a single pair of legs on each body segment

mill·race \'mil-ˌrās\ *n* **1** : a canal in which water flows to and from a mill wheel **2** : the current which drives a mill wheel

mill·stone \'mil-ˌstōn\ *n* **1** : either of two circular stones used for grinding grain **2** : a crushing burden

mill wheel *n* : a waterwheel that drives a mill

mim·e·o·graph \'mim-ē-ə-ˌgraf\ *n* : a machine for making copies of typewritten, written, or drawn matter by means of stencils

¹mim·ic \'mim-ik\ *adj* 1 : IMITATIVE 2 : not real : IMITATION, MOCK ⟨a *mimic* battle⟩

²mimic *n* : one that mimics

³mimic *vb* **mim·icked; mim·ick·ing** 1 : to imitate very closely 2 : to ridicule by imitating ⟨*mimic* a person's speech⟩ **syn** see IMITATE

min·a·ret \ˌmin-ə-'ret\ *n* : a tall slender tower of a mosque from a balcony of which the people are called to prayer

minaret

mince \'mins\ *vb* **minced; minc·ing** 1 : to cut or chop very fine ⟨*minced* ham⟩ 2 : to act or speak in an unnaturally dainty way ⟨*minced* her words⟩

mince·meat \'mins-ˌmēt\ *n* : a mixture of finely chopped and cooked raisins, apples, suet, spices, and sometimes meat that is used chiefly as a filling for pie (**mince pie**)

¹mind \'mīnd\ *n* 1 : MEMORY ⟨out of sight, out of *mind*⟩ 2 : the part of a person that feels, perceives, thinks, wills, and especially reasons ⟨he has a fine *mind*⟩ 3 : INTENTION ⟨changed her *mind*⟩ 4 : OPINION ⟨spoke his *mind*⟩

²mind *vb* 1 : REMEMBER 2 : to pay attention to : HEED ⟨*mind* what you're doing⟩ 3 : OBEY ⟨*minds* her parents⟩ 4 : to be bothered about ⟨never *mind* that mistake⟩ 5 : to object to : DISLIKE ⟨I don't *mind* the cold⟩ 6 : to take charge of : TEND ⟨*mind* the children⟩

mind·ed \'mīn-dəd\ *adj* 1 : having a specified kind of mind ⟨small-*minded*⟩ 2 : DISPOSED, INCLINED

mind·ful \'mīnd-fəl\ *adj* : keeping in mind : HEEDFUL

¹mine \'mīn\ *pron* 1 : one or the one belonging to me 2 : some or the ones belonging to me

²mine *n* 1 : a pit or tunnel from which minerals (as coal, gold, or diamonds) are taken 2 : a hole that is dug in the earth under an enemy position and contains an explosive charge 3 : an explosive buried in the ground and set to explode when disturbed (as by an enemy soldier or vehicle) 4 : an explosive placed in a case and sunk in the water to sink enemy ships 5 : a rich source of supply ⟨a *mine* of information⟩

³mine *vb* **mined; min·ing** 1 : to dig a mine 2 : to obtain from a mine ⟨*mine* coal⟩ 3 : to work in a mine 4 : to dig or form mines under a place 5 : to lay military mines in or

under ⟨*mine* a field⟩ ⟨*mine* a harbor⟩ — **min·er** *n*

¹min·er·al \'min-ə-rəl\ *n* 1 : a naturally occurring usually crystalline substance (as diamond or quartz) that results from processes other than those of plants and animals 2 : a naturally occurring substance (as ore, coal, petroleum, natural gas, or water) obtained for man's use usually from the ground 3 : a chemical compound not containing carbon

²mineral *adj* 1 : of or relating to a mineral 2 : containing gases or mineral salts ⟨*mineral* water⟩

min·gle \'ming-gəl\ *vb* **min·gled; min·gling** 1 : to mix or be mixed so that the components can still be distinguished : COMBINE 2 : to come together in a company or group : ASSOCIATE **syn** see MIX

¹min·i·a·ture \'min-ē-ə-ˌchùr\ *n* 1 : a copy on a much reduced scale 2 : a very small portrait especially on ivory or metal

²miniature *adj* : very small : represented on a small scale

min·i·mize \'min-ə-ˌmīz\ *vb* **min·i·mized; min·i·miz·ing** : to make as small as possible ⟨*minimize* the risks of an undertaking⟩

¹min·i·mum \'min-ə-məm\ *n*, *pl* **min·i·mums** *or* **min·i·ma** \-mə\ : the lowest quantity or amount

²minimum *adj* : as low as possible in amount or degree ⟨*minimum* time needed⟩

min·ing \'mī-ning\ *n* : the process or business of working mines

¹min·is·ter \'min-əs-tər\ *n* 1 : a Protestant clergyman : PASTOR 2 : a high government-official at the head of a department of government activities ⟨*minister* of war⟩ 3 : a person who represents his government in a foreign country

²minister *vb* : to give aid or service ⟨*minister* to the sick⟩

min·is·try \'min-əs-trē\ *n*, *pl* **min·is·tries** 1 : the act of ministering 2 : the office or duties of a minister 3 : a body of ministers 4 : a government department headed by a minister

mink \'mingk\ *n* : the soft rich typically brown fur of a slender animal that resembles the related weasels and has partly webbed feet and a bushy tail

min·now \'min-ō\ *n* 1 : any of various small freshwater fishes (as a shiner) related to the carps 2 : a fish that resembles a true minnow

¹mi·nor \'mī-nər\ *adj* : less in size, importance, or value : SMALLER, INFERIOR

²minor *n* : a person who is under twenty-one years of age

mi·nor·i·ty \mə-'nȯr-ət-ē\ *n, pl* **mi·nor·i·ties**
1 : the condition of being a minor **2** : a
number less than half of a total **3** : a part of a
population differing from other groups in
some characteristics and sometimes dis-
criminated against

min·strel \'min-strəl\ *n* **1** : a medieval singer
of verses often to the accompaniment of a
harp **2** : one of a group of entertainers
usually blacked in imitation of Negroes

¹mint \'mint\ *n* **1** : a place where metals are
made into coins **2** : a great amount ⟨made a
mint of money⟩

²mint *vb* **1** : COIN ⟨*mint* silver dollars⟩ **2** : to
make into coin ⟨*mint* silver⟩

³mint *n* **1** : any of a group of mostly aromatic
fragrant herbs and shrubs (as catnip or
peppermint) with square stems **2** : a piece of
candy flavored with mint

min·u·end \'min-yə-,wend\ *n* : a number
from which another number is to be subtracted

min·u·et \,min-yə-'wet\ *n* **1** : a slow graceful
dance marked by balancing, bowing, and toe
pointing **2** : a piece of music suitable for a
minuet

¹mi·nus \'mī-nəs\ *prep* **1** : diminished by
: LESS ⟨seven *minus* four is three⟩ **2** : WITHOUT
⟨*minus* his hat⟩

²minus *adj* : falling low in a specified range ⟨a
grade of C *minus*⟩

minus sign *n* : a sign — used especially in
mathematics to indicate subtraction (as in
$8-6=2$) or a negative quantity (as in $-10°$)

¹min·ute \'min-ət\ *n* **1** : the sixtieth part of
an hour or of a degree : sixty seconds **2** : MO-
MENT ⟨wait a *minute*⟩ **3** *pl* : a brief record of
the proceedings of a meeting ⟨the *minutes* of
the last meeting were read⟩

²mi·nute \mī-'nüt, mə-, -'nyüt\ *adj* **mi·nut·er**;
mi·nut·est **1** : very small : TINY **2** : paying
attention to small details ⟨a *minute* descrip-
tion⟩ — **mi·nute·ly** *adv*

min·ute·man \'min-ət-,man\ *n, pl* **min·ute-
men** \-,men\ : a member of a group of armed
men pledged to be ready to fight at a minute's
notice immediately before and during the
American Revolution

mir·a·cle \'mir-ə-kəl\ *n* **1** : an event or
effect that cannot be explained by any known
law of nature **2** : something so rare or unusual as to seem like a miracle

mi·rac·u·lous \mə-'rak-yə-ləs\ *adj* **1** : of the
nature of a miracle : SUPERNATURAL **2** : resembling a miracle : MARVELOUS — **mi·rac·u-
lous·ly** *adv*

mi·rage \mə-'räzh\ *n* : an effect that is sometimes seen at sea, in the desert, or over a hot

pavement and has the appearance of a pool
of water or a mirror in which distant objects
are seen inverted

¹mire \'mīr\ *n* : heavy deep mud

²mire *vb* **mired; mir·ing** : to stick or cause to
stick fast in mire

¹mir·ror \'mir-ər\ *n* **1** : a glass backed with
some reflecting substance (as mercury) **2** : a
polished surface that reflects an image
3 : something that reflects a true likeness or
gives a true description

²mirror *vb* : to reflect in or as if in a mirror

mirth \'mərth\ *n* : gladness or gaiety as
shown by or accompanied with laughter

mirth·ful \'mərth-fəl\ *adj* : full of or expressing mirth — **mirth·ful·ly** *adv*

mis- *prefix* **1** : badly : wrongly ⟨*mis*judge⟩
: unfavorably ⟨*mis*esteem⟩ : in a suspicious
manner ⟨*mis*doubt⟩ **2** : bad : wrong ⟨*mis*-
deed⟩ **3** : opposite or lack of ⟨*mis*trust⟩

mis·ad·ven·ture \,mis-əd-'ven-chər\ *n* : MIS-
FORTUNE, MISHAP

mis·be·have \,mis-bi-'hāv\ *vb* **mis·be·haved;
mis·be·hav·ing** : to behave badly

mis·car·ry \mis-'kar-ē\ *vb* **mis·car·ried; mis-
car·ry·ing** : to go wrong : FAIL ⟨the plan
miscarried⟩

mis·cel·la·ne·ous \,mis-ə-'lā-nē-əs\ *adj* : consisting of many things of different sorts
: MIXED

syn MISCELLANEOUS, ASSORTED, MOTLEY all
refer to variety among things that make up a
group or collection. MISCELLANEOUS suggests a
mixture of many kinds which shows almost no
signs of selection and which very often is a
result of chance ⟨the teacher's desk was a
storehouse for the *miscellaneous* supplies we
left behind on our desks⟩ ASSORTED is used to
describe a mixture that was made by choice,
and stresses a selection that often was intended to include a wide variety ⟨we like
assorted chocolates better than all of one
kind⟩ ⟨the crayons come in sixteen *assorted*
colors⟩ MOTLEY is a fairly derogatory term
that suggests a mixture that is not only wildly
variegated in makeup ⟨a *motley* collection of
stray and abandoned animals⟩ but is also composed of inferior or inadequate units ⟨a
motley crew of ballplayers that lost every
game⟩

mis·chance \mis-'chans\ *n* **1** : bad luck
2 : a piece of bad luck : MISHAP

mis·chief \'mis-chəf\ *n* **1** : injury or damage
caused by human agency **2** : conduct that
causes annoyance or trouble ⟨keep out of
mischief⟩

mis·chie·vous \'mis-chə-vəs\ *adj* **1** : causing mischief : intended to do harm ⟨*mischievous* gossip⟩ **2** : causing or inclined to cause petty injury or annoyance ⟨a *mischievous* youngster⟩ **3** : showing a spirit of irresponsible playfulness ⟨*mischievous* behavior⟩ — **mis·chie·vous·ly** *adv* — **mis·chie·vous·ness** *n*

¹mis·con·duct \mis-'kän-,dəkt\ *n* : wrong conduct : bad behavior

²mis·con·duct \,mis-kən-'dəkt\ *vb* : to manage badly

mis·cre·ant \'mis-krē-ənt\ *n* : VILLAIN, RASCAL

mis·deal \mis-'dēl\ *vb* **mis·dealt** \-'delt\; **mis·deal·ing** \-'dē-ling\ : to deal incorrectly or wrongly ⟨*misdeal* cards⟩

mis·deed \mis-'dēd\ *n* : a bad deed

mi·ser \'mī-zər\ *n* : a mean grasping person who lives miserably in order to hoard his money

mis·er·a·ble \'miz-ə-rə-bəl\ *adj* **1** : wretchedly unsatisfactory ⟨a *miserable* dinner⟩ **2** : causing great discomfort ⟨a *miserable* cold⟩ **3** : very unhappy : WRETCHED — **mis·er·a·bly** \-blē\ *adv*

mi·ser·ly \'mī-zər-lē\ *adj* : of, relating to, or characteristic of a miser **syn** see STINGY

mis·er·y \'miz-ə-rē\ *n, pl* **mis·er·ies** : suffering or distress due to poverty, pain, or unhappiness : WRETCHEDNESS

mis·fit \mis-'fit, 'mis-,fit\ *n* **1** : something that fits badly **2** : a person poorly adjusted to his environment

mis·for·tune \mis-'fòr-chən\ *n* **1** : bad luck **2** : an unfortunate condition or event

mis·giv·ing \mis-'giv-ing\ *n* : a feeling of distrust or doubt especially about what is going to happen

mis·hap \'mis-,hap\ *n* : an unfortunate accident

mis·judge \mis-'jəj\ *vb* **mis·judged; mis·judg·ing** : to judge incorrectly or unjustly

mis·lay \mis-'lā\ *vb* **mis·laid** \-'lād\; **mis·lay·ing** : to put in a place later forgotten : LOSE **syn** see MISPLACE

mis·lead \mis-'lēd\ *vb* **mis·led** \-'led\; **mis·lead·ing** **1** : to lead in a wrong direction : lead astray **2** : to lead into error : DECEIVE

mis·place \mis-'plās\ *vb* **mis·placed; mis·plac·ing** **1** : to put in a wrong place or position ⟨*misplace* a comma⟩ **2** : MISLAY

syn MISPLACE, MISLAY both mean to put in the wrong place. MISPLACE may mean to put an object somewhere other than its usual location ⟨someone seems to have *misplaced* the maps, as they're not here⟩ but usually suggests an original setting or fixing of some-

thing where it should not be ⟨we trusted him but discovered our confidence was *misplaced;* he turned out to be a spy⟩ MISLAY stresses not only placing an object in the wrong location but also forgetting where it has been put ⟨he started late because he had *mislaid* his car keys⟩

mis·pro·nounce \,mis-prə-'naùns\ *vb* **mis·pro·nounced; mis·pro·nounc·ing** : to pronounce in a way regarded as incorrect

mis·pro·nun·ci·a·tion \,mis-prə-,nən-sē-'ā-shən\ *n* : incorrect pronunciation

mis·read \mis-'rēd\ *vb* **mis·read** \-'red\; **mis·read·ing** \-'rēd-ing\ **1** : to read incorrectly **2** : MISUNDERSTAND

mis·rep·re·sent \,mis-,rep-ri-'zent\ *vb* : to give a false or misleading representation of

¹miss \'mis\ *vb* **1** : to fail to hit, catch, reach, or get ⟨*miss* a target⟩ ⟨*miss* the ball⟩ **2** : ESCAPE, AVOID ⟨*missed* being hurt by a narrow margin⟩ **3** : to fail to have or attend : OMIT ⟨*missed* his lunch⟩ **4** : to be aware of the absence of : feel the want or need of ⟨*miss* an absent friend⟩

²miss *n* : failure to hit or catch

³miss *n* **1** — used as a title before the name of an unmarried woman or girl ⟨*Miss* Doe⟩ **2** : a young woman or girl ⟨*misses'* clothing⟩

mis·shap·en \mis-'shā-pən\ *adj* : DEFORMED

mis·sile \'mis-əl\ *n* [from Latin *missilis* "capable of being thrown", from *miss-*, stem of *mittere* "to throw", "to send"] **1** : an object (as a stone, arrow, bullet, or rocket) that is dropped, thrown, projected, or launched usually so as to strike something at a distance **2** : a missile whose course may be changed during flight

miss·ing \'mis-ing\ *adj* **1** : ABSENT **2** : LOST

mis·sion \'mish-ən\ *n* **1** : a group of missionaries **2** : a place where the work of missionaries is carried on **3** : a group of persons sent by a government to conduct negotiations in a foreign country **4** : a task or function assigned or undertaken

¹mis·sion·ar·y \'mish-ə-,ner-ē\ *adj* : of or relating to religious missions ⟨a *missionary* society⟩

²missionary *n, pl* **mis·sion·ar·ies** : one sent to spread a religious faith among unbelievers

mis·sive \'mis-iv\ *n* : a written communication : LETTER

mis·spell \mis-'spel\ *vb* : to spell incorrectly

mis·step \mis-'step\ *n* **1** : a wrong step **2** : MISTAKE, SLIP

¹mist \'mist\ *n* **1** : particles of water floating in the air or falling as fine rain **2** : something that blurs or hinders vision : HAZE, FILM

ə abut ər further a ax ā age ä father, cot à (see key page) aù out ch chin e less ē easy g gift i trip I life

²**mist** *vb* **1** : to be or become misty **2** : to become or cause to become dim or blurred ⟨eyes *misted* with tears⟩ **3** : to cover with mist ⟨the windshield was *misted* over⟩

¹**mis·take** \mə-'stāk\ *vb* **mis·took** \mə-'stu̇k\; **mis·tak·en** \mə-'stā-kən\; **mis·tak·ing** **1** : to take in a wrong sense : MISUNDERSTAND **2** : to fail to recognize correctly ⟨*mistook* him for someone else⟩

²**mistake** *n* **1** : a wrong judgment **2** : a wrong action : BLUNDER **syn** *see* ERROR

mis·tak·en \mə-'stā-kən\ *adj* **1** : being in error : having a wrong opinion : judging wrongly ⟨*mistaken* about the time⟩ **2** : WRONG, INCORRECT ⟨a *mistaken* idea⟩ — **mis·tak·en·ly** *adv*

mis·ter \'mis-tər\ *n* **1** — used as a title before the name of a man or the designation of an office and usually written *Mr.* or in the plural *Messrs.* ⟨*Mr.* Doe⟩ ⟨*Mr.* President⟩ ⟨*Messrs.* Barnum and Bailey⟩ **2** : SIR ⟨look here, *mister*⟩

mis·tle·toe \'mis-əl-ˌtō\ *n* : a green plant with waxy white berries that grows on the branches and trunks of trees

mis·treat \mis-'trēt\ *vb* : to treat badly : ABUSE

mis·tress \'mis-trəs\ *n* : a woman who has power, authority, or position like that of a master : HEAD ⟨the *mistress* of a household⟩

mistletoe

¹**mis·trust** \mis-'trəst\ *n* : lack of confidence : SUSPICION

²**mistrust** *vb* **1** : SUSPECT **2** : to lack confidence in ⟨*mistrusts* his own abilities⟩

mist·y \'mis-tē\ *adj* **mist·i·er**; **mist·i·est** **1** : full of mist ⟨a *misty* valley⟩ **2** : blurred by or as if by mist ⟨through *misty* eyes⟩ **3** : VAGUE, INDISTINCT ⟨a *misty* memory⟩ — **mist·i·ly** \-tə-lē\ *adv* — **mist·i·ness** \-tē-nəs\ *n*

mis·un·der·stand \ˌmis-ˌən-dər-'stand\ *vb* **mis·un·der·stood** \-'stu̇d\; **mis·un·der·stand·ing** **1** : to fail to understand **2** : to take in a wrong sense or way

mis·un·der·stand·ing *n* **1** : a failure to understand **2** : DISAGREEMENT, QUARREL

¹**mis·use** \mis-'yüz\ *vb* **mis·used**; **mis·us·ing** **1** : to use improperly **2** : to treat badly or cruelly : ABUSE

²**mis·use** \mis-'yüs\ *n* : incorrect or improper use ⟨*misuse* of public funds⟩

mite \'mīt\ *n* **1** : any of various tiny spiderlike animals

mite 1

often living on plants, animals, and stored foods **2** : a very small coin or sum of money **3** : a very small object or creature

mi·to·sis \mī-'tō-səs\ *n* : a process of cell division in which two new nuclei are formed each containing the original number of chromosomes

mitt \'mit\ *n* **1** : a glove that leaves the fingers uncovered **2** : MITTEN **3** : a baseball glove (as for the catcher)

mit·ten \'mit-n\ *n* : a covering for the hand and wrist without separate divisions for the fingers other than the thumb

mix \'miks\ *vb* **1** : to make into one mass by stirring together : BLEND **2** : to make by blending different things ⟨*mix* a salad dressing⟩ **3** : to become one mass through blending ⟨oil will not *mix* with water⟩ **4** : CONFUSE ⟨all *mixed* up⟩ — **mix·er** *n*

syn MIX, MINGLE, BLEND all mean to combine two or more things. MIX is the most general of these words and suggests a fairly thorough combining in which the original elements may or may not lose their individual identity ⟨*mix* blue and yellow to make green⟩ ⟨she *mixed* peas and mushrooms and added a cream sauce⟩ MINGLE refers to a loose mixing in which the elements remain distinct ⟨some bad writing *mingled* with much of excellent quality⟩ BLEND suggests a complete uniting of similar things so that the original parts cannot be separated or distinguished ⟨*blended* equal amounts of black and green tea⟩

mixed \'mikst\ *adj* **1** : made up of two or more kinds ⟨*mixed* candy⟩ **2** : made up of persons of both sexes ⟨a *mixed* quartet⟩

mixed number *n* : a number (as 1⅔) made up of a whole number and a fraction

mix·ture \'miks-chər\ *n* **1** : the act of mixing **2** : something mixed or being mixed **3** : two or more substances mixed together but not united chemically so that each remains unchanged ⟨sand and sugar form a *mixture*⟩

mix–up \'miks-ˌəp\ *n* : an instance of confusion ⟨a *mix-up* about who was to meet the train⟩

miz·zen \'miz-n\ *n* **1** : a fore-and-aft sail set on the mizzenmast **2** : MIZZENMAST

miz·zen·mast \'miz-n-ˌmast, -məst\ *n* : the mast aft or next aft of the mainmast

¹**moan** \'mōn\ *n* **1** : a low drawn-out sound showing pain or grief **2** : a sound like a moan

²**moan** *vb* **1** : to utter a moan **2** : COMPLAIN

moat \'mōt\ *n* : a deep wide ditch around the walls of a castle or fortress that is usually filled with water

¹mob \'mäb\ n [by shortening from Latin *mobile vulgus* "the fickle crowd"] **1** : the common masses of people **2** : a disorderly excited crowd

²mob vb **mobbed; mob·bing** : to crowd about and attack or annoy

mo·bile \'mō-bəl\ adj **1** : readily moved : MOVABLE ⟨*mobile* homes⟩ **2** : changing quickly in expression ⟨*mobile* features⟩

mo·bi·lize \'mō-bə-ˌlīz\ vb **mo·bi·lized; mo·bi·liz·ing** : to assemble and make ready for action

moc·ca·sin \'mäk-ə-sən\ n **1** : a soft heelless shoe with the sole and sides made of one piece **2** : a poisonous snake of the southern United States

moccasin flower n : LADY'S SLIPPER

moccasin

¹mock \'mäk\ vb **1** : to laugh at scornfully : RIDICULE **2** : to make fun of by mimicking

²mock n : an object of ridicule

³mock adj : not real : PRETENDED, SHAM ⟨*mock* grief⟩ ⟨a *mock* battle⟩

mock·er·y \'mäk-ə-rē\ n, pl **mock·er·ies 1** : the act of mocking **2** : an object of ridicule **3** : an insincere or poor imitation

mock·ing·bird \'mäk-ing-ˌbərd\ n : a songbird of the southern United States noted for its sweet song and imitations of other birds

mock orange n : SYRINGA

¹mode \'mōd\ n **1** : a particular form or variety of something **2** : a form or manner of expression : STYLE **3** : a manner of doing something ⟨*mode* of travel⟩

²mode n : a prevailing fashion or style (as of dress)

¹mod·el \'mäd-l\ n **1** : a small but exact copy of a thing **2** : a pattern or figure of something that may be made **3** : a person who sets a good example ⟨a *model* of politeness⟩ **4** : a person who poses for an artist **5** : a person who wears garments that are for sale in the presence of customers **6** : a specific type or design of a product ⟨the latest *model* of an automobile⟩

²model vb **mod·eled** or **mod·elled; mod·el·ing** or **mod·el·ling 1** : to plan or shape after a pattern ⟨a sports car *modeled* on a racing car⟩ **2** : to make a model of : MOLD ⟨*model* a dog in clay⟩ **3** : to act or serve as a model ⟨*model* for an artist⟩

³model adj **1** : worthy of being imitated ⟨a *model* student⟩ **2** : being a miniature representation ⟨a *model* airplane⟩

¹mod·er·ate \'mäd-ə-rət\ adj **1** : neither too

much nor too little : not extreme ⟨*moderate* heat⟩ **2** : neither very good nor very bad : ORDINARY ⟨*moderate* success⟩ **3** : not expensive : REASONABLE ⟨*moderate* rates⟩ **syn** see TEMPERATE — **mod·er·ate·ly** adv

²mod·er·ate \'mäd-ə-ˌrāt\ vb **mod·er·at·ed; mod·er·at·ing** : to make or become less violent or severe

mod·er·a·tion \ˌmäd-ə-'rā-shən\ n **1** : the act of moderating **2** : the condition of being moderate : the avoidance of extremes

mod·ern \'mäd-ərn\ adj **1** : of, relating to, or characteristic of the present time or times not long past ⟨*modern* machinery⟩ **2** : of the period from about 1500 ⟨*modern* history⟩

mod·ern·ize \'mäd-ərn-ˌīz\ vb **mod·ern·ized; mod·ern·iz·ing** : to make or become modern

mod·est \'mäd-əst\ adj **1** : having a moderate opinion of one's own good qualities and abilities : not boastful ⟨a *modest* winner⟩ **2** : showing moderation : not excessive ⟨a *modest* request⟩ **3** : pure and decent in thought, conduct, and dress — **mod·est·ly** adv

mod·es·ty \'mäd-əs-tē\ n : the quality of being modest

mod·i·fi·ca·tion \ˌmäd-ə-fə-'kā-shən\ n **1** : the act of modifying **2** : the result of modifying : a slightly changed form

mod·i·fi·er \'mäd-ə-ˌfī-ər\ n : a word (as an adjective or adverb) joined to another word to limit or qualify its meaning

mod·i·fy \'mäd-ə-ˌfī\ vb **mod·i·fied; mod·i·fy·ing 1** : to make changes in ⟨*modify* a plan⟩ **2** : to lower or reduce in extent or degree ⟨*modify* a punishment⟩ **3** : to limit in meaning : QUALIFY ⟨green in the phrase "green gloves" *modifies* the word *gloves*⟩

mod·u·late \'mäj-ə-ˌlāt\ vb **mod·u·lat·ed; mod·u·lat·ing 1** : to adjust or regulate to a certain proportion **2** : to tone down : SOFTEN ⟨*modulate* your voice⟩

mo·hair \'mō-ˌhaər\ n : a fabric or yarn made from the long silky hair of an Asiatic goat

Mo·ham·med·an \mō-'ham-əd-ən\, **Mo·ham·med·an·ism** var of MUHAMMADAN, MUHAMMADANISM

moist \'moist\ adj : slightly wet : DAMP — **moist·ness** n

moist·en \'mois-n\ vb : to make moist

mois·ture \'mois-chər\ n : the small amount of liquid that causes moistness : DAMPNESS

mo·lar \'mō-lər\ n : a tooth with a broad surface adapted for grinding : a back tooth

mo·las·ses \mə-'las-əz\ n : the thick brown syrup that drains from sugar as it is being manufactured

¹mold \'mōld\ n : light rich crumbly earth

containing decayed matter (as leaves or manure)

²mold *n* **1** : a hollow from which something poured in takes its shape ⟨a candle *mold*⟩ **2** : something shaped in a mold ⟨a *mold* of ice cream⟩

³mold *vb* **1** : to knead into shape ⟨*mold* loaves of bread⟩ **2** : to form in or as if in a mold ⟨*mold* butter⟩ ⟨his character was *molded* by his early life⟩

⁴mold *n* **1** : an often woolly surface growth of fungus on damp or decaying matter **2** : a fungus that forms mold

⁵mold *vb* : to become moldy

mol·der \'mōl-dər\ *vb* : to crumble into dust by natural decay

mold·ing \'mōl-ding\ *n* **1** : the act or work of a person who molds **2** : a strip of material having a shaped surface and used as a decoration (as on a wall or the edge of a table)

moldings

mold·y \'mōl-dē\ *adj* **mold·i·er; mold·i·est** : overgrown with or containing mold

¹mole \'mōl\ *n* : a small usually brown lasting spot on the skin

²mole *n* : a small burrowing animal with very soft fur and very tiny eyes

mo·lec·u·lar \mə-'lek-yə-lər\ *adj* : of or relating to a molecule

mol·e·cule \'mäl-i-ˌkyül\ *n* **1** : one of the tiniest particles of a substance that is the same as the mass of the substance ⟨a *molecule* of water⟩ **2** : a very small particle

mole·hill \'mōl-ˌhil\ *n* **1** : a little ridge of earth pushed up by moles as they burrow underground **2** : an unimportant obstacle ⟨make a mountain out of a *molehill*⟩

mo·lest \mə-'lest\ *vb* : to injure or disturb by interfering : ANNOY

mol·li·fy \'mäl-ə-ˌfī\ *vb* **mol·li·fied; mol·li·fy·ing** : CALM, APPEASE

mol·lusk \'mäl-əsk\ *n* : any of a large group of mostly water-dwelling animals (as clams, snails, and octopuses) of which the body is not divided into segments and is usually enclosed in a limy shell

molt \'mōlt\ *vb* : to shed the hair, feathers, outer skin, or horns that will be replaced by a new growth

mol·ten \'mōlt-n\ *adj* : melted especially by intense heat ⟨*molten* metal⟩

mo·lyb·de·num \mə-'lib-də-nəm\ *n* : a white metallic chemical element used in steel alloys to give greater strength and hardness

mo·ment \'mō-mənt\ *n* **1** : a very brief time

: INSTANT ⟨it vanished in a *moment*⟩ **2** : IMPORTANCE ⟨a matter of great *moment*⟩

mo·men·tar·y \'mō-mən-ˌter-ē\ *adj* : lasting only a moment : SHORT-LIVED — **mo·men·tar·i·ly** \ˌmō-mən-'ter-ə-lē\ *adv*

mo·men·tous \mō-'ment-əs\ *adj* : very important ⟨a *momentous* decision⟩ — **mo·men·tous·ness** *n*

mo·men·tum \mō-'ment-əm\ *n* : the force that a moving body has because of its weight and motion

mon- *or* **mono-** *prefix* : one : single ⟨*mono*plane⟩

mon·arch \'män-ərk, -ˌärk\ *n* **1** : a person who reigns over a kingdom or empire usually for life and by hereditary succession **2** : something resembling a ruler ⟨the oak is the *monarch* of the forest⟩ **3** : a large orange and black American butterfly

mon·ar·chy \'män-ər-kē\ *n, pl* **mon·ar·chies** **1** : the system of government by a monarch **2** : a state or country having a monarch

mon·as·ter·y \'män-əs-ˌter-ē\ *n, pl* **mon·as·ter·ies** : an establishment in which a community of monks live and work

mo·nas·tic \mə-'nas-tik\ *adj* : of or relating to monks or monasteries

Mon·day \'mən-dē\ *n* : the second day of the week

mon·e·tar·y \'män-ə-ˌter-ē\ *adj* : of or relating to coinage or currency ⟨*monetary* policy⟩

mon·ey \'mən-ē\ *n, pl* **mon·eys** *or* **mon·ies** \-ēz\ **1** : metal (as gold, silver, or copper) coined or stamped and issued for use in buying and selling **2** : a written or stamped certificate (**paper money**) lawfully used in place of metal money **3** : wealth reckoned in terms of money

money order *n* : an order purchased at a post office, bank, or express or telegraph office directing another office to pay a specified sum of money to a named payee

Mon·gol \'mäng-gəl\ *n* : a member of a people of Mongolia

¹Mon·go·lian \män-'gōl-yən\ *adj* : of or relating to Mongolia or the Mongolians

²Mongolian *n* : MONGOL

mon·goose \'män-ˌgüs, 'mäng-ˌgüs\ *n, pl* **mon·goos·es** : an Indian mammal about the size of a ferret that feeds on snakes and rodents

¹mon·grel \'məng-grəl, 'mäng-\ *n* : one (as a plant, person, or thing) of mixed or uncertain ancestry or origin

²mongrel *adj* **1** : of mixed or uncertain ancestry or origin **2** : impossible to place in a particular class or group

¹mon·i·tor \'män-ət-ər\ *n* **1** : a pupil in a

school selected for a special duty (as keeping order) **2** : a person or device that warns or advises **3** : one that monitors **4** : a heavily armored warship with low sides and one or more revolving gun turrets

²monitor *vb* : to watch or check for a special purpose ⟨*monitor* a radio broadcast for quality of sound⟩

monk \'məngk\ *n* : a member of a religious order of men taking vows of poverty, chastity, and obedience and living in a community

¹mon·key \'məng-kē\ *n, pl* **mon·keys 1** : any of a group of mostly tropical furry animals in many respects resembling man and nearest to man in the animal kingdom — used especially of the smaller longer-tailed forms as distinguished from the apes **2** : a mischievous child

²monkey *vb* **mon·keyed; mon·key·ing 1** : to act in a mischievous manner ⟨just *monkeying* around⟩ **2** : TRIFLE, FOOL ⟨don't *monkey* with the lawn mower⟩

mon·key·shine \'məng-kē-,shīn\ *n* : a mischievous trick : PRANK

monkey wrench *n* : a wrench with one fixed and one adjustable jaw

monks·hood \'məngks-,hùd\ *n* : a tall poisonous Old World plant related to the buttercups that is grown for its spikes of hood-shaped white or purplish flowers or as a source of drugs

mono- — see MON-

mon·o·gram \'män-ə-,gram\ *n* : a design usually made by combining two or more letters (as a person's initials)

monkshood

mon·o·graph \'män-ə-,graf\ *n* : a learned treatise on a particular subject

mon·o·plane \'män-ə-,plān\ *n* : an airplane with only one main supporting surface

mo·nop·o·lize \mə-'näp-ə-,līz\ *vb* **mo·nop·o·lized; mo·nop·o·liz·ing** : to exercise or enjoy exclusive control or enjoyment of ⟨*monopolized* the conversation⟩

mo·nop·o·ly \mə-'näp-ə-lē\ *n, pl* **mo·nop·o·lies 1** : the sole or exclusive control of the entire supply of a commodity or service in a given market **2** : a commodity controlled by a single party **3** : a company that has a monopoly

mon·o·syl·la·ble \'män-ə-,sil-ə-bəl\ *n* : a word of one syllable

mo·not·o·nous \mə-'nät-n-əs\ *adj* : tiresome because of sameness : lacking variety — **mo·not·o·nous·ly** *adv*

mo·not·o·ny \mə-'nät-n-ē\ *n, pl* **mo·not·o·nies**

1 : sameness of tone or sound **2** : tiresome lack of variety

mon·soon \män-'sün\ *n* **1** : a wind in the Indian ocean and southern Asia that blows from the southwest from April to October and from the northeast from October to April **2** : the rainy season that accompanies the southwest monsoon

mon·ster \'män-stər\ *n* **1** : an animal or plant that differs greatly from the usual type **2** : a creature of strange or horrible form **3** : a huge animal or thing **4** : an extremely wicked or cruel person

mon·strous \'män-strəs\ *adj* **1** : unusually large : ENORMOUS **2** : shockingly wrong **3** : greatly different from the natural form : ABNORMAL — **mon·strous·ly** *adv*

month \'mənth\ *n* : one of the twelve parts into which the year is divided

¹month·ly \'mənth-lē\ *adj* **1** : occurring, done, produced, or issued every month **2** : computed in terms of one month **3** : lasting a month

²monthly *n, pl* **month·lies 1** : a monthly periodical **2** *pl* : a menstrual period

mon·u·ment \'män-yə-mənt\ *n* **1** : a physical object (as a building, pillar, stone, or statue) erected to preserve the memory of a person or event **2** : a work, saying, or deed that lasts or that is worth preserving ⟨the book is a *monument* of scholarship⟩

¹moo \'mü\ *vb* **mooed; moo·ing** : to make a moo : LOW

²moo *n, pl* **moos** : the sound made by a cow

¹mood \'müd\ *n* : a state or frame of mind : HUMOR, DISPOSITION ⟨in a good *mood*⟩

²mood *n* : a set of inflectional forms of a verb that show whether the action or state expressed is to be thought of as a fact, a command, or a wish or possibility

mood·y \'müd-ē\ *adj* **mood·i·er; mood·i·est** : subject to fits of depression or bad temper — **mood·i·ly** \'müd-l-ē\ *adv* — **mood·i·ness** \'müd-ē-nəs\ *n*

¹moon \'mün\ *n* **1** : the natural heavenly body that shines by the sun's reflected light and revolves about the earth in about 29½ days **2** : SATELLITE 2 **3** : MONTH **4** : MOONLIGHT

²moon *vb* : to wander or gaze about in a stupid or dreamy way

moon·beam \'mün-,bēm\ *n* : a ray of light from the moon

moon·light \'mün-,līt\ *n* : the light of the moon

moon·stone \'mün-,stōn\ *n* : a somewhat transparent lustrous stone used in jewelry

¹moor \'mur\ *n* : an area of open and usually infertile or wet wasteland

²moor *vb* : to fasten in place with cables, lines, or anchors ⟨*moor* a boat⟩

moor·ing \'mur-ing\ *n*   **1** : a place where or an object to which a boat can be made fast   **2** : a chain or line by which an object is moored

moor·land \'mur-lənd\ *n* : land consisting of moors

moose \'müs\ *n* : a large animal related to the deer that has broad flat-tened antlers and humped shoulders and lives in forests of Canada and the northern United States

moose

¹mop \'mäp\ *n*   **1** : an imple-ment for cleaning made of a bundle of cloth or yarn fastened to a handle   **2** : an implement for cleaning consisting of a long-handled sponge   **3** : something resembling a mop ⟨a *mop* of hair⟩

²mop *vb* **mopped; mop·ping** : to wipe or clean with or as if with a mop ⟨*mop* the floor⟩ ⟨*mopped* his brow with a handkerchief⟩

¹mope \'mōp\ *vb* **moped; mop·ing** : to be dull and without spirit

²mope *n* : a dull listless person

mo·raine \mə-'rān\ *n* : a pile of earth and stones deposited by a glacier

¹mor·al \'mȯr-əl\ *adj*   **1** : concerned with or relating to what is right and wrong in human behavior ⟨*moral* problems⟩ ⟨a *moral* code⟩   **2** : serving to teach a lesson ⟨a *moral* story⟩   **3** : VIRTUOUS, GOOD ⟨lead a *moral* life⟩   **4** : capable of right and wrong action ⟨man is a *moral* being⟩ — **mor·al·ly** *adv*

²moral *n*   **1** : the lesson to be learned from a story or experience   **2** *pl* : moral conduct ⟨men of bad *morals*⟩   **3** *pl* : moral teachings or principles

mo·rale \mə-'ral\ *n* : mental and emotional condition that is affected especially by enthusiasm, spirit, or hope ⟨an army's *morale*⟩

mo·ral·i·ty \mə-'ral-ət-ē\ *n, pl* **mo·ral·i·ties**   **1** : moral quality or character : VIRTUE ⟨judge the *morality* of an action⟩   **2** : principles of conduct : MORALS

mo·rass \mə-'ras\ *n* : MARSH, SWAMP

mor·bid \'mȯr-bəd\ *adj*   **1** : having to do with disease   **2** : not healthy : DISEASED ⟨a *morbid* lung condition⟩   **3** : characterized by gloomy or unwholesome ideas or feelings ⟨a *morbid* interest in horror stories⟩ — **mor·bid·ly** *adv*

¹more \'mōr\ *adj*   **1** : greater in amount or degree ⟨you like *more* sugar in your tea than I do⟩   **2** : ADDITIONAL ⟨have some *more* sugar⟩

²more *adv*   **1** : in addition ⟨wait one day *more*⟩   **2** : to a greater degree — often used with an adjective or adverb to form the comparative ⟨*more* active⟩ ⟨*more* actively⟩

³more *n*   **1** : a greater amount or number ⟨got *more* than he expected⟩   **2** : an additional amount ⟨too full to eat any *more*⟩

more·over \mōr-'ō-vər\ *adv* : in addition to what has been said : BESIDES

morn \'mȯrn\ *n* : DAWN

morn·ing \'mȯr-ning\ *n* : the early part of the day : the time from sunrise to noon

morning glory *n* : a twining vine with large showy funnel-shaped flowers that close in the sunshine

morning star *n* : any of the planets Venus, Jupiter, Mars, Mercury, or Saturn when rising before the sun

morning glory

mo·ron \'mȯr-,än\ *n* : a person with less than ordinary mental ability but able to be happy in doing simple monotonous work

mor·pheme \'mȯr-,fēm\ *n* : a meaningful unit in language that contains no smaller meaningful parts

mor·phine \'mȯr-,fēn\ *n* : a habit-forming drug made from opium and used mostly to relieve pain

mor·row \'mär-ō\ *n* : the next following day

mor·sel \'mȯr-səl\ *n*   **1** : a small bit of food : BITE   **2** : a small quantity : a little piece

¹mor·tal \'mȯrt-l\ *adj*   **1** : capable of causing death : FATAL ⟨a *mortal* wound⟩   **2** : subject to death ⟨all men are *mortal*⟩   **3** : unrelentingly hostile ⟨a *mortal* enemy⟩   **4** : very intense or severe ⟨*mortal* fear⟩   **5** : HUMAN ⟨*mortal* power⟩ — **mor·tal·ly** *adv*

²mortal *n* : a human being

¹mor·tar \'mȯrt-ər\ *n*   **1** : a strong bowl-shaped container in which sub-stances are pounded or rubbed with a pestle   **2** : a short light cannon used to throw shells high into the air

mortar and pestle

²mortar *n* : a building material made of lime and cement mixed with sand and water that is spread between bricks or stones so as to hold them together when it hardens

mor·ti·fy \'mȯrt-ə-,fī\ *vb* **mor·ti·fied; mor·ti·fy·ing** : HUMILIATE, SHAME ⟨the child's naughti-ness *mortified* the mother⟩

mo·sa·ic \mō-'zā-ik\ *n* : a surface decoration made by setting small pieces of glass or stone of different colors into some other material so as to make patterns or pictures

Mos·lem \'mäz-ləm\ *var of* MUSLIM

---

j job   ng sing   ō low   ȯ moth   ȯi coin   th thin   th this   ü boot   u̇ foot   y you   yü few   yu̇ furious   zh vision

mosque \\'mäsk\ *n* : a Muslim place of worship

mos·qui·to \məs-'kēt-ō\ *n, pl* **mos·qui·toes** : a small two-winged insect the female of which punctures the skin of people and animals to suck their blood

mosquito

moss \\'mòs\ *n* **1** : any of a class of flowerless plants with small leafy often tufted stems growing in cushionlike patches and clinging to rocks, bark, or damp ground **2** : any of various plants (as lichens) resembling moss

moss·y \\'mòs-ē\ *adj* **moss·i·er**; **moss·i·est** : covered with moss

¹most \\'mōst\ *adj* **1** : the majority of ⟨*most* men believe this⟩ **2** : greatest in quantity, extent, or degree ⟨the youngest of the boys had the *most* courage⟩

²most *adv* **1** : to the greatest or highest degree — often used with an adjective or adverb to form the superlative ⟨*most* active⟩ ⟨*most* actively⟩ **2** : to a very great degree ⟨a *most* careful driver⟩

³most *n* : the greatest amount, number, or part

-most \ˌmōst\ *adj suffix* : most ⟨inner*most*⟩ : most toward ⟨head*most*⟩

most·ly \\'mōst-lē\ *adv* : for the greatest part

mote \\'mōt\ *n* : a small particle : SPECK

mo·tel \mō-'tel\ *n* : a building or group of buildings used as a hotel in which the rooms are reached directly from an outdoor parking area for automobiles

moth \\'mòth\ *n, pl* **moths** \\'mòthz, 'mòths\ **1** : CLOTHES MOTH **2** : a usually night-flying insect with mostly feathery antennae and stouter body, duller coloring, and smaller wings than the related butterflies

¹moth·er \\'məth-ər\ *n* **1** : a female parent **2** : a nun in charge of a convent **3** : SOURCE, ORIGIN ⟨necessity is the *mother* of invention⟩ — **moth·er·hood** \-ˌhùd\ *n*

²mother *adj* **1** : of or having to do with a mother ⟨*mother* love⟩ **2** : being in the relation of a mother to others ⟨a *mother* church⟩ ⟨his *mother* country⟩ **3** : derived from or as if from one's mother ⟨our *mother* tongue⟩

³mother *vb* : to be or act as a mother to

⁴mother *n* : a slimy mass that forms in an alcoholic liquid (as wine or cider) undergoing an acid fermentation (as in the production of vinegar) and that contains the bacteria which cause the fermentation

moth·er–in–law \\'məth-ər-ən-ˌló\ *n, pl* **moth·ers–in–law** : the mother of one's husband or wife

moth·er–of–pearl \ˌməth-ər-əv-'pərl\ *n* : a hard pearly material that lines the shell of some mollusks (as mussels) and is often used for ornamental objects and buttons

¹mo·tion \\'mō-shən\ *n* **1** : a formal proposal for action made in an assembly of people ⟨a *motion* to adjourn⟩ **2** : the act or process of changing place or position : MOVEMENT — **mo·tion·less** \-ləs\ *adj* — **mo·tion·less·ness** *n*

²motion *vb* : to direct or signal by a movement or gesture ⟨*motioned* him to come forward⟩

motion picture *n* **1** : a series of pictures projected on a screen in rapid succession with objects shown in successive positions slightly changed so as to produce the effect of a continuous picture in which the objects move **2** : a representation of a story or other subject matter by means of motion pictures

mo·ti·vate \\'mōt-ə-ˌvāt\ *vb* **mo·ti·vat·ed**; **mo·ti·vat·ing** : to provide with a motive : INDUCE

¹mo·tive \\'mōt-iv\ *n* : a need, desire, or purpose that prompts one to do something ⟨the boy's *motive* in running away was to avoid trouble⟩ **syn** see CAUSE

²motive *adj* : causing motion ⟨*motive* power⟩

¹mot·ley \\'mät-lē\ *adj* **1** : having various colors **2** : composed of various often inharmonious kinds or parts ⟨a *motley* collection of junk⟩ **syn** see MISCELLANEOUS

²motley *n* : a garment of mixed colors formerly worn by court jesters

¹mo·tor \\'mōt-ər\ *n* **1** : a machine that produces motion or power for doing work ⟨an electric *motor*⟩ ⟨a *motor* run by gasoline⟩ **2** : AUTOMOBILE — **mo·tored** \\'mōt-ərd\ *adj*

²motor *adj* **1** : causing or imparting motion **2** : equipped with or driven by a motor **3** : of or relating to an automobile **4** : designed for motor vehicles or motorists

³motor *vb* : to travel by automobile

mo·tor·boat \\'mōt-ər-ˌbōt\ *n* : an often small boat propelled by a motor

mo·tor·car \\'mōt-ər-ˌkär\ *n* : AUTOMOBILE

mo·tor·cy·cle \\'mōt-ər-ˌsī-kəl\ *n* : a bicyclelike vehicle propelled by a motor

mo·tor·ist \\'mōt-ə-rəst\ *n* : a person who travels by automobile

motorcycle

mo·tor·ize \\'mōt-ə-ˌrīz\ *vb* **mo·tor·ized**; **mo·tor·iz·ing** : to equip with a motor or motor-driven vehicles

motor scooter *n* : a two- or three-wheeled motorized vehicle resembling a child's scooter but having a seat

mo·tor·truck \\'mōt-ər-ˌtrək\ *n* : an automotive truck for transporting freight

motor vehicle *n* : a motorized vehicle (as an automobile or motorcycle) not operated on rails

mot·tled \'mät-ld\ *adj* : marked with spots or blotches of several colors or shades : SPOTTED

mot·to \'mät-ō\ *n, pl* **mot·toes** : a short expression that suggests a guiding rule of conduct and is suitable for inscription (as on seals, coins, badges, and public buildings)

mould \'mōld\ *var of* MOLD

moult \'mōlt\ *var of* MOLT

mound \'maund\ *n* **1** : a small hill or heap of dirt (as made by man to mark a grave or to serve as a fort) **2** : the slightly elevated ground on which a baseball pitcher stands

¹mount \'maunt\ *n* : a high hill : MOUNTAIN — used especially before a proper name ⟨*Mount* Everest⟩

²mount *vb* **1** : ASCEND, CLIMB ⟨*mount* a ladder⟩ **2** : to get up onto something ⟨*mount* a platform⟩ ⟨*mount* a horse⟩ **3** : to increase rapidly in amount ⟨*mounting* debts⟩ **4** : to prepare for use or display by fastening in proper position on a support ⟨*mount* a picture on cardboard⟩ **syn** see ASCEND

³mount *n* : that upon which a person or thing is mounted

moun·tain \'maunt-n\ *n* **1** : an elevation higher than a hill **2** : a great mass or vast number ⟨a *mountain* of mail⟩

moun·tain·eer \,maunt-n-'iər\ *n* **1** : a person who lives in the mountains **2** : a mountain climber

mountain goat *n* : a goatlike animal of the mountains of western North America with thick white hairy coat and slightly curved black horns

mountain lion *n* : COUGAR

moun·tain·ous \'maunt-n-əs\ *adj* **1** : having many mountains ⟨*mountainous* country⟩ **2** : resembling a mountain in size : HUGE

mountain goat

moun·tain·side \'maunt-n-,sīd\ *n* : the side of a mountain

mount·ing \'maunt-ing\ *n* : something that serves as a mount : SUPPORT ⟨a *mounting* for an engine⟩

mourn \'mōrn\ *vb* : to feel or show grief or sorrow and especially over someone's death — **mourn·er** *n*

mourn·ful \'mōrn-fəl\ *adj* **1** : full of sorrow or sadness ⟨a *mournful* face⟩ **2** : causing sorrow ⟨*mournful* news⟩ — **mourn·ful·ly** *adv* — **mourn·ful·ness** *n*

mourn·ing \'mōr-ning\ *n* **1** : the act of sor-

rowing **2** : an outward sign (as black clothes or an arm band) of grief for a person's death ⟨she wore *mourning* for a year⟩

mourning cloak *n* : a brownish black butterfly with yellow-bordered wings

mourning dove *n* : a wild dove of the United States named from its mournful cry

mouse \'maus\ *n, pl* **mice** \'mīs\ : a furry gnawing animal resembling but smaller than the related rats

mous·er \'mau-zər\ *n* : a cat good at catching mice

mous·tache \'məs-,tash\ *n* : the hair allowed to grow on a man's upper lip

¹mouth \'mauth\ *n, pl* **mouths** \'mauthz, 'mauths\ **1** : the opening through which a person or an animal takes food or makes speech sounds : the opening containing the tongue and teeth **2** : an opening that is like a mouth ⟨the *mouth* of a cave⟩ **3** : the place where a stream enters a larger body of water

²mouth \'mauth\ *vb* : to repeat insincerely or without understanding

mouth·ful \'mauth-,ful\ *n* **1** : as much as the mouth will hold **2** : the amount put into the mouth at one time

mouth organ *n* : HARMONICA

mouth·piece \'mauth-,pēs\ *n* : a part that goes in the mouth or to which the mouth is applied ⟨the *mouthpiece* of a trumpet⟩ ⟨the *mouthpiece* of a telephone⟩

mov·able *or* **move·a·ble** \'mü-və-bəl\ *adj* **1** : capable of being moved : not fixed ⟨*movable* desks⟩ **2** : changing from one date to another ⟨Easter is a *movable* feast⟩

¹move \'müv\ *vb* **moved; mov·ing** **1** : to change the place or position of : SHIFT **2** : to go from one place to another ⟨*move* into the shade⟩ **3** : to set in motion : STIR ⟨*move* the head⟩ **4** : to cause to act : INFLUENCE ⟨*moved* him to change his mind⟩ **5** : to affect the feelings of ⟨the sad story *moved* the children to tears⟩ **6** : to propose formally in a meeting ⟨*move* to adjourn⟩ **7** : to change residence **8** : to change position ⟨*moved* in his chair⟩

²move *n* **1** : the act of moving a piece in a game **2** : the turn of a player to move ⟨it's your *move*⟩ **3** : a step taken to accomplish a purpose : MANEUVER **4** : the action of moving : MOVEMENT

move·ment \'müv-mənt\ *n* **1** : the act or process of moving : an instance of moving **2** : a program or series of acts working toward a desired end ⟨a *movement* for political reform⟩ **3** : a mechanical arrangement (as of wheels) for causing a particular motion (as in a clock or watch) **4** : RHYTHM, METER **5** : a section of a longer piece of music ⟨a *move-ment* in a symphony⟩ **6** : an emptying of the bowels : the matter emptied from the bowels

mov·ie \'mü-vē\ *n* : MOTION PICTURE

mov·ing \'mü-ving\ *adj* **1** : changing place or position ⟨a *moving* target⟩ **2** : having the power to affect the feeling or sympathies ⟨a *moving* song⟩ — **mov·ing·ly** *adv*

moving picture *n* : MOTION PICTURE

¹mow \'mau̇\ *n* : the part of a barn where hay or straw is stored

²mow \'mō\ *vb* **mowed; mowed** *or* **mown** \'mōn\; **mow·ing** **1** : to cut down with a scythe or machine ⟨*mow* grass⟩ **2** : to cut the standing plant cover from ⟨*mow* the lawn⟩ **3** : to cause to fall in great numbers ⟨machine guns *mowed* down the attackers⟩ — **mow·er** \'mō-ər\ *n*

¹much \'məch\ *adj* **more** \'mōr\; **most** \'mōst\ : great in amount, extent, or degree ⟨*much* money⟩

²much *adv* **more; most** **1** : to a great degree or extent ⟨*much* happier⟩ **2** : APPROXIMATELY, NEARLY ⟨looks *much* as he did years ago⟩

³much *n* : a great quantity or amount ⟨*much* that he said was false⟩

mu·ci·lage \'myü-sə-lij\ *n* : a water solution of a gum or similar substance used especially to stick things together

muck \'mək\ *n* **1** : soft wet soil or barnyard manure **2** : DIRT, FILTH

mu·cous \'myü-kəs\ *adj* **1** : of, relating to, or resembling mucus **2** : containing or producing mucus ⟨a *mucous* membrane⟩

mu·cus \'myü-kəs\ *n* : a slippery sticky animal secretion produced especially by mucous membranes (as of the nose and throat) which it moistens and protects

mud \'məd\ *n* : soft wet earth or dirt

¹mud·dle \'məd-l\ *vb* **mud·dled; mud·dling** **1** : CONFUSE, BEWILDER ⟨*muddled* by too much advice⟩ **2** : to mix up in a confused manner ⟨*muddle* the household accounts⟩ **3** : BUNGLE

²muddle *n* : a state of confusion

¹mud·dy \'məd-ē\ *adj* **mud·di·er; mud·di·est** **1** : filled or covered with mud **2** : looking like mud ⟨a *muddy* color⟩ **3** : not clear or bright : DULL, CLOUDY ⟨a *muddy* complexion⟩ **4** : CONFUSED ⟨*muddy* thinking⟩ — **mud·di·ly** \'məd-l-ē\ *adv* — **mud·di·ness** \'məd-ē-nəs\ *n*

²muddy *vb* **mud·died; mud·dy·ing** **1** : to soil or stain with or as if with mud **2** : to make cloudy or dull

¹muff \'məf\ *n* : a soft thick cover into which both hands

muff

may be thrust to protect them from cold

²muff *n* : a bungling performance : a clumsy failure

³muff *vb* : to handle awkwardly : BUNGLE

muf·fin \'məf-ən\ *n* : a bread made of batter containing eggs and baked in a small cup-shaped container

muf·fle \'məf-əl\ *vb* **muf·fled; muf·fling** **1** : to wrap up so as to conceal or protect or to prevent seeing, hearing, or speaking **2** : to deaden the sound of

muf·fler \'məf-lər\ *n* **1** : a scarf for the neck **2** : something that deadens noises ⟨the *muffler* on the exhaust pipe of an automobile⟩

mug \'məg\ *n* : a large drinking cup usually made of metal or thick earthen-ware

mug·gy \'məg-ē\ *adj* **mug·gi·er; mug·gi·est** : being warm, damp, and stifling ⟨*muggy* weather⟩ — **mug·gi·ness** *n*

mug

Mu·ham·mad·an \mō-'ham-əd-ən, mü-\ *n* : MUSLIM

Mu·ham·mad·an·ism \mō-'ham-əd-ən-,iz-əm, mü-\ *n* : ISLAM

mul·ber·ry \'məl-,ber-ē\ *n, pl* **mul·ber·ries** : a tree that bears edible usually purple or white berrylike fruits and has leaves on which silkworms can be fed

¹mulch \'məlch\ *n* : a material (as straw, sawdust, leaves, or paper) spread upon the ground to protect the roots of plants from heat, cold, or drought or to keep fruit clean

²mulch *vb* : to cover with mulch

mule \'myül\ *n* **1** : an animal that is an offspring of a donkey and a horse **2** : a spinning machine

mule skinner *n* : a driver of mules

mu·le·teer \,myü-lə-'tiər\ *n* : a driver of mules

mu·ley \'myü-lē\ *adj* : having no horns ⟨a *muley* cow⟩

mule 1

mul·ish \'myü-lish\ *adj* : stubborn like a mule — **mul·ish·ly** *adv* — **mul·ish·ness** *n*

mul·let \'məl-ət\ *n* : any of various freshwater or saltwater food fishes some mostly gray (**gray mullets**) and others red or golden (**red mullets**)

mul·ti- \-,məl-ti-\ *prefix* **1** : many : multiple : much ⟨*multi*colored⟩ **2** : more than two ⟨*multi*lateral⟩ ⟨*multi*racial⟩ **3** : many times over ⟨*multi*millionaire⟩

¹mul·ti·ple \'məl-tə-pəl\ *adj* : consisting of more than one ⟨*multiple* copies of a document⟩

²multiple *n* : the product of a quantity by an integer ⟨35 is a *multiple* of 7⟩

mul·ti·pli·cand \ˌməl-tə-plə-'kand\ *n* : a number that is to be multiplied by another number

mul·ti·pli·ca·tion \ˌməl-tə-plə-'kā-shən\ *n* : a short way of finding out what would be the result of adding a figure the number of times indicated by another figure ⟨the *multiplication* of 7 by 3 gives 21⟩

mul·ti·pli·er \'məl-tə-ˌplī-ər\ *n* : a number by which another number is multiplied

mul·ti·ply \'məl-tə-ˌplī\ *vb* **mul·ti·plied; mul·ti·ply·ing** **1** : to increase in number : make or become more numerous **2** : to find the product of by means of multiplication ⟨*multiply* 7 by 8⟩

mul·ti·tude \'məl-tə-ˌtüd, -ˌtyüd\ *n* : a great number of persons or things : CROWD

mum \'məm\ *adj* : SILENT ⟨keep *mum*⟩

¹**mum·ble** \'məm-bəl\ *vb* **mum·bled; mum·bling** : to speak indistinctly

²**mumble** *n* : a low indistinct utterance

mum·my \'məm-ē\ *n, pl* **mum·mies** : a dead body embalmed in the manner of the ancient Egyptians

mumps \'məmps\ *n sing or pl* : an infectious disease marked by fever and the inflammation and swelling of certain glands and especially of those around the jaw

munch \'mənch\ *vb* : to chew with a crunching sound ⟨*munch* crackers⟩

mu·nic·i·pal \myu̇-'nis-ə-pəl\ *adj* : having to do with the government of a town or city

mu·nic·i·pal·i·ty \myu̇-ˌnis-ə-'pal-ət-ē\ *n, pl* **mu·nic·i·pal·i·ties** : an incorporated town or city having local self-government

mu·ni·tions \myu̇-'nish-ənz\ *n pl* : military equipment and supplies : AMMUNITION

¹**mu·ral** \'myu̇r-əl\ *adj* **1** : having to do with a wall **2** : being on a wall ⟨*mural* paintings⟩

²**mural** *n* : a mural painting

¹**mur·der** \'mərd-ər\ *n* : the intentional and unlawful killing of a human being

²**murder** *vb* **1** : to kill unlawfully : commit murder **2** : to spoil by performing or using in a wretched manner ⟨*murder* a song⟩ ⟨*murder* English⟩ **syn** see KILL — **mur·der·er** *n*

mur·der·ous \'mərd-ə-rəs\ *adj* : characterized by, causing, or appearing to have the purpose of murder — **mur·der·ous·ly** *adv*

murk \'mərk\ *n* : DARKNESS, GLOOM

murk·y \'mər-kē\ *adj* **murk·i·er; murk·i·est** **1** : marked by darkness or gloom **2** : FOGGY, MISTY — **murk·i·ness** *n*

¹**mur·mur** \'mər-mər\ *n* : a low indistinct sound ⟨the *murmur* of voices⟩

²**murmur** *vb* **1** : to make a murmur **2** : to say in a low indistinct voice

mus·ca·dine \'məs-kə-ˌdīn\ *n* : a grape of the southern United States

mus·cle \'məs-əl\ *n* **1** : an animal body tissue consisting of long cells (**muscle cells**) that can contract and produce motion **2** : a bodily organ that is a mass of muscle tissue attached at either end (as to bones) so that it can make a body part (as an arm) move **3** : muscular strength or development

mus·cle–bound \'məs-əl-ˌbau̇nd\ *adj* : having muscles enlarged (as from excessive exercise) and lacking in elasticity

mus·cu·lar \'məs-kyə-lər\ *adj* **1** : of, relating to, or constituting muscle **2** : performed by the muscles **3** : STRONG

muse \'myüz\ *vb* **mused; mus·ing** : PONDER

mu·se·um \myu̇-'zē-əm\ *n* : a building in which are displayed objects of interest in one or more of the arts or sciences

¹**mush** \'məsh\ *n* : cornmeal boiled in water

²**mush** *vb* : to travel across snow with a sled drawn by dogs

¹**mush·room** \'məsh-ˌrüm, -ˌru̇m\ *n* **1** : a fleshy above-ground umbrella-like part of a fungus that bears spores **2** : a fungus that produces mushrooms

mushrooms

²**mushroom** *adj* : springing up suddenly or multiplying rapidly ⟨*mushroom* growth of filling stations⟩

³**mushroom** *vb* : to spring up suddenly or multiply rapidly

mu·sic \'myü-zik\ *n* **1** : the art of combining tones so that they are pleasing, expressive, or intelligible **2** : compositions made according to the rules of music **3** : agreeable sounds **4** : the score of a musical composition set down on paper ⟨bring your *music*⟩

mu·si·cal \'myü-zi-kəl\ *adj* **1** : having to do with music or the writing or performance of music ⟨*musical* instruments⟩ **2** : having the pleasing qualities of music ⟨a *musical* voice⟩ **3** : fond of or talented in music ⟨a *musical* family⟩ **4** : set to music — **mu·si·cal·ly** *adv*

music box *n* : a box enclosing an apparatus that reproduces music mechanically when activated by clockwork

mu·si·cian \myu̇-'zish-ən\ *n* : a person who writes, sings, or plays music skillfully and especially as a profession

musk \'məsk\ *n* **1** : a strong-smelling material from a gland of an Asiatic deer (**musk deer**) used in perfumes **2** : any of several plants with musky odors

mus·ket \'məs-kət\ *n* : a hand firearm formerly carried by infantry soldiers

mus·ke·teer \ˌməs-kə-'tiər\ *n* : a soldier armed with a musket

musk·mel·on \'məsk-ˌmel-ən\ *n* : a small round to oval melon with sweet usually green or orange flesh

musk–ox \'məsk-ˌäks\ *n* : a shaggy animal like an ox found in Greenland and northern North America

musk·rat \'məsk-ˌrat\ *n* : a North American water animal related to the rats that has webbed hind feet and a long scaly tail and is valued for its glossy usually dark brown fur

muskrat

musk·y \'məs-kē\ *adj* **musk·i·er; musk·i·est** : resembling musk especially in odor — **musk·i·ness** *n*

Mus·lim \'məz-ləm\ *n* : one whose religion is Islam

mus·lin \'məz-lən\ *n* : a cotton fabric of plain weave

¹muss \'məs\ *n* : DISORDER, CONFUSION

²muss *vb* : to make untidy ⟨*mussed* his hair⟩

mus·sel \'məs-əl\ *n* **1** : a sea mollusk that has a long dark two-part shell and is sometimes used as food **2** : any of various American freshwater clams with shells that yield mother-of-pearl

must \'məst\ *helping verb, pres & past all persons* **must 1** : is obliged or required to ⟨a man *must* eat to live⟩ ⟨you *must* not make a noise in the library⟩ **2** : is inferred by reasoning to ⟨it *must* be time⟩ ⟨I *must* have lost it⟩

mus·tache *var of* MOUSTACHE

mus·tang \'məs-ˌtang\ *n* : a small hardy half-wild horse of western North America

mus·tard \'məs-tərd\ *n* : a sharp-tasting yellow powder used as a seasoning for foods and in medicine that is prepared from the seeds of a yellow-flowered plant related to the turnips

¹mus·ter \'məs-tər\ *vb* **1** : to assemble (as troops or a ship's company) for roll call or inspection **2** : to call forth : COLLECT

mustard

²muster *n* **1** : a formal military inspection **2** : critical examination ⟨his slipshod work will never pass *muster*⟩

must·n't \'məs-nt\ : must not

must·y \'məs-tē\ *adj* **must·i·er; must·i·est** : bad in odor or taste from being kept in a damp place : MOLDY — **must·i·ness** *n*

mu·tate \'myü-ˌtāt\ *vb* **mu·tat·ed; mu·tat·ing** : to undergo great changes (as in hereditary makeup)

¹mute \'myüt\ *adj* **1** : unable to speak : DUMB **2** : not speaking : SILENT

²mute *n* **1** : a person who cannot or does not speak **2** : a device on a musical instrument which deadens, softens, or muffles its tone

³mute *vb* **mut·ed; mut·ing** : to muffle or reduce the sound of

mutes 2: for violin and for trumpet

mu·ti·late \'myüt-l-ˌāt\ *vb* **mu·ti·lat·ed; mu·ti·lat·ing 1** : to deprive of an essential part (as a limb) : MAIM **2** : to make imperfect by cutting or alteration ⟨*mutilate* a book⟩

mu·ti·neer \ˌmyüt-n-'iər\ *n* : a person who is guilty of mutiny

mu·ti·nous \'myüt-n-əs\ *adj* : being disposed to or in a state of mutiny — **mu·ti·nous·ly** *adv*

¹mu·ti·ny \'myüt-n-ē\ *n, pl* **mu·ti·nies 1** : willful refusal to obey rightful authority **2** : concerted revolt of a group against a superior officer

²mutiny *vb* **mu·ti·nied; mu·ti·ny·ing** : to refuse to obey rightful authority

mutt \'mət\ *n* : a mongrel dog

mut·ter \'mət-ər\ *vb* **1** : to speak in a low indistinct voice with lips partly closed **2** : GRUMBLE

mut·ton \'mət-n\ *n* : the flesh of a mature sheep

mu·tu·al \'myü-chə-wəl\ *adj* **1** : given and received in equal amount ⟨*mutual* favors⟩ **2** : having the same relation to one another ⟨*mutual* enemies⟩ **3** : shared by two or more at the same time ⟨our *mutual* friend⟩ — **mu·tu·al·ly** *adv*

¹muz·zle \'məz-əl\ *n* **1** : the nose and jaws of an animal **2** : a covering for the nose and jaws of an animal to prevent it from biting **3** : the open end of a gun from which the bullet is discharged

²muzzle *vb* **muz·zled; muz·zling 1** : to put a muzzle on ⟨*muzzle* your dog⟩ **2** : to restrain from free expression ⟨the dictator *muzzled* the press⟩

my \'mī, mə\ *adj* : of or relating to me or myself ⟨*my* head⟩ ⟨*my* injuries⟩

my·na *or* **my·nah** \'mī-nə\ *n* : an Asiatic starling

¹myr·i·ad \'mir-ē-əd\ *n* **1** : ten thousand **2** : an indefinitely large number ⟨*myriads* of stars visible⟩

²myriad *adj* : extremely numerous ⟨the *myriad* grains of sand on the beach⟩

myr·i·a·pod \'mir-ē-ə-ˌpäd\ *n* : any of a group of long-bodied many-legged animals including the centipedes and millipedes

myrrh \'mər\ *n* : a brown slightly bitter aromatic material obtained from African and Arabian trees and used especially in perfumes or formerly in incense

myr·tle \'mərt-l\ *n* **1** : a bushy evergreen shrub of southern Europe **2** : ¹PERIWINKLE

my·self \mī-'self, mə-\ *pron* : my own self ⟨I hurt *myself*⟩ ⟨I *myself* did it⟩

mys·te·ri·ous \mis-'tir-ē-əs\ *adj* : containing a mystery : hard to understand : SECRET — **mys·te·ri·ous·ly** *adv* — **mys·te·ri·ous·ness** *n*

mys·ter·y \'mis-tə-rē\ *n, pl* **mys·ter·ies** **1** : something that is beyond man's power to understand **2** : something that has not been explained **3** : a piece of fiction dealing with a mysterious crime

mys·ti·fy \'mis-tə-ˌfī\ *vb* **mys·ti·fied; mys·ti·fy·ing** : PUZZLE

myth \'mith\ *n* **1** : a legendary story that describes a supernatural being or event or explains a religious belief or practice **2** : a person or thing existing only in the imagination

myth·i·cal \'mith-i-kəl\ *adj* **1** : based on or described in a myth **2** : IMAGINARY **syn** see FABULOUS

my·thol·o·gy \mi-'thäl-ə-jē\ *n, pl* **my·thol·o·gies** : a collection of myths

n \'en\ *n, often cap* : the fourteenth letter of the English alphabet

nab \'nab\ *vb* **nabbed; nab·bing** : SEIZE, ARREST

na·bob \'nā-ˌbäb\ *n* : a man of great wealth or prominence

na·cre \'nā-kər\ *n* : MOTHER-OF-PEARL

¹nag \'nag\ *n* : a usually old or inferior horse

²nag *vb* **nagged; nag·ging** : to find fault continually : irritate by constant scolding

na·iad \'nā-əd\ *n, pl* **na·iads** *or* **na·ia·des** \'nā-ə-ˌdēz\ **1** : a nymph in ancient mythology living in lakes, rivers, and springs **2** : the aquatic larva of some insects (as a dragonfly)

¹nail \'nāl\ *n* **1** : the horny scale at the end of each finger and toe **2** : a slender pointed piece of metal driven into or through something for fastening

²nail *vb* : to fasten with or as if with a nail

nail·brush \'nāl-ˌbrəsh\ *n* : a brush for cleaning the hands and fingernails

nails 2

nain·sook \'nān-ˌsu̇k\ *n* : a soft lightweight muslin

na·ive \nä-'ēv\ *adj* **1** : marked by unaffected simplicity : ARTLESS **2** : showing lack of informed judgment : CREDULOUS — **na·ive·ly** *adv*

na·iv·e·té \nä-ˌē-və-'tā\ *n* : the quality or state of being naïve

na·ked \'nā-kəd\ *adj* **1** : having no clothes on : NUDE **2** : lacking a usual or natural covering ⟨*naked* trees⟩ **3** : not in its sheath ⟨a *naked* sword⟩ **4** : stripped of anything misleading : PLAIN ⟨the *naked* truth⟩ **5** : not aided by artificial means ⟨seen by the *naked* eye⟩ — **na·ked·ly** *adv* — **na·ked·ness** *n*

syn NAKED, BARE both mean being without natural or conventional covering. NAKED indicates absence of all covering, protective or ornamental ⟨a *naked* baby⟩ and may stress the resulting exposure and openness ⟨trees so gaunt and *naked* in their leafless state⟩ ⟨wanted the *naked* facts and no excuses⟩ BARE stresses the absence or removal of additional or unnecessary covering ⟨went about with *bare* head and legs all winter⟩ ⟨*bare* walls without pictures and *bare* windows lacking even shades⟩

nam·by–pam·by \ˌnam-bē-'pam-bē\ *adj* : lacking in character : INDECISIVE

¹name \'nām\ *n* **1** : a word or combination of words by which a person or thing is regularly known **2** : REPUTATION ⟨made a *name* for himself⟩

²name *vb* **named; nam·ing** **1** : to give a name to : CALL **2** : to refer to by name **3** : to nominate for or appoint to office **4** : CHOOSE **5** : MENTION ⟨*name* a price⟩

³name *adj* : having an established reputation ⟨*name* brands⟩

name·less \'nām-ləs\ *adj* **1** : having no name **2** : not marked with a name ⟨a *nameless* grave⟩ **3** : UNKNOWN, ANONYMOUS ⟨a *nameless* hero⟩ **4** : not to be described ⟨*nameless* fears⟩ — **name·less·ness** *n*

name·ly \'nām-lē\ *adv* : that is to say ⟨the cat family, *namely*, lions, tigers, and similar animals⟩

name·plate \'nām-ˌplāt\ *n* : a plate bearing a name

name·sake \'nām-ˌsāk\ *n* : one that has the same name as another and especially one named for another

nan·keen \nan-'kēn\ *n* : a durable brownish yellow cotton fabric

nan·ny goat \'nan-ē-\ *n* : a female goat

¹nap \'nap\ *vb* **napped; nap·ping** **1** : to sleep briefly especially during the day **2** : to be off guard ⟨was caught *napping*⟩

²**nap** *n* : a short sleep especially during the day ⟨take a *nap*⟩

³**nap** *n* : a hairy or downy surface of some cloth

nape \'nāp\ *n* : the back of the neck

na·per·y \'nā-pə-rē\ *n* : household linen especially for the table

naph·tha \'naf-thə, 'nap-thə\ *n* : any of various volatile often flammable liquids prepared from coal or petroleum and used as solvents or to thin paint

nap·kin \'nap-kən\ *n* : a small square of cloth or paper used at table to wipe the lips or fingers and protect the clothes

nar·cis·sus \när-'sis-əs\ *n, pl* **narcissus** *or* **nar·cis·sus·es** *or* **nar·cis·si** \-'sis-ˌī, -ē\ : a daffodil with white, yellow, or two-colored short-tubed flowers usually borne singly on the stalk

¹**nar·cot·ic** \när-'kät-ik\ *n* : a drug (as opium) that in moderate doses dulls the senses, relieves pain, and brings on sleep but in larger doses is a dangerous poison

narcissus

²**narcotic** *adj* 1 : having the properties of or being the source of a narcotic ⟨the opium poppy is a *narcotic* plant⟩ 2 : of or relating to narcotics or their use or control

nar·rate \'nar-ˌāt, na-'rāt\ *vb* **nar·rat·ed; nar·rat·ing** : to relate the details of (as a story) : TELL — **nar·ra·tor** *or* **nar·rat·er** *n*

nar·ra·tion \na-'rā-shən\ *n* 1 : the art or process or an instance of narrating 2 : STORY, NARRATIVE

¹**nar·ra·tive** \'nar-ət-iv\ *n* 1 : something (as a story) that is narrated 2 : the art or practice of narrating

²**narrative** *adj* : of or relating to narration : having the form of a story

¹**nar·row** \'nar-ō\ *adj* 1 : of slender or less than usual width 2 : limited in size or scope ⟨a *narrow* space⟩ 3 : not liberal or broad-minded 4 : barely successful : CLOSE ⟨a *narrow* escape⟩ — **nar·row·ly** *adv* — **nar·row·ness** *n*

²**narrow** *n* : a narrow passage connecting two bodies of water — usually used in plural

³**narrow** *vb* : to lessen in width or extent

nar·row–mind·ed \ˌnar-ō-'mīn-dəd\ *adj* : not tolerant or broad-minded — **nar·row–mind·ed·ly** *adv* — **nar·row–mind·ed·ness** *n*

nar·whal \'när-ˌhwäl\ *n* : an arctic sea animal about twenty feet long that is related to the dolphin and in the male has a long twisted ivory tusk

¹**na·sal** \'nā-zəl\ *n* : a nasal sound

²**nasal** *adj* 1 : of or relating to the nose 2 : uttered through the nose — **na·sal·ly** *adv*

nas·tur·tium \nəs-'tər-shəm, nas-\ *n* : an herb with a pungent juicy stem, roundish leaves, and showy red, yellow, or white flowers

nas·ty \'nas-tē\ *adj* **nas·ti·er; nas·ti·est** 1 : very dirty : FILTHY 2 : INDECENT, VILE 3 : DISAGREEABLE ⟨*nasty* weather⟩ 4 : MEAN, ILL-NATURED ⟨a *nasty* temper⟩ 5 : DISHONORABLE ⟨a *nasty* trick⟩ 6 : HARMFUL, DANGEROUS ⟨a *nasty* fall⟩ — **nas·ti·ly** \-tə-lē\ *adv* — **nas·ti·ness** \-tē-nəs\ *n*

nasturtium

na·tal \'nāt-l\ *adj* : of, relating to, or associated with birth ⟨*natal* day⟩

na·tion \'nā-shən\ *n* 1 : a people connected either by ties of blood or by a common language, customs, and traditions 2 : a usually large independent territorial division : COUNTRY

¹**na·tion·al** \'nash-ən-l\ *adj* : of or relating to a nation — **na·tion·al·ly** *adv*

²**national** *n* : a citizen or subject of a nation

na·tion·al·ism \'nash-ən-l-ˌiz-əm\ *n* : devotion to the interests of a particular country

na·tion·al·ist \'nash-ən-l-əst\ *n* : an advocate of or a believer in nationalism

na·tion·al·is·tic \ˌnash-ən-l-'is-tik\ *adj* 1 : of or relating to nationalism 2 : NATIONAL — **na·tion·al·is·ti·cal·ly** \-ti-kə-lē\ *adv*

na·tion·al·i·ty \ˌnash-ə-'nal-ət-ē\ *n, pl* **na·tion·al·i·ties** 1 : the fact or state of belonging to a nation 2 : existence as a separate nation 3 : a group of people having a common racial and cultural background

na·tion·al·ize \'nash-ən-l-ˌīz\ *vb* **na·tion·al·ized; na·tion·al·iz·ing** : to make national : place under government control

na·tion·wide \ˌnā-shən-'wīd\ *adj* : extending throughout a nation

¹**na·tive** \'nāt-iv\ *adj* 1 : INBORN, NATURAL ⟨*native* ability⟩ 2 : born in a particular place or country 3 : belonging to one because of his place of birth ⟨*native* language⟩ 4 : grown, produced, or originating in a particular place ⟨*native* art⟩

²**native** *n* : one that is native

na·tiv·i·ty \nə-'tiv-ət-ē, nā-\ *n, pl* **na·tiv·i·ties** 1 : BIRTH 2 *cap* : the birth of Christ : CHRISTMAS

nat·ty \'nat-ē\ *adj* **nat·ti·er; nat·ti·est** : trimly neat and tidy — **nat·ti·ly** \'nat-l-ē\ *adv* — **nat·ti·ness** \'nat-ē-nəs\ *n*

¹**nat·u·ral** \'nach-ə-rəl\ *adj* 1 : born in or with one : determined by nature ⟨*natural*

abilities⟩ **2** : being such by nature : BORN ⟨a *natural* musician⟩ **3** : existing in or produced by nature ⟨*natural* woodland⟩ **4** : of or relating to nature ⟨*natural* causes⟩ **5** : not made by man ⟨*natural* rubber⟩ **6** : marked by simplicity and sincerity ⟨*natural* manners⟩ **7** : LIFELIKE **8** : having neither sharps nor flats in the key signature or having a sharp or a flat changed in pitch by a natural sign — **nat·u·ral·ly** *adv* — **nat·u·ral·ness** *n*

²natural *n* : a character ♮ placed on a line or space of the musical staff to take away the effect of a sharp or flat

nat·u·ral·ist \'nach-ə-rə-ləst\ *n* : a student of nature and especially of plants and animals in their natural situation

nat·u·ral·i·za·tion \ˌnach-ə-rə-lə-'zā-shən\ *n* : the act or process of naturalizing : the state of being naturalized

nat·u·ral·ize \'nach-ə-rə-ˌlīz\ *vb* **nat·u·ral·ized; nat·u·ral·iz·ing** **1** : to become or cause to become established as if native ⟨*naturalize* a plant⟩ **2** : to admit to citizenship

natural number *n* : the number 1 : any number (as 3, 12, 432) obtained by repeatedly adding 1 to 1

natural resource *n* : something (as a mineral, waterpower source, forest, or kind of animal) that occurs in nature and is valuable to man

na·ture \'nā-chər\ *n* **1** : the peculiar quality or character of a person or thing ⟨man's *nature*⟩ **2** : KIND, SORT ⟨things of that *nature*⟩ **3** : natural feelings : DISPOSITION, TEMPERAMENT ⟨a generous *nature*⟩ **4** : the physical universe ⟨the study of *nature*⟩ **5** : the working of a living body : LIFE ⟨leave a cure to *nature*⟩ **6** : natural scenery

¹naught \'nȯt\ *pron* : NOTHING

²naught *n* **1** : NOTHING, NOTHINGNESS **2** : ZERO, CIPHER

naught·y \'nȯt-ē\ *adj* **naught·i·er; naught·i·est** : behaving badly or improperly — **naught·i·ly** \'nȯt-l-ē\ *adv* — **naught·i·ness** \'nȯt-ē-nəs\ *n*

nau·se·a \'nȯ-zē-ə, 'nȯ-shə\ *n* **1** : stomach distress with distaste for food and an urge to vomit **2** : deep disgust : LOATHING

nau·se·ate \'nȯ-zē-ˌāt, 'nȯ-shē-\ *vb* **nau·se·at·ed; nau·se·at·ing** : to affect or become affected with nausea — **nau·se·at·ing** *adj* — **nau·se·at·ing·ly** *adv*

nau·seous \'nȯ-shəs, 'nȯ-zē-əs\ *adj* **1** : NAUSEATED **2** : NAUSEATING

nau·ti·cal \'nȯt-i-kəl\ *adj* : of or relating to seamen, navigation, or ships — **nau·ti·cal·ly** *adv*

na·val \'nā-vəl\ *adj* : of or relating to a navy or warships ⟨*naval* vessels⟩

nave \'nāv\ *n* : the central part of the interior of a church running lengthwise

na·vel \'nā-vəl\ *n* : a depression in the middle of the abdominal wall

nav·i·ga·bil·i·ty \ˌnav-i-gə-'bil-ət-ē\ *n* : the quality or state of being navigable

nav·i·ga·ble \'nav-i-gə-bəl\ *adj* **1** : deep enough and wide enough to permit passage of ships ⟨a *navigable* river⟩ **2** : capable of being steered ⟨a *navigable* balloon⟩

nav·i·gate \'nav-ə-ˌgāt\ *vb* **nav·i·gat·ed; nav·i·gat·ing** **1** : to travel by water **2** : to sail over, on, or through **3** : to direct one's course in a ship or airplane **4** : to steer or direct the course of (as a boat)

nav·i·ga·tion \ˌnav-ə-'gā-shən\ *n* **1** : the act or practice of navigating **2** : the science of figuring out the position and course of a ship or airplane

nav·i·ga·tor \'nav-ə-ˌgāt-ər\ *n* : an officer on a ship or airplane responsible for its navigation

na·vy \'nā-vē\ *n, pl* **na·vies** **1** : a nation's ships of war **2** : the complete naval equipment and organization of a nation **3** : a grayish purplish blue

¹nay \'nā\ *adv* : NO

²nay *n* : a negative reply or vote

Na·zi \'nät-sē\ *n* : a member of a German fascist party controlling Germany from 1933 to 1945

ne- *or* **neo-** *prefix* **1** : new : recent ⟨*neophyte*⟩ **2** : New World ⟨*Nearctic*⟩

Ne·an·der·thal man \nē-ˌan-dər-ˌthȯl-\ *n* : an extinct primitive man who made tools of stone and lived by hunting

¹near \'niər\ *adv* **1** : at, within, or to a short distance or time **2** : NEARLY

²near *prep* : close to

³near *adj* **1** : closely related or associated ⟨a *near* relative⟩ **2** : not far away **3** : coming close : NARROW ⟨a *near* escape⟩ **4** : being the closer of two ⟨the *near* side⟩ **5** : DIRECT, SHORT ⟨the *nearest* route⟩ — **near·ly** *adv* — **near·ness** *n*

⁴near *vb* : to draw near : APPROACH

near·by \niər-'bī\ *adv (or adj)* : close at hand

near·sight·ed \'niər-'sīt-əd\ *adj* : able to see near things more clearly than distant ones — **near·sight·ed·ly** *adv* — **near·sight·ed·ness** *n*

neat \'nēt\ *adj* **1** : marked by simplicity and good taste ⟨a *neat* dress⟩ **2** : SKILLFUL ⟨a *neat* reply⟩ **3** : TIDY ⟨a *neat* room⟩ — **neat·ly** *adv* — **neat·ness** *n*

neb·u·la \'neb-yə-lə\ *n, pl* **neb·u·las** *or* **neb·u·lae** \-ˌlē\ : any of many clouds of gas or dust seen in the sky among the stars

---

j job   ng sing   ō low   ȯ moth   ȯi coin   th thin   <u>th</u> this   ü boot   u̇ foot   y you   yü few   yu̇ furious   zh vision

neb·u·lous \'neb-yə-ləs\ *adj* : HAZY, IN-DISTINCT — **neb·u·lous·ly** *adv* — **neb·u·lous·ness** *n*

¹**nec·es·sar·y** \'nes-ə-,ser-ē\ *adj* : positively needed : impossible to do without : ESSENTIAL, UNAVOIDABLE — **nec·es·sar·i·ly** \,nes-ə-'ser-ə-lē\ *adv*

²**necessary** *n, pl* **nec·es·sar·ies** : a necessary thing

ne·ces·si·tate \ni-'ses-ə-,tāt\ *vb* **ne·ces·si·tat·ed; ne·ces·si·tat·ing** : to make necessary or un-avoidable : DEMAND, COMPEL

ne·ces·si·ty \ni-'ses-ət-ē\ *n, pl* **ne·ces·si·ties** 1 : very great need of help or relief ⟨call in case of *necessity*⟩ 2 : a necessary thing : some-thing badly needed 3 : lack of necessary things : WANT, POVERTY 4 : conditions that cannot be changed ⟨compelled by *necessity*⟩

neck \'nek\ *n* 1 : the part of the body con-necting the head and the trunk 2 : the part of a garment covering or nearest to the neck 3 : something like a neck in shape or position ⟨the *neck* of a bottle⟩ — **necked** \'nekt\ *adj* — **neck and neck** : so nearly equal (as in a race) that one cannot be said to be ahead of the other

neck·er·chief \'nek-ər-chif\ *n* : a square of cloth worn folded about the neck like a scarf

neck·lace \'nek-ləs\ *n* : an ornament (as a string of beads) worn about the neck

neck·line \'nek-,līn\ *n* : the outline of the neck opening of a garment

neck·tie \'nek-,tī\ *n* : a narrow length of material worn about the neck and tied in front

nec·tar \'nek-tər\ *n* 1 : the drink of the Greek and Roman gods 2 : a sweet liquid secreted by plants and used by bees in making honey

nec·tar·ine \,nek-tə-'rēn\ *n* : a smooth-skinned peach

née *or* **nee** \'nā\ *adj* : BORN — used to identify a woman by her maiden family name ⟨Mrs. Jane Doe, *née* Roe⟩

¹**need** \'nēd\ *n* 1 : necessary duty : OBLIGA-TION ⟨the *need* to be careful⟩ 2 : a lack of something necessary, useful, or desired ⟨in great *need*⟩ 3 : something necessary or desired ⟨our daily *needs*⟩

²**need** *vb* 1 : to be in want ⟨give to those who *need*⟩ 2 : to be needful : be necessary ⟨some-thing *needs* to be done⟩ 3 : to be in need of : REQUIRE ⟨*need* advice⟩

need·ful \'nēd-fəl\ *adj* : NECESSARY — **need-ful·ly** *adv* — **need·ful·ness** *n*

¹**nee·dle** \'nēd-l\ *n* 1 : a slender pointed usually steel implement used in sewing 2 : a slender rod (as for knitting) 3 : a needle-shaped leaf (as of a pine) 4 : an indi-cator on a dial 5 : a slender hollow instrument by which material is introduced into or withdrawn from the body

needles 3

²**needle** *vb* **nee·dled; nee·dling** 1 : to pierce with or as if with a needle 2 : TAUNT, GOAD

nee·dle·point \'nēd-l-,point\ *n* : embroidery done on canvas usually in simple even stitches across counted threads

need·less \'nēd-ləs\ *adj* : UNNECESSARY — **need·less·ly** *adv* — **need·less·ness** *n*

nee·dle·wom·an \'nēd-l-,wùm-ən\ *n, pl* **nee·dle·wom·en** \-,wim-ən\ : SEAMSTRESS

nee·dle·work \'nēd-l-,wərk\ *n* : work done with a needle : SEWING, EMBROIDERY

need·n't \'nēd-nt\ : need not

needs \'nēdz\ *adv* : NECESSARILY ⟨must *needs* be recognized⟩

need·y \'nēd-ē\ *adj* **need·i·er; need·i·est** : being in want : very poor — **need·i·ness** *n*

ne'er \near\ *adv* : NEVER

ne'er–do–well \'near-dù-,wel\ *n* : an idle worthless person

ne·far·i·ous \ni-'far-ē-əs\ *adj* : WICKED, EVIL — **ne·far·i·ous·ness** *n*

ne·gate \ni-'gāt\ *vb* **ne·gat·ed; ne·gat·ing** 1 : to deny the existence or truth of 2 : to cause to be ineffective

ne·ga·tion \ni-'gā-shən\ *n* 1 : the action of negating : DENIAL 2 : CONTRADICTION

¹**neg·a·tive** \'neg-ət-iv\ *adj* 1 : expressing or showing denial ⟨a *negative* reply⟩ 2 : not positive or constructive ⟨a *negative* test⟩ ⟨a *negative* attitude⟩ 3 : less than zero : indicated by a minus sign ⟨−2 is a *negative* number⟩ : being a number that when added to a like number greater than zero yields zero ⟨the *negative* number −5 added to 5 = 0⟩ 4 : of, being, or relating to electricity of which the electron is the unit and which predominates in a hard rubber rod that has been rubbed with wool ⟨a *negative* charge⟩ 5 : having more electrons than protons ⟨a *negative* parti-cle⟩ 6 : being the part toward which the elec-tric current flows from the external circuit ⟨the *negative* pole of a storage battery⟩ — **neg·a·tive·ly** *adv*

²**negative** *n* 1 : a reply that indicates denial or contradiction : REFUSAL 2 : something that is the opposite of something else 3 : a negative number 4 : an expression (as the word *no*) of negation or denial 5 : the side that argues or votes against something

neg·a·tiv·i·ty \,neg-ə-'tiv-ət-ē\ *n* : the quality or state of being negative

¹ne·glect \ni-'glekt\ *vb* **1** : to give little attention or respect to : DISREGARD **2** : to fail to do or attend to especially through carelessness

syn NEGLECT, DISREGARD, SLIGHT all mean to pass over something without giving it any or enough attention. NEGLECT indicates a failure, either deliberate or unintentional, to give proper attention to something that deserves or requires attention ⟨*neglected* his chores⟩ ⟨*neglected* a wound until it became infected⟩ DISREGARD suggests deliberately overlooking some matter, often from a feeling that it is not worth noticing ⟨*disregarded* the dog's growls⟩ or because one prefers not to notice it ⟨*disregarded* the "no smoking" sign⟩ SLIGHT suggests a rude and scornful disregard of a person ⟨he went straight to his room, *slighting* the guests⟩ or a disdainful neglect of a thing ⟨*slighted* his homework all spring⟩

²neglect *n* **1** : an act or instance of neglecting something **2** : the condition of being neglected

ne·glect·ful \ni-'glekt-fəl\ *adj* : given to neglecting : CARELESS — **ne·glect·ful·ly** *adv* — **ne·glect·ful·ness** *n*

neg·li·gee \ˌneg-lə-'zhā\ *n* **1** : a woman's loose robe worn especially while dressing or resting **2** : carelessly informal or incomplete attire

neg·li·gence \'neg-lə-jəns\ *n* : the quality or an instance of being negligent

neg·li·gent \'neg-lə-jənt\ *adj* **1** : inclined to neglect things : CARELESS **2** : NONCHALANT — **neg·li·gent·ly** *adv*

neg·li·gi·ble \'neg-lə-jə-bəl\ *adj* : fit to be neglected or disregarded : TRIFLING — **neg·li·gi·bly** \-blē\ *adv*

ne·go·tia·bil·i·ty \ni-ˌgō-shə-'bil-ət-ē\ *n* : the quality or state of being negotiable

ne·go·tia·ble \ni-'gō-shə-bəl\ *adj* : capable of being negotiated

ne·go·ti·ate \ni-'gō-shē-ˌāt\ *vb* **ne·go·ti·at·ed**; **ne·go·ti·at·ing** [taken from the Latin verb *negotiari* "to carry on business", formed from the noun *negotium* "business", which originally meant "a being busy", and was formed from the prefix *neg-* "not" and the noun *otium* "leisure"] **1** : to have a discussion with another for the purpose of settling some matter ⟨*negotiate* for the purchase of a house⟩ **2** : to arrange for by discussing ⟨*negotiate* a loan⟩ **3** : to transfer to another in exchange for something of equivalent value ⟨*negotiate* a check⟩ **4** : to get through, around, or over successfully ⟨*negotiate* a turn⟩ — **ne·go·ti·a·tor** *n*

ne·go·ti·a·tion \ni-ˌgō-shē-'ā-shən\ *n* : the act or process of negotiating or being negotiated

¹Ne·gro \'nē-grō\ *n, pl* **Ne·groes** : a member of the black race of mankind native to Africa

²Negro *adj* : of or relating to Negroes

¹neigh \'nā\ *vb* : to utter a neigh

²neigh *n* : the long loud cry of a horse

¹neigh·bor \'nā-bər\ *n* : one living or located near another

²neighbor *vb* : to be near or next to : ADJOIN — **neigh·bor·ing** *adj*

neigh·bor·hood \'nā-bər-ˌhůd\ *n* **1** : the quality or state of being neighbors : NEARNESS **2** : a place or region near : VICINITY **3** : an approximate amount, extent, or degree ⟨cost in the *neighborhood* of ten dollars⟩ **4** : the people living nearby **5** : a section lived in by neighbors

neigh·bor·ly \'nā-bər-lē\ *adj* : befitting congenial neighbors : FRIENDLY ⟨*neighborly* help⟩ — **neigh·bor·li·ness** *n*

¹nei·ther \'nē-thər, 'nī-\ *pron* : not the one and not the other

²neither *conj* **1** : not either : equally not **2** : also not

³neither *adj* : not either

neo- — see NE-

ne·on \'nē-ˌän\ *n* [from Greek *neon* "a new thing", derived from the adjective *neos* "new"] : a colorless gaseous chemical element found in very small quantities in the air and used in electric lamps for signs

ne·o·phyte \'nē-ə-ˌfīt\ *n* **1** : a new convert **2** : BEGINNER, NOVICE

neph·ew \'nef-yü\ *n* : a son of one's brother, sister, brother-in-law, or sister-in-law

Nep·tune \'nep-ˌtün, -ˌtyün\ *n* : the planet that is 8th in order of distance from the sun and has a diameter of about 28,000 miles

nep·tu·ni·um \nep-'tü-nē-əm, -'tyü-\ *n* : a radioactive chemical element similar to uranium

¹nerve \'nərv\ *n* **1** : SINEW, TENDON **2** : one of the strands of nerve fibers that join centers (as the brain) of the nervous system with other parts of the body and conduct nerve impulses **3** : power of endurance or control **4** : BOLDNESS, IMPUDENCE **5** *pl* : NERVOUSNESS, JITTERS **6** : the sensitive soft inner part of a tooth — **nerve·less** \-ləs\ *adj*

²nerve *vb* **nerved**; **nerv·ing** : to give strength or courage to

nerve cell *n* : a cell of the nervous system with fibers that conduct nerve impulses

nerve fiber *n* : a process of a nerve cell : AXON, DENDRITE

nerve impulse *n* : a progressive alteration of

a nerve fiber by which information is carried to or orders from the central nervous system

nerv·ous \'nər-vəs\ *adj* **1** : of or relating to nerve cells ⟨*nervous* tissue⟩ **2** : of or relating to nerves or to nervous tissue ⟨the *nervous* system⟩ **3** : easily excited or irritated ⟨a *nervous* person⟩ **4** : FEARFUL, TIMID ⟨*nervous* about answering in class⟩ — **nerv·ous·ly** *adv* — **nerv·ous·ness** *n*

nerv·y \'nər-vē\ *adj* **nerv·i·er; nerv·i·est 1** : showing calm courage : BOLD **2** : IMPUDENT, FORWARD **3** : EXCITABLE, NERVOUS — **nerv·i·ness** *n*

-ness \nəs\ *n suffix* : state : condition : quality : degree ⟨good*ness*⟩ ⟨sick*ness*⟩

¹nest \'nest\ *n* **1** : a bed or shelter prepared by a bird for its eggs and young **2** : a place where the eggs of some animals other than birds are laid and hatched ⟨a snake's *nest*⟩ **3** : a cozy home : a snug retreat **4** : the occupants of a nest

²nest *vb* **1** : to build or occupy a nest ⟨*nesting* birds⟩ **2** : to fit compactly together

nes·tle \'nes-əl\ *vb* **nes·tled; nes·tling** \'nes-ling, -ə-ling\ **1** : to lie close and snug (as in a nest) **2** : to settle as if in a nest ⟨the bird *nestled* its head under its wing⟩

nest·ling \'nest-ling\ *n* : a young bird not yet able to leave the nest

¹net \'net\ *n* **1** : a fabric with a loose mesh made of intersecting threads, cords, ropes, or wires **2** : something (as a device for catching fish) made of net **3** : something that traps like a net ⟨a *net* of lies⟩ **4** : a system of crisscrossing lines or channels ⟨a *net* of canals⟩

²net *vb* **net·ted; net·ting 1** : to cover with or as if with a net **2** : to catch in or as if in a net

³net *adj* : free from all charges or deductions ⟨*net* profit⟩

⁴net *vb* **net·ted; net·ting** : to gain or produce as profit : CLEAR ⟨each sale *nets* ten cents⟩

neth·er \'neth-ər\ *adj* : being situated below

neth·er·most \'neth-ər-,mōst\ *adj* : LOWEST

neth·er·world \'neth-ər-,wərld\ *n* : the world of the dead

net·ting \'net-ing\ *n* **1** : NETWORK **2** : the making of nets

¹net·tle \'net-l\ *n* : any of several tall coarse herbs with stinging hairs

²nettle *vb* **net·tled; net·tling 1** : to sting with or as if with nettles ⟨a *nettling* rash⟩ **2** : PROVOKE, VEX

net·work \'net-,wərk\ *n* **1** : a net fabric or structure **2** : an arrangement of lines or channels crossing in the manner of

nettle

a net **3** : a group of connected radio or television stations

neu·ron \'nü-,rän, 'nyü-\ *n* : NERVE CELL

neu·ter \'nüt-ər, 'nyüt-\ *adj* : lacking sex organs : having imperfectly developed sex organs

¹neu·tral \'nü-trəl, 'nyü-\ *adj* **1** : not favoring either side in a quarrel, contest, or war **2** : of or relating to a neutral country ⟨*neutral* ships⟩ **3** : neither one thing nor the other ⟨a *neutral* character⟩ **4** : possessing no hue : GRAYISH **5** : neither acid nor basic **6** : not electrically charged ⟨a *neutral* atom⟩

²neutral *n* **1** : one that is neutral **2** : a state of adjustment in which the gears that transmit motion are not in contact ⟨put the automobile into *neutral*⟩

neu·tral·i·ty \nü-'tral-ət-ē, nyü-\ *n* : the quality or state of being neutral

neu·tral·i·za·tion \,nü-trə-lə-'zā-shən, ,nyü-\ *n* : an act or process of neutralizing

neu·tral·ize \'nü-trə-,līz, 'nyü-\ *vb* **neu·tral·ized; neu·tral·iz·ing 1** : to make chemically neutral ⟨*neutralize* an acid with lime⟩ **2** : to destroy the effectiveness of — **neu·tral·iz·er** *n*

neu·tri·no \nü-'trē-nō, nyü-\ *n, pl* **neu·tri·nos** : an uncharged particle having a very small mass

neu·tron \'nü-,trän, 'nyü-\ *n* : an uncharged particle that has a mass nearly equal to that of the proton and is present in all atomic nuclei except those of hydrogen

nev·er \'nev-ər\ *adv* **1** : not ever : at no time **2** : not in any degree, way, or condition ⟨*never* fear⟩

nev·er·more \,nev-ər-'mōr\ *adv* : never again

nev·er·the·less \,nev-ər-thə-'les\ *adv* : in spite of that : HOWEVER **syn** see BUT

¹new \'nü, 'nyü\ *adj* **1** : not old : RECENT, MODERN **2** : not the same as the former : taking the place of one that came before ⟨a *new* teacher⟩ **3** : recently discovered or learned about ⟨*new* lands⟩ **4** : not formerly known or experienced ⟨*new* feelings⟩ **5** : not accustomed ⟨a person *new* to her work⟩ **6** : beginning as a repetition of some previous act or thing ⟨a *new* year⟩ **7** : being in a position or place for the first time ⟨a *new* member⟩ — **new·ness** *n*

syn NEW, NOVEL, FRESH all mean having or seeming to have very recently come into being, use, or one's own experience. NEW is the general term and may describe something not known, thought of, or experienced before ⟨a *new* coat⟩ ⟨a *new* idea⟩ ⟨a *new* baby⟩ ⟨a *new* classmate⟩ NOVEL suggests something not only new but also notably unusual or strange ⟨a *novel* idea for a party⟩ and may suggest that more emphasis was placed on making something unusual than on making it worthwhile ⟨gadgets that are *novel* but a nuisance⟩ ⟨*novel* styles of dress⟩ FRESH can apply to something old or new that has the qualities of liveliness, brightness, spotlessness, or vigor that are associated with newness ⟨made a *fresh* start⟩ ⟨put on a *fresh* shirt⟩

²new *adv* : NEWLY, RECENTLY ⟨*new*-mown hay⟩

new·born \'nü-'bòrn, 'nyü-\ *adj* 1 : recently born 2 : born again : RENEWED ⟨*newborn* hopes⟩

new·com·er \'nü-,kəm-ər, 'nyü-\ *n* 1 : one recently arrived 2 : BEGINNER

new·el \'nü-əl, 'nyü-\ *n* : a post at the foot or at a turn of a stairway

new·fan·gled \'nü-'fang-gəld, 'nyü-\ *adj* : of the newest style : NOVEL ⟨*newfangled* ideas⟩

newel

new·ly \'nü-lē, 'nyü-\ *adv* 1 : LATELY, RECENTLY ⟨a *newly* married couple⟩ 2 : ANEW ⟨a *newly* decorated room⟩

new moon *n* 1 : the moon's phase when its dark side is toward the earth 2 : the thin crescent moon seen shortly after sunset for a few days after the new moon

news \'nüz, 'nyüz\ *n* 1 : a report of recent events ⟨school *news*⟩ 2 : material reported in a newspaper or news periodical or on a newscast 3 : matter that is interesting enough to warrant reporting

news·boy \'nüz-,bòi, 'nyüz-\ *n* : a person who delivers or sells newspapers

news·cast \'nüz-,kast, 'nyüz-\ *n* : a radio or television broadcast of news

news·man \'nüz-mən, 'nyüz-\ *n, pl* **news·men** \-mən\ : one who gathers or reports news

news·pa·per \'nüz-,pā-pər, 'nyüz-\ *n* : a paper that is printed and distributed at regular intervals and contains news, articles, features, and usually advertising

news·pa·per·man \'nüz-,pā-pər-,man, 'nyüz-\ *n, pl* **news·pa·per·men** \-,men\ : one who owns or is employed by an organization publishing a newspaper

news·reel \'nüz-,rēl, 'nyüz-\ *n* : a short moving picture showing current events

news·stand \'nüz-,stand, 'nyüz-\ *n* : a place where newspapers and periodicals are sold

news·y \'nü-zē, 'nyü-\ *adj* **news·i·er; news·i·est** : filled with news ⟨a *newsy* letter⟩

newt \'nüt, 'nyüt\ *n* : a small salamander that lives mostly in water

New World *n* : the western hemisphere including North America and South America

New Year's Day *n* : January 1 observed as a legal holiday

¹next \'nekst\ *adj* : immediately preceding or following : NEAREST

²next *adv* 1 : in the nearest place, time, or order following ⟨do this *next*⟩ 2 : at the first time after this ⟨when *next* we meet⟩

³next *prep* : next to

¹next to *prep* : immediately following : adjacent to ⟨*next to* the head of his class⟩

²next to *adv* : very nearly : ALMOST ⟨*next to* impossible to win⟩

nib \'nib\ *n* 1 : a pointed object (as the bill of a bird) 2 : the point of a pen

¹nib·ble \'nib-əl\ *vb* **nib·bled; nib·bling** : to bite or chew gently or bit by bit

²nibble *n* : an act of nibbling : a small or cautious bite — **nib·bler** \'nib-lər\ *n*

nib 2

nice \'nīs\ *adj* 1 : very particular about things (as appearance, manners, and food) : REFINED 2 : having the power to show or to feel small or fine differences between things : delicately sensitive ⟨have a *nice* ear for music⟩ 3 : PLEASING, AGREEABLE ⟨a *nice* time⟩ 4 : well behaved : WELL-BRED ⟨*nice* people⟩ — **nice·ly** *adv* — **nice·ness** *n*

ni·ce·ty \'nī-sət-ē\ *n, pl* **ni·ce·ties** 1 : a dainty, delicate, or elegant thing ⟨the *niceties* of life⟩ 2 : a fine detail ⟨*niceties* of workmanship⟩ 3 : EXACTNESS, ACCURACY

niche \'nich\ *n* 1 : a recess in a wall (as for a statue) 2 : a place, work, or use for which a person or a thing is best fitted

¹nick \'nik\ *n* 1 : a small groove : NOTCH, CHIP ⟨a *nick* in a cup⟩ 2 : the final possible moment ⟨in the *nick* of time⟩

²nick *vb* : to make a nick in : NOTCH, CHIP

niche

¹nick·el \'nik-əl\ *n* 1 : a hard silver-white metallic chemical element that can be highly polished, resists corrosion, and is used in alloys 2 : a United States five-cent piece made of copper and nickel

²nickel *vb* : to plate with nickel

¹nick·er \'nik-ər\ *vb* : NEIGH, WHINNY

²nicker *n* : NEIGH

¹nick·name \'nik-,nām\ *n* [in earlier English *a nekename* was the result of misunderstanding the phrase *an ekename*, which meant "an additional name", coming from *eke* "also"] 1 : a usually descriptive name given instead of or in addition to the one belonging to an individual 2 : a familiar form of a proper name

²nickname *vb* **nick·named; nick·nam·ing** : to give a nickname to

nic·o·tine \'nik-ə-ˌtēn\ n : a poisonous substance found in small amounts in tobacco and used as an insecticide

niece \'nēs\ n : a daughter of one's brother, sister, brother-in-law, or sister-in-law

nig·gard·ly \'nig-ərd-lē\ adj 1 : STINGY, MISERLY 2 : SCANTY — **nig·gard·li·ness** n

nig·gling \'nig-ling\ adj : PETTY

¹nigh \'nī\ adv 1 : near in time or place 2 : NEARLY, ALMOST

²nigh adj : CLOSE, NEAR

night \'nīt\ n 1 : the time between dusk and dawn when there is no sunlight 2 : NIGHTFALL 3 : the darkness of night

night·club \'nīt-ˌkləb\ n : a place of entertainment open at night usually serving food and liquor and providing music for dancing

night·fall \'nīt-ˌfȯl\ n : the coming of night

night·gown \'nīt-ˌgaùn\ n : a long loose garment worn in bed

night·hawk \'nīt-ˌhȯk\ n 1 : an insect-eating bird flying mostly at twilight and related to the whippoorwill 2 : a person who stays up late at night

night·ie \'nīt-ē\ n : NIGHTGOWN

night·in·gale \'nīt-n-ˌgāl\ n : a reddish brown Old World thrush noted for the sweet song of the male

¹night·ly \'nīt-lē\ adj 1 : of or relating to the night or every night 2 : happening or done at night or every night

²nightly adv : every night : at or by night ⟨mail is collected *nightly*⟩

night·mare \'nīt-ˌmaər\ n 1 : a frightening oppressive dream 2 : a horrible experience — **night·mar·ish** \'nīt-ˌmaər-ish\ adj

night·shirt \'nīt-ˌshərt\ n : a nightgown resembling a shirt

night·time \'nīt-ˌtīm\ n : the time from dusk to dawn

nil \'nil\ n : NOTHING, ZERO

nim·ble \'nim-bəl\ adj **nim·bler; nim·blest** 1 : quick and light in motion : AGILE ⟨*nimble* movements⟩ 2 : quick in understanding and learning : CLEVER ⟨a *nimble* mind⟩ — **nim·ble·ness** n — **nim·bly** \-blē\ adv

nim·bus \'nim-bəs\ n, pl **nim·bi** \-ˌbī\ or **nim·bus·es** : a rain cloud of uniform grayness that extends over the whole sky

nin·com·poop \'nin-kəm-ˌpüp\ n : FOOL

¹nine \'nīn\ adj : being one more than eight

²nine n 1 : one more than eight 2 : the ninth in a set or series

nine·pins \'nīn-ˌpinz\ n : a bowling game played with nine wooden pins set on end

¹nine·teen \nīn-'tēn\ adj : being one more than eighteen

²nineteen n : one more than eighteen

¹nine·teenth \nīn-'tenth\ adj : being next after the eighteenth

²nineteenth n : number nineteen in a series

¹nine·ti·eth \'nīnt-ē-əth\ adj : being next after the eighty-ninth

²ninetieth n : number ninety in a series

¹nine·ty \'nīnt-ē\ adj : being nine times ten

²ninety n : nine times ten

nin·ny \'nin-ē\ n, pl **nin·nies** : FOOL, SIMPLETON

¹ninth \'nīnth\ adj : being next after the eighth

²ninth n 1 : number nine in a series 2 : one of nine equal parts

¹nip \'nip\ vb **nipped; nip·ping** 1 : to catch hold of and squeeze sharply though not severely 2 : to sever by or as if by pinching sharply : CLIP 3 : to check (as growth) by or as if by pinching off ⟨*nip* plans in the bud⟩ 4 : to injure or make numb with cold

²nip n 1 : something that nips : STING, TANG 2 : the act of nipping 3 : a small portion

³nip n : a small drink

nip and tuck \ˌnip-ən-'tək\ adj (or adv) : so close that the lead or advantage shifts rapidly from one contestant to another

nip·per \'nip-ər\ n : a device (as pincers) for nipping — usually used in plural

nip·ple \'nip-əl\ n 1 : the part of the breast from which a baby or young animal sucks milk 2 : something (as the mouthpiece of a baby's bottle) resembling a nipple

nippers

nip·py \'nip-ē\ adj **nip·pi·er; nip·pi·est** 1 : NIMBLE, BRISK 2 : CHILLY ⟨a *nippy* day⟩

nit \'nit\ n : the egg of a louse or similar insect

ni·trate \'nī-ˌtrāt\ n : a substance that is made from or has a composition as if made from nitric acid ⟨*nitrates* are used as fertilizers and explosives⟩

ni·tric acid \ˌnī-trik-\ n : a strong liquid acid composed of hydrogen, nitrogen, and oxygen used in making fertilizers, explosives, and dyes

ni·tro·gen \'nī-trə-jən\ n : a colorless odorless gaseous chemical element that makes up 78 percent of the atmosphere and is a constituent of all living tissues

nitrogen cycle n : a continuous series of natural processes from the air to soil to organisms and back through processes of nitrogen fixation, metabolism, and decay

nitrogen fix·a·tion \-fik-'sā-shən\ n : the conversion of free nitrogen into combined forms especially by bacteria (**nitrogen-fixing bacteria**)

ə abut   ər further   a ax   ā age   ä father, cot   á (see key page)   aù out   ch chin   e less   ē easy   g gift   i trip   ī life

ni·tro·glyc·er·in *or* **ni·tro·glyc·er·ine** \ˌnī-trō-ˈglis-ə-rən\ *n* : a heavy oily liquid explosive from which dynamite is made

nit·wit \ˈnit-ˌwit\ *n* : a very silly or stupid person

¹no \nō\ *adv* **1** : in no respect or degree : not any ⟨he is *no* better than he should be⟩ **2** : not so — used to express disagreement or refusal ⟨*no*, I'm not hungry⟩ **3** — used to express surprise, doubt, or disbelief ⟨*no*—you don't say⟩

²no *adj* **1** : not any ⟨has *no* money⟩ **2** : hardly any : very little ⟨finished in *no* time⟩ **3** : not a ⟨he's *no* champion⟩

³no *n, pl* **noes** *or* **nos** **1** : an act or instance of refusing or denying by the use of the word *no* : DENIAL **2** : a negative vote or decision **3** *pl* : persons voting in the negative

no·bil·i·ty \nō-ˈbil-ət-ē\ *n, pl* **no·bil·i·ties** **1** : the quality or state of being noble ⟨*nobility* of character⟩ **2** : noble rank ⟨confer *nobility* on a person⟩ **3** : the class or a group of nobles ⟨a member of the *nobility*⟩

¹no·ble \ˈnō-bəl\ *adj* **no·bler; no·blest** **1** : ILLUSTRIOUS, FAMOUS **2** : of high birth or exalted rank **3** : possessing superior qualities **4** : grand and impressive in appearance ⟨a *noble* building⟩ — **no·ble·ness** *n* — **no·bly** \-blē\ *adv*

²noble *n* : a person of noble rank or birth

no·ble·man \ˈnō-bəl-mən\ *n, pl* **no·ble·men** \-mən\ : a member of the nobility : PEER

no·ble·wom·an \ˈnō-bəl-ˌwùm-ən\ *n, pl* **no·ble·wom·en** \-ˌwim-ən\ : a woman of noble rank

¹no·body \ˈnō-ˌbäd-ē\ *pron* : no person

²nobody *n, pl* **no·bod·ies** : a person of no importance

noc·tur·nal \näk-ˈtərn-l\ *adj* **1** : of, relating to, or happening at night : NIGHTLY **2** : active at night ⟨*nocturnal* insects⟩ — **noc·tur·nal·ly** *adv*

noc·turne \ˈnäk-ˌtərn\ *n* : a dreamy pensive composition for the piano

¹nod \ˈnäd\ *vb* **nod·ded; nod·ding** **1** : to bend the head downward or forward (as in bowing or going to sleep or as a sign of assent) **2** : to move up and down ⟨daisies *nodded* in the breeze⟩ **3** : to show by a nod of the head ⟨*nod* agreement⟩

²nod *n* : the action of nodding ⟨a *nod* of the head⟩

node \ˈnōd\ *n* : a thickened or swollen enlargement (as of a plant stem where a leaf develops)

nod·ule \ˈnäj-ül\ *n* : a small node (as of a clover root)

no·el \nō-ˈel\ *n* [from French *noël*, from Latin *natalis* "birthday", used in the Middle Ages especially of the birthday of Christ; the Latin noun was originally an adjective meaning "relating to birth" and derived from *nasci* "to be born"] **1** : a Christmas carol **2** *cap* : the Christmas season

¹noise \ˈnȯiz\ *n* **1** : loud confused unpleasant sound **2** : SOUND ⟨the *noise* of the wind⟩ — **noise·less** \-ləs\ *adj* — **noise·less·ly** *adv* — **noise·less·ness** *n*

²noise *vb* **noised; nois·ing** : to spread by rumor or report ⟨the story was *noised* about⟩

noise·mak·er \ˈnȯiz-ˌmā-kər\ *n* : a device used to make noise at parties

noi·some \ˈnȯi-səm\ *adj* **1** : UNWHOLESOME, NOXIOUS **2** : OFFENSIVE, DISGUSTING — **noi·some·ness** *n*

nois·y \ˈnȯi-zē\ *adj* **nois·i·er; nois·i·est** : making noise : full of noises ⟨a *noisy* street⟩ — **nois·i·ly** \-zə-lē\ *adv* — **nois·i·ness** \-zē-nəs\ *n*

¹no·mad \ˈnō-ˌmad\ *n* **1** : a member of a people that has no fixed home but wanders from place to place **2** : WANDERER

²nomad *adj* : ROVING, NOMADIC ⟨*nomad* tribes⟩

no·mad·ic \nō-ˈmad-ik\ *adj* **1** : of or relating to nomads **2** : roaming about aimlessly

nom de plume \ˌnäm-di-ˈplüm\ *n, pl* **noms de plume** \ˌnämz-\ : PEN NAME

nom·i·nal \ˈnäm-ən-l\ *adj* **1** : existing in name only ⟨the *nominal* president⟩ **2** : very small : INSIGNIFICANT ⟨a *nominal* price⟩ — **nom·i·nal·ly** *adv*

nom·i·nate \ˈnäm-ə-ˌnāt\ *vb* **nom·i·nat·ed; nom·i·nat·ing** : to choose as a candidate for election, appointment, or honor ⟨*nominated* her for president⟩ — **nom·i·na·tor** *n*

nom·i·na·tion \ˌnäm-ə-ˈnā-shən\ *n* **1** : the act or an instance of nominating **2** : the state of being nominated ⟨win the *nomination*⟩

nom·i·na·tive \ˈnäm-ə-nət-iv\ *adj* : marking typically the subject of a verb ⟨a noun in the *nominative* case⟩

nom·i·nee \ˌnäm-ə-ˈnē\ *n* : a person nominated for an office, duty, or position

non- *prefix* : not : reverse of : absence of ⟨*non*resident⟩ ⟨*non*fiction⟩

non·al·co·hol·ic \ˌnän-ˌal-kə-ˈhȯl-ik, -ˈhäl-\ *adj* : not containing alcohol

nonce \ˈnäns\ *n* : the one, particular, or present occasion or use ⟨for the *nonce*⟩

non·cha·lance \ˌnän-shə-ˈläns\ *n* : the state of being nonchalant

non·cha·lant \ˌnän-shə-ˈlänt\ *adj* : being without self-consciousness or embarrassment : having a confident and easy manner

non·com·bat·ant \ˌnän-kəm-ˈbat-nt, ˈnän-

---

j **job** ng **sing** ō **low** ȯ **moth** ȯi **coin** th **thin** <u>th</u> **this** ü **boot** ù **foot** y **you** yü **few** yù **furious** zh **vision**

'käm-bət-ənt\ *n* **1** : a member (as a chaplain) of the armed forces whose duties do not include fighting **2** : CIVILIAN

non·com·mis·sioned officer \ˌnän-kə-ˌmish-ənd-\ *n* : a subordinate officer in a branch of the armed forces appointed from enlisted personnel and holding one of various grades (as staff sergeant)

non·com·mit·tal \ˌnän-kə-'mit-l\ *adj* : not telling or showing what a person thinks or has decided ⟨a *noncommittal* answer⟩ — **non·com·mit·tal·ly** *adv*

non·con·duc·tor \ˌnän-kən-'dək-tər\ *n* : a substance that conducts heat, electricity, or sound only in very small degree

non·con·form·ist \ˌnän-kən-'fȯr-məst\ *n* **1** *often cap* : a person who does not conform to a certain church (as the Church of England) : DISSENTER **2** : a person who does not conform to prevailing standards or customs

non·con·form·i·ty \ˌnän-kən-'fȯr-mət-ē\ *n* : refusal to conform to an established or conventional creed, rule, or practice

non·de·script \ˌnän-di-'skript\ *adj* : not easy to describe : of no particular class or kind ⟨a *nondescript* house⟩

¹**none** \'nən\ *pron* : not any : not one

²**none** *adv* : by no means : not at all : to no extent ⟨arrived *none* too soon⟩

non·en·ti·ty \nän-'ent-ət-ē\ *n, pl* **non·en·ti·ties** : one of no importance

¹**non·es·sen·tial** \ˌnän-ə-'sen-chəl\ *adj* : not fundamentally needed

²**nonessential** *n* : something nonessential

none·the·less \ˌnən-thə-'les\ *adv* : NEVERTHELESS

non·ex·ist·ent \ˌnän-ig-'zis-tənt\ *adj* : not having existence

non·fic·tion·al \'nän-'fik-shən-l\ *adj* : not fictional

non·flam·ma·ble \'nän-'flam-ə-bəl\ *adj* : not flammable

non·liv·ing \'nän-'liv-ing\ *adj* : not living or characterized by life

¹**non·pa·reil** \ˌnän-pə-'rel\ *adj* : having no equal : PEERLESS

²**nonpareil** *n* : an individual of unequaled excellence : PARAGON

non·par·ti·san \'nän-'pärt-ə-zən\ *adj* : not partisan : free from party membership or bias

non·plus \'nän-'pləs\ *vb* **non·plussed; non·plus·sing** : to cause to be at a loss as to what to say, think, or do : PERPLEX

non·poi·son·ous \'nän-'pȯiz-n-əs\ *adj* : not poisonous ⟨*nonpoisonous* snakes⟩

non·pro·duc·tive \ˌnän-prə-'dək-tiv\ *adj* : not productive

non·prof·it \'nän-'präf-ət\ *adj* : not conducted or maintained for the purpose of making a profit ⟨*nonprofit* organization⟩

¹**non·res·i·dent** \'nän-'rez-ə-dənt\ *adj* **1** : not having one's permanent residence in a certain place ⟨*nonresident* student⟩ **2** : of or relating to a nonresident person ⟨*nonresident* license⟩

²**nonresident** *n* : a nonresident person

non·sched·uled \'nän-'skej-üld\ *adj* : licensed to carry passengers or freight by air without a regular schedule ⟨*nonscheduled* airline⟩

non·sec·tar·i·an \ˌnän-sek-'ter-ē-ən\ *adj* : not restricted to a particular religious group

non·sense \'nän-ˌsens\ *n* **1** : foolish or meaningless words or actions **2** : things of no importance or value : TRIFLES

non·sen·si·cal \nän-'sen-si-kəl\ *adj* : ABSURD, FOOLISH — **non·sen·si·cal·ly** *adv*

non·stan·dard \'nän-'stan-dərd\ *adj* : not standard

non·stop \'nän-'stäp\ *adv (or adj)* : without a stop ⟨fly *nonstop* to London⟩ ⟨a *nonstop* flight to London⟩

noo·dle \'nüd-l\ *n* : a food like macaroni but shaped into long flat strips and made with egg — usually used in plural

nook \'nuk\ *n* **1** : an interior corner : RECESS ⟨chimney *nook*⟩ **2** : a sheltered or hidden place ⟨a shady *nook*⟩

noon \'nün\ *n* : the middle of the day : twelve o'clock in the daytime

noon·day \'nün-ˌdā\ *n* : MIDDAY

noon·tide \'nün-ˌtīd\ *n* **1** : the time of noon **2** : the highest or culminating point

noon·time \'nün-ˌtīm\ *n* : NOONTIDE

noose \'nüs\ *n* : a loop with a slipknot that binds closer the more it is drawn ⟨the *noose* of a lasso⟩

nor \nər, nȯr\ *conj* : and not — used between two words or phrases preceded by *neither* ⟨neither here *nor* there⟩

norm \'nȯrm\ *n* : AVERAGE, STANDARD

¹**nor·mal** \'nȯr-məl\ *adj* **1** : of the regular or usual kind : REGULAR, NATURAL **2** : of average intelligence **3** : sound of body or mind : SANE — **nor·mal·ly** *adv*

²**normal** *n* **1** : one that is normal **2** : the usual condition or degree : AVERAGE

nor·mal·cy \'nȯr-məl-sē\ *n* : NORMALITY

nor·mal·i·ty \nȯr-'mal-ət-ē\ *n* : the quality or state of being normal

Nor·man \'nȯr-mən\ *n* **1** : one of the Scandinavians conquering Normandy in the tenth century **2** : one of the people of mixed Norman and French blood conquering England in 1066

Norse \'nȯrs\ *n pl* **1** : SCANDINAVIANS
2 : NORWEGIANS
¹north \'nȯrth\ *adv* : to or toward the north
²north *adj* : situated toward or coming from
the north
³north *n* **1** : the direction to the left of one
facing east : the compass point opposite to
south **2** *cap* : regions or countries north of a
specified or implied point
¹North American *n* : a native or inhabitant of
North America
²North American *adj* : of or relating to
North America or its inhabitants
north·bound \'nȯrth-ˌbau̇nd\ *adj* : going
north
¹north·east \nȯrth-'ēst\ *adv* : to or toward
the northeast
²northeast *n* **1** : the direction between north
and east **2** *cap* : regions or countries northeast of a specified or implied point
³northeast *adj* : situated toward or coming
from the northeast
north·east·ern \nȯrth-'ēs-tərn\ *adj* **1** *often
cap* : of or relating to a region usually called
Northeast **2** : lying toward or coming from
the northeast
north·er·ly \'nȯr-thər-lē\ *adv (or adj)* **1** : from
the north ⟨a *northerly* wind⟩ **2** : toward the
north
north·ern \'nȯr-thərn\ *adj* **1** *often cap* : of
or relating to a region usually called North
2 : lying toward or coming from the north
northern lights *n pl* : AURORA BOREALIS
north·land \'nȯrth-ˌland\ *n, often cap* : land
in the north : the north of a country or region
north pole *n* **1** *often cap N&P* : the most
northern point of the earth : the northern end
of the earth's axis **2** : the end of a magnet
that points toward the north when the magnet
is free to swing
North Star *n* : the star toward which the
northern end of the earth's axis very nearly
points
¹north·ward \'nȯrth-wərd\ *adv (or adj)*
: toward the north
²northward *n* : a northward direction or part
¹north·west \nȯrth-'west\ *adv* : to or toward
the northwest
²northwest *n* **1** : the direction between north
and west **2** *cap* : regions or countries northwest of a specified or implied point
³northwest *adj* : situated toward or coming
from the northwest
north·west·ern \nȯrth-'wes-tərn\ *adj* **1** *often
cap* : of or relating to a region usually called
Northwest **2** : lying toward or coming from
the northwest

¹Nor·we·gian \nȯr-'wē-jən\ *adj* : of or relating to Norway, the people of Norway, or
Norwegian
²Norwegian *n* **1** : a native or inhabitant of
Norway **2** : the language of the Norwegians
¹nose \'nōz\ *n* **1** : the part of a person's face
or an animal's head that con-
tains the nostrils **2** : the sense
or organ of smell ⟨a dog with
a good *nose*⟩ **3** : something
(as a point, edge, or the front
of an object) that resembles a nose ⟨the *nose*
of an airplane⟩ — **nosed** \'nōzd\ *adj*

nose

²nose *vb* **nosed; nos·ing** **1** : to detect by or as
if by smell : SCENT **2** : to touch or rub with
the nose : NUZZLE **3** : to search inquisitively
: PRY **4** : to move ahead slowly ⟨the ship
nosed into her berth⟩
nose·bleed \'nōz-ˌblēd\ *n* : a bleeding at the
nose
nose dive *n* **1** : the downward nose-first
plunge of an airplane **2** : a sharp sudden
drop (as in prices)
nose–dive \'nōz-ˌdīv\ *vb* **nose–dived; nose–
div·ing** : to plunge headlong
nose·gay \'nōz-ˌgā\ *n* : a small bunch of
flowers
nos·tal·gia \näs-'tal-jə\ *n* : a
wistful yearning for something
past or beyond recall
nos·tal·gic \näs-'tal-jik\ *adj*
: characterized by nostalgia —
nos·tal·gi·cal·ly \-ji-kə-lē\ *adv*

nosegay

nos·tril \'näs-trəl\ *n* : either of
the outer openings of the nose through which
one breathes
nos·trum \'näs-trəm\ *n* : a medicine of
secret formula and no official standing : a
questionable remedy
nos·y *or* **nos·ey** \'nō-zē\ *adj* **nos·i·er; nos·i·est**
: INQUISITIVE
not \'nät\ *adv* **1** — used to make negative a
word or group of words ⟨the books are *not*
here⟩ **2** — used to stand for the negative of a
preceding group of words ⟨sometimes hard to
see and sometimes *not*⟩
no·ta·bil·i·ty \ˌnōt-ə-'bil-ət-ē\ *n, pl* **no·ta-
bil·i·ties** **1** : the quality or state of being
notable **2** : a notable person
¹no·ta·ble \'nōt-ə-bəl\ *adj* **1** : worthy of
note : REMARKABLE ⟨a *notable* sight⟩ **2** : DIS-
TINGUISHED, PROMINENT — **no·ta·bly** \-blē\ *adv*
²notable *n* : a person of great reputation
no·ta·rize \'nōt-ə-ˌrīz\ *vb* **no·ta·rized; no-
ta·riz·ing** : to make legally authentic through
the use of the powers granted to a notary
public

no·ta·ry pub·lic \ˌnōt-ə-rē-\ *n, pl* **no·ta·ries pub·lic** *or* **no·ta·ry pub·lics** : a public officer who attests or certifies writings (as a deed) as authentic

no·ta·tion \nō-'tā-shən\ *n* **1** : the act of noting **2** : something noted ⟨make *notations* on a paper⟩ **3** : a system of signs, marks, figures, or characters used to express facts, quantities, or actions ⟨musical *notation*⟩

¹notch \'näch\ *n* **1** : a V-shaped cut in an edge or surface : NICK **2** : a narrow pass between mountains **3** : DEGREE, STEP ⟨turn the volume of the radio up a *notch*⟩

²notch *vb* : to cut or make notches in

¹note \'nōt\ *vb* **not·ed; not·ing 1** : to notice or observe with care **2** : to record or preserve in writing **3** : to make special mention of : REMARK

²note *n* **1** : a musical sound **2** : the musical call of a bird **3** : a special tone of voice ⟨a *note* of warning⟩ **4** : a brief informal record : MEMORANDUM **5** : a printed comment or explanation (as in a book) **6** : a brief informal letter **7** : a written promise to pay a debt **8** : a character in music that by its shape shows the length of time a tone is to be held and by its place on the staff shows the pitch of a tone **9** : a characteristic feature : MOOD ⟨a *note* of optimism⟩ **10** : DISTINCTION, REPUTATION ⟨a man of *note*⟩ **11** : NOTICE, HEED ⟨take *note* of the time⟩

note·book \'nōt-ˌbu̇k\ *n* : a book for notes or memoranda

not·ed \'nōt-əd\ *adj* : WELL-KNOWN, FAMOUS

note·wor·thy \'nōt-ˌwər-t͟hē\ *adj* : worthy of note : REMARKABLE — **note·wor·thi·ness** *n*

¹noth·ing \'nəth-ing\ *pron* **1** : not anything ⟨there's *nothing* in the box⟩ **2** : one of no interest, value, or consequence ⟨she's *nothing* to me⟩

²nothing *adv* : not at all : in no degree

³nothing *n* **1** : something that does not exist **2** : ZERO **3** : something of little or no worth or importance — **noth·ing·ness** *n*

¹no·tice \'nōt-əs\ *n* **1** : WARNING, ANNOUNCEMENT **2** : notification of the ending of an agreement at a specified time **3** : ATTENTION, HEED ⟨brought the matter to my *notice*⟩ **4** : a written or printed announcement **5** : a brief published criticism (as of a book)

²notice *vb* **no·ticed; no·tic·ing 1** : to make mention of **2** : to take notice of : OBSERVE

no·tice·a·ble \'nōt-ə-sə-bəl\ *adj* : capable of being or likely to be noticed : CONSPICUOUS — **no·tice·a·bly** \-blē\ *adv*

syn NOTICEABLE, CONSPICUOUS, PROMINENT all refer to something that attracts or com-

pels attention. NOTICEABLE applies to that which is unlikely to escape observation ⟨the dog had a *noticeable* limp⟩ or to what can be noticed by an observant person ⟨wondered if the erasures were *noticeable*⟩ CONSPICUOUS refers to that which is so obvious or open that it cannot escape observation ⟨*conspicuous* bravery⟩ and often stresses being unpleasantly or undesirably noticeable ⟨wore *conspicuous* clothes⟩ ⟨try not to be *conspicuous*⟩ PROMINENT normally applies to things that are noticeable because they protrude from their backgrounds ⟨had *prominent* eyebrows⟩ and when applied to people often suggests a desirable position well above the average ⟨his father is a *prominent* judge⟩

no·ti·fi·ca·tion \ˌnōt-ə-fə-'kā-shən\ *n* **1** : the act or an instance of notifying **2** : written or printed matter that gives notice

no·ti·fy \'nōt-ə-ˌfī\ *vb* **no·ti·fied; no·ti·fy·ing** : to give notice to : inform by a notice

no·tion \'nō-shən\ *n* **1** : IDEA, IMPRESSION **2** : VIEW, OPINION **3** : WHIM, FANCY ⟨a sudden *notion* to go home⟩ **4** *pl* : small useful articles (as buttons, needles, and thread) ⟨*notions* counter⟩

no·tion·al \'nō-shən-l\ *adj* **1** : IMAGINARY, UNREAL **2** : inclined to have foolish or visionary fancies or moods

no·to·ri·e·ty \ˌnōt-ə-'rī-ət-ē\ *n* : the quality or state of being notorious

no·to·ri·ous \nō-'tōr-ē-əs\ *adj* : widely and unfavorably known ⟨a *notorious* thief⟩ **syn** see FAMOUS — **no·to·ri·ous·ly** *adv*

¹not·with·stand·ing \ˌnät-with-'stan-ding, -with-\ *prep* : in spite of

²notwithstanding *adv* : NEVERTHELESS, HOWEVER

³notwithstanding *conj* : ALTHOUGH

nou·gat \'nü-gət\ *n* : a candy consisting of a sugar paste with nuts or fruit pieces

nought \'nȯt\ *var of* NAUGHT

noun \'nau̇n\ *n* : a word that is the name of something (as a person, place, or thing) that can be talked about

nour·ish \'nər-ish\ *vb* : to cause to grow or survive in a healthy state especially by providing with enough and suitable food — **nour·ish·ing** *adj*

nour·ish·ment \'nər-ish-mənt\ *n* **1** : something (as food) that nourishes **2** : the act of nourishing : the state of being nourished

¹nov·el \'näv-əl\ *adj* **1** : not resembling something formerly known **2** : original or striking in design or appearance **syn** see NEW

²novel *n* : a long prose narrative dealing usually with imaginary characters and events

nov·el·ist \'näv-ə-ləst\ *n* : a writer of novels

nov·el·ty \'näv-əl-tē\ *n, pl* **nov·el·ties** **1** : something new or unusual **2** : the quality or state of being novel **3** : a small article of unusual design intended mainly for decoration or adornment

No·vem·ber \nō-'vem-bər\ *n* : the eleventh month of the year

nov·ice \'näv-əs\ *n* **1** : a new member of a religious order who is preparing to take the vows of religion **2** : one who has no previous training or experience in a field or activity : BEGINNER

¹now \naù\ *adv* **1** : at the present time **2** : in the time immediately before the present ⟨left just *now*⟩ **3** : in the time immediately to follow ⟨will leave *now*⟩ **4** — used with the sense of present time weakened or lost (as to express command or introduce an important point) ⟨*now* do this⟩ **5** : SOMETIMES ⟨*now* one and *now* another⟩ **6** : under the present circumstances ⟨*now* what can we do⟩ **7** : at the time referred to ⟨*now* the trouble began⟩

²now *conj* : SINCE

³now *n* : the present time : PRESENT

⁴now *adj* : of or relating to the present time : EXISTING ⟨the *now* president⟩

now·a·days \'naù-ə-,dāz\ *adv* : at the present time

¹no·where \'nō-,hweər\ *adv* **1** : not in or at any place **2** : to no place

²nowhere *n* : a place that does not exist

no·wise \'nō-,wīz\ *adv* : in no way : not at all

nox·ious \'näk-shəs\ *adj* : HARMFUL, UNWHOLESOME ⟨*noxious* fumes⟩

noz·zle \'näz-əl\ *n* **1** : a projecting part with an opening that serves as an outlet ⟨the *nozzle* of a gun⟩ **2** : a short tube with a taper or constriction used on a hose or pipe to direct or speed up a flow of fluid

nozzles

-n't \nt, -nt, ənt\ *adv suffix* : not ⟨can't⟩ ⟨isn't⟩

nu·ance \'nü-,äns, 'nyü-\ *n* : a shade of difference in feeling or in meaning

nub·bin \'nəb-ən\ *n* : a small shriveled or imperfectly developed fruit

nu·cle·ar \'nü-klē-ər, 'nyü-\ *adj* **1** : of, relating to, or being a nucleus (as of a cell) **2** : of, relating to, or utilizing the atomic nucleus, atomic energy, the atom bomb, or atomic power

nuclear energy *n* : ATOMIC ENERGY

nu·cle·us \'nü-klē-əs, 'nyü-\ *n, pl* **nu·cle·i** \-klē-,ī\ *also* **nu·cle·us·es** [a use by modern scientists of the old Latin word meaning

"kernel", which was derived from the word *nux* "nut"] **1** : a central point, group, or mass **2** : a part of cell protoplasm enclosed in a nuclear membrane, containing chromosomes and genes, and concerned especially with the control of vital functions and heredity **3** : the central part of an atom that comprises nearly all of the atomic mass and that consists of protons and neutrons except in hydrogen which consists of one proton only

nude \'nüd, 'nyüd\ *adj* : not clothed : NAKED — **nude·ness** *n*

¹nudge \'nəj\ *vb* **nudged**; **nudg·ing** : to touch or push gently (as with the elbow) especially in order to attract attention

²nudge *n* : a slight push, poke, or jog

nu·di·ty \'nüd-ət-ē, 'nyüd-\ *n* : the quality or state of being nude

nug·get \'nəg-ət\ *n* : a solid lump usually of precious metal

nui·sance \'nüs-ns, 'nyüs-\ *n* : an annoying or troublesome person or thing

null \'nəl\ *adj* **1** : having no legal or binding force : VOID **2** : amounting to nothing : NIL

null and void *adj* : having no force, binding power, or validity

nul·li·fi·ca·tion \,nəl-ə-fə-'kā-shən\ *n* : the act of nullifying : the state of being nullified

nul·li·fy \'nəl-ə-,fī\ *vb* **nul·li·fied**; **nul·li·fy·ing** : to make null or valueless

nul·li·ty \'nəl-ət-ē\ *n* : the quality or state of being null

¹numb \'nəm\ *adj* **1** : lacking in sensation especially from cold **2** : lacking emotion : INDIFFERENT — **numb·ly** *adv* — **numb·ness** *n*

²numb *vb* : to make or become numb

¹num·ber \'nəm-bər\ *n* **1** : the total of persons, things, or units taken together : AMOUNT ⟨the *number* of people in a room⟩ **2** : a distinction of word form to denote reference to one or more than one ⟨a verb agrees in *number* with its subject⟩ **3** : NUMERAL ⟨the *number* 5⟩ **4** : a particular numeral for telling one person or thing from another or others ⟨a house *number*⟩ **5** : GROUP, MANY ⟨a *number* of presents⟩ **6** : one of a series of things ⟨the March *number* of a magazine⟩

²number *vb* **1** : COUNT, ENUMERATE **2** : INCLUDE ⟨was *numbered* among the guests⟩ **3** : to restrict to a definite number ⟨vacation days are *numbered* now⟩ **4** : to assign a number to ⟨*number* the pages of a scrapbook⟩ **5** : COMPRISE, CONTAIN ⟨our group *numbered* ten in all⟩

num·ber·less \'nəm-bər-ləs\ *adj* : too many to count : INNUMERABLE ⟨the *numberless* stars in the sky⟩

nu·mer·al \\'nü-mə-rəl, 'nyü-\\ *n* : a symbol or group of symbols representing a number

nu·mer·a·tion \\,nü-mə-'rā-shən, ,nyü-\\ *n* : a system of counting

nu·mer·a·tor \\'nü-mə-,rāt-ər, 'nyü-\\ *n* : the part of a fraction that is above the line ⟨3 is the *numerator* of the fraction 3/5⟩

nu·mer·i·cal \\nu̇-'mer-i-kəl, nyu̇-\\ *adj* : of or relating to number : expressed in numbers — **nu·mer·i·cal·ly** *adv*

nu·mer·ous \\'nü-mə-rəs, 'nyü-\\ *adj* : consisting of, including, or relating to a large number ⟨*numerous* friends⟩ ⟨a *numerous* family⟩ — **nu·mer·ous·ly** *adv*

nu·mis·mat·ics \\,nü-məz-'mat-iks, ,nyü-\\ *n* : the study or collecting of coins, tokens, medals, or paper money

nu·mis·ma·tist \\nü-'miz-mət-əst, nyü-\\ *n* : a student or collector of coins, tokens, medals, or paper money

num·skull \\'nəm-,skəl\\ *n* : a stupid person : DUNCE

nun \\'nən\\ *n* : a woman belonging to a religious order and usually living in a convent

nun·ci·o \\'nən-sē-,ō, 'nun-\\ *n, pl* **nun·ci·os** : a papal emissary to a civil government

¹nup·tial \\'nəp-shəl\\ *adj* : of or relating to marriage or a wedding

²nuptial *n* : MARRIAGE, WEDDING — usually used in plural

¹nurse \\'nərs\\ *n* **1** : a woman employed for the care of a young child **2** : a person skilled or trained in the care of the sick

²nurse *vb* **nursed; nurs·ing** **1** : to feed at the breast **2** : to take care of (as a young child or a sick person) **3** : to treat with special care ⟨*nurse* a plant⟩

nurse·maid \\'nərs-,mād\\ *n* : NURSE 1

nurs·er·y \\'nər-sə-rē\\ *n, pl* **nurs·er·ies** **1** : a place set aside or designed for small children or for the care of small children **2** : a place where young trees, vines, and plants are grown and usually sold

nurs·er·y·man \\'nər-sə-rē-mən\\ *n, pl* **nurs·er·y·men** \\-mən\\ : one whose occupation is the cultivation of trees, shrubs, and plants

¹nur·ture \\'nər-chər\\ *n* **1** : TRAINING, UP-BRINGING, EDUCATION **2** : something (as food) that nourishes

²nurture *vb* **nur·tured; nur·tur·ing** **1** : to supply with nourishment **2** : EDUCATE **3** : to further the development of

¹nut \\'nət\\ *n* **1** : a hard-shelled dry fruit or seed with a firm inner kernel **2** : the often edible kernel of a nut **3** : a piece of metal with a hole in it that is fastened to a bolt by means of a screw thread within the hole

²nut *vb* **nut·ted; nut·ting** : to gather or seek nuts

nut·crack·er \\'nət-,krak-ər\\ *n* **1** : an instrument for cracking the shells of nuts **2** : a bird related to the crows that lives mostly on the seeds of pine trees

nut·hatch \\'nət-,hach\\ *n* : a small insect-eating bird that creeps on tree trunks and branches

nut·let \\'nət-lət\\ *n* **1** : a small nut **2** : a small fruit resembling a nut

nut·meg \\'nət-,meg\\ *n* : a spice consisting of the ground nutlike seeds of a tree grown in the East and West Indies and Brazil

nu·tri·ent \\'nü-trē-ənt, 'nyü-\\ *n* : a substance used in nutrition ⟨green plants make their food from simple *nutrients* such as carbon dioxide and water⟩

nu·tri·ment \\'nü-trə-mənt, 'nyü-\\ *n* : something that nourishes or promotes growth

nu·tri·tion \\nü-'trish-ən, nyü-\\ *n* : the act or process of nourishing or being nourished : the processes by which a living being takes in and uses nutrients

nu·tri·tious \\nü-'trish-əs, nyü-\\ *adj* : NOUR-ISHING

nu·tri·tive \\'nü-trət-iv, 'nyü-\\ *adj* **1** : of or relating to nutrition **2** : NUTRITIOUS

nut·ty \\'nət-ē\\ *adj* **nut·ti·er; nut·ti·est** **1** : containing or suggesting nuts (as in flavor) **2** : mentally unbalanced : ECCENTRIC

nuz·zle \\'nəz-əl\\ *vb* **nuz·zled; nuz·zling** **1** : to push or rub with the nose **2** : to lie close : NESTLE

ny·lon \\'nī-,län\\ *n* : a synthetic material used in the making of stockings, cloth, carpets, brush bristles, and molded objects

nymph \\'nimf\\ *n* **1** : one of the minor divinities of nature in ancient mythology represented as beautiful maidens dwelling in the mountains, forests, meadows, and waters **2** : an immature insect that differs from the adult chiefly in size and bodily proportions

nuts 3

o \\'ō\\ *n, often cap* **1** : the fifteenth letter of the English alphabet **2** : ZERO

O *var of* OH

oaf \\'ōf\\ *n* : a stupid or awkward person — **oaf·ish** *adj*

oak \\'ōk\\ *n* : any of various trees and shrubs related to the beech and chestnut whose fruits are acorns and whose tough durable wood is much used for furniture and flooring

oak·en \'ō-kən\ *adj* : made of or resembling oak

oar \'ōr\ *n* **1** : a long slender wooden implement with a broad blade for rowing or steering a boat **2** : OARSMAN

oak: leaf and acorns

oar·lock \'ōr-,läk\ *n* : a usually U-shaped device for holding an oar in place

oars·man \'ōrz-mən\ *n, pl* **oars·men** \-mən\ : one who rows a boat

oarlock

o·a·sis \ō-'ā-səs\ *n, pl* **o·a·ses** \-,sēz\ : a fertile or green spot in a desert

oat \'ōt\ *n* **1** : a cereal grass grown for its loose clusters of seeds that are used for human food and animal feed **2** *pl* : a crop or the seed of the oat

oath \'ōth\ *n, pl* **oaths** \'ō<u>th</u>z, 'ōths\ **1** : a solemn appeal to God or to some revered person or thing to bear witness to the truth of one's word or the sacredness of a promise ⟨under *oath* to tell the truth⟩ **2** : a careless or profane use of a sacred name

oats

oat·meal \'ōt-,mēl\ *n* **1** : oats husked and crushed into meal or flattened into flakes **2** : porridge made from meal or flakes of oats

o·be·di·ence \ō-'bēd-ē-əns\ *n* : the act of obeying : willingness to obey

o·be·di·ent \ō-'bēd-ē-ənt\ *adj* : willing to obey : inclined to mind — **o·be·di·ent·ly** *adv*

ob·e·lisk \'äb-ə-,lisk\ *n* [from Greek *obeliskos* meaning originally "a little spit for roasting meat"] : a four-sided pillar that tapers toward the top and ends in a pyramid

o·bese \ō-'bēs\ *adj* : excessively fat

o·bey \ō-'bā\ *vb* **o·beyed; o·bey·ing** **1** : to follow the commands or guidance of ⟨*obeys* his parents⟩ **2** : to comply with : carry out ⟨*obey* an order⟩ ⟨*obey* the rules⟩

o·bit·u·ar·y \ō-'bich-ə-,wer-ē\ *n, pl* **o·bit·u·ar·ies** : a notice of a person's death (as in a newspaper)

obelisk

¹ob·ject \'äb-jikt\ *n* **1** : something that may be seen or felt ⟨tables and chairs are *objects*⟩ **2** : something (as affection, hatred, or pity) that arouses emotions ⟨he is the *object* of envy⟩ **3** : AIM, PURPOSE ⟨the *object* is to raise money⟩ **4** : a noun or noun equivalent that receives the action of a verb or completes the meaning of a preposition

²ob·ject \əb-'jekt\ *vb* **1** : to offer or cite as an objection ⟨the treasurer *objected* that the funds were too low for another expenditure⟩ **2** : to state one's opposition to or oppose something ⟨*object* to a plan⟩

ob·jec·tion \əb-'jek-shən\ *n* **1** : an act of objecting **2** : a reason for or a feeling of disapproval

ob·jec·tion·a·ble \əb-'jek-shə-nə-bəl\ *adj* : arousing objection : DISPLEASING, OFFENSIVE

¹ob·jec·tive \əb-'jek-tiv\ *adj* **1** : existing outside of the mind and independent of it **2** : treating or dealing with facts without allowing one's feelings to color them ⟨an *objective* report⟩ **3** : marking typically the object of a verb or preposition ⟨a noun in the *objective* case⟩ — **ob·jec·tive·ly** *adv*

²objective *n* : AIM, GOAL

ob·jec·tiv·i·ty \,äb-,jek-'tiv-ət-ē\ *n* : the quality or state of being objective

ob·li·gate \'äb-lə-,gāt\ *vb* **ob·li·gat·ed; ob·li·gat·ing** : to bind legally or morally

ob·li·ga·tion \,äb-lə-'gā-shən\ *n* **1** : an act of binding oneself to do something **2** : something (as the constraining power of a promise or contract) that binds one to do something **3** : something one is bound to do : DUTY **4** : indebtedness for an act of kindness

syn OBLIGATION and DUTY both denote some action or behavior that is demanded or expected of a person. OBLIGATION is used of specific responsibilities ⟨the *obligation* to repair the window he broke⟩ and suggests the involvement of some outside force or pressure ⟨financial *obligations* he had to meet each month⟩ DUTY, on the other hand, is used chiefly when discussing less specific responsibilities ⟨*duty* should be put before pleasure⟩ and suggests that the pressure comes from one's own conscience or standards rather than any outside force ⟨took the *duties* of a citizen seriously⟩

o·blig·a·to·ry \ə-'blig-ə-,tōr-ē\ *adj* : legally or morally binding : REQUIRED

o·blige \ə-'blīj\ *vb* **o·bliged; o·blig·ing** **1** : FORCE, COMPEL ⟨the soldiers were *obliged* to retreat⟩ **2** : to place under a debt of gratitude ⟨you will *oblige* me by coming early⟩ **3** : to do a favor for or do something as a favor ⟨I'll be glad to *oblige*⟩

o·blig·ing \ə-'blī-jing\ *adj* : willing to do favors — **o·blig·ing·ly** *adv*

o·blique \ō-'blēk, ə-\ *adj* : SLANTING, INCLINED — **o·blique·ly** *adv*

o·blit·er·ate \ə-'blit-ə-ˌrāt\ *vb* **o·blit·er·at·ed; o·blit·er·at·ing** : to remove or destroy completely : wipe out

o·bliv·i·on \ə-'bliv-ē-ən\ *n* **1** : an act of forgetting **2** : the quality or state of being forgotten

o·bliv·i·ous \ə-'bliv-ē-əs\ *adj* : UNAWARE, FORGETFUL ⟨*oblivious* to his danger⟩ ⟨*oblivious* of the crowd⟩

¹ob·long \'äb-ˌlông\ *adj* : longer in one direction than the other with opposite sides parallel : RECTANGULAR

²oblong *n* : an oblong figure or object

ob·nox·ious \äb-'näk-shəs, əb-\ *adj* : extremely disagreeable : HATEFUL

o·boe \'ō-bō\ *n* [from Italian, where it was an attempt to represent the sound of the French word for the instrument, *hautbois*, derived from *haut* "high" and *bois* "wood"] : a musical instrument in the form of a slender cone-shaped tube with holes and keys that is played by blowing into a reed mouthpiece

ob·scene \äb-'sēn, əb-\ *adj* : disgustingly offensive to modesty or decency

ob·scen·i·ty \äb-'sen-ət-ē, əb-\ *n, pl* **ob·scen·i·ties** **1** : the quality or state of being obscene **2** : something that is obscene

¹ob·scure \äb-'skyůr, əb-\ *adj* **1** : DARK, GLOOMY **2** : REMOTE ⟨an *obscure* village in the country⟩ **3** : not readily understood or clearly expressed ⟨an *obscure* passage in a book⟩ **4** : not prominent : INCONSPICUOUS, HUMBLE ⟨an *obscure* poet⟩

²obscure *vb* **ob·scured; ob·scur·ing** : to make obscure

ob·scu·ri·ty \äb-'skyůr-ət-ē, əb-\ *n, pl* **ob·scu·ri·ties** **1** : the quality or state of being obscure ⟨lived in *obscurity*⟩ **2** : something that is obscure ⟨his poems are filled with *obscurities*⟩

ob·serv·a·ble \əb-'zər-və-bəl\ *adj* : NOTICE-ABLE — **ob·serv·a·bly** \-blē\ *adv*

ob·serv·ance \əb-'zər-vəns\ *n* **1** : a customary practice or ceremony ⟨religious *observances*⟩ **2** : an act of following a custom, rule, or law ⟨careful *observance* of the speed laws⟩

ob·serv·ant \əb-'zər-vənt\ *adj* : quick to take notice : WATCHFUL, ALERT — **ob·serv·ant·ly** *adv*

ob·ser·va·tion \ˌäb-sər-'vā-shən, -zər-\ *n* **1** : an act or the power of seeing or fixing the mind upon something **2** : the gathering of information by noting facts or occurrences ⟨weather *observations*⟩ **3** : COMMENT **4** : the fact of being observed **syn** see REMARK

ob·serv·a·to·ry \əb-'zər-və-ˌtōr-ē\ *n, pl* **ob·serv·a·to·ries** : a place that has instruments for making observations of the stars

ob·serve \əb-'zərv\ *vb* **ob·served; ob·serv·ing** **1** : to comply with : OBEY ⟨*observe* the law⟩ **2** : CELEBRATE ⟨*observe* a religious holiday⟩ **3** : to pay attention to : NOTICE ⟨*observe* military maneuvers⟩ ⟨please *observe* what happens when we add this chemical⟩ **4** : REMARK, SAY ⟨*observed* that it was a fine day⟩ — **ob·serv·er** *n*

ob·sess \əb-'ses\ *vb* : to occupy the mind of completely or abnormally ⟨he is *obsessed* with his new scheme⟩

ob·ses·sion \əb-'sesh-ən\ *n* : a disturbing and often unreasonable idea or feeling that cannot be put out of the mind

ob·sid·i·an \əb-'sid-ē-ən\ *n* : a smooth dark-colored rock formed by the cooling of lava

ob·so·lete \ˌäb-sə-'lēt\ *adj* : no longer in use : OUT-OF-DATE ⟨*obsolete* words⟩

ob·sta·cle \'äb-stə-kəl\ *n* : something that stands in the way or opposes : HINDRANCE

ob·sti·na·cy \'äb-stə-nə-sē\ *n* : STUBBORNNESS

ob·sti·nate \'äb-stə-nət\ *adj* **1** : clinging unreasonably to an opinion or purpose : STUBBORN **2** : not easily subdued or removed ⟨an *obstinate* fever⟩ — **ob·sti·nate·ly** *adv*

ob·struct \əb-'strəkt\ *vb* **1** : to block or stop up by an obstacle **2** : to be or come in the way of : IMPEDE

ob·struc·tion \əb-'strək-shən\ *n* **1** : an act of obstructing : the state of being obstructed **2** : something that hinders or impedes : OBSTACLE

ob·tain \əb-'tān\ *vb* : to gain or get hold of with effort ⟨*obtain* a ticket⟩ ⟨*obtained* the prisoner's release⟩

ob·tain·a·ble \əb-'tā-nə-bəl\ *adj* : able to be obtained ⟨tickets were not *obtainable*⟩

ob·tuse \äb-'tüs, -'tyüs\ *adj* **1** : not quick or keen of understanding or feeling : DULL **2** : not pointed or acute : BLUNT

obtuse angle *n* : an angle that is greater than a right angle

ob·vi·ous \'äb-vē-əs\ *adj* : easily found, seen, or understood — **ob·vi·ous·ly** *adv* — **ob·vi·ous·ness** *n*

obtuse angle

oc·ca·sion \ə-'kā-zhən\ *n* **1** : a favorable opportunity : a good chance ⟨take the first *occasion* to write⟩ **2** : the time of an event ⟨on the *occasion* of the coronation⟩ **3** : a special event ⟨a great *occasion*⟩

oc·ca·sion·al \ə-'kā-zhən-l\ *adj* **1** : happening or met with now and then ⟨went to an *occasional* movie⟩ ⟨barren except for an *occasional* tree⟩ **2** : used or meant for a special

oboe

occasion ⟨an *occasional* poem⟩ — **oc·ca·sion·al·ly** *adv*

Oc·ci·dent \'äk-sə-dənt\ *n* : Europe and the western hemisphere : WEST

oc·ci·den·tal \ˌäk-sə-'dent-l\ *adj, often cap* : of or relating to the Occident

Occidental *n* : a member of any of the native peoples of the Occident

oc·cu·pan·cy \'äk-yə-pən-sē\ *n* : the act of occupying or taking possession

oc·cu·pant \'äk-yə-pənt\ *n* : a person who occupies or takes possession

oc·cu·pa·tion \ˌäk-yə-'pā-shən\ *n* **1** : one's business or vocation ⟨a tailor by *occupation*⟩ **2** : the taking possession and control of an area ⟨*occupation* of a conquered country⟩

oc·cu·pa·tion·al \ˌäk-yə-'pā-shən-l\ *adj* : of or relating to one's occupation — **oc·cu·pa·tion·al·ly** *adv*

oc·cu·py \'äk-yə-ˌpī\ *vb* **oc·cu·pied; oc·cu·py·ing** **1** : to engage the attention or energies of ⟨*occupied* himself with reading⟩ **2** : to fill up (an extent of time or space) ⟨sports *occupy* his spare time⟩ ⟨a gallon of water *occupies* 231 cubic inches of space⟩ **3** : to take or hold possession of ⟨enemy troops *occupied* the town⟩ **4** : to reside in as an owner or tenant ⟨*occupied* the house three years⟩

oc·cur \ə-'kər\ *vb* **oc·curred; oc·cur·ring** **1** : to be found or met with : APPEAR ⟨a disease that *occurs* among animals⟩ **2** : to take place : HAPPEN ⟨an accident *occurred* here last week⟩ **3** : to come into the mind ⟨it just *occurred* to me⟩

oc·cur·rence \ə-'kər-əns\ *n* **1** : something that takes place **2** : the action or process of taking place   **syn** see INCIDENT

o·cean \'ō-shən\ *n* **1** : the whole body of salt water that covers nearly three fourths of the earth **2** : one of the large bodies of water into which the great ocean is divided

o·ce·an·ic \ˌō-shē-'an-ik\ *adj* : of or relating to the ocean

o·cean·og·ra·phy \ˌō-shə-'näg-rə-fē\ *n* : a science that deals with the ocean

oc·e·lot \'äs-ə-ˌlät, 'ō-sə-\ *n* : a medium-sized American wildcat that is tawny or grayish and blotched with black

o'clock \ə-'kläk\ *adv* : according to the clock ⟨the time is one *o'clock*⟩

octa- *or* **octo-** *also* **oct-** *prefix* : eight ⟨*octagon*⟩ ⟨*octopus*⟩ ⟨*octave*⟩

oc·ta·gon \'äk-tə-ˌgän\ *n* : a flat figure with eight angles and eight sides

oc·tag·o·nal \äk-'tag-ən-l\ *adj* : having eight sides

octagon

oc·tave \'äk-tiv\ *n* **1** : a musical interval of eight degrees or steps **2** : a tone or note at the interval of an octave **3** : the whole series of notes, tones, or keys within an octave

oc·tet \äk-'tet\ *n* **1** : a musical composition for eight instruments or voices **2** : a group or set of eight

Oc·to·ber \äk-'tō-bər\ *n* : the tenth month of the year

oc·to·pus \'äk-tə-pəs\ *n, pl* **oc·to·pus·es** *or* **oc·to·pi** \-ˌpī\ : a sea animal that is a mollusk without a shell and with a rounded body at the base of which are eight flexible arms bearing suckers used to hold on to something (as prey)

octopus

oc·u·lar \'äk-yə-lər\ *adj* : of or relating to the eye or eyesight : VISUAL

odd \'äd\ *adj* **1** : not one of a pair or a set ⟨an *odd* glove⟩ **2** : not divisible by two without leaving a remainder ⟨the *odd* numbers 1, 3, 5, and 7⟩ **3** : numbered with an odd number ⟨an *odd* year⟩ **4** : some more than the number mentioned ⟨fifty *odd* years ago⟩ **5** : OCCASIONAL ⟨*odd* jobs⟩ **6** : UNUSUAL, STRANGE ⟨an *odd* thing to do⟩   **syn** see ABNORMAL — **odd·ly** *adv* — **odd·ness** *n*

odd·i·ty \'äd-ət-ē\ *n, pl* **odd·i·ties** **1** : something odd **2** : the quality or state of being odd

odds \'ädz\ *n pl* **1** : a difference in favor of one thing over another ⟨the *odds* are in our favor⟩ **2** : DISAGREEMENT, QUARRELING ⟨friends who are at *odds*⟩

odds and ends *n pl* : things left over : miscellaneous things or matters

odds–on \'ädz-'ȯn, -'än\ *adj* : thought to have a better than even chance to win ⟨the *odds-on* favorite in a race⟩

ode \'ōd\ *n* : a lyric poem that expresses a noble feeling in dignified style

o·di·ous \'ōd-ē-əs\ *adj* : causing hatred or strong dislike : worthy of hatred — **o·di·ous·ly** *adv* — **o·di·ous·ness** *n*

o·dom·e·ter \ō-'däm-ət-ər\ *n* : an instrument for measuring the distance traveled (as by a vehicle)

o·dor \'ōd-ər\ *n* **1** : a quality of something perceived by receptors in the nose as smell **2** : a smell whether pleasant or unpleasant **3** : REPUTE, REGARD ⟨in bad *odor*⟩ — **o·dored** \'ōd-ərd\ *adj* — **o·dor·less** \'ōd-ər-ləs\ *adj*

o·dor·ous \'ōd-ə-rəs\ *adj* : having or giving off an odor

o'er \'ȯr\ *adv or prep* : OVER

of \əv, 'əv, 'äv\ *prep* **1** : proceeding from : belonging to ⟨*of* royal blood⟩ **2** : CONCERNING ⟨boast *of* success⟩ **3** — used to indicate what one is delivered, rid, or freed of ⟨cured *of* a disease⟩ ⟨a tree bare *of* leaves⟩ **4** : FROM — used to indicate the material or parts used ⟨a house made *of* brick⟩ **5** : which is : BEING ⟨the continent *of* Asia⟩ ⟨the city *of* Rome⟩ **6** — used to indicate a quality in a person or thing ⟨a man *of* courage⟩

¹off \'òf\ *adv* **1** : from a place or position ⟨marched *off*⟩ **2** : from a course : ASIDE ⟨turned *off* onto a side street⟩ **3** : into an unconscious state ⟨dozed *off*⟩ **4** : so as not to be supported, covering or enclosing, or attached ⟨rolled to the edge of the table and *off*⟩ ⟨the lid blew *off*⟩ ⟨the handle fell *off*⟩ ⟨took his coat *off*⟩ **5** : so as to be discontinued or finished ⟨turn the radio *off*⟩ ⟨paid *off* his debts⟩ **6** : away from work ⟨took the day *off*⟩

²off *prep* **1** : away from the surface or top of ⟨*off* the table⟩ **2** : at the expense of ⟨lived *off* his sister⟩ **3** : released or freed from ⟨*off* duty⟩ **4** : below the usual level of ⟨he's *off* his game⟩ **5** : away from ⟨just *off* the highway⟩

³off *adj* **1** : REMOVED ⟨his shoes were *off*⟩ **2** : RIGHT ⟨the *off* horse⟩ **3** : CANCELED ⟨the game is *off*⟩ **4** : not operating ⟨the radio is *off*⟩ **5** : not correct ⟨his figures are *off*⟩ **6** : SLIGHT, FAINT ⟨an *off* chance⟩ **7** : provided for ⟨quite well *off*⟩

of·fend \ə-'fend\ *vb* : to cause anger, dislike, or annoyance : DISPLEASE

syn OFFEND, OUTRAGE, INSULT all mean to hurt or vex another person. OFFEND suggests unintentionally displeasing someone by hurting his feelings or violating his sense of what is proper ⟨his remark about foreigners *offended* me⟩ ⟨some people are too easily *offended*⟩ OUTRAGE carries the idea of offending someone beyond endurance, often by violating his principles or attacking his pride ⟨he was *outraged* when his friend betrayed him⟩ INSULT implies intentionally, often maliciously, offending a person so as to cause him humiliation or shame ⟨a good teacher can correct a student without *insulting* him⟩

of·fend·er \ə-'fen-dər\ *n* **1** : one that offends **2** : a person who breaks a law or rule

of·fense *or* **of·fence** \ə-'fens\ *n* **1** : an act of attacking : ASSAULT **2** : an offensive team **3** : the act of offending or being offended **4** : SIN, WRONGDOING

¹of·fen·sive \ə-'fen-siv\ *adj* **1** : relating to or made for or suited to attack ⟨*offensive* weapons⟩ **2** : of or relating to the attempt to score in a game or contest ⟨the *offensive* team⟩ **3** : causing displeasure or resentment ⟨an *offensive* smell⟩ ⟨an *offensive* remark⟩ — **of·fen·sive·ly** *adv* — **of·fen·sive·ness** *n*

²offensive *n* **1** : the state or attitude of one who is making an attack ⟨on the *offensive*⟩ **2** : ATTACK ⟨launch an *offensive*⟩

¹of·fer \'òf-ər\ *vb* **1** : to present as an act of worship : SACRIFICE **2** : to present for acceptance or rejection **3** : to present for consideration : SUGGEST **4** : to declare one's willingness ⟨*offered* to help⟩ **5** : to put up ⟨*offer* resistance⟩

²offer *n* **1** : an act of offering **2** : a price made by one proposing to buy : BID

of·fer·ing \'òf-ə-ring\ *n* **1** : the act of one who offers **2** : something offered **3** : a sacrifice offered as part of worship **4** : a contribution to the support of a church

off·hand \'òf-'hand\ *adv* (*or adj*) : without previous thought or preparation ⟨can't say *offhand* how many there are⟩ ⟨*offhand* remarks⟩

of·fice \'òf-əs\ *n* **1** : a special duty or position and especially a position of authority in government ⟨run for *office*⟩ **2** : a prescribed form or service of worship **3** : a place where business is done or a service is supplied ⟨ticket *office*⟩ ⟨a doctor's *office*⟩

of·fice·hold·er \'òf-əs-,hōl-dər\ *n* : a person who holds public office

of·fi·cer \'òf-ə-sər\ *n* **1** : a person charged with enforcement of the law ⟨police *officer*⟩ **2** : a person who holds an office ⟨an *officer* of the company⟩ **3** : a person who holds a commission in the armed forces ⟨navy *officer*⟩

¹of·fi·cial \ə-'fish-əl\ *n* : one who holds an office : OFFICER

²official *adj* **1** : of or relating to an office or position ⟨*official* duties⟩ **2** : holding an office ⟨an *official* referee⟩ **3** : AUTHORIZED, APPROVED ⟨an *official* American League baseball⟩ **4** : befitting or proper to a person in office ⟨an *official* greeting⟩ — **of·fi·cial·ly** *adv*

of·fi·ci·ate \ə-'fish-ē-,āt\ *vb* **of·fi·ci·at·ed**; **of·fi·ci·at·ing** **1** : to perform a ceremony or duty ⟨*officiated* at the wedding⟩ **2** : to act as an officer : PRESIDE ⟨*officiated* at the annual meeting⟩

of·fi·cious \ə-'fish-əs\ *adj* : volunteering one's services where they are neither asked for nor needed : MEDDLESOME — **of·fi·cious·ly** *adv* — **of·fi·cious·ness** *n*

off·ing \'òf-ing\ *n* : the near future or distance ⟨see trouble in the *offing*⟩

¹off·set \'òf-,set\ *n* **1** : a shoot from the base of a plant often able to produce a new plant **2** : an abrupt bend (as in a pipe) by which one part is turned aside or out of line

offset

3 : something that serves to compensate or make up for something else

²**offset** *vb* offset; off·set·ting : to make up for : BALANCE ⟨gains in one state *offset* losses in another⟩

off·shoot \'òf-,shüt\ *n* 1 : a branch of a main stem of a plant 2 : something arising or developing from or branching out of something else ⟨*offshoots* from the old trail⟩

¹**off·shore** \'òf-'shōr\ *adv* : from the shore : at a distance from the shore

²**off·shore** \'òf-,shōr\ *adj* 1 : coming or moving away from the shore ⟨an *offshore* breeze⟩ 2 : located off the shore ⟨*offshore* fisheries⟩

off·spring \'òf-,spring\ *n, pl* offspring *also* off·springs : the young of a person, animal, or plant : PROGENY

off·stage \'òf-'stāj\ *adv (or adj)* : off or away from the stage

off–the–rec·ord \,òf-thə-'rek-ərd\ *adj* : given or made in confidence and not for publication ⟨the candidate's *off-the-record* remarks⟩

oft \'òft\ *adv* : OFTEN

of·ten \'òf-ən, -tən\ *adv* : many times

of·ten·times \'òf-ən-,tīmz, 'òf-tən-\ *adv* : OFTEN

o·gle \'ō-gəl\ *vb* o·gled; o·gling : to look at in a flirting way ⟨*ogling* the pretty girls⟩

o·gre \'ō-gər\ *n* 1 : an ugly giant of fairy tales and folklore who eats people 2 : a dreaded person or object

oh \'ō\ *interj* 1 — used to express various emotions (as surprise or pain) 2 — used in direct address ⟨*Oh*, John, you forgot your cap⟩

¹**-oid** \,òid\ *n suffix* : something resembling a specified object or having a specified quality ⟨plan*etoid*⟩

²**-oid** *adj suffix* : resembling : having the form or appearance of ⟨petal*oid*⟩

¹**oil** \'òil\ *n* 1 : any of numerous greasy combustible and usually liquid substances from plant, animal, or mineral sources that are not soluble in water and are used especially as lubricants, fuels, and food 2 : PETROLEUM 3 : artists' paints made of pigments and oil 4 : a painting in oils

²**oil** *vb* : to put oil on or in

oil·cloth \'òil-,klòth\ *n* : cloth treated with oil or paint so as to be waterproof and used for shelf and table coverings

oil·skin \'òil-,skin\ *n* 1 : an oiled waterproof cloth used for garments and coverings 2 *pl* : an oilskin suit of coat and trousers

oilskins

oil well *n* : a well from which petroleum is obtained

oil·y \'òi-lē\ *adj* oil·i·er; oil·i·est 1 : of, relating to, or containing oil 2 : covered or soaked with oil ⟨*oily* rags⟩ 3 : too smooth in manner ⟨an *oily* salesman⟩ — **oil·i·ness** *n*

oint·ment \'òint-mənt\ *n* : a semisolid usually greasy and medicated preparation for use on the skin

¹**OK** *or* **o·kay** \ō-'kā\ *adv (or adj)* : all right

²**OK** *or* **okay** *vb* OK'd *or* o·kayed; OK'·ing *or* o·kay·ing : APPROVE, AUTHORIZE

³**OK** *or* **okay** *n* : APPROVAL

o·ka·pi \ō-'kä-pē\ *n* : a giraffelike animal of the African forests

o·kra \'ō-krə\ *n* : a plant related to the hollyhocks and grown for its edible green pods which are used in soups and stews

¹**old** \'ōld\ *adj* 1 : dating from the distant past : ANCIENT ⟨an *old* custom⟩ 2 : being of long standing ⟨an *old* friend⟩ 3 : having existed for a specified length of time ⟨a girl three years *old*⟩ 4 : advanced in age ⟨an *old* man⟩ 5 : FORMER ⟨his *old* students⟩ 6 : showing the effects of age or use ⟨wore an *old* coat⟩

²**old** *n* : old or earlier time ⟨in days of *old*⟩

old·en \'ōl-dən\ *adj* : of or relating to a bygone era : ANCIENT

Old English *n* : the language of the English people from the earliest documents in the seventh century to about 1100

old–fash·ioned \'ōld-'fash-ənd\ *adj* 1 : of, relating to, or characteristic of a past era 2 : holding fast to old ways : CONSERVATIVE

Old French *n* : the French language from the ninth to the thirteenth century

Old Glory *n* : the flag of the United States

old·ish \'ōl-dish\ *adj* : somewhat old

old maid *n* 1 : an elderly unmarried woman 2 : a prim fussy person 3 : a card game in which the player holding the odd queen at the end is called an "old maid"

old·ster \'ōld-stər\ *n* : an old or elderly person

old–tim·er \'ōld-'tī-mər\ *n* 1 : VETERAN 2 : OLDSTER 3 : something old-fashioned : ANTIQUE

Old World *n* 1 : the eastern hemisphere 2 : the continent of Europe

old–world \'ōld-'wərld\ *adj* : OLD-FASHIONED, PICTURESQUE

o·le·o·mar·ga·rine \,ō-lē-ō-'mär-jə-rən\ *n* : MARGARINE

ol·fac·to·ry \äl-'fak-tə-rē\ *adj* : of, relating to, or concerned with the sense of smell ⟨the *olfactory* nerve⟩

ol·ive \'äl-iv\ *n* 1 : an oily fruit that is eaten

both ripe and unripe, is the source of an edible oil (**olive oil**), and grows on an evergreen tree noted for its hard smooth lustrous wood (**olive wood**) 2 : a yellowish green

om·e·let *also* **om·e·lette** \'äm-ə-lət\ *n* : eggs beaten with milk or water, cooked without stirring until set, and folded over

o·men \'ō-mən\ *n* : a happening believed to be a sign or warning of a future event

om·i·nous \'äm-ə-nəs\ *adj* : foretelling evil : THREATENING — **om·i·nous·ly** *adv* — **om·i·nous·ness** *n*

o·mis·sion \ō-'mish-ən\ *n* 1 : something omitted 2 : the act of omitting : the state of being omitted

o·mit \ō-'mit\ *vb* **o·mit·ted**; **o·mit·ting** 1 : to leave out : fail to include ⟨*omit* a name from a list⟩ 2 : to leave undone : NEGLECT ⟨but he *omitted* to tell us how to do it⟩

¹om·ni·bus \'äm-ni-ˌbəs\ *n* [a French term taken from Latin *omnibus* meaning "for everybody"] : BUS

²omnibus *adj* : of, relating to, or providing for many things at once ⟨an *omnibus* bill before the congress⟩

om·nip·o·tent \äm-'nip-ət-ənt\ *adj* : having unlimited authority or influence : ALMIGHTY

om·ni·scient \äm-'nish-ənt\ *adj* : knowing all things — **om·ni·scient·ly** *adv*

¹on \ȯn, än\ *prep* 1 : over and in contact with ⟨a book *on* the table⟩ 2 : AGAINST ⟨shadows *on* the wall⟩ 3 : connected with or near ⟨a town *on* the river⟩ 4 : AT ⟨*on* the east⟩ 5 : DURING ⟨*on* Monday⟩ 6 : in the state or process of ⟨*on* fire⟩ ⟨*on* sale⟩ 7 : ABOUT, CONCERNING ⟨a book *on* minerals⟩ 8 : by means of ⟨talk *on* the phone⟩

²on *adv* 1 : in or into a position of contact with or attachment to a surface ⟨slipped the ring *on*⟩ ⟨jammed *on* his hat⟩ 2 : forward in time, space, or action ⟨went *on* home⟩ ⟨the argument went *on* for weeks⟩ 3 : in continuance or succession ⟨and so *on*⟩ 4 : into operation or into a position to permit operation ⟨flicked the light switch *on*⟩

³on *adj* 1 : situated on or in contact with a surface ⟨his hat was *on*⟩ 2 : OPERATING ⟨the radio is *on*⟩ 3 : placed so as to permit operation ⟨the light switch is *on*⟩ 4 : taking place ⟨the game is *on*⟩ 5 : PLANNED ⟨there's nothing *on* for tonight⟩

¹once \'wəns\ *adv* 1 : one time only ⟨it happened just *once*⟩ 2 : at any one time : EVER ⟨if *once* the truth becomes known, there will be trouble⟩ 3 : at some one time : FORMERLY ⟨it was *once* done that way⟩

²once *n* : one single time ⟨please, just this *once*⟩ — **at once** 1 : at the same time ⟨two people talking *at once*⟩ 2 : IMMEDIATELY ⟨must leave *at once*⟩

once–o·ver \'wəns-ˌō-vər\ *n* : a quick examination or survey

on·com·ing \'ȯn-ˌkəm-ing, 'än-\ *adj* : APPROACHING

¹one \'wən\ *adj* 1 : being a single unit or thing ⟨*one* dollar⟩ 2 : being a particular unit or thing ⟨early *one* morning⟩ 3 : being the same in kind or quality ⟨members of *one* race⟩ 4 : not specified or fixed ⟨at *one* time or another⟩

²one *pron* 1 : a single member or specimen ⟨saw *one* of his friends⟩ 2 : a person in general ⟨*one* never knows⟩

³one *n* 1 : the number denoting a single unit 2 : the first in a set or series 3 : a single person or thing

one·self \ˌwən-'self\ *pron* : one's own self

one–sid·ed \'wən-'sīd-əd\ *adj* 1 : having or occurring on one side only 2 : having one side prominent or more developed 3 : UNEQUAL ⟨a *one-sided* game⟩ 4 : favoring one side : PARTIAL ⟨a *one-sided* view of the case⟩

one·time \'wən-ˌtīm\ *adj* : FORMER ⟨*onetime* marbles champion⟩

one–way \'wən-'wā\ *adj* : moving, allowing movement, or functioning in one direction only

on·go·ing \'ȯn-ˌgō-ing, 'än-\ *adj* : continuously moving forward : GROWING

on·ion \'ən-yən\ *n* : the pungent edible bulb of a plant related to the lilies that is used as a vegetable and to season foods

onion

on·look·er \'ȯn-ˌlu̇k-ər, 'än-\ *n* : SPECTATOR

¹on·ly \'ōn-lē\ *adj* 1 : undoubtedly the best ⟨the *only* girl for me⟩ 2 : alone in its class or kind : SOLE ⟨the *only* survivor⟩

²only *adv* 1 : as a single fact or instance and nothing more or different ⟨worked *only* in the mornings⟩ 2 : EXCLUSIVELY ⟨*only* you know⟩ 3 : in the end ⟨it will *only* make you sick⟩ 4 : as recently as ⟨saw her *only* last week⟩

³only *conj* : except that ⟨I would go to the movies with you, *only* I'm too tired⟩

on·rush \'ȯn-ˌrəsh, 'än-\ *n* : a rushing onward

on·set \'ȯn-ˌset, 'än-\ *n* 1 : ATTACK 2 : BEGINNING

on·slaught \'än-ˌslȯt, 'ȯn-\ *n* : a furious attack

on·to \'ȯn-tə, 'än-, -ˌtü\ *prep* : to a position on or against

¹**on·ward** \'òn-wərd, 'än-\ *also* **on·wards** \-wərdz\ *adv* : toward or at a point lying ahead in space or time : FORWARD

²**onward** *adj* : directed or moving onward ⟨the *onward* march of time⟩

oo·dles \'üd-lz\ *n pl* : a great quantity

¹**ooze** \'üz\ *n* : soft mud : SLIME

²**ooze** *vb* **oozed; ooz·ing** : to flow or leak out gradually

³**ooze** *n* : something that oozes

o·pal \'ō-pəl\ *n* : a mineral having delicate changeable colors

o·paque \ō-'pāk\ *adj* **1** : not letting light through : not transparent **2** : not reflecting or giving off light : DARK

¹**o·pen** \'ō-pən\ *adj* **1** : not closed or blocked : not shut ⟨*open* window⟩ ⟨*open* book⟩ **2** : not enclosed or covered ⟨an *open* boat⟩ ⟨an *open* fire⟩ **3** : not secret : PUBLIC ⟨an *open* dislike⟩ **4** : free to the use, entry, or participation of all ⟨an *open* golf tournament⟩ ⟨an *open* meeting⟩ **5** : easy to enter, get through, or see ⟨*open* country⟩ **6** : not drawn together : spread out ⟨an *open* flower⟩ ⟨*open* umbrellas⟩ **7** : not decided or settled ⟨an *open* question⟩ **8** : ready to consider appeals or ideas ⟨an *open* mind⟩ — **o·pen·ly** *adv* — **o·pen·ness** *n*

²**open** *vb* **1** : to change or move from a shut condition ⟨*open* a book⟩ ⟨the door *opened*⟩ **2** : to clear by or as if by removing obstacles ⟨*open* a road blocked with snow⟩ **3** : to make or become functional ⟨*open* a store⟩ ⟨office *opens* at eight⟩ **4** : to give access ⟨the rooms *open* onto a hall⟩ **5** : BEGIN, START ⟨*open* talks⟩ ⟨*open* fire⟩

³**open** *n* : open space : OUTDOORS

o·pen–air \,ō-pən-'aər\ *adj* : OUTDOOR

o·pen–and–shut\,ō-pən-ən-'shət*adj* : PLAIN, OBVIOUS ⟨an *open-and-shut* case of murder⟩

o·pen·hand·ed \,ō-pən-'han-dəd\ *adj* : generous in giving

o·pen·ing \'ō-pə-ning\ *n* **1** : an act of opening ⟨the grand *opening* of a new department store⟩ **2** : an open place : CLEARING **3** : START, BEGINNING ⟨the *opening* of the speech⟩ **4** : CHANCE, OCCASION ⟨waiting for an *opening* to tell the joke⟩ **5** : a job opportunity ⟨an *opening* in the personnel department⟩

open letter *n* : a letter of protest or appeal intended for the general public and printed in a newspaper or periodical

o·pen ses·a·me \,ō-pən-'ses-ə-mē\ *n* : something that brings about a desired end without fail

o·pen·work \'ō-pən-,wərk\ *n* : something made or work done so as to show openings through the fabric or material

¹**o·per·a** \'ō-pə-rə, 'äp-ə-\ *pl of* OPUS

²**op·er·a** \'äp-ə-rə\ *n* : a play set to music made up of vocal pieces with orchestral accompaniment and orchestral pieces

opera glass *n* : a small binocular similar to a field glass — often used in plural

opera glasses

op·er·ate \'äp-ə-,rāt\ *vb* **op·er·at·ed; op·er·at·ing 1** : to perform or cause to perform a function ⟨a machine *operating* smoothly⟩ ⟨learn to *operate* a car⟩ **2** : to take effect ⟨a drug that *operates* quickly⟩ **3** : CONDUCT, MANAGE ⟨*operate* a farm⟩ ⟨*operates* a business⟩ **4** : to perform surgery : do an operation on (as a person)

op·er·a·tion \,äp-ə-'rā-shən\ *n* **1** : the act, process, method, or result of operating ⟨does the whole *operation* without thinking⟩ **2** : an exertion of power or influence ⟨the *operation* of a drug⟩ **3** : a procedure (as of cutting or manipulating) used by a surgeon to correct a disorder or improve the functioning of the body or one of its parts ⟨an *operation* for appendicitis⟩ **4** : a process (as addition or multiplication) of deriving one mathematical expression from others according to a rule **5** : a military or naval action, mission, or maneuver ⟨naval *operations* in the South China sea⟩

op·er·a·tion·al \,äp-ə-'rā-shən-l\ *adj* **1** : of or relating to operation or an operation **2** : ready for operation ⟨the new plant will be *operational* next week⟩

op·er·a·tor \'äp-ə-,rāt-ər\ *n* **1** : one that operates ⟨radio *operator*⟩ **2** : a person in charge of a telephone switchboard ⟨dial the *operator*⟩

op·er·et·ta \,äp-ə-'ret-ə\ *n* : a light amusing play set to music with spoken dialogue and dancing scenes

o·pin·ion \ə-'pin-yən\ *n* **1** : a belief stronger than an impression but less strong than knowledge ⟨in my *opinion*⟩ **2** : a judgment about a person or thing ⟨a high *opinion* of himself⟩ **3** : a statement by an expert after careful study ⟨get an *opinion* from a lawyer before filing suit⟩

o·pin·ion·at·ed \ə-'pin-yə-,nāt-əd\ *adj* : holding too strongly to one's own opinions

o·pi·um \'ō-pē-əm\ *n* : a bitter brownish narcotic drug that is the dried juice of one kind of poppy

opossum

o·pos·sum \ə-'päs-əm\ *n* : a

common American animal related to the kangaroos that lives mostly in trees and is active at night

op·po·nent \ə-'pō-nənt\ *n* : a person or thing that opposes another : FOE, RIVAL

op·por·tu·ni·ty \ˌäp-ər-'tü-nət-ē, -'tyü-\ *n, pl* **op·por·tu·ni·ties** **1** : a favorable combination of circumstances, time, and place ⟨write when you have an *opportunity*⟩ **2** : a chance for advancement ⟨his biggest *opportunity*⟩

op·pose \ə-'pōz\ *vb* **op·posed**; **op·pos·ing** **1** : to place against something to provide resistance or contrast ⟨wool as *opposed* to cotton⟩ **2** : to offer resistance to : stand against : RESIST ⟨*opposes* the plan⟩

syn OPPOSE and RESIST both mean to set oneself against something, but they differ in implication and application. OPPOSE suggests actively moving against something (as existing conditions) ⟨the voters *oppose* high taxes⟩ RESIST emphasizes standing up to something or exerting efforts against a change in existing conditions ⟨*resisted* the enemy attacks⟩ ⟨*resists* attempts to change the tax rate⟩

¹op·po·site \'äp-ə-zət\ *n* : one that is opposite

²opposite *adj* **1** : being at the other end, side, or corner ⟨house at the *opposite* end of town⟩ ⟨live on *opposite* sides of the street⟩ ⟨a clock standing in the *opposite* corner⟩ **2** : being contradictory, conflicting, or mutually exclusive ⟨the *opposite* side of the question⟩ ⟨ions with *opposite* charges⟩ ⟨went to the *opposite* extreme⟩ **3** : being as different as possible : CONTRARY ⟨went in *opposite* directions⟩ ⟨came to *opposite* conclusions⟩

³opposite *adv* : on opposite sides

⁴opposite *prep* : across from and usually facing or on the same level with

op·po·si·tion \ˌäp-ə-'zish-ən\ *n* **1** : a setting opposite : a being set opposite **2** : the action of resisting ⟨offered *opposition* to the plan⟩ **3** : a group of persons that oppose someone or something ⟨defeated our *opposition* easily⟩ **4** *often cap* : a political party opposed to the party in power

op·press \ə-'pres\ *vb* **1** : to weigh down : BURDEN ⟨*oppressed* by debts⟩ **2** : to crush by harsh rule : rule with cruelty ⟨a country *oppressed* by a dictator⟩

op·pres·sion \ə-'presh-ən\ *n* **1** : cruel or unjust use of power or authority **2** : a feeling of dullness and low spirits

op·pres·sive \ə-'pres-iv\ *adj* **1** : unjustly cruel, harsh, or burdensome ⟨*oppressive* taxes⟩ **2** : causing a feeling of oppression ⟨*oppressive* heat⟩ — **op·pres·sive·ly** *adv*

op·tic \'äp-tik\ *adj* : of or relating to seeing or the eye ⟨the *optic* nerve⟩

op·ti·cal \'äp-ti-kəl\ *adj* : OPTIC

op·ti·mal \'äp-tə-məl\ *adj* : OPTIMUM

op·ti·mism \'äp-tə-ˌmiz-əm\ *n* : a tendency to look on the bright side or to expect things to turn out for the best

op·ti·mist \'äp-tə-məst\ *n* : an optimistic person

op·ti·mis·tic \ˌäp-tə-'mis-tik\ *adj* **1** : inclined to look on the bright side of things ⟨an *optimistic* person⟩ **2** : expecting things to come out right : HOPEFUL ⟨takes an *optimistic* view⟩

op·ti·mum \'äp-tə-məm\ *adj* : most desirable or satisfactory ⟨under *optimum* conditions⟩

op·tion \'äp-shən\ *n* **1** : the power or right to choose ⟨have an *option* between black or gold lettering⟩ **2** : a right to buy or sell something at a specified price during a specified period ⟨a stock *option*⟩

op·tion·al \'äp-shən-l\ *adj* : left to one's choice : not required

op·u·lence \'äp-yə-ləns\ *n* **1** : WEALTH, RICHES **2** : PLENTY, PROFUSION

op·u·lent \'äp-yə-lənt\ *adj* **1** : WEALTHY **2** : richly abundant : PROFUSE

o·pus \'ō-pəs\ *n, pl* **o·per·a** \'ō-pə-rə, 'äp-ə-\ : a usually musical composition : WORK

or \ər, ȯr\ *conj* — used between two words or phrases that represent alternatives

¹-or \ər\ *n suffix* : one that does a specified thing ⟨actor⟩ ⟨elevator⟩

²-or *n suffix* : condition : activity ⟨demeanor⟩

or·a·cle \'ȯr-ə-kəl\ *n* **1** : a person (as a priestess in ancient Greece) through whom a god is held to speak **2** : the place where a god speaks through an oracle **3** : the answer or revelation given by an oracle **4** : a person who gives wise advice

o·rac·u·lar \ȯ-'rak-yə-lər\ *adj* **1** : of, relating to, or serving as an oracle ⟨*oracular* inscriptions⟩ **2** : resembling an oracle in solemnity or obscurity ⟨a poet's *oracular* sayings⟩

o·ral \'ōr-əl\ *adj* **1** : SPOKEN ⟨an *oral* agreement⟩ **2** : of, relating to, given by, or located near the mouth ⟨*oral* medication⟩ — **o·ral·ly** *adv*

syn ORAL, VERBAL both refer to words and their use in communicating, but the first applies to speech only. When the distinction to be made is between words and something else VERBAL is appropriate ⟨very young children cannot be given *verbal* tests⟩ ⟨had mechanical ability but little *verbal* ability⟩ and where the distinction is between words that are spoken and words that are written ORAL is appropriate ⟨received an *oral* invitation⟩ ⟨gave each student an *oral* exam⟩

or·ange \'ȯr-inj\ *n* **1** : a sweet juicy edible fruit with a reddish yellow rind that is borne by an evergreen citrus tree with shining leaves and fragrant white flowers **2** : the color in the rainbow between red and yellow : the color of a ripe orange

or·ange·ade \,ȯr-inj-'ād\ *n* : a drink made of orange juice, sugar, and water

o·rang·u·tan *or* **o·rang·ou·tan** \ə-'rang-ə-,tang, -,tan\ *n* [from Malay *orang hutan*, literally "man of the forest", from *orang* "man" and *hutan* "forest"] : a plant-eating and tree-dwelling manlike ape of Borneo and Sumatra

o·ra·tion \ə-'rā-shən\ *n* : an elaborate speech delivered in a dignified manner on a special occasion

or·a·tor \'ȯr-ət-ər\ *n* : a public speaker noted for skill and power in speaking

or·a·tor·i·cal \,ȯr-ə-'tȯr-i-kəl\ *adj* : of, relating to, or characteristic of an orator or of oratory — **or·a·tor·i·cal·ly** *adv*

or·a·to·ri·o \,ȯr-ə-'tōr-ē-,ō\ *n, pl* **or·a·to·ri·os** : a vocal and orchestral work usually on a biblical subject performed without scenery or action

¹or·a·to·ry \'ȯr-ə-,tōr-ē\ *n, pl* **or·a·to·ries** : a place for prayer : a small chapel for private worship

²oratory *n* **1** : the art of an orator **2** : oratorical language

orb \'ȯrb\ *n* : a spherical body (as a heavenly body or the eye) : BALL, GLOBE

¹or·bit \'ȯr-bət\ *n* **1** : the bony socket of the eye **2** : the path taken by one body revolving around another body ⟨the *orbit* of the earth around the sun⟩ ⟨the *orbit* of a man-made satellite around the earth⟩

²orbit *vb* **1** : to revolve in an orbit around : CIRCLE ⟨the moon *orbits* the earth⟩ **2** : to send up and make revolve in an orbit ⟨*orbit* a man-made satellite around the earth⟩

or·bit·al \'ȯr-bət-l\ *adj* : of or relating to an orbit ⟨the *orbital* velocity of a satellite⟩

or·chard \'ȯr-chərd\ *n* [from Old English *ortgeard*, where it was put together from Latin *hortus* "garden" and Old English *geard* "yard", the source of modern English *yard;* both *hortus* and *geard* are derived from the same noun meaning "enclosure" in the language from which both Latin and English are descended] **1** : a place where fruit trees are grown **2** : the trees in an orchard

or·ches·tra \'ȯr-kəs-trə\ *n* **1** : an organized group of musicians who play various musical instruments and especially stringed instruments **2** : the front part of the main floor in a theater

or·ches·tral \ȯr-'kes-trəl\ *adj* : of, relating to, or composed for an orchestra

or·chid \'ȯr-kəd\ *n* : any of a large group of plants with usually showy three-petaled flowers of which the middle petal is enlarged into a lip and differs from the others in shape and color

or·dain \ȯr-'dān\ *vb* **1** : to make a person a Christian minister or priest by a special ceremony **2** : ORDER, DECREE

or·deal \ȯr-'dēl\ *n* **1** : an old way of finding out the innocence or guilt of a person by submitting him to extremely dangerous tests with failure or injury held to show guilt ⟨*ordeal* by fire⟩ **2** : a severe trial or experience

¹or·der \'ȯrd-ər\ *n* **1** : a group of people united (as by living under the same religious rules or by loyalty to common interests or obligations) ⟨an *order* of monks⟩ ⟨fraternal *orders*⟩ **2** *pl* : the office and dignity of a person in the Christian ministry ⟨holy *orders*⟩ **3** : a group of related plants or animals ranking in classification below a class and above a family **4** : the arrangement or sequence of objects or events in space or time ⟨the *order* of the seasons⟩ ⟨a list of names in alphabetical *order*⟩ ⟨the cast in *order* of their appearance⟩ **5** : regular or harmonious arrangement : a condition marked by such arrangement ⟨kept the room in *order*⟩ **6** : the rule of law or proper authority ⟨restored *order* after the riot⟩ **7** : a specific rule or direction : COMMAND ⟨an executive *order*⟩ **8** : a written direction to pay money to someone **9** : goods or items bought or sold ⟨an *order* of groceries⟩ ⟨an *order* of fried eggs⟩ — **in order to** : for the purpose of

²order *vb* : to give an order to or for ⟨*order* troops to the front⟩ ⟨*order* groceries⟩

¹or·der·ly \'ȯrd-ər-lē\ *adj* **1** : being in good order : NEAT, TIDY ⟨an *orderly* room⟩ **2** : obeying orders or rules : well-behaved ⟨an *orderly* meeting⟩ ⟨*orderly* children⟩ — **or·der·li·ness** *n*

²orderly *n, pl* **or·der·lies** **1** : a soldier who attends a superior officer to carry messages and perform various services **2** : an attendant in a hospital who does general work

or·di·nal \'ȯrd-n-əl\ *n* : ORDINAL NUMBER

or·di·nal·i·ty \,ȯrd-n-'al-ət-ē\ *n* : the ordinal number of an element in a mathematical sequence

ordinal number *n* : a number that is used to indicate the place (as first, fifth, twenty-second) occupied by an element in a sequence

---

j job ng sing ō low ȯ moth ȯi coin th thin th this ü boot u̇ foot y you yü few yu̇ furious zh vision

or·di·nance \'òrd-n-əns\ *n* **1** : ORDER, DE-CREE **2** : a law made by a town or city government

or·di·nar·i·ly \‚òrd-n-'er-ə-lē\ *adv* **1** : in the ordinary course of events : USUALLY ⟨*ordinarily* goes to bed at nine o'clock⟩ **2** : in an ordinary commonplace way ⟨an *ordinarily* furnished apartment⟩

¹or·di·nar·y \'òrd-n-‚er-ē\ *n* : regular or customary condition or course of things ⟨nothing out of the *ordinary* about that⟩

²ordinary *adj* **1** : to be expected : NORMAL, USUAL ⟨an *ordinary* day⟩ **2** : neither good nor bad : AVERAGE ⟨an *ordinary* student⟩ ⟨just *ordinary* people⟩ **3** : of mediocre to poor quality ⟨a very *ordinary* speech⟩ — **or·di·nar·i·ness** *n*

ord·nance \'òrd-nəns\ *n* **1** : military supplies (as guns, ammunition, trucks, tanks) **2** : CANNONS, ARTILLERY

ore \'ōr\ *n* : a mineral containing a constituent for which it is mined and worked

or·gan \'òr-gən\ *n* **1** : a musical instrument played by means of one or more keyboards and having pipes sounded by compressed air **2** : a part of a person, plant, or animal that is specialized to perform a particular task ⟨the eye is an *organ* of sight⟩ **3** : a means of performing some function ⟨*organs* of government⟩

organ 1

or·gan·dy \'òr-gən-dē\ *n, pl* **or·gan·dies** : a fine thin muslin with a stiff finish

or·gan·ic \òr-'gan-ik\ *adj* **1** : relating to a bodily organ **2** : ORGANIZED ⟨an *organic* whole⟩ **3** : relating to living things **4** : relating to carbon compounds

or·gan·ism \'òr-gə-‚niz-əm\ *n* **1** : a living being made up of organs and able to carry on the activities of life : a living person, animal, or plant **2** : something like a living organism in having many related parts

or·gan·ist \'òr-gə-nəst\ *n* : a person who plays an organ

or·ga·ni·za·tion \‚òr-gə-nə-'zā-shən\ *n* **1** : the act or process of organizing ⟨the *organization* of a new club⟩ **2** : the condition or manner of being organized ⟨study the *organization* of city government⟩ **3** : a group of persons united for a common purpose ⟨a business *organization*⟩

or·ga·nize \'òr-gə-‚nīz\ *vb* **or·ga·nized**; **or·ga·niz·ing** : to make separate parts into one united whole

o·ri·ent \'ōr-ē-‚ent\ *vb* **1** : to set or arrange in a definite position especially in relation to the points of the compass **2** : to acquaint with an existing situation or environment — **o·ri·en·ta·tion** \‚ōr-ē-ən-'tā-shən\ *n*

O·ri·ent \'ōr-ē-ənt\ *n* : the countries of Asia and especially of eastern Asia : EAST

o·ri·en·tal \‚ōr-ē-'ent-l\ *adj, often cap* : of or relating to the Orient

Oriental *n* : a member of any of the native peoples of the Orient

or·i·gin \'òr-ə-jən\ *n* **1** : a person's parentage or ancestry **2** : rise, beginning, or derivation from a source **3** : primary source or cause

¹o·rig·i·nal \ə-'rij-ən-l\ *n* : something from which a copy, reproduction, or translation is made ⟨paintings that are *originals*⟩ ⟨read the Russian novel in the *original*⟩

²original *adj* **1** : of or relating to the origin or beginning : FIRST, EARLIEST ⟨the *original* part of an old house⟩ ⟨*original* inhabitants⟩ **2** : not copied from anything else : not translated : NEW ⟨an *original* painting⟩ ⟨an *original* idea⟩ **3** : able to think up new things : INVENTIVE ⟨an *original* mind⟩ — **o·rig·i·nal·ly** *adv*

o·rig·i·nal·i·ty \ə-‚rij-ə-'nal-ət-ē\ *n* **1** : the quality or state of being original ⟨the *originality* of an idea⟩ **2** : the power or ability to think, act, or do something in ways that are new ⟨an artist of great *originality*⟩

o·rig·i·nate \ə-'rij-ə-‚nāt\ *vb* **o·rig·i·nat·ed**; **o·rig·i·nat·ing** **1** : to bring into existence : cause to be : INVENT, INITIATE ⟨*originated* the idea⟩ **2** : to take or have origin : come into existence ⟨a custom that *originated* in ancient times⟩ — **o·rig·i·na·tor** *n*

o·ri·ole \'ōr-ē-‚ōl\ *n* [from French *oriol*, taken from Latin *aureolus* "golden", a derivative of *aurum* "gold"] **1** : an Old World yellow and black bird related to the crow **2** : an American songbird related to the blackbird and bobolink that has a showy orange and black male : a related smaller chestnut and black bird (the **orchard oriole**)

¹or·na·ment \'òr-nə-mənt\ *n* **1** : something that adorns or adds beauty : DECORATION ⟨a Christmas-tree *ornament*⟩ **2** : addition of something that beautifies ⟨added for *ornament*⟩

²or·na·ment \'òr-nə-‚ment\ *vb* : ADORN, DECORATE

¹or·na·men·tal \‚òr-nə-'ment-l\ *adj* : serving to ornament : DECORATIVE

²ornamental *n* : a plant grown for its beauty (as of foliage or flowers)

or·na·men·ta·tion \‚òr-nə-mən-'tā-shən\ *n* **1** : the act or process of ornamenting : the state of being ornamented **2** : ORNAMENTS

or·nate \ȯr-'nāt\ *adj* : decorated in an elaborate way — **or·nate·ly** *adv* — **or·nate·ness** *n*

or·ner·y \'ȯr-nə-rē, 'än-ə-\ *adj* **or·ner·i·er; or·ner·i·est** : having a bad disposition

¹or·phan \'ȯr-fən\ *n* : a child whose parents are dead

²orphan *vb* : to cause to become an orphan ⟨*orphaned* in childhood⟩

or·phan·age \'ȯr-fə-nij\ *n* : an institution for the care of orphans

or·ris \'ȯr-əs\ *n* : a European iris with a fragrant root (**orris root**) used especially in perfume and powder

or·tho·dox \'ȯr-thə-ˌdäks\ *adj* **1** : holding established beliefs especially in religion ⟨an *orthodox* Christian⟩ **2** : approved as measuring up to some standard : USUAL, CONVENTIONAL ⟨take an *orthodox* approach to a problem⟩

or·tho·dox·y \'ȯr-thə-ˌdäk-sē\ *n*, *pl* **or·tho·dox·ies** **1** : the quality or state of being orthodox **2** : an orthodox belief or practice

or·thog·ra·phy \ȯr-'thäg-rə-fē\ *n* : correct spelling

¹-o·ry \ˌȯr-ē, ə-rē\ *n suffix*, *pl* **-o·ries** : place of or for ⟨observat*ory*⟩

²-ory *adj suffix* : of, relating to, serving for, or characterized by ⟨prohibit*ory*⟩

os·cil·late \'äs-ə-ˌlāt\ *vb* **os·cil·lat·ed; os·cil·lat·ing** : to swing back and forth like a pendulum : VIBRATE

os·mo·sis \äs-'mō-səs, äz-\ *n* : a passing of material and especially water through a membrane (as of a living cell) that will not allow all kinds of molecules to pass

os·prey \'äs-prē\ *n*, *pl* **os·preys** : a large hawk that feeds chiefly on fish

os·ten·si·ble \äs-'ten-sə-bəl\ *adj* : DECLARED, PROFESSED, APPARENT ⟨his *ostensible* purpose⟩ — **os·ten·si·bly** \-blē\ *adv*

os·ten·ta·tion \ˌäs-tən-'tā-shən\ *n* : unnecessary or pretentious show

os·ten·ta·tious \ˌäs-tən-'tā-shəs\ *adj* : marked by or fond of unnecessary display

os·trich \'äs-trich\ *n* : a very large bird of Africa and Arabia that often weighs 300 pounds and is very swift-footed but unable to fly

¹oth·er \'əth-ər\ *adj* **1** : being the one (as of two or more) left ⟨broke his *other* arm⟩ **2** : SECOND, ALTERNATE ⟨every *other* page⟩ **3** : ADDITIONAL ⟨some *other* guests are coming⟩

²other *pron* **1** : remaining one or ones ⟨lift one foot and then the *other*⟩ **2** : another thing : another one ⟨something or *other*⟩

oth·er·wise \'əth-ər-ˌwīz\ *adv* **1** : in another way : DIFFERENTLY ⟨could not do *otherwise*⟩ **2** : in different circumstances ⟨*otherwise* he might have won⟩ **3** : in other respects ⟨an *otherwise* busy street⟩

ot·ter \'ät-ər\ *n* : a fish-eating web-footed animal related to the minks that is valued for its dense dark brown fur

ouch \'aůch\ *interj* — used to express sudden pain or displeasure

¹ought \'ȯt\ *helping verb* — used to express moral obligation ⟨*ought* to obey our parents⟩, what is advisable ⟨you *ought* to take better care of yourself⟩, what is naturally expected ⟨he *ought* to be here by now⟩, or what is logically correct ⟨the answer *ought* to be 9⟩

²ought *var of* AUGHT

ought·n't \'ȯt-nt\ : ought not

ounce \'aůns\ *n* [from medieval French *unce*, which came from Latin *uncia* "a twelfth part", a word which older English had already borrowed directly from Latin in the form *ynce* as the name for "one twelfth of a foot", now spelled *inch*] **1** : a unit of weight equal to 1/16 pound **2** : a unit of liquid capacity equal to 1/16 pint

our \aůr, är\ *adj* : of or relating to us : done, given, or felt by us ⟨*our* house⟩ ⟨*our* fault⟩

ours \'aůrz\ *pron* **1** : one or the one that belongs to us **2** : some or the ones that belong to us

our·selves \aůr-'selvz, är-\ *pron* : our own selves ⟨we amused *ourselves*⟩ ⟨we did it *ourselves*⟩

-ous \əs\ *adj suffix* : full of : having : possessing the qualities of ⟨clamor*ous*⟩ ⟨poison*ous*⟩

oust \'aůst\ *vb* : to force or drive out (as from office or from possession of something)

oust·er \'aůs-tər\ *n* : an act or instance of ousting

¹out \'aůt\ *adv* **1** : in a direction away from the inside, center, or surface ⟨looked *out* at the snow⟩ ⟨quills stuck *out* in all directions⟩ **2** : away from home, business, or the usual or proper place ⟨went *out* for lunch⟩ ⟨left a word *out* of the sentence⟩ **3** : beyond control or possession ⟨let a secret *out*⟩ **4** : so as to be exhausted, completed, or discontinued ⟨food supply ran *out*⟩ ⟨filled the form *out*⟩ ⟨turn *out* the lights⟩ **5** : in or into the open ⟨the sun came *out*⟩ **6** : ALOUD ⟨cried *out* in pain⟩ **7** : so as to put out or be put out in baseball ⟨the shortstop threw the runner *out*⟩

²out *vb* : to become known ⟨the truth will *out*⟩

³out *adj* **1** : situated outside or at a distance **2** : no longer in fashion, use, or power ⟨a style that is *out* this year⟩ ⟨lights are *out*⟩ ⟨the *out* party⟩ **3** : not confined : not concealed or covered ⟨the secret is *out*⟩ ⟨the sun is *out*⟩ **4** : ABSENT, MISSING ⟨a basket with its bottom *out*⟩ ⟨the barber is *out* today⟩ **5** : being no longer at bat and not successful in reaching base ⟨strike three — you're *out*⟩

⁴out *prep* **1** : outward through ⟨looked *out* the window⟩ **2** : outward on or along ⟨drove *out* the river road⟩

⁵out *n* **1** : PUTOUT **2** : a baseball player who has been put out

out- *prefix* : in a manner that goes beyond, surpasses, or excels ⟨*out*number⟩

out–and–out \ˌaut-n-ˈaut\ *adj* : COMPLETE, THOROUGHGOING ⟨an *out-and-out* crook⟩

out·board motor \ˌaut-ˌbȯrd-\ *n* : a small gasoline engine with an attached propeller that can be fixed to the stern of a small boat

out·break \ˈaut-ˌbrāk\ *n* : something that breaks out ⟨an *outbreak* of measles⟩

outboard motor

out·build·ing \ˈaut-ˌbil-ding\ *n* : a building smaller than and separate from a main building

out·burst \ˈaut-ˌbərst\ *n* **1** : a sudden violent expression of strong feeling **2** : a surge of activity or growth

¹out·cast \ˈaut-ˌkast\ *adj* : cast out : EXILED, REJECTED

²outcast *n* : a person who is cast out or expelled (as from home or country)

out·class \aut-ˈklas\ *vb* : EXCEL, SURPASS

out·come \ˈaut-ˌkəm\ *n* : RESULT

out·cry \ˈaut-ˌkrī\ *n, pl* **out·cries** **1** : a loud cry (as of distress or alarm) **2** : a strong protest ⟨raised an *outcry* against the law⟩

out·dat·ed \aut-ˈdāt-əd\ *adj* : OLD-FASHIONED, OBSOLETE ⟨*outdated* methods of farming⟩

out·dis·tance \aut-ˈdis-təns\ *vb* **out·dis·tanced; out·dis·tanc·ing** : to go far ahead of (as in a race)

out·do \aut-ˈdü\ *vb* **out·did** \-ˈdid\; **out·done** \-ˈdən\; **out·do·ing** \-ˈdü-ing\ : to do better than : EXCEL, SURPASS

out·door \ˌaut-ˌdōr\ *adj* **1** : of or relating to the outdoors ⟨an *outdoor* man⟩ **2** : done outdoors ⟨*outdoor* activities⟩

¹out·doors \aut-ˈdōrz\ *adv* : outside a building : in or to the open air ⟨play *outdoors*⟩

²outdoors *n* **1** : the open air **2** : the world away from human dwellings

out·er \ˈaut-ər\ *adj* **1** : situated on the outside or farther out ⟨an *outer* wall⟩ **2** : being beyond the earth's atmosphere or beyond the solar system ⟨*outer* space⟩

out·er·most \ˈaut-ər-ˌmōst\ *adj* : farthest out

out·field \ˈaut-ˌfēld\ *n* **1** : the part of a baseball field beyond the infield and between the foul lines **2** : the players who play in the outfield

out·field·er \ˈaut-ˌfēl-dər\ *n* : a baseball player who plays in the outfield

out·fight \aut-ˈfīt\ *vb* **out·fought** \-ˈfȯt\; **out·fight·ing** : to outdo in fighting : DEFEAT

¹out·fit \ˈaut-ˌfit\ *n* **1** : the articles forming the equipment for a special purpose ⟨a camping *outfit*⟩ ⟨a sports *outfit*⟩ **2** : a group of persons working together or associated in the same undertaking ⟨soldiers from the same *outfit*⟩

²outfit *vb* **out·fit·ted; out·fit·ting** : to furnish with an outfit : EQUIP ⟨*outfit* an expedition⟩ — **out·fit·ter** *n*

out·go \ˈaut-ˌgō\ *n, pl* **out·goes** : EXPENDITURE, PAYMENT ⟨income must exceed *outgo*⟩

out·go·ing \ˈaut-ˌgō-ing\ *adj* **1** : going out ⟨the *outgoing* tide⟩ **2** : retiring from a place or position ⟨the *outgoing* president⟩ **3** : FRIENDLY ⟨an *outgoing* person⟩

out·grow \aut-ˈgrō\ *vb* **out·grew** \-ˈgrü\; **out·grown** \-ˈgrōn\; **out·grow·ing** **1** : to grow faster than ⟨a plant that *outgrows* all the others⟩ **2** : to grow out of or away from : grow too large for ⟨*outgrew* his clothes⟩

out·growth \ˈaut-ˌgrōth\ *n* : something that grows out of or develops from another : CONSEQUENCE

out·ing \ˈaut-ing\ *n* : a brief trip or excursion often with a picnic ⟨an *outing* at the shore⟩

out·land·ish \aut-ˈlan-dish\ *adj* : very strange or unusual : BIZARRE ⟨*outlandish* behavior⟩ ⟨*outlandish* clothes⟩

out·last \aut-ˈlast\ *vb* : to last longer than

¹out·law \ˈaut-ˌlȯ\ *n* : a lawless person or a fugitive from the law

²outlaw *vb* : to make illegal ⟨*outlaw* war⟩ ⟨dueling was *outlawed*⟩

out·lay \ˈaut-ˌlā\ *n* : EXPENDITURE, PAYMENT

out·let \ˈaut-ˌlet\ *n* **1** : a place or opening for letting something out ⟨a lake with several *outlets*⟩ **2** : a means of release or satisfaction for an emotion or impulse ⟨needs an *outlet* for his anger⟩ **3** : a device (as in a wall) into which the prongs of an electrical plug are inserted for making connection with an electrical circuit

¹out·line \ˈaut-ˌlīn\ *n* **1** : a line that traces or forms the outer limits of an object or figure and shows its shape **2** : a drawing or picture giving only the outlines of a thing : this method of drawing **3** : a brief statement or sketch (as of a plan or speech)

outline of tree

²**outline** *vb* **out·lined; out·lin·ing** : to make or prepare an outline of ⟨*outlined* a plan⟩

out·live \aut-'liv\ *vb* **out·lived; out·liv·ing** : to live longer than ⟨*outlived* his brother⟩

out·look \'aut-ˌluk\ *n* **1** : a view seen by a person who looks out ⟨the *outlook* through a window⟩ **2** : a particular way of thinking about or looking at a thing ⟨a person with a broad *outlook*⟩ **3** : prospect for the future ⟨the *outlook* for business⟩

out·ly·ing \'aut-ˌlī-ing\ *adj* : being far from a central point : REMOTE ⟨an *outlying* suburb⟩

out·mod·ed \aut-'mōd-əd\ *adj* **1** : no longer in style ⟨an *outmoded* dress⟩ **2** : OUTDATED, OBSOLETE ⟨*outmoded* equipment⟩

out·most \'aut-ˌmōst\ *adj* : farthest out : OUTERMOST

out·num·ber \aut-'nəm-bər\ *vb* : to exceed in number ⟨girls *outnumber* boys in the class⟩

out–of–bounds \ˌaut-əv-'baundz\ *adv (or adj)* : outside the limits of the playing field

out–of–date \ˌaut-əv-'dāt\ *adj* : no longer in fashion or in use : OUTMODED, OBSOLETE

out–of–door \ˌaut-əv-'dōr\ *or* **out–of–doors** \-'dōrz\ *adj* : OUTDOOR

out–of–doors \ˌaut-əv-'dōrz\ *n* : OUTDOORS

out·pa·tient \'aut-ˌpā-shənt\ *n* : a person who visits a hospital for diagnosis or treatment but who does not stay overnight at the hospital

out·play \aut-'plā\ *vb* : to play better than

out·post \'aut-ˌpōst\ *n* **1** : a soldier or group of soldiers stationed at some distance from a force or camp to guard against enemy attack **2** : the position occupied by an outpost **3** : a settlement on a frontier or in an outlying place

¹**out·rage** \'aut-ˌrāj\ *n* **1** : an act of violence or brutality **2** : INJURY, INSULT **3** : the resentment aroused by injury or insult

²**outrage** *vb* **out·raged; out·rag·ing** **1** : to subject to violent injury or gross insult ⟨an act that *outraged* his sense of decency⟩ **2** : to arouse anger or extreme resentment in ⟨*outraged* by the way he was treated⟩ **syn** *see* OFFEND

out·ra·geous \aut-'rā-jəs\ *adj* : being beyond all bounds of decency or justice

¹**out·right** \aut-'rīt\ *adv* **1** : in entirety : COMPLETELY ⟨sold the business *outright*⟩ **2** : without holding back ⟨laughed *outright* at the story⟩ **3** : on the spot : INSTANTLY ⟨killed *outright*⟩

²**out·right** \'aut-ˌrīt\ *adj* **1** : going to the full extent ⟨an *outright* lie⟩ **2** : given without reservation ⟨an *outright* gift⟩

out·run \aut-'rən\ *vb* **out·ran** \-'ran\; **out·run; out·run·ning** : to run faster than

out·sell \aut-'sel\ *vb* **out·sold** \-'sōld\; **out·sell·ing** : to exceed in sales

out·set \'aut-ˌset\ *n* : BEGINNING, START

out·shine \aut-'shīn\ *vb* **out·shone** \-'shōn\; **out·shin·ing** **1** : to shine brighter than **2** : OUTDO, SURPASS

¹**out·side** \aut-'sīd\ *n* **1** : a place or region beyond an enclosure or boundary ⟨looking in from the *outside*⟩ **2** : an outer side or surface ⟨painted white on the *outside*⟩ **3** : the utmost limit or extent ⟨will take a week at the *outside*⟩

²**outside** *adj* **1** : of, relating to, or being on the outside : OUTER ⟨the *outside* edge⟩ **2** : coming from outside : not belonging to a place or group ⟨*outside* influences⟩

³**outside** *adv* : on or to the outside : OUTDOORS

⁴**outside** *prep* : on or to the outside of : beyond the limits of ⟨*outside* the door⟩ ⟨*outside* the law⟩

out·sid·er \aut-'sīd-ər\ *n* : a person who does not belong to a particular party or group

out·size \'aut-ˌsīz\ *adj* : unusually large or heavy

out·skirts \'aut-ˌskərts\ *n pl* : the outlying parts of a place or town

out·smart \aut-'smärt\ *vb* : OUTWIT

out·spo·ken \aut-'spō-kən\ *adj* : direct or open in speech or expression : FRANK, BLUNT ⟨*outspoken* criticism⟩ ⟨an *outspoken* man⟩ — **out·spo·ken·ness** *n*

out·spread \aut-'spred\ *vb* **out·spread; out·spread·ing** : to spread out or stretch out : EXTEND

out·stand·ing \aut-'stan-ding\ *adj* **1** : UNPAID ⟨several bills *outstanding*⟩ **2** : standing out from a group : CONSPICUOUS ⟨has *outstanding* talent⟩ **3** : DISTINGUISHED, EMINENT ⟨a most *outstanding* musician⟩ — **out·stand·ing·ly** *adv*

out·stay \aut-'stā\ *vb* : to stay beyond or longer than ⟨*outstayed* our welcome⟩

out·stretch \aut-'strech\ *vb* : to stretch out : EXTEND ⟨*outstretched* arms⟩

out·strip \aut-'strip\ *vb* **out·stripped; out·strip·ping** **1** : to go faster or farther than ⟨*outstripped* the other runners⟩ **2** : EXCEL, SURPASS

¹**out·ward** \'aut-wərd\ *adj* **1** : moving or directed toward the outside or away from a center ⟨an *outward* journey⟩ **2** : showing outwardly : EXTERNAL ⟨gave no *outward* signs of fear⟩

²**outward** *or* **out·wards** \'aut-wərdz\ *adv* : toward the outside ⟨the city stretches *outward* for miles⟩

out·ward·ly \'aut-wərd-lē\ *adv* : on the outside : in outward appearance ⟨*outwardly* calm⟩

out·weigh \aȯt-'wā\ *vb* : to exceed in weight or importance ⟨challenger *outweighs* the champion⟩ ⟨single fact *outweighs* all other considerations⟩

out·wit \aȯt-'wit\ *vb* **out·wit·ted; out·wit·ting** : to get the better of by cleverness

out·worn \aȯt-'wōrn\ *adj* : no longer useful or accepted ⟨*outworn* ideas⟩

¹o·val \'ō-vəl\ *adj* 1 : having the shape of a hen's egg 2 : having the shape of an elongated circle : ELLIPTICAL

²oval *n* : an oval figure or object

o·va·ry \'ō-və-rē\ *n, pl* **o·va·ries** 1 : the organ of the body in female animals in which eggs are produced 2 : the enlarged lower part of the pistil of a flower in which the seeds are formed

oval

o·va·tion \ō-'vā-shən\ *n* : a public expression of praise : enthusiastic applause

ov·en \'əv-ən\ *n* : a heated chamber (as in a stove) for baking, heating, or drying

¹o·ver \'ō-vər\ *adv* 1 : across a barrier or space ⟨flew *over* to London⟩ 2 : in a direction down or forward and down ⟨fell *over*⟩ 3 : across the brim ⟨soup boiled *over*⟩ 4 : so as to bring the underside up ⟨turned the cards *over*⟩ 5 : beyond a limit ⟨show runs a minute *over*⟩ 6 : in or to excess : EXCESSIVELY ⟨has two cards left *over*⟩ ⟨not *over* fond of parsnips⟩ 7 : once more : AGAIN ⟨please do it *over*⟩

²over *prep* 1 : above in place : higher than ⟨the sky *over* us⟩ ⟨towers *over* his sister⟩ 2 : above in power or value ⟨respected those *over* him⟩ 3 : on or along the surface of ⟨glide *over* the ice⟩ 4 : on or to the other side of : ACROSS ⟨jump *over* a puddle⟩ ⟨climb *over* a fence⟩ 5 : down from the top or edge of ⟨fell *over* a cliff⟩ 6 : DURING ⟨read the book *over* the weekend⟩ 7 : on account of ⟨trouble *over* money⟩ ⟨fought *over* a girl⟩ 8 : by means of ⟨heard it *over* the radio⟩

³over *adj* 1 : being more than needed : SURPLUS 2 : FINISHED, ENDED ⟨the game is *over*⟩ ⟨those days are *over*⟩

¹o·ver·all \ˌō-vər-'ȯl\ *adv* : as a whole : GENERALLY ⟨did a nice job *overall*⟩

²overall *adj* : including everything ⟨*overall* expenses⟩

o·ver·alls \'ō-vər-ˌȯlz\ *n pl* : loose trousers usually having a piece extending up to cover the chest that are worn over other clothes to protect them from soiling

o·ver·anx·ious \ˌō-vər-'angk-shəs\ *adj* : excessively or needlessly anxious

o·ver·bear·ing \ˌō-vər-'baər-ing\ *adj* : acting in a proud or domineering way toward other people : ARROGANT

o·ver·board \'ō-vər-ˌbōrd\ *adv* 1 : over the side of a ship into the water ⟨fall *overboard*⟩ 2 : to extremes of enthusiasm ⟨go *overboard* for a popular singer⟩

¹o·ver·cast \'ō-vər-ˌkast\ *vb* **overcast; o·ver·cast·ing** 1 : to spread over so as to cover : CLOUD, DARKEN 2 : to sew long slanting stitches over the raw edge of a seam to prevent raveling

²overcast *adj* : clouded over : GLOOMY

o·ver·charge \ˌō-vər-'chärj\ *vb* **o·ver·charged; o·ver·charg·ing** : to charge too much ⟨*overcharged* us for the meat⟩

o·ver·coat \'ō-vər-ˌkōt\ *n* : a warm heavy coat worn over indoor clothing

o·ver·come \ˌō-vər-'kəm\ *vb* **o·ver·came** \-'kām\; **overcome; o·ver·com·ing** 1 : to get the better of : CONQUER ⟨*overcome* the enemy⟩ 2 : to make helpless or exhausted ⟨were *overcome* by gas⟩

o·ver·con·fi·dent \ˌō-vər-'kän-fə-dənt\ *adj* : overly confident : excessively sure of oneself

o·ver·cooked \ˌō-vər-'ku̇kt\ *adj* : cooked too long : OVERDONE

o·ver·crowd \ˌō-vər-'krau̇d\ *vb* : to cause to be too crowded ⟨schools were *overcrowded*⟩

o·ver·do \ˌō-vər-'dü\ *vb* **o·ver·did** \-'did\; **o·ver·done** \-'dən\; **o·ver·do·ing** \-'dü-ing\ 1 : to do too much ⟨she *overdoes* it getting ready for a party⟩ 2 : EXAGGERATE ⟨*overdo* praise⟩ 3 : to cook too long ⟨the meat is *overdone*⟩

o·ver·dose \'ō-vər-ˌdōs\ *n* : too large a dose (as of medicine)

o·ver·due \ˌō-vər-'dü, -'dyü\ *adj* 1 : unpaid when due ⟨*overdue* bills⟩ 2 : delayed beyond a certain time ⟨an hour *overdue*⟩

o·ver·eat \ˌō-vər-'ēt\ *vb* **o·ver·ate** \-'āt\; **o·ver·eat·en** \-'ēt-n\; **o·ver·eat·ing** : to eat too much

o·ver·es·ti·mate \ˌō-vər-'es-tə-ˌmāt\ *vb* **o·ver·es·ti·mat·ed; o·ver·es·ti·mat·ing** : to estimate too highly ⟨*overestimated* the amount of paper needed⟩

o·ver·flight \'ō-vər-ˌflīt\ *n* : a passage over an area in an airplane

¹o·ver·flow \ˌō-vər-'flō\ *vb* 1 : to cover with or as if with water ⟨visitors *overflowed* the town⟩ 2 : to flow over the brim or top of ⟨the river *overflowed* its banks⟩ 3 : to flow over bounds ⟨the creek *overflows* every spring⟩

²o·ver·flow \'ō-vər-ˌflō\ *n* 1 : a flowing over : FLOOD 2 : something that flows over : SURPLUS 3 : an outlet or container for surplus liquid

o·ver·graze \,ō-vər-'grāz\ *vb* **o·ver·grazed;**
o·ver·graz·ing : to allow animals to graze on
(as pasture) to the point that vegetation is
damaged or killed

o·ver·grow \,ō-vər-'grō\ *vb* **o·ver·grew**
\-;'grü\; **o·ver·grown** \-'grōn\; **o·ver·grow·ing**
: to grow over so as to cover

o·ver·grown \,ō-vər-'grōn\ *adj* : grown too
big ⟨just an *overgrown* boy⟩

¹o·ver·hand \'ō-vər-,hand\ *adj* : made with a
downward movement of the hand or arm
⟨threw an *overhand* curve⟩

²overhand *adv* : with an overhand movement
⟨pitches better *overhand*⟩

overhand knot *n* : a small knot often used to
prevent the end of a cord
from fraying

¹o·ver·hang \'ō-vər-,hang\ *vb*
o·ver·hung \-,həng\; **o·ver-**
hang·ing : to jut, project, or be
suspended over ⟨an *overhang-*
ing cliff⟩

overhand knot

²overhang *n* : a part that overhangs ⟨the
second-story *overhang* of
a house⟩

¹o·ver·haul \,ō-vər-
'hȯl\ *vb* **1** : to make a
thorough examination of
and make necessary re-
pairs and adjustments

overhang

on ⟨*overhaul* an automobile engine⟩ **2** : to
catch up with : OVERTAKE ⟨*overhauled* by a
coast guard cutter before they could escape⟩

²o·ver·haul \'ō-vər-,hȯl\ *n* : an instance of
overhauling

¹o·ver·head \,ō-vər-'hed\ *adv* : above one's
head : ALOFT ⟨a plane flying *overhead*⟩

²o·ver·head \'ō-vər-,hed\ *adj* : placed or
passing overhead ⟨*overhead* garage doors⟩

³o·ver·head \'ō-vər-,hed\ *n* : the general expenses (as for rent or heat) of a business

o·ver·hear \,ō-vər-'hiər\ *vb* **o·ver·heard**
\-'hərd\; **o·ver·hear·ing** \-'hiər-ing\ : to hear
something said to someone else and not intended for one's own ears

o·ver·heat \,ō-vər-'hēt\ *vb* : to heat too much
: become too hot ⟨an *overheated* engine⟩

o·ver·joy \,ō-vər-'jȯi\ *vb* : to make very joyful

¹o·ver·land \'ō-vər-,land\ *adv* : by land
rather than by water ⟨travel *overland*⟩

²overland *adj* : going overland ⟨an *overland*
route⟩

o·ver·lap \,ō-vər-'lap\ *vb* **o·ver·lapped;** **o·ver-**
lap·ping : to place or be placed so that a part
of one covers a part of another : lap over

¹o·ver·lay \,ō-vər-'lā\ *vb* **o·ver·laid** \-'lād\;
o·ver·lay·ing **1** : to lay or spread over or across

something : SUPERIMPOSE ⟨*overlay* silver or
gold⟩ **2** : to lay or spread something over or
across : COVER ⟨*overlay* silver with gold⟩

²o·ver·lay \'ō-vər-,lā\ *n* : something (as a
veneer on wood) that is overlaid

o·ver·load \,ō-vər-'lōd\ *vb* : to put too great a
load on ⟨*overload* a truck⟩ ⟨*overload* an electrical circuit⟩

o·ver·look \,ō-vər-'lùk\ *vb* **1** : to look over
: INSPECT **2** : to look down upon from a
higher position ⟨house that *overlooks* a valley⟩
3 : to fail to see : MISS ⟨*overlook* a name on
the list⟩ **4** : to pass over without notice or
blame : EXCUSE ⟨*overlook* a beginner's mistake⟩

o·ver·lord \'ō-vər-,lȯrd\ *n* **1** : a lord over
other lords **2** : an absolute or supreme ruler

o·ver·ly \'ō-vər-lē\ *adv* : EXCESSIVELY, TOO

¹o·ver·night \,ō-vər-'nīt\ *adv* : on or during
the night ⟨stay *overnight*⟩

²overnight *adj* **1** : done or lasting through
the night ⟨an *overnight* journey⟩ **2** : staying
for the night ⟨an *overnight* guest⟩ **3** : for use
on short trips ⟨an *overnight* bag⟩

o·ver·pass \'ō-vər-,pas\ *n* : a crossing (as of
two highways or a highway and a railroad)
at different levels usually by means of a bridge

o·ver·pow·er \,ō-vər-'pau̇-ər\ *vb* **1** : to overcome by superior force : DEFEAT ⟨*overpowered*
his attacker⟩ **2** : to affect by being too strong
or intense ⟨an *overpowering* personality⟩

o·ver·rate \,ō-vər-'rāt\ *vb* **o·ver·rat·ed;** **o·ver-**
rat·ing : to value, rate, or praise too highly.

o·ver·ride \,ō-vər-'rīd\ *vb* **o·ver·rode** \-'rōd\;
o·ver·rid·den \-'rid-n\; **o·ver·rid·ing** \-'rīd-
ing\ **1** : to prevail over : DOMINATE ⟨the *over-*
riding consideration⟩ **2** : to set aside : annul
by contrary decision ⟨*overrode* the president's
veto⟩

o·ver·ripe \,ō-vər-'rīp\ *adj* : passed beyond
ripeness toward decay ⟨*overripe* fruit⟩

o·ver·rule \,ō-vər-'rül\ *vb* **o·ver·ruled;** **o·ver-**
rul·ing **1** : to decide against ⟨the chairman
overruled the suggestion⟩ **2** : to reverse or set
aside a decision or ruling made by someone
having less authority ⟨the superior court *over-*
ruled the decision of a lower court⟩

o·ver·run \,ō-vər-'rən\ *vb* **o·ver·ran** \-'ran\;
overrun; o·ver·run·ning **1** : to run over : OVER-
SPREAD ⟨a garden *overrun* with weeds⟩ **2** : to
take over and occupy by force ⟨the outpost
was *overrun* by the enemy⟩ **3** : to run further
than : go beyond ⟨*overran* second base⟩

o·ver·sea \,ō-vər-'sē\ *adj (or adv)* : OVERSEAS

¹o·ver·seas \,ō-vər-'sēz\ *adv* : beyond or
across the sea : ABROAD ⟨soldiers sent *over-*
seas⟩

²overseas *adj* : of, relating to, or intended for

lands across the sea ⟨*overseas* trade⟩ ⟨American *overseas* libraries⟩

o·ver·see \ˌō-vər-'sē\ *vb* **o·ver·saw** \-'sȯ\; **o·ver·seen** \-'sēn\; **o·ver·see·ing** 1 : SURVEY, WATCH 2 : INSPECT, EXAMINE 3 : SUPERINTEND, SUPERVISE

o·ver·seer \'ō-vər-ˌsiər\ *n* : a person whose business it is to oversee something

o·ver·shad·ow \ˌō-vər-'shad-ō\ *vb* 1 : to throw a shadow over : DARKEN 2 : to be more important than

o·ver·shoe \'ō-vər-ˌshü\ *n* : a shoe (as of rubber) worn over another for protection

o·ver·sight \'ō-vər-ˌsīt\ *n* 1 : the act or duty of overseeing : watchful care 2 : an omission or error resulting from carelessness or haste

overshoe

o·ver·sim·pli·fy \ˌō-vər-'sim-plə-ˌfī\ *vb* **o·ver·sim·pli·fied**; **o·ver·sim·pli·fy·ing** : to give an untrue account or picture of by making too simple ⟨*oversimplify* a complicated problem⟩ ⟨*oversimplify* a famous event in history⟩

o·ver·size \ˌō-vər-'sīz\ *or* **o·ver·sized** \-'sīzd\ *adj* : larger than the usual or normal size

o·ver·sleep \ˌō-vər-'slēp\ *vb* **o·ver·slept** \-'slept\; **o·ver·sleep·ing** : to sleep beyond the usual time for waking or beyond the time set for getting up

o·ver·spread \ˌō-vər-'spred\ *vb* **overspread**; **o·ver·spread·ing** : to spread over or above

o·ver·state \ˌō-vər-'stāt\ *vb* **o·ver·stat·ed**; **o·ver·stat·ing** : to put in too strong terms : EXAGGERATE ⟨*overstated* the case⟩

o·ver·step \ˌō-vər-'step\ *vb* **o·ver·stepped**; **o·ver·step·ping** : to step over or beyond : EXCEED ⟨*overstepped* his authority⟩

o·ver·stuffed \ˌō-vər-'stəft\ *adj* : covered completely and deeply with upholstery ⟨an *overstuffed* chair⟩

o·ver·sup·ply \ˌō-vər-sə-'plī\ *n, pl* **o·ver·sup·plies** : an excessive supply

o·vert \ō-'vərt, 'ō-ˌvərt\ *adj* : open to view : not secret — **o·vert·ly** *adv*

o·ver·take \ˌō-vər-'tāk\ *vb* **o·ver·took** \-'tȯk\; **o·ver·tak·en** \-'tā-kən\; **o·ver·tak·ing** 1 : to catch up with ⟨*overtook* the car ahead⟩ 2 : to come upon suddenly or unexpectedly ⟨*overtaken* by rain⟩

¹o·ver·throw \ˌō-vər-'thrō\ *vb* **o·ver·threw** \-'thrü\; **o·ver·thrown** \-'thrōn\; **o·ver·throw·ing** 1 : to throw over : UPSET 2 : to bring down : DEFEAT, DESTROY ⟨a government *overthrown* by rebels⟩

²o·ver·throw \'ō-vər-ˌthrō\ *n* : an act of overthrowing : the state of being overthrown : DEFEAT, RUIN ⟨advocated the violent *overthrow* of the government⟩

o·ver·time \'ō-vər-ˌtīm\ *n* : working time in excess of a standard day or week

o·ver·ture \'ō-vər-ˌchùr\ *n* 1 : an opening offer : a first proposal ⟨made *overtures* of peace⟩ 2 : a musical composition played by the orchestra at the beginning of an opera or musical play

o·ver·turn \ˌō-vər-'tərn\ *vb* 1 : to turn over : UPSET 2 : OVERTHROW, DESTROY

¹o·ver·weight *n* 1 \'ō-vər-ˌwāt\ : weight over what is required or allowed 2 \ˌō-vər-'wāt\ : bodily weight that is greater than what is considered normal or healthy

²o·ver·weight \ˌō-vər-'wāt\ *adj* : weighing more than is right, necessary, or allowed

o·ver·whelm \ˌō-vər-'hwelm\ *vb* 1 : to cover over completely : SUBMERGE ⟨a boat *overwhelmed* by a wave⟩ 2 : to bear down upon so as to crush or destroy : OVERPOWER ⟨*overwhelmed* by the superior force of the enemy⟩

¹o·ver·work \ˌō-vər-'wərk\ *vb* 1 : to work or cause to work too much or too hard 2 : to make excessive use of ⟨*overworked* phrases⟩

²overwork *n* : too much work

o·vip·a·rous \ō-'vip-ə-rəs\ *adj* : reproducing by eggs that hatch outside the parent's body ⟨birds are *oviparous* animals⟩

o·vule \'ō-vyül\ *n* : any of the tiny egglike structures in a plant ovary that can develop into seeds

o·vum \'ō-vəm\ *n, pl* **o·va** \'ō-və\ : EGG CELL

owe \'ō\ *vb* **owed**; **ow·ing** 1 : to be under obligation to pay, give, or return ⟨*owe* money⟩ ⟨*owed* allegiance to his country⟩ 2 : to be in debt to ⟨*owe* the grocer for food⟩ 3 : to be indebted or obliged for ⟨*owes* his success to hard work⟩

ow·ing \'ō-ing\ *adj* : due to be paid : OWED

owing to *prep* : because of ⟨absent *owing to* illness⟩

owl \'aùl\ *n* : a soft-feathered bird with large head and eyes, hooked bill, and strong claws that is active at night and lives on rats and mice, insects, and small birds — **owl·ish** *adj*

owl·et \'aù-lət\ *n* : a young or small owl

¹own \'ōn\ *adj* : belonging to oneself or itself ⟨has his *own* room⟩

²own *vb* 1 : to have or hold as property : POSSESS ⟨*own* a house⟩ 2 : to acknowledge or admit to be one's own : CONFESS ⟨*own* a mistake⟩ — **own up** : CONFESS, ADMIT ⟨if you break a window, *own up*⟩ ⟨won't *own up* to the mistake⟩

own·er \'ō-nər\ *n* : one that owns

own·er·ship \'ō-nər-,ship\ *n* : the state or fact of being an owner

ox \'äks\ *n, pl* **ox·en** \'äk-sən\ *also* **ox** : the adult castrated male of domestic cattle used especially for meat or for hauling loads : STEER

ox·bow \'äks-,bō\ *n* 1 : a U-shaped collar worn by an ox 2 : a U-shaped bend in a river

ox·cart \'äks-,kärt\ *n* : a cart drawn by oxen

oxbows

ox·ford \'äks-fərd\ *n* : a low shoe laced or tied over the instep

ox·i·da·tion \,äk-sə-'dā-shən\ *n* : the process of oxidizing

ox·ide \'äk-,sīd\ *n* : a compound of oxygen with another element or with a group of elements

ox·i·dize \'äk-sə-,dīz\ *vb* **ox·i·dized; ox·i·diz·ing** : to combine with oxygen : add oxygen to

ox·y·gen \'äk-si-jən\ *n* : a chemical element found in the air as a colorless odorless tasteless gas that is essential to life and involved in the burning process

oys·ter \'òis-tər\ *n* : a soft gray shellfish with a shell made up of two hinged parts that lives on stony bottoms (**oyster beds**) in shallow seawater and is used as food

o·zone \'ō-,zōn\ *n* 1 : a faintly blue form of oxygen that is present in the air in small quantities 2 : pure and refreshing air

p \'pē\ *n, often cap* : the sixteenth letter of the English alphabet

pa \'pä, 'pò\ *n* : FATHER

¹pace \'pās\ *n* 1 : rate of moving or progressing especially on foot 2 : a manner of walking : GAIT 3 : a horse's gait in which the legs on the same side move at the same time 4 : a single step or a measure based on the length of a step in walking

²pace *vb* **paced; pac·ing** 1 : to walk with slow measured steps 2 : to move at a pace ⟨a *pacing* horse⟩ 3 : to measure by paces ⟨*pace* off 300 feet⟩ 4 : to set or regulate the pace of

pach·y·derm \'pak-i-,dərm\ *n* : a thick-skinned hoofed animal (as an elephant or a rhinoceros)

pa·cif·ic \pə-'sif-ik\ *adj* 1 : making peace : PEACEABLE 2 : CALM, PEACEFUL 3 *cap* : relating to or bordering on the Pacific ocean

pac·i·fy \'pas-ə-,fī\ *vb* **pac·i·fied; pac·i·fy·ing** : to make peaceful or quiet : CALM, SOOTHE ⟨*pacify* a crying baby⟩

¹pack \'pak\ *n* 1 : a bundle arranged for carrying especially on the back of a man or animal 2 : a group of like persons or things : BAND, SET ⟨a *pack* of thieves⟩ ⟨a *pack* of cards⟩

²pack *vb* 1 : to put articles into for transporting or storage ⟨*pack* a suitcase⟩ 2 : to arrange closely and securely in a container or bundle 3 : to crowd into so as to fill full : CRAM ⟨a *packed* auditorium⟩ 4 : to send away ⟨*pack* boys off to school⟩

pack·age \'pak-ij\ *n* 1 : a bundle made up for delivery or for the mail or express : PARCEL 2 : a box or case in which goods are shipped or delivered

pack·et \'pak-ət\ *n* 1 : a small parcel or bundle 2 : a ship that carries passengers, mail, and goods and has fixed days for sailing

pack·ing·house \'pak-ing-,haůs\ *n* : a building for processing and packing foodstuffs and especially meat and its by-products

pact \'pakt\ *n* : AGREEMENT, TREATY

¹pad \'pad\ *n* 1 : a cushioned part or thing : CUSHION 2 : a piece of material that holds ink used in inking rubber stamps 3 : the hairy foot of some animals (as a fox or hare) 4 : a floating leaf of a water plant 5 : a tablet of writing or drawing paper

²pad *vb* **pad·ded; pad·ding** 1 : to stuff or cover with soft material 2 : to expand with unnecessary or trivial matter ⟨*pad* a speech⟩

³pad *vb* **pad·ded; pad·ding** 1 : to travel on foot : TRUDGE 2 : to walk or run with steady quiet steps ⟨a lion *padding* about its cage⟩

pad·ding \'pad-ing\ *n* : material used to pad

¹pad·dle \'pad-l\ *n* 1 : an oarlike implement used in moving and steering a small craft (as a canoe) 2 : one of the broad boards at the outer rim of a waterwheel or a paddle wheel 3 : an implement for beating, stirring, or mixing

²paddle *vb* **pad·dled; pad·dling** 1 : to move or propel by or as if by a paddle 2 : to stir or mix with a paddle 3 : to beat or punish with or as if with a paddle

³paddle *vb* **pad·dled; pad·dling** : to dabble in shallow water with the hands or feet : WADE

paddle wheel *n* : a wheel with paddles near its outer edge used to propel a boat

pad·dock \'pad-ək\ *n* 1 : an enclosed area where animals are put for pasturing or exercise 2 : an enclosure where racehorses are saddled and paraded

¹pad·lock \'pad-ˌläk\ *n* : a removable lock that has a hinged curved piece that snaps in or out of a catch

²padlock *vb* : to fasten with a padlock

padlock

pae·an \'pē-ən\ *n* : a song of joy, praise, or triumph

¹pa·gan \'pā-gən\ *n* [Latin *paganus* "country dweller" wa derived from *pagus* "country district", and in later Latin came to mean "pagan" because idol worship persisted longer in the country areas than in cities] : HEATHEN

²pagan *adj* : of or relating to pagans or their worship : HEATHEN ⟨*pagan* temple⟩

¹page \'pāj\ *n* 1 : a boy in medieval times in training for knighthood and serving as an attendant to a person of rank 2 : one employed (as by a hotel) especially to deliver messages or perform personal services for patrons

²page *vb* **paged; pag·ing** 1 : to act as a page 2 : to summon (as in a hotel lobby) by calling out the name of

³page *n* 1 : one side of a printed or written leaf 2 : the matter that is printed or written on a page

⁴page *vb* **paged; pag·ing** : to mark or number the pages of

pag·eant \'paj-ənt\ *n* 1 : an elaborate exhibition or spectacle 2 : an entertainment consisting of scenes based on history or legend ⟨a Christmas *pageant*⟩

pa·go·da \pə-'gōd-ə\ *n* : a Far Eastern tower of several stories erected as a temple or memorial

paid *past of* PAY

pail \'pāl\ *n* 1 : a round container usually with an arched handle mainly for holding or carrying liquids : BUCKET ⟨a water *pail*⟩ 2 : PAILFUL

pail·ful \'pāl-ˌful\ *n, pl* **pail·fuls** \-ˌfulz\ *or* **pails·ful** \'pālz-ˌful\ : the amount a pail holds

¹pain \'pān\ *n* 1 : PUNISHMENT, PENALTY ⟨forbidden on *pain* of death⟩ 2 : suffering from disease, injury, or bodily disorder that usually affects a particular part of the body ⟨*pain* in the chest⟩ 3 : a basic bodily sensation that is induced by a harmful stimulus, characterized by physical discomfort (as burning, throbbing, or aching), and serves as a warning to the body 4 : mental or emotional distress : GRIEF 5 *pl* : great care or effort ⟨took *pains* with his garden⟩ — **pain·ful** \'pān-fəl\ *adj* — **pain·ful·ly** *adv*

pagoda

²pain *vb* 1 : to cause pain in or to 2 : to give or experience pain

pains·tak·ing \'pānz-ˌtā-king\ *adj* : taking pains : showing care ⟨a *painstaking* workman⟩ — **pains·tak·ing·ly** *adv*

¹paint \'pānt\ *vb* 1 : to cover a surface with paint ⟨*paint* a wall⟩ 2 : to represent on a surface by applying colors : make a picture or design of by means of paints ⟨*paint* a dog on the sign⟩ 3 : to put on or apply like paint ⟨*paint* a throat with iodine⟩ 4 : to describe vividly — **paint·er** *n*

²paint *n* : a mixture of coloring matter with a suitable liquid that forms a dry coating when spread on a surface

¹pair \'paər\ *n, pl* **pairs** *also* **pair** 1 : two things of a kind naturally matched or intended to be used together ⟨a *pair* of gloves⟩ 2 : a thing having two connected similar parts ⟨a *pair* of scissors⟩ 3 : two of a sort : a set of two : COUPLE ⟨a *pair* of horses⟩ 4 : a mated couple ⟨a *pair* of robins⟩ **syn** see COUPLE

²pair *vb* 1 : to arrange or unite in pairs ⟨the guests *paired* off for dancing⟩ 2 : to form a pair : MATCH ⟨this glove doesn't *pair* with that one⟩

pa·ja·mas \pə-'jä-məz, -'jam-əz\ *n pl* [from Hindi *pājāma*, a compound of Persian *pā* "leg" and *jāma* "garment"] : a loose-fitting usually two-piece suit for lounging or sleeping

¹Pak·i·stan·i \ˌpak-i-'stan-ē, ˌpä-ki-'stä-nē\ *n* : a native or inhabitant of Pakistan

²Pakistani *adj* : of or relating to Pakistan or the Pakistanis

pal \'pal\ *n* : a close friend or associate

pal·ace \'pal-əs\ *n* 1 : the official residence of a ruler 2 : a large or elaborate mansion

pal·at·a·ble \'pal-ət-ə-bəl\ *adj* : pleasant to the taste : AGREEABLE, ACCEPTABLE

pal·ate \'pal-ət\ *n* 1 : the roof of the mouth consisting of a bony front part (**hard palate**) and a soft flexible back part (**soft palate**) 2 : the sense of taste

¹pale \'pāl\ *adj* **pal·er; pal·est** 1 : not having the warm color of a healthy person : WAN 2 : not bright or brilliant ⟨a *pale* star⟩ 3 : light in color : not vivid or deep ⟨*pale* pink⟩ — **pale·ness** *n*

²pale *vb* **paled; pal·ing** : to grow or turn pale

³pale *n* 1 : a stake or picket of a fence 2 : an enclosed place 3 : a district or territory with clearly marked bounds

Pa·le·o·zo·ic \ˌpā-lē-ə-'zō-ik\ *n* : an era of geological history ending about 230,000,000 years ago that preceded the Mesozoic and is marked by the appearance of vertebrates and land plants

pal·ette \'pal-ət\ *n* 1 : a thin often oval board or tablet on which a painter lays his colors and mixes them 2 : the set of colors that a painter lays on his palette

palette

pal·frey \'pȯl-frē\ *n, pl* **pal·freys** 1 : a saddle horse for the road as distinguished from a war horse 2 : a small saddle horse for ladies

pal·ing \'pā-ling\ *n* 1 : PALE, PICKET 2 : a fence of pales

pal·i·sade \,pal-ə-'sād\ *n* 1 : a high fence of stout pales or stakes especially for defense 2 : a line of steep cliffs

¹**pall** \'pȯl\ *n* 1 : a heavy cloth covering for a coffin, hearse, or tomb 2 : something that covers and darkens ⟨a *pall* of smoke⟩

²**pall** *vb* : to become dull or uninteresting : lose the ability to give pleasure

pall·bear·er \'pȯl-,bar-ər\ *n* : a person who helps to carry or follows a coffin at a funeral

pal·let \'pal-ət\ *n* : a bed of straw : a small poor bed often on the floor

pal·lid \'pal-əd\ *adj* : PALE, WAN

pal·lor \'pal-ər\ *n* : paleness of face

¹**palm** \'päm\ *n* [from Old English *palm* "palm tree", taken from Latin *palma* "palm of the hand" and also "palm tree"; the second meaning in Latin developed because the palm leaf resembles an outstretched hand] 1 : any of a group of mostly tropical trees, shrubs, and vines with a simple but often tall woody stem topped with a crown of large feathery or fan-shaped leaves that are often used or displayed as a religious symbol or an emblem of victory 2 : a symbol of victory or success

²**palm** *n* 1 : the under part of the hand between the fingers and the wrist 2 : a measure of length of about three to four inches 3 : a palm-shaped thing or part

³**palm** *vb* 1 : to hide in the hand ⟨*palm* a coin⟩ 2 : to get rid of or pass on by trickery ⟨*palm* off imitation fur as real⟩

pal·mate \'pal-,māt\ *adj* : resembling a hand with the fingers spread ⟨*palmate* leaves⟩

pal·met·to \pal-'met-ō\ *n, pl* **pal·met·tos** or **pal·met·toes** : a low-growing palm with fan= shaped leaves

Palm Sunday *n* : the Sunday before Easter celebrated in commemoration of Christ's triumphal entry into Jerusalem

pal·o·mi·no \,pal-ə-'mē-nō\ *n, pl* **pal·o·mi·nos** : a compact slender-legged horse of light tan or cream color with lighter mane and tail

pal·pi·tate \'pal-pə-,tāt\ *vb* **pal·pi·tat·ed; pal·pi·tat·ing** : THROB, QUIVER

pal·sy \'pȯl-zē\ *n* 1 : PARALYSIS 2 : an uncontrollable trembling or shaking of the head or hands

pal·try \'pȯl-trē\ *adj* **pal·tri·er; pal·tri·est** : PETTY, WORTHLESS

pam·pas \'pam-pəz\ *n pl* : wide treeless plains of South America : PRAIRIES

pam·per \'pam-pər\ *vb* : to let a person have his own way : SPOIL

pam·phlet \'pam-flət\ *n* : an unbound printed publication

¹**pan** \'pan\ *n* 1 : a shallow open vessel used in cooking 2 : a vessel or article somewhat like a cooking pan ⟨the *pans* of a pair of scales⟩ ⟨a screening *pan* used by gold miners⟩

pan 1

²**pan** *vb* **panned; pan·ning** : to wash earthy material so as to concentrate bits of metal (as gold) — **pan out** : to yield a result : SUCCEED

pan·cake \'pan-,kāk\ *n* : GRIDDLE CAKE

pan·cre·as \'pang-krē-əs\ *n* : a large abdominal gland that secretes and discharges a pancreatic digestive juice into the intestine and contains special cells that produce insulin

pan·cre·at·ic \,pang-krē-'at-ik\ *adj* : of or relating to the pancreas ⟨the *pancreatic* duct⟩

pan·da \'pan-də\ *n* : either of two animals of Tibet which are related to the raccoon and of which the smaller is reddish with black feet and a bushy ringed tail and the larger (**giant panda**) is black and white and bearlike

pan·de·mo·ni·um \,pan-də-'mō-nē-əm\ *n* : a state of wild uproar : TUMULT ⟨*pandemonium* broke loose in the stands as the winning run scored⟩

pane \'pān\ *n* : a sheet of glass (as in a window)

¹**pan·el** \'pan-l\ *n* 1 : a group of persons appointed for some service ⟨a jury *panel*⟩ 2 : a group of persons taking part in a discussion or quiz program 3 : a section of something (as a door or a wall) often sunk below the level of the frame 4 : a piece of material (as plywood) made to form part of a surface (as of a wall) 5 : a board on which instruments or controls are mounted

²**panel** *vb* **pan·eled** or **pan·elled; pan·el·ing** or **pan·el·ling** : to furnish or decorate with panels ⟨*panel* a wall⟩ ⟨a *paneled* ceiling⟩

pan·el·ing \'pan-l-ing\ *n* : panels joined in a continuous surface

pang \'pang\ *n* : a sudden sharp attack or feeling (as of pain or emotional distress)

¹**pan·ic** \'pan-ik\ *n* [from Greek *panikos*, literally, "of Pan", from *Pan*, Greek god of forests and pastures who was believed to

cause sudden unreasonable fear] : a sudden terrifying fright especially without reasonable cause

²**panic** *vb* **pan·icked; pan·ick·ing** : to affect or be affected by panic

pan·icky \'pan-i-kē\ *adj* **1** : resembling or caused by panic ⟨*panicky* fear⟩ **2** : feeling or likely to feel panic

pan·o·ram·a \ˌpan-ə-'ram-ə\ *n* [formed in English from *pan-* "all" and Greek *horama* "sight"] **1** : a picture that is unrolled little by little as a person looks at it **2** : a clear complete view in every direction **3** : a complete view of any subject ⟨a *panorama* of the war⟩

pan·pipe \'pan-ˌpīp\ *n* : a primitive flute consisting of a series of short pipes bound together with the mouthpieces in an even line — usually used in plural

panpipe

pan·sy \'pan-zē\ *n, pl* **pan·sies** : a garden plant related to the violets that has large velvety five-petaled flowers usually in shades of yellow, purple, or brownish red

¹**pant** \'pant\ *vb* **1** : to breathe hard or quickly ⟨*pant* from running⟩ **2** : to make a puffing sound **3** : to want intensely : LONG

²**pant** *n* **1** : a panting breath **2** : a throbbing puffing sound

pan·ta·lets *or* **pan·ta·lettes** \ˌpant-l-'ets\ *n pl* : long loose drawers with ruffles around each ankle once worn by women and girls

pan·ta·loons \ˌpant-l-'ünz\ *n pl* : TROUSERS

pan·ther \'pan-thər\ *n* **1** : LEOPARD **2** : COUGAR **3** : JAGUAR

pantalets

pant·ie *or* **pant·y** \'pant-ē\ *n, pl* **pant·ies** : a woman's or child's undergarment with short legs

pan·to·mime \'pant-ə-ˌmīm\ *n* **1** : a play in which the actors use few or no words **2** : expression of something by facial and bodily movements only

pan·try \'pan-trē\ *n, pl* **pan·tries** : a small room where food and dishes are kept

pants \'pants\ *n pl* **1** : TROUSERS **2** : PANTIES

pap \'pap\ *n* : soft digestible food fit for a baby or invalid

pa·pa \'pä-pə\ *n* : FATHER

pa·pal \'pā-pəl\ *adj* : of or belonging to the pope

pa·paw *for 1* pə-'pò, *for 2* 'pä-pò *or* 'pò-pò\ *n* **1** : PAPAYA **2** : the greenish or yellow edible fruit of a North American tree with shiny leaves and purple flowers

pa·pa·ya \pə-'pī-ə\ *n* : the oblong yellow black-seeded melonlike edible fruit of a tropical American tree

¹**pa·per** \'pā-pər\ *n* **1** : a pliable substance made in thin sheets from rags, wood, straw, or bark and used to write or print on, to wrap things in, or cover walls **2** : a sheet or piece of paper **3** : something printed or written on paper ⟨read a *paper* before a club⟩ ⟨the pupils handed their *papers* to the teacher⟩ **4** : an official document that proves who a person is or what position he holds ⟨an ambassador's *papers*⟩ **5** : NEWSPAPER **6** : WALLPAPER

papaya tree

²**paper** *vb* : to cover or line with paper (as wallpaper) ⟨*paper* a room⟩

³**paper** *adj* **1** : relating to or made of paper ⟨*paper* carton⟩ **2** : resembling paper in thinness or weakness ⟨a *paper*-shelled pecan⟩

pa·per·y \'pā-pə-rē\ *adj* : resembling paper ⟨the *papery* nest of a wasp⟩

pa·poose \pa-'püs\ *n* : a baby of North American Indian parents

pa·pri·ka \pə-'prē-kə\ *n* : a mild red spice made from the fruit of some sweet peppers

pa·py·rus \pə-'pī-rəs\ *n, pl* **pa·py·rus·es** *or* **pa·py·ri** \-rē, -ˌrī\ **1** : a tall African sedge that grows especially in Egypt **2** : a substance like paper made from papyrus by the ancients and used by them to write on **3** : a writing on or written scroll of papyrus

par \'pär\ *n* **1** : a set or stated value (as of money or stocks) **2** : an equally high or common level ⟨two people with talents on a *par*⟩ **3** : the score standard set for each hole of a golf course

par·a·ble \'par-ə-bəl\ *n* : a simple story told to illustrate a moral truth

¹**par·a·chute** \'par-ə-ˌshüt\ *n* : a folding umbrella-shaped device of light fabric used for making a safe descent from an airplane

²**parachute** *vb* **par·a·chut·ed; par·a·chut·ing** : to convey or descend by parachute : bail out

¹**pa·rade** \pə-'rād\ *n* **1** : pompous show or display ⟨the wedding reception was a *parade* of wealth⟩ **2** : the formation of troops before an officer for inspection **3** : a public procession ⟨a circus *parade*⟩ **4** : a crowd of people strolling along ⟨the Easter *parade*⟩

parachute

²**parade** *vb* **pa·rad·ed; pa·rad·ing** **1** : to march in procession **2** : to show off **syn** *see* SHOW

ə abut   ər further   a ax   ā age   ä father, cot   ȧ (see key page)   au̇ out   ch chin   e less   ē easy   g gift   i trip   ī life

par·a·dise \'par-ə-ˌdīs, -ˌdīz\ *n* **1** : the garden of Eden **2** : HEAVEN **3** : a place or state of bliss

par·a·dox \'par-ə-ˌdäks\ *n* : a statement that seems to contradict itself or to be contrary to common sense and yet is perhaps true ⟨a *paradox:* the poor pay more taxes than the rich⟩

par·af·fin \'par-ə-fən\ *n* : a white odorless tasteless substance obtained from wood, coal, or petroleum and used as a waterproof coating, in candles, and for sealing jars of canned food

par·a·gon \'par-ə-ˌgän\ *n* : a model of excellence or perfection ⟨a *paragon* of virtue⟩

¹par·a·graph \'par-ə-ˌgraf\ *n* : a subdivision of a piece of writing that consists of one or more sentences and deals with one point or gives the words of one speaker

²paragraph *vb* : to divide into paragraphs

par·a·keet *var of* PARRAKEET

¹par·al·lel \'par-ə-ˌlel\ *adj* **1** : lying or moving in the same direction but always the same distance apart ⟨*parallel* lines⟩ ⟨train tracks are *parallel*⟩ **2** : LIKE, SIMILAR ⟨*parallel* situations⟩

²parallel *n* **1** : a parallel line or surface **2** : one of the imaginary circles on the earth's surface parallel to the equator that mark latitude ⟨a boundary drawn along the thirty-eighth *parallel*⟩ **3** : a comparison showing resemblance ⟨draw a *parallel* between the course of two different wars⟩ **4** : a thing or event that is like another

parallels

³parallel *vb* **1** : COMPARE **2** : to correspond to **3** : to move, run, or extend in a direction parallel with ⟨the road *parallels* the river⟩

par·al·lel·o·gram \ˌpar-ə-'lel-ə-ˌgram\ *n* : a four-sided plane figure whose opposite sides are parallel and equal

pa·ral·y·sis \pə-'ral-ə-səs\ *n, pl* **pa·ral·y·ses** \-ˌsēz\ : loss of the sense of touch or of the power of voluntary motion

parallelograms

par·a·lyze \'par-ə-ˌlīz\ *vb* **par·a·lyzed; par·a·lyz·ing** **1** : to affect with paralysis **2** : to destroy or lessen the effectiveness or energy of something

par·a·me·ci·um \ˌpar-ə-'mē-shē-əm\ *n, pl* **par·a·me·ci·a** \-shē-ə\ *also* **par·a·me·ci·ums** : a tiny slipper-shaped one-celled water animal that swims by means of tiny hairlike extensions of its body surface

par·a·mount \'par-ə-ˌmaunt\ *adj* : SUPREME, CHIEF ⟨an event of *paramount* importance⟩

par·a·pet \'par-ə-pət, -ˌpet\ *n* **1** : a wall of earth or stone to protect soldiers : BREASTWORK **2** : a low wall or railing at the edge of a platform, roof, or bridge

parapet

par·a·pher·na·lia \ˌpar-ə-fər-'nāl-yə\ *n sing or pl* **1** : personal belongings **2** : EQUIPMENT, FURNISHINGS

¹par·a·phrase \'par-ə-ˌfrāz\ *n* : a restatement of something giving the meaning in different words

²paraphrase *vb* **par·a·phrased; par·a·phras·ing** : to make a paraphrase of : give the meaning of in different words

par·a·site \'par-ə-ˌsīt\ *n* **1** : a person who lives at the expense of another **2** : a plant or animal that lives in or on some other living creature and gets food and sometimes shelter from it

par·a·sit·ic \ˌpar-ə-'sit-ik\ *adj* : of or relating to parasites or their way of life : being a parasite

par·a·sol \'par-ə-ˌsȯl\ *n* : a light umbrella used as a protection against the sun

par·a·troop·er \'par-ə-ˌtrü-pər\ *n* : a soldier trained and equipped to parachute from an airplane

¹par·cel \'pär-səl\ *n* **1** : PORTION, FRAGMENT **2** : a tract or plot of land **3** : BUNDLE, PACKAGE

²parcel *vb* **par·celed** *or* **par·celled; par·cel·ing** *or* **par·cel·ling** **1** : to divide and distribute by parts **2** : to wrap up into a parcel

parch \'pärch\ *vb* : to dry up : shrivel with heat and dryness

parch·ment \'pärch-mənt\ *n* **1** : the skin of a sheep or goat prepared so that it can be written on **2** : a paper similar to parchment **3** : something written on parchment

¹par·don \'pärd-n\ *n* **1** : FORGIVENESS **2** : an official release from legal punishment

²pardon *vb* **1** : to free from penalty for a fault or crime **2** : to allow (an offense) to pass without punishment : FORGIVE **syn** see EXCUSE

pare \'paer\ *vb* **pared; par·ing** **1** : to cut or shave off the outside or the ends of **2** : to reduce as if by cutting ⟨*pare* the cost of a trip⟩

par·ent \'par-ənt, 'per-\ *n* **1** : a father or mother of a child **2** : an animal or plant that produces offspring or seed **3** : SOURCE, ORIGIN

par·ent·age \'par-ənt-ij, 'per-\ *n* : descent from parents or ancestors : LINEAGE ⟨a man of noble *parentage*⟩

pa·ren·tal \pə-'rent-l\ *adj* : of, typical of, or being in the position of parents ⟨*parental* affection⟩

pa·ren·the·sis \pə-'ren-thə-səs\ *n, pl* **pa·ren·the·ses** \-ˌsēz\ **1** : a word, phrase, or sentence inserted in a passage to explain or modify the thought **2** : one of a pair of punctuation marks ( ) used chiefly to enclose a parenthesis or to group mathematical terms to be treated as a unit

par·fait \pär-'fā\ *n* **1** : a flavored custard containing whipped cream and syrup frozen without stirring **2** : a cold dessert made of layers of fruit, syrup, ice cream, and whipped cream

par·ish \'par-ish\ *n* **1** : a section of a diocese committed to the care of a priest or minister **2** : the persons who live in a parish and attend the parish church **3** : the members of a church **4** : a division in the state of Louisiana corresponding to a county in other states

parish house *n* : a building for the educational and social activities of a church

pa·rish·io·ner \pə-'rish-ə-nər\ *n* : a member of a parish

¹park \'pärk\ *n* **1** : an area of land set aside for recreation or for its beauty **2** : an enclosed field for ball games **3** : an outdoor area for the parking of automobiles

²park *vb* : to leave a vehicle standing

par·ka \'pär-kə\ *n* : a warm windproof jacket with a hood

park·way \'pärk-ˌwā\ *n* : a wide road which is beautified with grass and trees and from which heavy vehicles (as trucks) are usually excluded

¹par·ley \'pär-lē\ *vb* **par·leyed; par·ley·ing** : to hold a discussion of terms with an enemy

²parley *n, pl* **par·leys** : a discussion with an enemy ⟨a truce *parley*⟩

par·lia·ment \'pär-lə-mənt\ *n* : an assembly that constitutes the supreme lawmaking body of a country (as the United Kingdom)

par·lor \'pär-lər\ *n* **1** : a room for receiving guests and for conversation **2** : a room or group of rooms fitted up for use in a business ⟨a beauty *parlor*⟩

pa·ro·chi·al \pə-'rō-kē-əl\ *adj* : of or supported by a parish or religious body ⟨*parochial* school⟩

par·ox·ysm \'par-ək-ˌsiz-əm\ *n* : a sudden violent outbreak (as of anger) or attack (as of a recurring disease) ⟨a *paroxysm* of coughing⟩

par·ra·keet \'par-ə-ˌkēt\ *n* : a small long-tailed parrot

par·rot \'par-ət\ *n* : a bright-colored tropical bird with a strong hooked bill often having the ability to imitate human speech

¹par·ry \'par-ē\ *vb* **par·ried; par·ry·ing** **1** : to turn aside an opponent's weapon or blow

2 : AVOID, SIDESTEP ⟨skillfully *parried* the embarrassing questions of the reporters⟩

²parry *n, pl* **par·ries** : an act or instance of parrying

pars·ley \'pärs-lē\ *n, pl* **pars·leys** : a garden plant of the carrot family with finely divided leaves used in cooking and for decorating various dishes

pars·nip \'pärs-nəp\ *n* : a vegetable that is the long white root of a plant related to the carrot

par·son \'pärs-n\ *n* : CLERGYMAN, MINISTER

par·son·age \'pärs-n-ij\ *n* : a house provided for the pastor by a parish or congregation

parsnip

¹part \'pärt\ *n* **1** : one of the portions into which something is divided : something less than a whole : SECTION, SHARE **2** : a spare piece for a machine **3** : a portion of a plant or animal body : MEMBER, ORGAN ⟨wash the injured *part*⟩ **4** : a person's share, duty, or concern ⟨did his *part*⟩ **5** : one of the sides in a disagreement ⟨took her *part* in a quarrel⟩ **6** : the parting or dividing of one's hair **7** : one particular voice or instrument **8** : the music for a particular voice or instrument ⟨the soprano *part*⟩ **9** : a character in a play ⟨the *part* of the hero⟩ **10** : the words or acts of a character in a play or in life ⟨play the *part* of an old lady⟩

²part *vb* **1** : to separate from or leave someone : go away : DEPART **2** : to divide into parts **3** : to hold apart ⟨the fighting boys were *parted* by friends⟩ **4** : to come apart : give way ⟨the anchor cable *parted* in the storm⟩

par·take \pär-'tāk\ *vb* **par·took** \-'tůk\; **par·tak·en** \-'tā-kən\; **par·tak·ing** : to have a share or part : take a portion ⟨*partake* of a dinner⟩ ⟨*partake* in a ceremony⟩

part·ed \'pärt-əd\ *adj* **1** : divided into parts **2** : cleft so that the divisions reach nearly but not quite to the base ⟨three-*parted* corolla⟩

par·tial \'pär-shəl\ *adj* **1** : inclined to favor one side of a question over another : BIASED ⟨a *partial* judge⟩ **2** : fond or too fond of some person or thing ⟨*partial* to ice cream sodas⟩ **3** : of one part or portion only : not complete ⟨*partial* deafness⟩ — **par·tial·ly** *adv*

par·ti·al·i·ty \ˌpär-shē-'al-ət-ē\ *n, pl* **par·ti·al·i·ties** **1** : the quality of being partial : BIAS, PREJUDICE **2** : a particular fondness

par·tic·i·pant \pər-'tis-ə-pənt, pär-\ *n* : a person who takes a part or share ⟨*participants* in a fight⟩

par·tic·i·pate \pər-'tis-ə-ˌpāt, pär-\ *vb* **par·tic·i·**

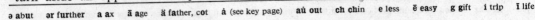

pat·ed; par·tic·i·pat·ing : to have a share in common with others : take part : SHARE

par·tic·i·pa·tion \pär-ˌtis-ə-'pā-shən\ n : the act of participating

par·ti·ci·ple \'pärt-ə-ˌsip-əl\ n : a word formed from a verb and used partly like a verb and partly like an adjective

par·ti·cle \'pärt-i-kəl\ n : a very small bit of something : the smallest possible portion ⟨not a *particle* of sense⟩ ⟨a *particle* of sand⟩

par·ti–col·ored \ˌpärt-ē-'kəl-ərd\ adj : having different colors in different parts ⟨*parti-colored* cows⟩

¹par·tic·u·lar \pər-'tik-yə-lər\ adj 1 : of or relating to the separate parts of a whole ⟨each *particular* item of a report⟩ 2 : of or relating to a single person, class, or thing ⟨each city's own *particular* problem⟩ 3 : SPECIAL ⟨a storm of *particular* violence⟩ 4 : attentive to details : PRECISE, FASTIDIOUS ⟨a *particular* boss⟩ — par·tic·u·lar·ly adv

²particular n : an individual fact, point, or detail ⟨his account was correct in every *particular*⟩

part·ing \'pärt-ing\ n 1 : SEPARATION, DIVISION 2 : a place where a division or separation occurs ⟨the *parting* of the ways⟩ 3 : DEPARTURE ⟨shake hands at *parting*⟩

par·ti·san \'pärt-ə-zən\ n 1 : a supporter of a party, cause, or person ⟨a *partisan* of the governor⟩ 2 : a member of a guerrilla force that works within enemy lines to impede the enemy by sabotage and raids — par·ti·san·ship \-ˌship\ n

¹par·ti·tion \pər-'tish-ən, pär-\ n 1 : an act of dividing into parts ⟨the *partition* of a defeated country⟩ 2 : something that divides ⟨a *partition* between two rooms⟩

²partition vb 1 : to divide into shares ⟨*partition* an estate⟩ 2 : to make into separate parts ⟨*partitioned* the basement into three rooms⟩

part·ly \'pärt-lē\ adv : in part or in some degree : not wholly ⟨the rain was *partly* to blame for the accident⟩

part·ner \'pärt-nər\ n 1 : a person who shares something with another 2 : either one of a married pair 3 : either of a couple who dance together 4 : one who plays with another person on the same side in a game 5 : one of two or more persons who run a business together and share the profits or losses

syn PARTNER, ALLY, CONFEDERATE all mean an associate. PARTNER normally refers to an associate in business ⟨added a third *partner* to the law firm⟩ or else to one of two individuals paired in some other association or activity

⟨tennis *partners*⟩ ⟨his *partner* at a dance⟩ ⟨marriage *partner*⟩ ALLY commonly refers to an associate joined with one for some common purpose and often for mutual protection ⟨the United States and Russia were *allies* in World War II⟩ ⟨my dog was the only *ally* I needed when the tramp followed me⟩ CONFEDERATE definitely implies that the purpose of the association is improper ⟨one man was caught but his *confederate* got away⟩

part·ner·ship \'pärt-nər-ˌship\ n 1 : the condition of being a partner : the relation between partners 2 : the contract by which a partnership is created 3 : an association of people joined for business

part of speech : a traditional class of words (as adjectives, adverbs, conjunctions, interjections, nouns, prepositions, pronouns, or verbs) distinguished according to the kind of idea denoted and the function performed in a sentence

partook past of PARTAKE

par·tridge \'pär-trij\ n, pl partridge or par·tridg·es : any of several stout-bodied game birds related to the domestic fowl

par·ty \'pärt-ē\ n, pl par·ties 1 : a group of persons who take one side of a question or believe in one set of principles ⟨a political *party*⟩ 2 : a social gathering or the entertainment provided for it 3 : a person or group concerned in an affair : one who takes part in something ⟨*party* to a lawsuit⟩

¹pass \'pas\ vb 1 : MOVE, PROCEED ⟨cars *passing* along the street⟩ 2 : DIE ⟨*pass* away⟩ 3 : to go by or move past ⟨*passes* our house on the way to school⟩ 4 : to go or allow to go across, over, or through ⟨*pass* only those who have tickets⟩ 5 : to go away ⟨the pain will soon *pass*⟩ 6 : to move from one place or condition to another ⟨the business has *passed* into other hands⟩ ⟨the throne *passed* to his son⟩ 7 : to go successfully through an examination or inspection ⟨all the candidates *passed* the physical fitness test⟩ 8 : to secure the approval of a legislative body ⟨the bill *passed* both houses of the legislature⟩ 9 : to take place : OCCUR ⟨thoughts *passing* in his mind⟩ 10 : to be recognized or generally known ⟨*pass* as an expert on finance⟩ 11 : to cause to be accepted ⟨*passed* himself off as a war hero⟩ 12 : to throw or transfer (as a ball) to a teammate

²pass n 1 : an opening or way for passing along or through 2 : a gap in a mountain range

³pass n 1 : the act of passing : PASSAGE 2 : condition of affairs : SITUATION ⟨things

have come to a strange *pass*⟩ **3** : a written permit to go or come **4** : an instance of throwing the ball to a teammate (as in football)

pass·a·ble \'pas-ə-bəl\ *adj* **1** : capable of being traveled on ⟨*passable* roads⟩ **2** : barely good enough ⟨a *passable* imitation⟩ — **pass·a·bly** \-blē\ *adv*

pas·sage \'pas-ij\ *n* **1** : the act of passing, going, or proceeding **2** : a means of passing or reaching : HALL, LOBBY, CORRIDOR **3** : JOURNEY, VOYAGE ⟨have a smooth *passage* over the sea⟩ **4** : a right or permission to go as a passenger ⟨*passage* at a reduced rate⟩ **5** : a brief portion of a whole speech or written work

pas·sage·way \'pas-ij-ˌwā\ *n* : a road or way by which a person or thing may pass

pas·sen·ger \'pas-n-jər\ *n* : a person who travels on a public or private vehicle (as a boat, car, bus, or train)

passenger pigeon *n* : a North American wild pigeon formerly abundant but now extinct

pass·er \'pas-ər\ *n* : one that passes

pass·er·by \ˌpas-ər-'bī\ *n, pl* **pass·ers·by** \-ərz-'bī\ : one who passes by

¹pass·ing \'pas-ing\ *n* **1** : the act of passing ⟨spring comes with the *passing* of winter⟩ **2** : DEPARTURE **3** : DEATH

²passing *adj* **1** : going by, beyond, through, or away **2** : lasting only for a short time : not enduring ⟨a *passing* fancy⟩ **3** : HASTY ⟨a *passing* glance⟩ **4** : indicating satisfactory completion of an examination or course of study ⟨a *passing* mark⟩

³passing *adv* : EXCEEDINGLY, VERY ⟨*passing* strange⟩

pas·sion \'pash-ən\ *n* **1** *cap* : the suffering of Christ between the night of the Last Supper and his death **2** : strong feeling or emotion : an outburst of feeling **3** *pl* : the feelings in contrast to reason **4** : strong liking or desire : LOVE ⟨a *passion* for music⟩ **5** : an object of one's love, liking, or desire

pas·sion·ate \'pash-ə-nət\ *adj* **1** : easily moved or excited : QUICK-TEMPERED **2** : ardent in feeling or desire : showing strong emotion

pas·sive \'pas-iv\ *adj* **1** : not active but acted upon ⟨*passive* spectators⟩ **2** : enduring without resistance : PATIENT ⟨*passive* obedience⟩ — **pas·sive·ly** *adv*

Pass·o·ver \'pas-ˌō-vər\ *n* : a Jewish holiday celebrated in March or April in commemoration of the liberating of the Hebrews from slavery in Egypt

pass·port \'pas-ˌpōrt\ *n* : an official docu-

ment issued upon request to a citizen desiring to travel abroad authorizing him to leave his own country and requesting protection for him abroad

pass·word \'pas-ˌwərd\ *n* : a secret word that must be uttered by a person before he is allowed to pass a guard

¹past \'past\ *adj* **1** : of or relating to a time that has gone by ⟨for the *past* month⟩ **2** : expressing a time gone by ⟨the *past* tense of a verb⟩ **3** : no longer serving ⟨a *past* president⟩

²past *prep* : BEYOND

³past *n* **1** : a former time or condition **2** : past life or history ⟨heroes of the nation's glorious *past*⟩

⁴past *adv* : so as to pass by ⟨a deer fled *past*⟩

¹paste \'pāst\ *n* **1** : dough for pies or tarts **2** : a smooth food product made by grinding substances and mixing them with a liquid ⟨almond *paste*⟩ ⟨sardine *paste*⟩ **3** : a preparation of flour or starch and water used for sticking things together **4** : a soft mixture of solid and liquid

²paste *vb* **past·ed; past·ing** : to stick on or together with paste or mucilage

paste·board \'pāst-ˌbōrd\ *n* : a stiff material made of sheets of paper pasted together or of pulp pressed and dried

¹pas·tel \pas-'tel\ *n* **1** : a crayon made of a paste of ground coloring matter **2** : a drawing made with pastel crayons **3** : a soft pale color

²pastel *adj* **1** : made with pastels **2** : light and pale in color

pas·teur·i·za·tion \ˌpas-chə-rə-'zā-shən, ˌpas-tə-\ *n* : the process or an instance of pasteurizing

pas·teur·ize \'pas-chə-ˌrīz, 'pas-tə-\ *vb* **pas·teur·ized; pas·teur·iz·ing** : to keep a fluid (as milk) for a time at a temperature high enough to kill many harmful germs and then cool it rapidly — **pas·teur·iz·er** *n*

pas·time \'pas-ˌtīm\ *n* : something that helps to make time pass pleasantly

pas·tor \'pas-tər\ *n* : a minister or priest in charge of a church or parish

pas·to·ral \'pas-tə-rəl\ *adj* **1** : of or relating to shepherds or peaceful rural scenes ⟨*pastoral* poetry⟩ **2** : relating to the pastor of a church ⟨*pastoral* duties⟩

past·ry \'pās-trē\ *n, pl* **past·ries** **1** : sweet baked goods (as pies, puffs, and tarts) made of enriched dough **2** : a piece of pastry

¹pas·ture \'pas-chər\ *n* **1** : plants (as grass) for feeding grazing animals **2** : land on which animals graze

²pasture *vb* **pas·tured; pas·tur·ing** **1** : GRAZE **2** : to supply (as cattle) with pasture

past·y \'pās-tē\ *adj* **past·i·er; past·i·est 1** : resembling paste : STICKY, DOUGHY **2** : pale and unhealthy in appearance ⟨*pasty* complexion⟩

¹pat \'pat\ *n* **1** : a light blow or tap with the open hand or a flat instrument **2** : the sound of a pat or tap **3** : a small mass (as of butter) shaped by patting

²pat *vb* **pat·ted; pat·ting** : to strike or tap gently with a flat surface (as the open hand)

³pat *adj* **pat·ter; pat·test 1** : exactly suitable : TIMELY, APT ⟨a *pat* answer⟩ **2** : learned or memorized exactly ⟨get a lesson down *pat*⟩ **3** : FIRM, STEADFAST ⟨stand *pat* against argument and persuasion⟩

¹patch \'pach\ *n* **1** : a piece of material used to mend or cover a torn or worn place **2** : a small piece or area distinguished from its surroundings ⟨a *patch* of oats⟩ ⟨a *patch* of snow⟩ **3** : a spot of color : BLOTCH ⟨a *patch* of white on a dog's head⟩

²patch *vb* **1** : to mend or cover with a patch **2** : SETTLE, ADJUST ⟨*patch* up a quarrel⟩ **syn** see MEND

pate \'pāt\ *n* **1** : HEAD **2** : the crown of the head ⟨a bald *pate*⟩

¹pat·ent \ *for 1* 'pat-nt, *for 2* 'pat- *or* 'pāt-\ *adj* **1** : protected by a patent ⟨*patent* medicines⟩ **2** : EVIDENT, OBVIOUS ⟨a *patent* lie⟩

²pat·ent \'pat-nt\ *n* **1** : an official document conferring a right or privilege **2** : a writing that secures to an inventor for a period of years the exclusive right to make, use, and sell his invention **3** : a patented article or process

³pat·ent \'pat-nt\ *vb* : to secure by patent

pa·ter·nal \pə-'tərn-l\ *adj* **1** : of or relating to a father : FATHERLY **2** : received or inherited from a father **3** : related through the father ⟨a *paternal* grandfather⟩

path \'path, 'påth\ *n, pl* **paths** \'pathz, 'påthz\ **1** : a track made by foot travel ⟨a *path* through the woods⟩ **2** : the way or track in which something moves ⟨the *path* of a planet⟩ **3** : a course or way of life or thought

pa·thet·ic \pə-'thet-ik\ *adj* : evoking pity, tenderness, or sorrow

pa·thos \'pā-ˌthäs\ *n* : the quality in an artistic or literary representation of life or in life itself which arouses pity, sympathy, or sorrow

path·way \'path-ˌwā, 'påth-\ *n* : PATH

pa·tience \'pā-shəns\ *n* : the state or quality of being patient

¹pa·tient \'pā-shənt\ *adj* **1** : bearing pain or trials without complaint **2** : showing calm self-control **3** : CONSTANT, PERSEVERING — **pa·tient·ly** *adv*

²patient *n* : a person under medical care and treatment

pat·i·o \'pat-ē-ˌō\ *n, pl* **pat·i·os 1** : an inner open court of a house **2** : an often paved open terrace attached to a house

pa·tri·arch \'pā-trē-ˌärk\ *n* **1** : the father and ruler of a family or tribe **2** : a venerable old man

pa·tri·cian \pə-'trish-ən\ *n* : a person of high birth : ARISTOCRAT

pat·ri·mo·ny \'pat-rə-ˌmō-nē\ *n, pl* **pat·ri·mo·nies** : an estate inherited from one's father or ancestors : HERITAGE

pa·tri·ot \'pā-trē-ət\ *n* [English *patriot* originally meant "fellow countryman" and was derived from Greek *patriōtēs*, from *patrios* "of one's forefathers", which in turn came from *patēr* "father"] : a person who loves his country and zealously supports it

pa·tri·ot·ic \ˌpā-trē-'ät-ik\ *adj* : of or befitting a patriot : having or showing patriotism

pa·tri·ot·ism \'pā-trē-ə-ˌtiz-əm\ *n* : love of one's country and devotion to its welfare

¹pa·trol \pə-'trōl\ *n* **1** : the action of going the rounds of an area for observation or guard **2** : a person or group performing the act of patrolling **3** : a subdivision of a troop of boy scouts that consists of eight scouts

²patrol *vb* **pa·trolled; pa·trol·ling** : to go the rounds of an area for the purpose of watching or protecting

pa·trol·man \pə-'trōl-mən\ *n, pl* **pa·trol·men** \-mən\ : a policeman assigned to a beat

pa·tron \'pā-trən\ *n* **1** : a person chosen as a special guardian or supporter ⟨a *patron* of poets⟩ **2** : a person who gives generous support or approval **3** : CUSTOMER **4** : a saint to whom a church or society is dedicated

pat·ron·age \'pat-rə-nij, 'pā-trə-\ *n* **1** : the act or position of a patron : the support or aid given by a patron **2** : a body of patrons (as of a shop or theater) **3** : the control by officials of appointments to jobs, contracts, and favors

pa·tron·ize \'pā-trə-ˌnīz, 'pat-rə-\ *vb* **pa·tron·ized; pa·tron·iz·ing 1** : to act as a patron to or of : FAVOR, SUPPORT ⟨*patronize* the arts⟩ **2** : to do business with : be a customer of ⟨*patronize* a neighborhood store⟩ **3** : to treat with a superior air

¹pat·ter \'pat-ər\ *vb* **1** : to strike with a quick succession of light blows ⟨rain *pattering* on a roof⟩ **2** : to run with quick light steps

²patter *n* : a quick succession of light sounds ⟨the *patter* of little feet⟩

¹pat·tern \'pat-ərn\ *n* **1** : something fit to be imitated or copied ⟨he is a *pattern* of good behavior⟩ **2** : a model, guide, or set of guiding pieces for making something ⟨a dressmaker's *pattern*⟩ **3** : a form or figure used in decoration : DESIGN ⟨a rug with an elaborate *pattern*⟩ **4** : a natural formation or marking ⟨frost *patterns* on the window⟩ — **pat·terned** \-ərnd\ *adj*

²pattern *vb* : to make or design according to a pattern

pat·ty \'pat-ē\ *n, pl* **pat·ties** : a small flat cake of chopped food ⟨a chicken *patty*⟩

paunch \'pȯnch\ *n* : BELLY

pau·per \'pȯ-pər\ *n* : a very poor person

¹pause \'pȯz\ *n* **1** : a temporary stop **2** : a sign ⌢ or ⌣ above or below a musical note or rest to show that the note or rest is to be prolonged

²pause *vb* **paused**; **paus·ing** : to stop for a time : make a pause

pave \'pāv\ *vb* **paved**; **pav·ing** **1** : to make a hard surface on (as with concrete or asphalt) ⟨*pave* a street⟩ **2** : to make smooth or easy ⟨*pave* the way for others to follow⟩

pave·ment \'pāv-mənt\ *n* **1** : something used to pave a street or floor **2** : a paved surface

pa·vil·ion \pə-'vil-yən\ *n* **1** : a large tent with a peaked or rounded top **2** : a lightly constructed orna- mented building serving as a shelter in a park or garden

pav·ing \'pā-ving\ *n* : PAVEMENT

¹paw \'pȯ\ *n* : the foot of a four= footed animal (as the lion, dog, or cat) that has claws

pavilion 2

²paw *vb* **1** : to touch clumsily or rudely **2** : to beat or scrape with a hoof

¹pawn \'pȯn\ *n* **1** : something of value given as a pledge or guarantee **2** : the condi- tion of being pledged ⟨have a watch in *pawn*⟩

²pawn *vb* : to deposit as security for a loan : PLEDGE

³pawn *n* : the piece of least value in the game of chess

pawn·bro·ker \'pȯn-,brō-kər\ *n* : a person who makes a business of lending money on personal property pledged in his keeping

paw·paw \'pȯ-pȯ\ *var of* PAPAW

pawn

¹pay \'pā\ *vb* **paid** \'pād\ *also in sense 6* **payed**; **pay·ing** **1** : to give (as money) in return for services received or for something bought ⟨*pay* the taxi driver⟩ ⟨*pay* for a ticket⟩ **2** : to discharge a debt ⟨*pay* a tax⟩ **3** : to get even with ⟨*pay* someone back for an injury⟩ **4** : to give or offer freely ⟨*pay* a compliment⟩ ⟨*pay* attention⟩ **5** : to make or secure suitable

return for expense or trouble : be worth the effort or pains required ⟨it *pays* to drive care- fully⟩ **6** : to allow (as a rope) to run out ⟨*pay* out more cable⟩

²pay *n* **1** : the act of paying : PAYMENT **2** : the state of being paid or employed for money ⟨in the *pay* of the company⟩ **3** : WAGES, SALARY

pay·a·ble \'pā-ə-bəl\ *adj* : that may, can, or must be paid

pay·ee \pā-'ē\ *n* : one to whom money is or is to be paid

pay·ment \'pā-mənt\ *n* **1** : the act of pay- ing **2** : money given to discharge a debt **3** : WAGES, SALARY

pay·roll \'pā-,rōl\ *n* **1** : a list of persons en- titled to receive pay **2** : the amount of money necessary to pay the employees of an enterprise

pea \'pē\ *n, pl* **peas** *also* **pease** \'pēz\ **1** : a vegetable that is the round seed found in the pods of a garden plant related to the clovers **2** : a plant (as the sweet pea) resembling or re- lated to the garden pea

peas

peace \'pēs\ *n* **1** : freedom from public disturbance or war **2** : agreement and harmony among persons **3** : a pact or agreement to end a war **4** : freedom from disturbing thoughts or emotions

peace·a·ble \'pē-sə-bəl\ *adj* **1** : inclined to- ward peace : not quarrelsome **2** : PEACEFUL

peace·ful \'pēs-fəl\ *adj* **1** : liking peace : not easily provoked to argue or fight ⟨a *peaceful* people⟩ **2** : CALM, QUIET **3** : not involving argument or fighting ⟨settle a dispute by *peaceful* means⟩ — **peace·ful·ly** *adv* — **peace· ful·ness** *n*

peace·mak·er \'pēs-,mā-kər\ *n* : a person who settles an argument or stops a fight

peach \'pēch\ *n* **1** : a fruit with a juicy sweet edible pulp that differs from the related plum in having a hairy skin and a very rough pitted stone and is borne on a low spreading tree of Chinese origin **2** : a pale yellowish pink color

pea·cock \'pē-,käk\ *n* : the male of a very large Asiatic pheasant with a very long shimmering tail that can be spread or raised at will, a small crest, and in most forms iridescent blue or green feathers on the neck and shoulders

peach 1: fruit and leaves

peak \'pēk\ *n* **1** : a projecting point **2** : the

top of a hill or mountain ⟨the *peak* of a hill⟩
3 : an isolated mountain itself ⟨the solitary
snow-capped *peak* rising from the plain⟩
4 : the projecting front part of a cap **5** : the
highest point of development or activity ⟨at
the *peak* of his career⟩

peaked *for 1* 'pēkt, *for 2* 'pē-kəd\ *adj*
1 : having a peak : POINTED **2** : THIN, SICKLY
⟨looked *peaked* after his illness⟩

¹peal \'pēl\ *n* **1** : a set of bells **2** : the sound
of bells **3** : a loud sound : a series of loud
sounds ⟨a *peal* of thunder⟩

²peal *vb* : to give out peals ⟨bells *pealing* in the
distance⟩

pea·nut \'pē-,nət\ *n* : a yellow-flowered
plant related to the peas grown for its underground pods of oily nutlike edible seeds that
yield a valuable oil (**peanut oil**) or are crushed
to form a spread (**peanut butter**)

pear \'paər\ *n* : the fleshy fruit of a tree related to the apple that is com-
monly larger at the end opposite the stem

pearl \'pərl\ *n* **1** : a dense
lustrous smooth body formed
within the shell of some mollusks (as the **pearl oyster** of
tropical seas) usually around
something irritating (as a sand
grain) that has gotten into the shell
2 : MOTHER-OF-PEARL **3** : something likened
to a pearl in shape, color, or value **4** : a pale
bluish gray color

pear: fruit
and leaves

pearl·y \'pər-lē\ *adj* **pearl·i·er; pearl·i·est** : resembling a pearl especially in softly lustrous
surface

peas·ant \'pez-nt\ *n* : a small farmer or farm
laborer in European countries

peas·ant·ry \'pez-n-trē\ *n* : PEASANTS

pease *pl of* PEA

peat \'pēt\ *n* : a blackish or dark brown material that is the remains of plants partly
decomposed in water and is dug and dried for
use as fuel

peat moss *n* : a spongy brownish moss of
wet areas that is often the chief plant constituent of peat

peb·ble \'peb-əl\ *n* : a small rounded stone

pe·can \pi-'kän, -'kan\ *n* : an oval edible and
usually thin-shelled nut that is the fruit of a
tall tree of the central and southern United
States related to the walnuts

pec·ca·ry \'pek-ə-rē\ *n, pl* **pec·ca·ries** : either
of two mostly tropical American animals that
gather in herds, are active at night, and resemble but are much smaller than the related
pigs

¹peck \'pek\ *n* **1** : a unit of dry capacity
equal to one quarter of a bushel **2** : a great
deal : a large quantity ⟨a *peck* of trouble⟩

²peck *vb* **1** : to strike with the bill **2** : to
strike with a sharp instrument (as a pick)
3 : to pick up food with the bill

³peck *n* **1** : the act of pecking **2** : the mark
made by pecking

pec·to·ral \'pek-tə-rəl\ *adj* : of or relating to
the chest ⟨*pectoral* muscles⟩

pe·cu·liar \pi-'kyül-yər\ *adj* **1** : one's own
: belonging to or characteristic of some one
person, thing, or place : PARTICULAR ⟨a custom *peculiar* to England⟩ **2** : different from
the usual : ODD **syn** *see* QUEER

pe·cu·li·ar·i·ty \pi-,kyü-lē-'ar-ət-ē\ *n, pl* **pe-
cu·li·ar·i·ties** **1** : the quality or condition of
being peculiar **2** : something that is peculiar
: a distinguishing characteristic

ped·a·gogue \'ped-ə-,gäg\ *n* : TEACHER,
SCHOOLMASTER

¹ped·al \'ped-l\ *n* : a lever worked by the foot
or feet

²pedal *adj* : of or relating to the foot or feet

³pedal *vb* **ped·aled** *or* **ped·alled; ped·al·ing** *or*
ped·al·ling : to use or work the pedals of something ⟨*pedal* a bicycle⟩

ped·dle \'ped-l\ *vb* **ped·dled; ped·dling** : to go
about in the street or from house to house
with goods for sale

ped·dler *or* **ped·lar** \'ped-lər\ *n* : one that
peddles

ped·es·tal \'ped-əst-l\ *n* **1** : the support or
foot of a column or of an upright structure
(as a statue, vase, or lamp) **2** : a position of
high regard ⟨placed his father on a *pedestal*⟩

pe·des·tri·an \pə-'des-trē-ən\ *n* : a person
who goes on foot : WALKER

ped·i·gree \'ped-ə-,grē\ *n* **1** : a table or list
showing the line of ancestors of a person or
animal **2** : an ancestral line

pe·dom·e·ter \pi-'däm-ət-ər\ *n* : an instrument that measures the distance one covers in
walking

¹peek \'pēk\ *vb* **1** : to look slyly or cautiously **2** : to take a brief glance — **peek·er** *n*

²peek *n* : a brief or furtive look

¹peel \'pēl\ *vb* **1** : to strip off the skin, bark,
or rind of **2** : to strip or tear off **3** : to come
off smoothly or in bits

²peel *n* : a skin or rind especially of a fruit

¹peep \'pēp\ *vb* : to make a feeble shrill
sound such as a young bird makes — **peep·er** *n*

²peep *n* : a feeble shrill sound : CHEEP

³peep *vb* **1** : to look through or as if through
a small hole or a crack : PEEK **2** : to show
slightly ⟨crocuses *peeping* through the grass⟩

⁴peep *n* **1** : a brief or furtive look   **2** : the first appearance ⟨the *peep* of dawn⟩

¹peer \'piər\ *n* **1** : a person of the same rank or character : EQUAL   **2** : a member (as a duke, marquis, earl, viscount, or baron) of one of the five ranks of the British nobility

²peer *vb* **1** : to look curiously or narrowly   **2** : to come slightly into view : peep out

peer·age \'piər-ij\ *n* **1** : the body of peers   **2** : the rank or dignity of a peer

peer·less \'piər-ləs\ *adj* : having no equal : MATCHLESS

pee·vish \'pē-vish\ *adj* **1** : STUBBORN   **2** : FRETFUL, COMPLAINING ⟨a *peevish* remark⟩ — **pee·vish·ly** *adv* — **pee·vish·ness** *n*

¹peg \'peg\ *n* **1** : a small pointed piece (as of wood) used to fasten things together   **2** : a projecting piece for hanging things on ⟨a clothes *peg*⟩   **3** : a piece of wood to be driven into the ground to mark a boundary or to hold something ⟨a *peg* for a tent rope⟩   **4** : STEP, DEGREE ⟨took him down a *peg*⟩   **5** : THROW ⟨a quick *peg* to third base⟩

²peg *vb* **pegged; peg·ging** **1** : to mark, plug, or fasten with pegs   **2** : THROW   **3** : to work hard ⟨*pegging* away at his job⟩

pel·i·can \'pel-i-kən\ *n* : a bird with a large bill, webbed feet, and a great pouch on the lower jaw that is used to scoop in fish for food

pel·lag·ra \pə-'lag-rə\ *n* : a disease caused by a diet deficient in protein and in an essential vitamin

pelican

pel·let \'pel-ət\ *n* **1** : a little ball (as of food or medicine)   **2** : a piece of small shot

pell–mell \'pel-'mel\ *adv* **1** : in crowded confusion   **2** : in great haste : HEADLONG

¹pelt \'pelt\ *n* : a skin of an animal especially with its fur or wool

²pelt *vb* **1** : to strike with repeated blows   **2** : HURL, THROW ⟨apples *pelted* to the ground by the wind⟩   **3** : to beat or pound repeatedly against something ⟨rain *pelting* on the roof⟩

pelt

¹pen \'pen\ *n* **1** : a small enclosure for animals   **2** : a small place of confinement or storage

²pen *vb* **penned; pen·ning** : to shut in or as if in a pen

³pen *n* : an instrument for writing with ink

⁴pen *vb* **penned; pen·ning** : to write with a pen

pe·nal \'pēn-l\ *adj* : of or relating to punishment, penalties, or punitive institutions ⟨*penal* laws⟩ ⟨a *penal* colony⟩

pe·nal·ize \'pēn-l-,īz, 'pen-\ *vb* **pe·nal·ized; pe·nal·iz·ing** : to subject to a penalty ⟨*penalize* an athlete for a foul⟩

pen·al·ty \'pen-l-tē\ *n, pl* **pen·al·ties** **1** : punishment for an offense or crime   **2** : loss or handicap imposed for breaking a rule in a sport or game

pence *pl of* PENNY

¹pen·cil \'pen-səl\ *n* : an implement for writing or drawing consisting of a stick of black or colored material encased in wood, plastic, or metal

²pencil *vb* **pen·ciled** *or* **pen·cilled; pen·cil·ing** *or* **pen·cil·ling** : to write, mark, or draw with a pencil

pen·dant \'pen-dənt\ *n* : a hanging ornament (as an earring)

¹pend·ing \'pen-ding\ *prep* **1** : DURING   **2** : while awaiting

²pending *adj* : not yet decided ⟨a question that is *pending*⟩

pen·du·lum \'pen-jə-ləm, -dyə-\ *n* : a body suspended from a fixed point so as to swing freely to and fro under the action of gravity ⟨the *pendulum* of a clock⟩

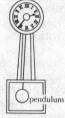

pendulum

pen·e·trate \'pen-ə-,trāt\ *vb* **pen·e·trat·ed; pen·e·trat·ing** **1** : to pass into or through : PIERCE   **2** : to see into or understand ⟨ideas too difficult to *penetrate*⟩

pen·e·tra·tion \,pen-ə-'trā-shən\ *n* **1** : the act or process of penetrating   **2** : sharp insight

pen·guin \'pen-gwən\ *n* : a short-legged flightless seabird found in the cold regions of the southern hemisphere

pen·i·cil·lin \,pen-ə-'sil-ən\ *n* : an antibiotic produced by a mold that is used especially against disease-causing spherical bacteria

pen·in·su·la \pə-'nin-sə-lə, -chə-lə\ *n* [from Latin *paeninsula*, from *paene* "almost" and *insula* "island"] : a piece of land extending out into a body of water

pe·nis \'pē-nəs\ *n, pl* **pe·nes** \-,nēz\ *or* **pe·nis·es** : a male organ used in sexual intercourse

pen·i·tence \'pen-ə-təns\ *n* : REPENTANCE

¹pen·i·tent \'pen-ə-tənt\ *adj* : REPENTANT

²penitent *n* : a penitent person

pen·i·ten·tia·ry \,pen-ə-'ten-chə-rē\ *n, pl* **pen·i·ten·tia·ries** : a prison for criminals

pen·knife \'pen-,nīf\ *n, pl* **pen·knives** \-,nīvz\ : a small pocketknife

pen·man \'pen-mən\ *n, pl* **pen·men** \-mən\ : a person who uses a pen : WRITER

pen·man·ship \'pen-mən-,ship\ *n* : writing with a pen : style or quality of handwriting

pen name *n* : a name assumed by an author ⟨a professor who wrote novels under a *pen name*⟩

pen·nant \'pen-ənt\ *n* 1 : a tapering flag used for identification, signaling, or decoration 2 : a flag that is the emblem of championship ⟨won the league *pennant*⟩

pen·ni·less \'pen-i-ləs\ *adj* : extremely poor : having no money

pen·ny \'pen-ē\ *n, pl* **pen·nies** \'pen-ēz\ *or* **pence** \'pens\ 1 : a coin of Great Britain equal to 1/12 shilling 2 *pl* **pennies** : a cent of the United States or Canada

¹pen·sion \'pen-chən\ *n* : a fixed sum paid regularly to a person retired from service

²pension *vb* : to grant or give a pension to

pen·sive \'pen-siv\ *adj* : dreamily thoughtful : MUSING ⟨a *pensive* mood⟩ — **pen·sive·ly** *adv* — **pen·sive·ness** *n*

pen·stock \'pen-,stäk\ *n* : a pipe for conducting water (as to a waterwheel)

pent \'pent\ *adj* : penned up : shut up

pen·ta·gon \'pent-ə-,gän\ *n* : a flat figure having five angles and five sides

pen·tag·o·nal \pen-'tag-ən-l\ *adj* : having five sides

pentagon

pen·tath·lon \pen-'tath-lən\ *n* : an athletic contest in which each competitor takes part in each of a series of five track-and-field contests

pent·house \'pent-,haùs\ *n* : an apartment built on the roof of a building

pe·on \'pē-,än\ *n* : a member of the landless laboring class in Spanish America

pe·o·ny \'pē-ə-nē\ *n, pl* **pe·o·nies** [through Latin and French from Greek *paiōnia*, derived from *Paiōn* "Paeon", the physician of the gods in Greek mythology, probably because of its use in medicine] : a perennial plant related to the buttercup that is widely grown for its very large usually double white, pink, or red flowers

peonies

¹peo·ple \'pē-pəl\ *n, pl* **people** *or* **peo·ples** 1 : a body of persons making up a race, tribe, or nation ⟨the *peoples* of Asia⟩ 2 : human beings : PERSONS 3 : the persons of some particular group or place ⟨the *people* of this state⟩ 4 : the mass of persons in a community without respect to special classes

²people *vb* **peo·pled; peo·pling** 1 : to supply or fill with people 2 : to dwell on or in : INHABIT

¹pep \'pep\ *n* : brisk energy or liveliness

²pep *vb* **pepped; pep·ping** : to put pep into ⟨cool weather *peps* us up⟩

¹pep·per \'pep-ər\ *n* 1 : a sharp-flavored product from the fruit of an East Indian climbing shrub that is used as a seasoning or in medicine and consists of the whole ground dried berry (**black pepper**) or of the ground seeds alone (**white pepper**) 2 : a plant related to the tomato that is grown for its fruits which may be very sharp-flavored and red when

pepper 2

ripe (**hot peppers**) and used mostly in pickles or dried and ground as a seasoning or be mild and sweet (**sweet peppers**) and used mostly as a vegetable

²pepper *vb* 1 : to season with pepper 2 : to hit with a shower of blows or missiles

pep·per·mint \'pep-ər-,mint\ *n* : a sharp-flavored aromatic mint with spikes of small pink flowers that yields an oil (**peppermint oil**) used especially to flavor candies

per \pər, ,pər\ *prep* 1 : to or for each ⟨ten dollars *per* day⟩ 2 : according to ⟨it was done *per* instructions⟩

per an·num \pər-'an-əm\ *adv* : by the year : in or for each year : ANNUALLY

per·cale \pər-'kāl, -'kal\ *n* : a fine closely woven cotton fabric

per cap·i·ta \pər-'kap-ət-ə\ *adv (or adj)* : by or for each person ⟨the *per capita* wealth of a country⟩

per·ceive \pər-'sēv\ *vb* **per·ceived; per·ceiv·ing** 1 : to become aware of through the senses and especially through sight 2 : UNDERSTAND

¹per·cent \pər-'sent\ *adv (or adj)* : out of every hundred : measured by the number of units as compared with one hundred

²percent *n, pl* **percent** 1 : one part in a hundred 2 : a part or fraction of a whole expressed in hundredths : PERCENTAGE ⟨thirty *percent* of the class failed the test⟩

per·cent·age \pər-'sent-ij\ *n* 1 : a part of a whole expressed in hundredths 2 : a share of winnings or profits

per·cep·ti·ble \pər-'sep-tə-bəl\ *adj* : capable of being perceived ⟨a *perceptible* change⟩

per·cep·tion \pər-'sep-shən\ *n* 1 : the act of perceiving 2 : the power or ability to perceive 3 : a judgment formed by perceiving

¹perch \'pərch\ *n* 1 : a place where birds roost : ROOST 2 : a raised seat or position

²perch *vb* : to sit or rest on or as if on a perch

³perch *n, pl* **perch** *or* **perch·es** 1 : a largely olive green and yellow European freshwater food fish 2 : any of numerous fishes related to or resembling the European perch

per·chance \pər-'chans\ *adv* : PERHAPS

per·co·late \'pər-kə-ˌlāt\ *vb* **per·co·lat·ed;
per·co·lat·ing** **1** : to trickle or cause to trickle
through a porous substance : OOZE ⟨water
percolating through sand⟩ **2** : to prepare
(coffee) by repeatedly passing hot water
through ground coffee beans — **per·co·la·tor** *n*

per·co·la·tion \ˌpər-kə-'lā-shən\ *n* : the act or
process of percolating

per·cus·sion \pər-'kəsh-ən\ *n* **1** : a striking
together : BLOW **2** : the striking of an explosive cap in order to set off the charge in a
gun **3** : the striking of sound waves against
the eardrum **4** : percussion instruments that
form a section of a band or orchestra

percussion instrument *n* : a musical instrument sounded by striking

¹pe·ren·ni·al \pə-'ren-ē-əl\ *adj* **1** : lasting
through the whole year ⟨*perennial* springs⟩
2 : CONTINUOUS, UNCEASING ⟨*perennial* joy⟩
3 : living from year to year ⟨a *perennial* plant⟩

²perennial *n* : a perennial plant

¹per·fect \'pər-fikt\ *adj* **1** : lacking nothing
: WHOLE, COMPLETE ⟨a *perfect* set of teeth⟩
2 : thoroughly skilled or trained : meeting the
highest standards of excellence ⟨practice
makes *perfect*⟩ **3** : having no mistake, error,
or flaw ⟨a *perfect* diamond⟩ — **per·fect·ly** *adv*
 syn PERFECT, INTACT both refer to something
that is not defective or deficient in any way.
PERFECT indicates that something is complete,
sound, and excellent in quality ⟨a *perfect*
replica of the old castle⟩ or that it measures
up to an extremely high standard of excellence
⟨a *perfect* June day⟩ INTACT refers to something that has retained its perfect, natural, or
original condition ⟨is this chess set *intact*⟩
especially after passing through an experience
or situation that might easily have injured it
⟨few houses were *intact* after the earthquake⟩

²per·fect \pər-'fekt\ *vb* : to make perfect
: REFINE

per·fec·tion \pər-'fek-shən\ *n* **1** : completeness in all parts or details **2** : the highest
excellence or skill **3** : a quality or thing that
cannot be excelled or improved

per·fo·rate \'pər-fə-ˌrāt\ *vb* **per·fo·rat·ed;
per·fo·rat·ing** **1** : to bore through : PIERCE
2 : to make many small holes in

per·form \pər-'förm\ *vb* **1** : to carry out
: ACCOMPLISH, DO **2** : to do something needing special skill ⟨*perform* on the piano⟩ —
per·form·er *n*

per·form·ance \pər-'för-məns\ *n* **1** : the
carrying out of an action ⟨the *performance* of
daily chores⟩ **2** : a public entertainment or
presentation

¹per·fume \'pər-ˌfyüm\ *n* **1** : a pleasing
odor : FRAGRANCE **2** : a fluid preparation
used for scenting

²per·fume \pər-'fyüm\ *vb* **per·fumed; per-
fum·ing** : to add a pleasing smell to : fill with a
pleasing odor

per·haps \pər-'haps\ *adv* : possibly but not
certainly : MAYBE

per·il \'per-əl\ *n* **1** : exposure to injury, loss,
or destruction : DANGER ⟨in *peril* of death⟩
2 : a cause or source of danger **syn** see DANGER

per·il·ous \'per-ə-ləs\ *adj* : HAZARDOUS,
DANGEROUS

pe·rim·e·ter \pə-'rim-ət-ər\ *n* **1** : the whole
outer boundary of a body or area **2** : the sum
of the lengths of all sides of a polygon

pe·ri·od \'pir-ē-əd\ *n* **1** : a punctuation mark
. used chiefly to mark the end of a declarative
sentence or an abbreviation **2** : the completion of a cycle or of a series of events **3** : a
portion of time marked by some stated characteristic ⟨a *period* of cool weather⟩ **4** : a
portion of time that constitutes a stage in the
history of something ⟨the colonial *period*⟩
5 : one of the divisions of a school day
 syn PERIOD, ERA, AGE all refer to a portion of
time. PERIOD is a very general term that can
be used of an extent of time of any length or
description ⟨we have a fifteen-minute rest
period after lunch⟩ ⟨the country was in a
period of prosperity⟩ ERA is used of a period
that is set apart or distinguished by some new
order or notable characteristic ⟨the *era* of the
common man⟩ AGE is stronger and more
specific, and usually denotes a period dominated by a central figure ⟨the *age* of Shake-
speare⟩ or by a central feature ⟨the Stone
Age⟩

pe·ri·od·ic \ˌpir-ē-'äd-ik\ *adj* : occurring at
regular intervals

¹pe·ri·od·i·cal \ˌpir-ē-'äd-i-kəl\ *adj* **1** : PERI-
ODIC **2** : published at regular intervals —
pe·ri·od·i·cal·ly *adv*

²periodical *n* : a periodical publication

per·i·scope \'per-ə-ˌskōp\ *n* : a tubular
instrument containing lenses and
mirrors by which an observer
(as on a submerged submarine
or around a corner) obtains an
otherwise obstructed view

per·ish \'per-ish\ *vb* : to pass
away completely : be destroyed
: DIE ⟨races that have *perished*
from the earth⟩

per·ish·a·ble \'per-ish-ə-bəl\
adj : liable to spoil or decay ⟨*perishable* foods
such as milk and eggs⟩

periscope
in diagram

ə abut   ər further   a ax   ā age   ä father, cot   á (see key page)   au̇ out   ch chin   e less   ē easy   g gift   i trip   ī life

¹per·i·win·kle \'per-i-,wing-kəl\ *n* : a trailing evergreen plant with shining leaves and blue or white flowers

²periwinkle *n* : a small edible snail that lives along rocky seashores

perk \'pərk\ *vb* : to lift quickly, sau017cily, or boldly ⟨a dog *perking* its ears⟩ — **perk up** **1** : to make oneself pretty or trim **2** : to be or become lively and alert

perk·y \'pər-kē\ *adj* **perk·i·er**; **perk·i·est** : JAUNTY, SAUCY

periwinkle

per·ma·nence \'pər-mə-nəns\ *n* : the quality or condition of being permanent

per·ma·nent \'pər-mə-nənt\ *adj* : lasting or intended to last for a very long time : not temporary : not changing **syn** see LASTING — **per·ma·nent·ly** *adv*

per·me·a·ble \'pər-mē-ə-bəl\ *adj* : having pores or openings that permit liquids or gases to pass through

per·me·ate \'pər-mē-,āt\ *vb* **per·me·at·ed**; **per·me·at·ing** **1** : to pass through something which has pores or small openings or is of loose texture ⟨water *permeates* sand⟩ **2** : to spread throughout ⟨a room *permeated* with the odor of tobacco⟩

per·mis·sion \pər-'mish-ən\ *n* : the consent of a person in authority : LEAVE

¹per·mit \pər-'mit\ *vb* **per·mit·ted**; **per·mit·ting** **1** : to give permission : ALLOW **2** : to make possible : give an opportunity ⟨if time *permits*⟩

²per·mit \'pər-,mit\ *n* : a statement of permission : LICENSE, PASS

per·ni·cious \pər-'nish-əs\ *adj* : very destructive or injurious ⟨a *pernicious* disease⟩ ⟨a *pernicious* habit⟩

¹per·pen·dic·u·lar \,pər-pən-'dik-yə-lər\ *adj* **1** : exactly vertical or upright **2** : being at right angles to a given line or plane — **per·pen·dic·u·lar·ly** *adv*

²perpendicular *n* : a perpendicular line, plane, or position

per·pe·trate \'pər-pə-,trāt\ *vb* **per·pe·trat·ed**; **per·pe·trat·ing** : to be guilty of doing : COMMIT ⟨*perpetrate* a crime⟩

horizontal | perpendicular

per·pet·u·al \pər-'pech-ə-wəl\ *adj* **1** : lasting forever : ETERNAL **2** : continuing without interruption ⟨*perpetual* arguments⟩ — **per·pet·u·al·ly** *adv*

per·pet·u·ate \pər-'pech-ə-,wāt\ *vb* **per·pet·u·at·ed**; **per·pet·u·at·ing** : to make perpetual : cause to last indefinitely

per·plex \pər-'pleks\ *vb* : to disturb mentally : BEWILDER, CONFUSE **syn** see BAFFLE

per·plex·i·ty \pər-'plek-sət-ē\ *n, pl* **per·plex·i·ties** **1** : the state of being perplexed : a puzzled or anxious state of mind **2** : something that perplexes

per·se·cute \'pər-si-,kyüt\ *vb* **per·se·cut·ed**; **per·se·cut·ing** **1** : to pursue in order to harm or destroy : keep on inflicting injuries or torture upon **2** : OPPRESS

per·se·cu·tion \,pər-si-'kyü-shən\ *n* **1** : the act of persecuting **2** : the state of being persecuted

per·se·ver·ance \,pər-sə-'vir-əns\ *n* : the act or power of persevering

per·se·vere \,pər-sə-'viər\ *vb* **per·se·vered**; **per·se·ver·ing** : to keep at something in spite of difficulties or opposition

per·sim·mon \pər-'sim-ən\ *n* : a plumlike usually orange-colored fruit that has soft pulp that puckers the mouth if eaten before fully ripe and that is borne by a tree related to the ebonies

persimmon: fruit and leaves

per·sist \pər-'sist\ *vb* **1** : to keep on doing or saying something : continue stubbornly **2** : to last on and on : continue to exist ⟨rain *persisting* for days⟩

per·sist·ence \pər-'sis-təns\ *n* **1** : the act or fact of persisting **2** : the quality of being persistent : PERSEVERANCE

per·sist·ent \pər-'sis-tənt\ *adj* : continuing to act or exist longer than usual : LASTING ⟨a *persistent* cold⟩ — **per·sist·ent·ly** *adv*

per·son \'pərs-n\ *n* **1** : a human being **2** : the body of a human being ⟨keeps his *person* neat⟩ **3** : bodily presence ⟨appear in *person*⟩ **4** : reference of a segment of discourse to the speaker, to one spoken to, or to one spoken of as indicated especially by means of certain pronouns

per·son·age \'pərs-n-ij\ *n* : a person of rank or importance : a famous person

per·son·al \'pərs-n-əl\ *adj* **1** : of, relating to, or belonging to a person : not public : not general ⟨*personal* property⟩ **2** : of the person or body ⟨*personal* appearance⟩ **3** : relating to a particular person or his character or conduct ⟨make *personal* remarks⟩ **4** : intended for one particular person ⟨a *personal* letter⟩ **5** : relating to oneself ⟨*personal* pride⟩ **6** : made or done in person ⟨*personal* attention⟩ — **per·son·al·ly** *adv*

per·son·al·i·ty \,pərs-n-'al-ət-ē\ *n, pl* **per·son·al·i·ties** **1** : the characteristics or traits of a person that make him different from other persons : INDIVIDUALITY **2** : pleasing qualities of character ⟨gifted with *personality*⟩ **3** : a person who has strongly marked qualities ⟨a great *personality*⟩ **4** : a personal remark : a slighting reference to a person ⟨use *personalities* in an argument⟩

per·son·i·fy \pər-'sän-ə-ˌfī\ *vb* **per·son·i·fied; per·son·i·fy·ing** : to think of or represent as a person

per·son·nel \ˌpərs-n-'el\ *n* : a group of persons employed in a service or an organization

per·spec·tive \pər-'spek-tiv\ *n* **1** : the art of painting or drawing a scene so that objects in it have their right shape and the appearance of distance **2** : the power to see or think of things in their true relationship to each other **3** : the true relationship of objects or events to one another

per·spi·ra·tion \ˌpər-spə-'rā-shən\ *n* **1** : the act or process of perspiring **2** : salty liquid given off from skin glands : SWEAT

per·spire \pər-'spīr\ *vb* **per·spired; per·spir·ing** : to give off perspiration

per·suade \pər-'swād\ *vb* **per·suad·ed; per·suad·ing** : to win over to a belief by argument or earnest request : argue into an opinion or course of action

per·sua·sion \pər-'swā-zhən\ *n* **1** : the act of persuading **2** : the power to persuade **3** : a way of believing : BELIEF ⟨two persons of the same *persuasion*⟩

per·sua·sive \pər-'swā-siv\ *adj* : having the power or effect of persuading — **per·sua·sive·ly** *adv*

pert \'pərt\ *adj* **1** : saucily bold **2** : LIVELY

per·tain \pər-'tān\ *vb* **1** : to belong to as a part, quality, or function ⟨duties *pertaining* to the office of sheriff⟩ **2** : to relate to a person or thing ⟨laws *pertaining* to hunting⟩

per·ti·nent \'pərt-n-ənt\ *adj* : relating to the subject that is being considered

per·turb \pər-'tərb\ *vb* : to disturb in mind : trouble greatly : AGITATE

pe·ruse \pə-'rüz\ *vb* **pe·rused; pe·rus·ing** **1** : READ **2** : to read through carefully or critically

per·vade \pər-'vād\ *vb* **per·vad·ed; per·vad·ing** : to pass through all parts of : spread through ⟨a life *pervaded* by fear⟩

per·verse \pər-'vərs\ *adj* : obstinate in being or doing wrong : WILLFUL

pe·se·ta \pə-'sāt-ə\ *n* : a coin of Spain

pe·so \'pā-sō\ *n, pl* **pe·sos** **1** : an old silver coin of Spain and Spanish America **2** : a coin of the Philippines or of any of various Latin American countries

pes·si·mis·tic \ˌpes-ə-'mis-tik\ *adj* **1** : lacking in hope that one's troubles will end or that success or happiness will come : GLOOMY **2** : having the belief that evil is more common or powerful than good

pest \'pest\ *n* **1** : an epidemic disease that causes many deaths : PESTILENCE **2** : a plant or animal damaging to man or his goods

pes·ter \'pes-tər\ *vb* : to annoy repeatedly

pes·ti·lence \'pes-tə-ləns\ *n* : a contagious often fatal disease that spreads quickly

pes·tle \'pes-əl\ *n* : a club-shaped implement for crushing substances in a mortar

¹pet \'pet\ *n* **1** : a domesticated animal kept for pleasure rather than service **2** : a person who is treated with special kindness or consideration

mortar and pestle

²pet *adj* **1** : kept or treated as a pet **2** : expressing fondness ⟨a *pet* name⟩ **3** : FAVORITE

³pet *vb* **pet·ted; pet·ting** **1** : to stroke or pat gently or lovingly **2** : PAMPER **3** : to engage in kissing and caressing

⁴pet *n* : a fit of peevishness or sulky anger

pet·al \'pet-l\ *n* : one of the often brightly colored specialized leaves that form the corolla of a flower — **pet·aled** *or* **pet·alled** \-ld\ *adj* — **pet·al·less** \-l-ləs\ *adj*

petal

pet·i·ole \'pet-ē-ˌōl\ *n* : the stalk of a leaf

pe·tite \pə-'tēt\ *adj* : small and trim of figure

¹pe·ti·tion \pə-'tish-ən\ *n* **1** : a formal written request addressed to an official person or group **2** : an earnest request : PRAYER

²petition *vb* **1** : to make a petition to **2** : to make a formal request for — **pe·ti·tion·er** *n*

pet·rel \'pet-rəl\ *n* : a small long-winged seabird that flies far from land

pet·ri·fy \'pet-rə-ˌfī\ *vb* **pet·ri·fied; pet·ri·fy·ing** **1** : to change plant or animal matter into stone or a stonelike substance : turn as hard as stone ⟨*petrified* trees⟩ **2** : to stun with fear

pe·tro·le·um \pə-'trō-lē-əm\ *n* : a raw oil that is obtained from wells drilled in the ground and that is the source of gasoline, kerosene, and fuel oils

petrel

pet·ti·coat \'pet-ē-ˌkōt\ *n* : a skirt worn under a dress or outer skirt

pet·ty \'pet-ē\ *adj* **pet·ti·er; pet·ti·est** **1** : being small and of no importance : TRIFLING ⟨*petty* details⟩ **2** : MINOR, INFERIOR ⟨*petty* princes⟩ — **pet·ti·ly** \'pet-l-ē\ *adv* — **pet·ti·ness** \'pet-ē-nəs\ *n* syn PETTY and TRIVIAL both mean little and insignificant. PETTY refers to things that are of minor importance in comparison with other things of the same general kind ⟨*petty* troubles⟩ and normally indicates a small= minded concern with unworthy matters ⟨*petty* gossip⟩ ⟨*petty* economies⟩ TRIVIAL is used of things so commonplace and insignificant that they are barely worthy of notice or consideration ⟨*trivial* mistakes⟩ and when used of people or their behavior suggests a shallow- ness of mind ⟨*trivial* comments⟩

petty officer *n* : an enlisted man in the navy of a rank corresponding to a noncommissioned officer in the army

pet·u·lant \'pech-ə-lənt\ *adj* : easily put in a bad humor : PEEVISH, FRETFUL

pe·tu·nia \pə-'tü-nyə, -'tyü-\ *n* : a plant re- lated to the potato that is grown for its velvety brightly colored funnel-shaped flowers

pew \'pyü\ *n* : one of the benches with backs and some- times doors set in rows in a church

petunia

pe·wee \'pē-,wē\ *n* : a small grayish or green- ish brown fly-catching bird (as a phoebe)

pe·wit \'pē-,wit\ *n* : any of several birds (as a small black-headed gull or a pewee)

pew·ter \'pyüt-ər\ *n* **1** : any of various metallic substances that have tin as the chief ingredient and sometimes contain also copper or antimony and are used in making utensils (as pitchers and bowls) **2** : utensils of pewter

phantasy *var of* FANTASY

phan·tom \'fant-əm\ *n* **1** : an image or figure apparent to sense but with no sub- stantial existence : APPARITION **2** : a person or thing existing in appearance only

phar·aoh \'feər-ō\ *n* : a ruler of ancient Egypt

phar·ma·cist \'fär-mə-səst\ *n* : one skilled or engaged in pharmacy

phar·ma·cy \'fär-mə-sē\ *n, pl* **phar·ma·cies** **1** : the art, practice, or profession of mixing and preparing medicines usually according to a doctor's prescriptions **2** : the place of business of a pharmacist : DRUGSTORE

phar·ynx \'far-ingks\ *n, pl* **pha·ryn·ges** \fə- 'rin-,jēz\ *also* **phar·ynx·es** : the space behind the mouth into which the nostrils, gullet, and windpipe open — **pha·ryn·ge·al** \fə-'rin-jē-əl, ,far-ən-'jē-əl\ *adj*

phase \'fāz\ *n* **1** : the way that the moon or a planet looks to the eye at any time in its series of changes with respect to illumination ⟨the new moon and the full moon are two *phases* of the moon⟩ **2** : a step or part in a

series of events or actions : STAGE **3** : a par- ticular part or feature : ASPECT

pheas·ant \'fez-nt\ *n* : a large long-tailed brilliantly colored game bird related to the domestic fowl

phe·nom·e·nal \fi-'näm-ən-l\ *adj* : REMARK- ABLE, EXTRAORDINARY ⟨a *phenomenal* memory⟩

phe·nom·e·non \fi-'näm-ə-,nän\ *n, pl* **phe- nom·e·na** \-nə\ **1** : an observable fact or event **2** : a fact or feature characteristic of something **3** : a rare or significant fact or event **4** *pl* **phe·nom·e·nons** : an extraordinary or exceptional person or thing

¹**-phil** \,fil\ *or* **-phile** \,fīl\ *n suffix* : lover : one having a strong attraction to ⟨Anglo- *phile*⟩

²**-phil** *or* **-phile** *adj suffix* : having a fondness or affinity for ⟨Franco*phile*⟩

phil·an·throp·ic \,fil-ən-'thräp-ik\ *adj* : of, relating to, or characterized by philanthropy : CHARITABLE — **phil·an·throp·i·cal·ly** \-i-kə- lē\ *adv*

phi·lan·thro·pist \fə-'lan-thrə-pəst\ *n* : a philanthropic person

phi·lan·thro·py \fə-'lan-thrə-pē\ *n, pl* **phi- lan·thro·pies** **1** : goodwill to fellowmen especially as shown by generous giving to charity **2** : a philanthropic gift **3** : an organi- zation supported by charitable gifts

phil·o·den·dron \,fil-ə-'den-drən\ *n* : any of several shade-tolerant plants often grown for their showy leaves

phi·los·o·pher \fə-'läs-ə-fər\ *n* **1** : a student of philosophy : SCHOLAR, THINKER **2** : a person who takes misfortunes with calmness and courage

phil·o·soph·i·cal \,fil-ə-'säf-i-kəl\ *or* **phil·o- soph·ic** \-'säf-ik\ *adj* **1** : of or relating to philosophy **2** : showing the wisdom and calm of a philosopher — **phil·o·soph·i·cal·ly** *adv*

phi·los·o·phy \fə-'läs-ə-fē\ *n, pl* **phi·los·o- phies** **1** : the study of the nature of knowl- edge, the principles of right and wrong, and the principles of value **2** : the philosophical teachings or principles of a man or a group of men **3** : calmness of temper and judgment

phlox \'fläks\ *n, pl* **phlox** *or* **phlox·es** : any of a group of American plants widely grown for their showy clusters of white, pink, purplish, or varie- gated flowers

-phobe \,fōb\ *n suffix* : one fear- ing or averse to something speci- fied ⟨Franco*phobe*⟩ — **-pho·bic** \'fō-bik, 'fäb-ik\ *adj comb form*

phoe·be \'fē-bē\ *n* : a slightly crested American fly-catching bird

phlox

that is grayish brown above and yellowish white below

¹phone \'fōn\ *n* : TELEPHONE

²phone *vb* **phoned; phon·ing** : TELEPHONE

pho·neme \'fō-ˌnēm\ *n* : one of the smallest units of speech that distinguish one utterance from another

pho·net·ic \fə-'net-ik\ *adj* : of or relating to spoken language or speech sounds

phon·ics \'fän-iks\ *n* : a method of teaching beginners to read and pronounce words by learning the phonetic value of letters, letter groups, and especially syllables

pho·no·graph \'fō-nə-ˌgraf\ *n* : an instrument that reproduces sounds recorded on a grooved disk (**phonograph record**)

phos·pho·rus \'fäs-fə-rəs\ *n* : a white or yellowish waxlike chemical element that gives a faint glow in moist air and is necessary in some form to plant and animal life

¹pho·to \'fōt-ō\ *n, pl* **pho·tos** : PHOTOGRAPH

²photo *vb* : PHOTOGRAPH

¹pho·to·graph \'fōt-ə-ˌgraf\ *n* : a picture or likeness made by photography

²photograph *vb* : to take a picture of with a camera — **pho·tog·ra·pher** \fə-'täg-rə-fər\ *n*

pho·to·graph·ic \ˌfōt-ə-'graf-ik\ *adj* : obtained by or used in photography

pho·tog·ra·phy \fə-'täg-rə-fē\ *n* : the making of pictures by means of a camera that directs the image of an object onto a film made sensitive to light

pho·to·play \'fōt-ə-ˌplā\ *n* : MOTION PICTURE

pho·to·syn·the·sis \ˌfōt-ə-'sin-thə-səs\ *n* : the process by which green plants form carbohydrates from carbon dioxide and water in the presence of light — **pho·to·syn·thet·ic** \-sin-'thet-ik\ *adj*

pho·tot·ro·pism \fō-'tät-rə-ˌpiz-əm\ *n* : attraction or turning (as of a plant) toward a source of light

¹phrase \'frāz\ *n* **1** : a brief expression **2** : a musical unit usually of two to four measures **3** : a group of two or more words that express a single idea but do not form a complete sentence ⟨"of the city" in "the streets of the city" is a *phrase*⟩

²phrase *vb* **phrased; phras·ing** : to express in words

phy·lum \'fī-ləm\ *n, pl* **phy·la** \-lə\ : a group (as one of the primary divisions of the animal kingdom) set apart by features that suggest descent from a common ancestor

phys·ic \'fiz-ik\ *n* : a medicine that purges

phys·i·cal \'fiz-i-kəl\ *adj* **1** : of or relating to nature or the world as we see it : being material and not mental, spiritual, or imaginary **2** : of the body : BODILY ⟨*physical* strength⟩ **3** : of or relating to physics — **phys·i·cal·ly** *adv*

phy·si·cian \fə-'zish-ən\ *n* : a specialist in healing human disease : a doctor of medicine

phys·i·cist \'fiz-ə-səst\ *n* : a specialist in the science of physics

phys·ics \'fiz-iks\ *n* : a science that deals with the facts about matter and motion and includes the subjects of mechanics, heat, light, electricity, sound, and the atomic nucleus

phys·i·o·log·i·cal \ˌfiz-ē-ə-'läj-i-kəl\ *or* **phys·i·o·log·ic** \-'läj-ik\ *adj* : of, relating to, or affecting physiology

phys·i·ol·o·gist \ˌfiz-ē-'äl-ə-jəst\ *n* : a specialist in physiology

phys·i·ol·o·gy \ˌfiz-ē-'äl-ə-jē\ *n* **1** : a branch of biology that deals with the functioning of the living body and its parts (as organs and cells) **2** : the functional processes and activities of a living being or any of its parts

phy·sique \fə-'zēk\ *n* : the build of a person's body : physical makeup : FIGURE

pi \'pī\ *n, pl* **pis** \'pīz\ : the symbol π denoting the ratio of the circumference of a circle to its diameter or about 3.1416

pi·an·ist \pē-'an-əst, 'pē-ə-nəst\ *n* : one who plays the piano

¹pi·an·o \pē-'an-ō\ *adv (or adj)* : SOFTLY, QUIETLY — used as a direction in music

²piano *n, pl* **pi·an·os** : a large stringed percussion instrument having steel wire strings that sound when struck by felt-covered hammers operated through a keyboard

pi·an·o·forte \pē-'an-ə-ˌfōrt, -ˌfòrt-ē\ *n* : PIANO

pi·as·ter \pē-'as-tər\ *n* : a coin of any of various Asian and north African countries

pianos

pi·az·za \pē-'az-ə, *1 is usually* -'at-sə\ *n* **1** : a large open square in an Italian town **2** : a roofed and arched gallery along one side of a house **3** : VERANDA, PORCH

pic·co·lo \'pik-ə-ˌlō\ *n, pl* **pic·co·los** : a small flute whose tones are an octave higher than those of the ordinary flute

piccolo

¹pick \'pik\ *vb* **1** : to strike or work on with a pointed tool **2** : to clear away or cleanse by plucking ⟨*pick* feathers off a chicken⟩ **3** : to gather one by one ⟨*pick* cherries⟩ **4** : CHOOSE, SELECT **5** : to eat sparingly or daintily **6** : to steal from ⟨*pick* a pocket⟩ **7** : PROVOKE

⟨*pick* a fight⟩   **8** : to unlock without a key ⟨*pick* a lock⟩   **9** : to pluck with a plectrum ⟨*pick* a banjo⟩ — **pick·er** *n*

²pick *n*   **1** : PICKAX   **2** : a slender pointed instrument ⟨ice *pick*⟩   **3** : PLECTRUM   **4** : the act or opportunity of choosing   **5** : the choicest ones ⟨bought only the *pick* of the crop⟩

pick·a·nin·ny \'pik-ə-ˌnin-ē\ *n, pl* **pick·a·nin·nies** : a Negro child

pick·ax *or* **pick·axe** \'pik-ˌaks\ *n* : a heavy tool with a wooden handle and a curved or straight blade pointed at one or both ends that is used in loosening or breaking up soil or rock

pick·er·el \'pik-ə-rəl\ *n* : any of several rather small fishes resembling the pike

pickerel

¹pick·et \'pik-ət\ *n*   **1** : a pointed stake or slender post (as for making a fence)   **2** : a soldier or detachment posted to stand guard   **3** : a person posted before a place of work where there is a strike

²picket *vb*   **1** : to fence in with pickets   **2** : to tie to a picket ⟨*picket* a horse⟩   **3** : to post pickets at or around : walk or stand in front of as a picket ⟨*picket* a factory⟩

¹pick·le \'pik-əl\ *n*   **1** : a mixture of salt and water for preserving foods : BRINE   **2** : vinegar with or without spices for preserving foods   **3** : something (as a cucumber) that has been preserved in a pickle   **4** : a difficult or very unpleasant condition : PREDICAMENT

²pickle *vb* **pick·led**; **pick·ling** : to soak in a pickle : preserve in pickle

pick·pock·et \'pik-ˌpäk-ət\ *n* : one who steals from pockets

¹pic·nic \'pik-ˌnik\ *n* : an outdoor party with food taken along usually by the members and eaten in the open air

²picnic *vb* **pic·nicked**; **pic·nick·ing** : to go on a picnic : eat in the open

pic·to·graph \'pik-tə-ˌgraf\ *n* : a diagram representing statistics in pictorial form

pic·to·ri·al \pik-'tōr-ē-əl\ *adj*   **1** : of or relating to pictures ⟨*pictorial* art⟩   **2** : using pictures : ILLUSTRATED ⟨a *pictorial* magazine⟩   **3** : resembling a picture in vividness ⟨*pictorial* description⟩

¹pic·ture \'pik-chər\ *n*   **1** : a representation of something real or imagined made (as by painting, drawing, or engraving) on a surface   **2** : a very vivid description   **3** : an exact likeness : COPY ⟨a boy who is almost the *picture* of his father⟩   **4** : MOTION PICTURE   **5** : an image on the screen of a television set

²picture *vb* **pic·tured**; **pic·tur·ing**   **1** : to draw or paint a picture of   **2** : to show as clearly as in a picture : describe vividly   **3** : to form a mental image of : IMAGINE

pic·tur·esque \ˌpik-chə-'resk\ *adj* : resembling a picture : suitable for a painting or drawing ⟨a *picturesque* lake⟩ **syn** see GRAPHIC

¹pie \'pī\ *n* : MAGPIE

²pie *n* : a food consisting of a pastry crust and a filling (as of fruit or meat)

pie·bald \'pī-ˌbȯld\ *adj* : of two colors and especially black and white : MOTTLED ⟨a *piebald* horse⟩

¹piece \'pēs\ *n*   **1** : a part cut, torn, or broken from a thing : FRAGMENT ⟨a *piece* of string⟩   **2** : one of a group, set, or mass of things ⟨a *piece* of mail⟩ ⟨a chess *piece*⟩   **3** : a portion marked off ⟨a *piece* of land⟩   **4** : a single item, example, or instance ⟨a *piece* of news⟩   **5** : a definite quantity or size in which various articles are made for sale or use ⟨buy lumber by the *piece*⟩   **6** : a finished product : something made, composed, or written ⟨a *piece* of music⟩   **7** : COIN ⟨a fifty-cent *piece*⟩

²piece *vb* **pieced**; **piec·ing**   **1** : to repair, complete, or extend by adding a piece or pieces ⟨*pieced* out a sweater with old yarn⟩   **2** : to make a whole out of pieces ⟨*piece* a puzzle together⟩

piece·meal \'pēs-ˌmēl\ *adv*   **1** : piece by piece : little by little   **2** : in or into pieces

pied \'pīd\ *adj* : of two or more colors in blotches

pier \'piər\ *n*   **1** : a support for a bridge span   **2** : a structure built out into the water for use as a landing place or walk or to protect or form a harbor   **3** : a single pillar or a structure used to support something

pier

pierce \'piərs\ *vb* **pierced**; **pierc·ing**   **1** : to run into or through as a pointed instrument does : STAB   **2** : to make a hole in or through   **3** : to break into or through ⟨*pierce* the enemy's line⟩   **4** : to penetrate with the eye or mind : DISCERN — **pierc·ing·ly** *adv*

pi·e·ty \'pī-ət-ē\ *n, pl* **pi·e·ties**   **1** : the quality or state of being pious : loyal devotion to one's parents or family   **2** : dutifulness in religion : DEVOUTNESS

pig \'pig\ *n*   **1** : a swine especially when not yet sexually mature   **2** : one resembling a pig (as in greediness)   **3** : a casting of metal (as iron or lead) run directly from the smelting furnace into a mold

pi·geon \'pij-ən\ *n* : a bird with a stout body, short legs, and smooth compact plumage

¹pi·geon·hole \'pij-ən-ˌhōl\ *n* **1** : a hole or small place for pigeons to nest **2** : a small open compartment (as in a desk or cabinet) for keeping letters or papers

²pigeonhole *vb* **pi·geon·holed; pi·geon·hol·ing** : to place in a pigeonhole : FILE, CLASSIFY

pi·geon–toed \ˌpij-ən-'tōd\ *adj* : having the toes turned in

pig·ger·y \'pig-ə-rē\ *n, pl* **pig·ger·ies** : a place where swine are kept

pig·gish \'pig-ish\ *adj* : resembling a pig especially in greed or dirtiness

pig·gy bank \'pig-ē-\ *n* : a coin bank often in the shape of a pig

pig·head·ed \'pig-'hed-əd\ *adj* : STUBBORN, OBSTINATE

pig·ment \'pig-mənt\ *n* **1** : a substance that gives color to other substances **2** : a powder mixed with a suitable liquid to form and give color to paint or enamel **3** : coloring matter in persons, animals, and plants

pigmy *var of* PYGMY

pig·pen \'pig-ˌpen\ *n* **1** : a pen for pigs **2** : a dirty place

pig·tail \'pig-ˌtāl\ *n* : a tight braid of hair

¹pike \'pīk\ *n, pl* **pike** *or* **pikes** : a long slender large-mouthed freshwater fish

²pike *n* : a long wooden staff with a steel point formerly used as a weapon by infantry

³pike *n* : TURNPIKE, ROAD

¹pile \'pīl\ *n* : a large wooden or metal stake or pointed post driven into the ground to support a foundation or to resist pressure

²pile *n* **1** : a mass of things heaped together : HEAP ⟨a *pile* of stones⟩ **2** : REACTOR

³pile *vb* **piled; pil·ing** **1** : to heap up or place in a pile : STACK ⟨*pile* firewood⟩ **2** : to heap on in abundance ⟨*pile* a table with food⟩

⁴pile *n* **1** : a coat of short fine furlike hair **2** : a velvety surface of fine short raised fibers (as on velvet or carpets)

pil·fer \'pil-fər\ *vb* : to steal small amounts at a time or articles of small value

pil·grim \'pil-grəm\ *n* [Latin *per* "through" and *ager* "land" were combined into the adverb *peregre* "abroad", which then developed a noun *peregrinus* "one who is abroad"; this was altered to *pelegrinus* in later Latin and became *peligrin* in Old French and *pilgrim* in English] **1** : WANDERER, TRAVELER **2** : a person who travels to a holy place or shrine as an act of religious devotion **3** *cap* : one of the English colonists founding the first permanent settlement in New England at Plymouth in 1620

pil·grim·age \'pil-grə-mij\ *n* : a journey made by a pilgrim

pil·ing \'pī-ling\ *n* : a structure of piles

pill \'pil\ *n* : a medicine in the form of a little ball to be taken whole

¹pil·lage \'pil-ij\ *n* : the act of plundering especially in war

²pillage *vb* **pil·laged; pil·lag·ing** : to take plunder : LOOT

pil·lar \'pil-ər\ *n* **1** : a firm upright shaftlike support (as for a roof) **2** : a column or shaft standing alone (as for a monument) **3** : something suggesting a pillar : a main support ⟨he is a *pillar* of local society⟩

pil·lo·ry \'pil-ə-rē\ *n, pl* **pil·lo·ries** : a device once used for punishing someone publicly consisting of a wooden frame having holes in which the head and hands can be locked

pillory

¹pil·low \'pil-ō\ *n* : a bag filled with soft or springy material (as feathers) used as a cushion for the head of a person lying down

²pillow *vb* **1** : to lay on or as if on a pillow **2** : to serve as a pillow for

pil·low·case \'pil-ō-ˌkās\ *n* : a removable covering for a pillow

¹pi·lot \'pī-lət\ *n* **1** : one who steers a ship **2** : a person especially qualified to conduct ships into and out of a port or in dangerous waters **3** : GUIDE **4** : one who flies or is qualified to fly an aircraft

²pilot *vb* : to act as pilot of : GUIDE, CONDUCT

pi·mien·to \pə-'ment-ō, pəm-'yent-\ *also* **pi·men·to** *n, pl* **pi·mien·tos** *also* **pi·men·tos** : a sweet pepper with mild thick flesh

pim·ple \'pim-pəl\ *n* : a very small inflamed swelling of the skin often containing pus : a small boil — **pim·pled** \-pəld\ *adj* — **pim·ply** \-plē\ *adj*

¹pin \'pin\ *n* **1** : a slender usually cylindrical and pointed piece (as of wood or metal) used to fasten articles together or in place **2** : a small pointed piece of wire with a head used for fastening or holding cloth or paper **3** : an ornament (as a brooch or badge) fastened to the clothing by a pin ⟨a girls' club *pin*⟩ **4** : one of the pieces set up as the target in bowling

²pin *vb* **pinned; pin·ning** **1** : to fasten, join, or make secure with a pin **2** : to hold as if with a pin ⟨*pinned* his opponent's arms to his sides⟩

pin·a·fore \'pin-ə-ˌfōr\ *n* : a sleeveless low=necked garment worn as an apron or a dress by girls and women

pincers

pin·cer \'pin-chər, 'pin-sər\ *n*

1 *pl* : a gripping instrument with two handles and two grasping jaws **2** : a claw (as of a lobster) resembling pincers

¹**pinch** \'pinch\ *vb* **1** : to squeeze between the finger and thumb or between the jaws of an instrument **2** : to squeeze painfully ⟨get a finger *pinched* in a door⟩ **3** : to cause to look thin or shrunken ⟨a face *pinched* with cold⟩ **4** : to be economical : be stingy ⟨*pinch* and save⟩

²**pinch** *n* **1** : a critical time or point : EMERGENCY **2** : a painful pressure or stress ⟨felt the *pinch* of hunger⟩ **3** : an act of pinching : NIP, SQUEEZE **4** : as much as may be picked up between the finger and the thumb ⟨a *pinch* of salt⟩

pinch hitter *n* **1** : a baseball player who is sent in to bat for another **2** : a person who does another's work in an emergency

pin·cush·ion \'pin-,kush-ən\ *n* : a small cushion in which pins may be stuck when not in use

¹**pine** \'pīn\ *vb* **pined; pin·ing 1** : to lose vigor, health, or weight through distress (as grief or worry) **2** : to long for intensely ⟨*pining* for home⟩

²**pine** *n* : a cone-bearing evergreen tree that has narrow needles for leaves and a durable wood that ranges from very soft to hard

pine·ap·ple \'pīn-,ap-əl\ *n* : a tropical plant with stiff spiny leaves that is widely grown for its large juicy edible fruit

pin·feath·er \'pin-,feth-ər\ *n* : an immature feather just breaking through the skin of a bird

pineapple

¹**pin·ion** \'pin-yən\ *n* **1** : the end part of a bird's wing **2** : WING **3** : FEATHER, QUILL

²**pinion** *vb* : to disable or restrain by binding the arms usually to the body

¹**pink** \'pingk\ *vb* : to cut cloth, leather, or paper in an ornamental pattern or with a saw-toothed edge

²**pink** *n* **1** : any of a group of plants with thick stem joints and narrow leaves that are grown for their showy often variegated or fragrant flowers **2** : the highest degree ⟨athletes in the *pink* of condition⟩

³**pink** *n* : a light red

⁴**pink** *adj* : of the color pink

pink·eye \'pingk-,ī\ *n* : a very contagious inflammatory disease of the eyes

pink·ish \'ping-kish\ *adj* : somewhat pink

pin·na \'pin-ə\ *n* : the projecting outer part of the ear

pin·na·cle \'pin-ə-kəl\ *n* **1** : a slender turret generally ending in a small spire **2** : a lofty peak : a pointed summit **3** : the highest point of development or achievement

pint \'pīnt\ *n* : a unit of capacity equal to 1/2 quart or sixteen ounces

pin·to \'pin-tō\ *n, pl* **pin·tos** : a spotted horse or pony

pinnacle 1

pin·y *or* **pin·ey** \'pī-nē\ *adj* : of, relating to, or characteristic of pine ⟨a *piny* odor⟩

¹**pi·o·neer** \,pī-ə-'niər\ *n* **1** : a person who goes before and prepares the way for others to follow **2** : an early settler

²**pioneer** *vb* **1** : to explore or open up paths or regions for others to follow **2** : to originate or take part in the early development of something new

pi·ous \'pī-əs\ *adj* **1** : showing reverence toward God : DEVOUT **2** : marked by self-conscious virtue

¹**pip** \'pip\ *n* : a dot or spot (as on dice) to indicate numerical value

²**pip** *n* : a small fruit seed ⟨orange *pip*⟩

¹**pipe** \'pīp\ *n* **1** : a musical instrument consisting of a tube of reed, wood, or metal played by blowing : a tube producing a musical sound ⟨organ *pipe*⟩ **2** : BAGPIPE **3** : a whistle, call, or note especially of a bird or an insect **4** : a long tube or hollow body for conducting a substance (as water, steam, or gas) **5** : a tube with a small bowl at one end for smoking tobacco or for blowing bubbles

²**pipe** *vb* **piped; pip·ing 1** : to play on a pipe **2** : to have or speak in a shrill voice **3** : to equip with pipes **4** : to convey by means of pipes ⟨*pipe* water from a spring⟩ — **pip·er** *n*

pipe·line \'pīp-,līn\ *n* **1** : a line of pipe with pumps, valves, and control devices (as for conveying liquids or gases) **2** : a direct channel for information

¹**pip·ing** \'pī-ping\ *n* **1** : the music or sound of a person or thing that pipes ⟨the *piping* of frogs⟩ **2** : a quantity or system of pipes **3** : a narrow fold of material sometimes covering a cord used to decorate edges or seams

²**piping** *adj* : having a high shrill sound : high-pitched

pip·it \'pip-ət\ *n* : a small bird like a lark

pip·pin \'pip-ən\ *n* : a dessert apple with a yellow or greenish skin flushed with red

pi·ra·cy \'pī-rə-sē\ *n, pl* **pi·ra·cies 1** : robbery on the high seas **2** : the using of another's work or invention without permission

pi·rate \'pī-rət\ *n* : a robber on the high seas : a person who commits piracy

pis·tach·i·o \pə-'stash-ē-,ō\ *n, pl* **pis·tach·i·os** : the green hard-shelled edible seed of a small tree related to the sumacs

pis·til \'pist-l\ *n* : the central organ in a flower that consists of stigma, style, and ovary and produces the seed

pistil

pis·tol \'pist-l\ *n* : a short gun made to be aimed and fired with one hand

pis·ton \'pis-tən\ *n* : a disk or short cylinder that slides back and forth inside a larger cylinder and is moved by steam in steam engines and by the explosion of fuel in automobiles

¹**pit** \'pit\ *n* **1** : a cavity or hole in the ground ⟨gravel *pit*⟩ **2** : a concealed hole for trapping animals **3** : a deep place : ABYSS **4** : a hollow or indented area usually at the surface of the body ⟨the *pit* of the stomach at the base of the breastbone⟩ **5** : an indented scar (as from a boil or smallpox) — **pit·ted** \'pit-əd\ *adj*

²**pit** *vb* **pit·ted**; **pit·ting** **1** : to put into or store in a pit **2** : to make pits in or scar with pits **3** : to set into opposition or rivalry ⟨*pitting* his speed and skill against his opponent's greater size and strength⟩

³**pit** *n* : a hard seed or stone (as of a cherry)

⁴**pit** *vb* **pit·ted**; **pit·ting** : to remove the pits from

¹**pitch** \'pich\ *n* **1** : a dark sticky substance left over from distilling tar used in making roofing paper, in caulking seams, and in paving **2** : resin from pine trees

²**pitch** *vb* **1** : to place and set up or erect ⟨*pitched* a tent⟩ **2** : THROW, TOSS ⟨*pitching* hay⟩ **3** : to throw a baseball to a batter **4** : to plunge or fall forward ⟨*pitch* from a cliff⟩ **5** : SLOPE **6** : to fix or set at a particular pitch or level ⟨*pitch* a tune higher⟩ **7** : to plunge so that the front and back ends (of a ship or plane) alternately rise and fall

³**pitch** *n* **1** : the action or manner of pitching **2** : highness or lowness of sound **3** : degree of slope ⟨*pitch* of a roof⟩ **4** : a high point : PEAK ⟨high *pitch* of success⟩ — **pitched** \'picht\ *adj*

pitch·blende \'pich-,blend\ *n* : a dark mineral that is a source of radium and uranium

¹**pitch·er** \'pich-ər\ *n* : a container usually with a handle and a lip used for holding and pouring out liquids

²**pitcher** *n* : a baseball player who pitches

pitch·fork \'pich-,fòrk\ *n* : a usually long-handled fork used in pitching hay or grain

pitchfork

pit·e·ous \'pit-ē-əs\ *adj* : seeking or deserving pity ⟨*piteous* cries for help⟩ — **pit·e·ous·ly** *adv*

pit·fall \'pit-,fòl\ *n* **1** : TRAP, SNARE **2** : a danger, difficulty, or error into which one may fall unknowingly

pith \'pith\ *n* **1** : the loose spongy tissue occupying the center of the stem in some plants **2** : a loose pithlike tissue ⟨the *pith* of a feather⟩ **3** : the necessary or important part ⟨the *pith* of the problem⟩

pith·e·can·thro·pus \,pith-i-'kan-thrə-pəs\ *n* : a primitive and long extinct man known from bones found in Java

pith·y \'pith-ē\ *adj* **pith·i·er**; **pith·i·est** : consisting of, containing, or resembling pith

pit·i·a·ble \'pit-ē-ə-bəl\ *adj* **1** : deserving or exciting pity **2** : CONTEMPTIBLE, INSIGNIFICANT

pit·i·ful \'pit-i-fəl\ *adj* **1** : arousing pity or sympathy ⟨a *pitiful* sight⟩ **2** : deserving pitying contempt ⟨a *pitiful* excuse⟩

pit·i·less \'pit-i-ləs\ *adj* : lacking pity : MERCILESS

pit·ter–pat·ter \'pit-ər-,pat-ər\ *n* : a rapid succession of light sounds or beats

¹**pity** \'pit-ē\ *n* **1** : a sympathetic feeling for the sufferings or distress of others : COMPASSION **2** : a reason or cause of pity, grief, or regret

²**pity** *vb* **pit·ied**; **pit·y·ing** : to feel pity for

¹**piv·ot** \'piv-ət\ *n* **1** : a point or a fixed pin on the end of which something turns **2** : something on which something else turns or depends : a central member, part, or point

²**pivot** *vb* **1** : to turn on or as if on a pivot **2** : to provide with, mount on, or attach by a pivot

pix·ie *or* **pix·y** \'pik-sē\ *n, pl* **pix·ies** : a mischievous sprite or fairy

plac·ard \'plak-,ärd\ *n* : a large card for announcing or advertising something : POSTER

pla·cate \'plā-,kāt\ *vb* **pla·cat·ed**; **pla·cat·ing** : to calm the anger of : SOOTHE, PACIFY

¹**place** \'plās\ *n* **1** : SPACE, ROOM ⟨make a *place* for the newcomer⟩ **2** : REGION, LOCALITY, SPOT ⟨a *place* on the map⟩ **3** : an inhabited area (as a village, town, or city) **4** : a space (as a seat in a theater) set aside for one's use **5** : a spot or locality on which there is a dwelling ⟨a *place* in the country⟩ **6** : POSITION, RANK **7** : DUTY ⟨it is my *place* to tell you⟩ **8** : a building or spot set apart for a special purpose ⟨a *place* of worship⟩ **9** : a short street or court **10** : position in the order of taking up matters ⟨in the first *place*⟩ **11** : the position of a numeral in relation to others of a series and especially of a numeral to the right of a decimal point **12** : usual

space or use : STEAD ⟨paper towels take the *place* of linen⟩

²place *vb* **placed; plac·ing** **1** : to put or arrange in a particular place or position **2** : to appoint to a position or find employment for **3** : to identify by connecting with a particular time place, or circumstance

place·hold·er \'plās-ˌhōl-dər\ *n* : a symbol (as *x*, △, *) used in mathematics in the place of a numeral not yet determined

place–kick \'plās-ˌkik\ *n* : a kick in football made with the ball in a stationary position

pla·cen·ta \plə-'sent-ə\ *n* : a vascular organ by which the fetus of a mammal is joined to its mother's uterus

¹plague \'plāg\ *n* **1** : something that causes much distress ⟨a *plague* of locusts⟩ **2** : NUISANCE **3** : a destructive epidemic disease

²plague *vb* **plagued; plagu·ing** **1** : to strike or afflict with disease or calamity **2** : TEASE, TORMENT

plaid \'plad\ *n* **1** : a rectangular shawl serving as a cloak in the Scottish national dress **2** : a pattern consisting of rectangles formed by crossed lines of various widths **3** : a fabric woven or printed with a plaid pattern

plaid 2

¹plain \'plān\ *adj* **1** : open and clear to the sight ⟨in *plain* view⟩ **2** : easily understood : clear to the mind ⟨in *plain* words⟩ **3** : lacking pattern or decoration ⟨*plain* dress⟩ **4** : FRANK, OUTSPOKEN ⟨*plain* speaking⟩ **5** : not luxurious or rich : SIMPLE ⟨*plain* food⟩ **6** : not handsome : HOMELY ⟨a *plain* woman⟩ **7** : not highly born, educated, or gifted by nature ⟨*plain* people⟩ **8** : of simple weave or of solid color ⟨a *plain* cloth⟩ **9** : not hard to do : not complicated ⟨*plain* sewing⟩ — **plain·ly** *adv* — **plain·ness** *n*

²plain *n* : an extensive area of level or rolling treeless land ⟨the *plains* of the West⟩

³plain *adv* : in a plain manner

plain·tive \'plānt-iv\ *adj* : expressing or suggesting sorrow : MOURNFUL, SAD ⟨a *plaintive* sigh⟩

¹plait \'plāt, 'plat\ *n* **1** : a flat fold : PLEAT **2** : a flat braid (as of hair)

²plait *vb* **1** : PLEAT **2** : BRAID ⟨*plaited* her hair⟩ **3** : to make by braiding ⟨*plaiting* a basket⟩

plaits 2

¹plan \'plan\ *n* **1** : a drawing or diagram showing the parts or outline of a thing **2** : a method or scheme of acting, doing, or arranging ⟨vacation *plans*⟩

²plan *vb* **planned; plan·ning** **1** : to form a plan of or for : arrange the parts or details of in advance ⟨*plan* a bridge⟩ ⟨*plan* a picnic⟩ **2** : INTEND

¹plane \'plān\ *vb* **planed; plan·ing** **1** : to smooth or level off with a plane **2** : to remove with or as if with a plane

²plane *n* : a tool for smoothing wood

³plane *adj* **1** : LEVEL, FLAT ⟨*plane* surface⟩ **2** : of, relating to, or dealing with planes ⟨*plane* curve⟩

plane

⁴plane *n* **1** : a level or flat surface **2** : a level of development ⟨exists on a low *plane*⟩ **3** : AIRPLANE

plan·et \'plan-ət\ *n* [from Greek *planēt-*, stem of *planēs* "planet", literally, "wanderer"; so named because the planets seemed to wander among the fixed stars] : a heavenly body except a comet or meteor that revolves about the sun

plan·e·tar·i·um \ˌplan-ə-'ter-ē-əm\ *n* : a building in which there is a device for projecting the images of heavenly bodies on a dome-shaped ceiling

plan·e·tar·y \'plan-ə-ˌter-ē\ *adj* **1** : of or relating to a planet **2** : having a motion like that of a planet

plank \'plangk\ *n* : a heavy thick board

¹plant \'plant\ *vb* **1** : to put or set in the ground to grow ⟨*plant* seeds in the spring⟩ **2** : to set firmly in or as if in the ground : FIX ⟨*plant* posts for a fence⟩ **3** : to introduce as a habit : IMPLANT **4** : ESTABLISH, SETTLE ⟨*plant* colonies⟩ **5** : to stock with something ⟨*plant* a stream with trout⟩

²plant *n* **1** : any member (as a grass, tree, seaweed, or fungus) of the natural kingdom that includes living things with cellulose cell walls, without obvious nervous system or sense organs, and usually without ability to move about **2** : the buildings and equipment of an industrial business or an institution ⟨a power *plant*⟩ — **plant·like** \-ˌlīk\ *adj*

¹plan·tain \'plant-n\ *n* : any of several common short-stemmed or stemless weeds having leaves with parallel veins and a long spike of tiny greenish flowers

²plantain *n* : a banana plant having greenish fruit that is larger, less sweet, and more starchy than the ordinary banana

plan·ta·tion \plan-'tā-shən\ *n* **1** : a group of plants and especially trees planted and being tended **2** : a planted area (as an estate) cultivated by laborers **3** : COLONY

plantain

plant·er \'plant-ər\ *n* **1** : one that plants or cultivates **2** : a person who owns or manages a plantation **3** : a container in which ornamental plants are grown

plant louse *n* : any of various small insects that are related to the true bugs and suck the juices of plants : APHID

plant louse

plaque \'plak\ *n* : a flat thin piece (as of metal) used for ornament or for bearing an inscription

plas·ma \'plaz-mə\ *n* : the watery part of blood, lymph, or milk

¹plas·ter \'plas-tər\ *n* **1** : an often medicated preparation stiffer than ointment, spread on cloth or plastic, and applied to the body 〈adhesive *plaster*〉 **2** : a paste (as of lime, sand, and water) that hardens on drying and is used for coating walls and ceilings

²plaster *vb* **1** : to cover or smear with or as if with plaster **2** : to paste or fasten on especially so as to cover 〈*plaster* the wall with posters〉 — **plas·ter·er** *n*

plaster of par·is \-'par-əs\ *often cap 2d P* : a white powder that mixes with water to form a quickly hardening paste used for casts and molds

¹plas·tic \'plas-tik\ *adj* **1** : characterized by giving form to a mass 〈sculpture is a *plastic* art〉 **2** : capable of being molded or modeled 〈*plastic* clay〉 **3** : made of plastic 〈a *plastic* radio cabinet〉 〈a *plastic* raincoat〉

²plastic *n* : any of numerous manufactured materials that can be molded into objects or formed into films or fibers

¹plat \'plat\ *n* **1** : a small plot of ground **2** : a plan or map of a piece of land

²plat *vb* **plat·ted; plat·ting** : to make a plat of 〈*plat* a building project〉

¹plate \'plāt\ *n* **1** : a thin flat piece of an unbending material **2** : metal in sheets 〈steel *plate*〉 **3** : a piece of metal on which something is engraved or molded 〈a license *plate*〉 **4** : an illustration often covering a full page of a book **5** : household utensils made of or plated with gold or silver **6** : a shallow usually round dish **7** : a main course of a meal 〈a vegetable *plate*〉 〈two dollars a *plate*〉 **8** : HOME PLATE **9** : a sheet of glass coated with a chemical sensitive to light for use in a camera

plate 6

²plate *vb* **plat·ed; plat·ing** : to cover with a thin layer of metal (as gold or silver)

pla·teau \pla-'tō\ *n, pl* **pla·teaus** *or* **pla·teaux** \-'tōz\ : a broad flat tract of high land

plat·form \'plat-ˌfȯrm\ *n* **1** : a level usually raised surface (as in a railway station) **2** : a raised floor or stage for performers or speakers **3** : a statement of principles for which a group stands

plat·i·num \'plat-n-əm\ *n* : a heavy grayish white metallic chemical element used in jewelry

pla·toon \plə-'tün\ *n* : a subdivision of a military company or troop commanded by a lieutenant

platoon sergeant *n* : SERGEANT FIRST CLASS

plat·ter \'plat-ər\ *n* : a large plate especially for serving meat

plat·y·pus \'plat-i-pəs\ *n* [from Greek *platypous* "broad-footed", from *platys* "broad" and *pous* "foot"] : DUCKBILL

plau·si·ble \'plȯ-zə-bəl\ *adj* : apparently reasonable or worthy of belief — **plau·si·bly** \-blē\ *adv*

¹play \'plā\ *n* **1** : brisk handling or motion (as of a weapon) 〈the *play* of a sword〉 **2** : exercise or activity for amusement **3** : the action of or a particular action in a game 〈rain held up *play*〉 〈a great *play* by the shortstop〉 **4** : one's turn to take part in a game **5** : ACTION, BEHAVIOR 〈fair *play*〉 **6** : OPERATION, ACTIVITY 〈a job that gave full *play* to his talents〉 **7** : brisk, fitful, or light movement 〈the light *play* of a breeze through the room〉 **8** : freedom of motion 〈this jacket gives more *play* for your shoulders〉 **9** : the stage representation of an action or story **10** : a dramatic composition : DRAMA **syn** see GAME

²play *vb* **1** : to move swiftly or lightly 〈leaves *play* in the wind〉 **2** : to engage in sport or recreation : amuse oneself **3** : PRETEND 〈*play* school〉 **4** : TRIFLE, FINGER 〈*play* with a watch〉 **5** : to perform on a musical instrument : produce music 〈*play* the piano〉 **6** : ACT, BEHAVE 〈*play* fair〉 **7** : to act on or as if on the stage 〈*play* a part〉 **8** : to put or keep in action 〈*play* a fish〉 **9** : to take part in 〈*play* ball〉 〈*play* cards〉 — **play·er** *n* — **play hook·y** \-'hůk-ē\ : to stay out of school without permission

play·fel·low \'plā-ˌfel-ō\ *n* : PLAYMATE

play·ful \'plā-fəl\ *adj* **1** : full of play : MERRY **2** : HUMOROUS, FANCIFUL — **play·ful·ly** *adv* — **play·ful·ness** *n*

play·ground \'plā-ˌgraůnd\ *n* : a piece of ground used for games and recreation

play·house \'plā-ˌhaůs\ *n* **1** : THEATER **2** : a small house for children to play in

playing card *n* : one of a set

playing cards

of cards marked to show its rank and suit (**spades, hearts, diamonds,** or **clubs**) and used in playing various games

play·mate \'plā-ˌmāt\ *n* : a companion in play

play·thing \'plā-ˌthing\ *n* : TOY

play·wright \'plā-ˌrīt\ *n* : a writer of plays

plaz·a \'plaz-ə, 'plä-zə\ *n* : a public square in a city or town

plea \'plē\ *n* 1 : an argument in defense : EXCUSE 2 : an earnest entreaty : APPEAL

plead \'plēd\ *vb* **plead·ed** *or* **pled** \'pled\; **plead·ing** 1 : to argue for or against a claim : argue at the bar ⟨*plead* a case before a jury⟩ 2 : to answer to a charge ⟨*plead* guilty⟩ 3 : to offer as a defense, an excuse, or an apology ⟨*plead* illness⟩ 4 : to appeal earnestly : IMPLORE

pleas·ant \'plez-nt\ *adj* 1 : giving pleasure : AGREEABLE 2 : having pleasing manners, behavior, or appearance — **pleas·ant·ly** *adv* — **pleas·ant·ness** *n*

please \'plēz\ *vb* **pleased; pleas·ing** 1 : to give pleasure or satisfaction : GRATIFY 2 : to be willing : LIKE, CHOOSE ⟨if you *please*⟩ ⟨do as you *please*⟩ ⟨*please* come in⟩

pleas·ing \'plē-zing\ *adj* : giving pleasure : AGREEABLE — **pleas·ing·ly** *adv*

plea·sur·a·ble \'plezh-ə-rə-bəl\ *adj* : PLEASANT

plea·sure \'plezh-ər\ *n* 1 : a feeling of satisfaction : ENJOYMENT, JOY 2 : WILL, WISH ⟨await the king's *pleasure*⟩ 3 : something that pleases or delights

¹**pleat** \'plēt\ *n* : a fold (as in cloth) made by doubling material over on itself

²**pleat** *vb* : to fold or arrange in pleats

plec·trum \'plek-trəm\ *n, pl* **plec·tra** \-trə\ *or* **plec·trums** : a thin stiff piece (as of ivory or metal) used to pluck a stringed instrument

pled *past of* PLEAD

plectrums

¹**pledge** \'plej\ *n* 1 : something given or considered as a security for the fulfillment of a promise 2 : the state of being held as a security : PAWN ⟨given in *pledge*⟩ 3 : something considered as a token, sign, or evidence of something else 4 : an assurance of goodwill given by drinking to another's health : TOAST 5 : a binding promise or agreement

²**pledge** *vb* **pledged; pledg·ing** 1 : to give as a pledge : PAWN 2 : to drink to the health of : TOAST 3 : to bind by a pledge : PROMISE

plen·te·ous \'plent-ē-əs\ *adj* : PLENTIFUL

plen·ti·ful \'plent-i-fəl\ *adj* 1 : yielding or containing plenty : FRUITFUL 2 : existing in plenty : ABUNDANT — **plen·ti·ful·ly** *adv*

plen·ty \'plent-ē\ *n* : a full or abundant supply : more than enough : ABUNDANCE

pleu·ri·sy \'plùr-ə-sē\ *n* : an inflammation of the membrane lining the chest often with fever, painful breathing, and coughing

plex·us \'plek-səs\ *n, pl* **plex·us·es** *or* **plex·us** \-səs, -ˌsüs\ : a network usually of nerves or blood vessels

pli·a·ble \'plī-ə-bəl\ *adj* 1 : capable of being bent without breaking : FLEXIBLE 2 : easily influenced

pli·ant \'plī-ənt\ *adj* 1 : FLEXIBLE 2 : easily influenced : YIELDING ⟨a *pliant* disposition⟩

pli·ers \'plī-ərz\ *n pl* : small pincers with long jaws used for bending or cutting wire or handling small objects

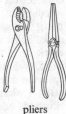

pliers

plight \'plīt\ *n* : a usually bad condition or state : PREDICAMENT ⟨an unhappy *plight*⟩

plod \'pläd\ *vb* **plod·ded; plod·ding** : to move or travel slowly but steadily : TRUDGE

¹**plot** \'plät\ *n* 1 : a small area of ground 2 : a plan of the ground floor of a building or of an area : MAP, CHART 3 : a secret usually evil scheme 4 : the plan or main story of a play or novel

syn PLOT, INTRIGUE, CONSPIRACY all mean a secret plan. PLOT suggests a carefully worked out plan to accomplish an evil, mischievous, or unlawful deed, and may involve one or many plotters ⟨a *plot* to kidnap the prince⟩ INTRIGUE often refers to a plan to gain a selfish or personal advantage and usually involves complicated scheming and the use of petty or underhanded methods ⟨political *intrigue* took up much of his time⟩ CONSPIRACY suggests a plot in which a large group of schemers participate and is especially apt when treason or great treachery is the purpose ⟨several of his friends were involved in the *conspiracy* to murder Caesar⟩

²**plot** *vb* **plot·ted; plot·ting** 1 : to make a plot, map, or plan of 2 : to plan or scheme secretly — **plot·ter** *n*

plov·er \'pləv-ər\ *n* : any one of several shorebirds having shorter and stouter bills than the sandpipers

¹**plow** *or* **plough** \'plaù\ *n* 1 : an implement used to cut, lift, and turn over soil 2 : an implement (as a snowplow) used to spread or clear away matter on the ground

²**plow** *or* **plough** *vb* 1 : to open, break up, or work with a plow ⟨*plow* a furrow⟩ ⟨*plow* the soil⟩ 2 : to move through or cut as a plow does

plow·share \'plaù-ˌsheər\ *n* : the part of a plow that cuts the earth

j job   ng sing   ō low   ȯ moth   ȯi coin   th thin   th this   ü boot   u̇ foot   y you   yü few   yu̇ furious   zh vision

¹pluck \'plək\ *vb* **1** : to pull off : PICK ⟨*pluck* grapes⟩ **2** : to remove something (as feathers) from by or as if by plucking ⟨*pluck* a fowl⟩ **3** : to seize and remove sharply : SNATCH **4** : to pull at (a string) and let go : TWANG

²pluck *n* **1** : a sharp pull : TUG, TWITCH **2** : COURAGE, SPIRIT

pluck·y \'plək-ē\ *adj* **pluck·i·er**; **pluck·i·est** : COURAGEOUS, BRAVE

¹plug \'pləg\ *n* **1** : a piece (as of wood or metal) used to stop or fill a hole **2** : a device usually on a cord for making an electrical connection by insertion into another part (as a receptacle or socket)

²plug *vb* **plugged**; **plug·ging** **1** : to stop or make tight with a plug **2** : to keep steadily at work or in action ⟨*plugged* away at his homework⟩ **3** : to connect to an electric circuit ⟨*plug* in a lamp⟩

plum \'pləm\ *n* **1** : a round to oval smooth-skinned edible fruit with an oblong stone that is borne by a tree related to the peaches and cherries **2** : something like a plum (as in shape or sweetness) **3** : a dark reddish purple **4** : a choice or desirable thing : REWARD, PRIZE

plums

plum·age \'plü-mij\ *n* : the feathers of a bird

¹plumb \'pləm\ *n* : a little weight of lead or other heavy material attached to a line and used by builders to show a vertical direction

²plumb *vb* **1** : to sound, adjust, or test with a plumb ⟨*plumb* the depth of a well⟩ ⟨*plumb* a wall⟩ **2** : to examine deeper or hidden parts of something

plumb

plumb·er \'pləm-ər\ *n* : one that installs or repairs pipes, fittings, and fixtures involved in the supply and use of water in a building

plumb·ing \'pləm-ing\ *n* **1** : a plumber's work **2** : a system of pipes for supplying and carrying off water in a building

¹plume \'plüm\ *n* **1** : a large or conspicuous feather of a bird **2** : an ornamental feather or tuft of feathers (as on a hat)

²plume *vb* **plumed**; **plum·ing** **1** : to attach feathers to **2** : PREEN **3** : to be proud of (oneself) ⟨*pluming* herself on her cooking⟩

¹plum·met \'pləm-ət\ *n* **1** : PLUMB **2** : a line with a plumb at one end

²plummet *vb* : to plunge straight down

¹plump \'pləmp\ *vb* : to drop or fall heavily or suddenly ⟨*plumped* down on the couch⟩

²plump *adv* **1** : with a sudden or heavy drop **2** : DIRECTLY ⟨ran *plump* into the wall⟩

³plump *n* : a sudden plunge, fall, or heavy blow

⁴plump *adj* : having a pleasingly full rounded form : well filled out — **plump·ness** *n*

⁵plump *vb* : to make or become plump ⟨*plump* up the pillows⟩

¹plun·der \'plən-dər\ *vb* : to rob or steal especially openly and by force (as during war)

²plunder *n* : something taken by plundering : LOOT

¹plunge \'plənj\ *vb* **plunged**; **plung·ing** **1** : to thrust or force into quickly ⟨*plunge* the family into debt⟩ **2** : to leap or dive into water **3** : to rush with reckless haste **4** : to dip, descend, or move forward and downward rapidly or suddenly

²plunge *n* : a sudden dive, rush, or leap

¹plu·ral \'plùr-əl\ *adj* : of, relating to, or constituting a word form used to indicate more than one ⟨*plural* nouns⟩

²plural *n* : a form of a word used to show that more than one person or thing is meant

plu·ral·ize \'plùr-əl-ˌīz\ *vb* **plu·ral·ized**; **plu·ral·iz·ing** : to make plural or express in the plural form

¹plus \'pləs\ *prep* **1** : increased by : with the addition of ⟨4 *plus* 5 is 9⟩ **2** : WITH ⟨a wife *plus* four children⟩

²plus *adj* : falling high in a specified range ⟨a grade of C *plus*⟩

plush \'pləsh\ *n* : a fabric like velvet but with a deeper and softer pile

plus sign *n* : a sign + used in mathematics to indicate addition (as in $8+6=14$) or a positive quantity (as in $+10°$)

Plu·to \'plüt-ō\ *n* : the planet that is most remote from the sun and has a diameter of about 3600 miles

plu·to·ni·um \plü-'tō-nē-əm\ *n* : a radioactive metallic chemical element formed from neptunium and used for releasing atomic energy

¹ply \'plī\ *n, pl* **plies** : one of the folds, layers, or strands of which something (as yarn or plywood) is made up

²ply *vb* **plied**; **ply·ing** **1** : to use something steadily or forcefully ⟨*ply* an ax⟩ **2** : to press or harass with something ⟨*ply* a man with questions⟩ **3** : to keep supplying ⟨*ply* a guest with food⟩ **4** : to work hard and steadily at ⟨*plied* his trade⟩ **5** : to go back and forth regularly ⟨the ferry *plies* between the two cities⟩

ply·wood \'plī-ˌwùd\ *n* : a strong board made by gluing together thin sheets of wood under heat and pressure

pneu·mat·ic \nù-'mat-ik, nyù-\ *adj* **1** : of, relating to, or using air, gas, or wind **2** : moved or worked by the pressure of air ⟨a *pneumatic* drill⟩ **3** : holding or inflated with compressed air ⟨a *pneumatic* tire⟩

pneu·mo·nia \nu̇-'mō-nyə, nyu̇-'mō-\ *n* : a serious disease in which the lungs are inflamed

¹**poach** \'pōch\ *vb* : to cook in simmering liquid ⟨*poach* fish in milk⟩ ⟨*poached* eggs⟩

²**poach** *vb* : to hunt or fish unlawfully on private property

pock \'päk\ *n* : a small pimplelike swelling on the skin (as in smallpox) or the mark it leaves

¹**pock·et** \'päk-ət\ *n* **1** : a small bag fastened into a garment for carrying small articles or money **2** : a place or thing like a pocket ⟨*pocket* of gold in a mine⟩ **3** : a condition of the air that causes an airplane to drop suddenly ⟨an air *pocket*⟩

²**pocket** *vb* **1** : to put something in a pocket : take for oneself especially dishonestly ⟨*pocket* the profits⟩ **2** : to accept quietly ⟨*pocket* an insult⟩ **3** : to put aside : SUPPRESS ⟨*pocketed* his pride and took the job⟩

pock·et·book \'päk-ət-,bu̇k\ *n* **1** : a case for carrying money or papers in the pocket **2** : PURSE, HANDBAG **3** : MONEY, INCOME ⟨a price suited to his *pocketbook*⟩

pock·et·knife \'päk-ət-,nīf\ *n, pl* **pock·et·knives** \-,nīvz\ : a small knife with folding blade or blades to be carried in the pocket

pock·et–size \'päk-ət-,sīz\ *adj* : of a size convenient for carrying in the pocket

pod \'päd\ *n* : a fruit (as of the pea or bean) that is dry when ripe and then splits open to release its seeds

pod

po·em \'pō-əm\ *n* : a composition in verse

po·et \'pō-ət\ *n* : a writer of poetry

po·et·ic \pō-'et-ik\ *or* **po·et·i·cal** \-i-kəl\ *adj* **1** : of, relating to, or characteristic of poets or poetry **2** : written in verse

po·et·ry \'pō-ə-trē\ *n* **1** : metrical writing : VERSE **2** : the productions of a poet : POEMS

poi·gnant \'pȯi-nyənt\ *adj* : keenly affecting the feelings : PIERCING ⟨*poignant* grief⟩

poin·set·ti·a \pȯin-'set-ē-ə\ *n* : a tropical plant much used at Christmas with dark green foliage and red leaves that grow like petals around its small greenish flowers

poinsettia

¹**point** \'pȯint\ *n* **1** : a separate or particular detail : ITEM ⟨explained the main *points* of the plan⟩ **2** : TRAIT, CHARACTERISTIC ⟨he has many good *points*⟩ **3** : the chief part or meaning (as of a story or a speech) **4** : AIM, PURPOSE ⟨keep to the *point*⟩ ⟨no *point*

in trying any more⟩ **5** : a small mark or dot **6** : PUNCTUATION MARK **7** : an item in geometry that has position but no dimensions and is pictured as a small dot **8** : a particular place or position ⟨*points* of interest in the city⟩ **9** : a single unit used in giving a value or score **10** : the tapering or sharp end (as of a sword, pin, or pencil) **11** : a projecting piece of land **12** : one of the thirty-two pointed marks indicating direction on a mariner's compass — **point·ed** \-əd\ *adj*

²**point** *vb* **1** : to put a point on ⟨*point* a pencil⟩ **2** : PUNCTUATE **3** : to indicate the position or direction of something by the finger or by standing in a fixed position ⟨*pointed* to the door⟩ ⟨the dog was *pointing* a pheasant⟩ **4** : AIM, DIRECT ⟨*point* a gun⟩ **5** : to separate figures into groups by placing decimal points ⟨*pointed* off three decimal places⟩ **6** : to face toward a certain direction ⟨the ship was *pointed* south⟩

¹**point–blank** \'pȯint-'blangk\ *adj* **1** : aimed straight for the mark ⟨a *point-blank* shot⟩ **2** : DIRECT, BLUNT ⟨a *point-blank* refusal⟩

²**point–blank** *adv* : in a point-blank manner

point·er \'pȯint-ər\ *n* **1** : something that points or is used for pointing **2** : a large long-eared short= haired hunting dog usually white with colored spots that hunts by scent and points game **3** : HINT, TIP ⟨get a few *pointers* on diving⟩

pointer

¹**poise** \'pȯiz\ *vb* **poised; pois·ing** **1** : to hold or make firm or steady by balancing **2** : to hang or be held motionless in a steady position : HOVER ⟨the bird *poised* in the air⟩

²**poise** *n* **1** : the state of being balanced : EQUILIBRIUM **2** : easy self-control and composure ⟨a speaker of great *poise*⟩ **3** : BEARING, CARRIAGE

¹**poi·son** \'pȯiz-n\ *n* : a substance that by its chemical action can injure or kill a living thing

²**poison** *vb* **1** : to injure or kill with poison **2** : to put poison on or in ⟨gas fumes *poisoned* the air⟩ **3** : CORRUPT ⟨*poisoned* their minds with suspicion⟩

poison hemlock *n* : HEMLOCK 1

poison ivy *n* : a common climbing or sprawling plant related to the sumacs that has leaves with three leaflets and is poisonous to touch

poison oak *n* : a shrubby poison ivy

poi·son·ous \'pȯiz-n-əs\ *adj* : containing poison : having or causing an effect of poison

poison ivy

poison sumac *n* : a poison oak that grows in wet places

¹poke \'pōk\ *n* : BAG, SACK

²poke *vb* **poked; pok·ing** **1** : PROD, JAB **2** : to stir or urge by prodding **3** : to thrust out or into ⟨*poking* his nose in other people's business⟩ **4** : to be idle : move lazily

³poke *n* : a quick thrust : JAB

¹pok·er \'pō-kər\ *n* : a metal rod used for stirring a fire

²po·ker \'pō-kər\ *n* : a card game in which each player bets on the value of his hand

po·lar \'pō-lər\ *adj* **1** : of or relating to a pole of the earth or the region around it : coming from or having the characteristics of such a region **2** : of or relating to a pole of a magnet

polar bear *n* : a large creamy-white bear of arctic regions

Po·lar·is \pə-'lar-əs\ *n* : NORTH STAR

¹pole \'pōl\ *n* : a long slender piece of wood or metal

polar bear

²pole *vb* **poled; pol·ing** : to push or impel with a pole ⟨*pole* a boat⟩

³pole *n* **1** : either the north or south end of the earth's axis **2** : either of the two ends of a magnet **3** : either of the terminals of an electric battery

Pole \'pōl\ *n* : a native or inhabitant of Poland

pole·cat \'pōl-,kat\ *n* **1** : a small dark flesh-eating European animal related to the weasel **2** : SKUNK

pole·star \'pōl-,stär\ *n* **1** : NORTH STAR **2** : a constant guiding principle **3** : a center of attraction

pole vault *n* : a track-and-field contest in which each contestant vaults for height with the use of a pole

¹po·lice \pə-'lēs\ *n, pl* **police** **1** : the department of government that keeps order and enforces law, investigates crimes, and makes arrests **2** *pl* : POLICEMEN **3** *pl* : soldiers appointed to keep order

²police *vb* **po·liced; po·lic·ing** **1** : to keep order in or among ⟨*police* a city⟩ **2** : to clean up ⟨*police* a camp area⟩

police dog *n* : a dog trained to assist police

po·lice·man \pə-'lēs-mən\ *n, pl* **po·lice·men** \-mən\ : a member of a police force

¹pol·i·cy \'päl-ə-sē\ *n, pl* **pol·i·cies** : a course of action selected to guide and determine decisions ⟨our country's foreign *policy*⟩ ⟨honesty is the best *policy*⟩

²policy *n, pl* **pol·i·cies** : a document that contains the agreement made by an insurance company with a person whose life or property is insured

po·li·o \'pō-lē-,ō\ *n* : POLIOMYELITIS

po·li·o·my·e·li·tis \,pō-lē-,ō-,mī-ə-'līt-əs\ *n* : an infectious disease affecting children especially and sometimes causing paralysis : INFANTILE PARALYSIS

¹pol·ish \'päl-ish\ *vb* **1** : to make smooth and glossy usually by rubbing ⟨*polish* glass⟩ **2** : to smooth or improve in manners or condition ⟨*polished* behavior of a diplomat⟩

²polish *n* **1** : a smooth glossy surface **2** : social good manners : REFINEMENT **3** : a preparation used for producing a shiny surface

¹Pol·ish \'pō-lish\ *adj* : of or relating to Poland, the Poles, or Polish

²Polish *n* : the language of the Poles

po·lite \pə-'līt\ *adj* **po·lit·er; po·lit·est** **1** : relating to or having the characteristics of advanced culture ⟨customs of a *polite* society⟩ **2** : showing courtesy or good breeding syn see CIVIL — **po·lite·ly** *adv* — **po·lite·ness** *n*

po·lit·i·cal \pə-'lit-i-kəl\ *adj* : of or relating to politics, government, or the conduct of government — **po·lit·i·cal·ly** *adv*

po·li·ti·cian \,päl-ə-'tish-ən\ *n* : one who is actively engaged in party politics or in conducting government affairs

pol·i·tics \'päl-ə-,tiks\ *n sing or pl* **1** : the science and art of government : the management of public affairs **2** : activity in or management of the affairs of political parties **3** : political theory, practice, or opinion

pol·ka \'pōl-kə\ *n* : a lively dance of Bohemian origin or the music for it

¹poll \'pōl\ *n* **1** : the hair-covered top and back part of the head **2** : the casting or recording of the votes or opinions of a number of persons ⟨a *poll* of the persons in the room⟩ **3** : the place where votes are cast — usually used in plural ⟨go to the *polls*⟩

²poll *vb* **1** : to cut off : cut short : CROP, SHEAR **2** : to receive and record the votes of **3** : to receive (votes) in an election **4** : to cast one's vote or ballot at a poll

pol·lack *or* **pol·lock** \'päl-ək\ *n* : an Atlantic food fish resembling the related cod

pol·len \'päl-ən\ *n* : the usually yellow dust-like material in the anthers of a flower that is made up of male spores which effect the fertilization of the seeds

pol·li·nate \'päl-ə-,nāt\ *vb* **pol·li·nat·ed; pol·li·nat·ing** : to place pollen on the stigma of ⟨bees *pollinating* clover⟩

pol·li·na·tion \,päl-ə-'nā-shən\ *n* : the act or process of pollinating

pol·li·wog *or* **pol·ly·wog** \'päl-ē-ˌwäg\ *n*
: TADPOLE

pol·lute \pə-'lüt\ *vb* **pol·lut·ed; pol·lut·ing** : to
make impure ⟨*pollute* a water supply⟩

po·lo \'pō-lō\ *n* : a game played by teams of
players on horseback who drive a wooden ball
with long-handled mallets

pol·o·naise \ˌpäl-ə-'nāz\ *n* : a stately Polish
dance : the music for it in moderate 3/4 time

poly- *prefix* : many : much : MULTI- ⟨*poly*-
syllable⟩

pol·y·gon \'päl-i-ˌgän\ *n* : a closed plane
figure bounded by straight
lines

pol·yp \'päl-əp\ *n* : a
small sea animal (as a
coral) having a tubelike
body closed and attached

polygons

at one end and opening at the other with a
mouth surrounded by tentacles

pome·gran·ate \'päm-ˌgran-ət, 'päm-ə-\ *n*
: a thick-skinned reddish fruit about the size
of an orange that has many seeds in a pulp of
acid flavor and is borne by a tropical Old
World tree

¹**pom·mel** \'pəm-əl\ *n* : a rounded often
ornamental knob on the handle
of a sword or at the front and
top of a saddle

²**pommel** *vb* **pom·meled** *or*
pom·melled; pom·mel·ing *or*
pom·mel·ling : PUMMEL

pommel→

pomp \'pämp\ *n* : a show of
wealth and splendor : a showy
display

pom·pa·dour \'päm-pə-ˌdōr\
n : a style of dressing the hair high over the
forehead

pom·pon \'päm-ˌpän\ *n* : a rounded tuft of
silk, feathers, or wool used as trimming on
costumes, hats, or shoes

pomp·ous \'päm-pəs\ *adj* **1** : making an
appearance of importance or dignity **2** : SELF-
IMPORTANT — **pomp·ous·ly** *adv* — **pomp·ous-
ness** *n*

pon·cho \'pän-chō\ *n, pl* **pon·chos** **1** : a
Spanish-American cloak like a blanket with a
slit in the middle for the head **2** : a waterproof garment like a poncho worn as a raincoat

pond \'pänd\ *n* : a body of water usually
smaller than a lake

pon·der \'pän-dər\ *vb* : to consider carefully

pon·der·ous \'pän-də-rəs\ *adj* **1** : very
heavy **2** : lacking lightness or liveliness : DULL
⟨a *ponderous* speech⟩

pond scum *n* : a mass of algae in stagnant

water or an alga that grows in such masses

pon·iard \'pän-yərd\ *n* : a slender dagger

pon·toon \pän-'tün\ *n* **1** : a small flat-
bottomed boat **2** : a light
watertight float used as one
of the supports for a floating
bridge **3** : a float attached to
the bottom of an airplane for
landing on water

pontoon

po·ny \'pō-nē\ *n, pl* **po·nies** : a small horse

poo·dle \'püd-l\ *n* [from German *pudel*, short
for *pudelhund*, from *pudeln* "to splash" and
hund "dog"; so named because they were
once used by hunters to bring back game from
water] : one of an old breed of active intelligent heavy-coated solid-colored dogs

pooh \'pü\ *interj* — used to express contempt,
disapproval, or impatience

¹**pool** \'pül\ *n* **1** : a small rather deep natural
or artificial body of water ⟨the *pool* below the
rock⟩ ⟨a swimming *pool*⟩ **2** : a small body of
standing liquid : PUDDLE

²**pool** *n* **1** : a game of billiards played on a
table with six pockets **2** : all the money contributed by a group of bettors or investors or
by the players of a game

³**pool** *vb* : to put together in a common fund

poor \'pur\ *adj* **1** : lacking riches : NEEDY
2 : SCANTY, INSUFFICIENT ⟨a *poor* crop⟩
3 : not good in quality or workmanship
4 : FEEBLE ⟨*poor* health⟩ **5** : lacking fertility
⟨*poor* land⟩ **6** : lacking in signs of wealth or
good taste ⟨*poor* furnishings⟩ **7** : not efficient
or capable : not satisfactory ⟨a *poor* carpenter⟩
8 : worthy of pity or sympathy ⟨the *poor* child
hurt herself⟩ — **poor·ly** *adv* — **poor·ness** *n*

¹**pop** \'päp\ *vb* **popped; pop·ping** **1** : to burst
or cause to burst with a pop **2** : to move
quickly or unexpectedly ⟨*pop* into bed⟩
3 : to fire a gun : SHOOT ⟨*popping* at tin cans⟩
4 : to stick out ⟨his eyes *popping* with surprise⟩

²**pop** *n* **1** : a small explosive sound **2** : a shot
from a rifle or pistol **3** : a bottled soft drink

pop·corn \'päp-ˌkorn\ *n* : corn that swells up
and bursts open into a white mass when
heated

pope \'pōp\ *n, often cap* : the head of the
Roman Catholic Church

pop·lar \'päp-lər\ *n* : a tree that has rough
bark, catkins for flowers, and a
white cottonlike substance a-
round its seeds

pop·lin \'päp-lən\ *n* : a strong
silk or worsted cloth ribbed like
corduroy

pop·py \'päp-ē\ *n, pl* **pop·pies**
: a hairy-stemmed plant with

poppy

flowers that are usually red, yellow, or white

pop·u·lace \'päp-yə-ləs\ *n* : the common people : MASSES, CROWD

pop·u·lar \'päp-yə-lər\ *adj* **1** : of, relating to, or coming from the whole body of people ⟨*popular* government⟩ **2** : suitable to the average person : easy to understand ⟨*popular* science⟩ **3** : pleasing to many people : approved by many people ⟨a *popular* game⟩ — **pop·u·lar·ly** *adv*

pop·u·lar·i·ty \,päp-yə-'lar-ət-ē\ *n* : the quality or state of being popular

pop·u·late \'päp-yə-,lāt\ *vb* **pop·u·lat·ed; pop·u·lat·ing** : to furnish with inhabitants

pop·u·la·tion \,päp-yə-'lā-shən\ *n* **1** : the whole number of people in a country, city, or area **2** : the people inhabiting a country or region

pop·u·lous \'päp-yə-ləs\ *adj* : thickly populated

por·ce·lain \'pōr-sə-lən\ *n* : a fine hard pottery that allows light to pass through it and is not porous

porch \'pōrch\ *n* : a covered entrance to a building usually with a separate roof

por·cu·pine \'pȯr-kyə-,pīn\ *n* : a gnawing animal having stiff sharp quills mingled with its hair

porcupine

¹pore \'pōr\ *vb* **pored; por·ing** : to gaze, study, or think long or earnestly ⟨*pore* over a book⟩

²pore *n* : a tiny opening (as in the skin or in the soil)

por·gy \'pȯr-gē\ *n, pl* **por·gies** : any of several food fishes of the Mediterranean sea and the Atlantic ocean

pork \'pōrk\ *n* : the fresh or salted flesh of swine dressed for food

po·rous \'pōr-əs\ *adj* **1** : full of pores ⟨*porous* wood⟩ **2** : capable of absorbing liquids ⟨*porous* blotting paper⟩

por·poise \'pȯr-pəs\ *n* [Latin *porcus* "pig" and *piscis* "fish" were combined in medieval Latin to make *porcopiscis* "porpoise"; this was modified to *porpois* in early French, and from there taken into English] **1** : a sea animal somewhat like a small whale with a blunt rounded snout **2** : DOLPHIN 1

porpoise 1

por·ridge \'pȯr-ij\ *n* : a food made by boiling meal of a grain or a vegetable (as peas) in water or milk until it thickens

porringer

por·rin·ger \'pȯr-ən-jər\ *n* : a small one-handled bowl for children

¹port \'pōrt\ *n* **1** : a place where ships may ride secure from storms **2** : a harbor where ships load or unload cargo **3** : AIRPORT

²port *n* **1** : an opening (as in machinery) for gas, steam, or water to go in or out **2** : PORTHOLE

³port *n* : the left side of a ship or airplane looking forward

⁴port *n* : a strong rich usually dark red wine

por·ta·ble \'pōrt-ə-bəl\ *adj* : capable of being carried : easily moved from one place to another

por·tage \'pōrt-ij\ *n* : the carrying of boats or goods overland from one body of water to another

por·tal \'pōrt-l\ *n* : a grand or elaborate door or gate : ENTRANCE

port·cul·lis \pōrt-'kəl-əs\ *n* : a heavy iron grating which can be let down to prevent entrance to a castle or fortress

por·tend \pȯr-'tend\ *vb* : to give a sign or warning of beforehand

por·tent \'pȯr-,tent\ *n* : a sign or warning usually of something evil

portcullis

por·ter \'pōrt-ər\ *n* **1** : a man who carries baggage (as at a terminal) **2** : an attendant on a train

port·fo·li·o \pōrt-'fō-lē-,ō\ *n, pl* **port·fo·li·os** : a case for carrying papers or drawings without having to fold them

port·hole \'pōrt-,hōl\ *n* : an opening in the side of a ship or airplane

por·ti·co \'pōrt-i-,kō\ *n, pl* **por·ti·coes** *or* **por·ti·cos** : a row of columns supporting a roof around or at the entrance of a building

¹por·tion \'pōr-shən\ *n* **1** : SHARE, PART ⟨a *portion* of time⟩ ⟨a *portion* of food⟩ **2** : DOWRY ⟨marriage *portion*⟩

²portion *vb* : to divide into portions : DISTRIBUTE

por·trait \'pōr-trət, -,trāt\ *n* **1** : a picture of a person **2** : a portrayal in words

por·tray \pōr-'trā\ *vb* **1** : to make a portrait of **2** : to picture in words : DESCRIBE **3** : to represent by acting

por·tray·al \pōr-'trā-əl\ *n* : the act or result of portraying : DESCRIPTION, REPRESENTATION

¹Por·tu·guese \,pōr-chə-'gēz\ *adj* : of or relating to Portugal, the people of Portugal, or Portuguese

²Portuguese *n* **1** : a native or inhabitant of Portugal **2** : the language of Portugal and Brazil

¹pose \'pōz\ *vb* **posed; pos·ing** **1** : to hold or

cause to hold a special position of the body ⟨*pose* for the painting of a picture⟩ **2** : to pretend to be what one is not ⟨*pose* as a hero⟩

²**pose** *n* **1** : a position of the body held for a special purpose ⟨photographed in different *poses*⟩ **2** : an assumed attitude or character ⟨a *pose* of innocence⟩

po·si·tion \pə-'zish-ən\ *n* **1** : the manner in which something is placed or arranged **2** : a way of looking at or considering things **3** : the place where a person or thing is : SITUATION ⟨a map showing the *position* of the treasure⟩ **4** : social or official rank ⟨persons of *position*⟩ **5** : EMPLOYMENT, JOB

¹**pos·i·tive** \'päz-ət-iv\ *adj* **1** : definitely and clearly stated ⟨the police had *positive* orders⟩ **2** : filled with confidence : CERTAIN ⟨*positive* that he would win⟩ **3** : of, relating to, or having the form of an adjective or adverb that shows no degree of comparison **4** : having a real position or effect ⟨a *positive* influence for good in the school⟩ **5** : having the light and shade as existing in the original subject ⟨a *positive* photograph⟩ **6** : being greater than zero and often indicated by a plus sign ⟨2 or +2 is a *positive* number⟩ **7** : of, being, or relating to electricity of a kind that predominates in a glass rod rubbed with silk ⟨a *positive* charge⟩ **8** : having a deficiency of electrons ⟨a *positive* particle⟩ **9** : being the part from which the electric current flows to the external circuit ⟨the *positive* pole of a storage battery⟩ **10** : APPROVING, AFFIRMATIVE ⟨a *positive* answer⟩ **11** : showing the presence of what is looked for or suspected to be present ⟨the test for tuberculosis was *positive*⟩ — **pos·i·tive·ly** *adv*

²**positive** *n* : the positive degree or a positive form in a language

pos·sess \pə-'zes\ *vb* **1** : to have and hold as property : OWN **2** : CONTROL, DOMINATE ⟨acted as if *possessed* by a devil⟩ — **pos·ses·sor** *n*

pos·ses·sion \pə-'zesh-ən\ *n* **1** : the act of possessing or holding as one's own : OWNERSHIP ⟨charged with the *possession* of stolen goods⟩ **2** : CONTROL **3** : something that is held as one's own property : something possessed

¹**pos·ses·sive** \pə-'zes-iv\ *adj* **1** : of, relating to, or being the form of a word that shows possession **2** : showing the desire to possess or keep

²**possessive** *n* : a form of a word (as *man's*) used to show possession

pos·si·bil·i·ty \ˌpäs-ə-'bil-ət-ē\ *n, pl* **pos·si·bil·i·ties** **1** : the condition or fact of being possible ⟨face the *possibility* of failure⟩ **2** : something that may happen

pos·si·ble \'päs-ə-bəl\ *adj* **1** : being within the limits of one's ability : being in a state that can be done or brought about ⟨a task *possible* only to skilled workmen⟩ **2** : being likely to occur ⟨*possible* dangers⟩ **3** : able or fitted to be or to become ⟨a *possible* site for a camp⟩ syn see PROBABLE

pos·sum \'päs-əm\ *n* : OPOSSUM

¹**post** \'pōst\ *n* **1** : a piece of solid substance (as metal or timber) fixed firmly in an upright position and used especially as a support ⟨a fence *post*⟩ **2** : a pole or stake set up to mark or indicate something ⟨starting *post*⟩

²**post** *vb* **1** : to fasten on a post, wall, or bulletin board ⟨*post* examination results⟩ **2** : to publish or announce as if by posting a notice **3** : to forbid persons from entering or using by putting up warning notices ⟨*post* a trout stream⟩

³**post** *n, chiefly Brit* : a delivery of mail : MAIL ⟨I expect a letter in the morning *post*⟩

⁴**post** *vb* **1** : to ride or travel with haste **2** : to send by mail : MAIL

⁵**post** *n* **1** : the place at which a soldier or sentry is stationed **2** : a place where a body of troops is stationed **3** : a place or office to which a person is appointed **4** : a trading settlement

⁶**post** *vb* : to station at a post ⟨*post* a guard⟩

post- *prefix* **1** : after : later : following : behind ⟨*post*date⟩ **2** : subsequent to : later than ⟨*post*war⟩

post·age \'pōs-tij\ *n* : the charge fixed by law for carrying something (as a letter or parcel) by mail

post·al \'pōst-l\ *adj* : of or relating to the post office or the handling of mail

postal card *n* **1** : a blank card with a postage stamp printed on it **2** : POSTCARD

post·card \'pōst-ˌkärd\ *n* **1** : a card on which a message may be sent by mail without an envelope **2** : POSTAL CARD

post·er \'pōs-tər\ *n* **1** : a notice or advertisement intended to be posted in a public place **2** : a person who posts notices

pos·ter·i·ty \päs-'ter-ət-ē\ *n* **1** : the line of persons who are descended from one ancestor **2** : all future generations ⟨leave a record for *posterity*⟩

post·haste \'pōst-'hāst\ *adv* : with great speed or promptness

post·man \'pōst-mən\ *n, pl* **post·men** \-mən\ : MAILMAN

post·mark \'pōst-ˌmärk\ *n* : a mark officially put on a piece of mail especially for canceling the postage stamp and giving the time and place of sending

post·mas·ter \'pōst-ˌmas-tər\ *n* : one in charge of a post office

post·mis·tress \'pōst-ˌmis-trəs\ *n* : a woman in charge of a post office

post office *n* 1 : an office under the charge of a government official where mail is received, handled, and sent out 2 : the department of the government in charge of the mail

post·pone \pōst-'pōn\ *vb* **post·poned; post·pon·ing** : to put off till some later time : DELAY — **post·pone·ment** *n*

post·script \'pōst-ˌskript\ *n* : a note added at the end of a finished letter or book

¹**pos·ture** \'päs-chər\ *n* : the position of one part of the body with relation to other parts : the general way of holding the body

²**posture** *vb* **pos·tured; pos·tur·ing** : to assume a particular posture : POSE

po·sy \'pō-zē\ *n, pl* **po·sies** 1 : FLOWER 2 : BOUQUET

¹**pot** \'pät\ *n* 1 : a deep rounded container made of metal or earthenware and used chiefly for domestic purposes 2 : the contents of a pot : the amount a pot will hold ⟨a *pot* of soup⟩

²**pot** *vb* **pot·ted; pot·ting** 1 : to place, keep, or preserve in a pot 2 : to plant (as a flower) in a pot to grow — often used with *up* ⟨*pot* up begonias⟩

pot·ash \'pät-ˌash\ *n* : potassium or a potassium compound

po·tas·si·um \pə-'tas-ē-əm\ *n* : a silver-white soft light metallic chemical element found especially in minerals

po·ta·to \pə-'tāt-ō\ *n, pl* **po·ta·toes** : the thick edible underground tuber of a widely grown American plant related to the tomato and egg-plant

po·tent \'pōt-nt\ *adj* 1 : POWER-FUL, MIGHTY ⟨a *potent* ruler⟩ 2 : very effective : STRONG ⟨*potent* medicine⟩

po·ten·tial \pə-'ten-chəl\ *adj* : capable of becoming real : POSSIBLE — **po·ten·tial·ly** *adv*

potato plant

pot·herb \'pät-ˌərb, -ˌhərb\ *n* : a plant whose leaves and stems are cooked for use as greens

pot·hole \'pät-ˌhōl\ *n* : a deep round hole (as in a stream bed or a road)

po·tion \'pō-shən\ *n* : a drink especially of a liquid medicine or of a poison : DOSE

¹**pot·ter** \'pät-ər\ *n* : one that makes pottery

²**potter** *vb* : PUTTER

pot·tery \'pät-ə-rē\ *n, pl* **pot·ter·ies** 1 : a

place where earthen articles (as pots, dishes, and vases) are made 2 : the art of making earthen articles : CERAMICS 3 : articles made usually from clay that is shaped while moist and hardened by heat

¹**pouch** \'paùch\ *n* 1 : a small drawstring bag ⟨a tobacco *pouch*⟩ 2 : a bag often with a lock for carrying goods or valuables ⟨mail *pouch*⟩ 3 : a bag or sac of folded skin or flesh especially for carrying the young (as on the abdomen of a kangaroo) or for carrying food (as in the cheek of many animals of the rat family)

²**pouch** *vb* : to put or form into a pouch

poul·tice \'pōl-təs\ *n* : a soft and usually medicated and heated mass applied to the body surface especially to relieve pain, inflammation, or congestion

poul·try \'pōl-trē\ *n* : domestic birds (as chickens, turkeys, ducks, and geese) that furnish meat or eggs for human food

¹**pounce** \'paùns\ *vb* **pounced; pounc·ing** 1 : to swoop down on and seize with or as if with talons ⟨the hawk *pounced* on a chicken⟩ 2 : to leap on or attack very quickly

²**pounce** *n* : an act of pouncing : a sudden swooping or springing on something

¹**pound** \'paùnd\ *n* 1 : a measure of weight equal to sixteen ounces 2 : the basic monetary unit of Great Britain

²**pound** *vb* 1 : to crush to a powder or pulp by striking heavily again and again ⟨*pound* almonds into a paste⟩ 2 : to strike heavily and repeatedly : BEAT, HAMMER ⟨*pound* a piano⟩ 3 : to walk, run, or move heavily ⟨horses *pounding* through mud⟩

³**pound** *n* : a public enclosure where stray animals are kept ⟨a dog *pound*⟩

pour \'pōr\ *vb* 1 : to flow or cause to flow in a stream 2 : to let loose something without restraint ⟨*poured* out his troubles⟩ 3 : to rain very hard

¹**pout** \'paùt\ *vb* : to show displeasure by pushing out one's lips : look sullen or sulky

²**pout** *n* 1 : an act of pouting 2 *pl* : a fit of bad humor

pov·er·ty \'päv-ərt-ē\ *n* 1 : the condition of being poor : lack of money : WANT, NEED 2 : a lack of something desirable : poor quality ⟨*poverty* of the soil⟩

¹**pow·der** \'paùd-ər\ *n* 1 : the fine particles made (as by pounding or crushing) from a dry substance : DUST 2 : something (as a food, medicine, or cosmetic) made in or changed to the form of a powder ⟨milk *powder*⟩ 3 : an explosive used in gunnery and blasting

²**powder** *vb* 1 : to sprinkle with or as if with

powder **2** : to reduce to powder **3** : to use face powder

powder horn *n* : a cow or ox horn made into a flask for carrying gunpowder

pow·der·y \\'paud-ə-rē\\ *adj* **1** : made of or like powder **2** : CRUMBLY **3** : sprinkled with powder : DUSTY

powder horn

¹pow·er \\'pau-ər\\ *n* **1** : the ability to act or to do ⟨lose the power to walk⟩ **2** : CONTROL, AUTHORITY ⟨in the *power* of an enemy⟩ **3** : one that has power or influence : a nation that has control or influence among the nations **4** : physical might : STRENGTH, VIGOR **5** : force or energy used to do work ⟨electric *power*⟩ **6** : the number of times an optical instrument magnifies the apparent size of the object viewed **7** : the number of times as indicated by an exponent a number is used as a factor to obtain a product ⟨10^3 is the third *power* of 10 and means $10 \times 10 \times 10$⟩ **8** : the rate of speed at which work is done — **pow·er·less** \\-ləs\\ *adj*

²power *adj* **1** : relating to or supplying power **2** : utilizing mechanical or electrical power ⟨*power* drill⟩ ⟨*power* mower⟩

³power *vb* : to supply with power

pow·er·ful \\'pau-ər-fəl\\ *adj* : full of or having power, strength, or influence : STRONG, MIGHTY — **pow·er·ful·ly** *adv*

pow·er·house \\'pau-ər-ˌhaus\\ *n* **1** : a building in which electric power is generated **2** : a source of power, energy, or influence

pow·wow \\'pau-ˌwau\\ *n* **1** : a North American Indian ceremony (as for victory in war) **2** : a conference of or with Indians **3** : a meeting for discussion

prac·ti·ca·ble \\'prak-ti-kə-bəl\\ *adj* : capable of being done, put into practice, or accomplished

prac·ti·cal \\'prak-ti-kəl\\ *adj* **1** : of or relating to action and practice rather than ideas or thought **2** : capable of being employed : USEFUL ⟨a *practical* knowledge of carpentry⟩ **3** : engaged in some work : WORKING ⟨a *practical* farmer⟩ **4** : inclined to do things rather than just plan or think about them ⟨a *practical* mind⟩

practical joke *n* : a joke consisting of something done rather than said : a trick played on someone for amusement

prac·ti·cal·ly \\'prak-ti-kə-lē\\ *adv* **1** : REALLY, ACTUALLY ⟨a clever but *practically* worthless scheme⟩ **2** : to all practical purposes though not absolutely ⟨a *practically* inert gas⟩ **3** : NEARLY, ALMOST ⟨*practically* friendless⟩

¹prac·tice *or* **prac·tise** \\'prak-təs\\ *vb* **prac·ticed** *or* **prac·tised**; **prac·tic·ing** *or* **prac·tis·ing** **1** : to do or observe often or usually ⟨*practice* politeness⟩ **2** : to do repeated exercises in so as to learn or improve ⟨*practice* music⟩ **3** : to follow or work at as a profession ⟨*practice* medicine⟩

²practice *also* **practise** *n* **1** : actual performance : USE ⟨put into *practice*⟩ **2** : CUSTOM, HABIT ⟨follow the local *practice*⟩ **3** : repeated action for gaining skill ⟨*practice* makes perfect⟩ **syn** see HABIT

prai·rie \\'prear-ē\\ *n* : a large area of level or rolling land with few or no trees

prairie chicken *n* : a grouse of the Mississippi valley

prairie dog *n* : a burrowing colonial animal related to the marmots but about the size of a large squirrel

prairie schooner *n* : a long covered wagon used by pioneers to cross the prairies

prairie schooner

¹praise \\'prāz\\ *vb* **praised**; **prais·ing** **1** : to express approval of : COMMEND **2** : to glorify God or a saint especially in song : WORSHIP **syn** see COMPLIMENT

²praise *n* **1** : an act of praising : approval given because of worth or excellence **2** : WORSHIP

praise·wor·thy \\'prāz-ˌwər-thē\\ *adj* : worthy of praise ⟨*praiseworthy* action⟩

prance \\'prans\\ *vb* **pranced**; **pranc·ing** **1** : to rise on the hind legs or move by so doing **2** : to ride on a prancing horse : ride gaily or proudly **3** : to walk proudly

prank \\'prangk\\ *n* : a playful or mischievous act : PRACTICAL JOKE, TRICK

prate \\'prāt\\ *vb* **prat·ed**; **prat·ing** : to talk a great deal and to little purpose : talk foolishly : BABBLE

prat·tle \\'prat-l\\ *vb* **prat·tled**; **prat·tling** : to talk a great deal without much meaning : CHATTER

prawn \\'pron\\ *n* : an edible shellfish resembling a shrimp

pray \\'prā\\ *vb* **1** : to ask earnestly : BEG ⟨*pray* a judge for a lenient decision⟩ **2** : to address God with adoration, pleading, or thanksgiving

prayer \\'praer\\ *n* **1** : a request or entreaty addressed to God ⟨a *prayer* for peace⟩ **2** : the act of praying to God **3** : a set form of words used in praying **4** : a religious service that is mostly prayers ⟨evening *prayer*⟩

pray·ing mantis \ˌprā-ing-\ *n* : MANTIS

pre- *prefix* **1** : earlier than : before ⟨*pre-historic*⟩ : preparatory or prerequisite to ⟨a *premedical* course⟩ **2** : in advance : beforehand ⟨*prepay*⟩ **3** : in front of : front ⟨*premolar*⟩

preach \ˈprēch\ *vb* **1** : to talk on a religious subject : deliver a sermon **2** : to urge publicly : ADVOCATE ⟨*preach* patience⟩

preach·er \ˈprē-chər\ *n* **1** : a person who preaches **2** : MINISTER

pre·am·ble \ˈprē-ˌam-bəl\ *n* : an introduction (as to a law) that often states the reasons and purpose for the matter that follows

pre·car·i·ous \pri-ˈkar-ē-əs\ *adj* **1** : depending on unknown conditions or chance circumstances : UNCERTAIN **2** : lacking stability or security ⟨*precarious* balance⟩ ⟨*precarious* state of health⟩ — **pre·car·i·ous·ly** *adv* — **pre·car·i·ous·ness** *n*

pre·cau·tion \pri-ˈkȯ-shən\ *n* **1** : caution or care taken beforehand **2** : something done beforehand to prevent evil or bring about good results ⟨take all possible *precautions* against fire⟩

pre·cede \pri-ˈsēd\ *vb* **pre·ced·ed; pre·ced·ing** [from Latin *praecedere*, a compound of the prefix *prae-* "pre-" and *cedere* "to go"] : to be or go before in rank, importance, position, or time

prec·e·dent \ˈpres-ə-dənt\ *n* : something that may serve as a rule or as a pattern to be followed in the future

pre·ced·ing \pri-ˈsēd-ing\ *adj* : going before : PREVIOUS

pre·cious \ˈpresh-əs\ *adj* **1** : very valuable ⟨diamonds, emeralds, and other *precious* stones⟩ **2** : greatly loved : DEAR, CHERISHED

prec·i·pice \ˈpres-ə-pəs\ *n* : a very steep and high face of rock or mountain : CLIFF

¹pre·cip·i·tate \pri-ˈsip-ə-ˌtāt\ *vb* **pre·cip·i·tat·ed; pre·cip·i·tat·ing** **1** : to throw or dash headlong **2** : to cause to happen suddenly or unexpectedly ⟨the misunderstanding *precipitated* a quarrel⟩ **3** : to change from a vapor to a liquid and fall as hail, mist, rain, sleet, or snow **4** : to separate from a solution ⟨*precipitate* salt from seawater⟩

²pre·cip·i·tate \pri-ˈsip-ət-ət\ *adj* : HASTY, RASH

pre·cip·i·ta·tion \pri-ˌsip-ə-ˈtā-shən\ *n* **1** : HASTE, RASHNESS **2** : water or the amount of water that falls to the earth as hail, mist, rain, sleet, or snow

pre·cise \pri-ˈsīs\ *adj* **1** : exactly stated or defined ⟨follow *precise* rules⟩ **2** : very clear and distinct ⟨a *precise* voice⟩ **3** : very exact : ACCURATE — **pre·cise·ly** *adv* — **pre·cise·ness** *n*

pre·ci·sion \pri-ˈsizh-ən\ *n* : the quality or condition of being precise : EXACTNESS

pre·co·cious \pri-ˈkō-shəs\ *adj* : showing mature qualities or abilities at an unusually early age — **pre·co·cious·ly** *adv* — **pre·co·cious·ness** *n*

pred·a·tor \ˈpred-ət-ər\ *n* : an animal that lives primarily by killing and eating other animals

pred·a·to·ry \ˈpred-ə-ˌtōr-ē\ *adj* : living by preying upon other animals

pred·e·ces·sor \ˈpred-ə-ˌses-ər\ *n* : a person who has held a position or office before another

pre·dic·a·ment \pri-ˈdik-ə-mənt\ *n* : a bad or difficult situation : FIX

pred·i·cate \ˈpred-i-kət\ *n* : the part of a sentence or clause that tells something about the subject

predicate adjective *n* : an adjective in the predicate that tells something about the subject ⟨*sweet* in "sugar is sweet" is a *predicate adjective*⟩

predicate noun *n* : a noun in the predicate that refers to the same person or thing as the subject ⟨*father* in "the president is my father" is a *predicate noun*⟩

pre·dict \pri-ˈdikt\ *vb* : to tell beforehand : foretell on the basis of experience or reasoning ⟨*predict* the weather⟩ **syn** *see* FORETELL

pre·dic·tion \pri-ˈdik-shən\ *n* **1** : an act of predicting **2** : PROPHECY, FORECAST

pre·dom·i·nance \pri-ˈdäm-ə-nəns\ *n* : the quality or state of being predominant

pre·dom·i·nant \pri-ˈdäm-ə-nənt\ *adj* : superior to others in number, strength, influence, authority, or importance

pre·dom·i·nate \pri-ˈdäm-ə-ˌnāt\ *vb* **pre·dom·i·nat·ed; pre·dom·i·nat·ing** : to be predominant : be of greatest importance or influence

preen \ˈprēn\ *vb* **1** : to smooth with or as if with the bill ⟨the peacock *preened* his feathers⟩ **2** : to make one's appearance neat and tidy

pre·fab·ri·cate \prē-ˈfab-ri-ˌkāt\ *vb* **pre·fab·ri·cat·ed; pre·fab·ri·cat·ing** : to manufacture the parts of something in advance so that it can be built by putting together the parts ⟨*prefabricate* houses⟩

pref·ace \ˈpref-əs\ *n* : an introductory section at the beginning of a book or a speech

pre·fer \pri-ˈfər\ *vb* **pre·ferred; pre·fer·ring** : to hold in greater favor : like better ⟨*prefer* dark clothes⟩

pref·er·a·ble \ˈpref-ə-rə-bəl\ *adj* : more desirable — **pref·er·a·bly** \-blē\ *adv*

pref·er·ence \'pref-ə-rəns\ n **1** : a choosing of or special liking for one person or thing rather than another **2** : the power or chance to choose : CHOICE **3** : one that is preferred
syn see CHOICE

¹**pre·fix** \'prē-ˌfiks\ vb : to put or attach at the beginning of a word : add as a prefix

²**prefix** n : a sound or sequence of sounds or a letter or sequence of letters occurring at the beginning of a word and having meaning in itself

preg·nant \'preg-nənt\ adj **1** : carrying unborn offspring **2** : full of meaning

pre·hen·sile \prē-'hen-səl\ adj : adapted for grasping ⟨a monkey's prehensile tail⟩

pre·his·tor·ic \ˌprē-his-'tȯr-ik\ adj : of, relating to, or existing in the period before written history began ⟨prehistoric animals⟩

¹**prej·u·dice** \'prej-ə-dəs\ n **1** : injury or damage to a case at law or to one's rights **2** : a favoring or dislike of one over another without good reason : BIAS

²**prejudice** vb **prej·u·diced; prej·u·dic·ing 1** : to cause damage to (as a case at law) **2** : to cause prejudice in

prel·ate \'prel-ət\ n : a clergyman (as a bishop) of high rank and authority

¹**pre·lim·i·nar·y** \pri-'lim-ə-ˌner-ē\ n, pl **pre·lim·i·nar·ies** : something that precedes or is introductory or preparatory

²**preliminary** adj : preceding the main part : INTRODUCTORY

prel·ude \'prel-ˌyüd\ n **1** : something preceding and preparing for the principal or more important matter **2** : a short musical piece or introductory section (as of an opera) **3** : a piece (as an organ solo) played at the beginning of a church service

pre·ma·ture \ˌprē-mə-'tùr, -'tyùr\ adj : happening, coming, or done before the usual or proper time : too early — **pre·ma·ture·ly** adv

pre·med·i·tate \pri-'med-ə-ˌtāt\ vb **pre·med·i·tat·ed; pre·med·i·tat·ing** : to think about and plan beforehand

¹**pre·mier** \pri-'miər, 'prē-mē-ər\ adj : first in position or importance : CHIEF, LEADING

²**premier** n : the chief minister of government : PRIME MINISTER

¹**pre·miere** \pri-'myeər, -'miər\ n : a first showing or performance ⟨premiere of a movie⟩

²**premiere** adj : CHIEF, LEADING ⟨the premiere -dancer of a group⟩

prem·ise \'prem-əs\ n **1** : a statement of fact made as a basis for argument or reasoning **2** pl : a piece of land with the buildings on it ⟨clean up the premises⟩

pre·mi·um \'prē-mē-əm\ n **1** : a prize to be gained by some special act or merit **2** : a sum over and above the stated or par value ⟨sell stock at a premium⟩ **3** : the amount paid for a contract of insurance

pre·mo·lar \'prē-'mō-lər\ n : any of the teeth that come between the canines and the molars and in man are normally two in each side of each jaw

pre·mo·ni·tion \ˌprē-mə-'nish-ən, ˌprem-ə-\ n : FOREBODING ⟨a premonition of danger⟩

pre·oc·cu·pied \prē-'äk-yə-ˌpīd\ adj : lost in thought : ABSORBED

prepaid past of PREPAY

prep·a·ra·tion \ˌprep-ə-'rā-shən\ n **1** : the act of making ready in advance for some special purpose **2** : something that prepares ⟨finish preparations for a journey⟩ **3** : something prepared for a particular purpose ⟨a preparation for burns⟩

pre·par·a·to·ry \pri-'par-ə-ˌtȯr-ē\ adj : preparing or serving to prepare for something ⟨a preparatory student⟩ ⟨a preparatory school⟩

pre·pare \pri-'paər\ vb **pre·pared; pre·par·ing 1** : to make ready beforehand for some particular purpose ⟨prepare for college⟩ **2** : EQUIP ⟨well prepared for a month's camping trip⟩ **3** : to put together the elements of : COMPOUND ⟨prepare a sauce⟩ ⟨prepare a vaccine⟩

pre·pay \'prē-'pā\ vb **pre·paid** \-'pād\; **pre·pay·ing** : to pay or pay for in advance ⟨prepay the shipping charges⟩

prep·o·si·tion \ˌprep-ə-'zish-ən\ n : a word or expression that combines with a noun or pronoun to form a phrase

prep·o·si·tion·al \ˌprep-ə-'zish-ən-l\ adj : of, relating to, or containing a preposition

pre·pos·ter·ous \pri-'päs-tə-rəs\ adj : contrary to common sense : FOOLISH

pre·req·ui·site \prē-'rek-wə-zət\ n : something that is required beforehand or is necessary as a preliminary to something else

pre·scribe \pri-'skrīb\ vb **pre·scribed; pre·scrib·ing 1** : to lay down as a rule of action : ORDER ⟨prescribe longer hours of rest⟩ **2** : to order or direct the use of as a remedy

pre·scrip·tion \pri-'skrip-shən\ n **1** : a written direction or order for the preparation and use of a medicine **2** : a medicine that is prescribed

pres·ence \'prez-ns\ n **1** : the fact or condition of being present ⟨no one noticed the stranger's presence⟩ **2** : immediate nearness or vicinity of a person ⟨took off his hat in the presence of a lady⟩ **3** : a person's appearance or bearing ⟨a man of noble presence⟩

presence of mind : ability to think clearly and act quickly in an emergency

j job   ng sing   ō low   ȯ moth   ȯi coin   th thin   th this   ü boot   ù foot   y you   yü few   yù furious   zh vision

¹pres·ent \'prez-nt\ *n* : something presented or given : GIFT

²pre·sent \pri-'zent\ *vb* **1** : to introduce one person to another **2** : to take (oneself) into another's presence ⟨*presented* himself before the chairman⟩ **3** : to bring before the public ⟨*present* a play⟩ **4** : to make a gift to **5** : to give as a gift **6** : to offer to view : SHOW, DISPLAY ⟨he *presents* a fine appearance⟩

³pres·ent \'prez-nt\ *adj* **1** : being before a person, in his sight, or near at hand : being at a certain place and not elsewhere **2** : not past or future : now going on **3** : pointing out or relating to time that is not past or future ⟨*present* tense of a verb⟩

pre·sent·a·ble \pri-'zent-ə-bəl\ *adj* : having an acceptable or pleasing appearance

pre·sen·ta·tion \,prē-,zen-'tā-shən, ,prez-n-\ *n* **1** : formal introduction of one person to another **2** : an act of presenting **3** : GIFT

pres·ent·ly \'prez-nt-lē\ *adv* **1** : SOON, SHORTLY **2** : at the present time : NOW ⟨*presently* at work on his second novel⟩

pres·er·va·tion \,prez-ər-'vā-shən\ *n* : a keeping from injury, loss, or decay

¹pre·serve \pri-'zərv\ *vb* **pre·served**; **pre·serv·ing** **1** : to keep or save from injury or ruin : PROTECT **2** : to prepare (as by canning or pickling) fruits or vegetables for keeping ⟨*preserved* peaches⟩ **3** : MAINTAIN ⟨*preserve* silence⟩ — **pre·serv·er** *n*

²preserve *n* **1** : fruit cooked in sugar or made into jam or jelly — often used in plural ⟨strawberry *preserves*⟩ **2** : an area where game or fish are protected

pre·side \pri-'zīd\ *vb* **pre·sid·ed**; **pre·sid·ing** **1** : to act as chairman of a meeting **2** : to exercise guidance or control

pres·i·den·cy \'prez-ə-dən-sē\ *n, pl* **pres·i·den·cies** **1** : the office of president **2** : the term during which a president holds office

pres·i·dent \'prez-ə-dənt\ *n* **1** : one who presides over a meeting **2** : the chief officer of a company or society **3** : the chief executive officer and chief of state of a modern republic

pres·i·den·tial \,prez-ə-'den-chəl\ *adj* : of or relating to a president or presidency

¹press \'pres\ *n* **1** : CROWD, THRONG **2** : a machine for exerting pressure for shaping, flattening, squeezing, or stamping (as for a book) **3** : the act of pressing : PRESSURE **4** : a closet for clothing **5** : a printing or publishing establishment **6** : the newspapers and magazines of a country

press 2

²press *vb* **1** : to bear down upon : push steadily against **2** : FORCE, COMPEL ⟨business *pressed* them to return⟩ **3** : to squeeze so as to force out the juice or contents ⟨*press* oranges⟩ : squeeze out ⟨*press* juice from grapes⟩ **4** : to flatten out or smooth by bearing down upon especially by ironing ⟨*press* clothes⟩ **5** : to request earnestly : urge strongly ⟨*press* someone to go along⟩

press·ing \'pres-ing\ *adj* : URGENT

pres·sure \'presh-ər\ *n* **1** : the action of pressing or bearing down upon : SQUEEZE **2** : a painful feeling : OPPRESSION, DISTRESS **3** : a burdensome force or influence ⟨*pressure* of taxes⟩ **4** : URGENCY ⟨the *pressure* of business⟩ **5** : the force exerted by a body over the surface of another body **6** : the condition of being pressed or of exerting force over a surface

pres·tige \pres-'tēzh\ *n* : importance or estimation in the eyes of people : REPUTE

pres·to \'pres-tō\ *adv* (*or adj*) **1** : QUICKLY, SUDDENLY **2** : at a very fast tempo — used as a direction in music

pre·sume \pri-'züm\ *vb* **pre·sumed**; **pre·sum·ing** **1** : to undertake without leave or right : VENTURE ⟨*presume* to question a judge's decision⟩ **2** : to suppose to be true without proof ⟨*presume* a person innocent until proven guilty⟩ **3** : to act or behave boldly without reason for doing so ⟨*presumed* to advise his superiors⟩

pre·sump·tion \pri-'zəmp-shən\ *n* **1** : presumptuous conduct or attitude **2** : a strong reason for believing something to be so **3** : something believed to be so but not proved

pre·sump·tu·ous \pri-'zəmp-chə-wəs\ *adj* : overstepping due bounds : taking liberties — **pre·sump·tu·ously** *adv* — **pre·sump·tu·ous·ness** *n*

pre·tend \pri-'tend\ *vb* [from Latin *praetendere* "to give as an excuse", literally, "to stretch in front like a curtain", a compound of *prae-* "pre-" and *tendere* "to stretch"] **1** : to make believe : SHAM **2** : to represent falsely : put forward as true something that is not true ⟨*pretend* friendship⟩ — **pre·tend·er** *n*

pre·tense *or* **pre·tence** \'prē-,tens, pri-'tens\ *n* **1** : a claim usually not supported by facts **2** : mere ostentation : PRETENTIOUSNESS ⟨a man free from *pretense*⟩ **3** : AIM, ATTEMPT ⟨no *pretense* at completeness⟩ **4** : false show : pretended action

pre·ten·tious \pri-'ten-chəs\ *adj* : SHOWY, OSTENTATIOUS ⟨a *pretentious* house⟩ — **pre·ten·tious·ly** *adv* — **pre·ten·tious·ness** *n*

¹**pret·ty** \'prit-ē\ *adj* **pret·ti·er; pret·ti·est**
: delicately or gracefully pleasing : attractive
to the eye or ear ⟨a *pretty* face⟩ ⟨a *pretty*
tune⟩ — **pret·ti·ly** \'prit-l-ē\ *adv*

²**pret·ty** \ˌpùrt-ē, ˌprit-ē\ *adv* : in some degree
: FAIRLY ⟨*pretty* good⟩

pret·zel \'pret-səl\ *n* : a brittle, glazed, salted,
and usually twisted cracker

pre·vail \pri-'vāl\ *vb* **1** : to win a victory
: TRIUMPH ⟨*prevailed* over his enemies⟩ **2** : to
urge successfully ⟨he was *prevailed* upon to
play the piano for us⟩ **3** : to be or become
usual, common, or widespread ⟨west winds
prevail in that region⟩

prev·a·lence \'prev-ə-ləns\ *n* : the condition
of being widespread in acceptance, use, or
occurrence

prev·a·lent \'prev-ə-lənt\ *adj* : accepted,
practiced, or occurring often or over a wide
area ⟨colds are *prevalent* in winter⟩

pre·vent \pri-'vent\ *vb* : to keep from happening : HINDER, STOP ⟨help to *prevent* acci-
dents⟩ — **pre·vent·a·ble** \-ə-bəl\ *adj*

pre·ven·tion \pri-'ven-chən\ *n* : the act of
preventing or hindering

pre·vi·ous \'prē-vē-əs\ *adj* : EARLIER, PRE-
CEDING — **pre·vi·ous·ly** *adv*

¹**prey** \'prā\ *n* **1** : an animal hunted or
killed by another animal for food **2** : a person that is helpless and unable to resist attack : VICTIM **3** : the act or habit of seizing
or pouncing upon ⟨birds of *prey*⟩

²**prey** *vb* **1** : to seize and devour something
as prey ⟨dogs *preying* on small game⟩ **2** : to
have a harmful or wasting effect ⟨fears
preyed upon his mind⟩

¹**price** \'prīs\ *n* **1** : the quantity of one thing
given or demanded for something else : the
amount of money paid or to be paid **2** : RE-
WARD **3** : the cost at which something is obtained or done ⟨win a victory at the *price* of
many lives⟩

syn PRICE, CHARGE, COST all mean the amount
asked or given in payment for something.
PRICE usually refers to what is asked for goods
⟨the *price* of wheat⟩ and CHARGE to what is
asked for services ⟨no delivery *charge*⟩ and
both are normally stated in terms of specific
units (as of weight or time) ⟨the *price* is a
dollar a pound⟩ ⟨the *charge* for baby-sitting
went up to fifty cents an hour⟩ COST is usually
used to state what is paid for something by
the buyer rather than what is asked by the
seller ⟨the *cost* of our dinner seemed unusually
high⟩ and may be used to mean the total of a
large number of individual expenses ⟨the
cost of the trip⟩ ⟨the *cost* of living⟩

²**price** *vb* **priced; pric·ing 1** : to set a price on
2 : to ask the price of

price·less \'prīs-ləs\ *adj* : too valuable to
have a price : not to be bought at any price

¹**prick** \'prik\ *n* **1** : a mark or small wound
made by a pointed instrument : POINT, DOT
⟨the *prick* of a pin⟩ **2** : something sharp or
pointed **3** : a sensation of being pricked

²**prick** *vb* **1** : to pierce slightly with a sharp
point **2** : to have or to cause a feeling of or
as if of being pricked : SMART, TINGLE **3** : to
urge on a horse by spurs **4** : to point upward
⟨the horse *pricked* up his ears⟩

prick·er \'prik-ər\ *n* : PRICKLE, THORN

¹**prick·le** \'prik-əl\ *n* **1** : a small sharp point
: THORN, SPINE **2** : a slight stinging pain

²**prickle** *vb* **prick·led; prick·ling** : TINGLE,
PRICK

prick·ly \'prik-lē\ *adj* **prick·li·er; prick·li·est**
1 : having prickles ⟨a *prickly* cactus⟩ **2** : PRICK-
ING, STINGING ⟨a *prickly* sensation⟩

prickly pear *n* : a branching flat-jointed
usually spiny cactus that has a
pulpy pear-shaped edible fruit

¹**pride** \'prīd\ *n* **1** : too high
an opinion of one's own ability
or worth : a feeling of being better than others **2** : a reasonable
and justifiable sense of one's
own worth : SELF-RESPECT ⟨*pride*
in doing good work⟩ **3** : a sense
of pleasure that comes from some

prickly pear

act or possession ⟨takes *pride* in his son's
high marks⟩ **4** : something of which one is
proud

²**pride** *vb* **prid·ed; prid·ing** : to rate (oneself)
highly ⟨*prided* herself on her apple pies⟩

priest \'prēst\ *n* : a person who has the authority to conduct religious rites

priest·ess \'prēs-təs\ *n* : a female priest

prim \'prim\ *adj* **prim·mer; prim·mest** : very
particular about one's appearance or conduct
: very neat or precise

pri·mar·i·ly \prī-'mer-ə-lē\ *adv* : in the first
place

¹**pri·mar·y** \'prī-ˌmer-ē, -mə-rē\ *adj* **1** : first
in time or development ⟨the *primary* grades⟩
2 : most important : PRINCIPAL ⟨*primary*
duties⟩ **3** : not made or derived from something else : BASIC ⟨*primary* road⟩ **4** : of, relating to, or being the strongest of three degrees of stress

²**primary** *n, pl* **pri·mar·ies** : an election in
which members of a political party nominate
candidates for office

primary color *n* : any of a set of colors from
which all other colors may be produced with

the colors for light being red, green, and blue and for pigments or paint being red, yellow, and blue

pri·mate \'prī-ˌmāt\ *n* : any of a group of mammals that includes man together with the apes and monkeys and a few related forms

¹prime \'prīm\ *n* 1 : the first part : the earliest stage 2 : the period in life when a person is best in health, looks, or strength ⟨a man in his *prime*⟩ 3 : the best individual or part ⟨the *prime* of the flock⟩

²prime *adj* 1 : first in time : ORIGINAL ⟨*prime* cost⟩ 2 : having no factor except itself and one ⟨3 is a *prime* number⟩ 3 : first in importance, rank, or quality ⟨*prime* beef⟩

³prime *vb* **primed**; **prim·ing** 1 : to put into working order by priming or filling ⟨*prime* a pump⟩ 2 : to instruct beforehand : COACH ⟨*prime* a witness⟩ 3 : to apply a first color, coating, or preparation to (an unpainted surface)

prime minister *n* : the chief officer of the government in some countries : PREMIER

¹prim·er \'prim-ər\ *n* 1 : a small book for teaching children to read 2 : a book of first instructions on a subject

²prim·er \'prī-mər\ *n* 1 : a device (as a cap) for setting off an explosive charge 2 : a priming coat or application

pri·me·val \prī-'mē-vəl\ *adj* : belonging to the first ages : PRIMITIVE ⟨a *primeval* forest⟩

prim·i·tive \'prim-ət-iv\ *adj* 1 : of or belonging to very early times ⟨*primitive* men⟩ 2 : resembling or representing early times in simplicity or crudeness ⟨*primitive* weapons⟩

primp \'primp\ *vb* : to dress, adorn, or arrange in a careful or finicky manner

prim·rose \'prim-ˌrōz\ *n* : a perennial plant six to eight inches tall with large leaves growing from the base of the stem and showy often yellow or pink flowers

primrose

prince \'prins\ *n* [from Old French *prince*, a modification of Latin *princeps*, literally, "one who takes the first part", from *primus* "first" (source of English *prime* and *primer*) and *capere* "to take"] 1 : a sovereign ruler : MONARCH 2 : a nobleman of very high or the highest rank 3 : the son of a king

prin·cess \'prin-səs, -ˌses\ *n* : a daughter or granddaughter of a monarch : a female member of a royal family

¹prin·ci·pal \'prin-sə-pəl\ *adj* : highest in rank or importance : CHIEF ⟨the *principal* act in the show⟩ — **prin·ci·pal·ly** *adv*

²principal *n* 1 : a leading or most important person or thing 2 : the head of a school 3 : a sum of money placed so as to earn interest, owed as a debt, or used as a fund

prin·ci·pal·i·ty \ˌprin-sə-'pal-ət-ē\ *n*, *pl* **prin·ci·pal·i·ties** : a small territory that is ruled by a prince or gives a prince his title ⟨the *principality* of Monaco⟩

principal parts *n pl* : the present infinitive, past tense, and past participle of an English verb

prin·ci·ple \'prin-sə-pəl\ *n* 1 : a general or fundamental truth that is the basis of other truths or theories ⟨scientific *principles*⟩ 2 : a rule of conduct ⟨a man of high *principles*⟩ 3 : a law or fact of nature which underlies the working of a machine or device ⟨the *principle* of magnetism⟩ ⟨the *principle* of the lever⟩

¹print \'print\ *n* 1 : a mark made by pressure 2 : a stamp or die for molding 3 : something which has been stamped with an impression ⟨a *print* of butter⟩ 4 : printed matter 5 : printed letters ⟨clear *print*⟩ 6 : a picture, copy, or design taken from an engraving or photographic negative 7 : cloth upon which a design is stamped ⟨a cotton *print*⟩

²print *vb* 1 : to put, stamp, or impress in or on : mark with a print 2 : to produce impressions from an inked surface (as of type or engraved plates) 3 : to publish in printed form ⟨*print* a newspaper⟩ 4 : to stamp with a design by pressure ⟨*print* wallpaper⟩ 5 : to write in separate letters like those made by a printing press 6 : to make (a positive picture) from a photographic negative

print·er \'print-ər\ *n* : a person whose business is printing

print·ing \'print-ing\ *n* 1 : reproduction in printed form 2 : the art, practice, or business of a printer

printing press *n* : a machine that produces printed copies automatically

¹pri·or \'prī-ər\ *n* : the head of a priory of monks

²prior *adj* 1 : being or happening before something else 2 : taking priority in importance or value

pri·or·ess \'prī-ə-rəs\ *n* : a nun corresponding in rank to a prior

pri·or·i·ty \prī-'òr-ət-ē\ *n*, *pl* **pri·or·i·ties** 1 : the quality or state of coming before another in time or importance 2 : the possession of first place or of certain rights or advantages over others

prior to *prep* : in advance of : BEFORE

pri·o·ry \'prī-ə-rē\ *n*, *pl* **pri·o·ries** : a religious house under a prior or prioress

prism \'priz-əm\ *n* : a transparent usually three-sided object that bends light and breaks it up into rainbow colors

pris·on \'priz-n\ *n* : a place of involuntary confinement especially for criminals

prism

pris·on·er \'priz-n-ər\ *n* : a person held under restraint or in prison or captured in war

pri·va·cy \'prī-və-sē\ *n, pl* **pri·va·cies** 1 : the condition of being out of sight and hearing of all other people 2 : SECRECY ⟨talk together in *privacy*⟩

¹**pri·vate** \'prī-vət\ *adj* 1 : having to do with or for the use of a single person, company, or special group : not public ⟨*private* property⟩ 2 : not holding any public office ⟨a *private* citizen⟩ 3 : SECRET ⟨*private* meetings⟩ — **pri·vate·ly** *adv* — **pri·vate·ness** *n*

²**private** *n* : an enlisted man in the army ranking next below a private first class — **in private** : SECRETLY

pri·va·teer \ˌprī-və-'tiər\ *n* 1 : an armed private ship permitted by its government to make war on ships of an enemy country 2 : a sailor on a privateer

private first class *n* : an enlisted man in the army ranking next below a corporal

priv·et \'priv-ət\ *n* : a white-flowered shrub related to the lilac that is often used for hedges

priv·i·lege \'priv-ə-lij\ *n* : a right or liberty granted as a favor or benefit especially to some and not others

priv·i·leged \'priv-ə-lijd\ *adj* : having one or more privileges ⟨*privileged* classes of society⟩

¹**prize** \'prīz\ *n* 1 : something won or to be won in a competition 2 : something unusually valuable or eagerly sought

²**prize** *adj* 1 : awarded a prize ⟨a *prize* essay⟩ 2 : worthy of a prize : OUTSTANDING ⟨a *prize* student⟩ ⟨a *prize* fool⟩

³**prize** *vb* **prized; priz·ing** 1 : to estimate the value of : RATE 2 : to value highly ⟨*prize* a picture⟩

⁴**prize** *n* : something taken (as in war) by force especially at sea : BOOTY

prize·fight·er \'prīz-ˌfīt-ər\ *n* : a professional boxer

¹**pro** \'prō\ *adv* : on the affirmative side : FOR ⟨argue *pro* and con⟩

²**pro** *n or adj* : PROFESSIONAL

¹**pro-** *prefix* : located in front of or at the front of : front ⟨*pro*thorax⟩

²**pro-** *prefix* 1 : taking the place of : substituting for ⟨*pro*cathedral⟩ 2 : favoring : supporting : championing ⟨*pro*-American⟩

prob·a·bil·i·ty \ˌpräb-ə-'bil-ət-ē\ *n, pl* **prob·a·bil·i·ties** 1 : the quality or condition of being probable : LIKELIHOOD 2 : something probable or likely

prob·a·ble \'präb-ə-bəl\ *adj* : reasonably sure but not certain of happening or being true : LIKELY

syn PROBABLE, POSSIBLE, LIKELY all refer to something that may or may not be real or true. PROBABLE is used of something that seems so reasonable or has behind it so much evidence that one tends to accept it without absolute proof ⟨no will has been found, but the son is the *probable* heir⟩ ⟨the weather report said rain is *probable*⟩ POSSIBLE is used of something that is conceivable but that presents no particular case for being believed, supported, or considered ⟨it's *possible* that humanlike life exists on Mars⟩ ⟨we thought of several *possible* explanations for his odd behavior⟩ LIKELY is normally applied to what falls between the other two; it suggests too little support or evidence to term something probable but enough so that it is more than just a possibility ⟨it is not *likely* that any life exists on Mars⟩ ⟨the *likely* outcome of this fight is two crying children⟩

prob·a·bly \'präb-ə-blē\ *adv* : in all likelihood : very likely

pro·ba·tion \prō-'bā-shən\ *n* : a period of trial for finding out or testing a person's character or fitness

¹**probe** \'prōb\ *n* 1 : a slender instrument for examining a cavity (as a deep wound) 2 : an investigation to discover evidence of wrongdoing

probe 1

²**probe** *vb* **probed; prob·ing** 1 : to examine with or as if with a probe 2 : INVESTIGATE, EXPLORE

prob·lem \'präb-ləm\ *n* 1 : something to be worked out or solved ⟨a *problem* in arithmetic⟩ 2 : a question, matter, or person that is hard to understand or deal with

pro·bos·cis \prə-'bäs-əs\ *n* : a long flexible hollow bodily process (as the trunk of an elephant or the beak of a mosquito)

proboscis

pro·ce·dure \prə-'sē-jər\ *n* 1 : the manner or method in which a business or action is carried on 2 : an action or series of actions : PROCEEDING ⟨the *procedure* of swearing in a club member⟩

pro·ceed \prō-'sēd\ *vb* 1 : to go forward or

onward : ADVANCE   **2** : to come forth from a source ⟨light *proceeds* from the sun⟩   **3** : to go or act by an orderly method ⟨*proceed* according to plan⟩

pro·ceed·ing \prō-'sēd-ing\ *n*   **1** *pl* : EVENTS, HAPPENINGS   **2** : a suit or action at law — usually used in plural

pro·ceeds \'prō-ˌsēdz\ *n pl* : the money or profit that comes from a business venture

¹proc·ess \'präs-ˌes\ *n*   **1** : PROGRESS, ADVANCE ⟨the *process* of time⟩   **2** : a series of actions, motions, or operations leading to some result ⟨a *process* of manufacture⟩   **3** : a projecting part : OUTGROWTH ⟨a bony *process* on the elbow⟩

²process *vb* : to subject to a special process or treatment ⟨*process* cheese⟩

pro·ces·sion \prə-'sesh-ən\ *n*   **1** : continuous forward movement : PROGRESSION   **2** : a group of individuals moving along in an orderly often ceremonial way ⟨a funeral *procession*⟩

pro·claim \prō-'klām\ *vb* : to announce publicly : DECLARE ⟨*proclaim* a holiday⟩

proc·la·ma·tion \ˌpräk-lə-'mā-shən\ *n*   **1** : the act of proclaiming   **2** : something proclaimed

pro·cure \prə-'kyùr\ *vb* **pro·cured; pro·cur·ing**   **1** : to get possession of : OBTAIN   **2** : to bring about or cause to be done ⟨*procured* his friend's release from jail⟩

¹prod \'präd\ *vb* **prod·ded; prod·ding**   **1** : to thrust a pointed thing into : poke or prick with something sharp or blunt   **2** : to arouse a person or animal to action

²prod *n*   **1** : a pointed instrument for prodding   **2** : an act of prodding   **3** : a sharp urging or reminder

¹prod·i·gal \'präd-i-gəl\ *adj* : recklessly wasteful ⟨a *prodigal* spender⟩

²prodigal *n* : SPENDTHRIFT

prod·i·gy \'präd-ə-jē\ *n, pl* **prod·i·gies**   **1** : an amazing deed or performance : WONDER   **2** : an unusually gifted or precocious child

¹pro·duce \prə-'düs, -'dyüs\ *vb* **pro·duced; pro·duc·ing**   **1** : to bring to view : EXHIBIT ⟨*produce* more evidence⟩   **2** : to bring forth : YIELD   **3** : MAKE, MANUFACTURE ⟨a city that *produces* steel⟩   **4** : to prepare (as a play) for public presentation — **pro·duc·er** *n*

²prod·uce \'präd-ˌüs, 'prōd-, -ˌyüs\ *n*   **1** : something produced   **2** : fresh fruits and vegetables

prod·uct \'präd-əkt\ *n*   **1** : something produced by manufacture, labor, thought, or growth   **2** : the number resulting from the multiplication of two or more numbers ⟨the *product* of 3 and 5 is 15⟩

pro·duc·tion \prə-'dək-shən\ *n*   **1** : the act of producing ⟨*production* of cars⟩   **2** : something produced ⟨a television *production* of a play⟩   **3** : total output ⟨annual *production* of coal⟩

pro·duc·tive \prə-'dək-tiv\ *adj*   **1** : having the power to produce plentifully : FERTILE ⟨*productive* soil⟩   **2** : producing something ⟨an age *productive* of great men⟩

¹pro·fane \prō-'fān\ *vb* **pro·faned; pro·fan·ing**   **1** : to violate or treat with irreverence, abuse, or contempt   **2** : to put to a wrong, unworthy, or vulgar use — **pro·fan·er** *n*

²profane *adj*   **1** : not holy or sacred : not concerned with or suitable for religious purposes ⟨*profane* history⟩   **2** : using or marked by oaths : SWEARING ⟨*profane* language⟩ — **pro·fane·ly** *adv* — **pro·fane·ness** *n*

pro·fan·i·ty \prō-'fan-ət-ē\ *n, pl* **pro·fan·i·ties** : profane language

pro·fess \prə-'fes\ *vb*   **1** : to declare openly one's own beliefs or actions ⟨*profess* confidence in a person⟩   **2** : PRETEND, CLAIM ⟨*professed* to be a gentleman⟩

pro·fes·sion \prə-'fesh-ən\ *n*   **1** : an open declaration or claim ⟨a *profession* of religious faith⟩   **2** : an occupation (as medicine, law, or teaching) that is not mechanical or agricultural and that requires special education   **3** : the people engaged in a profession   **syn** see TRADE

pro·fes·sion·al \prə-'fesh-ən-l\ *adj*   **1** : of, relating to, or characteristic of a profession   **2** : engaging in an occupation (as a sport) for money — **pro·fes·sion·al·ly** *adv*

pro·fes·sor \prə-'fes-ər\ *n* : a teacher especially of the highest academic rank at a college or university

prof·fer \'präf-ər\ *vb* : OFFER

pro·fi·cient \prə-'fish-ənt\ *adj* : SKILLED, EXPERT ⟨a *proficient* pianist⟩ — **pro·fi·cient·ly** *adv*

pro·file \'prō-ˌfīl\ *n* : the outline of a thing (as a head) seen or drawn from the side

¹prof·it \'präf-ət\ *n*   **1** : the gain, advantage, or benefit from something ⟨study something with *profit*⟩   **2** : the gain after all the expenses are subtracted from the total amount received ⟨a business that shows a *profit* of $100 a week⟩ — **prof·it·less** \-ləs\ *adj*

²profit *vb*   **1** : to derive benefit : GAIN ⟨*profit* by experience⟩   **2** : BENEFIT ⟨a business deal that *profited* no one⟩

prof·it·a·ble \'präf-ət-ə-bəl\ *adj* : yielding profit : USEFUL   **syn** see BENEFICIAL — **prof·it·a·bly** \-blē\ *adv*

pro·found \prə-'faùnd\ *adj*   **1** : very scholarly or intellectual ⟨a *profound* thinker⟩   **2** : very deep : INTENSE ⟨*profound* sorrow⟩ — **pro-found·ly** *adv* — **pro·found·ness** *n*

pro·fuse \prə-'fyüs\ *adj* : very generous : BOUNTIFUL, LAVISH — **pro·fuse·ly** *adv* — **pro·fuse·ness** *n*

pro·fu·sion \prə-'fyü-zhən\ *n* : lavish supply : ABUNDANCE, PLENTY

prog·e·ny \'präj-ə-nē\ *n, pl* **prog·e·nies** : DE-SCENDANTS, OFFSPRING

pro·gram \'prō-ˌgram, -grəm\ *n* **1** : a brief statement or written outline (as of a concert or play) **2** : PERFORMANCE ⟨a television *program*⟩ **3** : a plan of action

¹prog·ress \'präg-rəs, -ˌres\ *n* **1** : movement forward : ADVANCE ⟨a ship's *progress*⟩ **2** : gradual betterment

²pro·gress \prə-'gres\ *vb* **1** : to move forward : ADVANCE ⟨the story *progresses*⟩ **2** : to develop to a higher, better, or more advanced stage : IMPROVE

pro·gres·sion \prə-'gresh-ən\ *n* **1** : the act of progressing or moving forward **2** : a continuous and connected series (as of acts, events, or steps)

pro·gres·sive \prə-'gres-iv\ *adj* **1** : of, relating to, or characterized by progress ⟨a *progressive* city⟩ **2** : taking place gradually or step by step ⟨*progressive* erosion of the soil⟩ **3** : of, relating to, or favoring moderate political change and social improvement by governmental action — **pro·gres·sive·ly** *adv* — **pro·gres·sive·ness** *n*

pro·hib·it \prō-'hib-ət\ *vb* **1** : to forbid by law or authority ⟨parking *prohibited*⟩ **2** : to make impossible ⟨the high walls *prohibit* escape⟩

pro·hi·bi·tion \ˌprō-ə-'bish-ən\ *n* **1** : the act of prohibiting something **2** : the forbidding by law of the sale or manufacture of alcoholic liquids as beverages

¹proj·ect \'präj-ˌekt, -ikt\ *n* **1** : a specific plan or scheme **2** : a task or problem in school **3** : a group of houses or apartment buildings built and arranged according to a single plan and especially one built with government help to provide low-cost housing

²pro·ject \prə-'jekt\ *vb* **1** : to cause to fall on a surface ⟨*project* motion pictures on a screen⟩ ⟨*project* a shadow on the wall⟩ **2** : to jut out : stick out ⟨a rock that *projects* above the ground⟩

pro·jec·tile \prə-'jek-təl\ *n* : a thing (as a bullet, cannon shell, or rocket) that is thrown or driven forward with great force especially from a weapon

pro·jec·tion \prə-'jek-shən\ *n* **1** : something that projects or sticks out **2** : the act or

process of projecting on a surface (as by means of motion pictures or slides)

pro·jec·tor \prə-'jek-tər\ *n* : a machine for projecting images on a screen

pro·lif·ic \prə-'lif-ik\ *adj* : producing young or fruit abundantly : PRODUCTIVE

pro·logue \'prō-ˌlóg\ *n* **1** : the preface or introduction to a story, poem, or performance **2** : an act or event that serves as an introduction

pro·long \prə-'lóng\ *vb* : to make a thing longer than usual : continue or lengthen in time ⟨*prolong* a person's life⟩

prom·e·nade \ˌpräm-ə-'nād, -'näd\ *n* **1** : a walk or ride for pleasure, display, or exercise **2** : a place for walking **3** : a grand march serving to open a formal ball

prom·i·nence \'präm-ə-nəns\ *n* **1** : the quality, condition, or fact of being prominent : DISTINCTION ⟨a person of *prominence*⟩ **2** : something (as a mountain) that is prominent

prom·i·nent \'präm-ə-nənt\ *adj* **1** : sticking out beyond the surface : PROJECTING **2** : attracting attention (as by size or position) : CONSPICUOUS ⟨his tiny eyes are his most *prominent* feature⟩ **3** : WELL-KNOWN, DISTINGUISHED *syn* see NOTICEABLE — **prom·i·nent·ly** *adv*

¹prom·ise \'präm-əs\ *n* **1** : a statement assuring someone that the person making the statement will do or not do something ⟨a *promise* to pay within a month⟩ **2** : a cause or ground for hope ⟨these plans give *promise* of success⟩

²promise *vb* **prom·ised; prom·is·ing** **1** : to give a promise about one's own actions ⟨*promise* to pay within a month⟩ **2** : to assure someone about a thing that does not depend on one's own actions ⟨the people will come, I *promise* you⟩ **3** : to suggest beforehand ⟨the clouds *promise* rain⟩

prom·is·ing \'präm-ə-sing\ *adj* : full of promise : giving hope or assurance (as of success) ⟨a very *promising* pupil⟩

prom·on·to·ry \'präm-ən-ˌtōr-ē\ *n, pl* **prom·on·to·ries** : a high point of land jutting out into the sea

pro·mote \prə-'mōt\ *vb* **pro·mot·ed; pro·mot·ing** **1** : to advance in position or rank **2** : to help the growth or development of ⟨good food *promotes* health⟩

pro·mo·tion \prə-'mō-shən\ *n* **1** : advance in position or rank ⟨*promotion* to a higher grade in school⟩ **2** : the helping of the growth or development of something

¹prompt \'prämpt\ *vb* **1** : to move to action ⟨curiosity *prompted* him to ask the question⟩

2 : to remind of something forgotten or poorly learned ⟨*prompt* an actor⟩ 3 : SUGGEST, INSPIRE ⟨pride *prompted* the act⟩

²**prompt** *adj* 1 : quick and ready to act ⟨*prompt* to answer⟩ 2 : being on time : PUNCTUAL ⟨*prompt* in arriving⟩ 3 : done at once : given without delay ⟨*prompt* assistance⟩ — **prompt·ly** *adv* — **prompt·ness** *n*

prone \'prōn\ *adj* 1 : having a tendency or inclination : DISPOSED ⟨*prone* to laziness⟩ 2 : lying belly or face downward ⟨*prone* on the floor⟩ 3 : flattened out on a surface ⟨the wind blew the trees *prone*⟩ — **prone·ness** *n*

prong \'prȯng\ *n* 1 : one of the sharp points or tines of a fork 2 : a slender projecting part (as a point of an antler)

prong·horn \'prȯng-ˌhȯrn\ *n* : a cud-chewing animal of the treeless parts of the western United States and Mexico that resembles an antelope

pronghorn

pro·noun \'prō-ˌnaun\ *n* : a word used as a substitute for a noun

pro·nounce \prə-'nauns\ *vb* **pro·nounced; pro·nounc·ing** 1 : to utter officially or solemnly : DECLARE ⟨the minister *pronounced* them man and wife⟩ 2 : to speak aloud especially clearly and correctly

syn PRONOUNCE, ENUNCIATE both mean to form or utter the sounds of speech. PRONOUNCE has to do chiefly with how the sounds given to a word relate to the spelling or to the sounds of other words in the language ⟨*colonel* is *pronounced* as if it were spelled *kernel*⟩ ⟨he *pronounces* the word *deaf* to rhyme with *leaf*, not with *clef*⟩ ENUNCIATE has to do with the speech sounds actually produced by a particular speaker and especially with the distinctness of these sounds ⟨actors learn to *enunciate* very distinctly without sounding unnatural or artificial⟩

pro·nounced \prə-'naunst\ *adj* : strongly marked : DECIDED

pro·nun·ci·a·tion \prə-ˌnən-sē-'ā-shən\ *n* : the act or manner of pronouncing a word or words

¹**proof** \'prüf\ *n* 1 : evidence of truth or correctness ⟨find *proof* of a statement⟩ 2 : the means by which something is proved : TEST, TRIAL 3 : an impression (as from type) taken for correction or examination 4 : a test made from a photographic negative

²**proof** *adj* : having or marked by defenses or resistance ⟨*proof* against tampering⟩

proof·read \'prüf-ˌrēd\ *vb* **proof·read** \-ˌred\; **proof·read·ing** \-ˌrēd-ing\ : to read and make corrections (as in printer's proof)

¹**prop** \'präp\ *n* : something that props or sustains : SUPPORT

²**prop** *vb* **propped; prop·ping** 1 : to keep from falling or slipping by placing a support under or against 2 : to give help, encouragement, or support to

prop·a·gan·da \ˌpräp-ə-'gan-də\ *n* : an organized spreading of certain ideas or the ideas spread in such a way

prop·a·gate \'präp-ə-ˌgāt\ *vb* **prop·a·gat·ed; prop·a·gat·ing** 1 : to have or cause to have offspring : REPRODUCE, MULTIPLY ⟨*propagate* a winter apple by grafting⟩ 2 : to cause (as an idea or belief) to spread out and affect a greater number or wider area ⟨*propagate* a faith⟩

prop·a·ga·tion \ˌpräp-ə-'gā-shən\ *n* : an act or process of propagating

pro·pel \prə-'pel\ *vb* **pro·pelled; pro·pel·ling** : to push or drive usually forward or onward ⟨*propel* a bicycle⟩

pro·pel·ler \prə-'pel-ər\ *n* : a device consisting of a hub fitted with blades that is made to revolve rapidly by an engine and that drives a ship, power boat, or airplane

prop·er \'präp-ər\ *adj* 1 : belonging naturally to something : SPECIAL ⟨every animal has its *proper* instincts⟩ 2 : considered in an exact and accurate sense ⟨England *proper* is about the size of Pennsylvania⟩ 3 : SUITABLE, RIGHT ⟨the *proper* pay for the job⟩ 4 : obeying the social rules ⟨*proper* conduct⟩

proper fraction *n* : a fraction in which the numerator is smaller than the denominator

prop·er·ly \'präp-ər-lē\ *adv* 1 : in a fit or suitable way : in a proper manner 2 : according to fact : CORRECTLY

prop·er·ty \'präp-ərt-ē\ *n, pl* **prop·er·ties** 1 : a special quality or characteristic of a thing ⟨sweetness is a *property* of sugar⟩ 2 : something (as land, goods, or money) that is owned ⟨that chair is my aunt's *property*⟩ 3 : an article other than the artificial scenery and the costumes used on the stage during a play or on the set of a motion picture

proph·e·cy \'präf-ə-sē\ *n, pl* **proph·e·cies** 1 : the sayings of a prophet 2 : something foretold : PREDICTION

proph·e·sy \'präf-ə-ˌsī\ *vb* **proph·e·sied; proph·e·sy·ing** 1 : to speak or write as a prophet 2 : FORETELL, PREDICT

proph·et \'präf-ət\ *n* 1 : a person who declares publicly a message that he believes has been divinely inspired 2 : one who prophesies or predicts the future

pro·phet·ic \prə-'fet-ik\ *adj* : of or relating to a prophet or prophecy

¹pro·por·tion \prə-'pōr-shən\ *n* **1** : the size, number, or amount of one thing or group of things as compared to the size, number, or amount of another thing or group of things ⟨the *proportion* of boys to girls in our class is three to one⟩ **2** *pl* : the length and width or length, breadth, and height : DIMENSIONS ⟨the *proportions* of this room are very good⟩ **3** : a balanced or pleasing arrangement ⟨out of *proportion*⟩ **4** : fair or just share ⟨each did his *proportion* of the work⟩ **5** : a statement of the equality of two ratios (as 4/2 = 10/5)

²proportion *vb* **1** : to adjust (a part or thing) in size relative to other parts or things **2** : to make the parts of harmonious or symmetrical

pro·por·tion·ate \prə-'pōr-shə-nət\ *adj* : being in proportion to something else — **pro·por·tion·ate·ly** *adv*

pro·pos·al \prə-'pō-zəl\ *n* **1** : a proposing or setting forth for consideration **2** : something proposed : PLAN **3** : an offer of marriage

pro·pose \prə-'pōz\ *vb* **pro·posed**; **pro·pos·ing** **1** : to offer for consideration or discussion : SUGGEST **2** : to make plans : INTEND ⟨*propose* to buy a new house⟩ **3** : NAME, NOMINATE ⟨*propose* someone for membership in the club⟩ **4** : to make an offer of marriage

prop·o·si·tion \ˌpräp-ə-'zish-ən\ *n* **1** : something proposed : PROPOSAL **2** : a statement to be proved, explained, or discussed

pro·pri·e·tor \prə-'prī-ət-ər\ *n* : a person who holds something as his property or possession : OWNER

pro·pri·e·ty \prə-'prī-ət-ē\ *n*, *pl* **pro·pri·e·ties** **1** : the quality or state of being proper **2** : correctness in manners or behavior ⟨behave with *propriety*⟩ **3** *pl* : the rules and customs of good or polite society

pro·pul·sion \prə-'pəl-shən\ *n* **1** : the act or process of propelling **2** : something that propels : a driving or operating power

prose \'prōz\ *n* : the ordinary language of men in speaking or writing

pros·e·cute \'präs-i-ˌkyüt\ *vb* **pros·e·cut·ed**; **pros·e·cut·ing** **1** : to follow up to the end : keep at : persist in ⟨*prosecute* a war⟩ **2** : to seek to punish through an appeal to the courts : carry on a legal action against an accused person to prove his guilt

pros·e·cu·tion \ˌpräs-i-'kyü-shən\ *n* **1** : the act of prosecuting especially a criminal suit in court **2** : the party bringing charges of crime or serious misdeeds against a person being tried **3** : the state's lawyers in a criminal case

pros·e·cu·tor \'präs-i-ˌkyüt-ər\ *n* : a person who prosecutes especially a criminal case as lawyer for the state

¹pros·pect \'präs-ˌpekt\ *n* **1** : a wide view ⟨a *prospect* of sea and land⟩ **2** : the act of looking forward **3** : a mental vision of something to come **4** : something that is awaited or expected : probable or possible result **5** : a likely candidate or a potential buyer or customer

²prospect *vb* : to explore especially for mineral deposits

pro·spec·tive \prə-'spek-tiv, 'präs-ˌpek-\ *adj* **1** : likely to come about : EXPECTED ⟨*prospective* benefits⟩ **2** : likely to be or become ⟨a *prospective* bride⟩ — **pro·spec·tive·ly** *adv*

pros·pec·tor \'präs-ˌpek-tər\ *n* : one who explores a region in search of valuable deposits (as of metals or oil)

pros·per \'präs-pər\ *vb* **1** : to succeed especially financially **2** : FLOURISH, THRIVE

pros·per·i·ty \präs-'per-ət-ē\ *n* : the state of being prosperous or successful

pros·per·ous \'präs-pə-rəs\ *adj* **1** : marked by success or economic good fortune **2** : FLOURISHING, THRIVING — **pros·per·ous·ly** *adv*

pros·the·sis \präs-'thē-səs\ *n*, *pl* **pros·the·ses** \-ˌsēz\ : an artificial device used to replace a missing part of the body

¹pros·trate \'präs-ˌtrāt\ *adj* **1** : stretched out with face on the ground **2** : extended in a horizontal position : FLAT ⟨a *prostrate* shrub⟩ **3** : laid low : weak and powerless as though overthrown ⟨*prostrate* with a cold⟩

²prostrate *vb* **pros·trat·ed**; **pros·trat·ing** **1** : to throw or put into a prostrate position **2** : to bring to a weak and powerless condition

pro·tect \prə-'tekt\ *vb* : to cover or shield from something that would destroy or injure : GUARD **syn** see DEFEND

pro·tec·tion \prə-'tek-shən\ *n* **1** : the act of protecting : the state of being protected **2** : a protecting person or thing

pro·tec·tive \prə-'tek-tiv\ *adj* : giving or intended to give protection — **pro·tec·tive·ly** *adv* — **pro·tec·tive·ness** *n*

pro·tec·tor \prə-'tek-tər\ *n* : one that protects or is designed to protect

pro·tein \'prō-ˌtēn\ *n* : a nitrogen-containing nutrient that is found in all living plant or animal cells, is a necessary element in diet, and is supplied especially by such foods as meat, milk, or eggs

¹pro·test \'prō-ˌtest\ *n* **1** : the act of protesting **2** : a complaint or objection against an idea, an act, or a course of action

²pro·test \prə-'test\ *vb* **1** : to declare positively : ASSERT ⟨the accused man *protested* his innocence⟩ **2** : to object strongly : make a protest against ⟨the boys *protested* the umpire's decision⟩

¹Prot·es·tant \'prät-əs-tənt\ *n* : a member of one of most Christian churches other than the Eastern Orthodox Church and the Roman Catholic Church

²Protestant *adj* : of or relating to Protestants

pro·ton \'prō-,tän\ *n* : a very small particle that occurs in the nucleus of every atom and has a positive charge of electricity

pro·to·plasm \'prōt-ə-,plaz-əm\ *n* : the complex usually colorless and jellylike living part of cells

pro·to·zo·an \,prōt-ə-'zō-ən\ *n* : any of a large group of mostly microscopic animals whose body consists of a single cell

pro·to·zo·on \,prōt-ə-'zō-,än\ *n, pl* **pro·to·zo·a** \-'zō-ə\ : PROTOZOAN

pro·tract \prō-'trakt\ *vb* : to make longer : draw out in time or space

pro·trude \prō-'trüd\ *vb* **pro·trud·ed; pro·trud·ing** : to stick out : jut out : PROJECT

proud \'praùd\ *adj* **1** : having or showing a feeling that one is better than others : HAUGHTY **2** : having a feeling of delight or satisfaction : highly pleased ⟨the father was *proud* of his heroic son⟩ **3** : having proper self-respect ⟨too *proud* to beg⟩ **4** : GLORIOUS ⟨a *proud* occasion⟩ — **proud·ly** *adv*

prove \'prüv\ *vb* **proved; proved** *or* **prov·en** \'prü-vən\; **prov·ing** **1** : to test by experiment or by a standard **2** : to convince others of the truth of something by argument or evidence **3** : to show to be genuine **4** : to test the answer to and to check the means of solving an arithmetic problem

prov·erb \'präv-,ərb\ *n* : a brief popular saying expressing a wise thought : MAXIM, ADAGE ⟨"all work and no play makes Jack a dull boy" is a *proverb*⟩

pro·ver·bi·al \prə-'vər-bē-əl\ *adj* : of, relating to, or of the nature of a proverb — **pro·ver·bi·al·ly** *adv*

pro·vide \prə-'vīd\ *vb* **pro·vid·ed; pro·vid·ing** **1** : to look out for in advance : take measures beforehand ⟨*provide* for a rainy day⟩ **2** : SUPPLY ⟨well *provided* with books⟩ **3** : to make as a condition ⟨the rules *provide* that all players must do good work in school⟩

pro·vid·ed \prə-'vīd-əd\ *conj* : IF ⟨we'll go *provided* it doesn't rain⟩

prov·i·dence \'präv-ə-dəns\ *n* **1** *often cap* : divine guidance or care **2** *cap* : God as the guide and protector of all human beings **3** : an instance of divine help **4** : PRUDENCE, THRIFT

prov·ince \'präv-əns\ *n* **1** : a district or division of a country having a government of its own (as one of the divisions of the Dominion of Canada) **2** *pl* : the part or parts of a country far from the capital or chief city

pro·vin·cial \prə-'vin-chəl\ *adj* **1** : of, relating to, or coming from a province **2** : limited in outlook : NARROW **3** : lacking the polish and refinement of the city

¹pro·vi·sion \prə-'vizh-ən\ *n* **1** : the act of providing **2** : a measure taken beforehand **3** : a stock or store of food — usually used in plural ⟨lay in *provisions* for a holiday⟩ **4** : CONDITION ⟨the *provisions* of the contract⟩

²provision *vb* : to supply with provisions

prov·o·ca·tion \,präv-ə-'kā-shən\ *n* **1** : the act of provoking **2** : something that provokes

pro·voc·a·tive \prə-'väk-ət-iv\ *adj* : serving or tending to provoke or arouse (as interest, curiosity, or anger) — **pro·voc·a·tive·ly** *adv*

pro·voke \prə-'vōk\ *vb* **pro·voked; pro·vok·ing** **1** : to arouse to action or feeling and especially to anger ⟨warned the boy not to *provoke* him⟩ **2** : to bring about : stir up ⟨*provoke* a smile⟩ ⟨*provoke* an argument⟩

pro·vok·ing \prə-'vō-king\ *adj* : ANNOYING, VEXING — **pro·vok·ing·ly** *adv*

prow \'praù\ *n* : the bow of a ship

prow·ess \'praù-əs\ *n* **1** : great bravery especially in battle **2** : very great ability

¹prowl \'praùl\ *vb* : to move about quietly and secretly like a wild animal hunting prey — **prowl·er** *n*

²prowl *n* : an act of prowling ⟨a tiger on the *prowl*⟩

prox·y \'präk-sē\ *n, pl* **prox·ies** **1** : authority held by one person to act for another or a paper giving such authority **2** : a person holding authority to act for another

prude \'prüd\ *n* : a person having or showing extreme often merely pretended modesty in speech and conduct — **prud·ish** *adj*

pru·dence \'prüd-ns\ *n* : skill and good sense in taking care of oneself or of one's affairs

pru·dent \'prüd-nt\ *adj* **1** : shrewd and careful in action or judgment **2** : cautious in trying not to make mistakes : not reckless — **pru·dent·ly** *adv*

¹prune \'prün\ *n* : a plum dried or capable of being dried without fermentation

²prune *vb* **pruned; prun·ing** **1** : to cut off the dead or unwanted branches, twigs, or parts of a bush or tree : TRIM **2** : to cut out useless or unwanted parts (as unnecessary words or phrases in a composition)

¹pry \'prī\ *vb* **pried; pry·ing** : to look closely or inquisitively especially into the affairs of others : peer searchingly

---

ə abut   ər further   a ax   ā age   ä father, cot   à (see key page)   aù out   ch chin   e less   ē easy   g gift   i trip   ī life

²**pry** *vb* **pried; pry·ing** **1** : to raise or open or try to do so with a lever **2** : to get at with great difficulty ⟨*pry* a secret out of a person⟩

pry·ing \'prī-ing\ *adj* : impertinently inquisitive **syn** see CURIOUS

psalm \'säm\ *n* **1** : a sacred song or poem **2** *cap* : one of the hymns that make up the Old Testament Book of Psalms

psy·cho·log·i·cal \,sī-kə-'läj-i-kəl\ *adj* **1** : of or relating to psychology **2** : directed toward or intended to influence the will or mind ⟨*psychological* warfare⟩

psy·chol·o·gist \sī-'käl-ə-jəst\ *n* : a specialist in psychology

psy·chol·o·gy \sī-'käl-ə-jē\ *n* : the science that studies facts about the mind and its activities especially in human beings

pter·o·dac·tyl \,ter-ə-'dak-tl\ *n* : an ancient extinct winged reptile related to the dinosaurs

pu·ber·ty \'pyü-bərt-ē\ *n* : the age at or period during which an individual becomes able to reproduce sexually

¹**pub·lic** \'pəb-lik\ *adj* **1** : of or relating to the people as a whole ⟨*public* opinion⟩ **2** : of or relating to activities for the people especially in government ⟨*public* prosecutor⟩ ⟨holds *public* office⟩ **3** : open to all ⟨a *public* library⟩ **4** : generally known : not kept secret ⟨the story became *public*⟩ **5** : WELL-KNOWN, PROMINENT ⟨*public* figures⟩ — **pub·lic·ly** *adv*

²**public** *n* **1** : the people as a whole ⟨open to the *public*⟩ **2** : a group of people having common interests ⟨a novelist's *public*⟩

pub·li·ca·tion \,pəb-lə-'kā-shən\ *n* **1** : the act or process of publishing **2** : a printed work (as a book, pamphlet, or magazine) produced for sale or distribution

pub·lic·i·ty \,pəb-'lis-ət-ē\ *n* **1** : information with news value given out to gain public attention or support **2** : the state of being known to the public : public attention ⟨seek *publicity*⟩

pub·li·cize \'pəb-lə-,sīz\ *vb* **pub·li·cized; pub·li·ciz·ing** : to give publicity to

pub·lish \'pəb-lish\ *vb* **1** : to make generally known : announce publicly **2** : to bring especially printed matter before the public for sale or distribution **3** : to have one's work accepted for publication — **pub·lish·er** *n*

¹**puck** \'pək\ *n* : a mischievous sprite — **puck·ish** *adj*

²**puck** *n* : a rubber disk used in hockey

¹**puck·er** \'pək-ər\ *vb* : to draw up into folds or wrinkles ⟨*puckered* his brow⟩

²**pucker** *n* : a fold or wrinkle in a normally even surface

pud·ding \'pùd-ing\ *n* : a soft spongy or creamy dessert having a foundation of starch (as flour) with other ingredients (as milk, sugar, eggs, or flavoring) added

pud·dle \'pəd-l\ *n* : a very small pool (as of dirty or muddy water)

pudg·y \'pəj-ē\ *adj* **pudg·i·er; pudg·i·est** : being short and plump : CHUBBY

pu·eb·lo \pü-'eb-lō\ *n, pl* **pu·eb·los** : an Indian village of Arizona or New Mexico consisting of flat-roofed stone or adobe houses

¹**Puer·to Ri·can** \,pwert-ə-'rē-kən, ,pȯrt-\ *adj* : of or relating to Puerto Rico or the Puerto Ricans

²**Puerto Rican** *n* : a native or inhabitant of Puerto Rico

¹**puff** \'pəf\ *vb* **1** : to blow in short gusts **2** : to breathe hard : PANT **3** : to send out small whiffs or clouds **4** : to distend or become distended with or as if with air : SWELL ⟨the injured eye *puffed* up⟩ ⟨*puffed* out his cheeks⟩

²**puff** *n* **1** : a quick short sending or letting out of air, smoke, or steam ⟨*puffs* from a locomotive⟩ **2** : a very light pastry that has puffed in cooking **3** : a slight swelling **4** : a soft pad for applying powder to the skin **5** : a quilted bed covering

puf·fin \'pəf-ən\ *n* : a seabird related to the auks that has a short thick neck and a deep grooved bill marked with several colors

puff·y \'pəf-ē\ *adj* **puff·i·er; puff·i·est** **1** : blowing in puffs ⟨a *puffy* locomotive⟩ **2** : BREATHLESS **3** : SWOLLEN, DISTENDED **4** : resembling a puff : FLUFFY

puffin

pug \'pəg\ *n* **1** : a small stocky usually short-haired dog having a massive round head, a blunt square snout, and a tightly curled tail **2** : a nose turning up at the tip and usually short and thick

pug·na·cious \,pəg-'nā-shəs\ *adj* : fond of fighting : QUARRELSOME — **pug·na·cious·ly** *adv* — **pug·na·cious·ness** *n*

pug 1

¹**pull** \'pùl\ *vb* **1** : to separate from a firm or a natural attachment ⟨*pull* a tooth⟩ ⟨*pull* up carrots⟩ **2** : to exert force on so as to cause or tend to cause motion toward the force ⟨*pulled* the rope⟩ ⟨*pulling* a wagon⟩ **3** : to stretch repeatedly ⟨*pull* taffy⟩ **4** : MOVE ⟨a train *pulling* out of the station⟩ **5** : to draw apart : TEAR, REND ⟨*pull* a flower to pieces⟩ — **pull through** : to survive a very difficult or dangerous period ⟨was seriously ill but *pulled through*⟩

²pull _n_ **1** : the act or an instance of pulling ⟨two _pulls_ on the cord⟩ **2** : the effort put forth in moving ⟨a long _pull_ up the hill⟩ **3** : a device for pulling something **4** : a force that pulls ⟨the _pull_ of gravity⟩

pul·let \'pùl-ət\ _n_ : a young hen

pul·ley \'pùl-ē\ _n, pl_ **pul·leys** : a wheel with a grooved rim in which a belt, rope, or chain runs that is used to change the direction of a pulling force and in combination to increase the force applied for lifting

pulley

pull·o·ver \'pùl-ˌō-vər\ _n_ : a garment (as a sweater) that is put on by being pulled over the head

pul·mo·nar·y \'pùl-mə-ˌner-ē, 'pəl-\ _adj_ : of or relating to the lungs

¹pulp \'pəlp\ _n_ **1** : the soft juicy or fleshy part of a fruit or vegetable ⟨the _pulp_ of an apple⟩ **2** : a mass of vegetable matter from which the moisture has been squeezed **3** : the soft sensitive tissue inside a tooth **4** : a material prepared usually from wood or rags and used in making paper

²pulp _vb_ : to form into a pulp

pul·pit \'pùl-ˌpit\ _n_ **1** : an elevated place in which a clergyman stands at a religious service especially while preaching **2** : the preaching profession

pulp·wood \'pəlp-ˌwùd\ _n_ : wood (as of aspen or spruce) from which wood pulp is made

pulp·y \'pəl-pē\ _adj_ **pulp·i·er; pulp·i·est** : resembling or consisting of pulp

pul·sate \'pəl-ˌsāt\ _vb_ **pul·sat·ed; pul·sat·ing** : to have or show a pulse or beats : THROB

pul·sa·tion \ˌpəl-'sā-shən\ _n_ : pulsating movement or action : PULSE

¹pulse \'pəls\ _n_ : the edible seeds of a legume (as peas, beans, or lentils)

²pulse _n_ **1** : a regular beating or throbbing (as of the arteries) **2** : one complete beat of a pulse or the number of these in a given period (as a minute) ⟨a normal _pulse_ is about seventy beats to the minute⟩

pul·ver·ize \'pəl-və-ˌrīz\ _vb_ **pul·ver·ized; pul·ver·iz·ing** : to beat or grind into a powder or dust

pu·ma \'pyü-mə, 'pü-\ _n_ : COUGAR

pum·ice \'pəm-əs\ _n_ : a very light porous volcanic glass that is used in powder form for smoothing and polishing

pum·mel \'pəm-əl\ _vb_ **pum·meled** _or_ **pum·melled; pum·mel·ing** _or_ **pum·mel·ling** : BEAT, POUND

¹pump \'pəmp\ _n_ : a device for raising, transferring, or compressing fluids

²pump _vb_ **1** : to raise, transfer, or compress by means of a pump ⟨_pump_ water⟩ **2** : to free (as from water or air) by the use of a pump ⟨_pump_ a boat dry⟩ **3** : to fill by means of a pump ⟨_pump_ up tires⟩ **4** : to draw, force, or drive onward in the manner of a pump ⟨heart _pumping_ blood into the arteries⟩ **5** : to subject to persistent questioning to find out something — **pump·er** _n_

³pump _n_ : a low-cut shoe without fastenings

pum·per·nick·el \'pəm-pər-ˌnik-əl\ _n_ : a dark rye bread

pump·kin \'pəng-kən, 'pəmp-kən\ _n_ : a large round orange or yellow fruit of a vine related to the squash vine that is used as a vegetable and fed to farm animals

pumpkin

¹pun \'pən\ _n_ : a form of joking in which a person uses a word in two senses

²pun _vb_ **punned; pun·ning** : to make a pun

¹punch \'pənch\ _vb_ **1** : PROD, POKE **2** : DRIVE, HERD ⟨_punch_ cattle⟩ **3** : to strike with the fist **4** : to press or strike by or as if by punching ⟨_punch_ a typewriter⟩ **5** : to pierce or stamp with a punch

²punch _n_ : a blow with or as if with the fist

³punch _n_ : a tool for piercing, stamping, or cutting

⁴punch _n_ : a drink made of several ingredients often including wine or liquor

punch

punc·tu·al \'pəngk-chə-wəl\ _adj_ : acting at the proper time : not late : PROMPT

punc·tu·ate \'pəngk-chə-ˌwāt\ _vb_ **punc·tu·at·ed; punc·tu·at·ing** : to mark or divide (as a sentence) with punctuation marks

punc·tu·a·tion \ˌpəngk-chə-'wā-shən\ _n_ **1** : the act of punctuating **2** : a system of using standardized marks (**punctuation marks**) in written matter to clarify the meaning and separate structural units

¹punc·ture \'pəngk-chər\ _n_ **1** : the act of puncturing **2** : a hole or wound made by puncturing

²puncture _vb_ **punc·tured; punc·tur·ing** **1** : to pierce with something pointed **2** : to take the force out of something ⟨_puncture_ an argument⟩

pun·gent \'pən-jənt\ _adj_ : giving a sharp or biting sensation — **pun·gent·ly** _adv_

pun·ish \'pən-ish\ _vb_ **1** : to cause to suffer for a fault or crime ⟨_punished_ for breaking a window⟩ **2** : to inflict punishment for (as a crime)

syn PUNISH and DISCIPLINE both mean to inflict some kind of pain or suffering on an individual because of a misdeed he has committed. PUNISH stresses imposing a specific penalty for a wrongdoing or violation of law and is especially apt when the emphasis is on exacting payment for the crime rather than reforming the criminal ⟨treason is generally *punished* by death⟩ DISCIPLINE on the other hand stresses penalizing an offender either to bring him under control ⟨the warden had to *discipline* unruly prisoners⟩ or to impress better behavior or habits upon him ⟨*discipline* the dog for chasing cars⟩

pun·ish·a·ble \'pən-ish-ə-bəl\ *adj* : deserving or liable to be punished ⟨a *punishable* offense⟩

pun·ish·ment \'pən-ish-mənt\ *n* **1** : the act of punishing : the state or fact of being punished **2** : the penalty for a fault or crime

pu·ni·tive \'pyü-nət-iv\ *adj* : of, relating to, or designed to inflict punishment

punk \'pəngk\ *n* : a dry spongy material prepared from fungi and used to light fuses (as of fireworks)

¹punt \'pənt\ *vb* : to kick a football dropped from the hands before it hits the ground — **punt·er** *n*

²punt *n* : an act or instance of punting a ball

pu·ny \'pyü-nē\ *adj* **pu·ni·er**; **pu·ni·est** [the original meaning of *puny* in English was "younger", "inferior", taken from early French *puisné* "younger", a compound of *puis* "afterward" and *né* "born"] : slight or inferior in size or power

pup \'pəp\ *n* : a young dog

pu·pa \'pyü-pə\ *n, pl* **pu·pae** \-₁pē\ : an insect (as a bee, moth, or beetle) in an intermediate inactive stage of its growth in which it is enclosed in a cocoon or case

pu·pal \'pyü-pəl\ *adj* : of, relating to, or being a pupa

pu·pate \'pyü-₁pāt\ *vb* **pu·pat·ed**; **pu·pat·ing** : to change from an active larva into a pupa

¹pu·pil \'pyü-pəl\ *n* : a boy or girl in school or under the care of a teacher

²pupil *n* [from Latin *pupilla* "little doll", "pupil", from *pupa* "doll"; so named because of the tiny image of oneself seen reflected in another's eye] : the dark central usually round adjustable opening in the iris through which light enters the eye

pupil

pup·pet \'pəp-ət\ *n* **1** : a doll moved by hand or by strings or wires **2** : a person whose acts are controlled by another

puppet

pup·py \'pəp-ē\ *n, pl* **pup·pies** : PUP

¹pur·chase \'pər-chəs\ *vb* **pur·chased**; **pur·chas·ing** : BUY

²purchase *n* **1** : an act of purchasing ⟨the *purchase* of supplies⟩ **2** : something purchased ⟨an extravagant *purchase*⟩ **3** : a secure hold or grasp or place to stand ⟨could not get a *purchase* on the ledge⟩

pure \'pyúr\ *adj* **pur·er**; **pur·est** **1** : not mixed with anything else : free from everything that might taint or lower the quality ⟨*pure* water⟩ ⟨*pure* French⟩ **2** : free from sin : INNOCENT, CHASTE **3** : nothing other than : MERE, ABSOLUTE ⟨*pure* nonsense⟩ — **pure·ly** *adv* — **pure·ness** *n*

pure·bred \'pyúr-'bred\ *adj* : bred from ancestors of unmixed breed or strain for many generations

¹pu·ree \pyú-'rā\ *n* **1** : a paste made of food boiled to a pulp and forced through a sieve ⟨tomato *puree*⟩ **2** : a thick soup made with pureed vegetables

²puree *vb* **pu·reed**; **pu·ree·ing** : to boil soft and then force through a sieve

¹purge \'pərj\ *vb* **purged**; **purg·ing** **1** : CLEANSE, PURIFY **2** : to have or cause frequent passage of loose or watery feces ⟨*purge* a person with castor oil⟩ **3** : to get rid of by a purge ⟨*purged* the party of disloyal members⟩

²purge *n* **1** : an act or instance of purging **2** : a ridding of persons regarded as treacherous or disloyal **3** : something that purges

pu·ri·fi·ca·tion \₁pyúr-ə-fə-'kā-shən\ *n* : an act or instance of purifying or of being purified

pu·ri·fy \'pyúr-ə-₁fī\ *vb* **pu·ri·fied**; **pu·ri·fy·ing** : to make pure : free from impurities

pu·ri·tan \'pyúr-ət-n\ *n* **1** *cap* : a member of a sixteenth and seventeenth century Protestant group in England and New England opposing formal usages of the Church of England **2** : one who practices or preaches or follows a stricter moral code than that which prevails

pu·ri·ty \'pyúr-ət-ē\ *n* **1** : the quality of being pure : freedom from impurities **2** : freedom from sin or guilt

pur·loin \₁pər-'lóin\ *vb* : STEAL

pur·ple \'pər-pəl\ *n* : a bluish red

pur·plish \'pər-plish\ *adj* : somewhat purple

¹pur·pose \'pər-pəs\ *n* : something set up to be achieved or attained : an end in view : INTENTION — **on purpose** : PURPOSELY, INTENTIONALLY

²purpose *vb* **pur·posed**; **pur·pos·ing** : to have as one's intention : INTEND

pur·pose·ful \'pər-pəs-fəl\ *adj* : having a purpose : guided by a definite aim — **pur·pose·ful·ly** *adv* — **pur·pose·ful·ness** *n*

---

j job   ng sing   ō low   ȯ moth   ȯi coin   th thin   th̲ this   ü boot   ú foot   y you   yü few   yú furious   zh vision

pur·pose·ly \'pər-pəs-lē\ *adv* : with a clear or known purpose : INTENTIONALLY

purr \'pər\ *vb* : to make the low murmuring sound of a contented cat or a similar sound

¹**purse** \'pərs\ *n* **1** : a bag or pouch for money **2** : the contents of a purse : MONEY, FUNDS **3** : a sum of money offered as a prize or collected as a present

purse

²**purse** *vb* **pursed; purs·ing** : to pucker up ⟨*pursed* her lips⟩

pur·sue \pər-'sü\ *vb* **pur·sued; pur·su·ing** **1** : to follow after in order to capture or destroy : CHASE ⟨*pursued* the retreating enemy⟩ **2** : to follow with an end in view : proceed with ⟨*pursue* a wise course⟩ **3** : to be engaged in ⟨*pursue* medical studies⟩ **syn** see CHASE — **pur·su·er** *n*

pur·suit \pər-'süt\ *n* **1** : the act of pursuing **2** : ACTIVITY, OCCUPATION

pus \'pəs\ *n* : yellowish white creamy matter (as in a ripe abscess or a boil)

¹**push** \'pùsh\ *vb* **1** : to press against with force so as to drive or move away ⟨*push* a car to get it started⟩ **2** : to thrust forward, downward, or outward ⟨a tree *pushing* its roots deep in the soil⟩ **3** : to press or urge forward ⟨*push* a task to completion⟩

²**push** *n* **1** : a sudden thrust : SHOVE ⟨gave him a *push* and he fell over⟩ **2** : a steady application of force in a direction away from the body exerting it ⟨gave the car a *push* up the hill⟩

push–but·ton \ˌpùsh-ˌbət-n\ *adj* : using or depending on complicated automatic mechanisms ⟨*push-button* warfare⟩

push·cart \'pùsh-ˌkärt\ *n* : a cart pushed by hand

push·o·ver \'pùsh-ˌō-vər\ *n* **1** : an opponent that is easy to defeat ⟨thought the first team they played would be a *pushover*⟩ **2** : something easily done ⟨the exam was a *pushover*⟩

push·y \'pùsh-ē\ *adj* **push·i·er; push·i·est** : aggressive to an objectionable degree : FORWARD

puss \'pùs\ *n* : PUSSY

puss·y \'pùs-ē\ *n, pl* **puss·ies** : CAT

puss·y willow \ˌpùs-ē-\ *n* : a willow with large cylindrical silky catkins

pus·tule \'pəs-chül\ *n* : a small raised inflamed place in the skin containing pus

put \'pùt\ *vb* **put; put·ting** **1** : to place in or move into a particular position ⟨*put* the book on the table⟩ ⟨*put* your hand up⟩ **2** : to bring into a specified state or condition ⟨*puts* his money to good use⟩ ⟨*put* the room in

pussy willow

order⟩ **3** : to cause to endure or suffer something ⟨was *put* to death⟩ ⟨*puts* them to shame⟩ **4** : EXPRESS ⟨*puts* his feelings into words⟩ ⟨*puts* the idea clearly⟩ **5** : to devote or urge to an activity ⟨if he *puts* his mind to it⟩ ⟨*putting* us to work⟩ **6** : ATTACH, ATTRIBUTE ⟨*puts* a high value on friendship⟩ **7** : to begin a voyage ⟨the ship *put* to sea⟩ — **put away** **1** : DISCARD, RENOUNCE ⟨*put away* his childish things⟩ **2** : EAT, DRINK ⟨*put* a big meal *away*⟩ — **put by** : to lay aside : SAVE ⟨*put by* a little money for an emergency⟩ — **put down** **1** : to bring to an end by force ⟨*put* the riot *down*⟩ **2** : to assign to a particular category or cause ⟨*put* him *down* as lazy⟩ ⟨*puts* his laziness *down* to spring fever⟩ — **put forth** **1** : EXERT ⟨*put forth* a lot of effort⟩ **2** : to send out by growth ⟨*put forth* leaves⟩ — **put forward** : PROPOSE ⟨*put forward* a new plan⟩ — **put in** **1** : to make a request ⟨*put in* for a job at the store⟩ **2** : to spend (time) at an activity or place ⟨*put* six hours *in* at the office⟩ — **put off** : POSTPONE, DEFER ⟨kept *putting off* his visit to the dentist⟩ — **put on** **1** : to dress oneself in ⟨*put* her new dress *on*⟩ **2** : FEIGN, SHAM ⟨*put on* a show of anger⟩ **3** : to give a performance of : PRODUCE ⟨*put on* a skit⟩ — **put out** **1** : EXERT, USE ⟨*put out* all his strength to move the piano⟩ **2** : EXTINGUISH ⟨*put* the fire *out*⟩ **3** : PRODUCE ⟨*put out* a new book⟩ **4** : IRRITATE, ANNOY ⟨was *put out* by the curt answer⟩ **5** : to cause to be out (as in baseball) ⟨was *put out* at third base⟩ — **put through** : to bring to a successful conclusion ⟨*put through* needed reforms⟩ — **put up** **1** : to prepare for later use ⟨*put up* a lunch⟩ **2** : NOMINATE ⟨was *put up* for mayor⟩ **3** : to give or obtain shelter and often food ⟨*put* them *up* for the night⟩ **4** : BUILD ⟨*put up* a new building⟩ **5** : to carry on ⟨*put up* a fight⟩ — **put up to** : to urge or cause to do (something wrong or unexpected) ⟨ringleader who *put* the others *up to* mischief⟩ — **put up with** : to stand for : ENDURE, TOLERATE ⟨won't *put up with* any nonsense⟩

put·out \'pùt-ˌaùt\ *n* : the retiring of a batter or runner in baseball

pu·trid \'pyü-trəd\ *adj* **1** : ROTTEN, DECAYED ⟨*putrid* meat⟩ **2** : coming from decayed matter : FOUL ⟨a *putrid* smell⟩

put·ter \'pət-ər\ *vb* : to act or work aimlessly ⟨*puttering* around the garden⟩

¹**put·ty** \'pət-ē\ *n, pl* **put·ties** : a soft cement (as for holding glass in a window frame) usually made of powdered chalk and boiled linseed oil

²**putty** *vb* **put·tied; put·ty·ing** : to cement or seal up with putty

¹**puz·zle** \'pəz-əl\ *vb* **puz·zled; puz·zling**
1 : PERPLEX, CONFUSE ⟨*puzzled* by his answer⟩
2 : to solve by thought or by clever guessing
⟨*puzzle* out a mystery⟩

²**puzzle** *n* 1 : something that puzzles : MYS-
TERY 2 : a question, problem, or device designed to test the ingenuity

¹**pyg·my** \'pig-mē\ *n, pl* **pyg·mies** : a person or
thing very small for its kind : DWARF

²**pygmy** *adj* : very small

py·lo·rus \pī-'lōr-əs\ *n* : the opening between
the stomach and intestine which is closed
when at rest by a muscular ring

¹**pyr·a·mid** \'pir-ə-,mid\ *n* 1 : a massive
structure built especially in
ancient Egypt that usually has a
square base and four triangular
faces meeting at a point and
contains tombs 2 : something
that has the shape of a pyramid

pyramid

²**pyramid** *vb* : to build up in the form of a
pyramid

pyre \'pīr\ *n* : a heap of wood for burning a
dead body

py·re·thrum \pī-'rē-thrəm\ *n* : a chrysanthemum whose powdered flower heads (**pyre-
thrum powder**) are used as an insecticide

py·thon \'pī-,thän\ *n* : any of various large
snakes of the Old World tropics that are related to the boas

q \'kyü\ *n, often cap* : the
seventeenth letter of the English alphabet

¹**quack** \'kwak\ *vb* : to make
the characteristic cry of a duck

²**quack** *n* : a cry made by or as
if by quacking

³**quack** *n* 1 : an ignorant person who pretends
to have medical knowledge and skill 2 : one
who pretends to have knowledge of things he
really knows nothing about

⁴**quack** *adj* : of, relating to, or typical of a
quack : pretending to cure disease ⟨*quack*
remedies⟩

quad·ri- \'kwäd-rə\ *or* **quadr-** *or* **quad·ru-**
\'kwäd-rə\ *prefix* 1 : four ⟨*quadri*lateral⟩
2: fourth ⟨*quadri*centennial⟩

quad·ri·lat·er·al \,kwäd-
rə-'lat-ə-rəl\ *n* : a plane
figure of four sides and
four angles

quadrilaterals

quad·ru·ped \'kwäd-rə-
,ped\ *n* : an animal having four feet

qua·drup·let \kwä-'drəp-lət\ *n* 1 : one of
four offspring born at one birth 2 : a combination of four of a kind

quaff \'kwäf, 'kwaf\ *vb* : to drink deeply or
repeatedly

¹**quail** \'kwāl\ *n, pl* **quail** *or* **quails** : any of
various mostly small stocky game birds (as the
bobwhite) that are related to the common
domestic fowl

²**quail** *vb* : to lose courage : shrink fearfully
: COWER

quaint \'kwānt\ *adj* 1 : unusual or different
in character or appearance 2 : pleasingly
old-fashioned or unfamiliar — **quaint·ly** *adv* —
quaint·ness *n*

¹**quake** \'kwāk\ *vb* **quaked; quak·ing** 1 : to
shake or vibrate usually from shock or in-
stability 2 : to tremble or shudder usually
from cold or fear

²**quake** *n* : an instance (as an earthquake) of
shaking or trembling

qual·i·fi·ca·tion \,kwäl-ə-fə-'kā-shən\ *n*
1 : the act or an instance of qualifying 2 : the
state of being qualified 3 : a special skill,
knowledge, or ability that fits a person for a
particular work or position : FITNESS ⟨lacks
the *qualifications* for teaching⟩ 4 : LIMITATION
⟨agree without *qualification*⟩

qual·i·fy \'kwäl-ə-,fī\ *vb* **qual·i·fied; qual·i·fy·
ing** 1 : to make less general or more definite
in meaning : LIMIT ⟨*qualify* a statement⟩
⟨adjectives *qualify* nouns⟩ 2 : to make less
harsh or strict : SOFTEN ⟨*qualify* a punishment⟩
3 : to fit by training, skill, or ability for a
special purpose ⟨*qualified* himself to be a
doctor⟩ 4 : to show the skill or ability necessary to be on a team or take part in a contest

qual·i·ty \'kwäl-ət-ē\ *n, pl* **qual·i·ties** 1 : peculiar and essential character : NATURE
2 : degree of excellence : GRADE ⟨the *quality* of
the food⟩ 3 : high social status ⟨a gentleman
of *quality*⟩ 4 : a distinguishing attribute
: CHARACTERISTIC ⟨a man's good and bad
qualities⟩

qualm \'kwäm\ *n* 1 : a sudden attack of illness, faintness, or nausea 2 : a sudden fear or
misgiving 3 : a feeling of doubt or hesitation
in matters of conscience : SCRUPLE — **qualm-
ish** *adj*

quan·da·ry \'kwän-də-rē\ *n, pl* **quan·da·ries**
: a state of doubt or perplexity ⟨in a *quandary*
as to what to do next⟩

quan·ti·ty \'kwänt-ət-ē\ *n, pl* **quan·ti·ties**
1 : AMOUNT, NUMBER ⟨a *quantity* of informa-
tion⟩ 2 : a considerable amount or number
⟨a *quantity* of shoes⟩ ⟨*quantities* of money⟩

¹**quar·an·tine** \'kwȯr-ən-,tēn\ *n* [from Italian

quarantina "quarantine of a ship", from French *quarantaine* "period of forty days", from *quarante* "forty"] **1 :** a restraint on the movement of people or things to prevent the spread of disease or pests **2 :** a period during which a person with a contagious disease is under quarantine **3 :** a place (as a hospital) where persons are kept in quarantine

²quarantine *vb* **quar·an·tined; quar·an·tin·ing** **:** to put in quarantine **:** hold in quarantine

¹quar·rel \'kwȯr-əl\ *n* **1 :** a ground of dispute or complaint **2 :** an angry dispute

²quarrel *vb* **quar·reled** *or* **quar·relled; quar·rel·ing** *or* **quar·rel·ling** **1 :** to find fault **2 :** to contend or dispute actively **:** SQUABBLE

quar·rel·some \'kwȯr-əl-səm\ *adj* **:** inclined to quarrel

¹quar·ry \'kwȯr-ē\ *n, pl* **quar·ries :** a hunted animal or bird **:** GAME, PREY

²quarry *n, pl* **quar·ries :** an open excavation usually for obtaining building stone, slate, or limestone

³quarry *vb* **quar·ried; quar·ry·ing** **1 :** to dig or take from or as if from a quarry **2 :** to make a quarry in — **quar·ri·er** *n*

quart \'kwȯrt\ *n* **:** a measure of capacity that equals two pints

¹quar·ter \'kwȯrt-ər\ *n* **1 :** one of four equal parts into which something is divisible **:** a fourth part **2 :** a coin worth a fourth of a dollar **3 :** one limb of a four-limbed animal or carcass with the parts near it ⟨a *quarter* of beef⟩ **4 :** someone or something (as a place, direction, or group) not definitely specified ⟨expects trouble from another *quarter*⟩ **5 :** a particular division or district of a city ⟨a residential *quarter*⟩ **6** *pl* **:** living accommodations ⟨winter *quarters*⟩ **7 :** MERCY ⟨show no *quarter* to the enemy⟩

²quarter *vb* **1 :** to divide into four usually equal parts **2 :** to provide with lodgings or shelter

³quarter *adj* **:** consisting of or equal to a quarter ⟨give it a *quarter* turn⟩

quar·ter·back \'kwȯrt-ər-,bak\ *n* **:** a back who calls the signals for a football team

quar·ter·deck \'kwȯrt-ər-,dek\ *n* **:** the stern area of a ship's upper deck

quarter horse *n* **:** a stocky muscular saddle horse capable of high speed over short distances

¹quar·ter·ly \'kwȯrt-ər-lē\ *adv* **:** at three= month intervals ⟨interest compounded *quarterly*⟩

²quarterly *adj* **:** coming during or at the end of each three-month interval ⟨*quarterly* meeting⟩

³quarterly *n, pl* **quar·ter·lies :** a periodical published four times a year

quar·ter·mas·ter \'kwȯrt-ər-,mas-tər\ *n* **1 :** a petty officer who attends to a ship's steering and signals **2 :** an army officer who provides clothing and supplies for troops

quar·ter·staff \'kwȯrt-ər-,staf\ *n* **:** a long stout staff formerly used as a weapon

quar·tet *also* **quar·tette** \kwȯr-'tet\ *n* **1 :** a musical composition for four instruments or voices **2 :** a group or set of four

quartz \'kwȯrts\ *n* **:** a common mineral often found in the form of colorless transparent crystals but sometimes (as in amethysts, agates, and jaspers) brightly colored

qua·ver \'kwā-vər\ *vb* **1 :** TREMBLE, SHAKE ⟨*quavering* inwardly⟩ **2 :** TRILL **3 :** to utter sound in tremulous tones ⟨his voice *quavered*⟩

quay \'kē, 'kwā\ *n* **:** a paved bank or a solid artificial landing place beside the water **:** WHARF

quea·sy \'kwē-zē\ *adj* **quea·si·er; quea·si·est** **1 :** somewhat nauseated **2 :** UNEASY, UNCOMFORTABLE

queen \'kwēn\ *n* **1 :** the wife or widow of a king **2 :** a female monarch **3 :** a woman of high rank, power, or attractiveness ⟨a society *queen*⟩ **4 :** the most powerful piece in the game of chess **5 :** a playing card bearing the figure of a queen **6 :** an adult functional female of social bees, ants, or termites — **queen·ly** *adj*

Queen Anne's lace \-'anz-\ *n* **:** a plant with finely divided leaves and flat lacy heads of white flowers that is the wild form of the carrot

¹queer \'kwiər\ *adj* **:** differing from the usual or normal **:** PECULIAR, STRANGE — **queer·ly** *adv*

Queen Anne's lace

syn QUEER, PECULIAR, CURIOUS all refer to something out of the ordinary. QUEER applies to what seems extremely odd or whimsical and includes the suggestion that there might be something questionable involved ⟨told us a *queer* story to account for the missing money⟩ or that one disapproves of the thing ⟨he had some *queer* ideas about how money should be spent⟩ PECULIAR emphasizes the distinctive, often singular, characteristics that belong to a thing or person, and normally suggests neither approval nor disapproval of them ⟨each child has his *peculiar* abilities to develop⟩ ⟨studied the customs *peculiar* to the various religions⟩ CURIOUS refers to anything so remarkably odd or hard to explain that it invites closer attention or investigation ⟨found several *curious* shells on the beach⟩ ⟨I thought his remarks rather *curious* and tried to ask what he meant⟩

²queer *adv* : QUEERLY

³queer *vb* **1** : to spoil the effect or success of : DISRUPT ⟨the rain *queered* his plans⟩ **2** : to put or get into an embarrassing or disadvantageous situation ⟨*queered* himself with the authorities⟩

quell \'kwel\ *vb* **1** : to put down : SUPPRESS ⟨*quell* a riot⟩ **2** : QUIET, PACIFY ⟨*quelled* his fears⟩

quench \'kwench\ *vb* **1** : to put out : EXTINGUISH **2** : SUBDUE, OVERCOME ⟨*quench* hatred⟩ **3** : to end by satisfying ⟨*quenched* his thirst⟩

¹que·ry \'kwiər-ē\ *n, pl* **que·ries** **1** : QUESTION, INQUIRY **2** : DOUBT

²query *vb* **que·ried**; **que·ry·ing** **1** : to put as a question ⟨*queried* the matter to his teacher⟩ **2** : to ask questions about especially in order to resolve a doubt ⟨*queried* the procedure⟩ **3** : to ask questions of especially to obtain authoritative information ⟨*query* the professor⟩

¹quest \'kwest\ *n* **1** : PURSUIT, SEARCH ⟨in *quest* of fame⟩ **2** : a knightly expedition

²quest *vb* **1** : to go on a quest : SEEK **2** : to search for : PURSUE

¹ques·tion \'kwes-chən\ *n* **1** : something asked : QUERY ⟨try to make your *questions* short⟩ **2** : a subject of argument or inquiry ⟨an important *question* of the day⟩ **3** : a proposal to be voted on ⟨put the *question* to the members⟩ **4** : an act or instance of asking : INQUIRY **5** : OBJECTION, DISPUTE ⟨obey without *question*⟩

²question *vb* **1** : to ask questions of or about **2** : DOUBT, DISPUTE ⟨*question* a decision⟩

ques·tion·a·ble \'kwes-chə-nə-bəl\ *adj* **1** : not certain or exact : DOUBTFUL **2** : not believed to be true, sound, or moral ⟨*questionable* motives⟩

question mark *n* : a punctuation mark ? used chiefly at the end of a sentence to indicate a direct question

ques·tion·naire \ˌkwes-chən-'aər\ *n* : a set of questions to be asked of a number of persons to collect facts showing knowledge or opinions

quet·zal \ket-'säl\ *n, pl* **quet·zals** *or* **quet·za·les** \-'sä-lās\ : a Central American bird with narrow crest and brilliant plumage and in the male tail feathers often over two feet long

¹queue \'kyü\ *n* [from French, meaning literally "tail", derived from Latin *cauda*]

1 : PIGTAIL **2** : a waiting line ⟨a *queue* at a ticket window⟩

²queue *vb* **queued**; **queu·ing** *or* **queue·ing** **1** : to braid the hair in a queue **2** : to line up or wait in a queue ⟨*queuing* up for tickets⟩

quib·ble \'kwib-əl\ *vb* **quib·bled**; **quib·bling** **1** : to evade the issue **2** : to find fault especially over trivial points — **quib·bler** \'kwib-lər\ *n*

¹quick \'kwik\ *adj* **1** : RAPID, SPEEDY ⟨*quick* steps⟩ **2** : mentally alert **3** : SENSITIVE ⟨a *quick* ear for music⟩ **4** : easily aroused ⟨*quick* temper⟩ — **quick·ly** *adv* — **quick·ness** *n*

²quick *adv* : QUICKLY

³quick *n* **1** : a very sensitive area of flesh (as under a fingernail) **2** : the inmost sensibilities ⟨hurt to the *quick* by the remark⟩

quick·en \'kwik-ən\ *vb* **1** : to make or become alive : REVIVE **2** : AROUSE, STIMULATE ⟨curiosity *quickened* her interest⟩ **3** : to make or become more rapid : HASTEN ⟨*quickened* his steps⟩ **4** : to begin or exhibit active growth

quick·sand \'kwik-ˌsand\ *n* : a deep mass of loose sand mixed with water into which heavy objects sink

quick·sil·ver \'kwik-ˌsil-vər\ *n* : MERCURY

quick–tem·pered \'kwik-'tem-pərd\ *adj* : easily angered

quick–wit·ted \'kwik-'wit-əd\ *adj* : mentally alert

¹qui·et \'kwī-ət\ *n* : the quality or state of being quiet : TRANQUILLITY

²quiet *adj* **1** : marked by little or no motion or activity : CALM **2** : GENTLE, MILD ⟨a *quiet* disposition⟩ **3** : UNDISTURBED, PEACEFUL ⟨a *quiet* lunch⟩ **4** : free from noise or uproar : STILL ⟨a *quiet* day⟩ **5** : not showy (as in color or style) ⟨*quiet* dress⟩ **6** : SECLUDED ⟨a *quiet* nook⟩ — **qui·et·ly** *adv* — **qui·et·ness** *n*

³quiet *adv* : QUIETLY ⟨*quiet*-running engine⟩

⁴quiet *vb* **1** : to cause to be quiet : CALM ⟨*quieted* the crowd⟩ **2** : to become quiet ⟨*quieted* down after her exciting day⟩

qui·e·tude \'kwī-ə-ˌtüd, -ˌtyüd\ *n* : the state of being quiet : REST, REPOSE

quill \'kwil\ *n* **1** : a large stiff feather **2** : the hollow tubelike part of a feather **3** : a spine of a hedgehog or porcupine **4** : a pen made from a feather

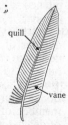

quill

vane

¹quilt \'kwilt\ *n* : a bed coverlet made of two pieces of cloth with a filling of wool, cotton, or down held together by patterned stitching or by tufting

²quilt *vb* **1** : to stitch or sew

---

j job   **ng** sing   **ō** low   **ȯ** moth   **ȯi** coin   **th** thin   **th̲** this   **ü** boot   **u̇** foot   **y** you   **yü** few   **yu̇** furious   **zh** vision

together as in making a quilt **2** : to make quilts ⟨a *quilting* party⟩

quince \'kwins\ *n* : the hard yellow rounded or pear-shaped fruit of a shrub-by tree related to the apple that is used especially in preserves

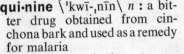
quince

qui·nine \'kwī-ˌnīn\ *n* : a bit-ter drug obtained from cin-chona bark and used as a remedy for malaria

quin·tet \kwin-'tet\ *n* **1** : a musical compo-sition for five instruments or voices **2** : a group or set of five

quin·tup·let \kwin-'təp-lət\ *n* **1** : a combina-tion of five of a kind **2** : one of five offspring born at one birth

quire \'kwīr\ *n* : a collection of twenty-four or sometimes twenty-five sheets of paper of the same size and quality

quirk \'kwərk\ *n* **1** : a sudden turn, twist, or curve (as a flourish in writing) **2** : a peculiar-ity of action or behavior

quit \'kwit\ *vb* **quit**; **quit·ting** **1** : BEHAVE, ACQUIT **2** : to finish doing, using, dealing with, working on, or handling : LEAVE ⟨*quit* a job⟩

quite \'kwīt\ *adv* **1** : COMPLETELY, WHOLLY ⟨*quite* alone⟩ **2** : POSITIVELY ⟨*quite* sure⟩ **3** : to a considerable extent : RATHER ⟨live *quite* near the school⟩

quit·ter \'kwit-ər\ *n* : a person who shirks or gives up too easily

¹**quiv·er** \'kwiv-ər\ *n* : a case for carrying arrows

²**quiver** *vb* : to move with a slight trembling motion ⟨leaves *quivering* in the breeze⟩

³**quiver** *n* : the act or ac-tion of quivering ⟨the *quiver* of a leaf⟩

quiver

¹**quiz** \'kwiz\ *n, pl* **quiz·zes** : a short oral or written test ⟨a *quiz* in history⟩

²**quiz** *vb* **quizzed**; **quiz·zing** : to question closely

quiz·zi·cal \'kwiz-i-kəl\ *adj* : QUESTIONING ⟨a *quizzical* look⟩ — **quiz·zi·cal·ly** *adv*

quoit \'kwāt, 'kwȯit\ *n* : a ring (as of rope) pitched at a peg in a game (**quoits**)

quo·rum \'kwȯr-əm\ *n* : the number of members of a body needed at a meeting in order for business to be legally transacted

quo·ta \'kwōt-ə\ *n* : a propor-tional share assigned to each member of a body ⟨the *quota* of delegates from each state⟩

quoits

quo·ta·tion \kwō-'tā-shən\ *n* **1** : something (as a passage from a book) that is quoted **2** : the act or process of quoting

quotation mark *n* : one of a pair of punctu-ation marks " " or ' ' used chiefly to indicate the beginning and end of a direct quotation

quote \'kwōt\ *vb* **quot·ed**; **quot·ing** **1** : to speak or write a passage from another usually with acknowledgment ⟨*quoted* his favorite poem⟩ **2** : to repeat a passage from especially as authority or illustration ⟨*quoted* the presi-dent's speech⟩

quo·tient \'kwō-shənt\ *n* : the number re-sulting from the division of one number by another

r \'är\ *n, often cap* : the eighteenth letter of the En-glish alphabet

rab·bi \'rab-ˌī\ *n, pl* **rabbis** **1** : MASTER, TEACHER — used as a term of address for Jewish religious leaders **2** : a Jew trained and ordained for professional religious leadership

rab·bit \'rab-ət\ *n* : a burrowing gnawing mammal that is smaller and has shorter ears than the related hare

rab·ble \'rab-əl\ *n* **1** : a noisy and unruly crowd : MOB **2** : a group of people looked down upon as ignorant and disorderly

rab·ble–rous·er \'rab-əl-ˌraủ-zər\ *n* : a per-son who stirs up the masses of the people es-pecially to hatred or violence

rab·id \'rab-əd\ *adj* **1** : VIOLENT, FURIOUS **2** : going to extreme lengths (as in interest or opinion) **3** : affected with rabies ⟨a *rabid* dog⟩ — **rab·id·ly** *adv* — **rab·id·ness** *n*

ra·bies \'rā-bēz\ *n* : HYDROPHOBIA

rac·coon \ra-'kün\ *n* : a small tree-dwelling North American flesh-eating animal that is active mostly at night and is sometimes hunted for sport, for its edible flesh, or for its coat of long fluffy usually mostly gray fur

¹**race** \'rās\ *n* **1** : a strong or rapid current of water **2** : an onward course (as of time or life) **3** : a contest of speed (as in running or sailing) **4** : a contest involving progress toward a goal ⟨the *race* for the governorship⟩

²**race** *vb* **raced**; **rac·ing** **1** : to take part in a race **2** : to go, move, or drive at top speed **3** : to cause to go too fast ⟨*race* an automobile engine⟩

³race *n* **1** : a group of individuals of common ancestry or stock **2** : a group of people unified by community of interests, habits, or characteristics **3** : one of the three, four, or five primary divisions commonly recognized in mankind and based on readily observable traits (as skin color) that are transmitted by heredity ⟨the white *race*⟩

race·course \'rās-,kōrs\ *n* : a place for racing

race·horse \'rās-,hȯrs\ *n* : a horse bred or kept for racing

rac·er \'rā-sər\ *n* **1** : one that races **2** : any of several long slender active snakes (as a common American blacksnake)

race·track \'rās-,trak\ *n* : a usually oval course on which races are run

ra·cial \'rā-shəl\ *adj* : of, relating to, or based on race — **ra·cial·ly** *adv*

¹rack \'rak\ *n* **1** : a framework on or in which articles are placed (as for display or storage) ⟨bicycle *rack*⟩ ⟨magazine *rack*⟩ **2** : an instrument of torture for stretching the body — **on the rack** : under great mental or emotional stress

²rack *vb* **1** : to cause to suffer torture, pain, or anguish **2** : to stretch or strain violently

³rack *n* : DESTRUCTION ⟨*rack* and ruin⟩

¹rack·et \'rak-ət\ *n* : a light bat consisting of a handle and an oval frame with a netting stretched across it

²racket *n* **1** : a confused noise : DIN **2** : a dishonest scheme (as for obtaining money through threats of violence)

rack·e·teer \,rak-ə-'tiər\ *n* : a person who extorts money or advantages (as by threats of violence)

ra·con·teur \,rak-,än-'tər\ *n* : a person good at telling anecdotes

rac·y \'rā-sē\ *adj* **rac·i·er; rac·i·est** **1** : having the distinctive quality of something in its original or most characteristic form **2** : full of zest or vigor

ra·dar \'rā-,där\ *n* [from the first letters of *ra*dio *d*etecting *a*nd *r*anging] : a radio device for detecting the position of distant masses and the course of moving objects (as distant airplanes or ships)

ra·di·ance \'rād-ē-əns\ *n* : the quality or state of being radiant : SPLENDOR

ra·di·ant \'rād-ē-ənt\ *adj* **1** : giving out or reflecting rays of light : SHINING ⟨the *radiant* sun⟩ **2** : glowing with love, confidence, or joy ⟨a *radiant* smile⟩ **3** : transmitted by radiation ⟨*radiant* heat from the sun⟩

radiant energy *n* : energy transmitted in the form of electromagnetic waves ⟨heat, light, radio waves are forms of *radiant energy*⟩

ra·di·ate \'rād-ē-,āt\ *vb* **ra·di·at·ed; ra·di·at·ing** **1** : to send out rays : SHINE **2** : to come forth in the form of rays ⟨light *radiates* from shining bodies⟩ **3** : to spread around as from a center ⟨the news *radiated* through the crowd⟩

ra·di·a·tion \,rād-ē-'ā-shən\ *n* **1** : the process of radiating and especially of emitting radiant energy in the form of waves or particles **2** : something that is radiated

ra·di·a·tor \'rād-ē-,āt-ər\ *n* : a device to heat air (as in a room) or to cool an object (as in an automobile engine)

radiators

¹rad·i·cal \'rad-i-kəl\ *adj* [this originally meant "of a root" in English, and was derived from Latin *radic-*, stem of *radix* "root"] **1** : of or relating to the origin : FUNDAMENTAL **2** : departing sharply from the usual or traditional : EXTREME ⟨a *radical* change⟩ **3** : of or relating to radicals in politics — **rad·i·cal·ly** *adv*

²radical *n* : a person who favors rapid and sweeping changes (as in laws and methods of government)

radii *pl of* RADIUS

¹ra·di·o \'rād-ē-,ō\ *n, pl* **ra·di·os** **1** : the sending or receiving of messages or effects and especially of sound by means of electromagnetic waves without a connecting wire **2** : a radio receiving set **3** : a radio message

²radio *adj* **1** : of or relating to radiant energy **2** : of, relating to, or used in radio

³radio *vb* : to communicate or send a message to by radio

ra·di·o·ac·tive \,rād-ē-ō-'ak-tiv\ *adj* : of, caused by, or exhibiting radioactivity

ra·di·o·ac·tiv·i·ty \,rād-ē-ō-ak-'tiv-ət-ē\ *n* : the property possessed by some elements (as uranium) of spontaneously emitting rays or tiny particles by the disintegration of the nuclei of atoms

radio wave *n* : an electromagnetic wave used in radio, television, or radar communication

rad·ish \'rad-ish\ *n* : the fleshy root of a plant of the mustard family eaten raw

ra·di·um \'rād-ē-əm\ *n* : a very strongly radioactive element found in minute quantities in various minerals (as pitchblende) and used in luminous materials and in the treatment of cancer

ra·di·us \'rād-ē-əs\ *n, pl* **ra·di·i** \-ē-,ī\ **1** : a straight line extending from the center of a circle to the circumference or from the center of a sphere to

radius

the surface : half of a diameter **2** : a roughly circular area defined by a radius ⟨within a *radius* of one mile from the school⟩

raf·fle \'raf-əl\ *n* : a lottery in which the prize is won by one of a number of persons buying chances

¹raft \'raft\ *n* **1** : a collection of logs or timber fastened together for conveyance by water **2** : a flat structure for support or transportation on water

²raft *n* : a large amount or number

raf·ter \'raf-tər\ *n* : one of the usually sloping timbers that support a roof

rag \'rag\ *n* **1** : a waste or worn piece of cloth **2** *pl* : shabby or tattered clothing ⟨dressed in *rags*⟩

rag·a·muf·fin \'rag-ə-ˌməf-ən\ *n* : a ragged dirty man or child

rafters

¹rage \'rāj\ *n* [from early French *rage*, a modification of Latin *rabies* "rage", "madness", the source of English *rabies*] **1** : violent and uncontrolled anger : FURY **2** : violent action (as of wind or sea) **3** : VOGUE, FASHION ⟨was all the *rage*⟩

²rage *vb* raged; rag·ing **1** : to be in a rage **2** : to continue out of control ⟨the fire *raged* for hours⟩

rag·ged \'rag-əd\ *adj* **1** : having an irregular edge or outline ⟨*ragged* cliffs⟩ **2** : TORN, TATTERED ⟨*ragged* clothes⟩ **3** : wearing tattered clothes **4** : done in an uneven way ⟨a *ragged* performance⟩ — **rag·ged·ly** *adv* — **rag·ged·ness** *n*

rag·man \'rag-ˌman\ *n, pl* rag·men \-ˌmen\ : a collector of or dealer in rags and waste

rag·time \'rag-ˌtīm\ *n* : music in which the accented notes of the melody fall on beats that are not usually accented

rag·weed \'rag-ˌwēd\ *n* : a common coarse weed whose pollen is irritating to the eyes and nasal passages of some persons

¹raid \'rād\ *n* **1** : a sudden attack or invasion by troops or aircraft as a military operation **2** : a sudden invasion by officers of the law

²raid *vb* : to make a raid on — **raid·er** *n*

ragweed

¹rail \'rāl\ *n* **1** : a bar extending from one support to another and serving as a guard or barrier **2** : a bar of steel forming a track for wheeled vehicles **3** : RAILROAD ⟨travel by *rail*⟩

²rail *vb* : to provide with a railing : FENCE

³rail *n* : any of a family of wading birds related to the cranes and hunted as game birds

⁴rail *vb* : to scold or complain in harsh or bitter language

rail·ing \'rā-ling\ *n* **1** : a barrier (as a fence or balustrade) consisting of rails and their supports **2** : material for making rails

railing

rail·ler·y \'rā-lə-rē\ *n, pl* rail·ler·ies **1** : good-natured ridicule **2** : JEST

¹rail·road \'rāl-ˌrōd\ *n* **1** : a permanent road that has parallel steel rails that make a track for cars **2** : a railroad together with the lands, buildings, locomotives, cars, and other equipment that belong to it

²railroad *vb* **1** : to work on a railroad **2** : to push (as a law) through without due consideration **3** : to convict with undue haste and often by means of insufficient evidence

rail·way \'rāl-ˌwā\ *n* : RAILROAD

rai·ment \'rā-mənt\ *n* : CLOTHING, GARMENTS

¹rain \'rān\ *n* **1** : water falling in drops from the clouds **2** : a fall of rain **3** : rainy weather **4** : a heavy fall of objects ⟨a *rain* of bullets⟩

²rain *vb* **1** : to fall as water in drops from the clouds **2** : to send down rain **3** : to fall like rain ⟨ashes *rained* from the volcano⟩ **4** : to bestow abundantly

rain·bow \'rān-ˌbō\ *n* : an arc of colors that appears in the sky opposite the sun and is caused by the sun shining through rain, mist, or spray

rain·coat \'rān-ˌkōt\ *n* : a coat of waterproof or water-resistant material

rain·drop \'rān-ˌdräp\ *n* : a drop of rain

rain·fall \'rān-ˌfȯl\ *n* **1** : RAIN **2** : amount of precipitation ⟨an annual *rainfall* of forty inches⟩

rain·proof \'rān-ˈprüf\ *adj* : impervious to rain

rain·storm \'rān-ˌstȯrm\ *n* : a storm of or with rain

rain·wa·ter \'rān-ˌwȯt-ər, -ˌwät-\ *n* : water falling or fallen as rain

raincoat

rain·y \'rā-nē\ *adj* rain·i·er; rain·i·est : having much rain : SHOWERY ⟨a *rainy* season⟩

¹raise \'rāz\ *vb* raised; rais·ing **1** : to cause to rise : LIFT ⟨*raise* a window⟩ **2** : to give life to : AROUSE ⟨enough noise to *raise* the dead⟩ **3** : BUILD, ERECT ⟨*raise* a monument⟩ **4** : ELEVATE, PROMOTE ⟨was *raised* to captain⟩ **5** : COLLECT ⟨*raise* money⟩ **6** : to foster the growth and development of : GROW ⟨*raise* hogs for market⟩ **7** : to give rise to : PROVOKE ⟨*raise* a laugh⟩ **8** : to bring to notice ⟨*raise* an objection〉 **9** : INCREASE 〈*raise* the rent〉 **10** : to make light and porous 〈*raise* dough〉 **11** : END 〈*raise* a siege〉 **12** : to cause to form on the skin 〈*raise* a blister〉 — **rais·er** *n*

²raise *n* : an increase in amount (as of pay)

rai·sin \'rāz-n\ *n* : a sweet grape dried for food

ra·ja *or* **ra·jah** \'räj-ə\ *n* : an Indian prince

¹rake \'rāk\ *n* : a long-handled garden tool having a bar with teeth or prongs

²rake *vb* **raked; rak·ing** **1** : to gather, loosen, or smooth with a rake 〈*rake* leaves〉 **2** : to search through : RANSACK **3** : to sweep the length of with gunfire

rakes

³rake *n* : a dissolute person

¹rak·ish \'rā-kish\ *adj* : DISSOLUTE

²rakish *adj* **1** : having a smart stylish appearance **2** : JAUNTY

¹ral·ly \'ral-ē\ *vb* **ral·lied; ral·ly·ing** **1** : to bring or come together for a common purpose **2** : to bring back to order 〈a leader *rallying* his forces〉 **3** : to rouse from depression or weakness 〈the patient *rallied*〉 **4** : RECOVER, REBOUND

²rally *n, pl* **ral·lies** **1** : the act of rallying **2** : a mass meeting held to arouse enthusiasm

¹ram \'ram\ *n* **1** : a male sheep **2** : BATTERING RAM

²ram *vb* **rammed; ram·ming** **1** : to strike or strike against with violence **2** : to force in, down, or together by driving or pressing 〈*ram* clothes into a suitcase〉 **3** : to force passage or acceptance of 〈*ram* a bill through congress〉

ram 1

¹ram·ble \'ram-bəl\ *vb* **ram·bled; ram·bling** **1** : to go aimlessly from place to place : WANDER **2** : to talk or write in an aimless way **3** : to grow or extend irregularly 〈a *rambling* vine〉

²ramble *n* : a long walk : HIKE

ram·bler \'ram-blər\ *n* : a hardy climbing rose with large clusters of small flowers

ram·bunc·tious \ram-'bəngk-shəs\ *adj* : UNRULY — **ram·bunc·tious·ly** *adv* — **ram·bunc·tious·ness** *n*

ram·i·fi·ca·tion \ˌram-ə-fə-'kā-shən\ *n* **1** : a branching out **2** : OUTGROWTH, CONSEQUENCE 〈the *ramifications* of a problem〉

ram·i·fy \'ram-ə-ˌfī\ *vb* **ram·i·fied; ram·i·fying** : to spread out or split up into branches or divisions

ramp \'ramp\ *n* : a sloping passage or roadway connecting different levels

ram·page \'ram-ˌpāj\ *n* : a course of violent or reckless action or behavior

ram·pant \'ram-pənt\ *adj* : not checked in growth or spread : RIFE 〈fear was *rampant* in the town〉 — **ram·pant·ly** *adv*

ram·part \'ram-ˌpärt\ *n* : a broad bank or wall used as a fortification or protective barrier

ram·rod \'ram-ˌräd\ *n* **1** : a rod for ramming the charge into a muzzle-loading firearm **2** : a cleaning rod for small arms

ram·shack·le \'ram-ˌshak-əl\ *adj* : ready to fall down : TUMBLEDOWN 〈a *ramshackle* barn〉

ran *past of* RUN

¹ranch \'ranch\ *n* **1** : an establishment for the grazing and raising of livestock (as cattle) **2** : a farm devoted to a special crop 〈a fruit *ranch*〉

²ranch *vb* : to live or work on a ranch — **ranch·er** *n*

ran·cid \'ran-səd\ *adj* : having the strong disagreeable smell or taste of old stale oil or fat 〈*rancid* butter〉 — **ran·cid·ness** *n*

ran·cor \'rang-kər\ *n* : deep hatred

ran·cor·ous \'rang-kə-rəs\ *adj* : marked by rancor — **ran·cor·ous·ly** *adv*

¹ran·dom \'ran-dəm\ *n* : a haphazard course — **at random** : without definite aim, direction, or method

²random *adj* : lacking a definite plan, purpose, or pattern

rang *past of* RING

¹range \'rānj\ *n* **1** : a series of things in a line 〈*range* of mountains〉 **2** : a cooking stove **3** : open land over which livestock may roam and feed **4** : the distance a gun will shoot **5** : a place where shooting is practiced 〈a rifle *range*〉 **6** : the space or extent included, covered, or used : SCOPE 〈the *range* of his knowledge〉 **7** : a variation within limits 〈a great *range* in prices〉

²range *vb* **ranged; rang·ing** **1** : to set in a row or in proper order **2** : to set in place among others of the same kind **3** : to roam over or through **4** : to correspond in direction or line **5** : to vary within limits 〈the temperature *ranged* from fifty to eighty degrees〉

rang·er \'rān-jər\ *n* **1** : the keeper of a British royal park or forest **2** : a warden who patrols forest lands **3** : a member of a body of troops who range over a region **4** : a soldier trained in close-range fighting and raiding tactics

rang·y \'rān-jē\ *adj* **rang·i·er; rang·i·est** : tall and slender in body build — **rang·i·ness** *n*

¹rank \'rangk\ *adj* **1** : strong and vigorous and usually coarse in growth 〈*rank* weeds〉 **2** : unpleasantly strong-smelling : RANCID 〈*rank* butter〉 **3** : EXTREME, UTTER 〈*rank* dishonesty〉 — **rank·ly** *adv* — **rank·ness** *n*

²rank *n* **1** : ROW, SERIES ⟨*ranks* of houses⟩ **2** : a line of soldiers ranged side by side **3** *pl* : a group of individuals classed together ⟨the *ranks* of the unemployed⟩ **4** : relative position : STANDING ⟨his *rank* was fifth in his class⟩ **5** : official grade or status ⟨the *rank* of major⟩ **6** : high social position ⟨a man of *rank*⟩ **7** *pl* : the body of enlisted men in an army ⟨rose from the *ranks*⟩

³rank *vb* **1** : to arrange in lines or in a regular formation **2** : to arrange according to classes **3** : to rate above (as in official standing) **4** : to take or have a relative position

ran·kle \'rang-kəl\ *vb* **ran·kled; ran·kling** : to cause anger, irritation, or bitterness

ran·sack \'ran-,sak\ *vb* **1** : to search thoroughly **2** : to search through in order to rob ⟨a burglar *ransacked* the house⟩

¹ran·som \'ran-səm\ *n* **1** : something (as money) paid or demanded for the freedom of a captured person **2** : the act of ransoming

²ransom *vb* : to free from captivity or punishment by paying a price — **ran·som·er** *n*

rant \'rant\ *vb* **1** : to talk loudly and wildly **2** : to scold violently — **rant·er** *n*

¹rap \'rap\ *n* : a sharp blow or knock

²rap *vb* **rapped; rap·ping** : to give a quick sharp blow : KNOCK

ra·pa·cious \rə-'pā-shəs\ *adj* **1** : extremely greedy or covetous **2** : PREDATORY **3** : RAVENOUS — **ra·pa·cious·ly** *adv* — **ra·pa·cious·ness** *n*

¹rape \'rāp\ *n* : a plant related to the mustards that is grown for forage and for its seeds used as birdseed and as a source of oil

²rape *vb* **raped; rap·ing** : to commit rape on

³rape *n* **1** : a seizing by force **2** : sexual intercourse with a woman without her consent and especially by force

rap·id \'rap-əd\ *adj* : very fast : SWIFT — **rap·id·ly** *adv*

ra·pid·i·ty \rə-'pid-ət-ē\ *n* : the quality or state of being rapid

rap·ids \'rap-ədz\ *n pl* : a part of a river where the current flows very fast

ra·pi·er \'rā-pē-ər\ *n* : a two-edged sword with a narrow pointed blade

rap·port \ra-'pōr\ *n* : harmonious relationship : ACCORD

rap·proche·ment \,rap-,rōsh-'män\ *n* : the establishment or a state of cordial relations

rap·scal·lion \rap-'skal-yən\ *n* : RASCAL, SCAMP

rapt \'rapt\ *adj* : showing complete delight or interest ⟨*rapt* attention⟩

rap·ture \'rap-chər\ *n* : a deep feeling of joy, delight, or love

rapier

¹rare \'raər\ *adj* **rar·er; rar·est** : cooked a short time ⟨*rare* roast beef⟩

²rare *adj* **rar·er; rar·est 1** : not thick or dense : THIN ⟨a *rare* atmosphere at high altitudes⟩ **2** : unusually fine : EXCELLENT ⟨a *rare* treat⟩ **3** : very uncommon ⟨*rare* books⟩

syn RARE, SCARCE both refer to something that is not common or ordinary. RARE is used of things of which there are only a few examples or instances ⟨a *rare* tropical disease⟩ and may suggest that there is a value attached because of the rarity ⟨a *rare* postage stamp much sought by collectors⟩ SCARCE applies to something that for the time being is in short supply ⟨cabs were *scarce* during the sudden downpour⟩ or that might be but isn't produced in sufficient quantity to fulfill needs ⟨food is *scarce* and starvation common in many countries⟩

rar·e·fy \'rar-ə-,fī\ *vb* **rar·e·fied; rar·e·fy·ing** : to make or become thin, porous, or less dense

rare·ly \'raər-lē\ *adv* **1** : not often : SELDOM **2** : with unusual skill **3** : EXTREMELY

rar·i·ty \'rar-ət-ē\ *n, pl* **rar·i·ties 1** : THINNESS ⟨the *rarity* of the atmosphere at great heights⟩ **2** : SCARCITY ⟨the *rarity* of holidays⟩ **3** : something rare : an uncommon thing

ras·cal \'ras-kəl\ *n* **1** : a mean or dishonest person **2** : a mischievous person

¹rash \'rash\ *adj* : too hasty in decision, action, or speech — **rash·ly** *adv* — **rash·ness** *n*

²rash *n* : a breaking out of the skin with red spots (as in measles)

rash·er \'rash-ər\ *n* : a thin slice of bacon or ham broiled or fried

¹rasp \'rasp\ *vb* **1** : to rub with or as if with a rough file ⟨*rasp* off the rough edges⟩ **2** : to grate harshly : IRRITATE ⟨a *rasping* voice⟩

²rasp *n* **1** : a coarse file with cutting points instead of lines **2** : a rasping sound, sensation, or effect

rasp 1

rasp·ber·ry \'raz-,ber-ē\ *n, pl* **rasp·ber·ries 1** : a sweet edible red, black, or purple berry that is usually smaller and less sour than the related blackberry **2** : a sound of contempt made by protruding the tongue between the lips and expelling air forcibly so as to produce a vibration

¹rat \'rat\ *n* **1** : a gnawing animal with brown, black, white, or grayish fur that resembles but is larger than the mouse **2** : a person who betrays his associates

²rat *vb* **rat·ted; rat·ting 1** : to betray one's associates **2** : to hunt or catch rats

rat

¹rate \'rāt\ *n* **1** : quantity, amount, or degree measured by some standard ⟨a *rate* of forty miles an hour⟩ **2** : an amount (as of payment) measured by its relation to some other amount (as of time) ⟨a wage *rate* of a dollar an hour⟩ **3** : a charge, payment, or price fixed according to a ratio, scale, or standard ⟨tax *rate*⟩ **4** : RANK, CLASS — **at any rate** : in any case

²rate *vb* **rat·ed; rat·ing 1** : CONSIDER, REGARD ⟨*rated* a good player⟩ **2** : to set an estimate or value on **3** : to determine the rank, class, or position of : GRADE **4** : to have a rating : RANK **5** : to have a right to : DESERVE ⟨*rates* a promotion⟩

rath·er \'rath-ər\ *adv* [from Old English *hrathor*, comparative of *hrathe* "quickly"] **1** : PREFERABLY ⟨would *rather* not go⟩ **2** : on the contrary : INSTEAD ⟨not for better but *rather* for worse⟩ **3** : with better reason : more exactly or precisely ⟨to be pitied *rather* than blamed⟩ **4** : SOMEWHAT ⟨a *rather* cold day⟩

rat·i·fi·ca·tion \ˌrat-ə-fə-'kā-shən\ *n* : the act or process of ratifying

rat·i·fy \'rat-ə-ˌfī\ *vb* **rat·i·fied; rat·i·fy·ing** : to approve and sanction formally ⟨*ratify* a treaty⟩

rat·ing \'rāt-ing\ *n* **1** : a classification according to grade : RANK **2** : a relative estimate or evaluation ⟨credit *rating*⟩

ra·tio \'rā-shō\ *n, pl* **ra·tios** : the relation in number, quantity, or degree between two or more things ⟨women outnumbered men in the *ratio* of three to one or 3/1 or 3:1⟩

¹ra·tion \'rash-ən, 'rā-shən\ *n* **1** : a food allowance for one day **2** : FOOD, PROVISIONS, DIET ⟨a salt-free *ration*⟩ **3** : a share as determined usually by supply or allotment by authority

²ration *vb* **1** : to supply with rations ⟨*ration* cattle⟩ **2** : to distribute or allot as a ration ⟨the government *rationed* gas⟩ **3** : to use or allot sparingly

ra·tio·nal \'rash-ən-l\ *adj* **1** : having the ability to reason ⟨man is a *rational* creature⟩ **2** : relating to, based on, or showing reason ⟨*rational* thinking⟩ **3** : SANE, SENSIBLE — **ra·tio·nal·ly** *adv*

ra·tio·nale \ˌrash-ə-'nal\ *n* : a fundamental explanation or underlying reason : BASIS

ra·tio·nal·ize \'rash-ən-l-ˌīz\ *vb* **ra·tio·nal·ized; ra·tio·nal·iz·ing 1** : to provide a natural explanation of (as a myth) **2** : to find plausible but untrue reasons for conduct

rational number *n* : a number that may be expressed as an integer or as the quotient of two integers ⟨7, 3/4, 2/3 are *rational numbers*⟩

rat·tan \ra-'tan\ *n* : a strong flexible material

that is a section of the stem of a climbing palm (**rattan palm**) and is used for walking sticks and wickerwork

rat·ter \'rat-ər\ *n* : a rat-catching dog or cat

¹rat·tle \'rat-l\ *vb* **rat·tled; rat·tling 1** : to make or cause to make a rapid succession of short sharp sounds **2** : to move with a clatter **3** : to say or do in a brisk lively way ⟨*rattle* off the answers⟩ **4** : CONFUSE, UPSET ⟨*rattle* a witness⟩

²rattle *n* **1** : a series of short sharp sounds **2** : a device (as a toy) for making a rattling sound **3** : a rattling organ at the end of a rattlesnake's tail made up of horny joints

rat·tler \'rat-lər\ *n* : RATTLESNAKE

rat·tle·snake \'rat-l-ˌsnāk\ *n* : a poisonous American snake with a rattle at the end of its tail

rat·tle·trap \'rat-l-ˌtrap\ *n* : something (as an old car) rickety and full of rattles

rau·cous \'ro-kəs\ *adj* **1** : disagreeably harsh **2** : boisterously disorderly — **rau·cous·ly** *adv* — **rau·cous·ness** *n*

¹rav·age \'rav-ij\ *n* **1** : an act of ravaging **2** : damage resulting from ravaging

²ravage *vb* **rav·aged; rav·ag·ing 1** : to lay waste : PLUNDER **2** : DESTROY, RUIN ⟨*ravaged* by disease⟩ — **rav·ag·er** *n*

rave \'rāv\ *vb* **raved; rav·ing 1** : to talk wildly (as in delirium) **2** : to talk with great enthusiasm ⟨*raved* about the new play⟩

rav·el \'rav-əl\ *vb* **rav·eled** *or* **rav·elled; rav·el·ing** *or* **rav·el·ling** : to undo something knitted or tangled : UNRAVEL

¹ra·ven \'rā-vən\ *n* : a glossy black crowlike bird about two feet long of northern regions

²raven *adj* : glossy and black like a raven's feathers

rav·en·ous \'rav-ə-nəs\ *adj* **1** : RAPACIOUS, VORACIOUS **2** : very eager for food — **rav·en·ous·ly** *adv*

ra·vine \rə-'vēn\ *n* : a small narrow steep-sided valley larger than a gully and smaller than a canyon

rav·ish \'rav-ish\ *vb* **1** : to seize and take away by force **2** : to overcome with emotion and especially with joy or delight **3** : RAPE

raw \'ro\ *adj* **1** : not cooked **2** : being in or nearly in the natural state ⟨*raw* materials⟩ **3** : lacking a normal or usual finish ⟨*raw* edge of a seam⟩ **4** : having the skin rubbed off **5** : not trained or experienced ⟨*raw* recruits⟩ **6** : disagreeably damp or cold ⟨a *raw* day⟩ — **raw·ly** *adv* — **raw·ness** *n*

raw·boned \'ro-'bōnd\ *adj* : GAUNT

raw·hide \'rȯ-ˌhīd\ *n* **1** : untanned cattle skin **2** : a whip of untanned hide

¹ray \'rā\ *n* : a flat broad fish related to the sharks that has its eyes on the top of its head

²ray *n* [from French *rai*, taken from Latin *radius* "spoke of a wheel", "ray", "radius"] **1** : one of the lines of light that appear to radiate from a bright object ⟨*rays* of sunlight⟩ **2** : a thin beam of radiant energy (as light) **3** : light from a beam **4** : a thin line suggesting a ray **5** : a straight line extending from a point in one direction only **6** : a plant or animal structure (as a petallike part of a daisy or an arm of a starfish) resembling a ray **7** : PARTICLE ⟨a *ray* of hope⟩

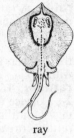
ray

ray·on \'rā-ˌän\ *n* : a textile fabric made from fibers produced chemically from cellulose

raze \'rāz\ *vb* **razed**; **raz·ing** : to destroy completely by laying level with the ground : DEMOLISH ⟨*raze* a building⟩

ra·zor \'rā-zər\ *n* : a sharp cutting instrument used to shave off hair

razz \'raz\ *vb* : to ridicule usually in fun : TEASE

re \'rā\ *n* : the second note of the musical scale

razors

re- *prefix* **1** : again : anew ⟨*retell*⟩ **2** : back : backward ⟨*recall*⟩

¹reach \'rēch\ *vb* **1** : to stretch out : EXTEND **2** : to touch or move to touch or seize by extending a part of the body (as the hand) or something held in the hand **3** : to extend or stretch to ⟨his land *reaches* the river⟩ **4** : to arrive at : COME ⟨*reached* home late⟩ **5** : to communicate with ⟨tried to *reach* her on the phone⟩

²reach *n* **1** : the act of reaching especially to grasp something **2** : ability to stretch (as an arm) so as to touch something ⟨a boy with a long *reach*⟩ **3** : COMPREHENSION, RANGE **4** : an unbroken stretch or expanse (as of a river)

re·act \rē-'akt\ *vb* **1** : to have a return effect or influence : act in return **2** : to act or behave in response (as to stimulation or an influence) ⟨*reacted* violently to his suggestion⟩ **3** : to undergo a chemical reaction

re·ac·tion \rē-'ak-shən\ *n* **1** : a return effect of an action upon the person or thing that originally started the action **2** : a response (as of body or mind) to a stimulus (as a treatment, situation, or stress) ⟨studied the patient's *reaction* to the drug⟩ ⟨his shocked *reaction* to the news⟩ **3** : a chemical change that is brought about by the action of one substance on another and results in the formation of a new substance

re·ac·tion·ar·y \rē-'ak-shə-ˌner-ē\ *adj* : of, relating to, or favoring an outmoded political or social order or policy

re·ac·tor \rē-'ak-tər\ *n* **1** : one that reacts **2** : an apparatus for the controlled release of atomic energy (as for the generation of heat)

read \'rēd\ *vb* **read** \'red\; **read·ing** \'rēd-ing\ **1** : to understand language by interpreting written symbols for speech sounds **2** : to utter aloud written or printed words ⟨*read* a poem to the class⟩ **3** : to learn from what one has seen in writing or printing ⟨*read* about the fire⟩ **4** : to discover or interpret the meaning of ⟨*read* palms⟩ **5** : to attribute as an assumption or conjecture ⟨*read* guilt in the boy's manner⟩ **6** : to make a study of ⟨*read* law⟩ **7** : INDICATE, REGISTER ⟨the thermometer *reads* zero⟩ **8** : to consist of specific words, phrases, or symbols ⟨the two versions *read* quite differently⟩ — **read between the lines** : to understand more than is directly stated — **read the riot act** : to give a stern warning or reprimand

read·er \'rēd-ər\ *n* **1** : one that reads **2** : a book for learning or practicing reading

read·ing \'rēd-ing\ *n* **1** : something read or for reading **2** : the form in which something is written : VERSION **3** : something that is registered (as on a gauge) **4** : a particular interpretation or performance ⟨an actor's *reading* of his part⟩

¹read·y \'red-ē\ *adj* **read·i·er**; **read·i·est** **1** : prepared for use or action ⟨dinner is *ready*⟩ **2** : APT, LIKELY ⟨*ready* to cry⟩ **3** : WILLING ⟨*ready* to give aid⟩ **4** : QUICK, PROMPT ⟨a *ready* answer⟩ **5** : AVAILABLE, HANDY ⟨*ready* money⟩ — **read·i·ly** \'red-l-ē\ *adv* — **read·i·ness** \'red-ē-nəs\ *n*

²ready *vb* **read·ied**; **read·y·ing** : to make ready : PREPARE

³ready *n* : the state of being ready ⟨guns at the *ready*⟩

read·y–made \ˌred-ē-'mād\ *adj* : made beforehand for general sale ⟨*ready-made* suit⟩

re·al \'rē-əl\ *adj* **1** : of, relating to, or constituting fixed, permanent, or immovable things ⟨*real* property⟩ **2** : not imaginary : ACTUAL ⟨*real* life⟩ **3** : not artificial : GENUINE ⟨*real* diamonds⟩ — **re·al·ness** *n*

real estate *n* : property in houses and land

re·al·ism \'rē-ə-ˌliz-əm\ *n* **1** : a disposition to face facts and to deal with them practically **2** : true and faithful portrayal of nature and of men in art or literature

re·al·is·tic \ˌrē-ə-'lis-tik\ *adj* **1** : true to life or nature ⟨a *realistic* painting⟩ **2** : having or showing an inclination to see things as they really are and to deal with them sensibly — **re·al·is·ti·cal·ly** \-ti-kə-lē\ *adv*

re·al·i·ty \rē-'al-ət-ē\ *n, pl* **re·al·i·ties 1** : actual existence : GENUINENESS **2** : someone or something real or actual ⟨the *realities* of life⟩

re·al·i·za·tion \ˌrē-ə-lə-'zā-shən\ *n* : the action of realizing : the state of being realized

re·al·ize \'rē-ə-ˌlīz\ *vb* **re·al·ized; re·al·iz·ing 1** : to make actual : ACCOMPLISH ⟨*realize* a lifelong ambition⟩ **2** : to obtain as a result of effort : GAIN ⟨*realize* a large profit⟩ **3** : to be aware of : UNDERSTAND ⟨*realized* his danger⟩

re·al·ly \'rē-ə-lē\ *adv* : ACTUALLY, TRULY

realm \'relm\ *n* **1** : KINGDOM **2** : SPHERE, DOMAIN ⟨the *realm* of fancy⟩

real number *n* : any number (as −2, 3, 7/8, .25) used in ordinary mathematics

re·al·ty \'rē-əl-tē\ *n, pl* **re·al·ties** : REAL ESTATE

¹ream \'rēm\ *n* **1** : a quantity of paper that is variously 480, 500, or 516 sheets **2** *pl* : a great amount ⟨*reams* of notes⟩

²ream *vb* **1** : to enlarge or shape with a reamer **2** : to clean or clear with a reamer

ream·er \'rē-mər\ *n* : a rotating tool with cutting edges

re·an·i·mate \rē-'an-ə-ˌmāt\ *vb* **re·an·i·mat·ed; re·an·i·mat·ing** : REVIVE

reap \'rēp\ *vb* **1** : to cut or clear with a sickle, scythe, or machine **2** : to gather by or as if by cutting : HARVEST

reap·er \'rē-pər\ *n* **1** : one that reaps **2** : a machine for harvesting grain

re·ap·pear \ˌrē-ə-'piər\ *vb* : to appear again

¹rear \'riər\ *vb* **1** : to erect by building : CONSTRUCT **2** : to raise or set upright **3** : to undertake the breeding and raising of ⟨*rear* cattle⟩ **4** : to bring up ⟨*rear* children⟩ **5** : to rise high **6** : to rise up on the hind legs ⟨the horse *reared* in fright⟩

²rear *n* **1** : the unit (as of an army) or area farthest from the enemy **2** : the space or position at the back

³rear *adj* : being at the back

rear admiral *n* : a commissioned officer in the navy ranking next below a vice admiral

re·ar·range \ˌrē-ə-'rānj\ *vb* **re·ar·ranged; re·ar·rang·ing** : to arrange again usually in a different way

rear·ward \'riər-wərd\ *adj (or adv)* **1** : located at, near, or toward the rear **2** : BACKWARD

¹rea·son \'rēz-n\ *n* **1** : a statement offered to explain or justify a belief or an act ⟨gave a *reason* for his absence⟩ **2** : GROUND, CAUSE

⟨has *reasons* for what he did⟩ **3** : the power to think : INTELLECT **4** : a sane or sound mind **syn** see CAUSE

²reason *vb* **1** : to talk with another so as to influence his actions or opinions **2** : to use the faculty of reason : think logically **3** : to state or formulate by the use of reason

rea·son·a·ble \'rēz-n-ə-bəl\ *adj* **1** : not extreme or excessive : MODERATE **2** : INEXPENSIVE **3** : able to reason : RATIONAL — **rea·son·a·ble·ness** *n* — **rea·son·a·bly** \-blē\ *adv*

re·as·sure \ˌrē-ə-'shùr\ *vb* **re·as·sured; re·as·sur·ing 1** : to assure again **2** : to restore confidence to : free from fear

¹re·bate \'rē-ˌbāt\ *vb* **re·bat·ed; re·bat·ing** : to make or give a rebate

²rebate *n* : a return of part of a payment ⟨*rebate* on a ticket⟩

¹reb·el \'reb-əl\ *adj* [from Old French *rebelle*, taken from Latin *rebellis*, literally, "that makes war again", from the prefix *re*- "again" and *bellum* "war"] **1** : opposing or taking arms against one's government or ruler **2** : DISOBEDIENT

²rebel *n* : a person who rebels against authority

³re·bel \ri-'bel\ *vb* **re·belled; re·bel·ling 1** : to oppose or resist authority and especially the authority of one's government **2** : to feel or exhibit anger or strong aversion

re·bel·lion \ri-'bel-yən\ *n* **1** : opposition and resistance to authority and especially to one's government **2** : an instance of rebellion : REVOLT

re·bel·lious \ri-'bel-yəs\ *adj* **1** : engaged in rebellion ⟨*rebellious* troops⟩ **2** : inclined to resist or disobey authority — **re·bel·lious·ly** *adv* — **re·bel·lious·ness** *n*

re·birth \'rē-'bərth\ *n* **1** : a new or second birth **2** : RENAISSANCE, REVIVAL

re·born \'rē-'bòrn\ *adj* : born again : REVIVED

¹re·bound \'rē-'baùnd\ *vb* **1** : to spring back on striking something **2** : to recover from a setback or frustration

²re·bound \'rē-ˌbaùnd\ *n* **1** : the action of rebounding : RECOIL **2** : an immediate reaction to a setback or frustration

¹re·buff \ri-'bəf\ *vb* **1** : SNUB **2** : to drive or beat back ⟨*rebuff* an attack⟩

²rebuff *n* **1** : an abrupt refusal to meet an advance or offer **2** : REPULSE

re·build \'rē-'bild\ *vb* **re·built** \-'bilt\; **re·build·ing 1** : to make extensive repairs to or changes in ⟨*rebuild* an old house⟩ **2** : to build again

¹re·buke \ri-'byük\ *vb* **re·buked; re·buk·ing** : to scold or criticize severely **syn** REBUKE, ADMONISH, SCOLD all mean to criticize severely especially in order to correct a fault. REBUKE suggests a sharp and stern expression of disapproval intended to put an immediate stop to undesirable behavior ⟨she *rebuked* the children for playing in the street⟩ ADMONISH emphasizes the issuing of a warning, often in a mild tone but usually with serious intent ⟨*admonished* the noisy children about disturbing their grandfather⟩ SCOLD stresses the delivering of a rebuke in a tone of ill temper or irritation ⟨perhaps it was the heat that made him nag and *scold* all day⟩

²rebuke *n* : REPRIMAND, REPROOF

re·but \ri-'bət\ *vb* **re·but·ted; re·but·ting** : to refute especially by formal argument or contrary proof

re·cal·ci·trant \ri-'kal-sə-trənt\ *adj* **1** : stubbornly resisting authority **2** : not responsive to handling or treatment

¹re·call \ri-'kȯl\ *vb* **1** : to ask or order to come back **2** : to bring back to mind ⟨*recall* an address⟩ **3** : CANCEL, REVOKE ⟨*recall* an order⟩

²recall *n* **1** : a summons to return **2** : remembrance of what has been learned or experienced **3** : the act of revoking

re·cant \ri-'kant\ *vb* : to repudiate an opinion or belief formally and publicly : RETRACT

re·ca·pit·u·late \ˌrē-kə-'pich-ə-ˌlāt\ *vb* **re·ca·pit·u·lat·ed; re·ca·pit·u·lat·ing** : to repeat briefly : SUMMARIZE

re·cap·ture \'rē-'kap-chər\ *vb* **re·cap·tured; re·cap·tur·ing** **1** : to capture again **2** : to experience again ⟨*recapture* his youth⟩

re·cede \ri-'sēd\ *vb* **re·ced·ed; re·ced·ing** **1** : to move back or away **2** : to slant backward **3** : DIMINISH, CONTRACT

¹re·ceipt \ri-'sēt\ *n* **1** : RECIPE **2** : the act of receiving **3** *pl* : something received ⟨the *receipts* from the sale⟩ **4** : a written acknowledgment of goods or money received

²receipt *vb* **1** : to give a receipt for **2** : to mark as paid

re·ceive \ri-'sēv\ *vb* **re·ceived; re·ceiv·ing** **1** : to take or get something that is given, paid, or sent ⟨*receive* the money⟩ ⟨*receive* a letter⟩ **2** : to permit to enter one's household or company : WELCOME ⟨*receive* friends⟩ **3** : to hold a reception **4** : to be the subject of : EXPERIENCE ⟨*receive* a shock⟩ **5** : to change incoming radio waves into sounds or pictures

re·ceiv·er \ri-'sē-vər\ *n* **1** : one that receives **2** : an apparatus for changing an electrical effect into an audible or visual effect ⟨a telephone *receiver*⟩ ⟨a radio *receiver*⟩

receiver

re·cent \'rēs-nt\ *adj* **1** : of or relating to a time not long past ⟨*recent* events⟩ **2** : having lately appeared or come into existence : NEW — **re·cent·ly** *adv* — **re·cent·ness** *n*

re·cep·ta·cle \ri-'sep-tə-kəl\ *n* : something used to receive and contain smaller objects : CONTAINER

re·cep·tion \ri-'sep-shən\ *n* **1** : the act or manner of receiving ⟨a warm *reception*⟩ **2** : a social gathering at which guests are formally welcomed **3** : the receiving of a radio or television broadcast

re·cep·tion·ist \ri-'sep-shə-nəst\ *n* : an office employee who greets callers

re·cep·tive \ri-'sep-tiv\ *adj* **1** : able or inclined to receive ideas **2** : able to receive and transmit stimuli — **re·cep·tive·ly** *adv* — **re·cep·tive·ness** *n*

re·cep·tor \ri-'sep-tər\ *n* : a cell or group of cells that receives stimuli : SENSE ORGAN

¹re·cess \'rē-ˌses, ri-'ses\ *n* **1** : an indentation in a line or surface **2** : a secret or secluded place **3** : an intermission between work periods

²recess *vb* **1** : to put into a recess ⟨*recessed* lighting⟩ **2** : to interrupt for or take a recess

re·ces·sion \ri-'sesh-ən\ *n* **1** : a departing procession (as of clergy and choir at the end of a church service) **2** : a period of reduced business activity

rec·i·pe \'res-ə-pē\ *n* [from Latin *recipe* "take", imperative form of *recipere* "to take"; used toward the end of the Middle Ages by physicians on prescriptions and later abbreviated to ℞] : a set of instructions for making something (as a food dish) from various ingredients

re·cip·i·ent \ri-'sip-ē-ənt\ *n* : one that receives

¹re·cip·ro·cal \ri-'sip-rə-kəl\ *adj* **1** : MUTUAL, SHARED ⟨*reciprocal* affection⟩ **2** : mutually corresponding — **re·cip·ro·cal·ly** *adv*

²reciprocal *n* : one of a pair of numbers (as 9 and 1/9, 2/3 and 3/2) whose product is one

re·cip·ro·cate \ri-'sip-rə-ˌkāt\ *vb* **re·cip·ro·cat·ed; re·cip·ro·cat·ing** **1** : to give and take mutually **2** : to make a return for something done or given

rec·i·proc·i·ty \ˌres-ə-'präs-ət-ē\ *n, pl* **rec·i·proc·i·ties** : mutual dependence, cooperation, or exchange (as between persons or nations)

re·cit·al \ri-'sīt-l\ *n* **1** : a reciting of something ⟨the *recital* of his troubles⟩ **2** : a program of one kind of music ⟨piano *recital*⟩ **3** : a public performance by pupils (as dancing pupils)

rec·i·ta·tion \ˌres-ə-'tā-shən\ *n* **1** : an enumerating or telling in detail **2** : the delivery before an audience of something memorized **3** : a student's oral reply to questions

re·cite \ri-'sīt\ *vb* **re·cit·ed; re·cit·ing 1** : to repeat from memory ⟨*recite* a poem⟩ **2** : to give a detailed account of **3** : to answer questions about a lesson

reck·less \'rek-ləs\ *adj* : CARELESS, NEGLIGENT **syn** see DARING — **reck·less·ly** *adv* — **reck·less·ness** *n*

reck·on \'rek-ən\ *vb* **1** : COUNT, COMPUTE ⟨*reckon* the days till vacation⟩ **2** : CONSIDER, REGARD ⟨was *reckoned* among the leaders⟩ **3** : to make up or settle an account

re·claim \ri-'klām\ *vb* **1** : to recall from wrong conduct : REFORM **2** : to change to a desirable condition or state ⟨*reclaim* a swamp⟩ **3** : to obtain from a waste product : RECOVER ⟨*reclaimed* rubber⟩

rec·la·ma·tion \,rek-lə-'mā-shən\ *n* : the act or process of reclaiming : the state of being reclaimed

re·cline \ri-'klīn\ *vb* **re·clined; re·clin·ing 1** : to lean or incline backward **2** : to lie down

rec·luse \'rek-,lüs\ *n* : a person (as a hermit) who lives away from others

rec·og·ni·tion \,rek-əg-'nish-ən\ *n* **1** : the act of recognizing **2** : special attention or notice ⟨won *recognition* for his paintings⟩ **3** : acknowledgment of something done or given ⟨got a medal in *recognition* of his bravery⟩

rec·og·nize \'rek-əg-,nīz\ *vb* **rec·og·nized; rec·og·niz·ing 1** : to know and remember upon seeing ⟨*recognize* an old friend⟩ **2** : to consent to admit : ACKNOWLEDGE ⟨*recognized* her own faults⟩ **3** : to take approving notice of ⟨*recognize* an act of bravery by the award of a medal⟩ **4** : to acknowledge acquaintance with ⟨*recognize* someone with a nod⟩

¹re·coil \ri-'kȯil\ *vb* **1** : to draw back ⟨*recoil* in horror⟩ **2** : to spring back to a former position ⟨the gun *recoiled* upon firing⟩

²recoil *n* **1** : the act or action of recoiling **2** : a springing back (as of a discharged gun) **3** : the distance through which something (as a spring) recoils

rec·ol·lect \,rek-ə-'lekt\ *vb* : to call to mind : REMEMBER ⟨*recollect* what happened⟩

rec·ol·lec·tion \,rek-ə-'lek-shən\ *n* **1** : the act or power of recalling to mind : MEMORY ⟨a good *recollection*⟩ **2** : something remembered ⟨my earliest *recollections*⟩

rec·om·mend \,rek-ə-'mend\ *vb* **1** : to make a statement in praise of ⟨*recommend* him for a promotion⟩ **2** : to put forward as one's advice, as one's choice, or as having one's

support ⟨*recommend* that the matter be dropped⟩ **3** : to cause to receive favorable attention ⟨a man *recommended* by his good manners⟩

rec·om·men·da·tion \,rek-ə-mən-'dā-shən\ *n* **1** : the act of recommending **2** : something that recommends ⟨a written *recommendation*⟩ **3** : a thing or course of action recommended

¹rec·om·pense \'rek-əm-,pens\ *vb* **rec·om·pensed; rec·om·pens·ing** : to give compensation to or for : PAY

²recompense *n* : COMPENSATION, PAYMENT

rec·on·cile \'rek-ən-,sīl\ *vb* **rec·on·ciled; rec·on·cil·ing 1** : to make friendly again ⟨*reconcile* friends who have quarreled⟩ **2** : SETTLE, ADJUST ⟨*reconcile* differences of opinion⟩ **3** : to make agree ⟨a story that cannot be *reconciled* with the facts⟩ **4** : to cause to submit or accept ⟨*reconcile* oneself to a loss⟩

re·con·di·tion \,rē-kən-'dish-ən\ *vb* : to restore to good condition (as by repairing or replacing parts)

re·con·firm \,rē-kən-'fərm\ *vb* : to confirm again ⟨*reconfirmed* his reservation⟩

re·con·nais·sance \ri-'kän-ə-zəns\ *n* : a preliminary survey (as of enemy territory)

re·con·noi·ter \,rē-kə-'nȯit-ər, ,rek-ə-\ *vb* : to make a reconnaissance (as in preparation for military action)

re·con·sid·er \,rē-kən-'sid-ər\ *vb* : to consider again especially with a view to change or reversal

re·con·sid·er·a·tion \,rē-kən-,sid-ə-'rā-shən\ *n* : the act of reconsidering : the state of being reconsidered

re·con·struct \,rē-kən-'strəkt\ *vb* : to construct again : REBUILD, REMODEL

¹re·cord \ri-'kȯrd\ *vb* **1** : to set down in writing **2** : to register permanently **3** : to cause (as sound images) to be registered (as on a phonograph disc) in reproducible form

²rec·ord \'rek-ərd\ *n* **1** : the state or fact of being recorded ⟨a matter of *record*⟩ **2** : something written to preserve an account **3** : the known or recorded facts about a person or thing ⟨has a good school *record*⟩ **4** : an attested top performance ⟨broke the home run *record*⟩ **5** : something on which sound or visual images have been recorded for later reproduction

³rec·ord \'rek-ərd\ *adj* : outstanding among other like things ⟨a *record* crop⟩

re·cord·er \ri-'kȯrd-ər\ *n* **1** : a person or device that records **2** : a flute with a whistle mouthpiece and eight finger holes

recorder 2

¹re·count \ri-'kaunt\ vb : to relate in detail : NARRATE ⟨recount an adventure⟩

²re·count \'rē-'kaunt\ vb : to count again

³re·count \'rē-,kaunt, -'kaunt\ n : a counting again (as of election votes)

re·coup \ri-'küp\ vb : to make up for : RECOVER ⟨recoup a loss⟩

re·course \'rē-,kōrs\ n 1 : a turning for help or protection 2 : a source of help or strength

re·cov·er \ri-'kəv-ər\ vb 1 : to get back : REGAIN ⟨recover a lost wallet⟩ 2 : to regain normal health, poise, or status 3 : RECLAIM ⟨recover land from the sea⟩ 4 : RECOUP

re–cov·er \'rē-'kəv-ər\ vb : to cover again

re·cov·er·y \ri-'kəv-ə-rē\ n, pl re·cov·er·ies : the act, process, or an instance of recovering

rec·re·ant \'rek-rē-ənt\ adj 1 : COWARDLY, CRAVEN 2 : UNFAITHFUL, FALSE

rec·re·a·tion \,rek-rē-'ā-shən\ n 1 : a refreshing of strength or spirits after work or anxiety 2 : a means of diversion

re·crim·i·nate \ri-'krim-ə-,nāt\ vb re·crim·i·nat·ed; re·crim·i·nat·ing : to make an accusation against an accuser

re·crim·i·na·tion \ri-,krim-ə-'nā-shən\ n : an accusation made against an accuser

¹re·cruit \ri-'krüt\ n [from French recrute "fresh growth", "new levy of soldiers", derived from an early French verb taken from Latin recrescere "to grow up again", from re- "again" and crescere "to grow"] 1 : a newcomer to a field of activity 2 : an enlisted man of the lowest rank in the army

²recruit vb 1 : to form or strengthen with new members ⟨recruit an army⟩ 2 : to secure the services of ⟨recruit engineers⟩ 3 : to restore or increase in health or vigor

rect·an·gle \'rek-,tang-gəl\ n : a four-sided plane figure with right angles and with opposite sides parallel

rect·an·gu·lar \rek-'tang-gyə-lər\ adj : shaped like a rectangle   rectangle

rec·ti·fy \'rek-tə-,fī\ vb rec·ti·fied; rec·ti·fy·ing : to set or make right

rec·ti·tude \'rek-tə-,tüd, -,tyüd\ n : moral integrity : RIGHTEOUSNESS

rec·tor \'rek-tər\ n : a clergyman who is in charge of a church or parish

rec·tum \'rek-təm\ n, pl rec·tums or rec·ta \-tə\ : the last part of the large intestine

re·cum·bent \ri-'kəm-bənt\ adj : lying down : RECLINING — **re·cum·bent·ly** adv

re·cu·per·ate \ri-'kyü-pə-,rāt\ vb re·cu·per·at·ed; re·cu·per·at·ing : to regain health or strength

re·cu·per·a·tion \ri-,kyü-pə-'rā-shən\ n : restoration to health or strength

re·cur \ri-'kər\ vb re·curred; re·cur·ring : to occur or appear again ⟨the fever recurred⟩

re·cur·rence \ri-'kər-əns\ n : the state of occurring again and again

¹red \'red\ adj red·der; red·dest 1 : of the color red 2 : REVOLUTIONARY 3 : of or relating to Communism or Communists — **red·ness** n

²red n 1 : the color of blood or of the ruby 2 : something red in color 3 : an advocate of revolutionary doctrines 4 cap : COMMUNIST

red·bird \'red-,bərd\ n : any of several birds (as a cardinal) with mostly red plumage

red blood cell n : one of the tiny reddish cells of the blood that have no nuclei and carry oxygen from the lungs to the tissues

red·breast \'red-,brest\ n : a bird (as a robin) with a reddish breast

red·cap \'red-,kap\ n : a baggage porter

red cell n : RED BLOOD CELL

red·coat \'red-,kōt\ n : a British soldier especially during the Revolutionary War

red corpuscle n : RED BLOOD CELL

red deer n : the common deer of Europe and Asia related to but smaller than the elk

red·den \'red-n\ vb : to make or become red

red·dish \'red-ish\ adj : somewhat red

re·ded·i·ca·tion \,rē-,ded-ə-'kā-shən\ n : an act or instance of dedicating again

re·deem \ri-'dēm\ vb 1 : to buy back ⟨redeem a watch from the pawnbroker⟩ 2 : to ransom, free, or rescue through payment or effort 3 : to atone for 4 : to make good : FULFILL ⟨redeem a promise⟩ 5 : to free from sin — **re·deem·er** n

re·demp·tion \ri-'demp-shən\ n : the act or process or an instance of redeeming

red–hand·ed \'red-'han-dəd\ adv (or adj) : in the act of committing a crime or misdeed ⟨was caught red-handed⟩

red·head \'red-,hed\ n : a person having red hair

red–hot \'red-'hät\ adj 1 : glowing red with heat 2 : EXCITED, FURIOUS ⟨a red-hot campaign for governor⟩

re·di·rect \,rē-də-'rekt, -dī-\ vb : to change the course or direction of

re·dis·cov·er \,rē-dis-'kəv-ər\ vb : to discover again or anew

red–let·ter \'red-'let-ər\ adj : of special significance : MEMORABLE ⟨a red-letter day in his life⟩

re·do \'rē-'dü\ vb re·did \-'did\; re·done \-'dən\; re·do·ing \-'dü-ing\ : to do over or again

red·o·lent \'red-l-ənt\ adj 1 : FRAGRANT, AROMATIC 2 : REMINISCENT, SUGGESTIVE — **red·o·lent·ly** adv

re·doubt·a·ble \ri-'daut-ə-bəl\ *adj* : FORMIDABLE ⟨a *redoubtable* warrior⟩

re·dound \ri-'daund\ *vb* : to have an effect ⟨actions that *redound* to a man's credit⟩

re·dress \ri-'dres\ *vb* : to make amends for : REMEDY

red·skin \'red-,skin\ *n* : a North American Indian

red tape *n* : official routine or procedure marked by delay

re·duce \ri-'düs, -'dyüs\ *vb* **re·duced; re·duc·ing 1** : LESSEN ⟨*reduce* expenses⟩ **2** : to bring to a specified state or condition ⟨*reduce* chaos to order⟩ **3** : to force to surrender ⟨*reduce* a fort⟩ **4** : to lower in grade or status : DEMOTE **5** : to change from one form into another ⟨*reduce* fractions to lowest terms⟩ **6** : to lose weight by dieting

re·duc·tion \ri-'dək-shən\ *n* **1** : the act of reducing : the state of being reduced **2** : the amount by which something is reduced ⟨a ten-cent *reduction* in price⟩ **3** : something made by reducing ⟨a *reduction* of a picture⟩

re·dun·dant \ri-'dən-dənt\ *adj* : using more words than necessary : SUPERFLUOUS — **re·dun·dant·ly** *adv*

red·wing blackbird \,red-,wing-\ *or* **red–winged blackbird** \-,wingd\ *n* : a blackbird with a brilliant red spot on the wing

red·wood \'red-,wud\ *n* : a tall coniferous timber tree of California with light durable brownish red wood

reed \'rēd\ *n* **1** : a tall slender grass of wet areas that has prominently jointed stems **2** : a stem or a growth or mass of reeds **3** : a musical instrument made of the hollow joint of a plant **4** : a thin elastic tongue of cane, wood, or metal fastened to the mouthpiece or over an air opening in a musical instrument (as a clarinet or accordion) and set in vibration by an air current (as the breath)

reef \'rēf\ *n* : a chain of rocks or ridge of sand at or near the surface of water

¹reek \'rēk\ *n* : a strong or disagreeable smell

²reek *vb* : to have a strong or unpleasant smell

¹reel \'rēl\ *n* **1** : a device that can be revolved on which yarn, thread, wire, hose, or film may be wound **2** : a quantity of something wound on a reel ⟨two *reels* of wire⟩

²reel *vb* **1** : to wind on a reel **2** : to draw by the use of a reel ⟨*reel* in a fish⟩ — **reel off** : to tell rapidly or fluently ⟨*reeled off* the right answers⟩

³reel *vb* **1** : to whirl around

reel for
a hose

2 : to be in a whirl ⟨heads *reeling* with excitement⟩ **3** : to fall back : WAVER **4** : to walk or move unsteadily : STAGGER

⁴reel *n* : a reeling motion

⁵reel *n* : a lively dance

re·e·lect \,rē-ə-'lekt\ *vb* : to elect for another term

re·en·ter \'rē-'ent-ər\ *vb* : to enter again

re·es·tab·lish \,rē-əs-'tab-lish\ *vb* : to establish again

re·ex·am·i·na·tion \,rē-ig-,zam-ə-'nā-shən\ *n* : a second or new examination

re·fec·to·ry \ri-'fek-tə-rē\ *n, pl* **re·fec·to·ries** : a dining hall especially in a monastery

re·fer \ri-'fər\ *vb* **re·ferred; re·fer·ring 1** : to go or send to some person or place for treatment, help, or information ⟨*refer* a boy to a dictionary⟩ **2** : to submit or hand over to someone else ⟨*refer* a patient to a specialist⟩ **3** : to call attention ⟨the teacher *referred* to a story in the newspaper⟩ **syn** see ALLUDE

¹ref·er·ee \,ref-ə-'rē\ *n* **1** : a person to whom something is referred for investigation or settlement **2** : a sports official with final authority (as in a boxing match)

²referee *vb* **ref·er·eed; ref·er·ee·ing** : to act or supervise as referee

ref·er·ence \'ref-ə-rəns\ *n* **1** : the act of referring **2** : RELATION, RESPECT ⟨with *reference* to what was said⟩ **3** : something that refers (as to a person or a book) **4** : a person of whom questions can be asked about the character or ability of another person **5** : a written statement about someone's character or ability ⟨the girl's employer gave her a good *reference*⟩

reference mark *n* : a conventional mark (as *, †, or ‡) used in printing or writing to mark a reference

ref·er·en·dum \,ref-ə-'ren-dəm\ *n, pl* **ref·er·en·da** \-də\ *or* **ref·er·en·dums** : the principle or practice of referring legislative measures to the voters for approval or rejection

¹re·fill \'rē-'fil\ *vb* : to fill or become filled again

²re·fill \'rē-,fil\ *n* : a new or fresh supply of something

re·fine \ri-'fīn\ *vb* **re·fined; re·fin·ing 1** : to come or bring to a pure state **2** : to make or become improved or perfected

re·fined \ri-'fīnd\ *adj* **1** : freed from impurities : PURE ⟨*refined* gold⟩ **2** : WELL-BRED, CULTURED ⟨*refined* manners⟩

re·fine·ment \ri-'fīn-mənt\ *n* **1** : the act or process of refining **2** : excellence of manners, feelings, or tastes : CULTURE ⟨a man of *refinement*⟩ **3** : a refined feature or method

re·fin·er·y \ri-'fī-nə-rē\ *n, pl* **re·fin·er·ies** : a building and equipment for refining metals, oil, or sugar

re·fin·ish \'rē-'fin-ish\ *vb* : to give (as furniture) a new surface

re·fit \'rē-'fit\ *vb* **re·fit·ted; re·fit·ting** : to get ready for use again ⟨*refit* a ship⟩

re·flect \ri-'flekt\ *vb* **1** : to bend or throw back waves of light, sound, or heat ⟨a polished surface *reflects* light⟩ **2** : to give back an image or likeness of in the manner of a mirror **3** : to bring as a result ⟨the boy's scholarship *reflects* credit on his school⟩ **4** : to cast reproach or blame ⟨our bad conduct *reflects* upon our training⟩ **5** : to think seriously

re·flec·tion \ri-'flek-shən\ *n* **1** : the return of light or sound waves from a surface **2** : an image produced by or as if by a mirror **3** : REPROACH, BLAME ⟨a *reflection* on his honesty⟩ **4** : a thought, idea, or opinion formed or a remark made after careful thought **5** : careful thought ⟨much *reflection* upon the problem⟩

re·flec·tor \ri-'flek-tər\ *n* : a polished surface for reflecting light or heat

re·flex \'rē-ˌfleks\ *n* : an automatic and usually unlearned action in response to a stimulus

re·for·est \'rē-'fȯr-əst\ *vb* : to renew forest growth by planting seeds or young trees

re·for·es·ta·tion \ˌrē-ˌfȯr-əs-'tā-shən\ *n* : the act of reforesting

¹re·form \ri-'fȯrm\ *vb* **1** : to make better or improve by removal of faults ⟨*reform* a prisoner⟩ **2** : to correct or improve one's own character or habits

²reform *n* **1** : correction of what is bad or corrupt **2** : a removal or correction of an abuse, a wrong, or an error

ref·or·ma·tion \ˌref-ər-'mā-shən\ *n* : the act of reforming : the state of being reformed

¹re·for·ma·to·ry \ri-'fȯr-mə-ˌtōr-ē\ *adj* : aiming at or tending toward reformation

²reformatory *n, pl* **re·for·ma·to·ries** : an institution for reforming young or first offenders or women

re·form·er \ri-'fȯr-mər\ *n* : a person who works for or urges reform

re·fract \ri-'frakt\ *vb* : to subject to refraction

re·frac·tion \ri-'frak-shən\ *n* : the bending of a ray when it passes obliquely from one medium into another in which its speed is different (as when light passes from air into water)

re·frac·to·ry \ri-'frak-tə-rē\ *adj* **1** : resisting control or authority : STUBBORN **2** : difficult to melt, corrode, or draw out — **re·frac·to·ri·ly** \-rə-lē\ *adv* — **re·frac·to·ri·ness** \-rē-nəs\ *n*

¹re·frain \ri-'frān\ *vb* : to hold oneself back

syn REFRAIN, ABSTAIN, FORBEAR all mean to hold back voluntarily from something one is inclined toward. REFRAIN suggests the checking of a momentary or temporary impulse ⟨he *refrained* from speaking out in class⟩ ⟨couldn't *refrain* from laughter⟩ ABSTAIN is stronger than REFRAIN because it stresses a deliberate self-denial often on principle and usually for some length of time ⟨*abstained* from sweets during Lent⟩ ⟨*abstained* from tobacco until he was twenty-one⟩ FORBEAR emphasizes self-restraint rather than self-denial, and often the exercise of extreme patience ⟨he *forbore* from crying out during the whole frightening descent⟩

²refrain *n* : a phrase or verse recurring regularly in a poem or song

re·fresh \ri-'fresh\ *vb* **1** : to make or become fresh or fresher : REVIVE ⟨sleep *refreshes* the body⟩ **2** : to supply or take refreshment — **re·fresh·er** *n*

re·fresh·ment \ri-'fresh-mənt\ *n* **1** : the act of refreshing : the state of being refreshed **2** *pl* : a light meal

re·frig·er·ate \ri-'frij-ə-ˌrāt\ *vb* **re·frig·er·at·ed; re·frig·er·at·ing** : to make or keep cold or cool

re·frig·er·a·tor \ri-'frij-ə-ˌrāt-ər\ *n* : a box or room for keeping articles (as food) cool

re·fu·el \'rē-'fyü-əl\ *vb* : to provide with or take on additional fuel

ref·uge \'ref-yüj\ *n* **1** : shelter or protection from danger or distress **2** : a place that provides shelter or protection ⟨wildlife *refuge*⟩

ref·u·gee \ˌref-yu̇-'jē\ *n* : a person who flees for safety especially to a foreign country

re·ful·gence \ri-'fu̇l-jəns\ *n* : BRILLIANCE

¹re·fund \ri-'fənd\ *vb* : to give back : REPAY ⟨*refund* the cost⟩

²re·fund \'rē-ˌfənd\ *n* : a sum of money refunded

re·fur·bish \ri-'fər-bish\ *vb* : RENOVATE

re·fus·al \ri-'fyü-zəl\ *n* : the act of refusing

¹re·fuse \ri-'fyüz\ *vb* **re·fused; re·fus·ing** **1** : to decline to accept ⟨*refuse* a job⟩ **2** : to decline to do, give, or grant : DENY ⟨*refused* to help⟩ **syn** see DECLINE

²ref·use \'ref-ˌyüs\ *n* : rejected or worthless material : RUBBISH

re·fute \ri-'fyüt\ *vb* **re·fut·ed; re·fut·ing** : to prove wrong by argument or evidence — **re·fut·er** *n*

re·gain \ri-'gān\ *vb* **1** : to gain or get again : get back ⟨*regained* her health⟩ **2** : to get back to : reach again ⟨*regain* the shore⟩

re·gal \'rē-gəl\ *adj* : of, relating to, or suitable for a king : ROYAL — **re·gal·ly** *adv*

re·gale \ri-'gāl\ *vb* **re·galed; re·gal·ing 1** : to entertain richly or agreeably **2** : to feast oneself : FEED

re·gal·ia \ri-'gāl-yə\ *n sing or pl* **1** : the emblems and symbols of royalty **2** : the insignia of an office or order **3** : special dress : FINERY

¹re·gard \ri-'gärd\ *n* **1** : CONSIDERATION, HEED ⟨*regard* for others⟩ **2** : LOOK, GAZE **3** : ESTEEM, RESPECT ⟨held in high *regard*⟩ **4** *pl* : friendly greetings implying esteem and respect ⟨give him my *regards*⟩ **5** : an aspect to be considered : PARTICULAR

²regard *vb* **1** : to pay attention to **2** : to show respect or consideration for **3** : ESTEEM **4** : to look at steadily or attentively **5** : to relate to : touch on **6** : to think of : CONSIDER ⟨*regarded* him as a friend⟩

re·gard·ing \ri-,gärd-ing\ *prep* : CONCERNING

re·gard·less \ri-'gärd-ləs\ *adj* : having or taking no regard : HEEDLESS

re·gat·ta \ri-'gät-ə, -'gat-\ *n* : a rowing, speedboat, or sailing race or a series of such races

re·gen·er·ate \ri-'jen-ə-,rāt\ *vb* **re·gen·er·at·ed; re·gen·er·at·ing 1** : to renew spiritually **2** : to reform completely **3** : to give or gain new life

re·gent \'rē-jənt\ *n* **1** : one who governs a kingdom (as when the sovereign is a child) **2** : a member of a governing board (as of a state university)

re·gime \rā-'zhēm\ *n* **1** : REGIMEN **2** : a form or system of government or administration

reg·i·men \'rej-ə-mən\ *n* : a systematic course of treatment

¹reg·i·ment \'rej-ə-mənt\ *n* : a military unit consisting of a variable number of units (as battalions)

²reg·i·ment \'rej-ə-,ment\ *vb* : to organize rigidly especially for regulation or central control

reg·i·men·ta·tion \,rej-ə-mən-'tā-shən\ *n* : the act or process of regimenting

re·gion \'rē-jən\ *n* **1** : an often indefinitely bounded part or area **2** : VICINITY ⟨a pain in the *region* of the heart⟩ **3** : a broad continuous area (as of the earth)

¹reg·is·ter \'rej-əs-tər\ *n* **1** : a written record or list containing regular entries of items or details **2** : a book or system of public records ⟨a *register* of deeds⟩ **3** : a device for regulating ventilation or flow of heat from a furnace **4** : a mechanical device (as a **cash register**) that records items **5** : the range of a voice or instrument

cash register

²register *vb* **1** : to enter or enroll in a register (as in a list of voters, students, or guests) **2** : to record automatically ⟨the thermometer *registered* zero⟩ **3** : to secure special protection for by paying additional postage ⟨*register* a letter⟩ **4** : to convey by expression and bodily movements ⟨*register* surprise⟩

reg·is·trar \'rej-əs-,trär\ *n* : an official recorder or keeper of records

reg·is·tra·tion \,rej-əs-'trā-shən\ *n* **1** : the act of registering **2** : an entry in a register **3** : the number of persons registered **4** : a document certifying an act of registering

reg·is·try \'rej-əs-trē\ *n, pl* **reg·is·tries 1** : a ship's nationality as determined by its registration **2** : a place of registration **3** : an official record book or an entry in one

re·gress \ri-'gres\ *vb* : to go or cause to go back especially to a former level or condition

¹re·gret \ri-'gret\ *vb* **re·gret·ted; re·gret·ting 1** : to mourn the loss or death of **2** : to be sorry for

²regret *n* **1** : sorrow aroused by circumstances beyond one's power to remedy **2** : an expression of sorrow **3** *pl* : a note politely declining an invitation ⟨send *regrets*⟩

re·gret·ful \ri-'gret-fəl\ *adj* : full of regret — **re·gret·ful·ly** *adv*

re·gret·ta·ble \ri-'gret-ə-bəl\ *adj* : deserving or demanding regret — **re·gret·ta·bly** \-blē\ *adv*

¹reg·u·lar \'reg-yə-lər\ *adj* **1** : formed, built, or arranged according to an established rule, law, principle, or type **2** : even or symmetrical in form or structure **3** : ORDERLY, METHODICAL **4** : following or conforming to established or prescribed usages, rules, or discipline **5** : NORMAL, CORRECT **6** : COMPLETE, THOROUGH **7** : of, relating to, or being a permanent standing army — **reg·u·lar·ly** *adv*

²regular *n* : a player on an athletic team who usually starts every game

reg·u·lar·i·ty \,reg-yə-'lar-ət-ē\ *n* : the quality or state of being regular

reg·u·late \'reg-yə-,lāt\ *vb* **reg·u·lat·ed; reg·u·lat·ing 1** : to govern or direct according to rule **2** : to bring under the control of authority ⟨*regulate* prices⟩ **3** : to reduce to order, method, or uniformity ⟨*regulated* his habits⟩ **4** : to fix or adjust the time, amount, degree, or rate of — **reg·u·la·tor** *n*

reg·u·la·tion \,reg-yə-'lā-shən\ *n* **1** : the act of regulating : the state of being regulated **2** : a rule or order dealing with details of procedure or having the force of law

re·ha·bil·i·tate \,rē-ə-'bil-ə-,tāt\ *vb* **re·ha·bil·i·tat·ed; re·ha·bil·i·tat·ing 1** : REINSTATE **2** : to put into good condition again

re·hash \'rē-'hash\ *vb* : to present again in another form without real change or improvement

re·hears·al \ri-'hər-səl\ *n* 1 : something told again 2 : a private performance or practice session in preparation for a public appearance

re·hearse \ri-'hərs\ *vb* **re·hearsed; re·hears·ing** 1 : to say again : REPEAT 2 : to recount in order : ENUMERATE 3 : to practice in private in preparation for a public performance ⟨*rehearse* a play⟩

¹**reign** \'rān\ *n* 1 : the authority or rule of a sovereign 2 : the time during which a sovereign rules

²**reign** *vb* 1 : to rule as a sovereign 2 : to be predominant or prevalent

re·im·burse \ˌrē-əm-'bərs\ *vb* **re·im·bursed; re·im·burs·ing** : to pay back : REPAY — **re·im·burse·ment** *n*

¹**rein** \'rān\ *n* 1 : a line or strap attached at either end of the bit of a bridle to control an animal — usually used in plural 2 : a restraining influence ⟨kept his son under a tight *rein*⟩ 3 : controlling or guiding power ⟨seized the *reins* of government⟩

reins

²**rein** *vb* : to check, control, or stop by or as if by reins

re·in·car·na·tion \ˌrē-in-ˌkär-'nā-shən\ *n* : rebirth of the soul in a new body

rein·deer \'rān-ˌdiər\ *n, pl* **reindeer** : a large antlered deer found in northern regions

re·in·force \ˌrē-ən-'fōrs\ *vb* **re·in·forced; re·in·forc·ing** 1 : to strengthen with new force, assistance, material, or support ⟨*reinforce* a wall⟩ 2 : to strengthen with additional troops or ships

reindeer

re·in·force·ment \ˌrē-ən-'fōrs-mənt\ *n* 1 : the act of reinforcing : the state of being reinforced 2 : something that reinforces

re·in·state \ˌrē-ən-'stāt\ *vb* **re·in·stat·ed; re·in·stat·ing** : to place again in a former position, condition, or capacity — **re·in·state·ment** *n*

re·in·ter·pret \ˌrē-ən-'tər-prət\ *vb* : to give a new or different interpretation to

re·it·er·ate \rē-'it-ə-ˌrāt\ *vb* **re·it·er·at·ed; re·it·er·at·ing** : to say or do over again or repeatedly

re·it·er·a·tion \rē-ˌit-ə-'rā-shən\ *n* : REPETITION

¹**re·ject** \ri-'jekt\ *vb* 1 : to refuse to acknowledge, believe, or receive 2 : to throw away as useless or unsatisfactory 3 : to refuse to grant or consider ⟨*reject* a request⟩

²**re·ject** \'rē-ˌjekt\ *n* : a rejected person or thing

re·jec·tion \ri-'jek-shən\ *n* 1 : the act of rejecting : the state of being rejected 2 : something rejected

re·joice \ri-'jȯis\ *vb* **re·joiced; re·joic·ing** 1 : to give joy to : GLADDEN ⟨news that *rejoices* the heart⟩ 2 : to feel joy ⟨*rejoice* over his good luck⟩

re·join \ri-'jȯin\ *vb* 1 : to join again : return to ⟨*rejoined* his family after his trip⟩ 2 : REPLY, RETORT

re·join·der \ri-'jȯin-dər\ *n* : REPLY

re·ju·ve·nate \ri-'jü-və-ˌnāt\ *vb* **re·ju·ve·nat·ed; re·ju·ve·nat·ing** : to make young or youthful again

¹**re·lapse** \ri-'laps\ *n* : a recurrence of illness after a period of improvement

²**relapse** *vb* **re·lapsed; re·laps·ing** : to slip or fall back into a former condition after a change for the better

re·late \ri-'lāt\ *vb* **re·lat·ed; re·lat·ing** 1 : to give an account of : NARRATE ⟨*related* his experiences⟩ 2 : to show or establish a relationship between : CONNECT ⟨the events are in no way *related*⟩ 3 : REFER

re·la·tion \ri-'lā-shən\ *n* 1 : NARRATION, ACCOUNT 2 : CONNECTION, RELATIONSHIP 3 : a related person : RELATIVE 4 : relationship by blood or marriage 5 : REFERENCE, RESPECT ⟨in *relation* to this matter⟩ 6 *pl* : DEALINGS, AFFAIRS ⟨foreign *relations*⟩

re·la·tion·ship \ri-'lā-shən-ˌship\ *n* 1 : a being related or interrelated 2 : connection by blood or marriage

¹**rel·a·tive** \'rel-ət-iv\ *n* : an individual connected with another by blood or marriage

²**relative** *adj* 1 : RELEVANT, PERTINENT 2 : not absolute or independent : COMPARATIVE ⟨the *relative* value of two houses⟩ — **rel·a·tive·ly** *adv*

re·lax \ri-'laks\ *vb* 1 : to make or become less tense or rigid : SLACKEN ⟨*relaxed* his attention⟩ 2 : to make or become less severe or strict ⟨*relax* discipline⟩ 3 : to seek rest or recreation

re·lax·a·tion \ˌrē-ˌlak-'sā-shən\ *n* 1 : the act or fact of relaxing or of being relaxed 2 : RECREATION, DIVERSION

¹**re·lay** \'rē-ˌlā\ *n* 1 : a fresh supply (as of horses or men) arranged to relieve others 2 : a race between teams in which each team member covers a specified part of the course

²**re·lay** \'rē-ˌlā, ri-'lā\ vb **re·layed; re·lay·ing** : to pass along by relays

¹**re·lease** \ri-'lēs\ vb **re·leased; re·leas·ing** 1 : to set free (as from confinement) 2 : to relieve from something that holds, burdens, or oppresses 3 : to give up in favor of another ⟨*release* a claim to property⟩ 4 : to permit to be published, sold, or shown ⟨*release* a news story⟩ — **re·leas·er** n

²**release** n 1 : relief or deliverance from sorrow, suffering, or trouble 2 : a discharge from an obligation 3 : a relinquishing of a right or claim 4 : a setting free (as from physical restraint) : the state of being freed 5 : a device for holding or releasing a mechanism as required 6 : the act of permitting publication or performance 7 : matter released for publication or performance

rel·e·gate \'rel-ə-ˌgāt\ vb **rel·e·gat·ed; rel·e·gat·ing** 1 : to remove or dismiss to a less important or prominent place ⟨*relegate* some old books to the attic⟩ 2 : to submit or refer for judgment, decision, or execution

re·lent \ri-'lent\ vb : to become less severe, harsh, or strict

re·lent·less \ri-'lent-ləs\ adj : extremely hard or harsh — **re·lent·less·ly** adv — **re·lent·less·ness** n

rel·e·vance \'rel-ə-vəns\ n : relation to the matter at hand

rel·e·vant \'rel-ə-vənt\ adj : having something to do with the case being considered ⟨a *relevant* question⟩ — **rel·e·vant·ly** adv

re·li·a·bil·i·ty \ri-ˌlī-ə-'bil-ət-ē\ n : the quality or state of being reliable

re·li·a·ble \ri-'lī-ə-bəl\ adj : fit to be trusted : DEPENDABLE — **re·li·a·bly** \-blē\ adv

re·li·ance \ri-'lī-əns\ n 1 : the act of relying 2 : the condition or attitude of one who relies 3 : one that is relied on

rel·ic \'rel-ik\ n 1 : an object that is venerated because of its association with a saint or martyr 2 : SOUVENIR, MEMENTO 3 : a remaining trace : VESTIGE ⟨*relics* of an ancient civilization⟩

re·lief \ri-'lēf\ n 1 : removal or lightening of something oppressive, painful, or distressing 2 : aid in the form of money or necessities (as for the aged) 3 : military assistance in or rescue from a position of difficulty 4 : release from a post or from performance of a duty 5 : legal remedy or redress 6 : projection of figures or ornaments from the background (as in sculpture) 7 : elevations of a land surface ⟨map showing *relief*⟩

re·lieve \ri-'lēv\ vb **re·lieved; re·liev·ing** 1 : to free partly or wholly from a burden or from

distress ⟨*relieve* pain⟩ 2 : to release from a post or duty ⟨*relieve* a sentry⟩ 3 : to break the monotony of ⟨black dress *relieved* by a white collar⟩ 4 : to stand out in relief — **re·liev·er** n

re·li·gion \ri-'lij-ən\ n 1 : the service and worship of God or the supernatural 2 : belief in or devotion to religious faith or observance 3 : a set or system of religious attitudes, beliefs, and practices

re·li·gious \ri-'lij-əs\ adj 1 : devoted to God or to the powers or principles believed to govern life ⟨a very *religious* person⟩ 2 : of or relating to religion ⟨*religious* books⟩ 3 : DEPENDABLE, FAITHFUL — **re·li·gious·ly** adv — **re·li·gious·ness** n

re·lin·quish \ri-'ling-kwish\ vb 1 : to withdraw or retreat from 2 : RENOUNCE 3 : to let go of : RELEASE

¹**rel·ish** \'rel-ish\ n [an alteration of earlier English *reles* "taste", from Old French *reles* "something left behind", from *relessier* "to release", derived from Latin *relaxare* "to relax"] 1 : a pleasing appetizing taste 2 : keen enjoyment ⟨eats with *relish*⟩ 3 : a highly seasoned food eaten with other food to add flavor

²**relish** vb 1 : to be pleased by : ENJOY 2 : to eat or drink with pleasure

re·live \'rē-'liv\ vb **re·lived; re·liv·ing** : to live over again (as in imagination)

re·luc·tance \ri-'lək-təns\ n : UNWILLINGNESS

re·luc·tant \ri-'lək-tənt\ adj : showing hesitation or unwillingness ⟨*reluctant* to answer⟩ — **re·luc·tant·ly** adv

re·ly \ri-'lī\ vb **re·lied; re·ly·ing** : to place faith or confidence : DEPEND

¹**re·main** \ri-'mān\ vb 1 : to be left after others have been removed, subtracted, or destroyed ⟨little *remained* after the fire⟩ 2 : to be something yet to be done or considered ⟨a fact that *remains* to be proved⟩ 3 : to stay after others have gone 4 : to continue unchanged ⟨the weather *remained* cold⟩

²**remain** n 1 : a remaining part or trace — usually used in plural 2 pl : a dead body

re·main·der \ri-'mān-dər\ n 1 : a remaining group, part, or trace 2 : the number left after a subtraction 3 : the final undivided part after division that is less than the divisor 4 : a book sold at a reduced price by the publisher after sales have slowed

re·make \'rē-'māk\ vb **re·made** \-'mād\; **re·mak·ing** : to make in a different form

re·mand \ri-'mand\ vb : to order back (as to a lower court for further action)

¹**re·mark** \ri-'märk\ *vb* **1** : to take note of : OBSERVE **2** : to make an observation or comment : SAY

²**remark** *n* **1** : OBSERVATION, NOTICE **2** : a passing comment : STATEMENT

syn REMARK, OBSERVATION, COMMENT all mean some kind of very brief expression in speech or writing. REMARK usually refers to a casual or passing thought not intended to express deep consideration or final judgment ⟨he made several *remarks* about the heavy traffic⟩ OBSERVATION may indicate a carefully considered opinion based on a thoughtful examination of a situation ⟨after watching us learning to swim he made a few *observations* that proved extremely helpful⟩ COMMENT may refer to a remark or observation made to explain, interpret, or criticize something ⟨the senator made several *comments* on the new law⟩ ⟨he made only one *comment* on their rude behavior⟩

re·mark·a·ble \ri-'mär-kə-bəl\ *adj* : worthy of being noticed : UNUSUAL — **re·mark·a·ble·ness** *n* — **re·mark·a·bly** \-blē\ *adv*

re·mar·riage \'rē-'mar-ij\ *n* : a second or later marriage

re·match \'rē-'mach\ *n* : a second match between the same contestants

re·me·di·al \ri-'mēd-ē-əl\ *adj* : intended to remedy or improve ⟨*remedial* measures⟩ — **re·me·di·al·ly** *adv*

¹**rem·e·dy** \'rem-ə-dē\ *n, pl* **rem·e·dies** **1** : a medicine or treatment that cures or relieves **2** : something that corrects an evil, rights a wrong, or makes up for a loss

²**remedy** *vb* **rem·e·died; rem·e·dy·ing** : to provide or serve as a remedy for : CURE

re·mem·ber \ri-'mem-bər\ *vb* **1** : to bring to mind or think of again **2** : to keep in mind ⟨*remember* your promise⟩ **3** : to convey greetings from ⟨*remember* us to your mother⟩

re·mem·brance \ri-'mem-brəns\ *n* **1** : the act of remembering **2** : something remembered ⟨a vivid *remembrance*⟩ **3** : something (as a souvenir) that brings to mind

re·mind \ri-'mīnd\ *vb* : to cause to remember — **re·mind·er** *n*

rem·i·nisce \,rem-ə-'nis\ *vb* **rem·i·nisced; rem·i·nisc·ing** : to engage in reminiscence

rem·i·nis·cence \,rem-ə-'nis-ns\ *n* **1** : a recalling or telling of a past experience **2** *pl* : an account of one's memorable experiences

rem·i·nis·cent \,rem-ə-'nis-nt\ *adj* **1** : of, relating to, or engaging in reminiscence **2** : SUGGESTIVE ⟨a house *reminiscent* of his home⟩

re·miss \ri-'mis\ *adj* : negligent in the performance of work or duty : CARELESS — **re·miss·ly** *adv* — **re·miss·ness** *n*

re·mit \ri-'mit\ *vb* **re·mit·ted; re·mit·ting** **1** : FORGIVE, PARDON **2** : to send money (as in payment) — **re·mit·ter** *n*

rem·nant \'rem-nənt\ *n* : something that remains or is left over ⟨a *remnant* of cloth⟩

re·mod·el \'rē-'mäd-l\ *vb* **re·mod·eled** *or* **re·mod·elled; re·mod·el·ing** *or* **re·mod·el·ling** : to alter the structure of

re·mon·strate \ri-'män-,strāt\ *vb* **re·mon·strat·ed; re·mon·strat·ing** : PROTEST

re·morse \ri-'mòrs\ *n* : deep regret for one's sins or for acts that wrong others — **re·morse·ful** \-fəl\ *adj* — **re·morse·less** \-ləs\ *adj*

re·mote \ri-'mōt\ *adj* **1** : far off in place or time ⟨*remote* countries⟩ ⟨*remote* ages⟩ **2** : located out of the way : SECLUDED ⟨a *remote* valley⟩ **3** : not closely connected or related ⟨a *remote* kinsman⟩ **4** : distant in manner : ALOOF — **re·mote·ly** *adv* — **re·mote·ness** *n*

re·mount \'rē-,maunt\ *n* : a fresh horse to replace one disabled or exhausted

re·mov·a·ble \ri-'mü-və-bəl\ *adj* : capable of being removed

re·mov·al \ri-'mü-vəl\ *n* : the act of removing : the fact of being removed

¹**re·move** \ri-'müv\ *vb* **re·moved; re·mov·ing** **1** : to move from one place to another **2** : to move by lifting or taking off or away **3** : DISMISS, DISCHARGE **4** : to get rid of ⟨*remove* the causes of poverty⟩

²**remove** *n* **1** : a change of residence or location **2** : a degree or stage of separation

re·mu·ner·ate \ri-'myü-nə-,rāt\ *vb* **re·mu·ner·at·ed; re·mu·ner·at·ing** : to pay an equivalent for or to : RECOMPENSE

Re·nais·sance \,ren-ə-'säns\ *n* **1** : the period of European history between the fourteenth and seventeenth centuries marked by a rebirth of interest in ancient art and literature and by the beginnings of modern science **2** *often not cap* : a movement or period of vigorous artistic and intellectual activity

re·nal \'rēn-l\ *adj* : of, relating to, or located near the kidneys

rend \'rend\ *vb* **rent** \'rent\; **rend·ing** **1** : to remove by violence : WREST **2** : to tear forcibly apart

ren·der \'ren-dər\ *vb* **1** : DELIVER, GIVE ⟨*render* thanks⟩ **2** : to extract by heating ⟨*render* lard from fat⟩ **3** : to give up : SURRENDER ⟨*rendered* his life⟩ **4** : to cause to be or become ⟨was *rendered* helpless by the blow⟩ **5** : FURNISH, CONTRIBUTE ⟨*render* aid⟩ **6** : PRESENT, PERFORM ⟨*render* a song⟩

ren·dez·vous \'rän-di-ˌvü\ *n, pl* **ren·dez·vous** \-ˌvüz\ **1** : a place set for a meeting **2** : a planned meeting

ren·di·tion \ren-'dish-ən\ *n* : an act or a result of rendering

ren·e·gade \'ren-i-ˌgād\ *n* : a person who deserts a faith, cause, or party

re·nege \ri-'nig\ *vb* **re·neged; re·neg·ing 1** : to fail to follow suit in a card game in violation of the rules **2** : to go back on a promise or commitment

re·new \ri-'nü, -'nyü\ *vb* **1** : to make or become new, fresh, or strong again **2** : to make, do, or begin again ⟨*renew* a complaint⟩ **3** : to put in a fresh supply of ⟨*renew* the water in a tank⟩ **4** : to continue in force for a new period ⟨*renew* a lease⟩

re·new·al \ri-'nü-əl, -'nyü-\ *n* **1** : the act of renewing : the state of being renewed **2** : something renewed

re·nounce \ri-'naúns\ *vb* **re·nounced; re·nounc·ing 1** : to give up, abandon, or resign usually by formal declaration ⟨*renounced* the throne⟩ **2** : to cast off : DISOWN

ren·o·vate \'ren-ə-ˌvāt\ *vb* **ren·o·vat·ed; ren·o·vat·ing** : to put in good condition again — **ren·o·va·tor** *n*

re·nown \ri-'naún\ *n* : FAME

re·nowned \ri-'naúnd\ *adj* : having renown : CELEBRATED **syn** *see* FAMOUS

¹rent \'rent\ *n* : money paid for the use of another's property — **for rent** : available for use at a price

²rent *vb* **1** : to take and hold property under an agreement to pay rent **2** : to give the possession and use of in return for rent ⟨*rented* a cottage to friends⟩ **3** : to be for rent ⟨the house *rents* for $125 a month⟩

³rent *n* : an opening (as in cloth) made by rending

¹rent·al \'rent-l\ *n* : an amount paid or collected as rent

²rental *adj* : of, relating to, or available for rent

re·nun·ci·a·tion \ri-ˌnən-sē-'ā-shən\ *n* : the act or practice of renouncing

¹re·pair \ri-'paər\ *vb* : GO ⟨*repair* to an inner office⟩

²repair *vb* **1** : to restore to good condition ⟨*repair* a broken toy⟩ **2** : REMEDY ⟨*repair* a wrong⟩ **syn** *see* MEND

³repair *n* **1** : the act or process of repairing **2** : general condition ⟨a house in bad *repair*⟩

rep·a·ra·tion \ˌrep-ə-'rā-shən\ *n* **1** : the act of making amends for a wrong **2** : money paid (as by one country) in compensation (as for damages in war)

rep·ar·tee \ˌrep-ər-'tē\ *n* : a succession of clever witty remarks

re·past \ri-'past\ *n* : MEAL

re·pa·tri·ate \rē-'pā-trē-ˌāt\ *vb* **re·pa·tri·at·ed; re·pa·tri·at·ing** : to send or bring back to one's own country

re·pay \rē-'pā\ *vb* **re·paid** \-'pād\; **re·pay·ing 1** : to pay back ⟨*repay* a loan⟩ **2** : to make a return payment to ⟨*repay* a creditor⟩

re·pay·ment \rē-'pā-mənt\ *n* : the act or an instance of paying back

re·peal \ri-'pēl\ *vb* : to do away with especially by legislative action ⟨*repeal* a law⟩

¹re·peat \ri-'pēt\ *vb* **1** : to say or state again ⟨*repeat* a question⟩ **2** : to say from memory : RECITE ⟨*repeat* a poem⟩ **3** : to make or do again ⟨*repeat* a mistake⟩ **4** : to tell to others ⟨*repeat* gossip⟩ — **re·peat·er** *n*

²repeat *n* **1** : the act of repeating **2** : something repeated

re·peat·ed \ri-'pēt-əd\ *adj* : done or happening again and again — **re·peat·ed·ly** *adv*

re·pel \ri-'pel\ *vb* **re·pelled; re·pel·ling 1** : to drive back : REPULSE ⟨*repel* the enemy⟩ **2** : to turn away : REJECT ⟨*repel* a suggestion⟩ **3** : to keep out : RESIST ⟨cloth treated to *repel* water⟩ **4** : DISGUST ⟨a sight that *repelled* everyone⟩

re·pel·lent \ri-'pel-ənt\ *n* : a substance used to repel pests (as insects)

re·pent \ri-'pent\ *vb* **1** : to feel sorrow for one's sin and determine to do what is right **2** : to feel sorry for something done : REGRET ⟨*repent* a rash decision⟩

re·pent·ance \ri-'pent-ns\ *n* : a feeling of regret for something done or said and especially for something wrong or evil

re·pent·ant \ri-'pent-nt\ *adj* : feeling or showing repentance — **re·pent·ant·ly** *adv*

re·per·cus·sion \ˌrē-pər-'kəsh-ən\ *n* **1** : a reciprocal action or effect **2** : a widespread, indirect, or unexpected effect of something said or done

rep·er·toire \'rep-ər-ˌtwär\ *n* : a list or supply of plays, operas, or pieces that a company or person is prepared to perform

rep·er·to·ry \'rep-ər-ˌtōr-ē\ *n, pl* **rep·er·to·ries 1** : a stock or store of something **2** : REPERTOIRE

rep·e·ti·tion \ˌrep-ə-'tish-ən\ *n* **1** : the act or an instance of repeating **2** : something repeated

re·place \ri-'plās\ *vb* **re·placed; re·plac·ing 1** : to put back in a former or proper place ⟨*replace* a card in a file⟩ **2** : to take the place of : SUPPLANT ⟨paper money has *replaced* gold coins⟩ **3** : to fill the place of ⟨*replace* a broken dish⟩

re·place·ment \ri-'plās-mənt\ *n* **1** : the act of replacing : the state of being replaced **2** : one that replaces

re·plen·ish \ri-'plen-ish\ *vb* : to fill again : bring back to a condition of being full or complete ⟨*replenish* a supply of fuel⟩ — **re·plen·ish·er** *n* — **re·plen·ish·ment** *n*

re·plete \ri-'plēt\ *adj* **1** : filled to capacity **2** : fully provided — **re·plete·ness** *n*

rep·li·ca \'rep-li-kə\ *n* **1** : a close reproduction (as of a statue) **2** : COPY, DUPLICATE

¹re·ply \ri-'plī\ *vb* **re·plied**; **re·ply·ing** : to say or do in answer : RESPOND

²reply *n, pl* **re·plies** : ANSWER, RESPONSE

¹re·port \ri-'pōrt\ *n* **1** : common talk : RUMOR **2** : REPUTATION, FAME **3** : a usually detailed account or statement ⟨weather *report*⟩ **4** : an explosive noise ⟨the *report* of a gun⟩

²report *vb* **1** : to give an account of : RELATE, TELL **2** : to give an account of in a newspaper article ⟨*report* a baseball game⟩ **3** : to make a charge of misconduct against **4** : to present oneself ⟨*report* for duty⟩ **5** : to make known to the proper authorities ⟨*report* a fire⟩ — **re·port·er** *n*

report card *n* : a report on a student's grades that is periodically submitted by a school to the student's parents or guardian

¹re·pose \ri-'pōz\ *vb* **re·posed**; **re·pos·ing** : to put without hesitation : SET ⟨*repose* trust in a friend⟩

²repose *vb* **re·posed**; **re·pos·ing** **1** : to lay at rest : put in a restful position **2** : to lie at rest : take rest ⟨*reposing* on the couch⟩

³repose *n* **1** : a state of resting and especially sleep after exertion or strain **2** : CALM, PEACE **3** : cessation or absence of activity, movement, or animation

re·pos·i·to·ry \ri-'päz-ə-ˌtōr-ē\ *n, pl* **re·pos·i·to·ries** **1** : a place where something is deposited or stored **2** : a person to whom something is entrusted

rep·re·hend \ˌrep-ri-'hend\ *vb* : to express disapproval of : CENSURE

rep·re·hen·si·ble \ˌrep-ri-'hen-sə-bəl\ *adj* : deserving blame or censure

rep·re·sent \ˌrep-ri-'zent\ *vb* **1** : to present a picture, image, or likeness of : PORTRAY ⟨this picture *represents* a scene at King Arthur's court⟩ **2** : to serve as a sign or symbol of ⟨the flag *represents* our country⟩ **3** : to act for or in place of ⟨we elect men and women to *represent* us in Congress⟩ **4** : to describe as having a specified character or quality ⟨*represented* himself as a friend of the people⟩ **5** : to serve as a specimen, example, or instance of

rep·re·sen·ta·tion \ˌrep-ri-ˌzen-'tā-shən\ *n* **1** : one (as a picture, image, symbol, or emblem) that represents something else **2** : a usually formal protest **3** : the act of representing : the state of being represented (as in a legislative body)

¹rep·re·sen·ta·tive \ˌrep-ri-'zent-ət-iv\ *adj* **1** : serving to represent ⟨a painting *representative* of a battle⟩ **2** : standing or acting for another **3** : founded on the principle of representation : carried on by elected representatives ⟨a *representative* government⟩ **4** : serving as a typical or characteristic example of ⟨a *representative* housewife⟩

²representative *n* **1** : a typical example of a group, class, or quality **2** : one that represents another (as in a state legislature)

re·press \ri-'pres\ *vb* : to hold in check by or as if by pressure

¹re·prieve \ri-'prēv\ *vb* **re·prieved**; **re·priev·ing** **1** : to delay the punishment of (as a condemned prisoner) **2** : to give temporary relief to

²reprieve *n* **1** : a temporary suspension of a sentence and especially a death sentence **2** : a temporary respite

¹rep·ri·mand \'rep-rə-ˌmand\ *n* : a severe or formal reproof

²reprimand *vb* : to reprove severely or formally

re·pri·sal \ri-'prī-zəl\ *n* : action or an act in retaliation for something done by another

¹re·proach \ri-'prōch\ *n* **1** : a cause or occasion of blame or disgrace **2** : REBUKE

²reproach *vb* **1** : to find fault with : BLAME **2** : to bring into discredit

rep·ro·bate \'rep-rə-ˌbāt\ *n* : a thoroughly bad person

re·pro·duce \ˌrē-prə-'düs, -'dyüs\ *vb* **re·pro·duced**; **re·pro·duc·ing** **1** : to produce again ⟨the cooling of steam *reproduces* water⟩ **2** : to produce another living thing : bear offspring ⟨many plants *reproduce* by means of seeds⟩ — **re·pro·duc·er** *n*

re·pro·duc·i·ble \ˌrē-prə-'dü-sə-bəl, -'dyü-\ *adj* : capable of being reproduced

re·pro·duc·tion \ˌrē-prə-'dək-shən\ *n* **1** : the act or process of reproducing **2** : COPY

re·pro·duc·tive \ˌrē-prə-'dək-tiv\ *adj* : of, relating to, capable of, or concerned with reproduction ⟨*reproductive* cells⟩

re·proof \ri-'prüf\ *n* : blame or censure for a fault : REBUKE

re·prove \ri-'prüv\ *vb* **re·proved**; **re·prov·ing** : to express blame or disapproval of : SCOLD ⟨*reprove* a child⟩

rep·tile \'rep-təl\ *n* [from later Latin *reptile*,

derived from *reptilis* "creeping"] : any of a group of air-breathing cold-blooded vertebrates (as snakes, lizards, turtles, and alligators) that usually have the skin covered with scales or bony plates

re·pub·lic \ri-'pəb-lik\ *n* **1** : a government having a chief of state who is not a monarch and who is usually a president **2** : a government in which supreme power resides in the citizens entitled to vote **3** : a state or country having a republican government

¹re·pub·li·can \ri-'pəb-li-kən\ *adj* : of, relating to, or resembling a republic ⟨a *republican* form of government⟩

²republican *n* : a person who favors a republican form of government

re·pu·di·ate \ri-'pyüd-ē-,āt\ *vb* **re·pu·di·at·ed**; **re·pu·di·at·ing** **1** : to refuse to have anything to do with : DISOWN **2** : to refuse to accept, acknowledge, or pay

re·pug·nant \ri-'pəg-nənt\ *adj* : DISTASTEFUL, REPULSIVE — **re·pug·nant·ly** *adv*

¹re·pulse \ri-'pəls\ *vb* **re·pulsed**; **re·puls·ing** **1** : to drive or beat back : REPEL **2** : to repel by discourtesy : REBUFF

²repulse *n* **1** : REBUFF, REJECTION **2** : a repelling or being repelled in hostile encounter

re·pul·sion \ri-'pəl-shən\ *n* : the action of repulsing : the state of being repulsed

re·pul·sive \ri-'pəl-siv\ *adj* : causing disgust : OFFENSIVE ⟨a *repulsive* sight⟩ — **re·pul·sive·ly** *adv* — **re·pul·sive·ness** *n*

rep·u·ta·ble \'rep-yət-ə-bəl\ *adj* : having a good reputation : RESPECTED ⟨*reputable* citizens⟩ — **rep·u·ta·bly** \-blē\ *adv*

rep·u·ta·tion \,rep-yə-'tā-shən\ *n* **1** : overall quality or character as seen or judged by people in general ⟨this car has a good *reputation*⟩ **2** : recognition by other people of some characteristic or ability ⟨have the *reputation* of being a good tennis player⟩ **3** : good name ⟨lost her *reputation*⟩ **4** : FAME ⟨a worldwide *reputation*⟩

¹re·pute \ri-'pyüt\ *vb* **re·put·ed**; **re·put·ing** : BELIEVE, CONSIDER ⟨a man *reputed* to be a millionaire⟩

²repute *n* **1** : REPUTATION **2** : FAME

¹re·quest \ri-'kwest\ *n* **1** : an asking for something **2** : something asked for ⟨grant every *request*⟩ **3** : the condition of being requested ⟨tickets are available on *request*⟩

²request *vb* **1** : to make a request to or of ⟨*request* her to sing⟩ **2** : to ask for ⟨*request* a loan⟩ **syn** see ASK

req·ui·em \'rek-wē-əm\ *n* : a mass for a dead person

re·quire \ri-'kwīr\ *vb* **re·quired**; **re·quir·ing**

1 : ORDER, COMMAND ⟨the law *requires* drivers to observe traffic lights⟩ **2** : to call for : NEED ⟨a trick that *requires* skill⟩

re·quire·ment \ri-'kwīr-mənt\ *n* **1** : something (as a condition or quality) required ⟨comply with all *requirements*⟩ **2** : NECESSITY, NEED ⟨sleep is a *requirement* for health⟩

¹req·ui·site \'rek-wə-zət\ *adj* : NECESSARY

²requisite *n* : REQUIREMENT

re·quite \ri-'kwīt\ *vb* **re·quit·ed**; **re·quit·ing** **1** : REPAY **2** : AVENGE

re·scind \ri-'sind\ *vb* : to make void : ANNUL

¹res·cue \'res-kyü\ *vb* **res·cued**; **res·cu·ing** : to free from confinement, danger, or evil : SAVE — **res·cu·er** *n*

²rescue *n* : an act of rescuing

re·search \ri-'sərch, 'rē-,sərch\ *n* : studious and critical inquiry and examination aimed at the discovery and interpretation of new knowledge

re·sem·blance \ri-'zem-bləns\ *n* : SIMILARITY, LIKENESS

re·sem·ble \ri-'zem-bəl\ *vb* **re·sem·bled**; **re·sem·bling** : to be like or similar to

re·sent \ri-'zent\ *vb* : to feel annoyance or indignation at ⟨*resent* criticism⟩

re·sent·ment \ri-'zent-mənt\ *n* : a feeling of indignant displeasure at something regarded as a wrong, insult, or injury

res·er·va·tion \,rez-ər-'vā-shən\ *n* **1** : an act of reserving **2** : an arrangement to have something (as a hotel room) held for one's use **3** : something (as land) reserved for a special use ⟨an Indian *reservation*⟩ **4** : a limiting condition ⟨agree without *reservations*⟩

¹re·serve \ri-'zərv\ *vb* **re·served**; **re·serv·ing** **1** : to keep in store for future or special use **2** : to retain or hold over to a future time or place : DEFER **3** : to arrange to have set aside and held for one's use ⟨*reserve* a hotel room⟩

²reserve *n* **1** : something stored or available for future use ⟨oil *reserves*⟩ **2** *pl* : military forces withheld or available for later decisive use **3** : a tract set apart : RESERVATION **4** : an act of reserving **5** : restraint or caution in one's words and bearing **6** : money or its equivalent kept in hand or available (as to meet liabilities) **7** : SUBSTITUTE

re·served \ri-'zərvd\ *adj* **1** : restrained in words and actions **2** : kept or set apart for future or special use

res·er·voir \'rez-ərv-,wär\ *n* : a place where something (as water) is kept in store for future use

re·set \'rē-'set\ *vb* : to set again or afresh

re·ship·ment \'rē-'ship-mənt\ *n* : an act of shipping again

re·side \ri-'zīd\ vb **re·sid·ed; re·sid·ing 1** : to live permanently and continuously : DWELL **2** : to be present as an element, quality, or right ⟨the power of veto *resides* in the president⟩

res·i·dence \'rez-ə-dəns\ n **1** : the act or fact of residing **2** : the place where one actually lives **3** : HOUSE, DWELLING **4** : the period of a person's residing in a place

¹res·i·dent \'rez-ə-dənt\ adj **1** : living in a place for some length of time **2** : living in a place while discharging official duties ⟨*resident* physician⟩

²resident n : a person who resides in a place

res·i·den·tial \,rez-ə-'den-chəl\ adj **1** : used as a residence or by residents ⟨a *residential* hotel⟩ **2** : adapted to or occupied by residences ⟨a *residential* section⟩

re·sid·u·al \ri-'zij-ə-wəl\ adj : left over — **re·sid·u·al·ly** adv

res·i·due \'rez-ə-,dü, -,dyü\ n : whatever remains after a part is taken, set apart, or lost

re·sign \ri-'zīn\ vb **1** : to give up by a formal or official act ⟨*resign* an office⟩ **2** : to commit or give over or up ⟨*resigned* herself to a disappointment⟩

res·ig·na·tion \,rez-ig-'nā-shən\ n **1** : an act of resigning **2** : a letter or written statement that gives notice of resignation **3** : the quality or the feeling of a person who is resigned : SUBMISSION

re·signed \ri-'zīnd\ adj : submitting patiently (as to loss or sorrow) : SUBMISSIVE — **re·sign·ed·ly** \-'zī-nəd-lē\ adv

re·sil·ience \ri-'zil-yəns\ or **re·sil·ien·cy** \-yən-sē\ n : ELASTICITY

re·sil·ient \ri-'zil-yənt\ adj : ELASTIC, SPRINGY — **re·sil·ient·ly** adv

res·in \'rez-n\ n **1** : a yellowish or brownish substance obtained from the gum or sap of some trees (as the pine) and used in varnishes and medicine **2** : any of various synthetic products that are similar to natural resins in properties and are used especially as plastics

re·sist \ri-'zist\ vb **1** : to withstand the force or effect of : ward off ⟨*resist* disease⟩ **2** : to fight against : OPPOSE ⟨*resist* arrest⟩ **syn** see OPPOSE

re·sist·ance \ri-'zis-təns\ n **1** : an act or instance of resisting **2** : the ability to resist ⟨the body's *resistance* to disease⟩ **3** : an opposing or retarding force ⟨the *resistance* of air to an airplane in motion⟩ **4** : the opposition offered by a substance to the passage through it of an electric current

re·sist·ant \ri-'zis-tənt\ adj : giving or capable of resistance

res·o·lute \'rez-ə-,lüt\ adj : firmly determined

: RESOLVED — **res·o·lute·ly** adv — **res·o·lute·ness** n

res·o·lu·tion \,rez-ə-'lü-shən\ n **1** : the act of resolving **2** : the act of solving : SOLUTION ⟨the *resolution* of a problem⟩ **3** : something resolved or decided on ⟨New Year *resolutions*⟩ **4** : FIRMNESS, DETERMINATION **5** : a statement expressing the feelings, wishes, or decisions of a group

¹re·solve \ri-'zälv\ vb **re·solved; re·solv·ing 1** : to break up into component parts : ANALYZE **2** : to find an answer to : SOLVE ⟨*resolve* a difficulty⟩ **3** : DECIDE, DETERMINE ⟨*resolve* to work hard⟩ **4** : to declare or decide by a formal resolution and vote

²resolve n **1** : something resolved **2** : resoluteness of purpose

re·solved \ri-'zälvd\ adj : DETERMINED

res·o·nance \'rez-n-əns\ n : the quality or state of being resonant

res·o·nant \'rez-n-ənt\ adj : marked by vibrant richness of sound — **res·o·nant·ly** adv

¹re·sort \ri-'zòrt\ n **1** : one that is looked to for help : REFUGE **2** : RECOURSE ⟨have *resort* to force⟩ **3** : a frequently visited place : HAUNT **4** : a place providing recreation especially to vacationers

²resort vb **1** : to go often or habitually **2** : to have recourse ⟨*resorted* to force in order to check the mob⟩

re·sound \ri-'zaůnd\ vb **1** : to become filled with sound : REVERBERATE ⟨the hall *resounded* with cheers⟩ **2** : to sound loudly ⟨the organ *resounds* through the hall⟩

re·source \'rē-,sòrs\ n **1** : a new or a reserve source of supply or support **2** pl : a usable stock or supply (as of money or products) ⟨America has great natural *resources*⟩ **3** : the ability to meet and handle situations : RESOURCEFULNESS

re·source·ful \ri-'sòrs-fəl\ adj : able to meet situations — **re·source·ful·ly** adv — **re·source·ful·ness** n

¹re·spect \ri-'spekt\ n **1** : relation to or concern with something specified ⟨with *respect* to your last letter⟩ **2** : high or special regard : ESTEEM **3** pl : an expression of regard or deference **4** : PARTICULAR, DETAIL ⟨perfect in all *respects*⟩

²respect vb **1** : to consider worthy of high regard : ESTEEM **2** : HEED ⟨*respected* their wishes⟩ **3** : to have reference to : CONCERN — **re·spect·er** n

re·spect·a·ble \ri-'spek-tə-bəl\ adj **1** : worthy of respect **2** : decent or correct in conduct : PROPER **3** : fair in size or quantity ⟨a *respectable* amount⟩ **4** : fit to be seen

: PRESENTABLE ⟨*respectable* clothes⟩ — **re·spect·a·bly** \-blē\ *adv*

re·spect·ful \ri-'spekt-fəl\ *adj* : marked by or showing respect ⟨a *respectful* manner⟩ — **re·spect·ful·ly** *adv* — **re·spect·ful·ness** *n*

re·spect·ing \ri-ˌspek-ting\ *prep* : with regard to : ABOUT

re·spec·tive \ri-'spek-tiv\ *adj* : relating to particular persons or things each to each : SEVERAL ⟨their *respective* homes⟩ — **re·spec·tive·ly** *adv*

re·spell \'rē-'spel\ *vb* : to spell again or in another way ⟨*respelled* pronunciations⟩

res·pi·ra·tion \ˌres-pə-'rā-shən\ *n* 1 : the act or process of breathing 2 : the physical and chemical processes (as breathing and oxidation) by which a living being obtains the oxygen it needs to live 3 : an oxidation by which an organism gains energy

res·pi·ra·tor \'res-pə-ˌrāt-ər\ *n* 1 : a device covering the mouth or nose especially to prevent the inhalation of harmful vapors 2 : a device used for aiding one to breathe

respirator 1

res·pi·ra·to·ry \'res-pə-rə-ˌtōr-ē\ *adj* : of, relating to, or concerned with respiration ⟨the *respiratory* system⟩

re·spire \ri-'spīr\ *vb* **re·spired; re·spir·ing** : to engage in respiration : BREATHE

res·pite \'res-pət\ *n* 1 : a temporary delay 2 : an interval of rest or relief

re·splen·dent \ri-'splen-dənt\ *adj* : shining brilliantly : SPLENDID — **re·splen·dent·ly** *adv*

re·spond \ri-'spänd\ *vb* 1 : to say something in return : REPLY 2 : to act in response : REACT ⟨*respond* to surgery⟩

re·sponse \ri-'späns\ *n* 1 : the act of replying : ANSWER 2 : words said or sung by the people or choir in a religious service 3 : a reaction of a living being (as to a drug or stimulus)

re·spon·si·bil·i·ty \ri-ˌspän-sə-'bil-ət-ē\ *n, pl* **re·spon·si·bil·i·ties** 1 : the quality or state of being responsible 2 : RELIABILITY, TRUSTWORTHINESS 3 : something for which one is responsible : BURDEN

re·spon·si·ble \ri-'spän-sə-bəl\ *adj* 1 : liable to be called upon to answer for one's acts or decisions ⟨held *responsible* for the damage⟩ 2 : TRUSTWORTHY, RELIABLE ⟨*responsible* persons⟩ 3 : requiring a person to take charge of or be trusted with important matters ⟨a *responsible* job⟩ — **re·spon·si·bly** \-blē\ *adv*

re·spon·sive \ri-'spän-siv\ *adj* 1 : RESPONDING, ANSWERING 2 : quick to respond or

react in a sympathetic way — **re·spon·sive·ly** *adv* — **re·spon·sive·ness** *n*

¹rest \'rest\ *n* 1 : REPOSE, SLEEP 2 : freedom from activity : QUIET 3 : a state of motionlessness or inactivity 4 : a place for resting or lodging 5 : a silence in music 6 : a character representing a musical silence 7 : something used for support ⟨a chin *rest* for a violin⟩

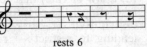
rests 6

²rest *vb* 1 : to get rest by lying down : SLEEP 2 : to give rest to ⟨*rested* himself on the couch⟩ 3 : to lie dead 4 : to refrain from work or activity 5 : to sit or lie fixed or supported ⟨a house *rests* on its foundation⟩ 6 : DEPEND ⟨the success of the flight *rests* on the wind⟩ 7 : to fix or be fixed in trust or confidence ⟨*rested* her hopes on his promise⟩

³rest *n* : something that is left over : REMAINDER

re·state·ment \'rē-'stāt-mənt\ *n* : a stating again or in another way

res·tau·rant \'res-tə-rənt\ *n* : a public eating place

rest·ful \'rest-fəl\ *adj* 1 : giving rest ⟨a *restful* chair⟩ 2 : giving a feeling of rest : QUIET ⟨a *restful* scene⟩ — **rest·ful·ly** *adv* — **rest·ful·ness** *n*

rest·ing \'res-ting\ *adj* : DORMANT ⟨a *resting* spore⟩

res·ti·tu·tion \ˌres-tə-'tü-shən, -'tyü-\ *n* : the restoring of something to its rightful owner or the giving of an equivalent (as for damage)

res·tive \'res-tiv\ *adj* 1 : BALKY 2 : UNEASY, FIDGETY — **res·tive·ly** *adv* — **res·tive·ness** *n*

rest·less \'rest-ləs\ *adj* 1 : having or giving no rest 2 : never resting or settled ⟨the *restless* sea⟩ — **rest·less·ly** *adv* — **rest·less·ness** *n*

res·to·ra·tion \ˌres-tə-'rā-shən\ *n* 1 : an act of restoring : the condition of being restored 2 : something (as a building) that has been restored

re·store \ri-'stōr\ *vb* **re·stored; re·stor·ing** 1 : to give back : RETURN ⟨*restore* a purse to its owner⟩ 2 : to put back into use or service 3 : to put or bring back into a former or original state ⟨*restore* an old house⟩

re·strain \ri-'strān\ *vb* 1 : to prevent from doing something 2 : to keep in check : CURB ⟨*restrain* anger⟩ — **re·strain·er** *n*

re·straint \ri-'strānt\ *n* 1 : the act of restraining : the state of being restrained 2 : a restraining force or influence 3 : control over one's thoughts or feelings

re·strict \ri-'strikt\ *vb* 1 : to keep within

bounds : LIMIT **2** : to place under restrictions as to use

re·stric·tion \ri-'strik-shən\ *n* **1** : something (as a law or rule) that restricts **2** : an act of restricting : the condition of being restricted

re·stric·tive \ri-'strik-tiv\ *adj* : serving or tending to restrict — **re·stric·tive·ly** *adv* — **re·stric·tive·ness** *n*

¹re·sult \ri-'zəlt\ *vb* **1** : to come about as an effect ⟨disease *results* from infection⟩ **2** : to end as an effect : FINISH ⟨the disease *results* in death⟩

²result *n* **1** : something that comes about as a consequence, issue, or conclusion ⟨the *results* of war⟩ **2** : a good effect ⟨this method gets *results*⟩

¹re·sume \ri-'züm\ *vb* **re·sumed; re·sum·ing** **1** : to take again : occupy again ⟨*resume* your seats⟩ **2** : to begin again ⟨*resume* play⟩

²ré·su·mé *or* **re·su·me** \'rez-ə-ˌmā\ *n* : a summing up (as of something said) : SUMMARY

re·sump·tion \ri-'zəmp-shən\ *n* : the act of resuming ⟨*resumption* of work⟩

re·sur·gence \ri-'sər-jəns\ *n* : a rising again into life, activity, or prominence

res·ur·rect \ˌrez-ə-'rekt\ *vb* **1** : to raise from the dead : bring back to life **2** : to bring to view or into use again ⟨*resurrect* an old song⟩

res·ur·rec·tion \ˌrez-ə-'rek-shən\ *n* **1** *cap* : the rising of Christ from the dead **2** *often cap* : the rising again to life of all human dead before the final judgment **3** : REVIVAL, RE-SURGENCE

re·sus·ci·tate \ri-'səs-ə-ˌtāt\ *vb* **re·sus·ci·tat·ed; re·sus·ci·tat·ing** : to revive from apparent death or unconsciousness — **re·sus·ci·ta·tor** *n*

¹re·tail \'rē-ˌtāl\ *vb* : to sell in small quantities directly to the consumer — **re·tail·er** *n*

²retail *n* : the sale of commodities or goods in small quantities directly to consumers

³retail *adj* : of, relating to, or engaged in the sale of commodities in small quantities

re·tain \ri-'tān\ *vb* **1** : to keep in possession or use ⟨*retain* knowledge⟩ **2** : to hold secure or intact ⟨lead *retains* heat⟩

re·tal·i·ate \ri-'tal-ē-ˌāt\ *vb* **re·tal·i·at·ed; re·tal·i·at·ing** : to get revenge by returning like for like

re·tal·i·a·tion \ri-ˌtal-ē-'ā-shən\ *n* : the act or an instance of retaliating

re·tal·ia·to·ry \ri-'tal-yə-ˌtōr-ē\ *adj* : of or relating to retaliation

re·tard \ri-'tärd\ *vb* : to slow up : keep back : HINDER, DELAY — **re·tard·er** *n*

retch \'rech, 'rēch\ *vb* : to vomit or try to vomit

re·ten·tion \ri-'ten-chən\ *n* **1** : the act of retaining : the state of being retained **2** : RETENTIVENESS

re·ten·tive \ri-'tent-iv\ *adj* : having the power of retaining especially in the mind — **re·ten·tive·ly** *adv* — **re·ten·tive·ness** *n*

ret·i·cent \'ret-ə-sənt\ *adj* : inclined to be silent or secretive — **ret·i·cent·ly** *adv*

ret·i·na \'ret-n-ə\ *n, pl* **ret·i·nas** *or* **ret·i·nae** \-n-ˌē\ : the membrane that lines the back part of the eyeball and is the sensitive part for seeing

ret·i·nue \'ret-n-ˌü, -ˌyü\ *n* : the body of attendants or followers of a distinguished person

re·tire \ri-'tīr\ *vb* **re·tired; re·tir·ing** **1** : RETREAT **2** : to withdraw especially for privacy **3** : to withdraw from one's occupation or position **4** : to go to bed **5** : to withdraw from circulation **6** : to put out (as a batter) in baseball — **re·tire·ment** *n*

re·tired \ri-'tīrd\ *adj* **1** : QUIET, HIDDEN ⟨a *retired* spot in the woods⟩ **2** : withdrawn from active duties or business

re·tir·ing \ri-'tīr-ing\ *adj* : SHY, RESERVED

¹re·tort \ri-'tȯrt\ *vb* **1** : to answer back : reply angrily or sharply **2** : to reply with a counter argument

²retort *n* : a quick, witty, or cutting reply

re·trace \rē-'trās\ *vb* **re·traced; re·trac·ing** : to trace again or back

re·tract \ri-'trakt\ *vb* **1** : to draw or pull back or in ⟨a cat can *retract* its claws⟩ **2** : to take back (as an offer or accusation) : WITHDRAW

re·tread \'rē-'tred\ *vb* **re·tread·ed; re·tread·ing** : to put a new tread on the bare cord fabric of (a pneumatic tire)

¹re·treat \ri-'trēt\ *n* **1** : an act of withdrawing especially from something dangerous, difficult, or disagreeable **2** : a military signal for withdrawal **3** : a military flag-lowering ceremony **4** : a place of privacy or safety : REFUGE **5** : a period of group withdrawal for prayer, meditation, and study

²retreat *vb* : to make a retreat : WITHDRAW

re·trench \ri-'trench\ *vb* **1** : REDUCE, CURTAIL **2** : to cut down expenses — **re·trench·ment** *n*

ret·ri·bu·tion \ˌret-rə-'byü-shən\ *n* : something given in payment for an offense

re·trieve \ri-'trēv\ *vb* **re·trieved; re·triev·ing** **1** : to find and bring in killed or wounded game ⟨a dog that *retrieves* well⟩ **2** : to make good a loss or damage : RECOVER — **re·triev·er** *n*

ret·ro·spect \'ret-rə-ˌspekt\ *n* : a looking back on things past

¹re·turn \ri-'tərn\ *vb* **1** : to come or go back **2** : REPLY, ANSWER **3** : to report officially ⟨the jury *returned* a verdict⟩ **4** : to bring, carry, send, or put back : RESTORE ⟨*return* a book to the library⟩ **5** : YIELD, PRODUCE ⟨the farm *returned* a poor crop⟩ **6** : REPAY ⟨*return* borrowed money⟩

²return *n* **1** : the act of coming back to or from a place or condition **2** : RECURRENCE ⟨the *return* of spring⟩ **3** : a report of the results of balloting ⟨election *returns*⟩ **4** : a formal statement of taxable income **5** : the profit from labor, investment, or business **6** : the act of returning something (as to a former place or condition) **7** : something given (as in repayment)

³return *adj* : played, delivered, or given in return ⟨a *return* game⟩

re·un·ion \rē-'yü-nyən\ *n* **1** : the act of reuniting : the state of being reunited **2** : a reuniting of persons after separation ⟨class *reunion*⟩

re·u·nite \₁rē-yù-'nīt\ *vb* **re·u·nit·ed; re·u·nit·ing** : to come or bring together again after a separation

rev \'rev\ *vb* **revved; rev·ving** : to increase the number of revolutions per minute of (a motor)

re·vamp \'rē-'vamp\ *vb* **1** : RENOVATE, RECONSTRUCT **2** : to work over : REVISE

re·veal \ri-'vēl\ *vb* [from Latin *revelare*, literally, "to uncover", from *re-* "back", "un-" and *velare* "to cover", "to veil", from *velum* "veil"] **1** : to make known : DIVULGE ⟨*reveal* a secret⟩ **2** : to show plainly : DISPLAY

rev·eil·le \'rev-ə-lē\ *n* : a signal sounded at about sunrise on a bugle or drum to call soldiers or sailors to duty

¹rev·el \'rev-əl\ *vb* **rev·eled** *or* **rev·elled; rev·el·ing** *or* **rev·el·ling** **1** : to take part in a revel **2** : to take great delight ⟨*reveling* in success⟩

²revel *n* : a noisy or merry celebration

rev·e·la·tion \₁rev-ə-'lā-shən\ *n* **1** : an act of revealing **2** : something revealed

rev·el·ry \'rev-əl-rē\ *n, pl* **rev·el·ries** : rough and noisy merrymaking

¹re·venge \ri-'venj\ *vb* **re·venged; re·veng·ing** : to inflict harm or injury in return for (a wrong) : AVENGE

²revenge *n* **1** : an act or instance of revenging **2** : a desire to repay injury for injury **3** : an opportunity for getting satisfaction

re·venge·ful \ri-'venj-fəl\ *adj* : inclined to seek revenge

rev·e·nue \'rev-ə-ₜnü, -ₜnyü\ *n* [from early French *revenue*, from *revenir* "to come back", taken from Latin *revenire*, a compound of *re-*

"back" and *venire* "to come"] **1** : the income from an investment **2** : money collected by a government (as through taxes and duties)

re·ver·ber·ate \ri-'vər-bə-ₜrāt\ *vb* **re·ver·ber·at·ed; re·ver·ber·at·ing** : RESOUND, ECHO

re·vere \ri-'viər\ *vb* **re·vered; re·ver·ing** : to regard with reverence

¹rev·er·ence \'rev-ə-rəns\ *n* **1** : honor and respect mixed with love and awe **2** : a gesture of respect (as a bow)

²reverence *vb* **rev·er·enced; rev·er·enc·ing** : to regard or treat with reverence

rev·er·end \'rev-ə-rənd\ *adj* **1** : worthy of honor and respect **2** — used as a title for clergymen

rev·er·ent \'rev-ə-rənt\ *adj* : very respectful — **rev·er·ent·ly** *adv*

rev·er·ie *or* **rev·er·y** \'rev-ə-rē\ *n, pl* **rev·er·ies** **1** : DAYDREAM **2** : the condition of being lost in thought

re·vers·al \ri-'vər-səl\ *n* : an act or the process of reversing

¹re·verse \ri-'vərs\ *adj* **1** : opposite or contrary to a previous or normal condition **2** : acting or operating in a manner contrary to the usual — **re·verse·ly** *adv*

²reverse *vb* **re·versed; re·vers·ing** **1** : to turn completely about or upside down or inside out **2** : ANNUL ⟨*reverse* a legal decision⟩ **3** : to go or cause to go in the opposite direction

³reverse *n* **1** : something contrary to something else : OPPOSITE **2** : an act or instance of reversing **3** : the back part of something **4** : an adjustment of gears causing backward movement

re·vert \ri-'vərt\ *vb* : to come or go back ⟨*reverted* to savagery⟩

¹re·view \ri-'vyü\ *n* **1** : a formal military inspection **2** : a general survey **3** : a critical evaluation (as of a book) **4** : a renewed study of previously studied material

²review *vb* **1** : to look at a thing again : study or examine again ⟨*review* a lesson⟩ **2** : to make a formal inspection of (as troops) **3** : to give a criticism of (as a book) **4** : to look back on ⟨*review* accomplishments⟩ — **re·view·er** *n*

re·vile \ri-'vīl\ *vb* **re·viled; re·vil·ing** : to abuse verbally : rail at — **re·vil·er** *n*

re·vise \ri-'vīz\ *vb* **re·vised; re·vis·ing** **1** : to look over again in order to correct or improve ⟨*revise* an essay⟩ **2** : to make a new version of ⟨*revise* a dictionary⟩

re·viv·al \ri-'vī-vəl\ *n* **1** : a reviving of interest (as in art) **2** : a new publication or presentation (as of a book or play) **3** : a renewed flourishing ⟨a *revival* of business⟩

---

j job   **ng** sing   **ō** low   **ȯ** moth   **ȯi** coin   **th** thin   **th̲** this   **ü** boot   **ù** foot   **y** you   **yü** few   **yù** furious   **zh** vision

4 : a meeting or series of meetings conducted by a preacher to arouse religious emotions or to make converts

re·vive \ri-'vīv\ *vb* **re·vived; re·viv·ing 1** : to bring back or come back to life, consciousness, or activity : make or become fresh or strong again **2** : to bring back into use ⟨*revive* an old custom⟩

re·voke \ri-'vōk\ *vb* **re·voked; re·vok·ing** : to put an end to by withdrawing, repealing, or canceling ⟨*revoke* a driver's license⟩

¹re·volt \ri-'vōlt\ *vb* **1** : to renounce allegiance or subjection (as to a government) : REBEL **2** : to experience or cause to experience disgust or shock

²revolt *n* : REBELLION, INSURRECTION

rev·o·lu·tion \,rev-ə-'lü-shən\ *n* **1** : the action by a celestial body of going round in a fixed course **2** : completion of a course (as of years) : CYCLE **3** : a turning round a center or axis : ROTATION **4** : a single complete turn (as of a wheel) **5** : a sudden, radical, or complete change (as in manner of living or working) **6** : the overthrow of one government and the substitution of another by the governed

rev·o·lu·tion·ar·y \,rev-ə-'lü-shə-,ner-ē\ *adj* **1** : of, relating to, or tending to revolution ⟨*revolutionary* war⟩ **2** : RADICAL ⟨*revolutionary* ideas⟩

rev·o·lu·tion·ist \,rev-ə-'lü-shə-nəst\ *n* : one engaged in or advocating a revolution

rev·o·lu·tion·ize \,rev-ə-'lü-shə-,nīz\ *vb* **rev·o·lu·tion·ized; rev·o·lu·tion·iz·ing** : to change fundamentally or completely (as by revolution)

re·volve \ri-'välv\ *vb* **re·volved; re·volv·ing 1** : to think over carefully ⟨*revolve* a plan in the mind⟩ **2** : to go round or cause to go round in an orbit ⟨planets *revolving* around the sun⟩ **3** : ROTATE **4** : RECUR **5** : to move in response to or dependence on a specified agent ⟨the whole household *revolves* about the baby⟩

re·volv·er \ri-'väl-vər\ *n* : a pistol having a revolving cylinder holding several bullets all of which may be shot without loading again

revolver

re·vue \ri-'vyü\ *n* : a theatrical production consisting usually of brief often satirical sketches and songs

¹re·ward \ri-'wȯrd\ *vb* **1** : to give a reward to or for **2** : RECOMPENSE

²reward *n* : something (as money) given or offered in return for a service (as the return of something lost)

re·word \'rē-'wərd\ *vb* : to state in different words ⟨*reword* a question⟩

re·write \'rē-'rīt\ *vb* **re·wrote** \-'rōt\; **re·writ·ten** \-'rit-n\; **re·writ·ing** \-'rit-ing\ : to write over again especially in a different form

rhap·so·dy \'rap-sə-dē\ *n, pl* **rhap·so·dies 1** : a written or spoken expression of extravagant praise or rapture **2** : a musical composition of irregular form

rhe·a \'rē-ə\ *n* : a tall flightless three-toed South American bird resembling but smaller than the ostrich

rheu·mat·ic \rù-'mat-ik\ *adj* : of, relating to, or affected with rheumatism — **rheu·mat·i·cal·ly** \-i-kə-lē\ *adv*

rheu·ma·tism \'rü-mə-,tiz-əm\ *n* : any of various disorders characterized by inflammation or pain in muscles or joints

rhi·noc·er·os \rī-'näs-ə-rəs\ *n, pl* **rhi·noc·er·os·es** *or* **rhinoceros** [from Greek *rhinokerōs*, a compound of *rhin-*, stem of *rhis* "nose", and *keros* "horn"] : a large thick-skinned three-toed mammal of Africa and Asia with one or two heavy upright horns on the snout

rho·do·den·dron \,rōd-ə-'den-drən\ *n* : a shrub or tree with long usually shiny and evergreen leaves and showy clusters of white, pink, or purple flowers

rhom·bus \'räm-bəs\ *n* : a parallelogram whose sides are equal

rhu·barb \'rü-,bärb\ *n* : a plant with broad green leaves and thick juicy pinkish stems that are used for food

rhombus

¹rhyme \'rīm\ *n* **1** : correspondence in final sounds of two or more words or lines of verse **2** : a verse composition that rhymes

²rhyme *vb* **rhymed; rhym·ing 1** : to make rhymes **2** : to end with the same sound **3** : to cause lines or words to end with a similar sound

rhythm \'rith-əm\ *n* **1** : a flow of rising and falling sounds produced in verse by a regular recurrence of stressed and unstressed syllables **2** : a flow of sound in music marked by accented beats coming at regular intervals **3** : a movement or activity in which some action recurs regularly ⟨the *rhythm* of breathing⟩

rhyth·mic \'rith-mik\ *or* **rhyth·mi·cal** \-mi-kəl\ *adj* : marked by rhythm — **rhyth·mi·cal·ly** *adv*

¹rib \'rib\ *n* **1** : one of the series of curved bones that are joined in pairs to the spine of man and animals and help to stiffen the body wall **2** : something (as a structural member of a ship) that is like a rib in shape or use **3** : one of the parallel ridges in a knitted or woven fabric — **ribbed** \'ribd\ *adj*

²rib *vb* **ribbed; rib·bing** **1** : to furnish or enclose with ribs **2** : to form ribs in (a fabric) in knitting or weaving

rib·bon \'rib-ən\ *n* **1** : a narrow strip of fabric (as silk) used for trimming, for tying or ornamenting packages, or for badges **2** : a long narrow strip resembling a ribbon ⟨typewriter *ribbon*⟩ **3** : TATTER, SHRED ⟨torn to *ribbons*⟩

rice \'rīs\ *n* : an annual cereal grass widely grown in warm wet regions for its grain that is a chief food in many parts of the world

rich \'rich\ *adj* **1** : having great wealth ⟨a *rich* man⟩ **2** : VALUABLE, EXPENSIVE ⟨*rich* robes⟩ **3** : containing much sugar, fat, or seasoning ⟨*rich* food⟩ **4** : high in combustible content ⟨a *rich* fuel mixture⟩ **5** : deep and pleasing in color or tone **6** : ABUNDANT ⟨*rich* harvest⟩ **7** : FERTILE, FRUITFUL ⟨*rich* soil⟩ — **rich·ly** *adv* — **rich·ness** *n*

rice

rich·es \'rich-əz\ *n pl* : WEALTH

rick·ets \'rik-əts\ *n* : a disease that especially attacks the young, is characterized by soft deformed bones, and is caused by lack of the vitamin that controls the use of calcium and phosphorus

rick·et·y \'rik-ət-ē\ *adj* : FEEBLE, SHAKY

rick·sha *or* **rick·shaw** \'rik-ˌshò\ *n* : JINRIKISHA

¹ric·o·chet \'rik-ə-ˌshā, *British also* -ˌshet\ *n* : a glancing rebound (as of a bullet off a wall)

²ricochet *vb* **ric·o·cheted** *or* **ric·o·chet·ted; ric·o·chet·ing** *or* **ric·o·chet·ting** : to skip with or as if with glancing rebounds

rid \'rid\ *vb* **rid** *also* **rid·ded; rid·ding** : to make free : RELIEVE ⟨*rid* a dog of fleas⟩

rid·dance \'rid-ns\ *n* : the act of ridding : the state of being rid of

¹rid·dle \'rid-l\ *n* : a puzzling question to be solved or answered by guessing

²riddle *vb* **rid·dled; rid·dling** : to pierce with many holes

¹ride \'rīd\ *vb* **rode** \'rōd\; **rid·den** \'rid-n\; **rid·ing** \'rīd-ing\ **1** : to go on an animal's back or in a conveyance (as a car) **2** : to sit on and control so as to be carried along ⟨*ride* a bicycle⟩ **3** : to float or move on water **4** : to travel over a surface **5** : CARRY ⟨*rode* him on their shoulders⟩ **6** : OBSESS, OPPRESS — **rid·er** \'rīd-ər\ *n*

²ride *n* **1** : a trip on horseback or by vehicle **2** : a mechanical device (as a merry-go-round) for riding on **3** : a means of transportation ⟨wants a *ride* to school⟩

ridge \'rij\ *n* **1** : a range of hills or mountains **2** : a raised strip (as of plowed ground) **3** : the line made where two sloping surfaces come together ⟨the *ridge* of a roof⟩ — **ridged** \'rijd\ *adj*

ridge·pole \'rij-ˌpōl\ *n* : the highest horizontal timber in a sloping roof to which the upper ends of the rafters are fastened

ridgepole

¹rid·i·cule \'rid-ə-ˌkyül\ *n* : the act of exposing to laughter : DERISION

²ridicule *vb* **rid·i·culed; rid·i·cul·ing** : to make fun of : DERIDE

ri·dic·u·lous \rə-'dik-yə-ləs\ *adj* : arousing or deserving ridicule : ABSURD **syn** *see* LAUGHABLE — **ri·dic·u·lous·ly** *adv* — **ri·dic·u·lous·ness** *n*

rife \'rīf\ *adj* **1** : WIDESPREAD, PREVALENT **2** : ABOUNDING ⟨*rife* with rumors⟩

riff·raff \'rif-ˌraf\ *n* : RABBLE

¹ri·fle \'rī-fəl\ *vb* **ri·fled; ri·fling** **1** : to ransack especially in order to steal **2** : STEAL

²rifle *n* : a gun having a long barrel with spiral grooves in its bore

rift \'rift\ *n* **1** : an opening made by splitting or separation : CLEFT **2** : ESTRANGEMENT, BREACH

¹rig \'rig\ *vb* **rigged; rig·ging** **1** : to fit out (as a ship) with rigging **2** : CLOTHE, DRESS **3** : EQUIP **4** : to set up especially as a makeshift

²rig *n* **1** : the distinctive shape, number, and arrangement of sails and masts of a ship **2** : DRESS, CLOTHING **3** : apparatus for a specified purpose ⟨oil-drilling *rig*⟩

rig·ging \'rig-ing\ *n* **1** : the ropes and chains that hold and move the masts, sails, and spars of a ship **2** : TACKLE, GEAR

¹right \'rīt\ *adj* **1** : RIGHTEOUS, UPRIGHT **2** : being in accordance with what is just or proper **3** : CORRECT ⟨*right* answer⟩ **4** : SUITABLE, APPROPRIATE ⟨*right* man for the job⟩ **5** : STRAIGHT ⟨*right* line⟩ **6** : GENUINE, REAL **7** : of, relating to, or being the stronger hand in most persons **8** : located nearer to the right hand **9** : made to be placed or worn outward **10** : physically or mentally well — **right·ly** *adv* — **right·ness** *n*

²right *n* **1** : qualities (as adherence to duty and obedience to authority) that constitute the ideal of moral propriety **2** : something to which one has a just claim ⟨the *right* to freedom⟩ **3** : the cause of truth or justice **4** : the side or part that is on or toward the right side

³right *adv* **1** : according to what is right **2** : EXACTLY, PRECISELY ⟨*right* now⟩ **3** : DI-

---

j job   **ng** sing   **ō** low   **ò** moth   **òi** coin   **th** thin   **th̲** this   **ü** boot   ** u̇** foot   **y** you   **yü** few   **yu̇** furious   **zh** vision

RECTLY ⟨went *right* home⟩ **4** : according to truth or fact **5** : COMPLETELY ⟨*right* to the end⟩ **6** : IMMEDIATELY ⟨*right* after lunch⟩ **7** : EXTREMELY, VERY **8** : on or to the right

⁴right *vb* **1** : to relieve from wrong **2** : to adjust or restore to a proper state or condition **3** : to bring or restore to an upright position **4** : to become upright

right angle *n* : an angle formed by two lines that are perpendicular to each other — **right–an·gled** \'rīt-'ang-gəld\ *adj*

righ·teous \'rī-chəs\ *adj* : acting or being in accordance with what is right — **righ·teous·ly** *adv* — **righ·teous·ness** *n*

right angle

right·ful \'rīt-fəl\ *adj* : LAWFUL, JUST — **right·ful·ly** *adv* — **right·ful·ness** *n*

right–hand \,rīt-,hand\ *adj* **1** : situated on the right **2** : RIGHT-HANDED **3** : chiefly relied on ⟨his *right-hand* man⟩

right–hand·ed \'rīt-'han-dəd\ *adj* **1** : using the right hand more easily than the left ⟨a *right-handed* pitcher⟩ **2** : done or made with or for the right hand **3** : CLOCKWISE

right triangle *n* : a triangle having a right angle

rig·id \'rij-əd\ *adj* **1** : not flexible : STIFF **2** : STRICT, SEVERE — **rig·id·ly** *adv* — **rig·id·ness** *n*

rig·or \'rig-ər\ *n* : SEVERITY, STRICTNESS

right triangle

rig·or·ous \'rig-ə-rəs\ *adj* **1** : very strict **2** : HARSH, SEVERE — **rig·or·ous·ly** *adv* — **rig·or·ous·ness** *n*

rill \'ril\ *n* : a very small brook : RIVULET

rim \'rim\ *n* **1** : an outer edge especially of something curved : BORDER **2** : the outer part of a wheel

¹rime \'rīm\ *n* : white frost

²rime *var of* RHYME

rind \'rīnd\ *n* : a usually hard or tough outer layer ⟨bacon *rind*⟩

¹ring \'ring\ *n* **1** : a circular band worn as an ornament or token or used for holding or fastening **2** : something circular in shape ⟨smoke *ring*⟩ **3** : a place for exhibitions (as at a circus) or contests (as boxing) **4** : a group of persons who work together for selfish or dishonest purposes — **ringed** \'ringd\ *adj*

²ring *vb* **ringed; ring·ing** **1** : ENCIRCLE **2** : to provide with a ring **3** : to throw a ring over (a mark) in a game (as quoits)

³ring *vb* **rang** \'rang\; **rung** \'rəng\; **ring·ing** **1** : to sound resonantly when struck **2** : to cause to make a clear metallic sound by strik-

ing **3** : to sound a bell ⟨*ring* for the waiter⟩ **4** : to announce by or as if by striking a bell **5** : RESOUND ⟨their cheers *rang* out⟩ **6** : to be filled with talk or report **7** : to repeat loudly and persistently **8** : to have a specified quality ⟨his story *rings* true⟩ **9** : to call on the telephone

⁴ring *n* **1** : a clear resonant sound made by vibrating metal **2** : resonant tone **3** : a loud resounding noise **4** : a sound or character expressive of a specified quality **5** : a telephone call

ring·lead·er \'ring-,lēd-ər\ *n* : a leader especially of a group of persons who cause trouble

ring·let \'ring-lət\ *n* : a long curl

rink \'ringk\ *n* : a place for skating

¹rinse \'rins\ *vb* **rinsed; rins·ing** **1** : to wash lightly with water **2** : to cleanse (as of soap) with clear water **3** : to treat (hair) with a rinse

²rinse *n* **1** : an act of rinsing **2** : a liquid used for rinsing **3** : a solution that temporarily tints hair

¹ri·ot \'rī-ət\ *n* **1** : public violence, tumult, or disorder **2** : a random or disorderly profusion especially of color

²riot *vb* : to create or engage in a riot

¹rip \'rip\ *vb* **ripped; rip·ping** : to cut or tear open — **rip·per** *n*

²rip *n* : TEAR

ripe \'rīp\ *adj* **rip·er; rip·est** **1** : fully grown and developed ⟨*ripe* fruit⟩ **2** : having mature knowledge, understanding, or judgment **3** : READY ⟨*ripe* for action⟩ **4** : brought by aging to full flavor — **ripe·ness** *n*

rip·en \'rī-pən\ *vb* : to make or become ripe

¹rip·ple \'rip-əl\ *vb* **rip·pled; rip·pling** **1** : to become or cause to become lightly ruffled on the surface **2** : to make a sound like that of water flowing in small waves

²ripple *n* **1** : the ruffling of the surface of water **2** : a sound like that of rippling water

¹rise \'rīz\ *vb* **rose** \'rōz\; **ris·en** \'riz-n\; **ris·ing** \'rī-zing\ **1** : to get up from lying, kneeling, or sitting **2** : to get up from sleep or from one's bed **3** : to return from death **4** : to take up arms **5** : ADJOURN **6** : to appear above the horizon **7** : ASCEND ⟨smoke *rises*⟩ **8** : to swell in size or volume **9** : to become heartened ⟨their spirits *rose*⟩ **10** : to attain a higher rank or position **11** : INCREASE ⟨*rising* prices⟩ **12** : to come about : HAPPEN **13** : ORIGINATE **14** : to exert oneself to meet a challenge — **ris·er** \'rī-zər\ *n*

²rise *n* **1** : an act of rising : a state of being risen **2** : BEGINNING, ORIGIN **3** : the elevation of one point above another **4** : an increase in amount, number, or volume **5** : an upward slope   **6** : a spot higher than surrounding ground   **7** : an angry reaction

¹risk \'risk\ *n* : exposure to possible loss or injury   **syn** see DANGER

²risk *vb*   **1** : to expose to danger   **2** : to incur the danger of

risk·y \'ris-kē\ *adj* **risk·i·er; risk·i·est** : DANGEROUS

rite \'rīt\ *n*   **1** : a set form of conducting a ceremony   **2** : a ceremonial act or action

rit·u·al \'rich-ə-wəl\ *n*   **1** : an established form especially for a religious ceremony   **2** : a system of rites

¹ri·val \'rī-vəl\ *n*   **1** : one of two or more trying to get what only one can have   **2** : PEER

²rival *adj* : COMPETING ⟨*rival* claims⟩

³rival *vb* **ri·valed** *or* **ri·valled; ri·val·ing** *or* **ri·val·ling**   **1** : to be in competition with   **2** : EQUAL, MATCH

ri·val·ry \'rī-vəl-rē\ *n, pl* **ri·val·ries** : COMPETITION

riv·er \'riv-ər\ *n*   **1** : a natural stream of water larger than a brook or creek   **2** : a large stream ⟨a *river* of oil⟩

riv·et \'riv-ət\ *n* : a headed pin or bolt of metal used for uniting two or more pieces by passing the shank through a hole in each piece and then beating or pressing down the plain end so as to make a second head

rivets

riv·u·let \'riv-yə-lət\ *n* : a small stream

¹roach \'rōch\ *n* : any of several fishes related to or resembling the carp

²roach *n* : COCKROACH

road \'rōd\ *n*   **1** : a place less enclosed than a harbor where ships may ride at anchor   **2** : an open way for vehicles, persons, and animals   **3** : ROUTE, PATH ⟨the *road* to prosperity⟩

road·bed \'rōd-,bed\ *n*   **1** : the foundation of a road or railroad   **2** : the traveled surface of a road

road·way \'rōd-,wā\ *n*   **1** : the strip of land over which a road passes   **2** : the part of the surface of a road traveled by vehicles

roam \'rōm\ *vb* : to go from place to place with no fixed purpose or direction : WANDER — **roam·er** *n*

¹roan \'rōn\ *adj* : of a dark color (as black or brown) with white hairs interspersed

²roan *n*   **1** : an animal (as a horse) with a roan coat   **2** : roan color

¹roar \'rōr\ *vb*   **1** : to utter a full loud prolonged sound   **2** : to make a loud confused sound — **roar·er** *n*

²roar *n* : a prolonged shout, bellow, or loud confused noise

¹roast \'rōst\ *vb*   **1** : to cook by exposing to dry heat (as in an oven)   **2** : to criticize severely — **roast·er** *n*

²roast *n*   **1** : a piece of meat roasted or suitable for roasting   **2** : an outing at which food is roasted

³roast *adj* : ROASTED ⟨*roast* beef⟩

rob \'räb\ *vb* **robbed; rob·bing**   **1** : to take something away from a person or place by force, threat, stealth, or trickery   **2** : to deprive of something due, expected, or desired — **rob·ber** *n*

rob·ber·y \'räb-ə-rē\ *n, pl* **rob·ber·ies** : theft from a person by use of violence or terror

¹robe \'rōb\ *n*   **1** : a long loose or flowing garment ⟨a judge's *robe*⟩   **2** : a covering or wrap for the lower part of the body

²robe *vb* **robed; rob·ing**   **1** : to clothe with a robe   **2** : DRESS ⟨*robed* in white⟩

rob·in \'räb-ən\ *n*   **1** : a small European thrush with a yellowish red throat and breast   **2** : a large North American thrush with a grayish back and dull reddish breast

ro·bot \'rō-,bät\ *n*   **1** : a machine that looks and acts like a human being   **2** : an efficient but insensitive person

ro·bust \rō-'bəst\ *adj* : strong and vigorously healthy — **ro·bust·ly** *adv* — **ro·bust·ness** *n*

¹rock \'räk\ *vb*   **1** : to move back and forth as in a cradle   **2** : to sway or cause to sway back and forth ⟨an earthquake *rocked* the town⟩

²rock *n* : a rocking movement

³rock *n*   **1** : a large mass of stone   **2** : solid mineral deposits   **3** : something (as a support) like a rock in firmness

rock·er \'räk-ər\ *n*   **1** : a curving piece of wood or metal on which an object (as a **rocking chair**) rocks   **2** : a structure or device that rocks on rockers   **3** : a mechanism that works with a rocking motion

¹rock·et \'räk-ət\ *n*   **1** : a firework consisting of a case containing a combustible substance that is propelled through the air as a result of the rearward discharge of gases produced by burning   **2** : a jet engine that operates like a firework rocket but carries the oxygen needed for burning its fuel   **3** : a rocket-propelled bomb, missile, or vehicle

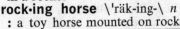

rockers

²rocket *vb*   **1** : to rise swiftly   **2** : to travel rapidly in or as if in a rocket

rocking horse

rock·ing horse \'räk-ing-\ *n* : a toy horse mounted on rockers

---

rock·y \'räk-ē\ *adj* **rock·i·er; rock·i·est 1 :** a-bounding in or consisting of rocks **2 :** HARD — **rock·i·ness** *n*

rod \'räd\ *n* **1 :** a straight slender stick or bar **2 :** a stick or bundle of twigs used in punishing a person **3 :** a measure of length equal to 16½ feet

rode *past of* RIDE

ro·dent \'rōd-nt\ *n* : any of a group of mammals (as squirrels, rats, mice, or beavers) with sharp front teeth used in gnawing

ro·de·o \'rōd-ē-,ō\ *n, pl* **ro·de·os** [formed in Spanish from *rodear* "to surround"; this in turn came from Latin *rota* "wheel"] **1 :** a roundup of cattle **2 :** an exhibition that features cowboy skills (as riding and roping)

¹roe \'rō\ *n, pl* **roe** *or* **roes :** DOE

²roe *n* : the eggs of a fish especially while still bound together in a membrane

roe·buck \'rō-,bək\ *n* : a male roe deer

roe deer *n* : a small nimble deer of Europe and Asia that has erect antlers forked at the tip and is reddish brown in summer and grayish in winter

rogue \'rōg\ *n* **1 :** SCOUNDREL **2 :** a pleasantly mischievous person

rogu·ish \'rō-gish\ *adj* : having the characteristics of a rogue — **rogu·ish·ly** *adv* — **rogu·ish·ness** *n*

roil \'rȯil\ *vb* **1 :** to make cloudy or muddy by stirring up sediment **2 :** VEX

role *also* **rôle** \'rōl\ *n* **1 :** an assigned or assumed character **2 :** a part played by an actor or singer **3 :** FUNCTION

¹roll \'rōl\ *n* **1 :** a written document that may be rolled up **2 :** an official list of names **3 :** something (as a bun) that is rolled up or rounded as if rolled

²roll *vb* **1 :** to move by turning over and over on a surface without sliding **2 :** to shape or become shaped in rounded form **3 :** to make smooth, even, or compact with a roller **4 :** to move on rollers or wheels **5 :** to sound with a full reverberating tone or with a continuous beating sound **6 :** TRILL **7 :** ELAPSE, PASS **8 :** to flow in a continuous stream **9 :** to move with a side-to-side sway ⟨the ship *rolled*⟩

³roll *n* **1 :** a sound produced by rapid strokes on a drum **2 :** a heavy reverberating sound **3 :** a rolling movement or action

roll·er \'rō-lər\ *n* **1 :** a revolving cylinder over or on which something is moved or which is used to press, shape, or smooth something **2 :** a rod on which something (as a map) is rolled up **3 :** a small wheel **4 :** a long heavy wave on the sea

roller skate *n* : a skate that has wheels instead of a runner

rol·lick \'räl-ik\ *vb* : to move or behave in a carefree joyous manner : FROLIC

roll·ing pin *n* : a cylinder (as of wood) used to roll out dough

¹Ro·man \'rō-mən\ *n* **1 :** a native or resident of Rome **2 :** a citizen of the Roman Empire **3** *not cap* : roman characters or type

rolling pin

²Roman *adj* **1 :** of or relating to Rome or the Romans **2** *not cap* : of or relating to a type style with upright characters (as in "these definitions")

¹ro·mance \rō-'mans\ *n* **1 :** a medieval tale of knights and noble ladies **2 :** a prose narrative dealing with heroic or mysterious events **3 :** a love story **4 :** an emotional attraction or appeal ⟨the *romance* of the sea⟩

²romance *vb* **ro·manced; ro·manc·ing 1 :** to exaggerate or invent detail or incident **2 :** to have romantic thoughts or ideas

roman numeral *n, often cap R* : a numeral in a system of notation based on the ancient Roman system ⟨some *roman numerals* with corresponding arabic numerals are I = 1; IV = 4; V = 5; IX = 9; X = 10; XI = 11; L = 50; C = 100; D = 500; M = 1000⟩

ro·man·tic \rō-'mant-ik\ *adj* **1 :** IMAGINARY **2 :** VISIONARY **3 :** emphasizing or appealing to the imagination and emotions **4 :** of, relating to, or associated with love — **ro·man·ti·cal·ly** \-'mant-i-kə-lē\ *adv*

¹romp \'rämp\ *n* : boisterous play : FROLIC

²romp *vb* : to play in a boisterous manner

romp·ers \'räm-pərz\ *n pl* : a child's one-piece garment with the lower part shaped like bloomers

¹roof \'rüf, 'rùf\ *n, pl* **roofs 1 :** the upper covering part of a building **2 :** something resembling a roof in form, position, or function — **roofed** \'rüft, 'rùft\ *adj*

²roof *vb* : to cover with a roof

roof·ing \'rüf-ing, 'rùf-\ *n* : material for a roof

roof·tree \'rüf-,trē, 'rùf-\ *n* : RIDGEPOLE

¹rook \'rùk\ *n* : an Old World bird similar to the related crows

²rook *vb* : CHEAT, SWINDLE

³rook *n* : one of the pieces in the game of chess

rook·ie \'rùk-ē\ *n* : RECRUIT

¹room \'rüm, 'rùm\ *n* **1 :** SPACE **2 :** a partitioned part of the inside of a building **3 :** the people in a room **4** *pl* : LODGINGS **5 :** OPPORTUNITY

rook

²room *vb* : to provide with or occupy lodgings

room·er \'rüm-ər, 'rùm-\ *n* : LODGER

rooming house *n* : a house for renting furnished rooms to lodgers

room·mate \'rüm-,māt, 'rùm-\ *n* : one of two or more persons occupying a room

room·y \'rüm-ē, 'rùm-\ *adj* **room·i·er; room·i·est** : SPACIOUS — **room·i·ness** *n*

¹**roost** \'rüst\ *n* : a support on which birds rest

²**roost** *vb* : to settle on a roost : PERCH

roost·er \'rüs-tər\ *n* : an adult male domestic fowl

¹**root** \'rüt, 'rùt\ *n* **1** : a leafless underground part of a plant that absorbs and stores nourishment and holds the plant in place **2** : the part of something by which it is attached **3** : something resembling a root especially as a source of support or growth **4** : SOURCE ⟨the *root* of evil⟩ **5** : the essential core ⟨get to the *root* of the matter⟩ **6** : a word or part of a word from which other words are derived by adding a prefix or suffix ⟨*hold* is the *root* of *holder*⟩ — **root·ed** \-əd\ *adj*

rooster

²**root** *vb* **1** : to form or enable to form roots **2** : to fix or implant by roots **3** : UPROOT

³**root** *vb* : to turn up or dig with the snout

⁴**root** \'rüt\ *vb* : CHEER — **root·er** *n*

¹**rope** \'rōp\ *n* **1** : a large stout cord of strands (as of fiber or wire) twisted or braided together **2** : a hangman's noose **3** : a row or string (as of beads) made by braiding, twining, or threading

²**rope** *vb* **roped; rop·ing 1** : to bind, fasten, or tie with a rope **2** : to separate or divide by a rope ⟨*rope* off a street⟩ **3** : LASSO — **rop·er** *n*

ro·sa·ry \'rō-zə-rē\ *n, pl* **ro·sa·ries** : a string of beads used in counting prayers

¹**rose** *past of* RISE

²**rose** \'rōz\ *n* **1** : any of various prickly shrubs with compound leaves and showy white, yellow, pink, or red often fragrant flowers **2** : a moderate purplish red

rose·mar·y \'rōz-,mer-ē\ *n* : a fragrant shrubby Old World mint used in cooking and in perfumes

ro·sette \rō-'zet\ *n* **1** : a badge or ornament of ribbon gathered in the shape of a rose **2** : a circular architectural ornament filled with representations of leaves

rosette 2

rose·wood \'rōz-,wùd\ *n* : the reddish or purplish black-streaked wood of tropical trees valued for furniture

Rosh Ha·sha·nah \,rōsh-hə-'shō-nə\ *n* : the Jewish New Year observed as a religious holiday in September or October

ros·in \'räz-n\ *n* : a hard brittle yellow to dark red substance obtained especially from pine trees and used in varnishes and on violin bows

ros·ter \'räs-tər\ *n* : a list of personnel

ros·trum \'räs-trəm\ *n, pl* **ros·trums** *or* **ros·tra** \-trə\ : a stage or platform for public speaking

ros·y \'rō-zē\ *adj* **ros·i·er; ros·i·est 1** : of the color rose **2** : HOPEFUL, PROMISING ⟨*rosy* prospects⟩

¹**rot** \'rät\ *vb* **rot·ted; rot·ting 1** : to undergo decomposition **2** : DETERIORATE, DEGENERATE

²**rot** *n* **1** : the process of rotting : the state of being rotten **2** : a disease of plants or of animals in which the breaking down of tissue occurs

ro·ta·ry \'rōt-ə-rē\ *adj* **1** : turning on an axis like a wheel **2** : having a rotating part

ro·tate \'rō-,tāt\ *vb* **ro·tat·ed; ro·tat·ing 1** : to turn about an axis or a center **2** : to do or cause to do something in turn **3** : to pass in a series

ro·ta·tion \rō-'tā-shən\ *n* **1** : the act of rotating especially on an axis **2** : return or succession in a series ⟨*rotation* of crops⟩

rote \'rōt\ *n* : repetition from memory of forms or phrases with little or no attention to meaning

ro·tor \'rōt-ər\ *n* **1** : a part that revolves in a stationary part **2** : a system of rotating horizontal blades for supporting a helicopter

rot·ten \'rät-n\ *adj* **1** : having rotted **2** : morally corrupt **3** : extremely unpleasant or inferior ⟨a *rotten* game⟩ — **rot·ten·ly** *adv* — **rot·ten·ness** *n*

ro·tund \rō-'tənd\ *adj* : ROUND, ROUNDED — **ro·tund·ly** *adv* — **ro·tund·ness** *n*

rouge \'rüzh\ *n* : a cosmetic used to give a red color to cheeks or lips

¹**rough** \'rəf\ *adj* **1** : uneven in surface **2** : not calm ⟨*rough* seas⟩ **3** : marked by harshness or violence ⟨*rough* treatment⟩ **4** : coarse or rugged in character or appearance **5** : done or made hastily or tentatively — **rough·ly** *adv* — **rough·ness** *n*

²**rough** *n* **1** : uneven ground covered with high grass **2** : a crude, unfinished, or preliminary state

³**rough** *vb* **1** : ROUGHEN **2** : to handle roughly : BEAT ⟨*roughed* up by hoodlums⟩ **3** : to make or shape roughly — **rough it** : to live without ordinary comforts

rough·age \'rəf-ij\ *n* : coarse food (as bran) whose bulk stimulates the activity of the intestines

rough·en \'rəf-ən\ *vb* : to make or become rough

rough·neck \'rəf-ˌnek\ *n* : ROWDY, TOUGH

¹**round** \'raủnd\ *adj* **1** : having every part of the surface or circumference the same distance from the center **2** : CYLINDRICAL **3** : PLUMP, SHAPELY **4** : COMPLETE, FULL ⟨a *round* dozen⟩ **5** : approximately correct or exact ⟨in *round* numbers⟩ **6** : AMPLE, LARGE ⟨a good *round* sum⟩ **7** : BLUNT, OUTSPOKEN **8** : moving in or forming a circle **9** : curved rather than angular — **round·ish** *adj* — **round·ly** *adv* — **round·ness** *n*

²**round** *adv* : AROUND

³**round** *prep* : AROUND

⁴**round** *n* **1** : something (as a circle or globe) that is round **2** : a song in which three or four singers follow one after another at intervals and sing the same melody and words **3** : a round or curved part (as of a ladder) **4** : a circuitous path or course **5** : an habitually covered route **6** : a series or cycle of recurring actions or events **7** : one shot fired by a soldier or a gun **8** : ammunition for one shot **9** : a unit of play in a contest or game **10** : a cut of beef especially between the rump and the lower leg — **in the round 1** : FREESTANDING **2** : with a center stage surrounded by an audience on all sides

⁵**round** *vb* **1** : to make or become round **2** : to go or pass around **3** : COMPLETE ⟨*round* out a career⟩ **4** : to express as a round number **5** : to follow a winding course — **round up 1** : to collect cattle by riding around them and driving them in **2** : to gather in or bring together

round·a·bout \'raủn-də-ˌbaủt\ *adj* : INDIRECT, CIRCUITOUS

round·up \'raủnd-ˌəp\ *n* **1** : the gathering together of cattle on the range by riding around them and driving them in **2** : a gathering together of scattered persons or things **3** : SUMMARY

round·worm \'raủnd-ˌwərm\ *n* : any of a group of round-bodied worms that are not segmented and that include serious parasites of man and animals

rouse \'raủz\ *vb* **roused; rous·ing 1** : AWAKEN **2** : to stir up : EXCITE

¹**rout** \'raủt\ *n* **1** : a state of wild confusion or disorderly retreat **2** : a disastrous defeat

²**rout** *vb* **1** : to put to flight **2** : to defeat decisively

¹**route** \'rüt, 'raủt\ *n* : an established, selected, or assigned course of travel

²**route** *vb* **rout·ed; rout·ing 1** : to send or transport by a selected route **2** : to arrange

and direct the order of (as a series of factory operations)

¹**rou·tine** \rü-'tēn\ *n* : a regular or customary course of procedure

²**routine** *adj* **1** : COMMONPLACE, ORDINARY **2** : done or happening in accordance with established procedure — **rou·tine·ly** *adv*

rove \'rōv\ *vb* **roved; rov·ing** : to wander without definite direction

rov·er \'rō-vər\ *n* : WANDERER, ROAMER

¹**row** \'rō\ *vb* **1** : to propel a boat by means of oars **2** : to travel or transport in a rowboat

²**row** *n* : an act or instance of rowing

³**row** *n* **1** : a series of persons or things in an orderly sequence **2** : WAY, STREET

⁴**row** \'raủ\ *n* : a noisy disturbance or quarrel

row·boat \'rō-ˌbōt\ *n* : a boat designed to be rowed

¹**row·dy** \'raủd-ē\ *adj* **row·di·er; row·di·est** : coarse or boisterous in behavior — **row·di·ness** *n*

²**rowdy** *n, pl* **row·dies** : a rowdy person

rowboat

roy·al \'rȯi-əl\ *adj* **1** : of or relating to a king or sovereign : REGAL **2** : suitable for a king — **roy·al·ly** *adv*

roy·al·ty \'rȯi-əl-tē\ *n, pl* **roy·al·ties 1** : royal status or power **2** : regal character or bearing **3** : persons of royal lineage **4** : a share of a product or profit (as of a mine) claimed by the owner for allowing another to use the property **5** : payment made to the owner of a patent or copyright for the use of it

¹**rub** \'rəb\ *vb* **rubbed; rub·bing 1** : to move along the surface of a body with pressure **2** : to fret or chafe with friction **3** : to cause discontent, irritation, or anger **4** : to scour, polish, erase, or smear by pressure and friction

²**rub** *n* **1** : OBSTRUCTION, DIFFICULTY **2** : something that grates on the feelings **3** : the application of friction with pressure

rub·ber \'rəb-ər\ *n* **1** : something used in rubbing **2** : an elastic substance obtained from the milky juice of various tropical plants **3** : a synthetic rubberlike substance **4** : something (as an overshoe) made of rubber

rub·bish \'rəb-ish\ *n* : TRASH

rub·ble \'rəb-əl\ *n* **1** : broken stones or bricks used in masonry **2** : a mass of rubble

ru·ble \'rü-bəl\ *n* : a Russian coin

ru·by \'rü-bē\ *n, pl* **ru·bies** : a precious stone of a deep red color

ruck·sack \'rək-ˌsak\ *n* : KNAPSACK

ruck·us \'rək-əs\ *n* : ROW, DISTURBANCE

rud·der \'rəd-ər\ *n* : a movable flat piece attached vertically at the rear of a ship or aircraft for steering

rudder

rud·dy \'rəd-ē\ *adj* **rud·di·er; rud·di·est** : having a healthy reddish color — **rud·di·ness** *n*

rude \'rüd\ *adj* **rud·er; rud·est** 1 : roughly made   2 : not refined or cultured   3 : DISCOURTEOUS, IMPOLITE — **rude·ly** *adv* — **rude·ness** *n*

ru·di·ment \'rüd-ə-mənt\ *n* : an elementary principle

ru·di·men·ta·ry \,rüd-ə-'ment-ə-rē\ *adj* 1 : ELEMENTARY, SIMPLE   2 : imperfectly developed

¹**rue** \'rü\ *vb* **rued; ru·ing** : to feel remorse or regret for

²**rue** *n* : REGRET, SORROW

³**rue** *n* : a woody plant with yellow flowers, a strong smell, and bitter-tasting leaves

rue·ful \'rü-fəl\ *adj* 1 : arousing pity or sympathy   2 : MOURNFUL, REGRETFUL

ruff \'rəf\ *n* 1 : a wheel-shaped collar of pleated muslin or linen worn by men and women in the sixteenth and seventeenth centuries   2 : a fringe of long hair or feathers on the neck of an animal or bird

rue

ruf·fi·an \'rəf-ē-ən\ *n* : a brutal cruel fellow

¹**ruf·fle** \'rəf-əl\ *vb* **ruf·fled; ruf·fling** 1 : to disturb the smoothness of   2 : TROUBLE, VEX   3 : to erect (as feathers) in or like a ruff   4 : to draw into or provide with pleats or folds

²**ruffle** *n* : a strip of fabric gathered or pleated on one edge

rug \'rəg\ *n* : a piece of thick heavy fabric usually with a nap or pile used as a floor covering or as a lap robe or blanket

rug·ged \'rəg-əd\ *adj* 1 : having a rough uneven surface   2 : STORMY, TURBULENT   3 : STRONG, STURDY — **rug·ged·ly** *adv* — **rug·ged·ness** *n*

¹**ru·in** \'rü-ən\ *n* 1 : complete collapse or destruction   2 *pl* : the remains of something destroyed   3 : a cause of destruction

²**ruin** *vb* 1 : to reduce to ruins   2 : to damage beyond repair   3 : BANKRUPT

ru·in·ous \'rü-ə-nəs\ *adj* : causing or tending to cause ruin : DESTRUCTIVE — **ru·in·ous·ly** *adv*

¹**rule** \'rül\ *n* 1 : a guide or principle for governing action   2 : an accepted procedure, custom, or habit   3 : the exercise of authority or control : GOVERNMENT   4 : the time of a particular king's reign   5 : a straight strip of material (as wood or metal) marked off in units and used for measuring or as a guide in drawing straight lines

²**rule** *vb* **ruled; rul·ing** 1 : CONTROL, DIRECT   2 : to exercise authority over : GOVERN   3 : to be supreme or outstanding in   4 : to give or state as a considered decision   5 : to mark with lines drawn along the straight edge of a rule

rul·er \'rü-lər\ *n* 1 : SOVEREIGN   2 : RULE 5

rum \'rəm\ *n* : an alcoholic liquor distilled from a fermented cane product (as molasses)

¹**rum·ble** \'rəm-bəl\ *vb* **rum·bled; rum·bling** 1 : to make a low heavy rolling sound   2 : to travel with a low reverberating sound

²**rumble** *n* : a low heavy reverberating sound

¹**ru·mi·nant** \'rü-mə-nənt\ *n* : an animal (as a cow) that chews the cud

²**ruminant** *adj* 1 : chewing the cud   2 : of or relating to the group of hoofed mammals that chew the cud

ru·mi·nate \'rü-mə-,nāt\ *vb* **ru·mi·nat·ed; ru·mi·nat·ing** 1 : to engage in thought : MEDITATE   2 : to bring up and chew again what has been previously swallowed

¹**rum·mage** \'rəm-ij\ *n* : a thorough search especially among a confusion of objects

²**rummage** *vb* **rum·maged; rum·mag·ing** 1 : to make a thorough search especially by moving about, turning over, or looking through the contents of a place or receptacle   2 : to discover by searching

rum·my \'rəm-ē\ *n* : a card game in which each player tries to assemble his cards in groups of three or more

¹**ru·mor** \'rü-mər\ *n* 1 : common talk : HEARSAY   2 : a statement or report that is current but not verified

²**rumor** *vb* : to tell or spread by rumor

rump \'rəmp\ *n* 1 : the back part of an animal's body where the hips and thighs join   2 : a cut of beef between the loin and round

rum·ple \'rəm-pəl\ *vb* **rum·pled; rum·pling** : WRINKLE, MUSS

rum·pus \'rəm-pəs\ *n* : DISTURBANCE, FRACAS

¹**run** \'rən\ *vb* **ran** \'ran\; **run; run·ning** 1 : to go at a pace faster than a walk   2 : to take to flight   3 : to move freely about at will   4 : to go rapidly or hurriedly   5 : to do something by or as if by running ⟨*run* errands⟩   6 : to contend in a race   7 : to move on or as if on wheels   8 : to go back and forth often according to a fixed schedule   9 : to migrate or move in schools   10 : FUNCTION, OPERATE   11 : to continue in force   12 : to pass into a specified condition   13 : FLOW   14 : DISSOLVE

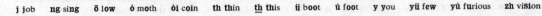

⟨colors guaranteed not to *run*⟩ **15** : to discharge matter ⟨a *running* sore⟩ **16** : to tend to develop a specified feature or quality **17** : EXTEND **18** : to be current **19** : to be in a certain form or expression or order of succession **20** : TRACE **21** : TRAVERSE **22** : to slip through or past **23** : to cause to penetrate **24** : to cause to go **25** : INCUR **26** : PRINT

²run *n* **1** : an act or the action of running **2** : a continuous series especially of similar things **3** : persistent heavy demands from depositors, creditors, or customers **4** : the quantity of work turned out in a continuous operation **5** : the usual or normal kind **6** : the distance covered in a period of continuous traveling **7** : a regular course or trip **8** : freedom of movement **9** : a way, track, or path frequented by animals **10** : an enclosure for livestock where they may feed and exercise **11** : a score made in baseball by a base runner reaching home plate **12** : an inclined course (as for skiing) **13** : a ravel in a knitted fabric

¹run·a·way \'rən-ə-ˌwā\ *n* **1** : FUGITIVE **2** : a horse that is running out of control

²runaway *adj* **1** : running away ⟨*runaway* slaves⟩ **2** : accomplished by elopement or during flight

run–down \'rən-'daùn\ *adj* **1** : being in poor repair **2** : being in poor health

¹rung \'rəng\ *past part of* RING

²rung *n* **1** : a rounded part placed as a crosspiece between the legs of a chair **2** : one of the crosspieces of a ladder

run–in \'rən-ˌin\ *n* : ALTERCATION, QUARREL

run·ner \'rən-ər\ *n* **1** : one that runs **2** : MESSENGER **3** : a thin piece or part on or in which something slides **4** : a slender creeping branch of a plant that roots at the end or at the joints to form new plants **5** : a plant that forms or spreads by runners **6** : a long narrow carpet (as for a hall)

runner

runt \'rənt\ *n* : an unusually small person or animal

run·way \'rən-ˌwā\ *n* **1** : a path beaten by animals in going to and from feeding grounds **2** : RUN 10 **3** : an artificially surfaced strip of ground for the landing and takeoff of airplanes

ru·pee \rü-'pē\ *n* : any of several coins (as of India or Pakistan)

¹rup·ture \'rəp-chər\ *n* **1** : a breach of peace or concord **2** : a breaking or tearing apart (as of body tissue) **3** : a condition in which a body part (as a loop of intestine) protrudes through the weakened wall of the cavity that contains it

²rupture *vb* **rup·tured; rup·tur·ing 1** : to part by violence : BREAK **2** : to produce a rupture in **3** : to have a rupture

ru·ral \'rùr-əl\ *adj* : of or relating to the country, country people or life, or agriculture
syn RURAL and RUSTIC both refer to the country and country life as opposed to the city. RURAL emphasizes the more pleasant aspects ⟨*rural* calm and peace⟩ but is used also simply as a general term for country ⟨*rural* schools⟩ RUSTIC stresses the less pleasant aspects ⟨*rustic* cabins without lights or plumbing⟩ and conveys a definite suggestion of roughness and lack of polish ⟨told of Lincoln's *rustic* schooling⟩ ⟨*rustic* speech may seem odd to city people⟩

rural free delivery *n* : the free delivery of mail on routes in country districts

ruse \'rüs, 'rüz\ *n* : TRICK, ARTIFICE

¹rush \'rəsh\ *n* : a grasslike marsh plant with hollow stems used in chair seats and mats

²rush *vb* **1** : to move forward or act with great haste or eagerness **2** : to perform in a short time or at high speed **3** : ATTACK, CHARGE — **rush·er** *n*

³rush *n* **1** : a violent forward motion **2** : a burst of activity or speed **3** : a crowding together of people usually at a new place and in search of wealth ⟨gold *rush*⟩

⁴rush *adj* : demanding special speed or urgency ⟨*rush* order⟩

¹Rus·sian \'rəsh-ən\ *adj* : of or relating to Russia, the people of Russia, or Russian

²Russian *n* **1** : a native or inhabitant of Russia **2** : a language of the Russians

¹rust \'rəst\ *n* **1** : a reddish coating formed on metal (as iron) when it is exposed especially to moist air **2** : a plant disease caused by fungi that makes spots on plants **3** : a fungus that causes a rust

²rust *vb* : to make or become rusty

¹rus·tic \'rəs-tik\ *adj* **1** : of, relating to, or suitable for the country **2** : PLAIN, SIMPLE
syn see RURAL

²rustic *n* : a country person

¹rus·tle \'rəs-əl\ *vb* **rus·tled; rus·tling 1** : to make or cause to make a rustle **2** : to steal (as cattle) from the range — **rus·tler** \'rəs-lər\ *n*

²rustle *n* : a quick succession of small sounds

rust·y \'rəs-tē\ *adj* **rust·i·er; rust·i·est 1** : affected by rust ⟨*rusty* nail⟩ **2** : inept and slow through lack of practice or old age — **rust·i·ness** *n*

¹rut \'rət\ *n* **1** : a track worn by a wheel or by habitual passage **2** : ROUTINE

²rut *vb* **rut·ted; rut·ting** : to make a rut in

ruth·less \'rüth-ləs\ *adj* : having no pity : CRUEL — **ruth·less·ly** *adv* — **ruth·less·ness** *n*

-ry \rē\ *n suffix* : -ERY ⟨wizard*ry*⟩

rye \'rī\ *n* : a hardy cereal grass grown especially for its edible seeds that are used in flour and animal feeds and in making whiskey

s \'es\ *n, often cap* **1** : the nineteenth letter of the English alphabet **2** : a grade rating a student's work as satisfactory

¹-s \s *after sounds* f, k, p, t, th; əz *after sounds* ch, j, s, sh, z, zh; z *after other sounds*\ *n pl suffix* **1** — used to form the plural of most nouns that do not end in *s, z, sh, ch,* or *y* following a consonant ⟨head*s*⟩ ⟨book*s*⟩ ⟨belief*s*⟩, to form the plural of proper nouns that end in *y* following a consonant ⟨Mary*s*⟩, and with or without a preceding apostrophe to form the plural of abbreviations, numbers, letters, and symbols used as nouns ⟨4*s*⟩ ⟨#*s*⟩ ⟨B'*s*⟩ **2** — used to form adverbs denoting usual or repeated action or state ⟨always at home Sunday*s*⟩

²-s *vb suffix* — used to form the third person singular present of most verbs that do not end in *s, z, sh, ch,* or *y* following a consonant ⟨fall*s*⟩ ⟨take*s*⟩ ⟨play*s*⟩

Sab·bath \'sab-əth\ *n* **1** : the seventh day of the week beginning in the Jewish calendar at sundown on Friday and lasting until sundown on Saturday **2** : the first day of the week (as Sunday) kept for rest and worship

sa·ber *or* **sa·bre** \'sā-bər\ *n* : a cavalry sword with a curved blade

sa·ber–toothed tiger \,sā-bər-,tütht-\ *n* : a very large prehistoric cat with long sharp curved upper canine teeth

Sa·bin vaccine \'sā-bən-\ *n* : a polio vaccine that is taken by mouth

sa·ble \'sā-bəl\ *n* **1** : the color black **2** : a meat-eating animal of northern Europe and Asia that is related to the marten and valued for its soft rich brown fur **3** : a North American animal related and similar to the true marten

sa·bot \sa-'bō\ *n* : a wooden shoe worn chiefly by peasants in Europe

¹sab·o·tage \'sab-ə-,täzh\ *n* **1** : destruction of an employer's property by discontented workmen **2** : destruc-

sabot

tion by enemy agents or sympathizers to hinder a nation's war effort or defenses

²sabotage *vb* **sab·o·taged; sab·o·tag·ing** : to practice sabotage on : WRECK

sac \'sak\ *n* : a baglike part of a plant or animal often containing a liquid

sa·chem \'sā-chəm\ *n* : a North American Indian chief

¹sack \'sak\ *n* **1** : a container of flexible material (as paper) for holding and carrying goods **2** : the quantity contained in a sack

²sack *vb* : to put into a sack

³sack *n* : the plundering of a city by its conquerors

⁴sack *vb* : to plunder after capture

sack·ing \'sak-ing\ *n* : a strong coarse cloth (as burlap) from which sacks are made

sac·ra·ment \'sak-rə-mənt\ *n* : a religious act, ceremony, or practice that is considered especially sacred

sa·cred \'sā-krəd\ *adj* **1** : HOLY ⟨the *sacred* name of God⟩ **2** : RELIGIOUS ⟨*sacred* songs⟩ **3** : entitled to respect and reverence : not to be violated or misused ⟨a *sacred* right⟩ — **sa·cred·ness** *n*

¹sac·ri·fice \'sak-rə-,fīs\ *n* **1** : the act or ceremony of making an offering to God or a god especially on an altar **2** : something offered up as a religious act **3** : an unselfish giving up ⟨a *sacrifice* of our time to help others⟩ **4** : a loss of profit

²sacrifice *vb* **sac·ri·ficed; sac·ri·fic·ing** **1** : to offer up or kill as a sacrifice **2** : to give up for the sake of something else ⟨*sacrificed* his life for his country⟩ **3** : to sell at a loss

sad \'sad\ *adj* **sad·der; sad·dest** **1** : filled with sorrow or unhappiness **2** : causing sorrow or gloom — **sad·ly** *adv* — **sad·ness** *n*

sad·den \'sad-n\ *vb* : to make or become sad

¹sad·dle \'sad-l\ *n* **1** : a leather-covered padded seat (as for a rider on horseback) **2** : a cut of meat (as lamb or veal) consisting of both sides of the back and including the two loins **3** : something that resembles a saddle in shape, position, or use

²saddle *vb* **sad·dled; sad·dling** **1** : to put a saddle on **2** : to put a load on : BURDEN

saddle

saddle horse *n* : a horse suited for or trained for riding

¹safe \'sāf\ *adj* **1** : freed or secure from harm or danger **2** : successful in reaching base in baseball **3** : giving protection or security against danger **4** : HARMLESS **5** : RELIABLE, TRUSTWORTHY — **safe·ly** *adv* — **safe·ness** *n*

---

j job ng sing ō low ȯ moth ȯi coin th thin th̲ this ü boot u̇ foot y you yü few yu̇ furious zh vision

²safe *n* : a steel or metal chest for keeping something (as money) safe

¹safe·guard \'sāf-,gärd\ *n* : something that protects and gives safety

safe

²safeguard *vb* : to keep safe
syn see DEFEND

safe·keep·ing \'sāf-'kē-ping\ *n* : the act of keeping safe : protection from danger or loss

safe·ty \'sāf-tē\ *n* 1 : freedom from danger : SECURITY ⟨the *safety* of citizens⟩ 2 : SAFE-NESS, RELIABILITY

saf·fron \'saf-rən\ *n* 1 : a pungent aromatic orange powder used especially to color or flavor foods that consists of the dried stigmas of a purple-flowered crocus 2 : an orange to orange yellow

¹sag \'sag\ *vb* **sagged; sag·ging** 1 : to droop below the natural or right level ⟨a *sagging* rope⟩ 2 : to lose firmness, resiliency, or vigor ⟨a *sagging* wall⟩

²sag *n* : a sagging part or area

sa·ga \'sä-gə\ *n* 1 : a narrative of historic or legendary figures and events especially of Norway and Iceland 2 : a story of heroic deeds

sa·ga·cious \sə-'gā-shəs\ *adj* : quick and shrewd in understanding and judging — **sa-ga·cious·ly** *adv* — **sa·ga·cious·ness** *n*

¹sage \'sāj\ *adj* : WISE, PRUDENT — **sage·ly** *adv* — **sage·ness** *n*

²sage *n* : a wise man

³sage *n* 1 : a shrubby mint with strong-smelling grayish green leaves used to flavor foods 2 : a mint related to the true sage that is grown for its showy usually scarlet flowers 3 : SAGEBRUSH

sage·brush \'sāj-,brəsh\ *n* : a low shrubby western American plant related to the daisies that has a bitter juice and a sagelike smell

sage

sa·gua·ro \sə-'gwä-rō\ *n, pl* **sa·gua·ros** : a giant cactus of the southwestern United States

said *past of* SAY

¹sail \'sāl\ *n* 1 : a three-sided or four-sided piece of canvas or cloth by means of which the wind is used to move boats through the water or over ice 2 : the sails of a ship 3 : a sailing ship 4 : something (as a wing or a fin) resembling a sail 5 : a voyage or trip on a sailing ship

²sail *vb* 1 : to travel on a boat propelled by the wind 2 : to travel by water 3 : to move or pass over by ship 4 : to manage or direct the motion of 5 : to move or glide along

sail·boat \'sāl-,bōt\ *n* : a boat equipped with sails

sail·fish \'sāl-,fish\ *n* : a fish related to the swordfish but distinguished by a large saillike fin on its back

sail·or \'sā-lər\ *n* : one that sails : SEAMAN

¹saint \'sānt\ *n* 1 : a holy and godly person and especially one who is declared to be worthy of public veneration throughout the church 2 : a person who is sweet-tempered, self-sacrificing, and righteous

²saint *vb* : to make a saint of

Saint Ber·nard \,sānt-bər-'närd\ *n* : a giant powerful dog bred originally in the Swiss Alps

saint·ed \'sānt-əd\ *adj* : SAINTLY

saint·hood \'sānt-,hud\ *n* : the quality or state of being a saint

saint·ly \'sānt-lē\ *adj* : HOLY, PIOUS — **saint-li·ness** *n*

sake \'sāk\ *n* 1 : END, PURPOSE ⟨for the *sake* of argument⟩ 2 : GOOD, BENEFIT ⟨for the *sake* of his country⟩

sal·a·ble *or* **sale·a·ble** \'sā-lə-bəl\ *adj* 1 : fit to be sold 2 : likely to be bought

sal·ad \'sal-əd\ *n* 1 : a cold dish of green vegetables usually served with oil, vinegar, and seasonings 2 : a cold dish of meat, shellfish, fruit, or vegetables served alone or in combinations with a dressing

sal·a·man·der \'sal-ə-,man-dər\ *n* : any of a group of animals that are related to the frogs but superficially resemble lizards

sal·a·ry \'sal-ə-rē\ *n, pl* **sal·a·ries** : money paid at regular times for work done

sale \'sāl\ *n* 1 : an exchange of goods or property for money 2 : the purpose of selling or being sold ⟨a house offered for *sale*⟩ 3 : AUCTION 4 : a selling of goods at reduced prices

sales·man \'sālz-mən\ *n, pl* **sales·men** \-mən\ : one that sells either in a territory or in a store — **sales·wom·an** \-,wum-ən\ *n*

sa·li·va \sə-'lī-və\ *n* : a watery fluid that contains salt, protein, and enzymes which break down starch and is secreted into the mouth from glands in the neck

sal·i·var·y \'sal-ə-,ver-ē\ *adj* : of, relating to, or producing saliva ⟨*salivary* glands⟩

Salk vaccine \'sȯk-\ *n* : a polio vaccine that is given by injection

sal·low \'sal-ō\ *adj* : of a grayish greenish yellow color ⟨*sallow* skin⟩

sailboat

¹sal·ly \'sal-ē\ *n, pl* **sal·lies** **1** : a rushing or bursting forth especially by besieged soldiers **2** : a witty or amusing remark

²sally *vb* **sal·lied; sal·ly·ing** : to leap or rush forth

salm·on \'sam-ən\ *n* : a large food fish with pinkish or reddish flesh

sa·loon \sə-'lün\ *n* **1** : a large public room (as on a passenger ship) **2** : a shop where liquors are sold and drunk

¹salt \'sȯlt\ *n* **1** : a colorless or white crystalline substance that consists of sodium and chlorine and is used in seasoning foods, preserving meats and fish, and in making soap and glass **2** : a compound formed by replacement of hydrogen in an acid by a metal or group of elements that act like a metal

²salt *vb* : to preserve, season, treat, or feed with salt

³salt *adj* **1** : SALTED, SALTY **2** : coming from, living in, or covered by salt or sea water

salt·wa·ter \'sȯlt-,wȯt-ər, -,wät-\ *adj* : of, relating to, or living in salt water

salt·y \'sȯl-tē\ *adj* **salt·i·er; salt·i·est** : of, tasting of, or containing salt

sal·u·ta·tion \,sal-yə-'tā-shən\ *n* **1** : an act or action of greeting **2** : a word or phrase of greeting used at the beginning of a letter

¹sa·lute \sə-'lüt\ *vb* **sa·lut·ed; sa·lut·ing** **1** : to address with expressions of kind wishes, courtesy, or honor **2** : to honor by a conventional military ceremony **3** : to show respect and recognition to (a military superior) by a prescribed position (as of the hand)

²salute *n* **1** : GREETING, SALUTATION **2** : the formal position assumed in saluting a superior

¹sal·vage \'sal-vij\ *n* **1** : money paid for saving a wrecked or endangered ship or its cargo or passengers **2** : the act of saving a ship **3** : the saving of possessions in danger of being lost **4** : something that is saved (as from a wreck)

²salvage *vb* **sal·vaged; sal·vag·ing** : to rescue or save especially from wreckage or ruin

sal·va·tion \sal-'vā-shən\ *n* **1** : the saving of a person from the power and the effects of sin **2** : the saving from danger or evil **3** : something that saves, preserves, or redeems

¹salve \'sav, 'sȧv\ *n* : a healing or soothing ointment

²salve *vb* **salved; salv·ing** : to quiet or soothe with or as if with a salve

¹same \'sām\ *adj* **1** : not another : IDENTICAL ⟨lived in the *same* house all his life⟩ **2** : very much alike : of one kind ⟨eat the *same* breakfast every day⟩ **3** : UNCHANGED ⟨is always the *same* no matter what happens⟩

²same *pron* : the same one or ones

³same *adv* : in the same manner

same·ness \'sām-nəs\ *n* **1** : the quality or state of being the same **2** : MONOTONY, UNIFORMITY

sam·pan \'sam-,pan\ *n* : a flat-bottomed Chinese skiff usually propelled by two short oars

¹sam·ple \'sam-pəl\ *n* : a part or piece that shows the quality of the whole

²sample *vb* **sam·pled; sam·pling** : to judge the quality of by samples : TEST

sampan

sam·pler \'sam-plər\ *n* : a decorative piece of needlework with letters or verses embroidered on it

san·a·to·ri·um \,san-ə-'tōr-ē-əm\ *n* : a place for the care and treatment of usually convalescent or chronically ill people

sanc·tion \'sangk-shən\ *n* : authoritative approval

sanc·tu·ar·y \'sangk-chə-,wer-ē\ *n, pl* **sanc·tu·ar·ies** **1** : a holy or sacred place **2** : a building for religious worship **3** : the most sacred part (as near the altar) of a place of worship **4** : a place of refuge or safety **5** : PROTECTION, REFUGE

sanc·tum \'sangk-təm\ *n* **1** : a sacred place **2** : a private place : STUDY

¹sand \'sand\ *n* **1** : loose granular material produced by the natural breaking up of rocks **2** : a soil consisting mostly of sand

²sand *vb* **1** : to sprinkle with sand **2** : to smooth or scour with sand or sandpaper

san·dal \'san-dl\ *n* **1** : a shoe consisting of a sole strapped to the foot **2** : a very low or open slipper held in place by straps

sandal 2

san·dal·wood \'san-dl-,wu̇d\ *n* : the close-grained fragrant yellowish heartwood of an Asiatic tree

sand·bag \'sand-,bag\ *n* : a bag filled with sand and used as ballast or as part of a fortification wall or of a temporary dam

sand·bar \'sand-,bär\ *n* : a ridge of sand formed in water by tides or currents

sand·bur \'sand-,bər\ *n* : a weed of waste places with prickly fruit

sand dollar *n* : a flat circular sea urchin

sand·man \'sand-,man\ *n, pl* **sand·men** \-,men\ : a genie who makes children sleepy by sprinkling sand in their eyes

¹sand·pa·per \'sand-,pā-pər\ *n* : paper with sand glued on one side that is used in rubbing surfaces to smooth or polish them

²sandpaper *vb* : to rub with sandpaper

---

sand·pip·er \'sand-ˌpī-pər\ *n* : a small shore-bird related to the plovers

sand·stone \'sand-ˌstōn\ *n* : rock made of sand held together by a natural cement

sand·storm \'sand-ˌstorm\ *n* : a storm of wind (as in a desert) that drives clouds of sand

sand·wich \'sand-ˌwich\ *n* : two or more slices of bread with a filling (as of meat or cheese) between them

sand·y \'san-dē\ *adj* 1 : consisting of, containing, or covered with sand 2 : of a yellowish gray color

sane \'sān\ *adj* **san·er; san·est** 1 : mentally healthy and sound 2 : very sensible

sang *past of* SING

san·i·tar·i·um \ˌsan-ə-'ter-ē-əm\ *n* : SANATORIUM

san·i·tar·y \'san-ə-ˌter-ē\ *adj* 1 : of or relating to health or hygiene 2 : free from filth, infection, or other dangers to health

san·i·ta·tion \ˌsan-ə-'tā-shən\ *n* 1 : the act or process of making sanitary 2 : the promotion of health and hygiene by maintenance of sanitary conditions

san·i·ty \'san-ət-ē\ *n* : soundness of mind

sank *past of* SINK

San·ta Claus \'sant-ə-ˌkloz\ *n* : the holiday spirit of Christmas personified as a jolly old man in a red suit who distributes toys

¹sap \'sap\ *n* : a watery juice that circulates through a higher plant and carries food and nutrients

²sap *vb* **sapped; sap·ping** 1 : to destroy by digging under : UNDERMINE 2 : to weaken or exhaust gradually

sap·ling \'sap-ling\ *n* : a young tree

sap·phire \'saf-ˌīr\ *n* : a transparent bright blue precious stone

sap·suck·er \'sap-ˌsək-ər\ *n* : a small American woodpecker with a white patch that runs lengthwise of its wings

sap·wood \'sap-ˌwud\ *n* : young porous wood found just beneath the bark of a tree and usually lighter colored than the heartwood

sa·ra·pe \sə-'rä-pē\ *n* : a blanket worn as an outer garment by some Spanish Americans

sar·casm \'sär-ˌkaz-əm\ *n* : the use of bitter or stinging remarks

sar·cas·tic \sär-'kas-tik\ *adj* 1 : having the habit of sarcasm 2 : containing, characterized by, or related to sarcasm — **sar·cas·ti·cal·ly** \-ti-kə-lē\ *adv*

sar·dine \sär-'dēn\ *n* : a young or very small fish often preserved in oil and used for food

sa·ri \'sä-rē\ *n* : a garment worn chiefly by Indian women that consists of a long lightweight cloth draped on the body

sar·sa·pa·ril·la \ˌsas-ə-pə-'ril-ə, ˌsär-sə-\ *n* : the dried root of a tropical American plant used especially as a flavoring

¹sash \'sash\ *n* : a broad band (as of silk) worn around the waist or over the shoulder

²sash *n* 1 : a frame for a pane of glass in a door or window 2 : the movable part of a window

sas·sa·fras \'sas-ə-ˌfras\ *n* : a tall tree of eastern North America whose dried root bark is used in medicine or as a flavoring

sash

sash 2

sat *past of* SIT

Sa·tan \'sāt-n\ *n* : DEVIL

satch·el \'sach-əl\ *n* : a small bag for carrying clothes or books

sat·el·lite \'sat-l-ˌīt\ *n* 1 : a servile follower of a great person (as a prince) 2 : a smaller body that revolves around a planet 3 : a vehicle sent out from the earth to revolve around the earth, moon, sun, or a planet 4 : a country dominated by another more powerful country

sa·ti·ate \'sā-shē-ˌāt\ *vb* **sa·ti·at·ed; sa·ti·at·ing** : GLUT

sat·in \'sat-n\ *n* : a cloth (as of silk) with a shiny surface

sat·ire \'sat-ˌīr\ *n* : biting wit, irony, or sarcasm used to expose and discredit vice or folly

sa·tir·i·cal \sə-'tir-i-kəl\ *adj* : of, relating to, or marked by satire

sat·is·fac·tion \ˌsat-əs-'fak-shən\ *n* 1 : the act of satisfying : the condition of being satisfied 2 : something that satisfies

sat·is·fac·to·ry \ˌsat-əs-'fak-tə-rē\ *adj* : causing satisfaction : SATISFYING — **sat·is·fac·to·ri·ly** \-rə-lē\ *adv* — **sat·is·fac·to·ri·ness** \-rē-nəs\ *n*

sat·is·fy \'sat-əs-ˌfī\ *vb* **sat·is·fied; sat·is·fy·ing** 1 : to give what is wanted or expected 2 : QUIET, APPEASE 3 : to give what is due : PAY 4 : CONVINCE

syn SATISFY, FULFILL, ANSWER all mean to measure up in some respect. SATISFY is used of things and occasionally persons that are subjected to certain conditions or requirements and are found to meet the test ⟨this water will *satisfy* our present need⟩ ⟨your experience doesn't *satisfy* the requirements for this job⟩ FULFILL suggests not only coming up to but surpassing basic requirements ⟨the book *fulfilled* all my expectations⟩ ⟨the new catcher didn't *fulfill* the coach's hopes⟩ ANSWER, on the other hand, suggests measuring up in the least satisfactory way with at best only minimum requirements having been met ⟨sleeping bags will *answer* the purpose until the beds arrive⟩

sat·u·rate \'sach-ə-,rāt\ *vb* **sat·u·rat·ed; sat·u·rat·ing** : to soak or fill full

Sat·ur·day \'sat-ər-dē\ *n* : the seventh day of the week

Sat·urn \'sat-ərn\ *n* : the planet that is sixth in order of distance from the sun and has a diameter of about 71,500 miles

sa·tyr \'sāt-ər, 'sat-\ *n* : a forest god in Greek mythology represented as having the ears and the tail of a horse or goat

sauce \'sȯs\ *n* **1** : a tasty often liquid mixture to be added to meats, salads, and puddings **2** : stewed fruit ⟨cranberry *sauce*⟩

sauce·pan \'sȯs-,pan\ *n* : a small deep cooking pan with a handle

sau·cer \'sȯ-sər\ *n* : a small shallow dish usually with a slightly depressed center for holding a cup at table

saucepan

sauc·y \'sas-ē, 'sȯs-\ *adj* **sauc·i·er; sauc·i·est** **1** : being bold and not respectful **2** : IRREPRESSIBLE, PERT **3** : SMART, TRIM — **sauc·i·ly** \-ə-lē\ *adv* — **sauc·i·ness** \-ē-nəs\ *n*

sau·er·kraut \'saù-ər-,kraùt\ *n* [from German, a compound of *sauer* "sour" and *kraut* "cabbage"] : finely cut cabbage fermented in brine

saun·ter \'sȯnt-ər\ *vb* : to walk along slowly and idly : STROLL

sau·sage \'sȯ-sij\ *n* **1** : highly seasoned ground meat (as pork) usually stuffed in casings **2** : a roll of sausage in a casing

¹sav·age \'sav-ij\ *adj* **1** : not tamed : WILD **2** : being cruel and brutal : FIERCE — **sav·age·ly** *adv* — **sav·age·ness** *n*

²savage *n* **1** : a brutal person **2** : a person belonging to a primitive uncivilized society

sav·age·ry \'sav-ij-rē\ *n, pl* **sav·age·ries** **1** : an uncivilized condition or state of being **2** : savage disposition or action

¹save \'sāv\ *vb* **saved; sav·ing** **1** : to free from danger or peril **2** : GUARD, KEEP ⟨*save* fruits from spoiling⟩ **3** : to lay by or aside **4** : to keep from being spent ⟨a device that *saves* labor⟩ **5** : to avoid unnecessary waste or expense

²save *prep* : EXCEPT

¹sav·ing \'sā-ving\ *n* **1** : the act of rescuing or delivering **2** : something saved especially through a period of years ⟨lost his *savings*⟩

²saving *adj* **1** : ECONOMICAL, THRIFTY **2** : COMPENSATING ⟨a *saving* sense of humor⟩

sav·ior *or* **sav·iour** \'sāv-yər\ *n* **1** : one that saves from ruin or danger **2** *cap* : JESUS

¹sa·vor·y \'sā-və-rē\ *adj* : pleasing to the taste or smell ⟨*savory* sausages⟩

²sa·vo·ry \'sā-və-rē\ *n, pl* **sa·vo·ries** : an aromatic mint often dried for use as a seasoning

¹saw \'sȯ\ *past of* SEE

²saw *n* **1** : a tool or instrument with a tooth-edged blade for cutting hard material **2** : a machine that operates a toothed blade

³saw *vb* **sawed; sawed** *or* **sawn** \'sȯn\; **saw·ing** : to cut or shape with a saw

⁴saw *n* : a common saying

saw·dust \'sȯ-,dəst\ *n* : fine particles (as of wood) which fall from something being sawed

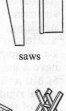
saws

saw·horse \'sȯ-,hȯrs\ *n* : a frame or rack on which wood is rested while being sawed

saw·mill \'sȯ-,mil\ *n* : a mill or factory having machinery for sawing logs

sawhorses

saw–toothed \'sȯ-'tütht\ *adj* : having an edge or outline like the teeth of a saw

sax·i·frage \'sak-sə-frij\ *n* : a low-growing plant with tufts of leaves and showy five-parted flowers

sax·o·phone \'sak-sə-,fōn\ *n* : a musical wind instrument with a reed mouthpiece and a bent conical metal body

¹say \'sā\ *vb* **said** \'sed\; **say·ing** \'sā-ing\ **1** : to express in words : UTTER **2** : to state as one's opinion or decision : DECLARE **3** : REPEAT, RECITE ⟨*said* his prayers every night⟩

saxophone

²say *n* **1** : an expression of opinion ⟨everybody had his *say* at the meeting⟩ **2** : the power to decide or help decide

say·ing \'sā-ing\ *n* : PROVERB

scab \'skab\ *n* **1** : SCABIES **2** : a plant disease characterized by crusted spots on stems or foliage **3** : a crust that forms over and protects a sore or wound

scab·bard \'skab-ərd\ *n* : a protective case or sheath for the blade of a sword or dagger

scab·by \'skab-ē\ *adj* **scab·bi·er; scab·bi·est** **1** : having scabs **2** : diseased with scab

sca·bies \'skā-bēz\ *n, pl* **scabies** : an itch or mange caused by mites living as parasites in the skin

---

j job   ng sing   ō low   ȯ moth   ȯi coin   th thin   <u>th</u> this   ü boot   ù foot   y you   yü few   yù furious   zh vision

scaf·fold \'skaf-əld\ *n* **1** : an elevated platform built as a support for workmen and their tools and materials **2** : a platform on which a criminal is executed

scaffold 1

scald \'skȯld\ *vb* **1** : to burn with hot liquid or steam **2** : to pour very hot water over **3** : to bring to a heat just below the boiling point **4** : to pain as though by scalding

¹scale \'skāl\ *n* **1** : either pan of a balance or the balance itself **2** : an instrument or machine for weighing

²scale *vb* **scaled; scal·ing** **1** : to weigh on scales **2** : to have a weight of

scales

³scale *n* **1** : one of the many small rigid plates that cover part of the body of some animals (as fish and snakes) **2** : a thin layer or part (as a special leaf that protects a plant bud) resembling a fish scale — **scaled** \'skāld\ *adj* — **scale·less** \'skāl-ləs\ *adj*

⁴scale *vb* **scaled; scal·ing** **1** : to strip or clear of scales **2** : to shed scales : FLAKE

⁵scale *n* **1** : something divided into regular spaces as a help in drawing, measuring, or finding distances **2** : a number of like things arranged in order from the highest to the lowest **3** : the size of a picture, plan, or model of a thing in proportion to the size of the thing itself **4** : a standard for measuring or judging **5** : a series of tones going up or down in pitch according to a certain scheme

⁶scale *vb* **scaled; scal·ing** **1** : to climb by or as if by a ladder **2** : to arrange in a graded series

scale insect *n* : any of a group of insects related to the plant lice that suck the juices of plants and have winged males and scale-covered wingless females which remain attached to the plant

¹scal·lop \'skäl-əp\ *n* **1** : an edible shellfish that is a mollusk with a ribbed shell in two parts **2** : one of a continuous series of rounded or angular projections forming a border (as on lace)

²scallop *vb* **1** : to bake with crumbs, butter, and milk **2** : to embroider, cut, or edge with scallops

scallop 1

¹scalp \'skalp\ *n* : the part of the skin and flesh of the head usually covered with hair

²scalp *vb* : to remove the scalp from

scal·y \'skā-lē\ *adj* **scal·i·er; scal·i·est** : covered with or resembling scales ⟨a *scaly* skin⟩

scamp \'skamp\ *n* : RASCAL

¹scam·per \'skam-pər\ *vb* : to run or move lightly and playfully

²scamper *n* : a playful scampering or scurrying

scan \'skan\ *vb* **scanned; scan·ning** **1** : to read or mark verses so as to show metrical structure **2** : to look over

scan·dal \'skan-dəl\ *n* **1** : something that causes a general feeling of shame : DISGRACE **2** : talk that injures a person's good name

scan·dal·ous \'skan-də-ləs\ *adj* **1** : causing scandal **2** : shockingly offensive : DISGRACEFUL

Scan·di·na·vi·an \ˌskan-də-'nā-vē-ən\ *n* : a native or inhabitant of Scandinavia

¹scant \'skant\ *adj* **1** : scarcely enough ⟨a *scant* lunch⟩ **2** : just short of ⟨a *scant* quart of milk⟩ **3** : having a small or inadequate supply ⟨*scant* of money⟩

²scant *vb* : SKIMP, STINT

scant·y \'skant-ē\ *adj* **scant·i·er; scant·i·est** : scant especially in amount : MEAGER **syn** see MEAGER

scape \'skāp\ *n* : a leafless flower stalk

¹scar \'skär\ *n* **1** : a mark left after a wound or sore has healed **2** : an ugly mark (as on furniture) **3** : the lasting effect of some unhappy experience

²scar *vb* **scarred; scar·ring** : to mark or become marked with a scar

scar·ab \'skar-əb\ *n* : a large dark beetle used in ancient Egypt as a symbol of immortality

scarce \'skeərs\ *adj* **scarc·er; scarc·est** **1** : not plentiful or abundant **2** : hard to find : RARE **syn** see RARE — **scarce·ness** *n*

scarce·ly \'skeərs-lē\ *adv* **1** : not quite ⟨*scarcely* enough to eat⟩ **2** : certainly not

scar·ci·ty \'sker-sət-ē\ *n, pl* **scar·ci·ties** : the condition of being scarce : a very small supply

¹scare \'skeər\ *vb* **scared; scar·ing** **1** : to frighten suddenly **2** : to be scared

²scare *n* **1** : a sudden fright **2** : a widespread state of alarm

scare·crow \'skeər-ˌkrō\ *n* : a crude manlike figure set up to scare away birds and animals from crops

scarf \'skärf\ *n, pl* **scarves** \'skärvz\ *or* **scarfs** **1** : a piece of cloth worn loosely around the neck or on the head **2** : a long narrow strip of cloth used as a cover (as on a bureau)

scarf

scar·la·ti·na \ˌskär-lə-'tē-nə\ *n* : a mild scarlet fever

¹scar·let \'skär-lət\ *n* : a bright red

²scarlet *adj* : of the color scarlet

scarlet fever *n* : a contagious disease marked by sore throat, a high fever, and a rash

scar·y \'skeər-ē\ *adj* **scar·i·er; scar·i·est** : causing fright ⟨a *scary* movie⟩

scath·ing \'skā-thing\ *adj* : bitterly severe

scat·ter \'skat-ər\ *vb* **1** : to throw, cast, sow, or place here and there **2** : to separate and go in different ways ⟨the crowd *scattered*⟩

scav·en·ger \'skav-ən-jər\ *n* **1** : a person who picks over junk or garbage for useful items **2** : an animal that lives on decayed matter

scene \'sēn\ *n* **1** : a division of an act in a play **2** : a single striking happening in a play or story **3** : the place and time of the action in a play or story **4** : the painted screens and slides used as backgrounds on the stage : SCENERY **5** : something that attracts or holds one's gaze : VIEW **6** : an exhibition of anger or unbecoming behavior

scen·er·y \'sē-nə-rē\ *n* **1** : the painted scenes used on a stage and the furnishings that go with them **2** : outdoor scenes or views

sce·nic \'sē-nik\ *adj* **1** : of or relating to stage scenery **2** : giving views of natural scenery

¹scent \'sent\ *vb* **1** : to become aware of or follow by means of the sense of smell **2** : to get a hint of **3** : to fill with an odor : PERFUME

²scent *n* **1** : an odor left by some animal or person no longer in a place or given forth (as by flowers) at a distance **2** : power or sense of smell **3** : a course followed by someone in search or pursuit of something **4** : PERFUME

scep·ter *or* **scep·tre** \'sep-tər\ *n* : a staff borne by a ruler as a sign of authority

¹sched·ule \'skej-ül\ *n* **1** : a written or printed list **2** : a list of the times set for certain events : TIMETABLE **3** : PROGRAM, AGENDA

²schedule *vb* **sched·uled; sched·ul·ing** : to form into or add to a schedule

¹scheme \'skēm\ *n* **1** : a plan or program of something to be done : PROJECT **2** : a secret plan : PLOT **3** : an arrangement that shows method

²scheme *vb* **schemed; schem·ing** : to form a scheme — **schem·er** *n*

Schick test \'shik-\ *n* : a test to determine whether a person is susceptible to diphtheria

schol·ar \'skäl-ər\ *n* **1** : a student in a school : PUPIL **2** : a person who knows a great deal about one or more subjects

schol·ar·ly \'skäl-ər-lē\ *adj* : characteristic of or suitable to learned persons

schol·ar·ship \'skäl-ər-,ship\ *n* **1** : the qualities of a scholar : LEARNING **2** : money given a student to help pay for further education

scho·las·tic \skə-'las-tik\ *adj* : of or relating to schools, pupils, or education

¹school \'skül\ *n* [from Old English *scōl*, taken from Latin *schola*, from Greek *scholē*, which meant originally "leisure" and then especially "leisure devoted to learning" and so finally "school"] **1** : a place for teaching and learning **2** : the body of teachers and pupils in a school **3** : a session of school **4** : SCHOOLHOUSE **5** : a body of persons who share the same opinions and beliefs

²school *vb* : TEACH, TRAIN

³school *n* : a large number of one kind of fish or water animals swimming together

school·bag \'skül-,bag\ *n* : a bag for carrying schoolbooks

school·book \'skül-,bùk\ *n* : a book used in schools

school·boy \'skül-,bòi\ *n* : a boy who goes to school

school·girl \'skül-,gərl\ *n* : a girl who goes to school

school·house \'skül-,haùs\ *n* : a building used as a school

school·ing \'skü-ling\ *n* : EDUCATION

school·mas·ter \'skül-,mas-tər\ *n* : a man who has charge of a school or teaches in a school

school·mate \'skül-,māt\ *n* : a fellow pupil

school·mis·tress \'skül-,mis-trəs\ *n* : a woman who has charge of a school or teaches in a school

school·room \'skül-,rüm, -,rùm\ *n* : CLASSROOM

school·teach·er \'skül-,tē-chər\ *n* : a person who teaches in a school

schoo·ner \'skü-nər\ *n* : a ship usually having two masts with the mainmast located amidships and the shorter mast forward

schwa \'shwä\ *n* **1** : an unstressed vowel that is the usual sound of the first and last vowels of the English word *America* **2** : the symbol ə commonly used for a schwa and sometimes also for a similarly articulated stressed vowel (as in *cut*)

schooner

sci·ence \'sī-əns\ *n* [from medieval French, from Latin *scientia* meaning literally "knowledge", a derivative of *scire* "to know"] **1** : a branch of knowledge in which what is known is presented in an orderly way **2** : a branch of study that is concerned with collecting facts and forming laws to explain them

sci·en·tif·ic \ˌsī-ən-'tif-ik\ *adj* **1** : of or relating to science or scientists **2** : using or applying the laws of science — **sci·en·tif·i·cal·ly** \-'tif-i-kə-lē\ *adv*

sci·en·tist \'sī-ən-təst\ *n* : a person who knows much about science or is engaged in scientific work

scim·i·tar \'sim-ət-ər\ *n* : a sword with a curved blade used chiefly in Muhammadan countries

sci·on \'sī-ən\ *n* **1** : the piece of plant that develops twigs and leaves in a graft **2** : DESCENDANT, CHILD

scimitar

scis·sors \'siz-ərz\ *n sing or pl* : a cutting instrument with two blades so fastened that the sharp edges slide against each other

scoff \'skäf\ *vb* : RIDICULE, JEER

syn SCOFF, JEER, SNEER all mean to show scorn or contempt through mockery. SCOFF stresses insolence, disrespect, or disbelief as the motive for the mockery ⟨only fools *scoff* at whatever they don't understand⟩ JEER carries a stronger suggestion of coarse laughter and loud ridicule and often implies a vulgar unthinking attitude ⟨the delegates *jeered* at every speaker they disagreed with⟩ SNEER strongly suggests ill-natured contempt often clothed in irony or satire and emphasizes an insulting manner ⟨he made our trip miserable by *sneering* at every suggestion anyone else made⟩

¹scold \'skōld\ *n* : a person who often scolds others

²scold *vb* : to find fault with or criticize angrily **syn** see REBUKE

¹scoop \'sküp\ *n* **1** : a large shovel (as for shoveling coal) **2** : a shovellike tool or utensil for digging into a soft substance and lifting out a portion **3** : a motion made with or as if with a scoop **4** : the amount held by a scoop **5** : a hole made by scooping

²scoop *vb* **1** : to take out or up with or as if with a scoop **2** : to make by scooping

scoop 2

scoot \'sküt\ *vb* : DART

scoot·er \'sküt-ər\ *n* **1** : a vehicle consisting of a narrow base mounted between two tandem wheels and guided by a handle attached to the front wheel **2** : MOTOR SCOOTER

scope \'skōp\ *n* **1** : space or opportunity for action or thought **2** : extent covered, reached, or viewed

scooter 1

scorch \'skòrch\ *vb* **1** : to burn on the surface **2** : to burn so as to brown, dry, or shrivel **syn** see SINGE

¹score \'skōr\ *n* **1** : a group of twenty things : TWENTY **2** : a line (as a scratch) made with or as if with a sharp instrument **3** : a record of points made or lost (as in a game) **4** : DEBT **5** : an obligation or injury kept in mind for settlement **6** : REASON, GROUND **7** : the written or printed form of a musical composition — **score·less** \-ləs\ *adj*

²score *vb* **scored; scor·ing** **1** : to set down in an account : RECORD **2** : to keep the score in a game **3** : to cut or mark with a line, scratch, or notch **4** : to make or cause to make a point in a game **5** : ACHIEVE, WIN **6** : GRADE, MARK

¹scorn \'skòrn\ *n* **1** : bitter contempt **2** : a person or thing held in contempt

²scorn *vb* : to hold in scorn

scorn·ful \'skòrn-fəl\ *adj* : feeling or showing scorn — **scorn·ful·ly** *adv*

scor·pi·on \'skòr-pē-ən\ *n* : an animal related to the spiders that has a long jointed body ending in a slender tail with a poisonous sting at the tip

Scot \'skät\ *n* : a native or inhabitant of Scotland

¹Scotch \'skäch\ *adj* : of or relating to Scotland or the Scotch

²Scotch *n pl* : the people of Scotland

scorpion

scot–free \'skät-'frē\ *adj* : completely free from obligation, harm, or penalty

Scot·tish \'skät-ish\ *adj* : SCOTCH

scoun·drel \'skaùn-drəl\ *n* : a wicked rascal

¹scour \'skaùr\ *vb* : to go or move swiftly about in search

²scour *vb* **1** : to rub hard with a gritty substance in order to clean **2** : to free or clear from impurities by or as if by rubbing

³scour *n* : an action or result of scouring

¹scourge \'skərj\ *n* **1** : WHIP, LASH **2** : AFFLICTION

²scourge *vb* **scourged; scourg·ing** **1** : to whip severely : FLOG **2** : to inflict severe suffering on : AFFLICT

¹scout \'skaùt\ *vb* **1** : to go about in search of information **2** : LOOK, SEARCH

²scout *n* **1** : a person, group, boat, or plane that scouts **2** : the act of scouting **3** : BOY SCOUT **4** : GIRL SCOUT

scout·ing \'skaùt-ing\ *n* **1** : the act of one that scouts **2** : the general activities of boy scout and girl scout movements

scout·mas·ter \'skaùt-ˌmas-tər\ *n* : the leader of a troop of boy scouts

scow \\'skau\\ *n* : a large flat-bottomed boat with square ends used chiefly for loading and unloading ships and for carrying refuse

¹scowl \\'skaul\\ *vb* : FROWN

²scowl *n* : an angry look

¹scram·ble \\'skram-bəl\\ *vb* **scram·bled; scram-bling** **1** : to move or climb on the knees or on hands and knees **2** : to strive or struggle for something **3** : to cook the mixed whites and yolks of eggs by stirring them while frying **4** : to mix together in disorder

²scramble *n* : the act or result of scrambling

¹scrap \\'skrap\\ *n* **1** *pl* : fragments of leftover food **2** : a small bit **3** : material discarded as useless

²scrap *vb* **scrapped; scrap·ping** **1** : to break up into scrap **2** : to discard as worthless

scrap·book \\'skrap-,buk\\ *n* : a blank book in which clippings or pictures are kept

¹scrape \\'skrāp\\ *vb* **scraped; scrap·ing** **1** : to remove by repeated strokes of an edged tool **2** : to clean or smooth by rubbing **3** : to rub or cause to rub so as to make a grating noise : SCUFF **4** : to hurt or roughen by dragging against a rough surface **5** : to get with difficulty and little by little

²scrape *n* **1** : the act of scraping **2** : a grating sound made by scraping **3** : SCRATCH **4** : a disagreeable or trying situation

¹scratch \\'skrach\\ *vb* **1** : to scrape or rub with the claws or nails **2** : to scrape with claws, nails, or an instrument so as to leave a mark **3** : to make a scraping noise **4** : to erase by scraping : CANCEL

²scratch *n* **1** : the act of scratching **2** : a mark or injury made by scratching **3** : the line from which contestants start in a race

scratch·y \\'skrach-ē\\ *adj* **scratch·i·er; scratch-i·est** : likely to scratch or irritate

¹scrawl \\'skrȯl\\ *vb* : to write hastily and carelessly : SCRIBBLE

²scrawl *n* : something written carelessly or without skill

scraw·ny \\'skrȯ-nē\\ *adj* **scraw·ni·er; scraw-ni·est** : THIN, LEAN, SKINNY

¹scream \\'skrēm\\ *vb* : to cry out (as in fright) loudly and shrilly

²scream *n* : a loud shrill prolonged cry

¹screech \\'skrēch\\ *vb* : to make an outcry usually in terror or pain

²screech *n* : a shrill harsh cry usually expressing pain or terror

¹screen \\'skrēn\\ *n* **1** : a curtain or partition used to hide or to protect **2** : a sieve set in a frame

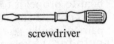

screen 1

for separating finer parts from coarser parts (as of sand) **3** : the curtain or wall on which motion pictures are projected **4** : the motion-picture industry **5** : the part of a television set on which the picture appears

²screen *vb* **1** : to hide or shield with or as if with a screen **2** : to separate or sift with a screen

¹screw \\'skrü\\ *n* **1** : a nail-shaped or rod-shaped piece of metal with a winding ridge around its length used for fastening and holding pieces together **2** : the thread of a screw **3** : the act of screwing tight : TWIST **4** : PROPELLER

screws

²screw *vb* **1** : to attach or fasten with a screw **2** : to operate, tighten, or adjust with a screw **3** : to turn or twist on a screwlike thread

screw·driv·er \\'skrü-,drī-vər\\ *n* : a tool for turning screws

¹scrib·ble \\'skrib-əl\\ *vb* **scrib·bled; scrib·bling** : to write hastily or carelessly

screwdriver

²scribble *n* : something scribbled

scribe \\'skrīb\\ *n* **1** : a teacher of Jewish law **2** : a copier of writing (as in a book)

scrim·mage \\'skrim-ij\\ *n* **1** : a confused struggle **2** : the play between two football teams that begins with the snap of the ball

script \\'skript\\ *n* **1** : HANDWRITING **2** : a type used in printing that resembles handwriting **3** : the manuscript or written form of a play or motion picture or the lines to be said by a radio or television performer

scrip·ture \\'skrip-chər\\ *n* **1** *cap* : BIBLE **2** : writings held sacred by a religious group

scroll \\'skrōl\\ *n* **1** : a roll of paper or parchment on which something is written or engraved **2** : an ornament resembling a roll of paper usually partly rolled

scroll 1

¹scrub \\'skrəb\\ *n* **1** : a thick growth of small or stunted shrubs or trees **2** : one that is inferior or second-rate (as in size)

²scrub *vb* **scrubbed; scrub·bing** : to rub hard in washing

³scrub *n* : the act or an instance of scrubbing

scrub·by \\'skrəb-ē\\ *adj* **scrub-bi·er; scrub·bi·est** **1** : inferior in size or quality : STUNTED **2** : covered with scrub

scrolls 2

scruff \'skrəf\ *n* : the loose skin of the back of the neck

scru·ple \'skrü-pəl\ *n* : an ethical consideration or principle that makes one uneasy or inhibits action

scru·pu·lous \'skrü-pyə-ləs\ *adj* : having or showing very careful and strict regard for what is right and proper : CONSCIENTIOUS

¹scud \'skəd\ *vb* **scud·ded; scud·ding** : to move or run swiftly

²scud *n* **1** : the act of scudding **2** : light clouds driven by the wind

scuff \'skəf\ *vb* **1** : to scrape the feet while walking **2** : to become rough or scratched through wear

¹scuf·fle \'skəf-əl\ *vb* **scuf·fled; scuf·fling 1** : to struggle in a confused way at close quarters **2** : to shuffle one's feet

²scuffle *n* : a rough confused struggle

scull \'skəl\ *n* **1** : an oar used at the stern of a boat to propel it forward **2** : one of a pair of short oars **3** : a boat propelled by one or more pairs of sculls

sculp·tor \'skəlp-tər\ *n* : one that sculptures ·

¹sculp·ture \'skəlp-chər\ *n* **1** : the act or process of making statues by carving or chiseling (as in wood or stone), by modeling (as in clay), or by casting (as in molten metals) **2** : work produced by sculpture

²sculpture *vb* **sculp·tured; sculp·tur·ing** : to make sculptures : CARVE

scum \'skəm\ *n* **1** : a film of matter that rises to the top of a liquid that is boiling or fermenting **2** : a coating on stagnant water

scurf \'skərf\ *n* : thin dry scales or a coating of these (as on a leaf or the skin)

¹scur·ry \'skər-ē\ *vb* **scur·ried; scur·ry·ing** : to hurry briskly

²scurry *n, pl* **scur·ries** : the act or an instance of scurrying

¹scur·vy \'skər-vē\ *adj* **scur·vi·er; scur·vi·est** : MEAN, CONTEMPTIBLE

²scurvy *n* : a disease marked by loose teeth, softened gums, and bleeding under the skin and caused by lack of vitamin C

¹scut·tle \'skət-l\ *n* : a pail or bucket for carrying coal

²scuttle *n* : a small opening with a lid or cover (as in the deck of a ship)

³scuttle *vb* **scut·tled; scut·tling** : to sink by cutting holes through the bottom or sides

scuttle

⁴scuttle *vb* **scut·tled; scut·tling** : to run rapidly from view

scythe \'sīth\ *n* : an implement consisting of a curved blade on a long curved handle for mowing grass or grain by hand

scythe

sea \'sē\ *n* **1** : a body of salt water not as large as an ocean and often nearly surrounded by land **2** : OCEAN **3** : rough water **4** : something suggesting a sea's great size or depth

sea anemone *n* : a tubular sea animal with a flowerlike cluster of tentacles about its mouth

sea·bird \'sē-,bərd\ *n* : a bird (as a gull) that frequents the open ocean

sea·coast \'sē-,kōst\ *n* : the shore of the sea

sea cucumber *n* : a sea animal related to the starfishes and sea urchins that has a long flexible muscular body resembling a cucumber

sea cucumber

sea dog *n* : an experienced sailor

sea·far·er \'sē-,far-ər\ *n* : a person who travels over the ocean : MARINER

¹sea·far·ing \'sē-,far-ing\ *adj* : of, given to, or employed in seafaring

²seafaring *n* : a traveling over the sea as work or as recreation

sea·go·ing \'sē-,gō-ing\ *adj* : adapted or used for sea travel

sea gull *n* : a gull that frequents the sea

sea horse *n* **1** : a fabulous animal half horse and half fish **2** : a small fish with a head which looks like that of a horse

sea horse 2

¹seal \'sēl\ *n* **1** : a flesh-eating sea mammal that has flippers for swimming, is found mostly in cold regions, and is hunted for fur, hides, or oil **2** : the soft dense fur of a northern seal

²seal *n* **1** : a device with a cut or raised design or figure that can be stamped or pressed into wax or paper **2** : a piece of wax stamped with a design and used to seal a letter or package **3** : a stamp that may be used to close a letter or package ⟨Christmas *seals*⟩ **4** : something (as a pledge) that makes safe or secure **5** : a tight perfect closure **6** : something that closes tightly

³seal *vb* **1** : to mark with a seal **2** : to close or make fast with or as if with a seal **3** : to settle forever — **seal·er** *n*

sea level *n* : the surface of the sea midway between high and low tide

sea lion *n* : a very large seal of the Pacific ocean

seal·skin \'sēl-ˌskin\ *n* : ¹SEAL 2

¹**seam** \'sēm\ *n* **1** : the fold, line, or groove made by sewing together or joining two edges or two pieces of material **2** : WRINKLE, FURROW **3** : a layer of a mineral or metal ⟨a *seam* of coal⟩

²**seam** *vb* **1** : to join with a seam **2** : to mark with a line, scar, or wrinkle ⟨a face *seamed* with age⟩

sea·man \'sē-mən\ *n, pl* **sea·men** \-mən\ **1** : a person who helps in the handling of a ship at sea : MARINER, SAILOR **2** : an enlisted man in the navy ranking next below a petty officer third class

seaman apprentice *n* : an enlisted man in the navy ranking next below a seaman

seaman recruit *n* : an enlisted man of the lowest rank in the navy

seam·stress \'sēm-strəs\ *n* : a woman who sews especially for a living

sea·plane \'sē-ˌplān\ *n* : an airplane that can rise from and land on water

sea·port \'sē-ˌpōrt\ *n* : a port, harbor, or town within reach of seagoing ships

seaplane

sear \'siər\ *vb* **1** : to dry by or as if by heat : PARCH, WITHER **2** : to burn, scorch, or brown especially on the surface (as in cooking meat)

¹**search** \'sərch\ *vb* **1** : to go through carefully and thoroughly in an effort to find something ⟨*search* the house⟩ **2** : to look in the pockets or the clothing of for something hidden ⟨all the men were *searched*⟩ — **search·ing·ly** *adv*

²**search** *n* : an act of searching : an attempt to get, find, or seek out

search·light \'sərch-ˌlīt\ *n* : a lamp for sending a beam of bright light toward objects at a distance

sea·shore \'sē-ˌshōr\ *n* : the shore of a sea

sea·sick \'sē-ˌsik\ *adj* : nauseated by the pitching or rolling of a ship — **sea·sick·ness** *n*

¹**sea·son** \'sēz-n\ *n* **1** : one of the four quarters into which a year is commonly divided **2** : a period of time that has some special character ⟨the Christmas *season*⟩

²**season** *vb* **1** : to make pleasant to the taste by use of seasoning **2** : to make suitable for use (as by aging or drying) ⟨*seasoned* lumber⟩

sea·son·a·ble \'sēz-n-ə-bəl\ *adj* : TIMELY

sea·son·al \'sēz-n-əl\ *adj* : of, relating to, or restricted to a particular season

sea·son·ing \'sēz-n-ing\ *n* : something (as salt or pepper) that seasons

¹**seat** \'sēt\ *n* **1** : the place on or at which a person sits **2** : a chair, bench, or stool **3** : the part (as of a chair) on which a person sits **4** : the part of the body or outer garment (as trousers) on which a person sits **5** : a place that serves as a capital or a center ⟨a *seat* of learning⟩ — **seat·ed** \'sēt-əd\ *adj*

²**seat** *vb* **1** : to place in or on a seat **2** : to provide seats for ⟨the hall *seats* 500 persons⟩

sea urchin *n* : a rounded spine-covered shellfish related to the starfishes that lives on or burrows in the sea bottom

sea·wall \'sē-ˌwòl\ *n* : a bank or a wall to prevent sea waves from cutting away the shore

sea urchin

sea·wa·ter \'sē-ˌwòt-ər, -ˌwät-\ *n* : water in or from the sea

sea·weed \'sē-ˌwēd\ *n* : an alga (as a kelp) that grows in the sea

se·clud·ed \si-'klüd-əd\ *adj* : hidden from sight : not much visited

se·clu·sion \si-'klü-zhən\ *n* **1** : the act of secluding : the condition of being secluded **2** : a secluded or isolated place

¹**sec·ond** \'sek-ənd\ *adj* **1** : being next after the first ⟨the *second* time⟩ **2** : next lower in rank, value, or importance than the first ⟨*second* prize⟩

²**second** *adv* : in the second place or rank

³**second** *n* : one that is second

⁴**second** *vb* : to give support to a motion or nomination in order that it may be debated or voted on

⁵**second** *n* **1** : a sixtieth part of a minute of time or of a degree **2** : MOMENT, INSTANT

sec·ond·ar·y \'sek-ən-ˌder-ē\ *adj* **1** : second in rank, value, or occurrence : INFERIOR, LESSER **2** : of, relating to, or being the second of three degrees of stress **3** : coming after the primary : higher than the elementary ⟨*secondary* schools⟩

sec·ond·hand \ˌsek-ənd-'hand\ *adj* **1** : not new : having had a previous owner ⟨a *secondhand* automobile⟩ **2** : selling used goods ⟨a *secondhand* store⟩

second lieutenant *n* : a commissioned officer (as in the army) ranking next below a first lieutenant

sec·ond·ly \'sek-ənd-lē\ *adv* : in the second place

sec·ond–rate \ˌsek-ənd-'rāt\ *adj* : MEDIOCRE

se·cre·cy \'sē-krə-sē\ *n, pl* **se·cre·cies** **1** : the practice of keeping things secret **2** : the quality or state of being secret or hidden

¹**se·cret** \'sē-krət\ *adj* **1** : hidden from the

knowledge of others ⟨keep your plans *secret*⟩
2 : done or working in secrecy : STEALTHY
3 : keeping certain things secret ⟨a *secret*
society⟩ — **se·cret·ly** *adv*

syn SECRET, STEALTHY, FURTIVE all refer to
something that is made or done so as not to
attract any attention. SECRET is the most
general term and applies to a hiding or concealing for any reason, good or bad ⟨the *secret*
meeting places of cats that roam at night⟩
STEALTHY suggests an intent to spy upon or
elude someone or to pursue one's own
purpose without arousing notice and is usually
a term of censure ⟨the stalking panther moves
with *stealthy* grace⟩ FURTIVE agrees in stressing determination to escape observation but
carries a clearer suggestion of sneaky watchfulness or slyness and is applied not only to
actions and movements ⟨the *furtive* walk of
the stranger made me suspicious⟩ but also to
features and expressions ⟨he feared most the
bloodthirsty weasel with its *furtive* eyes⟩

²secret *n* **1** : something kept or intended to
be kept from others' knowledge **2** : something
that cannot be explained : MYSTERY

sec·re·tary \'sek-rə-ˌter-ē\ *n, pl* **sec·re·tar·ies**
1 : a person who is employed
to take care of records and
letters of a private or confidential nature **2** : an officer of
a business corporation or society who has charge of the
correspondence and records
and who keeps minutes of
meetings **3** : a government
official in charge of the affairs
of a department **4** : a writing
desk especially with a top section for books

secretary 4

¹se·crete \si-'krēt\ *vb* **se·cret·ed; se·cret·ing**
: to produce and give off as a secretion ⟨glands
that *secrete* mucus⟩

²secrete *vb* **se·cret·ed; se·cret·ing** : to deposit
or conceal in a hiding place

se·cre·tion \si-'krē-shən\ *n* **1** : a concealing
or hiding of something **2** : the act or process
of secreting some substance **3** : a substance
formed in and given off by a gland that
typically performs a particular useful function
in the body ⟨digestive *secretions* contain
enzymes⟩

se·cre·tive \'sē-krət-iv, si-'krēt-\ *adj* : disposed to secrecy or concealment

¹sec·tion \'sek-shən\ *n* **1** : a part cut off or
separated ⟨a *section* of an orange⟩ **2** : a part
of a written work ⟨a chapter divided into
sections⟩ **3** : the appearance that a thing has
or would have if cut straight through ⟨a

drawing of a gun in *section*⟩ **4** : a part of a
country, people, or community ⟨a suburban
section⟩

²section *vb* : to cut into sections

sec·u·lar \'sek-yə-lər\ *adj* **1** : not sacred or
ecclesiastical **2** : not bound by monastic vows
: not belonging to a religious order ⟨*secular*
priest⟩

¹se·cure \si-'kyùr\ *adj* [from Latin *securus*,
derived from the prefix *se-* "without" and the
noun *cura* "care", "worry"] **1** : SAFE
2 : CERTAIN, ASSURED ⟨the final victory is
secure⟩ — **se·cure·ly** *adv* — **se·cure·ness** *n*

²secure *vb* **se·cured; se·cur·ing** **1** : to make
safe : GUARD ⟨*secure* troops against attack⟩
2 : to get or make sure of ⟨*secure* information⟩
3 : to fasten tightly ⟨*secure* a door⟩

se·cu·ri·ty \si-'kyùr-ət-ē\ *n, pl* **se·cu·ri·ties**
1 : the state of being secure : SAFETY **2** : something given as a pledge of payment ⟨*security*
for a loan⟩ **3** *pl* : STOCKS, BONDS

se·dan \si-'dan\ *n* **1** : a portable often
covered chair that is de-
signed to carry one person
and is borne on two poles
by two men **2** : a closed
automobile seating four or
more persons that has two
or four doors and full-width
front and rear seats

sedan 1

se·date \si-'dāt\ *adj* : QUIET, SOBER ⟨too
sedate for her age⟩ — **se·date·ly** *adv* — **se·
date·ness** *n*

¹sed·a·tive \'sed-ət-iv\ *adj* : tending to calm
or to relieve tension or irritability

²sedative *n* : a sedative medicine

sedge \'sej\ *n* : a plant that is like grass but
has solid stems and grows in tufts in marshes

sed·i·ment \'sed-ə-mənt\ *n* **1** : the material
from a liquid that settles to the bottom
: DREGS **2** : the material (as stones and sand)
deposited by water, wind, or a glacier

sed·i·men·ta·ry \ˌsed-ə-'ment-ə-rē\ *adj* : of,
relating to, or formed from sediment ⟨sand-
stone is a *sedimentary* rock⟩

se·duce \si-'düs, -'dyüs\ *vb* **se·duced; se·duc·
ing** : to persuade to do wrong : lead astray
⟨was *seduced* into crime⟩

¹see \'sē\ *vb* **saw** \'sò\; **seen** \'sēn\; **see·ing**
1 : to perceive with the eyes or have the power
of sight **2** : to have experience of : UNDERGO
⟨*saw* some action during the war⟩ **3** : to
perceive the meaning or importance of : UN-
DERSTAND **4** : to make sure ⟨*see* that the job
gets done⟩ **5** : to attend to ⟨I'll *see* to your
order at once⟩ **6** : to meet with ⟨the doctor
will *see* you now⟩ **7** : ACCOMPANY, ESCORT

²see *n* **1** : the city in which a bishop's church is located **2** : DIOCESE

¹seed \'sēd\ *n* **1** : a miniature dormant plant in a protective coating and often with its own food supply that is capable of developing under suitable conditions into a plant like the one that produced it **2** : a small structure (as a spore or a tiny dry fruit) other than a true seed by which a plant reproduces itself **3** : DESCENDANTS ⟨the *seed* of David⟩ **4** : a source of development or growth : GERM — **seed·ed** \-əd\ *adj* — **seed·less** \-ləs\ *adj*

²seed *vb* **1** : to sprinkle with or as if with seed : PLANT ⟨*seed* a field⟩ **2** : to bear or shed seeds ⟨a plant that *seeds* early⟩ **3** : to take the seeds out of ⟨*seed* raisins⟩

seed·case \'sēd-ˌkās\ *n* : a dry hollow fruit (as a pod) that contains seeds

seed·ling \'sēd-ling\ *n* **1** : a plant grown from seed **2** : a young plant (as a tree younger than a sapling)

seed plant *n* : a plant that reproduces by true seeds

seed·pod \'sēd-ˌpäd\ *n* : POD

seed·y \'sēd-ē\ *adj* **seed·i·er; seed·i·est** **1** : containing or full of seeds ⟨a *seedy* fruit⟩ **2** : inferior in condition or quality

see·ing \'sē-ing\ *conj* : in view of the fact that

seek \'sēk\ *vb* **sought** \'sȯt\; **seek·ing** **1** : to try to find ⟨*seek* help⟩ **2** : to try to reach a person or place : try to get something ⟨*seek* fame⟩ **3** : TRY, ATTEMPT ⟨*seek* to end a war⟩

seem \'sēm\ *vb* **1** : to give the impression of being : APPEAR ⟨*seem* pleased⟩ **2** : to appear to exist ⟨there *seems* no reason for worry⟩ **3** : to appear to a person's own mind ⟨this tooth *seems* to ache⟩

seem·ing \'sē-ming\ *adj* : APPARENT ⟨suspicious of his *seeming* enthusiasm⟩

seem·ing·ly \'sē-ming-lē\ *adv* : APPARENTLY

seen *past part of* SEE

seep \'sēp\ *vb* : to leak through : OOZE ⟨water *seeped* into the basement⟩

seer \'sir\ *n* : a person who foresees or foretells events

¹see·saw \'sē-ˌsȯ\ *n* **1** : a children's game of riding on the ends of a plank balanced in the middle with one end going up while the other goes down **2** : the plank used in seesaw **3** : an action or motion like that of a seesaw

seesaw

²seesaw *vb* **1** : to ride on a seesaw **2** : to move like a seesaw

seethe \'sēth\ *vb* **seethed; seeth·ing** : to stir up as if by boiling ⟨the *seething* water of the rapids⟩

seg·ment \'seg-mənt\ *n* **1** : any of the parts into which a thing is divided or naturally separates **2** : a part cut off from a figure (as a circle) by means of a line **3** : a part of a straight line included between two points — **seg·ment·ed** \-ˌment-əd\ *adj*

segment 2

seg·re·ga·tion \ˌseg-rə-'gāsh-ən\ *n* : the separation or isolation (as of a race) by discriminatory means

seize \'sēz\ *vb* **seized; seiz·ing** **1** : to take possession of by force ⟨*seize* a fortress⟩ **2** : to take hold of suddenly or with force : GRASP

sei·zure \'sē-zhər\ *n* : a seizing or being seized (as by an illness)

sel·dom \'sel-dəm\ *adv* : not often : RARELY

¹se·lect \sə-'lekt\ *adj* **1** : PICKED, CHOSEN ⟨a *select* group⟩ **2** : CHOICE, EXCLUSIVE ⟨a *select* hotel⟩

²select *vb* : to take by preference from a number or group : CHOOSE

se·lec·tion \sə-'lek-shən\ *n* **1** : the act of selecting **2** : the thing chosen

se·lec·tive \sə-'lek-tiv\ *adj* : involving or based on selection

self \'self\ *n, pl* **selves** \'selvz\ **1** : a person regarded as an individual apart from everyone else ⟨a man's *self*⟩ **2** : a particular side of a person's character ⟨his better *self*⟩

self- *prefix* **1** : oneself or itself ⟨*self*-supporting⟩ **2** : of or by oneself or itself ⟨*self*-abasement⟩ ⟨*self*-propelled⟩ **3** : to, with, for, or toward oneself or itself ⟨*self*-addressed⟩ ⟨*self*-satisfaction⟩ **4** : of, in, from, or by means of oneself or itself ⟨*self*-evident⟩

self-act·ing \'self-'ak-ting\ *adj* : acting or capable of acting of or by itself

self-con·fi·dence \'self-'kän-fə-dəns\ *n* : confidence in oneself and in one's powers and abilities

self-con·scious \'self-'kän-chəs\ *adj* : too much aware of one's feelings or appearance when in the presence of other people : ill at ease — **self-con·scious·ness** *n*

self-con·tained \ˌself-kən-'tānd\ *adj* : sufficient in itself

self-con·trol \ˌself-kən-'trōl\ *n* : control over one's own impulses, emotions, or acts

self-de·ni·al \ˌself-di-'nī-əl\ *n* : a going without something that one wants or needs

self-ev·i·dent \'self-'ev-ə-dənt\ *adj* : evident without proof or argument

self-gov·ern·ing \'self-'gəv-ər-ning\ *adj* : not subject to outside authority

self-gov·ern·ment \'self-'gəv-ərn-mənt\ *n* **1** : SELF-CONTROL **2** : government by action of the people making up a community : democratic government

self–im·por·tant \‚self-im-'pȯrt-nt\ *adj* : believing or acting as if one's importance is greater than it actually is

self·ish \'sel-fish\ *adj* : taking care of one's own desires or advantage without regard for the interests of others

self·less \'self-ləs\ *adj* : UNSELFISH — **self·less·ly** *adv* — **self·less·ness** *n*

self–pos·sessed \‚self-pə-'zest\ *adj* : having or showing self-control : CALM

self–pro·pelled \‚self-prə-'peld\ *adj* : containing within itself the means for its own propulsion

self–reg·is·ter·ing \'self-'rej-əs-tə-ring\ *adj* : registering automatically

self–reg·u·lat·ing \'self-'reg-yə-‚lāt-ing\ *adj* : regulating oneself

self–re·li·ance \‚self-ri-'lī-əns\ *n* : reliance upon one's own efforts and abilities

self–re·spect \‚self-ri-'spekt\ *n* **1** : a proper respect for oneself as a human being **2** : regard for one's own standing or position

self–re·straint \‚self-ri-'strānt\ *n* : restraint imposed upon oneself

self–righ·teous \'self-'rī-chəs\ *adj* : strongly convinced of one's own righteousness

self–sac·ri·fic·ing \'self-'sak-rə-‚fī-sing\ *adj* : marked by sacrifice of one's own interest (as for others)

self·same \'self-‚sām\ *adj* : exactly the same

self–serv·ice \'self-'sər-vəs\ *n* : the serving of oneself with things to be paid for at a cashier's desk usually upon leaving

sell \'sel\ *vb* **sold** \'sōld\; **sell·ing** **1** : to betray a person or duty (the traitors *sold* their king to the enemy) **2** : to exchange in return for money or something else of value (*sell* groceries) **3** : to be sold or priced (corn *sells* high) — **sell·er** *n*

syn SELL, VEND, BARTER all mean to transfer property to another in exchange for something else of value. SELL usually refers to the transferring of property for a fixed price with the payment made in money (I *sold* my old bike for five dollars) VEND applies chiefly to the selling or peddling of small and inexpensive items (a machine that *vends* cold drinks automatically) (heard the cry of a peddler *vending* berries along the street) BARTER usually indicates the exchange of one sort of commodity for another of equal value with no money being involved (the trappers *bartered* with the Indians and Eskimos)

selves *pl of* SELF

sem·a·phore \'sem-ə-‚fȯr\ *n* **1** : an apparatus for visual signaling **2** : a system of visual signaling by two flags

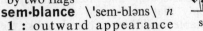

semaphore signals

sem·blance \'sem-bləns\ *n* **1** : outward appearance **2** : LIKENESS, IMAGE

se·mes·ter \sə-'mes-tər\ *n* : one of two terms of about eighteen weeks each into which a school year is divided

semi- *prefix* **1** : precisely half (*semi*circle) **2** : half of or occurring halfway through a specified period of time (*semi*annual) **3** : to some extent : partly : incompletely (*semi*civilized) **4** : partial : incomplete (*semi*darkness)

sem·i·cir·cle \'sem-i-‚sər-kəl\ *n* : half of a circle

sem·i·cir·cu·lar \‚sem-i-'sər-kyə-lər\ *adj* : having the form of a semicircle

semicircle

sem·i·co·lon \'sem-i-‚kō-lən\ *n* : a punctuation mark ; used chiefly in a coordinating function between major sentence elements

sem·i·con·duc·tor \‚sem-i-kən-'dək-tər\ *n* : a solid that conducts electricity well at high temperatures but practically not at all at low temperatures

¹sem·i·fi·nal \'sem-i-‚fīn-l\ *adj* : coming before the final round in a tournament

²semifinal *n* : a semifinal match or game

sem·i·nar·y \'sem-ə-‚ner-ē\ *n, pl* **sem·i·nar·ies** **1** : a private school of high school rank **2** : an institution for training clergymen

sem·i·sol·id \‚sem-i-'säl-əd\ *adj* : having the qualities of both a solid and a liquid

sen·ate \'sen-ət\ *n* **1** : the upper and smaller branch of the legislature in many countries **2** : an official lawmaking group or council

sen·a·tor \'sen-ət-ər\ *n* : a member of a senate — **sen·a·tor·ship** \-‚ship\ *n*

send \'send\ *vb* **sent** \'sent\; **send·ing** **1** : to cause to go : DISPATCH (*sent* the pupil home) **2** : to drive or propel physically (*sent* the ball into right field) **3** : to cause to happen or occur (asked the Lord to *send* some rain) **4** : to have an agent, order, or request go or be transmitted (*send* out for coffee) **5** : to transmit an order or request to come or return (the principal *sent* for the boy) **6** : to put or bring into a certain condition (her request *sent* him into a state of agitation) — **send·er** *n*

¹se·nior \'sē-nyər\ *n* **1** : a person older or higher in rank than someone else **2** : a student in the final year of high school or college

²senior *adj* **1** : OLDER — used to distinguish a father from a son with the same name ⟨John Doe, *Senior*⟩ **2** : higher in rank or office ⟨the *senior* partner of the law firm⟩ **3** : of or relating to seniors in an educational institution

senior chief petty officer *n* : a petty officer in the navy ranking next below a master chief petty officer

senior master sergeant *n* : a noncommissioned officer in the air force ranking next below a chief master sergeant

sen·sa·tion \sen-'sā-shən\ *n* **1** : awareness (as of noise or heat) or a mental process (as seeing or smelling) resulting from stimulation of a sense organ **2** : an indefinite bodily feeling ⟨a *sensation* of flying⟩ **3** : a state of excited interest or feeling ⟨the rumor caused a *sensation*⟩ **4** : a cause or object of sensation ⟨the play was a *sensation*⟩

sen·sa·tion·al \sen-'sā-shən-l\ *adj* **1** : of or relating to sensation or the senses **2** : arousing an intense and usually superficial interest or emotional reaction

¹sense \'sens\ *n* **1** : a specialized function or mechanism (as sight, taste, or touch) of the body basically involving interaction of a stimulus and a sense organ ⟨the pain *sense*⟩ **2** : a particular sensation or kind or quality of sensation ⟨a good *sense* of balance⟩ **3** : AWARENESS, FEELING ⟨a vague *sense* of danger⟩ **4** : intellectual appreciation ⟨*sense* of humor⟩ **5** : INTELLIGENCE, JUDGMENT **6** : good reason or excuse ⟨no *sense* in waiting⟩ **7** : one of the different meanings a word or phrase can have : MEANING

²sense *vb* **sensed**; **sens·ing** : to be or become conscious of ⟨*sense* the approach of a storm⟩

sense·less \'sens-ləs\ *adj* **1** : UNCONSCIOUS ⟨was knocked *senseless*⟩ **2** : STUPID — **sense·less·ly** *adv* — **sense·less·ness** *n*

sense organ *n* : a bodily structure (as the retina of the eye) that reacts to a stimulus (as light) and activates associated nerves so that they carry impulses to the brain

sen·si·bil·i·ty \,sen-sə-'bil-ət-ē\ *n*, *pl* **sen·si·bil·i·ties** **1** : the ability to receive or feel sensations **2** : the emotion or feeling of which a person is capable ⟨a woman of acute *sensibility*⟩

sen·si·ble \'sen-sə-bəl\ *adj* **1** : capable of being perceived by the senses or mind ⟨*sensible* impressions⟩ **2** : capable of feeling or perceiving ⟨*sensible* to pain⟩ **3** : AWARE **4** : showing or containing good sense or reason ⟨a *sensible* argument⟩ — **sen·si·ble·ness** *n* — **sen·si·bly** \-blē\ *adv*

sen·si·tive \'sen-sət-iv\ *adj* **1** : capable of responding to stimulation ⟨*sensitive* structures of the ear⟩ **2** : easily or strongly affected, impressed, or hurt ⟨a *sensitive* child⟩ **3** : readily changed or affected by the action of a certain thing ⟨plants *sensitive* to light⟩ — **sen·si·tive·ly** *adv* — **sen·si·tive·ness** *n*

sen·si·tiv·i·ty \,sen-sə-'tiv-ət-ē\ *n* : the quality or state of being sensitive

sen·so·ry \'sen-sə-rē\ *adj* : of or relating to sensation or the senses ⟨*sensory* nerves⟩

sen·su·al \'sen-chə-wəl\ *adj* **1** : relating to the pleasing of the senses **2** : devoted to the pleasures of the senses

sent *past of* SEND

¹sen·tence \'sent-ns\ *n* **1** : DECISION, JUDGMENT **2** : punishment imposed by a court ⟨served a *sentence* for robbery⟩ **3** : a group of words that makes a statement, asks a question, or expresses a command, wish, or exclamation

²sentence *vb* **sen·tenced**; **sen·tenc·ing** **1** : to pass sentence on : declare formally the punishment of ⟨the judge will *sentence* him today⟩ **2** : to condemn to a specified punishment ⟨*sentenced* him to die⟩

sen·ti·ent \'sen-chē-ənt\ *adj* : capable of feeling or perceiving

sen·ti·ment \'sent-ə-mənt\ *n* **1** : thought or mental attitude influenced by feeling ⟨a strong religious *sentiment*⟩ **2** : OPINION **3** : tender feelings of affection or nostalgia

sen·ti·men·tal \,sent-ə-'ment-l\ *adj* **1** : influenced strongly by sentiment **2** : primarily affecting the emotions ⟨*sentimental* music⟩

sen·ti·nel \'sent-n-əl\ *n* : SENTRY, GUARD

sen·try \'sen-trē\ *n*, *pl* **sen·tries** : a person and especially a soldier standing guard

se·pal \'sē-pəl, 'sep-əl\ *n* : one of the modified leaves that form the calyx of a flower

¹sep·a·rate \'sep-ə-,rāt\ *vb* **sep·a·rat·ed**; **sep·a·rat·ing** **1** : to take or put apart : DIVIDE ⟨*separate* an egg yolk from the white⟩ **2** : to keep apart by putting something in between ⟨*separate* the pages with a slip of paper⟩ **3** : to occupy the space between ⟨a valley *separates* the two mountains⟩ **4** : to cease to be together : PART

sepal

²sep·a·rate \'sep-ə-rət\ *adj* **1** : not connected ⟨two *separate* apartments⟩ **2** : divided from each other **3** : not shared ⟨live in *separate* rooms⟩ **4** : SINGLE, PARTICULAR ⟨the *separate* pieces of a puzzle⟩

sep·a·ra·tion \,sep-ə-'rā-shən\ *n* **1** : the act of separating **2** : a point or line of division

sep·a·ra·tor \'sep-ə-,rāt-ər\ *n* : a machine for separating cream from milk

Sep·tem·ber \sep-'tem-bər\ *n* : the ninth month of the year

sep·tet \sep-'tet\ *n* 1 : a musical composition for seven instruments or voices 2 : a group or set of seven

sep·ul·cher *or* **sep·ul·chre** \'sep-əl-kər\ *n* : GRAVE, TOMB

se·quel \'sē-kwəl\ *n* 1 : an event that follows or comes afterward : RESULT 2 : a book that continues a story begun in another

se·quence \'sē-kwəns\ *n* 1 : the condition or fact of following or coming after something else 2 : RESULT, SEQUEL 3 : the order in which things are or should be connected, related, or dated

se·quoi·a \si-'kwȯi-ə\ *n* 1 : a California tree that grows about 300 feet tall and has pointed leaves and small oval cones 2 : REDWOOD

se·ra·pe *var of* SARAPE

sere \'siər\ *adj* : DRY, WITHERED

ser·e·nade \,ser-ə-'nād\ *n* : music as sung or played in the open air at night under the window of a lady

sequoia: leaves and cone

se·rene \sə-'rēn\ *adj* 1 : BRIGHT, CLEAR 2 : QUIET, CALM ⟨a *serene* manner⟩ — **se·rene·ly** *adv* — **se·rene·ness** *n*

se·ren·i·ty \sə-'ren-ət-ē\ *n* : the quality or state of being serene

serf \'sərf\ *n* : a member of a servile feudal class bound to the soil

serge \'sərj\ *n* : woolen cloth woven with raised diagonal ribs

ser·geant \'sär-jənt\ *n* 1 : a noncommissioned officer (as in the army) ranking next below a staff sergeant 2 : an officer in a police force

sergeant first class *n* : a noncommissioned officer in the army ranking next below a master sergeant

sergeant major *n* : a noncommissioned officer (as in the army) of the highest rank

se·ri·al \'sir-ē-əl\ *adj* : arranged in or appearing in parts or numbers that follow regularly ⟨a *serial* story⟩ — **se·ri·al·ly** *adv*

se·ries \'siər-ēz\ *n, pl* **series** : a number of things or events arranged in order and connected by being alike in some way

se·ri·ous \'sir-ē-əs\ *adj* 1 : SOLEMN, THOUGHTFUL 2 : requiring much thought or work ⟨a *serious* task⟩ 3 : DANGEROUS, HARMFUL ⟨a *serious* accident⟩ — **se·ri·ous·ly** *adv* — **se·ri·ous·ness** *n*

syn SERIOUS, SOLEMN, EARNEST all apply to people or to things that concern people, and mean being actually or apparently involved in deep thought, important work, or weighty matters. SERIOUS stresses general absorption in and concern for things that really matter rather than things that merely amuse ⟨that piano teacher takes only pupils with a *serious* interest in music⟩ SOLEMN stresses the idea of impressive dignity along with the presence of weighty concerns ⟨the *solemn* moment when the president takes the oath of office⟩ EARNEST stresses sincerity and often zealousness along with seriousness of purpose ⟨the mayor made an *earnest* plea for calm during the emergency⟩

ser·mon \'sər-mən\ *n* 1 : a public speech usually by a clergyman for the purpose of giving religious instruction 2 : a serious talk to a person about his conduct

ser·pent \'sər-pənt\ *n* [from Latin *serpent-*, stem of *serpens* meaning literally "a creeping thing", from the present participle of *serpere* "to creep"] : a usually large snake

se·rum \'sir-əm\ *n* : the liquid part that can be separated from coagulated blood, contains antibodies, and is sometimes used to prevent or cure disease

serv·ant \'sər-vənt\ *n* : a person hired by and under the command of someone else and especially one (as a maid) hired to perform household or personal services

¹**serve** \'sərv\ *vb* **served**; **serv·ing** 1 : to be a servant : ATTEND 2 : to give the service and respect due 3 : WORSHIP ⟨*serve* God⟩ 4 : to put in : SPEND, UNDERGO ⟨*served* three years in the army⟩ 5 : to officiate as a clergyman or priest 6 : to be of use : answer some purpose ⟨the tree *served* as shelter⟩ 7 : BENEFIT 8 : to be enough for ⟨a pie that will *serve* eight people⟩ 9 : to hold an office : discharge a duty or function ⟨*serve* on a jury⟩ 10 : to help persons to food or set out portions of food or drink 11 : to furnish or supply with something needed or desired 12 : to make a serve (as in tennis)

²**serve** *n* : an act of putting the ball or shuttlecock in play (as in tennis or badminton)

¹**serv·ice** \'sər-vəs\ *n* 1 : the occupation or function of serving or working as a servant 2 : the work or action of one that serves ⟨gives quick *service*⟩ 3 : HELP, USE ⟨be of *service* to them⟩ 4 : a religious ceremony or rite ⟨the Sunday *service*⟩ 5 : a helpful act : good turn ⟨he did me a *service*⟩ 6 : SERVE 7 : a set of dishes or silverware ⟨a silver tea *service*⟩ 8 : a branch of public employment or the people working in it 9 : a nation's armed forces ⟨he went into the *service*⟩ 10 : a facility supplying some public demand or mainte-

nance and repair of something ⟨bus *service*⟩ ⟨TV sales and *service*⟩

²service *vb* **ser·viced; ser·vic·ing** : to do some work in taking care of or repairing

ser·vice·a·ble \'sər-və-sə-bəl\ *adj* **1** : prepared for or capable of service : USEFUL **2** : lasting or wearing well in use ⟨*serviceable* shoes⟩ — **ser·vice·a·ble·ness** *n*

ser·vice·man \'sər-vəs-ˌman\ *n, pl* **ser·vice·men** \-ˌmen\ : a male member of the armed forces

ser·vile \'sər-vəl\ *adj* **1** : of or befitting a slave ⟨*servile* work⟩ **2** : lacking spirit or independence

serv·ing \'sər-ving\ *n* : a helping of food

ser·vi·tude \'sər-və-ˌtüd, -ˌtyüd\ *n* : the condition of a slave : BONDAGE

ses·sion \'sesh-ən\ *n* **1** : a single meeting (as of a court, lawmaking body, or school) **2** : a whole series of meetings ⟨congress was in *session* for six months⟩ **3** : the time during which a court, congress, or school meets

¹set \'set\ *vb* **set; set·ting 1** : to cause to sit **2** : to cover and warm eggs to hatch them ⟨*setting* hens⟩ **3** : to put or fix in a place, condition, or position ⟨*set* the dish down⟩ ⟨*set* out seedlings⟩ ⟨*set* a watch⟩ **4** : to arrange in a desired and especially a normal position ⟨*set* a broken bone⟩ **5** : START ⟨*set* a fire⟩ **6** : to cause to be, become, or do ⟨*set* the prisoner free⟩ **7** : FIX, SETTLE ⟨*set* a price⟩ **8** : to furnish as a pattern or model ⟨*set* an example for others⟩ **9** : to put in order for immediate use ⟨*set* the table⟩ **10** : to provide (as words or verses) with music **11** : to fix firmly ⟨*set* his jaw in determination⟩ **12** : to become or cause to become firm or solid ⟨wait for the cement to *set*⟩ **13** : to form and bring to maturity ⟨the old tree still *sets* a good crop of apples⟩ **14** : to pass below the horizon : go down ⟨the sun is *setting*⟩ — **set about** : to begin to do — **set forth** : to start out ⟨*set forth* on a journey⟩ — **set in** : BEGIN ⟨winter *set in* early⟩ — **set off 1** : to show up by contrast ⟨her pale face *sets off* her dark eyes⟩ **2** : to separate from a whole : set apart ⟨words *set off* by commas⟩ **3** : to cause to begin ⟨that story always *sets* her *off* laughing⟩ **4** : EXPLODE ⟨*set off* a charge of dynamite⟩ **5** : to start on one's way ⟨*set off* for home⟩ — **set on 1** : ATTACK **2** : to urge to attack or pursue

²set *adj* **1** : fixed by authority ⟨a *set* rule⟩ **2** : INTENTIONAL, PREMEDITATED ⟨*set* purpose⟩ **3** : reluctant to change : OBSTINATE ⟨very *set* in his ways⟩ **4** : FIXED, RIGID ⟨a *set* smile⟩ **5** : PREPARED, READY ⟨are you all *set* to go⟩

³set *n* **1** : the act or action of setting : the con-

dition of being set **2** : a number of persons or things of the same kind that belong or are used together **3** : form or carriage of the body or of its parts ⟨the *set* of his shoulders⟩ **4** : an artificial setting for a scene of a play or motion picture **5** : a group of tennis games **6** : a collection of mathematical elements **7** : an electronic apparatus ⟨a television *set*⟩

set·back \'set-ˌbak\ *n* : a checking of progress

set·tee \se-'tē\ *n* : a long seat with a back

set·ter \'set-ər\ *n* **1** : one that sets **2** : a large long-coated dog used in hunting birds

settee

set·ting \'set-ing\ *n* **1** : the act of one that sets ⟨*setting* of type⟩ **2** : that in which something is set or mounted ⟨a gold *setting* for a ruby⟩ **3** : the background (as time and place) of the action of a story or play : SCENERY, SURROUNDINGS **4** : a batch of eggs for hatching

¹set·tle \'set-l\ *n* : a long wooden bench with arms and a high solid back

²settle *vb* **set·tled; set·tling 1** : to place so as to stay ⟨*settle* oneself in a chair⟩ **2** : ALIGHT ⟨the birds *settled* on the roof⟩ **3** : to sink gradually to a lower level ⟨the foundations of the house *settled*⟩ **4** : to sink in a liquid **5** : to become established : make one's home ⟨*settle* in the country⟩ **6** : to apply oneself ⟨*settle* down to work⟩ **7** : to fix by agreement **8** : to put in order ⟨*settled* his affairs⟩ **9** : to make quiet : CALM ⟨*settled* his nerves⟩ **10** : DECIDE ⟨*settle* a question⟩ **11** : to complete payment on ⟨*settle* a bill⟩ **12** : to adjust differences ⟨*settle* a quarrel⟩

settle

set·tle·ment \'set-l-mənt\ *n* **1** : the act of settling : the condition of being settled **2** : final payment (as of a bill) **3** : COLONIZING **4** : a place or region newly settled **5** : a small village **6** : an institution that gives help to people in a crowded part of a city

set·tler \'set-lər\ *n* : a person who settles in a new region : COLONIST

set·tling \'set-ling\ *n* : something that settles at the bottom of a liquid : SEDIMENT — usually used in plural

¹sev·en \'sev-ən\ *adj* : being one more than six

²seven *n* **1** : one more than six **2** : the seventh in a set or series

¹sev·en·teen \ˌsev-ən-'tēn\ *adj* : being one more than sixteen

²seventeen *n* : one more than sixteen

¹sev·en·teenth \ˌsev-ən-'tēnth\ *adj* : being next after the sixteenth

²**seventeenth** *n* : number seventeen in a series

¹**sev·enth** \'sev-ənth\ *adj* : being next after the sixth

²**seventh** *n* **1** : number seven in a series **2** : one of seven equal parts

¹**sev·en·ti·eth** \'sev-ən-tē-əth\ *adj* : being next after the sixty-ninth

²**seventieth** *n* : number seventy in a series

¹**sev·en·ty** \'sev-ən-tē\ *adj* : being seven times ten

²**seventy** *n* : seven times ten

sev·er \'sev-ər\ *vb* **1** : to put or keep apart : DIVIDE **2** : to come or break apart

¹**sev·er·al** \'sev-ə-rəl\ *adj* **1** : separate or distinct from others : DIFFERENT ⟨federal union of the *several* states⟩ **2** : consisting of more than two but not very many ⟨*several* persons⟩

²**several** *pron* : a small number : more than two but not many

se·vere \sə-'viər\ *adj* **se·ver·er; se·ver·est 1** : serious in feeling or manner : GRAVE, AUSTERE **2** : very strict : HARSH ⟨a *severe* ruler⟩ **3** : not using unnecessary ornament : PLAIN ⟨a *severe* style⟩ **4** : SHARP, DISTRESSING ⟨*severe* pain⟩ **5** : hard to endure ⟨a *severe* test⟩ — **se·vere·ly** *adv* — **se·vere·ness** *n*

se·ver·i·ty \sə-'ver-ət-ē\ *n, pl* **se·ver·i·ties** : the quality or state of being severe

sew \'sō\ *vb* **sewed; sewed** *or* **sewn** \'sōn\; **sew·ing** : to join or fasten by stitches : work with needle and thread

sew·age \'sü-ij\ *n* : waste liquids and waste matter carried off by sewers

¹**sew·er** \'sō-ər\ *n* : one that sews

²**sew·er** \'sü-ər\ *n* : a covered usually underground drain to carry off water and waste

sew·er·age \'sü-ə-rij\ *n* **1** : SEWAGE **2** : the removal and disposal of sewage by sewers **3** : a system of sewers

sew·ing \'sō-ing\ *n* **1** : the act, method, or occupation of one that sews **2** : material being sewed or to be sewed

sex \'seks\ *n* **1** : either of two divisions of living things distinguished respectively as male and female **2** : the characteristics that distinguish males from females **3** : sexual activity

sex·tet \seks-'tet\ *n* **1** : a musical composition for six instruments or voices **2** : a group or set of six

sex·ton \'seks-tən\ *n* : an official of a church who takes care of church buildings and property

sex·u·al \'sek-shə-wəl\ *adj* **1** : of or relating to sex or the sexes **2** : of, relating to, or being the form of reproduction in which germ cells

from two parents fuse in fertilization to form a new individual — **sex·u·al·ly** *adv*

shab·by \'shab-ē\ *adj* **shab·bi·er; shab·bi·est 1** : threadbare and faded from wear **2** : dressed in worn clothes **3** : MEAN ⟨*shabby* treatment⟩ — **shab·bi·ly** \'shab-ə-lē\ *adv* — **shab·bi·ness** \'shab-ē-nəs\ *n*

shack \'shak\ *n* : HUT, SHANTY

¹**shack·le** \'shak-əl\ *n* **1** : something (as a fetter) that confines the legs or arms **2** : something that prevents free action as if by fetters ⟨the *shackles* of superstition⟩ **3** : a device for making something fast or secure

²**shackle** *vb* **shack·led; shack·ling 1** : to bind or fasten with a shackle **2** : HINDER

shad \'shad\ *n, pl* **shad** : any of several deep‑bodied sea fishes related to the herrings that ascend rivers to spawn and are important food fish

¹**shade** \'shād\ *n* **1** : partial darkness or obscurity **2** : space sheltered from light or heat and especially from the sun **3** : a secluded place **4** : a dark color : a special variety of a color : the degree of darkness' or lightness of a color ⟨four *shades* of brown⟩ ⟨maroon is a *shade* of red⟩ **5** : a very small difference, variation, or degree of thought, belief, or expression ⟨*shades* of meaning⟩ **6** : the shadows that gather as darkness falls **7** : SPIRIT, GHOST **8** : a thing that shades : SCREEN, SHELTER **9** : an adjustable screen usually on a roller used to shut out or regulate the light **10** : the representation in painting or drawing of the effect of shade

²**shade** *vb* **shad·ed; shad·ing 1** : to shelter from light or heat : SCREEN **2** : to mark with degrees of light or color ⟨*shade* a drawing⟩ **3** : to undergo or show slight differences or variations of color, value, or meaning

¹**shad·ow** \'shad-ō\ *n* **1** : shade within certain boundaries **2** : a reflected image **3** : shelter from danger or observation **4** : an imperfect and faint representation or imitation **5** : the image made by an obscured space on a surface that cuts across it usually representing in silhouette the form of the interposed body **6** : PHANTOM **7** *pl* : DARKNESS **8** : a shaded part of a picture **9** : a small degree or portion : TRACE ⟨not a *shadow* of a doubt⟩ **10** : a gloomy influence

²**shadow** *vb* **1** : to cast a shadow upon **2** : to cast gloom over : CLOUD **3** : to follow and watch closely **4** : to pass gradually or by degrees

shad·ow·y \'shad-ə-wē\ *adj* **1** : being like a shadow : UNREAL ⟨*shadowy* dreams of glory⟩ **2** : full of shadow ⟨a *shadowy* lane⟩ **3** : DIM

ə abut   ər further   a ax   ā age   ä father, cot   á (see key page)   aú out   ch chin   e less   ē easy   g gift   i trip   ī life

shad·y \'shād-ē\ *adj* **shad·i·er; shad·i·est**
1 : abounding in shade : sheltered from the
sun's rays **2** : QUESTIONABLE, DISHONORABLE
— **shad·i·ness** *n*

shaft \'shaft\ *n* **1** : the long handle of a
weapon (as a spear) **2** : the
slender stem of an arrow
: ARROW **3** : POLE, FLAGPOLE
4 : one of two poles between
which a horse is hitched to
pull a wagon or carriage
5 : a narrow beam of light **6** : something
suggestive of the shaft of an arrow or spear : a
long slender part especially when round ⟨the
straight *shaft* of a pine⟩ **7** : the handle of a
tool or instrument **8** : a tall monument (as a
column) **9** : a vertical opening or passage
through the floors of a building ⟨an air *shaft*⟩
10 : a bar to support rotating pieces of machinery or to transmit motion to them **11** : a
mine opening made for finding or mining ore

shaft

shag·gy \'shag-ē\ *adj* **shag·gi·er; shag·gi·est**
1 : covered with or made up of a long, coarse,
and tangled growth (as of hair or vegetation)
⟨a dog with a *shaggy* coat⟩ **2** : having a rough
or hairy surface ⟨a *shaggy* tweed⟩ — **shag·gi·ly**
\'shag-ə-lē\ *adv* — **shag·gi·ness** \'shag-ē-
nəs\ *n*

¹shake \'shāk\ *vb* **shook** \'shůk\; **shak·en**
\'shā-kən\; **shak·ing** **1** : to tremble or make
tremble : QUIVER **2** : to make less firm
: WEAKEN ⟨had his confidence *shaken*⟩
3 : to move back and forth or to and fro
⟨*shake* your head⟩ **4** : to cause to be, become,
go, or move by or as if by a shake ⟨*shake*
apples from a tree⟩

²shake *n* : the act or motion of shaking

shak·er \'shā-kər\ *n* : one that shakes or is
used in shaking ⟨salt *shaker*⟩

shak·y \'shā-kē\ *adj* **shak·i·er; shak·i·est**
: easily shaken : UNSOUND — **shak·i·ly** \-kə-lē\
adv — **shak·i·ness** \-kē-nəs\ *n*

shall \shəl, shal\ *helping verb, past* **should**
\shəd, shůd\; *pres sing & pl* **shall** **1** : am or
are going to or expecting to ⟨I *shall* write
today⟩ **2** : is or are compelled to : MUST ⟨they
shall not pass⟩

shal·lop \'shal-əp\ *n* : a light open boat

¹shal·low \'shal-ō\ *adj* **1** : not
deep **2** : SUPERFICIAL

²shallow *n* : a shallow place
in a body of water — usually
used in plural — **shal·low-
ness** *n*

shallop

¹sham \'sham\ *n* : COUNTER-
FEIT, IMITATION

²sham *vb* **shammed; sham·ming** : PRETEND

³sham *adj* : FALSE, PRETENDED ⟨*sham* battle⟩

sham·ble \'sham-bəl\ *vb* **sham·bled; sham-
bling** : to walk awkwardly and unsteadily
: shuffle along

sham·bles \'sham-bəlz\ *n sing or pl* : a place
or scene of slaughter or destruction

¹shame \'shām\ *n* **1** : a painful emotion
caused by having done something wrong,
improper, or immodest **2** : DISGRACE, DIS-
HONOR **3** : something that brings disgrace or
reproach

²shame *vb* **shamed; sham·ing** **1** : to make
ashamed **2** : DISHONOR, DISGRACE **3** : to
bring or drive (a person) by shame ⟨was
shamed into confessing⟩

shame·faced \'shām-'fāst\ *adj* : ASHAMED —
shame·fac·ed·ly \-'fā-səd-lē\ *adv* — **shame-
fac·ed·ness** \-səd-nəs\ *n*

shame·ful \'shām-fəl\ *adj* : bringing shame
or disgrace : DISGRACEFUL ⟨*shameful* behavior⟩
— **shame·ful·ly** *adv* — **shame·ful·ness** *n*

shame·less \'shām-ləs\ *adj* : without shame
: BRAZEN ⟨a *shameless* liar⟩ — **shame·less·ly**
adv — **shame·less·ness** *n*

sham·my \'sham-ē\ *var of* CHAMOIS

¹sham·poo \sham-'pü\ *vb* : to wash the hair
and scalp

²shampoo *n, pl* **sham·poos** **1** : a shampooing
of the hair **2** : a preparation used in shampooing

sham·rock \'sham-,räk\ *n* : a plant (as some
clovers) that has leaves with
three leaflets and is used as a
floral emblem by the Irish

shank \'shangk\ *n* **1** : the
lower part of the leg : the
human shin : the corresponding part of a lower animal
2 : the part of a tool or instrument (as a key, anchor, or
knob) that connects the acting part with
another part (as a handle) by which it is
held or moved

shamrocks

shan't \shant\ : shall not

shan·ty \'shant-ē\ *n, pl* **shan·ties** : a small
roughly built shelter or cabin

¹shape \'shāp\ *vb* **shaped; shap·ing** **1** : to
form or create in a particular shape **2** : DE-
VISE, PLAN **3** : to make fit : ADAPT, ADJUST
4 : to take on a definite form or quality
: DEVELOP — often used with *up* — **shap·er** *n*

²shape *n* **1** : external appearance : FORM ⟨the
shape of a pear⟩ **2** : bodily outline : FIGURE
⟨a gnome of rotund *shape*⟩ **3** : definite arrangement and form ⟨beginning to take
shape⟩ **4** : CONDITION **5** : a thing having a
particular form — **shaped** \,shāpt\ *adj*

---

j job   ng sing   ō low   ȯ moth   ȯi coin   th thin   <u>th</u> this   ü boot   ů foot   y you   yü few   yů furious   zh vision

shape·less \'shāp-ləs\ *adj* **1** : being without shape or regular form **2** : not shapely — **shape·less·ly** *adv* — **shape·less·ness** *n*

shape·ly \'shāp-lē\ *adj* **shape·li·er; shape·li·est** : having a pleasing shape : TRIM — **shape·li·ness** *n*

¹share \'shear\ *n* **1** : a portion belonging to one person : the part given or belonging to one of a number of persons owning something together ⟨sold his *share* of the business⟩ **2** : any of the equal portions or interests into which a property or corporation is divided ⟨100 *shares* of stock⟩

²share *vb* **shared; shar·ing** **1** : to divide and distribute in portions ⟨*shared* her lunch⟩ **2** : to use, experience, or enjoy with others ⟨*share* a room⟩ **3** : to have a share ⟨*share* in planning the program⟩

³share *n* : the earth-cutting blade of a plow

share·crop \'shear-ˌkräp\ *vb* **share·cropped; share·crop·ping** : to farm another's land for a share of the produce or profit — **share·crop·per** *n*

shark \'shärk\ *n* : any of a group of fierce greedy sea fishes that are typically gray, have skeletons of cartilage, and include some large forms that may attack man

shark

¹sharp \'shärp\ *adj* **1** : having a very thin edge or fine point : KEEN **2** : ending in a point or edge ⟨a *sharp* peak⟩ **3** : STEEP, ABRUPT ⟨a *sharp* ascent⟩ ⟨a *sharp* curve⟩ **4** : clearly defined : DISTINCT **5** : affecting the senses as if pointed or cutting ⟨a *sharp* taste⟩ **6** : COLD, NIPPING ⟨*sharp* weather⟩ **7** : very trying to the feelings : PIERCING, PAINFUL **8** : showing rebuke or anger ⟨a *sharp* reply⟩ **9** : keen in spirit or action : having quick perception ⟨a *sharp* eye⟩ **10** : EAGER, KEEN ⟨a *sharp* appetite⟩ **11** : FIERCE, VIOLENT ⟨a *sharp* clash⟩ **12** : BRISK, ENERGETIC ⟨a *sharp* run⟩ **13** : very attentive ⟨keep a *sharp* watch⟩ **14** : QUICK-WITTED, CLEVER **15** : raised in pitch by a half step **16** : higher than the true pitch — **sharp·ly** *adv* — **sharp·ness** *n*

²sharp *vb* **1** : to raise (a note) in pitch by a half step **2** : to sing or play above the true pitch

³sharp *adv* **1** : in a sharp manner : SHARPLY **2** : EXACTLY ⟨four o'clock *sharp*⟩

⁴sharp *n* **1** : a note or tone that is a half step higher than the note named **2** : a sign # that indicates that a note is to be made higher by a half step

sharp·en \'shär-pən\ *vb* : to make or become sharp or sharper — **sharp·en·er** *n*

shat·ter \'shat-ər\ *vb* **1** : to dash, burst, or part violently into fragments **2** : RUIN, WRECK ⟨*shattered* hopes⟩

¹shave \'shāv\ *vb* **shaved; shaved** *or* **shav·en** \'shā-vən\; **shav·ing** **1** : to cut or pare off (as whiskers) by means of an edged instrument (as a razor) **2** : to make bare or smooth by cutting the hair from ⟨*shave* the face⟩ **3** : to cut off closely ⟨a lawn *shaven* close⟩ **4** : to pass close to : touch lightly in passing ⟨*shave* the curb in parking a car⟩

²shave *n* **1** : an operation of shaving **2** : a narrow escape ⟨a close *shave*⟩

shav·ing \'shā-ving\ *n* : a thin slice or strip pared off with a cutting tool ⟨wood *shavings*⟩

shawl \'shol\ *n* : a square or oblong piece of cloth (as wool or cotton) used especially by women as a loose covering for the head or shoulders

shawl

she \shē\ *pron* : that female one

sheaf \'shēf\ *n, pl* **sheaves** \'shēvz\ *also* **sheafs** **1** : a bundle of stalks and ears of grain **2** : a collection of things bound together ⟨a *sheaf* of arrows⟩ — **sheaf·like** \'shēf-ˌlīk\ *adj*

sheaf of wheat

shear \'shiər\ *vb* **sheared; sheared** *or* **shorn** \'shorn\; **shear·ing** **1** : to cut the hair or wool from : CLIP ⟨*shear* sheep⟩ **2** : to deprive of as if by cutting ⟨*shorn* of his powers⟩ **3** : to cut or break sharply ⟨a telephone pole *sheared* off by an automobile⟩ — **shear·er** *n*

shears \'shiərz\ *n pl* : a cutting tool like a pair of scissors but larger

sheath \'shēth\ *n, pl* **sheaths** \'shēthz\ **1** : a case for a blade (as of a sword or knife) **2** : a covering (as the outer wings of a beetle) like a sheath in form or use

sheath and knife

sheathe \'shēth\ *vb* **sheathed; sheath·ing** **1** : to put into a sheath ⟨*sheathe* your sword⟩ **2** : to cover with something that guards or protects

sheath·ing \'shē-thing\ *n* : the first covering of boards or of waterproof material on the outside wall of a frame house or on a timber roof

sheave \'shēv\ *vb* **sheaved; sheav·ing** : to gather and tie up (stalks of grain) into a sheaf

¹shed \'shed\ *vb* **shed; shed·ding** **1** : to pour forth or down in drops ⟨*shed* tears⟩ **2** : to cause to flow from a cut or wound ⟨*shed* blood⟩ **3** : to spread abroad ⟨the sun *sheds* light and heat⟩ **4** : to throw off ⟨raincoats *shed* water⟩ **5** : to cast aside (as some natural covering) ⟨a snake *sheds* its skin⟩

²shed *n* : a slight structure built for shelter or storage ⟨a tool *shed*⟩

she'd \shēd\ : she had : she would

sheen \'shēn\ *n* **1** : subdued shininess **2** : GLITTER, GLOSS

sheep \'shēp\ *n, pl* **sheep 1** : an animal related to the goat that is raised for its flesh, wool, and skin **2** : a timid weak defenseless person **3** : SHEEPSKIN

sheep·fold \'shēp-ˌfōld\ *n* : a pen for sheep

sheep·herd·er \'shēp-ˌhərd-ər\ *n* : a worker in charge of a flock of sheep

sheep·ish \'shē-pish\ *adj* **1** : being like a sheep (as in meekness or stupidity) **2** : embarrassed especially over being found out in a fault — **sheep·ish·ly** *adv* — **sheep·ish·ness** *n*

sheep·skin \'shēp-ˌskin\ *n* : the skin of a sheep or leather prepared from it

¹sheer \'shiər\ *adj* **1** : very thin or transparent ⟨*sheer* stockings⟩ **2** : UTTER, ABSOLUTE ⟨*sheer* nonsense⟩ **3** : very steep ⟨a *sheer* cliff⟩ — **sheer·ly** *adv* — **sheer·ness** *n*

²sheer *adv* **1** : COMPLETELY **2** : straight up or down

³sheer *vb* : to turn aside : SWERVE

¹sheet \'shēt\ *n* **1** : a broad piece of cloth (as an article of bedding used next to the body) **2** : a broad piece of paper (as for writing or printing) **3** : a broad surface ⟨a *sheet* of water⟩ **4** : something that is very thin as compared with its length and width ⟨a *sheet* of iron⟩

²sheet *n* : a rope or chain used to adjust the angle at which the sail of a boat is set to catch the wind

sheikh *or* **sheik** \'shēk\ *n* : an Arab chief

shek·el \'shek-əl\ *n* **1** : any of various ancient units of weight (as of the Hebrews) **2** : a coin weighing one shekel

shelf \'shelf\ *n, pl* **shelves** \'shelvz\ **1** : a thin, flat, and usually long and narrow piece of board or metal fastened against a wall above the floor to hold things **2** : a projecting ledge of rock : REEF, SHOAL

¹shell \'shel\ *n* **1** : a stiff hard covering of an animal (as a turtle, oyster, or beetle) **2** : the tough outer covering of an egg **3** : the outer covering of a nut, fruit, or seed especially when hard or tough and fibrous **4** : something resembling a shell (as in shape, function, or material) ⟨a pastry *shell*⟩ **5** : a narrow light racing boat rowed by one or more oars-

men **6** : a metal or paper case holding the explosive charge and the shot or projectile to be fired from a gun or cannon — **shelled** \'sheld\ *adj*

²shell *vb* **1** : to take out of the shell or husk ⟨*shell* peas⟩ **2** : to remove the kernels of grain from a cob or husk ⟨*shell* Indian corn⟩ **3** : to shoot shells at or upon

she'll \'shēl\ : she shall : she will

¹shel·lac \shə-'lak\ *n* : a varnish made from the secretion of an Asian insect dissolved usually in alcohol

²shellac *vb* **shel·lacked; shel·lack·ing** : to coat with shellac

shell·fish \'shel-ˌfish\ *n, pl* **shellfish** : an invertebrate animal that lives in water and has a shell — used mostly of edible forms (as oysters or crabs)

¹shel·ter \'shel-tər\ *n* **1** : something that covers or protects **2** : the condition of being protected ⟨find *shelter* with friends⟩

²shelter *vb* **1** : to be a shelter for : provide with a shelter **2** : to find and use a shelter

shelve \'shelv\ *vb* **shelved; shelv·ing** : to place or store on shelves

¹shep·herd \'shep-ərd\ *n* : a man who tends and guards sheep

²shepherd *vb* **1** : to tend as a shepherd **2** : to guide or guard in the manner of a shepherd

shep·herd·ess \'shep-ərd-əs\ *n* : a woman who takes care of sheep

sher·bet \'shər-bət\ *n* **1** : a drink made of sweetened fruit juice **2** : a frozen dessert of fruit juice to which milk, the white of egg, or gelatin is added before freezing

sher·iff \'sher-əf\ *n* : the chief law-enforcing officer of a county

she's \shēz\ : she is : she has

¹shield \'shēld\ *n* **1** : a defensive plate or framework (as of metal) carried on the arm to protect oneself in battle **2** : something that serves as a defense or protection

²shield *vb* : to cover or screen with or as if with a shield

¹shift \'shift\ *vb* **1** : to exchange for another of the same kind **2** : to change or remove from one person or place to another ⟨*shift* a bag to the other shoulder⟩ **3** : to change the arrangement of gears transmitting power (as in an automobile) **4** : to get along : FEND ⟨*shift* for himself⟩

²shift *n* **1** : the act of shifting : TRANSFER **2** : a group of workers who work together alternating with other groups **3** : the period during which one group of workers is working

shift·less \'shift-ləs\ *adj* : lacking in initiative

and energy : LAZY — **shift·less·ly** *adv* — **shift·less·ness** *n*

shift·y \'shif-tē\ *adj* **shift·i·er; shift·i·est** : TRICKY, UNRELIABLE — **shift·i·ly** \-tə-lē\ *adv* — **shift·i·ness** \-tē-nəs\ *n*

shil·ling \'shil-ing\ *n* : a coin of Great Britain equal to 1/20 pound

shim·mer \'shim-ər\ *vb* : to shine with a wavering light : GLIMMER ⟨*shimmering* silks⟩

¹shin \'shin\ *n* : the front part of the leg below the knee

²shin *vb* **shinned; shin·ning** : to climb (as a pole) by grasping with arms and legs and hitching oneself gradually upward

¹shine \'shīn\ *vb* **shone** \'shōn\ *or* **shined; shin·ing** 1 : to give light ⟨the sun *shone*⟩ 2 : to be glossy : GLEAM 3 : to make glossy ⟨he *shined* his shoes⟩

²shine *n* 1 : BRIGHTNESS, RADIANCE 2 : fair weather : SUNSHINE ⟨rain or *shine*⟩ 3 : POLISH

shin·er \'shī-nər\ *n* : a small silvery American freshwater fish related to the carp

¹shin·gle \'shing-gəl\ *n* 1 : a small thin piece of building material (as wood or an asbestos composition) for laying in overlapping rows as a covering for the roof or sides of a building 2 : a small sign (as on a doctor's office)

²shingle *vb* **shin·gled; shin·gling** : to cover with shingles

shin·ny \'shin-ē\ *vb* **shin·nied; shin·ny·ing** : SHIN

shin·y \'shī-nē\ *adj* **shin·i·er; shin·i·est** 1 : BRIGHT, RADIANT 2 : POLISHED, GLOSSY — **shin·i·ness** *n*

¹ship \'ship\ *n* 1 : a large seagoing boat 2 : a ship's crew 3 : AIRSHIP, AIRPLANE 4 : a vehicle for traveling beyond the earth's atmosphere ⟨a rocket *ship*⟩

²ship *vb* **shipped; ship·ping** 1 : to put or receive on board for transport by water 2 : to cause to be transported ⟨*ship* grain by rail⟩ 3 : to put in place for use ⟨*ship* the tiller⟩ 4 : to take into a ship or boat ⟨*ship* oars⟩ 5 : to sign on as a crew member on a ship

-ship \,ship\ *n suffix* 1 : state : condition : quality ⟨friend*ship*⟩ 2 : office : dignity : profession ⟨clerk*ship*⟩ ⟨lord*ship*⟩ ⟨author*ship*⟩ 3 : art : skill ⟨horseman*ship*⟩ 4 : something showing, exhibiting, or made of or formed by ⟨member*ship*⟩ ⟨town*ship*⟩ 5 : one entitled to a specified rank or title ⟨your Lord*ship*⟩

ship·board \'ship-,bōrd\ *n* 1 : a ship's side 2 : SHIP ⟨met on *shipboard*⟩

ship·ment \'ship-mənt\ *n* 1 : the act of shipping 2 : the goods shipped

ship·ping \'ship-ing\ *n* 1 : the body of ships in one place or belonging to one port or country 2 : the act or business of a person who ships goods

ship·shape \'ship-'shāp\ *adj* : TRIM, TIDY

ship·worm \'ship-,wərm\ *n* : a wormlike clam that burrows in wood and is destructive to wooden ships, piles, and wharves

¹ship·wreck \'ship-,rek\ *n* 1 : a wrecked ship 2 : the loss or destruction of a ship 3 : total loss : RUIN

²shipwreck *vb* 1 : to destroy (a ship) by grounding or foundering 2 : to cause to undergo shipwreck

ship·yard \'ship-,yärd\ *n* : a place where ships are built or repaired

shirk \'shərk\ *vb* 1 : to get out of doing what one ought to do 2 : AVOID

shirt \'shərt\ *n* 1 : a garment for the upper part of the body usually with a collar, sleeves, a front opening, and a tail long enough to be tucked inside trousers or a skirt 2 : UNDERSHIRT

shirt·waist \'shərt-,wāst\ *n* : a woman's tailored garment (as a dress or blouse) with details copied from men's shirts

¹shiv·er \'shiv-ər\ *vb* : to undergo trembling (as from cold or fear) : QUIVER

²shiver *n* : an instance of shivering : TREMBLE

¹shoal \'shōl\ *adj* : SHALLOW ⟨*shoal* water⟩

²shoal *n* 1 : a place where a sea, lake, or river is shallow 2 : a bank or bar of sand just below the surface of the water

³shoal *vb* : to become shallow gradually

⁴shoal *n* : a large number (as of fish) gathered together : SCHOOL

¹shock \'shäk\ *n* : a bunch of sheaves of grain or cut stalks of corn set upright in the field

²shock *n* 1 : the sudden violent collision of bodies in a fight ⟨the *shock* of battle⟩ 2 : a violent shake or jar ⟨an earthquake *shock*⟩ 3 : a sudden and violent agitation of mind or feelings ⟨a *shock* of surprise⟩ 4 : the effect of a charge of electricity passing through the body of man or animal 5 : a state of extreme bodily depression that is associated with escape of liquid from the blood vessels and that usually follows severe crushing injuries, burns, or hemorrhage

³shock *vb* 1 : to strike with surprise, terror, or disgust ⟨the man's violence *shocked* his friends⟩ 2 : to drive into or out of by or as if by a shock ⟨*shocked* the public into action⟩

⁴shock *n* : a thick bushy mass (as of hair)

shock·ing \'shäk-ing\ *adj* : causing horror or disgust ⟨a *shocking* crime⟩ — **shock·ing·ly** *adv*

shod·dy \'shäd-ē\ *adj* **shod·di·er**; **shod·di·est** : being inferior and without lasting quality ⟨*shoddy* construction⟩ — **shod·di·ly** \'shäd-l-ē\ *adv* — **shod·di·ness** \'shäd-ē-nəs\ *n*

¹shoe \'shü\ *n* **1** : an outer covering for the human foot usually having a thick and somewhat stiff sole and heel and a lighter upper **2** : something (as a horseshoe) resembling a shoe in appearance or use

²shoe *vb* **shod** \'shäd\; **shoe·ing** : to put a shoe on : furnish with shoes

shoe·horn \'shü-ˌhȯrn\ *n* : a curved piece (as of metal) to aid in slipping on a shoe

shoe·lace \'shü-ˌlās\ *n* : a lace or string for fastening a shoe

shoe·mak·er \'shü-ˌmā-kər\ *n* : a person who makes or repairs shoes

shoe·string \'shü-ˌstring\ *n* : SHOE-LACE

shoehorn

shone *past of* SHINE

shoo \'shü\ *vb* : to wave, scare, or send away by or as if by crying *shoo*

shook *past of* SHAKE

¹shoot \'shüt\ *vb* **shot** \'shät\; **shoot·ing** **1** : to let fly or cause to be driven forward with force ⟨*shoot* an arrow⟩ **2** : to cause a missile to be driven forth from ⟨*shoot* a gun⟩ **3** : to cause a weapon to discharge a missile ⟨*shoot* at a target⟩ **4** : to propel (a marble) by snapping the thumb **5** : to propel (as a ball or puck) toward a goal **6** : to score by shooting ⟨*shoot* a basket⟩ **7** : PLAY ⟨*shot* a round of golf⟩ **8** : to strike with a missile from a bow or gun ⟨*shot* a burglar⟩ **9** : to push or slide into or out of a fastening ⟨*shoot* the door bolt⟩ **10** : to thrust forward swiftly ⟨lizards *shooting* out their tongues⟩ **11** : to sprout or grow rapidly ⟨boys *shooting* up into manhood⟩ **12** : to go, move, or pass rapidly ⟨they *shot* past on skis⟩ **13** : to pass swiftly along or through ⟨*shot* the rapids in a canoe⟩ **14** : to stream out suddenly : SPURT — **shoot·er** *n*

²shoot *n* **1** : the part of a plant that grows above ground or as much of this as arises from a single bud **2** : a hunting party or trip ⟨a duck *shoot*⟩

shooting star *n* : a meteor appearing as a temporary streak of light in the night sky

¹shop \'shäp\ *n* **1** : a workman's place of business **2** : a building or room where goods are sold at retail : STORE **3** : a place in which workmen are doing a particular kind of work or the whole factory ⟨a machine *shop*⟩

²shop *vb* **shopped**; **shop·ping** : to visit shops for the purpose of looking over and buying goods — **shop·per** *n*

¹shore \'shōr\ *n* : the land along the edge of a body of water (as the sea)

²shore *vb* **shored**; **shor·ing** : to support with one or more bracing timbers

shore·bird \'shōr-ˌbərd\ *n* : any of a group of birds that frequent the seashore

shore·line \'shōr-ˌlīn\ *n* : the line where a body of water touches the shore

shorn *past part of* SHEAR

¹short \'shȯrt\ *adj* **1** : not long or tall ⟨a *short* dress⟩ **2** : not great in distance ⟨a *short* journey⟩ **3** : brief in time ⟨a *short* delay⟩ **4** : cut down to a brief length : CURT **5** : not coming up to the regular standard ⟨give *short* measure⟩ **6** : less in amount than expected or called for ⟨the cash in his pocket was three dollars *short*⟩ **7** : less than : not equal to ⟨little *short* of perfect⟩ **8** : not having enough ⟨*short* of money⟩ **9** : FLAKY, CRUMBLY ⟨a *short* biscuit⟩ **10** : having the sound of *a, e, i, o, oo, u* as pronounced in *add, end, ill, odd, foot,* and *up* — **short·ness** *n*

²short *adv* **1** : BRIEFLY, SUDDENLY ⟨stop *short*⟩ **2** : so as to reach less than the regular distance ⟨fall *short* of the mark⟩

³short *n* **1** : something shorter than the usual or regular length **2** *pl* : knee-length or less than knee-length trousers **3** *pl* : short underpants **4** : SHORT CIRCUIT

short·age \'shȯrt-ij\ *n* : a lack in the amount needed : DEFICIT ⟨a *shortage* in the accounts⟩

short·cake \'shȯrt-ˌkāk\ *n* : a dessert made usually of very short baking-powder-biscuit dough baked and served with sweetened fruit

short circuit *n* : an electric connection accidentally or intentionally made between points in an electric circuit between which current does not normally flow

short·com·ing \'shȯrt-ˌkəm-ing\ *n* : DEFECT

short·en \'shȯrt-n\ *vb* : to make or become short or shorter

syn SHORTEN, CURTAIL, ABRIDGE all mean to reduce in extent, especially by cutting. SHORTEN commonly implies a reduction in length, either in dimension ⟨*shorten* a skirt⟩ or in duration ⟨*shorten* a visit⟩ CURTAIL adds the idea of making cuts that leave something impaired or incomplete ⟨a sudden storm forced them to *curtail* the band concert⟩ ABRIDGE refers to a reduction in size that is accomplished by a careful elimination of parts not considered essential to relative completeness ⟨*abridge* a dictionary⟩ ⟨*abridged* the book for younger readers⟩

short·en·ing \'shȯrt-n-ing\ *n* : a food substance (as butter, lard, or cream) that shortens pastry, cake, or dough

short·hand \'shȯrt-ˌhand\ *n* : a method of rapid writing by using characters or symbols for sounds or words

short·horn \'shȯrt-ˌhȯrn\ *n* : any of a breed of red, roan, or white beef cattle originating in England and including strains from which a separate dairy breed of milking shorthorns has been developed

short–lived \'shȯrt-'līvd, -'livd\ *adj* : living or lasting but a short time

short·ly \'shȯrt-lē\ *adv* **1** : in or within a short time : SOON **2** : in a few words : BRIEFLY **3** : ABRUPTLY

short·stop \'shȯrt-ˌstäp\ *n* : a baseball infielder whose position is between second and third base

¹shot \'shät\ *n* **1** : the act of shooting **2** : a bullet or ball for a gun or cannon **3** : something forcefully thrown, cast forth, or let fly **4** : GUESS, ATTEMPT ⟨take another *shot* at that job⟩ **5** : the flight of a missile or the distance it travels : RANGE ⟨within rifle *shot*⟩ **6** : a person who shoots ⟨that man is a good *shot*⟩ **7** : a heavy metal ball thrown for distance in a track-and-field contest (**shot put**) **8** *pl* **shot** : a small round pellet of lead fired along with others like it from a gun ⟨the duck was riddled with *shot*⟩ **9** : a stroke or throw at a goal ⟨a long *shot* in basketball⟩ **10** : an injection of something (as medicine) into the body

²shot *past of* SHOOT

shot·gun \'shät-ˌgən\ *n* : a gun with a smooth bore used to fire shot at short range

should \shəd, shu̇d\ *past of* SHALL — used as a helping verb to express condition, obligation or propriety, probability, or futurity from a point of view in the past

¹shoul·der \'shōl-dər\ *n* **1** : the part of the body of a person or animal where the arm or foreleg joins the body **2** : the part of a coat or dress at the wearer's shoulder **3** : a part that resembles a person's shoulder ⟨the *shoulder* of a bottle⟩ **4** : the edge of a road **5** : a cut of meat including the upper joint of the foreleg and adjacent parts

²shoulder *vb* **1** : to push or to thrust with one's shoulder : JOSTLE **2** : to take upon one's shoulders

shoulder blade *n* : the flat triangular bone in a person's shoulder

should·n't \'shu̇d-nt\ : should not

¹shout \'shau̇t\ *vb* : to utter a sudden loud cry (as of joy, pain, or sorrow)

shotgun

²shout *n* : a sudden loud cry

¹shove \'shəv\ *vb* **shoved**; **shov·ing** **1** : to push with steady force **2** : to push along or away carelessly or rudely ⟨*shove* a person out of the way⟩

²shove *n* : the act or an instance of shoving

¹shov·el \'shəv-əl\ *n* **1** : a broad scoop used to lift and throw loose material (as snow, earth, or coal) **2** : as much as a shovel will hold ⟨toss up a *shovel* of earth⟩

²shovel *vb* **shov·eled** *or* **shov·elled**; **shov·el·ing** *or* **shov·el·ling** **1** : to lift or throw with a shovel **2** : to dig or clean out with a shovel ⟨*shovel* a ditch⟩ **3** : to throw or carry roughly or in a mass as if with a shovel ⟨*shoveled* food into his mouth⟩

shovels

¹show \'shō\ *vb* **showed**; **shown** \'shōn\ *or* **showed**; **show·ing** **1** : to place in sight : DISPLAY **2** : REVEAL ⟨*showed* himself a coward⟩ **3** : GRANT, GIVE ⟨*show* them no mercy⟩ **4** : TEACH ⟨*showed* him how to play⟩ **5** : PROVE ⟨that *shows* he's right⟩ **6** : DIRECT, USHER ⟨*showed* him to the door⟩ **7** : APPEAR ⟨anger *showed* in his face⟩ **8** : to be noticeable ⟨the patch hardly *shows*⟩

syn SHOW, EXHIBIT, PARADE all mean to display something in a way that allows or invites attention. SHOW merely means to enable something to be seen or noticed ⟨*showed* the bruise to the doctor⟩ ⟨*showed* his temper by shouting⟩ EXHIBIT means to display something prominently with the purpose of attracting the interest and attention of others ⟨the museum *exhibits* the work of a few very young artists⟩ PARADE usually refers to exhibiting in an ostentatious often vulgar manner ⟨girls *parading* their finery up and down the sidewalks⟩ — **show off** : to make a conspicuous display of one's abilities or possessions — **show up** **1** : to reveal the true nature of : EXPOSE ⟨*shown* up for what he really was⟩ **2** : APPEAR ⟨didn't *show up* for work today⟩

²show *n* **1** : a demonstrative display ⟨a *show* of strength⟩ **2** : a deceptive manifestation : PRETENSE ⟨he made a *show* of friendship⟩ **3** : a true indication : SIGN ⟨a *show* of reason⟩ **4** : an impressive or ostentatious display **5** : a ridiculous spectacle **6** : an entertainment or exhibition especially by performers (as on TV or the stage)

show·boat \'shō-ˌbōt\ *n* : a river steamboat used as a traveling theater

show·case \'shō-ˌkās\ *n* : a protective glass case in which things are displayed

¹**show·er** \'shaù-ər\ *n* **1** : a short fall of rain over a small area **2** : something like a shower ⟨a *shower* of sparks⟩ **3** : a party where gifts are given especially to a bride or expectant mother **4** : a bath in which water is showered on a person or a device for providing such a bath — **show·er·y** *adj*

²**shower** *vb* **1** : to wet with fine spray or drops **2** : to fall in or as if in a shower **3** : to provide abundantly ⟨*showered* her with presents⟩ **4** : to bathe in a shower

show·man \'shō-mən\ *n, pl* **show·men** \-mən\ **1** : the producer of a theatrical show **2** : a person having a knack for dramatization or visual effectiveness

show·y \'shō-ē\ *adj* **show·i·er; show·i·est** **1** : attracting attention : STRIKING **2** : OSTENTATIOUS, GAUDY — **show·i·ly** \'shō-ə-lē\ *adv* — **show·i·ness** \'shō-ē-nəs\ *n*

shrap·nel \'shrap-nl\ *n* **1** : a shell designed to burst and scatter the metal balls with which it is filled along with jagged fragments of the case **2** : metal from an exploded projectile or mine

¹**shred** \'shred\ *n* **1** : a long narrow piece torn or cut off : STRIP **2** : BIT, PARTICLE ⟨not a *shred* of evidence⟩

²**shred** *vb* **shred·ded; shred·ding** : to cut or tear into shreds — **shred·der** *n*

shrew \'shrü\ *n* **1** : a small mouselike animal with a long pointed snout and tiny eyes that lives on insects and worms **2** : a woman who scolds or quarrels constantly

shrewd \'shrüd\ *adj* : sharp-witted : KEEN — **shrewd·ly** *adv* — **shrewd·ness** *n*

¹**shriek** \'shrēk\ *vb* : to utter a sharp shrill cry

²**shriek** *n* : a sharp shrill cry

shrike \'shrīk\ *n* : a grayish or brownish bird that catches grasshoppers, mice, and small birds and often sticks them on thorns before eating them

¹**shrill** \'shril\ *vb* : to make a high sharp piercing sound : SCREAM

²**shrill** *adj* : having a sharp high sound ⟨a *shrill* whistle⟩ — **shrill·ness** *n* — **shril·ly** \'shril-lē\ *adv*

shrimp \'shrimp\ *n* **1** : a small edible shellfish related to the crabs and lobsters **2** : a small puny person or thing

shrine \'shrīn\ *n* **1** : a case or box for sacred relics (as the bones of saints) **2** : the tomb of a holy person (as a saint) **3** : a place that is considered sacred ⟨the Lincoln Memorial is a *shrine* to all lovers of freedom⟩

shrimp

shrink \'shringk\ *vb* **shrank** \'shrangk\ *also* **shrunk** \'shrəngk\; **shrunk; shrink·ing** **1** : to curl up or withdraw in or as if in fear or pain ⟨*shrink* in horror⟩ **2** : to make or become smaller ⟨the dress *shrank* when it got wet⟩

shrink·age \'shring-kij\ *n* : the amount by which something shrinks or becomes smaller

shriv·el \'shriv-əl\ *vb* **shriv·eled** *or* **shriv·elled; shriv·el·ing** *or* **shriv·el·ling** : to shrink and become dry and wrinkled

¹**shroud** \'shraùd\ *n* **1** : the cloth placed over or around a dead body **2** : something that covers or shelters like a shroud **3** : one of the ropes that go from the masthead of a boat to the sides to support the mast

shroud

²**shroud** *vb* : to cover with or as if with a shroud

shrub \'shrəb\ *n* : a woody plant having several stems and smaller than a typical tree

shrub·ber·y \'shrəb-ə-rē\ *n, pl* **shrub·ber·ies** : a group or planting of shrubs

shrub·by \'shrəb-ē\ *adj* **shrub·bi·er; shrub·bi·est** : resembling a shrub especially in woody branched growth

shrug \'shrəg\ *vb* **shrugged; shrug·ging** : to draw or hunch up the shoulders especially to express doubt, uncertainty, or lack of interest

shrunk·en \'shrəng-kən\ *adj* **1** : diminished or contracted especially in size or value ⟨*shrunken* dollar⟩ **2** : subjected to a shrinking process ⟨*shrunken* human heads⟩

¹**shuck** \'shək\ *n* : a covering shell or husk (as of a nut)

²**shuck** *vb* : to free (as an ear of corn) from the shuck

¹**shud·der** \'shəd-ər\ *vb* : to tremble convulsively : SHIVER ⟨*shudder* from cold⟩

²**shudder** *n* : an act of shuddering : TREMOR

¹**shuf·fle** \'shəf-əl\ *vb* **shuf·fled; shuf·fling** **1** : to mix in a disorderly mass ⟨odds and ends *shuffled* in a drawer⟩ **2** : to mix cards to change their order in the pack **3** : to shift from place to place ⟨*shuffle* chairs⟩ **4** : to move with a clumsy dragging gait ⟨*shuffled* his feet⟩ **5** : to dance in a slow lagging manner

²**shuffle** *n* **1** : an act of shuffling **2** : JUMBLE **3** : a dragging sliding movement : a clumsy dragging gait

shun \'shən\ *vb* **shunned; shun·ning** : to avoid deliberately or habitually

shunt \'shənt\ *vb* **1** : to turn off to one side or out of the way : SHIFT ⟨*shunt* cattle into a corral⟩ **2** : to switch (as a train) from one track to another

shut \'shət\ *vb* **shut**; **shut·ting** **1** : to close or become closed ⟨*shut* the door⟩ **2** : to forbid entrance to or passage to or from : BAR **3** : to confine by enclosing or by blocking the way out : IMPRISON ⟨*shut* him in his room⟩ **4** : to fold together : close by bringing parts together ⟨*shut* his eyes⟩ — **shut out** : to prevent (an opponent) from scoring in a game

shut·out \'shət-ˌaut\ *n* : a game in which one side fails to score

shut·ter \'shət-ər\ *n* **1** : one that shuts **2** : a movable cover for a window **3** : a device in a camera that opens to let in light when a picture is taken

shutters 2

¹**shut·tle** \'shət-l\ *n* **1** : an instrument used in weaving to carry the thread back and forth from side to side through the threads that run lengthwise **2** : a thread holder in a sewing machine that slides or rotates to carry the lower thread up to the top thread to make a stitch **3** : a vehicle (as a bus or train) that goes back and forth over a short route

²**shuttle** *vb* **shut·tled**; **shut·tling** : to move back and forth rapidly or frequently

shut·tle·cock \'shət-l-ˌkäk\ *n* : a light feathered object (as of cork) used in badminton

shuttlecock

¹**shy** \'shī\ *adj* **shi·er** *or* **shy·er**; **shi·est** *or* **shy·est** **1** : easily frightened : TIMID **2** : having a retiring manner : BASHFUL **3** : SCANT, LACKING ⟨the coat is *shy* a button⟩ — **shy·ly** *adv* — **shy·ness** *n*

syn SHY and BASHFUL both mean being ill at ease or awkward in the presence of others. SHY suggests either a permanent or a temporary shrinking from familiarity with other people and usually includes timidness or reserve in approaching people ⟨a *shy* little man who much preferred to be alone⟩ ⟨the strange school made her *shy* at first⟩ BASHFUL suggests a shrinking from public attention that often results in notable awkwardness of manner and behavior that is quite characteristic of young people; when it is applied to adults it suggests excessive or abnormal shyness ⟨the *bashful* children disappeared whenever a stranger approached⟩

²**shy** *vb* **shied**; **shy·ing** **1** : to draw back in dislike or distaste ⟨*shied* from publicity⟩ **2** : to start suddenly aside in fright ⟨the horse *shied*⟩

sick \'sik\ *adj* **1** : affected with disease or ill health : not well **2** : of, relating to, or intended for use in illness ⟨*sick* pay⟩ **3** : affected with or accompanied by nausea : QUEASY ⟨a *sick* headache⟩ **4** : sickened by strong emotion (as shame or fear) **5** : tired of something from having too much of it : SATIATED ⟨*sick* of flattery⟩ **6** : DISGUSTED

sick·bed \'sik-ˌbed\ *n* : a bed on which a sick person lies

sick·en \'sik-ən\ *vb* : to make or become sick

sick·le \'sik-əl\ *n* : a tool with a sharp curved metal blade and a short handle used to cut grass

sickle

sick·ly \'sik-lē\ *adj* **sick·li·er**; **sick·li·est** **1** : somewhat sick : often ailing **2** : caused by or associated with ill health ⟨a *sickly* complexion⟩ **3** : seeming as if sick : WEAK ⟨*sickly* plants⟩

sick·ness \'sik-nəs\ *n* **1** : ill health : ILLNESS **2** : a specific disease : MALADY **3** : NAUSEA

¹**side** \'sīd\ *n* **1** : the right or left part of the trunk of the body **2** : a place, space, or direction away from or beyond a central point or line ⟨set something to one *side*⟩ **3** : a surface forming a border or face of an object **4** : an outer portion of a thing considered as facing in a particular direction ⟨the upper *side*⟩ **5** : a position viewed as opposite to another ⟨the affirmative *side* of the question⟩ **6** : a body of contestants ⟨victory for neither *side*⟩ **7** : a line of descent traced from either parent ⟨French on his mother's *side*⟩

²**side** *adj* **1** : of, relating to, or situated on the side ⟨*side* pockets⟩ **2** : directed toward or from the side ⟨a *side* thrust⟩ **3** : INCIDENTAL, INDIRECT ⟨a *side* remark⟩

³**side** *vb* **sid·ed**; **sid·ing** : to take the same side ⟨*sided* with his friend in the argument⟩

¹**side·arm** \'sīd-ˌärm\ *adj* : made with a sideways movement of the hand or arm ⟨*sidearm* fast ball⟩

²**sidearm** *adv* : with a sidearm movement

side·board \'sīd-ˌbōrd\ *n* : a piece of diningroom furniture for holding dishes, silverware, and table linen

sid·ed \'sīd-əd\ *adj* : having sides often of a specified number or kind ⟨a four-*sided* figure⟩

side·line \'sīd-ˌlīn\ *n* **1** : a line marking the side of a playing field or court **2** : a line of goods sold in addition to one's main article of trade **3** : a business or activity carried on in addition to one's regular occupation

¹**side·long** \'sīd-ˌlȯng\ *adv* **1** : OBLIQUELY, SIDEWAYS **2** : on the side

²side·long *adj* **1** : lying or inclining to one side : SLANTING **2** : directed to one side ⟨*sidelong* looks⟩ **3** : INDIRECT

side·show \'sīd-ˌshō\ *n* : a small show near or accompanying a main exhibition (as of a circus)

side·step \'sīd-ˌstep\ *vb* **side-stepped; side-step·ping** **1** : to take a step to the side **2** : to avoid by a step to the side **3** : to avoid meeting issues : EVADE ⟨adept at *sidestepping* awkward questions⟩

side·track \'sīd-ˌtrak\ *vb* **1** : to transfer from a main railroad line to a side line **2** : to turn aside from a main purpose or use ⟨*sidetrack* the conversation⟩

side·walk \'sīd-ˌwȯk\ *n* : a usually paved walk at the side of a street or road

side·way \'sīd-ˌwā\ *adv (or adj)* : SIDEWAYS

side·ways \'sīd-ˌwāz\ *adv (or adj)* **1** : from one side **2** : with one side forward **3** : to, toward, or at one side

side·wise \'sīd-ˌwīz\ *adv (or adj)* : SIDEWAYS

sid·ing \'sīd-ing\ *n* **1** : a short railroad track connected with the main track **2** : material (as boards or metal pieces) used to cover the outside walls of frame buildings

si·dle \'sīd-l\ *vb* **si·dled; si·dling** : to go or move with one side forward ⟨the crab *sidled* away⟩

siege \'sēj\ *n* **1** : the placing of an army around or before a fortified place to force its surrender **2** : a continued attempt to gain possession of something **3** : a persistent attack (as of illness)

si·er·ra \sē-'er-ə\ *n* : a range of mountains especially with jagged peaks

si·es·ta \sē-'es-tə\ *n* [from Spanish, from Latin *sexta* "noon", from earlier *sexta hora* "sixth hour", because the ancient Romans reckoned the hours of the day from sunrise] : a nap or rest especially at midday

sieve \'siv\ *n* : a utensil with meshes or perforations to separate the finer particles from the coarser or solids from liquids

sift \'sift\ *vb* **1** : to pass or cause to pass through a sieve **2** : to separate with or as if with a sieve : SELECT **3** : to test or examine carefully ⟨*sift* facts⟩ **4** : to scatter by or as if by sifting — **sift·er** *n*

sieve

¹sigh \'sī\ *vb* **1** : to take a long deep breath that can be heard especially as an expression of grief or weariness **2** : to make a sound like sighing ⟨wind *sighing* in the branches⟩ **3** : GRIEVE, YEARN ⟨*sighing* for the days of his youth⟩

²sigh *n* **1** : the act of sighing **2** : a sound like a sigh

¹sight \'sīt\ *n* **1** : something that is seen : SPECTACLE **2** : something that is worth seeing or that is peculiar, funny, or disorderly in appearance **3** : the function, process, or power of seeing : the sense by which the position, form, and color of objects is perceived **4** : the act of seeing or looking **5** : INSPECTION ⟨a letter for your *sight* only⟩ **6** : VIEW, GLIMPSE **7** : the entrance or presence of an object within the field of vision ⟨can't bear the *sight* of him⟩ **8** : the distance a person can see **9** : a device (as a small metal bead on a gun barrel) that aids the eye in aiming or in determining the direction of an object **10** : an aim or observation taken by means of a sight **11** : a position from which a person can see a certain thing ⟨in *sight* of land⟩

²sight *vb* **1** : to get sight of : SEE **2** : to look at through or as if through a sight

sight·less \'sīt-ləs\ *adj* : lacking sight : BLIND

sight·se·er \'sīt-ˌsē-ər\ *n* : a person who goes about to see places and things of interest

¹sign \'sīn\ *n* **1** : something that stands for something else : SYMBOL ⟨the *sign* of the cross⟩ **2** : a motion, action, or gesture that expresses something **3** : a publicly displayed notice that advertises something or gives information **4** : something showing the existence of a thing **5** : something that indicates what is to come : OMEN **6** : TRACE ⟨no *signs* of life⟩

²sign *vb* **1** : to make or place a sign on **2** : to represent or indicate by a sign **3** : to write one's name on in token of assent, responsibility, or obligation ⟨*sign* a check⟩ **4** : to hire by getting the signature of ⟨*sign* a new player⟩

¹sig·nal \'sig-nl\ *n* **1** : a sign, event, or word that serves to start some action **2** : a sound or gesture made to give warning or command **3** : something that stirs to action ⟨one blow was the *signal* for a general fight⟩ **4** : a sign that gives notice ⟨a traffic *signal*⟩

²signal *vb* **sig·naled** *or* **sig·nalled; sig·nal·ing** *or* **sig·nal·ling** **1** : to notify by a signal **2** : to communicate by signals

³signal *adj* **1** : UNUSUAL ⟨a *signal* honor⟩ **2** : used for signaling ⟨a *signal* light⟩

sig·na·ture \'sig-nə-ˌchu̇r\ *n* **1** : the name of a person written by himself : AUTOGRAPH **2** : a sign placed at the beginning of a staff in music to show the key or time **3** : a tune, musical number, or sound effect or in television a characteristic title or picture used to identify a program, entertainer, or orchestra

sign·board \'sīn-ˌbōrd\ *n* : a board bearing a sign or notice

sig·nif·i·cance \sig-'nif-i-kəns\ *n* **1** : something signified : MEANING **2** : SUGGESTIVENESS **3** : IMPORTANCE

sig·nif·i·cant \sig-'nif-i-kənt\ *adj* **1** : having meaning and especially a special or hidden meaning **2** : IMPORTANT

sig·ni·fy \'sig-nə-ˌfī\ *vb* **sig·ni·fied; sig·ni·fy·ing** **1** : MEAN, DENOTE **2** : to show especially by a sign : make known **3** : to have importance ⟨a statement that *signified* nothing⟩

sign·post \'sīn-ˌpōst\ *n* : a post with a sign (as for directing travelers)

si·lage \'sī-lij\ *n* : fodder fermented (as in a silo) to produce a succulent feed for livestock

¹si·lence \'sī-ləns\ *n* **1** : the state of keeping or being silent **2** : absence of sound or noise : STILLNESS **3** : absence of mention : SECRECY

²silence *vb* **si·lenced; si·lenc·ing** **1** : to stop the noise or speech of : reduce to silence **2** : SUPPRESS ⟨*silence* objections⟩

si·lent \'sī-lənt\ *adj* **1** : not speaking : not talkative ⟨a *silent* person⟩ **2** : free from noise or sound : STILL **3** : performed or borne without utterance ⟨*silent* disapproval⟩ **4** : making no mention ⟨the boy was *silent* about that part of his plan⟩ **5** : INACTIVE ⟨a *silent* partner⟩ **6** : not pronounced ⟨the *e* in *came* is *silent*⟩

¹sil·hou·ette \ˌsil-ə-'wet\ *n* **1** : a drawing or picture of the outline of an object filled in with a solid usually black color : a profile portrait of this kind **2** : OUTLINE

²silhouette *vb* **sil·hou·ett·ed; sil·hou·ett·ing** : to represent by a silhouette : show against a light background ⟨an airplane *silhouetted* against the sky⟩

silhouette

sil·i·con \'sil-i-kən\ *n* : a chemical element that occurs combined as the most abundant element next to oxygen in the earth's crust

silk \'silk\ *n* **1** : fine protein fiber that is spun by many insect larvae usually to form their cocoon and that includes some kinds used for weaving cloth **2** : thread, yarn, or fabric made from silk **3** : something like silk ⟨the *silk* of an ear of corn⟩

silk·en \'sil-kən\ *adj* **1** : made or consisting of silk **2** : resembling silk especially in soft lustrous smoothness ⟨*silken* hair⟩

silk·worm \'silk-ˌwərm\ *n* : a yellowish hairless caterpillar that is the larva of an Asiatic moth (**silk moth** or **silkworm moth**), is raised in cap-

silkworm and moth

tivity on mulberry leaves, and produces a strong silk that is the chief silk of commerce

silk·y \'sil-kē\ *adj* **silk·i·er; silk·i·est** **1** : resembling silk : SILKEN **2** : having or covered with fine soft hairs, plumes, or scales

sill \'sil\ *n* **1** : a heavy horizontal piece (as of wood) that forms the bottom member of a window frame or a doorway **2** : a horizontal supporting piece at the base of a structure

sil·ly \'sil-ē\ *adj* **sil·li·er; sil·li·est** **1** : weak in intellect : FOOLISH **2** : contrary to reason **3** : TRIFLING, FRIVOLOUS — **sil·li·ness** *n*

  syn SILLY, FOOLISH, ASININE all refer to a seeming deficiency in intelligence. SILLY is the mildest term and simply suggests a lack of ordinary good judgment ⟨it was *silly* of me to come without a coat⟩ FOOLISH adds the idea of being so deficient in common sense that one is blind to dangers and consequences ⟨he was *foolish* enough to go canoeing when he couldn't swim⟩ ASININE is a term of extreme contempt that suggests a complete failure to use any intelligence or judgment ⟨it's *asinine* to elect as captain a boy who doesn't even show up for practice⟩

si·lo \'sī-lō\ *n, pl* **si·los** : a covered trench, pit, or especially a tall cylindrical building in which silage is made and stored

silo and barn

¹silt \'silt\ *n* **1** : particles of small size deposited as sediment from water **2** : a soil consisting mostly of silt and containing little clay

²silt *vb* : to choke, fill, cover, or block with silt

¹sil·ver \'sil-vər\ *n* **1** : a soft white metallic chemical element that takes a high polish and is used for money, jewelry and ornaments, and table utensils **2** : coin made of silver **3** : SILVERWARE ⟨table *silver*⟩ **4** : a medium gray

²silver *adj* **1** : made of or coated or plated with silver **2** : having the color of silver **3** : resembling silver (as in being shiny or precious)

³silver *vb* : to coat with or as if with silver

sil·ver·smith \'sil-vər-ˌsmith\ *n* : a person who makes articles of silver

sil·ver·ware \'sil-vər-ˌwaər\ *n* : articles (as knives, forks, and spoons) made of silver, silver-plated metal, or stainless steel

sil·ver·y \'sil-və-rē\ *adj* : having the luster of silver

sim·i·lar \'sim-ə-lər\ *adj* : closely resembling or corresponding ⟨houses *similar* in design⟩ — **sim·i·lar·ly** *adv*

sim·i·lar·i·ty \ˌsim-ə-'lar-ət-ē\ *n, pl* **sim·i·lar·i·ties** : RESEMBLANCE, CORRESPONDENCE

sim·i·le \'sim-ə-ˌlē\ *n* : a figure of speech in which two dissimilar things are compared by the use of *like* or *as* (as in "cheeks like roses")

sim·mer \'sim-ər\ *vb* **1** : to stew gently at or just below the boiling point **2** : to be on the point of bursting out with violence or emotional disturbance 〈*simmered* with anger at the insult〉

sim·ple \'sim-pəl\ *adj* **sim·pler; sim·plest** **1** : INNOCENT, MODEST **2** : of humble origin 〈*simple* folk〉 **3** : lacking in education, experience, or intelligence **4** : not elaborate 〈neat *simple* clothing〉 **5** : having few parts : not complex 〈a *simple* machine〉 **6** : UTTER, ABSOLUTE 〈the *simple* truth〉 **7** : not hard to understand or solve **8** : STRAIGHTFORWARD, EASY 〈a *simple* explanation〉

sim·ple·ton \'sim-pəl-tən\ *n* : a foolish or silly person

sim·plic·i·ty \sim-'plis-ət-ē\ *n, pl* **sim·plic·i·ties** **1** : the quality or state of being simple and not complex or difficult **2** : HONESTY, STRAIGHTFORWARDNESS **3** : directness or clearness of expression **4** : PLAINNESS **5** : FOOLISHNESS

sim·pli·fy \'sim-plə-ˌfī\ *vb* **sim·pli·fied; sim·pli·fy·ing** : to make simple or simpler : make easier

sim·ply \'sim-plē\ *adv* **1** : CLEARLY 〈explain *simply*〉 **2** : PLAINLY 〈dressed *simply*〉 **3** : DIRECTLY, CANDIDLY 〈told the story as *simply* as a child would〉 **4** : MERELY, ONLY 〈ask a question *simply* out of curiosity〉 **5** : REALLY, TRULY 〈*simply* marvelous〉

si·mul·ta·ne·ous \ˌsī-məl-'tā-nē-əs\ *adj* : existing or taking place at the same time — **si·mul·ta·ne·ous·ly** *adv*

¹sin \'sin\ *n* **1** : an offense against God **2** : MISDEED, FAULT

²sin *vb* **sinned; sin·ning** : to commit a sin

¹since \sins\ *adv* **1** : from a definite past time until now 〈has stayed there ever *since*〉 **2** : before the present time : AGO 〈long *since* dead〉 **3** : after a time in the past : SUBSEQUENTLY 〈has *since* become rich〉

²since *prep* **1** : in the period after 〈has changed *since* his marriage〉 **2** : continuously from 〈have lived here *since* 1959〉

³since *conj* **1** : in the period after **2** : seeing that : BECAUSE

sin·cere \sin-'siər\ *adj* **1** : HONEST, STRAIGHTFORWARD 〈a *sincere* person〉 **2** : being what it seems to be : GENUINE 〈*sincere* good wishes〉 — **sin·cere·ly** *adv*

sin·cer·i·ty \sin-'ser-ət-ē\ *n* : freedom from pretense : HONESTY, GENUINENESS

sin·ew \'sin-yü\ *n* **1** : a tough cord or band that connects a muscle with some other part (as a bone) : TENDON **2** : a tendon used as a thread or cord

sin·ew·y \'sin-yə-wē\ *adj* **1** : having many sinews : TOUGH, STRINGY 〈a *sinewy* piece of meat〉 **2** : STRONG, POWERFUL 〈*sinewy* arms〉

sin·ful \'sin-fəl\ *adj* : marked by or full of sin : WICKED

sing \'sing\ *vb* **sang** \'sang\ *or* **sung** \'səng\; **sung; sing·ing** **1** : to produce musical sounds by means of the voice 〈*sing* for joy〉 **2** : to utter with musical sounds 〈*sing* a song〉 **3** : CHANT, INTONE 〈*sing* mass〉 **4** : to make pleasing musical sounds 〈birds *singing* at dawn〉 **5** : to make a small shrill sound 〈arrows *singing* through the air〉 **6** : to express with enthusiasm 〈*sing* her praises〉 **7** : HUM, BUZZ 〈ears *singing* from the sudden descent〉 **8** : to do something with song 〈*sing* a baby to sleep〉

¹singe \'sinj\ *vb* **singed; singe·ing** **1** : to burn superficially or lightly : SCORCH **2** : to remove the hair, down, or fuzz from by passing briefly over a flame 〈*singe* a plucked chicken〉
syn SINGE, SCORCH, CHAR all refer to some degree of burning. SINGE suggests a very light burning with little damage involved 〈the dog edged up to the fire and *singed* his whiskers〉 SCORCH indicates a more serious burning that changes the color of the exposed area 〈the sun had *scorched* the earth and left the grass a grim brown〉 CHAR refers to a serious burning that reduces the burned area to charcoal or carbon 〈the tree was *charred* in seconds by the lightning〉

²singe *n* : a slight burn

sing·er \'sing-ər\ *n* : one that sings

¹sin·gle \'sing-gəl\ *adj* **1** : UNMARRIED **2** : being alone : being the only one **3** : consisting of or having only one **4** : having but one whorl of petals or rays 〈a *single* rose〉 **5** : consisting of a separate whole : INDIVIDUAL 〈a *single* thread〉 **6** : of, relating to, or involving only one person **7** : not broken or divided 〈a *single* world〉 **8** : done or taken part in by one person or by one person on each side 〈fight in *single* combat〉 **9** : designed for the use of one person or family only 〈a *single* house〉

²single *n* **1** : a separate individual person or thing **2** : a hit in baseball that enables the batter to reach first base

³single *vb* **sin·gled; sin·gling** : to select or distinguish (as one person or thing) from a number or group 〈*singled* out for praise〉

sin·gle–hand·ed \ˌsing-gəl-'han-dəd\ *adj* **1** : done or managed by one person or with one hand **2** : working alone : lacking help

j job   ng sing   ō low   ȯ moth   ȯi coin   th thin   t͟h this   ü boot   u̇ foot   y you   yü few   yu̇ furious   zh vision

¹sin·gu·lar \'sing-gyə-lər\ *adj* **1** : of, relating to, or constituting a word form used to indicate not more than one ⟨a *singular* noun⟩ **2** : SUPERIOR, EXCEPTIONAL **3** : of unusual quality : UNIQUE **4** : ODD, STRANGE ⟨*singular* habits⟩

²singular *n* : a form of a word used to show that only one person or thing is meant

sin·is·ter \'sin-əs-tər\ *adj* **1** : EVIL, CORRUPT **2** : threatening evil, harm, or danger ⟨*sinister* rumors⟩

¹sink \'singk\ *vb* **sank** \'sangk\ *or* **sunk** \'səngk\; **sunk**; **sink·ing** **1** : to move or cause to move downward so as to be submerged or swallowed up ⟨the ship *sank*⟩ **2** : to descend lower and lower ⟨the sun *sank* behind the hills⟩ **3** : to fall to a lower level : SETTLE ⟨the lake *sank* during the drought⟩ **4** : to lessen in amount or intensity ⟨his courage *sank*⟩ **5** : to penetrate or cause to penetrate ⟨*sank* his ax into the tree⟩ **6** : to become absorbed ⟨the water *sank* into the ground⟩ **7** : to form by digging or boring ⟨*sink* a well⟩ **8** : to invest (as money) often unwisely

²sink *n* : a basin usually with water faucets and a drain fixed to a wall or floor

Si·no- \'sī-nō\ *prefix* **1** : Chinese ⟨*Sino*phile⟩ **2** : Chinese and ⟨*Sino*-American⟩

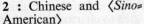

sink

si·nus \'sī-nəs\ *n* : any of several cavities in the skull mostly connected with the nostrils

¹sip \'sip\ *vb* **sipped**; **sip·ping** : to take small drinks of

²sip *n* **1** : the act of sipping **2** : a small amount taken by sipping

¹si·phon \'sī-fən\ *n* **1** : a bent pipe or tube through which a liquid can be drawn by means of air pressure up and over the edge of one container and into another container at a lower level **2** : a tubular organ in an animal and especially a mollusk or arthropod used to draw in or eject a fluid

²siphon *vb* : to draw off by siphon

sir \sər,'sər\ *n* **1** : a title put before the given name of a knight or baronet ⟨*Sir* John Doe⟩ **2** : a title of respect used in addressing a man without using his name

siphon 1

¹sire \'sīr\ *n* **1** : FATHER **2** : FOREFATHER **3** : the male parent of an animal

²sire *vb* **sired**; **sir·ing** : to become the father of

si·ren \'sī-rən\ *n* **1** : a womanlike creature in ancient Greek and Roman stories that lured a sailor and his ship to destruction on a rock or reef by her sweet singing **2** : an alluring but dangerous woman **3** : an often electrically operated whistle that makes a loud shrill fluctuating sound used as a signal or to give warning of present or approaching danger ⟨an ambulance *siren*⟩

sir·loin \'sər-,loin\ *n* : a cut of beef taken from the part just in front of the rump

sirup *var of* SYRUP

si·sal \'sī-səl\ *n* **1** : a West Indian agave **2** : the long durable white fiber of sisal used to make rope and twine

sis·ter \'sis-tər\ *n* **1** : a female person or animal related to another person or animal having one or both parents in common **2** : a member of a religious society of women : NUN **3** : a woman related to another by a common tie or interest — **sis·ter·ly** *adj*

sis·ter·hood \'sis-tər-,hüd\ *n* **1** : the state of being a sister : sisterly relationship **2** : women joined in a group especially for charitable or religious purposes

sis·ter–in–law \'sis-tər-ən-,lò\ *n, pl* **sis·ters–in–law** **1** : the sister of one's spouse **2** : the wife of one's brother

sit \'sit\ *vb* **sat** \'sat\; **sit·ting** **1** : to rest upon the buttocks or haunches : occupy a seat **2** : to cause (as oneself) to be seated ⟨*sat* him down to write a letter⟩ **3** : PERCH, ROOST **4** : to occupy a place as a member of an official group ⟨*sit* in congress⟩ **5** : to hold a session ⟨the court *sat* last month⟩ **6** : to pose for a portrait or photograph **7** : to be located : LIE, REST ⟨the vase *sits* on the table⟩ **8** : to remain quiet or inactive ⟨the car *sits* in the garage⟩

site \'sīt\ *n* : the local position of something (as a town, monument, or event) ⟨famous battle *sites*⟩

¹sit·ting \'sit-ing\ *n* **1** : an act of one that sits : the time occupied in such a sitting **2** : SESSION ⟨a *sitting* of the legislature⟩

²sitting *adj* : relating to or used in or for sitting ⟨a *sitting* position⟩

sitting room *n* : LIVING ROOM

sit·u·at·ed \'sich-ə-,wāt-əd\ *adj* **1** : LOCATED **2** : placed in a particular place or environment or in certain circumstances ⟨not rich but comfortably *situated*⟩

sit·u·a·tion \,sich-ə-'wā-shən\ *n* **1** : PLACE, LOCATION **2** : position or place of employment : JOB, POST **3** : position in life : STATUS **4** : position with respect to conditions and circumstances ⟨an embarrassing *situation*⟩

ə abut   ər further   a ax   ā age   ä father, cot   á (see key page)   aù out   ch chin   e less   ē easy   g gift   i trip   ī life

¹six \'siks\ *adj* : being one more than five

²six *n* **1** : one more than five **2** : the sixth in a set or series

six·pence \'siks-pəns\ *n* **1** : the sum of six pence **2** : an English coin worth six pence or half a shilling

¹six·teen \siks-'tēn\ *adj* : being one more than fifteen

²sixteen *n* : one more than fifteen

¹six·teenth \siks-'tēnth\ *adj* : being next after the fifteenth

²sixteenth *n* : number sixteen in a series

¹sixth \'siksth\ *adj* : being next after the fifth

²sixth *n* **1** : number six in a series **2** : one of six equal parts

¹six·ti·eth \'siks-tē-əth\ *adj* : being next after the fifty-ninth

²sixtieth *n* : number sixty in a series

¹six·ty \'siks-tē\ *adj* : being six times ten

²sixty *n* : six times ten

siz·a·ble *or* **size·a·ble** \'sī-zə-bəl\ *adj* : fairly large

size \'sīz\ *n* **1** : amount of space occupied : BULK **2** : the measurements of a thing ⟨the *size* of a book⟩ **3** : one of a series of measures especially of manufactured articles (as of clothing) ⟨a *size* 8 shoe⟩ — **sized** \'sīzd\ *adj*

siz·zle \'siz-əl\ *vb* **siz·zled; siz·zling** : to make a hissing or sputtering sound in or as if in frying or burning

¹skate \'skāt\ *n* : a very flat fish related to the sharks that has wide-spreading long fins

²skate *n* **1** : a metal runner fitting the sole of the shoe or a fixed combination of shoe and metal runner used for gliding on ice **2** : ROLLER SKATE

skate 1

³skate *vb* **skat·ed; skat·ing 1** : to glide along on skates **2** : to slide or move as if on skates

skein \'skān\ *n* : a quantity of yarn or thread arranged in a loose coil

skel·e·tal \'skel-ət-l\ *adj* : of, relating or attached to, forming, or resembling a skeleton ⟨*skeletal* muscles⟩

skel·e·ton \'skel-ət-n\ *n* **1** : a firm supporting or protecting structure or framework of an organism : the usually bony framework of a vertebrate (as a fish, bird, or man) **2** : FRAMEWORK ⟨the steel *skeleton* of a building⟩

skep·ti·cal \'skep-ti-kəl\ *adj* : having or showing doubt

¹sketch \'skech\ *n* **1** : a rough outline or drawing showing the main features of something to be written, painted, or built **2** : a short literary composition (as a story or essay) **3** : a comic vaudeville act

²sketch *vb* **1** : to make a sketch, rough draft, or outline of **2** : to draw or paint sketches

sketch·y \'skech-ē\ *adj* **sketch·i·er; sketch·i·est 1** : resembling a sketch : roughly outlined **2** : lacking completeness or clearness ⟨a *sketchy* description⟩

¹ski \'skē\ *n, pl* **skis** *or* **ski** : one of a pair of narrow wooden, metal, or plastic strips bound one on each foot and used in gliding over snow or water

²ski *vb* **skied; ski·ing** : to glide on skis

¹skid \'skid\ *n* **1** : a log or plank for supporting something above the ground ⟨put a boat on *skids*⟩ **2** : one of the logs, planks, or rails along or on which something heavy is rolled or slid **3** : a device attached to a wheel for checking motion **4** : a runner on which an airplane or helicopter lands **5** : the act of skidding : SLIDE

²skid *vb* **skid·ded; skid·ding 1** : to roll or slide on skids **2** : to slide sideways **3** : SLIDE, SLIP ⟨*skid* across the ice⟩

skiff \'skif\ *n* **1** : a small light rowboat **2** : a sailboat light enough to be rowed

skiff

ski·ing \'skē-ing\ *n* : the art or sport of sliding and jumping on skis

skill \'skil\ *n* **1** : ability or dexterity that comes from training or practice **2** : a developed or acquired ability : ACCOMPLISHMENT ⟨*skills* of swimming and diving⟩

skilled \'skild\ *adj* **1** : having skill : EXPERT ⟨a *skilled* mason⟩ **2** : requiring skill and training ⟨a *skilled* trade⟩

skil·let \'skil-ət\ *n* : a frying pan

skill·ful *or* **skil·ful** \'skil-fəl\ *adj* **1** : having or showing skill : EXPERT **2** : accomplished with skill — **skill·ful·ly** *adv*

skillet

syn SKILLFUL, ADEPT, EXPERT all mean having the knowledge and experience necessary to succeed in some endeavor. SKILLFUL suggests a highly developed dexterity in performing a job ⟨a *skillful* driver⟩ ADEPT stresses the element of unusual cleverness added to the skill that comes from experience and training ⟨*adept* at most card games⟩ EXPERT usually implies having a thorough knowledge as well as highly developed skill in a particular field or enterprise ⟨an *expert* automobile mechanic⟩ ⟨an *expert* trainer of racehorses⟩

skim \'skim\ *vb* **skimmed; skim·ming 1** : to clean a liquid of scum or floating substance : remove (as cream or film) from the top part of a liquid **2** : to read or examine superficially and rapidly **3** : to throw so as to ricochet along the surface of water **4** : to pass swiftly or lightly over

skim milk *n* : milk from which the cream has been taken

skimp \'skimp\ *vb* : to give insufficient or barely sufficient attention or effort to or funds for

skimp·y \'skim-pē\ *adj* **skimp·i·er; skimp·i·est** : deficient (as in supply) especially through skimping : SCANTY **syn** see MEAGER

¹skin \'skin\ *n* **1** : the hide especially of a small or fur-bearing animal **2** : the outer limiting layer of an animal body that in vertebrate animals (as man) is made up of two cellular layers constituting an inner dermis and an outer epidermis **3** : an outer or surface layer (as of a fruit) : RIND, PEEL — **skin·less** \-ləs\ *adj* — **skinned** \'skind\ *adj*

²skin *vb* **skinned; skin·ning 1** : to strip, scrape, or rub off the skin of ⟨*skinned* his knee⟩ **2** : to strip or peel off

skin dive *vb* : to swim deep below the surface of water with a face mask and portable breathing device

skin·ny \'skin-ē\ *adj* **skin·ni·er; skin·ni·est 1** : resembling skin **2** : very thin

¹skip \'skip\ *vb* **skipped; skip·ping 1** : to move lightly with leaps and bounds **2** : to bound or cause to bound off one point after another : SKIM **3** : to leap over lightly and nimbly **4** : to pass over : OMIT ⟨*skip* a page⟩ **5** : to pass to the grade beyond the next higher ⟨*skip* third grade⟩

²skip *n* **1** : a light bounding step **2** : a gait of alternating hops and steps **3** : OMISSION

skip·per \'skip-ər\ *n* [from medieval Dutch *schipper* "boatman", from *schip* "boat", "ship", a word coming from the same source as English *ship*] : the master of a ship and especially of a fishing, trading, or pleasure boat

¹skir·mish \'skər-mish\ *n* **1** : a minor fight in war **2** : a brisk preliminary conflict

²skirmish *vb* : to take part in a skirmish

¹skirt \'skərt\ *n* **1** : a woman's or girl's garment or part of a garment that hangs from the waist down **2** : either of two flaps on a saddle covering the bars on which the stirrups are hung **3** *pl* : OUTSKIRTS **4** : a part or attachment serving as a rim, border, or edging

²skirt *vb* **1** : BORDER **2** : to go or pass around or about the outer edge of

skit \'skit\ *n* : a brief sketch in play form

skit·tish \'skit-ish\ *adj* : easily frightened : NERVOUS ⟨a *skittish* horse⟩

skulk \'skəlk\ *vb* : to hide or move in a stealthy or sneaking way ⟨*skulked* behind a fence⟩ **syn** see LURK

skull \'skəl\ *n* : the bony or cartilaginous case that forms most of the skeleton of the head and face, encloses the brain, and supports the jaws

skunk \'skəngk\ *n* **1** : a North American animal related to the weasels and minks that has coarse black and white fur and can eject a fluid having an extremely offensive odor **2** : a contemptible person

sky \'skī\ *n, pl* **skies 1** : the upper air : the vast arch or dome that seems to spread over the earth **2** : HEAVEN **3** : WEATHER, CLIMATE ⟨sunny *skies* are predicted⟩

sky·lark \'skī-,lärk\ *n* : a European lark noted for its song

sky·light \'skī-,līt\ *n* : a window or group of windows in a roof or ceiling

sky·line \'skī-,līn\ *n* **1** : the line where earth and sky or water and sky seem to meet : HORIZON **2** : an outline against the sky ⟨buildings forming the *skyline*⟩

sky·rock·et \'skī-,räk-ət\ *n* : a firework rocket that shoots upward and explodes high in the air

sky·scrap·er \'skī-,skrā-pər\ *n* : a very tall building

sky·writ·ing \'skī-,rīt-ing\ *n* : the forming of words in the sky by means of smoke or vapor released from an airplane

slab \'slab\ *n* **1** : a flat thick piece or slice (as of stone, wood, or bread) **2** : the outside piece taken from a log in sawing it into boards

¹slack \'slak\ *adj* **1** : CARELESS, NEGLIGENT **2** : lacking vitality : SLOW ⟨a *slack* pace⟩ **3** : not tight or firm : not taut ⟨a *slack* rope⟩ **4** : not busy or active ⟨business is *slack*⟩

²slack *vb* : to make or become looser, slower, or less energetic : LOOSEN, SLACKEN

³slack *n* **1** : cessation in movement or flow **2** : a part (as of a rope or sail) that hangs loose without strain **3** *pl* : trousers especially for informal wear

slack·en \'slak-ən\ *vb* **1** : to make slower or less energetic : slow up ⟨*slacken* speed at a crossing⟩ **2** : to make less taut : LOOSEN ⟨*slacken* the reins⟩

slag \'slag\ *n* : the waste left after the melting of ores and the separation of the metal from them

slain *past part of* SLAY

slake \'slāk\ *vb* **slaked; slak·ing 1** : QUENCH ⟨*slaked* his thirst⟩ **2** : to cause solid lime to crumble by treating it with water or by exposing it to the air

¹**slam** \'slam\ *vb* **slammed; slam·ming 1 :** to strike or beat hard **2 :** to shut noisily and forcibly : BANG ⟨*slam* the door⟩ **3 :** to put or place forcibly ⟨*slam* down the money⟩ **4 :** to criticize harshly

²**slam** *n* **1 :** a heavy impact **2 :** a noisy violent closing : BANG

¹**slan·der** \'slan-dər\ *n* : a false statement maliciously uttered that damages another person's reputation

²**slander** *vb* : to utter slander against : DEFAME

slang \'slang\ *n* : an informal nonstandard vocabulary composed chiefly of coined words, arbitrarily changed words, and exaggerated or humorous figures of speech

¹**slant** \'slant\ *vb* : to turn or incline from a straight line or level : SLOPE

²**slant** *n* **1 :** a slanting direction, line, or plane : SLOPE **2 :** something that slants

³**slant** *adj* : not level or erect in line : SLOPING

slant·wise \'slant-ˌwīz\ *adv (or adj)* : so as to slant : at a slant : in a slanting direction or position

¹**slap** \'slap\ *n* **1 :** a quick sharp blow especially with the open hand **2 :** a noise suggesting that of a slap

²**slap** *vb* **slapped; slap·ping 1 :** to strike with or as if with the open hand **2 :** to make a sound like that of slapping **3 :** to put, place, or throw with haste or force

¹**slash** \'slash\ *vb* **1 :** to cut by sweeping and aimless blows : GASH **2 :** to whip or strike with or as if with a cane **3 :** to reduce sharply ⟨*slash* prices⟩

²**slash** *n* **1 :** an act of slashing **2 :** a long cut or slit made by slashing **3 :** a sharp reduction ⟨a *slash* in prices⟩

slat \'slat\ *n* : a thin narrow strip of wood, plastic, or metal ⟨the *slats* of a blind⟩

slate \'slāt\ *n* **1 :** a fine-grained usually bluish gray rock that splits into thin layers or plates and is used for roofing and blackboards **2 :** a framed piece of slate used to write on

¹**slaugh·ter** \'slȯt-ər\ *n* **1 :** the act of killing **2 :** the butchering of animals for food **3 :** destruction of many lives especially in battle

²**slaughter** *vb* **1 :** to kill an animal for food : BUTCHER **2 :** MASSACRE

slaugh·ter·house \'slȯt-ər-ˌhaús\ *n* : an establishment where animals are butchered

Slav \'släv, 'slav\ *n* : a person speaking a Slavic language as his native tongue

¹**slave** \'slāv\ *n* [an alteration of older *sclave*, from medieval Latin *sclavus*, meaning originally "a Slav"; it came to mean "slave" because so many Slavic peoples were reduced to slavery in the Middle Ages] **1 :** a person who is owned by another person and can be sold at his master's will **2 :** one who is like a slave in not being his own master ⟨a *slave* to alcohol⟩ **3 :** DRUDGE

²**slave** *vb* **slaved; slav·ing** : to work like a slave : DRUDGE

slav·er·y \'slā-və-rē\ *n* **1 :** long-continued and tiring labor : DRUDGERY **2 :** the state of being a slave : BONDAGE **3 :** the custom or practice of owning slaves

Slav·ic \'slav-ik, 'släv-\ *adj* : of, relating to, or characteristic of the Slavs or their languages

slav·ish \'slā-vish\ *adj* **1 :** of or characteristic of slaves : SERVILE ⟨*slavish* tasks⟩ **2 :** lacking in independence or originality especially of thought ⟨*slavish* imitators⟩

slay \'slā\ *vb* **slew** \'slü\; **slain** \'slān\; **slay·ing :** KILL — **slay·er** *n*

¹**sled** \'sled\ *n* **1 :** a vehicle on runners for carrying goods especially over snow **2 :** a small vehicle with runners used especially by children for sliding on snow and ice

sled 2

²**sled** *vb* **sled·ded; sled·ding :** to travel on a sled

¹**sledge** \'slej\ *n* : SLEDGEHAMMER

²**sledge** *n* : a strong heavy sledlike vehicle for heavy loads

sledge·ham·mer \'slej-ˌham-ər\ *n* : a large heavy hammer usually used with both hands

¹**sleek** \'slēk\ *vb* : to make smooth and glossy by rubbing, polishing, or brushing

sledgehammer

²**sleek** *adj* **1 :** smooth and glossy as if polished ⟨*sleek* dark hair⟩ **2 :** having a smooth healthy carefully groomed look ⟨*sleek* cattle⟩

¹**sleep** \'slēp\ *n* **1 :** a natural periodic suspension of consciousness during which the body rests and restores its powers **2 :** an inactive state (as hibernation or trance) resembling true sleep **3 :** DEATH — **sleep·less** \-ləs\ *adj*

²**sleep** *vb* **slept** \'slept\; **sleep·ing :** to take rest in sleep : be or lie asleep

sleep·er \'slē-pər\ *n* **1 :** one that sleeps **2 :** a horizontal beam to support something on or near ground level **3 :** a railroad car with berths for sleeping

sleep·y \'slē-pē\ *adj* **sleep·i·er; sleep·i·est 1 :** ready to fall asleep : DROWSY **2 :** INACTIVE, QUIET ⟨a *sleepy* town⟩ — **sleep·i·ness** *n*

¹**sleet** \'slēt\ *n* **1 :** partly frozen rain : a mixture of rain and snow **2 :** the icy coating formed by freezing rain

²**sleet** *vb* : to shower sleet

sleeve \'slēv\ *n* **1** : the part of a garment covering the arm **2** : something like a sleeve in shape or use — **sleeved** \'slēvd\ *adj* — **sleeve·less** \'slēv-ləs\ *adj*

¹sleigh \'slā\ *n* : a vehicle on runners for use on snow or ice

²sleigh *vb* : to drive or travel in a sleigh

sleigh

sleight of hand \ˌslīt-əv-'hand\ **1** : skill and quickness in the use of the hands especially in juggling or tricks **2** : a trick requiring sleight of hand

slen·der \'slen-dər\ *adj* **1** : THIN, SLIM **2** : not strong or great : WEAK ⟨a *slender* hope⟩ **3** : INSUFFICIENT, MEAGER ⟨a *slender* income⟩

slew *past of* SLAY

¹slice \'slīs\ *n* : a thin flat piece cut from something ⟨a *slice* of bread⟩

²slice *vb* **sliced; slic·ing** **1** : to cut with or as if with a knife **2** : to cut into slices

¹slick \'slik\ *vb* : to make sleek or smooth

²slick *adj* **1** : SMOOTH, SLIPPERY **2** : CLEVER, TRICKY

slick·er \'slik-ər\ *n* : a long loose raincoat

¹slide \'slīd\ *vb* **slid** \'slid\; **slid·ing** \'slīd-ing\ **1** : to move or cause to move smoothly over a surface : GLIDE, SLIP ⟨*slide* over the ice⟩ **2** : to slip and fall by a loss of footing, balance, or support **3** : to move or pass smoothly or so as not to be noticed ⟨*slid* into his seat⟩

²slide *n* **1** : the act or motion of sliding **2** : a loosened mass that slides ⟨a *slide* of rock⟩ **3** : a surface down which a person or thing slides **4** : something that operates or adjusts by sliding **5** : a transparent picture that can be thrown on a screen by means of a projector **6** : a glass plate on which is placed an object to be examined under a microscope

¹slight \'slīt\ *adj* **1** : SLENDER, SLIM ⟨a trim *slight* figure⟩ **2** : FLIMSY, FRAIL **3** : TRIVIAL, UNIMPORTANT ⟨a *slight* wound⟩ **4** : small of its kind or in amount : SCANTY, MEAGER — **slight·ly** *adv*

²slight *vb* **1** : to treat as slight or unimportant **2** : to ignore discourteously **3** : to perform or attend to carelessly **syn** *see* NEGLECT

³slight *n* **1** : an act or an instance of slighting **2** : a humiliating discourtesy

slight·ing \'slīt-ing\ *adj* : showing dislike, disrespect, or indifference ⟨a *slighting* remark⟩

¹slim \'slim\ *adj* **slim·mer; slim·mest** **1** : SLENDER, THIN **2** : SLIGHT **3** : SCANTY, SMALL

²slim *vb* **slimmed; slim·ming** : to make or become slender

slime \'slīm\ *n* **1** : soft slippery mud **2** : a soft slippery material (as a skin secretion of a slug or catfish)

slim·y \'slī-mē\ *adj* **slim·i·er; slim·i·est** : having the feel or appearance of slime : covered with slime

¹sling \'sling\ *vb* **slung** \'sləng\; **sling·ing** **1** : to toss casually or forcibly : FLING **2** : to hurl with a sling

²sling *n* **1** : a device (as a short strap with a string attached at each end) for hurling stones and other missiles **2** : SLINGSHOT **3** : a device (as a rope or chain) by which something is lifted or carried **4** : a hanging bandage put around the neck to hold up the arm or hand

³sling *vb* **slung** \'sləng\; **sling·ing** **1** : to put in or move or support with a sling **2** : to cause to become suspended ⟨*sling* a hammock⟩

sling·shot \'sling-ˌshät\ *n* : a forked stick with an elastic band attached for shooting small stones

slink \'slingk\ *vb* **slunk** \'sləngk\; **slink·ing** : to move or go stealthily : creep along (as in fear or shame)

¹slip \'slip\ *vb* **slipped; slip·ping** **1** : to move easily and smoothly : SLIDE ⟨*slip* the knife into its sheath⟩ **2** : to move or place quietly : STEAL ⟨*slipped* from the room⟩ **3** : to pass or let pass or escape without being noted, used, or done ⟨time *slipped* by⟩ **4** : to get away from ⟨*slipped* his pursuers⟩ **5** : to escape the attention of ⟨*slipped* his mind⟩ **6** : RELEASE ⟨*slip* a bolt⟩ **7** : to slide out of place or away from a support or so as to lose balance ⟨*slipped* to the floor⟩ **8** : to cause to slide especially in putting, passing, or inserting easily or quickly ⟨*slip* into a coat⟩ **9** : to fall from some level or standard ⟨*slipping* prices⟩

²slip *n* **1** : a ramp that serves for landing or repairing ships **2** : a berth for a ship between two piers **3** : a secret or hurried departure, escape, or evasion **4** : a small mistake : BLUNDER **5** : the act or an instance of slipping down or out of place ⟨a *slip* on the ice⟩ **6** : a sudden mishap **7** : a fall from some level or standard : DECLINE ⟨a *slip* in stock prices⟩ **8** : an undergarment made in dress length with shoulder straps **9** : PILLOWCASE

³slip *n* **1** : a piece of a plant cut for planting or grafting **2** : a long narrow piece of material **3** : a piece of paper used for a memorandum or record ⟨sales *slip*⟩ **4** : a young and slender person ⟨*slip* of a girl⟩

⁴slip *vb* **slipped; slip·ping** : to take slips from (a plant)

slip·cov·er \'slip-ˌkəv-ər\ *n* : a cover (as for

an article of furniture) that may be slipped off and on

slip·knot \'slip-ˌnät\ *n* : a knot made by tying the end of a line around the line itself to form a loop so that the size of the loop may be changed by slipping the knot

slipknot

slip·per \'slip-ər\ *n* : a light low shoe without laces that is easily slipped on or off

slip·per·y \'slip-ə-rē\ *adj* **slip·per·i·er; slip·per·i·est** **1** : having a surface smooth enough to cause one to fall or lose one's footing or hold **2** : not worthy of trust : TRICKY, UNRELIABLE

slip·shod \'slip-'shäd\ *adj* : very careless : SLOVENLY

¹slit \'slit\ *vb* **slit; slit·ting** **1** : to make a slit in : SLASH **2** : to cut off or away : SEVER **3** : to cut into long narrow strips

²slit *n* : a long narrow cut or opening

slith·er \'slith-ər\ *vb* : SLIP, SLIDE ⟨a snake *slithering* along⟩

¹sliv·er \'sliv-ər\ *n* : a long slender piece cut or torn off : SPLINTER

²sliver *vb* : to cut or form into slivers

¹slob·ber \'släb-ər\ *vb* **1** : to let saliva or liquid dribble from the mouth **2** : to show feeling to excess : GUSH

²slobber *n* **1** : dripping saliva **2** : silly excessive show of feeling

slo·gan \'slō-gən\ *n* **1** : a word or phrase that calls to battle **2** : a word or phrase used by a party, a group, or a business to attract attention

sloop \'slüp\ *n* : a sailing boat with one mast and a fore-and-aft mainsail and jib

¹slop \'släp\ *n* **1** : thin tasteless drink or liquid food ⟨prison *slops*⟩ **2** : liquid spilled or splashed **3** : food waste or a thin gruel fed to animals : GARBAGE **4** : body waste ⟨emptying other people's *slops*⟩

²slop *vb* **slopped; slop·ping** **1** : to spill on or over ⟨*slopped* her dress with gravy⟩ **2** : to feed slop to ⟨*slop* the pigs⟩

¹slope \'slōp\ *vb* **sloped; slop·ing** : to take a slanting direction : SLANT, INCLINE

²slope *n* **1** : ground that forms a natural or artificial incline **2** : upward or downward slant **3** : the part of a continent draining its water into a particular ocean

slop·py \'släp-ē\ *adj* **slop·pi·er; slop·pi·est** **1** : wet with slush, standing water, or slop **2** : SLOVENLY, CARELESS

slosh \'släsh\ *vb* : to flounder through or splash about in or with water, mud, or slush

¹slot \'slät\ *n* : a long narrow opening, groove, or passage : SLIT

²slot *vb* **slot·ted; slot·ting** : to cut a slot in

sloth \'slòth, 'slōth\ *n* **1** : LAZINESS **2** : a slow-moving mammal of Central and South America that hangs back downward from the branches of trees and feeds on leaves, shoots, and fruits

¹slouch \'slauch\ *n* **1** : a lazy slovenly incompetent person **2** : a loose or drooping gait or posture

²slouch *vb* : to walk, stand, or sit with a slouch

¹slough \'slü, 'slau\ *n* : a wet marshlike or muddy place

²slough \'sləf\ *n* : something (as the skin of a snake or a mass of dead tissue) that separates and is shed from the body

slov·en·ly \'sləv-ən-lē\ *adj* : untidy especially in dress or person

¹slow \'slō\ *adj* **1** : dull in mind : STUPID, SLUGGISH **2** : not quickly aroused or excited ⟨*slow* to anger⟩ **3** : moving, flowing, or going at less than the usual speed **4** : registering behind or below what is correct ⟨my watch is *slow*⟩ — **slow·ly** *adv* — **slow·ness** *n*

²slow *adv* : SLOWLY

³slow *vb* : to make or go slow or slower

slow·poke \'slō-ˌpōk\ *n* : a very slow person

¹slug \'sləg\ *n* : a long wormlike land mollusk that is related to the snails but has a rudimentary shell or none at all

²slug *n* **1** : a small piece of shaped metal **2** : BULLET **3** : a metal disk for use in place of a coin

³slug *n* : a heavy blow especially with the fist

⁴slug *vb* **slugged; slug·ging** : to strike heavily with or as if with the fist or a bat

slug·gard \'sləg-ərd\ *n* : a lazy person

slug·gish \'sləg-ish\ *adj* : slow in movement or reaction — **slug·gish·ly** *adv* — **slug·gish·ness** *n*

¹sluice \'slüs\ *n* **1** : an artificial passage for water with a gate for controlling its flow or changing its direction **2** : a device for controlling the flow of water **3** : a channel that carries off surplus water **4** : an inclined trough for washing ore or floating logs

²sluice *vb* **sluiced; sluic·ing** **1** : to wash in a stream of water running through a sluice **2** : DRENCH, FLUSH

slum \'sləm\ *n* : a thickly populated section especially of a city marked by wretched living conditions

¹slum·ber \'sləm-bər\ *vb* : to sleep usually lightly : DOZE

²slumber *n* : SLEEP

¹slump \'sləmp\ *vb* **1** : to drop or slide down suddenly : COLLAPSE **2** : SLOUCH **3** : to decline sharply

²slump *n* : a marked or continued decline especially in prices or values or in business

slung *past of* SLING

slunk *past of* SLINK

¹slur \'slər\ *vb* **slurred; slur·ring** **1** : to pass over without due mention or emphasis **2** : to perform two or more successive musical notes of different pitch in a smooth or connected way **3** : to speak indistinctly

²slur *n* **1** : a curved line in music connecting notes to be sung or performed without a break **2** : the combination of two or more slurred tones **3** : a slurring manner of speech

slur 1

³slur *n* **1** : REPROACH, STIGMA **2** : a slighting remark

slush \'sləsh\ *n* : partly melted snow

sly \'slī\ *adj* **sli·er** *or* **sly·er; sli·est** *or* **sly·est** **1** : CRAFTY, CUNNING ⟨a *sly* fox⟩ **2** : SECRETIVE, FURTIVE **3** : ROGUISH, ARTFUL — **sly·ly** *adv* — **sly·ness** *n* — **on the sly** : SECRETLY, UNDERHANDEDLY

¹smack \'smak\ *n* **1** : characteristic taste or flavor **2** : a slight taste, trace, or touch

²smack *vb* : to have a flavor, trace, or suggestion ⟨it *smacks* of garlic⟩

³smack *vb* **1** : to close and open the lips noisily especially in eating **2** : to kiss usually loudly or boisterously **3** : to make or give a smack : SLAP

⁴smack *n* **1** : a quick sharp noise made by the lips (as in enjoyment of some taste) **2** : a loud kiss **3** : a noisy slap or blow

⁵smack *n* : a sailing ship (as a sloop) used in fishing

¹small \'smȯl\ *adj* **1** : little in size **2** : few in numbers or members ⟨a *small* crowd⟩ **3** : little in amount ⟨a *small* supply⟩ **4** : not very much ⟨*small* success⟩ **5** : UNIMPORTANT **6** : operating on a limited scale ⟨*small* dealers⟩ **7** : GENTLE, SOFT ⟨a *small* voice⟩ **8** : not generous : MEAN, PETTY **9** : made up of small units ⟨*small* change⟩ **10** : HUMBLE, MODEST ⟨a *small* beginning⟩ **11** : HUMILIATED, HUMBLED **12** : relating to letters that are not capital letters — **small·ness** *n*

²small *n* : a part smaller and especially narrower than the remainder ⟨the *small* of the back⟩

small intestine *n* : the long narrow upper part of the intestine in which food is largely digested and from which digested food is absorbed into the body

small·pox \'smȯl-ˌpäks\ *n* : an acute contagious virus disease marked by fever and skin eruptions

¹smart \'smärt\ *vb* **1** : to cause or feel a sharp stinging pain **2** : to feel or endure distress ⟨*smart* under criticism⟩

²smart *adj* **1** : causing smarting : STINGING **2** : very active and able **3** : quick to learn or do : BRIGHT **4** : WITTY **5** : PERT, SAUCY **6** : stylish or elegant in dress or appearance — **smart·ly** *adv* — **smart·ness** *n*

³smart *n* : a stinging usually local pain

¹smash \'smash\ *vb* **1** : to break in pieces : SHATTER **2** : to drive or move violently ⟨the ball *smashed* through the window⟩ **3** : to destroy completely : WRECK **4** : to go to pieces : COLLAPSE

²smash *n* **1** : a smashing blow or attack **2** : the condition of being smashed : RUIN, COLLAPSE **3** : the action or sound of smashing

¹smear \'smiər\ *n* : a spot made by or as if by an oily or sticky substance : SMUDGE

²smear *vb* **1** : to spread or daub with something oily or sticky **2** : to spread over a surface **3** : SMUDGE, SOIL **4** : to blacken the reputation of

¹smell \'smel\ *vb* **smelled** \'smeld\ *or* **smelt** \'smelt\; **smell·ing** **1** : to perceive the odor of by means of sense organs located in the nose **2** : to detect by means or use of the sense of smell **3** : to have or give forth an odor

²smell *n* **1** : the sense by which a person or animal smells **2** : the sensation perceived through the sense of smell : ODOR, SCENT

¹smelt \'smelt\ *n, pl* **smelts** *or* **smelt** : a small food fish that resembles the related trouts, lives in coastal sea waters, and ascends rivers to spawn

²smelt *vb* : to melt or fuse (as ore) in order to separate the metal : REFINE

smelt·er \'smel-tər\ *n* **1** : a person whose work or business is smelting **2** : a place where ores or metals are smelted

¹smile \'smīl\ *vb* **smiled; smil·ing** **1** : to have, produce, or show a smile **2** : to look with amusement or ridicule **3** : to be favorable or agreeable ⟨the weather *smiled* on our plans⟩ **4** : to express by a smile ⟨*smile* approval⟩

²smile *n* : a change of facial expression in which the eyes brighten and the lips curve upward especially in expression of amusement, pleasure, approval, or sometimes scorn

smite \'smīt\ *vb* **smote** \'smōt\; **smit·ten** \'smit-n\; **smit·ing** \'smīt-ing\ **1** : to strike hard especially with the hand or a weapon **2** : to kill or injure by smiting **3** : to affect like a sudden hard blow ⟨*smitten* with terror⟩

smith \'smith\ *n* **1** : a worker in metals **2** : BLACKSMITH

smith·y \'smith-ē\ *n, pl* **smith·ies** : the workshop of a smith and especially of a blacksmith

smock \'smäk\ *n* : a light loose coatlike garment worn usually over regular clothing for protection from dirt

smog \'smäg\ *n* [from a blend of *smoke* and *fog*] : a fog made heavier and darker by the smoke or chemical fumes of a city

smock

¹**smoke** \'smōk\ *n* **1** : the gas of burning materials (as coal, wood, or tobacco) made visible by particles of carbon floating in it **2** : a mass or column of smoke : SMUDGE **3** : the act of smoking a cigar, pipe, or cigarette

²**smoke** *vb* **smoked**; **smok·ing** **1** : to give forth smoke **2** : to draw into and expel from the mouth the fumes of burning tobacco **3** : to drive away by smoke **4** : to cure (as fish) by smoke

smoke·stack \'smōk-,stak\ *n* : a pipe serving as a chimney (as on a factory or ship) : CHIMNEY

smok·y \'smō-kē\ *adj* **smok·i·er**; **smok·i·est** **1** : giving off smoke especially in large amounts ⟨*smoky* stoves⟩ **2** : resembling smoke in nature or appearance ⟨a *smoky* flavor⟩ **3** : filled with or darkened by smoke ⟨a *smoky* room⟩

¹**smol·der** *or* **smoul·der** \'smōl-dər\ *n* : a slow smoky fire

²**smolder** *or* **smoulder** *vb* **1** : to burn sluggishly with smoke and usually without flame ⟨a fire *smoldering* in the grate⟩ **2** : to burn inwardly ⟨anger *smoldered* in his heart⟩

¹**smooth** \'smüth\ *adj* **1** : not rough or uneven in surface ⟨a *smooth* board⟩ **2** : not hairy **3** : free from obstacles or difficulties ⟨a *smooth* path⟩ **4** : not jerky or jolting : even and uninterrupted in flow or flight ⟨*smooth* sailing⟩ **5** : fluent in speech and agreeable in manner ⟨a *smooth* salesman⟩ **6** : BLAND, MILD — **smooth·ly** *adv* — **smooth·ness** *n*

²**smooth** *vb* **1** : to make smooth **2** : POLISH, REFINE ⟨*smoothed* out his style⟩ **3** : to make calm : SOOTHE ⟨*smoothed* his anger⟩ **4** : to free from trouble or difficulty

smote *past of* SMITE

¹**smoth·er** \'sməth-ər\ *n* **1** : a thick stifling smoke **2** : a dense cloud (as of fog or dust)

²**smother** *vb* **1** : to overcome by depriving of air or exposing to smoke or fumes : SUFFOCATE **2** : to become suffocated **3** : to cover up : SUPPRESS ⟨*smother* a yawn⟩ **4** : to cover thickly ⟨steak *smothered* with onions⟩

¹**smudge** \'sməj\ *vb* **smudged**; **smudg·ing** : to soil or blur by rubbing or smearing

²**smudge** *n* **1** : a blurred spot or streak : SMEAR, STAIN **2** : a smoky fire (as to drive away mosquitoes or protect fruit from frost)

smug \'sməg\ *adj* **smug·ger**; **smug·gest** : highly satisfied with oneself : COMPLACENT

smug·gle \'sməg-əl\ *vb* **smug·gled**; **smug·gling** **1** : to export or import secretly and unlawfully especially to avoid paying duty ⟨*smuggle* jewels⟩ **2** : to take, bring, or introduce secretly or stealthily — **smug·gler** \'sməg-lər\ *n*

¹**smut** \'smət\ *vb* **smut·ted**; **smut·ting** : to affect or become affected with smut

²**smut** *n* **1** : something (as a particle of soot) that soils or blackens **2** : a destructive disease of plants (as cereal grasses) in which plant parts (as seeds) are replaced by masses of dark spores of the fungus that causes the disease **3** : a smut-causing fungus

snack \'snak\ *n* : a light meal : LUNCH

¹**snag** \'snag\ *n* **1** : a stump or stub of a tree branch especially when hidden under water **2** : a rough or broken projection from something otherwise smooth **3** : an unexpected difficulty or hindrance

²**snag** *vb* **snagged**; **snag·ging** : to catch or damage on or as if on a snag ⟨*snagged* her dress on a nail⟩

snail \'snāl\ *n* **1** : a small slow-moving mollusk with a spiral shell into which it can withdraw itself for protection **2** : a slow-moving person

snail 1

¹**snake** \'snāk\ *n* **1** : a long-bodied limbless crawling reptile that lives usually on large insects or small animals and birds **2** : a contemptible or treacherous person

²**snake** *vb* **snaked**; **snak·ing** : to crawl or move like a snake

snak·y \'snā-kē\ *adj* **snak·i·er**; **snak·i·est** **1** : of or like a snake **2** : abounding in snakes

¹**snap** \'snap\ *vb* **snapped**; **snap·ping** **1** : to grasp or grasp at something suddenly with the mouth or teeth ⟨fish *snapping* at the bait⟩ **2** : to grasp at something eagerly ⟨*snapped* at the chance to go⟩ **3** : to get, take, or buy promptly ⟨*snap* up a bargain⟩ **4** : to speak or utter sharply or irritably ⟨*snap* out a command⟩ **5** : to break or break apart suddenly with a cracking noise ⟨the branch *snapped*⟩ **6** : to make or cause to make a sharp or crackling sound ⟨*snap* a whip⟩ **7** : to close or fit in place with an abrupt movement ⟨the lid *snapped* shut⟩ **8** : to put into or remove from a position suddenly or with a snapping sound ⟨*snap* off a switch⟩ **9** : to close by means of snaps or fasteners **10** : FLASH ⟨eyes *snapping*

in anger〉 **11** : to act or be acted on with snap 〈*snapped* to attention〉 **12** : to take a snapshot of

²snap *n* **1** : the act or sound of snapping **2** : something that is easy and presents no problems 〈that job is a *snap*〉 **3** : a small amount : BIT 〈doesn't care a *snap*〉 **4** : a sudden interval of harsh weather 〈cold *snap*〉 **5** : a catch or fastening that closes or locks with a click 〈the *snap* on a purse〉 **6** : a thin brittle cookie **7** : SNAPSHOT **8** : smartness of movement or speech : ENERGY **9** : the act of putting the ball in play in football

³snap *adj* **1** : made suddenly or without deliberation 〈*snap* judgment〉 **2** : closing with a click or by means of a device that snaps 〈*snap* lock〉 **3** : unusually easy 〈*snap* course〉

snap·drag·on \'snap-ˌdrag-ən\ *n* : a garden plant with spikes of mostly white, pink, crimson, or yellow two-lipped flowers

snap·per \'snap-ər\ *n* **1** : one that snaps **2** : SNAPPING TURTLE **3** : an active flesh-eating sea fish important for sport and food

snap·ping tur·tle \ˌsnap-ing-'tərt-l\ *n* : a large American turtle that catches its prey with a snap of the powerful jaws

snapdragon

snap·py \'snap-ē\ *adj* **snap·pi·er**; **snap·pi·est** **1** : full of snap or life **2** : STYLISH, SMART

snap·shot \'snap-ˌshät\ *n* : a photograph taken with fast camera action and a hand-held camera

¹snare \'snaər\ *n* **1** : a trap (as a noose) for catching small mammals and birds **2** : something by which one is entangled, trapped, or deceived **3** : one of the catgut strings or metal spirals of a snare drum

²snare *vb* **snared**; **snar·ing** **1** : to capture or entangle by or as if by use of a snare **2** : LURE

snare drum *n* : a small double-headed drum with one or more snares stretched across its lower head

¹snarl \'snärl\ *n* **1** : a tangle especially of hairs or thread : KNOT **2** : a tangled situation 〈a traffic *snarl*〉

snares

snare drum

²snarl *vb* : to get into a tangle

³snarl *vb* **1** : to growl with a snapping and showing of teeth **2** : to express anger in surly language **3** : to utter with a growl

⁴snarl *n* : a surly angry growl

¹snatch \'snach\ *vb* **1** : to seize or try to seize something quickly or suddenly **2** : to grasp or take suddenly or hastily : GRAB

²snatch *n* **1** : an act of snatching **2** : a brief period 〈slept in *snatches*〉 **3** : something brief, hurried, or in small bits 〈*snatches* of old songs〉

¹sneak \'snēk\ *vb* : to move, act, bring, or put in a sly or secret way **syn** see LURK

²sneak *n* **1** : a person who acts in a stealthy or shifty manner **2** : the act or an instance of sneaking — **sneak·y** *adj*

¹sneer \'sniər\ *vb* **1** : to smile or laugh with facial contortions that show scorn or contempt **2** : to speak or write in a scornfully jeering manner **syn** see SCOFF

²sneer *n* : a sneering expression or remark

¹sneeze \'snēz\ *vb* **sneezed**; **sneez·ing** : to force out the breath in a sudden violent audible spasm

²sneeze *n* : an act or instance of sneezing

¹snick·er \'snik-ər\ *or* **snig·ger** \'snig-ər\ *vb* : to laugh in a slight, hidden, or partly suppressed manner

²snicker *or* **snigger** *n* : an act or sound of snickering

¹sniff \'snif\ *vb* **1** : to inhale in short breaths **2** : to show or express disdain or scorn **3** : to smell by taking short breaths

²sniff *n* **1** : the act or sound of sniffing **2** : something that is sniffed

¹snif·fle \'snif-əl\ *vb* **snif·fled**; **snif·fling** **1** : to sniff repeatedly **2** : to speak with sniffs

²sniffle *n* **1** : an act or sound of sniffling **2** *pl* : a common cold in which excessive nasal discharge is the chief symptom

¹snip \'snip\ *n* **1** : a small piece that is snipped off : FRAGMENT **2** : an act or sound of snipping **3** : an impertinent person

²snip *vb* **snipped**; **snip·ping** : to cut or cut off with or as if with shears or scissors

¹snipe \'snīp\ *n, pl* **snipes** *or* **snipe** : a game bird that lives in marshes and has a long straight bill

²snipe *vb* **sniped**; **snip·ing** : to shoot at individual enemy soldiers especially when there is no mass fighting

snob \'snäb\ *n* : one who imitates, admires, or seeks friendship with people who are of higher rank or position than himself and looks down on people whom he considers of lower rank or position

snob·bish \'snäb-ish\ *adj* : characteristic of or befitting a snob

¹snoop \'snüp\ *vb* : to look or pry especially in a sneaking or meddlesome manner

²snoop *n* : SNOOPER

snoop·er \'snü-pər\ *n* : one that snoops

¹snooze \'snüz\ *vb* **snoozed**; **snooz·ing** : to take a nap

²snooze *n* : a short sleep : NAP

snore \'snōr\ *vb* **snored; snor·ing** : to breathe with a rough hoarse noise while sleeping

¹snort \'snȯrt\ *vb* : to force air vigorously through the nose with a rough harsh sound

²snort *n* : an act or sound of snorting

snout \'snaut\ *n* **1** : a long projecting nose or muzzle (as of a swine) **2** : the projecting front of the head of an animal **3** : a usually large or grotesque human nose

¹snow \'snō\ *n* **1** : small white crystals of ice formed directly from the water vapor of the air **2** : a fall of snowflakes : a mass of snow-flakes fallen to earth

²snow *vb* **1** : to fall or cause to fall in or as snow ⟨it's *snowing*⟩ ⟨*snowed* messages on their congressman⟩ **2** : to cover or shut in with snow

snow·ball \'snō-,bȯl\ *n* : a round mass of snow pressed or rolled together

snow·bird \'snō-,bərd\ *n* : a small bird (as a junco) seen mostly in winter

snow·bound \'snō-'baund\ *adj* : shut in by snow

snow·drift \'snō-,drift\ *n* : a bank of drifted snow

snow·fall \'snō-,fȯl\ *n* **1** : a fall of snow **2** : the amount of snow that falls in a single storm or in a certain period

snow·flake \'snō-,flāk\ *n* : a snow crystal : a small mass of snow crystals

snow·plow \'snō-,plau\ *n* : any of various devices used for clearing away snow

¹snow·shoe \'snō-,shü\ *n* : a light frame of wood strung with rawhide leather worn under the shoe to prevent sinking into soft snow

²snowshoe *vb* **snow·shoed; snow·shoe·ing** : to go on snow-shoes

snow·storm \'snō-,stȯrm\ *n* : a storm of falling snow

snowshoes

snow·y \'snō-ē\ *adj* **snow·i·er; snow·i·est** **1** : having or covered with snow **2** : white like snow

¹snub \'snəb\ *vb* **snubbed; snub·bing** : to slight purposely : treat rudely

²snub *n* : an act or an instance of snubbing

snub–nosed \'snəb-'nōzd\ *adj* : having a stubby and usually slightly turned-up nose

¹snuff \'snəf\ *vb* **1** : to cut or pinch off the burned end of the wick of a candle **2** : EX-TINGUISH

²snuff *vb* **1** : to draw forcibly through or into the nose **2** : to sniff inquiringly

³snuff *n* : the act of snuffing : SNIFF

⁴snuff *n* : tobacco powdered and prepared to be chewed, placed against the gums, or in-haled through the nostrils

¹snuf·fle \'snəf-əl\ *vb* **snuf·fled; snuf·fling** : to breathe noisily through an obstructed nose

²snuffle *n* : the sound made in snuffling

snug \'snəg\ *adj* **snug·ger; snug·gest** **1** : fitting closely and comfortably ⟨a *snug* coat⟩ **2** : COMFORTABLE, COZY ⟨a *snug* corner⟩ **3** : CONCEALED ⟨a *snug* harbor⟩ — **snug·ly** *adv*

snug·gle \'snəg-əl\ *vb* **snug·gled; snug·gling** **1** : to curl up comfortably or cozily : CUDDLE **2** : NESTLE

¹so \sō\ *adv* **1** : in a manner indicated ⟨said he'd go and did *so*⟩ **2** : in the same way : ALSO ⟨he wrote well and *so* did she⟩ **3** : THEN, SUBSEQUENTLY ⟨and *so* to bed⟩ **4** : to an indicated degree or way ⟨had never felt *so* well⟩ **5** : VERY, EXTREMELY ⟨loved her *so*⟩ **6** : to a definite but unspecified extent ⟨can do only *so* much in a day⟩ **7** : most certainly : INDEED ⟨you did *so* say it⟩ **8** : THEREFORE ⟨is honest and *so* returned the wallet⟩

²so *conj* **1** : in order (that) ⟨be quiet *so* I can sleep⟩ **2** : and therefore ⟨we were hungry, *so* we ate⟩

³so *pron* **1** : the same : THAT ⟨became chair-man and remained *so*⟩ **2** : approximately that ⟨I'd been there a month or *so*⟩

¹soak \'sōk\ *vb* **1** : to remain in a liquid **2** : to place in a liquid to wet or as if to wet thoroughly : STEEP **3** : to enter or pass through something by or as if by pores or tiny holes : PERMEATE **4** : to penetrate or affect the mind or feelings ⟨the words *soaked* in⟩ **5** : to extract by or as if by steeping ⟨*soak* the dirt out⟩ **6** : to draw in by or as if by absorption ⟨*soaked* up the sunshine⟩

²soak *n* : the act or process of soaking : the state of being soaked

¹soap \'sōp\ *n* : a substance that is usually made by the action of alkali on fat, dissolves in water, and is used for washing

²soap *vb* : to rub soap over or into something

soap·stone \'sōp-,stōn\ *n* : a soft stone having a soapy or greasy feeling

soap·suds \'sōp-,sədz\ *n pl* : SUDS

soap·y \'sō-pē\ *adj* **soap·i·er; soap·i·est** **1** : smeared with or full of soap **2** : containing or combined with soap **3** : resembling soap

soar \'sōr\ *vb* : to fly upward on or as if on wings

¹sob \'säb\ *vb* **sobbed; sob·bing** **1** : to cry, sigh, or utter with heavings of the chest or with catching in the throat **2** : to make a sobbing sound ⟨the wind *sobs* in the trees⟩

²sob *n* **1** : an act of sobbing **2** : a sound of or like that of sobbing

---

j **job**   ng **sing**   ō **low**   ȯ **moth**   ȯi **coin**   th **thin**   <u>th</u> **this**   ü **boot**   u̇ **foot**   y **you**   yü **few**   yu̇ **furious**   zh **vision**

¹**so·ber** \'sō-bər\ *adj* **1** : not drinking too much : TEMPERATE **2** : not drunk **3** : SERIOUS, SOLEMN ⟨a *sober* child⟩ **4** : subdued in tone or color **5** : not fanciful or emotional ⟨a *sober* decision⟩

²**sober** *vb* : to make or become sober

so–called \'sō-'kȯld\ *adj* : commonly or popularly but often inaccurately so termed ⟨his *so-called* friend⟩

soc·cer \'säk-ər\ *n* : a football game in which a round inflated ball is moved usually by kicking toward a goal

¹**so·cia·ble** \'sō-shə-bəl\ *adj* **1** : liking companionship : FRIENDLY **2** : characterized by pleasant social relations ⟨enjoyed a *sociable* evening⟩

²**sociable** *n* : an informal friendly gathering frequently for a special activity or interest

¹**so·cial** \'sō-shəl\ *adj* **1** : FRIENDLY, SOCIABLE ⟨a *social* evening⟩ **2** : living or growing naturally in groups or communities ⟨bees are *social* insects⟩ **3** : of or relating to human beings as a group or to their conditions or welfare ⟨*social* institutions⟩ **4** : of, relating to, or based on rank in a particular society ⟨different *social* circles⟩ **5** : of or relating to fashionable society ⟨a *social* leader⟩ — **so·cial·ly** *adv*

²**social** *n* : SOCIABLE

so·ci·e·ty \sə-'sī-ət-ē\ *n, pl* **so·ci·e·ties** **1** : COMPANIONSHIP, COMPANY **2** : community life : people in general **3** : an association of persons for some purpose ⟨a mutual benefit *society*⟩ **4** : a part of a community that is regarded as a unit distinguished by certain interests or standards : the group or set of fashionable persons

sock \'säk\ *n, pl* **socks** *or* **sox** \'säks\ : a knitted or woven covering for the foot usually extending above the ankle and sometimes to the knee

sock·et \'säk-ət\ *n* : a hollow thing or place that receives and holds something ⟨an electric light *socket*⟩

sock·eye \'säk-ˌī\ *n* : a small Pacific salmon that is the source of most of the red-fleshed salmon of commerce

¹**sod** \'säd\ *n* : the layer of the soil filled with roots (as of grass) : TURF

²**sod** *vb* **sod·ded; sod·ding** : to cover with sod

so·da \'sōd-ə\ *n* **1** : a powdery saltlike substance used in washing and in making glass or soap **2** : SODIUM BICARBONATE **3** : SODA WATER **4** : a sweet drink of soda water, flavoring, and ice cream

soda fountain *n* : a counter where soda water, soft drinks, and ice cream are served

soda pop *n* : SODA WATER 2

soda water *n* **1** : water with carbon dioxide added **2** : a beverage of soda water with flavoring and sweetening

sod·den \'säd-n\ *adj* : SOGGY

so·di·um \'sōd-ē-əm\ *n* : a soft waxy silver‑white chemical element occurring in nature in combined form (as in salt)

sodium bicarbonate *n* : a white crystalline substance used in cooking and medicine

sodium chlo·ride \-'klōr-ˌīd\ *n* : SALT

so·fa \'sō-fə\ *n* : a long upholstered seat usually with a back and arms

sofa

¹**soft** \'sȯft\ *adj* **1** : having a pleasing, comfortable, or sooth‑ ing quality or effect : MILD **2** : not harsh : GENTLE ⟨*soft* breezes⟩ **3** : pleasing to the ear : QUIET ⟨*soft* voices⟩ **4** : not bright or glaring ⟨*soft* lights⟩ **5** : EASY ⟨a *soft* job⟩ **6** : smooth or delicate in appearance or texture ⟨a *soft* silk⟩ **7** : easily moved : KIND, TOLERANT ⟨a *soft* heart⟩ **8** : lacking in strength or vigor ⟨*soft* from good living⟩ **9** : not hard, solid, or firm ⟨a *soft* mattress⟩ **10** : sounding as in *ace* and *gem* — used of *c* and *g* **11** : not containing substances that prevent lathering of soap **12** : not containing alcohol — **soft·ness** *n*

²**soft** *adv* : SOFTLY

soft·ball \'sȯft-ˌbȯl\ *n* **1** : a game like base‑ ball played with a larger softer ball **2** : the ball used in softball

soft·en \'sȯf-ən\ *vb* : to make or become soft or softer — **soft·en·er** *n*

soft·ly \'sȯft-lē\ *adv* : QUIETLY, GENTLY

soft·wood \'sȯft-ˌwu̇d\ *n* : the wood of a cone-bearing tree (as a pine or spruce)

sog·gy \'säg-ē\ *adj* **sog·gi·er; sog·gi·est** **1** : heavy with water or moisture : SOAKED ⟨*soggy* ground⟩ **2** : heavy or doughy because of imperfect cooking ⟨*soggy* bread⟩

¹**soil** \'sȯil\ *vb* : to make or become dirty

²**soil** *n* **1** : STAIN **2** : CORRUPTION **3** : something that soils or pollutes

³**soil** *n* **1** : firm land : EARTH **2** : the loose finely divided surface material of the earth in which plants have their roots — **soil·less** \'sȯil-ləs\ *adj*

¹**so·journ** \'sō-ˌjərn\ *n* : a temporary stay

²**sojourn** *vb* : to stay as a temporary resident

sol \'sōl\ *n* : the fifth note of the musical scale

so·lar \'sō-lər\ *adj* **1** : of or relating to the sun ⟨the *solar* system includes the sun and the planets, comets, and meteors that revolve around it⟩ **2** : measured by the earth's course in relation to the sun ⟨a *solar* year⟩ **3** : produced or operated by the action of the sun's light or heat ⟨a *solar* furnace⟩

sold *past of* SELL

¹sol·der \'säd-ər\ *n* : a metal or a metallic alloy used when melted to join or mend surfaces of metal

²solder *vb* : to join together or repair with solder

sol·dier \'sōl-jər\ *n* **1** : a person in military service : an enlisted man who is not a commissioned officer **2** : a worker in a cause

¹sole \'sōl\ *n* **1** : the underside of the foot **2** : the bottom of a shoe, slipper, or boot

²sole *vb* **soled; sol·ing** : to furnish with a sole ⟨*sole* shoes⟩

³sole *n* : a flatfish that has a small mouth and small eyes set close together

⁴sole *adj* **1** : SINGLE, ONLY ⟨the *sole* heir⟩ **2** : belonging exclusively or limited to the one named ⟨gave him *sole* authority⟩

sole·ly \'sōl-lē\ *adv* **1** : without another : ALONE **2** : ENTIRELY ⟨done *solely* for money⟩

sol·emn \'säl-əm\ *adj* **1** : celebrated with religious rites or ceremony : SACRED **2** : FORMAL, CEREMONIOUS ⟨a *solemn* procession⟩ **3** : done or made seriously and thoughtfully ⟨a *solemn* promise⟩ **4** : GRAVE, SOBER **5** : SOMBER ⟨robe of *solemn* black⟩ **syn** see SERIOUS — **sol·emn·ly** *adv*

so·lem·ni·ty \sə-'lem-nət-ē\ *n*, *pl* **so·lem·ni·ties** **1** : a solemn ceremony or rite : a solemn event, day, or speech **2** : formal dignity : SERIOUSNESS

so·lic·it \sə-'lis-ət\ *vb* **1** : ENTREAT, BEG **2** : to approach with a request or plea **3** : to appeal for ⟨*solicited* the help of his neighbors⟩

¹sol·id \'säl-əd\ *adj* **1** : not hollow **2** : being without a break, interruption, or change ⟨practiced for three *solid* hours⟩ **3** : not loose or spongy : COMPACT ⟨a *solid* mass of rock⟩ **4** : neither liquid nor gaseous : HARD, RIGID ⟨*solid* ice⟩ **5** : of good substantial quality or kind ⟨a *solid* chair⟩ **6** : UNANIMOUS, UNITED ⟨the *solid* South⟩ **7** : DEPENDABLE, RELIABLE ⟨a *solid* citizen⟩ **8** : of one material, kind, or color ⟨*solid* gold⟩ — **sol·id·ly** *adv*

²solid *n* **1** : something (as a log) that has length, breadth, and thickness **2** : a solid substance

so·lid·i·fy \sə-'lid-ə-,fī\ *vb* **so·lid·i·fied; sol·id·i·fy·ing** : to make or become solid

so·lid·i·ty \sə-'lid-ət-ē\ *n*, *pl* **so·lid·i·ties** : the quality or state of being solid : HARDNESS, FIRMNESS

sol·i·tar·y \'säl-ə-,ter-ē\ *adj* **1** : all alone ⟨a *solitary* traveler⟩ **2** : seldom visited : LONELY **3** : SINGLE, SOLE **4** : growing or living alone : not one of a group or cluster ⟨*solitary* insects⟩

sol·i·tude \'säl-ə-,tüd, -,tyüd\ *n* **1** : the quality or state of being alone or away from others : SECLUSION **2** : a lonely place

¹so·lo \'sō-lō\ *n*, *pl* **so·los** **1** : a musical composition for a single instrument or voice **2** : an action (as in a dance) in which there is only one performer

²solo *adv* (*or adj*) : ALONE ⟨fly *solo*⟩ ⟨a *solo* dancer⟩

³solo *vb* : to fly solo in an airplane

so·lo·ist \'sō-lō-əst\ *n* : one who performs a solo

sol·stice \'säl-stəs\ *n* : the time of the year when the sun is farthest north (**summer solstice**, about June 22) or south (**winter solstice**, about December 22) of the equator

sol·u·ble \'säl-yə-bəl\ *adj* **1** : capable of being dissolved in liquid ⟨sugar is *soluble* in water⟩ **2** : capable of being solved or explained ⟨a *soluble* mystery⟩ ⟨a *soluble* problem⟩

so·lu·tion \sə-'lü-shən\ *n* **1** : the act or process of solving ⟨*solution* of a problem⟩ **2** : the result of solving a problem ⟨a correct *solution*⟩ **3** : the act or process by which a solid, liquid, or gaseous substance is dissolved in a liquid **4** : a liquid in which something has been dissolved

solve \'sälv\ *vb* **solved; solv·ing** : to find the answer to or a solution for

sol·vent \'säl-vənt\ *n* : a usually liquid substance capable of dissolving another substance ⟨water is a *solvent* for sugar⟩

som·ber *or* **som·bre** \'säm-bər\ *adj* **1** : being dark and gloomy : DULL ⟨*somber* colors⟩ **2** : GRAVE, MELANCHOLY ⟨a *somber* mood⟩

som·bre·ro \səm-'brear-ō\ *n*, *pl* **som·bre·ros** [from Spanish, derived from *sombra* "shade"] : a high-crowned hat of felt or straw with a very wide brim worn especially in the Southwest and Mexico

sombrero

¹some \'səm *or, for 3, without stress*\ *adj* **1** : being one unknown or not specified ⟨*some* man called⟩ **2** : being one, a part, or an unspecified or indefinite number of something named or implied ⟨*some* gems are hard⟩ **3** : being of an unspecified amount or number ⟨buy *some* flour⟩ **4** : being at least one and sometimes all of ⟨*some* years ago⟩

²some \'səm\ *pron* : a certain number or portion ⟨you can fool *some* of the people *some* of the time⟩

¹-some \səm\ *adj suffix* : characterized by a specified thing, quality, state, or action ⟨awe*some*⟩ ⟨burden*some*⟩

---

j job   ng sing   ō low   ȯ moth   ȯi coin   th thin   th̲ this   ü boot   u̇ foot   y you   yü few   yu̇ furious   zh vision

²-some *n suffix* : group of a specified number of members and especially persons ⟨four*some*⟩

¹some·bod·y \'səm-ˌbäd-ē\ *pron* : some person

²somebody *n, pl* **some·bod·ies** : a person of importance ⟨thinks himself a *somebody*⟩

some·how \'səm-ˌhau̇\ *adv* : in one way or another

some·one \'səm-ˌwən\ *pron* : some person

¹som·er·sault \'səm-ər-ˌsȯlt\ *n* : a leap or roll in which a person turns his heels over his head

²somersault *vb* : to turn a somersault

som·er·set \'səm-ər-ˌset\ *n or vb* : SOMER-SAULT

some·thing \'səm-thiŋ\ *pron* **1** : a thing that is not decided, settled, or understood **2** : a thing or amount that is definite but not named

some·time \'səm-ˌtīm\ *adv* **1** : at a future time ⟨will pay *sometime*⟩ **2** : at a time not known or not specified

some·times \'səm-ˌtīmz\ *adv* : now and then : OCCASIONALLY

¹some·what \'səm-ˌhwät\ *pron* : a little bit ⟨he's *somewhat* of a coward⟩

²somewhat *adv* : in some degree ⟨*somewhat* relieved⟩

some·where \'səm-ˌhweər\ *adv* **1** : in, at, or to a place not known or named **2** : at some unspecified time ⟨*somewhere* about two o'clock⟩

son \'sən\ *n* **1** : a male offspring or descendant **2** *cap* : the second person of the Trinity **3** : a man or boy closely associated with or thought of as a child of something (as a country, race, or religion) ⟨hardy *sons* of the soil⟩

song \'sȯŋ\ *n* **1** : vocal music **2** : poetic composition : POETRY **3** : a short musical composition of words and music **4** : a small amount ⟨can be bought for a *song*⟩

song·bird \'sȯŋ-ˌbərd\ *n* : a bird that sings

song·ster \'sȯŋ-stər\ *n* : a person or a bird that sings

son-in-law \'sən-ən-ˌlȯ\ *n, pl* **sons-in-law** : the husband of one's daughter

son·ny \'sən-ē\ *n, pl* **son·nies** : a young boy — used chiefly as a term of address

so·no·rous \sə-'nȯr-əs, 'sän-ə-rəs\ *adj* **1** : producing sound (as when struck) **2** : loud, deep, or rich in sound : RESONANT **3** : imposing or impressive in effect or style

soon \'sün\ *adv* **1** : without delay : before long **2** : PROMPTLY, QUICKLY **3** : EARLY ⟨arrived too *soon*⟩ **4** : READILY, WILLINGLY ⟨he would as *soon* do it now as later⟩

soot \'su̇t, 'sət\ *n* : a black powder formed when something is burned : the very fine powder that colors smoke

soothe \'süth\ *vb* **soothed; sooth·ing 1** : to please by flattery or attention **2** : RELIEVE **3** : to calm down : REASSURE, COMFORT

sooth·say·er \'süth-ˌsā-ər\ *n* : a person who claims to foretell events

soot·y \'su̇t-ē, 'sət-\ *adj* **soot·i·er; soot·i·est 1** : soiled with soot **2** : resembling soot especially in color

sop \'säp\ *vb* **sopped; sop·ping 1** : to steep or dip in or as if in liquid : SOAK **2** : to mop up (as water)

soph·o·more \'säf-ə-ˌmȯr\ *n* : a student in his second year at a college or high school

so·pran·o \sə-'pran-ō\ *n, pl* **so·pran·os 1** : the part in music sung by the highest female voice **2** : a voice or a singer that sings the soprano part

sor·cer·er \'sȯr-sər-ər\ *n* : a person who practices sorcery or witchcraft : WIZARD

sor·cer·ess \'sȯr-sə-rəs\ *n* : a woman sorcerer : WITCH

sor·cer·y \'sȯr-sə-rē\ *n, pl* **sor·cer·ies** : the use of magic : WITCHCRAFT

sor·did \'sȯrd-əd\ *adj* **1** : FILTHY, DIRTY ⟨*sordid* surroundings⟩ **2** : VILE ⟨a *sordid* life⟩

¹sore \'sȯr\ *adj* **1** : causing pain or distress ⟨*sore* news⟩ **2** : painfully sensitive : TENDER ⟨muscles *sore* from exercise⟩ **3** : hurt or inflamed so as to be or seem painful **4** : ANGERED, VEXED — **sore·ly** *adv* — **sore·ness** *n*

²sore *n* : a sore spot (as an ulcer) on the body usually with the skin broken or bruised and often with infection

sor·ghum \'sȯr-gəm\ *n* **1** : a tall grass similar to Indian corn that includes sorgo and other forms used for forage and grain **2** : syrup from sorgo juice

sor·go \'sȯr-gō\ *n, pl* **sor·gos** : a sorghum grown primarily for its sweet juice from which syrup is made and for fodder and silage

sorghum

so·ror·i·ty \sə-'rȯr-ət-ē\ *n, pl* **so·ror·i·ties** [from medieval Latin *sororitas* "sisterhood", from Latin *soror* "sister"] : a club of girls or women especially at a college

¹sor·rel \'sȯr-əl\ *n* **1** : an animal (as a horse) of a sorrel color **2** : a brownish orange to light brown

²sorrel *n* : any of several plants with sour juice

¹sor·row \'sär-ō\ *n* **1** : sadness or anguish caused by loss (as of something loved) **2** : a cause of grief or sadness **3** : REPENTANCE

²**sorrow** *vb* : to feel or express sorrow : GRIEVE

sor·row·ful \'sär-ō-fəl\ *adj* 1 : full of or marked by sorrow 2 : expressive of or arousing sorrow

sor·ry \'sär-ē\ *adj* **sor·ri·er; sor·ri·est** 1 : feeling sorrow, repentance, or regret ⟨*sorry* for his mistake⟩ 2 : inspiring sorrow, pity, scorn, or ridicule : WRETCHED ⟨a *sorry* sight⟩

¹**sort** \'sȯrt\ *n* 1 : a group of persons or things that have similar characteristics : CLASS ⟨all *sorts* of people⟩ 2 : general character or disposition : NATURE ⟨people of an evil *sort*⟩ 3 : PERSON, INDIVIDUAL ⟨he's not a bad *sort*⟩ — **out of sorts** 1 : IRRITABLE 2 : not well

²**sort** *vb* : to separate and arrange according to kind, class, or nature : CLASSIFY ⟨*sort* mail⟩

SOS \ˌes-ō-'es\ *n* : an international radio code distress signal used especially by ships and airplanes calling for help : a call for help

¹**so-so** \'sō-'sō\ *adv* : PASSABLY

²**so-so** *adj* : neither very good nor very bad

sought *past of* SEEK

soul \'sōl\ *n* 1 : the spiritual part of man believed to give life to his body 2 : man's moral and emotional nature : FERVOR 3 : the essential part of something 4 : the moving spirit : LEADER ⟨the *soul* of an enterprise⟩ 5 : a human being : PERSON ⟨a kind *soul*⟩

¹**sound** \'saund\ *adj* 1 : free from flaw or decay ⟨*sound* timbers⟩ 2 : free from disease or weakness : HEALTHY ⟨a *sound* body⟩ 3 : SOLID, FIRM ⟨a building of *sound* construction⟩ 4 : STABLE 5 : not faulty : RIGHT ⟨a *sound* argument⟩ 6 : showing good sense : WISE ⟨*sound* advice⟩ 7 : HONORABLE, HONEST ⟨*sound* principles⟩ 8 : THOROUGH ⟨a *sound* beating⟩ 9 : UNDISTURBED, DEEP ⟨a *sound* sleep⟩ **syn** see VALID — **sound·ly** *adv* — **sound·ness** *n*

²**sound** *adv* : SOUNDLY ⟨*sound* asleep⟩

³**sound** *n* 1 : the sensation experienced through the sense of hearing : an instance or occurrence of this : NOISE 2 : one of the noises that together make up human speech ⟨the *sound* of *th* in *this*⟩ 3 : a mental impression carried or given by something heard or read ⟨this excuse has a suspicious *sound*⟩ 4 : hearing distance — **sound·less** \'saund-ləs\ *adj* — **sound·less·ly** *adv*

⁴**sound** *vb* 1 : to make or cause to make a sound or noise ⟨*sound* the trumpet⟩ 2 : to make known : PROCLAIM ⟨*sound* the alarm⟩ 3 : to order, signal, or indicate by a sound ⟨*sound* the words clearly⟩ 4 : to make or give an impression : SEEM ⟨the story *sounds* false⟩ 5 : to examine the condition of by causing to emit sounds ⟨*sound* the lungs⟩

⁵**sound** *n* : a long passage of water that is wider than a strait and often connects two larger bodies of water or forms a channel between the mainland and an island

⁶**sound** *vb* 1 : to measure the depth of (as by a weighted line dropped down from the surface) : FATHOM 2 : to find or try to find the thoughts or motives of a person : PROBE ⟨*sounded* him out on the idea⟩

sound·proof \'saund-'prüf\ *adj* : capable of keeping sound from entering or escaping ⟨a *soundproof* room⟩

sound wave *n* : a wave that somewhat resembles a wave in water, is produced when a sound is made, and is responsible for carrying the sound to the ear

soup \'süp\ *n* : a liquid food made of vegetable, meat, or fish stock often containing pieces of solid food

¹**sour** \'saur\ *adj* 1 : having an acid or tart taste 2 : having become acid through fermentation ⟨*sour* milk⟩ 3 : indicating decay ⟨a *sour* smell⟩ 4 : UNPLEASANT, DISAGREEABLE ⟨a *sour* look⟩ 5 : acid in reaction ⟨*sour* soil⟩ — **sour·ish** *adj* — **sour·ly** *adv* — **sour·ness** *n*

²**sour** *vb* : to make or become sour

source \'sōrs\ *n* 1 : the beginning of a stream of water 2 : BEGINNING, ORIGIN 3 : one that supplies information

¹**south** \'sauth\ *adv* : to or toward the south

²**south** *adj* : situated toward or coming from the south

³**south** *n* 1 : the direction to the right of one facing east : the compass point opposite to north 2 *cap* : regions or countries south of a specified or implied point

¹**South American** *adj* : of or relating to South America or the South Americans

²**South American** *n* : a native or inhabitant of South America

south·bound \'sauth-ˌbaund\ *adj* : going south

¹**south·east** \sauth-'ēst\ *adv* : to or toward the southeast

²**southeast** *n* 1 : the direction between south and east 2 *cap* : regions or countries southeast of a specified or implied point

³**southeast** *adj* : situated toward or coming from the southeast

south·east·ern \sauth-'ēs-tərn\ *adj* 1 *often cap* : of or relating to a region usually called Southeast 2 : lying toward or coming from the southeast

south·er·ly \'səth-ər-lē\ *adv (or adj)* 1 : from the south ⟨a *southerly* wind⟩ 2 : toward the south

---

j job   ng sing   ō low   ȯ moth   ȯi coin   th thin   t͟h this   ü boot   u̇ foot   y you   yü few   yu̇ furious   zh vision

south·ern \'səth-ərn\ *adj* **1** *often cap* : of or relating to a region usually called South **2** : lying toward or coming from the south

south·paw \'saůth-ˌpȯ\ *n* : a person (as a baseball pitcher) who is left-handed

south pole *n, often cap S & P* **1** : the most southern point of the earth : the southern end of the earth's axis **2** : the end of a magnet that points toward the south when the magnet is free to swing

¹south·ward \'saůth-wərd\ *adv* (*or adj*) : toward the south

²southward *n* : a southward direction or part

¹south·west \saůth-'west\ *adv* : to or toward the southwest

²southwest *n* **1** : the direction between south and west **2** *cap* : regions or countries southwest of a specified or implied point

³southwest *adj* : situated toward or coming from the southwest

south·west·ern \saůth-'wes-tərn\ *adj* **1** *often cap* : of or relating to a region usually called Southwest **2** : lying toward or coming from the southwest

sou·ve·nir \'sü-və-ˌniər\ *n* : something that serves as a reminder : REMEMBRANCE

sou'·west·er \saů-'wes-tər\ *n* **1** : a long oilskin coat worn especially at sea during stormy weather **2** : a waterproof hat with wide slanting brim longer in back than in front

sou'wester

¹sov·er·eign \'säv-ə-rən\ *n* **1** : a person (as a king) or body of persons possessing the supreme power and authority in a state **2** : a gold coin of Great Britain worth one pound sterling

²sovereign *adj* **1** : CHIEF, HIGHEST ⟨our *sovereign* interest⟩ **2** : supreme in power or authority ⟨a *sovereign* prince⟩ **3** : having independent authority ⟨a *sovereign* state⟩ **4** : EFFECTIVE, EXCELLENT ⟨a *sovereign* remedy⟩

sov·er·eign·ty \'säv-ə-rən-tē\ *n, pl* **sov·er·eign·ties 1** : the condition of being sovereign or a sovereign : supreme rule or power **2** : freedom from external control **3** : one that is sovereign

¹sow \'saů\ *n* : an adult female swine

²sow \'sō\ *vb* **sowed**; **sown** \'sōn\ *or* **sowed**; **sow·ing 1** : to plant or scatter (as seed) for growing **2** : to strew with or as if with seed for growing ⟨*sow* a field to oats⟩ **3** : to spread abroad : DISPERSE ⟨*sow* discontent⟩ — **sow·er** *n*

sow bug \'saů-\ *n* : WOOD LOUSE

sox *pl of* SOCK

soy·bean \'sȯi-'bēn\ *n* : a hairy annual Asiatic plant related to the clovers that is widely grown especially for its edible seeds which yield a valuable oil (**soybean oil**) and a protein-rich residue (**soybean oil meal** or **soybean meal**) much used in animal feeds and in the chemical industry

¹space \'spās\ *n* **1** : a period of time **2** : the limitless area in which all things exist and move **3** : a measurable part of a distance, area, or volume **4** : a definite place set apart or available ⟨parking *space*⟩ **5** : one of the degrees between or above or below the lines of a musical staff **6** : the region beyond the earth's atmosphere **7** : an empty place

²space *vb* **spaced**; **spac·ing** : to place at intervals

space·craft \'spās-ˌkraft\ *n* : a man-carrying vehicle for travel beyond the earth's atmosphere

space·ship \'spās-ˌship\ *n* : SPACECRAFT

spa·cious \'spā-shəs\ *adj* : very large in extent

¹spade \'spād\ *n* : a tool with a flat blade for turning over earth

²spade *vb* **spad·ed**; **spad·ing** : to dig with or use a spade

spa·ghet·ti \spə-'get-ē\ *n* [from Italian, where it is a plural meaning literally "little strings"] : a food paste made chiefly of wheat flour dried in thin, solid, stringlike form

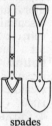
spades

¹span \'span\ *n* **1** : the space from the end of the thumb to the end of the little finger when the hand is stretched wide open **2** : an English unit of length equal to nine inches **3** : a limited portion of time ⟨*span* of life⟩ **4** : the spread (as of an arch) from one support to another

²span *vb* **spanned**; **span·ning 1** : to measure by or as if by the hand stretched wide open **2** : to reach or extend across **3** : to place or construct a span over

³span *n* : two animals (as mules) worked or driven as a pair

span·gle \'spang-gəl\ *n* : a bit of shiny metal used as an ornament (as on a dress)

Span·iard \'span-yərd\ *n* : a native or inhabitant of Spain

span·iel \'span-yəl\ *n* : a small or medium-sized dog with profuse wavy coat, long drooping ears, and usually short legs

¹Span·ish \'span-ish\ *adj* : of or relating to Spain, the people of Spain, or Spanish

²Spanish *n* **1** : the language of

spaniel

Spain and the countries colonized by Span-
iards **2 Spanish** *pl* : the people of Spain

spank \'spangk\ *vb* : to strike on the buttocks
usually with the open hand

spank·ing \'spang-king\ *adj* : BRISK, LIVELY

¹spar \'spär\ *n* : a long rounded piece of wood
or metal (as a mast, yard, or boom) to which a
sail is fastened

²spar *vb* **sparred; spar·ring** **1** : to box with the
fists especially cautiously **2** : SKIRMISH

¹spare \'spaər\ *vb* **spared; spar·ing** **1** : to
keep from being punished or harmed **2** : to
exempt or free from something ⟨be *spared* the
work⟩ **3** : to refrain from : AVOID ⟨*spare* no
cost⟩ **4** : to use frugally ⟨*spare* the rod and
spoil the child⟩ **5** : to give up as not strictly
needed ⟨unable to *spare* a dollar⟩ **6** : to have
left over ⟨time to *spare*⟩

²spare *adj* **1** : not being used : held in reserve ⟨a *spare* tire⟩ **2** : SUPERFLUOUS ⟨*spare*
time⟩ **3** : not liberal or profuse : SPARING ⟨a
spare diet⟩ **4** : somewhat thin **5** : SCANTY

³spare *n* **1** : a spare or duplicate piece or
part **2** : the knocking down of all ten bowling
pins with the first two bowls

spare·ribs \'spaər-,ribz\ *n pl* : a cut of pork
ribs separated from the bacon strip

spar·ing \'spaər-ing\ *adj* : SAVING, FRUGAL —
spar·ing·ly *adv*

¹spark \'spärk\ *n* **1** : a small particle of a
burning substance **2** : a hot glowing particle
struck from a mass (as by steel on flint) **3** : a
bright electric discharge of short duration between two conductors **4** : the mechanism that
controls the electric discharge igniting the
mixture of gasoline and air in an automobile
engine **5** : SPARKLE, FLASH **6** : something that
sets off a sudden force ⟨the *spark* that set off
the rebellion⟩ **7** : a latent particle capable of
growth or development ⟨not a *spark* of life was
found on the island⟩

²spark *vb* **1** : to produce sparks **2** : INCITE

¹spar·kle \'spär-kəl\ *vb* **spar·kled; spar·kling**
1 : to throw off sparks : FLASH, GLISTEN
2 : to perform brilliantly **3** : BUBBLE ⟨a
sparkling wine⟩ **4** : to be lively or active ⟨the
conversation *sparkled*⟩

²sparkle *n* **1** : a little spark : GLEAM, GLITTER
2 : BRILLIANCE, LIVELINESS

spar·kler \'spär-klər\ *n* : a firework that
throws off brilliant sparks on burning

spark plug *n* : a device that produces a spark
for combustion (as in an automobile engine
cylinder)

spar·row \'spar-ō\ *n* : any of various small
dull-colored finches or birds related to the
finches

sparrow hawk *n* : any of various small hawks
or falcons

sparse \'spärs\ *adj* **spars·er; spars·est** : not
thickly grown or settled ⟨*sparse* vegetation⟩
— **sparse·ly** *adv*

spasm \'spaz-əm\ *n* **1** : a sudden involuntary
and usually violent muscular contraction
2 : a sudden, violent, and temporary effort,
emotion, or outburst ⟨a *spasm* of coughing⟩

spas·mod·ic \spaz-'mäd-ik\ *adj* **1** : relating
to or affected or characterized by spasm
⟨*spasmodic* breathing⟩ **2** : going by fits and
starts : FITFUL ⟨*spasmodic* interest⟩ **3** : EX-
CITABLE — **spas·mod·i·cal·ly** \-i-kə-lē\ *adv*

spas·tic \'spas-tik\ *adj* : of, relating to, or
marked by spasm

¹spat \'spat\ *past of* SPIT

²spat *n* : a cloth or leather gaiter covering the
instep and ankle

³spat *n* : a brief petty quarrel
: DISPUTE

⁴spat *vb* **spat·ted; spat·ting** : to
quarrel pettily or briefly : DISPUTE

spat

spa·tial \'spā-shəl\ *adj* : relating
to, occupying, or of the nature of space

¹spat·ter \'spat-ər\ *vb* **1** : to splash with or
as if with a wet substance : SOIL, SPOT ⟨*spatter*
a clean floor⟩ **2** : to scatter by splashing
3 : to injure by slander ⟨*spatter* a good reputa-
tion⟩ **4** : to spurt in drops ⟨water *spattered*
from the faucet⟩ **5** : to drop with a sound like
rain

²spatter *n* **1** : the act or sound of spattering
2 : a drop or splash spattered on something
: a spot or stain due to spattering **3** : a small
number or quantity : SPRINKLE ⟨a *spatter* of
rain⟩

spat·u·la \'spach-ə-lə\ *n* : a knifelike instrument with a broad blade
that bends easily used
especially for spreading
or mixing soft substances

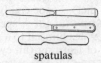

spatulas

¹spawn \'spòn\ *vb* **1** : to
produce or deposit eggs
or spawn ⟨salmon go up rivers to *spawn*⟩
2 : to produce young in large numbers

²spawn *n* **1** : the eggs of a water animal (as an
oyster or fish) that produces many small eggs
2 : offspring especially in large numbers

spay \'spā\ *vb* : to remove the ovaries of (a
female animal) ⟨a *spayed* cat⟩

speak \'spēk\ *vb* **spoke** \'spōk\; **spo·ken**
\'spō-kən\; **speak·ing** **1** : to utter words
: TALK **2** : to utter by means of words ⟨*speak*
the truth⟩ **3** : to mention in speech or writing
⟨*speak* of being ill⟩ **4** : to carry a meaning as
if by speech ⟨clothes that *spoke* of poverty⟩

5 : to use or be able to use in talking ⟨*speak* French⟩

syn SPEAK, TALK, CONVERSE all mean to express oneself orally. SPEAK is the broadest term and applies to any utterance, whether understandable or not and whether heard or not ⟨we didn't know what language he was *speaking*⟩ ⟨*speak* in whispers, please⟩ TALK implies both a listener and somewhat intelligible expression ⟨the principal wanted to *talk* to us⟩ and very often refers to an actual exchange of ideas ⟨we *talked* well into the night about vacation plans⟩ CONVERSE is used only of an actual interchange of thoughts and opinions ⟨I had hoped for a chance to *converse* with your guest⟩

speak·er \'spē-kər\ *n* **1** : one that speaks **2** : one that presides over a meeting

¹spear \'spiər\ *n* **1** : a weapon with a long shaft and sharp head or blade for throwing or thrusting **2** : a sharp-pointed instrument with barbs used in spearing fish

²spear *vb* : to strike or pierce with or as if with a spear

³spear *n* : a usually young blade, shoot, or sprout (as of grass)

¹spear·head \'spiər-,hed\ *n* **1** : the head or point of a spear **2** : the foremost point, person, or body in an attack or undertaking

²spearhead *vb* : to serve as leader or spearhead of ⟨*spearhead* an undertaking⟩

spear·mint \'spiər-,mint\ *n* : a common mint used for flavoring

spe·cial \'spesh-əl\ *adj* **1** : UNUSUAL, EXTRAORDINARY ⟨a *special* occasion⟩ **2** : regarded with particular favor ⟨a *special* friend⟩ **3** : PECULIAR, UNIQUE ⟨a *special* case⟩ **4** : ADDITIONAL, EXTRA ⟨a *special* edition⟩ **5** : meant for a particular purpose or occasion ⟨a *special* diet⟩ — **spe·cial·ly** *adv*

spe·cial·ist \'spesh-ə-ləst\ *n* : one who devotes himself to a special occupation or branch of learning ⟨an eye *specialist*⟩

spe·cial·ize \'spesh-ə-,līz\ *vb* **spe·cial·ized**; **spe·cial·iz·ing** **1** : to limit one's attention or energy to one business, subject, or study ⟨*specialize* in jet airplanes⟩ **2** : to alter and develop so as to be suited for some particular use or living conditions ⟨*specialized* sense organs⟩

spe·cial·ty \'spesh-əl-tē\ *n, pl* **spe·cial·ties** **1** : a particular quality or detail **2** : a product of a special kind or of special excellence ⟨pancakes were the cook's *specialty*⟩ **3** : a branch of knowledge, business, or professional work in which one specializes

spe·cies \'spē-shēz\ *n, pl* **species** **1** : a class

of things with common qualities and a common name : KIND, SORT **2** : a group of plants or animals that forms a subdivision of a genus and that consists of related individuals potentially able to breed one with another

spe·cif·ic \spi-'sif-ik\ *adj* **1** : of, relating to, or constituting a species **2** : DEFINITE, EXACT ⟨*specific* directions⟩

spec·i·fi·ca·tion \,spes-ə-fə-'kā-shən\ *n* **1** : the act or process of making specific **2** : a single specified item **3** : a description of work to be done or materials to be used — often used in plural ⟨the architect's *specifications* for a new building⟩

spec·i·fy \'spes-ə-,fī\ *vb* **spec·i·fied**; **spec·i·fy·ing** **1** : to mention or name exactly or in detail ⟨*specify* the cause⟩ **2** : to include as an item in a specification ⟨*specify* oak flooring⟩

spec·i·men \'spes-ə-mən\ *n* : a part or a single thing that shows what the whole thing or group is like : SAMPLE

speck \'spek\ *n* **1** : a small spot, stain, or blemish **2** : a small piece or bit : PARTICLE

¹speck·le \'spek-əl\ *n* : a little speck

²speckle *vb* **speck·led**; **speck·ling** : to mark with speckles

spec·ta·cle \'spek-tə-kəl\ *n* **1** : something exhibited to view as unusual or notable **2** : an impressive public display (as a pageant) **3** *pl* : a pair of glasses held in place by parts passing over the ears

spec·tac·u·lar \spek-'tak-yə-lər\ *adj* : STRIKING, SHOWY ⟨a *spectacular* sunset⟩

spec·ta·tor \'spek-,tāt-ər\ *n* : one who looks on (as at a football game)

spec·ter *or* **spec·tre** \'spek-tər\ *n* : GHOST, APPARITION

spec·tral \'spek-trəl\ *adj* : GHOSTLY

spec·trum \'spek-trəm\ *n, pl* **spec·tra** \-trə\ *or* **spec·trums** : the group of different colors including red, orange, yellow, green, blue, indigo, and violet seen when light passes through a prism and falls on a surface or when sunlight is affected by drops of water (as in a rainbow)

spec·u·late \'spek-yə-,lāt\ *vb* **spec·u·lat·ed**; **spec·u·lat·ing** **1** : REFLECT, MEDITATE **2** : to engage in a business deal in which a large profit may be made although at considerable risk

spec·u·la·tion \,spek-yə-'lā-shən\ *n* **1** : THOUGHT, MEDITATION **2** : GUESS **3** : an uncertain business venture

speech \'spēch\ *n* **1** : the communication or expression of thoughts in spoken words **2** : CONVERSATION **3** : something that is spoken **4** : a public or formal talk **5** : LAN-

GUAGE, DIALECT **6** : the power of expressing or communicating thoughts by speaking

speech·less \'spēch-ləs\ *adj* **1** : lacking or deprived of the power of speaking **2** : not speaking for a time : SILENT ⟨*speechless* with surprise⟩

¹speed \'spēd\ *n* **1** : SWIFTNESS, RAPIDITY **2** : rate of motion or performance **syn** see HASTE

²speed *vb* **sped** \'sped\ *or* **speed·ed**; **speed·ing** **1** : to move or cause to move rapidly : HURRY, HASTEN **2** : to go or drive at excessive or illegal speed **3** : to increase the speed of : ACCELERATE **4** : to wish good luck to

speed·boat \'spēd-ˌbōt\ *n* : a fast launch or motorboat

speed·om·e·ter \spi-'däm-ət-ər\ *n* **1** : an instrument that measures speed **2** : an instrument that measures speed and records distance traveled

speed·y \'spēd-ē\ *adj* **speed·i·er**; **speed·i·est** : rapid in motion : FAST, SWIFT — **speed·i·ly** \'spēd-l-ē\ *adv*

¹spell \'spel\ *n* **1** : a spoken word or group of words believed to have magic power : CHARM **2** : a strong compelling influence ⟨an evil *spell*⟩

²spell *vb* **1** : to read slowly and with difficulty ⟨*spell* out the page⟩ **2** : to name, write, or print in order the letters of a word **3** : to constitute the letters of ⟨*c-a-t spells* the word *cat*⟩ **4** : MEAN, SIGNIFY ⟨another drought may *spell* famine⟩

³spell *vb* **1** : to take the place of for a time : RELIEVE ⟨*spell* a person at shoveling⟩ **2** : to allow rest to ⟨the man *spelled* his horse⟩

⁴spell *n* **1** : one's turn at work or duty **2** : a period spent in a job or occupation **3** : a short period of time **4** : a stretch of a specified kind of weather **5** : a period of bodily or mental distress or disorder : ATTACK ⟨fainting *spell*⟩

spell·bound \'spel-'baùnd\ *adj* : ENTRANCED, FASCINATED

spell·er \'spel-ər\ *n* **1** : one that spells words **2** : a book with exercises for teaching spelling

spell·ing \'spel-ing\ *n* **1** : the forming of words from letters according to accepted usage **2** : the letters composing a word

spend \'spend\ *vb* **spent** \'spent\; **spend·ing** **1** : to use up : pay out : EXPEND **2** : to wear out : EXHAUST **3** : to use wastefully : SQUANDER **4** : to cause or permit to elapse : PASS ⟨*spend* the evening at home⟩ **5** : to make use of : EMPLOY

spend·thrift \'spend-ˌthrift\ *n* : one who spends lavishly or wastefully

spent \'spent\ *adj* **1** : used up : CONSUMED **2** : drained of energy : EXHAUSTED

sperm \'spərm\ *n* : SPERM CELL

sper·ma·ce·ti \ˌspər-mə-'set-ē\ *n* : a waxy solid found mixed with oil in a cavity in the head of a sperm whale and used in ointments, cosmetics, and candles

sperm cell *n* : a male germ cell

sperm whale *n* : a large whale of warm seas hunted for its spermaceti and its oil (**sperm oil**)

spew \'spyü\ *vb* : to pour forth : VOMIT

sphere \'sfiər\ *n* **1** : a figure so shaped that every point on its surface is an equal distance from the center of the figure **2** : a ball-shaped body (as the moon) **3** : place or scene of action or life ⟨a subject outside one's *sphere*⟩

spher·i·cal \'sfir-i-kəl, 'sfer-\ *adj* : relating to or having the form of a sphere

sphinx \'sfingks\ *n* **1** : a monster in ancient Greek mythology having a lion's body, wings, and the head and bust of a woman **2** : a person whose character and motives are hard to understand **3** : an Egyptian figure having the body of a lion and the head of a man, a ram, or a hawk

sphinx 3

¹spice \'spīs\ *n* **1** : a pungent or aromatic plant product (as pepper or nutmeg) used to season or flavor food **2** : something that adds interest or relish ⟨variety is the *spice* of life⟩

²spice *vb* **spiced**; **spic·ing** : to season with or as if with spices

spick–and–span \ˌspik-ən-'span\ *adj* **1** : FRESH, BRAND-NEW **2** : spotlessly clean and neat

spic·y \'spī-sē\ *adj* **spic·i·er**; **spic·i·est** **1** : flavored with or containing spice **2** : SHARP, KEEN ⟨a *spicy* debate⟩ **3** : somewhat scandalous or obscene

spi·der \'spīd-ər\ *n* **1** : a wingless animal resembling a true insect but having eight legs instead of six and a body divided into two parts instead of three **2** : a cast-iron frying pan

spider

spi·der·web \'spīd-ər-ˌweb\ *n* : the silken web spun by most spiders and used as a resting place and a trap for prey

spig·ot \'spig-ət, 'spik-\ *n* **1** : a pin or peg used to stop the vent in a cask **2** : FAUCET

¹spike \'spīk\ *n* **1** : a very large nail **2** : one of the metal projections set in the heel and sole of a shoe to prevent slipping (as in some sports) **3** : something shaped like a very large nail

spikes 2

²**spike** *vb* **spiked; spik·ing** **1** : to fasten or furnish with spikes **2** : to suppress or block completely ⟨*spike* a rumor⟩ **3** : to pierce or cut with or on a spike

³**spike** *n* **1** : an ear of grain ⟨*spikes* of wheat⟩ **2** : a long usually rather narrow flower cluster in which the blossoms grow very close to a central stem

spike of barley

¹**spill** \'spil\ *vb* **spilled** \'spild\ *also* **spilt** \'spilt\; **spill·ing** **1** : to cause blood to flow : SHED **2** : to cause or allow accidentally to fall, flow, or run out ⟨*spill* water⟩ **3** : to fall or run out with resulting loss or waste ⟨the milk *spilled*⟩ **4** : to let out : DIVULGE ⟨*spill* a secret⟩

²**spill** *n* **1** : an act or instance of spilling **2** : a fall from a horse or vehicle **3** : something spilled

¹**spin** \'spin\ *vb* **spun** \'spən\; **spin·ning** **1** : to draw out and twist into yarn or thread ⟨*spin* flax⟩ **2** : to produce by drawing out and twisting fibers ⟨*spin* thread⟩ **3** : to form threads or a web or cocoon by giving off a sticky fluid that quickly hardens into silk **4** : to revolve rapidly : TWIRL ⟨*spin* a top⟩ **5** : to be dizzy ⟨my head was *spinning*⟩ **6** : to make up and extend to great length : PROLONG ⟨*spin* out a story⟩ **7** : to move swiftly on wheels or in a vehicle **8** : to make, shape, or produce as if by spinning ⟨*spun* glass⟩

²**spin** *n* **1** : a rapid rotating motion : WHIRL **2** : an excursion in a wheeled vehicle

spin·ach \'spin-ich\ *n* [from early French *espinache*, from Spanish *espinaca*, from Arabic *isbānākh*, from Persian *isfānākh*] : a leafy plant that is grown for use as food

spi·nal \'spīn-l\ *adj* : of, relating to, or located near the backbone or spinal cord — **spi·nal·ly** *adv*

spinal column *n* : BACKBONE

spinal cord *n* : the thick cord of nervous tissue that extends from the brain down the back, occupies the cavity of the spinal column, and is concerned especially with reflex action

spin·dle \'spin-dl\ *n* **1** : a slender round rod or stick with tapered ends by which thread is twisted in spinning and on which it is wound **2** : something (as an axle or shaft) which is shaped or turned like a spindle or on which something turns

spin·dling \'spin-dling\ *adj* : being long or tall and thin and usually feeble or frail

spin·dly \'spin-dlē\ *adj* **spin·dli·er; spin·dli·est** : SPINDLING

spine \'spīn\ *n* **1** : BACKBONE **2** : a stiff pointed outgrowth of a plant or animal

spine·less \'spīn-ləs\ *adj* **1** : lacking spines **2** : having no backbone **3** : lacking spirit, courage, or determination : WEAK

spin·et \'spin-ət\ *n* : a small upright piano

spin·ning jen·ny \'spin-ing-,jen-ē\ *n* : a machine for spinning wool or cotton by means of many spindles

spinet

spinning wheel *n* : a small hand-driven or foot-driven machine that is used to spin yarn or thread

spin·ster \'spin-stər\ *n* : an unmarried woman past the common age for marrying

spinning wheel

spin·y \'spī-nē\ *adj* **spin·i·er; spin·i·est** : covered with or resembling spines : THORNY

spir·a·cle \'spir-ə-kəl\ *n* : an opening (as in the head of a whale or the abdomen of an insect) for breathing

¹**spi·ral** \'spī-rəl\ *adj* **1** : circling around a center like the thread of a screw ⟨a *spiral* staircase⟩ **2** : winding or circling around a center and gradually getting closer to or farther away from it ⟨*spiral* curve of a watch spring⟩ — **spi·ral·ly** *adv*

²**spiral** *n* **1** : a single turn or coil in a spiral object **2** : something that has a spiral form

³**spiral** *vb* **spi·raled** *or* **spi·ralled; spi·ral·ing** *or* **spi·ral·ling** **1** : to move in a spiral course **2** : to form into a spiral

spire \'spīr\ *n* **1** : a slender tapering blade or stalk (as of grass) **2** : a sharp pointed tip (as of an antler) **3** : STEEPLE

spi·re·a *or* **spi·rae·a** \spī-'rē-ə\ *n* : a shrub related to the roses that bears clusters of small white or pink flowers

¹**spir·it** \'spir-ət\ *n* **1** : a force within man held to give his body life, energy, and power : SOUL **2** *cap* : the active presence of God in human life : the third person of the Trinity **3** : a supernatural being : GHOST **4** : a supernatural being that enters into and controls a person **5** : MOOD, DISPOSITION ⟨in good *spirits*⟩ **6** : mental vigor or animation : VIVACITY **7** : real meaning or intention ⟨the *spirit* of the law⟩ **8** : an emotion, frame of mind, or inclination governing one's actions ⟨said in a *spirit* of fun⟩ **9** : PERSON ⟨a bold *spirit*⟩ **10** : a distilled alcoholic liquor — usually used in plural **11** *pl* : a solution in alcohol ⟨*spirits* of camphor⟩ — **spir·it·less** \-ləs\ *adj*

²**spirit** *vb* : to carry off secretly or mysteriously

spir·it·ed \'spir-ət-əd\ *adj* : full of spirit, courage, or energy : LIVELY, ANIMATED

¹spir·i·tu·al \'spir-i-chə-wəl\ *adj* **1** : of, relating to, or consisting of spirit : not bodily or material **2** : SACRED, RELIGIOUS — **spir·i·tu·al·ly** *adv*

²spiritual *n* : a Negro religious song especially of the southern United States usually of a deeply emotional character

¹spit \'spit\ *n* **1** : a thin pointed rod for holding meat to be roasted over a fire **2** : a small point of land that runs out into a body of water

²spit *vb* **spit·ted; spit·ting** : to pierce with or as if with a spit

³spit *vb* **spit** *or* **spat** \'spat\; **spit·ting** **1** : to eject (as saliva) from the mouth **2** : to express by or as if by spitting ⟨*spitting* a sarcastic reply⟩ **3** : to give off usually briskly : EMIT ⟨the fire is *spitting* sparks⟩ **4** : to rain or snow in flurries

⁴spit *n* **1** : SALIVA **2** : the act of spitting **3** : a secretion given out by some insects **4** : perfect likeness ⟨the boy was the *spit* and image of his father⟩

¹spite \'spīt\ *n* : dislike or hatred for another person with a wish to annoy, anger, or defeat — **in spite of** : in defiance or contempt of.

²spite *vb* **spit·ed; spit·ing** **1** : to treat with spite **2** : ANNOY, OFFEND ⟨did it to *spite* me⟩

spite·ful \'spīt-fəl\ *adj* : filled with or showing spite : MALICIOUS

spit·tle \'spit-l\ *n* : ⁴SPIT 1, 3

¹splash \'splash\ *vb* **1** : to strike a liquid or semifluid substance and cause it to move and scatter roughly ⟨*splash* water⟩ **2** : to wet or soil by dashing water or mud on : SPATTER ⟨*splashed* by a passing car⟩ **3** : to move or strike with a splashing sound ⟨*splash* through a puddle⟩ **4** : to spread or scatter like a splashed liquid ⟨a painting *splashed* with color⟩ **5** : to display prominently ⟨*splashed* the news all over the front page⟩

²splash *n* **1** : splashed material **2** : a spot or daub from or as if from splashed liquid : SPATTER **3** : the sound or action of splashing

¹splat·ter \'splat-ər\ *vb* : SPLASH, SPATTER

²splatter *n* : SPLASH

splen·did \'splen-dəd\ *adj* **1** : having or showing splendor : SHINING, BRILLIANT **2** : SHOWY, MAGNIFICENT ⟨a *splendid* palace⟩ **3** : GRAND **4** : EXCELLENT ⟨a *splendid* idea⟩ — **splen·did·ly** *adv*

splen·dor \'splen-dər\ *n* **1** : great brightness : BRILLIANCY ⟨the *splendor* of the sun⟩ **2** : POMP, GLORY ⟨the *splendors* of ancient Rome⟩

¹splice \'splīs\ *vb* **spliced; splic·ing** **1** : to unite (as two ropes) by weaving the strands

together **2** : to unite (as rails or timbers) by lapping the ends together and making them fast

²splice *n* : a joining or joint made by splicing

splint \'splint\ *n* **1** : a thin flexible strip of wood interwoven with others in making a chair seat or basket **2** : SPLINTER **3** : a device made of stiff material for keeping in proper position a broken or displaced bone in a limb

splice

¹splin·ter \'splint-ər\ *n* : a thin piece split or torn off lengthwise : SLIVER

²splinter *vb* : to divide or break into splinters ⟨a *splintered* board⟩

¹split \'split\ *vb* **split; split·ting** **1** : to divide lengthwise or by layers : CLEAVE ⟨*split* a log⟩ **2** : to separate the parts of by putting something between ⟨the river *split* the town⟩ **3** : to burst or break apart or in pieces **4** : to divide into shares, parts, or sections — **split hairs** : to make very fine or too fine distinctions

²split *n* **1** : a product or result of splitting : CRACK **2** : the act or process of splitting : DIVISION ⟨a *split* in a political party⟩ **3** : the feat of lowering oneself to the floor or leaping into the air with the legs extended in a straight line and in opposite directions

³split *adj* : divided by or as if by splitting ⟨a *split* lip⟩

splotch \'spläch\ *n* : BLOTCH, SPOT

¹spoil \'spȯil\ *n* : things taken by violence : stolen goods : BOOTY

²spoil *vb* **spoiled** \'spȯild\ *or* **spoilt** \'spȯilt\; **spoil·ing** **1** : PLUNDER, ROB **2** : to damage seriously : RUIN **3** : to damage the quality or effect of ⟨a quarrel *spoiled* the celebration⟩ **4** : to decay or lose freshness, value, or usefulness by being kept too long **5** : to damage or injure the character or disposition of by pampering ⟨*spoil* a child⟩

¹spoke \'spōk\ *past of* SPEAK

²spoke *n* **1** : one of the bars or rods extending from the hub of a wheel to the rim **2** : a rung of a ladder

¹spo·ken \'spō-kən\ *past part of* SPEAK

spoke

²spoken *adj* **1** : delivered by word of mouth : ORAL **2** : used in speaking : UTTERED ⟨the *spoken* word⟩ **3** : speaking in a specified manner ⟨soft-*spoken*⟩

spokes·man \'spōks-mən\ *n, pl* **spokes·men** \-mən\ : a person who speaks for another or for others

¹sponge \'spənj\ *n* **1** : a springy porous mass of horny fibers that forms the skeleton of a group of sea animals, is able to absorb water freely, and is used for cleaning 2 : any of a group of lowly water animals that are essentially two-layered cell colonies and that include those whose skeletons are sponges 3 : a manufactured product (as of rubber or plastic) having the elastic porous quality of natural sponge 4 : a pad of folded gauze used in surgery and medicine 5 : a spongelike substance (as raised dough or a whipped dessert)

²**sponge** *vb* **sponged; spong·ing 1** : to bathe, clean, or wipe with a sponge 2 : to absorb with or as if with or like a sponge 3 : to get something from or live on another by imposing on hospitality or good nature

spong·y \'spən-jē\ *adj* **spong·i·er; spong·i·est** : resembling a sponge in appearance or in absorbency : being soft and full of holes or moisture : not firm

¹**spon·sor** \'spän-sər\ *n* [from Latin, literally "one who promises", from *spondēre* "to pledge", "promise"] **1** : a person who takes the responsibility for some other person or thing ⟨agreed to be his *sponsor* at the club⟩ **2** : GODPARENT **3** : a person or an organization that pays for or plans and carries out a project or activity **4** : a person or an organization that pays the cost of a radio or television program — **spon·sor·ship** \-,ship\ *n*

²**sponsor** *vb* : to act as sponsor for

spon·ta·ne·ous \spän-'tā-nē-əs\ *adj* **1** : done, said, or produced freely and naturally ⟨*spontaneous* laughter⟩ **2** : acting or taking place without external force or cause — **spon·ta·ne·ous·ly** *adv*

spontaneous combustion *n* : a bursting into flame of material by the heat produced within itself through chemical action

spook \'spük\ *n* : GHOST, SPECTER

spook·y \'spü-kē\ *adj* **spook·i·er; spook·i·est 1** : resembling a spook ⟨a *spooky* figure⟩ **2** : suggesting the presence of spooks ⟨a *spooky* place⟩

¹**spool** \'spül\ *n* : a small cylinder with rimmed or ridged ends on which thread or wire is wound

²**spool** *vb* : to wind on a spool

¹**spoon** \'spün\ *n* **1** : a utensil with a shallow bowl and a handle used especially in cooking and eating **2** : something that resembles a spoon

spool

²**spoon** *vb* : to take up in or as if in a spoon

spoon·bill \'spün-,bil\ *n* : a long-legged wading bird related to the ibises and having a bill that widens and flattens at the tip

spoon·ful \'spün-,ful\ *n, pl* **spoon·fuls** \-,fulz\ *or* **spoons·ful** \'spünz-,ful\ : as much as a spoon can hold

spore \'spōr\ *n* : a primitive and usually one-celled reproductive body of various plants and some lower animals that can produce a new individual — **spored** \'spōrd\ *adj*

¹**sport** \'spōrt\ *vb* **1** : to amuse oneself : FROLIC **2** : to speak or act in fun or in jest **3** : to make usually ostentatious display of ⟨*sport* new shoes⟩

²**sport** *n* **1** : RECREATION, PASTIME **2** : physical activity (as hunting or an athletic game) engaged in for pleasure **3** : JEST **4** : MOCKERY, DERISION **5** : LAUGHINGSTOCK, BUTT **6** : SPORTSMAN **7** : a person devoted to a gay easy life **syn** see GAME

sports·man \'spōrts-mən\ *n, pl* **sports·men** \-mən\ **1** : a person who engages in or is interested in sports and especially outdoor sports **2** : a person who is fair and generous and a good loser and a modest winner

sports·man·ship \'spōrts-mən-,ship\ *n* : conduct befitting a good sportsman

¹**spot** \'spät\ *n* **1** : a blemish or stain on character or reputation : FAULT **2** : a small part different (as in color) from the main part **3** : an area marred or marked (as by dirt) **4** : PLACE, POSITION ⟨a good *spot* for a picnic⟩ — **spot·ted** \'spät-əd\ *adj* — **on the spot 1** : IMMEDIATELY **2** : at the place of action **3** : in difficulty or danger

²**spot** *vb* **spot·ted; spot·ting 1** : to mark or be marked with spots : BLEMISH, STAIN **2** : to single out : IDENTIFY ⟨*spot* a friend in the crowd⟩

spot·less \'spät-ləs\ *adj* : free from spot or blemish : immaculately clean or pure ⟨kept his name *spotless*⟩ — **spot·less·ly** *adv* — **spot·less·ness** *n*

¹**spot·light** \'spät-,līt\ *n* **1** : a spot of light used to show up a particular area, person, or thing (as on a stage) **2** : conspicuous public notice **3** : a light designed to direct a narrow intense beam of light on a small area

²**spotlight** *vb* **1** : to light up with a spotlight **2** : to bring to public notice : EMPHASIZE

spot·ty \'spät-ē\ *adj* **spot·ti·er; spot·ti·est 1** : SPOTTED **2** : not uniform especially in quality : UNEVEN ⟨*spotty* attendance⟩

spouse \'spaus\ *n* : a married person : HUSBAND, WIFE

¹**spout** \'spaut\ *vb* **1** : to throw out liquid in a jet or stream ⟨wells *spouting* oil⟩ **2** : to speak or utter readily, pompously, and at length **3** : to flow out with force or in a jet : SPURT ⟨blood *spouted* from the wound⟩

ə abut ər further a ax ā age ä father, cot à (see key page) aù out ch chin e less ē easy g gift i trip ī life

²spout *n* **1** : a tube, pipe, or hole through which something (as rainwater) spouts **2** : a jet of liquid

¹sprain \'sprān\ *n* **1** : a sudden or violent twisting of a joint with stretching or tearing of ligaments **2** : a sprained condition

²sprain *vb* : to subject to sprain ⟨*sprain* an ankle⟩

sprang *past of* SPRING

¹sprawl \'sprȯl\ *vb* **1** : to lie or sit with arms and legs spread out carelessly or awkwardly **2** : to spread out irregularly or awkwardly ⟨a *sprawling* city⟩

²sprawl *n* : the act or posture of sprawling

¹spray \'sprā\ *n* : a green or flowering branch or a usually flat arrangement of these

²spray *n* **1** : liquid flying in fine drops or particles like water blown from a wave **2** : a jet of fine vapor (as from an atomizer) **3** : a device (as an atomizer) for scattering a spray of liquid or vapor

³spray *vb* **1** : to scatter, blow out, or let fall in a spray ⟨*spray* paint⟩ **2** : to discharge spray on or into ⟨*spray* an orchard⟩ — **spray-er** *n*

spray gun *n* : a device for spraying paints, varnishes, or insect poisons

¹spread \'spred\ *vb* **spread; spread-ing** **1** : to open or expand over a larger area ⟨*spread* out a map⟩ **2** : to stretch out : EXTEND ⟨*spread* her arms wide⟩ **3** : SCATTER, STREW ⟨*spread* fertilizer⟩ **4** : to distribute over a period of time or among a group ⟨*spread* work to make it last⟩ **5** : to apply on a surface ⟨*spread* butter on bread⟩ **6** : COVER, OVERLAY ⟨*spread* a floor with carpet⟩ **7** : to prepare for a meal : SET ⟨*spread* a table⟩ **8** : to pass on from person to person : TRANSMIT ⟨the news *spread* rapidly⟩ ⟨flies *spread* disease⟩ **9** : to stretch or move apart ⟨*spreads* his fingers⟩

spray gun

²spread *n* **1** : the act or process of spreading ⟨the *spread* of education⟩ **2** : EXPANSE, EXTENT ⟨the *spread* of a bird's wings⟩ **3** : a prominent display in a magazine or newspaper **4** : a food to be spread on bread or crackers **5** : a sumptuous meal : FEAST **6** : a cloth cover for a table or bed **7** : distance between two points : GAP

sprig \'sprig\ *n* : a small shoot or twig

spright·ly \'sprīt-lē\ *adj* **spright·li·er; spright-li·est** : LIVELY, SPIRITED

¹spring \'spring\ *vb* **sprang** \'sprang\ *or* **sprung** \'sprəng\; **sprung; spring·ing** **1** : to move suddenly upward or forward : LEAP **2** : to move quickly by elastic force ⟨the lid

sprang shut⟩ **3** : WARP **4** : to shoot up or out ⟨weeds *sprang* up overnight⟩ **5** : to issue by birth or descent ⟨*sprang* from poor parents⟩ **6** : to come into being ⟨hope *springs* eternal⟩ **7** : SPLIT, CRACK ⟨winds *sprang* the masts⟩ **8** : to undergo the opening of (a leak) **9** : to cause to operate suddenly ⟨*spring* a trap⟩ **10** : to make lame : SPRAIN

²spring *n* **1** : a source of supply (as of water issuing from the ground) **2** : SOURCE, CAUSE **3** : the season between winter and summer comprising in the northern hemi-sphere usually the months of March, April, and May or as reckoned as-tronomically extending from the March equinox to the June solstice **4** : a time or season of growth or development **5** : an elastic body or device that recovers its original shape when it is released after being distorted **6** : LEAP, JUMP **7** : ELASTICITY, VIGOR ⟨a *spring* in his step⟩

springs 5

spring·board \'spring-ˌbōrd\ *n* : a flexible board usually secured at one end and used for gymnastics or diving

spring peep·er \-ˈpē-pər\ *n* : a small tree toad of eastern North America whose shrill call is heard in early spring

spring·tide \'spring-ˌtīd\ *n* : SPRINGTIME

spring·time \'spring-ˌtīm\ *n* : the season of spring

spring·y \'spring-ē\ *adj* **spring·i·er; spring·i-est** : ELASTIC, RESILIENT

¹sprin·kle \'spring-kəl\ *vb* **sprin·kled; sprin-kling** **1** : to scatter in drops or particles ⟨*sprinkle* water⟩ **2** : to scatter over or at intervals in or among : wet lightly **3** : to rain lightly — **sprin·kler** \-klər\ *n*

²sprinkle *n* **1** : a light rain **2** : SPRINKLING

sprin·kling \'spring-kling\ *n* : a limited quantity or amount : SCATTERING

¹sprint \'sprint\ *vb* : to run at top speed espe-cially for a short distance — **sprint·er** *n*

²sprint *n* **1** : a short run at top speed **2** : a short-distance race

sprite \'sprīt\ *n* **1** : GHOST, SPIRIT **2** : ELF, FAIRY

sprock·et \'spräk-ət\ *n* : a projection on the rim of a wheel (**sprocket wheel**) shaped so as to interlock with the links of a chain

sprocket

¹sprout \'spraut\ *vb* **1** : to push out or bring forth new shoots : grow rapidly like young shoots　**2** : to cause to sprout ⟨rain *sprouts* seed⟩

²sprout *n* : a plant shoot especially when young and arising directly from a seed or root

¹spruce \'sprüs\ *n* : a conical evergreen tree with a dense foliage of short needles, drooping cones, and light soft wood

²spruce *adj* **spruc·er; spruc·est** : neat or smart in appearance : TRIM

³spruce *vb* **spruced; spruc·ing** : to make or make oneself spruce ⟨*spruce* up a room⟩ ⟨*spruce* up a bit before an interview⟩

spruce: leaves and cones

sprung *past of* SPRING

spry \'sprī\ *adj* **spri·er** *or* **spry·er; spri·est** *or* **spry·est** : NIMBLE, ACTIVE

spun *past of* SPIN

spunk \'spəngk\ *n* : SPIRIT, COURAGE

¹spur \'spər\ *n*　**1** : a pointed device fastened to a rider's boot and used to urge on a horse　**2** : something that stirs or urges to action　**3** : a stiff sharp projection (as a horny spine on the leg of a rooster)　**4** : a ridge or crag extending sideways from a mountain　**5** : a short branch of railway track extending from the main line — **spurred** \'spərd\ *adj*

spur

²spur *vb* **spurred; spur·ring**　**1** : to urge a horse on with spurs　**2** : INCITE, STIMULATE

spurn \'spərn\ *vb*　**1** : to kick aside　**2** : to reject with contempt ⟨*spurn* an offer⟩　**syn** *see* DECLINE

¹spurt \'spərt\ *n* : a burst of increased effort or activity

²spurt *vb* : to make a spurt

³spurt *vb*　**1** : to gush forth : SPOUT　**2** : SQUIRT

⁴spurt *n* : a sudden gush : JET

¹sput·ter \'spət-ər\ *vb*　**1** : to spit or squirt particles of food or saliva noisily from the mouth　**2** : to speak or utter hastily or explosively in confusion or excitement ⟨*sputtered* out his protests⟩　**3** : to make explosive popping sounds ⟨the motor *sputtered* and died⟩

²sputter *n* : the act or sound of sputtering

¹spy \'spī\ *vb* **spied; spy·ing**　**1** : to watch, inspect, or examine secretly ⟨*spy* on an enemy⟩　**2** : to catch sight of : SEE ⟨*spy* land from a ship⟩　**3** : to discover by close examination or search ⟨*spied* out the secrets of the atom⟩

²spy *n, pl* **spies**　**1** : one that watches the conduct of others especially in secret　**2** : one that tries secretly to obtain information for one country in the territory of another usually hostile country

spy·glass \'spī-ˌglas\ *n* : a small telescope

squab \'skwäb\ *n* : a young pigeon especially when about four weeks old and ready for market or table

¹squab·ble \'skwäb-əl\ *n* : a noisy quarrel usually over trifles

²squabble *vb* **squab·bled; squab·bling** : to quarrel noisily and to no purpose : WRANGLE

squad \'skwäd\ *n*　**1** : a small unit of soldiers　**2** : a small group engaged in a common effort or occupation ⟨a football *squad*⟩

squad car *n* : CRUISER 2

squad·ron \'skwäd-rən\ *n*　**1** : a group in regular formation　**2** : a cavalry unit　**3** : a group of naval vessels　**4** : an air fleet or a division of an air fleet

squal·id \'skwäl-əd\ *adj*　**1** : filthy or degraded from neglect or poverty　**2** : SORDID, DEBASED

¹squall \'skwòl\ *vb* : to cry out or scream violently

²squall *n* : a sudden violent gust of wind often with rain or snow

squal·or \'skwäl-ər\ *n* : the quality or state of being squalid ⟨lived in *squalor*⟩

squan·der \'skwän-dər\ *vb* : to spend foolishly : WASTE

¹square \'skwaər\ *n*　**1** : an instrument having at least one right angle and two or more straight edges used to lay out or test right angles ⟨a carpenter's *square*⟩　**2** : a flat figure that has four equal sides and four right angles　**3** : something formed like a square ⟨the *squares* of a checkerboard⟩　**4** : the product of a number or quantity multiplied by itself　**5** : an open place or area where two or more streets meet　**6** : BLOCK 6, 7

square 1

square 2

²square *adj*　**1** : having four equal sides and four right angles　**2** : forming a right angle ⟨a *square* corner⟩　**3** : multiplied by itself　**4** : having a shape that suggests strength and solidity ⟨a *square* jaw⟩　**5** : converted from a linear unit into a square unit of area having the same length of side : SQUARED ⟨a *square* foot is the area of a square each side of which is a foot⟩　**6** : being of a specified length in each of two equal dimensions ⟨ten feet *square*⟩　**7** : exactly adjusted　**8** : JUST, FAIR ⟨a *square* deal⟩　**9** : leaving no balance : EVEN ⟨make accounts *square*⟩　**10** : SUBSTANTIAL, SATISFYING ⟨three *square* meals a day⟩ — **square·ly** *adv*

³square *vb* **squared; squar·ing**　**1** : to make

ə abut　ər further　a ax　ā age　ä father, cot　ȧ (see key page)　au̇ out　ch chin　e less　ē easy　g gift　i trip　ī life

square : form with four equal sides and right angles or with right angles and straight lines or with flat surfaces ⟨*square* a timber⟩ **2** : to bring to a right angle ⟨*squared* his shoulders⟩ **3** : to multiply a number by itself **4** : AGREE ⟨his story does not *square* with the facts⟩ **5** : BALANCE, SETTLE ⟨*square* an account⟩

square knot *n* : a knot made of two reverse half-knots and typically used to join the ends of two cords

square–rigged \'skwaər-'rigd\ *adj* : having the principal sails extended on yards fastened to the masts horizontally and at their center

square knot

square root *n* : a factor of a number that when multiplied by itself gives the number ⟨the *square root* of 9 is 3⟩

¹squash \'skwäsh\ *vb* **1** : to beat or press into a pulp or a flat mass : CRUSH ⟨*squash* a beetle⟩ **2** : to put down : SUPPRESS ⟨*squash* a revolt⟩

²squash *n* **1** : the sudden fall of a heavy soft body : the sound of such a fall **2** : a crushed mass **3** : SQUASH RACQUETS

³squash *n* : the fruit of any of several plants related to the gourds that is cooked as a vegetable or used for animal feed

squash racquets *n* : a game played with a racket and ball on a court with four walls

squashes

¹squat \'skwät\ *vb* **squat-ted; squat-ting** **1** : to sit on one's haunches or heels : CROUCH **2** : to settle without any right on land that one does not own

²squat *n* **1** : the act of squatting **2** : a squatting posture

³squat *adj* **squat-ter; squat-test** **1** : CROUCHING **2** : low to the ground **3** : short and thick in stature

squaw \'skwȯ\ *n* : an American Indian woman

¹squawk \'skwȯk\ *vb* **1** : to make a harsh abrupt scream **2** : to complain or protest loudly or vehemently

²squawk *n* **1** : a harsh abrupt scream **2** : a noisy complaint

¹squeak \'skwēk\ *vb* **1** : to make a short shrill cry or sound like that of a mouse **2** : to pass, succeed, or win by a narrow margin ⟨barely *squeaked* by⟩

²squeak *n* **1** : a sharp shrill cry or sound **2** : ESCAPE ⟨a close *squeak*⟩

squeak·y \'skwē-kē\ *adj* **squeak·i·er; squeak·i·est** : making squeaks ⟨a *squeaky* door⟩

¹squeal \'skwēl\ *vb* **1** : to make a sharp prolonged shrill cry or noise **2** : to turn informer **3** : COMPLAIN, PROTEST

²squeal *n* : a shrill sharp cry or noise

¹squeeze \'skwēz\ *vb* **squeezed; squeez·ing** **1** : to press together from the opposite sides or parts of : COMPRESS **2** : to get by squeezing ⟨*squeeze* juice from a lemon⟩ **3** : to force or thrust by squeezing ⟨*squeeze* into a box⟩

²squeeze *n* **1** : an act or instance of squeezing : COMPRESSION **2** : HANDCLASP **3** : EMBRACE

squid \'skwid\ *n* : a sea mollusk that is related to the octopus but has a long body and ten arms

¹squint \'skwint\ *adj* : not parallel in viewing or seeing : not looking in the same direction — used of the two eyes

²squint *vb* **1** : to have squint eyes **2** : to look or peer with the eyes partly closed

³squint *n* **1** : the condition of being cross=eyed **2** : SQUINTING

¹squire \'skwīr\ *n* [from Old French *escuier*, from Latin *scutarius* "shield bearer", from *scutum* "shield"] **1** : one who bears the shield or armor of a knight **2** : a male attendant on a great personage **3** : ESCORT **4** : an owner of a country estate especially in England

²squire *vb* **squired; squir·ing** : to attend as a squire or escort

squirm \'skwərm\ *vb* **1** : to twist about like an eel or a worm **2** : to feel extremely embarrassed

squir·rel \'skwər-əl\ *n* : a small gnawing animal (as the common American **red squirrel** and **gray squirrel**) typically with a bushy tail and soft fur and strong hind legs for leaping

squirrel

¹squirt \'skwərt\ *vb* : to eject liquid in a thin stream : SPURT

²squirt *n* **1** : an instrument (as a syringe) for squirting a liquid **2** : a small forcible stream of liquid : JET **3** : the action of squirting

¹stab \'stab\ *n* **1** : a wound produced by or as if by a pointed weapon **2** : a quick thrust **3** : EFFORT, TRY ⟨make a *stab* at it⟩

²stab *vb* **stabbed; stab·bing** **1** : to wound or pierce by or as if by the thrust of a pointed weapon **2** : THRUST, DRIVE ⟨*stab* a fork into meat⟩

sta·bil·i·ty \stə-'bil-ət-ē\ *n, pl* **sta·bil·i·ties** : the condition of being stable : FIRMNESS ⟨*stability* of character⟩

sta·bi·lize \'stā-bə-ˌlīz\ *vb* **sta·bi·lized; sta·bi·liz·ing** **1** : to make or become stable **2** : to hold steady — **sta·bi·liz·er** *n*

¹**sta·ble** \'stā-bəl\ *n* : a building in which domestic animals are fed and sheltered

²**stable** *vb* **sta·bled; sta·bling** : to put, keep, or lodge in a stable

³**stable** *adj* **sta·bler; sta·blest** **1** : firmly established : STEADFAST ⟨a *stable* government⟩ **2** : not changing or fluctuating ⟨a *stable* income⟩ **3** : LASTING, ENDURING ⟨*stable* institutions⟩ **4** : steady in purpose ⟨a man of *stable* character⟩

stac·ca·to \stə-'kät-ō\ *adj* [from Italian, literally "detached", from the past participle of *staccare* "to detach", from older *distaccare*, from Old French *destachier*, the source also of English *detach*] **1** : cut short or apart in performing : DISCONNECTED ⟨*staccato* notes⟩ **2** : marked by short clear-cut playing or singing of tones or chords ⟨a *staccato* passage⟩

¹**stack** \'stak\ *n* **1** : a large usually cone‑shaped pile (as of hay) **2** : an orderly pile of objects usually one on top of the other **3** : CHIMNEY, SMOKESTACK **4** : a rack with shelves for storing books

²**stack** *vb* : to arrange in or form a stack : PILE

sta·di·um \'stād-ē-əm\ *n, pl* **sta·di·ums** *or* **sta·di·a** \'stād-ē-ə\ : a large structure with tiers of seats for spectators at sports events

staff \'staf\ *n, pl* **staffs** *or* **staves** \'stavz\ **1** : a pole, stick, rod, or bar used as a support or as a sign of authority ⟨the *staff* of a flag⟩ ⟨a bishop's *staff*⟩ **2** : the long handle of a weapon **3** : CLUB, CUDGEL **4** : something that props or sustains ⟨bread is the *staff* of life⟩ **5** : the five horizontal lines with their four spaces on which music is written **6** *pl* **staffs** : a group of assistants to a superintendent or manager ⟨a hospital *staff*⟩ **7** *pl* **staffs** : a group of military officers who plan and manage for a commanding officer

staff 5

staff sergeant *n* : a noncommissioned officer ranking in the army next below a sergeant first class and in the air force next below a technical sergeant

¹**stag** \'stag\ *n* **1** : an adult male deer especially of the larger kind **2** : a social gathering of men only **3** : a man at a social gathering unaccompanied by a woman

²**stag** *adj* : intended or suitable for a gathering of men only ⟨a *stag* party⟩

¹**stage** \'stāj\ *n* **1** : a raised platform or scaffold (as for speaking or presenting plays) **2** : a center of attention : scene of action **3** : the theatrical profession or art **4** : a stopping place or place of rest (as for a stagecoach) on a traveled road **5** : the distance between two stopping places in a journey **6** : a degree of advance in a journey or in an undertaking, process, or development ⟨an early *stage* of a disease⟩ **7** : STAGECOACH

²**stage** *vb* **staged; stag·ing** : to produce or show publicly on or as if on the stage ⟨*stages* two plays each year⟩

stage·coach \'stāj-ˌkōch\ *n* : a horse-drawn coach running regularly between stations to carry passengers and mail

¹**stag·ger** \'stag-ər\ *vb* **1** : to move unsteadily from side to side as if about to fall : REEL **2** : to cause to reel or totter **3** : to begin or cause to doubt, waver, or hesitate **4** : to place or arrange in a zigzag or alternate but regular way ⟨*stagger* the nails along either edge of the board⟩

²**stagger** *n* : a reeling or unsteady gait or movement

stag·nant \'stag-nənt\ *adj* **1** : not flowing : MOTIONLESS ⟨a *stagnant* pool⟩ **2** : not active or brisk : DULL ⟨*stagnant* business⟩

stag·nate \'stag-ˌnāt\ *vb* **stag·nat·ed; stag·nat·ing** : to be or become stagnant

¹**staid** \'stād\ *adj* **1** : SETTLED, FIXED ⟨a *staid* opinion⟩ **2** : SERIOUS, SEDATE

²**staid** *past of* STAY

¹**stain** \'stān\ *vb* **1** : SOIL, DISCOLOR **2** : COLOR, TINGE **3** : TAINT, CORRUPT **4** : DISGRACE

²**stain** *n* **1** : SPOT, DISCOLORATION **2** : a taint of guilt : STIGMA **3** : a preparation (as of dye or pigment) used in staining

stair \'staər\ *n* **1** : a series of steps or flights of steps for going from one level to another — often used in plural ⟨ran down the *stairs*⟩ **2** : one step of a stairway

stair·case \'staər-ˌkās\ *n* : a flight of stairs with their supporting framework, casing, and balusters

stair·way \'staər-ˌwā\ *n* : one or more flights of stairs usually with connecting landings

¹**stake** \'stāk\ *n* **1** : a pointed piece (as of wood) driven or to be driven into the ground as a marker or support **2** : a post to which a person is tied for execution by burning ⟨death at the *stake*⟩ **3** : execution by burning at a stake **4** : something that is staked or risked for gain or loss ⟨play cards for high *stakes*⟩ **5** : the prize in a contest **6** : SHARE, INTEREST ⟨a *stake* in the business⟩ — **at stake** : in a position to be lost or won ⟨his job is *at stake*⟩

²**stake** *vb* **staked; stak·ing** **1** : to mark the limits of by stakes ⟨*stake* out a mining claim⟩ **2** : to fasten or support (as plants) with stakes **3** : RISK, BET **4** : to back financially

sta·lac·tite \stə-'lak-ˌtīt\ *n* : an icicle-shaped deposit hanging from the roof or side of a cave formed by the partial evaporating of dripping water containing lime

sta·lag·mite \stə-'lag-,mīt\ *n* : a deposit like an inverted stalactite formed by the dripping of water containing lime on the floor of a cave

¹stale \'stāl\ *adj* **stal·er; stal·est 1** : tasteless, unpleasant, or unwholesome from age ⟨*stale* food⟩ **2** : tedious from familiarity ⟨*stale* news⟩ **3** : impaired in vigor or effectiveness — **stale·ly** *adv* — **stale·ness** *n*

²stale *vb* **staled; stal·ing** : to make or become stale

¹stalk \'stȯk\ *vb* **1** : to hunt stealthily ⟨*stalk* deer⟩ **2** : to walk in a stiff or haughty manner **3** : to move through or follow usually in a persistent or furtive way ⟨famine *stalked* the land⟩ — **stalk·er** *n*

²stalk *n* **1** : the act of stalking **2** : a stalking gait

³stalk *n* **1** : a plant stem especially when not woody ⟨*stalks* of asparagus⟩ **2** : a slender upright or supporting structure ⟨the *stalk* of a goblet⟩ — **stalked** \'stȯkt\ *adj* — **stalk·less** \'stȯk-ləs\ *adj*

¹stall \'stȯl\ *n* **1** : a compartment for one animal in a stable **2** : a space set off (as for parking an automobile) **3** : a seat in a church choir : a church pew **4** : a booth, stand, or counter where business may be conducted or articles may be displayed for sale

²stall *vb* **1** : to put or keep in a stall **2** : to bring or come to a standstill usually unintentionally ⟨*stall* an engine⟩

³stall *n* : a ruse to deceive or delay

⁴stall *vb* : to hold off, divert, or delay in order to evade or deceive

stal·lion \'stal-yən\ *n* : a male horse

stal·wart \'stȯl-wərt\ *adj* : STRONG, BRAVE

sta·men \'stā-mən\ *n* : any of a row of organs at the center of a flower that consist of a pollen-bearing anther at the tip of a slender filament

stamen

stam·i·na \'stam-ə-nə\ *n* : VIGOR, ENDURANCE

¹stam·mer \'stam-ər\ *vb* : to speak or utter with involuntary stops and repetitions — **stam·mer·er** *n*

²stammer *n* : an act or instance of stammering

¹stamp \'stamp\ *vb* **1** : to pound or crush with a heavy instrument **2** : to strike or beat forcibly with the bottom of the foot **3** : to extinguish or destroy by or as if by stamping with the foot **4** : to walk heavily and noisily **5** : IMPRESS, IMPRINT ⟨*stamp* the bill *paid*⟩ **6** : to attach a stamp to **7** : to cut out or indent with a stamp or die **8** : CHARACTERIZE

²stamp *n* **1** : a device or instrument for stamping **2** : the mark or impression made by stamping **3** : a distinctive character, indication, or mark ⟨the *stamp* of genius⟩ **4** : the act of stamping **5** : a paper or mark affixed to show that a required charge (as a tax) has been paid or that certain conditions have been fulfilled ⟨a postage *stamp*⟩

¹stam·pede \stam-'pēd\ *n* **1** : a wild headlong rush or flight of frightened animals ⟨a cattle *stampede*⟩ **2** : a sudden rush of a group of people ⟨a *stampede* from a burning building⟩

²stampede *vb* **stam·ped·ed; stam·ped·ing 1** : to run or cause (as cattle) to run away in panic **2** : to act or cause to act together suddenly and without thought ⟨refused to be *stampeded* by threats⟩

stance \'stans\ *n* : way of standing : POSTURE

¹stanch \'stȯnch\ *vb* : to stop or check the flow of (as blood)

²stanch *var of* STAUNCH

¹stand \'stand\ *vb* **stood** \'stu̇d\; **stand·ing 1** : to be in or take an upright position ⟨*stood* on his feet all morning⟩ **2** : to take up or maintain a specified position ⟨*stands* first in his class⟩ **3** : to maintain a position : be firm or steadfast in support or opposition ⟨*stands* for democracy⟩ **4** : to be in a particular state or situation ⟨*stands* accused⟩ **5** : to rest, remain, or set upright ⟨*stand* a box on end⟩ **6** : to occupy a place or location ⟨a house *standing* on a hill⟩ **7** : to remain unchanged or inactive ⟨the machines *stood* idle⟩ **8** : to remain in effect ⟨the order still *stands*⟩ **9** : ENDURE, WITHSTAND ⟨*stand* pain⟩ **10** : to submit to : UNDERGO ⟨*stand* trial⟩ **11** : to perform the duty of ⟨*stand* guard⟩ **12** : to pay for ⟨*stand* the cost of desserts⟩ — **stand by** : to be or remain present, available, or loyal to — **stand for 1** : to be a symbol for : REPRESENT **2** : to put up with : PERMIT ⟨will not *stand for* any nonsense⟩ — **stand up 1** : to remain sound and intact **2** : to fail to keep an appointment with — **stand up for** : DEFEND — **stand up to 1** : to meet fairly and fully **2** : to face boldly

²stand *n* **1** : an act of standing **2** : HALT, STOP ⟨made a last *stand* against the enemy⟩ **3** : a place or post where one stands : STATION ⟨took the witness *stand*⟩ **4** : a tier of seats for spectators of a sport or spectacle **5** : a raised platform (as for speakers or performers) **6** : a stall or booth for a small retail business **7** : a sup-

stand for music

port (as a rack or table) on or in which something may be placed ⟨an umbrella *stand*⟩

¹**stan·dard** \'stan-dərd\ *n* **1** : a figure adopted as an emblem by an organized body of people **2** : the personal flag of the ruler of a state **3** : something set up as a rule for measuring or as a model ⟨a *standard* of weight⟩ ⟨*standards* of good manners⟩ **4** : an upright support ⟨a lamp *standard*⟩

²**standard** *adj* **1** : used as or agreeing with a standard for comparison or judgment ⟨*standard* weight⟩ **2** : regularly and widely used ⟨*standard* practice in the trade⟩ **3** : having recognized and permanent value ⟨*standard* authors⟩

stan·dard·ize \'stan-dər-ˌdīz\ *vb* **stan·dard·ized; stan·dard·iz·ing** : to make standard or uniform

standard time *n* : the time established by law or by general usage over a region or country

¹**stand·ing** \'stan-ding\ *adj* **1** : upright on the feet or base : ERECT ⟨*standing* grain⟩ **2** : not flowing : STAGNANT ⟨a *standing* pool⟩ **3** : remaining at the same level, degree, or amount for an indefinite period ⟨a *standing* offer⟩ **4** : PERMANENT ⟨a *standing* army⟩ **5** : done from a standing position ⟨a *standing* jump⟩

²**standing** *n* **1** : the action or position of one that stands **2** : DURATION ⟨a custom of long *standing*⟩ **3** : length of service or experience ⟨a farmer of long *standing*⟩ **4** : POSITION ⟨had the highest *standing* in his class⟩ ⟨a man of high *standing* in the community⟩

stand·point \'stand-ˌpȯint\ *n* : a mental position from which things are viewed and judged

stand·still \'stand-ˌstil\ *n* : a state marked by absence of motion or activity : STOP ⟨business was at a *standstill*⟩

stank *past of* STINK

stan·za \'stan-zə\ *n* : a group of lines forming a division of a poem

¹**sta·ple** \'stā-pəl\ *n* **1** : a U-shaped piece of metal with sharp points to be driven into a surface to hold something (as a hook, rope, or wire) **2** : a U-shaped piece of thin wire to be driven through papers and bent over at the ends to fasten them together or through thin material to fasten it to a surface ⟨fasten cardboard to wood with *staples*⟩

staples

²**staple** *vb* **sta·pled; sta·pling** : to fasten with staples

³**staple** *n* **1** : a chief commodity or product of a place **2** : something in widespread and con-

stant use or demand **3** : the chief element of a thing **4** : unmanufactured or raw material **5** : textile fiber (as wool or rayon) suitable for spinning into yarn

⁴**staple** *adj* **1** : used, needed, or enjoyed constantly usually by many individuals **2** : produced regularly or in large quantities **3** : PRINCIPAL, CHIEF ⟨*staple* foods⟩

sta·pler \'stā-plər\ *n* : a device that staples

¹**star** \'stär\ *n* **1** : any of those heavenly bodies except planets which are visible at night as apparently fixed points of light

stars 3

2 : a star or especially a planet that is supposed in astrology to influence one's fortune or destiny : FORTUNE ⟨born under a lucky *star*⟩ **3** : a figure with five or more points that represents or resembles a star **4** : an often star-shaped ornament or medal **5** : the principal member of a theatrical or operatic company **6** : an outstandingly talented performer

²**star** *vb* **starred; star·ring** **1** : to sprinkle or adorn with stars **2** : to mark with a star as being superior **3** : to mark with an asterisk **4** : to present in the role of a star **5** : to play the most important role ⟨*star* in a new play⟩ **6** : to perform outstandingly

star·board \'stär-bərd\ *n* [from Old English *stēorbord*, from *stēor-* "steering oar" and *bord* "ship's side"; so called because ships used to be steered by means of an oar held in the water over the right side] : the right side of a ship or airplane looking forward

¹**starch** \'stärch\ *vb* : to stiffen with starch

²**starch** *n* : a white odorless tasteless carbohydrate that is the chief storage form of carbohydrates in plants, is an important element of food, and has also various household and commercial uses (as for stiffening clothes)

starch·y \'stär-chē\ *adj* **starch·i·er; starch·i·est** **1** : resembling or containing starch **2** : FORMAL

¹**stare** \'staər\ *vb* **stared; star·ing** : to look fixedly at often with wide-open eyes

²**stare** *n* : the act or an instance of staring

star·fish \'stär-ˌfish\ *n* : any of a group of sea animals having typically five arms that radiate from a central disk and feeding mostly on mollusks

starfish

¹**stark** \'stärk\ *adj* **1** : STRONG, ROBUST **2** : STIFF, MOTIONLESS ⟨*stark* in death⟩ **3** : UNBENDING, STRICT ⟨*stark* discipline⟩ **4** : SHEER, UTTER ⟨*stark* nonsense⟩ **5** : BARREN, DESOLATE ⟨a *stark* landscape⟩ **6** : having few or no ornaments : BARE **7** : HARSH ⟨*stark* realism⟩

²stark *adv* : WHOLLY, QUITE ⟨*stark* mad⟩

star·light \'stär-,līt\ *n* : the light given by the stars

star·ling \'stär-ling\ *n* : a bird about the size of a robin with dark brown plumage that turns greenish black in summer and with yellowish white spots

star·lit \'stär-,lit\ *adj* : lighted by the stars

star·ry \'stär-ē\ *adj* **star·ri·er**; **star·ri·est** **1** : adorned or studded with stars ⟨*starry* heavens⟩ **2** : of, relating to, or consisting of stars ⟨*starry* light⟩ **3** : shining like stars : SPARKLING ⟨*starry* eyes⟩

Stars and Stripes *n sing or pl* : the flag of the United States

¹start \'stärt\ *vb* **1** : to move suddenly and quickly : give an involuntary twitch or jerk (as in surprise) **2** : to set out : BEGIN ⟨*start* to school⟩ **3** : to become or cause to become loosened or forced out of place **4** : to protrude or seem to protrude ⟨his eyes *started* from their sockets⟩ **5** : to set going ⟨*start* the motor⟩

²start *n* **1** : a sudden involuntary movement ⟨a *start* of surprise⟩ **2** : a brief act, movement, or effort ⟨by fits and *starts*⟩ **3** : a sudden impulse or outburst **4** : a beginning of movement, activity, or development ⟨got an early *start*⟩ **5** : a lead or handicap at the beginning of a race or competition **6** : a place of beginning

start·er \'stärt-ər\ *n* **1** : one who goes first **2** : one that causes something to begin

star·tle \'stärt-l\ *vb* **star·tled**; **star·tling** **1** : to cause to move or jump (as in alarm, surprise, or fear) **2** : to frighten suddenly and usually not seriously

star·va·tion \stär-'vā-shən\ *n* : the act or an instance of starving : the condition of being starved

starve \'stärv\ *vb* **starved**; **starv·ing** **1** : to suffer or die or cause to suffer or die from extreme hunger or lack of nourishment **2** : to suffer or die or cause to suffer or die from deprivation ⟨a cat *starving* for affection⟩

¹state \'stāt\ *n* **1** : manner or condition of being ⟨water in the gaseous *state*⟩ **2** : condition of mind or temperament ⟨in a nervous *state*⟩ **3** : a social position befitting a person of rank or wealth ⟨travel in *state*⟩ **4** : a body of people occupying a definite territory and politically organized under one government : the government of such a body of people **5** : one of the units of a nation having a federal government ⟨the United *States* of America⟩

²state *vb* **stat·ed**; **stat·ing** **1** : to set by regulation or authority : FIX ⟨at *stated* times⟩ **2** : to express especially in words ⟨*state* an opinion⟩

state·house \'stāt-,haůs\ *n* : the building where a state legislature performs its legislative functions

state·ly \'stāt-lē\ *adj* **state·li·er**; **state·li·est** **1** : HAUGHTY **2** : having lofty dignity **3** : impressive in size or proportions : IMPOSING ⟨a *stately* building⟩ — **state·li·ness** *n*

state·ment \'stāt-mənt\ *n* **1** : something that is stated : REPORT, ACCOUNT **2** : a brief summarized record of a financial account ⟨a monthly bank *statement*⟩

state·room \'stāt-,rüm, -,rům\ *n* : a private room on a ship or on a railroad car

states·man \'stāts-mən\ *n, pl* **states·men** \-mən\ : a person who is engaged in fixing the policies and conducting the affairs of a government especially by showing unusual wisdom in these matters

¹stat·ic \'stat-ik\ *adj* **1** : relating to bodies that are at rest or that balance each other **2** : not moving : not active **3** : of or relating to stationary charges of electricity (as produced by friction)

²static *n* : disturbing effects produced in a radio or television receiver by atmospheric or electrical disturbances

¹sta·tion \'stā-shən\ *n* **1** : the place or position where a person or thing stands or is assigned to stand or remain **2** : a regular stopping place (as on a railroad line or bus line) : DEPOT **3** : a post or area of duty or occupation ⟨military *station*⟩ **4** : a stock farm or ranch in Australia or New Zealand **5** : STANDING, RANK ⟨a woman of high *station*⟩ **6** : a place for specialized observation or for public service ⟨weather *station*⟩ ⟨police *station*⟩ **7** : a complete assemblage of radio or television equipment for transmitting or receiving

²station *vb* : to assign to or set in a station or position : POST

sta·tion·ar·y \'stā-shə-,ner-ē\ *adj* **1** : fixed in a certain place, post, or course : IMMOBILE ⟨a *stationary* laundry tub⟩ **2** : not changing : STABLE ⟨his weekly income remained *stationary*⟩

sta·tion·er·y \'stā-shə-,ner-ē\ *n* **1** : materials (as paper, pens, and ink) for writing or typing **2** : writing paper and envelopes

station wagon *n* : an automobile for passengers or light trucking that has an interior longer than a sedan's, one or more folding or removable seats, and no separate luggage compartment

stat·ue \'stach-ü\ *n* : an image or likeness (as of a person or animal) sculptured, modeled, or cast in a solid substance (as marble or bronze)

stat·ure \'stach-ər\ *n* **1** : natural height (as of a person) ⟨a man of average *stature*⟩ **2** : quality or status gained (as by growth or development) ⟨reached man's *stature*⟩

sta·tus \'stāt-əs, 'stat-\ *n* **1** : position or rank of a person or thing ⟨lost his *status* as an amateur tennis player⟩ **2** : CONDITION, SITUATION ⟨the economic *status* of a country⟩

stat·ute \'stach-üt\ *n* : a law enacted by a legislative body

¹staunch \'stonch\ *var of* STANCH

²staunch *adj* **1** : WATERTIGHT, SOUND ⟨a *staunch* ship⟩ **2** : strongly built : SUBSTANTIAL ⟨*staunch* foundations⟩ **3** : STEADFAST, LOYAL ⟨*staunch* friends⟩ — **staunch·ly** *adv*

¹stave \'stāv\ *n* **1** : a wooden stick : STAFF **2** : one of a number of narrow strips of wood or iron plates placed edge to edge to form the sides, covering, or lining of something (as a barrel or keg) **3** : STANZA **4** : a musical staff

stave

²stave *vb* **staved** *or* **stove** \'stōv\; **stav·ing** **1** : to break in the staves of ⟨*stave* in a boat⟩ **2** : to smash a hole in : crush or break inward ⟨*staved* in several ribs⟩ **3** : to drive or thrust away : ward off ⟨*stave* off trouble⟩

staves *pl of* STAFF

¹stay \'stā\ *n* : a strong rope or wire used to steady or brace something (as a mast)

²stay *vb* : to fasten (as a smokestack) with stays

stay

³stay *vb* **stayed** *or* **staid** \'stād\; **stay·ing** **1** : to stop going forward : PAUSE **2** : REMAIN ⟨*stayed* at home⟩ **3** : to stand firm **4** : DWELL, LIVE ⟨*stayed* at a hotel⟩ **5** : WAIT, DELAY **6** : to last out (as a race) **7** : CHECK, HALT ⟨*stay* an execution⟩ **8** : ALLAY, SATISFY

⁴stay *n* **1** : the action of halting : the state of being stopped **2** : a residence or sojourn in a place

⁵stay *n* **1** : PROP, SUPPORT **2** : a thin firm strip (as of whalebone, steel, or plastic) used for stiffening a garment (as a corset) or part of a garment (as a shirt collar) **3** *pl* : a corset stiffened with stays

⁶stay *vb* : to hold up : PROP, SUSTAIN ⟨*stay* a person who is about to fall⟩

stead \'sted\ *n* **1** : ADVANTAGE, SERVICE ⟨the captain's knowledge of the sea stood him in good *stead*⟩ **2** : the place or function ordinarily occupied or carried out by another ⟨acted in his brother's *stead*⟩

stead·fast \'sted-,fast\ *adj* **1** : firmly fixed in place **2** : not changing : RESOLUTE ⟨a *steadfast* purpose⟩ **3** : LOYAL ⟨*steadfast* friends⟩ — **stead·fast·ness** *n*

¹stead·y \'sted-ē\ *adj* **stead·i·er; stead·i·est** **1** : firm in position : FIXED **2** : DIRECT ⟨took a *steady* aim⟩ **3** : REGULAR, UNIFORM ⟨a *steady* pace⟩ **4** : CONTINUOUS, UNINTERRUPTED **5** : not changing or varying widely (as in price) **6** : not easily moved or upset : RESOLUTE **7** : CONSTANT, DEPENDABLE **8** : not given to excess : SOBER ⟨*steady* habits⟩ — **stead·i·ly** \'sted-l-ē\ *adv* — **stead·i·ness** \'sted-ē-nəs\ *n*

²steady *vb* **stead·ied; stead·y·ing** : to make, keep, or become steady

steak \'stāk\ *n* **1** : a slice of meat cut from a fleshy part of a beef carcass : a similar slice of a specified meat other than beef **2** : a slice of a large fish (as salmon)

¹steal \'stēl\ *vb* **stole** \'stōl\; **sto·len** \'stō-lən\; **steal·ing** **1** : to come or go secretly, gradually, or quietly ⟨*stole* out of the room⟩ **2** : to take and carry away without right and with intent to keep the property of another : ROB **3** : to take entirely to oneself or beyond one's proper share ⟨he *stole* the show⟩ **4** : SMUGGLE **5** : to accomplish or get for oneself in a concealed or unobserved manner ⟨*steal* a nap⟩

²steal *n* **1** : the act or an instance of stealing **2** : BARGAIN

stealth \'stelth\ *n* : sly or secret action

stealth·y \'stel-thē\ *adj* **stealth·i·er; stealth·i·est** : acting slyly or secretly : done in a sly manner : FURTIVE ⟨*stealthy* glances⟩ **syn** see SECRET — **stealth·i·ly** \-thə-lē\ *adv*

¹steam \'stēm\ *n* **1** : the vapor into which water is changed when heated to the boiling point **2** : steam when kept under pressure so that it supplies heat and power ⟨houses heated by *steam*⟩ **3** : the mist formed when water vapor cools **4** : driving force : POWER, ENERGY ⟨arrived under their own *steam*⟩

²steam *vb* **1** : to rise or pass off as steam **2** : to give off steam or vapor **3** : to move or travel by or as if by the power of steam

steam·boat \'stēm-,bōt\ *n* : a boat driven by steam

steam engine *n* : an engine driven by steam

steam·er \'stē-mər\ *n* **1** : a container in which something is steamed **2** : a ship propelled by steam **3** : an engine, machine, or vehicle operated by steam

steam·roll·er \'stēm-'rō-lər\ *n* : a steam-driven machine with wide heavy rollers for pressing down and smoothing roads

---

ə abut   ər further   a ax   ā age   ä father, cot   à (see key page)   aů out   ch chin   e less   ē easy   g gift   i trip   ī life

steam·ship \'stēm-,ship\ *n* : STEAMER 2

steam shovel *n* : a power shovel operated by steam

steed \'stēd\ *n* : a usually spirited horse

¹steel \'stēl\ *n* **1** : a hard and tough metal made by treating iron with intense heat and mixing carbon with it **2** : an article (as a sword or a dagger) or group of articles of steel **3** : a piece of steel (as for striking sparks from flint)

²steel *adj* : made of or resembling steel

³steel *vb* **1** : to overlay or edge with steel **2** : to make resemble steel **3** : to make bold, strong, or able to resist

steel·y \'stē-lē\ *adj* **steel·i·er; steel·i·est** **1** : made of steel **2** : resembling steel (as in hardness or color)

¹steep \'stēp\ *adj* **1** : having a very sharp slope : almost perpendicular **2** : too great or high ⟨*steep* prices⟩ — **steep·ly** *adv* — **steep·ness** *n*

²steep *vb* **1** : to soak in a liquid (as for softening, bleaching, or extracting a flavor) ⟨*steep* tea⟩ **2** : to saturate with or subject thoroughly to ⟨*steeped* in learning⟩

stee·ple \'stē-pəl\ *n* **1** : a tall tapering structure usually having a spire and built on top of a church tower **2** : a church tower

stee·ple·chase \'stē-pəl-,chās\ *n* **1** : a horse race across country by a number of riders **2** : a race on a course obstructed by hurdles (as hedges, walls, or ditches)

¹steer \'stiər\ *n* : a castrated domestic bull usually raised for beef

²steer *vb* **1** : to direct the course or the course of : GUIDE ⟨*steer* by the stars⟩ ⟨*steer* a boat⟩ **2** : to pursue a course of action **3** : to be guided ⟨this car *steers* well⟩

steer·age \'stiər-ij\ *n* **1** : the act or practice of steering : DIRECTION **2** : the part of a ship occupied by passengers paying the lowest fares

steers·man \'stiərz-mən\ *n, pl* **steers·men** \-mən\ : one who steers

¹stem \'stem\ *n* **1** : the main shaft of a plant that develops buds and shoots and usually grows above ground **2** : a plant part (as a leafstalk or flower stalk) that supports some other part **3** : the bow of a ship **4** : a line of ancestry : STOCK **5** : something that resembles a stem or shaft ⟨the *stem* of a goblet⟩ **6** : the part of an inflected word that remains unchanged throughout an inflection — **stem·less** \-ləs\ *adj*

²stem *vb* **stemmed; stem·ming** **1** : to make headway against ⟨*stem* the current⟩ **2** : to go counter to something adverse ⟨*stem* the tide of public opinion⟩

³stem *vb* **stemmed; stem·ming** **1** : to have or trace an origin or development : DERIVE ⟨illness that *stems* from an accident⟩ **2** : to remove the stem from

⁴stem *vb* **stemmed; stem·ming** **1** : to stop, check, or restrain by or as if by damming ⟨*stem* the flow of blood⟩ **2** : to become checked or stanched

¹stemmed \'stemd\ *adj* : having a stem

²stemmed *adj* : having the stem removed

stench \'stench\ *n* : STINK

¹sten·cil \'sten-səl\ *n* **1** : a material (as a sheet of paper, thin wax, or woven fabric) perforated with lettering or a design through which ink, paint, or metallic powder is forced onto a surface to be printed **2** : a pattern, design, or print produced by means of a stencil

²stencil *vb* **sten·ciled** *or* **sten·cilled; sten·cil·ing** *or* **sten·cil·ling** **1** : to produce by stencil **2** : to mark or paint with a stencil

ste·nog·ra·pher \stə-'näg-rə-fər\ *n* : one employed chiefly to take and transcribe dictation

¹step \'step\ *n* **1** : a rest or place for the foot in going up or down : STAIR, RUNG **2** : an advance or a movement made by raising one foot and putting it down in another spot **3** : a combination of foot and body movements that forms a unit or a repeated pattern ⟨a waltz *step*⟩ **4** : manner of walking : STRIDE **5** : FOOTPRINT **6** : the sound of a footstep **7** : the space passed over in one step **8** : a short distance **9** : the height of one stair **10** *pl* : COURSE, WAY ⟨directed his *steps* down the path⟩ **11** : a degree, grade, or rank in a scale or series : a stage in a process **12** : MEASURE, ACTION ⟨took *steps* to correct the condition⟩ **13** : a musical scale degree

²step *vb* **stepped; step·ping** **1** : to move by a step or steps ⟨*stepped* ashore⟩ **2** : DANCE **3** : WALK ⟨*step* outside⟩ **4** : to move briskly ⟨the horse *stepped* along⟩ **5** : to press down with the foot ⟨*step* on the pedal⟩ **6** : to come as if at a single step or by a simple effort ⟨*step* into a good job⟩ **7** : to measure by steps ⟨*step* off ten yards⟩ — **step up** : to change the rank, degree, or measure of by a series of gradual steps ⟨*step up* production⟩

step·child \'step-,chīld\ *n, pl* **step·chil·dren** \-,chil-drən\ : a child of one's husband or wife by a former marriage

step·fa·ther \'step-,fä-<u>th</u>ər\ *n* : the husband of one's mother by her remarriage

steeple

step·lad·der \'step-,lad-ər\ *n* : a light portable set of steps with a hinged
frame for steadying

step·moth·er \'step-,məth-ər\ *n*
: the wife of one's father by his
remarriage

steppe \'step\ *n* : dry and usually rather level and grass=
covered land in regions (as much
of southeastern Europe and parts
of Asia) of wide temperature
range

stepladder

step·ping–stone \'step-ing-,stōn\ *n* **1** : a
stone on which to step (as in crossing a
stream) **2** : a means of progress or advancement ⟨a *stepping-stone* to success⟩

-ster \stər\ *n suffix* **1** : one that does or
handles or operates ⟨team*ster*⟩ **2** : one that
makes or uses ⟨song*ster*⟩ ⟨pun*ster*⟩ **3** : one
that is associated with or participates in
⟨gang*ster*⟩ **4** : one that is ⟨young*ster*⟩

ster·e·o·scope \'ster-ē-ə-,skōp\ *n* : an optical
instrument that blends two
slightly different pictures of
the same subject to give the
effect of solidity and depth

ster·ile \'ster-əl\ *adj* **1** : not
able to bear fruit, crops, or
offspring : not fertile : BARREN
⟨*sterile* soil⟩ **2** : free from living germs : DISINFECTED

stereoscope

ster·i·lize \'ster-ə-,līz\ *vb* **ster·i·lized**; **ster·i·-
liz·ing** : to make sterile and especially free
from harmful germs

¹ster·ling \'stər-ling\ *n* **1** : British money
2 : sterling silver : articles made from sterling
silver

²sterling *adj* **1** : of, relating to, or calculated
in terms of British sterling **2** : having a fixed
standard of purity represented by an alloy of
925 parts of silver with 75 parts of copper
⟨*sterling* silver⟩ **3** : made of sterling silver
4 : having a high standard : GENUINE ⟨a man of
sterling quality⟩

¹stern \'stərn\ *adj* **1** : hard and
severe in nature or manner ⟨a
stern judge⟩ **2** : STOUT, RESOLUTE
⟨*stern* resolve⟩

²stern *n* : the rear end of a boat

ster·num \'stər-nəm\ *n, pl* **ster-
nums** *or* **ster·na** \-nə\ : BREASTBONE

steth·o·scope \'steth-ə-,skōp\ *n*
: an instrument used by doctors
for listening to sounds produced
in the body and especially in the
chest

stethoscope

¹stew \'stü, 'styü\ *vb* **1** : to boil

slowly : cook in liquid over a low heat **2** : FRET

²stew *n* **1** : food (as meat with vegetables)
prepared by slow boiling **2** : a state of excitement, worry, or confusion

stew·ard \'stü-ərd, 'styü-\ *n* **1** : a manager of
a very large home, an estate, or an organization **2** : a person employed to supervise the
provision and distribution of food (as on a
ship) **3** : a worker who serves and attends the
needs of passengers (as on a train or ship)

stew·ard·ess \'stü-ərd-əs, 'styü-\ *n* : a
female steward

¹stick \'stik\ *n* **1** : a cut or broken branch or
twig **2** : a long slender piece of wood : CLUB,
STAFF **3** : WALKING STICK **4** : something resembling a stick in shape or use ⟨a *stick* of
dynamite⟩ **5** : a dull, stiff, or uninteresting
person

²stick *vb* **stuck** \'stək\; **stick·ing** **1** : PIERCE,
STAB **2** : to kill by piercing **3** : to cause to
penetrate ⟨*stuck* a needle in her finger⟩
4 : FASTEN, ATTACH **5** : to push out, up, into,
or under : THRUST ⟨*stuck* out his hand⟩
6 : to put in a specified place or position
⟨*stuck* a cap on his head⟩ **7** : to halt the
movement or action of **8** : BAFFLE, STUMP
9 : CHEAT, DEFRAUD **10** : to burden with
something disagreeable or disadvantageous
⟨*stuck* with the job of washing the dishes⟩
11 : to remain in a place, situation, or environment : ADHERE, CLING **12** : to become
blocked, wedged, or jammed **13** : PROJECT,
PROTRUDE

stick·er \'stik-ər\ *n* : something (as paper)
with a gummed back that when moistened
sticks to a surface

stick·le·back \'stik-əl-,bak\ *n* : a small scale-
less nest-building fish having two or more
sharp spines on its back

stick·pin \'stik-,pin\ *n* : an ornamental pin
to be worn in a necktie

stick·y \'stik-ē\ *adj* **stick·i·er**; **stick·i·est**
1 : GLUEY, ADHESIVE **2** : coated with a sticky
substance **3** : HUMID, MUGGY ⟨a *sticky* day⟩
4 : tending to stick ⟨*sticky* valve⟩

stiff \'stif\ *adj* **1** : not easily bent : RIGID
2 : not easily moved : not limber ⟨*stiff*
muscles⟩ **3** : not flowing easily : being thick
and heavy ⟨*stiff* glue⟩ **4** : FIRM, RESOLUTE
5 : hard fought : STUBBORN ⟨a *stiff* fight⟩
6 : not natural and easy : FORMAL ⟨a *stiff*
manner⟩ **7** : STRONG, POWERFUL ⟨a *stiff* wind⟩
⟨a *stiff* dose⟩ **8** : HARSH, SEVERE ⟨a *stiff*
penalty⟩ **9** : DIFFICULT ⟨a *stiff* test⟩ — **stiff·ly**
adv — **stiff·ness** *n*

stiff·en \'stif-ən\ *vb* : to make or become stiff
or stiffer — **stiff·en·er** *n*

ə abut   ər further   a ax   ā age   ä father, cot   á (see key page)   aů out   ch chin   e less   ē easy   g gift   i trip   ī life

sti·fle \'stī-fəl\ *vb* **sti·fled; sti·fling** **1** : to kill by depriving of or die from lack of oxygen or air : SMOTHER **2** : to keep in check by deliberate effort : REPRESS **3** : to restrain firmly or forcibly ⟨*stifled* the freedom of the press⟩

stig·ma \'stig-mə\ *n, pl* **stig·ma·ta** \-mət-ə\ *or* **stig·mas** **1** : a mark of disgrace or discredit : STAIN **2** : the upper part of the pistil of a flower which receives the pollen grains and on which they mature

stile \'stīl\ *n* **1** : a step or set of steps for crossing a fence or wall **2** : TURNSTILE

sti·let·to \stə-'let-ō\ *n, pl* **sti·let·tos** *or* **sti·let·toes** : a slender pointed dagger

¹still \'stil\ *adj* **1** : MOTIONLESS **2** : QUIET, SILENT **3** : CALM, TRANQUIL **4** : PEACEFUL — **still·ness** *n*

²still *vb* : to make or become still : QUIET

³still *adv* **1** : without motion ⟨sit *still*⟩ **2** : up to this or that time ⟨he *still* lives there⟩ **3** : in spite of that : NEVERTHELESS ⟨they know it's not true, but they *still* believe it⟩ **4** : EVEN, YET — used as an intensive to stress the comparative degree ⟨ran *still* faster⟩

⁴still *n* : QUIET, SILENCE

⁵still *n* **1** : a place where distilling of alcoholic liquors is carried on **2** : apparatus used in distillation

still·born \'stil-'bȯrn\ *adj* : born dead

stilt \'stilt\ *n* **1** : one of a pair of tall poles each with a high step or loop for the support of a foot used to elevate the wearer above the ground in walking **2** : a tall post or log used as one of the supports for a shed or for a structure (as a pier) built over water

stiletto

stilts

stilt·ed \'stil-təd\ *adj* : stiffly formal : not easy and natural ⟨a *stilted* speech⟩

¹stim·u·lant \'stim-yə-lənt\ *n* **1** : something (as a drug) that temporarily increases the activity of the body or one of its parts ⟨a heart *stimulant*⟩ **2** : STIMULUS 1 **3** : an alcoholic beverage

²stimulant *adj* : stimulating or tending to stimulate

stim·u·late \'stim-yə-ˌlāt\ *vb* **stim·u·lat·ed; stim·u·lat·ing** **1** : to make active or more active : ANIMATE, AROUSE **2** : to act toward as a physiological stimulus or stimulant

stim·u·la·tion \ˌstim-yə-'lā-shən\ *n* : an act, instance, or result of stimulating

stim·u·lus \'stim-yə-ləs\ *n, pl* **stim·u·li** \-ˌlī\

1 : something that rouses or incites to activity : INCENTIVE **2** : an influence that acts usually from outside the body to alter bodily activity (as by exciting a sense organ) ⟨light, heat, and sound are common physical *stimuli*⟩

¹sting \'sting\ *vb* **stung** \'stəng\; **sting·ing** **1** : to prick painfully usually with a sharp or poisonous process ⟨a bee *stung* her hand⟩ **2** : to suffer or affect with sharp quick burning pain : SMART ⟨hail *stung* their faces⟩ **3** : to cause to suffer acutely ⟨*stung* with remorse⟩

²sting *n* **1** : an act of stinging **2** : a wound or pain caused by or as if by stinging **3** : STINGER

sting·er \'sting-ər\ *n* : a sharp organ by which an animal (as a wasp or scorpion) wounds by piercing and injecting a poison

sting·ray \'sting-ˌrā\ *n* : a very flat fish with a stinging spine on its whiplike tail

stin·gy \'stin-jē\ *adj* **stin·gi·er; stin·gi·est** **1** : not generous : sparing in giving or spending **2** : SCANTY, MEAGER ⟨a *stingy* portion⟩ — **stin·gi·ly** \-jə-lē\ *adv* — **stin·gi·ness** \-jē-nəs\ *n*

syn STINGY, CLOSE, MISERLY all mean being reluctant or unwilling to give or share one's possessions. STINGY simply indicates the lack of a generous and giving nature ⟨we were taught to be frugal but never *stingy*⟩ CLOSE adds the idea of being determined to keep a tight grip on whatever one has acquired ⟨he's rich enough, but too *close* to contribute to charity⟩ MISERLY suggests being so abnormally stingy and grasping that one lives and acts miserably in order to accumulate money ⟨he was a mean and *miserly* old man who loved only money and was loved by no one⟩

¹stink \'stingk\ *vb* **stank** \'stangk\ *or* **stunk** \'stəngk\; **stunk; stink·ing** **1** : to give forth or cause to have a strong and offensive smell **2** : to be offensive or of extremely bad quality

²stink *n* : a strong offensive odor : STENCH

¹stint \'stint\ *vb* **1** : to limit in share or portion **2** : to be sparing or frugal

²stint *n* **1** : RESTRAINT, LIMITATION **2** : a definite quantity of work assigned

¹stir \'stər\ *vb* **stirred; stir·ring** **1** : to make or cause to make an especially slight movement or change of position **2** : to disturb the quiet of : AGITATE **3** : to move to activity (as by pushing, beating, or prodding) ⟨*stir* up the fire⟩ **4** : to mix, dissolve, or make by a continued circular movement ⟨*stir* sugar in coffee⟩ **5** : AROUSE, EXCITE ⟨*stir* up trouble⟩

²stir *n* **1** : a state of disturbance, agitation, or activity **2** : widespread notice : IMPRESSION **3** : a slight movement **4** : a stirring movement

stir·ring \'stər-ing\ *adj* **1** : BUSY, ACTIVE **2** : LIVELY, INSPIRING

---

j job   ng sing   ō low   ȯ moth   ȯi coin   th thin   th this   ü boot   u̇ foot   y you   yü few   yu̇ furious   zh vision

stir·rup \'stər-əp\ *n* [from Old English *stigrāp*, literally "mounting rope"] : either of a pair of small light frames often of metal hung by straps from a saddle and used as a support for the foot of a horseback rider

stirrups

¹**stitch** \'stich\ *n* **1** : a sudden sharp pain especially in the side **2** : one in-and-out movement of a threaded needle in sewing : a portion of thread left in the material after one stitch **3** : a single loop of thread or yarn around an implement (as a knitting needle or crochet hook) **4** : a method of stitching

²**stitch** *vb* **1** : to fasten or join with stitches **2** : to make, mend, or decorate with or as if with stitches **3** : SEW

¹**stock** \'stäk\ *n* **1** : a stump of a tree : a block of wood **2** : a stupid person : a dull lifeless person or thing **3** : a part of a thing that serves as its support, frame, or handle ⟨the *stock* of a gun⟩ **4** *pl* : a wooden frame with holes to confine the feet or the feet and hands

stocks 4

of an offender undergoing public punishment **5** : a plant or plant part that contributes mostly underground parts to a graft **6** : the family from which others descend : ANCESTRY, SOURCE **7** : the whole supply or amount on hand **8** : farm animals : LIVESTOCK, CATTLE **9** : the sum of money or capital invested in a large business ⟨ten shares of *stock*⟩ **10** : raw material for making something ⟨soup *stock*⟩ **11** : a company of actors playing at a particular theater and presenting a series of plays

²**stock** *vb* **1** : to provide with or acquire stock or a stock ⟨*stock* a farm⟩ ⟨*stock* up on groceries⟩ **2** : to procure or keep a stock of ⟨that store *stocks* only the best merchandise⟩

³**stock** *adj* **1** : kept regularly in stock ⟨comes in *stock* sizes⟩ **2** : commonly used : STANDARD ⟨gave a *stock* answer⟩

stock·ade \stäk-'ād\ *n* **1** : a line of strong posts set in the ground to form a defense **2** : a pen or enclosure made of posts and stakes

stock·ing \'stäk-ing\ *n* : a close-fitting usually knit covering for the foot and leg

stocking cap *n* : a long knitted cone-shaped cap usually with a tassel or pompon worn especially for winter sports or play

stock·y \'stäk-ē\ *adj* **stock·i·er; stock·i·est** : compact, sturdy, and relatively thick in build : THICKSET

stock·yard \'stäk-ˌyärd\ *n* : a yard for stock and especially for keeping livestock about to be slaughtered or shipped

stole *past of* STEAL

stolen *past part of* STEAL

¹**stom·ach** \'stəm-ək\ *n* **1** : the pouch into which food goes after it leaves the mouth and has passed down the throat **2** : ABDOMEN, BELLY **3** : APPETITE, DESIRE

²**stomach** *vb* : to bear without showing disgust or resentment : ENDURE ⟨unable to *stomach* the smell⟩

¹**stone** \'stōn\ *n* **1** : earth or mineral matter hardened in a mass : ROCK **2** : a piece of rock not as fine as gravel ⟨throw *stones*⟩ **3** : JEWEL, GEM ⟨precious *stones*⟩ **4** : a stony mass sometimes present in a diseased organ **5** : the hard kernel of a fruit **6** *pl usu* **stone** : an English measure of weight equaling fourteen pounds

stone
stone 5

²**stone** *vb* **stoned; ston·ing** **1** : to throw stones at : pelt to death with stones **2** : to remove the stones of ⟨*stone* cherries⟩

³**stone** *adj* : of, relating to, or made of stone

Stone Age *n* : the oldest period in which man is known to have existed : the age during which man used stone tools

ston·y \'stō-nē\ *adj* **ston·i·er; ston·i·est** **1** : full of stones : having the nature of stone ⟨*stony* soil⟩ **2** : insensitive as stone : UNFEELING ⟨a *stony* stare⟩

stood *past of* STAND

stool \'stül\ *n* **1** : a seat without back or arms supported by three or four legs or by a central post **2** : FOOTSTOOL

stools

¹**stoop** \'stüp\ *vb* **1** : to bend down or over **2** : to carry the head and shoulders or the upper part of the body bent forward **3** : to descend to doing something that is beneath one ⟨*stoop* to lying⟩

²**stoop** *n* **1** : an act of bending the body forward **2** : a forward bend of the head and shoulders ⟨walks with a *stoop*⟩

³**stoop** *n* : a porch, platform, entrance stairway, or small veranda at a house door

¹**stop** \'stäp\ *vb* **stopped; stop·ping** **1** : to close an opening by filling or blocking it : PLUG ⟨*stopped* her ears with cotton⟩ **2** : CHECK, RESTRAIN ⟨*stop* a person from going⟩ **3** : to halt the movement or progress of ⟨*stop* the car⟩ **4** : to come to an end : cease activity or operation **5** : to make a visit : STAY ⟨*stopping* with friends for a week⟩

²**stop** *n* **1** : END, CESSATION **2** : a set of organ pipes of one tone quality : a control knob for such a set **3** : a means of regulating the tone or pitch of a musical instrument (as a violin) **4** : something that impedes, obstructs, or brings to a halt **5** : STOPPER, PLUG **6** : the act of stopping : the state of being stopped : CHECK **7** : a halt in a journey : STAY ⟨made a *stop* in the mountains⟩ **8** : a stopping place **9** : a punctuation mark (as a period)

stop·light \'stäp-ˌlīt\ *n* **1** : a light on the rear of a motor vehicle that is illuminated when the driver presses the brake pedal **2** : a signal light used in controlling traffic

stop·page \'stäp-ij\ *n* : the act of stopping : the state of being stopped : HALT, OBSTRUCTION

stop·per \'stäp-ər\ *n* : something (as a cork, plug, or bung) used to stop openings

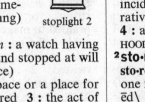
stoplight 2

stop·watch \'stäp-ˌwäch\ *n* : a watch having a hand that can be started and stopped at will for exact timing (as of a race)

stor·age \'stōr-ij\ *n* **1** : space or a place for storing **2** : an amount stored **3** : the act of storing : the state of being stored **4** : the price charged for storing something

storage battery *n* : a battery that can be renewed by passing an electric current through it

¹**store** \'stōr\ *vb* **stored; stor·ing 1** : FURNISH, SUPPLY ⟨*store* a ship with provisions⟩ **2** : to lay away for future use : ACCUMULATE ⟨*store* food in the freezer⟩ **3** : to put in a place (as a warehouse) for safekeeping

storage battery

²**store** *n* **1** : something accumulated or kept for future use : STOCK ⟨ship's *stores*⟩ **2** : a large or ample quantity **3** : a place where goods are sold : SHOP — **in store** : in readiness for use

store·house \'stōr-ˌhaůs\ *n* **1** : a building for storing goods **2** : an abundant supply or source : a place having a large supply of something

store·keep·er \'stōr-ˌkē-pər\ *n* **1** : an owner or manager of a store or shop **2** : a person in charge of stores

store·room \'stōr-ˌrüm, -ˌrům\ *n* : a room for storing things not in use

stork \'stork\ *n* : a large Old World wading bird that resembles the related herons and includes one European form (the **white stork**) that commonly nests on roofs and chimneys

¹**storm** \'storm\ *n* **1** : a heavy fall of rain, snow, or sleet with much wind **2** : a violent outbreak, disturbance, or turmoil ⟨a *storm* of anger⟩ **3** : a determined mass attack by soldiers ⟨take a place by *storm*⟩

²**storm** *vb* **1** : to blow hard and rain or snow heavily **2** : to make a mass attack against **3** : to be very angry : RAGE **4** : to rush about violently ⟨the mob *stormed* through the streets⟩

storm·y \'stor-mē\ *adj* **storm·i·er; storm·i·est 1** : relating to or characterized by a storm ⟨a *stormy* day⟩ **2** : being angry and excited : TURBULENT ⟨a *stormy* meeting⟩ — **storm·i·ness** *n*

¹**sto·ry** \'stōr-ē\ *n, pl* **sto·ries** [from Old French *estorie*, from Latin *historia* "history", "story", from Greek, where it originally meant "investigation", "research"] **1** : an account of incidents or events **2** : ANECDOTE **3** : a narrative shorter than a novel ⟨a fairy *story*⟩ **4** : a widely circulated rumor **5** : LIE, FALSEHOOD

²**sto·ry** *or* **sto·rey** \'stōr-ē\ *n, pl* **sto·ries** *or* **sto·reys** : a set of rooms or area making up one floor level of a building — **sto·ried** \'stōr-ēd\ *adj*

stout \'staůt\ *adj* **1** : strong of character or purpose : BRAVE, FIRM **2** : physically or materially strong : STURDY, TOUGH **3** : FORCEFUL **4** : bulky in body : THICKSET, FLESHY — **stout·ly** *adv* — **stout·ness** *n*

¹**stove** \'stōv\ *n* : a structure of iron or steel that burns fuel or uses electricity to provide heat (as for cooking or heating)

²**stove** *past of* STAVE

stove·pipe \'stōv-ˌpīp\ *n* **1** : a metal pipe to carry away smoke from a stove **2** : a tall silk hat

stow \'stō\ *vb* **1** : to put away : STORE, HIDE **2** : ARRANGE, PACK **3** : LOAD **4** : to cram in ⟨*stow* away a big meal⟩

stow·a·way \'stō-ə-ˌwā\ *n* : one who hides (as in a ship or airplane) to obtain free passage

strad·dle \'strad-l\ *vb* **strad·dled; strad·dling 1** : to stand, sit, or walk with the legs spread wide apart **2** : to stand, sit, or ride astride of ⟨*straddle* a horse⟩ **3** : to favor or seem to favor two apparently opposite sides ⟨*straddle* a question⟩

strag·gle \'strag-əl\ *vb* **strag·gled; strag·gling 1** : to wander from the direct course or way : STRAY **2** : to trail off from others of its kind : spread out far or irregularly — **strag·gler** \'strag-lər\ *n*

¹**straight** \'strāt\ *adj* **1** : following the same direction throughout its length : not curved or

wavy : not crooked or bent : DIRECT **2** : not wandering from the main point or proper course ⟨*straight* thinking⟩ **3** : not wandering from what is right, honest, or upright : FRANK ⟨a *straight* answer⟩ **4** : properly ordered or arranged ⟨keep accounts *straight*⟩ **5** : not modified or varying — **straight·ness** *n*

²straight *adv* : in a straight manner, course, or line

straight·en \'strāt-n\ *vb* **1** : to make or become straight **2** : to put in order ⟨*straighten* up a room⟩

straight·for·ward \strāt-'fȯr-wərd\ *adj* **1** : proceeding in a straight course or manner : DIRECT **2** : OUTSPOKEN, CANDID ⟨gave a *straightforward* reply⟩ — **straight·for·ward·ly** *adv* — **straight·for·ward·ness** *n*

syn STRAIGHTFORWARD, ABOVEBOARD, FORTHRIGHT all mean honest and open. STRAIGHTFORWARD is the general term and refers to something that is both direct and free from evasiveness ⟨gave a *straightforward* account of the accident⟩ ABOVEBOARD stresses the aspect of being free from any trace of deception or underhandedness ⟨we read the contract carefully and found it completely *aboveboard*⟩ FORTHRIGHT emphasizes the aspect of directness that goes immediately to the point without swerving or hesitating ⟨a *forthright* request for help⟩ ⟨we liked his *forthright* manner but it sometimes got him into trouble⟩

straight·way \'strāt-ˌwā\ *adv* : IMMEDIATELY

¹strain \'strān\ *n* **1** : LINEAGE, ANCESTRY **2** : a group of individuals that cannot be distinguished from related kinds by appearance alone ⟨a high-yielding *strain* of wheat⟩ **3** : a quality or disposition that runs through a family or race **4** : STREAK, TRACE ⟨a *strain* of sadness⟩ **5** : AIR, MELODY **6** : the general tone of an utterance (as a song or speech) or of a course of action or conduct

²strain *vb* **1** : to make taut ⟨*strain* a rope⟩ **2** : to stretch or be stretched, pulled, or used to maximum limit ⟨muscles *straining* under a load⟩ **3** : to stretch beyond a proper limit ⟨*strain* the truth⟩ **4** : to exert to the utmost : STRIVE ⟨*strain* to lift a heavy box⟩ **5** : to injure or be injured by too much or too hard use or effort ⟨*strained* his heart⟩ **6** : to squeeze or clasp tightly : HUG **7** : to press or pass through a strainer : FILTER

³strain *n* **1** : the act of straining **2** : the state of being strained **3** : OVERWORK, WORRY **4** : bodily injury resulting from strain or from a wrench or twist that stretches muscles and ligaments

strained \'strānd\ *adj* **1** : not easy or natural

: FORCED ⟨a *strained* smile⟩ **2** : pushed by antagonism near to open conflict ⟨*strained* relations between countries⟩

strain·er \'strā-nər\ *n* : a device (as a screen, sieve, or filter) to retain solid pieces while a liquid passes through

strait \'strāt\ *n* **1** : a narrow channel connecting two bodies of water **2** : DISTRESS, NEED — often used in plural ⟨in dire *straits*⟩

strainer

¹strand \'strand\ *n* : the land bordering a body of water : SHORE, BEACH

²strand *vb* **1** : to run, drive, or cause to drift onto a strand : run aground **2** : to leave in a strange or unfavorable place especially without means to depart ⟨*stranded* in a strange city⟩

³strand *n* **1** : one of the fibers, threads, strings, or wires twisted or braided to make a cord, rope, or cable : the cord, rope, or cable into which these strands are twisted **2** : an elongated or twisted and plaited body resembling a rope ⟨a *strand* of pearls⟩ ⟨a *strand* of hair⟩

strands

strange \'strānj\ *adj* **strang·er**; **strang·est** [from Old French *estrange* "foreign", from Latin *extraneus*, literally, "belonging outside", from *extra* "outside", from *ex* "out"] **1** : of or relating to some other person, place, or thing ⟨the cuckoo lays her eggs in a *strange* nest⟩ **2** : exciting curiosity, surprise, or wonder because of its not being usual or ordinary : QUEER ⟨*strange* clothes⟩ **3** : UNFAMILIAR ⟨*strange* surroundings⟩ **4** : ill at ease : SHY ⟨felt *strange* on his first day at school⟩ — **strange·ly** *adv* — **strange·ness** *n*

strang·er \'strān-jər\ *n* **1** : a person not in the place where his home is : FOREIGNER **2** : GUEST, INTRUDER **3** : a person that is unknown or with whom one is not acquainted

stran·gle \'strang-gəl\ *vb* **stran·gled**; **strangling** **1** : to choke to death by squeezing the throat **2** : to choke in any way : STIFLE, SUFFOCATE — **stran·gler** \-glər\ *n*

¹strap \'strap\ *n* **1** : a narrow strip of flexible material (as leather) used especially for fastening, binding, or wrapping **2** : a strip of leather used for flogging **3** : STROP

²strap *vb* **strapped**; **strap·ping** **1** : to secure with or attach by means of a strap **2** : BIND, CONSTRICT **3** : to beat or punish with a strap **4** : STROP

strap·ping \'strap-ing\ *adj* : LARGE, STRONG

strat·a·gem \'strat-ə-jəm\ *n* **1** : a trick in war to deceive or outwit the enemy : a deceptive scheme **2** : skill in deception

stra·te·gic \strə-'tē-jik\ *adj* **1** : of, relating to, or marked by strategy **2** : useful or important in strategy **3** : showing careful choice : ADVANTAGEOUS

strat·e·gy \'strat-ə-jē\ *n, pl* **strat·e·gies** **1** : the art of using military, naval, and air forces to gain victory in war **2** : a clever plan or method

strat·o·sphere \'strat-ə-,sfiər\ *n* : an upper portion of the atmosphere more than seven miles above the earth where temperature changes little and clouds rarely form

stra·tum \'strāt-əm\ *n, pl* **stra·ta** \-ə\ : LAYER ⟨a *stratum* of rock⟩

stra·tus \'strāt-əs\ *n* : a cloud extending over a large area at an altitude of from 2000 to 7000 feet

straw \'stro\ *n* **1** : stalks especially of grain after threshing : dry stalks or stalklike plant residue ⟨pine *straw*⟩ **2** : a single dry coarse plant stalk : a piece of straw **3** : a thing of small worth : TRIFLE **4** : a slender tube for sucking up a beverage

straw·ber·ry \'stro-,ber-ē\ *n, pl* **straw·ber·ries** : the juicy edible usually red fruit of a low herb (**strawberry vine**) with white flowers and long slender runners

¹stray \'strā\ *vb* **1** : to wander from company, restraint, or proper limits : ROAM **2** : to wander from a direct course or at random : ERR

²stray *n* : a person or animal that strays

³stray *adj* **1** : WANDERING ⟨a *stray* cow⟩ **2** : occurring at random : OCCASIONAL, INCIDENTAL ⟨*stray* remarks⟩

¹streak \'strēk\ *n* **1** : a line or mark of a different color or texture from its background **2** : a narrow band of light : a lightning bolt **3** : TRACE, STRAIN ⟨a *streak* of humor⟩ **4** : a brief run (as of luck) **5** : an unbroken series ⟨a winning *streak*⟩ **6** : a narrow layer ⟨a *streak* of ore⟩ — **streaked** \'strēkt, 'strē-kəd\ *adj*

²streak *vb* **1** : to form streaks in or on **2** : to move swiftly : RUSH

¹stream \'strēm\ *n* **1** : a body of water (as a brook or river) flowing on the earth **2** : a flow of liquid ⟨a *stream* of blood⟩ **3** : a steady flow ⟨a *stream* of words⟩

²stream *vb* **1** : to flow or cause to flow in or as if in a stream **2** : to pour out streams of liquid ⟨a face *streaming* with sweat⟩ **3** : to stretch or trail out at full length ⟨hair *streaming* in the wind⟩ **4** : to move forward in a steady stream

stream·er \'strē-mər\ *n* **1** : a flag that streams in the wind : PENNANT **2** : a long narrow wavy strip (as of ribbon on a hat) suggesting a banner floating in the wind **3** : a column of light (as from the aurora borealis)

stream·lined \'strēm-'līnd\ *also* **stream·line** \-'līn\ *adj* **1** : designed or constructed to reduce resistance to motion through water or air or as if for this purpose ⟨a *streamlined* automobile⟩ **2** : SIMPLIFIED, COMPACT ⟨a *streamlined* version of a play⟩ **3** : MODERNIZED

street \'strēt\ *n* [from Old English *strǣt* "paved road", from Latin *strata*, from the past participle of *sternere* "to spread flat"] **1** : a public way or thoroughfare especially in a city, town, or village **2** : the people occupying property on a street ⟨the whole *street* was excited⟩

street·car \'strēt-,kär\ *n* : a passenger vehicle running on rails and typically operating on city streets

strength \'strength\ *n* **1** : the quality of being strong : POWER **2** : TOUGHNESS, FIRMNESS ⟨the *strength* of a rope⟩ **3** : power to resist attack **4** : intensity of light, color, sound, or odor **5** : force as measured in numbers ⟨the full *strength* of an army⟩

strength·en \'streng-thən\ *vb* : to make, grow, or become stronger

stren·u·ous \'stren-yə-wəs\ *adj* **1** : VIGOROUS, ENERGETIC ⟨a *strenuous* supporter⟩ **2** : marked by or requiring energy or stamina : ARDUOUS ⟨a *strenuous* trip⟩

strep·to·my·cin \,strep-tə-'mīs-n\ *n* : an antibiotic produced by a soil microorganism and used especially in treating tuberculosis

¹stress \'stres\ *n* **1** : a force that tends to distort a body : PRESSURE, STRAIN **2** : a factor that induces bodily or mental tension : a state of tension resulting from a stress **3** : EMPHASIS, WEIGHT **4** : relative prominence of sound : a syllable carrying this stress : ACCENT

²stress *vb* **1** : ACCENT ⟨*stress* the first syllable⟩ **2** : to subject to physical stress : STRAIN **3** : EMPHASIZE

¹stretch \'strech\ *vb* **1** : to reach out : EXTEND, SPREAD ⟨*stretched* out his hand for the apple⟩ ⟨*stretched* himself out on the bed⟩ **2** : to draw out in length or breadth or both : EXPAND, ENLARGE **3** : to draw up from a cramped, stooping, or relaxed position ⟨awoke and *stretched* himself⟩ **4** : to pull taut : STRAIN **5** : to cause to reach or continue ⟨*stretch* a wire between two posts⟩ **6** : EXAGGERATE **7** : to become extended without breaking ⟨rubber *stretches* easily⟩

²stretch *n* **1** : the act of extending or drawing

out beyond ordinary or normal limits ⟨a *stretch* of the imagination⟩ **2** : a continuous extent in length, area, or time ⟨a fine *stretch* of country⟩ **3** : the extent to which something may be stretched **4** : a walk especially to relieve fatigue

stretch·er \'strech-ər\ *n* **1** : a person or thing that stretches ⟨a curtain *stretcher*⟩ **2** : a light bedlike arrangement for carrying sick or wounded persons

strew \'strü\ *vb* **strewed**; **strewed** *or* **strewn** \'strün\; **strew·ing** **1** : to spread by scattering ⟨*strew* crumbs for the birds⟩ **2** : to cover by or as if by scattering something over or on **3** : DISSEMINATE

strick·en \'strik-ən\ *adj* **1** : hit or wounded by or as if by a missile **2** : afflicted with disease, misfortune, or sorrow

strict \'strikt\ *adj* **1** : permitting no evasion or escape ⟨*strict* discipline⟩ **2** : COMPLETE, ABSOLUTE ⟨*strict* secrecy⟩ **3** : carefully conforming (as to a rule or principle) : EXACT, PRECISE ⟨a *strict* Catholic⟩ — **strict·ly** *adv* — **strict·ness** *n*

¹stride \'strīd\ *vb* **strode** \'strōd\; **strid·den** \'strid-n\; **strid·ing** \'strīd-ing\ **1** : to walk or run with long regular steps **2** : to step over : STRADDLE

²stride *n* **1** : a long step : the distance covered by such a step **2** : a manner of striding ⟨a mannish *stride*⟩ **3** : a stage of progress : ADVANCE ⟨made great *strides* in his studies⟩

stri·dent \'strīd-nt\ *adj* : harsh sounding : GRATING

strife \'strīf\ *n* **1** : bitter and sometimes violent conflict **2** : FIGHT, STRUGGLE

¹strike \'strīk\ *vb* **struck** \'strək\; **struck** *or* **strick·en** \'strik-ən\; **strik·ing** \'strī-king\ **1** : GO, PROCEED ⟨*strike* across the field⟩ **2** : to touch or hit forcibly ⟨waves *striking* the shore⟩ **3** : to come into contact or collision with ⟨the ship *struck* a rock⟩ **4** : to remove or cancel with or as if with the stroke of a pen ⟨*strike* his name from the list⟩ **5** : to produce by or as if by a blow ⟨*strike* fear into the enemy⟩ **6** : to lower (as a flag or sail) usually in salute or surrender **7** : to make known by sounding or cause to sound ⟨the clock *struck* one⟩ ⟨*strike* a bell⟩ **8** : to make a military attack : FIGHT ⟨*strike* for freedom⟩ **9** : to stop work in order to obtain a change in conditions of employment **10** : to afflict or affect especially suddenly ⟨*stricken* with a high fever⟩ **11** : to produce by impressing : IMPRESS ⟨*strike* a medal⟩ ⟨the sight *struck* him as strange⟩ **12** : to cause to ignite by striking or rubbing ⟨*strike* a match⟩ **13** : to agree on the terms of ⟨*strike* a bargain⟩ **14** : to reach or arrive at by reckoning ⟨*strike* an average⟩ **15** : to come to : run across ⟨*strike* oil⟩ **16** : to take on : ASSUME ⟨*strike* a pose⟩ — **strike out** : to retire or be retired on a strikeout

²strike *n* **1** : an act or instance of striking **2** : a work stoppage by workers to force an employer to comply with demands : a temporary stoppage of activities in protest against an act or condition **3** : a stroke of good luck **4** : a discovery of a valuable mineral deposit **5** : a pitch that counts against a batter in baseball **6** : DISADVANTAGE, HANDICAP **7** : the knocking down of all ten bowling pins with the first bowl **8** : a military attack

strike·out \'strīk-,aùt\ *n* : an out in baseball that results from a batter's being charged with three strikes

strike zone *n* : the area (as between the knees and shoulders of a batter in his natural stance) over home plate through which a pitched baseball must pass to be called a strike

strik·ing \'strī-king\ *adj* : attracting attention : REMARKABLE ⟨a *striking* resemblance⟩

¹string \'string\ *n* **1** : a small cord used to bind, fasten, or tie **2** : a thin tough plant structure (as the fiber connecting the halves of a bean pod) **3** : the gut or wire cord of a musical instrument **4** *pl* : the stringed instruments of an orchestra : the players of such instruments **5** : a group, series, or line of objects threaded on a string or arranged as if strung together ⟨a *string* of automobiles⟩ **6** : the cord of a necklace

²string *vb* **strung** \'strəng\; **string·ing** **1** : to provide with strings ⟨*string* a tennis racket⟩ **2** : to tune the strings of : TIGHTEN **3** : to make tense ⟨her nerves were *strung* up⟩ **4** : to thread on or as if on a string ⟨*string* beads⟩ **5** : to tie, hang, or fasten with string **6** : to remove the strings of ⟨*string* beans⟩ **7** : to extend or stretch like a string ⟨*string* wires from tree to tree⟩

string bean *n* : a bean grown primarily for its pods which are eaten before the seeds mature

stringed instrument \'stringd-\ *n* : a musical instrument (as a violin, harp, or piano) sounded by plucking or striking or by drawing a bow across tightly drawn strings

string beans

string·er \'string-ər\ *n* : a long strong piece of wood or metal used for support or strengthening in building (as under a floor)

string·y \'string-ē\ *adj* **string·i·er**; **string·i·est**

1 : containing, consisting of, or resembling string ⟨*stringy* meat⟩ ⟨*stringy* hair⟩ 2 : lean and sinewy in build : WIRY 3 : capable of being drawn out to form a string ⟨*stringy* molasses⟩

¹**strip** \'strip\ *vb* **stripped; strip·ping** 1 : to remove clothing, covering, or surface matter from : UNDRESS 2 : SKIN, PEEL ⟨*strip* bark from a tree⟩ 3 : to remove honors, privileges, or duties from 4 : PLUNDER, SPOIL ⟨*stripped* the captured town⟩ 5 : to make bare or clear (as by cutting or grazing)

²**strip** *n* : a long narrow piece or area ⟨*strips* of bacon⟩

strip–crop·ping \'strip-ˌkräp-ing\ *n* : the growing of a cultivated crop (as potatoes) in alternate strips with a sod-forming crop (as grass) to reduce soil erosion

¹**stripe** \'strīp\ *n* : a stroke or blow with a rod or lash

²**stripe** *n* 1 : a line or long narrow division or section of something different in color or appearance from the background 2 : a piece of braid (as on a sleeve) indicating military rank or length of service

³**stripe** *vb* **striped; strip·ing** : to make stripes on

striped \'strīpt, 'strī-pəd\ *adj* : having stripes

strip·ling \'strip-ling\ *n* : a youth just passing from boyhood to manhood

strive \'strīv\ *vb* **strove** \'strōv\; **striv·en** \'striv-ən\ *or* **strived; striv·ing** \'strī-ving\ 1 : to struggle in opposition : CONTEND 2 : to try hard ⟨*strive* to win⟩

strode *past of* STRIDE

¹**stroke** \'strōk\ *vb* **stroked; strok·ing** : to rub gently in one direction

²**stroke** *n* 1 : the act of striking : BLOW, KNOCK 2 : a single unbroken movement : one of a series of repeated movements 3 : the hitting of a ball in a game (as golf or tennis) 4 : a sudden action or process producing an impact or unexpected result ⟨a *stroke* of lightning⟩ 5 : an abrupt weakening or loss of consciousness and powers of voluntary movement that results from the breaking or obstruction of an artery in the brain 6 : one of a series of propelling movements ⟨a swimming *stroke*⟩ 7 : a vigorous effort ⟨not a *stroke* of work⟩ 8 : the sound of striking (as of a clock or bell) ⟨at the *stroke* of two⟩ 9 : a mark made by a single movement of a tool ⟨the *stroke* of a pen⟩ 10 : one of the lines of a letter of the alphabet

¹**stroll** \'strōl\ *vb* : to walk in a leisurely or idle manner : RAMBLE

²**stroll** *n* : a leisurely walk : RAMBLE

strong \'strȯng\ *adj* **strong·er** \'strȯng-gər\;

strong·est \'strȯng-gəst\ 1 : physically powerful : HEALTHY, ROBUST 2 : morally or intellectually powerful 3 : having great numbers or wealth ⟨*strong* armies⟩ 4 : of a specified number ⟨an army 10,000 *strong*⟩ 5 : FORCEFUL ⟨*strong* arguments⟩ 6 : not mild or weak 7 : moving with rapidity or force ⟨a *strong* wind⟩ 8 : ARDENT, ZEALOUS 9 : not easily injured, damaged, or subdued : SOLID 10 : well established : FIRM ⟨*strong* beliefs⟩ — **strong·ly** \'strȯng-lē\ *adv*

strong·hold \'strȯng-ˌhōld\ *n* : FORTRESS

¹**strop** \'sträp\ *n* : a strap used especially for sharpening a razor

²**strop** *vb* **stropped; strop·ping** : to sharpen (a razor) on a strop

strove *past of* STRIVE

struck *past of* STRIKE

struc·tur·al \'strək-chə-rəl\ *adj* 1 : of, relating to, or affecting structure ⟨*structural* defects⟩ 2 : used or formed for use in construction ⟨*structural* steel⟩

struc·ture \'strək-chər\ *n* 1 : something built (as a house or dam) 2 : the manner in which something is built : CONSTRUCTION 3 : the arrangement or relationship of parts or organs ⟨the *structure* of the body⟩

¹**strug·gle** \'strəg-əl\ *vb* **strug·gled; strug·gling** 1 : to make strenuous effort against opposition : STRIVE ⟨*struggle* for a living⟩ 2 : to proceed with difficulty or with great effort ⟨*struggled* through the snow⟩

²**struggle** *n* 1 : a violent effort or exertion 2 : CONTEST, FIGHT

strum \'strəm\ *vb* **strummed; strum·ming** : to play on a stringed instrument by brushing the strings with the fingers ⟨*strum* a guitar⟩

strung *past of* STRING

¹**strut** \'strət\ *vb* **strut·ted; strut·ting** : to walk with a proud or haughty gait : SWAGGER

²**strut** *n* 1 : a bar or brace used to resist lengthwise pressure 2 : a pompous step or walk

¹**stub** \'stəb\ *n* 1 : a tree stump 2 : something having or worn to a short or blunt shape : a short part left after a larger part has been broken off or used up ⟨a pencil *stub*⟩ 3 : a pen with a short blunt point 4 : a small part of a check kept as a record of the contents of the detached check

²**stub** *vb* **stubbed; stub·bing** : to strike (as the toe) against an object

stub·ble \'stəb-əl\ *n* 1 : the stem ends of herbs and especially cereal grasses left in the ground after harvest 2 : a rough growth or surface resembling stubble : a short growth of beard

---

stub·born \'stəb-ərn\ *adj* **1** : having a firm idea or purpose : OBSTINATE ⟨*stubborn* as a mule⟩ **2** : done or continued in an obstinate or persistent manner ⟨a *stubborn* refusal⟩ **3** : difficult to handle, manage, or treat ⟨*stubborn* hair⟩ — **stub·born·ly** *adv* — **stub·born·ness** *n*

stub·by \'stəb-ē\ *adj* **stub·bi·er; stub·bi·est** **1** : resembling a stub especially in shortness and thickness ⟨*stubby* fingers⟩ **2** : BRISTLY

¹stuc·co \'stək-ō\ *n, pl* **stuc·cos** *or* **stuc·coes** : a plaster for coating walls

²stucco *vb* : to coat or decorate with stucco

stuck *past of* STICK

¹stud \'stəd\ *n* **1** : one of the smaller uprights in a building to which sheathing, paneling, or laths are fastened **2** : a removable device like a button used as a fastener or ornament ⟨shirt *studs*⟩ **3** : a nail, pin, or rod that sticks out

²stud *vb* **stud·ded; stud·ding** **1** : to supply or adorn with or as if with studs **2** : to set thickly together ⟨water *studded* with islands⟩

stu·dent \'stüd-nt, 'styüd-\ *n* : a person who studies especially in school : a careful observer : PUPIL, SCHOLAR

stu·di·o \'stüd-ē-,ō, 'styüd-\ *n, pl* **stu·di·os** **1** : the place where an artist works **2** : a place for the study of an art **3** : a place where motion pictures are made **4** : a place from which radio or television programs are broadcast

stu·di·ous \'stüd-ē-əs, 'styüd-\ *adj* : devoted to and fond of study ⟨a *studious* boy⟩

¹stud·y \'stəd-ē\ *n, pl* **stud·ies** **1** : deep or puzzled thought : CONTEMPLATION **2** : application of the mind to obtain knowledge **3** : a careful examination of something ⟨the *study* of a disease⟩ **4** : a room especially for study, reading, or writing **5** : a branch of learning : SUBJECT

²study *vb* **stud·ied; stud·y·ing** **1** : to apply the mind to a thing by reading, investigation, or memorizing : examine closely **2** : to fix the attention on closely ⟨*studied* the matter carefully⟩

¹stuff \'stəf\ *n* **1** : personal property : household goods : BAGGAGE **2** : material out of which something is made **3** : a finished textile fabric (as wool or worsted material) **4** : writing, talk, or ideas of little worth : NONSENSE **5** : matter of a particular kind often unspecified ⟨sold tons of the *stuff*⟩ **6** : the basic part of something :· SUBSTANCE ⟨he lacks the *stuff* of manhood⟩

²stuff *vb* **1** : to fill by packing or crowding things into : CRAM **2** : OVEREAT, GORGE ⟨*stuffed* himself on candy⟩ **3** : to fill with a

stuffing ⟨*stuff* a turkey⟩ **4** : to stop up : PLUG ⟨a *stuffed* nose⟩ **5** : THRUST, PRESS ⟨*stuffed* the clothes into the drawer⟩

stuff·ing \'stəf-ing\ *n* **1** : material used in filling up or stuffing something **2** : a mixture (as of bread crumbs and seasonings) used to stuff meat, vegetables, eggs, or poultry

stuff·y \'stəf-ē\ *adj* **stuff·i·er; stuff·i·est** **1** : needing fresh air : CLOSE ⟨a *stuffy* room⟩ **2** : stuffed or choked up ⟨a *stuffy* nose⟩ **3** : DULL **4** : SELF-RIGHTEOUS

¹stum·ble \'stəm-bəl\ *vb* **stum·bled; stum·bling** **1** : to trip in walking or running **2** : to walk unsteadily **3** : to speak or act in a blundering or clumsy manner : blunder morally **4** : to happen unexpectedly or by chance ⟨*stumbled* on a discovery⟩

²stumble *n* **1** : the act of tripping **2** : BLUNDER

¹stump \'stəmp\ *n* **1** : the base of something (as an arm, a tooth, or a pencil) that remains after the rest has been removed, lost, or worn away : STUB **2** : the part of a tree that remains in the ground after the tree is cut down **3** : a place or occasion for political public speaking

²stump *vb* **1** : STUB **2** : to walk or walk over heavily, stiffly, or clumsily **3** : CHALLENGE, DARE **4** : PERPLEX, CONFOUND ⟨*stumped* the experts with his question⟩ **5** : to go about making political speeches or supporting a cause ⟨*stumped* the state for his candidate⟩

stump·y \'stəm-pē\ *adj* **stump·i·er; stump·i·est** **1** : full of stumps **2** : being short and thick : SQUAT

stun \'stən\ *vb* **stunned; stun·ning** **1** : to make dizzy or senseless by or as if by a blow **2** : BEWILDER, STUPEFY ⟨*stunned* by the news⟩

stung *past of* STING

stunk *past of* STINK

stun·ning \'stən-ing\ *adj* **1** : tending or able to stupefy or bewilder ⟨a *stunning* blow⟩ **2** : unusually lovely or attractive : STRIKING

¹stunt \'stənt\ *vb* : to hinder the normal growth of : DWARF ⟨*stunt* a tree⟩

²stunt *n* : an unusual or difficult performance or feat ⟨acrobatic *stunts*⟩

stu·pe·fy \'stü-pə-,fī, 'styü-\ *vb* **stu·pe·fied; stu·pe·fy·ing** **1** : to make stupid, dull, or numb by or as if by drugs **2** : ASTONISH, BEWILDER

stu·pen·dous \stu̇-'pen-dəs, styu̇-\ *adj* : stupefying or amazing especially because of great size or height

stu·pid \'stü-pəd, 'styü-\ *adj* **1** : slow or dull of mind **2** : marked by or resulting from dullness : SENSELESS ⟨a *stupid* mistake⟩ **3** : DREARY, BORING ⟨a *stupid* plot⟩ **syn** see IGNORANT — **stu·pid·ly** *adv*

ə abut   ər further   a ax   ā age   ä father, cot   à (see key page)   au̇ out   ch chin   e less   ē easy   g gift   i trip   ī life

stu·pid·i·ty \stu̇-'pid-ət-ē, styu̇-\ *n, pl* **stu·pid·i·ties** **1** : the quality or state of being stupid **2** : a stupid thought, action, or remark

stu·por \'stü-pər, 'styü-\ *n* : a condition in which the senses or feelings are dulled ⟨in a drunken *stupor*⟩

stur·dy \'stərd-ē\ *adj* **stur·di·er; stur·di·est** **1** : firmly built or made : SUBSTANTIAL **2** : physically strong : ROBUST **3** : RESOLUTE — **stur·di·ly** \'stərd-l-ē\ *adv*

stur·geon \'stər-jən\ *n* : a large food fish with tough skin and rows of bony plates

¹stut·ter \'stət-ər\ *vb* : to speak or say jerkily with involuntary repetition or interruption of sounds

²stutter *n* : the act of one who stutters

¹sty \'stī\ *n, pl* **sties** : a pen for swine

²sty *or* **stye** \'stī\ *n, pl* **sties** *or* **styes** : an inflamed swelling on the edge of an eyelid

¹style \'stīl\ *n* **1** : the stalklike middle part of the pistil of a flower **2** : a way of speaking or writing that is characteristic of a person, period, or nation ⟨ornate *style*⟩ **3** : a distinctive manner of doing something ⟨a batter's *style* of holding his bat⟩ **4** : a method or manner that is thought elegant, fashionable, or in accord with some standard : FASHION ⟨dine in *style*⟩ ⟨a dress that is out of *style*⟩

style 1

²style *vb* **styled; styl·ing** **1** : NAME, CALL ⟨*styles* himself an artist⟩ **2** : to design and make in accord with an accepted or a new style ⟨well-*styled* hats⟩

styl·ish \'stī-lish\ *adj* : having style : FASHIONABLE — **styl·ish·ly** *adv* — **styl·ish·ness** *n*

sty·lus \'stī-ləs\ *n, pl* **sty·li** \-,lī\ *or* **sty·lus·es** : a pointed instrument used by the ancients for writing on wax tablets

suave \'swäv\ *adj* : persuasively pleasing : smoothly polite and agreeable ⟨*suave* manners⟩

¹sub \'səb\ *n* : SUBSTITUTE

²sub *vb* **subbed; sub·bing** : to act as a substitute

³sub *n* : SUBMARINE

sub- *prefix* **1** : under : beneath : below ⟨*subsoil*⟩ ⟨*subnormal*⟩ **2** : subordinate : secondary ⟨*substation*⟩ **3** : subdivision of ⟨*subcommittee*⟩ **4** : so as to form, stress, or deal with subordinate parts or relations ⟨*sublet*⟩ **5** : less than completely, perfectly, or typically : somewhat ⟨*subacid*⟩

sub·di·vide \,səb-də-'vīd\ *vb* **sub·di·vid·ed; sub·di·vid·ing** **1** : to divide the parts of into more parts **2** : to divide (as a tract of land) into several parts

sub·di·vi·sion \,səb-də-'vizh-ən\ *n* **1** : the act of subdividing **2** : one of the parts into which something is subdivided

sub·due \səb-'dü, -'dyü\ *vb* **sub·dued; sub·du·ing** **1** : CONQUER, VANQUISH **2** : to bring under control : CURB **3** : REDUCE, SOFTEN ⟨a *subdued* light⟩

¹sub·ject \'səb-jikt\ *n* **1** : a person under the authority or control of another **2** : a person who is subject to a monarch or state **3** : an individual subjected to an operation or process ⟨the *subject* of an experiment⟩ **4** : the person or thing discussed or treated : TOPIC **5** : the word or word group about which the predicate makes a statement

²subject *adj* **1** : owing obedience or allegiance to the power or rule of another **2** : EXPOSED, LIABLE **3** : PRONE, DISPOSED **4** : dependent upon ⟨*subject* to approval⟩

³sub·ject \səb-'jekt\ *vb* **1** : to bring under control or rule **2** : to make liable or accountable **3** : to cause to undergo or submit to ⟨*subjected* to many inconveniences⟩

sub·junc·tive \səb-'jəngk-tiv\ *adj* : representing a denoted act or state not as fact but as contingent or possible ⟨a verb in the *subjunctive* mood⟩

sub·lime \sə-'blīm\ *adj* **1** : grand or noble in thought, expression, or manner ⟨*sublime* truths⟩ **2** : having awe-inspiring beauty or grandeur ⟨*sublime* scenery⟩

¹sub·ma·rine \'səb-mə-,rēn\ *adj* : being, acting, growing, or used under water especially in the sea

²submarine *n* : a naval ship able to operate under the surface of the water

sub·merge \səb-'mərj\ *vb* **sub·merged; sub·merg·ing** **1** : to put under or plunge into water **2** : to cover or become covered with or as if with water ⟨floods *submerged* the town⟩

sub·mis·sion \səb-'mish-ən\ *n* **1** : the act of submitting something (as for consideration or comment) **2** : the condition of being humble or obedient **3** : the act of submitting to power or authority

sub·mis·sive \səb-'mis-iv\ *adj* : inclined or willing to submit to others : MEEK

sub·mit \səb-'mit\ *vb* **sub·mit·ted; sub·mit·ting** **1** : to leave to the judgment or approval of someone else ⟨*submit* a plan for consideration⟩ **2** : to put forward as an opinion, reason, or idea **3** : YIELD, SURRENDER

¹sub·or·di·nate \sə-'bȯrd-n-ət\ *adj* **1** : placed in or occupying a lower class or rank : INFERIOR **2** : submissive to or controlled by authority

²subordinate *n* : one that is subordinate

³**sub·or·di·nate** \sə-'bȯrd-n-,āt\ *vb* **sub·or·di·nat·ed; sub·or·di·nat·ing 1** : to make subordinate **2** : SUBDUE

sub·scribe \səb-'skrīb\ *vb* **sub·scribed; sub·scrib·ing 1** : to sign one's name or a document to indicate approval, obligation, or awareness of something written **2** : to signify approval by or as if by signing one's name ⟨we *subscribe* to your plan⟩ **3** : to agree to give or contribute by signing one's name with the amount promised ⟨*subscribe* fifty dollars to the building fund⟩ **4** : to place an order (as for a magazine) with payment or promise to pay

sub·scrip·tion \səb-'skrip-shən\ *n* **1** : an act or instance of subscribing **2** : a thing or amount subscribed ⟨a *subscription* of ten dollars⟩

sub·se·quent \'səb-si-kwənt\ *adj* : following in time, order, or place ⟨*subsequent* events⟩ — **sub·se·quent·ly** *adv*

sub·set \'səb-,set\ *n* : a mathematical set each of whose members is also a member of a more inclusive set

sub·side \səb-'sīd\ *vb* **sub·sid·ed; sub·sid·ing 1** : to become lower : SINK ⟨the flood *subsided*⟩ **2** : to become quiet or less ⟨the pain *subsided*⟩

sub·sist \səb-'sist\ *vb* **1** : to continue living or being : EXIST, PERSIST **2** : to receive maintenance (as food and clothing) : LIVE ⟨*subsist* on charity⟩

sub·sist·ence \səb-'sis-təns\ *n* **1** : EXISTENCE **2** : means of subsisting : the minimum (as of food and clothing) necessary to support life

sub·soil \'səb-,sȯil\ *n* : a layer of weathered mineral soil lying just under the organic surface soil

sub·stance \'səb-stəns\ *n* **1** : the real part of a thing : ESSENCE **2** : the most important part ⟨the *substance* of a speech⟩ **3** : the material of which something is made **4** : PROPERTY, WEALTH ⟨a man of *substance*⟩

sub·stan·tial \səb-'stan-chəl\ *adj* **1** : consisting of or relating to substance : REAL, TRUE **2** : IMPORTANT, ESSENTIAL **3** : SATISFYING, NOURISHING ⟨a *substantial* meal⟩ **4** : WELL-TO-DO **5** : firmly constructed **6** : considerable in quantity

sub·stan·ti·ate \səb-'stan-chē-,āt\ *vb* **sub·stan·ti·at·ed; sub·stan·ti·at·ing 1** : PROVE ⟨*substantiated* his claims in court⟩ **2** : EMBODY

¹**sub·sti·tute** \'səb-stə-,tüt, -,tyüt\ *n* : a person or thing that takes the place of another

²**substitute** *vb* **sub·sti·tut·ed; sub·sti·tut·ing 1** : to put in the place of another **2** : to serve as a substitute

sub·sti·tu·tion \,səb-stə-'tü-shən, -'tyü-\ *n* : the act or process of substituting

sub·ti·tle \'səb-,tīt-l\ *n* : a secondary or explanatory title (as of a book)

sub·tle \'sət-l\ *adj* **sub·tler** \'sət-lər\; **subtlest** \'sət-ləst\ **1** : DELICATE, REFINED ⟨a *subtle* fragrance⟩ **2** : SHREWD, KEEN ⟨*subtle* questions⟩ **3** : CLEVER, SLY ⟨*subtle* flattery⟩

sub·top·ic \'səb-,täp-ik\ *n* : a secondary or less important topic (as in a composition)

sub·tract \səb-'trakt\ *vb* : to take away (as one part or number from another) : DEDUCT

sub·trac·tion \səb-'trak-shən\ *n* **1** : an act or instance of subtracting **2** : the operation of deducting one number from another

sub·tra·hend \'səb-trə-,hend\ *n* : a number that is to be subtracted from a minuend

sub·urb \'səb-,ərb\ *n* **1** : an outlying part of a city or town **2** : a smaller community adjacent to a city **3** *pl* : the residential area adjacent to a city or large town — **sub·ur·ban** \sə-'bər-bən\ *adj or n*

sub·way \'səb-,wā\ *n* **1** : an underground passage **2** : a usually electric underground railway

suc·ceed \sək-'sēd\ *vb* **1** : to come after : FOLLOW **2** : to take the throne or assume power after the death or removal of someone else **3** : to get possession of a thing next ⟨*succeed* to the ownership⟩ **4** : to be successful

suc·cess \sək-'ses\ *n* **1** : satisfactory completion of something **2** : the gaining of wealth, favor, or fame **3** : a person or thing that succeeds

suc·cess·ful \sək-'ses-fəl\ *adj* **1** : resulting or ending favorably or in success **2** : gaining or having gained success — **suc·cess·ful·ly** *adv*

suc·ces·sion \sək-'sesh-ən\ *n* **1** : the order, act, or right of succeeding to a throne, title, or property **2** : a repeated following of one person or thing after another **3** : a series of persons or things that follow one after another

suc·ces·sive \sək-'ses-iv\ *adj* : following in order and without gaps : CONSECUTIVE — **suc·ces·sive·ly** *adv*

suc·ces·sor \sək-'ses-ər\ *n* : one that succeeds to a throne, title, estate, or office

¹**suc·cor** \'sək-ər\ *n* : AID, RELIEF

²**succor** *vb* : to help or relieve when in need

suc·cu·lent \'sək-yə-lənt\ *adj* : JUICY

suc·cumb \sə-'kəm\ *vb* **1** : to yield to force or pressure ⟨*succumb* to temptation⟩ **2** : DIE

¹**such** \'səch, səch\ *adj* **1** : of a kind just specified or to be specified ⟨bag *such* as a doctor carries⟩ **2** : of the same class, type, or sort : SIMILAR ⟨opened three *such* stores⟩ **3** : so great : so remarkable ⟨*such* courage⟩

²**such** *pron* : that sort of thing, person, or group : THAT ⟨has a plan, if it may be called *such*⟩ ⟨boards and nails and *such*⟩

suck \'sək\ *vb* **1** : to draw in liquid and especially mother's milk with the mouth **2** : to draw liquid from by action of the mouth ⟨*suck* an orange⟩ **3** : to consume by applying the lips or tongue to ⟨*suck* a lollipop⟩ **4** : ABSORB ⟨plants *suck* moisture from the soil⟩

suck·er \'sək-ər\ *n* **1** : one that sucks **2** : a structure (as a muscular disk) by which an animal clings by suction **3** : a freshwater fish related to the carps that has thick soft lips for sucking in food **4** : a shoot from the roots or lower part of a plant **5** : LOLLIPOP

suck·le \'sək-əl\ *vb* **suck·led; suck·ling** : to feed directly from the breast or udder

suck·ling \'sək-ling\ *n* : a young mammal not yet weaned

suc·tion \'sək-shən\ *n* **1** : the act or process of sucking **2** : the process of drawing something (as liquid or dust) into a space (as in a pump) by removing air from the space **3** : the process of causing adhesion of surfaces by removing air from a space between them **4** : the force exerted during suction

sud·den \'səd-n\ *adj* **1** : happening or coming quickly and unexpectedly ⟨a *sudden* shower⟩ **2** : met with unexpectedly ⟨a *sudden* turn in the road⟩ **3** : ABRUPT, STEEP ⟨a *sudden* descent to the sea⟩ **4** : HASTY, RASH ⟨a *sudden* decision⟩ **5** : made or brought about in a short time ⟨a *sudden* cure⟩ — **sud·den·ly** *adv*

suds \'sədz\ *n pl* **1** : soapy water especially when frothy **2** : the froth on soapy water

sue \'sü\ *vb* **sued; su·ing** **1** : to seek justice or right by bringing legal action **2** : to make a request or application : PLEAD ⟨*sue* for peace⟩

suede \'swād\ *n* [from French *Suède* "Sweden", in the phrase *gants de Suède* "gloves of Sweden"] : leather tanned and rubbed so that it is soft and has a slight nap

su·et \'sü-ət\ *n* : the hard fat about the kidneys and loins in beef and mutton that yields tallow

suf·fer \'səf-ər\ *vb* **1** : to feel or endure pain **2** : EXPERIENCE, UNDERGO ⟨*suffer* a defeat⟩ **3** : to bear loss or damage ⟨his business *suffered* during his illness⟩ **4** : ALLOW, PERMIT

suf·fer·ing \'səf-ə-ring\ *n* **1** : the state or experience of one that suffers **2** : PAIN, HARDSHIP

suf·fice \sə-'fīs\ *vb* **suf·ficed; suf·fic·ing** **1** : to satisfy a need **2** : to be enough for

suf·fi·cient \sə-'fish-ənt\ *adj* : enough to accomplish a purpose or fill a need — **suf·fi·cient·ly** *adv*

suf·fix \'səf-,iks\ *n* : a sound or sequence of sounds or a letter or sequence of letters occurring at the end of a word and having meaning in itself

suf·fo·cate \'səf-ə-,kāt\ *vb* **suf·fo·cat·ed; suf·fo·cat·ing** **1** : to kill by stopping the breath : deprive of air : STIFLE, CHOKE **2** : to be or become choked, stifled, or smothered **3** : to have or cause to have a feeling of smothering

suf·frage \'səf-rij\ *n* : the right to vote

¹**sug·ar** \'shug-ər\ *n* **1** : a sweet substance obtained from sugarcane, sugar beets, or maple syrup **2** : any of numerous sweet substances obtained from grapes, corn, or milk

²**sugar** *vb* **1** : to mix, cover, or sprinkle with sugar **2** : to make something less hard to take or bear ⟨*sugar* advice with flattery⟩ **3** : to change to crystals of sugar

sugar beet *n* : a large white-rooted beet grown as a source of sugar

sug·ar·cane \'shug-ər-,kān\ *n* : a tall strong grass with jointed stems widely raised in tropical regions for the sugar it yields

sugar maple *n* : an American maple tree with hard close-grained wood and a sweet sap that yields maple syrup and maple sugar

sug·gest \səg-'jest, sə-'jest\ *vb* **1** : to put (as a thought or desire) into a person's mind **2** : to propose as an idea ⟨*suggest* going for a walk⟩ **3** : to bring to mind through close connection or association ⟨smoke *suggests* fire⟩

sugarcane

sug·ges·tion \səg-'jes-chən, sə-'jes-\ *n* **1** : the act or process of suggesting **2** : a thought or plan that is suggested **3** : TRACE, HINT

sug·ges·tive \səg-'jes-tiv, sə-'jes-\ *adj* **1** : INDICATIVE **2** : PROVOCATIVE **3** : arousing mental associations

su·i·cide \'sü-ə-,sīd\ *n* **1** : the act of killing oneself purposely **2** : a person who commits suicide

¹**suit** \'süt\ *n* **1** : an action in court for enforcing a right or claim **2** : an act or instance of suing or entreating : APPEAL **3** : COURTSHIP, WOOING **4** : a number of things used together : SET ⟨a *suit* of clothes⟩ **5** : all the playing cards of one kind (as spades) in a pack

²**suit** *vb* **1** : to be appropriate or satisfactory **2** : ACCOMMODATE, ADAPT ⟨*suit* the action to the word⟩ **3** : to be proper for or becoming to **4** : to meet the needs or desires of

suit·a·bil·i·ty \,süt-ə-'bil-ət-ē\ *n* : the quality or state of being suitable

suit·a·ble \'süt-ə-bəl\ *adj* : capable of suiting : PROPER — **suit·a·bly** \-blē\ *adv*

suit·case \'süt-ˌkās\ *n* : a flat rectangular traveling bag

suite *n* 1 \'swēt\ : a company of attendants : RETINUE ⟨an ambassador's *suite*⟩ 2 \'swēt, 'süt\ : a number of things that make up a series or a set ⟨*suite* of rooms⟩

suit·or \'süt-ər\ *n* 1 : one that sues or petitions 2 : one who courts a woman or seeks to marry her

sul·fur *or* **sul·phur** \'səl-fər\ *n* : a yellow chemical element that is found widely in nature and is used in making chemicals and paper

sul·fu·rous *or* **sul·phu·rous** \'səl-fə-rəs\ *adj* 1 : containing or resembling sulfur 2 : FIERY ⟨*sulphurous* language⟩

¹sulk \'səlk\ *vb* : to be moodily silent or irritable

²sulk *n* 1 : the state of one sulking ⟨had a case of the *sulks*⟩ 2 : a sulky mood or spell ⟨in a *sulk*⟩

¹sulk·y \'səl-kē\ *adj* **sulk·i·er; sulk·i·est** 1 : inclined to sulk 2 : SULLEN, GLOOMY

²sulky *n, pl* **sulk·ies** : a light two-wheeled vehicle with a seat for the driver only and usually without a body

sul·len \'səl-ən\ *adj* 1 : not sociable : SULKY 2 : GLOOMY, DISMAL ⟨a *sullen* sky⟩

sul·tan \'səlt-n\ *n* : a sovereign especially of a Muslim state

sul·tan·a \ˌsəl-'tan-ə\ *n* : the wife, mother, sister, or daughter of a sultan

sul·try \'səl-trē\ *adj* **sul·tri·er; sul·tri·est** 1 : very hot and moist : SWELTERING 2 : burning hot : TORRID

¹sum \'səm\ *n* 1 : a quantity of money : AMOUNT 2 : the whole amount ⟨the *sum* of man's experience⟩ 3 : the chief points when taken together : SUMMARY ⟨the *sum* of the evidence⟩ 4 : the result obtained by adding numbers ⟨the *sum* of 4 and 5 is 9⟩ 5 : a problem in arithmetic

²sum *vb* **summed; sum·ming** 1 : to find the sum of by adding or counting 2 : SUMMARIZE ⟨*sum* up a report⟩

su·mac *or* **su·mach** \'shü-ˌmak, 'sü-\ *n* 1 : any of a group of trees, shrubs, or woody vines with feathery compound leaves and loose clusters of red or white berries 2 : a material made of the leaves and other parts of sumac and used in tanning and dyeing

sum·ma·rize \'səm-ə-ˌrīz\ *vb*

sumac

sum·ma·rized; sum·ma·riz·ing : to tell in or reduce to a summary

¹sum·ma·ry \'səm-ə-rē\ *adj* 1 : expressing or covering the main points briefly : CONCISE ⟨a *summary* account⟩ 2 : done without delay or formality ⟨*summary* punishment⟩

²summary *n, pl* **sum·ma·ries** *n* : a brief or concise statement of the main points (as in a book or report)

¹sum·mer \'səm-ər\ *n* 1 : the season between spring and autumn comprising in the northern hemisphere usually the months of June, July, and August or as reckoned astronomically extending from the June solstice to the September equinox 2 : YEAR ⟨a girl of sixteen *summers*⟩

²summer *vb* : to pass the summer

sum·mer·time \'səm-ər-ˌtīm\ *n* : the summer season

sum·mer·y \'səm-ə-rē\ *adj* : of, relating to, or characteristic of summer

sum·mit \'səm-ət\ *n* : the highest point (as of a mountain) : TOP

sum·mon \'səm-ən\ *vb* 1 : to call or send for : order to convene 2 : to order to appear before a court of law 3 : to call forth : AROUSE ⟨*summon* up courage⟩ — **sum·mon·er** *n*

sum·mons \'səm-ənz\ *n, pl* **sum·mons·es** 1 : the act of summoning 2 : a call by authority to appear at a place named or to attend to some duty 3 : a written order to appear in court

sump·tu·ous \'səmp-chə-wəs\ *adj* : involving large expense : LUXURIOUS ⟨a *sumptuous* feast⟩

¹sun \'sən\ *n* 1 : the heavenly body whose light makes our day : the member of the solar system round which the planets revolve 2 : a heavenly body like our sun 3 : SUNSHINE

²sun *vb* **sunned; sun·ning** 1 : to expose to or as if to the rays of the sun 2 : to sun oneself

sun·beam \'sən-ˌbēm\ *n* : a ray of sunlight

sun·bon·net \'sən-ˌbän-ət\ *n* : a bonnet with a wide brim framing the face and usually a ruffle at the back to protect the neck from the sun

¹sun·burn \'sən-ˌbərn\ *vb* : to burn or discolor by the sun

²sunburn *n* : skin inflammation caused by too much exposure to sunlight

sun·dae \'sən-dē\ *n* : a serving of ice cream topped with fruit, syrup, or nuts

Sun·day \'sən-dē\ *n* : the first day of the week : the Christian Sabbath

sun·di·al \'sən-ˌdī-əl\ *n* : a device to show the time of

sundial

day by the position of the shadow cast typically by a straight-edged object on a marked plate or disk

sun·down \'sən-ˌdaún\ *n* : SUNSET

sun·dries \'sən-drēz\ *n pl* : various small articles or items

sun·dry \'sən-drē\ *adj* : MISCELLANEOUS, VARIOUS ⟨for *sundry* reasons⟩

sun·fish \'sən-ˌfish\ *n, pl* **sunfish** *or* **sun·fish·es**
1 : a large sea fish with a very deep, short, and flat body, high fins, and a small mouth **2** : any of numerous mostly small and brightly colored American freshwater fishes related to the perches

sun·flow·er \'sən-ˌflaú-ər\ *n* : a tall daisylike plant often grown for its large flower heads with brown center and yellow petals or for its edible oil-rich seeds

sung *past of* SING

sunk *past of* SINK

sunk·en \'səng-kən\ *adj* **1** : SUBMERGED ⟨*sunken* ships⟩ **2** : fallen in : HOLLOW ⟨*sunken* cheeks⟩ **3** : lying in a depression ⟨*sunken* gardens⟩ **4** : constructed below the general floor level ⟨a *sunken* living room⟩

sun·light \'sən-ˌlīt\ *n* : SUNSHINE

sun·lit \'sən-ˌlit\ *adj* : lighted by the sun

sun·ny \'sən-ē\ *adj* **sun·ni·er; sun·ni·est**
1 : bright with sunshine ⟨a *sunny* day⟩
2 : MERRY, BRIGHT ⟨a *sunny* smile⟩

sun·rise \'sən-ˌrīz\ *n* **1** : the apparent rise of the sun above the horizon : the light and color that go with this **2** : the time at which the sun rises

sun·set \'sən-ˌset\ *n* **1** : the apparent descent of the sun below the horizon : the light and color that go with this **2** : the time at which the sun sets

sun·shade \'sən-ˌshād\ *n* : something (as a parasol or an awning) used as a protection from the sun's rays

sun·shine \'sən-ˌshīn\ *n* **1** : the sun's light or direct rays : the warmth and light given by the sun's rays **2** : something that radiates warmth, cheer, or happiness

sun·stroke \'sən-ˌstrōk\ *n* : a disorder marked by high fever and collapse and caused by too great exposure to the sun

sun·up \'sən-ˌəp\ *n* : SUNRISE

sun·ward \'sən-wərd\ *adj* : facing the sun

super- *prefix* **1** : over and above ⟨*super*structure⟩ : higher in quality, quantity, or degree than : more than ⟨*super*human⟩ **2** : in addition ⟨*super*tax⟩ **3** : exceeding or so as to exceed the normal ⟨*super*heat⟩ **4** : in excessive degree : VERY ⟨*super*sensitive⟩ **5** : surpassing all or most others of its kind ⟨*super*highway⟩

su·perb \sú-'pərb\ *adj* **1** : MAJESTIC, NOBLE **2** : RICH, SUMPTUOUS **3** : of supreme excellence or beauty

su·per·fi·cial \ˌsü-pər-'fish-əl\ *adj* **1** : of or relating to the surface or appearance only ⟨a *superficial* cut⟩ **2** : not thorough : SHALLOW ⟨a *superficial* piece of work⟩ — **su·per·fi·cial·ly** *adv*

su·per·flu·i·ty \ˌsü-pər-'flü-ət-ē\ *n, pl* **su·per·flu·i·ties 1** : EXCESS, OVERSUPPLY **2** : something unnecessary or more than enough

su·per·flu·ous \sú-'pər-flə-wəs\ *adj* : exceeding what is sufficient or necessary : EXTRA

su·per·hu·man \ˌsü-pər-'hyü-mən\ *adj* : exceeding normal human power, size, or capability ⟨*superhuman* effort⟩

su·per·im·pose \ˌsü-pər-im-'pōz\ *vb* **su·per·im·posed; su·per·im·pos·ing** : to place or lay over or above something

su·per·in·tend \ˌsü-pər-in-'tend\ *vb* : to have or exercise the charge of : OVERSEE, DIRECT

su·per·in·tend·ent \ˌsü-pər-in-'ten-dənt\ *n* : a person who oversees or manages something (as schools or a building)

¹**su·pe·ri·or** \sú-'pir-ē-ər\ *adj* **1** : situated higher up : higher in rank, importance, numbers, or quality **2** : courageously or serenely indifferent ⟨*superior* to pain⟩ **3** : excellent of its kind : BETTER **4** : feeling that one is better or more important than others : ARROGANT

²**superior** *n* **1** : one that is higher than another in rank, station, or quality **2** : the head of a religious house or order — **su·pe·ri·or·i·ty** \sú-ˌpir-ē-'ȯr-ət-ē\ *n*

¹**su·per·la·tive** \sú-'pər-lət-iv\ *adj* **1** : of, relating to, or being the form of an adjective or adverb that shows the highest or lowest degree of comparison **2** : better than all others : SUPREME

²**superlative** *n* : the superlative degree or a superlative form in a language

su·per·nat·u·ral \ˌsü-pər-'nach-ə-rəl\ *adj* : of or relating to something beyond or outside of nature or the visible observable universe

su·per·sede \ˌsü-pər-'sēd\ *vb* **su·per·sed·ed; su·per·sed·ing** : to take the place or position of : REPLACE, DISPLACE

su·per·son·ic \ˌsü-pər-'sän-ik\ *adj* **1** : relating to vibrations too rapid to be heard **2** : having a speed from one to five times that of sound ⟨a *supersonic* airplane⟩

su·per·sti·tion \ˌsü-pər-'stish-ən\ *n* : beliefs or practices resulting from ignorance, fear of the unknown, or trust in magic or chance

su·per·sti·tious \ˌsü-pər-'stish-əs\ *adj* : of, relating to, showing, or influenced by superstition

---

j job **ng** sing **ō** low **ȯ** moth **ȯi** coin **th** thin **th̲** this **ü** boot **ú** foot **y** you **yü** few **yú** furious **zh** vision

su·per·vise \'sü-pər-,vīz\ *vb* **su·per·vised; su·per·vis·ing** : SUPERINTEND, OVERSEE

su·per·vi·sion \,sü-pər-'vizh-ən\ *n* : the act of supervising : MANAGEMENT

su·per·vi·sor \'sü-pər-,vī-zər\ *n* **1** : one that supervises **2** : an officer in charge of a business, government, or school unit or operation

sup·per \'səp-ər\ *n* **1** : the evening meal especially when dinner is eaten at midday **2** : refreshments served late in the evening especially at a social gathering

sup·plant \sə-'plant\ *vb* **1** : to take the place of another especially by trickery or force **2** : REPLACE, SUPERSEDE

sup·ple \'səp-əl\ *adj* **sup·pler** \'səp-lər\; **sup·plest** \'səp-ləst\ **1** : adapting easily : ADAPTABLE ⟨a *supple* mind⟩ **2** : capable of being bent or folded without creases or breaks : PLIANT ⟨*supple* leather⟩ **3** : LIMBER ⟨*supple* legs of a dancer⟩

¹sup·ple·ment \'səp-lə-mənt\ *n* : something that supplies a want or makes an addition ⟨the *supplement* at the back of the book⟩

²sup·ple·ment \'səp-lə-,ment\ *vb* : to add to : COMPLETE ⟨*supplements* his income by doing odd jobs⟩

sup·ple·men·ta·ry \,səp-lə-'ment-ə-rē\ *adj* : added as a supplement : ADDITIONAL

sup·pli·cate \'səp-lə-,kāt\ *vb* **sup·pli·cat·ed; sup·pli·cat·ing 1** : to make a humble entreaty : pray to God **2** : to ask earnestly and humbly : BESEECH

sup·pli·ca·tion \,səp-lə-'kā-shən\ *n* : the act of supplicating : earnest humble entreaty

¹sup·ply \sə-'plī\ *vb* **sup·plied; sup·ply·ing 1** : to add as a supplement ⟨*supply* an explanation⟩ **2** : to provide for : SATISFY ⟨enough to *supply* the demand⟩ **3** : PROVIDE, FURNISH ⟨*supplied* the sandwiches for the picnic⟩

²supply *n, pl* **sup·plies 1** : the quantity or amount that is needed or can be obtained : STOCK **2** : PROVISIONS, STORES **3** : the act or process of filling a want or need : PROVISION **4** : the quantities of goods or services offered for sale at a particular time or at one price

¹sup·port \sə-'pōrt\ *vb* **1** : to endure bravely or quietly : BEAR **2** : to take sides with : ASSIST ⟨*support* a candidate⟩ **3** : VERIFY ⟨his actions *support* his promises⟩ **4** : to pay the costs of : MAINTAIN ⟨*supports* a large family⟩ **5** : to hold up or in position : serve as a foundation or prop for ⟨pillars *support* the porch roof⟩ **6** : to keep going : SUSTAIN — **sup·port·er** *n*

²support *n* **1** : the act of supporting : the condition of being supported **2** : one that supports

sup·pose \sə-'pōz\ *vb* **sup·posed; sup·pos·ing**

1 : to take as true or as a fact for the sake of argument **2** : BELIEVE, THINK ⟨I *suppose* he is honest⟩ **3** : GUESS ⟨who do you *suppose* won⟩

sup·posed \sə-'pōzd\ *adj* **1** : BELIEVED **2** : mistakenly believed **3** : EXPECTED, REQUIRED ⟨I am *supposed* to be home early⟩ — **sup·pos·ed·ly** \-'pō-zəd-lē\ *adv*

sup·press \sə-'pres\ *vb* **1** : to put down (as by authority or force) : SUBDUE ⟨*suppress* a revolt⟩ **2** : to hold back : REPRESS ⟨could hardly *suppress* a smile⟩

sup·pres·sion \sə-'presh-ən\ *n* : an act or instance of suppressing : the state of being suppressed

su·prem·a·cy \su̇-'prem-ə-sē\ *n, pl* **su·prem·a·cies** : supreme rank, power, or authority

su·preme \su̇-'prēm\ *adj* **1** : highest in rank or authority **2** : highest in degree or quality : UTMOST ⟨*supreme* confidence⟩ **3** : ULTIMATE, FINAL ⟨the *supreme* sacrifice⟩ — **su·preme·ly** *adv*

Supreme Being *n* : ²GOD

supreme court *n* : the highest court of the United States consisting of a chief justice and eight associate justices

sur- *prefix* : over : SUPER- ⟨*surprint*⟩ ⟨*surtax*⟩

¹sure \'shu̇r\ *adj* **sur·er; sur·est 1** : firmly established : STEADFAST **2** : RELIABLE, TRUSTWORTHY ⟨a *sure* remedy⟩ **3** : ASSURED, CONFIDENT **4** : not to be disputed : CERTAIN **5** : bound to happen ⟨*sure* disaster⟩ **6** : DESTINED, BOUND ⟨he is *sure* to win⟩

²sure *adv* : SURELY

sure·ly \'shu̇r-lē\ *adv* **1** : with assurance : CONFIDENTLY **2** : without doubt : CERTAINLY **3** : INDEED, REALLY ⟨I *surely* do miss them⟩

surf \'sərf\ *n* **1** : the swell of the sea that splashes upon the shore **2** : the sound, splash, and foam of breaking waves

¹sur·face \'sər-fəs\ *n* **1** : the outside of an object : one face of an object **2** : the mere outside : outside appearance ⟨on the *surface* the plan seems good⟩

²surface *adj* **1** : of or relating to a surface : acting on a surface **2** : not deep or real ⟨*surface* scratches⟩

³surface *vb* **sur·faced; sur·fac·ing 1** : to give a surface to : make smooth (as by planing, paving, or varnishing) **2** : to come to the surface ⟨the submarine *surfaced*⟩

¹surge \'sərj\ *vb* **surged; surg·ing 1** : to rise and fall actively : TOSS **2** : to move in or as if in waves : SWELL ⟨crowds *surging* through the streets⟩

²surge *n* **1** : an onward rush, roll, or sweep like that of a wave ⟨a *surge* of anger⟩ **2** : a large wave or billow ⟨*surges* of water⟩

sur·geon \'sər-jən\ *n* : a doctor who specializes in surgery

sur·ger·y \'sər-jə-rē\ *n, pl* **sur·ger·ies** [from Old French *cirurgerie*, fr. Latin *chirurgia*, from Greek *cheirourgia*, from *cheirourgos* "working with the hand", from *cheir* "hand" and *ergon* "work"] **1** : a branch of medicine concerned with the correction of defects, the repair and healing of injuries, and the treatment of diseased conditions by operation **2** : the work done by a surgeon

sur·gi·cal \'sər-ji-kəl\ *adj* : of, relating to, or associated with surgery or surgeons ⟨*surgical* dressings⟩

sur·ly \'sər-lē\ *adj* **sur·li·er; sur·li·est** **1** : ILL= NATURED, DISAGREEABLE **2** : MENACING, THREATENING ⟨a *surly* dog⟩

¹sur·mise \sər-'mīz\ *vb* **sur·mised; sur·mis·ing** : to form an idea without proof that it is true : GUESS

²surmise *n* : a thought or idea based on scanty evidence : GUESS, CONJECTURE

sur·mount \sər-'maůnt\ *vb* **1** : CONQUER, OVERCOME ⟨*surmount* an obstacle⟩ **2** : to get to the top of **3** : to stand or lie at the top of ⟨a castle *surmounts* the cliff⟩

¹sur·name \'sər-ˌnām\ *n* : a family name : a last name

²surname *vb* **sur·named; sur·nam·ing** : to give a surname to ⟨a man *surnamed* Smith⟩

sur·pass \sər-'pas\ *vb* **1** : to be greater, better, or stronger than : EXCEED **2** : to go beyond the reach or powers of ⟨a task that *surpassed* his strength⟩

¹sur·plus \'sər-pləs\ *n* : an amount left over : EXCESS

²surplus *adj* : left over : EXTRA ⟨*surplus* wheat⟩

¹sur·prise \sər-'prīz\ *n* **1** : an attack made without warning **2** : an act or instance of taking unawares **3** : something that surprises **4** : ASTONISHMENT, AMAZEMENT

²surprise *vb* **sur·prised; sur·pris·ing** **1** : to attack unexpectedly : capture by an unexpected attack **2** : to take unawares : come upon unexpectedly **3** : to bring about by means of a surprise ⟨*surprise* a thief into confessing⟩ **4** : to strike with wonder or amazement because unexpected

syn SURPRISE, ASTONISH, AMAZE all mean to impress by being unexpected or unusual. SURPRISE means no more than this, but does stress the element of the unexpected ⟨his improved pitching *surprised* us all⟩ ASTONISH means to surprise greatly with something that is difficult or impossible to believe ⟨we were *astonished* by the young girl's thorough knowledge of space flights⟩ AMAZE carries the general idea of astonishment but emphasizes the bewilderment and wonder involved ⟨the magician *amazed* the children by making the rabbit disappear⟩

sur·pris·ing \sər-'prī-zing\ *adj* : ASTONISHING, AMAZING — **sur·pris·ing·ly** *adv*

¹sur·ren·der \sə-'ren-dər\ *vb* **1** : to give oneself or something over to the power, control, or possession of another especially under compulsion : YIELD ⟨*surrender* the fort⟩ **2** : RELINQUISH ⟨*surrendered* his place in line⟩

²surrender *n* : the act of giving up or yielding oneself or something into another's possession or control

sur·rey \'sər-ē\ *n, pl* **sur·reys** : a four-wheeled two-seated horse-drawn pleasure carriage

sur·round \sə-'raůnd\ *vb* : to enclose on all sides : ENCIRCLE, ENCOMPASS

surrey

sur·round·ings \sə-'raůn-dingz\ *n pl* : the circumstances, conditions, or objects around a person : ENVIRONMENT

¹sur·vey \sər-'vā\ *vb* **sur·veyed; sur·vey·ing** **1** : to look over and examine closely **2** : to determine the form, extent, or position of (as a tract of land) **3** : to view or study as a whole : make a survey of

²sur·vey \'sər-ˌvā\ *n, pl* **sur·veys** **1** : the action or an instance of surveying **2** : something that is surveyed **3** : a careful examination to learn certain facts ⟨a *survey* of the school system⟩ **4** : a history or description that covers a large subject briefly ⟨a *survey* of English literature⟩ **5** : the process of determining and making a record of the outline, measurements, or position of any part of the earth's surface

sur·vey·ing \sər-'vā-ing\ *n* **1** : the act or occupation of a person who makes surveys **2** : a branch of mathematics that teaches how to measure the earth's surface and record these measurements accurately

sur·vey·or \sər-'vā-ər\ *n* : one that surveys : a person whose occupation is surveying

sur·viv·al \sər-'vī-vəl\ *n* **1** : a living or continuing longer than another person or thing **2** : one that survives

sur·vive \sər-'vīv\ *vb* **sur·vived; sur·viv·ing** **1** : to remain alive : continue to exist **2** : OUTLIVE, OUTLAST ⟨*survived* his son⟩ ⟨*survived* the flood⟩

sur·vi·vor \sər-'vī-vər\ *n* : one that outlives or outlasts ⟨the only *survivor* of a large family⟩

sus·cep·ti·ble \sə-'sep-tə-bəl\ *adj* **1** : of such a nature as to permit ⟨words *susceptible* of being misunderstood⟩ **2** : having little resistance ⟨*susceptible* to colds⟩ **3** : easily affected or impressed ⟨*susceptible* to flattery⟩

¹sus·pect \'səs-ˌpekt, sə-'spekt\ *adj* : regarded with suspicion : SUSPECTED ⟨a person whose honesty is *suspect*⟩

²sus·pect \'səs-ˌpekt\ *n* : one who is suspected

³sus·pect \sə-'spekt\ *vb* **1** : to have doubts of : DISTRUST **2** : to imagine to be guilty without proof **3** : SURMISE, GUESS

sus·pend \sə-'spend\ *vb* **1** : to bar temporarily from a privilege or office ⟨*suspended* from school⟩ **2** : to stop or do away with for a time : WITHHOLD ⟨*suspend* a rule⟩ **3** : to cease for a time from operation or activity ⟨all business *suspended* during the storm⟩ **4** : to hang especially so as to be free except at one point ⟨*suspend* a ball by a thread⟩

sus·pend·er \sə-'spen-dər\ *n* : one of two supporting straps which pass over the shoulders and to which trousers or a skirt are fastened

sus·pense \sə-'spens\ *n* : uncertainty, anxiety, or worry about the result of something

sus·pen·sion \sə-'spen-chən\ *n* **1** : temporary forced withdrawal from a privilege or office ⟨*suspension* from school⟩ **2** : temporary removal of a rule or condition **3** : the state of being suspended

suspenders

sus·pi·cion \sə-'spish-ən\ *n* **1** : the act or an instance of suspecting or being suspected ⟨he was above *suspicion*⟩ **2** : a feeling that something is wrong : DOUBT **3** : a slight trace ⟨just a *suspicion* of garlic⟩ **syn** see DOUBT

sus·pi·cious \sə-'spish-əs\ *adj* **1** : tending to arouse suspicion ⟨*suspicious* actions⟩ **2** : inclined to suspect or distrust ⟨*suspicious* of everything new⟩ **3** : showing distrust ⟨a *suspicious* glance⟩

sus·tain \sə-'stān\ *vb* **1** : to give support or relief to **2** : to provide with nourishment **3** : to keep up : PROLONG **4** : to support the weight of : PROP **5** : to buoy up ⟨*sustained* by hope⟩ **6** : to bear up under **7** : to support as true, legal, or just **8** : PROVE, CONFIRM

sus·te·nance \'səs-tə-nəns\ *n* **1** : a means of support or nourishment : FOOD **2** : the act of sustaining : the state of being sustained **3** : something that gives support, endurance, or strength

¹swab \'swäb\ *n* **1** : MOP **2** : a small piece of sponge, gauze, or absorbent cotton usually on the end of a small stick and used to apply medicine or to clean a sore or wound

swab 2

²swab *vb* **swabbed; swab·bing** : to use a swab on : clean, wash, or bathe with a swab

¹swag·ger \'swag-ər\ *vb* **1** : to walk with a conceited strut **2** : BOAST, BRAG

²swagger *n* : an act or instance of swaggering

¹swal·low \'swäl-ō\ *n* : any of a group of small long-winged migratory birds with graceful flight and forked tails

²swallow *vb* **1** : to take into the stomach through the mouth and throat **2** : to perform the actions used in swallowing something ⟨cleared his throat and *swallowed* before answering⟩ **3** : to envelop or take in as if by swallowing : ENGULF ⟨a ship *swallowed* by the waves⟩ **4** : to accept or believe without question, protest, or resentment ⟨he *swallows* everything he hears⟩ ⟨*swallow* an insult⟩ **5** : to keep from expressing or showing : REPRESS ⟨*swallowed* his anger⟩

³swallow *n* **1** : an act of swallowing **2** : an amount that can be swallowed at one time

swam *past of* SWIM

¹swamp \'swämp\ *n* : wet spongy land often partly covered with water

²swamp *vb* **1** : to cause to capsize in water or fill with water and sink **2** : to fill with or as if with water : sink after filling with water **3** : OVERWHELM ⟨was *swamped* with work⟩

swamp·y \'swäm-pē\ *adj* **swamp·i·er; swamp·i·est** : of, relating to, or resembling a swamp

swan \'swän\ *n* : a heavy-bodied long-necked usually white water bird related to but larger than the geese

¹swap \'swäp\ *vb* **swapped; swap·ping** : to give in exchange : make an exchange : TRADE

²swap *n* : EXCHANGE, TRADE

swan

¹swarm \'sworm\ *n* **1** : a large number of bees that leave a hive together to form a new colony elsewhere **2** : a large crowd usually in motion : THRONG

²swarm *vb* **1** : to form and depart from the hive in a swarm ⟨*swarming* bees⟩ **2** : to migrate, move, or gather in a swarm or large crowd : THRONG **3** : to contain or fill with a swarm : TEEM ⟨a floor *swarming* with ants⟩

swar·thy \'swor-thē, -thē\ *adj* **swar·thi·er; swar·thi·est** : dark in color or complexion : dark-skinned : DUSKY

¹swat \'swät\ *vb* **swat·ted; swat·ting** : to hit with a quick hard blow

²swat *n* : a hard blow

swath \'swäth\ *or* **swathe** \'swäth\ *n* **1** : a sweep of a scythe or machine in mowing or the path cut in one course **2** : a row of cut grass (as grain) **3** : a long broad strip or belt

swathe \'swäth\ *vb* **swathed; swath·ing 1 :** to bind or wrap with or as if with a bandage **2 :** ENVELOP

¹sway \'swā\ *vb* **1 :** to swing slowly back and forth or from side to side **2 :** to bend or be bent to one side : LEAN **3 :** to fluctuate between one point, position, or opinion and another **4 :** INFLUENCE

²sway *n* **1 :** the action or an instance of swaying or of being swayed **2 :** a controlling influence or force : RULE

swear \'swaər\ *vb* **swore** \'swōr\; **sworn** \'swȯrn\; **swear·ing 1 :** to make a solemn statement or promise under oath : VOW 〈*swear* allegiance〉 **2 :** to administer an oath to 〈*swear* a witness〉 **3 :** to bind by an oath 〈*swore* him to secrecy〉 **4 :** to take an oath **5 :** to use profane or obscene language : CURSE

¹sweat \'swet\ *vb* **sweat** *or* **sweat·ed; sweat·ing 1 :** to give off salty moisture through the pores of the skin : PERSPIRE **2 :** to give off or cause to give off moisture **3 :** to collect drops of moisture 〈stones *sweat* at night〉 **4 :** to work so hard that one perspires : TOIL 〈*sweat* over a lesson〉 **5 :** to get rid of or lose by perspiring 〈*sweat* out a fever〉 **6 :** to drive hard : OVERWORK

²sweat *n* **1 :** PERSPIRATION **2 :** moisture issuing from or gathering in drops on a surface **3 :** the condition of one sweating or sweated

sweat·er \'swet-ər\ *n* : a knitted or crocheted jacket or pullover

sweat gland *n* : any of numerous small skin glands that secrete perspiration

Swede \'swēd\ *n* : a native or inhabitant of Sweden

¹Swed·ish \'swēd-ish\ *adj* : of or relating to Sweden, the Swedes, or Swedish

²Swedish *n* : the language of the Swedes

¹sweep \'swēp\ *vb* **swept** \'swept\; **sweep·ing 1 :** to remove by brushing 〈*sweep* up dirt with a broom〉 **2 :** to clean by brushing 〈*sweep* a floor〉 **3 :** to strip or clear by blows or gusts 〈the storm *swept* the decks clean〉 **4 :** to move across with swiftness, force, or destruction 〈a raging torrent *swept* the fields〉 **5 :** to gather or take up with a single swift movement 〈*sweep* the money from the counter〉 **6 :** to touch a surface with an action or result like that of a brush 〈the musician's fingers *swept* the piano keys〉 **7 :** to move across, extend across, or cover a wide range 〈*sweep* the horizon with a glance〉 — **sweep·er** *n*

²sweep *n* **1 :** something (as a long oar) that sweeps or operates with a sweeping motion **2 :** an act or instance of sweeping : a clearing out or away with or as if with a broom **3 :** an overwhelming victory **4 :** a movement of great range and force **5 :** a curving or circular course or line 〈the *sweep* of a scythe〉 **6 :** RANGE, SCOPE **7 :** CHIMNEY SWEEP

¹sweep·ing \'swē-ping\ *n* **1 :** the act or action of one that sweeps **2** *pl* : things collected by sweeping : REFUSE

²sweeping *adj* **1 :** moving or extending in a wide curve or over a wide area 〈gave the audience a *sweeping* glance〉 **2 :** EXTENSIVE 〈*sweeping* reforms〉

¹sweet \'swēt\ *adj* **1 :** pleasing to the taste **2 :** having a relatively large sugar content **3 :** pleasing to the mind or feelings : AGREEABLE 〈*sweet* memories〉 **4 :** KINDLY, MILD 〈a *sweet* disposition〉 **5 :** FRAGRANT 〈a *sweet* smell〉 **6 :** delicately pleasing to the ear or eye **7 :** much loved : DEAR **8 :** not sour, stale, or rancid 〈*sweet* milk〉 **9 :** not salt or salted : FRESH 〈*sweet* butter〉 — **sweet·ish** *adj* — **sweet·ly** *adv* — **sweet·ness** *n*

²sweet *n* **1 :** something (as candy) that is sweet to the taste **2 :** DARLING, DEAR

sweet corn *n* : an Indian corn with sugar-rich kernels that is cooked as a vegetable while young

sweet·en \'swēt-n\ *vb* : to make or become sweet

sweet·en·ing \'swēt-n-ing\ *n* **1 :** the act or process of making sweet **2 :** something that sweetens

sweet·heart \'swēt-‚härt\ *n* : one who is loved

sweet·meat \'swēt-‚mēt\ *n* : a delicacy (as a piece of candy or candied fruit) rich in sugar

sweet pea *n* : a climbing plant related to the peas that is grown for its fragrant flowers of many colors

sweet potato *n* : the large sweet mealy edible root of a tropical vine somewhat like a morning glory

sweet wil·liam \-'wil-yəm\ *n, often cap W* : a European pink grown for its thick flat clusters of many‑colored flowers

¹swell \'swel\ *vb* **swelled; swelled** *or* **swol·len** \'swō-lən\; **swell·ing 1 :** to enlarge abnormally especially by internal pressure or growth 〈a *swollen* ankle〉 **2 :** to grow or make bigger : increase in size, quantity, value, or intensity **3 :** to extend upward or outward : BULGE 〈a heavy wind *swelled* the sails〉 **4 :** to fill or become filled with emotion 〈a heart *swelling* with gratitude〉

sweet william

²**swell** *n* **1** : an increase in size, quantity, value, or intensity **2** : a long rolling wave or succession of waves in the open sea **3** : a person dressed in the height of fashion **4** : a person of high social position or outstanding competence

³**swell** *adj* **1** : STYLISH, FASHIONABLE **2** : EXCELLENT, FIRST-RATE

swel·ter \'swel-tər\ *vb* **1** : to suffer, sweat, or be faint from heat **2** : to oppress with heat

swept *past of* SWEEP

¹**swerve** \'swərv\ *vb* **swerved**; **swerv·ing** : to turn aside suddenly from a straight line or course ⟨*swerved* to avoid an oncoming car⟩

²**swerve** *n* : an act or instance of swerving

¹**swift** \'swift\ *adj* **1** : moving or capable of moving with great speed **2** : occurring suddenly **3** : READY, ALERT — **swift·ly** *adv* — **swift·ness** *n*

²**swift** *adv* : SWIFTLY

³**swift** *n* **1** : a small very active lizard **2** : a small usually sooty black bird that is related to the hummingbirds but resembles a swallow

¹**swill** \'swil\ *vb* **1** : to eat or drink greedily or to excess **2** : to feed (as pigs) with swill

²**swill** *n* **1** : food for animals (as pigs) made up of edible refuse mixed with liquid **2** : GARBAGE, REFUSE

¹**swim** \'swim\ *vb* **swam** \'swam\; **swum** \'swəm\; **swim·ming** **1** : to move through or in water by moving arms, legs, fins, or tail **2** : to glide smoothly and quietly **3** : to float on or in or be covered with or as if with a liquid ⟨meat *swimming* in gravy⟩ **4** : to be dizzy : move or seem to move dizzily ⟨his head *swam* in the smoky room⟩ **5** : to cross by swimming ⟨*swim* the river⟩ — **swim·mer** *n*

²**swim** *n* **1** : an act or period of swimming ⟨enjoyed a good *swim*⟩ **2** : the main current of activity ⟨in the social *swim*⟩

swim·ming \'swim-ing\ *adj* **1** : capable of or used to swimming ⟨*swimming* birds⟩ **2** : used in or for swimming

¹**swin·dle** \'swin-dəl\ *vb* **swin·dled**; **swin·dling** : to get money or property from by fraud or deceit : CHEAT, DEFRAUD

²**swindle** *n* : an act or instance of swindling

swin·dler \'swin-dlər\ *n* : one that swindles

swine \'swīn\ *n, pl* **swine** : a hoofed domestic animal derived from the wild boar that has a long snout and bristly skin and is widely raised for meat

swine·herd \'swīn-,hərd\ *n* : one who tends swine

¹**swing** \'swing\ *vb* **swung** \'swəng\; **swing·ing** **1** : to move rapidly in a sweeping curve ⟨*swing* a bat⟩ **2** : to throw or toss in a circle or back

and forth ⟨*swing* a lasso⟩ **3** : to sway to and fro ⟨a basket *swung* on the girl's arm⟩ **4** : to hang or be hung so as to move freely back and forth or in a curve ⟨*swing* a hammock between two trees⟩ **5** : to move or turn around an axis or about a point of suspension ⟨the door *swung* open⟩ **6** : to manage or handle successfully ⟨unable to *swing* the job⟩ **7** : to march or walk with free swaying movements

²**swing** *n* **1** : an act of swinging **2** : a swinging movement, blow, or rhythm **3** : the distance through which something swings ⟨measured the *swing* of the pendulum⟩ **4** : a swinging seat usually hung by overhead ropes **5** : a style of jazz marked by lively rhythm in which the melody is freely interpreted and improvised on by the individual players

swipe \'swīp\ *n* : a strong sweeping blow

¹**swirl** \'swərl\ *n* **1** : a whirling mass or motion : EDDY **2** : whirling confusion **3** : a twisting shape or mark ⟨wore her hair in a *swirl*⟩

²**swirl** *vb* : to move with a whirling or twisting motion : WHIRL, EDDY

¹**swish** \'swish\ *vb* : to make, move, or strike with a rustling or hissing sound

²**swish** *n* **1** : a hissing sound (as of a whip cutting the air) or a light sweeping or rustling sound (as of a silk skirt) **2** : a swishing movement

¹**Swiss** \'swis\ *n, pl* **Swiss** : a native or inhabitant of Switzerland

²**Swiss** *adj* : of or relating to Switzerland or the Swiss

¹**switch** \'swich\ *n* **1** : a slender flexible whip, rod, or twig **2** : an act of switching **3** : a blow with a switch or whip **4** : a change or shift from one thing to another ⟨a *switch* in plans⟩ **5** : a tuft of long hairs on the tail of an animal (as a cow) **6** : a device for adjusting the rails of a track so that a train or streetcar may be turned from one track to another **7** : a railroad siding **8** : a device for making, breaking, or changing the connections in an electrical circuit **9** : a strand of added or artificial hair

switch 8

²**switch** *vb* **1** : to strike or whip with or as if with a switch **2** : to lash from side to side : WHISK ⟨a cow *switching* its tail⟩ **3** : to turn, shift, or change by operating a switch ⟨*switch* off the light⟩ **4** : CHANGE, EXCHANGE ⟨*switched* to a new barber⟩

switch·board \'swich-,bōrd\ *n* : an apparatus consisting of a board or panel on which are mounted electric switches so arranged that a number of circuits may be connected, combined, and controlled ⟨the *switchboards* of a telephone exchange⟩

¹swiv·el \'swiv-əl\ *n* : a device joining two parts so that one or both can pivot freely (as on a bolt or pin)

swivel in a chain

²swivel *vb* **swiv·eled** *or* **swiv·elled; swiv·el·ing** *or* **swiv·el·ling** : to turn on or as if on a swivel

swollen *past part of* SWELL

¹swoon \'swün\ *vb* : FAINT

²swoon *n* **1** : a partial or total loss of consciousness : FAINT **2** : DAZE, RAPTURE

¹swoop \'swüp\ *vb* : to rush down or pounce suddenly like a hawk attacking its prey

²swoop *n* : an act or instance of swooping

sword \'sōrd\ *n* : a weapon having a long and usually sharp-pointed and sharp-edged blade

sword·fish \'sōrd-,fish\ *n, pl* **swordfish** *or* **sword·fish·es** : a very large ocean food fish having a long swordlike beak formed by the bones of the upper jaw

swordfish

swords·man \'sōrdz-mən\ *n, pl* **swords·men** \-mən\ **1** : one who fights with a sword **2** : FENCER

swore *past of* SWEAR

sworn *past part of* SWEAR

swum *past part of* SWIM

swung *past of* SWING

syc·a·more \'sik-ə-,mōr\ *n* **1** : the common fig tree of Egypt and Asia Minor **2** : a maple tree of Europe and Asia **3** : a broad= leaved American tree with flaky bark and round fruits

sycamore twig

syl·lab·i·cate \sə-'lab-ə-,kāt\ *vb* **syl·lab·i·cat·ed; syl·lab·i·cat·ing** : SYLLABIFY

syl·lab·i·ca·tion \sə-,lab-ə-'kā-shən\ *n* : the forming of syllables : the dividing of words into syllables

syl·lab·i·fi·ca·tion \sə-,lab-ə-fə-'kā-shən\ *n* : SYLLABICATION

syl·lab·i·fy \sə-'lab-ə-,fī\ *vb* **syl·lab·i·fied; syl·lab·i·fy·ing** : to form or divide into syllables

syl·la·ble \'sil-ə-bəl\ *n* **1** : a unit of spoken language consisting of an uninterrupted utterance and forming either a whole word (as *man*) or a commonly recognized division of a word (as *syl* in *syl·la·ble*) **2** : one or more letters representing a syllable

sym·bol \'sim-bəl\ *n* **1** : something that stands for and represents something else : EMBLEM ⟨the cross is the *symbol* of Christianity⟩ **2** : a letter, character, or sign used instead of a word to represent a quantity, position, relationship, direction, or something to be done ⟨the sign + is the *symbol* for addition⟩ **syn** see EMBLEM

sym·bol·ic \sim-'bäl-ik\ *or* **sym·bol·i·cal** \-i-kəl\ *adj* : of, relating to, or using symbols or symbolism ⟨a *symbolic* meaning⟩

sym·bol·ize \'sim-bə-,līz\ *vb* **sym·bol·ized; sym·bol·iz·ing** : to serve as a symbol of : TYPIFY ⟨a lion *symbolizes* courage⟩

sym·met·ri·cal \sə-'met-ri-kəl\ *or* **sym·met·ric** \-rik\ *adj* : having or showing symmetry : BALANCED ⟨a *symmetrical* design⟩

sym·me·try \'sim-ə-trē\ *n, pl* **sym·me·tries** : correspondence in size, shape, and position of parts that are on opposite sides of a dividing line or center : an arrangement marked by regularity and balanced proportions ⟨the *symmetry* of the human body⟩

sym·pa·thet·ic \,sim-pə-'thet-ik\ *adj* **1** : fitting one's mood or disposition : CONGENIAL ⟨a *sympathetic* atmosphere⟩ **2** : feeling sympathy ⟨*sympathetic* friends⟩ **3** : favorably inclined or disposed ⟨*sympathetic* to their ambitions⟩ — **sym·pa·thet·i·cal·ly** \-i-kə-lē\ *adv*

sym·pa·thize \'sim-pə-,thīz\ *vb* **sym·pa·thized; sym·pa·thiz·ing** **1** : to feel or show sympathy ⟨*sympathize* with a person in his sorrow⟩ **2** : to be in accord with something ⟨*sympathized* with his friend's ambitions⟩

sym·pa·thy \'sim-pə-thē\ *n, pl* **sym·pa·thies** [from Latin *sympathia*, from Greek *sympatheia*, from *syn-* or *sym-* "together" and *pathos* "state of being affected", "feelings"] **1** : a relationship between persons or things wherein whatever affects one similarly affects the other **2** : inclination to think or feel alike : agreement of likes, interest, or aims forming a bond of goodwill ⟨*sympathy* between friends⟩ **3** : tendency to favor or support ⟨political *sympathies*⟩ **4** : the act of or capacity for entering into or sharing the feelings or interests of another **5** : COMPASSION, PITY **6** : an expression of sorrow for another's loss, grief, or misfortune

sym·phon·ic \sim-'fän-ik\ *adj* : of, relating to, or suggesting a symphony or symphony orchestra

sym·pho·ny \'sim-fə-nē\ *n, pl* **sym·pho·nies** **1** : harmonious arrangement (as of sound or color) **2** : a usually long and complex musical composition for a full orchestra **3** : a large orchestra of winds, strings, and percussion that plays symphonies and similar compositions

symp·tom \'simp-təm\ *n* **1** : a noticeable change in the body or its functions indicating disease **2** : SIGN, INDICATION ⟨*symptoms* of fear⟩

syn·a·gogue *or* **syn·a·gog** \'sin-ə-ˌgäg\ *n* : a Jewish house of worship

syn·apse \'sin-ˌaps\ *n* : the point at which a nerve impulse passes from one nerve cell to another

syn·o·nym \'sin-ə-ˌnim\ *n* : a word having the same meaning as another word in the same language

syn·on·y·mous \sə-'nän-ə-məs\ *adj* : having the character of a synonym

syn·tax \'sin-ˌtaks\ *n* : the way in which words are put together to form phrases, clauses, or sentences

syn·thet·ic \sin-'thet-ik\ *adj* : produced artificially especially by chemical means : not genuine : ARTIFICIAL

sy·rin·ga \sə-'ring-gə\ *n* : an ornamental garden shrub with white or cream-colored often fragrant flowers

¹**sy·ringe** \sə-'rinj\ *n* : a device used to inject fluid into or withdraw it from the body or its cavities

²**syringe** *vb* **sy·ringed; sy·ring·ing** : to cleanse or flush with or as if with a syringe

syringa

syr·up \'sər-əp, 'sir-\ *n* [from medieval Latin *syrupus*, from Arabic *sharāb* "drink", "syrup"; a related Arabic word for "drink", *sharbah*, was the source of English *sherbet*] **1** : a thick sticky solution of sugar and water often flavored or medicated **2** : the concentrated juice of a fruit or plant

sys·tem \'sis-təm\ *n* **1** : a group of objects or units so combined as to form a whole and operate or move interdependently and in harmony ⟨a heating *system*⟩ **2** : a body that functions as a whole ⟨the disease affected his entire *system*⟩ **3** : a group of bodily organs that together carry on some vital function ⟨the nervous *system*⟩ **4** : a definite scheme or method of governing or arranging : a method of procedure or classification ⟨a democratic *system* of government⟩ **5** : regular method or order : ORDERLINESS

sys·tem·at·ic \ˌsis-tə-'mat-ik\ *adj* **1** : having or using a system : METHODICAL **2** : carrying out a plan with thoroughness or regularity ⟨*systematic* efforts⟩ — **sys·tem·at·i·cal·ly** \-i-kə-lē\ *adv*

sys·tem·ic \sis-'tem-ik\ *adj* : of or relating to the body as a whole ⟨*systemic* disease⟩

t \'tē\ *n, often cap* : the twentieth letter of the English alphabet — **to a T** : PRECISELY, EXACTLY

tab \'tab\ *n* **1** : a short flap or tag attached to or projecting from something (as for hanging up) **2** : a close watch ⟨keep *tabs* on the weather⟩

tab·by \'tab-ē\ *n, pl* **tab·bies** **1** : a domestic cat with a gray or tawny coat striped and mottled with black **2** : a female domestic cat

tab·er·na·cle \'tab-ər-ˌnak-əl\ *n* **1** *often cap* : a structure of wood hung with curtains used in worship by the Israelites during their wanderings in the wilderness under Moses **2** : a dwelling place **3** : a house of worship

¹**ta·ble** \'tā-bəl\ *n* **1** : a piece of furniture having a smooth flat top fixed on legs **2** : FOOD, FARE ⟨sets a good *table*⟩ **3** : the people around a table **4** : a condensed statement in list form ⟨a *table* of contents⟩ **5** : a collection and arrangement of data in rows or columns for ready reference

²**table** *vb* **ta·bled; ta·bling** **1** : to put in the form of a table **2** : to put on a table

tab·leau \'tab-ˌlō\ *n, pl* **tab·leaus** *or* **tab·leaux** \-ˌlōz\ : a lifelike representation of a scene or event by a grouping of persons who remain motionless and silent

ta·ble·cloth \'tā-bəl-ˌklȯth\ *n* : a covering spread over a dining table before the places are set

ta·ble·land \'tā-bəl-ˌland\ *n* : PLATEAU

ta·ble·spoon \'tā-bəl-ˌspün\ *n* **1** : a large spoon used especially for measuring ingredients in cooking **2** : TABLESPOONFUL

ta·ble·spoon·ful \ˌtā-bəl-'spün-ˌfu̇l\ *n, pl* **ta·ble·spoon·fuls** \-ˌfu̇lz\ *or* **ta·ble·spoons·ful** \-'spünz-ˌfu̇l\ **1** : as much as a tablespoon will hold **2** : a unit of measure used in cooking equal to three teaspoonfuls

tab·let \'tab-lət\ *n* **1** : a thin flat slab of stiff material used for writing, painting, or drawing **2** : a thin slab usually of marble or bronze fastened to a wall to bear inscriptions ⟨a memorial *tablet*⟩ **3** : a number of sheets of writing paper glued together at one edge at the top or side **4** : a compressed or molded mass of a dry material ⟨vitamin *tablets*⟩

ta·ble·ware \'tā-bəl-ˌwaər\ *n* : utensils (as of china, glass, or silver) for use at the table

tab·u·late \'tab-yə-ˌlāt\ *vb* **tab·u·lat·ed; tab·u·lat·ing** : to put in the form of a table

tac·it \'tas-ət\ *adj* : expressed or understood without being put into words — **tac·it·ly** *adv*

¹tack \'tak\ *n* **1** : a small sharp-pointed nail usually with a broad flat head for fastening a light object or material to a solid surface **2** : a rope used to hold in place the forward lower corner of the lowest sail on a square-rigged mast of a ship **3** : the lower forward corner of a fore-and-aft sail **4** : the direction a ship is sailing as shown by the way the sails are trimmed or the run of a ship as trimmed in one way **5** : a change of course from one tack to another **6** : a zigzag movement or course **7** : a course of action **8** : any of various temporary stitches

tacks

²tack *vb* **1** : to fasten with tacks **2** : to attach or join loosely **3** : to change from one tack to another in sailing **4** : to follow a zigzag course

¹tack·le \'tak-əl\ *n* **1** : a set of equipment used in a particular activity 〈fishing *tackle*〉 **2** : the rigging of a ship **3** : an arrangement of ropes and pulleys for hoisting or pulling heavy objects **4** : an act of tackling **5** : a football lineman stationed between guard and end

²tackle *vb* **tack·led; tack·ling 1** : to attach or fasten with or as if with tackle **2** : to seize and throw down or stop (as in football) **3** : to set about dealing with 〈*tackle* a job〉

tackles 3

tact \'takt\ *n* : a keen understanding of how to get along with other persons

tact·ful \'takt-fəl\ *adj* : having or showing tact — **tact·ful·ly** *adv* — **tact·ful·ness** *n*

tac·tic \'tak-tik\ *n* : a planned action for gaining an end

tac·tics \'tak-tiks\ *n sing or pl* **1** : the science and art of arranging and moving troops or warships in action in such a way as to use them to advantage **2** : a system or method for gaining an end

tac·tile \'tak-təl\ *adj* : of or relating to the sense of touch

tact·less \'takt-ləs\ *adj* : having or showing no tact — **tact·less·ly** *adv* — **tact·less·ness** *n*

tad·pole \'tad-ˌpōl\ *n* [from older English *taddepol*, from *tade* or *tode* "toad" and *pol*

tadpoles

"head"] : the water-dwelling larva of frogs and toads that has a long tail and breathes with gills

taf·fy \'taf-ē\ *n, pl* **taf·fies** : a candy made usually of molasses or brown sugar boiled and pulled until porous

¹tag \'tag\ *n* **1** : a metal or plastic binding on the end of a shoelace **2** : a small flap or tab fixed or hanging on something 〈price *tag*〉 **3** : an often quoted saying

²tag *vb* **tagged; tag·ging 1** : to put a tag on **2** : to follow closely and persistently

³tag *n* : a game in which one player who is it chases the others and tries to make one of them it by touching him

⁴tag *vb* **tagged; tag·ging** : to touch in or as if in a game of tag

¹tail \'tāl\ *n* **1** : the rear end or the lengthened growth extending from the rear end of an animal **2** : something that in shape, appearance, or position is like an animal's tail 〈*tail* of a coat〉 **3** : the back, last, or lower part of something 〈*tail* of an airplane〉 **4** : the side or end opposite the head — **tailed** \'tāld\ *adj* — **tail·less** \'tāl-ləs\ *adj* — **tail·like** \'tāl-ˌlīk\ *adj*

tail

²tail *adj* : being at or coming from the rear

³tail *vb* **1** : to make or furnish with a tail **2** : to follow closely especially to keep watch on

tail·board \'tāl-ˌbōrd\ *n* : TAILGATE

tail·gate \'tāl-ˌgāt\ *n* : a board at the back end of a vehicle that can be let down for loading and unloading

tail·light \'tāl-ˌlīt\ *n* : a red warning light mounted at the rear of a vehicle

¹tai·lor \'tā-lər\ *n* [from Old French *tailleur*, literally, "one who cuts", from *taillier* "to cut"] : a person whose business is making or altering men's or women's outer garments

²tailor *vb* **1** : to make or fashion as the work of a tailor **2** : to make to fit a special need

tail·spin \'tāl-ˌspin\ *n* : a spiral dive or plunge by an airplane

¹taint \'tānt\ *vb* **1** : to touch or affect slightly with something bad **2** : to rot slightly 〈*tainted* meat〉 **3** : to make morally impure

²taint *n* **1** : a touch of decay **2** : a tainting or corrupting influence

¹take \'tāk\ *vb* **took** \'tuk\; **tak·en** \'tā-kən\; **tak·ing 1** : to get into one's hands : GRASP **2** : CAPTURE 〈*take* a fort〉 **3** : WIN 〈*take* first prize〉 **4** : to get possession of 〈*take* a cottage for the summer〉 **5** : to seize and affect suddenly 〈was *taken* ill〉 **6** : CHARM, DELIGHT 〈was much *taken* with his new acquaintance〉 **7** : REMOVE, SUBTRACT 〈*take* six from ten〉

---

j job   ng sing   ō low   ȯ moth   ȯi coin   th thin   th this   ü boot   u̇ foot   y you   yü few   yu̇ furious   zh vision

8 : to find out by testing ⟨*take* the patient's temperature⟩ **9** : SELECT, CHOOSE ⟨*took* the blue suit⟩ **10** : ASSUME, UNDERTAKE ⟨*take* office⟩ **11** : ABSORB ⟨this cloth *takes* dye well⟩ **12** : to be affected by : CATCH ⟨*took* cold⟩ **13** : ACCEPT ⟨*take* my advice⟩ **14** : to introduce into the body ⟨*take* medicine⟩ **15** : to submit to ⟨*took* his punishment⟩ **16** : to subscribe for ⟨*takes* three magazines⟩ **17** : UNDERSTAND ⟨*took* his nod to mean *yes*⟩ **18** : EXPERIENCE ⟨*take* offense⟩ **19** : to be formed or used with ⟨verbs that *take* objects⟩ **20** : CONDUCT, CARRY ⟨*take* a parcel to the post office⟩ **21** : USE, OCCUPY ⟨*take* this chair⟩ **22** : NEED, REQUIRE ⟨the job will *take* an hour⟩ **23** : to make an image, copy, or record of ⟨*take* a photograph⟩ **24** : to proceed to undertake and do ⟨*take* a walk⟩ **25** : to have effect ⟨the vaccination *took*⟩ — **tak·er** *n* — **take advantage of 1** : to use to advantage **2** : to impose upon — **take after** : RESEMBLE ⟨*takes after* his father⟩ — **take back** : WITHDRAW, RETREAT ⟨*take back* a rude remark⟩ — **take care** : to be careful — **take care of** : to attend to — **take effect 1** : to go into effect **2** : to have its intended or expected effect — **take hold** : to become attached or established — **take in 1** : to make smaller ⟨*take in* a dress⟩ **2** : ADMIT, RECEIVE ⟨*take in* new members⟩ **3** : to receive work into one's house ⟨*take in* washing⟩ **4** : INCLUDE ⟨camp *took in* six acres⟩ **5** : to go to ⟨*take in* a movie⟩ **6** : to grasp the meaning of ⟨*took in* the situation at a glance⟩ **7** : CHEAT, DECEIVE — **take off 1** : REMOVE **2** : DEDUCT **3** : IMITATE, MIMIC **4** : to start off or away **5** : to begin a leap or spring **6** : to leave the surface — **take on 1** : to accept or come to grips with as an opponent ⟨*took on* the champion⟩ **2** : to assume or acquire as or as if one's own ⟨*took on* dignity with age⟩ **3** : ENGAGE, HIRE ⟨*take on* more workmen⟩ **4** : to behave in an excited manner especially from grief or anger — **take part** : JOIN, PARTICIPATE — **take place** : HAPPEN, OCCUR — **take to** : to be drawn or attracted to — **take up 1** : to take or accept as one's own **2** : to pull up or in so as to tighten or shorten **3** : to respond favorably to (as a challenge) **4** : to make a beginning where another has left off — **take up for** : to take the part or side of — **take up with** : to begin to associate with

²take *n* **1** : the act of taking **2** : something that is taken **3** : a bodily reaction indicating a successful smallpox vaccination

take·off \'tāk-ˌȯf\ *n* **1** : an imitation especially to mimic the original **2** : an act or instance of taking off from the ground (as by an airplane) **3** : a spot at which one takes off

tak·ing \'tā-king\ *adj* **1** : ATTRACTIVE ⟨*taking* ways⟩ **2** : CONTAGIOUS, CATCHING

talc \'talk\ *n* : a soft mineral much like soap to the touch used in making talcum powder and as a pigment

tal·cum powder \'tal-kəm-\ *n* : a perfumed toilet powder made of talc

tale \'tāl\ *n* **1** : ACCOUNT, RECITAL ⟨*tale* of woe⟩ **2** : a story about an imaginary event **3** : LIE **4** : a piece of harmful gossip

tale·bear·er \'tāl-ˌbar-ər\ *n* : one who spreads gossip or scandal — **tale·bear·ing** \-ˌbaər-ing\ *n*

tal·ent \'tal-ənt\ *n* **1** : any of several ancient units of weight and money value (as of Palestine) **2** : superior natural ability **3** : a natural gift for mastering some skill or pursuit **4** : persons of ability and skill **syn** see ABILITY — **tal·ent·ed** \-ən-təd\ *adj*

tal·is·man \'tal-əs-mən\ *n, pl* **tal·is·mans** : a ring or stone carved with symbols and held to have magical powers : CHARM

¹talk \'tȯk\ *vb* **1** : to express in speech : SPEAK **2** : to speak about : DISCUSS ⟨*talk* business⟩ **3** : to affect, influence, or cause by talking ⟨*talked* him into agreeing⟩ **4** : to use a language for communicating **5** : to exchange ideas by means of spoken words : CONVERSE **6** : to convey information (as by signs) **7** : GOSSIP **8** : to reveal secret or confidential information **syn** see SPEAK — **talk·er** *n*

²talk *n* **1** : the act of talking : SPEECH **2** : a way of speaking : LANGUAGE **3** : a formal discussion or exchange of views : CONFERENCE **4** : RUMOR, GOSSIP **5** : the topic of comment or gossip **6** : an informal address or lecture

talk·a·tive \'tȯk-ət-iv\ *adj* : fond of talking — **talk·a·tive·ness** *n*

talk·ing-to \'tȯk-ing-ˌtü\ *n* : SCOLDING

tall \'tȯl\ *adj* **1** : high in stature **2** : of a stated height ⟨six feet *tall*⟩ **3** : LARGE ⟨a *tall* order to fill⟩ **4** : IMPROBABLE — **tall·ness** *n*

tal·low \'tal-ō\ *n* : a white solid fat obtained by heating fatty tissues of cattle and sheep

¹tal·ly \'tal-ē\ *n, pl* **tal·lies 1** : a device (as a notched stick) for keeping a count **2** : a recorded count or reckoning **3** : a score or point made (as in a game)

²tally *vb* **tal·lied; tal·ly·ing 1** : to keep a reckoning of : COUNT **2** : SCORE **3** : CORRESPOND

tal·on \'tal-ən\ *n* : the claw of a bird of prey — **tal·oned** \-ənd\ *adj*

ta·ma·le \tə-'mä-lē\ *n* : a mixture of ground meat and red peppers rolled in cornmeal, wrapped in corn husks, and steamed

---

ə abut   ər further   a ax   ā age   ä father, cot   à (see key page)   aü out   ch chin   e less   ē easy   g gift   i trip   ī life

tam·bou·rine \ˌtam-bə-'rēn\ *n* : a small shallow one-headed drum with loose metallic disks at the sides played by shaking or striking with the hand

tambourine

¹**tame** \'tām\ *adj* **tam·er; tam·est 1** : made useful and obedient to man : DO-MESTICATED **2** : not afraid of man : GENTLE **3** : lacking in spirit or interest : DULL — **tame·ly** *adv* — **tame·ness** *n*

²**tame** *vb* **tamed; tam·ing 1** : to make or become tame, gentle, or obedient **2** : to subject land to cultivation **3** : SUBDUE — **tam·a·ble** *or* **tame·a·ble** \'tā-mə-bəl\ *adj* — **tam·er** *n*

tam-o'-shan·ter \'tam-ə-ˌshant-ər\ *n* : a woolen cap of Scottish origin with a wide flat circular crown and usually a pompon in the center

tamp \'tamp\ *vb* : to drive down or in by a series of slight blows

tam·per \'tam-pər\ *vb* : to meddle or interfere secretly or improperly **syn** see MEDDLE

tam-o'-shanter

¹**tan** \'tan\ *vb* **tanned; tan·ning 1** : to convert hide into leather by soaking in a tannin solution **2** : to make or become brown or tan in color **3** : BEAT, THRASH

²**tan** *n* **1** : the brown color of the skin caused by exposure to the sun or weather **2** : a light yellowish brown color

³**tan** *adj* **tan·ner; tan·nest** : of the color tan

tan·a·ger \'tan-ij-ər\ *n* : a brilliantly colored bird related to the finches

¹**tan·dem** \'tan-dəm\ *n* **1** : a two-seated carriage drawn by horses harnessed one behind the other **2** : a bicycle for two persons sitting tandem

tandem 2

²**tandem** *adv* (*or adj*) : one after or behind another

tang \'tang\ *n* : a sharp distinctive flavor or smell ⟨the *tang* of salt air⟩

tan·ger·ine \'tan-jə-ˌrēn\ *n* : a Chinese orange with a loose rind and sweet pulp

tan·gi·ble \'tan-jə-bəl\ *adj* **1** : capable of being touched **2** : capable of being understood and appreciated — **tan·gi·bly** \-blē\ *adv*

¹**tan·gle** \'tang-gəl\ *vb* **tan·gled; tan·gling** : to twist or become twisted together into a mass hard to straighten out again : ENTANGLE ⟨a *tangled* skein of wool⟩

²**tangle** *n* **1** : a tangled twisted mass (as of yarn) **2** : a complicated or confused state

¹**tank** \'tangk\ *n* **1** : a usually large artificial container for a liquid **2** : an enclosed heavily armed and armored combat vehicle supported,

driven, and steered by endless-belt treads

²**tank** *vb* : to put, store, or treat in a tank

tan·kard \'tang-kərd\ *n* : a tall one-handled drinking vessel (as of pewter) often with a lid

tank·er \'tang-kər\ *n* : a vehicle (as a ship) equipped with tanks for transporting a liquid

tan·ner \'tan-ər\ *n* : one that tans hides

tankard

tan·ner·y \'tan-ə-rē\ *n, pl* **tan·ner·ies** : a place where hides are tanned

tan·nin \'tan-ən\ *n* : a substance commonly made from oak bark or sumac and used in tanning, dyeing, and making ink

tan·ta·lize \'tant-l-ˌīz\ *vb* **tan·ta·lized; tan·ta·liz·ing** [from the name *Tantalus*, a king in Greek mythology who after death was punished for his sins by being made to stand up to his chin in water which sank away whenever he lowered his head to drink] : to tease or torment by or as if by presenting something desirable to the view but keeping it out of reach — **tan·ta·liz·er** *n*

tan·trum \'tan-trəm\ *n* : a fit of bad temper

¹**tap** \'tap\ *n* : FAUCET, SPIGOT — **on tap** : on hand : AVAILABLE

²**tap** *vb* **tapped; tap·ping 1** : to let out or cause to flow by piercing or by drawing out a plug ⟨*tap* wine from a cask⟩ **2** : to pierce or open so as to draw off a fluid ⟨*tap* a cask⟩ **3** : to draw from or upon ⟨*tap* a nation's natural resources⟩ **4** : to connect into a telephone or telegraph wire to get information — **tap·per** *n*

³**tap** *vb* **tapped; tap·ping 1** : to strike, knock, or rap lightly **2** : to make by striking lightly again and again **3** : to repair a shoe by putting a half sole on it — **tap·per** *n*

⁴**tap** *n* : a light blow or its sound

¹**tape** \'tāp\ *n* **1** : a narrow band of woven fabric **2** : a narrow strip or band of material (as paper, steel, or plastic) **3** : a string stretched above the finishing line of a race **4** : a coated paper or plastic tape used for making a record (as of sound) by magnetic means

²**tape** *vb* **taped; tap·ing 1** : to fasten, cover, or support with tape **2** : to measure with a tape measure **3** : to make a record of on tape

tape·line \'tāp-ˌlīn\ *n* : TAPE MEASURE

tape measure *n* : a tape marked off usually in inches and used for measuring

¹**ta·per** \'tā-pər\ *n* **1** : a long waxed wick used especially for lighting lamps or fires **2** : a slender candle **3** : a small light **4** : a gradual decrease in thickness or width in a long object

²**taper** *vb* **1** : to make or become gradually

smaller toward one end **2** : to grow gradually less and less : DIMINISH

tap·es·try \'tap-əs-trē\ *n, pl* **tap·es·tries** : a heavy usually hand-woven decorative fabric used especially as a wall hanging — **tap·es·tried** \-trēd\ *adj*

tape·worm \'tāp-ˌwərm\ *n* : a worm with a long flat segmented body that lives as a parasite in human or animal intestines

tap·i·o·ca \ˌtap-ē-ˈō-kə\ *n* : grains or flakes of starch from cassava roots used especially in puddings

ta·pir \'tā-pər\ *n* : a large hoofed mammal of tropical America, Malaya, and Sumatra that has thick legs, a short tail, and a long flexible snout

tap·root \'tap-ˌrüt, -ˌrut\ *n* : a main root of a plant that grows straight down and gives off smaller side roots

taps \'taps\ *n sing or pl* : the last bugle call at night blown as a signal to put out the lights

¹tar \'tär\ *n* : a thick dark sticky liquid distilled from wood, coal, or peat

²tar *vb* **tarred; tar·ring** : to treat or smear with or as if with tar

³tar *n* : SAILOR

taproot

ta·ran·tu·la \tə-ˈran-chə-lə\ *n* **1** : a large European spider whose bite was once believed to cause an overwhelming desire to dance **2** : any of several large hairy American spiders mistakenly believed to be dangerous

tar·dy \'tärd-ē\ *adj* **tar·di·er; tar·di·est** **1** : moving slowly : SLUGGISH **2** : not on time : LATE — **tar·di·ly** \'tärd-l-ē\ *adv* — **tar·di·ness** \'tärd-ē-nəs\ *n*

tar·get \'tär-gət\ *n* **1** : a mark to shoot at **2** : a person or thing that is made the object of remarks, criticisms, or jokes **3** : a goal to be achieved

tar·iff \'tar-əf\ *n* **1** : a schedule of duties imposed by a government on goods coming into a country **2** : the duty or the rate of duty imposed in a tariff schedule

target for archery

¹tar·nish \'tär-nish\ *vb* : to make or become dull, dim, or discolored

²tarnish *n* **1** : tarnished condition **2** : a surface film formed in tarnishing

tar·pau·lin \tär-ˈpo-lən\ *n* : a sheet of waterproofed canvas

¹tar·ry \'tar-ē\ *vb* **tar·ried; tar·ry·ing** **1** : to be slow in coming or going **2** : SOJOURN

²tar·ry \'tär-ē\ *adj* : of, resembling, or covered with tar

¹tart \'tärt\ *adj* **1** : agreeably sharp to the

taste **2** : BITING, SHARP ⟨a *tart* manner⟩ — **tart·ly** *adv* — **tart·ness** *n*

²tart *n* : a small pie or shell of pastry containing a filling of jelly, custard, or fruit

tar·tan \'tärt-n\ *n* : a twilled woolen cloth with a plaid design of Scottish origin consisting of stripes of varying width and color against a solid ground

tar·tar \'tärt-ər\ *n* **1** : a substance found in the juice of grapes and deposited on the inside of wine casks as a reddish crust or sediment **2** : a purified form of tartar used in making baking powder and in medicine **3** : a crust that forms on the teeth consisting of deposits of saliva, food, and calcium

task \'task\ *n* : a piece of work to be done especially as assigned by another

task·mas·ter \'task-ˌmas-tər\ *n* : one that imposes a task or labor on another

¹tas·sel \'tas-əl\ *n* **1** : a hanging ornament made of a bunch of cords of even length fastened at one end **2** : something resembling a tassel ⟨the *tassel* of Indian corn⟩

²tassel *vb* **tas·seled** *or* **tas·selled; tas·sel·ing** *or* **tas·sel·ling** **1** : to adorn with tassels **2** : to put forth tassels

tassel

¹taste \'tāst\ *vb* **tast·ed; tast·ing** **1** : EXPERIENCE, UNDERGO **2** : to test or determine the flavor of something by taking a little into the mouth **3** : to eat or drink usually in small quantities **4** : to perceive by the sense of taste **5** : to have a particular flavor — **tast·er** *n*

²taste *n* **1** : a small amount tasted or experienced **2** : the one of the special senses that perceives the sweet, sour, bitter, or salty quality of a dissolved substance and that acts through sense organs (**taste buds**) in the tongue **3** : the quality of something perceived by the sense of taste or by this together with smell and touch : FLAVOR **4** : individual preference or inclination ⟨has very expensive *tastes*⟩ **5** : the ability to appreciate, enjoy, and judge beauty or excellence

taste·ful \'tāst-fəl\ *adj* : having or showing good taste — **taste·ful·ly** *adv* — **taste·ful·ness** *n*

taste·less \'tāst-ləs\ *adj* **1** : lacking flavor **2** : not having or showing good taste — **taste·less·ly** *adv* — **taste·less·ness** *n*

tast·y \'tās-tē\ *adj* **tast·i·er; tast·i·est** **1** : pleasing to the taste ⟨a *tasty* dessert⟩ **2** : showing good taste : TASTEFUL — **tast·i·ness** *n*

tat·ter \'tat-ər\ *n* **1** : a part torn and left hanging : SHRED **2** *pl* : ragged clothing

tat·tered \'tat-ərd\ *adj* **1** : torn in shreds : RAGGED **2** : dressed in ragged clothes

¹**tat·tle** \'tat-l\ *vb* **tat·tled; tat·tling 1** : CHAT-
TER **2** : to tell secrets : inform on someone —
tat·tler \'tat-lər\ *n*
²**tattle** *n* : idle talk
tat·tle·tale \'tat-l-ˌtāl\ *n* : one that tattles
¹**tat·too** \ta-'tü\ *n, pl* **tat·toos 1** : a call
sounded shortly before taps as notice to go to
quarters **2** : a rapid rhythmic rapping
²**tattoo** *n, pl* **tat·toos** : a mark or figure made by
tattooing
³**tattoo** *vb* **tat·tooed; tat·too·ing** : to mark the
body with a pattern or figure by inserting
coloring matter under the skin — **tat·too·er** *n*
taught *past of* TEACH
¹**taunt** \'tȯnt\ *vb* : to jeer at : RIDICULE
²**taunt** *n* : a spiteful jeering remark
taut \'tȯt\ *adj* **1** : tightly drawn ⟨make a rope
taut⟩ **2** : TENSE, HIGH-STRUNG **3** : TRIM,
SHIPSHAPE — **taut·ly** *adv* — **taut·ness** *n*
tav·ern \'tav-ərn\ *n* **1** : an establishment
where alcoholic drinks are sold to be drunk
on the premises **2** : INN
taw·dry \'tȯ-drē\ *adj* **taw·dri·er; taw·dri·est**
: cheap and gaudy in appearance and quality
— **taw·dri·ly** \-drə-lē\ *adv* — **taw·dri·ness**
\-drē-nəs\ *n*
taw·ny \'tȯ-nē\ *adj* : of a brownish orange
color
¹**tax** \'taks\ *vb* **1** : to require to pay a tax
2 : to call to account for something ⟨*taxed*
him with neglect⟩ **3** : to cause a strain on
⟨*taxed* his strength⟩ — **tax·er** *n*
²**tax** *n* **1** : a charge usually of money laid on
persons or property for public purposes **2** : a
demanding task or duty : STRAIN
tax·a·ble \'tak-sə-bəl\ *adj* : subject to taxation
tax·a·tion \tak-'sā-shən\ *n* **1** : the action of
taxing **2** : money obtained from taxes
¹**tax·i** \'tak-sē\ *n, pl* **tax·is** : TAXICAB
²**taxi** *vb* **tax·ied; tax·i·ing** *or* **tax·y·ing 1** : to go
by taxicab **2** : to run an airplane slowly along
the ground or water under its own power
tax·i·cab \'tak-sē-ˌkab\ *n* : a chauffeur-driven
automobile that carries passengers for a fare
often registered automatically by a meter
tax·i·der·my \'tak-sə-ˌdər-
mē\ *n* : the art of stuffing and
mounting the skins of animals
tax·on·o·my \tak-'sän-ə-mē\
n **1** : the study of classification
2 : an orderly classification
(as of animals) usually based
on relationship
tea \'tē\ *n* **1** : the cured leaves
and leaf buds of a white=
flowered shrub widely grown
in eastern and southern Asia

tea: leaves
and blossoms

2 : a mildly stimulating aromatic drink made
by steeping tea in boiling water **3** : a medicinal or other drink made by steeping plant
parts (as dried roots) ⟨ginger *tea*⟩ **4** : refreshments usually including tea served in late
afternoon **5** : a party or reception at which
tea is served
teach \'tēch\ *vb* **taught** \'tȯt\; **teach·ing**
1 : to act as a teacher **2** : to show how ⟨*teach*
a child to swim⟩ **3** : to guide the studies of
4 : to cause to know the disagreeable consequences of an action **5** : to give lessons in
teach·a·ble \'tē-chə-bəl\ *adj* **1** : capable of
being taught **2** : well adapted for use in
teaching
teach·er \'tē-chər\ *n* : a person who teaches
teach·ing \'tē-ching\ *n* **1** : the act, practice,
or profession of a teacher **2** : something
taught
tea·cup \'tē-ˌkəp\ *n* : a cup used with a saucer
for hot beverages
teak \'tēk\ *n* : the hard yellowish brown decay-resistant
wood of a tall Indian tree
tea·ket·tle \'tē-ˌket-l\ *n* : a
covered kettle with a handle
and spout for boiling water

teacup and
saucer

teal \'tēl\ *n* : a small wild duck that is very
swift in flight
¹**team** \'tēm\ *n* **1** : two or more animals (as
horses) harnessed to pull the same vehicle or
implement **2** : a group of persons who work,
play, or act together
²**team** *vb* **1** : to haul with or drive a team
2 : to form a team
team·mate \'tēm-ˌmāt\ *n* : a fellow member
of a team
team·ster \'tēm-stər\ *n* : one who drives a
team or motortruck especially as a job
team·work \'tēm-ˌwərk\ *n* : the work or activity of a group of persons playing or acting
together as a unit
tea·pot \'tē-ˌpät\ *n* : a vessel with a spout for
brewing and serving tea
¹**tear** \'tiər\ *n* : a drop of the
salty liquid that keeps the eye-
balls and inner eyelids moist
²**tear** \'taər\ *vb* **tore** \'tōr\;

teapot

torn \'tōrn\; **tear·ing 1** : to separate by force
⟨*tore* a page from the book⟩ **2** : LACERATE
3 : to divide or disrupt by the pull of opposing
forces ⟨a mind *torn* with doubts⟩ **4** : to remove by force ⟨children *torn* away from their
mothers⟩ **5** : to effect by force or violence
6 : to move with haste or force
³**tear** \'taər\ *n* **1** : the act of tearing **2** : a
hole or flaw made by tearing

tear·ful \'tiər-fəl\ *adj* : flowing with, accompanied by, or causing tears — **tear·ful·ly** *adv*

tea·room \'tē-ˌrüm, -ˌrum\ *n* : a small restaurant serving light meals

¹**tease** \'tēz\ *vb* **teased; teas·ing** **1** : to annoy persistently **2** : TANTALIZE — **teas·er** *n*

²**tease** *n* **1** : the act of teasing : the state of being teased **2** : one that teases

tea·spoon \'tē-ˌspün\ *n* : a small spoon used especially for stirring beverages

tea·spoon·ful \'tē-ˌspün-ˌful\ *n, pl* **tea·spoon·fuls** \-ˌfulz\ *or* **tea·spoons·ful** \-ˌspünz-ˌful\ : as much as a teaspoon can hold

teat \'tit, 'tēt\ *n* : NIPPLE 1

tech·ni·cal \'tek-ni-kəl\ *adj* **1** : having special knowledge particularly of a mechanical or scientific subject **2** : of or relating to a particular and especially a practical or scientific subject **3** : according to a strict interpretation of the rules **4** : of or relating to technique — **tech·ni·cal·ly** *adv*

tech·ni·cal·i·ty \ˌtek-nə-'kal-ət-ē\ *n, pl* **tech·ni·cal·i·ties** **1** : the quality or state of being technical **2** : a detail meaningful only to a specialist

technical sergeant *n* : a noncommissioned officer in the air force ranking next below a master sergeant

tech·nique \tek-'nēk\ *n* **1** : the manner in which technical details are treated or used in accomplishing a desired aim **2** : technical methods

tech·nol·o·gy \tek-'näl-ə-jē\ *n, pl* **tech·nol·o·gies** **1** : applied science **2** : a technical method of achieving a practical purpose

ted·dy bear \'ted-ē-\ *n* : a stuffed toy bear

te·di·ous \'tēd-ē-əs, 'tē-jəs\ *adj* : tiring because of length or dullness — **te·di·ous·ly** *adv* — **te·di·ous·ness** *n*

teem \'tēm\ *vb* : to be full to the point of overflowing : ABOUND

teen·age \'tēn-ˌāj\ *or* **teen·aged** \-ˌājd\ *adj* : of, being, or relating to persons in their teens

teen·ag·er \'tēn-ˌā-jər\ *n* : a person in his teens

teens \'tēnz\ *n pl* : the years thirteen through nineteen in a person's life

tee·ny \'tē-nē\ *adj* **tee·ni·er; tee·ni·est** : TINY

tee·pee *var of* TEPEE

tee shirt *var of* T-SHIRT

tee·ter \'tēt-ər\ *vb* **1** : to move unsteadily : WOBBLE **2** : SEESAW

teeth *pl of* TOOTH

teethe \'tēth\ *vb* **teethed; teeth·ing** : to cut one's teeth : grow teeth

teddy bear

tele- *or* **tel-** *prefix* **1** : at a distance ⟨telegram⟩ **2** : television ⟨telecast⟩

¹**tel·e·cast** \'tel-i-ˌkast\ *n* : a broadcasting or a program broadcast by television

²**telecast** *vb* **telecast** *also* **tel·e·cast·ed; tel·e·cast·ing** : to broadcast by television — **tel·e·cast·er** *n*

tel·e·gram \'tel-ə-ˌgram\ *n* : a message sent by telegraph

¹**tel·e·graph** \'tel-ə-ˌgraf\ *n* : an electric apparatus or system for sending messages by a code over connecting wires

²**telegraph** *vb* **1** : to send by telegraph **2** : to send a telegram to

te·leg·ra·phy \tə-'leg-rə-fē\ *n* : the use or operation of a telegraph apparatus or system

te·lep·a·thy \tə-'lep-ə-thē\ *n* : apparent communication from one mind to another without speech or signs

¹**tel·e·phone** \'tel-ə-ˌfōn\ *n* : an instrument for receiving and reproducing sounds (as of the human voice) transmitted from a distance over wires by electricity

²**telephone** *vb* : to speak to by telephone

telephone

¹**tel·e·scope** \'tel-ə-ˌskōp\ *n* : a long tube-shaped instrument equipped with lenses for viewing objects at a distance and especially for observing the heavenly bodies

²**telescope** *vb* **tel·e·scoped; tel·e·scop·ing** : to slide or force one part into another like the sections of a hand telescope

tel·e·vise \'tel-ə-ˌvīz\ *vb* **tel·e·vised; tel·e·vis·ing** : to send (a program) by television

tel·e·vi·sion \'tel-ə-ˌvizh-ən\ *n* : the sending of scenes with sound over wire or through space by devices that convert light and sound into electrical effects and then convert these back into light and sound

tell \'tel\ *vb* **told** \'tōld\; **tell·ing** **1** : COUNT, ENUMERATE **2** : to relate in detail : NARRATE **3** : SAY, UTTER **4** : to make known ⟨tell a secret⟩ **5** : to report to : INFORM **6** : ORDER, DIRECT **7** : to ascertain by observing ⟨learned to tell time⟩ **8** : to act as a tattletale **9** : to have a marked effect

tell·er \'tel-ər\ *n* **1** : NARRATOR **2** : a person who counts votes (as in a legislative body) **3** : a bank employee who receives and pays out money

te·mer·i·ty \tə-'mer-ət-ē\ *n* : BOLDNESS

¹**tem·per** \'tem-pər\ *vb* **1** : MODERATE, SUBDUE **2** : to bring (a substance) to a desired state of consistency **3** : to bring (as steel) to a desired hardness, toughness, or flexibility by heating and cooling

²temper *n* **1** : characteristic tone **2** : the hardness or toughness of a substance (as metal) **3** : frame of mind **4** : COMPOSURE **5** : MOOD, HUMOR **6** : a proneness to anger — **tem·pered** \'tem-pərd\ *adj*

tem·per·a·ment \'tem-pə-rə-mənt\ *n* **1** : a person's disposition as it affects what he says or does **2** : excessive sensitiveness or irritability

tem·per·a·men·tal \,tem-pə-rə-'ment-l\ *adj* : having or showing a nervous sensitive temperament — **tem·per·a·men·tal·ly** *adv*

tem·per·ance \'tem-pə-rəns\ *n* **1** : RESTRAINT **2** : moderation in or abstinence from the use of intoxicating drink

tem·per·ate \'tem-pə-rət\ *adj* **1** : not excessive or extreme **2** : moderate in satisfying one's needs or desires **3** : moderate in the use of liquor **4** : RESTRAINED **5** : not having extremes of heat or cold

syn TEMPERATE and MODERATE both mean not being excessive, but MODERATE indicates the lack or avoidance of excess and may thus apply to anything ⟨a *moderate* allowance⟩ or may carry the idea of indifference or lack of interest ⟨*moderate* applause⟩ TEMPERATE stresses deliberate restraint or restriction and thus applies to people or their actions ⟨*temperate* spending habits⟩ and may suggest an existing but controlled enthusiasm ⟨tried to give a *temperate* opinion⟩

tem·per·a·ture \'tem-pə-rə-,chùr\ *n* **1** : degree of hotness or coldness as shown by a thermometer **2** : a degree of heat above that which is normal for the human body : FEVER

tem·pest \'tem-pəst\ *n* **1** : a violent wind often accompanied by rain, hail, or snow **2** : TUMULT, UPROAR

tem·pes·tu·ous \tem-'pes-chə-wəs\ *adj* : extremely stormy — **tem·pes·tu·ous·ly** *adv*

¹tem·ple \'tem-pəl\ *n* **1** : a building for the worship of a deity **2** *often cap* : one of three successive sanctuaries in ancient Jerusalem

²temple *n* : the space between the eye and forehead and the upper part of the ear

tem·po \'tem-pō\ *n, pl* **tem·pi** \-,pē\ *or* **tempos** : the rate of speed at which a musical composition is played or sung

tem·po·ral \'tem-pə-rəl\ *adj* **1** : of, relating to, or limited by time **2** : of or relating to earthly life or secular concerns

tem·po·rar·y \'tem-pə-,rer-ē\ *adj* : not permanent — **tem·po·rar·i·ly** \,tem-pə-'rer-ə-lē\ *adv*

tem·po·rize \'tem-pə-,rīz\ *vb* **tem·po·rized**; **tem·po·riz·ing** **1** : to adapt one's actions to the time or the dominant opinion **2** : DELAY

tempt \'tempt\ *vb* **1** : to entice to do wrong

(as by promise of gain) **2** : PROVOKE **3** : to risk the dangers of **4** : INCITE — **tempt·er** *n*

temp·ta·tion \temp-'tā-shən\ *n* **1** : a tempting or being tempted **2** : something tempting

¹ten \'ten\ *adj* : being one more than nine

²ten *n* **1** : one more than nine **2** : the tenth in a set or series

ten·a·ble \'ten-ə-bəl\ *adj* : capable of being held, maintained, or defended

te·na·cious \tə-'nā-shəs\ *adj* **1** : not easily pulled apart **2** : tending to adhere to another substance **3** : PERSISTENT ⟨*tenacious* in his beliefs⟩ **4** : RETENTIVE — **te·na·cious·ly** *adv*

te·nac·i·ty \tə-'nas-ət-ē\ *n* : the quality or state of being tenacious

ten·an·cy \'ten-ən-sē\ *n* : the temporary possession or occupancy of another's property

¹ten·ant \'ten-ənt\ *n* **1** : a person who rents or leases property (as a house) from a landlord **2** : DWELLER, OCCUPANT

²tenant *vb* : to hold or occupy as a tenant

¹tend \'tend\ *vb* **1** : to apply oneself **2** : to take care of **3** : to manage the operation of

²tend *vb* **1** : to move or turn in a certain direction : LEAD **2** : to have a tendency

tend·en·cy \'ten-dən-sē\ *n, pl* **tend·en·cies** **1** : DRIFT, TREND **2** : an inclination toward a particular kind of thought or action

¹ten·der \'ten-dər\ *adj* **1** : having a soft or yielding texture ⟨a *tender* steak⟩ **2** : DELICATE **3** : IMMATURE **4** : LOVING **5** : very sensitive — **ten·der·ly** *adv* — **ten·der·ness** *n*

²tend·er \'ten-dər\ *n* **1** : one that tends or takes care **2** : a car attached to a locomotive for carrying fuel or water **3** : a ship employed (as to supply provisions) to attend other ships **4** : a boat that carries passengers or freight to a larger ship

³ten·der \'ten-dər\ *n* **1** : an offer or proposal made for acceptance **2** : something (as money) that may be offered in payment

⁴ten·der *vb* **1** : to offer in payment **2** : to present for acceptance : PROFFER

ten·der·foot \'ten-dər-,fùt\ *n, pl* **ten·der·feet** \-,fēt\ *also* **ten·der·foots** : a person who is not hardened to a rough outdoor life

ten·der·heart·ed \,ten-dər-'härt-əd\ *adj* : easily moved to love, pity, or sorrow

ten·der·loin \'ten-dər-,lòin\ *n* : a strip of tender meat on each side of the backbone in beef or pork

ten·don \'ten-dən\ *n* : a cord or band of tough white fiber connecting a muscle to another part (as a bone) : SINEW

ten·dril \'ten-drəl\ *n* **1** : a slender leafless coiling stem by

tendril

which some climbing plants (as grapevines) fasten themselves to a support **2** : something that curls like a tendril

ten·e·ment \'ten-ə-mənt\ *n* **1** : a house used as a dwelling **2** : a dwelling house divided into separate apartments for rent to families and often meeting only minimum standards of safety and comfort

ten·nis \'ten-əs\ *n* : a game played on a level court by two or four players who use rackets to hit a ball back and forth across a low net dividing the court

ten·or \'ten-ər\ *n* **1** : the general drift of something **2** : the highest natural adult male voice **3** : TREND, TENDENCY

tennis racket

ten·pins \'ten-ˌpinz\ *n* : a bowling game played with ten bottle-shaped pins

¹tense \'tens\ *n* [from medieval French *tens*, meaning literally "time", from Latin *tempus*] : a form of a verb used to show the time of the action or state

²tense *adj* [from Latin *tensus*, the past participle of the verb *tendere* "to stretch"] **1** : stretched tight : RIGID **2** : feeling or showing nervous tension **3** : marked by strain or suspense — **tense·ly** *adv* — **tense·ness** *n*

³tense *vb* **tensed; tens·ing** : to make or become tense

ten·sion \'ten-chən\ *n* **1** : the act of straining or stretching : the condition of being strained or stretched **2** : a state of mental unrest **3** : a state of latent hostility or opposition

¹tent \'tent\ *n* : a collapsible shelter (as of canvas) stretched and supported by poles

²tent *vb* : to live or lodge in a tent — **tent·er** *n*

ten·ta·cle \'tent-ə-kəl\ *n* **1** : one of the long thin flexible projections from the head or the mouth of an animal (as an insect or fish) used especially for feeling or grasping **2** : a sensitive hair on a plant

tent

ten·ta·tive \'tent-ət-iv\ *adj* **1** : not final ⟨*tentative* plans⟩ **2** : HESITANT, UNCERTAIN ⟨a *tentative* smile⟩ — **ten·ta·tive·ly** *adv*

tent caterpillar *n* : any of several caterpillars that spin tentlike webs in which they live in colonies

¹tenth \'tenth\ *adj* : being next after the ninth

²tenth *n* **1** : number ten in a series **2** : one of ten equal parts

te·pee \'tē-ˌpē\ *n* : a cone-

tepee

shaped tent used by some American Indians

tep·id \'tep-əd\ *adj* : moderately warm : LUKEWARM ⟨*tepid* water⟩

te·re·do \tə-'rēd-ō\ *n, pl* **te·re·dos** : SHIPWORM

¹term \'tərm\ *n* **1** : END, TERMINATION **2** : a period of time fixed especially by law or custom ⟨a school *term*⟩ **3** *pl* : provisions determining the nature and scope of something (as a treaty or a will) **4** : a word or expression that has a precise meaning in some uses or is peculiar to a subject or field ⟨legal *terms*⟩ **5** : the numerator or denominator of a fraction **6** : any one of the numbers in a series **7** *pl* : mutual relationship **8** *pl* : AGREEMENT, CONCORD

²term *vb* : to apply a term to

¹ter·mi·nal \'tər-mən-l\ *adj* : of, relating to, or forming an end, limit, or terminus

²terminal *n* **1** : a part that forms the end : EXTREMITY **2** : a device at the end of a wire or on an apparatus for making an electrical connection **3** : either end of a carrier line or a passenger or freight station located at it

ter·mi·nate \'tər-mə-ˌnāt\ *vb* **ter·mi·nat·ed; ter·mi·nat·ing** : END, CLOSE

ter·mi·na·tion \ˌtər-mə-'nā-shən\ *n* **1** : END, CONCLUSION **2** : the act of terminating

ter·mi·nus \'tər-mə-nəs\ *n, pl* **ter·mi·ni** \-ˌnī\ *or* **ter·mi·nus·es** **1** : final goal : END **2** : either end of a transportation line or travel route

ter·mite \'tər-ˌmīt\ *n* : a pale-colored chewing antlike insect that lives in large colonies and feeds on wood

tern \'tərn\ *n* : any of numerous small slender narrow-winged sea gulls with black cap and white body

termite

¹ter·race \'ter-əs\ *n* **1** : a flat roof or open platform **2** : a level area next to a building **3** : a raised embankment with the top leveled **4** : a row of houses on raised ground or a slope **5** : a strip of park in the middle of a street

²terrace *vb* **ter·raced; ter·rac·ing** : to form into a terrace or supply with terraces

ter·rain \tə-'rān\ *n* : the surface features of a tract of land

ter·ra·pin \'ter-ə-pən\ *n* : a North American flesh-eating turtle that lives in water

ter·rar·i·um \tə-'rar-ē-əm\ *n, pl* **ter·rar·i·a** \-ē-ə\ *or* **ter·rar·i·ums** : a usually glass-enclosed box for keeping and observing small animals and plants

ter·res·tri·al \tə-'res-trē-əl\ *adj* **1** : of or relating to the earth or its inhabitants **2** : living or growing on land

ter·ri·ble \'ter-ə-bəl\ *adj* **1** : causing terror : FEARFUL **2** : hard to bear : DISTRESSING **3** : extreme in degree : INTENSE **4** : of very poor quality — **ter·ri·bly** \-blē\ *adv*

ter·ri·er \'ter-ē-ər\ *n* : any of various usually small dogs originally used by hunters to drive small game from holes

ter·rif·ic \tə-'rif-ik\ *adj* **1** : TERRIBLE, FRIGHTFUL **2** : EXTRAORDINARY, ASTOUNDING **3** : unusually fine — **ter·rif·i·cal·ly** \-i-kə-lē\ *adv*

ter·ri·fy \'ter-ə-ˌfī\ *vb* **ter·ri·fied; ter·ri·fy·ing** : to fill with terror : FRIGHTEN

ter·ri·to·ri·al \ˌter-ə-'tōr-ē-əl\ *adj* **1** : of or relating to a territory **2** : of or relating to an assigned area ⟨*territorial* commanders⟩

ter·ri·to·ry \'ter-ə-ˌtōr-ē\ *n, pl* **ter·ri·to·ries** **1** : a geographical area belonging to or under the jurisdiction of a government **2** : a part of the United States not included within any state but organized with a separate legislature **3** : REGION, DISTRICT **4** : a field of knowledge or interest **5** : an assigned area

ter·ror \'ter-ər\ *n* **1** : a state of intense fear **2** : a cause of intense fear

ter·ror·ism \'ter-ər-ˌiz-əm\ *n* : systematic use of terror especially as a means of coercing

ter·ror·ize \'ter-ər-ˌīz\ *vb* **ter·ror·ized; ter·ror·iz·ing** **1** : to fill with terror **2** : to coerce by threat or violence

terse \'tərs\ *adj* : being brief and effective : CONCISE — **terse·ly** *adv* — **terse·ness** *n*

¹test \'test\ *n* **1** : a critical examination, observation, or evaluation : TRIAL **2** : a school examination

²test *vb* **1** : to put to test or proof : TRY **2** : to undergo or score on a test

tes·ta·ment \'tes-tə-mənt\ *n* **1** : either of two chief divisions (**Old Testament** and **New Testament**) of the Bible **2** : EVIDENCE, WITNESS **3** : an expression of conviction **4** : WILL

tes·ti·fy \'tes-tə-ˌfī\ *vb* **tes·ti·fied; tes·ti·fy·ing** **1** : to make a solemn statement of what is true **2** : to give outward proof

tes·ti·mo·ni·al \ˌtes-tə-'mō-nē-əl\ *n* **1** : a statement testifying to a person's good character or to the worth of something **2** : an expression of appreciation

tes·ti·mo·ny \'tes-tə-ˌmō-nē\ *n, pl* **tes·ti·mo·nies** **1** : evidence based on observation or knowledge **2** : a statement made by a witness under oath especially in a court **3** : an open acknowledgment or profession

tes·tis \'tes-təs\ *n, pl* **tes·tes** \'tes-ˌtēz\ : a male reproductive gland

test tube *n* : a plain tube of thin glass closed at one end

tet·a·nus \'tet-n-əs\ *n* : an acute and dangerous disease marked by spasms of the muscles often with rigid locking of the jaws and caused by poison from a germ that enters wounds and grows in damaged tissue

¹teth·er \'teth-ər\ *n* : a line by which an animal is fastened so as to restrict its range

²tether *vb* : to fasten or restrain by a tether

text \'tekst\ *n* **1** : the actual words of an author's work ⟨the *text* of Shakespeare⟩ **2** : the main body of printed or written matter on a page **3** : a passage from the Bible chosen as the subject of a sermon **4** : TEXTBOOK **5** : THEME, TOPIC

text·book \'tekst-ˌbùk\ *n* : a book that presents the principles of a subject and is used as a basis of instruction

tex·tile \'tek-ˌstīl, 'teks-təl\ *n* : a woven or knit cloth

tex·ture \'teks-chər\ *n* **1** : the structure, feel, and appearance of something (as cloth) **2** : an essential part or quality

-th \th\ *or* **-eth** \əth\ *adj suffix* — used to form ordinal numbers ⟨hundred*th*⟩ ⟨forti*eth*⟩

than \thən, than\ *conj* : when compared to the way, extent, or degree in or to which ⟨it's colder *than* it was yesterday⟩

thank \'thangk\ *vb* **1** : to express gratitude to **2** : to hold responsible

thank·ful \'thangk-fəl\ *adj* : feeling or showing thanks : GRATEFUL — **thank·ful·ly** *adv* — **thank·ful·ness** *n*

thank·less \'thangk-ləs\ *adj* **1** : UNGRATEFUL **2** : not likely to earn thanks

thanks \'thangks\ *n pl* **1** : GRATITUDE **2** : an expression of gratitude (as for a gift)

thanks·giv·ing \thangks-'giv-ing\ *n* **1** : the act of giving thanks **2** : a prayer expressing gratitude **3** *cap* : THANKSGIVING DAY

Thanksgiving Day *n* : the fourth Thursday in November observed as a legal holiday for public thanksgiving to God

¹that \that\ *pron, pl* **those** \thōz\ **1** : the one indicated, mentioned, or understood ⟨*that*'s my book⟩ **2** : the one farther away ⟨this is an elm, *that*'s a maple⟩ **3** : what has been indicated or mentioned ⟨after *that*, we left⟩ **4** : the one or ones : the kind ⟨the richest ore is *that* found higher up⟩

²that *adj, pl* **those** **1** : being the one mentioned, indicated, or understood ⟨*that* boy⟩ **2** : being the one farther away ⟨this book or *that* one⟩

³that \thət, that\ *conj* **1** : the following, namely ⟨he said *that* he'd go⟩ **2** : which is, namely ⟨there's a chance *that* it may rain⟩ **3** : to this end or purpose ⟨shouted *that* all might hear⟩ **4** : as to result in the following, namely ⟨so heavy *that* it can't be moved⟩

---

j job   **ng** sing   **ō** low   **ȯ** moth   **ȯi** coin   **th** thin   **th** this   **ü** boot   **ù** foot   **y** you   **yü** few   **yù** furious   **zh** vision

5 : for this reason, namely ⟨glad *that* you came⟩

⁴that \thət, that\ *pron* **1** : WHO, WHOM, WHICH ⟨the man *that* saw you⟩ ⟨the dog *that* you saw⟩ **2** : in, on, or at which ⟨the way *that* he drives⟩

⁵that \'that\ *adv* : to such an extent or degree ⟨need a nail about *that* long⟩

¹thatch \'thach\ *vb* : to cover with thatch

²thatch *n* : a plant material (as straw) for use as roofing

¹thaw \'thȯ\ *vb* **1** : to melt or cause to melt **2** : to become so warm as to melt ice or snow **3** : to grow less cold or reserved in manner

²thaw *n* **1** : the action, fact, or process of thawing **2** : a period of weather warm enough to thaw ice and snow

¹the \thə (*especially before consonant sounds*), thē (*before vowel sounds*); 4 is often 'thē\ *definite article* **1** : that or those previously mentioned or clearly understood ⟨put *the* cat out⟩ **2** : that or those near in space, time, or thought ⟨news of *the* day⟩ **3** : in, to, or for each ⟨a dollar *the* bottle⟩ **4** : that or those considered best, most typical, or most worth singling out ⟨*the* poet of his day⟩ **5** : any one typical of or standing for the entire class named ⟨courtesy distinguishes *the* gentleman⟩ **6** : all those that are ⟨*the* Greeks⟩

²the *adv* **1** : than before ⟨none *the* wiser⟩ **2** : to what extent ⟨*the* sooner the better⟩ **3** : to that extent ⟨the sooner *the* better⟩

the·a·ter *or* **the·a·tre** \'thē-ət-ər\ *n* [through Latin and French from Greek *theatron* " a place for a spectacle", "theater", from the verb *theasthai* "to view"] **1** : a building in which plays or motion pictures are presented **2** : a place resembling a theater in form or use **3** : a place or area where some important action is carried on ⟨a *theater* of war⟩ **4** : dramatic literature or performance

the·at·ri·cal \thē-'at-ri-kəl\ *adj* **1** : of or relating to the theater or the presentation of plays **2** : not natural and simple

the·at·ri·cals \thē-'at-ri-kəlz\ *n pl* : the performance of plays ⟨amateur *theatricals*⟩

thee *pron, objective case of* THOU

theft \'theft\ *n* : the act of stealing

their \thər, theər\ *adj* : of or relating to them or themselves especially as possessors, agents, or objects of an action ⟨*their* clothes⟩ ⟨*their* deeds⟩ ⟨*their* pain⟩

theirs \'theərz\ *pron* **1** : one or the one belonging to them ⟨the house is *theirs*⟩ **2** : some or the ones belonging to them ⟨the books are *theirs*⟩

them \thəm, them\ *pron, objective case of* THEY

theme \'thēm\ *n* **1** : a subject of discourse, of artistic representation, or of musical composition **2** : a written exercise

them·selves \thəm-'selvz\ *pron* : their own selves

¹then \then\ *adv* **1** : at that time **2** : soon after that : NEXT **3** : in addition : BESIDES **4** : in that case **5** : as a necessary consequence

²then *n* : that time ⟨wait until *then*⟩

³then *adj* : existing or acting at that time ⟨the *then* king⟩

thence \'thens\ *adv* **1** : from that place **2** : from that fact or circumstance

thence·forth \'thens-ˌfȯrth\ *adv* : from that time forward

thence·for·ward \thens-'fȯr-wərd\ *adv* : onward from that place or time

the·ol·o·gy \thē-'äl-ə-jē\ *n, pl* **the·ol·o·gies** : the study and interpretation of religious faith, practice, and experience

the·o·ret·i·cal \ˌthē-ə-'ret-i-kəl\ *adj* **1** : ABSTRACT **2** : confined to theory or speculation **3** : HYPOTHETICAL — **the·o·ret·i·cal·ly** *adv*

the·o·ry \'thē-ə-rē\ *n, pl* **the·o·ries** **1** : the general or abstract principles of a body of fact, a science, or an art **2** : a general principle or body of principles offered to explain phenomena ⟨wave *theory* of light⟩ **3** : a hypothesis assumed for the sake of argument or investigation **4** : SPECULATION

ther·a·peu·tic \ˌther-ə-'pyüt-ik\ *adj* : MEDICINAL

ther·a·pist \'ther-ə-pəst\ *n* : a specialist in therapy and especially in methods of treatment other than drugs and surgery

ther·a·py \'ther-ə-pē\ *n, pl* **ther·a·pies** : treatment of bodily, mental, or social disorders or maladjusted states

¹there \thaər\ *adv* **1** : in or at that place ⟨stand over *there*⟩ **2** : to or into that place ⟨take the basket *there* and leave it⟩ **3** : in that matter or respect ⟨*there* you have a choice⟩

²there *pron* — used to introduce a sentence in which the subject comes after the verb ⟨*there*'s a lot to do⟩

³there *n* : that place ⟨get away from *there*⟩

there·a·bouts \ˌthar-ə-'baüts\ *or* **there·a·bout** \-'baüt\ *adv* **1** : near that place or time **2** : near that number, degree, or quantity

there·af·ter \thar-'af-tər\ *adv* : after that

there·at \thar-'at\ *adv* **1** : at that place **2** : on that account

there·by \thaər-'bī\ *adv* **1** : by that means **2** : connected with or with reference to that

there·for \thaər-'fȯr\ *adv* : for or in return for that ⟨issued bonds *therefor*⟩

there·fore \'thaər-ˌfȯr\ *adv* : for that reason

there·from \thaər-'frəm, -'främ\ *adv* : from that or it ⟨learned much *therefrom*⟩

there·in \thar-'in\ *adv* **1** : in or into that place, time, or thing ⟨the world and all that is *therein*⟩ **2** : in that matter or respect

there·of \thar-'əv, -'äv\ *adv* **1** : of that or it **2** : from that cause : THEREFROM

there·on \thar-'ȯn, -'än\ *adv* : on that

there·to \thaər-'tü\ *adv* : tŏ that

there·up·on \ˌthar-ə-'pȯn, -'pän\ *adv* **1** : on that matter : THEREON **2** : on account of that **3** : immediately after that : at once

there·with \thaər-'with, -'with\ *adv* : with that

ther·mal \'thər-məl\ *adj* : of, relating to, or caused by heat : WARM, HOT

ther·mom·e·ter \thər-'mäm-ət-ər\ *n* [from French *thermomètre*, from Greek *thermē* "heat" and *-mètre* "-meter"] : an instrument for measuring temperature commonly in the form of a glass tube with mercury or alcohol sealed within and with a scale marked in degrees on the outside

thermometer

ther·mo·stat \'thər-mə-ˌstat\ *n* : a device that automatically controls temperature (as by regulating a flow of electricity)

these *pl of* THIS

the·sis \'thē-səs\ *n, pl* **the·ses** \-ˌsēz\ **1** : a proposition that a person advances and offers to maintain by argument **2** : an essay embodying results of original research

they \thā\ *pron* : those individuals

they'd \thād\ : they had : they would

they'll \thāl\ : they shall : they will

they're \thər, theər\ : they are

they've \thāv\ : they have

¹thick \'thik\ *adj* **1** : having relatively great depth or extent from one surface to its opposite **2** : heavily built **3** : densely massed **4** : FREQUENT, NUMEROUS **5** : dense or viscous in consistency **6** : marked by haze, fog, or mist **7** : measuring in the smallest of three dimensions **8** : not clearly articulated **9** : OBTUSE, STUPID **10** : INTIMATE **11** : EXCESSIVE — **thick·ly** *adv* — **thick·ness** *n*

²thick *n* **1** : the most crowded or active part **2** : the part of greatest thickness

thick·en \'thik-ən\ *vb* : to make or become thick — **thick·en·er** *n*

thick·et \'thik-ət\ *n* : a thick usually restricted growth of bushes or small trees

thick·set \'thik-'set\ *adj* **1** : closely placed or planted **2** : being short and stout

thief \'thēf\ *n, pl* **thieves** \'thēvz\ : a person who steals : ROBBER

thieve \'thēv\ *vb* **thieved; thiev·ing** : STEAL, ROB

thiev·er·y \'thē-və-rē\ *n, pl* **thiev·er·ies** : THEFT

thiev·ish \'thē-vish\ *adj* **1** : given to stealing **2** : of, relating to, or characteristic of a thief

thigh \'thī\ *n* : the part of a leg between the knee and the main part of the body

thim·ble \'thim-bəl\ *n* [probably from Old English *thȳmel* "a protective covering for the thumb", from *thūma* "thumb"] : a cap or cover used in sewing to protect the finger that pushes the needle

thimble

¹thin \'thin\ *adj* **thin·ner; thin·nest** **1** : having relatively little extent from one surface to its opposite ⟨*thin* paper⟩ **2** : not dense in arrangement or distribution ⟨*thin* hair⟩ **3** : not well fleshed : LEAN **4** : more fluid or rarefied than normal ⟨*thin* air⟩ **5** : having less than the usual number ⟨*thin* attendance⟩ **6** : lacking substance or strength ⟨*thin* excuse⟩ **7** : somewhat weak, shrill, and lacking in resonance ⟨*thin* voice⟩ — **thin·ly** *adv* — **thin·ness** *n*

syn THIN, LEAN, GAUNT all mean having no superfluous flesh. THIN is a general term for having no excess fat or flesh ⟨*thin* people are often healthier than fat ones⟩ but often suggests having less flesh than is desirable for good health or appearance ⟨*thin* children with hungry eyes roamed the streets⟩ LEAN stresses a lack of fat and suggests an angular figure ⟨a *lean* girl wearing jeans and looking like a boy⟩ but carries no suggestion of undesirable thinness and may indicate exceptional physical fitness ⟨*lean* and vigorous hounds with shiny coats⟩ GAUNT refers to an extreme thinness that results in an undernourished appearance ⟨appeared *gaunt* and haggard after his long illness⟩

²thin *vb* **thinned; thin·ning** : to make or become thin

thine \thīn\ *pron, archaic* **1** : one or the one belonging to thee **2** : some or the ones belonging to thee

thing \'thing\ *n* **1** : a matter of concern : AFFAIR ⟨*things* to do⟩ **2** *pl* : state of affairs ⟨*things* are improving⟩ **3** : EVENT, CIRCUMSTANCE ⟨the accident was a terrible *thing*⟩ **4** : DEED, ACT ⟨expect great *things* from him⟩ **5** : a distinct entity : OBJECT **6** : an inanimate object distinguished from a living being **7** *pl* : POSSESSIONS, EFFECTS ⟨packed his *things*⟩ **8** : an article of clothing ⟨not a *thing* to wear⟩ **9** : DETAIL, POINT **10** : IDEA

think \'thingk\ *vb* **thought** \'thȯt\; **think·ing** **1** : to form or have in the mind **2** : to have as an opinion : BELIEVE **3** : to reflect on : PONDER ⟨*think* the matter over⟩ **4** : to call to mind **5** : to form a mental picture of **6** : to exercise the powers of judgment, conception, or inference **7** : to have the mind engaged in reflection **8** : to have a view or opinion ⟨*thinks* of himself as a poet⟩ **9** : to have concern **10** : EXPECT, SUSPECT — **think·er** *n*

thin·ner \'thin-ər\ *n* : a volatile liquid (as turpentine) used to thin paint

¹third \'thərd\ *adj* : being next after the second

²third *n* **1** : number three in a series **2** : one of three equal parts

¹thirst \'thərst\ *n* **1** : a feeling of dryness in the mouth and throat associated with a desire for liquids **2** : the bodily condition that produces thirst ⟨die of *thirst*⟩ **3** : a strong desire

²thirst *vb* **1** : to feel thirsty : suffer thirst **2** : to have a strong desire : CRAVE

thirst·y \'thərs-tē\ *adj* **thirst·i·er**; **thirst·i·est** **1** : feeling thirst **2** : needing moisture **3** : having a strong desire : EAGER

¹thir·teen \ˌthər-'tēn\ *adj* : being one more than twelve

²thirteen *n* : one more than twelve

¹thir·teenth \ˌthər-'tēnth\ *adj* : being next after the twelfth

²thirteenth *n* : number thirteen in a series

¹thir·ti·eth \'thərt-ē-əth\ *adj* : being next after the twenty-ninth

²thirtieth *n* : number thirty in a series

¹thir·ty \'thərt-ē\ *adj* : being three times ten

²thirty *n* : three times ten

¹this \this\ *pron, pl* **these** \thēz\ **1** : the one close or closest in time or space ⟨*this* is your book⟩ **2** : what is in the present or under immediate observation or discussion ⟨*this* is bad⟩

²this *adj, pl* **these** **1** : being the one present, near, or just mentioned ⟨*this* morning⟩ ⟨friends all *these* years⟩ **2** : being the one nearer at hand or more immediately under observation or discussion ⟨*this* book or that one⟩

³this *adv* : to the degree or extent indicated by something immediately present ⟨didn't expect to wait *this* long⟩

this·tle \'this-əl\ *n* : a prickly plant related to the daisies that has usually purplish often showy heads of mostly tubular flowers

¹thith·er \'thith-ər\ *adv* : to that place : THERE

²thither *adj* : being on the farther side : more remote

tho *var of* THOUGH

thong \'thȯng\ *n* : a strip of leather used especially for fastening something

thistle

tho·rax \'thȯr-ˌaks\ *n, pl* **tho·rax·es** *or* **tho·ra·ces** \'thȯr-ə-ˌsēz\ [from Greek *thōrax*, originally meaning "armor for the chest", "breastplate"] **1** : the part of the body of a mammal that lies between the neck and the abdomen and contains the heart and lungs **2** : the middle of the three chief divisions of the body of an insect

thorn \'thȯrn\ *n* **1** : a woody plant (as hawthorn) with sharp processes (as briers, prickles, or spines) **2** : a short hard sharp-pointed leafless branch on a woody plant **3** : something that causes distress or irritation

thorn

thorn·y \'thȯr-nē\ *adj* **thorn·i·er**; **thorn·i·est** **1** : full of or covered with thorns **2** : full of difficulties

thor·ough \'thər-ō\ *adj* **1** : being such to the fullest degree : COMPLETE ⟨a *thorough* search⟩ **2** : careful about detail ⟨a *thorough* workman⟩ — **thor·ough·ly** *adv* — **thor·ough·ness** *n*

¹thor·ough·bred \'thər-ō-ˌbred\ *adj* **1** : bred from the best blood through a long line **2** *cap* : of, relating to, or being a member of the Thoroughbred breed of horses **3** : marked by high-spirited grace and elegance

²thoroughbred *n* **1** *cap* : any of an English breed of light speedy horses kept chiefly for racing **2** : a purebred or pedigreed animal **3** : a person of sterling qualities

thor·ough·fare \'thər-ō-ˌfaər\ *n* **1** : a street or road open at both ends **2** : a main road

thor·ough·go·ing \ˌthər-ə-'gō-ing\ *adj* : THOROUGH

those *pl of* THAT

thou \thau̇\ *pron, archaic* : the person addressed

¹though \thō\ *adv* : HOWEVER, NEVERTHELESS ⟨not for long, *though*⟩

²though *conj* **1** : despite the fact that ⟨*though* it was raining, he went hiking⟩ **2** : even if : even supposing ⟨determined to tell the truth *though* he should die for it⟩

¹thought \'thȯt\ *past of* THINK

²thought *n* **1** : the act or process of thinking **2** : serious consideration ⟨give *thought* to the future⟩ **3** : power of reasoning and judging **4** : power of imagining or comprehending **5** : a product (as an idea or fancy) of thinking ⟨idle *thoughts*⟩ **6** : the intellectual product or the organized views and principles of a period, place, group, or individual

thought·ful \'thȯt-fəl\ *adj* **1** : absorbed in thought **2** : marked by careful thinking ⟨a *thoughtful* essay⟩ **3** : considerate of others — **thought·ful·ly** *adv* — **thought·ful·ness** *n*

thought·less \'thȯt-ləs\ *adj* **1** : insufficiently alert : CARELESS **2** : RECKLESS, RASH ⟨*thoughtless* acts⟩ **3** : not considerate of others — **thought·less·ly** *adv* — **thought·less·ness** *n*

¹thou·sand \'thau̇z-nd\ *n* **1** : ten times 100 **2** : a very large number ⟨*thousands* of things to do⟩

²thousand *adj* : being 1000

¹thou·sandth \'thau̇z-nth\ *adj* : being next after the 999th

²thousandth *n* : number 1000 in a series

thrall \'thrȯl\ *n* **1** : SLAVE **2** : SLAVERY

thrash \'thrash\ *vb* **1** : THRESH 1 **2** : to beat soundly : FLOG **3** : to move about violently **4** : to go over again and again

¹thrash·er \'thrash-ər\ *n* : one that thrashes

²thrasher *n* : an American long-tailed bird (as the common reddish brown **brown thrasher**) related to the thrushes and noted for its song

¹thread \'thred\ *n* **1** : a thin fine cord formed by spinning and twisting short textile fibers into a continuous strand **2** : something suggesting a thread ⟨a *thread* of light⟩ **3** : the ridge or groove that winds around a screw **4** : a line of reasoning or train of thought that connects the parts of an argument or story — **thread·y** *adj*

thread

thread 3

²thread *vb* **1** : to put a thread in working position (as in a needle) **2** : to pass through like a thread ⟨*thread* a pipe with wire⟩ **3** : to make one's way through or between : wind a way **4** : to put together on a thread : STRING **5** : to interweave with threads

thread·bare \'thred-,baȯr\ *adj* **1** : worn so that the thread shows : SHABBY **2** : TRITE

threat \'thret\ *n* **1** : an expression of an intent to do harm **2** : something that threatens ⟨the *threat* of punishment⟩

threat·en \'thret-n\ *vb* **1** : to utter threats : make threats against **2** : to give warning of by a threat or sign **3** : to give signs of trouble to come — **threat·en·ing·ly** *adv*

¹three \'thrē\ *adj* : being one more than two

²three *n* **1** : one more than two **2** : the third in a set or series

three·fold \'thrē-,fōld\ *adj* : being three times as great or as many

three·score \'thrē-,skōr\ *adj* : SIXTY

thresh \'thrash, 'thresh\ *vb* **1** : to separate (as grain from straw) by beating **2** : THRASH

thresh·er \'thrash-ər, 'thresh-\ *n* **1** : one (as a machine for separating grain from straw) that threshes **2** : a large shark having a long curved upper lobe on its tail with which it is said to thrash the water to stir up fish

thresh·old \'thresh-,ōld\ *n* **1** : the sill of a door **2** : a point or place of beginning or entering ⟨at the *threshold* of an adventure⟩

threw *past of* THROW

thrice \'thrīs\ *adv* : three times

thrift \'thrift\ *n* : careful management especially of money

thrift·y \'thrif-tē\ *adj* **thrift·i·er**; **thrift·i·est** **1** : inclined to save : SAVING **2** : thriving in health and growth ⟨*thrifty* cattle⟩

¹thrill \'thril\ *vb* **1** : to have or cause to have a sudden sharp feeling of excitement **2** : VIBRATE, TREMBLE — **thrill·er** *n*

²thrill *n* **1** : a feeling of being thrilled **2** : VIBRATION

thrive \'thrīv\ *vb* **throve** \'thrōv\ *or* **thrived**; **thriv·en** \'thriv-ən\ *also* **thrived**; **thriv·ing** \'thrī-ving\ **1** : to grow vigorously : FLOURISH **2** : to gain in wealth or possessions

throat \'thrōt\ *n* **1** : the part of the neck in front of the backbone **2** : the passage from the mouth to the stomach and lungs ⟨a sore *throat*⟩ **3** : something resembling the throat (as in being an entrance or a narrowed part)

throat·y \'thrōt-ē\ *adj* **throat·i·er**; **throat·i·est** **1** : uttered or produced from low in the throat ⟨a *throaty* voice⟩ **2** : heavy, thick, and deep as if from the throat ⟨the *throaty* notes of a horn⟩

¹throb \'thräb\ *vb* **throbbed**; **throb·bing** **1** : to pulsate or pound with abnormal force or rapidity **2** : to beat or vibrate rhythmically

²throb *n* : BEAT, PULSE

throe \'thrō\ *n* **1** : PANG, SPASM ⟨death *throes*⟩ **2** *pl* : a hard or painful struggle

throne \'thrōn\ *n* **1** : the chair of state especially of a king or bishop **2** : royal power and dignity : SOVEREIGNTY

¹throng \'thrȯng\ *n* **1** : a multitude of assembled persons : CROWD **2** : a crowding together of many individuals

²throng *vb* : CROWD

¹throt·tle \'thrät-l\ *vb* **throt·tled**; **throt·tling** **1** : CHOKE, STRANGLE **2** : to reduce the speed of (an engine) by closing the throttle

²throttle *n* **1** : a valve for regulating the flow of steam or fuel in an engine **2** : a lever that controls the throttle valve

¹through \thrü\ *prep* **1** : into at one side and out at the other side of ⟨go *through* the door⟩ **2** : by way of ⟨entered *through* a window⟩ **3** : AMONG ⟨a path *through* the trees⟩ **4** : by means of ⟨succeeded *through* hard work⟩ **5** : over the whole of ⟨rumors swept *through* the school⟩ **6** : during the whole of ⟨*through* the night⟩

²through *adv* **1** : from one end or side to the other ⟨his arm was pierced *through*⟩ **2** : from beginning to end ⟨read the book *through* in one evening⟩ **3** : to completion ⟨see the job *through*⟩ **4** : to the core ⟨he was wet *through*⟩ **5** : into the open ⟨break *through*⟩

³through *adj* **1** : admitting free or continuous passage : DIRECT ⟨a *through* road⟩ **2** : going from point of origin to destination without change or reshipment ⟨*through* trains⟩ **3** : initiated at and destined for points outside a local zone ⟨*through* traffic⟩ **4** : FINISHED ⟨he is *through* with the job⟩

¹through·out \thrü-'aut\ *adv* **1** : EVERY-WHERE ⟨of one color *throughout*⟩ **2** : from beginning to end ⟨remained loyal *throughout*⟩

²throughout *prep* **1** : in or to every part of **2** : during the whole period of

throve *past of* THRIVE

¹throw \'thrō\ *vb* **threw** \'thrü\; **thrown** \'thrōn\; **throw·ing** **1** : to propel through the air with a quick forward motion of the arm ⟨*throw* a ball⟩ **2** : to propel through the air in any way ⟨*threw* a glance at his wife⟩ **3** : to cause to fall ⟨the horse *threw* the rider⟩ **4** : to put suddenly in a certain position or condition ⟨was *thrown* out of work⟩ **5** : to put on or take off hastily ⟨*throw* on a coat⟩ **6** : to move quickly ⟨*throw* in reinforcements⟩ **7** : PROJECT **8** : to move (as a switch) to an open or closed position **9** : to lose (a game or contest) intentionally — **throw·er** *n*

²throw *n* **1** : an act of throwing **2** : the distance a missile is or may be thrown

thrum \'thrəm\ *vb* **thrummed; thrum·ming** : to play a stringed instrument idly : STRUM

thrush \'thrəsh\ *n* : any of numerous insect-eating songbirds that are usually of a plain color sometimes with spotted underparts

¹thrust \'thrəst\ *vb* **thrust; thrust·ing** **1** : to push or drive with force : SHOVE **2** : STAB, PIERCE **3** : to push forth : EXTEND **4** : to press the acceptance of on someone

²thrust *n* **1** : a lunge with a pointed weapon **2** : a military assault **3** : a strong continued pressure **4** : a forward or upward push

thru·way *or* **through·way** \'thrü-,wā\ *n* : EXPRESSWAY

¹thud \'thəd\ *vb* **thud·ded; thud·ding** : to move or strike so as to make a dull sound

²thud *n* : a dull sound : THUMP

thug \'thəg\ *n* : a brutal ruffian

¹thumb \'thəm\ *n* **1** : the short thick finger next to the forefinger **2** : the part of a glove covering the thumb

²thumb *vb* **1** : to leaf through with the thumb **2** : to request or obtain (a ride) in a passing automobile by signaling with the thumb

¹thump \'thəmp\ *vb* **1** : to strike or beat with something thick or heavy so as to cause a dull sound **2** : POUND, KNOCK

²thump *n* **1** : a blow with something blunt or heavy **2** : the sound made by a thump

¹thun·der \'thən-dər\ *n* **1** : the loud sound that follows a flash of lightning **2** : a noise like thunder ⟨the *thunder* of guns⟩

²thunder *vb* **1** : to produce thunder **2** : to make a sound like thunder **3** : ROAR, SHOUT

thun·der·bolt \'thən-dər-,bōlt\ *n* : a flash of lightning and the thunder that follows it

thun·der·cloud \'thən-dər-,klaud\ *n* : a dark storm cloud that produces lightning and thunder

thun·der·head \'thən-dər-,hed\ *n* : a rounded mass of dark cloud with white edges often appearing before a thunderstorm

thun·der·storm \'thən-dər-,stȯrm\ *n* : a storm accompanied by thunder and lightning

thun·der·struck \'thən-dər-,strək\ *adj* : stunned as if struck by a thunderbolt

Thurs·day \'thərz-dē\ *n* : the fifth day of the week

thus \'thəs\ *adv* **1** : in this or that way **2** : to this degree or extent : SO ⟨a mild winter *thus* far⟩ **3** : because of this or that : HENCE **4** : as an example

¹thwack \'thwak\ *vb* : to strike with something flat or heavy

²thwack *n* : a heavy blow : WHACK

¹thwart \'thwȯrt\ *adv* : ATHWART

²thwart *adj* : situated or placed across something else

³thwart *vb* **1** : BAFFLE **2** : BLOCK, DEFEAT

thy \thī\ *adj, archaic* : of, relating to, or done by or to thee or thyself

thyme \'tīm, 'thīm\ *n* : a mint with tiny pungent aromatic leaves used to season foods or formerly in medicine

thy·roid \'thī-,rȯid\ *n* : a ductless gland at the base of the neck that produces a secretion that affects growth, development, and metabolism

thyme

thy·self \thī-'self\ *pron, archaic* : thy own self

ti \'tē\ *n* : the seventh note of the musical scale

ti·ar·a \tē-'ar-ə\ *n* : a decorative band or semicircular ornament for the head for formal wear by women

¹tick \'tik\ *n* **1** : a bloodsucking eight-legged animal related to the spiders that attaches itself to man and animals **2** : a bloodsucking wingless fly that feeds on sheep

tick 1

²tick *n* **1** : a light rhythmic

---

audible tap or beat (as of a clock) **2** : a small mark used chiefly to draw attention to something or to check an item on a list

³tick *vb* **1** : to make a tick or a series of ticks ⟨a *ticking* clock⟩ **2** : to mark, count, or announce by the ticks of a clock or of a telegraph instrument **3** : OPERATE, RUN ⟨tried to understand what makes him *tick*⟩ **4** : CHECK

¹tick·et \'tik-ət\ *n* **1** : CERTIFICATE, LICENSE **2** : a summons or warning issued to a traffic offender **3** : a document or token showing that a fare or an admission fee has been paid **4** : a list of candidates for nomination or election **5** : a slip or card recording a transaction or giving instructions

²ticket *vb* **1** : to attach a ticket to : LABEL **2** : to serve with a traffic ticket

¹tick·le \'tik-əl\ *vb* **tick·led; tick·ling 1** : to have a tingling or prickling sensation ⟨my foot *tickles*⟩ **2** : to excite or stir up agreeably **3** : AMUSE **4** : to touch a body part lightly so as to excite the surface nerves and cause uneasiness, laughter, or spasmodic movements

²tickle *n* : a tickling sensation

tick·lish \'tik-lish\ *adj* **1** : sensitive to tickling **2** : extremely sensitive : TOUCHY ⟨*ticklish* about his baldness⟩ **3** : requiring delicate handling ⟨a *ticklish* situation⟩

tid·al \'tīd-l\ *adj* : of or relating to tides : flowing and ebbing like tides

tidal wave *n* **1** : a great wave that sometimes rolls in from the sea following an earthquake **2** : an unusual rise of water along a shore due to strong winds

tid·bit \'tid-ˌbit\ *n* **1** : a choice morsel of food **2** : a choice or pleasing bit (as of news)

¹tide \'tīd\ *n* **1** : the rising and falling of the surface of the ocean caused twice daily by the attraction of the sun and the moon **2** : the flow of the incoming or outgoing tide ⟨carried away by the *tide*⟩ **3** : something that rises and falls like the tides of the sea

²tide *vb* **tid·ed; tid·ing** : to enable to surmount or endure a difficulty ⟨a loan to *tide* him over⟩

tid·ings \'tīd-ingz\ *n pl* : NEWS

¹ti·dy \'tīd-ē\ *adj* **ti·di·er; ti·di·est 1** : well ordered and cared for : NEAT **2** : LARGE, SUBSTANTIAL ⟨a *tidy* sum⟩

²tidy *vb* **ti·died; ti·dy·ing 1** : to put in order **2** : to make things tidy ⟨*tidied* up after supper⟩

¹tie \'tī\ *n* **1** : a line, ribbon, or cord used for fastening, uniting, or closing **2** : a structural element (as a beam or rod) holding two pieces together **3** : one of the cross supports to which railroad rails are fastened **4** : a connecting link : BOND ⟨family *ties*⟩ **5** : an equality in number (as of votes or scores)

6 : an undecided or deadlocked contest **7** : NECKTIE

²tie *vb* **tied; ty·ing** \'tī-ing\ *or* **tie·ing 1** : to fasten, attach, or close by means of a tie **2** : to form a knot or bow in ⟨*tie* your necktie⟩ **3** : to bring together firmly : UNITE **4** : to restrain from freedom of action **5** : to make or have an equal score with in a contest

tier \'tiər\ *n* : a row, rank, or layer usually arranged in a series one above the other

tiff \'tif\ *n* : a petty quarrel

ti·ger \'tī-gər\ *n* : a large tawny black-striped Asiatic flesh-eating animal of the cat family

¹tight \'tīt\ *adj* **1** : so close in structure as not to permit passage of a liquid or gas ⟨a *tight* roof⟩ **2** : fixed or held very firmly in place ⟨a *tight* jar cover⟩ **3** : TAUT ⟨a *tight* rope⟩ **4** : fitting too closely ⟨*tight* shoes⟩ **5** : difficult to get through or out of ⟨in a *tight* spot⟩ **6** : firm in control ⟨keeps a *tight* hand on affairs⟩ **7** : STINGY **8** : set close together : COMPACT ⟨a *tight* formation⟩ **9** : low in supply : SCARCE ⟨money is *tight*⟩ — **tight·ly** *adv* — **tight·ness** *n*

²tight *adv* **1** : TIGHTLY, FIRMLY ⟨shut the door *tight*⟩ **2** : SOUNDLY ⟨sleep *tight*⟩

tight·en \'tīt-n\ *vb* : to make or become tight

tight·fist·ed \'tīt-'fis-təd\ *adj* : STINGY

tight·rope \'tīt-ˌrōp\ *n* : a taut rope or wire on which an acrobat performs

tights \'tīts\ *n pl* : a close-fitting garment covering the body especially from the waist down

tight·wad \'tīt-ˌwäd\ *n* : a stingy person

ti·gress \'tī-grəs\ *n* : a female tiger

¹tile \'tīl\ *n* **1** : a thin piece of baked clay, stone, concrete, or rubber used for roofs, walls, floors, or drains **2** : an earthenware pipe used for a drain

²tile *vb* **tiled; til·ing** : to cover with tiles

¹till \til\ *prep or conj* : UNTIL

²till \'til\ *vb* : to work by plowing, sowing, and raising crops from : CULTIVATE

³till \'til\ *n* : a drawer for money

till·age \'til-ij\ *n* : cultivated land

til·ler \'til-ər\ *n* : a lever used to turn the rudder of a boat from side to side

tiller

¹tilt \'tilt\ *vb* **1** : to move or shift so as to incline : TIP ⟨*tilted* his chair⟩ **2** : to engage in a combat with lances : JOUST **3** : to make an impetuous attack

²tilt *n* **1** : an exercise on horseback in which two combatants charging with lances try to unhorse one another : JOUST **2** : an encounter bringing about a sharp verbal conflict **3** : SPEED ⟨going at full *tilt*⟩ **4** : SLANT, TIP

¹tim·ber \'tim-bər\ *n* **1** : wood for use in making something **2** : a usually large or thick piece of squared or dressed lumber **3** : wooded land or growing trees forming a source of lumber

²timber *vb* : to frame, cover, or support with timbers

tim·ber·line \'tim-bər-ˌlīn\ *n* : the upper limit of tree growth (as on mountains)

¹time \'tīm\ *n* **1** : a period during which an action, process, or condition exists or continues **2** : LEISURE ⟨found *time* to read⟩ **3** : a point or period when something occurs : OCCASION **4** : a set or customary moment or hour for something to occur ⟨arrived on *time*⟩ **5** : AGE, ERA **6** : state of affairs — usually used in plural ⟨hard *times*⟩ **7** : rate of speed : TEMPO **8** : RHYTHM **9** : a moment, hour, day, or year as indicated by a clock or calendar ⟨what *time* is it⟩ **10** : a system of reckoning time ⟨solar *time*⟩ **11** : one of a series of recurring instances or repeated actions ⟨told him many *times*⟩ **12** *pl* : multiplied instances ⟨five *times* greater⟩ **13** : a person's experience during a particular period

²time *vb* **timed; tim·ing 1** : to arrange or set the time of **2** : to set the tempo or duration of ⟨*time* a performance⟩ **3** : to cause to keep time with something **4** : to determine or record the time, duration, or rate of — **tim·er** *n*

time·keep·er \'tīm-ˌkē-pər\ *n* **1** : a clerk who keeps records of the time worked by employees **2** : one appointed to mark and announce the time (as in an athletic game)

time·less \'tīm-ləs\ *adj* **1** : UNENDING, ETERNAL **2** : not affected by time : AGELESS

time·ly \'tīm-lē\ *adj* **time·li·er; time·li·est 1** : coming early or at the right time **2** : appropriate to the time ⟨a *timely* book⟩

time·piece \'tīm-ˌpēs\ *n* : a device (as a clock or watch) to measure the passage of time

times \tīmz\ *prep* : multiplied by ⟨two *times* seven is fourteen⟩

time·ta·ble \'tīm-ˌtā-bəl\ *n* : a table of departure and arrival times (as of trains or buses)

tim·id \'tim-əd\ *adj* : feeling or showing a lack of courage or self-confidence : SHY — **tim·id·ly** *adv* — **tim·id·ness** *n*

tim·o·rous \'tim-ə-rəs\ *adj* : of a timid disposition : FEARFUL — **tim·o·rous·ly** *adv*

tin \'tin\ *n* **1** : a soft bluish white metallic chemical element used chiefly in combination with other metals or as a coating to protect other metals **2** : TINPLATE **3** : a box, can, vessel, or sheet made from tinplate

tin·der \'tin-dər\ *n* : a very flammable substance that can be used as kindling

tine \'tīn\ *n* : a slender pointed part (as of a fork or an antler) : PRONG

tin·foil \'tin-ˌfȯil\ *n* : a thin metal sheeting usually of aluminum or tin-lead alloy

¹tinge \'tinj\ *vb* **tinged; tinge·ing** *or* **ting·ing** \'tin-jing\ **1** : to color slightly : TINT **2** : to affect or modify especially with a slight odor or taste

tine

²tinge *n* **1** : a slight coloring **2** : a modifying property or influence : TOUCH

¹tin·gle \'ting-gəl\ *vb* **tin·gled; tin·gling** : to feel or cause a prickling or thrilling sensation

²tingle *n* : a tingling sensation or condition

¹tin·ker \'ting-kər\ *n* : a usually itinerant mender of household utensils (as pans)

²tinker *vb* : to repair or adjust something in an unskilled or experimental manner

¹tin·kle \'ting-kəl\ *vb* **tin·kled; tin·kling** : to make or cause to make a tinkle

²tinkle *n* : a series of short high ringing or clinking sounds

tin·plate \'tin-'plāt\ *n* : thin steel sheets covered with tin

tin·sel \'tin-səl\ *n* **1** : a thread, strip, or sheet of metal, paper, or plastic used to produce a glittering effect **2** : something that seems attractive but is of little worth

tin·smith \'tin-ˌsmith\ *n* : a worker in tin or sometimes other metal

¹tint \'tint\ *n* **1** : a slight or pale coloring : TINGE **2** : a light color or shade ⟨*tints* of red⟩

²tint *vb* : to impart a tint to : COLOR

tin·ware \'tin-ˌwaər\ *n* : articles of tinplate

ti·ny \'tī-nē\ *adj* **ti·ni·er; ti·ni·est** : very small

¹tip \'tip\ *n* **1** : the pointed or rounded end of something **2** : a small piece or part serving as an end, cap, or point

²tip *vb* **tipped; tip·ping 1** : to furnish with a tip **2** : to cover or adorn the tip of

³tip *vb* **tipped; tip·ping 1** : OVERTURN, UPSET **2** : LEAN, SLANT **3** : to raise and tilt forward

⁴tip *n* : the act or an instance of tipping : TILT

⁵tip *n* : a light glancing blow ⟨foul *tip*⟩

⁶tip *vb* **tipped; tip·ping** : to give a gratuity to

⁷tip *n* : a small sum of money given for a service performed or anticipated : GRATUITY

⁸tip *n* : a piece of expert or confidential information

⁹tip *vb* **tipped; tip·ping** : to give a piece of expert or confidential information about or to

¹tip·toe \'tip-ˌtō\ *n* : the end of the toes

²tiptoe *adv* (*or adj*) : on or as if on tiptoe

³tiptoe *vb* **tip·toed; tip·toe·ing** : to walk tiptoe

¹tip·top \'tip-'täp\ *n* : the highest point

²tiptop *adj* : EXCELLENT, FIRST-RATE

¹tire \'tīr\ *vb* **tired; tir·ing** **1** : to make or become weary : FATIGUE **2** : to wear out the patience or attention of : BORE

syn TIRE, FATIGUE, EXHAUST all refer to a loss of strength or endurance. TIRE suggests losing so much energy, endurance, patience, or interest that one is reluctant to continue ⟨my dog is old and *tires* easily⟩ ⟨he quickly *tired* of collecting stamps and switched to coins⟩ FATIGUE suggests great weariness, often from extreme effort or strain, and may indicate an inability to go on without undesirable consequences ⟨a fifty-mile hike is painfully *fatiguing* to most civilians⟩ EXHAUST is the strongest of these terms and stresses such a complete draining of energy that it becomes impossible to exert effort in any direction ⟨the ranger collapsed, *exhausted* from seventy-two hours of fire fighting⟩ ⟨the fox was *exhausted* and couldn't escape the dogs any longer⟩

²tire *n* **1** : a metal band that forms the tread of a wheel **2** : a rubber cushion usually containing compressed air that encircles a wheel (as of an automobile)

tired \'tīrd\ *adj* : WEARY

tire·less \'tīr-ləs\ *adj* : capable of working a long time without tiring : UNTIRING — **tire·less·ly** *adv* — **tire·less·ness** *n*

tire·some \'tīr-səm\ *adj* : BORING, TEDIOUS — **tire·some·ly** *adv*

tis·sue \'tish-ü\ *n* **1** : a fine lightweight fabric **2** : MESH, NETWORK ⟨a *tissue* of lies⟩ **3** : a piece of soft absorbent paper **4** : a mass or layer of cells usually of one kind that together with their supporting structures form a fundamental structural material of an animal or plant body ⟨muscular *tissue*⟩

tit \'tit\ *n* : TEAT

ti·tan·ic \tī-'tan-ik\ *adj* : enormous in size, force, or power : COLOSSAL

ti·tle \'tīt-l\ *n* **1** : a legal right to the ownership of property **2** : the distinguishing name of a written, printed, or filmed production, of a musical composition, or of a work of art **3** : an appellation of honor, rank, or office **4** : CHAMPIONSHIP ⟨won the batting *title*⟩

TNT \,tē-,en-'tē\ *n* : a high explosive used in artillery shells and bombs and in blasting

¹to \tə, tü\ *prep* **1** : so as to reach or gain ⟨drove *to* town⟩ **2** : in the direction of ⟨was walking *to* school⟩ **3** : ON, AGAINST ⟨apply salve *to* a burn⟩ **4** : as far as ⟨will pay up *to* a dollar⟩ **5** : and thus brought into the state of or changed into ⟨broken *to* pieces⟩ **6** : BEFORE ⟨it's ten *to* six⟩ **7** : UNTIL ⟨from May *to* December⟩ **8** : fitting or being a part of ⟨a key *to* the lock⟩ **9** : with the accompaniment of ⟨sing *to* the music⟩ **10** : in relation or comparison with ⟨similar *to* that one⟩ ⟨won ten *to* six⟩ **11** : in accordance with ⟨add salt *to* taste⟩ **12** : within the range of ⟨*to* my knowledge⟩ **13** : contained, occurring, or included in ⟨two pints *to* a quart⟩ **14** : as regards ⟨our attitude *to* our friends⟩ **15** : affecting as the receiver or beneficiary ⟨whispered *to* her⟩ ⟨gave it *to* me⟩ **16** : for no one except ⟨a room *to* himself⟩ **17** : into the action of ⟨we got *to* talking⟩

²to \'tü\ *adv* **1** : in a direction toward ⟨run *to* and fro⟩ **2** : into contact, position, or attachment especially with a frame ⟨the wind blew the door *to*⟩ **3** : to the matter or business at hand ⟨fell *to* and ate heartily⟩ **4** : to a state of consciousness or awareness ⟨came *to* an hour after the accident⟩

toad \'tōd\ *n* : a rough-skinned tailless leaping amphibian that usually lives on land

toad·stool \'tōd-,stül\ *n* : a mushroom especially when poisonous or unfit for food

toad·y \'tōd-ē\ *n, pl* **toad·ies** : a person who flatters another in the hope of receiving favors

¹toast \'tōst\ *vb* **1** : to make (as bread) crisp, hot, and brown by heat **2** : to warm thoroughly — **toast·er** *n*

²toast *n* **1** : sliced toasted bread **2** : one in whose honor persons drink **3** : a highly admired person ⟨the *toast* of the town⟩ **4** : an act of drinking in honor of a toast

³toast *vb* : to propose or drink to as a toast

toast·mas·ter \'tōst-,mas-tər\ *n* : a person who presides at a banquet

to·bac·co \tə-'bak-ō\ *n* : a tall plant related to the tomato and potato that has pink or white tubular flowers and broad sticky leaves which are dried and processed for use in smoking or chewing or as snuff

¹to·bog·gan \tə-'bäg-ən\ *n* : a long flat-bottomed light sled made without runners and curved up at the front

tobacco

²toboggan *vb* **1** : to coast on a toboggan **2** : to decline suddenly (as in value)

¹to·day \tə-'dā\ *adv* **1** : on or for this day **2** : at the present time

²today *n* : the present day, time, or age

¹toe \'tō\ *n* **1** : one of the separate parts of the front end of a foot **2** : the front end or part of a foot or hoof — **toed** \'tōd\ *adj*

²toe *vb* **toed; toe·ing** : to touch, reach, or drive with the toes

toe·hold \'tō-ˌhōld\ *n* : a slight footing

toe·nail \'tō-ˌnāl\ *n* : the hard covering at the end of a toe

to·ga \'tō-gə\ *n* : the loose outer garment worn in public by citizens of ancient Rome

toga

to·geth·er \tə-'geth-ər\ *adv* **1** : in or into one group, body, or place ⟨gathered *together*⟩ **2** : in or into contact or association ⟨in business *together*⟩ **3** : at one time ⟨they all cheered *together*⟩ **4** : in succession ⟨for days *together*⟩ **5** : in or by combined effort ⟨worked *together* to clear the road⟩ **6** : in or into agreement ⟨get *together* on a plan⟩ **7** : considered as a whole ⟨gave more than all the others *together*⟩

togs \'tägz\ *n pl* : CLOTHING

¹toil \'tȯil\ *n* : long hard tiring labor : DRUDGERY **syn** see WORK

²toil *vb* **1** : to work hard and long **2** : to proceed with effort : PLOD

toi·let \'tȯi-lət\ *n* **1** : the act or process of dressing and grooming oneself **2** : BATHROOM **3** : a plumbing device consisting essentially of a hopper that can be flushed with water

to·ken \'tō-kən\ *n* **1** : an outward sign ⟨*tokens* of her grief⟩ **2** : an object used to suggest something that cannot be pictured **3** : SOUVENIR **4** : INDICATION ⟨a mere *token* of future benefits⟩ **5** : a piece resembling a coin issued as money or for use by a particular group ⟨bus *token*⟩

told *past of* TELL

tol·er·a·ble \'täl-ə-rə-bəl\ *adj* **1** : capable of being borne or endured **2** : moderately good : FAIR — **tol·er·a·bly** \-blē\ *adv*

tol·er·ance \'täl-ə-rəns\ *n* : sympathy or indulgence for beliefs or practices differing from one's own

tol·er·ant \'täl-ə-rənt\ *adj* : showing tolerance — **tol·er·ant·ly** *adv*

syn TOLERANT, LENIENT, INDULGENT all mean being gentle or humane toward people or their acts. TOLERANT stresses being neither narrow≠minded about opinion and behavior that differ from one's own nor overly critical of human failings ⟨the old woman was *tolerant* of children but disapproved of most adults⟩ LENIENT emphasizes a mild or soft temperament and a tendency to relax discipline and deal easily with offenders or those under one's control ⟨this country tends to be *lenient* toward conquered enemies⟩ INDULGENT may merely indicate being excessively lenient and inclined to pamper or show favor ⟨*indulgent* parents who

can't say no⟩ but may also imply a general inclination to make concessions out of mercy or charity ⟨Lincoln was known as a gentle man, *indulgent* of human foibles⟩

tol·er·ate \'täl-ə-ˌrāt\ *vb* **tol·er·at·ed; tol·er·at·ing 1** : to allow something to be done or to exist without making a move to stop it **2** : to endure or resist the action of (as a drug)

¹toll \'tōl\ *n* **1** : a tax paid for a privilege (as the use of a highway or bridge) **2** : a charge paid for a service **3** : a grievous or ruinous price especially in life or health

²toll *vb* **1** : to announce (as a death) or summon (as defenders) by the sounding of a bell **2** : to sound with slow measured strokes

³toll *n* : the sound of a tolling bell

¹tom·a·hawk \'täm-ə-ˌhȯk\ *n* : a light ax used as a weapon by North American Indians

²tomahawk *vb* : to cut, strike, or kill with a tomahawk

tomahawk

to·ma·to \tə-'māt-ō, -'mät-\ *n, pl* **to·ma·toes** : a red or yellow juicy pulpy fruit that is used as a vegetable or in salads and is produced by a hairy yellow-flowered plant related to the potato

tomb \'tüm\ *n* **1** : GRAVE **2** : a house, chamber, or vault for the dead

tom·boy \'täm-ˌbȯi\ *n* : a girl of boyish behavior

tomb·stone \'tüm-ˌstōn\ *n* : GRAVESTONE

tom·cat \'täm-ˌkat\ *n* : a male cat

¹to·mor·row \tə-'mär-ō\ *adv* : on or for the day after today

²tomorrow *n* : the day after today

tom–tom \'täm-ˌtäm\ *n* : a small-headed drum usually beaten with the hands

ton \'tən\ *n* : a measure of weight equal either to 2000 pounds (**short ton**) or 2240 pounds (**long ton**) with the short ton being more commonly used in the United States and Canada

¹tone \'tōn\ *n* [from Greek *tonos*, literally, "a stretching", because the tone or pitch of a musical string depends on how much it is stretched] **1** : quality of vocal or musical sound **2** : a sound of definite pitch **3** : accent or inflection expressive of an emotion ⟨an angry *tone*⟩ **4** : a style or manner of speaking or writing ⟨reply in a friendly *tone*⟩ **5** : general character, quality, or trend **6** : color quality or value ⟨decorated in soft *tones*⟩ **7** : a color that modifies another ⟨gray with a blue *tone*⟩ **8** : a healthy state of the body or any of its parts **9** : RESILIENCE

tom-tom

²tone *vb* **toned; ton·ing 1 :** to give tone to **:** STRENGTHEN ⟨medicine to *tone* up the system⟩ **2 :** to soften, blend, or harmonize in color, appearance, or sound

tongs \ˈtängz\ *n pl* **:** a scissorslike device for taking hold of something

tongue \ˈtəng\ *n* **1 :** an organ of the mouth used in tasting, in taking and swallowing food, and by human beings in speaking **2 :** the power of communication **:** SPEECH **3 :** LANGUAGE ⟨a foreign *tongue*⟩ **4 :** manner or quality of utterance **5 :** something resembling an animal's tongue in being elongated and fastened at one end

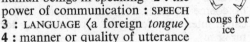

tongs for ice

tongue–tied \ˈtəng-ˌtīd\ *adj* **:** unable to speak clearly or freely (as from shyness)

¹ton·ic \ˈtän-ik\ *adj* **1 :** improving or restoring physical or mental tone **:** INVIGORATING **2 :** of or relating to tones

²tonic *n* **:** a tonic medicine

¹to·night \tə-ˈnīt\ *adv* **:** on this present night or the night following this present day

²tonight *n* **:** the present or the coming night

ton·nage \ˈtən-ij\ *n* **1 :** a duty on ships based on tons carried **2 :** ships in terms of the total number of tons registered or carried **3 :** the cubical content of a ship in units of 100 cubic feet **4 :** total weight in tons shipped, carried, or mined

ton·sil \ˈtän-səl\ *n* **:** either of a pair of oval masses of spongy tissue at the back of the mouth

ton·sil·li·tis \ˌtän-sə-ˈlīt-əs\ *n* **:** inflammation of the tonsils

too \ˈtü\ *adv* **1 :** in addition **:** ALSO **2 :** EXCESSIVELY ⟨the dress was *too* short⟩ **3 :** to such a degree as to be regrettable ⟨has gone *too* far⟩ **4 :** VERY ⟨would be *too* glad to help⟩

took *past of* TAKE

¹tool \ˈtül\ *n* **1 :** an instrument (as a saw, file, knife, or wrench) used by the hands or worked by a machine **2 :** a means to an end **3 :** a person used or manipulated by another

²tool *vb* **1 :** to shape, form, or finish with a tool **2 :** to equip a plant or industry with machines and tools for production

tool·box \ˈtül-ˌbäks\ *n* **:** a chest for tools

¹toot \ˈtüt\ *vb* **1 :** to sound a short blast **2 :** to blow or sound an instrument (as a horn) especially in short blasts

²toot *n* **:** a short blast (as on a horn)

tooth \ˈtüth\ *n, pl* **teeth** \ˈtēth\ **1 :** one of the hard bony structures borne in sockets on the jaws of most vertebrates and used in seizing and chewing food and in fighting

tooth

2 : something resembling or suggesting an animal's tooth in shape, arrangement, or action ⟨the *teeth* of a comb⟩ **3 :** one of the projections around the rim of a wheel that fit between the projections on another part causing the wheel or the other part to move along **:** COG — **tooth·less** \ˈtüth-ləs\ *adj*

tooth·ache \ˈtüth-ˌāk\ *n* **:** pain in or about a tooth

tooth·brush \ˈtüth-ˌbrəsh\ *n* **:** a brush for cleaning the teeth

toothed \ˈtütht\ *adj* **1 :** having teeth or such or so many teeth **2 :** NOTCHED, JAGGED

tooth·paste \ˈtüth-ˌpāst\ *n* **:** a paste for cleaning the teeth

tooth·pick \ˈtüth-ˌpik\ *n* **:** a pointed instrument for removing substances lodged between the teeth

¹top \ˈtäp\ *n* **1 :** the highest point, level, or part of something **2 :** the upper end, edge, or surface **3 :** the stalk and leaves of a plant and especially of one with edible roots **4 :** an upper piece, lid, or covering ⟨pajama *top*⟩ **5 :** the highest position or rank **:** ACME

²top *vb* **topped; top·ping 1 :** to remove or cut the top of ⟨*top* a tree⟩ **2 :** to cover with a top or on the top **:** CROWN, CAP **3 :** to supply with a decorative or protective finish or a final touch ⟨*top* the meal off with coffee⟩ **4 :** to be superior to **5 :** to go over the top of **6 :** to strike above the center ⟨*top* a golf ball⟩

³top *adj* **:** of, relating to, or at the top **:** HIGHEST

⁴top *n* **:** a child's toy having a tapering point on which it can be made to spin

to·paz \ˈtō-ˌpaz\ *n* **:** a mineral that when occurring as perfect yellow crystals is valued as a gem

top

top·coat \ˈtäp-ˌkōt\ *n* **:** a lightweight overcoat

top·ic \ˈtäp-ik\ *n* **1 :** a heading in an outlined argument or exposition **2 :** the subject of a discourse or a section of it

top·i·cal \ˈtäp-i-kəl\ *adj* **1 :** of, relating to, or arranged by topics ⟨a *topical* outline⟩ **2 :** relating to current or local events

top·knot \ˈtäp-ˌnät\ *n* **:** a crest of feathers or hair on the top of the head

top·mast \ˈtäp-ˌmast, -məst\ *n* **:** the second mast above a ship's deck

top·most \ˈtäp-ˌmōst\ *adj* **:** highest of all

top–notch \ˈtäp-ˈnäch\ *adj* **:** FIRST-RATE

top·ple \ˈtäp-əl\ *vb* **top·pled; top·pling 1 :** to fall from being too heavy at the top **2 :** to push over **:** OVERTURN

topsail

top·sail \ˈtäp-ˌsāl, -səl\ *n* **1 :** the sail next above the lowest sail on a mast in a square-rigged ship   **2** : the sail above the large sail on a mast in a ship with a fore-and-aft rig

top·soil \'täp-ˌsȯil\ *n* : the organic upper layer of soil in which plants have most of their roots

top·sy-tur·vy \ˌtäp-sē-'tər-vē\ *adv (or adj)* **1** : upside down   **2** : in utter confusion

torch \'tȯrch\ *n*   **1** : a flaming light that is made of something (as a twist of tow) which burns brightly and is usually carried in the hand   **2** : something that resembles a torch in giving light, heat, or guidance   **3** : a portable device for producing a hot flame

tore *past of* TEAR

¹tor·ment \'tȯr-ˌment\ *n*   **1** : extreme pain or anguish of body or mind : AGONY   **2** : a source of vexation or pain

²tor·ment \tȯr-'ment\ *vb*   **1** : to cause severe suffering of body or mind to   **2** : VEX, HARASS

torn *past part of* TEAR

tor·na·do \tȯr-'nād-ō\ *n, pl* **tor·na·does** *or* **tor·na·dos** : a violent whirling wind accompanied by a funnel-shaped cloud that moves overland in a narrow path

¹tor·pe·do \tȯr-'pēd-ō\ *n, pl* **tor·pe·does** [from Latin, a word meaning originally "numbness", from the verb *torpēre* "to be numb", because shock given by the fish produces numbness]   **1** : a fish related to the rays that has a pair of organs near the head capable of giving its prey an electric shock   **2** : a cigar-shaped metal case filled with an explosive charge and made so that it directs and propels itself under water   **3** : a bit of explosive clasped to a railroad rail to give a loud report as a signal when run over

²torpedo *vb* **tor·pe·doed; tor·pe·do·ing** : to hit with or destroy by a torpedo

tor·pid \'tȯr-pəd\ *adj*   **1** : having lost motion or the power of exertion or feeling (a bear *torpid* in his winter sleep)   **2** : lacking in energy or vigor : DULL (a *torpid* mind)

tor·por \'tȯr-pər\ *n* : extreme sluggishness

tor·rent \'tȯr-ənt\ *n*   **1** : a rushing stream (as of water or lava)   **2** : a tumultuous outburst

tor·rid \'tȯr-əd\ *adj*   **1** : parched with heat especially of the sun   **2** : very warm

tor·so \'tȯr-sō\ *n, pl* **tor·sos** *or* **tor·si** \-ˌsē\ : the human trunk

tor·ti·lla \tȯr-'tē-ə\ *n* : a round flat unleavened cake of cornmeal baked on a heated stone or iron

tor·toise \'tȯrt-əs\ *n* : any of various turtles (as a land turtle or large sea turtle)

tor·toise-shell \'tȯrt-əs-ˌshel\ *n*   **1** : the mottled brown and yellow horny covering of

the shell of a sea tortoise used for ornamental objects   **2** : any of several brightly colored butterflies

tor·tu·ous \'tȯr-chə-wəs\ *adj*   **1** : marked by repeated twists or turns : WINDING   **2** : CROOKED, TRICKY

¹tor·ture \'tȯr-chər\ *n*   **1** : the infliction of intense pain especially to punish or to obtain a confession   **2** : anguish of body or mind

²torture *vb* **tor·tured; tor·tur·ing**   **1** : to punish or coerce by inflicting intense pain   **2** : to cause intense suffering to : TORMENT — **tor·tur·er** *n*

¹toss \'tȯs\ *vb*   **1** : to fling to and fro or up and down (waves *tossed* the ship about)   **2** : to throw with a quick light motion   **3** : to lift with a sudden motion (*toss* the head)   **4** : to pitch or bob about rapidly (a canoe *tossing* on the waves)   **5** : to be restless   **6** : to stir or mix lightly (*tossed* salad)

²toss *n* : an act or instance of tossing

tot \'tät\ *n* : a small child

¹to·tal \'tōt-l\ *adj*   **1** : of or relating to the whole of something (a *total* eclipse of the sun)   **2** : making up the whole : ENTIRE   **3** : COMPLETE, UTTER (*total* ruin)   **4** : making use of every means to carry out an objective (*total* war) — **to·tal·ly** *adv*

²total *n*   **1** : a product of addition : SUM   **2** : an entire quantity : AMOUNT

³total *vb* **to·taled** *or* **to·talled; to·tal·ing** *or* **to·tal·ling**   **1** : to add up : COMPUTE   **2** : to amount to : NUMBER

tote \'tōt\ *vb* **tot·ed; tot·ing** : CARRY, HAUL

to·tem \'tōt-əm\ *n*   **1** : an object (as an animal or plant) serving as the emblem of a family or clan   **2** : a usually carved or painted representation of a totem (as on a **totem pole**)

tot·ter \'tät-ər\ *vb*   **1** : to tremble or rock as if about to fall : SWAY   **2** : to move unsteadily : STAGGER

tou·can \'tü-ˌkan\ *n* : a bright-colored fruit-eating tropical bird with a very large beak

¹touch \'təch\ *vb*   **1** : to feel or handle (as with the fingers) especially so as to perceive with the tactile sense   **2** : to be or cause to be in contact with something   **3** : to be or come next to : ADJOIN   **4** : to hit lightly   **5** : DISTURB, HARM (no one will dare to *touch* you)   **6** : to make use of (never *touches* meat)   **7** : to refer to in passing : MENTION   **8** : to affect the interest of (a matter that *touches* every parent)   **9** : to move emotionally (*touched* by his friend's

totem pole

kindness⟩ **10** : to make a usually brief or incidental stop in port **11** : to induce to give or lend **12** : to improve or alter with slight strokes of a brush or pencil

²touch *n* **1** : a light stroke or tap **2** : the act or fact of touching or being touched **3** : the special sense by which light pressure is perceived ⟨soft to the *touch*⟩ **4** : a particular impression conveyed by the sense of touch ⟨the soft *touch* of silk⟩ **5** : a state of contact or communication ⟨keep in *touch* with friends⟩ **6** : a characteristic or distinguishing trait or quality **7** : a small amount : TRACE

touch·down \'təch-,daun\ *n* : a score made in football by carrying or catching the ball over the opponent's goal line

touch·ing \'təch-ing\ *adj* : arousing tenderness or compassion

touch·y \'təch-ē\ *adj* **touch·i·er; touch·i·est** **1** : easily offended **2** : calling for tactful or careful treatment ⟨a *touchy* subject⟩

¹tough \'təf\ *adj* **1** : strong or firm in texture but flexible and not brittle ⟨*tough* fibers⟩ **2** : not easily chewed ⟨*tough* meat⟩ **3** : able to endure strain or hardship ⟨a *tough* body⟩ **4** : hard to influence : STUBBORN **5** : very difficult ⟨a *tough* problem⟩ **6** : ROWDY, LAWLESS ⟨a *tough* neighborhood⟩ **7** : marked by severity and determination — **tough·ness** *n*

²tough *n* : ROWDY

tough·en \'təf-ən\ *vb* : to make or become tough

¹tour \'tur\ *n* **1** : a period (as of duty) under an orderly schedule **2** : a trip usually ending at the starting point **syn** see JOURNEY

²tour *vb* : to make a tour of : travel as a tourist

tour·ist \'tur-əst\ *n* : a person who travels for pleasure

tour·na·ment \'tur-nə-mənt\ *n* **1** : a contest of skill and courage between armored knights fighting with blunted lances or swords **2** : a series of athletic contests, sports events, or games for a championship

tour·ni·quet \'tur-ni-kət\ *n* : a device (as a bandage twisted tight) for checking bleeding or blood flow

tou·sle \'tau-zəl\ *vb* **tou·sled; tou·sling** : to put into disorder by rough handling

¹tow \'tō\ *vb* : to draw or pull along behind

tourniquet

²tow *n* **1** : an act or instance of towing : the fact or condition of being towed **2** : a line or rope for towing **3** : something (as a barge) that is towed

³tow *n* : the coarse and broken parts of flax, hemp, or jute separated for spinning

to·ward \'tō-ərd, tə-'word\ *or* **to·wards** \'tō-ərdz, tə-'wordz\ *prep* **1** : in the direction of ⟨heading *toward* town⟩ **2** : along a course leading to ⟨efforts *toward* peace⟩ **3** : in regard to ⟨tolerance *toward* minorities⟩ **4** : so as to face ⟨his back was *toward* me⟩ **5** : close upon : NEAR ⟨along *toward* sundown⟩ **6** : for part payment of ⟨paid $100 *toward* his tuition⟩

tow·el \'tau-əl\ *n* : a cloth or piece of absorbent paper for wiping or drying

¹tow·er \'tau-ər\ *n* **1** : a building or structure that is higher than its length or width, is high relative to its surroundings, and may stand by itself or be attached to a larger structure **2** : CITADEL **3** : a tall framework or mast resembling a tower

²tower *vb* : to reach or rise to a great height

tow·er·ing \'tau-ə-ring\ *adj* **1** : LOFTY, TALL **2** : INTENSE, OVERWHELMING ⟨*towering* rage⟩ **3** : EXCESSIVE ⟨*towering* ambition⟩

tow·head \'tō-,hed\ *n* : a person having soft whitish hair

town \'taun\ *n* **1** : a compactly settled area that is usually larger than a village but smaller than a city **2** : CITY **3** : city life **4** : the people of a town

town·ship \'taun-,ship\ *n* **1** : a unit of local government in some northeastern and north central states **2** : a division of territory in surveys of United States public lands containing thirty-six square miles

tow·path \'tō-,path, -,path\ *n* : a path traveled by men or animals towing boats

tox·ic \'täk-sik\ *adj* : of, relating to, or caused by a poison ⟨*toxic* effects⟩

tox·in \'täk-sən\ *n* : a poison produced by an animal, a plant, or germs ⟨a snake *toxin*⟩

¹toy \'tói\ *n* **1** : something (as a trinket) of little or no value **2** : something for a child to play with **3** : something small of its kind

²toy *vb* : to amuse oneself as if with a toy

¹trace \'trās\ *n* **1** : a mark left by something that has passed : TRAIL **2** : a sign or evidence of some past thing **3** : a minute amount

²trace *vb* **traced; trac·ing** **1** : SKETCH **2** : to form (as letters) carefully or painstakingly **3** : to copy (as a drawing) by following the lines or letters as seen through a transparent sheet placed over the thing copied **4** : to follow the footprints, track, or trail of **5** : to study out or follow the development and progress of in detail

³trace *n* : either of the two straps, chains, or ropes of a harness that fasten a horse to a vehicle

trace·a·ble \'trā-sə-bəl\ *adj* : capable of being traced

trac·er·y \'trā-sə-rē\ *n, pl* **trac·er·ies** : ornamental work having a design done with branching or interlacing lines

tra·che·a \'trā-kē-ə\ *n, pl* **tra·che·ae** \-kē-,ē\ **1** : WINDPIPE **2** : a breathing tube of an insect

trac·ing \'trā-sing\ *n* **1** : the act of a person that traces **2** : something that is traced

tracery

¹track \'trak\ *n* **1** : a mark left in passing ⟨rabbit *tracks*⟩ **2** : PATH, TRAIL **3** : a course laid out for racing **4** : a way for a wheeled vehicle ⟨railroad *track*⟩ **5** : awareness of a fact or progression ⟨lose *track* of time⟩ **6** : either of two endless metal belts on which a vehicle travels **7** : track-and-field sports

²track *vb* **1** : to follow the tracks or traces of **2** : to make tracks on or with

track–and–field *adj* : of or relating to sports performed on a racing track or the adjacent field

¹tract \'trakt\ *n* : a pamphlet of political or religious propaganda

²tract *n* **1** : an indefinite stretch of land **2** : a defined area of land **3** : a system of body parts or organs that serve some special purpose ⟨the digestive *tract*⟩

trac·tor \'trak-tər\ *n* **1** : a self-propelled vehicle with large rear wheels or with beltlike tracks that is used especially for drawing farm implements **2** : a short motortruck for hauling a trailer

¹trade \'trād\ *n* **1** : the business or work in which one engages regularly : OCCUPATION **2** : an occupation requiring manual or mechanical skill : CRAFT **3** : the persons engaged in a business or industry **4** : the business of buying and selling or bartering commodities : COMMERCE **5** : an act of trading : TRANSACTION **6** : a firm's customers

syn TRADE, BUSINESS, PROFESSION all mean an occupation requiring skill or training by which one earns a living. TRADE applies chiefly to occupations requiring skilled labor and usually the handling of tools or machinery ⟨a carpenter by *trade*⟩ ⟨works at the printer's *trade*⟩ BUSINESS applies mainly to occupations concerned with the buying or selling of goods and services or with related occupations such as transportation and finance ⟨his father is in the hotel *business*⟩ ⟨baby-sitting has become a recognized *business*⟩ PROFESSION normally applies to occupations that require a higher education and considerable training along with a degree or other proof of qualification, and usually implies a certain devotion and adherence to standards and ideals upheld in the practice ⟨the *profession* of law⟩

²trade *vb* **trad·ed; trad·ing** **1** : to give in exchange for another commodity **2** : to engage in the exchange, purchase, or sale of goods **3** : to deal regularly as a customer

trade·mark \'trād-,märk\ *n* : a device (as a word) that points distinctly to the origin or ownership of merchandise or service to which it is applied and that is legally reserved for the exclusive use of the owner

trad·er \'trād-ər\ *n* **1** : a person who trades **2** : a ship engaged in trade

trades·man \'trādz-mən\ *n, pl* **trades·men** \-mən\ **1** : one who runs a retail store **2** : CRAFTSMAN

trade wind *n* : a wind blowing steadily toward the equator from an easterly direction

trad·ing post \'trād-ing-\ *n* : a station or store of a trader or trading company established in a sparsely settled region

tra·di·tion \trə-'dish-ən\ *n* **1** : the handing down of information, beliefs, or customs from one generation to another **2** : a belief or custom handed down by tradition

tra·di·tion·al \trə-'dish-ən-l\ *adj* **1** : handed down from age to age **2** : CONVENTIONAL — **tra·di·tion·al·ly** *adv*

¹traf·fic \'traf-ik\ *n* **1** : the business of carrying passengers or goods ⟨the tourist *traffic*⟩ **2** : the business of buying and selling : COMMERCE **3** : DEALINGS, FAMILIARITY ⟨*traffic* with the enemy⟩ **4** : the persons or goods carried by train, boat, or airplane or passing along a road, river, or air route **5** : the movement (as of vehicles) along a route

²traffic *vb* **traf·ficked; traf·fick·ing** : TRADE

trag·e·dy \'traj-ə-dē\ *n, pl* **trag·e·dies** **1** : a serious play that has a sorrowful or disastrous ending **2** : a disastrous event

trag·ic \'traj-ik\ *adj* **1** : of, relating to, or characteristic of tragedy ⟨a *tragic* actress⟩ **2** : LAMENTABLE, UNFORTUNATE

¹trail \'trāl\ *vb* **1** : to drag or draw along behind ⟨the horse *trailed* its reins⟩ **2** : to lag behind **3** : to follow in the tracks of : PURSUE **4** : to hang or let hang so as to touch the ground **5** : to form a trail **6** : DWINDLE

²trail *n* **1** : something that trails or is trailed ⟨a *trail* of smoke⟩ **2** : a trace or mark left by something that has passed or been drawn along **3** : a beaten path **4** : a marked path through a forest or mountainous region

trail·er \'trā-lər\ *n* **1** : a vehicle designed to be hauled (as by a tractor) **2** : a vehicle designed to serve wherever parked as a dwelling or a place of business

¹train \'trān\ *n* [from medieval French, derived from the verb *trainer* "to draw", "to drag"] **1** : a part of a gown that trails behind the wearer **2** : RETINUE **3** : a moving file of persons, vehicles, or animals **4** : a connected series ⟨*train* of thought⟩ **5** : accompanying circumstances **6** : a connected series of railway cars usually hauled by a locomotive

train

²train *vb* **1** : to direct the growth of (a plant) usually by bending, pruning, and tying **2** : to undergo or cause to undergo instruction, discipline, or drill **3** : to teach in an art, profession, or trade ⟨*train* radio operators⟩ **4** : to make ready (as by exercise) for a test of skill **5** : to aim (as a gun) at a target — **train·er** *n*

train·ing \'trā-ning\ *n* **1** : the course followed by one who trains or is being trained : EDUCATION **2** : the condition of one who has trained for a test or contest

trait \'trāt\ *n* : a distinguishing quality (as of personality) : CHARACTERISTIC

trai·tor \'trāt-ər\ *n* **1** : one who betrays another's trust or is false to an obligation or duty **2** : one who commits treason

trai·tor·ous \'trāt-ə-rəs\ *adj* **1** : guilty or capable of treason **2** : constituting treason — **trai·tor·ous·ly** *adv*

¹tramp \'tramp\ *vb* **1** : to walk heavily **2** : to tread on forcibly and repeatedly **3** : to travel or wander through on foot

²tramp *n* **1** : a begging or thieving vagrant **2** : HIKE **3** : the succession of sounds made by the beat of marching feet **4** : a ship not making regular trips but taking cargo to any port

tram·ple \'tram-pəl\ *vb* **tram·pled**; **tram·pling** **1** : to tramp or tread heavily so as to bruise, crush, or injure **2** : to tread underfoot **3** : to inflict injury or loss by ruthless treatment

tram·po·line \,tram-pə-'lēn\ *n* : a resilient canvas sheet or web supported by springs in a metal frame used as a springboard in tumbling

trampoline

trance \'trans\ *n* [from medieval French *transe*, derived from the verb *transir* "to die", "to faint", from Latin *transire* "to cross over", "to pass away", from *trans-* "across" and *ire* "to go"] **1** : DAZE, STUPOR **2** : a sleeplike condition (as of deep hypnosis) **3** : a state of profound abstraction or absorption

tran·quil \'trang-kwəl\ *adj* : very calm and quiet : PEACEFUL ⟨a *tranquil* life⟩

tran·quil·iz·er \'trang-kwə-,lī-zər\ *n* : a drug used to ease anxiety and nervous tension

tran·quil·li·ty *or* **tran·quil·i·ty** \tran-'kwil-ət-ē\ *n* : CALMNESS, QUIET

trans- *prefix* **1** : on or to the other side of : across : beyond ⟨*trans*atlantic⟩ **2** : so or such as to change or transfer ⟨*trans*ship⟩

trans·act \trans-'akt\ *vb* **1** : to bring about : NEGOTIATE **2** : to carry on : CONDUCT

trans·ac·tion \trans-'ak-shən\ *n* **1** : an act or process of transacting **2** : a business deal **3** *pl* : the record of the meeting of a society

trans·at·lan·tic \,trans-ət-'lant-ik\ *adj* : crossing or situated beyond the Atlantic ocean

tran·scend \tran-'send\ *vb* **1** : to rise above the limits of **2** : SURPASS

trans·con·ti·nen·tal \,trans-,känt-n-'ent-l\ *adj* : crossing, extending across, or situated on the farther side of a continent

tran·scribe \tran-'skrīb\ *vb* **tran·scribed**; **tran·scrib·ing** **1** : to make a copy of **2** : to record for later broadcast

tran·script \'tran-,skript\ *n* **1** : COPY **2** : an official copy of a student's educational record

¹trans·fer \trans-'fər\ *vb* **trans·ferred**; **trans·fer·ring** **1** : to pass or cause to pass from one person, place, or situation to another **2** : to make over the possession or ownership of : CONVEY **3** : to copy (as by printing) from one surface to another by contact **4** : to move to a different place, region, or situation **5** : to change from one vehicle or transportation line to another

²trans·fer \'trans-,fər\ *n* **1** : conveyance of right, title, or interest in property from one person to another **2** : an act or process of transferring **3** : one that transfers or is transferred **4** : a ticket entitling a passenger on a public conveyance to continue his journey on another route

trans·fix \trans-'fiks\ *vb* : to pierce through with or as if with a pointed weapon

trans·form \trans-'fòrm\ *vb* : to change completely in form or in nature ⟨*transform* waterpower into electric power⟩ — **trans·form·er** *n*

trans·for·ma·tion \,trans-fər-'mā-shən\ *n* : the act or process of transforming

trans·fu·sion \trans-'fyü-zhən\ *n* **1** : a passing of one thing into another : TRANSMITTING **2** : a transferring (as of blood or salt solution) into a vein of a person or animal

¹tran·sient \'tran-chənt\ *adj* : not lasting or staying long ⟨*transient* guests⟩

²transient *n* : one that is transient

tran·sis·tor \tran-'zis-tər\ *n* : a small solid

electronic device used especially in radios for amplifying an electric current

tran·sit \'trans-ət, 'tranz-\ *n* **1** : a passing through or across **2** : conveyance from one place to another **3** : local transportation of people by public conveyance **4** : a surveyor's instrument for measuring angles

transit 4

tran·si·tion \trans-'ish-ən, tranz-\ *n* : a passing from one state, stage, place, or subject to another : CHANGE

tran·si·tive \'trans-ət-iv, 'tranz-\ *adj* : having or containing a direct object

trans·late \trans-'lāt\ *vb* **trans·lat·ed**; **trans·lat·ing** **1** : to bear or change from one place, state, or form to another **2** : to turn from one language into another

trans·la·tion \trans-'lā-shən\ *n* **1** : the act or process of translating **2** : a rendering from one language into another

trans·lu·cent \trans-'lüs-nt\ *adj* : not transparent but clear enough to allow rays of light to pass through — **trans·lu·cent·ly** *adv*

trans·mis·sion \trans-'mish-ən\ *n* **1** : an act or process of transmitting ⟨the *transmission* of a disease⟩ **2** : the gears by which the power is transmitted from the engine to the axle that gives motion to an automobile

trans·mit \trans-'mit\ *vb* **trans·mit·ted**; **trans·mit·ting** **1** : to transfer from one person or place to another **2** : to convey by or as if by inheritance **3** : to pass or cause to pass through space or a medium (as glass) **4** : to send out by means of radio waves

trans·mit·ter \trans-'mit-ər\ *n* **1** : one that transmits **2** : the instrument in a telegraph system that sends out messages **3** : the part of a telephone that includes the mouthpiece and a device that picks up sound waves and sends them over the wire **4** : the apparatus that sends out radio or television signals

tran·som \'tran-səm\ *n* **1** : a piece that lies crosswise in a structure (as in the frame of a window or of a door that has a window above it) **2** : a window above a door or other window

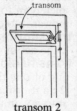

transom 2

trans·par·en·cy \trans-'par-ən-sē\ *n* : the quality or state of being transparent

trans·par·ent \trans-'par-ənt\ *adj* **1** : clear enough to be seen through **2** : fine or sheer enough to be seen through ⟨a *transparent* fabric⟩ **3** : easily detected : OBVIOUS — **trans·par·ent·ly** *adv*

trans·pi·ra·tion \ˌtrans-pə-'rā-shən\ *n* : an act or instance of transpiring

trans·pire \trans-'pīr\ *vb* **trans·pired**; **trans·pir·ing** **1** : to give off or pass off in the form of a vapor usually through pores **2** : to become known or apparent **3** : to come to pass

trans·plant \trans-'plant\ *vb* **1** : to remove and reset in another soil or location ⟨*transplant* seedlings⟩ **2** : to remove from one place and settle or introduce elsewhere

¹trans·port \trans-'pōrt\ *vb* **1** : to convey from one place to another : CARRY **2** : to fill with delight **3** : to send to a penal colony overseas

²trans·port \'trans-ˌpōrt\ *n* **1** : the act of transporting : TRANSPORTATION **2** : ECSTASY, RAPTURE ⟨*transports* of joy⟩ **3** : a ship for carrying soldiers or military equipment **4** : a vehicle used to transport persons or goods

trans·por·ta·tion \ˌtrans-pər-'tā-shən\ *n* **1** : an act, instance, or means of transporting or being transported **2** : means of conveyance or travel from one place to another **3** : public conveyance of passengers or goods especially as a commercial enterprise

trans·pose \trans-'pōz\ *vb* **trans·posed**; **trans·pos·ing** **1** : to change the position or order of ⟨*transpose* the letters in a word⟩ **2** : to write or perform in a different musical key

trans·verse \trans-'vərs\ *adj* : lying or being across : set crosswise — **trans·verse·ly** *adv*

¹trap \'trap\ *n* **1** : a device for catching animals **2** : something by which one is caught or stopped unawares **3** : a light one-horse carriage with springs **4** : a device that allows something to pass through but keeps other things out ⟨a *trap* in a drain⟩ **5** *pl* : a set of drums and accessory percussion instruments in an orchestra

trap 4

²trap *vb* **trapped**; **trap·ping** **1** : to catch in a trap ⟨*trap* game⟩ **2** : to provide or set (a place) with traps **3** : to set traps for animals especially as a business — **trap·per** *n*

trap·door \'trap-'dōr\ *n* : a lifting or sliding door covering an opening in a floor or roof

tra·peze \tra-'pēz\ *n* : a short horizontal bar suspended by two parallel ropes and used by acrobats and gymnasts

trap·e·zoid \'trap-ə-ˌzȯid\ *n* : a four-sided plane figure having only two sides parallel

trap·pings \'trap-ingz\ *n pl* **1** : ornamental covering especially for a horse **2** : outward decoration or dress

trapezoid

trash \'trash\ *n* **1** : something of little or no worth **2** : worthless or disreputable persons

¹trav·el \'trav-əl\ *vb* **trav·eled** *or* **trav·elled**; **trav·el·ing** *or* **trav·el·ling** **1** : to journey from place to place or to a distant place **2** : to journey from place to place selling or taking orders **3** : to move from point to point **4** : to journey through or over : TRAVERSE — **trav·el·er** *or* **trav·el·ler** *n*

²travel *n* **1** : the act of traveling : PASSAGE **2** : JOURNEY, TRIP — often used in plural **3** : the number traveling : TRAFFIC

traveling bag *n* : a bag carried by hand and designed to hold a traveler's clothing and personal articles

tra·verse \trə-'vərs\ *vb* **tra·versed**; **tra·vers·ing** : to pass through, across, or over

traveling bag

¹trawl \'trȯl\ *vb* : to fish or catch with a trawl

²trawl *n* : a large cone-shaped net dragged along the sea bottom in fishing

tray \'trā\ *n* : an open receptacle with a flat bottom and low rim for holding, carrying, or exhibiting articles ⟨a waiter's *tray*⟩

treach·er·ous \'trech-ə-rəs\ *adj* **1** : guilty of or inclined to treachery **2** : not trustworthy or reliable **3** : giving a false appearance of safety — **treach·er·ous·ly** *adv*

treach·er·y \'trech-ə-rē\ *n, pl* **treach·er·ies** : violation of allegiance or trust : TREASON

¹tread \'tred\ *vb* **trod** \'träd\; **trod·den** \'träd-n\ *or* **trod**; **tread·ing** **1** : to step or walk on or over **2** : to move on foot : WALK **3** : to beat or press with the feet : TRAMPLE **4** : to execute by stepping or dancing

²tread *n* **1** : a mark made by or as if by treading **2** : the action, manner, or sound of treading **3** : the part of something (as a shoe or tire) that bears on a surface **4** : the horizontal part of a step

trea·dle \'tred-l\ *n* : a device worked by the foot to drive a machine

tread·mill \'tred-,mil\ *n* **1** : a device moved by persons treading on steps around the rim of a wheel or by animals walking on an endless belt **2** : a tiresome routine

treadle

trea·son \'trēz-n\ *n* **1** : the betraying of a trust **2** : the offense of attempting or helping to overthrow the government of the state to which one owes allegiance or to bring about its defeat in war

¹trea·sure \'trezh-ər\ *n* **1** : wealth (as money or jewels) stored up or held in reserve **2** : something of great value

²treasure *vb* **trea·sured**; **trea·sur·ing** **1** : HOARD **2** : to keep as precious : CHERISH

trea·sur·er \'trezh-ər-ər\ *n* : a person (as an officer of a club) who has charge of the receipt, care, and disbursement of funds

trea·sur·y \'trezh-ə-rē\ *n, pl* **trea·sur·ies** **1** : a place in which stores of wealth are kept **2** : the place of deposit and disbursement of collected funds **3** *cap* : a governmental department in charge of finances

¹treat \'trēt\ *vb* **1** : to discuss terms of accommodation or settlement : NEGOTIATE **2** : to deal with especially in writing **3** : HANDLE **4** : to pay for the food or entertainment of **5** : to behave or act toward ⟨*treat* a horse cruelly⟩ **6** : to regard in a specified manner ⟨*treat* as confidential⟩ **7** : to give medical or surgical care to **8** : to subject to some action (as of a chemical) ⟨*treat* soil with lime⟩

²treat *n* **1** : an entertainment given without expense to those invited **2** : a source of pleasure or amusement

trea·tise \'trēt-əs\ *n* : a systematic written exposition or argument on a subject

treat·ment \'trēt-mənt\ *n* **1** : the act or manner of treating someone or something **2** : a substance or method used in treating

trea·ty \'trēt-ē\ *n, pl* **trea·ties** : an agreement or arrangement made by negotiation especially between two or more states or sovereigns

¹tre·ble \'treb-əl\ *n* **1** : the highest of the four voice parts in vocal music : SOPRANO **2** : a singer or instrument taking a soprano part **3** : a high-pitched voice or sound **4** : the upper half of the musical pitch range

²treble *adj* **1** : triple in number or amount **2** : relating to or having the range of a musical treble **3** : high-pitched : SHRILL

³treble *vb* **tre·bled**; **tre·bling** : to make or become three times as much

¹tree \'trē\ *n* **1** : a woody perennial plant having a single usually tall main stem with few or no branches on its lower part **2** : a plant of treelike form ⟨a banana *tree*⟩ **3** : a piece of wood usually adapted to a particular use or forming part of a structure or implement ⟨clothes *tree*⟩ **4** : something resembling a tree — **tree·less** \-ləs\ *adj*

²tree *vb* **treed**; **tree·ing** : to drive to or up a tree

tree fern *n* : a tropical fern with a tall woody stalk and a crown of often feathery leaves

tre·foil \'trē-,fȯil\ *n* [from medieval French *trefeuil*, from Latin *trifolium*, from *tri-* "tri-" and *folium* "leaf"] **1** : a clover or related plant having leaves

trefoil 2

---

j job   **ng** sing   **ō** low   **ȯ** moth   **ȯi** coin   **th** thin   **th** this   **ü** boot   **u̇** foot   **y** you   **yü** few   **yu̇** furious   **zh** vision

with three leaflets **2** : a decorative design with three leaflike parts

¹trek \'trek\ *n* : a slow or difficult journey or migration

²trek *vb* **trekked; trek·king** : to make one's way arduously

trel·lis \'trel-əs\ *n* : a frame of lattice used especially as a screen or a support for climbing plants

¹trem·ble \'trem-bəl\ *vb* **trem·bled; trem·bling** **1** : to move involuntarily (as with fear or cold) : SHIVER **2** : to move, sound, pass, or come to pass as if shaken or tremulous **3** : to be affected with fear or doubt

trellis

²tremble *n* : a spell of shaking or quivering

tre·men·dous \tri-'men-dəs\ *adj* **1** : TERRIFYING, DREADFUL **2** : astonishingly large, powerful, or great — **tre·men·dous·ly** *adv*

trem·or \'trem-ər\ *n* **1** : a trembling or shaking especially from weakness or disease **2** : a quivering motion of the earth (as during an earthquake)

trem·u·lous \'trem-yə-ləs\ *adj* **1** : marked by trembling or tremors : QUIVERING ⟨a *tremulous* voice⟩ **2** : FEARFUL, TIMID **3** : UNSTEADY

trench \'trench\ *n* **1** : a long narrow ditch **2** : a long ditch protected by mounds of earth thrown before it and used to shelter soldiers

tren·chant \'tren-chənt\ *adj* **1** : having a sharp edge or point **2** : sharply perceptive

¹trend \'trend\ *vb* **1** : to have or take a general direction **2** : to show a tendency

²trend *n* **1** : general direction taken **2** : a prevailing tendency : DRIFT

¹tres·pass \'tres-pəs\ *n* **1** : SIN, OFFENSE **2** : unlawful entry upon the land of another

²trespass *vb* **1** : ERR, SIN **2** : to enter unlawfully upon the land of another — **tres·pass·er** *n*

tress \'tres\ *n* : a long lock of hair — usually used in plural

tres·tle \'tres-əl\ *n* **1** : a braced frame consisting usually of a horizontal piece with spreading legs at each end that supports something (as the top of a table) **2** : a framework of timbers or steel for carrying a road or railroad over a depression

tri- *prefix* **1** : three : having three or three parts ⟨*tri*motor⟩ **2** : into three ⟨*tri*sect⟩ **3** : thrice ⟨*tri*weekly⟩ : every third ⟨*tri*monthly⟩

tri·al \'trī-əl\ *n* **1** : the action or process of trying or putting to the proof : TEST **2** : the hearing and judgment of a matter in issue before a competent tribunal **3** : a test of faith, patience, or stamina **4** : an experiment to test quality, value, or usefulness **5** : ATTEMPT

tri·an·gle \'trī-,ang-gəl\ *n* **1** : a plane figure that has three sides and three angles **2** : an object that has three sides and three angles ⟨a *triangle* of land⟩ **3** : a musical instrument made of a steel rod bent in the shape of a triangle with one open angle

triangle

tri·an·gu·lar \trī-'ang-gyə-lər\ *adj* **1** : of, relating to, or having the form of a triangle **2** : having three angles, sides, or corners ⟨a *triangular* building⟩ **3** : of, relating to, or involving three parts or persons

trib·al \'trī-bəl\ *adj* : of, relating to, or characteristic of a tribe ⟨*tribal* customs⟩

tribe \'trīb\ *n* **1** : a social group comprising numerous families, clans, or generations **2** : a group of persons having a common character, occupation, or interest **3** : a group of related plants or animals ⟨the cat *tribe*⟩

tribes·man \'trībz-mən\ *n, pl* **tribes·men** \-mən\ : a member of a tribe

trib·u·la·tion \,trib-yə-'lā-shən\ *n* **1** : distress or suffering resulting from oppression, persecution, or affliction **2** : a trying experience

tri·bu·nal \trī-'byün-l\ *n* **1** : a court of justice **2** : something that decides or determines ⟨the *tribunal* of public opinion⟩

¹trib·u·tar·y \'trib-yə-,ter-ē\ *adj* **1** : paying tribute to another : SUBJECT **2** : flowing into a larger stream or a lake

²tributary *n, pl* **trib·u·tar·ies** **1** : a ruler or state that pays tribute **2** : a stream flowing into a larger stream or a lake

trib·ute \'trib-yüt\ *n* **1** : a payment made by one ruler or state to another to show submission or to secure peace or protection **2** : a tax put on the people to raise money for tribute **3** : the obligation to pay tribute ⟨nations under *tribute*⟩ **4** : a gift or service showing respect, gratitude, or affection

tri·chi·na \trə-'kī-nə\ *n, pl* **tri·chi·nae** \-nē\ : a small parasitic roundworm which enters the body with infected meat and whose larvae form cysts in the muscles and cause a painful and dangerous disease (**trichinosis**)

¹trick \'trik\ *n* **1** : a crafty procedure intended to deceive or defraud **2** : a mischievous act : PRANK **3** : an indiscreet or childish action **4** : a deceptive or ingenious feat designed to puzzle or amuse **5** : MANNERISM **6** : an artful expedient **7** : the cards played in one round of a game **8** : a tour of duty

²trick *vb* **1** : to deceive by cunning or artifice : CHEAT **2** : to dress ornately : ADORN

trick·er·y \'trik-ə-rē\ *n, pl* **trick·er·ies** : the use of tricks to deceive or defraud

¹**trick·le** \'trik-əl\ *vb* **trick·led; trick·ling** **1** : to run or fall in drops **2** : to flow in a thin slow stream

²**trickle** *n* : a thin slow stream

trick·ster \'trik-stər\ *n* : one who tricks

trick·y \'trik-ē\ *adj* **trick·i·er; trick·i·est** **1** : inclined to trickery **2** : requiring skill, aptitude, or caution **3** : UNRELIABLE

tri·cy·cle \'trī-,sik-əl\ *n* : a three-wheeled vehicle propelled by pedals, hand levers, or a motor

tri·dent \'trīd-nt\ *n* : a three‗pronged spear

¹**tried** \'trīd\ *past of* TRY

²**tried** *adj* : found good or trustworthy through experience or testing

tricycle

¹**tri·fle** \'trī-fəl\ *n* **1** : something of little importance **2** : a small amount (as of money)

²**trifle** *vb* **tri·fled; tri·fling** **1** : to talk in a jesting or mocking manner **2** : to act in a frivolous or playful manner **3** : to waste time : DALLY **4** : to handle something idly : TOY

tri·fling \'trī-fling\ *adj* **1** : lacking in seriousness : FRIVOLOUS **2** : of little value : TRIVIAL

trig·ger \'trig-ər\ *n* **1** : a movable catch that when released by pulling or pressure allows a mechanism to go into action **2** : the part of the lock of a firearm that is pressed to release the hammer and so fire the gun

¹**trill** \'tril\ *n* **1** : the alternation of two musical tones a scale degree apart **2** : WARBLE 1 **3** : the rapid vibration of one speech organ against another ⟨pronounces his *r*'s with a *trill*⟩

²**trill** *vb* : to utter as or with a trill

tril·lion \'tril-yən\ *n* : a thousand billions

tril·li·um \'tril-ē-əm\ *n* : a spring-blooming plant related to the lilies that has three leaves and a single three-petaled flower

¹**trim** \'trim\ *vb* **trimmed; trim·ming** **1** : to put ornaments on : ADORN ⟨*trim* a Christmas tree⟩ **2** : to defeat decisively **3** : to get the better of in a bargain **4** : to make trim and neat especially by cutting or clipping ⟨*trim* a hedge⟩ **5** : to free of excess or extraneous matter ⟨*trim* a budget⟩ **6** : to cause (a ship) to assume a desirable position in the water by arrangement of ballast, cargo, or passengers **7** : to adjust (as an airplane or submarine) for horizontal movement or for motion upward or downward **8** : to adjust (as a sail) to a desired position **9** : to change one's views for safety or convenience — **trim·mer** *n*

²**trim** *adj* **trim·mer; trim·mest** : neat, orderly, and compact in line or structure — **trim·ly** *adv*

³**trim** *n* **1** : the readiness of a ship for sailing **2** : good condition : FITNESS **3** : material used for ornament or trimming **4** : the woodwork in the finish of a building especially around doors and windows **5** : something that is trimmed off or cut out

trim·ming \'trim-ing\ *n* **1** : the action of one that trims **2** : BEATING, DEFEAT **3** : something that trims, ornaments, or completes **4** *pl* : parts removed by trimming

Trin·i·ty \'trin-ət-ē\ *n* : the unity of Father, Son, and Holy Spirit

trin·ket \'tring-kət\ *n* **1** : a small ornament (as a jewel) **2** : a thing of small value

tri·o \'trē-ō\ *n, pl* **tri·os** **1** : a musical composition for three instruments or voices **2** : a group or set of three

¹**trip** \'trip\ *vb* **tripped; trip·ping** **1** : to move (as in dancing) with light quick steps **2** : to catch the foot against something so as to stumble : cause to stumble **3** : to make or cause to make a mistake **4** : to catch in a misstep, fault, or blunder **5** : to release (as a spring) by moving a catch **6** : ACTIVATE

²**trip** *n* **1** : a traveling from one place to another : VOYAGE ⟨a *trip* to Europe⟩ **2** : a brief errand having a specific aim or recurring regularly ⟨a *trip* to the dentist⟩ **3** : the action of tripping mechanically **4** : a device for tripping a mechanism

tripe \'trīp\ *n* : a part of the stomach of a cow used for food

¹**tri·ple** \'trip-əl\ *vb* **tri·pled; tri·pling** : to make or become three times as great or as many

²**triple** *n* **1** : a triple sum, quantity, or number **2** : a combination, group, or series of three **3** : a hit in baseball that enables the batter to reach third base

³**triple** *adj* **1** : having three units or members **2** : being three times as great or as many **3** : three times repeated

tri·plet \'trip-lət\ *n* **1** : three successive rhyming lines of verse **2** : a combination, set, or group of three **3** : one of three offspring born at one birth **4** : a group of three musical notes played in the time of two of the same value

tri·pod \'trī-,päd\ *n* **1** : something (as a container or stool) resting on three legs **2** : a three-legged stand (as for a camera)

trite \'trīt\ *adj* : so common that the novelty has worn off : STALE ⟨*trite* remarks⟩ — **trite·ness** *n*

¹**tri·umph** \'trī-əmf\ *n* **1** : the joy of victory or success **2** : VICTORY, CONQUEST

²**triumph** *vb* **1** : to celebrate victory or success exultantly **2** : to obtain victory : WIN

tripod 2

tri·um·phal \trī-'əm-fəl\ *adj* : of or relating to a triumph

tri·um·phant \trī-'əm-fənt\ *adj* **1** : CON-QUERING, VICTORIOUS **2** : rejoicing for or celebrating victory — **tri·um·phant·ly** *adv*

triv·et \'triv-ət\ *n* **1** : a three-legged metal stand used especially to hold a kettle near the fire **2** : an ornamental metal plate on very short legs used under a hot dish to protect the table

trivet 2

triv·i·al \'triv-ē-əl\ *adj* [from Latin *trivialis*, derived from *trivium* "place where three roads meet", "crossroads", from *tri-* "tri-" and *via* "way"; things found at a busy cross-roads could not be called "out of the way" but rather "commonplace"] **1** : ORDINARY, COMMONPLACE **2** : of little worth or importance : INSIGNIFICANT **syn** see PETTY

triv·i·al·i·ty \,triv-ē-'al-ət-ē\ *n, pl* **triv·i·al·i·ties** : the quality or state of being trivial

trod *past of* TREAD

trodden *past part of* TREAD

¹troll \'trōl\ *vb* **1** : to sing the parts of (a song) in succession **2** : to fish with a hook and line drawn through the water

²troll *n* **1** : a lure or a line with its lure and hook used in trolling **2** : a song sung in parts successively : ROUND

³troll *n* : a dwarf or giant of folklore inhabiting caves or hills

trol·ley *or* **trol·ly** \'träl-ē\ *n, pl* **trol·leys** *or* **trol·lies** **1** : a device (as a grooved wheel on the end of a pole) to carry current from a wire to an electrically driven vehicle **2** : a passenger car that runs on tracks and gets its power through a trolley **3** : a wheeled carriage running on an overhead track

trom·bone \träm-'bōn\ *n* [from Italian *trombone*, meaning literally "a big trumpet", from *tromba* "trumpet"] : a musical instrument that has a cupped mouthpiece, consists of a long cylindrical metal tube bent twice upon itself and ending in a bell, and has a movable slide with which to vary the pitch

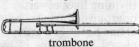
trombone

¹troop \'trüp\ *n* **1** : a cavalry unit corresponding to an infantry company **2** : armed forces : SOLDIERS — usually used in plural **3** : a collection of beings or things : COMPANY **4** : a unit of boy or girl scouts under a leader

²troop *vb* **1** : to move or gather in crowds **2** : ASSOCIATE

troop·er \'trü-pər\ *n* **1** : a soldier in a cavalry

unit **2** : a mounted policeman **3** : a state policeman

tro·phy \'trō-fē\ *n, pl* **tro·phies** **1** : something taken in battle or conquest especially as a memorial **2** : something given to commemorate a victory or as an award for achievement **3** : SOUVENIR, MEMENTO

trop·ic \'träp-ik\ *n* **1** : either of two parallels of the earth's latitude that are about 23½ degrees north of the equator and about 23½ degrees south of the equator **2** *pl, often cap* : the region lying between the two tropics

trop·i·cal \'träp-i-kəl\ *adj* : of, relating to, or occurring in the tropics

tropical fish *n* : any of various small often brightly colored fishes kept in aquariums

¹trot \'trät\ *n* **1** : a moderately fast gait of a four-footed animal in which a front foot and the opposite hind foot move as a pair **2** : a human jogging pace between a walk and a run

²trot *vb* **trot·ted; trot·ting** **1** : to ride, drive, or go at a trot **2** : to cause to go at a trot **3** : to go along briskly : HURRY

troth \'trȯth, 'träth, 'trōth\ *n* **1** : pledged faithfulness : FIDELITY **2** : one's pledged word

¹trou·ble \'trəb-əl\ *vb* **trou·bled; trou·bling** **1** : to agitate or become agitated mentally or spiritually : WORRY **2** : to produce physical disorder in : AFFLICT **3** : to put to inconvenience **4** : RUFFLE ⟨wind *troubled* the sea⟩ **5** : to make an effort ⟨do not *trouble* to write⟩

²trouble *n* **1** : the quality or state of being troubled : MISFORTUNE ⟨people in *trouble*⟩ **2** : an instance of distress or annoyance **3** : a cause of disturbance or distress **4** : EXERTION, PAINS ⟨took the *trouble* to write⟩ **5** : ill health : AILMENT **6** : failure to function normally

trou·ble·some \'trəb-əl-səm\ *adj* **1** : giving trouble or anxiety **2** : DIFFICULT, BURDEN-SOME — **trou·ble·some·ly** *adv*

trough \'trȯf\ *n* **1** : a long shallow open boxlike or basinlike container especially for water or feed for livestock **2** : a channel for water : GUTTER **3** : a long channel or hollow

trounce \'traůns\ *vb* **trounced; trounc·ing** **1** : BEAT, THRASH **2** : to defeat decisively

troupe \'trüp\ *n* : a company especially of performers on the stage

trou·sers \'traů-zərz\ *n pl* : an outer garment extending from the waist to the ankle or only to the knee, covering each leg separately, and worn typically by men and boys

trout \'traůt\ *n* **1** : any of various fishes (as the eastern **brook trout** or the European **brown trout**) mostly smaller than the related salmon and often speckled with dark colors **2** : any of various fishes (as a **rock trout** or greenling or a **sea trout** or weakfish) that somewhat resemble the true trouts

trow·el \'traů-əl\ *n* **1** : a small hand tool with a flat blade used by masons and plasterers for spreading and smoothing mortar or plaster **2** : a small hand tool with a curved blade used by gardeners

trowels

tru·ant \'trü-ənt\ *n* **1** : a person who shirks his duty **2** : a student who stays out of school without permission

truce \'trüs\ *n* **1** : ARMISTICE **2** : a temporary rest : RESPITE

¹truck \'trək\ *vb* : to exchange goods : BARTER

²truck *n* **1** : BARTER **2** : goods for barter or for small trade **3** : close association **4** : small articles of little value **5** : RUBBISH

³truck *n* **1** : a vehicle (as a small flat-topped car on wheels, a two-wheeled barrow with long handles, or a strong heavy wagon or automobile) for carrying heavy articles **2** : a swiveling frame with springs and one or more pairs of wheels used to carry an end of a railroad car

truck 1

⁴truck *vb* **1** : to transport on a truck **2** : to be employed as a truck driver

trudge \'trəj\ *vb* **trudged; trudg·ing** : to walk or march steadily and usually laboriously

¹true \'trü\ *adj* **tru·er; tru·est** **1** : FAITHFUL, LOYAL **2** : that can be relied on : CERTAIN **3** : agreeing with the facts : ACCURATE ⟨a *true* story⟩ **4** : SINCERE ⟨*true* friendship⟩ **5** : properly so called : GENUINE ⟨lichens have no *true* stems⟩ **6** : placed or formed accurately : EXACT ⟨a *true* square⟩ ⟨*true* pitch⟩ **7** : RIGHTFUL, LEGITIMATE ⟨the *true* owner⟩

²true *n* **1** : something that is true : REALITY **2** : the quality or state of being accurate (as in alignment) ⟨out of *true*⟩

³true *vb* **trued; tru·ing** *also* **tru·ing** : to bring to exactly correct condition as to place, position, or shape

⁴true *adv* **1** : TRUTHFULLY **2** : ACCURATELY ⟨the bullet flew straight and *true*⟩ **3** : without variation from type ⟨breed *true*⟩

true–blue \'trü-'blü\ *adj* : highly faithful

truf·fle \'trəf-əl\ *n* : the edible usually dark and wrinkled underground fruiting body of a European fungus

tru·ism \'trü-,iz-əm\ *n* : an obvious truth

tru·ly \'trü-lē\ *adv* **1** : SINCERELY **2** : TRUTHFULLY **3** : ACCURATELY

¹trum·pet \'trəm-pət\ *n* **1** : a wind instrument consisting of a long cylindrical metal tube commonly once or twice curved and ending in a bell **2** : something that resembles a trumpet or its tonal quality

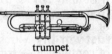

trumpet

²trumpet *vb* **1** : to blow a trumpet **2** : to sound or proclaim on a trumpet — **trum·pet·er** *n*

trumpet creeper *or* **trumpet vine** *n* : a North American woody vine having red trumpet-shaped flowers

¹trun·dle \'trən-dəl\ *n* **1** : a small wheel or roller **2** : a low-wheeled cart or truck

²trundle *vb* **trun·dled; trun·dling** : to roll along : WHEEL

trundle bed *n* : a low bed on casters that can be pushed under a higher bed

trunk \'trəngk\ *n* **1** : the main stem of a tree apart from branches and roots **2** : the body of a man or animal apart from the head, arms, and legs **3** : a box or chest for holding clothes or other goods especially for traveling **4** : the enclosed space usually in the rear of an automobile for carrying articles **5** : the long round muscular nose of an elephant **6** *pl* : men's shorts worn chiefly for sports

trundle bed

¹truss \'trəs\ *vb* **1** : to bind or tie firmly **2** : to prepare for cooking by binding close the wings or legs of (a fowl) **3** : to support, strengthen, or stiffen by a truss

²truss *n* **1** : a rigid framework of beams or bars used in building and engineering **2** : a device worn to hold a ruptured body part in place

¹trust \'trəst\ *n* **1** : assured reliance on the character, strength, or truth of someone or something **2** : one in which confidence is placed **3** : confident hope **4** : financial credit **5** : a property interest held by one person or concern (as a bank) for the benefit of another **6** : a combination of firms or corporations formed by a legal agreement and often held to reduce competition **7** : something (as a public office) entrusted to one to be cared for in the interest of another **8** : CARE

²trust *vb* **1** : to place confidence : DEPEND **2** : to be confident : HOPE **3** : to place in one's care or keeping : ENTRUST **4** : to rely on or on the truth of : BELIEVE **5** : to extend credit to

trust·ee \,trəs-'tē\ *n* : a person to whom property is legally committed in trust

trust·ful \\'trəst-fəl\\ *adj* : full of trust — **trust·ful·ly** *adv* — **trust·ful·ness** *n*

trust·ing \\'trəs-ting\\ *adj* : having trust, faith, or confidence

trust·wor·thy \\'trəst-ˌwər-thē\\ *adj* : worthy of confidence — **trust·wor·thi·ness** *n*

¹**trust·y** \\'trəs-tē\\ *adj* **trust·i·er; trust·i·est** : TRUSTWORTHY, RELIABLE

²**trusty** *n, pl* **trust·ies** : a convict considered trustworthy and allowed special privileges

truth \\'trüth\\ *n, pl* **truths** \\'trü<u>th</u>z\\ 1 : TRUTHFULNESS, HONESTY 2 : the state of being true : FACT 3 : the body of real events or facts 4 : a true or accepted statement or proposition 5 : agreement with fact or reality

truth·ful \\'trüth-fəl\\ *adj* : telling or disposed to tell the truth — **truth·ful·ly** *adv* — **truth·ful·ness** *n*

¹**try** \\'trī\\ *vb* **tried** \\'trīd\\; **try·ing** 1 : to examine or investigate judicially 2 : to conduct the trial of 3 : to put to test or trial 4 : to test to the limit 5 : to melt down and procure in a pure state 6 : to make an effort to do

²**try** *n, pl* **tries** : an experimental trial : ATTEMPT

try·ing \\'trī-ing\\ *adj* : hard to bear or endure

try·out \\'trī-ˌaút\\ *n* : an experimental performance or demonstration

T–shirt \\'tē-ˌshərt\\ *n* 1 : a collarless short-sleeved cotton undershirt 2 : a cotton or wool jersey outer shirt of a design like a T-shirt

¹**tub** \\'təb\\ *n* 1 : a wide low vessel 2 : an old or slow boat 3 : BATH 4 : the amount that a tub will hold

²**tub** *vb* **tubbed; tub·bing** : to wash or bathe in a tub

T-shirt

tu·ba \\'tü-bə, 'tyü-\\ *n* : a large low-pitched brass wind instrument

tube \\'tüb, 'tyüb\\ *n* 1 : a hollow elongated cylinder used especially to convey fluids 2 : a slender channel within a plant or animal body : DUCT 3 : a round metal container from which a paste is dispensed by squeezing 4 : TUNNEL 5 : ELECTRON TUBE — **tubed** \\'tübd, 'tyübd\\ *adj* — **tube·less** \\'tüb-ləs, 'tyüb-\\ *adj*

tu·ber \\'tü-bər, 'tyü-\\ *n* : a short fleshy usually underground stem (as of a potato plant) bearing minute scalelike leaves each with a bud at its base

tu·ber·cu·lo·sis \\tù-ˌbər-kyə-'lō-səs, tyù-\\ *n* : a communicable disease (as of man or cattle)

tuba

caused by a bacillus and marked by fever, wasting, and formation of cheesy nodules especially in the lungs

tube·rose \\'tüb-ˌrōz, 'tyüb-\\ *n* : a plant that grows from a bulb and is cultivated for its spikes of fragrant white lilylike flowers

tu·ber·ous \\'tü-bə-rəs, 'tyü-\\ *adj* : of, relating to, or resembling a tuber

tu·bu·lar \\'tü-byə-lər, 'tyü-\\ *adj* 1 : having the form of or consisting of a tube 2 : made with tubes

¹**tuck** \\'tək\\ *vb* 1 : to pull up into a fold 2 : to make tucks in 3 : to put or fit into a snug position or place 4 : to secure in place by pushing the edges under 5 : to cover by tucking in bedclothes

²**tuck** *n* : a fold stitched into cloth to shorten, decorate, or control fullness

Tues·day \\'tüz-dē, 'tyüz-\\ *n* : the third day of the week

¹**tuft** \\'təft\\ *n* 1 : a small cluster of long flexible outgrowths (as hairs) 2 : a bunch of soft fluffy threads cut off short and used for ornament 3 : CLUMP, CLUSTER

²**tuft** *vb* 1 : to provide or adorn with a tuft 2 : to grow in tufts 3 : to make (as a mattress) firm by stitching at intervals and sewing on tufts

¹**tug** \\'təg\\ *vb* **tugged; tug·ging** 1 : to pull hard ⟨*tug* at a rope⟩ 2 : to move by pulling hard : DRAG 3 : to struggle in opposition : CONTEND 4 : to tow with a tugboat

²**tug** *n* 1 : an act of tugging : PULL 2 : STRUGGLE 3 : a straining effort 4 : TUGBOAT

tug·boat \\'təg-ˌbōt\\ *n* : a strongly built powerful boat used for towing ships

tug–of–war \\ˌtəg-əv-'wòr\\ *n, pl* **tugs–of–war** 1 : a struggle for supremacy 2 : an athletic contest in which two teams pull against each other at opposite ends of a rope

tu·i·tion \\tù-'ish-ən, tyù-\\ *n* : the price of or payment for instruction (as at a college)

tu·lip \\'tü-ləp, 'tyü-\\ *n* [from modern Latin *tulipa*, taken from Turkish *tülbend* meaning "turban", because the flower resembles a turban in shape] : a spring-flowering plant of the lily family that grows from a bulb and has a large cup-shaped flower

tulle \\'tül\\ *n* : a sheer silk, rayon, or nylon net

¹**tum·ble** \\'təm-bəl\\ *vb* **tum·bled; tum·bling** 1 : to perform gymnastic feats of rolling and turning 2 : to fall suddenly and helplessly 3 : COLLAPSE 4 : to move or go hurriedly or confusedly 5 : to come to understand 6 : to toss together into a confused mass

²**tumble** *n* 1 : a disorderly state or collection 2 : an act or instance of tumbling

tum·ble·down \'təm-bəl-,daun\ *adj* : DILAPIDATED, RAMSHACKLE

tum·bler \'təm-blər\ *n* **1** : one (as an acrobat) that tumbles **2** : a drinking glass without foot or stem **3** : a movable part of a lock that must be adjusted (as by a key) before the lock will open

tumbler 2

tum·ble·weed \'təm-bəl-,wēd\ *n* : a plant that breaks away from its roots in autumn and is tumbled about by the wind

tu·mult \'tü-,məlt, 'tyü-\ *n* **1** : violent commotion or disturbance **2** : violent agitation of mind or feelings

tu·mul·tu·ous \tü-'məl-chə-wəs, tyü-\ *adj* : marked by tumult

tu·na \'tü-nə, 'tyü-\ *n* : any of several large sea fishes related to the mackerels and valued for food and sport

tun·dra \'tən-drə\ *n* : a treeless plain of northern arctic regions

¹tune \'tün, 'tyün\ *n* **1** : a succession of pleasing musical tones : MELODY **2** : the musical setting of a song **3** : correct musical pitch **4** : AGREEMENT, HARMONY **5** : general attitude **6** : AMOUNT — **tune·ful** \-fəl\ *adj*

²tune *vb* **tuned; tun·ing** **1** : to come or bring into harmony **2** : to adjust in musical pitch **3** : to adjust a radio or television set so that it receives clearly **4** : to put (as an engine) in good working order — **tun·er** *n*

tung·sten \'təng-stən\ *n* [a name formed in Swedish from *tung* "heavy" and *sten* "stone"] : a gray-white hard metallic chemical element used especially for electrical purposes and in hardening alloys (as steel)

tu·nic \'tü-nik, 'tyü-\ *n* **1** : a usually knee-length belted garment worn by ancient Greeks and Romans **2** : a blouse or jacket reaching to or just below the hips

tuning fork *n* : a metal instrument that gives a fixed tone when struck and is useful for tuning musical instruments

tuning fork

¹tun·nel \'tən-l\ *n* : an underground passage

²tunnel *vb* **tun·neled** *or* **tun·nelled; tun·nel·ing** *or* **tun·nel·ling** : to make a tunnel

tun·ny \'tən-ē\ *n, pl* **tun·nies** : TUNA

tur·ban \'tər-bən\ *n* **1** : a headdress worn especially by Muslims and made of a cap around which is wound a long cloth **2** : a woman's close-fitting brimless hat

tur·bid \'tər-bəd\ *adj* **1** : having the sediment stirred up **2** : heavy with smoke or mist : DENSE **3** : CONFUSED, MUDDLED

tur·bine \'tər-bən\ *n* : an engine whose central driving shaft is fitted with a series of winglike projections whirled around by the pressure of water, steam, or gas

tur·bot \'tər-bət\ *n* : a large brownish flatfish

tur·bu·lent \'tər-byə-lənt\ *adj* **1** : causing unrest, violence, or disturbance **2** : marked by agitation or tumult

tu·reen \tə-'rēn\ *n* : a deep bowl from which food (as soup) is served

turf \'tərf\ *n* : the upper layer of soil bound by grass and plant roots into a thick mat

tureen

Turk \'tərk\ *n* : a native or inhabitant of Turkey

tur·key \'tər-kē\ *n, pl* **tur·keys** : a large American bird related to the common fowl and widely raised for food

¹Turk·ish \'tər-kish\ *adj* : of or relating to Turkey, the Turks, or Turkish

²Turkish *n* : the language of the Turks

tur·moil \'tər-,moil\ *n* : an extremely confused or agitated state or condition

¹turn \'tərn\ *vb* **1** : to move or cause to move around an axis or center : ROTATE **2** : to twist so as to bring about a desired end **3** : WRENCH ⟨*turn* an ankle⟩ **4** : to change or cause to change position by moving through an arc of a circle **5** : to cause to move around a center so as to show another side of **6** : PONDER **7** : to become dizzy : REEL **8** : to reverse the sides or surfaces of ⟨*turn* a pancake⟩ **9** : UPSET, DISORDER ⟨*turned* his stomach⟩ **10** : to set in another and especially an opposite direction **11** : to change one's course or direction **12** : TRANSFER **13** : to go around **14** : to reach or pass beyond **15** : to direct toward or away from something **16** : to have recourse ⟨*turned* to an agency for help⟩ **17** : to become or make hostile **18** : to make or become spoiled : SOUR **19** : to cause to become of a specified nature or appearance **20** : to pass from one state to another **21** : CONVERT, TRANSFORM **22** : TRANSLATE, PARAPHRASE **23** : to give a rounded form to (as with a lathe) **24** : to gain by passing in trade — **turn a hair** : to be or become upset or frightened — **turn tail** : to run away — **turn the trick** : to bring about the desired result or effect — **turn turtle** : OVERTURN

²turn *n* **1** : a turning about a center or axis **2** : a change or changing of direction, course, or position **3** : a change or changing of condition or trend **4** : a place at which something turns **5** : a short walk or ride **6** : an act affecting another **7** : place or appointed time in a succession or scheduled order **8** : a period of action or activity : SPELL **9** : a special purpose or requirement **10** : distinctive quality or character **11** : the form according to which something is fashioned : CAST **12** : a single round (as of rope passed around an object) **13** : natural or special aptitude **14** : a usually sudden and brief disorder of body or spirits — **at every turn** : CONSTANTLY, CONTINUOUSLY — **to a turn** : precisely right

tur·nip \'tərn-nəp\ *n* : the thick white or yellow edible root of a plant related to the cabbage

turn·out \'tərn-ˌaut\ *n* : a gathering of people for a special purpose

turn·pike \'tərn-ˌpīk\ *n* **1** : a road for the use of which a toll is charged **2** : a main road

turn·stile \'tərn-ˌstīl\ *n* : a post with four pivoted arms set in a passageway so that persons can pass through only on foot one by one

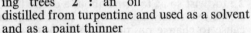

turnstile

tur·pen·tine \'tər-pən-ˌtīn\ *n* **1** : a mixture of oil and resin obtained from various cone-bearing trees **2** : an oil distilled from turpentine and used as a solvent and as a paint thinner

tur·quoise \'tər-ˌkȯiz, -ˌkwȯiz\ *n* : a blue to greenish gray mineral used as a gem

tur·ret \'tər-ət\ *n* **1** : a little tower often at a corner of a building **2** : a low usually revolving structure (as in a tank, warship, or airplane) in which guns are mounted

turrets

tur·tle \'tərt-l\ *n* : a reptile having a horny beak and a bony shell that encloses the body

tur·tle·dove \'tərt-l-ˌdəv\ *n* : any of several small wild pigeons

tusk \'təsk\ *n* : a long enlarged protruding tooth (as of an elephant) usually growing in pairs and used in digging and fighting — **tusked** \'təskt\ *adj*

¹**tus·sle** \'təs-əl\ *vb* **tus·sled**; **tus·sling** : to struggle roughly : SCUFFLE

²**tussle** *n* **1** : a physical contest or struggle **2** : a rough argument, controversy, or struggle against difficult odds

tus·sock \'təs-ək\ *n* : a compact tuft or clump (as of grass)

tu·te·lage \'tüt-l-ij, 'tyüt-\ *n* **1** : GUARDIANSHIP **2** : instruction especially of an individual

¹**tu·tor** \'tüt-ər, 'tyüt-\ *n* : a person charged with the instruction and guidance of another

²**tutor** *vb* : to teach usually individually

TV \ˈtē-ˈvē\ *n* : TELEVISION

twad·dle \'twäd-l\ *n* : silly idle talk

twain \'twān\ *n* **1** : TWO **2** : COUPLE, PAIR

¹**twang** \'twang\ *n* **1** : a harsh quick ringing sound like that of a plucked bowstring **2** : nasal speech or resonance

²**twang** *vb* **1** : to sound or cause to sound with a twang **2** : to speak with a nasal twang

¹**tweak** \'twēk\ *vb* : to pinch and pull with a sudden jerk and twist

²**tweak** *n* : an act of tweaking

tweed \'twēd\ *n* **1** : a rough woolen fabric made usually in twill weaves **2** *pl* : tweed clothing (as a suit)

¹**tweet** \'twēt\ *n* : a chirping note

²**tweet** *vb* : CHIRP

tweez·ers \'twē-zərz\ *n pl* : a small pincerlike instrument for grasping or pulling something

¹**twelfth** \'twelfth\ *adj* : being next after the eleventh

²**twelfth** *n* : number twelve in a series

¹**twelve** \'twelv\ *adj* : being one more than eleven

²**twelve** *n* : one more than eleven

tweezers

twelve·month \'twelv-ˌmənth\ *n* : YEAR

¹**twen·ti·eth** \'twent-ē-əth\ *adj* : being next after the nineteenth

²**twentieth** *n* : number twenty in a series

¹**twen·ty** \'twent-ē\ *adj* : being two times ten

²**twenty** *n* : two times ten

twice \'twīs\ *adv* : two times

twid·dle \'twid-l\ *vb* **twid·dled**; **twid·dling** **1** : to be busy with trifles **2** : TWIRL

twig \'twig\ *n* : a small shoot or branch

twi·light \'twī-ˌlīt\ *n* **1** : the light from the sky between full night and sunrise or between sunset and full night **2** : a state of indistinctness or of deepening darkness or gloom

¹**twill** \'twil\ *n* **1** : a fabric with a twill weave **2** : a textile weave that produces a pattern of diagonal lines or ribs

²**twill** *vb* : to make (cloth) with a twill weave

¹**twin** \'twin\ *adj* **1** : born with one another or as a pair at one birth ⟨*twin* girls⟩ **2** : made up of two similar, related, or connected members or parts **3** : being one of a pair

²**twin** *n* **1** : either of two offspring produced at a birth **2** : one of two persons or things closely related to or resembling each other

¹**twine** \'twīn\ *n* **1** : a strong string of two or more strands twisted together **2** : an act of entwining or interlacing

²**twine** *vb* **twined**; **twin·ing** **1** : to twist together **2** : to coil about a support **3** : WIND

¹**twinge** \'twinj\ *vb* **twinged**; **twing·ing** *or*

twinge·ing : to affect with or feel a sudden sharp pain

²**twinge** *n* : a sudden sharp stab (as of pain)

¹**twin·kle** \'twing-kəl\ *vb* **twin·kled; twin·kling** **1** : to shine or cause to shine with a flickering or sparkling light **2** : to appear bright with merriment **3** : to move or flutter rapidly

²**twinkle** *n* **1** : a wink of the eyelids **2** : the duration of a wink **3** : SPARKLE, FLICKER

twin·kling \'twing-kling\ *n* **1** : a winking of the eye **2** : INSTANT, MOMENT

¹**twirl** \'twərl\ *vb* **1** : to revolve or cause to revolve rapidly **2** : CURL, TWIST — **twirl·er** *n*

²**twirl** *n* **1** : an act of twirling **2** : COIL, WHORL

¹**twist** \'twist\ *vb* **1** : to unite by winding one thread, strand, or wire around another **2** : TWINE, COIL **3** : to turn so as to sprain or hurt **4** : to turn from the true form or meaning **5** : to pull off, rotate, or break by a turning force **6** : MEANDER **7** : to turn around

²**twist** *n* **1** : something (as thread) formed by twisting or winding **2** : an act of twisting : the state of being twisted **3** : a spiral turn or curve **4** : a turning aside : DEFLECTION **5** : a strong individual tendency or bent **6** : a distortion of meaning **7** : an unexpected turn or development **8** : DEVICE, TRICK

twist·er \'twis-tər\ *n* **1** : one that twists **2** : TORNADO, WATERSPOUT

twit \'twit\ *vb* **twit·ted; twit·ting** : to subject to light ridicule or reproach

¹**twitch** \'twich\ *vb* **1** : to move or pull with a sudden motion **2** : PLUCK **3** : QUIVER

²**twitch** *n* **1** : an act of twitching **2** : a short sharp contraction of muscle fibers

¹**twit·ter** \'twit-ər\ *vb* **1** : to make a succession of chirping noises **2** : to talk in a chattering fashion **3** : GIGGLE **4** : to tremble or cause to tremble with agitation

²**twitter** *n* **1** : a trembling agitation **2** : the chirping of birds **3** : a light chattering

¹**two** \'tü\ *adj* : being one more than one

²**two** *n* **1** : one more than one **2** : the second in a set or series

two·fold \'tü-,fōld\ *adj* : being twice as great or as many

two–winged fly \,tü-,wingd-\ *n* : an insect belonging to the same group as the housefly

ty·coon \tī-'kün\ *n* : a businessman of great wealth and power

tying *pres part of* TIE

tyke \'tīk\ *n* : a small child

¹**type** \'tīp\ *n* **1** : a person or thing believed to foreshadow or symbolize another **2** : one having qualities of a higher category : MODEL **3** : a rectangular block

type 3

(as of metal) that has its face so shaped as to produce a letter or figure when inked and pressed against a surface (as paper) **4** : a collection of printing types or the letters or figures printed from them **5** : qualities of form or character shared by a number of individuals that set them apart as an identifiable group ⟨horses of draft *type*⟩ **6** : a particular kind, class, or group ⟨a seedless *type* of orange⟩ **7** : KIND, SORT

²**type** *vb* **typed; typ·ing** **1** : TYPIFY **2** : TYPE-WRITE **3** : to identify as belonging to a type

type·write \'tīp-,rīt\ *vb* **type·wrote** \-,rōt\; **type·writ·ten** \-,rit-n\; **type·writ·ing** \-,rīt-ing\ : to write with a typewriter

type·writ·er \'tīp-,rīt-ər\ *n* : a machine for writing letters or figures like those produced by printer's type

type·writ·ing \'tīp-,rīt-ing\ *n* **1** : the use of a typewriter **2** : writing done with a typewriter

typewriter

¹**ty·phoid** \'tī-,fȯid\ *adj* **1** : of, relating to, or suggestive of typhus **2** : of, relating to, or being typhoid

²**typhoid** *n* : a communicable disease caused by a bacterium (**typhoid bacillus**), transmitted usually by contaminated food or water, and marked by fever, diarrhea, prostration, and intestinal inflammation

ty·phoon \tī-'fün\ *n* : a tropical cyclone in the region of the Philippines or the China Sea

ty·phus \'tī-fəs\ *n* : a communicable disease transmitted especially by body lice and marked by high fever, stupor and delirium, intense headache, and a dark red rash

typ·i·cal \'tip-i-kəl\ *adj* **1** : being of or having the nature of a type ⟨*typical* species⟩ **2** : combining or exhibiting the essential characteristics of a group — **typ·i·cal·ly** *adv*

typ·i·fy \'tip-ə-,fī\ *vb* **typ·i·fied; typ·i·fy·ing** **1** : REPRESENT **2** : to have or embody the essential or main characteristics of

typ·ist \'tī-pəst\ *n* : a person who uses a typewriter

ty·pog·ra·phy \tī-'päg-rə-fē\ *n* **1** : the use of type for printing **2** : the style or arrangement of matter printed from type

tyr·an·ny \'tir-ə-nē\ *n, pl* **tyr·an·nies** **1** : a government in which absolute power is vested in a single ruler **2** : rigorous, cruel, and oppressive government **3** : a tyrannical act

ty·rant \'tī-rənt\ *n* **1** : a ruler who has no legal limits on his power **2** : a ruler who exercises absolute power oppressively **3** : one who uses authority or power harshly

u \'yü\ *n, often cap* **1** : the twenty-first letter of the English alphabet **2** : a grade rating a student's work as unsatisfactory

ud·der \'əd-ər\ *n* : an organ (as of a cow) consisting of two or more milk glands enclosed in a common pouch but opening by separate nipples

ugh \'əg\ *interj* — used to indicate the sound of a cough or to express disgust or horror

ug·ly \'əg-lē\ *adj* **ug·li·er; ug·li·est** **1** : FRIGHTFUL, TERRIBLE **2** : unpleasant or offensive to the sight **3** : unpleasant to any sense ⟨*ugly* smells⟩ **4** : morally objectionable **5** : TROUBLESOME **6** : SURLY, QUARRELSOME — **ug·li·ness** *n*

u·ku·le·le \,yü-kə-'lā-lē\ *n* : a small guitar strung usually with four strings

ul·cer \'əl-sər\ *n* **1** : an open eroded sore that may discharge pus **2** : something that festers and corrupts like an open sore

ul·cer·ate \'əl-sə-,rāt\ *vb* **ul·cer·at·ed; ul·cer·at·ing** : to cause or become affected with an ulcer

ul·cer·a·tion \,əl-sə-'rā-shən\ *n* **1** : the process of becoming or state of being ulcerated **2** : ULCER 1

ul·cer·ous \'əl-sə-rəs\ *adj* : being or marked by ulceration

ukulele

ul·te·ri·or \,əl-'tir-ē-ər\ *adj* **1** : situated farther away **2** : HIDDEN ⟨*ulterior* motives⟩

¹**ul·ti·mate** \'əl-tə-mət\ *adj* **1** : most distant in space or time ⟨the *ultimate* stars⟩ **2** : last in a progression : FINAL **3** : EXTREME, UTMOST **4** : FUNDAMENTAL, ABSOLUTE ⟨*ultimate* reality⟩ **5** : not capable of further division or separation **syn** see LAST — **ul·ti·mate·ly** *adv*

²**ultimate** *n* : something ultimate

ul·ti·ma·tum \,əl-tə-'māt-əm\ *n, pl* **ul·ti·ma·tums** *or* **ul·ti·ma·ta** \-'māt-ə\ : a final proposition, condition, or demand whose rejection is likely to bring about an end of negotiations

ul·tra \'əl-trə\ *adj* : EXTREME, EXCESSIVE

ultra- *prefix* **1** : beyond in space : on the other side ⟨*ultra*violet⟩ **2** : beyond the range or limits of : SUPER- ⟨*ultra*microscopic⟩ **3** : beyond what is ordinary, proper, or moderate : excessively ⟨*ultra*modern⟩

ul·tra·vi·o·let \,əl-trə-'vī-ə-lət\ *adj* : relating to or producing ultraviolet light

ultraviolet light *n* : waves that are similar to light but are invisible, lie beyond the violet end of the spectrum, and are found especially along with light from the sun

um·bil·i·cal cord \,əm-,bil-i-kəl-\ *n* : a cord joining a fetus to its placenta

um·brel·la \,əm-'brel-ə\ *n* [from Italian *ombrella*, a modification of Latin *umbella*, literally "little shade", from *umbra* "shade", "shadow"] : a fabric covering stretched over ribs attached to a rod or pole and used as a protection against rain or sun

u·mi·ak \'ü-mē-,ak\ *n* : an open Eskimo boat made of a hide-covered wooden frame

um·pire \'əm-,pīr\ *n* : a sports official who rules on plays

umiak

¹**un-** \,ən, 'ən\ *prefix* **1** : not : IN-, NON- ⟨*un*skilled⟩ **2** : opposite of : contrary to ⟨*un*constitutional⟩ ⟨*un*believing⟩ ⟨*un*rest⟩

²**un-** *prefix* **1** : do the opposite of : reverse a specified action : DE- 1, DIS- 1 ⟨*un*dress⟩ ⟨*un*fold⟩ **2** : deprive of, remove a specified thing from, or free or release from ⟨*un*leash⟩ ⟨*un*hand⟩ **3** : cause to cease to be ⟨*un*man⟩ **4** : completely ⟨*un*loose⟩

un·able \,ən-'ā-bəl\ *adj* : not able

un·ac·com·pa·nied \,ən-ə-'kəm-pə-nēd\ *adj* : not accompanied

un·ac·count·a·ble \,ən-ə-'kaunt-ə-bəl\ *adj* : not accountable : not to be explained : STRANGE — **un·ac·count·a·bly** \-blē\ *adv*

un·ac·cus·tomed \,ən-ə-'kəs-təmd\ *adj* : not accustomed : not customary

un·af·fect·ed \,ən-ə-'fek-təd\ *adj* **1** : not influenced or changed **2** : free from affectation : GENUINE — **un·af·fect·ed·ly** *adv*

un·a·fraid \,ən-ə-'frād\ *adj* : not afraid

un·aid·ed \,ən-'ād-əd\ *adj* : not aided

un·al·loyed \,ən-l-'oid\ *adj* : PURE

u·na·nim·i·ty \,yü-nə-'nim-ət-ē\ *n* : the quality or state of being unanimous

u·nan·i·mous \yü-'nan-ə-məs\ *adj* **1** : being of one mind **2** : agreed to by all ⟨a *unanimous* vote⟩ — **u·nan·i·mous·ly** *adv*

un·armed \,ən-'ärmd\ *adj* : not armed or armored

un·asked \,ən-'askt\ *adj* : not asked or asked for

un·as·sum·ing \,ən-ə-'sü-ming\ *adj* : not putting on airs : MODEST

un·at·tached \,ən-ə-'tacht\ *adj* : not attached

un·a·void·a·ble \,ən-ə-'void-ə-bəl\ *adj* : INEVITABLE — **un·a·void·a·bly** \-blē\ *adv*

¹**un·a·ware** \,ən-ə-'waər\ *adv* : UNAWARES

²**unaware** *adj* : not aware : IGNORANT ⟨*unaware* of danger⟩ — **un·a·ware·ness** *n*

un·a·wares \,ən-ə-'waərz\ *adv* **1** : without warning : by surprise ⟨taken *unawares*⟩ **2** : without knowing : UNINTENTIONALLY

un·bal·anced \,ən-'bal-ənst\ *adj* **1** : not balanced **2** : disordered in mind

un·bear·a·ble \ˌən-'bar-ə-bəl\ *adj* : not bearable : greater than can be borne ⟨*unbearable* pain⟩ — **un·bear·a·bly** \-blē\ *adv*

un·beat·en \ˌən-'bēt-n\ *adj* : not beaten

un·be·com·ing \ˌən-bi-'kəm-ing\ *adj* : not becoming : not suitable or proper — **un·be·com·ing·ly** *adv*

un·be·known \ˌən-bi-'nōn\ *or* **un·be·knownst** \-'nōnst\ *adj* : happening without one's knowledge

un·be·lief \ˌən-bə-'lēf\ *n* : lack of belief

un·be·liev·a·ble \ˌən-bə-'lē-və-bəl\ *adj* : too improbable for belief — **un·be·liev·a·bly** \-blē\ *adv*

un·be·liev·er \ˌən-bə-'lē-vər\ *n* **1** : DOUBTER **2** : INFIDEL

un·bend \ˌən-'bend\ *vb* **un·bent** \-'bent\; **un·bend·ing** : RELAX

un·bend·ing \ˌən-'ben-ding\ *adj* : formal and distant in manner : INFLEXIBLE

un·bi·ased \ˌən-'bī-əst\ *adj* : free from bias

un·bind \ˌən-'bīnd\ *vb* **un·bound** \-'baund\; **un·bind·ing** **1** : to remove a band from : UNTIE **2** : to set free

un·born \ˌən-'bȯrn\ *adj* : not born : FUTURE

un·bos·om \ˌən-'bùz-əm\ *vb* : to disclose one's own thoughts or feelings

un·bound \ˌən-'baund\ *adj* : not bound

un·bound·ed \ˌən-'baun-dəd\ *adj* : having no bounds or limits ⟨*unbounded* enthusiasm⟩

un·break·a·ble \ˌən-'brā-kə-bəl\ *adj* : not easily broken

un·bro·ken \ˌən-'brō-kən\ *adj* **1** : not damaged : WHOLE **2** : not subdued or tamed ⟨an *unbroken* colt⟩ **3** : not interrupted

un·buck·le \ˌən-'bək-əl\ *vb* **un·buck·led**; **un·buck·ling** : to unfasten the buckle of (as a belt)

un·bur·den \ˌən-'bərd-n\ *vb* **1** : to free from a burden **2** : to relieve oneself of (as cares)

un·but·ton \ˌən-'bət-n\ *vb* : to unfasten the buttons of (as a garment)

un·called–for \ˌən-'kȯld-ˌfȯr\ *adj* : not needed or wanted : not proper ⟨*uncalled-for* remarks⟩

un·can·ny \ˌən-'kan-ē\ *adj* **1** : MYSTERIOUS, EERIE **2** : suggesting superhuman or supernatural powers ⟨an *uncanny* sense of direction⟩ — **un·can·ni·ly** \-'kan-l-ē\ *adv*

un·ceas·ing \ˌən-'sē-sing\ *adj* : never ceasing : CONTINUOUS — **un·ceas·ing·ly** *adv*

un·cer·tain \ˌən-'sərt-n\ *adj* **1** : not determined or fixed ⟨an *uncertain* quantity⟩ **2** : subject to chance or change : not dependable ⟨*uncertain* weather⟩ **3** : not sure **4** : not definitely known — **un·cer·tain·ly** *adv*

un·cer·tain·ty \ˌən-'sərt-n-tē\ *n, pl* **un·cer-**

tain·ties **1** : lack of certainty : DOUBT **2** : something uncertain

un·change·a·ble \ˌən-'chān-jə-bəl\ *adj* : not changing : not to be changed : IMMUTABLE

un·changed \ˌən-'chānjd\ *adj* : not changed

un·chang·ing \ˌən-'chān-jing\ *adj* : CHANGELESS

un·charged \ˌən-'chärjd\ *adj* : having no electric charge

un·civ·il \ˌən-'siv-əl\ *adj* : lacking in courtesy : IMPOLITE — **un·civ·il·ly** *adv*

un·civ·i·lized \ˌən-'siv-ə-ˌlīzd\ *adj* **1** : not civilized : BARBAROUS **2** : remote from civilization : WILD

un·cle \'əng-kəl\ *n* **1** : the brother of one's father or mother **2** : the husband of one's aunt

un·clean \ˌən-'klēn\ *adj* **1** : morally or spiritually impure **2** : prohibited by ritual law for use or contact **3** : DIRTY, FILTHY — **un·clean·ness** *n*

¹**un·clean·ly** \ˌən-'klen-lē\ *adj* : morally or physically unclean — **un·clean·li·ness** *n*

²**un·clean·ly** \ˌən-'klēn-lē\ *adv* : in an unclean manner

un·cleared \ˌən-'kliərd\ *adj* : not cleared especially of trees or brush

Un·cle Sam \ˌəng-kəl-'sam\ *n* : the American government, nation, or people personified

un·clothed \ˌən-'klōthd\ *adj* : not clothed

un·com·fort·a·ble \ˌən-'kəm-fərt-ə-bəl\ *adj* **1** : causing discomfort ⟨an *uncomfortable* chair⟩ **2** : feeling discomfort : UNEASY — **un·com·fort·a·bly** \-blē\ *adv*

un·com·mon \ˌən-'käm-ən\ *adj* **1** : not ordinarily encountered : UNUSUAL **2** : REMARKABLE, EXCEPTIONAL — **un·com·mon·ly** *adv* — **un·com·mon·ness** *n*

un·com·pli·men·ta·ry \'ən-ˌkäm-plə-'ment-ə-rē\ *adj* : not complimentary : DEROGATORY

un·com·pro·mis·ing \ˌən-'käm-prə-ˌmī-zing\ *adj* : not making or accepting a compromise — **un·com·pro·mis·ing·ly** *adv*

un·con·cern \ˌən-kən-'sərn\ *n* **1** : lack of care or interest : INDIFFERENCE **2** : freedom from excessive concern or anxiety

un·con·cerned \ˌən-kən-'sərnd\ *adj* **1** : not having any part or interest : not involved **2** : not anxious or upset : free of worry — **un·con·cern·ed·ly** \-'sər-nəd-lē\ *adv*

un·con·di·tion·al \ˌən-kən-'dish-ən-l\ *adj* : without any conditions or exceptions ⟨*unconditional* surrender⟩ — **un·con·di·tion·al·ly** *adv*

un·con·quer·a·ble \ˌən-'käng-kə-rə-bəl\ *adj* : not capable of being conquered or overcome

¹**un·con·scious** \ˌən-'kän-chəs\ *adj* **1** : deprived usually temporarily of mental aware-

ness ⟨knocked *unconscious* by a fall⟩ **2** : not aware ⟨*unconscious* of having made a mistake⟩ **3** : not consciously done — **un·con·scious·ly** *adv* — **un·con·scious·ness** *n*

²unconscious *n* : the part of one's mental life of which one is not ordinarily actively aware

un·con·sti·tu·tion·al \'ən-,kän-stə-'tü-shən-l, -'tyü-\ *adj* : not according to the constitution of a government or society

un·con·trol·la·ble \,ən-kən-'trō-lə-bəl\ *adj* : incapable of being controlled — **un·con·trol·la·bly** \-blē\ *adv*

un·con·trolled \,ən-kən-'trōld\ *adj* : not being under control

un·con·ven·tion·al \,ən-kən-'ven-chən-l\ *adj* : not conventional

un·couth \,ən-'küth\ *adj* [in earlier English this meant "unknown", "strange", being derived from Old English *uncūth*, a compound of *un-* and *cūth* "known"] **1** : strange or clumsy in shape or appearance **2** : vulgar in conduct or speech — **un·couth·ly** *adv*

un·cov·er \,ən-'kəv-ər\ *vb* **1** : to make known **2** : to expose to view by removing some covering **3** : to take off the hat

un·cul·ti·vat·ed \,ən-'kəl-tə-,vāt-əd\ *adj* : not put under cultivation

un·curl \,ən-'kərl\ *vb* : to make or become straightened out from a curled position

un·daunt·ed \,ən-'dȯnt-əd\ *adj* : not discouraged or dismayed : FEARLESS

un·de·cid·ed \,ən-di-'sīd-əd\ *adj* **1** : not settled **2** : not having decided

un·de·clared \,ən-di-'klaərd\ *adj* : not announced or openly acknowledged

un·de·fined \,ən-di-'fīnd\ *adj* : not defined

un·de·ni·a·ble \,ən-di-'nī-ə-bəl\ *adj* : plainly true — **un·de·ni·a·bly** \-blē\ *adv*

¹un·der \'ən-dər\ *adv* **1** : in or into a position below or beneath something ⟨the diver went *under* again⟩ **2** : below some quantity or level ⟨ten dollars or *under*⟩ **3** : so as to be covered or hidden ⟨turned *under* by the plow⟩

²under *prep* **1** : lower than and overhung, surmounted, or sheltered by ⟨*under* a tree⟩ **2** : below the surface of ⟨*under* the sea⟩ **3** : in or into such a position as to be covered or concealed by ⟨a vest *under* his jacket⟩ ⟨the moon went *under* a cloud⟩ **4** : subject to the authority or guidance of ⟨served *under* a colonel⟩ **5** : with the guarantee of ⟨*under* the royal seal⟩ **6** : controlled, limited, or oppressed by ⟨*under* lock and key⟩ **7** : subject to the action or effect of ⟨*under* an anesthetic⟩ **8** : within the division or grouping of **9** : less or lower than (as in size, amount, or rank)

³under *adj* ▸**1** : lying or placed below or be-

neath **2** : SUBORDINATE **3** : lower than usual or proper in amount, quality, or degree

un·der·brush \'ən-dər-,brəsh\ *n* : shrubs and small trees growing among large trees

un·der·clothes \'ən-dər-,klōz, -,klōthz\ *n pl* : UNDERWEAR

un·der·cloth·ing \'ən-dər-,klō-thing\ *n* : UNDERWEAR

un·der·foot \,ən-dər-'fu̇t\ *adv* **1** : under the feet ⟨flowers trampled *underfoot*⟩ **2** : close about one's feet ⟨a puppy always *underfoot*⟩

un·der·gar·ment \'ən-dər-,gär-mənt\ *n* : a garment to be worn under another

un·der·go \,ən-dər-'gō\ *vb* **un·der·went** \-'went\; **un·der·gone** \-'gȯn\; **un·der·go·ing** \-'gō-ing\ **1** : to submit to or be subjected to ⟨*undergo* an operation⟩ **2** : EXPERIENCE

¹un·der·ground \,ən-dər-'grau̇nd\ *adv* **1** : beneath the surface of the earth **2** : in or into hiding or secret operation

²un·der·ground \'ən-dər-,grau̇nd\ *adj* **1** : being or growing under the surface of the ground **2** : done or occurring secretly

³un·der·ground \'ən-dər-,grau̇nd\ *n* **1** : a space under the surface of the ground **2** : an underground railway **3** : a secret political movement or group

un·der·growth \'ən-dər-,grōth\ *n* : UNDERBRUSH

¹un·der·hand \'ən-dər-,hand\ *adv* : in an underhand or secret manner

²underhand *adj* **1** : marked by secrecy and deception : not honest : SLY **2** : made with an upward movement of the hand or arm

un·der·hand·ed \,ən-dər-'han-dəd\ *adj* : UNDERHAND — **un·der·hand·ed·ly** *adv* — **un·der·hand·ed·ness** *n*

un·der·lie \,ən-dər-'lī\ *vb* **un·der·lay** \-'lā\; **un·der·lain** \-'lān\; **un·der·ly·ing** \-'lī-ing\ **1** : to lie or be situated under **2** : to be at the basis of : SUPPORT ⟨*underlying* principles⟩

un·der·line \'ən-dər-,līn\ *vb* **un·der·lined**; **un·der·lin·ing** **1** : to draw a line under : UNDERSCORE **2** : EMPHASIZE

un·der·mine \,ən-dər-'mīn\ *vb* **un·der·mined**; **un·der·min·ing** **1** : to dig out or wear away the supporting earth beneath ⟨*undermine* a wall⟩ **2** : to weaken secretly or gradually

¹un·der·neath \,ən-dər-'nēth\ *prep* **1** : directly under **2** : under subjection to

²underneath *adv* **1** : below a surface or object : BENEATH **2** : on the lower side

un·der·nour·ished \,ən-dər-'nər-isht\ *adj* : supplied with insufficient nourishment — **un·der·nour·ish·ment** \-ish-mənt\ *n*

un·der·pants \'ən-dər-,pants\ *n pl* : pants worn under an outer garment

un·der·part \ˈən-dər-ˌpärt\ *n* : a part lying on the lower side especially of a bird or mammal

un·der·pass \ˈən-dər-ˌpas\ *n* : a passage underneath something (as for a road passing under a railroad or another road)

un·der·priv·i·leged \ˌən-dər-ˈpriv-ə-lijd\ *adj* : having fewer economic and social privileges than others ⟨*underprivileged* children⟩

un·der·rate \ˌən-dər-ˈrāt\ *vb* **un·der·rat·ed**; **un·der·rat·ing** : to rate too low : UNDERVALUE

un·der·score \ˈən-dər-ˌskōr\ *vb* **un·der·scored**; **un·der·scor·ing** : UNDERLINE

¹**un·der·sea** \ˌən-dər-ˌsē\ *adj* **1** : being or carried on under the sea or under the surface of the sea **2** : designed for use under the surface of the sea ⟨*undersea* fleet⟩

²**un·der·sea** \ˌən-dər-ˈsē\ *or* **un·der·seas** \-ˈsēz\ *adv* : under the surface of the sea

un·der·sell \ˌən-dər-ˈsel\ *vb* **un·der·sold** \-ˈsōld\; **un·der·sell·ing** : to sell articles cheaper than ⟨*undersell* a competitor⟩

un·der·shirt \ˈən-dər-ˌshərt\ *n* : a collarless undergarment with or without sleeves

un·der·shot \ˌən-dər-ˌshät\ *adj* : having the lower incisor teeth or lower jaw projecting beyond the upper when the mouth is closed

un·der·side \ˈən-dər-ˌsīd\ *n* : the side or surface lying underneath

un·der·skirt \ˈən-dər-ˌskərt\ *n* : PETTICOAT

un·der·stand \ˌən-dər-ˈstand\ *vb* **un·der·stood** \-ˈstůd\; **un·der·stand·ing** **1** : to get the meaning of : COMPREHEND **2** : to have thorough acquaintance with ⟨*understand* music⟩ **3** : to get an impression of : INFER ⟨I *understand* that he will come today⟩ **4** : INTERPRET ⟨*understand* the letter to be a refusal⟩ **5** : to have a sympathetic attitude **6** : to accept as settled **7** : to supply in thought as though expressed

un·der·stand·a·ble \ˌən-dər-ˈstan-də-bəl\ *adj* : capable of being readily understood — **un·der·stand·a·bly** \-blē\ *adv*

¹**un·der·stand·ing** \ˌən-dər-ˈstan-ding\ *n* **1** : ability to comprehend and judge **2** : a mutual agreement

²**understanding** *adj* : SYMPATHETIC

un·der·stud·y \ˈən-dər-ˌstəd-ē\ *n, pl* **un·der·stud·ies** : one who stands prepared to act another's part or take over another's duties

un·der·take \ˌən-dər-ˈtāk\ *vb* **un·der·took** \-ˈtůk\; **un·der·tak·en** \-ˈtā-kən\; **un·der·tak·ing** **1** : to take upon oneself as a task : set about **2** : CONTRACT, PROMISE

un·der·tak·er \ˈən-dər-ˌtā-kər\ *n* : a person whose business is to prepare the dead for burial and to take charge of funerals

un·der·tak·ing \ˈən-dər-ˌtā-king\ *n* **1** : the act of a person who undertakes something **2** : the business of an undertaker **3** : something undertaken **4** : PROMISE, GUARANTEE

un·der·tone \ˈən-dər-ˌtōn\ *n* **1** : a low or subdued tone **2** : a subdued or underlying color

un·der·tow \ˈən-dər-ˌtō\ *n* : a current beneath the surface of the water that moves away from or along the shore while the surface water above it moves toward the shore

un·der·val·ue \ˌən-dər-ˈval-yü\ *vb* **un·der·val·ued**; **un·der·val·u·ing** : to value below the real worth

¹**un·der·wa·ter** \ˌən-dər-ˌwȯt-ər, -ˌwät-\ *adj* : lying, growing, worn, or operating below the surface of the water

²**un·der·wa·ter** \ˌən-dər-ˈwȯt-ər, -ˈwät-\ *adv* : under the surface of the water

un·der·wear \ˈən-dər-ˌwaər\ *n* : clothing worn next to the skin and under other clothing

un·der·weight \ˌən-dər-ˈwāt\ *adj* : weighing less than what is normal, average, or necessary

underwent *past of* UNDERGO

un·der·wood \ˈən-dər-ˌwůd\ *n* : UNDERBRUSH

un·der·world \ˈən-dər-ˌwərld\ *n* **1** : the place of departed souls : HADES **2** : the world of organized crime

¹**un·de·sir·a·ble** \ˌən-di-ˈzī-rə-bəl\ *adj* : not desirable — **un·de·sir·a·bly** \-blē\ *adv*

²**undesirable** *n* : one that is undesirable

un·de·vel·oped \ˌən-di-ˈvel-əpt\ *adj* : not developed

un·dig·ni·fied \ˌən-ˈdig-nə-ˌfīd\ *adj* : not dignified

un·dis·cov·ered \ˌən-dis-ˈkəv-ərd\ *adj* : not discovered

un·dis·put·ed \ˌən-dis-ˈpyüt-əd\ *adj* : not disputed

un·dis·turbed \ˌən-dis-ˈtərbd\ *adj* : CALM

un·do \ˌən-ˈdü\ *vb* **un·did** \-ˈdid\; **un·done** \-ˈdən\; **un·do·ing** \-ˈdü-ing\ **1** : UNFASTEN, OPEN **2** : to make of no effect or as if not done : REVERSE **3** : to ruin the worldly means, reputation, or hopes of

un·do·ing \ˌən-ˈdü-ing\ *n* **1** : LOOSING, UNFASTENING **2** : RUIN **3** : REVERSAL

un·done \ˌən-ˈdən\ *adj* : not done : NEGLECTED

un·doubt·ed \ˌən-ˈdaůt-əd\ *adj* : not doubted

un·doubt·ed·ly \ˌən-ˈdaůt-əd-lē\ *adv* : SURELY

¹**un·dress** \ˌən-ˈdres\ *vb* : to remove the clothes or covering of : DISROBE

²**undress** *n* : informal or ordinary dress

un·due \ˌən-ˈdü, -ˈdyü\ *adj* **1** : not due : not yet payable **2** : INAPPROPRIATE, UNSUITABLE **3** : EXCESSIVE, EXTREME

un·du·late \ˈən-jə-ˌlāt, ˈən-dyə-\ *vb* **un·du·lat·ed**; **un·du·lat·ing** **1** : to form or move in waves **2** : to present a wavy appearance

un·du·la·tion \ˌən-jə-'lā-shən, ˌən-dyə-\ *n* 1 : the action of undulating 2 : a wavelike motion : VIBRATION 3 : a wavy appearance

un·du·ly \ˌən-'dü-lē, -'dyü-\ *adv* : in an undue manner

un·dy·ing \ˌən-'dī-ing\ *adj* : IMMORTAL

un·earth \ˌən-'ərth\ *vb* 1 : to drive or draw from the earth : dig up 2 : to bring to light

un·earth·ly \ˌən-'ərth-lē\ *adj* 1 : not of or belonging to the earth 2 : SUPERNATURAL, WEIRD ⟨an *unearthly* cry⟩

un·eas·y \ˌən-'ē-zē\ *adj* **un·eas·i·er; un·eas·i·est** 1 : not easy in manner : AWKWARD 2 : disturbed by pain or worry : RESTLESS — **un·eas·i·ly** \-zə-lē\ *adv* — **un·eas·i·ness** \-zē-nəs\ *n*

un·ed·u·cat·ed \ˌən-'ej-ə-ˌkāt-əd\ *adj* : not educated

un·em·ployed \ˌən-im-'plȯid\ *adj* : not employed : not engaged in a gainful occupation

un·em·ploy·ment \ˌən-im-'plȯi-mənt\ *n* : the state of being unemployed

un·end·ing \ˌən-'en-ding\ *adj* : having no ending : ENDLESS — **un·end·ing·ly** *adv*

un·en·dur·a·ble \ˌən-in-'dùr-ə-bəl, -'dyùr-\ *adj* : not capable of being endured : UNBEARABLE — **un·en·dur·a·bly** \-blē\ *adv*

¹**un·e·qual** \ˌən-'ē-kwəl\ *adj* 1 : not alike (as in size or value) 2 : badly balanced or matched ⟨an *unequal* fight⟩ 3 : INADEQUATE, INSUFFICIENT — **un·e·qual·ly** *adv*

²**unequal** *n* : one that is not equal to another

un·e·qualed \ˌən-'ē-kwəld\ *adj* : not equaled

un·e·ven \ˌən-'ē-vən\ *adj* 1 : ODD ⟨*uneven* numbers⟩ 2 : not level or smooth ⟨*uneven* surface⟩ 3 : IRREGULAR ⟨*uneven* teeth⟩ 4 : varying in quality ⟨an *uneven* performance⟩ — **un·e·ven·ly** *adv* — **un·e·ven·ness** *n*

un·e·vent·ful \ˌən-i-'vent-fəl\ *adj* : not eventful : lacking interesting or noteworthy happenings ⟨an *uneventful* vacation⟩ — **un·e·vent·ful·ly** *adv*

un·ex·pect·ed \ˌən-iks-'pek-təd\ *adj* : not expected ⟨an *unexpected* happening⟩ — **un·ex·pect·ed·ly** *adv* — **un·ex·pect·ed·ness** *n*

un·fail·ing \ˌən-'fā-ling\ *adj* : not failing or liable to fail — **un·fail·ing·ly** *adv*

un·fair \ˌən-'faər\ *adj* : marked by partiality, dishonesty, or injustice — **un·fair·ly** *adv* — **un·fair·ness** *n*

un·faith·ful \ˌən-'fāth-fəl\ *adj* 1 : DISLOYAL 2 : INACCURATE — **un·faith·ful·ly** *adv* — **un·faith·ful·ness** *n*

un·fa·mil·iar \ˌən-fə-'mil-yər\ *adj* 1 : not well known : STRANGE 2 : not well acquainted ⟨*unfamiliar* with the subject⟩ — **un·fa·mil·iar·i·ty** \ˌən-fə-ˌmil-'yar-ət-ē\ *n*

un·fas·ten \ˌən-'fas-n\ *vb* : to make or become loose : UNDO

un·fa·vor·a·ble \ˌən-'fā-və-rə-bəl\ *adj* 1 : OPPOSED, NEGATIVE 2 : DISADVANTAGEOUS — **un·fa·vor·a·bly** \-blē\ *adv*

un·feel·ing \ˌən-'fē-ling\ *adj* 1 : lacking feeling 2 : lacking kindness or sympathy : CRUEL — **un·feel·ing·ly** *adv*

un·feigned \ˌən-'fānd\ *adj* : not feigned

un·fin·ished \ˌən-'fin-isht\ *adj* : not finished

¹**un·fit** \ˌən-'fit\ *adj* 1 : UNSUITABLE 2 : not qualified 3 : UNSOUND — **un·fit·ness** *n*

²**unfit** *vb* **un·fit·ted; un·fit·ting** : to make unfit

un·fledged \ˌən-'flejd\ *adj* : not feathered or ready for flight ⟨a nest of *unfledged* robins⟩

un·fold \ˌən-'fōld\ *vb* 1 : to open the folds of : open up 2 : to lay open to view : REVEAL ⟨*unfold* a plan⟩ 3 : BLOSSOM, DEVELOP

un·fold·ed \ˌən-'fōl-dəd\ *adj* 1 : opened out 2 : not folded

un·fore·seen \ˌən-fōr-'sēn\ *adj* : not foreseen

un·for·get·ta·ble \ˌən-fər-'get-ə-bəl\ *adj* : not to be forgotten : lasting in memory — **un·for·get·ta·bly** \-blē\ *adv*

un·for·giv·a·ble \ˌən-fər-'giv-ə-bəl\ *adj* : not to be forgiven or pardoned — **un·for·giv·a·bly** \-blē\ *adv*

¹**un·for·tu·nate** \ˌən-'fȯr-chə-nət\ *adj* 1 : not fortunate : UNLUCKY 2 : UNSUITABLE 3 : DEPLORABLE — **un·for·tu·nate·ly** *adv*

²**unfortunate** *n* : an unfortunate person

un·found·ed \ˌən-'faùn-dəd\ *adj* : lacking a sound basis ⟨an *unfounded* accusation⟩

un·friend·ly \ˌən-'frend-lē\ *adj* **un·friend·li·er; un·friend·li·est** : not friendly or favorable : HOSTILE — **un·friend·li·ness** *n*

un·fruit·ful \ˌən-'früt-fəl\ *adj* 1 : not bearing fruit or offspring 2 : not producing a desired result ⟨*unfruitful* efforts⟩

un·furl \ˌən-'fərl\ *vb* : to loose from a furled state : UNFOLD ⟨*unfurl* a flag⟩

un·gain·ly \ˌən-'gān-lē\ *adj* **un·gain·li·er; un·gain·li·est** : CLUMSY, AWKWARD ⟨an *ungainly* walk⟩ — **un·gain·li·ness** *n*

un·gen·tle·man·ly \ˌən-'jent-l-mən-lē\ *adj* : unworthy of a gentleman

un·god·ly \ˌən-'gäd-lē\ *adj* **un·god·li·er; un·god·li·est** 1 : IMPIOUS, IRRELIGIOUS 2 : SINFUL, WICKED 3 : OUTRAGEOUS — **un·god·li·ness** *n*

un·gov·erned \ˌən-'gəv-ərnd\ *adj* : not subjected to regulation or control

un·gra·cious \ˌən-'grā-shəs\ *adj* : not gracious : DISCOURTEOUS — **un·gra·cious·ly** *adv*

un·grate·ful \ˌən-'grāt-fəl\ *adj* : not grateful — **un·grate·ful·ly** *adv* — **un·grate·ful·ness** *n*

un·guent \'əng-gwənt\ *n* : a soothing or healing salve : OINTMENT

¹un·gu·late \'əng-gyə-lət\ *adj* : having hooves ⟨horses and cows are *ungulate* animals⟩

²ungulate *n* : a hoofed animal

un·hand \ˌən-'hand\ *vb* : to remove the hand from : let go

un·hand·y \ˌən-'han-dē\ *adj* **un·hand·i·er; un·hand·i·est** **1** : hard to handle : INCONVENIENT **2** : not skillful ⟨*unhandy* with tools⟩

un·hap·py \ˌən-'hap-ē\ *adj* **un·hap·pi·er; un·hap·pi·est** **1** : not fortunate : UNLUCKY ⟨an *unhappy* mistake⟩ **2** : not cheerful : SAD **3** : INAPPROPRIATE — **un·hap·pi·ly** \-'hap-ə-lē\ *adv* — **un·hap·pi·ness** \-'hap-ē-nəs\ *n*

un·health·ful \ˌən-'helth-fəl\ *adj* : not healthful

un·health·y \ˌən-'hel-thē\ *adj* **un·health·i·er; un·health·i·est** **1** : not good for one's health ⟨an *unhealthy* climate⟩ **2** : not in good health : SICKLY **3** : BAD, HARMFUL ⟨an *unhealthy* situation⟩ — **un·health·i·ly** \-thə-lē\ *adv*

un·heard \ˌən-'hərd\ *adj* : not heard

un·heard-of \ˌən-'hərd-ˌəv, -ˌäv\ *adj* : previously unknown

un·hin·dered \ˌən-'hin-dərd\ *adj* : not hindered : not kept back ⟨*unhindered* progress⟩

un·hitch \ˌən-'hich\ *vb* : to free from being hitched

un·ho·ly \ˌən-'hō-lē\ *adj* **un·ho·li·er; un·ho·li·est** : not holy : WICKED — **un·ho·li·ness** *n*

un·hook \ˌən-'hůk\ *vb* **1** : to remove from a hook **2** : to unfasten by disengaging a hook

un·horse \ˌən-'hȯrs\ *vb* **un·horsed; un·hors·ing** : to dislodge from or as if from a horse

un·hur·ried \ˌən-'hər-ēd\ *adj* : not hurried

u·ni- \'yü-ni\ *prefix* : one : single ⟨*unicellular*⟩

u·ni·corn \'yü-nə-ˌkȯrn\ *n* : a fabulous animal with one horn in the middle of the forehead

un·i·den·ti·fied \ˌən-ī-'dent-ə-ˌfīd\ *adj* : not identified

u·ni·fi·ca·tion \ˌyü-nə-fə-'kā-shən\ *n* : the act, process, or result of unifying : the state of being unified

¹u·ni·form \'yü-nə-ˌfȯrm\ *adj* **1** : having always the same form, manner, or degree : not varying **2** : of the same form with others ⟨hats of *uniform* style⟩ — **u·ni·form·ly** *adv*

²uniform *vb* : to clothe with a uniform — **u·ni·formed** \-ˌfȯrmd\ *adj*

³uniform *n* : distinctive dress worn by members of a particular group (as an army)

u·ni·form·i·ty \ˌyü-nə-'fȯr-mət-ē\ *n, pl* **u·ni·form·i·ties** : the quality or state or an instance of being uniform

u·ni·fy \'yü-nə-ˌfī\ *vb* **u·ni·fied; u·ni·fy·ing** : to make into or become a unit : UNITE

un·im·por·tant \ˌən-im-'pȯrt-nt\ *adj* : not important : of no consequence

un·in·hab·it·ed \ˌən-in-'hab-ət-əd\ *adj* : having no inhabitants ⟨an *uninhabited* island⟩

un·in·tel·li·gi·ble \ˌən-in-'tel-ə-jə-bəl\ *adj* : not intelligible : OBSCURE

un·in·ten·tion·al \ˌən-in-'ten-chən-l\ *adj* : not intentional — **un·in·ten·tion·al·ly** *adv*

un·in·ter·est·ed \ˌən-'in-trəs-təd, -'int-ə-rəs-\ *adj* : not interested

syn UNINTERESTED, DISINTERESTED have often been used interchangeably but they are now usually sharply distinguished in meaning. UNINTERESTED has only the negative implication of being indifferent to something, of lacking sympathy or curiosity toward something ⟨the group neither agreed nor disagreed with what the speaker was saying; they were simply bored and *uninterested*⟩ DISINTERESTED is useful in describing a freedom from concern for personal or financial advantage that enables one to act or to judge fairly and impartially ⟨his advice to buy the house was *disinterested*, since he had nothing to gain or lose by the sale⟩

un·in·ter·est·ing \ˌən-'in-trəs-ting, -'int-ə-rəs-\ *adj* : not attracting interest or attention

un·in·ter·rupt·ed \'ən-ˌint-ə-'rəp-təd\ *adj* : not interrupted

u·nion \'yü-nyən\ *n* **1** : an act or instance of uniting two or more things into one **2** : something (as a nation) formed by a combining of parts or members **3** : a device for connecting parts (as of a machine) **4** : a group of workers organized to advance or protect their rights and interests

Union *adj* : of or relating to the side favoring the federal union in the American Civil War

u·nique \yů-'nēk\ *adj* **1** : being the only one of its kind **2** : very unusual : NOTABLE — **u·nique·ly** *adv* — **u·nique·ness** *n*

u·ni·son \'yü-nə-sən\ *n* **1** : sameness of musical pitch **2** : the condition of being tuned or sounded at the same pitch or at an octave **3** : exact agreement : ACCORD

u·nit \'yü-nət\ *n* **1** : the least whole number : ONE **2** : a definite quantity (as of length, time, or value) adopted as a standard of measurement **3** : a single thing or person or group forming part of a whole **4** : a part of a school course with a central theme

u·nite \yů-'nīt\ *vb* **u·nit·ed; u·nit·ing** **1** : to put or come together to form a single unit **2** : to link by a legal or moral bond ⟨nations *united* by a treaty⟩ **3** : to join in action

u·nit·ed \yů-'nīt-əd\ *adj* **1** : made one : COMBINED **2** : being in agreement : HARMONIOUS

u·ni·ty \'yü-nət-ē\ *n, pl* **u·ni·ties** **1** : the quality or state of being one **2** : CONCORD,

HARMONY ⟨live in *unity* with one another⟩
3 : reference of all the parts of an artistic or literary composition to a single main idea

u·ni·valve \'yü-ni-ˌvalv\ *n* : a mollusk (as a snail) having a shell made of a single usually spirally coiled piece

u·ni·ver·sal \ˌyü-nə-'vər-səl\ *adj* **1** : including, covering, or affecting the whole without limit or exception **2** : present or occurring everywhere — **u·ni·ver·sal·ly** *adv*

u·ni·verse \'yü-nə-ˌvərs\ *n* : all created things including the earth and heavenly bodies viewed as making up one system

u·ni·ver·si·ty \ˌyü-nə-'vər-sət-ē\ *n, pl* **u·ni·ver·si·ties** : an institution of higher learning granting degrees in special fields (as law and medicine) as well as in the arts and sciences

un·just \ˌən-'jəst\ *adj* : WRONGFUL, UNFAIR — **un·just·ly** *adv*

un·kempt \ˌən-'kempt\ *adj* [from *un-* and *kempt*, past participle of *kemb*, a verb now found only in dialect speech meaning "to comb", and coming from Old English *cemban*] : not combed ⟨*unkempt* hair⟩

un·kind \ˌən-'kīnd\ *adj* : not kind or sympathetic — **un·kind·ly** *adv* — **un·kind·ness** *n*

un·know·ing \ˌən-'nō-ing\ *adj* : not knowing — **un·know·ing·ly** *adv*

¹un·known \ˌən-'nōn\ *adj* : not known : UNFAMILIAR ⟨*unknown* lands⟩

²unknown *n* : one (as a quantity) that is unknown

un·lace \ˌən-'lās\ *vb* **un·laced**; **un·lac·ing** : to loose by undoing a lacing ⟨*unlace* a shoe⟩

un·latch \ˌən-'lach\ *vb* : to open by lifting a latch ·

un·law·ful \ˌən-'lò-fəl\ *adj* : not lawful : ILLEGAL — **un·law·ful·ly** *adv*

un·learned *adj* **1** \ˌən-'lər-nəd\ : not educated : ILLITERATE **2** \-'lərnd\ : not based on experience : INSTINCTIVE

un·leash \ˌən-'lēsh\ *vb* : to free from or as if from a leash ⟨a storm *unleashed* its fury⟩

un·leav·ened \ˌən-'lev-ənd\ *adj* : not leavened

un·less \ən-'les\ *conj* : except on condition that

¹un·like \ˌən-'līk\ *prep* **1** : different from ⟨he's *unlike* his brother⟩ **2** : unusual for ⟨it's *unlike* him to be late⟩ **3** : differently from ⟨behaves *unlike* his brothers⟩

²unlike *adj* : DIFFERENT, UNEQUAL — **un·like·ness** *n*

un·like·li·hood \ˌən-'līk-lē-ˌhùd\ *n* : IMPROBABILITY

un·like·ly \ˌən-'līk-lē\ *adj* **un·like·li·er**; **un·like·li·est** **1** : not likely : IMPROBABLE **2** : likely to fail — **un·like·li·ness** *n*

un·lim·it·ed \ˌən-'lim-ət-əd\ *adj* **1** : lacking any controls **2** : BOUNDLESS, INFINITE

un·load \ˌən-'lōd\ *vb* **1** : to take away or off : REMOVE **2** : to take a load from **3** : to get rid of or be relieved of a load or burden

un·lock \ˌən-'läk\ *vb* **1** : to open or unfasten through release of a lock **2** : RELEASE ⟨*unlock* a flood of emotions⟩ **3** : REVEAL

un·looked–for \ˌən-'lùkt-ˌfòr\ *adj* : UNEXPECTED

un·loose \ˌən-'lüs\ *vb* **un·loosed**; **un·loos·ing** **1** : to relax the strain of ⟨*unloose* a grip⟩ **2** : to set free **3** : UNTIE

un·loos·en \ˌən-'lüs-n\ *vb* : UNLOOSE

un·lucky \ˌən-'lək-ē\ *adj* **un·luck·i·er**; **un·luck·i·est** **1** : UNFORTUNATE **2** : likely to bring misfortune **3** : REGRETTABLE — **un·luck·i·ly** \-'lək-ə-lē\ *adv* — **un·luck·i·ness** \-'lək-ē-nəs\ *n*

un·man·age·a·ble \ˌən-'man-ij-ə-bəl\ *adj* : not capable of being managed

un·man·ner·ly \ˌən-'man-ər-lē\ *adj* : IMPOLITE

un·marked \ˌən-'märkt\ *adj* **1** : lacking a mark **2** : not noticed

un·mar·ried \ˌən-'mar-ēd\ *adj* : not married

un·mis·tak·a·ble \ˌən-mə-'stā-kə-bəl\ *adj* ʾ : not capable of being misunderstood : CLEAR — **un·mis·tak·a·bly** \-blē\ *adv*

un·moved \ˌən-'müvd\ *adj* **1** : not moved : remaining in the same place **2** : FIRM, RESOLUTE **3** : not disturbed emotionally

un·mu·si·cal \ˌən-'myü-zi-kəl\ *adj* : HARSH, DISCORDANT

un·nat·u·ral \ˌən-'nach-ə-rəl\ *adj* **1** : not natural **2** : ARTIFICIAL **3** : STRANGE — **un·nat·u·ral·ly** *adv* — **un·nat·u·ral·ness** *n*

un·nec·es·sary \ˌən-'nes-ə-ˌser-ē\ *adj* : not necessary : NEEDLESS — **un·nec·es·sar·i·ly** \'ən-ˌnes-ə-'ser-ə-lē\ *adv*

un·nerve \ˌən-'nərv\ *vb* **un·nerved**; **un·nerv·ing** : to deprive of nerve, courage, or self-control

un·num·bered \ˌən-'nəm-bərd\ *adj* : not numbered or counted : INNUMERABLE

un·ob·served \ˌən-əb-'zərvd\ *adj* : not observed

un·oc·cu·pied \ˌən-'äk-yə-ˌpīd\ *adj* **1** : not busy : UNEMPLOYED **2** : not occupied : EMPTY

un·of·fi·cial \ˌən-ə-'fish-əl\ *adj* : not official — **un·of·fi·cial·ly** *adv*

un·pack \ˌən-'pak\ *vb* **1** : to separate and remove things packed **2** : to open and remove the contents of ⟨*unpack* a suitcase⟩

un·paid \ˌən-'pād\ *adj* : not paid

un·paint·ed \ˌən-'pānt-əd\ *adj* : not painted

un·par·al·leled \ˌən-'par-ə-ˌleld\ *adj* : having no parallel : UNSURPASSED

un·plant·ed \ˌən-'plant-əd\ *adj* : not planted

un·pleas·ant \ˌən-'plez-nt\ *adj* : not pleasant or agreeable : DISPLEASING — **un·pleas·ant·ly** *adv* — **un·pleas·ant·ness** *n*

un·pop·u·lar \ˌən-'päp-yə-lər\ *adj* : not popular : disliked by many people — **un·pop·u·lar·i·ty** \'ən-ˌpäp-yə-'lar-ət-ē\ *n*

un·pre·dict·a·ble \ˌən-pri-'dik-tə-bəl\ *adj* : not capable of being foretold

un·prej·u·diced \ˌən-'prej-ə-dəst\ *adj* : not prejudiced : IMPARTIAL

un·pre·pared \ˌən-pri-'paərd\ *adj* : not prepared

un·prin·ci·pled \ˌən-'prin-sə-pəld\ *adj* : lacking moral principles

un·pro·voked \ˌən-prə-'vōkt\ *adj* : not provoked

un·ques·tion·a·ble \ˌən-'kwes-chə-nə-bəl\ *adj* : beyond question or doubt — **un·ques·tion·a·bly** \-blē\ *adv*

un·rav·el \ˌən-'rav-əl\ *vb* **un·rav·eled** *or* **un·rav·elled**; **un·rav·el·ing** *or* **un·rav·el·ling** **1** : to separate the threads of : UNTANGLE ⟨*unravel* a snarl⟩ **2** : SOLVE ⟨*unravel* a mystery⟩

un·re·al \ˌən-'rē-əl\ *adj* : not real

un·re·al·is·tic \'ən-ˌrē-ə-'lis-tik\ *adj* : not realistic — **un·re·al·is·ti·cal·ly** \-ti-kə-lē\ *adv*

un·re·al·i·ty \ˌən-rē-'al-ət-ē\ *n, pl* **un·re·al·i·ties** **1** : the quality or state of being unreal **2** : something unreal or insubstantial

un·rea·son·a·ble \ˌən-'rēz-n-ə-bəl\ *adj* **1** : not reasonable : not governed by reason **2** : EXCESSIVE ⟨an *unreasonable* price⟩ — **un·rea·son·a·ble·ness** *n* — **un·rea·son·a·bly** \-blē\ *adv*

un·re·lat·ed \ˌən-ri-'lāt-əd\ *adj* **1** : not having any connection or relationship ⟨*unrelated* facts⟩ **2** : not told

un·re·lent·ing \ˌən-ri-'lent-ing\ *adj* **1** : not softening or yielding in determination : STERN **2** : not letting up or weakening in vigor or pace — **un·re·lent·ing·ly** *adv*

un·re·li·a·ble \ˌən-ri-'lī-ə-bəl\ *adj* : not reliable

un·rest \ˌən-'rest\ *n* : lack of rest : a disturbed or uneasy state

un·re·strict·ed \ˌən-ri-'strik-təd\ *adj* : not restricted

un·righ·teous \ˌən-'rī-chəs\ *adj* : not righteous — **un·righ·teous·ly** *adv* — **un·righ·teous·ness** *n*

un·ripe \ˌən-'rīp\ *adj* : not ripe or mature

un·ri·valed *or* **un·ri·valled** \ˌən-'rī-vəld\ *adj* : having no rival : UNEQUALED

un·roll \ˌən-'rōl\ *vb* **1** : to unwind a roll of **2** : to become unrolled or spread out

un·ruf·fled \ˌən-'rəf-əld\ *adj* **1** : not upset or agitated **2** : SMOOTH ⟨*unruffled* water⟩

un·rul·y \ˌən-'rü-lē\ *adj* **un·rul·i·er**; **un·rul·i·est** : not yielding readily to rule or restraint — **un·rul·i·ness** *n*

un·safe \ˌən-'sāf\ *adj* : not safe

un·san·i·tar·y \ˌən-'san-ə-ˌter-ē\ *adj* : not sanitary

un·sat·is·fac·to·ry \'ən-ˌsat-əs-'fak-tə-rē\ *adj* : not satisfactory — **un·sat·is·fac·to·ri·ly** \-rə-lē\ *adv*

un·sat·is·fied \ˌən-'sat-əs-ˌfīd\ *adj* : not satisfied

un·say \ˌən-'sā\ *vb* **un·said** \-'sed\; **un·say·ing** \-'sā-ing\ : to take back (something said)

un·schooled \ˌən-'sküld\ *adj* : not taught

un·sci·en·tif·ic \'ən-ˌsī-ən-'tif-ik\ *adj* : not scientific — **un·sci·en·tif·i·cal·ly** \-i-kə-lē\ *adv*

un·screw \ˌən-'skrü\ *vb* **1** : to draw the screws from **2** : to loosen or withdraw by turning

un·scru·pu·lous \ˌən-'skrü-pyə-ləs\ *adj* : not scrupulous — **un·scru·pu·lous·ly** *adv*

un·seal \ˌən-'sēl\ *vb* : to break or remove the seal of : OPEN

un·sea·son·a·ble \ˌən-'sēz-n-ə-bəl\ *adj* : not seasonable : happening or coming at the wrong time ⟨*unseasonable* weather⟩ — **un·sea·son·a·bly** \-blē\ *adv*

un·sea·soned \ˌən-'sēz-nd\ *adj* **1** : not matured or made ready or fit for use (as by the passage of time) ⟨*unseasoned* lumber⟩ **2** : INEXPERIENCED ⟨an *unseasoned* leader⟩

un·seat \ˌən-'sēt\ *vb* **1** : to dislodge from one's seat **2** : to remove from office

un·seem·ly \ˌən-'sēm-lē\ *adj* **un·seem·li·er**; **un·seem·li·est** : not seemly : UNBECOMING **syn** see INAPPROPRIATE

un·seen \ˌən-'sēn\ *adj* : not seen or perceived : INVISIBLE

un·self·ish \ˌən-'sel-fish\ *adj* : not selfish — **un·self·ish·ly** *adv* — **un·self·ish·ness** *n*

un·set·tle \ˌən-'set-l\ *vb* **un·set·tled**; **un·set·tling** : to move or loosen from a settled position : DISTURB

un·set·tled \ˌən-'set-ld\ *adj* **1** : not fixed in position or character ⟨*unsettled* weather⟩ **2** : DISTURBED ⟨*unsettled* waters⟩ **3** : not decided in mind **4** : not paid ⟨an *unsettled* account⟩ **5** : not occupied by settlers

un·shak·a·ble \ˌən-'shā-kə-bəl\ *adj* : FIRM

un·shaped \ˌən-'shāpt\ *adj* **1** : not dressed or finished to final form **2** : imperfect especially in form ⟨*unshaped* ideas⟩

un·sheathe \ˌən-'shēth\ *vb* **un·sheathed**; **un·sheath·ing** : to draw from or as if from a sheath or scabbard

un·sight·ly \ˌən-'sīt-lē\ *adj* : unpleasant to the sight : UGLY — **un·sight·li·ness** *n*

un·skilled \,ən-'skild\ *adj* **1** : not skilled **2** : not requiring skill ⟨*unskilled* jobs⟩

un·skill·ful \,ən-'skil-fəl\ *adj* : not skillful : lacking in skill — **un·skill·ful·ly** *adv*

un·sound \,ən-'saund\ *adj* **1** : not healthy or whole **2** : not mentally normal **3** : not firmly made or placed **4** : not valid or true — **un·sound·ly** *adv* — **un·sound·ness** *n*

un·speak·a·ble \,ən-'spē-kə-bəl\ *adj* **1** : impossible to express in words ⟨*unspeakable* thoughts⟩ **2** : extremely bad ⟨*unspeakable* conduct⟩ — **un·speak·a·bly** \-blē\ *adv*

un·spec·i·fied \,ən-'spes-ə-,fīd\ *adj* : not specified

un·spoiled \,ən-'spoild\ *adj* : not spoiled

un·sta·ble \,ən-'stā-bəl\ *adj* **1** : not stable : FLUCTUATING **2** : FICKLE

un·stead·y \,ən-'sted-ē\ *adj* **un·stead·i·er**; **un·stead·i·est** : not steady : UNSTABLE — **un·stead·i·ly** \-'sted-l-ē\ *adv*

un·stressed \,ən-'strest\ *adj* : not stressed

un·suc·cess·ful \,ən-sək-'ses-fəl\ *adj* : not successful — **un·suc·cess·ful·ly** *adv*

un·suit·a·ble \,ən-'süt-ə-bəl\ *adj* : not suitable

un·sup·port·ed \,ən-sə-'pōrt-əd\ *adj* **1** : not supported or verified **2** : not sustained

un·sur·passed \,ən-sər-'past\ *adj* : not surpassed (as in excellence)

un·sus·pect·ing \,ən-sə-'spek-ting\ *adj* : having no suspicion

un·tan·gle \,ən-'tang-gəl\ *vb* **un·tan·gled**; **un·tan·gling** **1** : to remove a tangle from **2** : to straighten out ⟨*untangle* a problem⟩

un·tanned \,ən-'tand\ *adj* : not put through a tanning process

un·think·a·ble \,ən-'thing-kə-bəl\ *adj* : not to be thought of or considered as possible

un·think·ing \,ən-'thing-king\ *adj* : not thinking : THOUGHTLESS

un·ti·dy \,ən-'tīd-ē\ *adj* **un·ti·di·er**; **un·ti·di·est** : not neat : SLOVENLY — **un·ti·di·ly** \-'tīd-l-ē\ *adv* — **un·ti·di·ness** \-'tīd-ē-nəs\ *n*

un·tie \,ən-'tī\ *vb* **un·tied**; **un·ty·ing** *or* **un·tie·ing** **1** : to free from something that ties, fastens, or restrains **2** : DISENTANGLE

¹un·til \ən-,til\ *prep* : up to the time of ⟨worked *until* five o'clock⟩

²until *conj* **1** : up to the time that ⟨wait *until* he calls⟩ **2** : up to the point that ⟨ran *until* he was breathless⟩

un·tilled \,ən-'tild\ *adj* : not tilled

¹un·time·ly \,ən-'tīm-lē\ *adv* **1** : at an inopportune time **2** : PREMATURELY

²untimely *adj* **1** : occurring or done before the due, natural, or proper time **2** : INOPPORTUNE, UNSEASONABLE — **un·time·li·ness** *n*

un·tir·ing \,ən-'tī-ring\ *adj* : not becoming or making tired : TIRELESS — **un·tir·ing·ly** *adv*

un·to \'ən-tə, -tü\ *prep* : TO

un·told \,ən-'tōld\ *adj* **1** : not told : not revealed ⟨*untold* secrets⟩ **2** : not counted : VAST ⟨*untold* resources⟩

un·tow·ard \,ən-'tō-ərd\ *adj* : INCONVENIENT, UNFORTUNATE ⟨an *untoward* accident⟩

un·true \,ən-'trü\ *adj* **1** : not faithful : DISLOYAL **2** : not exact **3** : not according with the facts : FALSE — **un·tru·ly** *adv*

un·truth \,ən-'trüth\ *n* **1** : lack of truthfulness : FALSITY **2** : FALSEHOOD

un·truth·ful \,ən-'trüth-fəl\ *adj* : not containing or telling the truth : FALSE — **un·truth·ful·ly** *adv* — **un·truth·ful·ness** *n*

un·used \,ən-'yüzd, *1 often* -'yüst *before* "*to*"\ *adj* **1** : not accustomed **2** : FRESH, NEW **3** : not being in use : IDLE

un·u·su·al \,ən-'yü-zhə-wəl\ *adj* : not usual **syn** *see* ABNORMAL — **un·u·su·al·ly** *adv*

un·ut·ter·a·ble \,ən-'ət-ə-rə-bəl\ *adj* **1** : not capable of being pronounced **2** : not capable of being put into words : INEXPRESSIBLE

un·veil \,ən-'vāl\ *vb* **1** : to remove a veil or covering from ⟨*unveil* a statue⟩ **2** : to remove a veil : reveal oneself

un·want·ed \,ən-'wȯnt-əd\ *adj* : not wanted

un·war·y \,ən-'waər-ē\ *adj* **un·war·i·er**; **un·war·i·est** : not alert — **un·war·i·ness** *n*

un·wea·ried \,ən-'wiər-ēd\ *adj* : not tired

un·well \,ən-'wel\ *adj* : being in poor health

un·whole·some \,ən-'hōl-səm\ *adj* : not good for physical, mental, or moral welfare

un·wield·y \,ən-'wēl-dē\ *adj* **un·wield·i·er**; **un·wield·i·est** : not easily handled or managed because of size or weight — **un·wield·i·ness** *n*

un·will·ing \,ən-'wil-ing\ *adj* : not willing — **un·will·ing·ly** *adv* — **un·will·ing·ness** *n*

un·wind \,ən-'wīnd\ *vb* **un·wound** \-'waund\; **un·wind·ing** **1** : to cause to uncoil **2** : to become uncoiled or disentangled

un·wise \,ən-'wīz\ *adj* : not wise : FOOLISH — **un·wise·ly** *adv*

un·wor·thy \,ən-'wər-thē\ *adj* **un·wor·thi·er**; **un·wor·thi·est** : not worthy — **un·wor·thi·ly** \-thə-lē\ *adv* — **un·wor·thi·ness** \-thē-nəs\ *n*

un·wrap \,ən-'rap\ *vb* **un·wrapped**; **un·wrap·ping** : to remove the wrapping from

un·writ·ten \,ən-'rit-n\ *adj* **1** : not in writing : ORAL **2** : BLANK

un·yield·ing \,ən-'yēl-ding\ *adj* **1** : characterized by lack of softness or flexibility **2** : characterized by firmness or determination

un·yoke \,ən-'yōk\ *vb* **un·yoked**; **un·yok·ing** : to free (as oxen) from a yoke

¹up \'əp\ *adv* **1** : in or to a higher position

: away from the center of the earth **2** : from beneath a surface (as ground or water) ⟨come *up* for air⟩ **3** : from below the horizon **4** : in or into an upright position ⟨stand *up*⟩ **5** : out of bed **6** : with greater force or intensity ⟨speak *up*⟩ **7** : in or into a better or more advanced state ⟨bring *up* a child⟩ **8** : in or into a state of greater intensity or activity ⟨stir *up* a fire⟩ **9** : into existence, evidence, or knowledge ⟨the missing ring turned *up*⟩ **10** : into consideration ⟨bring the matter *up*⟩ **11** : into possession or custody ⟨gave himself *up*⟩ **12** : ENTIRELY ⟨the house burned *up*⟩ **13** — used for emphasis ⟨clean *up* a room⟩ **14** : ASIDE, BY ⟨lay *up* supplies⟩ **15** : into a state of enclosure or confinement ⟨seal *up* a package⟩ **16** : so as to approach, arrive, or overtake ⟨came *up* the street⟩ **17** : in or into pieces ⟨tear *up* paper⟩ **18** : to a stop ⟨pull *up*⟩

²up *adj* **1** : risen above the horizon or ground ⟨the corn is *up*⟩ **2** : being out of bed **3** : relatively high ⟨the river is *up*⟩ **4** : RAISED ⟨windows are *up*⟩ **5** : BUILT ⟨the house is *up*⟩ **6** : moving, inclining, or directed upward ⟨an *up* escalator⟩ **7** : marked by activity or excitement ⟨eager to be *up* and doing⟩ **8** : READY, PREPARED ⟨felt *up* to the task⟩ **9** : going on : taking place ⟨find out what is *up*⟩ **10** : EXPIRED, ENDED ⟨time is *up*⟩ **11** : well informed : SKILLED ⟨was *up* on the news⟩

³up *vb* **upped; up·ping 1** : to act abruptly or surprisingly ⟨she *upped* and left home⟩ **2** : to rise from a lying or sitting position **3** : ASCEND **4** : RAISE

⁴up *prep* **1** : to, toward, or at a higher point of ⟨*up* a ladder⟩ **2** : to or toward the source of ⟨*up* a river⟩ **3** : along toward the higher or farther end ⟨walk *up* an alley⟩

⁵up *n* : a period or state of prosperity or success ⟨had his *ups* and downs⟩

up·braid \ˌəp-'brād\ *vb* : to criticize, reproach, or scold severely

up·bring·ing \'əp-ˌbring-ing\ *n* : the process of bringing up and training

up·com·ing \ˌəp-ˌkəm-ing\ *adj* : FORTHCOMING

up·draft \'əp-ˌdraft\ *n* : an upward movement of gas (as air)

up·end \ˌəp-'end\ *vb* : to set, stand, or rise on end

¹up·grade \'əp-ˌgrād\ *n* **1** : an upward grade or slope (as of a road) **2** : INCREASE, RISE

²upgrade *vb* **up·grad·ed; up·grad·ing** : to raise to a higher grade or position

up·heav·al \ˌəp-'hē-vəl\ *n* **1** : the action or an instance of upheaving **2** : an instance of violent agitation or change

up·heave \ˌəp-'hēv\ *vb* **up·heaved; up·heav·ing** : to heave or lift up from beneath

¹up·hill \'əp-'hil\ *adv* **1** : upward on a hill or incline **2** : against difficulties

²up·hill \ˌəp-ˌhil\ *adj* **1** : going up : ASCENDING ⟨an *uphill* trail⟩ **2** : DIFFICULT

up·hold \ˌəp-'hōld\ *vb* **up·held** \-'held\; **up·hold·ing 1** : to give support to **2** : to lift up

up·hol·ster \ˌəp-'hōl-stər\ *vb* : to furnish with or as if with upholstery — **up·hol·ster·er** *n*

up·hol·ster·y \ˌəp-'hōl-stə-rē\ *n, pl* **up·hol·ster·ies** : materials used to make a soft covering for a seat

up·keep \'əp-ˌkēp\ *n* : the act or cost of keeping something in good condition

up·land \'əp-lənd\ *n* : high land especially at some distance from a coast or sea

¹up·lift \ˌəp-'lift\ *vb* **1** : to lift up **2** : to improve morally, mentally, or physically **3** : RISE

²up·lift \'əp-ˌlift\ *n* : an act, process, or result of uplifting

up·on \ə-'pȯn, -'pän\ *prep* : ON

¹up·per \'əp-ər\ *adj* **1** : higher in position or rank **2** : being toward the interior or source ⟨the *upper* river⟩

²upper *n* : something (as the parts of a shoe above the sole) that is upper

upper hand *n* : MASTERY, ADVANTAGE

up·per·most \'əp-ər-ˌmōst\ *adj* **1** : farthest up **2** : occupying the most prominent or most important position

up·raise \ˌəp-'rāz\ *vb* **up·raised; up·rais·ing** : to raise or lift up

¹up·right \'əp-ˌrīt\ *adj* **1** : PERPENDICULAR, VERTICAL **2** : erect in carriage or posture **3** : morally correct : HONORABLE — **up·right·ly** *adv* — **up·right·ness** *n*

²upright *n* **1** : the state of being upright **2** : something upright

up·rise \ˌəp-'rīz\ *vb* **up·rose** \-'rōz\; **up·ris·en** \-'riz-n\; **up·ris·ing** \-'rī-zing\ **1** : RISE **2** : to get up (as from sleep)

up·ris·ing \'əp-ˌrī-zing\ *n* : REBELLION

up·roar \'əp-ˌrȯr\ *n* : a state of commotion, excitement, or violent disturbance

up·root \ˌəp-'rüt, -'rút\ *vb* **1** : to remove by or as if by pulling up by the roots **2** : to displace from a country or a traditional habitat

¹up·set \ˌəp-'set, 'əp-ˌset\ *adj* : UNSETTLED, DISTURBED ⟨an *upset* stomach⟩

²up·set \ˌəp-'set\ *vb* **up·set; up·set·ting 1** : to force or be forced out of the usual upright, level, or proper position : OVERTURN **2** : to disturb emotionally **3** : to make somewhat ill **4** : DISARRANGE **5** : to defeat unexpectedly

³up·set \'əp-ˌset\ *n* : an act or result of upsetting : a state of being upset

---

j job   ng sing   ō low   ȯ moth   ȯi coin   th thin   <u>th</u> this   ü boot   ú foot   y you   yü few   yú furious   zh vision

up·shot \'əp-ˌshät\ *n* : RESULT, OUTCOME

up·side \'əp-ˌsīd\ *n* : the upper side or part

up·side down \ˌəp-ˌsīd-'daůn\ *adv* **1** : with the upper and the lower parts reversed in position **2** : in or into great disorder

upside–down *adj* **1** : having the upper and the lower parts reversed in position **2** : marked by great disorder

up·stage \'əp-'stāj\ *adv (or adj)* : toward or at the rear of a theatrical stage

¹up·stairs \'əp-'staərz\ *adv* : up the stairs : on or to a higher floor

²up·stairs \'əp-ˌstaərz\ *adj* : situated on or relating to an upper floor

³up·stairs \'əp-'staərz\ *n* : the part of a building above the ground floor

up·stand·ing \ˌəp-'stan-ding\ *adj* **1** : ERECT **2** : STRAIGHTFORWARD, HONEST

up·start \'əp-ˌstärt\ *n* **1** : one who has risen suddenly to wealth or power **2** : one who claims more personal importance than he deserves

up·stream \'əp-'strēm\ *adv* : at or toward the source of a stream ⟨rowed *upstream*⟩

up·swing \'əp-ˌswing\ *n* : an upward swing : a marked increase

up–to–date \ˌəp-tə-'dāt\ *adj* **1** : extending up to the present time **2** : abreast of the times

up·town \'əp-'taůn\ *adv* : to, toward, or in the upper part of a town or city

¹up·turn \'əp-ˌtərn, əp-'tərn\ *vb* **1** : to turn up or over **2** : to turn or direct upward

²up·turn \'əp-ˌtərn\ *n* : an upward turn

¹up·ward \'əp-wərd\ *or* **up·wards** \-wərdz\ *adv* **1** : in a direction from lower to higher **2** : toward a higher or better condition **3** : toward a greater amount or higher number, degree, or rate

²upward *adj* : directed toward or situated in a higher place or level — **up·ward·ly** *adv*

up·wind \'əp-'wind\ *adv (or adj)* : in the direction from which the wind is blowing

u·ra·ni·um \yů-'rā-nē-əm\ *n* [named in 1789 after *Uranus*, the most recently discovered planet] : a radioactive metallic chemical element used as a source of atomic energy

U·ra·nus \'yůr-ə-nəs\ *n* : the planet that is seventh in order of distance from the sun and has a diameter of about 29,400 miles

ur·ban \'ər-bən\ *adj* : of, relating to, or being a city ⟨*urban* life⟩

ur·bane \ˌər-'bān\ *adj* : polite or polished in manner — **ur·ban·i·ty** \-'ban-ət-ē\ *n*

ur·chin \'ər-chən\ *n* **1** : a pert or roguish youngster **2** : SEA URCHIN

u·re·a \yů-'rē-ə\ *n* : a soluble compound of nitrogen that is the chief solid component of the urine of a mammal and is formed by the breakdown of protein

¹urge \'ərj\ *vb* **urged**; **urg·ing** **1** : to present, advocate, or demand earnestly ⟨*urge* a plan⟩ **2** : to try to persuade or influence ⟨*urge* a guest to stay⟩ **3** : to force or impel to some course or action ⟨the dog *urged* the sheep onward⟩

²urge *n* : a force or impulse that urges

ur·gen·cy \'ər-jən-sē\ *n, pl* **ur·gen·cies** **1** : the quality or state of being urgent **2** : URGE

ur·gent \'ər-jənt\ *adj* **1** : calling for immediate attention ⟨an *urgent* need⟩ **2** : conveying a sense of urgency ⟨an *urgent* manner⟩ **3** : urging insistently — **ur·gent·ly** *adv*

u·ri·nal \'yůr-ən-l\ *n* **1** : a receptacle for urine **2** : a place for urinating

u·ri·nate \'yůr-ə-ˌnāt\ *vb* **u·ri·nat·ed**; **u·ri·nat·ing** : to discharge urine

u·rine \'yůr-ən\ *n* : the yellowish fluid secreted by the kidneys and discharged from the body as waste

urn \'ərn\ *n* **1** : a vessel usually in the form of a vase resting on a pedestal **2** : a closed vessel with a spigot used for serving a hot beverage ⟨coffee *urn*⟩

urn 1

us \əs, 'əs\ *pron, objective case of* WE

us·a·ble \'yü-zə-bəl\ *adj* : suitable or fit for use

us·age \'yü-sij, -zij\ *n* **1** : customary practice or procedure **2** : the way in which words and phrases are actually used **3** : the action of using : USE **4** : manner of treating ⟨hard *usage*⟩

¹use \'yüs\ *n* **1** : the act or practice of employing something ⟨put knowledge to *use*⟩ **2** : the fact or state of being used ⟨a book in daily *use*⟩ **3** : way of using ⟨the proper *use* of tools⟩ **4** : the ability or power to use something ⟨have the *use* of the limbs⟩ **5** : USEFULNESS **6** : the occasion or need to employ **7** : LIKING ⟨had no *use* for him⟩

urn 2

²use \'yüz\ *vb* **used**; **us·ing** **1** : to put into action or service : EMPLOY **2** : to consume or take (as a drug) regularly **3** : to carry out a purpose or action by means of ⟨*use* tact⟩ **4** : to behave toward : TREAT ⟨*used* the horse cruelly⟩ **5** — used with *to* to indicate a former practice, fact, or state ⟨said winters *used* to be harder⟩ — **us·er** *n*

used \'yüzd, 3 *often* 'yüst *before* "to"\ *adj* **1** : employed in accomplishing something **2** : SECONDHAND **3** : ACCUSTOMED

use·ful \'yüs-fəl\ *adj* : capable of being put to use : USABLE ⟨*useful* scraps of material⟩ — **use·ful·ly** *adv* — **use·ful·ness** *n*

use·less \'yüs-ləs\ *adj* : having or being of no use — **use·less·ly** *adv* — **use·less·ness** *n*

¹ush·er \'əsh-ər\ *n* : one who escorts persons to seats

²usher *vb* **1** : to conduct to a place **2** : to precede as a harbinger or forerunner

u·su·al \'yü-zhə-wəl\ *adj* : being in common use : CUSTOMARY — **u·su·al·ly** *adv*

   syn USUAL, CUSTOMARY, HABITUAL all mean commonly or ordinarily found or practiced. USUAL stresses the absence of any strangeness, newness, or unexpectedness ⟨the *usual* spring rains did not come⟩ ⟨the *usual* rush of last-minute customers⟩ CUSTOMARY applies to what agrees with the established practices or usages of a particular person or community ⟨it is *customary* for the bride's family to pay for the wedding⟩ ⟨taking his *customary* short early morning walk with the dog⟩ HABITUAL describes acts or ways of acting that are fixed by long repetition so that they are followed without conscious intent ⟨*habitual* disregard of speed laws⟩

u·surp \yu̇-'sərp, -'zərp\ *vb* : to seize and hold by force or without right ⟨*usurp* a throne⟩ — **u·surp·er** *n*

u·ten·sil \yu̇-'ten-səl\ *n* **1** : an instrument or vessel used in a household and especially a kitchen **2** : an article serving a useful purpose

u·ter·us \'yüt-ə-rəs\ *n, pl* **u·ter·i** \'yüt-ə-,rī\ : the organ of a female mammal in which the young develop before birth

u·til·i·ty \yu̇-'til-ət-ē\ *n, pl* **u·til·i·ties** **1** : USEFULNESS **2** : something useful or designed for use **3** : a business organization performing a public service and subject to special governmental regulation

u·ti·li·za·tion \,yüt-l-ə-'zā-shən\ *n* : the action of utilizing : the state of being utilized

u·ti·lize \'yüt-l-,īz\ *vb* **u·ti·lized; u·ti·liz·ing** : to make use of especially for a practical purpose

¹ut·most \'ət-,mōst\ *adj* **1** : situated at the farthest point : EXTREME **2** : of the greatest or highest degree, quantity, or amount

²utmost *n* : the most possible

¹ut·ter \'ət-ər\ *adj* : ABSOLUTE, TOTAL ⟨an *utter* impossibility⟩ ⟨*utter* strangers⟩ — **ut·ter·ly** *adv*

²utter *vb* **1** : to send forth as a sound **2** : to express in usually spoken words

ut·ter·ance \'ət-ə-rəns\ *n* **1** : something uttered **2** : the action of uttering : SPEECH

ut·ter·most \'ət-ər-,mōst\ *adj* : UTMOST

v \'vē\ *n, often cap* **1** : the twenty-second letter of the English alphabet **2** : the roman numeral 5

va·can·cy \'vā-kən-sē\ *n, pl* **va·can·cies** **1** : a vacating of an office, position, or piece of property **2** : a vacant office, position, or tenancy **3** : empty space : VOID **4** : the state of being vacant

va·cant \'vā-kənt\ *adj* **1** : not occupied or used **2** : free from business or care **3** : FOOLISH **syn** see EMPTY

va·cate \'vā-,kāt\ *vb* **va·cat·ed; va·cat·ing** **1** : to make void : ANNUL **2** : to make vacant

¹va·ca·tion \vā-'kā-shən\ *n* **1** : a period during which activity (as of a school) is suspended **2** : a period spent away from home or business in travel or recreation

²vacation *vb* : to take or spend a vacation — **va·ca·tion·er** *n*

vac·ci·nate \'vak-sə-,nāt\ *vb* **vac·ci·nat·ed; vac·ci·nat·ing** : to inoculate with weak germs in order to produce immunity to a disease

vac·ci·na·tion \,vak-sə-'nā-shən\ *n* **1** : the act of vaccinating **2** : the scar left by vaccinating

vac·cine \vak-'sēn, 'vak-,sēn\ *n* [from Latin *vaccinus*, an adjective meaning "of cows", from *vacca* "cow", because the first vaccine was produced from cows] : material (as a preparation of killed or weakened bacteria or virus) used in vaccinating

vac·il·late \'vas-ə-,lāt\ *vb* **vac·il·lat·ed; vac·il·lat·ing** **1** : FLUCTUATE **2** : to incline first to one course or opinion and then to another

va·cu·i·ty \va-'kyü-ət-ē\ *n, pl* **va·cu·i·ties** **1** : an empty space **2** : EMPTINESS, HOLLOWNESS **3** : vacancy of mind **4** : a foolish or inane remark

vac·u·ous \'vak-yə-wəs\ *adj* **1** : EMPTY, VACANT **2** : DULL, STUPID — **vac·u·ous·ly** *adv* — **vac·u·ous·ness** *n*

¹vac·u·um \'vak-yə-wəm\ *n, pl* **vac·u·ums** or **vac·u·a** \-yə-wə\ **1** : a space completely empty of matter **2** : a space almost exhausted of air (as by a pump) **3** : VOID, GAP

²vacuum *adj* : of, containing, producing, or using a partial vacuum

³vacuum *vb* : to use a vacuum cleaner on

vacuum bottle *n* : a cylindrical container with a vacuum between an inner and an outer wall used to keep liquids hot or cold

vacuum cleaner *n* : an electrical appliance for cleaning (as floors or rugs) by suction

vacuum tube *n* : an electron tube having a high degree of vacuum

¹vag·a·bond \'vag-ə-ˌbänd\ *adj* : moving from place to place without a fixed home

²vagabond *n* : one who leads a vagabond life

va·ga·ry \'vā-gə-rē, və-'geər-ē\ *n, pl* **va·ga·ries** : an odd or eccentric idea or action : CAPRICE

va·gi·na \və-'jī-nə\ *n* : a canal leading out from the uterus

¹va·grant \'vā-grənt\ *n* : a person who wanders idly from place to place without a home or apparent means of support

²vagrant *adj* **1** : wandering about from place to place usually with no means of support **2** : RANDOM, CAPRICIOUS

vague \'vāg\ *adj* **1** : not clearly expressed **2** : not clearly understood **3** : not sharply outlined — **vague·ly** *adv* — **vague·ness** *n*

vain \'vān\ *adj* **1** : WORTHLESS **2** : not succeeding : FUTILE **3** : proud of one's looks or abilities — **vain·ly** *adv* — **in vain** **1** : without success **2** : IRREVERENTLY

vain·glo·ri·ous \vān-'glōr-ē-əs\ *adj* : being vain and boastful — **vain·glo·ri·ous·ly** *adv* — **vain·glo·ri·ous·ness** *n*

vain·glo·ry \'vān-ˌglōr-ē\ *n* : excessive pride especially in one's achievements

vale \'vāl\ *n* : VALLEY

val·e·dic·tion \ˌval-ə-'dik-shən\ *n* : FAREWELL

val·e·dic·to·ri·an \ˌval-ə-ˌdik-'tōr-ē-ən\ *n* : a student usually of the highest rank in a graduating class who delivers the farewell speech at commencement

val·en·tine \'val-ən-ˌtīn\ *n* **1** : a sweetheart chosen or complimented on St. Valentine's Day **2** : a gift or greeting sent or given on St. Valentine's Day

val·et \'val-ət, va-'lā\ *n* : a male servant or hotel employee who takes care of a man's clothes and performs personal services

val·iant \'val-yənt\ *adj* **1** : boldly brave : COURAGEOUS **2** : performed with valor : HEROIC — **val·iant·ly** *adv*

val·id \'val-əd\ *adj* **1** : founded on truth or fact **2** : binding in law — **val·id·ly** *adv*

syn VALID, SOUND, CONVINCING are all applied to whatever gives the impression of being true, real, or based on sound information or judgment. VALID is used of something about which no objection can be made because it is supported or justified by fact, law, or reason ⟨a *valid* contract⟩ ⟨illness is a *valid* excuse for missing school⟩ SOUND emphasizes being free from imperfections and errors and also stresses being based on a solid foundation of right or truth ⟨wrote a *sound* report on the class project⟩ CONVINCING refers to something that seems so valid or sound that it demands agreement ⟨gave a *convincing* speech against using animals for medical experiments⟩ but of the three words is the only one in which the soundness may be apparent rather than real ⟨his story was *convincing* but turned out to be totally untrue⟩

val·i·date \'val-ə-ˌdāt\ *vb* **val·i·dat·ed; val·i·dat·ing** **1** : to make valid **2** : CONFIRM

va·lid·i·ty \və-'lid-ət-ē\ *n* : the quality or state of being valid

va·lise \və-'lēs\ *n* : TRAVELING BAG

val·ley \'val-ē\ *n, pl* **val·leys** : a tract of lowland between ranges of hills or mountains

val·or \'val-ər\ *n* : COURAGE

val·or·ous \'val-ə-rəs\ *adj* : BRAVE — **val·or·ous·ly** *adv*

¹val·u·a·ble \'val-yə-wə-bəl\ *adj* **1** : worth a great deal of money **2** : of great use or service

²valuable *n* : a personal possession (as a jewel) of relatively great value

¹val·ue \'val-yü\ *n* **1** : a fair return or equivalent in goods, services, or money for something exchanged **2** : worth in money **3** : relative worth, utility, or importance **4** : something (as an ideal) inherently valuable or desirable — **val·ue·less** \-ləs\ *adj*

²value *vb* **val·ued; val·u·ing** **1** : to estimate the worth of : APPRAISE **2** : to rate highly : ESTEEM

valve \'valv\ *n* **1** : a structure in a bodily channel (as a vein) that closes temporarily to obstruct passage of material or permits movement of a fluid in one direction only **2** : a mechanical device by which the flow of liquid, gas, or loose material in bulk may be started, stopped, or regulated by a movable part **3** : one of the distinct pieces of which the shell of some animals (as clams) consists and which are often hinged — **valve·less** \-ləs\ *adj*

valve 2

vam·pire \'vam-ˌpīr\ *n* **1** : the body of a dead person believed to come from the grave at night and suck the blood of persons asleep **2** : a person who preys on other people **3** : a bat that feeds or is held to feed on blood

¹van \'van\ *n* : VANGUARD

²van *n* : a usually enclosed wagon or truck for moving goods or animals

va·na·di·um \və-'nād-ē-əm\ *n* : a grayish metallic chemical element used in making a strong alloy of steel

van

van·dal \'van-dəl\ *n* : a person who willfully destroys or defaces property

van·dal·ism \'van-dəl-ˌiz-əm\ *n* : willful destruction or defacement of property

vane \'vān\ *n* **1** : a movable device attached to something high to show which way the wind blows **2** : a flat or curved extended surface attached to an axis and moved by wind or water **3** : the web or flat expanded part of a feather

quill

vane

vane 3

van·guard \'van-ˌgärd\ *n* **1** : the troops moving at the front of an army **2** : the forefront of an action or movement

va·nil·la \və-'nil-ə\ *n* : a flavoring extract made from the long beanlike pods of a tropical American climbing orchid

van·ish \'van-ish\ *vb* : to pass from sight or existence : DISAPPEAR

van·i·ty \'van-ət-ē\ *n, pl* **van·i·ties** **1** : something that is vain **2** : the quality or fact of being vain **3** : a small box for cosmetics

van·quish \'vang-kwish\ *vb* : CONQUER

vap·id \'vap-əd\ *adj* : INSIPID, FLAT — **vap·id·ly** *adv*

va·por \'vā-pər\ *n* **1** : fine particles of matter (as fog or smoke) floating in the air and clouding it **2** : the gaseous state of a substance and especially of a liquid ⟨water *vapor*⟩

va·por·ize \'vā-pə-ˌrīz\ *vb* **va·por·ized; va·por·iz·ing** : to turn from a liquid or solid into vapor

¹var·i·a·ble \'ver-ē-ə-bəl\ *adj* **1** : able or apt to vary : CHANGEABLE **2** : characterized by variations **3** : not true to type — **var·i·a·ble·ness** *n* — **var·i·a·bly** \-blē\ *adv*

²variable *n* **1** : something that is variable **2** : PLACEHOLDER

var·i·ant \'ver-ē-ənt\ *n* **1** : one that exhibits variation from a type or norm **2** : one of two or more different spellings or pronunciations of a word

var·i·a·tion \ˌver-ē-'ā-shən\ *n* **1** : a change in form, position, or condition : ALTERATION **2** : extent of change or difference **3** : divergence in qualities from those typical or usual to a group

var·ied \'veər-ēd\ *adj* **1** : CHANGED, ALTERED **2** : having many forms or types **3** : VARIEGATED

var·i·e·gat·ed \'ver-ē-ə-ˌgāt-əd\ *adj* **1** : having patches, stripes, or marks of different colors **2** : full of variety

va·ri·e·ty \və-'rī-ət-ē\ *n, pl* **va·ri·e·ties** **1** : the quality or state of having different forms or types : DIVERSITY **2** : a collection of different things : ASSORTMENT **3** : something differing from others of the same general kind **4** : entertainment consisting of successive unrelated performances (as dances or skits)

var·i·ous \'ver-ē-əs\ *adj* **1** : of differing kinds **2** : differing one from another : UNLIKE **3** : of an indefinite number — **var·i·ous·ly** *adv*

¹var·nish \'vär-nish\ *n* : a liquid preparation that is spread on a surface and dries into a hard glossy coating

²varnish *vb* : to cover with or as if with varnish

var·si·ty \'vär-sət-ē\ *n, pl* **var·si·ties** : a first team representing a college, school, or club

var·y \'veər-ē\ *vb* **var·ied; var·y·ing** **1** : ALTER, CHANGE **2** : to make or be of different kinds **3** : DEVIATE, SWERVE **4** : to diverge from typical members of a group

vas·cu·lar \'vas-kyə-lər\ *adj* : of, relating to, containing, or being anatomical vessels

vase \'vās, 'vāz\ *n* : a usually round vessel of greater depth than width used chiefly for ornament or for flowers

vas·sal \'vas-əl\ *n* **1** : a person acknowledging another as his feudal lord and protector to whom he owes homage and loyalty **2** : one occupying a dependent or subordinate position

vast \'vast\ *adj* : very great in extent, amount, or degree — **vast·ly** *adv* — **vast·ness** *n*

vase

vat \'vat\ *n* : a large vessel (as a tub) especially for holding liquids in manufacturing processes

vau·de·ville \'vȯd-ə-vəl\ *n* : light theatrical entertainment featuring songs, dances, and comic acts

¹vault \'vȯlt\ *n* **1** : an arched structure of masonry forming a ceiling or roof **2** : an arch suggesting a vault **3** : a room or compartment for storage or safekeeping **4** : a burial chamber

vault 1

²vault *vb* : to form or cover with a vault

³vault *vb* : to leap with the aid of the hands or a pole

⁴vault *n* : LEAP

vaunt \'vȯnt\ *vb* : BRAG, BOAST

veal \'vēl\ *n* : a young calf or its flesh for use as meat

vec·tor \'vek-tər\ *n* : an organism (as a fly) that transmits disease germs

veer \'viər\ *vb* : to change direction or course

vee·ry \'viər-ē\ *n, pl* **vee·ries** : a common brownish woodland thrush of the eastern United States

¹veg·e·ta·ble \'vej-ət-ə-bəl\ *adj* **1** : of, relating to, or made up of plants **2** : obtained from plants **3** : suggesting that of a plant ⟨a *vegetable* existence⟩

²vegetable *n* **1** : PLANT 1 **2** : a plant or plant

part grown for use as human food and usually eaten with the principal course of a meal

veg·e·tar·i·an \,vej-ə-'ter-ē-ən\ n : a person who lives on plants and their products

veg·e·tate \'vej-ə-,tāt\ vb **veg·e·tat·ed; veg·e·tat·ing** : to live or grow in the seemingly effortless passive way of a plant

veg·e·ta·tion \,vej-ə-'tā-shən\ n 1 : the act or process of vegetating 2 : plant life or cover (as of an area)

veg·e·ta·tive \'vej-ə-,tāt-iv\ adj 1 : of, relating to, or functioning in nutrition and growth rather than reproduction 2 : of, relating to, or involving reproduction by other than sexual means

ve·he·mence \'vē-ə-məns\ n : the quality or state of being vehement

ve·he·ment \'vē-ə-mənt\ adj 1 : marked by great force or energy 2 : intensely emotional 3 : strong in effect — **ve·he·ment·ly** adv

ve·hi·cle \'vē-,ik-əl\ n 1 : a medium through which something is transmitted, expressed, or achieved 2 : something used to transport persons or goods

¹veil \'vāl\ n 1 : a length of cloth or net worn by women over the head and shoulders and sometimes over the face 2 : a concealing curtain or cover of cloth 3 : something that covers or conceals like a veil ⟨a veil of secrecy⟩ 4 : the vows or life of a nun ⟨chose to take the veil⟩

²veil vb : to cover or provide with a veil

vein \'vān\ n 1 : a fissure in rock filled with mineral matter ⟨a vein of gold⟩ 2 : one of the blood vessels that carry the blood back to the heart 3 : one of the bundles of fine tubes that make up the framework of a leaf and carry food, water, and nutrients in the plant 4 : one of the thickened parts that support the wing of an insect 5 : a streak of different color or texture (as in marble) 6 : STYLE ⟨spoke in a witty vein⟩ 7 : a pervading element — **veined** \'vānd\ adj

veld or **veldt** \'felt, 'velt\ n : a tract of grassy land especially in southern Africa

vel·lum \'vel-əm\ n 1 : a fine-grained skin of a lamb, kid, or calf prepared for writing on or for binding books 2 : a strong cream-colored paper resembling vellum

ve·loc·i·ty \və-'läs-ət-ē\ n, pl **ve·loc·i·ties** : quickness of motion : SPEED

¹vel·vet \'vel-vət\ n : a usually silk or synthetic fabric with a short thick soft pile

²velvet adj 1 : made of or covered with velvet 2 : VELVETY

vel·vet·y \'vel-vət-ē\ adj : soft and smooth like velvet ⟨a velvety skin⟩

ve·na·tion \vā-'nā-shən, vē-\ n : an arrangement or system of veins

venation in leaves

vend \'vend\ vb : to sell or offer for sale **syn** see SELL — **vend·er** or **ven·dor** \'ven-dər\ n

ven·det·ta \ven-'det-ə\ n : a feud in which the relatives of a murdered man try to take vengeance by killing the murderer or his relatives

¹ve·neer \və-'niər\ n 1 : a thin layer of wood bonded to other wood usually to provide a finer surface or a stronger structure 2 : a protective or ornamental facing (as of brick) 3 : a superficial or false show

²veneer vb : to overlay with a veneer

ven·er·a·ble \'ven-ə-rə-bəl\ adj 1 : deserving to be venerated — often used as a religious title 2 : deserving honor or respect

ven·er·ate \'ven-ə-,rāt\ vb **ven·er·at·ed; ven·er·at·ing** : to regard with reverence or respect

ven·er·a·tion \,ven-ə-'rā-shən\ n 1 : the act of venerating : the state of being venerated 2 : a feeling of reverence or deep regard

ve·ne·re·al \və-'nir-ē-əl\ adj : of or relating to sexual intercourse or to diseases transmitted by it

ve·ne·tian blind \və-,nē-shən-\ n : a blind having thin horizontal slats that can be set to overlap to keep out light or tipped to let light come in between them

ven·geance \'ven-jəns\ n : punishment inflicted in return for an injury or offense : RETRIBUTION

venge·ful \'venj-fəl\ adj : VINDICTIVE — **venge·ful·ly** adv — **venge·ful·ness** n

ve·ni·al \'vē-nē-əl\ adj : capable of being forgiven or excused

venetian blind

ven·i·son \'ven-ə-sən, -ə-zən\ n [from Old French veneison, from Latin venation-, stem of venatio "hunting", and then "the hunted animal"; the Latin noun is from the verb venari "to hunt"] : the flesh of a deer used as food

ven·om \'ven-əm\ n 1 : poisonous matter secreted by an animal (as a snake) and transmitted usually by biting or stinging 2 : something that poisons or embitters the mind or spirit

ven·om·ous \'ven-ə-məs\ adj 1 : full of

venom : POISONOUS 2 : full of spite or malice

ve·nous \'vē-nəs\ *adj* : of, relating to, or full of veins ⟨*venous* blood⟩

¹**vent** \'vent\ *vb* 1 : to provide with an outlet 2 : to serve as an outlet for 3 : to give expression to

²**vent** *n* 1 : OUTLET 2 : an opening for the escape of a gas or liquid

³**vent** *n* : a slit in a garment and especially in the lower part of a seam

ven·ti·late \'vent-l-ˌāt\ *vb* **ven·ti·lat·ed; ven·ti·lat·ing** 1 : to discuss freely and openly 2 : to expose to air and especially to a current of fresh air 3 : to provide with ventilation

ven·ti·la·tion \ˌvent-l-'ā-shən\ *n* 1 : the act or process of ventilating 2 : circulation of air 3 : a system or means of providing fresh air

ven·ti·la·tor \'vent-l-ˌāt-ər\ *n* : a device for introducing fresh air or expelling foul or stagnant air

ven·tral \'ven-trəl\ *adj* : of, relating to, or being on or near the surface of the body that in man is the front but in most animals is the lower surface ⟨a fish's *ventral* fins⟩

ventilator

ven·tri·cle \'ven-tri-kəl\ *n* : a large lower chamber of the heart from which blood is forced into the arteries

ven·tril·o·quist \ven-'tril-ə-kwəst\ *n* : a person skilled in speaking in such a way that the voice seems to come from a source other than the speaker

¹**ven·ture** \'ven-chər\ *vb* **ven·tured; ven·tur·ing** 1 : to expose to risk 2 : to face the risks and dangers of 3 : to offer at the risk of rebuff or censure 4 : to proceed despite danger

²**venture** *n* 1 : an undertaking involving chance, risk, or danger 2 : a venturesome act

ven·ture·some \'ven-chər-səm\ *adj* 1 : inclined to venture : BOLD 2 : involving risk — **ven·ture·some·ly** *adv* — **ven·ture·some·ness** *n*

ven·tur·ous \'ven-chə-rəs\ *adj* : VENTURESOME — **ven·tur·ous·ly** *adv* — **ven·tur·ous·ness** *n*

Ve·nus \'vē-nəs\ *n* : the planet that is second in order of distance from the sun and has a diameter of about 7600 miles

ve·ra·cious \və-'rā-shəs\ *adj* : marked by veracity — **ve·ra·cious·ly** *adv*

ve·rac·i·ty \və-'ras-ət-ē\ *n* 1 : devotion to the truth 2 : ACCURACY, CORRECTNESS

ve·ran·da *or* **ve·ran·dah** \və-'ran-də\ *n* 1 : PORCH 2 : a long roofed gallery extending along one or more sides of a building

verb \'vərb\ *n* : a word that expresses an act, occurrence, or mode of being

¹**ver·bal** \'vər-bəl\ *adj* 1 : of, relating to, or consisting of words 2 : of, relating to, or formed from a verb ⟨*verbal* adjective⟩ 3 : spoken rather than written 4 : word-for-word : VERBATIM **syn** see ORAL — **ver·bal·ly** *adv*

²**verbal** *n* : a word that combines characteristics of a verb with those of a noun or adjective

ver·ba·tim \vər-'bāt-əm\ *adv* (*or adj*) : in the same words used by another

ver·be·na \vər-'bē-nə\ *n* : a garden plant with fragrant leaves and heads of five-petaled white, pink, red, blue, or purple flowers

ver·bi·age \'vər-bē-ij\ *n* : superfluity of words in proportion to sense or content : WORDINESS

ver·bose \vər-'bōs\ *adj* : excessively wordy — **ver·bose·ly** *adv* — **ver·bose·ness** *n*

verbena

ver·bo·ten \vər-'bōt-n\ *adj* : forbidden usually by authority and often unreasonably

ver·dant \'vərd-nt\ *adj* 1 : green in color 2 : green with growing plants — **ver·dant·ly** *adv*

ver·dict \'vər-dikt\ *n* 1 : the decision reached by a jury 2 : OPINION, JUDGMENT

ver·dure \'vər-jər\ *n* : green vegetation

¹**verge** \'vərj\ *n* 1 : something that borders, limits, or bounds : EDGE 2 : BRINK, THRESHOLD

²**verge** *vb* **verged; verg·ing** : to be on the verge

³**verge** *vb* **verged; verg·ing** 1 : to move in a particular direction : INCLINE 2 : to be in transition or change

ver·i·fi·ca·tion \ˌver-ə-fə-'kā-shən\ *n* : the act or process of verifying : the state of being verified

ver·i·fy \'ver-ə-ˌfī\ *vb* **ver·i·fied; ver·i·fy·ing** 1 : to prove to be true or correct : CONFIRM 2 : to check or test the accuracy of

ver·i·ly \'ver-ə-lē\ *adv* : in fact : CERTAINLY

ver·i·si·mil·i·tude \ˌver-ə-sə-'mil-ə-ˌtüd, -ˌtyüd\ *n* : the quality or state of appearing to be true : PROBABILITY

ver·i·ta·ble \'ver-ət-ə-bəl\ *adj* : ACTUAL, TRUE — **ver·i·ta·bly** \-blē\ *adv*

ver·i·ty \'ver-ət-ē\ *n, pl* **ver·i·ties** 1 : TRUTH, REALITY 2 : a true fact or statement

ver·mi·cel·li \ˌvər-mə-'chel-ē\ *n* : a food similar to but of smaller diameter than spaghetti

ver·min \'vər-mən\ *n, pl* **vermin** : small common harmful or objectionable animals (as fleas or mice) that are difficult to get rid of

ver·nal \'vərn-l\ *adj* : of, relating to, or characteristic of spring

ver·sa·tile \'vər-sət-l\ *adj* 1 : turning with ease from one thing or position to another 2 : having many uses or applications

---

j job **ng** sing **ō** low **ȯ** moth **ȯi** coin **th** thin **th** this **ü** boot **u̇** foot **y** you **yü** few **yu̇** furious **zh** vision

ver·sa·til·i·ty \ˌvər-sə-'til-ət-ē\ *n* : the quality or state of being versatile

verse \'vərs\ *n* **1** : a line of metrical writing **2** : metrical writing **3** : STANZA **4** : one of the short divisions of a chapter in the Bible

versed \'vərst\ *adj* : familiar from experience, study, or practice : SKILLED

ver·si·fy \'vər-sə-ˌfī\ *vb* **ver·si·fied; ver·si·fy·ing** **1** : to write verse **2** : to turn into verse

ver·sion \'vər-zhən\ *n* **1** : a translation especially of the Bible **2** : an account or description from a particular point of view **3** : an adaptation of a literary or musical work **4** : a form or variant of an original

ver·sus \'vər-səs\ *prep* : AGAINST

ver·te·bra \'vərt-ə-brə\ *n, pl* **ver·te·brae** \-brē\ : one of the bony segments making up the backbone

¹ver·te·brate \'vərt-ə-brət\ *adj* **1** : having vertebrae or a backbone **2** : of or relating to the vertebrates ⟨*vertebrate* anatomy⟩

²vertebrate *n* : any of a large group of animals that includes the fishes, amphibians, reptiles, birds, and mammals and is characterized by a segmented backbone that extends down the back of the body

ver·tex \'vər-ˌteks\ *n, pl* **ver·ti·ces** \'vərt-ə-ˌsēz\ *or* **ver·tex·es** **1** : the common endpoint of two rays that intersect **2** : the point opposite to and farthest from the base of a geometrical figure

¹ver·ti·cal \'vərt-i-kəl\ *adj* **1** : directly overhead **2** : rising perpendicularly from a level surface : UPRIGHT — **ver·ti·cal·ly** *adv*

²vertical *n* : something (as a line or plane) that is vertical

ver·ti·go \'vərt-i-ˌgō\ *n* : DIZZINESS, GIDDINESS

¹ver·y \'ver-ē\ *adj* **1** : EXACT, PRECISE ⟨the *very* heart of the city⟩ **2** : exactly suitable or necessary **3** : MERE, BARE ⟨the *very* thought frightened him⟩ **4** : SELFSAME, IDENTICAL **5** — used as an intensive ⟨the *very* dogs refused the food⟩

²very *adv* **1** : EXTREMELY **2** : in actual fact : TRULY

ves·per \'ves-pər\ *adj* : of or relating to vespers or the evening

ves·pers \'ves-pərz\ *n pl, often cap* : a late afternoon or evening church service

ves·sel \'ves-əl\ *n* **1** : a hollow or concave utensil (as a cup or bowl) for holding something **2** : a craft larger than a rowboat for navigation of the water **3** : a tube or canal (as an artery) in which a body fluid is contained and conveyed or circulated

¹vest \'vest\ *vb* **1** : to place or give into the possession or discretion of some person or authority **2** : to clothe in vestments

²vest *n* : a man's sleeveless garment worn under a suit coat

ves·ti·bule \'ves-tə-ˌbyül\ *n* : a passage, hall, or room between the outer door and the interior of a building : LOBBY

ves·tige \'ves-tij\ *n* : a trace or visible sign left by something lost or vanished

ves·tig·i·al \ves-'tij-ē-əl\ *adj* : of, relating to, or being a vestige

vest

vest·ment \'vest-mənt\ *n* : an outer garment especially for ceremonial or official wear

¹vet \'vet\ *n* : VETERINARIAN

²vet *vb* **vet·ted; vet·ting** : to examine fully or carefully especially in the capacity of a veterinarian or physician

³vet *n* : VETERAN

¹vet·er·an \'vet-ə-rən\ *n* **1** : a person who has had long experience **2** : a former member of the armed forces especially in war

²veteran *adj* : skilled through experience

Veterans Day *n* : November 11 observed as a legal holiday in commemoration of the end of hostilities in 1918 and 1945

vet·er·i·nar·i·an \ˌvet-ə-rə-'ner-ē-ən\ *n* : a person qualified and authorized to treat diseases and injuries of animals

¹vet·er·i·nar·y \'vet-ə-rə-ˌner-ē\ *adj* : of, relating to, or being the medical care of animals and especially domestic animals

²veterinary *n, pl* **vet·er·i·nar·ies** : VETERINARIAN

¹ve·to \'vēt-ō\ *n, pl* **ve·toes** [from Latin *veto* meaning "I forbid"] **1** : an authoritative prohibition **2** : the power of a chief executive to prevent the enactment of measures passed by a legislature

²veto *vb* **1** : FORBID, PROHIBIT **2** : to refuse assent to (a legislative bill) so as to prevent enactment or cause reconsideration

vex \'veks\ *vb* **1** : to bring trouble, distress, or agitation to **2** : to irritate or annoy by petty provocations **3** : to shake or toss about

vex·a·tion \vek-'sā-shən\ *n* **1** : the quality or state of being vexed **2** : the act of vexing **3** : a cause of trouble or worry

vi·a \ˌvī-ə, ˌvē-ə\ *prep* : by way of ⟨goods shipped *via* the Panama Canal⟩

vi·a·ble \'vī-ə-bəl\ *adj* **1** : capable of living or growing **2** : capable of being put into practice

vi·a·duct \'vī-ə-ˌdəkt\ *n* : a bridge for carrying a road or railroad over something (as a gorge or highway)

viaduct

vi·al \ˈvī-əl\ *n* : a small vessel for liquids (as medicines)

vi·and \ˈvī-ənd\ *n* **1** : an article of food **2** *pl* : FOOD

vi·brant \ˈvī-brənt\ *adj* **1** : VIBRATING, PULSING **2** : pulsating with life, vigor, or activity **3** : readily set in vibration **4** : RESONANT — **vi·brant·ly** *adv*

vi·brate \ˈvī-ˌbrāt\ *vb* **vi·brat·ed; vi·brat·ing** **1** : to swing or move back and forth **2** : to set or be in vibration **3** : to respond sympathetically **4** : FLUCTUATE, WAVER

vi·bra·tion \vī-ˈbrā-shən\ *n* **1** : the action of vibrating : the state of being vibrated **2** : a rapid back-and-forth motion of the particles of an elastic body or medium (as a stretched cord) that produces sound **3** : a trembling motion **4** : wavering in opinion or action

vi·bur·num \vī-ˈbər-nəm\ *n* : any of a group of shrubs often grown for their broad clusters of usually white flowers

vic·ar \ˈvik-ər\ *n* **1** : an administrative deputy **2** : a clergyman who serves as the deputy of a higher church authority

vi·car·i·ous \vī-ˈker-ē-əs, -ˈkar-\ *adj* **1** : acting for another **2** : done or suffered by one person on behalf of another **3** : realized or experienced through sympathetic sharing in the experience of another — **vi·car·i·ous·ly** *adv* — **vi·car·i·ous·ness** *n*

vice \ˈvīs\ *n* **1** : evil conduct : WICKEDNESS **2** : a moral fault or failing

vice- \ˈvīs\ *prefix* : one that takes the place of ⟨*vice*-consul⟩

vice admiral *n* : a commissioned officer in the navy ranking next below an admiral

vice–pres·i·dent \ˈvīs-ˈprez-ə-dənt\ *n* : an official (as of a government) whose rank is next below that of the president and who takes the place of the president when necessary

vice·roy \ˈvīs-ˌròi\ *n* : the governor of a country or province who rules as the representative of a king or queen

vice ver·sa \ˌvī-si-ˈvər-sə, ˈvīs-ˈvər-\ *adv* : with the order reversed

vi·cin·i·ty \və-ˈsin-ət-ē\ *n, pl* **vi·cin·i·ties** **1** : NEARNESS **2** : a surrounding area

vi·cious \ˈvish-əs\ *adj* **1** : given to vice : WICKED **2** : DEFECTIVE, FAULTY **3** : dangerously aggressive **4** : MALICIOUS, SPITEFUL — **vi·cious·ly** *adv* — **vi·cious·ness** *n*

vi·cis·si·tude \və-ˈsis-ə-ˌtüd, -ˌtyüd\ *n* : a change or succession from one thing to another

vic·tim \ˈvik-təm\ *n* **1** : a living being offered as a sacrifice in a religious rite **2** : an individual injured or killed (as by disease)

3 : a person who is cheated, fooled, or damaged by another or by some impersonal force

vic·tim·ize \ˈvik-tə-ˌmīz\ *vb* **vic·tim·ized; vic·tim·iz·ing** : to make a victim of : CHEAT

vic·tor \ˈvik-tər\ *n* : WINNER, CONQUEROR

vic·to·ri·ous \vik-ˈtōr-ē-əs\ *adj* : having won a victory : CONQUERING — **vic·to·ri·ous·ly** *adv*

vic·to·ry \ˈvik-tə-rē\ *n, pl* **vic·to·ries** **1** : the overcoming of an enemy or opponent **2** : achievement of success in a struggle against odds or difficulties

¹**vict·ual** \ˈvit-l\ *n* **1** : food usable by man **2** *pl* : supplies of food

²**victual** *vb* **vict·ualed** *or* **vict·ualled; vict·ual·ing** *or* **vict·ual·ling** **1** : to supply with food **2** : to lay in provisions

vict·ual·ler *or* **vict·ual·er** \ˈvit-l-ər\ *n* **1** : the keeper of a restaurant or tavern **2** : one that furnishes provisions (as to an army)

vi·cu·na \vī-ˈkü-nə, vi-ˈkü-nyə\ *n* : a wild animal of the Andes that is related to the llama and produces a fine lustrous wool

¹**vid·e·o** \ˈvid-ē-ˌō\ *adj* : relating to or used in the transmission or reception of the television image

²**video** *n* : TELEVISION

vie \ˈvī\ *vb* **vied; vy·ing** : CONTEND

¹**view** \ˈvyü\ *n* **1** : the act of seeing or examining **2** : OPINION, JUDGMENT **3** : SCENE, PROSPECT **4** : extent or range of vision **5** : PURPOSE **6** : a pictorial representation

²**view** *vb* **1** : SEE, BEHOLD **2** : to look at carefully **3** : to survey mentally — **view·er** *n*

view·point \ˈvyü-ˌpòint\ *n* : a position from which something is considered

vig·il \ˈvij-əl\ *n* **1** : the day before a religious feast **2** : the act of keeping awake when sleep is customary **3** : WATCH

vig·i·lance \ˈvij-ə-ləns\ *n* : WATCHFULNESS

vig·i·lant \ˈvij-ə-lənt\ *adj* : alertly watchful especially to avoid danger — **vig·i·lant·ly** *adv*

vig·i·lan·te \ˌvij-ə-ˈlant-ē\ *n* : a member of a local volunteer committee organized to suppress and punish crime (as when the processes of law seem inadequate)

vig·or \ˈvig-ər\ *n* **1** : strength or energy of body or mind **2** : INTENSITY, FORCE

vig·or·ous \ˈvig-ə-rəs\ *adj* **1** : having vigor **2** : done with vigor — **vig·or·ous·ly** *adv*

Vi·king \ˈvī-king\ *n* : one of the Scandinavian pirates plundering the coasts of Europe in the eighth to tenth centuries

vile \ˈvīl\ *adj* **vil·er; vil·est** **1** : of little worth or account **2** : WICKED **3** : highly objectionable — **vile·ly** \ˈvīl-lē\ *adv* — **vile·ness** *n*

vil·i·fy \ˈvil-ə-ˌfī\ *vb* **vil·i·fied; vil·i·fy·ing** **1** : DEGRADE **2** : DEFAME

---

j job   ng sing   ō low   ò moth   òi coin   th thin   <u>th</u> this   ü boot   ù foot   y you   yü few   yù furious   zh vision

vil·la \\'vil-ə\\ *n* **1** : a country estate **2** : the rural or suburban residence of a person of wealth

vil·lage \\'vil-ij\\ *n* : a settlement usually larger than a hamlet and smaller than a town

vil·lag·er \\'vil-ij-ər\\ *n* : a resident of a village

vil·lain \\'vil-ən\\ *n* **1** : VILLEIN **2** : a deliberate scoundrel or criminal

vil·lain·ous \\'vil-ə-nəs\\ *adj* **1** : befitting a villain **2** : highly objectionable

vil·lain·y \\'vil-ə-nē\\ *n, pl* **vil·lain·ies** **1** : villainous conduct **2** : a villainous act **3** : WICKEDNESS

vil·lein \\'vil-ən, vi-'lān\\ *n* : a serf of a feudal class gradually changing its status to that of free peasants

vil·lus \\'vil-əs\\ *n, pl* **vil·li** \\'vil-ˌī\\ : one of the tiny finger-shaped processes that line the small intestine and are active in absorbing nutrients

vim \\'vim\\ *n* : ENERGY, VIGOR

vin·di·cate \\'vin-də-ˌkāt\\ *vb* **vin·di·cat·ed; vin·di·cat·ing** **1** : ABSOLVE **2** : CONFIRM, SUBSTANTIATE **3** : to provide defense for : JUSTIFY **4** : to maintain a right to : ASSERT

vin·dic·tive \\vin-'dik-tiv\\ *adj* **1** : disposed to seek revenge **2** : VICIOUS, SPITEFUL — **vin·dic·tive·ly** *adv* — **vin·dic·tive·ness** *n*

vine \\'vīn\\ *n* **1** : GRAPEVINE **2** : a plant whose stem requires support and which climbs by tendrils or twining or creeps along the ground

vin·e·gar \\'vin-i-gər\\ *n* [from Old French *vinaigre*, literally "sour wine", from *vin* wine and *aigre* "sharp", "sour"] : a sour liquid obtained by the fermentation of cider, wine, or malt and used to flavor or preserve foods

vin·e·gar·y \\'vin-i-gə-rē\\ *adj* **1** : resembling vinegar **2** : DISAGREEABLE, CRABBED

vine·yard \\'vin-yərd\\ *n* : a planting of grapevines

vin·tage \\'vint-ij\\ *n* **1** : the grapes or wine produced during one season **2** : a usually superior wine of a particular type, region, and year **3** : a period of origin or manufacture

vi·ol \\'vī-əl\\ *n* : a bowed stringed musical instrument with a fretted neck and usually six strings

vi·o·la \\vē-'ō-lə, *2 is also* vī-\\ *n* **1** : an instrument of the violin family slightly larger and tuned lower than a violin **2** : a hybrid garden flower resembling but smaller than a typical pansy

vi·o·late \\'vī-ə-ˌlāt\\ *vb* **vi·o·lat·ed; vi·o·lat·ing** **1** : to fail to keep : BREAK **2** : PROFANE, DESECRATE **3** : INTERRUPT, DISTURB — **vi·o·la·tor** *n*

viola

vi·o·la·tion \\ˌvī-ə-'lā-shən\\ *n* : an act or instance of violating : the state of being violated

vi·o·lence \\'vī-ə-ləns\\ *n* **1** : the use of physical force so as to do harm to a person or his property **2** : injury especially to something that merits respect or reverence **3** : vigor in physical and especially in destructive action **4** : vehement feeling or expression

vi·o·lent \\'vī-ə-lənt\\ *adj* **1** : marked by extreme force or intense activity **2** : notably furious or vehement **3** : EXTREME, INTENSE **4** : caused by force — **vi·o·lent·ly** *adv*

vi·o·let \\'vī-ə-lət\\ *n* **1** : a wild or garden plant related to the pansies and violas that has small often fragrant and usually solid-colored white, blue, purple, or yellow flowers **2** : a reddish blue

violets

vi·o·lin \\ˌvī-ə-'lin\\ *n* : a bowed stringed musical instrument with four strings that has a shallower body and a more curved bridge than a viol

vi·o·lin·ist \\ˌvī-ə-'lin-əst\\ *n* : a violin player

vi·o·lon·cel·lo \\ˌvī-ə-lən-'chel-ō, ˌvē-\\ *n* : CELLO

vi·per \\'vī-pər\\ *n* : a snake that is or is held to be poisonous

vir·e·o \\'vir-ē-ˌō\\ *n, pl* **vir·e·os** : a small insect-eating songbird that is olive-green or grayish in color

¹vir·gin \\'vər-jən\\ *n* **1** : an unmarried woman devoted to religion **2** : a girl or woman who has not had sexual intercourse

²virgin *adj* **1** : being a virgin : CHASTE **2** : not soiled **3** : not altered by human activity

vir·ile \\'vir-əl\\ *adj* **1** : having the nature, powers, or qualities of a man **2** : ENERGETIC, VIGOROUS **3** : MASTERFUL, FORCEFUL

vir·tu·al \\'vər-chə-wəl\\ *adj* : being in essence or effect but not in fact or name ⟨the *virtual* ruler of the country⟩ — **vir·tu·al·ly** *adv*

vir·tue \\'vər-chü\\ *n* [from Old French *vertu*, from Latin *virtus*, meaning originally "manliness", being derived from *vir* "man"] **1** : moral excellence **2** : a particular moral excellence **3** : an active beneficial power **4** : a desirable or praiseworthy quality

vir·tu·o·so \\ˌvər-chə-'wō-sō\\ *n, pl* **vir·tu·o·sos** *or* **vir·tu·o·si** \\-sē\\ : one who excels in the technique of an art and especially in musical performance

vir·tu·ous \\'vər-chə-wəs\\ *adj* : having or showing virtue — **vir·tu·ous·ly** *adv*

vir·u·lent \\'vir-ə-lənt\\ *adj* : DEADLY

vi·rus \\'vī-rəs\\ *n* **1** : a disease-causing agent too tiny to be seen by the ordinary microscope that may be a living organism or may be a very special kind of protein molecule 2 : a disease caused by a virus

vis·age \'viz-ij\ *n* : FACE, COUNTENANCE

vis·cid \'vis-əd\ *adj* : VISCOUS

vis·count \'vī-ˌkaùnt\ *n* : a member of the British peerage ranking below an earl and above a baron

vis·count·ess \'vī-ˌkaùnt-əs\ *n* 1 : the wife or widow of a viscount 2 : a woman who holds the rank of a viscount in her own right

vis·cous \'vis-kəs\ *adj* : somewhat sticky

vise \'vīs\ *n* : a device with two jaws operated by a screw or lever for hold- ing or clamping work

vise

vis·i·bil·i·ty \ˌviz-ə-'bil-ət-ē\ *n* 1 : the quality or state of being visible 2 : the degree of clearness of the atmosphere

vis·i·ble \'viz-ə-bəl\ *adj* 1 : capable of being seen 2 : readily apparent

¹**vi·sion** \'vizh-ən\ *n* 1 : something seen otherwise than by ordinary sight (as in a dream) 2 : a vivid picture created by the imagination 3 : the act or power of imagina- tion 4 : unusual discernment or foresight 5 : the act or power of seeing : SIGHT 6 : the special sense by which the qualities of an object (as color) are perceived

²**vision** *vb* : IMAGINE

¹**vi·sion·ar·y** \'vizh-ə-ˌner-ē\ *adj* 1 : given to dreaming or imagining 2 : resembling a vision (as in fanciful or impractical quality)

²**visionary** *n, pl* **vi·sion·ar·ies** 1 : one who sees visions 2 : one whose ideas or projects are impractical

¹**vis·it** \'viz-ət\ *vb* 1 : to go to see in order to comfort or help 2 : to call on as an act of courtesy or in a professional capacity 3 : to dwell with for a time as a guest 4 : to come to or upon as a reward, affliction, or punishment 5 : INFLICT 6 : CHAT, CONVERSE

²**visit** *n* 1 : a brief stay : CALL 2 : a stay as a guest 3 : a professional call

vis·i·tor \'viz-ət-ər\ *n* : one that visits

syn VISITOR, GUEST, CALLER all mean someone who visits a person or place. VISITOR is a loose term that can be applied to anyone who visits but it does suggest that something other than business is the purpose of the visit ⟨she had many *visitors* while in the hospital⟩ ⟨thousands of *visitors* throng the fairgrounds⟩ GUEST applies to a visitor who is making a social call usually as a result of an invitation and stresses the idea of hospitality or entertainment ⟨we had four weekend *guests*⟩ ⟨invited the whole

class to be his *guests* at a barbecue⟩ CALLER applies to anyone who seeks entrance to a house or office and it gives no idea of the pur- pose of the visit or the status of the visitor ⟨she would see no *callers* until afternoon⟩

vi·sor \'vī-zər\ *n* 1 : the movable front upper piece of a helmet 2 : a projecting part to protect or shade the eyes

vis·ta \'vis-tə\ *n* : a distant view through or along an avenue or opening

visor on a windshield

vi·su·al \'vizh-ə-wəl\ *adj* 1 : of, relating to, or used in vision 2 : based or depending on sight 3 : appealing to the sense of sight ⟨*visual* aids⟩ — **vi·su·al·ly** *adv*

vi·su·al·ize \'vizh-ə-wə-ˌlīz\ *vb* **vi·su·al·ized**; **vi·su·al·iz·ing** : to see or form a mental image

vi·tal \'vīt-l\ *adj* 1 : of, relating to, or char- acteristic of life 2 : concerned with or necessary to the maintenance of life ⟨*vital* organs⟩ 3 : full of life and vigor 4 : very im- portant — **vi·tal·ly** *adv*

vi·tal·i·ty \vī-'tal-ət-ē\ *n, pl* **vi·tal·i·ties** 1 : the peculiarity distinguishing the living from the nonliving 2 : ENERGY

vi·tals \'vīt-lz\ *n pl* 1 : the vital organs (as heart, lungs, and liver) of the body 2 : the essential parts of something

vi·ta·min \'vīt-ə-mən\ *n* : any of a group of organic substances that are found in natural foods, are essential in small quantities to health, and include one (**vitamin A**) found mostly in animal products and needed for good vision, several (**vitamin B complex**) found in many foods and needed especially for growth, one (**vitamin C**) found in fruits and leafy vegetables and used as an enzyme and to prevent scurvy, and another (**vitamin D**) found in fish-liver oils, eggs, and milk and needed for healthy bone development

vi·ti·ate \'vish-ē-ˌāt\ *vb* **vi·ti·at·ed**; **vi·ti·at·ing** 1 : SPOIL, DEBASE 2 : INVALIDATE

vi·tu·per·a·tion \vī-ˌtü-pə-'rā-shən, -ˌtyü-\ *n* : sustained and bitter verbal abuse

vi·va·cious \və-'vā-shəs, vī-\ *adj* : LIVELY, SPRIGHTLY — **vi·va·cious·ly** *adv*

vi·vac·i·ty \və-'vas-ət-ē, vī-\ *n* : the quality or state of being vivacious

viv·id \'viv-əd\ *adj* 1 : having the appear- ance of vigorous life 2 : very strong or intense ⟨*vivid* red⟩ 3 : producing distinct mental images 4 : acting clearly and vigor- ously syn see GRAPHIC — **viv·id·ly** *adv* — **viv·id·ness** *n*

vi·vip·a·rous \vī-'vip-ə-rəs\ *adj* : giving birth to living young rather than laying eggs

viv·i·sec·tion \ˌviv-ə-'sek-shən\ *n* : the cutting of or operating on a living animal usually for scientific investigation

vix·en \'vik-sən\ *n* 1 : a female fox 2 : an ill-tempered woman

vi·zor *var of* VISOR

vo·cab·u·lar·y \vō-'kab-yə-ˌler-ē\ *n, pl* **vo·cab·u·lar·ies** 1 : a list or collection of words defined or explained 2 : a stock of words used in a language, by a class or individual, or in relation to a subject

vo·cal \'vō-kəl\ *adj* 1 : uttered by the voice : ORAL 2 : composed or arranged for or sung by the human voice 3 : of, relating to, or having the power of producing voice 4 : full of voices : RESOUNDING 5 : expressing oneself freely or insistently in speech — **vo·cal·ly** *adv*

vocal cords *n pl* : membranes at the top of the windpipe that produce vocal sounds when drawn tight and vibrated by the outgoing breath

vo·cal·ist \'vō-kə-ləst\ *n* : SINGER

vo·ca·tion \vō-'kā-shən\ *n* 1 : a summons or strong inclination to a particular state or course of action 2 : the work in which a person is regularly employed : OCCUPATION

vo·ca·tion·al \vō-'kā-shən-l\ *adj* 1 : of, relating to, or concerned with a vocation 2 : concerned with choice of or training in a vocation — **vo·ca·tion·al·ly** *adv*

vo·cif·er·ous \vō-'sif-ə-rəs\ *adj* : NOISY — **vo·cif·er·ous·ly** *adv* — **vo·cif·er·ous·ness** *n*

vod·ka \'väd-kə\ *n* : a colorless alcoholic liquor distilled from a mash (as of rye)

vogue \'vōg\ *n* 1 : popular acceptance or favor 2 : a period of popularity 3 : one that is in fashion at a particular time

¹**voice** \'vȯis\ *n* 1 : sound produced through the mouth by vertebrates and especially by human beings in speaking or shouting 2 : musical sound produced by the vocal cords 3 : the faculty of utterance : SPEECH 4 : a sound resembling or suggesting vocal utterance 5 : a medium of expression 6 : CHOICE

²**voice** *vb* **voiced; voic·ing** : UTTER

voice box *n* : LARYNX

¹**void** \'vȯid\ *adj* 1 : containing nothing : EMPTY 2 : WANTING, DEVOID 3 : NULL

²**void** *n* 1 : empty space 2 : a feeling of want or hollowness

³**void** *vb* 1 : to make empty or vacant 2 : DISCHARGE, EMIT 3 : NULLIFY, ANNUL

vol·a·tile \'väl-ət-l\ *adj* 1 : readily becoming a vapor at a relatively low temperature 2 : LIGHTHEARTED, LIVELY 3 : CHANGEABLE

vol·can·ic \väl-'kan-ik\ *adj* 1 : of or relating to a volcano 2 : explosively violent

vol·ca·no \väl-'kā-nō\ *n, pl* **vol·ca·noes** *or* **vol·ca·nos** 1 : a hole in the earth's crust from which molten or hot rock and steam issue 2 : a hill or mountain composed of material ejected in a volcanic eruption

vole \'vōl\ *n* : any of various small rodents that resemble stocky short-tailed mice or rats and are sometimes destructive to crops

vo·li·tion \vō-'lish-ən\ *n* : the act or power of making one's own choices or decisions : WILL

¹**vol·ley** \'väl-ē\ *n, pl* **vol·leys** 1 : a flight of missiles (as arrows or bullets) 2 : simultaneous discharge of a number of missile weapons (as rifles) 3 : a bursting forth of many things at once 4 : the act of volleying

²**volley** *vb* **vol·leyed; vol·ley·ing** 1 : to discharge in a volley 2 : to hit an object (as a ball) while it is in the air before it touches the ground

vol·ley·ball \'väl-ē-ˌbȯl\ *n* : a game played by volleying a large inflated ball across a net

volt \'vōlt\ *n* : a unit for measuring the force exerted to produce an electric current

volt·age \'vōl-tij\ *n* : electric power measured in volts ⟨the *voltage* of a current⟩

vol·u·ble \'väl-yə-bəl\ *adj* : fluent and smooth in speech — **vol·u·bly** \-blē\ *adv*

vol·ume \'väl-yəm\ *n* 1 : BOOK 2 : any of a series of books forming a complete work or collection 3 : space included within limits as measured in cubic units ⟨the *volume* of a cylinder⟩ 4 : a large amount : MASS 5 : intensity or quantity of tone

vo·lu·mi·nous \və-'lü-mə-nəs\ *adj* 1 : of great volume or bulk 2 : filling or capable of filling a large volume or several volumes

vol·un·tary \'väl-ən-ˌter-ē\ *adj* 1 : done, given, or made in accordance with one's own free will or choice 2 : not accidental : INTENTIONAL 3 : of, relating to, or controlled by the will — **vol·un·tar·i·ly** \ˌväl-ən-'ter-ə-lē\ *adv*
syn VOLUNTARY, INTENTIONAL, DELIBERATE all refer to something done of one's own free will. VOLUNTARY indicates lack of obvious force or pressure ⟨a *voluntary* confession⟩ and may stress the aspect of complete freedom of choice ⟨*voluntary* enlistment⟩ INTENTIONAL emphasizes the fact of doing something on purpose and after giving it at least some thought ⟨an *intentional* insult⟩ DELIBERATE refers to an intentional act in which there is full knowledge and awareness of its nature and probable results ⟨a *deliberate* attempt to stampede the cattle⟩

¹**vol·un·teer** \ˌväl-ən-'tiər\ *n* 1 : one who enters into or offers himself for any service of his own free will 2 : a plant growing spon-

taneously without direct human care especially from seeds lost from a previous crop

²**volunteer** *adj* : of, relating to, or consisting of volunteers ⟨*volunteer* fire department⟩

³**volunteer** *vb* **1** : to offer or bestow voluntarily **2** : to offer oneself as a volunteer

vo·lup·tu·ous \və-'ləp-chə-wəs\ *adj* : giving pleasure to the senses — **vo·lup·tu·ous·ly** *adv* — **vo·lup·tu·ous·ness** *n*

¹**vom·it** \'väm-ət\ *n* : the contents of the stomach thrown up through the mouth

²**vomit** *vb* **1** : to throw up the contents of the stomach through the mouth **2** : to spew forth

vo·ra·cious \vȯ-'rā-shəs, və-\ *adj* **1** : greedy in eating **2** : very eager — **vo·ra·cious·ly** *adv*

vo·ta·ry \'vȯt-ə-rē\ *n, pl* **vo·ta·ries 1** : EN-THUSIAST **2** : a devout or zealous worshiper

¹**vote** \'vōt\ *n* **1** : a formal expression of opinion or will (as by ballot) **2** : the decision reached by voting **3** : the right to vote **4** : the act or process of voting **5** : a group of voters with some common characteristics ⟨the farm *vote*⟩

²**vote** *vb* **vot·ed; vot·ing 1** : to express one's wish or choice by a vote **2** : to make into law by a vote **3** : ELECT **4** : to declare by common consent **5** : PROPOSE, SUGGEST

vot·er \'vōt-ər\ *n* : a person who votes or who has the legal right to vote

vo·tive \'vōt-iv\ *adj* : offered or performed in fulfillment of a vow or in petition, gratitude, or devotion — **vo·tive·ly** *adv*

vouch \'vauch\ *vb* **1** : PROVE **2** : to give a guarantee **3** : to supply supporting evidence

vouch·safe \vauch-'sāf\ *vb* **vouch·safed; vouch·saf·ing** : to grant in a condescending manner

¹**vow** \'vau\ *n* : a solemn promise or assertion

²**vow** *vb* **1** : to make a vow **2** : to bind or commit by a vow

vow·el \'vau-əl\ *n* **1** : a speech sound produced without obstruction or audible friction in the mouth **2** : a letter (as *a, e, i, o, u*) representing a vowel

¹**voy·age** \'vȯi-ij\ *n* : a journey especially by water from one place or country to another

²**voyage** *vb* **voy·aged; voy·ag·ing 1** : to take a trip **2** : SAIL, TRAVERSE — **voy·ag·er** *n*

vul·can·ize \'vəl-kə-ˌnīz\ *vb* **vul·can·ized; vul·can·iz·ing** : to treat rubber or similar material chemically in order to give it useful properties (as strength)

vul·gar \'vəl-gər\ *adj* **1** : of or relating to the common people **2** : lacking cultivation or taste : COARSE **3** : offensive in language

vul·gar·i·ty \ˌvəl-'gar-ət-ē\ *n, pl* **vul·gar·i·ties 1** : the quality or state of being vulgar **2** : a vulgar utterance or action

vul·ner·a·ble \'vəl-nə-rə-bəl\ *adj* **1** : capable of being wounded **2** : open to attack or damage — **vul·ner·a·bly** \-blē\ *adv*

vul·ture \'vəl-chər\ *n* : a large bird related to the hawks and eagles that has a naked head and feeds mostly on animals found dead

vying *pres part of* VIE

w \'dəb-əl-yü\ *n, often cap* : the twenty-third letter of the English alphabet

wab·ble \'wäb-əl\ *var of* WOBBLE

¹**wad** \'wäd\ *n* **1** : a small mass or lump **2** : a soft plug or stopper to retain a charge of powder (as in cartridges) **3** : a soft mass of cotton, cloth, or fibers used to plug up a hole or pad a garment

²**wad** *vb* **wad·ded; wad·ding** : to form into a wad

¹**wad·dle** \'wäd-l\ *vb* **wad·dled; wad·dling** : to walk with short steps swaying like a duck

²**waddle** *n* : a waddling walk

wade \'wād\ *vb* **wad·ed; wad·ing 1** : to walk or step through a substance (as water, mud, or sand) that offers more resistance than air **2** : to move, pass, or go with difficulty **3** : to pass or cross by stepping through water

wading bird *n* : a long-legged shorebird or water bird that wades in water in search of food

wa·fer \'wā-fər\ *n* : a thin crisp cake or cracker

waf·fle \'wäf-əl\ *n* : a crisp cake of pancake batter baked in a waffle iron

waffle iron *n* : a kitchen utensil with two metal parts hinged together and shutting upon each other used for cooking waffles

¹**waft** \'wäft, 'waft\ *vb* : to cause to move or go lightly by the action of waves or winds

²**waft** *n* : a slight breeze

¹**wag** \'wag\ *vb* **wagged; wag·ging** : to swing to and fro or from side to side

²**wag** *n* **1** : a wagging movement **2** : a person full of jokes and humor

¹**wage** \'wāj\ *vb* **waged; wag·ing** : to engage in

²**wage** *n* **1** : payment for labor or services **2** *pl* : RECOMPENSE, REWARD

¹**wa·ger** \'wā-jər\ *n* **1** : BET **2** : the act of betting

²**wager** *vb* : to bet on the result of a contest or question — **wa·ger·er** *n*

wag·gish \'wag-ish\ *adj* **1** : pleasantly mischievous **2** : done in a spirit of harmless mischief

wag·gle \'wag-əl\ *vb* **wag·gled; wag·gling** : to move backward and forward or from side to side

wag·on \'wag-ən\ *n* : a four-wheeled vehicle used for carrying goods

waif \'wāf\ *n* : a stray person or animal

wagon

¹wail \'wāl\ *vb* : to utter a mournful cry : WEEP

²wail *n* : a cry of grief

wain·scot \'wān-skət, -ˌskōt, -ˌskät\ *n* **1** : a wooden and usually paneled lining for a wall of a room **2** : the bottom three or four feet of an inside wall especially when consisting of material different from the rest

wain·scot·ing \'wān-ˌskōt-ing\ *or* **wain·scot·ting** \-ˌskät-\ *n* : WAINSCOT

waist \'wāst\ *n* **1** : the narrow part of the body between the chest and the hips **2** : the central part of a thing when it is narrower or thinner than the rest **3** : a garment or part of a garment covering the body from the neck to the waist

waist

waist·coat \'wāst-ˌkōt, 'wes-kət\ *n, chiefly Brit* : VEST

¹wait \'wāt\ *vb* **1** : to remain in a place looking forward to something that is expected to happen **2** : to be a waiter or waitress at **3** : DELAY — **wait upon 1** : to attend as a servant **2** : to visit on business, out of courtesy, or for purposes of ceremony

²wait *n* **1** : AMBUSH — used chiefly in the expression *lie in wait* **2** : an act or period of waiting

wait·er \'wāt-ər\ *n* : a man who waits on tables (as in a restaurant)

waiting room *n* : a room for the use of persons waiting (as for a train)

wait·ress \'wā-trəs\ *n* : a girl or woman who waits on table

waive \'wāv\ *vb* **waived; waiv·ing** : to give up claim to

¹wake \'wāk\ *vb* **waked** *or* **woke** \'wōk\; **waked** *or* **wo·ken** \'wō-kən\; **wak·ing 1** : to be or remain awake **2** : to remain awake on watch especially over a corpse **3** : AWAKE

²wake *n* **1** : WAKEFULNESS **2** : a watch held over the body of a dead person before burial

³wake *n* **1** : the track left by something moving in the water **2** : a track or path left

wake·ful \'wāk-fəl\ *adj* : SLEEPLESS, ALERT — **wake·ful·ness** *n*

wak·en \'wā-kən\ *vb* : AWAKE

¹walk \'wȯk\ *vb* **1** : to move or cause to move

along on foot at a natural slow gait **2** : to cover or pass over at a walk **3** : to take or cause to take first base with a base on balls

²walk *n* **1** : a going on foot **2** : a place or path for walking **3** : distance to be walked often measured in time required by a walker to cover **4** : social or economic status **5** : manner of walking **6** : BASE ON BALLS

walking stick *n* **1** : a stick used in walking **2** : a sticklike insect with a long round body and long thin legs

walk·out \'wȯk-ˌaȯt\ *n* **1** : a labor strike **2** : the leaving of a meeting or organization as an expression of disapproval

walk·over \'wȯk-ˌō-vər\ *n* : an easy victory

¹wall \'wȯl\ *n* **1** : a structure (as of stone) raised to some height and meant to enclose or shut off a space **2** : something like a wall that separates one thing from another **3** : the side or inner surface of a cavity or vessel — **walled** \'wȯld\ *adj*

²wall *vb* : to build a wall in or around

wall·board \'wȯl-ˌbȯrd\ *n* : a structural material (as of wood pulp) made in large rigid sheets and used for inside walls, paneling, or counter tops

wal·let \'wäl-ət\ *n* : a small flat pocket-size case for carrying paper money and personal papers

wall·eye \'wȯl-ˌī\ *n* : a large vigorous American freshwater sport and food fish that is related to the perches but resembles a pike

¹wal·lop \'wäl-əp\ *n* **1** : a powerful blow **2** : the ability to hit hard

²wallop *vb* : to hit hard

¹wal·low \'wäl-ō\ *vb* **1** : to roll oneself about in or as if in deep mud **2** : to live with vulgar pleasure in some condition

²wallow *n* : a muddy or dust-filled hollow where animals wallow

wall·pa·per \'wȯl-ˌpā-pər\ *n* : decorative paper for the walls of a room

wal·nut \'wȯl-ˌnət\ *n* : the edible nut (as the rough-shelled American **black walnut** or the smoother-shelled Old World **English walnut**) of trees that are related to the hickories and include some valued also for their wood

wal·rus \'wȯl-rəs\ *n* : a large mammal of northern seas related to the seals and hunted for its hide, for the ivory tusks of the males, and for oil

¹waltz \'wȯlts\ *n* : a gliding dance done to music having three beats to a measure

²waltz *vb* : to dance a waltz — **waltz·er** *n*

wam·pum \'wäm-pəm\ *n* : beads made of shells and used formerly for money or ornament by North American Indians

wan \ˈwän\ *adj* : having a pale or sickly color — **wan·ly** *adv* — **wan·ness** *n*

wand \ˈwänd\ *n* : a fairy's, diviner's, or magician's staff

wan·der \ˈwän-dər\ *vb* **1** : to move about aimlessly : RAMBLE **2** : to take a slow round-about way **3** : to go astray — **wan·der·er** *n*

wan·der·lust \ˈwän-dər-ˌləst\ *n* : a strong wish or longing to travel

wane \ˈwān\ *vb* **waned; wan·ing** **1** : to grow smaller or less **2** : to lose power, prosperity, or brilliance

¹want \ˈwȯnt\ *vb* **1** : to be without : LACK **2** : to feel or suffer the need of something **3** : to desire, wish, or long for something

²want *n* **1** : LACK, SHORTAGE **2** : extreme poverty ⟨the old man died in *want*⟩ **3** : a wish for something : DESIRE **4** : NEED

want·ing \ˈwȯnt-ing\ *adj* **1** : ABSENT **2** : falling below a standard, hope, or need

wan·ton \ˈwȯnt-ⁿ\ *adj* **1** : not restrained : UNRULY **2** : PLAYFUL **3** : IMMORAL **4** : having no real or just cause : MERCILESS — **wan·ton·ly** *adv* — **wan·ton·ness** *n*

wa·pi·ti \ˈwäp-ət-ē, wə-ˈpēt-ē\ *n* : the American elk

¹war \ˈwȯr\ *n* **1** : a state or period of armed conflict between states or nations **2** : the art or science of warfare **3** : a state of hostility, conflict, or antagonism **4** : a struggle between opposing forces

²war *vb* **warred; war·ring** : to make war : FIGHT

¹war·ble \ˈwȯr-bəl\ *n* **1** : a melodious succession of low pleasing sounds **2** : a musical trill **3** : the action of warbling

²warble *vb* **war·bled; war·bling** **1** : to sing with trills **2** : to express by warbling

war·bler \ˈwȯr-blər\ *n* **1** : one that warbles : SONGSTER **2** : any of a group of Old World birds related to the thrushes and noted for their melodious song **3** : any of a group of brightly colored insect-eating American migratory songbirds usually with a weak and unmusical call

¹ward \ˈwȯrd\ *n* **1** : the act of guarding **2** : a division of a hospital **3** : a district of a town or city for administrative purposes **4** : a person under the protection of a guardian

²ward *vb* **1** : to keep watch over : GUARD **2** : to turn aside — usually used with *off*

¹-ward \wərd\ *also* **-wards** \wərdz\ *adj suffix* **1** : that moves, tends, faces, or is directed toward ⟨wind*ward*⟩ **2** : that occurs or is situated in the direction of ⟨left*ward*⟩

²-ward *or* **-wards** *adv suffix* **1** : in a specified direction ⟨up*wards*⟩ **2** : toward a specified point, position, or area ⟨earth*ward*⟩

war·den \ˈwȯrd-ⁿ\ *n* **1** : WATCHMAN **2** : a person who sees that certain laws are followed **3** : the chief official of a prison **4** : an officer in certain colleges and churches

ward·er \ˈwȯrd-ər\ *n* : WARDEN

ward·robe \ˈwȯrd-ˌrōb\ *n* **1** : a room or closet where clothes are kept **2** : personal stock or supply of clothing

ware \ˈwaər\ *n* **1** : manufactured articles or products of art or craft **2** : an article of merchandise **3** : items (as dishes) of fired clay : POTTERY

ware·house \ˈwaər-ˌhaus\ *n* : a building for storing goods and merchandise

war·fare \ˈwȯr-ˌfaər\ *n* **1** : military combat between enemies **2** : STRUGGLE, CONFLICT

war·like \ˈwȯr-ˌlīk\ *adj* **1** : fond of war **2** : of or relating to war **3** : threatening war

¹warm \ˈwȯrm\ *adj* **1** : having a moderate degree of heat ⟨*warm* milk⟩ **2** : giving off heat **3** : making a person feel heat or suffer no loss of bodily heat ⟨*warm* clothing⟩ **4** : having a feeling of heat **5** : showing or marked by strong feeling ⟨a *warm* welcome⟩ **6** : newly made : FRESH **7** : near the object sought **8** : giving a pleasant impression of warmth, cheerfulness, or friendliness — **warm·ly** *adv*

²warm *vb* **1** : to make warm **2** : to give an impression of warmth **3** : to become more interested than at first ⟨a speaker *warming* to his subject⟩ — **warm up** **1** : to exercise or practice before entering a game or athletic contest **2** : to run (as a motor) at slow speed or without a load before using to full capacity

warm–blood·ed \ˈwȯrm-ˈbləd-əd\ *adj* **1** : able to maintain a relatively high body temperature that is independent of the temperature of the surroundings **2** : warm in feeling : FERVENT — **warm–blood·ed·ness** *n*

warmth \ˈwȯrmth\ *n* **1** : gentle heat **2** : strong feeling

warn \ˈwȯrn\ *vb* **1** : to put on guard : CAUTION **2** : to notify especially in advance

warn·ing \ˈwȯr-ning\ *n* : something that warns ⟨storm *warnings*⟩

¹warp \ˈwȯrp\ *n* **1** : the threads that go lengthwise in a loom and are crossed by the woof **2** : a twist or curve that has developed in something originally flat or straight **3** : a mental twist or abnormality

²warp *vb* **1** : to curve or twist out of shape **2** : to cause to judge, choose, or act wrongly **3** : FALSIFY, DISTORT

war·path \ˈwȯr-ˌpath, -ˌpàth\ *n* **1** : the course taken by a party of American Indians going on a warlike expedition **2** : a hostile course of action or frame of mind

war·plane \'wȯr-ˌplān\ *n* : a military or naval airplane

¹war·rant \'wȯr-ənt\ *n* **1** : an authorizing or being authorized **2** : a document giving legal power **3** : a person or thing that vouches for something **4** : JUSTIFICATION, RIGHT

²warrant *vb* **1** : to declare positively **2** : to give power to do or keep from doing something : AUTHORIZE **3** : to give reason for something **4** : GUARANTEE

warrant officer *n* : an officer in the armed forces ranking next below a commissioned officer

war·ren \'wȯr-ən\ *n* **1** : a place for keeping or breeding small game (as rabbits) **2** : a crowded tenement or district

war·rior \'wȯr-yər, 'wȯr-ē-ər\ *n* : SOLDIER

war·ship \'wȯr-ˌship\ *n* : a ship used in war

wart \'wȯrt\ *n* : a small hard lump of thickened skin — **wart·y** *adj*

war·y \'waər-ē\ *adj* **war·i·er**; **war·i·est** : very cautious **syn** see CAREFUL — **war·i·ly** \'war-ə-lē\ *adv* — **war·i·ness** \'war-ē-nəs\ *n*

was *past 1st & 3d sing of* BE

¹wash \'wȯsh, 'wäsh\ *vb* **1** : to cleanse with water **2** : to wet thoroughly with liquid (as water) **3** : FLOW, FLOOD **4** : to remove or carry away by the action of water **5** : to bear washing without injury ⟨linen *washes* well⟩ **6** : to be worn away by washing

²wash *n* **1** : articles (as of clothing) in the laundry **2** : the flow, sound, or action of water **3** : a disturbance of water (as displaced by the motion of a boat) **4** : material carried or set down by water

wash·board \'wȯsh-ˌbȯrd, 'wäsh-\ *n* : a grooved board to scrub clothes on

wash·bowl \'wȯsh-ˌbōl, 'wäsh-\ *n* : a large bowl for water to wash one's hands and face

wash·er \'wȯsh-ər, 'wäsh-\ *n* **1** : one (as a machine) that washes **2** : a ring (as of metal or leather) used to make something fit tightly or to prevent rubbing

washers 2

wash·er·wom·an \'wȯsh-ər-ˌwùm-ən, 'wäsh-\ *n, pl* **wash·er·wom·en** \-ˌwim-ən\ : a woman who works at washing clothes

wash·ing \'wȯsh-ing, 'wäsh-\ *n* : articles (as of clothing) in the wash

washing machine *n* : a machine used especially for washing clothes and household linen

wash·out \'wȯsh-ˌaut, 'wäsh-\ *n* **1** : the washing away of earth (as from a road) **2** : a place where earth is washed away **3** : a complete failure

wash·tub \'wȯsh-ˌtəb, 'wäsh-\ *n* : a tub for washing clothes or for soaking them before washing

was·n't \'wəz-nt, 'wäz-\ : was not

wasp \'wäsp\ *n* : a winged insect that is related to the bees and ants, that has a slender body with the abdomen attached by a narrow stalk, and that in females and workers is capable of producing a very powerful sting

wasp

wasp·ish \'wäs-pish\ *adj* : IRASCIBLE, IRRITABLE — **wasp·ish·ly** *adv* — **wasp·ish·ness** *n*

was·sail \'wäs-əl, wä-'sāl\ *n* [from an old Scandinavian toast *ves heill* meaning "be healthy", the first word being a form of the verb meaning "to be" and descended from the same source as English *was*, while the second is from the same source as English *whole* and *hale*] : an ancient expression of good wishes at a festivity and especially at the drinking of a toast to one's health

¹waste \'wāst\ *n* **1** : DESERT, WILDERNESS **2** : bare or uncultivated land **3** : the action of wasting : the state of being wasted **4** : material left over, rejected, or discarded **5** : material (as feces) produced in and of no further use to the living body

²waste *vb* **wast·ed**; **wast·ing** **1** : DEVASTATE **2** : to spend or use carelessly or uselessly **3** : to lose or cause to lose substance or vitality

³waste *adj* **1** : being wild and uninhabited : BARREN, DESOLATE **2** : of no further use

waste·bas·ket \'wāst-ˌbas-kət\ *n* : an open receptacle for unwanted odds and ends and especially for discarded paper

waste·ful \'wāst-fəl\ *adj* **1** : wasting or causing waste **2** : spending in a needless or useless manner — **waste·ful·ly** *adv* — **waste·ful·ness** *n*

waste·land \'wāst-ˌland\ *n* : barren uncultivated land

¹watch \'wäch\ *vb* **1** : to stay awake **2** : to be on one's guard **3** : to take care of : TEND **4** : to be on the lookout ⟨*watching* for a signal⟩ **5** : to keep one's eyes on — **watch·er** *n*

²watch *n* **1** : a watching especially as a long steady vigil **2** : a close lookout (as for guarding) **3** : SENTRY **4** : the time during which one is on duty to watch **5** : a small timepiece to be worn or carried

watch·dog \'wäch-ˌdȯg\ *n* : a dog kept to watch and guard property

watch

watch·ful \'wäch-fəl\ *adj* : ATTENTIVE, VIGILANT — **watch·ful·ly** *adv* — **watch·ful·ness** *n*

watch·man \'wäch-mən\ *n, pl* **watch·men** \-mən\ : a person who is assigned to watch

watch·tow·er \'wäch-ˌtaů-ər\ *n* : a tower on which a sentinel or watchman is placed

watch·word \'wäch-ˌwərd\ *n* : PASSWORD

¹**wa·ter** \'wȯt-ər, 'wät-\ *n* **1** : the liquid that comes from the clouds as rain and forms streams, lakes, and seas **2** : a liquid that contains or is like water

²**water** *vb* **1** : to wet or supply with water **2** : to treat with water **3** : to add water to : DILUTE **4** : to fill with liquid

water buffalo *n* : a common oxlike work animal of Asia

water clock *n* : a device or machine for measuring time by the fall or flow of water

wa·ter·col·or \'wȯt-ər-ˌkəl-ər, 'wät-\ *n* **1** : a paint whose liquid part is water **2** : a picture painted with watercolor **3** : the art of painting with watercolor

wa·ter·course \'wȯt-ər-ˌkōrs, 'wät-\ *n* **1** : a bed or channel in which water flows **2** : a stream of water (as a river or brook)

wa·ter·cress \'wȯt-ər-ˌkres, 'wät-\ *n* : a plant related to the mustards that grows in cold flowing waters and is used especially in salads

watercress

wa·ter·fall \'wȯt-ər-ˌfȯl, 'wät-\ *n* : a fall of water from a height

water flea *n* : a small active often brightly colored freshwater crustacean

wa·ter·fowl \'wȯt-ər-ˌfaůl, 'wät-\ *n* **1** : a bird that frequents water **2 waterfowl** *pl* : swimming game birds as distinguished from shorebirds and upland game birds

wa·ter·front \'wȯt-ər-ˌfrənt, 'wät-\ *n* : land or a section of a town that borders on a body of water

water hyacinth *n* : a floating water plant that often clogs streams in the southern United States

water lily *n* : any of a group of water plants with rounded floating leaves and many-petaled showy often fragrant flowers

water lily

wa·ter·line \'wȯt-ər-ˌlīn, 'wät-\ *n* : any of several lines that are marked on the outside of a ship and correspond with the surface of the water when it is afloat on an even keel

wa·ter·logged \'wȯt-ər-ˌlȯgd, 'wät-, -ˌlägd\ *adj* : so filled or soaked with water as to be heavy or hard to manage

wa·ter·mark \'wȯt-ər-ˌmärk, 'wät-\ *n* **1** : a mark that indicates a level to which water has risen **2** : a mark (as the maker's name) made in paper during manufacture and visible when the paper is held up to the light

wa·ter·mel·on \'wȯt-ər-ˌmel-ən, 'wät-\ *n* : a large edible fruit with a hard rind and a sweet red juicy pulp

water moccasin *n* : MOCCASIN 2

water polo *n* : a game played in water by teams of swimmers with an inflated ball

wa·ter·pow·er \'wȯt-ər-ˌpaů-ər, 'wät-\ *n* : the power of moving water used to run machinery

¹**wa·ter·proof** \ˌwȯt-ər-'prüf, ˌwät-\ *adj* : not letting water through ⟨a *waterproof* tent⟩

²**waterproof** *vb* : to make waterproof

wa·ter·shed \'wȯt-ər-ˌshed, 'wät-\ *n* **1** : a dividing ridge (as a mountain range) separating one drainage area from others **2** : the whole area that drains into a lake or river

wa·ter·spout \'wȯt-ər-ˌspaůt, 'wät-\ *n* **1** : a pipe for carrying off water from a roof **2** : a slender funnel-shaped cloud that extends down to a cloud of spray torn up from the surface of a body of water by a whirlwind

wa·ter·tight \ˌwȯt-ər-'tīt, ˌwät-\ *adj* : so tight as to be waterproof

wa·ter·way \'wȯt-ər-ˌwā, 'wät-\ *n* : a channel or a body of water by which ships can travel

wa·ter·wheel \'wȯt-ər-ˌhwēl, 'wät-\ *n* : a wheel rotated by a flow of water against it

wa·ter·works \'wȯt-ər-ˌwərks, 'wät-\ *n pl* : a system of dams, reservoirs, pumps, and pipes for supplying water (as to a city)

wa·ter·y \'wȯt-ə-rē, 'wät-\ *adj* **1** : of or relating to water **2** : full of or giving out water ⟨*watery* eyes⟩ **3** : being like water **4** : being soft and soggy

watt \'wät\ *n* [named in honor of James *Watt* (1736-1819), the Scotch engineer who invented the modern steam engine] : a unit for measuring electric power

¹**wat·tle** \'wät-l\ *n* **1** : a framework of flexible sticks used for walls, fences, or roofs **2** : a fleshy flap of skin that hangs from the throat (as of a bird) **3** : ACACIA

²**wattle** *vb* **wat·tled; wat·tling** **1** : to form or build with wattle **2** : to interlace (as reeds) to form wattle

¹**wave** \'wāv\ *vb* **waved; wav·ing** **1** : to move like a wave : FLOAT **2** : to move to and fro as a signal **3** : to curve like a wave

²**wave** *n* **1** : a moving ridge or swell on the surface of water **2** : a wavelike shape **3** : a waving motion (as of the hand) **4** : FLOW **5** : a rapid increase : SURGE ⟨a *wave* of prosperity⟩ **6** : a disturbance that is somewhat like a wave in water and transfers energy ⟨sound *waves*⟩

wave·length \'wāv-,length\ *n* : the distance in the line of advance of a wave from any one point (as a crest) to the next corresponding point

wave·let \'wāv-lət\ *n* : a little wave

wa·ver \'wā-vər\ *vb* **1** : to sway one way and the other **2** : to be unsettled in opinion **3** : FALTER

wav·y \'wā-vē\ *adj* **wav·i·er; wav·i·est** : having waves : moving in waves — **wav·i·ness** *n*

¹wax \'waks\ *n* **1** : a dull yellow sticky substance made by bees and used in building honeycomb : BEESWAX **2** : a substance resembling beeswax

²wax *vb* : to treat with wax

³wax *vb* **1** : to grow larger or stronger **2** : BECOME, GROW

wax bean *n* : a string bean with yellow waxy pods

wax·en \'wak-sən\ *adj* : of or resembling wax

wax myrtle *n* : the bayberry shrub

wax·wing \'waks-,wing\ *n* : a crested mostly brown smooth-feathered bird (as the American **cedar waxwing** with yellowish underparts)

wax·y \'wak-sē\ *adj* **wax·i·er; wax·i·est** **1** : being like wax **2** : made of or covered with wax

¹way \'wā\ *n* **1** : a track for travel or passage : PATH, STREET **2** : the course traveled from one place to another : ROUTE **3** : a course of action ⟨chose the easy *way*⟩ **4** : personal preference as to situation or behavior : WISH **5** : MANNER, METHOD **6** : FEATURE, RESPECT **7** : STATE, CONDITION **8** : a particular or characteristic mode of behavior **9** : DISTANCE **10** : progress along a course **11** : NEIGHBORHOOD, DISTRICT, LOCALITY ⟨used to live out our *way*⟩ **12** : room for movement or existence **13** *pl* : an inclined support on which a ship is built and from which it is launched **14** : CATEGORY, KIND **15** : motion or speed of a boat through the water

²way *adv* : AWAY, FAR

way·far·er \'wā-,far-ər\ *n* : a traveler especially on foot

way·lay \'wā-,lā\ *vb* **way·laid** \-,lād\; **way·lay·ing** : to attack from ambush

-ways \,wāz\ *adv suffix* : in a specified way, course, direction, or manner ⟨side*ways*⟩

way·side \'wā-,sīd\ *n* : the edge or border of a road

way·ward \'wā-wərd\ *adj* **1** : DISOBEDIENT **2** : contrary to one's wishes or hopes

we \wē\ *pron* : I and at least one other person

weak \'wēk\ *adj* **1** : lacking physical strength : FEEBLE **2** : not able to bear or exert a great weight or pressure **3** : easily overcome ⟨a *weak* argument⟩ **4** : lacking force : LOW

5 : not containing the usual amount or a large amount of the main ingredients **6** : lacking mental or moral strength **7** : coming from or showing lack of judgment or firmness : UNWISE **8** : lacking experience or skill

syn WEAK, FEEBLE, FRAIL all refer to something not strong enough to endure the stress or pressure normally placed on it. WEAK is the broadest term and suggests a temporary or permanent loss or lack of strength, power, vigor, or influence ⟨a *weak* throwing arm⟩ ⟨a *weak* argument⟩ ⟨Pierce was a *weak* president and Lincoln a strong one⟩ FEEBLE stresses an extreme and pitiful weakness and is applied most frequently to people or their actions ⟨the old man grew more *feeble* each day⟩ ⟨oversleeping is a *feeble* excuse for being tardy⟩ FRAIL suggests not loss or impairment of strength but rather a natural delicacy and lack of power to resist pressure or attack ⟨a *frail* child who was often ill⟩ ⟨we had to trust our lives to a *frail* boat in a wild sea⟩

weak·en \'wē-kən\ *vb* : to make or become weak or weaker

weak·fish \'wēk-,fish\ *n* : any of several sea fishes related to the perches (as a common sport and market fish of the eastern coast of the United States)

weak·ling \'wēk-ling\ *n* : a person or creature lacking strength

¹weak·ly \'wēk-lē\ *adv* : in a weak manner

²weakly *adj* **weak·li·er; weak·li·est** : not robust

weak·ness \'wēk-nəs\ *n* **1** : lack of strength : FEEBLENESS **2** : FAULT, DEFECT

wealth \'welth\ *n* : large possessions : RICHES

wealth·y \'wel-thē\ *adj* **wealth·i·er; wealth·i·est** : having wealth : RICH

wean \'wēn\ *vb* **1** : to accustom a child or young animal to take food other than its mother's milk **2** : to turn a person away from desiring a thing he has been fond of

weap·on \'wep-ən\ *n* : something (as a gun, knife, or club) to fight with

¹wear \'waər\ *vb* **wore** \'wōr\; **worn** \'wōrn\; **wear·ing** **1** : to use as an article of clothing or decoration **2** : to carry on the body : BEAR **3** : SHOW ⟨*wear* a smile⟩ **4** : to harm, waste, or lessen by use or by scraping or rubbing **5** : to make tired : WEARY **6** : to cause or make by rubbing ⟨*wear* a hole in a coat⟩ **7** : to endure use : LAST ⟨a cloth that *wears* well⟩ — **wear·er** *n* — **wear out** : to use up the useful life of

²wear *n* **1** : the act of wearing : the state of being worn **2** : things worn or meant to be worn **3** : wearing quality : lasting quality **4** : the result of wearing or use

wea·ri·some \'wir-ē-səm\ *adj* : TIRESOME

¹wea·ry \'wiər-ē\ *adj* **wea·ri·er; wea·ri·est**
1 : worn out : TIRED   **2** : expressing or caused
by weariness   **3** : having one's patience, pleasure, or interest worn out   **4** : causing weariness : TIRESOME — **wea·ri·ness** *n*

²weary *vb* **wea·ried; wea·ry·ing** : to make or become weary

wea·sel \'wē-zəl\ *n* : a small slender active
fur-bearing animal related to the
minks that feeds on small birds and
animals (as mice)

¹weath·er \'weth-ər\ *n* : the state
of the air and atmosphere with
respect to warmth, cold, dryness,
wetness, storminess, or clearness

²weather *adj* : WINDWARD

weasel

³weather *vb* **1** : to expose to or
endure the action of the elements   **2** : to alter
(as in color) by exposure   **3** : to sail or pass to
the windward of   **4** : to bear up against and
come safely through

weath·er·cock \'weth-ər-,käk\ *n* : a weather
vane shaped like a rooster

weath·er·man \'weth-ər-
,man\ *n, pl* **weath·er·men**
\-,men\ : one who reports and
forecasts the weather

weather vane *n* : VANE 1

weathercock

¹weave \'wēv\ *vb* **wove** \'wōv\;
wo·ven \'wō-vən\; **weav-
ing** **1** : to form by interlacing
strands of material : make
cloth on a loom by interlacing yarns   **2** : SPIN 3
3 : to make by or as if by interlacing   **4** : to
unite or entwine as if by weaving   **5** : to move
to and fro or up and down

²weave *n* : a method or pattern of weaving

¹web \'web\ *n* **1** : a woven fabric on a loom
or coming from a loom   **2** : COB-
WEB   **3** : something flimsy or
entangling like a cobweb   **4** : a
membrane especially when uniting toes (as of a bird)

web 4

²web *vb* **webbed; web·bing** : to
unite or surround with a web

web·bing \'web-ing\ *n* : a strong closely
woven tape

web·foot \'web-,fut\ *n, pl* **web·feet** \-,fēt\ : a
foot (as of a duck) having the toes joined by
webs — **web–foot·ed** \-'fut-əd\ *adj*

wed \'wed\ *vb* **wed·ded** *also* **wed; wed·ding**
1 : MARRY   **2** : to attach firmly

we'd \wēd\ : we had : we should : we would

wed·ding \'wed-ing\ *n* : a marriage ceremony

¹wedge \'wej\ *n* **1** : a piece of wood or metal
tapered to a thin edge and used to split wood
or rocks or to lift a heavy weight   **2** : some-

thing (as a piece of cake, a piece of land,
or wild geese flying) shaped
like a wedge   **3** : something (as
a policy) that serves to make
a gradual opening or change

wedge

²wedge *vb* **wedged; wedg·ing**
1 : to separate or split by means
of a wedge   **2** : to fasten or tighten with a
wedge   **3** : to crowd in tightly

wedge 1

wed·lock \'wed-,läk\ *n* : MARRIAGE

Wednes·day \'wenz-dē\ *n* : the fourth day of
the week

wee \'wē\ *adj* : very small : LITTLE, TINY

¹weed \'wēd\ *n* : a coarse worthless plant that
often tends to choke out more desirable plants

²weed *vb* **1** : to remove weeds from   **2** : to get
rid of as undesirable

³weed *n* : dress worn (as by a widow) as a sign
of mourning — usually used in plural

weed·y \'wēd-ē\ *adj* **weed·i·er; weed·i·est**
1 : full of or consisting of weeds   **2** : resembling a weed especially in coarse vigorous
growth   **3** : noticeably lean and scrawny

week \'wēk\ *n* **1** : seven successive days especially beginning with Sunday and ending with
Saturday   **2** : the working or school days of
the calendar week

week·day \'wēk-,dā\ *n* : a day of the week except Sunday or sometimes except Saturday
and Sunday

¹week·end \'wēk-,end\ *n* : the period between the close of one working or school week
and the beginning of the next

²weekend *vb* : to spend the weekend

¹week·ly \'wēk-lē\ *adj* **1** : occurring, done,
produced, or issued every week   **2** : computed
in terms of one week

²weekly *n, pl* **week·lies** : a weekly publication

weep \'wēp\ *vb* **wept** \'wept\; **weep·ing** **1** : to
show grief by shedding tears : CRY   **2** : LAMENT

weep·ing \'wē-ping\ *adj* **1** : TEARFUL
2 : RAINY   **3** : having slender drooping
branches

wee·vil \'wē-vəl\ *n* : any of various small
hard-shelled beetles having a
long snout and including many
which are injurious to fruits,
nuts, grain, or trees

weigh \'wā\ *vb* **1** : to determine the weight of   **2** : to
examine as if by weighing
⟨*weigh* a question⟩   **3** : to

weevil

measure out on or as if on scales   **4** : to balance something in one's hands to determine
its weight   **5** : to heave up (as an anchor) before sailing   **6** : to have weight or a specified
weight ⟨*weigh* 100 pounds⟩   **7** : to be con-

sidered important — **weigh down** : to bear heavily down upon

¹weight \'wāt\ *n* **1** : quantity as determined by weighing **2** : the property of a body measurable by weighing **3** : the amount that something weighs **4** : a unit (as a pound or kilogram) of weight : a system of such units **5** : an object (as a piece of metal) of known weight for balancing a scale in weighing other objects **6** : a heavy object used to hold, press down, or counterbalance something **7** : BURDEN ⟨a *weight* on his mind⟩ **8** : PRESSURE ⟨*weight* of an attack⟩ **9** : IMPORTANCE **10** : the greater or more impressive part

²weight *vb* **1** : to load or make heavy with a weight **2** : to oppress with a burden

weight·y \'wāt-ē\ *adj* **weight·i·er; weight·i·est** **1** : having much weight : HEAVY **2** : having importance or consequence **3** : SOLEMN

weird \'wiərd\ *adj* **1** : UNEARTHLY, MYSTERIOUS **2** : of strange or extraordinary character

¹wel·come \'wel-kəm\ *vb* **wel·comed; wel·com·ing** **1** : to greet with friendship or courtesy **2** : to receive or accept with pleasure

²welcome *adj* **1** : received gladly **2** : giving pleasure : PLEASING **3** : willingly permitted to do, have, or enjoy something **4** — used in the phrase "You're welcome" as a reply to an expression of thanks

³welcome *n* : a friendly greeting or reception

¹weld \'weld\ *vb* **1** : to join two pieces of metal or plastic by heating and allowing the edges to flow together or by hammering or pressing together **2** : to join closely **3** : to become or be capable of being welded

²weld *n* : a welded joint

wel·fare \'wel-ˌfaər\ *n* **1** : the state of doing well especially in respect to happiness, well‌being, or prosperity **2** : RELIEF 2

¹well \'wel\ *n* **1** : a source of supply **2** : a hole made in the earth to reach a natural deposit (as of water, oil, or gas) **3** : an open space extending vertically through floors (as for stairs) **4** : something suggesting a well

²well *vb* : to rise to the surface and flow forth

³well *adv* **bet·ter** \'bet-ər\; **best** \'best\ **1** : in a pleasing or desirable manner ⟨the party turned out *well*⟩ **2** : in a good or proper manner ⟨do your work *well*⟩ **3** : ABUNDANTLY, FULLY ⟨eat *well*⟩ **4** : with reason or courtesy **5** : COMPLETELY, THOROUGHLY **6** : INTIMATELY, CLOSELY **7** : CONSIDERABLY, FAR ⟨rode *well* ahead⟩ **8** : without trouble or difficulty : EASILY **9** : EXACTLY, DEFINITELY

⁴well *interj* **1** — used to express surprise or indignation **2** — used to begin a discourse or to resume one that was interrupted

⁵well *adj* **1** : FORTUNATE, SATISFACTORY **2** : free or recovered from ill health : HEALTHY

we'll \'wēl\ : we shall : we will

well-be·ing \'wel-'bē-ing\ *n* : WELFARE

well-bred \'wel-'bred\ *adj* : having or showing good breeding : REFINED, POLITE

well-known \'wel-'nōn\ *adj* : widely known

well-nigh \'wel-'nī\ *adv* : ALMOST, NEARLY

well-to-do \ˌwel-tə-'dü\ *adj* : PROSPEROUS

¹Welsh \'welsh\ *adj* : of or relating to Wales or the people of Wales

²Welsh *n pl* : the people of Wales

Welsh rabbit *n* : a dish made of melted cheese poured over toast or crackers

Welsh rare·bit \-'raər-bət\ *n* : WELSH RABBIT

welt \'welt\ *n* **1** : the narrow strip of leather between a shoe upper and sole to which other parts are stitched **2** : a ridge raised on the skin by a blow

¹wel·ter \'wel-tər\ *vb* **1** : to twist or roll one's body about **2** : to rise and fall or toss about in or with waves

²welter *n* : a confused jumble

wend \'wend\ *vb* : to direct one's course : GO

went *past of* GO

wept *past of* WEEP

were *past 2d sing, past pl, or past subjunctive of* BE

we're \'wiər, 'wər\ : we are

weren't \'wərnt\ : were not

were·wolf \'wiər-ˌwu̇lf, 'wər-\ *n, pl* **were·wolves** \-ˌwu̇lvz\ : a person in folklore who is changed or is able to change into a wolf

¹west \'west\ *adv* : to or toward the west

²west *adj* : situated toward or coming from the west

³west *n* **1** : the direction of sunset : the compass point opposite to east **2** *cap* : regions or countries west of a specified or implied point

west·bound \'west-ˌbau̇nd\ *adj* : going west

west·er·ly \'wes-tər-lē\ *adv (or adj)* **1** : from the west ⟨a *westerly* wind⟩ **2** : toward the west

west·ern \'wes-tərn\ *adj* **1** *often cap* : of or relating to a region usually called West **2** : lying toward or coming from the west

¹west·ward \'west-wərd\ *adv (or adj)* : toward the west

²westward *n* : a westward direction or part

¹wet \'wet\ *adj* **wet·ter; wet·test** **1** : containing, covered with, or soaked with liquid (as water) ⟨a *wet* cloth⟩ **2** : RAINY ⟨*wet* weather⟩ **3** : not yet dry ⟨*wet* paint⟩ — **wet·ness** *n*

²wet *n* **1** : WATER **2** : WETNESS, MOISTURE **3** : rainy weather : RAIN

³wet *vb* **wet** *or* **wet·ted; wet·ting** : to make wet

we've \'wēv\ : we have

¹whack \'hwak\ *vb* : to strike with a whack

²whack *n* **1** : a sharp noisy blow **2** : the sound of a whack

¹whale \'hwāl\ *n* : a warm-blooded sea animal that looks like a huge fish but breathes air and suckles its young and that is hunted for its oil

²whale *vb* **whaled; whal·ing** : to hunt whales

whale·boat \'hwāl-ˌbōt\ *n* : a long rowboat once used by whalers

whale·bone \'hwāl-ˌbōn\ *n* : a horny substance from the upper jaw of some whales

whal·er \'hwā-lər\ *n* **1** : a person or ship that hunts whales **2** : WHALEBOAT

wharf \'hwȯrf\ *n, pl* **wharves** \'hwȯrvz\ *or* **wharfs** : a structure built on the shore (as of a river) for loading and unloading ships

¹what \'hwät\ *pron* **1** : which thing or things ⟨*what* did you say⟩ **2** : which sort or kind of thing ⟨*what* is this⟩ **3** : which sort of person ⟨*what* is he, a salesman⟩ **4** : which in name or kind ⟨*what* is your trade⟩ **5** : that which ⟨do *what* you're told⟩

²what *adv* **1** : in what way : HOW ⟨*what* does it matter⟩ **2** : in part ⟨*what* with the cold and *what* with hunger the man nearly perished⟩

³what *adj* **1** — used to inquire about the identity or nature of a person, object, or matter ⟨*what* books does he read⟩ **2** : how remarkable or surprising ⟨*what* an idea⟩ **3** : WHATEVER

¹what·ev·er \hwät-'ev-ər\ *pron* **1** : anything that ⟨take *whatever* you need⟩ **2** : no matter what ⟨*whatever* you do, don't cheat⟩ **3** : what in the world ⟨*whatever* made you say that⟩

²whatever *adj* **1** : any and all : any . . . that ⟨take *whatever* money you need⟩ **2** : of any kind at all ⟨there's no food *whatever*⟩

wheat \'hwēt\ *n* : a cereal grain that is borne in dense spikes by a widely grown grass, yields a fine white flour, is the chief source of bread in temperate regions, and is also important in animal feeds

whee·dle \'hwēd-l\ *vb* **whee·dled; whee·dling** **1** : to entice by gentle flattery : COAX **2** : to gain or get by coaxing or flattery

wheat

¹wheel \'hwēl\ *n* **1** : a disk or circular frame capable of turning on a central axis **2** : something that is like a wheel (as in being round or in turning on an axis) **3** : a device the main part of which is a wheel ⟨a spinning *wheel*⟩ **4** *pl* : moving power or mechanism ⟨the *wheels* of government⟩ — **wheeled** \'hwēld\ *adj*

²wheel *vb* **1** : to carry or move on wheels or in a vehicle with wheels **2** : ROTATE **3** : to change direction as if revolving on an axis

wheel·bar·row \'hwēl-ˌbar-ō\ *n* : a small vehicle with two handles and usually one wheel for carrying small loads

wheel·chair \'hwēl-ˌcheər\ *n* : a chair mounted on wheels in which a crippled person or invalid can get about

wheel·house \'hwēl-ˌhaus\ *n* : a small house containing a ship's steering wheel that is built on or above the top deck

wheelchair

¹wheeze \'hwēz\ *vb* **wheezed; wheez·ing** **1** : to breathe with difficulty and usually with a whistling sound **2** : to make a sound like wheezing

²wheeze *n* : a wheezing sound

whelk \'hwelk\ *n* : a large sea snail with a spiral shell used in Europe for food

¹whelp \'hwelp\ *n* : one of the young of a flesh-eating animal and especially of a dog

²whelp *vb* : to give birth to whelps

¹when \'hwen, hwən\ *adv* **1** : at what time ⟨*when* did you leave⟩ **2** : the time at which ⟨unsure of *when* they'd come⟩ **3** : at, in, or during which ⟨came at a time *when* things were upset⟩

²when *conj* **1** : at, during, or just after the time that ⟨leave *when* I do⟩ **2** : in the event that : IF ⟨the batter is out *when* he bunts foul with two strikes⟩ **3** : ALTHOUGH ⟨why do you tease *when* you know he doesn't like it⟩

³when \'hwen\ *pron* : what or which time ⟨since *when* have you known that⟩

whence \'hwens\ *adv* **1** : from what place, source, or cause ⟨*whence* come all these questions⟩ **2** : from or out of which ⟨the land *whence* he came⟩

when·ev·er \hwen-'ev-ər, hwən-\ *conj or adv* : at whatever time

¹where \'hweər, hwər\ *adv* **1** : at, in, or to what place ⟨*where* is he⟩ **2** : the place to or in which ⟨spoke of *where* they'd been⟩ **3** : at or in which ⟨this is the dock *where* you get the ferry⟩

²where *conj* **1** : in or to the point or place in or to which ⟨sit *where* the light's better⟩ **2** : every place that ⟨goes *where* he wants to⟩

³where *pron* : what place ⟨*where*'s he from⟩

¹where·a·bouts \'hwer-ə-ˌbauts\ *adv* : about where

²whereabouts *n sing or pl* : the place where someone or something is

where·as \hwer-'az\ *conj* **1** : since it is true that **2** : while on the contrary ⟨water quenches fire, *whereas* gasoline feeds it⟩

where·at \hwer-'at\ *conj* **1** : at or toward which **2** : in consequence of which

where·by \hweər-'bī\ *adv* : by or through which

¹where·fore \'hweər-ˌfōr\ *adv* **1** : for what reason or purpose : WHY **2** : THEREFORE

²wherefore *n* : REASON

where·in \hwer-'in\ *adv* **1** : in what way **2** : in which

where·of \hwer-'əv, -'äv\ *conj* : of what : that of which ⟨knows *whereof* he speaks⟩

where·on \hwer-'ȯn, -'än\ *adv* : on which

where·up·on \'hwer-ə-ˌpȯn, -ˌpän\ *conj* : and then : at which time

¹wher·ev·er \hwer-'ev-ər\ *adv* : where in the world

²wherever *conj* **1** : at, in, or to whatever place **2** : in any circumstance in which

whet \'hwet\ *vb* **whet·ted; whet·ting 1** : to sharpen the edge of by rubbing on or with a stone **2** : to make (as the appetite) keen : STIMULATE

wheth·er \'hweth-ər\ *conj* : if it be the case that : IF ⟨see *whether* he can come⟩

whet·stone \'hwet-ˌstōn\ *n* : a natural or artificial stone on which blades are sharpened

whew *n* : a sound like a half-formed whistle uttered as an exclamation — used as an interjection chiefly to express amazement, discomfort, or relief

whey \'hwā\ *n* : the watery part of milk that separates after the milk sours and thickens

¹which \hwich\ *adj* : what one or ones in particular : what specific one or ones

²which *pron* **1** : which one or ones ⟨*which* are yours⟩ ⟨*which* is his⟩ **2** — used like the relative pronoun *that* but not in reference to human beings ⟨we found the horse *which* got away⟩ ⟨here's the house *which* we bought⟩

¹which·ev·er \hwich-'ev-ər\ *pron* : whatever one or ones : any that

²whichever *adj* : no matter which : any . . . that ⟨take *whichever* book you want⟩

¹whiff \'hwif\ *n* **1** : a slight gust : BREATH **2** : an inhalation of odor, gas, or smoke **3** : a slight trace : HINT

²whiff *vb* : to puff, blow out, or blow away in whiffs

¹while \'hwīl\ *n* **1** : a space of time **2** : time spent in doing something : TROUBLE

²while *conj* **1** : during the time that ⟨she called *while* you were out⟩ **2** : ALTHOUGH ⟨*while* the book is famous, it is seldom read⟩

³while *vb* **whiled; whil·ing** : to cause to pass especially in a pleasant way ⟨*while* away time⟩

whim \'hwim\ *n* : a sudden wish, desire, or notion : a sudden change of mind

¹whim·per \'hwim-pər\ *vb* : to cry in low broken tones : WHINE

²whimper *n* : a whining cry

whim·si·cal \'hwim-zi-kəl\ *adj* **1** : full of whims : CAPRICIOUS **2** : DROLL

¹whine \'hwīn\ *vb* **whined; whin·ing 1** : to make a low complaining cry or a sound like such a cry **2** : to complain in a childish way

²whine *n* : a whining cry or sound

¹whin·ny \'hwin-ē\ *vb* **whin·nied; whin·ny·ing** : to neigh usually in a low gentle way

²whinny *n, pl* **whin·nies** : NEIGH

¹whip \'hwip\ *vb* **whipped; whip·ping 1** : to move, snatch, or jerk quickly or forcibly **2** : to strike with something lithe and slender : LASH **3** : to punish by striking or lashing **4** : to beat to a froth ⟨*whip* cream⟩ **5** : to thrash about

²whip *n* **1** : an instrument used in whipping **2** : a light dessert blended with whipped cream or whipped whites of eggs

whip·pet \'hwip-ət\ *n* : a small swift greyhoundlike dog often used for racing

whippet

whip·poor·will \ˌhwip-ər-'wil\ *n* : a night-flying insect-eating bird of eastern North America named from its peculiar call

¹whir \'hwər\ *vb* **whirred; whir·ring** : to fly, move, or revolve rapidly with a buzzing whizzing sound

²whir *n* : a whirring sound

¹whirl \'hwərl\ *vb* **1** : to turn or move rapidly in circles **2** : to feel giddiness : REEL ⟨my head *whirls*⟩ **3** : to move or carry around or about very rapidly

²whirl *n* **1** : a whirling movement **2** : something caused by whirling : BUSTLE

whirl·pool \'hwərl-ˌpül\ *n* : a rapid swirl of water with a low place in the center into which floating objects are drawn : EDDY

whirl·wind \'hwərl-ˌwind\ *n* : a small rotating windstorm with an inward and upward spiral motion of the air

¹whisk \'hwisk\ *n* **1** : a quick sweeping or brushing motion **2** : a kitchen utensil of wire made for whipping eggs or cream

whisk 2

²whisk *vb* **1** : to move suddenly and speedily ⟨*whisk* around the corner⟩ **2** : to beat into a froth **3** : to brush with a whisk ⟨*whisked* dust off his clothes⟩

whisk broom *n* : a small broom with a short handle used especially as a clothes brush

whisk broom

whis·ker \'hwis-kər\ *n* **1** *pl* : the

part of the beard that grows on the sides of the face and on the chin **2** : one hair of the beard **3** : a long bristle or hair growing near the mouth of an animal

whis·key or **whis·ky** \'hwis-kē\ n, pl **whis·keys** or **whis·kies** : a distilled alcoholic liquor made from fermented mash of grain

¹**whis·per** \'hwis-pər\ vb **1** : to speak very low or under the breath **2** : to tell by whispering **3** : to make a low rustling sound

²**whisper** n **1** : a low soft utterance that can be heard only by persons who are near **2** : the act of whispering **3** : something said in a whisper **4** : HINT, RUMOR

¹**whis·tle** \'hwis-əl\ n **1** : a device by which a shrill sound is produced **2** : a shrill sound of or like whistling

²**whistle** vb **whis·tled**; **whis·tling** **1** : to make a shrill sound by forcing the breath through the teeth or lips **2** : to move, pass, or go with a sharp shrill sound **3** : to sound a whistle **4** : to utter by whistling ⟨*whistle* a tune⟩

whit \'hwit\ n : the least particle : BIT

¹**white** \'hwīt\ adj **1** : of the color white **2** : light or pale in color ⟨*white* wine⟩ **3** : pale gray : SILVERY **4** : having a light skin ⟨the *white* races⟩ **5** : BLANK ⟨*white* spaces in printed matter⟩ **6** : not intended to cause harm ⟨*white* lies⟩ **7** : SNOWY ⟨*white* Christmas⟩

²**white** n **1** : the color of fresh snow : the opposite of black **2** : the white part of something (as an egg) **3** : white clothing **4** : a member of a light-skinned race

white blood cell n : one of the tiny whitish cells of the blood that contain a nucleus and help fight infection

white·cap \'hwīt-ˌkap\ n : the top of a wave breaking into foam

white·fish \'hwīt-ˌfish\ n : an important freshwater food fish related to the trouts that is greenish above and silvery below

white flag n : a flag of plain white raised as a request for a truce or as a sign of surrender

whit·en \'hwīt-n\ vb : to make or become white : BLEACH ⟨*whiten* sheets⟩

white oak n : a large oak tree noted for its hard strong durable moisture-resistant wood

white·tail \'hwīt-ˌtāl\ n : the common deer of eastern North America with the underside of the tail white

¹**white·wash** \'hwīt-ˌwȯsh, -ˌwäsh\ vb **1** : to cover with whitewash **2** : to try to clear (someone) of a charge of wrongdoing by offering excuses or hiding facts **3** : to hold (a sports opponent) scoreless

²**whitewash** n **1** : a composition (as of lime

and water) for whitening a surface (as a wall) **2** : the act or fact of whitewashing

whith·er \'hwith-ər\ adv **1** : to what place **2** : to which place or destination

whit·ish \'hwīt-ish\ adj : somewhat white

whit·tle \'hwit-l\ vb **whit·tled**; **whit·tling** **1** : to pare or cut off chips from wood : shape or form by such paring or cutting **2** : to reduce little by little

¹**whiz** or **whizz** \'hwiz\ vb **whizzed**; **whiz·zing** : to move, pass, or fly rapidly with a hissing or whirring sound

²**whiz** n : a whizzing sound

who \'hü\ pron **1** : what person or persons ⟨*who* did it⟩ **2** : the person or persons that ⟨we know *who* did it⟩ **3** — used like the relative pronoun *that* but in reference to persons only ⟨the man *who* lives there is my brother⟩

who·ev·er \hü-'ev-ər\ pron **1** : whatever person **2** : who in the world

¹**whole** \'hōl\ adj [from Old English hāl; modern English hale comes from the same Old English word, but from a northern dialect where the pronunciation developed differently] **1** : perfectly healthy or sound in condition : INTACT **2** : not cut up or ground ⟨a *whole* pepper⟩ **3** : containing all its essential elements in being made ready for the market ⟨*whole* milk⟩ **4** : made up of all its parts : TOTAL ⟨the *whole* family⟩ **5** : not scattered or divided ⟨his *whole* attention⟩ **6** : each one of the ⟨the *whole* ten days⟩ — **whole·ness** n

²**whole** n **1** : something that is whole **2** : a sum of all the parts and elements — **on the whole** **1** : all things considered **2** : in most instances

whole·heart·ed \'hōl-'härt-əd\ adj : not holding back : SINCERE

whole number n : a number that is zero or any of the natural numbers

¹**whole·sale** \'hōl-ˌsāl\ n : the sale of goods in large quantities to retail dealers

²**wholesale** adj **1** : of, relating to, or engaged in wholesaling **2** : being large-scale and extensive ⟨*wholesale* slaughter⟩

³**wholesale** vb **whole·saled**; **whole·sal·ing** : to sell to retail dealers usually in large lots

whole·some \'hōl-səm\ adj **1** : promoting well-being of body, mind, or spirit ⟨*wholesome* food⟩ **2** : sound in body, mind, or morals **syn** see HEALTHY — **whole·some·ness** n

whol·ly \'hō-lē\ adv **1** : ENTIRELY, COMPLETELY **2** : SOLELY, EXCLUSIVELY

whom \'hüm\ pron, objective case of WHO

whom·ev·er \hüm-'ev-ər\ pron, objective case of WHOEVER

¹**whoop** \'hüp\ vb **1** : to shout or cheer loudly

and vigorously **2** : to make the sound that follows a coughing attack in whooping cough

²whoop *n* : a whooping sound or utterance

whooping cough *n* : an infectious bacterial disease especially of children marked by violent bouts of coughing often followed by a crowing intake of breath

whooping crane *n* : a large white nearly extinct North American crane noted for its loud whooping note

whop·per \'hwäp-ər\ *n* **1** : something huge of its kind **2** : a monstrous lie

whorl \'hwȯrl, 'hwərl\ *n* **1** : something that whirls **2** : COIL, SPIRAL **3** : a row of parts (as leaves or petals) encircling a stem

¹whose \hüz\ *adj* **1** — used as a question word to draw forth an answer like *mine* or *John's* ⟨*whose* book is this⟩ **2** : the . . . of whom or belonging to whom ⟨the boy *whose* car broke down had to walk home⟩

²whose *pron* : whose one : whose ones

¹why \'hwī\ *adv* : for what cause, reason, or purpose ⟨*why* did you do it⟩

²why *conj* **1** : the cause, reason, or purpose for which ⟨we know *why* you did it⟩ **2** : for which ⟨here's the reason *why* he did it⟩

³why *n, pl* **whys** : REASON, CAUSE

⁴why \wī\ *interj* — used to express surprise, hesitation, approval, disapproval, or impatience

wick \'wik\ *n* : a cord, strip, or ring of loosely woven material through which a liquid (as oil) is drawn to the top in a candle, lamp, or oil stove for burning

wick

wick·ed \'wik-əd\ *adj* **1** : guilty of serious wrongdoing (as breaking a criminal law) **2** : DANGEROUS, VILE — **wick·ed·ly** *adv* — **wick·ed·ness** *n*

¹wick·er \'wik-ər\ *n* **1** : a flexible twig (as of willow) used in basketry **2** : WICKERWORK

²wicker *adj* : made of wicker

wick·er·work \'wik-ər-ˌwərk\ *n* : basketry made of wicker

wick·et \'wik-ət\ *n* **1** : a small gate or door in or near a larger gate or door **2** : a small window with a grate (as in a bank or ticket office) **3** : either of the two sets of three rods topped by two crosspieces at which the ball is bowled in cricket **4** : an arch (as of wire) through which the ball is hit in the game of croquet

¹wide \'wīd\ *adj* **wid·er; wid·est** **1** : covering a vast area **2** : measured across or at right angles to length ⟨cloth fifty-four inches *wide*⟩ **3** : having a generous measure across : BROAD

4 : opened as far as possible ⟨eyes *wide* with wonder⟩ **5** : not limited : EXTENSIVE ⟨*wide* reading⟩ **6** : far from the goal, mark, or truth ⟨a *wide* guess⟩ — **wide·ly** *adv* — **wide·ness** *n*

²wide *adv* **wid·er; wid·est** **1** : over a wide area ⟨travel far and *wide*⟩ **2** : far off ⟨*wide* of the mark⟩ **3** : ASTRAY ⟨the ball went *wide*⟩

wide–a·wake \ˌwīd-ə-'wāk\ *adj* : not sleepy, dull, or listless : ALERT, KEEN

wid·en \'wīd-n\ *vb* : to make or become wide or wider

wide·spread \'wīd-'spred\ *adj* **1** : widely extended **2** : widely scattered

¹wid·ow \'wid-ō\ *n* : a woman who has lost her husband by death

²widow *vb* : to make a widow of ⟨women *widowed* by a disaster⟩

wid·ow·er \'wid-ə-wər\ *n* : a man who has lost his wife by death

width \'width\ *n* **1** : dimension at right angles to length **2** : BREADTH

wield \'wēld\ *vb* **1** : to use (as a tool) effectively ⟨*wield* a baton⟩ **2** : EXERCISE ⟨*wield* authority⟩

wie·ner \'wē-nər\ *n* : FRANKFURTER

wife \'wīf\ *n, pl* **wives** \'wīvz\ : a woman united to a man in marriage

wig \'wig\ *n* : a manufactured covering of hair for the head usually made of human hair

¹wig·gle \'wig-əl\ *vb* **wig·gled; wig·gling** **1** : to move to and fro jerkily **2** : to proceed with a twisting turning movement

²wiggle *n* : a wiggling motion

wig·gler \'wig-lər\ *n* **1** : one that wiggles **2** : a larval or pupal mosquito

wig·gly \'wig-lē\ *adj* **wig·gli·er; wig·gli·est** **1** : tending to wiggle **2** : WAVY ⟨*wiggly* lines⟩

wig·wag \'wig-ˌwag\ *vb* **wig·wagged; wig·wagging** : to move from side to side or up and down and especially to signal by such movements of a flag or light

wig·wam \'wig-ˌwäm\ *n* : an Indian hut made of poles overlaid with bark, rush mats, or hides

¹wild \'wīld\ *adj* **1** : living in a state of nature and not under human control and care : not tame or domesticated ⟨*wild* game animals⟩ **2** : growing or produced in nature : not cultivated or nurtured by man ⟨*wild* honey⟩ ⟨*wild* grapes⟩ **3** : not civilized : SAVAGE **4** : not kept within bounds or under control ⟨*wild* rage⟩ **5** : DESOLATE ⟨*wild* country⟩ **6** : wide of the mark ⟨a *wild* guess⟩ — **wild·ly** *adv*

²wild *n* : WILDERNESS

wild boar *n* : an Old World wild hog from which most domestic swine derive

wild·cat \'wīld-ˌkat\ *n* : any of various small or medium-sized cats (as an ocelot or lynx)

wil·der·ness \'wil-dər-nəs\ *n* : an uncultivated and uninhabited region

wild·fire \'wīld-ˌfīr\ *n* : a sweeping and destructive conflagration

wild flower *n* : a wild or uncultivated plant esteemed for its flowers

wild·life \'wīld-ˌlīf\ *n* : creatures that are neither human nor domesticated : the wild animals of field and forest

¹wile \'wīl\ *n* : a trick intended to deceive or tempt

²wile *vb* **wiled; wil·ing** : LURE, ENTICE

¹will \wəl, wil\ *helping verb, past* **would** \wəd, wùd\; *pres sing & pl* **will** **1** : wish to ⟨what *will* you have⟩ **2** : am, is, or are willing to ⟨I *will* go if you ask me⟩ **3** : am, is, or are determined to ⟨he *will* go in spite of the storm⟩ **4** : is or are going to ⟨everyone *will* be there⟩ **5** : is or are commanded to ⟨you *will* come here to the desk at once⟩

²will \'wil\ *n* **1** : wish or desire often combined with determination ⟨the *will* to win⟩ **2** : the power to decide or control what one will do or how one will act **3** : a legal paper in which a person states to whom his possessions are to be given after his death

³will \'wil\ *vb* **1** : to command or order sometimes in the form of a wish ⟨the king so *wills* it⟩ **2** : to bring to a certain condition by the power of the will ⟨*will* yourself to sleep⟩ **3** : to leave or bequeath (as property) by will

will·ful *or* **wil·ful** \'wil-fəl\ *adj* **1** : STUBBORN **2** : INTENTIONAL — **will·ful·ly** *adv* — **will·ful·ness** *n*

will·ing \'wil-ing\ *adj* **1** : favorably inclined ⟨*willing* to go⟩ **2** : not slow or lazy **3** : made, done, or given of one's own choice : VOLUNTARY — **will·ing·ly** *adv* — **will·ing·ness** *n*

wil·low \'wil-ō\ *n* **1** : a tree or bush with narrow leaves, catkins for flowers, and tough pliable shoots used in making baskets **2** : the wood of the willow tree used in making baseball bats

wilt \'wilt\ *vb* **1** : to lose freshness and become limp ⟨*wilting* roses⟩ **2** : to grow weak

wil·y \'wī-lē\ *adj* **wil·i·er; wil·i·est** : CUNNING, CRAFTY

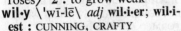
willow: twig and leaves

win \'win\ *vb* **won** \'wən\; **win·ning** **1** : to gain the victory in a contest or competition **2** : to get by effort or skill : GAIN ⟨*win* praise⟩ **3** : to obtain by victory ⟨*win* a prize in a contest⟩ **4** : to be the victor in ⟨*win* a race⟩ **5** : to solicit and gain the favor of

wince \'wins\ *vb* **winced; winc·ing** : to draw back (as from pain) : FLINCH

winch \'winch\ *n* : a machine that has a roller on which rope is coiled for hauling or hoisting and that is operated by a crank

winch

¹wind \'wind\ *n* **1** : a movement of the air : BREEZE ⟨there is a strong *wind* tonight⟩ **2** : power to breathe ⟨the fall knocked the *wind* out of the boy⟩ **3** : air carrying a scent (as of game) **4** : limited advance knowledge : HINT ⟨the girls got *wind* of the club's plans⟩ **5** : wind instruments especially as distinguished from strings and percussion

²wind *vb* **1** : to get a scent of ⟨the dogs *winded* game⟩ **2** : to cause to be out of breath

³wind \'wīnd, 'wind\ *vb* **wound** \'waùnd\; **wind·ing** : to sound (as a horn) by blowing

⁴wind \'wīnd\ *vb* **wound** \'waùnd\; **wind·ing** **1** : to twist or coil around ⟨*wind* thread on a spool⟩ **2** : to cover with something twisted around : WRAP ⟨*wind* an arm with a bandage⟩ **3** : to tighten the spring of ⟨*wound* his watch⟩ **4** : CURVE ⟨a road that *winds*⟩ — **wind up** **1** : to bring to a conclusion : END **2** : to swing the arm before pitching a baseball

⁵wind \'wīnd\ *n* : BEND, COIL

wind·break \'wind-ˌbrāk\ *n* : something (as a planting of trees and shrubs) that breaks the force of the wind

wind·fall \'wind-ˌfôl\ *n* **1** : something (as fruit from a tree) blown down by the wind **2** : an unexpected legacy or gift

wind instrument \'wind-\ *n* : a musical instrument (as a flute or horn) sounded by wind and especially by the breath

wind·lass \'wind-ləs\ *n* : a winch used especially on ships for hauling and hoisting

wind·mill \'wind-ˌmil\ *n* : a mill or a machine (as for pumping water) worked by the wind turning sails or vanes at the top of a tower

win·dow \'win-dō\ *n* [from an old Scandinavian word *vindauga*, put together from *vindr* "wind", "air" and *auga* "eye"] **1** : an opening in a wall to admit light and air **2** : the glass and framework that fill a window opening

window box *n* : a box for growing plants in or by a window

win·dow·pane \'win-dō-ˌpān\ *n* : a pane in a window

wind·pipe \'wind-ˌpīp\ *n* : a firm-walled tube extending from the pharynx to the lungs and used in breathing

wind·proof \'wind-'prüf\ *adj* : proof against the wind

wind·shield \'wind-ˌshēld\ *n* : a transparent

screen (as of glass) attached to the body of a vehicle (as a car) in front of the occupants to protect them from the wind

wind·storm \'wind-,stòrm\ *n* : a storm with strong wind and little or no rain

wind·up \'wīnd-,əp\ *n*   **1** : CONCLUSION, END   **2** : a swing of a baseball pitcher's arm before he pitches

¹wind·ward \'wind-wərd\ *adj* : moving or situated toward the direction from which the wind is blowing

²windward *n* : the side or direction from which the wind is blowing

wind·y \'win-dē\ *adj* **wind·i·er**; **wind·i·est**   **1** : having wind : exposed to winds ⟨a *windy* day⟩   **2** : indulging in useless talk

wine \'wīn\ *n* [from Old English *wīn*, probably borrowed by the ancestors of the English long before they came to England from the Latin word *vinum* "wine"]   **1** : fermented grape juice containing varying percentages of alcohol   **2** : the usually fermented juice of a plant product (as a fruit) used as a beverage

¹wing \'wing\ *n*   **1** : one of the paired limbs or limblike parts by means of which a bird, bat, or insect flies   **2** : something like a wing in appearance, use, or motion ⟨the *wings* of an airplane⟩   **3** : a part (as of a building) that projects from the main part   **4** : a division of an army or fleet   **5** *pl* : an area just off the stage of a theater

²wing *vb* : to go with wings : FLY

winged \'wingd, 'wing-əd\ *adj* : having wings or winglike parts ⟨*winged* insects⟩

wing·less \'wing-ləs\ *adj* : having no wings

wing·spread \'wing-,spred\ *n* : the distance between the tips of the spread wings

¹wink \'wingk\ *vb*   **1** : to close and open the eyelids quickly : BLINK   **2** : to pretend not to see ⟨*wink* at a violation of the law⟩   **3** : FLICKER, TWINKLE   **4** : to close and open one eye quickly as a signal or hint

²wink *n*   **1** : a brief period of sleep : NAP   **2** : a hint or sign given by winking   **3** : an act of winking   **4** : the time of a wink : INSTANT

win·ner \'win-ər\ *n* : one that wins

¹win·ning \'win-ing\ *n*   **1** : the act of one that wins   **2** : something won especially in gambling — often used in plural

²winning *adj* : ATTRACTIVE, CHARMING

win·now \'win-ō\ *vb* : to remove (as chaff from grain) by a current of air

win·some \'win-səm\ *adj* : WINNING, CHEERFUL ⟨a *winsome* girl⟩ ⟨a *winsome* smile⟩

¹win·ter \'wint-ər\ *n*   **1** : the season between autumn and spring comprising in the northern hemisphere usually the months of December,

January, and February or as reckoned astronomically extending from the December solstice to the March equinox   **2** : YEAR ⟨a man of seventy *winters*⟩

²winter *vb*   **1** : to pass the winter ⟨*wintered* in Florida⟩   **2** : to keep, feed, or manage during the winter ⟨*winter* livestock on silage⟩

win·ter·green \'wint-ər-,grēn\ *n* : a low‑growing evergreen plant bearing white bell-shaped flowers followed by red berries and yielding an oil (**oil of wintergreen**) used in medicine and flavoring

win·ter·time \'wint-ər-,tīm\ *n* : the winter season

win·try \'win-trē\ *adj* **win·tri·er**; **win·tri·est**   **1** : of, relating to, or characteristic of winter   **2** : COLD, CHEERLESS ⟨a *wintry* welcome⟩

wintergreen

¹wipe \'wīp\ *vb* **wiped**; **wip·ing**   **1** : to clean or dry by rubbing ⟨*wipe* dishes⟩   **2** : to remove by or as if by rubbing ⟨*wipe* away tears⟩   **3** : to erase completely : DESTROY ⟨the regiment was *wiped* out⟩ — **wip·er** *n*

²wipe *n* : an act of wiping : RUB

¹wire \'wīr\ *n*   **1** : metal in the form of a thread or slender rod   **2** : something made of wire   **3** : a telephone or telegraph wire or system   **4** : TELEGRAM, CABLEGRAM

²wire *vb* **wired**; **wir·ing**   **1** : to provide or equip with wire   **2** : to bind, string, or mount with wire   **3** : to telegraph or telegraph to

¹wire·less \'wīr-ləs\ *adj*   **1** : having no wire   **2** : relating to communication by electric waves but without connecting wires : RADIO

²wireless *n*   **1** : wireless telegraphy   **2** : RADIO

wir·y \'wīr-ē\ *adj* **wir·i·er**; **wir·i·est**   **1** : of or resembling wire   **2** : being slender yet strong and active

wis·dom \'wiz-dəm\ *n* : knowledge and the ability to utilize it to benefit oneself or others

wisdom tooth *n* : the last tooth of the full set on each half of each jaw of an adult

¹wise \'wīz\ *n* : WAY, MANNER — used in such phrases as *in any wise*, *in no wise*, *in this wise*

²wise *adj*   **1** : having or showing good sense or good judgment : SENSIBLE   **2** : aware of what is going on : INFORMED — **wise·ly** *adv*

-wise \,wīz\ *adv suffix*   **1** : in the manner of ⟨crab*wise*⟩   **2** : in the position or direction of ⟨clock*wise*⟩   **3** : with regard to ⟨dollar*wise*⟩

¹wish \'wish\ *vb*   **1** : DESIRE, WANT ⟨*wish* to be rich⟩   **2** : to form or express a desire concerning ⟨*wished* her a merry Christmas⟩

²wish *n*   **1** : an act or instance of wishing : WANT   **2** : something wished ⟨got his *wish*⟩

3 : a desire for happiness or good fortune ⟨send her best *wishes*⟩

wish·bone \'wish-ˌbōn\ *n* : the forked bone in front of a bird's breastbone

wish·ful \'wish-fəl\ *adj* **1 :** having a wish : DESIROUS **2 :** according with wishes rather than fact ⟨*wishful* thinking⟩

wish·y–wash·y \'wish-ē-ˌwȯsh-ē, -ˌwäsh-\ *adj* **1 :** being thin and pale **2 :** being weak and spiritless

wisp \'wisp\ *n* **1 :** a small bunch of hay or straw **2 :** a thin piece or strand ⟨*wisps* of hair⟩ **3 :** a thready streak ⟨*wisps* of smoke⟩

wisp·y \'wis-pē\ *adj* **wisp·i·er; wisp·i·est** : being thin, slight, and filmy

wis·tar·i·a \wis-'tir-ē-ə, -'ter-\ *n* : WISTERIA

wis·te·ri·a \wis-'tir-ē-ə\ *n* : a woody vine related to the beans that is grown for its long showy clusters of violet, white, or pink flowers

wist·ful \'wist-fəl\ *adj* : feeling or showing longing ⟨a *wistful* expression⟩

wit \'wit\ *n* **1 :** power to think, reason, or decide ⟨a person of little *wit*⟩ **2 :** mental soundness : SANITY **3 :** cleverness in expressing connections between words or things not usually connected **4 :** witty remarks, expressions, or passages **5 :** a witty person

witch \'wich\ *n* **1 :** a woman believed to have magic powers : SORCERESS **2 :** an ugly old woman

witch·craft \'wich-ˌkraft\ *n* : the power or practices of a witch : SORCERY

witch·er·y \'wich-ə-rē\ *n, pl* **witch·er·ies** **1 :** WITCHCRAFT **2 :** power to charm or fascinate

witch ha·zel \'wich-ˌhā-zəl\ *n* **1 :** a common shrub with small yellow flowers borne in late fall or very early spring **2 :** a soothing alcoholic lotion made from witch hazel bark

witch·ing \'wich-ing\ *adj* : BEWITCHING, ENCHANTING

with \with, with\ *prep* **1 :** AGAINST ⟨fought *with* his brother⟩ **2 :** in mutual relation to ⟨talk *with* friends⟩ **3 :** in regard to : TOWARD ⟨patient *with* children⟩ **4 :** compared to ⟨on equal terms *with* the rest⟩ **5 :** as well as ⟨plays *with* the best of them⟩ **6 :** at the same time as ⟨get up *with* the sun⟩ **7 :** in support of ⟨I'm *with* you all the way⟩ **8 :** in the opinion or judgment of ⟨their arguments had weight *with* him⟩ **9 :** because of : THROUGH ⟨pale *with* anger⟩ **10 :** in a way that shows ⟨work *with* a will⟩ **11 :** GIVEN, GRANTED ⟨*with* your permission, I'll leave⟩ **12 :** in the com-

witch hazel
flower clusters

pany of ⟨a boy *with* his friends⟩ **13 :** HAVING ⟨came *with* good news⟩ ⟨stood there *with* his mouth open⟩ **14 :** DESPITE ⟨*with* all his cleverness, he failed⟩ **15 :** at the time of ⟨*with* that statement, he paused⟩ **16 :** CONTAINING ⟨coffee *with* cream and sugar⟩ **17 :** FROM ⟨parting *with* friends⟩ **18 :** by means of ⟨hit him *with* a ruler⟩ **19 :** so as to go along with or follow rather than oppose ⟨sailed *with* the tide⟩

with·al \with-'ȯl, with-\ *adv* **1 :** BESIDES **2 :** for all that ⟨pleasant but stubborn *withal*⟩

with·draw \with-'drȯ, with-\ *vb* **with·drew** \-'drü\; **with·drawn** \-'drȯn\; **with·draw·ing** **1 :** to draw back : take away : REMOVE ⟨*withdraw* money from the bank⟩ ⟨the allies *withdrew* their troops⟩ **2 :** to take back (as something said or proposed) : RECALL ⟨*withdraw* a charge⟩ **3 :** to go away : RETREAT ⟨the enemy *withdrew*⟩ **4 :** to quit a position or the presence of others : cease an activity

with·draw·al \with-'drȯ-əl, with-\ *n* : an act or instance of withdrawing

with·er \'with-ər\ *vb* : to shrivel from or as if from loss of natural body moisture : WILT

with·ers \'with-ərz\ *n pl* : the ridge between the shoulder bones of a horse

with·hold \with-'hōld, with-\ *vb* **with·held** \-'held\; **with·hold·ing** : to refrain from giving, granting, or allowing

¹with·in \with-'in, with-\ *adv* **1 :** in or into the interior : INSIDE ⟨inquire *within*⟩ **2 :** INWARDLY ⟨raging *within*⟩

²within *prep* **1 :** inside of ⟨stay *within* the house⟩ **2 :** not beyond the bounds or limits of ⟨live *within* your income⟩

¹with·out \with-'aut, with-\ *prep* **1 :** at, to, or on the outside of ⟨*without* the gate⟩ **2 :** LACKING ⟨he's *without* hope⟩ **3 :** unaccompanied or unmarked by ⟨he spoke *without* thinking⟩

²without *adv* **1 :** on the outer sides : OUTSIDE ⟨the house is shabby *without*⟩ **2 :** out of doors ⟨the wind *without*⟩

with·stand \with-'stand, with-\ *vb* **with·stood** \-'stud\; **with·stand·ing** **1 :** to stand against **2 :** to oppose (as an attack) successfully

wit·less \'wit-ləs\ *adj* : lacking in wit or intelligence : FOOLISH

¹wit·ness \'wit-nəs\ *n* **1 :** TESTIMONY ⟨give false *witness*⟩ **2 :** PROOF, EVIDENCE ⟨a deed bears *witness* of a person's ownership⟩ **3 :** a person who sees or otherwise has direct knowledge of something ⟨*witnesses* of an accident⟩ **4 :** a person who gives testimony in court **5 :** a person who is present at an action (as the signing of a will) so that he can testify who performed it

²witness *vb* **1 :** to be a witness to **2 :** to give testimony to : testify as a witness **3** : to be or give proof of ⟨the man's actions *witness* his guilt⟩

wit·ted \'wit-əd\ *adj* : having wit or understanding ⟨quick-*witted*⟩ ⟨slow-*witted*⟩

wit·ty \'wit-ē\ *adj* **wit·ti·er; wit·ti·est** : having or showing wit ⟨a *witty* person⟩

wives *pl of* WIFE

wiz·ard \'wiz-ərd\ *n* [from medieval English *wysard* meaning "wise man", from *wys* "wise" with a suffix -*ard* derived from French and used to form names for persons having certain qualities, as in *drunkard*] **1** : MAGICIAN, SORCERER **2** : a very clever or skillful person

¹wob·ble \'wäb-əl\ *vb* **wob·bled; wob·bling** **1** : to be unsteady or move unsteadily : SHAKE **2** : to be undecided — **wob·bly** \'wäb-lē\ *adj*

²wobble *n* : a rocking motion from side to side

woe \'wō\ *n* : great sorrow, grief, or misfortune : TROUBLE, AFFLICTION ⟨a tale of *woe*⟩

woe·be·gone \'wō-bi-ˌgȯn\ *adj* **1** : looking sorrowful : MISERABLE **2** : DISMAL, DESOLATE

woe·ful \'wō-fəl\ *adj* **1** : full of grief or misery ⟨*woeful* heart⟩ **2** : bringing woe or misery ⟨a *woeful* day⟩

woke *past of* WAKE

woken *past part of* WAKE

¹wolf \'wu̇lf\ *n, pl* **wolves** \'wu̇lvz\ **1** : a large doglike flesh-eating wild animal with erect ears and bushy tail that is often destructive to game and domestic animals **2** : a person resembling a wolf (as in ferocity or guile) — **wolf·ish** *adj*

²wolf *vb* : to eat greedily : DEVOUR

wolf dog *n* **1** : WOLFHOUND **2** : the hybrid offspring of a wolf and a domestic dog **3** : a large wolflike domestic dog

wolf·hound \'wu̇lf-ˌhau̇nd\ *n* : any of several large dogs used in hunting large animals

wol·fram \'wu̇l-frəm\ *n* : TUNGSTEN

wol·ver·ine \ˌwu̇l-və-'rēn\ *n* : a blackish shaggy-furred flesh-eating wild animal related to the martens and sables and found chiefly in the northern parts of North America

wom·an \'wu̇m-ən\ *n, pl* **wom·en** \'wim-ən\ **1** : an adult female person **2** : a female attendant or servant **3** : WOMANHOOD

wom·an·hood \'wu̇m-ən-ˌhu̇d\ *n* **1** : the state of being a woman **2** : womanly qualities **3** : WOMEN

wom·an·kind \'wu̇m-ən-ˌkīnd\ *n* : WOMEN

wom·an·ly \'wu̇m-ən-lē\ *adj* **1** : having the qualities (as gentleness or modesty) becoming a woman **2** : no longer childish or girlish ⟨a *womanly* figure⟩

womb \'wüm\ *n* : UTERUS

wom·bat \'wäm-ˌbat\ *n* : a

wombat

brownish gray burrowing animal of Australia that carries its young in a pouch and resembles a small bear

wom·en·folk \'wim-ən-ˌfōk\ *or* **wom·en·folks** \-ˌfōks\ *n pl* : women especially of one family or group

won *past of* WIN

¹won·der \'wən-dər\ *n* **1** : something extraordinary : MARVEL **2** : a feeling (as of astonishment) aroused by something extraordinary

²wonder *vb* **1** : to feel surprise or amazement **2** : to have some doubt and curiosity

won·der·ful \'wən-dər-fəl\ *adj* **1** : exciting wonder : MARVELOUS, ASTONISHING **2** : unusually good or fine — **won·der·ful·ly** *adv*

won·der·land \'wən-dər-ˌland\ *n* **1** : a fairylike imaginary realm **2** : a place of wonders

won·der·ment \'wən-dər-mənt\ *n* : SURPRISE, AMAZEMENT

won·drous \'wən-drəs\ *adj* : WONDERFUL

¹wont \'wȯnt, 'wōnt\ *adj* : being in the habit of doing ⟨slept longer than he was *wont*⟩

²wont *n* : usual practice : CUSTOM, HABIT

won't \wōnt\ : will not

woo \'wü\ *vb* **wooed; woo·ing** **1** : to try to gain the love of : COURT **2** : to try to gain ⟨*woo* wealth and success⟩ ⟨*woo* public favor⟩

¹wood \'wu̇d\ *n* **1** : a thick growth of trees : a small forest — often used in plural **2** : a hard fibrous material that makes up most of the substance of a tree or shrub within the bark **3** : plant wood prepared or suitable for some use (as burning or building)

²wood *adj* **1** : WOODEN **2** : used for or on wood ⟨a *wood* chisel⟩ **3** *or* **woods** \'wu̇dz\ : living or growing in woodland ⟨*woods* herbs⟩

wood·bine \'wu̇d-ˌbīn\ *n* : any of several climbing vines of Europe and America (as honeysuckle or the Virginia creeper)

wood·carv·er \'wu̇d-ˌkär-vər\ *n* : a person who carves ornamental objects of wood

woodbine

wood·chuck \'wu̇d-ˌchək\ *n* : a reddish brown hibernating rodent : GROUNDHOG

wood·cock \'wu̇d-ˌkäk\ *n* : a long-billed brown game bird related to the snipe

wood·craft \'wu̇d-ˌkraft\ *n* : knowledge about the woods and how to take care of oneself in them

wood·cut·ter \'wu̇d-ˌkət-ər\ *n* : one that cuts wood especially as an occupation

wood·ed \'wu̇d-əd\ *adj* : covered with trees

wood·en \'wu̇d-n\ *adj* **1** : made of wood **2** : stiff like wood : AWKWARD ⟨a *wooden* posture⟩ **3** : SPIRITLESS, DULL ⟨a *wooden* expression⟩

wood·land \'wùd-lənd\ *n* : land covered with trees and shrubs : FOREST

wood louse *n* : a small flat gray crustacean that lives usually under stones or bark

wood·peck·er \'wùd-ˌpek-ər\ *n* : a bird that climbs trees and drills holes in them with its bill in search of insects

wood·pile \'wùd-ˌpīl\ *n* : a pile of wood especially for making fires

wood pulp *n* : wood processed for use in making cellulose derivatives (as paper)

wood·shed \'wùd-ˌshed\ *n* : a shed for storing wood and especially firewood

woods·man \'wùdz-mən\ *n, pl* **woods·men** \-mən\ **1** : a man who cuts down trees as an occupation **2** : one skilled in woodcraft

wood thrush *n* : a large thrush of eastern North America noted for its loud clear song

wood·wind \'wùd-ˌwind\ *n* : one of the group of wind instruments consisting of the flutes, oboes, clarinets, bassoons, and sometimes saxophones

wood·work \'wùd-ˌwərk\ *n* : work (as fittings for house interiors) made of wood

wood·work·ing \'wùd-ˌwər-king\ *n* : the art or process of shaping or working with wood

wood·y \'wùd-ē\ *adj* **wood·i·er; wood·i·est**
1 : abounding with woods **2** : of or containing wood or wood fibers ⟨*woody* stem⟩ **3** : typical of or resembling wood ⟨*woody* texture⟩

woof \'wùf, 'wüf\ *n* **1** : the threads that cross the warp in a fabric **2** : a woven fabric or its texture

wool \'wùl\ *n* **1** : soft heavy wavy or curly hair especially of the sheep **2** : a substance light and fleecy like wool ⟨glass *wool*⟩ **3** : a material (as yarn) made from wool

wool·en *or* **wool·len** \'wùl-ən\ *adj* **1** : made of wool **2** : of or relating to wool or cloth made of wool ⟨a *woolen* mill⟩

wool·ly \'wùl-ē\ *adj* **wool·li·er; wool·li·est**
: consisting of or resembling wool

¹word \'wərd\ *n* **1** : a meaningful sound or combination of sounds spoken by a human being **2** : a written or printed letter or letters standing for a spoken word **3** : a brief remark or conversation **4** : COMMAND, ORDER **5** : NEWS **6** : PROMISE **7** *pl* : quarrelsome remarks ⟨he and his brother had *words*⟩

²word *vb* : to express in words : PHRASE

word·ing \'wərd-ing\ *n* : the way something is put into words

word·y \'wərd-ē\ *adj* **word·i·er; word·i·est**
: using or containing many words or more words than are needed — **word·i·ness** *n*

wore *past of* WEAR

¹work \'wərk\ *n* **1** : the use of a person's strength or ability in order to get something done or get some desired result : LABOR ⟨the *work* of a carpenter⟩ **2** : EMPLOYMENT, OCCUPATION **3** : something that needs to be done : TASK, JOB ⟨have *work* to do⟩ **4** : DEED, ACHIEVEMENT ⟨honor a man for his good *works*⟩ **5** : something produced by toil or labor ⟨an author's latest *work*⟩ **6** *pl* : a place where industrial labor is carried on : PLANT, FACTORY ⟨a locomotive *works*⟩ **7** *pl* : the working or moving parts of a mechanical device ⟨the *works* of a watch⟩ **8** : manner of working : WORKMANSHIP ⟨a job spoiled by careless *work*⟩

syn WORK, LABOR, TOIL all mean effort or exertion directed toward achieving a particular result. WORK is the general term for any physical or mental effort aimed toward a certain end and may be applied whether the effort is itself enjoyable or is merely a means of accomplishing something ⟨we always share the *work* at parties and picnics⟩ ⟨he does a lot of *work* on antique cars⟩ LABOR suggests great exertion, especially hard or unpleasant physical effort, and usually indicates work done from necessity rather than choice ⟨it took several hours of *labor* to uproot the bush⟩ ⟨sentenced to five years at hard *labor*⟩ TOIL is likely to indicate extremely hard, fatiguing, and prolonged work ⟨years of *toil* showed on the old man's face⟩

²work *vb* **worked** *or* **wrought** \'ròt\; **work·ing**
1 : to do work especially for money or other gain or under necessity instead of for pleasure : labor or cause to labor **2** : to perform or act or to cause to act as intended : OPERATE ⟨a plan that *worked* well⟩ ⟨*work* a machine⟩ **3** : to move or cause to move slowly or with effort ⟨*work* the liquid into a cloth⟩ ⟨the screw *worked* loose⟩ **4** : MAKE, SHAPE ⟨a vase beautifully *wrought*⟩ **5** : to bring to pass : CAUSE **6** : to carry on one's occupation in, through, or along ⟨two salesmen *worked* the city⟩ **7** : EXCITE, PROVOKE ⟨*worked* himself into a rage⟩ **8** : FERMENT

work·a·ble \'wər-kə-bəl\ *adj* : capable of being worked or done

work·bench \'wərk-ˌbench\ *n* : a bench on which work is performed (as by mechanics)

work·book \'wərk-ˌbük\ *n* : a student's exercise book made up of a series of problems or exercises intended as part of a course of study

work·er \'wər-kər\ *n* **1** : one that works **2** : one of the members of a colony of bees, ants, wasps, or termites that are sexually im-

j job   ng sing   ō low   ȯ moth   ȯi coin   th thin   tẖ this   ü boot   ù foot   y you   yü few   yü furious   zh vision

perfectly developed and that perform most of the labor and protective activity of the community

work·ing \'wər-king\ *adj* **1** : doing work especially for a living ⟨a *working* girl⟩ **2** : relating to work ⟨*working* hours⟩ **3** : good enough to allow work or further work to be done

work·ing·man \'wər-king-,man\ *n, pl* **work·ing·men** \-,men\ : one who works for wages usually at manual labor or in industry

work·man \'wərk-mən\ *n, pl* **work·men** \-mən\ **1** : WORKINGMAN **2** : a skilled craftsman (as an electrician or carpenter)

work·man·ship \'wərk-mən-,ship\ *n* **1** : the art or skill of a workman **2** : the quality or character of a piece of work ⟨take pride in good *workmanship*⟩

work·out \'wərk-,aůt\ *n* : an exercise or practice intended to test or increase ability or performance ⟨give the team a *workout*⟩

work·shop \'wərk-,shäp\ *n* : a shop where work and especially skilled manual work is carried on

world \'wərld\ *n* **1** : UNIVERSE, CREATION **2** : EARTH **3** : people in general : MANKIND **4** : a state of existence ⟨a future *world*⟩ **5** : a great number or quantity ⟨a *world* of troubles⟩ **6** : a part or section of the earth or its inhabitants by itself

world·ly \'wərld-lē\ *adj* **world·li·er; world·li·est** : of or relating to this world

¹worm \'wərm\ *n* **1** : any of various long usually soft-bodied creeping or crawling animals **2** : a person despised because of his wretched condition or humble manner **3** *pl* : the presence of or disease caused by parasitic worms in the body ⟨a dog with *worms*⟩

²worm *vb* : to move, go, or work slowly in the manner of a worm

worm·y \'wər-mē\ *adj* **worm·i·er; worm·i·est** : containing worms

worn *past part of* WEAR

worn–out \'wōrn-'aůt\ *adj* **1** : useless from long or hard wear **2** : extremely weary **3** : TRITE

wor·ri·some \'wər-ē-səm\ *adj* **1** : inclined to worry **2** : causing worry

¹wor·ry \'wər-ē\ *vb* **wor·ried; wor·ry·ing 1** : to shake and tear or mangle with the teeth **2** : to torment with anxiety **3** : to feel or express great anxiety

²worry *n, pl* **wor·ries 1** : ANXIETY **2** : a cause of anxiety

¹worse \'wərs\ *adj, comparative of* BAD *or of* ILL **1** : bad or evil in a greater degree : poorer in quality or worth **2** : being in poorer health

²worse *n* : something worse

³worse *adv, comparative of* BAD *or of* BADLY *or of* ILL : not as well : in a worse degree

¹wor·ship \'wər-shəp\ *n* [from Old English *weorthscipe* meaning the quality of being worthy, from *weorth* "worth", "worthy" and the suffix *-scipe* "-ship"] **1** : reverence toward God, a god, or a sacred object **2** : extravagant respect or admiration

²worship *vb* **wor·shiped** *or* **wor·shipped; wor·ship·ing** *or* **wor·ship·ping 1** : to pay divine honors to : ADORE **2** : to regard with extravagant respect, honor, or devotion **3** : to perform or take part in worship or an act of worship — **wor·ship·er** *or* **wor·ship·per** *n*

¹worst \'wərst\ *adj, superlative of* BAD *or of* ILL : bad, ill, or evil in the highest degree : POOREST

²worst *n* : a person or thing that is worst

³worst *adv, superlative of* ILL *or of* BAD *or of* BADLY : in the worst way or to the worst extent possible ⟨treated him *worst* of all⟩

⁴worst *vb* : to get the better of : DEFEAT

wor·sted \'wůs-təd, 'wərs-\ *n* **1** : a smooth yarn spun from pure wool **2** : a fabric woven from a worsted yarn

wort \'wərt, 'wȯrt\ *n* : a dilute solution of sugars obtained by infusion from malt and fermented to form beer

¹worth \'wərth\ *prep* **1** : equal in value to ⟨a ring *worth* $1000⟩ **2** : having possessions or income equal to ⟨he's *worth* a lot of money⟩ **3** : deserving of ⟨it was well *worth* the effort⟩ **4** : capable of ⟨ran for all he was *worth*⟩

²worth *n* **1** : the quality or sum of qualities of a thing making it valuable or useful **2** : value as expressed in money **3** : EXCELLENCE, VIRTUE

worth·less \'wərth-ləs\ *adj* : USELESS

worth·while \'wərth-'hwīl\ *adj* : being worth the time spent or effort put forth

wor·thy \'wər-thē\ *adj* **wor·thi·er; wor·thi·est 1** : having worth or excellence ⟨a *worthy* goal⟩ **2** : MERITING, DESERVING ⟨*worthy* of promotion⟩ — **wor·thi·ness** *n*

would \wəd, wůd\ *past of* WILL **1** : strongly desire : WISH ⟨I *would* I were young again⟩ **2** — used as a helping verb to express preference, wish or desire, intention, habitual action, a contingency or possibility, probability, capability, a request, or simple futurity from a point of view in the past **3** : COULD ⟨the barrel *would* hold 20 gallons⟩ **4** : SHOULD ⟨*would* be glad to know the answer⟩

would·n't \'wůd-nt\ : would not

¹wound \'wünd\ *n* **1** : an injury cutting or breaking bodily tissue usually by violence, accident, or surgery **2** : an injury or hurt to feelings or reputation

²**wound** *vb* **1** : to hurt by cutting or breaking tissue **2** : to hurt the feelings or pride of

³**wound** \'wau̇nd\ *past of* WIND

wove *past of* WEAVE

woven *past part of* WEAVE

wraith \'rāth\ *n* **1** : a ghostly appearance of a living person believed to be seen just before his death **2** : GHOST

¹**wran·gle** \'rang-gəl\ *vb* **wran·gled; wran·gling 1** : to dispute angrily : BICKER **2** : ARGUE **3** : to herd and care for livestock and especially horses on the range

²**wrangle** *n* : QUARREL

wran·gler \'rang-glər\ *n* **1** : one that wrangles or bickers **2** : a ranch worker who tends the saddle horses

¹**wrap** \'rap\ *vb* **wrapped; wrap·ping 1** : to cover by winding or folding **2** : to enclose in a package **3** : to wind or roll together : FOLD **4** : ENGROSS, ABSORB

²**wrap** *n* : a warm loose outer garment (as a shawl, cape, or coat)

wrap·per \'rap-ər\ *n* **1** : what something is wrapped in **2** : one that wraps

wrap·ping \'rap-ing\ *n* : something used to wrap an object : WRAPPER

wrath \'rath\ *n* : violent anger : RAGE

wrath·ful \'rath-fəl\ *adj* **1** : full of wrath **2** : showing wrath ⟨a *wrathful* look⟩

wreak \'rēk\ *vb* **1** : to exact as a punishment : INFLICT **2** : to give free scope to

wreath \'rēth\ *n, pl* **wreaths** \'rēthz, 'rēths\ : something twisted or intertwined into a circular shape ⟨a *wreath* of flowers⟩

wreathe \'rēth\ *vb* **wreathed; wreath·ing 1** : to twist so as to show folds or creases **2** : to fold or coil around : ENTWINE **3** : to form into wreaths

wreath

¹**wreck** \'rek\ *n* **1** : broken remains (as of a ship or vehicle) after heavy damage by storm, collision, or fire **2** : a person or beast broken in health or in strength **3** : the action of breaking up or destroying something

²**wreck** *vb* **1** : to cause to suffer shipwreck **2** : to damage or ruin by breaking up

wreck·age \'rek-ij\ *n* **1** : a wrecking or being wrecked **2** : the remains of a wreck

wreck·er \'rek-ər\ *n* **1** : one that wrecks **2** : a person who works on wrecks of ships for rescue or for plunder **3** : a ship used in salvaging wrecks **4** : a truck equipped to remove wrecked or disabled cars

wren \'ren\ *n* : any of a group of small brown songbirds (as the **house wren**) with short rounded wings and short erect tail

¹**wrench** \'rench\ *n* **1** : a forcible twist to one side or out of shape **2** : an injury caused by twisting or straining : SPRAIN **3** : a tool used in turning nuts or bolts

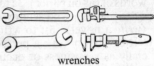

wrenches

²**wrench** *vb* **1** : to pull or twist with or as if with a wrench : WREST **2** : to injure or disable by a sudden sharp twisting or straining

wrest \'rest\ *vb* **1** : to pull away by twisting or wringing **2** : to obtain only by strenuous effort against great odds

¹**wres·tle** \'res-əl\ *vb* **wres·tled; wres·tling 1** : to grapple with an opponent in an attempt to trip him or throw him down **2** : to struggle for mastery (as with something hard to do)

²**wrestle** *n* : STRUGGLE

wres·tling \'res-ling\ *n* : a sport in which two opponents wrestle each other

wretch \'rech\ *n* **1** : a miserable unhappy person **2** : a base vile degraded person

wretch·ed \'rech-əd\ *adj* **1** : very miserable or unhappy **2** : causing misery and distress **3** : hatefully contemptible **4** : very poor in quality or workmanship — **wretch·ed·ly** *adv* — **wretch·ed·ness** *n*

wrig·gle \'rig-əl\ *vb* **wrig·gled; wrig·gling 1** : to twist or move like a worm : SQUIRM **2** : to advance by twisting dodging ways

wrig·gler \'rig-lər\ *n* **1** : one that wriggles **2** : WIGGLER 2

wring \'ring\ *vb* **wrung** \'rəng\; **wring·ing 1** : to twist so as to squeeze out moisture **2** : to get by or as if by twisting or pressing **3** : to affect as if by wringing ⟨their distress *wrung* our hearts⟩ **4** : to twist so as to strangle

wring·er \'ring-ər\ *n* **1** : one that wrings **2** : a machine or device for squeezing water out of clothes

¹**wrin·kle** \'ring-kəl\ *n* **1** : a crease or small fold (as in the skin or in cloth) **2** : a clever notion or trick

²**wrinkle** *vb* **wrin·kled; wrin·kling** : to mark or become marked with wrinkles : CREASE

wrist \'rist\ *n* : the joint or the region of the joint between the hand and arm

wrist·band \'rist-,band\ *n* : a band that encircles the wrist (as for support or warmth)

wrist·watch \'rist-,wäch\ *n* : a small watch attached to a bracelet or strap and worn on the wrist

writ \'rit\ *n* **1** : a piece of writing **2** : an order in writing signed by a court or judicial officer

write \'rīt\ *vb* **wrote** \'rōt\; **writ·ten** \'rit-n\; **writ·ing** \'rīt-ing\ **1** : to form letters or words with pen or pencil **2** : to form the letters or the words of (as on paper) **3** : to put down on paper **4** : to make up and set down for others to read ⟨*write* a novel⟩ **5** : to write a letter to

writ·er \'rīt-ər\ *n* : a person who writes especially as a business or occupation

writhe \'rīth\ *vb* **writhed; writh·ing 1** : to twist and turn this way and that **2** : to suffer as if twisting with pain

writ·ing \'rīt-ing\ *n* **1** : the act of one who writes **2** : HANDWRITING **3** : something (as a letter or book) that is written

¹wrong \'ròng\ *n* **1** : a harmful, unfair, or unjust act **2** : wrong principles, practices, or acts ⟨knows right from *wrong*⟩

²wrong *adj* **1** : not right morally : SINFUL **2** : not correct or true : FALSE **3** : not the one wanted or intended ⟨the *wrong* train⟩ **4** : not suitable or appropriate ⟨what is *wrong* with this dress⟩ **5** : made so as to be placed down or under ⟨the *wrong* side of a ribbon⟩ **6** : not proper — **wrong·ly** *adv* — **wrong·ness** *n*

³wrong *adv* : in the wrong direction, manner, or way : not in the right way ⟨answer *wrong*⟩

⁴wrong *vb* : to do wrong to

wrong·do·er \'ròng-'dü-ər\ *n* : a person who does wrong and especially a moral wrong

wrong·do·ing \'ròng-'dü-ing\ *n* : bad behavior or action ⟨guilty of *wrongdoing*⟩

wrong·ful \'ròng-fəl\ *adj* **1** : WRONG, UNJUST **2** : UNLAWFUL

wrote *past of* WRITE

wroth \'ròth\ *adj* : ANGRY

¹wrought \'ròt\ *past of* WORK

²wrought *adj* **1** : worked into shape **2** : STIRRED, EXCITED

wrung *past of* WRING

wry \'rī\ *adj* **wri·er; wri·est 1** : turned abnormally to one side : CONTORTED **2** : made by twisting the features ⟨a *wry* smile⟩

¹x \'eks\ *n, often cap* **1** : the twenty-fourth letter of the English alphabet **2** : the roman numeral 10 **3** : an unknown quantity

²x *vb* **x–ed** \'ekst\; **x–ing** \'ek-sing\ **1** : to mark with an *x* **2** : to cancel with a series of *x*'s

Xmas \'kris-məs\ *n* : CHRISTMAS

X ray \'eks-,rā\ *n* **1** : a powerful invisible ray of very short wavelength that is somewhat similar to light and that is able to penetrate various thicknesses of solids and act' on photographic film like light **2** : a photograph taken by the use of X rays

x–ray *vb, often cap X* : to examine, treat, or photograph with X rays

xy·lo·phone \'zī-lə-,fōn\ *n* [from Greek *xylon* "wood" and *phōnein* "to sound"] : a musical instrument consisting of a series of wooden bars graduated in length

xylophone

to sound the musical scale and played with two wooden hammers

xy·lo·phon·ist \'zī-lə-,fō-nəst\ *n* : a person who plays the xylophone

y \'wī\ *n, often cap* : the twenty-fifth letter of the English alphabet

¹-y *also* **-ey** \ē\ *adj suffix* **-i·er; -i·est 1** : characterized by, full of, or consisting of ⟨dirt*y*⟩ ⟨mudd*y*⟩ ⟨ic*y*⟩ **2** : like : like that of ⟨wintr*y*⟩ **3** : devoted to : enthusiastic over ⟨outdoors*y*⟩ **4** : tending or inclined to ⟨sleep*y*⟩ **5** : giving occasion for or performing specified action ⟨tear*y*⟩ **6** : somewhat : rather : -ISH ⟨chill*y*⟩ **7** : having specified characteristics to a marked degree or in an affected or superficial way ⟨French*y*⟩

²-y \ē\ *n suffix, pl* **-ies 1** : state : condition : quality ⟨jealous*y*⟩ **2** : activity, place of business, or goods dealt with ⟨laundr*y*⟩ **3** : whole body or group ⟨soldier*y*⟩

³-y *n suffix, pl* **-ies** : instance of a specified action ⟨entreat*y*⟩ ⟨inquir*y*⟩

⁴-y — see -IE

¹yacht \'yät\ *n* : any of various relatively small ships that usually have a sharp prow and graceful lines and are used especially for pleasure cruising or racing

²yacht *vb* : to race or cruise in a yacht

yacht·ing \'yät-ing\ *n* : the action, fact, or pastime of racing or cruising in a yacht

yachts·man \'yäts-mən\ *n, pl* **yachts·men** \-mən\ : a person who owns or sails a yacht

yak \'yak\ *n* : a long-haired wild or domesticated ox of the uplands of Asia

yam \'yam\ *n* **1** : the starchy edible root of a plant related to the lilies that is a staple food in much of the tropics **2** : a moist-fleshed and usually orange-fleshed sweet potato

---

ə abut   ər further   a ax   ā age   ä father, cot   á (see key page)   aù out   ch chin   e less   ē easy   g gift   i trip   ī life

¹yank \'yangk\ *n* : a strong sudden pull : JERK

²yank *vb* : JERK ⟨*yanked* the drawer open⟩

Yan·kee \'yang-kē\ *n* **1** : a native or inhabitant of New England **2** : a native or inhabitant of the northern United States **3** : a native or inhabitant of the United States

¹yap \'yap\ *vb* **yapped; yap·ping 1** : to bark in yaps : YELP **2** : CHATTER, SCOLD

²yap *n* **1** : a quick sharp bark : YELP **2** : often complaining chatter

¹yard \'yärd\ *n* **1** : a measure of length equal to three feet or thirty-six inches **2** : a long spar tapered toward the ends that supports and spreads the head of a sail

²yard *n* **1** : a small usually enclosed area open to the sky and adjacent to a building **2** : the grounds of a building **3** : an enclosure for livestock **4** : an area set aside for a particular business or activity ⟨a navy *yard*⟩ **5** : a system of railroad tracks especially for storage and maintenance of cars

yard·age \'yärd-ij\ *n* **1** : an aggregate number of yards **2** : the length, extent, or volume of something as measured in yards

yard·arm \'yärd-ͺärm\ *n* : either end of the yard of a square-rigged ship

yard goods *n pl* : fabrics sold by the yard

yard·mas·ter \'yärd-ͺmas-tər\ *n* : the man in charge of operations in a railroad yard

yard·stick \'yärd-ͺstik\ *n* **1** : a measuring stick a yard long **2** : a rule or standard by which something is measured or judged

¹yarn \'yärn\ *n* **1** : natural or synthetic fiber (as cotton, wool, or rayon) prepared as a continuous strand for use in knitting or weaving **2** : an interesting or exciting story

²yarn *vb* : to tell a yarn

yar·row \'yar-ō\ *n* : a strong-scented weedy plant with white or rarely pink flowers in flat clusters

yawl \'yòl\ *n* : a two-masted sailboat with the shorter mast aft of the point at which the stern enters the water

¹yawn \'yòn\ *vb* **1** : to open wide : GAPE ⟨a *yawning* cavern⟩ **2** : to open the mouth wide usually as an involuntary reaction to fatigue or boredom

yawl

²yawn *n* : a deep usually involuntary intake of breath through the wide-open mouth

ye \yē\ *pron, archaic* : YOU

¹yea \'yā\ *adv* **1** : YES — used in oral voting **2** : INDEED, TRULY

²yea *n* **1** : an affirmative vote **2** : a person casting a yea vote

year \'yiər\ *n* **1** : the period of about 365¼ solar days required for one revolution of the earth around the sun **2** : a period of 365 days or in leap year 366 days beginning January 1 **3** : a period of time other than a calendar year ⟨the school *year*⟩

year·book \'yiər-ͺbuk\ *n* **1** : a book published yearly especially as a report : ANNUAL **2** : a school publication recording the history and activities of a graduating class

year·ling \'yiər-ling\ *n* : one that is or is rated a year old

year·ly \'yiər-lē\ *adj* : ANNUAL

yearn \'yərn\ *vb* : to feel a longing

yearn·ing \'yər-ning\ *n* : a tender or urgent longing ⟨a *yearning* for his family⟩

year–round \'yiər-'raùnd\ *adj* : effective, employed, or operating for the full year

yeast \'yēst\ *n* **1** : a sediment or a surface froth that occurs usually in sweet liquids in which it causes an alcohol-producing fermentation and that consists largely of the cells of a tiny fungus **2** : a commercial product containing living yeast plants and used especially to make bread dough rise **3** : any of a group of mostly one-celled fungi some of which occur in yeast sediments or froths

¹yell \'yel\ *vb* : to utter a loud cry or scream

²yell *n* **1** : SCREAM, SHOUT **2** : a cheer used especially in schools or colleges to encourage athletic teams

¹yel·low \'yel-ō\ *adj* **1** : of the color yellow **2** : having a yellow complexion or skin ⟨the *yellow* races⟩ **3** : COWARDLY

²yellow *vb* : to turn yellow

³yellow *n* **1** : the color in the rainbow between green and orange **2** : something yellow in color

yellow fever *n* : an infectious disease carried by mosquitoes in hot countries

yel·low·ish \'yel-ə-wish\ *adj* : somewhat yellow

yellow jacket *n* : a small social wasp with yellow markings that usually nests in the ground

¹yelp \'yelp\ *vb* : to utter a sharp quick shrill cry ⟨a dog *yelping* in pain⟩

²yelp *n* : a sharp shrill bark or cry

yen \'yen\ *n* : an intense desire : LONGING

yellow jacket

yeo·man \'yō-mən\ *n, pl* **yeo·men** \-mən\ **1** : an attendant or officer in a royal or noble household **2** : a naval petty officer who performs clerical duties **3** : a small farmer who cultivates his own land

-yer — see -ER

¹yes \'yes\ *adv* **1** — used as a function word to express assent or agreement ⟨are you ready? *Yes*, I am⟩ **2** — used as a function word to introduce a more emphatic or explicit phrase ⟨we are glad, *yes*, very glad to see you⟩ **3** — used as a function word to indicate interest or attentiveness ⟨*yes*, what can I do for you⟩

²yes *n* : an affirmative reply

¹yes·ter·day \'yes-tər-dē\ *adv* : on the day preceding today

²yesterday *n* **1** : the day next before this day **2** : time not long past ⟨fashions of *yesterday*⟩

yes·ter·year \'yes-tər-,yiər\ *n* : the recent past

¹yet \'yet\ *adv* **1** : in addition : BESIDES ⟨gives *yet* another reason⟩ **2** : EVEN **3** ⟨a *yet* higher speed⟩ **3** : up to now : so far ⟨hasn't done much *yet*⟩ **4** : so soon as now ⟨not time to go *yet*⟩ **5** : STILL ⟨is *yet* a new country⟩ **6** : EVENTUALLY ⟨may *yet* decide to go⟩ **7** : NEVERTHELESS, HOWEVER

²yet *conj* : but nevertheless

yew \'yü\ *n* : a tree or shrub with stiff poisonous evergreen leaves, a fleshy fruit, and tough fine-grained wood used especially for bows and small articles

Yid·dish \'yid-ish\ *n* : a language derived from German and spoken by Jews especially of eastern Europe

yew

¹yield \'yēld\ *vb* **1** : to give up possession of on claim or demand : SURRENDER **2** : to give (oneself) up to an inclination, temptation, or habit **3** : to bear as a natural product ⟨trees that *yielded* many apples last year⟩ **4** : to furnish as return or result of expended effort ⟨a play that *yielded* a good profit⟩ **5** : to be fruitful or productive ⟨his peas did not *yield* well⟩ **6** : to give way (as to influence) ⟨*yielded* to his friend's pleas⟩ **7** : to give way under physical force so as to bend, stretch, or break ⟨the rope *yielded* under the strain⟩ **8** : to acknowledge another's superiority

²yield *n* : the amount or quantity produced or returned ⟨a good *yield* of wheat per acre⟩

¹yip \'yip\ *vb* **yipped**; **yip·ping** : to yelp especially from eagerness

²yip *n* : a noise made by or as if by yipping

¹yo·del \'yōd-l\ *vb* **yo·deled** *or* **yo·delled**; **yo·del·ing** *or* **yo·del·ling** **1** : to make sudden changes from a natural voice in singing to one pitched much higher **2** : to call or shout in the manner of yodeling — **yo·del·er** *n*

²yodel *n* **1** : a song or refrain sung by yodeling **2** : a yodeled shout

¹yoke \'yōk\ *n* **1** : a wooden bar or frame by which two work animals (as oxen) are coupled at the heads or necks for drawing a plow or load **2** : a frame fitted to a person's shoulders to carry a load in two equal portions

yoke and oxbows

3 : a clamp that joins two parts to hold or unite them in position **4** *pl usu* **yoke** : two animals yoked together **5** : something that reduces to hardship, humiliation, or servitude ⟨throw off the *yoke* of oppression⟩ **6** : BONDAGE **7** : TIE, LINK ⟨the *yoke* of matrimony⟩ **8** : a fitted or shaped piece at the shoulder of a garment or at the top of a skirt

²yoke *vb* **yoked**; **yok·ing** **1** : to put a yoke on **2** : to attach a work animal to ⟨*yoke* a plow⟩

yo·kel \'yō-kəl\ *n* : a simple country person

yolk \'yōk\ *n* [from Old English *geoloca*, from *geolu* "yellow"] **1** : the yellow inner mass of the egg of a bird or reptile containing stored food material for the developing embryo **2** : oily material in raw wool — **yolked** \'yōkt\ *adj*

Yom Kip·pur \yòm-'kip-ər\ *n* : a Jewish holiday observed in September or October with fasting and prayer as a day of atonement

¹yon \'yän\ *adj* : YONDER

²yon *adv* **1** : YONDER **2** : THITHER ⟨ran hither and *yon*⟩

¹yon·der \'yän-dər\ *adv* : at or in that place

²yonder *adj* **1** : more distant ⟨the *yonder* side of the hill⟩ **2** : being at a distance within view

yore \'yōr\ *n* : time long past ⟨men of *yore*⟩

you \yü, yə\ *pron* **1** : the person or group addressed **2** : ONE ⟨*you* never know what will happen⟩

you'd \yüd\ : you had : you would

you'll \yül\ : you shall : you will

¹young \'yəng\ *adj* **young·er** \'yəng-gər\; **young·est** \'yəng-gəst\ **1** : being in the first or an early stage of life, growth, or development **2** : INEXPERIENCED **3** : recently come into being : NEW **4** : YOUTHFUL

²young *n, pl* **young** **1** *pl* : young persons **2** *pl* : immature offspring ⟨a cat and her *young*⟩ **3** : a single recently born or hatched animal

young·est \'yəng-gəst\ *n, pl* **youngest** : one that is the least old especially of a family

young·ish \'yəng-ish\ *adj* : somewhat young

young·ster \'yəng-stər\ *n* **1** : a young person : YOUTH **2** : CHILD

your \yər, yùr\ *adj* **1** : of or belonging to you ⟨*your* book⟩ **2** : by or from you ⟨*your* gifts⟩ **3** : affecting you ⟨*your* enemies⟩ **4** : of or relating to one ⟨when you face the north, east is at *your* right⟩ **5** — used before a title of honor in address ⟨*your* Majesty⟩

you're \yər, yur\ : you are

yours \yurz\ *pron* **1** : one or the one belonging to you **2** : ones or the ones belonging to you

your·self \yər-'self\ *pron, pl* **your·selves** \-'selvz\ : your own self

youth \'yüth\ *n, pl* **youths** \'yüthz, 'yüths\ **1** : the period of life between childhood and maturity **2** : a young man **3** : young people ⟨the *youth* of today⟩ **4** : YOUTHFULNESS

youth·ful \'yüth-fəl\ *adj* **1** : of, relating to, or appropriate to youth **2** : being young and not yet mature **3** : FRESH, VIGOROUS — **youth·ful·ly** *adv* — **youth·ful·ness** *n*

syn YOUTHFUL and JUVENILE both mean belonging to or being suitable for someone not yet mature. YOUTHFUL is normally complimentary, stressing the desirable characteristics of youth ⟨*youthful* appearance⟩ ⟨*youthful* vigor⟩ or is used when no special disapproval is intended ⟨*youthful* mistakes are often understandable⟩ JUVENILE may merely refer to a product especially suitable for young people ⟨*juvenile* book department⟩ but when applied to things other than goods tends to suggest undesirable lack of maturity ⟨a *juvenile* and reckless point of view⟩

youth hostel *n* : HOSTEL 2

you've \yüv\ : you have

¹yowl \'yaul\ *vb* : WAIL

²yowl *n* : a loud long mournful cry (as of a cat)

yuc·ca \'yək-ə\ *n* : a plant related to the lilies that grows in dry regions and has stiff fibrous leaves at the base of a tall stiff spike of usually whitish flowers

yule \'yül\ *n, often cap* : CHRISTMAS

yule log *n, often cap Y* : a large log formerly put on the hearth on Christmas Eve as the foundation of the fire

yucca

yule·tide \'yül-,tīd\ *n, often cap* : the Christmas season

z \'zē\ *n, often cap* : the twenty-sixth letter of the English alphabet

¹za·ny \'zā-nē\ *n, pl* **za·nies** **1** : CLOWN **2** : a silly or foolish person

²zany *adj* **za·ni·er; za·ni·est** **1** : being or having the characteristics of a zany **2** : CRAZY, FOOLISH

zeal \'zēl\ *n* : eager and ardent interest in the pursuit of something

zeal·ous \'zel-əs\ *adj* : filled with, characterized by, or due to zeal — **zeal·ous·ly** *adv* — **zeal·ous·ness** *n*

ze·bra \'zē-brə\ *n* : an African wild animal related to the horses that has a hide striped in black and white or black and buff

ze·bu \'zē-byü\ *n* : an Asiatic domesticated ox that differs from the related European cattle in having a large fleshy hump over the shoulders and a loose skin with hanging folds

ze·nith \'zē-nəth\ *n* **1** : the point in the heavens directly overhead **2** : APEX

zeph·yr \'zef-ər\ *n* **1** : a breeze from the west **2** : a gentle breeze

zep·pe·lin \'zep-ə-lən\ *n* : a huge cigar-shaped balloon that has a metal framework and is driven through the air by engines carried on its underside

ze·ro \'zē-rō\ *n, pl* **ze·ros** *or* **ze·roes** [from Italian, from medieval Latin *zephirum*, from Arabic *ṣifr*, originally an adjective meaning "empty" and then used as a name for "nothing" in arithmetic and for its symbol] **1** : the numerical symbol 0 denoting the absence of all size or quantity : CIPHER **2** : the number represented by the symbol 0 that leaves unchanged any number to which it is added **3** : the point on a graduated scale (as on a thermometer) from which reckonings are made **4** : the temperature represented by the zero mark on a thermometer **5** : a state of total absence or neutrality : NOTHING ⟨a face that indicated *zero*⟩ **6** : the lowest point

zero hour *n* **1** : the hour at which a previously planned military movement is scheduled to start **2** : the moment at which an ordeal is to begin : the moment of crisis

zest \'zest\ *n* **1** : a quality of enhancing enjoyment **2** : keen enjoyment : RELISH ⟨eats with *zest*⟩ — **zest·ful** \-fəl\ *adj* — **zest·ful·ly** *adv* — **zest·ful·ness** *n* — **zest·y** *adj*

¹zig·zag \'zig-,zag\ *n* **1** : one of a series of short sharp turns or angles in a course **2** : a line, path, or pattern that bends sharply this way and that

zigzags

²zigzag *adv* : in or by a zigzag path or course ⟨ran *zigzag* across the field⟩

³zigzag *adj* : having short sharp turns or angles ⟨a *zigzag* road⟩

⁴zigzag *vb* **zig·zagged; zig·zag·ging** : to form into or proceed along a zigzag

zinc \'zingk\ *n* : a bluish white metal that

tarnishes only slightly in moist air and is used as roofing, to make alloys, and to give iron a protective coating

zing \'zing\ *n* **1** : a shrill humming noise **2** : VITALITY, VIM

zin·ni·a \'zin-ē-ə\ *n* : a tropical American herb related to the daisies that is widely grown for its bright showy long-lasting flower heads

zinnias

¹**zip** \'zip\ *vb* **zipped; zip·ping 1** : to move or act with speed and vigor **2** : to travel with a sharp hissing or humming sound

²**zip** *n* **1** : a sudden sharp hissing sound ⟨the *zip* of a bullet by his ear⟩ **2** : ENERGY, VIM

³**zip** *vb* **zipped; zip·ping** : to close or open with a zipper

zip·per \'zip-ər\ *n* : a fastener (as for a jacket) consisting of two rows of metal or plastic teeth on strips of tape and a sliding piece that closes an opening by drawing the teeth together — **zip·pered** \-ərd\ *adj*

zip·py \'zip-ē\ *adj* **zip·pi·er; zip·pi·est** : BRISK

zith·er \'zith-ər, 'zith-\ *n* : a many-stringed musical instrument played with the tips of the fingers and a pick

¹**zone** \'zōn\ *n* **1** : any of the five great divisions of the earth's surface with respect to latitude and temperature ⟨two frigid *zones*, two temperate *zones*, and one torrid *zone*⟩ **2** : an encircling band or girdle ⟨*zone* of trees⟩ **3** : an area set off or distinguished in some way from adjoining parts ⟨the Canal *Zone*⟩ ⟨a war *zone*⟩

²**zone** *vb* **zoned; zon·ing 1** : ENCIRCLE **2** : to arrange in or mark off in zones and especially into sections for different purposes

zones 1

zoo \'zü\ *n, pl* **zoos** : a collection of living animals for display : ZOOLOGICAL GARDEN

zo·o·log·i·cal \,zō-ə-'läj-i-kəl\ *adj* : of or relating to zoology

zoological garden *n* : a garden or park where wild animals are kept for exhibition

zo·ol·o·gist \zō-'äl-ə-jəst\ *n* : a specialist in zoology

zo·ol·o·gy \zō-'äl-ə-jē\ *n* **1** : a branch of biology dealing with animals and animal life **2** : animal life (as of a geographic region)

¹**zoom** \'züm\ *vb* **1** : to speed along with a loud hum or buzz **2** : to climb sharply and briefly by means of momentum

²**zoom** *n* **1** : an act or process of zooming **2** : a zooming sound

zwie·back \'swē-,bak\ *n* : a usually sweetened bread enriched with eggs that is baked and then sliced and toasted until dry and crisp

zy·gote \'zī-,gōt\ *n* : the new cell produced when a sperm cell fertilizes an egg

ə abut   ər further   a ax   ā age   ä father, cot   à (see key page)   aù out   ch chin   e less   ē easy   g gift   i trip   ī life
j job   ng sing   ō low   ȯ moth   ȯi coin   th thin   th this   ü boot   ù foot   y you   yü few   yù furious   zh vision

ABBREVIATIONS

Most of these abbreviations are shown in one form only.
Variation in use of periods, in kind of type, and in capitalization
is frequent and widespread (as *mph, MPH, m.p.h., Mph*)

abbr   abbreviation
AD   anno Domini (Latin, in the year of our Lord)
adj   adjective
adv   adverb, advertisement
AK   Alaska
AL, Ala   Alabama
alt   alternate, altitude
a.m.   ante meridiem (Latin, before noon)
amt   amount
anon   anonymous
ans   answer
AR   Arkansas
Ariz   Arizona
Ark   Arkansas
assn   association
asst   assistant
atty   attorney
Aug   August
ave   avenue
AZ   Arizona
BC   before Christ
bldg   building
blvd   boulevard
Brit   Britain, British
Bro   brother
bros   brothers
bu   bushel
c   cape, carat, cent, centimeter, century, chapter, cup
C   centigrade
CA, Cal, Calif   California
cap   capital, capitalize, capitalized
capt   captain
ch   chapter, church
co   company, county
CO   Colorado
COD   cash on delivery, collect on delivery
col   colonel, column
Colo   Colorado
conj   conjunction
Conn   Connecticut
ct   cent, court
CT   Connecticut
cu   cubic
CZ   Canal Zone
d   penny
DC   District of Columbia
DDS   doctor of dental science, doctor of dental surgery
DE   Delaware
Dec   December
Del   Delaware
dept   department
DMD   doctor of dental medicine
doz   dozen

Dr   doctor
DST   daylight saving time
E   east, eastern
ea   each
e.g.   exempli gratia (Latin, for example)
etc   et cetera
f   forte
F   Fahrenheit
FBI   Federal Bureau of Investigation
Feb   February
fem   feminine
FL, Fla   Florida
Fri   Friday
ft   feet, foot, fort
g   gram
Ga, GA   Georgia
gal   gallon
gen   general
gov   governor
govt   government
GU   Guam
HI   Hawaii
hr   hour
ht   height
IA   Iowa
ID   Idaho
i.e.   id est (Latin, that is)
IL, Ill   Illinois
in   inch
IN   Indiana
inc   incorporated
Ind   Indiana
interj   interjection
Jan   January
jr   junior
Kans, KS   Kansas
Ky, KY   Kentucky
La, LA   Louisiana
lb   pound
lt   lieutenant
ltd   limited
MA   Massachusetts
maj   major
Mar   March
masc   masculine
Mass   Massachusetts
Md   Maryland
MD   Doctor of Medicine, Maryland
Me, ME   Maine
Mex   Mexico
mi   mile
MI, Mich   Michigan
min   minute
Minn   Minnesota
Miss   Mississippi

MN   Minnesota
mo   month
Mo, MO   Missouri
Mon   Monday
Mont   Montana
mph   miles per hour
Mr   mister
Mrs   mistress
Ms   miss, Mrs.
MS   Mississippi
mt   mount, mountain
MT   Montana
mtn   mountain
MV   motor vessel
n   noun
N   north, northern
NC   North Carolina
ND, N Dak   North Dakota
NE   Nebraska, northeast
Neb, Nebr   Nebraska
Nev   Nevada
NH   New Hampshire
NJ   New Jersey
NM, N Mex   New Mexico
no   north, number
Nov   November
NV   Nevada
NW   northwest
NY   New York
Oct   October
off   office
OH   Ohio
OK, Okla   Oklahoma
OR, Ore, Oreg   Oregon
oz   ounce
p   page, piano
Pa, PA   Pennsylvania
part   participle
pat   patent
Penn, Penna   Pennsylvania
pg   page
PI   Philippine Islands
pk   park, peck
pkg   package
pl   plural
p.m.   post meridiem (Latin, afternoon)
PO   post office
pp   pages
pr   pair
PR   Puerto Rico
prep   preposition
pres   present, president
prof   professor
pron   pronoun
PS   postscript, public school
pt   pint, point
qt   quart
rd   road, rod

recd   received
reg   registered
rev   reverend
RFD   rural free delivery
RI   Rhode Island
rpm   revolutions per minute
RR   railroad
RSVP   répondez s'il vous plaît (French, please reply)
S   south, southern
Sat   Saturday
SC   South Carolina
Scot   Scotland, Scottish
SD, S Dak   South Dakota
SE   southeast
sec   second
Sept   September
sing   singular
so   south
sq   square
sr   senior
Sr   sister
SS   steamship
st   saint, state, strait, street
Sun   Sunday
SW   southwest
tbsp   tablespoon
Tenn   Tennessee
Tex   Texas
Thurs, Thur, Thu   Thursday
TN   Tennessee
tsp   teaspoon
Tues, Tue   Tuesday
TV   television
TX   Texas
UN   United Nations
US   United States
USA   United States of America
USSR   Union of Soviet Socialist Republics
UT   Utah
v   verb
Va, VA   Virginia
var   variant
vb   verb
VI   Virgin Islands
vol   volume
vs   versus
Vt, VT   Vermont
W   west, western
WA, Wash   Washington
Wed   Wednesday
WI, Wis, Wisc   Wisconsin
wk   week
wt   weight
WV, W Va   West Virginia
WY, Wyo   Wyoming
yd   yard
yr   year

PRESIDENTS OF THE U. S. A.

Number	Name and Pronunciation of Surname	Life Dates	Birthplace	Term
1	George Washington \'wȯsh-ing-tən, 'wäsh-\	1732–1799	Virginia	1789–1797
2	John Adams \'ad-əmz\	1735–1826	Massachusetts	1797–1801
3	Thomas Jefferson \'jef-ər-sən\	1743–1826	Virginia	1801–1809
4	James Madison \'mad-ə-sən\	1751–1836	Virginia	1809–1817
5	James Monroe \mən-'rō\	1758–1831	Virginia	1817–1825
6	John Quincy Adams \'ad-əmz\	1767–1848	Massachusetts	1825–1829
7	Andrew Jackson \'jak-sən\	1767–1845	South Carolina	1829–1837
8	Martin Van Buren \van-'byür-ən\	1782–1862	New York	1837–1841
9	William Henry Harrison \'har-ə-sən\	1773–1841	Virginia	1841
10	John Tyler \'tī-lər\	1790–1862	Virginia	1841–1845
11	James Knox Polk \'pōk\	1795–1849	North Carolina	1845–1849
12	Zachary Taylor \'tā-lər\	1784–1850	Virginia	1849–1850
13	Millard Fillmore \'fil-,mōr\	1800–1874	New York	1850–1853
14	Franklin Pierce \'piərs\	1804–1869	New Hampshire	1853–1857
15	James Buchanan \byü-'kan-ən\	1791–1868	Pennsylvania	1857–1861
16	Abraham Lincoln \'ling-kən\	1809–1865	Kentucky	1861–1865
17	Andrew Johnson \ jän-sən\	1808–1875	North Carolina	1865–1869
18	Ulysses Simpson Grant \'grant\	1822–1885	Ohio	1869–1877
19	Rutherford Birchard Hayes \'hāz\	1822–1893	Ohio	1877–1881
20	James Abram Garfield \'gär-,fēld\	1831–1881	Ohio	1881
21	Chester Alan Arthur \'är-thər\	1830–1886	Vermont	1881–1885
22	Grover Cleveland \'klēv-lənd\	1837–1908	New Jersey	1885–1889
23	Benjamin Harrison \'har-ə-sən\	1833–1901	Ohio	1889–1893
24	Grover Cleveland \'klēv-lənd\	1837–1908	New Jersey	1893–1897
25	William McKinley \mə-'kin-lē\	1843–1901	Ohio	1897–1901
26	Theodore Roosevelt \'rō-zə-,velt\	1858–1919	New York	1901–1909
27	William Howard Taft \'taft\	1857–1930	Ohio	1909–1913
28	Woodrow Wilson \'wil-sən\	1856–1924	Virginia	1913–1921
29	Warren Gamaliel Harding \'härd-ing\	1865–1923	Ohio	1921–1923
30	Calvin Coolidge \'kü-lij\	1872–1933	Vermont	1923–1929
31	Herbert Clark Hoover \'hü-vər\	1874–1964	Iowa	1929–1933
32	Franklin Delano Roosevelt \'rō-zə-,velt\	1882–1945	New York	1933–1945
33	Harry S Truman \'trü-mən\	1884–1972	Missouri	1945–1953
34	Dwight David Eisenhower \'īz-n-,haü-ər\	1890–1969	Texas	1953–1961
35	John Fitzgerald Kennedy \'ken-ə-dē\	1917–1963	Massachusetts	1961–1963
36	Lyndon Baines Johnson \'jän-sən\	1908–1973	Texas	1963–1969
37	Richard Milhous Nixon \'nik-sən\	1913–	California	1969–1974
38	Gerald Rudolph Ford \'fōrd\	1913–	Nebraska	1974–

VICE-PRESIDENTS OF THE U. S. A.

Number	Name and Pronunciation of Surname	Life Dates	Birthplace	Term
1	John Adams \'ad-əmz\	1735–1826	Massachusetts	1789–1797
2	Thomas Jefferson \'jef-ər-sən\	1743–1826	Virginia	1797–1801
3	Aaron Burr \'bər\	1756–1836	New Jersey	1801–1805
4	George Clinton \'klint-n\	1739–1812	New York	1805–1812
5	Elbridge Gerry \'ger-ē\	1744–1814	Massachusetts	1813–1814
6	Daniel D. Tompkins \'tämp-kənz\	1774–1825	New York	1817–1825
7	John C. Calhoun \kal-'hün\	1782–1850	South Carolina	1825–1832
8	Martin Van Buren \van-'byür-ən\	1782–1862	New York	1833–1837
9	Richard M. Johnson \'jän-sən\	1780–1850	Kentucky	1837–1841
10	John Tyler \'tī-lər\	1790–1862	Virginia	1841
11	George M. Dallas \'dal-əs\	1792–1864	Pennsylvania	1845–1849
12	Millard Fillmore \'fil-,mōr\	1800–1874	New York	1849–1850
13	William R. King \'king\	1786–1853	North Carolina	1853
14	John C. Breckinridge \'brek-ən-rij\	1821–1875	Kentucky	1857–1861
15	Hannibal Hamlin \'ham-lən\	1809–1891	Maine	1861–1865
16	Andrew Johnson \'jän-sən\	1808–1875	North Carolina	1865
17	Schuyler Colfax \'kōl-,faks\	1823–1885	New York	1869–1873
18	Henry Wilson \'wil-sən\	1812–1875	New Hampshire	1873–1875
19	William A. Wheeler \'hwē-lər\	1819–1887	New York	1877–1881
20	Chester A. Arthur \'är-thər\	1830–1886	Vermont	1881
21	Thomas A. Hendricks \'hen-driks\	1819–1885	Ohio	1885
22	Levi P. Morton \'mȯrt-n\	1824–1920	Vermont	1889–1893
23	Adlai E. Stevenson \'stē-vən-sən\	1835–1914	Kentucky	1893–1897
24	Garret A. Hobart \'hō-,bärt\	1844–1899	New Jersey	1897–1899
25	Theodore Roosevelt \'rō-zə-,velt\	1858–1919	New York	1901
26	Charles W. Fairbanks \'faər-,bangks\	1852–1918	Ohio	1905–1909
27	James S. Sherman \'shər-mən\	1855–1912	New York	1909–1912
28	Thomas R. Marshall \'mär-shəl\	1854–1925	Indiana	1913–1921
29	Calvin Coolidge \'kü-lij\	1872–1933	Vermont	1921–1923
30	Charles G. Dawes \'dȯz\	1865–1951	Ohio	1925–1929
31	Charles Curtis \'kərt-əs\	1860–1936	Kansas	1929–1933
32	John N. Garner \'gär-nər\	1868–1967	Texas	1933–1941
33	Henry A. Wallace \'wäl-əs\	1888–1965	Iowa	1941–1945
34	Harry S Truman \'trü-mən\	1884–1972	Missouri	1945
35	Alben W. Barkley \'bär-klē\	1877–1956	Kentucky	1949–1953
36	Richard M. Nixon \'nik-sən\	1913–	California	1953–1961
37	Lyndon B. Johnson \'jän-sən\	1908–1973	Texas	1961–1963
38	Hubert H. Humphrey \'həm-frē\	1911–	South Dakota	1965–1969
39	Spiro T. Agnew \'ag-nü, -nyü\	1918–	Maryland	1969–1973
40	Gerald R. Ford \'fōrd\	1913–	Nebraska	1973–1974
41	Nelson A. Rockefeller \'räk-i-,fel-ər\	1908–	Maine	1974–

THE STATES OF THE U. S. A.

Name and Pronunciation	State Capital and Pronunciation	Name and Pronunciation	State Capital and Pronunciation
Alabama \,al-ə-'bam-ə\	Montgomery \mənt-'gəm-ə-rē\	Missouri \mə-'zùr-ē, -'zùr-ə\	Jefferson City \,jef-ər-sən-\
Alaska \ə-'las-kə\	Juneau \'jü-nō\	Montana \män-'tan-ə\	Helena \'hel-ə-nə\
Arizona \,ar-ə-'zō-nə\	Phoenix \'fē-niks\	Nebraska \nə-'bras-kə\	Lincoln \'ling-kən\
Arkansas \'är-kən-,sò\	Little Rock \'lit-l-,räk\	Nevada \nə-'vad-ə, -'väd-\	Carson City \,kärs-n-\
California \,kal-ə-'fòr-nyə\	Sacramento \,sak-rə-'ment-ō\	New Hampshire \-'hamp-shər\	Concord \'käng-kərd\
Colorado \,käl-ə-'rad-ō, -'räd-\	Denver \'den-vər\	New Jersey \-'jər-zē\	Trenton \'trent-n\
Connecticut \kə-'net-i-kət\	Hartford \'härt-fərd\	New Mexico \-'mek-si-,kō\	Santa Fe \,sant-ə-'fā\
Delaware \'del-ə-,waər\	Dover \'dō-vər\	New York \-'yòrk\	Albany \'òl bə-nē\
Florida \'flòr-ə-də\	Tallahassee \,tal-ə-'has-ē\	North Carolina \-,kar-ə-'lī-nə\	Raleigh \'ròl ē, 'räl-\
Georgia \'jòr-jə\	Atlanta \ət-'lant-ə\	North Dakota \-də-'kōt-ə\	Bismarck \'bi, ,märk\
Hawaii \hə-'wä-ē\	Honolulu \,hän-l-'ü-lü\	Ohio \ō-'hī-ō\	Columbus \kə-'ləm-bəs\
Idaho \'īd-ə-,hō\	Boise \'bòi-sē, -zē\	Oklahoma \,ō-klə-'hō-mə\	Oklahoma City
Illinois \,il-ə-'nòi\	Springfield \'spring-,fēld\	Oregon \'òr-i-gən\	Salem \'sā-ləm\
Indiana \,in-dē-'an-ə\	Indianapolis \,in-dē-ə-'nap-ə-ləs\	Pennsylvania \,pen-səl-'vā-nyə\	Harrisburg \'har-əs ,bərg\
Iowa \'ī-ə-wə\	Des Moines \di-'mòin\	Rhode Island \rō-'dī-lənd\	Providence \'präv-ə-dəns\
Kansas \'kan-zəs\	Topeka \tə-'pē-kə\	South Carolina \-,kar-ə-'lī-nə\	Columbia \kə-'ləm-bē-ə\
Kentucky \kən-'tək-ē\	Frankfort \'frangk-fərt\	South Dakota \-də-'kōt-ə\	Pierre \'piər\
Louisiana \lü-,ē-zē-'an-ə, ,lü-ə-zē-\	Baton Rouge \,bat-n-'rüzh\	Tennessee \,ten-ə-'sē\	Nashville \'nash-,vil\
Maine \'mān\	Augusta \ò-'gəs-tə\	Texas \'tek-səs\	Austin \'òs-tən\
Maryland \'mer-ə-lənd\	Annapolis \ə-'nap-ə-ləs\	Utah \'yü-,tò\	Salt Lake City
Massachusetts \,mas-ə-'chü-səts\	Boston \'bòs-tən\	Vermont \vər-'mänt\	Montpelier \mänt-'pēl-yər\
Michigan \'mish-i-gən\	Lansing \'lan-sing\	Virginia \vər-'jin-yə\	Richmond \'rich-mənd\
Minnesota \,min-ə-'sōt-ə\	St. Paul \sānt-'pòl\	Washington \'wòsh-ing-tən, 'wäsh-\	Olympia \ə-'lim-pē-ə\
Mississippi \,mis-ə-'sip-ē\	Jackson \'jak-sən\	West Virginia \-vər-'jin-yə\	Charleston \'chärl-stən\
		Wisconsin \wis-'kän-sən\	Madison \'mad-ə-sən\
		Wyoming \wī-'ō-ming\	Cheyenne \shī-'an\

THE PROVINCES OF CANADA

Name and Pronunciation	Provincial Capital and Pronunciation	Name and Pronunciation	Provincial Capital and Pronunciation
Alberta \al-'bərt-ə\	Edmonton \'ed-mən-tən\	Nova Scotia \,nō-və-'skō-shə\	Halifax \'hal-ə-,faks\
British Columbia \-kə-'ləm-bē-ə\	Victoria \vik-'tōr-ē-ə\	Ontario \än-'ter-ē-,ō\	Toronto \tə-'ränt-ō\
Manitoba \,man-ə-'tō-bə\	Winnipeg \'win-ə-,peg\	Prince Edward Island \-,ed-wərd-\	Charlottetown \'shär-lət-,taùn\
New Brunswick \-'brənz-wik\	Fredericton \'fred-rik-tən\		
Newfoundland \'nü-fən-lənd, 'nyü-, -,land\	St. John's \sānt-'jänz\	Quebec \kwi-'bek, ki-, kā-\	Quebec
		Saskatchewan \sə-'skach-ə-wən, -,wän\	Regina \ri-'jī-nə\

NATIONS OF THE WORLD

Name and Pronunciation	Location	Name and Pronunciation	Location
Afghanistan \af-'gan-ə-,stan\	Asia	Cuba \'kyü-bə\	West Indies
Albania \al-'bā-nē-ə\	Europe	Cyprus \'sī-prəs\	Asia
Algeria \al-'jir-ē-ə\	Africa	Czechoslovakia \,chek-ə-slō-'vä-kē-ə\	Europe
Andorra \an-'dòr-ə\	Europe	Dahomey \də-'hō-mē\	Africa
Angola \ang-'gō-lə\	Africa	Denmark \'den-,märk\	Europe
Argentina \,är-jən-'tē-nə\	South America	Dominican Republic \də-,min-i-kən-\	West Indies
Australia \òs-'trāl-yə\	Between Indian and Pacific oceans	Ecuador \'ek-wə-,dòr\	South America
Austria \'òs-trē-ə\	Europe	Egypt \'ē-jəpt\	Africa
Bahamas \bə-'häm-əs\	North Atlantic	El Salvador \el-'sal-və-,dòr\	Central America
Bahrain \bä-'rān\	Asia	Equatorial Guinea \-'gin-ē\	Africa
Bangladesh \,bäng-glə-'desh\	Asia	Ethiopia \,ē-thē-'ō-pē-ə\	Africa
Barbados \bär-'bād-ōs\	West Indies	Fiji \'fē-jē\	South Pacific
Belgium \'bel-jəm\	Europe	Finland \'fin-lənd\	Europe
Bermuda \bər-'myüd-ə\	North Atlantic	France \'frans\	Europe
Bhutan \bü-'tan\	Asia	Gabon \ga-'bōn\	Africa
Bolivia \bə-'liv-ē-ə\	South America	Gambia \'gam-bē-ə\	Africa
Botswana \bät-'swän-ə\	Africa	Germany, East \-'jər-mə-nē\	Europe
Brazil \brə-'zil\	South America	Germany, West	Europe
British Honduras (Belize) \-hän-'dùr-əs, -'dyùr-\ \bə-'lēz\	Central America	Ghana \'gä-nə\	Africa
		Greece \'grēs\	Europe
Bulgaria \,bəl-'gar-ē-ə, bùl-\	Europe	Guatemala \,gwät-ə-'mä-lə\	Central America
Burma \'bər-mə\	Asia	Guinea \'gin-ē\	Africa
Burundi \bù-'rün-dē\	Africa	Guinea-Bissau (formerly Portuguese Guinea) \'gin-ē-bis-'aù\	Africa
Cambodia (Khmer Republic) \kam-'bōd-ē-ə\ \kə-'mer-\	Asia	Guyana \gī-'an-ə\	South America
Cameroon \,kam-ə-'rün\	Africa	Haiti \'hāt-ē\	West Indies
Canada \'kan-ə-də\	North America	Honduras \hän-'dùr-əs, -'dyùr-\	Central America
Central African Republic \-'af-ri-kən-\	Africa	Hungary \'həng-gə-rē\	Europe
Chad \'chad\	Africa	Iceland \'īs-lənd\	North Atlantic
Chile \'chil-ē\	South America	India \'in-dē-ə\	Asia
China \'chī-nə\	Asia	Indonesia \,in-də-'nē-zhə\	Asia
Colombia \kə-'ləm-bē-ə\	South America	Iran (Persia) \i-'ran, -'rän\ \'pər-zhə\	Asia
Congo Republic \'käng-gō-\	Africa	Iraq \i-'rak, -'räk\	Asia
Costa Rica \,käs-tə-'rē-kə\	Central America	Ireland, Republic of \-'īr-lənd\	Europe
			(continued on next page)

NATIONS OF THE WORLD

(continued from preceding page)

Name and Pronunciation	Location
Israel \'iz-rē-əl\	Asia
Italy \'it-l-ē\	Europe
Ivory Coast	Africa
Jamaica \jə-'mā-kə\	West Indies
Japan \jə-'pan\	Asia
Jordan \'jȯrd-n\	Asia
Kenya \'ken-yə, 'kēn-\	Africa
Korea, North \kə-'rē-ə\	Asia
Korea, South	Asia
Kuwait \kə-'wät\	Asia
Laos \'laus, 'lä-ōs\	Asia
Lebanon \'leb-ə-nən\	Asia
Lesotho \lə-'sō-tō\	Africa
Liberia \lī-'bir-ē-ə\	Africa
Libya \'lib-ē-ə\	Africa
Liechtenstein \'lik-tən-,stīn\	Europe
Luxembourg \'lùk-səm-,bùrg\	Europe
Malagasy Republic \,mal-ə-,gas-ē-\	Africa
Malawi \mə-'lä-wē\	Africa
Malaysia \mə-'lā-zhə\	Asia
Maldives \'mȯl-,dēvz\	Indian Ocean
Mali \'mä-lē\	Africa
Malta \'mȯl-tə\	Central Mediterranean
Mauritania \,mȯr-ə-'tā-nē-ə\	Africa
Mauritius \mȯ-'rish-əs\	Indian Ocean
Mexico \'mek-si-,kō\	North America
Monaco \'män-ə-,kō\	Europe
Mongolian Republic \män-,gōl-yən-\	Asia
Morocco \mə-'räk-ō\	Africa
Mozambique \,mō-zəm-'bēk\	Africa
Nauru \nä-'ü-rü\	South Pacific
Nepal \nə-'pȯl\	Asia
Netherlands \'neth-ər-ləndz\	Europe
New Zealand \-'zē-lənd\	Southwest Pacific
Nicaragua \,nik-ə-'räg-wə\	Central America
Niger \'nī-jər\	Africa
Nigeria \nī-'jir-ē-ə\	Africa
Norway \'nȯr-,wā\	Europe
Oman \ō-'män\	Asia
Pakistan \,pak-i-'stan, ,päk-i-'stän\	Asia
Panama \'pan-ə-,mä, -,mȯ\	Central America
Papua New Guinea \'pap-yə-wə-, -'gin-ē\	Asia
Paraguay \'par-ə-,gwī, -,gwä\	South America
Peru \pə-'rü\	South America
Philippines \'fil-ə-,pēnz\	Asia
Poland \'pō-lənd\	Europe
Portugal \'pōr-chi-gəl\	Europe
Qatar \'kät-ər\	Asia
Rhodesia \rō-'dē-zhə\	Africa
Rumania \rù-'mā-nē-ə\	Europe
Rwanda \rù-'än-də\	Africa
San Marino \,san-mə-'rē-nō\	Europe
Saudi Arabia \,saùd-ē-ə-'rā-bē-ə\	Asia
Senegal \,sen-i-'gȯl\	Africa
Seychelles \sā-'shelz\	Indian Ocean
Sierra Leone \sē-,er-ə-lē-'ōn\	Africa
Singapore \'sing-ə-,pōr, 'sing-gə-\	Asia
Somalia \sō-'mä-lē-ə\	Africa
South Africa, Republic of \-'af-ri-kə\	Africa
Southern Yemen \-'yem-ən\	Asia
Spain \'spān\	Europe
Sri Lanka (Ceylon) \srē-'läng-kə \si-'län\	Asia
Sudan \sü-'dan\	Africa
Swaziland \'swäz-ē-,land\	Africa
Sweden \'swēd-n\	Europe
Switzerland \'swit-sər-lənd\	Europe
Syria \'sir-ē-ə\	Asia
Tanzania \,tan-zə-'nē-ə\	Africa
Thailand \'tī-,land\	Asia
Togo \'tō-gō\	Africa
Tonga \'täng-ə, -gə\	South Pacific
Trinidad and Tobago \'trin-ə-,dad, tə-'bā-gō\	West Indies
Tunisia \tü-'nē-zhə, tyü-, -'nizh-ə\	Africa
Turkey \'tər-kē\	Asia and Europe
Uganda \yü-'gan-də\	Africa
Union of Soviet Socialist Republics (U.S.S.R.) \-'sō-vē-,et-\	Asia and Europe
United Arab Emirates \-,ar-əb-i-'mir-əts\	Asia
United Kingdom of Great Britain and Northern Ireland \-grāt-'brit-n, 'īr-lənd\	Europe
England \'ing-glənd\	
Northern Ireland	
Scotland \'skät-lənd\	
Wales \'wālz\	
United States of America \-ə-'mer-ə-kə\	North America
Upper Volta \-'vōl-tə\	Africa
Uruguay \'yùr-ə-,gwī, -,gwä\	South America
Vatican City State \,vat-i-kən-\	Europe
Venezuela \,ven-ə-zə-'wä-lə, -'wē-\	South America
Vietnam, North \-vē-,et-'näm\	Asia
Vietnam, South	Asia
Western Samoa \-sə-'mō-ə\	Southwest Pacific
Yemen Arab Republic \'yem-ən-\	Asia
Yugoslavia \,yü-gō-'slä-vē-ə\	Europe
Zaire \'zī-ər, zä-'iər\	Africa
Zambia \'zam-bē-ə\	Africa

LARGEST CITIES OF THE WORLD

These cities all have over 150,000 inhabitants; cities marked * have over 1,000,000 inhabitants.

Name and Pronunciation	Location
Aachen \'ä-kən\	West Germany
Abadan \,ä-bə-'dän\	Iran
Aberdeen \,ab-ər-'dēn\	Scotland
Abidjan \,ab-i-'jän\	Ivory Coast
Acapulco \,äk-ə-'pül-kō, ,ak-\	Mexico
Accra \ə-'krä\	Ghana
Adana \'äd-n-ə\	Turkey
Addis Ababa \,ad-əs-'ab-ə-bə\	Ethiopia
Adelaide \'ad-l-,ād\	Australia
Aden \'äd-ən\	Southern Yemen
Agra \'ä-grə\	India
Aguascalientes \,äg-wə-,skäl-'yen-,täs\	Mexico
*Ahmadabad \'ä-məd-ə-,bäd\	India
Ajmer \,əj-'miər\	India
Akita \ä-'kēt-ə\	Japan
Akron \'ak-rən\	Ohio
Albuquerque \'al-bə-,kər-kē\	New Mexico
Aleppo \ə-'lep-ō\	Syria
*Alexandria \,al-ig-'zan-drē-ə\	Egypt
Algiers \al-'jiərz\	Algeria
Aligarh \,al-i-'gär\	India
Allahabad \'al-ə-hə-,bad\	India
Alleppey \ə-'lep-ē\	India
Alma-Ata \,al-mə-ə-'tä\	U.S.S.R.
Amagasaki \,am-ə-gə-'sä-kē\	Japan
Amman \ä-'man\	Jordan
Amoy \ä-'mȯi\	China
Amravati \əm-'räv-ət-ē\	India
Amritsar \əm-'rit-sər\	India
Amsterdam \'am-stər-,dam\	Netherlands
Anaheim \'an-ə-,hīm\	California
Andizhan \,an-di-'zhan\	U.S.S.R.
Angarsk \än-'gärsk\	U.S.S.R.
*Ankara \'ang-kə-rə\	Turkey
Annaba (Bône) \ə-'näb-ə\ \'bōn\	Algeria
Anshan \'än-'shän\	China
Antung \'än-'dùng\	China
Antwerp \'ant-,wərp\	Belgium
Aomori \aù-mə-rē\	Japan
Arequipa \,ar-ə-'kē-pə\	Peru
Arkhangelsk \är-'kan-,gelsk\	U.S.S.R.
Asahikawa \,ä-sə-hē-'kä-wə\	Japan
Ashkhabad \'ash-kə-,bad\	U.S.S.R.
Asmara \az-'mär-ə\	Ethiopia
Astrakhan \'as-trə-,kan, -kən\	U.S.S.R.
Asunción \ə-,sün-sē-'ōn\	Paraguay
*Athens \'ath-ənz\	Greece
Atlanta \ət-'lant-ə\	Georgia
Auckland \'ȯk-lənd\	New Zealand
Augsburg \'ȯgz-,bərg\	West Germany
Austin \'ȯs-tən\	Texas
Avellaneda \,av-ə-zhə-'nä-thə\	Argentina
Bacolod \bə-'kō-,lȯd\	Philippines
Baghdad \'bag-,dad\	Iraq
*Baku \bä-'kü\	U.S.S.R.
Baltimore \'bȯl-tə-,mōr\	Maryland
Bamako \'bam-ə-,kō\	Mali

(continued on next page)

Name and Pronunciation	Location
Banaras \bə-'nä-rəs\	India
*Bandung \'bän-ˌdu̇ng\	Indonesia
Bangalore \'bang-gə-ˌlōr\	India
*Bangkok \'bang-ˌkäk\	Thailand
Bangui \bäng-'gē\	Central African Republic
*Barcelona \ˌbär-sə-'lō-nə\	Spain
Bareilly \bə-'rā-lē\	India
Bari \'bä-rē\	Italy
Barnaul \ˌbär-nə-'ül\	U.S.S.R.
Baroda \bə-'rōd-ə\	India
Barquisimeto \ˌbär-ki-sə-'mät-ō\	Venezuela
Barranquilla \ˌbar-ən-'kē-yə\	Colombia
Basel \'bä-zəl\	Switzerland
Basilan \bə-'sē-ˌlän\	Philippines
Basra \'bäs-rə\	Iraq
Baton Rouge \ˌbat-n-'rüzh\	Louisiana
Beirut \bā-'rüt\	Lebanon
Belém \bə-'lem\	Brazil
Belfast \'bel-ˌfast\	Northern Ireland
Belgaum \bel-'gaüm\	India
Belgrade \'bel-ˌgräd\	Yugoslavia
*Belo Horizonte \'bel-ō-ˌhȯr-ə-'zänt-ē\	Brazil
*Berlin \bər-'lin\	Germany
Bern \'bərn, 'beərn\	Switzerland
Bhagalpur \'bäg-əl-ˌpür\	India
Bhavnagar \baü-'nəg-ər\	India
Bhopal \bō-'päl\	India
Bielefeld \'bē-lə-ˌfelt\	West Germany
Bikaner \ˌbik-ə-'neər\	India
Bilbao \bil-'bä-ˌō\	Spain
Birmingham \'bər-ming-ˌham\	Alabama
*Birmingham \'bər-ming-əm\	England
Bisk \'bisk\	U.S.S.R.
Blackpool \'blak-ˌpül\	England
Bochum \'bō-ˌkum\	West Germany
*Bogotá \ˌbō-gə-'tȯ, -'tä\	Colombia
Bologna \bə-'lōn-yə\	Italy
Bolton \'bōlt-n\	England
*Bombay \bäm-'bā\	India
Bonn \'bän\	West Germany
Bordeaux \bȯr-'dō\	France
Boston \'bȯs-tən\	Massachusetts
Bournemouth \'bȯrn-məth, 'bərn-\	England
Bradford \'brad-fərd\	England
Brasilia \brə-'zil-yə\	Brazil
Brasov \brä-'shȯv\	Rumania
Bratislava \ˌbrat-ə-'slä-və\	Czechoslovakia
Brazzaville \'braz-ə-ˌvil, 'bräz-\	Congo Republic
Bremen \'brem-ən, 'brā-mən\	West Germany
Brescia \'bresh-ə\	Italy
Bridgeport \'brij-ˌpȯrt\	Connecticut
Brighton \'brīt-n\	England
Brisbane \'briz-bən\	Australia
Bristol \'brist-l\	England
Brno \'bər-nō\	Czechoslovakia
Brunswick \'brənz-wik\	West Germany
*Brussels \'brəs-əlz\	Belgium
Bryansk \brē-'ansk\	U.S.S.R.
Bucaramanga \ˌbü-kə-rə-'mäng-gə\	Colombia
*Bucharest \'bü-kə-ˌrest\	Rumania
*Budapest \'büd-ə-ˌpest\	Hungary
*Buenos Aires \ˌbwä-nəs-'aər-ēz\	Argentina
Buffalo \'bəf-ə-ˌlō\	New York
Bulawayo \ˌbul-ə-'wä-ō\	Rhodesia
Bursa \bür-'sä, 'bər-sə\	Turkey
Bydgoszcz \'bid-ˌgȯshch\	Poland
Bytom \'bē-ˌtȯm\	Poland
Cagliari \'käl-yə-rē\	Italy
*Cairo \'kī-rō\	Egypt
*Calcutta \kal-'kət-ə\	India
Calgary \'kal-gə-rē\	Alberta
Cali \'kä-lē\	Colombia
Callao \kə-'yä-ō\	Peru
Camagüey \ˌkam-ə-'gwä\	Cuba
Canberra \'kan-bər-ə, -brə\	Australia
*Canton \'kan-ˌtän\	China
Cape Town \'kāp-ˌtaün\	South Africa
*Caracas \kə-'rak-əs, -'rä-kəs\	Venezuela
Cardiff \'kärd-əf\	Wales
Cartagena \ˌkärt-ə-'gä-nə\	Colombia
*Casablanca \ˌkas-ə-'blang-kə\	Morocco
Catania \kə-'tän-yə\	Italy
Cebu \sā-'bü\	Philippines
Chandigarh \'chən-dē-gər\	India
Changchow \'jäng-jō\	China
*Changchun \'chäng-'chun\	China
Changsha \'chäng-'shä\	China
Changteh \'chäng-'də\	China
Charlotte \'shär-lət\	North Carolina

Name and Pronunciation	Location
Cheboksary \ˌcheb-ˌäk-'sär-ē\	U.S.S.R.
Chelyabinsk \chel-'yä-bənsk\	U.S.S.R.
Chengchow \'jəng-jō\	China
Chengteh \'chəng-'də\	China
*Chengtu \'chəng-'dü\	China
Cherepovets \ˌcher-ə-pə-'vets\	U.S.S.R.
Chernovtsy \chər-'nȯft-sē\	U.S.S.R.
Chiba \'chē-bə\	Japan
*Chicago \shə-'käg-ō, -'kȯg-\	Illinois
Chihuahua \chə-'wä-wä\	Mexico
Chimkent \chim-'kent\	U.S.S.R.
Chinchow (Chinhsien) \'jin-jō\ \'jin-shē-'en\	China
Chinkiang \'jin-jē-'äng\	China
Chinwangtao \'chin-'wäng-'daü\	China
Chita \chi-'tä\	U.S.S.R.
Chittagong \'chit-ə-ˌgäng\	Bangladesh
Christchurch \'krīst-ˌchərch\	New Zealand
*Chungking \'chùng-'king\	China
Cincinnati \ˌsin-sə-'nat-ē, -'nat-ə\	Ohio
Ciudad Juárez \sē-ü-ˌthä-'hwär-ˌes\	Mexico
Cleveland \'klēv-lənd\	Ohio
Cluj \'klüzh\	Rumania
Cochabamba \ˌkō-chə-'bäm-bə\	Bolivia
Coimbatore \ˌkȯim-bə-'tōr\	India
Cologne \kə-'lōn\	West Germany
Colombo \kə-'ləm-bō\	Sri Lanka
Columbus \kə-'ləm-bəs\	Georgia
Columbus	Ohio
Conakry \'kän-ə-krē\	Guinea
Concepción \kən-ˌsep-sē-'ōn\	Chile
Constantine \'kän-stən-ˌtēn\	Algeria
Copenhagen \ˌkō-pən-'hä-gən, -'hä-\	Denmark
Córdoba \'kȯrd-ə-bə\	Argentina
Córdoba	Spain
Corpus Christi \ˌkȯr-pəs-'kris-tē\	Texas
Coventry \'käv-ən-trē, 'kəv-\	England
Cuernavaca \ˌkwer-nə-'väk-ə\	Mexico
Culiacan \ˌkül-yə-'kän\	Mexico
Curitiba \ˌkür-ə-'tē-bə\	Brazil
Cuttack \'kət-ək\	India
Czestochowa \ˌchen-stə-'kō-və\	Poland
Dacca \'dak-ə\	Bangladesh
Dakar \də-'kär\	Senegal
Dallas \'dal-əs\	Texas
Damascus \də-'mas-kəs\	Syria
Da Nang \dä-'näng\	South Vietnam
Dar es Salaam \ˌdär-ˌes-sə-'läm\	Tanzania
Davao \'dä-ˌvaü\	Philippines
Dayton \'dāt-n\	Ohio
Debrecen \'deb-rət-ˌsen\	Hungary
*Delhi \'del-ē\	India
Denver \'den-vər\	Colorado
Derby \'där-be\	England
Des Moines \di-'mȯin\	Iowa
*Detroit \di-'trȯit\	Michigan
Dneprodzerzhinsk \ˌnep-rō-dər-'zhinsk\	U.S.S.R.
Dnepropetrovsk \ˌnep-rō-pə-'trȯfsk\	U.S.S.R.
Donetsk \də-'netsk\	U.S.S.R.
Dortmund \'dȯrt-ˌmùnt\	West Germany
Douala \dü-'äl-ə\	Cameroon
Dresden \'drez-dən\	East Germany
Dublin \'dəb-lən\	Ireland
Dudley \'dəd-lē\	England
Duisburg \'düs-ˌbùrg\	West Germany
Duluth \də-'lüth\	Minnesota
Dundee \ˌdən-'dē\	Scotland
Durango \dü-'rang-gō\	Mexico
Durban \'dər-bən\	South Africa
Dushanbe \dü-'shäm-bə\	U.S.S.R.
Düsseldorf \'düs-səl-ˌdȯrf\	West Germany
Dzerzhinsk \dər-'zhinsk\	U.S.S.R.
Edinburgh \'ed-n-ˌbər-ə\	Scotland
Edmonton \'ed-mən-tən\	Alberta
Eindhoven \'īnt-ˌhō-vən\	Netherlands
El Mansûra \ˌel-man-'sùr-ə\	Egypt
El Paso \el-'pas-ō\	Texas
Erfurt \'eər-fərt\	East Germany
Eskisehir \ˌes-ki-shə-'hiər\	Turkey
Essen \'es-n\	West Germany
Fatshan \'fät-'shän\	China
Ferrara \fə-'rär-ə\	Italy
Fez \'fez\	Morocco
Flint \'flint\	Michigan
Florence \'flȯr-əns\	Italy
Foochow \'fü-jō\	China
Fortaleza \ˌfȯrt-l-'ā-zə\	Brazil
Fort Wayne \ˌfȯrt-'wān\	Indiana

(continued on next page)

607

LARGEST CITIES OF THE WORLD

(continued from preceding page)

Name and Pronunciation	Location
Fort Worth \fȯrt-'wərth\	Texas
Frankfurt \'frangk-fərt\	West Germany
Freetown \'frē-,taùn\	Sierra Leone
Fresno \'frez-nō\	California
Frunze \'frün-zə\	U.S.S.R.
Fukuoka \,fü-kə-'wō-kə\	Japan
Fukushima \,fü-kə-'shē-mə\	Japan
Fukuyama \,fü-kə-'yäm-ə\	Japan
Funabashi \,fü-nə-'bäsh-ē\	Japan
Fuse \'fü-,sā\	Japan
Fushun \'fü-'shùn\	China
Fusin \'fü-'shin\	China
Galati \gə-'lät-sē\	Rumania
Gary \'gaər-ē\	Indiana
Gaya \gə-'yä\	India
Gdansk (Danzig) \gə-'dänsk\ \'dänt-sig\	Poland
Gelsenkirchen \,gel-zən-'kiər-kən\	West Germany
General San Martín \,hā-nä-,räl-,sän-mär-'tēn\	Argentina
Geneva \jə-'nē-və\	Switzerland
Genoa \'jen-ə-wə\	Italy
George Town \'jȯrj-,taùn\	Malaysia
Germiston \'jər-məs-tən\	South Africa
Ghent (Gent) \'gent\	Belgium
Gifu \'gē-fü\	Japan
Giza \'gē-zə\	Egypt
*Glasgow \'glas-kō, -gō\	Scotland
Gomel \'gō-məl\	U.S.S.R.
Gorakhpur \'gōr-ək-,pùr\	India
*Gorki \'gȯr-kē\	U.S.S.R.
Gorlovka \gȯr-'lȯf-kə\	U.S.S.R.
Göteborg \,yərt-ə-'bȯr-yə\	Sweden
Granada \grə-'näd-ə\	Spain
Grand Rapids	Michigan
Graz \'gräts\	Austria
Grenoble \grə-'nō-bəl\	France
Groningen \'grō-ning-ən\	Netherlands
Grozny \'grȯz-nē\	U.S.S.R.
*Guadalajara \,gwäd-ə-lə-'här-ə\	Mexico
Guatemala City \,gwät-ə-,mä-lə-\	Guatemala
Guayaquil \,gwī-ə-'kēl\	Ecuador
Guntur \gùn-'tùr\	India
Gwalior \'gwä-lē-,ȯr\	India
Haarlem \'här-ləm\	Netherlands
Hachioji \,häch-ē-'ō-jē\	Japan
Hagen \'hä-gən\	West Germany
Hague, The \thə-'häg\	Netherlands
Haifa \'hī-fə\	Israel
Haiphong \'hī-'fȯng\	North Vietnam
Hakodate \,hä-kə-'dät-ē\	Japan
Halifax \'hal-ə-,faks\	Nova Scotia
Halle \'häl-ə\	East Germany
Hama \'ham-ə\	Syria
Hamadan \,ham-ə-'dan\	Iran
Hamamatsu \,hä-mə-'mät-sü\	Japan
*Hamburg \'ham-,bərg\	West Germany
Hamilton \'ham-əl-tən\	Ontario
Hangchow \'hang-'chaù, 'häng-'jō\	China
Hannover \'han-ə-vər\	West Germany
Hanoi \hä-'nȯi, ha-\	North Vietnam
*Harbin \'här-bən\	China
Hartford \'härt-fərd\	Connecticut
*Havana \hə-'van-ə\	Cuba
Helsinki \'hel-,sing-kē\	Finland
Hendon \'hen-dən\	England
Hengyang \'həng-'yäng\	China
Hermosillo \,er-mə-'sē-yō\	Mexico
Higashiosaka \hē-,gä-shē-ō-'säk-ə\	Japan
Himeji \hi-'mej-ē\	Japan
Hiroshima \,hir-ə-'shē-mə, hi-'rō-shə-\	Japan
Hofei \'hə-'fā\	China
Holguín \ȯl-'gēn\	Cuba
Homs \'hȯmz\	Syria
Hong Kong (see Victoria)	
Honolulu \,hän-l-'ü-lü\	Hawaii
Houston \'hyüs-tən\	Texas
Howrah \'haù-rə\	India
Hubli-Dharwar \,hùb-lē-där-'wär\	India
Hue \'hwā\	South Vietnam
Huhehot (Kweisui) \'hü-hä-,hōt\ \'gwā-'swā\	China
Hull \'həl\	England
Hwainan \'hwī-'nän\	China
*Hyderabad \'hīd-ə-rə-,bad\	India
Hyderabad	Pakistan
Iasi (Jassy) \'yäsh-i\ \'yäs-ē\	Rumania
Ibadan \ē-'bäd-n\	Nigeria
Iloilo \,ē-lə-'wē-lō\	Philippines
Inchon \'in-,chän\	South Korea

Name and Pronunciation	Location
Indianapolis \,in-dē-ə-'nap-ə-ləs\	Indiana
Indore \in-'dōr\	India
Ipin \'ē-'pin\	China
Irapuato \,ir-ə-'pwä-tō\	Mexico
Irkutsk \iər-'kütsk\	U.S.S.R.
Isfahan \,is-fə-'hän\	Iran
*Istanbul \,is-,täm-'bül\	Turkey
Ivanovo \i-'vä-nə-və\	U.S.S.R.
Iwaki \i-'wäk-ē\	Japan
Izhevsk \'ē-,zhefsk\	U.S.S.R.
Izmir \iz-'miər\	Turkey
Jackson \'jak-sən\	Mississippi
Jacksonville \'jak-sən-,vil\	Florida
Jaipur \'jī-,pùr\	India
*Jakarta \jə-'kärt-ə\	Indonesia
Jamnagar \jäm-'nəg-ər\	India
Jamshedpur \'jäm-,shed-,pùr\	India
Jersey City \,jər-zē-\	New Jersey
Jerusalem \jə-'rü-sə-ləm\	Israel and Jordan
Jhansi \'jän-sē\	India
Jidda (Jedda) \'jid-ə\ \'jed-ə\	Saudi Arabia
João Pessoa \,zhwaùn-pə-'sō-ə\	Brazil
Jodhpur \'jäd-pər\	India
*Johannesburg \jō-'han-əs-,bərg\	South Africa
Jokjakarta \,jōk-jə-'kärt-ə\	Indonesia
Jubbulpore (Jabalpur) \'jəb-əl-,pōr\ \-,pùr\	India
Jullundur \'jəl-ən-dər\	India
Kabul \'kä-bəl, kə-'bül\	Afghanistan
Kadiyevka \kə-'dē-yəf-kə\	U.S.S.R.
Kagoshima \,kä-gə-'shē-mə\	Japan
Kaifeng \'kī-'fəng\	China
Kalgan \'kal-'gan\	China
Kalinin \kə-'lē-nən\	U.S.S.R.
Kaliningrad \kə-'lē-nən-,grad\	U.S.S.R.
Kaluga \kə-'lü-gə\	U.S.S.R.
Kamensk-Uralski \,kä-mənsk-ù-'ral-skē\	U.S.S.R.
Kampala \käm-'päl-ə\	Uganda
Kanazawa \kə-'nä-zə-wə\	Japan
Kano \'kän-ō\	Nigeria
Kanpur (Cawnpore) \'kän-,pùr\ \'kȯn-,pōr\	India
Kansas City \,kan-zəs-\	Kansas
Kansas City	Missouri
Kaohsiung \'kaù-shē-'ùng\	China (Taiwan)
*Karachi \kə-'rä-chē\	Pakistan
Karaganda \,kar-ə-gən-'dä\	U.S.S.R.
Karl-Marx-Stadt (Chemnitz) \kärl-'märk-,shtät\ \'kem-nits\	East Germany
Karlsruhe \'kärlz-,rü-ə\	West Germany
Kassel \'kas-əl, 'käs-\	West Germany
Katmandu \,kat-,man-'dü\	Nepal
Katowice \,kät-ə-'vēt-sə\	Poland
Kaunas (Kovno) \'kaù-nəs\ \'kȯv-nō\	U.S.S.R.
Kawaguchi \,kä-wə-'gü-chē\	Japan
Kawasaki \,kä-wə-'sä-kē\	Japan
Kazan \kə-'zan\	U.S.S.R.
Keelung \'kē-'lùng\	China (Taiwan)
Kemerovo \'kem-ə-rə-,vō\	U.S.S.R.
Khabarovsk \kə-'bä-rəfsk\	U.S.S.R.
Kharagpur \'kər-əg-,pùr\	India
*Kharkov \'kär-,kȯf\	U.S.S.R.
Khartoum \kär-'tüm\	Sudan
Kherson \ker-'sȯn\	U.S.S.R.
Kiamusze \jē-'ä-'mü-'sü\	China
Kiel \'kēl\	West Germany
*Kiev \'kē-,ef\	U.S.S.R.
*Kinshasa \kin-'shäs-ə\	Zaire
Kirin \'kē-'rin\	China
Kirkuk \kir-'kük\	Iraq
Kirov \'kē-,rȯf\	U.S.S.R.
Kirovagrad \ki-'rō-və-,grad\	U.S.S.R.
Kisangani \,kē-sən-'gän-ē\	Zaire
Kishinev \'kish-ə-,nef\	U.S.S.R.
*Kitakyushu \kē-'tä-'kyü-shü\	Japan
Kitchener \'kich-ə-nər\	Ontario
Knoxville \'näks-,vil\	Tennessee
*Kobe \'kō-bē\	Japan
Kochi \'kō-chē\	Japan
Kofu \'kō-fü\	Japan
Kolar Gold Fields \kō-'lär-\	India
Kolhapur \'kō-lə-,pùr\	India
Komsomolsk \,käm-sə-'mȯlsk\	U.S.S.R.
Kopeisk \kō-'päsk\	U.S.S.R.
Koriyama \,kȯr-ə-'yäm-ə\	Japan
Kostroma \,käs-trə-'mä\	U.S.S.R.
Kotah \'kōt-ə\	India

(continued on next page)

LARGEST CITIES OF THE WORLD

(continued from preceding page)

Name and Pronunciation	Location
Kowloon \'kaù-'lün\	China
Kozhikode (Calicut) \'kō-zhə-,kōd\ \'kal-i-kət\	India
Krakow \'krä-,kaù, -,küf\	Poland
Kramatorsk \,kräm-ə-'tórsk\	U.S.S.R.
Krasnodar \,kras-nə-,där\	U.S.S.R.
Krasnoyarsk \,kras-nə-'yärsk\	U.S.S.R.
Krefeld \'krā-,felt\	Germany
Krivoi Rog \,kriv-,ói-'rōg\	U.S.S.R.
Kuala Lumpur \,kwä-lə-'lùm-,pùr\	Malaysia
*Kuibyshev \'kwē-bə-,shef\	U.S.S.R.
Kumamoto \,kü-mə-'mōt-ō\	Japan
Kumasi \kü-'mä-sē\	Ghana
*Kunming \'kùn-'ming\	China
Kurashiki \kü-'rä-shē-kē\	Japan
Kure \'kùr-ē\	Japan
Kurgan \kùr-'gan\	U.S.S.R.
Kursk \'kùrsk\	U.S.S.R.
Kutaisi \kù-'tī-sē\	U.S.S.R.
Kwangju \'gwäng-jü, 'kwäng-\	South Korea
Kweilin \'gwā-'lin\	China
*Kweiyang \'gwä-'yäng\	China
*Kyoto \kē-'ōt-ō\	Japan
La Coruña \,lä-kə-'rü-nyə\	Spain
Lagos \'lā-,gäs\	Nigeria
*Lahore \lə-'hōr\	Pakistan
*Lanchow \'län-'jō\	China
Lanús \lə-'nüs\	Argentina
La Paz \lə-'paz\	Bolivia
La Plata \lə-'plät-ə\	Argentina
Las Palmas \läs-'päl-məs\	Spain (Canary Is.)
Leeds \'lēdz\	England
Leghorn \'leg-,hórn\	Italy
Le Havre \lə-'häv-rə\	France
Leicester \'les-tər\	England
Leipzig \'līp-sig\	East Germany
*Leningrad \'len-ən-,grad\	U.S.S.R.
León \lā-'ōn\	Mexico
Liège \lē-'āzh\	Belgium
Lille \'lēl\	France
*Lima \'lē-mə\	Peru
Linz \'lints\	Austria
Lipetsk \'lē-,petsk\	U.S.S.R.
Lisbon \'liz-bən\	Portugal
Liuchow \lē-'ü-'jō\	China
Liverpool \'liv-ər-,pül\	England
Ljubljana \lē-'ü-blē-ə-,nä\	Yugoslavia
Lodz \'lüj\	Poland
Lomé \lō-'mā\	Togo
*London \'lən-dən\	England
London	Ontario
Long Beach \'lóng-,bēch\	California
*Los Angeles \lós-'an-jə-ləs\	California
Louisville \'lü-ē-,vil\	Kentucky
Lourenço Marques \lə-,ren-sō-,mär-'kēs\	Mozambique
Loyang \'lō-'yäng\	China
Luanda \lù-'an-də\	Angola
Lübeck \'lü-,bek\	West Germany
Lublin \'lü-blən\	Poland
Lubumbashi \,lü-büm-'bäsh-ē\	Zaire
Luchow \'lü-'jō\	China
Lucknow \'lək-,naù\	India
Ludhiana \,lüd-ē-'ä-nə\	India
Ludwigshafen \,lüd-vigz-'hä-fən\	West Germany
Lusaka \lü-'säk-ə\	Zambia
Lü-ta (Port Arthur-Dairen) \'lü-'dä\ \-'är-thər-,dī-'ren\	China
Luton \'lüt-ən\	England
Lvov \lə-'vóf\	U.S.S.R.
Lyallpur \'lī-əl-,pùr\	Pakistan
Lyons (Lyon) \lē-'ōn\	France
Macao \mə-'kaù\	Macao
Maceió \,mas-ā-'ō\	Brazil
Madison \'mad-ə-sən\	Wisconsin
*Madras \mə-'dras\	India
*Madrid \mə-'drid\	Spain
Madurai \,mad-ə-'rī\	India
Maebashi \mī-'bäsh-ē\	Japan
Magdeburg \'mäg-də-,bùrg\	East Germany
Magnitogorsk \mag-'nēt-ə-,górsk\	U.S.S.R.
Mahalla el Kubra \mə-,hal-ə-,el-'kü-brə\	Egypt
Makassar \mə-'kas-ər\	Indonesia
Makeevka \mə-'kā-əf-kə\	U.S.S.R.
Málaga \'mal-ə-gə\	Spain
Malang \mə-'läng\	Indonesia
Malegaon \,mäl-ə-'gaùn\	India
Malmö \'mal-,mər\	Sweden
Managua \mə-'nä-gwə\	Nicaragua

Name and Pronunciation	Location
Manaus \mə-'naùs\	Brazil
Manchester \'man-,ches-tər\	England
Mandalay \,man-də-'lā\	Burma
Mangalore \'mäng-gə-,lòr\	India
*Manila \mə-'nil-ə\	Philippines
Manizales \,man-ə-'zä-ləs\	Colombia
Mannheim \'man-,hīm\	West Germany
Maracaibo \,mar-ə-'kī-bō\	Venezuela
Marianao \,mä-rē-ə-'naù\	Cuba
Marrakesh \mə-'rä-kish\	Morocco
Marseilles (Marseille) \mär-'sā\	France
Matamoros \,mat-ə-'mōr-əs\	Mexico
Matsudo \mät-'sü-dō\	Japan
Matsuyama \,mät-sù-'yä-mə\	Japan
Mazatlan \,mäz-ət-'län\	Mexico
Mecca \'mek-ə\	Saudi Arabia
Medan \mā-'dän\	Indonesia
Medellín \,med-l-'ēn\	Colombia
Meerut \'mā-rət\	India
Meknes \mek-'nes\	Morocco
*Melbourne \'mel-bərn\	Australia
Memphis \'mem-fəs\	Tennessee
Mérida \'mer-ə-də\	Mexico
Meshed (Mashhad) \mə-'shed\ \mə-'shad\	Iran
Messina \mə-'sē-nə\	Italy
Mexicali \,mek-sə-'kal-ē\	Mexico
*Mexico City \,mek-si-,kō-\	Mexico
Miami \mī-'am-ē, -'am-ə\	Florida
*Milan \mə-'lan\	Italy
Milwaukee \mil-'wò-kē\	Wisconsin
Minneapolis \,min-ē-'ap-ə-ləs\	Minnesota
Minsk \'minsk\	U.S.S.R.
Miskolc \'mish-,kōlts\	Hungary
Mobile \mō-'bēl\	Alabama
Mogadishu \,mä-gə-'dish-ü\	Somalia
Mogilev \'mäg-ə-,lef\	U.S.S.R.
Mombasa \mäm-'bäs-ə\	Kenya
Mönchen-Gladbach \,men-kən-'glät-,bäk\	West Germany
Monterrey \,mänt-ə-'rā\	Mexico
*Montevideo \,mänt-ə-və-'dā-ō\	Uruguay
*Montreal \,män-trē-'ól\	Quebec
Moradabad \mə-'räd-ə-,bäd\	India
Morelia \mə-'rāl-yə\	Mexico
*Moscow \'mäs-,kaù, -,kō\	U.S.S.R.
Mosul \mō-'sül, 'mō-səl\	Iraq
Mülheim \'myül-,hīm\	West Germany
Multan \mùl-'tän\	Pakistan
*Munich \'myü-nik\	West Germany
Münster \'myün-stər\	West Germany
Murcia \'mər-shē-ə\	Spain
Murmansk \mùr-'mansk\	U.S.S.R.
Mutankiang \'mü-'dän-jē-'äng\	China
Mysore \mī-'sōr\	India
Nagano \nə-'gä-nō\	Japan
Nagasaki \,nä-gə-'sä-kē\	Japan
*Nagoya \nə-'gói-ə\	Japan
Nagpur \'näg-,pùr\	India
Nairobi \nī-'rō-bē\	Kenya
Namangan \,näm-ən-'gän\	U.S.S.R.
Nanchang \'nän-'chäng\	China
Nanchung \'nän-'chùng\	China
*Nanking \'nan-'king\	China
Nanning \'nän-'ning\	China
Nantes \'nants\	France
Nantung \'nän-'tùng\	China
*Naples \'nā-pəlz\	Italy
Nashville \'nash-,vil\	Tennessee
Nasik \'näs-ik\	India
Neikiang \'nä-jē-'äng\	China
Newark \'nü-ərk, 'nyü-\	New Jersey
Newcastle \'nü-,kas-əl, 'nyü-\	Australia
Newcastle upon Tyne \-'tīn\	England
New Orleans \-'ór-lē-ənz\	Louisiana
*New York \-'yórk\	New York
Nice \'nēs\	France
Niigata \nē-'gät-ə\	Japan
Nikolaev \,nik-ə-'lī-əf\	U.S.S.R.
Ningpo \'ning-'pō\	China
Nishinomiya \,nish-i-'nō-mē-,yä\	Japan
Niterói \,nēt-ə-'rói\	Brazil
Nizhni Tagil \,nizh-nē-tə-'gil\	U.S.S.R.
Norfolk \'nór-fək\	Virginia
Nottingham \'nät-ing-əm\	England
Novi Sad \,nō-vē-'säd\	Yugoslavia
Novocherkassk \,nō-vō-chər-'kask\	U.S.S.R.
Novokuznetsk \,nō-vō-küz-'netsk\	U.S.S.R.
*Novosibirsk \,nō-vō-sə-'birsk\	U.S.S.R.
Nuevo Laredo \nù-,ā-vō-lə-'rād-ō\	Mexico

(continued on next page)

609

Name and Pronunciation	Location
Nuremberg \'nür-əm-,bərg, 'nyür-\	West Germany
Oakland \'ōk-lənd\	California
Oberhausen \'ō-bər-,haúz-n\	West Germany
Odessa \ō-'des-ə\	U.S.S.R.
Ogbomosho \,äg-bə-'mō-shō\	Nigeria
Oita \'ō-i-,tä\	Japan
Okayama \,ō-kə-'yä-mə\	Japan
Oklahoma City \,ō-klə-,hō-mə-\	Oklahoma
Omaha \'ō-mə-,hȯ, -,hä\	Nebraska
Omdurman \,äm-dər-'man\	Sudan
Omiya \ō-'mē-ə\	Japan
Omsk \'ȯmsk\	U.S.S.R.
Omuta \'ō-mə-,tä\	Japan
Oporto (Porto) \ō-'pȯrt-ō\ \'pȯrt-ō\	Portugal
Oran \ȯ-'rän\	Algeria
Ordzhonikidze \,ȯr-,jän-ə-'kid-zə\	U.S.S.R.
Orel \ȯ-'rel\	U.S.S.R.
Orenburg (Chkalov) \'ȯr-ən-,bərg\ \chə-'kä-ləf\	U.S.S.R.
Orsk \'ȯrsk\	U.S.S.R.
*Osaka \ō-'sä-kə\	Japan
Oshogbo \ō-'shäg-bō\	Nigeria
Oslo \'äz-,lō\	Norway
Ostrava \'ȯs-trə-və\	Czechoslovakia
Otaru \ō-'tä-rü\	Japan
Ottawa \'ät-ə-wə\	Ontario
Padua \'paj-ə-wə\	Italy
Palembang \,pä-ləm-'bäng\	Indonesia
Palermo \pə-'lər-mō\	Italy
Palma de Mallorca \,päl-mə-thä-mə-'yȯr-kə\	Spain
Panama City \,pan-ə-,mä-, -,mȯ-\	Panama
Paoting \'baú-'ding\	China
Paotow \'baú-'dō\	China
Paraná \,par-ə-'nä\	Argentina
*Paris \'par-əs\	France
Patiala \,pət-ē-'äl-ə\	India
Patna \'pət-nə\	India
Pavlodar \,pav-lə-'där\	U.S.S.R.
*Peking (Peiping) \'pē-'king\ \'pā-'ping\	China
Penang \pə-'nang\	Malaysia
Pengpu \'pəng-'pü\	China
Penki \'bən-'chē\	China
Penza \'pen-zə\	U.S.S.R.
Perm \'pərm\	U.S.S.R.
Perth \'pərth\	Australia
Peshawar \pə-'shä-wər\	Pakistan
Petropavlovsk \,pe-trə-'pav-,löfsk\	U.S.S.R.
Petropavlovsk-Kamchatski \-kam-'chat-skē\	U.S.S.R.
*Philadelphia \,fil-ə-'del-fē-ə\	Pennsylvania
Phnom Penh \pə-'nȯm-'pen\	Cambodia
Phoenix \'fē-niks\	Arizona
Piraeus \pī-'rē-əs\	Greece
Pittsburgh \'pits-,bərg\	Pennsylvania
Ploesti \plȯ-'esht-ē\	Rumania
Plovdiv \'plȯv-,dif\	Bulgaria
Plymouth \'plim-əth\	England
Podolsk \pə-'dȯlsk\	U.S.S.R.
Poltava \pȯl-'tä-və\	U.S.S.R.
Poona \'pü-nə\	India
Port-au-Prince \,pȯrt-ō-'prins\	Haiti
Port Elizabeth \-i-'liz-ə-bəth\	South Africa
Port Harcourt \-'här-,kȯrt\	Nigeria
Portland \'pȯrt-lənd\	Oregon
Pôrto Alegre \,pȯrt-ō-ə-'leg-rə\	Brazil
Port Said \-'sīd\	Egypt
Portsmouth \'pȯrts-məth\	England
Poznan \'pȯz-,nän\	Poland
*Prague \'präg\	Czechoslovakia
Pretoria \pri-'tȯr-ē-ə\	South Africa
Prokopevsk \prə-'kȯ-pəfsk\	U.S.S.R.
Providence \'präv-ə-dəns\	Rhode Island
Puebla \pü-'eb-lə\	Mexico
*Pusan \'pü-,sän\	South Korea
Pyongyang \pē-'ȯng-,yäng\	North Korea
Quebec \kwi-'bek\	Quebec
Quezon City \,kā-,sȯn-\	Philippines
Quito \'kē-,tō\	Ecuador
Rabat \rə-'bät\	Morocco
Rajahmundry \,räj-ə-'mùn-drē\	India
Rajkot \'räj-,kōt\	India
*Rangoon \'ran-'gün\	Burma
Rawalpindi \,rä-wəl-'pin-dē\	Pakistan
*Recife \rə-'sē-fə\	Brazil
Reggio di Calabria \,rej-ō-,dē-kə-'lä-brē-ə\	Italy
Rennes \'ren\	France
Richmond \'rich-mənd\	Virginia

Name and Pronunciation	Location
Riga \'rē-gə\	U.S.S.R.
*Rio de Janeiro \'rē-ō-,dā-zhə-'neər-ō\	Brazil
Riyadh \rē-'yäd\	Saudi Arabia
Rochester \'räch-əs-tər\	New York
*Rome \'rōm\	Italy
Rosario \rō-'zär-ē-,ō\	Argentina
Rostock \'räs-,täk\	East Germany
Rostov \rə-'stȯf\	U.S.S.R.
Rotterdam \'rät-ər-,dam\	Netherlands
Ryazan \,rē-ə-'zan\	U.S.S.R.
Rybinsk \'rib-ənsk\	U.S.S.R.
Sacramento \,sak-rə-'ment-ō\	California
Saharanpur \sə-'hä-rən-,pùr\	India
*Saigon \sī-'gän\	South Vietnam
Saint-Étienne \,san-tā-'tyen\	France
Saint Louis \,sānt-'lü-əs\	Missouri
Saint Paul \,sānt-'pȯl\	Minnesota
Saint Petersburg \sānt-'pēt-ərz-,bərg\	Florida
Sakai \sä-'kī\	Japan
Salem \'sā-ləm\	India
Salisbury \'sȯlz-,ber-ē\	Rhodesia
Saltillo \säl-'tē-yō\	Mexico
Salt Lake City	Utah
Salvador \'sal-və-,dȯr\	Brazil
Samarkand \'sam-ər-,kand\	U.S.S.R.
San Antonio \,san-ən-'tō-nē-,ō\	Texas
San Diego \,san-dē-'ā-gō\	California
San Francisco \,san-frən-'sis-kō\	California
San Jose \,san-ə-'zā\	California
San José \,san-ə-'zā\	Costa Rica
San Juan \san-'wän\	Puerto Rico
San Luis Potosí \,sän-lù-'ēs-,pōt-ə-'sē\	Mexico
San Miguel de Tucumán \,san-mig-,el-də-,tü-kə-'män\	Argentina
San Salvador \san-'sal-və-,dȯr\	El Salvador
Santa Ana \,sant-ə-'an-ə\	California
Santa Ana	El Salvador
Santa Fe \,sant-ə-'fā\	Argentina
Santander \,sän-,tän-'deər\	Spain
*Santiago \,sant-ē-'ä-gō\	Chile
Santiago de Cuba \-də-'kyü-bə\	Cuba
Santiago de los Caballeros \-də-,lȯs-,kä-bə-'yeər-ōs\	Dominican Republic
Santo Domingo \,sant-ə-də-'ming-gō\	Dominican Republic
Santos \'sant-əs\	Brazil
*São Paulo \saùm-'paù-lü\	Brazil
*Sapporo \sə-'pȯr-ō\	Japan
Sarajevo \'sä-rə-ye-,vȯ\	Yugoslavia
Saransk \sə-'ränsk\	U.S.S.R.
Saratov \sə-'rät-əf\	U.S.S.R.
Sasebo \'sä-sə-,bō\	Japan
Seattle \sē-'at-l\	Washington
Semarang \sə-'mä-,räng\	Indonesia
Semipalatinsk \,sem-i-pə-'lä-,tinsk\	U.S.S.R.
Sendai \sen-'dī\	Japan
*Seoul \'sōl\	Korea
Sevastopol \sə-'vas-tə-,pōl\	U.S.S.R.
Seville \sə-'vil\	Spain
Shakhty \'shäk-tē\	U.S.S.R.
*Shanghai \shang-'hī\	China
Shcherbakov \,sher-bə-'kȯf\	U.S.S.R.
Sheffield \'shef-,ēld\	England
*Shenyang \'shən-'yäng\	China
Shihkiachwang \'shiər-jē-'äj-'wäng\	China
Shimonoseki \,shim-ə-nō-'sek-ē\	Japan
Shiraz \shi-'räz\	Iran
Shizuoka \,shiz-ə-'wō-kə\	Japan
Sholapur \'shō-lə-,pùr\	India
Shreveport \'shrēv-,pȯrt\	Louisiana
Sialkot \sē-'äl-,kōt\	Pakistan
*Sian \'shē-'än\	China
Siangtan \shē-'äng-'tän\	China
Simferopol \,sim-fə-'rȯ-pəl\	U.S.S.R.
*Singapore \'sing-ə-,pȯr, 'sing-gə-\	Malaysia
Sinhailien \'shin-'hī-lē-'en\	China
Sinsiang \'shin-shē-'äng\	China
Skopje (Skoplje) \'skäp-,yä\ \'skäp-əl-,yä\	Yugoslavia
Smolensk \smō-'lensk\	U.S.S.R.
Sochi \'sō-chē\	U.S.S.R.
Sofia \'sō-fē-ə, sō-'fē-ə\	Bulgaria
Solingen \'zō-ling-ən\	West Germany
Soochow \'sü-'jō\	China
Southampton \saùth-'amp-tən\	England
Southend on Sea \,saùth-,end-\	England
Spokane \spō-'kan\	Washington
Springfield \'spring-,fēld\	Massachusetts
Srinagar \sri-'nəg-ər\	Kashmir
Sterlitamak \,ster-li-tə-'mak\	U.S.S.R.

(continued on next page)

LARGEST CITIES OF THE WORLD

(continued from preceding page)

Name and Pronunciation	Location
Kowloon \'kaù-'lün\	China
Kozhikode (Calicut) \'kō-zhǝ-,kōd\ \'kal-i-kǝt\	India
Krakow \'krä-,kaù, -,küf\	Poland
Kramatorsk \,kräm-ǝ-'tórsk\	U.S.S.R.
Krasnodar \,kras-nǝ-,där\	U.S.S.R.
Krasnoyarsk \,kras-nǝ-'yärsk\	U.S.S.R.
Krefeld \'krā-,felt\	Germany
Krivoi Rog \,kriv-,ói-'rōg\	U.S.S.R.
Kuala Lumpur \,kwä-lǝ-'lüm-,pùr\	Malaysia
*Kuibyshev \'kwē-bǝ-,shef\	U.S.S.R.
Kumamoto \,kü-mǝ-'mōt-ō\	Japan
Kumasi \kü-'mä-sē\	Ghana
*Kunming \'kùn-'ming\	China
Kurashiki \kù-'rä-shē-kē\	Japan
Kure \'kùr-ē\	Japan
Kurgan \kùr-'gan\	U.S.S.R.
Kursk \'kùrsk\	U.S.S.R.
Kutaisi \kù-'tī-sē\	U.S.S.R.
Kwangju \'gwäng-jü, 'kwäng-\	South Korea
Kweilin \'gwā-'lin\	China
*Kweiyang \'gwä-'yäng\	China
*Kyoto \kē-'ōt-ō\	Japan
La Coruña \,lä-kǝ-'rü-nyǝ\	Spain
Lagos \'lā-,gäs\	Nigeria
Lahore \lǝ-'hōr\	Pakistan
*Lanchow \'län-jō\	China
Lanús \lǝ-'nüs\	Argentina
La Paz \lǝ-'paz\	Bolivia
La Plata \lǝ-'plät-ǝ\	Argentina
Las Palmas \läs-'päl-mǝs\	Spain (Canary Is.)
Leeds \'lēdz\	England
Leghorn \'leg-,hórn\	Italy
Le Havre \lǝ-'häv-rǝ\	France
Leicester \'les-tǝr\	England
Leipzig \'līp-sig\	East Germany
*Leningrad \'len-ǝn-,grad\	U.S.S.R.
León \lā-'ōn\	Mexico
Liège \lē-'āzh\	Belgium
Lille \'lēl\	France
*Lima \'lē-mǝ\	Peru
Linz \'lints\	Austria
Lipetsk \'lē-,petsk\	U.S.S.R.
Lisbon \'liz-bǝn\	Portugal
Liuchow \lē-'ü-'jō\	China
Liverpool \'liv-ǝr-,pül\	England
Ljubljana \lē-'ü-blē-ǝ-,nä\	Yugoslavia
Lodz \'lüj\	Poland
Lomé \lō-'mā\	Togo
*London \'lǝn-dǝn\	England
London	Ontario
Long Beach \'lóng-,bēch\	California
*Los Angeles \lós-'an-jǝ-lǝs\	California
Louisville \'lü-ē-,vil\	Kentucky
Lourenço Marques \lǝ-,ren-sō-,mär-'kēs\	Mozambique
Loyang \'lō-'yäng\	China
Luanda \lù-'an-dǝ\	Angola
Lübeck \'lü-,bek\	West Germany
Lublin \'lü-blǝn\	Poland
Lubumbashi \,lü-büm-'bäsh-ē\	Zaire
Luchow \'lü-jō\	China
Lucknow \'lǝk-,naù\	India
Ludhiana \,lüd-ē-'ä-nǝ\	India
Ludwigshafen \,lüd-vigz-'hä-fǝn\	West Germany
Lusaka \lü-'säk-ǝ\	Zambia
Lü-ta (Port Arthur-Dairen) \'lü-'dä\ \-'är-thǝr-,dī-'ren\	China
Luton \'lüt-ǝn\	England
Lvov \lǝ-'vóf\	U.S.S.R.
Lyallpur \'lī-ǝl-,pùr\	Pakistan
Lyons (Lyon) \lē-'ōn\	France
Macao \mǝ-'kaù\	Macao
Maceió \,mas-ā-'ō\	Brazil
Madison \'mad-ǝ-sǝn\	Wisconsin
*Madras \mǝ-'dras\	India
*Madrid \mǝ-'drid\	Spain
Madurai \,mad-ǝ-'rī\	India
Maebashi \mī-'bäsh-ē\	Japan
Magdeburg \'mäg-dǝ-,bùrg\	East Germany
Magnitogorsk \mag-'nēt-ǝ-,górsk\	U.S.S.R.
Mahalla el Kubra \mǝ-,hal-ǝ-,el-'kü-brǝ\	Egypt
Makassar \mǝ-'kas-ǝr\	Indonesia
Makeevka \mǝ-'kā-ǝf-kǝ\	U.S.S.R.
Málaga \'mal-ǝ-gǝ\	Spain
Malang \mǝ-'läng\	Indonesia
Malegaon \,mäl-ǝ-'gaùn\	India
Malmö \'mal-,mǝr\	Sweden
Managua \mǝ-'nä-gwǝ\	Nicaragua

Name and Pronunciation	Location
Manaus \mǝ-'naùs\	Brazil
Manchester \'man-,ches-tǝr\	England
Mandalay \,man-dǝ-'lā\	Burma
Mangalore \'mäng-gǝ-,lór\	India
*Manila \mǝ-'nil-ǝ\	Philippines
Manizales \,man-ǝ-'zä-lǝs\	Colombia
Mannheim \'man-,hīm\	West Germany
Maracaibo \,mar-ǝ-'kī-bō\	Venezuela
Marianao \,mä-rē-ǝ-'naù\	Cuba
Marrakesh \mǝ-'rä-kish\	Morocco
Marseilles (Marseille) \,mär-'sā\	France
Matamoros \,mat-ǝ-'mōr-ǝs\	Mexico
Matsudo \mät-'sü-dō\	Japan
Matsuyama \,mät-sù-'yä-mǝ\	Japan
Mazatlan \,mäz-ǝt-'län\	Mexico
Mecca \'mek-ǝ\	Saudi Arabia
Medan \mä-'dän\	Indonesia
Medellín \,med-l-'ēn\	Colombia
Meerut \'mā-rǝt\	India
Meknes \mek-'nes\	Morocco
*Melbourne \'mel-bǝrn\	Australia
Memphis \'mem-fǝs\	Tennessee
Mérida \'mer-ǝ-dǝ\	Mexico
Meshed(Mashhad) \mǝ-'shed\ \mǝ-'shad\	Iran
Messina \mǝ-'sē-nǝ\	Italy
Mexicali \,mek-sǝ-'kal-ē\	Mexico
*Mexico City \,mek-si-,kō-\	Mexico
Miami \mī-'am-ē, -'am-ǝ\	Florida
*Milan \mǝ-'lan\	Italy
Milwaukee \mil-'wó-kē\	Wisconsin
Minneapolis \,min-ē-'ap-ǝ-lǝs\	Minnesota
Minsk \'minsk\	U.S.S.R.
Miskolc \'mish-,kōlts\	Hungary
Mobile \mō-'bēl\	Alabama
Mogadishu \,mä-gǝ-'dish-ü\	Somalia
Mogilev \'mäg-ǝ-,lef\	U.S.S.R.
Mombasa \mäm-'bäs-ǝ\	Kenya
Mönchen-Gladbach \,men-kǝn-'glät-,bäk\	West Germany
Monterrey \,mänt-ǝ-'rā\	Mexico
*Montevideo \,mänt-ǝ-vǝ-'dā-ō\	Uruguay
*Montreal \,män-trē-'ól\	Quebec
Moradabad \mǝ-'räd-ǝ-,bäd\	India
Morelia \mǝ-'rāl-yǝ\	Mexico
*Moscow \'mäs-,kaù, -,kō\	U.S.S.R.
Mosul \mō-'sül, 'mō-sǝl\	Iraq
Mülheim \'myül-,hīm\	West Germany
Multan \mùl-'tän\	Pakistan
*Munich \'myü-nik\	West Germany
Münster \'myün-stǝr\	West Germany
Murcia \'mǝr-shē-ǝ\	Spain
Murmansk \mùr-'mansk\	U.S.S.R.
Mutankiang \'mü-'dän-jē-'äng\	China
Mysore \mī-'sōr\	India
Nagano \nǝ-'gä-nō\	Japan
Nagasaki \nä-gǝ-'sä-kē\	Japan
*Nagoya \nǝ-'gói-ǝ\	Japan
Nagpur \'näg-,pùr\	India
Nairobi \nī-'rō-bē\	Kenya
Namangan \,näm-ǝn-'gän\	U.S.S.R.
Nanchang \'nän-'chäng\	China
Nanchung \'nän-'chùng\	China
*Nanking \'nan-'king\	China
Nanning \'nän-'ning\	China
Nantes \'nants\	France
Nantung \'nän-'tùng\	China
*Naples \'nā-pǝlz\	Italy
Nashville \'nash-,vil\	Tennessee
Nasik \'näs-ik\	India
Neikiang \'nā-jē-'äng\	China
Newark \'nü-ǝrk, 'nyü-\	New Jersey
Newcastle \'nü-,kas-ǝl, 'nyü-\	Australia
Newcastle upon Tyne \-'tīn\	England
New Orleans \-'ór-lē-ǝnz\	Louisiana
*New York \-'yòrk\	New York
Nice \'nēs\	France
Niigata \nē-'gät-ǝ\	Japan
Nikolaev \,nik-ǝ-'lī-ǝf\	U.S.S.R.
Ningpo \'ning-,pō\	China
Nishinomiya \,nish-i-'nō-mē-,yä\	Japan
Niterói \,nēt-ǝ-'rói\	Brazil
Nizhni Tagil \,nizh-nē-tǝ-'gil\	U.S.S.R.
Norfolk \'nór-fǝk\	Virginia
Nottingham \'nät-ing-ǝm\	England
Novi Sad \,nō-vē-'säd\	Yugoslavia
Novocherkassk \,nō-vō-chǝr-'kask\	U.S.S.R.
Novokuznetsk \,nō-vō-kùz-'netsk\	U.S.S.R.
*Novosibirsk \,nō-vō-sǝ-'birsk\	U.S.S.R.
Nuevo Laredo \nù-,ā-vō-lǝ-'räd-ō\	Mexico

(continued on next page)

609

Name and Pronunciation	Location
Nuremberg \'nùr-əm-,bərg, 'nyùr-\	West Germany
Oakland \'ōk-lənd\	California
Oberhausen \'ō-bər-,haùz-n\	West Germany
Odessa \ō-'des-ə\	U.S.S.R.
Ogbomosho \,äg-bə-'mō-shō\	Nigeria
Oita \'ō-i-,tä\	Japan
Okayama \,ō-kə-'yä-mə\	Japan
Oklahoma City \,ō-klə-,hō-mə-\	Oklahoma
Omaha \'ō-mə-,hȯ, -,hä\	Nebraska
Omdurman \,äm-dər-'man\	Sudan
Omiya \ō-'mē-ə\	Japan
Omsk \'ȯmsk\	U.S.S.R.
Omuta \'ō-mə-,tä\	Japan
Oporto (Porto) \ō-'pȯrt-ō\ \'pȯrt-ō\	Portugal
Oran \ȯ-'rän\	Algeria
Ordzhonikidze \,ȯr-,jän-ə-'kid-zə\	U.S.S.R.
Orel \ȯ-'rel\	U.S.S.R.
Orenburg (Chkalov) \'ȯr-ən-,bərg\ \chə-'kä-ləf\	U.S.S.R.
Orsk \'ȯrsk\	U.S.S.R.
*Osaka \ō-'sä-kə\	Japan
Oshogbo \ō-'shäg-bō\	Nigeria
Oslo \'äz-,lō\	Norway
Ostrava \'ȯs-trə-və\	Czechoslovakia
Otaru \ō-'tä-rü\	Japan
Ottawa \'ät-ə-wə\	Ontario
Padua \'paj-ə-wə\	Italy
Palembang \,pä-ləm-'bäng\	Indonesia
Palermo \pə-'lər-mō\	Italy
Palma de Mallorca \,päl-mə-thä-mə-'yȯr-kə\	Spain
Panama City \,pan-ə-,mä-, -,mȯ-\	Panama
Paoting \'baù-'ding\	China
Paotow \'baù-'dō\	China
Paraná \,par-ə-'nä\	Argentina
*Paris \'par-əs\	France
Patiala \,pət-ē-'äl-ə\	India
Patna \'pət-nə\	India
Pavlodar \,pav-lə-'där\	U.S.S.R.
*Peking (Peiping) \'pē-'king\ \'pā-'ping\	China
Penang \pə-'nang\	Malaysia
Pengpu \'pəng-'pü\	China
Penki \'bən-chē\	China
Penza \'pen-zə\	U.S.S.R.
Perm \'pərm\	U.S.S.R.
Perth \'pərth\	Australia
Peshawar \pə-'shä-wər\	Pakistan
Petropavlovsk \,pe-trə-'pav-,lȯfsk\	U.S.S.R.
Petropavlovsk-Kamchatski \-kam-'chat-skē\	U.S.S.R.
*Philadelphia \,fil-ə-'del-fē-ə\	Pennsylvania
Phnom Penh \pə-'nȯm-'pen\	Cambodia
Phoenix \'fē-niks\	Arizona
Piraeus \pī-'rē-əs\	Greece
Pittsburgh \'pits-,bərg\	Pennsylvania
Ploesti \plȯ-'esht-ē\	Rumania
Plovdiv \'plȯv-,dif\	Bulgaria
Plymouth \'plim-əth\	England
Podolsk \pə-'dȯlsk\	U.S.S.R.
Poltava \pȯl-'tä-və\	U.S.S.R.
Poona \'pü-nə\	India
Port-au-Prince \,pȯrt-ō-'prins\	Haiti
Port Elizabeth \-i-'liz-ə-bəth\	South Africa
Port Harcourt \-'här-,kōrt\	Nigeria
Portland \'pȯrt-lənd\	Oregon
Pôrto Alegre \,pȯrt-ō-ə-'leg-rə\	Brazil
Port Said \-'sīd\	Egypt
Portsmouth \'pȯrts-məth\	England
Poznan \'pȯz-,nän\	Poland
*Prague \'präg\	Czechoslovakia
Pretoria \pri-'tōr-ē-ə\	South Africa
Prokopevsk \prə-'kȯ-pəfsk\	U.S.S.R.
Providence \'präv-ə-dəns\	Rhode Island
Puebla \pü-'eb-lə\	Mexico
*Pusan \'pü-'sän\	South Korea
Pyongyang \pē-'ȯng-,yäng\	North Korea
Quebec \kwi-'bek\	Quebec
Quezon City \,kā-,són-\	Philippines
Quito \'kē-,tō\	Ecuador
Rabat \rə-'bät\	Morocco
Rajahmundry \,räj-ə-'mùn-drē\	India
Rajkot \'räj-,kōt\	India
*Rangoon \ran-'gün\	Burma
Rawalpindi \,rä-wəl-'pin-dē\	Pakistan
*Recife \rə-'sē-fə\	Brazil
Reggio di Calabria \,rej-ō-,dē-kə-'lä-brē-ə\	Italy
Rennes \'ren\	France
Richmond \'rich-mənd\	Virginia
Riga \'rē-gə\	U.S.S.R.
*Rio de Janeiro \'rē-ō-,dā-zhə-'neər-ō\	Brazil
Riyadh \rē-'yäd\	Saudi Arabia
Rochester \'räch-əs-tər\	New York
*Rome \'rōm\	Italy
Rosario \rō-'zär-ē-,ō\	Argentina
Rostock \'räs-,täk\	East Germany
Rostov \rə-'stȯf\	U.S.S.R.
Rotterdam \'rät-ər-,dam\	Netherlands
Ryazan \,rē-ə-'zan\	U.S.S.R.
Rybinsk \'rib-ənsk\	U.S.S.R.
Sacramento \,sak-rə-'ment-ō\	California
Saharanpur \sə-'hä-rən-,pùr\	India
*Saigon \,sī-'gän\	South Vietnam
Saint-Étienne \,san-tā-'tyen\	France
Saint Louis \sänt-'lü-əs\	Missouri
Saint Paul \sänt-'pȯl\	Minnesota
Saint Petersburg \sänt-'pēt-ərz-,bərg\	Florida
Sakai \sä-'kī\	Japan
Salem \'sä-ləm\	India
Salisbury \'sȯlz-,ber-ē\	Rhodesia
Saltillo \säl-'tē-yō\	Mexico
Salt Lake City	Utah
Salvador \'sal-və-,dȯr\	Brazil
Samarkand \'sam-ər-,kand\	U.S.S.R.
San Antonio \,san-ən-'tō-nē-,ō\	Texas
San Diego \,san-dē-'ā-gō\	California
San Francisco \,san-frən-'sis-kō\	California
San Jose \,san-ə-'zā\	California
San José \,san-ə-'zā\	Costa Rica
San Juan \san-'wän\	Puerto Rico
San Luis Potosí \,sän-lù-'ēs-,pōt-ə-'sē\	Mexico
San Miguel de Tucumán \,san-mig-,el-də-,tü-kə-'män\	Argentina
San Salvador \san-'sal-və-,dȯr\	El Salvador
Santa Ana \,sant-ə-'an-ə\	California
Santa Ana	El Salvador
Santa Fe \,sant-ə-'fā\	Argentina
Santander \,sän-,tän-'deər\	Spain
*Santiago \,sant-ē-'ä-gō\	Chile
Santiago de Cuba \-də-'kyü-bə\	Cuba
Santiago de los Caballeros \-də-,lōs-,kä-bə-'yeər-ōs\	Dominican Republic
Santo Domingo \,sant-ə-də-'ming-gō\	Dominican Republic
Santos \'sant-əs\	Brazil
*São Paulo \saùm-'paù-lü\	Brazil
*Sapporo \sə-'pōr-ō\	Japan
Sarajevo \'sä-rə-ye-,vȯ\	Yugoslavia
Saransk \sə-'ränsk\	U.S.S.R.
Saratov \sə-'rät-əf\	U.S.S.R.
Sasebo \'sä-sə-,bō\	Japan
Seattle \sē-'at-l\	Washington
Semarang \sə-'mä-,räng\	Indonesia
Semipalatinsk \,sem-i-pə-'lä-,tinsk\	U.S.S.R.
Sendai \sen-'dī\	Japan
*Seoul \'sōl\	Korea
Sevastopol \sə-'vas-tə-,pōl\	U.S.S.R.
Seville \sə-'vil\	Spain
Shakhty \'shäk-tē\	U.S.S.R.
*Shanghai \shang-'hī\	China
Shcherbakov \,sher-bə-'kȯf\	U.S.S.R.
Sheffield \'shef-,ēld\	England
*Shenyang \'shən-'yäng\	China
Shihkiachwang \'shiər-jē-'äj-'wäng\	China
Shimonoseki \,shim-ə-nō-'sek-ē\	Japan
Shiraz \shi-'räz\	Iran
Shizuoka \,shiz-ə-'wō-kə\	Japan
Sholapur \'shō-lə-,pùr\	India
Shreveport \'shrēv-,pōrt\	Louisiana
Sialkot \sē-'äl-,kōt\	Pakistan
*Sian \'shē-'än\	China
Siangtan \shē-'äng-'tän\	China
Simferopol \,sim-fə-'rȯ-pəl\	U.S.S.R.
*Singapore \'sing-ə-,pōr, 'sing-gə-\	Malaysia
Sinhailien \'shin-'hī-lē-ən\	China
Sinsiang \'shin-shē-'äng\	China
Skopje (Skoplje) \'skäp-,yä\ \'skäp-əl-,yä\	Yugoslavia
Smolensk \smō-'lensk\	U.S.S.R.
Sochi \'sō-chē\	U.S.S.R.
Sofia \'sō-fē-ə, sō-'fē-ə\	Bulgaria
Solingen \'zō-ling-ən\	West Germany
Soochow \'sü-'jō\	China
Southampton \saùth-'amp-tən\	England
Southend on Sea \,saùth-,end-\	England
Spokane \spō-'kan\	Washington
Springfield \'spring-,fēld\	Massachusetts
Srinagar \sri-'nəg-ər\	Kashmir
Sterlitamak \,ster-li-tə-'mak\	U.S.S.R.

(continued on next page)

Name and Pronunciation	Location
Stockholm \'stäk-,hōm\	Sweden
Stoke on Trent \,stōk, 'trent\	England
Strasbourg \'sträs-,bûrg\	France
Stuttgart \'stût-,gärt\	West Germany
Subotica \'sü-bə-,tēt-sə\	Yugoslavia
Suchow \'sü-'jō\	China
Suez \sü-'ez\	Egypt
Suita \sü-'ēt-ə\	Japan
Sumy \'sü-mē\	U.S.S.R.
Sunderland \'sən-dər-lənd\	England
*Surabaja \,sûr-ə-'bī-ə\	Indonesia
Surakarta (Solo) \,sûr-ə-'kärt-ə\ \'sō-lō\	Indonesia
Surat \'sûr-ət\	India
*Sverdlovsk \sferd-'lófsk\	U.S.S.R.
Swansea \'swän-zē\	Wales
Swatow \'swä-'taú\	China
*Sydney \'sid-nē\	Australia
Syracuse \'sir-ə-,kyüs\	New York
Syzran \'siz-rən\	U.S.S.R.
Szczecin (Stettin) \'shchet-,sēn\ \shte-'tēn\	Poland
Tabriz \tə-'brēz\	Iran
Tacoma \tə-'kō-mə\	Washington
Taegu \ta-'gü, tī-\	Korea
Taejon \tä-'jón, tī-\	South Korea
Taganrog \'tag-ən-,räg\	U.S.S.R.
Taichow \'tī-'jō\	China
Taichung \'tī-'chùng\	China (Taiwan)
Tainan \'tī-'nän\	China (Taiwan)
Taipeh \'tī-'pā\	China (Taiwan)
*Taiyuan \'tī-yü-'än\	China
Takamatsu \,tä-kə-'mät-sü\	Japan
Tallin \'tal-ən\	U.S.S.R.
Tambov \täm-'bóf\	U.S.S.R.
Tampa \'tam-pə\	Florida
Tampere \'tam-pə-,rā\	Finland
Tampico \tam-'pē-kō\	Mexico
Tananarive \tə-'nan-ə-,rēv\	Malagasy Republic
Tangier \tan-'jiər\	Morocco
Tangshan \'täng-'shän\	China
Tanta \'tänt-ə\	Egypt
Taranto \'tä-rən-,tō\	Italy
*Tashkent \tash-'kent\	U.S.S.R.
Tatung \'dä-'tùng\	China
Tegucigalpa \ti-,gü-sə-'gal-pə\	Honduras
*Tehran \,te-ə-'ran\	Iran
Tel Aviv \,tel-ə-'vēv\	Israel
Temirtau \'tä-mir-,taú\	U.S.S.R.
Thana \'tän-ə\	India
Thessaloniki \,thes-ə-lə-'nē·kē\	Greece
Thon Buri \tən-'bùr-ē\	Thailand
*Tientsin \tē-'ent-'sin\	China
Tiflis (Tbilisi) \'tif-ləs\ \tə-'bil-ə-sē\	U.S.S.R.
Tijuana \tē-'wä-nə\	Mexico
Timisoara \,tē-mē-shə-'wä-rə\	Rumania
Tirana \ti-'rän-ə\	Albania
Tiruchchirappalli \,tir-ə-chə-'rä-pə-lē\	India
Tlalnepantla \tə-,läl-nə-'pänt-lə\	Mexico
Tokushima \,tō-kə-'shē-mə\	Japan
*Tokyo \'tō-kē-,ō\	Japan
Toledo \tə-'lēd-ō\	Ohio
Tollygunge \'täl-ē-,gənj\	India
Tolyatti (Stavropol) \tól-'yät-ē\ \stav-'ró-pəl\	U.S.S.R.
Tomsk \'tämsk\	U.S.S.R.
*Toronto \tə-'ränt-ō\	Ontario
Torreón \,tór-ē-'ōn\	Mexico
Toulon \tü-'lōn\	France
Toulouse \tü-'lüz\	France
Toyama \tō-'yä-mə\	Japan
Toyohashi \,tō-yə-'hä-shē\	Japan
Toyonaka \,tō-yō-'näk-ə\	Japan
Trieste \trē-'est, -'es-tē\	Italy
Tripoli \'trip-ə-lē\	Libya
Trivandrum \tri-'van-drəm\	India
Tsamkong \'jäm-'góng\	China
Tselinograd \se-'lin-ə-,grad\	U.S.S.R.
Tsinan \'jē-'nän\	China
*Tsingtao \'ching-'daú\	China
Tsitsihar \'tsēt-sē-,här\	China
Tucson \'tü-,sän, tü-'sän\	Arizona
Tula \'tü-lə\	U.S.S.R.
Tulsa \'təl-sə\	Oklahoma
Tunis \'tü-nəs, 'tyü-\	Tunisia

Name and Pronunciation	Location
*Turin \'tùr-ən, 'tyùr-\	Italy
Turku \'tùr-,kü\	Finland
Tuticorin \,tüt-i-kə-'rin\	India
Tyumen \tyü-'men\	U.S.S.R.
Tzekung \'dzə-'gùng\	China
Tzepo \'dzə-'pō\	China
Ube \'ü-bē\	Japan
Ufa \ü-'fä\	U.S.S.R.
Ujjain \'ü-,jīn\	India
Ulan Bator (Urga) \,ü-,län-'bä-,tór\ \'ùr-gə\	Mongolian People's Republic
Ulan-Ude \,ü-,län-ù-'dā\	U.S.S.R.
Ulyanovsk \ül-'yä-nəfsk\	U.S.S.R.
Urawa \ù-'rä-wə\	Japan
Ust-Kamenogorsk \,üst-kə-'men-ə-,górsk\	U.S.S.R.
Utrecht \'yü-,trekt\	Netherlands
Utsunomiya \,üt-sə-'nō-mē-yə\	Japan
Valencia \və-'len-chē-ə\	Spain
Valencia	Venezuela
Valladolid \,val-ə-də-'lid, -'lē\	Spain
Valparaíso \,val-pə-'rī-zō, ,väl-pä-rä-'ē-sō\	Chile
Vancouver \van-'kü-vər\	British Columbia
Varna \'vär-nə\	Bulgaria
Venice \'ven-əs\	Italy
Veracruz \,ver-ə-'krüz, -'krüs\	Mexico
Verona \və-'rō-nə\	Italy
*Victoria (Hong Kong) \vik-'tōr-ē-ə\ \'häng-,käng\	Hong Kong Colony
*Vienna \vē-'en-ə\	Austria
Vigo \'vē-gō\	Spain
Vijayavada \,vij-ə-yə-'väd-ə\	India
Vilnius (Vilna) \'vil-nē-əs\ \'vil-nə\	U.S.S.R.
Vinnitsa \'vin-ət-sə\	U.S.S.R.
Virginia Beach \vər-,jin-yə-\	Virginia
Visakhapatnam \vi-,sä-kə-'pət-nəm\	India
Vitebsk \'vē-,tepsk\	U.S.S.R.
Vladimir \'vlad-ə-,miər, vlə-'dē-,miər\	U.S.S.R.
Vladivostok \,vlad-ə-vəs-'täk\	U.S.S.R.
Vologda \'vó-ləg-də\	U.S.S.R.
Voronezh \və-'rö-nish\	U.S.S.R.
Voroshilovgrad \,vór-ə-'shē-ləf-,grad\	U.S.S.R.
Wakayama \,wä-kə-'yä-mə\	Japan
Walsall \'wól-,sól, -səl\	England
Warangal \'wər-ən-gəl\	India
Warren \'wór-ən\	Michigan
Warrington \'wór-ing-tən\	England
*Warsaw \'wór-,só\	Poland
Washington \'wósh-ing-tən, 'wäsh-\	District of Columbia
Wenchow \'wən-'jō\	China
West Bromwich \'brəm-ij, 'bräm-\	England
Wichita \'wich-ə-,tó\	Kansas
Wiesbaden \'vēs-,bäd-n\	Germany
Willesden \'wilz-dən\	England
Windsor \'win-zər\	Ontario
Winnipeg \'win-ə-,peg\	Manitoba
Wolverhampton \'wùl-vər-,hamp-tən\	England
Worcester \'wùs-tər\	Massachusetts
Wroclaw \'vróts-,läf\	Poland
Wuchang \'wü-'chäng\	China
*Wuhan \'wü-'hän\	China
Wuhu \'wü-'hü\	China
Wuppertal \'vùp-ər-,täl\	West Germany
Wusih \'wü-'shē\	China
Wutungkiao \'wü-'tùng-chē-'aú\	China
Yamagata \yä-'mä-gə-,tä\	Japan
Yangchow \'yäng-'jō\	China
Yangchuan \'yäng-chù-'än\	China
Yaroslavl \,yä-rə-'släv-əl\	U.S.S.R.
Yerevan \,yer-ə-'vän\	U.S.S.R.
Yingkow \'ying-'kaú\	China
Yokkaichi \yō-'kī-chē\	Japan
*Yokohama \,yō-kə-'hä-mə\	Japan
Yokosuka \yō-'kó-sə-kə\	Japan
Yonkers \'yäng-kərz\	New York
Yoshkar-Ola \yosh-,kär-ə-'lä\	U.S.S.R.
Zabrze \'zäb-,zhä\	Poland
Zagreb \'zä-,greb\	Yugoslavia
Zaporozhe \,zä-pə-'ró-zhə\	U.S.S.R.
Zaragoza \,zar-ə-'gō-zə\	Spain
Zhdanov \'zhdä-nəf\	U.S.S.R.
Zhitomir \zhi-'tó-,mir\	U.S.S.R.
Zlatoust \,zlät-ə-'üst\	U.S.S.R.
Zurich \'zùr-ik\	Switzerland

SIGNS AND SYMBOLS

Astronomy

⊙ the sun; Sunday
◑, ☾, or ☽ the moon; Monday
● new moon
☽, ◐, ☽, ☽ first quarter
○ or Ⓜ full moon
☾, ◑, ☾, ☾ last quarter
☿ Mercury; Wednesday
♀ Venus; Friday
⊕, ⊖, or ♁ the earth
♂ Mars; Tuesday
♃ Jupiter; Thursday
♄ or ♄ Saturn; Saturday
♂, ⛢, or ♅ Uranus
♆, ♆, or ♆ Neptune
♇ Pluto
⚹ comet
* or ✳ fixed star

Business

@ at; each ⟨4 apples @ 5¢ = 20¢⟩
℀ per
number if it precedes a numeral ⟨track #3⟩; pounds if it follows ⟨a 5# sack of sugar⟩
℔ pound; pounds
% percent
‰ per thousand
$ dollars
¢ cents
£ pounds
/ shillings
© copyrighted
® registered trademark

Mathematics

+ plus; positive ⟨a+b=c⟩
− minus; negative
± plus or minus ⟨the square root of 4a² is ±2a⟩; more or less than ⟨an error of ±2⟩
× multiplied by; times ⟨6×4=24⟩—also indicated by placing a dot between the numbers ⟨6·4=24⟩
÷ or : divided by ⟨24÷6=4⟩—also indicated by writing the divisor under the dividend with a line between ⟨$\frac{24}{6}=4$⟩ or by writing the divisor after the dividend with a diagonal between ⟨3/8⟩
= equals ⟨6+2=8⟩
≠ or ≐ is not equal to
> is greater than ⟨6>5⟩
< is less than ⟨3<4⟩
≧ or ≥ is greater than or equal to
≦ or ≤ is less than or equal to
≯ is not greater than
≮ is not less than
≈ is approximately equal to
: is to; the ratio of
∴ therefore
∞ infinity
0 zero
∠ angle; the angle ⟨∠ ABC⟩
∟ right angle ⟨∟ ABC⟩
⊥ the perpendicular; is perpendicular to ⟨AB⊥CD⟩
‖ parallel; is parallel to ⟨AB‖CD⟩
⊙ or ○ circle
⌒ arc of a circle
△ triangle
□ square
▭ rectangle
√ or √ square root ⟨as in √4=2⟩
() parentheses ⎫ indicate that the quantities
[] brackets ⎬ enclosed by them
{} braces ⎭ are to be taken together
π pi; the number 3.14159265+; the ratio of the circumference of a circle to its diameter
° degree ⟨60°⟩

' minute; foot ⟨30'⟩
" second, inch ⟨30"⟩
²,³, etc.—used as exponents placed above and at the right of an expression to indicate that it is raised to a power indicated by the figure ⟨a², the square of a⟩
∪ union of two sets
∩ intersection of two sets
⊂ is included in, is a subset of
⊃ contains as a subset
∈ or ϵ is an element of
∉ is not an element of
Λ or 0 or ∅ or {} empty set

Miscellaneous

& and
&c et cetera; and so forth
/ diagonal or slant; used to mean "or" (as in and/or), "per" (as in feet/second), indicates end of a line of verse; separates the figures of a date (9/29/73)
† died—used esp. in genealogies
☧ monogram from Greek XP signifying Jesus
LXX Septuagint
✡ Star of David
* —used in Roman Catholic and Anglican service books to divide each verse of a psalm indicating where the response begins
✠ or + —used in some service books to indicate where the sign of the cross is to be made; also used by certain Roman Catholic and Anglican prelates as a sign of the cross preceding their signatures
f/ or f: relative aperture of a photographic lens
☠ poison
℞ take—used on prescriptions
♀ female
♂ male
☢ civil defense
☮ peace

Reference marks

* asterisk or star ⎫
† dagger ⎪ These marks are
‡ double dagger ⎪ placed in written
§ section or numbered clause ⎬ or printed text to
‖ parallels ⎪ direct attention to
¶ or ‖ paragraph ⎭ a footnote.

Weather

barometer, changes of:
∧ Rising, then falling
⌒ Rising, then steady; or rising, then rising more slowly
／ Rising steadily, or unsteadily
√ Falling or steady, then rising; or rising, then rising more quickly
— Steady, same as 3 hours ago
∨ Falling, then rising, same or lower than 3 hours ago
＼ Falling, then steady; or falling, then falling more slowly
＼ Falling steadily, or unsteadily
∧ Steady or rising, then falling; or falling, then falling more quickly
◉ calm
○ clear
◐ cloudy (partly)
● cloudy (completely overcast)

+ drifting or blowing snow
⌇ drizzle
≡ fog
⌒⌒ freezing rain
▲▲ cold front
●● warm front
▲●▲ stationary front
)(funnel clouds
∞ haze
● hurricane
⟲ tropical storm
: rain
⁖ rain and snow
⋎ rime
⤳ sandstorm or dust storm
∇ shower(s)
⍩ shower of rain
⍩ shower of hail
△ sleet
* snow
⧧ thunderstorm
⌇ visibility reduced by smoke

612